# HANDBOOK OF AFFECTIVE SCIENCES

# Series in Affective Science

*Series Editors*
Richard J. Davidson
Paul Ekman
Klaus Scherer

*The Nature of Emotion: Fundamental Questions*
edited by Paul Ekman and Richard J. Davidson

*Boo!: Culture, Experience, and the Startle Reflex*
Ronald Simons

*Emotions in Psychopathology:*
*Theory and Research*
edited by William F. Flack Jr. and James D. Laird

*What the Face Reveals:*
*Basic and Applied Studies of Spontaneous Expression*
*Using the Facial Action Coding System (FACS)*
edited by Paul Ekman and Erika Rosenberg

*Shame:*
*Interpersonal Behavior, Psychopathology, and Culture*
edited by Paul Gilbert and Bernice Andrews

*Affective Neuroscience:*
*The Foundations of Human and Animal Emotions*
Jaak Panksepp

*Extreme Fear, Shyness, and Social Phobia:*
*Origins, Biological Mechanisms, and Clinical Outcomes*
edited by Louis A. Schmidt and Jay Schulkin

*Cognitive Neuroscience of Emotion*
edited by Richard D. Lane and Lynn Nadel

*The Neuropsychology of Emotion*
edited by Joan C. Borod

*Anxiety, Depression, and Emotion*
edited by Richard J. Davidson

*Persons, Situations, and Emotions:*
*An Ecological Approach*
edited by Hermann Brandstätter and Andrzej Eliasz

*Emotion, Social Relationships, and Health*
edited by Carol D. Ryff and Burton H. Singer

*Appraisal Processes in Emotion:*
*Theory, Methods, Research*
edited by Klaus R. Scherer, Angela Schorr,
and Tom Johnstone

*Music and Emotion:*
*Theory and Research*
edited by Patrik N. Juslin and John A. Sloboda

# Handbook of
# AFFECTIVE SCIENCES

*Edited by*

Richard J. Davidson

Klaus R. Scherer

H. Hill Goldsmith

OXFORD

UNIVERSITY PRESS

2003

# OXFORD
## UNIVERSITY PRESS

Oxford   New York
Auckland   Bangkok   Buenos Aires   Cape Town   Chennai
Dar es Salaam   Delhi   Hong Kong   Istanbul   Karachi   Kolkata
Kuala Lumpur   Madrid   Melbourne   Mexico City   Mumbai   Nairobi
São Paulo   Shanghai   Taipei   Tokyo   Toronto

Published by Oxford University Press, Inc.
198 Madison Avenue, New York, New York 10016

www.oup.com

Library of Congress Cataloging-in-Publication Data
Handbook of affective sciences / edited by Richard J. Davidson,
Klaus R. Scherer, H. Hill Goldsmith.
    p.   cm.—(Series in affective science)
Includes bibliographical references and index.
ISBN 0-19-512601-7
1. Affect (Psychology)   2. Emotions.   I. Davidson, Richard J.   II. Scherer, Klaus R.
III. Goldsmith, H. Hill.   IV. Series.
BF511 .H35 2002
152.4—dc21      2001045163

9 8 7 6 5 4 3 2 1

Printed in the United States of America
on acid-free paper

# CONTENTS

Contributors   ix

Introduction   xiii

## Part I. Neuroscience

1   Introduction: Neuroscience   3
    *Richard J. Davidson, Klaus R. Scherer,*
    *H. Hill Goldsmith*

2   Parsing the Subcomponents of Emotion and
    Disorders of Emotion: Perspectives from
    Affective Neuroscience   8
    *Richard J. Davidson, Diego Pizzagalli,*
    *Jack B. Nitschke, Ned H. Kalin*

3   Comparing the Emotional Brains of Humans and
    Other Animals   25
    *Kent C. Berridge*

4   Emotional Learning Circuits in Animals
    and Humans   52
    *Kevin S. LaBar, Joseph E. LeDoux*

5   The Contributions of the Lesion Method to the
    Functional Neuroanatomy of Emotion   66
    *Antonio R. Damasio, Ralph Adolphs, H. Damasio*

6   Emotion and Memory: Central and Peripheral
    Contributions   93
    *James L. McGaugh, Larry Cahill*

7   Functional Neuroimaging of Depression: A Role for
    Medial Prefrontal Cortex   117
    *Rebecca Elliott, Raymond J. Dolan*

## Part II. Autonomic Psychophysiology

8   Introduction: Autonomic Psychophysiology   131
    *Gerhard Stemmler*

9   The Autonomic Nervous System and Its Coordination
    by the Brain   135
    *Wilfrid Jänig*

10  Motivational Organization of Emotions:
    Autonomic Changes, Cortical Responses, and
    Reflex Modulation   187
    *Alfons O. Hamm, Harald T. Schupp,*
    *Almut I. Weike*

11  Autonomic Specificity and Emotion   212
    *Robert W. Levenson*

12  Methodological Considerations in the
    Psychophysiological Study of Emotion   225
    *Gerhard Stemmler*

13  On the Automaticity of Autonomic Responses in
    Emotion: An Evolutionary Perspective   256
    *Arne Öhman, Stefan Wiens*

14  Emotional Modulation of Selective
    Attention: Behavioral and Psychophysiological
    Measures   276
    *Kenneth Hugdahl, Kjell Morten Stormark*

## Part III. Genetics and Development

15  Introduction: Genetics and Development  295
    *H. Hill Goldsmith*

16  Genetics of Emotional Development  300
    *H. Hill Goldsmith*

17  Behavioral Inhibition as a Temperamental
    Category  320
    *Jerome Kagan*

18  Emotional Development in Early Childhood: A Social
    Relationship Perspective  332
    *Judy Dunn*

19  Emotional Development During Infancy  347
    *Claire B. Kopp, Susan J. Neufeld*

20  Dynamic Development of Component Systems of
    Emotions: Pride, Shame, and Guilt in China and the
    United States  375
    *Michael F. Mascolo, Kurt W. Fischer, Jin Li*

## Part IV. Expression of Emotion

21  Introduction: Expression of Emotion  411
    *Dacher Keltner, Paul Ekman*

22  Facial Expression of Emotion  415
    *Dacher Keltner, Paul Ekman, Gian C. Gonzaga,
    Jennifer Beer*

23  Vocal Expression of Emotion  433
    *Klaus R. Scherer, Tom Johnstone,
    Gundrun Klasmeyer*

24  Expression of Emotion in Nonhuman Animals  457
    *Charles T. Snowdon*

25  Creative Expression and Communication of Emotions
    in the Visual and Narrative Arts  481
    *Keith Oatley*

26  Emotional Expression in Music  503
    *Alf Gabrielsson, Patrik N. Juslin*

27  Language and Emotion  535
    *Judy Reilly, Laura Seibert*

## Part V. Cognitive Components of Emotion

28  Introduction: Cognitive Components of Emotion  563
    *Klaus R. Scherer*

29  Appraisal Processes in Emotion  572
    *Phoebe C. Ellsworth, Klaus R. Scherer*

30  Affective Influences on Attitudes and Judgments  596
    *Joseph P. Forgas*

31  The Role of Affect in Decision Making  619
    *George Loewenstein, Jennifer S. Lerner*

32  Remembering Emotional Events: A Social Cognitive
    Neuroscience Approach  643
    *Kevin N. Ochsner, Daniel L. Schacter*

33  Information Processing Approaches to Emotion  661
    *Tim Dalgleish*

## Part VI. Personality

34  Introduction: Personality  677
    *H. Hill Goldsmith, Richard J. Davidson*

35  Information Processing Approaches to Individual
    Differences in Emotional Reactivity  681
    *Douglas Derryberry, Marjorie A. Reed*

36  Individual Differences in Emotional Reactions and
    Coping  698
    *Heinz W. Krohne*

37  Emotion and Life-Span Personality Development  726
    *Laura L. Carstensen, Susan T. Charles,
    Derek M. Isaacowitz, Quinn Kennedy*

## Part VII. Emotion and Social Processes

38  Introduction: Emotion and Social Processes  747
    *Peter Salovey*

39  Emotional Factors in Attitudes and Persuasion  752
    *Richard E. Petty, Leandre R. Fabrigar,
    Duane T. Wegener*

40  The Self and Emotion: The Role of Self-Reflection
    in the Generation and Regulation of
    Affective Experience  773
    *Mark R. Leary*

**41**   Affect and Prosocial Responding   787
*Nancy Eisenberg, Sandy Losoya, Tracy Spinrad*

**42**   Affect, Aggression, and Antisocial Behavior   804
*Leonard Berkowitz*

**43**   Two Types of Relationship Closeness and Their
Influence on People's Emotional Lives   824
*Margaret S. Clark, Ian Brissette*

**Part VIII. Evolutionary and Cultural Perspectives
on Affect**

**44**   Introduction: Evolutionary and Cultural Perspectives
on Affect   839
*Paul Rozin*

**45**   The Moral Emotions   852
*Jonathan Haidt*

**46**   Emotions as Dynamic Cultural Phenomena   871
*Batja Mesquita*

**47**   Adaptive Rationality and the Moral Emotions   891
*Robert H. Frank*

**Part IX. Emotion and Psychopathology**

**48**   Introduction: Emotion and Psychopathology   899
*Robert M. Post*

**49**   Response Modulation and Emotion Processing:
Implications for Psychopathy and Other Dysregulatory
Psychopathology   904
*Joseph P. Newman, Amanda R. Lorenz*

**50**   Physiological and Pharmacological Induction
of Affect   930
*Terence A. Ketter, Po W. Wang, Anna Lembke,
Nadia Sachs*

**51**   Neuroimaging and the Neurobiology of
Anxiety Disorders   963
*Scott L. Rauch*

**52**   Cognitive Biases in Emotional Disorders:
Information Processing and Social-Cognitive
Perspectives   976
*Susan Mineka, Eshkol Rafaeli, Iftah Yovel*

**53**   The Neurobiology of Affiliation: Implications
for Autism   1010
*Thomas R. Insel*

**54**   Neurobiology of Depressive Disorders   1021
*Steven J. Garlow, Charles B. Nemeroff*

**Part X. Emotion and Health**

**55**   Introduction: Emotion and Health   1047
*John T. Cacioppo*

**56**   Emotional Expression and Cancer Progression   1053
*Janine Giese-Davis, David Spiegel*

**57**   The Role of Emotion on Pathways to
Positive Health   1083
*Carol D. Ryff, Burton H. Singer*

**58**   Bottom-Up: Implications for Neurobehavioral
Models of Anxiety and Autonomic Regulation   1105
*Gary G. Berntson, John T. Cacioppo,
Martin Sarter*

**59**   Stress and Affect: Applicability of the Concepts of
Allostasis and Allostatic Load   1117
*Bruce S. McEwen, Teresa Seeman*

Index   1139

*Color insert follows page 414*

# CONTRIBUTORS

Richard J. Davidson
Department of Psychology
University of Wisconsin-Madison

Klaus R. Scherer
Department of Psychology
University of Geneva

H. Hill Goldsmith
Department of Psychology
University of Wisconsin-Madison

Ralph Adolphs
Department of Neurology
The University of Iowa

Jennifer Beer
Department of Psychology
University of California-Berkeley

Leonard Berkowitz
Department of Psychology
University of Wisconsin-Madison

Gary G. Berntson
Department of Psychology
The Ohio State University

Kent C. Berridge
Department of Psychology
University of Michigan

Ian Brissette
Department of Psychology
Carnegie Mellon University

John T. Cacioppo
Department of Psychology
University of Chicago

Larry Cahill
Department of Neurobiology and Behavior, Center for the
    Neurobiology of Learning and Memory
University of California-Irvine

Laura L. Carstensen
Department of Psychology
Stanford University

Susan T. Charles
Department of Psychology and Social Behavior
University of California-Irvine

Margaret S. Clark
Department of Psychology
Carnegie Mellon University

Tim Dalgleish
Cognition and Brain Sciences Unit
Medical Research Council

Antonio R. Damasio
Department of Neurology
The University of Iowa

H. Damasio
Department of Neurology
The University of Iowa

Douglas Derryberry
Department of Psychology
Oregon State University

Raymond J. Dolan
Wellcome Department of Cognitive Neurology, London

Judy Dunn
Institute of Psychiatry; Social, Genetic, and
    Developmental Psychiatry Research Centre
King's College

Nancy Eisenberg
Department of Psychology
Arizona State University

Paul Ekman
Department of Psychiatry
University of California-San Francisco

Rebecca Elliott
Neuroscience and Psychiatry Unit
University of Manchester

Phoebe C. Ellsworth
Department of Psychology
University of Michigan

Leandre R. Fabrigar
Department of Psychology
Queen's University

Kurt W. Fischer
Graduate School of Education
Harvard University

Joseph P. Forgas
Department of Psychology
University of New South Wales

Robert H. Frank
Cornell University

Alf Gabrielsson
Department of Psychology
Uppsala University

Steven J. Garlow
Department of Psychiatry and Behavioral Sciences
Emory University School of Medicine

Janine Geise-Davis
Department of Psychiatry and Behavioral Sciences
Stanford University, School of Medicine

Gian C. Gonzaga
Department of Psychology
University of California-Berkeley

Jonathan Haidt
Department of Psychology
University of Virginia

Alfons O. Hamm
Department of Psychology
University of Griefswald

Kenneth Hugdahl
Department of Biological and Medical Psychology
University of Bergen

Thomas R. Insel
Center for Behavioral Neuroscience
Emory University

Derek M. Isaacowitz
Department of Psychology
University of Pennsylvania

Wilfrid Jänig
Psychologisches Institut
Christian-Albrechts-Universität zu Kiel

Tom Johnstone
Department of Psychology
University of Wisconsin-Madison

Patrik N. Juslin
Department of Psychology
Uppsala University

Jerome Kagan
Department of Psychology
Harvard University

Ned H. Kalin
Department of Psychiatry
University of Wisconsin-Madison

Dacher Keltner
Department of Psychology
University of California-Berkeley

Quinn Kennedy
Department of Psychology
Stanford University

Terence A. Ketter
Department of Psychiatry and Behavioral Sciences
Stanford University School of Medicine

Gundrun Klasmeyer
Department of Psychology
University of Geneva

Claire B. Kopp
School of Behavioral and Organizational Sciences
Claremont Graduate University

Heinz W. Krohne
Department of Psychology
University of Mainz

Kevin S. LaBar
Center for Cognitive Neuroscience and Department of
    Psychology: Experimental
Duke University

Mark R. Leary
Department of Psychology
Wake Forest University

Joseph E. LeDoux
Center for Neural Science
New York University

Anna Lembke
Department of Psychiatry and Behavioral Sciences
Stanford University School of Medicine

Jennifer S. Lerner
Department of Social and Decision Sciences
Carnegie Mellon University

Robert W. Levenson
Department of Psychology
University of California-Berkeley

Jin Li
Department of Education
Brown University

George Loewenstein
Department of Social and Decision Sciences
Carnegie Mellon University

Amanda R. Lorenz
Department of Psychology
University of Wisconsin-Madison

Sandy Losoya
Department of Psychology
Arizona State University

Michael F. Mascolo
Department of Psychology
Merrimack College

Bruce S. McEwen
Laboratory of Neuroendocrinology
The Rockefeller University

James L. McGaugh
Department of Neurobiology and Behavior, Center for the
    Neurobiology of Learning and Memory
University of California-Irvine

Batja Mesquita
Department of Psychology
Wake Forest University

Susan Mineka
Department of Psychology
Northwestern University

Charles B. Nemeroff
Department of Psychiatry and Behavioral Sciences
Emory University School of Medicine

Susan J. Neufeld
School of Behavioral and Organizational Sciences
Claremont Graduate University

Joseph P. Newman
Department of Psychology
University of Wisconsin-Madison

Jack B. Nitschke
Department of Psychology
University of Wisconsin-Madison

Keith Oatley
Ontario Institute for Studies in Education
University of Toronto

Kevin N. Ochsner
Department of Psychology
Harvard University

Arne Öhman
Department of Clinical Neuroscience
Karolinska Institutet

Richard E. Petty
Department of Psychology
The Ohio State University

Diego Pizzagalli
Department of Psychology
University of Wisconsin-Madison

Robert M. Post
Biological Psychiatry Branch
National Institute of Mental Health

Eshkol Rafaeli
Department of Psychology
Northwestern University

Scott L. Rauch
Departments of Psychiatry and Radiology & Harvard
    Medical School, Department of Psychiatry
Massachusetts General Hospital

Marjorie A. Reed
Department of Psychology
Oregon State University

Judy Reilly
Department of Psychology
San Diego State University

Paul Rozin
Department of Psychology
University of Pennsylvania

Carol D. Ryff
Department of Psychology
University of Wisconsin-Madison

Nadia Sachs
Department of Psychiatry and Behavioral Sciences
Stanford University School of Medicine

Peter Salovey
Department of Psychology
Yale University

Martin Sarter
Department of Psychology
The Ohio State University

Daniel L. Schacter
Department of Psychology
Harvard University

Harold T. Schupp
Department of Psychology
University of Griefswald

Teresa Seeman
Department of Medicine
UCLA School of Medicine, Division of Geriatrics

Laura Seibert
Department of Psychology
San Diego State University

Burton H. Singer
Woodrow Wilson School of Public and International
    Affairs
Princeton University

Charles T. Snowdon
Department of Psychology
University of Wisconsin-Madison

David Spiegel
Department of Psychology
Stanford University

Tracy Spinrad
Department of Family and Human Development
Arizona State University

Gerhard Stemmler
Department of Psychology
University of Marburg

Kjell Morten Stormark
Regional Competence Center for Child and Adolescent
    Psychiatry
University of Bergen

Po W. Wang
Department of Psychiatry and Behavioral Sciences
Stanford University School of Medicine

Duane T. Wegener
Department of Psychological Sciences
Purdue University

Almut I. Weike
Department of Psychology
University of Griefswald

Stefan Wiens
Department of Clinical Neuroscience
Karolinska Institutet

Iftah Yovel
Department of Psychology
Northwestern University

# INTRODUCTION

## Affective Sciences

Between the covers of this *Handbook* readers will find what we consider to be the core material, in terms of theory, methods, and empirical evidence, of an emergent scientific domain, affective science. It is not a "Handbook of Emotion." Affective science is a considerably broader concept that subsumes emotion but is not restricted to it. The purpose of this *Handbook* is to illustrate how many different disciplines are making fundamental contributions to the development of affective science and to provide a compendium for scholars inside and outside of this rapidly developing field. In addition, the chapters in this *Handbook* bring into focus the many specific areas in the neural, behavioral, and social sciences that are impacted by research on affective processes.

It is useful at the outset to offer working definitions of the various phenomena that are targets of inquiry within affective science, addressed in this *Handbook*. We distinguish among six major affective phenomena (see Scherer & Peper, in press, for a more detailed discussion of definitional issues). This is not meant to be an exhaustive list, but rather a catalog of the most frequently studied of the affective phenomena, prominently treated here. *Emotion* refers to a relatively brief episode of coordinated brain, autonomic, and behavioral changes that facilitate a response to an external or internal event of significance for the organism. *Feelings* are the subjective representation of emotions. Note that they can reflect any or all of the components that constitute emotion. *Mood* typically refers to a diffuse affective state that is often of lower intensity than emotion, but considerably longer in duration. Moods are not usually associated with the patterned expressive signs that typically accompany emotion and sometimes occur

without apparent cause. *Attitudes* are relatively enduring, affectively colored beliefs, preferences, and predispositions toward objects or persons. *Affective style* refers to relatively stable dispositions that bias an individual toward perceiving and responding to people and objects with a particular emotional quality, emotional dimension, or mood. *Temperament* refers to particular affective styles that are apparent early in life, and thus may be determined by genetic factors.

These are working definitions that provide a roadmap to the terrain that will be covered in this *Handbook*. There are some partial overlaps among these phenomena, and they are not offered as orthogonal constructs. For example, there are claims in the literature that moods and affective style will differentially weight the probability of experiencing particular emotions. Thus, an individual in a hostile mood may show an increased probability for experiencing anger. By distinguishing among these phenomena, we also do not wish to imply that they are necessarily generated by separate neural substrates. In fact, there is good evidence to suggest that at least some of the circuitry that underlies the episodic arousal of fear is also at work in producing an anxious mood or affective style.

## Scope of the *Handbook*

When we collectively first had the vision for this *Handbook*, we each had a conception of affective science that was considerably broader and more inclusive than was represented in any existing publication on emotion. Bringing different, but partially overlapping and complementary perspectives to bear, we were acutely aware that even though affective processes pervade much of the cognitive, biobehavioral, and social sciences, only a very small slice of this scholarship is generally identified as "emotion research." Indeed, many of the researchers who are doing cutting-edge work that we all considered to be within the rubric of affective science do not currently consider themselves to be affective scientists, let alone emotion psychologists. This is reminiscent of the early days of a number of multidisciplinary areas of science. For example, prior to appearance of Neisser's classic text in 1967 entitled *Cognitive Psychology*, many of the scientists who Neisser considered to be prototypic examples of cognitive psychologists did not identify themselves in this way. Neisser's volume helped to focus, integrate, and catalyze that field, which has since become the dominant approach in academic psychology. Similarly, when neuroscience first came on the scene as a discipline, many of the practitioners did not consider themselves to be neuroscientists, but rather pharmacologists, endocrinologists, cell biologists, or physiological psychologists. It was not until the Society for Neuroscience was founded, and specialized journals in neuroscience appeared in print, that this discipline experienced the extraordinary growth that we have witnessed over the past two decades. One other example is pertinent here—the emergence of cognitive neuroscience. Probably the most rapidly growing multidisciplinary field in the biobehavioral sciences today, cognitive neuroscience barely existed a decade ago. The publication of the *Handbook of Cognitive Neurosciences* (which just appeared in a new and expanded second edition; Gazzaniga, 2000), along with the publication of the *Journal of Cognitive Neuroscience*, helped to propel this field into the forefront of academic and popular interest. Many of the individuals who have become important voices in this movement were conducting research similar to what they are still doing now, though it was not being performed under the banner of cognitive neuroscience and was likely appreciated by a considerably smaller and less interdisciplinary audience.

Similarly, while there has been an enormous expansion of research on affective phenomena in the social sciences (and the humanities, for that matter), this research is rarely considered as part of the affective sciences. Rather, the widespread tendency toward compartmentalization within established classical disciplines such as anthropology, sociology, or social psychology prevents scholars working on affective processes from sharing information and integrating their approaches. However, there have been some pioneering efforts to cross boundaries, as in the establishment of a research society for emotion research (International Society for Research on Emotions), the establishment of a new interdisciplinary journal published by the American Psychological Association called *Emotion*, and the development of the nascent fields of affective (e.g., Davidson & Sutton, 1995) and social neuroscience (e.g., Cacioppo, Berntson, Sheridan, & McClintock, 2000).

Based on these examples from recent history, we suggest that the formal constitution of the area of affective science can have a seminal effect on research in this area and lead to a degree of scientific exchange and research collaboration that could revolutionize our approach to studying affective phenomena.

Affective science today can be likened to cognitive science at the end of the 1960s. We believe it is just on the threshold of major new insights that will profoundly influence many areas of the biobehavioral and social sciences. Affective processes are responsible for mobilizing the individual's resources to cope with the unexpected, to avoid punishment, and to secure nourishment and pleasure. They are key to social interaction, reproductive success, personality development, and vulnerability to psychopathology. Given their strategic role in the adaptation to the physical and social environment, they are likely to have been selected for over the course of evolution, as suggested first by Charles Darwin in 1872.

One of the most important roles of affective phenomena is their regulatory function in relationships, social interaction, and group organization. The expressive signals that accompany many affective processes allow efficient communication of significant information among conspecifics in a rapid and flexible fashion. Therefore, the expression of emotional reactions in face, voice, and body has often been considered as a royal road to the understanding of affect. Thus, it is not surprising that research on affective expression lies at the core of affective science, particularly because it is directly observable and thus can be measured objectively.

Finally, affective processes are relevant to health. The age-old adage that stress leads to illness is likely to contain an important nugget of truth, although it is unlikely that there is a simple, unidirectional relationship. Of course, the mechanisms by which such effects occur are not fully understood, but today there is little disagreement that affective processes play a major role in the inception of and recovery from physical illness. Dysfunctions in affective processes also lie at the core of virtually all forms of psychopathology, and differences among individuals in certain parameters of affective functioning are likely associated with differential vulnerability to particular types of pathology.

## The Organization of the *Handbook*

In this *Handbook*, we attempt to cover this vast terrain and to provide representative, albeit not exhaustive, reviews of areas that we consider key to each of the major domains enumerated or implied above. We have grouped these areas into parts, each of which has been edited by a specialist in the areas represented in the part. In addition, each part editor has contributed an introduction to this domain, which outlines the major issues and research approaches. The first two parts on the neuroscience and autonomic psychophysiology of emotion address the biological underpinnings of affective phenomena, with the first section devoted to the brain mechanisms underlying affective processes and the second addressing the autonomic concomitants of affect. There has been great progress in the biological study of emotion, with remarkable convergence occurring for the first time in the human and animal research traditions. The detailed circuitry that has been the subject of painstaking research with laboratory animals at the molecular and systems levels in the past few decades is now being addressed for the first time in humans, mostly through brain imaging studies. The autonomic correlates of emotion are being studied in their appropriate biological context with an appreciation for the functional role that autonomic nervous system (ANS) activity might be playing. Moreover, the mechanisms by which the central circuitry underlying affective processes exert downstream effects on the ANS and other bodily systems (e.g., the endocrine and immune systems) are now being elucidated in exquisite detail. We know that once ANS activation occurs in the periphery, it feeds back to the brain and may modulate ongoing brain activity. The brain and body are probably more intimately linked in affective processes than they are in any other major domain of psychological function, reflecting the importance of system coordination or synchronization as a constitutive factor of affect. Ever since the pioneering emotion theory suggested by William James (1890), theorists in this area have afforded feedback from the periphery a primary role in the production of affective tone.

Major transitions occur in affective processes over the course of development and are the subject of the third part, "Genetics and Development." The role of emotional development has been a central issue in developmental psychology since its inception (e.g., Campos, Barrett, Lamb, Goldsmith, & Stenberg, 1983), and a special role has been assigned to the study of facial and vocal expression in infants unable to self-report on their affective states. Relatedly, both quantitative behavior genetics and more recently, molecular genetics, have made enormous strides in helping us to appreciate the role of genetic factors in affective processes and to illustrate the dynamic relationship between genes and environment. Variations in gene expression can be produced by early social and emotional events, and these effects can then have profound consequences for the biology and experience of emotion that can persist for a lifetime (e.g., Francis, Diorio, Liu, & Meany, 1999).

Another feature that distinguishes emotion from other psychological processes is the public nature of the expressive signals that accompany at least some affective phenomena. What are the determinants of facial and vocal signs of emotion? When and how are they socially controlled or regulated? Are there expressive signs of mood and affective traits? Are there continuities between expressive signals in humans and nonhuman primates? What are the mechanisms and biases in the perception of emotional expression and the inference of underlying affect? These are some of the key questions addressed in part IV on the expression of emotion.

Affect does not occur in a vacuum in the human mind and/or body. It typically co-occurs with other classes of psychological processes, the most important of which is cognition. The study of affect-cognition relations, particularly the cognitive antecedents of emotion and the cognitive consequences of affect for diverse functions such as memory, decision making, and language, is a central focus of research in the affective sciences. The neural circuitry underlying components of affect and cognition largely overlaps, and this overlap provides important clues for how the processes will interact. All of these questions are taken up in part V on the cognitive components of emotion. This is a core area in affective science addressing many issues that are fundamental for both cognitive and affective science, providing a meeting point for scholars from many different traditions.

Affective processes are central to our understanding of both personality and social behavior. Virtually all dimensions of personality that have received empirical attention over the past 50 years have affective components at their core. And much of the phenomena of social psychology—attitudes, prejudice, prosocial behavior, and aggression—include important affective components. Parts VI (personality) and VII (emotion and social processes) highlight some of the most important developments in these areas. Given the important role of emotion in social interaction, particularly for social relationships, it is not surprising that social psychological theorizing and research play increasingly important roles in the affective sciences. Their influence is particularly noticeable in the area of emotion-cognition interaction, owing to the dominant role of the cognitive approach in current social psychology.

Cultural influences on the various components of emotion and other affective processes are the subject of part VIII. All affective processes occur in a sociocultural context, and there may be profound influences by culture on affective processes. These influences are not limited to the semantic or subjective level; they can "get under the skin" and influence the biological processes underlying emotion in significant ways. Apart from examining cultural variability, cross-cultural comparisons can also reveal regularities that allow us to make inferences about universal features of emotion. As shown by the contributions in part VIII, the data from intercultural research on emotional antecedents and reactions provide some of the most compelling evidence for the presence of biologically based, species-general features of affective responding.

Historically there has been little interchange between

basic research on affective processes and clinical concerns with psychopathology. Even work on mood or emotional disorders has rarely appealed to the corpus of basic research on emotion and mood for insights, and vice versa. One goal of part IX on emotion and psychopathology is to begin to redress this imbalance and to call for a more integrative strategy for research in this area. In this section are featured some of the most promising trends in this emerging integration, ranging from cognitive to neurobiological to developmental approaches. We believe that future research on mood and anxiety disorders will need to make contact with the growing corpus of relevant work on cognitive and neural underpinnings of emotion and mood. This is beginning to occur in the neuroscience area where insights from research on the neural substrates of basic processes of emotion and emotion regulation help to better understand abnormalities in affective processing in different forms of psychopathology (e.g., Davidson, Putnam, & Larson, 2000).

Finally, part X contains contributions on the relations between emotion and health. The popular press is replete with descriptions of putative relations between stress and illness, and there are also some suggestions that positive affect may have salubrious effects. What are the mechanisms by which this type of influence might occur? Are individuals who exhibit high levels of emotional stability and of well-being also those who are resilient with respect to physical health and illness? Can different types of "emotion work" in patients with a terminal illness like cancer improve or impair their prognosis and influence the course of the disease? What makes these questions particularly exciting is that newly developed, powerful methods in the biobehavioral sciences hold promise for an unprecedented increase in our understanding of the mechanisms by which affective processes can influence health.

## Some Limitations

In the course of planning and editing this volume, we quickly realized that even the most comprehensive handbook could not possibly encompass all the material that is pertinent to theory and research, particularly in the case of a multidisciplinary domain. We decided to privilege depth rather than exhaustiveness and asked the part editors to invite contributors to write synthetic chapters that illustrate the respective phenomena in their context and that render the underlying mechanisms comprehensible to a wide readership rather than providing compendia of research summaries. This required some selectivity and thus some topics and some research traditions are absent from particular sections. At the same time, part editors tried hard to ensure that most major theoretical approaches and the most important classic and recent research findings are represented. Where necessary, they have also noted in their section introductions specific topics of import that could not be included.

There are also a number of broad themes that we had decided not to include in this *Handbook*. For example, given the large diversity of the foundational sources in the many disciplines that contribute to affective science, we have not included a section on the history of theory and research in this area. However, many of the chapters include some historical review of the literature pertinent to a particular theme.

Relatedly, we have not included a section on the grand theories of emotion because other recent surveys are available (e.g., Scherer, 2000). We also believe that the field has matured since the days of the preeminence of grand theories of emotion. Much of current research, while sometimes inspired by grand theories, or more often middle-range theories and models, focus on more limited, but more precisely defined, topics within affective science. As a consequence, while we have endeavored to include chapters rich in theoretical content, these contributions are mostly focused on specific phenomena and do not reflect the breadth of the grand theories more typical of scholarship in the early stages of research on emotion. The data generated by affective science research in recent years have highlighted the complexity of affective processing and the failure of the grand theories to account for much of this complexity. An effort to achieve this would be analogous to proposing a grand theory of cognition, a project that would not be looked upon favorably by modern cognitive science. There is also no special section on methods in affective science. Affective science has now attracted such a plethora of sophisticated methods that it would be difficult to cover all of the relevant methods in a single section, short of attempting an overview of the methods of all of the biobehavioral and social sciences. The absence of a methods section is also justified by the fact that quite a number of handbooks on methods are currently available—for example, on psychophysiological measurement (Cacioppo, Berntson, & Tassinary, 2000), neuroimaging (Toga, 1996), measurement of nonverbal behavior (Scherer & Ekman, 1984), and many others. Furthermore, throughout the *Handbook*, specific methods are introduced where appropriate to a particular question.

Another broad domain that is conspicuously absent in this *Handbook* is application (with the exception of health-related research). Affective science approaches have now made major inroads into research on applied problems such as sports, organizational behavior and management, travel and leisure, traffic and city planning, and law and crime, to name but a few. Again, a separate volume would have been required to do justice to the wide variety of important research activity on affective phenomena in these applied areas.

## Outlook

Having gone through the long but rewarding process of assembling this handbook, we are surprised ourselves at just how vibrant and diverse affective science really is. From cultural value systems to assemblies of molecules in the brain, the reach of affective science is extraordinary and its import for vast domains of the biobehavioral and social sciences is inestimable. We hope that this handbook will serve as the major reference compendium for research in affective science for the next decade. We also hope that the next generation of scholars, our current graduate students and postdoctoral fellows, will benefit from finding united in a single volume the full panoply of scholarship in affective science and will glean the importance of interdisciplinary training so central to progress in affective science. Most important, we hope that the scholarly reviews of the issues and the challenge of the unresolved puzzles will spark new affective science research that will firmly establish this field as the primary home for work on the behavioral and neural components of affective processes that has defied systematic scientific inquiry for the past two centuries.

## REFERENCES

Cacioppo, J. T., Berntson, G. G., Sheridan, J. F., & McClintock, M. K. (2000). Multi-level integrative analyses of human behavior: Social neuroscience and the complementing nature of social and biological approaches. *Psychological Bulletin, 126,* 829–843.

Cacioppo, J. T., Berntson, G., & Tassinary, L. (Eds.). (2000). *Principles of psychophysiology,* 2nd ed. New York: Cambridge University Press.

Campos, J. J., Barrett, K., Lamb, M. E., Goldsmith, H. H., & Stenberg, C. (1983). Socioemotional development. In M. M. Haith & J. J. Campos (Eds.), *Infancy and developmental psychobiology (Vol. 2).* In P. H. Mussen (Series Ed.), *Handbook of Child Psychology,* 4th ed. (pp. 783–915). New York: Wiley.

Darwin, C. (1998). *The expression of emotion in man and animals* (3rd ed.). New York: Oxford University Press.

Davidson, R. J., Putnam, K. M., & Larson, C. L. (2000). Dysfunction in the neural circuitry of emotion regulation—A possible prelude to violence. *Science, 289,* 591–594.

Davidson, R. J., & Sutton, S. K. (1995). Affective neuroscience: The emergence of a discipline. *Current Opinion in Neurobiology 5,* 217–224.

Francis, D., Diorio, J., Liu, D., & Meany, M. J. (1999). Nongenomic transmission across generations of maternal behavior and stress responses in the rat. *Science, 286,* 1155–1158.

Gazzaniga, M. S. (Ed.). (2000). *The new cognitive neuroscience,* 2nd ed. Cambridge, MA: MIT Press.

James, W. (1890) *The principles of psychology.* New York: Holt.

Neisser, U. (1967) *Cognitive psychology.* Englewood, NJ: Appleton-Century Crofts.

Scherer, K. R. (2000). Psychological models of emotion. In J. Borod (Ed.), *The neuropsychology of emotion* (pp. 137–162). Oxford/New York: Oxford University Press.

Scherer, K. R., & Ekman, P. (1984). *Handbook of methods in nonverbal behavioral research (Studies in Emotion and Social Interaction).* Cambridge: Cambridge University Press.

Scherer, K. R., & Peper, M. (in press). Psychological theories of emotion and neuropsychological research. In F. Boller & J. Grafman (Eds.), *Handbook of Neuropsychology. Vol. 5 (Emotional behavior and its disorders,* ed. G. Gainotti). Amsterdam: Elsevier.

Toga, A. W. (1996). *Brain mapping methods.* San Diego: Academic Press.

# Neuroscience

# INTRODUCTION: NEUROSCIENCE

Richard J. Davidson, Klaus R. Scherer, and H. Hill Goldsmith

Over the past decade there has been a remarkable explosion of research on the neural substrates of affective processing. This work has involved a diverse range of species and has included many different methods. The chapters in this first part of the *Handbook* provide a roadmap and overview of this growing area. We place this part first because it provides the foundation for the parts that follow. We also wish to call attention to the possibility that neuroscience approaches to affective processes offer the potential of providing new ways of parsing the landscape of affect and have implications for many of the domains of affective science that follow in this *Handbook*.

For many years, the study of emotion lay dormant in the biobehavioral sciences. While both William James (1890) and Walter Cannon (1929) described changes in brain function that accompanied emotion, it has only been during the past 30 years when the corpus of literature at the animal level has developed significantly (see LeDoux, 1987, for review). Similarly, while case reports of emotional changes in patients with localized lesions have been in the literature for more than 100 years (e.g., Harlow, 1868), it is only recently that more systematic studies of the emotional behavior of patients with discrete lesions have been published.

The past decade has witnessed a veritable plethora of new texts on the neuroscience of emotion including Damasio (1994), LeDoux (1996), Panksepp (1998), and Rolls (1999). There has been a general recognition in the scientific community that the study of the neural substrates of at least some affective processes is tractable and has the potential of informing our understanding of the etiology of certain forms of psychopathology, of the relations between emotions and health, and of normal processes of emotional development and personality. This body of research is giving rise to the development of a new subdiscipline that has been termed affective neuroscience (Davidson & Sutton, 1995). Affective neuroscience shares many of the same conceptual and methodological approaches with its cognate discipline cognitive neuroscience. And in fact, as will be made more explicit below, the study of the neural substrates of affective and cognitive processes must proceed hand-in-hand since these processes are not clearly segregated in the brain, and are integrated seamlessly in everyday behavior and experience.

## The Chapters of This Part

The chapters that were selected for this part provide a broad overview of the different approaches, perspectives, methods, and levels of analysis in contemporary research on the neuroscience of emotion. One of the most important general themes that will emerge from reading this section is that the literature on nonhumans and humans is converging and integrated. There was a period earlier in the 1900s when research on emotion and motivation in nonhuman species was quite segregated from our understanding of the neural substrate of human emotion. More systematic examination of the emotional behavior of patients with discrete lesions and the advent of neuroimaging studies of emotion in humans has helped to bridge the chasm between these research traditions.

The chapter by Davidson and colleagues provides a broad overview of the circuitry underlying emotion and emotion regulation. Emphasis is placed on the different territories of the prefrontal cortex (PFC), anterior cingulate, hippocampus, and amygdala. Information is drawn from experiments in nonhuman species as well as in human lesion and neuroimaging studies. This circuitry is used to parse different subcomponents of emotion and affective style. *Affective style* refers to individual differences in parameters of emotional reactivity. These findings are then used to illuminate potential targets for understanding disorders of emotion, particularly mood and anxiety disorders.

The chapter by Kent Berridge in this part explicitly integrates the literature on nonhuman and human research and focuses on a number of subcortical and cortical regions that have been implicated in different aspects of affective phenomena. Berridge's chapter also provides a brief introduction to the various methods of interrogating the brain that have been featured in modern affective neuroscience research. An important issue addressed by Berridge, and one that has not received sufficient attention, is the similarities and differences in the study of affective neuroscience in nonhumans and humans. The issue of species differences in the functional neuroanatomy and the constraints on causal mechanisms in many human studies are crucial problems for the student of this topic to be aware of when reading this literature.

LaBar and LeDoux also illustrate how similar mechanisms can be studied in both humans and animals. They specifically focus on fear conditioning in their chapter since it is this experimental model that has probably yielded the largest corpus of evidence in affective neuroscience to date. One of the virtues of this experimental model is that very similar procedures can be used in both animals and humans. In nonhuman animals, they illustrate how some of the molecular mechanisms of emotional learning can be studied; and in humans, they show how fear conditioning can be used in conjunction with both the lesion method and with neuroimaging to investigate the role of the amygdala in human fear learning.

Damasio and his colleagues have effectively exploited the lesion method in humans to illuminate the contributions of different components of cortical and subcortical circuitry to particular types of affective processes. Their chapter highlights the role of right-hemisphere cortical regions and the amygdala and prefrontal cortices to particular components of emotional processing. Using their extensive registry of patients, they are able to identify those with very selective focal lesions to examine the impact of damage in these areas on performance of particular types of emotion-related tasks. This type of work provides a very important bridge between invasive studies in nonhuman animals and human neuroimaging studies. As will be discussed below, while human imaging studies have provided very important new information, they are also limited because they are essentially restricted to providing correlational evidence.

The chapter by McGaugh and Cahill provides an overview of an important body of work on the neural substrates of the links between emotion and memory. Our memories for emotional events are often more robust than memory for nonemotional events. Emotional episodes tend to be salient and to be better recalled. McGaugh and Cahill have amassed a considerable corpus of data on this topic to elucidate the mechanisms by which emotionally arousing events are encoded. They show that both central and peripheral processes contribute to these effects and that endogenous stress hormones affect the amgydala to modulate memory storage in other parts of the brain in response to emotionally arousing events.

Elliott and Dolan provide an overview of the role of the medial prefrontal cortex in aspects of mood and mood regulation and its implications for understanding the neural abnormalities in depression. This region of the brain has important upstream projections from brain neuromodulating systems (e.g., the dopaminergic system). In addition, there are two-way projections between this region and the limbic structures implicated in emotion such as the amygdala. Medial PFC abnormalities have been found in depression, and this region is activated in response to emotion inductions in normal subjects.

## Relations to Other Sections of the *Handbook*

The second part of this *Handbook* is devoted to autonomic nervous system (ANS) function in emotion. While the central nervous system obviously represents and controls the autonomic nervous system, there is also important feedback from the ANS to the central nervous system that serves to modulate central function. In addition, there is a large literature on ANS function in emotion that has emerged somewhat independently of research on the central mechanisms of emotion. However, in any complete accounting of the brain and emotion, the ANS should have a prominent role. Since the time of James (1890), the ANS has figured importantly in many influential theoretical accounts of emotion.

The third part, on "Genetics and Development," contains chapters that present evidence related to central mechanisms underlying temperament (e.g., Kagan, chapter 17). There is a growing literature on developmental changes in brain structure and function that bear importantly on understanding emotional development. Much of this work is still in the embryonic stages since the tools for investigating brain function in humans are still quite new. We expect that in 10 years, the knowledge in this area will grow considerably.

The chapter by Davidson et al. in this part presents an overview of their research program on affective style, or individual differences in different parameters of emotional reactivity. This section could just as easily have been placed in part VI, "Personality." The study of individual differences in the central circuitry of emotion and its relation to personality differences is a burgeoning area. While some of this work is reviewed in the Davidson et al. chapter, there is other work that could not be included because of limitations on space. Included among this latter category are studies on individual differences in neurochemical function and their relation to affective traits (e.g., Depue & Collins, 1999), and studies of individual differences in genetic polymorphisms related to affective function (e.g., Manuck, Flory, Ferrell, Mann, & Muldoon, 2000).

The final two parts of the *Handbook* contain chapters on emotion and health and emotion and psychopathology. Each of these parts contains material of direct relevance to the neuroscience of emotion, and in some cases, placement of chapters in one or another section is arbitrary. The Elliott and Dolan chapter in this section could just as easily have been placed in part IX, "Emotion and Psychopathology." It is included here because it draws upon the literature on the neural substrates of normal mood in formulating a model of dysfunctions in depression. Similarly, the Rauch and Insel chapters in part IX could have been placed in the neuroscience section. The last part of the *Handbook* on health and emotion also contains chapters that could well have appeared in this first part. Chapters 58 and 59 both address the central substrates of stress, allostatis, and their relation to peripheral biology that is relevant to health. The conceptual approaches advanced in these latter chapters underscore the importance of the connections between the central circuitry of emotion and the periphery. The growing corpus of data on this topic is providing the beginning of a mechanistic account of how emotions may affect physical health and illness.

## Some General Lessons from Research on the Neuroscience of Emotion

There are some important generalities that can now be offered regarding the neuroscience of emotion. First, the classic concept of the "limbic system" as being the seat of emotion has now effectively been challenged (see LeDoux, 1987). Along with challenging the limbic system concept, modern research illustrates how there is no single region of the brain dedicated to emotion but, rather, different aspects of emotion processing are distributed in different brain circuits. The notion that emotions were somehow limbic and subcortical and cognitions cortical is giving way to a much more refined and complex view. The older notions helped to perpetuate anachronistic dichotomies

between thought and feeling. More modern approaches exemplified in the chapters in this part clearly indicate that the substrates of complex emotion and cognition overlap considerably. It is simply not possible to identify regions of the brain devoted exclusively to affect or exclusively to cognition. This fact should dispel claims about their independence and help to foster a more nuanced appreciation of the ways in which affect and cognition interact. The work of Damasio and his colleagues (see chapter in this part) has helped to cogently illustrate why emotion is essential for certain types of cognition functioning. In particular, they illustrate how complex decision making is deleteriously affected if a patient has a lesion in the ventromedial PFC, an important area that subserves both affective and cognitive functions. Certain types of complex decisions in life, such as who to marry, what house to buy, are the types of decisions that simply cannot be made on the basis of a cold cognitive calculus. These decisions, as Damasio and colleagues argue, require emotion. In evaluating the potential choices such decisions present, we will typically "consult our emotions" and forecast our emotional reactions. Patients with lesions to the ventromedial PFC are impaired in their ability to affectively forecast and thus are deficient in their decision-making capacities.

Second, modern brain research on emotion illustrates how many emotion-related processes occur implicitly. For example, autonomic and expressive changes in response to emotional stimuli and components of emotional learning can occur without much effort and sometimes without awareness (e.g., Ohman & Soares, 1998). It is clear that some components of our emotional behavior and expression do not require explicit processing. Observations of this type have important implications for research that seeks to relate brain function and the subjective experience of emotion and suggest that at least some neural events are unlikely to have correlates in experience. It also underscores the fact that research strategies that rely upon self-reports of emotion are likely to miss a substantial portion of important affective processing.

Third, work on the neuroscience of emotion is providing new schemes for parsing emotional processes. Such schemes are likely to be different from the typologies that we have inherited from work on the self-report of emotion or research on facial expressions of emotions. The self-report tradition has largely emphasized dimensions such as valence and arousal while the facial expression tradition places greater emphasis on discrete emotions such as happiness, sadness, anger, fear, and disgust. There are notable exceptions to these generalizations, but by and large they represent the normative traditions in these areas. Research on the neuroscience of emotion is leading to different ways of parsing aspects of emotional processing. This is not to imply that there is unlikely to be found circuitry associated with dimensional and discrete components of emotion. Rather, it is meant to underscore the fact that there will be other ways of parsing the landscape of emotion processing when we use neural circuitry as our starting point. For example, we used information on brain circuitry to help identify different aspects of emotion regulation (Davidson, Jackson, & Kalin, 2000; Davidson, Putnam, & Larson, 2000). They have argued that some forms of emotion regulation are autonomic, such as modulating emotional responses on the basis of contextual information. The hippocampus is likely to play a role in this form of regulation, and variations in hippocampal structure and function likely contribute to individual differences in the context-modulation of emotional reactivity. Another example from my own work is the distinction between pre- and post-goal attainment positive affect (Davidson, 2000). Pre-goal attainment positive affect is that form of positive affect that arises as one gets progressively closer to a desired goal while post-goal attainment positive affect is aroused following the acquisition of a desired goal. I have suggested (Davidson, 2000) that regions of the prefrontal cortex are required for pre-goal attainment positive affect since this requires the instantiation of an appetitive goal toward which behavior is directed. There are data and theory that suggest that pre-goal attainment positive affect may be particularly impaired in at least a subgroup of patients with major depressive disorder (Davidson, Pizzagalli, Nitschke, & Putnam, 2002).

One of the principles derived from research on the neuroscience of emotion is that clues to the contribution of a particular brain region to affective processes can be gleaned from other domains of investigation where that brain region has been a target of study. For example, there is now a large corpus of data on the role of different territories of the PFC in emotion. It seems that one function of at least some regions of the PFC in emotion is to provide an affective working memory. Much of the affect of everyday life occurs in the absence of the physical stimuli that elicit affect. We either maintain emotion following the offset of affective events or we anticipate the occurrence of particular events that are affectively salient. In both of these cases, emotion is generated in the absence of physically present elicitors. The PFC in these cases likely plays an important role in sustaining the affect. Such affective working memory likely plays an important role in motivation and in guiding behavior on the avoidance of potentially harmful situations and the approach toward potentially appetitive situations.

## Modern Methodological Innovations of Relevance to Affective Neuroscience

It is important in an introduction of this sort to acknowledge the importance of methodological innovations in the evolution of research in this area and to call attention to methodological developments on the horizon that are likely to be featured in research in affective neuroscience. At the nonhuman level, major developments in molecular genetics are having an enormous impact (e.g., Watson, Meng, Thompson, & Akil, 2000). Gene chips are enabling investigators to examine gene expression in thousands of genes simultaneously from localized brain tissue. This work is greatly facilitating our understanding of how social-emotional events get "under the skin" and actually change gene expression to alter the emotional circuitry of the brain (Meaney, 2001).

There are important new developments in human brain imaging that will also play an important role in affective neuroscience. One of these is the development of diffusion tensor imaging (DTI), a technique that enables tract tracing noninvasively (Melhem et al., 2002). Using DTI, investigators can now trace white matter connections among different brain regions. When this information is combined with functional activation maps, circuitry can be more clearly identified and delineated. This work will help to establish the role of distributed circuits in complex affective processes and will lead to more sophisticated hypotheses about the interactions among different regions of the brain that participate in specific subcomponents of emotion.

Another important method that is just now being used in studies of normal and disordered emotion is transcranial magnetic stimulation (TMS). TMS is a method that enables an investigator to temporarily activate or inactivate a cortical region selectively using an exogenously imposed high field strength magnetic field (e.g., Post & Keck, 2001). There is currently a plethora of research using this method to examine its potential efficacy in the treatment of mood disorders. In addition, it can be used as a powerful research tool to examine causal hypotheses about the potential role of different cortical regions in emotion by manipulating the activity of those regions and observing their impact on tasks that reflect mood. TMS can also be used together with neuroimaging (both PET and fMRI) to probe the functional connectivity between brain regions. For example, the effects of prefrontal cortical stimulation on the amygdala and other limbic structures can be studied.

## Conclusions

Reading the chapters in this part should be sufficient to persuade the reader that this is an area of the affective sciences that is burgeoning with new information. The convergence in methods, approaches, and concepts between research in nonhuman animals and humans is providing the beginnings of an integrated understanding of the neuroscience of emotion for the first time. This work is promising to yield new insights, provide new ways of parsing the terrain of emotion, and offer new targets for therapeutic interventions for patients suffering from disorders of emotion. The new methods involving both molecular genetic approaches and brain imaging underscore the possibilities for the development of this area in the near future. I expect that within the next decade, the scientific literature on the neuroscience of emotion will be so extensive as to warrant an entire handbook just on this topic.

## REFERENCES

Cannon, W. B. (1929). *Bodily changes in pain, hunger, fear and rage.* New York: Appleton.

Damasio, A. R. (1994). *Descartes-error: Emotion, reason, and the human brain.* New York: Avon Books.

Darwin, C. (1998) *The expression of emotion in man and animals* (3rd ed.). New York: Oxford University Press.

Davidson, R. J. (2000). Affective style, psychopathology and resilience: Brain mechanisms and plasticity. *American Psychologist, 55,* 1196–1214.

Davidson, R. J., Jackson, D. C., & Kalin, N. H. (2000). Emotion, plasticity, context, and regulation: Perspectives from affective neuroscience. *Psychological Bulletin, 126,* 890–909.

Davidson, R. J., Pizzagalli, D., Nitschke, J. B., & Putnam, K. M. (2002). Depression: Perspectives from affective neuroscience. *Annual Review of Psychology, 53,* 545–574.

Davidson, R. J., Putnam, K. M., & Larson, C. L. (2000). Dysfunction in the neural circuitry of emotion regulation—a possible prelude to violence. *Science, 289,* 591–594.

Davidson, R. J., & Sutton, S. K. (1995). Affective neuroscience: The emergence of a discipline. *Current Opinion in Neurobiology, 5,* 217–224.

Depue, R. A., & Collins, P. F. (1999). Neurobiology of the structure of personality: Dopamine, facilitation of incentive motivation, and extraversion. *Behavioral and Brain Sciences, 22,* 491–569.

Harlow, J. M. (1868). Recovery from the passage of an iron bar through the head. *Publications of the Massachusetts Medical Society, 3,* 1–21.

James, W. (1890). *The principles of psychology.* New York: Holt.

LeDoux, J. E. (1987). Emotion. In F. Plum (Ed.), *Handbook of physiology. 1: The nervous system. Vol. V. Higher functions of the brain* (pp. 419–460). Bethesda, MD: American Physiological Society.

LeDoux, J. E. (1996). *The emotional brain: The mysterious underpinnings of emotional life.* New York: Simon & Schuster.

Manuck, S. B., Flory, J. D., Ferrell, R. E., Mann, J. J., & Muldoon, M. F. (2000). A regulatory polymorphism of the monoamine oxidase-A gene may be associated with variability in aggression, impulsivity, and central nervous system serotonergic responsivity. *Psychiatry Research, 95,* 9–23.

Meaney, M. J. (2001). Maternal care, gene expression, and the transmission of individual differences in stress reactivity across generations. *Annual Review of Neuroscience, 24,* 1161–1192.

Melhem, E. R., Mori, S., Mukundan, G., Kraut, M. A., Pomper, M. G., & van Zijl, P. C. (2002). Diffusion tensor MR imaging of the brain and white matter tractography. *American Journal of Roentgenology, 178,* 3–16.

Ohman, A., & Soares, J. J. F. (1998). Emotional conditioning to masked stimuli: Expectancies for aversive outcomes following nonrecognized fear-relevant stimuli. *Journal of Experimental Psychology: General, 127,* 69–82.

Panksepp, J. (1998). *Affective neuroscience: The foundations of human and animal emotions.* New York: Oxford University Press.

Post, A., & Keck, M. E. (2001). Transcranial magnetic stimulation as a therapeutic tool in psychiatry: What do we know about the neurobiological mechanisms? *Journal of Psychiatric Research, 35,* 193–215.

Rolls, E. T. (1999). *The brain and emotion.* New York: Oxford University Press.

Watson, S. J., Meng, F., Thompson, R. C., & Akil, H. (2000). The "chip" as a specific genetic tool. *Biological Psychiatry, 48,* 1147–1156.

# PARSING THE SUBCOMPONENTS OF EMOTION AND DISORDERS OF EMOTION: PERSPECTIVES FROM AFFECTIVE NEUROSCIENCE

Richard J. Davidson, Diego Pizzagalli,
Jack B. Nitschke, and Ned H. Kalin

Affective neuroscience is the subdiscipline of the biobehavioral sciences that examines the underlying neural bases of mood and emotion. The application of this body of theory and data to the understanding of individual differences in affective style, mood regulation, and mood disorders is helping to generate a new understanding of the brain circuitry underlying these phenomena. At a more general level, this approach is helping to bridge the wide chasm between the literatures that have focused on normal emotion and the disorders of emotion. Historically, these research traditions have had little to do with one another and have emerged completely independently. However, affective neuroscience has helped to integrate these approaches into a more unified project that is focused on the understanding of normal and pathological individual differences in affective style, its constituent components, and their neural bases (see, e.g., Davidson, Jackson, & Kalin, 2000; Davidson, 2000).

Affective neuroscience takes as its overall aims a project that is similar to that pursued by its cognate discipline, cognitive neuroscience, though focused instead on affective processes. The decomposition of cognitive processes into more elementary constituents that can then be studied in neural terms has been remarkably successful. We no longer query subjects about the contents of their cognitive processes since many of the processes so central to important aspects of cognitive function are opaque to consciousness. Instead, modern cognitive scientists and neuroscientists have developed laboratory tasks to interrogate and reveal more elementary cognitive function. These more elementary processes can then be studied using imaging methods in humans, lesion methods in animals, and the study of human patients with focal brain damage. Affective neuroscience approaches emotion using the same strategy. Global constructs of emotion are giving way to more specific and elementary constituents that can be examined with objective laboratory measures. For example, the time course of emotional responding and the mechanisms that are brought into play during the regulation of emotion can now be probed using objective laboratory measures. These constructs may be particularly important for understanding individual differences in affective style since the key characteristic of variations in mood among individuals is the extent to which negative affect persists versus subsides rapidly. Moreover, these ideas have significant import for understanding disorders of mood. Some patients with mood disorders may have a particular problem with persistence of negative affect while other patients may have a primary deficit in reactivity to positive incentives.

Previously, constructs such as emotion regulation have mostly been gleaned from self-report measures whose validity has been seriously questioned (e.g., Kahneman, 1999). While the phenomenology of emotion provides critical information to the subject that helps guide behavior, it may not be a particularly good source for making inferences about the processes and mechanisms that underlie emotion and its regulation. Though it is still tempting and often important to obtain measures of subjects' conscious experience of the contents of their emotional states and traits, these no longer constitute the sole source of information about emotion.

Since there are recent reviews of the basic literature on the circuitry underlying emotion and emotion regulation (e.g., Davidson & Irwin, 1999; Davidson, Jackson, et al., 2000; Davidson, Putnam, & Larson, 2000; Rolls, 1999), these data will not be systematically reviewed in this chapter. We emphasize studies that have been published in the past three years since two recent reviews cover much of the literature prior to this time (Davidson, Abercrombie, Nitschke, & Putnam, 1999; Drevets, 1998). A major focus of this chapter will be on individual differences in affective style and how such variability across individuals can be captured using objective laboratory probes rather than relying exclusively upon self-report data.

We have two broad goals for this chapter:

1. To review the functional role of the prefrontal cortices, anterior cingulate, hippocampus, and amygdala in affect and emotion regulation (see Figure 2.1 for a depiction of these structures and their locations).
2. To review the functional and structural variations in these regions that have been linked to affective style and affective disorders.

## The Circuitry of Emotion

### Prefrontal Cortex (PFC)

PFC: Functional and Anatomical Considerations for Understanding Its Role in Affect

Although the prefrontal cortex is often considered to be the province of higher cognitive control, it has also consistently been linked to various features of affective processing (see, e.g., Nauta, 1971, for an early preview). Miller and Cohen (2001) have recently outlined a comprehensive theory of prefrontal function based on nonhuman primate anatomical and neurophysiological studies, human neuroimaging findings, and computational modeling. The core feature of their model holds that the PFC maintains the rep-

resentation of goals and the means to achieve them. Particularly in situations that are ambiguous, the PFC sends bias signals to other areas of the brain to facilitate the expression of task-appropriate responses in the face of competition with potentially stronger alternatives. In the affective domain, we often confront situations where the arousal of emotion is inconsistent with other goals that are have already been instantiated. For example, the availability of an immediate reward may provide a potent response alternative that may not be in the best service of the overall goals of the person. In such a case, the PFC is required to produce a bias signal to other brain regions that guide behavior toward the acquisition of a more adaptive goal, which in this case would entail delay of gratification. Affect-guided planning and anticipation that involves the experience of emotion associated with an anticipated choice is the hallmark of adaptive, emotion-based decision making that has repeatedly been found to become impaired in patients with lesions of ventromedial PFC (Damasio, 1994). Affect-guided anticipation is most often accomplished in situations that are heavily laden with competition from potentially stronger alternatives. In such cases in particular, we would expect PFC activation to occur. Certain disorders of emotional processing such as depression may be caused by abnormalities of affect-guided anticipation. For example, the failure to anticipate positive incentives and direct behavior toward the acquisition of appetitive goals are symptoms of depression that may arise from abnormalities in the circuitry that implements positive affect-guided anticipation. Our laboratory has contributed extensively to the literature on asymmetries in PFC function associated with approach- and withdrawal-related emotion and mood (e.g., Davidson & Irwin, 1999; Davidson, Jackson, et al., 2000). In this context, we suggest that left-sided PFC regions are particularly involved in approach-related, appetitive goals. The instantiation of such goals, particularly in the face of strong alternative responses, requires left-sided PFC activation and hypoactivation in these circuits has been linked to depression. Right-sided PFC regions, alternatively, are hypothesized to be particularly important in the maintenance of goals that require behavioral inhibition and withdrawal in situations that involve strong alternative response options to approach. The prototype of such a process has recently been captured in several neuroimaging studies that involve variants of a go/no-go task where a dominant response set is established to respond quickly, except those trials on which a cue to inhibit the response is presented. Two recent studies using event-related fMRI have found a lateralized focus of activation in the right lateral PFC (inferior frontal sulcus) to cues that signaled response inhibition that were presented in the context of other stimuli toward which a strong approach set was established (Garavan, Ross, & Stein, 1999; Konishi et al., 1999).

Depressed individuals with hypoactivation in certain

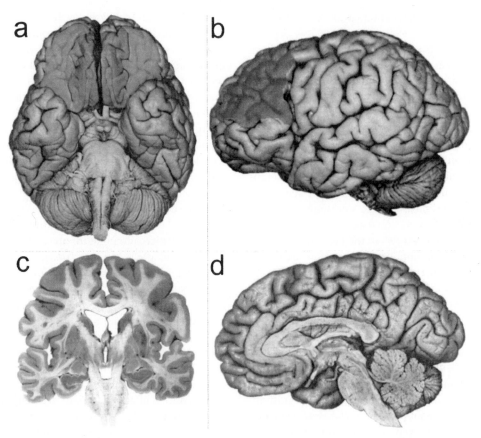

Figure 2.1 Key brain regions involved in affect and mood disorders. (A) Orbital prefrontal cortex (green) and the ventromedial prefrontal cortex (red). (B) Dorsolateral prefrontal cortex (blue). (C) Hippocampus (purple) and amygdala (orange). (D) Anterior cingulate cortex (yellow). (*See color insert.*)

regions of the PFC may be deficient in the instantiation of goal-directed behavior and in the overriding of more automatic responses that may involve the perseveration of negative affect and dysfunctional attitudes. Such deficits would be expected to be unmasked in situations where decision making is ambiguous and where the maintenance of goal-directed behavior is required in the face of potentially strong alternative responses. As we will argue below, when the strong alternative responses involve affect, which they often do, the ventromedial PFC is particularly implicated.

Recent neuroimaging and electrophysiological studies suggest that the orbital and ventral frontal cortex in particular may be especially important for the representation of rewards and punishments, and different sectors within this cortex may emphasize reward versus punishment (Kawasaki et al., 2001; O'Doherty, Kringelbach, Rolls, Hornak, & Andrews, 2001). In particular, a left-sided medial region of the oribitalfrontal cortex (OFC) appears particularly responsive to rewards while a lateral right-sided region appears particularly responsive to punishments (O'Doherty et al., 2001). Kawasaki and colleagues (2001) recorded from single units in the right ventral PFC of patients with implanted depth electrodes for presurgical planning. They found these neurons in healthy tissue to exhibit short-latency responses to aversive visual stimuli. Such studies provide important clues regarding the circuitry that might be most relevant to understanding differences among individuals in affective style. For example, there are individual differences in responsivity to rewards versus punishments that can probed behaviorally using signal detection methods (Henriques, Glowacki, & Davidson, 1994; Henriques & Davidson, 2000). Most normal individuals exhibit systematic modification of response bias to monetary reward, but some do not. Those who do not showed elevated depressed mood. We would also predict that left-medial OFC would be hyporesponsive to manipulations of reward in such individuals while right-lateral OFC to punishment would either be normal or perhaps accentuated.

### Anterior Cingulate Cortex (ACC): Functional and Anatomical Considerations for Understanding Its Role in Affect

Several theories have proposed that the ACC acts as a bridge between attention and emotion (Devinsky, Morrell,

& Vogt, 1995; Ebert & Ebmeier, 1996; Mayberg, 1997; Vogt, Nimchinsky, Vogt, & Hof, 1995). In their recent review, Thayer and Lane (2000) described the ACC as "a point of integration for visceral, attentional, and affective information that is critical for self-regulation and adaptability" (p. 211). In light of its anatomical connections (see below), the ACC appears well equipped for assessing and responding to the behavioral significance of external stimuli. Critical roles of the ACC in selective attention (i.e., prioritizing incoming information), affect, and specific characteristic mammalian social behaviors have been described (Devinsky et al., 1995; Vogt, Finch, & Olson, 1992). However, in order to fully understand the role of the ACC in psychopathology, affective states, and emotional processing, it is critical to recognize that the ACC is far from being a functionally homogeneous region, and at least two subdivisions can be discerned (Devinsky et al., 1995; Vogt et al., 1992, 1995). The first, referred to as the "affect subdivision," encompasses rostral and ventral areas of the ACC (areas 25, 32, 33, and rostral area 24). The second, referred to as the "cognitive subdivision," involves dorsal regions of the ACC (caudal area 24' and 32', cingulate motor area). The affect subdivision possesses extensive connections with limbic and paralimbic regions—such as the amygdala, nucleus accumbens, OFC, periaqueductal grey, anterior insula, and autonomic brainstem motor nuclei—and is assumed to be involved in regulating visceral and autonomic responses to stressful behavioral and emotional events, emotional expression, and social behavior. Owing to its strong connections with the lateral hypothalamus, the subgenual ACC (BA25) is considered the most important region within the frontal cortex for regulating autonomic function (Öngür, An, & Price, 1998).

Conversely, the cognitive subdivision is intimately connected with the DLPFC (BA46/9), posterior cingulate, parietal cortex (BA7), supplementary motor area, and spinal cord, and plays an important role in response selection and processing of cognitively demanding information. In functional neuroimaging studies, evidence suggesting a functional differentiation between ventral (affective) and dorsal (cognitive) ACC subdivisions is emerging (Bush et al., 1998; Bush, Luu, & Posner, 2000; Whalen et al., 1998; see Figure 2.2).

From a functional perspective, activation of the cognitive subdivision of the ACC has been reported during interference between competing information (Pardo, Pardo, Janer, & Kaichle, 1990), visual attention (Nobre et al., 1997), monitoring of cognitive (Carter et al., 2000; MacDonald, Cohen, Stenger, & Carter, 2000) and reward-related (Rogers et al., 1999) conflicts, task difficulty (Paus et al., 1997), and increased risk-associated outcome uncertainty (Critchley, Mathias, & Dolan, 2001), among other experimental manipulations. A common denominator among these experimental conditions is that they all required modulation of attention or executive functions and

monitoring of competition (Bush et al., 2000). The role of the ACC in conflict monitoring has been especially emphasized by Cohen and colleagues (Carter, Botvinick, & Cohen, 1999; Carter et al., 2000; Miller & Cohen, 2001). These authors proposed that the ACC may serve an evaluative function, reflecting the degree of response conflict elicited by a given task. Conflict occurs when two or more possible task-related decisions compete with or interfere with each other. According to the "competition monitoring hypothesis," the cognitive subdivision of the ACC monitors conflicts or crosstalk between brain regions. If a signal of competition emerges, this output signals the need for controlled processing. The DLPFC (BA 9) is assumed to be critical for this form of controlled processing, in that it represents and maintains task demands necessary for such control *and* inhibits (see, e.g., Garavan et al., 1999) or increases neural activity in brain regions implicated in

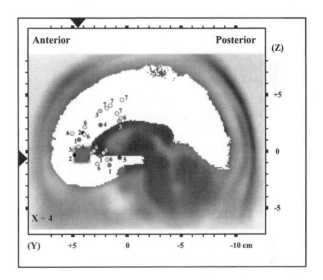

Figure 2.2 Summary of functional brain imaging studies of anterior cingulate cortex (ACC) involvement in depression as well as during various cognitive and affective task manipulations. Foci of ACC activation or deactivation were registered to a common stereotaxic brain atlas (Talairach & Tournoux, 1988) and plotted on a sagittal brain slice (anterior part of the head to the left). The large red area and the black triangles show the location of the ACC cluster found to be associated with degree of treatment response in our previous EEG study (Pizzagalli et al., 2001). The studies of depressed subjects showed pretreatment hyperactivity among patients who responded to treatment (1); posttreatment decreased activity in responders (2); hypoactivity in depressed subjects (3); increased activity with remission of depression (4); decreased activity with remission of depression (5). Studies involving emotional (6) and cognitive (7) tasks in nonpsychiatric subjects are also reported. Coordinates in mm (Talairach & Tournoux, 1988), origin at anterior commissure; (X)=left(−) to right(+); (Y)=posterior(−) to anterior(+); (Z)=inferior(−) to superior(+). Adapted from Pizzagalli et al. (2001). (*See color insert.*)

the competition. Thus, dorsal ACC activation leading to a call for further processing by other brain regions may represent a mechanism for effortful control.

From a functional perspective, activation of the affective subdivision of the ACC has been reported during various emotional states and manipulations (for reviews, see Reiman, 1997; Bush et al., 2000; see also Figure 2.2).

What could be a common denominator underlying activation of the rostral/ventral ACC in such disparate experimental conditions, such as pain, classical conditioning, transient mood, primal affect, Stroop task, and perceiving facial expressions, all of which have been reported in the literature? A possible answer to this question is that the affective subdivision of the ACC may be critical for assessing the presence of possible conflicts between the current functional state of the organism and incoming information with potentially relevant motivational and emotional consequences. This suggestion is based on the observation that the affective subdivision of the ACC is involved in behaviors characterized by monitoring and evaluation of performance, internal states, and presence or reward or punishment, which often require change in behavior.

Extant evidence suggests that ACC activation may be present when effortful emotional regulation is required in situations where behavior is failing to achieve a desired outcome or when affect is elicited in contexts that are not normative, which includes most laboratory situations (Bush et al., 2000; Ochsner & Barrett, 2001). Relatedly, it is not surprising that the ACC is one of the most consistently activated regions in patients with different anxiety disorders, such as OCD (Breiter et al., 1996; Rauch et al., 1997), simple phobia (Rauch et al., 1995), and PTSD (Rauch et al., 1996; Shin et al., 1997), in which conflicts between response tendencies and environments are prominent. Interestingly, psychosurgical lesions of the ACC has been used as a treatment for mood and anxiety disorders (e.g., Baer et al., 1995; for review, Binder & Iskandar, 2000), possibly because of a reduction of conflict monitoring and uncertainty that otherwise characterize these psychiatric conditions.

The interplay between the affective and cognitive subdivision of the ACC is presently unknown. From a theoretical perspective, several authors have suggested that the affective subdivision of the ACC may integrate salient affective and cognitive information (such as that derived from environmental stimuli or task demands), and subsequently modulate attentional processes within the cognitive subdivision accordingly (Mega, Cummings, Galloway, & Malloy, 1997; Mayberg, 1997; Mayberg et al., 1999; Pizzagalli et al., 2001). In agreement with this hypothesis, dorsal anterior and posterior cingulate pathways devoted to attentional processes and amygdalar pathways devoted to affective processing converge within area 24 (Mega et al., 1997). These mechanisms may be especially important

for understanding the now replicated finding in depressed patients that increased *pre*-treatment activity in the rostral ACC is associated with eventual better treatment response (Mayberg et al., 1997; Ebert, Feistel, & Barocka, 1991; Pizzagalli et al., 2001; Wu et al., 1992, 1999). In an influential paper, Mayberg and colleagues (1997) reported that unipolar depressed patients who responded to treatment after six weeks showed higher pre-treatment glucose metabolism in a rostral region of the ACC (BA 24a/b) compared to both nonresponders and nonpsychiatric comparison subjects. Recently, we (Pizzagalli et al., 2001) replicated this finding with EEG source localization techniques and demonstrated that even among those patients who respond to treatment, the magnitude of treatment response was predicted by baseline levels of activation in the same region of the ACC as identified by Mayberg et al. (1997). In addition, we suggested that hyperactivation of the rostral ACC in depression might reflect an increased sensitivity to affective conflict such that the disparity between one's current mood and the responses expected in a particular context activates this region of ACC, which then in turn issues a call for further processing to help resolve the conflict. This call for further processing is hypothesized to aid the treatment response. In other words, individuals exhibiting high levels of activation in the rostral ACC may be affectively resilient since these individuals would be motivated to resolve discrepancies between their current mood state and the behavior that is most appropriate for the situation at hand.

One of the major outputs from the ACC is a projection to PFC. This pathway may be the route via which the ACC issues a call to the PFC for further processing to address a conflict that has been detected. Individual differences in PFC function that are relevant to affective style may arise as a consequence of variations in signals from ACC, or may be intrinsic to the PFC, or both. There may ACC-based variations in affective style that may be reflected phenomenologically in the motivation or "will-to-change" certain habits or patterns of affective reactivity. Individuals with low levels of rostral ACC activation would not experience conflict between their current state and the demands of everyday life and would thus be unmotivated to alter their behavior. PFC-based variations in affective style may predominantly revolve around differences among individuals in the capacity to organize and guide behavior in a goal-directed fashion.

An important issue not considered above is the anatomical and functional connectivity between the different regions of PFC and ACC. Future studies need to examine both structural and functional variation in these connections since it is likely that some individual differences in affective style are primarily associated with connectivity between PFC, ACC, and amygdala, rather than with activation differences in any single or even multiple regions. We comment on this issue in more detail below.

## Hippocampus: Functional and Anatomical Considerations for Understanding Its Role in Affect

The hippocampus is critically involved in episodic, declarative, contextual, and spatial learning and memory (Squire & Knowlton, 2000; Fanselow, 2000). Additionally, it is also importantly involved in the regulation of adrenocorticotropic hormone secretion (Jacobson & Sapolsky, 1991). With respect to conditioning, in recent years, rodent studies have convincingly shown that the hippocampus plays a key role in the formation, storage, and consolidation of contextual fear conditioning (see Fanselow, 2000, for review). In this form of hippocampal-dependent Pavlovian conditioning, fear (e.g., expressed in increased freezing) is acquired to places or contexts (e.g., a specific cage) previously associated with aversive events (e.g., shock). This fact has important implications for our understanding of the abnormalities in affective function that may arise as a consequence of hippocampal dysfunction.

In functional neuroimaging studies, hippocampal/parahippocampal activation has been reported during perception of several negatively valenced stimuli and/or experiencing of negatively valenced affective states, such as trace conditioning (Büchel, Dolan, Armong, & Friston, 1999), perception of aversive complex stimuli (Lane, Fink, Chau, & Dolan, 1997), threat-related words (Isenberg et al., 1999), increasing music dissonance (Blood, Zatorre, Bermudez, & Evans, 1999), tinnitus-like aversive auditory stimulation (Mirz, Gjedde, Sodkilde-Jørgensen, & Pedersen, 2000), vocal expressions of fear (Phillips et al., 1998), aversive taste (Zald, Lee, Fluegel, & Pardo, 1998), anticipatory anxiety (Javanmard et al., 1999), procaine-induced affect (Ketter et al., 1996; Servan-Schreiber & Perlstein 1997), and monetary penalties (Elliott & Dolan, 1999). However, it seems that valence is not the critical variable for evoking hippocampal activation. Indeed, hippocampal activation has been also reported during experimental manipulation of positive affect, such as re-evoking pleasant affective autobiographical memories (Fink et al., 1996), increases in winning in a game-like task (Zalla et al., 2000), and perception of the loved person (Bartels & Zeki, 2000). Also, hippocampal activation was correlated with long-term recognition memory for pleasant films (Hamann, Eby, Grafton, & Kitts, 1999).

In order to reconcile these findings, we suggest that most of the experimental manipulations leading to hippocampal activation contain contextual cues. That is, we assume that they involve the consolidation of a memory for an integrated representation of a context similar to that associated with the presented stimulus (Fanselow, 2000). This is clearly the case during Pavlovian and trace conditioning, for instance, but also during presentation of both positively and negatively valenced visual, olfactory, and auditory cues that may induce reevocation and consolidation of contextual information associated with similar situation in the past (see, e.g., Nader, Schafe, & LeDoux, 2000).

Although in humans the mechanisms underlying contextual conditioning are still unclear, it is possible that plasticity in functional connectivity between the hippocampus and regions crucially involved in decoding the behavioral significance of incoming information, such as the amygdala and the pulvinar, may critically contribute to contextual learning (Morris, Friston, & Dolan, 1997; Morris, Ohman, & Dolan, 1999), even when the information is presented below the level of conscious awareness (Morris et al., 1999). As recently reviewed by Davis and Whalen (2001), animal studies clearly suggest that the amygdala exerts a modulatory influence on hippocampal-dependent memory systems, possibly through direct projections from the basolateral nucleus of the amygdala. Consistent with this view, stimulation of the amygdala causes LTP induction in the dentate gyrus of the hippocampus (Ikegaya, Abe, Saito, & Nishiyama, 1995). Conversely, lesions to (Ikegaya, Saito, & Abe, 1994) or local anesthetics within (Ikegaya, Saito, & Abe, 1995) the basolateral nucleus of the amygdala attenuate long-term potentiation in the dentate gyrus. Although drawing conclusions from these rodent studies to humans is at this stage speculative, it is intriguing that most of the human neuroimaging studies reporting hippocampal activation during aversive affective manipulations also found amygdalar activation (Büchel et al., 1999; Isenberg et al., 1999; Ketter et al., 1996; Mirz et al., 2000; Servan-Schreiber & Perlstein, 1997; Zald et al., 1998). Future neuroimaging studies should directly test the interplay between the hippocampus and the amygdala in these processes and in fear-related learning and memory, especially in light of recent animal data suggesting an interplay between these regions for modulating extinction of conditioned fear (Corcoran & Maren, 2001).

In their recent review, Davidson and colleagues (Davidson, Jackson, et al., 2000) noted that various form of psychopathology involving disorders of affect could be characterized as disorders in context-regulation of affect. That is, patients with mood and anxiety disorders often display normative affective responses but in *inappropriate* contexts. For example, fear that may be appropriate in response to an actual physical threat but persists following the removal of that threat, or sadness that may be appropriate in the acute period following a loss but persists for a year following that loss are both examples of context-inappropriate emotional responding. In these examples, the intensity and form of the emotion would be perfectly appropriate in response to the acute challenges, but when they occur in the absence of those acute stresses they can be viewed as context-inappropriate.

In a series of studies with non-human primates, Kalin and colleagues (Kalin & Shelton, 2000) have used the human intruder paradigm to probe the context specificity of emotional responding. In this paradigm, the monkey is exposed to different contexts that elicit a specific normative pattern of affective responses. In response to the profile of a human intruder (no eye contact, or NEC condition), the animals tend to freeze while in response to the same human staring at the animal, agonistic, aggressive behavior is elicited. When the animal is alone, freezing and aggression decline and the animals vocalize. These very well-defined normative patterns can be used to identify responses that are context-inappropriate. In a large group of monkeys ($N$ = 100), approximately five show highly context-inappropriate responding. The most dramatic example of this is the small group of animals that freeze during the Alone condition at levels that are comparable to what they exhibit during the NEC condition. These are the animals that we predict would have hippocampal dysfunction since they are regulating their emotions in a context-appropriate fashion. These animals do have high levels of cortisol and extreme right-sided prefrontal activation derived from a noninvasive EEG measurement (see Figure 2.3).

Given the preclinical and functional neuroimaging literature reviewed above, one may hypothesize that subjects

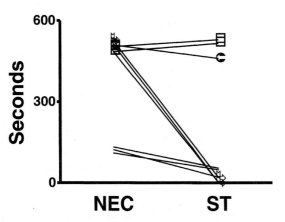

Figure 2.3 Freezing duration in seconds (out of a total of 600 seconds) in response to the No Eye Contact (NEC—exposure of the monkey to a profile of a human) and the Stare (ST) conditions in four groups of animals: One group shows very long durations of freezing during the normative context (NEC) but then freezes little during ST. Another group shows moderately elevated freezing during NEC and then shows little during ST. A third group shows virtually no freezing during either NEC or ST. Finally, the fourth group exhibits high levels of freezing in response to both NEC and ST. This is the group that displays out-of-context freezing (i.e., during ST). The group of three animals who show the out-of-context freezing are the only animals in a group of 100 to exhibit this pattern. From Kalin and Shelton (2000), copyright © 2000 by Oxford University Press, Inc. Used by permission of Oxford University Press, Inc.

displaying inappropriate context-regulation of affect may be characterized by hippocampal dysfunction. Consistent with this conjecture, recent morphometric studies using MRI indeed reported smaller hippocampal volumes in patients with major depression (Sheline, Wang, Gado, Csernausky, & Vannier, 1996; Sheline, Sanghaui, Mintun, & Gado, 1999; Shah, Ebmeier, Glabus, & Goodwin, 1998; Bremner et al., 2000; von Gunten, Fox, Cipolotti, & Ron 2000; Steffens et al., 2000; Mervaala et al., 2000; but see Vakili et al., 2000; Ashtari et al., 1999), bipolar disorder (Noga, Vladar, & Torrey, 2001), posttraumatic stress disorder (Bremner et al., 1995; Bremner, Randall, et al., 1997; Stein, Koverola, Hanna, Torchia, & McClarty, 1997), and borderline personality disorder (Driessen et al., 2000) (for review, see Sapolsky, 2000; Sheline, 2000). Where hippocampal volume reductions in depression have been found, the magnitude of reduction ranges from 8 to 19%. Recently, functional hippocampal abnormalities in major depression have been also reported at baseline using PET measures of glucose metabolism (Saxena et al., 2001). Whether hippocampal dysfunction precedes or follows onset of depressive symptomatology is still unknown.

In depression, inconsistencies across studies may be explained by several methodological considerations. First, as pointed out by Sheline (2000), studies reporting positive findings generally used MRI with higher spatial resolution (~0.5–2 mm) compared to those reporting negative findings (~3–10 mm). Second, it seems that age, severity of depression, and most significantly, duration of recurrent depression may be important moderator variables. Indeed, studies reporting negative findings either studied younger cohorts [e.g., Vakili et al. (2000): 38 ± 10 years vs. Sheline et al. (1996): 69 ± 10 years; von Gunten et al. (2000): 58 ± 9 years; Steffens et al. (2000): 72 ± 8 years] or less severe and less chronic cohorts (Ashtari et al., 1999, vs. Sheline et al., 1996; Shah et al., 1998; Bremner et al., 2000). In a recent study from our laboratory (Rusch, Abercrombie, Oakes, Schaefer, & Davidson, 2001), we also failed to find hippocampal atrophy in a relatively young subject sample (33.2 ± 9.5 years) with moderate depression severity. Notably, in normal early adulthood (18–42 years), decreased bilateral hippocampal volume has been reported with increasing age in male but not female healthy subjects (Pruessner, Collins, Pruessner, & Evans, 2001). Finally, in females, initial evidence suggests that total life-time duration of depression, rather than age, is associated with hippocampal atrophy (Sheline et al., 1999), inviting the possibility that hippocampal atrophy may be a symptom rather than a cause of depression. Future studies should carefully assess the relative contribution of these possible modulatory variables in the hippocampal pathophysiology and examine hippocampal changes longitudinally in individuals at risk for mood disorders.

Structurally, the hippocampal changes may arise due to neuronal loss through chronic hypercortisolemia, glial cell loss, stress-induced reduction in neurotrophic factors, or stress-induced reduction in neurogenesis, but the precise mechanisms are not completely known (Sheline, 2000). In depression, the hypothesis of an association between sustained, stress-related elevations of cortisol and hippocampal damage has received considerable attention. This hypothesis is based on the observation that the pathophysiology of depression involves dysfunction in negative feedback of the hypothalamic-pituitary-adrenal (HPA) axis (see Pariante & Miller, 2001, for a review), which results in increased levels of cortisol during depressive episodes (e.g., Carroll, Curtis, & Mendela, 1976). Higher levels of cortisol may, in turn, lead to neuronal damage in the hippocampus, since this region possesses high levels of glucocorticoid receptors (Reul & De Kloet, 1986) and glucocorticoids are neurotoxic (Sapolsky, Krey, & McEwan, 1986). Since the hippocampus is involved in negative-feedback control of cortisol (Jacobson & Sapolsky, 1991), hippocampal dysfunction may result in reduction of the inhibitory regulation of the hypothalamic-pituitary-adrenal axis, which could then lead to hypercortisolemia. Consistent with this view, chronic exposure to increased glucocorticoid concentrations has been shown to lower the threshold for hippocampal neuronal degeneration in animals (Gold, Goodwin, & Chrousos, 1988; Sapolsky, Uno, Robert, & Finch, 1990; McEwen, 1998) and humans (Lupien et al., 1998). At least in nonhuman primates, this association is qualified by the observation that chronically elevated cortisol concentrations in the absence of chronic "psychosocial" stress do not produce hippocampal neuronal loss (Leverenz et al., 1999). Conversely, naturalistic, chronic psychosocial stress has been shown to induce structural changes in hippocampal neurons of subordinate animals (Magarinos, McEwen, Flugge, & Fuchs, 1996). In depression, hippocampal volume loss has been shown to be associated with lifetime duration of depression (Sheline et al., 1999), consistent with the assumption that long-term exposure to high cortisol levels may lead to hippocampal atrophy. However, this conjecture has not been empirically verified in humans.

Although intriguing, these findings cannot inform us about the causality between hippocampal dysfunction, elevated levels of cortisol, and most important, inappropriate context-regulation of affect. Unfortunately, none of the structural neuroimaging studies in depression investigating hippocampal volume were prospective and took into account cortisol data in an effort to unravel the causal link between cortisol output and hippocampal dysfunction.

The possibility of plasticity in the hippocampus deserves particular comment. In rodents, recent studies have shown hippocampal neurogenesis as a consequence of antidepressant pharmacological treatment (Chen, Rajkowska, Du, Seraji-Bozorgzad, & Manji, 2000; Malberg, Eisch, Nestler, & Duman, 2000), electroconvulsive shock (Madhav, Pei, Grahame-Smith, & Zetterstrom, 2000), and most intri-

guingly, as a consequence of positive handling, learning, and exposure to an enriched environment (Kempermann, Kuhn, & Cage, 1997; see Gould, Tanepat, Rydel, & Hastings, 2000, for review). In humans, neurogenesis in the adult human hippocampus has been also reported (Eriksson et al., 1998). Further, in patients with Cushing's disease, who are characterized by very high levels of cortisol, increases in hippocampal volume were significantly associated with magnitude cortisol decrease produced by microadrenomectomy (Starkman et al., 1999). As a corpus, these animal and human data clearly suggest that plasticity in the human hippocampus is possible (for reviews, see Duman, Malberg, & Nakagawa, 2000; Jacobs, Praag, & Gage, 2000; Gould et al., 2000), a finding that suggests that structural and functional changes in the hippocampus of depressed patients may be reversible.

In summary, preclinical and clinical studies converge in suggesting an association between context-modulation of affective responding and hippocampal function. Future studies should (1) assess whether hippocampal atrophy precedes or follows onset of depression or other sydromes of affective dysregulation; (2) assess the causal relation between hypercortisolemia and hippocampal volume reduction; (3) directly test a putative link between inappropriate context-dependent affective responding and hippocampal atrophy; and (4) assess putative treatment-mediated plastic changes in the hippocampus.

## Amygdala: Functional and Anatomical Considerations for Understanding Its Role in Affect

Although a link between amygdala activity and negative affect has been a prevalent view in the literature, particularly when examined in response to exteroceptive aversive stimuli (e.g., LeDoux, 2000), recent findings from invasive animal studies, human lesion, and functional neuroimaging studies are converging on a broader view that regards the amygdala's role in negative affect as a special case of its more general role in directing attention to affectively salient stimuli and issuing a call for further processing of stimuli that have major significance for the individual. Extant evidence is consistent with the argument that the amygdala is critical for recruiting and coordinating cortical arousal and vigilant attention for optimizing sensory and perceptual processing of stimuli associated with underdetermined contingencies, such as novel, "surprising" or "ambiguous" stimuli (see also Davis & Whalen, 2001; Holland & Gallagher, 1999; Whalen, 1998). Most stimuli in this class may be conceptualized as having an aversive valence since we tend to have a negativity bias in the face of uncertainty (Taylor, 1991).

Both structural and functional differences in the amygdala have been reported in disorders of emotion, particularly depression. Structurally, several recent studies reported an association between enlargement of amygdala volume and depression. This association has been found in depressed patients with bipolar disorders (Altshuler, Bartzokis, Grieder, Curran, & Mintz, 1998; Strakowski et al., 1999) as well as temporal lobe epilepsy (TLE; Tebartz van Elst, Woermann, Lemieux, & Trimble, 1999, 2000). In a recent study, Mervaala et al. (2000) observed significant asymmetry in amygdalar volumes (right smaller than left) in patients with major depressive disorder (MDD) but not in the controls. In TLE patients with dysthymia, left amygdala volume was positively correlated with depression severity, as assessed with the BDI (Tebartz van Elst et al., 1999). Although these findings depict a relation between increased amygdalar volume and depression, it is important to stress that (1) the causal relations between the two entities are still unknown, and (2) some inconsistencies among studies are present. Indeed, some studies reported either *decreased* bilateral volume in the amygdala core nuclei (Sheline et al., 1998) or null findings (Coffey et al., 1993; Pantel et al., 1997; Ashtari et al., 1999). Although the reasons are still unclear, it is interesting to note that two null findings were found in geriatric depression (Pantel et al., 1997; Ashtari et al., 1999).

Functionally, abnormal elevations of resting rCBF or glucose metabolism in the amygdala have been reported in depression during both wakefulness (Drevets et al., 1992) and sleep (Ho et al., 1996; Nofzinger et al., 1999). In an FDG-PET study, Ho et al. (1996) reported increased absolute cerebral glucose metabolic in several brain regions, particularly the amygdala (+44%), in 10 unmedicated men with unipolar depression during non-REM sleep period. Further, in his recent review, Drevets (2001) reports data from five consecutive studies, in which increased rCBF or glucose metabolism has been consistently replicated in depressives with familial MDD or melancholic features. In a postmortem study, 5-HT2 receptor density was significantly increased in the amygdala of depressive patients committing suicide (Hrdina, Demeter, Vu, Sotonyi, Palkovits, 1993). Abnormally increased amygdalar activation has also been recently reported in bipolar depression (Ketter et al., 2001) and anxiety disorders, which often show a high degree of comorbidity with depression (Birbaumer et al., 1998; Liberzon et al., 1999; Rauch et al., 1996, 2000; Schneider et al., 1999; Semple et al., 2000; Shin et al., 1997). Further establishing a link between depression and amygdalar activation, two studies have reported a positive correlation between amygdalar activation and depression severity or dispositional negative affect in patients with MDD (Drevets et al., 1992; Abercrombie et al., 1998). After pharmacologically induced remission from depression, amygdalar activation has been observed to decrease to normative values (Drevets, 2001). In familial pure depressive disease, however, increased (left) amygdalar activation persists during the remitted

phases (Drevets et al., 1992), suggesting at least in some subtypes of depression amygdalar dysfunction may be traitlike. Interestingly, remitted MDD patients showing symptom relapse as a consequence of serotonin depletion showed increased amygdalar activation *prior* to the depletion compared to those who will not relapse (Bremner, Innis, et al., 1997). Finally, in one of the first fMRI studies using an activation paradigm, Yurgelun-Todd et al. (2000) reported higher left amygdalar activation for bipolar patients than controls in response to fearful faces.

In light of the pivotal role of the amygdala in recruiting and coordinating vigilant behavior toward stimuli with underdetermined contingencies, hyperactivation of the amygdala in major depression may bias initial evaluation of and response to incoming information. Although still speculative, this mechanism may rely on norepinephrine, which (1) is oftentimes abnormally elevated in depression (e.g., Veith et al., 1994), (2) is involved in amygdala-mediated emotional learning (Ferry, Roozendaal, & McGough, 1999), and (3) is affected by glucocorticoid secretion, which is often elevated in MDD (e.g., Carroll et al., 1976). Thus, these findings may explain cognitive biases toward aversive or emotionally arousing information observed in depression.

Increased amygdalar activation in depression may also represent a possible biological substrate for anxiety, which is often comorbid with depression. In this respect, elevated levels of glucocortocoid hormones—which characterize at least some subgroups of patients with depression—may be especially relevant, since elevated glucocorticoid hormones have been shown to be associated with increased corticotropin-releasing hormone (CRH) in the amygdala. Increased CHR availability may increase anxiety, fear and expectation for adversity (Schulkin, 1994).

In light of evidence suggesting a link between amygdalar activation, on one hand, and memory consolidation and acquisition of long-term declarative knowledge about emotionally salient information, on the other hand, the observations of dysfunctionally increased amygdalar activation in major depression are intriguing. As recently pointed out by Drevets (2001), tonically *increased* amygdalar activation during depressive episodes may favor the emergence of rumination based on increased availability of emotionally negative memories. Although still untested, it is possible that these aberrant processes may rely on dysfunctional interactions between the amygdala, the PFC, and the ACC. Notably, structural abnormalities have been reported in territories of the PFC intimately connected with the ACC (Drevets et al., 1997; Öngür, Drevets, & Price, 1998). ACC dysfunction, in particular, may lead to a decreased capability of monitoring potential conflict between memory-based ruminative processes and sensory information coming from the environment.

## Summary and Conclusions

This chapter reviewed circuitry that underlies the representation and regulation of emotion. It is this circuitry that is responsible for many of the emotional variations among people and for governing vulnerability and resilience in the face of stressful events. Different territories of the PFC and ACC, the hippocampus, and the amygdala were considered. These structures are all interconnected in regionally specific ways and exhibit bi-directional feedback. Variations in the morphometry and functioning of each of these structures have been reported in disorders of emotion, and functional variations are associated with several parameters of affective style in normal individuals. The establishment of differences in brain function or structure in cross-sectional studies that involve only a single assessment have been informative. However, such studies cannot specify which variations may be primary and which may be a consequence of primary variations. For example, an individual may have a low threshold for activation in the amygdala that will predispose him to react with more intense and more prolonged negative affect in response to a stressful event. Territories of the prefrontal cortex may display accentuated activation as part of a regulatory strategy to attenuate activation in the amygdala. In this instance, one might refer to the amygdala difference as primary and the PFC difference as secondary. In the absence of longitudinal research, however, it will be difficult to tease apart.

In addition, a paucity of work has examined functional and/or structural connectivity among these regions. Some of the variations in affective style that have been identified may arise as a consequence of variations in connectivity, either functional, structural, or both. Future research should include measures of both functional (e.g., Cordes et al., 2000) and structural connectivity. The latter can be measured with diffusion tensor imaging (Le Bihan et al., 2001).

We have drawn upon the animal and human literature on basic processes in emotion and emotion regulation to help interpret normal and pathological variations in affective style and to highlight the kinds of studies that have not yet been performed but are important to conduct. The findings on the basic processes in animals and normal humans provide the foundation for a model of the major components in affect representation and regulation. The input to affect representation can be either a sensory stimulus or a memory. Most sensory stimuli are relayed through the thalamus and from there they can take a short route to the amygdala (LeDoux, 2000) and/or go up to cortex. From both association cortex and from subcortical regions including the amygdala, information is relayed to different zones of the PFC. The PFC plays a crucial role in the representation of goals. In the presence of ambiguous situations, the PFC sends bias signals to other brain regions to facilitate the expression of task-appropriate responses in the face of competition with potentially stronger alternatives. We argued that in the affective domain, the PFC implements affect-guided anticipatory processes. Left-sided PFC regions are particularly involved in approach-related appetitive goals while right-sided PFC regions are involved in the maintenance of goals that require behavioral inhibition. Abnormalities in PFC function would be expected to compromise goal-instantiation in patients with depression. Left-sided hypoactivation would result in deficits specifically in pre-goal attainment forms of positive affect while right-sided hyperactivation would result in excessive behavioral inhibition and anticipatory anxiety. Hypoactivation in regions of the PFC with which the amygdala is interconnected may result in a decrease in the regulatory influence on the amygdala and a prolonged time course of amygdala activation in response to challenge. This might be expressed phenomenologically as perseveration of negative affect and rumination.

The ACC is critically involved in conflict monitoring and is activated whenever an individual is confronted with a challenge that involves conflict among two or more response options. According to an influential theory of ACC function (Carter et al., 1999), the ACC monitors the conflicts among brain regions. When such conflict is detected, the ACC issues a call for further processing to the PFC that then adjudicates among the various response options and guides behavior toward a goal. The ACC is very frequently activated in neuroimaging studies of human emotion (see Bush et al., 2000, for review) in part because when emotion is elicited in the laboratory it produces response conflict. There is the general expectation to behave in an unemotional fashion since subjects are participating in a scientific experiment, yet there are the responses that are pulled for by the emotional challenge, such as certain patterns of facial expression. This is commonly reported by subjects and is associated with ACC activation. The ACC is also activated when an individual is exposed to a conflict among different channels of emotional communication. For example, when the face and voice each express inconsistent emotions simultaneously, a conflict in the viewer is created and the ACC is activated (Dolan, Morris, & de Gelder, 2001). Individuals with low levels of ACC activation would be expected to be less sensitive to or less reactive to these inconsistent affective cues.

There is sometimes a conflict between an individual's mood state and the behavior that is expected of the individual in a particular social or role context. For example, among depressed individuals, their dispositional mood state may predispose them to set few goals and engage in little intentional action, yet the demands of their environments may include expectations to behave and act in specific ways. In an individual with normal levels of ACC activation, the signal from ACC would issue a call to other brain regions, the PFC being the most important, to resolve the conflict and engage in the appropriate goal-directed behavior. However, in an individual with abnormally low levels of ACC activation, the conflict between her dispositional mood state and the expectations of her context would not be effectively monitored and thus, the usual call for further processing would not be issued. The data on ACC function in depression most consistently reveal a pattern of decreased activation in certain regions of the ACC. Interestingly, those depressed patients with greater activation in the ventral ACC before antidepressant treatment are the ones most likely to show the largest treatment responses. In normal individuals, activation of the affective subdivision of the ACC may also be associated phenomonologically with the "will to change."

The hippocampus appears to play an important role in encoding context. Lesions to the hippocampus in animals impair context conditioning. In addition, this structure has a high density of glucocorticoid receptors, and elevated levels of cortisol in animal models have been found to produce hippocampal cell death. In humans, various stress-related disorders, including depression, have been found to be associated with hippocampal volume reductions. Whether such hippocampal volume differences are a cause or a consequence of the depression cannot be answered from extant data. However, to the extent that hippocampal dysfunction is present, we would expect that such individuals would show abnormalities in the context-appropriate modulation of emotional behavior. This type of abnormality would be expressed as the display of normal emotion in inappropriate contexts. Thus, the persistence of sadness in situations that would ordinarily engender happiness could in part arise as a consequence of a hippocampally dependent problem in the context-modulation of emotional responses. We have shown such effects in rhesus monkeys (see Davidson, Jackson, et al., 2000, a for review) though they have not yet been studied systematically in humans. The extensive connections between hippocampus and PFC would presumably provide the requisite anatomical substrate for conveying the contextual information to PFC to regulate emotional behavior in a context-appropriate fashion. The connections between hippocampus and PFC are another potential target of dysfunction in depression and other disorders of emotion. It is possible that a certain subtype of individual exists wherein contextual encoding is intact and PFC-implemented goal-directed behavior is intact, but context fails to adequately guide and reprioritize goals. In such cases, the functional and/or anatomical connectivity between hippocampus and PFC might be a prime candidate for dysfunction. The tools are now available to examine both types of connectivity using noninvasive measures.

The amygdala has long been viewed as a key site for both the perception of cues that signal threat and the production of behavioral and autonomic responses associated with aversive responding. As we have noted above, current evidence suggests that the amygdala's role in negative affect may be a special case of its more general role in directing attention and resources to affectively salient stimuli and issuing a call for further processing of stimuli that have potentially major significance for the individual. As with other parts of the circuit we have addressed, there are extensive connections between the amygdala and each of the other structures we have considered. The amygdala receives input from a wide range of cortical zones and has even more extensive projections back to cortex, enabling the biasing of cortical processing as a function of the early evaluation of a stimulus as affectively salient. Also, like the other components of the circuit we have described, there are individual differences in amygdala activation both at baseline (Schaefer et al., 2000) and in response to challenge (see Davidson & Irwin, 1999, for review). Moreover, it is likely that regions of the PFC play an important role in modulating activation in the amygdala and thus influencing the time course of amygdala-driven negative affective responding. In light of the associations that have been reported between individual differences in amygdala activation and affect measures, it is likely that when it occurs, hyperactivation of the amygdala in depression is associated more with the fear-like and anxiety components of the symptoms than with the sad mood and anhedonia. In our own work, we have found that amygdala activation predicts dispositional negative affect in depressed patients but is unrelated to variations in positive affect (Abercrombie et al., 1998). Excessive activation of the amygdala in depressed patients may also be associated with hypervigilance, particularly toward threat-related cues, which further exacerbates some of the symptoms of depression.

There are several types of studies that critically need to be performed in light of the extant evidence reviewed in this chapter. First, studies are needed that relate specific variations in activation in particular brain regions to objective laboratory tasks that are neurally inspired and designed to capture the particular kinds of processing that are hypothesized to be implemented in those brain regions. Relatively few studies of that kind have been conducted. Most studies that examine relations between individual differences in neural activity and affective style, either normal or abnormal, almost always relate such neural variation to either self-report or interview-based indices. In the future, it will be important to complement the phenomenological description with laboratory measures that are explicitly designed to highlight the processes implemented in different parts of the circuit that we described.

Such future studies should include measures of both functional and structural connectivity to complement the activation measures. It is clear that interactions among the various components of the circuitry we describe are likely to play a crucial role in determining behavioral output. Moreover, it is possible that connectional abnormalities may exist in the absence of abnormalities in specific structures.

Longitudinal studies of at-risk samples with the types of imaging measures that are featured in this review are crucial. We do not know if any of the variations discussed above, both of a structural and a functional variety, precede the onset of a disorder, co-occur with the onset of a disorder or follow by some time the expression of a disorder. It is likely that the timing of the abnormalities in relation to the clinical course of the disorder varies for different parts of the circuitry. For example, data showing a relation between the number of cumulative days depressed over the course of the lifetime and hippocampal volume (Sheline et al., 1996, 1999) suggest that this abnormality may follow the expression of the disorder and represent a consequence rather than a primary cause of the disorder. However, before such a conclusion is accepted, it is important to conduct the requisite longitudinal studies to begin to disentangle these complex causal factors.

Finally, we regard the evidence presented in this review as offering very strong support for the view that specific constituents of emotion regulation and affective style will be identified that have not been directly uncovered with self-report methods. For example, the rapidity of recovery from a stressful stimulus or variations in context-sensitivity of emotional responding are each separable processes that will influence self-reports of emotion, yet such reports will not be revealing with respect to the constituents that led to these influences. Thus, two individuals who each report high levels of dispositional negative affect may be doing so because of variations in different parts of the circuitry reviewed. It is also very likely that some of the important variations in affective style, such as individual differences in the rapidity of recovery from a negative event, may not map precisely onto extant personality or self-report descriptors. A major challenge for the future will be to build a more neurobiologically plausible scheme for parsing the heterogeneity of emotion, emotion regulation, disorders of emotion, and affective style, based on the location and nature of the abnormality in the featured circuitry. We believe that this ambitious effort will lead to considerably more consistent findings at the biological level and will also enable us to more rigorously characterize different endophenotypes that could then be exploited for genetic studies.

## ACKNOWLEDGMENTS

The authors wish to thank Alexander J. Shackman and William Irwin for invaluable comments, and Andrew M. Hendrick, Kathryn A. Horras, Megan Zuelsdorff, and Jenna Topolovich for skilled and dedicated assistance in the preparation of the manuscript. Additional thanks to William Irwin for preparation of Figure 2.2. This work was supported by NIMH grants (MH40747, P50-MH52354, MH43454, P50-MH61083) and by an NIMH Research Scientist Award (K05-MH00875) to Richard J. Davidson. Diego Pizzagalli was supported by grants from the Swiss National Research Foundation (81ZH-52864) and "Holderbank"-Stiftung zur Förderung der wissenschaftlichen Fortbildung. Jack B. Nitschke was supported by NIMH Training grant T32-MH18931 and Katherine Putnam was supported by a NARSAD Young Investigator Award.

## REFERENCES

Abercrombie, H. C., Schaefer, S. M., Larson, C. L., Oakes, T. R., Holden, J. E., Perlman, S. B., Krahn, D. D., Benca, R. M., & Davidson, R. J. (1998). Metabolic rate in the right amydala predicts negative affect in depressed patients. *NeuroReport, 9*, 3301–3307.

Altshuler, L. L., Bartzokis, G., Grieder, T., Curran, J., & Mintz, J. (1998). Amygdala enlargement in bipolar disorder and hippocampal reduction in schizophrenia: An MRI study demonstrating neuroanatomic specificity. *Archive of General Psychiatry, 55*, 663–664.

Ashtari, M., Greenwald, B. S., Kramer-Ginsberg, E., Hu, J., Wu, H., Patel, M., Aupperle, P., & Pollack, S. (1999). Hippocampal/amygdala volumes in geriatric depression. *Psychological Medicine, 29*, 629–638.

Baer, L., Rauch, S. L., Ballantine, H. T. J., Martuza, R., Cosgrove, R., Cassem, E., Giriunas, I., Manzo, P. A., Dimino, C., & Jenike, M. A. (1995). Cingulotomy for intractable obsessive-compulsive disorder. Prospective long-term follow-up of 18 patients. *Archives of General Psychiatry, 52*, 384–392.

Bartels, A., & Zeki, S. (2000). The neural basis of romantic love. *NeuroReport, 11*, 3829–3834.

Binder, D. K., & Iskandar, B. J. (2000). Modern neurosurgery for psychiatric disorders. *Neurosurgery, 47*, 9–21.

Birbaumer, N., Grodd, W., Diedrich, O., Klose, U., Erb, E., Lotze, M., Schneider, F., Weiss, U., & Flor, H. (1998). fMRI reveals amygdala activation to human faces in social phobics. *NeuroReport, 9*, 1223–1226.

Blood, A. J., Zatorre, R. J., Bermudez, P., & Evans A. C. (1999). Emotional responses to pleasant and unpleasant music correlate with activity in paralimbic brain regions. *Nature Neuroscience, 2*, 382–387.

Breiter, H. C., Rauch, S. L., Kwong, K. K., Baker, J. R., Weisskoff, R. M., Kennedy, D. N., Kendrick, A. D., Davis, T. L., Jiang, A., Cohen, M. S., Stern, C. E., Belliveau, J. W., Baer, L., O'Sullivan, R. L., Savage, C. R., Jenike, M. A., & Rosen, B. R. (1996). Functional magnetic resonance imaging of symptom provocation in obsessive-compulsive disorder. *Archives of General Psychiatry, 53*, 595–606.

Bremner, J. D., Innis, R. B., Salomon, R. M., Staib, L. H., Ng, C. K., Miller, H. L., Bronen, R. A., Krystal, J. H., Duncan, J., Rich, D., Price, L. H., Malison, R., Dey, H., Soufer, R., & Charney, D. S., (1997). Positron emission tomography measurement of cerebral metabolic correlates of tryptophan depletion-induced depressive relapse. *Archives of General Psychiatry, 54*, 364–374.

Bremner, J. D., Narayan, M., Anderson, E. R., Staib, L. H.

Miller, H. L., & Charney, D. S. (2000). Hippocampal volume reduction in major depression. *American Journal of Psychiatry, 157,* 115–118.

Bremner, J. D., Randall, P., Scott, T. M., Bronen, R. A., Seibyl, J. P., Southwick, S. M., Delaney, R. C., McCarthy, G., Charney, D. S., & Innis, R. B. (1995). MRI-based measurement of hippocampal volume in patients with combat-related posttraumatic stress disorder. *American Journal of Psychiatry, 152,* 972–981.

Bremner, J. D., Randall, P., Vermetten, E., Staib, L. H., Bronen, R. A., Mazure, C., Capelli, S., McCarthy, G., Innis, R. B., & Charney, D. S. (1997). Magnetic resonance imaging-based measurement of hippocampal volume in posttraumatic stress disorder related to childhood physical and sexual abuse—a preliminary report. *Biological Psychiatry, 41,* 23–32.

Büchel, C., Dolan, R., Armony, J. L., Friston, K. J. (1999). Amygdala-hippocampal involvement in human aversive trace conditioning revealed through event-related functional magnetic resonance imaging. *Journal of Neuroscience, 19,* 10869–10876.

Bush, G., Luu, P., & Posner, M. I. (2000). Cognitive and emotional influences in anterior cingulate cortex. *Trends in Cognitive Science, 4,* 215–222.

Bush, G., Whalen, P. J., Rosen, B. R., Jenike, M. A., McInerney, S. C., & Rauch, S. L. (1998). The counting Stroop: An interference task specialized for functional neuroimaging-validation study with functional MRI. *Human Brain Mapping, 6,* 270–282.

Carroll, B. J., Curtis, G. C., & Mendels, J. (1976). Cerebrospinal fluid and plasma free cortisol concentrations in depression. *Psychological Medicine, 6,* 235–244.

Carter, C. S., Botvinick, M. M., & Cohen, J. D. (1999). The contribution of the anterior cingulate cortex to executive processes in cognition. *Review of Neuroscience, 10,* 49–57.

Carter, C. S., Macdonald, A. M., Botvinick, M., Ross, L. L., Stenger, V. A., Noll, D., & Cohen, J. D. (2000). Parsing executive processes: Strategic vs. evaluative functions of the anterior cingulate cortex. *Proceedings of the National Academy of Sciences USA, 97,* 1944–1948.

Chen, G., Rajkowska, G., Du, F., Seraji-Bozorgzad, N., & Manji, H. K. (2000). Enhancement of hippocampal neurogenesis by lithium. *Journal of Neurochemistry, 75,* 1729–1734.

Coffey, C. E., Wilkinson, W. E., Weiner, R. D., Parashos, I. A., Djang, W. T., Webb, M. C., Figiel, G. S., & Spritzer, C. E. (1993). Quantitative cerebral anatomy in depression. A controlled magnetic resonance imaging study. *Archives of General Psychiatry, 50,* 7–16.

Corcoran, K. A., & Maren, S. (2001). Hippocampal inactivation disrupts contextual retrieval of fear memory after extinction. *Journal of Neuroscience, 21,* 1720–1726.

Cordes, D., Haughton, V. M., Arfanakis, K., Wendt, G., Turski, P. A., Moritz, C. H., Quigley, M. A., & Meyerand, M. E. (2000). Mapping functionally related regions of brain with functional connectivity MR imaging. *American Journal of Neuroradiology, 21,* 1636–1644.

Critchley, H. D., Mathias, C. J., & Dolan, R. J., (2001). Neural activity in the human brain relating to uncertainty and arousal during anticipation. *Neuron, 29,* 537–545.

Damasio, A. R. (1994). *Descartes-error: Emotion, reason, and the human brain.* New York: Avon Books.

Davidson, R. J., (2000). Affective style, psychopathology and resilience: Brain mechanisms and plasticity. *American Psychologist, 55,* 1193–1214.

Davidson, R. J., Abercrombie, H. C., Nitschke, J. B., & Putnam, K. M. (1999). Regional brain function, emotion and disorders of emotion. *Current Opinion in Neurobiology, 9,* 228–234.

Davidson, R. J., & Irwin, W. (1999). The functional neuroanatomy of emotion and affective style. *Trends in Cognitive Sciences, 3,* 11–21.

Davidson, R. J., Jackson, D. C., & Kalin, N. H. (2000). Emotion, plasticity, context and regulation. *Psychological Bulletin, 126,* 890–906.

Davidson, R. J., Putnam, K. M., & Larson, C. L. (2000). Dysfunction in the neural circuitry of emotion regulation—A possible prelude to violence. *Science, 289,* 591–594.

Davis, M., & Whalen, P. J. (2001). The amygdala: Vigilance and emotion. *Molecular Psychiatry, 6,* 13–34.

Devinsky, O., Morrell, M. J., & Vogt, B. A. (1995). Contributions of anterior cingulate cortex to behaviour. *Brain, 118,* 279–306.

Dolan, R. J., Morris, J. S., & de Gelder, B. (2001). Cross-modal binding of fear in voice and face. *Proceedings of the National Academy of Sciences, 98,* 10006–10010.

Drevets, W. C. (1998). Functional neuroimaging studies of depression: The anatomy of melancholia. *Annual Review of Medicine, 49,* 341–361.

Drevets, W. C. (2001). Neuroimaging and neuropathological studies of depression: Implications for the cognitive-emotional features of mood disorders. *Current Opinion in Neurobiology, 11,* 240–249.

Drevets, W. C., Price, J. L., Simpson, J. R. J., Todd, R. D., Reich, T., Vannier, M., & Raichle, M. E. (1997). Subgenual prefrontal cortex abnormalities in mood disorders. *Nature, 386,* 824–827.

Drevets, W. C., Videen, T. O., Price, J. L., Preskorn, S. H., Carmichael, S. T., & Raichle, M. E. (1992). A functional anatomical study of unipolar depression. *Journal of Neuroscience, 12,* 3628–3641.

Driessen, M., Hermann, J., Stahl, K., Zwaan, M., Meier, S., Hill, A., Osterheider, M., & Petersen, D. (2000). Magnetic resonance imaging volumes of the hippocampus and the amygdala in women with borderline personality disorder and early traumatization. *Archives of General Psychiatry, 57,* 1115–1122.

Duman, R. S., Malberg, J., Nakagawa, S., & D'Sa, C. (2000). Neuronal plasticity and survival in mood disorders. *Biological Psychiatry, 48,* 732–739.

Ebert, D., & Ebmeier, K. P. (1996). The role of the cingulate gyrus in depression: From functional anatomy to neurochemistry. *Biological Psychiatry, 39,* 1044–1050.

Ebert, D., Feistel, H., & Barocka, A. (1991). Effects of sleep deprivation on the limbic system and the frontal lobes in affective disorders: A study with Tc-99m-HMPAO SPECT. *Psychiatry Research, 40,* 247–251.

Elliott, R., & Dolan, R. J. (1999). Differential neural responses during performance of matching and non-matching to sample tasks at two delay intervals. *Journal of Neuroscience, 19,* 5066–5073.

Eriksson, P. S., Perfilieva, E., Bjork-Eriksson, T., Alborn, A., Nordborg, C., Peterson, D. A., & Gage, F. H. (1998). Neurogenesis in the adult human hippocampus. *Nature Medicine, 4,* 1313–1317.

Fanselow, M. S. (2000). Contextual fear, gestalt memories, and the hippocampus. *Behavioral and Brain Research, 110,* 73–81.

Ferry, B., Roozendaal, B., & McGaugh, J. L. (1999). Role of norepinephrine in mediating stress hormone regulation of long-term memory storage: A critical involvement of the amygdala. *Biological Psychiatry, 46,* 1140–1152.

Fink, G. R., Markowitsch, H. J., Reinkemeier, M., Bruckbauer, T., Kessler, J., & Heiss, W. (1996). Cerebral representation of one's own past: Neural networks involved in autobiographical memory. *Journal of Neuroscience, 16,* 4275–4282.

Garavan, H., Ross, R. H., & Stein, E. A. (1999). Right hemispheric dominance of inhibitory control: An event-related functional MRI study. *Proceeding of the National Academy of Sciences, USA, 96,* 8301–8306.

Gold, P. W., Goodwin, F. K., & Chrousos, G. P. (1988). Clinical and biochemical manifestations of depression: Relation to the neurobiology of stress. *New England Journal of Medicine, 314,* 348–353.

Gould, E., Tanapat, P., Rydel, T., & Hastings, N. (2000). Regulation of hippocampal neurogenesis in adulthood. *Psychiatry, 48,* 715–720.

Hamann, S. B., Ely, T. D., Grafton, S. T., & Kilts, C. D. (1999). Amygdala activity related to enhanced memory for pleasant and aversive stimuli. *Nature Neuroscience, 2,* 289–293.

Henriques, J. B., & Davidson, R. J. (2002). Decreased responsiveness to reward in depression. *Cognition and Emotion, 15,* 711–724.

Henriques, J. B., Glowacki, J. M., & Davidson, R. J. (1994). Reward fails to alter response bias in depression. *Journal of Abnormal Psychology, 103,* 460–466.

Ho, A. P., Gillin, J. C., Buchsbaum, M. S., Wu, J. C., Abel, L., & Bunney, W. E., Jr. (1996). Brain glucose metabolism during non-rapid eye movement sleep in major depression. A positron emission tomography study. *Archives of General Psychiatry, 53,* 645–652.

Holland, P. C., & Gallagher, M. (1999). Amygdala circuitry in attentional and representational processes. *Trends in Cognitive Sciences, 3,* 65–73.

Hrdina, P. D., Demeter, E., Vu, T. B., Sotonyi, P., & Palkovits, M. (1993). 5-HT uptake sites and 5-HT2 receptors in brain of antidepressant-free suicide victims/depressives: Increase in 5-HT2 sites in cortex and amygdala. *Brain Research, 614,* 37–44.

Ikegaya, Y., Abe., K., Saito, H., & Nishiyama, N. (1995). Medial amygdala enhances synaptic transmission and synaptic plasticity in the dentate gyrus of rats in vivo. *Journal of Neurophysiology, 74,* 2201–2203.

Ikegaya, Y., Saito, H., & Abe, K. (1994). Attenuated hippocampal long-term potentiation in basolateral amygdala-lesioned rats. *Brain Research, 656,* 157–164.

Ikegaya, Y., Saito, H., & Abe, K. (1995). Requirement of basolateral amygdala neuron activity for the induction of long-term potentiation in the dentate gyrus in vivo. *Brain Research, 671,* 351–354.

Isenberg, N., Silbergswieg, D., Engelien, A., Emmerich, S., Malavade, K., Beattie, B., & Leon, A. C. (1999). Linguistic threat activates the human amygdala. *Proceedings of the National Academy of Sciences USA, 96,* 10456–10459.

Jacobs, B. L., Praag, H., & Gage, F. H. (2000). Adult brain neurogenesis and psychiatry: A novel theory of depression. *Molecular Psychiatry, 5,* 262–269.

Jacobson, L., & Sapolsky, R. M. (1991). The role of the hippocampus in feedback regulation of the hypothalamic-pituitary-adrenocortical axis. *Endocrinology Review, 12,* 118–134.

Javanmard, M., Shlik, J., Kennedy, S. H., Vaccarino, F. J., Houle, S., & Bradwejn, J. (1999). Neuroanatomic correlates of CCK-4-induced panic attacks in healthy humans: A comparison of two time points. *Biological Psychiatry, 45,* 872–882.

Kahneman, D. (1999). Objective happiness. In E. Kahneman, E. Diener, & N. Schwartz (Eds.), *Well-being: The foundations of hedonic psychology* (pp. 3–25). New York: Russell Sage Foundation.

Kalin, N. H., & Shelton, S. E. (2000). The regulation of defensive behaviors in rhesus monkeys: Implications for understanding anxiety disorders. In R. J. Davidson (Ed.), *Anxiety, depression and emotion* (pp. 50–68). New York: Oxford University Press.

Kawasaki, H., Adolphs, R., Kaufman, O., Damasio, H., Damasio, A. R., Granner, M., Bakken, H., Hori, T., & Howard III, M. A. (2001). Single-neuron responses to emotional visual stimuli recorded in human ventral prefrontal cortex. *Nature Neuroscience, 4,* 15–16.

Kempermann, G., Kuhn, H. G., & Gage, F. H. (1997). More hippocampal neurons in adult mice living in an enriched environment. *Nature, 386,* 493–495.

Ketter, T. A., Andreason, P. J., George, M. S., Lee, C., Gill, D. S., Parekh, P. I., Willis, M. W., Herscovitch, P., & Post, R. M. (1996). Anterior paralimbic mediation of procaine-induced emotional and psychosensory experiences. *Archives of General Psychiatry, 53,* 59–69.

Ketter, T. A., Kimbrell. T. A., George, M. S., Dunn, R. T., Speer, A. M., Benson, B. E., Willis, M. W., Danielson, A., Frye, M. A., Herscovitch, P., & Post, R. M. (2001). Effects of mood and subtype on cerebral glucose metabolism in treatment-resistant bipolar disorder. *Biological Psychiatry, 49,* 97–109.

Konishi, S., Nakajima, K., Uchida, I., Kikyo, H., Kameyama, M., & Miyashita, Y. (1999). Common inhibitory mechanism in human inferior prefrontal cortex revealed by event-related functional MRI. *Brain, 122,* 981–991.

Lane, R. D., Fink, G. R., Chau, P. M., & Dolan, R. J. (1997). Neural activation during selective attention to subjective emotional responses. *Neuroreport, 8,* 3969–3972.

Le Bihan, D., Mangin, J. F., Poupon, C., Clark, C. A., Pappata, S., Molko, N., & Chabriat, H. (2001). Diffusion tensor imaging: Concepts and applications. *Journal of Magnetic Resonance Imaging, 13,* 534–546.

LeDoux, J. E., (2000). Emotion circuits in the brain. *Annu. Rev. Neurosci., 23,* 155–184.

Leverenz, J. B., Wilkinson, C. W., Wamble, M., Corbin, S., Grabber, J. E., Raskind, M. A., & Peskind, E. R. (1999). Effect of chronic high-dose exogenous cortisol on hippocampal neuronal number in aged nonhuman primates. *Journal of Neuroscience, 19,* 2356–2361.

Liberzon, I., Taylor, S. F., Amdur, R., Jung, T. D., Chamberlain, K. R., Minoshima, S., Koeppe, R. A., & Fig, L. M. (1999). Brain activation in PTSD in response to trauma-related stimuli. *Biological Psychiatry, 45,* 817–826.

Lupien, S. J., de Leon, M., de Santi, S., Convit, A., Tarshish, C., Nair, N. P., Thakur, M., McEwen, B. S., Hauger, R. L., & Meaney, M. J. (1998). Cortisol levels during human aging predict hippocampal atrophy and memory deficits. *Nature Neuroscience, 1,* 69–73.

MacDonald, A. W., Cohen, J. D., Stenger, V. A., & Carter, C. S. (2000). Dissociating the role of the dorsolateral prefrontal and anterior cingulate cortex in cognitive control. *Science, 288,* 1835–1838.

Madhav, T. R., Pei, Q., Grahame-Smith, D. G., & Zetterstrom, T. S. (2000). Repeated electroconvulsive shock promotes the sprouting of serotonergic axons in the lesioned rat hippocampus. *Neuroscience, 97*, 677–683.

Magarinos, A. M., McEwen, B. S., Flugge, G., & Fuchs, E. (1996). Chronic psychosocial stress causes apical dendritic atrophy of hippocampal CA3 pyramidal neurons in subordinate tree shrews. *Journal of Neuroscience, 16*, 3534–3540.

Malberg, J. E., Eisch, A. J., Nestler, E. J., & Duman, R. S. (2000). Chronic antidepressant treatment increases neurogenesis in adult rat hippocampus. *Journal of Neuroscience, 20*, 9104–9110.

Mayberg, H. S. (1997). Limbic-cortical dysregulation: A proposed model of depression. *Journal of Neuropsychiatry and Clinical Neuroscience, 9*, 471–481.

Mayberg, H. S., Liotti, M., Brannan, S. K., McGinnis, S., Mahurin, R. K., Jerabek, P. A., Silva, J. A., Tekell, J. L., Martin, C. C., Lancaster, J. L., & Fox, P. T. (1999). Reciprocal limbic-cortical function and negative mood: Converging PET findings in depression and normal sadness. *American Journal of Psychiatry, 156*, 675–682.

McEwen, B. S., (1998). Protective and damaging effects of stress mediators. *New England Journal of Medicine, 338*, 171–179.

Mega, M. S., Cummings, J. L., Salloway, S., & Malloy, P. (1997). The limbic system: An anatomic, phylogenetic, and clinical perspective. *Journal of Neuropsychiatry and Clinical Neuroscience, 9*, 315–330.

Mervaala, E., Fohr, J., Kononen, M., Valkonen-Korhonen, M., Vainio, P., Partanen, K., et al. (2000). Quantitative MRI of the hippocampus and amygdala in severe depression. *Psychological Medicine, 30*, 117–125.

Miller, E. K., & Cohen, J. D. (2001). An integrative theory of prefrontal cortex function. *Annual Review of Neuroscience, 24*, 167–202.

Mirz, F., Gjedde, A., Sodkilde-Jørgensen, H., & Pedersen, C. B. (2000). Functional brain imaging of tinnitus-like perception induced by aversive auditory stimuli. *NeuroReport, 11*, 633–637.

Morris, J. S., Friston, K. J., & Dolan, R. J. (1997). Neural responses to salient visual stimuli. *Proceedings of the Royal Society of London, 264*, 769–775.

Morris, J. S., Ohman, A., & Dolan, R. J. (1999). A subcoritcal pathway to the right amygdala mediating "unseen" fear. *Proceedings of the National Academy of Sciences USA, 96*, 1680–1685.

Nader, K., Schafe, G. E., & Le Doux, J. E. (2000). Fear memories require protein synthesis in the amygdala for reconsolidation after retrieval. *Nature, 406*, 722–726.

Nauta, W. H. (1971). The problem of the frontal lobe: A reinterpretation. *Journal of Psychiatric Research, 8*, 167–187.

Nobre, A. C., Sebestyen, G. N., Gitelman, D. R., Mesulam, M. M., Frackowiak, R. S., & Frith, C. D. (1997). Functional localization of the system for visuospatial attention using positron emission tomography. *Brain, 120*, 515–533.

Nofzinger, E. A., Nichols, T. E., Meltzer, C. C., Price, J., Steppe, D. A., Miewald, J. M., Kupfer, D. J., & Moore, R. Y. (1999). Changes in forebrain function from waking to REM sleep in depression: Preliminary analyses of [18F]FDG PET studies. *Psychiatry Research 91*, 59–78.

Noga, J. T., Vladar, K., & Torrey, E. F. (2001). A volumetric magnetic resonance imaging study of monozygotic twins discordant for bipolar disorder. *Psychiatry Research Neuroimaging, 106*, 25–34.

Ochsner, K. N., & Barrett, L. F. (2001). A multiprocess perspective on the neuroscience of emotion. In T. J. Mayne & G. A., Bonanno (Eds.), *Emotions: Current Issues and Future Directions* (vol 2, pp. 38–81). New York: Guilford Press.

O'Doherty, J., Kringelbach, M. L., Rolls, E. T., Hornak, J., & Andrews, C. (2001). Abstract reward and punishment representations in the human orbitofrontal cortex. *Nature Neuroscience, 4*, 95–102.

Öngür, D., An, X., & Price, J. L. (1998a). Prefrontal cortical projections to the hypothalamus in macaque monkeys. *Journal of Comparative Neurology, 401*, 480–505.

Öngür, D., Drevets, W. C., & Price, J. L. (1998). Glial reduction in the subgenual prefrontal cortex in mood disorders. *Proceedings of the National Academy of Sciences USA, 95*, 13290–13295.

Pantel, J., Schroder, J., Essig, M., Popp, D., Dech, H., Knopp, M. V., Schad, L. R., Eysenbach, K., Backenstrass, M., & Friedlinger, M. (1997) Quantitative magnetic resonance imaging in geriatric depression and primary degenerative dementia. *Journal of Affective Disorders, 42*, 69–83.

Pardo, J. V., Pardo, P. J., Janer, K. W., & Raichle, M. E. (1990). The anterior cingulate cortex mediates processing selection in the Stroop attentional conflict paradigm. *Proceedings of the National Academy of Sciences USA, 87*, 256–259.

Pariante, C. M., & Miller, A. H. (2001). Glucocorticoid receptors in major depression: Relevance to pathophysiology and treatment. *Biological Psychiatry, 49*, 391–404.

Paus, T., Zatorre, R. J., Hofle, N., Caramanos, Z., Gotman, J., Petrides, M., & Evans, A. C. (1997). Time-related changes in neural systems underlying attention and arousal during the performance of an auditory vigilance task. *Journal of Cognitive Neuroscience, 9*, 392–408.

Phillips, M. L., Bullmore, E. T., Howard, R., Woodruff, P. W., Wright, I. C., Williams, S. C., Simmons, A., Andrew, C., Brammer, M., & David A. S. (1998). Investigation of facial recognition memory and happy and sad facial expression perception: An fMRI study. *Psychiatry Research, 83*, 127–38.

Pizzagalli, D., Pascual-Marqui, R. D., Nitschke, J. B., Oakes, T. R., Larson, C. L., Abercrombie, H. C., Schaefer, S. M., Koger, J. V., Benca, R. M., & Davidson, R. J. (2001). Anterior cingulate activity as a predictor of degree of treatment response in major depression: Evidence from brain electrical tomography analysis. *American Journal of Psychiatry, 158*, 405–415.

Pruessner, J. C., Collins, D. L., Pruessner, M., & Evans, A. C. (2001). Age and gender predict volume decline in the anterior and posterior hippocampus in early adulthood. *Journal of Neuroscience, 21*, 194–200.

Rauch, S. L., Savage, C. R., Alpert, N. M., Fischman, A. J., & Jenike, M. A., (1997). A study of three disorders using positron emission tomography and symptom provocation. *Biological Psychiatry, 42*, 446–452.

Rauch, S. L., Savage, C. R., Alpert, N. M., Miguel, E. C., Baer, L., Breiter, H. C., Fischman, A. J., Manzo, P. A., Moretti, C., & Jenike, M. A. (1995). A positron emission tomographic study of simple phobic symptom provocation. *Archives of General Psychiatry, 52*, 20–28.

Rauch, S. L., van der Kolk, B. A., Fisler, R. E., Alpert, N. M., Orr, S. P., Savage, C. R., Fischman, A. J., Jenike, M. A., & Pitman, R. K. (1996). A symptom provocation study of posttraumatic stress disorder using positron emission tomography and script-driven imagery. *Archives of General Psychiatry, 53,* 380–387.

Rauch, S. L., Whalen, P. J., Shin, L. M., McInerney, S. C., Macklin, M. L., Lasko, N. B., Orr, S. P., & Pitman, R. K. (2000). Exaggerated amygdala response to masked facial stimuli in posttraumatic stress disorder: A functional MRI study. *Biological Psychiatry, 47,* 769–776.

Reiman, E. M. (1997). The application of positron emission tomography to the study of normal and pathologic emotions. *Journal of Clinical Psychiatry, 58,* 4–12.

Reul, J. M., & de Kloet, E. R. (1986). Anatomical resolution of two types of corticosterone receptor sites in rat brain with in vitro autoradiography and computerized image analysis. *Journal of Steroid Biochemical Molecular Biology, 24* (1), 269–272.

Rogers, R. D., Owen, A. M., Middleton, H. C., Williams, E. J., Pickens, J., Sahakian, B. J., & Robbins, T. W. (1999). Choosing between small, likely rewards and large, unlikely rewards activates inferior and orbital prefrontal cortex. *Journal of Neuroscience, 20,* 9029–9038.

Rolls, E. T. (1999). The functions of the orbitofrontal cortex. *Neurocase, 5,* 301–312.

Rusch, B. D., Abercrombie, H. C., Oakes, T. R., Schaefer, S. M., & Davidson, R. J. (2001). Hippocampal morphometry in depressed patients and controls: Relations to anxiety symptoms. *Biological Psychiatry, 50,* 960–964.

Sapolsky, R. M. (2000). Glucocorticoids and hippocampal atrophy in neuropsychiatric disorders. *Archives of General Psychiatry, 57,* 925–935.

Sapolsky, R. M., Krey, L. C., & McEwans, B. S. (1986). The neuroendocrinology of stress and aging: The glucocorticoid cascade hypothesis. *Endocrinology Review, 7,* 284–301.

Sapolsky, R. M., Uno, H., Rebert, C. S., & Finch, C. E. (1990). Hippocampal damage associated with prolonged glucocorticoid exposure in primates. *Journal of Neuroscience, 10,* 2897–2902.

Saxena, S., Brody, A. L., Ho, M. L., Alborzian, S., Ho, M. K., Maidment, K., Huang, S. C., Wu, H., Au, S. C., & Baxter, L. R., Jr. (2001). Cerebral metabolism in major depression and obsessive-compulsive disorder occurring separately and concurrently. *Biological Psychiatry, 50,* 159–170.

Schaefer, S. M., Abercrombie, H. C., Lindgren, K. A., Larson, C. L., Ward, R. T., Oakes, T. R., Holden, J. E., Perlman, S. B., Turski, P. A., & Davidson, R. J. (2000). Six-month test-retest reliability of MRI-defined PET measures of regional cerebral glucose metabolic rate in selected subcortical structures. *Human Brain Mapping, 10,* 1–9.

Schneider, F., Weiss, U., Kessler, C., Muller-Gartner, H. W., Posse, S., Salloum, J. B., Grodd, W., Himmelmann, F., Gaebel, W., & Birbaumer, N. (1999). Subcortical correlates of differential classical conditioning of aversive emotional reactions in social phobia. *Biological Psychiatry, 45,* 863–971.

Schulkin, J. (1994). Melancholic depression and the hormones of adversity—A role for the amygdala. *Current Directions in Psychological Science, 3,* 41–44.

Semple, W. E., Goyer, P. F., McCormick, R., Donovan, B., Muzic, R. F. J., Rugle, L., McCutcheon, K., Lewis, C., Liebling, D., Kowaliw, S., Vapenik, K., Semple, M. A., Flener, C. R., & Schulz, S. C. (2000). Higher brain blood flow at amygdala and lower frontal cortex blood flow in PTSD patients with comorbid cocaine and alcohol abuse compared with normals. *Psychiatry, 63,* 65–74.

Servan-Schreiber, D., & Perlstein, W. M. (1997). Pharmacologic activation of limbic structures and neuroimaging studies of emotions. *Journal of Clinical Psychiatry, 58,* 13–15.

Shah, P. J., Ebmeier, K. P., Glabus, M. F., & Goodwin, G. M. (1998). Cortical grey matter reductions associated with treatment-resistant chronic unipolar depression. Controlled magnetic resonance imaging study. *British Journal of Psychiatry, 172,* 527–532.

Sheline, Y. I. (2000). 3D MRI studies of neuroanatomic changes in unipolar major depression: The role of stress and medical comorbidity. *Biological Psychiatry, 48,* 791–800.

Sheline, Y. I., Gado, M. H., & Price, J. L. (1998). Amygdala core nuclei volumes are decreased in recurrent major depression. *NeuroReport, 9,* 2023–2028.

Sheline, Y. I., Sanghavi, M., Mintun, M. A., & Gado, M. H. (1999). Depression duration but not age predicts hippocampal volume loss in medically healthy women with recurrent major depression. *Journal of Neuroscience, 19,* 5034–5043.

Sheline, Y. I., Wang, P. W., Gado, M. H., Csernansky, J. G., & Vannier, M. W. (1996). Hippocampal atrophy in recurrent major depression. *Proc. Natl. Acad. Sci. USA, 93,* 3908–3913.

Shin, L. M., Kosslyn, S. M., McNally, R. J., Alpert, N. M., Thompson, W. L., Rauch, S. L., Macklin, M. L., & Pitman, R. K. (1997). Visual imagery and perception in posttraumatic stress disorder. A positron emission tomographic investigation. *Archives of General Psychiatry, 54;* 233–241.

Squire, L. R., & Knowlton, B. J. (2000). The medial temporal lobe, the hippocampus, and the memory systems of the brain. In M. S. Gazzaniga (Ed.), *The new cognitive neurosciences* (pp. 765–779). Cambridge, MA: MIT Press.

Starkman, M. N., Giordani, B., Gebarski, S. S., Berent, S., Schork, M. A., & Schteingart, D. E. (1999). Decrease in cortisol reverses human hippocampal atrophy following treatment of Cushing's disease. *Biological Psychiatry, 46,* 1595–1602.

Steffens, D. C., Byrum, C. E., McQuoid, D. R., Greenberg, D. L., Payne, M. E., Blitchington, T. F., MacFall, J. R., & Krishnan, K. R. (2000). Hippocampal volume in geriatric depression. *Biological Psychiatry, 48,* 301–309.

Stein, M. B., Koverola, C., Hanna, C., Torchia, M. G., & McClarty, B. (1997). Hippocampal volume in women victimized by childhood sexual abuse. *Psychological Medicine, 27,* 951–959.

Strakowski, S. M., DelBello, M. P., Sax, K. W., Zimmerman, M. E., Shear, P. K., Hawkins, J. M., & Larson, E. R. (1999). Brain magnetic resonance imaging of structural abnormalities in bipolar disorder. *Archives of General Psychiatry, 56,* 254–260.

Taylor, S. E. (1991). Asymmetrical effects of positive and negative events: The mobilization-minimization hypothesis. *Psychological Bulletin, 110,* 67–85.

Tebartz van Elst, L., Woermann, F. G., Lemieux, L., & Trimble, M. R. (1999). Amygdala enlargement in dysthymia: A volumetric study of patients with temporal lobe epilepsy. *Biological Psychiatry, 46,* 1614–1623.

Tebartz van Elst, L., Woermann, F., Lemieux, L., & Trimble, M. R. (2000). Increased amygdala volumes in female and depressed humans. A quantitative magnetic resonance imaging study. *Neuroscience Letters, 281,* 103–106.

Thayer, J. F., & Lane, R. D. (2000). A model of neurovisceral integration in emotion regulation and dysregulation. *Journal of Affective Disorders, 61,* 201–216.

Vakili, K., Pillay, S. S., Lafer, B., Fava, M., Renshaw, P. F., & Bonello-Cintron, C. M. (2000). Hippocampal volume in primary unipolar major depression: A magnetic resonance imaging study. *Biological Psychiatry, 47,* 1087–1090.

Veith, R. C., Lewis, N., Linares, O. A., Barnes, R. F., Raskind, M. A., Villacres, E. C., Murburg, M. M., Ashleigh, E. A., Castillo, S., & Peskind, E. R. (1994). Sympathetic nervous system activity in major depression. Basal and desipramine-induced alterations in plasma norepinephrine kinetics. *Archives of General Psychiatry, 51,* 411–422.

Vogt, B. A., Finch, D. M., & Olson, C. R. (1992). Functional heterogeneity in cingulate cortex: The anterior executive and posterior evaluative regions. *Cerebral Cortex, 2,* 435–443.

Vogt, B. A., Nimchinsky, E. A., Vogt, L. J., & Hof, P. R. (1995). Human cingulate cortex: Surface features, flat maps, and cytoarchitecture. *Journal of Comparative Neurology, 359,* 490–506.

Von Gunten, A., Fox, N. C., Cipolotti, L., & Ron, M. A. (2000). A volumetric study of hippocampus and amygdala in depressed patients with subjective memory problems. *Journal of Neuropsychiatry and Clinical Neuroscience, 12,* 493–498.

Whalen, P. J. (1998). Fear, vigilance, and ambiguity: Initial neuroimaging studies of the human amygdala. *Current Directions in Psychological Science, 7,* 177–188.

Whalen, P. J., Bush, G., McNally, R. J., Wilhelm, S., McInerney, S. C., Jenike, M. A., & Rauch, S. L. (1998). The emotional Stroop paradigm: A functional magnetic resonance imaging probe of the anterior cingulate affective division. *Biological Psychiatry, 44,* 1219–1228.

Wu, J., Buschbaum, M. S., Gillin, J. C., Tang, C., Cadwell, S., Wiegland, M., Najafi, A., Klein, E., Hazen, K., & Bunney, W. E. (1999). Prediction of antidepressant effects of sleep deprivation by metabolic rates in the ventral anterior cingulate and medical prefrontal cortex. *American Journal of Psychiatry, 156,* 1149–1158.

Wu, J. C., Gillin, J. C., Buchsbaum, M. S., Hershey, T., Johnson, J. C., & Bunney, W. E. (1992). Effect of sleep deprivation on brain metabolism of depressed patients. *American Journal of Psychiatry, 149,* 538–543.

Yurgelun-Todd, D. A., Gruber, S. A., Kanayama, G., Killgore, D. S., Baird, A. A., & Young, A. D. (2000). fMRI during affect discrimination in bipolar affective disorder. *Bipolar Disorders, 2,* 237–248.

Zald, D. H., Lee, J. T., Fluegel, K. W., & Pardo, J. V. (1998). Aversive gustatory stimulation activates limbic circuits in humans. *Brain, 121,* 1143–1154.

Zalla, T., Koechlin, E., Pietrini, P., Basso, G., Aquino, P., Sirigu, A., & Grafman, J. (2000). Differential amygdala responses to winning and losing: A functional magnetic resonance imaging study in humans. *European Journal of Neurosci, 12,* 1764–1770.

# 3

# COMPARING THE EMOTIONAL BRAINS OF HUMANS AND OTHER ANIMALS

Kent C. Berridge

How is emotion embodied in the brain? That is the question posed by affective neuroscience (Cacioppo & Gardner, 1999; Davidson & Sutton, 1995; LeDoux, 1996; Panksepp, 1991, 1998), an enterprise that comprises the efforts of psychologists of emotion and cognition and philosophers of mind, as well as biopsychologists, psychiatrists, neurologists, and other neuroscientists. Affective neuroscience seeks a better understanding of affect and emotion at both psychological and neurobiological levels.

Evidence regarding the brain substrates of feeling and emotion has grown substantially in recent years. But which brain structures are most important for emotion seems to depend to an extent on whom you read. This chapter is intended to address an apparent division in the affective neuroscience literature between views of brain organization that see emotion primarily as a product of the *neocortex* and views that see emotion as a product of *subcortical* brain structures (Figure 3.1). Not at all by coincidence, this corresponds largely to a distinction between those who study emotion and affect in human beings or primates and those who study brain mechanisms of emotion and affect in nonprimate animals.

A newcomer to the affective neuroscience literature would deserve to be forgiven for concluding that there are actually two emotional brains. One literature comes mainly from studies of human subjects, either from PET or fMRI brain imaging of normal individuals or from clinical studies of patients with brain damage. It depicts an emotional brain that is composed chiefly of regions of neo-cortex. The second literature stresses the role of subcortical systems in emotion and comes chiefly from studies of cats, rats, and other nonprimate animals. These animal studies often involved techniques of brain manipulation (stimulation, lesion, microinjection, etc.) and measured basic behavioral or physiological emotional reactions.

Upon a quick reading one might conclude that there are two different "emotional brains," depending on which species is being studied. Human and other primate emotion apparently starts at the amygdala and goes upward to the cortex, whereas emotion in most other animals seems to proceed downward from amygdala to the brain stem.

The conclusion that human emotion is cortical but that animal emotion is subcortical would be grossly mistaken, I believe, but it is important to understand why the difference in cortical versus subcortical emphasis has arisen in affective neuroscience. Why have human and animal studies of emotion tended to emphasize different brain structures? And how does the emotional brain of humans really compare to other animals?

I will begin by considering how the two subfields of affective neuroscience differ not only in the species of their subjects but also in their conceptual and methodological approaches. Then a brief review is given of evidence that implicates brain structures from its highest to lowest levels, which suggests that neural mechanisms of affective reaction are highly distributed in both human and animal brains. To understand how the difference in cortical versus subcortical emphases has arisen, we then

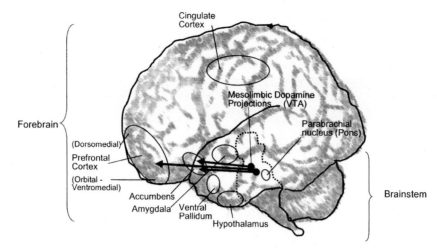

Figure 3.1 Important structures within a generalized emotional brain. The figure shows the placements of each brain structure with respect to front/back and top/bottom, but does not show the relative depth of any structure within the brain. Since the view is from the side, only one of each bilateral pairs of structures can be seen. See text for more detail.

consider various methodological and conceptual artifacts that have exaggerated the perceived difference between humans and other animals. Finally, we examine what real differences in affective neural organization are likely to exist between humans and other animals, and consider the implications of evolutionary encephalization for emotional processing in human brains.

## Affective Neuroscience of Humans: Brain Imaging and Brain-Damaged Patients

Most studies in human affective neuroscience either use brain imaging techniques to study normal human subjects or focus on emotional deficits of clinical patients who have suffered focal brain damage. Brain imaging studies include EEG measurements as well as PET or fMRI techniques. All use noninvasive measures to detect changes in large-scale electrical potentials or changes in regional blood flow in brain regions that are correlated to an emotion-related reaction. Human patient studies examine the psychological consequence of brain damage caused by vascular strokes, tumors, surgery, injury, or other disease. The damage is often unilateral, in which case it may be useful for evaluation of hemispheric specialization. For evaluation of the particular role of brain structures, such as prefrontal cortex or amygdala, however, the damage must usually be bilateral. This requirement has generally restricted patient studies to analyses of cortical regions that are often damaged by a single zone of injury, such as frontal, unilateral, or midline cortex areas, or to bilateral zones, such as the temporal lobe that contains the amyg-

dala, which are especially vulnerable to selective bilateral injury or to a disease such as epilepsy.

## Affective Neuroscience of Animals: Effect of Brain Manipulation of Emotional Reaction

The study of affective neuroscience in nonhuman animals has focused on behavioral and physiological emotional reactions in rodents such as rats, mice, or hamsters, occasionally in cats (though rarely in the past two decades), and in Old World monkeys, such as rhesus macaques. Studies of animals[1] have relied on manipulations of the brain that cause or alter the expression of emotion as much as on measures of neural activity correlated to naturally induced emotion. Common brain manipulation techniques are stereotactically placed lesions (often specific to particular types of neurons in the case of excitotoxin or neurochemical toxin lesions), electrical stimulation, and pharmacological activation or inhibition of neurotransmitter receptors by drugs delivered either systemically or by microinjection into a brain structure. Lesion studies employ a logic similar to that used in studies of brain-damaged humans. Electrical stimulation of the brain can produce the opposite consequence of lesions, exciting neural tissue in the vicinity of the electrode. Pharmacological stimulation provides a more naturalistic way of activating neuronal receptors and is neurochemically selective for neurons with a specific population of neurotransmitter receptors. Pharmacological inhibition by antagonist drugs uses a similar route to produce the opposite effect of receptor suppression. Affective neuroscience studies of animals also often use techniques to *monitor* neural activity. Electrophysiological measures use surgically implanted microelectrodes to record the neuronal firing patterns of single neurons or groups of neurons. Neurochemical measures, such as microdialysis or voltammetry, detect changes in the extracellular concentration of neurotransmitters. Neuronal metabolism measures, such as c-Fos or c-jun expression in a brain slice collected postmortem, detect the gene transcription or metabolic activation of internal second messenger systems within neurons, which often accompany sustained changes in functional activation of a neural system.

## Limbic System as the Emotional Brain

The term *limbic system* has often been taken to be synonymous with emotional brain. The neuroanatomical term offers a cloak of apparent objectivity. As developed originally by Broca, Papez, and Maclean, the limbic system included both cortical and subcortical structures: cingulate cortex, hippocampus, thalamus, and hypothalamus (Maclean, 1955; Papez, 1937/1995). But the original neuroanatomical definition has not stood the test of time. It was based on what was known prior to 1950 about neural connectivity. Anyone's definition of the emotional brain today would probably include some original structures not on the original list (e.g., amygdala, nucleus accumbens, orbitofrontal cortex) and might remove others from that list. An excellent history and cogent critique of the limbic system as a neuroanatomical concept has been provided by LeDoux (1996), who suggests the label limbic system is too flawed to be of future use. He argues that the emotional brain cannot be predefined on the basis of anatomical connections. Instead, he argues that the emotional brain can be identified only by functional studies—that is, studies that provide actual neurobehavioral evidence that a brain structure mediates some aspect of emotion.

LeDoux's criticisms of the limbic system as a neuroanatomical entity are undoubtedly right, and I believe he is correct to insist that the emotional brain can be identified only by functional studies. But although it would be more direct to simply say "emotional brain," the term *limbic system* will probably not fade from use. It is far too entrenched in current usage to be rooted out, and the apparent objectivity of its neuroanatomical concreteness—even if illusory—remains too powerfully attractive for neuroscientists to abandon it. It will forever be preferred by a group of investigators that is uncomfortable talking explicitly about emotional functions because it views terms of emotion as insufficiently concrete to serve as scientific labels and seeks an objective fig leaf. That the fig leaf is only an illusion in the mind of the wearer does not at all diminish the comfort it affords. This practice may not be entirely bad, however, since use of "limbic" (rather than,

say, the "fear brain") avoids the danger of identifying brain structures too closely with interim concepts of emotion, when either the identification or the concepts may turn out eventually to need modification. Still, both the emotions and the brain structures that mediate them must be identified by the empirical results of functional neurobehavioral studies. Even if we use the term *limbic system*, it must be defined based on functional evidence that a particular brain stem truly mediates a particular emotional process. Functional evidence reigns in deciding issues of this type. So what is the current functional evidence on the emotional or limbic brain?

## Review of Brain Structures in Emotion

### Orbitofrontal Cortex (Prefrontal Cortex)

Prefrontal cortex lies at the very front of the brain.[2] The ventral or bottom one-third of prefrontal cortex is called the orbitofrontal cortex, a name that derives from its position immediately above the eyes or orbits. Orbitofrontal cortex is most elaborately developed in humans and other primates, though it is present to some extent in all mammals. In his recent book on brain systems of emotion, Rolls writes concerning its role that "especially important for reward and punishment, emotion and motivation, are the orbitofrontal cortex and amygdala, where primary reinforcers are represented. These parts of the brain appear to be especially important in emotion and motivation not only because they are the parts of the brain where in primates the primary (unlearned) reinforcing value of stimuli is represented, but also because they are the parts of the brain that perform pattern-association learning between potential secondary reinforcers and primary reinforcers. They are thus the parts of the brain involved in learning the emotional and motivational value of stimuli" (Rolls, 1999, pp. 286–287).

In his popular and thoughtful books on human brain function, Damasio also singles out the orbital or ventromedial prefrontal cortex for special importance regarding emotion (Damasio, 1994, 1999). For example, "Primary emotions (read: innate, preorganized, Jamesian) depend on limbic system circuitry, the amygdala and anterior cingulate being the prime players. . . . But the mechanism of primary emotions does not describe the full range of emotional behaviors. . . . The network must be broadened, and it requires the agency of prefrontal and of somatosensory cortices" (Damasio, 1994, pp. 133–134).

For both Rolls and Damasio the neocortex, and especially the prefrontal cortex, is the emotional apex of the brain. Rolls's view is based on 25 years of important electrophysiological studies by him and his colleagues of orbitofrontal neurons in monkeys that have received rewards or associated stimuli. They have shown that orbitofrontal neurons fire vigorously when a monkey tastes a favorite food or when it sees the food or an associated stimulus (as do neurons in hypothalamus and amygdala; Rolls, 1997, 2000; Rolls & Baylis, 1994; Rolls, Critchley, Browning, Hernadi, & Lenard, 1999; Rolls, Yaxley, & Sienkiewicz, 1990). Orbitofrontal cortex neurons, these studies find, respond especially to the hedonic or affective reward properties of the taste or to the sight of the learned stimulus that predicts those reward properties. Most especially, if the predictive reward value of a learned stimulus is switched back and forth, orbitofrontal neurons uniquely track the switch and change their response to follow the current reward-signaling status of the stimulus (Rolls, 2000; Rolls, Scott, Sienkiewicz, & Yaxley, 1988). Also, if the monkey is allowed to eat its fill of a particular delicious food, orbitofrontal neurons cease firing to its sight or smell, showing a neural decrement that correlates to the food's diminished hedonic value (Rolls et al., 1988). Most "reward neurons" in other regions of the brain, by contrast, remain constant in response to the same situation, coding the "sensory quality" of the taste rather than the "affective quality," though hypothalamus and amygdala may also be affective exceptions (Rolls, 1999; Yan & Scott, 1996). When humans eat a food to repletion, the palatability or pleasure they report to further tastes of the food diminishes (Cabanac, 1979), and the decline in orbitofrontal neuron firing presumably reflects a related decrease in hedonic impact for the monkey.

Brain imaging PET and fMRI studies of normal human subjects have found changes in orbitofrontal cortex in response to pleasant or unpleasant tastes (Zald, Lee, Fluegel, & Pardo, 1998) and odors (Francis et al., 1999; Zald & Pardo, 1997) (although not all studies have found orbitofrontal changes in response to pleasant/unpleasant odors [Fulbright et al., 1998]). Similarly, human orbitofrontal activation has been found to pleasant touch (Francis et al., 1999), and even to pleasant music (Blood, Zatorre, Bermudez, & Evans, 1999) or to a monetary reward (Thut et al., 1997). Changes in human prefrontal cortex (containing orbitofrontal cortex) have also been reported to be evoked by traumatic photographs in former soldiers who suffered from posttraumatic stress disorder (Bremner et al., 1999; actually this study showed a *decrease* in PET measured blood flow during the emotion, but the relation of blood flow to neuronal or neurochemical activation is complex).

Basic rewarding stimuli such as cocaine or similar drugs also produce changes in human orbitofrontal cortex. Orbitofrontal responses have been found in humans to cocaine, opiates, and THC (the active ingredient in marijuana), especially in regular abusers (Breiter et al., 1997; Firestone et al., 1996; Volkow et al., 1996). Even stimuli associated with cocaine use, which evokes feelings of craving in addicts, may activate the prefrontal cortex (Maas et al., 1998), though not in all studies (Childress et al., 1999).

Most of the focus on the prefrontal cortex has come from studies of humans or monkeys, but other animals show prefrontal responses to emotional events too (Kolb & Tees, 1990). In rats, prefrontal cortex neurons have been shown to fire action potentials in response to cocaine or heroin (Chang, Janak, & Woodward, 1998) or in response to an odor that signals a reward (Schoenbaum, Chiba, & Gallagher, 1999). Rats will also work to administer a microinjection of cocaine or related drugs directly into their medial prefrontal cortex (Carlezon & Wise, 1996; Goeders & Smith, 1983). There are even neuroanatomical changes induced in the structure of dendrites on neurons in prefrontal cortex of rats after exposure to addictive drugs that produce neurobehavioral sensitization (Robinson & Kolb, 1997, 1999).

Neurochemical release of dopamine in the prefrontal cortex of rats, measured by microdialysis or in vivo voltammetry, occurs when a rat eats an especially palatable food (Bassareo & DiChiara, 1997) or when it works for a food reward (Richardson & Gratton, 1998). Expression of "immediate early gene" markers such as Fos protein, indicating rapid transcription of the c-Fos gene and probable metabolic activation of the neuron, is triggered in rat prefrontal cortex by rewarding electrical brain stimulation of the hypothalamus (Hunt & McGregor, 1998). Unpleasant shocks or other stressful events also elicit dopamine release in the prefrontal cortex of rats, as do associated stimuli that predict those stressful events (Davis et al., 1994; Yoshioka, Matsumoto, Togashi, & Saito, 1996). Thus, in humans, monkeys, and rats, affective stimuli are powerful elicitors of neural activation in prefrontal and orbitofrontal cortex.

What are the emotional consequences of losing orbitofrontal or entire prefrontal cortex? The answer to this is crucial for interpreting whether or not prefrontal cortex activation is truly a neural apex for emotion. Is orbitofrontal or other prefrontal cortex *necessary for causation of the emotion* triggered by affective events? If so, then loss of prefrontal cortex should disrupt the capacity for most emotional experiences and responses. However, the consequence of prefrontal cortex loss appears to be far more subtle than a loss of emotion. This is our first clue that prefrontal cortex plays a different causal role than to "mediate" emotion in a simple direct sense.

Rolls (1999, p. 115) writes that "in the human, euphoria, irresponsibility, and lack of affect can follow frontal lobe damage" (see Kolb & Whishaw, 1990; Damasio, 1994; Eslinger & Damasio, 1985), particularly orbitofrontal damage" (Rolls, Hornak, Wade, & McGrath, 1994a). Lack of affect is indeed what one might expect if the capacity for emotion were eliminated, though it is somewhat contradicted by the listing of euphoria as another consequence.

The paradox between euphoria versus flattened affect after damage to prefrontal cortex may be partly resolved by distinguishing subregions within it (Cummings, 1995;

Tucker, Luu, & Pribram, 1995). Lack of affect and general apathy are most often reported after damage to the dorsal region, especially to dorsomedial prefrontal cortex. Euphoria, impulsiveness, and general emotional disinhibition appears to be more commonly a consequence of damage to the ventral region, especially ventromedial and orbital prefrontal cortex (Tucker et al., 1995). Some neuroanatomists argue further that among ventral prefrontal cortex, the ventromedial region can be distinguished anatomically from the orbital region on the basis of connections with other structures, a distinction that appears to apply to monkeys and rats as well as to humans (Kolb & Tees, 1990; Ongur & Price, 2000). For example, taste and smell inputs appear to go most directly to the orbital region, whereas outputs to the nucleus accumbens originate primarily in the ventromedial region (Ongur & Price, 2000).

But how important is prefrontal cortex to the actual *causation* of an emotion? If by lack of affect is meant the utter loss of affective reactions, then that appears to be extremely rare and perhaps nonexistent in humans after prefrontal damage (Damasio, 1994, 1996). All prefrontal lesion patients still seek some simple pleasures: they choose palatable foods and eat them (and may even overeat); they react to some pains and avoid some unpleasant events; and they may become angry, or fearful, or sexually aroused in certain situations. Though their behavior regarding emotional events may be unquestionably odd in certain respects, it would clearly be an exaggeration to say that they have lost all emotion or are incapable of affective reaction (Damasio, 1994, 1996; Valenstein, 1986).

Animals, too, after prefrontal lesions react affectively to many emotional stimuli, even if their reactions are sometimes blunted or misdirected. Rolls writes (1999, p. 115) that rhesus monkeys after prefrontal lesions have "reduced aggression to humans and to stimuli such as a snake and a doll, a reduced tendency to reject foods such as meat [Butter, McDonald, & Snyder, 1969; Butter & Snyder, 1972; Butter, Snyder, & McDonald, 1970], and a failure to display the normal preference rankings for different foods" (Baylis & Gaffan, 1991). These emotional deficits seem relatively subtle, compared to the possibility of losing all emotion that might be expected if the prefrontal cortex were the chief site "where primary reinforcers are represented."

In a fascinating study of human patients after loss of the prefrontal cortex, Bechara and colleagues (Bechara, Damasio, Tranel, & Damasio, 1997) asked prefrontal patients to play a card game in which they could win or lose a reward, and in which they had to figure out the best strategy for winning on their own as they went along. Bechara and colleagues found that prefrontal patients were eventually able to figure out the strategy for winning of the game and to describe it explicitly, but they had several deficits. First, while normal subjects seemed to absorb and use the inferred strategy in relatively early trials, guided by hunches they could not explain even before they were able to explicitly describe what that strategy was, prefrontal patients were not able to follow these "nonconscious biases" prior to being able to describe the strategy. Second, even after they were able to explicitly describe the strategy, prefrontal patients sometimes still failed to follow it in their playing, and made unwise decisions and incurred losses even though in one sense they "knew" and could say what the best strategy was. From neuropsychological tests, such as the Wisconsin card-sorting task, prefrontal lesions are famous for inducing such perseverative errors (especially dorsolateral prefrontal lesions), such as continuing to employ a choice strategy even after it becomes wrong and a different strategy is called for—and even if the patient knows and can say that it is wrong (Hauser, 1999; Kolb & Whishaw, 1996). Finally, prefrontal patients had blunted autonomic skin conductance responses to outcomes while playing the game. In particular, they failed to show a skin conductance response when they played strategies that produced losses, in advance of the loss itself, unlike normal subjects who showed the autonomic response and may have used it as a cue to guide subsequent action (Bechara et al., 1997).

Damasio and colleagues interpret the lack of such anticipatory autonomic emotional reactions to loss to mean that prefrontal patients are unable to generate or to follow "somatic markers" that label emotional outcomes, and so the patients fail to devise and follow the strategies based on emotional outcome that often guide normal human behavior (Bechara, Damasio, & Damasio, 2000; Bechara et al., 1997; Damasio, 1994, 1996, 1998). Somatic markers, according to Damasio, are physiological reactions, such as the skin conductance response, often generated to an emotional event without conscious awareness (a view of affective reaction similar to that suggested by Zajonc [1980, 1998]). Damasio and colleagues suggest these reactions may function as crucial informational cues for further action. They may possibly influence the final conscious experience of the emotion (in a sense similar to the classic James-Lange hypothesis, in that they may cause sensations that are felt as part of the conscious emotion; James, 1884), but more certainly are posited to guide or trigger behavioral strategies on the basis of the emotion. It is the failure to use somatic markers, Damasio suggests, that makes prefrontal patients unable to benefit from normal "nonconscious biases" that provide useful hunches and that makes them choose wrongly even after they explicitly understand the rules (Bechara et al., 1997; Damasio, 1994, 1996, 1998).

The "somatic marker" hypothesis of emotion offered by Damasio and colleagues is remarkable in part for its specificity regarding the role of prefrontal cortex in emotion. This role is very different from a general loss of primary or even secondary emotion and is much more circumscribed than emotional loss. After loss of prefrontal cortex, people may fail to generate some emotional reactions and may fail in some way to incorporate the emotional consequences of their own actions into their everyday behavioral strategies. But they do not lose all capacity for affective reaction, they are not missing all primary emotions or any particular emotion, and they do not even lack capacity for learning emotion. They are still emotional creatures in virtually every sense—just, sometimes and in subtle ways, slightly odd in they way they act on their emotions.

An intriguing and related hypothesis has been suggested for prefrontal cortex—namely, that *emotional regulation* may be the psychological function most impaired (Davidson, Jackson, & Kalin, 2000; Tucker et al., 1995). Emotional regulation means to exercise deliberate voluntary control over the magnitude of an emotional or affective reaction. This can mean either to deliberately suppress an emotional reaction that might otherwise occur, or to deliberately induce an emotion in oneself by cognitive means (Davidson et al., 2000; Tucker et al., 1995). It has even been suggested that suppression versus induction types of emotional regulation might be mediated by different prefrontal regions, such that euphoria after ventral or orbital damage could reflect lack of regulatory suppression of emotional reaction, whereas lack of affect after dorsomedial damage could reflect loss of regulatory induction of emotion (Tucker et al., 1995). As yet, little experimental evidence exists concerning the role of prefrontal cortex in emotional regulation, although one promising approach has begun to compare cortical activity during voluntary changes in emotional reaction to that during spontaneously induced emotion (Davidson et al., 2000).

### Cingulate Cortex

Cingulate cortex consists of a longitudinal strip running front to back along the midline on each hemisphere of the brain. The anterior or front region of this strip is especially implicated in human emotion, as alluded to in the quote above from Damasio, and cingulate cortex has been implicated in human clinical conditions such as depression, anxiety, and other distressing states (Davidson, Abercrombie, Nitschke, & Putnam, 1999).

Pain and distress in many forms have been linked to cingulate cortex by PET and fMRI brain imaging studies (Davis, Taylor, Crawley, Wood, & Mikulis, 1997; Porro, Cettolo, Francescato, & Baraldi, 1998; Rainville, Duncan, Price, Carrier, & Bushnell, 1997; Tolle et al., 1999). Even the mere anticipation of pain may produce fMRI activation of (right) anterior cingulate cortex (Hsieh, Stone-Elander, & Ingvar, 1999). *Reduction* of pain via opiate fentanyl anesthesia has also been suggested to *increase* PET signal in cingulate cortex, somewhat paradoxically, even though it decreases the subjective conscious experience of the pain that by itself seems to produce cingulate activation (Adler

et al., 1997). Nitrous oxide anesthesia, by contrast, may abolish the cingulate PET response to pain (Gyulai, Firestone, Mintun, & Winter, 1997). Clearly, the neural encoding of pain and anesthesia must be complex, and the full story remains to be understood.

Analgesia induced by hypnosis has been reported to reduce the electrical potential evoked from human cingulate cortex by a painful skin stimulus (Kropotov, Crawford, & Polyakov, 1997). A favored neurosurgical approach to the treatment of intractable pain in human patients has long been surgical destruction of the cingulate cortex, and this appears effective often (Hurt & Ballantine, 1974; Kondziolka, 1999). For reasons that are less clear, cingulate cortex lesions have also been favored for a variety of other human psychological disorders such as depression and obsessive-compulsive disorder (Hay et al., 1993; Hay & Sachdev, 1992; Valenstein, 1986). Remarkably, cingulate cortex lesions have even been suggested as a possible psychosurgical "treatment" for human sex offenders (Brown, 1995), although the impaired ability to inhibit nonreward responses that follow cingulate cortex lesions in animals (below) raises the question as to whether cingulate lesions might instead exacerbate some sexual offences. It is worth noting that prescriptive psychosurgery applied to criminal or antisocial behavior in humans has had a very poor record in the past (Valenstein, 1974, 1986).

Brain imaging studies of cingulate cortex in other emotional situations have produced results similar to orbitofrontal or prefrontal cortex. Affectively rewarding drugs like cocaine, fentanyl, or marijuana's THC produced increased fMRI blood flow signal in cingulate when given intravenously (Breiter et al., 1997; Firestone et al., 1996; Mathew, Wilson, Coleman, Turkington, & DeGrado, 1997), though cingulate cortex was also activated by procaine HCI infusions that triggered panic attacks that were unpleasant (Servan-Schreiber, Perlstein, Cohen, & Mintun, 1998). Even mere craving for cocaine, induced by photographs of drug use, appears to produce cingulate activation in human drug addicts (Childress et al., 1999; Maas et al., 1998). Induction of sexual arousal or of competitive arousal, in men at least, also has been linked in one PET study to increased blood flow in anterior cingulate cortex (Rauch et al., 1999).

Transient sadness and clinical depression both have been associated with cingulate fMRI activation (Mayberg et al., 1999). Gustatory distaste for an unpleasant concentrated salt solution also activates cingulate cortex (Zald et al., 1998), and the cingulate cortex was the structure that showed the strongest PET signal in humans experiencing sensations of thirst (Denton et al., 1999).

There are intriguing suggestions that the recognition of emotional facial expression may involve cingulate cortex. Captioned photographs of both positive and negative emotional scenes produced fMRI activation in the right cingulate cortex, possibly with a special advantage for negative scenes (Teasdale et al., 1999). However, no special cingulate involvement was found to sad faces in a study of expression recognition, though happy faces produced left sided cingulate activation (Phillips et al., 1998). The laterality of these reported effects is consistent with Davidson's suggestion of left-hemisphere specialization for positive emotion, and right-hemisphere specialization for negative emotion, discussed below (Davidson, 1998a; Davidson & Sutton, 1995; Sutton & Davidson, 1997).

Although human subjects constitute the main source for a role of cingulate cortex in emotion, studies of rats also provide evidence for cingulate cortex activation in emotional situations. The c-Fos marker of neuronal activation is increased in cingulate cortex of rats that fear an impending electric shock (Beck & Fibiger, 1995). In positive emotional situations, cingulate cortex lesions in rats are reported to result in an increase in responses to a non-rewarded stimulus (Bussey, Everitt, & Robbins, 1997) and to increase perseverative responses to no-longer rewarded maze choice (Seamans, Floresco, & Phillips, 1995).

### Amygdala

The amygdala is one of the best known structures in animal and human affective neuroscience and features prominently in most brain-referenced theories of emotion (Cacioppo, Gardner, & Berntson, 1999; Damasio, 1994; Davidson et al., 1999; Gallagher & Chiba, 1996; Gray & McNaughton, 1996; Kagan & Schulkin, 1995; LeDoux, 1996; Panksepp, 1998; Rolls, 1999; Schulkin, 1994; Toates, 1994; Zajonc, 1998).

Kagan, Schulkin, and others have posited human anxiety disorders to be modulated by chronic hyperactivity in the amygdala (Kagan & Snidman, 1991; Schulkin, 1994; Schwartz, Snidman, & Kagan, 1996). In brain-imaging studies, human subjects who experienced an unpleasant taste or odor showed changes in PET signal in amygdala (Zald et al., 1998; Zald & Pardo, 1997), as did subjects who experienced intense feelings of thirst (Denton et al., 1999). The visual perception of an angry or fearful face also has been reported to trigger changes in blood flow to human amygdala (Baird et al., 1999; Phillips et al., 1997), though another PET study reported amygdala activation after visual perception of sad facial expressions but not of angry expressions (Blair, Morris, Frith, Perrett, & Dolan, 1999). In some cases, the amygdala change may occur even if the face is seen too briefly to be consciously perceived (i.e., in a subliminal priming paradigm; Morris, Ohman, & Dolan, 1998). Emotionally unpleasant photographs of other types also have been reported to elicit amygdala PET changes (Lane et al., 1997). Classical conditioning of responses to particular faces, induced by pairing neutral facial expressions with an unpleasant odor, induced suppression of fMRI signal in amygdala of normal subjects,

but an increase in signal in patients with social phobias (Schneider et al., 1999).

Adolphs and colleagues found that a human patient who had bilateral lesions of the amygdala showed impaired recognition of emotional facial expression, especially for fearful expressions (Adolphs, Tranel, Damasio, & Damasio, 1994; Adolphs, Tranel, Damasio, & Damasio, 1995). Similarly, auditory recognition of fear expressed by a human voice has been reported to be impaired after amygdala lesions (Scott et al., 1997). However, another study found normal recognition of vocal expression of fear in a patient with bilateral amygdala damaged, and suggested that deficits of auditory emotional recognition may actually be due to damage to basal ganglia (i.e., caudate-putamen or neostriatum) rather than to amygdala (Anderson & Phelps, 1998).

In rats, conditioned fear and anxiety reactions have long been known to depend on the amygdala (Davis, 1992; Fanselow & LeDoux, 1999; Gallagher & Chiba, 1996; LeDoux, 1996, 1992; Maren & Fanselow, 1996). In the literature on animal amygdala, a distinction is often made between subregions of the amygdala. In particular, the basolateral nucleus of the amygdala lies at the bottom outside edge of the amygdala on both sides, whereas the central nucleus of the amygdala lies slightly above and nearer the middle of the brain. The basolateral nucleus of the amygdala receives many sensory inputs from other brain structures, and it projects chiefly to the central nucleus of the amygdala in turn. This arrangement allows information to be processed in a serial fashion, first in basolateral nucleus and then in central nucleus (Fanselow & LeDoux, 1999; LeDoux, 1998; Maren, 1999a). However, there also exist some direct sensory inputs from other brain structures to amygdala central nucleus, which bypass the basolateral nucleus and direct outputs from basolateral nucleus to other brain structures, which bypass the central nucleus, and these pathways allow for the possibility of independent or parallel processing too (Everitt, Cardinal, Hall, Parkinson, & Robbins, 2000; Killcross, Robbins, & Everitt, 1997; Parkinson, Robbins, & Everitt, 2000). The relative roles of basolateral and central amygdala subregions in emotion is currently a topic of much research in animal affective neuroscience.

Lesions of the basolateral or central amygdala in rats often disrupt the acquisition of new conditioned fears, as well as the expression of "old" fears conditioned to previously trained sounds or places (Davis, 1992; Fanselow & LeDoux, 1999; Killcross et al., 1997; LeDoux, 1996; Maren & Fanselow, 1996). However, some investigators have suggested that basolateral amygdala and central amygdala play different roles in fear learning and that lesions of the two nuclei may disrupt different types of learned fear responses (Killcross et al., 1997).

Amygdala lesions alter many reactions of animals to emotionally *positive* events as well, as has been apparent since the Kluver and Bucy's original report of hyper-orality and hypersexuality in monkeys (Kluver & Bucy, 1939). Reaction to primary rewards is altered in other species as well. For example, rats fail to work for a salty reward when they are in a physiological state of sodium depletion (Schulkin, 1991; Schulkin, Marini, & Epstein, 1989) and fail to consume salt that is freely given after amygdala lesions, even though they emit normal positive hedonic reactions to a salty taste if it is put into their mouths (Galaverna et al., 1993; Schulkin, 1991; Seeley, Galaverna, Schulkin, Epstein, & Grill, 1993).

Everitt and Robbins and their colleagues have suggested aspects of reward *learning* to be especially disrupted by amygdala damage (Everitt et al., 2000; Everitt & Robbins, 1992; Parkinson et al., 2000). For example, male rats fail to perform a learned task to earn access to a sexual partner after amygdala damage, even though the same rats will engage in copulation if access to the female is freely granted (Everitt, 1990). Similarly, in a "conditioned reinforcement" task, lesions of the basolateral amygdala appear to reduce the value of learned rewards to rats. Ordinary rats will work for conditioned stimulus (a light or sound) that has been paired either with food or with a sexual partner, but amygdala lesions eliminate such "conditioned reinforcement" and disrupt some other appetitive learned responses (though the rats will still work for food reward itself; Everitt, 1990; Everitt et al., 2000; Everitt & Robbins, 1992; Parkinson et al., 2000).

The parenthetical caveat above signifies that destruction of the amygdala is clearly not sufficient to eliminate all reward or emotional learning, as there is much evidence that aspects of learned reward and learned fear persist after amygdala destruction. For example, monkeys still show fear to especially strong stimuli after bilateral amygdala lesions (Kling & Brothers, 1992), even though the original Kluver-Bucy syndrome emphasized the taming of monkeys and apparent elimination of fear in some situations (Kluver & Bucy, 1939). Many of the deficits of conditioned fear or conditioned reward produced by damage to the amygdala appear to be specific to a particular *type* of fearful or reward stimulus or to a particular task or measure of fear or reward learning (Everitt & Robbins, 1992; Hatfield, Han, Conley, Gallagher, & Holland, 1996; Kim & Davis, 1993; Pesold & Treit, 1995; Treit, Pesold, & Rotzinger, 1993).

Perhaps the most "typical" deficit after amygdala damage is the loss of Pavlovian conditioned fear responses such as freezing or startle in response to a shock paired sound. Pavlovian fear learning is considered by some to be a chief emotional function carried out by amygdala systems (Davis & Lee, 1998; Fanselow & LeDoux, 1999; LeDoux, 1996; Maren, 1999a). But even the "lost" capacity to learn some Pavlovian conditioned fear reactions may reemerge to relatively normal levels after central or baso-lateral amygdala lesions if rats are given many additional learning trials (Kim & Davis, 1993; Maren, 1999b), suggesting that fear learning is not lost but merely very slowed after the lesion. And a human patient who is unable to categorize the visual perception of a fearful facial expression may nonetheless recognize fear in verbal descriptions and even be able to produce excellent voluntary facial expressions of fear herself (Anderson & Phelps, 2000). Whether any particular type of fear learning or other psychological category of emotional learning or emotional reaction will eventually be found to be totally disrupted by amygdala lesions remains at present an open question.

An alternative view is that amygdala lesions do not eliminate any learned emotions or affective reactions of any type (Berridge, 1999; Gallagher & Holland, 1994; Weiskrantz, 1997). Instead, they appear to disturb a *targeting* of affective reaction to particular stimuli. As Weiskrantz (1956) put it in an early and perspicacious observation, what amygdala lesions appear to do is to disrupt an aspect of the "emotional significance of perceived stimuli." That may not be the same as disruption of emotion itself. The motivational targeting function would be instead a *nonaffective* process that controls the *triggering* of reward, fear, and other motivational and emotional processes by particular stimuli. The targeting function has been suggested by some to be an attentional mechanism that gates information processing (Gallagher & Holland, 1994) or to be an incentive salience assignment mechanism that attaches motivational significance to the perception of particular stimuli (Berridge, 1999). However, a complete account has not been formulated in terms of either of these frameworks, nor in terms of emotion (fear, reward, etc.), associative learning, or of emotional learning, which can satisfactorily account for the deficits that result from amygdala damage (see also Aggleton, 2000, and pp. 547–553 in Berridge, 1999). It remains a challenge for affective neuroscience to produce a proper characterization of the role of amygdala nuclei in fear and in other emotion.

## Accumbens and Mesolimbic Dopamine and Opioid Systems

The nucleus accumbens, which lies at the front of subcortical forebrain and is rich in dopamine and opioid neurotransmitter systems, is a brain structure as famous for *positive* affective states as the amygdala is for fear. Accumbens systems are often portrayed as reward and pleasure systems. Activation of dopamine projections to the accumbens and related targets has been viewed by many neuroscientists as a neural "common currency" for reward (Koob & Le Moal, 1997; Panksepp, 1998; Phillips, Blaha, Pfaus, & Blackburn, 1992; Rolls, 1999; Shizgal, 1997;

Wise, 1996). For example, Shizgal calls the neural system constituted by these brain structures an "affective channel" for positive reward (Shizgal, 1999).

Drugs, rather than lesions, have often been used to study the affective consequences of suppression or activation of accumbens-related dopamine and opioid systems (Koob & Le Moal, 1997). The simple social fact that billions of human beings have chosen to stimulate their own mesolimbic systems via the ingestion of drugs, beginning thousands of year ago with alcohol and opiates and continuing today with a vast array of natural and synthetic compounds, constitutes a kind of voluntary experiment by generations of human subjects whose results support a causal role of this brain system in positive emotion (Nesse & Berridge, 1997).

Dopamine (especially dopamine projections to accumbens) has often been called the "brain's pleasure neurotransmitter" (Nash, 1997; Pani & Gessa, 1997; Wickelgren, 1997; Wise, 1985). In rats, electrophysiological or neurochemical studies of accumbens neuronal activity or dopamine release have shown this neural system to be activated by many pleasant rewards. For example, accumbens activation and dopamine release occur in response to palatable food (Apicella, Ljungberg, Scarnati, & Schultz, 1991; Blackburn, Phillips, Jakubovic, & Fibiger, 1989; Richardson & Gratton, 1996; Schultz, Dayan, & Montague, 1997), to rewards such as heroin or amphetamine (Kiyatkin, Wise, & Gratton, 1993; Ranaldi, Pocock, Zereik, & Wise, 1999), and to the chance to engage in sexual copulation in both females and males (Fiorino, Coury, & Phillips, 1997; Mermelstein & Becker, 1995; Pfaus, Damsma, Wenkstern, & Fibiger, 1995). Accumbens activation and dopamine release are also elicited by secondary rewards, such as conditioned stimuli that have been paired with food, drugs, or sex (Apicella et al., 1991; Di Ciano, Blaha, & Phillips, 1998; Hoebel, Mark, & West, 1992; Hollerman, Tremblay, & Schultz, 1998; Kiyatkin & Gratton, 1994).

Rewarding electrical brain stimulation (typically delivered via hypothalamic electrodes) may be a related reward mediated by this system, though in some ways it is more difficult to interpret. Brain stimulation reward has long been viewed as mediated by mesoaccumbens dopamine systems (Gallistel, Boytim, Gomita, & Klebanoff, 1982; Phillips & Fibiger, 1973; Shizgal, 1997; Wise, 1998). However, direct measures indicate only weak neuronal activation of dopamine projections by electrical stimulation (Gallistel, 1986; Garris et al., 1999; Hunt & McGregor, 1998). Conversely, drugs that block dopamine receptors were once suggested to produce anhedonia (Wise, 1985), and certainly those drugs reduce some aspect of reward, as they decrease the willingness of animals to work for food rewards (Blackburn, Phillips, & Fibiger, 1987; Ettenberg & Camp, 1986; Salamone, Cousins, & Snyder, 1997; Smith, 1995; Wise, Spindler, deWit, & Gerberg, 1978), ad-

dictive drug rewards (De Wit & Wise, 1977; McFarland & Ettenberg, 1998; Roberts, Loh, & Vickers, 1989), and electrical brain stimulation rewards (Fouriezos & Wise, 1976; Gallistel & Karras, 1984; Nakajima & Patterson, 1997; Wise, 1991), among other reward-related effects.

In human imaging studies of accumbens or of dopamine projections, signal activation has been reported to be produced by many types of rewarding drugs of abuse that human addicts commonly take, including amphetamine, heroin, cocaine, and fentanyl (Breiter et al., 1997; Firestone et al., 1996; Sell et al., 1999; Vollenweider, Maguire, Leenders, Mathys, & Angst, 1998). Even mere craving for these drugs, induced by looking at photographs of people taking drugs, appears to modulate these neural systems (Childress et al., 1999; Sell et al., 1999). Purely psychological human recreations also appear to activate dopamine systems in the nucleus accumbens and related structures (sometimes called ventral striatum in humans). For example, human subjects in a PET study played a tank battle videogame in which they won money whenever they collected flags or destroyed the enemy tanks, and players showed an increase in the amount of dopamine released in their nucleus accumbens (indicated by a decrease in the binding of a radioactive drug to dopamine receptors, because extra dopamine presumably displaced the drug from the receptors; Koepp et al., 1998). Regarding this observation, the authors wrote: "We interpret changes in ventral striatal [11C] RAC binding to be related to affective components of the task" (Koepp et al., 1998, p. 267).

My colleagues and I have conducted a number of studies in rats on the role of dopamine in hedonic impact over the past decade, guided at first by the hypothesis that "dopamine = hedonia" (Gardner & Lowinson, 1993; Wise, 1985). We have measured behavioral affective reactions of rats to food reward, which are related to the facial expressions that human babies show to sweet tastes (Steiner, 1973; Steiner, Glaser, Hawilo, & Berridge, 2001). Those positive affective reactions provide a specific behavioral measure of the *hedonic impact* of a taste (Berridge, 2000). We originally expected to find that manipulations that suppressed dopamine neurotransmission would impair the hedonic impact of food rewards and suppress positive affective reactions to a sweet taste. Therefore, we were surprised to find that dopamine did not seem necessary for normal hedonic reaction to the reward property of sweet tastes. Neither anti-dopamine drugs nor massive 6-OHDA lesions of dopamine neurons impaired hedonic impact, as expressed by affective reactions (Berridge & Robinson, 1998; Berridge, Venier, & Robinson, 1989; Peciña, Berridge, & Parker, 1997).

That was puzzling because it seems quite clear that dopamine is needed for *some* aspect of reward (Panksepp, 1998; Rolls, 1999; Shizgal, 1997; Smith, 1995; Wise, 1982;

Wise, 1985). To help resolve the puzzle, my colleagues and I suggested that incentive salience or "wanting" for rewards better captures the psychological aspect of reward contributed by dopamine, rather than pleasure, hedonic impact, or "liking" for the same rewards (see Berridge & Robinson, 1998, for review). Consistent with our hypothesis that "dopamine is needed for wanting but not liking" are recent reports that suppression of dopamine neurotransmission in humans who take a pleasurable drug, such as amphetamine or cocaine, does not suppress their reported drug pleasure, even when it reduces their drug craving (Brauer & De Wit, 1997; Brauer, Goudie, & de Wit, 1997). Finally, I should also mention that dopamine accumbens systems are activated in aversive situations such as when rats expect or receive foot shock or other stressors (Gray et al., 1997; Rada, Mark, & Hoebel, 1998; Salamone, 1994; Young, Ahier, Upton, Joseph, & Gray, 1998). The psychological implications of this joint participation in positive and negative motivational states are complex, however, and do not necessarily rule out an important "wanting" role for dopamine in positive reward (see pp. 348–349 in Berridge & Robinson, 1998, for discussion of dopamine's shared role in positive and negative motivation).

Regardless of the role of dopamine in reward, accumbens neurons with receptors for *opioid* neurotransmitters do appear to mediate hedonic affect or "liking" as well as "wanting" for a drug or sugar reward. Rats will work to obtain microinjections of amphetamine, PCP (angel dust), and many other drugs directly into their nucleus accumbens (Carlezon & Wise, 1996). Microinjections in the nucleus accumbens of drugs that block opioid receptors can reduce the reward value of heroin or cocaine to rats, and microinjections that activate opioid receptors conversely enhance the reward value of such drugs (Stewart & Vezina, 1988). Further, activation of opioid receptors, unlike activation of dopamine receptors, does enhance the hedonic impact of sweet rewards, as measured by behavioral affective reactions elicited by the taste of sucrose (Berridge, 1996; Berridge, 2000; Peciña & Berridge, 1995; Peciña & Berridge, 2000; Rideout & Parker, 1996; Treit & Berridge, 1990).

It has recently become clear that one subregion of the nucleus accumbens in particular (an outer wrapping called the "shell") contains opioid receptors that can cause increases in the capacity of tasty food rewards to trigger "liking" or hedonic impact. Susana Peciña and I have found that microinjection of morphine, which activates opioid receptors, directly into a posterior and medial region of accumbens shell is sufficient to increase the ability of a sweet taste to elicit positive affective reactions (Peciña, 1998; Peciña & Berridge, 2000). Thus accumbens neurons that have opioid receptors seem to be a true hedonic substrate capable of enhancing a natural sensory pleasure.

## Lateral Hypothalamus

The hypothalamus was perhaps the first brain structure to be highlighted by functional affective neuroscience nearly a half-century ago. A host of discoveries in the 1950s and 1960s on the behavioral consequences of lesions and stimulation cemented the status of the hypothalamus as crucial to motivations such as sex or hunger, and to emotional displays (Stellar, 1954; Teitelbaum & Epstein, 1962). Lesions of the lateral hypothalamus in rats or cats abolish eating, drinking, sexual behavior, and several other forms of motivated behavior. Conversely, eating and social or defensive aggression are increased by lesions to the ventromedial hypothalamus.

When the firing patterns of lateral hypothalamic neurons in rats, rabbits, or monkeys have been studied by electrophysiological recording, neurons have been found that fire to the hedonic properties of food rewards, and even to the mere sight of food (Rolls, 1999; Schwartzbaum, 1988). Rolls and colleagues found that lateral hypothalamic neurons in monkeys responded to the reward properties of food, in that they fired more when the monkey was hungry than after it had eaten to satiation (Rolls, 1999; Rolls, Murzi, Yaxley, Thorpe, & Simpson, 1986). This sensitivity to hunger/satiety mirrors the increase in subjective or behavioral hedonic reactions to the taste of food, which occur in humans and animals when they are hungry (Berridge, 1991; Cabanac, 1992; Cabanac & Lafrance, 1990). Increases in hedonic palatability during hunger have been called alliesthesia by Cabanac (1979). The only other brain regions in monkeys known to show an electrophysiological alliesthesia response during hunger/satiation shifts are neurons in the orbitofrontal cortex (Rolls, 1999, 2000) and, to some degree, the amygdala (Yan & Scott, 1996).

Together with the discovery that electrical brain stimulation of the hypothalamus in animals could elicit motivated or emotional behavior (e.g., eating, maternal behavior towards infants, predatory attack, fearful freezing or defensive attack, hoarding behavior directed to food or other objects), the hypothalamus was firmly established as a prime substrate for the generation of motivation (Teitelbaum & Stricker, 1994). Originally, these behaviors were viewed as reflecting activation of neural circuits dedicated to hunger, sex, fear, and so on. However, a series of experiments by Valenstein and his colleagues around 1970 showed that the motivational state aroused by hypothalamic stimulation was actually quite flexible in nature and that its expression depended intimately on the predisposition of the individual and on past experience (Valenstein, 1971; Valenstein, Cox, & Kakolewski, 1969, 1970).

A further affective tone was added to hypothalamic electrical stimulation by the important discovery by Olds and Milner in 1954 of brain stimulation reward: rats would quickly learn to work in order to gain stimulation of the lateral hypothalamus or adjacent regions (Olds &

Milner, 1954). Brain stimulation reward has proved tremendously useful for identifying properties of neural circuits for reward (Gallistel, 1986; Shizgal, 1997, 1999; Yeomans, 1995). Humans, too, if they have electrodes implanted in their brains and given a button to activate them, will stimulate equivalent brain regions, sometimes thousands of times in a single session (Heath, 1972). However, whether electrical stimulation of the hypothalamus produces actual sensations of pleasure is open to doubt. For example, stimulation of the lateral hypothalamus in rats fails to enhance the ability of a sweet taste to elicit positive affective reactions (Berridge & Valenstein, 1991), even though lateral hypothalamic stimulation had earlier been suggested to increase the perceived palatability of foods because it typically causes rats to seek out and eat food (e.g., Hoebel, 1988). This discrepancy between pleasure and motivation induced by lateral hypothalamic stimulation may indicate that electrical stimulation actually evokes a more subtle psychological component of reward and incentive motivation than is captured by notions of sensory pleasure. For instance, stimulation might activate the psychological process of incentive salience or reward "wanting," perhaps by modulating mesolimbic dopamine systems, rather than hedonic pleasure or reward "liking." Although activation of these two processes might produce many similar consequences, they would still be different in important ways (Berridge, 1996; Berridge & Valenstein, 1991).

## Ventral Pallidum

Less famous than the hypothalamus, the ventral pallidum is at least as important to *affective* reactions and is responsible for some of the effects often attributed to hypothalamic manipulations. The ventral pallidum region borders the lateral hypothalamus at its front and lateral sides. The ventral pallidum is also sometimes called the substantia innominata, or unnamed substance, although this label has been criticized (Heimer, Harlan, Alheid, Garcia, & de Olmos, 1997). In recent years interest in the ventral pallidum has risen as it has been recognized as part of the forebrain configuration known as the extended amygdala (connecting the amygdala, nucleus accumbens, ventral pallidum, and other structures; Heimer et al., 1997).

The sight and taste of food activates neuronal firing in the ventral pallidum as in the lateral hypothalamus (Rolls, 1999). But more than this, the ventral pallidum is uniquely necessary (among forebrain structures) for tasty foods to cause normal positive affective reactions. Destruction of ventral pallidal neurons by excitotoxin lesions abolishes hedonic reactions and causes aversive reactions (e.g., gaping and headshakes) to be elicited even by normally palatable foods (Cromwell & Berridge, 1993). Lesions of the lateral hypothalamus, by contrast, do not cause aversion to food as long as ventral pallidal neurons

remain intact (Berridge, 1996). The ventral pallidum has the unique status of being the only spot in the brain where a discrete lesion can abolish the capacity of sweet food rewards to elicit any positive affective reactions from rats (for weeks to months). Instead, after ventral pallidal damage food elicits only negative or aversive affective reactions that are normally elicited by bitter tastes (Cromwell & Berridge, 1993), suggesting the ventral pallidal neurons are crucial to the normal positive affect of sweet tastes. Electrophysiological studies of animals have implicated the ventral pallidum in other types of reward too, such as cocaine reward (Gong, Neill, & Justice, 1997; McBride, Murphy, & Ikemoto, 1999) or brain stimulation reward (Johnson & Stellar, 1994; Panagis et al., 1997).

Less is known regarding the role of ventral pallidum in positive affect for humans, as the structure is too small to study in brain imaging studies and has not received much attention in clinical patient studies. However, there are a few intriguing observations that do suggest a role for ventral pallidum in human mood and positive affect. For example, electrical stimulation of the globus pallidus is sometimes used in treating symptoms of Parkinson's disease in human patients, and such electrodes might also stimulate neurons in the adjacent ventral pallidum. Electrical stimulation of the globus pallidus by a surgically implanted electrode contiguous to the ventral pallidum has been reported to sometimes induce bouts of affective mania that can last for days (Miyawaki, Perlmutter, Troster, Videen, & Koller, 2000). Also, the induction of a state of sexual or competitive arousal in normal men was found to be accompanied by increased blood flow in the ventral globus pallidus in the same PET study that found increased blood flow in the cingulate cortex (Rauch et al., 1999).

Thus, ventral pallidal neurons may play a special role in affective processing, especially in generating positive affective states. In animals, activity in the ventral pallidum plays a unique causal role in generating the core process of food pleasure, enabling the normal hedonic reaction to "liked" food rewards. In humans, ventral pallidal activation may be correlated with a number of types of positive affective states.

## Septum

The septum is known in animal affective neuroscience chiefly for the syndrome that results when it is damaged. In rats, "septal rage" is a consequence of septal lesions. Though ordinarily timid toward humans, after septal lesions rats have been reported to leap from their cages to attack their handlers and to persistently attack other rodents. The phenomenon, however, may not reflect release of pure aggression so much as a kind of heightened "defensive irritability." Animals from other species (mice, monkeys, etc.) do not show increased propensities to attack after septal lesions, but rather increases in the tendency to avoid or flee social partners, or other increased aspects of emotionality (Albert, Walsh, & Jonik, 1993).

In humans, the septum has been linked to *positive* affect evoked by brain stimulation by a few early reports primarily by Heath (1972). He emphasized positive mood shifts and pleasure evoked in schizophrenic and other patients, who had had electrodes or injection cannulae implanted in their brains, when electrical or pharmacological stimulation was delivered near the lateral septal nuclei (Heath, 1972). The septal location chosen by Heath may have been influenced by the fact that the title of the original 1954 report of brain stimulation reward by Olds and Milner emphasized "electrical stimulation of the septal area" in rats. However, it later became clear that Olds and Milner's brain stimulation reward effect was chiefly due to the lateral hypothalamus and associated pathways. It is likely also that the human stimulation similarly activated front and upper regions of the lateral hypothalamus and ventral pallidum, as well as the posterior region of the nucleus accumbens, and the fiber bundles that connect these regions, as much as septal structures. Heath emphasized the pleasure reported by his subjects, which often was sexual in nature, and sometimes orgasmic in intensity. But other investigators who studied brain stimulation in humans almost never reported producing similar reports of physical pleasure in their patients (Sem-Jacobsen, 1976), and even Heath reported only a few patients with intense affective reactions. In these patients, the most common and earliest effect was elevation of mood and interest and attraction to events and people. Whether the attraction was necessarily sexual is unclear, as Heath often seemed to take steps that would encourage channeling into sexual modes (providing pornographic films, etc.). As mentioned above, careful studies of brain stimulation in animals made clear that the motivation evoked was often much more flexible and subtle in nature than it appeared, and could be channeled by situational determinants (Valenstein, 1976; Valenstein et al., 1970). It is probably safe to conclude that intense pleasure produced by brain stimulation in humans is an exceedingly rare event and that its neuroanatomical basis remains unknown. Any pleasure produced by septal stimulation may actually be due to effect on neurons in other brain structures, and the relevant neural substrate for sensory pleasure has simply not yet been clearly identified for this general region of the brain.

### Brain Stem Sites

Conjunction of the words "affective" and "brain stem" might seem contradictory to those who hold a dogmatic view of the lower brain as merely reflexive. But it is worth keeping in mind that almost every feeling of physical pleasure or pain felt by your forebrain must climb its way there through the brain stem. Much can happen to ascending signals on the way, and there is compelling reason to believe that brain stem sites themselves make important contributions to affective experience.

Pain is clearly modulated in important ways by brain stem structures, notably by the periaqueductal gray and associated projections (Budai & Fields, 1998; Hosobuchi, 1987; Young, Bach, Van Norman, & Yaksh, 1993). An active form of analgesia is generated by the periaqueductal gray system, which sends descending influences to inhibit spinal processing of pain signals, prior to their ascent (Crofford & Casey, 1999; Willis & Westlund, 1997). The activation of this brain stem analgesia system is in turn controlled intimately by larger neural networks extending to the forebrain (King et al., 1999; Liebeskind, Sherman, & Cannon, 1982; Terman, Shavit, Lewis, Cannon, & Liebeskind, 1984).

Pleasures owe part of their hedonic impact to brain stem processing too, just as pains do. The hedonic palatability of the taste of food, for example, is enhanced in rats by brain stem administration of benzodiazepine drugs (Berridge & Peciña, 1995; Peciña & Berridge, 1996). These drugs cause indirect stimulation of receptors on neurons that use gamma-amino-butyric acid (GABA) as their neurotransmitter, via activation of a benzodiazepine receptor, which is coupled to the $GABA_A$ receptor. Benzodiazepine drugs are mostly used for their tranquilizing effects (probably at forebrain sites), but also act on the brain stem to enhance appetite and perceived palatability of foods. In humans, administration of benzodiazepine drugs can quickly lead to an increase by up to 25% in the amount of food consumed during a meal (Evans, Foltin, & Fischman, 1999). In rats, the same phenomenon of increased food intake has long been known to occur (Cooper, 1980; Wise & Dawson, 1974), and is known also to be accompanied by an increase in the positive behavioral affective reactions indicative of hedonic impact, which are normally elicited by palatable food (Berridge & Peciña, 1995; Berridge & Treit, 1986; Gray & Cooper, 1995; Parker, 1995). Microinjections of benzodiazepines are more effective at increasing positive hedonic reactions to food and eating if they are delivered to the brainstem than if delivered to the forebrain (Peciña & Berridge, 1996). The crucial brain stem site for taste pleasure enhancement appears to involve the parabrachial nucleus in the pons. Microinjection of midazolam (a benzodiazepine drug) directly into the parabrachial nucleus causes an increase in the behavioral positive affective reaction that is elicited from rats by a sweet taste (Söderpalm & Berridge, 2000), and microinjections also increase eating behavior more when delivered in the parabrachial nucleus than in other brainstem sites (Higgs & Cooper, 1996; Söderpalm & Berridge, 2000). Benzodiazepine stimulation of the parabrachial nucleus in the pons thus appears to magnify the hedonic impact of food, leading to an increase in motivation to eat. That is consistent with other evidence regarding a role for the parabrachial nucleus in mediating learned taste aversions that change the hedonic value of food (Grigson, Reilly, Shimura, & Norgren, 1998; Spector, 1995).

Other rewards also depend on brain stem sites. For example, the pedunculopontine nucleus, another nucleus of the pons, is important to brain stimulation reward and drug reward. Lesions of the pedunculopontine nucleus disrupt the ability of drugs like morphine or amphetamine to produce conditioned place preferences in rats, even when the drugs are given systemically and reach the entire brain (Bechara & van der Kooy, 1989). Interference with neuronal transmission in the pedunculopontine nucleus also disrupts the reward value to rats of electrical brain stimulation, even when the stimulation is delivered to the lateral hypothalamus, well above the pons (Waraczynski & Shizgal, 1995; Yeomans, Mathur, & Tampakeras, 1993), although not every study has found large disruption (Waraczynski & Perkins, 1998).

The idea that the brain stem may be important in mediating human emotions in general has been recently emphasized by Panksepp and by Damasio (Damasio, 1999; Panksepp, 1998). Panksepp argues for a brain stem role based on a concept of emotional primitives (Panksepp, 1998). He suggests that the capacity for emotional reactions is so fundamental a psychological feature that it must have appeared very early in vertebrate evolution when brain organization was dominated by the brain stem (Panksepp, 1998). Panksepp argues that basic emotional states must have been originally encoded by neural systems in the hindbrain and midbrain, and that the emotional organization of human and other modern mammalian brains remains rooted today to a large degree in brain stem neural systems. In particular, Panksepp suggests that opioid neurotransmitter receptors in the periaqueductal gray area of the midbrain are important to many emotional states, on the grounds that drugs that act on opioid receptors have been shown to alter many different types of motivation and emotion (pleasure, pain, hunger, sex, maternal behavior, etc), and the periaqueductal gray is site of a major opioid system that might influence those emotional states.

Damasio has arrived at a related conclusion about the importance of brain stem systems to human emotion and self-awareness (Damasio, 1999). His argument is based on the clinical neurological observation regarding human patients that the type of brain damage that most often causes an utter loss of all consciousness, and production of a deep coma or vegetative state, typically involves the brain stem, especially the area of the midbrain in front of the trigeminal cranial nerve (Damasio, 1999). This pretrigeminal area of the brain stem, Damasio argues, works in conjunction with forebrain structures, such as the cingulate cortex and prefrontal cortex, and is fundamentally important to the generation of consciously aware states of all types, including emotional states. Thus evidence from both humans and animals suggests the brain stem may be rather more important to pleasure and pain than has commonly been presumed.

## Left and Right: Hemisphere Specialization

Distinct from the question of the role played by particular brain structures or levels in affect and emotion is the question of whether structures on the left side of the brain make a contribution different from those on the right side. The lateralization question is important for understanding the organization of affect in the brain, however, and so it is interesting to compare it in humans and other animals. The issue of lateralization of affective function has arisen mostly but not exclusively from studies of humans and primates (Davidson, 1992). There appear to be two types of views regarding human hemispheric asymmetry and emotion (Habib, 1998). The original view arose from "split-brain" patient studies, and suggests that affective processes in general are largely mediated by the right hemisphere (Cacioppo & Gardner, 1999). It is part of the larger and well-known hypothesis of cognitive lateralization, which suggests that the left hemisphere is best at linguistic and analytic tasks, whereas the right hemisphere may be best at recognizing and expressing emotion, as well as at spatial and holistic tasks. However, recent split-brain patient evidence indicates that the left hemisphere may not have emotional deficits per se, as the left and right hemisphere may be equally able to identify emotional facial expression in such patients (Stone, Nisenson, Eliassen, & Gazzaniga, 1996).

A quite different lateralization theory of affect has been championed especially by Davidson, who suggests that the left hemisphere predominately mediates positive affect whereas the right hemisphere mediates negative affect (Davidson, 1992, 1998b). This hypothesis has its roots in early observations that catastrophic levels of depression were produced more often in neurological patients after damage to the left hemisphere than after damage to the right hemisphere (Gainotti, 1972; Goldstein, 1952), but the idea that positive and negative affect might be segregated among cortical hemispheres was not truly developed until the 1980s, when a number of studies began to provide converging evidence (for reviews see Davidson, 1992, 1998a). For example, normal human subjects may be more likely to recognize happy expressions when presented to their left hemisphere (Davidson, Mednick, Moss, Saron, & Schaffer, 1987). The left hemisphere may be more activated by EEG measures in human infants who experience a pleasant sweet taste (Fox & Davidson, 1986) or adults who view photographs of a positive emotional scene (Lane et al., 1997), or report positive emotional self-evaluations (Sutton & Davidson, 1997).

In support of the hypothesis that negative affect is a right-hemisphere specialization, recognition of fear expression has been reported to be most impaired after right-hemisphere damage (Adolphs, Damasio, Tranel, & Damasio, 1996). The right hemisphere may be more activated by EEG measures in human infants who are distressed (Davidson & Fox, 1989), or by PET or fMRI measures in adults who receive an unpleasantly salty taste (Zald et al., 1998), a repeated painful stimulus (Hsieh et al., 1999), or photographs of negative emotional scenes (Canli, Desmond, Zhao, Glover, & Gabrieli, 1998). Similarly, the right hemisphere is more activated in depressed adults who report sadness (Davidson et al., 1999; Mayberg et al., 1999).

The selective impairment of positive affect by left cortical damage, or impairment of fear by right cortical damage, seems often to be interpreted in terms of release of the *opposite hemisphere's* affective function. An alternative to that view is that the emotional change actually reflects release of *subcortical structures* below the damaged cortex but on its own side (Tucker, 1981; Tucker et al., 1995). By this alternative "within-hemisphere" interpretation, subcortical structures may have an emotional bias that is opposite to the bias of their cortex on the same side. Imaging studies of normal humans will typically reflect the cortical bias on one side (discussed below), whereas cortical damage by this view would release the opposite affective state mediated by subcortical structures on the damaged side. As yet, there is little basis on which to choose among these interesting alternative explanations.

There is some evidence from animals to support the hypothesis that manipulations of right neocortex, especially prefrontal and cingulate cortex, may alter emotional reactions, especially negative emotional reactions (Denenberg, 1983). For example, excitotoxin lesions of the right prefrontal cortex of rats, more than left prefrontal cortex, reduce the magnitude of stress hormone responses (corticosterone) evoked by physical restrain stressors, as well as the consequence of gastric ulcers that can follow (Sullivan & Gratton, 1999). Unilateral destruction of dopamine projections in the right prefrontal and cingulate regions of neocortex produces an increase in stress-induced gastric ulcers to a greater degree than unilateral destruction on the left side of the brain (Sullivan & Szechtman, 1995). The reason right prefrontal excitotoxin lesions *decrease* responses to stress whereas right dopamine-depleting lesions *increase* them may be that excitotoxin lesions destroy the cortical neurons themselves, whereas dopamine depletion leaves the cortical neurons intact and merely removes dopamine axons to them that might normally exert inhibitory effects. Whether right neocortical dominance for emotional responsiveness is specific in rats to responses with negative emotional valence is not yet entirely clear. The right hemisphere might also be important in reward, as more dopamine release has been suggested to occur in right prefrontal cortex than left prefrontal cortex of rats learning to press a bar to gain drug reward in the form of an intravenous morphine infusion (Glick et al., 1992).

Finally, some evidence also suggests a lateralization of function regarding reward mediated by *subcortical* brain systems at least in rats. This lateralization may not be consistently localized to the left or right side in particular, but instead localized to the same side of a rat's brain that is dominant for motor function (Glick, Weaver, & Meibach, 1980, 1981). Individual rats have one side of the brain specialized for motor dominance, as do individual humans, but the dominant side is distributed nearly equally between left and right hemispheres across the rat population (unlike humans, who most commonly are right-handed and left motor-dominant). The association of subcortical reward-dominance with motor-dominance has been suggested to reflect the involvement of both functions with mesolimbic/nigrostriatal dopamine projections (Glick et al., 1980, 1981).

A few other studies have also been interpreted as reflecting emotional lateralization in nonhuman animals (Davidson & Sutton, 1995). In Old World monkeys, Davidson and colleagues found that a shift from right to left EEG dominance was produced together with a reduction of fearful freezing after administration of a diazepam tranquilizer (Davidson, Kalin, & Shelton, 1993). In an interesting study of lateralized facial expression by New World monkeys, Hook-Costigan and colleagues reported that larger movements were made on the side of the mouth controlled by the left brain hemisphere (right side of the mouth) when they made emotionally positive vocalizations (social contact calls), but larger movements were made on the side of the mouth controlled by the right brain hemisphere (left side of the mouth) during emotionally negative facial expressions (fear; Hook-Costigan & Rogers, 1998). These results are consistent with the hypothesis that the right brain mediates negative affect, whereas the left brain mediates positive affect, and thus emotional lateralization may extend at least in primates. Finally, one study suggested that anxiety in rats may be increased by stimulation of the right amygdala but not of the left amygadala (Adamec & Morgan, 1994), suggesting a possible subcortical right bias for negative affect even in rats. The degree to which brain systems of affect are lateralized more generally in animals deserves to be explored further.

## Comparing Humans and Other Animals

### Human and Animal Similarities From This Review

A major point to be taken from this survey of brain systems in affective impact is that there is no qualitative difference between humans and other animals. Each brain structure surveyed here, from prefrontal cortex to brain stem, is similarly implicated in humans and other animals, whenever the evidence allows direct comparison. There is no substantial disagreement between the results of human imaging or clinical patient studies, on the one hand, and, on the other, animal electrophysiological recording, neurochemical measurement, brain stimulation, brain lesion, or pharmacological manipulation studies.

For both humans and other animals, brain mechanisms of affective reaction are distributed widely throughout the brain. Even in humans, the brain stem plays a potent role in modulating affective reactions. For example, the affective component of human pain is certainly modulated by opioid activity in the periaqueductal gray and associated regions (Budai & Fields, 1998; Hosobuchi, 1987; Young et al., 1993). Human appetite and the positive hedonic component of food palatability may also be modulated in part by benzodiazepine receptors in human brain stem, though crucial evidence from humans remains to be collected.

Conversely, even in rats, the prefrontal cortex plays a role in emotional responses. Lesions of prefrontal cortex disrupt delayed foraging for rewards (Seamans et al., 1995), and microinjections into prefrontal cortex are rewarding. Thus from prefrontal cortex to brain stem, each brain structure reviewed here can be seen to play a comparable role in all mammals, from humans to rats.

### Differences Between Human and Animal Affective Neuroscience

Yet there is an enormous gap between humans and other animals in the *relative weight* given to conclusions about the role of cortical regions and subcortical brain structures in the affective neuroscience literature, even if the difference is not all or none. The overwhelming majority of statements that *prefrontal or cingulate cortex* are important substrates for emotion comes from studies of humans, or at least, of primates. Investigators who study humans or primates are the authors of all theoretical formulations of brain and emotion that emphasize cortical areas (Damasio, 1994; Davidson et al., 1999; Rolls, 1999). It is no accident, by contrast, that authors who stress the importance of *subcortical brain structures* in affective reaction have been investigators whose research has primarily been on brain mechanisms of emotion and motivation in rats (Berridge, 1999; Davis & Lee, 1998; Gray, 1987; LeDoux, 1996; Panksepp, 1998; Toates, 1994).

In part, *artifactual differences* in technique and conceptual approaches may account for the discrepant emphases on "human cortical emotion" versus "animal subcortical emotion." The questions and methods used to approach brain substrates of feeling and emotion are quite different in studies of humans from studies of animals. This is partly why different brain structures have been highlighted in different species.

Human brain imaging studies of emotion are biased to concentrate on cortical brain regions rather than subcortical regions for several reasons: (1) human studies use *cognitive* tasks to evaluate emotion, which are more likely to recruit cortical regions; (2) the functional architecture of cortical modules is better suited to register on regional activation scans than is subcortical architecture; (3) *correlational* measures of emotion like functional brain imaging will include cortical regions that are activated during an emotion even if those regions may be incapable of causing the emotion, or may not actually be needed for the emotion; and (4) human patients with brain damage used in studies of emotion are more likely to present with lesions in cortical than subcortical sites. Conversely, animal studies of emotion are biased to focus on subcortical structures because (1) tests of emotion in animals involve relatively little abstract cognitive evaluation, and instead focus on a behavioral or physiological reaction to a strong innate or conditioned emotion-arousing stimulus; (2) *causation* of a particular emotional reaction by a brain event seems more likely to result from manipulation of subcortical regions than of cortical regions; (3) subcortical structures seem more likely than cortical regions to prove absolutely *necessary* to the induction of a particular emotional reaction.

### Emotional Cognition Versus Basic Emotional Reaction

Human brain imaging studies of emotion could be said typically to focus on *emotional cognition* (as opposed to cognition that is emotionally or affectively more neutral, which is the focus of other cognitive neuroscience studies). Such tasks often involve high-level cognitive evaluation of emotional meanings of language stories or of complex pictures, or cognitive induction of an emotional state through these cognitive symbols. Normal individuals or brain damaged patients are usually asked to judge the emotional *significance* of a face, voice, scene, or word. Can they recognize fearful from friendly or cheerful from sad? Such stimuli require complex perceptual and symbolic decoding, at least, and often further thematic and cultural decoding. Human studies of adult emotion are inevitably highly cognitive in this sense (Ellsworth, 1994a; Ellsworth & Scherer, this volume; Kitayama & Markus, 1994). A cognitive approach to emotion is most likely to highlight cortical involvement. It is interesting to note that in the rare psychological theory of human emotion in which affect is conceived as *separate* from cognition, such as that of Zajonc and colleagues (Zajonc, 1980, 1998), the most often referenced brain substrates for emotional reaction are the amygdala and its subcortical connections.

Animal studies of emotion, by contrast to most studies of humans, often aim to produce strong *emotional states* directly, either by presentation of a primary affective stimulus for fear, hunger, or the pleasure of sex or food, or by the brain manipulation itself. One does not measure the animal's emotional judgment or categorization but rather its behavioral or physiological *emotional reaction*. The question asked is not what motivational *meaning* a stimulus has but rather what emotional or motivational *state or reaction* has been produced or modulated by an event or brain manipulation.

Affective neuroscience studies of monkeys performing discriminative reward tasks may be exceptions to the rule that animal studies are always about emotional reaction rather than emotional cognition (Rolls, 1999; Schultz, 1998). Electrophysiological studies often ask the monkeys to recognize the emotional meaning of a stimulus, acquired by associative learning or by a cognitive rule. This may be one reason studies of monkeys have highlighted neocortical regions for mediating emotion to a greater degree than studies of other animals. The greater cognitive sophistication of monkeys allows use of tasks that rely on stimulus meaning rather than immediate emotional state. Behavioral neuroscientists are generally hesitant to induce strong emotional states such as fear or hunger in monkeys, partly for ethical reasons and partly because these investigators typically use the same monkeys in several consecutive experiments. A strong emotional manipulation in one experiment might alter results in subsequent experiments, and hence is avoided by investigators. For these reasons, the procedures from affective neuroscience studies of monkeys have tended to be as cognitive as possible, and so may have maximized the role of cortical areas.

## Brain Correlation Versus Causation of Emotion

Another artifactual source of the discrepancy between human and animal affective neuroscience comes from the fact that most current studies of humans tend to focus on brain activation that is *correlated* to emotion whereas studies of animals focus to a greater extent on manipulations that *cause* observable changes in emotional reactions. Both correlational and causal evidence indicate that a brain structure mediates emotion, but the word "mediates" has more than one meaning regarding brain-behavior relations (Sarter, Berntson, & Cacioppo, 1996).

To mediate can mean that activation of the brain structure is a reliable correlate to the emotion, independent of whether it causes the emotion. This is the case when studies of brain activation identify particular neural substrates as especially activated during an emotion. Mediate can mean alternatively that activation of the brain structure is causally *necessary* in order for the emotion to occur, and that the emotion never occurs in the absence of the structure, as when a lesion disrupts affective reaction. Mediate can also mean that activation of the brain structure is causally *sufficient* (all else being equal) to trigger the emotion. Or mediate can mean any combination of these. It can

mean even more complex and subtle mind-brain relations, such as those involved in distributed neural processing, or the dynamic capacity of neural systems for reorganization after damage (Farah, 1994; Sarter et al., 1996; Winkielman, Berntson, & Cacioppo, 2001). We often say that a brain structure mediates a particular psychological function, as though the term "mediate" had one clear meaning, which combined all of these senses equally: brain activation correlated to a function, necessary for the function, and sufficient to cause the function (all else being equal). But we make a mistake when we do so without recognizing the difference among these claims.

It can perhaps be stated as a general axiom that correlational studies, which measure neural activation correlated to a psychological function (PET, fMRI, EEG, electrophysiology, Fos, etc.), will always implicate a greater number of brain regions than causal studies, which measure changes in the function caused by brain manipulations (lesions, stimulation, drug microinjection, etc.). There are more correlates than causes. This is because the two approaches rely on entirely different senses of mediation. The two approaches mean different things when they say "brain area X mediates psychological function Y."

## Brain Imaging Biases for Cortical Spatial Segregation

Human brain imaging techniques such PET or fMRI have a special measurement-related feature that biases them toward neocortex, irrespective of the importance of subcortical structures (Sarter et al., 1996). PET and fMRI techniques are designed to detect changes in regional *blood flow*. These measures exploit the remarkable ability of the brain's vascular system to change blood delivery to cerebral blood vessels, based on the changing needs of active neurons, which increase their uptake of glucose and oxygen when they fire. They detect a change within one spatial region and compare it to other regions. The crucial word here is "region": the blood flow measure requires that the psychological functions of interest be parceled out to widely separated parts of the brain.

For this imaging technique to implicate a particular brain region in emotion, the neurons devoted to the emotional state must (1) be grouped together densely in one area and (2) separated from neurons devoted to other functions. Only then can an increase in the combined neuronal metabolic uptake be sufficient to trigger a vascular response. No signal would be detected if the neurons mediating a function either were distributed widely across the brain. Likewise, no signal would be detected if the neurons for one function were densely packed close together with neurons mediating functions activated by other tasks.

The neocortex is most likely to register on fMRI and PET imaging techniques partly because of its sheer size in human beings and partly because the neocortex segregates functions especially well across spatial regions. By contrast, even if the brain stem or hypothalamus had segregation of psychological functions across different neurons to an equal degree as in the cortex, the "labeled line" code of those dedicated neurons are less likely to appear on an fMRI or PET scans. The neurons in those structures are too closely packed together to allow subpopulations to impact on vascular blood flow. In upshot, human imaging studies of psychological function are biased to detect functional correlations to neocortical regions rather than to subcortical brain structures.

## Cortical Biases in Studies of Human Patients

To a lesser extent, studies of human patients with brain damage are also inherently better suited to specify contributions of neocortex than to reveal the role of subcortical structures (other than the amygdala, which is isolated in neocortex). First, lesions of neocortex are more likely to be localized to a *single region* than are subcortical lesions. Cortical lesions are more likely to produce a *single functional consequence*, rather than a host of many consequences. The neocortex is sufficiently large that a lesion in one cortical lobe may leave most other cortical lobes untouched, as well as most subcortical structures. Further, the neocortex is especially vulnerable to external injury. Wounds or other injury may sometimes destroy a cortical region without damaging deeper brain structures. Even some forms of brain disease tend to damage neocortex most, and these are the most prominent diseases in the clinical neuropsychological literature. For example, epilepsy, with its predilection for temporal lobe foci, often causes specific bilateral temporal lobe and amygdala damage. That allows analysis of the psychological functions of those structures, with a specificity of pathology that cannot be matched for most other brain structures.

Subcortical lesions, if they are large enough to cause bilateral damage to a particular subcortical structure, are more likely to destroy neighboring subcortical structures in addition. Parkinson's disease and medial hypothalamic tumors are two exceptions to this rule, as they can cause bilateral damage specifically in the nigrostriatal system or in the ventromedial hypothalamus. But, in most cases, subcortical lesions that are large enough to be interesting damage more than one subcortical structure. Subcortical brain lesions are also more likely to produce generalized or even catastrophic functional deficits, such as coma. Naturally such broad deficits tend to preclude psychological analyses.

For these reasons, studies of human patients after brain damage, just as studies of human brain imaging, have been better at providing information about the roles of cortical areas than about subcortical brain structures. Conclusions from such studies naturally are biased to emphasize the role of neocortex. Since these studies are conducted invariably in humans, it has produced an impression that human brain organization of emotion is disproportionately weighted toward the amygdala and neocortex.

## Encephalization Differences Between Human and Animal Emotional Brains

I have stressed the degree to which perceived animal/human differences in the brain's organization of feeling and emotion are probably due to artifacts rather than to a real gap between primates (including humans) and other mammalian orders. But that is not to say there is no real difference at all between humans and other animals. There may indeed be a real difference in brain organization of emotion. If so, however, it is quantitative in nature and moderate in degree—not a qualitative or massive difference.

The chief evidence for a difference is that emotional processes may be somewhat more susceptible to disruption by cortical damage in humans than in other animals. Humans can be devastated, rendered into vegetative states, by large neocortical lesions, whereas a rat can lose its entire neocortex and continue on remarkably normal (Panksepp, Normansell, Cox, & Siviy, 1994; Skinner et al., 1994; Whishaw, Schallert, & Kolb, 1981; Wirsig & Grill, 1982). To some extent this may reflect the increased influence of cognition on emotional processes in humans and primates to which we have already alluded. But alternatively it may also reflect a subtle primate reorganization of the neural bases for emotional core processes themselves. This difference may be captured by the term "encephalization" from the study of brain evolution.

*Encephalization* describes the physical expansion in evolution of human neocortex and forebrain structures compared to other animals (Jerison, 1977). It applies to primates in general, but especially to humans. Human neocortex is large compared to neocortex in other mammals. The only other mammals to own comparably large neocortices belong to the order of cetaceans, comprising dolphins and whales (Marino, 1998). But the internal microstructure of neocortex in cetaceans appears to be much simpler and primitive compared to primate neocortex (even compared to most other nonprimate land mammals; Morgane, Jacobs, & Galaburda, 1985). Thus primates probably have an uncontested lead in their net complexity of cortical computation. Humans are paramount in terms of *functional encephalization*, the relative degree of neural information processing given over to neocortex.

What is the psychological consequence of human functional encephalization? In one sense this question seems easy to answer: only humans read books about emotion. Human cognition is our distinguishing feature, and cognition exerts myriad influences over the human experience of emotion. Human emotional life is psychologically richer compared to that of other animals: it is laden with symbolism and culture, linguistically elaborated to ourselves and to each other (Cacioppo & Gardner, 1999; Ellsworth, 1994a; 1994b; Ellsworth & Scherer, in press; Kitayama & Markus, 1994; Nisbett & Wilson, 1978; Wilson, Hodges, & LaFleur, 1995; Winkielman et al., 2001; Zajonc, 1998). No doubt human neocortex plays a vital role in the cognitive elaboration of this psychological richness of human emotion. In this sense, cognition may feed back upon, and perhaps change, human emotional core processes.

### Emotional Re-Representation in Neocortex

But there may also have been a change in the neural organization of emotional core processes. Emotion has not "moved" in humans to the neocortex from subcortical structures, in this sense, but its center of gravity may have shifted slightly upward. Our understanding of functional encephalization owes a lot to the early insights and writings of John Hughlings Jackson, a 19th-century British neurologist. Hughlings Jackson surmised principles for the organization of functions embodied at different levels of the brain, based on the movement deficits of his patients with damage to those levels. The lowest portions of the brain, he suggested, simply *represented* the outside world and the programs needed for movement. By themselves, low levels were capable of triggering simple responses to appropriate simple stimuli. Higher levels of the brain, in turn, rerepresented those original neural representations. Higher levels were forced to work with the products of those lower levels, since there was no other way for them to get input about what was happening. But higher levels *transformed* the lower products they received: "They represent over again in more complex, etc., combinations, the parts which all middle centres have re-represented, and thus they represent the whole organism; they are re-re-representative" (Hughlings Jackson, 1958, p. 42).

*Re-re-representation* captures the iterative nature of hierarchical representation as one ascends the brain. High levels do not replace the lower levels in a hierarchical brain, nor take over themselves the representative functions originally performed by those lower levels (Gallistel, 1980). The lower levels remain responsible for their original representations. Higher levels rather reproduce those lower representations as re-representations, and in doing so add new and abstract features. Cortical re-representation of emotional signals, with increasingly abstract features at upper levels, provides one way to conceive of the elaboration of human emotional processes in terms of encephalization (Gallistel, 1980; Rolls, 1999).

Finally, the encephalized re-representation of emotion in humans has implications for a change in the *autonomy* of subcortical structures. Subcortical systems in a hierarchical system do not give up their emotional functions to higher levels. But subcortical systems do give up autonomy—their independence—in a hierarchical system as higher, abstract representations become increasingly dominant (Gallistel, 1980). Higher units can influence lower levels, and that happens in both humans and rats. A difference between humans and rats, however, is the *magnitude* of descending inputs that impinge ordinarily upon subcortical systems. Human subcortical systems receive greater cortical inputs ordinarily. But not only that, they are wired to a greater degree to *expect* that cortical input. There is a cost to this: greater vulnerability to disruption when the expected cortical input to a subcortical system suddenly disappears. The visible manifestation of this difference is that human psychological function, even for basic psychological processes, is relatively disturbed by a cortical lesion that would have minimal impact in the brain of another mammal. This is not to say that emotion has *moved* from subcortical structures to the cortex in humans. Human core processes of emotion may remain grounded in subcortical brain structures (Berridge, 1999; LeDoux, 1996; Panksepp, 1998; Zajonc, 1998). It may be truer to say instead that feeling in humans may have "spread upwards." The tendrils of emotional core processes extend from their original homes in subcortical structures to more fully integrate cingulate and orbitofrontal regions of the human neocortex into their subcortically based computations.

### Conclusion

Neural substrates of feeling and emotion are distributed throughout the brain, from front to back, and top to bottom. The same brain structures are implicated in affective reactions for both humans and other animals. Orbitofrontal and other prefrontal cortex, cingulate cortex, amygdala, nucleus accumbens, ventral pallidum, mesolimbic dopamine and opioid systems, hypothalamus, midbrain, and brain stem sites—all play a role in affective reaction, whether of a human, monkey, or rat. The divergence in relative emphasis placed on neocortical regions versus subcortical structures in the literature on emotion has occurred largely because of methodological differences between human affective neuroscience and animal affective neuroscience. Human affective neuroscience has been dominated by correlational studies of neural activation, whereas animal neuroscience has given greater weight to causal studies involving brain manipulation that change emotional states and reactions.

The difference in cortical/subcortical emphasis arises also because of conceptual differences in the kind of questions asked of its subject by each subfield. Human affective neuroscience studies have tended to measure emotional cognition and judgments, whereas animal affective neuroscience has tended to measure basic affective reactions. Finally, the relative emphasis on neocortex in human emotion may also stem in part from the greater role of cognitive evaluation in elaborating cognitive aspects of human emotion.

Human evolution has changed only one major aspect of the organization of emotional core processes within the brain—namely, the *degree of encephalization* for particular emotional functions. Encephalization has modified the autonomy of subcortical structures, so that neocortical inputs have become incorporated into subcortical function to a greater degree than in nonhuman animals, so much so that human subcortical function cannot be maintained normally when cortical inputs are suddenly removed. This encephalization has not *relocated* emotional core processes from subcortical to cortical structures, but it has *expanded* the penumbra of emotional core processing circuitry into upper layers of the brain. This is reflected in humans by pronounced cortical activation during affective reactions and by a special human vulnerability to disruption of psychological function after neocortical damage. Encephalization in humans reports an important evolutionary tweak of preexisting neural organization—a modification that transforms the capacity of the human emotional brain in fascinating ways but does not replace the basic emotional brain that we share with other animals.

## NOTES

I thank Professors J. Wayne Aldridge, Richard J. Davidson, Edward E. Smith, Stephen Maren, Terry E. Robinson, Elliot S. Valenstein, and Dr. Cindy L. Wyvell for their helpful comments on an earlier version of this manuscript, and Dr. Susana Peciña and Sheila Reynolds for help in correcting the final manuscript.

1. I accept the admonition of Dess and Chapman that the term "animals" should not be used to exclude humans, who in the most relevant sense are animals, too (Dess & Chapman, 1998). In most cases, I will try to make clear that I mean "animals other than humans," or sometimes "animals other than primates." In other cases I hope the reader will accept the use of "animals" as a shorthand for those phrases.

2. Every brain structure discussed in this chapter actually exists as a paired structure, with one half on the left side of the brain and one on the right side. Thus one should say that the left and right prefrontal cortices lie at the very front of the brain. For the sake of simplicity, I will speak of each brain structure as a singular entity (and leave implied the true bilateral symmetry).

## REFERENCES

Adamec, R. E., & Morgan, H. D. (1994). The effect of kindling of different nuclei in the left and right amygdala on anxiety in the rat. *Physiology and Behavior, 55*(1), 1–12.

Adler, L. J., Gyulai, F. E., Diehl, D. J., Mintun, M. A., Winter, P. M., & Firestone, L. L. (1997). Regional brain activity changes associated with fentanyl analgesia elucidated by positron emission tomography [published erratum appears in *Anesthesia & Analgesia, 84*(5), 949]. *Anesthesia & Analgesia, 84*(1), 120–126.

Adolphs, R., Damasio, H., Tranel, D., & Damasio, A. R. (1996). Cortical systems for the recognition of emotion in facial expressions. *Journal of Neuroscience, 16*(23), 7678–7687.

Adolphs, R., Tranel, D., Damasio, H., & Damasio, A. (1994). Impaired recognition of emotion in facial expressions following bilateral damage to the human amygdala. *Nature, 372*(6507), 669–672.

Adolphs, R., Tranel, D., Damasio, H., & Damasio, A. R. (1995). Fear and the human amygdala. *Journal of Neuroscience, 15*(9), 5879–5891.

Aggleton, J. P. (Ed.). (2000). *The amygdala* (2nd ed.). Oxford: Oxford University Press.

Albert, D. J., Walsh, M. L., & Jonik, R. H. (1993). Aggression in humans—What is its biological foundation? *Neuroscience and Biobehavioral Reviews, 17*(4), 405–425.

Anderson, A. K., & Phelps, E. A. (1998). Intact recognition of vocal expressions of fear following bilateral lesions of the human amygdala. *Neuroreport, 9*(16), 3607–3613.

Anderson, A. K., & Phelps, E. A. (2000). Expression without recognition: Contributions of the human amygdala to emotional communication. *Psychological Science, 11*, 106–111.

Apicella, P., Ljungberg, T., Scarnati, E., & Schultz, W. (1991). Responses to reward in monkey dorsal and ventral striatum. *Experimental Brain Research, 85*(3), 491–500.

Baird, A. A., Gruber, S. A., Fein, D. A., Maas, L. C., Steingard, R. J., Renshaw, P. F., Cohen, B. M., & Yurgelun-Todd, D. A. (1999). Functional magnetic resonance imaging of facial affect recognition in children and adolescents. *Journal of the American Academy of Child & Adolescent Psychiatry, 38*(2), 195–199.

Bassareo, V., & DiChiara, G. (1997). Differential influence of associative and nonassociative learning mechanisms on the responsiveness of prefrontal and accumbal dopamine transmission to food stimuli in rats fed ad libitum. *Journal of Neuroscience, 17*(2), 851–861.

Baylis, L. L., & Gaffan, D. (1991). Amygdalectomy and ventromedial prefrontal ablation produce similar deficits in food choice and in simple object discrimination learning for an unseen reward. *Experimental Brain Research, 86*(3), 617–622.

Bechara, A., Damasio, H., & Damasio, A. R. (2000). Emotion, decision making and the orbitofrontal cortex. *Cerebral Cortex, 10*(3), 295–307.

Bechara, A., Damasio, H., Tranel, D., & Damasio, A. R. (1997). Deciding advantageously before knowing the advantageous strategy. *Science, 275*(5304), 1293–1295.

Bechara, A., & van der Kooy, D. (1989). The tegmental pedunculopontine nucleus: A brain-stem output of the limbic system critical for the conditioned place preferences produced by morphine and amphetamine. *Journal of Neuroscience, 9*(10), 3400–3409.

Beck, C. H., & Fibiger, H. C. (1995). Conditioned fear-induced changes in behavior and in the expression of the immediate early gene c-fos: With and without diazepam pretreatment. *Journal of Neuroscience, 15*(1 Pt 2), 709–720.

Berridge, K. C. (1991). Modulation of taste affect by hunger, caloric satiety, and sensory-specific satiety in the rat. *Appetite, 16*(2), 103–120.

Berridge, K. C. (1996). Food reward: Brain substrates of wanting and liking. *Neuroscience and Biobehavioral Review, 20*(1), 1–25.

Berridge, K. C. (1999). Pleasure, pain, desire, and dread: Hidden core processes of emotion. In D. Kahneman, E. Diener, & N. Schwarz (Eds.), *Well-being: The foundations of hedonic psychology* (pp. 525–557). New York: Russell Sage Foundation.

Berridge, K. C. (2000). Taste reactivity: Measuring hedonic impact in human infants and animals. *Neuroscience and Biobehavioral Reviews, 24*, 173–198.

Berridge, K. C., & Peciña, S. (1995). Benzodiazepines, appetite, and taste palatability. *Neuroscience and Biobehavioral Reviews, 19*, 121–131.

Berridge, K. C., & Robinson, T. E. (1998). What is the role of dopamine in reward: Hedonic impact, reward learning, or incentive salience? *Brain Research—Brain Research Reviews, 28*(3), 309–369.

Berridge, K. C., & Treit, D. (1986). Chlordiazepoxide directly enhances positive ingestive reactions in rats. *Pharmacology Biochemistry and Behavior, 24*(2), 217–221.

Berridge, K. C., & Valenstein, E. S. (1991). What psychological process mediates feeding evoked by electrical stimulation of the lateral hypothalamus? *Behavioral Neuroscience, 105*(1), 3–14.

Berridge, K. C., Venier, I. L., & Robinson, T. E. (1989). Taste reactivity analysis of 6-hydroxydopamine-induced aphagia: Implications for arousal and anhedonia hypotheses of dopamine function. *Behavioral Neuroscience, 103*(1), 36–45.

Blackburn, J. R., Phillips, A. G., & Fibiger, H. C. (1987). Dopamine and preparatory behavior: I. Effects of pimozide. *Behavioral Neuroscience, 101*(3), 352–360.

Blackburn, J. R., Phillips, A. G., Jakubovic, A., & Fibiger, H. C. (1989). Dopamine and preparatory behavior: II. A neurochemical analysis. *Behavioral Neuroscience, 103*(1), 15–23.

Blair, R. J., Morris, J. S., Frith, C. D., Perrett, D. I., & Dolan, R. J. (1999). Dissociable neural responses to facial expressions of sadness and anger. *Brain, 122*(Pt 5), 883–893.

Blood, A. J., Zatorre, R. J., Bermudez, P., & Evans, A. C. (1999). Emotional responses to pleasant and unpleasant music correlate with activity in paralimbic brain regions. *Nature Neuroscience, 2*(4), 382–387.

Brauer, L. H., & De Wit, H. (1997). High dose pimozide does not block amphetamine-induced euphoria in normal volunteers. *Pharmacology Biochemistry and Behavior, 56*(2), 265–272.

Brauer, L. H., Goudie, A. J., & de Wit, H. (1997). Dopamine ligands and the stimulus effects of amphetamine: Animal models versus human laboratory data. *Psychopharmacology, 130*(1), 2–13.

Breiter, H. C., Gollub, R. L., Weisskoff, R. M., Kennedy, D. N., Makris, N., Berke, J. D., Goodman, J. M., Kantor, H. L., Gastfriend, D. R., Riorden, J. P., Mathew, R. T., Rosen, B. R., & Hyman, S. E. (1997). Acute effects of cocaine on human brain activity and emotion. *Neuron, 19*(3), 591–611.

Bremner, J. D., Staib, L. H., Kaloupek, D., Southwick, S. M., Soufer, R., & Charney, D. S. (1999). Neural correlates of exposure to traumatic pictures and sound in Vietnam combat veterans with and without posttraumatic stress disorder: A positron emission tomography study. *Biological Psychiatry, 45*(7), 806–816.

Brown, D. W. (1995). Felonious sex crime: The possibility of unilateral cerebral irradiation for the offenders. *Medical Hypotheses, 45*(4), 383–385.

Budai, D., & Fields, H. L. (1998). Endogenous opioid peptides acting at mu-opioid receptors in the dorsal horn contribute to midbrain modulation of spinal nociceptive neurons. *Journal of Neurophysiology, 79*(2), 677–687.

Bussey, T. J., Everitt, B. J., & Robbins, T. W. (1997). Dissociable effects of cingulate and medial frontal cortex lesions on stimulus-reward learning using a novel Pavlovian autoshaping procedure for the rat: Implications for the neurobiology of emotion. *Behavioral Neuroscience, 111*(5), 908–919.

Butter, C. M., McDonald, J. A., & Snyder, D. R. (1969). Orality, preference behavior, and reinforcement value of nonfood object in monkeys with orbital frontal lesions. *Science, 164*, 1306–1307.

Butter, C. M., & Snyder, D. R. (1972). Alterations in aversive and aggressive behaviors following orbital frontal lesions in rhesus monkeys. *Acta Neurobiologiae Experimentalis, 32*(2), 525–565.

Butter, C. M., Snyder, D. R., & McDonald, J. A. (1970). Effects of orbital frontal lesions on aversive and aggressive behaviors in rhesus monkeys. *Journal of Comparative & Physiological Psychology, 72*(1), 132–144.

Cabanac, M. (1979). Sensory pleasure. *Quarterly Review of Biology, 54*(1), 1–29.

Cabanac, M. (1992). Pleasure: The common currency. *Journal of Theoretical Biology, 155*, 173–200.

Cabanac, M., & Lafrance, L. (1990). Postingestive alliesthesia: The rat tells the same story. *Physiology and Behavior, 47*(3), 539–543.

Cacioppo, J. T., & Gardner, W. L. (1999). Emotion. *Annual Review of Psychology, 50*, 191–214.

Cacioppo, J. T., Gardner, W. L., & Berntson, G. G. (1999). The affect system has parallel and integrative processing components: Form follows function. *Journal of Personality and Social Psychology, 76*(5), 839–855.

Canli, T., Desmond, J. E., Zhao, Z., Glover, G., & Gabrieli, J. D. E. (1998). Hemispheric asymmetry for emotional stimuli detected with fMRI. *Neuroreport, 9*(14), 3233–3239.

Carlezon, W. A., Jr., & Wise, R. A. (1996). Rewarding actions of phencyclidine and related drugs in nucleus accumbens shell and frontal cortex. *Journal of Neuroscience, 16*(9), 3112–3122.

Chang, J. Y., Janak, P. H., & Woodward, D. J. (1998). Comparison of mesocorticolimbic neuronal responses during cocaine and heroin self-administration in freely moving rats. *Journal of Neuroscience, 18*(8), 3098–3115.

Childress, A. R., Mozley, P. D., McElgin, W., Fitzgerald, J., Reivich, M., & O'Brien, C. P. (1999). Limbic activation during cue-induced cocaine craving. *American Journal of Psychiatry, 156*(1), 11–18.

Cooper, S. J. (1980). Benzodiazepines as appetite-enhancing compounds. *Appetite, 1*, 7–19.

Crofford, L. J., & Casey, K. L. (1999). Central modulation of pain perception. *Rheumatic Disease Clinics of North America, 25*(1), 1–13.

Cromwell, H. C., & Berridge, K. C. (1993). Where does damage lead to enhanced food aversion: The ventral pallidum/substantia innominata or lateral hypothalamus? *Brain Research, 624*(1–2), 1–10.

Cummings, J. L. (1995). Anatomic and behavioral aspects

of frontal-subcortical circuits. *Annals of the New York Academy of Sciences, 769*, 1–13.

Damasio, A. R. (1994). *Descartes' error: Emotion, reason, and the human brain.* New York: G. P. Putnam.

Damasio, A. R. (1996). The somatic marker hypothesis and the possible functions of the prefrontal cortex. *Philosophical Transactions of the Royal society of London—Series B: Biological Sciences, 351*(1346), 1413–1420.

Damasio, A. R. (1998). Emotion in the perspective of an integrated nervous system. *Brain Research—Brain Research Reviews, 26*(2–3), 83–86.

Damasio, A. R. (1999). *The feeling of what happens: Body and emotion in the making of consciousness.* New York: Harcourt Brace.

Davidson, R. J. (1992). Anterior cerebral asymmetry and the nature of emotion. *Brain and Cognition, 20*(1), 125–151.

Davidson, R. J. (1998a). Affective style and affective disorders: Perspectives from affective neuroscience. *Cognition & Emotion, 12*(3), 307–330.

Davidson, R. J. (1998b). Anterior electrophysiological asymmetries, emotion, and depression: Conceptual and methodological conundrums. *Psychophysiology, 35*(5), 607–614.

Davidson, R. J., Abercrombie, H., Nitschke, J. B., & Putnam, K. (1999). Regional brain function, emotion and disorders of emotion. *Current Opinion in Neurobiology, 9*(2), 228–234.

Davidson, R. J., & Fox, N. A. (1989). Frontal brain asymmetry predicts infants' response to maternal separation. *Journal of Abnormal Psychology, 98*(2), 127–131.

Davidson, R. J., Jackson, D. C., & Kalin, N. H. (2000). Emotion, plasticity context, and regulation: Perspectives from affective neuroscience. *Psychological Bulletin, 126*(6), 890–909.

Davidson, R. J., Kalin, N. H., & Shelton, S. E. (1993). Lateralized response to diazepam predicts temperamental style in rhesus monkeys. *Behavioral Neuroscience, 107*(6), 1106–1110.

Davidson, R. J., Mednick, D., Moss, E., Saron, C., & Schaffer, C. E. (1987). Ratings of emotion in faces are influenced by the visual field to which stimuli are presented. *Brain and Cognition, 6*(4), 403–411.

Davidson, R. J., & Sutton, S. K. (1995). Affective neuroscience: The emergence of a discipline. *Current Opinion in Neurobiology, 5*(2), 217–224.

Davis, K. D., Taylor, S. J., Crawley, A. P., Wood., M. L., & Mikulis, D. J. (1997). Functional MRI of pain- and attention-related activations in the human cingulate cortex. *Journal of Neurophysiology, 77*(6), 3370–3380.

Davis, M. (1992). The amygdala and conditioned fear. In J. P. Aggleton (Ed.), *The amygdala: Neurobiological aspects of emotion, memory, and mental dysfunction.* (pp. 255–306). New York: John Wiley.

Davis, M., Hitchcock, J. M., Bowers, M. B., Berridge, C. W., Melia, K. R., & Roth, R. H. (1994). Stress-induced activation of prefrontal cortex dopamine turnover: Blockade by lesions of the amygdala. *Brain Research, 664*(1–2), 207–210.

Davis, M., & Lee, Y. (1998). Fear and anxiety: Possible roles of the amygdala and bed nucleus of the stria terminalis. *Cognition & Emotion, 12*(3), 277–305.

De Wit, H., & Wise, R. A. (1977). Blockade of cocaine reinforcement in rats with the dopamine receptor blocker pimozide, but not with the noradrenergic blockers phentolamine or phenoxybenzamine. *Canadian Journal of Psychology, 31*(4), 195–203.

Denenberg, V. H. (1983). Lateralization of function in rats. *American Journal of Physiology, 245*(4), R505–9.

Denton, D., Shade, R., Zamarippa, F., Egan, G., Blair-West, J., McKinley, M., Lancaster, J., & Fox, P. (1999). Neuroimaging of genesis and satiation of thirst and an interoceptor-driven theory of origins of primary consciousness. *Proceedings of the National Academy of Sciences of the United States of America, 96*(9), 5304–5309.

Dess, N. K., & Chapman, C. D. (1998). "Humans and animals"? On saying what we mean. *Psychological Science, 9*(2), 156–157.

Di Ciano, P., Blaha, C. D., & Phillips, A. G. (1998). Conditioned changes in dopamine oxidation currents in the nucleus accumbens of rats by stimuli paired with self-administration or yoked-administration of d-amphetamine. *European Journal of Neuroscience, 10*(3), 1121–1127.

Ellsworth, P. C. (1994a). Levels of thought and levels of emotion. In P. Ekman & R. J. Davidson (Eds.), *The nature of emotion: Fundamental questions* (pp. 192–196). New York: Oxford University Press.

Ellsworth, P. C. (1994b). Sense, culture, and sensibility. In H. Markus & S. Kitayama (Eds.), *Emotion and culture: Empirical studies of mutual influence* (pp. 23–50). Washington, DC: American Psychological Association.

Eslinger, P. J., & Damasio, A. R. (1985). Severe disturbance of higher cognition after bilateral frontal lobe ablation: Patient EVR. *Neurology, 35*(12), 1731–1741.

Ettenberg, A., & Camp, C. H. (1986). Haloperidol induces a partial reinforcement extinction effect in rats: Implications for a dopamine involvement in food reward. *Pharmacology Biochemistry and Behavior, 15*, 813–821.

Evans, S. M., Foltin, R. W., & Fischman, M. W. (1999). Food "cravings" and the acute effects of alprazolam on food intake in women with premenstrual dysphoric disorder. *Appetite, 32*(3), 331–349.

Everitt, B. J. (1990). Sexual motivation: A neural and behavioural analysis of the mechanisms underlying appetitive and copulatory responses of male rats. *Neuroscience and Biobehavioral Review, 14*(2), 217–232.

Everitt, B. J., Cardinal, R. N., Hall, J., Parkinson, J. A., & Robbins, T. R. (2000). Differential involvement of amygdala subsystems in appetitive conditioning and drug addiction. In J. P. Aggleton (Ed.), *The amygdala: A functional analysis* (pp. 353–390). Oxford: Oxford University Press.

Everitt, B. J., & Robbins, T. W. (1992). Amygdala-ventral striatal interactions and reward-related processes. In J. P. Aggleton (Ed.), *The amygdala: Neurobiological aspects of emotion, memory, and mental dysfunction* (pp. 401–429). New York: John Wiley.

Fanselow, M. S., & LeDoux, J. E. (1999). Why we think plasticity underlying Pavlovian fear conditioning occurs in the basolateral amygdala. *Neuron, 23*(2), 229–232.

Farah, M. J. (1994). Neuropsychological inference with an interactive brain—A critique of the locality assumption. *Behavioral and Brain Sciences, 17*(1), 43–61.

Fiorino, D. F., Coury, A., & Phillips, A. G. (1997). Dynamic changes in nucleus accumbens dopamine efflux during the Coolidge effect in male rats. *Journal of Neuroscience, 17*(12), 4849–4855.

Firestone, L. L., Gyulai, F., Mintun, M., Adler, L. J., Urso, K., & Winter, P. M. (1996). Human brain activity response to fentanyl imaged by positron emission tomography. *Anesthesia & Analgesia, 82*(6), 1247–1251.

Fouriezos, G., & Wise, R. A. (1976). Pimozide-induced extinction of intracranial self-stimulation: Response patterns rule out motor or performance deficits. *Brain Research, 103*(2), 377–380.

Fox, N. A., & Davidson, R. J. (1986). Taste-elicited changes in facial signs of emotion and the asymmetry of brain electrical activity in human newborns. *Neuropsychologia, 24*(3), 417–422.

Francis, S., Rolls, E. T., Bowtell, R., McGlone, F., O'Doherty, J., Browning, A., Clare, S., & Smith, E. (1999). The representation of pleasant touch in the brain and its relationship with taste and olfactory areas. *Neuroreport, 10*(3), 453–459.

Fulbright, R. K., Skudlarski, P., Lacadie, C. M., Warrenburg, S., Bowers, A. A., Gore, J. C., & Wexler, B. E. (1998). Functional MR imaging of regional brain responses to pleasant and unpleasant odors. *American Journal of Neuroradiology, 19*(9), 1721–1726.

Gainotti, G. (1972). Emotional behavior and hemispheric side of the lesion. *Cortex, 8*(1), 41–55.

Galaverna, O. G., Seeley, R. J., Berridge, K. C., Grill, H. J., Epstein, A. N., & Schulkin, J. (1993). Lesions of the central nucleus of the amygdala. I: Effects on taste reactivity, taste aversion learning and sodium appetite. *Behavioral Brain Research, 59*(1–2), 11–17.

Gallagher, M., & Chiba, A. A. (1996). The amygdala and emotion. *Current Opinion in Neurobiology, 6*(2), 221–227.

Gallagher, M., & Holland, P. C. (1994). The amygdala complex: Multiple roles in associative learning and attention. *Proc Natl Acad Sci USA, 91*(25), 11771–11776.

Gallistel, C. R. (1980). *The organization of action: A new synthesis*. Hillsdale, NJ: Erlbaum.

Gallistel, C. R. (1986). The role of the dopaminergic projections in MFB self-stimulation. *Behavioral Brain Research, 22*(2), 97–105.

Gallistel, C. R., Boytim, M., Gomita, Y., & Klebanoff, L. (1982). Does pimozide block the reinforcing effect of brain stimulation? *Pharmacology Biochemistry and Behavior, 17*(4), 769–781.

Gallistel, C. R., & Karras, D. (1984). Pimozide and amphetamine have opposing effects on the reward summation function. *Pharmacology Biochemistry and Behavior, 20*(1), 73–77.

Gardner, E. L., & Lowinson, J. H. (1993). Drug craving and positive-negative hedonic brain substrates activated by addicting drugs. *Seminars in the Neurosciences, 5*(5), 359–368.

Garris, P. A., Kilpatrick, M., Bunin, M. A., Michael, D., Walker, Q. D., & Wightman, R. M. (1999). Dissociation of dopamine release in the nucleus accumbens from intracranial self-stimulation. *Nature, 398*, 67–69.

Glick, S. D., Merski, C., Steindorf, S., Wang, S., Keller, R. W., & Carlson, J. N. (1992). Neurochemical predisposition to self-administer morphine in rats. *Brain Research, 578*(1–2), 215–220.

Glick, S. D., Weaver, L. M., & Meibach, R. C. (1980). Lateralization of reward in rats: Differences in reinforcing thresholds. *Science, 207*, 1093–1095.

Glick, S. D., Weaver, L. M., & Meibach, R. C. (1981). Amphetamine enhancement of reward asymmetry. *Psychopharmacology, 73*(4), 323–327.

Goeders, N. E., & Smith, J. E. (1983). Cortical dopaminergic involvement in cocaine reinforcement. *Science, 221*, 773–775.

Goldstein, K. (1952). The effect of brain damage on the personality. *Psychiatry, 15*, 41–45.

Gong, W., Neill, D., & Justice, J. B., Jr. (1997). 6-Hydroxydopamine lesion of ventral pallidum blocks acquisition of place preference conditioning to cocaine. *Brain Research, 754*(1–2), 103–12.

Gray, J. A. (1987). *The psychology of fear and stress* (2nd ed.). Cambridge and New York: Cambridge University Press.

Gray, J. A., & McNaughton, N. (1996). The neuropsychology of anxiety: Reprise. *Nebraska Symposium on Motivation, 43*, 61–134.

Gray, J. A., Moran, P. M., Grigoryan, G., Peters, S. L., Young, A. M., & Joseph, M. H. (1997). Latent inhibition: The nucleus accumbens connection revisited. *Behavioural Brain Research, 88*(1), 27–34.

Gray, R. W., & Cooper, S. J. (1995). Benzodiazepines and palatability: Taste reactivity in normal ingestion. *Physiology and Behavior, 58*(5), 853–859.

Grigson, P. S., Reilly S., Shimura, T., & Norgren, R. (1998). Ibotenic acid lesions of the parabrachial nucleus and conditioned taste aversion: Further evidence for an associative deficit in rats. *Behavioral Neuroscience, 112*(1), 160–171.

Gyulai, F. E., Firestone, L. L., Mintun, M. A., & Winter, P. M. (1997). In vivo imaging of nitrous oxide-induced changes in cerebral activation during noxious heat stimuli. *Anesthesiology, 86*(3), 538–548.

Habib, M. (1998). Hemispheric lateralization of emotion: Experimental paradigms and theoretical debates. *Revue De Neuropsychologie, 8*(4), 587–641.

Hatfield, T., Han, J. S., Conley, M., Gallagher, M., & Holland, P. (1996). Neurotoxic lesions of basolateral, but not central, amygdala interfere with Pavlovian second-order conditioning and reinforcer devaluation effects. *Journal of Neuroscience, 16*(16), 5256–5265.

Hauser, M. D., (1999). Perseveration, inhibition and the prefrontal cortex: A new look. *Current Opinion in Neurobiology, 9*(2) 214–222.

Hay, P., Sachdev, P., Cumming, S., Smith, J. S., Lee, T., Kitchener, P., & Matheson, J. (1993). Treatment of obsessive-compulsive disorder by psychosurgery. *Acta Psychiatrica Scandinavica, 87*(3), 197–207.

Hay, P. J., & Sachdev, P. S. (1992). The present status of psychosurgery in Australia and New Zealand [see comments]. *Medical Journal of Australia, 157*(1), 17–19.

Heath, R. G. (1972). Pleasure and brain activity in man. Deep and surface electroencephalograms during orgasm. *Journal of Nervous and Mental Disease, 154*(1), 3–18.

Heimer, L., Harlan, R. E., Alheid, G. F., Garcia, M. M., & de Olmos, J. (1997). Substantia innominata: A notion which impedes clinical-anatomical correlations in neuropsychiatric disorders. *Neuroscience, 76*(4), 957–1006.

Higgs, S., & Cooper, S. J. (1996). Hyperphagia induced by direct administration of midazolam into the parabrachial nucleus of the rat. *European Journal of Pharmacology, 313*(1–2), 1–9.

Hoebel, B. G. (1988). Neuroscience and motivation: Pathways and peptides that define motivational systems. In R. C. Atkinson, Herrnstein, R. J., Lindzey, G., & Luce, R. D. (Eds.), *Stevens' handbook of experimental psy-*

*chology* (2nd ed.; Vol. 1, pp. 547–626). New York: John Wiley.

Hoebel, B. G., Mark, G. P., & West, H. L. (1992). Conditioned release of neurotransmitters as measured by microdialysis. *Clinical Neuropharmacology, 15 Supplement 1(A)*, 704–705.

Hollerman, J. R., Tremblay, L., & Schultz, W. (1998). Influence od reward expectation on behavior-related neuronal activity in primate striatum. *Journal of Neurophysiology, 80(2)*, 974–963.

Hook-Costigan, M. A., & Rogers, L. J. (1998). Lateralized use of the mouth in production of vocalizations by marmosets. *Neuropsychologia, 36(12)*, 1265–1273.

Hosobuchi, Y. (1987). Dorsal periaqueductal gray-matter stimulation in humans. *Pacing & Clinical Electrophysiology, 10(1 Pt 2)*, 213–216.

Hsieh, J. C., Stone-Elander, S., & Ingvar, M. (1999). Anticipatory coping of pain expressed in the human anterior cingulate cortex: A positron emission tomography study. *Neuroscience Letters, 262(1)*, 61–64.

Hughlings Jackson, J. (Ed.). (1958). *Selected writings of John Hughlings Jackson* (Vols. 1 and 2). London: Staples Press.

Hunt, G. E., & McGregor, I. S. (1998). Rewarding brain stimulation induces only sparse Fos-like immunoreactivity in dopaminergic neurons. *Neuroscience, 83(2)*, 501–515.

Hurt, R. W., & Ballantine, H. T., Jr. (1974). Stereotactic anterior cingulate lesions for persistent pain: A report on 68 cases. *Clinical Neurosurgery, 21*, 334–351.

James, W. (1884). What is an emotion? *Mind, 9*, 188–205.

Jerison, H. J. (1977). The theory of encephalization. *Annals of the New York Academy of Sciences, 299*, 146–160.

Johnson, P. I., & Stellar, J. R. (1994). Comparison of delta opiate receptor agonist induced reward and motor effects between the ventral pallidum and dorsal striatum. *Neuropharmacology, 33(10)*, 1171–1182.

Kagan, J., & Schulkin, J. (1995). On the concepts of fear. *Harvard Review of Psychiatry, 3*, 231–234.

Kagan, J., & Snidman, N. (1991). Infant predictors of uninhibited profiles. *Psychological Science, 2*, 40–44.

Killcross, S., Robbins, T. W., & Everitt, B. J. (1997). Different types of fear-conditioned behaviour mediated by separate nuclei within amygdala. *Nature, 388*, 377–380.

Kim, M., & Davis, M. (1993). Electrolytic lesions of the amygdala block acquisition and expression of fear-potentiated startle even with extensive training but do not prevent reacquisition. *Behavioral Neuroscience, 107(4)*, 580–595.

King, T. E., Crown, E. D., Sieve, A. N., Joynes, R. L., Grau, J. W., & Meagher, M. W. (1999). Shock-induced hyperalgesia: Evidence forebrain systems play an essential role. *Behavioural Brain Research, 100(1–2)*, 33–42.

Kitayama, S., & Markus, H. R. (Eds.). (1994). *Emotion and culture*. Washington, DC: American Psychological Association.

Kiyatkin, E. A., & Gratton, A. (1994). Electrochemical monitoring of extracellular dopamine in nucleus accumbens of rats lever-pressing for food. *Brain Research, 652(2)*, 225–234.

Kiyatkin, E. A., Wise, R. A., & Gratton, A. (1993). Drug- and behavior-associated changes in dopamine-related electrochemical signals during intravenous heroin self-administration in rats. *Synapse, 14(1)*, 60–72.

Kling, A. S., & Brothers, L. A. (1992). The amygdala and social behavior. In J. P. Aggleton (Ed.), *The amygdala: Neurobiological aspects of emotion, memory, and mental dysfunction* (pp. 353–377). New York: John Wiley.

Kluver, H., & Bucy, P. C. (1939). Preliminary analysis of the temporal lobes in monkeys. *Archives of Neurology and Psychiatry, 42*, 979–1000.

Koepp, M. J., Gunn, R. N., Lawrence, A. D., Cunningham, V. J., Dagher, A., Jones, T., Brooks, D. J., Bench, C. J., & Grasby, P. M. (1998). Evidence for striatal dopamine release during a video game. *Nature, 393*, 266–268.

Kolb, B., & Tees, R. C. (1990). *The cerebral cortex of the rat*. Cambridge, MA: MIT Press.

Kolb, B., & Whishaw, I. Q. (1996). *Fundamentals of human neuropsychology* (4th ed.). New York: W. H. Freeman.

Kondziolka, D. (1999). Functional radiosurgery. *Neurosurgery, 44(1)*, 12–20; discussion 20–22.

Koob, G. F., & Le Moal, M. (1997). Drug abuse: Hedonic homeostatic dysregulation. *Science, 278(5335)*, 52–58.

Kropotov, J. D., Crawford, H. J., & Polyakov, Y. I. (1997). Somatosensory event-related potential changes to painful stimuli during hypnotic analgesia: Anterior cingulate cortex and anterior temporal cortex intracranial recordings. *International Journal of Psychophysiology, 27(1)*, 1–8.

Lane, R. D., Reiman, E. M., Bradley, M. M., Lang, P. J., Ahern, G. L., Davidson, R. J., & Schwartz, G. E. (1997). Neuroanatomical correlates of pleasant and unpleasant emotion. *Neuropsychologia, 35(11)*, 1437–1444.

LeDoux, J. (1996). *The emotional brain: The mysterious underpinnings of emotional life*. New York: Simon & Schuster.

LeDoux, J. (1998). Fear and the brain: Where have we been, and where are we going? *Biological Psychiatry, 44(12)*, 1229–1238.

LeDoux, J. E. (1992). Emotion and the amygdala. In J. P. Aggleton (Ed.), *The amygdala: Neurobiological aspects of emotion, memory, and mental dysfunction* (pp. 339–351). New-York: Wiley-Liss.

Liebeskind, J. C., Sherman, J. E., & Cannon, T. (1982). Neural and neurochemical mechanisms of pain inhibition. *Anaesthesia & Intensive Care, 10(2)*, 139–43.

Maas, L. C., Lukas, S. E., Kaufman, M. J., Weiss, R. D., Daniels, S. L., Rogers, V. W., Kukes, T. J., & Renshaw, P. F. (1998). Functional magnetic resonance imaging of human brain activation during cue-induced cocaine craving. *American Journal of Psychiatry, 155(1)*, 124–126.

Maclean, P. (1955). The limbic system ('visceral brain') and emotional behavior. *Archives of Neurology & Psychiatry, 73*, 120–133.

Maren, S. (1999a). Long-term potentiation in the amygdala: A mechanism for emotional learning and memory. *Trends in Neurosciences, 22(12)*, 561–567.

Maren, S. (1999b). Neurotoxic basolateral amygdala lesions impair learning and memory but not the performance of conditional fear in rats. *Journal of Neuroscience, 19(19)*, 8696–8703.

Maren, S., & Fanselow, M. S. (1996). The amygdala and fear conditioning: Has the nut been cracked? *Neuron, 16*, 237–240.

Marino, L. (1998). A comparison of encephalization between odontocete cetaceans and anthropoid primates. *Brain, Behavior & Evolution, 51(4)*, 230–238.

Mathew, R. J., Wilson, W. H., Coleman, R. E., Turkington, T. G., & DeGrado, T. R. (1997). Marijuana intoxication and brain activation in marijuana smokers. *Life Sciences, 60*(23), 2075–2089.

Mayberg, H. S., Liotti, M., Brannan, S. K., McGinnis, S., Mahurin, R. K., Jerabek, P. A., Silva, J. A., Tekell, J. L., Martin, C. C., Lancaster, J. L., & Fox, P. T. (1999). Reciprocal limbic-cortical function and negative mood: Converging PET findings in depression and normal sadness. *American Journal of Psychiatry, 156*(5), 675–682.

McBride, W. J., Murphy, J. M., & Ikemoto, S. (1999). Localization of brain reinforcement mechanisms: intracranial self-administration and intracranial place-conditioning studies. *Behavioural Brain Research, 101*(2), 129–52.

McFarland, K., & Ettenberg, A. (1998). Naloxone blocks reinforcement but not motivation in an operant runway model of heroin-seeking behavior. *Experimental and Clinical Psychopharmacology, 6*(4), 353–359.

Mermelstein, P. G., & Becker, J. B. (1995). Increased extracellular dopamine in the nucleus accumbens and striatum of the female rat during paced copulatory behavior. *Behavioral Neuroscience, 109*(2), 354–365.

Miyawaki, E., Perlmutter, J. S., Troster, A. I., Videen, T. O., & Koller, W. C. (2000). The behavioral complications of pallidal stimulation: A case report. *Brain & Cognition, 42*(3), 417–434.

Morgane, P. J., Jacobs, M. S., & Galaburda, A. (1985). Conservative features of neocortical evolution in dolphin brain. *Brain Behavior and Evolution, 26*(3–4), 176–184.

Morris, J. S., Ohman, A., & Dolan, R. J. (1998). Conscious and unconscious emotional learning in the human amygdala. *Nature, 393*(6684), 467–470.

Nakajima, S., & Patterson, R. L. (1997). The involvement of dopamine D2 receptors, but not D3 or D4 receptors, in the rewarding effect of brain stimulation in the rat. *Brain Research, 760*(1–2), 74–79.

Nash, M. J. (1997, May 8). Addicted: Why do people get hooked? Mounting evidence points to a powerful brain chemical called dopamine. *Time,* 68–76.

Nesse, R. M., & Berridge, K. C. (1997). Psychoactive drug use in evolutionary perspective. *Science, 278*(5335), 63–66.

Nisbett, R. W., & Wilson, T. D. (1978). Telling more than we can know: Verbal reports on mental processes. *Psychological Review, 84,* 231–259.

Olds, J., & Milner, P. (1954). Positive reinforcement produced by electrical stimulation of septal area and other regions of rat brain. *Journal of Comparative and Physiological Psychology, 47,* 419–427.

Ongur, D., & Price, J. L. (2000). The organization of networks within the orbital and medial prefrontal cortex of rats, monkeys and humans. *Cereb Cortex, 10*(3), 206–219.

Panagis, G., Nomikos, G. G., Miliaressis, E., Chergui, K., Kastellakis, A., Svensson, T. H., & Spyraki, C. (1997). Ventral pallidum self-stimulation induces stimulus dependent increase in c-Fos expression in reward-related brain regions. *Neuroscience, 77*(1), 175–186.

Pani, L., & Gessa, G. L. (1997). Evolution of the dopaminergic system and its relationships with the psychopathology of pleasure. *International Journal of Clinical Pharmacology Research, 17*(2–3), 55–58.

Panksepp, J. (1991). Affective neuroscience: A conceptual framework for the study of emotions. In K. Strongman (Ed.), *International reviews of studies in emotions* (Vol., 1; pp. 59–99). Chichester: John Wiley.

Panksepp, J. (1998). *Affective Neuroscience: The foundations of human and animal emotions.* New York: Oxford University Press.

Panksepp, J., Normansell, L., Cox, J. F., & Siviy, S. M. (1994). Effects of neonatal decortication on the social play of juvenile rats. *Physiology and Behavior, 56*(3), 429–443.

Papez, J. W. (1937/1995). A proposed mechanism of emotion. 1937 [classical article]. *Journal of Neuropsychiatry & Clinical Neurosciences, 7*(1), 103–112.

Parker, L. A. (1995). Chlordiazepoxide enhances the palatability of lithium-, amphetamine-, and saline-paired saccharin solution. *Pharmacology Biochemistry and Behavior, 50*(3), 345–349.

Parkinson, J. A., Robbins, T. W., & Everitt, B. J. (2000). Dissociable roles of the central and basolateral amygdala in appetitive emotional learning. *European Journal of Neuroscience, 12*(1), 405–413.

Peciña, S. (1998). *Contrasting roles of mesostriatal dopamine and opioid systems in food "wanting" and "liking."* Unpublished Ph.D. dissertation, University of Michigan, Ann Arbor.

Peciña, S., & Berridge, K. C. (1995). Central enhancement of taste pleasure by intraventricular morphine. *Neurobiology, 3*(3–4), 269–280.

Peciña, S., & Berridge, K. C. (1996). Brainstem mediates diazepam enhancement of palatability and feeding: Microinjections into fourth ventricle versus lateral ventricle. *Brain Research, 727*(1–2), 22–30.

Peciña, S., & Berridge, K. C. (2000). Opioid eating site in accumbens shell mediates food intake and hedonic 'liking': Map based on microinjection Fos plumes. *Brain Research, 863,* 71–86.

Peciña, S., Berridge, K. C., & Parker, L. A. (1997). Pimozide does not shift palatability: Separation of anhedonia from sensorimotor suppression by taste reactivity. *Pharmacology Biochemistry and Behavior, 58*(3), 801–811.

Pesold, C., & Treit, D. (1995). The central and basolateral amygdala differentially mediate the anxiolytic effects of benzodiazepines. *Brain Research, 67*(2), 213–221.

Pfaus, J. G., Damsma, G., Wenkstern, D., & Fibiger, H. C. (1995). Sexual activity increases dopamine transmission in the nucleus accumbens and striatum of female rats. *Brain Research, 693*(1–2), 21–30.

Phillips, A. G., Blaha, C. D., Pfaus, J. G., & Blackburn, J. R. (1992). Neurobiological correlates of positive emotional states: Dopamine, anticipation, and reward. In K. T. Strongman (Ed.), *International review of studies on emotion* (Vol. 2; pp. 31–50). New York: John Wiley.

Phillips, A. G., & Fibiger, H. C. (1973). Dopaminergic and noradrenergic substrates of positive reinforcement: Differential effects of *d-* and *l- amphetamine. Science, 258,* 750–751.

Phillips, M. L., Bullmore, E. T., Howard, R., Woodruff, P. W. R., Wright, I. C., Williams, S. C. R., Simmons, A., Andrew, C., Brammer, M., & David, A. S. (1998). Investigation of facial recognition memory and happy and sad facial expression perception: An fMRI study. *Psychiatry Research-Neuroimaging, 83*(3), 127–138.

Phillips, M. L., Young, A. W., Senior, C., Brammer, M., Andrew, C., Calder, A. J., Bullmore, E. T., Perrett, D. I., Rowland, D., Williams, S. C. R., Gray, J. A., & David, A. S. (1997). A specific neural substrate for perceiving facial expressions of disgust. *Nature, 389,* 495–498.

Porro, C. A., Cettolo, V., Francescato, M. P., & Baraldi, P. (1998). Temporal and intensity coding of pain in human cortex. *Journal of Neurophysiology, 80*(60), 3312–3320.

Rada, P. V., Mark, G. P., & Hoebel, B. G. (1998). Dopamine release in the nucleus accumbens by hypothalamic stimulation-escape behavior. *Brain Research, 782*(1–2), 228–234.

Rainville, P., Duncan, G. H., Price, D. D., Carrier, B., & Bushnell, M. C. (1997). Pain affect encoded in human anterior cingulate but not somatosensory cortex. *Science, 277*, 968–971.

Ranaldi, R., Pocock, D., Zereik, R., & Wise, R. A. (1999). Dopamine fluctuations in the nucleus accumbens during maintenance, extinction, and reinstatement of intravenous D-amphetamine self-administration. *Journal of Neuroscience, 19*(10), 4102–4109.

Rauch, S. L., Shin, L. M., Dougherty, D. D., Alpert, N. M., Orr, S. P., Lasko, M., Macklin, M. L., Fischman, A. J., & Pitman, R. K. (1999). Neural activation during sexual and competitive arousal in healthy men. *Psychiatry Research, 91*(1), 1–10.

Richardson, N. R., & Gratton, A. (1996). Behavior-relevant changes in nucleus accumbens dopamine transmission elicited by food reinforcement: An electrochemical study in rat. *Journal of Neuroscience, 16*, 8160–8169.

Richardson, N. R., & Gratton, A. (1998). Changes in medial prefrontal cortical dopamine levels associated with response-contingent food reward: An electrochemical study in rat. *Journal of Neuroscience, 18*(21), 9130–9138.

Rideout, H. J., & Parker, L. A. (1996). Morphine enhancement of sucrose palatability: Analysis by the taste reactivity test. *Pharmacology Biochemistry and Behavior, 53*(3), 731–734.

Roberts, D. C., Loh, E. A., & Vickers, G. (1989). Self-administration of cocaine on a progressive ratio schedule in rats: Dose-response relationship and effect of haloperidol pretreatment. *Psychopharmacology, 97*(4), 535–538.

Robinson, T. E., & Kolb, B. (1997). Persistent structural modifications in nucleus accumbens and prefrontal cortex neurons produced by previous experience with amphetamine. *Journal of Neuroscience, 17*(21), 8491–8497.

Robinson, T. E., & Kolb, B. (1999). Alterations in the morphology of dendrites and dendritic spines in the nucleus accumbens and prefrontal cortex following repeated treatment with amphetamine or cocaine. *European Journal of Neuroscience, 11*(5), 1598–1604.

Rolls, E. T. (1997). Taste and olfactory processing in the brain and its relation to the control of eating. *Critical Reviews in Neurobiology, 11*(4), 263–287.

Rolls, E. T. (1999). *The brain and emotion.* Oxford: Oxford University Press.

Rolls, E. T. (2000). The orbitofrontal cortex and reward. *Cerebral Cortex, 10*(3), 284–294.

Rolls, E. T., & Baylis, L. L. (1994). Gustatory, olfactory, and visual convergence within the primate orbitofrontal cortex. *Journal of Neuroscience, 14*(9), 5437–5452.

Rolls, E. T., Critchley, H. D., Browning, A. S., Hernadi, I., & Lenard, L. (1999). Responses to the sensory properties of fat of neurons in the primate orbitofrontal cortex. *Journal of Neuroscience, 19*(4), 1532–1540.

Rolls, E. T., Murzi, E., Yaxley, S., Thorpe, S. J., & Simpson, S. J. (1986). Sensory-specific satiety: Food-specific reduction in responsiveness of ventral forebrain neurons after feeding in the monkey. *Brain Research, 368*(1), 79–86.

Rolls, E. T., Scott, T. R., Sienkiewicz, Z. J., & Yaxley, S. (1988). The responsiveness of neurones in the frontal opercular gustatory cortex of the macaque monkey is independent of hunger. *Journal of Physiology, 397*, 1–12.

Rolls, E. T., Yaxley, S., & Sienkiewicz, Z. J. (1990). Gustatory responses of single neurons in the caudolateral orbitofrontal cortex of the macaque monkey. *Journal of Neurophysiology, 64*(4), 1055–1066.

Salamone, J. D. (1994). The involvement of nucleus accumbens dopamine in appetitive and aversive motivation. *Behavioral Brain Research, 61*, 117–133.

Salamone, J. D., Cousins, M. S., & Snyder, B. J. (1997). Behavioral functions of nucleus accumbens dopamine: Empirical and conceptual problems with the anhedonia hypothesis. *Neuroscience and Biobehavioral Review, 21*(3), 341–359.

Sarter, M., Berntson, G. G., & Cacioppo, J. T. (1996). Brain imaging and cognitive neuroscience: Toward strong inference in attributing function to structure. *American Psychologist, 51*(1), 13–21.

Schneider, F., Weiss, U., Kessler, C., Muller-Gartner, H. W., Posse, S., Salloum, J. B., Grodd, W., Himmelmann, F., Gaebel, W., & Birbaumer, N. (1999). Subcortical correlates of differential classical conditioning of aversive emotional reactions in social phobia. *Biological Psychiatry, 45*(7), 863–871.

Schoenbaum, G., Chiba, A. A., & Gallagher, M. (1999). Neural encoding in orbitofrontal cortex and basolateral amygdala during olfactory discrimination learning. *Journal of Neuroscience, 19*(5), 1876–1884.

Schulkin, J. (1991). *Sodium hunger: The search for a salty taste.* New York: Cambridge University Press.

Schulkin, J. (1994). Melancholic depression and the hormones of adversity: A role for the amygdala. *Current Directions in Psychological Science, 3*, 41–44.

Schulkin, J., Marini, J., & Epstein, A. N. (1989). A role for the medial region of the amygdala in mineralocorticoid-induced salt hunger. *Behavioral Neuroscience, 103*(1), 179–185.

Schultz, W. (1998). Predictive reward signal of dopamine neurons. *Journal of Neurophysiology, 80*(1), 1–27.

Schultz, W., Dayan, P., & Montague, P. R. (1997). A neural substrate of prediction and reward. *Science, 275*, 1593–1599.

Schwartz, C. E., Snidman, N., & Kagan, J. (1996). Early childhood temperament as a determinant of externalizing behavior in adolescence. *Development and Psychopathology, 8*, 527–537.

Schwartzbaum, J. S. (1988). Electrophysiology of taste, feeding and reward in lateral hypothalamus of rabbit. *Physiology and Behavior, 44*(4–5), 507–526.

Scott, S. K., Young, A. W., Calder, A. J., Hellawell, D. J., Aggleton, J. P., & Johnson, M. (1997). Impaired auditory recognition of fear and anger following bilateral amygdala lesions. *Nature, 385*, 254–257.

Seamans, J. K., Floresco, S. B., & Phillips, A. G. (1995). Functional differences between the prelimbic and anterior cingulate regions of the rat prefrontal cortex. *Behavioral Neuroscience, 109*(6), 1063–1073.

Seeley, R. J., Galaverna, O., Schulkin, J., Epstein, A. N., & Grill, H. J. (1993). Lesions of the central nucleus of the amygdala. II: Effects on intraoral NaCl intake. *Behavioral Brain Research, 59*(1–2), 19–25.

Sell, L. A., Morris, J., Bearn, J., Frackowiak, R. S. J., Friston, K. J., & Dolan, R. J. (1999). Activation of reward circuitry in human opiate addicts. *European Journal of Neuroscience, 11*(3), 1042–1048.

Sem-Jacobsen, C. W. (1976). Electrical stimulation and self-stimulation with chronic implanted electrodes: Interpretation and pitfalls of results. In A. Wauquier & E. T. Rolls (Eds.), *Brain-stimulation reward* (pp. 505–520). Amsterdam: Elsevier-North Holland.

Servan-Schreiber, D., Perlstein, W. M., Cohen, J. D., & Mintun, M. (1998). Selective pharmacological activation of limbic structures in human volunteers: A positron emission tomography study. *Journal of Neuropsychiatry and Clinical Neurosciences, 10*(2), 148–159.

Shizgal, P. (1997). Neural basis of utility estimation. *Current Opinion in Neurobiology, 7*, 198–208.

Shizgal, P. (1999). On the neural computation of utility: Implications from studies of brain stimulation reward. In *Well-being: The foundations of hedonic psychology* (pp. 500–524). New York: Russell Sage Foundation.

Skinner, D. M., Martin, G. M., Harley, C., Kolb, B., Pridgar, A., Bechara, A., & van der Kooy, D. (1994). Acquisition of conditional discriminations in hippocampal lesioned and decorticated rats: Evidence for learning that is separate from both simple classical conditioning and configural learning. *Behavioral Neuroscience, 108*(5), 911–926.

Smith, G. P. (1995). Dopamine and food reward. In A. M. Morrison & S. J. Fluharty (Eds.), *Progress in psychobiology and physiological psychology* (Vol. 15; pp. 83–144). New York: Academic Press.

Söderpalm, A. H. V., & Berridge, K. C. (2000). The hedonic impact and intake of food are increased by midazolam microinjection in the parabrachial nucleus. *Brain Research, 877*(2), 288–297.

Spector, A. C. (1995). Gustatory function in the parabrachial nuclei: Implications from lesion studies in rats. *Reviews in the Neurosciences, 6*(2), 143–175.

Steiner, J. E. (1973). The gustofacial response: Observation on normal and anencephalic newborn infants. *Symposium on Oral Sensation and Perception, 4*, 254–278.

Steiner, J. E., Glaser, D., Hawilo, M. E., & Berridge, K. C. (2001). Comparative expression of hedonic impact: Affective reactions to taste by human infants and other primates. *Neuroscience and Biobehavioral Reviews, 25*(1), 53–74.

Stellar, E. (1954). The physiology of motivation. *Psychological Review, 61*, 5–22.

Stewart, J., & Vezina, P. (1988). A comparison of the effects of intra-accumbens injections of amphetamine and morphine on reinstatement of heroin intravenous self-administration behavior. *Brain Research, 457*(2), 287–294.

Stone, V. E., Nisenson, L., Eliassen, J. C., & Gazzaniga, M. S. (1996). Left hemisphere representations of emotional facial expressions. *Neuropsychologia, 34*(1), 23–29.

Sullivan, R. M., & Gratton, A. (1999). Lateralized effects of medial prefrontal cortex lesions on neuroendocrine and autonomic stress responses in rats. *Journal of Neuroscience, 19*(7), 2834–2840.

Sullivan, R. M., & Szechtman, H. (1995). Asymmetrical influence of mesocortical dopamine depletion on stress ulcer development and subcortical dopamine systems in rats: Implications for psychopathology. *Neuroscience, 65*(3), 757–766.

Sutton, S. K., & Davidson, R. J. (1997). Prefrontal brain asymmetry: A biological substrate of the behavioral approach and inhibition systems. *Psychological Science, 8*(3), 204–210.

Teasdale, J. D., Howard, R. J., Cox, S. G., Ha, Y., Brammer, M. J., Williams, S. C. R., & Checkley, S. A. (1999). Functional MRI study of the cognitive generation of affect. *American Journal of Psychiatry, 156*(2), 209–215.

Teitelbaum, P., & Epstein, A. N. (1962). The lateral hypothalamic syndrome: Recovery of feeding and drinking after lateral hypothalamic lesions. *Psychological Review, 69*, 74–90.

Teitelbaum, P., & Stricker, E. M. (1994). Compound complementarities in the study of motivated behavior. *Psychological Review, 101*(2), 312–317.

Terman, G. W., Shavit, Y., Lewis, J. W., Cannon, J. T., & Liebeskind, J. C. (1984). Intrinsic mechanisms of pain inhibition: Activation by stress. *Science, 226*, 1270–1277.

Thut, G., Schultz, W., Roelcke, U., Nienhusmeier, M., Missimer, J., Maguire, R. P., & Leenders, K. L. (1997). Activation of the human brain by monetary reward. *Neuroreport, 8*(5), 1225–1228.

Toates, F. M. (1994). Comparing motivational systems—An incentive motivation perspective. In C. R. Legg & D. A. Booth (Eds.), *Appetite: Neural and behavioural bases* (pp. 305–327). New York: Oxford University Press.

Tolle, T. R., Kaufmann, T., Siessmeier, T., Lautenbacher, S., Berthele, A., Munz, F., Zieglgansberger, W., Willoch, F., Schwaiger, M., Conrad, B., & Bartenstein, P. (1999). Region-specific encoding of sensory and affective components of pain in the human brain: A positron emission tomography correlation analysis. *Annals of Neurology, 45*(1), 40–47.

Treit, D., & Berridge, K. C. (1990). A comparison of benzodiazepine, serotonin, and dopamine agents in the taste-reactivity paradigm. *Pharmacology Biochemistry and Behavior, 37*(3), 451–456.

Treit, D., Pesold, C., & Rotzinger, S. (1993). Dissociating the anti-fear effects of septal and amygdaloid lesions using two pharmacologically validated models of rat anxiety. *Behavioral Neuroscience, 107*(5), 770–785.

Tucker, D. M. (1981). Lateral brain function, emotion, and conceptualization. *Psychological Bulletin, 89*(1), 19–46.

Tucker, D. M., Luu, P., & Pribram, K. H. (1995). Social and emotional self-regulation. *Annals of the New York Academy of Science, 769*, 213–239.

Valenstein, E. S. (1971). Channeling of responses elicited by hypothalamic stimulation. *Journal of Psychiatric Research, 8*(3), 335–344.

Valenstein, E. S. (1974). *Brain control.* New York: John Wiley.

Valenstein, E. S. (1976). The interpretation of behavior evoked by brain stimulation. In A. Wauquier & E. T. Rolls (Eds.), *Brain-stimulation reward* (pp. 557–575). New York: Elsevier.

Valenstein, E. S. (1986). *Great and desperate cures: The rise and decline of psychosurgery and other radical treatments for mental illness.* New York: Basic Books.

Valenstein, E. S., Cox, V. C., & Kakolewski, J. W. (1969). Hypothalamic motivational systems: Fixed or plastic neural circuits? *Science, 163*(871), 1084.

Valenstein, E. S., Cox, V. C., & Kakolewski, J. W. (1970). Reexamination of the role of the hypothalamus in motivation. *Psychological Review, 77*(1), 16–31.

Volkow, N. D., Gillespie, H., Mullani, N., Tancredi, L.,

Grant, C., Valentine, A., & Hollister, L. (1996). B glucose metabolism in chronic marijuana users at baseline and during marijuana intoxication. *Psychiatry Research-Neuroimaging, 67*(1), 29–38.

Vollenweider, F. X., Maguire, R. P., Leenders, K. L., Mathys, K., & Angst, J. (1998). Effects of high amphetamine dose on mood and cerebral glucose metabolism in normal volunteers using positron emission tomography (PET). *Psychiatry Research-Neuroimaging, 83*(3), 149–162.

Waraczynski, M., & Perkins, M. (1998). Lesions of pontomesencephalic cholinergic nuclei do not substantially disrupt the reward value of medial forebrain bundle stimulation. *Brain Research, 800*(1), 154–69.

Waraczynski, M., & Shizgal, P. (1995). Self-stimulation of the MFB following parabrachial lesions. *Physiology and Behavior, 58*(3), 559–566.

Weiskrantz, L. (1956). Behavioral changes associated with ablation of the amygdaloid complex in monkeys. *Journal of Comparative and Physiological Psychology, 49*, 381–391.

Weiskrantz, L. (1997). *Consciousness lost and found: A neuropsychological exploration.* New York: Oxford University Press.

Whishaw, I. Q., Schallert, T., & Kolb, B. (1981). An analysis of feeding and sensorimotor abilities of rats after decortication. *Journal of Comparative and Physiological Psychology, 95*(1), 85–103.

Wickelgren, I. (1997). Getting the brain's attention [news]. *Science, 278*, 35–37.

Willis, W. D., & Westlund, K. N. (1997). Neuroanatomy of the pain system and of the pathways that modulate pain. *Journal of Clinical Neurophysiology, 14*(1), 2–31.

Wilson, T. D., Hodges, S. D., & LaFleur, S. J. (1995). Effects of introspecting about reasons: Inferring attitudes from accessible thoughts. *Journal of Personality and Social Psychology, 69*(1), 16–28.

Winkielman, P., Berntson, G. G., & Cacioppo, J. T. (2001). The psychophysiological perspective on the social mind. In A. Tesser & N. Schwarz (Eds.), *Blackwell handbook of social psychology* (pp. 89–108). Oxford: Blackwell.

Wirsig, C. R., & Grill, H. J. (1982). Contribution of the rat's neocortex to ingestive control: I. Latent learning for the taste of sodium chloride. *Journal of Comparative and Physiological Psychology, 96*(4), 615–627.

Wise, R. A. (1982). Neuroleptics and operant behavior: The anhedonia hypothesis. *Behavioral and Brain Sciences, 5*, 39–87.

Wise, R. A. (1985). The anhedonia hypothesis: Mark III. *Behavioral and Brain Sciences, 8*, 178–186.

Wise, R. A. (1991). Neuroleptic-induced anhedonia: Recent studies. In C. A. Tamminga & C. S. Schulz (Eds.), *Schizophrenia research. Advances in neuropsychiatry and psychopharmacology* (Vol. 1, pp. 323–331). New York: Raven Press.

Wise, R. A. (1996). Addictive drugs and brain stimulation reward. *Annual Review of Neuroscience, 19*, 319–340.

Wise, R. A. (1998). Drug-activation of brain reward pathways. *Drug & Alcohol Dependence, 51*(1–2), 13–22.

Wise, R. A., & Dawson, V. (1974). Diazepam-induced eating and lever pressing for food in sated rats. *Journal of Comparative and Physiological Psychology, 86*(5), 930–941.

Wise, R. A., Spindler, J., deWit, H., & Gerber, G. J. (1978). Neuroleptic-induced "anhedonia" in rats: Pimozide blocks reward quality of food. *Science, 201*(4352), 262–264.

Yan, J., & Scott, T. R. (1996). The effect of satiety on responses of gustatory neurons in the amygdala of alert cynomolgus macaques. *Brain Research, 740*(1-2), 193–200.

Yeomans, J. S. (1995). Role of tegmental cholinergic neurons in dopaminergic activation, antimuscarinic psychosis and schizophrenia. *Neuropsychopharmacology, 12*(1), 3–16.

Yeomans, J. S., Mathur, A., & Tampakeras, M. (1993). Rewarding brain stimulation: Role of tegmental cholinergic neurons that activate dopamine neurons. *Behavioral Neuroscience, 107*(6), 1077–1087.

Yoshioka, M., Matsumoto, M., Togashi, H., & Saito, H. (1996). Effect of conditioned fear stress on dopamine release in the rat prefrontal cortex. *Neuroscience Letters, 209*(3), 201–203.

Young, A. M., Ahier, R. G., Upton, R. L., Joseph, M. H., & Gray, J. A. (1998). Increased extracellular dopamine in the nucleus accumbens of the rat during associative learning of neutral stimuli. *Neuroscience, 83*(4), 1175–1183.

Young, R. F., Bach, F. W., Van Norman, A. S., & Yaksh, T. L. (1993). Release of beta-endorphin and methionine-enkephalin into cerebrospinal fluid during deep brain stimulation for chronic pain: Effects of stimulation locus and site of sampling. *Journal of Neurosurgery, 79*(6), 816–825.

Zajonc, R. B. (1980). Feeling and thinking: Preferences need no inferences. *American Psychologist, 35*, 151–175.

Zajonc, R. B. (1998). Emotions. In D. T. Gilbert, S. T. Fiske, & G. Lindzey (Eds.), *The handbook of social psychology* (4 ed., Vol. 2, pp. 591–632). Boston: McGraw-Hill.

Zald, D. H., Lee, J. T., Fluegel, K. W., & Pardo, J. V. (1998). Aversive gustatory stimulation activates limbic circuits in humans. *Brain, 121*, 1143–1154.

Zald, D. H., & Pardo, J. V. (1997). Emotion, olfaction, and the human amygdala: Amygdala activation during aversive olfactory stimulation. *Proceedings of the National Academy of Sciences of the United States of America, 94*(8), 4119–4124.

# 4

# EMOTIONAL LEARNING CIRCUITS IN ANIMALS AND HUMANS

Kevin S. LaBar and Joseph E. LeDoux

Imagine living in a world in which sensory events occurred haphazardly. Without a means to evaluate the predictability of stimuli in the environment, it would seem impossible to determine where to focus one's attention and how to use external cues to obtain behaviorally relevant goals. In the complex and changing real world, the regularity and salience of the environment must be established to handle the bombardment of sensory stimulation in a limited-capacity brain. A primary function of an emotional learning system is to assess the predictive outcome of external events relevant for the organism's survival and to mobilize the body's resources to coordinate appropriate actions. In particular, situations that warn of impending danger (or lead to unbridled pleasure) must be reacted to quickly and stored into long-term memory in the event that they are encountered again in the future.

Recent advances in neuroscience have enabled a detailed account of the brain circuits that underlie emotional learning and memory. Much of what we know has been discovered through studies of fear conditioning, a procedure in which animals learn that certain stimuli reliably predict noxious stimulation. In this chapter, we review the neural basis of fear conditioning, beginning with the systems-level anatomy and proceeding to the cellular and molecular substrates. Both simple and complex forms of conditioning are considered, including the control of conditioned responses as a function of their contextual relevance. We conclude with applications of

fear conditioning paradigms to human cognitive neuroscience and comment on the implications of this approach for understanding emotional psychopathology in clinical populations.

## Fear Conditioning: A Primer

Emotionally neutral stimuli can acquire affective properties when they occur in conjunction with a biologically significant event. As originally described by Pavlov (1927), the neutral stimulus is called a conditional (or conditioned) stimulus (CS) and the biologically significant event an unconditional (or unconditioned) stimulus (US). For the conditioning of fear responses, the US is some form of noxious stimulation, such as a mild electric shock or loud noise, and the CS is typically a transient sensory stimulus, such as a tone. By pairing the CS and US in time, innate physiological and behavioral responses to danger come under the control of the CS (Figure 4.1). As a result, the CS becomes a warning cue that prepares the animal for an impending threatening situation. The set of conditioned responses triggered by the CS include direct alterations in autonomic (heart rate, blood pressure), endocrine (hormone release), and skeletal (conditioned immobility, or "freezing") systems, as well as modulations of pain sensitivity (analgesia) and somatic reflexes (fear-potentiated startle). The bodily responses susceptible to fear condi-

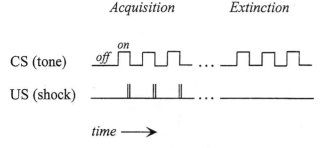

Figure 4.1 Classical conditioning involves learning the predictive relationship between an initially-neutral stimulus (CS) and an emotionally arousing event (US). The time line for three acquisition and three extinction trials is depicted.

tioning are largely species-typical defensive reactions that are hardwired into the brain. What is altered through the conditioning process is the accessibility of such reactions to previously innocuous stimuli.

One advantage of this approach is that the formation of novel emotional associations is investigated using relatively simple stimuli and well-defined behavioral responses. This feature of conditioning paradigms has two important repercussions. First, because the sensorimotor demands are minimal and operate via known anatomical pathways, the brain mechanisms for the learning component of the task, which is of primary interest, can be carefully identified. Second, the procedures can be carried out in a variety of preparations and compared across species, including human populations with compromised cognitive or motor faculties. Finally, since the experimenter has exquisite control over the parameters of the conditioning setting, the neuroscientific investigation of more intricate emotional associations is tractable. In this regard, the contextual specificity of conditioned responding has received increased interest in recent years. As we discuss below, this line of work exemplifies how brain regions specialized for emotional and cognitive functions normally interact to guide mental activity.

## Neural Pathways of Conditioned Fear

Consensus has emerged across several laboratories regarding the anatomic pathways mediating conditioned fear learning (reviewed in Kapp, Whalen, Supple, & Pascoe, 1992; Davis, 1994; Fendt & Fanselow, 1999; LeDoux, 1996, 2000). Irrespective of the stimulus modality and the behavioral response system under investigation, the amygdala is consistently implicated as the key brain region through which CS-US associations are formed. We discuss below the input pathways to the amygdala (particularly in the auditory domain), intra-amygdala processing of fear

signals, and output pathways from the amygdala to effector systems involved in generating conditioned responses.

### Unimodal Afferent Pathways

Most unimodal sensory information reaches the amygdala through the lateral amygdala (LA), which serves as the amygdala's sensory interface (LeDoux, Cicchetti, Xagoraris, & Romanski, 1990). Conditioning to a single tone involves transmission through the auditory pathways of the brain stem to the auditory thalamus, including the medial geniculate body and posterior intralaminar nucleus (LeDoux, Sakaguchi, & Reis, 1984). The auditory signal is then transmitted in parallel to LA and to the auditory cortex, which, in turn, projects to LA (Figure 4.2). The amygdala thus receives sensory input from two parallel routes: a direct thalamo-amygdala and an indirect thalamocortico-amygdala pathway. Either route is sufficient to mediate fear conditioning (Romanski & LeDoux, 1992), although the cortical pathway may be required for more complex stimulus computations (Jarrell, Gentile, Romanski, McCabe, & Schneiderman, 1987; but see Armony, Servan-Schreiber, Romanski, Cohen, & LeDoux, 1997). Lesions to LA disrupt fear conditioning (LeDoux et al., 1990; Campeau & Davis, 1995a), and LA is the earliest site of conditioned-induced plasticity observed within the amygdala (Quirk, Repa, & LeDoux, 1995; Quirk, Armony, & LeDoux, 1997).

The direct subcortical pathway allows the amygdala to detect threatening stimuli in the environment quickly, in the absence of a thorough analysis of the stimulus. This processing route may function to "prime" the amygdala to evaluate subsequent information received along the cortical pathway. Both pathways converge onto single neurons in LA (Li, Stutzmann, & LeDoux, 1996), providing a means whereby subcortical and cortical integration could take place. Differences in the organization of synapses from these afferent fibers onto LA are only beginning to be discovered and may yield clues as to the functional interactions of the parallel projection streams.

Many neurons in LA respond to auditory stimuli (Bordi & LeDoux, 1992), and a majority of these are also responsive to somatosensory cues (Romanski, Clugnet, Bordi, & LeDoux, 1993). Thus, LA is a region where unimodal CS and US information are integrated in the brain, as evidenced by electrophysiological studies of LA plasticity. Although neural convergence of the CS and US had been postulated as the basis of learning decades ago by learning theorists (Hebb, 1949; Konorski, 1967), only recently has such evidence emerged at the neural level for fear conditioning. Interestingly, the predominant auditory responses of cells in LA are in the range of vocalizations of conspecifics (Bordi & LeDoux, 1992). Defense calls characterized by species-typical vocalizations in mammals are vital for

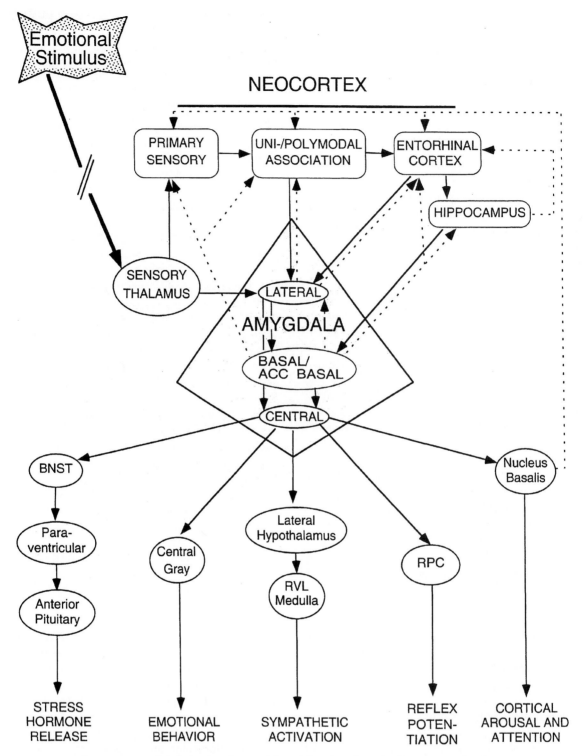

Figure 4.2 Emotional circuitry for conditioned fear learning. Simple sensory stimuli reach the lateral amygdala via parallel projections from the thalamus (subcortical route) and from neocortical association areas (cortical route). Spatial contextual cues enter the basal nuclei of the amygdala via the hippocampus. Neocortical feedback projections (indicated by dashed lines) originate primarily from these nuclei. Intra-amygdala processing is directed toward the central nucleus, which serves as the amygdala's output station. The central nucleus coordinates brainstem systems involved in defensive and arousal responses. BNST = bed nucleus of the stria terminalis, RPC = nucleus reticularis pontis caudalis, RVL = rostral ventrolateral medullary nuclei.

the social communication of threatening stimuli in the environment. Such vocalizations can be classically conditioned and may reflect the fear of pain in the immediate environment (Borszcz, 1995).

### Multimodal Afferent Pathways

In addition to discrete unimodal cues, more complex sensory stimuli can elicit conditioned fear responses. For example, in a typical conditioning experiment, a rat given tone-shock pairings will acquire fear reactions not only to the tone CS but also to the conditioning chamber in which the tone was presented. Both the amygdala and the hippocampus are critical for mediating conditioned responses to spatial contexts, although the hippocampus is not required for single cue conditioning (Kim & Fanselow, 1992; Phillips & LeDoux, 1992; Maren, Aharonov, & Fanselow, 1997; Figure 4.3). A potential route of spatial contextual information to the amygdala occurs through direct projections from the ventral hippocampus to the basal and accessory basal nuclei of the amygdala (B/BA; Canteras & Swanson, 1992; Figure 4.2). Moreover, long-term potentiation (LTP), currently the most popular model of neuronal plasticity during learning, has been observed along this hippocampal-amygdala pathway (Maren & Fanselow, 1995).

Multimodal projections also exist between the perirhinal cortex and amygdala (Stefanacci, Suzuki, & Amaral, 1996). Pretraining lesions of the perirhinal cortex, however, do not prevent acquisition of conditioning (Phillips & LeDoux, 1995). Posttraining lesions to this structure do impair the expression of fear conditioning (Campeau & Davis, 1995b; Corodimas & LeDoux, 1995) and implicate a role for the perirhinal cortex in the consolidation of fear memories (Corodimas & LeDoux, 1995; Sacchetti, Lorenzini, Baldi, Tassoni, & Bucherelli, 1999).

### Intra-Amygdala Pathways

It must be emphasized that the amygdala is a complex brain region composed of roughly a dozen nuclei, only some of which are involved in fear conditioning (Amaral, Price, Pitkänen, & Carmichael, 1992; Pitkänen, Savander, & LeDoux, 1997; Swanson & Petrovich, 1998). The information flow within the amygdala relevant for unimodal fear conditioning occurs via projections from LA to the central nucleus (CE), either directly or through B/BA (Figure 4.2). B/BA, in turn, is the entry point for contextual fear stimuli, which is further relayed to CE. Input from nociceptive pathways mediating US information arises through each of these nuclei, where it is integrated with CS- and context-specific computations (reviewed in LeDoux, 2000).

**(a)** *Non-lesioned (n = 12)*

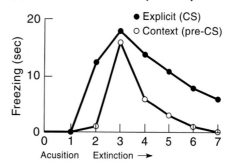

**(b)** *Cortex lesion (n = 11)*

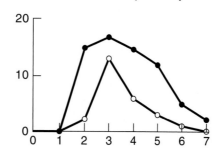

**(c)** *Amygdala lesion (n = 8)*

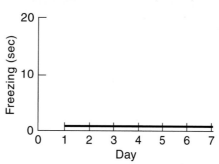

**(d)** *Hippocampus lesion (n = 25)*

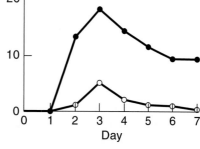

Figure 4.3 The amygdala and hippocampus make dissociable contributions to cued and contextual fear. In contrast to non-lesioned (a) and cortex-lesioned controls (b), rats with amygdala lesions (c) do not acquire conditioned freezing responses to either an explicit conditioned stimulus (CS) or to the context where conditioning takes place (pre-CS). Hippocampal lesions (d) selectively disrupt fear conditioning to spatial contextual cues. Adapted from Phillips & LeDoux (1992).

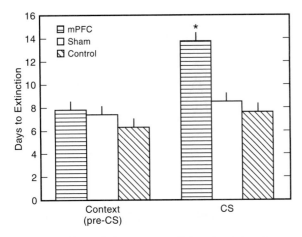

Figure 4.4 Lesions of the ventromedial prefrontal cortex (mPFC) selectively prolong the extinction of conditioned fear. Rats with pretraining mPFC lesions acquire conditioning at a normal rate (not shown) but take longer to extinguish their fear responses to an explicit CS. Adapted from Morgan et al. (1993).

## Efferent Pathways

The subcortical efferent projections from CE orchestrate brain stem systems involved in species-typical defensive reactions (reviewed in Kapp et al., 1992; Davis, 1994; LeDoux, 1996; Figure 4.2). Whereas lesions to the amygdala nuclei reviewed above interfere with fear conditioning regardless of how it is measured, damage to areas that CE projects to interferes with the expression of conditioned fear through individual response channels. For example, a double dissociation has been reported between lesions of the central gray, which selectively disrupt conditioned freezing, and lesions of the lateral hypothalamus, which selectively disrupt conditioned autonomic changes (LeDoux, Iwata, Cicchetti, & Reis, 1988). Both of these regions are targets of CE projections. CE thus serves as an output interface through which emotional associations computed within amygdala neurons converge to mediate the expression of fear via individual effector targets.

By contrast, most neocortical efferent projections arise directly from the basolateral nuclei (Amaral et al., 1992). The function of these cortical feedback pathways are not well understood, but they may contribute to cortical synaptic plasticity that underlies attentional maintenance of conditioned fear stimuli and memory consolidation for the conditioning episode (Weinberger, 1995; Armony, Quirk, & LeDoux, 1998; Cahill & McGaugh, 1998).

## Contextual Control of Conditioning Circuits

Once conditioned fear responses are acquired, they can be modified according to the spatial and temporal contexts in which the CS is encountered. An environmental stimulus that initially provokes a defensive response may turn out not to be threatening at all, or its emotional significance may change over space and time. In order to adapt to a changing world, it is necessary to have mechanisms in place for the perception of alterations in threat value, as a prolonged or generalized state of fear and stress is detrimental to the organism.

Temporal changes in emotional relevance have been studied through the extinction of conditioned fear responses and reversals of CS-US associations. Extinction refers to the process by which conditioned reactions to a CS are suppressed by repeated exposures to the CS in the absence of reinforcement (Figure 4.1). As the animal learns that a feared CS is no longer predictive of a threatening event, its fear reactivity to the CS decreases over time. When rats are given pretraining lesions of the ventromedial prefrontal or medial orbitofrontal cortex, the extinction process is selectively retarded (Morgan, Romanski, & LeDoux, 1993; Morgan & LeDoux, 1995; Quirk, Rosaly, Romero, Santini, & Muller, 1999; but see Gewirtz, Falls, & Davis, 1997; Figure 4.4). In addition, neurons within the orbitofrontal cortex are responsive to reversals of stimulus-reward associations (Thorpe, Rolls, & Maddison, 1983). In the absence of interactions with the prefrontal cortex and other cortical regions, conditioned responses established in the amygdala are relatively indelible (LeDoux, Romanski, & Xagoraris, 1989; Teich et al., 1989).

Fear reactions can also be triggered or modulated by the spatial context in which the CS is encountered. For example, seeing a snake in the woods typically evokes different visceral and behavioral responses than seeing one at the zoo. Conditioned fear can be recovered after extinction through several mechanisms that depend on spatial contextual cues (Bouton, 1993). One of these, called *reinstatement*, occurs when an extinguished CS is encountered in a spatial context whose fearfulness is independently established by US-alone presentations. In this case, the fear response returns to the CS but is specific to this fearful context. The hippocampus may play a critical role in this form of fear reinstatement, as well as establishing spatial context associations when conditioned responses are initially acquired (Wilson, Brooks, & Bouton, 1995; Frohardt, Guarraci, & Bouton, 1999; O'Connor, LaBar, & Phelps, 1999).

Therefore, the hippocampus, prefrontal cortex, and perhaps other cortical areas regulate the expression of learned fear based on temporal and spatial contextual information. These brain regions may be exerting their influences via connections with the B/AB nuclei of the amygdala, as reversible inactivation or blockade of NMDA receptors in this region also impairs contextual conditioning, extinction, and reinstatement (Falls, Miserendino, & Davis, 1992; Fanselow & Kim, 1994; Muller, Corodimas, Fridel, &

LeDoux, 1997; Lee & Kim, 1998; Falls & Pistell, 1999). Cortical control over the expression of defensive reactions may have evolved as a brain mechanism by which animals are protected from a prolonged state of fear. Malfunctions in these control operations could have profound implications for understanding the generalization and maintenance of fear and anxiety in clinical affective disorders.

## Cellular Substrates of Fear Learning

With the major components of the neural pathways involved in fear conditioning identified, researchers have begun to address questions concerning the cellular and molecular mechanisms that underlie the learning and memory functions of these pathways. We emphasize electrophysiological changes within the amygdala, particularly within LA, since this region is the sensory entry point and thus the first place where amygdala plasticity could occur.

The conditioning-induced firing patterns in LA have several important characteristics. First, the most prominent increases in firing rates in the dorsal LA occur at the earliest response latency window (< 15 msec after CS onset) within a few training trials, reflecting changes in the efficacy of signal processing along the direct thalamo-amygdala pathway (Quirk et al., 1995, 1997; Figure 4.5).

It is not likely that changes in LA are downstream from plasticity established in the auditory association cortex, since conditioned response latencies there tend to occur in later epochs (> 20 msec after CS onset) and emerge only after a larger number of training trials (Quirk et al., 1997). Plasticity established in LA, in turn, may contribute to subsequent changes in efferent structures, including the basal and central amygdala nuclei, where conditioned response latencies occur between 30 and 70 msec after CS onset (Pascoe & Kapp, 1985).

Second, convergent information arriving from the direct thalamo-amygdala and indirect thalamo-cortico-amygdala pathways onto single neurons in LA provide a cellular substrate for temporal summation of inputs (Li et al., 1996). While both pathways utilize glutamate as an excitatory transmitter (Li, Phillips, & LeDoux, 1995; Li et al., 1996), only the thalamic pathway requires both NMDA and non-NMDA (AMPA) receptor activation for routine transmission. Because of the slower kinetics of NMDA receptor function (Hestrin, Sah, & Nicoll., 1990), the effect of direct thalamic activation onto LA neurons is prolonged. Thus, LA cells driven by a crude thalamic input remain in an active state until cortical inputs arrive, thereby "priming" a subset of LA cells to receive more specific auditory information from the cortex regarding CS properties. The glutamatergic synapses from the thalamus onto LA neurons also have a smaller AMPA-to-NMDA ra-

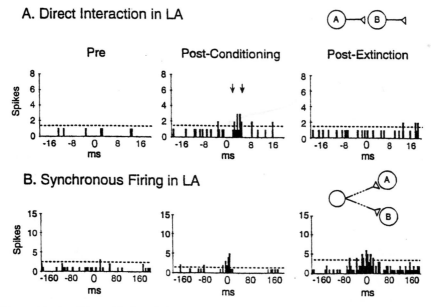

Figure 4.5 Conditioned-induced changes in simultaneously recorded unit responses in the lateral amygdala (LA). Cross-correlograms indicate (A) a rapid conditioned-induced direct interaction between LA neurons (indicated by double arrows). This interaction was reversed following extinction training. Conditioning also entrained synchronous firing between LA neurons (synchronicity peak at time = 0 ms), which persisted following 30 trials of extinction training (B). This latter finding suggests that the LA has access to an extinction-resistant memory trace for the conditioning episode. Dashed line indicates a confidence interval of p < 0.01. Adapted from Quirk et al. (1995).

tio and are more sensitive to magnesium than the synapses arising from the cortex (Weisskopf & LeDoux, 1999). These findings may have implications for understanding differential contributions of the input pathways to amygdala plasticity during emotional learning.

Finally, there is evidence for altered functional coupling among local neurons in LA as a result of the conditioning process (Quirk et al., 1995). The synchrony of spontaneous firing in LA is maintained long after conditioning has taken place, suggesting that this region may participate in the consolidation of emotional memories (see also Sacchetti et al., 1999; Schafe, Nadel, Sullivan, Harris, & LeDoux, 1999; Vazdarjanova & McGaugh, 1999). Because such changes are not obvious in CS-evoked firing patterns, their persistence may be overlooked by other techniques (e.g., functional neuroimaging). Neural populations within LA also exhibit conditioned-induced modification of receptive field properties, as evidenced by shifts in auditory tuning curves favoring the tuning frequency of the auditory cue used as a CS (Bordi & LeDoux, 1993). Similar adaptive frequency tuning is found in the auditory thalamus and auditory cortex during fear conditioning, and plasticity in each of these regions may have different functional consequences (Weinberger, 1995).

## The LTP–Conditioning Connection

Long-term potentiation (LTP), an activity-dependent enhancement of synaptic transmission, is a promising physiological substrate of learning and memory. In a typical preparation, LTP is induced by high-frequency stimulation of afferent fibers to a given brain structure and is measured as a long-lasting increase in evoked intracellular postsynaptic potentials or extracellular population field responses. Although several kinds of LTP have been identified, the classic form of LTP is dependent upon activation of glutamatergic NMDA receptors (Malenka & Nicoll, 1993). Due to the prevalence of NMDA receptors in LA, researchers have taken several approaches to determine whether an NMDA-dependent LTP mechanism underlies learning and memory functions of the amygdala during fear conditioning.

Intra-amygdala blockade of NMDA receptor function indeed disrupts conditioned fear acquisition (Miserendino, Sananes, Melia, & Davis 1990; Campeau, Miserendino, & Davis 1992; Fanselow & Kim, 1994; Lee & Kim, 1998). However, NMDA blockade has sometimes been found to affect the expression of conditioned responses as well (Maren, Aharonev, Stote, & Fanselow, 1996; Lee & Kim, 1998; but see Miserendino et al., 1990; Gewirtz & Davis, 1997). Given that NMDA receptors are involved in routine synaptic transmission along the thalamo-amygdala pathway (Li et al., 1996), their blockade may not selectively alter an NMDA-dependent *learning* process in LA. In other words, both routine synaptic transmission along

the thalamo-amygdala pathway and learning-related changes in the thalamo-amygdala and cortico-amygdala pathways may be altered by NMDA manipulations. The contribution of these receptors to plastic changes in other amygdala nuclei remains to be elucidated. Nonetheless, this pharmacologic approach has some limitations in specifying the cellular basis for an LTP-dependent mechanism in amygdala circuitry during fear learning.

Electrophysiological studies have shown LTP induction in the amygdala by stimulating various afferent inputs, including the thalamo-amygdala (Clugnet & LeDoux, 1990; Rogan & LeDoux, 1995; Weisskopf et al., 1999), cortico-amygdala (Chapman, Kairiss, Koenan, & Brown., 1990; Chapman & Bellavance, 1992; Gean, Chang, Huang, Lin, & Way., 1993; Huang & Kandel, 1998), and hippocampal-amygdala (Maren & Fanselow, 1995) pathways. The LTP induction appears to be NMDA-dependent under some circumstances (Huang & Kandel, 1998) but not others (Chapman & Bellavance, 1992; Weisskopf, Bauer, & LeDoux, 1999). Importantly, LTP enhances auditory evoked potentials along the thalamo-amygdala pathway (Rogan & LeDoux, 1995), and behavioral fear conditioning induces long-lasting potentiation of both LA synaptic currents *in vitro* (McKernan & Schinnick-Gallagher, 1997) and LA field potentials in vivo (Rogan, Stäubli, & LeDoux, 1997; Figure 4.6). Mechanistic links of this type have been dif-

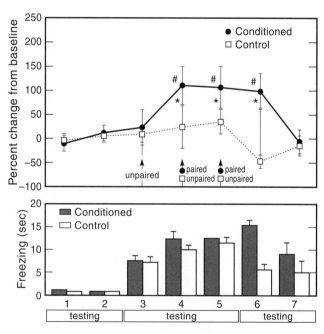

Figure 4.6 Fear conditioning induces associative long-term potentiation in the lateral amygdala (LA) in vivo. The slope (top) and amplitude (not shown) of CS-evoked field potentials in LA is significantly enhanced following associative CS-US training but not in pseudo-conditioned controls. Concomitant behavioral index of fear learning (freezing) is indicated in the bottom panel. Adapted from Rogan et al. (1997).

ficult to establish with LTP in other brain systems (e.g., the hippocampus), as the connection between the circuits studied and behavioral learning have not been as well characterized (Malenka & Nicoll, 1997; Stevens, 1998). These results provide strong evidence that LTP-like associative processes underlie the amygdala plasticity that mediates conditioned fear learning. Since the plastic changes do not always depend on the classic form of LTP that is associated with NMDA receptors, multiple cellular mechanisms may support emotional learning at different amygdala synapses.

## Fear Conditioning Circuitry in Humans

Animal models of conditioned learning have made remarkable advances, from the systems-level approach (Kapp et al., 1992; Davis, 1994; LeDoux, 1996, 2000; Fendt & Fanselow, 1999) to the microscopic details of the intracellular signaling pathways (Mayford et al., 1996; Bourtchouladze et al., 1998). In humans, the techniques of cognitive neuroscience have only recently been applied to the study of fear conditioning. The limitations in the spatiotemporal resolution of these methods currently restrict the level of analysis to the macroscopic circuits involved. Nonetheless, there has been some progress in this area, and the existing data suggest a large degree of conservation in the function of the fear networks across species.

### Role of the Human Amygdala

Human patients with amygdala lesions exhibit deficits in acquiring fear reactions to conditioned stimuli (Bechara et al., 1995; LaBar, LeDoux, Spencer, & Phelps, 1995; Phelps et al., 1998; Figure 4.7). The degree of impairment depends upon the extent of amygdala damage (unilateral vs. bilateral), a finding which parallels that seen in rats (LaBar & LeDoux, 1996). In the absence of concomitant bilateral hippocampal lesions, amygdala damage does not impair unconditioned responses to eliciting stimuli nor awareness of CS-US contingencies. Such observations demonstrate that the impairment is specific to an emotional learning system and not a general inability to generate arousal responses or a failure of declarative memory. With the advent of functional MRI, amygdala activation has been observed in normal human subjects during both the acquisition (Büchel, Morris, Dolan, & Friston, 1998; LaBar, Gatenby, Gore, LeDoux, & Phelps, 1998) and extinction (LaBar et al., 1998) of fear conditioning. The extent of amygdala activation selectively correlates with behavioral indices of learning in individual subjects (Furmark, Fischer, Wik, Larsson, & Fredrikson, 1997; LaBar et al., 1998). Interestingly, the signal strength elicited in the amygdala is strongest during the first few trials of acquisition and extinction, and decreases thereafter. This tem-

poral pattern shows that the amygdala is critical for learning about novel conditioned associations, but its role becomes less pronounced as the associations are well established. If the stimulus contingencies change (as in extinction), the amygdala once again plays a critical but time-limited role in updating the fear memory in an adaptive manner (Figure 4.7). These temporal dynamics are consistent with electrophysiological recordings of LA in rats (Quirk et al., 1995, 1997), although the hemodynamic signal in the human imaging studies is derived from a broader area than just the LA alone. The amygdala's response also covaries with activation of the auditory cortex during conditioning to tone CSs (Morris, Friston, & Dolan, 1998).

Additional positron emission tomography (PET) studies have examined blood flow changes to visual stimuli after conditioning has already taken place. These studies have yielded mixed results, with some studies reporting amygdala activation (Morris, Öhman, & Dolan, 1998) and others not (Fredrikson, Wik, Fischer, & Andersson, 1995; Hugdahl et al., 1995; Morris, Friston, & Dolan, 1997). Given that the amygdala's hemodynamic response tends to habituate over time, the temporal resolution of PET may be generally insufficient to yield positive findings. Moreover, postconditioning comparisons that are averaged over a large number of trials confound acquisition-related and extinction-related effects.

### Prefrontal Cortex Contributes to Extinction and Reversal Learning

In humans, as well as other mammals, the amygdala may interact with the ventral prefrontal cortex during extinction. Several lines of evidence support this hypothesis. First, a prefrontal source of extinction-related activity has been noted across human functional imaging (Hugdahl et al., 1995) and electrophysiological (LaBar, 1996) studies (Figure 4.7). As noted above, the amygdala is also engaged during fear extinction (LaBar et al., 1998). Second, amygdalar responses to masked stimuli that were previously conditioned vary inversely with activity in the orbitofrontal cortex, suggesting a reciprocity of neural interactions (Morris, Öhman, & Dolan, 1999). Third, patients with damage to the ventromedial prefrontal/orbitofrontal cortex are impaired at extinction and reversal of learned visual associations (Rolls, Hornak, Wade, & McGrath, 1994). Such forms of "emotional perseveration" accord with clinical observations in patients with damage to this region, highlighting the potential utility of conditioning models for assessing emotional regulation in the prefrontal cortex.

### The Hippocampus and Contextual Conditioning

Amnesic patients with hippocampal lesions (but spared amygdala function) are not impaired at acquiring fear re-

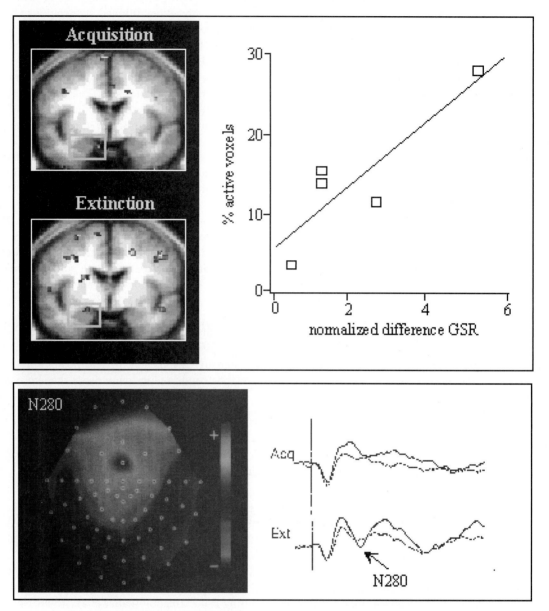

Figure 4.7 Mapping conditioned-related changes in the amygdala and prefrontal cortex of normal human subjects. *Top panel*: Hemodynamic changes in the amygdala (green box) during the early stages of fear acquisition and extinction is revealed by event-related functional magnetic resonance imaging (fMRI). The fMRI signal represents significant increases in CS-evoked responses relative to a control cue that was unpaired with a shock US. The hemodynamic activity decreased over additional training trials (data not shown). The degree to which the amygdala was engaged during acquisition significantly correlated with behavioral measures of conditioned fear in individual subjects (shown at right). GSR = galvanic skin response. Adapted from LaBar et al. (1998). *Bottom panel*: Conditioned-induced changes in event-related potential (ERP) activity measured at the scalp. Extinction (Ext) was characterized by an N280-P440 potential that was larger following paired CS-US training (solid line) than in pseudoconditioned controls (dashed line). The N280 component of this potential had a maximal scalp distribution over the prefrontal cortex (shown in purple at left). This potential may index extinction-specific learning, as it was not found during acquisition training (Acq). Vertical line indicates onset of the CS. Adapted from LaBar (1996). (*See color insert.*)

actions to simple conditioned stimuli (Bechara et al., 1995; O'Connor et al., 1999). If anything, these patients show some generalization of conditioned responses to unpaired stimuli (Bechara et al., 1995; LaBar & Disterhoft, 1998). Despite their ability to acquire conditioned responses, however, amnesics are insensitive to contextual reinstatement of fear reactions following extinction (O'Connor et al., 1999; Figure 4.8). These findings support the animal literature in revealing dissociable contributions of the amygdala and hippocampus to cued and contextual fear learning (Figure 4.3).

## Implications of Fear Conditioning Models for Emotional Psychopathology

The support for conditioning models in explaining clinical disorders of fear and anxiety has received variable support over the years. Many of the earlier objections to these models were based upon outdated concepts of conditioning (Rachman, 1991; LeDoux, 1996). Contemporary theories have encompassed modern conditioning principles as an important component to the genesis and maintenance of affective dysfunction in panic disorders, phobias, and posttraumatic stress disorders (Öhman, 1979; Wolpe & Rowan, 1988; Bouton & Swartzentruber, 1991; Charney, Deutch, Krystal, Southwick, & Davis, 1993; Pitman, Shalev, & Orr, 2000). Because the concept of fear is multifaceted, not all aspects of its regulation will be captured by a conditioning account. Nonetheless, we propose that the functional anatomy of conditioned fear can benefit the clinical arena in several ways.

First, the functional integrity of fear systems can be evaluated in patients through systematic applications of conditioning paradigms. As an example, the clinical symptomatology of human anxiety shares many features with measures of conditioned fear in animals (Davis, 1994), and anxiety patients generally show elevated conditioned fear responses (Welch & Kubis, 1947; Howe, 1958; Pitman & Orr, 1986; Ashcroft, Guimarães, Wang, & Deakin, 1991). The integrity of the brain circuits and neurotransmitter systems implicated in these disorders can now be directly explored using emotional challenges during functional imaging, rather than simply evaluating regional baseline metabolism rate changes. Studies that target specific features of anxiety, such as its reinstatement following extinction, can make use of the conditioning paradigms already developed, where much progress has been made in delineating the circuitry involved.

Second, the human cognitive neuroscience research has built a critical bridge from the animal studies to clinical applications. The initial findings are important in demonstrating the conservation of function in the networks for fear learning and memory across species. Pharmacological and genetic treatments of particular symp-

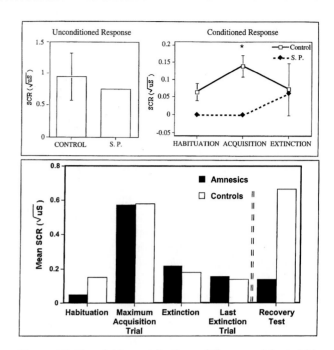

Figure 4.8 Dissociable contributions of the amygdala and hippocampus to cued and contextual fear in humans. *Top panel*: Impaired acquisition of fear in patient S. P., who sustained bilateral amygdala lesions without concomitant amnesia. Despite showing intact declarative memory of the CS-US contingency and normal skin conductance responses (SCRs) to the US, S. P. does not acquire conditioned SCRs to the CS. uS = microSiemens. Adapted from Phelps et al. (1998). *Bottom panel*: Contextual reinstatement of fear conditioning is impaired in amnesic patients with bilateral hippocampal lesions but spared amygdala function. In contrast to patient S. P., amnesics can acquire conditioned fear to simple CSs despite having no declarative memory for the CS-US contingency. However, they fail to recover conditioned responding to the CS after extinction when the fearfulness of the context is reestablished by repeated US-alone presentations (vertical dashed lines). Adapted from O'Connor et al. (1999).

toms of emotional dysregulation depend upon these experimental models to establish their relevance for human populations. If spatial or temporal contextual control over fear reactions is abnormal, clues may reside in the prefrontal-amygdala or hippocampal-amygdala circuits described above. Alternatively, if the coordination of subcortical and cortical streams of emotional information processing to the amygdala is imbalanced, pharmacological distinctions and integration of these pathways to LA must be understood at the cellular and molecular levels. Finally, dysfunctional alterations in the expression of particular emotional reactions, such as hyperventilation or excessive stress hormone release, can be probed at the connections between amygdalar output (via the central nucleus) and individual brainstem and diencephalic targets (Figure 4.2).

We have previously argued that a renewed neuropsychological theory of emotion may benefit from the decomposition of emotional constructs into component parts or subsystems (LeDoux, 1991; LaBar & LeDoux, 1997). The study of memory systems in the brain, for example, has dramatically changed in the past two decades through this kind of systematic approach. Even if fear conditioning does not account for all aspects of emotion-related psychopathology, the methodologies outlined herein should serve as a model for future investigations in this area. Only through the structured application of well-defined principles across all levels of neuroscientific investigation can a full account of emotional functions be advanced. Fortunately, with imminent technological developments, the mysteries behind the emotional brain are solvable, provided that the techniques are applied with the same kind of scientific integrity as that which has advanced our knowledge to its current state.

## Summary

The ability of an organism to detect and respond to danger is fundamental to survival across the phyla. The neural network that coordinates behavioral reactions to threatening cues in the environment has been well delineated in mammals using fear conditioning as a model system. The amygdala is a brain region that is essential for identifying fearful stimuli (via incoming parallel sensory projections from the thalamus and neocortex to the lateral nucleus), and for appropriating physiological responses to threat (via multiple efferent projections from the central nucleus). Other limbic forebrain regions, such as the hippocampus and medial prefrontal cortex, regulate the expression of conditioned fear responses with regard to spatial and temporal contexts. The role of the amygdala in emotional learning and memory is conserved across species, including humans. Conditioning-induced alterations in neuronal responsiveness, receptive field properties, and interactions with neighboring cells reveal mechanisms by which emotional associations are instantiated at the neural level. Fear conditioning induces long-term synaptic plasticity in the lateral amygdala, providing a link between behavioral learning and artificial LTP induction, which has been difficult to establish using other experimental approaches. Dysregulation of function along these information processing streams can lead to maladaptive defensive response tendencies and a prolonged or generalized state of fear.

## REFERENCES

Amaral, D. G., Price, J. L., Pitkänen, A., & Carmichael, S. T. (1992). Anatomical organization of the primate amygdaloid complex. In J. P. Aggleton (Ed.), *The amygdala: Neurobiological aspects of emotion, memory, and mental dysfunction* (pp. 1–66). New York: Wiley-Liss.

Armony, J. L., Quirk, G. J., & LeDoux, J. E. (1998). Differential effects of amygdala lesions on early and late plastic components of auditory cortex spiketrains during fear conditioning. *Journal of Neuroscience, 18,* 2592–2601.

Armony, J. L., Servan-Schreiber, D., Romanski, L. M., Cohen, J. D., & LeDoux, J. E. (1997). Stimulus generalization of fear responses: Effects of auditory cortex lesions in a computational model and in rats. *Cerebral Cortex, 7,* 157–165.

Ashcroft, K., Guimarães, F. S., Wang, M., & Deakin, J. F. W. (1991). Evaluation of a psychophysiological model of classical fear conditioning in anxious patients. *Psychopharmacology, 104,* 215–219.

Bechara, A., Tranel, D., Damasio, H., Adolphs, R., Rockland, C., & Damasio, A. R. (1995). Double dissociation of conditioning and declarative knowledge relative to the amygdala and hippocampus in humans. *Science, 269,* 1115–1118.

Bordi, F., & LeDoux, J. E. (1992). Sensory tuning beyond the sensory system: An initial analysis of auditory properties of neurons in the lateral amygdaloid nucleus and overlying areas of the striatum. *Journal of Neuroscience, 12,* 2493–2503.

Bordi, F., & LeDoux, J. E. (1993) Sensory-specific conditioned plasticity in lateral amygdala neurons. *Society for Neuroscience Abstracts, 19,* 1227.

Borszcz, G. (1995). Pavlovian conditional vocalizations of the rat: A model system for analyzing the fear of pain. *Behavioral Neuroscience, 109,* 648–662.

Bourtchouladze, R., Abel, T., Berman, N., Gordon, R., Lapidus, K., & Kandel, E. R. (1998). Different training procedures recruit either one or two critical periods for contextual memory consolidation, each of which requires protein synthesis and PKA. *Learning and Memory, 5,* 365–374.

Bouton, M. E. (1993). Context, time, and memory retrieval in the interference paradigms of Pavlovian learning. *Psychological Bulletin, 114,* 80–99.

Bouton, M. E., & Schwartzentruber, D. (1991). Sources of relapse after extinction in Pavlovian and instrumental learning. *Clinical Psychology Review, 11,* 123–140.

Büchel, C., Morris, J., Dolan, R. J., & Friston, K. J. (1998). Brain systems mediating aversive conditioning: An event-related fMRI study. *Neuron, 20,* 947–957.

Cahill, L., & McGaugh, J. L. (1998). Mechanisms of emotional arousal and lasting declarative memory. *Trends in Neurosciences, 21,* 294–299.

Campeau, S., & Davis, M. (1995a). Involvement of the central nucleus and basolateral complex of the amygdala in fear conditioning measured with fear-potentiated startle in rats trained concurrently with auditory and visual conditioned stimuli. *Journal of Neuroscience, 15,* 2301–2311.

Campeau, S., & Davis, M. (1995b). Involvement of subcortical and cortical afferents to the lateral nucleus of the amygdala in fear conditioning measured with fear-potentiated startle in rats trained concurrently with auditory and visual conditioned stimuli. *Journal of Neuroscience, 15,* 2312–2327.

Campeau, S., Miserendino, M. J., & Davis, M. (1992). Intra-amygdala infusion of the N-methyl-D-aspartate receptor antagonist AP5 blocks acquisition but not expression of fear-potentiated startle to an auditory conditioned stimulus. *Behavioral Neuroscience, 106*, 569–574.

Canteras, N. S., & Swanson, L. W. (1992). Projections of the ventral subiculum to the amygdala, septum, and hypothalamus: A PHA-L anterograde tract-tracing study in the rat. *Journal of Comparative Neurology, 324*, 180–194.

Chapman, P. F., & Bellavance, L. L. (1992). Induction of long-term potentiation in the basolateral amygdala does not depend on NMDA receptor activation. *Synapse, 11*, 310–318.

Chapman, P. F., Kairiss, E. W., Keenan, C. L., & Brown, T. H. (1990). Long-term synaptic potentiation in the amygdala. *Synapse, 6*, 271–278.

Charney, D. S., Deutch, A. Y., Krystal, J. H., Southwick, S. M., & Davis, M. (1993). Psychobiologic mechanisms of posttraumatic stress disorder. *Archives of General Psychiatry, 50*, 294–305.

Clugnet, M. C., & LeDoux, J. E. (1990). Synaptic plasticity in fear conditioning circuits: Induction of LTP in the lateral nucleus of the amygdala by stimulation of the medial geniculate body. *Journal of Neuroscience, 10*, 2818–2824.

Corodimas, K. P., & LeDoux, J. E. (1995). Disruptive effects of posttraining perirhinal cortex lesions on conditioned fear: Contributions of contextual cues. *Behavorial Neuroscience, 109*, 613–619.

Davis, M. (1994). The role of the amygdala in emotional learning. *International Review of Neurobiology, 36*, 225–266.

Falls, W. A., Miserendino, M. J. D., & Davis, M. (1992). Extinction of fear-potentiated startle: Blockade by infusion of an NMDA antagonist into the amygdala. *Journal of Neuroscience, 12*, 854–863.

Falls, W. A., & Pistell, P. (1999). Reversible inactivation of the amygdala interferes with reinstatement of extinguished fear as measured with the fear-potentiated startle paradigm. *Society for Neuroscience Abstracts, 25*, 1617.

Fanselow, M. S., & Kim, J. J. (1994). Acquisition of contextual Pavlovian fear conditioning is blocked by application of an NMDA receptor antagonist D,L-2-amino-5-phosphonovaleric acid to the basolateral amygdala. *Behavorial Neuroscience, 108*, 210–212.

Fendt, M., & Fanselow, M. S. (1999). The neuroanatomical and neurochemical basis of conditioned fear. *Neuroscience and Biobehavioral Reviews, 23*, 743–760.

Fredrikson, M., Wik, G., Fischer, H., & Andersson, J. (1995). Affective and attentive neural networks in humans: A PET study of Pavlovian conditioning. *Neuroreport, 7*, 97–101.

Frohardt, R. J., Guarraci, F. A., & Bouton, M. E. (1999). The role of the hippocampus in reinstatement and renewal. *Society for Neuroscience Abstracts, 25*, 1617.

Furmark, T., Fischer, H., Wik, G., Larsson, M., & Fredrikson, M. (1997). The amygdala and individual differences in human fear conditioning. *Neuroreport, 8*, 3957–3960.

Gean, P. W., Chang, F. C., Huang, C. C., Lin, J. H., & Way, L. J. (1993). Long-term enhancement of EPSP and NMDA receptor-mediated synaptic transmission in the amygdala. *Brain Research Bulletin, 31*, 7–11.

Gewirtz, J. C., & Davis, M. (1997). Second-order fear conditioning prevented by blocking NMDA receptors in amygdala. *Nature, 388*, 471–474.

Gewirtz, J. C., Falls, W. A., & Davis, M. (1997). Normal

conditioned inhibition and extinction of freezing and fear-potentiated startle following electrolytic lesions of the medial prefrontal cortex in rats. *Behavioral Neuroscience, 111*, 712–726.

Hebb, D. O. (1949). *The organization of behavior.* New York: John Wiley.

Hestrin, S., Sah, P., & Nicoll, R. A. (1990). Mechanisms generating the time course of dual component excitatory synaptic currents recorded in hippocampal slices. *Neuron 5*, 247–253.

Howe, E. S. (1958). GSR conditioning in anxiety states, normals, and chronic functional psychotic subjects. *Journal of Abnormal and Social Psychology, 56*, 183–189.

Huang, Y.-Y., & Kandel, E. R. (1998). Postsynaptic induction and PKA-dependent expression of LTP in the lateral amygdala. *Neuron, 21*, 169–178.

Hugdahl, K. Berardi, A., Thompson, W. L., Kosslyn, S. M., Macy, R., Baker, D. P., Alpert, N. M., & LeDoux, J. E. (1995). Brain mechanisms in human classical conditioning: A PET blood flow study. *Neuroreport, 6*, 1723–1728.

Jarrell, T. W., Gentile, C. G., Romanski, L. M., McCabe, P. M., & Schneiderman, N. (1987). Involvement of cortical and thalamic auditory regions in retention of differential bradycardia conditioning to acoustic conditioned stimuli in rabbits. *Brain Research, 412*, 285–294.

Kapp, B. S., Whalen, P. J., Supple, W. F., & Pascoe, J. P. (1992). Amygdaloid contributions to conditioned arousal and sensory information processing. In J. P. Aggleton (Ed.), *The amygdala: Neurobiological aspects of emotion, memory, and mental dysfunction* (pp. 229–254). New York: Wiley-Liss.

Kim, J. J., & Fanselow, M. S. (1992). Modality-specific retrograde amnesia of fear. *Science, 256*, 675–677.

Konorski, J. (1967). *Integrative activity of the brain: An interdisciplinary approach.* Chicago: University of Chicago Press.

LaBar, K. S. (1996). *The neural substrate of conditioned fear: Extension of an emotional memory network to the human brain.* Unpublished doctoral dissertation, New York University, New York.

LaBar, K. S., & Disterhoft, J. F. (1998). Conditioning, awareness, and the hippocampus. *Hippocampus, 8*, 620–626.

LaBar, K. S., Gatenby, J. C., Gore, J. C., LeDoux, J. E., & Phelps, E. A. (1998). Human amygdala activation during conditioned fear acquisition and extinction: A mixed-trial fMRI study. *Neuron, 20*, 937–945.

LaBar, K. S., & LeDoux, J. E. (1996). Partial disruption of fear conditioning in rats with unilateral amygdala damage: Correspondence with unilateral temporal lobectomy in humans. *Behavorial Neuroscience, 110*, 991–997.

LaBar, K. S., & LeDoux, J. E. (1997). Emotion and the brain: An overview. In T. E. Feinberg & M. Farah (Eds.), *Behavioral neurology and neuropsychology* (pp. 675–689). New York: McGraw-Hill.

LaBar, K. S., LeDoux, J. E., Spencer, D. D., & Phelps, E. A. (1995). Impaired fear conditioning following unilateral temporal lobectomy in humans. *Journal of Neuroscience, 15*, 6846–6855.

LeDoux, J. E. (1991). Emotion and the limbic system concept. *Concepts in Neuroscience, 2*, 169–199.

LeDoux, J. E. (1996). *The emotional brain.* New York: Simon & Schuster.

LeDoux, J. E. (2000). Emotion circuits in the brain. *Annual Review of Neuroscience, 23,* 155–184.

LeDoux, J. E., Cicchetti, P., Xagoraris, A., & Romanski, L. M. (1990). The lateral amygdaloid nucleus: Sensory interface of the amygdala in fear conditioning. *Journal of Neuroscience, 10,* 1062–1069.

LeDoux, J. E., Iwata, J., Cicchetti, P., & Reis, D. J. (1988). Different projections of the central amygdaloid nucleus mediate autonomic and behavioral correlates of conditioned fear. *Journal of Neuroscience, 8,* 2517–2529.

LeDoux, J. E., Romanski, L. M., & Xagoraris, A. E. (1989). Indelibility of subcortical emotional memories. *Journal of Cognitive Neuroscience, 1,* 238–243.

LeDoux, J. E., Sakaguchi, A., & Reis, D. J. (1984). Subcortical efferent projections of the medial geniculate nucleus mediate emotional responses conditioned by acoustic stimuli. *Journal of Neuroscience, 4,* 683–698.

Lee, H., & Kim, J. J. (1998). Amygdalar NMDA receptors are critical for new fear learning in previously fear-conditioned rats. *Journal of Neuroscience, 18,* 8444–8454.

Li, X.-F., Phillips, R. G., & LeDoux, J. E. (1995). NMDA and non-NMDA receptors contribute to synaptic transmission between the medial geniculate body and the lateral nucleus of the amygdala. *Experimental Brain Research, 105,* 87–100.

Li, X.-F., Stutzmann, G. E., & LeDoux, J. E. (1996). Convergent but temporally separated inputs to lateral amygdala neurons from the auditory thalamus and auditory cortex use different postsynaptic receptors: *in vivo* intracellular and extracellular recordings in fear conditioning pathways. *Learning and Memory, 3,* 229–242.

Malenka, R. C., & Nicoll, R. A. (1993). NMDA-receptor-dependent synaptic plasticity: Multiple forms and mechanisms. *Trends in Neuroscience, 16,* 521–527.

Malenka, R. C., & Nicoll, R. A. (1997). Never fear, LTP is hear. *Nature, 390,* 552–553.

Maren, S., Aharonov, G., & Fanselow, M. S. (1997). Neurotoxic lesions of the dorsal hippocampus and Pavlovian fear conditioning in rats. *Behavorial Brain Research, 88,* 261–274.

Maren, S., Aharonov, G., Stote, D. L., & Fanselow, M. S. (1996). N-methyl-D-aspartate receptors in the basolateral amygdala are required for both acquisition and expression of conditional fear in rats. *Behavioral Neuroscience, 110,* 1365–1374.

Maren, S., & Fanselow, M. S. (1995). Synaptic plasticity in the basolateral amygdala induced by hippocampal formation stimulation *in vivo. Journal of Neuroscience, 15,* 7548–7564.

Mayford, M., Bach, M. E., Huang, Y.-Y., Wang, L., Hawkins, R. D., & Kandel, E. R. (1996). Control of memory formation through regulated expression of a CaMKII transgene. *Science, 274,* 1678–1683.

McKernan, M. G., & Shinnick-Gallagher, P. (1997). Fear conditioning induces a lasting potentiation of synaptic currents *in vitro. Nature, 390,* 607–611.

Miserendino, M. J. D., Sananes, C. B., Melia, K. R., & Davis, M. (1990). Blocking of acquisition but not expression of conditioned fear-potentiated startle by NMDA antagonists in the amygdala. *Nature, 345,* 716–718.

Morgan, M. A., & LeDoux, J. E. (1995). Differential contribution of dorsal and ventral medial prefrontal cortex to the acquisition and extinction of conditioned fear in rats. *Behavioral Neuroscience, 109,* 681–688.

Morgan, M. A., Romanski, L. M., & LeDoux, J. E. (1993). Extinction of emotional learning: Contribution of medial prefrontal cortex. *Neuroscience Letters, 163,* 109–113.

Morris, J. S., Friston, K. J., & Dolan, R. J. (1997). Neural responses to salient visual stimuli. *Proceedings of the Royal Society London, Series B, 264,* 769–775.

Morris, J. S., Friston, K. J., & Dolan, R. J. (1998). Experience-dependent modulation of tonotopic neural responses in human auditory cortex. *Proceedings of the Royal Society London, Series B, 265,* 649–657.

Morris, J. S., Öhman, A., & Dolan, R. J. (1998). Conscious and unconscious emotional learning in the human amygdala. *Nature, 393,* 467–470.

Morris, J. S., Öhman, A., & Dolan, R. J. (1999). A subcortical pathway to the right amygdala mediating "unseen" fear. *Proceedings of the National Academy of Science USA, 96,* 1680–1685.

Muller, J., Corodimas, K. P., Fridel, Z., & LeDoux, J. E. (1997). Functional inactivation of the lateral and basal nuclei of the amygdala by muscimol infusion prevents fear conditioning to an explicit CS and to contextual stimuli. *Behavioral Neuroscience, 111,* 683–691.

O'Connor, K. J., LaBar, K. S., & Phelps, E. A. (1999). Impaired contextual fear conditioning in amnesics. *Journal of Cognitive Neuroscience, Supplement S,* 19.

Öhman, A. Fear-relevance, autonomic conditioning, and phobias: A laboratory model. In P. O. Sjödén, S. Bates, & W. S. Dockens (Eds.), *Trends in behavior therapy* (pp. 107–133). New York: Academic Press.

Pascoe, J. P., & Kapp, B. S. (1985). Electrophysiological characteristics of amygdaloid central nucleus neurons during Pavlovian fear conditioning in the rabbit. *Behavioral Brain Research, 16,* 117–133.

Pavlov, I. P. (1927). *Conditioned reflexes.* New York: Dover.

Phelps, E. A., LaBar, K. S., Anderson, A. K., O'Connor, K. J., Fulbright, R. K., & Spencer D. D. (1998). Specifying the contribution of the human amygdala to emotional memory: A case study. *Neurocase, 4,* 527–540.

Phillips, R. G., & LeDoux, J. E. (1992). Differential contribution of amygdala and hippocampus to cued and contextual fear conditioning. *Behavioral Neuroscience, 106,* 274–285.

Phillips, R. G., & LeDoux, J. E. (1995). Lesions of the fornix, but not the entorhinal or perirhinal cortex interfere with contextual fear conditioning. *Journal of Neuroscience, 15,* 5308–5315.

Pitkänen, A., Savander, V., & LeDoux, J. E. (1997). Organization of intra-amygdaloid circuitries: An emerging framework for understanding functions of the amygdala. *Trends in Neuroscience, 20,* 517–523.

Pitman, R. K., & Orr, S. P. (1986). Test of the conditioning model of neurosis: Differential aversive conditioning of angry and neutral facial expressions in anxiety disorder patients. *Journal of Abnormal Psychology, 95,* 208–213.

Pitman, R. K., Shalev, A. Y., & Orr, S. P. (2000). Posttraumatic stress disorder: Emotion, conditioning, and memory. In M. S. Gazzaniga (Ed.), *The new cognitive neurosciences* (pp. 1133–1147). Cambridge, MA: MIT Press.

Quirk, G. J., Armony, J. L., & LeDoux, J. E. (1997). Fear conditioning enhances different temporal components of tone-evoked spike trains in auditory cortex and lateral amygdala. *Neuron, 19,* 613–624.

Quirk, G. J., Repa, J. C., & LeDoux, J. E. (1995). Fear conditioning enhances short-latency auditory responses of lateral amygdala neurons: Parallel recordings in the freely behaving rat. *Neuron, 15,* 1029–1039.

Quirk G. J., Rosaly, E., Romero, R. V., Santini, E., & Muller, R. U. (1999). NMDA receptors are required for long-term but not short-term memory of extinction learning. *Society for Neuroscience Abstracts, 25,* 1620.

Rachman, S. (1991). Neo-conditioning and the classical theory of fear acquisition. *Clinical Psychology Review, 11,* 155–173.

Rogan, M. T., & LeDoux, J. E. (1995). LTP is accompanied by commensurate enhancement of auditory-evoked responses in a fear conditioning circuit. *Neuron, 15,* 127–136.

Rogan, M. T., Stäubli, U. V., & LeDoux, J. E. (1997). Fear conditioning induces associative long-term potentiation in the amygdala. *Nature, 390,* 604–607.

Rolls, E. T., Hornak, J., Wade, D., & McGrath, J. (1994). Emotion-related learning in patients with social and emotional changes associated with frontal lobe damage. *Journal of Neurology, Neurosurgery, and Psychiatry, 57,* 1518–1524.

Romanski, L. M., Clugnet, M. C., Bordi, F., & LeDoux, J. E. (1993). Somatosensory and auditory convergence in the lateral nucleus of the amygdala. *Behavorial Neuroscience, 107,* 444–450.

Romanski, L. M., & LeDoux, J. E. (1992). Equipotentiality of thalamo-amygdala and thalamo-cortico-amygdala projections as auditory conditioned stimulus pathways. *Journal of Neuroscience, 12,* 4501–4509.

Sacchetti, B., Lorenzini, C. A., Baldi, E., Tassoni, G., & Bucherelli, C. (1999). Auditory thalamus, dorsal hippocampus, basolateral amygdala, and perirhinal cortex role in the consolidation of conditioned freezing to context and to acoustic conditioned stimulus in the rat. *Journal of Neuroscience, 19,* 9570–9578.

Schafe, G. E., Nadel, N. V., Sullivan, G. M., Harris, A., & LeDoux, J. E. (1999). Memory consolidation for contextual and auditory fear conditioning is dependent on protein synthesis, PKA, and MAP kinase. *Learning and Memory, 6,* 97–110.

Stefanacci, L., Suzuki, W. A., & Amaral, D. G. (1996). Organization of connections between the amygdaloid complex and the perirhinal and parahippocampal cortices in macaque monkeys. *Journal of Comparative Neurology, 375,* 552–582.

Stevens, C. F. (1998). A million dollar question: Does LTP = memory? *Neuron, 20,* 1–2.

Swanson, L. W., & Petrovich, G. D. (1998). What is the amygdala? *Trends in Neuroscience, 21,* 323–331.

Teich, A. H., McCabe, P. M., Gentile, C. C., Schneiderman, L. S., Winters, R. W., Liskowsky, D. R., & Schneiderman N. (1989). Auditory cortex lesions prevent the extinction of Pavlovian differential heart rate conditioning to tonal stimuli in rabbits. *Brain Research, 480,* 210–218.

Thorpe, S. J., Rolls, E. T., & Maddison, S. (1983). Neuronal activity in the orbitofrontal cortex of the behaving monkey. *Experimental Brain Research, 49,* 93–115.

Vazdarjanova, A., & McGaugh, J. L. (1999). Basolateral amygdala is involved in modulating consolidation of memory for classical fear conditinoing. *Journal of Neuroscience, 19,* 6615–6622.

Weinberger, N. M. (1995). Retuning the brain by fear conditioning. In M. S. Gazzaniga (Ed.), *The cognitive neurosciences* (pp. 1071–1090). Cambridge, MA: MIT Press.

Weisskopf, M. G., Bauer, E. P., & LeDoux, J. E. (1999). L-type voltage-gated calcium channels mediate NMDA-independent associative long-term potentiation at thalamic input synapses to the amygdala. *Journal of Neuroscience, 19,* 10512–10519.

Weisskopf, M. G., & LeDoux, J. E. (1999). Distinct populations of NMDA receptors at subcortical and cortical inputs to principal cells of the lateral amygdala. *Journal of Neurophysiology, 81,* 930–934.

Welch, L., & Kubis, J. (1947). The effect of anxiety on the conditioning rate and stability of the PGR. *Journal of Psychology, 23,* 83–91.

Wilson, A., Brooks, D. C., & Bouton, M. E. (1995). The role of the rat hippocampal system in several effects of context in extinction. *Behavorial Neuroscience, 109,* 828–836.

Wolpe, J., & Rowan, V. C. (1988). Panic disorder: A product of classical conditioning. *Behavorial Research and Therapy, 26,* 441–450.

# 5

# THE CONTRIBUTIONS OF THE LESION METHOD TO THE FUNCTIONAL NEUROANATOMY OF EMOTION

Antonio R. Damasio, Ralph Adolphs,
and H. Damasio

Damage to the human brain has consequences for cognitive function, including emotional and social behavior. While the majority of impairments in brain function result from damage that is not focal, such as neurodegenerative disease or psychiatric disorders, there is a subset of cases that feature impaired processing of emotion as a result of focal damage in specific neural structures. It is these latter cases that are especially well suited to explore the relationships between particular structures and particular functions.

Historically, investigations of brain-cognition relationships on the basis of focal brain damage have relied on single, or a small number, of rare case studies. In the ideal case, such studies of individuals can provide the opportunity to link impairments in a particular domain of cognitive function to damage in a single structure. The single-case approach is complemented with approaches that utilize larger sample sizes and that examine patterns shared across many subjects whose lesions share a common focus, even though those lesions may not be restricted to a single structure of interest. We briefly discuss some of these developments in the analysis of lesions, before reviewing their contribution to the field of emotion research.

## The Logic of the Lesion Method

At the outset, it is important to bear in mind what the lesion method can and cannot demonstrate. Regardless of the specific methods used, inferences from impaired performances following brain damage always focus on the same conclusion: an inference regarding which structures are necessary to perform a given task. In most cases, the structures so revealed are only a subset of the structures that are sufficient to perform the task. This logic contrasts the lesion method with functional imaging of normal individuals. While functional imaging studies attempt to reveal all the structures that are engaged when normal subjects perform a certain task, the lesion method demonstrates which of these are critical, in the sense that normal performance is impossible in their absence.

The approach of the lesion method is connected with several caveats.

1. Neural structures contribute to cognitive function as components of distributed, large-scale neural systems. Consequently, identification of a structure that is critical to perform a task does not demonstrate that the task is carried out by that structure. On the contrary, essentially all higher cognitive functions, including the processing of emotion, rely on multiple, interdependent processes that are subserved by multiple neuroanatomical structures that operate as a system.

2. Impairments observed following brain damage must be interpreted in relation to the experimental task used. Any inferences about specific cognitive processes can only be as good as the task used. Experimental tasks should be considered as probes that tap one or (usually) multiple

cognitive processes. Depending on the specificity of the performance measure used, more or less specific inferences regarding cognitive processes may be possible. Numerous factors contribute to the power of an experimental task: specificity of the design, difficulty (avoidance of either floor or ceiling effects in performance), and sensitivity (wide performance range) are all important to consider.

3. Confounding factors on performance must be addressed. Human lesion studies have a between-subject design, rather than the within-subject design that is possible in animals. In most studies, investigators have compared subjects with lesions to control groups of normal subjects with no brain damage; in most of our studies we have added a second control group of subjects who have lesions that are outside of the structure under investigation. This design necessitates controls for possibly confounding factors that could also systematically vary between groups and affect their performances on the experimental task. For instance, one usually has to control for demographic factors, such as age, years of education, and gender ratio of the samples; additionally, one has to control for background neuropsychological profile, such as IQ and basic perceptual function.

## Analysis of the Contribution of Single Structures

In contrast to the lesion method as typically used in animals, human lesions cannot be experimentally introduced, but result from a variety of pathologies, including stroke, tumor, or other disorders. Conclusions regarding single structures or regions of the brain therefore require one of two approaches: investigation of rare cases whose lesions are confined to those structures or regions; or investigation of larger numbers of subjects and an analysis of how task performance varies with lesion location among multiple individuals. The first approach has been the historical one, and it is still enormously informative in generating specific hypotheses that can be tested in replications. The second approach has generally been confined to samples of modest size. We have recently undertaken a major extension of the group approach that relies on co-registration of lesions from relatively large numbers of subjects.

When one compares the performances of a sample of brain-damaged subjects to the performances of normal controls, one inevitably finds an increased variance in the brain-damaged group. Sometimes, but not always, this is also accompanied by a lower mean performance. The increased variance is not at all surprising: whatever are the sources of variance that contribute to task performance, the brain-damaged group has an additional source (their brain damage). The interesting research question is how the increased variance in task performance relates to the variance in the underlying neuroanatomical location of the brain damage. Are there specific locations at which brain damage systematically results in lower performance, and other locations at which brain damage does not result in lower performance?

This question can be approached in an exploratory fashion, as it has often been done historically, or it can be approached in a hypothesis-driven fashion, once enough data have accumulated to permit the formulation of neuroanatomical hypotheses. In many cases, initial findings provide the material on which to base more specific hypotheses that can be tested in additional, independent samples or subjects.

One empirical approach, as mentioned above, is to use single cases. If multiple single-case studies converge to show a systematic relationship between damage to a given structure and impaired performance on a given task, this can be taken in support of the idea that the structure in question is normally important (again, among other structures) to perform the task. Such a situation has now been reached with respect to the amygdala's role in recognizing emotions, a topic we review below.

The other way to approach the question is to examine a large group of subjects, some of whom are impaired and some of whom are not, and ask whether certain performances correlate with damage in certain brain regions. The most straightforward way to imagine doing this is to simply divide the subject sample in half: is there a significant difference in the lesion locations shared by that half of the subjects with the worst performances, as compared with the lesion locations shared by that half of the subjects with the best performances? This situation has been reached recently in investigations of the role of right hemisphere structures in emotion recognition, a set of regions whose importance to the processing of emotion we review next.

## Contributions of the Right Hemisphere to Emotion

The right hemisphere is an appropriate point at which to begin a review of the brain structures important to emotion because it has been the topic of the most numerous research studies. Despite this attention, the precise role of the right hemisphere, both neuroanatomically and in terms of a theory describing the component processes involved, is still very unclear.

A large number of clinical and experimental lesion studies have demonstrated that the right hemisphere is preferentially involved in processing emotion in humans (e.g., Blonder, Bowers, & Heilman, 1991; Borod, 1993; Borod et al., 1992; Bowers et al., 1991; Bowers et al., 1987; Darby, 1993; Ley & Bryden, 1979; Ross, 1985; Silberman & Weingartner, 1986; Van Strien & Morpurgo, 1992) as well as in nonhuman primates (Hamilton & Vermeire,

1988; Hauser, 1993; Morris & Hopkins, 1993). Lesions in right temporal and parietal cortices have been shown to impair emotional experience, arousal (Heller, 1993) and imagery (Blonder et al., 1991; Bowers, Blonder, Feinberg, & Heilman, 1991) for emotion. It has been proposed that the right hemisphere contains modules for nonverbal affect computation (Bowers et al., 1993), which may have evolved to subserve aspects of social cognition (Borod, 1993). Despite this consensus, it remains unclear for which aspects, or for which classes of emotions, the right hemisphere is specialized; one currently debated issue concerns the extent to which the right hemisphere might play a disproportionate role in processing all emotions, or only emotions with negative valence (this issue pertains primarily to the experience of emotions).

Lesion studies have focused on the processing of emotion from three classes of stimuli: visual nonlexical stimuli (mostly facial expressions of emotion), auditory nonlexical stimuli (mostly prosody), and lexical stimuli (both auditory and visual; e.g., Blonder et al., 1991; Borod, Andelman, Obler, Tweedy, Welkowitz, 1992).

With regard to facial expressions of emotion, data from normal subjects have provided evidence that there are six so-called basic emotional expressions: happiness, surprise, fear, anger, disgust, and sadness (Ekman, 1972; Ekman & Friesen, 1976). The six basic emotional expressions are recognized easily by normal subjects and are recognized consistently across very different cultures (Ekman, 1972, 1973, 1992). Selective impairments in recognizing facial expressions, with sparing of the ability to recognize identity, can occur following right temporoparietal lesions (Bowers, Bauer, Coslett, & Heilman, 1985; Bowers & Heilman, 1984), just as there can be selective impairments in recognition of facial identity with sparing of recognition of facial emotion (Tranel, Damasio, & Damasio, 1988). This double-dissociation argues for partly separate neural systems that process information about identity or about emotion from the face. Specific anomia for emotional facial expressions has been reported following right temporal lesions (Rapcsak, Comer, & Rubens 1993; Rapcsak, Kasal-niak, & Rubens, 1989; Bowers & Heilman, 1984), a finding that may be related, in part, by the demonstration of direct (monosynaptic) input to Broca's area in the left hemisphere from temporal cortex of the right hemisphere in humans (Di Virgilio & Clarke, 1997). The evidence that the right temporoparietal cortex is important in processing emotional facial expressions is corroborated by data from PET imaging (Gur Skalnick, & Gur, 1994) and neuronal recording (Ojemann, Ojemann, & Lettich, 1992).

In addition to facial expressions, a major channel for social communication is the human voice. As with facial expressions, prosody can most reliably communicate a subset of emotions, in particular a subset of so-called basic emotions, and, again like facial expressions, there is evidence that prosody can signal emotion reliably across different cultures (van Bezooijen, Otto, & Heenan, 1983). Studies with normal and brain-damaged subjects indicate that happiness, surprise, fear, anger, and sadness can all be recognized from prosody, independent of visual cues from faces or lexical cues from speech (Scherer, 1995). Several studies have reported impaired recognition of emotional prosody following damage in the right hemisphere (Blonder et al., 1991; Ryalls, 1988; Schmitt, Hartje, & Willmes, 1997; Ross, 1985), an impairment that may be augmented when the lexical semantic content of the stimuli does not match their prosodic content (Bowers, Coslett, Bauer, Speedie, & Heilman, 1987). Conversely, recognition of emotional prosody can be entirely preserved despite global aphasia following massive damage to the left hemisphere (Barrett, Crucian, Raymer, & Heilman 1999).

Some studies have provided evidence for more localized, particular regions within the right hemisphere that might be most critical for recognition of emotion from prosody. For instance, Darby (1993) reported impaired recognition of emotion from prosody following right MCA infarction, and Starkstein, Federoff, Price, Leiguardor, & Robinson (1994) found evidence for the involvement of right frontoparietal regions, among others. Ross (1985) has proposed that the right hemisphere may contain anatomical regions for processing prosody that are analogues of those in the left hemisphere for processing language. The critical role of the right frontal cortex that emerges across these studies appears to extend also to processing more complex social information, such as humor, from verbal stimuli (Shammi & Stuss, 1999). In addition to the strong evidence implicating structures in the right hemisphere, especially right frontal regions, there are also data to support a role for callosal white matter that subserves interhemispheric connection (Ross, Stark, & Yenkosky, 1997), as well as for left-hemisphere regions (Pell, 1998), although the details of this remain quite unclear.

These findings, together with those from facial expressions, have been used to argue for a set of nonverbal affect processes that subserve social communication in the right hemisphere (Bowers et al., 1993; Ross, 1985) and complement a large literature that shows impairments following right-hemisphere damage in understanding humor and other pragmatic conversational content (Shammi & Stuss, 1999; Brownell, Michel, Powelson, & Gardner, 1983; Kaplan, Brownell, Jacobs, & Gardner, 1990; Wapner, Hamby, & Gardner, 1981). Clearly, the neuroanatomical specification of the studies reviewed above leaves the story at a very macroscopic level and implicates a large number of different motor, sensory, and association cortices, as well as subcortical structures. In regard to the cortical regions critical to processing emotion in the right hemisphere, we have recently undertaken several large-scale lesion studies to address this issue. We review the data from these studies next.

We have investigated the recognition of facial emotion

and of prosody in a large and partly overlapping sample of subjects with focal brain damage ($N$ = 108 for faces; $N$ = 66 for prosody; $N$ = 46 for both). These studies build on earlier investigations in which we explored cortical (Adolphs, Damasio, Tranel, & Damasio, 1996) and subcortical regions (Adolphs, Bechara, Tranel, Damasio, & Damasio, 1995; Adolphs, Russell, & Tranel, 1999; Adolphs, Lee, Tranel, & Damasio, 1997) important for recognizing emotion from faces and prosody (Adolphs & Tranel, 1999).

## Recognition of Emotion from Facial Expressions

In this quantitative study of 108 subjects with focal brain lesions, we used three different tasks to assess recognition and naming of six basic emotions from facial expressions (Adolphs, Damasio, Tranel, Cooper, & Damasio, 2000). Lesions were analyzed as a function of task performance by coregistration in a common brain space, and statistical analyses of their joint volumetric density revealed specific regions wherein damage was significantly associated with impairment.

In the first task, we investigated recognition of emotion in 108 subjects with focal brain lesions, using a procedure (Adolphs et al., 1996; Adolphs, Tranel, Damasio, & Damasio, 1994; Adolphs et al., 1995; Hamann et al., 1996) in which subjects rated 36 facial expressions of basic emotions (Ekman & Friesen, 1976) (six each of happiness, surprise, fear, anger, disgust, and sadness) with respect to the intensity of each of the six emotions. We correlated the rating profile each subject produced for each face with the mean ratings given by normal controls. To investigate how different performances might vary systematically with brain damage in specific regions, we then partitioned the 108 subjects into two groups: the 54 with the lowest correlations (who gave the most abnormal ratings), and the 54 with the highest correlations (who gave the most normal ratings). We computed the density of lesions at a given voxel for each of the two groups of subjects, and then subtracted the two data sets from one another, yielding images that showed in which regions lesions were systematically associated with either a low or a high performance score.

The worst performances, averaged across all emotions, were associated with lesions in right somatosensory-related cortices, including right anterior supramarginal gyrus, the lower sector of SI, SII, and insula, as well as with lesions in left frontal operculum (red regions in Figure 5.1). We tested the statistical significance of these results using rerandomization computation, which confirmed that lesions in such regions significantly impair recognition of facial emotion (see Figure 5.1 for details). A multiple regression analysis with other neuropsychological performances demonstrated that the impairments in recognizing emotion could not be attributed to impaired language or visuoperceptual function (see Adolphs et al., 2000, for details).

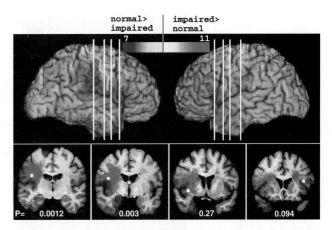

Figure 5.1 Distribution of lesions as a function of mean performance in recognizing emotion from faces in 108 subjects. Color codes the difference in density of lesions between those subjects with the lowest scores and those with the highest scores. Red regions correspond to locations where lesions resulted in impairment more often than not, and blue regions correspond to locations where lesions resulted in normal performance more often than not. P-values indicating statistical significance are shown for voxels in 4 regions (white squares), on coronal cuts (bottom) that correspond to the white lines in the 3-D reconstructions (top). These p-values were calculated by resampling methods and corrected for multiple comparisons. Figure from Adolphs et al. (2000), copyright Society for Neuroscience. (See color insert.)

To investigate emotion recognition with respect to individual basic emotions, we examined lesion density as a function of performance for each emotion category (Figure 5.2). We found that lesions in the right frontoparietal cortex impaired recognition of *all* emotions, consistent with other reports (Borod et al., 1992; Bowers et al., 1985; Adolphs et al., 1996), suggesting that emotion recognition may draw upon a common set of right-hemisphere structures related to processing somatic information. However, some emotions also relied on additional regions. Notably, damage to right, but not to left, anterior temporal lobe resulted in impaired recognition of fear in accord with a prior study (Anderson, LaBar, & Phelps, 1996), an effect that was statistically significant ($P$ = 0.036 by rerandomization).

The above recognition task (as most of the tasks used in the literature) requires both conceptual knowledge of the emotion shown in the face and lexical knowledge necessary for linking the concept to the name of the emotion. We investigated the possible dissociation of conceptual and lexical knowledge with two additional tasks. To assess lexical knowledge, subjects chose from a list of the six names for the emotions the name that best matched each of the 36 faces (Calder et al., 1996; Young et al., 1995). Examination of lesion density as a function of performance on this task revealed critical regions in bilateral

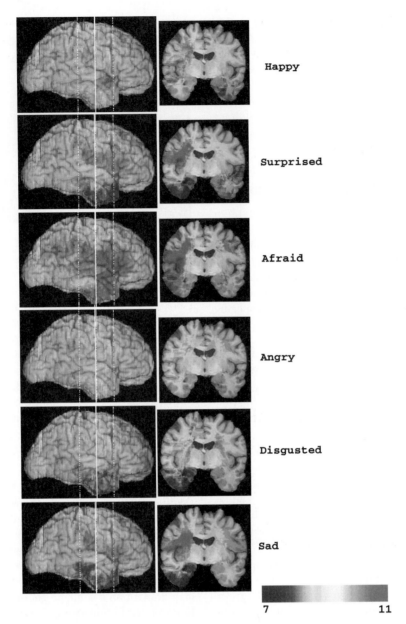

Figure 5.2 Recognition of different basic emotions draws upon overlapping but partially separable regions. Difference overlap images were calculated as described in Figure 5.1 for each of the 6 basic emotions in the same sample of 108 subjects. See Figure 5.1 caption for details. Data from Adolphs et al. (2000). (*See color insert.*)

frontal cortex, in right superior temporal gyrus, and in left inferior parietal cortex (Figure 5.3a), a subset of the structures important to recognize emotions also on the above rating task (cf. Figures 5.1 and 5.2).

To investigate conceptual knowledge, we asked subjects to sort photographs of 18 of the faces (3 of each basic emotion, a subset of the 36 used above) into piles according to similarity of the emotion displayed. Examination of lesion density as a function of performance on this task showed that right somatosensory-related cortices, includ-

ing S-1, S-2, insula and supramarginal gyrus, were critical to retrieve the conceptual knowledge that is required to sort facial expressions into emotion categories (Figure 5.3b). Again, these regions were a subset of the structures important to recognize emotions on the rating task.

### Recognition of Emotion from Prosody

We investigated recognition of emotion in prosody in a study with design analogous to that described above for

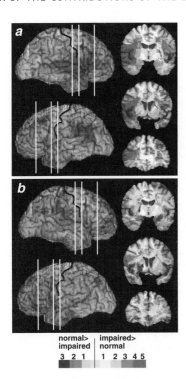

normal> | impaired>
impaired | normal
3  2  1  |  1  2  3  4  5

Figure 5.3 (a) Neuroanatomical regions for choosing the name of an emotion. Images were calculated as described in Figure 5.1. (b) Neuroanatomical regions for sorting emotions into categories without naming. Figures from Adolphs et al. (2000), copyright Society for Neuroscience. (*See color insert.*)

facial expressions. Briefly, 66 subjects with focal lesions were asked to rate the intensity of emotion expressed by prosodic stimuli, which had been carefully designed so that they varied only with respect to a single factor of interest: emotional prosody. The same four semantically neutral English sentences were spoken by the same female voice for each of five different prosodic emotions: happiness, sadness, anger, fear, and surprise. In a procedure identical to the one previously used with facial expressions, subjects heard the 20 sentences 8 times and rated them on a scale of 0 (= "not at all") to 5 (= "very much") with respect to the labels "awake," "happy," "sleepy," "sad," "angry," "afraid," "disgusted," "surprised" (one label per each of the 8 blocks).

We analyzed the distributions of subjects' correlations of ratings given across all emotion labels (Figure 5.4). Lesions in the right fronto-parietal regions, in the left frontal operculum, and in the right anterior temporal lobe were associated with impaired recognition of emotion from prosody.

To attempt to distinguish those regions that might be critical for retrieval of knowledge about emotions across modalities from those critical to recognize the emotion from a particular sensory modality, we compared the find-

ings from recognition of emotional prosody with the findings from recognition of emotional facial expressions. This analysis was limited to 46 subjects who had participated in both studies.

Low correlation scores on both prosody and facial expression recognition were associated with damage in right fronto-parietal cortices and with damage in the left frontal operculum, suggesting that these two regions are jointly important to recognize emotion with our task procedure. Whereas damage to the right temporal lobe was associated with normal recognition of facial expressions, damage to the left temporal lobe was associated with normal recognition of prosody (Figure 5.5a).

A within-subject comparison of performance on both tasks confirmed this impression and offered additional findings (Figure 5.5b). First, an analysis of the overlaps of lesions of subjects who had low scores on both prosody and facial emotion recognition ($N = 13$) revealed that anterior parietal and frontal cortices in the right hemisphere, and frontal operculum in the left hemisphere, were important to recognize emotion regardless of modality of the stimuli. Second, damage to the left temporal pole resulted in worse recognition of emotion from facial expressions than from prosody, whereas damage to the right temporal pole resulted in worse recognition of emotion from prosody than from facial expression. Out of 6 subjects with left anterior temporal lobe lesions, 5 had a lower correlation with normal ratings on faces than on prosody, whereas 5 out of 5 subjects with right anterior temporal lobe lesions had lower correlation scores on prosody than on faces. When comparing prosody and faces, the difference between performances resulting from left and right anterior temporal lobe damage was statistically significant (Mann-Whitney U test: $P < 0.01$). Thus, we found evidence of a double dissociation of recognizing emotion from visual or from auditory stimuli, relative to damage in the left or in the right temporal pole, respectively. Because of the within-subject measure used (prosody versus faces in the same subject), this double dissociation was statistically significant, even though differences between subjects with left and right anterior temporal damage were not significant when assessed for faces or for prosody in isolation (all $Ps > 0.1$, Mann-Whitney U tests).

## Emotion and Somatic Representation

To begin to think about how the structures identified in Figures 5.1–5.5 might be critical for various component processes in emotion, it is helpful to consider in detail the tasks we used. For both the recognition of emotion from faces and from prosody, at last two different strategies could be used by subjects. In one strategy, subjects might reason about the other person's emotion from knowledge he or she has acquired about which stimulus features are

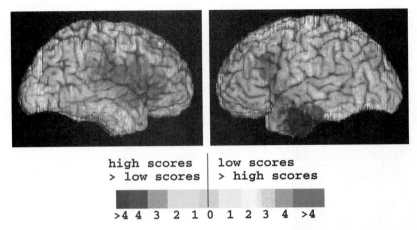

high scores | low scores
> low scores | > high scores

>4 4 3 2 1 0 1 2 3 4 >4

Figure 5.4 Recognition of emotion from prosody. MAP-3 images are shown in which the color at each voxel represents the difference in the overlaps of lesions from those subjects with performances in the bottom half of the distribution, compared to those subjects with performances in the top half (cf. Figure 5.1 for details on the general method). The scale at the bottom shows how color corresponds to number of subjects: blue colors correspond to a larger number of lesions from subjects with performances in the top half; red colors correspond to a larger number of lesions from subjects with performances in the bottom half. The dependent measure was the mean emotion recognition from prosody. From Adolphs, Tranel, and Damasio (in press). (*See color insert.*)

associated with which emotions. This knowledge could be at an explicit level and involve overt reasoning—for instance, knowledge regarding the facial configurations normally associated with certain emotions (e.g., reasoning that a smile signals happiness) or overt knowledge of certain prosodic contours that are reliably associated with specific emotions (e.g., reasoning that a loud voice signals anger). Or the knowledge could be retrieved at a more covert level: perceptual representations of the stimulus could trigger knowledge of the emotion with which the stimulus has been typically associated (of which the subject could then become aware).

However, there is yet another strategy that relies less on retrieval of prior associations and more on the construction of knowledge. Such a strategy might obtain information about another person's emotional state in part by internal simulation—for instance, by generating somatosensory imagery corresponding to the way one would feel if one were making the facial expression or producing the tone of voice given by the stimulus. We thus suggest that specific regions in the right hemisphere may serve to link (1) perceptual (visual or auditory) representations of the properties of the stimuli (at either the level of individual features or at the level of a more configural encoding) with (2) somatic representations of the feeling associated with such expressions. Such a mechanism could permit attribution of mental states to others by simulation of their body state.

This idea, that somatic simulation is important to retrieve knowledge about emotions signaled by other individuals, is related to the idea that mental simulation guides our knowledge of what goes on in the minds of others, a proposal that has been put forth by philosophers and cognitive scientists (Goldman, 1992). The proposal has received recent attention from the finding of so-called mirror neurons in monkey prefrontal cortex that respond only when the monkey observes another individual performing an action (Gallese & Goldman, 1999; Rizzolatti, Fadiga, Gallese, & Fogassi, 1996).

In addition to right parietal regions, performance on our tasks appeared to rely on left frontal operculum. There are two possible interpretations of this: tasks may draw explicitly upon lexical processing (certainly, the tasks we used do so), or they may draw upon motor imagery in left frontal operculum that need not be essentially lexical, but that is perhaps part of the same machinery on which language also relies (Iacoboni et al., 1999; Rizzolatti & Arbib, 1998). In humans, there is evidence from a recent functional imaging study that the translation of behavior observed in other people into one's own simulation or imitation of the same behavior relies on two cortical regions: left frontal operculum, and right anterior parietal cortex (Iacoboni et al., 1999), the two regions most important also to recognize emotion both from facial expressions and from prosody.

We thus suggest that left frontal operculum and right frontoparietal cortex are important to recognize emotion from prosody and from facial expressions for the same reasons. In our task, left frontal operculum may help to link knowledge about emotion to lexical performance and/or to motor imagery; right frontoparietal cortices may help to construct a somato-motor representation that simulates

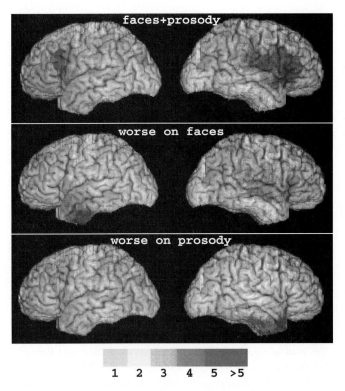

Figure 5.5 Comparisons between recognition of emotion from prosody and from facial expressions in 46 subjects who participated in rating both classes of stimuli. All data used were average correlation scores across all stimuli. MAP-3 images are shown in which color corresponds to the number of subjects with lesions at a given location, as indicated on the respective color scales. In all cases, the dependent measure was the mean correlation score across all stimuli. (a) Data from prosody and from facial expressions. Color represents the difference between the number of lesions from subjects in the top 50% compared to those in the bottom 50%. (b) Direct comparisons using within-subject difference scores. For clarity, only the overlaps of subjects in the bottom half of a distribution are shown. *Top panel*: Overlaps of subjects who were in the bottom partitions both for faces and for prosody (N = 13); red regions indicate lesions from the greatest number of subjects who were impaired in recognizing emotion from both faces and prosody. *Middle and bottom panels*: Overlaps of lesions from all subjects in the bottom partition (N = 23) for the derived difference in rank-orders of performances on prosody and on faces, showing differential performances in recognizing emotion from these two classes of stimuli. From Adolphs, Tranel, and Damasio (in press). (*See color insert.*)

some components of what it would be like to express and experience the emotion signaled by the stimulus.

## Expression and Experience of Emotion

While the experience of emotion is a topic that is difficult to operationalize, and also one that has been addressed primarily by functional imaging (Canli, 1999), there are some findings from lesion studies that inform it. Damage in the right hemisphere typically results not only in impaired recognition of emotions but also in impaired (usually flattened) expression and experience of emotions (Borod et al., 1996). Lesions of the right hemisphere can result in emotional hypoarousal that may be more apparent in autonomic responses (Meadows & Kaplan, 1994; Zoccolotti, Scabini, & Violani, 1982; Yoon, Morillo, Cechetto, & Hachinski, 1997) rather than in cognitive performance on rating tasks. These findings support the idea that the right hemisphere is disproportionately important for linking emotional experience to autonomic arousal (Tucker & Williamson, 1984).

The critical role of the right hemisphere in the expression of emotion is supported by findings in animals (Hauser, 1993) and humans (Davidson, 1993; Blonder, Burns, Bowers, Moore, & Heilman, 1993). Subjects with damage to the right hemisphere express posed emotions inaccurately, compared to normal controls or to subjects with left-hemisphere damage (Canino, Borod, Madigan, Tabert, & Schmidt, 1999). There is some evidence that the expression (Sackheim et al., 1982), experience, and perception (Borod, 1992) of negatively valenced emotions rely on the right hemisphere, whereas processing of positive emotions may rely on the left hemisphere, or bilaterally.

The data clearly indicate that the right hemisphere is disproportionately important in the processing of emotion. It remains an interesting and broad question why emotion processing should feature hemispheric lateralization—a question not unique to the domain of emotion. We have suggested elsewhere (Adolphs, 1999b) that much emotional processing puts a premium on processing speed and that therefore the localization of multiple processing components within the same hemisphere would avoid the relative delay introduced by interhemispheric transfer of information (cf. also Ringo, Doty, Demeter, & Simard, 1994). This argument, if valid, would predict that hemispherically lateralized processing of emotion should be even more important the larger the brain, and hence might be more lateralized in humans than in mammals with smaller brains.

## Contributions of the Amygdala to Emotion

The amygdala is a collection of nuclei in the anterior mesial temporal lobe that receive highly processed sensory information and that have extensive, reciprocal connections with a large number of other brain structures whose function can be modulated by emotion (Amaral, Price, Pitkanen, & Carmichael, 1992). These other structures importantly include the ventromedial frontal cortices, basal ganglia, basal forebrain, and the hypothalamus, as well as immediately adjacent structures such as the hippocampus, bed nucleus of the stria terminalis, rhinal cortex, and temporal polar cortex. Consequently, the amygdala is situated so as to link information about external stimuli conveyed by sensory cortices, on the one hand, with modulation of decision making, memory, and attention, as well as somatic, visceral, and endocrine processes, on the other hand. It is important to note that the amygdala is itself a complex and heterogeneous collection of nuclei that subserve extensive intrinsic processing (Pitkanen, Savander, & LeDoux, 1997); also, there is some debate concerning the functional and anatomical delineation of what are really multiple nuclei into a single structure termed "the amygdala" (cf. Swanson & Petrovich, 1998).

## Overview of Studies of the Amygdala in Animals

Unlike the case for the right hemisphere, whose contribution to emotion is most clear and has been the most intensively studied in humans, the contributions to emotion made by the amygdala have come primarily from studies in animals, a topic we briefly review first. These studies can be grouped into two rough categories: those that have investigated the amygdala in the context of ecologically valid (and usually highly complex) emotional and social behaviors (typically behaviors among animals in a group); and those that examined a presumably more basic, and more simple, function—the amygdala's role in motivated behavior in general.

Bilateral ablation of the monkey amygdala, in addition to large sectors of adjacent temporal lobe, results in a constellation of impairments in social and emotional functioning that is best described as an agnosia for the social and emotional meanings conveyed by external stimuli (Kluver & Bucy, 1939). Damage confined to the amygdala results in a more restricted set of behavioral impairments, which varies depending on the species and on whether the behavior is assessed in the laboratory or in the wild (Amaral, Capitanio, Machado, Mason, & Meudoza, 1997; Kling & Brothers, 1992; Weiskrantz, 1956; Zola-Morgan, Squire, Alvarez-Royo, & Clower, 1991). The most consistent finding is that the animals are more placid and tend to approach stimuli that normal monkeys would avoid. Detailed assessments of the effects of amygdala on various components of primate social and emotional behavior are currently underway (Emery & Amaral, 1999), and are pointing toward the finding that an explication of the amygdala's contribution to behavior in real life will need to take into account, on the one hand, the reciprocal interactions between a subject and other individuals and, on the other hand, also the neurofunctional interactions between amygdala and other anatomical structures.

However, the largest number of lesion studies of the amygdala in animals have focused on the role of the amygdala in regulating motivated behavior. Lesion studies in rats and other species have shown that the amygdala is required for the acquisition of conditioned behavioral responses to stimuli that have been previously paired with an intrinsically aversive event, a paradigm called fear conditioning (Davis, 1992a; Gewirtz & Davis, 1997; Le Doux, 1996; LeDoux, Cicchetti, Xagoraris, & Romanski, 1990). In such an experiment, an animal is presented with two different types of stimuli: a stimulus that has intrinsic emotional value to the animal (e.g., a rewarding stimulus, such as food, or an aversive stimulus, such as electric shock), and a stimulus that has no intrinsic value to the animal (e.g., the sound of a tone). When these two stimuli are presented together on several occasions, the animal learns that the presence of one can predict the presence of the other: if the tone sounds, it is likely that the shock (or the food) will also occur. This very basic form of associative emotional memory may be an important substrate for more complex forms of learning and of motivated behavior. Several different neuroanatomical structures in addition to the amygdala have been shown to be involved in emotionally motivated learning, depending on the details of the task: the amygdala (Davis, 1992a; LeDoux, 1996), the ventral striatum (Everitt & Robbins, 1992), and the orbitofrontal cortex (Gaffan, Morray, & Fabre-Thorpe, 1993; Rolls, 1999) all appear to play important roles and are likely to function as components of a distributed, large-scale neural system for associating stimuli with their rewarding or punishing contingencies.

Although many of the above structures are implicated in processing both reward and punishment, they appear to be disproportionately important along certain dimensions of emotion. For instance, the amygdala specifically mediates behaviors and responses correlated with arousal and stress, especially emotional arousal pertaining to negatively valenced, aversive situations (Davis, 1992b; Goldstein, Rasmusson, Burney, & Roth, 1996; Kesner, 1992). In this regard, its role bears some similarity to that of the right hemisphere reviewed earlier. While sensory cortices all project to the basolateral amygdala, the projections from the basolateral nucleus are diverse and subserve different functions (LeDoux, Iwata, Cicchetti, & Reis, 1988). Animal studies suggest that the amygdala circuitry underlying the processing of aversive stimuli depends on the central nucleus of the amygdala, whereas processing of stimuli that are rewarding appears to depend on projections from the basolateral nucleus of the amygdala to frontal cortex and ventral striatum (Killcross, Robbins, & Everitt, 1997). Furthermore, the role of the amygdala in Pavlovian conditioning and in motivating instrumental behavior depends on pathways from the basolateral nucleus to the central or to the basal nucleus, respectively (Amorapanth, LeDoux, & Nader, 2000).

It is critical to keep in mind that the amygdala is merely one nodal structure in a very distributed network that can modulate cognition on the basis of affect and, furthermore, that there are multiple neurotransmitter systems within these structures that can carry out different functional roles. The complexity of the systems is illustrated in the effects of emotion on modulating motivated learning in animals. A large number of studies have shown that aversively motivated learning can be modulated by multiple neurotransmitter systems acting within the amygdala. For instance, direct posttraining injections into the amygdala of a variety of drugs that modulate GABAergic, noradrenergic, or opiate-mediated neurotransmission influence long-term memory for inhibitory avoidance training. However, the amygdala influences memory by modulating consolidation that actually takes place within other brain structures, such as the hippocampus and basal ganglia (McGaugh, 2000).

In addition to its role in emotional memory, the amygdala, together with a collection of nuclei termed the basal forebrain, have been shown to make critical contributions to the effect that emotion has on attentional processes (Holland & Gallagher, 1999). One component of attention, orienting behavior toward cues that have become associated with rewarding contingencies, has been found to rely on a circuit involving the central nucleus of the amygdala and its connections with the substantia nigra and the dorsal striatum (Han, McMahan, Holland, & Gallagher, 1997). Another important component of attention, increased allocation of processing resources toward novel or surprising situations, appears to depend on the integrity of the central nucleus of the amygdala and its connections with cholinergic neurons in the substantia innominata and nucleus basalis, structures in the basal forebrain. Thus, the amygdala could influence cholinergic neuromodulatory functions of the basal forebrain nuclei and consequently modulate attention, vigilance, signal-to-noise, and other aspects of information processing that depend on cholinergic modulation of cognition (Everitt & Robbins, 1997). Through circuits including components of amygdala, striatum, and basal forebrain, emotion may thus help to select particular aspects of the stimulus environment for disproportionate allocation of cognitive processing resources—namely, an organism should be designed to preferentially process information about those aspects of its environment that are most salient to its immediate and long-term survival.

Finally, it is clear that structures in close association with the amygdala, notably the bed nucleus of the stria terminalis, the rhinal cortex, and the cortex of the temporal pole, are necessary for more prolonged emotional states that can influence information processing in a global and less stimulus-driven fashion. In rats, the bed nucleus of the stria terminalis, together with nuclei within the amygdala proper, appear to be involved in anxiety rather than in fear; moreover, specific neuropeptides, such as coricotropin-releasing hormone, have dramatic effects specifically on the bed nucleus of the stria terminalis and on anxiety, but not on fear (Davis, 1992a, 1992b, 1997;

Davis, Walker, & Lee, 1997). While the detailed neural structures involved in fear and in anxiety remain to be fully elucidated in humans, the findings from animal studies point toward anatomically and pharmacologically dissociable systems for fear and anxiety, and suggest particular avenues for further research as well as for therapeutic intervention (Davis, 1992b).

Lesion studies in monkeys have demonstrated that the temporal pole and the rhinal cortex contribute, together with the amygdala, to the animal's emotional behavior. Specifically, lesions in either of the two former structures exacerbate the hypoemotionality seen with bilateral amygdala lesions (Aggleton & Young, 2000); clearly, this was also the case with the original descriptions given by Kluver and Bucy. Despite this finding, it remains very unclear what the specific contribution of rhinal cortex and temporal pole are, and it is not even clear that lesions restricted to those structures cause any impairment in emotional behavior by themselves.

### Emotional Memory

The lesion method has been used to investigate the amygdala's contribution to emotion also in humans. Unlike the case for the right hemisphere, essentially all of these studies are case studies (or multiple case studies) because amygdala lesions resulting from stroke are very rare. There are three primary classes of etiology that give rise to amygdala damage in humans: (1) unilateral, nonselective, and usually incomplete damage resulting from neurosurgical temporal lobectomy for the treatment of epilepsy (such subjects are numerous); (2) bilateral, relatively selective but usually incomplete damage resulting from either Urbach-Wiethe disease or from neurosurgical bilateral amygdalotomy for treating psychiatric conditions (such subjects with clean lesions and no interfering psychiatric co-morbidity are very rare); (3) bilateral, complete, and nonselective amygdala damage resulting from encephalitis (there are several such subjects available, but the usually substantial extra-amygdala damage often makes interpretation of data difficult. Almost all of these subjects are densely amnesic).

Several recent lesion studies have reported impaired conditional discrimination (discrimination of sensory cues on the basis of their association with an unconditioned stimulus) in subjects with unilateral amygdala damage, using measures such as skin conductance response (LaBar, LeDoux, Spencer, & Phelps, 1995) or eyeblink magnitude (Daum, Channon, Polkey, & Gray, 1991). A correlation between amygdala activation and conditioned skin conductance response has been corroborated by functional imaging studies (Furmark, Fischer, Wik, & Fedrikson, 1997; Buechel, Morris, Dolan, & Friston, 1998; LaBar, Gatenby, Gore, LeDoux, & Phelps, 1998). Conditioned fear is also of clinical relevance in humans. Pathological conditions, such as anxiety disorders, panic attacks, or posttraumatic stress disorder, likely have as part of their cause the ability of conditioned stimuli to elicit fear via the amygdala (Davis, 1992b), consistent with the finding from animals that the amygdala plays a critical role in those behaviors and responses that are associated with high arousal and stress.

We carried out an experiment similar to fear conditioning in a human subject with bilateral amygdala lesions (Bechara et al., 1995). In one study, we tested the ability to acquire conditioned autonomic responses to stimuli that had been paired with an aversive startle stimulus. We found that the subject with bilateral amygdala damage failed to acquire conditioned skin-conductance responses, while she did acquire the declarative knowledge regarding the stimuli that had been paired with the startle stimulus. Conversely, an amnesic patient with damage to the hippocampus, tested in the same experiment, failed to acquire declarative knowledge but acquired normal conditioned skin conductance responses. The study showed that declarative and nondeclarative memory in this experiment depends, respectively, on the hippocampus and on the amygdala (Figure 5.6). However, there are two important wrinkles to this conclusion. First, the amygdala is not essential for learning all forms of nondeclarative emotional knowledge; an amnesic subject with complete bilateral amygala damage was able to learn to avoid people with whom he had unpleasant interactions and to approach people with whom he had pleasant interactions, even though he did not declaratively recall ever having met the people (Tranel & Damasio, 1993). Second, there is now evidence that the amygdala also participates in declarative emotional memory, a topic we review next.

Four case studies of rare patients with selective bilateral amygdala damage have provided evidence that the human amygdala is necessary for the enhanced memory normally seen with highly aversive, emotionally arousing stimuli (Adolphs et al., 1997; Babinsky et al., 1993; Cahill, Babinsky, Markowitsch, & McGaugh, 1995; Hamann, Lee, & Adolphs, (1999). In corroboration with these findings from lesion studies, functional imaging studies have shown that amygdala activation at the time that stimuli are first seen and encoded correlates with how well the same stimuli are remembered weeks later, but only in those cases where the stimuli are emotionally highly arousing (Cahill et al., 1996; Canli, Zhao, Desmond, Glover, & Gabrieli, 1998; Hamann, Ely, Grafton, & Kilts, 1999). There is thus good evidence that the human amygdala aids in the potentiation of memory traces for emotionally arousing stimuli during their acquisition and consolidation into long-term declarative memory. An example of the effect of amygdala damage on the normal potentiation of emotional memory is illustrated in Figure 5.7. In this experiment, a subject with bilateral amygdala damage (subject SM; see below) remembered emotionally arousing

stimuli only as well as neutral stimuli, whereas control subjects showed superior memory for the emotional stimuli over neutral stimuli.

It remains a difficult issue to disentangle the precise mechanisms whereby the amygdala might modulate declarative memory. On their own, most of the lesion studies are consistent with amygdala modulation of initial encoding, consolidation, forgetting, or even retrieval, or any combination of these. In light of the findings from human imaging studies, as well as from the studies in animals, a time-limited role in consolidation appears most plausible (this could include both elaboration and forgetting of material). In particular, the functional imaging studies have shown that amygdala activation at the time that stimuli are encoded correlates with subsequent recall of the same stimuli weeks later (e.g., Cahill et al., 1996; Hamann, Ely, Grafton, & Kilts, 1999). Studies in animals have demonstrated directly that the amygdala can modulate hippocampal-dependent memory consolidation, and they have pointed to a primary role for the amygdala in such modulation in tasks that are aversively motivated (Packard & Teather, 1996). Furthermore, the amygdala modulates memory consolidation over long periods of time (days; Sacchetti, Lorenzini, Baldi, Tassoni, & Bucherelli, 1999). A previous study in humans with amygdala damage reported a similar finding in regard to lexical stimuli (taboo words): enhanced memory for emotional words normally appears over an extended time course and is dependent on the amygdala (LaBar & Phelps, 1998).

As all studies found a role for the amygdala for consolidating emotional memories over a substantial time period, typically days or weeks in the studies reviewed above, one intriguing suggestion is that at least some of the amygdala-dependent modulation of memory consolidation might be occuring during sleep, perhaps especially REM sleep and dreaming. This idea is consonant with several observations: functional imaging studies of REM sleep have found profound activation of the amygdala (Maquet et al., 1996), and some studies have pointed toward a dependency for memory consolidation on REM sleep (Stickgold, 1999). The psychological aspects of dreams are notable for emotional experiences in which the amygdala has been implicated—notably, states of negative emotions related to threat and danger (cf. Revonsuo, 2000).

### Recognition of Emotion

There are now a number of studies demonstrating that the human amygdala plays an important, albeit not always essential, role in the recognition of emotions from facial expressions. These findings have been extensively reviewed elsewhere (Adolphs, 1999a), and we only summarize the salient findings here.

The only subject, to our knowledge, with complete bilateral amygdala damage that does not include substantial

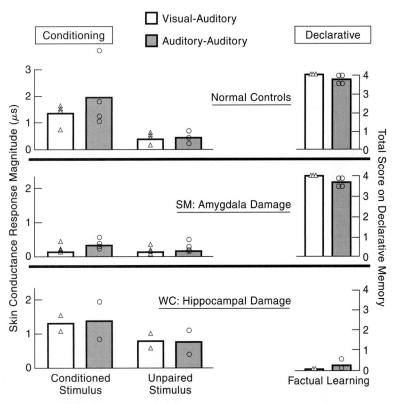

Figure 5.6 Amygdala damages blocks the acquisition of conditioned autonomic responses. In one study (visual-auditory conditioning; blue bars), subjects were shown slides of various colors. Only blue slides were paired with a loud auditory startle stimulus (unconditioned stimulus, US) that reliably evoked large skin conductance responses in all subjects (not shown). After several such paired presentations, subsequent presentations of blue slides presented *alone* (without the auditory startle stimulus) now evoked skin conductance responses in normal subjects (top panel; conditioned stimulus). This is a classical conditioning paradigm, in which a previously neutral stimulus (the blue slide) has acquired the ability to elicit reactions similar to those normally elicited by an emotional stimulus (the auditory startle sound) with which it has been paired in the past. Subsequent presentations of slides of other colors (unpaired stimuli) elicited no skin conductance response. Normal subjects also remembered that blue slides has been paired with the auditory startle stimulus (declarative; factual learning).

A second study used the same paradigm, substituting short auditory melodies for the colored slides (auditory-auditory conditioning; red bars). One of the melodies was paired with the auditory startle stimulus. Again, normal subjects showed conditioned skin conductance responses to the melody that had been paired with the startle stimulus but not to the unpaired melodies.

We compared normal responses to those of subject SM, who had complete bilateral amygdala damage but no damage to hippocampus, and to those of subject WC, who had bilateral hippocampal damage but no damage to amygdala. Unlike control subjects, SM failed to acquire conditioned skin conductance responses although she showed normal declarative knowledge regarding which stimulus had been paired with the startle sound. By contrast, subject WC failed to acquire declarative knowledge but showed normal conditioned skin conductance responses. The findings describe a double dissociation between a form of non-declarative learning (conditioned skin conductance response) and a form of declarative learning (verbal recall) and show that the two types of memory rely on the amygdala and the hippocampus, respectively.
Adapted from Bechara et al. (1995); copyright (1995) American Association for the Advancement of Science.

**(a)**

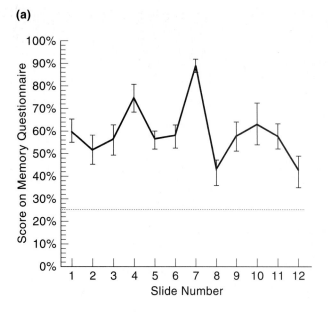

**(b)**

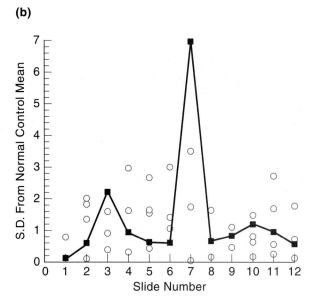

Figure 5.7  Bilateral damage to the human amygdala impairs declarative memory for emotionally arousing material. Subjects were shown a series of 12 slides that varied in emotional arousal. Slide 7 was the most arousing slide, showing surgically reattached legs of a car-crash victim. (a) Data from 7 normal controls, showing memory score on a questionnaire about each slide. Chance is at 25% (dotted line). (b) Data from 6 brain-damaged controls with no damage to amygdala (E) and from subject SM (B, solid lines), plotted as differences from the control data. SM differed most from controls on the most emotional slide, an impairment not shown by any of the brain-damaged control subjects. Data from Adolphs, Cahill, et al. (1997); copyright © 1997 Cold Spring Harbor Laboratory Press.

damage to other structures, is subject SM, whom we have studied in detail (Tranel & Hyman, 1990; Adolphs & Tranel, 2000). The subject SM is a 32-year-old woman with a very rare, heritable illness, Urbach-Wiethe disease, that affects primarily epithelial tissue. The disease, also known as lipoid proteinosis, typically exhibits a variable phenotype of thickened skin, thickened vocal cords, beaded appearance of the eyelids, and a diagnostic staining of epithelial tissue with lipophilic dyes (Hofer, 1973). In roughly half the cases, patients develop avascular and atrophic mineralizations of medial temporal neural tissue. This involves variable calcification of hippocampal, amygdaloid, and adjacent parahippocampal, periamygdaloid, entorhinal, and perirhinal cortices. The phenotype becomes evident in early childhood, although it is not known at what age central nervous system abnormalities may develop.

In the case of SM, we have reason to believe that she sustained her amygdala damage in early childhood, and perhaps earlier. Her neuroanatomical and neuropsychological profile has remained entirely stable during the time we have studied her (more than a decade). In particular, MR scans taken at various times show selective and complete bilateral damage of the amygdala, as well as some minor damage to anterior entorhinal cortices. There is no damage to other structures anywhere in her brain, and there is no damage to the hippocampal system, as also confirmed by her normal performance on standard tasks of declarative memory.

We averaged the signal from three coregistered volumetric MR sets (three sets of serial MR scans that cover the entire brain) to obtain a three-dimensional reconstruction of SM's brain with superior spatial resolution. This reconstruction and selected sections through it are shown in Figure 5.8. The amygdala shows a structural lesion in its entirety, and we confirmed that this structural lesion was in fact a functional lesion with a 14-deoxyglucose PET. The PET showed severe hypometabolism bilaterally in the amygdala (at rest), but normal glucose uptake elsewhere in the brain. It is important to reemphasize that all the findings we summarize below pertain to a subject with complete damage to all nuclei within the amygdala; however, the amygdala is not a homogeneous structure, either functionally or hodologically (Swanson & Petrovich, 1998), and the details of functional contributions made by different nuclei are important issues for future research.

SM's neuropsychological background has been described in detail (Tranel & Hyman, 1990; Adolphs & Tranel, 2000). Briefly, she has performance and verbal IQs in the low average range, a high-school education, and lives independently. Extensive neuropsychological assessment revealed normal declarative memory (e.g., on the Wechsler Memory Scale), although recognition memory for faces was somewhat inferior to recognition memory for words. Although lexical recall is normal, her recall of at least some visual, nonlexical information is impaired (e.g., Rey-

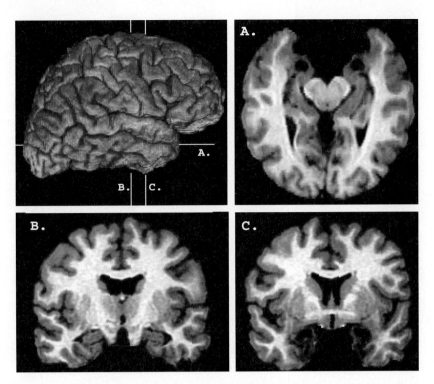

Figure 5.8 High resolution MR images of the brain of patient SM, who has selective bilateral amygdala damage. Extensive investigations with this subject have shown that the lesion is stable and chronic (there is no evidence of any progression in the last decade) and that SM's neuropsychological profile is also stable (her scores on all neuropsychological tasks, including those on which she is impaired, have remained essentially unchanged over the course of more than a decade). There is complete damage to both amygdalae, as well as some damage to anterior entorhinal cortex. All other brain structures are spared. *Top left*: 3-D reconstruction of SM's brain, showing planes of sections. (a) Horizontal section at level of amygdala. (b) Coronal section at level of hippocampus. (c) Coronal section at level of amygdala. All images were obtained by computing an average from three separate MR scans of SM's brain, providing superior resolution. Copyright Human Neuroimaging and Neuroanatomy Laboratory.

Osterrieth 30-minute recall), suggesting that there may be some impairments in memory for information that cannot be encoded into language.

The first clear demonstrations of the amygdala's role in recognition of facial emotion came from two lesion case studies (Adolphs et al., 1994; Young et al., 1995), although prior case studies had hinted at the same conclusion (e.g., Jacobson, 1986). When shown emotional facial expressions, subject SM consistently failed to rate the emotions surprise, fear, and anger as very intense. She was particularly impaired in rating the intensity of fear, on several occasions failing to recognize any fear whatsoever in prototypical facial expressions of fear. We examined SM's ability to recognize all the different basic emotions in facial expressions, and found a severe and specific impairment in recognizing emotions signalled by fearful facial expressions (Adolphs, Tranel, Damasio, & Damasio, 1995; Figure 5.9a), a finding that has now been replicated by other groups in several patients with bilateral amygdala

damage (Calder et al., 1996; Broks et al., 1998). Further investigations revealed that unilateral amygdala damage did not result in the same magnitude of impairment (Adolphs et al., 1995).

Although there remain puzzling exceptions to the reported impairments (Hamann et al., 1996), the findings have now been replicated in a relatively large number of cases (Adolphs et al., 1999; Broks et al., 1998). However, the majority of cases show impairments in multiple emotions, including surprise, fear, anger, disgust, and sadness (Adolphs et al., 1999; Figure 5.9b).

### Recognition of Arousal

Subject SM's impairment in recognizing emotional facial expressions is disproportionately severe with respect to fear. However, she also has lesser impairments in recognition of highly arousing emotions that are similar to fear, such as anger, consistent with findings from other subjects

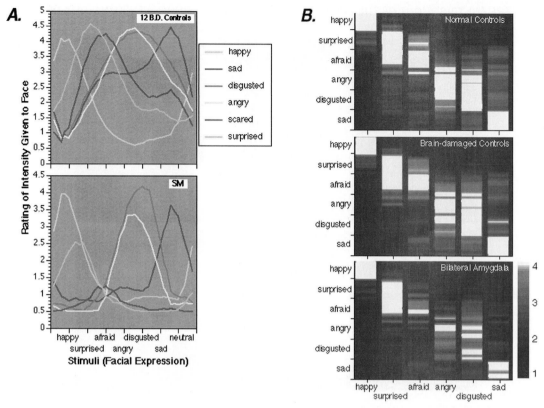

Figure 5.9 Recognition of facial emotion following bilateral amygdala damage. (a) Impaired recognition of fear in facial expressions in SM. Twelve brain-damaged control subjects (without damage to amygdala) and subject SM were shown 39 facial expressions of emotion from Ekman & Friesen, 1976, and asked to rate the 39 faces with respect to the intensity of one of the six basic emotions displayed (happiness, surprise, fear, anger, disgust, and sadness) on a scale of 0 (not at all showing this emotion) to 5 (most intense rating possible for this emotion). These data are shown for SM (bottom) and 12 brain-damaged controls (top), with the ratings that subjects gave to the 39 faces depicted by the colored lines. Each differently colored line corresponds to subjects' ratings on one of the six different emotions. The stimuli (39 facial expressions) are ordered along the x-axis by their judged similarity (more similar emotional expressions are adjacent on the x-axis while dissimilar ones are farther apart); the order of the stimuli on the x-axis corresponds to the order obtained by proceeding clockwise around a circumplex model of emotion (Adolphs et al., 1995). Modified from Adolphs, Tranel, et al., 1995; copyright Society for Neuroscience, 1995. (b) Impaired recognition of emotions from facial expressions in subjects with bilateral amygdala damage. Raw rating scores of facial expressions of emotion are shown from eight subjects with bilateral amygdala damage (from Adolphs, Tranel, et al., 1999). The emotional stimuli (36 faces; 6 each of each of the 6 basic emotions indicated) are ordered on the y-axis according to their perceived similarity (stimuli perceived to be similar [e.g., happy and surprised faces] are adjacent; stimuli perceived to be dissimilar [e.g., happy and sad faces] are distant; cf. Adolphs, Tranel, et al., 1995). The six emotion labels on which subjects rated the faces are displayed on the x-axis. Grayscale brightness codes the mean rating given to each face by a group of subjects, as indicated in the scale. A darker line indicates a lower mean rating than a brighter line for a given face, and a thin bright line for a given emotion category would indicate that few stimuli of that emotion received a high rating, whereas a thick bright line would indicate that many or all stimuli within that emotion category received high ratings. Because very few mean ratings were <1 or >4, we truncated the graphs outside these values. Data from subjects with bilateral amygdala damage indicate abnormally low ratings of negative emotions (thinner bright bands across any horizontal position corresponding to an expression of a negative emotion). From Adolphs, Tranel, et al. (1999); copyright Elsevier Science Publishers, 1999. (*See color insert.*)

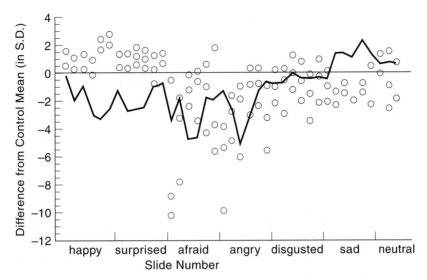

Figure 5.10 Impaired recognition of the arousal of stimuli with negative valence in subject SM. Each circle plots the difference between SM's arousal rating and control subjects' mean arousal rating for a given face in SD units. The solid black line on the plot indicates the measure expected for completely random ratings; that is, it represents the expected (average) difference of random ratings from the mean control ratings. SM gave abnormally low ratings of arousal to faces expressing negative emotions (open circles), and this finding could not be accounted for solely by larger variance in her ratings. From Adolphs, Russell, et al. (1999); copyright © 1999 Blackwell Scientific Publishers.

with bilateral amygdala damage, whose impairments include a variety of negative emotions, as mentioned above. The data so far are thus compatible both with neural systems that process a specific basic emotion, fear, and with neural systems specialized to process highly arousing, unpleasant emotions, of which fear may be one instance.

To investigate the amygdala's role in processing emotional arousal and valence directly, we asked subjects to rate facial expressions of emotion (the same stimuli used before) with respect to these two factors (Adolphs et al., 1999). In addition, we asked subjects to rate the arousal and the valence of the emotion depicted by single words and by sentences describing emotional events. We asked subjects to rate all these stimuli with respect to their valence (pleasantness/unpleasantness) and arousal on a 9-point scale. Our rating instrument consisted of a one-dimensional grid onto which the subject placed an "x"; this was a simpler modification of a previously developed rating instrument called the Affect Grid, which has demonstrated reliability and construct validity (Russell, Weiss, & Mendelsohn, 1989). Subjects were told that, for the valence scale, ratings greater than 5 corresponded to feelings that were more pleasant than neutral and that ratings less than 5 corresponded to feelings that were less pleasant than neutral. Similarly, for the arousal scale, subjects were told that ratings greater than 5 corresponded to a higher energy/arousal/wakefulness than one's average arousal state and that ratings lower than 5 corresponded to a lower

energy/arousal or greater sleepiness/relaxation than one's average arousal state. Subjects were told that any given level of arousal could be either a pleasant or an unpleasant emotion.

SM rated the valence of emotional facial expressions normally. Her ratings of valence were within 2 SD of the control mean for all six basic emotions. By contrast, she was severely impaired in her ratings of arousal, differing from the control mean by more than 4 SD for certain emotional facial expressions. We calculated the difference between SM's arousal rating and the mean rating given to that face by the 24 normal control subjects (Figure 5.10). This analysis showed clearly that she assigned abnormally low arousal ratings to negative emotions. The two negative emotions normally judged to be the most arousing, fear and anger, received the most abnormal ratings. The specificity of the impairment is especially striking when comparing pleasant and unpleasant emotions that are both highly arousing; for example, SM's ratings of the arousal of surprise were normal, whereas her ratings of fear were severely impaired. Additionally, this specificity for only certain emotions argues that SM's performance cannot be due simply to a failure to understand the rating attribute.

We carried out an additional experiment in which we asked subjects to rate the arousal and valence of lexical stimuli that denote emotions (Adolphs et al., 1999). SM showed a severe impairment in her ability to recognize the arousal signalled by stories and by words denoting negative emotions. She rated stories depicting anger or fear as "relaxing," ratings that were typically more than 5 SD below the mean for the normal controls. For two of the stories depicting fear every normal subject gave arousal ratings of 9 (the highest possible rating), whereas SM gave ratings of 6 (to the sentence, "As the car was speeding down the mountain, Mike stepped down to find that he had no brakes") and 3 (to the sentence, "Sally waved her hands in the air and called for help, as the boat was sinking"). However, she gave normal ratings of valence to all emotions.

In yet a third experiment, SM was shown short clips from movies designed to elicit specific, basic emotions (Adolphs & Tranel, 2000). We used stimuli that had been previously shown to elicit the most specific, negative emotional experiences in subjects (Gross & Levenson, 1995). In this experiment, SM was asked to indicate how the stimuli made her feel, a different question from the one asked with all other stimuli, and one which provides pilot data on the complex question of SM's emotional experience. When shown clips that normally elicit anger, disgust, or sadness, SM gave them normal ratings of negative valence (they all received the most negative rating possible), but endorsed average emotional arousal (ratings of 5 for all), just as we had found with respect to her recognition in the experiments above. When shown clips that normally elicit fear (*The Shining* and *The Silence of the Lambs*), SM gave neutral ratings (5) on both the valence scale and the arousal scale. When we asked her what emotion she felt while watching these two clips, she replied "neutral," but added that, in general, most people watching these clips would feel afraid. That is, it appears that SM is able to recognize the emotion that is intended by these complex stimuli but that she is not able to trigger a normal emotional response personally. It is possible that the latter impairment may account for some of her recognition impairment, and specifically for her impaired ability to attribute arousal to negatively valenced stimuli.

The data provide further detail to previously reported impairments in recognizing facial expressions of fear in subjects with bilateral amygdala damage. It is not the case that bilateral amygdala damage impairs *all* knowledge regarding fear; rather, it impairs the knowledge that fear is highly arousing, which may be an important correlate of the ability to predict potential harm or danger. This interpretation may explain impaired recognition of fear in subject SM (Adolphs et al., 1994, 1995). The amygdala may be of special importance in triggering, rapidly and automatically, a concerted physiological change in response to an emotionally salient stimulus. A key component of such an emotional response may be physiological arousal, including the well-documented increases in autonomic arousal that can be triggered by the amygdala (Chapman et al., 1954; Lee et al., 1988). A key issue for further research will be an elucidation of how emotional arousal, as a component of an emotional response triggered by the amygdala, can also come to depend on the amygdala as a component of conceptual knowledge regarding the emotion. One possibility deserving further investigation is that, in SM's case, amygdala damage early in life impaired her experience of emotional arousal in conjunction with certain classes of sensory stimuli and that she consequently failed to develop normal knowledge of which stimuli are emotionally arousing (cf. Adolphs, 1999a; Adolphs et al., 1999; Phelps & Anderson, 1997). Data from our laboratory that compared performances on the above task (rating the arousal of facial expressions) obtained from subjects who acquired amygdala damage early in life, and from subjects that acquired such damage in adulthood, provide preliminary support for this interpretation (Adolphs, Cahill, Schul, & Babinsky, 1997).

## Contribution of the Ventromedial Frontal Cortex to Emotion

The frontal lobes have a long history in emotional and social behavior, going back to the story of a rather horrible accident: the injury of the railroad worker Phineas Gage (Damasio, Grabowski, Frank, Galaburda, & Damasio, 1994). Gage received a large bilateral lesion of his frontal lobes, including the ventromedial prefrontal cortex, from an accidental explosion that shot a metal rod through his head. Whereas Gage had been a diligent, reliable, polite, and socially adept person before his accident, he subsequently became uncaring, profane, and socially inappropriate in his conduct. This change in his personality remained a mystery until it could be interpreted later in light of similar patients; like Gage, other subjects with bilateral damage to the ventromedial frontal lobes show a severely impaired ability to function in society, despite an entirely normal profile on standard neuropsychological measures, such as IQ, language, perception, and memory. More recently, it has become clear that the frontal lobes, specifically their ventromedial sectors, are critical in linking stimuli with their emotional significance (Damasio, 1994). This function bears some resemblance to that of the amygdala outlined above, but with two important differences. First, it is clear that the ventromedial frontal cortices play an equally important role in processing stimuli with either rewarding or aversive contingencies, whereas the amygdala's role, at least in humans, is clearest for aversive contingencies. Second, reward-related representations in the ventromedial frontal cortex are less stimulus driven than in the amygdala, and can be the substrate of more flexible computations, playing a general monitoring role in regard to both punishing and rewarding contingencies (Schoenbaum, Chiba, & Gallagher, 1998).

As with the amygdala, it is important to keep in mind that the prefrontal cortex consists of many different, interconnected sectors (Fuster, 1989; Pandya & Barnes, 1987). Although it is often difficult to distinguish their boundaries, a rough but robust division can be made between ventromedial sectors, which include more poorly laminated paralimbic mesocortex (Morecraft, Geula, & Mesulam, 1992), and dorsolateral sectors, which show the well-developed lamination of isocortex, and whose connections more clearly situate them within sensori-motor neocortical networks (Goldman-Racik, 1988). While there are numerous further subdivisions within these sectors, and while ventromedial and dorsolateral cortices are heavily interconnected, the utility of this division is borne out both by connectivity and function. In particular, there is a division of labor between these two sectors, in that the dorsolateral frontal cortices play a key role in working memory but not decision making, whereas the converse is true of the ventromedial sectors (Bechara, Damasio, Tranel, & Anderson, 1998).

Although damage to the human frontal cortices often encompasses several of the above sectors, investigations of some patients with lesions relatively restricted to the ventromedial sector, as well as a retrospective view of those larger lesions that were not so restricted, has clearly pointed to the ventromedial frontal lobe as most critical to the integration of emotionally relevant information with other aspects of cognition, such as social behavior and decision making (Damasio, 1994).

Historically, the impairments in social behavior following damage that includes the ventromedial frontal lobes have been described as "acquired sociopathy," or "pseudo-psychopathy." Like the more common developmental antisocial personality disorders, the impaired social behavior following ventromedial frontal lobe injury is notable for an inability to organize and plan future activity, a diminished capacity to respond to punishment, stereotyped and sometimes inappropriate social manners, and an apparent lack of concern for other individuals, all in the face of otherwise normal intellectual functioning (e.g., Ackerly & Benton, 1948; Brickner, 1932; Damasio, 1994). Particularly striking are the patients' often gross lack of concern for the well-being of others and remarkable lack of empathy (Brickner, 1932; Stuss & Benson, 1986). While the details of impaired emotional and social function following damage to the ventromedial frontal lobes can be complex, and can vary from case to case, the impairments share a core dysfunctional mechanism that no longer permits cognitive processes to incorporate certain types of emotional knowledge (Damasio, Tranel, & Damasio, 1991; Damasio, Tranel, & Damasio, 1990). We have proposed an account of the underlying defect in the somatic marker theory (Damasio, 1994, 1996).

The somatic marker theory hypothesizes that somatic states are engaged in many instances of decision making and reasoning. The function of these somatic states is to steer the decision-making process toward those outcomes that are advantageous for the subject, based on the subject's past experience with similar situations. This hypothesis was motivated by two findings: (1) the VM frontal cortex is situated anatomically such that it can receive highly processed sensory information from all sensory modalities and such that it can interact with neural systems that control skeletomotor, visceral, and neuroendocrine effectors; and (2) lesions of the VM frontal cortex in humans result in a profound inability to make successful decisions in real life, in the context of relatively spared memory, language, and most other cognitive functions. To test the hypothesis, we have conducted a number of studies with patients who have bilateral damage to the VM frontal cortex.

## Emotional Response to Salient Stimuli

First, we briefly summarize results of psychophysiological studies, which have been published in detail elsewhere (Damasio et al., 1990, 1991; Tranel, 1994; Tranel & Damasio, 1994). We wanted to test the hypothesis that patients with bilateral damage to the VM frontal cortex will be defective in their ability to engage somatic states in response to emotionally significant stimuli. Our reasoning was that the significance of complex stimuli with emotional significance would depend on the prior experiences subjects had with those stimuli and that the VM frontal cortex would be an essential node in the reconstitution of somatic states that had been elicited by these stimuli on previous occasions.

The experiments measured a robust autonomic variable as one index of somatic state: the change in skin conductance (SCR) in response to a stimulus. Three groups of subjects were used: (1) normal subjects with no evidence of brain damage; (2) subjects with lesions outside the frontal cortex; and (3) subjects with lesions of the ventromedial frontal cortex. Subjects in group 3 all had bilateral lesions and all exhibited defects in decision making in real life. Subjects were shown slides of two types: neutral slides (landscapes or abstract pictures) and emotionally significant target slides (scenes of nudity, social disaster, or mutilation). While all three groups of subjects showed robust SCRs to startling stimuli, such as a loud noise, or to behaviors that reliably elicit SCRs, such as a deep breath, the VM frontal group showed specific defects in response to emotionally significant stimuli (scenes of nudity or of mutilation). Control groups showed larger SCRs to target stimuli than to neutral slides, whereas the VM frontal group failed to show significantly different SCR magnitudes between the two classes of stimuli. These results suggest that VM frontal patients are defective in their

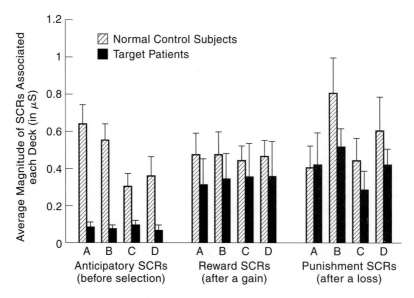

Figure 5.11 Impaired autonomic response and impaired decision making in subjects with damage to ventromedial frontal cortex. Shown are skin conductance responses while deliberating on a card-gambling task. Risky decks of cards, on which subjects can lose large sums of money, are decks A and B; safer decks, on which subjects win less money immediately, but make more in the long run, are decks C and D. Controls soon begin to show large skin conductance responses when about to choose from a risky deck and avoid decks A and B on future occasions. However, VM frontal patients, despite normal skin conductance responses to actually wining or losing money on the cards ("punishment" and "reward"), do not show the anticipatory responses that the controls show. Consequently, they do not avoid the risky decks and end up losing money in the task. From Bechara et al. (1996), copyright © Oxford University Press, Inc. Used by permission of Oxford University Press, Inc.

ability to trigger somatic responses to stimuli with emotional meaning.

## Decision Making

The specific role of the ventromedial prefrontal cortex in decision making has been explored in another series of studies by Antoine Bechara and colleagues, who used a task in which subjects had to gamble in order to win money. As with gambling in real life, the task involved probabilistic contingencies that required subjects to make choices based on incomplete information. Normal subjects learn to maximize their profits on the gambling task by building a representation of the statistical contingencies gleaned from prior experiences: certain choices tend to pay off better than others in the long run. The key ingredient that distinguishes the task of Bechara and colleagues from other tasks of probabilistic reasoning is that subjects discriminate choices by feeling; they develop hunches that certain choices are better than others, and these hunches can be measured both by asking subjects verbally and by measuring autonomic correlates of emotional arousal, such as skin conductance response. Subjects with damage to the ventromedial frontal cortex fail this task (Bechara, Damasio, Da-

masio, & Anderson, 1994), and they fail it precisely because they are unable to represent choice bias in the form of an emotional hunch (Bechara, Damasio, Tranel, & Damasio, 1997). Not only do subjects with VM frontal damage make poor choices on the task, they also acquire neither any subjective feeling regarding their choices (Bechara et al., 1997), nor any anticipatory autonomic changes (Bechara, Tranel, Damasio, & Damasio, 1996; Figure 5.11).

## Reasoning

The ventromedial frontal cortex plays a pervasive and general role in how we make decisions and how we reason, as already suggested by the impairments in real-life behaviors that follow damage to this structure. We carried out another series of studies in which we examined reasoning biases. Human reasoning strategies have been intensively investigated using the Wason selection task, the most popular experimental design for probing deductive reasoning. The Wason selection task consists of a conditional statement ("if P then Q"), often presented in some context (e.g., "If you are drinking beer, then you must be over the age of 18"), and subjects must use deductive reasoning in order to decide its truth. Typically, the proportion of logically correct choices made by normal subjects on this task is facilitated by conditionals about social rules, threats, and promises. It has been argued that these data provide evidence for evolved mechanisms for reasoning about social exchange (Cosmides & Tooby, 1992). Specifically, the findings from the Wason selection task support the hypothesis of an evolved skill to detect deception in the context of social contracts (cheating) because an ability to rapidly and reliably detect such deception would have been adaptive (although there is considerable debate regarding the interpretation of the data and alternative models have been proposed).

We investigated the role of the VM frontal cortex in such deductive reasoning, using three groups of subjects: patients with damage centered on the VM frontal cortex, patients with damage centered on the dorsolateral frontal cortex (specifically excluding the VM frontal cortex), and patients with damage outside the frontal cortex (Adolphs et al., 1995). Subjects with bilateral damage to the VM frontal cortex were disproportionately impaired in normal reasoning about social and familiar scenarios, whereas they showed no abnormality when reasoning about more abstract material (Figure 5.12). These findings are consonant with those presented above, and support a role for the VM frontal cortex in guiding reasoning and decision making by the elicitation of emotional states that serve to bias cognition. While the ventromedial frontal cortices, together with the amygdala, would participate in a more general function of linking stimuli to emotionally valued responses, they may be notably indispensable when reasoning and making decisions about social matters. Additional future studies that attempt to dissect the broad collection of processes that constitute social cognition will help to shed light on the question of the specificity and modularity of ventromedial frontal cortex function. The evolutionary implications that can be drawn from such a disproportionate importance to social cognition remain a difficult and open question.

Taken together, the findings to date support the idea that the VM frontal cortex is a critical component of the neural systems by which we acquire, represent, and retrieve the values of our actions. This mechanism includes the generation of overt somatic states, and/or the generation of internal representations of somatic states, that correspond to the anticipated future outcome of decisions. Such a mechanism may be of special importance in the social domain, where the enormous complexity of the decision space precludes an exhaustive analysis.

## Contribution of Other Structures

In addition to the structures detailed above, there are three categories of additional structures that are important to the processing of emotion:

1. Structures that directly regulate autonomic, somatomotor, and/or neuroendocrine components of an emotional response. This category would include hypothalamic nuclei (but see Weddell, 1994), brain stem nuclei, and basal ganglia (Cancelliere & Kertesz, 1990).

2. Structures that subserve various other cognitive functions whose function is directly modulated by emotion. We have already outlined some examples above—for instance, the hippocampus, whose function in memory consolidation is modulated by emotional arousal as a consequence of its connections with the amygdala. The basal forebrain's contribution to attentional processes is modulated in a similar way.

3. Structures that represent information about the body. This includes, in addition to somatosensory cortices, thalamic and brain stem nuclei that receive afferent information about somatic state; this category also importantly includes structures that represent such homeostatically critical parameters as pH, body temperature, blood pressure, and oxygen tension.

A more detailed review of the contributions of these structures is outside the scope of the present review. Less is known about the precise roles that these structures play in emotion, and human lesion studies exploring their role are quite rare. There are some neurodegenerative diseases—for instance, Parkinson's and Huntington's diseases—that have pointed to important roles of the basal ganglia in emotion; but the complexity of the structures concerned and their massive interconnectivity with other brain systems will necessitate future research to more accurately delineate the processes in which they participate. It should be pointed out that lesion studies in animals have indeed made considerable progress in understanding the functions of structures such as the ventral striatum, the hypothalamus, and others that are difficult to examine with human lesion studies (see, e.g., chapter 7, this volume).

## Conclusions

Although our understanding of the specific roles in emotion processing subserved by specific structures is still in its infancy, the rate of research progress is rapid. For some key structures, such as the ventromedial frontal cortices and the amygdala, a sizable set of data have accrued and we can begin to construct some rather detailed hypotheses regarding their contribution to emotion. For other sets of structures, notably thalamic nuclei and brain stem nuclei, our understanding of their function in human emotion is still rudimentary, in part due to the difficulty in anatom-

A.

B.

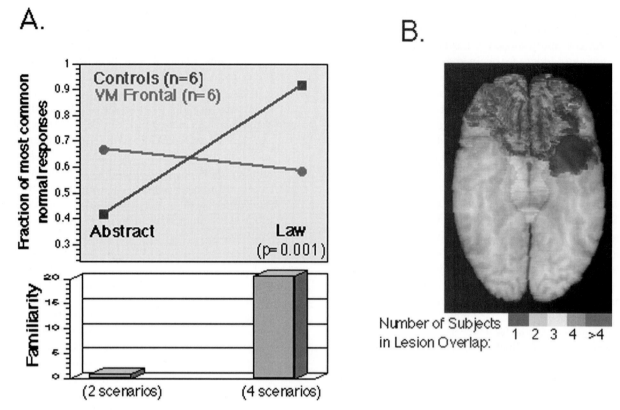

Figure 5.12 Reasoning on the Wason Selection Task by subjects with ventromedial frontal lobe lesions. (a) While subjects with VM frontal lesions gave the logically correct answer more often than did control subjects when reasoning about scenarios where the subject matter was logical and abstract (e.g., "If a student got an 'A' grade, then his card must be marked with the numeral 3"), they gave the logically correct answer less often than controls when the subject matter concerned familiar social situations, specifically social laws (e.g., "If you are drinking beer, then you must be over the age of 18"). These findings support the idea that, in normal subjects, the VM frontal cortices may be part of a system that facilitates correct reasoning about social matters. The results were especially striking, since the scenarios on which subjects with VM frontal damage fail are in fact the ones that are normally the easiest, and the most familiar, to reason about. When subjects were asked to indicate how familiar they found each of the scenarios, both VM frontal and normal control subjects judged the social laws to be much more familiar than the abstract scenarios (bar graph at bottom). (b) Volumetric overlap image of the lesions of all subjects with VM frontal lobe damage. Color codes the number of subjects who have a lesion at a given anatomical location, rendered onto a ventral view of the human brain. The anatomical sites shared in common by all subjects in the group were in the ventromedial frontal cortex, bilaterally. From Adolphs (1999c); copyright Elsevier Science Publishers. (See color insert.)

ical localization. The lesion method is particularly difficult to apply to the latter structures, in part because lesions restricted to particular nuclei are very rare, and in part because larger lesions often result in a complex constellation of impairments or in death.

The neural processes that constitute an emotion unfold in a complex, but ordered, fashion in time. Similarly, the order in which emotionally salient events unfold in time in the environment is not random, an issue that has been

addressed in regard to their appraisal. For instance, Scherer (1999) has found evidence to support the idea that appraisal of emotional scenarios capitalizes on the nonrandom order in which events typically succeed one another: scripts that unfold in a standard, predictable order mesh more closely with the order of stimulus evaluation checks in appraisal and are recognized more quickly and more accurately than random sequences of events. Some components of an emotional reaction can appear extremely rapidly—for instance, spider phobics will show potentiation of the startle reflex only 300 ms after seeing a spider picture (Globisch, Hamm, Esteves, & Ohman, 1999)—whereas some require more substantial processing time to appraise the significance of the stimuli. There is thus considerable complexity in the temporal structure of the organism-environment interaction, and also in the neural processes that represent the dynamics of body-state changes resulting from such interaction. This issue, of how multiple components of emotional processing interact in time, will be a critical issue for future research.

Despite the gaps in our knowledge of the function of many structures in the human brain that will no doubt matter to emotion, we can begin to sketch a framework for discussing their integrated action. This framework needs to provide a link between neuroanatomy and hodology, on the one hand, and emotional processes, on the other.

In essence, the neural processes contributing to an emotion consist of three overlapping functional domains: (1) reactions/responses to stimuli that have emotional salience for the organism (that are of biological value); (2) representations (both first and higher order) of such reactions, juxtaposed in relation to the baseline body-state of the organism and in relation to the environmental stimulus that triggered the emotion; and (3) emotional experience (feeling) resulting from the referral of representations of such body-state changes to a comprehensive representation of the self (these ideas are explicated in more detail in Damasio, 1999).

We would like to propose that amygdala and ventromedial frontal cortices are two components of a distributed, large-scale neural system that participate in triggering an emotional physiological state in response to a salient sensory stimulus. It is important to keep in mind that by "emotional physiological state" we intend to include changes in the state of the body (including somatomotor, visceral, and autonomic components), of the endocrine system, and also of the brain itself (e.g., through global neuromodulatory changes by transmitters, such as 5-HT, ACh, or dopamine in brain stem nuclei). The emotional state that is triggered can then be used to guide behavior, to reconstruct knowledge, or to influence decision making and reasoning. The amygdala may be especially important to trigger, in response to sensory stimuli, relatively basic, fast, and undifferentiated emotional responses. Moreover, there is evidence that suggests that the amygdala may be disproportionately important to trigger emotional responses to a restricted category of stimuli: those stimuli that signal potential threat or danger in the environment. By contrast, ventromedial frontal cortices would serve to link more complex and diverse categories of stimuli to more complex and diverse patterns of emotional response (both somatic and neural). Certain classes of stimuli may trigger activation of the amygdala relatively automatically, whereas the involvement of the ventrome-

dial frontal cortices may depend on the particular set of processes and the particular task strategy that the subject is engaging. Normally, in a typical, complex, emotionally salient situation in real life, both structures will operate in parallel: the amygdala will provide a quick and automatic bias with respect to those aspects of the response that pertain to evaluating the potentially threatening/dangerous nature of the situation; the ventromedial frontal cortex will associate elements of the situation with elements of previously encountered situations and trigger a reenactment of the corresponding emotional state.

Structures that represent the emotional responses and the consequent changes in body state will include somatosensory-related cortices in the right hemisphere. Right somatosensory-related cortices also will be called upon to the extent that a detailed, comprehensive representation of the body state associated with the emotion needs to be made available in certain tasks, such as those we described above.

A full account of the interplay of these different sets of processes, and of their concerted action through time, will also require more data than provided by the lesion method. In particular, we believe that a combination of findings from lesions, from functional imaging, and from techniques with excellent temporal resolution, such as evoked potential recordings, will be important to pursue in the future. Of special value will be the opportunity to use several of these methods jointly in the same subjects, research issues that are currently under investigation in our laboratory.

## NOTE

The work reviewed here draws upon research carried out jointly with our colleagues Daniel Tranel, Thomas Grabowski, Antoine Bechara, and Steven Anderson. Funding sources include a program project grant from NINDS to A.R.D., a grant from the Mathers Fund to A.R.D., and grants from NIMH, the EJLB Foundation, and the Sloan Foundation to R.A.

## REFERENCES

Ackerly, S. S., Benton, A. L. (1948). Report of a case of bilateral frontal lobe defect. *Res. Publ. Assoc. Res. NervMent Dis, 27*, 479–504.

Adolphs, R. (1999a). The human amygdala and emotion. *The Neuroscientist, 5*, 125–137.

Adolphs, R. (1999b). Neural systems for recognizing emotions in humans. In M. Hauser & M. Konishi (Eds.), *Neural mechanisms of communication*. Cambridge, MA: MIT Press.

Adolphs, R. (1999c). Social cognition and the human brain. *Trends in Cognitive Science, 3*, 469–479.

Adolphs, R., Bechara, A., Tranel, D., Damasio, H., & Damasio, A. (1995). Neuropsychological approaches to reasoning and decision-making. In Y. Christen, A. Damasio, & H. Damasio (Eds.), *Neurobiology of decision making*. New York: Springer.

Adolphs, R., Cahill, L., Schul, R., & Babinsky, R. (1997).

Impaired declarative memory for emotional material following bilateral amygdala damage in humans. *Learning and Memory, 4*, 291–300.

Adolphs, R., Damasio, H., Tranel, D., Cooper, G., & Damasio, A. R. (2000). A role for somatosensory cortices in the visual recognition of emotion as revealed by 3-D lesion mapping. *Journal of Neuroscience, 20*, 2683–2690.

Adolphs, R., Damasio, H., Tranel, D., & Damasio, A. R. (1996). Cortical systems for the recognition of emotion in facial expressions. *Journal of Neuroscience, 16*, 7678–7687.

Adolphs, R., Lee, G. P., Tranel, D., Damasio, A. R. (1997). Bilateral damage to the human amygdala early in life impairs knowledge of emotional arousal. *Society for Neuroscience Abstracts, 23*, 1582.

Adolphs, R., Russell, J. A., & Tranel, D. (1999). A role for the human amygdala in recognizing emotional arousal from unpleasant stimuli. *Psychological Science, 10*, 167–171.

Adolphs, R., Schul, R., & Tranel, D. (1997). Intact recognition of facial emotion in Parkinson's disease. *Neuropsychology, 12*, 253–258.

Adolphs, R., & Tranel, D. (1999). Intact recognition of emotional prosody following amygdala damage. *Neuropsychologia, 37*, 1285–1292.

Adolphs, R., & Tranel, D. (2000). Emotion recognition and the human amygdala. In J. Aggleton (Ed.), *The amygdala* (2nd ed.). New York: Oxford University Press.

Adolphs, R., Tranel, D., & Damasio, H. (in press). Neural systems for recognition of emotional prosody. *Emotion.*

Adolphs, R., Tranel, D., Damasio, H., & Damasio, A. (1994). Impaired recognition of emotion in facial expressions following bilateral damage to the human amygdala. *Nature, 372*, 669–672.

Adolphs, R., Tranel, D., Damasio, H., & Damasio, A. R. (1995). Fear and the human amygdala. *Journal of Neuroscience, 15*, 5879–5892.

Adolphs, R., Tranel, D., Hamann, S., Young, A., Calder, A., Anderson, A., Phelps, E., Lee, G. P., & Damasio, A. R. (1999). Recognition of facial emotion in nine subjects with bilateral amygdala damage. *Neuropsychologia, 37*, 1111–1117.

Aggleton, J. P., & Young, A. W. (2000). The enigma of the amygdala: On its contribution to human emotion. In L. Nadel and R. D. Lane (Eds.), *Cognitive neuroscience of emotion* (pp. 106–128). New York: Oxford University Press.

Amaral, D. G., Capitanio, J. P., Machado, C. J., Mason, W. A., & Mendoza, S. P. (1997). The role of the amygdaloid complex in rhesus monkey social behavior. *Society for Neuroscience Abstracts, 23*, 570.

Amaral, D. G., Price, J. L., Pitkanen, A., & Carmichael, S. T., (1992). Anatomical organization of the primate amygdaloid complex. In J. P. Aggleton (Ed.), *The amygdala: Neurobiological aspects of emotion, memory, and mental dysfunction* (pp. 1–66). New York: Wiley-Liss.

Amorapanth, P., LeDoux, J. E., & Nader, K. (2000). Different lateral amygdala outputs mediate reactions and actions elicited by a fear-arousing stimulus. *Nature Neuroscience, 3*, 74–79.

Anderson, A. K., LaBar, K. S., & Phelps, E. A. (1996). Facial affect processing abilities following unilateral temporal lobectomy. *Society for Neuroscience Abstracts, 22*, 1866.

Babinsky, R., Calabrese, P., Durwen, H. F., Markowitsch, H. J., Brechtelsbauer, D., Heuser, L., & Gehlen, W.

(1993). The possible contribution of the amygdala to memory. *Behavioral Neurology, 6*, 167–170.

Barrett, A. M., Crucian, G. P., Raymer, A. M., & Heilman, K. M. (1999). Spared comprehension of emotional prosody in a patient with global aphasia. *Neuropsychiatry Neuropsychol Behav Neurol, 12*, 117–120.

Bechara, A., Damasio, A. R., Damasio, H., & Anderson, S. W. (1994). Insensitivity to future consequences following damage to human prefrontal cortex. *Cognition, 50*, 7–15.

Bechara, A., Damasio, H., Tranel, D., & Anderson, S. W., (1998). Dissociation of working memory from decision making within the human prefrontal cortex. *Journal of Neuroscience, 18*, 428–437.

Bechara, A., Damasio, H., Tranel, D., & Damasio, A. (1997). Deciding advantageously before knowing the advantageous strategy. *Science, 275*, 1293–1295.

Bechara, A., Tranel, D., Damasio, H., Adolphs, R., Rockland, C., & Damasio, A. R. (1995). Double dissociation of conditioning and declarative knowledge relative to the amygdala and hippocampus in humans. *Science, 269*, 1115–1118.

Bechara, A., Tranel, D., Damasio, H., & Damasio, A. R. (1996). Failure to respond autonomically to anticipated future outcomes following damage to prefrontal cortex. *Cerebral Cortex, 6*, 215–225.

Blonder, L. X., Bowers, D., & Heilman, K. (1991). The role of the right hemisphere in emotional communication. *Brain, 114*, 1115–1127.

Blonder, L. X., Burns, A. F., Bowers, D., Moore, R. W., & Heilman, K. M. (1993). Right hemisphere facial expressivity during natural conversation. *Brain and Cognition, 21*, 44–56.

Borod, J. (1992). Interhemispheric and intrahemispheric control of emotion: A focus on unilateral brain damage. *Journal of Consulting and Clinical Psychology, 60*, 339–348.

Borod, J. C. (1993). Cerebral mechanisms underlying facial, prosodic, and lexical emotional expression: A review of neuropsychological studies and methodological issues. *Neuropsychology, 7*, 445–463.

Borod, J. C., Andelman, F., Obler, L. K., Tweedy, J. R., & Welkowitz, J. (1992). Right hemisphere specializations for the identification of emotional words and sentences: Evidence from stroke patients. *Neuropsychologia, 30*, 827–844.

Borod, J. C., Kashemi, D. R., Haywood, C. S., Andelman, F., Obler, L. K., Welkowitz, J., Bloom, R. L., & Tweedy, J. R. (1996). Hemispheric specialization for discourse reports of emotional experiences: Relationships to demographic, neurological, and perceptual variables. *Neuropsychologia, 34*, 351–359.

Bowers, D., Bauer, R. M., Coslett, H. B., & Heilman, K. M. (1985). Processing of faces by patients with unilateral hemisphere lesions. *Brain and Cognition, 4*, 258–272.

Bowers, D., Bauer, R. M., & Heilman, K. M. (1993). The nonverbal affect lexicon: Theoretical perspectives from neuropsychological studies of affect perception. *Neuropsychology, 7*, 433–444.

Bowers, D., Blonder, L. X., Feinberg, T., & Heilman, K. M. (1991). Differential impact of right and left hemisphere lesions on facial emotion and object imagery. *Brain, 114*, 2593–2609.

Bowers, D., Coslett, H. B., Bauer, R. M., Speedie, L. J., & Heilman, K. H. (1987). Comprehension of emotional prosody following unilateral hemispheric lesions: Processing defect versus distraction defect. *Neuropsychologia, 25,* 317–328.

Bowers, D., & Heilman, K. M. (1984). Dissociation between the processing of affective and nonaffective faces: A case study. *Journal of Clinical Neuropsychology, 6,* 367–379.

Brickner, R. M. (1932). An interpretation of frontal lobe function based upon the study of a case of partial bilateral frontal lobectomy. Localization of function in the cerebral cortex. *Proceedings of the Association for Research in Nervous and Mental Disease* (Baltimore), *13,* 259.

Broks, P., Young, A. W., Maratos, E. J., Coffey, P. J., Calder, A. J., Isaac, C., Mayes, A. R., Hodges, J. R., Montaldi, D., Cezayirli, E., Roberts, N., & Hadley D. (1998). Face processing impairments after encephalitis: Amygdala damage and recognition of fear. *Neuropsychologia, 36,* 59–70.

Brownell, H. H., Michel, D., Powelson, J. A., & Gardner, H. (1983). Surprise but not coherence: Sensitivity to verbal humor in right hemisphere patients. *Brain and Language, 18,* 20–27.

Buechel, C., Morris, J., Dolan, R. J., & Friston, K. J. (1998). Brain systems mediating aversive conditioning: An event-related fMRI study. *Neuron, 20,* 947–957.

Cahill, L., Babinsky, R., Markowitsch, H. J., & McGaugh, J. L. (1995). The amygdala and emotional memory. *Nature, 377,* 295–296.

Cahill, L., Haier, R. J., Fallon, J., Alkire, M. T., Tang, C., Keator, D., Wu, J., & McGaugh, J. L. (1996). Amygdala activity at encoding correlated with long-term, free recall of emotional information. *PNAS, 93,* 8016–8021.

Calder, A. J., Young, A. W., Rowland, D., Perrett, D. I., Hodges, J. R., & Etcoff, N. L. (1996). Facial emotion recognition after bilateral amygdala damage: Differentially severe impairment of fear. *Cognitive Neuropsychology, 13,* 699–745.

Cancelliere, A. E. B., & Kertesz, A. (1990). Lesion localization in acquired deficits of emotional expression and comprehension. *Brain and Cognition, 13,* 133–147.

Canino, E., Borod, J. C., Madigan, N., Tabert, M. H., & Schmidt, J. M. (1999). Development of procedures for rating posed emotional expressions across facial, prosodic, and lexical channels. *Perceptual and Motor Skills, 89,* 57–71.

Canli, T. (1999). Hemispheric asymmetry in the experience of emotion. *Neuroscientist, 5,* 201–207.

Canli, T., Zhao, Z., Desmond, J., Glover, G., & Gabrieli, J. D. E. (1998). Amygdala activation at encoding correlates with long-term recognition memory for emotional pictures: An fMRI study. *Society for Neuroscience Abstracts, 24,* 935.

Chapman, W. P., Schroeder, H. R., Geyer, G., Brazier, M. A. B., Fager, C. Poppen, J. L., Solomon, H. C., & Yakovlev, P. I. (1954). Physiological evidence concerning importance of the amygdaloid nuclear region in the integration of circulatory function and emotion in man. *Science, 120,* 949–950.

Cosmides, L., & Tooby, J. (1992). Cognitive adaptations for social exchange. In J. H. Barkow, L. Cosmides, & J. Tooby (Eds.), *The adapted mind: Evolutionary psychology and the generation of culture* (pp. 163–228). New York: Oxford University Press.

Damasio, A. R. (1994). *Descartes' error: Emotion, reason, and the human brain.* New York: Grosset/Putnam.

Damasio, A. R. (1996). The somatic marker hypothesis and the possible functions of the prefrontal cortex. *Phil. Trans. R. Soc. London Series B, 351,* 1413–1420.

Damasio, A. R. (1999). *The feeling of what happens: Body and emotion in the making of consciousness.* New York: Harcourt Brace.

Damasio, A. R., Tranel, D., & Damasio H. (1990). Individuals with sociopathic behavior caused by frontal damage fail to respond autonomically to social stimuli. *Behavorial Brain Research, 41,* 81–94.

Damasio, A. R., Tranel, D., & Damasio, H. (1991). Somatic markers and the guidance of behavior: Theory and preliminary testing. In H. S. Levin, H. M. Eisenberg, & A. L. Benton (Eds.), *Frontal lobe function and dysfunction* (pp. 217–229). New York: Oxford University Press.

Damasio, H., Grabowski, T., Frank, R., Galaburda, A. M., & Damasio, A. R. (1994). The return of Phineas Gage: Clues about the brain from the skull of a famous patient. *Science, 264,* 1102–1104.

Darby, D. G. (1993). Sensory aprosodia—A clinical clue to lesions of the inferior division of the right middle cerebral artery. *Neurology, 43,* 567–572.

Daum, I., Channon, S., Polkey, C. E., & Gray, J. A. (1991). Classical conditioning after temporal lobe lesions in man: Impairment in conditional discrimination. *Behavioral Neuroscience, 105,* 396–408.

Davidson, R. J. (1993). Parsing affective space: Perspectives from neuropsychology and psychophysiology. *Neuropsychology, 7,* 464–475.

Davis, M. (1992a). The role of the amygdala in conditioned fear. In J. P. Aggleton (Ed.), *The amygdala: Neurobiological aspects of emotion, memory, and mental dysfunction.* New York: Wiley-Liss.

Davis, M. (1992b). The role of the amygdala in fear and anxiety. *Annual Review of Neuroscience, 15,* 353–375.

Davis, M. (1997). Neurobiology of fear responses: The role of the amygdala. *Journal of Neuropsychiatry and Clinical Neurosciences, 9,* 382–402.

Davis, M., Walker, D. L., & Lee, Y. (1997). Amygdala and bed nucleus of the stria terminalis: Differential roles in fear and anxiety measured with the acoustic startle reflex. *Phil. Trans. R. Soc. London B, 352,* 1675–1687.

Di Virgilio, G., & Clarke, S. (1997). Direct interhemispheric visual input to human speech areas. *Human Brain Mapping, 5,* 347–354.

Ekman, P. (1972). Universals and cultural differences in facial expressions of emotion. In J. Cole (Ed.), *Nebraska Symposium on Motivation* (pp. 207–283). Lincoln: University of Nebraska Press.

Ekman, P. (1973). *Darwin and facial expression: A century of research in review.* New York: Academic Press.

Ekman, P. (1992). An argument for basic emotions. *Cognition and Emotion, 6,* 169–200.

Ekman, P., & Friesen, W. (1976). *Pictures of facial affect.* Palo Alto, CA: Consulting Psychologists Press.

Emery, N. J., & Amaral, D. G. (1999). The role of the amygdala in primate social cognition. In R. D. Lane & L. Nadel (Eds.), *Cognitive, neuroscience of emotion* (pp. 156–191). Oxford: Oxford University Press.

Everitt, B. J., & Robbins, T. W. (1992). Amygdala-ventral striatal interactions and reward-related processes. In J. P. Aggleton (Ed.), *The amygdala: Neurobiological aspects of emotion, memory, and mental dysfunction.* New York: Wiley-Liss.

Everitt, B. J., & Robbins, T. W. (1997). Central cholinergic systems and cognition. *Annual Review of Psychology, 48,* 649–684.

Frank, R. J., Damasio, H., & Grabowski, T. J. (1997). Brain-vox: An interactive, multi-modal visualization and analysis system for neuroanatomical imaging. *Neuroimage, 5,* 13–30.

Furmark, T., Fischer, H., Wik, G., & Fredrikson M. (1997). Individual differences in fear-conditioning and amygdalar activity: A PET study in humans. *Neuroimage, 5,* S596.

Fuster, J. M. (1989). *The prefrontal cortex: Anatomy, physiology, and neuropsychology of the frontal lobe.* New York: Raven Press.

Gaffan, D., Murray, E. A., & Fabre-Thorpe, M. (1993). Interaction of the amygdala with the frontal lobe in reward memory. *European Journal of Neuroscience, 5,* 968–975.

Gallese, V., & Goldman, A. (1999). Mirror neurons and the simulation theory of mind-reading. *Trends in Cognitive Sciences, 2,* 493–500.

Gewirtz, J. C., & Davis, M. (1997). Second-order fear conditioning prevented by blocking NMDA receptors in amygdala. *Nature, 388,* 471–474.

Globisch, J., Hamm, A. O., Esteves, F., & Ohman, A. (1999). Fear appears fast: Temporal course of startle reflex potentiation in animal fearful subjects. *Psychophysiology, 36,* 66–75.

Goldman, A. (1992). In defense of the simulation theory. *Mind and Language, 7,* 104–119.

Goldman-Racik, P. S. (1988). Topography of cognition: Parallel distributed networks in primate association cortex. *Annual Review of Neuroscience, 11,* 137–156.

Goldstein, L. E., Rasmusson, A. M., Bunney, B. S., & Roth, R. H. (1996). Role of the amygdala in the coordination of behavioral, neuroendocrine, and prefrontal cortical monoamine responses to psychological stress in the rat. *Journal of Neuroscience, 16,* 4787–4798.

Gross, J. J., & Levenson, R. W. (1995). Emotion elicitation using films. *Cognition and Emotion, 9,* 87–107.

Gur, R. C., Skolnick, B. E., & Gur, R. E. (1994). Effects of emotional discrimination tasks on cerebral blood flow: Regional activation and its relation to performance. *Brain and Cognition, 25,* 271–286.

Hamann, S. B., Ely, T. D., Grafton, S. T., & Kilts, C. D. (1999). Amygdala activity related to enhanced memory for pleasant and aversive stimuli. *Nature Neuroscience, 2,* 289–293.

Hamann, S. B., Lee, G. P., & Adolphs, R. (1999). Impaired declarative emotional memory but intact emotional responses following human bilateral amygdalotomy. *Society for Neuroscience Abstracts, 25,* 99.

Hamann, S. B., Stefanacci, L., Squire, L. R., Adolphs, R., Tranel, D., Damasio, H., & Damasio, A. (1996). Recognizing facial emotion. *Nature, 379,* 497.

Hamilton, C. R., & Vermeire, B. A. (1988). Complementary hemispheric specialization in monkeys. *Science, 242,* 1691–1694.

Han, J.-S., McMahan, R. W., Holland, P., & Gallagher M. (1997). The role of an amygdalo-nigrostriatal pathway in associative learning. *Journal of Neuroscience, 17,* 3913–3919.

Hauser, M. D. (1993). Right hemisphere dominance for the production of facial expression in monkeys. *Science, 261,* 475–477.

Heller, W. (1993). Neuropsychological mechanisms of individual differences in emotion, personality, and arousal. *Neuropsychology, 7,* 476–489.

Hofer, P.-A. (1973). Urbach-Wiethe disease: A review. *Acta Derm. Venerol, 53,* 5–52.

Holland, P. C., & Gallagher, M. (1999). Amygdala circuitry in attentional and representational processes. *TICS, 3,* 65–73.

Iacoboni, M., Woods, R. P., Brass, M., Bekkering, H., Mazziotta, J. C., & Rizzolatti G. (1999). Cortical mechanisms of human imitation. *Science, 286,* 2526–2528.

Jacobson, R. (1986). Disorders of facial recognition, social behavior and affect after combined bilateral amygdalotomy and subcaudate tractotomy—A clinical and experimental study. *Psychological Medicine, 16,* 439–450.

Kaplan, J. A., Brownell, H. H., Jacobs, J. R., & Gardner, H. (1990). The effects of right hemisphere damage on the pragmatic interpretation of conversational remarks. *Brain and Language, 38,* 315–333.

Kesner, R. P. (1992). Learning and memory in rats with an emphasis on the role of the amygdala. In J. P. Aggleton (Ed.), *The amygdala: Neurobiological aspects of emotion, memory, and mental dysfunction* (pp. 379–400). New York: Wiley-Liss.

Killcross, S., Robbins, T. W., & Everitt, B. J. (1997). Different types of fear-conditioned behavior mediated by separate nuclei within the amygdala. *Nature, 388,* 377–380.

Kling, A. S., & Brothers, L. A. (1992). The amygdala and social behavior. In J. P. Aggleton (Ed.), *The amygdala: Neurobiological aspects of emotion, memory, and mental dysfunction* New York: Wiley-Liss.

Kluver, H., & Bucy, P. C. (1939). Preliminary analysis of functions of the temporal lobes in monkeys. *Arch. Neurol. Psychiatry, 42,* 979–997.

LaBar, K. S., Gatenby, J. C., Gore, J. C., LeDoux, J. E., & Phelps, E. A. (1998). Human amygdala activation during conditioned fear acquisition and extinction: A mixed-trial fMRI study. *Neuron, 20,* 937–945.

LaBar, K. S., LeDoux, J. E., Spencer, D. D., & Phelps, E. A. (1995). Impaired fear conditioning following unilateral temporal lobectomy in humans. *Journal of Neuroscience, 15,* 6846–6855.

LaBar, K. S., & Phelps, E. A. (1998). Arousal-mediated memory consolidation: Role of the medial temporal lobe in humans. *Psychological Science, 9,* 490–494.

Le Doux, J. (1996). *The emotional brain.* New York: Simon & Schuster.

LeDoux, J. E., Cicchetti, P., Xagoraris, A., & Romanski, L. M. (1990). The lateral amygdaloid nucleus: Sensory interface of the amygdala in fear conditioning. *J. Neurosci, 10,* 1062–1069.

LeDoux, J. E., Iwata, J., Cicchetti, P., & Reis, D. J. (1988). Different projections of the central amygdaloid nucleus mediate autonomic and behavioral correlates of conditioned fear. *J. Neurosci, 8,* 2517–2529.

Lee, G. P., Arena, J. G., Meador, K. J., Smith, J. R., Loring, D. W., & Flanigin, H. F. (1988). Changes in autonomic responsiveness following bilateral amygdalotomy in humans. *Neuropsychiatry, Neuropsychology, and Behavioral Neurology, 1,* 119–129.

Ley, R. G., & Bryden, M. P. (1979). Hemispheric differences in processing emotion and faces. *Brain and Language, 7,* 127–138.

Maquet, P., Peters, J.-M., Aerts, J., Delfiore, G., Degueldre, C., Luxen, A., & Franck, G. (1996). Functional neuroanatomy of human rapid-eye-movement sleep and dreaming. *Nature, 383,* 163–166.

McGaugh, J. L. (2000). Memory—A century of consolidation. *Science, 287,* 248–251.

Meadows, M.-E., & Kaplan, R. F. (1994). Dissociation of autonomic and subjective responses to emotional slides in right hemisphere damaged patients. *Neuropsychologia, 32,* 847–856.

Morecraft, R. J., Geula, C., & Mesulam, M.-M. (1992). Cytoarchitecture and neural afferents of orbitofrontal cortex in the brain of the monkey. *J. Comp. Neurol, 323,* 341–358.

Morris, R. D., & Hopkins, W. D. (1993). Perception of human chimeric faces by chimpanzees: Evidence for a right hemisphere advantage. *Brain and Cognition, 21,* 111–122.

Ojemann, J. G., Ojemann, G. A., & Lettich, E. (1992). Neuronal activity related to faces and matching in human right nondominant temporal cortex. *Brain, 115,* 1–13.

Packard, M. G., & Teather, L. A. (1996). Amygdala modulation of multiple memory systems. *Soc. for Neurosci, Abstr, 22,* 1868.

Pandya, D. N., & Barnes, C. L. (1987). Architecture and connections of the frontal lobe. In E. Perecman (Ed.), *The frontal lobes revisited* (pp. 41–68). New York: IRBN Press.

Pell, M. D. (1998). Recognition of prosody following unilateral brain lesion: Influence of functional and structural attributes of prosodic contours. *Neuropsychologia, 36,* 701–715.

Phelps, E. A., & Anderson, A. K. (1997). What does the amygdala do? *Current Biology, 7,* R311–R314.

Pitkanen, A., Savander, V., & LeDoux, J. E. (1997). Organization of intra-amygdaloid circuitries in the rat: An emerging framework for understanding functions of the amygdala. *Trends in Neurosciences, 20,* 517–523.

Rapcsak, S. Z., Comer, J. F., & Rubens, A. B. (1993). Anomia for facial expressions: Neuropsychological mechanisms and anatomical correlates. *Brain and Language, 45,* 233–252.

Rapcsak, S. Z., Kaszniak, A. W., & Rubens, A. B. (1989). Anomia for facial expressions: Evidence for a category specific visual-verbal disconnection syndrome. *Neuropsychologia, 27,* 1031–1041.

Revonsuo, A. (2000). The reinterpretation of dreams: An evolutionary hypothesis of the function of dreaming. *Behavioral and Brain Sciences, 23.*

Ringo, J. L., Doty, R. W., Demeter, S., & Simard, P. Y. (1994). Time is of the essence: A conjecture that hemispheric specialization arises from interhemispheric conduction delay. *Cerebral Cortex, 4,* 331–343.

Rizzolatti, G., & Arbib, M. (1998). Language within our grasp. *TINS, 21,* 188–194.

Rizzolatti, G., Fadiga, L., Gallese, V., & Fogassi, L. (1996). Premotor cortex and the recognition of motor actions. *Cognitive Brain Research, 3,* 131–141.

Rolls, E. T. (1999). *The brain and emotion.* New York: Oxford University Press.

Ross, E. D. (1985). Modulation of affect and nonverbal communication by the right hemisphere. In M. M. Mesulam (Ed.), *Principles of behavioral neurology* (pp. 239–258). Philadelphia: F. A. Davis.

Ross, E. D., Stark, R. D., & Yenkosky, J. P. (1997). Lateralization of affective prosody in brain and the callosal integration of hemispheric language functions. *Brain and Language, 56,* 27–54.

Russell, J. A. (1980). A circumplex model of affect. *J. Pers. Soc. Psych, 39,* 1161–1178.

Russell, J. A., Weiss, A., & Mendelsohn, G. A. (1989). Affect grid: A single-item scale of pleasure and arousal. *Journal of Personality and Social Psychology, 57,* 493–502.

Ryalls, J. (1988). Concerning right-hemisphere dominance for affective language. *Archives of Neurology, 45,* 337–338.

Sacchetti, B., Lorenzini, C. A., Baldi, E., Tassoni, G., & Bucherelli, C. (1999). Auditory thalamus, dorsal hippocampus, basolateral amygdala, and perirhinal cortex role in the consolidation of conditioned freezing to context and to acoustic conditioned stimulus in the rat. *Journal of Neuroscience, 19,* 9570–9578.

Sackheim, H. A., Greenberg, M. S., Weiman, A. L., Gur, R. C., Hungerbuhler, J. P., & Geschwind, N. (1982). Hemispheric asymmetry in the expression of positive and negative emotions: Neurologic evidence. *Archives of Neurology, 39,* 210–218.

Scherer, K. R. (1995). Expression of emotion in voice and music. *Journal of Voice, 9,* 235–248.

Scherer, K. R. (1999). On the sequential nature of appraisal processes: Indirect evidence from a recognition task. *Cognition and Emotion, 13,* 763–794.

Schmitt, J. J., Hartje, W., & Willmes, K., (1997). Hemispheric asymmetry in the recognition of emotional attitude conveyed by facial expression, prosody and propositional speech. *Cortex, 33,* 65–81.

Schoenbaum, G., Chiba, A. A., & Gallagher, M. (1998). Orbitofrontal cortex and basolateral amygdala encode expected outcomes during learning. *Nature Neuroscience, 1,* 155–159.

Shammi, P., & Stuss, D. T. (1999). Humour appreciation: A role of the right frontal lobe. *Brain, 122,* 657–666.

Silberman, E. K., & Weingartner, H. (1986). Hemispheric lateralization of functions related to emotion. *Brain and Cognition, 5,* 322–353.

Sprent, P. (1998). *Data-driven statistical methods.* New York: Chapman and Hall.

Starkstein, S. E., Federoff, J. P., Price, T. R., Leiguarda, R. C., & Robinson, R. G. (1994). Neuropsychological and neuroradiologic correlates of emotional prosody comprehension. *Neurology, 44,* 515–522.

Stickgold, R. (1999). Sleep: Off-line memory reprocessing. *Trends in Cognitive Sciences, 2,* 484–492.

Stuss, D. T., & Benson, D. F. (1986). *The frontal lobes.* New York: Raven Press.

Swanson, L. W., & Petrovich, G. D. (1998). What is the amygdala? *TINS, 21,* 323–331.

Tranel, D. (1994). "Acquired sociopathy": The development of sociopathic behavior following focal brain damage. In D. C. Fowles. (Ed.), *Progress in experimental personality and psychopathology research.* New York: Springer.

Tranel, D., & Damasio, A. R. (1993). The covert learning of affective valence does not require structures in hippocampal system or amygdala. *Journal of Cognitive Neuroscience, 5,* 79–88.

Tranel, D., & Damasio, H. (1994). Neuroanatomical correlates of electrodermal skin conductance responses. *Psychophysiology, 31,* 427–438.

Tranel, D., Damasio, A. R., & Damasio, H. (1988). Intact recognition of facial expression, gender, and age in patients with impaired recognition of face identity. *Neurology, 38,* 690–696.

Tranel, D., & Hyman, B. T. (1990). Neuropsychological

correlates of bilateral amygdala damage. *Archives of Neurology, 47,* 349–355.

Tucker, D. M., & Williamson, P. A. (1984). Asymmetric neural control in human self-regulation. *Psychological Review, 91,* 185–215.

van Bezooijen, R., Otto, S. A., & Heenan, T. A. (1983). Recognition of vocal expressions of emotion. *Journal of Cross-Cultural Psychology, 14,* 387–406.

Van Strien, J. W., & Morpurgo, M. (1992). Opposite hemispheric activations as a result of emotionally threatening and non-threatening words. *Neuropsychologia, 30,* 845–848.

Wapner, W., Hamby, S., & Gardner, H. (1981). The role of the right hemisphere in the apprehension of complex linguistic materials. *Brain and Language, 14,* 15–33.

Weddell, R. A. (1994). Effects of subcortical lesion site on human emotional behavior. *Brain and Cognition, 25,* 161–193.

Weiskrantz, L. (1956). Behavioral changes associated with ablation of the amygdaloid complex in monkeys. *J. Comp. Physiol. Psychol, 49,* 381–391.

Yoon, B.-W., Morillo, C. A., Cechetto, D. F., & Hachinski, V. (1997). Cerebral hemispheric lateralization in cardiac autonomic control. *Archives of Neurology, 54,* 741–744.

Young, A. W., Aggleton, J. P., Hellawell, D. J., Johnson, M., Broks, P., & Hanley, J. R. (1995). Face processing impairments after amygdalotomy. *Brain, 118,* 15–24.

Zoccolotti, P., Scabini, D., & Violani, C. (1982). Electrodermal responses in patients with unilateral brain damage. *J. Clin. Neuropsych, 4,* 143–150.

Zola-Morgan, S., Squire, L. R., Alvarez-Royo, P., & Clower, R. P. (1991). Independence of memory functions and emotional behavior: Separate contributions of the hippocampal formation and the amygdala. *Hippocampus, 1,* 207–220.

# 6

# EMOTION AND MEMORY: CENTRAL AND PERIPHERAL CONTRIBUTIONS

James L. McGaugh and Larry Cahill

Every moment of our lives new information inundates our brains. Some of the information is preserved, perhaps for a lifetime. It has long been noted that memories of emotionally arousing experiences endure vividly (James, 1890; Christianson, 1992). We have enduring memories of significant personal experiences such as birthdays, weddings, holiday celebrations, the births of children, and the deaths of loved ones. We also tend to remember where we were and what we were doing when we witnessed a serious accident (Stratton, 1919; Bohannon, 1988), learned highly surprising and important information (Conway et al., 1994), or experienced an earthquake (Neisser, Winograd, Shreiber, Palmer, & Weldon, 1996). More common emotional experiences induced by praise, embarrassment, and insults are also not quickly forgotten. Emotional arousal thus appears to play a central and highly adaptive role in enabling the significance of events to influence the strength of the memories of events (McGaugh, 1992, 2000; Cahill & McGaugh, 1998). As William James commented, "An experience may be so exciting emotionally as to almost leave a scar on the cerebral tissue" (1890, p. 670).

This chapter reviews research investigating the neurobiological systems involved in creating such "scars on the cerebral tissue." The research is guided by the general hypothesis that emotional experiences activate processes that continue for some time after the experience and that those processes play critical roles in creating lasting memory. As noted by George Stratton, "When fear is relieved by the sudden disappearance of a menace, as when one

has killed a rattlesnake faced suddenly in the mountains, there is no instant calm. The alarm is gone, but the waters continue to be troubled as after a squall" (1928, p. 220). Livingston (1967) was the first, to our knowledge, to offer a general neurobiological hypothesis to account for the effects of emotional arousal on memory. He suggested that activation of specific brain systems might promote the storage of recently activated brain events by initiating a "neurohormonal influence (favoring) future repetitions of the same neural activities" (p. 576). Kety (1972) subsequently offered a similar yet more specific suggestion that adrenergic catecholamines released in emotional states may serve "to reinforce and consolidate new and significant sensory patterns in the neocortex" (p. 73). In support of those hypotheses there is now extensive evidence indicating that stress hormones released by emotional stimulation modulate memory consolidation and that stress hormones act, at least in part, by activating brain systems that modulate memory consolidation. More specifically, the evidence indicates that (1) stress hormones released from the adrenal medulla (epinephrine) and adrenal cortex (corticosterone in the rat) activate noradrenergic systems in the amygdala, and (2) the amygdala regulates the consolidation of long-term explicit memory by modulating neuroplasticity in other brain regions (McGaugh, Liang, Bennett, & Sternberg, 1984; McGaugh, Cahill, & Roozendaal, 1996; McGaugh, 1989c; Cahill & McGaugh, 1998; McGaugh et al., 2000). Although these conclusions are based primarily on findings of studies using rats, the conclusions are also supported by studies of memory in human subjects (Cahill, 1996; Cahill & McGaugh, 1998).

## Hormonal Modulation of Memory Consolidation

Adrenal stress hormones are released immediately after even relatively mild stressful stimulation of the kinds used in aversively motivated animal learning tasks (McCarty & Gold, 1981; McGaugh & Gold, 1989). The hypothesis that these hormones might influence memory by influencing consolidation was suggested by findings, first reported over four decades ago, that stimulant drugs enhance memory when administered to rats shortly after training (Breen & McGaugh, 1961; McGaugh, 1966, 1973, 1989a; McGaugh & Herz, 1972). Such findings strongly support the hypothesis that the drugs enhance memory by modulating the consolidation of recently acquired information (McGaugh, 1966, 2000). In discussing these early findings of drug enhancement of memory, Gerard (1961) suggested that the adrenal medullary hormone epinephrine might have enhancing effects on memory storage comparable to those of stimulant drugs. He proposed that as "epinephrine . . . is released in vivid emotional experiences, such an intense adventure should be highly memorable" (p. 30). Experiments by Gold and van Buskirk (1975) conducted in our laboratory were the first to report that epinephrine administered to rats immediately after inhibitory avoidance training enhanced long-term memory. As with stimulant drugs, the effect was dose dependent and time dependent. Greatest enhancement was obtained with low to moderate doses and with injections administered within an hour after training. In the inhibitory avoidance task, which is used extensively in studies of drugs and hormone influences on memory consolidation, rats are placed in a well-lit starting compartment in a straight alley and receive a footshock after entering a dark compartment. Retention of the training is tested, usually within a few days, by measuring the animals' latency to reenter the shock compartment.

These early findings, as well as those of subsequent experiments using many other types of training tasks, strongly support the hypothesis that endogenously released epinephrine modulates the strength of memories of experiences that induce epinephrine release (McGaugh, 1989b; McGaugh & Gold, 1989). Findings of a recent study of the effect of posttraining adrenergic blockade on memory for water-maze spatial training provide additional support for this view (Cahill, Pham, & Setlow, 2000). Systemic injections of the β-adrenoceptor antagonist propranolol administered immediately after training in a water-maze spatial task impaired 24-hour retention of the rats' memory of the location of the escape platform. Additionally, propranolol differentially impaired memory in rats that

exhibited good learning during the training session compared to those that exhibited poor learning.

As noted above, findings of many studies have shown that adrenocortical hormones also modulate memory consolidation (Bohus, 1994; de Kloet, 1991; Lupien & McEwen, 1997; McEwen & Sapolsky, 1995; Roozendaal, in press). As with epinephrine, posttraining administration of moderate doses of glucocorticoids induce dose- and time-dependent modulation of memory storage (Cottrell & Nakajima, 1977; Roozendaal & McGaugh, 1996a; Sandi & Rose, 1994). The memory-modulating effects of glucocorticoids appear to involve selective activation of glucocorticoid receptors (Lupien & McEwen, 1997; Oitzl & de Kloet, 1992; Roozendaal, Portillo-Marquez, & McGaugh, 1996). Such findings are consistent with the hypothesis that glucocorticoids released by emotionally arousing training enhance the storage of recent experiences (Roozendaal, 2000; Roozendaal, Quirarte, & McGaugh, 1997).

## Amygdala Modulation of Memory Consolidation

Considerable evidence suggests that epinephrine and glucocorticoid effects on memory are mediated, at least in part, by influences involving the amygdala. Additionally, as is discussed below, release of norepinephrine (NE) within the amygdala appears to be an essential step in mediating the effects of epinephrine and glucocorticoids on memory consolidation. Much current research investigating the role of the amygdala in learning and memory has its roots in early findings that, in rats, electrical stimulation of the amygdala shortly after aversive training induces retrograde amnesia (Goddard, 1964; Kesner & Doty, 1968; Kesner & Wilburn, 1974; McGaugh & Gold, 1976; Gold, Zornetzer, & McGaugh, 1974) as well as memory enhancement (Gold, Hankins, Edwards, Chester, & McGaugh, 1975). Such findings indicate that alterations in amygdala functioning modulate—that is, either impair or enhance memory consolidation.

It is of interest to note that Gerard (1961) offered the remarkably prescient suggestion that the amygdala may play a role in regulating memory consolidation several years before Goddard's paper (Goddard, 1964) and over a decade before those reporting memory enhancing effects of amygdala stimulation (Gold et al., 1974, 1975). In discussing the possible role of the limbic system in memory he proposed that "the amygdala [may act] directly on cortical neurones to alter . . . their responsiveness to the discrete impulses that reach the cortex. . . . These deep nuclei could easily modify the ease and completeness of experience fixation even if the nuclei were not themselves the loci of engrams" (Gerard, 1961, p. 30). But it should be noted that Gerard suggested that the amygdala influences would impair memory. It was in that chapter that Gerard also suggested, as noted above, that epinephrine might enhance memory consolidation. It is of interest that Gerard's suggestions did not directly affect research on systems involved in modulating memory consolidation. To our knowledge, Gerard's views were not discussed (or even cited) in studies investigating epinephrine and amygdala involvement in memory consolidation.

The hypothesis that endogenous stress hormones influence memory storage by activating the amygdala suggests that the impairing effects of amygdala lesions on memory should be most evident in emotionally arousing (i.e., sympathetic nervous system activating) learning situations. Findings of several experiments support this implication (Cahill & McGaugh, 1990). In one experiment (see Figure 6.1), control rats and rats with large excitotoxically induced amygdala lesions were trained on several days to find water in one arm of a Y-maze. In both groups, one-trial appetitively motivated learning was seen in significantly (and equivalently) decreased latencies, between days 1 and 2, to locate and drink the water. On day 3, rats received a footshock as they began to drink. In both groups, one-trial aversively motivated learning was evident in increased latencies on day four. However, the increases in latencies were smaller in the amygdala-lesioned animals. That is, the lesions attenuated but did not block inhibitory avoidance learning.

In another experiment, rats received a milder aversive stimulus (quinine solution) when they drank on day 3. In this experiment amygdala lesions affected neither the appetitively nor aversively motivated training. These findings

strongly suggest that amygdala involvement in learning depends upon the degree of training-induced arousal and not simply the aversive nature of the training. According to this view, sufficiently emotionally arousing (i.e., sympathetic nervous system activating) learning situations should engage amygdala participation in memory formation, independently of whether the particular emotions involved are positive or negative. This implication is supported by findings of amygdala involvement in human memory.

## Involvement of Norepinephrine in the Amygdala

Many findings suggest that activation of adrenergic receptors within the amygdala is of critical importance in mediating epinephrine as well as other neuromodulatory influences on memory storage (McGaugh, 1989b). Gallagher and her colleagues (1981) reported that posttraining infusions of β-adrenoceptor antagonists into the amygdala impair retention of inhibitory avoidance and that NE blocked the impairment. Subsequently, findings from our laboratory indicated that posttraining intra-amygdala infusions of the β-adrenoceptor antagonist propranolol block epinephrine induced enhancement of memory (Liang, Juler, & McGaugh, 1986). Infusions of β-adrenoceptor antagonists into the amygdala after training also block the memory-enhancing effects of NE administered concurrently (Liang et al. 1986; Liang, Chen, & Huang, 1995; Salinas, Introini-Collison, Dalmaz, & McGaugh, 1997) and attenuate the memory impairment induced by intra-amygdala infusions of the noradrenergic neurotoxin DSP4 (Liang, 1998). In contrast, infusions of NE or the β-adrenoceptor agonist clenbuterol into the amygdala after training produce dose-dependent enhancement of memory storage (Introini-Collison, Miyazaki, & McGaugh, 1991; Introini-Collison, Dalmaz, & McGaugh, 1996; Liang et al., 1986; Liang, McGaugh, & Yas, 1990; Liang et al., 1995; Ferry & McGaugh, 1999).

The pharmacological evidence of a critical role for NE receptor activation in the amygdala in modulating memory consolidation suggests that epinephrine, as well as footshock stimulation comparable to that used in inhibitory avoidance training, should induce NE release in the amygdala. In support of this implication results of studies using in vivo microdialysis indicate that levels of NE released in the amygdala following footshock stimulation vary directly with the footshock stimulation intensity (Galvez, Mesches, & McGaugh, 1996; Quirarte, Galvez, Roozendaal, & McGaugh, 1998) and that epinephrine enhances the release of NE in the amygdala (Williams, Men, Clayton, & Gold, 1998; Williams, 2001). Additionally, as is shown in Figure 6.2, the opioid peptidergic antagonist naloxone potentiates NE release induced by footshock (Quirarte et al., 1998), a finding consistent with evidence that intra-amygdala infusions of β-adrenoceptor antago-

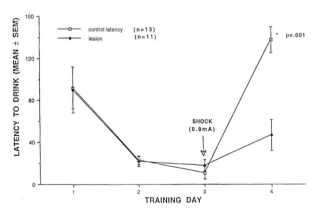

Figure 6.1 Effect of amygdala lesions on retention of one-trial appetitively motivated and one-trial aversively motivated learning. Amygdala lesions had no effect on retention of the appetitively motivated task (learning to find a water reward), seen in the decreased latencies to find water in a Y-maze between training days 1 and 2. Lesions significantly attenuated, but did not completely block, retention of one-trial aversive learning with a highly arousing stimulus (footshock); see the increased latencies to drink between days 3 and 4. From Cahill and McGaugh (1990), copyright 1990 by the American Psychological Association. Reprinted with permission.

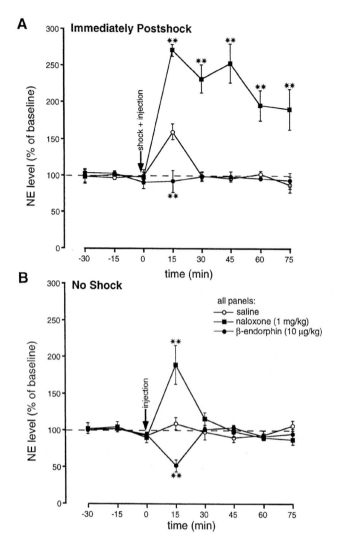

Figure 6.2 Effects of the opioid peptidergic agonist β-endorphin (10 μ/kg, i.p.) and antagonist naloxone (1 mg/kg, i.p.) on norepinephrine (NE) release in the amygdala when administered (A) immediately after footshock (0.55mA, 1s), (B) without prior footshock. NE levels are presented as means (± S.E.M.) of basal levels prior to footshock. $p < 0.01$ as compared to saline group ($n$ = 4–5 animals per group). From Quirarte et al. (1998), copyright 1998, with permission from Elsevier Science.

Table 6.1 Treatment Effects on Memory Storage and Amygdala NE Release

| Treatment | Effects on Memory Storage | Effect on Amygdala NE Release |
|---|---|---|
| Footshock | Varies directly with FS intensity | Increases |
| Epinephrine | Enhances | Increases |
| Picrotoxin | Enhances | Increases |
| Muscimol | Impairs | Decreases |
| Naloxone | Enhances | Increases |
| β-endorphin | Impairs | Decreases |

& Schulman, 1986) and that projections from the nucleus of the solitary tract release NE within the amygdala (Ricardo & Koh, 1978). The finding that inactivation of the nucleus of the solitary tract with lidocaine blocks epinephrine effects on memory storage, as well as epinephrine enhancement of NE release in the amygdala, are consistent with the hypothesis that epinephrine effects on memory are mediated by activation of β-adrenoceptors on vagal afferents projecting to the nucleus of the solitary tract (Williams & McGaugh, 1993; Williams et al., 1998). Additionally, in humans as well as in rats, posttraining electrical stimulation of vagal afferents enhances memory storage (Clark, Krahl, Smith, & Jensen, 1995; Clark, Naritoku, Smith, Browning, & Jensen, 1999; Jensen, 2001).

Noradrenergic projections from the locus coeruleus also influence memory consolidation. Posttraining infusions of the $\alpha_2$-adrenoceptor agonist clonidine into the locus coeruleus impair memory, and NE infused into the amygdala blocks the memory impairment (Liang & Chiang, 1994). Furthermore, clonidine infused into the locus coeruleus blocks the memory-enhancing effects of epinephrine. Perhaps, most importantly, infusions of the $\alpha_2$-adrenoceptor antagonist yohimbine into the locus coeruleus enhance retention and intra-amygdala infusions of propranolol block the enhancement (Liang & Chiang, 1994). These findings are consistent with the finding that stimulation of the locus coeruleus alters evoked potentials (induced by olfactory bulb stimulation) recorded from the amygdala and that administration of a β-adrenoceptor antagonist blocks this effect (Oishi, Watanabe, Ohmori, Shibata, & Veki, 1979). It is likely that locus coeruleus effects on memory are influenced by the nucleus of the solitary tract, as that nucleus projects to the nucleus paragigantacellularis, which provides excitatory afferents to the locus coeruleus. In support of this view a recent study (Clayton & Williams, 2000) reported that muscimol or lidocaine infused into the nucleus paragigantacellularis immediately after training impairs retention of inhibitory avoidance.

Other neuromodulatory influences on memory storage

nists block naloxone-induced enhancement of memory storage (Introini-Collison, Nagahara, & McGaugh, 1989; McGaugh, Introini-Collison, & Nagahara, 1988). Furthermore, findings indicating that GABAergic antagonist bicuculline enhances NE release and the GABAergic agonist muscimol impairs NE release (Hatfield, Spanis, & McGaugh, 1999) are consistent with evidence that GABAergic agonists and antagonists impair and enhance memory storage, respectively (Breen & McGaugh, 1961; Castellano & McGaugh, 1990) (see Table 6.1).

It is known that β-adrenoceptors are located on vagal afferents in the periphery that project to the nucleus of the solitary tract located in the brain stem (Schreurs, Seelig, are also mediated by noradrenergic activation in the amygdala. As is discussed below, the amygdala is also involved in mediating glucocorticoid influences on memory storage, and these effects, like those of epinephrine, involve noradrenergic activation in the amygdala (McGaugh, Roozendaal, & Cahill, 1999; Roozendaal, 2000). As briefly noted above, opioid peptides and opiates impair memory, and opiate antagonists enhance memory (Izquierdo & Diaz, 1983; McGaugh, 1989b; McGaugh, Introini-Collison, & Castellano, 1993). Furthermore, GABAergic antagonists and agonists administered posttraining enhance and impair retention, respectively (Brioni & McGaugh, 1988; Brioni, Nagahara, & McGaugh, 1989; Salinas McGaugh, 1995, 1996; Izquierdo & Medina, 1993; Jerusalinsky et al., 1994). Most importantly, intra-amygdala infusions of the β-adrenoceptor antagonist propranolol block opioid peptidergic and GABAergic influences on memory storage (McGaugh et al., 1988; Introini-Collison et al., 1989).

Considerable evidence indicates that memory is enhanced by glucose (Gold, 1988; White, 1991). As it is known that epinephrine induces the release of glucose and that glucose readily enters the brain, Gold has proposed that epinephrine effects on memory may be due, at least in part, to the effects of glucose (Gold, 1988). In support of this view, Ragozzino and Gold (1994) reported that glucose infused into the amygdala after inhibitory avoidance training blocked the memory-impairing effects of morphine infused into the amygdala. However, as glucose infused into the amygdala did not attenuate the memory-impairing effects of the β-adrenoceptor antagonist propranolol (McNay & Gold, 1998), it seems unlikely that glucose effects on memory of inhibitory avoidance training are mediated by noradrenergic influences within the amygdala. However, a recent study reported that blood glucose levels influence the activity of the NTS (Dallaporta, Himmi, Perrin, & Orsini, 1999). Thus, it may be that the effects of glucose on memory are mediated, at least in part, by the same vagal mechanism implicated in the effects of epinephrine on memory. Future work should explore these potential interactions.

## Selective Involvement of the Basolateral Amygdala Complex

Considerable evidence indicates that the basolateral amygdala complex (BLA; comprising the lateral, basolateral, and basomedial nuclei) selectively mediates the modulating influences of drugs and stress hormones on memory consolidation. It is well established that the memory-impairing effects of benzodiazepines involve potentiation of GABAergic mechanisms in the amygdala (Izquierdo et al., 1990a; Izquierdo, DaCunha, & Medina, 1990). Studies of benzodiazepine effects on memory provided the initial evidence suggesting the selective involvement of the BLA.

Lesions of the BLA block BZD-induced amnesia (Tomaz, Dickinson-Anson, & McGaugh, 1992). Infusions of a benzodiazepine selectively into the BLA induce amnesia (de Souza-Silva & Tomaz, 1995), whereas infusions of the benzodiazepine antagonist flumazenil enhance memory when administered selectively into the BLA (Da Cunha, Roozendaal, Vazdarjanova, & McGaugh, 1999). Studies of the effects of lidocaine infused into amygdala nuclei posttraining provide additional evidence that the BLA is selectively involved in modulating memory consolidation. Lidocaine infused selectively into the BLA immediately after inhibitory avoidance training or contextual fear conditioning impairs retention (Parent & McGaugh, 1994; Vazdarjanova & McGaugh, 1999). Infusions of clenbuterol administered into the BLA posttraining enhance inhibitory avoidance retention (Ferry & McGaugh, 1999). Additionally, infusions of NE into the BLA after training enhance spatial memory whereas infusions of propranolol into the BLA impair spatial memory (Hatfield & McGaugh, 1999).

The amygdala contains a high density of α-adrenoceptors (Unnerstal, Kopajtic, & Kuhar, 1984; Zilles, Qu, & Schleicher, 1993). Findings of several recent studies indicate that α-adrenoceptors within the BLA are involved in regulating memory storage processes. When infused selectively into the BLA posttraining, the $\alpha_1$-adrenoceptor antagonist prazosin impaired inhibitory avoidance retention. Posttraining intra-BLA infusions of the nonselective α-adrenoceptor agonist phenylephrine together with the presynaptic $\alpha_2$-adrenoceptor antagonist yohimbine enhanced retention. These findings suggest that activation of $\alpha_1$-adrenoceptors enhances memory storage and that activation of presynaptic $\alpha_2$-adrenoceptors impairs memory storage (Ferry, Roozendaal, & McGaugh, 1999a). As activation of presynaptic $\alpha_2$-adrenoceptors is known to block NE release (Langer, 1974; Starke, 1979), these findings provide additional evidence that memory storage is influenced by activation of NE receptors within the BLA.

Other evidence suggest that the $\alpha_1$-adrenergic influence on memory is mediated by an interaction with β-adrenoceptors within the BLA. Gallagher and colleagues (1981) reported that posttraining intra-amygdala infusions of the α-antagonist phentolamine enhanced retention and that the effect was blocked by the β-adrenoceptor antagonist propranolol. More recent studies using infusions restricted to the BLA found that posttraining intra-BLA infusions of the β-adrenoceptor antagonist atenolol blocked the memory enhancement induced by selective activation of $\alpha_1$-adrenoceptors (Ferry, Roozendaal, & McGaugh, 1999b). Additionally, the finding that higher doses of the β-adrenoceptor agonist clenbuterol were required to enhance memory when administered into the BLA together with the $\alpha_1$-adrenoceptor antagonist prazosin (Ferry et al., 1999b) suggests that $\alpha_1$-adrenergic activity in the BLA normally facilitates the effects of β-adrenergic activation on memory formation. Liang and his colleagues (1995) reported that posttraining infusions of the synthetic cAMP analog 8-bromo-cAMP administered into the amygdala enhanced inhibitory avoidance retention. Infusions of analog 8-bromo-cAMP also enhance retention when administered selectively into the BLA. However, unlike the findings obtained with clenbuterol, prazosin did not shift the dose-response effects induced by 8-bromo-cAMP (Ferry et al., 1999b). These findings are consistent with pharmacological evidence suggesting that β-adrenoceptors modulate memory storage by a direct coupling to adenylate cyclase and that $α_1$-adrenoceptors may act indirectly by modulating β-adrenergic-induced cAMP synthesis (Leblanc & Ciaranello, 1984; Perkins & Moore, 1973; Schultz & Daly, 1973). Previous studies from our laboratory found that low doses of α-antagonists infused into the amygdala did not block the memory-enhancing effects of naloxone (McGaugh et al., 1988). Such findings would be expected on the basis of studies showing that α-adrenoceptor activation in the amygdala modulates β-adrenergic receptors but is not critical for regulating memory consolidation.

Glucocorticoid influences on memory storage also selectively involve the BLA. As is shown in Figure 6.3, lesions of the amygdala restricted selectively to the BLA block the memory-enhancing effects of posttraining systemic injections of the synthetic glucocorticoid dexamethasone (Roozendaal & McGaugh, 1996a), and posttraining infusions of the specific glucocorticoid receptor agonist RU 28362 enhance retention when administered selectively into the BLA (Roozendaal & McGaugh, 1997a). BLA lesions also block glucocorticoid effects on memory for water-maze spatial learning (Roozendaal et al., 1996). Adrenalectomy before training impairs memory in this task, and immediate posttraining injections of dexamethasone attenuate the impairment. BLA lesions block the effect of both adrenalectomy and glucocorticoids (Roozendaal & McGaugh, 1996a; Roozendaal et al., 1996).

Glucocorticoid influences on memory storage involve β-adrenergic activation in the BLA. Beta-adrenoceptor antagonists infused selectively into the BLA block the memory-enhancing effects of systemically administered dexamethasone (Quirarte, Roozendaal, & McGaugh, 1997). The finding that infusions of a glucocorticoid receptor antagonist into the BLA attenuated the memory-enhancing effect of clenbuterol infused into the BLA concurrently provides further evidence that the BLA is a locus of interaction between glucocorticoids and noradrenergic activation affecting memory storage (Quirarte, Roozendaal, & McGaugh, 1997b). Glucocorticoid receptor activation in the BLA appears to influence the effectiveness of β-adrenoceptor stimulation in modulating memory storage. Glucocorticoid effects on memory storage also involve activation of glucocorticoid receptors in the ascending noradrenergic cell groups in the nucleus of the solitary tract and locus coeruleus that have high densities of glucocorticoid receptors (Harfstrand, et al., 1986). As discussed

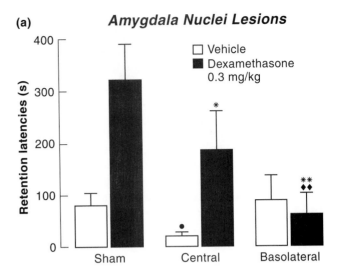

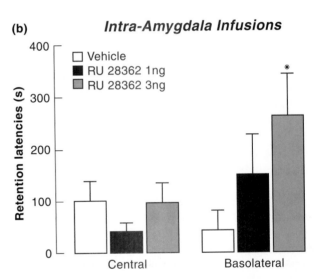

Figure 6.3 Step-through latencies (mean ± SEM) for a 48-hour inhibitory avoidance test. (A) Rats with sham or lesions of either the central or basolateral nucleus of the amygdala had been treated with dexamethasone (0.3 mg/kg, subcutaneous) or vehicle immediately after training. (B) Rats received posttraining infusions of the glucocorticoid receptor agonist RU 28362 (1.0 or 3.0 ng in 0.2 µl) into the central or basolateral nucleus. * $p < 0.05$; ** $p < 0.01$ as compared with the corresponding vehicle group; ● $p < 0.05$ as compared with the corresponding sham lesion-vehicle group; ♦ ♦ $p < 0.01$ as compared with the corresponding sham lesion-dexamethasone group. From Roozendaal & McGaugh (1996a, 1997a), with permission from Academic Press.

above, noradrenergic projections from these nuclei activate the amygdala. Findings of recent studies have shown that infusions of the glucocorticoid receptor agonist RU 28362 into the nucleus of the solitary tract posttraining enhance memory for inhibitory avoidance training (Roozendaal, Williams, & McGaugh, 1999) and that infusions of

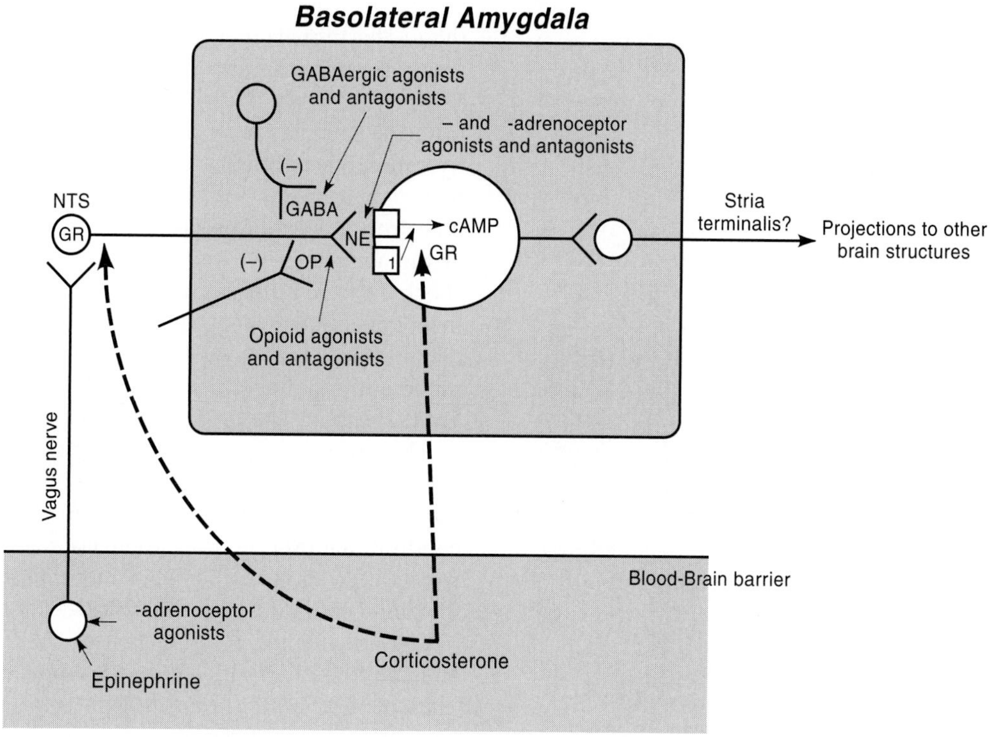

Figure 6.4 Schematic summarizing the interactions of neuromodulatory influences in the basolateral amygdala on memory storage as suggested by the findings of our experiments ($\alpha_1 = \alpha_1$-adrenoceptor; $\beta = \beta$-adrenoceptor; cAMP-cyclic 3'5' adenosine monophosphate; GR=glucocorticoid receptor; NE=norepinephrine; NTS=nucleus of the solitary tract; OP=opioids).

the β-adrenoceptor antagonist atenolol into the BLA block the enhancement. Figure 6.4 summarizes the interactions of neuromodulatory systems in the amygdala affecting memory consolidation.

## Role of the Amygdala in Modulating Memory Consolidation

As reviewed above, extensive evidence supports the hypothesis that the BLA is a critical locus of interactions of neuromodulatory systems influencing memory consolidation. Such findings do not, however, provide any information concerning the brain site(s) modulated by amygdala activity. Findings of many studies have been interpreted as suggesting that neural changes mediating aversively based conditioning may be located at least partly within the amygdala (Davis, 1992; LeDoux, 1995). However, extensive evidence suggests that the amygdala is not a unique site of aversively based memory (Cahill, Weinberger, Roozendaal, & McGaugh, 1999). Findings indicating that amygdala lesions induced either before or after training do not block memory for footshock-motivated escape training clearly indicate that the amyg-

dala is not a unique locus of aversive learning (Parent & McGaugh, 1994; Parent, Tomaz, & McGaugh, 1992; Parent, West, & McGaugh, 1994; Parent, Avila, & McGaugh, 1995). In one experiment examining this issue (Parent et al., 1995) rats were trained, with either 0, 1, or 10 trials to escape from footshock by running to a safe compartment in a straight alley and BLA lesions were induced one week later. Two weeks after the training they were placed in the safe compartment and received a footshock each time they entered the shock compartment. As is shown in Figure 6.5, for both the sham-lesioned controls and the BLA-lesioned group, animals given prior escape training made fewer entries into the shock compartment; those given 10 escape training trials made the fewest entries. It is important to note that the animals were first trained to move quickly to escape from footshock, and that memory was then tested by training them to refrain from moving. Clearly, the BLA lesions did not block either the memory of the escape training and/or the subsequent learning of the inhibitory avoidance response.

Although amygdala lesions impair the expression of conditioned fear as assessed by "freezing" behavior (LeDoux, 1995) or fear-potentiated startle (Davis, 1992), overtraining of fear conditioning attenuates the lesion-

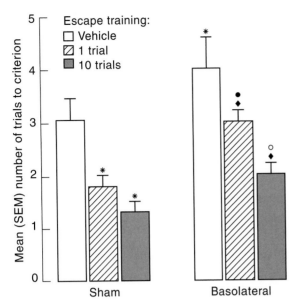

Figure 6.5 Basolateral amygdala lesions induced after escape training in a two-compartment alley do not block memory as assessed by subsequent training (inhibitory avoidance) to avoid entering the shock compartment. Mean (±S.E.M.) entries of shock compartment to reach criterion of remaining in safe compartment for 100 consecutive seconds. * $p < 0.05$ vs. sham-no shock; ● $p < 0.05$ vs. sham 1 trial; ◆ $p < 0.05$ vs. BLA-lesioned no shock; ○ $p < 0.05$ vs. BLA-lesioned 1 trial. From Parent, Avila, & McGaugh (1995), copyright 1995, with permission from Elsevier Science.

induced freezing deficit (Maren, 1998, 1999) and enables reacquisition of fear-potentiated startle (Kim & Davis, 1993). It is, of course, essential to distinguish the effects of amygdala lesions on performance of the response used as an index of fear from effects on learning of the significance of the cues inducing the fear (Cahill et al., 1999). This issue was addressed in an experiment using Pavlovian fear conditioning (Vazdarjanova & McGaugh, 1998). Sham-lesioned and BLA-lesioned rats were first allowed to explore a Y-maze and on the following day received a series of four footshocks in one arm of the Y-maze. The next day each rat was placed in one of the other arms— i.e., an arm where shock had *not* been delivered—and several behavioral measures were assessed for 8 minutes (see Figure 6.6). The sham-lesioned animals displayed freezing in the arm in which they were placed for approximately 75% of the test period. As a consequence they moved very little and spent only about 10% of the time in the other safe arm and almost no time in the shock arm. As was expected, the BLA lesions disrupted freezing behavior. However, in comparison with controls that did not receive footshock on the second day, the BLA-lesioned, like the sham-lesioned animals, had longer latencies to enter the arm where they had received shock and spent less time

there. The animals that had received no shock spent equal amounts of time in each of the arms during the 8-minute test period. Thus, these findings indicate that the BLA-lesioned animals very clearly learned that shock was delivered in one of the three arms of the maze and displayed that knowledge by subsequently avoiding that arm. Another recent study reported that large neurotoxic lesions of the amygdala induced four days after rats received a shock delivered through an electrified probe inserted into their cage did not block subsequent memory of the shock experience, as assessed by the latencies to contact the probe and number of contacts with the probe (Lehmann, Treit, & Parent, 2000).

The finding of an experiment examining conditioned neuroendocrine responses provides further evidence that the amygdala is not a unique locus of memory for fear conditioning (Roozendaal, Koolhaas, & Bohus, 1992). Lesions of the amygdala induced after training blocked rats' freezing behavior but did not block expression of conditioned neuroendocrine responses. Additionally, two strains of rats that differ in their response to shock stimulation, posttraining intra-amygdala infusions of NE enhanced memory of the aversive experience (mild shock delivered through a probe inserted into the cage). However, rats of the two strains differed in the behavior expressing memory of the experience. The NE infusions enhanced freezing in the strain of rats that normally displayed freezing but enhanced another natural defensive response (i.e., burying and biting of the probe) displayed by rats of the other strain (Roozendaal, Koolhaas, & Bohus, 1993). Such findings indicate that the amygdala has a comparable time-limited role in regulating memory storage for contextual fear conditioning and inhibitory avoidance learning.

Other recent studies clearly show that the central and basal amygdala nuclei are not necessary for acquisition and retention of Pavlovian fear conditioning. Electrolytic lesions of either of these nuclei induced before training do not prevent retention of memory for tone-footshock pairing (Amorapanth, LeDoux, & Nader, 2000). Central nucleus lesions selectively attenuated the expression of freezing to the tone CS where as basal nucleus lesions selectively attenuated fear-based escape learning elicited by the tone previously used as the CS. Another recent study reported that rats with complete, excitotoxin-induced BLA lesions readily acquire significant contextual Pavlovian fear conditioning, as assessed by freezing behavior, when given only two footshocks (Cahill, Vazdarjanova, & Setlow, 2000; see Figure 6.7). Freezing increased further after a single footshock given the following day, indicating clear savings of the previous day's training. BLA-lesioned rats given unpaired CS-US training showed no such effect, indicating that the increased freezing displayed by the paired CS-US group reflected acquisition of a specific CS-US association. Thus, it appears that neither the cen-

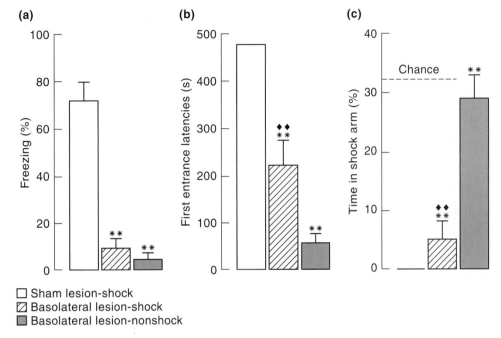

Figure 6.6 Effects of basolateral amygdala lesions on several measures of retention 24 hours after context footshock pairing in a three-arm maze. (A) Percent total time (mean ± SEM) rats spent in freezing behavior. (B) First entrance latency (mean ± SEM) to enter the former shock arm. (C) Percent total time (mean ± SEM) rats spent in the former shock arm. The dotted line depicts the level of chance. ** $p < 0.01$ as compared with the sham-lesion-shock group; ◆◆ $p < 0.01$ as compared between the basolateral nucleus lesion-nonshock and basolateral nucleus lesion-shock groups. From Vazdarjanova & McGaugh (1998), copyright 1998, National Academy of Sciences, U.S.A.

tral nucleus nor the BLA (lateral, basolateral, basomedial nuclei) is necessary for acquisition of Pavlovian fear conditioning associations. It remains possible that the lateral nucleus is specifically necessary for auditory fear conditioning. However, it seems unlikely that the lateral nucleus is a unique site of the learning as tone-shock pairings produce learning-specific alterations in the medial geniculate nucleus of the thalamus that projects to the lateral amygdala (Cahill et al., 1999; Weinberger, 1998a).

Previous findings of studies using inhibitory avoidance training indicate that posttraining intra-amygdala lidocaine or oxotremorine infusions impair and enhance memory, respectively (Parent & McGaugh, 1994; Introini-Collison et al., 1996). Recent studies of the effects of posttraining intra-BLA infusions of drugs on memory for contextual fear conditioning provide strong additional support for the hypothesis that the BLA has a time-limited role in modulating the consolidation of fear-based memory (Vazdarjanova & McGaugh, 1999). Rats received a series of footshocks in an arm of a Y-maze and immediately after training received intra-BLA infusions of a control solution, lidocaine, or the muscarinic receptor agonist oxotremorine. On the following day the rats were placed in one of the "safe" arms and allowed access to all arms. As indicated by several response measures—time spent freez-

ing, latency to enter the shock arm, and time spent in the shock arm—the posttraining lidocaine infusions impaired memory and the oxotremorine infusions enhanced memory (Vazdarjanova & McGaugh, 1998). These findings fit well with the evidence that in contextual fear conditioning (Vazdarjanova & McGaugh, 1998), as well as in inhibitory avoidance training, the rats learn that footshock is experienced in a particular context (i.e., a place in the apparatus).

Many of the experiments examining the role of the amygdala in memory have used inhibitory avoidance as the measure of memory. Several investigators (e.g., Maren Aharonov, & Fanselow, 1996; LeDoux, 1998; Wilensky, Schafe, & LeDoux, 1999) have suggested that the results of studies using inhibitory avoidance may differ from those using Pavlovian fear conditioning because inhibitory avoidance and Pavlovian contextual fear conditioning differ procedurally. It is not at all clear, however, that these two types of training differ in critical ways. As noted by Morgan and LeDoux (1999), inhibitory avoidance is essentially a version of contextual fear conditioning. For both types of training learning may occur with but a single training trial in which shock is delivered in a specific place in an apparatus. The critical difference appears to be the way in which memory of the training is assessed.

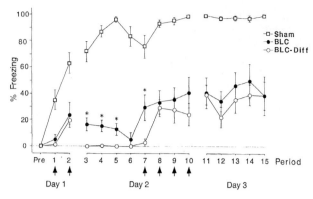

Figure 6.7 Contextual "fear conditioning" behavior in rats with complete lesions of the basolateral amygdala complex and sham-lesioned rats. Numbers on the abscissa refer to successive 55-second measurement periods. Black arrows indicate a footshock given at the start of the period. BLC-Diff refers to lesioned rats trained on day 1 in a box different from that in which all rats were tested on days 2 and 3. The BLC-lesioned rats clearly acquired the Pavlovian CS-US association as indexed by their freezing behavior, despite their overall freezing impairment. Note especially the retention savings in the BLC rats revealed by administration of a single footshock (period 7) on day 2. From Cahill, Vazdarjanova, & Setlow (2000), with permission from Blackwell Science.

Freezing is typically used as the measure for contextual fear conditioning, whereas latency to enter the place where shock was received is typically used as the inhibitory avoidance measure. It is well established that "place" learning is very rapidly acquired and that response learning typically requires extensive training (e.g., Packard & McGaugh, 1996; Packard, 1999). Thus, it is highly unlikely that one-trial inhibitory avoidance involves the learning of an instrumental response. Just as the learning of contextual fear conditioning based on a single training trial occurs too rapidly to be based on instrumental conditioning (Fanselow, 1980), the learning of inhibitory avoidance with only a single training trial also occurs too rapidly to be based on learning of an instrumental response. Additionally, and equally importantly, posttraining treatments selectively affecting the BLA have a highly comparable effect on memory for inhibitory avoidance training and contextual fear conditioning (Parent & McGaugh, 1994; Vazdarjanova & McGaugh, 1999).

Experiments examining the effects of posttraining intra-BLA infusions of drugs on fear conditioning and inhibitory avoidance do not, of course, directly address the issue of whether memory of the shock training is located in neural changes within the amygdala. They are not designed to address that issue. The findings merely indicate that such posttraining treatments modulate—that is, enhance or impair—such memory and thus provide additional evidence that the two types of training, fear conditioning and inhibitory avoidance, have common neural bases. Additionally, it is important to note that findings of posttraining intra-BLA infusions of drugs comparable to those found with inhibitory and contextual fear conditioning tasks have also been obtained in experiments using several other kinds of learning tasks.

## Amygdala Interactions with Other Brain Regions

As we emphasized above, considerable evidence indicates that the amygdala has a time-limited, modulatory role in memory consolidation (McGaugh et al., 1996). The findings of two experiments examining changes in unit activity in the amygdala and auditory cortex of rats induced by fear conditioning and extinction are consistent with this view. Quirk and colleagues (1997) reported that changes in cell firing in the auditory cortex generally occurred after changes recorded in the lateral amygdala. Importantly, the amygdala units extinguished relatively rapidly whereas the cortical units persisted in responding during the extinction. A second study reported that electrolytic lesions of the amygdala impair learning-related responses in the auditory cortex (Armony, Quirk, & LeDoux, 1998). In an extensive series of studies, Weinberger et al. (1990; Weinberger, 1995, 1998b) has shown that fear conditioning induced by pairing tones with footshock rapidly induces long-lasting changes in tone-specific receptive fields in the auditory cortex and has proposed that the changes are modulated by amygdala activation of the cholinergic basal forebrain. Cortical activation by the BLA appears to require the cholinergic basal forebrain. The amygdala is one of the principal sources of afferents to the basal forebrain cholinergic nuclei (Russchen, Amaral, & Price, 1985). Activation of cortical EEG activity by BLA stimulation is blocked both by systemic administration of the cholinergic antagonist scopolamine and by infusions of a local anesthetic (lidocaine) into the cholinergic basal forebrain (Dringenberg & Vanderwolf, 1996). Additionally, stimulation of the basal forebrain has been shown to enhance the duration of an EEG response evoked by somatosensory stimulation (Dykes, 1997). Thus, substantial evidence supports the view that the amygdala modulates cortical memory processes via activation of the cholinergic forebrain.

Other studies have reported that posttraining intra-amygdala infusions of many compounds, including NE and picrotoxin, as well as the NMDA antagonist AP5 and the muscarinic cholinergic receptor antagonist scopolamine, influence memory tested 24 hours after training but do not affect memory tested 90 minutes after training (Bianchin, Mello e Souza, Medina, & Izquierdo, 1999). These findings clearly indicate that the amygdala is not involved in mediating short-term aversively based memory. Furthermore, they are consistent with extensive evidence indicating that as time passes after training, different brain regions participate in memory storage (Izquierdo et al., 1992; Izquierdo & Medina, 1997).

As the amygdala is known to project directly or indirectly to many brain regions it is not surprising that many findings suggest that amygdala activation regulates memory consolidation occurring in other brain regions. The stria terminalis, a major amygdala pathway, seems to be critically involved in enabling amygdala regulation of memory storage as lesions of the stria terminalis block all of the drug and hormone effects on memory that we have examined to date (Liang & McGaugh, 1983; McGaugh, Introini-Collison, Juler, & Izquierdo, 1986; Introini-Collison et al., 1989; Roozendaal & McGaugh, 1996b; Packard, Introini-Collison, & McGaugh, 1996). It is of interest that, in the 1950s, Kaada and colleagues discovered that stimulation of BLA produces an arousal or orienting reaction associated with cortical desynchronization and that the arousal response is blocked by lesions of the stria terminalis (Kaada, 1972). Studies of brain regions activated by amygdala efferents mediated by the stria terminalis may help to reveal brain loci in which memory consolidation is modulated. The amygdala sends direct projections to the striatum via the stria terminalis. Lesions of the stria terminalis block the memory enhancement induced by posttraining infusions of the muscarinic cholinergic agonist oxotremorine into the medial caudate nucleus (Packard et al., 1996), suggesting that amygdala projections to the caudate via the stria terminalis are required for enabling such modulatory influences. N-methyl-D-aspartate infused into the amygdala induces the expression of the proto-oncogene c-fos in the caudate nucleus as well as the dentate gyrus of the dorsal hippocampus. Thus, the amygdala appears to be functionally connected with both of these brain regions (Cahill & McGaugh, 1993; Packard, Williams, Cahill, & McGaugh, 1995). These functional connections are of considerable interest in view of the results of "double-dissociation" studies suggesting that the caudate nucleus and hippocampus mediate different forms of memory (McDonald & White, 1993; Packard, 1999; Packard & McGaugh, 1992, 1996). Caudate lesions selectively impair visually cued learning in a water maze (Packard & McGaugh, 1992), whereas hippocampal lesions selectively impair spatial learning (Morris, Garrud, Rawlins, & O'Keefe 1982; Moser, Moser, & Andersen, 1993; Olton, Bicker, & Handelman, 1979).

Several studies have reported that the amygdala modulates memory consolidation in tasks known to be dependent on hippocampal or caudate nucleus functioning. Infusions of amphetamine administered into the dorsal hippocampus immediately after a single training session selectively enhanced memory of spatial training in a water maze, whereas amphetamine infused into the caudate nucleus selectively enhanced memory of a visually cued training task (Packard, Cahill, & McGaugh, 1994; Packard & Teather, 1998). In contrast, amphetamine infused into the amygdala posttraining enhanced memory for both kinds of training. Furthermore, the finding that inactivation of the amygdala prior to the retention tests did not block the enhanced retention of either type of training clearly indicates that the amygdala is not the locus of the enhanced memory (Packard et al., 1994). However, infusions of lidocaine into the hippocampus prior to retention testing selectively blocked the enhanced memory for the spatial training and infusions of lidocaine into the caudate selectively blocked the enhanced memory for the cued training (Packard & Teather, 1998) (see Table 6.2).

Findings of other recent experiments indicate that memory for inhibitory avoidance involves both the amygdala and the hippocampus and that the amygdala is not the neural locus of the memory (Barros et al., 1999). Infusions of the CaMKII inhibitor, KN-62, impairs memory when administered into either the amygdala or CA1 region of the hippocampus immediately after training. Furthermore, infusions of any of several drugs (including 8-bromo-cAMP and norepinephrine) into the hippocampus three hours after the training attenuate the memory-impairing effects of the previous KN-62 infusions administered into the amygdala. In contrast, the drugs infused into the hippocampus three hours after training did not attenuate the memory impairment induced by posttraining intra-hippocampal infusion of KN-62. These findings support the view that the amygdala influence on memory is modulatory whereas the hippocampus appears to be essential for consolidation of memory for training in this task.

Results of studies investigating the effects of BLA lesions and intra-BLA infusions of a β-adrenoceptor antagonist provide additional evidence that inputs from the BLA influence hippocampally dependent memory (Roozendaal & McGaugh, 1997b; Roozendaal, Nguyen, Power, & McGaugh 1999; see Figure 6.8). Infusions of a glucocorticoid receptor agonist into the dorsal hippocampus after inhibitory avoidance training enhanced memory. However, the memory enhancement was completely blocked in animals with BLA lesions as well as animals given intra-BLA infusions of the β-adrenoceptor atenolol. Other findings indicated that the memory-enhancing effects of unilateral intra-hippocampal infusions of the glucocorticoid were blocked only by treatments affecting the ipsilateral BLA (Roozendaal, 1999). Results indicating that the BLA modulates memory involving the hippocampus are of interest in relation to the finding of Ikegaya and colleagues that the BLA modulates LTP in the dentate gyrus of the hippocampus. Lesions of the BLA or infusions of a β-adrenoceptor antagonist into the BLA block the induction of LTP in the dentate gyrus (Ikegaya, Saito, & Abe, 1994, 1995a; Ikegaya, Saito, Abe, & Nakanishi, 1997). Fur-

Table 6.2  Amygdala Modulation of Hippocampal Dependent and Caudate Nucleus Dependent
Memory Processes

|  | Retention of Spatial Task | Retention of Cued Task |
| --- | --- | --- |
| **_Posttraining infusions_** | | |
| d-amphetamine, Hippocampus[1] | Enhanced | No effect |
| d-amphetamine, Caudate Nucleus[1] | No Effect | Enhanced |
| d-amphetamine, Amygdala[1] | Enhanced | Enhanced |
| d-amphetamine, Amygdala lidocaine, Hippocampus[2] | Enhancement Blocked | Enhanced |
| d-amphetamine, Amygdala lidocaine, Caudate Nucleus[2] | Enhanced | Enhancement Blocked |
| **_Posttraining and pretesting infusions_** | | |
| Post: d-amphetamine, Hippocampus Pre: lidocaine, Hippocampus[2] | Enhancement Blocked | (not tested) |
| Post: d-amphetamine, Caudate Nucleus Pre: lidocaine, Caudate Nucleus[2] | (not tested) | Enhancement Blocked |
| Post: d-amphetamine, Amygdala Pre: lidocaine, Amygdala[1] | Enhanced | Enhanced |

1. Packard, Cahill, & McGaugh, 1994; Packard & Teather, 1998.
2. Packard & Teather, 1998.

thermore, stimulation of the BLA enhances induction of LTP in the dentate gyrus (Ikegaya, Saito, & Abe, 1995b).

As the nucleus accumbens receives projections from both the BLA and the hippocampus (O'Donnell & Grace, 1995), the BLA might affect hippocampal functioning via the BLA-nucleus accumbens pathway. Lesions of the stria terminalis, which carries projections from the BLA to the nucleus accumbens, have effects comparable to those induced by amygdala or selective BLA lesions. The hypothesis that the nucleus accumbens mediates modulating influences of the amygdala is supported by recent findings indicating that excitotoxic lesions of the nucleus accumbens, like lesions of the BLA or stria terminalis, block the memory-modulating effects of posttraining systemic injections of dexamethasone (Setlow, Roozendaal, & McGaugh, 2000). Additionally, there is evidence suggesting that the amygdala may modulate information processing within the hippocampal formation via projections to the entorhinal cortex, hippocampus subiculum, and parasubiculum (Pikkarainen, Ronko, Savander, Insausti, & Pitkanen, 1999).

Other recent findings from several laboratories suggest that the medial prefrontal cortex may also be involved in influencing the expression of memory for aversively based learning. Lesions of the dorsomedial prefrontal cortex enhance freezing behavior elicited by a tone previously paired with footshock (Morgan & LeDoux, 1995). These results may reflect lesion effects on the expression of freezing rather than on learning, as retention is *impaired* in rats in which the prefrontal cortex is reversibly inactivated

with tetrodotoxin only before inhibitory avoidance training, and not before testing (Bermudez-Rattoni, Introini-Collison, & McGaugh, 1991). Large lesions of the amygdala that include the BLA block decreases in spontaneous unit activity in the prefrontal cortex as well as the freezing induced by presentation of a tone previously paired with footshock (Garcia, Voulmba, Baudry, & Thompson, 1999). These results are consistent with other evidence suggesting that affective stimulation attenuates medial prefrontal cortex inputs to the BLA and potentiates sensory inputs from sensory cortex, thus enhancing amygdala responsiveness to affective stimulation (Rosenkranz & Grace, 1999). There is also evidence that the amygdala and medial prefrontal cortex interact in modulating memory in inhibitory avoidance and are differentially involved at different posttraining stages of memory storage (Liang, in press; Izquierdo et al., 1997).

The amygdala also appears to influence memory processing in the insular cortex. It is well established that the insular cortex is important for the acquisition and retention of conditioned taste aversion (Braun, Slick, & Lorden, 1972; Bermudez-Rattoni, Sanchez, & Prado-Alcala, 1989; Bermudez-Rattoni & McGaugh, 1991). There is also evidence that the insular cortex is important for inhibitory avoidance learning and water-maze spatial learning. Reversible inactivation of the insular cortex either before or immediately after training in these tasks impairs retention (Bermudez-Rattoni et al., 1991; Lamprecht & Dudai, 2000). As the BLA projects directly to the insular cortex, the BLA may influence memory consolidation by modulating activ-

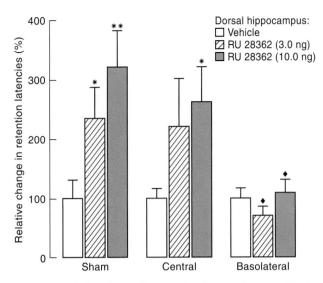

Figure 6.8 Relative change in retention latency (mean ± SEM) for the 48-hour inhibitory avoidance test of rats with sham or neurotoxic lesions of the central or basolateral amygdala nuclei given vehicle or the specific glucocorticoid receptor agonist RU 28362 (3.0 or 10.0 ng) in the dorsal hippocampus immediately after inhibitory avoidance training. * $p < 0.05$; ** $p < 0.01$ compared with the corresponding vehicle group; ◆ $p < 0.05$ compared with the corresponding sham-lesion group ($n$ = 6–15 per group). From Roozendaal & McGaugh (1997b), with permission from Blackwell Science.

ity in this brain region as well. The findings indicating that BLA stimulation induces NMDA-dependent LTP in the insular cortex support this hypothesis (Escobar, Chao, & Bermudez-Rattoni, 1998; Jones, French, Bliss, & Rosenblum, 1999). It is of interest that the muscarinic cholinergic antagonist atropine also attenuated BLA-induced LTP in the insular cortex. These findings are consistent with evidence that release cholinergic activation of the cortex is critical for aversively based learning (Metherate & Weinberger, 1990; Miranda & Bermudez-Rattoni, 1999).

The findings of animal studies summarized above leave little doubt that the amygdala is involved in regulating memory consolidation. Although most animal studies have used aversive training experiences, the involvement of the amygdala is clearly not restricted to aversively motivated learning. The findings also indicate that the BLA is the region of the amygdala that is critical for mediating the effects of stress-activated neuromodulatory influences on memory storage and that NE release within the amygdala is critical (see Figure 6.9). Finally, the evidence strongly suggests that the amygdala modulates memory storage processes in other brain regions. Future exploration of amygdala projections to other brain regions, including other cortical regions, will in all likelihood reveal that the amygdala influences memory processes in many brain regions. The evidence from animal studies indicat-

ing that the amygdala modulates the storage of different forms of memory would seem to require widespread modulation of brain processes involved in memory consolidation.

## Emotional Arousal and Human Memory

Findings comparable to those from studies using animals are emerging from studies of human subjects. Recent studies clearly support the view that the effect of emotional arousal on long-term explicit/declarative memory in human subjects involves β-adrenoceptor activation as well as activation of the amygdala complex (Cahill, 2000; Cahill & McGaugh, 1998).

### Role of the Adrenergic System

Few studies to date have examined the influence of direct catecholaminergic stimulation on human memory. Two studies (Christianson & Mjorndal, 1985; Christianson, Nilsson, Mjorndal, Perris, & Jellden, 1986) failed to find enhanced retention with injections of epinephrine administered before learning. However, both studies examined relatively short-term (12-minute) recall. The hypothesis that epinephrine modulates the consolidation of long-term memory (a process that likely lasts for at least several hours; McGaugh, 1966, 2000) makes no prediction about the effects of epinephrine on short-term retention. Thus, the negative findings of Christianson et al. are completely consistent with the hypothesis that epinephrine released by an emotional event modulates *long-term* memory for the event.

Two studies reported that postlearning catecholaminergic stimulation enhanced long-term memory consolidation in humans. In the first (Soetens, Caesar, D'Hooge, & Hueting, 1995), subjects learned lists of words and then received immediately an intramuscular injection of either amphetamine or vehicle. The results revealed a significant enhancing effect of the amphetamine injections on long-term (24-hour) memory for the words. It is not known whether the effects found in this study were due to influences on dopamine or adrenergic catecholamines. The second study (Cahill & Alkire, in preparation, 2001) provided evidence of epinephrine effects on memory. Healthy volunteers received an intravenous infusion of epinephrine or placebo immediately after they viewed a series of slides. Memory of the slides was assessed in a surprise free-recall test one week later. Compared to subjects given the placebo, subjects given epinephrine recalled significantly more of the initial slides in the series. A follow-up study demonstrated that the arousal response (measured by electrodermal skin responses) to the initial slides was significantly greater than it was to any of the later slides. These findings are important in two respects. First, they

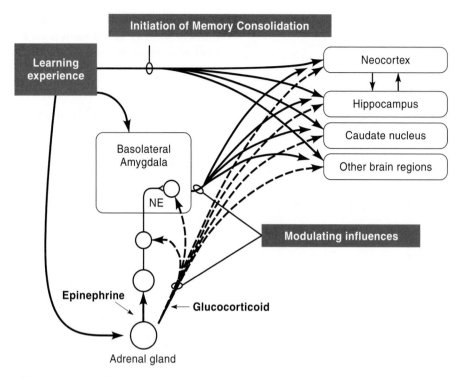

Figure 6.9 Neurobiological systems regulating memory consolidation. Experiences activate time-dependent cellular storage processes in various brain regions involved in the forms of memory represented. The experiences also initiate the release of the stress hormones from the adrenal medulla and adrenal cortex and activate the release of norepinephrine in the basolateral amygdala, an effect critical for enabling modulation of consolidation. The amygdala modulates memory consolidation by influencing neuroplasticity in other brain regions. From McGaugh (2000), copyright 2000, American Association for the Advancement of Science.

represent the first demonstration that epinephrine enhances human memory consolidation and thus provide important confirming support for the hypothesis that adrenergic activation modulates memory consolidation for emotional events. Second, the findings suggest that the effects of postlearning catecholamine activation on long-term memory depend upon the degree of arousal associated with the initial encoding of the material.

Several studies employing adrenergic blockade, rather than stimulation, in humans clearly implicate β-adrenergic activation in long-term memory for emotionally arousing events. In the first study examining this effect (Cahill, Prins, Weber, & McGaugh, 1994), subjects received either the β-adrenoceptor antagonist propranolol or a placebo one hour prior to viewing either an emotionally arousing story or a very similar, but more emotionally neutral story. Memory for the story was tested one week later (see Figure 6.10). Propranolol treatment selectively impaired the enhanced memory associated with the emotional story. The lack of effect of propranolol on memory for the neutral story indicates that the impairing effect on memory for the emotional story cannot be attributed to

nonspecific attentional or sedative effects of the drug. Also, as propranolol did not affect subjects' self-assessed emotional reaction to viewing either story, the memory impairing effects are not due to a lack of emotional responsiveness produced by propranolol. The findings therefore provide strong support for the view, derived from animal research, that catecholamine activation is preferentially involved with modulation of memory by emotional arousal. A second study of memory in elderly human subjects (Nielson & Jensen, 1994) demonstrated a similar impairing effect of chronic, as opposed to acute, propranolol treatment on enhanced memory associated with arousal.

A third study, using the general procedures used in the Cahill et al. (1994) study investigated whether the impairing effect of propranolol on memory for emotionally arousing material was due to actions at central or peripheral receptors (van Stegeren, Everaerd, Cahill, McGaugh, & Goeren, 1998). Those investigators confirmed the finding that propranolol selectively impaired memory for the emotionally arousing story. In contrast, they found that nadolol (a beta-adrenergic blocker like propranolol, but

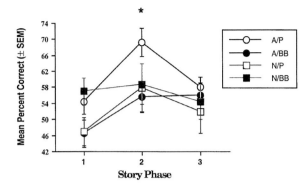

Figure 6.10 Effect of administration of the β-adrenergic blocking drug propranolol on long-term (one week) retention of an emotionally arousing story and of a closely matched, but relatively emotionally neutral, story. Propranolol significantly impaired memory only for phase 2 of the emotional story, the phase in which the emotionally arousing story elements were introduced. Propranolol had no significant effect on memory for the neutral story. From Cahill et al. (1994), by permission from *Nature,* copyright 1994, Macmillan Magazines Ltd.

which does not readily cross the blood-brain barrier) did not affect memory of either the emotionally arousing or neutral stories. These findings suggest that the impairing effect of propranolol on memory resulted from central, rather than peripheral, actions. However, the lack of effect of nadolol on memory leaves open the possibility, suggested by animal research, that an influence of peripheral adrenergic blockade on memory in humans may be found in more highly emotionally arousing learning situations.

The findings of another recent study (O'Carroll, Drysdale, Cahill, Shajahan, & Ebmeier, 1999) provide additional evidence for adrenergic modulation of memory in humans. Subjects in this study received either a placebo, metoprolol (a β$_1$ adrenoceptor antagonist), or yohimbine (which stimulates noradrenergic activity via blockade of the α$_2$-adrenergic autoreceptor) before viewing an emotionally arousing story. Retention of the story was tested one week later. Compared to the performance of placebo control subjects, the retention of subjects receiving metoprolol was significantly impaired, whereas the retention of the yohimbine treated subjects significantly enhanced. These findings therefore provide the first suggestion that selective β$_1$ receptor activation in humans influences memory for emotionally arousing material. More generally, they provide additional evidence that adrenergic stimulation can enhance memory for emotional material.

As discussed earlier, animal research implicates vagal nerve function in emotionally influenced memory (Clark et al., 1998). This hypothesis was recently confirmed in a study examining memory in subjects given vagal nerve stimulation immediately after acquisition of verbal material (Clark, Naritoku, Smith, Browning, & Jensen, 1999). Vagal nerve stimulation dose-dependently increased word

recognition as compared to word recognition in the same subjects when stimulation was not given. These findings thus converge with animal research in suggesting that epinephrine and other peripherally acting hormones influence memory consolidation via activation of vagal afferents to the brain.

## Role of the Amygdala in Emotionally Influenced Long-Term Declarative Memory

### Effects of Amygdala Damage

The animal research reviewed in detail in this chapter, some of which dates back over 40 years, clearly implicates amygdala function in the consolidation of long-term memory for emotionally arousing events. Despite this evidence, for many years it was generally considered that the amygdala had no role in explicit (or "declarative") memory formation (e.g., Scoville & Milner, 1957; Squire & Zola-Morgan, 1991; Bechara et al., 1995). Recent evidence from studies of human patients with amygdala damage, as well as studies of brain imaging in healthy individuals, has, however, provided strong confirming evidence that, in humans as well as animals, the amygdala is critical for enhanced long-term declarative memory associated with emotional arousal.

Although patients with selective amygdala damage are exceedingly rare, several studies have examined memory in a few patients. The findings provide clear evidence that long-term memory for emotionally arousing material is selectively impaired in these patients, despite the fact that they may experience normal emotional reactions to the material (Babinsky et al., 1993; Cahill, Babinsky, Markowitsch, & McGaugh, 1995; Adolphs, Cahill, Schul, & Babinsky, 1997) For example, in a study using the same paradigm previously shown to be sensitive to β-adrenergic blockade, a patient with selective amygdala damage failed to show the enhanced memory normally associated with emotional arousal (Cahill et al., 1995). This finding was subsequently confirmed in another patient with nearly selective amygdala damage (Adolphs et al., 1997). Additionally, amnesic subjects with intact amygdalae show relatively intact enhancement of memory for emotional material despite their overall impaired memory performance (Hamann, Cahill, McGaugh, & Squire, 1997).

Several studies reported that despite the fact that memory for the emotional material was impaired in the patients with amygdala damage, the reactions of patients with amygdala damage to emotionally provocative stimuli (both cognitive and physiological) did not differ significantly from those of control subjects (Cahill et al., 1995; Adolphs et al., 1997; Hamann, Cahill, & Squire, 1997). One subject spontaneously described to the experimenters her strong negative emotional reaction to a particular aver-

**(a)**

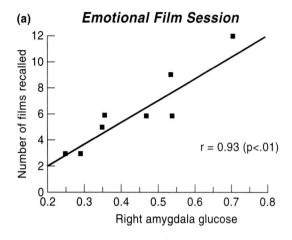

**(b)**

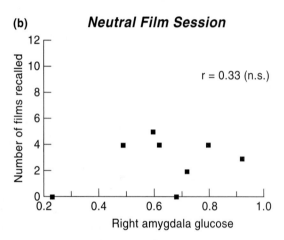

Figure 6.11 Positron emission tomography (PET) study of amygdala participation in memory storage in healthy humans. (A) Right amygdala activity (glucose levels) while subjects viewed a series of emotionally arousing films correlated highly with long-term (3 week) film recall. (B) Relationship between amygdala activity while viewing a series of relatively emotionally neutral films and later recall of the films. Right amygdala activity did not correlate significantly with recall of the relatively emotionally neutral films. From Cahill et al. (1996), copyright 1996, National Academy of Sciences, U.S.A.

sive stimulus, yet failed to demonstrate enhanced recall of that stimulus (Adolphs et al., 1997). Other evidence indicates that electrodermal responses to emotionally stressful events are intact in humans with amygdala damage (Bechara et al., 1995). These findings support the suggestion that amygdala functioning in humans "may be more important for the translation of an emotional reaction into heightened recall than it is for the generation of an emotional reaction *per se*" (Cahill et al., 1996, p. 8019). This important possibility warrants careful future study.

The amygdala exhibits severe degeneration in Alzheimer's disease (AD; Vereecken, 1993). A recent investigation of memory in AD patients provides further support for the "memory modulation" view of amygdala function

(Mori et al., 1999). This study investigated the memory of AD patients who had experienced a highly emotional event—the Kobe earthquake. They found that amygdala volume (measured with MRI) correlated significantly with retention of the personal events experienced during the earthquake, but not with retention of semantic knowledge of the earthquake (such as its size on the Richter scale). These findings suggest that the modulatory role for the amygdala in emotionally influenced long-term memory is a very robust phenomenon.

## Amygdala Activation and Enhanced Long-Term Memory

Complementing the research involving amygdala-damaged subjects, the findings of several brain imaging studies provide additional evidence supporting the view that amygdala modulates long-term declarative memory for emotionally arousing events. The first of these studies (Cahill et al., 1996) investigated amygdala activity (using PET imaging) while subjects viewed a series of emotionally arousing (aversive) films. In Figure 6.11, activity of the right amygdala during the encoding of the information correlated very highly with long-term recall of the films assessed several weeks later. Amygdala activity in the same subjects induced by viewing of relatively emotionally neutral films did not correlate with recall of those films.

The Cahill et al. (1996) study measured glucose activity in the amygdala with PET. A subsequent PET study using $O^{15}$ blood flow measurement confirmed the selective role of the amygdala in memory for emotional material (Hamann, Elt, Grafton, & Kilts, 1999). Additionally, in this study amygdala activity assessed while subjects viewed emotionally arousing, *positively* valenced (i.e., pleasant) material also correlated with long-term memory. These findings thus provide strong support for the hypothesis (Cahill & McGaugh, 1990) that the degree of arousal occurring in an emotional learning situation—and not the pleasant or unpleasant nature of the emotion—is the key determinant of amygdala participation in modulating memory storage. An additional important finding of that study (Hamann et al., 1999) is that amygdala activity during encoding did not correlate with memory tested shortly after learning. These findings fit with extensive evidence indicating that the amygdala is selectively involved in modulating the consolidation of long-term memory.

Two studies using functional magnetic resonance imaging (fMRI) have provided additional evidence indicating that the amygdala participates in the storage of long-term memory storage for emotional material in humans. Canli and colleagues (1998) reported that amygdala activity in response to emotionally negative pictures correlated with long-term (2–14 month) memory of the pictures. In a second study involving an individual-trial fMRI design, activity of the amygdala induced by individual stimuli was shown to relate only to memory for emotionally arousing stimuli. Furthermore, the degree to which amygdala activity at encoding correlated with long-term memory increased as the degree of arousal associated with the stimuli increased (Canli et al., 2000).

Thus, evidence from human brain imaging studies, including studies using PET, as well as fMRI imaging, converges with neuropsychological data and with findings from animal research in supporting the view that the amygdala is involved in regulating the long-term storage of explicit memory for emotionally arousing events (McGaugh et al., 1984; Cahill & McGaugh, 1990, 1998; McGaugh, 2000). The role of the amygdala in the production of emotional responses per se in humans remains less clear (Cahill et al., 1996; Cahill & McGaugh, 1998).

## Candidate Sites of Modulation

As discussed above, extensive evidence from animal subject studies strongly suggests that the amygdala influences memory storage processes in other brain regions (McGaugh et al., 1984, 1996; McGaugh, 2000). Although this issue has not as yet been systematically investigated in human brain studies, there are some suggestions regarding potential sites of modulation. In the PET study discussed above (Cahill et al., 1996), activity of the cholinergic basal forebrain region (substantia innominata), as well as activity of the amygdala, correlated significantly with recall of emotional but not neutral films. Similarly, Morris Friston, & Dolan (1998) reported that amygdala activity co-varied with basal forebrain activity during acquisition of classical conditioning. As discussed above, findings of animal studies suggest that the amygdala may influence cortical processing via the cholinergic basal forebrain (Gutierrez, Miranda, & Bermudez-Rattoni, 1997; Kapp, Whalen, Supple, & Pascol, 1992; Weinberger et al., 1990). Our findings regarding the substantia innominata (Cahill et al., 1996) fit well with this view.

The results of many animal studies implicate the hippocampal region as a brain region modulated by the amygdala in influencing consolidation (Packard et al., 1994; Packard & Teather, 1998; Packard & Chen, 1999). In the PET study reported by Cahill et al. (1996), activity of the parahippocampal cortex correlated with memory of both neutral and emotional films, a finding confirmed in subsequent PET (Alkire, Haier, Fallon, & Cahill, 1998; Hamann et al., 1999) and fMRI (Brewer, Zhao, Desmond, Glover, & Gabrieli, 1998; Wagner et al., 1998) studies. The finding that activity of both the amygdala and hippocampal regions relates to memory for emotional events is consistent with the hypothesis that the amygdala influences hippocampal participation in memory consolidation.

Findings of a recent fMRI study of Pavlovian "trace" conditioning provides additional evidence for amygdala-hippocampal interaction in human learning (Buchel, Dolan, Armony, & Friston, 1999). Activity of both the amygdala and hippocampus was examined as subjects were trained in an experiment using a differential (CS+/CS−) trace conditioning procedure. Consistent with previous reports involving "delay" conditioning (Buchel, Morris, Dolan, & Friston, 1998; LaBar, Gatenby, Gore, LeDoux, & Phelps, 1998), the amygdala was active in response to the CS+ only early in training as the association with the US was being acquired. These findings provide further support for the view that the amygdala plays a time-limited role in learning (Cahill & McGaugh, 1998). Activity in the anterior hippocampus displayed a similar time-limited involvement in the learning. Like the findings of the imaging studies mentioned above, these findings are consistent with the view that the amygdala and hippocampus interact in the consolidation of long-term memory.

## Summary

At least since the time of William James (1890), brain scientists have recognized the importance of understanding the mechanisms by which the brain modulates memory storage. An impressive amount of evidence now makes clear that interacting peripheral and central nervous processes are critical. Endogenous stress hormones appear to interact with the basolateral amygdala during and after emotionally arousing events to modulate memory storage processes occurring in other brain regions. It is presumably these other brain areas that serve as the loci of the "scars on the cerebral tissue" (James, 1890) that provide lasting memory of emotional experiences.

### NOTE

This research was supported by a research grant from the National Institute of Mental Health, MH12526 (JLM) and MH57508 (LC). We thank Nancy Collett, Benno Roozendaal, and Almira Vazdarjanova for their suggestions and assistance.

### REFERENCES

Adolphs, R., Cahill, L., Schul, R., & Babinsky, R. (1997). Impaired declarative memory for emotional stimuli following bilateral amygdala damage in humans. *Learning and Memory, 4*, 291–300.

Alkire, M., Haier, R., Fallon, J., & Cahill, L. (1998). Hippocampal, but not amygdala, activity at encoding correlates with long-term, free recall of non-emotional information. *Proceedings of the National Academy of Sciences, USA, 95*, 14506–14510.

Amorapanth, P., LeDoux, J. E., & Nader, K. (2000). Different lateral amygdala outputs mediate reactions and actions elicited by a fear-arousing stimulus. *Nature Neuroscience, 3*, 74–79.

Armony, J. L., Quirk, G. J., & LeDoux, J. E. (1998). Differential effects of amygdala lesions on early and late plastic components of auditory cortex spike trains during fear conditioning. *Journal of Neuroscience, 18,* 2592–2601.

Babinsky, R., Calabrese, P., Durwen, H. F., Markowitsch, H. J., Brechtelsbauer, D., Heuser, L., & Gehlen, W. (1993). The possible contribution of the amygdala to memory. *Behavioral Neurology, 6,* 167–170.

Barros, D. M., Izquierdo, L. A., Sant'Anna, M. K., Quevedo, J., Medina, J. H., McGaugh, J. L., & Izquierdo, I. (1999). Stimulators of the cAMP cascade reverse amnesia induced by intra-amygdala but not intrahippocampal KN-62 administration. *Neurobiology of Learning and Memory, 71,* 94–103.

Bechara, A., Tranel, D., Damasio, H., Adolphs, R., Rockland, C., & Damasio, A. (1995). Double dissociation of conditioning and declarative knowledge relative to the amygdala and hippocampus in humans. *Science, 269,* 1115–1118.

Bermudez-Rattoni, F., Introini-Collison, I. B., & McGaugh, J. L. (1991). Reversible inactivation of the insular cortex by tetrodotoxin produce retrograde and anterograde amnesia for inhibitory avoidance and spatial learning. *Proceedings of the National Academy of Sciences, USA, 88,* 5379–5382.

Bermudez-Rattoni, F., & McGaugh, J. L. (1991). Insular cortex and amygdala lesions differentially affect acquisition on inhibitory avoidance and conditioned taste aversion. *Brain Research, 549,* 165–170.

Bermudez-Rattoni, F., Sanchez, M. A., & Prado-Alcala, R. A. (1989). Learning of external and visceral cue consequences may be subserved by different neuroanatomical substrates. In T. Archer & N. Lars-Goran (Eds.), *Aversion avoidance and anxiety* (pp. 121–138). Hillsdale, NJ: Erlbaum.

Bianchin, M., Mello e Souza, T., Medina, J. H., & Izquierdo, I. (1999). The amygdala is involved in the modulation of long-term memory, but not in working or short-term memory. *Neurobiology of Learning and Memory, 71,* 127–131.

Bohannon, N. J. (1988). Flashbulb memories for the Space Shuttle disaster: A tale of two theories. *Cognition, 29,* 179–196.

Bohus, B. (1994). Humoral modulation of memory processes: Physiological significance of brain and peripheral mechanisms. In J. Delacour (Ed.), *The memory system of the brain* (Vol. 4; pp. 337–364). River Edge, NJ: World Scientific.

Braun, J. J., Slick, T. B., & Lorden, J. F. (1972). Involvement of the gustatory neocortex in the learning of taste aversion. *Physiological Behavior, 9,* 637–641.

Breen, R. A., & McGaugh, J. L. (1961). Facilitation of maze learning with posttrial injections of picrotoxin. *Journal of Comparative and Physiological Psychology, 54,* 498–501.

Brewer J. B., Zhao Z., Desmond J. E., Glover, G. H., & Gabrieli, J. D. (1998). Making memories: Brain activity that predicts how well visual experience will be remembered. *Science, 281,* 1185–1187.

Brioni, J. D., & McGaugh, J. L. (1988). Posttraining administration of GABAergic antagonists enhance retention of aversively motivated tasks. *Psychopharmacology, 96,* 505–510.

Brioni, J. D., Nagahara, A. H., & McGaugh, J. L. (1989). Involvement of the amygdala GABAergic system in the modulation of memory storage. *Brain Research, 487,* 105–112.

Buchel, C., Dolan, R. J., Armony, J. L., & Friston, K. J. (1999). Amygdala-hippocampal involvement in human aversive trace conditioning revealed through event-related functional magnetic resonance imaging. *Journal of Neuroscience, 19,* 10869–10876.

Buchel, C., Morris, J., Dolan, R. J., & Friston, K. J. (1998). Brain systems mediating aversive conditioning: An event-related fMRI study. *Neuron, 20,* 947–957.

Cahill, L. (1996). The neurobiology of memory for emotional events. Converging evidence from infra-human and human studies. In *Function and dysfunction in the nervous system, Symposium 61* (pp. 259–264). Cold Spring Harbor, NY: Cold Spring Harbor Press.

Cahill, L. (1999). A neurobiological perspective on long-term, emotionally influenced memory. *Seminars in Clinical Neuropsychiatry, 4,* 266–273.

Cahill, L. (2000). Emotional modulation of long-term memory storage in humans: Adrenergic activation and the amygdala. In J. Aggleton (Ed.), *The amygdala: A functional analysis* (pp. 425–441). London: Oxford University Press.

Cahill, L., & Alkire, M. (2001). *Epinephrine enhancement of human memory consolidation.* Manuscript in preparation.

Cahill, L., Babinsky, R., Markowitsch, H., & J. L. McGaugh. (1995). The amygdala and emotional memory. *Nature, 377,* 295–296.

Cahill, L., Haier, R., Fallon, J., Alkire, M., Tang, C., Keator, D., Wu, J., & McGaugh, J. L. (1996). Amygdala activity at encoding correlated with long-term, free recall of emotional information. *Proceedings of the National Academy of Sciences, USA, 93,* 8016–8021.

Cahill, L., & McGaugh, J. L. (1990). Amygdaloid complex lesions differentially affect retention of tasks using appetitive and aversive reinforcement. *Behavioral Neuroscience, 104,* 532–543.

Cahill, L., & McGaugh, J. L. (1993) The functional anatomy of amygdala efferent pathways. *Society for Neuroscience Abstracts, 19,* 226.

Cahill, L., & McGaugh J. L. (1998). Mechanisms of emotional arousal and lasting declarative memory. *Trends in Neuroscience, 21,* 294–299.

Cahill, L., Pham, C., & Setlow, B. (2000). Impaired memory consolidation in rats produced with β-adrenergic blockade. *Neurobiology of Learning and Memory.*

Cahill, L., Prins, B., Weber, M., & McGaugh, J. L. (1994). β-adrenergic activation and memory for emotional events. *Nature, 371,* 702–704.

Cahill, L., Vazdarjanova, A., & Setlow, B. (2000). The basolateral amygdala complex is not necessary for rapid acquisition of Pavlovian "fear conditioning." *European Journal of Neuroscience, 12,* 3044–3050.

Cahill, L., Weinberger, N. M., Roozendaal, B., & McGaugh, J. L. (1999). Is the amygdala a locus of "conditioned fear"? Some questions and caveats. *Neuron, 23,* 227–228.

Canli, T., Zhao, Z., Brewer, J., Gabrieli, J. D. E., & Cahill, L. (2000). Event-related activation in the human amygdala associates with later memory for individual emotional experience. *Journal of Neuroscience, 20,* RC99.

Canli, T., Desmond, J. E., Zhao, Z., Glover, G., & Gabrieli, J. D. E. (1998a). Hemispheric asymmetry for emotional stimuli detected with fMRI. *Neuroreport, 9,* 3233–3239.

Canli, T., Zhao, Z., Desmond, J., Glover, G., & Gabrieli, J. D. E. (1998b). Amygdala activation at encoding correlates with long-term recognition memory for emotional pictures: An fMRI study. *Society for Neuroscience Abstracts, 24,* 935.

Castellano, C., & McGaugh, J. L. (1990). Effects of post-training bicuculline and muscimol on retention: Lack of state dependency. *Behavioral and Neural Biology, 54,* 156–164.

Christianson, S.-A. (1992.). *Handbook of emotion and memory: Current research and theory.* Hillsdale, NJ: Lawrence Erlbaum.

Christianson, S.-A., & Mjorndal, T. (1985) Adrenalin, emotional arousal and memory. *Scandinavian Journal of Psychology, 26,* 237–248.

Christianson, S.-A., Nilsson, L.-G., Mjorndal, T., Perris, C., & Tjellden, G. (1986) Psychological versus physiological determinants of emotional arousal and its relationship to laboratory induced amnesia. *Scandinavian Journal of Psychology, 27,* 300–310.

Clark, K. B., Krahl, S. E, Smith, D. C, & Jensen, R. A. (1995). Post-training unilateral vagal stimulation enhances retention performance in the rat. *Neurobiology of Learning and Memory, 63,* 213–216.

Clark, K. B., Naritoku, D. K., Smith, D. C., Browning, R. A., & Jensen, R. A. (1999). Enhanced recognition memory following vagus nerve stimulation in human subjects. *Nature Neuroscience, 2,* 94–98.

Clark, K. B., Smith, D. C., Hassert, D. L., Browning R. A., Naritoku, D. K., & Jensen, R. A. (1998). Posttraining electrical stimulation of vagal efferent with concomitant vagal efferent inactivation enhances memory storage processes in the rat. *Neurobiology of Learning and Memory, 70,* 364–373.

Clayton, E. C., & Williams, C. L. (2000). Posttraining inactivation of excitatory afferent input to the locus coeruleus impairs retention in an inhibitory avoidance learning task. *Neurobiology of Learning and Memory, 73,* 127–140.

Conway, M. A., Anderson, S. J., Larsen, S. F., Donnelly, C. M., McDaniel, M. A., McClelland, A. G. R., Rawles, R. E., & Logie, R. H. (1994). *Memory and Cognition, 22,* 326–343.

Cottrell, G. A., & Nakajima, S. (1977). Effects of corticosteroids in the hippocampus on passive avoidance behavior in the rat. *Pharmacology, Biochemistry and Behavior, 7,* 277–280.

Da Cunha, C., Roozendaal, B., Vazdarjanova, A., & McGaugh, J. L. (1999). Microinfusions of flumazenil into the basolateral but not central nucleus of the amygdala enhance memory consolidation in rats. *Neurobiology of Learning and Memory, 72,* 107.

Dallaporta, M., Himmi, T., Perrin, J., Orsini, J. C. (1999). Solitary tract nucleus sensitivity to moderate changes in glucose level. *Neuroreport, 10,* 2657–2660.

Davidson, R. J., & Irwin, W. (1999). The functional neuroanatomy of emotion and affective style. *Trends in Cognitive Sciences, 3,* 11–21.

Davis, M. (1992). The role of the amygdala in conditioned fear. In J. Aggleton (Ed.), *The amgydala* (pp. 255–306). New York: Wiley-Liss.

De Kloet, E. R. (1991). Brain corticosteroid receptor balance and homeostatic control. *Frontiers of Neuroendocrinology, 12,* 95–164.

De Souza-Silva, M. A., & Tomaz, C. (1995). Amnesia after diazepam infusion into basolateral but not central amygdala of Rattus norvegicus. *Neuropsychobiology, 32,* 31–36.

Dringenberg, H., & Vanderwolf, C. (1996). Cholinergic activation of the electrocorticogram: An amygdaloid activating system. *Experimental Brain Research, 108,* 285–296.

Dykes, R. W. (1997). Mechanisms controlling neuronal plasticity in somatosensory cortex. *Canadian Journal of Physiology and Pharmacology, 75,* 535–545.

Escobar, M. L., Chao, V., & Bermudez-Rattoni, F. (1998). In vivo long-term potentiation in the insular cortex: NMDA receptor dependence. *Brain Research, 779,* 314–319.

Fanselow, M. S. (1980). Conditional and unconditional components of post-shock freezing. *Pavlovian Journal of Biological Science, 15,* 177–182.

Ferry, B., & McGaugh, J. L. (1999). Clenbuterol administration into the basolateral amygdala post-training enhances retention in an inhibitory avoidance task. *Neurobiology of Learning and Memory, 72,* 8–12.

Ferry, B., Roozendaal, B., & McGaugh, J. L. (1999a). Involvement of alpha$_1$-adrenergic receptors in the basolateral amygdala in modulation of memory storage. *European Journal of Pharmacology, 372,* 9–16.

Ferry, B., Roozendaal, B., & McGaugh, J. L. (1999b). Basolateral amygdala noradrenergic influences on memory storage are mediated by an interaction between beta- and alpha$_1$-receptors. *Journal of Neuroscience, 19,* 5119–5123.

Gallagher, M., Kapp, B. S., Pascoe, J. P., & Rapp, P. R. (1981). A neuropharmacology of amygdaloid systems which contribute to learning and memory. In Y. Ben-Ari (Ed.), *The amygdaloid complex* (pp. 343–354). Amsterdam: Elsevier/N. Holland.

Galvez, R., Mesches, M., & McGaugh, J. L. (1996). Norepinephrine release in the amygdala in response to footshock stimulation. *Neurobiology of Learning and Memory, 66,* 253–257.

Garcia, R., Voulmba, R.-M., Baudry, M., & Thompson, R. F. (1999). The amygdala modulates prefrontal cortex activity relative to conditioned fear. *Nature, 402,* 294–296.

Gerard, R. W. (1961). The fixation of experience. In A. Fessard, R. W. Gerard, and J. Konorski (Consulting Eds.), *Brain mechanisms and learning* (pp. 21–35). Springfield, IL: Charles C. Thomas.

Goddard, G. V. (1964). Amygdaloid stimulation and learning in the rat. *Journal of Comparative and Physiological Psychology, 58,* 23–30.

Gold, P. E. (1988). Plasma glucose regulation of memory storage processes. In C. D. Woody, D. L. Alkon, & J. L. McGaugh (Eds.), *Cellular mechanisms of conditioning and behavioral plasticity* (pp. 329–341). New York: Plenum.

Gold, P. E., Hankins, L., Edwards, R. M., Chester, J., & McGaugh, J. L. (1975). Memory interference and facilitation with posttrial amygdala stimulation: Effect on memory varies with footshock level. *Brain Research, 86,* 509–513.

Gold, P. E., & McGaugh, J. L. (1975). A single-trace, two process view of memory storage processes. In J. Deutsch & D. Deutsch (Eds.), *Short-term memory* (pp. 355–378). New York: Academic Press.

Gold, P. E., & van Buskirk, R. (1975). Facilitation of time-dependent memory processes with posttrial epinephrine injections. *Behavioral Biology, 13,* 145–153.

Gold, P. E., Zornetzer, S. F., & McGaugh, J. L. (1974). Electrical stimulation of the brain: Effects on memory storage. In G. Newton & A. Riesen (Eds.), *Advances in psychobiology* (Vol. 2; pp. 193–224). New York: Wiley Interscience.

Gutierrez, H., Miranda, M. I., & Bermudez-Rattoni, F. (1997). Learning impairment and cholinergic deafferentation after cortical nerve growth factor deprivation. *Journal of Neuroscience, 17*, 3796–3803.

Hamann, S., Cahill, L., McGaugh, J. L., & Squire, L. (1997). Intact enhancement of declarative memory by emotional arousal in amnesia. *Learning and Memory, 4*, 301–309.

Hamann, S. B., Cahill, L., & L. R. Squire. (1997). Emotional perception and memory in amnesia. *Neuropsychology, 11*, 1–10.

Hamann, S., Elt, T., Grafton, S., & Kilts, C. (1999). Amygdala activity related to enhanced memory for pleasant and unpleasant aversive stimuli. *Nature Neuroscience, 2*, 289–293.

Harfstrand, A., Fuxe, K., Cintra, A., Agnati, L., Mzini, L., Wikstrom, A. C., Okret, S., Yu, Z. Y., Goldstein, M., Steinbusch, H., Verhofstad, A., & Gustafsson, J.-A. (1986). Glucocorticoid receptor immunoreactivity in monoaminergic neurons of rat brain. *Proceedings of the National Academy of Sciences, USA, 83*, 9779–9783.

Hatfield, T., & McGaugh, J. L. (1999). Norepinephrine infused into the basolateral amygdala posttraining enhances retention in a spatial water maze task. *Neurobiology of Learning and Memory, 71*, 232–239.

Hatfield, T., Spanis, C., & McGaugh, J. L. (1999). Response of amygdalar norepinephrine to footshock and GABAergic drugs using *in vivo* microdialysis and HPLC. *Brain Research, 835*, 340–345.

Ikegaya, Y., Saito, H., & Abe, K. (1994). Attenuated hippocampal long-term potentiation in basolateral amygdala-lesioned rats. *Brain Research, 656*, 157–164.

Ikegaya, Y., Saito, H., & Abe, K. (1995a). Requirement of basolateral amygdala neuron activity for the induction of long-term potentiation in the dentate gyrus in vivo. *Brain Research, 671*, 351–354.

Ikegaya, Y., Saito, H., & Abe, K. (1995b). High-frequency stimulation of the basolateral amygdala facilitates the induction of long-term potentiation in the dentate gyrus in vivo. *Neuroscience Research, 22*, 203–207.

Ikegaya, Y., Saito, H., & Abe, K., & Nakanishi, K. (1997). Amygdala beta-noradrenergic influence on hippocampal long-term potentiation in the dentate gyrus in vivo. *Neuroreport, 8*, 3143–3146.

Introini-Collison, I. B., Arai, Y., & McGaugh, J. L. (1989). Stria terminalis lesions attenuate the effects of posttraining oxotremorine and atropine on retention. *Psychobiology, 17*, 397–401.

Introini-Collison, I. B., Dalmaz, C., & McGaugh, J. L. (1996). Amygdala β-noradrenergic influences on memory storage involve cholinergic activation. *Neurobiology of Learning and Memory, 65*, 57–64.

Introini-Collison, I. B., Miyazaki, B., & McGaugh, J. L. (1991). Involvement of the amygdala in the memory-enhancing effects of clenbuterol. *Psychopharmacology, 104*, 541–544.

Introini-Collison, I. B., Nagahara, A. H., & McGaugh, J. L. (1989). Memory-enhancement with intra-amygdala posttraining naloxone is blocked by concurrent administration of propranolol. *Brain Research, 476*, 94–101.

Izquierdo, I., DaCunha, C., Huang, C. H., Walz, R., Wolfman, C., & Medina, J. H. (1990). Post-training down regulation of memory consolidation by a GABA-A mechanism in the amygdala modulated by endogenous benzodiazepines. *Behavioral and Neural Biology, 54*, 105–109.

Izquierdo, I., DaCunha, C., & Medina, J. (1990). Endogenous benzodiazepine modulation of memory processes. *Neuroscience and Biobehavioral Review, 14*, 419–424.

Izquierdo, I., DaCunha, C., Rosat, R., Jerusalinsky, D., Ferreira, M. B. C., & Medina, J. H. (1992). Neurotransmitter receptors involved in memory processing by the amygdala, medial septum and hippocampus of rats. *Behavioral and Neural Biology, 58*, 16–25.

Izquierdo, I., & Diaz, R. D. (1983). Effect of ACTH, epinephrine, β-endorphin, naloxone, and of the combination of naloxone or β-endorphin with ACTH or epinephrine on memory consolidation. *Psychoneuroendocrinology, 8*, 81–87.

Izquierdo, I., & Medina, J. H. (1993). Neurotransmitter systems involved in memory consolidation: The role of GABA-A receptors. In I. Izquierdo (Ed.), *Naturally occurring benzodiazepines: Structure, distribution and function* (pp. 65–80). Chichester: Ellis Horwood.

Izquierdo, I., & Medina, J. H. (1997). Memory formation: The sequence of biochemical events in the hippocampus and its connection to activity in other brain structures. *Neurobiology of Learning and Memory, 68*, 285–316.

Izquierdo, I., Quillfeldt, J. A., Zanatta, M. S., Quevedo, J., Schaeffer, E., Schmitz, P. K., & Medina, J. H. (1997). Sequential role of hippocampus and amygdala, entorhinal cortex and parietal cortex in formation and retrieval of memory for inhibitory avoidance in rats. *European Journal of Neuroscience, 9*, 786–793.

James, W. (1890). *Principles of psychology*. New York: Henry Holt.

Jensen, R. A. (2001). Neural pathways mediating modulation of learning and memory by peripheral factors. In P. E. Gold & W. T. Greenough (Eds.), *Memory consolidation: Essays in honor of James L. McGaugh* (pp. 129–140). Washington, DC: American Psychological Association.

Jerusalinsky, D., Quillfeldt, J. A., Walz, R., Da Silva, R. C., Bueno e Silva, M., Bianchin, M., Zanatta, M. S., Ruschel, A. C., Schmitz, P. K., Paczko, N., Medina, J. H., & Izquierdo, I. (1994). Effect of the infusion of the GABA-A receptor agonist, muscimol, on the role of the entorhinal cortex, amygdala and hippocampus in memory processes. *Behavioral and Neural Biology, 61*, 132–138.

Jones, M. W., French, P. J., Bliss, T. V. P., & Rosenblum, K. (1999). Molecular mechanisms of long-term potentiation in the insular cortex in vivo. *Journal of Neuroscience, 19*, 74–79.

Kaada, B. R. (1972). Stimulation and regional ablation of the amygdaloid complex with reference to functional representations. In B. Eleftheriou (Ed.), *The neurobiology of the amygdala* (pp. 205–282). New York: Plenum.

Kapp, B. S., Whalen, P. J., Supple, W. F., & Pascoe, J. P. (1992). Amygdaloid contributions to conditioned arousal and sensory information processing. In J. P. Aggleton (Ed.), *The amygdala neurobiological aspects of emotion, memory, and mental dysfunction* (pp. 229–254). New York: Wiley-Liss.

Kesner, R. P., & Doty, R. W. (1968). Amnesia produced in cats by local seizure activity initiated from the amygdala. *Experimental Neurology, 21*, 58–68.

Kesner, R. P., & Wilburn, M. (1974). A review of electrical stimulation of the brain in the context of learning and retention. *Behavioral Biology, 10*, 259–293.

Kety, S. (1972). Brain catecholamines, affective states and memory. In J. L. McGaugh (Ed.), *The chemistry of mood, motivation and memory* (pp. 65–80). New York: Plenum.

Kim, M., & Davis, M. (1993). Electrolytic lesions of the amygdala block acquisition and expression of fear-potentiated startle even with extensive training but do not prevent reacquisition. *Behavioral Neuroscience, 7*, 580–595.

LaBar, K. S., Gatenby, J. C., Gore, J. C., LeDoux, J. E., & Phelps, E. A. (1998). Human amygdala activation during conditioned fear acquisition and extinction: A mixed trial fMRI study. *Neuron, 20*, 937–945.

Lamprecht, R., & Dudai, Y. (2000). The amygdala in conditioned taste aversions: It's there, but where. In J. P. Aggleton (Ed.), *The amygdala: A functional analysis* (pp. 331–352). Oxford: Oxford University Press.

Langer, S. Z. (1974). Presynaptic regulation of catecholamine release. *Biochemical Pharmacology, 23*, 1793–1800.

Leblanc, G. G., & Ciaranello, R. D. (1984). α-Noradrenergic potentiation of neurotransmitter-stimulated cAMP production in rat striatal slices. *Brain Research, 293*, 57–65.

LeDoux, J. E. (1995). Emotion: Clues from the brain. *Annual Review of Psychology, 46*, 209–235.

LeDoux, J. E. (1998) Fear and the brain: Where have we been, and where are we going. *Biological Psychiatry, 44*, 1229–1238.

Lehmann, H., Treit, D., & Parent, M. B. (2000). Amygdala lesions do not impair shock-probe avoidance retention performance. *Behavioral Neuroscience, 114*, 107–116.

Liang, K. C. (1998). Pretraining infusion of DSP-4 into the amygdala impaired retention in the inhibitory avoidance task: Involvement of norepinephrine but not serotonin in memory facilitation. *Chinese Journal of Physiology, 41*, 223–233.

Liang, K. C. (2001). Epinephrine modulation of memory: Amygdala activation and regulation of long-term storage. In P. E. Gold & W. T. Greenough (Eds.), *Memory consolidation: Essays in honor of James L. McGaugh* (pp. 165–184). Washington, DC: American Psychological Association.

Liang, K. C., & Chiang, T.-C. (1994). Locus coeruleus infusion of clonidine impaired retention and attenuated memory enhancing effects of epinephrine. *Society for Neuroscience Abstracts, 20*, 153.

Liang, K. C., Chen, L., & Huang, T.-E. (1995). The role of amygdala norepinephrine in memory formation, involvement in the memory enhancing effect of peripheral epinephrine. *Chinese Journal of Physiology, 38*, 81–91.

Liang, K. C., Juler, R., & McGaugh, J. L. (1986). Modulating effects of posttraining epinephrine on memory: Involvement of the amygdala noradrenergic system. *Brain Research, 368*, 125–133.

Liang, K. C., & McGaugh, J. L. (1983). Lesions of the stria terminalis attenuate the enhancing effect of posttraining epinephrine on retention of an inhibitory avoidance response. *Behavioural Brain Research, 9*, 49–58.

Liang, K. C., & McGaugh, J. L., & Yao, H. (1990). Involvement of amygdala pathways in the influence of post-training amygdala norepinephrine and peripheral epinephrine on memory storage. *Brain Research, 508*, 225–233.

Livingston, R. B. (1967). Reinforcement: A study program. In G. C. Quarton, T. Melnechuk, & F. O. Schmitt (Eds.), *The neuroscience* (pp. 568–576). New York: Rockefeller University Press.

Lupien, S. J., & McEwen, B. S. (1997). The acute effects of corticosteroids on cognition: Integration of animal and human model studies. *Brain Research Review, 24*, 1–27.

Maren, S. (1998). Overtraining does not mitigate contextual fear conditioning deficits produced by neurotoxic lesions of the basolateral amygdala. *Journal of Neuroscience, 18*, 3088–3097.

Maren, S. (1999). Neurotoxic basolateral amygdala lesions impair learning and memory but not the performance of conditional fear in rats. *Journal of Neuroscience, 19*, 8696–8703.

Maren, S., Aharonov, G., & Fanselow, M. S. (1996). Retrograde abolition of conditional fear after excitotoxic lesions in the basolateral amygdala of rats: Absence of a temporal gradient. *Behavioral Neuroscience, 110*, 718–726.

McCarty, R., & Gold, P. E. (1981). Plasma catecholamines: Effects of footshock level and hormonal modulators of memory storage. *Hormones and Behavior, 15*, 168–182.

McDonald, R. J., & White, N. M. (1993). A triple dissociation of memory systems: Hippocampus, amygdala and dorsal striatum. *Behavioral Neuroscience, 107*, 3–22.

McEwen, B. S., & Sapolsky, R. M. (1995). Stress and cognitive function. *Current Opinion in Neurobiology, 5*, 205–216.

McGaugh, J. L. (1966). Time-dependent processes in memory storage. *Science, 153*, 1351–1358.

McGaugh, J. L. (1973). Drug facilitation of learning and memory. *Annual Review of Pharmacology, 13*, 229–241.

McGaugh, J. L. (1983). Preserving the presence of the past: Hormonal influences on memory storage. *American Psychologist, 38*, 161–174.

McGaugh, J. L. (1989a). Dissociating learning and performance: Drug and hormone enhancement of memory storage. *Brain Research Bulletin, 23*, 339–345.

McGaugh, J. L. (1989b). Involvement of hormonal and neuromodulatory systems in the regulation of memory storage. *Annual Review of Neuroscience, 12*, 255–287.

McGaugh, J. L. (1989c). Modulation of memory storage processes. In P. R. Solomon, G. R. Goethals, C. M. Kelley, & B. R. Stephens (Eds.), *Memory: Interdisciplinary approaches* (pp. 33–64). New York: Springer-Verlag.

McGaugh, J. L. (1992) Affect, neuromodulatory systems and memory storage. In S.-A. Christianson (Ed.), *Handbook of emotion and memory: Current research and theory* (pp. 245–268). Hillsdale, NJ: Erlbaum.

McGaugh, J. L. (2000). Memory: A century of consolidation. *Science, 287*, 248–251.

McGaugh, J. L., Cahill, L., & Roozendaal, B. (1996). Involvement of the amygdala in memory storage: Interaction with other brain systems. *Proceedings of the National Academy of Sciences, USA, 93*, 13508–13514.

McGaugh, J. L., Ferry, B., Vazdarjanova, A., & Roozendaal, B. (2000). Amygdala: Role in modulation of memory storage. In J. P. Aggleton (Ed.), *The amygdala: A functional analysis* (pp. 391–423). Oxford: Oxford University Press.

McGaugh, J. L., & Gold, P. E. (1976). Modulation of memory by electrical stimulation of the brain. In M. R. Rosenzweig & E. L. Bennett (Eds.), *Neural mechanisms of learning and memory* (pp. 549–560). Cambridge, MA: MIT Press.

McGaugh, J. L., & Gold, P. E. (1989). Hormonal modulation of memory. In R. B. Brush & S. Levine (Eds.), *Psychoendocrinology* (pp. 305–339). New York; Academic Press.

McGaugh, J. L., & Herz, M. J. (1972). *Memory consolidation*. San Francisco: Albion.

McGaugh, J. L., Introini-Collison, I., & Castellano, C. (1993). Involvement of opioid peptides in learning and memory. In A. Herz, H. Akil, & E. J. Simon (Eds.), *Handbook of experimental pharmacology, opioids, part I and II* (pp. 419–477). Heidelberg: Springer-Verlag.

McGaugh, J. L., Introini-Collison, I. B., Juler, R. G., & Izquierdo, I. (1986). Stria terminalis lesions attenuate the effects of posttraining naloxone and β-endorphin on retention. *Behavioral Neuroscience, 100*, 839–844.

McGaugh, J. L., Introini-Collison, I. B., & Nagahara, A. H. (1988). Memory-enhancing effects of posttraining naloxone: Involvement of β-noradrenergic influences in the amygdaloid complex. *Brain Research, 446*, 37–49.

McGaugh, J. L., Liang, K. C., Bennett, C., & Sternberg, D. B. (1984). Adrenergic influences on memory storage: Interaction of peripheral and central systems. In G. L. Lynch, J. L. McGaugh, & N. M. Weinberger (Eds.), *Neurobiology of learning and memory* (pp. 313–333). New York: Guilford Press.

McGaugh, J. L., Roozendaal, B., & Cahill, L. (1999). Modulation of memory storage by stress hormones and the amygdaloid complex. In Gazzaniga, M. (Ed.), *Cognitive neuroscience* (2nd ed.; pp. 1081–1098). Cambridge, MA: MIT Press.

McNay, E. C., & Gold, P. E. (1998). Memory modulation across neural systems: Intra-amygdala glucose reverses deficits caused by intraseptal morphine on a spatial task but not on an aversive task. *Journal of Neuroscience, 18*, 3853–3858.

Metherate, R., & Weinberger, N. M. (1990). Cholinergic modulation of responses to single tones produces tone-specific receptive field alterations in cat auditory cortex. *Synapse, 6*, 133–145.

Miranda, M. I., & Bermudez-Rattoni, F. (1999). Reversible inactivation of the nucleus basalis magnocellularis induces disruption of cortical acetylcholine release and acquisition, but not retrieval, of aversive memories. *Proceedings of the National Academy of Sciences, USA, 96*, 6478–6482.

Morgan, M. A., & LeDoux, J. E. (1995). Differential contribution of dorsal and ventral medial prefrontal cortex to the acquisition and extinction of conditioned fear in rats. *Behavioral Neuroscience, 109*, 681–688.

Morgan, M. A., & LeDoux, J. E. (1999). Contribution of ventrolateral prefrontal cortex to the acquisition and extinction of conditioned fear in rats. *Neurobiology of Learning and Memory, 72*, 244–251.

Mori, E., Ikeda, M., Hirono, N., Kitagaki, H., Imamura, T., & Shimomura, T. (1999). Amygdalar volume and emotional memory in Alzheimer's disease. *American Journal of Psychiatry, 156*, 216–222.

Morris, J., Friston, K., & Dolan, R. (1998). Experience-dependent modulation of tonotopic neural responses in human auditory cortex. *Proceedings of the Royal Society of London, 265*, 649–657.

Morris, R. G. M., Garrud, P., Rawlins, J. N. P., & O'Keefe, J. (1982). Place navigation impaired in rats with hippocampal lesions. *Nature, 297*, 681–683.

Moser, E., Moser, M.-B., & Andersen, P. (1993). Spatial learning impairment parallels the magnitude of dorsal hippocampal lesions, but is hardly present following ventral lesions. *Journal of Neuroscience, 13*, 3916–3925.

Neisser, U., Winograd, E., Shreiber, C., Palmer, S., & Weldon, M. (1996). Remembering the earthquake: Direct experience vs. hearing the news. *Memory, 4*, 337–357.

Nielson, K. A., & Jensen, R. (1994). Beta-adrenergic receptor antagonist antihypertensive medications impair arousal-induced modulation of working memory in elderly humans. *Behavioral and Neural Biology, 62*, 190–200.

O'Carroll, R. E., Drysdale, E., Cahill, L., Shajahan, P., & Ebmeier, K. P. (1999). Stimulation of the noradrenergic system enhances and blockade reduces memory for emotional material in man. *Psychological Medicine, 29*, 1083–1088.

O'Donnell, P., & Grace, A. A. (1995). Synaptic interactions among excitatory afferents to nucleus accumbens neurons, hippocampal gating of prefrontal cortical input. *Journal of Neuroscience, 15*, 3622–3639.

Oishi, R., Watanabe, S., Ohmori, K., Shibata, S., & Ueki, S. (1979). Effect of stimulation of locus cooeruleus on the evoked potential in the amygdala in rats. *Japanese Journal of Pharmacology, 29*, 105–111.

Oitzl, M. S., & de Kloet, E. R. (1992). Selective corticosteroid antagonist modulate specific aspects of spatial orientation learning. *Behavioral Neuroscience, 106*, 62–71.

Olton, D. S., Becker, J. T., & Handelman, G. E. (1979). Hippocampus, space, and memory. *The Behavioural Brain Scientist, 2*, 313–365.

Packard, M. G. (1999). Glutamate infused posttraining into the hippocampus or caudate-putamen differentially strengthens place and response learning. *Proceedings of the National Academy of Sciences, USA, 96*, 12881–12886.

Packard, M. G., Cahill, L., & McGaugh, J. L. (1994). Amygdala modulation of hippocampal-dependent and caudate nucleus-dependent memory processes. *Proceedings of the National Academy of Sciences, USA, 91*, 8477–8481.

Packard, M. G., & Chen, S. A. (1999) The basolateral amygdala is a cofactor in memory enhancement produced by intrahippocampal glutamate injections. *Psychobiology, 27*, 377–385.

Packard, M. G., Introini-Collison, I., & McGaugh, J. L. (1996). Stria terminalis lesions attenuate memory enhancement produced by intra-caudate nucleus injections of oxotremorine. *Neurobiology of Learning and Memory, 65*, 278–282.

Packard, M. G., & McGaugh, J. L. (1992). Double dissociation of fornix and caudate nucleus lesions on acquisition of two water maze tasks, further evidence for multiple memory systems. *Behavioral Neuroscience, 106*, 439–446.

Packard, M. G., & McGaugh, J. L. (1996). Inactivation of hippocampus or caudate nucleus with lidocaine differentially affects expression of place and response learning. *Neurobiology of Learning and Memory, 65*, 65–72.

Packard, M. G., & Teather, L. (1998). Amygdala modulation of multiple memory systems: Hippocampus and caudate-putamen. *Neurobiology of Learning and Memory, 69*, 163–203.

Packard, M. G., Williams, C., Cahill, L., & McGaugh, J. L. (1995). The anatomy of a memory modulatory system: From periphery to brain. In N. Spear, L. Spear, & M. Woodruff (Eds.), *Neurobehavioral plasticity, learning development and response to Brain Insults* (pp. 149–184). Hillsdale, NJ: Erlbaum.

Parent, M., Avila, E., & McGaugh, J. L. (1995). Footshock facilitates the expression of aversively motivated memory in rats given post-training amygdala basolateral complex lesions. *Brain Research, 676*, 235–244.

Parent, M., & McGaugh, J. L. (1994). Posttraining infusion of lidocaine into the amygdala basolateral complex impairs retention of inhibitory avoidance training. *Brain Research, 661*, 97–103.

Parent, M., Tomaz, C., & McGaugh, J. L. (1992). Increased training in an aversively motivated task attenuates the memory impairing effects of posttraining N-methyl-D-aspartic acid-induced amygdala lesions. *Behavioral Neuroscience, 106*, 791–799.

Parent, M., West, M., & McGaugh, J. L. (1994). Memory of rats with amygdala lesions induced 30 days after footshock-motivated escape training reflects degree of original training. *Behavioral Neuroscience, 6*, 1080–1087.

Perkins, J. P., & Moore, M. M. (1973). Characterization of the adrenergic receptors mediating a rise in cyclic 3',5'-adenosine monophosphate in rat cerebral cortex. *Journal of Pharmacology and Experimental Therapeutics, 185*, 371–378.

Pikkarainen, M., Ronko, S., Savander, V., Insausti, R., & Pitkanen, A. (1999). Projections from the lateral, basal, and accessory basal nuclei of the amygdala to the hippocampal formation in rat. *Journal of Comparative Neurology, 403*, 229–260.

Quirarte, G. L., Galvez, R., Roozendaal, B., & McGaugh, J. L. (1998). Norepinephrine release in the amygdala in response to footshock and opioid peptidergic drugs. *Brain Research, 808*, 134–140.

Quirarte, G. L., Roozendaal, B., & McGaugh, J. L. (1997a). Glucocorticoid enhancement of memory storage involves noradrenergic activation in the basolateral amygdala. *Proceedings of the National Academy of Sciences, USA, 94*, 14048–14053.

Quirarte, G. L., Roozendaal, B., & McGaugh, J. L. (1997b). Glucocorticoid receptor antagonist infused into the basolateral amygdala inhibits the memory enhancing effects of the noradrenergic agonist infused clenbuterol. *Society for Neuroscience Abstracts, 23*, 1314.

Quirk, G. J., Armony, J. L., & LeDoux, J. E. (1997). Fear conditioning enhances different temporal components of tone-evoked spike trains in auditory cortex and lateral amygdala. *Neuron, 19*, 613–624.

Ragozzino, M. E., & Gold, P. E. (1994). Task-dependent effects of intra-amygdala morphine injections: Attenuation by intra-amygdala glucose injections. *Journal of Neuroscience, 14*, 7478–7485.

Ricardo, J., & Koh, E. (1978). Anatomical evidence of direct projections from the nucleus of the solitary tract to the hypothalamus, amygdala, and other forebrain structures in the rat. *Brain Research, 153*, 1–26.

Roozendaal, B. (2000). Glucocorticoids and the regulation of memory consolidation. *Psychoneuroendocrinology, 25*, 213–238.

Roozendaal, B., Koolhaas, J. M., & Bohus, B. (1992). Cen-tral amygdaloid involvement in neuroendocrine correlates of conditioned stress response. *Journal of Neuroendocrinology, 4*, 483–489.

Roozendaal, B., Koolhaas, J. M., & Bohus, B. (1993). Posttraining norepinephrine infusion into the central amygdala differentially enhances later retention in Roman high-avoidance and low-avoidance rats. *Behavioral Neuroscience, 7*, 575–579.

Roozendaal, B., & McGaugh, J. L. (1996a). Amygdaloid nuclei lesions differentially affect glucocorticoid-induced memory enhancement in an inhibitory avoidance task. *Neurobiology of Learning and Memory, 65*, 1–8.

Roozendaal, B., & McGaugh, J. L. (1996b). The memory-modulatory effects of glucocorticoids depend on an intact stria terminalis. *Brain Research, 709*, 243–250.

Roozendaal, B., & McGaugh, J. L. (1997a). Glucocorticoid receptor agonist and antagonist administration into the basolateral but not central amygdala modulates memory storage. *Neurobiology of Learning and Memory, 67*, 176–179.

Roozendaal, B., & McGaugh, J. L. (1997b). Basolateral amygdala lesions block the memory-enhancing effect of glucocorticoid administration in the dorsal hippocampus of rats. *European Journal of Neuroscience, 9*, 76–83.

Roozendaal, B., & Nguyen, B. T., Power, A. E., & McGaugh, J. L. (1996). Basolateral amygdala noradrenergic influence on the memory-enhancing effect of glucocorticoid receptor activation into the hippocampus. *Proceedings, National Academy of Sciences, USA, 96*, 11642–11647.

Roozendaal, B., Portillo-Marquez, G., & McGaugh, J. L. (1996). Basolateral amygdala lesions block glucocorticoid-induced modulation of memory for spatial learning. *Behavioral Neuroscience, 110*, 1074–1083.

Roozendaal, B., Quirarte, G. L., & McGaugh, J. L. (1997). Stress-activated hormonal systems and the regulation of memory storage. In R. Yehuda & A. C. McFarlane (Eds.), *Psychobiology of posttraumatic stress disorder* (pp. 247–258). New York: *Annals of the New York Academy of Sciences*.

Roozendaal, B., Williams, C. L., & McGaugh, J. L. (1999). Glucocorticoid receptor activation of noradrenergic neurons within the rat nucleus of the solitary tract facilitates memory consolidation: Involvement of the basolateral amygdala. *European Journal of Neuroscience, 11*, 1317–1323.

Rosenkranz, J. A., & Grace, A. A. (1999). Modulation of basolateral amygdala neuronal firing and afferent drive by dopamine receptor activation in vivo. *Journal of Neuroscience, 19*, 11027–11039.

Russchen, F. T., Amaral, D. G., & Price, J. L. (1985). The afferent connections of the substantia innominata in the monkey, Macaca fascicularis. *Journal of Comparative Neurology, 242*, 1–27.

Salinas, J., Introini-Collison, I. B., Dalmaz, C., & McGaugh, J. L. (1997). Posttraining intra-amygdala infusion of oxotremorine and propranolol modulate storage of memory for reduction in reward magnitude. *Neurobiology of Learning and Memory, 68*, 51–59.

Salinas, J., & McGaugh, J. L. (1995). Muscimol induces retrograde amnesia for changes in reward magnitude. *Neurobiology of Learning and Memory, 63*, 277–285.

Salinas, J., & McGaugh, J. L. (1996). The amygdala modulates memory for changes in reward magnitude, involvement of the amygdaloid GABAergic system. *Behavioural Brain Research, 80*, 87–98.

Sandi, C., & Rose, S. P. R. (1994). Corticosterone enhances long-term memory in one-day-old chicks trained in a weak passive avoidance learning paradigm. *Brain Research, 647*, 106–112.

Schultz J., & Daly, J. W. (1973). Accumulation of cyclic adenosine 3',5'-monophosphate in cerebral cortical slices from rat and mouse: Stimulatory effect of α- and β-adrenergic agents and adenosine. *Journal of Neurochemistry, 21*, 1319–1326.

Schreurs, J., Seelig, T., & Schulman, H. (1986). β₂-Adrenergic receptors on peripheral nerves. *Journal of Neurochemistry, 46*, 294–296.

Scoville, W. B., & Milner, B. (1957). Loss of recent memory after bilateral hippocampal lesions. *Journal of Neurology, Neurosurgery, and Psychiatry, 20*, 11–21.

Setlow, B., Roozendaal, B., & McGaugh, J. L. (2000). Involvement of a basolateral amygdala complex—nucleus accumbens pathway in glucocorticoid-induced modulation of memory storage. *European Journal of Neuroscience, 12*, 367–375.

Soetens, E., Casaer, S., D'Hooge, R., & Hueting, J. E. (1995). Effect of amphetamine on long-term retention of verbal material. *Psychopharmacology, 119*, 155–62.

Squire, L., & Zola-Morgan, S. (1991). The medial temporal lobe memory system. *Science, 253*, 1380–1386.

Starke, K. (1979). Presynaptic regulation of catecholamines release in the central nervous system. In D. M. Paton (Ed.), *The release of catecholamines from adrenergic neurons* (pp. 143–183). New York: Pergamon Press.

Stratton, G. (1919). Retroactive hypermnesia and other emotional effects on memory. *Psychology Review, 26*, 474–486.

Stratton, G. M. (1928). Excitement as undifferentiated emotion. In M. Reymert (Ed.), *Feelings and emotions: The Wittenberg symposium* (pp. 215–222). Worchester, MA: Clark University Press.

Tomaz, C., Dickinson-Anson, H., & McGaugh, J. L. (1992). Basolateral amygdala lesions block diazepam-induced anterograde amnesia in an inhibitory avoidance task. *Proceedings, National Academy of Sciences, USA, 89*, 3615–3619.

Unnerstal, J. R., Kopajtic, T. A., & Kuhar, M. J. (1984). Distribution of α₂-agonist binding sites in the rat and human central nervous system: Analysis of some functional, anatomic correlates of the pharmacological effects of clonidine and related adrenergic agents. *Brain Research, 319*, 69–101.

van Stegeren, A., Everaerd, W., Cahill, L., McGaugh, J. L., & Goeren, L. (1998). Memory for emotional events: Differential effects of centrally versus peripherally acting beta-blocking agents. *Psychopharmacology, 138*, 305–310.

Vazdarjanova, A., & McGaugh, J. L. (1998). Basolateral amygdala is not a critical locus for memory of contextual fear conditioning. *Proceedings of the National Academy of Sciences, USA, 95*, 15003–15007.

Vazdarjanova, A., & McGaugh, J. L. (1999). Amygdala modulates consolidation of memory for classical fear conditioning. *Journal of Neuroscience, 19*, 6615–6622.

Vereecken, T. (1993). *The amygdaloid complex in Alzheimer's disease.* Unpublished doctoral dissertation, Catholic University of Nijmegen, Nijmegen, The Netherlands.

Wagner, A. D., Schacter, D. L., Rotte, M., Koutstaal, W., Maril, A., Dale, A. M., Rosen, B. R., & Buckner, R. L. (1998). Building memories: Remembering and forgetting of verbal experiences as predicted by brain activity. *Science, 281*, 1188–1191.

Weinberger, N. M. (1995). Retuning the brain by fear conditioning. In M. S. Gazzaniga (Ed.), *The cognitive neurosciences* (pp. 1071–1089). Cambridge, MA: MIT Press.

Weinberger, N. M. (1998a). Physiological memory in primary auditory cortex, characteristics and mechanisms. *Neurobiology of Learning and Memory, 70*, 226–251.

Weinberger, N. M. (1998b). Tuning the brain by learning and by stimulation of the nucleus basalis. *Trends in Cognitive Sciences, 2*, 271–273.

Weinberger, N. M., Ashe, J. H., Metherate, R., McKenna, T., Diamond, D., & Bakin, J. (1990). Retuning auditory cortex by learning: A preliminary model of receptive field plasticity. *Concepts in Neuroscience, 1*, 91–132.

White, N. M. (1991) Peripheral and central memory enhancing actions of glucose. In R. C. A. Frederickson, J. L. McGaugh, & D. L. Felten (Eds.), *Peripheral signaling of the brain: Role of neural-immune interactions, learning and memory* (pp. 421–442). Toronto: Hogrefe and Huber.

Wilensky, A. E., Schafe, G. E., & LeDoux, J. E. (1999) Functional inactivation of the amygdala before but not after auditory fear conditioning prevents memory dormation *Journal of Neuroscience, 19*, 1–5.

Williams, C. L. (2001). Brainstem contributions to memory formation. In P. E. Gold & W. T. Greenough (Eds.), *Memory consolidation: Essays in honor of James L. McGaugh* (pp. 141–164). Washington, DC: American Psychological Association.

Williams, C. L., & McGaugh, J. L. (1993). Reversible lesions of the nucleus of the solitary tract attenuate the memory-modulating effects of posttraining epinephrine. *Behavioral Neuroscience, 107*, 1–8.

Williams, C. L., Men, D., Clayton, E. C., & Gold, P. E. (1998). Norepinephrine release in the amygdala following systemic injection of epinephrine or escapable footshock: Contribution of the nucleus of the solitary tract. *Behavioral Neuroscience, 112*, 1414–1422.

Zilles, K., Qu, M., & Schleicher, A. (1993). Regional distribution and heterogeneity of α-adrenoceptors in the rat and human central nervous system. *Journal für Hirnforschung, 2*, 123–132.

# FUNCTIONAL NEUROIMAGING OF DEPRESSION: A ROLE FOR MEDIAL PREFRONTAL CORTEX

Rebecca Elliott and Raymond J. Dolan

Functional imaging has proved an important tool in the study of depression with studies consistently reporting abnormalities. In this chapter we consider the converging findings from a number of positron emission tomography (PET) and functional magnetic resonance imaging (fMRI) studies that critically implicate regions of the medial prefrontal cortex in depression. The medial region of prefrontal cortex is extensively interconnected with other cortical and subcortical structures. More specifically, many of the connections of this region are to structures within the classically defined limbic system, a set of structures with a fundamental role in emotional aspects of processing. The medial prefrontal cortex also projects extensively to more lateral areas of cortex involved in the control of willed action and behavior. It thus provides a plausible substrate for mediating emotional determinants of cognition and behavior that may be dysfunctional in depression.

Results from lesion studies, in both animals and humans, are consistent with this proposition. Damage to the medial portion of prefrontal cortex produces a spectrum of deficits, many of which have an emotional component. Specifically, the deficits associated with medial prefrontal damage suggest that this region performs an interpretative role in response to emotional stimuli. Thus it is involved less in the experience of emotion per se and more in the incorporation of emotional factors in decision making and behavioral response. Functional imaging of normal emotional processing, including transiently induced mood changes, would also suggest that medial prefrontal regions are involved in a number of aspects of mood and emotional processing.

In this chapter we will briefly review this literature before considering data from recent neuroimaging studies of depression supporting a theory that medial prefrontal cortex dysfunction is the fundamental cortical manifestation of clinical depression. The evidence suggests that medial prefrontal function is abnormal in the resting state and that this abnormality can be related to clinical features of the disorder. Further, cognitive activation studies have demonstrated that depressed patients fail to show normal activation of this region in response to cognitive challenges. Finally, we discuss evidence suggesting that medial prefrontal abnormality can be related to response to various treatments in depressed patients and, indeed, that this region may be important in predicting treatment outcomes.

## Medial Prefrontal Cortex: Definitions

The term medial prefrontal cortex has not always been used consistently, with some authors considering a reasonably circumscribed region corresponding to Brodmann's area (BA) 10, while others have adopted an all-inclusive use of the term. Here we adopt the more general definition, to incorporate anterior cingulate extending forward to the medial frontal polar region and ventrally to the medial orbitofrontal cortex.

Within a broadly defined area of medial prefrontal cortex, the regions of particular relevance to depression are anterior cingulate (BA 24 and 32) and medial orbitofrontal cortex (BA 10, 11, and 25). The more caudal regions of the anterior cingulate are reciprocally connected with motor and premotor cortex (Dum & Strick, 1991; Morecraft & Van Hoesen, 1992) and with dorsolateral prefrontal cortex (Pandya & Yeterian, 1996). The more ventral regions of anterior cingulate are principally interconnected with other classical limbic structures including the amygdala (Konishio & Haber, 1994; Vogt & Pandya, 1987) and also projects to brain stem regions involved in control of autonomic function (Terreberry & Neafsey, 1983; Hurley, Herbert, Moga, & Saper, 1991). These patterns of cingulate connectivity are commensurate with a mediating role between emotion and behavior. It provides an interface between limbic and subcortical regions, involved in the instinctive and autonomic responses to emotionally salient information, and prefrontal and premotor regions, involved in the generation of willed action.

The medial orbitofrontal region is also diversely connected, receiving inputs from subcortical structures, including strong projections from the amygdala and mediodorsal nucleus of the thalamus (Krettek & Price, 1977; Ray & Price, 1993). In turn, the orbitofrontal cortex projects to inferior temporal and entorhinal cortices, anterior cingulate, hypothalamus, ventral tegmental area, and caudate nucleus (Insausti, Amaral, & Cowan, 1987; Kemp & Powell, 1970; Nauta, 1964). Again, this complex pattern of interconnectivity is consistent with a role for the orbitofrontal cortex in multimodal integration of stimulus information and behavioral guidance.

## Lesions of Medial Prefrontal Cortex in Humans and Animals

Lesions of medial prefrontal regions in animals and human give rise to an array of deficits with both cognitive and emotional components, many of which have clear links with the symptomatology of clinical depression. Recent evidence suggests that medial prefrontal lesions in rats have pronounced effects on neuroendocrine and autonomic stress responses (Sullivan & Gratton, 1999), responses that are also disturbed in depressed patients (Arborelius, Owens, Plotsky, & Nemeroff, 1999). Specific lesions to anterior cingulate in monkeys lead to significant changes in emotional behavior (Stern & Passingham, 1996), including increased responsiveness to frustration.

There are relatively few reports of restricted anterior cingulate damage in humans, however, Degos, da Fonseca, Gray, and Cesaro (1993) reported single case studies, suggesting that anterior cingulate is necessary for sustained goal-orientated responses to discriminated stimuli. More recently Cohen, Kaplan, Moser, Jenkins, and Wilkinson

(1999) reported lasting deficits in intention and spontaneous behavior in patients who had undergone cingulotomy as treatment for intractable pain. Impaired goal-oriented and spontaneously generated behavior is a feature of many patients with clinical depression, reflected in their impaired performance of many neuropsychological tests of executive function (e.g., Beats, Sahakian, & Levy, 1996; Dalla Barba, Parlato, Iavarone, & Boller, 1995; Moreaud et al., 1996).

Orbitofrontal cortex lesions in humans and animals also have pronounced emotional consequences. In monkeys, orbitofrontal lesions disrupt feeding and social behavior (Baylis & Gaffan, 1991; Butter & Snyder, 1972). Changes in appetite and weight loss or gain are important somatic symptoms of depression (*DSM-IV*; APA, 1994), and social behavior is also typically impaired. In humans, orbitofrontal lesions can lead to emotional abnormalities including inappropriate euphoria, lack of affect, and social irresponsibility (Rolls, Hornak, Wade, & McGrath, 1994; Bechara, Damasio, Damasio, & Anderson, 1994; Damasio, 1994)—deficits that have parallels in some aspects of the phenomenology of depression. These deficits resulting from orbitofrontal lesions have been hypothesized to arise from an impaired ability to process reward-related information and to adapt behavior in response to changing reinforcement contingencies (Jones & Mishkin 1972; Rolls 1975, 1990, 1994, 1996). In line with this account, orbitofrontal lesions cause deficits in tasks dependent on reward-related learning such as discrimination reversal learning and extinction (Butter, 1969; Jones & Mishkin, 1972; Rolls et al. 1994).

Patients with medial orbitofrontal lesions also show impairments in real-life decision making, in spite of otherwise preserved intellectual abilities (Damasio, 1994). Bechara et al. (1994) developed a gambling task that simulates aspects of real-life decision making. The task requires subjects to deal with uncertain premises and unpredictable outcomes in order to optimize reward—important components of many real-life decisions. Normal subjects performing the task learn to prioritize long-term consequences over immediate gain. Thus, they will accept smaller immediate rewards to avoid potentially larger penalties that will compromise long-term success. Patients with ventromedial prefrontal lesions, however, are oblivious to long-term outcomes, opting instead for higher immediate gain. Interestingly, when questioned, the patients can adequately describe the contingencies governing the task. Thus, their deficit is not in appreciating the optimum strategy; it is in acting upon it. A dissociation between understanding contingencies and translating this understanding into appropriate behavioral responses has also been reported by Rolls (1996). Bechara, Tranel, Damasio, and Damasio (1996) measured anticipatory skin conductance responses (SCRs) during performance of their gambling task. Both patients and controls generated SCRs in response to reward or punishment, but patients failed to develop the anticipatory SCRs *prior* to response selection, which are seen in normal subjects. This finding is further evidence that orbitofrontal cortex mediates the autonomic component of emotional response.

Studies of the effects of lesions to medial prefrontal regions thus suggest a role for these areas in several aspects of emotional processing, and also in using emotive or motivationally salient factors to guide cognitive performance. It is clear that the spectrum of symptoms associated with depression is distinct from that resulting from circumscribed lesions to regions of medial prefrontal cortex. Most significantly, although mood changes have been described in patients with medial prefrontal lesions, these patients do not typically demonstrate the consistently dysphoric mood that is at the core of depressive symptomatology. However, the emotional consequences of medial prefrontal lesions suggest that these structures may play a role in at least some aspects of affective disorders. An alternative approach to understanding the role of the medial prefrontal cortex in emotional processing is functional imaging of such processing in normal volunteers.

## Neuroimaging Findings of Anterior Cingulate Cortex Involvement in Emotional Processing

PET studies have associated activation of anterior cingulate with performance of a diverse range of cognitive tasks (Bench, Frith, et al., 1993a; Corbetta, Miezin, Shulman, & Peterson, 1993; Frith, Friston, Liddle & Frackowiak, 1991; Pardo, Pardo, Janer, & Raichle, 1990; Paus, Petrides, Evans, & Meyer, 1993), suggesting a functional heterogeneity consistent with the widespread connectivity of this region. There are numerous studies implicating anterior cingulate in attention, willed action, and goal-directed behavior, all of which are compromised in depression. However, there is also direct evidence that anterior cingulate is crucially involved in various aspects of emotional processing. Anterior cingulate response has been associated with subjective anxiety, either with anticipating electric shocks (Chua, Krams, Toni, Passingham, & Dolan, 1999) or with recalling anxiety-provoking life events (Kimbrell et al., 1999). The latter study also assessed response to anger-provoking events and again found anterior cingulate activity, a result confirmed by Dougherty et al. (1999). An anger-related response in anterior cingulate has also been reported in studies of response to facial expressions (Blair, Morris, Frith, Perrett, & Dolan, 1999). However, this finding would not appear to be specific to anger, as both fearful (Morris et al., 1998) and happy (Dolan et al., 1996) facial expressions have been associated with greater anterior cingulate response than neutral faces.

Anterior cingulate response to emotionally toned material appears not to be modality specific. Thus, Whalen et al. (1998) found that ventral regions of anterior cingulate responded preferentially to emotionally toned words in a version of the Stroop paradigm, while Lane, Fink, Chua, and Dolan (1997) found anterior cingulate response to emotionally charged pictures. The response also seems to cut across different emotions; it has been suggested (Teasdale et al., 1999) that the anterior cingulate response mediates the processing of affect-related meanings in general, rather than any individual emotion. There is also evidence to suggest that the region is involved in both internally cued (e.g., recalling emotional events) and externally cued (e.g., viewing emotional film clips) emotional experience (Lane et al., 1998).

A role for anterior cingulate in the control of autonomic function has also been demonstrated in neuroimaging studies. The regions activated in association with physical pain have been found to include anterior cingulate. This is a finding that has been replicated using both PET (Coghill et al., 1994; Jones, Brown, Friston, Qi, & Frackowiak, 1991; Talbot et al., 1991) and fMRI (Creac'h, Franconni, Henry, & Alland, 1997; Tracey et al., 1997). However, anterior cingulate has been associated not only with objectively painful levels of stimulation but also with "illusory pain." Touching spatially interlaced warm (40° C) and cold (20° C) bars, neither temperature being intrinsically painful alone, produces a painful sensation like that associated with intense, noxious cold. Craig, Reiman, Evans, and Bushnell (1996) showed that this so-called thermal grille illusion was associated with cingulate activity. Touching the component warm or cold stimuli, presented alone, did not activate this region. This demonstrates that the anterior cingulate may play a role in a more integrated level of emotional response. Results from Hsieh, Stone-Elander, & Ingvar (1999) suggest that anterior cingulate response to pain is decreased when subjects had learned to anticipate a painful stimulus, suggesting the region may mediate a form of coping mechanism.

## Neuroimaging Findings of Orbitofrontal Cortex Involvement in Emotional Processing

Unlike anterior cingulate, which has been activated in such a wide range of cognitive and emotional paradigm, the medial portion of orbitofrontal cortex has been activated relatively rarely. Rolls et al. (1997) studied activations associated with taste and olfaction in humans using fMRI. As predicted by the lesion literature on nonhuman primates, medial orbitofrontal cortex showed a significantly greater neural response to glucose or saline solutions than to tasteless solution. In a study on tactile stimulation (Francis et al., 1999), pleasant touch was associated with enhanced orbitofrontal activity compared to neutral touch. These findings can be interpreted in terms of orbitofrontal cortex mediating response to different rewarding or reinforcing properties of stimuli.

Using more abstract reinforcement (visual performance feedback), we have also identified orbitofrontal activation that may reflect responses to reinforcement (Elliott, Frith, & Dolan, 1997). Orbitofrontal response was associated with the presence compared to the absence of feedback in a guessing task, regardless of the valence of that feedback (positive or negative). These results can be interpreted in terms of orbitofrontal cortex mediating response to reinforcement contingencies in an incompletely specified (guessing) task and are consistent with the neuropsychological data of Damasio and colleagues, as discussed above. While our feedback study reported valence-independent medial orbitofrontal response, it should be noted that other studies have reported a valence specificity. For example, Paradiso et al. (1999) demonstrated orbitofrontal activation in association with emotional judgments for positively but not negatively valenced pictures.

## Functional Neuroimaging of Mood Induction in Normal Volunteers

The findings discussed above clearly suggest a role for medial prefrontal structures in affective processing. However, they do not explicitly address the question of whether these regions are involved in different mood states. One approach to this question is to study patients with mood disorders, as will be discussed below. However it is also possible to induce transient changes in mood in normal volunteers. Mood-induction procedures in normal volunteers can be considered as a possible model for mild retarded depression (Clark, 1983; Riskind & Rholes, 1985) and is associated with symptoms similar to those in clinical depression (Brown & Mankowski, 1993; Brown, Sirota, Niaura, & Engebretson, 1993), including cognitive disturbance (Ellis, Thomas, & Rodriguez, 1984; Ellis, Thomas, McFarland, & Lane, 1985).

In a PET study of mood induction, George et al. (1995) studied activation associated with depressed and elated moods induced by recall of sad and happy experiences from autobiographical memory. Subjects simultaneously viewed faces expressing the corresponding mood. Induction of transient depressed mood was associated with activation in regions including ventral anterior cingulate and orbitofrontal cortex. In a different approach, Fischer, Wik, and Fredrikson (1996) induced stress in a group of bank officials by playing them a video of a robbery they had experienced. The enhanced subjective and physiological responses to stress were paralleled by an increase in orbitofrontal activation.

These studies assessed regional cerebral blood flow (rCBF) during the mood-induction procedure. An alternative approach is to consider blood-flow changes in response to a cognitive challenge once mood induction is complete. Using this technique, Baker, Frith, and Dolan (1997) scanned subjects with neutral, elated, and depressed moods while performing a verbal fluency or a low-level control task (word repetition). Mood states were induced using the Velten procedure (Gerrard-Hesse, Spics, & Heese, 1994; Velten, 1968) where subjects are presented with mood-evocative statements. To enhance the effect, these statements were accompanied by mood-congruent music, a potent determinant of transient mood states. The main effect of induced mood (depressed or elated) was associated with activation in the lateral orbitofrontal cortex but not in more medial regions. Further, there was a significant interaction between induced mood and cognitive performance. Performance of the verbal fluency task, a classic test of spontaneous behavior generation, is usually associated with activation of anterior cingulate. When subjects were experiencing induced depression, this cingulate activation was significantly attenuated. Thus, transient depression suppressed the cingulate response to a cognitive challenge.

Mood induction is typically used to elicit transient sadness in normal controls; however, it can also be used to heighten negative affect in depressed patients. Beauregard et al. (1998) used emotionally laden film clips to produce sadness in both normal subjects and patients with unipolar depression. In both groups, significant medial prefrontal cortex activation was seen for the emotional clips compared to neutral ones. The film-induced enhancement of medial prefrontal activity was greater in patients who were already depressed. Medial prefrontal function was also associated with transient sadness in a PET study by Mayberg et al. (1999), who further proposed that an induced sad mood disrupted the reciprocal connectivity between limbic and cortical regions. Thus, blood flow increased in subgenual cingulate, a medial prefrontal component of the extended limbic system, and decreased in the right dorsolateral prefrontal cortex during transient sad mood. The reverse pattern of reciprocal change was observed in a parallel study of recovery from chronic dysphoria in depressed patients. This study demonstrates that medial prefrontal function mediates mood changes in patients as well as normal volunteers, a hypothesis that is discussed further below.

## Medial Prefrontal Cortex and Depression

Taken together, the consequences of medial prefrontal lesions in animals and humans, and the findings of neuroimaging studies in normal subjects, suggest important functions for medial prefrontal structures in mediating emotional experience, mood, and the impact of these factors on cognition. Various lines of evidence suggest that these regions may be involved in the interpretation of emotional and motivational factors and the use of these to guide behavior. It is thus intuitively plausible that these structures should be important in clinical depression, a disorder characterized by emotional and motivational disturbance and specific distortions of emotional interpretation (e.g., Teasdale & Barnard, 1993).

Various neurobiological hypotheses of the disorder have incorporated this view. The hypothesis that depression is critically associated with abnormal function of cingulate cortex has been extensively discussed (Dolan et al., 1994; Ebert & Ebmeier, 1996; George, Ketter, & Post 1993; Goodwin et al., 1993), largely based on imaging data reviewed below, although a role for orbitofrontal dysfunction has been less influential as a theory. It is noteworthy that subcaudate tractotomy, a surgical procedure disconnecting orbitofrontal cortex, is one of the most reliable surgical approaches to severe resistant depression (Bridges et al., 1994). Evidence from structural imaging studies has typically been inconclusive, except in elderly patients, leading to the suggestion that the neurobiological abnormality associated with depression is functional, rather than structural, in nature. Functional neuroimaging provides a tool to assess this contention.

## Resting State Studies

Perhaps the most obvious approach to the study of abnormal brain function associated with a particular disorder is to image patients with that disorder in the resting state. Thus, patients are scanned simply lying still in the scanner and the pattern of blood flow is compared with that of a matched control group. A number of early PET studies of depression adopted this approach. It should be noted that fMRI cannot be used to assess resting subjects; it is a technique that is critically dependent on a comparison between states.

One of the early PET studies of depression assessed a cohort of 33 patients, scanned at rest with eyes closed (Bench et al., 1992). Relative to normal control subjects, the patients showed a decrease in rCBF in left anterior cingulate. A subsequent study expanded the cohort of patients to 40 and, further, considered how blood-flow abnormalities may relate to clinical features of depression. In a follow-up study, expanding the cohort to 40 patients, Bench et al. (1993) again reported anterior cingulate abnormalities. This study also related resting-state blood flow to symptoms; findings that will be discussed further below.

Another seminal PET study of depressed patients in the resting state was that of Drevets et al. (1992); this study also reported abnormalities of medial prefrontal blood flow. However, the abnormality was *increased* blood flow relative to controls in contrast to the *decreased* blood flow reported by Bench et al. (1992). The most obvious reason

for this discrepancy was the different profile of the patients. The patients in the Drevets study had a particular form of unipolar depression (familial pure depressive disorder), were significantly younger than the patients in the Bench et al. study, and were all medication free at the time of scanning. Additionally, both studies interpreted the medial prefrontal abnormalities in terms of dysfunction of prefrontal-limbic-subcortical circuitry in depression, which would allow either decreases or increases to be accommodated under different circumstances.

Recent evidence has suggested a more focal resting-state dysfunction. Drevets et al. (1997) reported decreased blood flow in subgenual prefrontal cortex, a region of agranular cortex on the most ventral extent of the anterior cingulate gyrus. This functional abnormality was accompanied by a reduction in cortical gray-matter volume, measured by structural MRI. A similar finding has been reported in first-episode patients (Hirayasu et al., 1999), indicating that it is not a consequence of disease progression. Recent histopathological investigations have suggested that this cortical volume reduction is associated with reduced glial cell numbers (Drevets et al., 1998). These findings suggest a potentially pivotal role for this medial prefrontal region in the pathogenesis of depression. Interestingly, the finding was observed in both unipolar and bipolar depressed patients. Depression is a heterogeneous disorder, and an important application of functional neuroimaging has been to determine whether different symptom profiles are associated with different patterns of brain function.

## Functional Imaging Correlates of Depressive Symptoms

There have been relatively few attempts to characterize the functional imaging abnormalities associated with different subtypes of depression, and those that have been made have tended to adopt a correlational rather than a categorical approach. A straightforward approach to the issue of whether blood flow could be related to symptom profile in depression is to use statistical procedures to correlate resting-state blood flow. In the study of Bench et al. (1993), discussed above, a dimensional within-subjects comparison was used to determine which changes in regional cerebral blood flow (rCBF) correlated with clinical factors. The relevant clinical factors were determined by using a factor analytical technique to transform clinical symptom data into a limited number of psychopathological dimensions. Three significant dimensions were identified by this procedure, with high loadings for anxiety, psychomotor retardation/depressed mood, and cognitive performance. Each of these factors correlated significantly with the rCBF profile. Anxiety was positively correlated with activation of posterior cingulate and inferior parietal lobule; psychomotor retardation was negatively correlated with activation in dorsolateral prefrontal cortex and angular gyrus, and cognitive performance was correlated with activity in the left medial prefrontal cortex. This confirmed a post hoc finding from an earlier study that a selective subgroup of depressed patients with severe cognitive dysfunction showed decreased medial prefrontal blood flow (Bench et al., 1992).

Thus, medial prefrontal dysfunction was particularly associated with cognitive impairments. An obvious question is whether a greater degree of specificity is possible. The cognitive deficits associated with unipolar depression (Austin et al., 1992; Elliott, Sahakian, McKay, et al., 1996; Roy-Byrne, Weingarther, Bierer, Thompson & Post, 1986; Weingartner, Cohen, Martells, & Gerdt, 1981) are widespread and include deficits in a number of cognitive domains, including memory, attention, and executive function. Dolan et al. (1994) considered the relationship between rCBF measured by PET and by neuropsychological performance test on a comprehensive battery in 29 depressed patients. The results on tests where performance of patients was impaired relative to controls were entered into a principal components analysis. This identified two significant factors, one with high loading for memory items and one with high loading for attentional items. These factors were then related to resting rCBF, and it was found that both significantly correlated with activation in several frontal and posterior brain regions. However, the strongest correlation was in the medial prefrontal and anterior cingulate cortex, extending to the ventral precommissural region of the cingulate gyrus. This suggests that medial prefrontal activity is particularly associated with cognitive impairment, albeit in a relatively general way. This is consistent with the hypothesis that the medial prefrontal cortex may mediate the interface between emotional and cognitive aspects of abnormality in depressed patients. A more direct approach to studying this is to measure neural function during the performance of cognitive tasks.

## Cognitive Activation Studies

The majority of studies of neural function in depression have assessed subjects in the resting state. Although rest is a stable and reproducible state, it is also a poorly controlled one. It could, for example, be argued that differences between patients and controls may be exaggerated at rest, if this encourages patients to ruminate on their negative cognitions. Conversely, it is possible that the functional abnormalities associated with depression may become more pronounced in the face of a cognitive challenge. If this is the case, the neural correlates of impaired response to cognitive challenges may be more informative

concerning the precise functional nature of neural deficits seen in depression.

In a recent study (Elliott, Baker, et al., 1997), $H_2O^{15}$ PET was used to compare depressed patients and controls performing a high-level planning task. The task used was a computerised one-touch version (Owen et al., 1992) of the Tower of London task (Shallice, 1982). Evidence from various neuropsychological studies suggests that performance of this task depends on intact frontal cortices (Owen, Downes, Sahakian, Polkey, & Robbins, 1990; Owen et al., 1992; Shallice, 1982); indeed, the task has become accepted as a hallmark test of prefrontal function. Functional imaging studies of normal volunteers performing the task have confirmed the importance of the frontal, and particularly prefrontal, cortices in mediating performance (Andreasen et al., 1992; Morris, Ahmed, Syed, & Toone 1993; Baker et al., 1996). Furthermore, performance on the Tower of London, particularly the one-touch version, is a sensitive index of cognitive impairment in depression (Elliott et al., 1996), and preliminary evidence (Elliott, Sahakian, Herrod, Robbins, & Paykel, 1997) suggests that impairment on this task represents a state rather than a trait abnormality. The performance of depressed patients returned to control levels on remission of symptoms, even though many of the patients were still taking antidepressant medication.

The paradigm used in the functional imaging study of depressed patients performing this task (Elliott, Baker, et al., 1997) was identical to that developed in an earlier study of normal volunteers (Baker et al., 1996). Subjects were presented with two arrays of three colored balls and asked to determine the number of moves required to transform the bottom array into the top array according to certain rules. They responded by pressing one of six numbered buttons corresponding to the appropriate number of moves. Activations in easy and hard versions of this planning task were compared, in a factorial design, to those associated with a perceptuomotor control task.

In normal subjects, performance of this one-touch Tower task compared to the yoked control was associated with rCBF increases in lateral prefrontal cortex, anterior cingulate, occipito-parietal cortices, thalamus, caudate, and putamen. Activation throughout this network was attenuated in depressed patients, and there was a specific failure of activation in anterior cingulate. Closer investigation revealed that cingulate activation was higher for patients than normal subjects in the control task, but was not further activated in response to the cognitive challenge. Thus, this study again suggests a critical role for anterior cingulate dysfunction in depression, a role that is sensitive to the cognitive demands placed on subjects. The focus of cingulate abnormality in this study was caudal to the region of decreased resting rCBF in depression, indicating the dysfunction within the medial prefrontal region may be more extensive than revealed by resting-state studies. The focus, as well as the nature (i.e., increases or decreases in neural response), of this dysfunction may depend on the requirements of the particular study.

There are few reports of other cognitive activation studies in depression, although recent evidence is confirming the importance of medial prefrontal function. In a study of word generation, activation of a dorsal region of anterior cingulate was also decreased relative to controls (Stern et al., 1999). Word generation is a very different task to the Tower of London, which suggests that the cingulate dysfunction associated with cognitive performance may mediate some relatively general, rather than task-specific, aspect of impaired performance. In another cognitive activation study, Leschinger et al. (1999) reported decreased activation of regions including medial prefrontal cortex in depressed patients relative to controls performing an auditory working memory task. Further, they demonstrated that these abnormalities may be specific to depression. A group of schizophrenic patients showed abnormalities that overlapped to some extent those of the depressives but the medial prefrontal dysfunction was not seen.

These findings may be tentatively interpreted in terms of medial prefrontal cortex mediating the nonspecific effects of depressed mood and impaired motivation on cognitive performance. However, it is important to determine more explicitly whether motivational factors may depend on the medial prefrontal cortex. One form of motivational influence on performance is performance feedback. In many cognitive tests that have been used to study depression, subjects are given explicit feedback to responses, allowing them to monitor and assess how well they are doing. Preliminary neuropsychological evidence has suggested that depressed patients may show abnormal responses to negative feedback compared to controls (Beats et al., 1996; Elliott et al., 1996; Elliott, Sahakian, et al. 1997). More specifically, depressed patients may fail to respond to negative feedback, or failure, by improving performance on subsequent trials. Abnormal responsiveness to failure is consistent with cognitive and psychological accounts of depression (Beck, 1967; Teasdale & Barnard, 1993; Lewinsohn, Youngren, & Grosscup, 1979); however, it should be noted that the effect has not always been replicated (Shah et al., 1999). It is possible that the finding is only seen for some demographic profiles.

In our most recent $H_2O^{15}$ PET study, we recruited a group of patients from the same pool who had showed the abnormal response to failure in the earlier neuropsychological study. These patients were compared with a control group performing cognitive tasks under different feedback conditions. The cognitive paradigm used was again based on the one-touch Tower of London task described above, but with certain important differences. Most important, unlike in the version of the task used previously (Baker et al., 1996; Elliott, Baker, et al., 1997), subjects were given explicit visual feedback after each response. This feedback was actually independent of subjects' performance. In one condition, positive feedback was given to all responses, regardless of actual performance accuracy; in another, negative feedback was given to 80% of responses, and in a third no feedback was given. As in previous studies, the planning task was compared with a low-level perceptual control. This was a guessing task where subjects were required to monitor two identical arrays until they disappeared and then press any one of the six response buttons. They were told that half the buttons were randomly assigned as correct on each trial and were given feedback on the same positive, negative, and no feedback schedules as for the planning task.

For normal subjects, a key finding of this study was that the presence of feedback (either positive or negative) in the guessing, but not the planning, task was associated with activation of medial orbitofrontal cortex (Elliott, Frith, et al., 1997). These findings suggest that neural response to feedback, or reinforcement, in an incompletely specified guessing task (i.e., a task where there is no consistent relationship between responses and outcomes), but not a planning task, involves the ventromedial orbitofrontal region. There are several possible, and not mutually exclusive, interpretations of this pattern of activity. One explanation depends on the difference between the perceived controllability of the tasks. In the planning task subjects believed that they could control the type of feedback they received; by optimizing their performance they believed they could increase the amount of positive feedback they received. In the guessing task, by contrast, they believed they could not; they were led to think of positive or negative outcomes in terms of good or bad luck. This difference in controllability may be related to the phenomenon of learned helplessness (Seligman, 1975), which behavioral theories have suggested may be associated with, or even model, depression (e.g., Abramson, Seligman, & Teasdale, Abramson, 1978).

An alternative explanation of the finding is that orbitofrontal activity reflected an implicit requirement to process feedback across trials. For the planning task, each trial (incorporating problem, response, and feedback) is a discrete and meaningful entity. During guessing, by contrast, feedback to a single trial is less meaningful; it is only when feedback is assimilated across a number of trials that subjects can evaluate their performance against chance. In the face of uncertainty, subjects probably monitored performance across trials and (illogically) chose their responses in the light of previously rewarded responses. A proposed involvement of orbitofrontal cortex in acquiring and monitoring stimulus-reinforcement relations is consistent with findings from studies of monkeys (Thorpe, Rolls, & Maddison, 1983) and patients with orbitofrontal lesions as discussed above (Bechara et al., 1994, 1996; Damasio, 1994; Rolls et al., 1994).

Depressed patients scanned during this task showed significantly attenuated medial orbitofrontal activation compared to controls. This may suggest that depressed patients have a reduced tendency to monitor stimulus-reward relations, an interpretation that can be linked speculatively to learned helplessness. Passive "learned helplessness," a failure to actively initiate behavior to avoid negative reinforcement that provides a model for clinical depression, could be seen as a failure to attempt to determine response-outcome relations, which is reflected at a neural level by reduced orbitofrontal activity. This finding may also be consistent with the concept of "depressive realism," which suggests that depressed patients may be more accurate in assessing the extent to which they control a situation than controls (Pacini, Muir, Epstein, 1998). If normal subjects activate the orbitofrontal cortex during an attempt to seek a relationship between events that does not exist, failure to activate this region could be related to a greater acceptance of the uncontrollability of the situation by depressed subjects.

The extended discussion of this study reflects the fact that it is one of a few attempts to use functional imaging to study the impact of motivational factors on cognition in depression. Admittedly at a highly speculative level, it suggests possible links between neuropathological, neuropsychological, and cognitive behavioral accounts of the disorder. A theory of medial prefrontal dysfunction as the core cortical manifestation of depression should not only link aspects of phenomenology but also relate to the effects of treatment.

## Functional Imaging Studies of Treatment Response

In recent years, several studies have related medial prefrontal abnormalities to treatment response in depressed patients. Mayberg et al. (1997) demonstrated that regional cerebral glucose metabolism in ventral anterior cingulate uniquely distinguished eventual responders and nonresponders to antidepressant treatment. Patients were scanned prior to treatment and after several weeks of treatment, when the responding and nonresponding groups could be identified, and the scans were compared on this basis. There were no differences between the groups on any behavioral, demographic, or clinical measures recorded prior to treatment, and the neural differences were specific to the ventral cingulate region. Patients who subsequently responded showed enhanced cingulate metabolism relative to controls, while subsequent nonresponders showed relative hypometabolism.

A similar difference in anterior cingulate metabolism between subsequent responders and nonresponders was reported by Wu et al. (1999). These authors were assessing the effects of sleep deprivation, which has been found to exert an antidepressant effect in certain subgroups of patients. In a group of 36 patients, a third showed significant response to sleep deprivation, defined as a 40% or greater drop in Hamilton depression rating. This subgroup showed elevated pretreatment metabolic rates in medial prefrontal regions, including ventral anterior cingulate. Patients who responded to sleep deprivation were rescanned, and it was found that medial prefrontal metabolic rates were significantly decreased, toward normal levels. A similar finding was described by Smith et al. (1999), who performed a series of PET scans in elderly patients undergoing combined sleep deprivation and paroxetine treatment. These patients showed reduced ventral anterior cingulate metabolism following initial sleep deprivation that was sustained after recovery sleep and paroxetine treatment.

However, a converse pattern of changes after treatment has also been reported. In a group of patients with seasonal affective disorder, Vasile et al. (1997) found that responders to light treatment showed a significant increase in cingulate rCBF in response to treatment relative to nonresponders. Similarly, Buchsbaum et al. (1997) reported increases in metabolic rate in a number of regions, including medial frontal cortex, following treatment with sertraline. The direction of change in medial prefrontal regions thus seems to vary between studies, but the fact that the region is important in predicting treatment outcomes has been consistently demonstrated.

## Conclusions

The evidence discussed in this chapter points to a clear role for regions of the medial prefrontal cortex in the regulation of mood. The obvious prediction from these findings is that function within this region may be abnormal in depression, a disorder characterized by core deficits in mood. This finding has been borne out by functional imaging studies of depression. While a number of other regions have also been implicated in various studies, medial prefrontal cortex, and particularly ventral anterior cingulate, is probably the region that has been most consistently and reliably shown to function abnormally. Abnormalities are seen in the resting state, in response to cognitive challenges and in response to induced mood in depressed patients, as well as normal controls. Further, medial prefrontal abnormality in depression has been related to clinical profile and also has been shown to predict treatment response. This latter finding is particularly important not only in demonstrating a practical application of the neuroimaging approach but also in suggesting that medial prefrontal abnormality is crucial to the manifestation of depressive symptoms. The treatment studies suggest that normalizing medial prefrontal function goes hand in hand with clinical improvement.

Thus, we believe that a strong case can be made for the importance of medial prefrontal cortex in depression. However, there are clearly a number of outstanding issues. First, it should be noted that different studies have activated anatomically distinct foci within the medial prefrontal cortex. The recent evidence (Drevets et al., 1997, 1998; Mayberg et al., 1997) implicates the specific region of subgenual cingulate as particularly important. However, it is also clear that under other circumstances, particularly response to cognitive challenge, more dorsal regions of anterior cingulate or medial orbitofrontal regions may also be involved. While further systematic investigation may add clarity, it is plausible to conclude from existing evidence that medial prefrontal dysfunction in depression may be relatively extensive, with different subdivisions mediating different aspects of symptomatology.

A possibly more problematic issue is that there appear to be discrepancies regarding the nature of the abnormality. Some studies have reported hypometabolism in the medial prefrontal region in the resting state while others have reported hypermetabolism. Typically, medial prefrontal response to a cognitive challenge is attenuated in depressed patients, suggesting hypofunction. However, it is also possible that the region is hyperactive in the baseline state and cannot increase its activation further in the face of a challenge. There is also a discrepancy in the treatment studies, with some reporting decreases in medial prefrontal metabolism in response to treatment while others reporting increases. One possible explanation for these differences is that depression is mediated by a disruption of normal medial prefrontal function that may be manifest as *either* an increase *or* a decrease. It may be that the pattern varies between individuals or that it varies depending on the stage of disease within individuals. It is also possible that adjacent, interconnected regions of medial prefrontal cortex respond in different ways, such that hypofunction in one subdivision may be associated with hyperfunction in another. A final possibility is that the difference relates to the influence of neuromodulatory inputs. Deficits in, for example, serotonergic or dopaminergic influences may have opposite functional effects within a particular region. Future investigation is required to resolve this issue and gain a full understanding of exactly how medial prefrontal dysfunction mediates the disturbances of mood and cognition at the core of depression.

## REFERENCES

Abramson, L. Y., Seligman, M. E. P., & Teasdale, J. (1978). Learned helplessness in humans: Critique and reformulation. *Journal of Abnormal Psychology, 87,* 49–74.

American Psychiatric Association. (1994). *Diagnostic and statistical manual of mental disorders* (4th ed.). Washington, DC: Author.

Andreasen, N. C., Rezai, K., Alliger, R., Swayze, V. W., Flaum, M., Kirchner, P., Cohen, G., & O'Leary, D. S. (1992). Hypofrontality in neuroleptic-naive patients and in patients with chronic schizophrenia. *Archives of General Psychiatry, 49,* 943–958.

Arborelius, L., Owens, M. J., Plotsky, P. M., & Nemeroff, C. B., (1999). The role of corticotrophin-releasing factor in depression and anxiety disorders. *J. Endocrinology, 160,* 1–12.

Austin, M.-P., Ross, M., Murray, C., O'Carroll, R. E., Ebmeier, K. P., & Goodwin, G. M. (1992). Cognitive function in major depression. *J. Affective Disorders, 25,* 21–30.

Baker, S. C., Frith, C. D., & Dolan, R. J. (1997). The interaction between mood and cognitive function studied with PET. *Psych. Medicine, 27,* 565–578.

Baker, S. C., Rogers, R. D., Owen, A. M., Frith, C. D., Dolan, R. J., Frackowiak, R. S. J., & Robbins, T. W. (1996). Neural systems engaged by planning: A PET study of the Tower of London task. *Neuropsychologia, 6,* 515–526.

Baylis, L. L., & Gaffan, D. (1991). Amygdalectomy and ventromedical prefrontal ablation produce similar deficits in food choice and in simple object discrimination learning for an unseen reward. *Experimental Brain Research, 86,* 617–622.

Beauregard, M., Leroux, J. M., Bergman, S., Arzoumanian, Y., Beaudoin, G., Bourgouin, P., & Stip, E. (1998). The functional neuroanatomy of major depression: an fMRI study using an emotional activation paradigm. *Neuroreport, 9,* 3252–3258.

Beats, B. C., Sahakian, B. J., & Levy, R. (1996). Cognitive performance in tests sensitive to frontal lobe dysfunction in the elderly depressed. *Psych. Medicine, 26,* 591–603.

Bechara, A., Damasio, A. R., Damasio H., & Anderson, S. W. (1994). Insensitivity to future consequences following damage to human prefrontal cortex. *Cognition, 50,* 7–15.

Bechara, A., Tranel, D., Damasio, H., & Damasio, A. R. (1996). Failure to respond autonomically to anticipated future outcomes following damage to the prefrontal cortex. *Cerebral Cortex, 6,* 215–225.

Beck, A. T. (1967). *Depression: Clinical, experimental and theoretical aspects.* New York: Harper & Row.

Bench, C. J., Friston, K. J., Brown, R. G., Scott, L. C., Frackowiak, R. S. J., & Dolan, R. J. (1992). The anatomy of melancholia—Focal abnormalities of cerebral blood flow in major depression. *Psych. Medicine, 22,* 607–615.

Bench, C. J., Friston, K. J., Brown, R. G., Frackowiak, R. S. J., & Dolan, R. J. (1993). Regional cerebral blood flow in depression measured by positron emission tomography: the relationship with clinical dimensions. *Psychological Medicine, 23,* 579–590.

Bench, C. J., Frith, C. D., Grasby, P. M., Friston, K. J., Paulesu, E., Frackowiak, R. S. J., & Dolan, R. J. (1993). Investigations of the functional anatomy of attention using the Stroop test. *Neuropsychologia, 31* 907–922.

Blair, R. J., Morris, J. S., Frith, C. D., Perrett, D. I., & Dolan, R. J., (1999). Dissociable neural responses to facial expressions of sadness and anger. *Brain, 122,* 883–893

Bridges, P. K., Bartlett, J. R., Hale, A. S., Poynton, A. M., Malizia, A. L., & Hodgkiss, A. D. (1994). Psychosurgery: Stereotactic subcaudate tractomy. An indispensable treatment. *Brit. J. Psychiatry, 165,* 599–611.

Brown, J. D., & Mankowski, T. A. (1993). Self-esteem, mood and self-evaluation: Changes in mood and the way you see you. *Journal of Personality and Social Psychology, 64*, 421–430.

Brown, W. A., Sirota, A. D., Niaura, R., & Engebretson, T. O. (1993). Endocrine correlates of sadness and elation. *Psychosomatic Medicine 55*, 458–467.

Buchsbaum, M. S., Wu, J., Siegel, B. V., Hackett, E., Trenary, M., Abel, L., & Reynolds, C. (1997). Effect of sertraline on regional metabolic rate in patients with affective disorder. *Biol. Psychiatry, 41*, 15–22.

Butter, C. M., (1969). Perseveration in extinction and in discrimination reversal tasks following selective prefrontal ablations in Macaca mulatta. *Physiol. Behav, 4*, 163–171.

Butter, C. M., & Snyder, D. R., (1972). Alterations in aversive and aggressive behaviors following orbitofrontal lesions in rhesus monkeys. *Acta Neurobiol. Exp, 32*, 525–565.

Chua, P., Krams, M., Toni, I., Passingham, R., & Dolan, R. (1999). A functional anatomy of anticipatory anxiety. *Neuroimage, 6*, 563–571.

Clark, D. M. (1983). On the induction of depressed mood in the laboratory: Evaluation and comparison of the effects of the Velten and musical procedures. *Adv. Behavioural Research and Therapy, 5*, 27–49.

Coghill, R. C., Talbot, J. D., Evans, A. C., Meyer, E., Gjedde, A., Bushnell, M. C., & Duncan, G. H. (1994). Distributed processing of pain and vibration by the human brain. *Journal of Neuroscience, 14*, 4095–4108.

Cohen, R. A., Kaplan, R. F., Moser, D. J., Jenkins, M. A., & Wilkinson, H. (1999). Impairments of attention after cingulotomy. *Neurology, 53*, 819–824.

Corbetta, M., Miezin, F. M., Shulman, G. L., & Petersen, S. E. (1993). A PET study of visuospatial attention. *Journal of Neuroscience, 13*, 1202–1226.

Craig, A. D., Reiman, E. M., Evans, A., & Bushnell, M. C. (1996). Functional imaging of an illusion of pain. *Nature, 384*, 258–260.

Creac'h, C., Franconni, J. M., Henry, P., & Allard, M. (1997). Cerebral activation for pain processing in man: A functional magnetic resonance imaging study. *Neuroimage abstract, 5*, S223.

Dalla Barba, G., Parlato, V., Iavarone, A., & Boller, F. (1995). Anosognosia, intrusions and "frontal" functions in Alzheimer's disease and depression. *Neuropsychologia, 33*, 247–259.

Damasio, A. R. (1994). *Descartes's Error*. New York: Putnam.

Degos, J. D., da Fonseca, N., Gray, F., & Cesaro, P. (1993). Severe frontal syndrome associated with infarcts of the left anterior cingulate gyrus and the head of the right caudate nucleus: A clinico-pathological case. *Brain, 116*, 1541–1548.

Dolan, R. J., Bench, C. J., Brown, R. G., Scott, L. C., & Frackowiak, R. S. J. (1994). Neuropsychological dysfunction in depression: The relationship to regional cerebral blood flow. *Psych. Medicine, 24*, 849–857.

Dolan, R. J., Bench, C. J., Friston, K. J., Brown, R., Scott, L., & Frackowiak, R. S. J. (1992). Regional cerebral blood flow abnormalities in depressed patients with cognitive impairment. *J. Neurol. Neurosurg. Psychiatry, 55*, 768–773.

Dolan, R. J., Fletcher, P., Morris, J., Kapur, N., Deakin, J. F., & Frith, C. D. (1996). Neural activation during covert processing of positive emotional facial expressions. *Neuroimage, 3*, 194–200.

Dougherty, D. D., Shin, L. M., Alpert, N. M., Pitman, R. K., Orr, S. P., Lasko, M., Macklin, M. L., Fischman, A. J., & Rauch, S. L. (1999). Anger in healthy men: A PET study using script-driven imagery. *Biol. Psychiatry, 46*, 466–472.

Drevets, W. C., Ongur, D., & Prince, J. L. (1998). Neuroimaging abnormalities in the subgenual prefrontal cortex: Implications for the pathophysiology of familial mood disorders. *Mol. Psychiatry, 3*, 220–226, 190–191.

Drevets, W. C., Price, J. L., Simpson, J. R., Jr., Todd, R. D., Reich, T., Vannier, M., & Raichle, M. E. (1997). Subgenual prefrontal cortex abnormalities in mood disorders. *Nature, 386*, 824–827.

Drevets, W. C., Videen, T. O., Price, J. L., Preskorn, S. H., Carmichael, S. T., & Raichle, M. E. (1992). A functional anatomical study of unipolar depression. *Journal of Neuroscience,12*(9), 3628–3641.

Dum, R. P., & Strick, P. L. (1991). The origin of the corticospinal projections from the premotor areas in the frontal lobe. The *Journal of Neuroscience, 11*, 667–688.

Ebert, D., & Ebmeier, K. P. (1996). The role of the cingulate gyrus in depression: From functional anatomy to neurochemistry. *Biological Psychiatry, 39*, 1044–1050.

Elliott, R., Baker, S. C., Rogers, R. D., O'Leary, D. A., Paykel, E. S., Frith, C. D., Dolan, R. J., & Sahakian, B. J. (1997). Prefrontal dysfunction in depressed patients performing a planning task: A study using positron emission tomography. *Psych. Medicine, 27*, 931–942.

Elliott, R., Frith, C. D., & Dolan, R. J. (1997). Differential neural response to positive and negative feedback in planning and guessing tasks. *Neuropsychologia, 15*, 1395–1404.

Elliott, R., Sahakian, B. J., Herrod, J. J., Robbins, T. W., & Paykel, E. S. (1997). Abnormal response to negative feedback in unipolar depression: Evidence for a disease-specific impairment. *J. Neurol. Neurosurg. Psychiatry, 63*, 74–82.

Elliott, R., Sahakian, B. J., McKay, A. P., Herrod, J. J., Robbins, T. W., & Paykel, E. S.. (1996). Neuropsychological impairments in unipolar depression: The role of perceived failure on subsequent performance. *Psych. Medicine, 26*, 975–989.

Ellis, H. C., Thomas, R. L., McFarland, A. D., & Lane, J. W. (1985). Emotional mood states and retrieval in episodic memory. *J. Exp. Psychology: Learning, Memory and Cognition, 11*, 363–370.

Ellis, H. C., Thomas, R. L., & Rodriguez, I. A. (1984). Emotional mood states and memory: Elaborative encoding, semantic processing and cognitive effort. *J. Exp. Psychology: Learning, Memory and Cognition, 10*, 470–482.

Fischer, H., Wik, G., & Fredrikson, M. (1996). Functional neuroanatomy of robbery reexperience: Affective memories studied with PET. *Neuroreport, 7*, 2081–2086.

Francis, S., Rolls, E. T., Bowtell, R., McGlone, F., O'Doherty, J., Browning, A., Clare, S., & Smith, E. (1999). The representation of pleasant touch in the brain and its relationship with taste and olfactory areas. *Neuroreport, 10*, 453–459.

Frith, C. D., Friston, K. J., Liddle, P. F., & Frackowiak, R. S. J. (1991). Willed action and the prefrontal cortex in man: A study with PET. *Proceedings of the Royal Society London, Series B, B244*, 241–246.

George, M. S., Ketter, T. A., Parekh, P. I., Horwitz, B., Herscovitch, P., & Post, R. M. (1995). Brain activity during transient sadness and happiness in healthy women. *American J. Psychiatry, 152*, 341–351.

George, M. S., Ketter, T. A., & Post R. M. (1993). SPECT and PET in mood disorders. *J. Clinical Psychiatry, 54* (suppl.), 6–13.

Gerrards-Hesse, A., Spies, K., & Heese, F. W. (1994). Experimental induction of emotional states and their effectiveness: A review. *Brit. J. Psychology, 85*, 55–78.

Goodwin, G. M., Austin, M. P., Dougall, N., Ross, M., Murray, C., O'Carroll, R. E., Moffoot, A., Prentice, N., & Ebmeier, K. P. (1993). State changes in brain activity shown by the uptake of 99mTc-exametazime with single photon emission tomography in major depression before and after treatment. *J. Affective Disorders, 29*, 243–253.

Hirayasu, Y., Shenton, M. E., Salisbury, D. F., Kwon, J. S., Wible, C. G., Fischer, I. A., Yurgelun-Todd, D., Zarate, C., Kikinis, R., Jolesz, F. A., & McCarley, R. W. (1999). Subgenual cingulate cortex volume in first-episode psychosis. *Am J Psychiatry, 156*, 1091–1093.

Hsieh, J. C., Stone-Elander, S., & Ingvar M. (1999). Anticipatory coping of pain expressed in the human anterior cingulate cortex: A position emission tomography study. *Neuroscience Letters, 262*, 61–64.

Hurley, K. M., Herbert, H., Moga, M. M., & Saper, C. B., (1991). Efferent projections of the infralimbic cortex of the rat. *Journal of Comparative Neurology, 308*, 249–276.

Insausti, R., Amaral, D. G., & Cowan, W. M. (1987). The entorhinal cortex of the monkey: II. Cortical afferents. *Journal of Comparative Neurology, 264*, 356–394.

Jones, A. K., Brown, W. D., Friston, K. J., Qi, L. Y., & Frackowiak, R. S. J. (1991). Cortical and subcortical localisation of response to pain in man using position emission tomography. *Proceedings of the Royal Society London, Series B, 244*, 39–44.

Jones, B., & Mishkin, M. (1972). Limbic lesions and the problem of stimulus-reinforcement associations. *Expl. Neurology, 36*, 362–377.

Kemp, J. L., & Powell, T. P. S. (1970). The cortico-striate projections of the monkey. *Brain, 93*, 525–546.

Kimbrell, T. A., George, M. S., Parekh, P. I., Ketter, T. A., Podell, D. M., Danielson, A. L., Repella, J. D., Benson, B. E., Willis, M. W., Herscovitch, P., & Post, R. M. (1999). Regional brain activity during transient self-induced anxiety and anger in healthy adults. *Biol. Psychiatry, 46*, 454–465.

Krettek, J. E., & Price, J. L. (1977). The cortical projections of the mediodorsal nucleus and adjacent thalamic nuclei in the rat. *Journal of Comparative Neurology, 171*, 157–192.

Kunishio, K., & Haber, S. N. (1994). Primate cingulostriatal projection: Limbic striatal vs. sensorimotor striatal input. *Journal of Comparative Neurology, 250*, 337–356.

Lane, R. D., Fink, G. R., Chua, P. M., & Dolan, R. J. (1997). Neural activation during selective attention to subjective emotional responses. *Neuroreport, 8*, 3969–3972.

Lane, R. D., Reiman, E. M., Axelrod, B., Yun, L. S., Holmes, A., & Schwartz, G. E. (1998). Neural correlates of levels of emotional awareness: Evidence of an interaction between emotion and attention in the cingulate cortex. *Journal of Cognitive Neuroscience, 10*, 525–535.

Leschinger, A., Baumgart, F., Gaschler-Markefski, B., Burger, E., Northoff, G., Scheich, H., & Bogerts, B. (1999). Impaired cortical activation in patients with affective disorder during an auditory working memory task: A 3T-fMRI study. *Neuroimage, 9*, S611.

Lewinsohn, P. M., Youngren, M. A., & Grosscup, S. J. (1979). Reinforcement and depression. In R. A. Depue (Ed.), *The psychobiology of depressive disorders* (pp. 291–316). New York: Academic Press.

Mayberg, H. S., Brannan, S. K., Mahurin, R. K., Jerabek, P. A., Brickman, J. S., Tekell, J. L., Silva, J. A., McGinnis, S., Glass, T. G., Martin, C. C., & Fox, P. T. (1997). Cingulate function in depression: A potential predictor of treatment response. *Neuroreport, 8*, 1057–1061.

Mayberg, H. S., Liotti, M., Brannan, S. K., McGinnis, S., Mahurin, R. K., Jerabek, P. A., Silva, J. A., Tekell, J. L., Martin, C. C., Lancaster, J. L., & Fox, P. T. (1999). Reciprocal limbic-cortical function and negative mood: Converging PET findings in depression and normal sadness. *Am J Psychiatry, 156*, 675–682.

Moreaud, O., Naegele, B., Chabannes, J. P., Roulin, J. L., Garbolino B., & Pellat, J. (1996). Frontal lobe dysfunction and depressive state: Relation to endogenous character of depression. *Encephale, 22*, 47–51.

Morecraft, R. J., & Van Hoesen, G. W. (1992). Cingulate input to the primary and supplementary motor cortices in the rhesus monkey: Evidence for somatotopy in areas 24c and 23c. *Journal of Comparative Neurology, 322*, 471–489.

Morris, J. S., Friston, K. J., Buchel, C., Frith, C. D., Young, A. W., Calder, A. J., & Dolan, R. J. (1998). A neuromodulatory role for the human amygdala in processing emotional facial expressions. *Brain, 121*, 47–57.

Morris, R. G., Ahmed, S., Syed, G. M., & Toone, B. K. (1993). Neural correlates of planning ability: Frontal lobe activation during the Tower of London test. *Neuropsychologia 31*, 1367–1378.

Nauta, W. J. H. (1964). Some efferent connections of the prefrontal cortex in the monkey. In J. M. Warren & K. Akert (Eds.), *The frontal granular cortex and behavior* (pp. 397–407). New York: McGraw-Hill.

Owen, A. M., Downes, J. D., Sahakian, B. J., Polkey, C. E., & Robbins, T. W. (1990). Planning and spatial working memory following frontal lobe lesions in man. *Neuropsychologia, 28*, 1021–1034.

Owen, A. M., James, M., Leigh, P. N., Summers, B. A., Marsden, C. D., Quinn, N. P., Sahakian, B. J., & Robbins, T. W. (1992). Frontostriatal cognitive deficits at different stages of Parkinson's disease. *Brain, 115*, 1727–1751.

Pacini, R., Muir, F., & Epstein, S. (1998). Depressive realism from the perspective of cognitive-experiential self-theory. *J. Pers. Soc. Psychol., 74*, 1056–1068.

Pandya, D. N., & Yeterian, E. H. (1996). Comparison of prefrontal architecture and connections. *Philosophical Transactions of the Royal Society of London B, 351*, 1423–1432.

Paradiso, S., Johnson, D. L., Andreasen, N. C., O'Leary, D. S., Watkins, G. L., Ponto, L. L., & Hichwa, R. D. (1999). Cerebral blood flow changes associated with attribution of emotional valence to pleasant, unpleasant, and neutral visual stimuli in a PET study of normal subjects. *Am. J. Psychiatry, 156*, 1618–1629.

Pardo, J. V. Pardo, P. J., Janer, K. W., & Raichle, M. E. (1990). The anterior cingulate cortex mediates processing selection in the Stroop attentional conflict paradigm. *Proceedings of National Academy of Science USA, 87*, 256–259.

Paus, T., Petrides, M., Evans, A. C., & Meyer, E. (1993).

Role of human anterior cingulate cortex in the control of oculomotor, manual and speech responses: A positron emission tomography study. *Journal of Neurophysiology, 2,* 453–469.

Ray, J. P., & Price, J. L. (1993). The organization of projections from the mediodorsal nucleus of the thalamus to orbital and medical prefrontal cortex in macaque monkeys. *Journal of Comparative Neurology, 337,* 1–31.

Riskind, J. H., & Rholes, W. S. (1985). The Velten Mood Induction Procedure and cognitive manipulation: Our response to Clark (1985). *Behavioral Research and Therapy, 23,* 671–673.

Rolls, E. T. (1975). *The brain and reward.* Oxford: Pergamon.

Rolls, E. T. (1990). A theory of emotion and its application to understanding the neural basis of emotion. *Cog. Emotion, 4,* 161–190.

Rolls, E. T. (1994). Brain mechanisms for invariant visual recognition and learning. *Behav. Proc, 33,* 113–138.

Rolls, E. T. (1996). The orbitofrontal cortex. *Philosophical Transactions of the Royal Society of London B, 351,* 1433–1444.

Rolls, E. T., Francis, S., Bowtell, R., Browning, A. S., Clare, S., Smith, E., & McGlone, F. (1997). Taste and olfactory activity of the orbitofrontal cortex. *Neuroimage abstract, S199.*

Rolls, E. T., Hornak, J., Wade, D., & McGrath, J. (1994). Emotion related learning in patients with social and emotional changes associated with frontal lobe damage. *Journal of Neurology, Neurosurgery and Psychiatry, 57,* 1518–1524.

Roy-Byrne, P. P., Weingartner, H., Bierer, L. M., Thompson, K., & Post, R. M. (1986). Effortful and automatic cognitive processes in depression. *Arch. Gen. Psychiatry, 43,* 265–267.

Seligman, M. E. P. (1975). *Helplessness: On depression, development, and death.* San Francisco: Freeman.

Shah, P. J., O'Carroll, R. E., Rogers, A., Moffoot, A. P., & Ebmeier, K. P. (1999). Abnormal response to negative feedback in depression. *Psychol. Med., 29,* 63–72.

Shallice, T. (1982). Specific impairments in planning. *Phil. Transact. Royal Soc., B298,* 199–209.

Smith, G. S., Reynolds, C. F. 3rd, Pollock, B., Derbyshire, S., Nofzinger, E., Dew, M. A., Houck, P. R., Milko, D., Meltzer, C. C., & Kupfer, D. J. (1999). Cerebral glucose metabolic response to combined total sleep deprivation and antidepressant treatment in geriatric depression *Am. J. Psychiatry, 156,* 683–689.

Stern, C. E., & Passingham, R. E. (1996). The nucleus accumbens in monkeys (Macaca Fascicularis): II. Emotion and motivation. *Behaviorial Brain Research, 75,* 179–193.

Stern, E., DeAsis, J., Alexopoulos, G., Blumberg, H., Eidelberg, D., & Silbersweig, D. (1999). Decreased hippocampal and anterior cingulate activation in geriatric depression *Neuroimage, 9,* S665.

Sullivan, R. M., & Gratton, A. (1999). Lateralized effects of medial prefrontal cortex lesions on neuroendocrine and autonomic stress responses in rats. *Journal of Neuroscience, 19,* 2834–2840.

Talbot, J. D., Marrett, S., Evans, A. C., Meyer, E., Bushnell, M. C., & Duncan, G. H. (1991). Multiple representations of pain in human cerebral cortex. *Science, 251,* 1355–1358.

Teasdale, J. D., & Barnard, P. J. (1993). *Affect, cognition, and change.* Hillsdale, NJ: Erlbaum.

Teasdale, J. D., Howard, R. J., Cox, S. G., Ha, Y., Brammer, M. J., Williams, S. C., & Checkley, S. A. (1999). Functional MRI study of the cognitive generation of affect *Am. J. Psychiatry, 156,* 209–215.

Terreberry, R. R., & Neafsey, E. J. (1983). Rat medial frontal cortex: A visceral motor region with direct projection to a solitary nucleus. *Brain Research, 278,* 245–249.

Thorpe, S. J., Rolls, E. T., & Maddison, S. (1983). The orbitofrontal cortex: Neuronal activity in the behaving monkey. *Experimental Brain Research, 49,* 93–115.

Tracey, I., Becerra, L. R., Chang, I., Stojanovic, M., Edwards, A., Fishman, S., Boorsock, D., & Gonzalez, R. G. (1997). Functional MRI of pain: Noxious heat and cold stimuli. *Neuroimage Abstract, S222.*

Vasile, R. G., Sachs, G., Anderson, J. L., Lafer, B., Matthews, E., & Hill, T. (1997). Changes in regional cerebral blood flow following light treatment for seasonal affective disorder: Responders versus nonresponders. *Biol. Psychiatry, 42,* 1000–1005.

Velten, E. (1968). A laboratory task for induction of mood states. *Behavior Research and Therapy, 6,* 473–482.

Vogt, B. A., & Pandya, D. N. (1987). Cingulate cortex of the rhesus monkey: II. Cortical afferents. *Journal of Comparative Neurology, 262,* 271–289.

Weingartner, H., Cohen, R. M., Martello, J. Di., & Gerdt, C. (1981). Cognitive processes in depression. *Arch. Gen. Psychiatry, 38,* 42–47.

Whalen, P. J., Bush, G., McNally, R. J., Wilhelm, S., McInerney, S. C., Jenike, M. A., & Rauch, S. L. (1998). The emotional counting Stroop paradigm: A functional magnetic resonance imaging probe of the anterior cingulate affective division. *Biol. Psychiatry, 44,* 1219–1228.

Wu, J., Buchsbaum, M. S., Gillin, J. C. Tang, C., Cadwell, S., Wiegand, M., Najafi, A., Klein, E., Hazen, K., Bunney, W. E. Jr., Fallon, J. H., & Keator, D. (1999). Prediction of antidepressant effects of sleep deprivation by metabolic rates in the ventral anterior cingulate and medial prefrontal cortex. *Am. J. Psychiatry, 156,* 1149–1158.

# Autonomic Psychophysiology

# 8

# INTRODUCTION: AUTONOMIC PSYCHOPHYSIOLOGY

Gerhard Stemmler

The autonomic psychophysiology of emotion has a long thought tradition in philosophy but a short empirical tradition in psychological research. Yet the past 20 years or so have seen the accumulation of an impressive body of replicated findings in which autonomic variables acquire a well-validated psychological meaning. This is particularly true for research areas with well-developed experimental paradigms and an emergence of "minitheories" (some of which are reviewed in chapters 10, 13, and 14). The situation differs, however, if reverberations of specific emotions are sought in autonomic variables. Even though large-scale studies were initiated as long as 50 years ago, consensus among scholars about the psychological meaning of the registered somatovisceral "emotion" profiles is still low (see chapter 11). This ongoing debate is an indication that the field is still struggling with enormous complexities in understanding the psychobiology of emotions and even in studying it properly. An acknowledgment of today's changing view of the physiology of the autonomic nervous system (see chapter 9) and of methodological considerations (see chapter 12) might play a role in overcoming those complexities.

## Functions and Tasks of Emotions

Considering the functions of emotions and the tasks performed by the brain in processing an external or an internally generated emotion stimulus might help to distinguish among research areas in which the activity of autonomic systems during emotion is assessed. All of the contributors to this section mention one or more functions of the emotions. The function of an emotion can be recognized by its goals. To begin with, we have to introduce the terms *emotion goal, emotion strategy, emotion tactics*, and *emotion task*. Briefly, an emotion stimulus initiates a processing cascade, which results in solutions for a series of emotion tasks. Emotion tasks prepare the organism for approaching the goal of an emotion. Emotion strategies lead the way to a goal, whereas emotion tactics are specific actions on this way.

An emotion goal can be formulated on different levels of abstraction. The top level is a tribute to Charles Darwin: Emotions have the goal to secure survival and procreation. Still on a rather abstract level, emotions, defined as states elicited by rewards and punishers, function "as a mechanism for the genes to influence behavior . . . by specifying the stimuli or events that the animal is built to find rewarding or punishing, so that the genes specify the goals for action, not the actions themselves" (Rolls, 2000, p. 220). In another account, emotions deal with major adaptational dilemmas: The function of disgust is rejection; of anger, destruction; of fear, protection; of sadness, reintegration; of joy, reproduction (Plutchik, 1980). The goal of most (negative) emotions is to "maintain a relatively steady (or 'normal') state in the face of interpersonal challenges" (Plutchik, 1997, p. 20), for example, to reinstate one's dominance or, even more specifically, to win a fight. Emotions provide the cognitive and bodily means to accomplish these goals.

Emotion goals are approached by emotion strategies, which consist of one or several context-dependent decisions (Ciani, 2000) such as behavior plans (including a plan to postpone any action). Cognitive reappraisals can alter an emotion strategy. Thus strategies are more malleable than goals; one emotion encounter may engage different strategies in sequence. Emotion tactics are the specific, context-bound patterns of action (Lang, Bradley, & Cuthbert, 1990), which can be any instrumental response in the service of an emotion strategy.

In this account, neither goals nor strategies nor tactics are linked to autonomic physiological activity in any way that might illuminate emotion mechanisms. (However, autonomic activity could be used to inform about perceptual, cognitive, energetic, and behavior direction aspects of the organism's state.) One can question whether strategies are a part of emotions at all. Tactics are not, but strategies and tactics are in the service of an emotion's goal.

To my understanding, emotion tasks are steps in the processing of emotion stimuli. Current neurophysiological knowledge suggests that during emotions both unspecific and specific brain modules take command (on fear and anxiety, see Berntson, Sarter, & Cacioppo, 1998; on anger and anger control, see Davidson, Putnam, & Larson, 2000). Their duty is to prepare the organism for approaching the emotion goal (*emotion* from the Latin *ex movere* = to prepare). Included are the following tasks:

- Decoding a stimulus as positive or negative (Lang, Bradley, & Cuthbert, 1997) or, alternatively, as rewarding or punishing (Rolls, 1999)
- Interruption of ongoing behaviors and cognitions (Mandler, 1980); refocusing of attention (see chapter 14 in this volume)
- Scanning emotion memory for learned stimulus-response contingencies proven successful in one's species or one's own past (see chapter 13)
- Biasing broad behavioral response tendencies toward a particular motivational disposition such as approach or avoidance, including modulation of reflex circuits (see chapter 10)
- Invoking explicit and implicit processes for an evaluation of stimulus, environment, and memory (Rolls, 1999), as well as implicit appraisal processes (Lazarus, 1991)
- Preparing for behavior classes, such as defense, defeat, or attack, through a coordinated tuning of somatic, hormonal, immune, and autonomic systems (see chapters 9 and 11)
- Communicating one's intentions to others nonverbally through posture, skin color, facial expression, and so forth (see chapter 11)
- Communicating the activity of somatic and autonomic effectors back to integration centers in the brain (Damasio, 1994; see also chapter 9 in this volume)

- Readiness to counteract injuries threatening the body's integrity, that is, protecting the body and its most important organs from damage, for example, through blood loss (see chapter 9)

Emotions, at least some "basic" ones, could be characterized neurophysiologically by the sequence and outcomes of the separate tasks mentioned in the preceding list (and probably others, too) rather than by the postulate of separate "specific" brain centers for fear, anxiety, anger, happiness, and so forth. Still, even under this perspective, patterns of autonomic activity during emotions may inform us about the brain's specific processing cascade.

Each emotion task defines a separate pivotal area of research. Data assembled from well-developed experimental paradigms and associated minitheories have clearly demonstrated the involvement of autonomic variables in some of these tasks (see chapter 14 on attentional processes, chapter 13 on emotion memory and learning processes, and chapter 10 on motivational dispositions in this volume). Other emotion tasks make an even stronger use of the autonomic nervous systems (see chapters 9 and 11 on the preparation for broad behavioral classes; chapters 21–27 on the social display of emotions, in part 4 in this volume; and chapter 9 on the protection of the body). In each of these emotion tasks there is probably only a limited number of relatively fixed and hardwired choices.

But there are also research questions that deal with the net effect of all emotion tasks. These questions are usually rather broad and crystallize around the net effect that emotions have on the autonomic systems, for example, somatovisceral emotion specificity, the effects of emotion suppression, or emotion coping and coronary heart disease. Experimental paradigms are usually less well standardized in research areas such as these, and emotion tasks are often not specifically probed.

Choosing autonomic emotion specificity as an example for such rather broad research questions, I discuss two competing conceptual models, autonomic nonspecificity and autonomic specificity, in light of the definitions proposed previously. Research on the autonomic separability of at least some emotions is quite controversial these days (see chapter 11). Skeptics would argue (see chapter 10) that autonomic activity serves only emotion tactics, that is, the launching and subserving of specific somatic actions (e.g., Gray, 1994; Lang et al., 1990). Autonomic activity could therefore not reveal emotion goals.

This assertion obviously cannot be discussed without considering the time dimension. After introduction of the emotion stimulus, the cascade of emotion tasks is initiated. At least in a rudimentary fashion, context information from the environment is incorporated in the early processing stages. For example, if escape is not possible (and the animal has learned so in previous contingencies), threat produces behavioral inhibition; if escape is possible, active avoidance behavior will result. Likewise, "if an active behavioral response can occur to the omission of a positive reinforcer, then anger might be produced; but if only passive behavior is possible, then sadness, depression, or grief might occur" (Rolls, 2000, p. 179). Thus emotion tasks take into account the momentary behavioral options if the animal has already associated them with the environmental context. This means that autonomic responses evoked by the emotion tasks prepare for rather differentiated emotion goals before instrumental actions are launched.

Only extremely intense and abruptly presented emotion stimuli initiate nearly immediate motor responses such as flight or startle responses. Flight (William James's "bear-in-the-woods" threat comes to mind; James, 1884) is often taken to be the prototypical fear response. In this case only a very short moment of defensive orientation before flight onset could be used for autonomic specificity research, because with the onset of vigorous motor activity the autonomic systems are in service of motor activity. However, the immediate flight response might be better conceived as panic and is not the typical consequence of fear in the human condition. Thus, under most natural and experimental conditions, autonomic activity stemming from the emotion tasks is undisturbed by the onset of actions.

Even though for many researchers the traditional idea of separate neuronal structures for each basic emotion is highly improbable today, the idea of autonomic emotion specificity need not die with a perhaps outdated localization model. If on an abstract level emotions prepare for attaining emotion goals, and if this preparation is accomplished through rather specific solutions to a set of emotion tasks, then the "fingerprints" of these tasks could give rise to autonomic emotion specificity. (For a discussion of related assessment problems, see chapters 11 and 12.)

## New Physiological Concepts for the Autonomic Systems

Researchers using autonomic measures do so in the interpretative context they have learned to apply. Both the design of research and the interpretation of results are strongly influenced by this context. Interestingly, several highly influential physiological concepts used in psychophysiological work date back to Walter Cannon, even though new insights and discoveries have been available for more than 10 years. In chapter 9, Jänig gives a comprehensive account of these new insights and resulting changes in the view on autonomic systems. With them the psychophysiologist's toolbox looks somewhat different from the way it has traditionally.

The following new concepts support the notion of a rather differentiated patterning of autonomic responses:

- Both Cannon's and Walter R. Hess's views are too global (Cannon, 1929; Hess, 1948). What Cannon described as a general fight/flight response is better conceived of as a "defense" pattern. Transmitter substances or receptor types are too global for a functional classification of autonomic nervous system (ANS) effects. The ANS is constituted by building blocks, the "final autonomic pathways." The functional specificity of the peripheral autonomic pathways reflects the central organization of these systems.
- There exist at least six brain programs that regulate preformed constellations of somatomotor, autonomic, and hormonal adjustments. These programs provide for fast, integrated somatic, autonomic, and antinociceptive mechanisms during stress and pain. They are critical for survival because they serve to protect the body.

It is obvious that these findings are quite compatible with the view of emotion processing presented previously.

## Research Questions Ahead

Autonomic psychophysiology plays a pivotal role in the preparation of approaching emotion goals. A full understanding of the processes involved in the series of emotion tasks and how they recruit the ANS should be the agenda of future emotion research, with a focus on autonomic psychophysiology. Specific research questions include:

- What is the time course of emotion tasks and what factors contribute to its variability (see chapter 13 on the "threat imminence" continuum)? How long does it take to complete the preparation period and how long for ANS activity to dissipate (see chapter 11)? Determination of the optimal time window during which to measure emotion effects in the ANS is a crucial task to solve.
- What is the role of the situational context in the preparation period? The context affords behavioral options if stimulus and response associations had been established in previous learning or through observation of a model's behavior. There is only little experimental work with human participants in which behavioral options are systematically and emotion-specifically varied. Much could be learned from such investigations about the kind and diversity of specific ANS patterns during the preparation period. Such studies would also throw light on the

(limited) mapping of verbal categories on biological categories.

- How can we disentangle different contributions to ANS activity that originate from various emotion tasks from those that originate from the nonemotional context? The multicomponent model of somatovisceral emotion responses could be a first step (Stemmler, Heldmann, Pauls, & Scherer, 2001). It distinguishes effects of the "nonemotional" context (e.g., posture, ambient temperature, nonemotional cognitive processes, constitution) from those of the "emotional" context (the behavioral options afforded by the environment) and from the fixed, rather emotion-specific, programs that prepare behavior.

- What is the role of ANS afferents in the generation, amplification, and duration of an emotion? Since Damasio proposed the "somatic marker hypothesis" (1994), interest in the function of ANS feedback has revived. In particular, Damasio's contention that feelings give us cognitions about our visceral and musculoskeletal states should be put to a test.

- There is still little systematic knowledge about individual differences in ANS activity during emotion. Of interest are individual differences in emotion arousability, emotion intensity, emotion duration, and emotion plasticity (i.e., changes in emotion sequences). Are there correlates of these individual differences in the activity of specific brain circuits in positron emission tomography (PET) or magnetic resonance imaging (MRI), in personality, or in health variables?

- Is emotion processing experimentally induced in the laboratory distinct from processing during naturally occurring emotion encounters? Reliable multichannel ambulatory recordings in people's natural environment would be needed (Fahrenberg & Myrtek, 1996).

The branch of autonomic psychophysiology in affective science will substantially profit from insights into brain mechanisms that subserve emotion. As major output systems of the brain, the autonomic systems and their activity during emotion can be fully understood only after we have a firmer grasp of the interplay of brain modules included in emotion processing and of their respective emotion tasks. Then a surge of interest in the autonomic psychophysiology of emotion can be expected.

## REFERENCES

Berntson, G. G., Sarter, M., & Cacioppo, J. T. (1998). Anxiety and cardiovascular reactivity: The basal forebrain cholinergic link. *Behavioural Brain Research, 94,* 225–248.

Cannon, W. B. (1929). Bodily changes in pain, hunger, fear, and rage. New York: Appleton.

Ciani, A. C. (2000). When to get mad: Adaptive significance of rage in animals. *Psychopathology, 33,* 191–197.

Damasio, A. R. (1994). *Descartes's error: Emotion, reason, and the human brain.* New York: Avon Books.

Davidson, R. J., Putnam, K. M., & Larson, C. L. (2000). Dysfunction in the neural circuitry of emotion regulation: A possible prelude to violence. *Science, 289,* 591–594.

Fahrenberg, J., & Myrtek, M. (1996). *Ambulatory assessment.* Seattle, WA: Hogrefe & Huber.

Gray, J. A. (1994). Three fundamental emotion systems. In P. Ekman & R. J. Davidson (Eds.), *The nature of emotion: Fundamental questions* (pp. 243–247). New York: Oxford University Press.

Hess, W. R. (1948). *Die funktionelle organisation des vegetativen nerven systems [The functional organization of the vegetative nervous system].* Basel, Switzerland: Schwabe.

James, W. (1884). What is emotion? *Mind, 19,* 188–205.

Lang, P. J., Bradley, M. M., & Cuthbert, B. N. (1990). Emotion, attention, and the startle reflex. *Psychological Review, 97,* 377–395.

Lang, P. J., Bradley, M. M., & Cuthbert, B. N. (1997). Motivated attention: Affect, activation, and action. In P. J. Lang, R. F. Simons, & M. T. Balaban (Eds.), *Attention and orienting: Sensory and motivational processes* (pp. 97–135). Mahwah, NJ: Erlbaum.

Lazarus, R. S. (1991). *Emotion and adaptation.* New York: Oxford University Press.

Mandler, G. (1980). The generation of emotion: A psychological theory. In R. Plutchik & H. Kellerman (Eds.), *Emotion: Theory, research, and experience* (Vol. 1, pp. 219–243). New York: Academic Press.

Plutchik, R. (1980). *Emotion: A psychoevolutionary synthesis.* New York: Harper & Row.

Plutchik, R. (1997). The circumplex as a general model of the structure of emotions and personality. In R. Plutchik & H. R. Conte (Eds.), *Circumplex models of personality and emotion* (pp. 17–45). Washington, DC: American Psychological Association.

Rolls, E. T. (1999). *The brain and emotion.* New York: Oxford University Press.

Rolls, E. T. (2000). Précis of *The brain and emotion. Behavioral and Brain Sciences, 23,* 177–234.

Stemmler, G., Heldmann, M., Pauls, C. A., & Scherer, T. (2001). Constraints for emotion specificity in fear and anger: The context counts. *Psychophysiology, 36,* 275–291.

# 9

# THE AUTONOMIC NERVOUS SYSTEM AND ITS COORDINATION BY THE BRAIN

Wilfrid Jänig

The internal milieu of the body is controlled to keep the component cells, tissues, and organs (including the brain and skeletal muscles) maintained in an optimal environment for their function. This enables the organism to adjust its performance to the varying internal and external demands placed on the organism. In the short term the mechanisms involved include the control of:

- constancy of the fluid matrix of the body (fluid volume regulation, osmoregulation)
- gas exchange with the environment (regulation of airway resistance and the pulmonary circulation)
- ingestion and digestion of nutrients (regulation of the gastrointestinal tract, control of energy balance)
- excretion of substances (disposal of waste)
- transport of gases, nutrients, and other substances throughout the body (cardiovascular regulation)
- constancy of body temperature (thermoregulation)
- reproductive behavior (mechanics of sexual organs)
- defensive behaviors (adaptation of the body during fight, flight, and quiescence)

and in the long term the control of:

- recovery of the body (control of circadian rhythms, sleep, and wakefulness)
- development and maintenance of body organs and tissues
- protection of the organism at the cellular and sys-

tems levels (regulation of inflammatory processes, control of the immune system)

These body functions that maintain the internal milieu are controlled by the brain. This control is exerted by the autonomic nervous system and the endocrine systems. Specifically, the brain acts on many peripheral target tissues (smooth muscle cells of various organs, cardiac muscle cells, exocrine glands, endocrine cells, metabolic tissues, immune cells, etc.). The *efferent signals* from the brain to the periphery of the body by which this control is achieved are neural (by the autonomic nervous systems) and hormonal (by the neuroendocrine systems). The time scales of these controls differ by orders of magnitude: Autonomic regulation is normally fast and occurs within seconds, and neuroendocrine regulation is relatively slow (over tens of minutes, hours, or even days). The *afferent signals* from the periphery of the body to the brain are neural, hormonal (e.g., hormones from both endocrine organs and the gastrointestinal tract, cytokines from the immune system, leptin from adipocytes), and physicochemical (e.g., blood glucose level, temperature).

By analogy with the organization of the somatomotor system, the brain contains "sensorimotor programs" for the coordinated regulation of the internal environment of the body's tissues and organs and sends efferent commands to the peripheral target tissues through the autonomic and endocrine routes (see Figure 9.1). There is considerable overlap within the brain between the areas which are involved with the outputs of the autonomic, endocrine, and somato-motor systems. This overlap is essential for the coordination of behavior within the environment.

The role of the autonomic nervous system in these integrative programs for maintaining the body's internal environment is primarily to distribute specific signals to the various target organs. The signals need to be precisely patterned to implement reactions in each target tissue or organ. The essential role of distributing the message from the central nervous system to the target organs is the function of the autonomic nervous system. Some of these signals pass continuously to the periphery in the resting state; others are recruited during particular body behaviors and states of the internal milieu. The precision and biological importance of the control of peripheral target organs by the autonomic nervous system is accepted, but the mechanisms by which it comes about are not generally appreciated. Both of these aspects become quite obvious in the following cases:

- when the peripheral (efferent) autonomic neurons are damaged (e.g., as a consequence of metabolic disease, such as long-term diabetes)
- when certain types of peripheral autonomic neurons are inherently absent, such as in the rare cases of pure autonomic failure in which most of the neurons in autonomic ganglia are absent or in which one enzyme for synthesis of the transmitter noradrenaline, dopamine-β-hydroxylase, is deficient or absent (Mathias & Bannister, 1999) or in Hirsch-sprung's disease, in which some of the inhibitory neurons of the enteric nervous system of the gut are missing (Christensen, 1994)
- when the spinal cord is traumatically lesioned (leading to interruption of the connections from supraspinal centers to a large part of the autonomic outflow)
- when hypothalamic functions are impaired (e.g., in anorexia nervosa or as a consequence of tumor or trauma)
- when the autonomic nervous system fails to function during severe infectious diseases
- quite commonly in old age, when autonomic systems may be reduced in effectiveness or cease to function

It is commonly stated that we can principally live without the function of large parts of the autonomic nervous system. However, the lifestyle of an individual in such a state becomes severely constrained, so that many of the large range of actions for which our biology equips us, such as being sexually active, playing tennis, running a marathon, climbing mountains, diving in the sea, living in the tropics or in arctic climates, and being involved in intellectual activities, are not possible without a normally

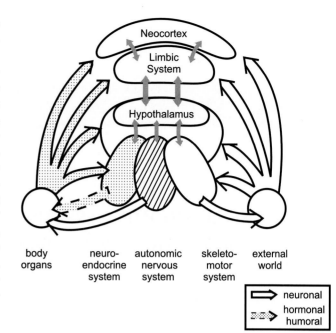

Figure 9.1 Autonomic nervous system, brain and body. *Right*, somatic nervous system (motor system and sensory systems) and environment. *Left*, autonomic nervous system, neuroendocrine system, and body organs. In the *middle* neuraxis, hypothalamus, and telencephalon. The afferent feedback from the body is neuronal, hormonal, and humonal (e.g., glucose concentration, osmolality) and of other types (e.g., body temperature). *Solid line arrows*, neuronal; *dotted line arrows* and *dotted arrows*, hormonal and humoral. Note that the feedback from the body organs to the brain is neuronal (visceral afferents), as well as hormonal and humoral. Adapted from Jänig & Häbler (1999).

functioning autonomic nervous system. Finally, all vertebrates are endowed with autonomic systems in order also to meet extreme environmental challenges; the development, anatomical differentiation, and functional differentiation probably correspond to the behavioral repertoire of the vertebrate species (Nilsson, 1983; Nilsson & Holmgren, 1994).

Autonomic regulation of body functions requires the existence of specific neuronal pathways in the periphery and relatively specific organization in the central nervous system; otherwise, it would not be possible to have the precision and flexibility of control that higher vertebrates possess to make rapid adjustments during diverse behaviors. This implies that the various autonomic systems must be centrally integrated and have multiple but distinct peripheral pathways. These pathways are defined according to the function they effect in the target cells they innervate. From this point of view, it is clear that the autonomic nervous system is the major efferent component of the peripheral nervous system, which outweighs in its diversity of function and size the somatic efferent pathways.

In this chapter, I first describe the neuronal basis for the precise regulation of the peripheral autonomic target organs in higher vertebrates. This description includes the functional organization of autonomic neurons in the periphery and how these neurons integrate and transmit the signals leading to target regulation. Then I describe some principles of organization of the autonomic control systems in the spinal cord, brain stem, and hypothalamus. Finally, the role of the autonomic system in protection of the body and in basic emotions is discussed. The properties of autonomic circuits, single autonomic neurons, or parts of autonomic neurons are described in the context of their biological functions in vivo to give the reader an idea about the principles of organization of the autonomic neurons and their interrelationships. This description should also help explain why the brain is able to adapt and coordinate the different functions of the body so precisely during our daily activities, during extreme exertion and physiological stress, as well as during various mental activities and while we experience emotions. For the detailed physiology of the various autonomic control systems, as well as their specific organization in the spinal cord, brain stem, and hypothalamus, the reader is referred to volume 70 of Appenzeller (1999), Appenzeller and Oribe (1997), Blessing (1997), Greger and Windhorst (1996), Jordan (1997), Loewy and Spyer (1990), Low (1993), Mathias and Bannister (1999), Randall (1984), Ritter, Ritter, and Barnes (1992), Rowell (1993), and Shepherd and Vatner (1996), as well as to special review articles (Dampney, 1994; Folkow, 2000; Häbler, Jänig, & Michaelis, 1994; Jänig, 1985, 1986, 1988a, 1995a, 1996b; Jänig & Häbler, 1999; Kirchheim, Just, & Ehmke, 1998; Spyer, 1994). The description of the enteric nervous system is not covered (see Furness & Bornstein, 1995; Furness & Costa, 1987).

## Functional Anatomy

Before developing the general concepts of the function of the autonomic nervous system, I provide some definitions. The limitations of present understanding and some aspects of the anatomy and function of the autonomic nervous system are described on the macroscopic level. This conventional approach is necessary to help to convey what is meant when we speak of the autonomic nervous system and its functions.

### Definitions and Limitations

Langley (1903, 1921) originally proposed the generic term *autonomic nervous system* to describe the system of nerves that regulates the function of all innervated tissues and organs throughout the vertebrate body except striated muscle fibers, that is, the innervation of the viscera, vasculature, glands, and some other tissues. This term is syn-

onymous with the term *vegetative nervous system*. Langley divided the autonomic nervous system into three parts: the parasympathetic nervous system, the sympathetic nervous system, and the enteric nervous system. This division has withstood the test of time and is now universally used in descriptions of the autonomic nervous system in vertebrates (Gibbins, 1994; Nilsson, 1983).

The definition of the *sympathetic* and the *parasympathetic nervous systems* is based on the specialized neuroanatomical arrangement of the autonomic outflow from the central nervous system to the peripheral target tissues (see Figure 9.2). This outflow is separated into a tectal, bulbar, and sacral system (craniosacral system = parasympathetic system) and a thoracolumbar system (sympathetic system). The separation made by Langley was based on several criteria: the distribution of innervated target organs, the opposing effects of nerve stimulation, embryological development, and the effects of exogenously applied substances (e.g., adrenaline, pilocarpine, atropine) on effector organs (Langley, 1903). The main feature distinguishing sympathetic and parasympathetic spinal outflows is their separation by the cervical and lumbar enlargements (which contain the innervation supplying the limbs), and so the definition is primarily an anatomical one. In some lower vertebrates, the distinction between sympathetic outflow and sacral parasympathetic outflow to pelvic organs is not clear. Therefore, it has been proposed to use the terms *cranial autonomic outflow* and *spinal autonomic outflow* rather than the terms *sympathetic* and *parasympathetic* (Nilsson, 1983). Although there is some merit in this idea, I do not use it in this chapter.

Langley defined the spinal levels of the functional outflow to different organs by examining organ function in response to ventral root stimulation at each segmental level. He then localized ganglionic synapses in each pathway by direct application of nicotine, a substance that excites postganglionic cell bodies. In this way, all the major efferent functional pathways to the peripheral tissues of several species of laboratory animal (cat, dog, and rabbit) were defined. It was evident that every organ receives a supply from one or both of the sympathetic and parasympathetic outflows and that the effects on each organ system are discrete and appear in some cases to be opposing each other. These experiments led to the concept of control of function of the autonomic target organs by independent peripheral autonomic pathways.

By the end of his life, Langley had also described the enteric nervous system, which is intrinsic to the wall of the gastrointestinal tract and is distinct from the sympathetic and parasympathetic nervous systems. Langley recognized that this system acts to a large extent independently of the central nervous system. It is composed of several types of afferent neurons, motoneurons, and inter-

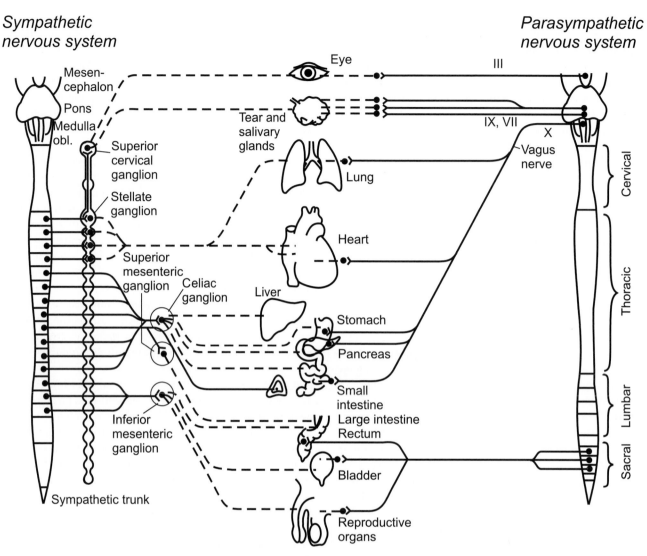

*Sympathetic nervous system*

*Parasympathetic nervous system*

Figure 9.2 The sympathetic and parasympathetic nervous systems. *Continuous lines*, preganglionic axons; *dotted lines*, postganglionic axons. The sympathetic outflows to skin and deep somatic structures of the extremities (upper extremity, T2 to T5; lower extremity, T12 to L3) and of the trunk are not shown. III, oculomotorius nerve; VII, facial nerve; IX, glossopharyngeal nerve; X, vagus nerve. Adapted from Jänig (2000).

neurons, which constitute reflex circuits controlling motility, secretion, absorption, and local blood flow in the gastrointestinal tract. The brain modifies and adapts the activity of the enteric nervous system to adjust the various gastrointestinal functions to the behavior of the organism via the sympathetic and the parasympathetic nervous systems. Astonishingly, the existence of the enteric nervous system as a functionally independent nervous system was almost entirely ignored until 1970 (see Furness & Bornstein, 1995; Furness & Costa, 1987).

Throughout the article I use the terms *sympathetic* and *parasympathetic* as defined anatomically by Langley. When peripheral autonomic neurons or neuron populations cannot unambiguously be assigned to one of these

systems, I speak of autonomic neurons. I do not use the terms *sympathetic* and *parasympathetic* in a global sense, as may be inferred from the work of Cannon (1939), Hess (1948), and others and as is still sometimes done in the literature. To speak of sympathetic or parasympathetic "functions" is a simplification which generates misunderstandings and gives a wrong impression of how these systems work.

### Gross Anatomy of the Peripheral Autonomic Nervous System

The basic feature of the sympathetic and parasympathetic systems is that each consists of two populations of neurons in series, which are connected synaptically in the periphery. The sympathetic and parasympathetic neurons that innervate the target issue lie entirely outside the central nervous system. The cell bodies of these neurons are grouped in autonomic ganglia. Their axons project from these ganglia to the target organs. Therefore, these neurons are called *ganglion cells* or *postganglionic neurons*. The efferent neurons that send axons from the CNS into the ganglia and form synapses on the dendrites and somata of the postganglionic neurons are called *preganglionic neurons*. Their somata and dendrites lie in the spinal cord or in the brain stem. The following section describes some aspects of the macroanatomical organization and function of both autonomic systems and some functional aspects of visceral afferents. Details of the anatomical organization are described in the literature (Pick, 1971; Williams & Warwick, 1980).

### Sympathetic Nervous System

The cell bodies of the preganglionic sympathetic neurons lie in the intermediate zone of the thoracic and upper lumbar spinal cord (the upper two to four lumbar segments, depending on the species). The axons of these neurons are either myelinated or unmyelinated and conduct action potentials at about 0.5–15 m/s. They leave the spinal cord in the ventral roots and white rami communicantes and project (1) either through the sympathetic chains, terminating in either of the bilateral paravertebral ganglia; (2) through the sympathetic chains and various splanchnic nerves (major, lesser, minor, lumbar), terminating in the (largely unpaired) prevertebral ganglia in the abdomen (celiac, superior mesenteric, and inferior mesenteric ganglion or plexus); or (3) further through the hypogastric nerves, terminating in the pelvic splanchnic ganglia. A preganglionic axon may travel through several paravertebral ganglia before making synaptic contacts (e.g., with postganglionic neurons in the superior cervical ganglion to the head and in lumbar prevertebral ganglia to the hindlimb) or form synapses with postganglionic neurons in several of them. However, there is no indication that individual preganglionic axons which innervate postganglionic neurons to the head and extremities project both up and down in the sympathetic chain, although they may do so in the midthoracic region. Furthermore, individual preganglionic axons most likely do not form synapses on postganglionic neurons in paravertebral, as well as prevertebral, ganglia. Finally, almost all preganglionic neurons projecting to paravertebral ganglia terminate only in ipsilateral ganglia; preganglionic neurons projecting to prevertebral ganglia terminate to about 80% on the ipsilateral side and to about 20% on the contralateral side (Baron, Jänig, & McLachlan, 1985b, 1985c, 1985d; Jänig & McLachlan, 1986a, 1986b).

The sympathetic ganglia are usually distinct in laboratory and smaller domestic animals, but some may become more like plexuses in larger species such as the human being (particularly the prevertebral ganglia and the lumbo-sacral sympathetic chains). This plexus-like organization probably contributed to the erroneous belief that the sympathetic nervous system is diffusely organized. Some aggregations of sympathetic postganglionic cell bodies are found more peripherally in ganglia in the vicinity of the pelvic organs (e.g., rectum, vas deferens, seminal vesicle, prostate). These ganglia belong to the pelvic plexus, which includes neurons that are innervated by either sympathetic or parasympathetic preganglionic axons or both (i.e., these neurons are simply autonomic). The preganglionic axons to these postganglionic neurons project through the hypogastric nerves (or plexuses).

The paravertebral ganglia are interconnected by nerve trunks to form a chain on either side of the vertebral column, extending from the base of the skull to the sacrum. These chains are called *sympathetic trunks*. Most sympathetic ganglia lie remote from the organs they supply, so that their postganglionic axons are long. The axons of postganglionic neurons are unmyelinated and conduct action potentials at less than 1 m/s; a few to the eye are myelinated.

- Overall, there is approximately one pair of ganglia per thoracic, lumbar, and sacral segment.
- The paravertebral ganglia are connected to the spinal nerves by white and gray rami. Preganglionic neurons project through the white rami and postganglionic neurons through the gray rami (but also the white rami).
- The paravertebral ganglia are named according to the spinal nerve from which the white ramus comes. Variations in the arrangement are described in the literature (Baron, Jänig, & Kollmann, 1988; Baron, Jänig, & McLachlan, 1985a; Baron, Jänig, & With, 1995; Pick, 1971).
- At the rostral end of the cervical sympathetic trunk lies the superior cervical ganglion (SCG), which contains the postganglionic neurons projecting to the head and the upper two or three cervical segments.
- At the rostral end of the thoracic sympathetic trunk lies the stellate ganglion, which contains the postganglionic neurons that project to the upper extremity in the brachial plexus and to the thoracic organs.
- Most postganglionic neurons in the paravertebral ganglia project through the gray rami, the respective spinal nerves, and the peripheral nerves to the effector cells in the somatic tissues. Some postganglionic neurons in the paravertebral ganglia project through the splanchnic nerves to the viscera.
- Postganglionic neurons in the SCG that project to the target organs in the head travel in perivascular bundles and join the nerves that project to the target

organs in the head. Some postganglionic neurons in the SCG project through special gray rami to the upper two or three cervical spinal nerves (Lichtman, Purves, & Yip, 1979).

- Postganglionic neurons in the stellate ganglion project through cardiac branches to the heart, through other branches to the lung, and through gray rami to the cervical spinal nerves C4–C8 (Pick, 1971).
- Postganglionic neurons in the prevertebral ganglia project in nerve bundles that accompany the relevant blood vessels or sometimes in special nerves (e.g., the hypogastric nerves) to the organs in the abdominal and pelvic cavity.

The effector cells and organs of the sympathetic nervous system are the smooth musculature of all organs (blood vessels, erector pili muscles, pupil, lung, evacuative organs), the heart, and some glands (sweat, salivary, and digestive glands). In addition, sympathetic postganglionic fibers innervate adipose tissue (white and brown), liver cells, the pineal gland, and lymphatic tissues (e.g., thymus, spleen, lymph nodes, and Peyer's patches in the gastrointestinal tract). Additionally, activity of the enteric nervous system is modulated by postganglionic sympathetic neurons.

Cells in the adrenal medulla are ontogenetically homologous to sympathetic postganglionic neurons. These cells are synaptically innervated by thoracic preganglionic neurons which project through the splanchnic nerves bypassing the celiac ganglion. The adrenal medulla is an endocrine gland that releases adrenaline and noradrenaline directly into the blood, which circulates to reach tissues throughout the body. The responses of these tissues depend on the characteristic adrenoceptors and postreceptor events which are present in each.

### Parasympathetic Nervous System

The cell bodies of preganglionic parasympathetic neurons are situated in the brain stem (dorsal motor vagus nucleus, nucleus ambiguus, superior salivary nucleus, visceral efferent oculomotor [Edinger-Westphal] nucleus) and in the intermediate zone of the sacral spinal cord. They project through the third (oculomotor), seventh (facial and intermediate), and ninth (glossopharyngeal) cranial nerves to the ocular muscles and glands of the head, through the tenth cranial (vagal) nerve to the target organs in the thoracic and abdominal cavity, and through the pelvic splanchnic nerves to the pelvic organs. The preganglionic axons can be very long and are either myelinated or unmyelinated. Discrete parasympathetic ganglia are found only in the head region (ciliary ganglion: eye; pterygopalatine ganglion: lachrymal, nasal, and palatal glands; otic and submandibular ganglion: salivary glands) and near or in the wall of the effector organs (heart: cardiac plexus;

airways: ganglia on the membranous part; pancreas; gallbladder; organs in the pelvic cavity: ganglia in the pelvic plexus; see McLachlan, 1995). Preganglionic neurons project to the gastrointestinal tract synapse with neurons and their presynaptic terminals that are part of the enteric nervous system.

The parasympathetic system innervates the exocrine glands of the head, the intraocular smooth muscles, the smooth muscles and glands of the airways, the smooth musculature, exocrine glands, and endocrine glands of the gastrointestinal tract (via the enteric nervous system), the heart (pacemaker cells and atria), the pelvic organs (lower urinary tract, hindgut, reproductive organs), and epithelia and mucosa throughout the body. Except for the helical arteries and sinusoids of the erectile tissues of the reproductive organs and some intracranial, uterine, and facial blood vessels, the parasympathetic system does not innervate blood vessels. The parasympathetic supply to these tissues is not involved in blood pressure regulation.

### Reactions of Autonomic Target Organs to Activation of Sympathetic and Parasympathetic Axons

Table 9.1 describes the overall reactions of the peripheral target organs and individual target tissues to activity in the sympathetic and parasympathetic neurons which innervate them. The responses have been defined by reflex activation or by electrical stimulation of the respective nerves. In some cases, the apparent effects of these nerves have been identified by changes in function after removing or blocking the nerve supply. The table shows that:

- Most target tissues react to only one of the autonomic systems.
- A few target tissues react to the activation of both autonomic systems (e.g., iris, pacemaker cells and atria of the heart, urinary bladder).
- Opposite reactions to the activation of sympathetic and parasympathetic neurons are more the exception than the rule (e.g., pacemaker and atria of the heart, erectile tissue of the reproductive organs, some exocrine digestive glands, insulin-producing islet cells of the pancreas).
- Most effects are excitatory; inhibition (e.g., relaxation of muscle, decreased secretion) is rare.

It is evident from Table 9.1 that both systems have some very specialized effects on particular organs but also generate functional effects that are similar in many tissues. For example, parasympathetic innervation of mucosae and glands is almost always responsible for the generation of watery secretions, whereas sympathetic innervation in most organs is at least in part associated with vasoconstriction.

Table 9.1. Effects of Activation of Sympathetic and Parasympathetic Neurons on Autonomic Target Organs. From Jänig and Häbler (1999), copyright 1999, with permission from Elsevier Science.

| Organ and Organ System | Activation of Parasympathetic Nerves | Activation of Sympathetic Nerves |
|---|---|---|
| Heart muscle | decrease of heart rate decrease of contractility (only atria) | increase of heart rate increase of contractility (atria, ventricles) |
| Blood vessels: Arteries | | |
| in skin of trunk and limbs | 0 | vasoconstriction |
| in skin and mucosa of face | vasodilatation (?) | vasoconstriction |
| in visceral domain | 0 | vasoconstriction |
| in skeletal muscle | 0 | vasoconstriction vasodilatation (cholinergic) |
| in heart (coronary arteries) | | vasoconstriction |
| in erectile tissue (helical arteries and sinusoids in penis and clitoris) | vasodilatation | vasoconstriction |
| in cranium | vasodilatation (?) | vasoconstriction |
| Blood vessels: Veins | 0 | vasoconstriction |
| Gastrointestinal tract | | |
| longitudinal and circular muscle | increase of motility | decrease of motility |
| sphincters | relaxation | contraction |
| Capsule of spleen | 0 | contraction |
| Urinary bladder | | |
| detrusor vesicae | contraction | relaxation (small) |
| trigone (internal sphincter) | 0 | contraction |
| Reproductive organs | | |
| seminal vesicle, prostate | 0 | contraction |
| vas deferens | 0 | contraction |
| uterus | 0 | contraction relaxation (depends on species and hormonal state) |
| Eye | | |
| dilator muscle of pupil | 0 | contraction (mydriasis) |
| sphincter muscle of pupil | contraction (miosis) | 0 |
| ciliary muscle | contraction (accommodation) | 0 |
| tarsal muscle | 0 | contraction (lifting of lid) |
| orbital muscle | 0 | contraction (protrusion of eye) |
| Tracheo-bronchial muscles | contraction | relaxation (probably mainly by adrenaline) |
| Piloerector muscles | 0 | contraction |
| Exocrine glands | | |
| salivary glands | copious serous secretion | weak mucous secretion (submandibular gland) |
| lachrymal glands | secretion | 0 |
| nasopharyngeal glands | secretion | ? |
| bronchial glands | secretion | ? |
| sweat glands | 0 | secretion (cholinergic) |
| digestive glands (stomach, pancreas) | secretion | decrease of secretion or 0 |
| mucosa (small, large intestine) | secretion | decrease of secretion or reabsorption |
| Pineal gland | 0 | increase in synthesis of melatonin |

(continued)

Table 9.1. Continued

| Organ and Organ System | Activation of Parasympathetic Nerves | Activation of Sympathetic Nerves |
|---|---|---|
| Brown adipose tissue | 0 | heat production |
| Metabolism | | |
| liver | 0 | glycogenolysis, gluconeo-genesis |
| fat cells | 0 | lipolysis (free fatty acids in blood increased) |
| beta-cells in islets of pancreas | secretion of insulin | decrease of secretion of insulin |
| Adrenal medulla | 0 | secretion of adrenaline and noradrenaline |
| Lymphoid tissue | 0 | depression of activity (e.g., of natural killer cells) |

Table 9.1 clearly shows that the universally propagated idea of an antagonism between the parasympathetic and sympathetic nervous systems is a misconception. Where there is a reciprocal effect of the two autonomic systems on the target cells, it can usually be shown either that the systems work synergistically or that they exert their influence under different functional conditions. For example, the opposite actions of sympathetic and parasympathetic systems on the size of the pupil is a consequence of the separate target cells (dilator pupillae for sympathetic, sphincter pupillae for parasympathetic) supplied by each system. Moreover, in larger mammals, fast changes of heart rate during changes of body position and emotional stress are generated via changes in activity in the parasympathetic neurons to the pacemaker cells; the sustained increase of heart rate during exercise is mainly generated by activation of sympathetic neurons supplying the heart. In addition, it is likely that some organs which can be affected by both systems under experimental conditions are primarily under the control of only one system in vivo (i.e., under physiological conditions).

In essence, Table 9.1 shows the macroscopic effects of activation of sympathetic and parasympathetic neurons on target organs; it does not show whether these responses have functional meaning nor how the autonomic systems work to regulate the behavior of these target organs. Finally, these nervous effects on the autonomic target organs are not necessarily the same as the reactions of the effector organs to application of exogenous transmitter substances or to circulating adrenaline from the adrenal medulla.

### Neuropeptides in Autonomic Neurons and the Idea of "Neurochemical Coding"

The presence of distinct functional subunits of the autonomic nervous system is supported by a substantial amount of histochemical evidence that autonomic neurons projecting to some specific targets contain particular combinations of neuropeptides with (and without) the classical transmitters, noradrenaline (NA) and acetylcholine (ACh). The patterns of coexistence of peptide and nonpeptide transmitters within the cell bodies in peripheral ganglia can often be correlated with combinations of coexisting substances that can be demonstrated in the nerve terminals associated with target tissues (see Gibbins, 1990, 1995; Morris & Gibbins, 1992). Various combinations of substances are present in, for example, the vascular innervation, the innervation of the vas deferens, and so forth; but there are many examples of species-specific neuropeptide expression (see Nilsson & Holmgren, 1994). The term *neurochemical coding* has been coined for the coexistence of a classical transmitter and one or a set of neuropeptides in the neurons associated with a particular target tissue. The patterns of coding can often be used to identify different functional populations of autonomic neurons. Examples of neuropeptide/neurotransmitter combinations in the cat are: Most postganglionic terminals on arterial blood vessels (vasoconstrictor neurons) in viscera, skin, and skeletal muscle contain, in addition to NA, neuropeptide Y (NPY) and galanin (GAL); skeletal muscle vessels with vasodilator innervation have, presumably in addition to acetylcholine (ACh), vasoactive intestinal peptide (VIP); and terminals in sweat glands (from sudomotor neurons) contain, again in addition to choline acetyl transferase (ChAT), the enzyme that synthesizes ACh, VIP, calcitonin gene-related peptide (CGRP), and substance P (Anderson, McAllen, & Edwards, 1995; Lindh, Lundberg, & Hökfelt, 1989; Lindh, Risling, Remahl, Terenius, & Hökfelt 1993; Lundberg et al., 1988; Moriarty, Gibbins, Potter, & McCloskey 1992). The principle of neurochemical coding has been exploited to unravel the connectivity and function of the enteric nervous system in the guinea pig (Furness & Bornstein, 1995; Furness & Costa, 1987) Although only a few preganglionic neurons have as yet been found to contain identified neuropeptides, this neurochemical coding is also present to a certain extent in preganglionic pathways (Gibbins, 1995; Lindh et al., 1993; Shafton, Old-field, & McAllen, 1992).

The concept of neurochemical coding of autonomic neurons is an interesting development, and at present it is a powerful experimental tool in the analysis of the pathways of the autonomic nervous system, that is, in the context of chemical neuroanatomy of the autonomic nervous system. The functions of most neuropeptides are unknown; however, they are beginning to be revealed for a few neuropeptides (Furness, Bornstein, Murphy, & Pompolo, 1992; Lundberg, 1981; Ulman, Potter, & McCloskey, 1992). In much of the published literature it is assumed that these neuropeptides act as transmitters, as the terms *transmitter, cotransmitter, neuromodulator*, and so forth are generally applied to them. However, the presence of a neuropeptide in an autonomic neuron, the release of that neuropeptide during nerve stimulation, and the presence of the receptors for the same neuropeptide on the target cells (neurons or effector cells) does not reveal whether the neuropeptide is normally or even pathophysiologically used during the neural regulation of that target tissue. For example, no convincing experiment has been performed that illustrates for autonomic neurons in which functional context NPY is physiologically important for the regulation of target tissues, although it has been shown that this peptide is released into the blood during activity of muscle vasoconstrictor neurons and that its concentration increases during exercise (Morris et al., 1986; Pernow, 1988). Another example is VIP, which is colocalized with ACh in sympathetic postganglionic neurons innervating sweat glands (Lundberg, 1981) and in parasympathetic postganglionic neurons innervating the erectile tissue of sexual organs (de Groat, 1999; de Groat & Booth, 1993). Thus it is important to appreciate (1) that the chemical coding of many functionally distinct autonomic pathways is not straightforward, (2) that the correlation between target tissue and neurochemistry is by no means absolute, (3) that the function of neurally released peptides is mostly unclear, and (4) that the neuropeptides expressed in particular functional pathways can differ markedly between species, even where a function has been demonstrated (Gibbins, 1992, 1995; Gibbins & Morris, 1987; Potter, 1991; Romano, Felten, Felten, & Olschowka, 1991; Ulman et al., 1992).

## Visceral Afferent Neurons and Autonomic Regulation

### Visceral Afferents: General Functions

Afferent neurons that innervate visceral organs in the thoracic, abdominal, and pelvic cavities and that have their cell bodies either in the spinal dorsal root ganglia or in the equivalent ganglia of the vagal and glossopharyngeal

nerves are called visceral afferent neurons. These afferent neurons encode mechanical and chemical events that occur in the visceral organs and convey this information to spinal cord and lower brain stem. They are the interface between the visceral body domain and the central nervous system. They are involved in specific organ regulations, multiple organ reflexes, general neuroendocrine regulations, specific and general visceral sensations (including visceral pain), shaping of emotional feelings, and other functions. Visceral afferent neurons that convey the information from the viscera to the neuraxis are distinguished from visceral afferent neurons of the enteric nervous system. These sensory neurons have their cell bodies in the wall of the gastrointestinal tract; some of them project to the prevertebral ganglia (Furness & Costa, 1987; Jänig, 1988b; Szurszewski & King, 1989).

Some visceral afferent neurons serve special functions related to distinct types of physiological control in which the autonomic nervous system is the efferent pathway—for example, cardiovascular afferents, afferents from the respiratory tract, and afferents from the gastrointestinal tract which project to the nucleus of the solitary tract and afferents from pelvic organs which project to the sacral spinal cord. These afferents monitor the inner state of the body and serve to maintain homeostasis and to adapt the internal milieu and the organ functions to the behavior of the organism. In this sense they belong functionally to the autonomic nervous system. However, the second-order neurons that the visceral afferents connect to are widespread and carry signals to higher levels of integration. The brain's knowledge of the body's inner state may influence behavior in the widest sense.

Although visceral afferents are anatomically and functionally closely associated with the autonomic nervous systems, it is preferred to call these afferent neurons *visceral* (qualified by *spinal* or *vagal*). The terms *sympathetic afferent* and *parasympathetic afferent neuron* are misleading because they imply that the afferents have functions that uniquely pertain to that particular part of the autonomic nervous system. No functional, morphological, or other criteria exist to associate any type of visceral afferent neuron that projects to the spinal cord or brain stem with only one of the autonomic systems. The label *sympathetic* or *parasympathetic* would lead to further complications as far as the function of these afferents is concerned. For example, pelvic organs are innervated by two sets of spinal visceral afferents, one entering the cord at lumbar levels and the other at sacral levels, and both are involved in visceral nociception (Cervero, 1994; Jänig, 1996b; Jänig & Koltzenburg, 1993; Jänig & Morrison, 1986; Ritter et al., 1992). It makes no sense to speak of "sympathetic" and "parasympathetic" visceral nociception.

This section focuses on functional aspects of vagal and spinal visceral afferent neurons. Anatomy and physiology of the afferent neurons for each organ are described in detail in the literature (Cervero, 1994; Cervero & Morrison, 1986; Coleridge & Coleridge, 1980, 1984; Grundy, 1988; Grundy & Scratcherd, 1989; Jänig, 1996a; Jänig & Koltzenburg, 1990, 1991, 1993; Malliani, 1982; Mei, 1983, 1985; Ritter et al., 1992; see Thorén, 1979).

### Reciprocal Neural Connections Between Brain and Viscera

The central nervous system (CNS) receives information from the internal organs by two sets of visceral afferents and sends efferent impulses to the internal organs by two sets of autonomic efferents (Figure 9.3).

About 80–85% of the nerve fibers in the vagus nerve are afferent. The cell bodies of afferent neurons projecting in the vagus nerve lie in the nodose (and some in the jugular) ganglion, those projecting in the glossopharyngeal nerve (including afferents from arterial baro- and chemoreceptors) lie in the petrosal ganglion. Most of these afferents are unmyelinated, some are myelinated, but this varies between organs. The fibers project viscerotopically to the nucleus of the solitary tract (NTS; Loewy & Spyer, 1990; Ritter et al., 1992). The second-order neurons in the NTS project to various sites in the lower brain stem, upper brain stem, hypothalamus, and amygdala, establishing well-organized neural pathways which are the basis for distinct organ regulation. It is assumed that vagal visceral afferents are normally not associated with the generation of visceral pain. This has been questioned as far as the heart is concerned (Mehler & Gebhart, 1992), and there are indications that some unmyelinated vagal afferents that innervate the mucosa of trachea and esophagus are involved in discomfort and possibly pain. Stimulation of these afferents induces vasodilatation and plasma extravasation in the mucosa of trachea and esophagus, both being proinflammatory reactions which are typical for some types of polymodal nociceptive afferents (see Barnes, 1991; Coleridge & Coleridge, 1984; McDonald, 1990). Otherwise it is likely that most impulses in visceral vagal afferents never reach consciousness; yet they are associated with general feelings like hunger, satiety, and nausea. Finally, experiments on animals show that vagal afferents may be involved in central inhibitory control of nociception and pain (see Foreman, 1989; Gebhart & Randich, 1992; Randich & Gebhart, 1992).

Spinal visceral afferent neurons project from the viscera through splanchnic nerves to the thoracic, upper lumbar, and sacral spinal cord and have their cell bodies in the corresponding dorsal root ganglia. There is no evidence that the peripheral axons of spinal afferents project along the sympathetic chain and the major distributing arteries (e.g., the subclavian, iliac, carotid artery) to the extremities or to the head. However, large vessels in some parts of the body are surrounded by the terminals of primary afferent neurons that form a plexus lying outside the perivascular noradrenergic plexus.

The spinal projections of visceral afferent neurons from the different organs are segmentally organized, although the afferent projections from each organ exhibit a wide segmental distribution (Jänig & Morrison, 1986). No distinct organotopic organization of this projection is present in the dorsal horn: The afferents project to laminae I and V of the dorsal horn, sparing lamina II (substantia gelatinosa Rolandi) and laminae III and IV (nucleus proprius). Occasionally they project to the contralateral laminae V and X. Single visceral afferent neurons with unmyelinated fibers project over 4–5 segments and over the whole mediolateral width of the dorsal horn. This projection contrasts with that of single cutaneous afferent neurons with unmyelinated fibers, which is spatially much more restricted (Sugiura, Terui, & Hosoa, 1989; for reviews of spinal projection of visceral and other afferents, see de Groat, 1986; Willis & Coggeshall, 1994).

About 1.5–2% of all spinal afferents which have their cell bodies in the dorsal root ganglia project to the viscera; the other spinal afferent neurons project to skin and deep somatic tissues (Jänig & Morrison, 1986). This illustrates that visceral organs are much less densely innervated by spinal afferents than the superficial and deep somatic domains. The low density of spinal visceral afferent innervation and the broad segmental projection of spinal afferents from different organs is one basis of the poor localization and graduation of visceral sensations mediated by spinal visceral afferent neurons.

Thoraco-lumbar spinal visceral afferent neurons encode events in their activity which may lead to pain and discomfort. Furthermore, these afferents are involved in extraspinal and spinal intestino-intestinal reflexes and probably also in specific organ reflexes, for example, to the heart and the kidney (see DiBona, 1982; Kopp & DiBona, 1992; Malliani, 1982). However, this has not been thoroughly studied.

Pelvic organs have a dual spinal visceral afferent innervation and a somewhat higher density of innervation by spinal afferents than the other organs. This is related to the precise control of these organs by the central nervous system (CNS). The sacral component of this afferent innervation is essential for the regulation of evacuation and storage functions and of the reproductive organs, as well as for the generation of nonpainful and most painful sensations associated with the pelvic organs. Thoraco-lumbar visceral afferents are not essential for the regulation of the pelvic organs and the associated nonpainful sensations but may be important for the generation of pain (see Jänig & Koltzenburg, 1993; Jänig & McLachlan, 1987; Jänig & Morrison, 1986).

Most or all neurons in the thoraco-lumbar spinal cord which are synaptically excited by visceral afferents re-

*Visceral Afferent Inputs*
*Autonomic Efferent Outputs*                                    *General Functions*

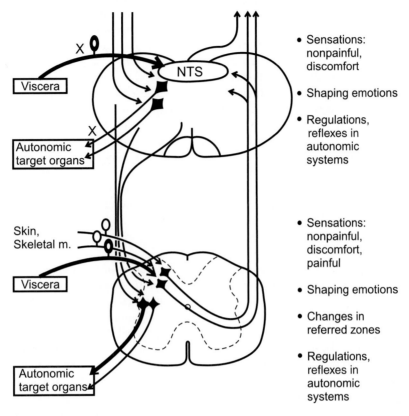

Figure 9.3 General scheme of visceral-autonomic relations. *Left*: Visceral afferent inputs and efferent (autonomic) outputs of lower brain stem and spinal cord. *Right*: General functions of visceral afferent neurons. *Upper part*: medulla oblongata; cell bodies of preganglionic neurons that project in the vagus nerve are located in the dorsal vagus motor nucleus and in the nucleus ambiguus; X, vagus nerve; NTS, nucleus of the solitary tract. *Lower part*: spinal cord, spinal visceral afferents converge on viscero-somatic neurons with afferent input from skin and skeletal muscle in laminae I and V of the dorsal horn; sensations are also referred to the segmentally corresponding body domains. Note that all efferent autonomic systems and that the transmission of impulses from visceral primary afferent neurons to second-order neurons (in the NTS and in the dorsal horn of the spinal cord) are under descending control from higher brain centers (see Jänig & Morrison, 1986; Jänig & Häbler, 1995). Adapted from Jänig & Häbler (1995).

ceive additional convergent synaptic input from afferents of the superficial (skin) and the deep somatic domains. They are viscero-somatic convergent neurons and are located in laminae I, V, and X (around the central canal) of the dorsal horn (Cervero & Tattersall, 1986). In the sacral spinal cord, the viscero-somatic convergent neurons are also situated in lamina I and close to the autonomic nuclei (laminae V–VII, dorsal commissure) to which the sacral visceral afferents project (see de Groat & Booth, 1993; de Groat, Booth, & Yoshimura, 1993). These neurons are ei-

ther local interneurons or they project to other spinal segments or to supraspinal brain structures (e.g., through the ventrolateral quadrant of the spinal cord to brain stem and thalamus).

Efferent vagal nerve fibers are preganglionic parasympathetic axons which have their cell bodies in the dorsal motor nucleus of the vagus nerve and in the nucleus ambiguus. The spinal autonomic efferents to the viscera are thoraco-lumbar (sympathetic) and sacral (parasympathetic; for details see the sections in this chapter on functional anatomy and on functional organization of the peripheral sympathetic and parasympathetic pathways).

### Visceral Primary Afferent Neurons as Interface Between Visceral Organs and Brain

Many spinal afferent neurons and some vagal afferent neurons, in particular those with unmyelinated axons and supplying viscera, seem to have multiple functions (Jänig, 1996b). The knowledge about some of these functions is well established; others are at best hypothetical. These functions do not apply to each type of visceral afferent neuron, and afferent neurons may be specialized not only with respect to their receptive properties but also with respect to the other putative functions (de Groat, 1987; Dockray, Green, & Varro, 1989; Maggi & Meli, 1988). Spinal visceral afferents might further be differentiated for mediating preferentially peripheral extraspinal reflexes or local regulations or trophic influences.

- The conventional function of the visceral afferent neuron is to encode physical (distension, contraction) and chemical events by centripetal impulses leading to organ regulations, reflexes, and distinct sensations.
- Collaterals of some spinal visceral afferent fibers form peptidergic synapses with noradrenergic neurons in prevertebral ganglia (celiac, mesenteric ganglia) which are particularly involved in gastrointestinal functions (regulation of secretion and motility), establishing in this way extraspinal reflexes. These neurons integrate activity in preganglionic neurons, peripheral afferent neurons of the enteric nervous system, and spinal visceral afferents (de Groat, 1987; Dockray et al., 1989; Furness & Costa, 1987; Jänig, 1988b, 1995b; Szurszewski & King, 1989).
- Visceral afferent neurons may participate in a variety of important "efferent" functions by release of neuropeptides (such as calcitonin gene-related peptide, substance P), within the viscera that are independent of CNS and prevertebral ganglia—for example, vasodilatation, bronchoconstriction, secretory processes in the gastrointestinal tract, regulation of gut and urinary tract motility, and protection of the gastric mucosa against acid back-diffusion and other functions (Holzer, 1992, 1995; Maggi, Giachetti, Dey, & Said, 1995; Santicioli & Maggi, 1998). These functions may be particularly important under pathophysiological conditions, for example, inflammatory changes of the peripheral tissue (de Groat, 1989; Dockray et al., 1989; Kumazawa, 1990).
- Visceral afferents may have trophic functions and could be important for the maintenance of the structure of the visceral tissues (e.g., the mucosa of the urogenital tract or of the stomach; cf. Lundgren, 1989).
- Afferent neurons transport retrogradely neurotrophic substances; this invites speculation that these substances might have long-term effects on the synaptic connections formed by primary afferent terminals in the spinal cord with second-order neurons (cf. Lewin & McMahon, 1993).

The cascade of functions of spinal visceral afferents may serve the same final general aim: the protection and maintenance of the integrity of visceral tissues. For example, excitation of thoracolumbar spinal visceral afferent neurons may elicit pain and discomfort, protective supraspinal, spinal, and extraspinal reflexes, and peripheral changes of target organ responses (such as increase of blood flow, change of motility, and secretion).

### Central Functions of Visceral Afferent Neurons

The degree of functional specificity of afferent neurons is generally described by way of their quantitative responses to physical and chemical stimuli. If an afferent neuron responds preferentially to a particular physiological stimulus applied to its receptive endings at low stimulus energy but not to other physiological stimuli, then this stimulus is considered to be an adequate stimulus and the receptive ending of the afferent neuron specific for this stimulus (see Cervero, 1994). Many visceral receptors are specific with respect to the adequate stimuli occurring in the visceral domain. Table 9.2 lists, separated for different organ systems, the physiologically distinct types of visceral afferent neurons and the sensations, organ functions, and general regulations that are associated with the activation of these afferent neurons. The activation of a particular type of afferent neuron does not *cause* a particular sensation, and the afferent signals generated in the periphery are not "carried through" to the cerebral cortex in a labeled-line system. Here three classes of events are involved which are not interchangeable: the anatomy of the neurons, the physiology of the neurons, and the "psychology" of the sensations. Detailed descriptions of the receptive properties of these afferent neurons are given in the literature quoted in Table 9.2:

- Many visceral afferents that project to the brain stem (nucleus of the solitary tract) and to the sacral spinal cord are involved in the regulation of internal organs (i.e., lungs, heart, gastrointestinal tract, evacuative organs, reproductive organs). Most of these afferents respond rather specifically and in a graded way to adequate peripheral stimuli, are mechanosensitive, and are activated by various types of mechanical distortion.

Table 9.2. Visceral Afferent Neurons, Sensations, Regulations, and Reflexes

| Organ[a] | | Afferent neuron[b] | Sensation[c] | Regulation/Reflex[d] |
|---|---|---|---|---|
| **Respiratory Tract** | | | | |
| Pharynx, larynx | V | Mech. rec. (pressure), irritant rec., cold rec., flow rec. | Rawness, irritation, desire to cough, pain, nausea | Aspiration reflex, cough reflex, swallowing, bronchodilatation, etc. |
| Trachea, bronchi, lung | V | Irritant rec., C-fiber (epithelial) rec. | Substernal rawness, irritation, urge to cough, tightness | Burn-cough reflex, laryngo-, bronchoconstriction, mucus secretion, hyperpnea |
| | V | Slowly adapting rec. | ?/no | Hering-Breuer reflex |
| | V | J-receptor | Irritation in throat, breathlessness, discomfort, pain | Respiratory-protective reflexes |
| | S | yes, function? | ?/no | ? |
| **Cardiovascular Organs** | | | | |
| Large blood vessels | V | Barorec., chemorec. | No | Cardiovascular regul., reflexes |
| | S | Mechanorec. | Discomfort, pain | Spinal reflexes |
| Heart | V | Mechanorec. (atrial, ventricular) | No | Cardiovascular regul., reflexes |
| | S | Atrial rec. | No | Cardiovascular reflexes |
| | S | Ventricular, coronary | Discomfort, pain, other sensations (?) | Cardio-cardial reflexes, other cardiovascular reflexes |
| **Gastrointestinal Tract** | | | | |
| Esophagus | V | Mechanorec. (tension) | Fullness, thermal sensations, heartburn | Propulsive peristalsis, vomiting |
| | S | Mechanorec. | Discomfort, (tension) pain | ? |
| Stomach | V | Mechanorec. (tension)[e] | Fullness/emptiness | Storage, relaxation |
| | V | Mucosarec. (mechano-, chemo-, thermo-)[f] | Satiety/hunger, thermal sensations (?) | Secretion, peristalsis, vomiting |
| | S | Mechanorec. (serosal)[g] | Discomfort, pain | Intestino-intestinal reflexes |
| Duodenum | V | Mechanorec. (tension)[e] | ? | Secretion, peristalsis |
| Ileum, jejunum | V | Mucosarec. (mechano-, chemo-, thermo-)[f] | ? | Secretion (?), peristalsis (?) |
| | S | Mechanorec. (serosal)[g] | Discomfort, pain | Intestino-intestinal reflexes |
| Liver | V | Osmorec. | Thirst | Osmoregulation (?) |
| Gallbladder | S | Mechanorec. | Discomfort, pain | ? |
| Pancreas | S | Mechanorec. | Discomfort, pain | |
| Colon, rectum | S1[h] | Mechanorec. (wall) | Fullness, call to defecate, discomfort; pain | Defecation, continence reflexes |
| | S2[h] | Mechanorec. (serosal)[g] | Discomfort, pain | ? |
| Anal canal | S1[h] | Mechanorec., thermorec., nociceptor (?) | Shearing sensation, thermal sensation (?), pain | Anorectal, anovesical reflexes |
| **Urinary Tract** | | | | |
| Kidney | S | Mechanorec., chemorec. | Pain | Renorenal reflexes, other reflexes |

*(continued)*

Table 9.2. *(continued)*

| Organ[a] | | Afferent neuron[b] | Sensation[c] | Regulation/Reflex[d] |
|---|---|---|---|---|
| ***Urinary Tract*** | | | | |
| Ureter | S1/S2[h] | Mechanorec. | Pain | ? |
| Urinary bladder, urethra | S1[h] | Mechanorec. | Fullness, urge to micturate, discomfort, pain | Micturition, continence reflexes |
| | S2[h] | Mechanorec. | Discomfort, pain | ? |
| Spleen | S | Mechanorec. | Discomfort, pain | ? |
| ***General*** | | | | |
| All organs, inclusive blood vessels, etc. | S | Mechanorec. (high threshold), chemorec. (?) (mechanoinsensitive afferents) | ?; pain under pathophysiological conditions | Defensive reactions/reflexes (?), trophic functions (?) |

*Note.* V: Visceral afferent neurons projecting through the vagal or glossopharyngeal nerves to the nucleus of the solitary tract in the medulla oblongata. The cell bodies of these afferent neurons lie in the nodose, jugular, and petrosal ganglia. S: Spinal afferent neurons projecting through the splanchnic nerves to the thoracic, upper lumbar, and sacral spinal cord. The cell bodies of these afferents lie in the thoracic, upper lumbar, and sacral dorsal root ganglia. Data from Andrews (1986), Coleridge and Coleridge (1984), Grundy (1988), Hertz (1911), Jänig and Koltzenburg (1993), Jänig and Morrison (1986), Malliani (1982), Mei (1983, 1985), Paintal (1986), Widdicombe (1986). Adopted from Jänig (1996b).

[a]Organ or organ system. [b]Functional type of afferent neuron. [c]Type of sensation(s) elicited when the respective afferent neuron(s) is (are) stimulated. [d]Type(s) of regulation and reflexes associated with the afferent neurons. [e]Receptors lying in the muscular wall of the gastrointestinal tract, responding to distension and contraction. [f]Stimulus specificity unclear. [g]Receptors lying particularly at the insertion of the mesenteries and responding to mechanical and chemical stimuli. [h]S1, sacral visceral afferent neurons; S2, lumbar visceral afferent neurons.

- Many vagal afferents innervate mucosal receptors of the stomach, duodenum, and small intestine and respond to chemical (glucose, amino acids, long/short-chain lipids), mechanical, and thermal stimuli. Whether these afferents are specific for one of the stimuli is a matter of debate and unclear (Grundy, 1988; Grundy & Scratcherd, 1989; Mei, 1983, 1985). Other chemosensory afferents that project to the nucleus of the solitary tract innervate secondary chemoreceptive cells in the carotid and aortic glomeruli, which are primarily sensitive to decrease in arterial oxygen pressure and osmosensors in the liver.
- The sensory receptors of thoraco-lumbar visceral afferents are situated in the serosa, at the attachment sites of the mesenteries, and in the walls of some organs. It is unclear whether these afferents also innervate the mucosa (e.g., of the gastrointestinal tract or the urinary bladder). Most of these afferents seem to be mechanosensitive and react to distension and contraction of the organs but also to chemical stimuli as they occur during inflammation and ischemia of the organs. They probably do not signal specific events to the spinal cord except that they are associated with a particular organ, but they trigger protective reflexes and regulation, pain, and local protective responses (see additional discussion in this section) when excited.
- Pain associated with the visceral organs (with the possible exception of the upper respiratory tract and the esophagus) is elicited by excitation of spinal visceral afferents (including sacral visceral afferents; see Jänig & Morrison, 1986). For some visceral organs it is very much debated whether these spinal visceral afferents are specific nociceptive afferents or whether the same afferents are involved in organ regulations, nonpainful sensations, as well as pain (Häbler, Jänig, & Koltzenburg, 1990, 1991, 1993a, 1993b; Jänig & Häbler, 1995; Jänig & Koltzenburg, 1990, 1993; Jänig & Morrison, 1986). The same reasoning may apply to the heart (Lombardi, Della Bella, Casati, & Malliani, 1981; Malliani, 1982; see also Coleridge & Coleridge, 1980) and the kidney (Recordati, Moss, Genovesi, & Rogenes, 1981). Other visceral organs (e.g., gallbladder and ureter) seem to be largely innervated only by mechanically high threshold afferents which also have chemosensitivity (for details see Cervero, 1994; Jänig, 1996b).
- Many organs and tissues in the visceral domain are probably innervated by mechano-insensitive spinal afferents that are not excited during normal regulation of the organs, not by stimuli that elicit pain under healthy conditions. These afferents may be recruited under pathophysiological conditions, such as, for example, inflammation (Häbler et al., 1990; Jänig & Koltzenburg, 1990, 1993; Michaelis, Häbler, & Jänig, 1996).
- There is indirect evidence that abdominal vagal afferents innervating the liver and small intestine are involved in the production of a general sickness be-

havior in rats which is characterized by protective illness responses (e.g., immobility, decrease in food intake, formation of taste aversion to novel food, decrease of digestion, loss of weight [anorexia], fever, increase of sleep, change in endocrine functions, malaise, hyperalgesia). These afferents are supposed to sense toxic events and agents in the intestine that are dangerous for the organism. They may serve as an early warning system for the body and may therefore be important for protective functions of the gastrointestinal tract and the body (for review see Jänig, Khasar, Levine, & Miao, 2000).

- Emotional feelings and their expression (by the somatomotor system in facial expression, by autonomic systems in the adaptive responses of the cardiovascular system, gastrointestinal tract, and evacuative organs, by neuroendocrine systems) are represented in the brain and generated in parallel by the brain without peripheral afferent input from visceral and deep somatic body domains. However, visceral afferent activity has strong influence by modulating centrally generated emotional feelings. It is virtually impossible to disprove that emotions are evoked ("caused") by afferent activity from viscera and deep somatic structures during bodily changes, as originally proposed by James and Lange (James & Lange, 1920; Meyers, 1986; see the subsection in this chapter on basic emotions and autonomic systems.

## General Concepts of Function of the Autonomic Nervous System

In the introduction, I alluded to the enormous range of vital functions which are under the control of the autonomic nervous system. This control is essential in order to maintain the state of the internal milieu within appropriate limits during various motor behaviors and to adjust the function of the component cells, tissues, and organs in the face of internal and external challenges. From the anatomy and macroscopic functions of the autonomic nervous system presented in the section on functional anatomy in this chapter, an overall concept of how the body functions in terms of the regulation of organ systems and how this is done by the various divisions of the autonomic nervous system and at different levels of the neuraxis can now be formulated. Table 9.3 lists the different controls which are represented in the spinal cord, brain stem, and hypothalamus. Autonomic regulation that is mainly dependent on integrative processes in spinal cord and brain stem involves predominantly either one or both parts of the autonomic outflows. More complex control is represented in the hypothalamus, which directs the autonomic control

systems represented in the spinal cord and brain stem, the neuroendocrine systems, and elementary motor behavior. The forebrain adapts the controls represented in the neuraxis to the needs of the organism.

Here I discuss some general concepts of the function of the autonomic nervous system that evolved from the experimental work of W. B. Cannon and W. R. Hess and others in the first half of the last century and that had and still have considerable impact on our thinking.

### Walter Bradford Cannon and the Concept of the Sympathico-Adrenal System

In the second half of the nineteenth century, Claude Bernard formulated the idea that "It is the fixity of the *milieu intérieur* which is the condition of free and independent life" and that "all the vital mechanisms, however varied they may be, have only one object, that of preserving constant the conditions of life in the internal environment" (cited in Cannon, 1939, p. 38). The American physiologist Walter Bradford Cannon was very much influenced by the ideas of Claude Bernard. He called the *milieu intérieur* the *fluid matrix* of the body. Cannon described the coordinated physiological processes which maintain the steady state of the organism with the term *homeostasis*. Cannon was convinced that the automatic corrections of the physiological parameters of the body are the primary function of the autonomic nervous system.

Cannon's ideas about how homeostasis is achieved and the role the autonomic nervous system plays in this were first presented in a review, "Organization for Physiological Homeostasis" (1929), and culminated in his famous and influential book, *The Wisdom of the Body* (1939). The title for this book was taken from the late E. H. Starling, who gave a Harvey Lecture with the same title before the Royal College of Physicians in London in 1923. Starling declared that, by understanding the wisdom of the body, we would attain the "mastery of disease and pain which enables us to relieve the burden of mankind" (quoted from the preface to Cannon's book, *The Wisdom of the Body*), and that tenet became also the belief of Cannon.

Cannon was originally influenced by ideas about the role of the sympathetic nervous system in strong emotions, pain, and stress. As an undergraduate he was in William James's philosophy course at Harvard. James contended that the mental state of the emotions is associated with afferent feedback from the deep body domains, notably from vascular and visceral structures (James, 1884). He believed that the brain triggers bodily changes by activity in the autonomic nervous system (particularly the sympathetic nervous system) and that the activity initiated in the afferent neurons from the disturbed organs leads to the felt emotions (see James & Lange, 1920). This is the essence of the James-Lange theory of emotions, which is

Table 9.3. Autonomic Nervous Systems and Regulation of Organs

### A. *Spinal cord and brain stem*

| Regulation of | Controlled by | |
| --- | --- | --- |
| | Parasympathetic System | Sympathetic System |
| eye | visual acuity accommodation secretion | ? |
| phasic arterial blood pressure | heart rate | peripheral resistance cardiac contractibility |
| tonic arterial blood pressure | heart rate | peripheral resistance cardiac contractibility |
| airways | resistance secretion | ? ? |
| heat transfer through skin | | blood flow, sweating |
| gastrointestinal tract | acid secretion increased motility mucosal secretion | decreased motility mucosal reabsorption |
| urinary bladder | micturition | continence |
| hindgut | defecation | continence |
| sexual organs, male female | erection congestion, secretion | ejaculation ? |

### B. *Hypothalamus*

| Regulation of | Behavior |
| --- | --- |
| body temperature | thermoregulatory behavior |
| body fluid (volume, osmoregulation) | thirst |
| metabolismus | hunger and satiety |
| sexual organs | reproductive behavior |
| circadian (endogenous) rhythm | sleep and wakefulness |
| heart, circulation, respiration | exercise |
| body resources during pain/stress | |
| cellular defense (immune system) | defensive behavior |

*Note.* Functions listed in A involve sympathetic and parasympathetic systems. Most of these are of a complex nature and require the coordination of several autonomic systems. Functions in A contribute to the complex functions in B, which are dependent on the functioning of autonomic, as well as neuroendocrine, systems. From Jänig and Häbler (1999), copyright 1999, with permission from Elsevier Science.

still mentioned in textbooks of psychology. Lange was a Danish physiologist who tried to provide a physiological basis to underpin the theory of James; he worked on the innervation of blood vessels. Cannon was intrigued by the general idea of this theory, which states that the brain generates activity of the internal organs and tissues via the autonomic nervous system and that the various emotional states are brought about by afferent signals from these organs. The consequence of this idea is that different felt emotions are generated by different patterns of activity in afferent neurons from the internal organs. However, Cannon critically argued:

If various strong emotions can thus be expressed in the diffused activities of a single division of the autonomic nervous system . . . it would appear that the bodily conditions which have been assumed, by some psychologists, to distinguish emotions from one another must be sought for elsewhere than in the viscera. We do not "feel sorry because we cry," as James contended, but we cry because, when we are sorry or overjoyed or violently angry or full of tender affection—when any of these diverse emotional states is present—there are nervous discharges by sympathetic channels to various viscera, including the lachrymal glands. And in terror and rage and intense elation, for example, the responses in the viscera seem too uniform [and therefore the discharges of sympathetic neurons to various target organs] to offer a satisfactory means of distinguishing emotional states which in man, at least, are subjectively very different. For this reason I am inclined to urge that the visceral changes merely contribute to an emotional complex more or less indefinite, but still pertinent, feelings of disturbance, in organs which we are not usually conscious of. (Cannon, 1914a, p. 280)

Instead, Cannon proposed (Cannon, 1914a) that the different emotional states are represented in the brain rather than being peripheral in origin and are expressed by changes of activity in sympathetic and parasympathetic neurons.

Later in the 1920s, this reasoning led to the famous experiments conducted by Philip Bard and Cannon on diencephalic cats, in which they had removed the cortex and most of the structures of the limbic system. These cats exhibited a behavior on stimulation of the skin which was phenomenologically very much reminiscent of a cat in rage, as was so beautifully described by Charles Darwin (1872/1998). Bard and Cannon called the behavior of their diencephalic cats "sham rage behavior" (Bard, 1928). These cats exhibited reactions with typical somatomotor components (tail arched backward, everted claws, hissing) and responses in target organs that are under control of the sympathetic nervous system (piloerection, dilatation of pupil, sweating of paw pads). Had they recorded other autonomic parameters, they would have observed increases in arterial blood pressure, heart rate, and blood flow through skeletal muscle and decreased blood flow through viscera and skin, decreased motility of the gastrointestinal tract, and increased secretion of adrenaline and noradrenaline by the adrenal medulla. These are all effects generated by activation of sympathetic pathways (see table 9.1), but they do not involve the entire sympathetic outflow. These changes are also associated with activation of the adrenal cortex via the anterior pituitary gland and an increase of corticosterone in the blood. On the basis of their experiments, Bard and Cannon created the thalamic theory of emotions (Bard, 1932; Cannon, 1929).

Cannon obtained his first experimental experience of the powerful influence the sympathetic nervous system can have on body functions when he studied movements of the stomach and intestines in conscious cats using X-rays. He was surprised to see that the movements of the gastrointestinal tract ceased under strong emotional stimuli and that when the cats were pacified or asleep the movements recommenced. He attributed these changes to the activation of the sympathetic nervous system (Cannon,

1911; Cannon & Murphy, 1906). Then, over the years, in experiments on cats, dogs, and rabbits, Cannon studied the role of the sympathetic nervous system in maintaining homeostasis during various disturbances of the body, such as hemorrhage, hypoglycemia, hypoxia, low and high body temperature, muscle exercise, emotional disturbances, and so forth. On the basis of these studies, he formulated his concept of the fundamental role of the sympathetic nervous system in maintaining homeostasis: The sympathetic nervous system acts promptly and directly to prevent serious changes of the internal environment. It serves to mobilize body energies. It exhibits a widespread discharge through the sympathetic channels and different sympathetic outflows act simultaneously in one direction. It is organized for diffuse effects (Cannon, 1939).

This generalization was extensively discussed by Cannon in his book *The Wisdom of the Body* (1939). Cannon obviously did not believe that individual sympathetic preganglionic neurons make functional synaptic contacts only with postganglionic neurons of the same function but, rather, that they diverge widely and form contacts with postganglionic neurons of many different functions. Generalized activation of the sympathetic nervous system included activation of the adrenal medulla causing the secretion of adrenaline and noradrenaline into the blood. It was assumed that the circulating adrenaline and noradrenaline reinforce the nervous effects on the target organs and mobilize glucose and free fatty acids from their stores, decrease the time for blood clotting, enhance gas exchange in the lung (by relaxation of the smooth muscles of the airways and subsequent reduction of airway resistance), and decrease fatigue of skeletal muscle. These broad functional effects are conceptualized under the term *sympathico-adrenal system*. In contrast, the parasympathetic functions were thought to be specialized. This system serves to conserve body energies and the stability and constancy of the internal environment of the body. It influences special viscera separately and its discharges are sharply directed to specific organs only. Different types of parasympathetic neurons are therefore not bound to act simultaneously but separately depending on the organ. Individual parasympathetic preganglionic neurons influence one target organ only. The effects of the sympathetic nervous system and of the parasympathetic nervous system are generally opposite (Cannon, 1939).

This clearly shows that Cannon's view of the autonomic nervous system was that of a system designed to preserve life during grave physical crises that require extreme effort. The sympathetic division of the autonomic nervous system was considered to mobilize bodily forces during struggle, the cranial (parasympathetic) division to preserve body energies, and the sacral (parasympathetic) division to function in emptying of the hollow organs and in reproduction of the species (Cannon, 1928, 1929). Animals from which he had removed the entire sympathetic paravertebral chains survived, suggesting that the sympathetic nervous system might not be important at all. However, these animals lived in the protected environment of the laboratory. They would not have been able to adapt to environmental extremes or even to maintain physiological stability in terms of body temperature, adequate arterial blood pressure for cerebral perfusion, constant fluid volume, and so forth, under more normal conditions (Cannon, Newton, Bright, Menkin, & Moore, 1929). Cannon was also aware that the autonomic nervous system is active during lesser disturbances. Cannon's idea of synchronized sympathetic activity in the "fright, fight, and flight" response (Cannon, 1929, 1939) is what we would today call the "defense reaction"; this idea was readily picked up by the scientific and clinical community and even by lay people. The coordinated response was taken to indicate that activity of all parts of the sympathetic system was linked so as to occur in an "all-or-none" fashion without distinction between the different effector organs. This activation of the sympathetic system was thought to be generally protective and the level of arousal to be expressed in the level of sympathetic discharge or *sympathetic tone.*

Cannon himself was surprised that the same unified action of the sympathetic nervous system could be useful in circumstances as diverse as hypoglycemia, hypotension, hypothermia, and so forth. He was aware that the unified system apparently produced responses which, although they were physiologically meaningful in certain states of the body, were useless in others (e.g., sweating in hypoglycemia, rise of blood sugar in asphyxia; Cannon, 1939). But he contented himself by assuming that the appearance of inappropriate features in the total complex of sympathico-adrenal function is made reasonable in the context of its emergency functions (*Notfallfunktionen*; Cannon, 1928) if one considers "first, that it is on the whole, a unitary system; second, that it is capable of producing effects in many different organs; and third, that among these effects are different combinations which are of the utmost utility in correspondingly different conditions of need" (Cannon, 1939, p. 298).

Great emphasis was placed in Cannon's research on the adrenal medulla (Cannon, 1914b). In his animals, under experimental conditions in which the body's ability to recover from major disturbances was tested, Cannon measured many effects that were responses to catecholamines (adrenaline and noradrenaline) released from the adrenal medulla. It is almost universally stated in textbooks that adrenaline and noradrenaline released from the adrenal medulla act on the same effector organs as the sympathetic postganglionic neurons and thereby enhance and support the effects of sympathetic neurons on target tissues. This statement is misleading as far as the function of the sympathetic nervous system is concerned, at least under normal conditions in higher vertebrates, not only because it

assumes widespread and uniform actions of the sympathetic nervous system on target tissues but also because catecholamines from the adrenal medulla often do *not* have the same effect on the target tissues as sympathetic nerve activity. About 92% to 98% of circulating noradrenaline originates from sympathetic nerve terminals (Esler et al., 1990), and all circulating adrenaline is released by the adrenal medulla. Adrenaline released from the adrenal medulla under physiological conditions is primarily a metabolic hormone and chiefly serves to catalyze the mobilization of glucose and lactic acid from glycogen and of free fatty acids from adipose tissue (see table 9.1); in physiological concentrations, it does not support the effect of sympathetic postganglionic neurons on target tissues (see Celander, 1954; Cryer, 1980; Shah, Tse, Clutter, & Cryer, 1984; Silverberg, Shah, Haymond, & Cryer, 1978).

This was a puzzling way of arguing, given that the precise and distinct control of, for example, body temperature, cerebral perfusion, and so forth, by the autonomic nervous system was already known at the time when Cannon was working. As mentioned in the introduction, such control systems could not work if Cannon's concept about the sympathico-adrenal system were true! Cannon's argument was even more surprising given the enormous amount of detailed experimental work described by Langley between 1890 and 1920, which supported the principle that each organ and tissue is innervated by distinct sympathetic and parasympathetic pathways (Langley, 1903, 1921). Moreover, Langley's conclusions were reinforced by further experiments in which he studied the regeneration of lesioned preganglionic axons (e.g., in the cervical sympathetic trunk to the superior cervical ganglion) and found orderly restitution of function (i.e., functionally appropriate synaptic connections; Langley, 1897).

## Walter Rudolf Hess and the Dichotomous Organization of the Autonomic Nervous System

In the 1920s, the Swiss physiologist Walter Rudolf Hess, influenced by Karplus and Kreidle (see Akert, 1981), started his famous experiments in which he observed the behavior elicited in conscious cats by local electrical stimulation of the hypothalamus. He implanted electrodes stereotactically and correlated the type of behavior (defensive behavior [*Abwehrverhalten*] consisting of confrontational defense [attack] or flight, submissive, nutritive, sexual and evacuative behaviors, and particular autonomic reactions, such as piloerection, sweating, dilatation of the pupil, micturition, defecation) which he could evoke from the anatomical sites he stimulated in cats that were freely moving. After the experiments, he left the electrodes in position and perfused the brains of the animals in order to locate the tips of the electrodes in the diencephalon, in particular in the hypothalamus. Over several years, Hess investigated the whole diencephalon and constructed maps for the different autonomic reactions, which he documented as integral components of the different elicited behaviors. Hess interpreted his results to mean that the hypothalamus integrates the activity of the autonomic nervous system so as to adapt body organs to somatomotor behavior (for translation of the key publications of Hess, see Akert, 1981).

Similar experiments were later conducted on chickens by von Holst and St. Paul (1960, 1962). These experimenters showed that electrical microstimulation of the different areas of the hypothalamus via implanted electrodes lead to species-specific (instinctive) behavior of the birds, including vocalization, which could not be discriminated from their natural behavior. These authors concluded that the different components of behavior, including the adaptive changes in the body that are dependent on the autonomic nervous system and the neuroendocrine system, are represented in the diencephalon.

On the basis of his experiments, Hess propagated generalizations similar to those of Cannon about how the autonomic nervous system works. Like Cannon, he believed that the cranial division of the parasympathetic nervous system promotes the conservation of energy and aids in the recovery of the body after stress (i.e., has "trophotropic" functions), whereas the sympathetic nervous system has "ergotropic" functions, mobilizing bodily energy and adapting the body to challenges from the outside world (Hess, 1948). These observations are based on the experimental evidence that stimulation of the parasympathetic system leads to an activation of gastrointestinal tract and pelvic organs, whereas stimulation of the sympathetic branch of the autonomic nervous system mediates all those reactions that are also seen during defensive behavior elicited from the caudal hypothalamus and the central gray matter of the midbrain (Hess, 1949; see also Akert, 1981).

Hess later transferred the idea of a generalized dichotomy of the functional organization of the autonomic nervous system to the hypothalamus (Hess, 1949): He hypothesized that the rostral parts of the hypothalamus integrate somatic, autonomic, and endocrine reactions and controls to promote recovery and conservation of energy, digestion, excretion, and evacuation of waste, as well as reproductive functions. He thought that these functions were associated with the excitation of the parasympathetic nervous system, and the entire process was subsumed under the umbrella term trophotropic reaction. He further hypothesized that activation of the caudal parts of the hypothalamus causes general excitation of the sympathetic nervous system, mobilization of body energy, and enhancement of performance capacity (ergotropic reaction). These concepts require that the hypothalamus consists of two functionally and anatomically different systems. Thus the unifying concept of the antagonistic function of the sympathetic and parasympathetic nervous systems was

applied to the hypothalamus. Today it is known that the concept itself is far too general to explain the complexities of the central control of autonomic systems.

## The Consequences of the Generalizing Concepts of Cannon and Hess

Both Cannon and Hess had enormous impact on thinking in the scientific community and in clinical medicine. Their influence was to some extent positive because it focused clinical practice, clinical research, and research in systems physiology on the importance of the effects the autonomic nervous system has in regulating body functions. Later the influence of Cannon and Hess was amplified as the pharmacology of the autonomic nervous system developed. This development was related to the detection of the principal transmitters of the autonomic nervous system, acetylcholine and noradrenaline, and their receptors. Even today, much of the progress in understanding neuroeffector mechanisms depends on our knowledge of pharmacological principles and of specific drug actions.

The ideas of Cannon and Hess soon became imprinted on the disciplines of physiology and pharmacology. Generalizations about the actions of the sympathetic nervous system also led to a change in the connotations of the terms sympathetic and parasympathetic from those originally defined by Langley: These terms began to imply particular types of function, that is, "sympathetic" function and "parasympathetic" function, in line with the generalists' ideas. This is best demonstrated by the commonly used term sympathico-adrenal system (Cannon, 1939). However, modern research shows that there is no justification for the generalizations made by Cannon and Hess and no justification (other than ontogenetic) to lump all the sympathetic systems functionally together.

The concept that the sympathetic system operates in a more or less unitary way was enhanced by the development of knowledge about the receptors (notably the adrenoceptors and muscarinic acetylcholine receptors) on which these transmitters act. Drugs were systematically developed for potential therapeutic use that interfere with or mimic actions of autonomic transmitter substances. This trend continues in modern molecular pharmacology. First, a plethora of receptors in the membranes of the autonomic neurons and their target cells have been detected and cloned and their molecular structure analyzed. For example, at present nine types of adrenoceptors and five types of muscarinic receptors have been identified by their molecular structure, their coupling to intracellular signaling pathways, and their genes. The function of these different receptors in the neural regulation of autonomic target tissues is known for only some tissues and specifically for the subtypes $\alpha_1$, $\alpha_2$, $\beta_1$, $\beta_2$. Second, many neuropeptides and other substances have been detected in autonomic neurons which are colocalized with the classical transmitters in the vesicles or the cytoplasm of the presynaptic terminals and which may have neurotransmitter functions. Molecular techniques are being used to demonstrate the distribution of mRNA for a range of identified receptors/binding sites, as well as for the pathways for synthesis and the peptides themselves (Alexander, Mathie, & Peters, 2000). The almost exponential expansion of molecular pharmacology has not necessarily led to a better understanding of how this system works in regulating the target organs. Care must be taken in drawing conclusions from this type of research as far as the biological meaning is concerned.

## Functional Organization of the Peripheral Sympathetic and Parasympathetic Pathways

### Functions of the Autonomic Nervous System and Levels of Integration

The autonomic nervous system is a nervous system in its own right, like the motor system or the sensory systems. It regulates body functions in order to enable the body to act in a coordinated way under various challenging conditions. The autonomic nervous pathways are hierarchically organized and represented in the peripheral and in the central nervous systems.

Figure 9.4 shows in a schematic form the different levels of function of the autonomic nervous system:

- The lowest level occurs at the *target tissue.* The effector responses of these cells may depend on several classes of signals which potentially impinge on them. The target cells are under the control of autonomic neurons, and some individual tissues are supplied by more than one type of efferent innervation (e.g., pacemaker cells of the heart, some blood vessels; see Table 9.1). The effectiveness of the neural signals in generating an effector response may also depend on signals arising from other sources (e.g., spontaneous myogenic activity of some smooth muscle cells; local physical factors, e.g., $P_{CO_2}$, pH, temperature), other neurons (e.g., nociceptive primary afferent terminals; see the subsection in this chapter on visceral primary afferent neurons as interface with the brain), remotely derived hormones (e.g., circulating angiotensin, adrenaline, vasopressin), endothelium-derived factors (e.g., nitric oxide), or local paracrine signals (e.g., cytokines).
- The next level of integration occurs in the *autonomic ganglia.* Postganglionic neurons may integrate signals derived from multiple preganglionic neurons. Some postganglionic neurons, particularly in prevertebral and possibly in some parasympathetic ganglia, also integrate signals from other peripheral neurons (e.g., branches of afferent neurons or interneurons of

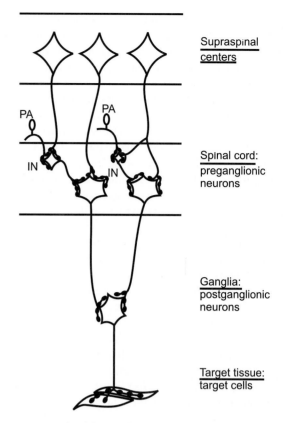

Figure 9.4 Levels of integration of the autonomic nervous system. IN, interneuron; PA, primary afferent neuron. From Jänig and Häbler (1999), copyright 1999, with permission from Elsevier Science.

the enteric nervous system or collateral branches of spinal primary visceral afferent neurons; see the subsection mentioned previously).
- The cell bodies and dendrites of *preganglionic neurons* are situated in the spinal cord and brain stem. These neurons integrate a diverse range of synaptic activity from interneurons, primary afferent neurons, and systems at higher levels in the central nervous system. This level of organization is associated with reflexes and regulating systems, which are represented in the spinal cord and lower brain stem (cardiovascular system, gastrointestinal tract, evacuative systems).
- *Central pathways* in the upper brain stem and hypothalamus are antecedent to the spinal and lower brain stem reflex centers. They integrate activity from several sources concerned with autonomic homeostatic regulation, neuroendocrine regulation, and regulation of the somatomotor system.
- *Pathways in the forebrain* (limbic system and neocortex) adapt the complex homeostatic regulations to the needs of the organism according to the environmental conditions and through memory processes according to previous experiences.

This type of functional hierarchical organization is, of course, a simplification as the afferent and efferent communication between levels of central integration does not occur only between adjacent levels but also across levels. For example, neurons from the hypothalamus project directly to preganglionic neurons in the spinal cord, and second-order neurons in lamina I of the spinal cord may directly project to the hypothalamus; second-order neurons in the nucleus of the solitary tract do project to nuclei in the brain stem, hypothalamus, and limbic system.

### The Final Autonomic Pathway

Physiologists have always known that the autonomic involvement in the regulation of functions of different organs is marked by the precision with which this occurs in relation to the overall behavior of the organism. This is the basis of homeostasis and its adaptation to various external and internal perturbations. Such precision of control implies that there are subgroups of pre- and postganglionic autonomic neurons that are discrete with respect to the function they control in their target organs.

The peripheral sympathetic and parasympathetic autonomic systems consist of several functionally distinct subsystems, each associated with a different type of target tissue (see Table 9.1). Each autonomic system is based on a set of preganglionic and postganglionic neurons that are synaptically connected in autonomic ganglia and constitute a pathway that transmits the central message to its target tissue. This pathway is therefore called, in analogy to the "final common motor path" (Sherrington, 1947), the *final autonomic pathway* (Jänig, 1986). The final autonomic pathways are the building blocks of the peripheral autonomic nervous system, and the concept described by this term probably applies to all sympathetic and parasympathetic pathways. Except for the vagal pathways to the gastrointestinal tract (see Furness & Bornstein, 1995; Furness & Costa, 1987), parasympathetic pathways appear to be more distinct and simpler in organization than the sympathetic ones. However, the simplicity results more from the relatively small size and simple anatomy of most target organs of the parasympathetic pathways compared with the target organs of most sympathetic pathways (e.g., vasoconstrictor pathways to various groups of blood vessels). The sympathetic pathways to organs such as the pineal gland and dilator pupillae are probably just as simple in their organization.

For the sympathetic pathways through the paravertebral ganglia to target organs in skeletal muscle and skin and those through the inferior mesenteric ganglion to the vasculature and smooth muscle of the pelvic organs, neurophysiological investigations suggest that there is functionally very little or no cross-talk between different peripheral pathways. Thus each autonomic target tissue or set of target tissues which is under central autonomic control is in principle supplied by one (sometimes two) separate final autonomic pathway(s).

As far as transmission of the central message to the target organs is concerned, the concept of the final autonomic pathway is for most autonomic systems similar to that of the final common motor path in the somatomotor system in the sense that it corresponds to the innervation of a skeletal muscle or group of muscles with the same function by a pool of α-motoneurons (see Figure 9.5). The main differences between the final motor path and the final autonomic pathway are the following:

- The same autonomic target organ can be innervated by more than one final autonomic pathway.
- The central message may undergo quantitative changes within autonomic ganglia because of convergence and divergence and the variable effectiveness of different preganglionic synaptic inputs (see the subsection in this chapter on transmission of signals to the effector tissue; see also Jänig, 1995a).
- In prevertebral ganglia and in some other ganglia, synaptic inputs from the periphery may summate with those from preganglionic neurons. Peripheral afferent neurons (of the enteric nervous system) and collateral branches of spinal visceral afferent neurons may establish peripheral autonomic circuits with postganglionic neurons which are integrated in

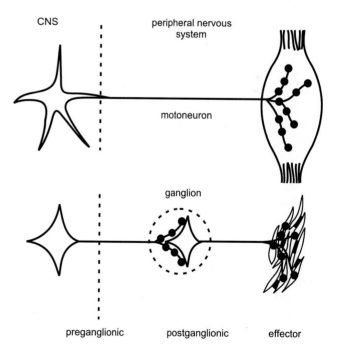

Figure 9.5 The final autonomic pathway (upper part) in comparison with the final common motor path (lower part) of the somatomotor system. CNS, central nervous system. From Jänig and Häbler (1999), copyright 1999, with permission from Elsevier Science.

the final autonomic pathways (see the subsection cited previously; see also Jänig, 1995a).

- The neurally derived signals may interact with other parameters in the target organ or in the ganglion. These include local neural influences (e.g., peptide release from activated afferent terminals), remote and local hormones, local metabolites and the endogenous activity of the target organ (e.g., myogenic activity), and substances released from local cells (e.g., nitric oxide from the vascular endothelium). Such factors vary in different functional pathways (see the subsection cited previously).

In the following two subsections, reflex patterns for different groups of autonomic neurons, in particular sympathetic ones, are described, showing that functional differences in the subgroups of pre- and postganglionic neurons are reflected in the discharge patterns elicited by afferent stimuli and can be measured in neurophysiological experiments. For other groups of autonomic neurons that have not yet been investigated in this way, I draw indirect conclusions by analogy to those that have been investigated. Using this approach, one gathers information about the functional specificity of different neurons, about the relation between activity in certain types of neuron and the responses of the target tissue, as well as information about the principal organization of the central circuits that determine the discharge pattern of these neurons, leading to the concept that the autonomic nervous system consists of functionally distinct building blocks (Jänig & McLachlan, 1992a, 1992b).

### Sympathetic Pathways

Many individual sympathetic pre- and postganglionic neurons are spontaneously active and/or can be activated or inhibited by appropriate physiological stimuli. This has been shown in anesthetized cats (and for some systems in rats) for neurons of the lumbar sympathetic outflow to skeletal muscles, skin, and pelvic viscera (Häbler, Jänig, Krummel, & Peters, 1993, 1994; Jänig, 1985, 1996a; Jänig & McLachlan, 1987; Jänig, Schmidt, Schnitzler, & Wesselmann, 1991) and for neurons of the thoracic sympathetic outflow to the head and neck (Boczek-Funcke et al., 1992), as well as in nonanesthetized humans for the sympathetic outflow to skeletal muscles and skin (Wallin, 1999; Wallin & Fagius, 1988). The reflexes observed correspond to the effector responses which are induced by changes of activity in these neurons. The reflex patterns elicited by stimulation of various afferent input systems are characteristic for each functional sympathetic pathway and therefore represent *physiological fingerprints* for each pathway. Some major classes of sympathetic neurons are characterized as follows:

- Reflex patterns in muscle and visceral vasoconstrictor neurons consist of inhibition by arterial baroreceptors but excitation by arterial chemoreceptors, cutaneous nociceptors, and spinal visceral nociceptors (see Figure 9.6).
- Most cutaneous vasoconstrictor neurons are inhibited by stimulation of cutaneous nociceptors of the distal extremities, spinal visceral afferents, arterial chemoreceptors, and central warm-sensitive neurons in the spinal cord and hypothalamus (see Figure 9.7).
- Sudomotor neurons are activated by stimulation of pacinian corpuscles in skin and by some other afferent stimuli (see Figure 9.7b).
- Motility-regulating neurons innervating pelvic organs are excited or inhibited by stimulation of sacral afferents from the urinary bladder, hindgut, or anal canal, but are not affected by arterial baroreceptor activation. Functionally different types of motility-regulating neurons can be discriminated by way of their reflex pattern.

So far, twelve different functional groups of postganglionic and preganglionic sympathetic neurons have been identified (Table 9.4). The same types of reflex patterns have been observed in both preganglionic and postganglionic neurons. The neurons in eight of these pathways (e.g., the vasoconstrictor neurons, sudomotor neurons, many motility regulating neurons, etc.; see Table 9.4) have ongoing activity, whereas in four pathways (e.g., the pilomotor and vasodilator pathways) the neurons are normally silent. The activity in the vasoconstrictor and sudomotor neurons exhibits distinct patterns of modulation with respect to central respiration, indicating a coupling between the respiratory network and the presympathetic pathways in the lower brain stem (Boczek-Funcke, Häbler, Jänig, & Michaelis, 1992; Boczek-Funcke, Dembowsky, Häbler, Jänig, & Michaelis, 1992; Häbler et al., 1993; Häbler, Bartsch, & Jänig, 1999, 2000; for review, see Häbler, Jänig, & Michaelis, 1994).

It is likely that other target cells are innervated by other functionally distinct groups of sympathetic neurons which have not been studied so far (kidney: blood vessels, juxtaglomerular cells producing renin [DiBona & Kopp, 1997; Kopp & DiBona, 1992]; spleen: immune tissue; heart: cardiomotor neurons; fat tissue: lipocytes of brown adipose tissue, Himms-Hagen, 1991; lipocytes of white adipose tissue, Frayn & Macdonald, 1996; salivary glands, pineal glands, Klein, Moore, & Reppert, 1991; Moore, 1996; dilator muscle of pupil, etc.).

To emphasize, most of the data have been obtained under standardized experimental conditions in anesthetized cats and some in anesthetized rats. In humans this type of standardized experimentation is not possible. Further-

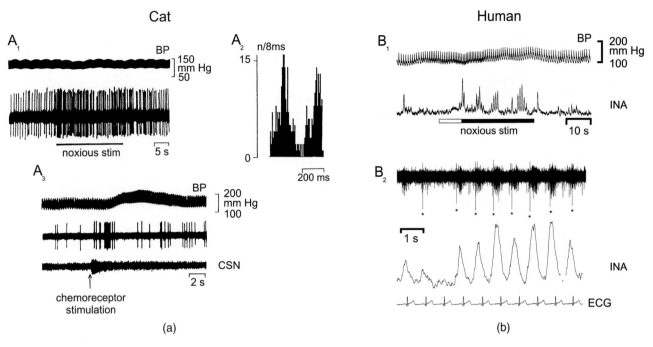

Figure 9.6 Reflexes in muscle vasoconstrictor neurons. (a) Cat. Recordings from a single thoracic preganglionic neuron projecting in the cervical sympathetic trunk of the anesthetized cat. Original neural activity in lower trace of $A_1$ and in middle trace of $A_3$. $A_1$ Excitation to mechanical noxious stimulation of the ear. $A_2$. Strong rhythmic changes of the activity with respect to phasic stimulation of arterial baroreceptors by the pulsatile blood pressure (and therefore phasic inhibition of activity; "cardiac rhythmicity" of the activity, 500 sweeps superimposed). $A_3$. Excitation to stimulation of arterial chemoreceptors projecting through the carotid sinus nerve (CSN) by retrograde bolus injection of 0.2 ml $CO_2$-enriched Ringer solution into the left lingual artery. BP, blood pressure. Modified from Boczek-Funcke et al. (1992). (b) Microneurographic recordings in human participants from bundles with muscle vasoconstrictor axons in the deep peroneal nerve. $B_1$. Activation by mechanical noxious stimulation (*black bar; open bar*, nonnoxious mechanical stimulation). Note pulsatile modulation of neural bursts and inhibition by slower blood pressure (BP) waves. Integrated multiunit activity. $B_2$ Activation during apnea (cessation of respiration). Note rhythmic multiunit and single unit(*) activity with respect to electrocardiogram (ECG). INA, integrated neural activity. Adapted from Nordin and Fagius (1995) and Macefield and Wallin (1999a).

more, no direct recording from autonomic preganglionic neurons and from autonomic neurons innervating viscera and head can be made in humans. However, by using microneurographic recordings from bundles with few or single postganglionic axons in human skin and muscle nerves, it is possible to study activity in peripheral afferent and efferent axons traveling in human skin and muscle nerves in conscious participants who can communicate freely with the experimenter. Activity in these neurons can be correlated with sensory perceptions, somatomotor responses, autonomic effector responses, central commands, and so forth. It has clearly been shown that muscle vasoconstrictor, cutaneous vasoconstrictor, and sudomotor neurons have distinct reflex patterns (Vallbo, Hagbarth,

Torebjörk, & Wallin, 1979; Wallin, 1999; Wallin & Fagius, 1988) and that there is also some (though controversial) evidence for the existence of sympathetic vasodilator neurons that supply skin and skeletal muscle in humans (Table 9.5). Figure 9.6b illustrates the behavior of muscle vasoconstrictor neurons during noxious stimulation and during apnea (cessation of breathing). Figure 9.8 illustrates the behavior of cutaneous vasoconstrictor neurons and sudomotor neurons during whole body warming and cooling to an arousal stimulus and to deep inspiration. Overall, it can be concluded that the behavior of muscle vasoconstrictor neurons, cutaneous vasoconstrictor neurons, and sudomotor neurons is at least as distinctive in human beings as it is in anesthetized animals, indicating that the

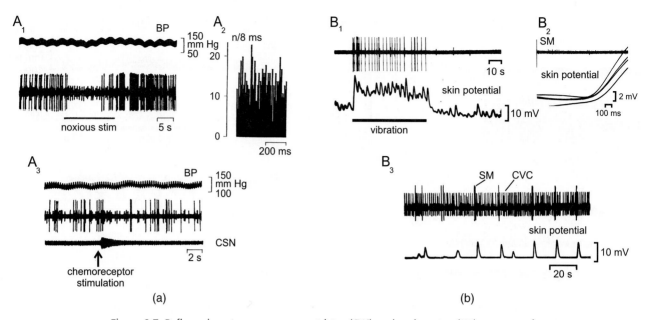

Figure 9.7 Reflexes in cutaneous vasoconstrictor (CVC) and sudomotor (SM) neurons of the cat. (A) CVC neuron. Recordings from a single thoracic preganglionic neurone projecting in the cervical sympathetic trunk of the anesthetized cat. $A_1$. Inhibition to mechanical noxious stimulation of the ear. $A_2$. No modulation of the activity with respect to phasic stimulation of arterial baroreceptors by the pulsatile blood pressure ("cardiac rhythmicity," 500 sweeps superimposed). $A_3$. Inhibition to stimulation of arterial chemoreceptors projecting through the carotid sinus nerve (CSN) by retrograde bolus injection of 0.2 ml $CO_2$-enriched Ringer solution into the left lingual artery. BP, blood pressure. Modified from Boczek-Funcke et al. (1992) (B). SM neuron. Recording from single SM axons isolated from fascicles of the medial plantar nerve innervating the hairless skin of the hindpaw; lower records skin potential. $B_1$. Reflex response to vibration stimulation (stimulation of the pacinian corpuscles in the paw by tapping). Note that most discharges of the SM axon are followed by a fast deflection of the skin potential (negativity up). $B_2$. Ongoing discharges in an SM axon are followed by deflection of the skin potential at about 600 ms latency. $B_3$. Ongoing activity in SM axon and CVC axons and skin potential. Most SM discharges are followed by transient skin potential changes. Adapted from Jänig and Kümmel (1977).

activity in these three populations of neurons is regulated by different central mechanisms. Furthermore, it is also important to remember that cutaneous vasoconstrictor neurons are likely to include functionally heterogeneous subtypes (e.g., innervating cutaneous blood vessels in the hands and feet or in the proximal parts of the extremities; innervating arteriovenous anastomoses or cutaneous nutritive blood vessels).

## Parasympathetic Pathways

Pre- and postganglionic parasympathetic neurons have always been presumed to constitute distinct peripheral pathways which transmit centrally derived signals to their target organs and exhibit distinct reflexes to afferent stimuli that are appropriate for their function. Compared with the amount of experimentation on the reflex discharge in single sympathetic pre- and postganglionic neurons, relatively few systematic studies have investigated the functional properties of parasympathetic pre- and postganglionic neurons with respect to their target organs. Table 9.6 lists experiments in which some reflexes elicited by physiological stimuli in pre- and postganglionic parasympathetic neurons innervating heart, tracheal smooth muscle, stomach, urinary bladder, colon, and iris have been investigated. The reasons for the lack of systematic studies probably include the following:

- Many parasympathetic ganglia are less well defined than sympathetic ganglia, being located close to or on the wall of their target organs. Those in the cranium are relatively inaccessible. The postganglionic

Table 9.4. Functional Classification of Sympathetic Neurons in the Cat Based on Reflex Behavior in Vivo

| Likely function | Location | Target organ | Likely target tissue | Major identifying stimulus | Ongoing activity[1] |
|---|---|---|---|---|---|
| **Vasoconstrictor Neurons** | | | | | |
| Muscle vasoconstrictor | Lumbar | Hindlimb muscles | Resistance vessels | Baro-inhibition | |
| | Cervical | Head and neck muscles | Resistance vessels | Baro-inhibition | Yes |
| Cutaneous vasoconstrictor | Lumbar | Hindlimb skin | Thermoregulatory blood vessels | Inhibited by CNS warming | Yes |
| | Cervical | Head and neck skin | Thermoregulatory blood vessels | Inhibited by CNS warming | Yes |
| Visceral vasoconstrictor | Lumbar splanchnic | Pelvic viscera | Resistance vessels | Baro-inhibition | Yes |
| Renal vasoconstrictor | Thoracic splanchnic | Kidney | Resistance vessels | Baro-inhibition | Yes |
| **Nonvasoconstrictor Neurons** | | | | | |
| Muscle vasodilator | Lumbar | Hindlimb muscles | Muscle arteries (feeding vessels) | Hypothalamic stim. emotional stim. | No |
| Cutaneous vasodilator | Lumbar | Hindlimb skin | Skin vasculature blood vessels | Excited by CNS warming | No |
| Sudomotor | Lumbar | Paw pads | Eccrine sweat glands | Vibration (in cat) | Yes |
| Pilomotor | Lumbar | Skin, tail, back | Piloerector muscles | Hypothalamic stim. emotional stim. | No |
| Inspiratory | Cervical | Airways? | Nasal mucosal vasculature | Inspiration | Yes |
| Pupillo-motor | Cervical | Iris | Dilator pupillae muscle | Inhibition by light | Yes |
| Motility-regulating | | | | | |
| Type 1 | Lumbar splanchnic | Hindgut, urinary tract | Visceral smooth muscle | Bladder distension | Yes |
| Type 2 | Lumbar splanchnic | Hindgut, urinary tract | Visceral smooth muscle | Inhibited by bladder distension | Yes |
| Reproduction | Lumbar | Reproductive organs | Visceral smooth muscle | Central stim. (?) | No |

*Note.* For details about rates of ongoing activity in pre- and postganglionic neurons, reflexes to various afferent stimuli, spinal and supraspinal reflex pathways, coupling to regulation of respiration and conduction velocities of pre- and postganglionic axons, see Jänig (1985, 1988a, 1995a, 1996a), Jänig and McLachlan (1987), Häbler et al. (1992), Häbler, Jänig, Krummel, & Peters (1993, 1994), Häbler, Jänig, & Michaelis (1994), Jänig et al. (1991), Grewe et al. (1995), Boczek-Funcke et al. (1992), Boczek-Funcke, Dembowsky, Häbler, Jänig, & Michaelis (1993). From Jänig and Häbler (1999), copyright 1999, with permission from Elsevier Science.

[1]Some vasoconstrictor neurons do not have spontaneous activity and are recruited under special functional conditions.

axons are therefore very short and often cannot be visualized for dissection.

- Parasympathetic preganglionic neurons are relatively difficult to record from and to separate with respect to their target organs (e.g., in the dorsal vagal motor nucleus, in the nucleus ambiguus, in the sacral spinal cord).
- It is widely accepted that the peripheral parasympathetic neurons constitute functionally and anatomically more discrete pathways to the target organs than the sympathetic neurons and that the

ganglia act as simple relay stations (i.e., without integration).

The main difference between the two autonomic systems is that each type of target organ of the parasympathetic system is spatially restricted (such as sphincter pupillae and ciliary body, salivary and other exocrine glands of the head, the heart), whereas many types of target organs of the sympathetic nervous system are widely distributed (e.g., blood vessels in skeletal muscle, in skin, in viscera, sweat glands, erector pili muscles, etc.). This has conse-

Table 9.5. Functional Classification of Sympathetic Neurons Innervating Skeletal Muscle and Skin in Human Beings Based on Microneurographic Studies

| Likely function | Target organ | Likely target tissue | Major identifying stimulus | Ongoing activity[1] |
|---|---|---|---|---|
| Muscle vasoconstrictor | Hindlimb, forelimb | Resistance vessels muscles | Baro-inhibition | Yes |
| Cutaneous vasoconstrictor | Hindlimb, forelimb | Thermoregul. blood vessels skin | Excited by general cooling | Yes |
| Sudomotor | Hindlimb | Sweat glands forelimb skin | Excited by general warming | Yes |
| Cutaneous vasodilator | Hindlimb, forelimb skin | Blood vessels | ? | No (?) |
| Pilomotor | Hairy skin | Piloerector muscles | ? | No (?) |

*Note.* All data are obtained from postganglionic neurons in awake humans. For details about rates of ongoing activity, reflexes to various stimuli and maneuvers, coupling to respiration, and conduction velocity of postganglionic axons, see Bini, Hagbarth, Hynninen, & Wallin (1980a, 1980b), Macefield, Wallin, & Vallbo (1994), Nordin and Fagius (1995), Macefield and Wallin (1996, 1999a, 1999b), Noll, Elam, Kunimoto, Karlsson, & Wallin (1994), Nordin (1990), Wallin, Batelsson, Kienbaum, Karlsson, Gazelius, & Elam (1998). From Jänig and Häbler (1999), copyright 1999, with permission from Elsevier Science.

[1]Some neurons do not have spontaneous activity and are recruited under special functional conditions.

quences for the organization of the autonomic ganglia in each of the systems.

## Transmission of Signals in the Final Autonomic Pathways to the Effector Tissue

### Autonomic Ganglia

A major function of the peripheral ganglia is to distribute the centrally integrated signals by connecting each preganglionic axon with several postganglionic neurons. The extent of divergence varies significantly, the ratio of pre- to postganglionic axons being, in pathways such as in the ciliary ganglion to the iris and ciliary body, as low as 1:4, and in others, such as in the superior cervical ganglion with many vasoconstrictor neurons, as high as 1:150. However, limited divergence and much divergence, respectively, are not characteristics of the parasympathetic and sympathetic systems (see Wang, Holst, & Powley, 1995). Probably, by analogy with somatic motor units, limited divergence is common in pathways to small targets with discrete functions (e.g., autonomic pathways to the inner muscles of the eye), whereas widespread divergence is a feature of pathways to anatomically extensive effectors that act more or less simultaneously (e.g., vasoconstrictor pathways).

*Sympathetic Paravertebral Ganglia.* Within sympathetic paravertebral ganglia (in the sympathetic chains), ganglionic neurons have uniform properties. Each convergent

cholinergic preganglionic axon produces an excitatory postsynaptic potential by activating nicotinic receptor channels. The amplitude of the potential varies between inputs, ranging from a few millivolt to suprathreshold. In most cases, one or a few inputs have, like the endplate potential at the skeletal neuromuscular junction, a high safety factor and always initiate an action potential. Thus the ganglion cell relays the incoming CNS-derived signals in only a few of its preganglionic inputs (McLachlan, Davies, Häbler, & Jamieson, 1997; McLachlan, Häbler, Jamieson, & Davies, 1998). The function of the subthreshold synapses in ganglia is not clear.

*Sympathetic Prevertebral Ganglia.* In prevertebral (sympathetic) ganglia, postganglionic neurons, at least in experimental animals, do not have uniform properties. Three broad groups differ electrophysiologically (by the $K^+$ channels that control excitability), morphologically (by their size and dendritic branching), and neurochemically (by their neuropeptide content; see Boyd, McLachlan, Keast, & Inokuchi, 1996). Two groups, like paravertebral neurons, have suprathreshold synaptic connections with one or two preganglionic axons which determine the firing pattern of these neurons. The mode of synaptic transmission in the third group is different. These neurons receive, in addition to preganglionic inputs that do not necessarily activate them, many nicotinic inputs from mechanosensitive afferents of the enteric nervous system and peptidergic synaptic inputs from visceral primary afferent collaterals. Temporal and spatial summation of

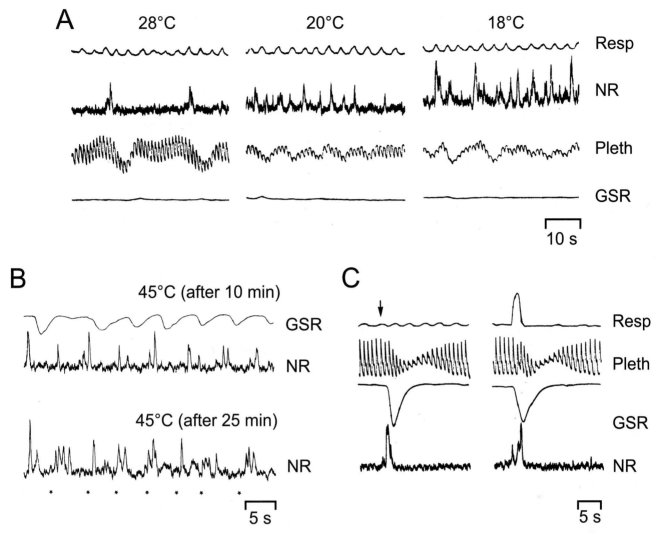

Figure 9.8 Activity in cutaneous vasoconstrictor neurons and sudomotor neurons in human participants. (A) Integrated cutaneous vasconstrictor activity (median nerve) at three different ambient temperatures in relation to finger pulse plethysmogram (Pleth, vasoconstriction downward and reduction of amplitude) and palmar skin resistance (GSR, galvanic skin response; reduction of skin resistance downward). Note increase of neural activity and decrease of pulse amplitude with decrease of ambient temperature and relation of neural bursts to phasic vasoconstriction. Upper record, respiration (Resp). (B) Integrated sudomotor activity at high central (and ambient) temperature in relation to skin resistance change (GSR). Activation of sudomotor neurons is accompanied by perception of heat waves (indicated by *). (C) Activation of both cutaneous vasoconstrictor neurons and sudomotor neurons by arousal stimulus (sudden shout, *arrow left*) and by deep inspiration (*right*). NR, integrated neural response (mean voltage neurogram). Adapted from Wallin and Fagius (1986) and Bini et al. (1980a).

synaptic potentials from peripheral and preganglionic inputs is necessary to initiate in these prevertebral neurons action potentials establishing peripheral (extracentral) reflexes.

*Parasympathetic Ganglia.* The structure of many parasympathetic ganglion cells, with few dendrites, is simpler than that of sympathetic neurons. The preganglionic input is correspondingly simple, often consisting of a single suprathreshold input. However, some parasympathetic ganglia in the body trunk contain, in addition to postganglionic neurons, neurons which behave as primary afferent and interneurons, that is, they have the potential for reflex activity independent of the CNS, like the enteric system

Table 9.6. Functional Classification of Parasympathetic Neurons in Animals Based on Reflex Behavior in Vivo

| Likely function | Location | Target organ | Likely target tissue | Major identifying stimulus | Ongoing activity |
|---|---|---|---|---|---|
| Pupillo-constrictor[1] | Ganglion ciliare, postggl. | Iris | Constrictor pupillae muscle | Excitation/inhibition by light | Yes |
| Cardiomotor[2] | N. ambig. preggl. | Heart | Pacemaker cells, atrial muscle cells | Excited by stim. baroreceptors | Yes |
| Bronchomotor[3] | N. ambig. preggl. | Trachea, bronchi | Smooth muscle cells | Stim. tracheal mucosa | Yes |
| Gastromotor excitatory[4] | NDNV preggl. | Stomach | Smooth muscle | Inhibition to duodenal distension | Yes |
| Gastromotor inhibitory[4] | NDNV preggl. | Stomach | Smooth muscle | Excitation to duodenal distension | Yes |
| Urinary bladder[5] | Sacral spinal cord, preggl. | Urinary bladder | Smooth muscle | Excitation to bladder distension | No |
| Colon[5] | Sacral spinal cord, preggl. | Colon | Smooth muscle | Excitation to colon distension | Yes |

*Note.* For details about rates of ongoing activity in pre- and postganglionic neurons and reflexes to various afferent stimuli, see:
[1] Inoue (1980), Johnson and Purves (1983), Melnitchenko and Skok (1970).
[2] Jewett (1964), Katona, Poitras, Barnett, and Terry (1970), Kunze (1972), Spyer (1981).
[3] Tomori and Widdicombe (1969), Widdicombe (1966).
[4] Grundy, Salih, and Scratcherd (1981), Roman and Gonella (1994).
[5] De Groat, Booth, Milner, and Roppolo (1982).
Abbreviations: preggl., preganglionic; postggl., postganglionic; stim., stimulation; N. ambig., Nucleus ambiguus; NDNV, Nucleus dorsalis nervi vagi. From Jänig and Häbler (1999), copyright 1999, with permission from Elsevier Science.

(intracardiac ganglia; Edwards, Hirst, Klemm, & Steele, 1995; see also Mawe, 1995).

The pelvic or hypogastric plexuses contain the neurons that innervate the pelvic organs. Some of these ganglion cells are noradrenergic and are innervated by lumbar sympathetic preganglionic axons; others are cholinergic and receive sacral parasympathetic inputs (Keast, Luckensmeyer, & Schemann, 1995). A proportion of pelvic neurons receive synaptic connections from both hypogastric and pelvic nerves. In bladder ganglia, noradrenaline from stimulated sympathetic postganglionic terminals can inhibit acetylcholine release from preganglionic parasympathetic axons and so depress transmission of sacral signals. Norepinephrine does not affect the parasympathetic neurons directly.

## Autonomic Neuroeffector Junctions

In peripheral tissues, the effects of activity in autonomic nerve terminals on autonomic effector cells are complex and may depend on the release of several different compounds and on the presence and distribution of the receptors in the effector membranes for these compounds. Anatomical investigations of neuroeffector junctions at arterioles, veins, pacemaker cells of the heart, and longitudinal muscle of the gastrointestinal tract have demonstrated that varicosities of autonomic nerve fibers that are not surrounded by Schwann cells form close synaptic contacts with the effector cells (Hirst, Bramich, Edwards, &

Klemm, 1992; Hirst, Choate, Cousins, Edwards, & Klemm, 1996). These structures are the morphological substrate for the precise transmission of the centrally generated signals in the postganglionic neurons to the effector cells.

Classically, chemical transmission at these neuroeffector junctions is based on the release of the "conventional" transmitters, acetylcholine and noradrenaline. However, it is now clear that several chemical substances are often contained within individual autonomic neurons, can be released by action potentials, and can have multiple actions on effector tissues (Furness, Morris, Gibbins, & Costa, 1989; Morris & Gibbins, 1992). The compounds which may be involved are nitric oxide (NO), ATP, or a neuropeptide (e.g., vasoactive intestinal peptide, neuropeptide, galanin, and others). Immunohistochemistry has revealed the presence of many peptides, although only a few of these have been demonstrated to modify function after release from nerve terminals in vivo (e.g., neuropeptide Y or vasoactive intestinal peptide).

Most sympathetic postganglionic axons release noradrenaline, but sympathetic sudomotor and muscle vasodilator axons are cholinergic. Cholinergic sympathetic muscle vasodilator neurons have been shown to exist in cat, dog, and some other mammal species (for a review see Uvnäs, 1960), yet not in rat, hare, and monkey (Bolme, Novotny, Uvnäs, & Wright, 1970). Whether they exist in humans is a controversial issue (Dietz et al., 1994; Joyner & Halliwell, 2000). Most, but not all, nerve-mediated effects can be antagonized by blockade of adrenoceptors or muscarinic acetycholine receptors. All parasympathetic neurons are cholinergic; that is, they release acetylcholine on stimulation (Keast et al., 1995). However, not all effects of stimulating parasympathetic nerves are blocked by muscarinic antagonists. This fact clearly implies that other transmitters and/or other receptors are involved.

Responses of tissues to nerve-released noradrenaline and acetylcholine usually only follow repetitive activation of many axons. High-frequency stimuli, particularly in bursts, may produce effector responses due to the concomitant release of a neuropeptide. Alternatively, when the effects of nerve activity are not blocked completely by an adrenoceptor or muscarinic antagonist at a concentration that entirely abolishes the response to an exogenous transmitter, it may not necessarily be the case that a transmitter other than acetylcholine or noradrenaline is involved. Although the effects of exogenously applied substances that have putative transmitter function on cellular functions are known for many tissues, the consequences of activation of postjunctional receptors by neurally released transmitters have rarely been investigated. When they have, the mechanisms of neuroeffector transmission have been found to be diverse, involving a range of cellular events (Jänig & McLachlan, 1999). One important concept that has emerged is that the cellular mechanisms utilized by an endogenously released transmitter are often not the same as they are when this transmitter substance or its analog is applied exogenously (Hirst et al., 1996).

## Conclusions

The autonomic nervous system supplies each target organ and tissue via a separate pathway that consists of sets of pre- and postganglionic neurons with distinct patterns of reflex activity. This has been established for the lumbar sympathetic outflow to skin, skeletal muscle, and viscera, for the thoracic sympathetic outflow to the head and neck, and for some parasympathetic pathways. There are good reasons to assume that the principle of organization into functionally discrete pathways is the same in the sympathetic nervous system and the parasympathetic nervous system, the only difference being that some targets of the sympathetic system are widely distributed throughout the body (e.g., muscle blood vessels, skin blood vessels, sweat glands, erector pili muscles, fat tissue). The neurons in many of these pathways have ongoing activity, but neurons in some pathways are normally silent and activated only under special behavioral conditions (see Figure 9.9).

- The reflex patterns observed in each group of autonomic neurons are the result of integrative processes in spinal cord, brain stem, and hypothalamus (these being again under the control of the forebrain). With the possible exception of some groups of postganglionic neurons in prevertebral and car-

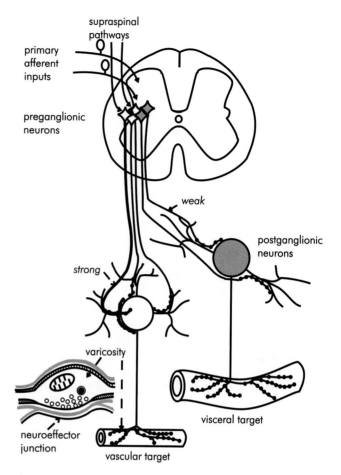

Figure 9.9 Organization of the peripheral autonomic nervous system into functional pathways. Separate functional pathways extend from the CNS to the effector organs. Preganglionic neurons located in the spinal cord and lower brain stem (here the intermediate zone of the thoraco-lumbar and sacral spinal cord) integrate signals descending from brain stem and hypothalamus and arising segmentally from primary afferent fibers. The preganglionic neurons project to peripheral ganglia and converge onto postganglionic neurons. Some preganglionic inputs to postganglionic neurons are always suprathreshold (or strong). Others are subthreshold (weak) and must summate to generate an action potential. The postganglionic axons form multiple neuroeffector junctions with their target cells. Many varicosities of the terminal axons that contain the synaptic vesicles with the transmitter(s) form close contacts with the target cells (neuroeffector junctions). Adapted from Jänig and McLachlan (1992a).

diac ganglia, which have functions other than vasoconstriction, postganglionic neurons do not generate spontaneous activity and do not have reflex activity independent of the synaptic activity from preganglionic neurons that is generated in the neuraxis.

- Functionally similar preganglionic and postganglionic neurons are synaptically connected in the autonomic ganglia, probably with little or *no* "cross-talk" between different peripheral pathways. The centrally generated reflex patterns are faithfully transmitted through the autonomic ganglia without distortion. However, modulation of impulse transmission may occur in these ganglia; this modulation varies between different autonomic (in particular sympathetic) ganglia. In prevertebral sympathetic ganglia, the central messages may be modulated by extraspinal synaptic inputs in pathways involved in the regulation of motility and secretion of the gastrointestinal tract.

- The messages in these functional pathways are transmitted to the autonomic effector cells by distinct neuroeffector mechanisms. This has clearly been shown for arterioles and the heart.

- The mechanisms of neuroeffector transmission are diverse in different targets. The classical transmitters noradrenaline and acetylcholine react with arrays of adrenoceptors and muscarinic receptors in the membranes of the effector cells, some of them being specific for functionally specific pathways. These transmitters may be colocalized with putative cotransmitters (acetylcholine with vasoactive intestinal peptide and nitric oxide; noradrenaline with ATP and/or neuropeptide Y).

- This anatomically and physiologically distinct organization of autonomic pathways is the basis for the precise neural regulation of homeostatic body functions during internal and external challenges. It is also the basis for the adaptive responses of the body during different types of behavior, including the responses during basic emotions. In this sense, the functioning of the sympathetic nervous system in an "all-or-none" fashion, without distinction between different effector organs, and the idea of simple functional antagonistic organization between sympathetic and parasympathetic nervous system are misleading, inadequate, and untenable.

## Principles of Spinal and Supraspinal Control of Autonomic Pathways

In the preceding section I described how sympathetic and parasympathetic systems consist of many *separate* pathways that supply the peripheral target organs. The neurons in these pathways have characteristic reflex discharge patterns. These discharge patterns are centrally generated and transmitted in the same form through the autonomic ganglia from the preganglionic to the postganglionic neurons and are the signals that are distributed from the autonomic ganglia to the effector cells at neuroeffector junctions. Integrative processes in general do not seem to occur between the autonomic pathways but only within the pathways. In the ganglia, the discharge rates appear to

be modified without changing the overall discharge pattern. At the neuroeffector junctions, temporal and spatial aspects of these signals to the effector cells contribute to the transmission. The final output neurons that integrate the neural processes in the central nervous system are the preganglionic neurons in the spinal cord and in the brain stem.

This section focuses on principles of central integration in the neuraxis (spinal cord, brain stem, hypothalamus) and therefore on principles of central regulation of autonomic functions. The reference point for this description is the *functional specificity* of the peripheral autonomic pathways with respect to the target organs. This functional specificity reflects the central organization of the systems. The main arguments to define the functional specificity of the neurons of the peripheral autonomic pathways are derived from the measurements of the reflexes in post- and preganglionic neurons (see the previous section). These reflexes are mostly isolated fragments of regulating systems and as such are in principle experimental artifacts. Some reflexes may easily be interpreted as functionally meaningful (e.g., baro- and chemoreceptor reflexes in vasoconstrictor neurons), whereas others may not. However, the application of the reflex concept provides an insight into the neuronal elements of the regulation of autonomic target organs. The advantages of this approach are obvious (Granit, 1981): (1) one knows the types of efferent neurons being controlled; (2) the afferent neurons stimulated are known; (3) the experimental conditions can be defined; (4) the reflexes can be studied in various types of preparation (e.g., in vivo brain-intact, decerebrate, or spinal animals; in vitro whole brain stem preparations with attached heart in which the afferent and efferent pathways are intact; Paton, 1996). Once the reflexes and their pathways (including interneurons) are well defined, one should be able to elucidate how these pathways function and interact during ongoing regulation of the autonomic target organs.

This section gives only an overview, without describing special functions, and primarily concentrates on the sympathetic systems. The organization of the sacral parasympathetic systems innervating pelvic organs and parasympathetic systems in the lower brain stem is described elsewhere (de Groat, 1999; de Groat, Vizzard, Araki, & Roppolo, 1996; Jänig, 1996c, 1996d; Loewy & Spyer, 1990; Ritter et al., 1992). The separation into spinal cord, brain stem, and hypothalamus is somewhat artificial because all three are closely integrated in the regulation of the peripheral autonomic systems (Blessing, 1997).

### Spinal Mechanisms

The spinal cord contains many autonomic reflex circuits that consist of preganglionic neurons, putative interneurons, and spinal afferent inputs. No monosynaptic connections between primary afferent and preganglionic neurons have been found so far. These reflex circuits are defined by the functions of the preganglionic neurons and the function of the afferent neurons. It has been shown for the lumbar sympathetic outflow to skin, skeletal muscle, and pelvic viscera in the cat that most sympathetic pathways are associated with two or more specific spinal reflex pathways each, indicating that there are several distinct classes of autonomic interneurons, none of which have been functionally identified so far (Jänig, 1996a), but some of them have been identified morphologically (Strack, Sawyer, Hughes, Platt, & Loewy, 1989). For the sacral parasympathetic system innervating pelvic organs the situation is similar; also here several distinct functional types of spinal segmental, propriospinal, and ascending tract interneurons have to be postulated to be involved in the regulation of the pelvic organs and in various types of spinal reflexes related to the pelvic organs (Bahr, Bartel, Blumberg, & Jänig, 1986a, 1986c; Bartel, Blumberg, & Jänig, 1986; de Groat, 1999; de Groat et al., 1996; Jänig, 1996c, 1996d; Jänig & Häbler, 1995; Jänig & Koltzenburg, 1993).

Some functional characteristics of the discharge pattern in spinal neurons of the autonomic pathways are dependent on spinal reflex circuits and some on supraspinal mechanisms (Jänig, 1985, 1986, 1988a). For example, discharge pattern and spontaneous activity ("tone") in vasoconstrictor neurons that regulate resistance vessels (e.g., muscle vasoconstrictor and visceral vasoconstrictor neurons, renal vasoconstrictor neurons; Bahr et al., 1986b, 1986c; Jänig, 1985, 1988a; Jänig et al., 1991) are largely dependent on activity generated in the medulla oblongata, on reflexes associated with cardiovascular afferents (notably baroreceptor and chemoreceptor afferents; Guyenet, 1990; Guyenet & Koshiya, 1995; Guyenet et al., 1996; Koshiya, Huangfu, & Guyenet, 1993) and on the coupling between respiratory neurons and "presympathetic" neurons in the medulla oblongata (Guyenet & Koshiya, 1992; Häbler & Jänig, 1995; Häbler, Jänig, & Michaelis, 1994; McAllen, 1987; Richter & Spyer, 1990). The discharge pattern and spontaneous activity in most cutaneous vasoconstrictor neurons (Grewe, Jänig, & Kümmel, 1995; Jänig, 1985, 1988a; Jänig & Kümmel, 1977, 1981) are mainly dependent on the hypothalamus (thermoregulation), on the spinal circuits (nociceptive and non-nociceptive somatosympathetic and viscerosympathetic reflexes, thermoregulatory reflexes) and on the medulla oblongata (cardiovascular reflexes, coupling to central respiratory generator). The discharge pattern and spontaneous activity in sympathetic motility-regulating neurons supplying pelvic organs are dependent on sacro-lumbar reflex pathways and relatively independent of brain stem and hypothalamus (Bartel et al., 1986).

Spinal autonomic interneurons are possibly located in laminae V, VII, and X of the spinal cord, as well as in the intercalated and central autonomic nuclei of the intermediate zone (Cabot, 1996; Strack et al., 1989a). These inter-neurons may be segmental and propriospinal. The segmental interneurons may be associated with the preganglionic neurons in the same and adjacent segments of a particular sympathetic outflow (e.g., the lumbar outflow to the pelvic organs, or the lumbar outflow to skin and skeletal muscle of the hindlimb). The propriospinal autonomic interneurons may be important for the communication between different spinal autonomic outflows and may project over many segments. For example, sacro-lumbar reflexes elicited in motility-regulating neurons of the lumbar sympathetic outflow to pelvic organs and colon are mediated by propriospinal neurons. Or many spinal somatosympathetic reflexes that are associated with the different types of cutaneous afferents are mediated by propriospinal interneurons. Candidates are lamina I neurons of the dorsal horn. These neurons may specifically project to the thoracolumbar sympathetic nuclei (Craig, 1993, 1996). The interneurons are probably important for the integration of spinal and supraspinal circuits in the regulation of autonomic functions.

Candidates for descending systems that are distinct with respect to their origin and histochemistry (monaminergic, peptidergic) and that project to the sympathetic preganglionic neurons have been described (Strack, Sawyer, Hughes, Platt, & Loewy, 1989; Strack, Sawyer, Platt, & Loewy, 1989; see also Dampney, 1994; Loewy & Spyer, 1990). They originate in the rostral ventrolateral medulla, the rostral ventromedial medulla, the caudal raphe nuclei, the pontine A5 area, the midbrain periaqueductal gray, the paraventricular hypothalamic nuclei, the lateral hypothalamic, and the zona incerta. For example, for the different types of vasoconstrictor neurons (muscle, visceral, renal, and cutaneous vasoconstrictor neurons), distinct descending pathways from the rostroventrolateral medulla, in which presympathetic neurons for these sympathetic systems are situated (Dampney & McAllen, 1988; McAllen & May, 1994a) and which mediate baroreceptor, chemoreceptor, and other cardiovascular reflex activities and components of coupling with the central respiratory generator (see Häbler & Jänig, 1995; Häbler, Jänig, & Michaelis, 1994) have been described or postulated. However, the functions of the other descending systems which project to the preganglionic sympathetic neurons are unknown.

It is hypothesized that integration of spinal and supraspinal circuits, which leads to the characteristic discharge patterns in the sympathetic neurons, occurs principally in the same way as in the somatomotor system (see Baldissera, Hultborn, & Illert, 1981). Preganglionic neurons, autonomic interneurons, spinal afferent neurons, and descending systems may be synaptically connected in a similar way as are the corresponding neurons of the somatomotor system (see Baldissera et al., 1981; Jankowska & Lundberg, 1981; Schomburg, 1990). In this sense spinal autonomic circuits are integrative mechanisms for the control of autonomic target organs. These may be called "spinal autonomic motor programs." Higher (supraspinal) centers use these spinal integrative mechanisms in the control of the peripheral sympathetic pathways. The signals originating from supraspinal centers are shaped by the spinal circuits before they are channeled into the peripheral sympathetic pathways. This shaping by the spinal autonomic programs varies between different spinal autonomic systems, and there are certainly also many monosynaptic connections between descending systems and preganglionic sympathetic neurons (McAllen, Häbler, Michaelis, Peters, & Jänig, 1994; Morrison, Callaway, Milner, & Reis, 1991; Strack, Sawyer, Platt, & Loewy, 1989; Zagoun & Smith, 1993). Thus this spinal component is probably very important for the understanding of the neural regulation of autonomic target organs (e.g., cardiovascular regulation, thermoregulation of blood flow through skin, regulation of evacuative organs).

In conclusion, the spinal cord is an integrative organ in its own right which determines many components of the discharge pattern in the autonomic neurons. Most of these responses are also present when the spinal cord is isolated from the brain stem (Jänig, 1985, 1996a). Thus these reflexes are based on a distinct organization of the sympathetic systems in the spinal cord. Visceral afferents (notably from pelvic organs) have strong uniform excitatory reflex effects on vasoconstrictor neurons of all vascular beds chronically after interrupting the connection between the spinal sympathetic systems and their supraspinal control centers.

## Regulation of Organ Systems by Lower Brain Stem Mechanisms

The lower brain contains the neuronal mechanisms for the homeostatic regulation of the cardiovascular system, the respiratory system, and the gastrointestinal tract. These global regulations are closely coordinated in different time domains and according to the external and internal demands on the organism. Thus regulation of respiration, heartbeat, and peripheral resistance are adjusted in the time domain of seconds, so as to adjust the gas transport precisely into the body and in the body to the peripheral tissues. Ingestion of food and fluid and respiration are precisely regulated in the time domain of milliseconds in order to prevent nutrients and fluid getting into the lungs. Digestion and absorption of nutrients is closely coordinated with regulation blood flow through the gastrointestinal tract to guarantee its transport to liver and body tissues. These differentiated regulations, their coordination, and their adaptation to the external and internal challenges of the body require (1) a variety of specialized primary afferent neurons which continuously inform the lower brain stem about the internal state of these systems, (2) a variety of specialized autonomic final pathways to the three systems (and somatic pathways to the respiratory

muscles), (3) distinct synaptic connections between the afferent inputs from and the efferent pathways to these three systems via distinct groups of interneurons, and (4) complex and differentiated neuronal controls of these reflex pathways by the centers in the upper brain stem, hypothalamus, and forebrain. It is clear that the different groups of interneurons are synaptically interconnected in a functionally specific way; otherwise the closely coordinated regulations of the three systems are not possible. We have only limited knowledge about the different types of interneurons, their transmitters, their synaptic connections, and their connections with supramedullary brain centers. Conceptually it is fair to say that the basic homeostatic regulations of the three global body functions and their coordination are represented in the lower brain stem. The specific components of these neuronal regulations become visible in the distinct reflexes elicited in the autonomic neurons by physiological stimulation of different groups of afferents (e.g., from the cardiovascular, gastrointestinal, or respiratory systems; see the previous section). This leads to the definition of a high number of reflexes which are the building blocks of the regulations (many of them not being functionally meaningful in isolation). It is to be expected that specific reflexes obtained under standardized experimental conditions change quantitatively and qualitatively in relation to the state in which the regulation systems are and according to the command signals from supramedullary centers. Details about the different reflexes, their integration in the homeostatic regulations, and their anatomical basis are to be found in the literature (Blessing, 1997 [see extensive literature here]; Brodal, 1998; Dampney, 1994; Guyenet, 1990; Guyenet & Koshiya, 1992, 1995; Guyenet et al., 1996; Jordan, 1997; Kirchheim et al., 1998; Loewy & Spyer, 1990; Ritter et al., 1992; Spyer, 1981, 1994). Some general principles of this organization are described by reference to the arterial baroreceptor reflexes and to gastrointestinal reflexes.

Arterial baroreceptor reflexes have fascinated cardiovascular physiologists since the beginning of the 19th century. The function of these reflexes is to minimize the fluctuations of arterial blood pressure during various actions of the body (e.g., exercise, change of position of body in earth gravity, mental activity) but not to regulate the height of blood pressure (see Cowley, Liard, & Guyton, 1973; Persson, Ehmke, Kirchheim, & Seller, 1988). There are several types of arterial baroreceptor reflexes which are related to the parasympathetic and sympathetic cardiomotor neurons and to the different types of vasoconstrictor neurons that innervate resistance vessels (mainly in skeletal muscle, kidney, other viscera). Phasic stimulation of the arterial baroreceptors (in the carotid sinus and aortic arch) leads to phasic activation of the parasympathetic cardiomotor neurons and phasic inhibition of the sympathetic cardiomotor and vasoconstrictor neurons. This is reflected in phasic changes of the activity in these peripheral cardiovascular neurons with respect to the pulse pressure wave in anesthetized and awake animals and humans (see cardiac rhythmicity of the activity in muscle vasoconstrictor neurons in Figures 9.6A$_2$ and 9.6B$_2$), but not in most other autonomic neurons, which do not innervate resistance vessels (e.g., cutaneous vasoconstrictor neurons; see Figure 9.7A$_2$). The neuronal components of these baroreceptor pathways have been worked out, although there remain many open questions as far as the synaptic transmission in the different "relay nuclei" (NTS, CVLM, RVLM, IML; see Figure 9.10), the specificity of these transmissions, and alternative reflex pathways are concerned. The baroreceptor pathway to the parasympathetic preganglionic cardiomotor neurons is most likely disynaptic and those to the sympathetic preganglionic cardiomotor and vasoconstrictor neurons trisynaptic. The inhibition in the latter pathways occurs in the RVLM by GABAergic interneurons, which are located in the CVLM. Neurons in the RVLM which project to the IML are called presympathetic cardiomotor and vasoconstrictor neurons. There is experimental evidence that these neurons are topically organized in the RVLM with respect to their targets (cardiomotor, muscle vasoconstrictor, renal vasoconstrictor, other visceral vasoconstrictor; Dampney & McAllen, 1988; Lovick, 1987; McAllen & May, 1994b; McAllen, May, & Shafton, 1995; Polson, Halliday, McAllen, Coleman, & Dampney, 1992). These presympathetic RVLM neurons or interneurons in the RVLM are supposed to be responsible for the resting activity in the sympathetic neurons associated with resistance vessels and heart (see Guyenet, 1990; Guyenet et al., 1996). However, other groups of neurons in the brain which project to the different relays (including the IML) of the baroreceptor pathways may contribute, too. The origin of the resting activity in the parasympathetic cardiomotor neurons is unknown. In this context it is important to note that the resting activity in other functional types of sympathetic neurons (see Tables 9.4–9.6) is unlikely to originate exclusively, if at all, in the RVLM. Thus, as mentioned earlier, the generalized term "sympathetic tone" lacks a physiological basis and should be avoided or at least be specified with respect to the functional type of sympathetic system. The relays of the baroreceptor reflex pathways are under powerful modulatory control exerted by other centers in the lower and upper brain stem, hypothalamus, and forebrain (shaded arrows in Figure 9.10). These influences lead to enhancement or depression of the baroreceptor reflexes. For example, during the hypothalamically induced defense behavior arterial baroreceptor-induced reflexes are depressed by inhibition in the NTS and probably elsewhere (Paton & Kasparov, 2000; Spyer 1981, 1994). This example of the baroreceptor pathways in the lower brain stem serves to illustrate how complex their organization and functioning really is. Similar complexities are present for the autonomic chemoreceptor pathways (Guyenet & Koshiya,

1992, 1995) and other reflex pathways related to the cardiovascular system, most of which are still unknown in their structure. These complexities are the basis for the high adaptability of the homeostatic cardiovascular regulation and its distortion during disease (see Eckberg & Sleight, 1992; Folkow & Neil, 1971; Kirchheim et al., 1998; Mathias & Bannister, 1999; Randall, 1984; Rowell, 1993).

The second example is related to neural regulation of the gastrointestinal tract (GIT; Figure 9.11). Various types of specific reflex pathways between functionally distinct primary afferent neurons from the GIT which sense mechanical, chemical, or other events and several functionally distinct preganglionic neurons in the dorsal motor nucleus of the vagus nerve (DMN) which are involved in regulation of motility, exocrine secretion, endocrine secretion, and other events in the GIT have to be postulated. These reflex pathways are at least disynaptic and include the second-order neurons of the nucleus of the solitary tract (NTS). Details of most of these pathways are still unknown. These reflex pathways are under control of neurons in supramedullary brain centers (so-called executive neurons; e.g., in the paraventricular nucleus of the hypothalamus, PVN, the central nucleus of the amygdala, CNA, the bed nucleus of the stria terminalis, BNST, etc.; see Figure 9.11), which also receive detailed afferent information from the GIT (via the NTS) and from other body domains. Executive neurons and basic autonomic circuits to the GIT represent part of the internal state of the body as far as the GIT is concerned. This internal state is adapted to the behavior of the organism by cortex and limbic system structures that monitor and represent the external state of the organism. However, the internal state modulates the central representation of the external state, too, leading to changes of sensory perception, body feeling, and experience of emotions. Also, this example shows conceptually that there is a close integration between homeostatic regulation of GIT functions and higher nervous system functions which are related to body perceptions, emotions, and adaptation of behavior, the basis of this integration being highly specific autonomic reflex pathways.

### Integration of Homeostatic Mechanisms in Upper Brain Stem and Limbic-Hypothalamic Centers

The upper brain stem, hypothalamus, and limbic system contain the neuronal programs which generate the response patterns to adjust species and individual in a continuously changing environment. These programs regulate preformed constellations of *somatomotor, autonomic,* and *hormonal adjustments,* which are organized in such a way that each motor behavior is accompanied by changes of inner organs, metabolism, and so forth, so as to optimize net performance. The brain is continuously informed about the environment via the sensory systems and selects

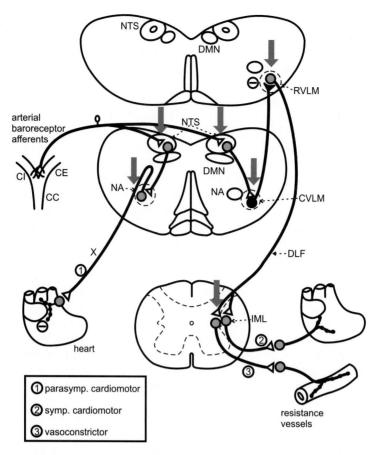

Figure 9.10 Arterial baroreceptor reflexes involving parasympathetic cardiomotor (PCM) neurons (pacemaker cells and atria of the heart), sympathetic cardiomotor (SCM) neurons (pacemaker cells, atria, and ventricles), and vasoconstrictor neurons (VC) innervating resistance blood vessels. Arterial baroreceptor afferents innervating the carotid bifurcation and aortic arch project bilaterally to the nucleus of the solitary tract (NTS). They encode in their activity arterial blood pressure and change of blood pressure. *Left*: Parasympathetic baroreceptor reflex pathway to the heart. Excitatory second-order neurons of the NTS project to the preganglionic PCM neurons in the nucleus ambiguus (NA). Activation of the baroreceptors leads to activation of the PCM neurons and subsequently to a decrease of heart rate (by inhibition of the pacemaker cells). *Right*: Sympathetic baroreceptor pathways to the heart and the resistance blood vessels. These baroreceptor pathways consist of a chain of minimally three neurons between the baroreceptor afferents and the preganglionic neurons in the intermediolateral nucleus (IML). "Presympathetic" neurons are located in the rostroventrolateral medulla (RVLM), project through the dorsolateral funiculus (DLF) of the spinal cord to the preganglionic SCM and VC neurons and excite these neurons. Excitatory second-order neurons of the NTS project to inhibitory interneurons in the caudal ventrolateral medulla (CVLM). These inhibitory interneurons project to the "presympathetic" neurons in the RVLM and inhibit them. Thus activation of arterial baroreceptors leads to decrease of activity in the SCM and VC neurons by inhibition in the RVLM. The transmitter mediating this inhibition is GABA (gamma-amino-butyric acid). The transmitter at all other central synapses of the baroreceptor pathways is glutamate. Ongoing activity in the SCM and VC neurons has its origin in the RVLM. Signal transmission through the baroreceptor pathways can be modulated (inhibited, enhanced) from other centers in brain stem, hypothalamus, and forebrain at all synapses (see *shaded arrows*). Adapted from Guyenet (1990).

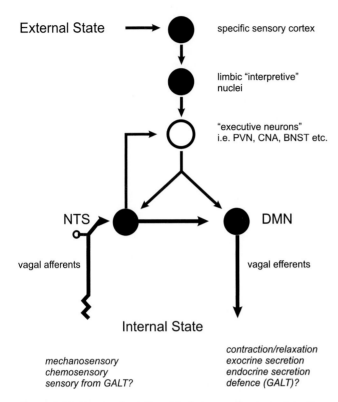

Figure 9.11 Proposed relationship between the gastrointestinal vago-vagal reflex pathways, forebrain autonomic "executive" neuronal circuits, limbic "interpretive" neuronal circuits, and exterosensory systems. Several functional specific vago-vagal reflex pathways are the basic neuronal building blocks. They are mediated through the medulla oblongata. Vagal afferents measure mechano-, chemo-, and other sensory events (e.g., sensing events in the gut-associated lymphoid tissue, GALT) and project to the nucleus of the solitary tract (NTS); vagal preganglionic neurons are located in the dorsal vagal motor nucleus (DMN) and are involved in regulation of motility, exocrine secretion, endocrine secretion, and other events (e.g., those associated with the GALT). Forebrain "executive" centers (e.g., paraventricular nucleus of the hypothalamus, PVN; central nucleus of the amygdala, CNA; bed nucleus of the stria terminalis, BNST) evaluate the state of the internal milieu (by way of inputs from vagal and other visceral afferents), as well as the current or anticipated behavioral state (via input from limbic nuclei which evaluate the significance of exteroceptive signals). These executive centers adapt the internal state (e.g., gastrointestinal functions) to the behavioral state of the organism. Adapted from Rogers & Hermann (1992).

the most appropriate among these reaction patterns for coping with the actual environmental situation. The number of these "preprogrammed" patterns probably is higher than those known. These patterns are of great physiological importance, and some of them are of pathophysiological importance as well, this, in particular, in order to understand "civilization disorders" such as primary hy-

pertension and the metabolic syndrome in humans in modern society (for reviews, see Björntorp, 1997; DiBona & Kopp, 1997; Folkow, 1982, 1987, 1993; Folkow, Schmidt, & Uvnäs-Moberg, 1997; Henry, 1994; Henry, Liu, & Meehan, 1995; Henry & Stephens, 1977; Kaplan, Manuck, & Clarkson, 1985). Here some of the response patterns are described briefly, illustrating the highly differentiated way in which CNS can engage the autonomic systems.

Changes of cardiovascular functions for six of these response patterns in which the autonomic systems are involved are summarized in Table 9.7 (the defense reaction, the vigilance [freezing] reaction, the defeat reaction, the playing-dead reaction, the feeding reaction, and the diving response). Most of these response patterns also affect in various ways other organ systems and many metabolic events (Folkow, 1987, 1993; McCabe et al., 1994). The forebrain "uses" these response patterns or combinations of them to adjust the body. Integrated in these patterns are the various spinal and bulbar reflexes and homeostatic regulations, which are related to the regulation of the cardiovascular system, the respiratory system, the gastrointestinal tract, the evacuative organs, and some other functions, as discussed in the following:

- In the *defense reaction* cardiac output increase is delivered preferentially to skeletal muscles, myocardium, and brain, whereas flow to gastrointestinal tract, kidneys, and skin is reduced and their functions suppressed (Folkow, 1987, 1993). These changes are mainly generated by sympathetic pathways.
- Organisms can within seconds shift from, for example, an initial *vigilance reaction* to a defense reaction or, if "cornered," to a *playing-dead reaction*. Alternatively, if a defense reaction on a more long-term basis becomes untenable because the situation is judged as "no way out," shifts to the *defeat reaction* are common, for example, among group-living (social) animals.
- In the *defeat reaction*, which is unfortunately less well explored than the defense reaction, activation of sympathetic vasoconstrictor systems leads to an increased systemic resistance combined with bradycardia generated by parasympathetic cardiomotor neurons while gastrointestinal functions are in several respects enhanced. In this reaction the hormonal side is dominated by enhanced and prolonged ACTH-glucocorticoid secretion, which can lead to far-reaching metabolic disturbances, as well as to suppression of the immune system (Björntorp, 1997; Folkow et al., 1997).
- In terms of magnitude and temporal precision of responses, the perhaps most spectacular response pattern is the *diving response*, used both for protection and food seeking in diving species (Schytte-Blix &

Table 9.7. Patterns of Activity in Functionally Specific Sympathetic (S) and Parasympathetic (P) Cardiovascular Neurons During Different Behavioral Reactions

|  |  | Defense reaction | Vigilance reaction | Defeat reaction | Playing-dead reaction | Feeding reaction | Diving response |
|---|---|---|---|---|---|---|---|
| Heart | $S_{CM}$ | ++ | Ø? | Ø? | −− | + | −− |
|  | $P_{CM}$ | −− | + | + | +++ | − | +++ |
| Skeletal muscle | $S_{VC}$ | − | + | +? | −− | + | +++ |
|  | $S_{VD}$ | ++ | Ø | Ø | +?/Ø | Ø | Ø |
| Skin | $S_{ord}$ | ++ | + | ? | −− | ? | +++ |
|  | $S_{A-V}$ | ++ | + | ? | −− | ? | −− |
| Kidney | $S_{VC}$ | ++ | +? | +? | −− | +? | +++ |
| G-I tract | $S_{VC}$ | ++ | + | −? | −− | − | +++ |
| MAP |  | + | + | + | −−− | + | Ø |
| CO |  | ++ | − | Ø? | −− | +/Ø | −−− |
| RESPIR. |  | −/Ø | + | + | −−− | -? | +++ |

*Note.* CM, cardiomotor neurons: VC, vasoconstrictor neurons; VD, vasodilatator neurons; ord, cutaneous vasoconstrictor neurons to nutritional blood vessels; A-V, cutaneous vasoconstrictor neurons to arteriovenous anastomoses. +, ++, +++/−,−−,−−−, increase/decrease of activity (or cardiovascular and respiratory parameters); Ø, relatively unchanged; ?, effect unknown; G-I, gastrointestinal; MAP, mean arterial blood pressure; CO, cardiac output; RESPIR., respiration. Adapted from Folkow (2000).

Folkow, 1983). In a few seconds the cardiovascular system is transformed into a "heart-brain circulation system." Major systemic circuits are virtually shut off by sympathetic vasoconstrictor fibers, while cardiac activity is profoundly reduced by activation of parasympathetic cardiomotor neurons and reduced activity in sympathetic cardiomotor neurons. In the skin, the apical nonnutritional arteriovenous anastomoses, which are under strict nervous control, are *left open* during submersion by inhibition of activity in cutaneous vasoconstrictor neurons, helping to slowly move the oxygen-containing blood in diverse huge venous "depots" to the pump, without any peripheral $O_2$ consumption, for subsequent nutritional delivery to brain and myocardium in a situation in which cardiac output is often reduced twentyfold.

- Stimulation of the *hypothalamic "hunger"* (appetite) center leads to food intake. This is paralleled by cardiovascular and gastrointestinal adjustments, which are mediated by the various types of sympathetic and parasympathetic pathways. In this way blood supply to, as well as activity of, the gastrointestinal tract is enhanced in combination with reduced muscle blood flow and increased blood pressure and heart activity (Folkow & Rubinstein, 1965).

The defense and defeat reactions probably are important for the gradual induction—often over decades—of primary hypertension and the metabolic syndrome in human beings (Björntorp, 1997; Folkow, 1982, 1987; Folkow et al., 1997; Kaplan et al., 1985). In this context the sympathetic nervous system not only is involved in cardiovascular adjustments (as shown in Table 9.7) but also

causes lipid and carbohydrate mobilization from nutritional depots, stimulates the immune system, enhances blood coagulability, and so forth. Furthermore, it engages the renin-angiotensin-aldosterone axis and contributes to fluid electrolyte conservation, probably by direct nervous influence on both glomerular and tubular functions of the kidney (DiBona & Kopp, 1997; Kopp & DiBona, 1992), whereas gastrointestinal functions are suppressed.

## Autonomic Nervous System and Body Protection

Responses of the organism during emotions, pain, and stress, whether elicited by external or internal stimuli, are integral components of an adaptive biological system and important for the organism to function in the confines of a dynamic and frequently challenging and dangerous environment (see Brown, Koob, & Rivier, 1991). These responses consist of autonomic, neuroendocrine, and somatomotor responses, which include the appropriate sensory perceptions and felt emotions. They serve to adapt organ functions to the changing behavior and the behavior to changing environments. The integrated responses displayed by the organism are states of the organism which are represented in the brain (brain stem, hypothalamus, limbic system, and neocortex). Perception of sensations, experience of emotions, autonomic responses, endocrine responses, and somatomotor responses occur principally in parallel and are therefore parallel readouts of these central representations. These central representations obtain continuous neuronal afferent, hormonal, and humoral signals that monitor the state of the different tissues (see Figure 9.12). Here I argue that adaptive and protective reactions of the body during defensive behaviors, adaptation of the immune system, control of inflammation and hyperalgesia, and basic emotions require autonomic nervous systems which function in a differentiated way.

### Defense Behavior During Pain and Stress Integrated in the Mesencephalon

Reactions of the autonomic (in particular sympathetic) nervous system to peripheral noxious stimuli are expressions of the state of the organism in pain. These reactions are well orchestrated, and the functional specificity resides in the individual responses which are associated with the functionally discrete autonomic pathways. They enable the organism to cope with dangerous situations and are presumably protective and adaptive under normal biological conditions and associated with the activation of the hypothalamo-pituitary-adrenal axis and the somatomotor system.

The general pattern of reaction when the organism is in pain and stress can best be exemplified by the different types of *defense behavior*, which are integrated responses consisting of autonomic, endocrine, and motor components and sensory (antinociceptive) adjustments. They are triggered by stimuli that challenge the integrity of the organism, such as noxious stimuli, as well as stimuli and situations which are perceived by the brain as threatening. In

the rat these stereotyped defense behaviors are labeled confrontational defense, flight, and quiescence, and they are integrated in the midbrain periaqueductal gray (PAG; Bandler, Carrive, & Zhang, 1991; Bandler & Keay, 1996; Bandler, Price, & Keay, 2000; Bandler & Shipley, 1994). *Confrontational defense* is characterized by hypertension, tachycardia, decrease of blood flow through the limb muscles and viscera, and increase of blood flow through the face; it is represented in the rostral part of the lateral PAG. *Flight* is characterized by hypertension, tachycardia, increase of blood flow through the limb muscles, and decrease of blood flow through the face; it is represented in the caudal part of the lateral PAG. Both types of defensive behaviors are accompanied by endogenous nonopioid analgesia. *Quiescence* (hyporeactivity) is characterized by hypotension, bradycardia, and endogenous opioid analgesia; it is represented in the ventrolateral PAG. The systemic cardiovascular changes (and probably other autonomic changes, such as blood flow through skin, piloerection, sweating, change of motility of the gastrointestinal tract, activation of the adrenal medulla, change of pupil size, etc.) are generated by activation or inhibition of specific sympathetic and parasympathetic pathways (see Figure 9.13).

These defensive behaviors represented in the lateral and ventrolateral columns of the PAG are basic neuronal substrates of the body to meet threatening demands from the environment and from the deep body domains. The following points support this idea (Bandler et al., 2000):

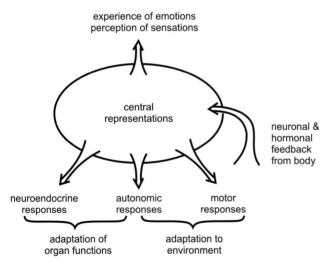

Figure 9.12 Scheme of somatomotor and autonomic emotional expression, experience of basic emotions, and afferent feedback from the viscera and the deep body domain. Activation of the central representation of the emotions leads to the emotional feelings and the specific expression of the emotions in the somatomotor system and in the autonomic nervous system. The afferent feedback from the deep body domains modulates the emotional feelings. From Jänig & Häbler (2000), copyright 2000, with permission from Elsevier Science.

- Neurons in the lateral and ventrolateral PAG columns project to various autonomic centers in the medulla oblongata which contain the parasympathetic and "presympathetic" neurons, neurons which are involved in regulating different types of autonomic target organs related to the cardiovascular system and gastrointestinal tract, neurons which are involved in control of respiration, and neurons which control transmission of nociceptive impulses in the dorsal horn and caudal trigeminal nuclei (Fields & Basbaum, 1999).
- Lateral and ventrolateral PAG columns receive afferent inputs from the superficial and deep body domains via spinal cord and trigeminal nuclei. The afferent input to the lateral PAG is somatotopically organized and derives preferentially from the body surface. The afferent input to the ventrolateral PAG derives preferentially from the deep somatic body structures and from viscera.
- Cortical structures and subcortical forebrain structures (e.g., the central nucleus of the amygdala and the medial preoptic area) have powerful projections to the PAG. These afferent projections from the forebrain also have a columnar organization, those from the neocortex probably being spatially more discrete than those from subcortical structures. Furthermore,

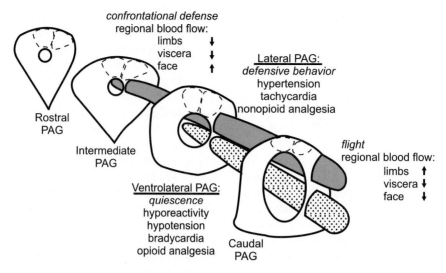

*confrontational defense*
regional blood flow:
limbs    ↓
viscera    ↓
face    ↑

Rostral PAG

Intermediate PAG

Lateral PAG:
*defensive behavior*
hypertension
tachycardia
nonopioid analgesia

*flight*
regional blood flow:
limbs    ↑
viscera    ↓
face    ↓

Ventrolateral PAG:
*quiescence*
hyporeactivity
hypotension
bradycardia
opioid analgesia

Caudal PAG

Figure 9.13 Representation of defensive behavior and quiescent behavior in the lateral and ventrolateral periaqueductal gray (lPAG, vlPAG). Schematic illustration of the lateral and ventrolateral columns within the rostral, intermediate, and caudal PAG. The dorso-medial and dorsolateral neuronal PAG columns are indicated in interrupted contours. Stimulation of neuron populations on the lPAG and vlPAG by microinjections of excitatory amino acids evoke distinct behaviors and the corresponding autonomic (changes of blood flows, blood pressure, heart rate) and sensory changes (analgesia): Confrontational defense from the intermediate lPAG; flight from the caudal lPAG; quiescence (cessation of spontaneous activity) from the vlPAG. Adapted from Bandler and Shipley (1994).

many projections from subcortical structures are more dense than those from the cortex (An, Bandler, Öngür, & Price, 1998; Bandler et al., 2000).

The attraction of the idea of Bandler and others is that the PAG contains the neural networks that enable the forebrain structures to coordinate, on a moment-to-moment basis, the integrated somatic, autonomic, and antinociceptive mechanisms and other sensory mechanisms during stress and pain. These fast neuronal adjustments are critical for the survival of the organism. Primitive strategies for coping with threatening events seem to be represented in the longitudinal columns of the PAG: Noxious events occurring at the body surface and deriving from the environment are associated with active coping strategies (e.g., confrontational defense and flight), whereas noxious events in the deep body domains are associated with passive coping strategies (quiescence). These fast neuronal protective mechanisms are coordinated with hypothalamic mechanisms that control homeostatic body functions, which include the associated behaviors and neuroendocrine processes (e.g., thermoregulation, regulation of energy balance, regulation of sexual behavior).

The fast neuronally directed protective adjustments of body functions require precisely working sympathetic and parasympathetic systems that are functionally specific, as described in the section of this chapter titled "Functional Organization of the Peripheral Sympathetic and Parasympathetic Pathways."

## Control of the Immune System by the Sympathetic Nervous System

A large body of evidence from anatomical, physiological, pharmacological, and behavioral experiments on animals supports the notion that the sympathetic nervous system can influence the immune system and therefore control protective mechanisms of the body at the cellular level (see Ader, Felten, & Cohen, 1991; Besedovsky & del Rey, 1992, 1995; Hori, Katafuchi, Take, Shimizu, & Niijima, 1995; Madden & Felten, 1995; Madden, Sanders, & Felten, 1995). Control of the immune system by the sympathetic nervous system would mean that the forebrain is principally able to influence immune responses, an assumption which is almost taken for granted by several groups without necessary experimental basis (see Ader et al., 1991; Schedlowski & Tewes, 1999). The mechanisms of this influence remain largely unsolved (Ader & Cohen, 1993; Besedovsky & del Rey, 1992; Saphier, 1993) for conceptual and methodological reasons. In view of the functional specificity of the sympathetic pathways, the key question which has to be addressed is this: Does a specific sympathetic subsystem exist which communicates signals from the brain to the immune system, or is this efferent communication a general function of the sympathetic system? In other words, is the immune system supplied by a sympathetic pathway which is distinct from other (classical) sympathetic pathways and mediates only an immunomodulatory effect?

Several observations support the idea that an important channel of efferent communication from the brain to the immune system occurs via the sympathetic nervous system:

- Primary and secondary lymphoid tissues are innervated by noradrenergic sympathetic neurons. Varicosities of the sympathetic terminals can be found in close proximity with T lymphocytes and macrophages (see Ader et al., 1991; Madden et al., 1995) as described for other neuroeffector junctions of the sympathetic nervous system (see Jänig & McLachlan, 1999).
- The spleen of the cat is innervated by approximately 12,000 sympathetic postganglionic neurons. This innervation is numerically, relative to the weight of the organs, three times the number of neurons that innervate the kidneys (Baron & Jänig, 1988). Functional neurophysiological studies have shown that the sympathetic innervation of the spleen is different from that of the kidney: Sympathetic neurons that innervate the kidney behave like "classical" vasoconstrictor neurons (Dorward, Burke, Jänig, & Cassell, 1987; Jänig, 1988a; Kopp & DiBona, 1992). Many sympathetic neurons innervating the spleen are not under control of the arterial baroreceptors and show distinct (spinal) reflexes to stimulation of afferents from the spleen and the gastrointestinal tract which are different from those in vasoconstrictor neurons (Meckler & Weaver, 1988; Stein & Weaver, 1988). These results suggest that many sympathetic neurons innervating the spleen have a function other than to elicit vasoconstriction or capsular contraction. This function may be related to the immune system.
- Functional studies performed on the spleen of rodents have shown the following (for review, see Hori et al., 1995, and references therein):
  1. Surgical and chemical sympathectomy alters the splenic immune responses (e.g., increase of natural killer cell cytotoxicity, lymphocyte proliferation responses to mitogen stimulation and production of interleukin-1β).
  2. Stimulation of the splenic nerve reduces the splenic immune responses.
  3. Lesions or stimulation, as well as microinjection of cytokines at distinct hypothalamic sites, activates some splenic immune responses. These changes are no longer present after denervation of the spleen.
  4. Activity in the splenic nerve is affected by these central manipulations, and changes in neural activity are correlated with the changes of the splenic immune responses. For example, activity in sympathetic neurons to the spleen elicited by interventions at the hypothalamus (in particular the ventromedial nucleus of the hypothalamus) is highly correlated with suppression of natural killer cell cytotoxicity in the spleen. This suppression is mediated by β-adrenoceptors (Katafuchi, Take, & Hori, 1993; Okamoto, Ibaraki, Hayashi, & Saito, 1996). It has been postulated that there is a hypothalamo-sympathetic neural system which controls the immune system.
- The skin is innervated by sympathetic vasoconstrictor, sudomotor, pilomotor, and vasodilator neurons. These neurons can functionally be recognized (see the section in this chapter titled "Functional Organization of the Peripheral Sympathetic and Parasympathetic Pathways"). It is, however, obvious from neurophysiological studies that there are many sympathetic neurons projecting in skin nerves which do not exhibit spontaneous and reflex activity and the function of which is unknown. It is possible that these postganglionic neurons do not innervate the "classical" sympathetic target organs but are associated with the skin immune system (Bos, 1989; Bos & Kapsenberg, 1986; Edelson & Fink, 1985; Williams & Kupper, 1996).

These observations suggest that the lymphoid tissue is innervated by a specific sympathetic system which is functionally distinct from all other sympathetic systems (such as the vasoconstrictor systems, etc.) and under control of the hypothalamus.

This hypothesis is testable in vivo using classical neurophysiological recordings of sympathetic neurons innervating spleen, kidney, skin, and skeletal muscle. It should be possible to decipher this neural code and to discriminate it from that of other functional types of sympathetic neurons (e.g., vasoconstrictor neurons to skin, skeletal muscle, kidney, or spleen). This is exemplified in Table 9.8, which shows the target cells in particular organs that are innervated and possibly controlled by sympathetic neurons and the functions of these neurons. One sympathetic channel in three of these organs projects potentially to the immune tissue and possibly regulates the immune response.

As described in the section on functional organization, the different types of sympathetic neurons are functionally characterized by their reflex patterns (elicited by physiological stimulation of afferent neurons), their discharge pattern with respect to effector organ responses, and responses with respect to central respiration and with respect to other criteria. These discharge patterns are their

Table 9.8. Examples of Function-Specific Sympathetic Pathways to Different Targets Within Some Organs

| Organ | Target cells | Function |
|---|---|---|
| Spleen | BV, IC | VC, IR |
| Hairy skin | $BV_{skin}$, IC | VC (VD?), IR |
| Hairless skin | $BV_{skin}$, SG, IC | VC (VD?), SM, IR |
| Kidney | BV, JGA | VC, renin release |
| Skeletal muscle | $BV_{muscle}$ | VC (VD?) |

*Abbreviations.* BV, blood vessel; VC, vasoconstriction; VD, vasodilatation; IC, immune cells; IR, immune response; SG, sweat gland; SM, sudomotor response; JGA, juxtraglomerular cells. Adapted from Jänig (1985, 1995a); Jänig and McLachlan (1987, 1992a).

*functional markers.* In analogy it should theoretically be possible to characterize the sympathetic neurons that innervate lymphoid tissues by using stimuli which are adequate to elicit immune responses (for review and references, see Hori et al., 1995). This idea leads to the formulation of two alternative testable hypotheses: (1) Neurons of sympathetic pathways are functionally specific for the immune tissues and can be characterized by distinct reflex patterns elicited in these neurons by adequate stimuli which are related to the immune system and therefore related to defense and protection of the organism. (2) The alternative hypothesis would be that reflex responses in sympathetic neurons which modulate immune responses are found indiscriminately in all sympathetic neurons; these responses would therefore not be functionally specific for the lymphoid tissue. This could mean that more or less all sympathetic pathways have, in addition to their specific target-organ-related functions, a general function which is related to defense and protection of the tissues. Also this result could be interesting because it would render an argument that unifies both Cannon's concept about the general function of the sympathetic nervous system and the concept of the specificity of the sympathetic nervous system.

## Control of Inflammation and Hyperalgesia by the Brain Involving the Sympatho-Adrenal System

Inflammation and hyperalgesia following tissue trauma are protective reactions that further healing. Mechanisms of inflammation are commonly considered to be confined to the periphery, involving immune-competent and related inflammatory cells, as well as vascular cells. The main mechanism of hyperalgesia during inflammation in this view is confined to the sensitization of nociceptors by inflammatory mediators leading to central changes (central sensitization) and appropriate protective behavior. However, using animal models of experimental inflammation and mechanical hyperalgesia, it has recently been shown that both inflammation and nociceptor sensitiza-

tion are potentially under the control of the sympatho-adrenal system, implying that the brain can influence both via this system.

For example, experimental inflammation in the rat knee joint generated by the inflammatory mediator bradykinin is dependent on the presence of the innervation of the knee joint synovia by sympathetic neurons, but not on activity in these neurons (Miao, Jänig, & Levine, 1996; Miao, Green, Coderre, Jänig, & Levine, 1996). This inflammatory process is potentially under the control of the hypothalamo-pituitary-adrenal (HPA) system (Green, Jänig, & Levine, 1997; Green, Miao, Jänig, & Levine, 1995) and of the sympatho-adrenal system. Noxious stimulation leads to depression of the experimental inflammation, which is, depending on the type of afferent stimulation used, mediated either by the HPA axis (Green et al., 1995, 1997) or by the sympatho-adrenal axis (Miao, Jänig, & Levine, 2000). These nociceptive neuroendocrine negative feedback circuits are based on reflex pathways in the spinal cord, brain stem, and hypothalamus. It has been shown that the sensitivity of these reflex control pathways can be changed by activity in vagal afferents from the abdominal viscera. This activity inhibits these reflex pathways, and removal of activity in the vagal afferents (by surgical interruption of the appropriate visceral nerves) leads to central disinhibition and therefore to an enhancement of the nociceptive-neuroendocrine negative feedback control (Miao, Jänig, & Levine, 1997; Miao, Jänig, Green, & Levine, 1997; Miao, Jänig, & Levine, 2000).

Bradykinin-induced mechanical hyperalgesic behavior is enhanced and baseline paw withdrawal threshold reduced in rats in which abdominal vagal afferents have been interrupted. The vagal afferents involved are those that innervate the small intestine. This enhancement is generated by activation of the sympatho-adrenal system. After denervation of the adrenal medullae (cutting the sympathetic preganglionic axons) the hyperalgesic behavior either does not develop following vagotomy or reverses in vagotomized animals (Khasar, Miao, Jänig, & Levine, 1998a, 1998b; Jänig et al., 2000). These results imply that there exists a vagosympathetic reflex pathway which controls the activity in the preganglionic neurons that innervate the adrenal medullae, that activity in vagal afferents inhibits this pathway and therefore these preganglionic neurons, and that removal of the vagal activity activates the sympatho-adrenal system. Activation of the adrenal medullae leads to release of a substance (possibly adrenaline) and subsequently to sensitization of cutaneous nociceptors for mechanical stimulation. This sensitization has a long time course: It develops slowly over 7 days following activation of the adrenal medullae and reverses slowly following denervation of the adrenal medullae. It is an entirely new form of nociceptor sensitization. Its detailed mechanism is so far unknown.

Overall, these findings mean that inflammatory pro-

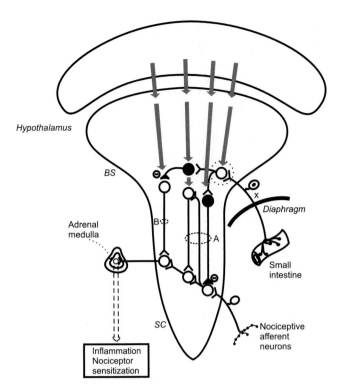

Figure 9.14 Schematic diagram showing the proposed neural circuits in spinal cord and brain stem which modulate inflammation and nociceptor sensitization via the symphato-adrenal system (adrenal medulla). (a) Stimulation of cutaneous nociceptors leads to depression of inflammation by activation of preganglionic neurons innervating the adrenal medullae via a spinal and a spino-bulbo-spinal excitatory circuit. The ascending limb of this spino-bulbo-spinal reflex loop projects through the contralateral dorsolateral funiculus of the spinal cord (DLF). The descending limb of this reflex loop projects through the dorsal quadrants. This circuit is inhibited by activity in abdominal vagal afferents from the small intestine, which is exerted at the level of the spinal cord. The descending limb of this inhibitory pathway projects through the ipsilateral DLF. (b) Sensitivity of cutaneous nociceptors for mechanical stimulation is modulated by a signal (probably adrenaline) from the adrenal medullae. Activation of the adrenal medullae increases sensitivity. Activity in preganglionic neurons that innervate the adrenal medullae depends on activity in vagal afferents from the small intestine, which has an inhibitory influence on the central pathway to the preganglionic neurons. Thus interruption of the vagal afferents leads to activation of the adrenal medullae. It is hypothesized that these neuronal (reflex) circuits in the brain stem are under the control of upper brain stem, hypothalamus, and forebrain (*shaded arrows*). For details, see text. BS, brain stem; SC, spinal cord. Adapted from Khasar et al. (1998b); Miao, Jänig, & Levine (2000); and Miao, Jänig, Jasmin, & Levine (2001).

cesses and sensitivity of nociceptors can be changed via the sympatho-adrenal system (adrenal medullae) by interventions at remote body domains, leading to activation of nociceptors and activation of vagal afferents. The changes are mediated by reflex circuits in the spinal cord and brain stem (see Figure 9.14) which connect the nociceptive afferent inputs and the vagal afferent inputs (to the nucleus of the solitary tract) with the sympathetic preganglionic neurons that innervate the adrenal medullae. It is postulated that the reflex circuits consist of excitatory spinal and spino-bulbo-spinal pathways associated with the nociceptive afferent input and inhibitory bulbo-spinal pathways associated with the vagal afferent input (Miao, Jänig, & Levine, 2000; Miao, Jänig, Jasmin, & Levine, 2001). Details of these reflex circuits have to be worked out. It is not farfetched to assume that these multiple reflex circuits are under the control of hypothalamus and forebrain; that is, these basic reflex circuits could be used by higher brain centers to control both inflammation and nociceptor sensitization via the sympathetic-adrenal system. By the same token it is possible that the HPA system is also integrated in this control (Green et al., 1995, 1997).

## Basic Emotions and Autonomic Systems: A Physiologist's View

Emotional feelings and the corresponding emotional expressions generated by the somatomotor system are highly integrated components of behavior in humans and animals which are important (externally and internally) for survival and for the regulation of social behavior and therefore for protection of the body (Darwin, 1872/1998). A very influential theory of emotions, which was first propagated by James (James & Lange, 1920; see also Meyers, 1986), states that the experience of the basic emotions is closely associated with the afferent feedback from the deep body domains. According to this theory, the brain triggers bodily changes by the activity in the autonomic systems (innervating cardiovascular target organs and visceral organs), and the conscious experience of these changes, which is generated by the afferent feedback from the visceral organs, leads to the felt emotions. It was assumed that without this afferent feedback, the emotional expressions are not accompanied by the internally experienced emotions and that the expressed emotions are, so to speak, "cold."

Interestingly, the James-Lange theory of emotions strictly requires that the autonomic efferent pathways are functionally specific. If this were not the case, it would barely be possible to generate the distinct basic emotions by functionally distinct patterns of afferent discharge from internal organs. Also, Cannon was intrigued by the general idea of this theory that the various emotional states are brought about by afferent signals from these organs and that different emotions are generated by different patterns of activity in afferent neurons from the internal organs. However, Cannon argued that the discharges of sympathetic neurons to various target organs were "too uniform to offer a satisfactory means of distinguishing emotional states which in man, at least, are subjectively very different. For this reason I am inclined to urge that the visceral changes merely contribute to an emotional complex more or less indefinite, but still pertinent, feelings of disturbance, in organs which we are not usually conscious of" (Cannon, 1914a). Instead, he proposed (Cannon, 1914a) that the different emotional states are represented in the brain rather than being peripheral in origin and are expressed by general changes of activity in sympathetic and parasympathetic neurons.

In its original form, the James-Lange theory is no longer tenable because experimentally it cannot be refuted. It appears to be impossible to design an experimental situation in which the perception of emotions can be investigated without afferent feedback from the body (viscera and deep somatic structures). However, it is generally accepted that the activity in afferents from the deep somatic and visceral body domains shapes the emotions. This afferent activity may be generated by activation of the efferent autonomic systems. From this point of view the James-Lange theory of emotions is, of course, in principle not at variance with the idea that different basic emotions (or groups of related affected states) can be characterized by specific autonomic motor patterns (see the following discussion).

There is some, although not general, consensus that six universal basic emotions exist that are the product of evolution: anger, fear, disgust, sadness, surprise, happiness. This idea goes back to Charles Darwin's famous book *The Expression of Emotions in Man and Animals* (1872/1998). The term *basic emotion* should not be taken too literally. Each emotion is, according to Ekman and Panksepp (see Ekman & Davidson, 1994), not a single discrete affective state but a group of related affected states. These states are universal and the result of evolution. They unfold and develop in specific environments. They are represented in central circuits, are not the result of associative learning, and cannot completely be changed or modified (for extensive discussion, see Ekman & Davidson, 1994). The relatively invariant expression of these basic emotions by the motor system (above all by the facial muscles in humans and primates) is represented in the central programs of the limbic system and neocortex (notably the amygdaloid complex and the orbitofrontal cortex; see Aggleton, 2000). These central programs are also responsible for the internal experience of the emotions (see Ekman & Davidson, 1994).

Psychologists are traditionally interested in whether the basic emotions are also expressed in and can be characterized by distinct autonomic reaction patterns, that is, patterned activation of autonomic final pathways and their effector organs. Ekman and his coworkers have measured

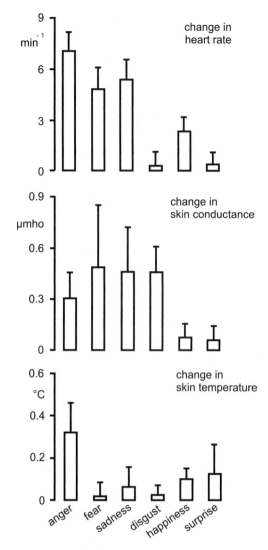

Figure 9.15 Changes of autonomic parameters during the six basic emotions. The facial motor expressions of the basic emotions were generated experimentally under visual control. The research participants did not know the type of emotion expressed. Changes of heart rate (dependent on changes in activity of parasympathetic cardiomotor neurons), of skin temperature at the fingertips (dependent on skin blood flow and therefore on activity in cutaneous vasoconstrictor neurons), and of skin conductance (dependent on activity of sweat glands and therefore on activity in sudomotor neurons) were measured simultaneously. The relived emotions experienced by the experimental participants were reported afterward. The patterns of the autonomic reactions and the type of relived emotions are highly correlated with each other. Data from 12 experimental participants. Mean + SEM. Adapted from Levenson et al. (1992).

on American actors, American college students, Americans in old age, and inhabitants of West Sumatra, whose cultural background is entirely different from that of the Americans, the subjective experience which was reported by the experimental participants and the patterns of autonomic responses (changes in heart rate, skin temperature [dependent on cutaneous vasoconstrictor activity], skin conductance [dependent on sudomotor activity]) when the participants followed muscle-by-muscle instructions and coaching to produce facial configurations that resemble the different types of basic emotions during instruction of the expression of the different types of basic emotions (Ekman, Levenson, & Friesen, 1983; Levenson, 1993; Levenson, Carstensen, Friesen, & Ekman, 1991; Levenson, Ekman, & Friesen, 1990; Levenson, Ekman, Heider, & Friesen, 1992). In their study of elderly Americans they also measured autonomic activity in another task in which participants attempted to relive past emotion experiences. They found that the patterns of autonomic reactions are principally specific for each basic emotion, that this specificity is independent of cultural background, age, and profession, and that the three parameters (expression of emotions, relived emotions, and autonomic patterns) correlate significantly with each other. All three, the emotional feelings, the somatomotor expression of the emotions, and the autonomic expression of the emotions, are parallel (not sequential) "readouts" of the same brain centers in which the emotions are represented (see Figure 9.15).

The authors came to the conclusion that the autonomic patterns which are specific for the different groups of affective states are functionally distinct adaptive autonomic motor responses that have developed during evolution (see also chapter 11 in this volume). The authors express their view in stating that there is an innate affect program for each emotion that, once activated, directs for each emotion changes in the organism's biological state by providing instructions to multiple response systems, including facial muscles, skeletal muscles, and the autonomic nervous system (Levenson et al., 1990, 1991; Ekman, 1992). Finally they come to the conclusion that a general arousal model of the sympathetic nervous system, as originally propagated by Cannon (1928, 1939), cannot account for differentiated autonomic responses seen during the basic emotions. This conclusion is fully compatible with the findings discussed in this chapter that the autonomic, and in particular also sympathetic, pathways are functionally specific.

## NOTES

This research was supported by the German Research Foundation and by the Max Planck Society.

The section titled "Integration of Homeostatic Mechanisms in Upper Brain Stem and Limbic Hypothalamic Centers" was adapted from Folkow (2000). I thank Professor Elspeth McLachlan and Professor Björn Folkow for their intellectual inputs.

## REFERENCES

Ader, A., & Cohen, N. (1993). Psychoneuroendocrinology: Conditioning and stress. *Annual Reviews of Psychology, 44*, 53–85.

Ader, A., Felton, D. L., & Cohen, N. (1991). *Psychoneuroimmunology*. Boston: Academic Press.

Aggleton, J. P. (2000). *The amygdala: A functional analysis* (2nd ed.). Oxford: Oxford University Press.

Akert, K. (1981). *Biological order and brain organization: Selected works of W. R. Hess*. Berlin: Springer.

Alexander, S. P. H., & Peters, J. A. (2001). Nomenclature supplement. *Trends in Pharmacological Sciences*, 12th ed., pp. 1–146

An, X., Bandler, R., Öngür, D., & Price, J. L. (1998). Medial and orbital prefrontal connections of the midbrain periaqueductal gray of the macaque. *Journal of Comparative Neurology, 461*, 455–479.

Anderson, C. R., McAllen, R. M., & Edwards, S. L. (1995). Nitric oxide synthase and chemical coding in cat sympathetic postganglionic neurons. *Neuroscience, 68*, 255–264.

Andrews, P. L. R. (1986). Vagal afferent innervation of the gastrointestinal tract. *Progress in Brain Research, 67*, 65–86.

Appenzeller, O. (Ed.). (1999). The autonomic nervous system: Part I. Normal functions. In P. J. Vinken & G. W. Bruyn (Series Eds.), *Handbook in clinical neurology* (Vol. 74, rev. ser. 30). Amsterdam: Elsevier.

Appenzeller, O., & Oribe, E. (1997). *The autonomic nervous system* (5th ed.) Amsterdam: Elsevier.

Bahr, R., Bartel, B., Blumberg, H., & Jänig, W. (1986a). Functional characterization of preganglionic neurons projecting in the lumbar splanchnic nerves: Neurons regulating motility. *Journal of the Autonomic Nervous System, 15*, 109–130.

Bahr, R., Bartel, B., Blumberg, H., & Jänig, W. (1986b). Functional characterization of preganglionic neurons projecting in the lumbar splanchnic nerves: Vasoconstrictor neurons. *Journal of the Autonomic Nervous System, 15*, 131–140.

Bahr, R., Bartel, B., Blumberg, H. & Jänig, W. (1986c). Secondary functional properties of lumbar visceral preganglionic neurons. *Journal of the Autonomic Nervous System, 15*, 141–152.

Baldissera, F., Hultborn, H., & Illert, M. (1981). Integration in spinal neuronal systems. In V. B. Brooks (Ed.), *Handbook of physiology. Section 1: The nervous system. Vol. 2: Motor control.* (pp. 509–595). Bethesda, MD: American Physiological Society.

Bandler, R., Carrive, P., & Zhang, S. P. (1991). Integration of somatic and autonomic reactions within the midbrain periaqueductal grey: Viscerotopic, somatotopic and functional organization. *Progress in Brain Research, 87*, 269–305.

Bandler, R., & Keay, K. A. (1996). Columnar organization in the midbrain periaqueductal gray and the integration of emotional expression. *Progress in Brain Research, 107*, 285–300.

Bandler, R., Price, J. L., & Keay, K. A. (2000). Brain mediation of active and passive emotional coping. *Progress in Brain Research, 122*, 333–349.

Bandler, R., & Shipley, M. T. (1994). Columnar organization in the midbrain periaqueductal gray: Modules for emotional expression? *Trends in Neuroscience, 17*, 379–389.

Bard, P. (1928). A diencephalic mechanism for the expression of rage with special reference to the sympathetic nervous system. *American Journal of Physiology, 84*, 490–515.

Bard, P. (1932). An emotional expression after decortication with some remarks on certain theoretical views (Pts. 1 & 2). *Psychological Reviews, 41*, 309–329; 424–449.

Barnes, P. J. (1991). Sensory nerves, neuropeptides, and asthma. *Annals of the New York Academy of Sciences, 629*, 359–370.

Baron, R., & Jänig, W. (1988). Sympathetic and afferent neurons projecting in the splenic nerve of the cat. *Neuroscience Letters, 94*, 109–113.

Baron, R., Jänig, W., & Kollmann, W. (1988). Sympathetic and afferent somata projecting in hindlimb nerves and the anatomical organization of the lumbar sympathetic nervous system of the rat. *Journal of Comparative Neurology, 275*, 460–468.

Baron, R., Jänig, W., & McLachlan, E. M. (1985a). On the anatomical organization of the lumbosacral sympathetic chain and the lumbar splanchnic nerves of the cat: Langley revisited. *Journal of the Autonomic Nervous System, 12*, 289–300.

Baron, R., Jänig, W., & McLachlan, E. M. (1985b). The afferent and sympathetic components of the lumbar spinal outflow to the colon and pelvic organs in the cat: I. The hypogastric nerve. *Journal of Comparative Neurology, 238*, 135–46.

Baron, R., Jänig, W., & McLachlan, E. M. (1985c). The afferent and sympathetic components of the lumbar spinal outflow to the colon and pelvic organs in the cat: II. The lumbar splanchnic nerves. *Journal of Comparative Neurology, 238*, 147–157.

Baron, R., Jänig, W., & McLachlan, E. M. (1985d). The afferent and sympathetic components of the lumbar spinal outflow to the colon and pelvic organs in the cat: III. The colonic nerves, incorporating an analysis of components of all lumbar prevertebral outflows. *Journal of Comparative Neurology, 238*, 158–168.

Baron, R., Jänig, W., & With, H. (1995). Sympathetic and afferent neurones projecting into forelimb and trunk nerves and the anatomical organization of the thoracic sympathetic outflow of the rat. *Journal of the Autonomic Nervous System, 53*, 205–214.

Bartel, B., Blumberg, H., & Jänig, W. (1986). Discharge patterns of motility-regulating neurons projecting in the lumbar splanchnic nerves to visceral stimuli in spinal cats. *Journal of the Autonomic Nervous System, 15*, 153–163.

Besedovsky, H. O., & del Rey, A. (1992). Immune-neuroendocrine circuits: Integrative role of cytokines. *Frontiers in Neuroendocrinology, 13*, 61–94.

Besedovsky, H. O., & del Rey, A. (1995). Immune-neuroendocrine interactions: Facts and hypotheses. *Endocrine Reviews, 17*, 64–102.

Bini, G., Hagbarth, K.-E., Hynninen, P., & Wallin, B. G. (1980a). Thermoregulatory and rhythm-generating mechanisms governing the sudomotor and vasoconstrictor outflow in human cutaneous nerves. *Journal of Physiology (London), 306*, 547–552.

Bini, G., Hagbarth, K.-E., Hynninen, P., & Wallin, B. G.

(1980b). Regional similarities and differences in thermoregulatory vasomotor and sudomotor tone. *Journal of Physiology (London), 306*, 553–565.

Björntorp, P. (1997). Behavior and metabolic disease. *International Journal of Behavior and Medicine, 3*, 285–302.

Blessing, W. W. (1997). *The brain stem and bodily homeostasis.* New York: Oxford University Press.

Boczek-Funcke, A., Dembowsky, K., Häbler, H.-J., Jänig, W., McAllen, R. M., & Michaelis, M. (1992). Classification of preganglionic neurones projecting into the cat cervical sympathetic trunk. *Journal of Physiology (London), 453*, 319–339.

Boczek-Funcke, A., Dembowsky, K., Häbler, H.-J., Jänig, W., & Michaelis, M. (1992). Respiratory related activity patterns in preganglionic neurones projecting into the cat cervical sympathetic trunk. *Journal of Physiology (London), 457*, 277–296.

Boczek-Funcke, A., Dembowsky, K., Häbler, H.-J., Jänig, W., & Michaelis, M. (1993). Spontaneous activity, conduction velocity and segmental origin of different classes of thoracic preganglionic neurons projecting into the cat cervical sympathetic trunk. *Journal of the Autonomic Nervous System, 43*, 189–200.

Boczek-Funcke, A., Häbler, H.-J., Jänig, W., & Michaelis, M. (1992). Respiratory modulation of the activity in sympathetic neurones supplying muscle, skin and pelvic organs in the cat. *Journal of Physiology (London), 449*, 333–361.

Bolme, B., Novotny, J., Uvnäs, B., & Wright, P. G. (1970). Species distribution of sympathetic cholinergic vasodilator nerves in skeletal muscle. *Acta Physiologica Scandinavica, 78*, 60–64.

Bos, J. D. (1989). *Skin immune system.* Boca Raton, FL: CRC Press.

Bos, J. D., & Kapsenberg, M. L. (1986). The skin immune: Its cellular constituents and their interactions. *Immunology Today, 7*, 235–240.

Boyd, H. D., McLachlan, E. M., Keast, J. R., & Inokuchi, H. (1996). Three electrophysiological classes of guinea pig sympathetic postganglionic neurone have distinct morphologies. *Journal of Comparative Neurology, 369*, 372–387.

Brodal, P. (1998). *The central nervous system* (2nd ed.). New York: Oxford University Press.

Brown, M. R., Koob, G. F., & Rivier, C. (1991). *Stress: Neurobiology and neuroendocrinology.* New York: Dekker.

Burnstock, G., & Hoyle, C. H. V. (Eds.). (1992). *Autonomic neuroeffector mechanisms.* In G. Burnstock (Series Ed.), *The autonomic nervous system* (Vol. 4). Chur, Switzerland: Harwood Academic.

Cabot, J. B. (1996). Some principles of the spinal organization of the sympathetic preganglionic outflow. *Progress in Brain Research, 107*, 29–43.

Cannon, W. B. (1911). *The mechanical factors of digestion.* New York: Longmans, Green, & Co.

Cannon, W. B. (1914a). The interrelations of emotions as suggested by recent physiological researches. *American Journal of Psychology, 25*, 252–282.

Cannon, W. B. (1914b). The emergency function of the adrenal medulla in pain and the major emotions. *American Journal of Physiology, 33*, 356–372.

Cannon, W. B. (1928). Die Notfallfunktion des sympathico-adrenalen Systems [The emergency function of the sympathico-adrenal system]. *Ergebnisse der Physiologie, 27*, 380–406.

Cannon, W. B. (1929). Organization for physiological homeostasis. *Physiological Reviews, 9*, 399–431.

Cannon, W. B. (1939). *The wisdom of the body.* New York: Norton.

Cannon, W. B., & Murphy, F. F. (1906). The movements of the stomach and intestines in some surgical conditions. *Annals of Surgery, 63*, 513–536.

Cannon, W. B., Newton, H. F., Bright, E. M., Menkin, V., & Moore, R. M. (1929). Some aspects of the physiology of animals surviving complete exclusion of sympathetic nerve impulses. *American Journal of Physiology, 89*, 84–107.

Celander, O. (1954). The range of control exercised by the sympatho-adrenal system. *Acta Physiologica Scandinavica 32* (Suppl. 116), 1–132.

Cervero, F. (1994). Sensory innervation of the viscera: Peripheral basis of visceral pain. *Physiological Reviews, 74*, 95–138.

Cervero, F., & Morrison, J. F. B. (Eds.). (1986). Visceral sensation. *Progress in Brain Research, 67.*

Cervero, F., & Tattersall, J. E. (1986). Somatic and visceral sensory integration in the thoracic spinal cord. *Progress in Brain Research, 67*, 189–205.

Christensen, J. (1994). The motility of the colon. In L. R. Johnson (Ed.), *Physiology of the gastrointestinal tract* (pp. 991–1024). New York: Raven Press.

Coleridge, H. M., & Coleridge, J. C. G. (1980). Cardiovascular afferents involved in regulation of peripheral vessels. *Annual Reviews of Physiology, 42*, 413–427.

Coleridge, J. C. G., & Coleridge, H. M. (1984). Afferent vagal C fibre innervation of the lungs and airways and its functional significance. *Reviews of Physiology, Biochemistry and Pharmacology, 99*, 1–110.

Cowley, A. W., Jr., Liard, J. F., & Guyton, A. C. (1973). Role of the baroreceptor reflex in daily control of arterial blood pressure and other variables in dogs. *Circulation Research, 32*, 564–576.

Craig, A. D. (1993). Propiospinal input to thoracolumbar sympathetic nuclei from cervical and lumbar lamina I neurons in the cat and the monkey. *Journal of Comparative Neurology, 331*, 517–530.

Craig, A. D. (1996). An ascending general homeostatic afferent pathway originating in lamina I. *Progress in Brain Research, 107*, 225–243.

Cryer, P. E. (1980). Physiology and pathophysiology of the human sympathoadrenal neuroendocrine system. *New England Journal of Medicine, 303*, 436–444.

Dampney, R. A. (1994). Functional organization of central pathways regulating the cardiovascular system. *Physiological Reviews, 74*, 323–364.

Dampney, R. A., & McAllen, R. M. (1988). Differential control of sympathetic fibres supplying hindlimb skin and muscle by subretrofacial neurones in the cat. *Journal of Physiology (London), 395*, 41–56.

Darwin, C. (1998). *The expression of the emotions in man and animals* (3rd ed.). London: HarperCollins. (Original work published 1872).

De Groat, W. C. (1986). Spinal cord projections and neuropeptides in visceral afferent neurons. *Progress in Brain Research, 67*, 165–187.

De Groat, W. C. (1987). Neuropeptides in pelvic afferent pathways. *Experientia, 43*, 801–813.

De Groat, W. C. (1989). Neuropeptides in pelvic afferent pathways. In J. M. Polak (Ed.), *Regulatory peptides* (pp. 334–361). Basel, Switzerland: Birkhauser Verlag.

De Groat, W. C. (1999). Neural control of the urinary bladder and sexual organs. In C. J. Mathias & R. Bannister (Eds.), *Autonomic failure* (4th ed., pp. 151–165). New York: Oxford University Press.

De Groat, W. C., & Booth, A. M. (1993). Neural control of penile erection. In G. Burnstock (Series Ed.) & C. A. Maggi (Vol. Ed.), *The autonomic nervous system. Vol. 3. Nervous control of the urogenital system* (pp. 467–524). Chur, Switzerland: Harwood Academic.

De Groat, W. C., Booth, A. M., Milne, R. J., & Roppolo, J. R. (1982). Parasympathetic preganglionic neurons in the sacral spinal cord. *Journal of the Autonomic Nervous System, 5*, 23–43.

De Groat, W. C., Booth, A. M., & Yoshimura, N. (1993). Neurophysiology of micturition and its modification in animal models in human disease. In G. Burnstock (Series Ed.) & C. A. Maggi (Vol. Ed.), *The autonomic nervous system. Vol. 3. Nervous control of the urogenital system* (pp. 227–290). Chur, Switzerland: Harwood Academic.

De Groat, W. C., Vizzard, M. A., Araki, I., & Roppolo, J. R. (1996). Spinal interneurons and preganglionic neurons in sacral autonomic reflex pathways. *Progress in Brain Research, 107*, 97–112.

DiBona, G. F. (1982). The functions of the renal nerves. *Reviews of Physiology, Biochemistry and Pharmacology, 94*, 75–181.

DiBona, G. F., & Kopp, U. C. (1997). Neural control of renal function. *Physiological Reviews, 77*, 75–197.

Dietz, N. M., Rivera, J. M., Eggener, S. E., Fix, R. T., Warner, D. O., & Joyner, M. J. (1994). Nitric oxide contributes to the rise in forearm blood flow during mental stress in humans. *Journal of Physiology (London), 480*, 361–368.

Dockray, G. J., Green, T., & Varro, A. (1989). The afferent peptidergic innervation of the upper gastrointestinal tract. In M. V. Springer & A. Goebel (Eds.), *Nerves and the gastrointestinal tract* (pp. 105–122). Boston: MTP Press.

Dorward, P. K., Burke, S. L., Jänig, W., & Cassell, J. (1987). Reflex responses to baroreceptor, chemoreceptor and nociceptor inputs in single renal sympathetic neurones in the rabbit and the effects of anaesthesia on them. *Journal of the Autonomic Nervous System, 18*, 39–54.

Eckberg, D. L., & Sleight, P. (1992). *Human baroreceptor reflexes in health and disease.* Oxford, England: Clarendon Press.

Edelson, R. L., & Fink, J. M. (1985). The immunologic function of skin. *Scientific American, 252/6*, 34–41.

Edwards, F. R., Hirst, G. D. S., Klemm, M. F., & Steele, P. A. (1995). Different types of ganglion cell in the cardiac plexus of guinea-pigs. *Journal of Physiology (London), 486*, 453–471.

Ekman, P. (1992). Facial expression of emotion: New findings, new questions. *Psychological Science, 3*, 34–38.

Ekman, P., & Davidson, R. J. (Eds.). (1994). *The nature of emotions.* New York: Oxford University Press.

Ekman, P., Levenson, R. W., & Friesen, M. V. (1983). Autonomic nervous system activity distinguishes between emotions. *Science, 221*, 1208–1210.

Esler, M., Jennings, G., Lambert, G., Meredith, I., Horne, M., & Eisenhofer, G. (1990). Overflow of catecholamine neurotransmitters to the circulation: Source, fate, and functions. *Physiological Reviews, 70*, 963–985.

Fields, H. L., & Basbaum, A. I. (1999). Central nervous system mechanisms of pain modulation. In P. D. Wall

& R. Melzack (Eds.), *Textbook of pain* (4th ed., pp. 309–329). Edinburgh, Scotland: Churchill Livingstone.

Folkow, B. (1982). Physiological aspects of primary hypertension. *Physiological Reviews, 62,* 347–504.

Folkow, B. (1987). Psychosocial and central nervous influences in primary hypertension. *Circulation, 76* (Suppl. 1), 10–19.

Folkow, B. (1993). Physiological organisation of neurohormonal responses to psychosocial stimuli: Implications for health and disease. *Annals Behavior of Medicine, 15,* 236–234.

Folkow, B. (2000). Perspectives on the integrative function of the "sympatho-adrenomedullary system." *Autonomic Neuroscience, 83,* 101–115.

Folkow, B., & Neil, E. (1971). *Circulation.* New York: Oxford University Press.

Folkow, B., & Rubinstein, E. H. (1965). Behavioural and autonomic patterns evoked by stimulation of the lateral hypothalamic area in the cat. *Acta Physiologica Scandinavica, 65,* 292–299.

Folkow, B., Schmidt, T., & Uvnäs-Moberg, K. (1997). Stress, health and the social environment. *Acta Physiologica Scandinavica, 161* (Suppl. 640), 1–179.

Foreman, R. D. (1989). Organization of the spinothalami tract as a relay for cardiopulmonary sympathetic afferent fiber activity. *Progress in Sensory Physiology, 9,* 1–51.

Frayn, K. N., & Macdonald, I. A. (1996). Adipose tissue circulation. In G. Burnstock (Series Ed.) & T. Bennett & S. M. Gardiner (Vol. Eds.), *The autonomic nervous system: Vol. 8. Nervous control of blood vessels* (pp. 505–539). Amsterdam: Harwood Academic.

Furness, J. B., & Bornstein, J. C. (1995). The enteric nervous system and its extrinsic connections. In T. Yamada (Ed.), *Textbook of gastroenterology* (2nd ed., pp. 2–20). Philadelphia: Lippincott.

Furness, J. B., Bornstein, J. C., Murphy, R., & Pompolo, S. (1992). Roles of peptides in transmission in the enteric nervous system. *Trends in Neurosciences, 15,* 66–71.

Furness, J. B., & Costa, M. (1987). *The enteric nervous system.* London: Churchill Livingston.

Furness, J. B., Morris, J. L., Gibbins, I. L., & Costa, M. (1989). Chemical coding of neurons and plurichemical transmission. *Annual Review of Pharmacology and Toxicology, 29,* 289–306.

Gebhart, G. F., & Randich, A. (1992). Vagal modulation of nociception. *American Pain Society Journal, 1,* 26–32.

Gibbins, I. L. (1990). Target-related patterns of co-existence of neuropeptide Y, vasoactive intestinal peptide, enkephalin and substance P in cranial parasympathetic neurons innervating the facial skin and glands of guinea-pigs. *Neuroscience, 38,* 541–560.

Gibbins, I. L. (1992). Vasoconstrictor, vasodilator and pilomotor pathways in sympathetic ganglia of guinea-pigs. *Neuroscience, 47,* 657–672.

Gibbins, I. L. (1994). Comparative anatomy and evolution of the autonomic nervous system. In G. Burnstock (Series Ed.) & S. Nilsson & S. Holmgren (Vol. Eds.), *The autonomic nervous system*: Vol. 4. *Comparative physiology and evolution of the autonomic nervous system* (pp. 1–67). Chur, Switzerland: Harwood Academic.

Gibbins, I. L. (1995). Chemical neuroanatomy of sympathetic ganglia. In G. Burnstock (Series Ed.) & E. M. McLachlan (Vol. Ed.), *The autonomic nervous system*: Vol. 6. *Autonomic ganglia* (pp. 73–122). Luxembourg: Harwood Academic.

Gibbins, I. L., & Morris, J. L. (1987). Co-existence of neuropeptides in sympathetic, cranial autonomic and sensory neurons innervating the iris of the guinea-pig. *Journal of the Autonomic Nervous System, 21,* 67–82.

Granit, R. (1981). Comments on history of motor control. In V. B. Brooks (Ed.), *Handbook of physiology: Part 1. Motor control. Section 1. The nervous system* (Vol. 2, pp. 1–16). Bethesda, MD: American Physiological Society.

Green, P. G., Jänig, W., & Levine, J. D. (1997). Negative feedback neuroendocrine control of inflammatory response in the rat is dependent on the sympathetic postganglionic neuron. *Journal of Neuroscience, 17,* 3234–3238.

Green, P. G., Miao, F. J.-P., Jänig, W., & Levine, J. D. (1995). Negative feedback neuroendocrine control of the inflammatory response in rats. *Journal of Neuroscience, 15,* 4678–4686.

Greger, R., & Windhorst, U. (Eds.). (1996). *Comprehensive human physiology: From cellular mechanisms to integration (Vols. 1 & 2).* Berlin, Germany: Springer Verlag.

Grewe, W., Jänig, W., & Kümmel, H. (1995). Effects of hypothalamic thermal stimuli on sympathetic neurones innervating skin and skeletal muscle of the cat hindlimb. *Journal of Physiology (London), 488,* 139–152.

Grundy, D. (1988). Speculation on the structure/function relationship for vagal and splanchic afferent endings supplying the gastrointestinal tract. *Journal of the Autonomic Nervous System, 22,* 175–180.

Grundy, D., Salih, A. A., & Scratcherd, T. (1981). Modulation of vagal efferent fibre discharge by mechanoreceptors in the stomach, duodenum and colon of the ferret. *Journal of Physiology (London), 319,* 43–52.

Grundy, D., & Scratcherd, T. (1989). Sensory afferents from the gastrointestinal tract. In *Handbook of Physiology: Section 6: The Gastrointestinal System.* Vol. 1 (ed. J. D. Wood): *Motility and circulation* (pp. 593–620). Bethesda, MD: American Physiological Society.

Guyenet, P. G. (1990). Role of the ventral medulla oblongata in blood pressure regulation. In A. D. Loewy & K. M. Spyer (Eds.), *Central regulation of autonomic functions* (pp. 145–167). New York: Oxford University Press.

Guyenet, P. G., & Koshiya, N. (1992). Respiratory-sympathetic integration in the medulla oblongata. In G. Kunos & J. Ciriello (Eds.), *Central neural mechanisms in cardiovascular regulation* (pp. 226–247). Boston: Birkhäuser.

Guyenet, P. G., & Koshiya, N. (1995). Working model of the sympathetic chemoreceptor reflex in rats. *Clinical and Experimental Hypertension, 17,* 167–179.

Guyenet, P. G., Koshiya, N., Huangfu, D., Baraban, R. L., Stornetta, R. L., & Li, Y.-W. (1996). Role of medulla oblongata in generation of sympathetic and vagal outflows. *Progress in Brain Research, 107,* 127–144.

Häbler, H.-J., Bartsch, T., & Jänig, W. (1999). Rhythmicity in single fiber postganglionic activity supplying the rat tail. *Journal of Neurophysiology, 81,* 2026–2036.

Häbler, H.-J., Bartsch, T., & Jänig, W. (2000). Respiratory rhythmicity in the activity of postganglionic neurones supplying the rat tail during hyperthermia. *Autonomic Neuroscience, 83,* 75–80.

Häbler, H.-J., Hilbers, K., Jänig, W., Koltzenburg, M., Kümmel, H., & Lobenberg-Khosravi, M. (1992). Viscero-sympathetic responses to mechanical stimulation of pelvic viscera in the cat. *Journal of the Autonomic Nervous System, 38*, 147–158.

Häbler, H.-J., & Jänig, W. (1995). Coordination of sympathetic and respiratory systems: Neurophysiological experiments. *Clinical and Experimental Hypertension, 17*, 223–235.

Häbler, H.-J., Jänig, W., & Koltzenburg, M. (1990). Activation of unmyelinated afferent fibres by mechanical stimuli and inflammation of the urinary bladder in the cat. *Journal of Physiology (London), 425*, 545–562.

Häbler, H.-J., Jänig, W., & Koltzenburg, M. (1993a). Myelinated primary afferents of the sacral spinal cord responding to slow filling and distension of the urinary bladder. *Journal of Physiology (London), 463*, 449–460.

Häbler, H.-J., Jänig, W., & Koltzenburg, M. (1993b). Receptive properties of myelinated primary afferents innervating the inflamed urinary bladder of the cat. *Journal of Neurophysiology, 69*, 395–405.

Häbler, H.-J., Jänig, W., Krummel, M., & Peters, O. A. (1993). Respiratory modulation of the activity in postganglionic neurons supplying skeletal muscle and skin of the rat hindlimb. *Journal of Neurophysiology, 70*, 920–930.

Häbler, H.-J., Jänig, W., Krummel, M., & Peters, O. A. (1994). Reflex patterns in postganglionic neurons supplying skin and skeletal muscle of the rat hindlimb. *Journal of Neurophysiology, 72*, 2222–2236.

Häbler, H.-J., Jänig, W., & Michaelis, M. (1994). Respiratory modulation of activity in sympathetic neurones. *Progress in Neurobiology, 43*, 567–606.

Henry, J. P. (1994). Psychosocial stress and hypertension: Theory and animal experimental evidence. In J. D. Swales (Ed.), *Textbook of hypertension* (pp. 633–639). London: Blackwell.

Henry, J. P., Liu, J., & Meehan, W. P. (1995). Psychosocial stress and hypertension. In J. H. Laragh & B. M. Brenner (Eds.), *Hypertension: Pathophysiology, diagnosis and management* (pp. 902–922). New York: Raven Press.

Henry, J. P., & Stephens, P. M. (1977). *Stress, health and the social environment: A sociobiologic approach to medicine.* Berlin, Germany: Springer.

Hertz, A. F. (1911). *The sensibility of the alimentary canal.* Oxford, England: Oxford University Press.

Hess, W. R. (1948). *Die Organisation des vegetativen Nervensystems.* Basel, Switzerland: Benno Schwabe.

Hess, W. R. (1949). *Das Zwishenhirn.* Basel, Switzerland: Benno Schwabe.

Himms-Hagen, J. (1991). Neural control of brown adipose tissue: Thermogenesis, hypertrophy, and atrophy. *Frontiers in Neuroendocrinology, 12*, 38–93.

Hirst, G. D. S., Bramich, N. J., Edwards, F. R., & Klemm, M. F. (1992). Transmission at autonomic neuroeffector junctions. *Trends in Neuroscience, 15*, 40–46.

Hirst, G. D. S., Choate, J. K., Cousins, H. M., Edwards, F. R., & Klemm, M. F. (1996). Transmission by postganglionic axons of the autonomic nervous system: The importance of the specialized neuroeffector junction. *Neuroscience, 73*, 7–23.

Holst, E. von, & St. Paul, U. (1960). Vom Wirkungsgefüge der Triebe [On the organization and structure of drives]. *Die Naturwissenschaften, 47*, 409–422.

Holst, E. von, & St. Paul, U. (1962). Electrically controlled behavior. *Scientific American, 206*, 50–60.

Holzer, P. (1992). Peptidergic sensory neurons in the control of vascular functions: Mechanisms and significance in the cutaneous and splanchnic vascular beds. *Reviews of Physiology, Biochemistry and Pharmacology, 121*, 49–146.

Holzer, P. (1995). Chemosensitive afferent nerves in the regulation of gastric blood flow and protection. *Advances in Experimental Medicine and Biology, 371B*, 891–895.

Hori, T., Katafuchi, T., Take, S., Shimizu, N., & Niijima, A. (1995). The autonomic nervous system as a communication channel between the brain and the immune system. *Neuroimmunomodulation, 2*, 203–215.

Inoue, T. (1980). Efferent discharge patterns in the ciliary nerve of rabbits and the pupillary light reflex. *Brain Research, 186*, 43–53.

James, W. (1884). What is an emotion? *Mind, 9*, 188–205.

James, W., & Lange, C. G. (1920). *The emotions.* Baltimore: Williams & Wilkins.

Jänig, W. (1985). Organization of the lumbar sympathetic outflow to skeletal muscle and skin of the cat hindlimb and tail. *Reviews of Physiology, Biochemistry and Pharmacology, 102*, 119–213.

Jänig, W. (1986). Spinal cord integration of visceral sensory systems and sympathetic nervous system reflexes. *Progress in Brain Research, 67*, 255–277.

Jänig, W. (1988a). Pre- and postganglionic vasoconstrictor neurons: Differentiation, types, and discharge properties. *Annual Reviews of Physiology, 50*, 525–539.

Jänig, W. (1988b). Integration of gut function by sympathetic reflexes. *Baillieres Clinical Gastroenterology, 2*, 45–62.

Jänig, W. (1995a). Ganglionic transmission in vivo. In G. Burnstock (Series Ed.) & E. M. McLachlan (Vol. Ed.), *The autonomic nervous system: Vol. 6. Autonomic ganglia* (pp. 349–395). Chur, Switzerland: Harwood Academic.

Jänig, W. (1995b). The sympathetic nervous system in pain. *European Journal of Anaesthesiology, 12* (Suppl. 10), 53–60.

Jänig, W. (1996a). Spinal cord reflex organization of sympathetic systems. *Progress in Brain Research, 107*, 43–77.

Jänig, W. (1996b). Neurobiology of visceral afferent neurons: Neuroanatomy, functions, organ regulations and sensations. *Biological Psychology, 42*, 29–51.

Jänig, W. (1996c). Regulation of the lower urinary tract. In R. Greger & U. Windhorst (Eds.), *Comprehensive human physiology: From cellular mechanism to integration* (Vol. 2, pp. 1611–1624). Berlin, Germany: Springer-Verlag.

Jänig, W. (1996d). Behavioral and neurovegetative components of reproductive functions. In R. Greger & U. Windhorst (Eds.), *Comprehensive human physiology: From cellular mechanism to integration* (Vol. 2, pp. 2253–2263). Berlin, Germany: Springer-Verlag.

Jänig, W. (2000). Vegetatives Nervensystem. In R. F. Schmidt, G. Thews, & T. Lang (Eds.), *Physiologie des Menschen* (28th ed., pp. 340–369). Heidelberg, Germany: Springer-Verlag.

Jänig, W., & Häbler, H.-J. (1995). Visceral-autonomic integration. In G. F. Gebhart (Ed.), *Visceral pain. Progress in pain research and management* (Vol. 5, pp. 311–348). Seattle, WA: IASP Press.

Jänig, W., & Häbler, H.-J. (1999). Organisation of the autonomic nervous system: Structure and function. In P. J. Vinken & G. W. Bruyn (Series Eds.) & O. Appenzeller (Vol. Ed.), *Handbook of clinical neurology: Vol. 74. The autonomic nervous system. Part 1. Normal functions* (pp. 1–52). Amsterdam: Elsevier.

Jänig, W., & Häbler, H.-J. (2000). Specificity in the organization of the autonomic nervous system: A basis for precise neural regulation of homeostatic and protective body functions. *Progress in Brain Research, 122,* 351–367.

Jänig, W., Khasar, S., Levine, J. D., & Miao, F. J.-P. (2000). The role of vagal afferents in the control of nociception. *Progress in Brain Research, 122,* 273–287.

Jänig, W., & Koltzenburg, M. (1990). On the function of spinal primary afferent fibres supplying colon and urinary bladder. *Journal of the Autonomic Nervous System, 30* (Suppl.), S89–S96.

Jänig, W., & Koltzenburg, M. (1991). Receptive properties of sacral primary afferent neurons supplying the colon. *Journal of Neurophysiology, 65,* 1067–1077.

Jänig, W., & Koltzenburg, M. (1993). Pain arising from the urogenital tract. In G. Burnstock (Series Ed.) & C. A. Maggi (Vol. Ed.), *The autonomic nervous system: Vol. 3. Nervous control of the urogenital system* (pp. 525–578). Chur, Switzerland: Harwood Academic.

Jänig, W., & Kümmel, H. (1977). Functional discrimination of postganglionic neurones to the cat's hindpaw with respect to the skin potentials recorded from the hairless skin. *Pflügers Archiv, 371,* 217–225.

Jänig, W., & Kümmel, H. (1981). Organization of the sympathetic innervation supplying the hairless skin of the cat's paw. *Journal of the Autonomic Nervous System, 3,* 215–230.

Jänig, W., & McLachlan, E. M. (1986a). The sympathetic and sensory components of the caudal lumbar sympathetic trunk in the cat. *Journal of Comparative Neurology, 245,* 62–73.

Jänig, W., & McLachlan, E. M. (1986b). Identification of distinct topographical distributions of lumbar sympathetic and sensory neurons projecting to end organs with different functions in the cat. *Journal of Comparative Neurology, 246,* 104–112.

Jänig, W., & McLachlan, E. M. (1987). Organization of lumbar spinal outflow to distal colon and pelvic organs. *Physiological Reviews, 67,* 1332–1404.

Jänig, W., & McLachlan, E. M. (1992a). Characteristics of function-specific pathways in the sympathetic nervous system. *Trends in Neurosciences, 15,* 475–481.

Jänig, W., & McLachlan, E. M. (1992b). Specialized functional pathways are the building blocks of the autonomic nervous system. *Journal of the Autonomic Nervous System, 41,* 3–13.

Jänig, W., & McLachlan, E. M. (1999). Neurobiology of the autonomic nervous system. In C. J. Mathias & R. Bannister (Eds.), *Autonomic failure* (4th ed., pp. 3–15). New York: Oxford University Press.

Jänig, W., & Morrison, J. F. B. (1986). Functional properties of spinal visceral afferents supplying abdominal and pelvic organs, with special emphasis on visceral nociception. *Progress in Brain Research, 67,* 87–114.

Jänig, W., Schmidt, M., Schnitzler, A., & Wesselmann, U. (1991). Differentiation of sympathetic neurones projecting in the hypogastric nerves in terms of their discharge patterns in cats. *Journal of Physiology (London), 437,* 157–179.

Jankowska, E., & Lundberg, A. (1981). Interneurones in the spinal cord. *Trends in Neurosciences, 4,* 230–233.

Jewett, D. L. (1964). Activity of single efferent fibres in the cervical vagus nerve of the dog, with special reference to possible cardio-inhibitory fibres. *Journal of Physiology (London), 175,* 321–357.

Johnson, D. A., & Purves, D. (1983). Tonic and reflex synaptic activity recorded in ciliary ganglion cells of anaesthetized rabbits. *Journal of Physiology (London), 339,* 599–613.

Jordan, D. (Ed.). (1997). *Central nervous control of the autonomic function.* In G. Burnstock (Series Ed.), *The autonomic nervous system* (Vol. 2). Amsterdam: Harwood Academic.

Joyner, M. J., & Halliwill, J. R. (2000). Sympathetic vasodilation in human limbs. *Journal of Physiology (London), 526,* 471–480.

Kaplan, J. R., Manuck, S. B., & Clarkson, T. B. (1985). Animal models of behavioural influences on atherogenesis. *Advances in Behavior and Medicine, 1,* 115–163.

Katafuchi, T., Take, S., & Hori, T. (1993). Roles of sympathetic nervous system in the suppression of cytotoxicity of splenic natural killer cells in the rat. *Journal of Physiology (London), 465,* 343–357.

Katona, P. G., Poitras, J. W., Barnett, G. O., & Terry, B. S. (1970). Cardiac vagal efferent activity and heart period in the carotid sinus reflex. *American Journal of Physiology, 218,* 1030–1037.

Keast, J. R., Luckensmeyer, G. B., & Schemann, M. (1995). All pelvic neurons in male rats contain immunoreactivity for the synthetic enzymes of either noradrenaline or acetylcholine. *Neuroscience Letters, 196,* 209–212.

Khasar, S. G., Miao, F. J.-P., Jänig, W., & Levine, J. D. (1998a). Modulation of bradykinin-induced mechanical hyperalgesia in the rat by activity in abdominal vagal afferents. *European Journal of Neuroscience, 10,* 435–444.

Khasar, S. G., Miao, F. J.-P., Jänig, W., & Levine, J. D. (1998b). Vagotomy-induced enhancement of mechanical hyperalgesia in the rat is sympathoadrenal-mediated. *Journal of Neuroscience, 18,* 3043–3049.

Kirchheim, H. R., Just, A., & Ehmke, H. (1998). Physiology and pathophysiology of baroreceptor function and neuro-hormonal abnormalities in heart failure. *Basic Research in Cardiology, 93* (Suppl. 1), 1–22.

Klein, D. C., Moore, R. Y., & Reppert, S. M. (Eds.). (1991). *Suprachiasmatic nucleus.* New York: Oxford University Press.

Kopp, U. C., & DiBona, G. F. (1992). The neural control of renal function. In G. Seldin & G. Giebisch (Eds.), *The kidney: Physiology and pathophysiology* (2nd ed., pp. 1157–1204). New York: Raven Press.

Koshiya, N., Huangfu, D. H., & Guyenet, P. G. (1993). Ventrolateral medulla and sympathetic chemoreceptor reflex in the rat. *Brain Research, 609,* 174–184.

Kumazawa, T. (1990). Functions of the nociceptive primary neurons. *Japanese Journal of Physiology, 40,* 1–14.

Kunze, D. L. (1972). Reflex discharge patterns of cardiac vagal efferent fibres. *Journal of Physiology (London), 222,* 1–15.

Langley, J. N. (1897). On the regeneration of pre-ganglionic and of post-ganglionic visceral nerve fibres. *Journal of Physiology (London), 22,* 215–230.

Langley, J. N. (1903). Das sympathische und verwandte nervöse Systeme der Wirbeltiere (autonomes nervöses System). *Ergebnisse der Physiologie, 27/II,* 818–827.

Langley, J. N. (1921). *The autonomic nervous system (Pt. 1).* Cambridge, England: Heffer.

Levenson, R. W. (1993). Autonomic nervous system differences among emotions. *Psychological Science, 3,* 23–27.

Levenson, R. W., Carstensen, L. L., Friesen, W. V., & Ekman, P. (1991). Emotion, physiology, and expression in old age. *Psychology and Aging, 6,* 28–35.

Levenson, R. W., Ekman, P., & Friesen, M. V. (1990). Voluntary facial action generates emotion-specific autonomic nervous system activity. *Psychophysiology, 27,* 363–384.

Levenson, R. W., Ekman, P., Heider, K., & Friesen, W. V. (1992). Emotion and autonomic nervous system activity in the Minangkabau of West Sumatra. *Journal of Personality and Social Psychology, 62,* 972–988.

Lewin, G. R., & McMahon, S. B. (1993). Muscle afferents innervating skin form somatotopically appropriate connections in the adult dorsal horn. *European Journal of Neuroscience, 5,* 1083–1092.

Lichtman, J. W., Purves, D., & Yip, J. W. (1979). On the purpose of selective innervation of guinea-pig superior cervical ganglion cells. *Journal of Physiology (London), 292,* 69–84.

Lindh, B., Lundberg, J. M., & Hökfelt, T. (1989). NPY-, galanin-, VIP/PHI-, CGRP- and substance P-immunoreactive neuronal subpopulations in the cat autonomic and sensory ganglia and their projections. *Cell Tissue Research, 256,* 259–273.

Lindh, B., Risling, M., Remahl, S., Terenius, L., & Hökfelt, T. (1993). Peptide-immunoreactive neurons and nerve fibres in lumbosacral sympathetic ganglia: Selective elimination of a pathway-specific expression of immunoreactivities following sciatic nerve resection in kittens. *Neuroscience, 55,* 545–562.

Loewy, A. D., & Spyer, K. M. (Eds.). (1990). *Central regulation of autonomic functions.* New York: Oxford University Press.

Lombardi, F., Della Bella, P., Casati, R., & Malliani, A. (1981). Effects of intracoronary administration of bradykinin on the impulse activity of afferent sympathetic unmyelinated fibers with left ventricular endings in the cat. *Circulation Research, 48,* 69–75.

Lovick, T. A. (1987). Differential control of cardiac and vasomotor activity by neurones in nucleus paragigantocellularis lateralis in the cat. *Journal of Physiology (London), 389,* 23–35.

Low, P. (Ed.). (1993). *Clinical autonomic disorders.* Boston: Brown.

Lundberg, J. M. (1981). Evidence for coexistence of vasoactive intestinal polypeptide (VIP) and acetylcholine in neurons of cat exocrine glands: Morphological, biochemical and functional studies. *Acta Physiologica Scandinavica, 496,* 1–57.

Lundberg, J. M., Hemsen, A., Rudehill, A., Harfstrand, A., Larsson, O., Sollevi, A., Saria, A., Hökfelt, T., Fuxe, K., & Fredholm, B. B. (1988). Neuropeptide Y- and alpha-adrenergic receptors in pig spleen: Localization, binding characteristics, cyclic AMP effects and functional responses in control and denervated animals. *Neuroscience, 24,* 659–672.

Lundgren, O. (1989). Enteric nervous control of mucosal functions of the small intestine in vivo. In M. V. Singer & A. Goebell (Eds.), *Nerves and the gastrointestinal tract* (pp. 275–285). Lancaster: MTP Press.

Macefield, V. G., & Wallin, B. G. (1996). The discharge behaviour of single sympathetic neurones supplying human sweat glands. *Journal of the Autonomic Nervous System, 61,* 277–286.

Macefield, V. G., & Wallin, B. G. (1999a). Firing properties of single vasoconstrictor neurones in human subjects with high level of muscle sympathetic activity. *Journal of Physiology (London), 516,* 293–301.

Macefield, V. G., & Wallin, B. G. (1999b). Respiratory and cardiac modulation of single sympathetic vasoconstrictor and sudomotor neurones to human skin. *Journal of Physiology (London) 516,* 303–314.

Macefield, V. G., Wallin, B. G., & Vallbo, A. B. (1994). The discharge behaviour of single vasoconstrictor motoneurones in human muscle nerves. *Journal of Physiology (London), 481,* 799–809.

Madden, K. S., & Felten, D. L. (1995). Experimental basis for neural-immune interactions. *Physiological Reviews, 75,* 77–106.

Madden, K. S., Sanders, V. M., & Felten, D. L. (1995). Catecholamine influences and sympathetic modulation of immune responsiveness. *Reviews of Pharmacology and Toxicology, 35,* 417–448.

Maggi, C. A., Giachetti, A., Dey, R. D., & Said, S. I. (1995). Neuropeptides as regulators for airway function: Vasoactive intestinal peptide and the tachykinins. *Physiological Reviews, 75,* 277–322.

Maggi, C. A., & Meli, A. (1988). The sensory-efferent function of capsaicin-sensitive sensory neurons. *General Pharmacology, 119,* 1–43.

Malliani, A. (1982). Cardiovascular sympathetic afferent fibers. *Reviews of Physiology, Biochemistry and Pharmacology, 94,* 11–74.

Mathias, C. J., & Bannister, R. (Eds.). (1999). *Autonomic failure* (4th ed.). Oxford, England: Oxford University Press.

Mawe, G. M. (1995). Prevertebral, pancreatic and gallbladder ganglia: Non-enteric ganglia that are involved in gastrointestinal function. In G. Burnstock (Series Ed.) & E. M. McLachlan (Vol. Ed.), *The autonomic nervous system: Vol. 6. Autonomic ganglia* (pp. 397–444).Luxembourg: Harwood Academic.

McAllen, R. M. (1987). Central respiratory modulation of subretrofacial bulbospinal neurones in the cat. *Journal of Physiology (London), 388,* 533–545.

McAllen, R. M., Häbler, H.-J., Michaelis, M., Peters, O. A., & Jänig, W. (1994). Monosynaptic excitation of preganglionic vasomotor neurons by subretrofacial (RVLM) neurons. *Brain Research, 634,* 227–234.

McAllen, R. M., & May, C. N. (1994a). Effects of preoptic warming on subretrofacial and cutaneous vasoconstrictor neurons in anaesthetized cats. *Journal of Physiology (London), 481,* 719–730.

McAllen, R. M., & May, C. N. (1994b). Differential drives from rostral ventrolateral medullary neurons to three identified sympathetic outflows. *American Journal of Physiology, 277,* R935–R944.

McAllen, R. M., May, C. N., & Shafton, A. D. (1995). Functional anatomy of sympathetic premotor cell groups in the medulla. *Clinical and Experimental Hypertension: Theory and Practice, 17,* 209–221.

McCabe, P. M., Duan, Y. F., Winters, R. W., Green, E. J., Huang, Y., & Schneiderman, N. (1994). Comparison of peripheral blood flow patterns associated with the defense reaction and the vigilance reaction in rabbits. *Physiological Behaviour, 56,* 1101–1106.

McDonald, D. M. (1990). The ultrastructure and permeability of tracheobronchial blood vessels in health and disease. *European Respiratory Journal* (Suppl. 12), 572s–585s.

McLachlan, E. M. (Ed.). (1995). *Autonomic ganglia.* In G. Burnstock (Series Ed.), *The autonomic nervous system* (Vol. 6). Luxembourg: Harwood Academic.

McLachlan, E. M., Davies, P. J., Häbler, H.-J., & Jamieson, J. (1997). Reflex synaptic events evoked in rat superior cerical ganglion cells. *Journal of Physiology (London), 501,* 165–182.

McLachlan, E. M., Häbler, H.-J., Jamieson, J., & Davies, P. J. (1998). Analysis of the periodicity of synaptic events in neurones in the superior cervical ganglion of anaesthetized rats. *Journal of Physiology (London), 511,* 461–478.

Meckler, R. L., & Weaver, L. C. (1988). Characteristics of ongoing and reflex discharge of single splenic and renal sympathetic postganglionic fibres in the cat. *Journal of Physiology (London), 396,* 139–153.

Mehler, S. T., & Gebhart, G. F. (1992). A critical review of the afferent pathways and the potential chemical mediators involved in cardiac pain. *Neuroscience, 48,* 501–524.

Mei, N. (1983). Sensory structures in the viscera. *Progress in Sensory Physiology, 4,* 1–42.

Mei, N. (1985). Intestinal chemosensitivity. *Physiological Reviews, 65,* 211–237.

Melnitchenko, L. V., & Skok, V. I. (1970). Natural electrical activity in mammalian parasympathetic ganglion neurones. *Brain Research, 23,* 277–279.

Meyers, G. E. (1986). *William James: His life and thought.* New Haven, CT: Yale University Press.

Miao, F. J.-P., Jänig, W., & Levine, J. D. (1996). Role of sympathetic postganglionic neurons in synovial plasma extravasation induced by bradykinin. *Journal of Neurophysiology, 75,* 715–724.

Miao, F. J.-P., Green, P., Coderre, T. J., Jänig, W., & Levine, J. D. (1996). Sympathetic-dependence in bradykinin-induced synovial plasma extravasation is dose-related. *Neuroscience Letters, 205,* 165–168.

Miao, F. J.-P., Jänig, W., Green, P. G., & Levine, J. D. (1997). Inhibition of bradykinin-induced synovial plasma extravasation produced by noxious cutaneous and visceral stimuli and its modulation by activity in the vagal nerve. *Journal of Neurophysiology, 78,* 1285–1292.

Miao, F. J.-P., Jänig, W., Jasmin, L., & Levine, J. D. (2001). Spino-bulbo-spinal pathway mediating vagal modulation of nociceptive-neuroendocrine control of inflammation in the rat. *Journal of Physiology (London), 532,* 811–852.

Miao, F. J.-P., Jänig, W., & Levine, J. D. (1997). Vagal branches involved in inhibition of bradykinin-induced synovial plasma extravasation by intrathecal nicotine and noxious stimulation in the rat. *Journal of Physiology (London), 498,* 473–481.

Miao, F. J.-P., Jänig, W., & Levine, J. D. (2000). Nociceptive neuroendocrine negative feedback control of neurogenic inflammation activated by capsaicin in the rat paw: Role of the adrenal medulla. *Journal of Physiology (London), 527,* 601–610.

Michaelis, M., Häbler, H.-J., & Jänig, W. (1996). Silent afferents: A further class of nociceptors? *Clinical and Experimental Pharmacology and Physiology, 23,* 14–20.

Moore, R. Y. (1996). Neural control of the pineal gland. *Behavioural Brain Research, 73,* 125–130.

Moriarty, M., Gibbins, I. L., Potter, E. K., & McCloskey, D. I. (1992). Comparison of the inhibitory roles of neuropeptide Y and galanin on cardiac vagal action in the dog. *Neuroscience Letters, 139,* 272–279.

Morris, J. L., & Gibbins, I. L. (1992). Co-transmission and neuromodulation. In G. Burnstock (Series Ed.) & G. Burnstock & C. H. V. Hoyle (Vol. Eds.), *The autonomic nervous system: Vol. 1. Autonomic neuroeffector mechanisms* (pp. 33–119). Chur, Switzerland: Harwood.

Morris, M. J., Russell, A. E., Kapoor, V., Cain, M. D., Elliott, J. M., West, M. J., Wing, L. M., & Chalmers, J. P. (1986). Increases in plasma neuropeptide Y concentrations during sympathetic activation in man. *Journal of the Autonomic Nervous System, 17,* 143–149.

Morrison, S. F., Callaway, J., Milner, T. A., & Reis, D. J. (1991). Rostral ventrolateral medulla: A source of the glutamatergic innervation of the sympathetic intermediolateral nucleus. *Brain Research, 562,* 126–135.

Nilsson, S. (1983). *Autonomic nerve function in the vertebrates.* Berlin, Germany: Springer Verlag.

Nilsson, S., & Holmgren, S. (Eds). (1994). *Comparative physiology and evolution of the autonomic nervous system.* In G. Burnstock (Series Ed.), *The autonomic nervous system* (Vol. 4). Chur, Switzerland: Harwood Academic.

Noll, G., Elam, M., Kunimoto, M., Karlsson, T., & Wallin, B. G. (1994). Skin sympathetic nerve activity and effector function during sleep in humans. *Acta Physiologica Scandinavica, 151,* 319–329.

Nordin, M. (1990). Sympathetic discharges in the human supraorbital nerve and their relation to sudo- and vasomotor response. *Journal of Physiology (London), 423,* 241–255.

Nordin, M., & Fagius, J. (1995). Effect of noxious stimulation on sympathetic vasoconstrictor outflow to human muscles. *Journal of Physiology (London), 489,* 885–894.

Okamoto, S., Ibaraki, K., Hayashi, S., & Saito, M. (1996). Ventromedial hypothalamus suppresses splenic lymphocyte activity through sympathetic innervation. *Brain Research, 39,* 308–313.

Paintal, A. S. (1986). The visceral sensations. Some basic mechanisms. *Progress in Brain Research, 67,* 3–19.

Paton, J. F. R. (1996). A working heart-brainstem preparation of the mouse. *Journal of Neuroscience Methods, 65,* 63–68.

Paton, J. F. R., & Kasparov, S. (2000). Sensory channel specific modulation in the nucleus of the solitary tract. *Journal of the Autonomic Nervous System, 80,* 117–129.

Pernow, J. (1988). Co-release and functional interactions of neuropeptide Y and noradrenaline in peripheral sympathetic vascular control. *Acta Physiologica Scandinavica Supplement, 568,* 1–56.

Persson, P., Ehmke, H., Kirchheim, H., & Seller, H. (1988). Effect of sino-aortic denervation in comparison to cardiopulmonary deafferentiation on long-term blood pressure in conscious dogs. *Pflügers Archiv, 411,* 160–166.

Pick, J. (1971). *The autonomic nervous system.* Philadelphia: Lippincott.

Polson, J. W., Halliday, G. M., McAllen, R. M., Coleman, M. J., & Dampney, R. A. L. (1992). Rostrocaudal differences in morphology and neurotransmitter content of cells in the subretrofacial vasomotor nucleus. *Journal of the Autonomic Nervous System, 38,* 117–138.

Potter, E. K. (1991). Neuropeptide Y as an autonomic neurotransmitter. In C. Bell (Ed.), *Novel peripheral neurotransmitter* (pp. 81–112). New York: Pergamon.

Randall, W. C. (Ed.). (1984). *Nervous control of cardiovascular function*. New York: Oxford University Press.

Randich, A., & Gebhart, G. F. (1992). Vagal afferent modulation of nociception. *Brain Research Reviews, 17*, 77–99.

Recordati, G., Moss, N. G., Genovesi, S., & Rogenes, P. (1981). Renal chemoreceptors. *Journal of the Autonomic Nervous System, 3*, 237–251.

Richter, D. W., & Spyer, K. M. (1990). Cardiorespiratory control. In A. D. Loewy & K. M. Spyer (Eds.), *Central regulation of autonomic functions* (pp. 189–207). New York: Oxford University Press.

Ritter, S., Ritter, R. C., & Barnes, C. D. (Eds.). (1992). *Neuroanatomy and physiology of abdominal vagal afferents*. Boca Raton, FL: CRC Press.

Rogers, R. C., & Hermann, G. E. (1992). Central regulation of brainstem gastric vago-vagal control circuits. In S. Ritter, R. C. Ritter, & C. D. Barnes (Eds.), *Neuroanatomy and physiology of abdominal vagal afference* (pp. 99–134). Boca Raton, FL: CRC Press.

Roman, C., & Gonella, J. (1994). Extrinsic control of digestive tract motility. In L. R. Johnson (Ed.), *Physiology of the gastrointestinal tract* (pp. 507–553). New York: Raven Press.

Romano, T. A., Felten, S. Y., Felten, D. L., & Olschowka, J. A. (1991). Neuropeptide-Y innervation of the rat spleen: Another potential immunomodulatory neuropeptide. *Brain, Behavior, and Immunity, 5*, 116–131.

Rowell, L. B. (1993). *Human cardiovascular control*. New York: Oxford University Press.

Santicioli, P., & Maggi, C. A. (1998). Myogenic and neurogenic factors in the control of pyeloureteral motility and ureteral peristalsis. *Pharmacological Reviews, 50*, 683–722.

Saphier, D. (1993). Psychoimmunology: The missing link. In J. Schulkin (Ed.), *Hormonally induced changes in mind and brain* (pp. 191–224). San Diego: Academic Press.

Schedlowski, M., & Tewes, U. (Eds.). (1999). *Psychoneuroimmunology: An interdisciplinary introduction*. New York: Kluwer Academic.

Schomburg, E. D. (1990). Spinal sensorimotor systems and their supraspinal control. *Neuroscience Research, 7*, 265–340.

Schytte-Blix, A., & Folkow, B. (1983). Cardiovascular adjustments to diving in mammals and birds. In J. T. Shepherd & F. M. Abboud (Eds.), *Handbook of physiology: Vol. 3. The cardiovascular system* (pp. 917–945). Bethesda, MD: American Physiological Society.

Shafton, A. D., Oldfield, B. J., & McAllen, R. M. (1992). CRF-like immunoreactivity selectively labels preganglionic sudomotor neurons in cat. *Brain Research, 599*, 253–260.

Shah, S. D., Tse, T. F., Clutter, W. E., & Cryer, P. E. (1984). The human sympathochromaffin system. *American Journal of Physiology, 247*, E380–E384.

Shepherd, J. Z., & Vatner, S. F. (Eds.). (1996). *Nervous control of the heart*. Amsterdam: Harwood Academic.

Sherrington, C. S. (1947). *The integrative action of the nervous system* (2nd ed.). New Haven, CT: Yale University Press.

Silverberg, A. B., Shah, S. D., Haymond, M. W., & Cryer, P. E. (1978). Norepinephrine: Hormone and neurotransmitter. *American Journal of Physiology, 234*, E252–E256.

Spyer, K. M. (1981). Neural organisation and control of the baroreceptor reflex. *Reviews of Physiology, Biochemistry and Pharmacology, 88*, 23–124.

Spyer, K. M. (1994). Central nervous mechanisms contributing to cardiovascular control. *Journal of Physiology (London), 474*, 1–19.

Stein, R. D., & Weaver, L. C. (1988). Multi- and single-fibre mesentric and renal sympathetic responses to chemical stimulation of intestinal receptors in cats. *Journal of Physiology (London), 396*, 155–172.

Strack, A. M., Sawyer, W. B., Hughes, J. H., Platt, K. B., & Loewy, A. D. (1989). A general pattern of CNS innervation of the sympathetic outflow demonstrated by transneuronal pseudorabies viral infections. *Brain Research, 491*, 156–162.

Strack, A. M., Sawyer, W. B., Platt, K. B., & Loewy, A. D. (1989). CNS cell groups regulating the sympathetic outflow to adrenal gland as revealed by transneuronal cell body labeling with pseudorabies virus. *Brain Research, 491*, 274–296.

Sugiura, Y., Terui, N., & Hosoya, Y. (1989). Differences in the distribution of central terminals between visceral and somatic unmyelinated (C) primary afferent fibers. *Journal of Neurophysiology, 62*, 834–847.

Szurszewski, J. H., & King, B. F. (1989). Physiology of prevertebral ganglia in mammals with special reference to the inferior mesentric ganglion. In J. D. Wood (Ed.), *Handbook of physiology: Section 6. The gastrointestinal system: Motility and circulation* (vol. 1, pp. 519–592). Bethesda, MD: American Physiological Society.

Thorén, P. (1979). Role of cardiac vagal C-fibers in cardiovascular control. *Reviews of Physiology, Biochemistry and Pharmacology, 86*, 1–94.

Tomori, Z., & Widdicombe, J. G. (1969). Muscular, bronchomotor and cardiovascular reflexes elicited by mechanical stimulation of the respiratory tract. *Journal of Physiology (London), 200*, 25–49.

Ulman, L. G., Potter, E. K., & McCloskey, D. I. (1992). Effects of sympathetic activity and galanin on cardiac vagal action in anaesthetized cats. *Journal of Physiology (London), 448*, 225–235.

Uvnäs, B. (1960). Sympathetic vasodilator system and blood flow. *Physiological Reviews, 40* (Suppl. 4), 68–75.

Vallbo, A. B., Hagbarth, K.-E., Torebjörk, H. E., & Wallin, B. G. (1979). Somatosensory, proprioceptive and sympathetic activity in human peripheral nerves. *Physiological Reviews, 59*, 919–957.

Wallin, B. G. (1999). Intraneural recordings of normal and abnormal sympathetic activity in humans. In C. J. Mathias & R. Bannister (Eds.), *Autonomic failure* (4th ed., pp. 224–231). Oxford, England: Oxford University Press.

Wallin, B. G., Batelsson, K., Kienbaum, P., Karlsson, T., Gazelius, B., & Elam, M. (1998). Two neural mechanisms for respiration-induced cutaneous vasodilatation in humans? *Journal of Physiology (London), 513*, 559–569.

Wallin, B. G., & Fagius, J. (1986). The sympathetic nervous system in man: Aspects derived from microelectrode recordings. *Trends in Neurosciences, 9*, 63–67.

Wallin, B. G., & Fagius, J. (1988). Peripheral sympathetic neural activity in conscious humans. *Annual Reviews of Physiology, 50*, 565–576.

Wang, F. B., Holst, M. C., & Powley, T. L. (1995). The ratio of pre- to postganglionic neurons and related issues in the autonomic nervous system. *Brain Research Review, 21*, 93–115.

Widdicombe, J. G. (1966). Action potentials in parasympathetic and sympathetic efferent fibres to the trachea and lungs of dogs and cats. *Journal of Physiology (London), 186,* 56–88.

Widdicombe, J. G. (1986). Sensory innervation of the lungs and airways. *Progress in Brain Research, 67,* 49–64.

Williams, I. R., & Kupper, T. S. (1996). Immunity at the surface: Homeostatic mechanisms of the skin immune system. *Life Sciences, 58,* 1485–1507.

Williams, P. L., & Warwick, R. (1980). *Gray's anatomy* (36th ed.). Edinburgh, Scotland: Churchill Livingstone.

Willis, W. D., & Coggeshall, R. E. (1994). *Sensory mechanisms of the spinal cord* (2nd ed.). New York: Plenum Press.

Zagoun, A., & Smith, A. D. (1993). Monosynaptic projections from the rostral ventrolateral medulla oblongata to identified sympathetic preganglionic neurons. *Neuroscience, 54,* 729–743.

# 10

# MOTIVATIONAL ORGANIZATION OF EMOTIONS: AUTONOMIC CHANGES, CORTICAL RESPONSES, AND REFLEX MODULATION

Alfons O. Hamm, Harald T. Schupp, and Almut I. Weike

"Everyone knows what an emotion is, until asked to give a definition" (Fehr & Russell, 1984). Thus, although it is difficult to define emotions in a way everybody would agree on, there is a general acceptance that emotions are episodes of a set of interrelated subevents which are elicited by a specific situation, person, or object (real or imagined; Russell & Feldman-Barrett, 1999). These subevents include changes in three different reactive systems (Lang, 1995). Usually emotions are experienced as *feelings*, and sometimes we are willing and able to report these affective experiences to others. Although rich in emotional terms (Averill, 1975; Clore, Ortony, & Foss, 1987), language sometimes fails to capture these feelings, so metaphors and sometimes art become vehicles for rendering these conscious states of mind (Cacioppo, Gardner, & Berntson, 1999). Furthermore, emotions are usually accompanied by *expressive displays* (postures, gestures, facial and vocal expressions) to communicate the emotions to others (Ekman, 1971; Scherer, 1986). Although some investigators claim that facial expression of emotion uses an innate, species-typical repertoire of movements of facial muscles that shows the same pattern in different cultures (Ekman & Friesen, 1971), it is also clear that emotional expressions are influenced by display rules that serve functions of social coordination (Buck, 1999). Whereas facial expressions and vocalizations are the most prominent indices of emo-

tional expression in humans, overt behavior such as running away, fighting, jumping, freezing, or grooming is used to study emotional expression in laboratory animals. Finally, emotions are accompanied by *bodily responses* that comprise changes in the somatic and autonomic nervous system, as well as in the endocrine and immune system, that modify specific psychophysiological responses such as reflex, cardiovascular, electrodermal, gastrointestinal, or pupillary activity (Cacioppo, Tassinary, & Berntson, 2000) and also changing hormone levels, as well as the number of immune and antibody cells (e.g., cortisol or cytokine levels in the blood; see Maier & Watkins, 1998). These peripheral components of emotions prepare the body for action. This readiness to act is often considered to be the core function of an emotion. Thus emotions are action dispositions giving priority to one kind of action, interrupting ongoing behavior or other mental processes (Frijda, 1986; Lang, 1995; Oatley & Jenkins, 1996). This preparatory function of emotion involves general arousal, which sensitizes the organism as a whole for action (an *energetic component*), as well as specific arousal, which prepares the body for a particular behavior (e.g., attack, flight, immobility, vomiting).

Because each of these indices of emotions serves such a different function, it is not really surprising that the correlations between and within these response systems often are quite modest (Lang, 1968, 1995; Mandler, 1980; see Cacioppo, Klein, Berntson, & Hatfield, 1993, for a review) when researchers confront participants with situations designed to evoke particular emotions (e.g., fear, anger, or disgust). This implies that the emotional experience can be neither an epiphenomenon of the autonomic changes and the facial responses nor based on visceral-autonomic or facial-somatic feedback, as stated in the still influential James-Lange view of emotion (James, 1894). Rather, emotional response patterns are often unreliable within participants and vary across different contexts of stimulation (see Lang, Bradley, & Cuthbert, 1990, for the distinction between strategic and tactical aspects of emotion). This context specificity of the physiological response pattern is illustrated by the cardiac waveforms obtained during encoding of disgusting pictures and during imagery of disgust-evoking scenes (see Figure 10.1). Whereas cardiac deceleration is obtained during viewing of disgusting pictures, imagery of scenes receiving the same disgust ratings as the slides prompted cardiac acceleration (Hamm, Gerlach, Globisch, & Vaitl, 1992).

In the same vein, participants who are afraid of snakes and spiders show a strong cardiac acceleration and blood pressure increase when confronted with their feared objects (Geer, 1966; Hamm, Cuthbert, Globisch, & Vaitl, 1997; Lang, Melamed, & Hart, 1970). These autonomic changes presumably prepare the organism for an active escape or flight response. By contrast, instead of responding to threatening stimuli with strong sympathetic activation, a remarkable number of animals, including humans, respond to fear stimuli with a profound bradycardia (see Campbell, Wood, & McBride, 1997, for a review; see also the subsection in this chapter titled "Startle Reflex Modulation During Picture Viewing"). Blood and injection phobics exhibit such fear bradycardia when continuously exposed to pictures of mutilations, film clips of thoracic surgery, or when anticipating a venipuncture (Graham, Kabler, & Lunsford, 1961; Lumley & Melamed, 1992; Öst, Sterner, & Lindahl, 1984). This fear bradycardia is a result

of vagally mediated parasympathetic inhibition of the heart (Campbell et al., 1997), and this autonomic response profile prepares the organism for tonic immobility, a robust defensive response documented in numerous animals (see Marks, 1987, for a review). In alligators, for example, the heart rate drops from 30 bpm to 2 to 5 bpm at an approach of a canoe, and the animal shows complete tonic immobility as well. Some investigators claim that this bradycardia might be a prominent component of the diving reflex, which can be observed in a variety of amphibians, reptiles, birds, and mammals. However, Gaunt and Gans (1969) convincingly showed that diving bradycardia was minimal in caimans during voluntary undisturbed dives but that it increased dramatically when the dive was triggered by the entry of a human into the laboratory room. Similarly, rats respond with a decrease in blood pressure and heart rate during shock anticipation when they are restrained but exhibit an increase in both autonomic indices when they can freely move around (Iwata & LeDoux, 1988). The findings discussed so far question the existence of fixed affective programs which then regulate specific peripheral response profiles for a limited number of discrete emotions. Instead, the autonomic changes of an emotion prepare the body for action, and the specific response patterns depend on the action tendency that is activated for a certain situational context (e.g., whether the organism activates the disposition for tonic immobility or headlong flight).

## The Biphasic Organization of Emotion

Although emotional expressions, bodily changes, and reported feelings vary idiosyncratically according to dispositional (e.g., temperament, social learning history) and situational factors, many theorists claim that the emotional or affect system (see Buck, 1999; Cacioppo et al., 1999) has evolved from a motivational basis that has a much simpler two-factor organization (see Lang, 1995; Lang, Bradley, & Cuthbert, 1997). As the perceptual and cognitive systems provide information about the organism's environment, the motivational-emotional systems sort out the relative importance of that information (Buck, 1999; Cacioppo et al., 1999). Evolution has primed the organism to be responsive to those stimuli that are related to survival and to the task of promoting one's genes to the next generation (e.g., priming motivated behavior such as escape, attack, etc., in the presence of hostile stimuli and grooming, sexual consummation, etc., in a hospitable environment; Cacioppo et al., 1999; Lang, 1995; Lang et al., 1997; Öhman, Hamm, & Hugdahl, 2000). Because motivated behavior is energetic and always goal directed (McSweeney & Swindell, 1999), numerous researchers proposed that the emotional-motivational system can be subdivided into an aversive and an appetitive motiva-

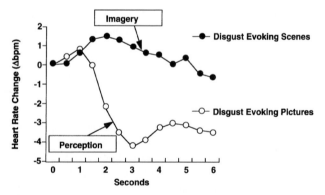

Figure 10.1 Heart rate waveforms during perception and imagery of disgusting scenes illustrate the context specificity of physiological responses.

tional system (Dickinson & Dearing, 1979; Schneirla, 1959; see also Lang et al., 1990, 1992, for integrative reviews). When the aversive motivational system is activated, defensive and protective behaviors (e.g., flight, avoidance, defense) are facilitated in order to withdraw from aversive stimulation as quickly as possible (Schneirla, 1959; Lang et al., 1990). Activation of the appetitive system primes approach behaviors (e.g., food intake, mating, exploration) to appetitive stimuli. This biphasic organization of emotion is also advocated in the conditioning literature. For example, Konorski (1967) categorized unconditioned responses according to their function as protective and appetitive reflex systems. Dickinson and Dearing (1979) took Konorski's dichotomy further, postulating two reciprocally inhibiting motivation systems, each of which can be activated by a broad range of unconditioned stimuli. This implies that during activation of the aversive system protective reflexes (such as the startle reflex) are potentiated, whereas appetitive reflexes (e.g., salivation) are simultaneously inhibited (see the section titled "The Emotional Priming Model" in this chapter for an elaboration of this theoretical approach). This reciprocal activation of the motivational systems is the rule when the modulation of simple protective (i.e., the startle reflex) and appetitive reflexes and their regulation by subcortical brain structures are investigated (for an extensive review of this literature, see the subsection in this chapter titled "The Startle Reflex and Emotional Priming"). When thinking about the human affect system as a whole, Cacioppo and Berntson (1994) claim, however, that both the aversive and the appetitive systems can be coactivated in parallel by certain stimuli that elicit intense ambivalence. This can be seen in certain behaviors when an organism stays motionless, circles a stimulus at a certain distance, or runs toward or away from a certain stimulus. Defining the critical parameters that contribute to reciprocal versus concurrent or separable activation of appetitive and aversive systems, however, remains to be worked out. Besides stimulus complexity, intensity of emotional activation might be an important factor, as recently suggested by Bradley (2000).

The motivational organization of emotions is not restricted to simple behavioral outputs (such as appetitive or protective reflexes). Researchers who tried to categorize emotional feelings, either by using the method of introspection (Wundt, 1896) or by asking people to report their emotional experiences, also found that knowledge about emotions or emotion language is hierarchically organized with pleasure and displeasure as a fundamental dimension (Osgood, Suci, & Tannenbaum, 1957; Russell & Feldman-Barrett, 1999; Watson & Tellegen, 1985). Factor analyses of the verbal reports of emotional experiences in several contexts (e.g., during imagery of emotional evocative situations, during viewing of affective slides) consistently found one fundamental pleasure-displeasure or valence dimension (Bradley & Lang, 1994; Hamm & Vaitl,

1993a; Mehrabian & Russell, 1974; Russell & Carroll, 1999). The second factor of the reported emotional experience is the activation dimension, which refers to the intensity of mobilization or energy. This two-dimensional structure of emotional experience has been replicated by many researchers, and although the basic dimensions are rotated 45° by some authors (Tellegen, Watson, & Clark, 1999; Thayer, 1989), the empirical structure of the emotional judgments remains the same (see Russell & Feldman-Barrett, 1999). In our view, both the categorical and dimensional views of emotions need not be incompatible but are directed to different levels of the hierarchy of the emotional systems. At the base of the hierarchy, activation and pleasure-displeasure dimensions are indeed fundamental (or strategic; Lang et al., 1990) in a sense. The behaviors of very primitive organisms vary along the arousal and the approach-withdrawal dimensions, and there are neural systems in the brain which are associated with these fundamental motivational systems. As will be demonstrated in the subsection titled "Neural Pathways for the Fear-Potentiated Startle," these neural systems are located in the phylogenetically older parts of the brain.

## The Picture-Viewing Paradigm

As noted previously, verbal reports of emotional feelings, affective expressions, and bodily changes vary substantially according to the contextual demand. Thus the emotional response patterns are highly idiosyncratic and have often proven to be unreliable across different contexts of stimulation (Cacioppo, Klein, et al., 1993). In part this is due to the variability of methods used for emotional instigation across experiments that reach from electrical and pharmacological stimulations of brain regions over shock anticipation to insults of the participants by experimenters' confederates (M. Martin, 1990; see also chapter 12 in this volume). Therefore it might be helpful, at least at first, to hold the procedure of emotional instigation constant and to use stimuli that are standardized within and between different laboratories. In the early 1980s Peter Lang and his colleagues started the effort to develop a set of calibrated stimuli for use in the study of emotion. Lang and collaborators chose photographs as emotional stimuli because picture viewing is a highly motivated human activity, one which may occupy 10% to 50% of the waking life of children and adults (Reeves & Hawkins, 1986). A majority of these pictorial images are intended to provoke emotions in the viewer. Indeed, many politicians, advocacy groups, and some social scientists have voiced major concerns about the emotional impact of media representations. Thus studying the perception of emotional images in the laboratory draws on a widespread human activity. Furthermore, during emotional perception, the organism is in a passive sensory intake posture (like the animal

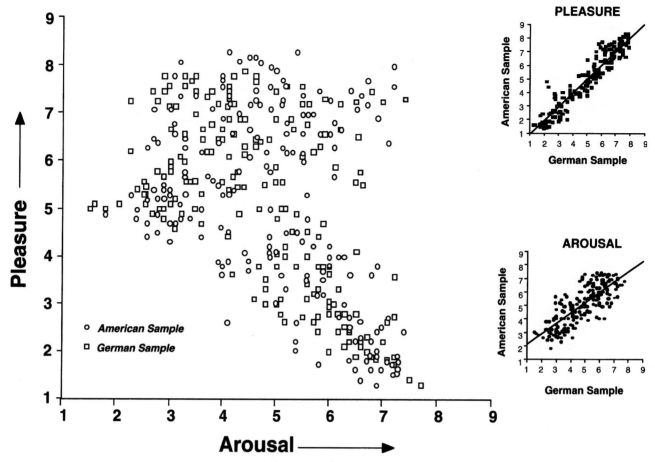

Figure 10.2  Mean ratings of valence and arousal are plotted for each of the 192 pictures selected from the IAPS (1–9 scale). Circles indicate the ratings from a U.S. sample, whereas the quadrants indicate ratings of the same pictures from a German sample (N = 492).

scanning its environment), with a common processing task in which motor interference is reduced. Moreover, exposure timing and physical intensity can be carefully controlled, and results can therefore be compared within and between different laboratories.

In a first step, a large group of participants in different laboratories rated their emotional experiences during viewing of the color photographs, using either bipolar adjective pairs (Bradley & Lang, 1994; Hamm & Vaitl, 1993a) or the Self-Assessment Manikin (SAM). The SAM is a nonverbal graphical procedure developed by Lang (1980) to assess experienced pleasure, arousal, and dominance. Factor analysis of the ratings with the semantic differential consistently resulted in a three-factor solution, with valence, arousal, and dominance accounting for 55% to 62% of the variance (see Bradley & Lang, 1994; Hamm & Vaitl, 1993a), supporting the findings of Mehrabian and Russell (1974). Furthermore, correlational analyses confirmed that the ratings obtained using the more time-consuming semantic differential (SD) are similar to those obtained using the SAM (intercorrelations between ratings obtained with

the SD and SAM are: for valence, $r = .97$; arousal, $r = .95$; dominance, $r = .86$). Therefore, in most studies that investigate the emotional evaluations evoked by the pictures, ratings are obtained using the SAM. Figure 10.2 shows a distribution of a representative sample of these pictures, which were rated by large groups of college students both in the United States and in Germany. In this figure each data point represents participants' mean pleasure and arousal ratings of each picture.

Overall, there is a boomerang-shaped distribution of these pictures, with the neutral pictures clustering in the center of the distribution, indicating that it is difficult to find neutral images that are simultaneously judged to be highly arousing. Departing from the center of the affective space, stimuli are rated as progressively more pleasant or unpleasant. To the extent that pictures are more affectively engaging, they also receive higher arousal ratings. Supporting recent findings from Ito, Cacioppo, and Lang (1998), the coupling of arousal and valence ratings is more pronounced for unpleasant pictures, demonstrating a steeper slope for the aversive motivation (or negativity; Ito et al., 1998; see also Bradley, 2000, for discussion). Furthermore, the data clearly demonstrate a substantial stability of the affective evaluations across laboratories in different countries, indicating that the stimuli are indeed suitable to serve as an International Affective Picture System (IAPS; Lang, Bradley, & Cuthbert, 1998b). The correlations between the SAM ratings obtained in the United States (Lang et al., 1998b) and the ratings from our sample of 492 participants were very high for each rating dimension: valence, $r = .94$; arousal, $r = .78$. Finally, the distribution of the affective ratings supports the fundamental biphasic organization of emotion along the hypothetical underlying appetitive and defensive motivational systems (as indicated by the arrows in Figure 10.2).

### Autonomic Changes and Facial Responses Elicited by Emotional Pictures

In addition to differential emotional experience, research has demonstrated that pictures of the IAPS evoke a broad range of emotional reactions, including characteristic autonomic changes, as well as facial reactions. A number of different studies explored the covariation between various physiological responses and subjective evaluations while participants viewed pleasant, neutral, and unpleasant pictures. In these studies autonomic measures such as heart rate, skin conductance, and sometimes blood pressure are recorded together with affective SAM ratings of valence and arousal (and sometimes dominance), which were obtained either immediately after picture presentation or in separate runs. Additionally, facial EMG activity is recorded while participants view the emotional pictures (Greenwald, Cook, & Lang, 1989; Hamm & Vaitl, 1993a; Lang, Greenwald, Bradley, & Hamm, 1993; for a review, see Bradley, 2000).

In these studies it has been consistently shown that the magnitude of the skin conductance responses covaries with the rated arousal level of the affective pictures, regardless of their valence. Both pleasant and unpleasant pictures elicit significantly larger skin conductance responses than neutral contents do (see Figure 10.3, top panel). The electrodermal response system is indeed a very good candidate to reflect general arousal because sweat gland activity—the basic mechanism of electrodermal phenomena (Fowles, 1986)—is entirely under the neural control of the sympathetic branch of the autonomic nervous system (see chapter 9, this volume). In contrast to the electrodermal system, the heart is dually innervated by the sympathetic and parasympathetic branches of the autonomic nervous system, and thus heart rate responses might indicate more or less activation of one or the other system (Berntson, Cacioppo, & Quigley, 1991). The time course of heart rate during picture viewing exhibits a triphasic pattern, with an initial deceleration followed by an accelerative component and subsequently a secondary de-

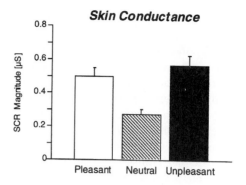

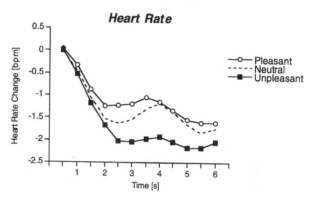

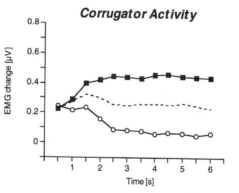

Figure 10.3 Autonomic and facial response patterns during presentation of pleasant, neutral, and unpleasant pictures. Skin conductance response data (*top*) included 222 participants and 93 different slides. Heart rate changes during slide viewing (*middle*) were pooled over 163 participants and 87 slides. Data from 133 participants and 75 different slides contributed to the analysis of the corrugator muscle activity (*bottom*).

celeration (see Figure 10.3, middle panel). Affective modulations of the heart rate include a more pronounced initial deceleration for unpleasant pictures and a larger accelerative peak for positive pictures, suggesting an association of the heart rate response with the valence dimension.

Facial expressive behavior plays a central role in many models of emotion. Different from natural social situations, facial responses are often weak or covert when there are no confederates present (Fridlund, 1991). Therefore, facial responses during "private" affective picture viewing have been assessed by means of electromyographic recordings that can detect more subtle, nonvisible changes in expression (Tassinary & Cacioppo, 1992). In most studies using the IAPS pictures, electromyogram (EMG) activity was recorded over the regions of corrugator supercilii and zygomatic muscles. As illustrated in Figure 10.3 (see bottom panel), corrugator activity shows a clear inverse covariation with picture pleasantness. After an initial general activation due to picture onset, the contraction of the corrugator muscle further increases while the participant is viewing unpleasant stimuli, although this contraction might not suffice to produce overt behavioral signs. By contrast, pleasant pictures tend to evoke a relaxation of that muscle, occasionally even below baseline. The zygomatic muscle is active when the cheek is drawn back or tightened. Consistent with its involvement in smiling behavior, the zygomatic muscle is activated during pleasant scenes, reflecting a covariation with the valence dimension. However, it was also found that the zygomatic muscle is activated for very unpleasant materials, including scenes of mutilations and death. Bradley (2000) reported that these aversive materials might elicit a facial grimace involving both high corrugator and zygomatic muscle activation, which can also be elicited by intense pain stimuli.

Taken together, evaluative judgments and physiological responses obtained during affective picture viewing are consistently related to the affective dimensions of valence and arousal. Several studies submitted these data to a factor analysis and reported stable two-factor solutions. One factor was characterized by high loadings of zygomatic and corrugator activity and heart rate acceleration, as well as valence judgments. This factor was consequently identified as a valence factor. The second factor had high loadings of skin conductance and arousal, as well as interest ratings, and therefore was assumed to reflect the arousal dimension (Bradley, 2000; Lang et al., 1993).

## Exploring Specific Patterns of Emotional Responding During Affective Picture Processing

Although emotional valence and arousal might account for a large proportion of the variance in the autonomic and facial responses elicited by the pictures, it is also clear that more specific content effects can influence the emotional responses (see the previous section on biphasic organization of emotion). Therefore, the dimensional analysis of the affective modulation of physiological measures needs to be complemented by analyses of the covariation of specific emotional response patterns with specific emotional states as identified by the participants.

To apply a specific-emotions account to the picture-viewing paradigm, a forced-choice procedure was used. Participants had to categorize the feeling state evoked by each picture either by selecting one of six different feeling states (happiness, surprise, fear, disgust, grief, anger) or by describing himself or herself as being in a neutral state. As illustrated in Figure 10.4, specific emotional feeling states were indeed associated with distinct physiological response patterns. For example, skin conductance responses varied consistently among the unpleasant categories, being more pronounced for experiences of fear and disgust than for grief and anger. However, discrete interpretations of skin conductance responses depend on considering the established association of this measure with arousal. Therefore, enhanced skin conductance responses to fear and disgust might reflect enhanced stimulus arousal rather than discrete emotional response patterns for these categories.

Interestingly, an analysis of heart rate revealed a differentiated response profile for emotional states of fear and disgust, respectively. As illustrated in Figure 10.4, a pronounced midacceleratory peak was found for pictures evoking fear, whereas this acceleratory peak was absent for experiences of disgust and other negative experiences such as grief or anger.

Facial activity, assessed over the corrugator region, also varied as a function of specific emotion states. In contrast to heart rate response patterning, experiences of disgust, but not of fear, were associated with pronounced corrugator activity, whereas grief and anger elicited moderate corrugator increases. The finding of strong corrugator activation during experiences of disgust supports previous findings of typical facial expressions of disgust (Vrana, 1993; see Figure 10.4). These patterns of results observed for specific emotions ratings converge with a complementary approach in which the effect of specific contents of the pictures was investigated (Bradley et al., in press). Drawing from the IAPS library, specific categories of human experience were selected. Among the pleasant contents were erotica, adventure, food, nature, family scenes, and babies, and the unpleasant categories involved pollution, illness, contamination, loss, threat, and mutilation.

Although physiological responses again covaried with the valence and arousal ratings of the stimuli as described previously, there were also clear effects of specific picture categories. For example, although all pleasant and unpleasant categories elicited modest skin conductance responses, only erotic images and threatening contents, as well as pictures of mutilations, elicited large skin conductance responses. Given the fact that these picture contents are associated with high arousal, Bradley et al. (in press) suggest a threshold model of affective activation in which only affectively engaging material extends sympathetic skin conductance responses beyond those that occur to

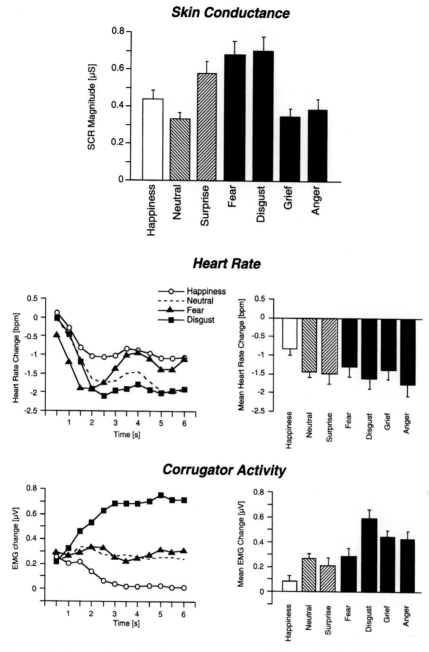

Figure 10.4 Autonomic and facial response patterns during presentation of emotional pictures evaluated to elicit feelings of happiness, surprise, fear, disgust, grief, anger, or no specific emotion (neutral). These plots were based on the same pooled-participant samples from which response patterns were derived according to a priori groupings of slides as pleasant, neutral, or unpleasant (see Figure 10.3).

moderately arousing novel stimuli. As mentioned previously, changes in the cardiovascular response system seem to index the organism's preparation for a specific action set that is associated with the emotion engaged; that is, threatening contents, which presumably prepare the organism for an overt motor behavior, elicit a stronger cardiac acceleration than the other unpleasant contents.

Facial muscles were indicative of the valence dimension, but they also revealed content-specific activity, which was most apparent in the corrugator muscle. Corrugator activity was most pronounced for specific aversive categories, including scenes of mutilations and contamination, and may be part of a disgust expression. Other specific aspects of facial muscle activity were observed for the zygomatic muscle, which was activated primarily when women viewed pictures of family scenes and babies.

## Cortical Processing of Affective Pictures

Various neuroimaging methods explored the cortical correlates of affective picture processing. Studies assessing brain activity indirectly through variations of blood flow and metabolic changes with positron emission tomography (PET) or functional magnetic resonance imaging (fMRI) try to localize where in the brain affective information processing is taking place. In addition to such structural approaches, event-related-potential studies (ERP) reveal insights into the temporal dimension of affective processing.

### Neural Imaging: PET and fMRI Studies

Brain activity to affective pictures was recently explored in a PET study in which 12 women were presented with blocks of pleasant, neutral, and unpleasant pictures (Lane et al., 1997).[1] Unpleasant pictures elicited increased regional blood flow in the thalamus and in the occipital regions (Brodman area 18 and 19) compared with neutral materials. Unexpectedly, there were no significant differences in occipital blood flow between pleasant and neutral pictures. Concurrent measurement of skin conductance activity, however, revealed that women also showed less pronounced skin conductance responses to the selected pleasant pictures than to the unpleasant contents, suggesting that both contents engaged different arousal levels in this sample. Following this line of research, Lang, Bradley, Fitzsimmons, Cuthbert, Scott, Moulder, and Nangia (1998) assessed brain activation during affective picture viewing using fMRI. Functional images were taken at four coronal slices, sampling occipital regions, while both male and female participants viewed blocks of pleasant, neutral, or unpleasant pictures. Data were collected during the 12 s picture period and compared with a 12 s intertrial interval in which no visual stimuli were presented. Again, more activation in the visual cortex (Brodman area 18 and 19, in the fusiform gyrus, and at parietal sites) was found during processing of unpleasant and pleasant pictures relative to neutral contents. Moreover, a larger area of activation was found in the right than in the left visual cortex. These results were recently replicated and extended in a study by Sabatinelli, Bradley, King, Desai, Fitzsimmons, Cuthbert, and Lang (1999) in which pictures of specific content categories were selected. Pleasant categories included erotic images and pictures of families; neutral images consisted of either household objects or pictures displaying neutral human faces; unpleasant categories were pictures of mutilations and angry facial expressions. Replicating previous findings, pleasant and aversive pictures elicited enhanced activation of the visual cortex with a larger area of activation of the occipital regions compared with neutral images. Moreover, high-arousing erotic pictures not only elicited more brain activation in the visual areas but also activated a larger area relative to the low-arousing pleasant pictures. The same effect of stimulus arousal was found for the unpleasant stimulus categories.

Taken together, assessment of regional brain activation during affective picture processing revealed that pleasant and unpleasant pictures prompt enhanced brain activation in cortical areas involved in visual information processing. Thus emotional stimuli seem to undergo more elaborated stimulus processing in the visual areas than nonaffective contents. This effect is more pronounced with increasing arousal mechanism. Some investigators suggest that these findings might be explained by a reentrant mechanism by which projections from the amygdala feed back to the visual cortex (Emery & Amaral, 2000; Lang, Bradley, & Cuthbert, 1998a).

### Event-Related Potential Studies

PET and fMRI measures depend on metabolic and hemodynamic processes, and ERPs reflect electrical brain activity. The blood flow response typically has a time lag of about 1–2 s compared with the actual electrical signal and reflects average activity integrated over a few hundred milliseconds. Considering the poorly understood link between electrical and hemodynamic processes (Kutas & Federmeier, 1998), it is interesting that ERP studies on affective picture processing are quite resonant to findings of the fMRI studies.

Numerous studies have demonstrated that late positive potentials (LPP) are sensitive to higher order aspects of perceptual and central information processing and covary with the perceived stimulus relevance (Kok, 1997). Accordingly, many studies investigating the cortical responses during affective picture processing found augmented late positive potentials for affective relative to neutral pictures (Cuthbert, Schupp, Bradley, Birbaumer, & Lang, 2000; Diedrich, Naumann, Maier, Becker, & Bartussek, 1997; Johnston, Miller, & Burleson, 1986; Palomba, Angrilli, & Mini, 1997; Schupp, Cuthbert, Bradley, Cacioppo, Ito, & Lang, 2000). As shown in Figure 10.5, affective pictures elicit enlarged late positive potentials peaking at around 700 ms, followed by sustained slow potential changes lasting several seconds, similarly pronounced over left and right hemispheric sites (Cuthbert et al., 2000). In addition, stimulus arousal critically interacts with picture valence. As shown in the lower panel of Figure 10.5, augmentation of positive potentials was considerably more pronounced for high-arousing pleasant and unpleasant pictures then for low-arousing pictures of the same affective categories.

Taken together, in line with the fMRI results, the data support the view that the large positive slow wave of the

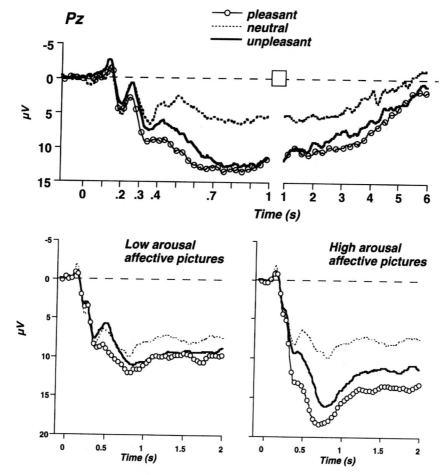

Figure 10.5 *Upper panel*: Stimulus synchronized grand average ERP waveforms for the Pz sensor (referenced to link mastoids) during viewing of affective pictures, separately for each valence category (pleasant, neutral, and unpleasant). *Lower panel*: Grand average ERPs separately for low- and high-arousing pleasant and unpleasant pictures.

event-related potential indexes the selective allocation of more attentional resources for a sustained and more elaborate processing due to the motivational significance of the stimuli. Recent evidence by Ito, Larsen, Smith, and Cacioppo (1998) suggests that the context in which these affective pictures are evaluated may also contribute to the late positive potentials.

## Dense Sensor ERPs and Affective Evaluation

Starting with these findings, several laboratories have recently investigated the cortical responses during affective picture processing using dense sensor arrays (Junghöfer, et al., 1999; Schupp, Stockburger, Weike, Mohrmann, & Hamm, 1999). Dense sensor arrays have a number of potential methodological advantages: (1) improved spatial resolution, (2) the reference-independent characterization of the brain potentials, and (3) application of deblurring methods (Junghöfer, Elbert, Leiderer, Berg, & Rockstroh, 1997; Srinivasan, Tucker, & Murias, 1998). However,

dense sensor arrays have an increased likelihood of artifacts restricted to a few sensors. Consequently, the procedure was modified to allow for an increased number of trials and for an improved statistical control procedure to identify artifacts (Junghöfer, Elbert, Tucker, & Rockstroh, 2000). Similar to the modified oddball paradigm (Cacioppo, Crites, Berntson, & Coles, 1993), pictures were shown for 1.5 s in sequence of six exemplars. Picture valence and arousal were varied randomly. Replicating previous results, viewing of emotional pictures resulted in a stronger late positive voltage shift relative to neutral contents. The approximated Laplacian calculations, which improve the spatial resolution, suggest that the generators of these scalp field potentials might be located over the posterior brain sites, which are involved in higher visual processing, consistent with the fMRI results (Schupp et al., 1999). Interestingly, affective pictures also elicited a distinct brain response already at about 300 ms after picture onset. The processing of unpleasant and pleasant pictures resulted in a substantial

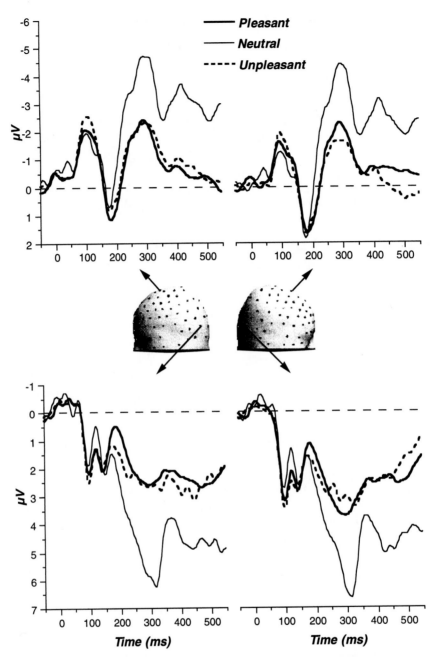

Figure 10.6 Grand-averaged ERPs recorded from selected central and occipital sensors, as indicated by arrows (applying an average reference), while viewing affective pictures. To control for picture complexity, only those pictures that displayed humans in pleasant (e.g., erotic pictures), neutral (e.g., family scenes), and unpleasant contexts (e.g., human violence) were selected for this analysis.

affect-related negativity over the temporo-occipital sensors. Such a selection negativity is also found for visual color stimuli if the participant is instructed to pay attention to one color and ignore the other. The current data suggest that such selection processes might also be triggered implicitly by the intrinsic emotional significance of the stimuli. The topographical analysis revealed bilateral centers of opposite voltage over anterior and poste-

rior regions with a coronal (temporal central) inversion line (see Figure 10.6).

Difference brain maps (affective–neutral) illustrate the spatial topography of this evaluative modulation in more detail (see Figure 10.7). Additional analyses were undertaken to explore whether the ERP effects vary as a function of stimulus arousal. Not surprisingly, the processing negativity of the ERP peak was more pronounced for highly

## Difference map (ERP peak at 312 ms): Pleasant - Neutral

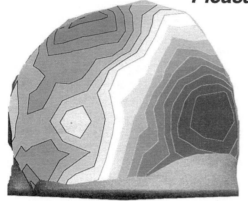
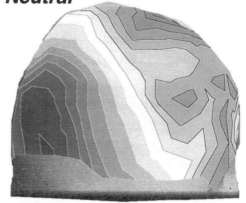

## Difference map (ERP peak at 312 ms): Unpleasant - Neutral

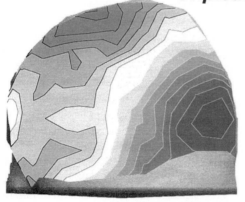
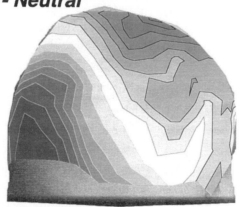

3.6
μV
-3.6

Figure 10.7 Topography of event-related-potential difference maps calculated by subtracting affective (pleasant and unpleasant) from neutral images. Voltages were interpolated to the scalp surface using spherical splines and back-projected to a model head. Contour lines were spaced every 0.4 μV. (*See color insert.*)

arousing erotic images than for family scenes (which are also rated as pleasant but receive lower arousal ratings). Both stimulus categories, however, exhibited stronger ERP negativity over the occipital regions than pictures of people, which were rated as affectively neutral. The same arousal effect was observed within the unpleasant picture category.

Affective evaluations, categorizing impinging stimuli as good or bad, can be conceptualized as a routine process, involved in virtually all perceptions (Cacioppo et al., 1999). The findings of the present study suggest that the processing negativity of the ERP over the occipital region around 300 ms after picture onset might be an index of this affective evaluation of the external stimuli. Interestingly, these ERP effects are observed in the same time region in which selective attention effects to nonspatial fea-

tures of visual stimuli (e.g., color, shape) appear (Näätänen, 1992). Future studies might explore the hypothesis that the early affective ERP modulation might be related to the selective call for continued and elaborated stimulus encoding.

### Summary

A large body of evidence now indicates that a consistent pattern of autonomic, somatic, and cortical responses is elicited during emotional picture viewing. These response patterns are highly reliable and show clear covariations with the emotional evaluations evoked by the different pictures. Cortical and electrodermal responses show a clear covariation with the arousal level of the stimuli and seem to be related to the intensity of emotional stimulation. By contrast, facial expression was related to the valence characteristics of the pictures and seems to indicate whether stimuli are perceived as hospitable or as hostile stimuli. The organization of the psychophysiological responses along valence and arousal dimensions of the stimuli might also reflect the engagement of neural structures that regulate appetitive or defensive motivational systems. This concept is elaborated in the emotional priming model proposed by Lang and collaborators (Lang, 1995; Lang et al., 1997, 1998a).

## The Emotional Priming Model

Priming is an automatic process (McKoon & Ratcliff, 1980) and comprises the facilitation in identifying or processing a stimulus as a result of having it processed before, even if an individual is unaware that the stimulus had previously been observed. Priming tasks have been extensively used to demonstrate implicit memory. For example, if participants are presented with a list of words and, after a delay period, view a few letters or fragments of words, memory performance is significantly better for words they had seen before, even though they might not be able to tell whether they had seen these words before or not (Tulving & Schacter, 1990). Priming can also be demonstrated with nonword stimuli. Object identification is improved when fragments of the objects had been seen before or if the objects had been previously presented subliminally (Bar & Biederman, 1998; Warrington & Weiskrantz, 1968). Although amnesic patients show clear deficits in recalling what they have recently seen or heard, these patients show as much priming as normal control subjects (Graf, Squire, & Mandler, 1984; Warrington & Weiskrantz, 1968). Thus, although patients with damage in the hippocampus and the medial temporal lobe show a clear impairment in explicit memory performance, implicit memory, which does not require a conscious memory search, is intact. Compared with explicit memory, implicit memory seems to involve different brain regions, because it builds up slowly through the repetition over many trials and because it is expressed primarily in performance (such as *perceptual priming*) and not in words (such as *explicit recall*).

Priming can also be demonstrated in a lexical decision task. In this task, participants are presented with a pair of words. The first word is the prime; the second "word," the target, can either be a real word (*fish*), a nonword (*sfih*), or a pseudoword (*fisch*). The participant has to decide as fast and as accurately as possible whether the target is a real word or not. Participants are faster and more accurate in their decisions if the target is semantically related to the prime (bread–roll). In this case of *semantic priming*, the facilitation or improvement of the performance might be a result of an automatic spread of activation in the men-

tal lexicon (Collins & Loftus, 1975). Again, patients with Wernicke's aphasia, who have severe difficulties in language comprehension, showed the same semantic priming effects in the lexical decision task as normal controls. Thus the lexical knowledge might be preserved, but aphasics cannot access it.

In the same vein, emotional priming means that certain memory associations, action programs, or other representations can either be facilitated or inhibited by appetitive or defensive emotional states (Lang, 1995; Lang et al., 1998a). Findings from Bower (1981) suggest that negative or positive affective moods occasion mood-congruent memories (for a review, see Blaney, 1986). Accordingly, depressive patients remember more affectively negative words (e.g., *hopeless, unwanted*) than normal controls in an association task. They also produce more negative words to a cue than normal controls, thus showing emotional priming in this implicit memory task (Watkins, Vache, Verney, Muller, & Mathews, 1996). Again, these emotional priming effects can take place outside awareness. For example, happy and angry faces presented subliminally as prime stimuli were able to generate significant shifts in participants' preferences for the target stimuli (Chinese ideographs; Murphy & Zajonc, 1993). According to the emotional priming model proposed by Lang and collaborators (Lang et al., 1998a), the most fundamental emotional priming can be demonstrated at the level of unconditioned reflexes. As described previously, Konorski (1967) categorized unconditioned reflexes according to their function and the reinforcement properties of their eliciting unconditioned stimuli as defensive or protective (e.g., withdrawal from noxious stimuli) and appetitive (e.g., saliva secretion or reflexes involved in copulation) reflex systems. The emotional priming model predicts that these fundamental reflexes are modulated depending on the organism's emotional state (see Bradley & Lang, 2000a; Lang, 1995; Lang et al., 1998a). An independently evoked defensive reflex should be facilitated when the organism is in a defensive emotional state (e.g., during processing of a threatening stimulus) and inhibited when the organism is in an appetitive state (e.g., during processing or anticipating of pleasant events). On the other hand, an appetitive reflex should be primed during pleasant states and inhibited when a defensive emotional state is activated (a dry mouth is a typical symptom of fear and anxiety). In the past decade, the startle response has become a prominent defensive reflex for investigating the emotional priming model.

## The Startle Reflex and Emotional Priming

In its full expression, the startle reflex is a cranial-to-caudal spreading wave of flexor movements along the neural axis that is elicited by an abruptly occurring sensory event of a certain intensity (Landis & Hunt, 1939; for a current review of methodological issues on startle elicitation, see Berg & Balaban, 1999). The startle response has been observed in many species and appears to be a protective reflex to prevent injury (e.g., by closure of the eyelid, limb flexion, stiffening of the neck muscles; see Pilz & Schnitzler, 1996). According to the emotional priming model, an induced defensive emotional state of an organism should facilitate an independently instigated defensive reflex. This affective modulation of the startle reflex is a basic example of priming, as it is in no sense a conscious or "controlled processing" mechanism. As we will show, the sensory encoding of the startle-eliciting stimulus as measured by evoked cortical responses is independent of the motor output. Moreover, animal data demonstrate that the acoustic startle response is a brain stem reflex whose output is modulated by subcortical structures.

Brown, Kalish, and Farber (1951) first demonstrated emotional priming of the startle reflex. In their pioneering fear-conditioning experiment with rodents, they used a light-tone compound stimulus as the conditioned stimulus (CS) and a footshock as the unconditioned stimulus (UCS). When the startle probes (pistol shot) were administered in the presence of the cue that had previously been paired with shock, animals responded with a stronger potentiation of the whole-body startle response than they did when the startle responses were elicited without the CS. A series of follow-up studies provided evidence that this so-called fear-potentiated startle effect was indeed caused by the emotional state and not by other factors. For example, Davis and Astrachan (1978) found a robust potentiation of the startle reflex after fear conditioning, independent of whether the shock UCS was applied to the back or to the foot of the animal. Thus the alternative explanation that a special body posture (e.g., crouching; Kurtz & Siegel, 1966) might have caused the potentiation effects was ruled out (for a review, see Davis, 1986). Pharmacological studies support this interpretation. Substances that have anxiolytic effects in humans (e.g., diazepam) also reduce fear-potentiated startle in rats (Davis, 1979). By contrast, substances that induce fear in nonanxious persons and increase symptoms in anxiety patients (e.g. yohimbine) lead to substantial potentiation of the startle reflex in animals (Davis, Redmond, & Baraban, 1979). Recent evidence by Schmid, Koch, and Schnitzler (1995) suggests that the acoustic startle response can also be attenuated when elicited during a cue which had previously been associated with a reward (a palatable food and sucrose), supporting the emotional priming model.

## Neural Pathways for the Fear-Potentiated Startle

The neural circuitry that underlies fear-induced potentiation of the startle response in the rat has been extensively investigated by Davis (for recent reviews, see Davis, 1997,

1998) and others (Koch, 1999). The *primary acoustic startle pathway* in rodents consists of three synapses[2] (Davis, 1998). When the ear is stimulated by the startle probe, the afferent neural volleys travel from the spiral ganglion cells in the cochlea to very large cells embedded in the cochlear nerve in rodents and humans, called "cochlear root neurons," and then proceed via thick axon collaterals directly to the caudal pontine reticular nucleus (PnC), the sensorimotor interface in the brain stem. Efferent projections pass from the PnC through the facial motor nucleus (pinna and blink reflex) or spinal cord (whole-body startle) to the reflex effectors (Davis, 1998). The anatomical structures that mediate the startle response in the rat are found in the human brain as well. In the human PnC large neurons are found that also project to the facial nuclei and to the spinal cord (Martin, Holstege, & Mehler, 1990). This obligatory circuit is schematically described in Figure 10.8.

The phenomenon of startle potentiation during fear conditioning suggests the existence of an additional modulatory circuit. Converging evidence now indicates that the amygdala and its many efferent projections may represent the key structure within this modulatory circuit. Sensory information from different modalities, transmitted via cortical and subcortical pathways (from the thalamus), converges on the lateral nucleus of the amygdala and is then transmitted via intra-amygdala connections to the basal and accessory basal nuclei (Pitkänen, Savander, & LeDoux, 1997), then continues to the central nucleus, the main output structure of the amygdala. The basal and accessory basal nuclei also project to the central nucleus (see Figure 10.8). Pathways from the central nucleus of the amygdala project to a variety of hypothalamic, midbrain, and brain stem target areas that directly mediate specific signs of aversively motivated behavior (e.g., fear; see Davis, 1992; Emery & Amaral, 2000; LeDoux, 2000; Rosen & Schulkin, 1998).

Electrical stimulation of the amygdala elicits many of the behaviors used to define a fear state (e.g., fear bradycardia, freezing, hypoalgesia), including startle potentiation. By contrast, lesions of the central nucleus of the amygdala block the expression of fear-potentiated startle (Hitchcock & Davis, 1986). Pharmacological blockade of glutamate receptors in the central nucleus of the amygdala disrupts the acquisition of conditioned fear but does not affect the expression of this response once it is acquired (Fanselow & Kim, 1994; Gerwitz & Davis, 1997). The central nucleus of the amygdala projects via the ventral amygdalofugal pathway to the PnC. Recent evidence suggests that a synapse of this pathway between the amygdala and the lateral periaqueductal gray may be required for the fear-potentiated startle (Koch, 1999). The multiple projections of the amygdala to various target areas in the brain have implications for the psychophysiology of emotions. It implies that there are hierarchically organized central networks that tie together structures that control various

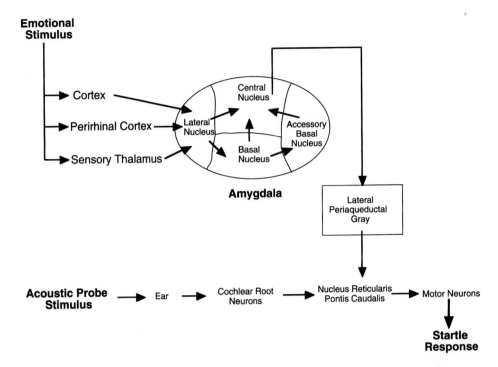

Figure 10.8 Schematic diagram of the neural structures involved in the startle reflex potentiation. As shown, previous aversive stimuli (unconditioned or learned) impinge on the primary startle circuit via projections from the central nucleus of the amygdala along the lateral periaqueductal gray. The intrinsic connections within the amygdala are simplified (see Davis, 1992; Emery & Amaral, 2000).

response outputs. These structures may also have inputs from and outputs to other networks. For example, cardiovascular responses are recruited by the fear network via nuclei in the lateral hypothalamus and the brain stem (for details, see chapter 9 in this volume). These nuclei, however, may also be recruited for other networks and may also receive inhibitory afferents (e.g., the baroreceptor control mechanism), working to keep blood pressure within preset limits. Therefore, it is not surprising that multiple influences impinge on the cardiovascular system, only some of which emanate from the brain's emotional systems (Stemmler, Heldmann, Pauls, & Scherer, 2001). Emotional priming as indexed by startle reflex modulation may provide a relatively unequivocal index of amygdala activation, which is independent of different task demands.

### Fear-Potentiated Startle in Humans

The phenomenon of fear-potentiated startle can be investigated in humans as well, although the methodology of recording the startle response is somewhat different. Although the "whole body" startle response—measured as cage floor displacement—is most often used in animal studies, the blink component of the startle reflex is re-

corded as the most reliable and fastest component of the reflex sequence in humans. Although many different procedures have been used to quantify the startle-eyeblink response, most investigators now record the electrical activity of the orbital portion of the orbicularis oculi muscle (Lang et al., 1990; Berg & Balaban, 1999). The most commonly used startle-eliciting stimulus in human research is a 50 ms burst of white noise at an intensity of around 95 to 100 dB. Hamm, Greenwald, Bradley, and Lang (1993) presented a subset of the IAPS stimuli (see the section "The Picture-Viewing Paradigm" in this chapter) as conditioned stimuli. During acquisition, one of two slide stimuli was paired with an electric shock. Acoustic startle probes were presented during slide viewing prior to and after conditioning. As in the animal experiments, there was a significant startle response potentiation as a consequence of fear conditioning. After conditioning, blinks elicited during the presentation of the stimulus, which had previously been paired with the electric shock (CS+), had larger magnitudes than blinks elicited during the presentation of the stimulus, which was never paired with shock (CS−), or during intertrial intervals (ITI). Moreover, there was dissociation among the various response systems measured. While the extent of startle potentiation covaried with the changes in the valence ratings of the conditioned stimuli, electrodermal response differentiation was associated with changes in the arousal ratings of the stimuli. These data suggest that startle potentiation might specifically index emotional learning, whereas electrodermal conditioning primarily reflects changes in stimulus significance as a result of contingency learning (Rescorla, 1968). This two-level account of human conditioning was tested more explicitly in two follow-up experiments by Hamm and Vaitl (1996). Two slide stimuli again served as conditioned stimuli; the aversiveness of the unconditioned stimulus was, however, varied systematically. In one experiment an aversive electric shock was used as the US; in the other experiment, a nonaversive but engaging reaction time task served as the UCS. The main results of these studies are summarized in Figure 10.9.

Startle response magnitudes to probes presented during the CS− did not differ from those presented during the intertrial interval; during the CS+, magnitudes were clearly augmented—but only if the UCS was *aversive*. With a nonaversive reaction time task, no startle enhancement was observed. In contrast to animal studies, in these studies with human research participants the shock intensity had to be adjusted individually to a level which the participant describes as highly annoying but not painful. This procedure risks that the UCS was not highly aversive for all participants. Indeed, only those participants showed clear potentiation of the startle response who also showed conditioned heart accelerations to the CS+ during acquisition. Participants who showed a heart rate deceleration to the CS+ (an index of enhanced orienting; see chapter 13 in this volume) did not evidence any potentiation of their startle response (Hamm & Vaitl, 1996). Finally, startle potentiation was independent of participants' contingency awareness. Participants who failed to report any explicit declarative knowledge of the CS–UCS contingencies showed the same fear-potentiated startle effect as those who correctly recalled the contingencies (see the upper panel of Figure 10.9).

By contrast, electrodermal response differentiation was independent of the UCS aversiveness but depended strongly on participants' awareness of the CS–UCS contingencies (see the lower panel of Figure 10.9). These findings suggest that skin conductance conditioning mainly indexes changes in stimulus significance, resulting in stronger orienting to the cue and reflecting explicit contingency learning, whereas startle response potentiation is a specific index of implicit emotional learning.

Recent neuropsychological data from our laboratory suggest that the amygdala might be the core structure for this implicit fear learning in humans as well. In this study, seven patients were studied who had undergone a unilateral removal of the amygdala to control epileptical seizures. Patients were studied either 3 or 24 months after

surgery, and the same differential conditioning procedure was employed as that reported by Hamm and Vaitl (1996). Nineteen nonepileptic adults served as controls. The main results of this study are depicted in Figure 10.10.

Replicating previous results, in control participants startle responses to probes presented during the CS+ were again augmented relative to those in the intertrial interval, during both acquisition and extinction. This fear-potentiated startle was again independent of participants' awareness of the stimulus contingencies (six participants were not able to recall the CS–UCS contingencies but showed the same amount of fear-potentiated startle as the other control participants). By contrast, although the acoustic probe stimuli were able to elicit clear startle responses in patients after unilateral amygdala removal, these startle responses were not modulated as a result of fear conditioning. Blink magnitudes to probes presented during the intertrial interval did not differ from those to probes administered during the cue, which was paired with the aversive shock. Because startle reflex modulation seems to be a more specific index for emotional learning than conditioned skin conductance differentiation and because the startle reflex might be less influenced by the anticholinergic side effects of anticonvulsant medication (e.g., carbamazepine) than the electrodermal system, these data are a valuable replication and extension of the findings reported by LaBar, LeDoux, Spencer, and Phelps (1995).

## Startle Reflex Modulation During Picture Viewing

According to the emotional priming model, the startle response is differentially modulated depending on an individual's ongoing emotional state. Thus, as demonstrated previously, the startle response is substantially potentiated if the defensive motivational system is activated by a cue that predicts an aversive event. On the other hand, startle response magnitudes should also be inhibited if elicited in the presence of cues, which activate an appetitive motivational state. As mentioned in the subsection "Autonomic Changes and Facial Responses Elicited by Emotional Pictures," differential autonomic and somatic physiological responses are elicited during viewing of emotional pictures, suggesting that defensive and appetitive motivational systems can indeed be activated in this observational intake task. Accordingly, the magnitude of the startle response to probes presented during viewing of unpleasant pictures should be enhanced, whereas responses to probes administered during viewing of pleasant pictures (activating appetitive motivational states) should be inhibited. A large body of evidence has been accumulated by Lang and his associates (for a review, see Lang, 1995; Lang, Bradley & Cuthbert, 1990, 1997, 1998a) and

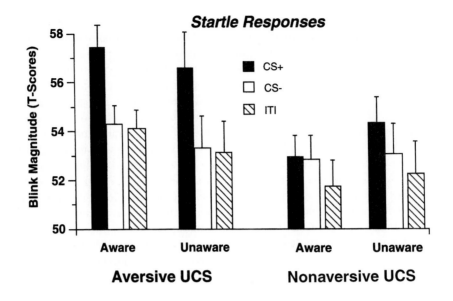

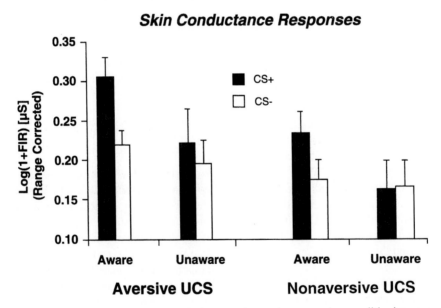

Figure 10.9 Differential responding during aversive and nonaversive conditioning as a function of the participants' awareness of CS-UCS contingencies. *Top*: Standardized mean blink magnitudes to probes presented during CS+, CS−, and the intertrial interval, respectively. *Bottom*: Skin conductance response magnitudes elicited by the CS+ and CS−. Note in the lower panel that skin conductance response primarily reflects awareness of the CS-UCS relationship; that is, only aware participants showed differential response to CS+ and CS−, regardless of the aversiveness of the US. According to the upper panel, however, startle response potentiation primarily reflects aversiveness of the US.

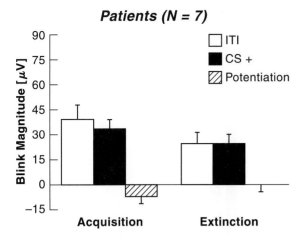

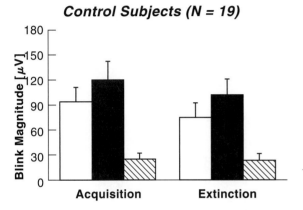

Figure 10.10 Startle blink magnitudes elicited during presentations of the CS+ and the intertrial interval (ITI) in an aversive conditioning procedure in epileptic patients after unilateral temporal lobectomy (*top*) and in healthy control participants (*bottom*).

others (see Cook, 1999; Hamm & Vaitl, 1993b; Patrick, 1994) in the past decade that consistently conforms to the emotional priming model. In the original experiment by Vrana, Spence, and Lang (1988), participants were presented with a set of color slides that were previously categorized into unpleasant, neutral, and pleasant pictures (see the section "The Picture-Viewing Paradigm" for extensive description of the IAPS). While viewing these slides, startle probes were presented, and the amplitudes of the eyeblink responses were recorded. As predicted by the emotional priming model, blink response magnitudes were enhanced during viewing of unpleasant pictures and inhibited during viewing of pleasant pictures, relative to neutral contents. In a follow-up study, Bradley, Cuthbert, and Lang (1990) found the same pattern of affective startle modulation using both visual (flashgun) and acoustic (burst of white noise) startle probes, disconfirming an alternative hypothesis that affective startle modulation might be secondary to differences in modality-directed attention (Anthony & Graham, 1985). More recently, Hawk

and Cook (1997) demonstrated that affective startle modulation was also observed if tactile startle-eliciting probes were used during picture viewing. Finally, Bradley and Lang (2000b) showed that startle responses to visual probe stimuli were significantly augmented when participants listening to unpleasant sounds and inhibited when they were processing pleasant sounds. These results support the view that affect-startle modulation is broadly motivational and independent of stimulus and probe modality. Moreover, affective startle modulation is a highly robust and reliable phenomenon that has been replicated by many other laboratories using slides (Cook, Davis, Hawk, Spence, & Gautier, 1992; Hamm & Stark, 1993; Larson, Ruffalo, Nietert, & Davidson, 2000; Patrick, 1994), video film clips (Jansen & Frijda, 1994), or odors (Ehrlichman, Brown, Zhu, & Warrenburg, 1995; Miltner, Matjak, Braun, Diekman, & Bodym, 1994) as emotionally evocative stimuli. Balaban (1995) found affective modulation of the startle reflex in 5-month-old infants looking at pictures of happy, neutral, or angry faces. Moreover, emotional modulation of the startle reflex shows familial resemblance in monozygotic twins and the lack thereof in dizygotic twins, suggesting that it may be under partial genetic control (Carlson, Katsanis, Iacono, & McGue, 1997).

Recent findings have extended and further clarified the affective modulation of the startle reflex. Cuthbert, Bradley, and Lang (1996) found that with increasing arousal, magnitude of the blink reflex first decreased and then increased for unpleasant pictures,[3] whereas for attractive pictures reflex inhibition increased progressively with arousal level. Supporting these findings, Bradley et al. (in press) found the strongest potentiation of the blink reflex during viewing of highly arousing threatening picture contents, whereas reflex potentiation was less pronounced during viewing of pictures of mutilations or pictures depicting contamination. Accordingly, strongest inhibition was found for highly arousing erotic pictures. In the same vein, participants with specific fears showed greater startle potentiation when exposed to pictures of their feared objects than during viewing of other unpleasant materials (Hamm et al., 1997). In this study, fear-potentiated startle was also independent of the autonomic pattern of the fear response. Participants who were afraid of snakes and spiders showed a clear fear tachycardia and an increase in blood pressure when exposed to pictures of their fear-relevant object. By contrast, individuals who were afraid of injections or the sight of blood showed a substantial fear bradycardia and a decrease in blood pressure when exposed to pictures of their phobia-relevant contents. Both groups of specific phobia patients, however, exhibited substantial startle potentiation during viewing of the phobia-relevant pictures (see Figure 10.11).

These data support the emotional priming model, suggesting that the probe startle response indexes the organism's basic motivational state. Moreover, other data sup-

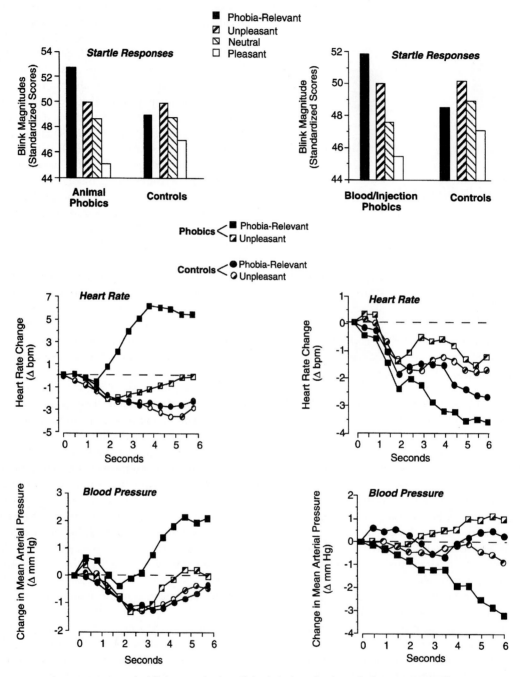

Figure 10.11 Startle blink magnitudes elicited during viewing of pleasant, neutral, unpleasant, and phobia-relevant slides for animal phobic participants and controls (*top left*: in this case, pictures of snakes and spiders served as phobia-relevant slides) and for blood/injection phobic participants and controls (*top right*: in this case, pictures of blood and mutilated bodies served as phobia-relevant stimuli), respectively. Lower panels illustrate the time course of mean heart rate and blood pressure changes during viewing of these materials.

port the hypothesis that the modulatory pattern described herein is specific for protective reflexes such as the startle response. Other reflexes, such as the spinal tendinous (T) reflex, are not modulated by the affective valence of the visual foreground stimulus but are rather facilitated in the context of arousing pictures, irrespective of whether they are pleasant or unpleasant (Bonnet, Bradley, Lang, & Requin, 1995). Accordingly, cortical responses that index the brain's attentional system might not show the same modulation pattern as the blink response.

## Cortical Responses to Startle-Eliciting Stimuli

The presentation of an intense, abrupt stimulus such as a startle probe elicits not only a reflexive eyeblink response but also a pronounced P3 wave of the event-related potential (e.g., Roth, Dorato, & Kopell, 1984; Sugawara, Sadeghpour, DeTraversay, & Ornitz, 1994). The P3 wave is considered to be sensitive to higher order perceptual/central information processing and varies among other variables with attention and stimulus relevance (e.g., Johnson, 1988; Kok, 1997). Several dual-task studies reported a reduced P3 wave to a target stimulus in a secondary (oddball) task when attention was directed to a primary task in the visual modality (Donchin, Kramer, & Wickens, 1986). For instance, Isreal, Chesney, Wickens, and Donchin (1980) found that increasing the perceptual difficulty of a primary visual task resulted in attenuated secondary P3 amplitudes. Following this line of research, Schupp, Cuthbert, Bradley, Birbaumer, and Lang (1997) assessed the attentional involvement to pleasant, neutral, and unpleasant pictures, measuring the P3 to secondary startle probes while the participant viewed the emotional pictures. As shown in Figure 10.12, P3 amplitudes were reduced during processing of the more arousing emotional pictures—both pleasant and unpleasant—compared with neutral stimuli.

As stated previously, activation of the motivational systems increases with increasing arousal level of the pictures. The cortical data indicate that this activation of the motivational systems also initiates processes of attention and selection to facilitate and serve related processing demands. Supporting this hypothesis, attenuation of the probe P3 was more pronounced for pleasant and unpleasant pictures high in arousal than for those of the same valence but judged as low in arousal (see right panel, Figure 10.12). These results demonstrate that attention manipulated by affective stimulus characteristics has similar effects on P3 amplitude to those observed in more traditional cognitive studies. However, although in these studies attention is manipulated by explicit instruction (e.g., attend to X but not Y, task priority), the intrinsic motivational significance of the affective pictures implicitly drives the allocation of attentional resources in the current task. This interaction of cognitive and affective variables was further investigated in a study by Cuthbert, Schupp, Bradley, and Lang (1998), who explored the impact of attention to the probe on P3 modulation. Another implicit manipulation of attention devoted to the probe can be achieved by varying probe intensity, either by a soft tone or an acoustic startle stimulus (50/50 probability). Explicit attentional manipulations compared a no-task group with a group conducting a reaction-time task. In this task, participants had to indicate whether a second tone stimulus was the same as or different from the tone presented during the picture probe. The probe P3 revealed comparable affective modulation for attended and unattended startle probes: Smaller P3s were observed during affective (pleasant and unpleasant) pictures than during neutral contents. The tone probe P3 was modulated by the affective foreground similar to the startle P3, although the effects were less pronounced. These results further support the hypothesis that the probe P3 reduction to affectively arousing pictures reflects less elaborated processing of the startle stimuli at the perceptual/central level. Importantly, the sensitivity of the P3 amplitude to the motivational/attentional characteristics of the foreground pictures was intact for soft tones, which did not elicit an eyeblink response. Thus varying explicitly and implicitly the attention paid to the probe stimuli explicitly and implicitly did not alter the observed modulation of the P3 amplitude as a function of affect.

Taken together, the studies on the affective modulation of the startle P3 consistently revealed attenuated P3 amplitudes while participants viewed affective—pleasant and unpleasant—compared with neutral pictures. In addition, P3 attenuation was more pronounced for high-arousing stimuli within both the positive and negative affect systems. One attractive feature of the startle probe methodology is that two separate responses to the same startle probe reveal insights into different processing components of the affect system (Cacioppo, Gardner, & Berntson, 1999).

## Summary

From the perspective of affective science, the study of emotion should be based on an operational definition of the phenomenon, which can then be investigated in the laboratory. We propose here that emotional states have two components—one evident in characteristic physical responses that can be measured; the other a consciously experienced feeling state. The peripheral autonomic changes have a preparatory function, and their pattern depends on the action tendency that is activated in a certain emotional context. Skeletomotor changes, such as gestures or facial expressions, primarily have a communicative

## Affective P3 Modulation

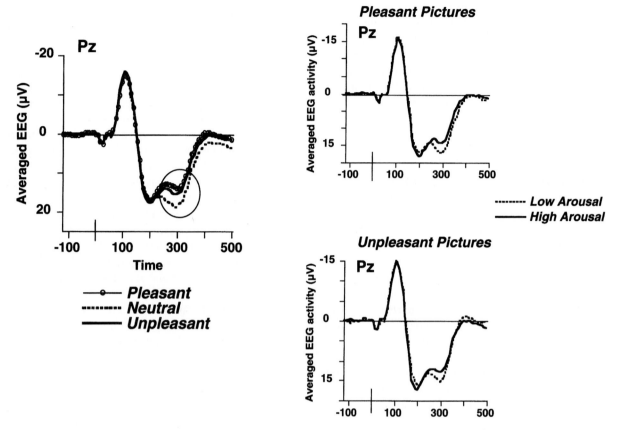

Figure 10.12 *Left panel*: Startle probe synchronized grand average waveforms for the Pz site during picture processing, separately for each valence category (pleasant, neutral, and unpleasant). *Right panel*: Startle probe ERPs for the Pz site during picture viewing, separately for pleasant and unpleasant pictures and high and low arousal categories.

function. To understand an emotion such as fear, anger, or pride, we need to understand the relationship between the cognitive feeling probably represented in the cortex and the associated physiological changes mainly orchestrated by subcortical brain structures. Some theorists claim that there is a close relationship between the two components. Consequently, a limited number of basic or prototypical emotional episodes is postulated, which are thought of as discrete categories that mostly stem from everyday folk categorization, captured by words such as *fear, anger, grief*, and so forth. The empirical evidence for such a close relationship between discrete feeling states and fixed emotion-specific physiological response patterns, however, is weak. According to our view, the emotional or affect system has evolved from a motivational basis that has a much simpler organization. Thus evolution has primed the organism to be responsive to those stimuli that are related to survival—for example, priming defensive behavior in the presence of hostile or threatening stimuli

and appetitive behavior in a hospitable environment. Such a dimensional view of emotions, however, need not oppose a categorical structure of emotional episodes but might be directed at different levels of the hierarchy of the emotional system. The appetitive and defensive dimensions are indeed fundamental, and the neural circuits for these functions are located in the phylogenetically older parts of the brain. Animal data suggest that the amygdala is a core structure within the defensive motivational system. Although emotional behavior is often more complex in humans, evidence suggests that simpler underlying patterns persist across different mammalian species. It is proposed that the modulation of the startle reflex by affective processes might be a good index for the activation of subcortical neural circuits. Startle potentiation probably occurs at an early stage of the defense cascade after the threat (e.g., the predator) has been detected. At this early stage of defensive orientation, the organism freezes, shows focused attention to the threat cue, and prepares for active flight and escape. These processes seem to operate in response to picture media when attention is focused on the cue and the organism is in an immobile sensory intake position. From this perspective it is clear that the subcortical structures which regulate affective mobilization (priming protective reflexes) interact with higher brain functions. The affect system stays in close contact with the perceptual or cognitive system and triggers natural selective attention to hostile and hospitable stimuli. Indeed, emotional stimuli elicit stronger activation of cortical areas that are involved in stimulus encoding. Moreover, emotional stimuli elicit augmented late positive potential amplitudes of the event-related potentials, suggesting that these cues prompt a selective attention process.

Interestingly, an early affective selection negativity can be observed for emotional-relevant stimuli, suggesting an implicit significance detection of these cues that is driven by the affective system. These findings also have implications for models that claim that specific biases in the cognitive system might be responsible for specific emotional disturbances, such as anxiety disorders. Our approach suggests, rather, that activation of the affect system changes the way stimuli from the environment are processed.

## NOTES

This research was supported by grants Ha 1593/6-2; Ha 1593/10-1; 10-2; Schu 1074/7-4 from the Deutsche Forschungsgemeinschaft (German Research Foundation).

1. Instead of using the picture-viewing paradigm, a number of studies investigated brain activity during emotional states employing film clips, imagery procedures, exposure to phobic stimuli, and pharmacological agents in normal and clinical participants (cf., Drevets & Raichle, 1998; Fredrikson et al., 1993; Rauch et al., 1996; Reiman, Lane, Ahern, & Schwartz, 1997; Servan-Schreiber & Perlstein, 1998).

2. In 1982, Davis and collaborators suggested that the acoustic startle pathway was mediated by four synapses, three in the brain stem and one in the spinal cord. With newly developed lesion techniques that allow destruction of the cell bodies without a concomitant loss of fiber passages, it now seems clear that there are only three synapses involved in the primary acoustic startle pathway (Davis, 1998).

3. For aversive pictures, there is an initial decrease in blink amplitude as arousal begins to increase. At a certain arousal level, the direction of reflex modulation is reversed; now the blink magnitude increases with increasing arousal level of the unpleasant slides. This pattern of results is consistent with Miller's (1959) classic conflict theory (for an extensive discussion of these results, see Bradley, 2000).

## REFERENCES

Anthony, B. J., & Graham, F. (1985). Blink modification by selective attention: Evidence for the modulation of "automatic" processing. *Biological Psychology, 21*, 43–59.

Averill, J. R. (1975). A semantic atlas of emotional concepts. *Catalog of Selected Documents in Psychology, 5*, 330.

Balaban, M. T. (1995). Affective influences on startle in five-month-old infants: Reactions to facial expressions of emotion. *Child Development, 66*, 28–36.

Bar, M., & Biederman, I. (1998). Subliminal visual priming. *Psychological Science, 9*, 464–469.

Berg, W. K., & Balaban, M. T. (1999). Startle elicitation: Stimulus parameters, recording techniques, and quantification. In M. E. Dawson, A. E. Schell, & A. H. Boehmelt (Eds.), *Startle modification* (pp. 21–50). New York: Cambridge University Press.

Berntson, G. G., Cacioppo, J. T., & Quigley, K. S. (1991). Autonomic determinism: The modes of autonomic control, the doctrine of autonomic space, and the laws of autonomic constraint. *Psychological Review, 98*, 459–487.

Blaney, P. H. (1986). Affect and memory: A review. *Psychological Bulletin, 99*, 229–246.

Bonnet, M., Bradley, M. M., Lang, P. J., & Requin, J. (1995). Modulation of spinal reflexes: Arousal, pleasure, and action. *Psychophysiology, 32*, 367–372.

Bower, G. H. (1981). Mood and memory. *American Psychologist, 36*, 129–148.

Bradley, M. M. (2000). Emotion and motivation. In J. T. Cacioppo, L. G. Tassinary, & G. G. Berntson (Eds.), *Handbook of psychophysiology* (pp. 602–642). New York: Cambridge University Press.

Bradley, M. M, Cuthbert, B. N., & Lang, P. J. (1990). Startle reflex modification: Attention or emotion. *Psychophysiology, 27*, 513–522.

Bradley, M. M., & Lang, P. J. (1994). Measuring emotion: The self-assessment manikin and the semantic differential. *Journal of Behavior Therapy and Experimental Psychiatry, 25*, 49–59.

Bradley, M. M., & Lang, P. J. (2000a). Measuring emotion: Behavior, feeling, and physiology. In R. D. Lane & L. Nadel (Eds.), *Cognitive neuroscience of emotion* (pp. 242–276). New York: Oxford University Press.

Bradley, M. M., & Lang, P. J. (2000b). Affective reactions to acoustic stimuli. *Psychophysiology, 37*, 204–215.

Bradley, M. M., Lang, P. J., Codispoti, M., Sabatinelli, D., Cuthbert, B. N., & McManis, M. (in press). Emotion and picture perception: Stimulus content and sex differences. *Psychophysiology*.

Brown, J. S., Kalish, H. I., & Farber, I. E. (1951). Conditioned fear as revealed by magnitude of startle response to an auditory stimulus. *Journal of Experimental Psychology, 41*, 317–328.

Buck, R. (1999). Typology of biological affects. *Psychological Review, 106*, 301–336.

Cacioppo, J. T., & Berntson, G. G. (1994). Relationships between attitudes and evaluative space: A critical review with emphasis on the separability of positive and negative substrates. *Psychological Bulletin, 115*, 401–423.

Cacioppo, J. T., Crites, S. L., Jr., Berntson, G. G., & Coles, M. G. H. (1993). If attitudes affect how stimuli are processed, should they not affect the event-related brain potential? *Psychological Science, 4*, 108–112.

Cacioppo, J. T., Gardner, W. L., & Berntson, G. G. (1999). The affect system has parallel and integrative processing components: Form follows function. *Journal of Personality and Social Psychology, 76*, 839–855.

Cacioppo, J. T., Klein, D. J., Berntson, G. G., & Hatfield, E.

(1993). The psychophysiology of emotion. In M. Lewis & J. M. Haviland (Eds.), *Handbook of emotions* (pp. 67–83). New York: Guilford Press.

Cacioppo, J. T., Tassinary, L. B., & Berntson, G. G. (2000). *Handbook of psychophysiology*. New York: Cambridge University Press.

Campbell, B. A., Wood, G., & McBride, T. (1997). Origins of orienting and defensive responses: An evolutionary perspective. In P. J. Lang, R. F. Simons, & M. Balaban (Eds.), *Attention and orienting* (pp. 41–67). Mahwah, NJ: Erlbaum.

Carlson, S. R., Katsanis, J., Iacono, W. G., & McGue, M. (1997). Emotional modulation of the startle reflex in twins: Preliminary findings. *Biological Psychology, 46*, 235–246.

Clore, G. L., Ortony, A., & Foss, M. A. (1987). The psychological foundations of the affective lexicon. *Journal of Personality and Social Psychology, 53*, 751–766.

Collins, A. M., & Loftus, E. F. (1975). A spreading-activation theory of semantic processing. *Psychological Review, 82*, 407–428.

Cook, E. W., III. (1999). Affective individual differences, psychopathology, and startle reflex modification. In M. E. Dawson, A. M. Schell, & A. H. Boehmelt (Eds.), *Startle modification* (pp. 187–208). New York: Cambridge University Press.

Cook, E. W., III., Davis, T. L., Hawk, L. W., Spence, E. L., & Gautier, C. H. (1992). Fearfulness and startle potentiation during aversive visual stimuli. *Psychophysiology, 29*, 633–645.

Cuthbert, B. N., Bradley, M. M., & Lang, P. J. (1996). Probing picture perception: Activation and emotion. *Psychophysiology, 33*, 103–111.

Cuthbert, B. N., Schupp, H. T., Bradley, M. M., Birbaumer, N., & Lang, P. J. (2000). Brain potentials in affective picture processing: Covariation with autonomic arousal and affective report. *Biological Psychology, 52*, 95–111.

Cuthbert, B. N., Schupp, H. T., Bradley, M. M., & Lang, P. J. (1998). Probing affective pictures: Attended startle and tone probes. *Psychophysiology, 95*, 344–347.

Davis, M. (1979). Diazepam and flurazepam: Effects on conditioned fear as measured with the potentiated startle paradigm. *Psychopharmacology, 62*, 1–7.

Davis, M. (1986). Pharmacological and anatomical analysis of fear conditioning using the fear-potentiated startle paradigm. *Behavioral Neuroscience, 100*, 814–824.

Davis, M. (1992). The role of the amygdala in conditioned fear. In J. P. Aggleton (Ed.), *The amygdala* (pp. 255–305). New York: Wiley-Liss.

Davis, M. (1997). Neurobiology of fear responses: The role of the amygdala. *Journal of Neuropsychiatry and Clinical Neurosciences, 9*, 382–402.

Davis, M. (1998). Are different parts of the extended amygdala involved in fear versus anxiety? *Biological Psychiatry, 44*, 1239–1247.

Davis, M., & Astrachan, D. I. (1978). Conditioned fear and startle magnitude: Effects of different footshock or backshock intensities used in training. *Journal of Experimental Psychology: Animal Behavior Processes, 4*, 95–103.

Davis, M., Redmond, D. E., Jr., & Baraban, J. M. (1979). Noradrenergic agonists and antagonists: Effects on conditioned fear as measured by the potentiated startle paradigm. *Psychopharmacology, 65*, 111–118.

Dickinson, A., & Dearing, M. F. (1979). Appetitive-aversive interactions and inhibitory processes. In A. Dickinson & R. A. Boakes (Eds.), *Mechanisms of learning and motivation* (pp. 203–231). Hillsdale, NJ: Erlbaum.

Diedrich, O., Naumann, E., Maier, S., Becker, G., & Bartussek, D. (1997). A frontal positive slow wave in the ERP associated with emotional slides. *Journal of Psychophysiology, 11*, 71–84.

Donchin, E., Kramer, A. F., & Wickens, C. (1986). Applications of brain event-related potentials to problems in engineering psychology. In M. G. H. Coles, E. Donchin, & S. W. Porges (Eds.), *Psychophysiology* (pp. 702–718). New York: Guilford Press.

Drevets, W. C., & Raichle, M. E. (1998). Reciprocal suppression of regional cerebral blood flow during emotional versus higher cognitive processes: Implications for interactions between emotion and cognition. *Cognition and Emotion, 12*, 353–385.

Ehrlichman, H., Brown, S., Zhu, J., & Warrenburg, S. (1995). Startle reflex modulation during exposure to pleasant and unpleasant odors. *Psychophysiology, 32*, 150–154.

Ekman, P. (1971). Universals and cultural differences in facial expression of emotion. In J. K. Cole (Ed.), *Nebraska Symposium on Motivation* (pp. 207–283). Lincoln: University of Nebraska Press.

Ekman, P., & Friesen, W. V. (1971). Constants across cultures in face and emotion. *Journal of Personality and Social Psychology, 17*, 124–129.

Emery, N. J., & Amaral, D. G. (2000). The role of the amygdala in primate social cognition. In R. D. Lane & L. Nadel (Eds.), *Cognitive neuroscience of emotion* (pp. 156–191). New York: Oxford University Press.

Fanselow, M. S., & Kim, J. J. (1994). Acquisition of contextual Pavlovian fear conditioning is blocked by the application of the NMDA receptor antagonist D,L-2-amino-5-phosphonovaleric acid to the basolateral amygdala. *Behavioral Neuroscience, 108*, 210–212.

Fehr, B., & Russell, J. A. (1984). Concept of emotion viewed from a prototype perspective. *Journal of Experimental Psychology: General, 113*, 464–486.

Fowles, D. C. (1986). The eccrine system and electrodermal activity. In M. G. H. Coles, E. Donchin, & S. W. Porges (Eds.), *Psychophysiology: Systems, processes, and applications* (pp. 51–96). New York: Guilford Press.

Fredrikson, M., Wik, G., Greitz, T., Eriksson, L., Stone, E. S., Ericson, K., & Sedvall, G. (1993). Regional cerebral blood flow during experimental phobic fear. *Psychophysiology, 30*, 126–130.

Fridlund, A. J. (1991). Sociality of solitary smiling: Potentiation by an implicit audience. *Journal of Personality and Social Psychology, 60*, 229–240.

Frijda, N. H. (1986). *The emotions*. New York: Cambridge University Press.

Gaunt, A. S., & Gans, C. (1969). Diving bradycardia and withdrawal bradycardia in *Caiman crocodilus*. *Nature, 223*, 207–208.

Geer, J. H. (1966). Fear and autonomic arousal. *Journal of Abnormal Psychology, 71*, 253–255.

Gerwitz, J. C., & Davis, M. (1997). Second-order fear conditioning prevented by blocking NMDA receptors in amygdala. *Nature, 388*, 471–473.

Graf, P., Squire, L. R., & Mandler, G. (1984). The information that amnestic patients do not forget. *Journal of Experimental Psychology: Learning, Memory, and Cognition, 22*, 552–571.

Graham, D. T., Kabler, J. D., & Lunsford, L. (1961). Vasovagal fainting: A diphasic response. *Psychosomatic Medicine, 23*, 319–336.

Greenwald, M. K., Cook, E. W., & Lang, P. J. (1989). Affective judgment and psychophysiological response: Dimensional covariation in the evaluation of pictorial stimuli. *Journal of Psychophysiology, 3*, 51–64.

Hamm, A. O., Cuthbert, B. N., Globisch, J., & Vaitl, D. (1997). Fear and the startle reflex: Blink modulation and autonomic response patterns in animal and mutilation fearful subjects. *Psychophysiology, 34*, 97–107.

Hamm, A. O., Gerlach, M., Globisch, J., & Vaitl, D. (1992). Phobia specific startle reflex modulation during affective imagery and slide viewing. *Psychophysiology, 29*, S36.

Hamm, A. O., Greenwald, M. K., Bradley, M. M., & Lang, P. J. (1993). Emotional learning, hedonic change, and the startle probe. *Journal of Abnormal Psychology, 102*, 453–465.

Hamm, A. O., & Stark, R. (1993). Sensitization and aversive conditioning: Effects on the startle reflex and electrodermal responding. *Integrative Physiological and Behavioral Science, 28*, 171–176.

Hamm, A. O., & Vaitl, D. (1993a). Emotionsinduktion durch visuelle Reize: Validierung einer Stimulationsmethode auf drei Reaktionsebenen [Emotion induction by visual stimuli: Validation of a method using three response systems]. *Psychologische Rundschau, 44*, 143–161.

Hamm, A. O., & Vaitl, D. (1993b). Affective associations: The conditioning model and the organization of emotions. In N. Birbaumer & A. Öhman (Eds.), *The structure of emotion* (pp. 205–217). Seattle, WA: Hogrefe & Huber.

Hamm, A. O., & Vaitl, D. (1996). Affective learning: Awareness and aversion. *Psychophysiology, 33*, 698–710.

Hawk, L. W., & Cook, E. W., III. (1997). Affective modulation of tactile startle. *Psychophysiology, 34*, 23–31.

Hitchcock, J. M., & Davis, M. (1986). Lesions of the amygdala, but not of the cerebellum or red nucleus, block conditioned fear as measured with the potentiated startle paradigm. *Behavioral Neuroscience, 100*, 11–22.

Isreal, J. B., Chesney, G. L., Wickens, C. P., & Donchin, E. (1980). P300 and tracking difficulty: Evidence for multiple resources in dual-task performance. *Psychophysiology, 17*, 259–273.

Ito, T. A., Cacioppo, J. T., & Lang, P. J. (1998). Eliciting affect using the international affective picture system: Trajectories through evaluative space. *Personality and Social Psychology Bulletin, 24*, 855–879.

Ito, T. A., Larsen, J. T., Smith, N. K., & Cacioppo, J. T. (1998). Negative information weighs more heavily on the brain: The negativity bias in evaluative categorizations. *Journal of Personality and Social Psychology, 75*, 887–900.

Iwata, J., & LeDoux, J. E. (1988). Dissociation of associative and nonassociative concomitants of classical fear conditioning in the freely behaving rat. *Behavioral Neuroscience, 102*, 66–76.

James, W. (1894). The physical basis of emotion. *Psychological Review, 1*, 516–529.

Jansen, D. M., & Frijda, N. H. (1994). Modulation of the acoustic startle response by film-induced fear and sexual arousal. *Psychophysiology, 31*, 565–571.

Johnson, R. J. (1988). The amplitude of the P300 component of the event-related potential: Review and synthesis. In P. K. Ackles, J. R. Jennings, & M. G. H. Coles (Eds.), *Advances in psychophysiology* (Vol. 3, pp. 69–137). Greenwich, CT: JAI Press.

Johnston, V. S., Miller, D. R., & Burleson, M. H. (1986). Multiple P3s to emotional stimuli and their theoretical significance. *Psychophysiology, 23*, 684–693.

Junghöfer, M., Elbert, T., Leiderer, P., Berg, P., & Rockstroh, B. (1997). Mapping EEG-potentials on the surface of the brain: A strategy for uncovering cortical sources. *Brain Topography, 9*, 203–217.

Junghöfer, M., Elbert, T., Tucker, D. M., & Rockstroh, B. (2000). Statistical control of artifacts in dense array EEG/MEG studies. *Psychophysiology, 37*, 523–532.

Junghöfer, M., Perlstein, W. M., Russmann, T., May, J. C., Cuthbert, B. N., Bradley, M. M., & Lang, P. J. (1999). Arousal sensitive slow wave in high-density EEG. *Psychophysiology, 36*, S64.

Koch, M. (1999). The neurobiology of startle. *Progress in Neurobiology, 59*, 107–128.

Kok, A. (1997). Event-related-potential (ERP) reflections of mental resources: A review and synthesis. *Biological Psychology, 45*, 19–56.

Konorski, J. (1967). *Integrative activity of the brain: An interdisciplinary approach*. Chicago: University of Chicago Press.

Kurtz, K. H., & Siegel, A. (1966). Conditioned fear and magnitude of startle response: A replication and extension. *Journal of Comparative and Physiological Psychology, 62*, 8–14.

Kutas, M., & Federmeier, K. D. (1998). Minding the body. *Psychophysiology, 35*, 135–150.

LaBar, K. S., LeDoux, J. E., Spencer, D. D., & Phelps, E. A. (1995). Impaired fear conditioning following unilateral temporal lobectomy in human. *Journal of Neuroscience, 15*, 6846–6855.

Landis, C., & Hunt, W. A. (1939). *The startle pattern*. New York: Farrar.

Lane, R. D., Reiman, E. M., Bradley, M. M., Lang, P. J., Ahern, G. L., Davidson, R. J., & Schwartz, G. E. (1997). Neuroanatomical correlates of pleasant and unpleasant emotion. *Neuropsychologia, 35*, 1437–1444.

Lang, P. J. (1968). Fear reduction and fear behavior: Problems in treating a construct. In J. Schlien (Ed.), *Research in psychotherapy* (Vol. 3, pp. 90–103). Washington, DC: American Psychological Association.

Lang, P. J. (1980). Behavioral treatment and the biobehavioral assessment: Computer applications. In J. B. Sidowski, J. H. Johnson, & T. A. Williams (Eds.), *Technology in mental health care delivery systems* (pp. 119–137). Norwood, NJ: Ablex.

Lang, P. J. (1995). The emotion probe. *American Psychologist, 50*, 372–385.

Lang, P. J., Bradley, M. M., & Cuthbert, B. N. (1990). Emotion, attention, and the startle reflex. *Psychological Review, 97*, 377–395.

Lang, P. J., Bradley, M. M., & Cuthbert, B. N. (1992). A motivational analysis of emotion: Reflex-cortex connections. *Psychological Science, 3*, 44–49.

Lang, P. J., Bradley, M. M., & Cuthbert, B. N. (1997). Motivated attention: Affect, activation, and action. In P. J. Lang, R. F. Simons, & M. Balaban (Eds.), *Attention and orienting: Sensory and motivational processes* (pp. 97–135). Mahwah, NJ: Erlbaum.

Lang, P. J., Bradley, M. M., & Cuthbert, B. N. (1998a). Emotion, motivation, and anxiety: Brain mechanisms and psychophysiology. *Biological Psychiatry, 44*, 1248–1263.

Lang, P. J., Bradley, M. M., & Cuthbert, B. N. (1998b). *International Affective Picture System (IAPS): Technical manual and affective ratings.* Gainesville, FL: Center for Research in Psychophysiology.

Lang, P. J., Bradley, M. M., Fitzsimmons, J. R., Cuthbert, B. N., Scott, J. D., Moulder, B., & Nangia, V. (1998). Emotional arousal and activation of the visual cortex: An fMRI analysis. *Psychophysiology, 35,* 199–210.

Lang, P. J., Greenwald, M. K., Bradley, M. M., & Hamm, A. O. (1993). Looking at pictures: Affective, facial, visceral, and behavioral reactions. *Psychophysiology, 30,* 261–273.

Lang, P. J., Melamed, B. G., & Hart, J. (1970). A psychophysiological analysis of fear modification using an automated desensitization procedure. *Journal of Abnormal Psychology, 176,* 220–234.

Larson, C., Ruffalo, D., Nietert, J. Y., & Davidson, R. J. (2000). Temporal stability of the emotion-modulated startle response. *Psychophysiology, 37,* 92–101.

LeDoux, J. E. (2000). Cognitive emotional interactions: Listen to the brain. In R. D. Lane & L. Nadel (Eds.), *Cognitive neuroscience of emotion* (pp. 129–155). New York: Oxford University Press.

Lumley, M. A., & Melamed, B. G. (1992). Blood phobics and nonphobics: Psychological differences and affect during exposure. *Behaviour Research and Therapy, 30,* 425–434.

Maier, S. F., & Watkins, L. R. (1998). Cytokines for psychologists: Implications of bidirectional immune-to-brain communication for understanding behavior, mood, and cognition. *Psychological Review, 105,* 83–107.

Mandler, G. (1980). The generation of emotion: A psychological theory. In R. Plutchik & H. Kellerman (Eds.), *Emotion: Theory, research, and experience* (Vol. 1, pp. 219–243). New York: Academic Press.

Marks, I. M. (1987). *Fears, phobias, and rituals.* Oxford, England: Oxford University Press.

Martin, G. F., Holstege, G., & Mehler, W. R. (1990). Reticular formation of the pons and medulla. In G. Paxinos (Ed.), *The human nervous system* (pp. 203–220). San Diego, CA: Academic Press.

Martin, M. (1990). On the induction of mood. *Clinical Psychology Review, 10,* 669–697.

McKoon, G., & Ratcliff, R. (1980). Priming in item recognition: The organization of propositions in memory for text. *Journal of Verbal Learning and Verbal Behavior, 19,* 369–386.

McSweeney, F. K., & Swindell, S. (1999). General-process theories of motivation revisited: The role of habituation. *Psychological Bulletin, 125,* 437–457.

Mehrabian, A., & Russell, J. A. (1974). *An approach to environmental psychology.* Cambridge, MA: MIT Press.

Miller, N. E. (1959). Liberalization of basic S-R concepts: Extensions to conflict behavior, motivation and social learning. In S. Koch (Ed.), *Psychology: A study of science* (Vol. 2, pp. 1–12) New York: McGraw-Hill.

Miltner, W., Matjak, M., Braun, C., Diekman, H., & Bodym, S. (1994). Emotional qualities of odors and their influence on the startle reflex in humans. *Psychophysiology, 31,* 107–110.

Murphy, S. T., & Zajonc, R. B. (1993). Affect, cognition, and awareness: Affective priming with optimal and suboptimal stimulus exposures. *Journal of Personality and Social Psychology, 64,* 723–739.

Näätänen, R. (1992). *Attention and brain function.* Hillsdale, NJ: Erlbaum.

Oatley, K., & Jenkins, J. M. (1996). *Understanding emotions.* Cambridge, MA: Blackwell.

Öhman, A., Hamm, A., & Hugdahl, K. (2000). Cognition and the autonomic nervous system: Orienting, anticipation, and conditioning. In J. T. Cacioppo, L. G. Tassinary, & G. G. Bernston (Eds.), *Handbook of psychophysiology* (pp. 533–575). New York: Cambridge University Press.

Osgood, C., Suci, G., & Tannenbaum, P. (1957). *The measurement of meaning.* Urbana: University of Illinois.

Öst, L.-G., Sterner, U., & Lindahl, I. L. (1984). Physiological responses in blood phobics. *Behaviour Research and Therapy, 22,* 109–117.

Palomba, D., Angrilli, A., & Mini, A. (1997). Visual evoked potentials, heart rate responses and memory to emotional pictorial stimuli. *International Journal of Psychophysiology, 27,* 55–67.

Patrick, C. J. (1994). Emotion and psychopathy: Startling new insights. *Psychophysiology, 31,* 319–330.

Pilz, P. K. D., & Schnitzler, H.-U. (1996). Habituation and sensitization of the acoustic startle response in rats: Amplitude, threshold, and latency measures. *Neurobiology of Learning and Memory, 66,* 67–79.

Pitkänen, A., Savander, V., & LeDoux, J. E. (1997). Organization of the intra-amygdaloid circuitries: An emerging framework for understanding functions of the amygdala. *Trends in Neurosciences, 20,* 517–523.

Rauch, S. L., van der Kolk, B. A., Fisler, R. E., Alpert, N. M., Orr, S. P., Savage, C. R., Fischman, A. J., Jenike, M. A., & Pitman, R. K. (1996). A symptom provocation study of posttraumatic stress disorder using positron emission tomography and script-driven imagery. *Archives of General Psychiatry, 53,* 380–387.

Reeves, B., & Hawkins, R. (1986). *Masscom: Modules of mass communication.* Chicago: Science Research Associates.

Reiman, E. M., Lane, R. D., Ahern, G. L., & Schwartz, G. E. (1997). Neuroanatomical correlates of externally and internally generated human emotion. *American Journal of Psychiatry, 154,* 918–925.

Rescorla, R. A. (1968). Probability of shock in the presence and absence of CS in fear conditioning. *Journal of Comparative and Physiological Psychology, 66,* 1–5.

Rosen, J. B., & Schulkin, J. (1998). From normal fear to pathological anxiety. *Psychological Review, 105,* 325–350.

Roth, W. T., Dorato, K. H., & Kopell, B. S. (1984). Intensity and task effects on evoked physiological response to noise bursts. *Psychophysiology, 21,* 466–481.

Russell, J. A., & Carroll, J. M. (1999). On the bipolarity of positive and negative affect. *Psychological Bulletin, 125,* 3–30.

Russell, J. A., & Feldman-Barrett, L. (1999). Core affect, prototypical emotional episodes, and other things called emotion: Dissecting the elephant. *Journal of Personality and Social Psychology, 76,* 805–819.

Sabatinelli, D., Bradley, M. M., King, D. W. M., Desai, J. R., Fitzsimmons, J. R., Cuthbert, B. N., & Lang, P. J. (1999). Functional activity in visual cortex: Pleasure and arousal. *Psychophysiology, 36,* S99.

Scherer, K. R. (1986). Vocal affect expression: A review and a model for future research. *Psychological Bulletin, 99,* 143–165.

Schmid, A., Koch, M., & Schnitzler, H.-U. (1995). Conditioned pleasure attenuates the startle response in rats. *Neurobiology of Learning and Memory, 64*, 1–3.

Schneirla, T. C. (1959). An evolutionary and developmental theory of biphasic processes underlying approach and withdrawal. In M. R. Jones (Ed.), *Nebraska Symposium on Motivation* (pp. 1–42). Lincoln: University of Nebraska Press.

Schupp, H. T., Cuthbert, B. N., Bradley, M. M., Birbaumer, N., & Lang, P. J. (1997). Probe P3 and blinks: Two measures of affective startle modulation. *Psychophysiology, 34*, 1–6.

Schupp, H. T., Cuthbert, B. N., Bradley, M. M., Cacioppo, J. T., Ito, T., & Lang, P. J. (2000). Affective picture processing: The late positive potential is modulated by motivational relevance. *Psychophysiology, 37*, 257–261.

Schupp, H. T., Stockburger, J., Weike, A., Mohrmann, H., & Hamm, A. O. (1999). Emotion and attention: High-density ERP recordings during picture processing. *Psychophysiology, 36*, S104.

Servan-Schreiber, D., & Perlstein, W. M. (1998). Selective limbic activation and its relevance to emotional disorders. *Cognition and Emotion, 12*, 331–352.

Srinivasan, R., Tucker, D. M., & Murias, M. (1998). Estimating the spatial Nyquist of the human EEG. *Behavior Research Methods, Instruments and Computers, 30*, 8–19.

Stemmler, G., Heldmann, M., Pauls, C. A., & Scherer, T. (2001). Constraints for emotion specificity in fear and anger: The context counts. *Psychophysiology, 38*, 275–291.

Sugawara, M., Sadeghpour, M., DeTraversay, J., & Ornitz, E. M. (1994). Prestimulation-induced modulation of the P300 component of the event-related potentials accompanying startle in children. *Journal of Electroencephalography and Clinical Neurophysiology, 90*, 201–213.

Tassinary, L. G., & Cacioppo, J. T. (1992). Unobservable facial actions and emotion. *Psychological Sciences, 2*, 28–33.

Tellegen, A., Watson, D., & Clark, L. A. (1999). On the dimensional and hierarchical structure of affect. *Psychological Science, 10*, 297–303.

Thayer, R. E. (1989). *The psychobiology of mood and activation.* New York: Oxford University Press.

Tulving, E., & Schacter, D. L. (1990). Priming and human memory systems. *Science, 247*, 301–306.

Vrana, S. R. (1993). The psychophysiology of disgust: Differentiating negative emotional contexts with facial EMG. *Psychophysiology, 30*, 279–286.

Vrana, S. R., Spence, E. L., & Lang, P. J. (1988). The startle probe response: A new measure of emotion? *Journal of Abnormal Psychology, 97*, 487–491.

Warrington, E. K., & Weiskrantz, L. (1968). New method of testing long-term retention with special reference to amnesic patients. *Nature, 217*, 972–974.

Watkins, P. C., Vache, K., Verney, S. P., Muller, S., & Mathews, A. (1996). Unconscious mood-congruent memory bias in depression. *Journal of Abnormal Psychology, 105*, 34–41.

Watson, D., & Tellegen, A. (1985). Toward a consensual structure of mood. *Psychological Bulletin, 98*, 219–238.

Wundt, W. (1896). *Grundriss der Psychologie.* Leipzig, Germany: Engelmann.

# AUTONOMIC SPECIFICITY AND EMOTION

Robert W. Levenson

Autonomic specificity refers to the notion that emotions can be distinguished in terms of their associated patterns of autonomic nervous system activity. This idea has a long history in psychology, tracing back at least to James's (1884) writings on the nature of emotion. Moreover, it is an idea that has always been shrouded in controversy, attracting many critics along the way (e.g., Cacioppo, Klein, Berntson, & Hatfield, 1993; Cannon, 1927; Schachter & Singer, 1962; Zajonc & McIntosh, 1992). The controversy has been framed by two immoderate assertions: (1) Every emotion is autonomically unique; and (2) every emotion is autonomically the same.

The uniqueness assertion is generally associated with Alexander's (1950) psychosomatic hypotheses. The second assertion of sameness arguably finds its clearest statement in Mandler's (1975) writings. Needless to say, these are both statements in extremis, and it would be difficult to find undiluted, unhedged versions of either in the contemporary literature. Nonetheless, they form the two poles around which participants in the debate over autonomic specificity have aggregated over the decades. In my view, both of these assertions are highly dubious.

Regarding the first assertion of uniqueness, as I hope this chapter makes clear, it is highly likely that reliable autonomic differences only exist for a small number of emotions. Moreover, where these differences do exist, they are likely to be "prototypical" in nature, with particular occurrences of a given emotion showing variation around these central tendencies.

Similarly, there is ample basis for rejecting the second assertion of no autonomic differences among emotions. An examination of the empirical literature reveals many studies that report evidence of autonomic specificity. A flurry of such studies appeared after Ax (1953) developed a paradigm for using "real life" inductions to study this issue in the laboratory. Another flurry appeared 30 years later following our report (Ekman, Levenson, & Friesen, 1983) that used directed facial actions and relived emotional memories to address the same question. In contrast, there are surprisingly few published empirical studies that report failures to find any evidence for autonomic specificity. Most of the support for the "sameness" position comes from a number of influential critiques that have either discounted autonomic specificity on a priori grounds (e.g., Cannon's argument that the autonomic nervous system was structurally incapable of supporting specificity; Cannon, 1927) or that have criticized existing data (e.g., Zajonc & McIntosh, 1992) without presenting any new data. The other source of "support" for the sameness position has derived from studies that have followed the paradigm introduced by Schachter and Singer (1962) in which the autonomic nervous system is activated by using some nonemotional agent (e.g., injection of epinephrine). Participants' emotional labeling of the resultant state is shown to be quite malleable, reflecting cues in the experimental environment. The original study and its progeny have been criticized on numerous grounds over the years (e.g., Plutchik & Ax, 1967; Reisenzein, 1983). However, beyond any methodological problems, the application of the findings from these studies to the question of autonomic specificity is logically flawed. A study that manipulates autonomic nervous system physiology (that is, in which autonomic physiology is the independent variable) cannot be used to study the autonomic concomitants of emotion (in which autonomic physiology has to be the dependent variable).

It would be useful to consider the empirical literature on autonomic specificity as a whole. However, to my knowledge there have been no formal meta-analyses of the research findings in the area. Several informal aggregations of results do exist, but these are much less useful in settling controversies. For example, a number of years ago, I took the four most reliable autonomic differences among emotions that were found in our work and reviewed quite a large body of relevant research from other laboratories, concluding that there was a substantial amount of evidence in support of these four instances of specificity (Levenson, 1992). In the same volume, Zajonc and McIntosh (1992) published a paper highlighting other, much less reliable, findings in our work. Needless to say, the conclusions of these two papers regarding the evidence for autonomic specificity were quite different. Thus it is not surprising that more than a century after James's initial proposals and more than a half century after Ax's initial empirical forays, the issue of whether there is autonomic specificity in emotion is still far from settled.

## Why Might Autonomic Specificity Exist?

The idea that emotions are likely to have different patterns of autonomic nervous system activity is grounded in an evolutionary view of emotion that suggests that emotions were selected for their ability to help the organism deal effectively and efficiently with a small set of problems that were critical for the species survival (for a thorough presentation of this position, see Tooby & Cosmides, 1990). Viewed from this perspective, emotions can be seen as time-tested solutions to timeless problems and challenges, such as defending what is ours, avoiding harm, attracting potential mates, regulating social distance, soothing and restoring equilibrium, and engendering help from conspecifics. With our emotions, evolution has provided us with at least one generalized response to these problems that has a high likelihood of being successful most of the time. In humans this emotional response encompasses multiple psychological and physiological systems, some of which serve to prepare the organism for action, some of which serve to regulate the behavior of conspecifics, and some of which do both. I have previously described these functions of emotion as follows:

> Emotions are short-lived psychological-physiological phenomena that represent efficient modes of adaptation to changing environmental de-

mands. Psychologically, emotions alter attention, shift certain behaviors upward in response hierarchies, and activate relevant associative networks in memory. Physiologically, emotions rapidly organize the response of disparate biological systems including facial expression, somatic muscular tonus, voice tone, autonomic nervous system activity, and endocrine activity to produce a bodily milieu that is optimal for effective response. Emotions serve to establish our position vis-à-vis our environment, pulling us toward certain people, objects, actions and ideas, and pushing us away from others. Emotions also serve as a repository for innate and learned influences, possessing certain invariant features, and others that show considerable variation across individuals, groups, and cultures. (Levenson, 1994, p. 123)

This view presupposes an emotion system in which there exists some central mechanism that continuously scans the incoming stream of information from the external and internal worlds in search of certain configurations that represent a small number of problems and challenges that have significant consequence for the species's survival and well-being. Having recognized one of these prototypical configurations (e.g., being cheated; Tooby & Cosmides, 1990), the system activates the appropriate emotion (e.g., anger), which efficiently orchestrates a coordinated multisystem response that is highly likely to deal successfully with the problem. This response package is crafted from a number of disparate elements, drawn from a palette that may include perceptual/attentional systems (e.g., Mathews & Bradley, 1983), gross motor behavior, purposeful behavior (e.g., Frijda, 1986), expressive behavior (e.g., Ekman, 1984; Izard, 1971), gating of higher mental processes (e.g., Bower, 1981), and physiological support (e.g., Davidson, Ekman, Saron, & Senulis, 1990; Levenson, 1992). The elements of this package are mixed in their proper proportions, and the elements are choreographed in terms of the timing of onset, duration, and offset to produce a coordinated response.

Figure 11.1 presents a schematic for this kind of model of emotion (for a similar model, see Levenson, 1994).[1] The model has been simplified to emphasize systems primarily involved in studies of autonomic specificity. In this model, the emotion that is activated functions like a computer program that activates a set of subroutines for the various response systems (Tomkins, 1962). Thus there are sets of instructions for the facial muscles, the vocal apparatus, the skeletal muscles, and for various physiological systems, including the autonomic nervous system. These patterns of activation have two broad classes of functions: (1) preparing the organism to activate the behavioral response[2] that represents the generalized solution most likely to deal successfully with the eliciting situation, and

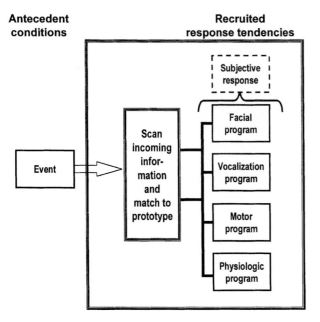

Figure 11.1 A schematic model of emotion.

(2) communicating the organism's emotional state to others in the service of altering their behavior. The likelihood that autonomic specificity exists derives support from both of these classes of functions.

The most commonly advanced argument for autonomic specificity derives from the first class of functions. If the emotion mobilizes a behavioral response or motor program (Frijda, 1986), it must also mobilize the configuration of autonomic nervous system activation necessary to provide optimal support for this particular set of behaviors. Moreover, this autonomic support should be produced on a "just in time" basis, so that the support will be there when needed and will not linger too long after the behavior is completed. Concluding the logic of this argument, if different emotions reliably call forth different patterns of behavior, and if these different behaviors require different configurations of autonomic support, then the pattern of autonomic nervous system activity should be different for different emotions.

The second argument for autonomic specificity, which is not emphasized as often as is the first, pertains to autonomically mediated appearance changes that accompany different emotions and that serve (along with changes in facial expression and in vocalization) as signals, communicating our emotional state to others. Many of these involve changes in coloration that result from alterations in local blood flow (e.g., flushing, blushing, blanching, bulging of arteries), whereas others involve additional detectable changes such as piloerection, sweating (and accompanying odors when apocrine sweat glands are involved), tearing and crying, and visible and audible changes in breathing. Of course, some of these autonomically mediated appearance changes are merely the ob-

servable manifestations of the previously discussed autonomic support for behavioral responses. Regardless, the specificity argument remains the same: If different emotions are reliably associated with different patterns of autonomically mediated appearance changes, then these should provide additional instantiation of autonomic specificity.

There is another aspect of this model that has important implications for autonomic specificity. Because the instructions associated with the emotion program create only tendencies to respond in certain ways, the observable emotional responses (which we measure in our laboratories in the form of changes in facial expression, vocalization, muscle tension, and autonomic and other forms of physiological activation) can vary in how closely they represent the response tendencies. If the onset gradient of the stimulus event is sharp, the match to prototype is close, and the stimulus intensity high, the activation of the emotion will be rapid and strong, with little opportunity for alteration of the response tendencies. Thus, in these situations, the observable emotional response would most closely resemble the generalized solution to the problem or challenge. In contrast, if the stimulus onset is gradual, the match to prototype only approximate, and the stimulus intensity low, then there will be ample opportunity for the person to alter (e.g., diminish, amplify, transform, mask) these response tendencies in accordance with learned emotional beliefs and practices (e.g., display and feeling rules; Ekman & Friesen, 1969; Hochschild, 1979). In these instances, the observable emotional response might be quite different from the prototype, depending on the person and situation. Thus, in terms of revealing autonomic specificity, stimulus situations of the first type, with sharp onset, close match to prototype, and high intensity, will be less vulnerable to interindividual "noise" and thus will be more likely to reveal any associated specificity of autonomic response. Unfortunately, in the laboratory, emotion elicitations are usually of the second type, with relatively gradual onset, approximate match to prototype, and mild intensity, and thus they are highly vulnerable to alteration, which works against finding evidence of autonomic specificity.

## Why Is the Idea of Autonomic Specificity So Compelling?

Arguably, autonomic specificity is one of those ideas that is just too good *not* to be true. Consider the following thought experiments:

- Does your body feel the same way when you are afraid as when you are happy?
- Is your heart just as likely to race when you are disgusted as when you are afraid?

- Are you just as likely to cry when you are angry as when you are sad?
- Are you just as likely to say that your "blood is boiling" when you are afraid as when you are angry?
- Is your face just as likely to turn white and drain of blood when you are angry as when you are afraid?

For most of us, the answer to all five of these questions will be "no." Each of these "no" answers depends, in its own way, on the existence of autonomic specificity. Of course, these thought experiments may prove little other than that we share a set of common beliefs about the autonomic organization of emotion. But if emotions were truly undifferentiated autonomically, then what would be the source of these beliefs? And would not some of these beliefs, especially those that could be disconfirmed by casual observation, be called more frequently into question?

The notion of autonomic specificity is quite ubiquitous in our culture. Our metaphorical language of emotion is replete with references to differentiated bodily states. Linguists such as Lakoff (1987) and Kovecses (1989) have elaborated sophisticated theories based on careful analysis of the representation of the body in emotional language. In Lakoff's analysis of anger metaphors, the themes of "heat" ("burning up," "turning red") and "pressure" ("blowing my top") are most representative. The rising temperature and reddening themes in anger directly contrast with those of fear, in which themes of dropping temperature and turning pale are regularly found. As Lakoff has pointed out, the same temperature difference between anger and fear that is found in language has also been found in empirical work (e.g., Ekman et al., 1983; Levenson, Ekman, & Friesen, 1990). Moreover, the differences in the metaphorical language of anger and fear concur with consistent empirical findings of peripheral vascular differences between these two emotions (see Levenson, 1992, for a review). And finally, providing some preliminary support for a direct link between the nature of physiological metaphors and underlying physiology, we (Marchitelli & Levenson, 1992) reported a study of the use of anger metaphors of heat and pressure during discussions of marital conflict in married couples ($N = 144$ spouses). In this study, we found small but reliable correlations between greater use of heat and pressure metaphors and autonomic nervous system changes that indicate greater temperature (finger temperature: $r$ [140] $= .17$, $p < .05$), greater blood flow (vasodilation: $r$ [142] $= .37$, $p < .001$), and faster blood velocity (pulse transmission time: $r$ [143] $= -.24$, $p < .01$).

Of course, such findings could merely reflect cultural conventions, socially constructed beliefs about emotion that would likely vary from culture to culture. However, recent cross-national surveys have also found marked consistencies in the autonomic sensations associated with different emotions, including the aforementioned temperature differences between anger and fear (Scherer & Wallbott, 1994).

## The Importance of Autonomic Specificity

### Implications for Emotion Theory

The question of whether emotions are associated with different patterns of autonomic nervous system activity is of fundamental importance to our understanding of the nature of emotion. Learning more about how the autonomic nervous system is organized in emotion would be of value in much the same way as would learning whether there are differences in patterns of regional brain activation or in patterns of facial muscle action in different emotions. Because emotions bridge mind and body and because they reflect both hardwired and learned influences, issues surrounding the biology of emotion often get caught up in larger theoretical controversies. This excess baggage has been a mixed blessing, drawing considerable attention to basic research on autonomic specificity but also increasing the likelihood that research findings will agitate one theoretical camp or another in a growing list of connected areas. I cite some examples here.

A case could be made that the "cognitive revolution" in psychology can be traced in some significant way to Schachter and Singer's (1962) study of cognition, physiology, and emotion. This study was widely interpreted as showing the primacy of cognition over emotion. If something as fundamental to the human condition as emotion could be made to dance like a puppet on the end of the strings of cognition, then cognition was clearly a force to be reckoned with. Schachter and Singer's two-factor model of emotion appeared to rest on the assumption of undifferentiated autonomic arousal in emotion. Thus, to many, any and all assertions that autonomic physiology was in fact differentiated in emotion would, at the very least, complicate the model and could in fact undermine one of its essential tenets.[3]

Autonomic specificity has also become involved in the controversy over the existence of "basic" emotions. In Ekman's model (Ekman, 1992), one characteristic of basic emotions is that they show differentiated autonomic nervous system activity (as well as unique facial signatures and other defining features). The entire notion of basic emotions was questioned by Ortony and Turner (Ortony & Turner, 1990; Turner & Ortony, 1992), thus setting off a spirited debate about whether there are some emotions that have special status by virtue of their unique biological features. Thus the issue of whether certain emotions have "autonomic signatures" whereas others do not has now become part of this controversy.

Another example is that of the universality of emotion.

After a long period in which emotions were considered to be socially constructed and thus culturally variable, evidence from cross-cultural studies suggested that facial expressions for emotions such as anger, fear, sadness, surprise, disgust, and happiness were universal (Ekman & Friesen, 1971; Ekman, Sorenson, & Friesen, 1969; Izard, 1971). A large part, but not all, of this evidence was based on studies in which participants in different cultures matched photographs of emotional expressions with emotion terms and emotion antecedents. The universalist position held sway in psychology until it was called into question by Russell (1994), setting off a heated controversy that still rages in some quarters. Evidence for the cross-cultural consistency of other aspects of emotion such as autonomic specificity would lend support to the universalist position. At this point there has been only one study that actually measured autonomic nervous system physiology during different emotions in more than one culture (Levenson, Ekman, Heider, & Friesen, 1992), and this study found evidence of cross-cultural consistency.

A final example derives from a number of controversies related to the parsing of emotional space. The major variant of this controversy is whether emotions are best organized in terms of *discrete* emotions or in terms of *dimensions* (usually a two-dimensional space consisting of valence and activation). Because most devotees of these models believe that they reflect the underlying biological organization of emotion, it is important to know whether autonomic nervous system differences reflect the discrete or the dimensional structure. Overwhelmingly, research on autonomic specificity has been carried out within the discrete-emotions tradition, but there have been a few exceptions, such as Winton and colleagues' work that attempted to map heart rate and skin conductance responses onto the pleasantness and intensity dimensions (Winton, Putnam, & Krauss, 1984). Evidence of autonomic differences among negative emotions, such as findings that disgust does not share the cardiac acceleratory characteristics of anger, fear, and sadness and that anger and fear differ in terms of peripheral vascular activity (Levenson, 1992), is more consistent with a discrete-emotions view than with a dimensional one.

### Implications for Health

A great deal of the early interest in autonomic specificity was stimulated by the psychosomatic literature, exploring Alexander's (1950) speculations about the relationship between particular psychosomatic disorders, particular emotions, and particular patterns of autonomic physiology. These ideas were tested in research by Graham and others (e.g., Graham, Stern, & Winokur, 1958, 1960), who found that evoking attitudes (which roughly mapped onto different emotions) thought to be associated with psychosomatic diseases produced subclinical changes in organ

systems relevant to the pathophysiology of the disease. Thus inducing an attitude thought to be associated with Reynaud's disease was found to produce decreases in hand temperature, whereas an attitude associated with hives was found to produce temperature increases.

Although these findings were quite promising, this line of research was not continued. Subsequent work on emotion and health, such as that showing the relationship between hostility and heart disease (e.g., Diamond, 1982; Williams et al., 1980), does not assume or test for autonomic specificity. Moreover, this subsequent work seems to mark a move away from the viewpoint that the *expression* of certain emotions is pathogenic toward the view that it is the chronic and repeated *restraint* of emotion that is most harmful. I base this assertion in part on the view that hostility is more closely associated with the suppression of anger than with its free expression. Interestingly, there is very little experimental work on the cardiovascular impact of restraining emotion (there is, however, a great deal of correlational research). Experimental work from our laboratory indicates that suppressing emotion (i.e., restraining emotional behavior once an emotion is stimulated) has profound effects on the cardiovascular system, essentially doubling the magnitude of sympathetically mediated cardiovascular responses over the level present when the emotion is freely expressed (Gross & Levenson, 1993, 1997). Importantly, there appears to be little autonomic specificity in this aspect of emotion—the inhibition of three quite different emotions (sadness, disgust, and amusement) all have similar cardiovascular effects.

## Research on Autonomic Specificity: Challenges and Obstacles

In previous work (Levenson, 1988), I addressed a number of methodological issues in autonomic specificity research in detail (see also chapter 12 in this volume). Here I address three more general problems that have historically plagued research in this area. Although I focus on the autonomic nervous system in this section, these same problems are also encountered in the emerging body of research on the role of other physiological systems in emotion (e.g., brain research using MEG, fMRI, and PET measures).

### Emotion Elicitation

It is ironic that humans have emotions all of the time in their everyday lives, yet getting participants to experience a particular emotion at a particular time in the laboratory can be very difficult. To study the physiology of emotion, regardless of whether it is autonomic, central, endocrine,

| ELICITOR | ECOLOGICAL VALIDITY | EXPERIMENTAL CONTROL | "DIFFICULT" EMOTIONS |
|---|---|---|---|
| Directed facial actions | Low | High | None (if subjects are good facial "athletes"); fear, sadness (if subjects are not) |
| Slides | Low-Medium | High | Anger, fear, sadness |
| Films | Medium | High | Anger |
| Relived emotions | Medium-High | Medium | None (if subjects are good imagers) |
| Staged manipulations | Medium-High | Medium | Sadness |
| Dyadic interaction among intimates | High | Low | None |

*Greater validity* (left arrow)  *Greater control* (right arrow)

Figure 11.2 Emotion elicitation: Trade-offs between ecological validity and experimental control.

or immunological, we must have effective ways of producing what, for lack of a better term, might be called "real" emotions. In this regard, we must distinguish between situations in which participants make emotional judgments (e.g., rating a photograph of a crying child in ragged clothing as being "5" on a 7-point sadness scale) and situations in which they actually experience sadness. Of course, participants may experience sadness when viewing such a photograph, but they may not—their ratings in the latter case indicate that they perceive the photograph as having sad qualities but *not* that it makes them actually experience sadness. For the purpose of studying the physiology of emotion, we need to produce "real" emotional experience in our participants, but the structure and demand characteristics of our experiments are such that I believe we often fail in pursuit of this goal. Even more disturbing, even when participants say they are "feeling" emotion in our studies, they may, as in the earlier example, merely be providing a readout of the emotional characteristics of the experimental stimuli. If this happens, we are in effect studying the physiology of emotional judgments rather than the physiology of emotion—introducing a source of error that will serve as a major impediment to progress in this field.

Researchers who enter into the study of the physiology of emotion immediately encounter the problem of how to elicit emotions in the laboratory. It is tempting to simply adopt some method of elicitation that has a modicum of a priori face validity and assume that this method will produce the full range of emotions of interest. In our work, we have struggled with this issue of how to produce emotions in the laboratory. Over the years we have worked with directed facial actions (constructing emotional facial configurations), slides, films, relived emotions (emotional imagery), staged manipulations (e.g., threatened electrical

shock at the hands of an incompetent experimenter; Ax, 1953), and dyadic interaction between intimates. Although historically most investigators have invented their own stimuli, investigators can now make use of standardized sets of slides (the International Affective Picture System [IAPS]; Lang, Greenwald, & Bradley, 1988) and films (Gross & Levenson, 1995).

Each of the methods commonly used for eliciting emotion has strengths and weaknesses. Figure 11.2 summarizes my experience with these methods. Invariably, the investigator is faced with a frustrating trade-off between ecological validity and experimental control. Thus tasks that are most similar to contexts in which human emotions typically occur (e.g., unrehearsed, minimally structured dyadic interactions between intimates) can be an experimental nightmare. In contrast, tasks with very tight experimental control (e.g., directed facial actions, which give the experimenter precise control of which emotion is displayed on the face and when) are not very representative of the ways in which emotions usually occur.

Furthermore, the six emotions commonly studied in autonomic specificity research (anger, disgust, fear, happiness, sadness, surprise) are not equally accessible using the different elicitors. Based on my own experience, and using a convergent criterion that considers an emotion most likely to have been successfully elicited if facial, autonomic, and subjective indicators are all present, I have included a column in Figure 11.2 that indicates the emotions that are particularly difficult to elicit using the various techniques.

Finally, there is the issue raised earlier about whether we are eliciting "real" emotions or not. With the directed facial action task, the experimental demand to report the emotion constructed on the face is high, even if that emotion is not actually felt. With external visual stimuli such as slides and films, it is common for participants actually to feel no emotion but to report feeling emotions that in reality represent their judgments of the emotional qualities of the stimuli. The "real-life" elicitors (staged manipulations and dyadic interactions) seem most likely to produce "real" emotions but not without incurring a number of costs, including loss of experimental control, appearance of complex sequences of emotions, and, in the case of staged manipulations, serious ethical and human-participants issues.

## Emotion Verification

Even if emotion elicitation tasks were usually successful in producing the desired emotion in most participants; even if the autonomic nervous system was inactive before and after being recruited in the service of emotion; even if emotion elicitations in the laboratory had the kind of sharp onset, close match to prototype, and high intensity that reliably produced full-blown emotional reactions; even if the autonomic concomitants of specific emotions were dramatically different; and even if effect sizes were huge, then it would still be critical to ensure that the autonomic physiology derived on a particular trial from a particular participant was in fact associated with the actual occurrence of the targeted emotion. In reality, none of these "ideal case" scenarios is likely to be true. Even the best of the available elicitation tasks often have unintended emotional outcomes; the autonomic nervous system is continually acting in the service of many masters other than emotion; laboratory-induced emotional elicitations are often pale comparisons of real-life ones; participants' emotional responses are often of low intensity and often include emotions other than the intended one; autonomic correlates of emotions are not unique but rather show complex patterns of overlap; and effect sizes are small.

For all of these reasons, it seems absolutely critical to verify the emotional state of participants on some independent basis and to derive conclusions about the autonomic correlates of emotional states from data obtained on trials on which participants are most likely to have actually experienced the targeted emotion. To fail to do this introduces a great deal of additional noise into an already noisy system and greatly undermines the value of such research in addressing the issue of autonomic specificity. The need for verification seems so compelling and so obvious that one would expect reasonable verification to be an important part of any study intending to assess autonomic specificity. With autonomic physiology serving as the dependent variable in these studies, verification of participants' emotional states needs to rely on some non-autonomic indicator such as emotional facial behavior or self-report or ideally both. And importantly, once the verification has been carried out, there must be some rational

plan to use it to inform the subsequent data analyses. Has this in fact been done? Examination of the "classic" literature on emotional specificity reveals few, if any, studies that have adequately verified the emotional states of participants and used this information in a meaningful way in subsequent data analyses.

Consider these examples. Ax (1953) used an interview procedure to determine the emotional states produced by elicitors that targeted fear and anger. However, the interview was conducted 10 minutes after the second elicitor; thus, in the case of the first elicitor, participants were making retrospective statements about emotions that had occurred 30 minutes earlier. Moreover, the decision rules to deal with elicitation failures were not stated. Sternbach (1962) used a single film to study sadness, fear, pleasantness, and amusement. Participants were interviewed about their feelings 10 minutes after the film—all data were used in the subsequent analyses. Schwartz and colleagues (Schwartz, Weinberger, & Singer, 1981) used emotional imagery to study happiness, anger, sadness, and fear. Self-reports of emotion were obtained 7 minutes after each image ended (within this 7-minute period, a 1-minute physical exercise task also occurred)—all data were used in subsequent analyses. Roberts and Weerts (1982) also used imagery to study anger and fear. Self-report ratings were obtained following each trial, but again all data were used in subsequent analyses.

As pertains to verification, probably the best of the early studies of autonomic specificity was conducted by Funkenstein and colleagues (Funkenstein, King, & Drolette, 1954). Using criticism of performance on a math task to elicit anger-in, anger-out, and anxiety, they interviewed participants 10 minutes after the task to determine which emotions they experienced. Based on these interviews, 25% of the data were excluded. This procedure did have one questionable feature, however; they included in the analyses participants who experienced both anger and anxiety, which would seem to compromise their ability to distinguish between the two emotions.

Although verification sounds as if it should be useful, it is certainly reasonable to ask whether it makes any appreciable difference. There is not much published research that directly addresses this issue other than our work using the directed facial action task (Levenson et al., 1990). In this work, we used two kinds of verification: (1) facial measurement to determine if the targeted facial configurations were produced, and (2) self-report of emotional experience. To simplify presentation of these data, I use an index of the extent of specificity among negative emotions that we used in this research. This index is derived by computing "hit rates" (which represent whether an individual participant showed or did not show each of four differences between pairs of emotions found in group data—heart rate greater during anger than during disgust, heart rate greater during fear than during disgust, heart rate greater during sadness than during disgust, finger temperature greater during anger than during fear).

In Figure 11.3 the hit rates are portrayed when the facial configurations in the comparisons are of low quality (i.e., they did not closely resemble the intended emotion prototype) versus high quality (i.e., they did closely resemble the intended emotion prototype). The hit rates (and thus the evidence of autonomic specificity) are significantly higher for data derived from the high-quality faces.

Figure 11.4 portrays hit rates when participants reported feeling the emotion associated with the facial configurations versus when they did not. Again, the hit rates are significantly higher for data derived when the targeted emotion is present.

These data, derived from one series of studies that used one eliciting task, are indicative of the potential clarity that can come from using reasonable verification procedures. Although we have not previously published these data, we found the same advantages when we used self-report verification criteria with the relived emotions task. Similar improvements over unverified data have been reported by others using verification procedures based on emotional facial behavior when examining EEG measures of regional brain activation obtained during a film eliciting task (Davidson et al., 1990)

### Emotion Timing

There are several theoretical and methodological issues related to timing that are of particular importance for research on autonomic specificity. The first of these pertains to the time course of affective phenomena. Ekman (1984) has provided a useful discussion of this issue in which he arrays affective phenomena in terms of their increasing duration, starting with emotions, then moods, emotional traits, emotional plots, and, finally, emotional disorders. Emotions are the briefest of these phenomena, usually lasting only a matter of seconds. Compared with emotions,

moods represent more enduring changes in affective tone, lasting from hours to days, with the stimulus conditions being less punctate and not always recognizable. Over the years, studies of autonomic correlations of affective states have addressed the entire range of affective phenomena. However, autonomic specificity, at least as it has been defined in the psychophysiological tradition, pertains to emotions and not to the longer affective phenomena. For that reason, it is important that attempts to aggregate data across multiple experiments do not mix apples and oranges (for example, comparing cardiovascular patterns during anger with those associated with being in an irritable mood or having a hostile personality).

The second issue is more practical, having to do with the temporal matching of autonomic measurement to the occurrence of emotion. As noted earlier, the autonomic nervous system is the slave to many masters, serving the needs of a host of bodily processes, including skeletal muscle demands, digestion, postural adjustments, thermoregulation, and so forth. According to the model I have proposed (Levenson, 1994, 1999), emotions such as anger, fear, sadness, and disgust briefly take the reins of the autonomic nervous system and alter its pattern of activation in service of behaviors that are likely to deal successfully with particular problems and challenges that face the organism. It is during this brief period in which the autonomic nervous system is under the control of emotion that we would expect to find autonomic specificity. Before the emotion asserts its influence and after it relinquishes control, autonomic activity will reflect other forces, and emotion-related patterning will not be found. In this regard, the autonomic nervous system is similar to other physiological systems that are taken over momentarily by emotion. For example, prior to the onset of emotion, the facial muscles may be serving a variety of functions, such as speech production and illustration; but in the throes of an emotion, a set of particular muscle actions can occur that signal the person's emotional state to others. After the emotion recedes, the facial muscle system, like the auto-

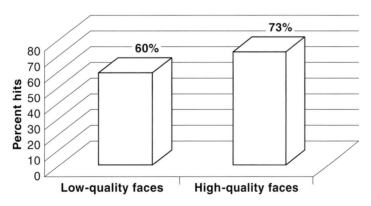

Figure 11.3  Impact of quality of facial configuration on extent of autonomic specificity.

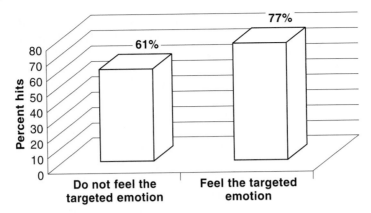

Figure 11.4 Impact of self-report of target emotion on extent of autonomic specificity.

nomic nervous system, goes back to its other activities with no residual sign that the emotion ever occurred.

In research using other physiological systems that show this kind of tight temporal linkage to the eliciting stimulus, great care is taken to ensure that measurements are time-locked to the stimulus onset. Thus, in measuring the electrocortical response evoked by a given stimulus, the EEG response is measured in a particular time window. Often with such systems, averaging over many stimulus presentations may be necessary to reveal the signal (e.g., a cortical event-related potential) against the background of noncontingent activity. In research on autonomic specificity, attempts to average across even two elicitations have been rare. Moreover, the temporal matching between measurement and emotion onset has often been lax, making it quite possible that the measured physiology has nothing to do with the elicited emotion.

Again, a look at the "classic" specificity literature will be illustrative. Ax (1953) induced fear and anger using complex manipulations (e.g., an incompetent experimenter) that stretched out over a 5-minute period. For each measured physiological function, the maximum and minimum levels reached during the 5-minute elicitation period plus the following 2 minutes were calculated and used to represent the targeted emotion. This is not an unreasonable approach, but it does have problems. For example, during the 7-minute period, one would expect a number of different emotions (targeted and nontargeted) to come and go. No attempt was made to match the autonomic responses to the occurrence of particular emotions. Nonetheless, the emotional induction and physiological measurement clearly had some amount of overlap.

In a number of other studies, the autonomic data that were analyzed were obtained *after* rather than *during* the emotion induction. Funkenstein and colleagues (Funkenstein et al., 1954) induced emotion by criticizing participants' performances, but all autonomic measures were obtained after the criticism was over. Similarly, Schwartz and colleagues (Schwartz et al., 1981) used imagery to induce emotion, but their autonomic data were obtained af-

ter the images ended. Stemmler (1989), in his "real life" inductions of fear, anger, and happiness, extracted physiological data during a 1-minute period following the end of the inductions.

In evaluating these studies, we unfortunately lack knowledge about the time course of any patterned autonomic response produced by an emotion. If this patterning continues long after the offset of the stimulus, then the reviewed studies were likely to be measuring the emotion-related autonomic response. If the patterning offsets rapidly, then they were likely measuring autonomic activity related to other, nonemotional activities of the organism.

## The Future of Specificity Research

### Specificity in the Autonomic Nervous System

Following the second flurry of research on this topic in the 1980s and early 1990s, activity in this area seems once again to have diminished. This is unfortunate for several reasons. First and foremost, it is my belief that despite more than 50 years of empirical work, we still do not have a definitive answer as to the extent of autonomic specificity in emotion. Despite the general belief in various cultures in autonomic specificity and a number of empirical findings that support its existence, there still does not exist a body of well-replicated, well-designed research that would settle this issue. Second, the extent of autonomic specificity is important to our understanding of the nature of emotion. As I pointed out earlier, autonomic specificity has profound implications for a number of theoretical formulations about the nature of emotion. Third, assuming that there is at least some degree of autonomic specificity for at least some emotions, then there are a host of interesting auxiliary issues that remain to be investigated.

### Specificity for Positive Emotions

In research on autonomic specificity, the positive emotions have received far less attention than the negative.

Often, when positive emotion has been studied, only a single positive emotion (e.g., happiness) has been included. In considering these issues a number of years ago (Levenson, 1988), I argued that the lack of association between positive emotions and behaviors that involve high-activity motor programs makes autonomic patterning for positive emotions less likely than for negative emotions. In that work, I proposed a model of positive emotions as efficient "undoers" of the autonomic activation provoked by negative emotion. Subsequently, Fredrickson and I were able to demonstrate that this was indeed the case for the positive emotions of amusement and contentment (Fredrickson & Levenson, 1998). Beyond this, the question of autonomic specificity for positive emotions remains unanswered. Subsequent work on this question should consider a broad range of positive emotions, including amusement and contentment, as well as calmness, excitement, joy, pride, awe, and love.

## Temporal Organization and Interrelations of Emotion Response Systems

Many biologically oriented emotion researchers specialize in a single response system, such as visible facial expression, subvisible facial electromyographic activity, subjective emotional experience, acoustic properties of speech, autonomic nervous system activity, electrocortical or hemodynamic brain activity, or neurohormonal activity. What is needed is integrative research that advances our understanding of how these response systems are coordinated in emotion. Very basic questions, such as the temporal organization of facial response, autonomic response, electrocortical response, and subjective experience in emotion, remain largely unexamined. A related set of issues concerns the duration of autonomic specificity. Our work suggests that the activation of individual components of the autonomic responses can continue for some time (Fredrickson & Levenson, 1998), but we do not know how long the emotion-specific *pattern* is maintained.

## Autonomic Concomitants of Blended and Sequential Emotions

In research on autonomic specificity, we often try to stimulate pure emotions—single emotions rather than a blend of emotions, and emotions that are isolated in time from other emotions. In this way, the autonomic activity associated with different emotions can be identified. In the natural world, however, emotions typically do not occur in such splendid isolation. Rather, they may occur in blends with other emotions or in sequences in which one emotion segues into another. Once we have identified emotions with different autonomic signatures, it will be important to determine what happens to this patterning when two emotions with different signatures combine or when they follow each other closely in time.

## Alternative Motor Programs for Different Emotions

If the basis for autonomic specificity is a mapping between emotions and motor programs (with their need for a particular configuration of autonomic support), then the simplest model of specificity would be a single pattern of autonomic activity for each emotion. However, if emotions have multiple associated motor programs (e.g., "flight" and "freezing" in fear), each requiring a different configuration of autonomic support, this begs the question of whether, at least for *some* emotions, there are multiple associated autonomic patterns, depending on the particular motor program that is activated.

## Generalizability Across Modes of Elicitation

The question of whether emotion-specific autonomic activity is consistent across modes of emotion elicitation has been nicely framed by Stemmler (1989), who argues for the importance of context in determining patterns of autonomic activity. In my review of four specific autonomic differences among negative emotions (Levenson, 1992), I found evidence for these same patterns in studies using quite different modes of elicitation. We (Levenson, Carstensen, Friesen, & Ekman, 1991) have also presented evidence in a single sample of participants exposed to multiple elicitors for this kind of generalizability across modes of elicitation for some autonomic differences among emotions. Generalizability to visual stimuli, such as films and slides, presents special challenges in this regard because there are strong autonomic correlates of orienting to the slides and films that can make it difficult to detect any emotion-specific autonomic activity. Clearly, this is an area in need of additional research.

## Generalizability Across Sources of Individual Variation

In our work we have demonstrated generalizability of emotion-specific autonomic activity across gender (Levenson et al., 1990), young and old age (Levenson et al., 1991), and U.S. and West Sumatran cultures (Levenson et al., 1992). Clearly, this is just a beginning—there are many important issues pertaining to development, personality, and culture that remain to be explored.

## Controlled Emotions

Emotions often occur in contexts in which the individual's learning history (e.g., cultural proscriptions) acts to limit free emotional expression. Such emotion control, whether it is conscious or unconscious, voluntary or involuntary, inhibition or exaggeration, could alter the patterns of autonomic activity usually associated with that emotion. In our work on emotion suppression (Gross, 1998; Gross & Levenson, 1993, 1997), it appears that there may be a general pattern that is consistent across emotions when emotional behavior is voluntarily suppressed, but beyond that we know little about this issue.

## Specificity in the Central Nervous System

In recent years, the spotlight in affective science has moved away from the autonomic nervous system and toward the brain. Localization of psychological functions in particular brain regions has always assumed an important role in brain research and continues to do so. New measurement methodologies offer the potential for studying activation sequences across different brain regions, which may go beyond mere localization and shed new light on the dynamics of the working brain.

Although human neuroscience maintains its longstanding interest in memory and other cognitive processes, there is clearly an explosion of interest in emotion and affective phenomena. At this juncture, most of this work has not been concerned with emotional specificity per se, perhaps reflecting the "traditional" undifferentiated model that places all emotional processing in the right hemisphere. However, a number of important challenges to this model now exist, especially models that situate certain classes of emotions (positive, approach-oriented) in left anterior brain regions (e.g., Davidson, 1993). To this point, however, most brain localization research has conceptualized emotion in terms of dimensions (positive-negative, approach-avoidance) rather than discrete emotions. Perhaps, with better experimental paradigms for eliciting discrete emotions repeatedly (or sustained over time), specificity of brain regions (and/or activation sequences) for some discrete emotions may be revealed. If not, we may be left with an interesting lack of parallelism, with emotional specificity in the central nervous system organized around dimensions and emotional specificity in the autonomic nervous system organized around discrete emotions.

Regardless of the ultimate organization, studies of specificity in the brain will have to address the same issues concerning emotion elicitation, verification, and temporal matching that beleaguer studies of autonomic specificity. As measures of brain functioning get more and more sophisticated and more precise in terms of temporal and spatial resolution, it may be tempting to become lax in the elicitation side of the research. However, the data derived from such studies will only be as good as their weakest link, and, as I hope this chapter has demonstrated, it is very easy to intend to study particular emotions but to end up missing the target. In fMRI studies, with participants lying on their backs in narrow tubes for hours on end, with

their heads in vises, with loud hammering sounds in the background, and with major constraints on the kinds of emotional stimuli that can be used, the challenges for those wishing to conduct serious studies of the organization of brain function in emotion will be enormous.

## NOTES

Preparation of this chapter was supported by grants from the National Institute of Mental Health (MH50841) and the National Institute on Aging (AG17766).

1. In the earlier model, there was another subprogram for subjective emotional experience. In the ensuing years, I have come to view subjective emotional experience as deriving primarily from sensations associated with activation of the other response systems such as the face, physiology, vocal apparatus, and muscles. This sensory information can subsequently be integrated with appraisals of the environmental conditions when we engage in the act of labeling our emotional states.

2. In chapter 9 in this volume, Jänig discusses the function that the autonomic nervous system plays in protective reactions of the body during defensive behaviors such as flight, quiescence, and confrontation. Jänig suggests that the autonomic concomitants of these behaviors are integrated in the lateral and ventrolateral columns of the periaqueductal gray.

3. This "either/or" mentality is quite unfortunate. I believe that Schachter and Singer's model does in fact describe *one* way that emotion can be elicited. A system as important to our survival as emotion would likely be designed with multiple methods of activation. Thus, surely, there are instances in which we find ourselves aroused for no immediately apparent reason and search for explanations as to why that might be. However, this is just one of a number of different ways in which emotions can be activated.

## REFERENCES

Alexander, F. (1950). *Psychosomatic medicine: Its principles and applications.* New York: Norton.

Ax, A. F. (1953). The physiological differentiation between fear and anger in humans. *Psychosomatic Medicine, 15,* 433–442.

Bower, G. H. (1981). Mood and memory. *American Psychologist, 36*(2), 129–148.

Cacioppo, J. T., Klein, D. J., Berntson, G. G., & Hatfield, E. (1993). The psychophysiology of emotion. In M. Lewis & J. M. Haviland (Eds.), *Handbook of emotions* (pp. 119–142). New York: Guilford Press.

Cannon, W. B. (1927). The James-Lange theory of emotions: A critical examination and an alternative theory. *American Journal of Psychology, 39,* 106–124.

Davidson, R. J. (1993). The neuropsychology of emotion and affective style. In M. Lewis & J. M. Haviland (Eds.), *Handbook of emotions* (pp. 143–154). New York: Guilford Press.

Davidson, R. J., Ekman, P., Saron, C. D., Senulis, J. A., & Friesen, W. V. (1990). Approach-withdrawal and cerebral asymmetry: Emotional expression and brain physiology. I. *Journal of Personality and Social Psychology, 58*(2), 330–341.

Diamond, E. L. (1982). The role of anger and hostility in

essential hypertension and coronary heart disease. *Psychological Bulletin, 92*, 410–433.

Ekman, P. (1984). Expression and the nature of emotion. In K. R. Scherer & P. Ekman (Eds.), *Approaches to emotion* (pp. 319–343). Hillsdale, NJ: Erlbaum.

Ekman, P. (1992). An argument for basic emotions. *Cognition and Emotion, 6*(3–4), 169–200.

Ekman, P., & Friesen, W. V. (1969). The repertoire of nonverbal behavior: Categories, origins, usage, and coding. *Semiotica, 1*, 49–98.

Ekman, P., & Friesen, W. V. (1971). Constants across cultures in the face and emotion. *Journal of Personality and Social Psychology, 17*, 124–129.

Ekman, P., Levenson, R. W., & Friesen, W. V. (1983). Autonomic nervous system activity distinguishes among emotions. *Science, 221*, 1208–1210.

Ekman, P., Sorenson, E. R., & Friesen, W. V. (1969). Pancultural elements in facial displays of emotion. *Science, 164*, 86–88.

Fredrickson, B. L., & Levenson, R. W. (1998). Positive emotions speed recovery from the cardiovascular sequelae of negative emotions. *Cognition and Emotion, 12*(2), 191–220.

Frijda, N. H. (1986). *The emotions.* Cambridge, England: Cambridge University Press.

Funkenstein, D. H., King, S. H., & Drolette, M. (1954). The direction of anger during a laboratory stress-inducing situation. *Psychosomatic Medicine, 16*, 404–413.

Graham, D. T., Stern, J. A., & Winokur, G. (1958). Experimental investigation of the specificity of attitude hypothesis in psychosomatic disease. *Psychosomatic Medicine, 20*, 446–457.

Graham, D. T., Stern, J. A., & Winokur, G. (1960). The concept of a different specific set of physiological changes in each emotion. *Psychiatric Research Reports, 12*, 8–15.

Gross, J. J. (1998). Antecedent- and response-focused emotion regulation: Divergent consequences for experience, expression, and physiology. *Journal of Personality and Social Psychology, 74*(1), 224–237.

Gross, J. J., & Levenson, R. W. (1993). Emotional suppression: Physiology, self-report, and expressive behavior. *Journal of Personality and Social Psychology, 64*(6), 970–986.

Gross, J. J., & Levenson, R. W. (1995). Emotion elicitation using films. *Cognition and Emotion, 9*(1), 87–108.

Gross, J. J., & Levenson, R. W. (1997). Hiding feelings: The acute effects of inhibiting negative and positive emotion. *Journal of Abnormal Psychology, 106*(1), 95–103.

Hochschild, A. R. (1979). Emotion work, feeling rules, and social structure. *American Journal of Sociology, 84*, 551–575.

Izard, C. E. (1971). *The face of emotion.* New York: Appleton-Century-Crofts.

James, W. (1884). What is an emotion? *Mind, 9*, 188–205.

Kovecses, Z. (1989). *Emotion concepts.* New York: Springer-Verlag.

Lakoff, G. (1987). *Women, fire, and dangerous things.* Chicago: University of Chicago Press.

Lang, P. J., Greenwald, M. K., & Bradley, M. M. (1988). *The International Affective Picture System (IAPS) standardization procedure and initial group results for affective judgments* (Tech. Rep. Nos. 1A–1D). Gainesville: University of Florida, Center for the Study of Emotion and Attention.

Levenson, R. W. (1988). Emotion and the autonomic nervous system: A prospectus for research on autonomic specificity. In H. L. Wagner (Ed.), *Social psychophysiology and emotion: Theory and clinical applications* (pp. 17–42). Chichester, England: Wiley.

Levenson, R. W. (1992). Autonomic nervous system differences among emotions. *Psychological Science, 3*(1), 23–27.

Levenson, R. W. (1994). Human emotion: A functional view. In P. Ekman & R. J. Davidson (Eds.), *The nature of emotion: Fundamental questions* (pp. 123–126). New York: Oxford University Press.

Levenson, R. W. (1999). The intrapersonal functions of emotion. *Cognition and Emotion, 13*, 481–504.

Levenson, R. W., Carstensen, L. L., Friesen, W. V., & Ekman, P. (1991). Emotion, physiology, and expression in old age. *Psychology and Aging, 6*(1), 28–35.

Levenson, R. W., Ekman, P., & Friesen, W. V. (1990). Voluntary facial action generates emotion-specific autonomic nervous system activity. *Psychophysiology, 27*(4), 363–384.

Levenson, R. W., Ekman, P., Heider, K., & Friesen, W. V. (1992). Emotion and autonomic nervous system activity in the Minangkabau of West Sumatra. *Journal of Personality and Social Psychology, 62*(6), 972–988.

Mandler, G. (1975). *Mind and emotion.* New York: Wiley.

Marchitelli, L., & Levenson, R. W. (1992, October). *When couples converse: The language and physiology of emotion.* Paper presented at the meeting of the Society for Psychophysiological Research, San Diego, CA.

Mathews, A., & Bradley, B. P. (1983). Mood and the self-reference bias in recall. *Behaviour Research and Therapy, 21*(3), 233–239.

Ortony, A., & Turner, T. J. (1990). What's basic about basic emotions? *Psychological Review, 97*(3), 315–331.

Plutchik, R., & Ax, A. F. (1967). A critique of "Determinants of Emotional State" by Schachter and Singer (1962). *Psychophysiology, 4*(1), 79–82.

Reisenzein, R. (1983). The Schachter theory of emotion: Two decades later. *Psychological Bulletin, 94*(2), 239–264.

Roberts, R. J., & Weerts, T. C. (1982). Cardiovascular responding during anger and fear imagery. *Psychological Reports, 50*(1), 219–230.

Russell, J. A. (1994). Is there universal recognition of emotion from facial expressions? A review of the cross-cultural studies. *Psychological Bulletin, 115*(1), 102–141.

Schachter, S., & Singer, J. E. (1962). Cognitive, social, and physiological determinants of emotional state. *Psychological Review, 69*, 379–399.

Scherer, K. R., & Wallbott, H. G. (1994). Evidence for universality and cultural variation of differential emotion response patterning. *Journal of Personality and Social Psychology, 66*(2), 310–328.

Schwartz, G. E., Weinberger, D. A., & Singer, J. A. (1981). Cardiovascular differentiation of happiness, sadness, anger, and fear following imagery and exercise. *Psychosomatic Medicine, 43*(4), 343–364.

Stemmler, G. (1989). The autonomic differentiation of emotions revisited: Convergent and discriminant validation. *Psychophysiology, 26*(6), 617–632.

Sternbach, R. A. (1962). Assessing differential autonomic patterns in emotions. *Journal of Psychosomatic Research, 6*, 87–91.

Tomkins, S. S. (1962). *Affect, imagery, consciousness. Volume 1. The positive affects.* New York: Springer.

Tooby, J., & Cosmides, L. (1990). The past explains the present: Emotional adaptations and the structure of ancestral environments. *Ethology and Sociobiology, 11*(4–5), 375–424.

Turner, T. J., & Ortony, A. (1992). Basic emotions: Can conflicting criteria converge? *Psychological Review, 99*(3), 566–571.

Williams, R. B., Jr., Haney, T. L., Lee, K. L., Kong, Y., Blumenthal, J. A., & Whalen, R. E. (1980). Type A behavior, hostility, and coronary atherosclerosis. *Psychosomatic Medicine, 42*, 539–549.

Winton, W. M., Putnam, L. E., & Krauss, R. M. (1984). Facial and autonomic manifestations of the dimensional structure of emotion. *Journal of Experimental Social Psychology, 20*(3), 195–216.

Zajonc, R. B., & McIntosh, D. N. (1992). Emotions research: Some promising questions and some questionable promises. *Psychological Science, 3*(1), 70–74.

# METHODOLOGICAL CONSIDERATIONS IN THE PSYCHOPHYSIOLOGICAL STUDY OF EMOTION

Gerhard Stemmler

What is an emotion? Ever since William James asked this four-word question (James, 1884), there have been heated debates about its answer. Actually, answers are plenty, but consensus is small. As we have gradually learned, cortical, subcortical, and peripheral neuronal and humoral networks at different system levels subserve the processing of emotions. Likewise, cognitive processing at preattentive and conscious levels is complex and multifaceted. Thus emotions have many sides and give rise to many views.

Studying emotions with psychophysiological methods seems straightforward. But simply registering physiological activity while an individual is in an affective state most certainly will not advance our knowledge about emotions. The reason for this assertion is that many decisions in setting up a psychophysiological study of emotion generate a particular perspective. Methodological considerations could disclose these often tacit implications of research decisions. They can also assist in the choice of methods, including the selection of emotion induction procedures, the sampling of variables and participants, the selection of an experimental design, and strategies of statistical analysis.

## Induction of Emotion—The Context of Emotion

By far most psychophysiological studies on emotion have been conducted in the laboratory. Although the lab may not be the best place to monitor emotions with high ecological validity (Fahrenberg & Myrtek, 1996), the lab provides for a wide range of more or less standardized induction procedures that can vary in the degree of subjective meaning and ego involvement they excite. Thus emotion inductions in the lab do have some degree of ecological validity. Admittedly, the social psychology of lab experimentation can be drastically different from that in the field.

Methodologically, the choice of an emotion induction procedure may be codetermined by the theoretical perspective in which emotions are primarily embedded. From an evolutionary perspective, one would emphasize classes of situational demands for which emotions facilitate adaptive and functionally adequate solutions. From an activation-theoretical perspective, one would titrate the intensity of an emotional stimulus such that the intensity of the resulting arousal is within an optimal range given the momentary task demands and the arousability of an individual's nervous system. From a neurophysiological perspective, one would construct conditions (including drugs) that have a proven agonist or antagonist effect on the activity of a specified neurobiological system. From a learning theory perspective, one would use the powerful tools of associative learning, which enable a separation of the physical properties of an unconditioned stimulus from the cue function of the conditioned stimulus. From a cognitive perspective, one would design emotional episodes that lead to desired appraisals or attributions. In practice, various goals associated with different perspectives may combine.

## Methods of Emotion Induction

Izard (1993) presented a fourfold distinction of mechanisms that may elicit an emotion (for a meta-analytic comparison of the effectiveness of induction procedures, see Westermann, Spies, Stahl, & Hesse, 1996). These mechanisms may operate on different hierarchically organized system levels:

- Neural systems are the basis for activity at all other system levels. Nevertheless, emotions can be activated solely on this level, that is, without contributions from higher system levels.
- The sensorimotor system may contribute to emotion elicitation through somatomotor efferences and their somaesthetic reafferences.
- The motivational system includes the regulation of emotions, pain, and cyclically changing drives such as hunger, thirst, fatigue, and sexuality.
- The cognitive system may activate emotions through attributions, emotionally laden memory networks, or appraisals.

### Emotion Modulation Through Neural Processes

Different mechanisms may modulate emotions through the direct experimental manipulation of neural processes. One experimental avenue is the use of neuropeptides or of psychoactive drugs, which modulate the activity of neurotransmitters in the central or in the peripheral nervous system (Erdmann, Ising, & Janke, 2000). Well-known examples are the anxiolytic actions of antidepressives, benzodiazepines, or alcohol through the blockade of noradrenergic and serotonergic afferents; the fear-inducing properties of yohimbine or benzodiazepine agonists (Berntson, Sarter, & Caccioppo, 1998); the effects of dopaminergic agonists on positive affectivity (Depue & Collins, 1999). Another experimental avenue is the electrical stimulation of the brain, as demonstrated by the classical experiments of Hess (1948; see also Bandler, 1982; Flynn, 1967) in the cat. But electrical brain stimulation in humans could also be performed, for example, during neurosurgery. Finally, variations of blood temperature in arteries supplying the brain were reported to change the valence of feelings (Zajonc, Murphy, & Inglehart, 1989), purportedly by indirectly influencing the activity of neurotransmitters. It should be noted that most of these mechanisms will not induce an acute emotion; instead, they may modulate emotions instigated otherwise, or they may alter mood states (for the distinction between emotions and moods, see Ekman & Davidson, 1994).

### Emotion Induction Through Sensorimotor Processes

One form of the facial feedback hypothesis states that voluntary expressions similar to those shown during acute emotions serve as input to emotion systems in the brain. Changes of body posture (e.g., Bloch, Orthous, & Santibanez-H., 1987; Duclos et al., 1989) or directed facial expressions (Levenson, Carstensen, Friesen, & Ekman, 1991; Levenson, Ekman, & Friesen, 1990; Levenson, Ekman, Heider, & Friesen, 1992) have induced rather specific emotions. For the validity of the "directed facial action task," it is important that (1) the research participants are blind to the purpose of the procedure, (2) the effort to produce certain facial expressions is controlled for, and (3) a modified respiratory activity would not have unwanted influences on physiological patterns (Boiten, 1996). Levenson and Ekman (submitted) make a convincing case that in their series of studies these prerequisites were fulfilled.

### Emotion Induction Through Motivational Processes

There are different ways in which emotions may be induced through motivational processes. One way is through gustatory, olfactory, or pain stimuli (e.g., Ehrlichman & Bastone, 1992; Freedman & Ianni, 1985; Rosenstein & Oster, 1988). Pain has been elicited by electric shocks, high sound pressures, the cold pressor test, venipuncture, or skin irritation with dull needles. The effectiveness of discrete stimuli to induce emotions is probably based on those stimulus properties that activate a motivationally aversive state. Berkowitz (1983, 1990) suggested that these aversive states would ignite cognitive processes that finally lead to anger and aggression. Another way is by using pictures of human faces, spiders, snakes, or other conditioned stimuli that allow for easy associability with unconditioned noxious or threatening stimuli (see chapter 13 in this volume). Finally, emotions can be triggered by other emotions, because they may be functionally related in an individual's goal structure (Frijda, Ortony, Sonnemans, & Clore, 1992; Lazarus, 1991). For example, sadness and depression are likely followed by anger, because, functionally, anger could mobilize resources to overcome obstacles (Izard, 1993).

### Emotion Induction Through Cognitive Processes

Most emotion inductions reported in the literature have made use of mechanisms that operate on the level of cognitive processes. These include appraisals and evaluations, comparisons and judgments, attributions and beliefs, and memory and anticipation. Sample induction procedures are:

- Interviews with a choice of emotionally relevant topics or with a particular form of conduct, as in a "stress interview" (e.g., Adsett, Schottstaedt, & Wolf, 1962; Cacioppo, Martzke, Petty, & Tassinary, 1988; Van Heck, 1988).
- The Velten method (Velten, 1968), in which participants twice read 60 self-referential mood statements, each printed on a card. Participants are instructed to really feel what they read. There are versions for depressed and elated moods, as well as a neutral comparison version. The Velten technique has the advantage of easy applicability, but it has also been criticized for weak effect sizes and possible demand or expectancy effects (Alloy, Abramson, & Viscusi, 1981; Brewer, Doughtie, & Lubin, 1980; Mecklenbräuker & Hager, 1986; Polivy, 1981; Sirota & Schwartz, 1982; Spies, Hesse, Gerrards-Hesse, & Ueffing, 1991).
- Fear and nervous tension have often been induced by announcing difficult tasks or threatening stimuli, such as electric shocks (Grillon, Ameli, Woods, Merikangas, & Davis, 1991; Miltner, Larbig, & Braun, 1988), loud noises (Foulds, McAllister, & Foulds, 1988), speech tasks (Erdmann & Baumann, 1996), sports (Fahrenberg, Foerster, Schneider, Müller, & Myrtek, 1986), pictures of mutilated bodies (Regan & Howard, 1991), handgrip tasks (Mäntysaari, Antila, & Peltonen, 1988), stress interviews (Papciak, Feuerstein, & Spiegel, 1985), blood donations (Chessick, Bassan, & Shattan, 1966), or defenses of doctoral theses (van Doornen & Turner, 1992).
- Presentation of films (Gross & Levenson, 1993), pictures (Hamm & Vaitl, 1993; Lang, Greenwald, Bradley, & Hamm, 1993), pieces of music (Nyklicek, Thayer, & van Doornen, 1997; Vaitl, Vehrs, & Sternagel, 1993), and radio plays (Davison, Williams, Nezami, Bice, & DeQuattro, 1991) have often been used. Presentation of emotional stimuli per se does not guarantee the production of an emotion in the perceiver; in the first place, the perceiver's task is to decode the material presented for emotional meaning (Davidson & Irwin, 1999).
- Interpersonal episodes, in which participants are deliberately enacting a role or in which—without knowing it in advance—they are part of a script ending in an emotional episode, may offer a somewhat more naturalistic context for the induction of emotions. Hence, these forms of emotion induction have been called "real-life" inductions. Simpler variants of real-life inductions use bogus feedback about the performance in a previous task, an intelligence test, a personality questionnaire, or the attitude of a confederate toward the participant. More elaborate variants rely on the acting skills of experimenters and confederates (Ax, 1953; Engebretson, Matthews, & Scheier, 1989; Schachter & Singer, 1962; Stemmler, 1989; Stemmler, Heldmann, Pauls, & Scherer, 2001; Suarez & Williams, 1989).
- Because real-life emotion inductions can pose ethical problems and often require good acting skills, imagery has been increasingly used for the induction of emotions. Participants are asked either to imagine standard scripts or to recollect prior emotional episodes (e.g., Fridlund, Schwartz, & Fowler, 1984; Lang, Levin, Miller, & Kozak, 1983; Roberts & Weerts, 1982; Sinha, Lovallo, & Parsons, 1992).
- Hypnosis has sometimes been used for the induction of emotions. In such studies, using suggestibility as the criterion, participants have often been highly selected (e.g., Gottlieb, Gleser, & Gottschalk, 1967; Graham, Kabler, & Graham, 1962; Maslach, 1979).
- Attribution theory (Weiner, 1990) emphasizes cognitive variables that are deemed to be relevant for the activation of emotion, for example, the locus of control for the activation of anger (Hodapp, Heiligtag, & Stormer, 1990).
- There have also been attempts to give participants the choice of which mechanism for emotion induction to employ, for example, gesture and facial expression or the imagination of personal emotion episodes (U. Hess, Kappas, McHugo, Lanzetta, & Kleck, 1992).

## Criteria for the Evaluation of Emotion Inductions

In addition to general evaluation criteria for emotion induction procedures, the emotion researcher using psychophysiological methods needs to consider specific criteria as well. General criteria (M. Martin, 1990) are the congruence of the actually elicited emotion with the intended emotion; the intensity, duration, and the patterning of the induced emotions; the number of participants successfully induced; interindividual differences in the patterning of emotions; and the ethical defensibleness of the emotion induction procedure, especially if a complete prior informing of participants would interfere with a successful induction, as, for example, in real-life induction settings. Additional evaluation criteria are decisive in psychophysiological emotion research, including differential effects of coping with an emotion, situational and social context effects, and demand effects.

Differential effects of coping with an emotion pose two problems. On the one hand, emotionally challenged individuals may make use of different habitual coping mechanisms (Carver, Scheier, & Weintraub, 1989; Gross, 1998a, 1998b)—for example, repression or sensitization

(Asendorpf & Scherer, 1983; Weinberger, 1990); vigilant or avoidant processing of threat (Krohne, 1989); or modes of anger coping (R. Martin & Watson, 1997). Such individual differences could easily dilute emotion effects through an increase of error variance. On the other hand, coping with emotions can lead to dissociations among behavioral, verbal, and physiological activations (Böddeker & Stemmler, 2000). Dissociations make it difficult to judge the success of an emotion induction because the results from different response systems may no longer converge.

A further aspect in the evaluation of emotion inductions that needs attention in psychophysiological investigations is the situational and social context of an induction. There is ample evidence that not only physical tasks, body postures, and their associated motor behaviors but also psychological influences, such as attention or mental effort, exert an effect on physiological responding. Thus, nonemotional physical, behavioral, and psychological factors influence physiological activation during emotion, and it is likely that many physiological variables contain confounds from both the nonemotional context and emotions or their direct effects.

A last aspect in the evaluation of emotion inductions in psychophysiological research concerns expectancy and demand effects. Expecting or even knowing the emotion to be induced may lead to wanted and unwanted consequences. A wanted effect could be the activation of emotion memory networks that facilitate the formation of an emotion proper (Lang, 1979). In contrast, in complying to a perceived demand, participants could be primed to report emotions they are not actually feeling, which is clearly an unwanted effect. Whenever the target emotion is concealed from the research participant, demand effects should be either assessed in a postexperimental interview or, preferably, experimentally controlled (Krantz & Ratliff-Crain, 1989; Parkinson, 1985). Emotion induction procedures that are probably susceptible to expectancy effects include emotion imagery, the Velten technique, positively or negatively valent pictures presented in blocks, real-life inductions gone awry, and self-generated emotions.

## Relative Nonselectivity of Emotion Inductions

A crucial problem with emotion induction procedures is the relative nonselectivity of the emotions elicited. With emotion self-reports on rating scales used as a criterion, it has often been demonstrated that, in addition to the target emotion, other emotions were elicited as well (Polivy, 1981). A questionable selectivity of the emotions induced may easily compromise the conclusions drawn from studies designed to investigate a specific emotion: Is the psychophysiological effect caused by an emotion induction attributable to, for example, aroused anger, as intended by the experimenter, or, rather, to coaroused guilt and de-

pression, or is the effect caused by the ensemble of elicited emotions?

On analyzing the problem of relative nonselectivity of emotion inductions, it quickly becomes apparent that several controversial theoretical issues are involved. The first issue involved is the psychobiological organization of emotions. If there are biologically separable basic emotions, emotion inductions should have a high selectivity to allow studying basic emotion families separately (on basic emotions and the concept of emotion families, see Ekman, 1994). If an organization of emotion along the dimensions of positive and negative affect (Watson, Wiese, Vaidya, & Tellegen, 1999) or valence and activation (Russell & Feldman Barrett, 1999) is stipulated, lack of selectivity of emotion inductions is a much smaller problem as long as the co-occurring emotions occupy the same region in affect space.

The second issue involved is the timing of emotions and the time window for which emotion self-reports are obtained. Clearly, emotions are aroused very fast; but without recurring emotional stimuli or reactivated memories of the primary event, they may last only seconds to a few minutes (Ekman, 1994). But it is unlikely that over an appraisal-reappraisal sequence initiated by an emotional stimulus (Lazarus, 1991; Smith & Lazarus, 1990) or over the sequence of stimulus evaluation checks (K. R. Scherer, 1999) just one emotion will be activated. Rather, according to the principle of emotion-emotion activation delineated earlier, "one emotion can almost instantaneously elicit another emotion that amplifies, attenuates, inhibits or interacts with the original emotional experience" (Izard, 1972, p. 77). Because the rating of emotions has a rather low time resolution, different feelings could merge into one rating, even though they represent distinct events. Or the assessment of feelings itself might initiate renewed appraisal-reappraisal cycles, paving the way for new feelings, for example, shame after anger. The effects of the emotional stimulus per se could have been governed, however, solely by the target emotion. But still, one would expect that a "modal" emotion stands out among the others (K. R. Scherer, 1994). Then the analytical problem remains to identify the modal emotion (see the demonstration that follows).

A third issue involved in the relative nonselectivity of emotion inductions is the organization of emotion output systems. Current neurophysiological conceptualizations of emotion systems (set out in particular for the fear system; see LeDoux, 1993) state that emotion output systems operate in a feed-forward fashion; that is, at a given point in time they are independent of one another. Disregarding feedback loops from the output systems' effectors back to the core emotion processors (e.g., the amygdala in fear), feelings and their self-reports would not need to match other output systems in a one-to-one fashion (Cacioppo & Tassinary, 1990b). Empirical research has actually shown only partial correspondences between major output systems of emotion, such as verbal reports, autonomic activity, and somatomotor activity (Cacioppo, Klein, Berntson, & Hatfield, 1993). Put into a systems-analytic framework, "the structure of the affect system depends on function, which varies across the level of the nervous system (neuraxis)" (Cacioppo, Gardner, & Berntson, 1999, p. 839). Thus a relative nonselectivity of emotion inductions as revealed through emotion self-reports does not preclude that other output systems are influenced by just one emotion.

A fourth issue involved in relative nonselectivity is the homogeneity of emotion self-report responses across participants. If one subset of the participants responds with the target emotion but another subset with some other emotion, the average response profile across all participants would demonstrate nonselectivity. In this case, an emotion induction is nonselective across individuals. If, however, participants respond homogeneously with both the target emotion and other self-reported emotions, an emotion induction is nonselective within individuals. In most experimental studies, nonselectivity of emotion responses across individuals is an undesirable outcome that can be "cured" only by appropriate participant selections. Participant selection with respect to self-reports may, however, obscure important relationships with respect to other data, as for example in emotion repression or suppression (the different topic of "nonresponders" is covered in a later section of this chapter). Origins for nonselectivity of emotion responses within individuals have already been discussed in the first two points presented in this section. To the extent that the target emotion coactivated other self-reported emotions, an analytic strategy could be to partial out the target emotion from other self-reports. Nonselectivity of emotion inductions within individuals would be revealed by a drop in the emotion induction effects in the partial variables.

In sum, it seems that the relative nonselectivity of emotion inductions poses questions more than it warrants firm conclusions. At present, a lack of selectivity does not necessarily speak against the successful induction of the target emotion during the presence of the emotional stimulus or shortly thereafter, provided the target emotion stands out as modal from the corona of coactivated emotions as assessed by self-reports.

To demonstrate the effect of nonselectivity and the identification of modal emotions, I use the data of a real-life fear and anger induction from a recent experiment in my lab (Stemmler, Heldmann, Pauls, & Scherer, 1998; Stemmler et al., 2001). To identify modal emotions, two experimental design characteristics are helpful. First, we used an emotion-induction group and a separate emotion-control group. Because the emotion-control group was receiving a treatment identical to the one of the emotion-induction group with the sole difference that control participants were debriefed *before* the procedure began,

differences in emotion self-reports between these groups were expected to reflect emotion induction effects. *Nonselectivity* of emotion inductions could be inferred if the group means for induction minus control were significantly different from zero in other than the target emotions. Second, two different target emotions—fear and anger—were induced. Compared with one positive and one negative emotion, the choice of two negatively valenced emotions increased the likelihood of finding nonselective induction effects. But more important, the comparison of fear and anger emotion induction effects would help to identify any modal emotion.

The sample of female participants ($N = 158$) were randomly assigned to a fear-induction ($N = 38$), fear-control ($N = 41$), anger-induction ($N = 40$), or anger-control group ($N = 39$). Fear induction used the announcement of a speech task; anger induction, provocations by an experimenter during mental tasks (for details, see Stemmler et al., 1998, 2001). Self-reports of emotion were obtained during three periods within the ongoing emotion induction protocol. Emotion ratings were performed on six unipolar and five bipolar scales tagged by one to four descriptive adjectives. Unipolar scales were labeled *shame, fear, sadness, happiness, anger,* and *pounding heart*; bipolar scales were labeled *tense vs. relaxed, active vs. tired, positive vs. negative, alert vs. confused,* and *interested vs. bored.*

Figure 12.1 shows raw self-report means for the fear (panel 12.1a) and the anger (panel 12.1b) induction and control groups. It is obvious that both fear and anger inductions led to many self-reported emotional changes, as is evident from the significant differences between induction and control groups. Both inductions led to feelings of shame, fear, sadness, anger, and pounding heart and to more tenseness, a negative valuation, less alertness, and decreased interest. Notably, self-reported fear also increased during the anger induction, as did self-reported anger during the fear induction. These are indeed clear signs for nonselective emotion inductions. However, there existed differences between the inductions that were superimposed on a general, negatively valenced background: Fear increases during the fear induction (effect size $d = 1.61$) were about 2.6 times larger than those during the anger induction ($d = 0.62$). Conversely, anger increases during the anger induction ($d = 1.88$) were about 3.8 times larger than those during the fear induction ($d = 0.49$). These results suggested that fear and anger inductions both produced a background of negative feelings and specific increases in the target emotions. This conclusion could be substantiated by forming tetrad differences,

$$\text{tetrad difference} = (\text{fear-induction} - \text{fear-control}) \quad (1)$$
$$- (\text{anger-induction} - \text{anger-control}),$$

and testing them against zero (see Figure 12.1, panel c). Differences between the fear and anger inductions could

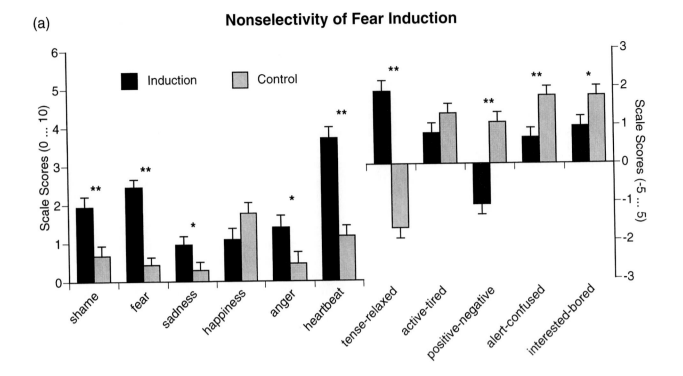

**(a) Nonselectivity of Fear Induction**

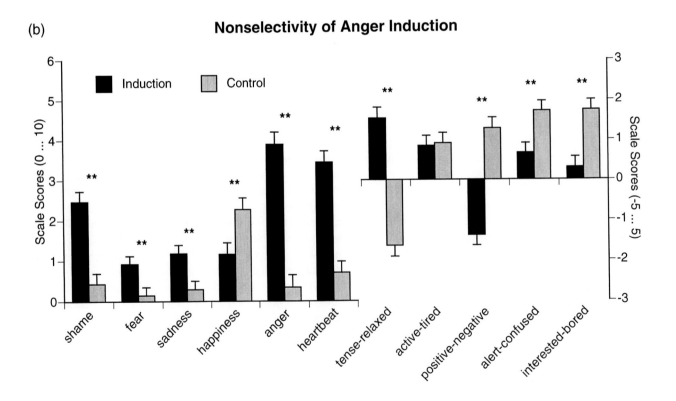

**(b) Nonselectivity of Anger Induction**

(c)
## Modal Emotion

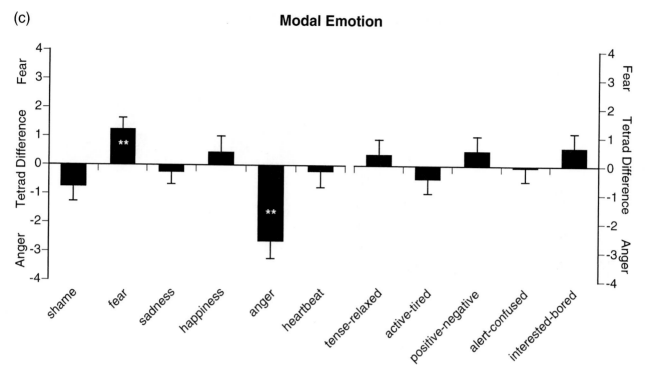

Figure 12.1 Demonstration in emotion self-reports of relative nonselectivity of real-life emotion inductions of fear (*panel a*) and anger (*panel b*). Fear-induction (*N* = 38) and anger-induction (*N* = 40) groups are contrasted with their respective fear-control (*N* = 41) and anger-control (*N* = 39) groups, which had been debriefed immediately before the induction started. Bars represent group means, error bars their standard errors. Asterisks denote significant differences between induction and respective control group means. Panel c demonstrates the identification of modal emotions by tetrad differences. Asterisks denote significant tetrad differences. Positive values denote larger induction–control group differences during fear than anger; negative values, larger differences during anger than fear. **p* ≤ .05. ***p* ≤ .01. All *t*-tests with *df* = 154.

be established only in the target emotions and in the expected direction. Clearly, self-reported fear and anger qualified as emotion-specific modal responses, whereas the other self-report scales did not.

Finally, coactivation of emotion self-reports are demonstrated with the same data set. Figure 12.2 shows emotion-induction and control-group means in the self-reports from which the target emotion had been partialed out. Partialing was performed using a heterogeneous regression slopes model, which, using, for example, self-reported shame as the dependent variable and self-reported anger as the regressor, read

$$shame = a + \beta_1 \text{ Emotion} + \beta_2 \text{ Group} + \beta_3 \text{ Emotion} \times \text{Group} + \beta_4 \text{ anger} + \beta_5 \text{ Emotion} \times \text{anger} + \beta_6 \text{ Group} \times \text{anger} + \beta_7 \text{ Emotion} \times \text{Group} \times \text{anger} \quad (2)$$

with *a* = intercept, β = regression weights, Emotion = fear versus anger induction, Group = induction versus control group.

Panel a of Figure 12.2 presents the fear induction data

with self-reports of fear partialed out of the other self-reports. In comparison with panel a of Figure 12.1, which presents the unpartialed raw data, differences between induction and control groups in nontarget emotions became less pronounced. Significant emotion induction effects vanished in self-reported shame, sadness, anger, and interest; effects, though reduced, remained in pounding heart, tenseness, negative valuation, and alertness. These results suggest that the fear induction produced coactivated, nonselective self-reports within individuals mainly in the discrete emotion rating scales (shame, sadness, anger) but nonselective self-reports across individuals predominantly in the bipolar rating dimensions of nervous tension, affective evaluation, and mental alertness. Panel b of Figure 12.2 (compare with panel b of Figure 12.1) shows the anger induction data with self-reports of anger partialed out of the other self-reports. In this case partialing led to a complete absence of emotion induction effects in self-reports other than the target emotion of anger. Again, this result confirms that in self-reports anger was the modal emotion elicited by the anger induction. It can

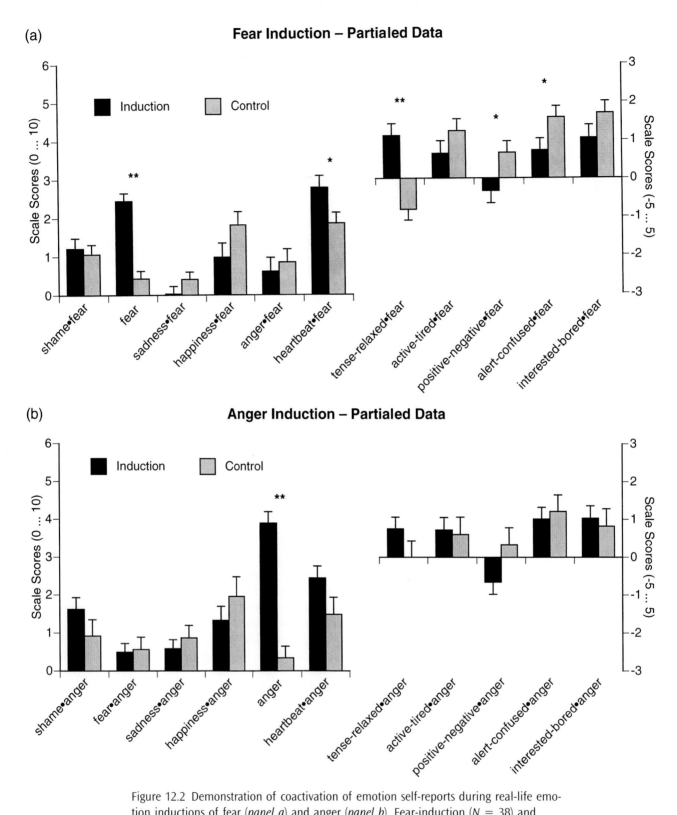

Figure 12.2 Demonstration of coactivation of emotion self-reports during real-life emotion inductions of fear (*panel a*) and anger (*panel b*). Fear-induction ($N = 38$) and anger-induction ($N = 40$) groups are contrasted with their respective fear-control ($N = 41$) and anger-control ($N = 39$) groups. Bars represent group means of self-reports from which the target emotion was partialed out. Error bars depict their standard errors. Asterisks denote significant differences between induction and respective control group means. *$p \leq .05$. **$p \leq .01$. All *t*-tests with $df = 150$.

be concluded that the anger induction produced coactivated, nonselective self-reports within individuals.

## The Challenge of Emotion-Context Confounds

What people tell us about their feelings or whether and how they express an emotion is obviously a function of an audience that can listen to and observe their affective responses. Many psychological concepts, such as emotion regulation (Gross, 1998a; Gross & John, 1997), repression (Asendorpf & Scherer, 1983; Mendolia, Moore, & Tesser, 1996), or suppression (Dimsdale et al., 1986; Gross & Levenson, 1997), make use of both individual differences in and situational determinants of affective responses. Physiological responses during emotions, on the other hand, are considered uncontrollable and unmodifiable (hence the term *passion* for emotion, from Latin *pati*, to suffer, in use for about 2,000 years of occidental history; see Averill, 1974). But even though physiological responses are hard to modify voluntarily, they are not an ongoing monitor of affective states. Too many influences place their demands on somatovisceral effectors for one specific influence, emotion effects, to pop out unconditionally. Such influences include body posture, ambient temperature, circadian rhythms, and motor activity but also psychological influences such as attention or mental effort. Collectively, these nonemotional influences are termed *context effects*. Some or all of these context effects on somatovisceral activation are certainly operating also during emotion episodes, which means that emotion and context effects are easily confounded and hard to disentangle (more on this subject can be found in the sections "Experimental Design" and "Statistical Analysis" later in this chapter).

For the emotion researcher, an obvious conclusion would be to select an emotion induction procedure that minimizes unwanted context effects. Imagining standard emotion scripts or personal recollections of prior emotional episodes in one's life come close to this objective (e.g., Sinha et al., 1992; Sinha & Parsons, 1996). A potential disadvantage of the imagination technique, however, is the small magnitude of somatovisceral responses during imagery. Real-life emotion inductions, on the contrary, try to engage the participant in diverse physical or mental tasks and should therefore introduce considerable context effects.

Using data from the experiment described previously (Stemmler et al., 1998, 2001), context effects can easily be demonstrated for both emotion self-reports and somatovisceral variables. Data from this experiment allow us to contrast the contexts of real-life inductions with those of an imagination session that took place 1 week later with the same participants. Context effects devoid of emotion effects should be apparent in the control groups that were debriefed before the emotion inductions. During the imag-

ination session, participants recalled the real-life induction from the previous week.

Figure 12.3 shows the data of the combined fear-control and anger-control groups for real-life and imagination contexts. The data are depicted as change scores from an initial rest period to the emotion induction periods and expressed in standard z-scores. In emotion self-reports (Figure 12.3, panel a), context effects were apparent in feelings of a pounding heart and in tenseness, which were more intense during imagination than during real life. An opposite picture emerged from the somatovisceral variables (Figure 12.3, panel b). During real-life sessions, physiological activation was considerably larger than during imagination sessions, as demonstrated in shorter heart period, smaller T-wave amplitude, larger Heather index (estimate of left-ventricular contractility), and higher number of skin conductance responses.

The illustrative data in Figure 12.3 suggest that context effects were indeed operating. However, emotion self-reports and somatovisceral activation seemed to connect to different aspects of the context. Somatovisceral activation was bound to the actual physical and cognitive task structure, which was more arousing during real life. Self-reports of emotion, however, primarily captured meaning structures, which despite large context differences did not much differ. The higher ratings of pounding heart and of tenseness during imagination sessions suggest that the quiet and introspective imagination context invited bodily attributions that were not, however, substantiated by the physiological data as valid interoceptions.

## Assessment of Emotions— Sampling Variables

### Self-Reports of Emotion

The assessment of subjectively felt emotions is perhaps the least standardized technique in the arsenal of the emotion researcher. It is telling that in the past decades the prestigious journal *Psychophysiology* has published several publication guidelines for physiological variables, but none for emotion self-reports. At the same time, emotion self-reports are considered the *via regia* to the assessment of emotions (Krause, 1972). In human participants, some sort of emotion rating is indispensable. But the *what* and *how* of the assessment of feelings is decisive for a study's interpretation.

What should be assessed? A researcher's stand between dimensional and categorical models of emotion is clearly reflected in his or her choice of dimensions of an affect space, a tradition that dates back to Wilhelm Wundt (1893), or of distinct feeling qualities, an approach embraced in particular by Charles Darwin (1872). One im-

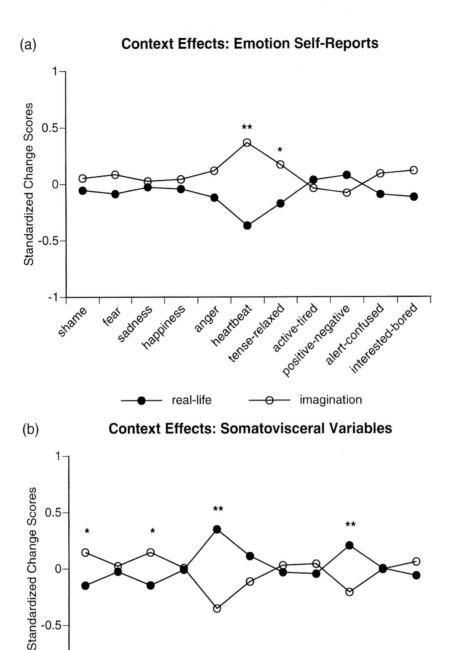

**(a)          Context Effects: Emotion Self-Reports**

*(Panel a: Standardized Change Scores plotted for shame, fear, sadness, happiness, anger, heartbeat, tense-relaxed, active-tired, positive-negative, alert-confused, interested-bored; with ** at heartbeat and * at tense-relaxed.)*

── real-life          ─○─ imagination

**(b)          Context Effects: Somatovisceral Variables**

*(Panel b: Standardized Change Scores plotted for Heart period, HP-variability, T-wave amplitude, PEP, Heather index, CO, SBP, DBP, SCR-No., EMG corrugator, EMG extensor; with * at Heart period, * at T-wave amplitude, ** at Heather index, ** at SCR-No.)*

── real-life          ─○─ imagination

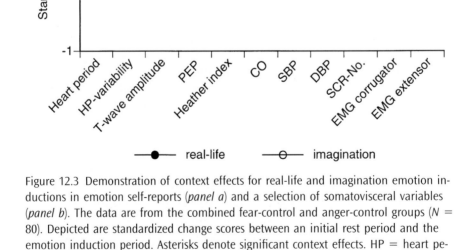

Figure 12.3 Demonstration of context effects for real-life and imagination emotion inductions in emotion self-reports (*panel a*) and a selection of somatovisceral variables (*panel b*). The data are from the combined fear-control and anger-control groups ($N = 80$). Depicted are standardized change scores between an initial rest period and the emotion induction period. Asterisks denote significant context effects. HP = heart period; PEP = preejection period; CO = cardiac output; SBP = systolic blood pressure; DBP = diastolic blood pressure; SCR-No. = Number of skin conductance responses. *$p \leq .05$. **$p \leq .01$. All *t*-tests with $df = 79$.

portant reasoning behind the dimensional model, for example, a valence–activation affect space (Lang, Bradley, & Cuthbert, 1990), is its mapping to some neurobiological circuit in the brain, as demonstrated with the startle probe paradigm for the valence dimension (Lang, Bradley, & Cuthbert, 1997). However, it is still quite unclear which rotational position of axes in the circumplex structure of affect space should be called "basic" (Watson et al., 1999, propose positive-negative activation). The shortcoming of the dimensional model is, of course, its lack of differentiation within the classes of negative and positive states. For example, even though there are marked differences in feelings, behaviors, postures, and facial expressions, anger and fear occupy quite similar positions in affect space.

The categorical model of emotion lends itself to the study of individual emotions. But which emotions should be rated, beyond those targeted in a particular study? Recourse to the notion of "basic emotions" may seem reasonable, but it is infected with the principal problem that what is "basic" cannot be determined with a priori criteria that are independent of our theoretical positions (see the excellent discussions by Ekman, 1992, 1994; Izard, 1992; Oatley & Johnson-Laird, 1987; Ortony & Turner, 1990; Panksepp, 1992, 1994). On the other hand, a fine-grained semantic differentiation of emotion words (Shaver, Schwartz, Kirson, & O'Connor, 1987; Storm & Storm, 1987) would yield an unwieldy assembly with high redundancy and low economy. A pragmatic compromise would perhaps be a collection of between 10 and 20 feeling states (see Table 12.1), such as those proposed by Ekman (1994), Izard (1991), or Plutchik (1989), and activation states (Thayer, 1996).

How should the selected feeling and activation states be assessed? The emotion researcher has a choice between one-item, multi-item, or parcel-item scales. One-item scales have the advantage of brevity and hence superior chances to capture elusive emotional states that with long, multi-item scales might get blurred in their semantic representation. A good compromise are scales with just a few items, such as Izard's (1991) Differential Emotion Scale, with three items per scale. An additional advantage of short multi-item scales is that they allow calculation of internal consistencies as reliability estimates. Parcel-item scales present several adjectival or noun descriptors that are rated as an ensemble on one single scale. This procedure builds on the prototypical meaning of the class of affective states targeted by the scale. It has, again, the advantage of brevity and allows one to determine the homogeneity of the scale descriptors if a test form with separately rated descriptors is constructed and analyzed for internal consistency. For example, the parcel-item scale "fear" made up of the descriptors *frightened/timid/afraid/ scared*, instead of being rated as an ensemble on one Likert-type scale, could be rated on four separate scales. In unpublished work, we found for this four-item scale high consistencies, which, however, were dependent on the condition in which the ratings were obtained: 0.94 for an anagram task, 0.60 for a rest period, 0.87 for an anger induction, and 0.93 for a relived anger episode (Glombiewski & Schirmbeck, 2000). In sum, either short multi-item or parcel-item scales can have a satisfactory psychometric quality and, at the same time, offer a differentiated description of brief emotional states.

### Physiological Variables

The sampling of somatovisceral variables in emotion research is often dictated more by the availability of particular recording equipment than by a priori considerations—somewhat like the simpleton who looks for his watch under a lamppost because it is brighter there than where he had lost it. However, a priori knowledge is often not available. In addition, single somatovisceral variables will seldom map one-to-one to psychological constructs (Cacioppo & Tassinary, 1990a). Therefore, a broad sampling of somatovisceral variables might be a good strategy. But what are the criteria by which to sample the variables?

A recurring response to this question is to sample those variables that are good estimators of basic activation components (Stemmler, 1992) or of autonomic space (Berntson, Cacioppo, & Quigley, 1991, 1993). For example, Wenger tried to identify emotions with patterns of the sympathetic and parasympathetic branch of the autonomic nervous system (Wenger, Jones, & Jones, 1956).

Table 12.1. Proposals for Basic Emotions

| Ekman (1994) | Izard (1991) | Plutchik (1989) |
|---|---|---|
| **Positive Emotions** | | |
| Contentment | Enjoyment | Acceptance/trust |
| Satisfaction | | Expectancy/curiosity |
| Pride in achievement | | Joy |
| Relief | | |
| Sensory pleasure | | |
| Excitement | | |
| **Negative Emotions** | | |
| Anger | Anger | Anger |
| Awe | | |
| Contempt | Contempt | |
| Disgust | Disgust | Disgust |
| Embarrassment | | |
| Fear | Fear | Fear |
| Guilt | Guilt | |
| Sadness | Sadness | Sadness |
| Shame | Shame/Shyness | |
| **Other** | | |
| Interest | Interest | |
| | Surprise | Surprise/Startle |

Gellhorn (Gellhorn, 1964a, 1964b, 1967) proposed that emotions were characterized by the specific balance of the ergotropic and trophotropic systems. These systems were thought of as hypothalamic activation states with widespread cortical, autonomic, and somatic effects. Another systematization of autonomic activity is through the neurotransmitters that carry nerve impulses to end organs (see chapter 9 in this volume). Predominantly cardiovascular responses during emotion have been described in terms of alpha-adrenergic, beta-adrenergic, and cholinergic activation (Nyklicek et al., 1997; Stemmler, Grossman, Schmid, & Foerster, 1991; Stemmler, 1992).

Figure 12.4 illustrates the use of cardiovascular activation components and partial autonomic receptor blockades to unmask the alpha-adrenergic contribution expected under anger arousal (see the noradrenaline hypothesis of anger; Funkenstein, King, & Drolette, 1954). The anger group, compared with a control group (which was presented the same task but without harassment), showed a significant increase of the beta-adrenergic component. Unexpectedly, alpha-adrenergic activation in anger was lacking (Figure 12.4, panel a). A separate experimental group received partial beta-adrenergic and cholinergic blockades and was also observed under anger and control conditions. As a consequence of the partial blockades, beta-adrenergic activation during anger was reduced to control-group levels. Importantly, the alpha-adrenergic component—now unmasked from beta-adrenergic influences (C. E. Martin et al., 1974; Stemmler, 1992)—could show its expected increase during anger.

Which cardiovascular variables could serve as indicators for these activation components? Studies using alpha-adrenergic, beta-adrenergic, and cholinergic antagonists (for a review, see Stemmler, 1992) clearly point out that different variables are activated by different autonomic receptor classes or combinations thereof. Table 12.2 summarizes previous reviews about the sensitivity of selected cardiovascular variables for adrenergic and cholinergic antagonists. A surprising result in Table 12.2 is the size of qualitative differences among variables in their sensitivity for autonomic neurotransmitters. Would it be a viable strategy to pick out those variables that seem to have a rather "pure" autonomic basis for their activity? For example, skin temperature at the finger could be used to index alpha-adrenergic tone; the Heather index and preejection period to capture beta-adrenergic tone; and

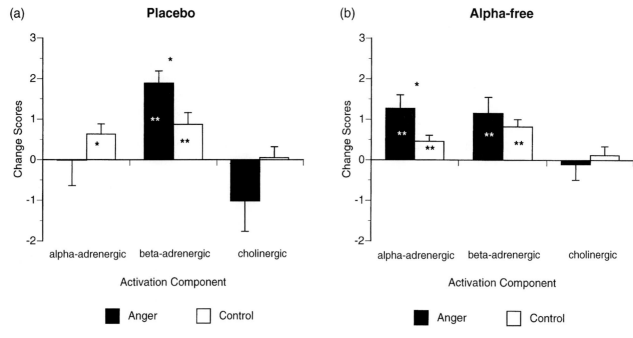

Figure 12.4 Effects on three cardiovascular activation components of an anger induction compared with a control condition with identical situational contexts (Stemmler, 1992). Panel a shows the data from a placebo condition. Panel b shows the data from a dual partial blockade group, which received a low-dose beta blocker (60 mg propranolol) plus a cholinergic blocker (1 mg atropine); alpha-adrenergic receptors were thus unblocked ("alpha-free"). Each bar represents the mean of $N = 12$ participants. Error bars depict standard errors of the mean. Asterisks denote significant differences of means from zero (within bars) or significant differences between anger and control. Change scores refer to differences between induction or control periods and a prestimulus phase. *$p \leq .05$. **$p \leq .01$.

Table 12.2. In Vivo Effects of Autonomic Receptor Activation on Selected Cardiovascular Variables

| Variable | Receptor Class | | |
| --- | --- | --- | --- |
|  | Alpha-adrenergic | Beta-adrenergic | Cholinergic |
| Heart rate | − | + | − |
| Respiratory sinus arrhythmia |  |  | + |
| P-Q time |  | − | + |
| P-wave amplitude |  | + | − |
| Q-T time (relative to heart rate) |  | + |  |
| ST segment |  | − | + |
| T-wave amplitude |  | − | + |
| Preejection period |  | − |  |
| Left-ventricular ejection time |  | − | + |
| Stroke volume[a] | + | − |  |
| Cardiac output |  | + | − |
| Heather index |  | + |  |
| R-Z time |  | − |  |
| Systolic blood pressure | + | + | − |
| Mean blood pressure | + | + | − |
| Diastolic blood pressure | + | − | − |
| Total peripheral resistance | + | − |  |
| Pulse wave velocity | + | + | − |
| Pulse volume amplitude | − | + |  |
| Skin temperature at finger | − |  |  |

Note: Based on Fahrenberg & Foerster (1989) and on a review of pharmacological blockade studies in Stemmler (1992). Increases denoted by +, decreases by −.

[a]Increases and decreases in stroke volume are a function of heart rate, ventricular filling, and contractility, and thus may change even under one receptor class activation.

Table 12.3. Cardiovascular Regulation Patterns During Physical Tasks

| Variable | Regulation Pattern | | | |
| --- | --- | --- | --- | --- |
|  | A | B | C | D |
| Heart rate | ++ |  | ++ |  |
| Respiratory sinus arrhythmia |  | − |  | − |
| P-Q time |  |  |  |  |
| P-wave amplitude | − |  |  | − |
| Relative Q-T time |  | + | + | ++ |
| ST segment | − | −−− |  |  |
| T-wave amplitude | − | −− | + | − |
| Preejection period | −−− |  |  |  |
| Left-ventricular ejection time |  |  | − | ++ |
| Stroke volume |  | + | −−− | + |
| Cardiac output | + |  | − | + |
| Heather index | +++ | + | − |  |
| Ejection speed | + | + | − |  |
| R-Z time | −−− |  |  | − |
| Systolic blood pressure | + |  |  | − |
| Diastolic blood pressure | − |  | + |  |
| Total peripheral resistance | − |  | ++ |  |
| Pulse wave velocity | ++ |  |  | + |
| Pulse volume amplitude |  | + |  |  |
| Skin temperature at forehead | ++ |  | − | + |
| Skin temperature at finger |  | − |  | − |
| Variance explained by |  |  |  |  |
|   Alpha-adrenergic tone | 20% | 26% | 14% | 38% |
|   Beta-adrenergic tone | 46% | 46% | 42% | 39% |
|   Cholinergic tone | 34% | 28% | 44% | 23% |

Note: Correlations of cardiovascular variables with regulation patterns derived by a redundancy analysis (for details, see Stemmler, 1992). Tasks were speech, handgrip, mental arithmetic, signal detection, loud noise, cold pressor, and anticipation of sentence completion. The symbols denote: $+, 0.20 \leq r < 0.40$; $++, 0.40 \leq r < 0.60$; $+++, 0.60 \leq r < 1.00$; $−, −0.20 \geq r > −0.40$; $−−, −0.40 \geq r > −0.60$; $−−−, −0.60 \geq r > −1.00$.

respiratory sinus arrhythmia to assess cholinergic tone. This strategy, however, is not recommended for the following reasons: (1) Autonomic changes more often than not are the result of interactions among the activation components. Such interactions have not yet been studied adequately (with single, dual, and triple autonomic antagonists). (2) The large differences between receptor subtypes and their specific effects are not adequately accounted for. (3) The type of receptor through which autonomic target organs are innervated does not necessarily correspond with the target's functions. Instead, the ultimate goal of the circulation—to establish an efficient transportation system under extremely varying conditions—can be secured only by the intricate interplay of broadly acting humoral (the catecholamines), local metabolic, and very specific neural influences (Jänig & McLachlan, 1992a, 1992b). Thus cardiovascular variables serve specific functions in an overall regulation pattern.

Single variables cannot adequately identify such regulation patterns. To illustrate this point, regulation patterns from an experiment with seven different physical tasks (speech, handgrip, mental arithmetic, signal detection, loud noise, cold pressor, sentence completion; see Stemmler, 1992), are presented in Table 12.3. Regulation pattern A describes a marked inotropic and chronotropic pattern with increases in contractility, heart rate, pulse wave velocity, and forehead skin temperature. This pattern has a beta-adrenergic dominance but also a sizable component of vagal withdrawal. Regulation pattern B displays a strong depression of the ST segment and of T-wave amplitude, together with signs of moderate inotropic activation but without a chronotropic contribution. Because heart rate does not increase, the blood volume entering the ventricles in the diastole is relatively large, forcing the heart to increase its stroke volume through a higher contractility (Frank-Starling mechanism). Under such conditions, the work load of the heart rises, which could lead to an unequal distribution of blood in the myocardium and finally to a depression of the ST segment. *Regulation pattern C* is characterized by strong vagal withdrawal and increased beta-adrenergic tone. But in contrast to pattern A, inotropic activation is missing; diastolic blood pressure and total peripheral resistance, however, are rising. *Regulation pattern D* presents prolonged systolic times, increased cardiac output, and vasoconstriction at finger sites. Thus this pattern describes a mixed alpha-adrenergic and beta-adrenergic activation.

This example underscores that single variables alone, even those with relatively pure neurotransmitter mediation, cannot give an adequate picture of a regulation pattern. A physiological reasoning in terms of regulation patterns rather than single variables could provide a strong basis for bridges to psychological concepts such as emotion, because at least some regulation patterns are coordinated by the brain (e.g., the defense, the pressor, the depressor, the dive patterns; Folkow, 1979; Hilton, 1982; Lisander, 1979) and because they serve specific organismic goals. Blascovich and Tomaka (1996) make a related point when they distinguish between a sympathetic-adrenomedullary (SAM) and a pituitary-adrenocortical (PAC) regulation pattern. The authors argue "that the SAM is an 'effort' system, responsible primarily for energy mobilization to support actual or anticipated behavioral coping. The PAC system, in contrast, is a 'distress' system associated with perceptions of actual or potential physical or psychological harm" (Blascovich & Tomaka, 1996, p. 20). These authors propose that SAM activation follows *challenge appraisals* and can be identified by strong increases in heart rate, cardiac output, and left-ventricular contractility and a drop in total peripheral resistance. In contrast, *threat appraisals* should lead to an increased PAC activity, which inhibits the adrenal medullary SAM release of catecholamines. The result is only moderate increases in heart rate, cardiac output, and left-ventricular contractility and a slight rise in total peripheral resistance.

My conclusion about the issue of sampling variables is probably clear by now: Register as many variables as are necessary to understand the physiological regulation on a macrolevel.

Hilton summarizes the argument most cogently: "the central nervous system is organized to produce not single, isolated variables but integrated patterns of response. Any variable which can be described or measured independently is actually a component of several such patterns" (Hilton, 1975, p. 215).

## Sampling Research Participants

### A Priori Selection

With a priori selection the research participants are selected by some attribute before the research itself begins.

Attributes could be group membership (e.g., gender or psychiatric diagnosis) or the standing on a score distribution (e.g., intelligence, personality, or hypnotic susceptibility). If experimental groups are formed by group membership, experimental outcomes may be difficult to interpret causally because preexisting groups in an unknown number of variables are nonequivalent. For example, the difference in emotion self-ratings after an experimental emotion induction between a clinical depression and a nonclinical control group could be described but not causally explained (Cook & Campbell, 1979; Huitema, 1980; Wainer, 1991).

Selection on the basis of a score distribution or a pretest is not unusual in psychophysiological emotion research (e.g., Boiten, 1996; Levenson et al., 1990; Levenson et al., 1992; Roberts & Weerts, 1982). The main purpose of this form of selection is to increase effect sizes, because it is expected that the success of an emotion induction or the amplitude of emotion responses is correlated with the selection variable. Another positive effect is the reduction of sample size needed to reject the null hypothesis, which may be important if an experiment is costly or participants difficult to recruit. For example, to detect a "small" effect (effect size $d = 0.20$) in the population for a given alpha error of .05 (two-tailed $t$-test) and statistical power of 0.95, a sample size of $N = 1,302$ is required; to detect a "large" effect under the same assumptions, sample size is dramatically reduced to $N = 84$ (Buchner, Faul, & Erdfelder, 1992). However, this selection procedure also has some disadvantages. First, the external validity of the experiment, that is, the generalizability of its findings, is impaired. Second, the well-known psychometric principle of the restriction of range applies. As a consequence, correlations with third variables decrease. Thus selection of participants may work against differential hypotheses, for example, in the study of personality correlates of emotion responses. Third, it is assumed—but practically never assessed—that the selection variable correlates with all of the important dependent variables encompassing emotion self-reports, physiological, behavioral, and observation data. However, the often only moderate to low correlations within and between these different response systems used for the assessment of emotion make this assumption quite implausible. Hence selecting participants according to one criterion variable probably implies a nonrandom selection of response systems.

### A Posteriori Selection

Emotion research is confronted with the problem of unresponsiveness of some of the research participants to experimental emotion inductions. For example, in a "real life" induction procedure, it is not uncommon to find only two-thirds of the participants reporting an emotional involvement ("true responders"; see Table 12.4). About one-

Table 12.4. Response Types in Induction and Control Groups

| | Response | |
| --- | --- | --- |
| Group | Emotion | No Emotion |
| Induction | True responders | False nonresponders |
| Control | False responders | True nonresponders |

third of the participants do not report the targeted emotion ("false nonresponders"). Thus there is a real danger that group averages reflect only blunted emotion effects, which in turn lead to an underestimate of the magnitude of emotion responses. In order to compensate for such adverse effects, a posteriori selections of participants, that is, selections for certain stages of the analysis after data collection, have been recommended (e.g., Levenson et al., 1991; Levenson et al., 1992). If the main focus of a study is on physiological emotion responses, a selection could be based on emotion self-reports, emotion appraisals, or behavioral (e.g., facial) expressions of emotion.

An a posteriori selection can also be applied to participants in a control group or in a within-subjects control condition. Some control participants might rate the target emotion above some criterion ("false responders"; see Table 12.4), even though in this group or condition target emotions of very low intensity or a complete absence of emotions is expected ("true nonresponders"). The data from the aforementioned study (Stemmler et al., 1998, 2001) will be used again for illustration. Setting, for example, the selection criterion on the 11-point target emotion self-report scale (i.e., self-reported fear for the fear induction; self-reported anger for the anger induction) to a value of 1, then in the control group all individuals with a score less than or equal to 1 will be selected ("true non-responders"), whereas in the induction group all individuals with a score greater than 1 will be selected ("true responders"). Increasing the selection criterion gradually leads to a rise in the number of "true nonresponders" and a decline in the number of "true responders"; that is, sample sizes of control and induction groups diverge more and more (see Figure 12.5, panel a).

The goal of a posteriori selection of cases is increased effect size through elimination of unresponsive participants. However, effect size is only one side of the coin. An effect of a given size also needs to be detected in the population. Probability of detection is the statistical power of a test. At a fixed alpha error, power increases with effect size and sample size. The potential problem with the a posteriori selection of cases is that the inevitable drop in sample size has to be overcompensated by a gain in effect size, should statistical power not decrease.

To illustrate the effects of a posteriori selection, the average absolute effect size across 29 somatovisceral variables and their associated statistical power were computed for the contrasts "fear-induction minus fear-control" and "anger-induction minus anger-control." Figure 12.5, panel b, shows that effect sizes for the fear induction are highest with no selection and decline with stricter selection criteria. Statistical power is acceptably high up to selection criterion 2. For the anger induction, effect sizes are considerably lower but quite steady over selection criteria. Statistical power is satisfactory only when no selection occurs.

Effect sizes of select somatovisceral variables were also determined to exclude the possibility that the grand average might hide strong effect size increases in but a few variables. Figure 12.5, panels c and d, show effect sizes of cardiac output, EMG extensor digitorum, heart period, diastolic blood pressure, and the Heather index during the fear and anger induction, respectively. These variables were expected to show medium ($d = 0.5$) or better effect sizes for fear or anger. During the fear induction, variables with high ($d > 0.8$) effect sizes did not gain from a posteriori selection. During anger induction, some variables obtained higher effect sizes with increasingly strict selection criteria, whereas others remained at about the same levels.

In sum, at least in this data set the expected advantage of an a posteriori selection of cases did not come true. However, more systematic research on the conditions under which selection is or is not appropriate should be conducted. Such research should include an investigation of other potential drawbacks of selection besides effect size, sample size, and statistical power, such as response fractionation. If the emotion response system from which the selection variable is derived (e.g., self-report of emotion) in some individuals becomes uncoupled from the response system under investigation (e.g., physiological variables), the selection of cases would risk severe misclassifications. For example, participants for different reasons might report that they are not feeling the target emotion even though the target emotion and its physiological manifestations actually existed: An individual could be blind to his or her feelings or might want to suppress any socially visible signs of an emotion. Such cases critically compromise the validity of a posteriori selections.

## Experimental Design

### Designs for the Assessment of Specific Emotion Effects

Experimental designs can be differently suited for the study of specific emotion effects. The primary goal of a design is to ensure high internal validity of an investigation (Campbell & Stanley, 1963). High internal validity means that the likelihood of the substantive hypothesis is large in comparison with rival hypotheses. In psycho-

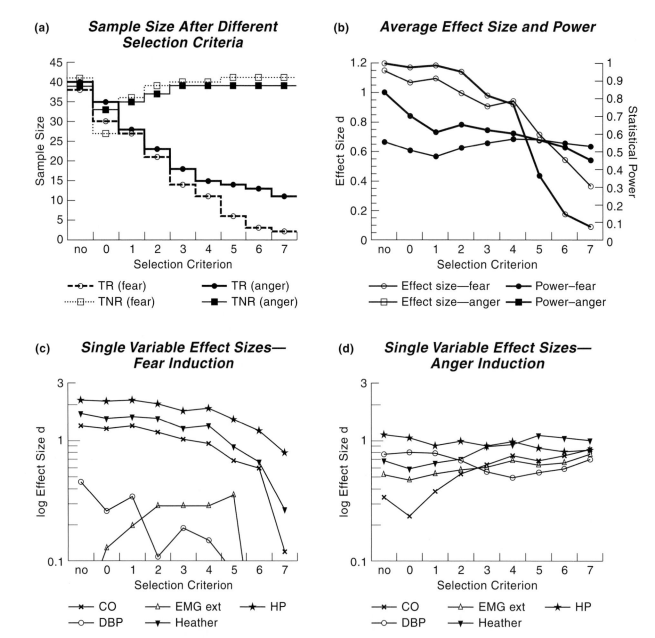

**(a) Sample Size After Different Selection Criteria**

**(b) Average Effect Size and Power**

**(c) Single Variable Effect Sizes— Fear Induction**

**(d) Single Variable Effect Sizes— Anger Induction**

Figure 12.5 Selection of research participants a posteriori with different selection criteria. Selection variable for the fear-induction and fear-control groups was self-reported fear; for the anger-induction and anger-control groups, self-reported anger. Rating scales had 11 categories, ranging from 0 to 10. Selection criteria were either "no," that is, no selection performed, or a digit (0 to 7), that is, (1) members of the control group with a score at or below the digit and (2) members of the induction group with a score larger than the digit were selected. Panel a shows the gradual depletion of the induction group and completion of the control group. TR = "true responders" and TNR = "true nonresponders" in the fear or anger group. Panel b shows effect sizes averaged over 29 somatovisceral variables (left ordinate) and their statistical power (right ordinate). Effect sizes were determined from induction-group minus control-group contrasts. Panels c and d show the effect sizes of select somatovisceral variables in the fear and anger induction, respectively. CO = Cardiac output; EMG ext = EMG extensor digitorum; HP = Heart period; DBP = Diastolic blood pressure; Heather = Heather index.

physiological studies of emotion, one of the most serious rival hypotheses is that influences other than the emotion per se produce the somatovisceral response pattern or that emotion effects are confounded with the effects of such influences. After all, unlike emotion self-reports, somatovisceral activity is the slave of many masters, including not only homeostatic regulations for ambient temperature, body posture, motor activity, or physical tasks but also the direction of attention (B. C. Lacey & Lacey, 1974), mental effort (Mulder, Mulder, & Veldeman, 1985), anticipation (Mäntysaari et al., 1988), thoughts and mental images (Lang, Kozak, Miller, Levin, & McLean, 1980)—and emotions. Thus the internal validity of psychophysiological studies on emotion is easily threatened. In this sense, experimental designs vary from weak to strong.

## Design 1: Comparison of Different Emotions in Different Contexts

In this design at least two emotions are compared, but each one is induced in a different situational context. Different contexts may evoke different perceptual, attentional, cognitive, and motor demands that could have specific psychophysiological effects quite independent of any emotion effect. Thus in this design context and emotion are thoroughly confounded. If, for example, fear were induced by films and anger by a role play, somatovisceral differences between fear and anger conditions could not be attributed to specific emotion effects.

## Design 2: Comparison of Different Emotions in the Same Context

This design has often been used in studies using emotional imagery (e.g., Grossberg & Wilson, 1968; Roberts & Weerts, 1982; Schwartz, Weinberger, & Singer, 1981).

## Design 3: Comparison of Different Emotions in Different Intensities

In analogy to a typical pharmacological dose-response experiment, the planned intensity variation of an emotion would constitute an important experimental strategy. However, this design presupposes a constant situational context and also an unchanged emotional quality which is very difficult to achieve experimentally. Intensity variations of emotions were targeted through cognitive sets (e.g., Dandoy & Goldstein, 1990; Lazarus & Alfert, 1964; Lazarus, Opton, Nomikos, & Rankin, 1965; Steptoe & Vögele, 1986), through varied stimulus intensities (Cacioppo, Petty, Losch, & Kim, 1986), or through the imagination of weaker or stronger emotion episodes (Roberts & Weerts, 1982). It should be noted that designs 1, 2, and 4 assume equal intensities of the emotions induced.

## Design 4: Comparison of One and the Same Emotion Across Different Contexts

In this design one emotion is induced in at least two different situational contexts. Thus this design tests for transsituational consistency of emotion profiles. Different contexts were, for example, imagination of emotion episodes versus directed facial actions (Ekman, Levenson, & Friesen, 1983; Fridlund et al., 1984; Levenson et al., 1990) or real-life inductions versus emotional imagery (Lang et al., 1983; Stemmler, 1989; Stemmler et al., 2001).

## Design 5: Comparison of an Emotion With Its Induction Context

This design permits the decomposition of a response profile into two parts, context and emotion. To achieve this goal, a control condition has to be established that can invoke the induction context without emotion. Most psychophysiological studies on emotion specificity have used some kind of control condition; it is, however, often questionable whether the control condition indeed represents the situational context of the emotion induction. For example, "neutral" control films do not necessarily control for all of the nonemotional aspects of induction films, such as vividness, change in scenery, or narrative complexity. Likewise, simple rest or baseline conditions cannot control for the situational context of any emotion induction. In recent years, two alternative experimental procedures were developed in my lab. In the within-subjects control technique, participants are first subjected to a real-life emotion induction, then they are debriefed, and finally they are presented with exactly the same emotion induction a second time. The first emotion induction captures context plus emotion effects; the second induction, context effects alone, because both the disclosure and the mere repetition will remove any personal meaning and, with it, emotional significance of the second induction (Koslowitz, 1993). A problem of this technique, however, is the fixed order of emotion induction and control induction; permutations of order are logically not possible. Therefore, in the between-subjects control technique, one experimental group is subjected to the emotion induction (induction group). A second experimental group is thoroughly debriefed before the emotion induction (control group). Again, the induction group captures context plus emotion effects, and the control group, context effects alone. (Most illustrations in this chapter are taken from Stemmler et al., 2001, which employed the between-subjects control technique.)

### Convergent and Discriminant Validity

The discussion of experimental designs suggests that construct validity (Campbell & Fiske, 1959) of emotion-specific physiological responses is rather difficult to obtain. Obviously, different experimental designs have to be combined to make a satisfactory claim for construct validity. In particular, three different tests of discriminant validity and one test of convergent validity compose the desirable set. As will become evident, a minimum of two emotions each induced in two intensities and in two different situational contexts would be required to allow for all of the desirable validity tests.

*Discriminant validity I* is given if an emotion differs from its induction context (design 5). Differences are expected in somatovisceral profile patterns and not just in profile levels. This test is a *necessary* condition for physiological emotion specificity.

*Discriminant validity II* is given if at least two emotions within one situational context (e.g., films, imagination, real life) differ from one another (design 2). This test is a *sufficient* condition for physiological emotion specificity. If the induction contexts of two emotions are not equal (as judged from the within-subjects or between-subjects control technique), responses to different emotions are not compared directly but relative to the control condition or control group. Forming tetrad differences (see equation 1) is straightforward.

*Discriminant validity III* is given if intensity variations within an emotion differ from one another (design 3). It should be noted that, with different emotion intensities, physiological profiles would be expected to change in their levels; however, because of nonlinearities in the transfer functions of somatovisceral variables (Stemmler, 1987), additional changes in their profile patterns cannot be excluded.

*Convergent validity* is given if an emotion in one induction context does not differ from the same emotion in a distinct context (design 4). Convergent validity ensures the generalizability of results across different contexts of emotion inductions. Claims for generalizability are at the core of the postulate of emotion specificity. The test for convergent validity usually has to allow for differences in the induction contexts, for instance, by considering appropriate control conditions or control groups.

## Control of Within-Group Variability

Within-group variability, or error variance, can be quite high in physiological data. As a consequence, statistical power is easily compromised. Therefore, it is important to think about ways of controlling within-group variability. Procedural and experimental design considerations may play a significant part in any solution.

One major cause of a large within-group variability is individual response specificity (Engel & Bickford, 1961; J. I. Lacey, 1956; Marwitz & Stemmler, 1998). This notion describes the fact that individuals (1) may have fairly consistent patterns of response across different conditions

that (2) are unique compared with consistent patterns of other individuals. Consistency has two aspects, arousal level and arousability. This means that individuals differ both in their somatovisceral baselines and in their response magnitudes. As I have demonstrated, reactivity is multicomponential activation. Somatovisceral arousability would then have to be observed under conditions that separately activate each relevant component or regulation pattern.

To control for individual differences in arousal levels, baselines are incorporated in practically all experimental designs. However, when to record baselines (Fahrenberg, Schneider, & Safian, 1987; Obrist, 1981) and for how long (Jennings, Kamarck, Stewart, Eddy, & Johnson, 1992; Saab et al., 1992) is still worth some consideration. To control for individual differences in arousability is still quite rare. Physical tasks such as the cold pressor, handgrip, exercise, or loud noise task seem to be well suited, because they are standardized and demand different physiological regulation patterns (Buell, Alpert, & McCrory, 1986). For reasons to be explained shortly, such "standard tests" should always be placed before any differential treatment of experimental groups begins.

In most published research, a reduction of within-group variability is achieved through change scores in which baseline levels are subtracted from task levels. Thus change scores control for individual differences in arousal level, provided the baseline is a good estimate of arousal level. A powerful generalization of difference scores is residual scores from a regression analysis of task levels on baseline levels,

$$residual = y - M_y - \beta_{yx}(x - M_x) \qquad (3)$$
$$= y - a - \beta_{yx}x,$$

which, with $a = 0$ and $\beta_{yx} = 1$, is the definition of the difference score. Thus the difference score implicitly residualizes from a line parallel to the main diagonal, whereas the residual score from regression analysis residualizes from the regression function. Another feature of regression analysis is that more than one regressor can be specified. Multiple regressors are needed for the control of individual differences in arousability in more than one regulation pattern (see Cronbach & Furby, 1970). A distinctive advantage of regression analysis is that with its extension—the analysis of covariance (ANCOVA)—random pretreatment differences of experimental groups can be equated. Such random pretreatment differences can easily distort posttreatment minus pretreatment effects.

How many regressors, or covariates in ANCOVA, should be used? No general recommendation is possible because empirical data are lacking. To illustrate, various analysis methods were compared using the example data set with 27 somatovisceral variables, two emotions (fear, anger), and two experimental groups (induction, control). The two sessions had identical standard tests before the real-life and imagination inductions; here the sessions were analyzed separately to allow comparison of results. Seven analysis methods were compared: (1) ANOVA on induction levels, (2) ANOVA on change scores (induction minus initial rest period), (3) ANCOVA with initial rest period, (4) ANCOVA with additional prestimulus period before a loud noise, (5) ANCOVA with additional task period loud noise, (6) ANCOVA with additional prestimulus period before handgrip, and (7) ANCOVA with additional task period handgrip. From each analysis, treatment sums of squares (SS) during induction (summed over Emotion, Experimental Group, and their interaction) and error SS were extracted. An analysis method is superior if, in comparison with the ANOVA on induction levels, the error SS are reduced and the treatment SS increased, equaled, or only moderately reduced. To describe the net efficiency of an analysis method, we calculated the $F$-ratio of treatment to error mean squares and divided it by the $F$-ratio of the ANOVA on induction levels.

Figure 12.6 shows the performance of analysis methods relative to the performance of an ANOVA on induction levels, separately for the real-life and the imagination emotion inductions. Each point in the plot represents the mean across the analyses of 27 somatovisceral variables. During real-life inductions, relative error SS dropped to 70% with an analysis of change scores but to 50% and down to 36% with ANCOVAs with one to five covariates. Relative treatment SS was around 80% for all analysis methods. Relative efficiency rose to 112% with change scores but to twice as much (221%) with an ANCOVA with five covariates. Thus in the real-life data set, ANCOVA with five covariates on average more than doubled the $F$-value of a simple ANOVA on levels. Put differently, a substantial reduction of within-group variability could be achieved. This reduction was not considerably countered by the moderate decline of treatment variance. During *imagination* inductions, the drop in relative error SS across analysis methods was very similar to the drop seen in the real-life data. However, the behavior of the relative treatment SS was quite different: Change scores boosted the relative treatment SS to 122%, whereas ANCOVA reduced it increasingly with the number of covariates employed. As a result, relative efficiency was highest for change scores (198%) and settled around 170% for ANCOVA analyses.

The relative efficiency of an ANCOVA with five covariates, compared with the change score ANOVA, was 198% for the real-life and 86% for the imagination induction. This comparison shows that general conclusions about *the* best analysis method to control for within-group variability cannot be drawn. Conclusions seem to depend on the actual choice of baselines and standard tests and on the covariance structure among responses to them and to

**Control of Within-Group Variance**

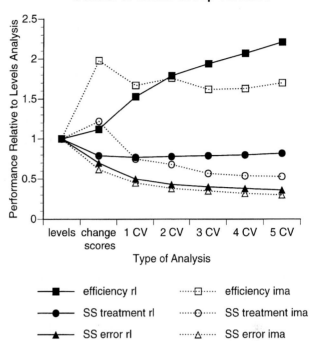

Figure 12.6 Performance of various analysis methods used to control within-group variance (error variance). Performance was measured relative to an ANOVA on levels. Analysis methods were change (difference) scores and ANCOVAs, with increasing numbers of covariates (CV) registered during an initial rest period and subsequent standard tests (see text). Two sets of analyses were conducted, with data from a session with real-life emotion inductions (rl) and with data from a session with the imagination (ima) of the prior rl emotion induction. Data are the averages across 27 somatovisceral variables. SS treatments are the sums of squares for Group (induction vs. control), Emotion (fear vs. anger), plus Group × Emotion. SS errors are the sums of squares after explaining treatment and, if present, covariate effects. Efficiency is the net effect achieved by a particular analysis method in relation to the levels of ANOVA; it is the ratio of their $F$-ratios. $N = 158$.

the inductions. Specifically, there was a marked covariance between standard test responses (i.e., covariates) and the independent variables (i.e., treatments) during the imagination session, which led to a continuous reduction of treatment SS with the addition of covariates. However, for experimental studies with (1) a random assignment of participants to experimental groups and (2) an identical treatment of groups during baselines and standard tests before any group-specific treatments are introduced, ANCOVA may be preferable to simple change scores, because ANCOVA equates for random pretreatment differences among groups. Thus ANCOVA tests conditional hypotheses of the form, "What are the effects of the differential treatments if the experimental groups start out equally?" If, by chance or by nonrandom assignment of participants to experimental groups, responses to baselines or standard tests are different, differences scores can easily run awry.

## Statistical Analysis

### The Measurement of Change

Conventional statistical wisdom has it that difference scores, $d = y - x$, are inherently unreliable and thus obsolete. However, there is a continuing practice of using difference scores because they are simple, they correspond to the usual ANOVA treatment of repeated measures data, and, unlike ANCOVA applications with $x$ as covariate and $y$ as dependent variable, they are sample independent. Among statisticians there is also a growing awareness that difference scores are better than often presented because they are unbiased estimators of true linear change (Rogosa, 1988; Rogosa, Brandt, & Zimowski, 1982) and because their purported unreliability occurs only under the most unfavorable conditions (Williams & Zimmerman, 1996). In this section, I present Williams and Zimmerman's clarifications, discuss initial value dependencies, and comment on conditions under which alternatives to $d$ are worth considering.

#### Factors Influencing the Reliability of $d$, $r_{dd}$

The reliability of $d$ is a function of (1) the reliabilities of $x$ and $y$, $r_{xx}$ and $r_{yy}$, respectively, (2) the stability of true scores, $r_{T_x T_y}$, (3) the ratio of standard deviations, $\lambda = s_x / s_y$, and (4) the correlation of errors in $x$ and $y$, $r_{E_x E_y}$:

$$r_{dd} = \frac{\lambda r_{xx} + \lambda^{-1} r_{yy} - 2 r_{T_x T_y}\sqrt{r_{xx} r_{yy}} + r_{E_x E_y}\sqrt{(1 - r_{xx})(1 - r_{yy})}}{\lambda + \lambda^{-1} - 2 r_{T_x T_y}\sqrt{r_{xx} r_{yy}}}.$$

(4)

The following conclusions can be drawn from equation 4 and the graphs in Figure 12.7:

- The higher the stability of true scores, the lower the reliability of $d$. The explanation for this rather counterintuitive derivation is that the more alike the rank orders of participants in $T_x$ and $T_y$ are, the more likely it is that random errors in $x$ and $y$ will lead to rank order fluctuations in $d$, that is, to unreliability of $d$. Conversely, the lower the stability of true scores is, the higher the reliability of $d$ is. Stability will be low if the stimuli intervening between measurements $x$ and $y$ are interindividually differentially effective, which in emotion research is often the case.

- The further apart $\lambda$ is from 1, that is, the more unequal the standard deviations of $x$ and $y$ are, the larger the reliability of $d$ is. As shown in Figure 12.7, panel a, the detrimental effect of approximately equal standard deviations on the reliability of difference scores is especially pronounced at large true score stabilities (compare "Rel 0.80, Stab 0.20" with "Rel 0.80, Stab 0.80" and note the marked drop in reliability of $d$ for $\lambda = 1.00$).

- The reliabilities of $x$ and $y$ have a prime effect on the reliability of $d$. Obviously, the larger $r_{xx}$ and $r_{yy}$ are, the larger $r_{dd}$ will be. What is less well known is that $r_{dd}$ will follow the larger of $r_{xx}$ and $r_{yy}$ provided $\lambda$ is small. This effect cannot be observed in Figure 12.7 because $r_{xx} = r_{yy}$ is assumed there.

- Positive correlations between the error variables $E_x$ and $E_y$ increase and negative ones decrease the reliability of $d$. If measurements are spaced closely, positive error correlations are likely. Surprisingly, the violation of the classical test theory assumption of uncorrelated errors is beneficial for the reliability of $d$. The change in $r_{dd}$ with increasing error correlation can be clearly seen in comparing Figure 12.7, panels a–c.

In sum, difference scores can have acceptable reliability if $x$ or $y$ can be reliably assessed and if true score stability is not high. Experiments should be planned to allow determination of reliability estimates of $x$; reliability estimates of $y$ are difficult, and in emotion research often impossible, to obtain, because retests after treatment would not assess the same latent dimension (Plewis, 1985).

To illustrate the determination of the reliability of $d$, I use the previously introduced data set. The reliability of $x$ was determined as the average correlation of three 1-minute periods within the initial rest phase (Minutes 1, 5, and 9). Initial measure $x$ was Minute 9 of the rest phase; final measure $y$ was recorded during a 105W exercise period on a bicycle ergometer. Table 12.5 shows the calculation of the reliability of $d$ under two different assumptions concerning the unknown reliability of $y$: (1) $r_{yy}$ is set equal to $r_{xx}$, and (2) $r_{yy}$ is reduced. The second assumption seems to be justified, given the higher amount of recording artifacts during exercise, especially with cuff-based blood pressure measurements. Three variables—heart period, systolic, and diastolic blood pressure—were selected for this demonstration. Due to the high reliability of $x$ and with moderate to high true score stabilities, the reliability under assumption (1) was moderate to high; under assumption (2) for diastolic blood pressure, barely acceptable.

#### Regression Toward the Mean

This effect is best seen in the context of two measurements $x$ and $x'$ without any intervening stimulus. Participants

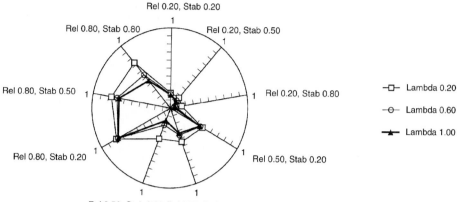

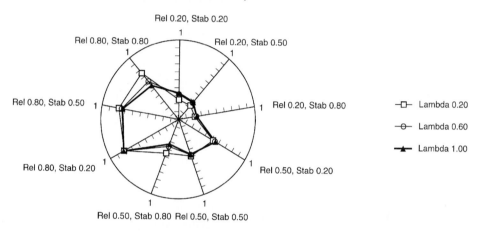

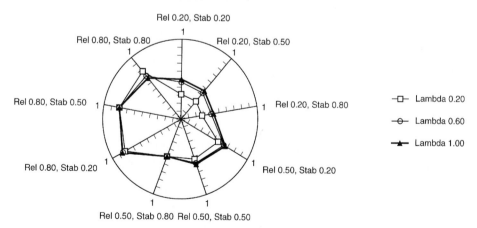

Figure 12.7 Reliability of the difference score as a function of (1) the reliability of $x$ and $y$ (Rel $= r_{xx} = r_{yy}$; in steps of 0.20, 0.50, and 0.80), (2) the true score stability $r_{T_xT_y}$ (Stab; in steps of 0.20, 0.50, and 0.80), (3) the ratio of true score standard deviations (Lambda $= s_{T_x} / s_{T_y}$; in steps of 0.20, 0.60, and 1.00), and (4) the correlation of errors $r_{E_xE_y}$ (panels a–c; in steps of 0.00, 0.40, and 0.80).

Table 12.5. Reliability of the Difference Score: Example

| Statistics | Variables | | |
|---|---|---|---|
| | HP (ms) | SBP (mmHg) | DBP (mmHg) |
| $M_x$ | 818 | 115 | 76 |
| $M_y$ | 434 | 143 | 76 |
| $M_d$ | −384 | 28 | 0 |
| $s_x$ | 119.0 | 10.2 | 10.1 |
| $s_y$ | 82.0 | 15.3 | 10.4 |
| $\lambda$ | 1.44 | 0.67 | 0.97 |
| $r_{xy}$ | .38 | .48 | .55 |
| $r_{xx}$ | .95 | .81 | .76 |
| **Assumption 1** | | | |
| $r_{yy}$ | .95 | .81 | .76 |
| $r_{T_xT_y}$ | .40 | .59 | .72 |
| $r_{dd}$ | .92 | .66 | .47 |
| **Assumption 2** | | | |
| $r_{yy}$ | .85 | .70 | .60 |
| $r_{T_xT_y}$ | .42 | .64 | .81 |
| $r_{dd}$ | .87 | .52 | .28 |

*Note:* Difference score $d$ between rest ($x$) and exercise ($y$). $M$ = mean; $s$ = standard deviation; $\lambda = s_x/s_y$; $r_{xx}$, $r_{yy}$, and $r_{dd}$ = reliabilities of $x$, $y$, and $d$, respectively; $r_{T_xT_y}$ = true score stability. It is assumed that error correlations are zero. $N = 158$. HP = heart period; SBP = systolic blood pressure; DBP = diastolic blood pressure.

with scores in $x$ above the population mean tend to have lower scores in $x'$; participants with scores in $x$ below the population mean tend to have higher scores in $x'$. Formally, the linear regression of $x'$ and $x$, $\beta_{x'x}$, has a slope of less than one (Nesselroade, Stigler, & Baltes, 1980). Because $r_{x'x}$ is an estimator of the reliability of $x$, it is evident that the regression-toward-the-mean effect is completely attributable to the unreliability of $x$. Difference scores with or without a stimulus intervening between two measurements are subject to this effect: Participants with scores above the mean tend toward smaller differences; participants with scores below the mean, toward larger differences. Thus there is an initial value dependency (IVD) which is larger the smaller $r_{xx}$ is. Because this IVD (another one will be introduced soon) is solely determined by random measurement error, Foerster (1995) called it the "Statistical IVD." The Statistical IVD contributes the following part to the difference score:

$$d_{\text{Statistical IVD}} = (r_{xx} - 1)(x - M_x). \tag{5}$$

### Detecting an Emotion or Other Intervention Effect in the Individual Case

The regression-toward-the-mean effect could easily mislead the investigator who wants to determine which participants actually responded to an emotion induction or to another intervention. With the regression-toward-the-

mean effect operating, participants with low initial values are expected to display larger difference scores than those with high initial values, even if an intervention effect is absent. Identifying responsive participants could be important if, for example, an a posteriori selection of participants is attempted. Hsu (1995) recommended the construction of a $(1 - \alpha) * 100\%$ confidence interval around the mean of the initial values,

$$M_x \pm z_{(1 - \alpha/2)}s_x \sqrt{1 - r_{xx}^2}, \tag{6}$$

with $z$ the standard normal variate at $1 - \alpha/2$. An individual with final value $y$ outside this confidence interval could be identified as a true responder.

### The "Law of Initial Value" (LIV)

Wilder (1931, 1967) postulated the LIV after observing that structure and function of biological systems prohibit unrestrained increases in activation. Physiological variables following the LIV would be expected to exhibit a negative correlation between the initial value $x$ and the difference $d$. The correlation $r_{xd}$, however, is not appropriate to gauge the LIV. The reason is that $r_{xd}$ is also affected by unreliability, that is, by the Statistical IVD (Rogosa et al., 1982, equation 11). Instead, the LIV acts to induce a negative correlation between the true scores of $x$ and $d$, $r_{T_xT_d}$ or, alternatively, a deviation from 1 of the regression coefficient $\beta_{T_yT_x}$ from the regression of $T_y$ on $T_x$, (Estimates are discussed by Foerster, 1995; Goldstein, 1979; Kendall & Stuart, 1967; Messick, 1981.) Because many physiological variables exhibit a positive correlation between the initial value $T_x$ and the difference $T_d$ (Myrtek & Foerster, 1986: Myrtek, Foerster, & Wittmann, 1977), a dependency opposite to the direction postulated by the LIV, Foerster (1995) suggested the generic term "True IVD" for cases in which $\beta_{T_yT_x}$ deviates from 1 in either direction. The True IVD contributes the following part to the difference score:

$$d_{\text{True IVD}} = (\beta_{T_yT_x} - 1)r_{xx}(x - M_x) \tag{7}$$
$$= (\beta_{yx} - r_{xx})(x - M_x).$$

The True IVD influences the difference score more the further $\beta_{yx}$ deviates from $r_{xx}$.

### A Variety of Difference Scores

A classical proposal to measure change in physiological variables was put forward by Lacey (1956), the Autonomic Lability Score (ALS). ALS scores are the residuals from the regression of final on initial values. In an unbiased form, ALS scores are defined as

$$d'' = ALS = y - \beta_{yx}(x - M_x) - M_x. \tag{8}$$

By definition, ALS scores are uncorrelated with initial values $x$; that is, they are free from influences of Statistical or True IVDs.

If an estimate for the reliability of initial values is available, an estimate of true change $T_d$ can be devised (e.g., Huitema, 1980).

$$d' = T_d = y - r_{xx}(x - M_x) - M_x. \tag{9}$$

By definition, $T_d$ scores are uncorrelated with the Statistical IVD because true initial values are used.

Now we are in a position to tie together the various loose ends in this section. The difference score $d$ can be decomposed into three parts, one due to the Statistical IVD, one due to the True IVD, and one due to change orthogonal to both IVDs. The true change score $T_d$ can be decomposed into two parts, one due to the True IVD and one due to change orthogonal to it. Finally, the ALS score represents any change orthogonal to either IVD. Thus

$$
\begin{aligned}
d &= d_{\text{Statistical IVD}} + d_{\text{True IVD}} + \text{ALS} \\
d' &= \qquad\qquad\qquad d_{\text{True IVD}} + \text{ALS} \\
d'' &= \qquad\qquad\qquad\qquad\qquad\qquad \text{ALS,}
\end{aligned} \tag{10}
$$

as can be confirmed by inserting equations 5 and 7–9 into equation 10.

Which of the three difference scores, or perhaps alternative response measures (Stemmler, 1987), to choose depends on substantial considerations of the investigator. With regard to $d$, $d'$, and $d''$, Foerster (1995) stated that

- The simple difference score $d$ is an unbiased estimate of change, easy to understand, and independent of the actual sample. It contains all three effects, $d_{\text{Statistical IVD}}$, $d_{\text{True IVD}}$, and ALS.
- The change score $d'$ is a true score difference if errors are uncorrelated. It contains the effects $d_{\text{True IVD}}$ and ALS.
- The change score $d''$ or ALS is uncorrelated with the initial value and thus describes the incremental variance in $d$ over and above all effects attributable to $x$.

### Detecting Initial Value Dependencies

Foerster (1995) discussed tests for IVD on the background of Kendall and Stuart's (1967) structural models. Under the assumption of equal error variances and uncorrelated errors, the test for equal variances (Geenen & Van de Vijver, 1993; Jamieson, 1993, 1995), $H_0$: $s_x^2 = s_y^2$,

$$F(1, N - 2) = \frac{(N - 2)(s_x^2 - s_y^2)^2}{4s_x^2 s_y^2(1 - r_{xy}^2)}, \tag{11}$$

together with the rest of a zero correlation between initial and final values (Foerster, 1995), $H_0$: $r_{xy} = 0$,

$$F(1, N - 2) = \frac{(N - 2)r_{xy}^2}{1 - r_{xy}^2}, \tag{12}$$

lead to the following conclusions:

- If $s_x^2 > s_y^2$, a True IVD exists, because the difference score is determined more by the initial than the final score. If, additionally, $r_{xy} > 0$, it can be concluded that the LIV holds: The higher the initial value, the smaller the response to an activating stimulus. If $r_{xy} = 0$, the responses of the participants tend toward a certain final value, but a prediction of final values based on initial values is not possible. If $r_{xy} < 0$, participants with high initial values tend to show decreased final values ("paradoxical responses"). This is rare in physiological data sets.
- If $s_x^2 = s_y^2$, the difference score is determined in equal parts by initial and final values. If $r_{xy} < 0$ (e.g., $y = -x$), a True IVD exists, though.
- If $s_x^2 < s_y^2$, the difference score depends more on the final than the initial value. If $r_{xy} > 0$, the change follows a "fan model" (Weisberg, 1979), which describes a condition opposite to the LIV ("Anti-LIV"; Myrtek et al., 1977).

Applying, for example, these rules to the data in table 12.5, we find that (1) heart period exhibits a strong True IVD according to the LIV, because $s_x^2 > s_y^2$, $F(1,156) = 26.48$, $p < .001$, and $r_{xy} > 0$, $F(1,156) = 26.33$, $p < .001$; (2) systolic blood pressure also exhibits a strong True IVD, according, however, to the Anti-LIV, because $s_x^2 < s_y^2$, $F(1,156) = 35.19$, $p < .001$, and $r_{xy} > 0$, $F(1,156) = 46.70$, $p < .001$; (3) diastolic blood pressure shows no True IVD, because $s_x^2 = s_y^2$, $F(1,156) = 0.19$, $ns$, and $r_{xy} > 0$.

### Somatovisceral Profiles and Their Configurational Representation

The choice of a measure of change is often only an intermediate step in the statistical analysis of one's data. The next step is hypothesis testing. However, when it comes to somatovisceral and emotion self-report *profiles*, separate univariate or a summary multivariate test tells us only that something is there, not what it is. The previous discussion in this chapter about the sampling of variables emphasized that not single variables but regulation patterns should be assessed, because only the latter point to the functional significance of organismic states. Thus the final step of data analysis should be a close inspection of profiles and of differences among experimental groups in their response profiles.

Techniques of exploratory data analysis can effectively assist in this task. One method, multistage discriminant analysis (Stemmler, 1988, 1992), identifies three aspects of profiles: profile level, that is, average intensity; profile scatter, that is, the magnitude of intensity differences among variables; and profile shape, that is, the configuration or quality of activation. These aspects are separable in certain geometrical properties of centroid plots in the space of maximal discrimination among the experimental groups, provided some rules are followed. (Centroids are representations of average group profiles as points in discriminant space.) An abbreviated procedure takes the following steps:

- It should be ensured that all variables have a comparable scaling and polarity. A comparable scaling can be achieved through z-standardization, centering plus standardization with the pooled within-group standard deviation, or the coefficient of variation (T. Scherer, 2000).
- Profile levels are formed for each experimental group and tested for no difference among groups with the main effect group in multivariate analysis of variance (MANOVA).
- The data matrix is semi-ipsatized; that is, for all cases within a group the respective group's profile level is subtracted. Semi-ipsatization eliminates differences in profile levels among groups.
- The semi-ipsatized data matrix is subjected to a MANOVA or a discriminant analysis (DA).
- If variables had not been set to a mean of zero, the origin of discriminant space has to be readjusted to coincide with the origin of variable space, which is at $(0, 0, \ldots, 0)$:

$$c^*_{gv} = c_{gv} + \sum_{k=1}^{p} (q_{vk}M_{xk}), \qquad (13)$$

with $c_{gv}$ the centroid of group $g$ on discriminant function (DF) $v$, $q_{vk}$ the unstandardized discriminant weight of variable $k$ on DF$v$, $p$ the number of variables, and $c^*$ the adjusted centroid. $M_{xk}$ is the mean of variable $x_k$.

- If the DFs are not yet scaled to a length of 1 (usually they are scaled such that their error variance is 1), the centroid matrix is rescaled to that effect,

$$c^{**}_{gv} = \frac{c^*_{gv}}{\sqrt{\sum_{k=1}^{p} q_{vk}^2}}, \qquad (14)$$

with $c^{**}$ the adjusted and rescaled centroid.

- Centroids are plotted in a low-dimensional discriminant space, along with the projection of variables into that space (coordinates of variables are given by the structure or correlation matrix of variables with DFs).

The previous steps allow the following interpretations. Distances among centroids are only a function of profile differences in scatter and shape, because profile levels were made equal through semi-ipsatization (Skinner, 1978). Profile scatters are proportional to the distance of centroids from the origin. The dissimilarity of profile shapes is represented in their angular separation. Centroids located at a 90° angle have uncorrelated profile shapes. Centroids located at a 180° angle, that is, opposite from the origin, have inverted profile shapes, or a correlation of −1. These interpretations are exact if the dimensionality of discriminant space is 2 or 3, for 2- or 3-dimensional centroid plots, respectively. If the dimensionality of discriminant space is larger than the dimensionality of the centroid plot, these interpretations are no longer exact.

However, each DF represents one "layer" of the total variation among profile patterns. The angular separations of centroids and their distances from the origin therefore reflect similarities of profile shapes and profile scatters, respectively, within particular layers of profile dissimilarity. Thus this technique may unveil sources of pattern dissimilarity.

As an example from the data set used throughout this chapter (Stemmler et al., 1998, 2001), I analyze somatovisceral profiles of real-life fear and anger inductions. Four experimental groups, fear induction, fear control, anger induction, and anger control, were formed. It was asked what the response patterns of emotion responses, that is, of induction minus control groups, would look like and how the difference between fear and anger emotion responses could be characterized. From the pool of 29 somatovisceral variables, 8 were selected for this demonstration. Because the variables have different units of measurement, ANCOVA-adjusted change scores were centered and standardized with the pooled within-group standard deviation. Finally, the polarity of heart period was inverted. The resulting profiles are depicted in Figure 12.8 (panel a); profile parameters are collected in Table 12.6. The profiles of fear control and anger control were quite similar. The anger-induction and especially the fear-induction profiles had higher levels and scatters than the control group profiles. Despite some differences, the profile shapes of fear induction and anger induction were very similar.

Next, standard profile tests (Morrison, 1976) were conducted. The flatness test indicated that the grand average profile was completely "flat," a consequence of centering. The null hypothesis of equal profile levels was rejected. Finally, profile parallelism was also rejected. Thus the profiles had different levels and patterns.

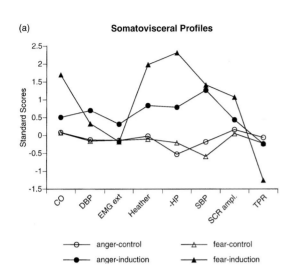

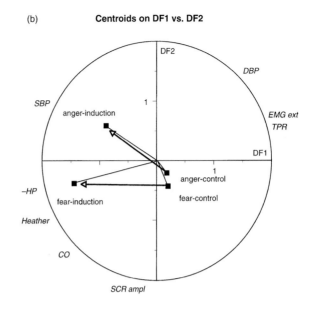

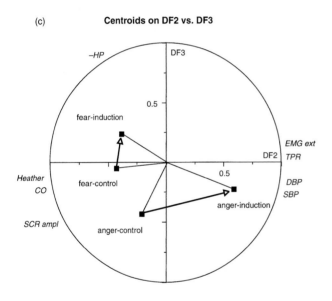

Figure 12.8 Visualization of profiles and their similarity. Depicted are responses to real-life fear and anger induction and control groups, adjusted for responses in standard tests. Panel a shows profiles of eight somatovisceral variables after centering and scaling of variables to the pooled within-group standard deviation. Panels b and c depict group centroids (black squares) in the space of discriminant functions (DF) 1 versus 2 and 2 versus 3, respectively. Arrows mark the difference between induction and control groups of the same emotion. Names of somatovisceral variables are inserted at positions that indicate their projection onto the plane. CO = cardiac output; DBP = diastolic blood pressure; EMG ext = EMG extensor digitorum; Heather = Heather index; −HP = heart period (reflected); SBP = systolic blood pressure; SCR ampl = amplitude of skin conductance response; TPR = total peripheral resistance.

After semi-ipsatization, the space discriminating maximally among the four experimental groups was determined through a discriminant analysis. Centroids were rescaled; the projection of variables into the discriminant space was derived from the variables × DF correlations across group means (named "Between Canonical Structure" in PROC CANDISC output; SAS Institute, 1989). Panels b and c of Figure 12.8 show the results of these calculations for the planes of DF1 by DF2 and DF2 by DF3, respectively. In panel b, the fear-induction centroid is located in the lower left quadrant extending toward the variables heart period (reflected), Heather index, and cardiac output and away from diastolic blood pressure, EMG extensor, and total peripheral resistance. Thus, in this layer of the response pattern, the former variables were markedly elevated in the fear-induction group, whereas the lat-

ter variables were subdued. The position of each of the centroids can be interpreted in a similar way.

I inspect the configuration of centroids in panel b of Figure 12.8 now. The control group centroids are very close to each other; that is, the control groups had very similar patterns in this response layer. Anger-induction and anger-control centroids are located on nearly opposite sides of the origin. This means that, in this response layer, the profile shapes were nearly inverse to each other. Fear-induction and fear-control centroids are nearly perpendicular to each other: Their profile shapes were thus nearly uncorrelated with each other in this response layer.

Of substantial interest was whether the emotion responses, that is, the induction minus control group difference, would be different for fear and anger. Geometrically, the difference between two vectors is a vector connecting

Table 12.6. Profile Parameters of Somatovisceral Profiles in Figure 12.8

| Group | Level | Scatter | Correlations | | |
| | | | a-i | f-c | f-i |
|---|---|---|---|---|---|
| anger-control[a] | −0.10 | 0.20 | −0.32 | 0.51 | −0.23 |
| anger-induction[b] | 0.58 | 0.44 | | −0.46 | 0.76 |
| fear-control[c] | −0.16 | 0.20 | | | 0.06 |
| fear-induction[d] | 0.92 | 1.21 | | | |

*Note:* a-i = anger-induction; f-c = fear-control; f-i = fear-induction. Correlations calculated across eight somatovisceral variables. [a]$N = 39$. [b]$N = 40$. [c]$N = 41$. [d]$N = 38$.

their endpoints, as can be seen in Figure 12.8 (panels b and c). The length and direction of these vectors can be interpreted exactly as previously. From the plane of DF1 and DF2, it is evident that fear and anger emotion response patterns were quite similar. Marker variables on this response layer are systolic blood pressure increases and heart period decreases, as well as Heather index and cardiac output increases. The plane of DF2 by DF3 shows a different picture. Fear and anger emotion response patterns are approaching orthogonality. Marker variables on this layer are heart period decreases for fear and EMG extensor, total peripheral resistance, and diastolic, as well as systolic, blood pressure increases for anger. This finding suggests that different and separable influences combine to form the observed response patterns (for a substantial interpretation, see Stemmler et al., 2001).

## Summary

This chapter has reviewed some topics in the design and analysis of psychophysiological investigations that are of particular importance in emotion research. My treatment of the topics covered was directed toward spelling out criteria for an evaluation of different options that researchers have rather than prescribing what in my opinion they should do.

Models guide methods. This certainly sounds like a commendable scientific principle. Methods should be selected such as to inform the researcher about the validity of his or her theoretical models as best possible. But even though strict methods have their roots in "hard" rather than "soft" science (Meehl, 1978), and even though criteria for the use (and misuse) of some statistical methods are unequivocally embraced by the scientific community, there is a wide range of acceptable answers to methodological questions. Some of these answers will be real gold mines, others will lead nowhere. Often there is no way to know in advance the best methodological decision. It follows that more often than not models do not guide methods, at least not completely. One, and perhaps the most important, reason is that models in psychology are often hopelessly underspecified and imprecise. Methods cannot be deduced from such models.

Methods inform models. Employed in a critical and scrupulous way, methods are tools in a context of discovery. They may lead to specifications of models dictated by empirical data. In this inductive loop of theory construction, methods are the *via regia* to progress. To foster such progress, methodological open-mindedness and a plurality of methods are helpful. Successful progress, however, also needs the creative mind that proposes new and better models. This is not an easy or quickly mastered task in an area as complex as emotion research.

## REFERENCES

Adsett, C. A., Schottstaedt, W. W., & Wolf, S. G. (1962). Changes in coronary blood flow and other hemodynamic indicators induced by stressful interviews. *Psychosomatic Medicine, 24*, 331–336.

Alloy, L. B., Abramson, L. Y., & Viscusi, D. (1981). Induced mood and the illusion of control. *Journal of Personality and Social Psychology, 41*, 1129–1140.

Asendorpf, J. B., & Scherer, K. R. (1983). The discrepant repressor: Differentiation between low anxiety, high anxiety, and repression of anxiety by autonomic-facial-verbal patterns of behavior. *Journal of Personality and Social Psychology, 45*, 1334–1346.

Averill, J. R. (1974). An analysis of psychophysiological symbolism and its influence on theories of emotion. *Journal for the Theory of Social Behaviour, 4*, 147–190.

Ax, A. F. (1953). The physiological differentiation between fear and anger in humans. *Psychosomatic Medicine, 15*, 433–442.

Bandler, R. (1982). Induction of "rage" following microinjections of glutamate into the midbrain but not hypothalamus of cats. *Neuroscience Letter, 30*, 183–188.

Berkowitz, L. (1983). Aversively stimulated aggression: Some parallels and differences in research with animals and humans. *American Psychologist, 38*, 1135–1144.

Berkowitz, L. (1990). On the formation and regulation of anger and aggression: A cognitive-neoassociationistic analysis. *American Psychologist, 45*, 494–503.

Berntson, G. G., Cacioppo, J. T., & Quigley, K. S. (1991). Autonomic determinism: The modes of autonomic control, the doctrine of autonomic space, and the laws of autonomic constraint. *Psychological Review, 98*, 459–487.

Berntson, G. G., Cacioppo, J. T., & Quigley, K. S. (1993). Cardiac psychophysiology and autonomic space in humans: Empirical perspectives and conceptual implications. *Psychological Bulletin, 114*, 296–322.

Berntson, G. G., Sarter, M., & Cacioppo, J. T. (1998). Anxiety and cardiovascular reactivity: The basal forebrain cholinergic link. *Behavioural Brain Research, 94*, 225–248.

Blascovich, J., & Tomaka, J. (1996). The biopsychosocial model of arousal regulation. In M. P. Zanna (Ed.), *Experimental social psychology* (pp. 1–51). New York: Academic Press.

Bloch, S., Orthous, P., & Santibanez-H., G. (1987). Effector patterns of basic emotions: A psychophysiological method for training actors. *Journal of Social and Biological Structures, 10*, 1–19.

Böddeker, I., & Stemmler, G. (2000). Who responds how and when to anger? The assessment of actual anger response styles and their relation to personality. *Cognition and Emotion, 14*, 737–762.

Boiten, F. (1996). Autonomic response patterns during voluntary facial action. *Psychophysiology, 33*(2), 123–131.

Brewer, D., Doughtie, E. B., & Lubin, B. (1980). Induction of mood and mood shift. *Journal of Clinical Psychology, 36*, 215–226.

Buchner, A., Faul, F., & Erdfelder, E. (1992). *GPOWER: A priori-, post hoc-, and compromise power analyses for the Macintosh*. Bonn, Germany: Bonn University.

Buell, J. C., Alpert, B. S., & McCrory, W. W. (1986). Physical stressors as elicitors of cardiovascular reactivity. In K. A. Matthews, S. M. Weiss, T. Detre, T. M. Dembrowski, B. Falkner, S. B. Manuck, & R. B. Williams (Eds.), *Handbook of stress, reactivity, and cardiovascular disease* (pp. 127–144). New York: Wiley.

Cacioppo, J. T., Gardner, W. L., & Berntson, G. G. (1999). The affect system has parallel and integrative processing components: Form follows function. *Journal of Personality and Social Psychology, 76*(5), 839–855.

Cacioppo, J. T., Klein, D. J., Berntson, G. G., & Hatfield, E. (1993). The psychophysiology of emotion. In M. Lewis & J. M. Haviland (Eds.), *Handbook of emotions* (pp. 119–142). New York: Guilford Press.

Cacioppo, J. T., Martzke, J. S., Petty, R. E., & Tassinary, L. G. (1988). Specific forms of facial EMG response index emotions during an interview: From Darwin to the continuous flow hypothesis of affect-laden information processing. *Journal of Personality and Social Psychology, 54*, 592–604.

Cacioppo, J. T., Petty, R. E., Losch, M. E., & Kim, H. S. (1986). Electromyographic activity over facial muscle regions can differentiate the valence and intensity of affective reactions. *Journal of Personality and Social Psychology, 50*, 260–268.

Cacioppo, J. T., & Tassinary, L. G. (1990a). Inferring psychological significance from physiological signals. *American Psychologist, 45*, 16–28.

Cacioppo, J. T., & Tassinary, L. G. (1990b). Psychophysiology and psychophysiological inference. In J. T. Cacioppo & L. G. Tassinary (Eds.), *Principles of psychophysiology* (pp. 3–33). Cambridge, England: Cambridge University Press.

Campbell, D. T., & Fiske, D. W. (1959). Convergent and discriminant validation by the multitrait–multimethod matrix. *Psychological Bulletin, 56*, 81–105.

Campbell, D. T., & Stanley, J. C. (1963). Experimental and quasi-experimental designs for research on teaching. In N. L. Gage (Ed.), *Handbook of research on teaching* (pp. 171–246). Chicago: Rand McNally.

Carver, C. S., Scheier, M. F., & Weintraub, J. K. (1989). Assessing coping strategies: A theoretically based approach. *Journal of Personality and Social Psychology, 56*, 267–283.

Chessick, R. D., Bassan, M., & Shattan, S. (1966). A comparison of the effect of infused catecholamines and certain affect states. *American Journal of Psychiatry, 123*, 156–165.

Cook, T. D., & Campbell, D. T. (1979). *Quasi-experimentation: Design and analysis issues for field settings*. Chicago: Rand McNally.

Cronbach, L. J., & Furby, L. (1970). How we should measure "change": Or should we? *Psychological Bulletin, 74*, 68–80.

Dandoy, A. C., & Goldstein, A. G. (1990). The use of cognitive appraisal to reduce stress reactions: A replication. *Journal of Social Behavior and Personality, 5*, 275–285.

Darwin, C. (1872). *The expression of the emotions in man and animals*. London: Murray.

Davidson, R. J., & Irwin, W. (1999). The functional neuroanatomy of emotion and affective style. *Trends in Cognitive Sciences, 3*(1), 11–21.

Davison, G. C., Williams, M. E., Nezami, E., Bice, T. L., & DeQuattro, V. L. (1991). Relaxation, reduction in angry articulated thoughts, and improvements in borderline hypertension and heart rate. *Journal of Behavioral Medicine, 14*, 453–468.

Depue, R. A., & Collins, P. F. (1999). Neurobiology of the structure of personality: Dopamine, facilitation of incentive motivation, and extraversion. *Behavioral and Brain Sciences, 22*(3), 491–569.

Dimsdale, J. E., Pierce, C., Schoenfeld, D., Brown, A., Zusman, R., & Graham, R. (1986). Suppressed anger and blood pressure: The effects of race, sex, social class, obesity, and age. *Psychosomatic Medicine, 48*, 430–436.

Duclos, S. E., Laird, J. D., Schneider, E., Sexter, M., Stern, L., & Van Lighten, O. (1989). Emotion-specific effects of facial expressions and postures on emotional experience. *Journal of Personality and Social Psychology, 57*(1), 100–108.

Ehrlichman, H., & Bastone, L. (1992). Olfaction and emotion. In M. Serby & K. Chobor (Eds.), *The science of olfaction* (pp. 410–438). New York: Springer.

Ekman, P. (1992). Are there basic emotions? *Psychological Review, 99*(3), 550–553.

Ekman, P. (1994). All emotions are basic. In P. Ekman & R. J. Davidson (Eds.), *The nature of emotion: Fundamental questions* (pp. 15–19). New York: Oxford University Press.

Ekman, P., & Davidson, R. J. (Eds.). (1994). *The nature of emotion: Fundamental questions*. New York: Oxford University Press.

Ekman, P., Levenson, R. W., & Friesen, W. V. (1983). Autonomic nervous system activity distinguishes among emotions. *Science, 221*, 1208–1210.

Engebretson, T. O., Matthews, K. A., & Scheier, M. F. (1989). Relations between anger expression and cardiovascular reactivity: Reconciling inconsistent findings through a matching hypothesis. *Journal of Personality and Social Psychology, 57*, 513–521.

Engel, B. T., & Bickford, A. F. (1961). Response specificity: Stimulus-response and individual-response specificity in essential hypertensives. *Archives of General Psychiatry, 5*, 478–489.

Erdmann, G., & Baumann, S. (1996). Sind psychophysiologische Veränderungen im Paradigma "Öffentliches Sprechen" Ausdruck emotionaler Belastung? [Do psychophysiological effects elicited by the "Public Speaking paradigm" reflect emotional stress?]. *Zeitschrift für Experimentelle Psychologie, 43*(2), 224–255.

Erdmann, G., Ising, M., & Janke, W. (2000). Pharmaka und Emotionen [Pharmacological agents and emotions]. In J. H. Otto, H. A. Euler, & H. Mandl (Eds.), *Handbuch der Emotionspsychologie* (2nd ed.). Weinheim, Germany: Psychologie Verlags Union.

Fahrenberg, J., & Foerster, F. (1989). *Nicht-invasive Methodik für die kardiovasculäre Psychophysiologie [Non-*

*invasive methods for cardiovascular psychophysiology*]. Frankfurt, Germany: Lang.

Fahrenberg, J., Foerster, F., Schneider, H.-J., Müller, W., & Myrtek, M. (1986). Predictability of individual differences in activation processes in a field setting based on laboratory measures. *Psychophysiology, 23*, 323–333.

Fahrenberg, J., & Myrtek, M. (1996). *Ambulatory assessment.* Seattle, WA: Hogrefe & Huber.

Fahrenberg, J., Schneider, H.-J., & Safian, P. (1987). Psychophysiological assessments in a repeated-measurement design extending over a one-year interval: Trends and stability. *Biological Psychology, 24*, 49–66.

Flynn, J. P. (1967). The neural basis of aggression in cats. In D. C. Glass (Ed.), *Neurophysiology and emotion* (pp. 40–60). New York: Rockefeller University Press and Russell Sage Foundation.

Foerster, F. (1995). On the problems of initial-value-dependencies and measurement of change. *Journal of Psychophysiology, 9*, 324–341.

Folkow, B. (1979). Relevance of cardiovascular reflexes. In R. Hainsworth, C. Kidd, & R. J. Linden (Eds.), *Cardiac receptors* (pp. 473–505). London: Cambridge University Press.

Foulds, J., McAllister, H., & Foulds, S. (1988). The relationship between socialisation and electrodermal activity in normal subjects. *Journal of Psychophysiology, 2*, 227–230.

Freedman, R. R., & Ianni, P. (1985). Effects of general and thematically relevant stressors in Raynaud's disease, *Journal of Psychosomatic Research, 29*, 275–280.

Fridlund, A. J., Schwartz, G. E., & Fowler, S. C. (1984). Pattern recognition of self-reported emotional state from multiple-site facial EMG activity during affective imagery. *Psychophysiology, 21*, 622–637.

Frijda, N. H., Ortony, A., Sonnemans, J., & Clore, G. L. (1992). The complexity of intensity: Issues concerning the structure of emotion intensity. In M. S. Clark (Ed.), *Emotion: Review of personality and social psychology* (pp. 60–89). Newbury Park, CA: Sage Publications.

Funkenstein, D. H., King, S. H., & Drolette, M. (1954). The direction of anger during a laboratory stress-inducing situation. *Psychosomatic Medicine, 16*, 404–413.

Geenen, R., & Van de Vijver, F. J. (1993). A simple test of the Law of Initial Values. *Psychophysiology, 30*(5), 525–530.

Gellhorn, E. (1964a). Motion and emotion: The role of proprioception in the physiology and pathology of the emotions. *Psychological Review, 71*, 457–472.

Gellhorn, E. (1964b). The significance of the state of the central autonomic nervous system for quantitative and qualitative aspects of some cardiovascular reactions. *American Heart Journal, 67*, 106–120.

Gellhorn, E. (1967). *Principles of autonomic-somatic integrations.* Minneapolis: University of Minnesota Press.

Glombiewski, J., & Schirmbeck, F. (2000). *Ärger-und Freudeinduktion: Vergleich zweier Fragebögen zur Befindlichkeitsmessung [The induction of anger and happiness: Comparison of two questionnaires for the assessment of emotion*]. Unpublished manuscript, University of Marburg, Germany.

Goldstein, H. (1979). *The design and analysis of longitudinal studies.* London: Academic Press.

Gottlieb, A. A., Gleser, G. C., & Gottschalk, L. A. (1967). Verbal and physiological responses to hypnotic suggestion of attitude. *Psychosomatic Medicine, 29*, 172–183.

Graham, D. T., Kabler, J. D., & Graham, F. K. (1962). Physiological response to the suggestion of attitudes specific for hives and hypertension. *Psychosomatic Medicine, 24*, 159–169.

Grillon, C., Ameli, R., Woods, S. W., Merikangas, K., & Davis, M. (1991). Fear-potentiated startle in humans: Effects of anticipatory anxiety on the acoustic blink reflex. *Psychophysiology, 28*, 588–595.

Gross, J. J. (1998a). Antecedent- and response-focused emotion regulation: Divergent consequences for experience, expression, and physiology. *Journal of Personality and Social Psychology, 74*(1), 224–237.

Gross, J. J. (1998b). The emerging field of emotion regulation: An integrative review. *Review of General Psychology, 2*, 271–299.

Gross, J. J., & John, O. P. (1997). Revealing feelings: Facets of emotional expressivity in self-reports, peer ratings, and behavior. *Journal of Personality and Social Psychology, 72*(2), 435–448.

Gross, J. J., & Levenson, R. W. (1993). Emotional suppression: Physiology, self-report, and expressive behavior. *Journal of Personality and Social Psychology, 64*, 970–986.

Gross, J. J., & Levenson, R. W. (1997). Hiding feelings: The acute effects of inhibiting negative and positive emotion. *Journal of Abnormal Psychology, 106*(1), 95–103.

Grossberg, J. M., & Wilson, H. K. (1968). Physiological changes accompanying the visualization of fearful and neutral situations. *Journal of Personality and Social Psychology, 10*, 124–133.

Hamm, A. O., & Vaitl, D. (1993). Emotionsinduktion durch visuelle Reize: Validierung einer Stimulationsmethode auf drei Reaktionsebenen. [Induction of emotions via visual stimuli: Validation of an induction method on three response levels]. *Psychologische Rundschau, 44*(3), 143–161.

Hess, U., Kappas, A., McHugo, G. J., Lanzetta, J. T., & Kleck, R. E. (1992). The facilitative effect of facial expression on the self-generation of emotion. *International Journal of Psychophysiology, 12*(3), 251–265.

Hess, W. R. (1948). *Die funktionelle Organisation des vegetativen Nervensystems* [The functional organization of the vegetative nervous system]. Basel, Switzerland: Schwabe.

Hilton S. M. (1975). Ways of viewing the central nervous control of the circulation: Old and new. *Brain Research, 87*, 213–219.

Hilton, S. M. (1982). The defence-arousal system and its relevance for circulatory and respiratory control. *Journal of Experimental Biology, 100*, 159–174.

Hodapp, V., Heiligtag, U., & Stormer, S. W. (1990). Cardiovascular reactivity, anxiety and anger during perceived controllability. *Biological Psychology, 30*, 161–170.

Hsu, L. M. (1995). Regression toward the mean associated with measurement error and the identification of improvement and deterioration in psychotherapy. *Journal of Consulting and Clinical Psychology, 63*(1), 141–144.

Huitema, B. E. (1980). *The analysis of covariance and alternatives.* New York: Wiley.

Izard. C. E. (1972). *Patterns of emotion: A new analysis of anxiety and depression.* New York: Academic Press.

Izard, C. E. (1991). *The psychology of emotions.* New York: Plenum.

Izard, C. E. (1992). Basic emotions, relations among emotions, and emotion-cognition relations. *Psychological Review, 99*(3), 561–565.

Izard, C. E. (1993). Four systems for emotion activation: Cognitive and noncognitive processes. *Psychological Review, 100*, 68–90.

James, W. (1884). What is an emotion? *Mind, 19*, 188–205.

Jamieson. J. (1993). The law of initial values: Five factors or two? *International Journal of Psychophysiology, 14*(3), 233–239.

Jamieson, J. (1995). Measurement of change and the law of initial values: A computer simulation study. *Educational and Psychological Measurement, 55*(1), 38–46.

Jänig, W., & McLachlan, E. M. (1992a). Characteristics of function-specific pathways in the sympathetic nervous system. *Trends in Neurosciences, 15*, 475–481.

Jänig, W., & McLachlan, E. M. (1992b). Specialized functional pathways are the building blocks of the autonomic nervous system. *Journal of the Autonomic Nervous System, 41*, 3–14.

Jennings, J. R., Kamarck, T., Stewart, C., Eddy, M., & Johnson, P. (1992). Alternate cardiovascular baseline assessment techniques: Vanilla or resting baseline. *Psychophysiology, 29*, 742–750.

Kendall, M. G., & Stuart, A. (1967). *The advanced theory of statistics*. London: Griffin.

Koslowitz, I. (1993). *Imagination emotionaler Erlebnisse. Eine Untersuchung zur psychophysiologischen Spezifität von Angst and Ärger. [Emotional imagery: A study on the psychophysiological specificity of fear and anger]*. Unpublished Diploma thesis, University of Freiburg, Germany.

Krantz, D. S., & Ratliff-Crain, J. (1989). The social context of stress and behavioral medicine research: Instructions, experimenter effects, and social interactions. In N. Schneiderman, S. M. Weiss, & P. G. Kaufmann (Eds.), *Handbook of research methods in cardiovascular behavioral medicine* (pp. 383–392). New York: Plenum.

Krause, M. S. (1972). The implications of convergent and discriminant validity data for instrument validation. *Psychometrika, 37*, 179–186.

Krohne, H. W. (1989). The concept of coping modes: Relating cognitive person variables to actual coping behavior. *Advances in Behaviour Research and Therapy, 11*(4), 235–248.

Lacey, B. C., & Lacey, J. I. (1974). Studies of heart rate and other bodily processes in sensorimotor behavior. In P. A. Obrist, A. H. Black, J. Brener, & L. V. DiCara (Eds.), *Cardiovascular psychophysiology* (pp. 538–564). Chicago: Aldine.

Lacey, J. I. (1956). The evaluation of autonomic responses: Toward a general solution. *Annals of the New York Academy of Sciences, 67*, 123–164.

Lang, P. J. (1979). A bio-informational theory of emotional imagery. *Psychophysiology, 16*, 495–512.

Lang, P. J., Bradley, M. M., & Cuthbert, B. N. (1990). Emotion, attention, and the startle reflex. *Psychological Review, 97*, 377–395.

Lang, P. J., Bradley, M. M., & Cuthbert, B. N. (1997). Motivated attention: Affect, activation, and action. In P. J. Lang, R. F. Simons, & M. T. Balaban (Eds.), *Attention and orienting: Sensory and motivational processes* (pp. 97–135). Mahwah, NJ: Erlbaum.

Lang, P. J., Greenwald, M. K., Bradley, M. M., & Hamm, A. O. (1993). Looking at pictures: Affective, facial, visceral, and behavioral reactions. *Psychophysiology, 30*(3), 261–273.

Lang, P. J. Kozak, M. J., Miller, G. A., Levin, D. N., & McLean, A. (1980). Emotional imagery: Conceptual structure and pattern of somato-visceral response. *Psychophysiology, 17*, 179–192.

Lang, P. J., Levin, D. N., Miller, G. A., & Kozak, M. J. (1983). Fear behavior, fear imagery, and the psychophysiology of emotion: The problem of affective response integration. *Journal of Abnormal Psychology, 92*, 276–306.

Lazarus, R. S. (1991). *Emotion and adaptation*. New York: Oxford University Press.

Lazarus, R. S., & Alfert, E. (1964). Short-circuiting of threat by experimentally altering cognitive appraisal. *Journal of Abnormal and Social Psychology, 69*, 195–205.

Lazarus, R. S., Opton, E. M. J., Nomikos, M. S., & Rankin, N. O. (1965). The principle of short-circuiting of threat: Further evidence. *Journal of Personality, 33*, 622–635.

LeDoux, J. E. (1993). Emotional networks in the brain. In M. Lewis & J. M. Haviland (Eds.), *Handbook of emotions* (pp. 109–118). New York: Guilford Press.

Levenson, R. W., Carstensen, L. L., Friesen, W. V., & Ekman, P. (1991). Emotion, physiology, and expression in old age. *Psychology and Aging, 6*, 28–35.

Levenson, R. W., & Ekman, P. *Difficulty does not account for emotion-specific heart rate changes in the directed facial action task*. Manuscript submitted for publication, 2000.

Levenson, R. W., Ekman, P., & Friesen, W. V. (1990). Voluntary facial action generates emotion-specific autonomic nervous system activity. *Psychophysiology, 27*, 363–384.

Levenson, R. W., Ekman, P., Heider, K., & Friesen, W. V. (1992). Emotion and autonomic nervous system activity in the Minangkabau of West Sumatra. *Journal of Personality and Social Psychology, 62*, 972–988.

Lisander, B. (1979). Somato-autonomic reactions and their higher control. In C. M. Brooks, K. Koizumi, & A. Sato (Eds.), *Integrative functions of the autonomic nervous system* (pp. 385–395). Amsterdam: Elsevier.

Mäntysaari, M. J., Antila, K. J., & Peltonen, T. E. (1988). Circulatory effects of anticipation in a light isometric handgrip test. *Psychophysiology, 25*, 179–184.

Martin, C. E., Shaver, J. A., Leon, D. F., Thompson, M. E., Reddy, P. S., & Leonard, J. J. (1974). Autonomic mechanisms in hemodynamic responses to isometric exercise. *Journal of Clinical Investigation, 54*, 104–115.

Martin, M. (1990). On the induction of mood. *Clinical Psychology Review, 10*(6), 669–697.

Martin, R., & Watson, D. (1997). Style of anger expression and its relation to daily experience. *Personality and Social Psychology Bulletin, 23*(3), 285–294.

Marwitz, M., & Stemmler, G. (1998). On the status of individual response specificity. *Psychophysiology, 35*, 1–15.

Maslach, C. (1979). Negative emotional biasing of unexplained arousal. *Journal of Personality and Social Psychology, 37*, 953–969.

Mecklenbräuker, S., & Hager, W. (1986). Zur experimentellen Variation von Stimmungen: Ein Vergleich einer deutschen Adaptation der selbstbezogenen Velten-Aussagen mit einem Musikverfahren [On the experimental variation of moods: A comparison of a German adaptation of the Velten-technique with the induction by music]. *Zeitschrift für Experimentelle und Angewandte Psychologie, 33*, 71–94.

Meehl, P. E. (1978). Theoretical risks and tabular asterisks: Sir Karl, Sir Ronald, and the slow progress of soft psychology. *Journal of Consulting and Clinical Psychology, 46*, 806–834.

Mendolia, M., Moore, J., & Tesser, A. (1996). Dispositional and situational determinants of repression. *Journal of Personality and Social Psychology, 70*(4), 856–867.

Messick, S. (1981). Denoting the base-free measure of change. *Psychometrika, 46*, 215–217.

Miltner, W., Larbig, W., & Braun, C. (1988). Attention and event-related potentials elicited by intracutaneous electrical stimulation of the skin. *Journal of Psychophysiology, 2*, 269–276.

Morrison, D. F. (1976). *Multivariate statistical methods.* New York: McGraw-Hill.

Mulder, G., Mulder, L. J. M., & Veldeman, J. B. P. (1985). Mental tasks as stressors. In A. Steptoe, H. Rüddel, & H. Neus (Eds.), *Clinical and methodological issues in cardiovascular psychophysiology* (pp. 30–44). Berlin, Germany: Springer.

Myrtek, M., & Foerster, F. (1986). The law of initial value: A rare exception. *Biological Psychology, 22*, 227–237.

Myrtek, M., Foerster, F., & Wittmann, W. (1977). Das Ausgangswertproblem [The initial value problem]. *Zeitschrift für Experimentelle und Angewandte Psychologie, 24*, 463–491.

Nesselroade, J. R., Stigler, S. M., & Baltes, P. B. (1980). Regression toward the mean and the study of change. *Psychological Bulletin, 88*, 622–637.

Nyklicek, I., Thayer, J. F., & van Doornen, L. J. P. (1997). Cardiorespiratory differentiation of musically induced emotions. *Journal of Psychophysiology, 11*, 304–321.

Oatley, K., & Johnson-Laird, P. (1987). Towards a cognitive theory of emotions. *Cognition and Emotion, 1*, 29–50.

Obrist, P. A. (1981). *Cardiovascular psychophysiology.* New York: Plenum.

Ortony, A., & Turner, T. J. (1990). What's basic about basic emotions? *Psychological Review, 97*, 315–331.

Panksepp, J. (1992). A critical role for "affective neuroscience" in resolving what is basic about basic emotions. *Psychological Review, 99*(3), 554–560.

Panksepp, J. (1994). The basics of basic emotion. In P. Ekman & R. J. Davidson (Eds.), *The nature of emotion: Fundamental questions* (pp. 20–24). New York: Oxford University Press.

Papciak, A. S., Feuerstein, M., & Spiegel, J. A. (1985). Stress reactivity in alexithymia: Decoupling of physiological and cognitive responses. *Journal of Human Stress, 11*, 135–142.

Parkinson, B. (1985). Emotional effects of false automatic feedback. *Psychological Bulletin, 98*, 471–494.

Plewis, I. (1985). *Analysing change.* New York: Wiley.

Plutchik, R. (1989). Measuring emotions and their derivatives. In R. Plutchik & H. Kellerman (Eds.), *The measurement of emotions* (Vol. 4, pp. 1–35). San Diego, CA: Academic Press.

Polivy, J. (1981). On the induction of emotion in the laboratory: Discrete moods or multiple affect states? *Journal of Personality and Social Psychology, 41*, 803–817.

Regan, M., & Howard, R. C. (1991). Controllability, predictability and event-related potentials to fear-relevant and fear-irrelevant stimuli. *Journal of Psychophysiology, 5*, 43–57.

Roberts, R. J., & Weerts, T. C. (1982). Cardiovascular responding during anger and fear imagery. *Psychological Reports, 50*, 219–230.

Rogosa, D. (1988). Myths about longitudinal research. In K. W. Schaie, R. T. Campbell, W. Meredith, & S. C. Rawlings (Eds.), *Methodological issues in aging research* (pp. 171–210). New York: Springer.

Rogosa, D., Brandt, D., & Zimowski, M. (1982). A growth curve approach to the measurement of change. *Psychological Bulletin, 92*, 726–748.

Rosenstein, D., & Oster, H. (1988). Differential facial responses to four basic tastes in newborns. *Child Development, 59*(6), 1555–1568.

Russell, J. A., & Feldman Barrett, L. (1999). Core affect, prototypical emotional episodes, and other things called emotion: Dissecting the elephant. *Journal of Personality and Social Psychology, 76*(5), 805–819.

Saab, P. G., Llabre, M. M., Hurwitz, B. E., Frame, C. A., Reineke, L. J., Fins, A. I., McCalla, J., Cieply, L. K., & Schneiderman, N. (1992). Myocardial and peripheral vascular responses to behavioral challenges and their stability in Black and White Americans. *Psychophysiology, 29*, 384–397.

SAS Institute. (1989). *SAS/STAT User's Guide, Version 6*, (4th ed.). Cary, NC: Author.

Schachter, S., & Singer, J. E. (1962). Cognitive, social, and physiological determinants of emotional state. *Psychological Review, 69*, 379–399.

Scherer, K. R. (1994). Toward a concept of "modal emotions." In P. Ekman & R. J. Davidson (Eds.), *The nature of emotion: Fundamental questions* (pp. 25–31). New York: Oxford University Press.

Scherer, K. R. (1999). On the sequential nature of appraisal processes: Indirect evidence from a recognition task. *Cognition and Emotion, 13*, 763–793.

Scherer, T. (2000). *Stimme, Emotion und Psyche [Voice, emotion, and psyche].* Unpublished doctoral dissertation, University of Marburg, Germany.

Schwartz, G. E., Weinberger, D. A., & Singer, J. A. (1981). Cardiovascular differentiation of happiness, sadness, anger, and fear following imagery and exercise. *Psychosomatic Medicine, 43*, 343–364.

Shaver, P., Schwartz, J., Kirson, D., & O'Connor, C. (1987). Emotion knowledge: Further exploration of a prototype approach. *Journal of Personality and Social Psychology, 52*, 1061–1086.

Sinha, R., Lovallo, W. R., & Parsons, O. A. (1992). Cardiovascular differentiation of emotions. *Psychosomatic Medicine, 54*, 422–435.

Sinha, R., & Parsons, O. A. (1996). Multivariate response patterning of fear and anger. *Cognition and Emotion, 10*(2), 173–198.

Sirota, A. D., & Schwartz, G. E. (1982). Facial muscle patterning and lateralization during elation and depression imagery. *Journal of Abnormal Psychology, 91*, 25–34.

Skinner, H. A. (1978). Differentiating the contribution of elevation, scatter and shape in profile similarity. *Educational and Psychological Measurement, 38*, 297–308.

Smith, C. A., & Lazarus, R. S. (1990). Emotion and adaptation. In L. A. Pervin (Ed.), *Handbook of personality: Theory and research* (pp. 609–637). New York: Guilford Press.

Spies, K., Hesse, F. W., Gerrards-Hesse, A., & Ueffing, E. (1991). *Experimentelle Induktion emotionaler Zustände: Verbessert die zusätzliche Darbietung von Musik die Wirksamkeit selbstbezogener Aussagen? [Experimental induction of emotional states: Improved effects of self-referential statements through an additional presentation of music?].* Zeitschrift für Experimentelle und Angewandte Psychologie, 38, 321–342.

Stemmler, G. (1987). Implicit measurement models in methods for scoring physiological reactivity. *Journal of Psychophysiology, 1*, 113–125.

Stemmler, G. (1988). Effects of profile elevation, scatter, and shape on discriminant analysis results. *Educational and Psychological Measurement, 48*, 853–871.

Stemmler, G. (1989). The autonomic differentiation of emotions revisited: Convergent and discriminant validation. *Psychophysiology, 26*, 617–632.

Stemmler, G. (1992). *Differential psychophysiology: Persons in situations.* New York: Springer.

Stemmler, G., Grossman, P., Schmid, H., & Foerster, F. (1991). A model of cardiovascular activation components for studies using autonomic receptor antagonists. *Psychophysiology, 28*, 367–382.

Stemmler, G. Heldmann, M., Pauls, C. A., & Scherer, T. (1998). *Fear and anger specificity in somatovisceral responses* (Berichte aus dem Fachbereich Psychologie Nr. 116). Marburg, Germany: Philipps-Universität.

Stemmler, G. Heldmann, M., Pauls, C. A., & Scherer, T. (2001). Constraints for emotion specificity in fear and anger: The context counts. *Psychophysiology, 36*, 275–291.

Steptoe, A., & Vögele, C. (1986). Are stress responses influenced by cognitive appraisal? An experimental comparison of coping strategies. *British Journal of Psychology, 77*, 243–255.

Storm, C., & Storm, T. (1987). A taxonomic study of the vocabulary of emotions. *Journal of Personality and Social Psychology, 53*, 805–816.

Suarez, E. C., & Williams, R. B. (1989). Situational determinants of cardiovascular and emotional reactivity in high and low hostile men. *Psychosomatic Medicine, 51*, 404–418.

Thayer, R. E. (1996). *The origin of everyday moods: Managing energy, tension, and stress.* New York: Oxford University Press.

Vaitl, D., Vehrs, W., & Sternagel, S. (1993). Prompts—Leitmotif—emotion: Play it again, Richard Wagner. In N. Birbaumer & A. Öhman (Eds.), *The structure of emotion: Psychophysiological, cognitive and clinical aspects* (pp. 169–189). Toronto: Hogrefe & Huber.

van Doornen, L. J. P., & Turner, J. R. (1992). The ecological validity of laboratory stress testing. In R. J. Turner, A. Sherwood, & K. C. Light (Eds.), *Individual differences in cardiovascular response to stress* (pp. 63–83). New York: Plenum.

Van Heck, G. L. (1988). Modes and models in anxiety. *Anxiety Research, 1*, 199–214.

Velten, E. (1968). A laboratory task for induction of mood states. *Behaviour Research and Therapy, 6*, 473–482.

Wainer, H. (1991). Adjusting for differential base rates: Lord's Paradox again. *Psychological Bulletin, 109*(1), 147–151.

Watson, D., Wiese, D., Vaidya, J., & Tellegen, A. (1999). The two general activation systems of affect: Structural findings, evolutionary considerations, and psychobiological evidence. *Journal of Personality and Social Psychology, 76*(5), 820–838.

Weinberger, D. A. (1990). The construct validity of the repressive coping style. In J. L. Singer (Ed.), *Repression and dissociation: Implications for personality theory, psychopathology, and health* (pp. 337–386). Chicago: University of Chicago Press.

Weiner, B. (1990). Attribution in personality psychology. In L. A. Pervin (Ed.), *Handbook of personality: Theory and research* (pp. 465–485). New York: Guilford Press.

Weisberg, H. I. (1979). Statistical adjustments and uncontrolled studies. *Psychological Bulletin, 86*, 1149–1164.

Wenger, M. A., Jones, F. N., & Jones, M. H. (1956). *Physiological psychology.* New York: Holt, Rinehart & Winston.

Westermann, R., Spies, K., Stahl, G., & Hesse, F. W. (1996). Relative effectiveness and validity of mood induction procedures: A meta-analysis. *European Journal of Social Psychology, 26*, 557–580.

Wilder, J. (1931). Das "Ausgangswert-Gesetz", ein unbeachtetes biologisches Gesetz und seine Bedeutung für Forschung und Praxis [The "Law of Initial Values," an unnoted biological law and its relevance for research and practice]. *Zeitschrift für Neurologie, 137*, 317–338.

Wilder, J. (1967). *Stimulus and response: The Law of Initial Value.* Bristol, England: Wright.

Williams, R. H., & Zimmerman, D. W. (1996). Are simple gain scores obsolete? *Applied Psychological Measurement, 20*(1), 59–69.

Wundt, W. (1893). *Grundzüge der physiologischen Psychologie (Band 2).* Leipzig, Germany: Engelmann.

Zajonc, R. B., Murphy, S. T., & Inglehart, M. (1989). Feeling and facial efference: Implications of the vascular theory of emotion. *Psychological Review, 96*, 395–416.

# 13

# ON THE AUTOMATICITY OF AUTONOMIC RESPONSES IN EMOTION: AN EVOLUTIONARY PERSPECTIVE

Arne Öhman and Stefan Wiens

An evolutionary perspective on emotions emphasizes their function in promoting survival and procreation. Because meeting evolutionary challenges often requires vigorous behavioral responding, metabolic resources must be recruited as a support for action. For example, to escape the attacking predator, the potential prey must activate energy-demanding flight-or-fight responses. By modulating the state of the autonomic nervous system, the emotion of fear can assure that there are metabolic resources at hand to cope with dangers through defense responses appropriate for a given situation. Furthermore, if the organism can learn to utilize cues that signal emotional events, autonomic responses can be recruited well before the actual occurrence of the event that has to be coped with. From this perspective, the flow of emotion that is inherent in the interaction between an organism and its environment results in a continuous adjustment of autonomic effectors to meet actual or potential demands posed by the situation. Attended stimuli, including those that are sensitized by emotional states, elicit autonomic responses, often as components of the orienting response. These unspecific responses alert the organism and can then be channeled into more specific response patterns to assist emotional actions that are invited by the situational contingencies. An important point is that much of this fine-tuning of the autonomic nervous system to meet situational demands is controlled from information processing

mechanisms that are inaccessible to conscious deliberations. Depending on circumstances, the body is automatically adjusted to meet whatever challenge may emerge.

In this chapter, we start out by giving emotion an important role in the control of evolutionarily derived behavioral systems. Much of the burden on emotion in an evolutionary perspective is to recruit metabolic support for action via the autonomic nervous system, which we discuss with particular reference to fear. We go on to discuss the interplay between attention and emotion, using the orienting response as a bridge between the two domains. We then focus on how fear can become attached to new stimuli through Pavlovian conditioning. We particularly emphasize the role of evolutionary constraints on associations in Pavlovian conditioning and the role of nonconscious processes in the recruitment and learning of fear. Finally we integrate the findings on fear into a concept of a fear module and discuss how activation of this module provides input to higher cognition, such as decision making, and to the conscious experience of emotion.

## Evolution and Emotion

As a result of biological evolution, information about successful solutions to environmental challenges has accumulated in the gene pools of species. "Successful solutions" in this context refers to more effective means of promoting procreation. For sexually reproducing organisms, more effective mediation of genes across generations requires that partners be found in order for eggs to be fertilized and a new generation to emerge and reproduce. Thus the emotionally charged activities of finding a partner, having sex, and caring for offspring are central to the biological perspective. The typical topics of contemporary soap operas, therefore, not only mirror human life at the transition between two millennia but also reflect central life themes originating far back in evolution. Indeed, the focus on emotionally absorbing relationships (between men and women and between parents and children) in different artistic representations of the human predicament attest to the fact that humans, regardless of their cultural identity, in the end are biological creatures for which different aspects of procreation are central purposes of life. Thus the convergence on sex as the central source of motivation by two of the great thinkers of the 19th century, Darwin and Freud, reflects their shared (but still widely different) insights into the basic dynamics of life.

However, even though procreation drives evolution, individuals must survive to reproduce. Thus survival is not a biological goal in itself but serves as a prerequisite for procreation. To survive, organisms must honor homeostatic needs by keeping their internal temperature within defined limits, and they must ingest nutrients and fluid from the environment and excrete waste products. Furthermore, organisms must defend themselves against life-threatening insults from the environment. Microbes may invade organisms, and immune systems evolved as a result of the continuing arms race between rapidly evolving microbes and ever more sophisticated bodily defense systems. Poison-avoidance systems evolved to get rid of, or avoid, polluted nutrients. The emotion of disgust, therefore, is a means of keeping individuals away from the taste or smell of substances that have caused nausea and stomach upset. Last but not least, there were threats to survival that could be dealt with only at the behavioral level, through fast action. For example, threatening predators or conspecifics seeking dominance had to be coped with through escape or avoidance or through aggressive attack, and natural disasters such as floods, extreme cold, storms, and lightning were recurrent threats putting demands on defense systems. Such behavioral defenses are closely related to fear, whose basic function is to motivate escape from, and avoidance of, life-threatening situations.

Homeostatic needs typically have been dealt with within the topic of motivation, but motivation and emotion are closely related constructs. Both denote dispositional states that sensitize organisms to stimuli and give priority to responses of relevance to the particular state. For example, when hungry, an animal preferentially attends to food-related stimuli; and if food is encountered, it is approached and consumed. Similarly, when in fear, animals show an attentional bias for threatening stimuli; and in the face of acute danger, escape responses are quickly activated. When there is a need to distinguish between emotion and motivation, motivation is typically associated with homeostatically controlled internal needs, whereas emotions are states typically evoked by external stimuli.

Emotion is primarily concerned with stimulus evaluation, to determine which stimuli are good and which bad and, consequently, which should be approached and which avoided (e.g., Lang, Bradley, & Cuthbert, 1990). Furthermore, emotions can be understood as action sets, as mechanisms for prioritizing among action alternatives (e.g., Frijda, 1986; Lang, 1984). Finally, emotions are complex phenomena incorporating diverse and partly independent components such as expressive behavior (e.g., facial expressions), action tendencies (e.g., avoidance), recruitment of autonomic responses (e.g., heart-rate increases), and feelings (e.g., an urge to get out of the situation; see Oatley & Jenkins, 1996, for a comprehensive discussion of the definition of emotion).

This overview suggests that at the heart of evolution there is emotion. Indeed, the basic dynamics of life are pervaded by emotion. Emotions are systems that evolved to make organisms adhere to time-proven strategies to survive and breed. Thus, rather than focusing on feeling states in humans, we view emotions as integral parts of evolved behavioral systems that solved crucial problems in the environment of evolutionary adaptiveness (Tooby & Cosmides, 1990).

## Evolution, Emotion, and the Autonomic Nervous System

Because a central function of emotions is to modulate the readiness to act, they tune the autonomic nervous system to ensure metabolic resources for action. This functional connection between emotion and the autonomic nervous system provides the basis for the popularity of autonomic responses as indicators of emotion.

The autonomic nervous system is composed of the sympathetic and the parasympathetic branches, the former generally functioning to mobilize and the latter to restore metabolic resources. The cardiovascular system provides a key to metabolic housekeeping, because the blood flow determines the distribution of oxygen and nutrients to muscles and brain, as well as the removal of waste products from tissue. In general, sympathetic activation results in increased blood flow, thus expediting the exchange of substances between blood and tissue. The parasympathetic branch, through the vagus nerve, has traditionally been conceived as having the opposite effect, mainly through its inhibitory influence on heart rate.

## Evolution of Neural Control of the Autonomic Nervous System

Far back in vertebrate evolution, the spontaneous activity of the heart was humorally modulated by catecholamines (adrenaline, noradrenaline) that were secreted from stores in the walls of the heart and the circulatory system to accelerate heart activity and constrict blood vessels. Thus, originally there was no neural control of the cardiovascular system. However, cholinergic neural control of the heart via the vagus nerve emerged in primitive fishes (Campbell, Wood, & McBride, 1997). This allowed neural tuning of heart rate through inhibitory vagal tone that could adjust cardiac output to allow for changes in environmental temperature or level of oxygen. Millions of years later excitatory neural control of the heart by sympathetic fibers emerged in amphibians. The dual nature of cardiovascular control seen in mammals appears essentially to have been established in reptiles (Campbell et al., 1997). Thus early primitive mammals had the capacity to mobilize their bodies to cope with life exigencies, and they could fine-tune their circulatory systems to acute behavioral demands through independent but interacting sympathetic and parasympathetic fibers to the heart. As a consequence, the emergence and progressive enlargement of neocortex in mammalian evolution, which allowed progressively more complex and flexible behavior repertoires, could rely on an already established autonomic nervous system to recruit the required metabolic support for ever more complex action in emotional circumstances.

## Interactions Between the Sympathetic and Parasympathetic Systems

Obrist (1981) proposed the cardiac-somatic coupling hypothesis to account for cardiovascular changes in behaviorally challenging situations. This hypothesis characterized the activation of the two branches of the autonomic nervous system in relation to the metabolic demands of the psychological circumstances. It postulated two distinct patterns of cardiovascular control that reflected different strategies to cope with the current (or anticipated) situation. According to Obrist (1981), in experimental situations that lacked options for active coping because organisms were denied the opportunity to influence emotionally important events, the organisms reverted to a strategy of passive coping, quietly enduring, for example, the stress of uncontrollable aversive stimulation. He proposed that the cardiovascular system is primarily under parasympathetic control during passive coping and that heart activity closely mirrors the metabolic demands of the situation. This was demonstrated by close correlations between heart rate and various indicators of general somatic activity under such conditions (e.g., Obrist, Sutterer, & Howard, 1972). Obrist (1981) further proposed that, if

the situation allows some control of aversive stimuli (even though uncertain and effort demanding), organisms actively attempt to cope with stressors, and then sympathetic activation of the cardiovascular system may be in excess of that motivated by somatic needs.

More recent conceptualizations of the interaction between the sympathetic and parasympathetic branches of the autonomic nervous system (Berntson, Cacioppo, & Quigley, 1991, 1994) emphasize their relative independence and allow for more variable response patterns than the reciprocal activation-deactivation implied in Obrist's (1981) theory. For example, in antagonistic coactivation of the two branches of the autonomic nervous system, inhibitory vagal effects may mask excitatory sympathetic effects on the heart (Quigley & Berntson, 1990). Furthermore, the mode of control of the heart in terms of interactions between the two branches of the autonomic nervous system may differ between individuals (Berntson et al., 1994).

## Active and Passive Defense in Fear-Inducing Situations

Obrist's (1981) analysis suggests that the topography of autonomic activation depends on the specific behaviors exhibited in emotional situations. This interdependence between autonomic and behavioral responses can be illustrated by fear activation. Fear is associated with widely different patterns of defense behaviors, some of which involve intense behavioral output and others of which are more passive. The former defense patterns center on the metabolically demanding fight-or-flight response related to the "emergency function" of sympathetic activation (Cannon, 1915), whereas the latter defense patterns center on immobility or "freezing."

Freezing is an evolved defense response that should not be misunderstood as the mere absence of active responses. Animals freeze primarily in locations providing shelter, for example, close to a wall (Fanselow & Lester, 1988). Immobility may help to prevent discovery by predators whose sensory systems are sensitive to motion. Furthermore, active escape responses may be risky because they often serve as a releasing stimulus for the predator to attack (Fendt & Fanselow, 1999). The freezing response may have its evolutionary origin in defensive diving in amphibians. For example, crocodiles dive in response to an approaching canoe (Campbell et al., 1997). Defensive dives are associated with pronounced heart-rate decelerations that exceed those during voluntary dives. This deceleration is of vagal origin, and it may reflect reduced blood oxygen utilization in order to allow longer protective submergence under water (Campbell et al., 1997). Consistent with this evolutionary scenario, freezing responses in mammals are accompanied by a pronounced "fear bradycardia" (i.e., a strong heart-rate deceleration). Heart-rate deceleration has been related to openness for intake of environmental stimuli (e.g., Graham & Clifton, 1966; Lacey & Lacey, 1970), and an important concomitant of freezing is active scanning of the environment (Rosen & Schulkin, 1998).

## Threat Imminence and Psychophysiological Responses

Fanselow (1994; Fanselow & Lester, 1988) used a notion of "predatory imminence" to specify the dynamics of defense responses in the encounter between a predator and a potential prey, arguing that different defenses are activated depending on the closeness of the predator. Although predatory imminence was conceptualized as a continuum, it was divided into three main stages (Fanselow & Lester, 1988) that may differ in the neural control of defensive responding (Fanselow, 1994).

The first stage of defensive responding occurs in the absence of predators. In this preencounter stage, potential prey animals may forage for food, partners, or whatever, with the readiness for defensive postures moderated only by the perceived risk of predator encounters according to past experience. Note that this is not a baseline, such as in a completely safe situation, but involves some level of perceived risk. Should a predator emerge on the scene, there is a switch to the postencounter stage. This stage is associated with defenses of the freezing type, with attention focused on the predator. If the predator attacks, the circa-strike stage is entered, and contact defenses such as flight or fight are elicited.

Inspired by Fanselow's model, Lang, Bradley, and Cuthbert (1997) identified different patterns of psychophysiological responding with these stages. Figure 13.1 illustrates the relationships between several psychophysiological measures and threat imminence. Although threat imminence refers to any situations that involve threat (Flykt, 1999), Figure 13.1 also identifies stages of preencounter, postencounter, and circa-strike that are specific to encounters with predators. In the absence or at a low level of threat (e.g., preencounter), fear stimuli, as well as other relevant or novel stimuli, elicit orienting. This is indexed by skin conductance responses (SCRs), decelerations in heart rate (HR), and inhibition of the startle reflex to irrelevant startle probe stimuli, which suggests that attention is allocated to the relevant stimulus (Lang et al., 1997). With more imminent threat, there is intensification of the orienting response (OR): larger SCRs and HR decelerations. Startle inhibition, however, is replaced by fear-potentiated startle (Lang et al., 1990); that is, startle amplitudes are larger to probes presented during the threat stimuli than to probes presented alone. Thus, as the animal freezes, in accordance with Obrist's (1981) cardiac-somatic coupling hypothesis, the HR deceleration associated with fear bradycardia exceeds the HR deceleration during orienting. When threat imminence increases fur-

ther, SCRs and startle potentiation continue to increase, but HR changes to acceleration, reflecting mobilization of the sympathetic branch of the autonomic nervous system for active coping with the danger (Obrist et al., 1974). As the fight-or-flight or panic stage is reached (e.g., when the predator strikes in circa-strike), the intense sympathetically dominated autonomic response of fight or flight appears.

## Predatory Defense and Social Submissiveness Systems

The concept of predatory imminence (Fanselow & Lester, 1988) fits nicely with the concept of a predatory defense system developed by Öhman, Dimberg, and Öst (1985; see also Öhman, 1986) to account for animal phobia in humans. They used a distinction introduced by Mayr (1974) to categorize the large number of stimuli that evoke fear in humans (e.g., Russell, 1979) into three main categories: animals, other humans, and physical objects or situations. These categories correspond to three classes of human phobias: animal phobias, social phobia, and nature phobias (cf. American Psychiatric Association, 1994).

Öhman et al. (1985) argued that fear of animals originates in the predatory defense system that resulted from the evolutionary arms race between predator and prey in which more effective hunting strategies by predators stimulated more effective defenses in prey animals and vice versa (Dawkins & Krebs, 1979). An important component of effective defense concerns early and reliable recognition of the predator. This process appears to be ecologically fine-tuned by evolution. For example, Hirsch and Bolles (1981) found that laboratory-reared offspring of mice captured in the wild in different habitats can distinguish between predators and nonpredators from only their own habitats. That is, mice from a grassland habitat differentiated between predatory and nonpredatory snakes from grasslands but responded fearfully to both predatory and nonpredatory mammals from other habitats. In contrast, mice from a woodland habitat differentiated between predatory and nonpredatory mammals from woodland habitats but did not respond fearfully to predatory and nonpredatory snakes from other habitats. Accordingly, when encountering the predatory snake, grassland mice survived longer (i.e., had more effective defense behaviors) than woodland mice. Öhman et al. (1985) suggested fthat the predatory defense system has its evolutionary origin in a prototypical fear of reptiles in early mammals. Remnants of this "original fear" make contemporary snakes and lizards powerful actual fear stimuli (e.g., Agras, Sylvester, & Oliveau, 1969) and dragons mythical embodiments of fear-arousing creatures throughout the history of mankind (Öhman, 1986; Sagan, 1977). Animal stimuli remain a prominent cluster of human fears that includes crawling and creeping animals, such as reptiles

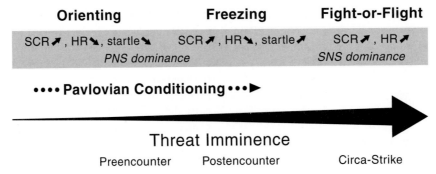

Figure 13.1 Effects of threat imminence on psychophysiological measures. When threat imminence increases, response changes from orienting to freezing to fight or flight. Orienting is mainly associated with skin conductance responses (SCRs) but also with heart-rate (HR) decreases and startle inhibition. Freezing is mainly associated with startle potentiation and HR decreases. Fight-or-flight responses are mainly associated with HR increases. The parasympathetic nervous system (PNS) dominates in orienting and freezing responses, and the sympathetic nervous system (SNS) dominates in fight-or-flight responses. When neutral stimuli are paired with an aversive stimulus (in Pavlovian conditioning), they gain in threat imminence and elicit freezing or fight-or-flight responses rather than orienting. Note that stages of preencounter, postencounter, and circa-strike refer to encounters with predators (Fanselow, 1994). Adapted from Lang, Bradley, and Cuthbert (1997).

and insects, but also many harmless small animals and domestic animals more generally (Arrindell, Pickersgill, Merckelbach, Ardon, & Cornet, 1991).

Stimuli that are central to the predatory defense system capture attention very effectively in humans. Öhman, Flykt, and Esteves (2001) demonstrated a bias to detect evolutionary fear-relevant animal stimuli (snakes and spiders) in a complex array of stimuli (various flowers and mushrooms). They used a visual search paradigm in which the participants looked for discrepant target stimuli among various exemplars of a background category of stimuli. For example, the target could be a snake picture presented among pictures of flowers. Normal nonfearful participants were faster to locate snakes and spiders among flowers and mushrooms than flowers and mushrooms among snakes and spiders. This fear-relevance advantage was independent of the number of distractors in the display, suggesting that fear-relevant stimuli automatically captured attention (see Hansen & Hansen, 1988). Further, in a separate experiment, snake-fearful participants detected snakes faster than they did spiders, whereas spider-fearful participants detected spiders faster than they did snakes. Thus people in general are sensitive to biologically fear-relevant stimuli (Öhman et al., 1985), and this sensitivity is further enhanced if the stimuli actually elicit fear.

A second evolved behavioral system that controls fear is the social submissiveness system (Öhman et al., 1985; Öhman, 1986). This system was proposed as the basis for the prevalence of social anxiety among humans. Many

people feel some degree of apprehension in social encounters, particularly if the interaction concerns novel acquaintances or persons with the insignia of power. For some, the fear is part of a debilitating social phobia. The social submissiveness system is part of a larger behavioral system that controls the interaction between individuals in a group. Such interaction centers on dominance hierarchies that define which group members boss or yield to which others. Once established, a hierarchy provides a vehicle for bringing order into the group and for minimizing further aggressive encounters. Dominance hierarchies are established in (more or less explicitly) aggressive contests in which individuals take measure of their relative strength. It is seldom, however, that such conflicts are allowed to escalate into physical fights. Most often they are fought at a symbolic level, with more or less impressive dominance displays and with submissive gestures from combatants about to lose a contest.

In primates, facial expressions of threat and submissiveness provide an important channel of communication in dominance contests, which make facial threat a powerful fear stimulus that elicits strong psychophysiological responses (Dimberg & Öhman, 1996; Öhman & Dimberg, 1984). For example, Boysen and Berntson (1989) reported that a young chimpanzee showed HR decelerations (i.e., low threat imminence) to slides of a chimpanzee face she did not know, little response to a well-known companion, but a pronounced heart rate acceleration (i.e., high threat imminence) to the face of a familiar chimpanzee who dominated her and used to attack her. Similarly, young chimpanzees (but not young orangutans) showed pronounced HR accelerations to chimpanzee vocal threat, and these responses were independent of somatic activity (Berntson & Boysen, 1989).

Facial stimuli capture attention also in humans. Öhman, Lundqvist, and Esteves (2001) used schematic faces in a visual search task similar to the one developed for animal stimuli by Öhman, Flykt, and Esteves (2001). They reported that normal nonanxious participants were quicker to detect a discrepant threatening face among neutral and friendly distractors than a friendly face against neutral or threatening distractors. Furthermore, studies found that, when participants are asked to respond to probes presented either at the location of a preceding emotional or neutral face, probe detection is faster to threatening faces, particularly for high-anxiety participants (e.g., Bradley, Mogg, White, Groom, & de Bono, 1999; see Mogg & Bradley, 1998, for review)

The behavioral defense systems discussed by Öhman and colleagues (Öhman, 1986; Öhman et al., 1985) imply that there are stimuli within both systems that owe at least part of their fear-evoking potential to evolutionary contingencies. Such biologically fear-relevant stimuli would include, for instance, snakes and angry faces. However, they may not necessarily be innate fear stimuli in the sense that they automatically elicit fear. For example, in a classical contribution to the psychology of fear, Miller (1951) suggested that "fear may be high in the innate hierarchy of responses to a stimulus without being the dominant response" (p. 445). In sum, although biologically fear-relevant stimuli may not be innate fear stimuli, stimuli of this type (snakes, spiders, angry faces) are effective in capturing attention, and they may be easily associated with aversive events (e.g., Öhman, 1993b; Öhman & Mineka, 2001; Seligman, 1971).

## Emotion, Orienting, and Attention

### Orienting to Novel Stimuli

As changes in the environment are relevant for the needs and goals of organisms, even in the absence of imminent threat, most organisms show orienting responses (ORs) to sudden environmental changes. The OR involves an arrest of ongoing behavior and orientation of sensory receptors toward the stimulus. It can be understood as a tactical mechanism, disrupting ongoing activity to process unexpected changes in the state of the world. It tunes the body for intake of information through modulations of autonomic effectors (Graham & Clifton, 1966; Lacey & Lacey, 1970; Sokolov, 1963). The OR is most conveniently measured by simple autonomic responses such as increases in skin conductance or HR decelerations (see Öhman,

Hamm, & Hugdahl, 2000; Siddle, 1983). However, it is also reflected in blocking of the EEG alpha rhythm (Sokolov, 1963) or the P300 component of the event-related potential (Donchin et al., 1984).

As novel stimuli elicit an OR, Sokolov (1963) postulated that the OR results from a mismatch between the actual stimulus and corresponding memory or neuronal models of the stimulus. When a stimulus is first encountered, there is no memory model available, and consequently a strong OR is elicited. If the stimulus is presented repeatedly, the brain learns about it, which results in an increasingly accurate memory model. The stimulus now has a matching model available in memory, and therefore the OR is no longer elicited by subsequent presentations of the stimulus. Thus the OR habituates with repeated stimulus presentation. However, if some characteristic, whether physical (e.g., Siddle & Heron, 1976) or conceptual (e.g., Siddle, Kyriacou, Heron, & Matthews, 1979), is changed after habituation, the OR reemerges (see Öhman, Hamm, & Hugdahl, 2000, for review). Thus Sokolov's (1963) neuronal model theory of the OR integrates this simple response into the development of perceptual representations of the world.

The sheer novelty of a suddenly and unexpectedly presented stimulus makes it emotionally significant. Because it is unexpected in the context, there is no routine way of handling it, and therefore one must attend to it to find out whether a reinforcement or a disaster is lurking in its aftermath. If surprise is recognized as an emotion (but see Ortony & Turner, 1992), it is the emotion associated with orienting. Although Izard (1991) included surprise-astonishment in his list of basic emotions, he acknowledged that it does not have all the characteristics of the other emotions. He described it as a rapidly passing, often mildly pleasant feeling with little thought content, elicited by any sudden and unexpected event. The mind goes blank, "as though ordinary thought processes are momentarily stopped" (Izard, 1991, p. 177). Its function is "to clear the nervous system of ongoing activity that would interfere with adjustment to a sudden change in our environment" (Izard, 1991, p. 182). Thus there is considerable overlap between orienting and the emotion of surprise-astonishment.

### Orienting to Significant Stimuli

Aside from novel stimuli, any "significant" stimuli elicit strong and slowly habituating ORs (Öhman, Hamm, & Hugdahl, 2000). For example, pictures of snakes and spiders elicit strong ORs (measured as SCRs), particularly in an aversive context (Öhman, Eriksson, Fredrikson, Hugdahl, & Olofsson, 1974). "Significant" should be given a broad interpretation. For Sokolov (1963) it primarily means that the stimulus is conditioned, either because it signals an aversive consequence or other important events or simply because the research participant is warned to pay attention to it. Often it means "task relevant"; that is, the stimulus must be attended to for participants to comply with the experimental instructions and solve their tasks (e.g., Bernstein & Taylor, 1979). However, a stimulus may also be regarded as significant and elicit strong ORs because it moves toward the observer (Bernstein, Taylor, Austen, Nathanson, & Scarpelli, 1971) or because it is related to personal interests of the participants (Wingard & Maltzman, 1980).

An OR is thus elicited by stimuli that are novel or significant. These two determinants may appear contradictory, particularly as viewed from the perspective of Sokolov's (1963) theory. A novel stimulus, according to this theory, elicits an OR because it fails to find a matching memory model. A significant stimulus, however, must be a known stimulus to be judged as significant. Yet, even though it matches a memory model, it elicits a strong OR. Öhman (1979) tried to reconcile this apparent paradox by arguing that what is common to both novel and significant stimuli is that they both require controlled processing at the focus of voluntary attention. He suggested that the comparison between stimulus and memory models occurs preattentively against the content of a short-term memory store defined as an activated subset of the long-term memory store. This automatic (effortless, resource independent, nonconscious) processing was contrasted with the controlled (effortful, resource demanding, usually conscious) cognitive processing to which the stimulus was allocated in case it failed to find a matching memory model in the first stage of processing. Öhman (1979) argued that the OR could be identified with a call for processing resources in the controlled central channel. He suggested that the OR could be viewed as marking a switch from automatic to controlled processing of a stimulus. Thus ORs are elicited when a stimulus cannot be handled at the automatic level, either because it lacks a matching memory model or, if it matches a model, because it signals consequences that require controlled processing. Thus the OR is an important mechanism of bringing important stimuli into focal, conscious attention (Öhman, 1987).

### Orienting to Emotional Stimuli

Although significant stimuli may not necessarily be associated with an emotional state (see Spinks & Siddle, 1983), a substantial subset of significant stimuli owe their significance to an emotion. Emotional stimuli, by definition, are significant because they are related to personal concerns (Frijda, 1986). Therefore, organisms typically show an OR to emotional stimuli. Part of the autonomic changes constituting the OR, such as a heart-rate deceleration (Graham & Clifton, 1966), are also related to anticipation and readiness to respond motorically (Jennings,

1992; Öhman, Hamm, & Hugdahl, 2000). Thus the OR, as related to an initial stage of evaluation of an emotional stimulus, is nonspecific with regard to the emotional quality of the stimulus. However, it may get the body ready for action by activating nonspecific autonomic responses that can be rechanneled into more specific patterns related to the specific emotion that eventually is evoked and the metabolic demands it implies.

The fact that orienting is the first response to virtually any abruptly presented emotional stimuli confounds assessment of psychophysiological response patterns hypothesized to be specific for a particular emotion. Indeed, this may be a reason that findings of reliable response specificity emerge primarily from situations in which the emotion is maintained over a considerable time period (e.g., Levenson, Ekman, & Friesen, 1990; Schwartz, Weinberger, & Singer, 1981).

According to Öhman (1979), an important function of the OR is to bring the eliciting, potentially emotional stimulus into the focus of conscious attention. Thus an emotionally relevant stimulus captures attention because of the same OR mechanism that guarantees focused attention to any significant stimulus. However, as the stimulus enters focused attention, the relatively unspecific activation associated with the OR can give way to the activation dynamics of specific emotions. The OR ensures that emotional stimuli receive active attention, and because emotional experience by definition has to occur in focal attention, the OR can be viewed as an important component in the activation of emotion (Öhman, 1987).

### Preattentive Mechanisms in the Activation of Emotion

More than most other emotions, fear is constrained by the defensive need for fast action. Fast response recruitment of fear responses, for example, provides an adaptive edge for a potential prey to escape a predator. Indeed, in humans, responses may be elicited even before persons become aware that they are experiencing fear, which suggests that preattentive processing is sufficient for fear activation (Öhman, 1986; Öhman, Dimberg, & Esteves, 1989; Öhman, Flykt, & Lundqvist, 2000; Robinson, 1998). In agreement with LeDoux's (1996) "low road" to emotional activation via a thalamus–amygdala route, Öhman (1993a) proposed a model in which fear-related autonomic responses to threatening stimuli can be activated in the absence of a full perceptual analysis of the eliciting stimulus.

According to this model, two routes of preattentive processing result in the activation of fear (Öhman, 1993a). A "bottom-up" or "stimulus-driven" route operates on simple perceptual features, primarily those defining evolutionarily shaped fear signals, such as snakes, spiders, or angry faces. Stimuli that involve such primary fear features automatically activate an arousal system that controls autonomic responses such as the components of the OR. A second, "top-down" or "conceptually driven" route involves the biasing of a significance-evaluating system by an expectancy system based on memory. Even though the expectancy system interacts with conscious perception of stimuli, its "attentional control setting" (Folk, Remington, & Johnston, 1992) of the significance evaluator results in the automatic capture of attention (Yantis, 1998) by threatening information. For example, anxious participants show attentional biases to words with threatening content (see Mathews & MacLeod, 1994; Mogg & Bradley, 1998). The models proposed by LeDoux (1996) and Öhman (1993a) suggest that autonomic responses to fear-relevant stimuli can be activated by a preattentive analysis of the fear-relevant stimuli without conscious representation of the eliciting stimuli. Studies testing this notion of preattentive fear activation have typically used backward masking to present stimuli outside of awareness.

### The Backward Masking Technique

Backward masking is an effective technique to present stimuli so that they remain unrecognized by the observer. Basically, it involves the presentation of a brief target stimulus that is immediately followed by a masking stimulus. If the interval between the onsets of these two stimuli (the stimulus-onset asynchrony, SOA) is long (e.g., > 100 ms), both stimuli are consciously perceived. However, if the SOA is sufficiently short, only the masking stimulus can be consciously recognized.

Öhman and Soares (1993, 1994) studied effects of the SOA on participants' ability to recognize masked pictures of snakes, spiders, flowers, and mushrooms. Masking stimuli were pictures of randomly cut, reorganized, and re-photographed pictures of the target stimuli. Thus masking stimuli were similar to target stimuli except that they had no central object. In the Öhman and Soares (1994) study, the SOA between target and masking stimuli varied between 20 and 180 ms. A control condition involved presentations of the masks without any target. Participants were instructed that on each trial two brief pictures would be presented consecutively, and that their task was to identify the first picture of each pair. After each presentation, participants used a forced-choice scale to indicate whether they saw snakes, spiders, flowers, or mushrooms. Participants also indicated their confidence in the answers. As shown in Figure 13.2, the SOA had strong effects on participants' ability to recognize targets, as well as on their confidence in the ratings. At long SOAs (80, 120, and 180 ms), participants recognized correctly almost all of the pictures and were sure of their answers. At shorter SOAs, however, participants' ability to recognize targets, as well as their confidence in their ratings, de-

creased sharply. At a 30-ms SOA, participants performed at chance and indicated that they were guessing. That is, performance in discriminating among the target stimuli did not differ significantly either from guessing (100/4 = 25%) or from the control condition. Similar results have been reported for facial stimuli (Esteves & Öhman, 1993). Furthermore, participants who were fearful of the target stimuli (snakes or spiders) did not differ significantly from nonfearful participants in their ability to recognize targets (Öhman & Soares, 1994), and shocks and task practice apparently had no effects on recognition of targets (Esteves, Parra, Dimberg, & Öhman, 1994; Öhman & Soares, 1993). Although these findings indicate that a 30-ms SOA produces effective masking, it is important to ascertain the effectiveness of the masking procedure for each study be-

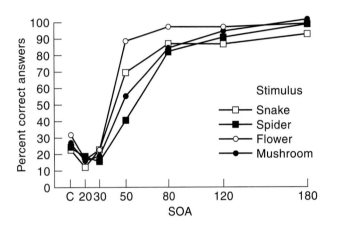

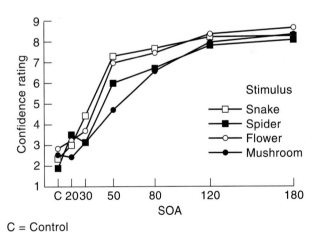

C = Control

Figure 13.2 Effects of stimulus onset asynchrony (SOA in ms) between target and masking stimuli on mean percent correct responses and mean confidence ratings. Target stimuli were images of snakes, spiders, flowers, and mushrooms. In the control condition (C), two masking stimuli were presented consecutively. Note that at a 30-ms SOA, which was employed in studies using backward masking, participants performed at chance (i.e., 25%) and tended to rate that they were guessing. Adapted from Öhman & Soares (1994).

cause masking is affected by numerous variables, such as picture size and brightness.

### Preattentive Bias for Threat in Anxiety

Research on attentional biases to threat in anxiety supports Öhman's (1993a) proposition that the threat value of stimuli can be determined at a preattentive level of information processing. With anxious participants and with both masked threatening words (Bradley, Mogg, Millar, & White, 1995; MacLeod & Rutherford, 1992) and masked threatening faces (Mogg & Bradley, 1999), the attentional bias is evident to stimuli presented outside of awareness. For example, Mogg and Bradley (1999) used a dot-probe paradigm in which pairs of faces were presented side by side on a screen. The pairs of faces portrayed the same individual in an emotional (threatening or happy) and a neutral pose. The faces were presented very briefly (14 ms) and were followed by masking stimuli (jumbled faces) that prevented conscious recognition of the target stimuli. The participants performed choice reaction times (RTs) by pressing different response keys depending on whether a dot-probe stimulus following the masking stimulus was presented behind the left or the right stimulus location on the screen. Participants were faster to decide the position of the probe if it was preceded by a masked threatening face, particularly if it was presented on the left half of the screen (suggesting a right cerebral hemisphere advantage for processing threat). This effect was evident in all participants, but it was particularly obvious for participants high in trait anxiety. These results clearly indicate that attention can be preattentively captured by an emotional stimulus. However, it remains to be determined, as predicted by Öhman's (1993a) model, whether autonomic responses such as the SCR can be activated from threat stimuli that are denied access to conscious recognition.

### Psychophysiological Responding Without Stimulus Recognition

Öhman and Soares (1994) used the well-established finding that phobics show elevated psychophysiological responses to phobic stimuli (e.g., Fredrikson, 1981; Globisch, Hamm, Esteves, & Öhman, 1999; Hamm, Cuthbert, Globisch, & Vaitl, 1997) to test whether elevated responses could be elicited by masked presentations of feared stimuli. Participants were selected on the basis of their self-reported fear of spiders and snakes and were assigned to one of three groups: participants afraid of snakes but not of spiders (snake fearful), participants afraid of spiders but not of snakes (spider fearful), and participants not afraid of either spiders or snakes (controls). These participants were presented with masked pictures of snakes, spiders, flowers, and mushrooms to assess individual differences in fear responses. As shown in Figure 13.3, SCRs were

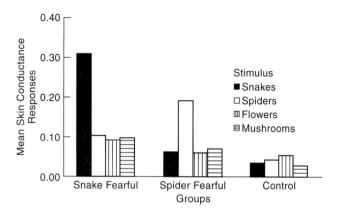

Figure 13.3 Mean skin conductance responses (SCRs in μS) to backward-masked images of snakes, spiders, flowers, and mushrooms for snake-fearful, spider-fearful, and control participants. Note that SCRs were elevated only in fearful participants with stimuli that were relevant to their specific fear. Adapted from Öhman & Soares (1994).

elevated only in fearful participants for stimuli that were relevant to their specific fear. That is, snake-fearful participants showed larger SCRs to masked pictures of snakes than to masked pictures of spiders, flowers, and mushrooms, whereas spider-fearful participants showed larger SCRs to masked pictures of spiders than to masked pictures of snakes, flowers, and mushrooms. These results indicate that participants selected for their fear of snakes and spiders showed enhanced SCRs to these stimuli even if they did not recognize them consciously.

The dependent variable in this study, the SCR, is widely used as an OR index, and it is closely related to the arousing effect of emotional stimuli (see review by Lang et al., 1997). However, the SCR is relatively insensitive to the emotional valence of stimuli; that is, large SCRs are seen to both positive-arousing (e.g., erotica) and negative-arousing (e.g., mutilated bodies) stimuli (e.g., Greenwald, Cook, & Lang, 1989; Lang, Greenwald, Bradley, & Hamm, 1993; Simons, Detenber, Roedema, & Reiss, 1999). Because the SCR shares variance not only with arousal ratings but also with ratings of interest and with self-controlled viewing time of stimuli (Lang et al., 1993), it is apparent that the SCR provides a direct index of the attention value of emotional stimuli. Thus, because emotion and attention are so intricately interwoven, it is hard to determine whether the enhanced SCR to masked fear stimuli in the Öhman and Soares (1994) study reflects merely a general relationship to attention manifested as an OR or a relationship that is specific to fear. However, there is one response system that may allow a decision as to whether psychophysiological responses to masked emotional stimuli reflect an unspecific OR or a patterned emotional response, and that is facial muscle responses as assessed by electromyography (EMG).

Dimberg (1982) reported that participants tended to

mimic the emotional expressions of stimulus faces in their facial muscle responses. Thus, when exposed to an angry face, they showed increases in activity of the *corrugator supercilii* muscle that mediates the frown and little change in the *zygomatic major* muscle, which connects the corner of the mouth and the cheekbone and mediates a smile. With a happy face, however, the opposite pattern was found, with increases in the zygomatic and no change or a decrease in the corrugator muscle. To examine whether this patterned EMG response could be elicited by stimuli presented outside awareness, Dimberg, Elmehed, and Thunberg (2000) examined facial responses to masked facial stimuli in nonanxious participants. They presented angry, neutral, and happy faces very briefly (30 ms) and immediately masked by a 5-s presentation of a neutral face. Even though participants consciously could perceive only the neutral masking face, they nevertheless showed differential facial EMG responses depending on the preceding target face. The masked happy face elicited a larger zygomatic response than the neutral or angry face, whereas the angry face elicited a larger corrugator response than the neutral or happy face. These differences, furthermore, emerged within the first 500 ms after stimulus onset. Thus it appears that not only a nonspecific response such as the SCR but also a more specific emotional response could be elicited by masked stimuli.

Further important data on fear responding to masked stimuli were reported by Whalen et al. (1998). To test the hypothesis that emotional responses are mediated by the amygdala (e.g., LeDoux, 1996), they used functional magnetic resonance imaging (fMRI) to measure responses of the human amygdala to masked presentations of facial stimuli. They contrasted regional blood flow in the amygdala during periods of repeated presentations of a masked fearful face with periods of repeated presentations of a masked happy face and reported specific increases in amygdala activation to the fearful faces. Thus, even though conscious recognition of the stimuli was prevented by backward masking, reliable activation of the central structure of the fear circuit, the amygdala (e.g., Fendt & Fanselow, 1999; LeDoux, 1996), was observed to the fearful faces.

In sum, results from studies that have examined attention and psychophysiological responses to fear-relevant stimuli show that such stimuli are effective both in capturing attention and in eliciting autonomic responses. Both processes appear to have a preattentive origin, because they can be observed to stimuli that are prevented from reaching conscious recognition by backward masking. Interpreted within an OR framework and in agreement with Öhman's (1979) model, the SCR results suggest that ORs are elicited as a call for processing in a central processing channel as a result of preattentive processing mechanisms. However, there are also data that suggest some emotional specificity in preattentively elicited responses, which indicates that stimuli can be positively or negatively evaluated without conscious recognition. Finally, brain imaging data suggest that the emotional effects of masked stimuli are mediated by the amygdala.

## Emotion and Learning

### Fear Conditioning

Emotionally significant events may be heralded by subtle cues. For example, a predator may provide clues to its presence by faint sounds or odors. Pavlov described the importance of these cues for survival:

> Under natural conditions the normal animal must respond not only to stimuli which themselves bring immediate benefit or harm, but also to other physical or chemical agencies—waves of sound, light, and the like—which in themselves only *signal* the approach of these stimuli; though it is not the sight and sound of the beast of prey which is in itself harmful to the smaller animal, but its teeth and claws. (1927, p. 14)

Therefore, organisms that learn to show fear responses in anticipation of a threatening encounter increase their chances for survival because they can mobilize resources either to avoid the encounter altogether or to escape potentially disastrous consequences of an encounter by early activation of defensive responses. This type of learning is commonly called classical or Pavlovian conditioning, and it is studied, for instance, by pairing a nonaversive stimulus with an aversive stimulus. When organisms learn that the nonaversive stimulus signals the occurrence of the aversive stimulus, fear responses that are elicited by the aversive stimuli (the "natural trigger") are transferred to the signal stimulus (the "learned trigger"; LeDoux, 1996). Pavlovian conditioning is a powerful mechanism for extending the range of events that can elicit emotions. Because of Pavlovian conditioning, "emotions of all shades eventually help connect homeostatic regulation and survival 'values' to numerous events and objects in our autobiographical experience" (Damasio, 1999, p. 54–55).

In terms of the dimension of threat imminence (see figure 13.1), conditioning implies that the learned trigger moves upward on the threat imminence continuum because it is predictive of the natural trigger that is associated with the circa-strike phase. As a consequence, the psychophysiological fear response to the learned trigger is strengthened, but the response pattern may also change. Implicit in the threat imminence notion is the suggestion that the conditioned and the unconditioned responses (CRs and UCRs, respectively) may be different. For example, contact with a natural trigger in the circa-strike region elicits active defenses (fight/flight) associated with HR accelerations. As a result of conditioning, a neutral stimulus signaling such a natural trigger would move upward on the threat imminence continuum, perhaps from the baseline to the postencounter area. As a result, HR decelerations to the conditioned stimulus (CS) would be enhanced, thus resulting in an HR-CR opposite in direction to the UCR.

## Fear Conditioning and Evolutionary Preparedness

Pavlov (1927) assumed that specific features of the stimuli do not affect learning in a Pavlovian contingency. Accordingly, any stimulus (e.g., lights or tones) paired with an unconditioned stimulus (UCS) was expected to result in similar degrees of learning. Seligman (1970) questioned this *premise of equipotentiality* and argued that evolutionary contingencies constrain learning in that animals learn some associations more easily than others. In particular, Seligman (1971) argued that cues that have been recurrently encountered in threatening contexts throughout evolution become learned triggers for fear more easily than cues that have been independent of threatening situations. This *preparedness* postulate pertained to the ease of associability between stimuli rather than to the effect of their individual features. Thus evolutionary recurring fear stimuli are expected to become easily associated with aversiveness but not to serve equally well as signals for nonaversive events such as food.

The preparedness hypothesis is strongly supported by research on fear learning in monkeys. Studies have shown that lab-reared monkeys do not show the fear of snakes that is typical of monkeys reared in the wild (Mineka, Keir, & Price, 1980). However, if lab-reared monkeys were exposed to a "model" wild-reared monkey that exhibited fear to a snake or a snakelike stimulus, they rapidly acquired a strong fear of snakes (Mineka, Davidson, Cook, & Keir, 1984; Mineka & Cook, 1993). Thus real snakes served as effective cues for observational conditioning of fear. This finding is further supported from studies that allow direct comparison between observational conditioning to snakes and conditioning to a neutral stimulus such as a flower. In these studies, videotapes were produced in which a model monkey exhibited identical fear responses to either a snake or a flower. These videotapes resulted in strong fear conditioning to the snake but little conditioning to the flower (Cook & Mineka, 1989, 1990). Furthermore, snakes and flowers served equally well as discriminative stimuli for food, thus showing that the superior conditioning to snakes was specific to the aversive context. These findings are inconsistent with the equipotentiality premise, but they provide good support for the preparedness postulate.

## Differential Conditioning of Human Autonomic Responses

Öhman and his colleagues have used differential conditioning tasks in humans to test Seligman's (1970, 1971) preparedness theory (see Dimberg & Öhman, 1996; Öhman, 1993b; Öhman & Mineka, 2001, for reviews). In these tasks, participants are presented with two nonaversive stimuli, one of which is paired with an unconditioned stimulus (UCS) that reliably elicits a fear response. During habituation, both nonaversive stimuli are presented repeatedly without the UCS to eliminate any differential responding before training. During acquisition, one of the nonaversive stimuli (CS+) is followed by the UCS, and the other stimulus (CS−) is not. During extinction, CS+ and CS− continue to be presented, but the CS+ is no longer followed by the US. Learning is indicated by differential responding to the CS+ and the CS− in acquisition or extinction. When organisms have learned that the CS+ is a signal stimulus for the UCS, it elicits a greater anticipatory SCR than the CS−, provided that the CS-UCS interval is long enough to allow observation of an anticipatory CR before the UCR is elicited by the UCS. Thus the CS− is a comparison stimulus to ensure that changes in responding to the CS+ are the result of learning (see Öhman, 1983, for a discussion of control procedures in conditioning). For example, participants are presented with pictures of spiders and snakes and receive mild electric shocks (UCS) after the spider pictures (CS+) but not after the snake pictures (CS−). When participants learn that only the spiders are followed by shocks, the spider pictures elicit a greater anticipatory SCR than the snake pictures. To test Seligman's preparedness theory, Öhman and his colleagues have employed pictures of snakes, spiders, and angry faces as evolutionary fear-relevant stimuli and pictures of flowers, mushrooms, and neutral and happy faces as fear-irrelevant stimuli (see Öhman & Mineka, 2001).

Results from differential conditioning experiments that compare conditioning to fear-relevant and fear-irrelevant stimuli show more robust conditioning to fear-relevant stimuli. For example, Öhman, Fredrikson, Hugdahl, and Rimmö (1976) conditioned participants either to snakes and spiders or to flowers and mushrooms. In two independent experiments they found marginally larger SCRs, if any, to fear-relevant than fear-irrelevant stimuli during habituation, reliable response acquisition to both classes of stimuli during the acquisition phase, and reliably larger differential responses to snakes/spiders than to flowers/mushrooms during extinction. Similar results were reported by Öhman and Dimberg (1978) for groups required to differentiate between two angry (fear-relevant stimuli) faces versus groups differentiating between neutral and happy (fear-irrelevant stimuli) faces. Similar SCR findings have been reported from several laboratories (see Cook, Hodes, & Lang, 1986; Davey, 1992; Dawson, Schell, & Banis, 1986; and Schell, Dawson, & Marinkovic, 1991, for animal stimuli, and Johnsen & Hugdahl, 1991, 1993; Mazurski, Bond, Siddle, & Lovibond, 1996; and Pitman & Orr, 1986, for facial stimuli). Similar findings have been reported also for finger pulse-volume responses (Fredrikson & Öhman, 1979) and slow cortical potentials (Regan & Howard, 1995).

Data on heart rate indicate that directionally different responses are conditioned to fear-relevant and fear-irrelevant stimuli (Öhman et al., 1985). With fear-relevant CSs (snakes and spiders), there is a pronounced heart rate acceleration to the CS+ during acquisition that contrasts with the large deceleration conditioned to the fear-irrelevant CS+ and the small response elicited by the CS− (whether fear-relevant or fear-irrelevant; Cook et al., 1986). These results suggest that different responses are conditioned to evolutionarily fear-relevant and fear-irrelevant stimuli. Fear-irrelevant stimuli that signal an aversive event appear to acquire a greater OR as a result of conditioning, because the HR deceleration reflects orienting and attention in the postencounter stage (Lang et al., 1997) of the threat imminence continuum. The HR acceleration conditioned to fear-relevant stimuli, on the other hand, reflects a defensive response (Graham, 1979) and perhaps the flight-fight response at the circa-strike region of the threat imminence continuum (Lang et al., 1997; see Öhman & Mineka, 2001, for further discussion of this issue).

### Eliciting Conditioned Fear Without Stimulus Recognition

The differential-conditioning experiments demonstrate more robust conditioning to biologically fear-relevant stimuli. In fact, in several respects, autonomic responses conditioned to snakes and spiders are similar to the responses to such stimuli in participants selected as fearful of snakes and spiders (Fredrikson, 1981). In view of Öhman and Soares's (1994) demonstration that SCRs in fearful participants could be elicited through masked presentations of the feared stimuli, an interesting question concerns whether such nonconscious elicitation of responses could be demonstrated for participants conditioned to fear snakes, spiders, or angry faces.

Öhman and Soares (1993) conditioned two groups of normal, nonfearful participants to nonmasked presentations of either spiders (snakes for half the group) or flowers (mushrooms for half the group) in a differential-conditioning paradigm in which snakes (spiders) and mushrooms (flowers) served as the CSs. Both groups showed similar differential SCRs to the CS+ and the CS− during acquisition. However, in the following extinction

phase, when the CSs were masked, participants conditioned to fear-relevant stimuli retained a significant conditioned SCR, whereas participants conditioned to fear-irrelevant stimuli did not (Figure 13.4). Several other studies have replicated this pattern of results (Öhman & Soares, 1993; Soares & Öhman, 1993a, 1993b). The retained differential response to masked fear-relevant stimuli was also obtained when participants were informed prior to extinction that they would receive no more shocks (Soares & Öhman, 1993b). There was also no evidence that the effect differed significantly between phobic and nonphobic participants conditioned to nonphobic but fear-relevant stimuli (e.g., spiders in snake phobics; Soares & Öhman, 1993a) or when pictures were presented to the left or the right visual field (Öhman & Soares, 1993). Taken together, these findings provide strong support for the idea of preparedness in a predatory defense system in that degraded input elicits fear responses, particularly so if the stimuli are fear relevant.

Öhman and his colleagues further postulated that preparedness applies also to facial expressions of anger as part of a social submissiveness system. Esteves, Dimberg, and Öhman (1994) presented evidence to support this postulate. In their study, nonphobic participants were conditioned to nonmasked pictures of angry and happy faces. When pictures were masked during extinction, only participants conditioned to angry faces showed a significant conditioned SCR; participants conditioned to happy faces did not. Taken together with findings that conditioned

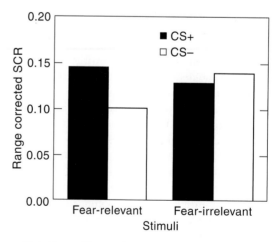

Figure 13.4 Mean skin conductance responses (SCRs in μS) during extinction to backward-masked presentations of stimuli that were or were not paired with electric shock in acquisition (CS+ and CS−, respectively) for participants conditioned to fear-relevant stimuli (i.e., spiders and snakes) or fear-irrelevant stimuli (i.e., flowers and mushrooms). Note that differential conditioning (i.e., CS+ significantly exceeded CS−) was observed only for participants conditioned to fear-relevant stimuli. Adapted from Öhman & Soares (1993).

SCRs to happy faces extinguish fast, even for nonmasked presentations (Dimberg & Öhman, 1996), these findings support the idea of preparedness in a social submissiveness system.

### Fear Learning Without Stimulus Recognition

Because of its evolutionary origin in animals with primitive brains, an effective fear system should form new associations even without the capacity for conscious awareness of stimuli, which is characteristic for brains of the recently evolved hominid lineage. This is consistent with Seligman's (1970) suggestion that prepared learning is noncognitive and can occur even with degraded input, such as minimal training or extremely long CS-UCS intervals. If masking is accepted as a method to degrade input during learning, then it follows that conditioning should be possible to masked stimuli, provided that the CSs are fear relevant. This prediction is contrary to widely held beliefs that the CS-UCS contingency has either to be represented in awareness (Dawson & Schell, 1985) or processed in a capacity-limited channel (Öhman, 1979; Wagner, 1976) for associations to be formed.

There is evidence that conditioning can occur to masked stimuli from both predatory defense and social submissiveness systems. In a study by Öhman and Soares (1998), participants were conditioned to masked pictures of either spiders and snakes or of flowers and mushrooms. The CSs were presented for 30 ms and were immediately followed by a 100-ms exposure of the mask. The same masking stimulus was used for both the CS+ and the CS− for a given person. The UCS followed 500 ms after onset of the stimulus designated as the CS+. To test for conditioning during acquisition, test trials without a UCS were occasionally presented. During extinction the CSs were presented for 130 ms without any masks. As shown in Figure 13.5, during acquisition only participants conditioned to fear-relevant stimuli (i.e., spiders or snakes) acquired a significant conditioned SCR. This conditioned response in the fear-relevant group was retained during extinction when the masks were removed (not shown in figure). Thus only participants who received shocks to fear-relevant stimuli acquired a significant conditioned SCR that was present during both acquisition and extinction. Similar data were reported from a second experiment by Öhman and Soares (1998) in which the CS-UCS interval was extended to allow measurement of the SCR on every trial. In contrast to participants conditioned to fear-relevant stimuli, participants who received shocks to either flowers or mushrooms did not show any evidence of a conditioned SCR during either acquisition or extinction. These findings support a preparedness effect for the predatory defense system.

Esteves et al. (1994) demonstrated that preparedness also applies to facial expressions of anger as part of the

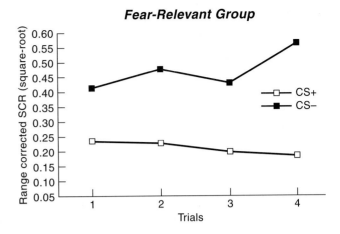

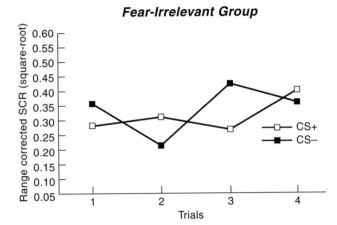

Figure 13.5 Mean skin conductance responses (SCRs in μS) on test trials in acquisition to backward masked stimuli that were or were not paired with electric shock (CS+ and CS−, respectively) for participants conditioned to fear-relevant stimuli (i.e., spiders and snakes; upper panel) or fear-irrelevant stimuli (i.e., flowers and mushrooms; lower panel). Note that differential conditioning (i.e., CS+ significantly exceeded CS−) was observed only for participants conditioned to fear-relevant stimuli. Adapted from Öhman & Soares (1998).

social submissiveness system. They reported two experiments in which angry and happy faces were effectively or ineffectively masked by neutral faces during conditioning. Control groups were conditioned only to the masks or were exposed to unpaired presentations of the masked CSs and the shocks. When the CSs were shown nonmasked during extinction, only participants who had the angry face as the CS+ showed reliable differential responding, both with effective (30 ms SOA) and ineffective (300 ms SOA) masking conditions. Participants conditioned to happy faces showed no evidence of conditioning, nor did any of the control groups. These results for stimuli belonging to the social submissiveness system parallel those for predatory stimuli reported by Öhman and Soares (1998).

### The Role of the Amygdala in Eliciting Human Fear Responses

Animal research demonstrates that the amygdala is a critical structure for fear conditioning (Fendt & Fanselow, 1999) and that the amygdala can be activated by a "low route" from the thalamus, bypassing the cortex (Armony & LeDoux, 2000; LeDoux, 1996). To directly test the role of the amygdala in human conditioning, Morris, Öhman, and Dolan (1998) used positron emission tomography (PET) to measure regional cerebral blood flow responses to conditioned angry faces. Immediately preceding PET scanning, participants were presented with pictures of four different male faces, two of which were angry and two neutral. One of the angry faces served as a CS+ (i.e., it was paired with an aversive noise), and the other angry face served as a CS−. During 1 minute of PET scanning, the same target-mask pair was repeatedly presented without the noise UCS. The nonconscious conditions involved presentations of the CS+ and the CS− in separate scans, each serving as a target stimulus of 30 ms duration that was masked by a 45 ms presentation of one of the neutral faces. In the conscious conditions, the order of the targets and the masks was reversed, so that the CS+ and the CS−, now serving as masks, could be consciously recognized. SCR data confirmed reliable differential responding to the CS+ and CS− in both the masked and the nonmasked extinction series during the PET scans. To test the hypothesis that human fear conditioning involves the amygdala, PET images to the CS+ and CS− were separately contrasted for the masked and nonmasked presentations. In support of this hypothesis, the overall contrasts between the CS+ and the CS− stimuli showed significant differential activation specifically in the amygdala regions. However, there was also an unpredicted interaction with brain laterality. For the masked CSs, only the right amygdala was activated, whereas for nonmasked CSs, reliable activation was observed only in the left amygdala.

Morris et al. (1999) analyzed the neural connectivity between the amygdala and other brain regions during masked stimulation to examine whether the activation of the amygdala occurred through a subcortical route, as predicted from LeDoux's (1996) model. In support of this hypothesis, they reported that masked activation of the right amygdala could be reliably predicted from activation in the superior colliculus and the right pulvinar in the thalamus, but not from any cortical regions. Such relationships were not obvious when the left amygdala was activated by nonmasked stimuli. The research by Morris et al. (1998, 1999) demonstrates that a system for fear conditioning similar to that in the rodent brain (see, e.g., LeDoux, 1996; Fendt & Fanselow, 1999, for reviews) appears to be operating also in the brains of humans. Consistent with Öhman's (1993a) model, furthermore, these data suggest that fear can be activated from a coarse perceptual analysis of biologically fear-relevant stimuli that is based on perceptual features rather than on a full meaning analysis.

## Emotional Modules and Emotional Experience

### The Fear Module

Our emphasis so far has been on emotional responses (particularly fear responses) that are shared among mammals. These responses reflect evolutionary coupling of autonomic function to behavioral demands to assure effective coping with emotional situations. Because of their ancient origin, they operate quite independently of the more recently evolved capacity for neural computations in primates and, most notably, in the hominid line of descent. As we have shown, there is strong experimental evidence that the autonomic responses associated with fear can be activated from stimuli that are not consciously processed. Indeed, as proposed in LeDoux's (1996) animal model, and as indicated by the results in humans reported by Morris et al. (1998, 1999), the central structure of the fear network, the amygdala, does not require cortical input for its activation by a fear stimulus. It appears, therefore, that the autonomic nervous system is continuously modulated by automatic appraisal processes that monitor the surroundings for threat, independent of the conscious awareness of the person. When these automatic perceptual processes encounter threatening (including novel) stimuli, an OR is elicited as selective attention is switched to the threat to evaluate it more thoroughly or to activate defense responses immediately if they have high threat imminence (e.g., in the circa-strike area).

Several authors have taken this automaticity and the speed of emotional activation (as exemplified in fear) to suggest that there are "automatic appraisal mechanisms" or "inescapable" affective responses that are independent of higher cognition (e.g., Ekman, 1994; Robinson, 1998; Zajonc, 1980; see also Griffith, 1997, for review). Öhman and Mineka (2001) postulated that fear activation can be understood in terms of a "fear module" (cf. Fodor, 1983; Griffith, 1997), that is, a relatively independent behavioral, psychophysiological, and neural system that evolved to solve adaptive problems related to potentially life-threatening situations. This fear module was proposed to have four important characteristics. First, in aversive contexts it is preferentially activated by evolutionarily relevant threatening stimuli, often as a result of the learning of selective associations between fear-relevant stimuli and aversive events. Second, it can be automatically activated by fear stimuli with no need for conscious recognition of the stimulus. Third, it is encapsulated in the sense that it is relatively impenetrable to cognition, so that, once activated, it runs its course with limited possibility for cognition to intervene. Finally, it reflects an independent and dedicated neural circuit that is centered on the amygdala and incorporates a series of subcortical structures that in concert control fear responses (e.g., LeDoux, 1996; Fendt & Fanselow, 1999).

### Experiencing the Fear Module

The fear module is primitive in the sense that it was assembled by evolutionary contingencies hundreds of millions of years ago to serve in brains with little cortices. However, it now operates in a human brain capable of advanced thought, language, and the conscious experience of emotion. Humans can talk about emotions, and they have emotional experiences. Awareness of an emotion not only depends on the recognition of an emotional stimulus but also originates primarily in feedback from the emotional responses that are elicited by the stimulus. For example, experiencing a racing heart when a shadow appears from the dark alley contributes to the feeling of fear. In fact, in perhaps the most classic of all the classical contributions to the psychology of emotion, William James (1884) proposed that such feedback *is* the emotion. To paraphrase, you feel the emotion when you experience its effect on your body. Thus the feeling of fear is the experience of an activated fear module (LeDoux, 1996).

The Jamesian idea has stood the test of time remarkably well, in spite of merciless critics (e.g., Cannon, 1927). Several decades ago, the role of bodily feedback in emotion was revived as a modulator of emotional intensity rather than as a determinant of emotional quality (Schachter & Singer, 1962). Later on, the effects of autonomic feedback provided the cornerstone to one of the most articulated cognitive theories of emotion (Mandler, 1975). More recently, on the basis of neuropsychological data, Damasio (1994) argued that bodily feedback, called *somatic markers* in his version, has a crucial role in cognitive activity such as decision making. For example, options that have led to negative outcomes in the past may be automatically discounted as viable alternatives when a decision is to be taken.

> Somatic markers do not deliberate for us. They assist the deliberation by highlighting some options (either dangerous or favorable). . . . You may think of it as a system for automated qualification of predictions, which acts, whether you want it or not, to evaluate the extremely diverse scenarios of the anticipated future before you. Think of it as a biasing device. (Damasio, 1994, p. 174)

### Effects of Feedback from the Autonomic Nervous System During Conditioning

Some unexpected results in the study by Öhman and Soares (1998) on conditioning to masked pictures of

snakes and spiders may be interpreted in terms of the somatic marker hypothesis. While being trained in a conditioning paradigm in which the UCS was presented 4 s after the CS+, participants were asked to rate their expectancy of shock immediately after each masked CS presentation. They indicated their rating by manipulating a lever between one endpoint designated "−100" ("sure of no shock") and another designated "+100" ("sure of shock"). The results showed that participants acquired a conditioned SCR that was retained in extinction (Öhman & Soares, 1998, Exp. 2). Furthermore, participants showed differential shock expectancies to masked pictures of CS+ and CS−. They rated shocks as more likely to occur on CS+ trials than on CS− trials, even though it is very unlikely that they recognized the stimuli (as shown by the chance-level performance of a separate group that was asked to indicate after each trial whether a spider or a snake preceded the mask). Thus, even though they could not recognize the stimuli, participants somehow appeared to have access to information allowing better than chance ratings of shock likelihood. Similarly, Parra, Esteves, Flykt, & Öhman (1997), albeit with less stringent recognition control, reported that when participants had been conditioned to nonmasked CSs they rated shocks as somewhat more likely to occur after the masked CS+ than after the masked CS− during extinction.

To account for these findings, Öhman and Soares (1998) invoked the somatic marker hypothesis, suggesting that participants may have been able to predict shocks based on autonomic cues associated with the conditioned fear response. This interpretation is weakened by the failure to find reliable correlations between SCRs and expectancy ratings (Öhman & Soares, 1998; Parra et al., 1997). However, Katkin, Wiens, and Öhman (2001) proposed that participants in the Öhman and Soares (1998) and Parra et al. (1997) studies based their shock expectancy on the sensation of the conditioned autonomic response and that it was the sensation that acted as a cue. Accordingly, participants who were sensitive to autonomic cues associated with the conditioned fear response predicted shocks more accurately than participants who did not perceive their own autonomic activity.

To test this hypothesis, Katkin et al. (2001) replicated Öhman and Soares's (1998) experiment, adding the assessment of the participants' ability to perceive their autonomic activity. This ability was indexed by performance on a heartbeat detection task (Katkin, 1985) in which participants were asked to judge the temporal relationship between sensations of their own heartbeats and tones that were triggered by the R-waves from an electrocardiogram. That is, participants judged whether or not they perceived the tones to be delayed from their own heartbeats. Participants who performed beyond chance were classified as *good* heartbeat detectors, whereas all other participants were classified as *poor* heartbeat detectors.

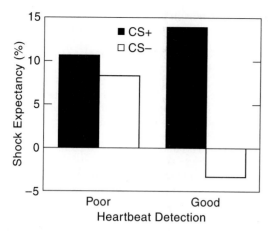

Figure 13.6 Mean shock expectancy ratings across acquisition for poor and good heartbeat detectors to backward-masked images of spiders and snakes that were or were not paired with electric shocks (CS+ and CS−, respectively). Positive ratings represent expectancies of shock, and negative ratings represent expectancies of no shock. Note that only good heartbeat detectors showed differential shock expectancy on CS+ and CS− trials.

Results reported by Katkin et al. (2001) showed, in acquisition, reliable conditioning to masked CSs, as well as a greater expectancy of shock after masked CS+ than masked CS− stimuli, thus replicating the results of Öhman and Soares (1998). However, as shown in Figure 13.6, only good heartbeat detectors differentially expected shock on CS+ trials and no shock on CS− trials, whereas poor detectors did not differentiate the CS+ and the CS− in their shock ratings. These results are consistent with the hypothesis that somatic markers can become associated with stimuli that are not recognized consciously. However, the results further suggest that somatic markers may have to be perceived to affect decision making.

## Implications

Because this chapter focuses on autonomic responses in emotion, we have emphasized evolutionarily derived mechanisms connecting autonomic responses to emotionally significant stimuli. The autonomic nervous system provides an avenue to get at the continuously ongoing interplay between organisms and environmental demands. Its activity is modulated by the automatic appraisal of situational contingencies that set the metabolic stage for potentially life-saving actions. This is a basic level of emotionality that we share with all mammals. But by focusing on this basic level (however justifiable that may be from a scientific point of view), one risks neglecting the embeddedness of human emotion in the complex computations that characterize the human brain. In humans, the fear module may be activated not only by external stimuli but

also by memories, thoughts, mental images, and conscious worries. Damasio (1999) has recently presented an integrated view of emotion and consciousness that includes the emotionally elicited autonomic responses that are discussed in this chapter as the biological core of emotion. As feelings, such emotional responses become manifested in "core consciousness," the experience of here and now, which in turn is integrated in the "extended consciousness" that relates experiences to a self that emerges from autobiographical memory.

Damasio's (1999) work illustrates that we are approaching an era in which the whole range of emotional phenomena can be discussed within an explicit neuroscience framework built on explicit anatomical hypotheses. To explicate this framework and to fill in the enormous number of details that are missing, specific empirical studies are necessary. For such studies of emotion, the psychophysiological methodologies that are discussed in this chapter provide important tools, particularly if they are combined with perceptual masking methods to control the level of cognitive elaboration of the emotional stimulus. By adding brain imaging, explicit anatomical hypotheses can be posed and tested, even for the highest levels of emotional awareness. Thus there is hope that we are eventually reaching a stage in the research of emotion in which we will be able to understand not only the neural correlates of emotion but also emotion in terms of neural mechanisms. This is the challenge of the emerging "affective neuroscience."

## NOTE

Preparation of this chapter was supported by grants to the first author from the Swedish Council for Research in Humanities and Social Science and the Bank of Sweden Tercentennial Foundation.

## REFERENCES

Agras, W. S., Sylvester, D., & Oliveau, D. (1969). The epidemiology of common fears and phobias. *Comprehensive Psychiatry, 10*, 151–156.

American Psychiatric Association. (1994). *Diagnostic and statistical manual of mental disorders* (4th ed.). Washington, DC: Author.

Armony, J. L., & LeDoux, J. E. (2000). How danger is encoded: Toward a systems, cellular, and computational understanding of cognitive-emotional interactions in fear. In M. S. Gazzaniga (Ed.), *The new cognitive neurosciences* (pp. 1067–1079). Cambridge, MA: MIT Press.

Arrindell, W. A., Pickersgill, M. J., Merckelbach, H., Ardon, M. A., & Cornet, F. C. (1991). Phobic dimensions: III. Factor analytic approaches to the study of common phobic fears: An updated review of findings obtained with adult subjects. *Advances in Behaviour Research and Therapy, 13*, 73–130.

Bernstein, A. S., & Taylor, K. W. (1979). The interaction of stimulus information with potential stimulus significance in eliciting the skin conductance orienting response. In H. D. Kimmel, E. H. van Olst, & J. F. Orlebeke (Eds.), *The orienting reflex in humans* (pp. 499–520). Hillsdale, NJ: Erlbaum.

Bernstein, A. S., Taylor, K., Austen, B. G., Nathanson, M., & Scarpelli, A. (1971). Orienting response and apparent movement toward or away from the observer. *Journal of Experimental Psychology, 87*, 37–45.

Berntson, G. G., & Boysen, S. T. (1989). Specificity of the cardiac response to conspecific vocalization in the chimpanzee. *Behavioral Neuroscience, 103*, 235–245.

Berntson, G. G., Cacioppo, J. T., Binkley, P. F., Uchino, B. N., Quigley, K. S., & Fieldstone, A. (1994). Autonomic cardiac control: III. Psychological stress and cardiac response in autonomic space as revealed by pharmacological blockades. *Psychophysiology, 31*, 599–608.

Berntson, G. G., Cacioppo, J. T., & Quigley, K. S. (1991). Autonomic determinism: The modes of autonomic control, the doctrine of autonomic space, and the laws of autonomic constraint. *Psychological Review, 98*, 459–487.

Berntson, G. G., Cacioppo, J. T., & Quigley, K. S. (1994). Autonomic cardiac control: I. Estimation and validation from pharmacological blockades. *Psychophysiology, 31*, 572–585.

Boysen, S. T., & Berntson, G. G. (1989). Conspecific recognition in the chimpanzee: Cardiac indices of significant others. *Journal of Comparative Psychology, 103*, 215–220.

Bradley, B. P., Mogg, K., Millar, N., & White, J. (1995). Selective processing of negative information: Effects of clinical anxiety, concurrent depression, and awareness. *Journal of Abnormal Psychology, 104*, 532–536.

Bradley, B. P., Mogg, K., White, J., Groom, C., & de Bono, J. (1999). Attentional bias for emotional faces in generalized anxiety disorder. *British Journal of Clinical Psychology, 38*, 267–278.

Campbell, B. A., Wood, G., & McBride, T. (1997). Origins of orienting and defensive responses: An evolutionary perspective. In P. J. Lang, R. F. Simons, & M. T. Balaban (Eds.), *Attention and orienting: Sensory and motivational processes* (pp. 41–68). Hillsdale, NJ: Erlbaum.

Cannon, W. B. (1915). *Bodily changes in pain, hunger, fear and rage*. New York: Appleton.

Cannon, W. B. (1927). The James-Lange theory of emotions: A critical examination and an alternative theory. *American Journal of Psychology, 39*, 106–124.

Cook, E. W., Hodes, R. L., & Lang, P. J. (1986). Preparedness and phobia: Effects of stimulus content on human visceral conditioning. *Journal of Abnormal Psychology, 95*, 195–207.

Cook, M., & Mineka, S. (1989). Observational conditioning of fear to fear-relevant versus fear-irrelevant stimuli in rhesus monkeys. *Journal of Abnormal Psychology, 98*, 448–459.

Cook, M., & Mineka, S. (1990). Selective associations in the observational conditioning of fear in rhesus monkeys. *Journal of Experimental Psychology: Animal Behavior Processes, 16*, 372–389.

Damasio, A. R. (1994). *Descartes' error: Emotion, reason, and the human brain*. New York: Putnam.

Damasio, A. R. (1999). *The feeling of what happens: Body and emotion in the making of consciousness*. New York: Harcourt Brace.

Davey, G. C. L. (1992). An expectancy model of laboratory preparedness effects. *Journal of Experimental Psychology: General, 121*, 24–40.

Dawkins, R., & Krebs, J. R. (1979). Arms race between and within species. *Proceedings of the Royal Society, B 205*, 489–511.

Dawson, M. E., & Schell, A. M. (1985). Information processing and human autonomic classical conditioning. *Advances in Psychophysiology, 1*, 89–165.

Dawson, M. E., Schell, A. M., & Banis, H. T. (1986). Greater resistance to extinction of electrodermal responses conditioned to potentially phobic CSs: A noncognitive process? *Psychophysiology, 23*, 552–561.

Dimberg, U. (1982). Facial reactions to facial expressions. *Psychophysiology, 19*, 643–647.

Dimberg, U., Elmehed, K., & Thunberg, M. (2000). Unconscious facial reactions to emotional facial expressions. *Psychological Science, 11*, 86–89.

Dimberg, U., & Öhman, A. (1996). Behold the wrath: Psychophysiological responses to facial stimuli. *Motivation and Emotion, 20*, 149–182.

Donchin, E., Heffley, E., Hillyard, S. A., Loveless, N., Maltzman, I., Öhman, A., Rösler, F., Ruchkin, D., & Siddle, D. (1984). Cognition and event-related potentials: The orienting reflex and P300. *Annals of the New York Academy of Sciences, 425*, 39–57.

Ekman, P. (1994). All emotions are basic. In P. Ekman & R. J. Davidson (Eds.), *The nature of emotion: Fundamental questions* (pp. 15–19) New York: Oxford University Press.

Esteves, F., Dimberg, U., & Öhman, A. (1994). Automatically elicited fear: Conditioned skin conductance responses to masked facial expressions. *Cognition and Emotion, 8*, 393–413.

Esteves, F., & Öhman, A. (1993). Masking the face: Recognition of emotional facial expressions as a function of the parameters of backward masking. *Scandinavian Journal of Psychology, 34*, 1–18.

Esteves, F., Parra, C., Dimberg, U., & Öhman, A. (1994). Nonconscious associative learning: Pavlovian conditioning of skin conductance responses to masked fear-relevant facial stimuli. *Psychophysiology, 31*, 375–385.

Fanselow, M. S. (1994). Neural organization of the defensive behavior system responsible for fear. *Psychonomic Bulletin and Review, 1*, 429–438.

Fanselow, M. S., & Lester, L. S. (1988). A functional behavioristic approach to aversively motivated behavior: Predatory imminence as a determinant of the topography of defensive behavior. In R. C. Bolles & M. D. Beecher (Eds.), *Evolution and learning* (pp. 185–212). Hillsdale, NJ: Erlbaum.

Fendt, M., & Fanselow, M. S. (1999). The neuroanatomical and neurochemical basis of conditioned fear. *Neuroscience and Biobehavioral Reviews, 23*, 743–760.

Flykt, A. (1999). A threat imminence approach to human fear responding. *Studie Psychologica Upsaliensis* [Psychological Studies from Uppsala University] Vol. 18; *Acta Universitatis Upsaliensis* [Records from Uppsala University]. Uppsala, Sweden: Almqvist & Wiksell International.

Fodor, J. (1983). *The modularity of mind*. Cambridge, MA: MIT Press.

Folk, C. L., Remington, R. W., & Johnston, J. C. (1992). Involuntary covert orienting is contingent on attentional control setting. *Journal of Experimental Psychology: Human Perception and Performance, 18*, 1030–1044.

Fredrikson, M. (1981). Orienting and defensive reactions

to phobic and conditioned fear stimuli in phobics and normals. *Psychophysiology, 18*, 456–465.

Fredrikson, M., & Öhman, A. (1979). Cardiovascular and electrodermal responses conditioned to fear-relevant stimuli. *Psychophysiology, 16*, 1–7.

Frijda, N. H. (1986). *The emotions.* Cambridge, England: Cambridge University Press.

Globisch, J., Hamm, A. O., Esteves, F., & Öhman, A. (1999). Fear appears fast: Temporal course of startle reflex potentiation in animal fearful subjects. *Psychophysiology, 36*, 66–75.

Graham, F. K. (1979). Distinguishing among orienting, defense, and startle reflexes. In H. D. Kimmel, E. H. van Olst, & J. F. Orlebeke (Eds.), *The orienting reflex in humans* (pp. 137–167). Hillsdale, NJ: Erlbaum.

Graham, F. K., & Clifton, R. K. (1966). Heart-rate change as a component of the orienting response. *Psychological Bulletin, 65*, 305–320.

Greenwald, M. K., Cook, E. W., III, & Lang, P. J. (1989). Affective judgement and psychophysiological response: Dimensional covariation in the evaluation of visual stimuli. *Journal of Psychophysiology, 3*, 347–363.

Griffith, P. E. (1997). *What emotions really are.* Chicago: University of Chicago Press.

Hamm, A. O., Cuthbert, B. N., Globisch, J., & Vaitl, D. (1997). Fear and the startle reflex: Blink modulation and autonomic response patterns in animal and mutilation fearful subjects. *Psychophysiology, 34*, 97–107.

Hansen, C. H., & Hansen, R. D. (1988). Finding the face in the crowd: An anger superiority effect. *Journal of Personality and Social Psychology, 54*, 917–924.

Hirsch, S. M., & Bolles, R. C. (1981). On the ability of prey to recognize predators. *Zeitschrift für Tierpsychologie, 54*, 71–84.

Izard, C. E. (1991). *The psychology of emotions.* New York: Plenum.

James, W. (1884). What is an emotion? *Mind, 9*, 188–205.

Jennings, J. R. (1992). Is it important that the mind is in a body? Inhibition and the heart. *Psychophysiology, 29*, 369–383.

Johnsen, B. H., & Hugdahl, K. (1991). Hemisphere asymmetry in conditioning to facial emotional expressions. *Psychophysiology, 28*, 154–162.

Johnsen, B. H., & Hugdahl, K. (1993). Right hemisphere representation of autonomic conditioning to facial emotional expressions. *Psychophysiology, 30*, 274–278.

Katkin, E. S. (1985). Blood, sweat, and tears: Individual differences in autonomic self-perception. *Psychophysiology, 22*, 125–137.

Katkin, E. S., Wiens, S., & Öhman, A. (2001). Nonconscious fear conditioning, visceral perception, and the development of gut feelings. *Psychological Science, 12*, 366–370.

Lacey, J. I., & Lacey, B. C. (1970). Some autonomic-central nervous system interrelationships. In P. Black (Ed.), *Physiological correlates of emotion* (pp. 205–228). New York: Academic Press.

Lang, P. J. (1984). Cognition and emotion: Concept and action. In C. E Izard, J. Kagan, & R. B. Zajonc (Eds.), *Emotion, cognition, and behavior* (pp. 192–226). New York: Cambridge University Press.

Lang, P. J., Bradley, M. M., & Cuthbert, B. N. (1990). Emotion, attention, and the startle reflex. *Psychological Review, 97*, 377–398.

Lang, P. J., Bradley, M. M., & Cuthbert, B. N. (1997). Mo-

tivated attention: Affect, activation, and action. In P. J. Lang, R. F. Simons, & M. T. Balaban (Eds.), *Attention and orienting: Sensory and motivational processes* (pp. 97–135). Hillsdale, NJ: Erlbaum.

Lang, P. J., Greenwald, M. K., Bradley, M. M., & Hamm, A. O. (1993). Looking at pictures: Affective, facial, visceral, and behavioral reactions. *Psychophysiology, 30*, 261–273.

LeDoux, J. E. (1996). *The emotional brain.* New York: Simon & Schuster.

Levenson, R. W., Ekman, P., & Friesen, W. V. (1990). Voluntary facial action generates emotion-specific autonomic nervous system activity. *Psychophysiology, 27*, 363–384.

MacLeod, C., & Rutherford, E. M. (1992). Anxiety and the selective processing of emotional information: Mediating roles of awareness, trait and state variables, and personal relevance of stimulus materials. *Behaviour Research and Therapy, 30*, 479–491.

Mandler, G. (1975). *Mind and emotion.* New York: Wiley.

Mathews, A., & MacLeod, C. (1994). Cognitive approaches to emotion and emotional disorders. *Annual Review of Psychology, 45*, 25–50.

Mayr, E. (1974). Behavior programs and evolutionary strategies. *American Scientist, 62*, 650–659.

Mazurski, E. J., Bond, N. W., Siddle, D.A.T., & Lovibond, P. F. (1996). Conditioning of facial expressions of emotion: Effects of CS sex and age. *Psychophysiology, 33*, 416–425.

Miller, N. E. (1951). Learnable drives and rewards. In S. S. Stevens (Ed.), *Handbook of experimental psychology* (pp. 435–472). New York: Wiley.

Mineka, S., & Cook, M. (1993). Mechanisms involved in the observational conditioning of fear. *Journal of Experimental Psychology: General, 122*, 23–38.

Mineka, S., Davidson, M., Cook, M., & Keir, R. (1984). Observational conditioning of snake fear in rhesus monkeys. *Journal of Abnormal Psychology, 93*, 355–372.

Mineka, S., Keir, R., & Price, V. (1980). Fear of snakes in wild- and laboratory-reared rhesus monkeys (*Macaca mulatta*). *Animal Learning and Behavior, 8*, 653–663.

Mogg, K., & Bradley, B. P. (1998). A cognitive-motivational analysis of anxiety. *Behavioural Research and Therapy, 36*, 809–848.

Mogg, K., & Bradley, B. P. (1999). Orienting of attention to threatening facial expressions presented under conditions of restricted awareness. *Cognition and Emotion, 13*, 713–740.

Morris, J., Öhman, A., & Dolan, R. J. (1998). Modulation of human amygdala activity by emotional learning and conscious awareness. *Nature, 393*, 467–470.

Morris, J. S., Öhman, A., & Dolan, R. J. (1999). A subcortical pathway to the right amygdala mediating "unseen" fear. *Proceedings of the National Academy of Sciences, 96*, 1680–1685.

Oatley, K., & Jenkins, J. M. (1996). *Understanding emotions.* Cambridge, MA: Blackwell.

Obrist, P. A. (1981). *Cardiovascular psychophysiology: A perspective.* New York: Plenum.

Obrist, P. A., Lawler, J. E., Howard, J. L., Smithson, K. W., Martin, P. A., & Manning, J. (1974). Sympathetic influences on the heart in humans: Effects on contractility and heart rate of acute stress. *Psychophysiology, 11*, 405–427.

Obrist, P. A., Sutterer, J. R., & Howard, J. L. (1972). Preparatory cardiac changes: A psychobiological approach. In A. H. Black & W. F. Prokasy (Eds.), *Classical conditioning: II. Current research and theory* (pp. 312–340). New York: Appleton-Century-Crofts.

Öhman, A. (1979). The orienting response, attention, and learning: An information-processing perspective. In H. D. Kimmel, E. H. van Olst, & J. F. Orlebeke (Eds.), *The orienting reflex in humans* (pp. 443–472). Hillsdale, NJ: Erlbaum.

Öhman, A. (1983). The orienting response during Pavlovian conditioning. In D. Siddle (Ed.), *Orienting and habituation: Perspectives in human research* (pp. 315–369). Chichester, England: Wiley.

Öhman, A. (1986). Face the beast and fear the face: Animal and social fears as prototypes for evolutionary analyses of emotion. *Psychophysiology, 23,* 123–145.

Öhman, A. (1987). The psychophysiology of emotion: An evolutionary-cognitive perspective. *Advances in Psychophysiology, 2,* 79–127.

Öhman, A. (1993a). Fear and anxiety as emotional phenomena: Clinical phenomenology, evolutionary perspectives, and information processing mechanisms. In M. Lewis & J. M. Haviland (Eds.), *Handbook of emotions* (pp. 511–536). New York: Guilford Press.

Öhman, A. (1993b). Stimulus prepotency and fear learning: Data and theory. In N. Birbaumer & A. Öhman (Eds.), *The structure of emotion: Psychophysiological, cognitive, and clinical aspects* (pp. 218–239). Seattle, WA: Hogrefe & Huber.

Öhman, A., & Dimberg, U. (1978). Facial expressions as conditioned stimuli for electrodermal responses: A case of "preparedness"? *Journal of Personality and Social Psychology, 36,* 1251–1258.

Öhman, A., & Dimberg, U. (1984). An evolutionary perspective on human social behavior. In W. M. Waid (Ed.), *Sociophysiology* (pp. 47–86). New York: Springer-Verlag.

Öhman, A., Dimberg, U., & Esteves, F. (1989). Preattentive activation of aversive emotions. In T. Archer & L.-G. Nilsson (Eds.), *Aversion, avoidance and anxiety* (pp. 169–193). Hillsdale, NJ: Erlbaum.

Öhman, A., Dimberg, U., & Öst, L.-G. (1985). Animal and social phobias: Biological constraints on learned fear responses. In S. Reiss & R. R. Bootzin (Eds.), *Theoretical issues in behavior therapy* (pp. 123–178). New York: Academic Press.

Öhman, A., Eriksson, A., Fredrikson, M., Hugdahl, K., & Olofsson, C. (1974). Habituation of the electrodermal orienting reaction to potentially phobic and supposedly neutral stimuli in normal human subjects. *Biological Psychology, 2,* 85–93.

Öhman, A., Flykt, A., & Esteves, F. (2001). Emotion drives attention: Detecting the snake in the grass. *Journal of Experimental Psychology: General, 130,* 466–478.

Öhman, A., Flykt, A., & Lundqvist, D. (2000). Unconscious emotion: Evolutionary perspectives, psychophysiological data, and neuropsychological mechanisms. In R. Lane & L. Nadel (Eds.), *The cognitive neuroscience of emotion* (pp. 296–327). New York: Oxford University Press.

Öhman, A., Fredrikson, M., Hugdahl, K., & Rimmö, P. A. (1976). The premise of equipotentiality in human classical conditioning: Conditioned electrodermal responses to potentially phobic stimuli. *Journal of Experimental Psychology: General, 103,* 313–337.

Öhman, A., Hamm, A., & Hugdahl, K. (2000). Cognition and the autonomic nervous system: Orienting, antici-

pation, and conditioning. In J. T. Cacioppo, L. G. Tassinary, & G. G. Berntson (Eds.), *Handbook of psychophysiology* (pp. 522–575). New York: Cambridge University Press.

Öhman, A., Lundqvist, D., & Esteves, F. (2001). The face in the crowd revisited: An anger superiority effect with schematic stimuli. *Journal of Personality and Social Psychology, 80,* 381–396.

Öhman, A., & Mineka, S. (2001). Fear, phobias, and preparedness: Toward an evolved module of fear and fear learning. *Psychological Review, 108,* 482–522.

Öhman, A., & Soares, J. J. F. (1993). On the automatic nature of phobic fear: Conditioned electrodermal responses to masked fear-relevant stimuli. *Journal of Abnormal Psychology, 102,* 121–132.

Öhman, A., & Soares, J. J. F. (1994). "Unconscious anxiety": Phobic responses to masked stimuli. *Journal of Abnormal Psychology, 103,* 231–240.

Öhman, A., & Soares, J. J. F. (1998). Emotional conditioning to masked stimuli: Expectancies for aversive outcomes following nonrecognized fear-relevant stimuli. *Journal of Experimental Psychology: General, 127,* 69–82.

Ortony, A., & Turner, T. J. (1992). What's basic about basic emotions? *Psychological Review, 97,* 315–331.

Parra, C., Esteves, F., Flykt, A., & Öhman, A. (1997). Pavlovian conditioning to social stimuli: Backward masking and the dissociation of implicit and explicit cognitive processes. *European Psychologist, 2,* 106–117.

Pavlov, I. P. (1927). *Conditioned reflexes.* Oxford, England: Oxford University Press.

Pitman, R. K., & Orr, S. P. (1986). Test of the conditioning model of neurosis: Differential aversive conditioning of angry and neutral facial expressions in anxiety disorder patients. *Journal of Abnormal Psychology, 95,* 208–213.

Quigley, K. S., & Berntson, G. G. (1990). Autonomic origins of cardiac responses to nonsignal stimuli in the rat. *Behavioral Neuroscience, 104,* 751–762.

Regan, M., & Howard, R. (1995). Fear conditioning, preparedness, and the contingent negative variation. *Psychophysiology, 32,* 208–214.

Robinson, M. D. (1998). Running from William James' bear: A review of preattentive mechanisms and their contributions to emotional experience. *Cognition and Emotion, 12,* 667–696.

Rosen, J. B., & Schulkin, J. (1998). From normal fear to pathological anxiety. *Psychological Review, 105,* 325–350.

Russell, P. A. (1979). Fear-evoking stimuli. In W. Sluckin (Ed.), *Fear in animals and man* (pp. 85–124). New York: Van Nostrand Reinhold.

Sagan, C. (1977). *The dragons of Eden: Speculations on the evolution of human intelligence.* London: Hodder & Stoughton.

Schachter, S., & Singer, J. E. (1962). Cognitive, social, and physiological determinants of emotional state. *Psychological Review, 69,* 379–399.

Schell, A. M., Dawson, M. E., & Marinkovic, K. (1991). Effects of the use of potentially phobic CSs on retention, reinstatement, and extinction of the conditioned skin conductance response. *Psychophysiology, 28,* 140–153.

Schwartz, G. E., Weinberger, D. A., & Singer, J. A. (1981). Cardiovascular differentiation of happiness, sadness, anger, and fear following imagery and exercise. *Psychosomatic Medicine, 43,* 343–364.

Seligman, M. E. P. (1970). On the generality of the laws of learning. *Psychological Review, 77*, 406–418.

Seligman, M. E. P. (1971). Phobias and preparedness. *Behavior Therapy, 2*, 307–320.

Siddle, D. A. T. (1983). *Orienting and habituation: Perspectives in human research.* Chichester, England: Wiley.

Siddle, D. A. T., & Heron, P. A. (1976). Effects of length of training and amount of tone frequency change on amplitude of autonomic components of the orienting response. *Psychophysiology, 13*, 281–287.

Siddle, D. A. T., Kyriacou, C., Heron, P. A., & Matthews, W. A. (1979). Effects of changes in verbal stimuli on the skin conductance response component of the orienting response. *Psychophysiology, 16*, 34–40.

Simons, R. F., Detenber, B. H., Roedema, T. M., & Reiss, J. E. (1999). Emotion processing in three systems: The medium and the message. *Psychophysiology, 36*, 619–628.

Soares, J. J. F., & Öhman, A. (1993a). Backward masking and skin conductance responses after conditioning to non-feared but fear-relevant stimuli in fearful subjects. *Psychophysiology, 30*, 460–466.

Soares, J. J. F., & Öhman, A. (1993b). Preattentive processing, preparedness, and phobias: Effects of instruction on conditioned electrodermal responses to masked and non-masked fear-relevant stimuli. *Behaviour Research and Therapy, 31*, 87–95.

Sokolov, E. N. (1963). *Perception and the conditioned reflex.* Oxford, England: Pergamon.

Spinks, J. A., & Siddle, D. (1983). The functional significance of the orienting response. In D. A. T. Siddle (Ed.), *Orienting and habituation: Perspectives in human research* (pp. 237–324). Chichester, England: Wiley.

Tooby, J., & Cosmides, L. (1990). The past explains the present: Emotional adaptations and the structure of ancestral environment. *Ethology and Sociobiology, 11*, 375–424.

Wagner, A. R. (1976). Priming in the STM: An information-processing mechanism for self-generated or retrieval-generated depression of performance. In T. J. Tighe & R. N. Leaton (Eds.), *Habituation: Perspectives from child development, animal behavior, and neurophysiology* (pp. 95–128). Hillsdale, NJ: Erlbaum.

Whalen, P. J., Rauch, S. L., Etcoff, N. L., McInerney, S. C., Lee, M. B., & Jenike, M. A. (1998). Masked presentations of emotional facial expression modulate amygdala activity without explicit knowledge. *Journal of Neuroscience, 18*, 411–418.

Wingard, J. A., & Maltzman, I. (1980). Interest as a predeterminer of the GSR index of the orienting reflex. *Acta Psychologica, 46*, 153–160.

Yantis, S. (1998). Control of visual attention. In H. Pashler (Ed.), *Attention* (pp. 223–256). Hove, England: Psychology Press.

Zajonc, R. B. (1980). Feeling and thinking: Preferences need no inferences. *American Psychologist, 35*, 151–175.

# 14

# EMOTIONAL MODULATION OF SELECTIVE ATTENTION: BEHAVIORAL AND PSYCHOPHYSIOLOGICAL MEASURES

Kenneth Hugdahl and Kjell Morten Stormark

## Attention, Cognition, and Emotion

The study of attention has been central to the understanding of human cognition. Although research on attention has led to an enhanced understanding of selective information processing, it has tended to treat human attention in terms of "cold cognition." As a consequence, researchers usually study attention to emotionally "neutral" stimuli, and the concept of attention is treated in terms of stages of information processing, as conscious, cognitive, rational activity.

This approach neglects, however, the fact that selective attention in the natural environment most often is driven by motivation and regulated by the emotional significance of stimuli (see Lang, Bradley, & Cuthbert, 1997). We argue that selective attention to a neutral or innocuous stimulus is the exception rather than the rule in everyday life and that orienting of attention in most instances means orienting toward a stimulus source that has some affective value for the individual. This argument also goes the other way—an emotional response is always followed by redirecting attention to the source of the emotion. In this chapter we focus on emotion-attention interaction by reviewing a series of studies from our laboratory, in which we have investigated emotional influences on selective attention.

## Attentional and Emotional Bias: The Stroop Paradigm

According to Posner (1995), selective attention can be understood in terms of three distinct mental processes: initial orienting following changes in sensory stimulation, detection of a stimulus that elicits orienting, and sustained attentiveness to the stimulus. One method by which behavioral consequences of selective processing have been investigated is the Stroop (1935) color naming interference task, in which participants are instructed to name the ink color of color words such as *red, blue*, and so forth printed on a sheet of paper or shown on a computer screen. The ink color of the words is either congruent (the word *red* typed in red ink) or incongruent (the word *red* written in blue ink).

A basic assumption when explaining performance on the Stroop task in terms of selective attention is that the participant initially focuses his or her attention on the content, not on the ink color, of the words. Reading is a highly automated skill, whereas color naming is a less practiced skill. This means that it is virtually impossible for participants not to read when they are presented with verbal material (MacLeod, 1991). The fact that naming the ink color of incongruent words takes more time than naming congruent words suggests that processing of the word interferes with the ability to simultaneously attend to the ink color. In terms of shifting attention, participants have to disengage attention from the task-irrelevant semantic information in order to engage attention to the task-relevant ink color (cf. Posner & Snyder, 1975).

Recent studies of emotional bias in a shifting-attention situation have used a modified version of the Stroop task to test the assumption that emotionally threatening words produce the same kind of cognitive interference as incongruent color words. Mathews and MacLeod (1985) found that anxiety words interfered with the ability of anxiety patients to name the color of the same words. Mathews and MacLeod (1985) studied a group of patients suffering from generalized anxiety disorder (GAD). They found that these patients were disproportionately slower in naming the color of social or physical threat words than neutral words, whereas there was no such difference in a group of healthy controls. These results were later replicated in another sample of GAD patients by Mogg, Mathews, and Weinman (1989), and similar results have also been demonstrated in specific (spider) phobia (Watts, McKenna, Sharrock, & Tresize, 1986), social phobia (Hope, Rapee, Heimberg, & Dombeck, 1990), obsessive-compulsive disorders (Foa, Illai, McCarthy, Shoyer, & Murdock, 1993), posttraumatic stress disorder (McNally, Kaspi, Riemann, & Zeitlin, 1990), and panic disorders (McNally, Reimann, & Kim, 1990).

It may thus seem as if anxious individuals find it difficult to disengage attention from words that contain threatening information. The cognitive system in patients with anxiety or depression is assumed to selectively filter emotionally relevant information through preexisting memory representations or schemata that are idiosyncratic for the individual's emotional concern (see Williams, Watts, MacLeod, & Mathews, 1988). According to this perspective, attention in anxiety patients is biased toward stimuli that are related to the specific emotional concern. Attentional bias results in facilitating identification of threatening information (Mathews & MacLeod, 1986), but it impairs the ability to shift attention away from threat-provoking stimuli (Mathews, 1990).

Several studies have, however, shown that the interference effect that is seen in the emotional Stroop situation occurs to both negative and positive emotional words (Martin, Williams, & Clark, 1991), as long as the words are specifically related to the individual's emotional concern (Mathews & Klug, 1993). This suggests that the emotional interference effect in the Stroop situation can be explained by assuming that words will be automatically processed for meaning and then disregarded if they are irrelevant to the task of naming the color of the word. However, when the word is related to an individual's emotional problem, it will be more difficult to disregard the word. It is as if task-irrelevant words that are emotionally relevant capture attention resources, which interferes with performance on the relevant task, that is, naming the ink color of the words.

The bias toward emotionally salient words in the emotional Stroop task can be attributed to several attention components: peripheral orientation, selective engagement, or disengagement (Cook & Turpin, 1997). The problem with disentangling the different components in attention is emphasized in the emotional Stroop task, because it does not involve a congruent condition, as in the original version of the Stroop task. It is thus not possible to compare responses to congruent and incongruent colors in the emotional Stroop task. Slower responses to the ink color of emotional words could reflect either an inability to shift attention away from the content of an emotional word or increased orienting to the word.

## Selective Attention: Posner's Cue-Target Paradigm

Attention orienting can occur either voluntarily (e.g., searching for a specific object or event) or involuntarily (when attention is elicited by an external event). The latter phenomenon is demonstrated in Posner's (1980) attention-orienting task (see Figure 14.1), in which attention is shifted in visual space either to the left or right spatial location through lateralized presentation of a peripheral stimulus (cue) on a computer screen. The cue is followed by a response target, presented either at the same location as the cue (referred to as valid trials, because the spatial location of the target is validly indicated by the cue) or at the opposite location from the cue (referred to as invalid trials).

Several studies have shown that manual reaction time (RT) is slower to targets on invalid than on valid trials (see Posner & Driver, 1992, for examples), demonstrating that responses to stimuli presented at the location of the cue are facilitated, whereas responses to stimuli at other locations are temporarily inhibited (Posner, 1988). A common interpretation of this finding is made in terms of a cognitive *cost-benefit* difference, reflecting a cognitive benefit of responding to targets at the attended location and a cognitive cost involved in responding to targets at the opposite location. When the target occurs in a different location from the cue, shifting attention to the target involves interruption and disengagement of ongoing attention to the location of the cue, moving attention from the cue location to the target location, and reengagement of attention to the target. The validity effect may be regarded as involving an expectation that the target will be presented at the same spatial location as the cue. The building up of such an expectation is facilitated by the fact that

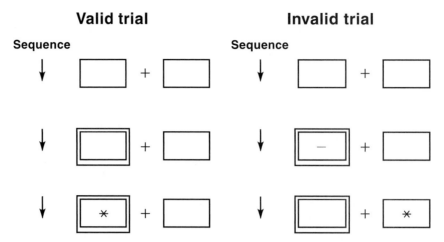

**Valid trial**    **Invalid trial**

Figure 14.1 Schematic outline of the attention-orienting task. The top row shows the fixation point and the two rectangles designating spatial locations. The middle row shows the presentation of the cue (extra frame indicating that one of the rectangles is lit up). The bottom row shows the presentation of the target. The left-hand column shows an example of a valid trial. The right-hand column shows an example of an invalid trial.

targets are presented at the same location as the cue on most of the trials.

## Emotional Cuing with Words

In a first study, Stormark, Nordby, and Hugdahl (1995) used emotionally negative and neutral words as cues. The purpose of this study was to assess to what extent an emotional cue would facilitate and/or impair attention disengagement, somewhat similar to the effects observed in the emotional Stroop situation. If delayed response latencies in naming the color of emotional words in the Stroop task reflect difficulties in disengaging attention from the semantic meaning of the word, one would also expect that responses to targets presented in the opposite location from an emotional word cue would be delayed.

The emotionally negative and neutral words were selected from a pool of Norwegian words that had been rated for their emotional valence. The experimental setup was similar to that of the classic Posner paradigm, with the exception that the typical rectangle brightening was replaced by emotional or neutral words as cues. Thus all parameters between conditions were the same except that in one condition a neutral word was presented and in another condition an emotional word was presented.

Scalp recordings of event-related potentials (ERPs) showed an overall enhanced P3 component (Hillyard & Picton, 1979) to the emotional words, reflecting that the

emotional words elicited increased orienting (see Figure 14.2).

There was a significant interaction between the word cues (emotional/neutral) and validity (valid/invalid cue). Follow-up tests showed significantly shorter RTs to valid compared to invalid trials for the emotional words (see Figure 14.3). This finding suggests that the emotional words on validly cued targets initially "attracted" attention to a stronger extent than the neutral words. The difference in RTs on valid and invalid trials in Figure 14.3 is in accordance with findings from the emotional Stroop task described earlier in this chapter.

## Emotional Conditioning of the Cue

It could, however, be questioned to what extent words can act as substitutes for genuine emotional stimuli (cf. McNally, 1995). This question could be empirically tested by using the same physical cue in both the neutral and emotional conditions and by applying a classical conditioning procedure to establish one of the cues as an emotional stimulus. In a series of studies (Stormark & Hugdahl, 1996, 1997; Stormark, Hugdahl, & Posner, 1999), we have investigated attention orienting to an emotional nonverbal cue in a classical conditioning situation in which the cue is paired with an aversive white-noise unconditioned stimulus (UCS) *before* the attention experiment. Thus in the typical paradigm we manipulate the intrinsic emotional valence while retaining the same extrinsic appearance of the cues.

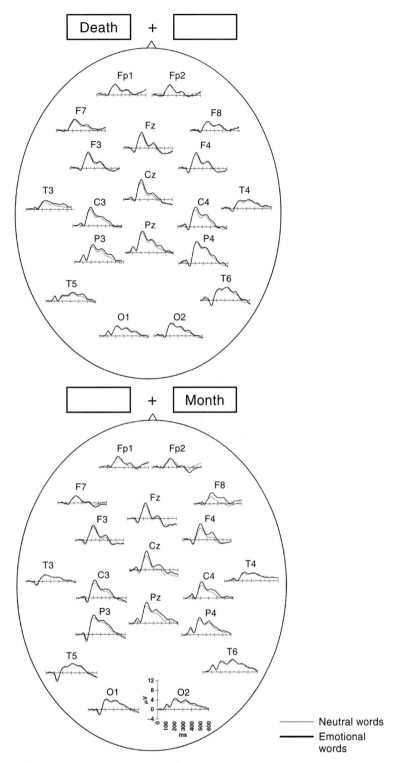

Figure 14.2 Grand-average scalp recordings of event-related potentials (ERPs) for all 21 leads during presentation of emotional (e.g., *death*) and neutral (e.g., *month*) cue words in the attention-orienting task. The words were presented for 600 milliseconds. The top diagram shows ERPs to presentation of the words in the left visual half-field (with an emotional word as an example). The bottom diagram shows ERPs to presentation of the words in the right visual half-field (with a neutral word as an example). Note the pronounced asymmetry in the early ERPs to the word presentation. Most important, however, is the enhanced positive peak with a latency around 200 ms to the emotional words. Data adapted from Stormark, Hugdahl, and Posner (1999).

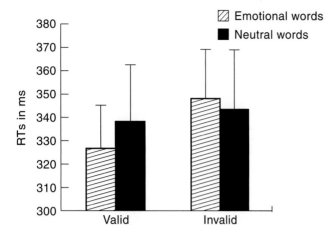

Figure 14.3 Mean reaction time (RT) on valid and invalid trials, separated for the emotional and the neutral words. Small bars = standard error of the mean. Data adapted from Stormark, Nordby, and Hugdahl (1995).

These experiments, then, consisted of two parts or phases, a *conditioning* part in which the attention cue is established as a conditioned stimulus (CS), and an *attention* part, in which the influence of the emotional cue on orienting attention is evaluated.

The results from the first studies were later applied to the study of emotion-attention reactivity in alcoholic participants, testing emotion-attention interactions in a clinical setting (e.g., Stormark, Field, Hugdahl, & Horowitz, 1997; Stormark, Laberg, Bjerland, Nordby, & Hugdahl, 1995; Stormark, Laberg, Nordby, & Hugdahl, 1998; Stormark, Laberg, Nordby, & Hugdahl, 2000).

Briefly, classical conditioning is a basic form of learning in which an emotionally neutral sensory stimulus gains signaling qualities through repeated associations with a strong emotional stimulus. The associative process thus transforms the neutral stimulus into a conditioned stimulus (CS), eliciting a similar response as that elicited by the emotional stimulus (UCS). The change in behavior that follows the presentation of the UCS is called the unconditioned response (UCR), and the response that accompanies the temporal pairing of the CS and UCS is called a conditioned response (CR; see Hugdahl, 1995, for an overview of classical conditioning).

## Psychophysiological Response Systems

In the classical conditioning studies, electrodermal (skin conductance) responses served as indices of emotionality, together with manual reaction time (RT) and scalp-recorded event-related potentials (ERPs), to evaluate the effects on attention. The electrodermal system, that is, skin conductance response (SCR), is sensitive to rapid change in hydration in the epidermis and dermis of the skin to a sensory stimulus; it is typically recorded from the surface of the palms (see Hugdahl, 1995, for a review). The physiological basis of the skin conductance response is the activity of the eccrine sweat gland. The eccrine sweat glands are uniquely innervated by the sympathetic branch of the autonomic nervous system (ANS). The final common neural pathway for skin conductance responses is, therefore, the sympathetic branch of the ANS, which in turn is regulated from the frontal cortex via hypothalamic-limbic pathways (Boucsein, 1993; Luria & Homskaya, 1970; Tranel & Damasio, 1994).

## Empirical Studies Using the Conditioning Paradigm

As previously stated, the initial experiments consisted of two separate parts: emotional conditioning and attention orienting. To recapitulate, in the emotional conditioning part, the stimulus that was to serve as cue in the attention-orienting part was paired with the white-noise UCS, and the influence on orienting of the emotional cue was assessed in the attention part of the experiment.

In the Stormark, Hugdahl, and Posner (1999) study, 10 male and 10 female right-handed students participated. A differential-conditioning paradigm was used, in which a 4-s presentation of the classic rectangle that served as the attention cue was paired with a 2-s 90-dB white-noise UCS for half of the participants (conditioning group) before the attention test. The cue which was paired with the noise was called a CS+. There were a total of 18 trials, 9 CS+ trials and 9 CS− trials (the CS− was another rectangle in which the frame was not lit up). The UCS followed the CS+ for 6 trials, and for 3 test trials the CS+ was presented without the UCS.

The other half of the participants (control group) received the same number of rectangle presentations (CS+ and CS−) and white-noise presentations during the conditioning part. However, the noise was always presented without a rectangle being seen on the screen; thus the noise was presented noncontingent on the presentation of both rectangles. To assess the extent to which the cue rectangle was established as an emotional cue, SCRs were scored as the first response within a 1–4 s period after onset of the CS, thus excluding any response to the white-noise UCS.

As is evident in Figure 14.4, the CS+ trials elicited significantly larger SCRs than the CS− trials. SCRs were also larger to the CS+ in the conditioning group compared with the CS+ in the control group, whereas there was no significant difference between the groups for the CS− trials. Moreover, SCRs to the CS+ in the conditioning group showed a pronounced increase during the last three trials in the conditioning part, whereas SCRs to the CS− and

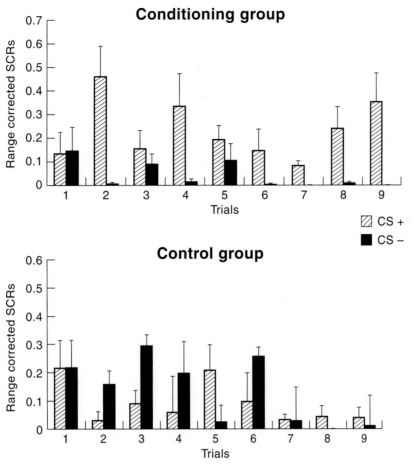

Figure 14.4  Mean range-corrected skin conductance responses (SCRs) during the conditioning phase in which the attention cue stimulus was classically conditioned to a white-noise-tone unconditioned stimulus (UCS) for the conditioning group. The attention cue stimulus is thus referred to as a conditioned stimulus (CS+), whereas the stimulus that was never paired with the UCS is referred to as CS−. Note that the control group had only noncontingent presentations of the UCS and the CS cues. The results show mean SCRs for all trials, separated for the two groups. Small bars = standard error of the mean. Data adapted from Stormark, Hugdahl, and Posner (1999).

the SCRs to both the CS+ and CS− in the control group were almost abolished on the last few conditioning trials. Responding to the CS+ and CS− in the control group was also like a "random walk" across trials, with no systematic difference. This suggests that SCRs to the CS− stimulus habituated or extinguished over trials, whereas SCRs to the CS+ in the conditioning group increased toward the end of the conditioning phase. This is exactly what would be expected if classical conditioning had occurred to the CS+ cue.

In the attention phase, spatial locations were designated by the "classic" single-frame rectangle (which had been conditioned for half of the participants), presented in the left and right visual hemifields (see Figure 14.1).

The horizontal distance from the central fixation point on the computer screen to the nearest edge of the rectangles was 6° of visual angle. The participants were instructed to maintain fixation at the center cross and to respond as quickly as possible by pressing a key on a keyboard whenever they saw the asterisk response target. Each trial started when one of the rectangles was lit up on the screen (identical to the stimulus established as the CS+ in the conditioning group during the conditioning phase). Making one of the rectangles suddenly brighter served as the cue to orient attention toward it. The cue was presented 600 ms before the target. Valid trials composed two-thirds of the trials, and the remaining one-third were invalid trials.

As can be seen in Figure 14.5, there was a two-way interaction between the Group and Validity factors, showing that although the control group evidenced the typical cost-benefit effect between valid and invalid trials, there was no significant invalidity effect in the conditioning group. The conditioning group actually responded faster to targets presented in the opposite location from the cue during the first trial block. Although the conditioning group overall tended to respond faster than the control group (see Figure 14.5), there were no significant overall differences in RTs between the two groups.

The conditioning group also showed an enhanced N1 component in the ERPs during the presentation of the cue, suggesting that the increased emotional significance attributed to the cue after it had been paired with the white-noise UCS triggered enhanced attention to the CS+ cue (cf. Näätänen, 1992). This is seen in Figure 14.6.

From the ERP data, it is unlikely that the lack of the cost-benefit valid-invalid difference in the RT-data was caused by the cue becoming less efficient in orienting attention. Instead, we believe that the participants voluntarily directed their attention away from the spatial location at which the CS+ cue was presented and that the lack of the cost-benefit effect between valid and invalid trials in the conditioning group may reflect the fact that attention was not summoned at the cued location at the time the target appeared on the screen. We would like to label this effect "cognitive avoidance," which may explain why the typical invalidity effect disappears to emotional cues. Cognitive avoidance may be conceptualized as hyperfacilitation of attentional disengagement with the result that shifts of attention away from the emotional cue are already initiated at the onset of target presentation. Cognitive avoidance is discussed in more detail later in the chapter.

## Attention Orienting Before and After Conditioning

A second study (Stormark & Hugdahl, 1996) also investigated attention orienting to the CS+ and CS− cues *before* and *after* conditioning had occurred. The hypothesis was that there should be no difference in orienting to the two cues before conditioning, with a clear difference after conditioning.

Sixteen male and 16 female right-handed students participated in the study, in which the standard frame-lit rectangle or a completely lit rectangle served as the attention cue on separate trials. In the conditioning part, half of the participants (conditioning group) received white-noise presentations contingent on the presentation of one of the rectangles (CS+) but not on presentations of the other rectangle. The other half of the participants (control group) received white noise noncontingent on presentations of the rectangles. Which rectangle served as the CS+ and CS− was counterbalanced across participants. By comparing attention orienting to the same physical cue *before* it had acquired emotional valence through conditioning with attention orienting to the same cue *after* conditioning, the effects of emotional valence on attention orienting could be further investigated.

The results showed that the CS+ rectangle again elicited significantly larger SCRs than the CS− rectangle in the conditioning group in the conditioning phase, whereas there was no significant difference between the cue rectangles in the control group. As can be seen in Figure 14.7, there was also a tendency toward smaller SCRs to the CS− in the conditioning group than in the control group. This suggests that the CS− may also have elicited conditioned inhibition, in addition to conditioned excitation to the CS+.

The RT data showed that the cognitive cost observed on invalid trials *before* conditioning disappeared *after* conditioning in the conditioning group. For the control group, there was no significant difference between valid and invalid trials before and after conditioning. This is seen in Figure 14.8. In general, both groups evidenced slower RTs on invalid than on valid trials in the attention-preconditioning part of the experiment, independent of whether the CS+ or CS− rectangle served as the attention cue. Thus, once again the conditioning group showed evidence of *reduced* cognitive cost of shifting attention on invalid trials after the cue had acquired emotional significance.

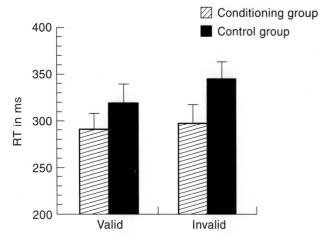

Figure 14.5 Mean reaction time (RT) on valid and invalid trials across four trial blocks, separated for the conditioning and the control groups. Small bars = standard error of the mean. Data from Stormark, Hugdahl, and Posner (1999).

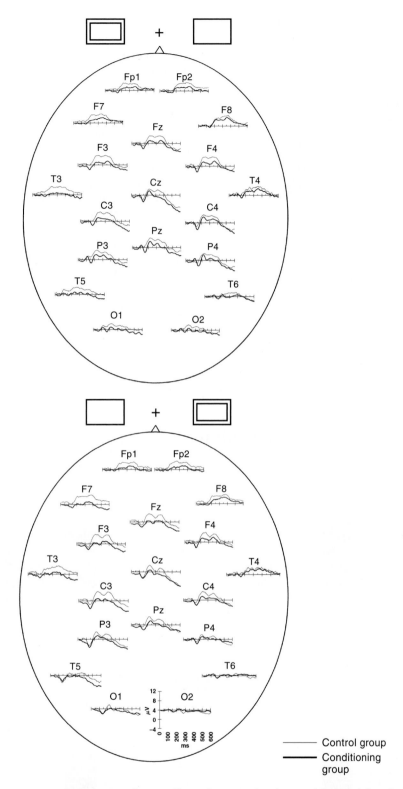

Figure 14.6 Grand-average scalp recordings of event-related potentials (ERPs) for all 21 leads during presentation of the cue in the attention-orienting task. The cue was presented for 600 ms. The top diagram shows ERPs to presentation of the cue in the left visual half-field. The bottom diagram shows ERPs to presentation of the cue in the right visual half-field. Note the enhanced negative peak with a latency of around 150 ms in the conditioning group, most pronounced at the parietal region of the scalp. Data adapted from Stormark, Hugdahl, and Posner (1999).

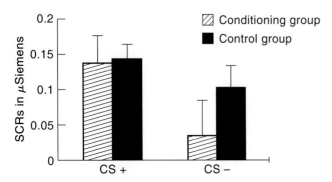

Figure 14.7 Mean skin conductance responses (SCRs) during the conditioning phase in which one of two attention cue stimuli was classically conditioned to the UCS in the conditioning group. The conditioned cue stimulus is referred to as CS+; the unconditioned attention cue stimulus is referred to as CS−. Note that the control group had only noncontingent presentations of the white noise and the attention cues. The results show mean SCRs for the three test trials (see text for further details). Small bars = standard error of the mean. Data adapted from Stormark and Hugdahl (1996).

As can also be seen in Figure 14.8, there was an overall decrease in RTs after conditioning than before conditioning. This could indicate that the absence of a difference between valid and invalid trials in the conditioning group may have been caused by a floor effect in the sense that *all* responses were automated, with no room for further response facilitation on invalid trials. However, Figure 14.8 shows that RTs on invalid trials were slower than on valid trials in the postconditioning phase except for those trials in which the CS+ served as cue. This was, furthermore, irrespective of the level of reduction of overall RTs obtained after, compared with before, conditioning. This would argue against the conclusion that the specific reduction in RTs on invalid trials where the CS+ had served as cue could be attributed to an overall reduction in RTs postconditioning. The absence of a difference between valid and invalid trials in the conditioning group may be regarded as a specific effect for attentional orienting to emotional stimuli, similar to the concept of cognitive avoidance that was discussed earlier.

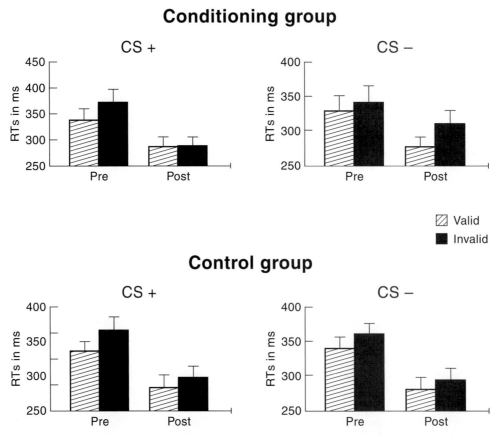

Figure 14.8 Mean reaction time (RT) on valid and invalid trials pre- and postconditioning, in which one of the attention cues (referred to as CS+) was conditioned to a white-noise tone. Small bars = standard error of the mean. Data adapted from Stormark and Hugdahl (1996).

## Attention and Response Automatization

To further investigate the issue of response automatization, we used the cue-conditioning paradigm in a go/no-go version of Posner's (1980) attention-orienting task (Stormark & Hugdahl, 1997). We did this because it could be argued that the absence of the invalidity effect to emotional cues could have been caused by a response bias rather than an attentional bias. The emotional cue could have had an energizing effect on all responses (cf. Eysenck & Calvo, 1992) so that responses were facilitated indiscriminantly. This possibility could be tested by having *two* cues that had been given emotional salience through conditioning; the participants would be instructed to respond to one of the cues ("go-cue") but to withhold responding to the other cue ("no-go cue"). In order to respond to the correct target, the participant must maintain information about the cue until the target appears on the screen.

Ten male and 10 female right-handed students participated. The frame-lit rectangle CS+ (which should be familiar to the reader by now) was again paired with a white-noise UCS, and the completely lit rectangle served as CS−. The control group received noncontingent presentations of both rectangles and the noise, identical to the conditioning procedure in the Stormark et al. (1999) study. In the subsequent attention-orienting phase, both the CS+ and CS− served as attention cues on separate trials. Half of the participants in each group were instructed to respond to targets cued by the CS+ (go-trials) and not to respond to targets cued by the CS− (no-go trials). The other half of each group responded to target cues by the CS− and ignored targets cued by the CS+.

In the conditioning phase, as expected, the conditioning group showed significantly greater SCRs to the CS+, demonstrating that the frame-lit rectangle was established as a conditioned emotional stimulus. In the attention-orienting phase, the conditioning subgroup that was instructed to "go" (i.e., to respond) to targets cued by the CS+ and "not to go" to targets cued by the CS− showed significantly faster RTs on invalid than on valid trials and also faster RTs on invalid trials than those observed in the control group. This effect was evident already on the first trial block (see Figure 14.9).

Again, the results suggest that attention was oriented *away* from the location at which the cue was presented before target onset. This would indicate that the aversive emotional quality associated with the cue actually *facilitated* attention shifting away from the cued location.

## Summary of Studies on Conditioned Emotional Cuing

To summarize so far, our findings indicate that the emotional quality that the cue acquired through conditioning reversed the cost-benefit difference between valid and invalid trials that was observed to a neutral cue. One may speculate whether the absence of the typical invalidity effect to the CS+ is a behavioral correlate of hyperfacilitation of attentional disengagement that limits further intake and processing of emotionally aversive information. If so, it would be in accordance with the findings by Hamm, Cuthbert, Globisch, and Vaitl (1997) that snake/spider phobics show *shorter* inspection times of pictures of the phobic object than of nonphobic objects.

## Rapid Disengagement: Approach-Avoidance Conflict

The rapid disengagement of attention from the CS+ contrasts with the findings from studies that have used the emotional Stroop task. These latter studies have in general shown increased difficulties in disengaging attention away from emotional stimuli (e.g. Williams et al., 1988). One factor that is likely to contribute to this difference between studies may be differences in the experimental setup in the Stroop interference task and in Posner's (1980) attention-orienting task. Naming the color words in the Stroop task takes generally a longer time than responding to the target in the attention-orienting task, showing that the Stroop task is more cognitively demanding. However, this is probably not the whole story, because recent studies using the emotional Stroop task in connection with exposing participants to fear-provoking stimuli have shown that exposure to the feared stimulus greatly reduces the cognitive interference effect. For example, Mathews and Sebastian (1993) found that exposing snake phobics to snakes abolished the color-naming interference effect to snake words. The same was found for spider phobics after they had been exposed to spiders (Lavy, Van den Hout, & Arntz, 1993). Similarly, using negative emotional words as cues in the attention-orienting paradigm has different effects on attention than using conditioned emotional cues. Whereas emotional words enhance both the validity and invalidity effects (e.g., Stormark, Nordby, & Hugdahl, 1995), conditioned emotional cues abolish the difference in RTs between valid and invalid trials.

### Emotional Words Versus Emotional Stimuli: A Paradoxical Effect?

It may thus seem a paradox that words that are descriptive of negative emotional stimuli elicit increased attentional *engagement* to the cue (slower RTs on invalid trials), whereas exposure to conditioned emotional cues elicit rapid attentional *disengagement* (faster RTs on invalid trials). From a functional perspective, however, the motivation to approach and avoid emotional stimuli is related.

## Conditioning group

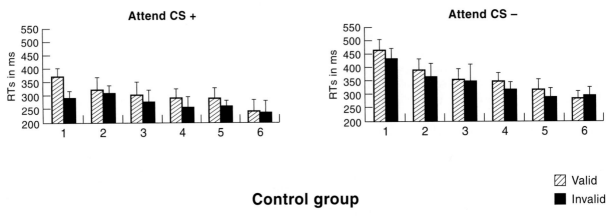

## Control group

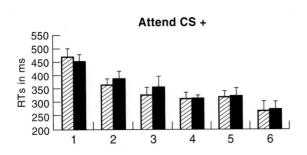
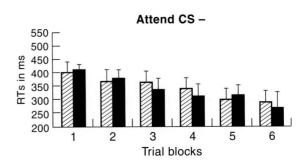

Figure 14.9 Mean reaction time (RT) on valid and invalid trials across six trial blocks, separated for the two conditioning and the two control groups. The left-hand panels show the results for the conditioning and control groups that were instructed to attend to targets cued by the CS+ and to ignore targets cued by the CS−. The right-hand panels show the results for the conditioning and the control groups that were instructed to attend to targets cued by the CS− and to ignore targets cued by the CS+. Note the reversed validity effect in the first trial block in the conditioning group that attended CS+ trials. Small bars = standard error of the mean. Data adapted from Stormark and Hugdahl (1997).

The experience of threat is related to the imminence and likelihood that an aversive event will occur (Tallis & Eysenck, 1994). Although negative emotional words may be highly salient, they are only referents to the emotional and/or physical harm the participant may experience; exposure to an emotional word (like *snake*) in itself is not harmful, whereas exposure to a real snake may in fact be lethal.

Thus slowing of RTs to emotional words in the Stroop task may reflect dysfunctional worrying, actually serving to limit the risk of exposing oneself to real threat (Mathews, 1990). Individuals who fixate on newspaper stories about crime downtown at night and worry that they themselves may be assaulted if they go there are probably more likely to avoid such situations than people who do not pay attention to this information. On the other hand, failure to disengage attention from threatening stimuli themselves may paralyze the individual and thus limit the possibility

of escape. According to this view, the most adaptive decision when confronted with an aversive stimulus would be to rapidly avert attention away from the situation. Thus the rapid RTs seen to targets invalidly cued by the CS+ could be a behavioral substrate of rapid attentional disengagement, similar to a defense response (DR; cf. Lacey, 1967).

Successful avoidance is, however, also contingent on rapid initial perception and identification of a threatening stimulus. Results from our studies have shown that rapid shifting of attention away from the spatial location of the cue was associated with larger amplitudes in the early components of the ERPs. This would suggest enhanced sensitivity for initial selective filtering of the attentional cue after it had become a CS. In a broader perspective this may indicate that attention to emotional stimuli may be thought of as an initial approach response, which is immediately followed by avoidance, in which attention is averted away from stimuli perceived to be emotionally aversive.

## Attentional Approach-Avoidance Conflicts in Alcoholics

To investigate whether it was possible to obtain behavioral indices of both approach and avoidance to the same stimulus, attention orienting was studied in a group of abstinent alcoholics. Abstinent alcoholics may be a good example of individuals who frequently experience approach-avoidance conflicts (cf. Tiffany, 1990). Alcoholics have a long history of repeated experience and practice with all aspects of alcohol intake and consumption. Thus it is reasonable to assume that the processing of alcohol stimuli elicits strong emotions in these individuals. One would expect that alcohol stimuli would attract increased attention, that is, initiate approach response tendencies. On the other hand, increased attention to alcohol stimuli may also represent a threat of eliciting unwanted urges to drink, and such stimuli would therefore be associated with negative emotions, that is, initiate avoidance response tendencies, particularly in abstinent alcoholics.

Attentional approach-avoidance was studied by Stormark, Field, Hugdahl, and Horowitz (1997), who presented abstinent alcoholics with alcohol and neutral words in the attention-orienting paradigm, with short (100 ms) and long (500 ms) cue-target intervals. A group of social drinkers served as the control group. The prediction was that short cue-target intervals would interfere with approach, whereas a longer interval would interfere with avoidance. Thus the presentation of an alcohol word would initially attract attention, but if the cue-target interval was long enough, the initial approach tendency would be replaced by a tendency to avoid by shifting attention away from the alcohol word. This would again mean that the typical invalidity effect on RTs should disappear.

In accordance with the predictions, the alcoholics showed significantly slower RTs to targets invalidly cued by the alcohol words with short duration (indicating reduced disengagement). However, they also showed significantly faster RTs to targets invalidly cued by the alcohol words with long duration (indicating enhanced disengagement). This suggests that the alcohol words elicited emotional responses that, subsequent to initial stimulus identification, triggered an interrupt function of the attentional system that resulted in rapid disengagement, similar to what was found in the conditioning experiments reviewed previously (see Figure 14.10; cf. Posner & Petersen, 1990).

It should be noted that attention orienting can be directed either voluntarily or involuntarily. To attend to words requires voluntary control over attention, because the participant has to decode the meaning of the word stimulus. Thus processing of emotional words is contingent on voluntary attention. On the other hand, processing of sensory stimuli does not necessarily require voluntary attention. For example, if the stimulus is fear provoking, it will involuntarily direct the participants' attention to the spatial location at which it appears. Nevertheless, the participant may *choose* to direct attention *away* from the emotional stimulus subsequent on stimulus identification, and this is what may have happened in the Stormark et al. (1997) study.

## The Orienting-Defense Response Distinction

The initial response on the first presentation of a stimulus is an *orienting response* (OR; Öhman, 1979; Sokolov, 1963). The OR is a kind of surprise, involving shift of attention to novel, unexpected stimuli. The OR consists of a complex of sensory, somatic, EEG, and autonomic changes (see, e.g., Graham, 1973), which interrupts ongoing behavior and increases sensory sensitivity. Thus the OR facilitates sensory input to the brain (Lacey & Lacey, 1974; Siddle, 1991). In terms of information-processing models, the OR reflects passive attention to stimulus input that is amplified in the nervous system to a level at which it interrupts ongoing activity. After repeated presentations of the same stimulus, the OR becomes smaller and smaller, finally disappearing. This is called habituation, and it represents one of the most powerful examples of plasticity, or "learning," in the nervous system (Thompson & Spencer, 1966).

A DR is similar to the OR but differs with respect to the types of events that elicit it. The DR is elicited by high-intensity stimuli, which have an inherent emotional valence (Graham & Clifton, 1966). The DR is associated with inhibition of sensory input and does not habituate on repeated stimulus presentations. In the present terminology, the DR reflects arousal amplification—an interruption of action plans due to increased arousal from limbic structures. A DR is usually differentiated from an OR by analyzing cardiovascular response patterns, particularly heart-rate changes and vasomotor responses.

Cardiovascular reactivity was defined by Carver and Matthews (1989) as a deviation of a cardiovascular response parameter from a comparison or control value that results from an individual's response to a discrete, environmental stimulus, either emotional or neutral. Change in cardiac rate after a sensory stimulus may be expressed in heart rate in beats per minute (BPM).

Cardiovascular reactivity to sensory stimuli is typically observed within the so-called triphasic heart-rate response, with initial deceleration following a few seconds after the stimulus, followed sometimes by acceleration and a second deceleration (see Hugdahl, 1995, for a more detailed overview). The initial deceleration is associated with the cognitive processes of focusing attention and ori-

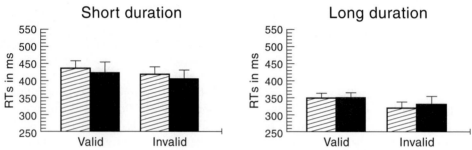

Figure 14.10 Mean reaction time (RT) for valid and invalid trials, separated for alcohol and neutral words. The top row shows RTs for the alcoholics; the bottom row shows the RTs for the social drinkers. The left-hand panels depict RTs on trials in which alcohol and neutral words with a short duration served as cues. The right-hand panels show RTs on trials in which alcohol and neutral words with a long duration served as cues. Small bars = standard error of the mean. Data adapted from Stormark, Field, Hugdahl, and Horowitz (1997).

enting to the stimulus. The acceleration is related to emotional aspects of the stimulus, as in a classical conditioning situation, or to the concept of environmental rejection proposed by Lacey (1967), reflecting internal processing. Thus, in the cardiovascular system, DRs are characterized by heart-rate *acceleration*, whereas ORs are characterized by heart-rate *deceleration* to an external stimulus (Graham & Clifton, 1966).

## Attentional Orienting and Defense in Alcoholics

From the distinctions between OR and DR and between voluntary and involuntary control of attention, we suggest that emotional nonverbal stimuli will produce a DR, whereas emotional verbal stimuli will produce an OR in an attention situation. This idea was tested in another series of studies on alcoholics, who were confronted with either real alcohol stimuli (smell, taste) or words referring to alcohol and drinking situations.

In a study by Stormark, Laberg, et al. (1995) study, we found that alcoholics evidenced greater SCR and more pronounced HR acceleration to the smell of distinct alcohol odors (such as beer) than nonalcoholic participants. They also demonstrated faster inhalation onset of the alcohol odors than of nonalcohol odors (such as vanilla and soap) through faster respiration inhalation rate. The observed HR acceleration probably reflects a cognitive concomitant to the DR, suggesting that exposure to the alcohol odors promoted a shift of focus from the environmental alcohol cues to internal thoughts and emotions. The alcoholic participants also showed a sustained elevated HR acceleration when they were exposed to drinks that contained alcohol compared with exposure to nonalcoholic beverages (Stormark et al., 1998).

In another study with alcoholic participants (Stormark et al., 2000), we investigated attention to alcohol words in a computerized version of the emotional Stroop task. The alcoholic participants used longer RTs to name the color of both alcohol and negative emotional words than neutral words, whereas there was no such difference in RTs in the social drinkers who served as control group. Both groups evidenced the typical (Stroop-like) interference effect to the color of incongruent color words. However, although both the emotional and alcohol words produced interference in the alcoholic participants, meaning delayed RTs, only the alcohol words had an effect on autonomic arousal. According to Lacey (1967), HR acceleration reflects rejection of sensory input. Decreased HR acceleration to alcohol words may therefore reflect problems for the alcoholics in disengaging attention. This is supported by the fact that RT latencies to the alcohol words were inversely related to response accuracy. Thus the longer time it took the alcoholics to respond to the color of alcohol words, the more likely that the response was inaccurate. These findings indicate that it is possible to differentiate alcoholics' attention between emotionally relevant verbal stimuli and stimuli (such as odor of alcohol) that have become "naturally" conditioned to the intake of alcoholic beverages.

## Summary

The main results from this series of studies may be summed up with respect to three main topics

1. A common feature of the results from the classical conditioning studies has been that the typical cognitive cost on invalid trials disappeared after the cue had been given emotional salience through classical conditioning. We believe that this effect may have been caused by cognitive avoidance in the sense that, after initial perception and registration of the cue, the participant actively avoids further processing if the stimulus is perceived as aversive. Thus there seems to be a mechanism of rapid disengagement of attention from the cue when it is aversive, moving attention to a different spatial location. This may perhaps be a blunting effect, minimizing the impact of an emotional event. The key aspect of the concept of cognitive avoidance is that attention is rapidly shifted, or moved, from one spatial location to another. Posner and Raichle (1994) suggested that the superior colliculus and the thalamic pulvinar nucleus are critical structures for "moving" and "enhancing" attention in space, being part of what they called the posterior, or "orienting," attention system. We would like to suggest that the pulvinar may selectively enhance the emotional component through a feedback loop from the posterior parietal lobe, which inhibits further input to the cortex, similar to the notion of a defensive response (DR) (cf. Lacey, 1967). The pulvinar may thus be regarded as the central gatekeeper for emotional arousal (see LeDoux, 1995). This is illustrated in Figure 14.11.

2. In general, our findings have shown *faster* RTs to targets cued by an emotional stimulus presented at a different spatial location from the cue. This may at first

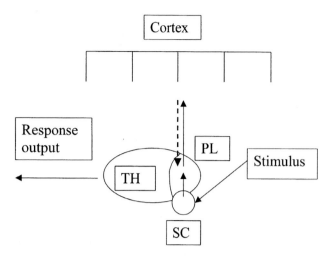

Figure 14.11 Schematic outline of the hyperfacilitation effect observed to emotionally charged cues. The model assumes that attentional selection and enhancement that is typically attributed to the superior colliculus (SC) and the pulvinar (PL) thalamus is gated to the prefrontal cortex when the cue has emotional charge while input to the posterior cortex is inhibited through a thalamo-cortico feedback loop (*dashed arrow*).

glance seem to be in conflict with previous studies on attention bias, for example, in anxiety patients (Mathews, 1990). However, as discussed at length in the chapter, although emotional words may be highly salient, they are only verbal descriptors of the emotional and/or physical harm the participant may experience, and exposure to emotional words such as *snake* in themselves are not harmful. Thus emotional words may engage attention processes in very different ways than do real emotional situations. Moreover, the typical findings in fearful patients is that they avoid the feared object or situation, which probably also means that they rapidly shift attention away from the same situation. Thus the emotional Stroop words situation may be an unrealistic situation with which to study attention-emotion interactions.

3. The findings of an approach-avoidance conflict in the alcoholic patients, depending on the length of the cue-target latency, may be an analogue to the typical ambivalence individuals often experience when in an emotional situation. This is a well-known phenomenon in clinical psychology and psychiatry, and our findings in the alcoholic participants show that it is possible to study emotional ambivalence under experimental control.

A concluding remark relates to possible future "research avenues" for attention-emotion interactions. An obvious route would be to include measures of localization in the brain of specific emotional neuronal networks that are modulated by attention and demands for attention shifting. Thus, we suggest that functional magnetic resonance imaging (fMRI) may prove an invaluable tool in this regard, specifically if so-called event-related fMRI could be used, thus looking for effects of attention on a single-trial basis. Hemodynamic neuroimaging may therefore reveal the underlying network "machinery" that cannot be observed in the studies described in this chapter.

## NOTE

This research was financially supported by grants to Kenneth Hugdahl from the Norwegian Research Council and to Kjell Morten Stormark and Kenneth Hugdahl from the Faculty of Psychology, University of Bergen.

## REFERENCES

Boucsein, W. (1993). Methodological issues in electrodermal measurement. In J. C. Roy, W. Boucsein, D. C. Fowles, & J. H. Gruzelier (Eds.), *Progress in electrodermal research* (pp. 31–43). New York: Plenum.

Carver, C. S., & Matthews, K. A. (1989). An overview of issues in psychometric assessment. In N. Schneiderman & S. M. Weiss (Eds.), *Handbook of research methods in cardiovascular behavioral medicine* (pp. 485–494). New York: Plenum.

Cook, E. III, & Turpin, G. (1997). Differentiating orienting, startle, and defense responses: The role of affect and its implications for psychopathology. In P. J. Lang, R. F. Simons, & M. Balaban (Eds.), *Attention and orienting: Sensory and motivational processes* (pp. 137–166). Mahwah, NJ: Lawrence Erlbaum.

Eysenck, M. W., & Calvo, M. G. (1992). Anxiety and performance: The processing efficiency theory. *Cognition and Emotion, 6*, 409–434.

Foa, E. B., Illai, D., McCarthy, P. R., Shoyer, B., & Murdock, T. (1993). Information processing in obsessive-compulsive disorder. *Cognitive Therapy and Research, 17*, 173–189.

Graham, F. K. (1973). Habituation and dishabituation of responses innervated by the autonomic nervous system. In H. S. Peeke & M. J. Hertz (Eds.), *Habituation* (Vol. 1, pp. 163–218). New York : Academic Press.

Graham, F. K., & Clifton, R. K. (1966). Heart-rate change as a component of the orienting response. *Psychological Bulletin, 65*, 305–320.

Hamm, A. O., Cuthbert, B. N., Globisch, J., & Vaitl, D. (1997). Fear and the startle reflex: Blink modulation and autonomic response patterns in animal and mutilation fearful subjects, *Psychophysiology, 34*, 97–107.

Hillyard, S. A., & Picton, T. W. (1979). Conscious perception and cerebral event-related potentials. In J. E. Desmedt (Ed.), *Progress in clinical neurophysiology: Vol. 6. Cognitive components in cerebral event-related potentials and selective attention* (pp. 1–52) Basel, Switzerland: Karger.

Hope, D. A., Rapee, R. M., Heimberg, R. G., & Dombeck, M. J. (1990). Representations of the self in social phobia: Vulnerability to social threat. *Cognitive Therapy and Research, 14*, 177–189.

Hugdahl, K. (1995). Psychophysiology. *The mind-body perspective.* Cambridge, MA: Harvard University Press.

Lacey, B. C., & Lacey, J. I. (1974). Studies of heart rate and other bodily processes in sensorimotor behavior. In P. A. Obrist, A. H. Black, J. Brener, & L. DiCara (Eds.), *Cardiovascular psychophysiology* (pp. 538–564). Chicago: Aldine Press.

Lacey, J. I. (1967). Somatic response patterning and stress: Some revisions of activation theory. In M. H. Appley & R. Trumbull (Eds.), *Psychological stress: Issues in research* (pp. 14–42). New York: Appleton-Century-Crofts.

Lang, P. J., Bradley, M. M., & Cuthbert, B. N. (1997). Motivated attention: Affect, activation, and action. In P. J. Lang, R. F. Simons, & M. Balaban (Eds.), *Attention and orienting: Sensory and motivational processes* (pp. 97–136). Mahwah, NJ: Erlbaum.

Lavy, E. H., & Van den Hout, M. A. (1994). Cognitive avoidance and attentional bias: Causal relationships. *Cognitive Therapy and Research, 18*, 179–191.

LeDoux, J. E. (1995). In search of an emotional system in the brain: Leaping from fear to emotion and consciousness. In M. S. Gazzaniga (Ed.), *The cognitive neurosciences* (pp. 1049–1061). Cambridge, MA: MIT Press.

Luria, A. R., & Homskaya, E. D. (1970). Frontal lobes and the regulation of arousal processes. In D. I. Mostofsky (Ed.), *Attention: Contemporary theory and analysis.* New York: Appleton-Century-Crofts.

MacLeod, C. M. (1991). Half a century of research on the Stroop effect: An integrative review. *Psychological Bulletin, 109*, 163–203.

Martin, M., Williams, R. M., & Clark, D. M. (1991). Does anxiety lead to selective processing of threat-related information? *Behaviour Research and Therapy, 28*, 455–468.

Mathews, A. (1990). Why worry? The cognitive function of anxiety. *Behaviour Research and Therapy, 28*, 455–468.

Mathews, A., & Klug, F. (1993). Emotionality and interference with color-naming in anxiety. *Behaviour Research and Therapy, 31*, 57–62.

Mathews, A., & MacLeod, C. (1985). Selective processing of threat cues in anxiety states. *Behaviour Research and Therapy, 23*, 563–569.

Mathews, A., & MacLeod, C. (1986). Discrimination of threat cues without awareness in anxiety states. *Journal of Abnormal Psychology, 98*, 31–34.

Mathews, A., & Sebastian, S. (1993). Suppression of emotional Stroop effects by fear-arousal. *Cognition and Emotion, 7*, 517–530.

McNally, R. J. (1995). Automaticity and the anxiety disorders. *Behaviour Research and Therapy, 33*, 747–754.

McNally, R. J., Kaspi, S. P., Riemann, B. C., & Zeitlin, S. B. (1990). Selective processing of threat cues in posttraumatic stress disorder. *Journal of Abnormal Psychology, 99*, 398–402.

McNally, R. J., Riemann, B. C., & Kim, E. (1990). Selective processing of threat cues in panic disorder. *Behaviour Research and Therapy, 28*, 407–412.

Mogg, K., Mathews, A., & Weinman, J. (1989). Selective processing of threat cues in anxiety states: A replication. *Behaviour Research and Therapy, 27*, 317–323.

Näätänen, R. (1992). *Attention and brain function.* Hillsdale, NJ: Erlbaum.

Öhman, A. (1979). The orienting response, attention, and learning: An information-processing perspective. In H. D. Kimmel, E. H. van Olst, & J. F. Orlebeke (Eds.), *The orienting reflex in humans* (pp. 443–471). Hillsdale, NJ: Erlbaum.

Posner, M. I. (1980). Orienting of attention. *Quarterly Journal of Experimental Psychology, 32*, 3–25.

Posner, M. I. (1988). Structures and functions of selective attention. In H. Bouman & D. Bowhuis (Eds.), *Clinical neuropsychology and brain function: Research, assessment and practice* (pp. 173–202). Washington, DC: American Psychological Association.

Posner, M. I. (1995). Attention in the cognitive neurosciences: An overview. In M. S. Gazzaniga (Ed.), *The cognitive neurosciences* (pp. 615–624). Cambridge, MA: MIT Press.

Posner, M. I., & Driver, J. (1992). The neurobiology of selective attention. *Current Opinion in Neurobiology, 2*(2), 165–169.

Posner, M. I., & Petersen, S. (1990). The attentional system of the human brain. *Annual Review of Neuroscience, 13*, 25–42.

Posner, M. I. & Raichle, M. E. (Eds.). (1994). *Images of mind*. New York: Scientific American Library.

Posner, M. I., & Snyder, C. R. R. (1975). Facilitation and inhibition in the processing of signals. In P. M. A. Rabbit & S. Dornic (Eds.), *Attention and performance* (Vol. 5, pp. 669–682). New York: Academic Press.

Siddle, D. A. T. (1991). Orienting, habituation, and resource allocation: An associative analysis. *Psychophysiology, 28*, 245–259.

Sokolov, E. N. (Ed.). (1963). *Perception and the conditioned reflex*. London: Pergamon Press.

Stormark, K. M., Field, N., Hugdahl, K., & Horowitz, M. (1997). Selective processing of visual alcohol cues: An approach-avoidance conflict? *Addictive Behaviors, 22*, 509–519.

Stormark, K. M., & Hugdahl, K. (1996). Peripheral cuing of covert spatial attention before and after emotional conditioning of the cue. *International Journal of Neuroscience, 86*, 225–240.

Stormark, K. M., & Hugdahl, K. (1997). Conditioned emotional cuing of spatial attentional shifts in a go/no-go discrimination task. *International Journal of Psychophysiology, 27*, 241–248.

Stormark, K. M., Hugdahl, K., & Posner, M. I. (1999). Emotional modulation of attention orienting: A classical conditioning study. *Scandinavian Journal of Psychology, 40*, 91–99.

Stormark, K. M., Laberg, J. C., Bjerland, T., Nordby, H., & Hugdahl, K. (1995). Autonomic cued reactivity in alcoholics: The effect of olfactory stimuli. *Addictive Behaviors, 20*, 571–584.

Stormark, K. M., Laberg, J. C., Nordby, H., & Hugdahl, K. (1998). Heart rate responses in alcoholics immediately prior to drinking. *Addictive Behaviors, 23*, 251–255.

Stormark, K. M., Laberg, J. C., Nordby, H., & Hugdahl, K. (2000). Alcoholics' selective attention to alcohol stimuli: Automated processing? *Journal of Studies on Alcohol, 61*, 18–23.

Stormark, K. M., Nordby, H., & Hugdahl, K. (1995). Attentional shifts to emotionally charged cues: Behavioral and ERP data. *Cognition and Emotion, 9*, 507–523.

Stroop, J. R. (1935). Studies of interference in serial verbal reactions. *Journal of Experimental Psychology, 18*, 643–662.

Tallis, F., & Eysenck, M. W. (1994). Worry-mechanisms and modulating influences. *Behavioral and Cognitive Psychotherapy, 22*, 37–56.

Thompson, R. F., & Spencer, W. A. (1966). Habituation: A model phenomenon for the study of neuronal substrates of behavior. *Psychological Review, 73*, 16–43.

Tiffany, S. T. (1990). A cognitive model of drug urges and drug-use behavior: Role of automatic and nonautomatic processes. *Psychological Review, 97*, 147–168.

Tranel, D., & Damasio, H. (1994). Neuroanatomical correlates of electrodermal skin conductance responses. *Psychophysiology, 31*, 427–438.

Watts, F. N., McKenna, P., Sharrock, R., & Tresize, L. (1986). Colour naming of phobia related words. *British Journal of Psychology, 77*, 97–108.

Williams, M., Watts, F. N., MacLeod, C., & Mathews, A. (1988). *Cognitive psychology and emotional disorders*. New York: Wiley.

# Genetics and Development

# 15

# INTRODUCTION: GENETICS AND DEVELOPMENT

H. Hill Goldsmith

In some more scientifically coherent future, almost every chapter in a handbook such as this would treat developmental issues in conjunction with its substantive focus, but the current reality is that developmental issues are the specialty of those, such as the authors represented in this section, who know the young organism well. A developmental perspective is largely missing from the treatment of many issues. However, this *Handbook* is distinctive in that nearly every section does have at least one chapter with significant developmental content.

One reason for the missing developmental perspective in much of affective science is that emotional development has proved to be complex. In a simpler world, the essentials of emotional development might have been distilled into a story something like this: "Shortly after the neonatal period, all of a set of basic emotions would become apparent, at least in some form. These basic emotions would be discernible via facial expressions and rudimentary behavioral reactions to situations with the same formal features that elicit adult emotions (e.g., goal-blocking, threat). The essential features of emotional development would concern how emotion is regulated and how appraisal of context becomes increasingly complex. Emotions that typically emerge in the second year of life or later could be understood via principles of straightforward combinations or differentiation of earlier, basic emotions. Genes would be more important for specification of early emotions, with later-emerging emotions and emotional regulation being largely molded by social experience. The individual differences aspect of emotion—

largely understood as temperament—would be very stable and highly heritable. There would be unambiguous convergence of different measures of emotional individuality during development, such that the perspectives of parents and teachers, as well as objective behavioral recording, would be interchangeable."

Unfortunately, this simple scenario does not recognize the complexity that is emerging from recent research, such as that reviewed in this part. Instead, it seems probable that *none* of the statements in the preceding paragraph are unambiguously true, and some are demonstrably false.

Perhaps Campos, Barrett, Lamb, Goldsmith, and Stenberg (1983) posed the organizing question in this field over the past two decades, "What develops in emotional development?" After positing a set of differentiated core emotion states that were present throughout the life span—which may be questionable for early infancy—Campos et al. (1983) offered six, still apt answers to this question:

1. As cognitive development proceeds and new goals appear in the life of the child, complex intercoordinated emotions become evident.
2. The effectiveness of specific eliciting circumstances changes as the organism develops.
3. The relationship between emotional expression and emotional experience changes as the organism develops.
4. Coping responses to emotion change as the organism develops.

295

5. Emotions become socialized as the organism develops.

6. Receptivity to others' emotional expressions changes as the organism develops.

A decade later, Davidson and Ekman (1994) posed the same question about emotional development to a panel of researchers and received a set of different, but largely compatible responses. These answers emphasized the roles of maturation of the central nervous system, of cognitive development, of regulatory and coping abilities, and of cultural factors. Of course, these are not orthogonal factors. Moreover, there was recognition that the relationship of each of these factors with emotional development was bidirectional. Not surprisingly, these same factors are also emphases of the chapters in this part.

In this introduction, I first provide some context for reading the five chapters in this part. Second, I note the developmental content in other sections of this *Handbook* and mention some facets of emotional development that are largely missing from the *Handbook*. Finally, I offer some thoughts about current and future challenges in this research area.

## The Chapters of This Part

The lead chapter in this part by Kagan offers some important philosophical orientations to the study of emotional development, including cautions regarding the uncritical use of the "folk language" of emotion. This chapter also highlights the dangers of overreliance on cheap-and-easy parental report measures of temperament. In many cases, there is simply no substitute for actually eliciting the child's emotional reactions under carefully constructed laboratory conditions or observing the child's behavior in carefully chosen natural contexts. Kagan's chapter also offers a synopsis of his lab's research on behavioral inhibition, which has become the best-studied feature of temperamental individuality. The pattern of continuity at the extremes and bounded change observed in this research led to Kagan's notion of temperament as constraint on development. The biological correlates of behavioral inhibition reported in this chapter and elsewhere by Kagan point to the necessity of an integrative affective neuroscience approach for fuller understanding of any aspect of emotional development.

Goldsmith's chapter surveys the genetics of emotional development, chiefly from the perspective of human quantitative genetics. A basic, replicated finding is that twin and family studies implicate genetic factors in human temperamental variability. This finding is extended and qualified by considering different methods of measuring temperament, longitudinal designs, and multivariate genetic analysis (where other phenotypes, such as psycho-pathology, are analyzed jointly with temperament). Although molecular genetic analysis of emotionality now lies primarily in the animal research domain, this chapter also considers molecular genetic approaches to human emotional traits.

Kopp and Neufeld situate their comprehensive treatment of emotional development during infancy within a decade-by-decade historical context. This treatment is a fascinating portrait of a field undergoing periods of quiescence and then explosive growth, as well as fundamental changes from descriptive to more process-oriented questions. Currently, many issues in the field revolve around the interplay of relationships with caregivers, individual differences in infants and toddlers, and developmental change. This chapter also offers one of the most concise, authoritative treatments of early emotion regulation available. Emotion regulation is dependent on perceptual and cognitive development, influenced by and influential upon social relationships, indexed by different behaviors as the child grows, and intimately related to the individual's adaptation. It is little wonder that a construct of this breadth has become a central focus of behavioral development, even beyond the infancy period.

Dunn builds on what we know about emotional development during infancy to elucidate the association between emotion understanding and children's social relationships in the succeeding years. The development of empathetic concern is an early accomplishment in this domain, followed by increasingly sophisticated understanding of emotions in their social context. After describing how cognitive growth (e.g., sense of self, ability to appreciate the perspectives of different persons) influences the development of social emotions, Dunn discusses the likelihood that affective phenomena such as the child's emotional state and emotion-motivated narratives in family contexts also facilitate new cognitive accomplishments. Dunn draws the deeply significant implication that "an understanding of cognitive states arises from an earlier understanding of emotional states." Like the previous chapters in this part, Dunn also emphasizes the importance of individual differences in affective development, and she makes a strong case that these individual differences should be studied in the contexts of parent-child, sibling, and peer relationships. Dunn concludes by noting that cultural factors are also a key context for the development of affect and relationships, and this theme is central to the next chapter.

Mascolo, Fischer, and Li carefully set out the tenets of a dynamic components systems approach to emotional development. This approach focuses on the roles of appraisal, action, and culture in emotion. One interesting feature of the approach is that it demonstrates that structurally similar conceptual frameworks, with a neo-Piagetian flavor, can account for both emotional development (this chapter) and the development of cognitive skills, as seen in Fischer's earlier work (e.g., Fischer, 1980). This approach draws from, and shows potential for integrating, several of the other leading theoretical approaches to emotional development, including componential approaches (e.g., Scherer, 1984; Ellsworth & Scherer, chapter 29, this volume), functionalist approaches (e.g., Campos et al., 1983), and other dynamic systems approaches with strong social emphases (e.g., Fogel et al., 1992). Much of the content of this chapter concerns the normative development of pride, shame, and guilt in American and Chinese cultures. The vast differences in the meaning and salience of these three emotions across these two cultures are intriguing, all the more if formally similar processes in both cases can explain their development.

## Developmental Content in Other Parts of This *Handbook*

The entire realm of research on emotional development could not be accommodated in a single section of this *Handbook*. For instance, this section has limited coverage of emotional development and psychopathology, of some traditional areas of intersection between cognitive and emotional development (e.g., Saarni & Harris, 1989), and of the history of research in this area, other than that offered by Kopp and Neufeld. Readers who are interested in a more detailed historical treatment might consult the monograph by Magai and McFadden (1995), who adroitly review the literature relevant to the role of emotions in the development of personality by drawing consistently upon detailed historical and biographical information. They especially emphasize the study of attachment and of discrete emotions as traditions that have crucially shaped the current study of emotional development. Fortunately, some of the other developmental topics that received limited coverage in this part are covered in chapters throughout the *Handbook*.

Eisenberg, Losoya, and Spinrad (chapter 41, this volume) treat the development of prosocial behavior during toddlerhood and early childhood (as well as during later development), and especially the role of empathy-related responding in prosocial behavior. The Eisenberg et al. chapter (chapter 41) discusses topics in common with the ones in this section: emotion regulation (Kopp and Neufeld); temperament (Kagan, Goldsmith); social and moral development (Dunn), and shame and guilt (Mascolo, Fischer, and Li). Chapter 41 is a good illustration of how the joint perspectives of developmental and social psychology can be focused on a single area of affective behavior.

A thoroughly developmental approach pervades Reilly and Seibert's chapter (chapter 27) on the interplay between language and emotion, particularly the communicative facet of emotion. The approach in this chapter

might be a good model for future inquiry. Reilly and Seibert first describe the multifaceted relations between affect and language as inferred from research with adults, including adults who use sign language. Then, they turn to the developmental relations between emotion and language during childhood for clues to the underlying organization of the more integrated adult system. They consider these emotion-language relations in both facial and vocalic domains, and they focus on the child as both sender and receiver of signals in both domains. As paradigms, these authors describe the (1) acquisition of English and of American Sign Language and (2) the development of the quality of evaluation—which often involves emotional expression—in both hearing and deaf children's narratives. The outcome is sufficiently tantalizing to encourage other efforts along this line of inquiry.

The study of emotional development during infancy and childhood is not well integrated with the same topic during middle and later adulthood, a point made in Carstensen's chapter (chapter 37). Carstensen begins her chapter by treating topics central to the developmental section—genetics, early temperament, emotion regulation, and attachment relationships—and then continues to consider emotions in the context of adult personality development. Ryff and Singer (chapter 57) also consider emotional development during adulthood and aging, with emphases on well-being and positive emotional health, from both behavioral and biological perspectives.

Developmental perspectives on the biological aspects of emotion are often somewhat implicit in the *Handbook*. For instance, there are clear developmental implications in Insel's chapter (chapter 53) describing the roles of oxytocin and vasopressin, and particularly their receptor distribution patterns, on pair bonding, social memory, and the affiliative aspects of parental behavior in prairie voles. The plausible molecular genetic bases of species differences offered in this chapter will depend on developmental mechanisms for their expression. The systematic study of developmental aspects of many other affective neuroscience topics is still in the early stages of progress. For instance, the pharmacological and lesion approaches to dissecting the components of the *development* of emotional behavior are largely stories remaining to be written.

## Challenges to Research on Emotional Development

One way to think about the challenges facing the developmental study of emotion is to consider the intersection of the more generic problems facing developmental science and affective science. In the broader field of developmental science, including motor, perceptual, cognitive, and affective domains, at least four overarching trends, or issues, can be discerned. The first trend is a halting movement from attempts to describe development to attempts to understand processes of change. The emphasis on processes of change is well illustrated in this part of the *Handbook*, as well as in other current work in the field. A single example is how researchers have investigated the shift from external (e.g., parental input) to internal (e.g., cognitive strategies) resources in the regulation of emotion (Eisenberg et al., chapter 41, this volume). While recognizing that this trend is necessary and overdue, we still cannot assume that the descriptive task is complete, and methodologically rigorous descriptive research continues to be of great value in some domains of the study of affective development. For example, systematic descriptive information on brain development from imaging studies is only beginning to be accumulated (Casey, Giedd, & Thomas, 2000; Giedd et al., 1999; Thompson et al., 2000), largely in the service of understanding findings from neuroimaging studies of pediatric disorders.

A second tension in the field is emphasis on individual and clinical group differences versus normative developmental processes. Often, this distinction is confounded with differences in dominant research paradigms, with individual differences and clinical work being observational or questionnaire- and interview-based, whereas the study of normative processes more likely occurs in the laboratory-based behavioral or physiological studies. Switching from the dominant paradigms—and particularly bringing the study of individual and clinical differences into the developmental laboratory—is a welcome trend.

Many of the topics discussed in this part lend themselves to both differential and normative study. For instance, emotional regulation has perhaps most typically been studied as a normative developmental phenomenon. However, learning the variety of ways that emotion is typically regulated would be a key to understanding individual differences in personality. Moreover, discovering the causes and consequences of dysregulation seems central to understanding the causes of anxiety, depression, and some externalizing forms of psychopathology. In general, exploring the boundary areas between normal and atypical affective development appears to be a promising but underexplored arena. For instance, it is normative for older infants and toddlers to show wariness in response to strangers and novel environments, just as it is normative for adults to show signs of fear and anxiety in potentially threatening situations. However, the display of fear in nonnovel, nonthreatening contexts may hold important predictive value for dysfunction. That is, behavioral inhibition in children and anxiety in adults might not in themselves be predictive of possible vulnerability, but may have particular relevance for psychopathology when displayed in context-inappropriate situations. This viewpoint about the role of context in affective style emerged

from observations in *Rhesus* monkeys (Kalin & Shelton, 2000).

The third issue is the ever-evolving nature-nurture question, which is the field's attempt to focus on the interplay of biology and experience as the conceptualizations of both biology and experience become more dynamic. One contemporary way to address this issue is to consider the interplay of individual traits, often conceptualized under the temperament rubric, and interpersonal relationships. However, measurement of a behavioral temperamental trait is generally a poor proxy for biology, and relationships should not be equated with the effects of experience (Reiss, 1995). One reason for these cautions is that biological and experiential influences unfold in the context of one another and are thus difficult to parse in normative development. Even in the realm of individual differences, we observe occasional low heritability of temperament traits—for example, infant positive affectivity (Goldsmith, Buss, & Lemery, 1997) and of affect-related childhood externalizing disorders, at least in some samples (Lyons et al., 1995). Also, maternal behavior—a key element of early relationships—has already been associated with at least nine individual genes (Leckman & Herman, 2002). Thus, the nature-nurture issue, far from being put to rest by the recognition that individuals are active agents in their own development and that interactive influences predominate during development, continues to be an organizing issue for students of affective development.

The final overarching issue is the nature of continuity and change. The various meanings of continuity and change have been explicated in detail by many developmentalists (e.g., Caspi, 1998) and increasingly sophisticated ways of measuring and modeling continuity and change have been implemented. This issue is multifaceted, and one of the more significant facets is the extent to which this issue can be subsumed under the biology/experience issue (above). The extent to which continuity is a function of biological effects and change is a function of experience is a difficult empirical issue. These linkages (continuity with biology, change with experience) should not be assumed, a point repeatedly emphasized by behavioral geneticists (Gottesman, 1974; Plomin, 1986). Such general laws about the roots of continuity and change might not exist. Another element of the continuity debate is the link between early and later development, and in particular between infant development and later life. While infancy might have been overemphasized as a crucial stage of development (Bruer, 1999), determining just what the degree of prediction from infancy to later period is for affective phenomena has proved difficult, in part owing to the problem of establishing measurement equivalence. Nonlinear dynamic systems approaches have provided new conceptual tools for thinking about the ingredients of change in the affective realm, modeled after principles largely investigated empirically in the motoric domain but capable of much broader extension (Thelen & Smith, 1994).

In summary, the field of affective development must still be considered a young one. The construction of this field by scientists is occurring in the context of the advances in neuroscience documented elsewhere in this volume, a context that requires continual rethinking of basic principles. The field is also developing while demands for the practical, societal application of knowledge about emotional development must be answered on the basis of our best current understandings (National Research Council, 2000).

## REFERENCES

Bruer, J. T. (1999). *The myth of the first three years*. New York: The Free Press.

Campos, J. J., Barrett, K., Lamb, M. E., Goldsmith, H. H., & Stenberg, C. (1983). Socioemotional development. In M. M. Haith & J. J. Campos (Eds.), *Infancy and developmental psychobiology (Vol. 2)*. In P. H. Mussen (Series Ed.), *Handbook of child psychology*, 4th ed. (pp. 783–915). New York: John Wiley.

Casey, B. J., Giedd, J. N., & Thomas, K. M. (2000). Structural and functional brain development and its relation to cognitive development. *Biological Psychology, 54*, 241–257.

Caspi, A. (1998). Personality development across the life course. In N. Eisenberg (Volume Ed.), *Social, emotional, and personality development (Vol. 3)*. In W. Damon (Ed.-in-Chief), *Handbook of child psychology*, 5th ed. (pp. 311–388). New York: John Wiley.

Davidson, R. J., & Ekman, P. (Eds.). (1994). *Questions about emotion*. New York: Oxford University Press.

Fischer, K. W. (1980). A theory of cognitive development: The control and construction of hierarchies of skills. *Psychological Review, 87*, 447–531.

Fogel, A., Nwokah, E., Dedo, J., Messinger, D., Dickson, L., Matusov, E., & Holt, S., (1992). Social process theory of emotion: A dynamic systems approach. *Social Development, 1*, 122–142.

Giedd, J. N., Blumenthal, J., Jeffries, N. O., Castellanos, F. X., Liu, H., Zijdenbos, A., Paus, T., Evans, A. C., & Rapoport, J. L. (1999). Brain development during childhood and adolescence: A longitudinal MRI study. *Nature Neuroscience, 10*, 861–863.

Goldsmith, H. H., Buss, K. A., & Lemery, K. S. (1997). Toddler and childhood temperament: Expanded content, stronger genetic evidence, new evidence for the importance of environment. *Developmental Psychology, 33*, 891–905.

Gottesman, I. I. (1974). Developmental genetics and ontogenetic psychology: Overdue détente and propositions from a matchmaker. In A. D. Pick (Ed.), *Minnesota symposia on child psychology* (Vol. 8; pp. 55–80). Minneapolis: University of Minnesota Press.

Kalin, N. H., & Shelton, S. E. (2000). The regulation of defensive behaviors in rhesus monkeys: Implications for understanding anxiety disorders. In R. J. Davidson (Ed.), *Anxiety, depression and emotion: The first Wisconsin Symposium on Emotion* (pp. 50–68). New York: Oxford University Press.

Leckman, J. F., & Herman, A. E. (2002). Maternal behavior and developmental psychopathology. *Biological Psychiatry, 51*, 27–43.

Lyons, M. J., True, W. R., Eisen, S. A., Goldberg, J., Meyer, J. M., Faraone, S. V., Eaves, L. J., & Tsuang, M. T. (1995). Differential heritability of adult and juvenile antisocial traits. *Archives of General Psychiatry, 52*, 906–915.

Magai, C., & McFadden, S. H. (1995). *The role of emotions in social and personality development: History, theory, and research*. New York: Plenum Press.

National Research Council (2000). *From neurons to neighborhoods: The science of early childhood development*. Washington, DC: National Academy Press.

Plomin, R. (1986). *Development, genetics and psychology*. Hillsdale, NJ: Lawrence Erlbaum.

Reiss, D. (1995). Genetic influence on family systems: Implications for development. *Journal of Marriage and the Family, 57*, 1–18.

Saarni, C., & Harris, P. L. (1989). *Children's understanding of emotion*. Cambridge, UK: Cambridge University Press.

Scherer, K. R. (1984). On the nature and function of emotion: A component process approach. In K. R. Scherer & P. Ekman (Eds.), *Approaches to emotion* (pp. 293–318). Hillsdale, NJ: Lawrence Erlbaum.

Thelen, E., & Smith, L. B. (1994). *A dynamic systems approach to the development of cognition and action*. Cambridge, MA: MIT Press.

Thompson, P. M., Giedd, J. N., Woods, R. P., MacDonald, D., Evans, A. C., & Toga, A. W. (2000). Growth patterns in the developing brain detected by using continuum mechanical tensor maps. *Nature, 9*, 190–193.

# 16

# GENETICS OF EMOTIONAL DEVELOPMENT

H. Hill Goldsmith

The genetics of early emotional development is both a big and a small topic. The literature is a small one when emotional development is defined narrowly as involving measurement of relatively "pure" emotion expression or reception. However, the literature is substantial when we turn to the genetics of emotion-relevant features of temperament and psychopathology in early development. Rather than a comprehensive review, this chapter samples the literature, noting how various aspects of temperament or psychopathology relate to emotion. The chapter depends on the four other contributions in this part of the *Handbook* to elaborate the nongenetic, developmental aspects of the emotional phenomena that it features. In practical research on genetics, however, these developmental issues need to be integrated into the design of studies and assessment of infants and children.

The chapter begins with a brief description of what is entailed in the behavior-genetic research paradigm. After this conceptual overview, both concepts of behavioral genetics and illustrative empirical findings on temperament and emotion-related psychopathology are treated. When possible, the examples in this lengthy section are drawn from typical infant and childhood development or from childhood psychopathology. The emphasis in this section is on quantitative genetic approaches.

The next section turns to molecular genetic approaches in humans and describes linkage and association studies. Recently, this has become a very large field, heavily weighted toward analyses of disorders rather than quantitative variation. Then, the chapter turns to a few examples of nonhuman animal research to illustrate the potential of complementary animal and human approaches. This section is highly selective and brief; fortunately, other chapters in this handbook provide much more detail on the animal studies. The chapter concludes with the prospects for integrating molecular and quantitative genetic approaches and for dealing with complex, nonlinear systems.

## The Behavior-Genetic Paradigm

To place any particular set of behavior-genetic results in proper perspective, it is well to have in mind the broader paradigm of research in this field. This paradigm, as outlined in Table 16.1, applies to any phenotypic behavioral pattern. The term "emotion phenotype" in the table can be understood as "emotional trait" or "emotional disorder" within the context of this chapter.

An overview of the stages in Table 16.1 is provided in this section, and aspects of these stages will be elucidated in sections to follow. Although the research paradigm outlined in Table 16.1 remains to be enacted in its totality for any emotion phenotype, it is important to realize that, for instance, twin studies, or genome screens, do not stand alone in this paradigm as a basis for inference. The numbered stages of the paradigm obviously are not always executed in the order provided. For instance, the discovery of a single-gene effect initiates more focused investigations, and the availability of markers spaced evenly across

Table 16.1 The Behavior-Genetic Paradigm, for Elucidating Emotion-related Traits

1. Definition and measurement of an emotion phenotype.
2. Observation that the emotion phenotype "runs in families."
3. Demonstration of heritable influence on the emotion phenotype, usually initially in twin studies.
4. Confirmation of initial (twin study) results in adoption studies or other family designs.
5. Possible decomposition of the emotion phenotype to highlight heritable or nonheritable features.
6. Longitudinal study with a genetically informative design of genetic influences on continuity and change of the emotion phenotype.
7. Examination of environmental influences on the emotion phenotype within a behavior-genetic context (possibly including study of gene-environment correlation and interaction).
8. Search for associated endophenotypes—e.g., neural substrates of the emotion phenotype.
9. Analysis of whether the emotion phenotype and its associated endophenotypes share genetic sources of variation.
10. If [8] is successful, possible further redefinition of the emotion phenotype in terms of etiological processes.
11. Given the availability of genetic probes, search for specific genes or chromosomal regions associated with the emotion phenotype (e.g., genome screens, association and linkage studies with candidate genes or markers, gene chips or expressed sequence arrays).
12. Development of animal models of the emotion phenotype or associated endophenotypes.

the chromosomes makes genome screens a more feasible early-stage approach. Historically, many programs of research stopped at steps 3 or 4 with the completion of twin and family studies.

The second stage of the paradigm, family studies, does not distinguish genetic from environmental transmission, but is nevertheless of major importance. Family studies establish vertical transmission of traits (from parent to offspring), and such demonstration is a key piece of evidence for genetic effects. Data on the risk to siblings of affected individuals also constitute crucial baseline information for other stages in the paradigm. It should be appreciated, however, that family history of a disorder is not synonymous with genetic risk, and negative family history cannot be equated with lack of genetic risk. For instance, although genetic influences in the liability to schizophrenia are widely appreciated, it is perhaps less well known that 89% of persons with schizophrenia do *not* have a parent with schizophrenia, and 63% do not have any first- or second-degree relative with schizophrenia (Gottesman, 1991). This is simply the expectation for complex disorders with multifactorial inheritance and environmental involvement. When individuals are chosen for study in high-risk designs by virtue of an affected parent, those offspring who eventually do become affected themselves are likely to be at greater genetic risk, and therefore unrepresentative of the full population of affected individuals in terms of etiological factors.

Twin and adoption studies (stages 3 and 4) are the traditional methods of human behavioral genetics, and results to be presented later in the chapter will illustrate their utility. The notion of decomposing a phenotype to highlight heritable and nonheritable features (stage 5) involves an interaction between genetic studies and the process of conceptualizing and measuring the phenotype. Stage 6 makes the point that the longitudinal extension of behavior-genetic designs allows inferences regarding genetic influences not only on the level of a trait but also on continuity and change. Stage 7 recognizes that controlling for genetic similarity allows for the investigation of environmental factors, including their interaction and covariance with genetic factors. Some illustrations of this step are provided later in the chapter.

Stages 8, 9, and 10 incorporate the idea of "endophenotypes." This term was apparently coined by John and Lewis (1966), in reference to genetics and insect populations, and introduced into psychiatric genetics by Gottesman and Shields (1972) in the context of searching for nonobservable traits causally associated with the liability to schizophrenia. The idea of endophenotypes suggests more productive investigation of simpler phenotypes than, say, a psychiatric diagnosis. Some of these investigations are mentioned later in the chapter.

Stage 11 represents perhaps the major focus of current activity for emotion-related disorders. The search for specific genes uses a set of rapidly evolving molecular and bioinformatic techniques, aided greatly by advances in the Human Genome Project.

Stage 12 of the paradigm, development of animal models, is a gross simplification. In fact, behavior-genetic research on animals has its own, rapidly evolving paradigm. There are multiple interfaces with human behavior-genetic research. Recently, there has been increasing consensus that conceptualizing and measuring the phenotype in both humans and animals, as well as linking the human and animal phenotypes, is perhaps the field's most significant challenge (Gold, 1999), as exemplified in the title of Crawley's (2000) volume, *What's Wrong With My Mouse? Behavioral Phenotyping of Transgenic and Knockout Mice*, and in the effort in psychiatric genetics to find phenotypes "closer to the genes" than current diagnostic categories.

Behavioral genetics and genetic epidemiology are rapidly evolving fields, and research activity is occurring for emotion-related phenotypes at each of the 12 stages. The nature of explicit and implicit assumptions for genetic inference is quite different for the various stages of the research paradigm. Some of the assumptions that pertain to certain earlier stages in the paradigm (e.g., linear genetic effects on the phenotype in some types of analysis of twin data) do not pertain to later stages. A fair evaluation of likely genetic influences on any phenotype requires consideration of the full paradigm.

# Concepts of Human Behavioral Genetics, With Illustrations From Early Temperament

## Genetic and Environmental Variance

We can infer the relative strength of various classes of genetic and environmental factors from patterns of covariation among family members who have varying degrees of genetic overlap and who have shared environments or not. The heritability statistic estimates the association between degree of genetic overlap and similarity on behavioral traits in relatives. The genetic component can be divided into additive and nonadditive effects, and the environmental component can be divided into effects shared versus nonshared by relatives. This basic biometric model can be expanded for longitudinal, multivariate analysis (Neale & Cardon, 1992).

The limitations of the concept of heritability require emphasis. Heritability applies only to differences among persons within populations, not to the development of single individuals or to differences between populations. Heritability may also change at different points in the life span, owing to the dynamic nature of gene action, changes in the effects of environmental factors, changes in the nature of the trait being measured, or other constellations of factors (Carey, 1988). Because heritability is a ratio involving both genetic and environmental effects, a relevant environment that varies widely across a population will reduce heritability whereas more nearly uniform environmental conditions increase it (Falconer, 1989). Another caveat is that similar heritability estimates for two traits, even conceptually related traits, do not imply common genetic underpinnings. In fact, the great majority of reliable heritability estimates for human behavioral traits lie in a 30–70% range.

The developmental implications of simple heritability estimates are also limited. Failures to appreciate distinctions between individual differences and the development of an individual are common in popular accounts of behavior-genetic research. Such failures also occur among scientists who sometimes fail to appreciate that classic behavior-genetic inferences are confined to genetic and environmental *effects on phenotypic variance*, not gene action and the direct action of environmental influences per se. Genes exert their effects on behavior via complex pathways that involve feedback loops, rate-limiting processes, and so on. Environments likewise probably exert many of their effects in inherently nonlinear ways. However, it is still informative to analyze individual differences by linear regression of outcome on sources of variation, even when the individual differences result from highly contingent, interactive developmental processes operating in the lives of individuals. Such linear models relating predictors and outcomes are used profitably in other fields, such as economics, where the underlying processes involved are also complex and interactive.

Behavior genetic methodology does allow for the estimation of nonadditive genetic effects, defined in a statistical sense. The additive value of a gene is the sum of the average effects of the individual alleles, or alternative forms of a gene at the same locus (Neale & Cardon, 1992). (Although estimates change with new molecular genetic information, polymorphic genes are estimated to have about 14 different alleles, on the average, with wide variation from gene to gene.) There are two main types of nonadditivity: dominance and epistasis. Dominance is the interaction between alleles at the same locus. It reflects deviation of heterozygotes from the mean of the genotypic values of the two relevant homozygotes, summed over the loci that influence the trait under study. Epistasis, on the other hand, is the interaction between alleles at different loci. It occurs when the effect of an allele depends on which allele is expressed at another locus. Taking nonadditivity into account in modeling is important in order to compare heritability estimates across twin, adoption, and family studies. Epistasis cannot be estimated separately from dominance in models for most human data. The twin method depends on the fact that MZ pairs share 100% of nonmutated genes, and thus additive and nonadditive genetic effects are completely shared, whereas DZ pairs share on average 50% of additive genetic variance and 25% or less of nonadditive genetic variance.

Environmental effects are also subject to behavior-genetic analysis. Environmental effects can be shared or nonshared by a particular set of family members. Shared environmental effects explain similarity between twins and relatives in addition to that accounted for by common genes. Shared environmental variance also accounts for the similarity of genetically unrelated individuals who are reared together. The nonshared environmental variance is the remainder of the variance not explained by genes or by shared environment (see Turkheimer & Waldron, 2000, for a conceptual review). It includes the effects of experiences that are unique to each individual and independent of genetic factors. Nonshared environmental variance can be directly estimated from differences between MZ co-twins. The estimate of nonshared environment is often confounded with measurement error. A common misunderstanding is that environmental effects are "what is left over" after genetic effects are estimated. Typical behavior-genetic methods treat genetic and shared environmental effects in an even-handed manner, given the assumptions about how these effects can be partitioned. The more cogent criticism is that the genetic partitioning is based on sound theories of Mendelian inheritance whereas the environmental partitioning is based on familial units that might not be the most important markers of environmental influence. Despite extensive explication of the issue (Plomin & Daniels, 1987), the meaning of "shared" and "nonshared" environments continues to create confusion. The variance component referred to as "shared environment" can differ from one kinship design to the next. That is, the environment shared by co-twins has a somewhat different quality from the environment shared by ordinary siblings or adopted siblings, and certainly different from the environment shared by parents and offspring. Of course, these differences in the quality of the shared environment might well be irrelevant to the behavior under study. Fortunately, many of these issues can be subjected to empirical tests, which are common in the more technical behavior-genetic literature (Loehlin, 1992).

Parents can exert strong experiential effects on their offspring behavior in the absence of a shared environmental factor in biometric analyses. For example, hypothetically, aggressive fathers might induce inhibited behavior in children of a certain age. Such a hypothetical effect would not emerge in a univariate analysis of parent-offspring data of either aggressiveness or inhibition. Part of the solution to problems like this is use of multivariate analysis (McArdle & Goldsmith, 1990; Neale & Cardon, 1992). A more important part of the solution is integrating theories of how the environment works into these multivariate designs. In summary, the distinctions between shared and nonshared environmental effects and transmitted environmental effects in behavior-genetic designs do not map well onto some issues concerning the nature and effects of interaction among family members (Hoffman, 1991). Testing for environmental risk and protective factors in ways that are also sensitive to genetic factors requires programmatic application of several research strategies (Rutter, Pickles, Murray, & Eaves, 2001).

We shall illustrate the investigation of genetic and environmental variance with data gathered using the classical twin method, wherein the phenotypic similarity of monozygotic and dizygotic pairs is contrasted. The assumptions of the twin method are portrayed carefully in textbooks (e.g., Plomin, DeFries, McClearn, & Rutter, 1997). The first assumption is that the twin sample is representative of the population and that the results can therefore be generalized. Second, the equal environments assumption holds that environmental similarity is the same for both types of twins reared in the same family. If identical twins experience more similar environments than fraternal twins for a given trait and this excess environmental similarity is not in reaction to their greater genetic similarity, then genetic variance estimates will be inflated. Although it is difficult to conclude that the equal environments assumption is completely valid, several methods for testing it exist. Another general assumption for most behavior genetic designs is the absence of assortative mating, which refers to the tendency for birth parents to be similar on the traits of interest. Assortative mating can be a problem because it inflates genetic resemblance between siblings and may thus reduce the differences be-

tween identical and fraternal twin correlations. However, most studies have found negligible spousal correlations for personality traits (Plomin et al., 1997), which often encompass individual differences in emotionality.

A rubric that is even more closely identified with individual differences in emotionality than personality is temperament, as suggested by many theorists (e.g., Goldsmith, 1993). Several reviews of the behavior-genetic literature on temperament from the perspective of parental report are in the literature (e.g., Goldsmith, 1983, 1989), and there is little need for a comprehensive review here. Instead, twin results from our research group, using a specific series of questionnaires with good psychometric properties, are provided. Table 16.2 illustrates twin similarity for temperament using the *Infant Behavior Questionnaire* (IBQ; Rothbart, 1981), *Toddler Behavior Assessment Questionnaire* (TBAQ; Goldsmith, 1996), and the *Children's Behavior Questionnaire* (CBQ; Rothbart & Ahadi, 1994; Rothbart, Ahadi, & Hershey, 1994). Only a subset of scales with parallel content across the age ranges is represented in Table 16.2. These age- and sex-corrected correlations come from different studies by our research group (Goldsmith, Buss, & Lemery, 1997; Goldsmith, Lemery, Buss, & Campos, 1999; Lemery, 1999). In some cases, the values in Table 16.2 are means from different studies, with appropriate weighting by sample size.

We found evidence for additive genetic effects for temperament scales and factors related to negative affect (e.g., fear and anger proneness) with little or no evidence for the shared environment. Moreover, two findings were relatively novel. First, we found evidence for moderate shared environmental variance for scales related to posi-

Table 16.2 Twin Similarity for Selected Temperament Scales (Fear and/or Shyness, Anger, Pleasure, Emotion Regulation)

|  | Monozygotic R | Dizygotic R |
|---|---|---|
| Rothbart's *Infant Behavior Questionnaire* | | |
| Distress to Novelty | .59 | .28 |
| Distress to Limitations | .66 | .28 |
| Smiling and Laughter | .72 | .52 |
| Duration of Orienting | .69 | .45 |
| Soothability | .53 | .61 |
| Goldsmith's *Toddler Behavior Assessment Questionnaire* | | |
| Social Fearfulness | .50 | .40 |
| Anger Proneness | .72 | .55 |
| Pleasure | .69 | .64 |
| Interest/Persistence | .81 | .26 |
| Rothbart's *Children's Behavior Questionnaire* (factor scales) | | |
| Negative Affect | .69 | .28 |
| Surgency (positive affect) | .60 | .11 |
| Effortful Control | .61 | .25 |

tive affect for infants, toddlers, and preschoolers. Perhaps because positive affect is not measured separately from negative affect in most other instruments, this finding of shared environmental variance is unusual in the behavior genetic literature for parental report of temperament. However, there is a variety of evidence in the literature for shared environmental effects on positive affect, such as person interest (Goldsmith & Gottesman, 1981), laboratory measures of smiling, questionnaire measures of smiling/laughter and pleasure (Goldsmith & Campos, 1986; Goldsmith, 1986), observations of positive activity (Lytton, 1980), and questionnaire measures of zestfulness (Cohen, Dibble, & Graw, 1977). What might be the substantive interpretation of this finding? The leading candidate is perhaps some feature of maternal behavior or personality common to the twins. The sources of this shared environmental variance remain to be identified. A reasonable speculation is that the primary caregiver might be the source of the common environment, as seen in some other cases where shared environment was a significant factor (Leve, Winebarger, Fagot, Reid, & Goldsmith, 1998). Even more speculatively, twin similarity for attachment security in respective twin-mother relationships might play a role because attachment security has been shown to relate to positive affectivity (e.g., Mangelsdorf, Diener, McHale, & Pilolla, 1993). On the other hand, other features of maternal personality such as extraversion could be influential as a source of common experience for the twins. We must also acknowledge the possibility of a social desirability explanation because preliminary research indicates that the TBAQ Pleasure scale is more strongly related to a trial measure of content-balanced social desirability than other TBAQ scales (Goldsmith, 1996).

Another notable result, in the third section of Table 16.2, is the genetic contribution to emotion regulation. The Effortful Control factor of the CBQ represents an understudied area in the behavior genetic literature; its constituents include measures of attention focusing and inhibitory control. The ability to allocate attention flexibly allows children to modulate or regulate their exposure to stressful situations or contexts (Ruff & Rothbart, 1996), and inhibitory control involves the ability to inhibit ongoing or prepotent behavior upon demand. Thus, effortful control is part of the domain of emotion regulation, currently one of the most intensively studied areas in the developmental literature (see Fox, 1994; Kopp & Neufeld, Chapter 19, this volume, for reviews). Despite the recent surge of interest in the topic, the origins of emotion regulation are largely unexplored, with this exception of the present results and some studies of the etiology of ADHD. As a whole, our results have demonstrated that emotion expression is mediated by genetic factors. Regulation of this expression is also apparently mediated by genetic factors, but the specificity of genetic contributions to emotion regulation requires additional study.

To summarize the full body of research using parental report temperament measures (including studies with instruments other than those shown in Table 16.2), studies have generally yielded evidence for genetic effects with MZ correlations ranging from .50 to .80 and DZ correlations ranging from zero to .50. Several questionnaires—not those in Table 16.2—show DZ correlations that are less than half the MZ correlations, and that typically are near zero. These "too-low" dizygotic twin correlations are problematic because, if a trait is heritable, dizygotic twins who share on average half their segregating genes should resemble each other if genetic effects are additive. These low DZ correlations may in part reflect genetic nonadditivity. However, behavioral geneticists more frequently interpret negative and zero DZ correlations as suggesting possible contrast effects in parental temperamental ratings of DZ twins. Parents may tend to exaggerate temperamental differences in DZ twins, for whom they can more easily discern differences than can parents of MZ pairs. It also may be that gene-environment interaction inflates the MZ correlations relative to the DZ correlations, in which case the low correlations may accurately reflect DZ similarity. In any case, these zero or negative DZ correlations make heritability estimates based on the traditional Falconer (1989) equation (doubling the MZ-DZ correlational difference) inaccurate. In these cases, model-fitting approaches to data analysis are necessary (Neale & Cardon, 1992).

In addition to the twin research using parental report temperament questionnaires, a handful of twin and adoption studies have used versions of Bayley's *Infant Behavior Record* (IBR; Bayley, 1969), mostly as a supplementary temperament measure during cognitive testing. In most implementations, the examiner using the IBR makes ratings of the infant or toddler on as many as 30 ratings scales, which are factor-analyzed to yield scores for broader domains that are then subjected to genetic analysis. The factors differ somewhat from study to study. The results for the three major twin studies that have reported IBR results are portrayed in Table 16.3, which includes data only for the assessment occasions closest to age 1 year and 3 years. The results are also confined to the major affect-related factor from each study, as well as the major interest/persistence factor from each study, with the latter perhaps representing rudimentary regulatory skills.

The first results tabulated are from the Louisville Twin Study (Matheny, 1990a). The second set of results are from Goldsmith and Gottesman (1981), and the final set are from the MacArthur Longitudinal Twin Study (Emde & Hewitt, 2001). All three studies were longitudinal, with IBR results available at three ages or more. Other than missing data, the same individuals are represented in both the upper (around 1 year) and lower (around 3 years) sections of Table 16.3. The results are fairly consistent when we bear in mind that sample sizes differ across the three studies, that the IBR factors are not defined exactly alike

Table 16.3 Twin Similarity at 1 and 3 Years of Age for Examiner Ratings of Temperament From Three Studies: Selected Emotion-related Factors

|  | Monozygotic R | Dizygotic R |
|---|---|---|
| **I. Twin Similarity at age closest to 1 year** | | |
| Louisville Twin Study (12 months, $N$ = 60-91 MZ, 35-54 DZ pairs) | | |
|    IBR Task Orientation | .49 | .23 |
|    IBR Test Affect/Extraversion | .43 | .07 |
| Goldsmith & Gottesman (8 months, $N$ = 115 MZ, 209 DZ pairs) | | |
|    IBR Person Interest | .28 | .20 |
|    IBR Activity | .57 | .35 |
| MALTS (14 months, $N$ = 118 MZ, 106 DZ pairs, and 167 MZ, 146 DZ pairs, for the two measures) | | |
|    IBR Task Orientation | .13* | .22* |
|    IBR Affect/Extraversion | .32* | .12* |
| **II. Twin Similarity at age closest to 3 years** | | |
| Louisville Twin Study (2 years, $N$ = 60-91 MZ, 35-54 DZ pairs) | | |
|    IBR Task Orientation | .48 | .21 |
|    IBR Test Affect/Extraversion | .53 | .03 |
| Goldsmith & Gottesman (4 years, $N$ = 110 MZ, 206 DZ pairs) | | |
|    IBR Task Persistence | .56 | .25 |
|    IBR Spontaneity/activity vs. Rigidity/passivity | .41 | .37 |
| MALTS (3 years, 2 years; $N$ = 118 MZ, 106 DZ pairs, and 167 MZ, 146 DZ pairs, for the two measures) | | |
|    IBR Task Orientation (3 years) | .42* | .23* |
|    IBR Affect/Extraversion (2 years) | .43* | .22* |

*Correlational values estimated from graphical presentation.

in each study, and that there is true developmental change in the phenotypes and possibly in the underlying genotypes. Monozygotic twin correlations do not rise above the .50s and are mostly below that level. Since the monozygotic twin correlations are an upper-bound estimate of heritability, we can conclude that the genetic variance is about 50% or less. Low and similar MZ and DZ correlations characterize some of the interest/persistence variables at the younger age. Comparing the results with those for parental report in Table 16.2, we note that genetic effects on temperament are clearly not confined to parental report. However, the lower monozygotic correlations and the occasional lack of a genetic effect distinguish IBR-like tester ratings from the parental rating data.

In addition to twin studies, the IBR has been used to study adoptive and nonadoptive siblings at 12 and 24 months. Braungart, Plomin, DeFries, and Fulker (1992) compared the correlations for the adoptive and nonadoptive siblings to the MZ and DZ twin correlations obtained in the Louisville Twin Study (Matheny, 1980). For the three main factors—affect-extraversion, activity, and task orientation—the order of correlations was MZ> DZ= nonadoptive siblings > adoptive siblings. These results suggest genetic influence and buttress the validity of the twin method. Model-fitting procedures indicated that, on average, 44% of the variance was accounted for by genetic factors.

Having covered the estimation of genetic and environmental variance from twin studies using parental report and observer rating methodology, we now turn to laboratory-based methods of assessing temperament and emotion-related behavior. There are a variety of observational measures of temperament (Goldsmith & Rieser-Danner, 1990), and a handful of twin studies have employed such methods. Among the first twin researchers to observe temperament-related reactions in the laboratory were Wilson and Matheny (1983), and others directly assessed behavior in the home (Lytton, 1980; Plomin & Rowe, 1979). Many reports in the infancy literature focus on only a single dimension, such as activity level (Eaton, McKeen, & Lam, 1988; Saudino & Eaton, 1991) or inhibition. In one early report on 3- and 4-year-old twins, Matheny (1987) reported substantial genetic contributions (heritabilities averaging 60%) to observed temperamental traits including surgency, responsiveness, activity, emotional tone, and attentiveness. Another early study reported greater monozygotic than dizygotic twin similarity for laboratory-based measures of fearful reactions to a stranger and to a perceived drop-off on a visual cliff for infants (Goldsmith & Campos, 1986).

One of the most widely studied temperamental traits has been behavioral inhibition (Kagan, Reznick, Clarke, Snidman, & Garcia-Coll, 1984; Kagan, Reznick, & Gibbons, 1989), which has also been examined using behavioral genetic methods. In addition to parental ratings and experimenter ratings, Matheny (1990b) investigated the genetic and environmental components of behavioral inhibition in toddlers. An observational rating of emotional tone was used to measure inhibition. Twin data demonstrated that a substantial portion of the variance in inhibition could be explained by genetic effects (MZ $r$ = .79, DZ $r$ = .26). Analyses from the MALTS have also shown genetic effects on behavioral inhibition. Robinson, Kagan, Reznick, and Corley (1992) found higher MZ than DZ similarity (average $r$ = .55 vs. .23, respectively) for observational measures of behavioral inhibition. DiLalla, Kagan, and Reznick (1994) replicated this finding in 24-month-olds using both correlational (MZ $r$ = .82 and DZ $r$ = .47) and multiple regression analyses. In more recent analyses of the same sample, Manke, Saudino, and Grant (2001) examined genetic and environmental effects on membership in high-inhibition and low-inhibition groups at the three ages under study, 14, 20, and 24 months. Generally, the degree of heritability was moderately high and consistent for high group membership, low group membership, and for individual differences in the sample as a whole. The only exception was membership in the low-inhibition group at the earliest age (14 months), which appeared to be associated solely with environmental sources of variance. A limitation to this conclusion is that the sample size limits the power to discern modest differences between the various heritability estimates.

In the MALTS, mentioned above, several observational measures of temperament/emotionality were analyzed. With as many as 400 twin pairs, Plomin, Emde, Hewitt, Kagan, and DeFries (2001) summarized evidence that several temperamental/emotional phenotypes showed evidence for both additive genetic effects and shared environmental effects. These dimensions include shyness, cheerfulness, and anger response to restraint. In contrast, behavioral inhibition and empathy showed only additive genetic effects.

A rarely used method of assessing temperament in children is self-report. However, Warren, Schmitz, and Emde (1999) administered an anxiety questionnaire verbally to a nonrisk sample of over 300 7-year-old twin pairs. Scales tapping the physical manifestations of anxiety and social concerns showed heritabilities in the .30s, but an index of frequency of worrying showed only shared and nonshared environmental influences.

In summary, it is fair to conclude that the finding of genetic variance associated with emotion-related phenotypes in twin studies is not dependent on the method of measurement, although parental report measures tend to suggest greater twin monozygotic similarity than other methods.

In the results reviewed above, shared environmental variance was implicated for some variables. However, we have not treated the nonshared environmental variance. Nonshared environmental variance, sometimes confounded with measurement error, is as ubiquitous as genetic variance in analyses of emotion-related phenotypes. Two examples will suffice to illustrate current findings. Both of these examples draw on the study of differences between monozygotic co-twins, which must arise from the nonshared environment. Deater-Deckard et al. (2001) studied intrapair differences in emotionality, behavior problems, and observed behavior in 62 pairs of 3.5-year-old twins. Differences in maternal behavior toward the two twins were rated by the mother herself and an interviewer, as well as observed directly in maternal behavior. Among other findings, more maternal negativity and more harsh discipline were associated with a variety of less-adaptive child behaviors. Thus, differential maternal behavior was implicated as a specific nonshared environmental factor. Lemery and Goldsmith (in press) explored the twin relationship as a factor in intrapair monozygotic differences. Co-twins with larger temperamental differences (in difficulty/negative affect) had more conflictual relationships, suggesting that the sibling relationship acted as a source of nonshared environmental effects.

## Endophenotypes

A concept with substantial currency is that of the "endophenotype" (Almasy & Blangero, 2001; LeBoyer et al., 1998). Despite its short history (see section on "The Behavior-Genetic Paradigm"), this concept has proved quite useful (Sing, Zerba, & Reilly, 1994). Among the desirable properties of a good endophenotype for genetic analysis are (1) an etiologic association with the complex behavioral phenotype; (2) presence in some unaffected relatives; and (3) being amenable to objective measurement. Endophenotypes can be biochemical, neurological, anatomical, psychophysiological, endocrine, sensorimotor, perceptual, cognitive, or affective in nature. Such phenotypes are available, especially for anxiety-related phenotypes (Bakshi & Kalin, 2000), but they have been subjected to genetic analysis mainly in mice to the present time.

Complex behavioral phenotypes such as schizophrenia, anxiety, and autism do not yield readily to genetic analysis. The same is true for complex medical disorders such as coronary artery disease and idiopathic generalized epilepsies. For these medical disorders, endophenotypic indicators such as plasma cholesterol and abnormal EEG patterns have facilitated genetic analyses. For instance, Klos et al. (2001) examined 11 endophenotypes for plasma lipid or apolipoprotein levels in genome-wide linkage scans (described below). Five chromosomal regions containing possible susceptibility genes for four of the lipid or apolipoprotein endophenotypes were identified. These genes, once identified more definitively, would not only be new potential genetic risk factors for coronary artery disease but might also signal opportunities for therapeutic interventions. Greenberg et al. (2000) and Durner et al. (2001) used both subtyping and endophenotypes to allow localization of genes involved in idiopathic generalized epilepsies. Studying juvenile myoclonic epilepsy (a subtype of idiopathic generalized epilepsy), Greenberg et al. (2000) included as "affected" in their analyses family members who were clinically normal but who showed an endophenotype (spike-and-wave EEG or paroxysmal bursts of generalized high-amplitude slow waves in the theta range) that is known to be genetically related to the disorder. These distinctions allowed the investigators to demonstrate genetic heterogeneity (see below) in juvenile myoclonic epilepsy and to confirm previous reports of linkage to the HLA region. In another study, this same research group (Durner et al., 2001) examined families containing probands with three clinical varieties of juvenile-onset idiopathic generalized epilepsies. A genome scan identified one chromosomal region that apparently contains a susceptibility gene that elevates risk for all three forms of epilepsy and other chromosomal regions that appeared to confer risks specific to the three clinical varieties. A genetic classification of the disorders was not isomorphic with the existing clinical classification.

The point of these medical examples is that a greater understanding of the disease processes yields endophenotypes, as well as subtypes, that can themselves become the focus of genetic analysis. For emotion-related disorders and traits, this level of analysis remains largely a future goal.

## Gene-Environment Covariance and Interaction

Upon first exposure to behavioral genetics, scientists often question how mutual or interactive processes are treated. The concepts of gene-environment (GE) covariance and interaction provide a partial answer. These two concepts figure into almost every "textbook" presentation of the behavior-genetic paradigm. However, in empirical research, both concepts are difficult to operationalize and are often simply uninvestigated.

### GE Covariance

Individuals can be differentially exposed to environments that contribute to further development of heritable traits. This gene-conditioned, differential exposure is often viewed as reflecting three types of gene-environment correlation: passive, reactive, and active (Plomin, DeFries, & Loehlin, 1977). If a child's genotype is correlated with the environment provided by parents and siblings, and such provision is associated with heritable traits of the parents or siblings, then "passive" GE correlation results. "Reactive," or evocative GE correlation refers to others' reacting to a particular child on the basis of the child's inherited characteristics. For example, children who are inattentive in school may be taught less material in a less effective manner. Thus, the environment becomes correlated with genotypic differences. Lastly, an active GE correlation refers to the situation in which a child seeks an environment conducive to further developing some of his or her heritable tendencies (cf. Buss, 1993, for further distinctions). Thus, aggressive youths may actively choose to become friends with peers who are also easily frustrated and prone to attribute hostile intent to benign actions of others, and these friendships would contribute to further development of the aggressive phenotype. Obviously, naturally occurring situations might reflect combinations of all three types of correlation. Scarr and McCartney (1983) postulate a shift from passive to reactive and then to active GE correlation during childhood, as children begin to select more of their own experiences and environments.

Versions of the idea of GE correlation have captured the attention of many behavioral scientists; however, some behavioral geneticists argue that active GE correlation cannot be meaningfully distinguished from "direct" genetic effects. That is, even "direct" genetic effects are always instances of genes correlated with environments although the environments might occasionally be entirely nonpsy-

chological in nature. In the case of social environments, suppose that genotypic differences are correlated with, say, antisocial behavioral tendencies. As described above, these tendencies might be manifest, in part, by seeking peers who are experienced in antisocial behaviors themselves. The association with peers might be the most proximal influence on antisocial acts. This scenario would usually be characterized as active gene-environment correlation, of the type in which the individual selects an environment on the basis of genetically influenced behavioral predispositions—that is, "birds of a feather flock together." But don't all genetic effects on behavior involve selection of relevant environments, in the sense that genes and their proximal and distal products must be expressed in a facilitative context, where the "context" may range from the physiological to the social? Perhaps so, but it may still be useful to retain the concept of active GE correlation for scenarios in which the environment is a measurable experience.

Although the idea is intuitively appealing, the importance of GE correlations for emotion-related phenotypes, including those related to affect and psychopathology, largely remain to be demonstrated. GE correlations may be negative correlations, such that caregivers and others provide, for example, inhibited children with extra opportunities to engage their environment without eliciting fear. On the other hand, GE correlations may be positive, such that emotionally labile children experience unsettled and unpredictable environments.

GE correlations will obviously increase phenotypic variance but in many cases may not bias heritability estimates greatly. If GE covariance is present but not accounted for in the data analytic model, it will bias the estimates of both genetic and environmental variance. Assuming that the direction of GE covariance is positive, it will inflate similarity of both monozygotic and dizygotic twins, and thus the shared environmental variance will be overestimated. Given their greater genetic similarity, identical twins' similarity will likely be more affected by GE covariance than fraternal similarity, thus inflating the genetic variance estimate as well. Depending on the size of the GE covariance and its association with linear (vs. nonadditive) genetic effects, heritability estimates may not be much affected. Of course, if the direction of the GE covariance is negative, both the genetic and the environmental variance components will be underestimated. The adoption study is unaffected by most GE correlations and is a convenient design for estimating their importance (Plomin et al., 1977).

One of the most informative human developmental studies of gene-environment correlation for an emotion-related phenomenon concerned parent-child mutuality (Deater-Deckard & O'Conner, 2000). Mutuality is the notion that healthy parent-child relationships exhibit emotional reciprocity and have a bidirectional, responsive quality (Hinde, 1987; Kochanska, 1997). Using explicitly dyadic observational measures such as shared positive emotion, mutual eye gaze, and responsiveness, Deater-Deckard and O'Conner (2000) examined mutuality with the same mother for two of her 3–4-year-old children, where the children were samples of MZ twins, DZ twins, full siblings, and genetically unrelated adopted siblings. The similarity of siblings for the mutuality measures with their mothers showed a pattern indicating genetic influence based on child characteristics: MZ, $r = .61$, DZ, $r = .26$; full siblings, $r = .25$; and adopted siblings, $r = -.04$. An interpretation of these findings is that qualities of parent-child mutuality become correlated with child-specific factors. Because the child-specific factors are heritable and the parent's contribution to mutuality constitutes an aspect of the child's environment, gene-environment correlation is induced in this situation.

## GE Interaction

Gene-environment interaction refers to the differential effects on the phenotype of an environmental factor for persons with different genotypes. In this sense, GE interaction is a statistical rather than a process-oriented interaction. For example, having poor sibling, peer, or adult models for the development of empathy might affect the development of aggressive tendencies primarily for those children with genes associated with, say, low frustration tolerance (assuming that lack of empathy and frustration tolerance are both precursors of aggressive behavior). The few attempts to isolate these interactions in human data have been largely unsuccessful (Plomin & Daniels, 1984). In principle, analyzing GE interaction effects need not be complicated. Plomin et al. (1977) introduced a $2 \times 2$ ANOVA method adapted from animal studies for human adoption studies. In brief, for a heritable trait, the parent's (or midparent's) phenotype may be taken as an estimate of the child's genotype. Of course, the parent's phenotype is an indirect and possibly poor estimate of the child's genotype, depending on the heritability and the association between the childhood and mature forms of the phenotype in question. The environmental measure can be, for example, a characteristic of the adoptive parents. In the simplest case, a $2 \times 2$ table is set up with one variable reflecting genotype and the other environment, and with the dependent variable being some behavioral pattern of the child. Each main effect indicates an independent effect of genotype or environment, and the interaction of the two yields the GE interaction. Likewise, multiple regression with family data can be used to analyze continuous data, and logistic regression can be used when only the outcome is discontinuous. The analysis of GE interaction in designs such as those described above requires large sample sizes.

The strongest promise of identifying GE interactions is on the horizon when genes associated with traits of interest can be assayed directly, as with quantitative trait loci (QTLs; see below). A simple first approach, already well established in studying maize and tomato genetics, would be to ask whether QTLs identified as affecting a trait in one environment also affect it in contrasting environments (Tanksley, 1993).

## Genetic Heterogeneity

The notion of genetic heterogeneity refers to subsets of a patently single clinical disorder having different genetic roots. At least in the early stages of understanding a disorder, genetic heterogeneity is probably the norm rather than the exception. That is, distinct genes (or distinct alleles at the same gene locus) can lead to the "same" disorder. Some genetic approaches initially assume that all cases of a disorder have a common cause, but empirical results often reveal unsuspected heterogeneity.

Two medical disorders illustrate clear cases of genetic heterogeneity. First, the autosomal dominant disorder neurofibromatosis can be divided clinically into two subgroups: the more common von Recklinghausen (NF1) type and the rarer acoustic type (NF2). Both subtypes run true in families. Linkage studies have demonstrated that NF1 is caused by a gene on chromosome 19 and that the NF2 gene is on chromosome 22. As a second example, the Duchenne (more severe) and Becker type muscular dystrophies are caused by different mutations of the same gene. In general, differences in the mode of inheritance and in the age of onset have proved useful in distinguishing subtypes of disorders that are more genetically homogeneous.

The situation changes when we consider complex emotion-related phenotypes. Results from a large population-based sample of female adult twins point to the etiologically heterogeneous nature of depression (Kendler et al., 1996). Concordant twin pairs had the same depressive syndrome (seven classes, of which three represent the clinical syndromes of mild typical depression, atypical depression, and severe typical depression) more often than chance, and resemblance was greater in MZ than DZ twin pairs. In this example, a genetic marker that cosegregates with depression in some families but not in others has not been found (the best standard of evidence for genetic heterogeneity), but Kendler et al. (1996) did fulfill another standard of evidence: demonstration that certain clinical features "run true" in families—in this case, in twins. Another type of evidence for genetic heterogeneity would be a finding that the risk to relatives differs by proband characteristics (e.g., as in early- and late-onset Alzheimer's disease).

The general idea of genetic heterogeneity applies not only to disorders but also more generally to traits. That is, it is possible that different genes affect traits in the low, medium, and high ranges of trait values. And it is also possible different combinations of genes can result in the same trait phenotype in different individuals or different subgroups of the population.

## Developmental Behavioral Genetics

To this point, the concepts reviewed apply largely to static views of behavior. However, these concepts can be supplemented with notions that help us to understand quantitative genetic aspects of development (Gottesman & Goldsmith, 1994). First, genetic analyses can be extended from the occurrence or strength of a disorder or trait to developmental (time-related) features of disorders or traits. Thus, we can analyze the genetics of the age of onset and of the clinical course of, say, schizophrenia, as Gottesman and Shields (1972) showed. Questions about whether the genetic liability to the disorder itself overlaps with the liability to age of onset can then be addressed. These questions can be framed for polygenic or single-gene effects.

Developmental behavioral genetics received a great boost from the development of multivariate methods, mostly using structural equation modeling. Multivariate methods, which involve the simultaneous biometric analysis of more than one phenotype, including the case of one or more phenotypes measured on multiple occasions. Even if cross-sectional studies show that a phenotype is heritable at two different ages, and other studies show that the phenotype is stable, we cannot assume that this stability is mediated genetically without longitudinal, genetically informative studies.

One example of this approach concerns conduct disorder (CD), which is diagnosed in children, and antisocial personality disorder (APD), which is diagnosed later in adolescence and in adulthood. Considering the similarities and differences between CD and APD, Lyons et al. (1995), with over 3,000 adult male Vietnam-era veteran twin pairs, estimated the heritability for the juvenile trait of CD at 7%, whereas for adult APD it was 43%. In addition, the shared environmental effect was 31% for CD and 5% for APD. Interestingly, the CD genetic influences completely overlapped with the APD genetic influences, and the APD shared environmental influences completely overlapped with the CD shared environmental influences. In another example from the MALTS project, using an observational measure of shyness in the laboratory and home (14- and 20-month-olds), Cherny, Fulker, Corley, Plomin, and DeFries (1994) reported that genetic effects accounted for a large proportion of the stability in shyness from 14 to 20 months. There was also apparent change in genetic and shared environmental influences on shyness during this period (Plomin et al., 1993). The genetic mediation of stability is a common finding in this literature.

Goldsmith and Lemery (2000) considered the association of earlier temperament and later anxiety symptoms within a twin study design. Here, the analysis takes the same form as the investigation of genetic or environmental mediation of stability of temperament, with the exception that the outcome is not later temperament, but rather symptoms of disorder. There are too few results from this line of inquiry to yield generalizations, but both genetic and environmental mediation of temperamental effects on later symptoms have been noted (Lemery, 1999; Goldsmith & Lemery, 2000).

It is especially important to consider the potential changing influences of genes and the environment across developmental transitions, when reorganization in one system is often followed by reorganization in another. Where such change is detected, many developmental factors are plausible correlates and perhaps causes, including locomotor and cognitive transitions or reorganizations. It is also important to note that the tendency to equate genetics or biology with "constraint" and experience with "possibility," while perhaps holding some validity, should probably be resisted. At best, these equations are oversimplifications.

## Non-Mendelizing Genetic Influences

Traditional behavior-genetic analysis of genetic variability using family, twin, and adoption studies is not the whole story of genes and behavior. An obvious and important aspect of genetic influence that is not encompassed by these designs comes from nonpolymorphic genes (genes that have only one allelic form in the population). Nonpolymorphic genes do not contribute to individual variability. Nonpolymorphic genes are, of course, transmitted via Mendelian principles. However, there are genetic sources of variability that are not transmitted via Mendelian principles and thus not captured by behavior-genetic designs. One list of such mechanisms includes mitochondrial inheritance, gonadal mosaicism, imprinting (wherein a gene's expression is modulated based on whether it is transmitted from the father or the mother), progressive amplification (Morton, 1992, 1993), and the degree of homozygosity. Here, we consider the last three of these mechanisms although their links to affective phenomena largely remain to be demonstrated.

### Progressive Amplification

The mechanism of progressive amplification has received tremendous attention over the past decade. Fragile X disorder, a leading cause of mental retardation, exemplifies the pattern of progressive amplification through pedigrees. A CGG trinucleotide in an untranslated segment of the FMR-1 gene on the X chromosome is normally repeated fewer than 50 times. When the gene mutates, these unstable CGG repeats are amplified, resulting in hundreds or even thousands of copies. The premutations are expanded to full mutations (termed "triplet repeats") only when transmitted by the mother. Fathers with the premutation have normal daughters who might be at risk to pass on the disorder.

The implications of triplet repeat mutations for psychopathology might be substantial. (Huntington's disease follows the same pattern of inheritance Huntington's Disease Collaborative Research Group, 1993). The extent of the amplified region (a CAG repeat) is associated with age of onset, with earlier onset cases having longer repeated regions. Early-onset cases are more likely to be those with the "at risk" allele transmitted from the father, an apparent example of genomic imprinting (see below). These associations of molecular processes with age of onset illustrate the need to incorporate developmental aspects of psychopathology into behavioral genetics.

### Imprinting

As mentioned above, genomic imprinting confers functional differences on specific genes derived from paternal versus maternal genomes during development. Only one of the two alleles is expressed in a particular tissue during a stage of development; the other is silenced. The epigenetic phenomenon of genomic imprinting has been well established in mice, and was hypothesized to be important in mammalian and primate forebrain evolution (Keverne, Martel, & Nevison, 1996). Supporting evidence for this hypothesis is accumulating (Reik & Walter, 1998, 2001). Experimental evidence from mice shows that maternally derived genes are expressed preferentially in cortex, striatum, and hippocampus, and paternally derived genes are expressed preferentially in certain hypothalamic regions (Keverne, Fundele, Narasimha, Barton, & Surani, 1996). Given the different roles of these regions in behavior, such differential expression could affect the behavioral resemblance of relatives if the genes involved are polymorphic. The question of whether imprinting is actually a significant and widespread factor in normal human development and for affective phenomena awaits further study, but studies of human mutations suggest that imprinted genes do affect brain development and behavior in some syndromes (Christian et al., 1995; Nicholls, 1993). Of some 35 human genes now thought to be imprinted, perhaps the best studied are those responsible for Prader-Willi and Angelman syndromes. These syndromes are due to deletions, rearrangements, or other anomalies in the region of chromosome 15q11-q13, which is a meiotically unstable, imprinted region of the genome (Amos-Landgraf et al., 1999; Hanel & Wevick, 2001). Current research in this field centers around elucidating the mechanisms of DNA methylation and de-methylation that presumably underlie imprinting (Reik, Dean, & Walter, 2001).

### Homozygosity

Recent empirical results and theorizing suggest the plausibility of variability in degree of homozygosity as a source of genetic variability for psychopathology. A key construct in this line of theorizing and research is "developmental instability" (see Yeo & Gangestad, 1993, for illustrations with human data). Indicators of developmental instability include some minor physical anomalies and fluctuating asymmetries (deviations from symmetry in bilateral physical characteristics). Among others, Markow and Gottesman (1989, 1993) and Yeo and Gangestad (1993) have documented associations between developmental instability—likely during the prenatal period—and psychopathology, including childhood disorders. These authors explain that genetic heterozygosity leads to multiple forms of proteins, and these multiple forms might buffer the organism by facilitating adaptation to changing environmental demands. Conversely, genetic homozygosity would reduce the organism's metabolic buffering and thus render it susceptible to insult from environmental perturbations.

The degree of genetic homozygosity is a function of the state of paired alleles, manifest only when the zygote is formed. Thus, homozygosity is not transmitted from parent to offspring and is not detectable as a genetic effect in traditional twin, family, or adoption studies. Effects of genetic homozygosity would be misidentified as environmental variance in parent-offspring analyses and as nonadditive genetic variance in twin studies.

These brief considerations of non-Mendelizing genetic effects caution us not to become paradigm-bound—even to useful paradigms such as the twin design and genome scans—if we wish to discern the entire panorama of genetic influences on behavior.

## Initial Molecular Genetic Approaches to Human Emotion-related Behavior: Linkage and Association Studies

Identifying individual genes involved in etiology is currently feasible although still in early stages for emotion-related phenotypes with complex inheritance. This task of identifying genes inevitably follows from the results of the Human Genome Project. In this chapter, only a brief review is feasible. Our attention is focused on "complex inheritance," a term that can encompass single genes of discernible effect operating in a background of both polygenic and environmental effects, as well as the possibility of genetic heterogeneity and environmentally molded phenotypes that resemble genetically influenced ones (phenocopies).

The methods that are applicable to complex inheritance are varieties of linkage analysis and association studies. These methods are reviewed at length and in technical detail by Ott (1991) and in many other sources (e.g., McGuffin, Owen, O'Donovan, Thapar, & Gottesman, 1994; Risch, 1990a, 1990b, 1990c; Sham, 1998). For humans, linkage methods include classic pedigree analysis in which statistical transmission models are tested in large families with many affected members. Also relevant to complex inheritance are the newer methods using gene chips and expressed sequence arrays (Watson & Akil, 1999), which can detect the expression (in mRNA) of hundreds or even thousands of genes simultaneously. These methods are currently used only in nonhuman animals.

A class of nonparametric analyses called "allele-sharing methods" (Lander & Schork, 1994) involve studying affected relatives to determine whether a gene or marker is shared, through inheritance from a common ancestor, by these affected relatives more frequently than expected. The most common implementation of allele-sharing methodology is the analysis of affected sib pairs in "genome scans," often with a finer-grained scan following an initial scan. For instance, this technique was used in several attempts to locate susceptibility genes for autism, with only modest success when no subtyping of autism was employed (see Maestrini, Paul, Monaco, & Bailey, 2000, for review). In a genome scan, linkage analysis is conducted using a series of anonymous polymorphisms, or genetic probes, spaced at relatively constant intervals over the entire genome (e.g., about 350 markers with an average spacing of 10 cM). The results of the scan are used to identify candidate chromosomal regions that are shared at rates greater than 50% (the rate expected for randomly selected markers for full siblings). (The two studies of juvenile onset idiopathic epilepsy and plasma lipids and apolipoprotein levels relevant to coronary artery disease, referred to earlier, were also examples of genome scans; however, they did not employ the affected sibling design.) Recently, much larger numbers of genetic probes have been used, trios rather than pairs have been studied, and highly discordant rather than concordant pairs of relatives have been employed. This approach offers the potential of identifying genes previously unsuspected of having an influence on the phenotype of interest. Genome scans are complicated by several factors, including these: (1) instead of a single test for linkage, one must conduct multiple tests across the entire genome; and (2) genetic heterogeneity and misdiagnosis can seriously distort results.

Allelic association studies compare the frequency of a marker (e.g., a blood group) in two samples (e.g., an affected versus a control group). A classic association is between the blood group O and duodenal ulcer. Unless the marker locus and the actual gene responsible for the disorder are very tightly linked, results from properly conducted association studies will be negative. Of course, association studies can be used to test candidate genes that might themselves be responsible for the disorder. A key

limitation of association studies is that spurious association can occur due to population stratification; that is, the samples studied might come from a population that contains groups with differing frequencies of the allele under study. If these groups differ for any reason in occurrence of the disorder, then a spurious association of allele and disorder will result. Some association studies have been conducted with genetic probes that systematically cover large expanses of the genome, thus allowing a search for association with so-called quantitative trait loci (QTLs). QTLs are genetic regions responsible for small but discernible quantitative effects on a polygenically based phenotype. The smallest QTL effect that can be detected by association with a marker depends on the distance from the marker to the QTL, the size of population, and the heritability of the trait or disorder. In plant genetics, QTLs accounting for as little as 0.3% of the phenotypic variance have been reported, as reviewed by Tanksley (1993).

At first blush, it would seem straightforward to compare extreme groups (e.g., highly inhibited versus uninhibited children) for different frequencies of a candidate gene or QTL. However, high levels of behavioral inhibition in one subset of individuals might have different roots from similarly high levels in another subset. This trait heterogeneity problem haunts current attempts to link behavior with specific genes. There are other practical difficulties in this genre of research. For instance, individuals at the extreme of the distribution might possess several alleles promoting higher trait values. The effect of any one allele may be more difficult to discern against this "high value" genetic background than in more typical genetic backgrounds.

In conceptualizing genes that have only small effects on the phenotype, it is important to realize that they might be related to major genes of large effect. That is, if a major gene leading to qualitative dysfunction is identified, other alleles at the same locus could affect more subtle quantitative variation. The allele that leads to qualitative dysfunction could code for an inactive protein whereas a different allelic variant of the same gene might lead to an active but physiologically nonoptimal protein.

One of the best known examples of an allelic association with an emotion-related trait in humans is a report that a polymorphism in a promoter of the serotonin transporter gene on chromosome 17q accounts for 3–4% of the variance in self-reported anxiety proneness. This finding held in two samples totaling 505 individuals, and the allele in question also differentiated affected from unaffected siblings (Lesch et al., 1996). Although enthusiasm for initial reports such as this one must be tempered for the reasons we have already discussed, some credence must be accorded this finding because of its consonance with known mechanisms of action of anti-anxiety drugs. Serotonin is, of course, involved in neurotransmission in regions of the limbic system and cortex associated with anxious behavior, and some antidepressant and anti-anxiety drugs inhibit uptake of serotonin. The serotonin transporter is a protein that helps "fine-tune" this neurotransmission. The allele of the serotonin transporter promoter that leads to decreased transporter activity—at least in lymphoblast cell lines—occurred at a high frequency, 43%, in the samples studied (Lesch et al., 1996). Persons with this allele would be expected to show increased serotonergic transmission, and they report higher neuroticism scores (but are not different on the other factors of the Big Five personality traits). Lesch et al. (1996) caution that their results, from a normal sample, may not generalize as a cause of clinically significant levels of anxiety in patients. There have been both replications and failures to replicate these results. Another issue is the nonspecificity of findings from candidate gene studies where the gene affects functioning in key pathways. For instance, a single poster session at the 1999 Society for Psychiatric Genetics conference included papers reporting association of serotonin receptor or transporter alleles (or their promoters) with these disorders or traits: schizophrenia, suicidal behavior, asocial personality traits in affective disorders, panic disorder, suicidal ideation in schizophrenia, negative symptoms in schizophrenia, seasonal affective disorders, unipolar affective disorder, antisocial personality and alcoholism, ADHD, obsessive-compulsive disorder, premenstrual dysphoric disorder, anorexia nervosa and bulimia, Tourette's syndrome and alcohol dependence, and pervasive developmental disorder (Seventh World Congress of Psychiatric Genetics, 1999). Such a lack of specificity is perhaps not surprising for genes mediating neurotransmitter function in circuitry central to affective processing. Population stratification is also a concern in these studies because Gelernter, Cubells, Kidd, Pakstis, and Kidd (1999) showed that the frequency of the serotonin transporter promoter allele under study in this research varies widely (from .29 to .89) in eight geographically distinct ethnic groups.

In addition to alleles coding to genes related to serotonin function, numerous studies have examined the association of emotion-related traits and disorders with genes for dopamine receptors and transporters. For instance, two studies in 1996 showed an association of the personality trait of novelty-seeking with the 7 repeat allele of the dopamine receptor D4 (DRD4) gene (Ebstein, Novick, Umansky, Priel, & Osher, 1996; Benjamin et al., 1996). However, a meta-analysis that includes eight subsequent studies, with varying characteristics, casts doubt on the validity or at least the generalizability of the association (Wahlsten, 1999). Several recent studies break new ground, in various ways. For instance, Lakatos, Toth, Nemoda, Ney, Sasvari-Szekely, and Gervai (2000) demonstrated an association of a DRD4 III allele with attachment disorganization in infants. Attachment disorganization is measured in a laboratory episode involving separations

and reunions with the primary caregiver; the disorganized behavioral pattern is associated with childhood behavioral problems. Thus, this study uses structured behavioral observations rather than questionnaire reports of behavior, and it taps a domain often ascribed to caregiving deficiencies. The same DRD4 receptor allele has been associated with attention deficit hyperactivity disorder (ADHD) in four studies and not confirmed in one (see Swanson, Flodman, et al., 2000, for review). The study that breaks new methodological ground uses this association as the basis for dividing severely affected ADHD children into subtypes based on presence of the specific DRD4 allele that appears to be a susceptibility gene (Swanson, Oosterlaan, et al., 2000). Then, those subjects (41%) who had at least one copy of the target allele were compared with subjects who had the allele absent on three neuropsychological tests intended to probe the functioning of three cortical regions implicated in attentional deficits in ADHD (anterior cingulate, right dorsolateral prefrontal, and posterior parietal). Compared with non-ADHD controls, the entire ADHD group showed slow and inefficient processing. However, the ADHD subgroup characterized by presence of the susceptibility allele (the 7-repeat allele of the DRD4-III gene) showed no attentional deficits, leading the authors to speculate that the presence of this allele marked cases of ADHD with an affective phenotype predisposing to the development of ADHD. Studies such as these two clearly require replication and tests of generalization, but they perhaps illustrate a trend away from "cheap phenotyping," as well as application to infants and children. One challenge for behavioral scientists is to take a role in such studies so that the assessment of the emotion-related phenotype incorporates developmental concerns and any available endophenotypic indicators. In other words, the behavioral side of the investigation should be at least as sophisticated as the genetic side.

## Animal Studies of the Genetics of Emotion-Related Behavior: A Sampler Introduction

The field of animal behavioral genetics has evolved rapidly and its synergism with human research is beginning to be realized for behavioral phenotypes. During what we now consider the "classical" period of animal research, researchers were able to selectively breed mice for behavioral characteristics, and to demonstrate differences in behavior between previously inbred strains raised under controlled conditions. Some of the very earliest rodent genetic research concerned emotionality (Hall, 1934), and this was followed by work on emotionality in other species, such as dogs (Murphree, Angel, DeLuca, & Newton, 1977). Recently, systematic approaches to using the mouse as a model for analysis of molecular pathways underlying psychiatric disorders, as well as relevant endophenotypes (e.g., anxiety, sensorimotor gating), have been pursued empirically (see Tarantino & Bucan, 2000, for review).

Two broad concepts that are key to understanding this work are forward and reverse genetics. "Reverse genetics" refers to moving from the identification of a gene to the phenotype, whereas "forward genetics" begins with the phenotype and moves to identify an unknown gene. Efficient reverse genetics requires the ability to selectively modify genes (as in transgenic "knockout," or "null mutant" preparations), and forward genetics requires efficient mutagenesis—several hundred germline mutations per mouse can be induced—and a system for isolating variants in the behavior of interest (e.g., anxious behavior). The availability of detailed genetic maps allows much quicker localization and identification of mutated genes in the forward genetics approach. Thus, in the mouse, the forward and reverse genetics approaches allow the study of both unknown and known genes affecting behavior (Takahashi, Pinto, & Vitaterna, 1994).

Mouse models have recently become much more feasible with the development of "knockout genetics" (Capecchi, 1994), techniques that allow for the inactivation, or knockout, of specific genes, as well as for changes in the efficiency of genes, short of complete inactivation. For example, separate mouse lines can be prepared that are deficient in each of the dopamine receptors, and the phenotypic effects of each deficiency can then be studied. Moreover, conditional knockout lines can be prepared to study developmental implications. That is, the gene's function can be knocked out after a period of normal expression. Conditional knockouts are useful when a gene has both developmental (e.g., neurotropic) and physiological functions.

Figure 16.1 depicts one of several ways in which human and mouse genetic analytic strategies can interact. In this diagram, the ultimate goal is viewed as the ability to conduct functional studies of the effects of a candidate gene in the mouse. Such studies would inform our understanding of the pathophysiology of the phenotype in humans. The diagram also indicates steps to increase the probability that the mouse and human genes being studied are homologous. In the figure, we assume that the phenotype is a complex one, with multiple genes involved. The upper part of the figure shows lines of human research, beginning with studies that establish the phenotype as heritable and proceeding to genome screens or other types of linkage analysis that establish chromosomal regions likely to contain susceptibility genes. Once specific genes have been identified within these regions, association studies in humans would be in order. At the same time, comparative mapping of human and mouse genes, which is becoming more routine with near-completion of genome-wide sequencing efforts in both species, allows functional studies of the candidate gene in mice, which was the goal of the work.

This line of research could also begin with the steps depicted in the lower section of Figure 16.1. In this case, a model phenotype is identified in a cross between two inbred strains of mice. This preparation allows genetic mapping to identify quantitative trait loci (QTLs) using microsatellite markers. Multiple genetic strategies can be employed to move from wider to narrower QTL intervals and ultimately to one, or a few, candidate genes. These strategies include genetic crosses, expressed sequence array approaches, and bioinformatic approaches (Belknap et al., 2001). As Belknap et al. (2001) point out, it has recently become possible to generate a list of strain differences (between two of the inbred strains commonly used in these crosses) in expression levels of 7,169 genes expressed in hippocampus (Sandberg et al., 2000). Such pre-existing information can greatly accelerate the process of isolating genes underlying QTLs. Obviously, genes isolated from mice can be checked for homologues in humans, leading to association studies in humans based solely on mouse research.

In actual practice, research is not as linear as Figure 16.1 might appear to suggest. For a given phenotype, research at many levels of the diagram might be ongoing simultaneously. Also, analysis of complex phenotypes is likely to involve some research on related endophenotypes or on subtypes of the phenotype, and uneven genetic information about different endophenotypes and subtypes is likely. Finally, it should be emphasized that Figure 16.1 only shows a subset of the genetic approaches that are possible in bringing mouse and human genetic approaches to bear on the same phenotype. For instance, genome-wide mutagenesis approaches (Nadeau & Frankel, 2000) are not considered.

## Overview of Research on Emotion-Related Phenotypes

In a review of only a subset of papers on targeted mutations (knockouts) published in 1998 and 1999, Tarantino and Bucan (2000) listed 23 reports of alterations in anxiety-related phenotypes that implicated 17 different genes. Of these, three genes showed replicated effects across 3–4 studies: (1) knockout of the corticotropin-releasing hormone (CRH) receptor 1 gene led to reduced anxiety-related behavior; (2) knockout of the serotonin 5-HT1A receptor led to elevated anxiety-related behavior; and (3) knockout of the serotonin 5-HT1B receptor was associated with less anxiety. The measures of anxiety (fear and stress reactivity) used in this rapidly expanding literature, unconditioned behavior in mazes and in light/dark emergence paradigms, depend on pitting rodents' exploratory drive against their wariness of lighted or open spaces. The findings related to CRH receptor 1 knockouts (Contarino et al., 1999; Smith et al., 1998; Timpl et al., 1998) are consistent with the primate findings reviewed

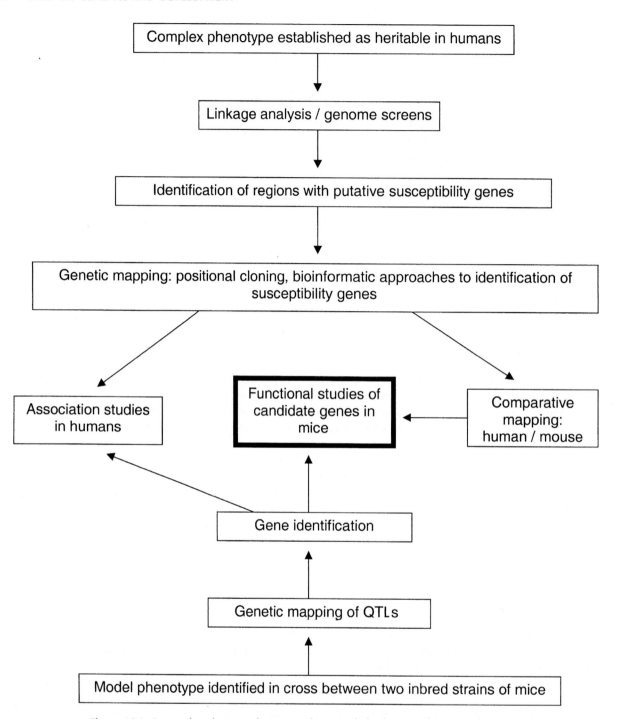

Figure 16.1 Connections between human and mouse behavior-genetic approaches.

by Davidson, Pizzagalli, Nitschke, and Kalin (chapter 2, this volume) on the association of higher cortisol levels with fearful temperament. An exception to the study of unconditioned fear responses in this literature is the study of contextual fear conditioning in mice, where a neutral stimulus is paired with an aversive stimulus. Using such approaches, chromosomal regions containing likely QTLs have been identified (Caldarone et al., 1997; Wehner et al., 1997).

Despite the momentum of this literature, a number of cautions pertain to these lines of research with rodents. First, putative anxiety measures from different experimental paradigms tend to be statistically independent (Belzung & LePape, 1994). Of even more concern, a methodological study showed different profiles of six behaviors in three labs for the same mouse strain. The labs were attempting to hold constant both environmental variables and the experimental procedures used to measure the behaviors, and they employed eight strains (Crabbe, Wahlsten, & Dudek, 1999). Thus, there is danger of lab-specific behavioral findings in this field.

Much relevant research in this area does not explicitly involve behavior at all but rather brain systems known from other research to affect behavior. To provide just one example, Janowsky et al. (2001) demonstrated significant strain differences in neostriatal dopamine transporter (DAT) density. Then, using 1,390 genetic markers, these investigators conducted a genome scan for QTLs that influenced the expression of the dopamine transporter. A QTL that accounted for slightly more than 50% of the genetic variance in DAT binding site density was identified on mouse chromosome 19. This unusually strong effect indicates the presence of a gene, yet unidentified, that modulates the expression of DAT (not the DAT gene itself). Because the homologous areas on the human chromosome to this region of the mouse genome are known, this finding, and others like it, can be exploited in the search for genetic bases of human behaviors known to be influenced by dopamine activity, especially when relevant human endophenotypes have been identified.

A reviewer of the mouse genetics literature is struck by how little research on emotionality exists outside the realm of anxiety, fear, and exploration and of aggression. The research of Insel and colleagues (chapter 53, this volume) illustrates how social behavior and pair bonding, in the prairie vole, can also be explicated with a genetic approach. Other lines of genetic research extend the research on emotionality to maternal-infant interactions (e.g., Brown, Ye, Bronson, Dikkes, & Greenberg, 1996; Brunner, Buhot, Hen, & Hofer, 1999).

## Summary and Prospects for Integration

Quantitative genetic research (twin, family, and adoption studies) has been undertaken increasingly over the past two decades, and projects are currently being extended longitudinally. Heritability seldom rises above a figure of about 60% of the observed variance. In longitudinal analyses, much of the stability—in some cases practically all the stability—of these traits is due to the stability of genetic influences rather than stability of environmental factors. Both genes and environments seem to influence change in most emotion-related traits. Adoption and stepfamily evidence still need to be integrated more fully with the more widely available twin results. A continuing need in quantitative genetic studies is for assessment other than self- or parental-report of emotion-related phenotypes. Some laboratory-based assessment of temperament/emotionality has occurred in twin and adoption studies, but much more is needed. Classic twin and family studies need to continue the present trend of becoming highly multivariate, incorporating both dimensional (e.g., temperament trait) and categorical (e.g., diagnosis) variables, and multiple, theoretically relevant occasions of study. Synthetic data analytic approaches exist for measuring specific genes within such classic quantitative designs (Fulker, Cherny, Sham, & Hewitt, 1999).

Another need in this area is integration of assessment of experiential processes into the twin and adoption studies to "actualize" the environmental component of the observed variation. On the social side of the environment, measures of specific interactional processes need to be refined and incorporated into studies. Environmental assessment needs to extend into the realm of biological measures as well. Identified environmental factors should be quantified (e.g., in terms of increases in relative risk) and compared with other known risk factors to evaluate their importance.

The genetic component of the variation is "actualized" by detecting specific genes associated with the trait. Molecular genetic studies have recently been initiated in this area, mostly as association studies and mostly for disorders. There is a question of whether investigation will more profitably be gene-centered (wherein the behavioral correlates of identified genes are sought) or behavior-centered (wherein the investigator begins with an emotion-related phenotype and searches for associated genetic markers). Progress in this area has been accelerated by the Human Genome Project, and in particular by mapping of genes that are expressed in the human brain. These efforts promise a new synergism with animal research, where gene function in the neurophysiological sense is more easily investigated.

Finally, genetic research on emotional development is one of the "missing links" in psychiatric epidemiology. Psychiatric epidemiology has yielded quite clear evidence of genetic input to common adult disorders such as schizophrenia, bipolar affective disorder, unipolar depression, and antisocial personality disorder. The genetics of rarer disorders, including some with relatively early onset, such as Tourette's syndrome, has also been clarified. However, the genetics of common childhood disorders such as attention deficit hyperactivity disorder (ADHD), childhood depression, and early conduct disorder are more poorly understood. Part of the reason is perhaps that diagnostic criteria for these childhood disorders are not fully satisfying. One route to addressing the issue—and moving the issue temporarily from clinical to basic behavioral research—is to study the genetics of poor impulse control, activity level, anger and emotional aggressiveness, inhibition, and other emotional/temperamental traits that are putative components of the childhood disorders in at-risk populations. The statistical methodology for such studies has been developed, but there are few extant data.

Perhaps the most general recipe for progress in the field is interdisciplinary research. The effect sizes in the prediction of most emotion-related behavior are modest, thus allowing ample room for multiple predictors from different domains. *Different* explanatory factors are not always *competing* explanatory factors. It should be clear that genetic methodology does not *fully* elucidate psychopathology. As in most areas of science, fuller understanding requires the joint perspectives of several methodologies, including epidemiology, neuroscience, and various approaches to investigating the effects of experience. Enthusiasm for reductionistic explanations based on genetics for the origins of the neural underpinnings of emotion should not overshadow the appreciation of developmental plasticity in the manifestation of emotional behavior.

## REFERENCES

Almasy, L., & Blangero, J. (2001). Endophenotypes as quantitative risk factors for psychiatric disease: Rationale and study design. *American Journal of Medical Genetics (Neuropsychiatric Genetics), 105,* 42–44.

Amos-Landgraf, J. M., Ji, Y., Gottlieb, W., Depinet, T., Wandstrat, A. E., Cassidy, S. B., Driscoll, D. J., Rogan, P. K., Schwartz, S., & Nicholls, R. D. (1999). Chromosome breakage in the Prader-Willi and Angelman syndromes involves recombination between large, transcribed repeats at proximal and distal breakpoints. *American Journal of Human Genetics, 65,* 370–386.

Bakshi, V. P., & Kalin, N. H. (2000). Corticotropin-releasing hormone and animal models of anxiety: Gene-environment interactions. *Society of Biological Psychiatry, 48,* 1175–1198.

Bayley, N. (1969). *Manual for the Bayley Scales of Infant Development.* New York: Psychological Corporation.

Belknap, J. K., Hitzemann, R., Crabbe, J. C., Phillips, T. J., Buck, K. J., & Williams, R. W. (2001). QTL analysis and genomewide mutagenesis in mice: Complementary genetic approaches to the dissection of complex traits. *Behavior Genetics, 31,* 5–15.

Belzung, C., & LePape, G. (1994). Comparison of different behavioral test situations used in psychopharmacology for measurement of anxiety. *Physiology & Behavior, 56,* 623–628.

Benjamin, L., Li, L., Patterson, C., Greenberg, B. D., Murphy, D. L., & Hamer, D. H. (1996). Population and familial association between the D4 dopamine receptor gene and measures of novelty seeking. *Nature Genetics, 12,* 81–84.

Braungart, J. M., Plomin, R., DeFries, J. C., & Fulker, D. W. (1992). Genetic influence on tester-rated infant temperament as assessed by Bayley's Infant Behavior Record: Nonadoptive and adoptive siblings and twins. *Developmental Psychology, 28,* 40–47.

Brown, J. R., Ye, H., Bronson, R. T., Dikkes, P., & Greenberg, M. E. (1996). A defect in nurturing in mice lacking the immediate early gene *fosB. Cell, 86,* 297–309.

Brunner, D., Buhot, M. C., Hen, R., & Hofer, M. (1999). Anxiety, motor activation and maternal-infant interactions in 5HT1B knockout mice. *Behavioral Neuroscience, 113,* 587–601.

Buss, D. M. (1993). Strategic individual differences: The evolutionary psychology of selection, evocation, and manipulation. In T. J. Bouchard, Jr. & P. Propping (Eds.), *Twins as a tool of behavior genetics* (pp. 121–138). Chichester, UK: John Wiley.

Caldarone, B., Saavedra, C., Tartaglia, K., Wehner, J. M., Dudek, B. C., & Flaherty, L. (1997). Quantitative trait loci analysis affecting contextual conditioning in mice. *Nature Genetics, 17,* 335–338.

Capecchi, M. R. (1994). Targeted gene replacement. *Scientific American, 270,* 52–59.

Carey, G. (1988). Inference about genetic correlations. *Behavior Genetics, 18,* 329–338.

Cherny, S. S., Fulker, D. W., Corley, R. P., Plomin, R., & DeFries, J. C. (1994). Continuity and change in infant shyness from 14 to 20 months. *Behavior Genetics, 24,* 365–379.

Christian, S. L., Robinson, W. P., Huang, B., et al. (1995). Molecular characterisation of two proximal deletion breakpoint regions in both Prader Willi and Angelman syndrome patients. *American Journal of Human Genetics, 46,* 857–873.

Cohen, D. J., Dibble, E., & Graw, J. M. (1977). Fathers' and mothers' perceptions of children's personality. *Archives of General Psychiatry, 34,* 480–487.

Contarino, A., Dellu, F., Koob, G. F., Smith, G. W., Lee, K. F., Vale, W., & Gold, L. H. (1999). Reduced anxiety-like and cognitive performance in mice lacking the corticotrophin-releasing factor receptor 1. *Brain Research, 835,* 1–9.

Crabbe, J. C., Wahlsten, D., & Dudek, B. C. (1999). Genetics of mouse behavior: Interactions with laboratory environment. *Science, 284,* 1670–1672.

Crawley, J. N. (2000). *What's wrong with my mouse? Behavioral phenotyping of transgenic and knockout mice.* New York: Wiley-Liss.

Deater-Deckard, K., & O'Connor, T. G. (2000). Parent-child mutuality in early childhood: Two behavioral genetic studies. *Developmental Psychology, 36,* 561–570.

Deater-Deckard, K., Pike, A., Petrill, S. A., Cutting, A. L., Hughes, C., & O'Connor, T. G. (2001). Nonshared environmental processes in social-emotional development: an observational study of identical twin differences in the preschool period. *Developmental Science, 4,* F1–F6.

DiLalla, L. F., Kagan, J., & Reznick, J. S. (1994). Genetic etiology of behavioral inhibition among 2-year-old children. *Infant Behavior and Development, 17,* 405–412.

Durner, M., Keddache, M. A., Tomasini, L., Shinnar, S., Resor, S. R., Cohen, J., Harden, C., Moshe, S., Yohai, D., Klotz, I., Dicker, E., & Greenberg, D. A. (2001). Genome scan of idiopathic generalized epilepsy: Evidence for major susceptibility gene and modifying genes influencing the seizure type. *Annals of Neurology, 49,* 328–335.

Eaton, W. O., McKeen, N. A., & Lam, C. S. (1988). Instrumented motor activity measurement of the young infant in the home: Validity and reliability. *Infant Behavior and Development, 11,* 375–378.

Ebstein, R. P., Novick, O., Umansky, R., Priel, B., & Osher, Y. (1996). Dopamine D4 receptor (D4DR) exon III polymorphism associated with the human personality trait of Novelty Seeking. *Nature Genetics, 12,* 78–80.

Emde, R. N., & Hewitt, J. K. (Eds.). (2001). *The transition from infancy to early childhood: Genetic and environmental influences in the MacArthur Longitudinal Twin Study.* New York: Oxford University Press.

Falconer, D. S. (1989). *Introduction to quantitative genetics* (3rd ed.). New York: Longman.

Fox, N. A. (1994). The development of emotion regulation: Biological and behavioral considerations. *Monographs of the Society for Research in Child Development 59,* (2–3, Serial No. 240).

Fulker, D. W., Cherny, S. S., Sham, P. C., & Hewitt, J. K. (1999). Combined linkage and association sib-pair analysis for quantitative traits. *American Journal of Human Genetics, 64,* 259–267.

Gelernter, J., Cubells, J. F., Kidd, J. R., Pakstis, A. J., & Kidd, K. K. (1999). Population studies of polymorphisms of the serotonin transporter protein gene. *American Journal of Medical Genetics, 88,* 61–66.

Gold, L. H. (1999). Hierarchical strategy for phenotypic analysis in mice. *Psychopharmacology, 147,* 2–4.

Goldsmith, H. H. (1983). Genetic influences on personality from infancy to adulthood. *Child Development, 54,* 331–355.

Goldsmith, H. H. (1986). Heritability of temperament: Cautions and some empirical evidence. In G. A. Kohnstamm (Ed.), *Temperament discussed: Temperament and development in infancy and childhood* (pp. 83–96). Lisse, The Netherlands: Swets & Zeitlinger.

Goldsmith, H. H. (1989). Behavior-genetic approaches to temperament. In G. A. Kohnstamm, J. E. Bates & M. K. Rothbart (Eds.), *Temperament in childhood* (pp. 111–132). Chichester, UK: John Wiley.

Goldsmith, H. H. (1993). Temperament: Variability in developing emotion systems. In M. Lewis & J. M. Haviland (Eds.), *Handbook of emotions* (pp. 353–364). New York: Guilford Press.

Goldsmith, H. H. (1996). Studying temperament via construction of the Toddler Behavior Assessment Questionnaire. *Child Development, 67,* 218–235.

Goldsmith, H. H., Buss, K. A., & Lemery, K. S. (1997). Toddler and childhood temperament: Expanded content, stronger genetic evidence, new evidence for the importance of environment. *Developmental Psychology, 33,* 891–905.

Goldsmith, H. H., & Campos, J. J. (1986). Fundamental issues in the study of early temperament: The Denver Twin Temperament Study. In M. E. Lamb, A. L. Brown, & B. Rogoff (Eds.), *Advances in developmental psychology* (Vol. 4, pp. 231–283). Hillsdale, NJ: Lawrence Erlbaum.

Goldsmith, H. H., & Gottesman, I. I. (1981). Origins of variation in behavioral style: A longitudinal study of temperament in young infants. *Child Development, 52,* 91–103.

Goldsmith, H. H., & Lemery, K. S. (2000). Linking temperamental fearfulness and anxiety symptoms: A behavior-genetic perspective. *Biological Psychiatry, 48,* 1199–1209.

Goldsmith, H. H., Lemery, K. S., Buss, K. A., & Campos, J. J. (1999). Genetic analyses of focal aspects of infant temperament. *Developmental Psychology, 35,* 972–985.

Goldsmith, H. H., & Rieser-Danner, L. (1990). Assessing early temperament. In C. R. Reynolds & R. Kamphaus (Eds.), *Handbook of psychological and educational assessment of children. Vol. 2: Personality, behavior, and context* (pp. 345–378). New York: Guilford Press.

Gottesman, I. I. (1991). *Schizophrenia genesis: Origins of madness.* New York: Freeman.

Gottesman, I. I., & Goldsmith, H. H. (1994). Developmental psychopathology of antisocial behavior: Inserting genes into its ontogenesis and epigenesis. In C. Nelson (Ed.), *Threats to optimal development: Integrating biological, social, and psychological risk factors. Vol. 27: Minnesota symposium on child development* (pp. 69–104). Hillsdale, NJ: Lawrence Erlbaum.

Gottesman, I. I., & Shields, J. (1972). *Schizophrenia and genetics: A twin study vantage point.* New York: Academic Press.

Greenberg, D. A., Durner, M., Keddache, M., Shinnar, S., Resor, S. R., Moshe, S. L., Rosenbaum, D., Cohen, J., Harden, C., Kang, H., Wallace, S., Luciano, D., Ballaban-Gil, K., Tomasini, L., Zhou, G., Klotz, I., & Dicker, E. (2000). Reproducibility and complications in gene searches: Linkage on chromosome 6, heterogeneity, association, and maternal inheritance in juvenile myoclonic epilepsy. *American Journal of Human Genetics, 66,* 508–516.

Hall, C. S. (1934). Emotional behavior in the rat. I. Defaecation and urination as measures of individual differences in emotionality. *Journal of Comparative Psychology, 18,* 385–403.

Hanel, M. I., & Wevrick, R. (2001). The role of genomic imprinting in human developmental disorders: Lessons from Prader-Willi syndrome. *Clinical Genetics, 59,* 159–164.

Hinde, R. A. (1987). *Individuals, relationships, and cultures.* Cambridge, England: Cambridge University Press.

Hoffman, L. W. (1991). The influence of the family environment on personality: Accounting for sibling differences. *Psychological Bulletin, 110,* 187–203.

Huntington's Disease Collaborative Research Group. (1993). A novel gene containing a trinucleotide repeat that is expanded and unstable on Huntington's disease chromosomes. *Cell, 72,* 971–983.

Janowsky, A., Mah, C., Johnson, R. A., Cunningham, C. L., Phillips, T. J., Crabbe, J. C., Eshleman, A. J., & Belknap, J. K. (2001). Mapping genes that regulate density of dopamine transporters and correlated behaviors in recombinant inbred mice. *Journal of Pharmacological and Experimental Therapeutics, 298,* 634–643.

John, B., & Lewis, K. R. (1966). Chromosome variability and geographic distribution in insects. *Science, 152,* 711–721.

Kagan, J., Reznick, J. S., Clarke, C., Snidman, N., & Garcia Coll, C. (1984). Behavioral inhibition to the unfamiliar. *Child Development, 55,* 2212–2225.

Kagan, J., Reznick, J. S., & Gibbons, J. (1989). Inhibited and uninhibited types of children. *Child Development, 60,* 838–845.

Kendler, K. S., Eaves, L. J., Walters, E. E., Neale, M. C., Heath, A. C., & Kessler, R. C. (1996). The identification and validation of distinct depressive syndromes in a population-based sample of female twins. *Archives of General Psychiatry, 53,* 391–399.

Keverne, E. B., Fundele, R., Narasimha, M., Barton, S. C., & Surani, M. A. (1996). Genomic imprinting and the differential roles of parental genomes in brain development. *Developmental Brain Research, 92,* 91–100.

Keverne, E. B., Martel, F. L., & Nevison, C. M. (1996). Primate brain evolution: Genetic and functional considerations. *Proceedings of the Royal Society London B, 262,* 689–696.

Klos, K. L., Kardia, S. L. R., Ferrell, R. E., Turner, S. T., Boerwinkle, E., & Sing, C. F. (2001). Genome-wide linkage analysis reveals evidence of multiple regions that influence variation in plasma lipid and apolipoprotein levels associated with risk of coronary heart disease.

*Arteriosclerosis, Thrombosis, and Vascular Biology, 21,* 971–978.

Kochanska, G. (1997). Mutually responsive orientation between mothers and their young children: Implications for early socialization. *Child Development, 68,* 94–112.

Lakatos, K., Toth, I., Nemoda, Z., Ney, K., Sasvari-Szekely, M., & Gervai, J. (2000). A genetic basis for attachment disorganization in infants. *Molecular Psychiatry, 5,* 633–637.

Lander, E. S., & Schork, N. J. (1994). Genetic dissection of complex traits. *Science, 265,* 2037–2048.

LeBoyer, M., Bellivier, F., Nosten-Bertrand, M., Jouvent, R., Pauls, D., & Mallet, J. (1998). Psychiatric genetics: Search for phenotypes. *Trends in Neuroscience, 21,* 102–105.

Lemery, K. S. (1999). *Exploring the etiology of the relationship between temperament and behavior problems in children.* Unpublished doctoral dissertation, University of Wisconsin-Madison.

Lemery, K. S., & Goldsmith, H. H. (in press). Genetic and environmental influences on preschool sibling cooperation and conflict: Associations with difficult temperament and parenting style. *Marriage and Family Review.*

Lesch, K.-P., Bengel, D., Heils, A., Sabol, S. Z., Greenberg, B. D., Petri, S., Benjamin, J., Muller, C. R., Hamer, D. H., & Murphy, D. L. (1996). Association of anxiety-related traits with a polymorphism in the serotonin transporter gene regulatory region. *Science, 274,* 1527–1531.

Leve, L. D., Winebarger, A. A., Fagot, B. I., Reid, J. B., & Goldsmith, H. H. (1998). Environmental and genetic variance in children's observed and reported maladaptive behavior. *Child Development, 69,* 1286–1298.

Loehlin, J. C. (1992). *Genes and environment in personality development.* Newbury Park, CA: Sage Publications.

Lyons, M. J., True, W. R., Eisen, S. A., Goldberg, J., Meyer, J. M., Faraone, S. V., Eaves, L. J., & Tsuang, M. T. (1995). Differential heritability of adult and juvenile antisocial traits. *Archives of General Psychiatry, 52,* 906–915.

Lytton, H. (1980). *Parent-child interaction: The socialization process observed in twin and singleton families.* New York: Plenum Press.

Maestrini, E., Paul, A., Monaco, A. P., & Bailey, A. (2000). Identifying autism susceptibility genes. *Neuron, 28,* 19–24.

Mangelsdorf, S., Diener, M., McHale, J., & Pilolla, L. (1993, June). *Temperament and attachment: Individual differences in emotionality and infant-caregiver attachment.* Paper presented at the American Psychological Society meetings, Chicago, IL.

Manke, B., Saudino, K. J., & Grant, J. D. (2001). Extremes analysis of observed temperament dimensions. In R. N. Emde & J. K. Hewitt (Eds.), *Infancy to early childhood: Genetic and environmental influences on developmental change* (pp. 52–72). New York: Oxford University Press.

Markow, T. A., & Gottesman, I. I. (1989). Dematoglyphic fluctuating asymmetry in psychotic twins. *Psychiatric Research, 29,* 37–43.

Markow, T. A., & Gottesman, I. I. (1993). Behavioral phenodeviance: A Lerneresque conjecture. *Genetica, 89,* 297–305.

Matheny, A. P. (1980). Bayley's Infant Behavior Record: Behavioral components and twin analysis. *Child Development, 51,* 1157–1167.

Matheny, A. P. (1987). Developmental research on twins' temperament. *Acta Geneticae Medicae et Gemellologiae, 36,* 135–143.

Matheny, A. P. (1990a). Children's behavioral inhibition over age and across situations: Genetic similarity for a trait during change. *Journal of Personality, 57,* 215–235.

Matheny, A. P. (1990b). Developmental behavior genetics: Contributions from the Louisville Twin Study. In M. E. Hahn, J. K. Hewitt, N. D. Henderson, & R. H. Denno (Eds.), *Developmental behavior genetics: Neural, biometrical, and evolutionary approaches* (pp. 25–39). New York: Oxford University Press.

McArdle, J. J., & Goldsmith, H. H. (1990). Alternative common factor models for multivariate biometric analyses. *Behavior Genetics, 20,* 569–608.

McGuffin, P., Owen, M. J., O'Donovan, M. C., Thapar, A., & Gottesman, I. I. (1994). *Seminars in psychiatric genetics.* London: Royal College of Psychiatrists.

Morton, N. E. (1992). The future of genetic epidemiology. *Annals of Medicine, 24,* 557–562.

Morton, N. E. (1993). Genetic epidemiology. *Annual Review of Genetics, 27,* 523–538.

Murphree, O. D., Angel, C., DeLuca, D. C., & Newton, J. E. (1977). Longitudinal studies of genetically nervous dogs. *Biological Psychiatry, 12,* 573–576.

Nadeau, J. H., & Frankel, W. N. (2000). The roads from phenotypic variation to gene discovery: Mutagenesis versus QTLs. *Nature Genetics, 25,* 381–384.

Neale, M. C., & Cardon, L. R. (1992). *Methodology for genetic studies of twins and families.* Dordrecht, The Netherlands: Kluwer.

Nicholls, R. D. (1993). Genomic imprinting and candidate syndromes. *Current Opinion in Genetics and Development, 3,* 445–456.

Ott, J. (1991). *Analysis of human genetic linkage.* Baltimore, MD: Johns Hopkins University Press.

Plomin, R., & Daniels, D. (1984). The interaction between temperament and environment: Methodological considerations. *Merrill Palmer Quarterly, 30,* 149–162.

Plomin, R., & Daniels, D. (1987). Why are children in the same family so different from each other? *Behavioral and Brain Sciences, 10,* 1–16.

Plomin, R., DeFries, J. C., & Loehlin, J. C. (1977). Genotype-environment interaction and correlation in the analysis of human behavior. *Psychological Bulletin, 84,* 309–322.

Plomin, R., DeFries, J. C., McClearn, G. E., & Rutter, M. (1997). *Behavioral genetics.* New York: W. H. Freeman.

Plomin, R., Emde, R. N., Braungart, J. M., Campos, J., Corley, R., Fulker, D. W., Kagan, J., Reznick, J. S., Robinson, J., Zahn-Waxler, C., & DeFries, J. C. (1993). Genetic change and continuity from fourteen to twenty months: The MacArthur Longitudinal Twin Study. *Child Development, 64,* 1354–1376.

Plomin, R., Emde, R. N., Hewitt, J. K., Kagan, J., & DeFries, J. C. (2001). An experiment in collaborative science. In R. N. Emde & J. K. Hewitt (Eds.), *Infancy to childhood: Genetic and environmental influences on developmental change.* New York: Oxford University Press.

Plomin, R., & Rowe, D. C. (1979). Genetic and environmental etiology of social behavior in infancy. *Developmental Psychology, 15,* 62–72.

Reik, W., Dean, W., & Walter, J. (2001). Epigenetic reprogramming in mammalian development. *Science, 293,* 1089–1093.

Reik, W., & Walter, J. (1998). Imprinting mechanisms in

mammals. *Current Opinion in Genetics and Development, 8,* 154–164.

Reik, W., & Walter, J. (2001). Genomic imprinting: Parental influence on the genome. *Nature Review Genetics, 2,* 21–32.

Risch, N. (1990a). Linkage strategies for genetically complex traits. I. Multilocus models. *American Journal of Human Genetics, 46,* 222–228.

Risch, N. (1990b). Linkage strategies for genetically complex traits. II. The power of affected relative pairs. *American Journal of Human Genetics, 46,* 229–241.

Risch, N. (1990c). Linkage strategies for genetically complex traits. III. The effect of marker polymorphism on analysis of affected relative pairs. *American Journal of Human Genetics, 46,* 242–253.

Robinson, J. L., Kagan, J., Reznick, J. S., & Corley, R. (1992). The heritability of inhibited and uninhibited behavior: A twin study. *Developmental Psychology, 28,* 1030–1037.

Rothbart, M. K. (1981). Measurement of temperament in infancy. *Child Development, 52,* 569–578.

Rothbart, M. K., & Ahadi, S. A. (1994). Temperament and the development of personality. *Journal of Abnormal Psychology, 103,* 55–66.

Rothbart, M. K., Ahadi, S. A., & Hershey, K. L. (1994). Temperament and social behavior in childhood. *Merrill-Palmer Quarterly, 40,* 21–39.

Ruff, H. A., & Rothbart, M. K. (1996). *Attention in early development: Themes and variations.* New York: Oxford University Press.

Rutter, M., Pickles, A., Murray, R., & Eaves, L. (2001). Testing hypotheses on specific environmental causal effects on behavior. *Psychological Bulletin, 127,* 291–324.

Sandberg, R., Yasuda, R., Pankratz, D. G., Carter, T. A., Del Rio, J. A., Wodicka, L., et al. (2000). Regional and strain-specific gene expression mapping in the adult mouse brain. *Proceedings of the National Academy of Sciences, USA, 97,* 11038–11043.

Saudino, K. J., & Eaton, W. O. (1991). Infant temperament and genetics: An objective twin study of motor activity level. *Child Development, 65,* 1167–1174.

Scarr, S., & McCartney, K. (1983). How people make their own environments: A theory of genotype–environment effects. *Child Development, 54,* 424–435.

Seventh World Congress of Psychiatric Genetics. (1999). Abstracts. *Molecular Psychiatry, 4* (Suppl. 1), S1–S134.

Sham, P. (1998). *Statistics in human genetics.* London: Arnold.

Sing, C. F., Zerba, K. E., & Reilly, S. L. (1994). Traversing the biological complexity in the hierarchy between genome and CAD endpoints in the population at large. *Clinical Genetics, 46,* 6–14.

Smith, G. W., Aubry, J. M., Dellu, F., Contarino, A., Bilezikjian, L. M., Gold, L. H., Chen, R., Marchuk, Y., Hauser, C., Bentley, C. A., et al. (1998). Corticotropin releasing factor receptor 1–deficient mice display decreased anxiety, impaired stress response and aberrant neuroendocrine development. *Neuroscience, 20,* 1092–1102.

Swanson, J. M., Flodman, P., Kennedy, J., Spence, M. A., Moyzis, R., Schuck, S., Murias, M., Moriarity, J., Barr, C., Smith, M., & Posner, M. (2000). Dopamine genes and ADHD. *Neuroscience and Biobehavioral Reviews, 24,* 21–25.

Swanson, J., Oosterlaan, J., et al. (2000). Attention deficit/hyperactivity disorder children with a 7-repeat allele of the dopamine receptor D4 gene have extreme behavior but normal performance on critical neuropsychological tests of attention. *Proceedings of the National Academy of Sciences, 97,* 4754–4759.

Takahashi, J. S., Pinto, L. H., & Vitaterna, M. H. (1995). Forward and reverse genetic approaches to behavior in the mouse. *Science, 6,* 1724–1733.

Tanksley, S. D. (1993). Mapping polygenes. *Annual Review of Genetics, 27,* 205–233.

Tarantino, L. M., & Bucan, M. (2000). Dissection of behavior and psychiatric disorders using the mouse as a model. *Human Molecular Genetics, 9,* 953–965.

Timpl, P., Spanagel, R., Sillaber, I., Kresse, A., Reul, J. M., Stalla, G. K., Blanquet, V., Steckler, T., Holsboer, F., & Wurst, W. (1998). Impaired stress response and reduced anxiety in mice lacking a functional corticotropin-releasing hormone receptor. *Nature Genetics, 19,* 162–166.

Turkheimer, E., & Waldron, M. C. (2000). Nonshared environment: A theoretical, methodological, and quantitative review. *Psychological Bulletin, 126,* 78–108.

Wahlsten, D. (1999). Single-gene influences on brain and behavior. *Annual Review of Psychology, 50,* 599–624.

Watson, S. J., & Akil, H. (1999). Gene chips and arrays revealed: A primer on their power and their uses. *Biological Psychiatry, 45,* 533–543.

Warren, S. L., Schmitz, S., & Emde, R. N. (1999). Behavioral genetic analyses of self-reported anxiety at seven years of age. *Journal of American Academy Child and Adolescent Psychiatry, 38,* 1403–1408.

Wehner, J. M., Radcliffe, R. A., Rosmann, S. T., Christensen, S. C., Rasmussen, D. L., Fulker, D. W., & Wiles, M. (1997). Quantitative trait locus analysis of contextual fear conditioning in mice. *Nature Genetics, 17,* 250–251.

Wilson, R. S., & Matheny, A. P. (1983). Assessment of temperament in infant twins. *Developmental Psychology, 19,* 172–183.

Yeo, R. A., & Gangestad, S. W. (1993). Developmental origins of variation in human hand preference. *Genetica, 89,* 281–296.

# 17

# BEHAVIORAL INHIBITION AS A TEMPERAMENTAL CATEGORY

Jerome Kagan

Historical changes in the sense meaning of the term *temperament* have been less dramatic than alterations in other important psychological concepts, such as emotion, memory, symptom, or perception. Most ancient and modern writers agreed that the human temperaments were combinations of psychological profiles (behaviors, thoughts, and emotions) and their presumed biological foundations, which, during this century, were assumed to be genetically mediated. A set of psychological features was not sufficient evidence to posit a temperamental disposition. Chronic shyness with strangers, for example, need not be due to a temperamental bias, because some shy adults could have acquired that trait during adolescence.

A combination of a psychological profile and its presumed biological foundation represents the ideal definition of a temperament. Combining behavior with biological measures is common in other domains. An individual born with the genes for compromised pancreatic function who has normal blood sugar levels is not diabetic. An adolescent born to two schizophrenic parents who displays one nondebilitating marker of this illness is not regarded as schizophrenic as long as he or she does not display any of the primary symptoms that define the category. However, the lack of insight into the biological contribution to temperament has meant that, at present, the psychological features compose the primary definition of temperament.

The definition of temperament offered here suggests the potential error in classifying a trait as temperamental simply because it is stable over long periods of time. Future research on the temperaments will gather biological data and, if possible, begin with observations of young children. As investigators discover sensitive biological markers for each of the temperamental types, they will be able to separate groups of children or adults who display similar behavioral phenotypes into those who probably do and probably do not possess the relevant temperaments. The research of Davidson (1994, 1995) and Fox, Schmidt, Calkins, Rubin, & Coplan (1996) on asymmetry of alpha power in frontal areas illustrates this point. These investigators suggest that greater activation in the right frontal area than in the left (that is, greater desynchronization of alpha frequencies on the right side) is a sensitive sign of a temperamental vulnerability to uncertainty and/or anxiety. As a result, scientists can gather the electroencephalograph (EEG) data on groups of anxious adults and parse these samples into distinct groups based on the presence or absence of right-hemisphere activation. This suggestion is not fanciful.

My laboratory has been following a large group of middle-class, Caucasian children who were evaluated initially at 4 months of age (see Kagan, 1994). Twenty percent of the infants, called high reactive, displayed high levels of motor activity and distress to a variety of unfamiliar stimuli; 40% of the sample, classified as low reactive, showed the complementary profile of minimal motor activity and distress. More children from the high-reactive group became shy and fearful in the second year, whereas most low reactives became relatively sociable and fearless. We gathered

320

EEG data on these children when they were 10 years old. As expected, significantly more children who had been high-rather than low-reactive infants showed right-hemisphere activation. However, a few low reactives who were bold as toddlers had become shy by 10 years of age; but these children did not display right-hemisphere activation, suggesting that their contemporary timidity was not a temperamental trait.

The definition of temperament as a moderately stable psychological profile under some genetic constraint that usually emerges during childhood is unduly permissive. Unusual musical and athletic ability are stable, have a genetic contribution, and emerge during childhood. However, most investigators do not regard these talents as temperamental because of the implicit understanding that specific affect states are a salient feature of a temperament. Indeed, Goldsmith and Campos (1990) proposed that, in infants, temperament refers to individual differences in the tendency to express the primary emotions. Musicians and athletes are not characterized by a restricted set of affective states.

Psychopathological categories are also excluded from the category of temperament, even though some are stable, under genetic control, and emerge during childhood. For example, most investigators do not place Williams syndrome in the temperament category, even though these patients have a specific emotional profile, due, in part, to a chromosomal anomaly, because Williams patients also display a special set of compromised cognitive abilities. Thus the sense meaning of *temperament* held by most contemporary scientists is a stable psychological profile, characteristic of only a proportion of the population, that has a biological foundation, that emerges during childhood, that is associated with particular affective states, and that is not a pathological category.

## The Measurement of Temperaments

The definition of temperament offered in the previous section is unlikely to provoke serious controversy. There is considerably more debate, however, on the number of temperaments, their referents, and whether some should be conceptualized as a continuum or as a category.

It is not possible at present to predict the number of temperaments that will be discovered. The first and principal reason for this agnostic claim is that the vast majority of studies, although not all, rely on questionnaires (or occasionally interviews) that require adults to describe their own emotions and behaviors or those of their children. This form of evidence, which Thomas and Chess (1977) used in their groundbreaking work, severely limits the number of temperaments. A person's verbal products, whether answers to interview questions or check marks on questionnaires, have special features that are not char-

acteristic of the phenomena that the sentences are intended to describe.

Osgood, Suci, and Tannenbaum (1957) demonstrated that people from different language communities use the evaluative contrast of good versus bad as the first dividing principle when categorizing people, objects, and events. Hence most individuals impose an evaluative construction on their behavior, as well as on the behavior of their children, that represents their representation of the ideal. Thus individuals who value sociability are likely to be threatened by extreme timidity and are apt to deny their own shyness, as well as shy behavior in their children. This evaluative frame colors verbal answers to all questions.

The second reason is that humans are sensitive to the logical consistency of a series of answers. A mother who says that her daughter is usually happy will resist acknowledging that her daughter occasionally feels sad, tense, or anxious. There is no such demand for consistency in a person's behavior, physiology, or stream-of-consciousness feelings.

Third, most English words and sentences refer to discrete categories of events; there are few words that describe blends. There is, for example, no word in English that describes the feeling generated when one hopes for good news about a hospitalized loved one but fears the worst, nor is there a term for the feeling provoked by learning that a misfortune has occurred to an enemy combined with guilt over the satisfaction the information produced. No language is rich enough to describe all the significant experiences that are within human competence.

Fourth, every sentence implicitly assumes a comparison. A parent who reads on a questionnaire, "Does your child like to go to parties?" unconsciously compares that preference with others. If one mother compares "going to parties" with an activity the child dislikes, whereas a second parent compares it with one that the child also prefers, the former is more likely to endorse the item than the latter, even though both children like parties to an equivalent degree. Parental descriptions of twins reveal that parents seriously distort their children's actual behavior by maximizing the similarity of identical twins and maximizing differences between fraternal twins. This fact led a set of researchers expert in behavioral genetics to conclude, "Twin studies employing maternal ratings probably overestimate heritability" (Saudino, McGuire, Reiss, Heatherington, & Plomin, 1993, p. 31).

Fifth, individuals differ in their understanding of the meanings of words. For example, the parents of nine-month-olds were asked to rate their infants on traits such as fearfulness, smiling, duration of attention, and activity level. Parental agreement was relatively low for all of these traits, but especially for activity level, because fathers interpreted high activity to mean a positive emotional mood, whereas the mothers of the same infants interpreted the same word as implying a tendency toward anger (Goldsmith & Campos, 1990). Individuals from different social class groups or cultural backgrounds often extract different meanings from the same words. That is why Weisz, Chaiyasit, Weiss, Eastman, and Jackson (1995) concluded from a study of Thai and American school-aged children that observations of behavior are superior to a sole reliance on reports of informants.

Finally, investigators cannot ask participants about qualities that are not observable, for example, asymmetry of cerebral activation, and cannot use words that are not part of a consensual folk vocabulary. There is a small group of children who are minimally irritable, who smile frequently, who have low heart rate and minimal muscle tension, and who show greater EEG activation in the left frontal area. A psychologist evaluating these data would be motivated to invent a novel temperamental category for this combination of qualities. However, mothers cannot rate their children on this quality because they do not have access to the biological information. These problems imply that scientists who rely only on questionnaires must restrict their temperamental categories to a small number of easily understood ideas, such as activity level, fearfulness, shyness, attentiveness, and ease of anger arousal, and thus are unable to detect the internal structure of the temperamental construct (Goldsmith & Campos, 1990).

These limitations on verbal self-reports also challenge the utility of contemporary personality constructs, such as extraversion or neuroticism, that are based on factor analyses of questionnaire data. If psychologists had gathered extensive behavioral observations on large samples of adults, they probably would have extracted different factors. Further, social class position, gender, vocation, and the local context of action would be significant correlates of these personality categories. It is not obvious that this set of personality types, extracted from behavioral observations, is less valid or less useful than those derived from verbal self-reports. Men who never graduated high school and who work in unskilled jobs have a personality profile that is distinctly different from that of men who are college deans, computer programmers, lawyers, and investment bankers. The differences between these two groups of adults are not captured well by relying on such terms as *extraversion, neuroticism,* or *harm/avoidance.* Psychologists and psychiatrists hold a deep, unquestioned belief in the validity and special significance of what people say to strangers. But the many limitations on the validity of verbal report, as noted, should motivate a more skeptical posture toward this belief.

Frege (1979) argued persuasively that language cannot always capture a thought accurately. Each individual possesses ensembles of schemata, feelings, and symbolic ideas about self and others, and it is often the case that no word or phrase is able to communicate the combinations of semantic meaning and perceptual schemata that make up each ensemble. It is likely that the personality constructs of the future that are most theoretically powerful will refer to processes that are available neither to consciousness nor to easy linguistic description by informants.

History casts aside popular methods in all sciences. Archaeologists now use carbon dating, not informed intuition, to establish the age of a fossil. Evolutionary biologists examine blood proteins, in addition to obvious physical similarities, to assign an animal to a species. Very few research psychologists continue to use replies to Rorschach inkblots to measure psychological conflict. Thus the recognition that questionnaires and interviews, when used alone, are not sufficiently sensitive indexes of all significant temperamental traits should be regarded as progress. When radio frequencies were added to the evidence from telescopes, astronomers learned about the existence of dark matter in the universe. Analogously, new temperaments will be discovered when test performances, biological measures, and direct behavioral observations are added to the information gained from questionnaires and interviews.

## Temperaments as Continua or Categories

The decision whether to regard temperaments as continuous dimensions or qualitative categories is both controversial and of theoretical significance. Thomas and Chess (1977) regarded easy, difficult, and slow-to-warm-up children as representing distinct categories, although they treated the variation within each of the nine dimensions on which these categories rest as continuous.

Most psychologists prefer continua over categories for several reasons. First, the use of inferential statistics became the mark of sophisticated social scientists during the late 1940s. Because correlation coefficients, *t*-tests, and analyses of variance are supposed to be computed on continuous variables, psychologists found it useful to assume that the entire range of values for a dependent variable was controlled by the same set of causes and produced by different experimental conditions. Current statistical procedures, such as regression, assume that the forces that produced the distribution of values for a set of variables under study vary only in magnitude and act similarly on the entire range of scores.

Meehl (1995), who has written persuasively on the utility of considering some profiles as qualitative categories, has described a data analytic technique that rests on the assumption that changing magnitudes of association between two indicators of a personality type indicate whether the population consists of two qualitative types or of only one type. Application of this analysis to infant data from our laboratory revealed that some infants are members of a discrete behavioral category and are not on a continuum with other children (Woodward, Lenzen-weger, Kagan, Snidman, & Arcus, 2000). Latent class analysis is another technique used to detect temperamental categories (see Loken, 2000).

The most important argument for categories is the fact that nonlinear functions are common in the life sciences. Unique functional relations between variables often emerge at transition points because a small number of participants with special qualities possess either high or low levels of a variable. These individuals are likely to be members of a category. I have frequently found relations with theoretical import between behavioral and biological measurements for participants with extreme scores, but not for the entire sample. For example, a positive relation between the magnitude of skin temperature asymmetry for the pair of index fingers, which reflects sympathetic activity on arteriovenous anastomoses, and inhibited behavior held only for children who had very high values on both variables. There was no relation between the two measurements for each of four samples nor for the entire group of almost 400 children.

A second example comes from the distribution of the average standard scores for heart rate period and heart rate period standard deviation of two hundred 14-month-old children during an initial sitting baseline. The distribution was divided into quintiles, and a low score represented a very high and stable heart rate (low vagal tone), whereas a high score represented a low and variable heart rate (high vagal tone). The frequency of smiling at an adult examiner during the subsequent hour of testing was similar for the children in Quintiles 2–5 but was significantly less frequent for the children in Quintile 1, who had the highest and most stable heart rates. The relation of heart rate to smiling was clearly nonlinear.

A large colony of ants has distinct qualities that cannot be predicted from or explained by an additive model that sums the behavior of a large number of ants considered one at a time: "The study of biological form begins to take us in the direction of a science of qualities that is not an alternative to but complements and extends the science of quantities" (Goodwin, 1994, p. 198).

## What Is Affect?

It is necessary to address the meaning of affect before describing the history of the idea of temperament, not only because emotional states are a salient feature of temperaments but also because affect is a critical concept in this volume.

Most philosophers have recognized that words often refer to heterogeneous phenomena (for example, *ill*), or to events that do not exist (for example, *ghosts*). It is surprising, therefore, that some social scientists and psychiatrists write about *emotion* as though the term referred to a unitary natural phenomenon with the intellectual challenge being to figure out the one correct definition and, subsequently, to discover ways to measure it. E. T. Rolls (1999), for example, accepts the utility of the concept of emotion and suggests that it is a state created by a reward or the sign of a reward. This broad definition could apply to almost any change in psychological state produced by almost any event, from the sight of a movie marquee to an almost imperceptible smile displayed by a partner in a conversation.

Scientists continue to use old, familiar words for emotions—*fear, angry, sad,* and *surprise* are examples—as if the communities that invented these contextually unconstrained terms eons ago possessed a special insight into the basic elements of human nature. Although *fear* is used frequently in everyday conversation, as well in technical reports, it refers to a family of emotional states that are mediated by different neural circuits. For example, the state created in a rat by a conditioned stimulus that had been associated in the past with pain involves a neural circuit that is different from the one that mediates the avoidance of a brightly lit alley (Treit, Pesold, & Rotzinger, 1993).

Some scientists who study humans have suggested that the abstract term *negative affect* has theoretical utility (Lang, Bradley, & Cuthbert, 1992). The extensive research on potentiated startle in humans, measured by the magnitude of the blink reflex to aversive versus nonaversive pictures, provides an example of the conceptual problems that trail a decision to treat this single response as a valid indicator of a negative affective state. Our laboratory has gathered startle data from 10-year-old children on whom extensive longitudinal information was available. The children were exposed to brief acoustic probes while they watched aversive, pleasant, and neutral pictures. There was no relation between the differential magnitudes of blink reflexes to unpleasant versus neutral or pleasant pictures on the one hand and the child's past or current mood or behavior on the other. However, the children who showed large startle reflexes to neutral and pleasant pictures, as well as to unpleasant ones, were most likely to show potentiation to the unpleasant pictures. These children were characterized by greater sympathetic reactivity in targets of the cardiovascular system (for example, a very cool tympanic membrane, reflecting constriction of nearby capillaries, constriction of arteriovenous anastomoses in the fingertips to cognitive challenge, and large heart rate acceleration to cognitive challenge). Further, the children who showed these sympathetic reactions also had more beta than alpha power in frontal areas under resting conditions. These data suggest that a large startle reflex is mediated by a special state of cortical/cognitive arousal, which some children experience more easily than others. It is not obvious, however, that this state should be described as negative or unpleasant or as reflecting a semblance of fear or anxiety. An exaggerated blink reflex to an aversive stimulus might, under some conditions and in some individuals, index a state of anxiety, but the magnitude of this reflex, considered alone, is not sufficient to infer a particular emotional state, especially one as general as "negative affect."

Scientists should begin their inquiry into affect with phenomena rather than with words. Four distinctly different phenomena are often given the same emotional name. I use the emotion of anxiety as an illustration, but the following statements apply to all emotions.

One referent for anxiety is a person's subjective judgment, whether private or told to an investigator, without the presence of any accompanying physiology. It is common for an individual to express worry or anxiety over an imminent storm or his or her child's high fever. However, if scientists had measured the individual's physiology at the time he or she made the statement, they would not detect any particular change in physiology. Let us call this meaning *subjective judgment*.

A second referent is the person's judgment of being anxious, accompanied by a physiological profile that is not the one scientists assume to be the theoretically relevant profile. An individual coming down with a viral infection may feel tense and, in an attempt to understand these intrusive sensations, may decide he is worried about his job. Let us call this meaning *constructed anxiety*.

The third referent is the one used most often by investigators working with animals. A stimulus event has provoked the limbic physiology appropriate for fear/anxiety (that is, activation of the amygdala and its projections). However, the individual either does not detect the consequences of this altered physiology or, if she does detect it, awards it another meaning. Let us call this meaning *physiological anxiety*.

The fourth referent is the one most scientists would like to believe occurs most of the time. An event, either a thought or an external provocation, has provoked the physiology believed to index fear or anxiety, and the individual detects this change and interprets it as anxiety. In the discussion that follows, I use this fourth definition of emotion. Let us call this meaning *anxiety*. The single term is selected to imply that it is the one most investigators want to understand.

The reader should note that most investigations of humans that use questionnaires rely on the first meaning of subjective judgment, whereas those who work with animals rely on the third meaning. There is probably very little relation between these two definitions. Thus the fear inferred when a rat avoids a place at which it was shocked is not equivalent to the state we attribute to an adult who says she is afraid of spiders.

The following discussion of affect assumes the fourth meaning. The phenomena that define each of the many acute affective states are correlated changes in physiology, thought, and behavior provoked by a particular class of incentive. The latter factor is critical. A rise in heart rate, increased sweating, irregular respiration, and shouting, for example, do not define a particular emotional state. If that combination occurred on a tennis court, the agent would be called excited; if during a quarrel with a stranger, the agent would be called angry. The failure to add the class of incentive to descriptions of the physiology and behavior of the agent is attributable to the fact that scientists have been unable to discover a persuasive a priori set of incentives.

Furthermore, the correlated changes in physiology that are components of each emotion require an additional parsing into those combinations that the agent detects consciously and those that are undetected. Most adults react to a punctate auditory stimulus with a time-locked series of event-related potentials, including the P3, which occurs at about 300 ms, and a decrease in heart rate that reaches its trough about 3 s after the onset of the event. It is unlikely that most persons are aware of a feeling state, either at 300 ms, or 3 s following the presentation of the stimulus. Similarly, reflex eye blinks and pupillary dilation usually accompany an attempt to solve a difficult problem, but most individuals do not report a conscious change in feeling during these brief biological reactions.

When a person with a tumor that has been growing for years becomes aware of the bodily changes created by the disease process, a special psychological state is provoked. Hence, it is necessary to invent different names for the states characterized by undetected and detected physiological changes. One possibility is to call the former state *internal tone* and the latter, *feeling state*. Imagine three women, each of whom has just realized that in a month her last child will go to college. Over the next few days, the first woman detects a loss of appetite and energy, thinks about these changes, decides they are due to the imminent loss, and concludes that she must be sad because her last child is leaving home. The second woman detects the same bodily changes but decides she has been working too hard and must be fatigued. Similar bodily changes in the third mother are undetected, even though she appears to her husband to be less affectionate and more likely to quarrel. The imminent loss of the child generated a bodily change in feeling tone in all three women, and, therefore, a similar physiological foundation for an emotion was present. But it is necessary to invent different terms for the emotional states of the three mothers. It is an error to regard all three as sad, because both the conscious state and the behaviors of each woman are qualitatively different. At the least it will be useful to call the states Sadness 1, Sadness 2, and Sadness 3. Because it is probable that conscious reflection on detected physiological changes is more extensive in humans than in animals, it is wise to distinguish between the emotional states of rats and those of humans and to resist the easy assumption that the same term can be used for all species.

Finally, it is necessary to differentiate between acute emotions provoked by specific incentives that are transient, on the one hand, and chronic moods that are less clearly linked to external events, on the other. Four different affective constructs are created by crossing the distinction between consciously detected versus undetected changes in physiology with the distinction between acute emotions and chronic moods. Each of the four phenomena requires a different name. Adults who report that they worry a lot but do not report detection of bodily changes show different EEG patterns than do those who are conscious of the physiological changes that usually accompany anxiety and uncertainty (Nitschke, Heller, Palmieri, & Miller, 1999).

Although it is too early in the history of this domain to posit with certainty a list of the major acute affective categories in humans, it is probably harmless to risk some guesses. The following set of possible affects, which is not meant to be complete, accommodates to particular classes of incentive because each incentive creates a specific profile of physiology and cognition that should be part of the definition of the emotional state. The need to specify the incentive is apparent even in work with animals; for example, different patterns of neural activity and behaviors are provoked when a rat is presented with a conditioned stimulus that was previously associated with electric shock or with the place in which the shock was administered (Belzung & LePape, 1994; Phillips & LeDoux, 1992). It is assumed that the incentive and the pattern of physiological and psychological changes the incentive provokes is, in theory, amenable to measurement.

In the list that follows, the phrase in parentheses is a suggested name for the emotion.

1. Novel, discrepant, or unexpected events alert the individual (surprise to the unexpected).
2. A novel, discrepant, or unexpected event is not assimilated easily, and the individual does not have a coping response to make to that failure (fear to the unfamiliar).
3. Anticipation of a possible future threat to the individual's physiological or psychological state (anxiety to threat).
4. The individual has violated a community norm in the presence of others (shame).
5. The individual has violated a personal moral standard and believes that the act could have been suppressed (guilt).
6. A person or situation has frustrated the individual's attempt to gain a desired goal (anger to frustration).

7. A person has implied that the individual possesses traits regarded as undesirable (anger to personal attack).
8. A source of pleasure or support has been withdrawn (sadness).
9. A source of pleasure or support has been withdrawn, and the agent feels that he or she has no response to cope with the loss (depression).
10. The individual attains a desired goal through effort (pride).
11. The individual witnesses an event that matches a personal standard of competence, beauty, or perfection (admiration).
12. The individual experiences sensory pleasure (joy).
13. The individual experiences sexual arousal to a person, surrogate symbol, or thought (sexual desire).
14. The individual experiences sexual arousal combined with a feeling of admiration for the qualities of another (love).
15. The individual experiences a loss of energy (fatigue).
16. The individual infers a state of distress in another (empathy).
17. The individual wishes an object or state believed to be possessed by another (envy).
18. The individual wishes the affection of a love object possessed by another (jealousy).

Each of these 18 acute emotional states will have a gloss, depending on whether the physiological components of the state are or are not detected consciously.

## History of the Concept of Temperament

The Greeks and Romans believed that a balance among the four humors—yellow and black bile, blood, and phlegm—present in all persons created an opposition between two pairs of qualities, called "warm" versus "cool" and "dry" versus "moist," resulting in four different states that bore a relation to the four fundamental substances in the world; namely, fire, air, earth, and water. The Greeks assumed that the balance among these opposed qualities explained the observed variation in emotionality, rationality, and behavior.

Galen, born in Asia Minor in the first century, elaborated these ideas by positing nine temperamental types derived from the four humors (Siegel, 1968). The ideal personality possessed a perfect balance among the complementary characteristics of warm versus cool and dry versus moist, but in each of the four less ideal types one of the four qualities was dominant. These were the temperamental categories Galen called *melancholic, sanguine, choleric,* and *phlegmatic.* Each type was the result of an excess of one of the four bodily humors which produced, in turn, an imbalance in the paired qualities. For example, the melancholic was cool and dry because of too much black bile; the sanguine was warm and moist because of an excess of blood.

Galen's ideas remained popular until the end of the nineteenth century. Alexander Bain, a philosopher at the University of Aberdeen, who wrote *On the Study of Character* in 1861, agreed with Galen that people differed biologically in their capacity for each of the major emotions. Although the blood and liver remained organs of importance, the watery lymph replaced phlegm and brain physiology replaced black bile as the basis for the melancholic type.

Two millennia before Galen, the Chinese view of human nature shared some features with the Greek theory but was different in several important ways (Yosida, 1973). First, the seminal balance was not among humors but among sources of energy. The energy of the universe, called *ch'i,* which was regulated by the complementary relationship between the active initiating force of yang and the passive completing force of yin, must be in balance for optimal functioning. The Chinese thought there were five, rather than four, basic elements: wood, fire, earth, metal, and water. The Chinese were far less interested than the Greeks in temperamental types because the energy of *ch'i* was always changing, and, therefore, a person's moods could not be permanent. The idea of inheriting a fixed emotional bias was inconsistent with the Chinese premise of continual transformation. A mood of melancholy might occur temporarily, but not because the person was a melancholic type.

Nineteenth-century essays on temperament moved the origin of cause from bodily humors to the brain. Franz Gall (1835) incurred the hostility of many scientists by suggesting that variations in human intention and emotion were based on differences in brain tissue that could be detected by measuring the skull. Spurzheim (1834) consolidated Gall's ideas while retaining the essential premise of a separate location for each important human characteristic.

Ernst Kretschmer (1925) invented the asthenic, pyknic, and athletic types, corresponding to the three classical body physiques, and suggested that each was differentially vulnerable to particular moods and mental illnesses. Asthenics, for example, were most likely to become schizophrenic; pyknics, manic-depressives. These speculations formed the basis for Sheldon's (1940) famous book on personality and its relation to the physiques called ectomorph, endomorph, and mesomorph.

Temperamental ideas were exiled during the first decades of the twentieth century because they posed a threat to the egalitarian premise necessary to assimilate the large number of poor European immigrants whose children were having difficulty adjusting to American society. In addition, Freud's changes to the remnants of Galen's views weakened the popularity of temperamental constructs. Although Freud did not deny the importance of temperament, he awarded extraordinary power to early family experience. Freud substituted the concept of libido for the four humors and assumed that a balance among id, ego, and superego, rather than among the humors, created different psychological profiles. Freud accepted the nineteenth-century belief that individuals varied in the amount of energy they possessed. This energy, called *vis nervosa,* resembled the Chinese notion of *ch'i.* The belief that individuals varied in the amount of energy they had available for brain activity and, therefore, in the ability to cope with stress was popular during the latter part of the nineteenth century. The term *neurasthenia* was applied to those who had depleted their brain energy more easily than others and, as a result, experienced symptoms of tension, anxiety, and worry.

Freud's ideas represented a novel conception of pathology and personality. Nineteenth-century experts on mental illness had focused primarily on the small number of adults with serious pathology rather than on the majority who worried occasionally about money, friends, illness, and death. Freud softened that division and persuaded many that a fear of walking in a park at night or worry over the possible death of a loved one were exemplars of the same state that produced a chronic phobia of heights and panic attacks. The suggestion that experiences that provoked the repression of libidinal urges was the primary basis for all fears implied that anyone could develop a phobia. Freud let his readers conclude that little Hans, the young child who developed a fear of horses, was no different temperamentally from any other child. Psychoanalytic theory turned minds away from categories of persons who, because of temperament, were especially vulnerable to acquiring a phobia to categories of environments that could produce fears in anyone. The adjective *fearful* now became a continuous dimension, varying only in intensity, on which any person could be placed.

Although the concept of temperament went underground from about 1910 to 1960, the ascendance of biology produced a change in the zeitgeist that permitted psychiatrists Alexander Thomas and Stella Chess (1977) to reintroduce the idea of infant temperament in the late 1950s. Thomas and Chess emphasized the distinctive style of a behavior rather than the goal sought or the competence with which a behavior was displayed. They inferred nine temperamental dimensions based on lengthy interviews with 85 middle-and upper-middle-class parents. The nine categories were (1) general activity level, (2) regularity of basic functions, (3) reactions to unfamiliarity, (4) ease of adapting to new situations, (5) responsiveness to stimulus events, (6) amount of energy associated with an activity, (7) dominant mood, (8) distractibility, and (9) attention span. Although the nine dimensions are not independent—the child who approaches a stranger is typically more adaptive than one who does not—Thomas and Chess used the correlations to create three abstract categories: the easy child, the slow-to-warm-up child, and the difficult child. Children in the latter category, making up 10% of their sample, were very irritable and minimally regular, showed poor adaptation, and were most likely to develop psychiatric symptoms in later childhood.

The dramatic progress in the neurosciences over the past decade has made the community more receptive to the significance of temperament. The brain contains over 150 different molecules, which, along with their receptors, influence the excitability of specific sites in the central nervous system. Individuals inherit different concentrations of these chemicals and their associated receptors, and it is easy to imagine how such persons might be especially vulnerable to a particular temperamental profile.

Investigators have posited different sets of adult temperamental types over the past 25 years. For example, Cloninger (1987) believes that avoidance of danger, seeking of novelty, and dependence on social rewards mark the three primary temperamental types. On the other hand, Buss and Plomin (1975) posit emotionality, activity, and sociability as three primary temperaments. Gray's writings (1994) imply that variation in three basic emotional systems accounts for the human temperaments. The *behavioral inhibition system*, which involves septohippocampal circuits and is activated by conditioned stimuli associated with punishment, omission, or termination of reward and novelty, produces cessation in ongoing behavior. Activation of the second system of *flight-fight* involves the amygdala, hypothalamus, and central gray and is activated by aversive events, such as pain, that lead to escape behavior. If escape is impossible, aggression is likely to occur. The *behavioral approach system*, activated by events associated with reward or the termination of punishment, involves the basal ganglia, dopaminergic tracts, and neocortical areas linked to the basal ganglia and usually elicits approach behavior.

A more conservative theoretical approach focuses on the neurochemical systems in the brain that can modulate mood and action profiles rather than on the behaviors. For example, infants born with high levels of brain norepinephrine might show unusual sensitivities to sensory events. Some children who find it difficult to sustain attention might have low levels of the enzyme dopamine hydroxylase, which is necessary for the synthesis of norepinephrine. Dopamine, an essential transmitter in limbic and striatal areas, serves motor behavior, as well as frontal areas that mediate planning, inhibition of impulsivity, and delay. It is possible that children with low levels of dopamine are characterized by impulsivity.

Children with high levels of endorphins or other endogenous opioids might show blunted sympathetic reactions to challenge, whereas those with low levels might show exaggerated sympathetic reactions to the same events. Children with low levels of serotonin might be susceptible to unusual mood states, including excitation, anger, or depression; some scientists believe that violent criminals have chronically low brain concentrations of serotonin. Finally, high levels of glucocorticoids, which exert powerful effects on the brain, could produce profiles related to fear and withdrawal.

These profiles of brain neurochemistry are difficult to quantify and, sadly, no peripheral physiological measure, such as heart rate, blood pressure, startle, or galvanic skin response (GSR), is likely to be an especially valid index of any of these temperamental types because each measure is subject to local influences at the level of the peripheral target that are not closely related to the central brain mechanisms.

## The Concept of Inhibition

The behavioral profiles characterized by avoidance of discrepancy or novelty and hesitation to challenge are usually nominated as a temperamental type. The concept of inhibition to the unfamiliar has attracted scientific attention because the relevant behaviors are observable and easily quantified in children and animals; because they appear early in development; because they have implications for social behavior and, therefore, adaptation; and because they differentiate among animal species, as well as among strains within a species.

My colleagues, Nancy Snidman, Mark McManis, Sue Woodward, Doreen Arcus, Cynthia Garcia-Coll, Steven Reznick, and I have been studying two temperamental categories of children that we call "inhibited" and "uninhibited to the unfamiliar." The corpus of data has led to a small set of relatively firm conclusions (Kagan, 1994). We regard shyness with strangers as only one feature of the broader temperamental category of inhibition to the unfamiliar. Inhibited children react to many different types of unfamiliarity with avoidance, distress, or subdued emotion when they reach the age at which discrepancies elicit uncertainty, usually a few months before the first birthday. The source of the unfamiliarity can be people, situations, objects, or events. The complementary category, called uninhibited, is defined by a sociable, affectively spontaneous reaction to unfamiliarity. As with the inhibited child, the term refers to an envelope of profiles whose exact form changes with development.

Observations of a large group of four-month-old infants administered visual, auditory, and olfactory stimuli revealed early predictors of the inhibited and uninhibited profiles that emerge after the first birthday. The infant behaviors that predict the two categories can be understood by assuming that some infants are born with a low threshold of excitability in the amygdala and its projections to the ventral striatum, hypothalamus, cingulate, central gray, and brain stem. Infants with low thresholds of excitability show vigorous motor activity, muscle tension, and frequent crying to a standard 40-minute battery of unfamiliar stimuli. The infants who display this profile, about 20% of an unselected, healthy, Caucasian sample, are called high reactive. The complementary group, who display low levels of motor arousal and minimal irritability to the same battery, make up about 40% of the sample and are called low reactive.

We have observed more than 450 four-month-old infants. More than 250 of these children were evaluated again when they were 14 and 21 months old. The high-reactive infants showed significantly more fear to a variety of unfamiliar events than did low-reactive infants. About one-third of high reactives were very fearful or avoidant, and only 3% showed minimal fear to unfamiliar people, objects, or procedures. By contrast, one-third of the low reactives were minimally fearful in the second year, and only 4% showed high levels of fear.

When these children were evaluated at 4½ years of age, high reactives were affectively more subdued than low reactives; they talked and smiled less often during a long interaction with an unfamiliar woman. The two groups also differed in their social behavior with two unfamiliar children of the same sex and age while the trios played in a laboratory room for a half hour. Almost two-thirds of the low reactive, but less than 10% of the high reactive, children were outgoing and sociable with the unfamiliar children. Forty percent of the high reactives were avoidant and shy, compared with only 10% of the low reactives. The parents of the high-reactive, inhibited preschool children described them as extremely sensitive to criticism and noted that they cried or had a tantrum when chastised. The minds of four-year-olds are continually generating representations of the present and the immediate future. An unexpected punishment is a discrepant event. If the amygdala and its projections are excited by discrepancy, these children should be expected to show an extreme emotional reaction to such events (Kagan, Snidman, & Arcus, 1998).

These children were evaluated again when they were 7½ years old. Thirty-one percent of the sample of 164 children had been high-reactive infants, 36% low-reactive, and 33% belonged to other temperamental categories. Questionnaires and interviews with the mothers and teachers of the children were used to determine which children met criteria for anxious symptoms (e.g., fear of harm, dark, animals, or separation and extreme shyness with strangers). Forty-three children who were classified as having anxious symptoms were compared with 107 control children from other temperamental groups who did not meet criteria for either anxiety, conduct disorder, or attention problems.

The children who had been high reactive were most likely to have acquired anxious symptoms; 45% of this group, compared with only 15% of low reactives, had anxious symptoms. These anxious, high-reactive children were the ones most likely to scream in terror during the assessment at age 21 months when a person dressed in a clown costume unexpectedly entered the room in which they were playing. The best predictor of anxious symptoms at 7 years was the temperamental profile of high reactivity at 4 months, not the degree of fear shown in the second year (Kagan, Snidman, Zentner, & Peterson, 1999).

It is important to note that only 18% of the group of high reactives showed consistent inhibition over time; that is, high levels of fear in the second year, shy behavior with peers at 4½ years of age, and anxious symptoms at 7½ years. However, not one high reactive showed the complementary profile of consistently uninhibited behavior from 14 months to 7½ years. By contrast, 29% of the children who had been low-reactive infants showed minimal fear in the second year bold, sociable behavior with the unfamiliar peers, and no anxious symptoms at 7½ years; only one child showed a consistently inhibited profile.

A comparison of the 23 high reactives who had anxious symptoms with the 27 high reactives who did not revealed that more members of the former group had a narrow facial skeleton, higher sitting diastolic blood pressure, and a greater magnitude of cooling of the temperature of the fingertips while listening to a series of digits they were asked to remember. These last two variables imply a more reactive sympathetic nervous system. The ability of the facial skeleton to differentiate the anxious from the nonanxious high reactives is in accord with an earlier report revealing that 14- and 21-month-old children with a narrow facial skeleton were more inhibited than those with broad faces (Arcus & Kagan, 1995). These results imply that the genes that control the growth of bones in the upper face, which are derivatives of the cells in the neural crest and, therefore, ectodermal in origin, are correlated with the genes that contribute to the display of inhibited behavior. The fact that diastolic blood pressure separated the anxious from the nonanxious high reactives is also in accord with other data showing greater sympathetic reactivity among high reactives. Fifty-seven percent of the high-reactive girls who had high and stable heart rates in the second year or at 4½ years displayed anxious symptoms at 7½ years. The fact that this relation was absent for boys implies that the link between sympathetic influence on the cardiovascular system and behavioral inhibition might be stronger in girls than in boys.

The magnitude of asymmetry in the temperature of the fingertips of the index fingers of the left and right hands, which is another index of sympathetic activity, also differentiated the two groups. The asymmetry in skin temperature is the result of the differential constriction of the arteriovenous anastomoses in the fingertips. The index fingers typically have much larger asymmetries than the other fingers (a mean difference of 0.3°C) and the asymmetry typically favors a cooler left hand. When the asymmetry was treated as a continuous variable across all participants, it did not differentiate the groups, but extreme values did separate the temperamental groups. We divided the distribution of asymmetries into terciles and found that more high than low reactives were either in the top or the bottom tercile; that is, they had large temperature asymmetries that favored either a cooler left or cooler right index finger.

The greater prevalence of anxious symptoms among the high reactives is in accord with the fact that 61% of children from another cohort who were selected as inhibited in the second year of life (Garcia-Coll, Kagan, & Reznick, 1984) were judged as having social anxiety at 13 years of age, compared with 27% of children who were classified as uninhibited in the second year. Almost 50% of the latter group told an interviewer that they had never experienced any sign of social anxiety (Schwartz, Snidman, & Kagan, 1999).

A group of 32 ten-year-olds who had been high-reactive and 31 children who had been low-reactive infants were evaluated recently (unpublished raw data). Data on asymmetry of 8–13 Hz power in the EEG during baseline conditions revealed that significantly more high than low reactives had greater activation on the right than on the left frontal area, as Davidson (1994) and Fox et al. (1996) would have predicted. In addition, the children with greater activation on the right side were emotionally subdued and made significantly fewer spontaneous comments while interacting with an examiner. It is also of interest that high reactives showed more power than low reactives in the 14–30 Hz band while sitting quietly in a chair, implying greater cortical arousal. The high-reactive children who showed less 14–30 Hz power in the right frontal area (more active on the right side) had higher fear scores at 14 and 21 months. The correlation between the mean fear score in the second year and the difference between right and left power for the 14–30 Hz band was .40.

Finally, the children who had been high-reactive infants possessed a physiological feature that implies the possession of a more reactive amygdala. The feature is a relatively large Wave 5 component in the brain stem auditory evoked potential, generated by neural activity of the inferior colliculus to a series of clicks (Woodward et al., 2001). Activity in the amygdala can influence the excitability of the inferior colliculus, and, therefore, a Wave 5 magnitude greater than 0.3 microvolts (in children this age) might reflect the priming of this midbrain structure by the amygdala. The logic of this inference resembles the logic of potentiated startle. In the case of the startle, the amygdala projects to the nucleus reticularis pontis caudalis in the brain stem. Rats show potentiated startle to an acoustic probe when a conditioned stimulus that had been associated with shock is presented prior to the probe because the conditioned stimulis activates the amygdala and the amygdala primes the brain stem nucleus that mediates the startle. Analogously, the amygdala influences the inferior colliculus through the ventral amygdalofugal pathway and, therefore, can enhance the magnitude of Wave 5.

Although high reactives, as a group, had a significantly larger Wave 5 component than low reactives, a small number of high reactives who were very fearful in the second year and showed a large Wave 5 were not particularly shy or timid when seen in the laboratory at 10 years of age. Furthermore, these children told an interviewer who talked with them at home that they were neither shy nor anxious, and their parents agreed with that description. This fact suggests the possibility of a dissociation between the biological processes that form part of the foundation of a temperamental category and the contemporary behavioral phenotype (see Dawson et al., 1999, for another example). This distinction, which Jung intended when he differentiated between anima and persona, is the sense meaning of the cliché, "You can't judge a book by its cover."

The possibility that some aspects of brain physiology that form the foundation of an inhibited temperamental type need not remain closely associated with inhibited behavior is analogous to the idea of penetrance in genetics. An individual who possesses the genes for a particular feature may not display that feature. These data on 10-year-olds, combined with other evidence, reminds us that experience can change an early behavioral profile of extreme timidity, linked originally to the excitability of the amygdala and its projections, to a more normative profile without eliminating completely the excitability of the limbic structures that contributed to the infant behavior.

## Internal Tone

Afferent feedback from cardiovascular targets, gut, lungs, and muscles ascends to the medulla, pons, and central nucleus of the amygdala and arrives finally at the ventromedial prefrontal cortex to form the foundation of a conscious perception of internal body tone. Inhibited children, who have a more reactive sympathetic nervous system, might be especially vulnerable to frequent or salient feedback from peripheral sympathetic targets, and the subsequent conscious perception of body tone might have special consequences. If these children are more likely to experience a tone that has an unpleasant sensory quality and learn with age that unfamiliar or challenging situations produce that feeling, some will learn eventually to avoid these contexts.

In addition, most adolescents and adults will want to understand the reasons for the sudden dysphoric feelings. A frequent first guess among members of our society is that they probably violated one of their ethical standards. The list of possible moral lapses is so long that few individuals will have trouble finding an ethical flaw to explain the unwelcome feeling and, as a consequence, will become vulnerable to a moment of guilt. This argument is similar to the view of emotions posited by Carl Lange and William James (1885), who suggested, independently, that each person used sensory feedback from his or her body to decide what emotion he or she is experiencing. The body tone each person lives with is so completely hidden from observers and, at the moment, so far beyond measurement that it does not enter into most theorizing. The biology that is a vital component of each temperament probably affects this internal tone and, as a consequence, modulates moods and acute emotions. It is here that temperament's darkest shadow may fall.

## Temperament as Constraint

Although relations between variables are always contingent, the tightness of any link can vary over a very broad range of probabilities, from the near-perfect relation between the force with which a stone is thrown and the distance it travels to the far-from-perfect relation between an infant's Apgar score and his or her grade point average in school. Because physics and chemistry began their growth before biology and psychology, the word *determine* became the preferred term to describe the relation between an incentive event and some outcome. When the probability of one event following a prior one is relatively high—for example, the probability is greater than 0.7—it is reasonable to conclude that the prior event influenced the latter one directly. But when the probability is low— say, less than 0.4—it is more likely that the prior event affected the consequent indirectly, only at extremes, or in combination with other factors. In most cases a significant correlation between psychological or biological variables of less than 0.4 is attributable to a small proportion of participants, usually less than 20%, who have extreme values. When this is the case, it is more accurate to use the verb *constrain* rather than *determine*. For example, consistent nurturance of young children during the first 5 years does not predict, at a high level of probability, quality of marriage, amount of education, or level of professional achievement. But consistent nurture during childhood probably constrains seriously the likelihood that the adults who enjoyed that experience will become criminals or homeless people.

Only 18% of the children who were high-reactive infants became highly fearful at 14 and 21 months and very shy with unfamiliar peers at 4½ years or developed anxious symptoms at 7½ years. But not one high-reactive infant developed the complementary profile. Because more than 80% of high-reactive infants did not become consistently inhibited, anxious children, it is misleading to suggest that a high-reactive temperament determines a consistently inhibited profile. It is more accurate to conclude that a high-reactive temperament constrains the probability of becoming a consistently uninhibited child. Replacing the word *determine* with the term *constrain* is not idle word play, for the connotations surrounding the two words are different. The term *determine* implies a particular consequence; *constrain* implies a restriction on a set of outcomes. The biology that humans inherit constrains the probability of incest, homicide, and deciding that nothing one does can affect one's personal future. But the human genome does not determine any one of these psychological outcomes. It is probably useful to regard each temperamental bias as imposing a constraint on the probability of developing a particular family of profiles rather than to assume that a temperamental bias determines the development of a particular trait.

## Summary

The return of the concept of temperamentally based variation is part of a broad interest in the contribution of an individual's biological states, whether stable or transient, to emotion and behavior. However, the enthusiasm for probing the biological contributions has been accompanied, unfortunately, by a loss of interest in each person's psychological interpretation of their experiences and indifference to the cultural influence on those private interpretations. The temperamental categories of inhibited and uninhibited are especially interesting because the critical incentive for inhibited behavior is encounter with an event that is discrepant from the individual's schematic or semantic representations. Therefore, each person's history influences the probability that an event will be treated as discrepant and, therefore, the likelihood of an emotional reaction and inhibited behavior. The probability that a high-reactive infant born with the biology that favors inhibition will display inhibited behavior at age 10 depends on the frequency of exposure to discrepant events, the ease with which the child can assimilate them, and the conscious decision to seek environments that are predictable.

Many inhibited children recognize, usually during adolescence, that they are especially vulnerable to uncertainty when unexpected events occur. As a result, they are likely to choose vocations and make life choices that permit them to manage the unexpected and to manage uncertainty. Temperamental dispositions and emotions are inextricably linked, as Galen understood, but the nature of those links is modulated by each individual's history and the cultural context in which each life is actualized.

## NOTE

The preparation of this chapter was supported, in part, by grants from the W. T. Grant Foundation, Bial Foundation, NIMH Grant #47077, and the Mind/Brain/Behavior Initiative at Harvard University.

## REFERENCES

Arcus, D., & Kagan, J. (1995). Temperament and craniofacial variation in the first two years. *Child Development, 66*, 1529–1540.

Bain, A. (1861). *On the study of character.* London: Parker Son & Bourn.

Belzung, C., & LePape, G. (1994). Comparison of different behavioral test situations used in psychopharmacology for the measurement of anxiety. *Physiology and Behavior, 56*, 623–628.

Buss, A. H., & Plomin, R. (1975). *A temperament theory of personality development.* New York: Wiley.

Cloninger, C. R. (1987). The systematic method for clinical description and classification of personality variants. *Archives of General Psychiatry, 44*, 573–588.

Davidson, R. J. (1994). Asymmetric brain function, affective style, and psychopathology. *Development and Psychopathology, 6*, 741–758.

Davidson, R. J. (1995). Cerebral asymmetry, emotion, and affective style. In R. J. Davidson & K. Hugdahl (Eds.), *Brain asymmetry* (pp. 361–388). Cambridge, MA: MIT Press.

Dawson, G., Frey, K., Self, J., Panagiotides, H., Hessl, D., Yamada, E., & Rinaldi, J. (1999). Frontal brain electrical activity in infants of depressed and nondepressed mothers. *Development and Psychopathology, 11*, 589–606.

Fox, N. A., Schmidt, L. A., Calkins, S. D., Rubin, K. H., & Coplan, R. J. (1996). The role of frontal activation in the regulation and disregulation of social behavior during the preschool years. *Development and Psychopathology, 8*, 89–102.

Frege, G. (1979). *Posthumous writings* (P. Long & R. White, Trans.). London: Oxford University Press.

Gall, F. J. (1835). *On the organ of moral qualities and intellectual faculties and the plurality of the cerebral organs* (W. Lewis, Trans.). Boston: Marsh, Copen, & Lyon.

Garcia-Coll, C., Kagan, J., & Reznick, J. S. (1984). Behavioral inhibition in young children. *Child Development, 55*, 1005–1019.

Goldsmith, H. H., & Campos, J. J. (1990). The structure of temperamental fear a pleasure in infants. *Child Development, 61*, 1944–1964.

Goodwin, B. (1994). *How the leopard changed its spots.* New York: Scribners.

Gray, J. A. (1994). Three fundamental emotional systems. In P. Ekman & R. J. Davidson (Eds.), *The nature of emotion* (pp. 243–247). New York: Oxford University Press.

Kagan, J. (1994). *Galen's prophecy.* New York: Basic Books.

Kagan, J., Snidman, N., & Arcus, D. (1998). Childhood derivatives of high and low reactivity in infancy. *Child Development, 69*, 1483–1493.

Kagan, J., Snidman, N., Zentner, M., & Peterson, E. (1999). Infant temperament and anxious symptoms in school age children. *Development and Psychopathology, 11*, 209–224.

Kretschmer, E. (1925). *Physique and character* (2nd ed., W. J. H. Sprott, Trans.). New York: Harcourt Brace.

Lang, P. J., Bradley, M. M., & Cuthbert, B. N. (1992). A motivational analysis of emotion. *Psychological Review, 97*, 377–395.

Lange, C. P., & James, W. (1885). *The emotions.* Baltimore: Williams & Wilkins.

Loken, E. (2000). *A latent class analysis of temperament.* Unpublished doctoral dissertation, Harvard University.

Meehl, P. E. (1995). Bootstrap taxometrics. *American Psychologist, 50*, 266–275.

Nitschke, J. B., Heller, W., Palmieri, P. A., & Miller, G. A. (1999). Contrasting patterns of brain activity in anxious apprehensive and anxious arousal. *Psychophysiology, 36*, 628–637.

Osgood, C. E., Suci, G. J., & Tannenbaum, P. H. (1957). *The measurement of meaning.* Urbana: University of Illinois Press.

Phillips, R. G., & LeDoux, J. E. (1992). Differential contribution of amygdala and hippocampus to cued and contextual fear conditioning. *Behavioral Neuroscience, 106*, 274–285.

Rolls, E. T. (1999). *The brain and emotion.* New York: Oxford University Press.

Saudino, K. J., McGuire, S., Reiss, D., Hetherington, E. M., & Plomin, R. (1993). *Clarifying the confusion.* Unpublished manuscript, Pennsylvania State University, Center for Developmental and Health Genetics.

Schwartz, C. E., Snidman, N., & Kagan, J. (1999). Adolescent social anxiety as an outcome of inhibited temperament in childhood. *Journal of the American Academy of Child and Adolescent Psychiatry, 38*, 1008–1015.

Sheldon, W. H. (1940). *The varieties of human physique.* New York: Harper.

Siegel, R. E. (1968). *Galen's system of physiology and medicine.* Basel: Karger.

Spurzheim, J. G. (1834). *Phrenology.* Boston: Marsh, Copen, & Lyon.

Thomas, A., & Chess, S. (1977). *Temperament and development.* New York: Brunner/Mazel.

Treit, D., Pesold, C., & Rotzinger, S. (1993). Dissociating the anti-fear effects of septal and amygdaloid lesions using two pharmacologically validated models of rat anxiety. *Behavioral Neuroscience, 107*, 770–785.

Weisz, J. R., Chaiyasit, W., Weiss, B., Eastman, K. L., & Jackson, E. W. (1995). A multimethod study of problem behavior among Thai and American children in school. *Child Development, 66*, 402–415.

Woodward, S. A., Lenzenweger, M. F., Kagan, J., Snidman, N., & Arcus, D. (2000). Taxonic structure of infant reactivity. *Psychological Science, 11*, 300–305.

Woodward, S. A., McManis, M. H., Kagan, J., Deldir, P., Snidman, N., Lewis, M., & Kahn, V. (2001). Infant temperament and the brain stem auditory evoked response in later childhood. *Developmental Psychology, 37*, 1–6.

Yosida, M. (1973). The Chinese concept of nature. In S. Nakayama & N. Sivin (Eds.), *Chinese science* (pp. 71–90). Cambridge, MA: MIT Press.

# 18

# EMOTIONAL DEVELOPMENT IN EARLY CHILDHOOD: A SOCIAL RELATIONSHIP PERSPECTIVE

Judy Dunn

In this chapter, children's affective development in childhood is considered within the framework of their close relationships. The striking developments in children's emotional expression and experience and in their understanding of emotions during early childhood take place in the context of these relationships and profoundly affect the nature of such relationships. In turn, children's experiences within their close relationships are related to both normative and individual differences in affective development. Three core themes in current developmental research are particularly important for our understanding of affective development and its links with children's social relationships. First, there has been major growth over the past decade in research on children's understanding of emotions—clearly of key significance for the nature of relationships. Second, a key theme in research on affective development in infancy and early childhood has been the significance of reciprocal emotional communication between child and caregiver and the growth of "intersubjectivity" (Braten, 1998). These developments are seen as setting the stage for relationship development in the childhood years that follow. Third, the work on links between affective development and social relationships has provided an exciting opportunity to bridge the gap between cognitive and social approaches to understanding children's development and to address major questions in psychology concerning links between affect and cognition (Dunn, 1996).

In infancy and childhood, changes in what causes babies' distress, comfort, amusement, and interest are intimately linked to the changes in their relationships with others. In parallel, parents' and siblings' emotional behavior with young children are intricately connected with the babies' increasingly differentiated response to their partners' affective communication. In terms of theoretical approaches, there has been growing interest in functional accounts of the significance of emotional development (Campos, Mumme, Kermoian, & Campos, 1994), in the development of ideas on affective communication, and in how such emotional communication sets a framework for the development of "shared meaning." Emotion, as Stern (1985) put it, is the primary medium and the primary subject of communication in infancy. The emotional communication between child and partner in the first two years is thought by many scholars to set up a framework for the growth of joint attention and shared reference, for the development of intentional action and the understanding of agency, and thus for the growth of language and the development of a sense of self (see, e.g., Hobson, 1993; Thompson, 1998). In terms of empirical research, advances have been made in documenting babies' and young children's sensitivity to their mothers' and fathers' emotional expressions, in the detailed analysis of how affective messages are carried by the voice and face and how they change with children's development, and in toddlers' and preschoolers' rapidly growing understanding of emotion and its role in relation to human action.

There is increasing interest not only in the normative

developmental patterns of such emotional communication and understanding but also in individual differences and the links between such individual differences and children's social experiences. In this chapter, we consider both. In the first section of the chapter, normative developmental changes in affective development and relationships in the early years are the focus; in the second section, the focus is on individual differences and the longer term significance of early individual differences in affective understanding and relationships.

## Normative Developments in Emotion and Relationships

### The Power of Emotion in Relationships

From birth onward, the impact of children's emotional expressions on those who interact with them is striking. Newborn babies may seem vulnerable and helpless, but in their crying they possess a signaling system of great power, which has an immediate effect on those around them. A newborn's crying is not an elaborately planned action (unlike the crying of older children, which may well be deliberately intended to get attention) nor a "message" of much specificity, but it is responded to by adults as a sign of distress or pain or upset. A few weeks later, babies' first smiles have a tremendous impact, in turn, on those who care for them; the way babies respond to calming and comforting actions, their contented cooing and vocalizing, their expressions of anger, wariness, and discomfort during the first months play a central role in the relationships that they develop, as does their changing responsiveness to other people's emotions. In the toddler years, the power of children's expressions of anger in the notorious "terrible twos," the delights of their new expressive powers of affection, and their evident concern for those they love mean that their relationships change markedly. In this section we look at how such developments in affect expression are linked to changes in children's relationships.

### Developments in Affect Expression and Recognition

#### Changes in the First Year

Even in the early months of infancy, babies' facial expressions of distress, of happiness, and of anger at frustration are remarkably like our own. Darwin's (1872) careful observation of his own son's facial expressions and his observations of the similarity in facial expressions in various cultures led to his argument that there is an innate, universal basis to the expression of emotions and indeed some continuity across different primate species. His proposal that emotional expression was a product of evolu-

tion because of its central role in social interaction continues to inspire research on infants' expression of emotion and cross-cultural studies of emotion (Ekman & Davidson, 1994). There is still controversy about the extent to which babies express (and experience) specific emotions at birth; however, from the careful analysis of babies' facial expressions, many think that the basic emotions of happiness, anger, fear, sadness, and disgust are present in the first weeks of life; these studies have shown that babies, even in the first months of life, systematically produce appropriate, discriminably different emotion expressions of distress, happiness, and anger—even though the range and selectivity of the repertoire still has to be established. But although there are disagreements about these early stages of children's emotional life, the effect on adults of the babies' emotional expressions is unquestionable.

Although the facial expressions of these "core" emotions of happiness, anger, and distress may show continuity over time as children grow up, it is important to note that what leads a seven-day-old baby to express (and presumably feel) distress can be markedly different from the circumstances that elicit distress in a seven-month-old and different again from what makes a seven-year-old express and feel distress. As children grow up and their goals, relationships, and understanding of other people change, so the circumstances that elicit anger, frustration, fear, or amusement also change. The changes in causes of babies' distress, for instance, were documented in a classic study by Wolff (1969). Even in the first week of life, babies responded by crying when he teased them by repeatedly removing a pacifier; in our own study we found this would happen by the eighth day after birth (Dunn, 1977). So as early as this, babies can be upset by circumstances that are psychologically frustrating, rather than simply by their physical states (such as cold or hunger). From very early on, babies can also be upset when someone with whom they are familiar behaves oddly, such as when their mother does not behave in her usual animated, conversational way, for instance. By their second or third week, they can often be calmed by the human voice: Their attention and interest is more drawn to this than to the sound of a rattle or bell. By a month or so, a fussing baby can often be calmed by someone looking at or talking to him or her, and indeed he or she will often cry at being left.

This crying at being left (which shows great individual variability) reveals babies' increasing sociability. Wolff showed that if a feeding was interrupted at five to six weeks, many babies were so interested in the person feeding them that they did not protest. Their distress at being left was not, at this age, related to a particular person's departure. But by the second half of the first year, being left by *particular individuals* causes distress. Babies have distinguished their familiar caregivers and family members from strangers much earlier than this, but it is in the second half of the year that they miss particular people in a different way, in their absence. The development reflects a profound change in the way children's memory works, in their ability to picture an absent person, and this capacity greatly changes the way a baby relates to family and friends. He or she can miss them when they are gone; his or her tie with them spans time and space. They are no longer "out of sight, out of mind." It means that there is a new dimension to babies' relationships, with a new source of distress and anxiety when they are left by those people that the babies love, and a transformation of the babies' state of contentment and happiness in the presence of these people.

A key change in babies' affective expression comes with the development of intentional crying and the instrumental use of displays of negative emotions. The crying of a newborn baby has a compelling effect on the adults around him or her, but the baby is not aware of this or able to use it intentionally. But during the first year, the expression of distress or anger comes to be used as a controllable way for getting attention and help. For a one-year-old, it is clear that crying is just one way among many for getting attention. Tracing the development of this deliberate control over the expression of anger or distress presents many problems. The difficulty is this: If we are to distinguish when the means to an end (crying to get attention) is being used deliberately, we have to be able to distinguish the means from the end. This is much easier to do in relation to a baby's wish for an object: We can see him or her try different ways to get it. But it is much harder to conclude, from simply observing them crying and being comforted, when babies have begun to cry intentionally to get attention. The beginnings of intentional behavior have been studied chiefly in the context of children's behavior with objects (Zelazo, Astington, & Olson, 1999). However, drawing conclusions about children's intentional use of emotional signals from what we know of their intentional use of objects may well be misleading.

For example, experiments show that a 9-month-old is not aware of the ways in which adults can help in the world of objects (Bates, Camaioni, & Volterra, 1975), but we should not conclude that a baby of this age is unaware of how his or her own emotional signals affect the people around him or her. The literature on the effects on babies of perturbations in their usual reciprocal exchanges with their caregivers (such as their mothers' posing a "still face" rather than their usual responses to the babies' own emotional expressions) shows that well before 6 months babies are extremely sensitive to such violations of their caregivers' usual expressions and responsiveness. It appears very likely that a nine-month-old will have been aware for many weeks that his or her distress signals are usually followed by attention and comfort from adults and will have been putting this awareness into practice. It has been plausibly argued by those in both behavioral and psycho-

analytic traditions that the capacity to act intentionally may develop initially in children's most significant and distressful interactions with other people—notably parents.

Developmental changes in what elicits babies' emotions have also been documented in research on fear and on smiling and laughter. The appearance of babies' smiling response to people's faces and voices at around 6 weeks of age, for instance, has a powerful effect on both adults and other children. When these smiles are accompanied a few weeks later by cooing (Sroufe & Waters, 1986), the impact is even more rewarding. Experiments that compared babies' reactions to puppets and to unfamiliar people showed that although they looked at the puppets as much as at the adults, they very rarely smiled at the puppets, even though these were moving "talking" puppets. The adults, in contrast, were treated to big smiles and much "talk" (Ellsworth, Muir, & Hains, 1993). After 7 months or so, it is *familiar* people in particular that make babies smile. And with the cognitive changes that take place toward the end of the first year, sources of amusement and happiness become still more differentiated. Shared games and jokes that involve unexpected or discrepant experiences become a potent source of pleasure to both baby and other. The sight of their mothers wearing funny hats or hearing them making a funny noise can make 10-month-olds roar with laughter. The more that babies understand of their social world and what is expected of other people, the more they find violations of "usual" behavior a source of amusement. And for their parents and their siblings, this means a new dimension of affectionate interaction—a sharing of amusement that we recognize as a crucial aspect of adult relationships—is already present in the first year.

### Responsiveness to Others' Emotions

These changes in the elicitors of babies' emotions are paralleled by the changes in their sensitivity to others' emotions. A number of lines of evidence suggest that very young infants do respond to certain emotional signals with a corresponding emotional state (Thompson, 1998)—in their response to other babies' crying, for instance. Research by Haviland and Lelwica (1987) showed that by 10 weeks of age babies responded differentially to their mothers' happy, sad, and angry facial and vocal expressions. The mothers sat facing their babies and were asked to show each emotion with face and voice. Each emotion was presented repeatedly, with rest periods. The babies were filmed, and the analysis of their facial reactions showed that they expressed more joy in response to mothers' expression of happiness, more "mouthing" in response to sadness, and less interest in response to anger. The authors argued that the evidence indicates the babies were not simply matching their mothers' expressions but were matching their mothers' affective states; it seemed that their mothers' expressions elicited an affective experience for the babies.

Babies are also differentially responsive to the affective message carried in the voice and are highly sensitive to the prosody of the human voice. Fernald (1993) used an auditory preference procedure to investigate the responses of five-month-old babies to positive and negative vocal affect, measuring the babies' facial expressions when they were played vocalizations in their own language and in an unfamiliar language. The babies showed differential and appropriate emotional responses, with more positive attention and smiling when they heard vocal "approvals" than when they heard "prohibitions." Even young infants, these results revealed, respond to the hedonic tone of the vocal messages they hear. Face, voice, and body posture all potentially provide important information to babies about others' emotion. And, from research within the social referencing paradigm, much has been learned about the extent to which babies understand and use such information.

## Social Referencing

A group of researchers in Denver in the mid-1970s noticed that, toward the end of their first year, babies who were faced with an unusual object or placed in a situation about which they were uncertain often glanced toward their mothers, as if they sought guidance or reassurance (Klinnert, Campos, Sorce, Emde, & Svejda, 1983). They investigated this observation in a series of studies in which they placed babies in such uncertain situations (for instance, on a "visual cliff," in which it appeared that there was a sudden drop in the floor level) and instructed the babies' mothers to express various emotions (smiling encouragement, expressing fear, or holding a neutral expression). The babies' response varied systematically and appropriately according to the emotion expressed by their mothers. They appeared to be emboldened by the mothers' happy and positive expressions and inhibited by the mothers' fearful expression. These initial observations raised a range of questions. Were the babies responding to the mothers' general emotional state—or to the specific facial expression? Was the babies' behavior a reflection of their own emotional states, which were affected in a general way by their mothers' emotional signals? Or were they sensitive to the source and direction of the mothers' emotional expression? That is, do babies of this age appreciate that their mothers' emotional state refers to a specific source?

A series of elegant studies by Mumme and Fernald (1995; Mumme, Fernald, & Herrera, 1996) and by Baldwin and Moses (1994, 1996) has clarified the picture. It seems that by the end of the first year babies are able to pick up what their mothers' emotional response (voice and face)

refers to and to regulate their own response appropriately, but also that the babies' emotional moods are influenced by their mothers' emotional states. The fundamental processes of emotional communication are in place: Another person's emotional message affects the baby's own emotions and provides information about the specific sources of emotion in the other person.

## Changes in the Second and Third Years

Just as the sources of children's happiness, fear, and anger change with the cognitive developments of the first year and affect the quality of their close relationships, so are there marked changes with the cognitive developments of the second and third years in children's emotional expressions and in the sources that elicit them. These carry profound implications for the children's close relationships. For example, as babies become more able to control their own actions and become more independent and autonomous, they are increasingly likely to be angry when their "plans" are frustrated. In a classic study in the 1930s, Goodenough (1931) documented a striking increase in the frequency with which children displayed anger toward their mothers, which peaked in the course of the second year and then decreased in the third year. The development of angry, assertive, "difficult" behavior between 18 months and 2 years of age has been commented on for centuries (the "terrible twos") and clearly documented (Dunn, 1988). In general terms, observational studies of children show that children take an increasing role as initiators of their interactions with their parents (Clarke-Stewart & Hevey, 1981) and also within the sibling relationship (Abramovitch, Corter, Pepler, & Stanhope, 1986; Dunn & Munn, 1986a, 1986b) between 18 months and 3 years.

Most notably, a range of new emotions that reflects an increasing and subtle sensitivity to others' reactions is shown over the course of the second year: pride, shame, embarrassment, and guilt (Tangney & Fischer, 1995). These are often termed the *social* or *self-conscious emotions*, as they relate to our sense of self and our consciousness of others' reactions to us. The first signs of pride are evident in children's "success" or "mastery" smiles as they glance at their parents when they have achieved a goal (Kagan, 1981; Lewis, 1993). Lewis and his colleagues showed that by 3 years old, children expressed more pride when they succeeded on difficult tasks than when they succeeded on easy ones. They also showed more shame at failure on easy than on difficult tasks. And during the second half of the second year, signs of embarrassment are seen. Children lower their eyes, hang their heads, blush, or hide their faces in their hands (Lewis, 1993; Stipek, Recchia, & McClintic, 1992; Tangney & Fischer, 1995). In relationship terms, such sensitivity and responsiveness to other people's responses to a child's own behavior is clearly of key significance for the growth of intimacy and self-disclosure. Seeds of this intimacy are shown in the second and third years, when children begin to talk (with their mothers initially, then increasingly with their siblings and friends) about feelings—their own and those of others (Brown, Donelan-McCall, & Dunn, 1996; Brown & Dunn, 1991, 1992).

This growing sensitivity to others' feelings, revealed in the expression of shame, guilt, and embarrassment, and in children's behavioral responses to others' emotions during infancy, toddlerhood, and the preschool years (for review, see Harris, 1994) has key implications for the quality of children's relationships. We consider this sensitivity next in terms of a series of relationship themes.

## Understanding Emotions and Close Relationships

### The Development of Empathetic Concern

Clearly, the growth of babies' sensitivity to their parents' and siblings' expressions of emotion is important for the quality of their relationships. But when do they show signs of empathic concern for these others, if they are distressed? A classic study by Zahn-Waxler and Radke-Yarrow (1982) charted the early development of empathic behavior. Mothers were trained to record their babies' behavior when in the presence of other people expressing emotions; the reliability of this methodology was carefully established, and the results showed that during the second year, when their parents showed distress, children began to behave in a way that indicated they recognized the distress and made an attempt to alleviate it. A similar developmental pattern is reported for young children's response to siblings' distress: During the second year, home observations showed that attempts to comfort siblings are made (as are attempts to exacerbate the distress; Dunn, 1988). The key developmental shift is away from simply reacting to others' emotions toward using these emotional cues as guides to others' internal states and to understanding the links between these states and people's behavior.

### Talking About Feelings

With the growth of language, a new dimension of connectedness and intimacy in relationships is possible: Talk about feelings between children and the other members of their families and their friends is a central part of this new aspect of their relationships. What we have learned from studies of children's talk about emotions includes the following two key points.

First, talk about emotions, which reflects children's interest in and curiosity about others' feelings, increases rapidly over the second and third years, as Bartsch and Wellman's (1995) meticulous analyses of a large data set of children's spontaneous naturally occurring talk has established (see also Brown et al., 1996). Questions about other people's feelings and wants and about why they behave the way they do increase markedly over the third year and are often focused on hurt and upset. Emotion features prominently in children's first essays into talking about other people's behavior and in their causal reasoning about why people behave the way they do (Dunn & Brown, 1993). This family discourse about emotions is central to the growth of understanding others' inner states (Bartsch & Estes, 1996; Bartsch & Wellman, 1995). The analysis of children's spontaneous conversations about the emotions of those with whom they are familiar shows that after the initial curiosity and interest in feelings in the second and third years, around four years they begin to understand that emotions can depend on beliefs, on what people expect will happen. They talk not only about current emotions but about both past and future emotions (Wellman, Harris, Banerjee, & Sinclair, 1995).

Second, both natural discourse data and experimental studies show that two- and three-year-olds appreciate that individual emotional reactions in others will diverge depending on the desires or preferences of the individual (e.g., Wellman et al., 1995). In the experimental studies, children are told stories in which the likes and dislikes of a character are first established; then the events of the narrative involve the character facing the liked or disliked experience, and the children are asked to explain or predict the story characters' reactions. In natural discourse, children often explicitly contrast their own and others' emotional responses to particular situations.

### The Development of Shared Humor

The dimension of shared humor in children's relationships with family members, which is evident in the first year, becomes increasingly elaborate and differentiated as their powers of communication and social understanding flower during the preschool years. Observations of children within their families reveal that they clearly differentiate what their parents and their siblings will find funny and exploit their rapidly increasing grasp of what is forbidden and what is expected in clowning and in verbal jokes. The significance of this joking and teasing lies both in the pleasure that they experience in sharing their positive feelings with particular others and in manipulating the emotions of the others through the new understanding that their jokes and teasing reflect. This new power of expression within close relationships, which is evident in the dimension of shared humor, is one aspect of a more general development that is central to the quality of children's relationships—the growth of emotion regulation.

## Emotion Regulation

The term *emotion regulation* is usually used to refer to the variety of processes (both internal and external) that are involved in the management of emotional arousal—on which communication and interaction will depend. Initially, parents are of key importance in helping babies in this respect (see chapter 19, this volume). Research on developments in emotional regulation has been chiefly focused on the increasing control that children exert over their frustration, anger, or distress. These changes have been studied in a variety of ways, including the use of maternal and nursery staff reports, naturalistic observations, and experimental studies in which babies' and toddlers' responses to standard, mildly frustrating situations are investigated (e.g., having their arms restrained when sitting in a high chair or being presented with a frustrating toy; Stifter & Braungart, 1995). These major changes in emotional control during the second year are clearly achievements of great importance for their relationships (Garber & Dodge, 1991; Goodenough, 1931).

But it is misleading to consider the development of children's emotion regulation only in terms of the "damping down" of extremes of distress or anger, as a homeostatic mechanism operating within the individual. What is striking is the growth of children's ability to influence not only their own emotions but those of others—as in their use of shared humor—and to use other people to meet their own emotional needs and influence their own affective states. These developments reflect profound changes in the nature of children's relationships. Through their increased communicative abilities and their grasp of what influences the behavior of their family members and friends, they are able to express their affection and ask for love, to explain their own feelings, and to enlist comfort or help. They are increasingly able to share positive experiences, draw attention to their successes, and start conversations about what interests them. They begin to be able to exert some control over their own future emotional states, for instance, by evading parental disapproval, by shifting blame to others, or by deception (Dunn, 1988; Newton, 1994). In their ability to influence the feelings and actions of their parents, siblings, and friends, preschool children reveal the richness and complexity of their close relationships and the increasing intimacy and power these relationships involve, even for children in their third and fourth years.

Does the decrease in outbursts of negative emotions during the third year imply a greater harmony in the children's close relationships? In one sense, yes: Overt anger is less vividly expressed. However, the greater understanding of other people's wishes, intentions, and feelings during the second and third years does not necessarily mean greater harmony in their relationships in terms of conflict and disputes, as we see in considering individual differences in the next section.

## Response to Emotions Between Other People

In their classic study of children's responses to the expression of emotion between other family members, Zahn-Waxler and Radke-Yarrow (1982) reported that, within a family setting, children were increasingly sensitive during the second year to expressions of affection or conflict between their parents. In a parallel way, the observational research on siblings has documented how vigilantly children as early as the second year monitor the interactions between their parents and their siblings; their reaction to those interactions between other family members are importantly linked to the emotions the others are expressing (Dunn & Munn, 1985). Important research within an experimental paradigm has focused on the significance of this interest and sensitivity to anger and conflict between others, including family members (Cummings & Davies, 1994). Children within a laboratory "apartment" were exposed to arguments between adults (in some experiments, their mother and an expert; in others, unfamiliar adults). Witnessing such conflict has both an immediate and a longer term impact on children's behavior and their interactions with others.

## Understanding Mixed Emotions

One of the hallmarks of children's understanding of emotions in middle childhood is their appreciation of the experience of mixed or ambivalent emotions (see Harris, 1989; chapter 20, this volume). In the early school years, children who are asked to comment on a series of vignettes in which the protagonists are likely to feel mixed emotions begin to acknowledge that such experiences may provoke a mix of both positive and negative emotions. Longitudinal research indicates that many children, by six years, understand the experience of mixed emotions in response to a single event (Brown & Dunn, 1996). This growing understanding is seen as essential for integrating emotional experience into a mature conceptualization of the self (Harter, 1986), in understanding how people who have transgressed feel. It is also of obvious importance for our conceptions of our own relationships: As adults we acknowledge that those we love may anger us as well as love us, and that we may feel both anger and affection within our close relationships.

## The Relationship Specificity of Understanding Emotions

Finally, we note that research into children's understanding of the emotions of those with whom they had close relationships showed that by age four, children gave quite differentiated accounts of causes of emotions experienced by their mothers, siblings, and friends (Dunn & Hughes, 1998). The children in these studies were asked, in a conversational way, "What makes Mommy sad/angry/happy/scared?" (after the researchers had established the children's recognition of these terms) and were similarly asked about causes of these emotions in themselves, their siblings, and their friends. Research into the understanding of emotions could usefully specify *whose* emotions are being assessed rather than treating this understanding as a child characteristic that is independent of the person whose emotions are the focus of attention.

### Emotions and Understanding More Broadly Considered

The evidence for children's understanding of the emotions and mental states of those with whom they have close relationships, drawn from naturalistic studies of toddlers and preschoolers and from the analyses of natural discourse, raises some central questions about the relationship of emotion to cognitive capacities and to developmental changes in those capacities. The naturalistic data on comforting, teasing, and deception and on children's causal talk about feelings provide a picture of the early development of these aspects of understanding that is in some respects in tension with the findings of experimental studies, which suggests that these abilities are evident only in older children. Why should there be a discrepancy between the capacities very young children demonstrate in the context of their close relationships with familiar others and their less successful performance in the more formal, standardized experimental assessments of emotion understanding and mind reading, all of which involve children's judgments and reasoning about hypothetical scenarios?

Both the familiarity of the people involved in the naturalistic setting and the emotional salience of the pragmatic context are relevant to the children's success in anticipating and manipulating the emotions of others. The situations in which children show their earliest powers of deception, comforting, teasing, or joking (all indicating some grasp of others' inner states) involve relationship settings that are far from affectively neutral. Rather, they are interactive situations in which the children and their interlocutors are feeling and expressing frustration, desire, amusement, or anger. It is in these emotional interactions with familiar others that the earliest signs of children's understanding of inner states are evident. We may misrepresent children's powers of understanding if we do not pay attention to such socioemotional and pragmatic issues.

Furthermore, the evidence suggests that such emotionally salient interactions, in the context of close relationships, may not only reveal children's capacities particularly clearly but also may well be implicated in the development of understanding of others' emotions and minds (Dunn, 1999). As we have seen, it is plausible to assume that the cognitive changes that underlie children's increasing understanding of emotions, appreciation of social rules, and sense of self lead to the emergence of the new emotions of shame, guilt, and embarrassment—that is, that the emotions develop as a result of the children's cognitive maturity. However, the relationship between emotion and cognitive change may be more complicated; the direction of causality may well go both ways. Emotional experiences in close relationships may well foster more mature understanding of others. A number of lines of evidence illustrate the support for this argument: the findings on children's conversations about inner states, on early narratives, and on deception.

First, the evidence on conversations: As we discuss in the section on individual differences, children who frequently participate in conversations in which feelings are referred to and discussed are much more successful on later assessments of emotion understanding and mind reading than those who have not had such conversational experience. In addition, experimental studies of children's performance on theory of mind tasks show that performance is enhanced if children are given a chance to engage in conversations about the behavior of the protagonists (Appleton & Reddy, 1996). What precipitates such conversations in real-life settings? Does the social partner matter? How is the emotional setting important for what is learned?

The evidence indicates that children's own emotional state is important in the initiation of talk about inner states. Dunn and Brown (1994) found, for instance, in naturalistic observations that mothers were more than twice as likely to talk about feelings with their children when the children were upset or angry than when they were happy or expressing neutral emotions. And the children were more likely to engage in causal talk about feelings when they were angry or upset (Dunn & Brown, 1993). The general point—that what is learned in particular interactions may be linked in a central way to the emotional context and the pragmatics of the interactions—is one that was made by Stein and her colleagues (Stein & Miller, 1993) in their analyses of arguments between mothers and their children. It can be argued that it is not simply the child's exposure to new information or to the viewpoint of another in such exchanges that is important for fostering cognitive change. Rather, the quality of the relationship between child and interlocutor, reflected in the emotion and pragmatics of their interaction, plays a key role. A parallel argument was powerfully made for taking account of the "contexts of practice" in children's acquisition of language (Bruner, 1983).

A second line of evidence on the significance of the emotional context for cognitive change comes from research on children's early narratives. It has been proposed that narrative plays a central part in the development of social understanding—that patterns of narrative scaffold the kind of metacognition about intentions that lies at the core of understanding how inner states are linked to human action (Bruner, 1990; Feldman, 1992). The argument is that we account for our own actions and those of others within the frame of narrative stories. Conversational narratives have a key place in children's close relationships—in children's explanations of events, their sharing of excitement or trouble, their amusement, or their concern about the future. We examined the occurrence of children's unsolicited narratives about the past in a longitudinal study over the second, third, and fourth years; the frequency of such narratives paralleled the development of children's talk about more broad psychological issues. The analysis of these narratives highlighted two issues relevant to the significance of emotion to the development of social understanding (Brown, 1995).

First, just as emotion figured importantly in the initiation of talk about feelings, so too was it important in the narratives of these very young children. Experiences involving anger, fear, and distress prompted the children to tell coherent stories about the past; the children showed their most sophisticated language skills (sequencing events causally and temporally, referring to inner states) in their narratives about such negative emotional experiences. Second, the pragmatic context in which these young children engaged in this sophisticated behavior was predominantly when the children attempted to influence another family member's behavior. Brown argued that there is a great pressure in family disputes and discussions for children to be able to construct their own compelling accounts of what happened and to persuade others. The urgency of getting their own accounts appreciated in such family discussions may well contribute to the growth of their communicative competence, as in Mannle and Tomasello's (1987) concept of "communicative pressure." The general point established by the study of conversations and narratives, as in the research on naturally occurring deception, is that children's relationship goals and the emotional context of the interactions involved are central to the children's developing understanding of emotions and to what is learned about others.

The argument that the emotional context is central not only to how children use their understanding but also to the development of that understanding is further supported by the general developmental account of children's understanding of the mind proposed by Bartsch and Estes (1996). The account, based on data from both experimental research within the theory of mind paradigm and natural language studies, is as follows. Very young children

explain people's actions at first in terms of emotions and desires. Through their social experiences, they come to incorporate the notion of belief in their explanations of why people behave the way they do. One important implication of this is that an understanding of cognitive states arises from an earlier understanding of emotional states. Bartsch and Estes (1996) argue that metacognitive understanding develops from the framework of understanding emotions—a framework which, we have seen, develops through close relationships. Such an argument relates to children's initial understanding of the mind. What remains unclear, and a fruitful issue for future research, is how far the significance of emotional relationships for cognitive development changes as children grow up. It is possible that the significance of heightened emotions for what is learned in particular interactions diminishes as children become less at the mercy of their own emotions.

A final general point concerning emotional development and social relations involves the consideration of cultural concepts of emotion. The remarkable developments in children's interest in and reflection on emotions, evident in their discourse about feelings with their families and friends during early childhood, are important for two rather different reasons. First, as we have seen, these developments in communication about emotion make it possible for children to understand emotional experiences (their own and those of others) and thus "to share their personal experience of the world with others, including 'being with' others in intimacy, isolation, loneliness, fear, awe, and love" (Stern, 1985, p. 182). Second, this engagement in talk about feelings within close relationships is the process through which children participate in the particular shared cultural concepts of their social world, and these concepts can differ widely across cultures (Lutz & White, 1986; Shweder & LeVine, 1984). It is through this discourse—central to close relationships—that children become members of particular cultures. For a discussion of how cultural influences on the perception and classification of experiences, including affective experiences, are mediated through relationships, see Hinde (1987).

## Individual Differences

So far, we have considered normative changes in affective development and their relation to children's developing relationships. But from birth, individual differences in emotional expression, regulation, and temperament are striking (see chapters 16 and 17, this volume, and Rothbart & Bates, 1998; Thompson, 1998, for recent reviews). How are these differences related to the development of close relationships? In this section, individual differences in children's emotional characteristics as contributors to parent-child relations are first considered; second, we discuss implications of the research on individual differences in sibling relationships; third, we consider links between these relationships and individual differences in emotion understanding.

## Parent-Child Relationships in Early Childhood

The marked individual differences in children's emotional behavior and responsiveness are central to differences in the early development of their social relationships. Such individual characteristics have been most widely studied in relation to parent-child relationships. Thus within attachment research a lively debate has taken place on the extent to which temperamental differences, especially in emotional behavior, contribute to the classification of the security aspects of babies' relationships with their parents (Goldsmith & Harman, 1994). The following conclusions appear justified. First, temperamental differences make a significant though modest contribution to children's behavior in the Strange Situation—the sequence of separations and reunions of child and parent that is standardly employed to assess the security of a child's relationship (Thompson, 1998). Second, and most important, both temperamental characteristics and family experiences act together to influence a child's behavior in the Strange Situation (e.g., Van den Boom & Hoeksma, 1994). Thus, for example, maternal personality and sensitivity are particularly clearly linked to the quality of the relationship that develops between child and mother for babies that are especially easily distressed or irritable (Mangelsdorf, Gunnar, Kestenbaum, Lang, & Andreas, 1990).

From the wealth of recent research on parent-child relationships, three general issues concerning individual differences in affective development stand out as key questions for future research. First, it is important to clarify further how children's emotional characteristics and their parents' (not only mothers') personalities interact—following the findings noted previously. This interaction needs to be studied in terms not only of the contribution to the quality of the relationship that develops between child and parent but also of the possible influence of that relationship on the children's later emotional behavior. We need to investigate the processes that underlie the connections between child and parent emotional characteristics. What, for instance, is the role of genetics in contributing to the patterns that link maternal personality, children's emotional responsiveness and regulation, and the quality of their relationships?

Although the genetic contribution to differences in emotional aspects of temperament is becoming clear (Goldsmith, Lemery, Buss, & Campos, 1999), the story regarding attachment needs further clarification. Sibling concordance of about 60% has been reported for attachment classification—that is, the categorization of the way

siblings react to the sequence of separation and reunion experiences with their parents (Van IJzendoorn et al., 2000; Ward, Vaughn, & Robb, 1988). However, the first systematic twin study of attachment using the Strange Situation focused on 110 twin pairs and found only modest genetic influence but substantial influence of the aspects of the twins' shared environment (O'Connor & Croft, 2001). Thus, for a continuous measure of attachment security, the correlations between the monozygotic (MZ) and dizygotic (DZ) twins were .48 and .38, respectively, whereas the concordance of the twins for attachment type were 70% and 64%, respectively. Another twin study that was based on observations rather than the twins' behavior in the Strange Situation reported evidence for greater genetic influence (Finkel, Wille, & Matheny, 1998).

Beyond the evidence for genetic influence on the emotional aspects of temperament, it should be noted that other individual characteristics that contribute to the quality of close relationships (and thus in turn play a part in children's affective development) are importantly influenced by genetics: for example, differences in empathy (Zahn-Waxler, Robinson, & Emde, 1992), emotion understanding and mind reading (Hughes & Cutting, 1999), and, in adolescence, humor (Manke et al., submitted), self-esteem, and self-confidence (McGuire et al., 1999). This is clearly a key area for future research in relationships, in both young children and adolescents.

A second general issue is the principle established by Hinde (1979) that is centrally important to acknowledge but that is all too often ignored in the interests of presenting simple models of relationship development—that no aspect of an individual's behavior in interaction with another person is independent of the shared history of their relationship. How a young child interacts with her parent is affected not only by both of their personalities and emotional responsiveness but also by their shared history and expectations of joint pleasures, conflict, humor, or control. Progress in understanding the significance of relationships for affective development and vice versa requires us, then, to deal with widely differing levels of influence: the level of the individual and what he or she brings to a relationship; the level of the interactions between the individuals, and the level of the relationship between the two individuals, which includes the patterns of their interactions over a long time span, their shared expectations, and the balance of their relative contributions to the relationship (which changes with development; Dunn, Creps, & Brown, 1996). Finally, the level of the social world beyond the dyad needs to be taken into account: the impact of other relationships within the family, the influence of social networks and social institutions on relationships within the family, and the norms and expectations concerning emotional behavior and relationships within the particular cultural group (Dunn, 1993; Hinde, 1992).

The third issue relates to the breadth of dimensions of relationships studied. If we are to understand either the part played by individual differences in children's emotional characteristics in the development of their relationships or the role of those relationships in the children's later affective development, a broad range of affective dimensions of parent-child relationships needs to be included in our studies, beyond the dimension of security of attachment. Parent-child relationships differ in mutual warmth, in the expression of affection and conflict, in the extent of shared communication about feelings, in shared humor and self-disclosure, and in shared involvement in activities. All these dimensions of relationships are considered important in adult-adult relationships, and they deserve to be included in investigations of affective development.

## Sibling Relationships and Emotion

Children's emotional behavior is often strikingly different within their relationships with their siblings and their parents. During the early preschool period, both anger and positive emotions are expressed much more frequently and intensely in sibling interactions than within the parent-child relationship (Dunn et al., 1996). The individual differences between siblings in the emotional quality of their relationships are also notable: Some brothers and sisters are affectionate, warm, and empathetic in their relations with each other; others are constantly irritable, angry, and aggressive; and still others are relatively uninterested and emotionally neutral (Boer & Dunn, 1990). Systematic study of individual differences in sibling and parent-child relationships has some key implications for those concerned with affective development.

First, the differences in the emotional behavior of children within their relationships with siblings and with parents remind us that we should move away from the notion of emotional characteristics (including responsiveness and regulation) as being solely within-child traits. Rather, children's affective behavior is closely bound to the context of particular relationships—indeed, it could be considered an emergent property of those relationships. Whereas temperamental characteristics contribute importantly to differences in the quality of sibling relationships (Brody, Stoneman, & McCoy, 1994), *different* temperamental characteristics may be important in a child's various relationships. Little overlap may be seen in the dimensions that are significant for a child's various relationships, and the same characteristic may have different implications for different relationships. Thus shy, emotionally inhibited girls were found in one study to have especially warm relationships with their parents, but such qualities were associated with relatively distant peer relationships (Hinde, 1979, 1987, 1992)

This general principle—that we should take a relationship perspective to the study of individual differences in emotional development—is further supported by a second implication of research on children within their different close relationships. This concerns the evidence that children use their emotion understanding differently within their different relationships. Findings from one study showed that there was no significant correlation between children's propensity to take account of their antagonist's feelings in conflict with their mothers and their propensity to do so when in conflict with their siblings or friends. The same child behaved quite differently in conflict with mother, sibling, or friend (Slomkowski & Dunn, 1992). Similarly, children's participation in discourse about inner states with mothers and with siblings and their discourse about inner states with friends were not correlated (Brown et al., 1996). Children's management of conflict and their discourse about feelings were each related to their performance on standard assessments of emotion understanding, but the *use* of this understanding in real-life interactions with mother, sibling, or friend was influenced by the emotional dynamics of the particular social relationship.

A third implication of the evidence on sibling relationships concerns individual differences in the development of this emotional understanding. Individual differences in understanding of feelings are marked, both in standard assessments of understanding and in children's "real-life" interactions with others. Interest in investigating the antecedents and sequelae of these individual differences has grown rapidly in recent years, and the role of social processes in their development has been of particular interest.

## Social Processes in the Development of Individual Differences in Emotion Understanding

A range of different aspects of early social relationships have been cited as important in the development of emotion understanding. These include (1) studies of the security of children's attachment to their mothers, parental socialization techniques, and the emotional expressiveness of parents with their children (Cassidy, Parke, Butkovsky & Braungart, 1992); (2) evidence that children's participation in family discourse about feelings is linked to individual differences in their emotion understanding later (Dunn, Brown, Slomkowski, Tesla, & Youngblade, 1991); and (3) evidence that children's experiences with other children, including siblings (Dunn et al., 1991), friends (Hughes & Dunn, 1998), and peers in the preschool period (Denham, McKinley, Couchoud, & Holt, 1990), are implicated in these later differences. Of particular interest here are recent findings that bring together the evidence on the significance of talk about emotions with information on both parent-child attachment and child-child relationships.

For example, recent studies of parent-child attachment relationships have begun to highlight links between the security of early mother-child attachment relationships, discourse about inner states, and children's social understanding—pursuing the hypothesis that securely attached children might be better able to reflect on metacognitive issues, including the relation of emotional states of others to their actions (Main, 1991). Meins and her colleagues reported that children who were securely attached in infancy were more successful on mind-reading tasks at age four and assessment of "mentalizing" abilities at five years (Meins, Fernyhough, Russell, & Clarke-Carter, 1998). Their account of the processes involved here was that the mothers of the securely attached children showed particular sensitivity to their children's current levels of understanding and used mental state terms in their interactions with them. Meins referred to this propensity as "mind-mindedness" (1997).

The research on child-child relationships highlights three points about the social processes involved in the development of individual differences in emotion understanding. First, individual differences in children's performances on assessments of social understanding (both emotion understanding and mind reading) have been shown to be linked to earlier experiences of cooperative play with an older sibling (Dunn et al., 1991). Children who had experienced frequent positive cooperative experiences with their siblings—especially joint pretend play—were more successful on assessments of social understanding later. Second, talk about feelings with a sibling quadrupled in frequency between ages 33 and 47 months, whereas such talk with mothers declined in frequency over this period; talk about inner states was much more frequent with siblings and especially friends than with mothers (Brown et al., 1996). Third, the positive quality of the sibling relationships and of the friendships of the children in these studies were linked positively to the children's engagement in talk about inner states and to their later social understanding (Hughes & Dunn, 1998). The findings indicate that some child-child relationships, those that are affectively close, have real potential as influences on the development of children's ability to understand the emotions and thoughts of others, especially in the third and subsequent years of life. These relationships are notably different from those with parents or teachers in terms of communicative demands and challenges. Children are communicative partners who do not make the allowances of a parent or sensitive adult, who is motivated to respond to a relatively inexperienced communicator. But they are more likely to share interests and fantasies than an adult partner, to be excited and amused by similar situations. The notion that certain kinds of interactions between young children who like each other may foster the growth of emotion understanding does not fit with accounts of cognitive development that emphasize

the significance of didactic encounters with expert adults (such as Vygotskian accounts). However, it is clear that in most cultures children spend much more of their childhood from infancy onward interacting with other children than they do with adults. The traditional view of adults as the key influences on social understanding may well need revision.

A major caveat that relates to all such correlational studies concerns direction of effects. Causal inferences cannot be made from such studies, and the findings are always open to the possibility that a third common causal factor may underlie any connections found. This note of caution applies to the numerous studies that are focused on connections between individual differences in affective development and later relationships and understanding of emotions. In the next section, the issue of patterns over time in emotion understanding is considered as one aspect of affective development that is currently of particular interest.

## Sequelae of Individual Differences in Emotion Understanding

Longitudinal studies of individual differences in emotion understanding have established four important points. The first is that continuities in emotion understanding over the preschool and early childhood years are substantial. An interesting point here is that the aspects of emotion understanding that are assessed are different at the various time points investigated (designed to be appropriate for preschool and school-aged children, respectively), yet the stability of individual differences remains relatively high. Thus two separate studies (with samples differing in socioeconomic and educational background from the United States and the United Kingdom) report that preschoolers' scores on assessments of affective perspective taking and emotion recognition were correlated with their scores years later on assessments of their understanding of mixed emotions (Brown & Dunn, 1996; Dunn & Cutting, 1999). Such data in themselves do not clarify what processes may be underlying the continuities: It could be continuity in the social relationships associated with fostering of emotion understanding that contribute to the patterns over time, or other characteristics of the children (such as general intelligence) could contribute.

The second point is that early emotion understanding is clearly associated with later differences in the quality of children's peer, parent-child, and sibling relationships, Success in understanding emotions as a preschooler, for example, is correlated with later cooperative, shared pretend games with friends (a central feature of friendship in childhood), with negotiating and compromise in conflict (Dunn & Herrera, 1997), with enjoying good peer relations at school (Cutting & Dunn, 2001; Dunn, 1995), and with moral sensibility (Dunn, Brown, & Maguire, 1995; Dunn,

Cutting, & Demetriou, 2000). Other research has shown that difficulties in peer relations (being rejected, isolated, or aggressive with peers) are related to problems in some aspects of social understanding, which include emotion understanding (Rubin, Bukowski, & Parker, 1998). Recent studies of preschoolers who are at risk for later problems in friendships have also implicated difficulties in emotion understanding in the poor quality of their dyadic friendships (Hughes, White, Sharpen, & Dunn, 2000).

The third point in considering these sequelae of early emotion understanding concerns the processes that explain such connections over time. Among the mechanisms suggested, it has been proposed that parental emotional expressiveness and responsiveness may influence children's emotional understanding and that this in turn influences their peer relationships (Cassidy et al., 1992; Pettit, Bates, & Dodge, 1997). It has also been proposed that emotion understanding may well play a mediating role in creating links across relationships within the family—for instance, between parent and child and sibling relationships. We still have much to learn about the processes that underlie these connections over time. At present, very different mechanisms have been postulated to explain, for instance, links between parent-child and child-friend relationships. Such associations could include, for instance, a third common causal factor, and genetic mediation could play such a role.

Fourth, it is increasingly clear that the later correlates of early emotion understanding include a wide range of developmental outcomes (Dunn, 1995). For instance, the associations that involve children's relationships with other children carry much significance for children's adjustment to school—in which the quality of peer relations plays such a major role. Emotion understanding is also a strong predictor of children's moral sensibility, a relatively neglected but clearly important developmental outcome; connections have been found for both normal and at-risk samples of children (Dunn et al., 2000; Hughes & Dunn, 2000).

## Challenges and Growing Points for Research on Affective Development

Research on children's emotional development within the framework of their close relationships has not only taught us much but has also raised a series of developmental questions that present important challenges for researchers. The lessons that we have learned include the following: (1) close attention has to be paid to the emotional context of particular interactions and to children's interactional goals if we are to clarify the way children use their affective understanding; (2) to understand the development of individual differences in children's affective development, the research framework must include both

the children's earlier emotional experiences and their cognitive abilities; (3) the social processes that are implicated in connections between relationships and emotional understanding need further investigation, which includes attention to both affective and communication dimensions of relationships. At a methodological level, if we are to make progress in understanding causal mechanisms implicated in the links between affective experience, emotional understanding and relationships, both experimental and naturalistic strategies are needed. Among the developmental issues the recent research has raised, the following are particularly exciting.

### How Is Understanding of Emotion Related to Children's Discovery of the Mind?

The issue of how far understanding of emotions should be differentiated from the understanding of other people's beliefs and thoughts—the question of children's understanding of mind that has been the central topic for cognitive developmental research over the past decade—is an important one. Is emotion understanding one aspect of more general cognitive development? Does it play a foundational role of key significance—as in the developmental account articulated by Bartsch and Estes (1996), in which an understanding of cognitive states arises from an earlier understanding of emotion? The suggestion that the sequelae of early mind-reading abilities and emotion understanding are different merits further investigation, as does the suggestion that differences in attachment relationships are related to some aspects of mind reading but not to others (e.g., Meins et al., 1998).

### What Developmental Changes Are There in the Significance of Affective Experiences for Children's Understanding of Others?

The significance of the affective context for the use children make of their developing understanding of others is clear in early childhood. But does this change as children grow up? Are they less at the mercy of their emotions as their powers of metacognition increase? Some research on children's handling of conflict indicates this may be so (Dunn & Herrera, 1997). However, whether the significance of emotion for what children learn in particular interactions changes as they grow up remains unclear and little studied.

### How Does Affective Development Differ for Children at the Extremes?

Most of the research on links between individual differences in affective understanding and their social relationships in early childhood has been conducted with children within the normal range, with the notable exception of studies of autism. Children in middle childhood who have language problems or conduct problems or who suffer from anxiety or disabilities are all at risk for difficulties in both social relationships and social understanding (e.g. Coie & Dodge, 1998). But little is known about the early development of these connections for children who are at the extremes in these domains. Research on preschool children at risk for attention and conduct problems indicates that there are interesting differences in the children's understanding of emotions, their emotional regulation and executive function, their antisocial behavior, and their problems in close relationships (Hughes & Dunn, 1998; Hughes & Dunn, 2000; Hughes et al., 2000). The social and theoretical importance of studying these links in other groups—such as children with language and communication problems—is clear.

### How Do the Developmental Patterns Differ for Children in Different Cultural and Social Class Groups?

Finally, it is evident that we need to learn more about the significance of cultural and social-class differences for the links between emotional experiences, understanding, and social relationships. The focus of most studies has been on a narrow band of middle-class families in the United States and Europe. It is clear that educational background is implicated in individual differences in emotion understanding and socialization practices and that cultures differ markedly in emotion expression and regulation. But children are cultural creatures from birth. The challenge of studying the connections between their cultural worlds, their close relationships, and the interactions in which their understanding is fostered is an exciting one.

### REFERENCES

Abramovitch, R., Corter, C., Pepler, D. J., & Stanhope, L. (1986). Sibling and peer interaction: A final follow-up and a comparison. *Child Development, 57,* 217–229.

Appleton, M., & Reddy, V. (1996). Teaching 3-year-olds to pass false-belief tests: A conversational approach. *Social Development, 5,* 275–291.

Baldwin, D., & Moses, L. J. (1994). Early understanding of referential intent and attentional focus: Evidence from language and emotion. In C. Lewis & P. Mitchell (Eds.), *Children's early understanding of mind: Origins and development* (pp. 133–156). Hove, England: Erlbaum.

Baldwin, D. A., & Moses, L. J. (1996). The ontogeny of social information-processing. *Child Development, 67,* 1915–1939.

Bartsch, K., & Estes, D. (1996). Individual differences in children's developing theory of mind and implications for metacognition. *Learning and Individual Differences, 8*(4), 281–304.

Bartsch, K., & Wellman, H. M. (1995). *Children talk about the mind.* Oxford, England: Oxford University Press.

Bates, E., Camaioni, L., & Volterra, V. (1975). The acquisition of performatives prior to speech. *Merrill Palmer Quarterly, 21,* 205–226.

Boer, F., & Dunn, J. (1990). *Children's sibling relationships: Developmental and clinical issues.* Hillsdale, NJ: Erlbaum.

Braten, S. (1998). *Intersubjective communication and emotion in early ontogeny.* Cambridge, England: Cambridge University Press.

Brody, G. H., Stoneman, Z., & McCoy, J. K. (1994). Forecasting sibling relationships in early adolescence from child temperaments and family processes in middle childhood. *Child Development, 65,* 771–784.

Brown, J. R. (1995). *What happened? Emotional experience and children's talk about the past.* Unpublished manuscript.

Brown, J. R., Donelan-McCall, N., & Dunn, J. (1996). Why talk about mental states? The significance of children's conversations with friends, siblings, and mothers. *Child Development, 67*(3), 836–849.

Brown, J. R., & Dunn, J. (1991). "You can cry, mum": The social and developmental implications of talk about internal states. *British Journal of Developmental Psychology, 9*(2), 237–256.

Brown, J. R., & Dunn, J. (1992). Talk with your mother or your sibling? Developmental changes in early family conversations about feelings. *Child Development, 63*(2), 336–349.

Brown, J. R., & Dunn, J. (1996). Continuities in emotion understanding from 3–6 yrs. *Child Development, 67*(3), 789–802

Bruner, J. (1983). *Child's talk.* Oxford, England: Oxford University Press.

Bruner, J. (1990). *Acts of meaning.* Cambridge, MA: Harvard University Press.

Campos, J. J., Mumme, D. L., Kermoian, R., & Campos, R. (1994). A functionalist perspective on the nature of emotion. *Monographs of the Society for Research in Child Development, 59*(2/3, Serial No. 240), 284–303.

Cassidy, J. C., Parke, R. D., Butkovsky, L., & Braungart, J. M. (1992). Family-peer connections: The roles of emotional expressiveness within the family and children's understanding of emotions. *Child Development, 63,* 603–618.

Clarke-Stewart, K. A., & Hevey, C. M. (1981). Longitudinal relations in repeated observations of mother-child interactions from 1 to 2 and a half years. *Developmental Psychology, 17,* 127–145.

Coie, J. D., & Dodge, K. A. (1998). Aggression and antisocial behavior. In W. Damon (Series Ed.) & N. Eisenberg (Vol. Ed.), *Handbook of child psychology: Vol. 3. Social, emotional, and personality development.* (pp. 779–862). New York: Wiley.

Cummings, E. M., & Davies, P. (1994). *Children and marital conflict: The impact of family dispute and resolution.* New York: Guilford Press.

Cutting, A., & Dunn, J. (2001). *Making the transition to school: Preschool predictors and personal perceptions.* Manuscript submitted for publication.

Darwin, C. (1872). *The expression of emotions in man and animals.* London: Murray.

Denham, S. A., McKinley, M., Couchoud, E. A., & Holt, R. (1990). Emotional and behavioral predictors of preschool peer ratings. *Child Development, 61,* 1145–1152.

Dunn, J. (1977). *Distress and comfort.* London: Open Books.

Dunn, J. (1988). *The beginnings of social understanding.* Cambridge, MA: Harvard University Press.

Dunn, J. (1993). *Young children's close relationships: Beyond attachment* (Vol. 4). Newbury Park, CA: Sage.

Dunn, J. (1995). Children as psychologists: The later correlates of individual differences in understanding of emotions and other minds. *Cognition and Emotion, 9*(2–3), 187–201.

Dunn, J. (1996). Children's relationships: Bridging the divide between cognitive and social development. *Journal of Child Psychology and Psychiatry, 37*(5), 507–518.

Dunn, J. (1999). Mindreading and social relationships. In M. Bennett (Ed.), *Developmental psychology: Achievements and prospects* (pp. 55–71). Philadelphia, PA: Psychology Press.

Dunn, J., & Brown, J. R. (1993). Early conversations about causality: Content, pragmatics and developmental change. *British Journal of Developmental Psychology, 11*(2), 107–123.

Dunn, J., & Brown, J. (1994). Affect expression in the family, children's understanding of emotions, and their interactions with others. *Merrill Palmer Quarterly, 40*(1), 120–137.

Dunn, J., Brown, J. R., & Maguire, M. (1995). The development of children's moral sensibility: Individual differences and emotion understanding. *Developmental Psychology, 31*(4), 649–659.

Dunn, J., Brown, J., Slomkowski, C., Tesla, C., & Youngblade, L. (1991). Young children's understanding of other people's feelings and beliefs: Individual differences and their antecedents. *Child Development, 62*(6), 1352–1366.

Dunn, J., Creps, C., & Brown, J. (1996). Children's family relationships between two and five: Developmental changes and individual differences. *Social Development, 5*(3), 230–250.

Dunn, J., & Cutting, A. (1999). Understanding others, and individual differences in friendship interactions in young children. *Social Development, 8*(2), 201–219.

Dunn, J., Cutting, A., & Demetriou, H. (2000). Moral sensibility, understanding other, and children's friendship interactions in the preschool period. *British Journal of Developmental Psychology, 18*(2), 159–177.

Dunn, J., & Herrera, C. (1997). Conflict resolution with friends, siblings, and mothers: A developmental perspective. *Aggressive Behavior, 23*, 343–357.

Dunn, J., & Hughes, C. (1998). Young children's understanding of emotions within close relationships. *Cognition and Emotion, 12*(2), 171–190.

Dunn, J., & Munn, P. (1985). Becoming a family member: Family conflict and the development of social understanding in the second year. *Child Development, 56*, 764–774.

Dunn, J., & Munn, P. (1986a). Sibling quarrels and maternal intervention: Individual differences in understanding and aggression. *Journal of Child Psychology and Psychiatry and Allied Disciplines, 27*(5), 583–595.

Dunn, J., & Munn, P. (1986b). Siblings and the development of prosocial behaviour. *International Journal of Behavioral Development, 9*(3), 265–284.

Ekman, P., & Davidson, R. (1994). *The nature of emotion.* New York: Oxford University Press.

Ellsworth, C. P., Muir, D. W., & Hains, S. M. J. (1993). Social competence and person-object differentiation: An analysis of the still-face effect. *Developmental Psychology, 29*, 63–73.

Feldman, C. F. (1992). The theory of theory of mind. *Human Development, 35*, 107–117.

Fernald, A. (1993). Approval and disapproval: Infant responsiveness to vocal affect in familiar and unfamiliar languages. *Child Development, 64*, 657–674.

Finkel, D., Wille, D. E., & Matheny, A. P. (1998). Preliminary results from a twin study of infant-caregiver attachment. *Behavior Genetics, 28*, 1–8.

Garber, J., & Dodge, K. (1991). *Affect regulation and dysregulation in childhood.* Cambridge, England: Cambridge University Press.

Goldsmith, H. H., & Harman, C. (1994). Temperament and attachment: Individuals and relationships. *Current Directions in Psychological Science, 3*, 53–57.

Goldsmith, H. H., Lemery, K. S., Buss, K. A., & Campos, J. (1999). Genetic analyses of focal aspects of infant temperament. *Developmental Psychology, 35*, 972–985.

Goodenough, F. L. (1931). *Anger in young children.* Minneapolis: University of Minnesota Press.

Harris, P. L. (1989). *Children and emotion.* Oxford, England: Blackwell.

Harris, P. L. (1994). The child's understanding of emotion: Developmental change and the family environment. *Journal of Child Psychology and Psychiatry, 35*(1), 3–28.

Harter, S. (1986). Cognitive-developmental processes in the integration of concepts about emotions and the self. *Social Cognition, 4*, 119–151.

Haviland, J. M., & Lelwica, M. (1987). The induced affect response: Ten-week-old infants' responses to three emotion expressions. *Developmental Psychology, 23*, 97–104.

Hinde, R. A. (1979). *Towards understanding relationships.* London: Academic Press.

Hinde, R. A. (1987). *Individuals, relationships, cultures.* Cambridge, England: Cambridge University Press.

Hinde, R. A. (1992). Developmental psychology in the context of other behavioral sciences. *Developmental Psychology, 28*, 1018–1029.

Hobson, P. (1993). *Autism and the development of mind.* Hove, England: Erlbaum.

Hughes, C., & Cutting, A. (1999). Nature, nurture and individual differences in early understanding of mind. *Psychological Science, 10*(5), 429–432.

Hughes, C., & Dunn, J. (1998). Understanding mind and emotion: Longitudinal associations with mental-state talk between young friends. *Developmental Psychology, 34*(5), 1026–1037.

Hughes, C., & Dunn, J. (2000). Hedonism or empathy? Hard-to-manage children's moral awareness, and links with cognitive and maternal characteristics. *British Journal of Developmental Psychology, 18*(2), 227–245.

Hughes, C., White, A., Sharpen, J., & Dunn, J. (2000). Antisocial, angry and unsympathetic: "Hard to manage" preschoolers' peer problems, and possible social and cognitive influences. *Journal of Child Psychology and Psychiatry, 41*(2), 169–179.

Kagan, J. (1981). *The second year.* Cambridge, MA: Harvard University Press.

Klinnert, M. D., Campos, J. J., Sorce, J. F., Emde, R. N., & Svejda, M. (1983). Emotions as behavior regulators: Social referencing in infancy. In P. Plutchik & H. Kellerman (Eds.), *Emotion: Theory, research, experience* (pp. 57–86). New York: Academic Press.

Lewis, M. (1993). Self-conscious emotions: Embarrassment, pride, shame, and guilt. In M. Lewis & J. Haviland (Eds.), *The handbook of emotions* (pp. 563–573). New York: Guilford Press.

Lutz, C., & White, G. M. (1986). The anthropology of emotions. *Annual Review of Anthropology, 15*, 405–436.

Main, M. (1991). Metacognitive knowledge, metacognitive monitoring, and singular (coherent) vs. multiple (incoherent) models of attachment: Findings and directions for future research. In C. M. Parkes, J. Stevenson-Hinde, & P. Morris (Eds.), *Attachment across the life cycle* (pp. 127–159). London: Routledge.

Mangelsdorf, S., Gunnar, M., Kestenbaum, R., Lang, S., & Andreas, D. (1990). Infant proneness to distress, temperament, maternal personality, and mother-infant attachment. *Child Development, 61*, 820–831.

Manke, B., Pike, A., Carson, C., Robertson, R., Dunn, J., & Plomin, R. *Associative and distancing humor in adolescent family relations: A genetic study of individual and dyadic relationship effects.* Manuscript submitted for publication.

Mannle, S., & Tomasello, M. (1987). Fathers, siblings and the bridge hypothesis. In K. E. Nelson & A. van Kleeck (Eds.), *Children's language* (Vol. 6, pp. 23–41). Hillsdale, NJ: Erlbaum.

McGuire, S., Manke, B., Saudino, K. J., Reiss, D., Hetherington, E. M., & Plomin, R. (1999). Perceived competence and self worth during adolescence: A longitudinal behavioral genetic study. *Child Development, 70*, 1283–1296.

Meins, E. (1997). *Security of attachment and the social development of cognition.* Hove, England: Psychology Press.

Meins, E., Fernyhough, C., Russell, J. T., & Clarke-Carter, D. (1998). Security of attachment as a predictor of symbolic and mentalising abilities: A longitudinal study. *Social Development, 7*, 1–24.

Mumme, D. L., & Fernald, A. (1995). *Infants' use of gaze in interpreting emotional signals.* Unpublished manuscript.

Mumme, D. L., Fernald, A., & Herrera, C. (1996). Infants' responses to facial and emotional signals in a social referencing paradigm. *Child Development, 67*, 3219–3237.

Newton, P. (1994). *Preschool prevarication: An investigation of the cognitive prerequisites for deception.* Unpublished doctoral dissertation, Portsmouth University, England.

O'Connor, T. G., & Croft, D. M. (2001). A twin study of attachment in preschool children. *Child Development, 72*, 1501–1511.

Pettit, G. S., Bates, J. E., & Dodge, K. A. (1997). Supportive parenting, ecological context, and children's adjustment: A seven-year longitudinal study. *Child Development, 68*, 908–923.

Rothbart, M. K., & Bates, J. E. (1998). Temperament. In W. Damon (Series Ed.) & N. Eisenberg (Vol. Ed.), *Handbook of child psychology: Vol. 3. Social, emotional and personality development* (pp. 105–176). New York: Wiley.

Rubin, K. H., Bukowski, W., & Parker, J. G. (1998). Peer interactions, relationships and groups. In W. Damon &

N. Eisenberg (Eds.), *Handbook of child psychology* (Vol. 3) *Social, emotional, and personality development* (pp. 619–700). New York: Wiley.

Shweder, R. A., & LeVine, R. A. (1984). *Culture theory.* Cambridge, England: Cambridge University Press.

Slomkowski, C. L., & Dunn, J. (1992). Arguments and relationships within the family: Differences in young children's disputes with mother and sibling. *Developmental Psychology, 28*(5), 919–924.

Sroufe, L. A., & Waters, E. (1986). The ontogenesis of smiling and laughter. *Psychological Review, 88*, 173–189.

Stein, N., & Miller, C. (1993). The development of memory and reasoning skill in argumentative contexts: Evaluating, explaining, and generating evidence. In R. Glaser (Ed.), *Advances in instructional psychology* (Vol. 4, pp. 284–334). Hillsdale, NJ: Erlbaum.

Stern, D. (1985). *The interpersonal world of the infant.* New York: Basic Books.

Stifter, C. A., & Braungart, J. M. (1995). The regulation of negative affectivity in infancy: Function and development. *Developmental Psychology, 31*, 448–455.

Stipek, D., Recchia, S., & McClintic, S. (1992). Self-evaluation in young children. *Monographs of the Society for Research in Child Development, 57*(1, Serial No. 226), 100.

Tangney, J., & Fischer, K. (1995). *Self-conscious emotions: The psychology of shame, guilt and embarrassment.* New York: Guilford Press.

Thompson, R. A. (1998). Early sociopersonality development. In W. Damon (Series Ed.) & N. Eisenberg (vol. Ed.), *Handbook of child psychology: Vol. 3. Social, emotional and personality development* (pp. 25–104). New York: Wiley.

Van den Boom, D. C., & Hoeksma, J. B. (1994). The effect of infant irritability on mother-infant interaction. *Developmental Psychology, 30*, 581–590.

Van IJzendoorn, M. H., Moran, G., Belsky, J., Pederson, D., Bakermans-Kranenburg, M. J., & Fisher, K. (2000). The similarity of siblings' attachments to their mother. *Child Development, 71*, 1086–1098.

Ward, M. J., Vaughn, B. E., & Robb, M. D. (1988). Socioemotional adaptation and infant-mother attachment in siblings: Role of the mother in cross-sibling consistency. *Child Development, 59*, 643–651.

Wellman, H., Harris, P., Banerjee, M., & Sinclair, A. (1995). Early understanding of emotion: Evidence from natural language. *Cognition and Emotion, 9*, 117–149.

Wolff, P. H. (1969). The natural history of crying and other vocalizations in infancy. In B. Foss (Ed.), *Determinants of infant behavior* (pp. 81–109). London: Methuen.

Zahn-Waxler, C., & Radke-Yarrow, M. (1982). The development of altruism: Alternative research strategies. In N. Eisenberg (ed.), *The development of prosocial behavior* (pp. 109–137). New York: Academic Press.

Zahn-Waxler, C., Robinson, J. L., & Emde, R. N. (1992). The development of empathy in twins. *Developmental Psychology, 28*, 1038–1047.

Zelazo, P. D., Astington, J. W., & Olson, D. R. (1999). *Developing theories of intention: Social understanding and self control.* Mahwah, NJ: Erlbaum.

# 19

# EMOTIONAL DEVELOPMENT DURING INFANCY

Claire B. Kopp and Susan J. Neufeld

*Emotions are* about *the life of an organism.*
—Damasio (1999)

Seven decades ago a small group of researchers sought to describe developmental trends in emotion expressions among infants and young children. What began as relatively modest research efforts evolved decades later into many hundreds of studies focused on broad research questions about infant emotional development. From the 1960s onward, research designs and coding systems have become more innovative and refined, and sophisticated analytic approaches have moved the field to causal inferences.

Instead of the single emphasis that characterized initial attempts to define infant emotions, six research themes now dominate the field: (1) the development of emotion expressions and experiences (e.g., fear, pleasure) during the first two years of life and the way those expressions influence the growth of social relationships; (2) the perception of others' emotion expressions and the role that increased understanding of these expressions has on self-organized behaviors; (3) the ways that development in other domains (e.g., cognition, motor development) influences the emotion repertoire; (4) the role that self-awareness has in emotion reorganization; (5) the impact of emotion language (e.g., *mad, afraid*) on young children's understanding of their own emotions and its effect on their social interactions, including conflict situations; and (6) the meaning of emotion regulation for

infants and toddlers and their caregivers, the way that emotion regulation changes during the first two years, and the role of individual differences in its manifestation.

History has also witnessed a shift in how the meaning of emotions is conceptualized. Once viewed as disruptive and incompatible with reason, emotions are now viewed as essential to developmental organization. Solomon (1993), in his historical review, notes that the "most enduring metaphor of reason and emotion has been the metaphor of master and slave, with the wisdom of reason firmly in control and the dangerous impulses of emotion safely suppressed" (p. 3). Whether this perspective actually extended down to infancy is uncertain; however, developmental theorists from the 1970s on have emphasized the organizing nature of infant emotions (see Campos, Barrett, Lamb, Goldsmith, & Stenberg, 1983; Sroufe, 1979, 1996). Emotions are not simply noise but contribute to and benefit from development in other domains (Kagan, 1994). Studies of infant and toddler perception, cognition, language, and selfhood underscore this point.

As the field recognized the importance of emotions to other developments, researchers began extending emotion research to include temperamental and social-emotional variables (see Campos et al., 1983; Sroufe, 1979, 1996; Stern, 1977) in research on specific emotion states (e.g., pleasure, fear, anger). The addition of other developmental domains to emotion research has been important from theoretical and applied vantage points: Interactions with caregivers underpin early emotion development, and evolving relationships may be influenced by a distinct temperamental style (e.g., Rothbart & Bates, 1998). Additionally, extending the focus in emotion research has resulted in the addition of individual-difference variables. Consequently, research efforts have largely moved away from developmental themes, although short-term longitudinal studies that identify developmental trends do occasionally resurface (e.g., Lewis, Koroshegyi, Douglas, & Kampe; 1997; Toda & Fogel, 1993). The emphasis on individual variability has been reinforced with the introduction of topics such as infant emotion and psychophysiology, brain and behavior, genetic contributions to emotions, and stress responses.

These changes and the productivity of recent decades have led to increasing expectations that research will be able to explain *what* develops in infant emotions, *when* transformations in emotion functioning take place and *why* they occur, and *how* different influences mediate infant emotion behaviors that then shape social interactions. A few of these questions have been answered, whereas others are still in a promissory-note stage. Sometimes methodological challenges slow progress, simply because it can be difficult to measure infant behavior. Other times, the field is confounded by unresolved ideational controversies, including questions about the definition of infant emotions (e.g., behaviors, states, experiences), the role of infant emotions (e.g., as regulators, relational processes, goal mediators), and how infant emotions change across the two years of infancy (e.g., the question of isomorphism between expression and feeling, the precise role of cognitive influences).

Reaching consensus about conceptual issues and understanding the *what, when, why,* and *how* questions are not solely academic concerns. Research findings have implications for the everyday lives of infants and their parents, in particular for the advice and interventions offered to parents. Consider that at least one state is attempting to provide various kinds of parenting education programs to its citizenry.[1] The American Academy of Pediatrics has made attempts to enhance pediatrician knowledge about parenting practices. However, applied issues in infant development tend to be complex: There is a need to acquire information useful to parents and infants and to convey that information accurately and clearly. Consider the topic of infant fear: Some researchers suggest fear is present at two months, whereas others indicate fear emerges five or six months later. How should a parent interpret these conflicting messages? Even when there is agreement about findings, there can be confusion about effective ways to translate complicated data for parents, such as findings that note the interrelation of infant temperament, regulation of emotion states, and the nature of interactions. Yet it is obvious that the way that caregivers interpret infant emotions influences the quality of social-emotional interactions.

## Taking Stock

Given the demands on the field of emotion development—those that come from within and those that arise elsewhere—it is appropriate to step back and ask key questions. Where has the field been with respect to ideas and research? What do we know definitively about emotions during the first two years of life? What are promising research areas? What big issues have yet to be resolved? This chapter attempts to chart our research history and, in so doing, to point to some answers, recognizing, of course, that the content reflects one point of view (alternatively, see Campos et al., 1983; Campos, Kermoian, & Witherington, 1996; Izard & Harris, 1995; Lewis, 1993a; Magai & McFadden, 1995; Malatesta, 1990; Sroufe, 1996; Thompson, 1990).

The first part of this chapter focuses on historical trends in programmatic research from the 1920s on.[2] This section contains a decade-by-decade historical table that calls attention to representative ideas and research. The decade approach imposes artificial boundaries but offers convenience in organizing a sizable database. It also allows a systematic view of important themes and researchers from earlier periods which might be overlooked in the rapidly changing study of infant emotions.

The text of this section and the table differ in important ways. The text highlights some of the most salient ideas from each decade's time frame, albeit there is some mention of research. The table, in contrast, offers a broad overview of each decade's research themes and includes examples of representative researchers. As can be seen each decade reveals increases in numbers of research themes. Thus an informal analysis of studies that emanated from the 1960s and of those conducted during the 1990s reveals impressive growth in intellectual and research interests.

A synthesis of themes represented in both the table and the text reveals several leitmotifs—infant emotions being fundamental to social relationships, the emergence of specific emotions and their effects on both infant and caregiver, the signaling power of infant and caregiver emotion communications, individual differences in infant emotions—many of which formed a research focus early on and continue to the present. Themes such as emotion regulation, the physiology of infant emotions, and emotion behaviors and brain functioning are relatively recent additions to the research lexicon.

Although it is important to ask where the field has been, it is equally as important to identify the current state of the art. Thus the historical summary leads to the second part of the chapter, which provides a compact, integrative synthesis that is organized by research focus. Recognizing that disagreements cut across every arena of infancy emotion research, the summary focuses on knowledge in which there is consensus, findings about which there is a lack of consensus, or themes yet unexplored. It will be clear that much has been learned about infancy and emotions.

The third section of the chapter focuses on emotion regulation, a topic that has received increased attention in the past decade because of its crucial role in individual adaptation (Gross, 1998; Heckhausen & Dweck, 1998). As Schore (1994) notes, emotion regulation "is one of the few theoretical constructs that is now being utilized by literally every developmental discipline" (p. 7). Research may eventually show that differences in the quality of emotion regulation during the first two years of life have a greater impact on later development than any other aspect of early emotion behavior. However, emotion regulation has been difficult to define and study, partly because of the advances, plateaus, and occasional disruptions that are intrinsic to early development. Recognizing these challenges, this part of the chapter focuses on definitions, emphasizes the purposes of emotion regulation with particular emphasis on infancy, and outlines themes that can facilitate an understanding of the developmental side of emotion regulation.

This developmental emphasis is both overdue and warranted. It is difficult to assess the meaning of individual differences in emotions and emotion regulation in the absence of developmental frames. Indeed, contemporary research that focuses on the other end of the age spectrum, namely middle-aged and aging adults, repeatedly reveals the heuristic value of a developmental focus for understanding social and emotional relationships (Carstensen, 1998).

## Historical and Thematic Trends

### Emergence of a Field: 1920s–1940s

As several historical accounts point out (see, for example, the extended discussion by Magai & McFadden, 1995), the study of emotions in infants has a venerable history. There is Charles Darwin, of course, along with the "baby biographers" (e.g., Dietrich Tiedemann, Wilhelm Preyer, and Millicent Shinn), the developmentally oriented Vienna-trained Charlotte Bühler, and the 1920s American research team of M. and I. C. Sherman. John B. Watson's study (Watson & Raynor, 1920) of conditioned fear in the infant Albert may be the most cited study of all the early writings. After Watson's departure from research, Mary Cover Jones, who had worked with Watson, continued the study of emotions in infants and young children (e.g., M. C. Jones, 1924a, 1924b; H. E. Jones & Jones, 1928, 1930). And it was Mary Cover Jones who later authored integrative chapters and monographs that included a focus on infants' emotions (M. C. Jones, 1930; Jones & Burks, 1936).

Prior to the 1930s, the study of infants' emotions was relatively sporadic; however, the decade of the 1930s witnessed consistent and programmatic research efforts. It is not clear why this occurred, but several factors likely played a role. Mary Cover Jones probably had an influential voice, along with her husband, Harold Jones, who became the director of the then-titled Institute of Child Welfare at the University of California, Berkeley. The creation of other child study centers probably played a role (Senn, 1975). Many of these centers also provided research quarters to a small group of well-trained female psychologists who seemed willing to tackle issues (e.g., emotions in infants and toddlers) eschewed by their more empirical, measurement-and laboratory-oriented male colleagues. Nancy Bayley, Katherine Bridges, Florence Goodenough, and Jean MacFarlane are a sampling of other pioneers who were associated with some of the child study centers and who studied the very young. Nowadays, historical accounts tend to cite Bridges's (1932) work because of her systematic attempts to define developmental trends in emotion differentiation (i.e., expression) from early infancy through the second year. Bridges's work was enormously important because it opened consideration of the question, What develops and when?

Measurement of stimuli conditions and changes in infant emotion states were also a concern in the 1930s. The Iowa Child Study group, among others, addressed neonatal states and newborn receptivity to various kinds of stimuli. Researchers (e.g., Irwin & Weiss, 1934a, 1934b; Stubbs, 1934) studied crying and noncrying young infants by exposing them to varying light, sound, and clothing conditions and carefully measuring state changes. The issue of soothability continues to this day. Along the way there have been some interesting controversies. During the 1960s, for example, Salk (1962) maintained that prenatal exposure to maternal heartbeats would promote later infant soothability to heartbeat stimuli. Salk's findings were called into question, although his theory garnered a great deal of media attention. However, most relevant to contemporary times, the issue of infant soothability has been recast into an analysis of individual differences, often within a conceptualization of emotion regulation. Within this framework, questions would be posed about irritability, the relative ease of soothing infants, and implications of soothability for social interactions.

Lastly, the 1940s contributed the writings of Rene Spitz. His observations of institutionalized infants can be considered one of the forerunners of the field of infant psychopathology that would come into being years later (Zeanah, 1993). Spitz's (1946) case reports of infants raised under conditions of marked deprivation revealed signs of emotion disorders akin to severe depression in older individuals. However, Spitz's ideas would form one of the underpinnings of infant emotion research—namely, how caregivers influence the nature of emotions even in young infants. The role of caregivers as a correlate of infant emotional well-being has been an important feature of research to this day.

### Reigniting the Field: 1950s and 1960s

Social, economic, and political catastrophes delayed major research efforts until the 1950s. Early in the decade, Sibylle Escalona (1953) presented a new view of infant emotions, with emphasis on relationships, development, and individual differences among infants and their mothers. Drawing on psychoanalytic perspectives and her experiences at the Menninger Foundation, Escalona described her mostly clinical observations of infants and their mothers. Infant development, she stated, was a systematic and organized process. However, individual patterns of behavior overlay the developmental process as a function of infants' sensory and perceptual characteristics and experiences, and their emotional and social responses to their immediate environs. Although an obvious influence came from mothers' interactive styles, Escalona noted how similarities in maternal approaches could have profoundly different effects as a function of infant characteristics. The relationship, ever dynamic, functioned as a mix of infant and maternal characteristics.[3]

Escalona represented one of many clinician-researchers—T. Berry Brazelton, Robert Emde, L. Alan Sroufe, Daniel Stern—whose voices would increasingly have a persuasive influence on research paths in infant emotions. There would be other, nontraditional psychology voices as well: Marian Radke-Yarrow (personal communication, January 2000), a student with Kurt Lewin, was neither a behaviorist nor a social learning adherent. In retrospect, it is not surprising that the three themes emphasized by Escalona, namely development, relationships, and individual variability, presaged later writings by Emde, Gaensbauer, and Harmon (1976) and Sroufe (1979), as well as Rothbart's (Rothbart, Ziaie, & O'Boyle, 1992) studies of infant temperament and Kochanska's (Kochanska, 1995; Kochanska & Aksan, 1995) research on the role of temperament, emotion, and mother and infant interactions.[4]

During the 1960s, descriptive, detailed studies of infant smiling, crying, and soothing and the stimuli conditions underlying emotion expressions recalled the research of the 1930s. The emphasis of the 1960s, however, differed in its explicit focus on situational factors that interact with level of infant development. Some of Schaffer's research (1963, 1966) suggested that infants' cognitive understanding of *unfamiliarity*, albeit a nascent understanding, played a key role in the emergence of infants' wary or fearful responses. This research began to get at the issue of *how*. How does developmental change in one domain (e.g., cognitive functioning) influence responses in another domain (e.g., emotion)? In succeeding decades, this particular question surfaced repeatedly.

### Measurement Issues and Developmental Models: 1970s

Examination of Table 19.1 reveals the dramatic growth of research that occurred during the 1970s. Infants' emotional lives gained status as a topic worthy of study, and concomitantly new theoretical and measurement models were introduced. Arguably, Izard's (Izard, 1971; Izard & Dougherty, 1980) introduction of the facial coding technique was a major catalyzing force for research on infant facial expressions. The MAX (Maximally Discriminative Facial Movement) offered a standardized approach to coding infant emotions with a system previously unavailable. Many researchers drew on the MAX as they formulated questions about expressions (e.g., smiling, crying), infant emotion expressivity in social interactions, and links between cognition and emotions. Despite the MAX's popularity, questions began to arise about defining emotion states by relying solely on facial expressions (e.g., Campos et al., 1983; Campos, Campos, & Barrett, 1989; Camras, 1986; Fogel & Thelen, 1987). In time, the MAX and Izard's (Izard & Dougherty, 1980) more global scoring system, the AFFEX, diminished in popularity. However, despite the expansiveness of more recent coding systems, it is notable that no standardized, comprehensive, universally agreed-on measurement system for infant emotions has emerged as a successor (see M. Lewis & Michalson, 1983; Sroufe, 1996).

Two principal conceptual issues dominated the 1970s. One focused on infants' emotion expressions in relation to the infant-parent relationship and the other on issues of developmental change. Within the relationship theme, discussions ranged from the theoretical, such as the evolutionary origins of infant facial expressions (e.g., Izard), to the practical, such as the disappointment mothers felt when infants responded to playful interactions with weak or noncontingent behaviors (see Emde, Katz, & Thorpe, 1978). Clinical observations by Stern (1977) added another point to the relationship theme. Stern suggested that infants used *coping mechanisms* (e.g., modulating gaze bouts) as a way to adapt to temporarily insensitive caregiver interactions. Continuing adverse interactions between mother and infant could, Stern said, subvert the infant's self-regulatory mechanisms. When this occurs, infants "develop more extreme regulating or terminating behaviors" (Stern, 1977, p. 114).

The attention directed to interpersonal interactions and infants' emotions was reflected in various other writings, as well (e.g., Bowlby, 1969; Mahler, Pine, & Bergman, 1975). This wealth of ideas was later echoed in seminal research. As one example, the studies by Tronick and colleagues (Tronick, Als, Adamson, Wise, & Brazelton, 1978) identified infants' responses to unresponsive maternal expressions and the nature of coordinated interactions between mother and infant (e.g., Tronick & Cohn, 1989;

Table 19.1 Historical Trends in Infant/Toddler Emotion Research

| Era | Representative Research Themes | Sources |
| --- | --- | --- |
| 1930s–1940s | Emotion expressions: descriptive, longitudinal studies of crying, smiling, fear, anger; difficulty in coding fear vs. anger expressions | Bayley, 1932; Bridges, 1932, 1934; Buhler, 1934; Buhler & Hetzer, 1929; Cattell, 1933; Gesell, 1928; Goodenough, 1929, 1931a, 1931b, 1932; Jersild & Holmes, 1935; Jones, 1930a, 1930b; Murphy, 1937 |
| | Deprivation: influence on development, including emotional functioning | Spitz, 1946 |
| 1950s–1960s | Emotion expressions: stimuli associated with crying, smiling in early months of life | Ahrens, 1954; Ambrose, 1963a, 1963b; Birns, Blank, Bridger, & Escalona, 1965; Brackbill, Adams, & Crowell, 1966; Brossard & Decarie, 1968; Gewirtz, 1965; Wolff, 1963, 1969 |
| | Emotion and cognitive development<br>the relation between arousal and attention<br>cognitively mediated changes in response to unfamiliar objects or people | Kagan, 1966; Korner & Grobstein, 1966; Schaffer, 1963; Stechler & Latz, 1966 |
| 1970s | Emotion expressions: physiological responses; elucidation of endogenous and exogenous smiling; development and transitions in emotions, 1st year | Campos & Brackbill, 1973; Campos et al., 1975; Emde & Harmon, 1972; Emde et al., 1976; Field, 1979; Meltzoff & Moore, 1977 |
| | Measurement of facial expressions: standardized coding system for infant facial expressions | Izard, 1971, 1977, 1979 |
| | Feeling states: anger, wariness, fear, happiness | Bronson, 1978; Brooks & Lewis, 1976; Campos et al., 1978; Decarie, 1974; Hiatt, Campos, & Emde, 1979; Scarr & Salapatek, 1970; Schaffer, 1974; Sroufe, Waters, & Matas, 1974; Sroufe & Wunsch, 1972 |
| | Emotion-based relationships: effects of infant crying on caregivers; infant responses to caregivers' facial expressions | Bell & Ainsworth, 1972; Caron, Caron, Caldwell, & Weiss, 1973; Frodi, Lamb, Leavitt, & Donovan, 1978; Tronick et al., 1978 |
| | Self-conscious emotions: the role of selfhood and cognition | Brooks & Lewis, 1976 |
| | Emotion regulation: independent control of a fearful stimulus | Gunnar-von Gnechten, 1978 |
| | Prosocial behaviors: independent attempts to remedy another's negative emotions | Radke-Yarrow & Zahn-Waxler, 1977 |
| | Developmental psychopathology: the link between emotion and cognition in atypical populations; readability of infant emotion expressions (e.g., Down syndrome) and effects on parents | Cicchetti & Sroufe, 1976; Emde, Katz, & Thorpe, 1978 |
| 1980s | Facial expressions: developmental trends, individual differences; stability of individual differences; socialization of emotion expressions | Demos, 1986; Malatesta, Cullver, Tesman, & Shepard, 1989; Malatesta, Grigoryev, Lamb, Albin, & Cullver, 1986; Malatesta & Haviland, 1982; Thompson & Lamb, 1984 |
| | Expression perception, understanding: use of expressions to inform behavior; developmental trends in expression discrimination | Bretherton & Beeghly, 1982; Bretherton, Fritz, Zahn-Waxler, & Ridgeway, 1986; Caron, Caron, & MacLean, 1988; Caron, Caron, & Myers, 1982; Cohn & Tronick, 1983; Feinman, 1982; Haviland & Lelwica, 1987; Klinnert, 1984; Nelson, 1987; Nelson, Morse, & Leavitt, 1979; Sorce et al., 1985; Walden & Ogan, 1984 |
| | Emotion-based relationships: effects of maternal depression on infant emotions; effect of irritable infants on maternal behavior | Connell & Thompson, 1986; Crockenberg & Smith, 1982 |
| | Self-conscious emotions: the role of selfhood and cognition | M. Lewis et al., 1989 |
| | Brain and emotions: developmental trends regarding frontal lobes; individual differences in patterning of responses to specific situations (e.g., separation) | Davidson & Fox, 1982, 1989; Fox & Davidson, 1987 |
| | Neurohormonal responses; emotion responses, control in fearful or stressful situations | Gunnar, Mangelsdorf, Larson, & Hertsgaard, 1989; Hornik et al., 1987 |
| | Psychopathology: readability of emotion expressions (e.g., children with Down syndrome); recognition of emotion expressions by abused children | Camras, Grow, & Ribordy, 1983; Field, 1984; Thompson, Cicchetti, Lamb, & Malkin, 1985 |

*(continued)*

Table 19.1 *(continued)*

| Era | Representative Research Themes | Sources |
| --- | --- | --- |
| 1990s | Facial expressions: developmental trends, individual differences, and stability of individual differences | Camras, 1992; Oster, Hegley, & Nagel, 1992 |
| | Perception; understanding: use of stimuli (near, distance receptors) or words to inform behavior | Blass & Ciaramitaro, 1994; Gustafson & Green, 1991; Mumme, Fernald, & Herrera, 1996; Soken & Pick, 1999; Weinberg & Tronick, 1994, 1996 |
| | Feeling states, behavior: anger, aggression | Keenan & Shaw, 1997; M. Lewis, Alessandri, & Sullivan, 1990 |
| | Emotion and cognitive development: the relation between arousal and memory, cognitive performance | Geva, Gardner, & Karmel, 1999; M. D. Lewis et al., 1997 |
| | Emotion-based relationships: attachment, temperament, social interactions | de Weerth, van Geert, & Hoijtink, 1999; van den Boom, 1994 |
| | Emotion regulatory mechanisms: individual differences and emotion regulation | Braungart & Stifter, 1991; Buss & Goldsmith, 1998; Calkins & Johnson, 1998; DeGangi, Porges, Sickel, & Greenspan, 1993; Friedlmeier & Trommsdorff, 1999; Grolnick, Bridges, & Connell, 1996; Mangelsdorf, Shapiro, & Marzolf, 1995; Rothbart et al., 1992; Stifter & Braungart, 1995; Stifter & Fox, 1990 |
| | Emotion regulation and social relationships: effects of mother-child interactions on emotion regulation | Braungart-Rieker, Garwood, Powers, & Notaro, 1998; Bridges, Grolnick, & Connell, 1997; Gable & Isabella, 1992; Nachmias, Gunnar, Mangelsdorf, Parritz, & Buss, 1996; Park, Belsky, Putnam, & Crnic, 1997 |
| | Prosocial behaviors: independent attempts to remedy another's negative emotions; group differences in prosocial behaviors | Barrett, Zahn-Waxler, & Cole, 1993; Zahn-Waxler, Radke-Yarrow, Wagner, & Chapman, 1992 |
| | Self-conscious emotions: effects of self-generated violations | Lewis, Alessandri, & Sullivan, 1990 |
| | Emotions across cultures: culturally mediated crying, emotion responses | Barr, Konner, Bakeman, & Adamson, 1991; Camras, Oster, Campos, & Miyake, 1992 |
| | Genetic factors: longitudinal studies of emotion, temperament, cognition | Emde et al., 1992; Goldsmith, Buss, & Lemery, 1997 |
| | Brain and emotions: developmental trends re frontal lobes; individual differences in patterning of responses to specific situations (e.g., separation) | Dawson, 1994; Fox, 1994; Fox & Davidson, 1991 |
| | Neurohormonal responses; emotion control, in fearful situations; stress responses | Gunnar, Brodersen, Krueger, & Rigatuso, 1996; Gunnar, Brodersen, Nachmias, Buss, & Rigatuso, 1996; Gunnar & Nelson, 1994; M. Lewis & Ramsay, 1995 |
| | Psychopathology: mothers with clinical depression; emotions and abused children; children with Down syndrome; infants with focal brain damage | Beeghly & Cicchetti, 1997; Reilly, Stiles, Larsen, & Trauner, 1995 |

Tronick & Field, 1987). Tronick's statement, "the affective communications of each infant and mother actually change the emotional experience and behavior of the other," has been an illuminating one (Tronick & Cohn, 1989, p. 112).

A second issue of the 1970s, developmental perspectives, was controversial because emotion researchers held somewhat different views about its relative importance. To some, such as Robert Emde and L. Alan Sroufe, a developmental perspective called attention to a dynamic and organized process that profoundly influenced infants' general competencies, motivations, and social interactions. Their writings addressed issues such as the emergence of specific emotions, the effect of emergence on the reorganization of existing abilities, and subsequent social and physical adaptations. Emde and colleagues (Emde et al., 1976), in particular, emphasized the nature and meaning of developmental transitions in the 1st year. Transitions occurred both behaviorally and physiologically. Defined as qualitative, these changes (e.g., the emergence of the infant's social smile) led to dramatically different interactions with others. In turn, infant behavior became richer and more complex. L. Alan Sroufe (1979) explicitly emphasized development, stating "the organization of development refers to the *nature of the developmental process* [italics added], the way in which behaviors are hierarchically organized into more complex patterns within developmental systems, the way in which later modes and functions evolve from earlier prototypes, and the way in which part functions are integrated into wholes" (p. 464). At a later date, Sroufe (1996) further elaborated a developmental and differentiated approach to infant emotions.

The organizational view argues that no single developmental entity (e.g., emotions, cognition, motivation) has a privileged role in development. All systems must work together to produce effective behavior. However, at some points in development, one or another system may have a more primary role for certain aspects of behavior. A telling example comes from M. Lewis and Brooks-Gunn (1979). The self, which drives so many toddler actions (e.g., autonomy), has a sizable cognitive basis and a major role in emotion experiences. Lewis and Brooks-Gunn described how self knowledge is essential for the emotional experiences of empathy, guilt, and embarrassment, which come into focus in the second year. Because shame and guilt reflect others' standards, the emotional experience of shame (or guilt) must involve consciousness of standards and evaluation of those standards with respect to one's actions.

Izard's[5] (1971, 1977) discrete emotions theory also contained reference to development, but primarily within an evolutionary, adaptive context. He suggested that neonates are born with emotional systems (e.g., expressions) such as disgust and distress, which are adaptive for survival and interactions. Soon after, infants show emotions of anger and joy. However, an emotion such as fear would emerge only when infants have motoric skills to adapt to fearful response. In Izard's view, emotional development changes in relation to perceptual, cognitive, and motor capabilities. Arguing for the isomorphism between emotion expressions and feeling states, Izard further emphasized the independence of early emotion states and cognitive appraisals. Izard's focus on developmental issues tended to describe in general terms the experiences that shape a particular emotion style. Thus his research increasingly emphasized individual differences and their stability. A focus on individual differences, rather than developmental processes, still drives many contemporary studies of infant emotions.

Finally, the 1970s offered innovative research that would leave additional ideational and methodological legacies. Far-reaching research included Gunnar-von Gnechten's study (1978) that showed how object control by infants serves as a mediator of their arousal levels. Toddler emotions were represented by resourceful observations of the prosocial/helping behaviors of young children (Radke-Yarrow & Zahn-Waxler, 1977). Also, psychophysiological measures related to infant emotions were introduced (e.g., Campos, Emde, Gaensbauer, Sorce, & Henderson, 1975).

### Expanding the Research Foci: The 1980s

The 1980s continued the great productivity of the 1970s, but with paradigmatic shifts, new waves of innovative research (e.g., social referencing), and an emphasis on individual differences. Several conceptual treatises appeared, some of which extended earlier views, whereas others focused on new themes in infant emotions (e.g., Kopp, 1989; Lewis & Michalson, 1983; Stern, 1985; Tronick, 1989).

The major paradigmatic shift was represented by Campos (Campos et al., 1983), who argued for a new view of infant emotions. Emotions, according to the researchers, are determinants and regulators of interpersonal processes and are influenced by attachments and temperament factors. This newer view claimed that infant emotions were a primary force in social interactions, a claim that superseded earlier statements about infants' contributory role to social interactions. The authors downplayed earlier descriptions of developmental trajectories and stimuli that elicit emotions (e.g., cognitive appraisal of certain situations). Rather, they emphasized that certain kinds of experiences and contexts endow particular stimuli with significance, a point that drew on findings from the famed visual cliff study (Campos, Hiatt, Ramsay, Henderson, & Svejda, 1978). Locomotor experiences endowed heights with emotional significance for infants. Undeniably, the most intriguing part of Campos's work concerned the role of goals in infants' emotion functioning (Campos et al., 1983).[6] Goals, the authors wrote, have different origins (e.g., biology, socialization) and different objectives, such as the maintenance of interactions with objects or the maintenance of self-integrity. Their key point was that goals had to have value to the individual and that these goals formed a major underpinning of infant emotions. In all, these ideas represented core elements of the *functionalist view* of emotions (see also Barrett & Campos, 1987). This functionalist perspective provided one impetus for the major shift in the study of infant emotions that occurred during the 1990s.

Campos et al.'s (1983) emphasis on infant emotions and temperament style fit nicely with Rothbart's ideas. Having studied temperament in infancy for a number of years, Rothbart now appeared to view temperament more broadly by including in its definition arousal/reactivity and regulatory processes (e.g., attention) that influence reactivity (Rothbart, 1981, 1986, 1989; Rothbart & Posner, 1985). This recasting of temperament had a profound influence on the study of emotions in infancy and childhood, and by the next decade infant temperament, emotion, and regulation were frequent underpinnings of research. As noted earlier, the interest in early temperament styles and the effects on relationships was part of the resurgence of interest in individual differences in infant emotion functioning.

In hindsight, the 1980s was a watershed period for the study of all aspects of infancy, including the study of emotion development. With respect to emotions, imaginative and meaningful research addressed topics such as social referencing (e.g., Hornik & Gunnar, 1988; Sorce, Emde, Campos, & Klinnert, 1985; Walden & Ogan, 1988), state-related language (e.g., Bretherton, McNew, & Beeghly-Smith, 1981), toddler's social emotions and caring behaviors (e.g., M. Lewis, Sullivan, Stanger, & Weiss, 1989; Rheingold & Emery, 1986), use of soothing mechanisms such as transitional objects (see Kopp, 1989), and more. Researchers explicitly linked the study of infant emotions to topics such as attention, temperament (e.g., Matheny, Wilson, & Nuss, 1984; Rothbart, 1981), social relationships (e.g., Vaughn, Lefever, Sifer, & Barglow, 1989), and locomotor development (e.g., Campos, Svejda, Campos, & Bertenthal, 1982). Taken together, the research exponentially increased the understanding of infant development, most particularly infant social and emotional development. Equally as important, findings from a host of studies increasingly supported a transition in infant functioning in the last quarter of the 1st year.

What Piaget (1952), Werner (1957), and others (e.g., Kagan, 1972; McCall, 1981) had earlier labeled intelligent and adaptive behavior with respect to cognitive functioning was now observed in transformed, newly integrated, or new social and emotional behaviors such as social referencing (e.g., Sorce et al., 1985; Feinman, 1982; Walden & Ogan, 1988), gestural communication (e.g., Rogoff, Malkin, & Gilbride, 1984), dyadic social play (e.g., Kaye, 1982), intentional crying, and more. These studies revealed how infants actively sought to gain information from others, to draw others into specific activities, or to draw attention from others. In the aggregate, findings from the 1980s studies built on earlier data that indicated qualitative changes in emotion responses such as fear at about 9 months.

If data unequivocally supported the occurrence of a major developmental transition at about 9 months of age, other findings revealed the nature of the developmental transformation. Research would show that by 12 months infants could take control of certain situations. An interesting example of this control was reflected in Gunnar's (1980) continuing studies: Infants appraise a situation for its negative properties and then act on their own to change the offending part of the situation. In other words, infants actively and purposefully control their emotions. Other research revealed how and when infants coped with, and controlled, fearful episodes (e.g., Hornik, Risenhoover, & Gunnar, 1987). Still other data showed the panoply of active control strategies engaged in by infants about a year of age, including: control of some caregiver behaviors by using joint attention and gestures (Adamson & Bakeman, 1984), control of communication (Bates, Bretherton, & Snyder, 1988), imitation (e.g., Meltzoff, 1988), and control and mastery of physical objects (Frodi, Grolnick, & Bridges, 1985; Sinclair, Stambak, Lezine, Rayna, & Verba, 1989). Many of these achievements rely on infants' knowledge about others' responsiveness, their ability to remember goals while going through several steps to achieve these same goals, the coordinated use of

their hands, and the memory of pleasurable and distressful events.

Figure 19.1 represents a number of important transition behaviors observed at nine months (or thereabouts) and the active control processes that come into place at about a year of age. Several points are worth noting. First, many control processes demand a form of behavioral inhibition so that nonessential actions are inhibited, which allows the activation of desired actions. This inhibitory control fits nicely with Diamond's thesis that inhibitory control linked with the maintenance of task-relevant information is associated with activation of dorsolateral prefrontal cortex (e.g., Diamond, 1990; Diamond, Prevor, Callender, & Druin, 1997). Dawson, (1994a), too, linked frontal cortex activation to behaviors, namely regulatory acts, many of which are noted herein. Second, the control processes that emerge at about 12 months reveal support for Campos's emphasis on the functional role of emotions in that both pleasure and fear have a role in activating these processes. Third, emotion control processes find additional expression during the second year, an achievement reflected in studies that address conflict and language (e.g., Dunn & Munn, 1985), help seeking when dealing with frustrating situations (van Lieshout, 1976), and upsets and use of transitional objects (e.g., Kopp, 1989). It seems, although research is wanting, that the antecedents of toddlers' emotion regulation is preceded by more general forms of control processes evidenced at about a year, which in turn are preceded by the emergence or transformation of key social, perceptual, cognitive, and motor behaviors. Fourth, there is an advantage to viewing behaviors as an aggregate of competencies rather than framing each behavior as an isolated achievement. By adopting an *ensemble* strategy, students of infant development are better able to interpret the meaning of behaviors and fit them into "a point in an epigenetic landscape" (Fischer & Biddell, 1991, p. 214).

Two other research themes emerged during the 1980s and then took hold during the 1990s. One dealt with emotion regulation (see Campos, Campos, & Barrett, 1989; Kopp, 1989; Tronick, 1989). The second area was represented by seminal brain and behavior studies by Davidson and Fox (e.g., Davidson & Fox, 1982, 1989; Fox & Davidson, 1987, 1988). Using electroencephalograph (EEG) recordings that linked frontal lobe activation with infant emotion expressions, they also reported patterns of EEG asymmetries (e.g., right frontal activation with distress) and characteristic individual patterns of asymmetries that were seemingly coupled with increased stress reactions to certain conditions.

In sum, this productive decade moved researchers closer to understanding what happens in infant emotions, when does it happen, and what the implications are of what happens. The productivity and understanding grew even more in the following decade.

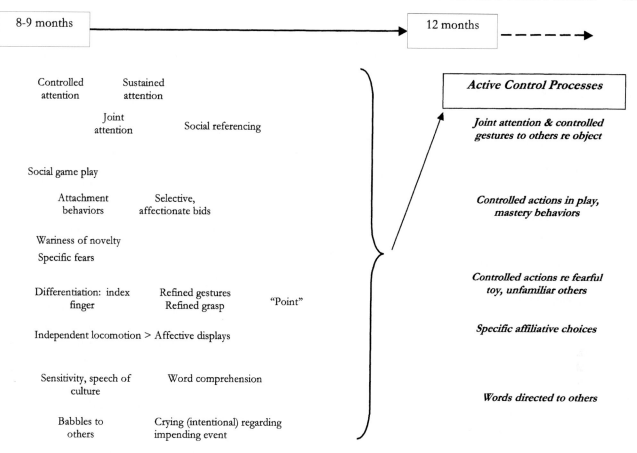

Figure 19.1 Developmental competencies between 8 and 12 months, and a "control" transition at 12 months.

## The 1990s: Brains, Emotion Regulation, Selfhood, and More

In the 1990s, conceptually oriented writings on infant emotions were represented by Lewis (1993a) and Sroufe (1996), who updated and expanded their developmental perspectives; by Dawson (1994a), Fox (1994), Schore (1994), and Thompson (1990) who focused on varied aspects of infant emotion regulation, including brain and behavior relations; by Marc Lewis (1995; M. D. Lewis & Douglas, 1998), who addressed cognitive and emotion interactions within a framework that integrated development and individual differences; by Kagan (1998) and Rothbart (Rothbart & Bates, 1998), who further consolidated their views on temperament and regulation; and by Gunnar (Gunnar, 1991; Stansbury & Gunnar, 1994), who expanded the conceptualization of behavioral stresses and hormonal functioning. Interesting and provocative research was done on infant brain functioning and behavior; on emotion regulation, as well as other regulatory processes; on the relation of infant temperament, caregiver interactions, and resultant behaviors such as compliance; and on heritable contributions to infant emotional functioning (see Table 19.1). The focus on individual differ-

ences in infants' emotional functioning was considerable and perhaps greater than during any other previous research period. As noted earlier, studies of infant temperament and stylistic variations (e.g., inhibited, irritable, fearful), associations with emotion regulation, and influences on social relationships contributed to this growth (e.g., Buss & Goldsmith, 1998; Kagan, Arcus, Snidman, & Feng, 1994; Kochanska, 1997; Rothbart, et al., 1992; Stifter & Fox, 1990).

On another front, writings about infant brains began to reveal a coherent and meaningful picture of development and individual differences. Three research themes prevailed: developmental changes that represented reorganization, frontal lobe activation and its implications for behavior, and individual differences in brain functioning and their presumed correlates. In relation to general development, Chugani (1994) summarized a series of positron emission tomography (PET) scan studies on regional brain glucose metabolism (primarily neocortex) and reported changes in glucose rates at various age periods during the first year. Notably, between 6 to 12 months, there were changes first in the lateral portions of the frontal lobes and then subsequently in the dorsal prefrontal regions. The presumption is that glucose levels are related to increases in the overproduction of synapses and nerve terminals as the aforementioned areas increasingly come on line. Huttenlocher (1994) also summarized his developmentally oriented research on synaptogenesis in the visual cortex using electron microscopic techniques on postmortem brain tissue. His visual cortex data reveal a marked increase in synaptic density and total synapses starting at about 2 months and reaching a peak at about 8 to 10 months, with fairly steep declines to age 10 years and then a leveling off. Using a limited data base, Huttenlocher suggests that synaptic elimination for the frontal cortex occurs later, likely between 7 years and adolescence. The significance of these findings is that they suggest that a "functional fine tuning" of brain systems is taking place as a result of experiences Huttenlocher, 1994, p. 146). Overall, the brain data go along with behavioral changes, specifically for behaviors such as inhibition, purposefulness, and control, as noted by Diamond (1990) and Rothbart (e.g., Rothbart & Bates, 1998; Ruff & Rothbart, 1996).

The emphasis on frontal lobes was exemplified by Schore's (1994) intriguing, although highly controversial discussion of right frontal lobe activation (specifically, the orbitofrontal cortex [OFC]) and emotion development. Schore maintained that the OFC is (1) an enlarged portion of the frontal cortex, (2) increasingly activated in late infancy, and (3) experience dependent in that its growth is influenced by the nature of infant and mother interaction. The OFC is presumed to modulate arousal mechanisms in late infancy and is therefore implicated in socioaffective regulatory activities. Schore argues for an increasing shift later in the second year from right to left hemisphere, along with increasing maturation of the dorsolateral cortex (also part of the prefrontal cortex). The regulation of emotional experiences, he added, is a behavioral manifestation of these brain changes.

Although Schore supports his thesis with a considerable amount of related research, there are as yet little data to support his points. Of importance, other recent perspectives about early brain and behavior relations adopt a markedly different approach. Johnson (1998, 2000) for example, in his discussions of infant neurocognitive development, adopts a far more relativistic approach to brain localization in early infancy. The dramatic growth in measurement of young brains that is certain to occur during the next decade should lead to increasingly sophisticated studies of numerous aspects of brain development during infancy and possible links with experiences and behavior.

Turning to the issue of individual differences, the findings initially reported by Davidson and Fox about differential patterns of asymmetries in the frontal lobes of infants, specific stimuli conditions, and behavioral responses were further explored by Fox and his colleagues (e.g., Calkins, 1997; Calkins, Fox, & Marshall, 1996; Fox,

Calkins, & Bell, 1994). In other research, right frontal asymmetry was linked to behavioral indices that reflect fear, along with psychophysiological responses that reflect behavioral inhibition. Relatedly, Dawson (e.g., Dawson, 1994b; Dawson, Frey, Panagiotides, Yamada, Hessl, & Osterling, 1999; Dawson, Klinger, Panagiotides, & Spieker, 1992) supported the finding that distinct patterns of electrical activity in the frontal lobes were associated with particular patterns of emotion expression among infants of depressed mothers. In all, findings suggest a role for temperament factors, as well as for the quality of social environments offered to infants. On the basis of these data, inferentially it seems that the most discordant frontal lobe hemispheric patterns should be observed among fearful or inhibited infants who are reared by depressed or socially withdrawn mothers. Whether or not these individual differences represent developmental patterns of brain and behavior or have long-term behavioral implications remains to be seen. Developmental inferences are limited, in part, by current measurement techniques that provide "snapshots" of brain and behavior as opposed to indicators of dynamic processes (Segalowitz, 2000).

In any event, the tapestry of research on brain, emotion regulation, and temperament was so compelling that other topics, such as the relation between selfhood and emotions, barely stood out. Yet selfhood continued to be a presence during the 1990s, probably because the emergence and growth of a consciously experienced self-identify has major implications for emotions and emotion regulatory behaviors (e.g., Kopp & Wyer, 1994; M. Lewis, 1993a, 1993b; Thompson, 1998). Consider how affective values influence the interpretation of emotional and social experiences when the young child has a sense of the temporal dimensions of the past, the here-and-now, and the future. How different it must be for the infant who views experiences only from *now*.

M. Lewis (1993a, 1993b) offered comprehensive depictions of the developmental trajectory of self-conscious (or social) emotions, the role of cognition in selfhood, the manifestations of shame, pride, and guilt, and addressed measurement issues. Other researchers studied toddlers' manifestations of shame and guilt, reparations, and self-evaluation (e.g., Stipek, Recchia, & McClintic, 1992; Zahn-Waxler, Cole, & Barrett, 1991).

Thompson (1998), adopting a somewhat different emphasis, noted the crucial links between self-awareness, the social emotions, and relationships, such as the successes that engender joy when sharing achievements with caregivers and failures when caregivers' requests are ignored. Thompson further described the complex interactions of child emotions reflected in successes and failures, the nature of the parent and child relationship, and the increasing parental socialization demands placed on young children.

Largely undescribed and unexplained to date, however, are the specific processes that are involved in the integration of emotion regulation and self-regulation to caregivers' standards (Kopp, 1989). Clearly, it is possible for young toddlers to comply to family norms while simultaneously demonstrating out-of-control emotions, albeit effective adaptations require the coherence of both forms of regulation. Overall, selfhood, emotions, and emotion regulation represent fertile areas for additional study, particularly for potential implications for child functioning in the preschool years and later.

In all, close to a century of research on infants and their emotions culminated in the 1990s with a decade of extraordinary research dynamism and breadth of focus. And although some topics of the 1990s connected to earlier themes (e.g., soothability and emotion regulation), there was originality in conceptualization and measurement.

## The New Millennium

Looking first backward and then to the present, even the most disinterested observer has to be impressed with the ideas and research that have focused on emotional functioning in the first two years of life. There has been convincing growth toward understanding the complexities involved in early emotional and social development and the many correlates and contributions to the process, which has increased appreciation of the challenges inherent in measuring emotion behavior and broadened sensitivity to the inferences that can be made about the nonverbal emotion-related behaviors of infants and toddlers. Given these achievements, what is unequivocally known?

## A Synthesis

This section offers a perspective on this question, beginning with an overall statement about the three major themes that are represented in research on infant emotions—relationships, development, individual differences—and then moving to specific areas of research.

Research findings incontrovertibly reveal that infants begin life with an impressive set of emotion behaviors that signal others to provide nurturance and soothing. The infant's emotion signaling system continues to have a powerful effect on caregiving throughout the first two years of life. From a developmental standpoint, all intact infants at some point develop emotion states akin to pleasure, anger, fear, and, later on, the social emotions. With development, intact infants are able to produce and regulate these emotions according to contextual demands. The broad configuration of emotion development stems from humans' evolutionary history represented by patterns of brain development in interaction with multiple kinds of experiences provided by caregivers. Thus emotion development is inextricably bound to the social relationships initially launched and maintained by caregivers. However, the emotional and social relationship is further maintained because infants and toddlers gradually learn to derive emotion meaning from their caregivers and then to act on this information in their ongoing social interactions and in their physical surroundings. Emotion development is a changing, dynamic process because it is inextricably linked to growth in perceptual, cognitive, motor, and social functioning. Thus the development of emotions reflects qualitative and quantitative change. Individual differences in infants' emotion functioning are associated with the quality and content of caregiving, caregiver attributes, and infant attributes, such as temperament or neurophysiological well-being.

Questions about infant and toddler emotions and relationships continue to arise. One, for example, turns on the complex interaction between toddlers' autonomy seeking and parental responses to accompanying behavioral changes in their toddlers. Some parents deal with frequent *I can*'s and *no*'s with equanimity, whereas others become annoyed and highly restrictive. Is it possible that some variations among parents are a function of their culturally mediated values concerning young children's acceptable behaviors? Also of interest is the magnitude of behavioral allowances that are made by different cultures for children's developmental status. Some socialization data from rural environments (e.g., LeVine et al., 1994) suggest that there is little behavioral leeway in certain cultural groups once young children begin to locomote and to comprehend simple requests.

A second intriguing relationship issue centers on parental responses to infant irritability and the mediating role of culture. In Western urban samples, data reveal that infant irritability has long-term adverse relationship consequences (e.g., Caspi, Henry, McGee, Moffitt, & Silva, 1995; Rothbart & Bates, 1998). However, it is unclear whether adverse parental responses to infant irritability are a function of the demands of urbanized societies (e.g., job responsibilities, spatial constraints), prevailing cultural norms (e.g., acceptance or rejection of acting out), or a combination of the two (e.g., low tolerance of irritability magnified in families who operate on tight schedules versus high tolerance for toddler irritability where family scheduling is loose). Stated another way, the issue is the extent to which infant and toddler irritability is differentially accepted as a function of cultural norms and the circumstances that must be present within a culture such that early irritability leads to later relationship and other problems.

Beyond this general summary of knowledge and identification of a few research questions, the field has pinpointed specifics. These follow, with a summary of agreements and disagreements about findings and uncertainties.

## Infants' Facial Expressions

This topic, which has been one of the most enduring research foci, shows consensus about these findings. Infants' facial expressions are used by caregivers to infer states and needs of infants; within each age period, individual differences exist in the readability of infant expressions and the caregiver's ability to interpret and use these expressions; hard-to-read infant expressions can cause maladaptation in interactions; disruptions in social interactions may stem from caregivers' interpretation (or misinterpretation) of infant emotion expressions. There is disagreement about the meaning of facial expression in young infants (i.e., is there equivalence between an expression and an experience of emotion?), about the reasons underlying the emergence and development of emotion expressions during the first two years of life, and about whether two or more neural substrates underlie the expressions of early infancy versus those that emerge during the second year. Little is known about the parents who are able to adapt to distortions of infant expressions and how parents accomplish this adaptation.

## Infants' Perception of Others' Facial Expressions

Agreement exists that infants begin to perceive differences in facial expressions between 3 and 7 months; toward the end of the first year, they recognize that others' facial expressions convey information, and this information can inform their own behavior; infants also begin to recognize unfamiliar faces, and this recognition also informs their own behavior; toddlers use others' expressions to engage in prosocial behaviors. There is little information about the long-term implications for individual variability in reading emotion expressions.

## Self-Awareness Influences Emotion Repertoire

There is consensus about the role of selfhood in emotional responses, such that self-awareness in certain situations may elicit an emotion response (e.g., embarrassment when violating social standards). There is disagreement, however, about the distinctiveness of social emotions. To some, social emotions represent a separate class of emotions, whereas others do not differentiate emotions. A topic largely ignored in the literature is a delineation of the ontogeny of functional changes in the social emotions in the late toddler period and into the preschool years.

## The Role of Emotion Language

There is consensus that emotion language (i.e., using words to describe emotional experiences) prompts major changes in toddler and parent emotional and social interactions and that emotion language reorganizes the intersubjective nature of the relationship. There is scant information about the implications of functional limitations or delay in the use of emotion language for relationships, selfhood, and emotion regulation.

## Emotion Regulation

There is consensus that emotion regulation serves as a self-protective, survival mechanism; caregivers serve as important external regulators during infancy; the nature and relative contribution of infants and caregivers to emotion regulation shifts with development; individual differences (e.g., temperament) influence the quality of emotion regulation and social relationships; strategies used for emotion regulation change across development. There is disagreement about the definitions of emotion regulation, how it develops, how it varies by context, and how to measure emotion regulation. Unknowns include its neural substrates, the long-term stability of adaptive or dysfunctional emotion regulation, and whether in the face of pathological caregiving some infants are able to develop effective emotion regulation. An even more basic unknown pertains to the role of specific aspects of emotion development that contribute to effective emotion regulation. It is likely, for example, that adaptive emotion regulation in toddlers is greatly influenced by their functional understanding of others' emotions and their functional use of the language of emotions.

Issues related to emotion regulation are addressed in the next section. The topic has become increasingly important in the study of infant emotions, and there is continuing recognition of its importance for other age groups. Moreover, emotion regulation has relevance for interventions directed to parents and infants.

## Emotion Regulation: Moving Toward an Integrated Perspective

Although it is a relatively new area of research, emotion regulation has historical roots. Freud's (1926/1977) theory of psychosexual development made reference to the "struggle between internal emotional impulses and attempts to control their expression" (Dodge & Garber, 1991, p. 3). Evolutionary biologists and animal behaviorists (e.g., Baker & Aureli, 1997; Clarke & Snipes, 1998; Johnson-Laird & Oatley, 1992; Panksepp, Knutson, & Pruitt, 1998; Tooby & Cosmides, 1990) have discussed the relevance of emotion expressions and the ability to control those expressions to basic survival. Thus emotion regulation resolves the "conflict between emotion centers of the brain that push for one action in a particular situation, and other parts of the brain (the cortical center in humans) that appreciate that the emotional impulse may not be well matched to [a] current situation" (Gross, 1998, p. 542). For infants, whose appraisal systems, understanding, and general neuropsychological development are in the process of *becoming*, emotion regulation involves a more fundamental aspect that is not fully understood. Infant patterns of emotion regulation may change dramatically across the first two years. The challenge is to determine the nature of adaptations that occur in the face of change, particularly when they accompany seemingly disorganized transition periods.

What exactly is emotion regulation? Table 19.2 reveals considerable diversity in its conceptualizations.[7] The definitions, by and large, are focused exclusively on the content (i.e., components or "ingredients" of emotion regulation), function (i.e., the activities involved in emotion regulation), or the processes (i.e., how emotion reg-

ulation happens) of emotion regulation. Thus there is fundamental disagreement over how to characterize early emotion regulation. Moreover, there are questions about the breadth of emotion regulation. Definitions that focus only on the content of emotion regulation (e.g., neurophysiological underpinnings) do not explicate the process by which regulatory functioning is promoted. Similarly, process-oriented definitions do not highlight individual behavioral or anatomical contributors to emotion regulation. Another unresolved definitional issue is the developmental one, with some definitions accounting for change and other ignoring the expanding nature of infant behavioral repertoires.

There are, however, common themes in the definitions outlined in Table 19.2. First, most definitions either explicitly or implicitly underscore the adaptive nature of emotion regulation. For example, all of the function-oriented definitions refer to emotion regulation as a vehi-

Table 19.2 Definitions of Emotion Regulation

| Approach | Researcher/Theorist | Definition of Emotion Regulation (ER) |
|---|---|---|
| Structure | Dawson (1994a) | Identifies frontal lobe as starting place for regulation; discriminates between source of primitive emotional responses (amygdala) and source of complex emotional responses (neocortex) |
| | Eisenberg & Fabes (1992) | Identifies four forms of ER: attentional and cognitive modes of emotion coping; approach, inhibitory, distracting, and avoidant behaviors; regulation via social communication; self-stimulation and self-soothing behavior (p. 133) |
| | Lyons-Ruth & Zeanah (1993) | Highlights parents' responsiveness to infant cognitive, linguistic, and social signals |
| | Radke-Yarrow (1986) | Discusses the three aspects of ER: expression, physiology, and subjective experience |
| | Rothbart, Ziaie, & O'Boyle (1992) | Defines ER (called self-regulation) as a component of temperament, with a particular focus on the role of attention mechanisms, activation, and inhibition in regulation. |
| Function | Brenner & Salovey (1997) | Defines ER as the relative capacity to manage one's emotional reactivity (including intensity and duration of arousal) such that alterations in one's physiological-biochemical system, behavioral-expressive system, and experiential-cognitive system are effected |
| | Diamond (1990) | Defines ER as the ability to inhibit prepotent responses |
| | Goldman-Rakic (1987) | Defines ER as the ability to guide one's behavior on the basis of internal representations |
| | Kopp (1989) | Defines ER as the ability to modulate emotions in accordance with situational demands |
| | | Highlights inhibition as a key component in ER |
| Process | Campos, Campos, & Barrett (1989) | Defines ER as the "control of emotional experience and expression by the self and others" |
| | | Uses a functionalist definition of emotions; emotions are "processes of establishing, maintaining, or disrupting the relations between the person and the internal or external environment, when such relations are significant to the individual" (p. 394) |
| | Cicchetti, Ganiban, & Barnett (1991) | Defines ER as the "intra- and extra-organismic factors by which emotional arousal is redirected, controlled, modulated, and modified to enable an individual to function adaptively in emotionally arousing situations" (p. 15) |
| | Dodge & Garber (1991) | Defines ER as the process by which activation in one response domain serves to alter, titrate, or modulate activation in another response domain |
| | Thompson (1994) | Defines ER as the "extrinsic and intrinsic processes responsible for monitoring, evaluating, and modifying emotional reactions to achieve one's goals" (pp. 27–28) |

cle for guiding behavior to meet situational demands. This theme is furthered by the process-oriented definitions, which suggest that emotion regulation is the means by which infants adapt to their surrounding environments. Recalling the work of Sroufe (1979), emotion regulation is highly organized and embedded in all other developments—a point that is revisited later in this section. There is also some overlap in the content of emotion regulation, with some definitions emphasizing attention and cognitive aspects (e.g., Cicchetti, Ganiban, & Barnett, 1991; Eisenberg & Fabes, 1992; Rothbart et al., 1992; Thompson, 1994), other definitions focusing on temperamental qualities of regulation (Derryberry & Rothbart, 1988; Rothbart et al., 1992), and some addressing the neurological underpinnings of emotion regulation (Dawson, 1994a). Still, overlapping aspects of definitions fall short of providing a complete, integrated, developmental model of early emotion regulation.

### Toward a Developmental Understanding of Emotion Regulation

One of the difficulties in understanding emotion regulation is that it represents many different things. Consider how Stern (1985) once described attachment. It is, at various levels, "a set of infant behaviors, a motivational system, a relationship between mother and infant, a theoretical construct, and a subjective experience for the infant in the form of 'working models' " (Stern, 1985, p. 25). These phrases could just as easily be translated to emotion regulation.

The definitions of Dante Cicchetti (Cicchetti et al., 1991) and Ross Thompson (1994) offer a starting point to approach an integrative definition of emotion regulation for the first two years of life. Cicchetti and colleagues define emotion regulation as the "intra-and extra-organismic factors by which emotional arousal is redirected, controlled, modulated, and modified to enable an individual to function adaptively in emotional situations" (Cicchetti et al., 1991, p. 15). Thompson (1994) views emotion regulation as the "extrinsic and intrinsic processes responsible for monitoring, evaluating, and modifying emotional reactions to achieve one's goals" (pp. 27–28). Unifying these correspondent definitions, we suggest that emotion regulation during the early years is a developmental process that represents the deployment of intrinsic and extrinsic processes—at whatever maturity level the young child is at—to (1) manage arousal states for effective biological and social adaptations and (2) achieve individual goals.

Intrinsic processes reflect an individual's physiological well-being, temperament style, levels of self-development, self-commitment, and motivation, and level of cognitive development. Extrinsic processes reflect social and emotional relationships, specific contexts and their demands, and informal, subjective cost-benefit analyses. Because intrinsic processes also reflect developmental transformations, they must represent interactions between changing and stable aspects of temperament, the growth of self-awareness, and changing levels of cognitive maturity. Examples of intrinsic processes involved in emotion regulation across three age periods in infancy are illustrated in Table 19.3. The table also makes clear that manifestations of temperament style are not isomorphic with emotion regulation, albeit temperament contributes to patterns of emotion regulation.

Irrespective of definitional preference, all of the aforementioned converge into common themes: (1) there is purpose to emotion regulation; (2) emotion regulation is not a specified collection of behavior but is a process that involves different constellations of behaviors across the first two years of life; (3) changes in individual capacities and social expectations underlie developmental shifts in regulatory functioning and (4) emotion regulation during infancy often sets the stage for future regulatory functioning. The first three themes are explored in the following section in an attempt to build a developmental model of emotion regulation.

### The Purpose of Emotion Regulation

The primary goal of emotion regulation during the first two years is arousal control, reflected by the ability to increase, decrease, or maintain arousal appropriate to context. Arousal control is fundamental to survival and future functioning and is manifested for three purposes, which are not mutually exclusive. First, infants must achieve a comfortable range of emotional homeostasis involving both positive and negative arousal states. Thus arousal control is essentially a self-protective mechanism that safeguards infants from uncomfortably high levels of pleasurable excitement or untoward distress. Young infants with their early special-purpose responses (Fischer & Biddell, 1991; Kopp, 1997) must work in tandem with sensitive caregivers to discover a comfortable range of arousal states. Over time, infants and toddlers develop preferred choices of control mechanisms as a function of their maturity and personal style (e.g., Stifter & Braungart, 1995). Arguably, one of the most crucial achievements of the first two years—that will have major implications for later competencies—involves increasing skill in managing independent arousal control.

A second purpose of arousal control is the establishment and maintenance of social relationships. In other words, infants must learn to manage their emotions (i.e., not crying) for the purpose of cementing close relationships. Thus the relationship takes precedence over individual needs, as, for example, when an infant discovers she can distract herself (rather than crying) when a parent is not immediately available for attention or play. Arousal

Table 19.3  Examples of Intrinsic Influences on Infant Emotion Regulation, Across Ages

| AGE | Temperament manifestations | Self-awareness | Cognitive resources | | Manifestations of Effective Emotion Regulation |
|---|---|---|---|---|---|
| 3 months | Perceptual sensitivity[1] Intensity of responses: fear, anger[2,3] Soothability[2] Predominant mood state; positive emotionality[2,3] Rhythmicity (sleep, eating patterns)[2] Activity level[2,3] | Ill-defined awareness of physical separateness from another | Special purpose responses Limited representation and memory systems | → | Self-soothing when bored, in mild states of upset |
| 12 months | Perceptual sensitivity Intensity of responses: fear, anger Soothability Predominant mood state; positive emotionality Rhythmicity (sleep, eating patterns) Effortful control[4] | Affectively invested experiences[5] Awareness of physical and social boundaries An affectional bond to specific others | Memory, including recall; elemental knowledge of scripts Emerging word comprehension Emergent understanding of means-end relationships | → | Active control of the environment[6] Use of caregiver Self-soothing techniques (e.g., distraction) |
| 24 months | Perceptual sensitivity Intensity of response Soothability Predominant mood state Rhythmicity (sleep, eating patterns) Effortful control Threshold of response to social norm demands Tolerance for self-related frustration | Awareness of a separate and continuous identity Autonomy goals Intersection of self-identity, affectional bonds, and parent socialization goals | Memory of affective and social experiences Memory for social expectations Spoken language around selfhood and self-desires Recognition of violation of expectations | → | Use of transitional objects Use of language to define feeling states, and context that is upsetting Avoidance of an unpleasant situation Attempts at reparation Cost-benefit analysis (e.g., attempt to make up to parent after violation) |

Note: 1. Escalona, 1968; 2. Thomas, Chess, & Birch, 1968; 3. Lemery, Goldsmith, Klinnert, & Mrazek, 1999; Rothbart, 1981; Goldsmith, 1996; 4. Derryberry & Rothbart, 1997; 5. Gunnar, 1980; 6. Uzgiris, 1967

control in the service of relationships differs in important ways for parents of infants, toddlers, and older children. Parents of toddlers become annoyed with excessive whining, whereas parents of young preschoolers are often annoyed when their children talk back or display out-of-control anger (Kopp & Bean, 1998).

Again caregivers are essential external regulators of infants' heightened arousal states (Fogel & Thelen, 1987; Sander, 1987, 1988), particularly until infants become more competent in emotion regulation for dyadic interactions. Individual variability has an important role vis-à-vis emotion regulation and relationships (see previous references). If the caregiver's ability to manage her or his own emotional state within the context of infant interactions is compromised (e.g., due to depression), then there will be effects on infant behavior. In similar manner, if the infant's ability to control emotional arousal is compromised (e.g., due to illness, physiological immaturity, difficult temperament style), then there can be untoward effects on the relationship, at least for the short term—and in some instances for the long term.

A third purpose of arousal control involves priming emotional readiness for learning. For this purpose, infants must alter their state to maximize attentiveness to surroundings and minimize the distractions that come from states of hyper- or hypoarousal (Escalona, 1963). A handful of studies indicate that infants attend, learn, and remember more effectively when they are in a neutral state than when they are in high or low arousal. Both Fagen (Singer & Fagen, 1992) and Rothbart (Rothbart & Bates, 1998) report findings that reveal that negative affect interferes with infants' cognitive processing skills (e.g., attention, memory). Similarly, heightened positive emotion states impede learning. Rose, Futterweit, and Jankowski (1999) found that neutral affect, rather than positive affect, was associated with faster learning of familiar and novel faces. Several issues beg for elucidation. Given that infants' and toddlers' experiences with their caregivers lead to considerable learning, does better learning take place when both members of the dyad are in neutral states or in heightened pleasure states of arousal? Given that pleasure is often a strong motivator for interest, exploring, and learning for infants and toddlers (as well as older individuals), is there a point when the heightened pleasure associated with interest in learning clashes with the more neutral states necessary for the actual implementation of learning?

## Emotion Regulation: Development of a Process

Defining a developmental approach to the process of emotion regulation is a singular and complex challenge, but a challenge that, when met, will pay dividends. Developmentally oriented questions are integral for (1) identifying how emotion regulation functions within and across age periods during the first two years of life; (2) determining when emotion regulation shows reorganization or disorganization and the associated implications; (3) identifying the varied processes that contribute to patterns of emotion regulation; and (4) identifying those aspects of emotion dysregulation during infancy or toddlerhood that are most likely to lead to long-term developmental and behavioral difficulties. Fundamentally, understanding patterns of emotion regulation development should further illuminate the significance of individual differences.

The literature suggests the potential usefulness of certain themes in building a developmental model of emotion regulation in the early years. In keeping with the definitions of emotion regulation offered previously, these themes address aspects of process, content, and context.

### The Process

Thelen and Smith (1998) used the metaphor of a mountain stream and its changing trajectories to illustrate the basic principles of dynamic systems theory. Development in some ways is like a stream. Just as streams always have two common elements—a body of water and a flow that navigates curves and turns—so human infants invariably share common features or elements. These include preprogrammed responses, such as those that prompt humans to social interaction (Bowlby, 1958); a social world that provides a setting for stimulation and exploration; and salient developmental challenges or *goals* that infants must manage for development to progress (Kopp & Coulson, 1999; Sroufe & Rutter, 1984). In emotion regulation, broad objectives range from physiological regulation during early infancy to effective social and emotional attachments by the end of the first year and, still later, to emotion regulation that is informed by conscious self-awareness.

Although shared human features are universal, the stream metaphor serves as a reminder of individual differences in emotion regulation in terms of pace, direction, and force. These differences manifest themselves because of the neurophysiological integrity of the young organism, the nature of preprogrammed responses and their transitions to more mature behaviors, the quality of social environments, temperament styles, individual niches, and

the relative effectiveness of infants and toddlers as they meet developmental challenges (see also Calkins, 1994).

Given the ubiquity of individual differences in early forms of emotion regulation, the issue becomes one of defining harmless variations and characterizing those that may mark increased risk for child and family (see, e.g., Stifter & Spinrad, in press).

### The Expanding Content of the Emotion Regulation Process

A fundamental issue for those interested in the ontogeny of infant emotion regulation turns on how to describe a process that begins in early infancy, that is dependent on the development of other skills (e.g., perception, cognition), and that must become increasingly adaptive for self, relationship, learning, and other needs. A beginning strategy involves the delineation of a developmental prototype that can be tested and refined with research. Such a prototype should highlight the resources and constraints of the infant's repertoire available for use in emotion regulation, the relative maturity of these behaviors (e.g., a newly emergent skill in contrast to one that is relatively functionally mature), and the overall level of caregiver support that is needed by infants to enact emotion regulation. To this end, an adaptation of Bremner (1997) serves as a point of departure.

Bremner (1997) describes behavioral reorganizations that occur during the first two years of life. Bremner's primary thesis is "that development in infancy is very much to do with the formation of links between pre-existing objective perception and emerging action, so that knowledge of the world implicit in perception eventually becomes explicit knowledge in the sense that it can be used to guide action" (p. 56).

In his model, the first knowledge is implicit knowledge, in that infants can perceive an objective world but are unable to use their knowledge to guide their behavior. We add that this knowledge stems from biological "givens," in that infants have sets of *predisposed* behaviors that allow them to function in their social and physical world. Implicit knowledge is transformed, often because of new developments in other domains (of course, partly as a function of varied experiences). As an example, Bremner (1997) describes how locomotor ability facilitates the growth of spatial perception, which in turn guides actions in new ways. New affordances are recognized; this changing representation of one's world, and how one can act on that world, is explicit knowledge. However important this transition is, Bremner takes care to distinguish explicit knowledge that is represented by automatic-type behaviors and explicit knowledge that is characterized by deliberate, purposeful, and varied actions. Seemingly, this level of explicit knowledge reflects consciousness of actions and interactions in the physical and social environments (Bremner, 1997). An example of infant automatic-explicit knowledge is random scanning for relief when distress is high. More purposeful behaviors might involve specific actions directed to another person (see Kopp, in press).

Bremner's conceptual approach has several important advantages. First, it places behaviors in a developmental framework that highlights behavioral resources and age-specific associations of skills at different age periods (M. D. Lewis et al., 1997), while simultaneously calling attention to behavioral constraints. This approach minimizes an emphasis on one or another specific behavior at a specific age as key to successful emotion regulation. Second, the model has application for documenting transitions in development in other domains, such as the onset of language. The point is simply that infants are "knowledge rich" (implicit knowledge) before they actively and effectively use words (explicit knowledge) to communicate with others about the events that cause fear or anger (see Bretherton et al., 1981). Much the same thesis can be made about selfhood. Infants and toddlers amass considerable information about themselves in relation to others (see Brownell & Kopp, 1991) before they are able to construct a personal identity and to use this identity in relation to autonomy-related emotion-regulatory acts such as maintaining possession of personal items that have emotional significance. Third, Bremner's (1997) approach is inherently organizational and calls for an analysis of how the shift from implicit to explicit knowledge furthers the reorganization of infant and toddler skills. Fourth, the conceptualization (i.e., implicit or explicit knowledge) can be used as a background developmental frame in which to evaluate individual contributors of emotion regulation (e.g., temperament, adaptability) and the dynamic features of emotion regulation, such as its range, timing, persistence, and lability (Thompson, 1998).

Translating Bremner's ideas to emotion regulation, implicit knowledge can be represented in content by the activation of special-purpose responses, such as infant facial expressions; mechanisms that reduce distress, such as nonnutritive sucking; and behavioral synchrony in positive affective states with caregivers. Implicit knowledge is preconscious, nonsymbolic, and goal-driven in a context-dependent setting and constrained by needs for interpersonal supports (Clyman, 1991; Emde, Biringen, Clyman, & Oppenheim, 1991; Kopp, 1997). Most important, total reliance on implicit knowledge means that infants are highly dependent on the extensive and varied experiences with their caregivers to facilitate emotion regulation. In time, they move beyond their sole reliance on implicit knowledge for effective emotion regulation.

Explicit, somewhat automatic, knowledge is demonstrated when infants' emotion regulatory behaviors are less tied to interpersonal supports and take into account another's actions but do not generalize and do not exemplify smoothly controlled actions (e.g., Calkins, Dedmon, Gill, Lomax, & Johnson, in press). The behaviors are in a *becoming* mode. An interesting regulatory example pertains to infants' initial, active negative responses to specific events, such as being fed a food with a displeasing taste (see Wenar, 1982). One type of response, observed at about five months, involves a side-to-side movement of the head while the infant looks at the caregiver. The infant's regulatory action is appropriate to the feeding context and occurs primarily with certain foods. However, the act itself is loosely controlled in terms of timing and duration and is not extended to other situations that the infant does not like (e.g., play is interrupted while a drippy nose is wiped). Typically in these other, nonfood situations, infants revert to crying. Overall, however, in this period of becoming, infants take a greater role in emotion regulation (see also Kaye, 1982), and their responses increasingly reveal behavioral integration (e.g., visual attention and head shaking) and organization. Caregiver inputs are still essential external supports for emotion regulation. Presumably, differences in the quality of caregiving may greatly influence the quality of infants' regulatory actions and may have implications for the next period, which involves a shift to more purposeful explicit knowledge.

Explicit, purposeful emotion knowledge is represented by infant acts that are specific to desired goals, that include recognition of obstacles in the way of goals, and that involve well-controlled actions taken to overcome obstacles. In terms of emotion regulation, examples from the literature reveal rich content of purposeful, situation-appropriate, modulated behavioral actions that cut across late infancy and include all of the toddler period. These include social referencing in the face of uncertainty, elemental control of bothersome toys, visual checks to a caregiver—while walking away—for emotional reassurance, looking at a caregiver's face while reaching for his hand when the special mechanism of a toy is too difficult to activate, bringing a toy to a caregiver for help when confronted with a problem (e.g., a difficult puzzle), initiating prosocial behaviors after discerning that a caregiver is upset, looking at a caregiver's face and offering descriptions of one's own emotional state, and offering excuses in the face of sibling conflicts. Certain behaviors, such as offering excuses, suggest the toddler's increasingly conscious understanding of others' needs, along with concerns for the self to maintain emotional equilibrium. The varied nature of these purposeful acts and the many contexts in which they are displayed signify ever widening active and independent forms of emotion regulation (see also Diener, Mangelsdorf, McHale, & Frosch, in press; Mangelsdorf, Shapiro, & Marzolf, 1994; Stifter & Braungart, 1995).

Bremner's (1997) account, however, does not emphasize the role of selfhood in explicit knowledge. Self-awareness in conjunction with cognitive and language growth (e.g., representation of others' needs, script knowledge about emotion reactions, nascent planning ability about emotion control strategies, comprehension of one's own and others' emotion states, the use of language to describe one's own and others' emotions) must reorganize explicit knowledge and, in particular, the process of adaptive emotion regulation. At approximately the midpoint of the second year dimensions of self-awareness are likely to influence emotion regulation. Examples include the more purposeful and appropriate responses to others' distress, judgments about the goodness and badness of events, justifications for conflict, expressions of anger directed to others, and strategies to handle anger in the face of caregivers' requests that go against personal wishes (e.g., Dunn, Bretherton, & Munn, 1987; Shatz, 1994; Stipek, Gralinski, & Kopp, 1990; Zahn-Waxler, 1998). Unquestionably, emotion regulation in the service of personal and social goals must have important ramifications for children's effective transitions to the expanding social environments that are central to the preschool years. Still, during toddlerhood, caregiver supports are essential, although these supports are likely to diminish in frequency or to change in focus and strategy (e.g., Calkins & Johnson, 1998).

Table 19.4 illustrates the shift from implicit to explicit knowledge by focusing on the emotion of anger. It includes developmentally relevant examples of anger-producing situations and of observable behaviors that mark anger for each age range. In addition, specific developmental resources, age-related associated abilities, and constraints are introduced to emphasize the competencies and limitations that infants bring to an emotionally laden situation. Specifically, the table details the developmental linkages between emotions and other domains of development. Given the various kinds of knowledge infants are utilizing, there are multiple sources of meaningful individual differences. The last column of Table 19.4 highlights some of these individual differences. An empirical question for research on infant emotions is the stability of these individual differences for longer term development.

Finally, it is important to emphasize that the model of development in emotion regulation described herein does not presume linear trends. Rather, there are likely to be plateaus and periods of disorganization. The latter is exemplified by the increase in crying and temper tantrums observed at midpoint of the second year (Kopp, 1992). Whether these emotional outbursts are due to an expansion in selfhood and understanding without concomitant growth in the ability to produce words is not known. These and a panoply of other questions could begin to be addressed with developmentally oriented studies of emotion regulation. The descriptive representation proposed here could serve as a reasonable preliminary conceptual framework for model building and additional research. At the very least, Bremner's (1997) approach forces us to consider the nature of infant resources with respect to emotion regulation.

### The Contexts of Emotion Regulation

Thompson (1998) wrote, "Individual differences in emotion regulation are not necessarily manifested in whether young children are competent peer partners or cooperate with their parents . . . but depend on the contextual demands and incentives that children perceive and their goals for managing emotions" (p. 79). Context is a particularly important issue in the study of infancy and toddlerhood because children of this age are often affected by fatigue, hunger, time of day, and age-related emotional disorganizations (e.g., see Brazelton, 1969). These factors differentially influence regulatory responses. Moving beyond the immediacy of these state variables, infants and toddlers must increasingly learn to adapt to different contexts that require emotion regulation. In addition, new context demands arise as a function of increasing developmental maturity and associated caregiver expectations. A challenge for researchers is how to frame the contexts of emotion regulation.

A reasonable starting point can be found in Siegler (1986), who described cognitive development as a "process of deploying limited processing resources increasingly effectively to meet task demands" (p. 380). This definition is not far afield from the developmental adaptations required in emotion regulation. Siegler further stated that children adapt to the demands of task environments by representing task environments in increasingly inclusive ways, by becoming more flexible processors, and by applying their "most sophisticated processing to a widening range of situations" (p. 380).

Siegler's "flexible processors" translates to emotion regulation adaptations that must occur during the first two years: (1) when infants and toddlers are engaged in social interactions, (2) when they are in social contexts but are not participants in social interactions, and (3) when they are alone and engaged in their surrounding physical world. Each of these task environments prompts different caregiver expectations, as well as different regulatory demands. Being alert and alone at 3 months and visually exploring objects when bored differs from the regulatory requirements of a social interaction. The latter involves regulation of attention to the caregiver's voice and face, arousal control for increases and decreases in state that accompany pleasurable interactions, and control of reciprocal social smiling. Here the regulatory aspects of emotion regulation are embedded in regulatory processes associated with attention and communication.

The specifics of task demands for regulatory behaviors vary with older infants and toddlers, yet whether they are alone, socially engaged, or asleep, each situation has requirements that must be met to achieve the state control,

Table 19.4  The Process of Regulation of Anger: A Developmental Perspective

| Types of behavioral reorganizations | Eliciting situations and responses | | Organization of the behavioral repertoire | | | Individual variability |
| | Anger-producing situation | Observable behavior | Age-specific domain associations | Resources (e.g., attention, perception, motor, cognitive, language) | Constraints | Sources of differences |
| --- | --- | --- | --- | --- | --- | --- |
| Implicit Approximately newborn–2 mos. | Bodily restraint (e.g., during a diaper change) | Fusses (e.g., facial flush, body tenses) | Perception-emotion (e.g., perception of bodily states) | Eye contact Gaze aversion | Limited understanding of offending stimulus or person enacting the 'offense' | Soothability Latency of response Vigor of response |
| Explicit—becoming Approximately 5–6 mos. | Parent selection of food vs. infant food preference (e.g., dislikes strained vegetables) | Side-to-side head movement (nascent) Directs action (e.g., shakes head toward object or person) | Perception-emotion (e.g., discrimination of emotional states) Motor-emotion Associative learning | Coordinated and expressive motor control (e.g., head shake) | Inability to use hands to push away offending food Limited ability to control the time and duration of behavioral response to offending act Situation-specific behavioral response | Motor quality Temperament style Associates act and effect (e.g., effect of head shake on caregiver's removal of food) |
| Explicit—understanding Approximately 12–15 mos. | Parent boundaries (e.g., parent stops toddler's play because of dinner time; inhibits toddler play in toilet) | Cries Attempts to push caregiver Toddles away from situation | Motor-emotion Cognitive-emotion (e.g., nascent framing of situation so that it has meaning; attention to detail of objects, others' actions) Motivation-emotion (e.g., goal seeking as a function of emotion state) | Nascent understanding of cause/effect Understanding the source of anger and situations that elicit anger | Limited ability to control various aspects of the situation (e.g., limited understanding of steps that lead to control of situation) Inability to effectively use language to express feelings about situation Limited understanding of how the self has a role in situation | Motor quality Temperament style "Learnability" Level of motivation Social-emotional bond that facilitates acceptance of caregiver standards |
| Explicit—self-understanding Approximately 18–24 mos. | Parent boundaries (e.g., removes toy from toddler, reinforces structure of bath routines, requires sharing with age-mates/siblings) | Cries Yells Tantrums Runs from scene Hits/bites another | Motor-emotion Cognitive-emotion Motivation-emotion Social-emotion Language-emotion Self-emotion | Improved understanding of cause/effect Memory (e.g., able to file information about offending events in memory) Language—used to explain feelings in relation to situations Protostrategies—used around 24 mos. to control anger (e.g., getting caregiver when upset with a peer) Understanding own identity and possessions Desire to please caregiver | Easily upset when perceives threat to self-directed activity or self-possessions Limited understanding of situations and parent needs or requirements Limited ability to express a full range of feelings/desires Limited understanding of how to act in diverse situations Limited understanding of own limitations in relation to certain objects/situations (e.g., scissors, heights) | Fragile social-emotional bonds Attention control Impulsivity Use of available resources Ability to 'read' situations or caregiver cues |

relational, or learning goals of emotion regulation. Within age periods, Siegler's theme of *sophisticated processing* also bears consideration. It could be examined as another meaningful dimension of individual differences in early emotion regulation. Also, it may be useful to examine in detail those young children who show sophisticated emotion regulation strategies across a wide range of situations compared with those children whose emotion regulation strategies are relatively immature across varied contexts.

Finally, the emphasis on contexts again points to the view that emotion regulation is not a stable set of behaviors recognizable across the first two years of life. Rather, it represents organized collections of behaviors that change as a function of development, caregiver demands, and situational factors. What is important in infant emotion regulation is how effectively these collections of emotion regulatory behaviors are implemented for different purposes and how caregivers support the emotion regulatory processes within and across age periods.

## Summary

Among the many topics addressed in this chapter, several merit additional comment. First, with a few notable exceptions (e.g., M. D. Lewis et al., 1997) the field has recently turned away from developmentally oriented models and longitudinal research. This movement has truly unfortunate consequences for the understanding of infant emotions and most particularly emotion regulation. Quoting Caspi (1998), "Only longitudinal studies can chart growth, identify developmental sequences, establish the temporal order of variables across time, trace behavioral connections across development, and reveal the implications of early behavior for later adjustment" (p. 370). We add that a sound understanding of infants' and toddlers' developmental competencies enhances the meaning of individual differences.

Second, the neuropsychological and neurophysiological research on infants and emotions has been extraordinarily productive and illuminating. These research areas could continue to provide important insights by including the study of infants and toddlers who are developing atypically. There has been seminal research on infants with diagnoses of phenylketonuria or with Down syndrome; however, research attention could profitably be directed to disorders that implicate right hemisphere functioning. Infants with localized brain damage or those who have an early diagnosis of Asperger's syndrome might provide important insights about emotion understanding and emotion regulation.

Third, there has been scant study of gender differences in the amount and quality of emotion regulation; the research that has been done often reveals equivocal findings. However, Keenan and Shaw (1997) raise intriguing issues in their analysis of young girls' problem behaviors. Noting that gender differences in problem behaviors are rarely observed before age 4 years, Keenan and Shaw suggest that earlier problems might be resolved for females. Buffering factors could include earlier physical maturation, lower stress reactivity, earlier language development, higher levels of prosocial behaviors, and the nature of parenting of girls. This confluence of factors is worthy of empirical test, if only for the practical implications the findings might have.

Fourth, as noted earlier, the study of infant emotions has been troubled by measurement issues for decades. Researchers often use their own coding systems for emotion states, with minimal acknowledgement of others' approaches. This tendency can be problematic for data interpretation, for example, when trying to extract meaning from the emotion states of young infants. Another measurement issue pertains to the extensive use of laboratory settings to measure emotions, reactivity, or emotion regulation in stressful situations. All three may be confounded in a single setting. Moreover, skills displayed in the laboratory may not accurately translate to real-life capabilities. In general, laboratory settings deny infants and their caregivers the opportunities to display the full range of their behavioral repertoires, their content and quality, and the use of affordances in the surrounding environment. The task for researchers, then, is to use measurement techniques that allow for an understanding of the richness of the repertoire, of the behaviors in the repertoire that are developmentally appropriate, those that are developmentally sophisticated, and those that are confounded with other developmental systems, including temperament, emotion expression and understanding, and maturity of cognitive or motor skills.

As pointed out earlier, emotion regulation can take place in different task environments, including those in which interactions with different partners take place and in which the infant or toddler is alone in one or another familiar setting. Because each setting may have different emotion regulatory task demands, it is most meaningful to identify the richness of emotion regulatory behaviors across settings and to note the types of settings that reveal the most adaptive and sophisticated regulatory repertoire. This approach can help elucidate the individual differences that may be most meaningful at a particular developmental age and highlight dysfunctional emotion regulatory processes that may be displayed by children who have cognitive, sensory, or motor impairments. Expansive research strategies, of course, can reveal how culture mediates the nature of task environments and expectations and emotion regulation in the first two years of life.

## NOTES

1. California passed an initiative (Proposition 10) by a small margin to tax tobacco use and apply the funds to parenting education. There was an attempt to appeal the measure in March 2000, which did not succeed.

2. Readers interested in biographical sketches of major researchers during the early decades, along with discussion of some of the themes they grappled with, will find fascinating material in Magai & McFadden, 1995.

3. To this day, the father's role in infant emotions receives scant attention in research.

4. Clearly, we do not mean to imply direct conceptual lineages between Escalona and later researchers. The topics of research interests are similar, but each later researcher went on to make unique contributions to the field.

5. Izard shared a rich intellectual history with Ekman, Tomkins, and others.

6. The motivational influence on adult emotions is a long-standing topic, albeit Lazarus's (1991) cognitive-motivational-relational theory is most closely related to Campos's thinking.

7. Because this chapter is focused on emotional development during infancy, definitions of emotion regulation from the adult literature are not included in Table 19.2.

## REFERENCES

Adamson, L. B., & Bakeman, R. (1984). Mothers' communicative acts: Changes during infancy. *Infant Behavior and Development, 7*, 467–478.

Ahrens, R. (1954). An ontogenetic study of reactions to facial expressions. *Zeitschrift Feur Experimentelle und Angewandte Psychologie, 2*, 412–454.

Ambrose, J. A. (1963a). The concept of a critical period for the development of social responsiveness in early infancy. In B. M. Foss (Ed.), *Determinants of infant behavior: II.* New York: Wiley.

Ambrose, J. A. (1963b). Age of onset of ambivalence in early infancy. *Journal of Child Psychology and Psychiatry and Allied Disciplines, 4*, 167–181.

Baker, K. C., & Aureli, F. (1997). Behavioural indicators of anxiety: An empirical test in chimpanzees. *Behaviour, 134*, 1031–1050.

Barr, R. G., Konner, M., Bakeman, R., & Adamson, L. (1991). Crying in !Kung San infants: A test of the cultural specificity hypothesis. *Developmental Medicine and Child Neurology, 33*, 601–610.

Barrett, K., & Campos, J. (1987). Perspectives on emotional development: II. A functionalist approach to emotions. In J. Osofsky (Ed.), *Handbook of infant development* (2nd ed., pp. 555–578). New York: Wiley.

Barrett, K. C., Zahn-Waxler, C., & Cole, P. M. (1993). Avoiders vs. amenders: Implications for the investigation of guilt and shame during toddlerhood. *Cognition and Emotion, 7*, 481–505.

Bates, E., Bretherton, I., & Snyder, L. (1988). *From first words to grammar: Individual differences and dissociable mechanisms.* Cambridge, MA: Cambridge University Press.

Bayley, N. (1932). A study of the crying of infants during mental and psychological tests. *Journal of Genetic Psychology, 40*, 306–329.

Beeghly, M., & Cicchetti, D. (1997). Talking about self and other: Emergence of an internal state lexicon in young children with Down syndrome. *Development and Psychopathology, 9*, 729–748.

Bell, S. M., & Ainsworth, M. D. (1972). Infant crying and maternal responsiveness. *Child Development, 43*, 1171–1190.

Birns, B., Blank, M., Bridger, W. H., & Escalona, S. (1965). Behavioral inhibition in neonates produced by auditory stimuli. *Child Development, 36*, 639–645.

Blass, E., & Ciaramitaro, V. (1994). A new look at some old mechanisms in human newborns: Taste and tactile determinants of state, affect, and action. *Monographs of the Society for Research in Child Development, 59*, (1, Serial No. 239).

Bowlby, J. (1958). The nature of the child's tie to his mother. *International Journal of Psycho-Analysis, 39*, 350–373.

Bowlby, J. (1969). Disruption of affectional bonds and its effects on behavior. *Canada's Mental Health Supplement*, No. 59, p. 12.

Brackbill, Y., Adams, G., & Crowell, D. H. (1966). Arousal level in neonates and preschool children under continuous auditory stimulation. *Journal of Experimental Child Psychology, 4*, 178–188.

Braungart, J., & Stifter, S. (1991). Regulation of negative reactivity during the Strange Situation: Temperament and attachment in 12-month-old infants. *Infant Behavior and Development, 14*, 349–364.

Braungart-Rieker, J., Garwood, M. M., Powers, B. P., & Notaro, P. C. (1998). Infant affect and affect regulation during the still-face paradigm with mothers and fathers: The role of infant characteristics and parental sensitivity. *Developmental Psychology, 24*, 1428–1437.

Brazelton, T. B. (1969). *Infants and mothers: Differences in development.* New York: Delacorte Press.

Bremner, J. G. (1997). From perception to cognition. In G. Bremner, A. Slater, & G. Butterworth (Eds.), *Infant development: Recent advances* (pp. 55–72). East Sussex, England: Psychology Press.

Brenner, E. M., & Salovey, P. (1997). Emotion regulation during childhood: Developmental, interpersonal, and individual considerations. In P. Salovey & D. J. Sluyter (Eds.), *Emotional development and emotional intelligence: Educational implications* (pp. 168–195). New York: Basic Books.

Bretherton, I., & Beeghly, M. (1982). Talking about internal states: The acquisition of an explicit theory of mind. *Developmental Psychology, 18*, 906–921.

Bretherton, I., Fritz, J., Zahn-Waxler, C., & Ridgeway, D. (1986). Learning to talk about emotions: A functionalist perspective. *Child Development, 57*, 529–548.

Bretherton, I., McNew, S., & Beeghly-Smith, M. (1981). Early person knowledge as expressed in gestural and verbal communication: When do infants acquire a "theory of mind"? In M. E. Lamb & L. R. Sherrod (Eds.), *Infant social cognition: Empirical and theoretical considerations* (pp. 333–374). Hillsdale, NJ: Erlbaum.

Bridges, K. M. B. (1932). Emotional development in early infancy. *Child Development, 3*, 324–341.

Bridges, K. M. B. (1934). Measuring emotionality in infants: A tentative experiment. *Child Development, 5*, 36–40.

Bridges, L., Grolnick, W., & Connell, J. (1997). Infant emotion regulation with mothers and fathers. *Infant Behavior and Development, 20*, 47–57.

Bronson, G. (1978). Aversive reactions to strangers: A dual process interpretation. *Child Development, 49,* 495–499.

Brooks, J., & Lewis, M. (1976). Infants' responses to strangers: Midget, adult, and child. *Child Development, 47,* 323–332.

Brossard, L. M., & Decarie, T. G. (1968). Comparative reinforcing of eight stimulations on the smiling response of infants. *Journal of Child Psychology and Psychiatry and Allied Disciplines, 9,* 51–59.

Brownell, C. A., & Kopp, C. B. (1991). Common threads, diverse solutions: Concluding commentary. *Developmental Review, 11,* 288–303.

Bühler, C. (1934). The curve of life as studies in biographies. *Journal of Applied Psychology, 3,* 27–41.

Bühler, C., & Hetzer, H. (1929). Individual differences among children in the first two years of life. *Child Study, 1,* 11–13.

Buss, K., & Goldsmith, H. H. (1998). Fear and anger regulation in infancy: Effects on the temporal dynamics of affective expression. *Child Development, 69,* 359–374.

Calkins, S. D. (1994). Origins and outcomes of individual differences in emotion regulation. *Monographs of the Society for Research in Child Development, 59* (2–3, Serial No. 240).

Calkins, S. D. (1997). Cardiac vagal tone indices of temperamental reactivity and behavioral regulation in young children. *Developmental Psychobiology, 31,* 125–135.

Calkins, S. D., Dedmon, S. E., Gill, K. L., Lomax, L. E., & Johnson, L. M. (in press). Frustration in infancy: Implications for emotion regulation, physiological processes, and temperament. *Infancy.*

Calkins, S. D., Fox, N. A., & Marshall, T. R. (1996). Behavioral and physiological antecedents of inhibited and uninhibited behavior. *Child Development, 67,* 523–540.

Calkins, S. D., & Johnson, M. C. (1998). Toddler regulation of distress to frustrating events: Temperamental and maternal correlates. *Infant Behavior and Development, 21,* 379–395.

Campos, J. J., Barrett, K. C., Lamb, M. E., Goldsmith, H. H., & Stenberg, C. (1983). Socioemotional development. In P. H. Mussen (Series Ed.) & M. Haith & J. Campos (Vol. Eds.), *Handbook of child development: Vol. 2. Infancy and developmental psychobiology* (4th ed., pp. 435–571). New York: Wiley.

Campos, J. J., & Brackbill, Y. (1973). Infant state: Relationship to heart rate, behavioral response and response decrement. *Developmental Psychobiology, 6,* 9–19.

Campos, J. J., Campos, R. G., & Barrett, K. C. (1989). Emergent themes in the study of emotional development and emotion regulation. *Developmental Psychology, 25,* 394–402.

Campos, J. J., Emde, R., Gaensbauer, T., Sorce, J., & Henderson, C. (1975). Cardiac behavioral interrelations in the reactions of infants to strangers. *Developmental Psychology, 11,* 589–601.

Campos, J. J., Hiatt, S., Ramsay, D., Henderson, C., & Svejda, M. (1978). The emergence of fear on the visual cliff. In M. Lewis & L. Rosenblum (Eds.), *The origins of affect* (pp. 149–182). New York: Wiley.

Campos, J. J., Kermoian, R., & Witherington, D. (1996). An epigenetic perspective on emotional development. In R. D. Kavanaugh & B. Zimmerberg (Eds.), *Emotion: Interdisciplinary perspectives* (pp. 119–138). Mahwah, NJ: Erlbaum.

Campos, J. J., Svejda, M. J., Campos, R. G., & Bertenthal, B. (1982). The emergence of self-produced locomotion: Its importance for psychological development in infancy. In D. Bricker (Ed.), *Intervention with at-risk and handicapped infants.* Baltimore, MD: University Park Press.

Camras, L. A. (1986). Judgments of emotion from facial expression and situational context. In C. E. Izard (Ed.), *Cambridge studies in social and emotional development: Vol. 2. Measuring emotions in infants and children* (pp. 75–89). New York: Cambridge University Press.

Camras, L. A. (1992). Expressive development and basic emotions. *Cognition and Emotion, 6,* 269–283.

Camras, L. A., Grow, J. G., & Ribordy, S. C. (1983). Recognition of emotional expression by abused children. *Journal of Clinical Child Psychology, 12,* 325–328.

Camras, L. A., Oster, H., Campos, J. J., & Miyake, K. (1992). Japanese and American infants' responses to arm restraint. *Developmental Psychology, 28,* 578–583.

Caron, A. J., Caron, R. F., Caldwell, R. C., & Weiss, S. J. (1973). Infant perception of the structural properties of the face. *Developmental Psychology, 9,* 385–399.

Caron, A. J., Caron, R. F., & MacLean, D. J. (1988). Infant discrimination of naturalistic emotional expressions: The role of face and voice. *Child Development, 59,* 604–616.

Caron, A. J., Caron, R. F., & Myers, R. S. (1982). Abstraction of invariant face expressions in infancy. *Child Development, 53,* 1008–1015.

Carstensen, L. L. (1998). A life-span approach to social motivation. In J. Heckhausen & C. S. Dweck (Eds.), *Motivation and self-regulation across the lifespan* (pp. 341–364). Cambridge, England: Cambridge University Press.

Caspi, A. (1998). Personality development across the life course. In W. Damon (Series Ed.) & N. Eisenberg (Vol. Ed.), *Handbook of child psychology: Vol. 3. Social, emotional, and personality development* (5th ed., pp. 311–388). New York: Wiley.

Caspi, A., Henry, B., McGee, R. O., Moffitt, T. E., & Silva, P. A. (1995). Temperamental origins of child and adolescent behavior problems: From age three to fifteen. *Child Development, 66,* 55–68.

Cattell, R. B. (1933). Temperament tests: I. Temperament. *British Journal of Psychology, 23,* 308–329.

Chugani, H. T. (1994). Development of regional brain glucose metabolism in relation to behavior and plasticity. In G. Dawson & K. Fischer (Eds.), *Human behavior and the developing brain* (pp. 153–175). New York: Guilford Press.

Cicchetti, D., Ganiban, J., & Barnett, D. (1991). Contributions from the study of high risk populations to understanding the development of emotion regulation. In K. Dodge & J. Garber (Eds.), *The development of emotion regulation* (pp. 15–48). New York: Cambridge University Press.

Cicchetti, D., & Sroufe, L. A. (1976). The relationship between affective and cognitive development in Down's syndrome infants. *Child Development, 47,* 920–929.

Clarke, A. S., & Snipes, M. (1998). Early behavioral development and temperamental traits in mother- vs. peer-reared rhesus monkeys. *Primates, 39,* 433–448.

Clyman, R. (1991). The procedural organization of emotions: A contribution from cognitive science to the psychoanalytic theory of therapeutic action. *Journal of the American Psychiatric Association, 39,* 349–382.

Cohn, J. F., & Tronick, E. Z. (1983). Three-month-old infants' reaction to simulated maternal depression. *Child Development, 54,* 185–193.

Connell, J. P., & Thompson, R. (1986). Emotion and social interaction in the Strange Situation: Consistencies and asymmetric influences in the second year. *Child Development, 57,* 733–745.

Crockenberg, S., & Smith, B. (1982). Antecedents of mother-infant interaction and infant irritability in the first three months of life. *Infant Behavior and Development, 5,* 105–119.

Damasio, A. (1999). *The feeling of what happens: Body and emotion in the making of consciousness.* New York: Harcourt Brace.

Davidson, R. J., & Fox, N. A. (1982). Asymmetrical brain activity discriminates between positive and negative affective stimuli in human infants. *Science, 218,* 1235–1237.

Davidson, R. J., & Fox, N. A. (1989). Frontal brain asymmetry predicts infants' responses to maternal separation. *Journal of Abnormal Psychology, 98,* 127–131.

Dawson, G. (1994a). Development of emotional expression and emotion regulation in infancy: Contributions of the frontal lobe. In G. Dawson & K. W. Fischer (Eds.), *Human behavior and the developing brain* (pp. 346–379). New York: Guilford Press.

Dawson, G. (1994b). Frontal electroencephalographic correlates of individual differences in emotion expression in infants: A brain systems perspective on emotion. *Monographs of the Society for Research in Child Development, 59* (Serial No. 240, 2–3).

Dawson, G., Frey, K., Panagiotides, H., Yamada, E., Hessl, D., & Osterling, J. (1999). Infants of depressed mothers exhibit atypical frontal electrical brain activity during interactions with mother and with a familiar, nondepressed adult. *Child Development, 70,* 1058–1066.

Dawson, G., Klinger, L. G., Panagiotides, H., & Spieker, S. (1992). Infants of mothers with depressive symptoms: Electrocephalographic and behavioral findings related to attachment status. *Development and Psychopathology, 4,* 67–80.

Decarie, T. (1974). *The infant's reaction to strangers.* New York: International Universities Press.

DeGangi, G., Porges, S., Sickel, R. Z., & Greenspan, S. (1993). Four-year follow-up of a sample of regulatory disordered infants. *Infant Mental Health Journal, 14,* 330–343.

Demos, V. (1986). Crying in early infancy: An illustration of the motivational function of affect. In T. B. Brazelton & M. W. Yogman (Eds), *Affective development in infancy* (pp. 39–73). Norwood, NJ: Ablex.

Derryberry, D., & Rothbart, M. K. (1988). Arousal, affect, and attention as components of temperament. *Journal of Personality and Social Psychology, 55,* 958–966.

Derryberry, D., & Rothbart, M. K. (1997). Reactive and effortful processes in the organization of temperament. *Development and Psychopathology, 9,* 633–652.

de Weerth, C., van Geert, P., & Hoijtink, H. (1999). Intraindividual variability in infant behavior. *Developmental Psychology, 35,* 1102–1112.

Diamond, A. (1990). Developmental time course in human infants and infant monkeys, and the neural bases of inhibitory control in reaching. In A. Diamond (Ed.), *Annals of the New York Academy of Sciences: Vol. 608.*

*The development and neural bases of higher cognitive functions* (pp. 637–676). New York: New York Academy of Sciences.

Diamond, A., Prevor, M. B., Callender, G., & Druin, D. P. (1997). Prefrontal cortex cognitive deficits in children treated early and continuously for PKU. *Monographs of the Society for Research in Child Development, 62* (4, Serial No. 252).

Diener, M. L., Mangelsdorf, S. C., McHale, J. L., & Frosch, C. A. (in press). Infants' behavioral strategies for emotion regulation with mothers and fathers. *Infancy.*

Dodge, K. A., & Garber, J. (1991). Domains of emotion regulation. In J. Garber & K. A. Dodge (Eds.), *The development of emotion regulation and dysregulation* (pp. 3–14). New York: Cambridge University Press.

Dunn, J., & Munn, P. (1985). Becoming a family member: Family conflict and the development of social understanding. *Child Development, 56,* 480–492.

Eisenberg, N., & Fabes, R. A. (1992). Emotion, regulation, and the development of social competence. In M. S. Clark (Ed.), *Emotion and social behavior: Review of personality and social psychology, Vol. 14* (pp. 119–150). Newbury Park, CA: Sage.

Emde, R. N., Biringen, Z., Clyman, R. B., & Oppenheim, D. (1991). The moral self of infancy: Affective core and procedural knowledge. *Developmental Review, 11,* 251–270.

Emde, R. N., Gaensbauer, T. J., & Harmon, R. J. (1976). Emotion expression in infancy: A biobehavioral study. *Psychological Issues, 10, Monograph 37.* New York: International Universities Press.

Emde, R. N., & Harmon, R. (1972). Endogenous and exogenous smiling systems in early infancy. *Journal of the American Academy of Child Psychiatry, 11,* 177–200.

Emde, R. N., Katz, E. I., & Thorpe, J. K. (1978). Emotional expression in infancy: II. Early deviations in Down's syndrome. In M. Lewis & L. A. Rosenblum (Eds.), *The development of affect* (pp. 351–360). New York: Plenum.

Emde, R. N., Plomin, R., Robinson, J. Corley, R., DeFries, J., Fulker, D., Reznick, J. S., Campos, J. J., Kagan, J., & Zahn-Waxler, C. (1992). Temperament, emotion, and cognition at fourteen months: The MacArthur Longitudinal Twin Study. *Child Development, 63,* 1437–1455.

Escalona, S. (1953). Emotional development in the first year of life. In M. Senn (Ed.), *Problems of infancy and childhood* (pp. 11–92). New York: Josiah Macy, Jr. Foundation.

Escalona, S. (1963). Patterns of infantile experience and the developmental process. In F. Eissler, A. Freud, H. Hartman, & M. Kris (Eds.), *The psychoanalytic study of the child* (Vol. 18, pp. 197–244). New York: International Universities Press.

Escalona, S. (1968). *The roots of individuality.* Chicago: Aldine.

Feinman, S. (1982). Social referencing in infancy. *Merrill-Palmer Quarterly, 28,* 445–470.

Field, T. (1979). Differential behavior and cardiac responses of 3-month-old infants to a mirror and peer. *Infant Behavior and Development, 2,* 179–184.

Field, T. (1984). Early interactions between infants and their postpartum depressed mothers. *Infant Behavior and Development, 7,* 517–522.

Fischer, K. W., & Biddell, T. (1991). Constraining nativist inferences about cognitive capacities. In S. Carey & R.

Gelman (Eds.), *The epigenesis of mind: Essays on biology and cognition* (pp. 199–235). Hillsdale, NJ: Erlbaum.

Fogel, A., & Thelen, E. (1987). Development of early expressive and communicative action: Reinterpreting the evidence from a dynamic systems perspective. *Developmental Psychology, 23*, 747–761.

Fox, N. A. (1994). Dynamic cerebral processes underlying emotion regulation. *Monographs of the Society for Research in Child Development, 59* (2–3, Serial No. 240).

Fox, N. A., Calkins, S. D., & Bell, M. A. (1994). Neural plasticity and development in the first two years of life: Evidence from cognitive and socioemotional domains of research. *Development and Psychopathology, 6*, 677–696.

Fox, N. A., & Davidson, R. J. (1987). Electroencephalogram asymmetry in response to the approach of a stranger and maternal separation in 10-month-old infants. *Developmental Psychology, 23*, 233–240.

Fox, N. A., & Davidson, R. J. (1988). Patterns of brain electrical activity during facial signs of emotion in 10-month-old infants. *Developmental Psychology, 24*, 230–236.

Fox, N. A., & Davidson, R. J. (1991). Hemispheric specialization and attachment behaviors: Developmental processes and individual differences in separation protest. In J. L. Gewirtz & W. M. Kurtines (Eds.), *Intersections with attachment* (pp. 147–167). Hillsdale, NJ: Erlbaum.

Freud, S. (1977). *Inhibition, symptoms, and anxiety.* New York: Norton. (Original work published 1926)

Friedlmeier, W., & Trommsdorff, G. (1999). Emotion regulation in early childhood: A cross-cultural comparison between German and Japanese toddlers. *Journal of Cross-Cultural Psychology, 30*, 684–711.

Frodi, A., Grolnick, W., & Bridges, L. (1985). Maternal correlates of stability and change in infant-mother attachment. *Infant Mental Health Journal, 6*, 60–67.

Frodi, A., Lamb, M. E., Leavitt, L. A., & Donovan, W. L. (1978). Fathers' and mothers' responses to the faces and cries of normal and premature infants. *Developmental Psychology, 14*, 490–498.

Gable, S., & Isabella, R. A. (1992). Maternal contributions to infant regulation of arousal. *Infant Behavior and Development, 15*, 95–107.

Gesell, A. (1928). *Infant and human growth.* New York: Macmillan.

Geva, R., Gardner, J. M., & Karmel, B. Z. (1999). Feeding-based arousal effects on visual-recognition memory in early infancy. *Developmental Psychology, 35*, 640–650.

Gewirtz, J. L. (1965). The course of infant smiling in four child-rearing environments in Israel. In B. M. Foss (Ed.), *Determinants of infant behavior* (Vol. 3, pp. 205–248). New York: Wiley.

Goldman-Rakic, P. S. (1987). Circuitry of primate prefrontal cortex and regulation of behavior by representational memory. In F. Plum & V. Mountcastle (Eds.), *Handbook of physiology: Sec. I. The nervous system. Vol. 5. Higher functions of the brain* (pp. 373–417). Bethesda, MD: American Physiological Society.

Goldsmith, H. H. (1996). Studying temperament via construction of the Toddler Behavior Assessment questionnaire. *Child Development, 67*, 218–235.

Goodenough, F. L. (1929). The emotional behavior of young children during mental tests. *Journal of Juvenile Research, 13*, 204–219.

Goodenough, F. L. (1931a). The expression of emotions in infancy. *Child Development, 2*, 96–101.

Goodenough, F. L. (1931b). *Anger in young children.* Minneapolis, MN: University of Minnesota Press.

Goodenough, F. L. (1932). Expression of the emotions in a blind-deaf child. *Journal of Abnormal and Social Psychology, 27*, 328–333.

Grolnick, W. S., Bridges, L. J., & Connell, J. P. (1996). Emotion regulation in two-year-olds: Strategies and emotional expression in four contexts. *Child Development, 67*, 928–941.

Gross, J. J. (1998). The emerging field of emotion regulation: An integrative review. *Review of General Psychology, 2*, 271–299.

Gunnar, M. R. (1980). Control, warning signals, and distress in infancy. *Developmental Psychology, 16*, 281–289.

Gunnar, M. R. (1991, July). Psychobiology of stress in early development: Reactivity and regulation. Paper presented at the meeting of the International Society for the Study of Behavioral Development, Minneapolis, MN.

Gunnar, M. R., Brodersen, L., Krueger, K., & Rigatuso, J. (1996). Dampening of adrenocortical responses during infancy: Normative changes and individual differences. *Child Development, 67*, 887–889.

Gunnar, M. R., Brodersen, L., Nachmias, M., Buss, K., & Rigatuso, J. (1996). Stress reactivity and attachment security. *Developmental Psychobiology, 29*, 191–204.

Gunnar, M. R., Mangelsdorf, S., Larson, M., & Hertsgaard, L. (1989). Attachment, temperament, and adrenocortical activity in infancy: A study of psychoendocrine regulation. *Developmental Psychology, 25*, 355–363.

Gunnar, M. R., & Nelson, C. A. (1994). Event-related potentials in year-old infants: Relations with emotionality and cortisol. *Child Development, 65*, 80–94.

Gunnar-von Gnechten, M. R. (1978). Changing a frightening toy into a pleasant toy by allowing the infant to control its actions. *Developmental Psychology, 14*, 157–162.

Gustafson, G. E., & Green, J. A. (1991). Developmental coordination of cry sounds with visual regard and gestures. *Infant Behavior and Development, 14*, 51–57.

Haviland, J. M., & Lelwica, M. (1987). The induced affect response: ten-week-olds infants' responses to three emotional expressions. *Developmental Psychology, 23*, 97–104.

Heckhausen, J., & Dweck, C. S. (1998). *Motivation and self-regulation across the life span.* New York: Cambridge University Press.

Hiatt, S. W., Campos, J. J., & Emde, R. N. (1979). Facial patterning and infant emotional expression: Happiness, surprise, and fear. *Child Development, 50*, 1020–1035.

Hornik, R., & Gunnar, M. (1988). A descriptive analysis of infant social referencing. *Child Development, 59*, 626–634.

Hornik, R., Risenhoover, N., & Gunnar, M. (1987). The effects of maternal positive, neutral, and negative affect communications on infant responses to new toys. *Child Development, 58*, 937–944.

Huttenlocher, P. R. (1994). Synaptogenesis in human cerebral cortex. In G. Dawson & K. Fischer (Eds.), *Human behavior and the developing brain* (pp. 137–152). New York: Guilford Press.

Irwin, O. C., & Weiss, L. A. (1934a). The effect of darkness on the activity of newborn infants. *University of Iowa Studies: Child Welfare, 9,* 163–175.

Irwin, O. C., & Weiss, L. A. (1934b). The effect of clothing on the general and vocal activity of the newborn infant. In *University of Iowa Studies: Vol. 9. Child Welfare* (pp. 149–162).

Izard, C. E. (1971). *The face of emotion.* New York: Appleton-Century-Crofts.

Izard, C. E. (1977). *Human emotions.* New York: Plenum.

Izard, C. E. (1979). *Emotions in personality and psychopathology.* New York: Plenum.

Izard, C. E., & Dougherty, L. M. (1980). *System for identifying affect expressions by holistic judgments (AFFEX).* Newark: University of Delaware Press.

Izard, C. E., & Harris, P. (1995). Emotional development and developmental psychopathology. In D. Cicchetti & D. J. Cohen (Eds.), *Developmental psychopathology: Vol. 1. Theory and methods* (pp. 467–503). New York: Wiley.

Jersild, A. T., & Holmes, F. B. (1935). Children's fears. *Child Development Monographs, 20.*

Johnson, M. H. (1998). The neural basis of cognitive development. In W. Damon (Series Ed.) & D. Kuhn & R. S. Siegler (Vol. Eds.), *Handbook of child psychology: Vol. 2. Cognition, perception, and language* (5th ed., pp. 1–50). New York: Wiley.

Johnson, M. H. (2000). Cortical specialization for higher cognitive functions: Beyond the maturational model. *Brain and Cognition, 42,* 124–127.

Johnson-Laird, P. N., & Oatley, K. (1992). Basic emotions, rationality, and folk theory. *Cognition and Emotion, 6,* 201–223.

Jones, H. E. (1930a). The galvanic skin reflex in infancy. *Child Development, 1,* 106–110.

Jones, H. E. (1930b). The retention of conditioned emotional reactions in infancy. *Journal of Genetic Psychology, 37,* 485–497.

Jones, H. E., & Jones, M. C. (1928). A study of fear. *Childhood Education, 5,* 136–143.

Jones, H. E., & Jones, M. C. (1930). Genetic studies of emotions. *Psychological Bulletin, 27,* 40–64.

Jones, M. C. (1924a). A laboratory study of fear: The case of Peter. *Pedagogical Seminary, 31,* 308–315.

Jones, M. C. (1924b). The elimination of children's fears. *Journal of Experimental Psychology, 7,* 382–390.

Jones, M. C. (1930). The conditioning of children's emotions. In C. Murchison (Ed.), *Handbook of child psychology* (pp. 71–93). Worcester, MA: Clark University Press.

Jones, M. C., & Burks, B. S. (1936). Personality development in childhood. *Monographs of the Society for Research in Child Development, 1* (No. 4).

Kagan, J. (1966). Infants' differential reactions to familiar and distorted faces. *Child Development, 37,* 519–532.

Kagan, J. (1972). Do infants think? *Scientific American, 226,* 74–82.

Kagan, J. (1994). On the nature of emotion. *Monographs of the Society for Research in Child Development, 59* (2–3, Serial No. 240).

Kagan, J. (1998). Biology and the child. In W. Damon (Series Ed.) & N. Eisenberg (Vol. Ed.), *Handbook of child psychology: Vol. 3. Social, emotional, and personality development* (5th ed., pp. 177–236). New York: Wiley.

Kagan, J., Arcus, D., Snidman, N., & Feng, W. Y. (1994). Reactivity in infants: A cross-national comparison. *Developmental Psychology, 30,* 342–345.

Kaye, K. (1982). *The mental and social life of babies: How parents create persons.* Chicago: University of Chicago Press.

Keenan, K., & Shaw, D. (1997). Developmental and social influences on young girls' early problem behavior. *Psychological Bulletin, 121,* 95–113.

Klinnert, M. D. (1984). The regulation of infant behavior by maternal facial expression. *Infant Behavior and Development, 7,* 447–465.

Kochanska, G. (1995). Children's temperament, mother's discipline, and security of attachment: Multiple pathways to emerging internalization. *Child Development, 66,* 597–615.

Kochanska, G. (1997). Multiple pathways to conscience for children with different temperaments: From toddlerhood to age 5. *Developmental Psychology, 33,* 228–240.

Kochanska, G., & Aksan, N. (1995). Mother-child mutually positive affect, the quality of child compliance to requests and prohibitions, and maternal control as correlates of early internalization. *Child Development, 66,* 236–254.

Kopp, C. B. (1989). Regulation of distress and negative emotions: A developmental view. *Developmental Psychology, 25,* 343–354.

Kopp, C. B. (1992). Emotional distress and control in young children. In N. Eisenberg & R. Fabes (Eds.), *New directions for child development: Vol. 55. Emotion and its regulation in early development* (pp. 41–56). San Francisco, CA: Jossey-Bass.

Kopp, C. B. (1997). Young children: Emotion management, instrumental control, and plans. In S. L. Friedman & E. K. Scholnick (Eds.), *The developmental psychology of planning* (pp. 103–126). Mahwah, NJ: Erlbaum.

Kopp, C. B. (in press). Commentary: Emotion regulation and attention. *Infancy.*

Kopp, C. B., & Bean, D. (1998, April). Maternal annoyances: Young children's everyday behaviors. Paper presented at the International Conference of Infant Studies, Atlanta, GA.

Kopp, C. B., & Coulson, S. (1999). Motivation: Contemporary research agendas. *Contemporary Psychology, 44,* 515–518.

Kopp, C. B., & Wyer, N. (1994). Self-regulation in normal and atypical development. In D. Cicchetti & S. L. Toth (Eds.), *Rochester Symposium on Developmental Psychopathology: Vol. 5. Disorders and dysfunctions of the self* (pp. 31–56). Rochester, NY: University of Rochester Press.

Korner, A. F., & Grobstein, R. (1966). Visual alertness as related to soothing in neonates: Implications for maternal stimulation and early deprivation. *Child Development, 37,* 867–876.

Lazarus, R. S. (1991). *Emotion and adaptation.* New York: Oxford University Press.

Lemery, K. S., Goldsmith, H. H., Klinnert, M. D., & Mrazek, D. A. (1999). Developmental models of infant and childhood temperament. *Developmental Psychology, 35,* 189–204.

LeVine, R., Dixon, S., LeVine, S., Richman, A., Leiderman, P. H., Keefer, C. H., & Brazelton, T. B. (1994). *Child care and culture: Lessons from Africa.* New York: Cambridge University Press.

Lewis, M. (1993a). The emergence of human emotions. In M. Lewis & J. Haviland (Eds.), *Handbook of emotions* (pp. 223–236). New York: Guilford Press.

Lewis, M. (1993b). Self-conscious emotions: Embarrassment, pride, shame, and guilt. In M. Lewis & J. Haviland (Eds.), *Handbook of emotions* (pp. 563–573). New York: Guilford Press.

Lewis, M., Alessandri, S. M., & Sullivan, M. W. (1990). Violation of expectancy, loss of control, and anger expressions in young infants. *Development Psychology, 26,* 745–751.

Lewis, M., & Brooks-Gunn, J. (1979). *Social cognition and the acquisition of self.* New York: Plenum.

Lewis, M., & Haviland, J. M. (Eds.) (1993). *Handbook of emotions.* New York: Guilford Press.

Lewis, M., & Michalson, L. (1983). *Children's emotions and moods: Developmental theory and measurement.* New York: Plenum Press.

Lewis, M., & Ramsay, D. S. (1995). Developmental change in infants' responses to stress. *Child Development, 66,* 657–670.

Lewis, M., Sullivan, M. W., Stanger, C., & Weiss, M. (1989). Self-development and self-conscious emotions. *Child Development, 60,* 146–156.

Lewis, M. D. (1995). Cognition-emotion feedback and the self-organization of developmental paths. *Human Development, 38,* 71–102.

Lewis, M. D., & Douglas, L. (1998). A dynamic systems approach to cognition-emotion interactions in development. In M. F. Mascolo & S. Griffin (Eds.), *What develops in emotional development? Emotions, personality, and psychotherapy* (pp. 159–188). New York: Plenum.

Lewis, M. D., Koroshegyi, C., Douglas, L., & Kampe, K. (1997). Age-specific associations between emotional responses to separation and cognitive performance in infancy. *Developmental Psychology, 33,* 32–42.

Lyons-Ruth, K., & Zeanah, C. H., Jr. (1993). The family context of infant mental health: I. Affective development in the primary caregiving relationship. In C. H. Zeanah, Jr. (Ed.), *Handbook of infant mental health* (pp. 14–37). New York: Guilford Press.

Magai, C., & McFadden, S. H. (1995). *The role of emotions and personality development: History, theory, and research.* New York: Plenum.

Mahler, M., Pine, F., & Bergman, A. (1975). *The psychological birth of the human infant.* New York: Basic Books.

Malatesta, C. Z. (1990). The role of emotions in the development of organization of personality. In R. A. Thompson (Ed.), *Socioemotional development* (pp. 1–56). Lincoln: University of Nebraska Press.

Malatesta, C. Z., Cullver, C., Tesman, J., & Shepard, B. (1989). The development of emotion expression during the first two years of life. *Monographs of the Society for Research in Child Development, 50,* (1–2, Serial No. 219).

Malatesta, C. Z., Grigoryev, P., Lamb, C., Albin, M., & Cullver, C. (1986). Emotion socialization and expressive development in preterm and full-term infants. *Child Development, 53,* 991–1003.

Malatesta, C. Z., & Haviland, J. M. (1982). Learning display rules: The socialization of emotion expressions in infancy. *Child Development, 53,* 991–1003.

Mangelsdorf, S. C., Shapiro, J. R., & Marzolf, D. (1995). Developmental and temperamental differences in emotion regulation during infancy. *Child Development, 66,* 1817–1828.

Matheny, A. P., Wilson, R. S., & Nuss, S. M. (1984). Toddler temperament: Stability across settings and over ages. *Child Development, 55,* 1200–1211.

McCall, R. B. (1981). Toward an epigenetic conception of mental development in the first year of life. In M. Lewis (Ed.), *Origins of intelligence* (pp. 97–122). New York: Plenum.

Meltzoff, A. N. (1988). Infant imitation and memory: Nine-month-olds in immediate and deferred tests. *Child Development, 59,* 217–225.

Meltzoff, A. N., & Moore, M. K. (1977). Imitation of facial and manual gestures by human neonates. *Science, 198,* 75–78.

Mumme, D. L., Fernald, A., & Herrera, C. (1996). Infants' responses to facial and vocal emotional signals in a social referencing paradigm. *Child Development, 67,* 3219–3237.

Murphy, L. B. (1937). *Social behavior and child personality: An exploratory study of some roots of sympathy.* New York: Columbia University Press.

Nachmias, M., Gunnar, M., Mangelsdorf, S., Parritz, R. H., & Buss, K. (1996). Behavioral inhibition and stress reactivity: The moderating role of attachment security. *Child Development, 67,* 508–522.

Nelson, C. A. (1987). The recognition of facial expressions in the first two years of life: Mechanisms of development. *Child Development, 58,* 889–909.

Nelson, C. A., Morse, P. A., &Leavitt, L. A. (1979). Recognition of facial expressions by seven-month-old infants. *Child Development, 50,* 1239–1242.

Oster, H., Hegley, D., & Nagel, L. (1992). Adult judgments and fine-grained analysis of infant facial expressions: Testing the validity of a priori coding formulas. *Developmental Psychology, 28,* 1115–1131.

Panksepp, J., Knutson, B., & Pruitt, D. L. (1998). Toward a neuroscience of emotion: The epigenetic foundations of emotional development. In M. Mascolo & S. Griffin (Eds.), *What develops in emotional development? Emotions, personality, and psychopathology, and psychotherapy* (pp. 53–84). New York: Plenum.

Park, S. Y., Belsky, J., Putnam, S., & Crnic, K. (1997). Infant emotionality, parenting, and 3-year inhibition: Exploring stability and lawful discontinuity in a male sample. *Developmental Psychology, 33,* 218–227.

Piaget, J. (1952). *The origins of intelligence in children.* New York: International Universities Press. (Original work published 1936.)

Radke-Yarrow, M. (1986). Affective development in infancy. In T. B. Brazelton & M. W. Yogman (Eds.), *Affective development in infancy* (pp. 145–152). Norwood, NJ: Ablex.

Radke-Yarrow, M., & Zahn-Waxler, C. (1977). The emergence and functions of prosocial behaviors in young children. In R. C. Smart & M. S. Smart (Eds.), *Readings in child development and relationships* (2nd ed., pp. 77–81). New York: Macmillan.

Reilly, J. S., Stiles, J., Larsen, J, & Trauner, D. (1995). Affective facial expression in infants with focal brain damage. *Neuropsychologia, 33,* 83–99

Rheingold, H. L., & Emery, G. N. (1986). The nurturant acts of very young children. In D. Olweus, J. Block, & M. Radke-Yarrow (Eds.), *The development of anti- and prosocial behavior* (pp. 75–94). San Diego, CA: Academic Press.

Rogoff, B., Malkin, C., & Gilbride, K. (1984). Interaction with babies as guidance in development. In B. Rogoff & J. V. Wertsch (Eds.), *Children's learning in the "zone of proximal development"* (pp. 31–44). San Francisco, CA: Jossey-Bass.

Rose, S. A., Futterweit, L. R., & Jankowski, J. J. (1999). The relation of affect to attention and learning in infancy. *Child Development, 70,* 549–559.

Rothbart, M. K. (1981). Measurement of temperament in infancy. *Child Development, 52,* 569–578.

Rothbart, M. K. (1986). A psychobiological approach to the study of temperament. In G. A. Kohnstamm (Ed.), *Temperament discussed: Temperament and development in infancy and childhood* (pp. 63–72). Lisse, Netherlands: Swets & Zeitlinger.

Rothbart, M. K. (1989). Biological processes in temperament. In G. A. Kohnstamm & J. E. Bates (Eds.), *Temperament in childhood* (pp. 77–110). Chichester, England: Wiley.

Rothbart, M. K., & Bates, E. (1998). Temperament. In W. Damon (Series Ed.) & N. Eisenberg (Vol. Ed.), *Handbook of child psychology: Vol. 3. Social, emotional, and personality development* (5th ed., pp. 105–176). New York: Wiley.

Rothbart, M. K., & Posner, M. (1985). Temperament and the development of self-regulation. In H. Hartlage & C. F. Telzrow (Eds.), *Neuropsychology of individual differences: A developmental perspective* (pp. 93–123). New York: Plenum.

Rothbart, M. K., Ziaie, H., & O'Boyle, C. G. (1992). Self-regulation and emotion in infancy. In N. Eisenberg & R. Fabes (Eds.), *Emotion and its regulation in early development. New directions for child development: Vol. 55. Emotion and its regulation in early development* (pp. 7–23). San Francisco, CA: Jossey-Bass.

Ruff, H. A., & Rothbart, M. K. (1996). *Attention in early development: Themes and variations.* New York: Oxford University Press.

Salk, L. (1962). Mothers' heartbeat as an imprinting stimulus. *Transactions of the New York Academy of Sciences, 24,* 753–763.

Sander, L. W. (1987). Awareness of inner experience: A systems perspective on self-regulatory process in early development. *Child Abuse and Neglect, 11,* 339–346.

Sander, L. W. (1988). Reflections on self psychology and infancy: The event-structure of regulation in the neonate-caregiving system as a biological background for early organization of psychic structure. In A. Goldberg (Ed.), *Frontiers in self psychology: Vol. 3. Progress in self psychology* (pp. 64–77). Hillsdale, NJ: Analytic Press.

Scarr, S., & Salapatek, P. (1970). Patterns of fear development during infancy. *Merrill-Palmer Quarterly, 16,* 53–90.

Schaffer, H. R. (1963). Some issues for research in the study of attachment behavior. In B. M. Foss (Ed.), *Determinants of infant behavior* (Vol. 2, pp. 179–199). New York: Wiley.

Schaffer, H. R. (1966). The onset of fear of strangers and the incongruity hypothesis. *Journal of Child Psychology and Psychiatry, 7,* 95–106.

Schaffer, H. R. (1974). Cognitive components of the infant's response to strangeness. In M. Lewis & L. A. Rosenblum (Eds.), *The origins of fear* (pp. 11–24). New York: Wiley.

Schore, A. N. (1994). *Affect regulation and the origin of the self: The neurobiology of emotional development.* Hillsdale, NJ: Erlbaum.

Segalowitz, S. J. (2000). Dynamics and variability of brain activation: Searching for neural correlates of skill acquisition. *Brain and Cognition, 42,* 163–165.

Senn, M. J. (1975). Insights on the child development movement in the United States. *Monographs of the Society for Research in Child Development, 40* (series no. 161, pp. 3–4).

Shatz, M. (1994). *A toddler's life: Becoming a person.* New York: Oxford University Press.

Siegler, R. S. (1986). *Children's thinking.* Englewood Cliffs, NJ: Prentice Hall

Sinclair, H., Stamback, M., Lezine, I., Rayna, S., & Verba, N. (1989). *Infants and objects: The creativity of cognitive development.* New York: Academic Press.

Singer, J. M., & Fagen, J. W. (1992). Negative affect, emotional expression, and forgetting in young infants. *Developmental Psychology, 28,* 48–57.

Soken, N. H., & Pick, A. (1999). Infants' perception of dynamic affective expressions: Do infants distinguish specific expressions? *Child Development, 70,* 1275–1282.

Solomon, R. C. (1993). The philosophy of emotions. In M. Lewis & J. M. Haviland (Eds.), *Handbook of emotions* (pp. 3–16). New York: Guilford Press.

Sorce, J. F., Emde, R. N., Campos, J., & Klinnert, M. D. (1985). Maternal emotional signaling: Its effect on the visual cliff behavior of 1-year-olds. *Developmental Psychology, 21,* 195–200.

Spitz, R. A. (1946). Hospitalism: A follow-up report on investigation described in Volume I, 1945. *Psychoanalytic Study of the Child, 2,* 113–117.

Sroufe, L. A. (1979). Socioemotional development. In J. Osofsky (Ed.), *Handbook of infant development* (pp. 462–516). New York: Wiley.

Sroufe, L. A. (1996). *Emotional development: The organization of emotional life in the early years.* New York: Cambridge University Press.

Sroufe, L. A., & Rutter, M. (1984). The domain of developmental psychopathology. *Child Development, 55,* 17–29.

Sroufe, L. A., Waters, E., & Matas, L. (1974). Contextual determinants of infant affective response. In M. Lewis & L. Rosenblum (Eds.), *The origins of fear* (pp. 49–72). New York: Wiley.

Sroufe, L. A., & Wunsch, J. P. (1972). The development of laughter in the first year of life. *Child Development, 43,* 1326–1344.

Stansbury, K., & Gunnar, M. (1994). Adrenocortical activity in emotion regulation. In N. Fox (Ed.), The development of emotion regulation: Biological and behavioral considerations. *Monographs of the Society for Research in Child Development, 59* (series no. 240, pp. 108–134).

Stechler, G., & Latz, E. (1966). Some observations on attention and arousal in the human infant. *Journal of the American Academy of Child Psychiatry, 5,* 517–525.

Stern, D. (1977). *The first relationship: Infant and mother.* Cambridge, MA: Harvard University Press.

Stern, D. (1985). *The interpersonal world of the infant.* New York: Basic Books.

Stifter, C. A., & Braungart, J. M. (1995). The regulation of negative reactivity in infancy: Function and development. *Developmental Psychology, 31,* 448–455.

Stifter, C. A., & Fox, N. A. (1990). Infant reactivity: Physiological correlates of newborn and 5-month temperament. *Developmental Psychology, 26*, 582–588.

Stifter, C. A. & Spinrad, T. L. (in press). The effect of excessive crying on the development of emotion regulation. *Infancy.*

Stipek, D., Gralinski, J. H., & Kopp, C. B. (1990). Self-concept development in the toddler years. *Developmental Psychology, 26*, 972–977.

Stipek, D., Recchia, S., & McClintic, S. (1992). Self-evaluation in young children. *Monographs of the Society for Research in Child Development, 57* (1, Serial No. 226).

Stubbs, E. M. (1934). The effect of the factors of duration, intensity, and pitch of sound stimuli on the responses of newborn infants. *University of Iowa Studies: Vol. 9. Child Welfare* (pp. 74–135).

Thelen, E., & Smith, L. B. (1998). Dynamic systems theory. In W. Damon (Series Ed.) & E. R. Lerner (Vol. Ed.), *Handbook of child psychology: Vol. 1. Theories and models of human development* (5th ed., pp. 563–634). New York: Wiley.

Thomas, A., Chess, S., & Birch, H. G. (1968). *Temperament and behavior disorders in children.* New York: New York University Press.

Thompson, R. A. (1990). Emotion and self-regulation. In R. A. Thompson (Ed.), *Nebraska Symposium on Motivation: Vol. 36. Current theory and research in motivation* (pp. 367–467). Lincoln: University of Nebraska Press.

Thompson, R. A. (1994). Emotion regulation: A theme in search of a definition. *Monographs of the Society for Research in Child Development, 59* (Serial No. 240, 2–3).

Thompson, R. A. (1998). Empathy and its origins in development. In S. Braten (Ed.), *Intersubjective communication and emotion in early ontogeny: Studies in emotion and social interaction* (pp. 144–157). New York: Cambridge University Press.

Thompson, R. A., Cicchetti, D., Lamb, M. E., & Malkin, C. (1985). Emotional responses of Down syndrome and normal infants to the Strange Situation: The organization of affective behavior in infants. *Developmental Psychology, 21*, 828–841.

Thompson, R. A., & Lamb, M. E. (1984). Assessing qualitative dimensions of emotional responsiveness in infants: Separation reactions in the strange situation. *Infant Behavior and Development, 7*, 423–445.

Toda, S., & Fogel, A. (1993). Infant response to the still-face situation at 3 and 6 months. *Developmental Psychology, 29*, 532–538.

Tooby, J., & Cosmides, L. (1990). On the universality of human nature and the uniqueness of the individual: The role of genetics and adaptation. *Journal of Personality, 58*, 17–67.

Tronick, E. Z. (1989). Emotions and emotional communication in infants. *American Psychologist, 44*, 112–119.

Tronick, E. Z., Als, H., Adamson, L., Wise, S., & Brazelton, T. B. (1978). The infant's response to entrapment between contradictory messages in fact-to-face interaction. *Journal of Child Psychiatry, 17*, 1–13.

Tronick, E. Z., & Cohn, J. F. (1989). Infant-mother face-to-face interaction: Age and gender differences in coordination and the occurrence of miscoordination. *Child Development, 60*, 85–92.

Tronick, E. Z., & Field, T. (1987). *Maternal depression and infant disturbance.* San Francisco: Jossey-Bass.

Uzgiris, I. (1967). Ordinality in the development of schemes for relating to objects. In J. Hellmuth (Ed.), *The exceptional infant: Vol 1. The normal infant.* Seattle, WA: Special Child Publications.

van den Boom, D. C. (1994). The influence of temperament and mothering on attachment and exploration: An experimental manipulation of sensitive responsiveness among lower-class mothers with irritable infants. *Child Development, 65*, 1457–1477.

van Lieshout, C. F. (1976). Young children's reactions to barriers placed by their mothers. *Child Development, 46*, 879–886.

Vaughn, B. E., Lefever, G. B., Sifer, R., & Barglow, P. (1989). Attachment behavior, attachment security, and temperament during infancy. *Child Development, 60*, 728–737.

Walden, T. A., & Ogan, T. A. (1988). The development of social referencing. *Child Development, 59*, 1230–1240.

Watson, J. B., & Raynor, R. (1920). Conditioned emotional reactions. *Journal of Experimental Psychology, 3*, 1–14.

Weinberg, K. M., & Tronick, E. Z. (1994). Beyond the face: An empirical study of infant affective configurations of facial, vocal, gestural, and regulatory behaviors. *Child Development, 65*, 1503–1515.

Weinberg, K. M., & Tronick, E. Z. (1996). Infant affective reactions to the resumption of maternal interaction after the Still-Face. *Child Development, 67*, 905–914.

Wenar, C. (1982). On negativism. *Human Development, 25*, 1–23.

Werner, H. (1957). The concept of development from a comparative organismic view. In D. Harris (Ed.), *The concept of development* (pp. 125–148). Minneapolis: University of Minnesota Press.

Wolff, P. H. (1963). The early development of smiling. In B. M. Foss (Ed.), *Determinants of infant behavior* (Vol. 2, pp. 113–134). New York: Wiley.

Wolff, P. H. (1969). The natural history of crying and other vocalizations in early infancy. In B. M. Foss (Ed.), *Determinants of infant behavior* (Vol. 4, pp. 81–109). London: Methuen.

Zahn-Waxler, C. (1998). From the enlightenment to the millennium: Changing conceptions of the moral sentiments. In "Developmental Psychologist," the newsletter of Div. 7, APA, Fall 1998, 1–7.

Zahn-Waxler, C., Cole, P. M., & Barrett, K. C. (1991). Guilt and empathy: Sex differences and implications for the development of depression. In J. Garber & K. Dodge (Eds.), *The development of emotion regulation and dysregulation* (pp. 243–272). New York: Cambridge University Press.

Zahn-Waxler, C., Radke-Yarrow, M., Wagner, E., & Chapman, M. (1992). Development of concern for others. *Developmental Psychology, 28*, 126–136.

Zeanah, C. H. (1993). *Handbook of infant mental health.* New York: Guilford Press.

# 20

# DYNAMIC DEVELOPMENT OF COMPONENT SYSTEMS OF EMOTIONS: PRIDE, SHAME, AND GUILT IN CHINA AND THE UNITED STATES

Michael F. Mascolo, Kurt W. Fischer, and Jin Li

Three-year-old Danny and his mother are putting together the pieces of a puzzle. Danny places a piece in its correct location. Immediately, he looks up to his mother, smiles, and says "Oh! I did it!" Looking up from her work, his mother smiles and says "You did it!" Danny claps his hands, after which his mother applauds and says, "That's great!" (Pride exhibited by U.S. child and mother).

Mother asks 3-year-old Lin to sing a song for guests. After she finishes, with smiles and exaggerated expressions, the guests say, "Wonderful! You sing nicer than my child!" Mother replies, "*Hai-hao*, she is O.K. Her voice is kind of off the tune, though. But she likes to sing." To Lin, "You did all right, but now you need more practice. Play down your success!" (Chinese mother and guests reacting to child's song).

Reactions of college students to compliments about their class presentations in science (Chen, 1993): "Thanks. I feel good about it. I'm so glad you enjoyed it" (American students). "No. It's not that great. I didn't do it well. I know I bored you. I'm embarrassed" (Chinese students).

These vignettes depict typical emotional reactions to accomplishment in American and Chinese children and adults. In so doing, they not only show the very different ways in which socialization agents react to children's accomplishments in the United States and China, but they also illustrate typical developmental outcomes spawned by these practices. The third set of responses described in the vignettes demonstrate differences in the ways in which American and Chinese adults respond in the context of being praised for producing worthy outcomes. The modal response in Americans is to accept praise and even to express their own pride in their accomplishments. In contrast, the modal response to praise among Chinese individuals is modest self-effacement and embarrassment (Chen, 1993). The first two vignettes suggest ways in which American and Chinese parents socialize these disparate emotional orientations. Parents of children in the United States tend to praise their children's accomplishments and encourage positive self-expression (Mascolo & Harkins, 1998; Stipek, 1995). In contrast, in the presence of their child, Chinese parents often make effacing remarks to others about their children's efforts. Guests and relatives, however, generally lavish praise on the child, often effacing their own children in the process.

These vignettes suggest that emotional reactions to accomplishment not only undergo considerable change in ontogenesis but also can develop along different pathways in different cultures. Whereas Americans often experience pride in their accomplishments (Mascolo & Fischer, 1995), pride is explicitly discouraged among the Chinese (Chen, 1993; Stipek, 1999; Wu, 1996). Instead, Chinese individuals are motivated to harmonize the self with others through self-effacement. These observations raise important questions. What does it mean to say that emotions develop? What are the processes by which emotions undergo change in ontogenesis? What are the contributions of biology, cognition, individual action, social interaction, and culture in promoting and shaping emotional development?

To address these questions we first develop a dynamic component-systems approach to understanding emotional development, an approach that is based in dynamic skill theory and that specifies how cognitive, emotional, and social processes work together in emotional development (Fischer & Bidell, 1998; Fischer, Shaver, & Carnochan, 1990; Mascolo & Fischer, 1995; Mascolo & Harkins, 1998; Mascolo, Harkins, & Harakal, 2000; Scherer, 1994). A component systems approach proceeds from the assertion that emotional states and experiences are composed of partially distinct appraisal, affective, and overt action systems that function within particular sociocultural contexts. As evidenced by research and theory, emotions arise through the mutual regulation of component systems within specific contexts and in ontogenesis. For example, experiences of pride in the United States are composed of a prototypical pattern of appraisal ("I am responsible for a valued outcome"), phenomenal experience (e.g., feeling bigger; joyful qualia), and action (e.g., showing one's worthy outcome to others). These component processes dynamically influence each other in the evolution and constitution of an emotional state. Component systems not only adjust themselves to each other within individuals but also mutually regulate each other between individuals. Although emotions emerge through the interaction among systems that exist within individuals, they do not consist of discrete states that are encased within individuals. Instead, they are context sensitive: Within a given context, emotions are modulated as appraisal-affect-action processes that adjust themselves not only to each other but also to the ongoing and anticipated actions of others (Fogel, 1993).

After articulating a dynamic component systems approach to emotions, we examine the ways in which emotions undergo development in ontogenesis. To the extent that emotions are composed of multiple component processes, it follows that they undergo developmental transformation as the systems that compose them change in relation to each other (Sroufe, 1996). Further, like all psychological processes, emotional assemblies develop through dynamic interactions among biological, individual, and sociocultural processes (Bidell & Fischer, 1997; Fischer & Bidell, 1998; Gottlieb, 1997; Mascolo, Pollack, & Fischer, 1997). As a result of variation in biological (e.g., temperament), individual (e.g., preferred goals and motives, skills), and sociocultural (e.g., cultural values and beliefs) processes, emotions can develop along a variety of pathways. To realize these principles in actual developing activities, we use dynamic skill theory (Fischer, 1980; Fischer et al., 1990; Mascolo & Fischer, 1995; Mascolo et al., 1997) to chart alternative pathways in the development of pride and shame in China and the United States. We first analyze similarities and differences in the cultural values and meaning systems that frame the development of pride and shame in the United States and China. Having articulated idealized forms of pride and shame in these cultures, we organize existing research within the dynamic skill framework and chart alternative pathways in the development of appraisal skills for pride and shame in China and the United States.

## A Dynamic Component Systems Approach to Emotion

A dynamic component systems approach (Fischer et al., 1990; Mascolo & Fischer, 1998; Mascolo & Harkins, 1998; Mascolo et al., 1997) proceeds from four basic assertions. The first is that emotional states and experiences are composed of *multiple component processes* (Scherer, 1994). Second, emotional experiences emerge and evolve both on-line and in development through the *mutual regulation* (Fischer & Bidell, 1998; Fogel, 1993; M. D. Lewis, 1995) of component systems over time and within particular social contexts. Third, component systems are *multileveled*, composed of hierarchies of skills that include social-emotional components of differing levels of complexity, as illustrated by analyses of skill development. In our discussion, this point is incorporated into the other assertions, because it is so pervasive. Fourth, component systems are *socially sensitive and coregulated*, meaning that they adjust themselves not only to each other but also to continuous changes in other people and events in a social interaction. As a result, within particular social contexts, emotional experiences self-organize (Fischer & Bidell, 1998; Fogel, 1993; M. D. Lewis, 1997; M. D. Lewis & Granic, 2000) into a series of more or less stable patterns that yield a large number of minor variations (Camras, 1992; Mascolo et al., 2000).

### Component Processes of Emotional States and Experiences

The first assertion of a dynamic component systems view is that emotional episodes are composed of multiple component processes. This is an assumption that is common to functionalist (Barrett, 1998; Campos, 1994; Frijda & Mesquita, 1998), social process (Dickson, Fogel, & Messinger, 1998; Fogel et al., 1992), and systems (M. D. Lewis

& Granic, 2000; Mascolo & Harkins, 1998) approaches to emotion.

One important class of component processes consists of *appraisal*. Appraisals refer to assessments of relations between perceived events and a person's goals, motives, and concerns (Frijda, 1986; Lazarus, 1991). Like the emotional syndromes of which they are a part, appraisals themselves are composed of multiple components, including sensory-perceptual, cognitive-representational, and motivational processes. It is important to note that although appraisal processes *involve* cognitive processes (i.e., the processing of information in terms of existing knowledge structures), appraisal is not simply a cognitive affair. Instead, in emotional appraisal, cognitive representations of events function in the service of an individual's goals, motives, and concerns (Smith & Lazarus, 1990). To be sure, cognitive processes are essential in representing one's motives and concerns and in mediating an individual's interpretation of any given event. Nonetheless, appraisals in emotion are more about the fate of one's motives than about cognitive processes per se (Roseman, 1991).

Further, appraisals are the products of both conscious and nonconscious processes. At any given time, an individual's appraisal systems are active in monitoring enormous amounts of sensory data that are made available from one's ongoing activity in the world. Much of this processing proceeds without conscious awareness. Persons only become aware of the products of such appraisal activity when those products have significance for them—that is, when they implicate one's most important goals, motives, and concerns (Roseman, 1984). Appraisals that events are consistent with an individual's goals, motives, and concerns play a role in the generation of positively valanced emotions; assessments that events are motive inconsistent participate in negatively valanced experiences. Distinctions among different categories of emotional experience are attributable, in part, to both gross and subtle differences in the ways in which persons appraise events (Lazarus, 1999; Mascolo & Griffin, 1998; Mikula, Scherer, & Athenstaedt, 1998; Parkinson, 1999; Robinson, 1998; Roseman, Antoniou, & Jose, 1996; Roseman, Spindel, & Jose, 1990).

From a component systems view, appraisals do not simply function as discrete "elicitors" that precede or "cause" an emotion to come into play. Instead, they are seen as part and parcel of the emotional experience itself. An important justification for this assertion is that emotions are intentional states (Brentano, 1874; Campos, 1994; Searle, 1980; Solomon, 1976). That is, emotions have objects; they are about something. A person is not simply angry or proud; Jan is angry that I was late for our appointment; I am proud of myself for having achieved a high grade in physics. The idea that emotions take objects suggests that emotions involve judgments or appraisals as

important, albeit not privileged, parts of their very constitution (Solomon, 1997).

A second class of emotion systems includes *affect systems*. From a component systems view, different emotional states are accompanied by distinct, emotion-typical feeling tones (Kagan, 1984) and phenomenal experiences (de Rivera, 1981). Affect systems refer to the biological and bodily processes that contribute to the experience of emotion-typical feeling tone and phenomenal states, including components in the central nervous system (CNS) and autonomic nervous system (ANS). Affect systems are partially distinct from appraisal and action components, which simply means that different brain and bodily structures and processes often, but not always, mediate their production.

A large and growing body of research indicates that diverse patterns of CNS and ANS activity contribute to variations in the constitution and phenomenal experience of different emotions and emotional behaviors. For example, Gray (1990, 1994; Gray, Feldon, Rawlins, Hemsley, & Smith, 1991) has described different anatomical structures in the brain (including the limbic system and basal ganglia) that appear to mediate each of three basic emotional systems he has proposed (i.e., behavioral approach, fight or flight, and behavioral inhibition systems; see also Davidson, 1992; Panksepp, Knutson, & Pruitt, 1998, for similar analyses). LeDoux (1994) has argued convincingly for the role of the amygdala in the mediation of fear and other emotional states. Panksepp (1998; Panksepp et al., 1998) has reviewed a large number of studies that demonstrate the role of specific anatomical, neurochemical, and hormonal systems in the mediation of different emotional behaviors and dispositions in mammals (e.g., distress, nurturance, dominance). Other researchers have demonstrated asymmetries in brain activation (e.g., frontal lobe activity) in the processing of different emotions (Dawson, 1994; Fox, 1994). Finally, although findings are inconsistent (Cacioppo, Berntson, Klein, & Poehlmann, 1998), researchers have demonstrated a degree of ANS specificity in the experience of different emotions (Ekman, Levenson, & Friesen, 1983; Levenson, Carstensen, Friesen, & Ekman, 1991; Levenson, Ekman, & Friesen, 1990).

Research suggests some modularity among appraisal, action, and affect-producing systems, but appraisal, affect, and action systems are not entirely separate and distinct. For example, the very brain areas that researchers have identified as emotion systems (e.g., the amygdala, hypothalamus, frontal lobe) are also heavily involved in the mediation of cognitive, memorial, and overt action processes (Bell & Fox, 1994; Davidson, 1994; Dawson, 1994; LeDoux, 1994). In this way, the biological mediators of affect, appraisal, and action are somewhat distinct yet fully intertwined, even in brain anatomy. Similarly, research on emotion physiology does not support a single undifferentiated state of physiological (ANS) arousal for different emotional experiences (Mandler, 1984; Schachter & Singer, 1962), but neither does it support the existence of unique neurobiological patterns for different emotional experiences. It is more likely that physiology discriminates emotional experiences in complex, nonlinear ways. For example, Cacioppo, Priester, and Berntson (1993) demonstrated that the same pattern of somatovisceral activity can be associated with reports of very different emotions. Conversely, reports of the same emotion can be sustained in the context of different patterns of somatovisceral activity. Thus, given the state of current evidence, it is most prudent to conclude that affect and appraisal systems are partially distinct and richly interactive.

A third class of component emotional experiences involves overt *action tendencies*, which consist of the propensity to want things and to do particular actions in the context of a given type of appraised event and affective experience. Like appraisal and affect systems, overt action systems are themselves composed of a series of interlocking subsystems. These include both emotion-typical involuntary (e.g. facial and vocal) and instrumental/communicative activity. Emotion-typical action tendencies serve adaptive functions for persons and their social groups. They function not only in the service of the local goals and concerns implicated in a person's appraisal of a given event but also to preserve broader psychological concerns beyond the immediate context, and they are affected by social and cultural contexts. They function to regulate social behavior and to maintain cultural and moral standards shared within a given social community.

A dynamic component systems approach differentiates between the concepts of emotional state and emotional experience (M. Lewis, 1998). An emotional *state* refers to the specific patterning of an individual's appraisal, affect, and action systems in the context of notable changes in one's relation to one's environs. An emotional *experience* refers to the phenomenal aspects of the various components of an emotional state.[1] Table 20.1 provides a representation of prototypical appraisals, phenomenal experiences, and action tendencies for several categories of emotion. For example, experiences of anger among Western adults often involve appraisals that events are contrary to the way they ought to be (de Rivera, 1981; Fischer et al., 1990; Mascolo & Griffin, 1998). Such appraisals may be accompanied by patterned bodily changes, including CNS and ANS activity, increased heart rate, perspiration, and bodily temperature (Barrett & Campos, 1987; Ekman et al., 1983). The phenomenal experience of anger characteristically involves "angry" feeling tone or qualia, as well as the bodily experience of "heat," "pressure," or "tension." Persons experience a strengthening of will, which supports the action tendency to remove the conditions judged as contrary to how they should be and to look for someone or something to blame (de Rivera, 1981; Shaver, Schwartz, Kirson, & O'Connor, 1987).

## Mutual Regulation Among Component Emotion Systems

A central principle of a component systems approach is that although component emotion systems function as relatively distinct systems, they are not independent of one another. Instead they mutually regulate each other in the formation of any given emotional state or experience (Fischer & Bidell, 1998; Fogel, 1993; M. D. Lewis, 1995, 1997; M. D. Lewis & Douglas, 1998; Mascolo & Harkins, 1998; Mascolo, Harkins, & Harakal, 2000). Mutual regulation refers to the processes by which component systems adjust themselves to the ongoing (and anticipated) outputs and activity of each other (Fogel, 1993). We use the concept of mutual regulation broadly to refer to both positive and negative feedback processes, which are central to the ways that emotions self-organize. Through mutual regulation, component systems modulate each other's activity simultaneously and continuously. As such, there is no fixed or preset sequence of psychological events that occurs in the generation and constitution of emotion; no single component system is privileged in the constitution of emotional events. Figure 20.1 depicts a dynamic component systems model of the emotion process. Each individual represented in the model is composed of three classes of component systems (appraisal, affect, and action) that mutually regulate each other. The double arrows between component systems denote mutual regulation. To explicate the concept of mutual regulation, we draw on existing theory and research to articulate the specific influences that each component system has on every other system throughout the emotion process.

### Appraisal-Affect Relations

At any given time, appraisal processes continuously monitor the significance of all classes of event-related input in parallel, as well as the activity of ongoing affect-producing systems; and much of this monitoring proceeds nonconsciously (Marcel, 1983). A large body of research demonstrates relations between different types of event appraisals and affective feeling tone (Lazarus, 1991; Mascolo & Griffin,

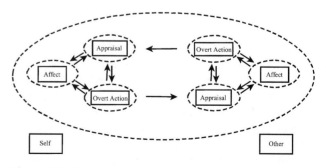

Figure 20.1 Emotion process.

Table 20.1  Anatomy of Some Emotional Syndromes in North American and Western European Culture

|  | Appraisal | Phenomenal Tone | Action Tendency | Personal and Social Functions |
|---|---|---|---|---|
| Joy | Motive-consistent event; getting what is wanted | Feeling joyful qualia, excitement | Approach others and/or wanted outcome or event | *Personal.* Alerts self of salient goal attainment; motivates continued goal-directed activity *Social.* Alerts others of goal attainment; brings self and others into closer proximity |
| Anger | Events are illegitimate or contrary to the way they should be; other is blameworthy and held responsible for violation. | Feeling "pressure," "heat," "tension," increase in will or resolve to move against offender; angry qualia. | Actions to remove violation of what ought to be (as manifested in 'angry' facial and vocal expressions, verbal or nonverbal threat or attack, etc.) | *Personal.* Removes violations to one's sense of what ought to be *Social.* Alerts others that they have violated conditions that self perceives ought to exist. |
| Sadness | Loss of desired object; loss of wanted state | Absence of will or resolve to change situation; lethargy; sad qualia. | Withdrawal from wanted event, activity, or social relations; motivates reflection on lost object and goal abandonment | *Personal.* Makes self aware of loss: facilitates goal abandonment. *Social.* Alerts others of self's sense of loss; others can assist self in managing loss. |
| Pride | I am responsible for performing a socially valued action/ being a valued person | Feeling bigger, taller, "expanding," "on top of the world," positive and excited feeling tone. | Celebrate the self; show worthy action or self to others (as manifested in smiling, celebratory gestures, social referencing) | *Personal.* Strengthens sense of personal worth, efficacy, and value in the eyes of others. *Social.* Alerts others of self's accomplishment and value. |
| Guilt | I am responsible for a wrongdoing | Feeling "heavy," "as if I am bad" | Fix wrongdoing; confess; apologize; make reparations to others; increase resolve to act in a moral fashion; atone for sins | *Personal.* Enhances self's sense of morality; motivates moral action; enables self to maintain moral agency and identity ("I am moral but I did a bad thing") *Social.* Regulates individual action in terms of social standards or appropriate moral conduct; helps restore interpersonal relations following transgressions |
| Shame | I see myself through the eyes of others and realize that I am an unworthy person and cannot be otherwise in their eyes | Feeling "small," feeling one's unworthy self exposed. | Hide the self; remove the self from social scrutiny (as manifested in gaze aversion, hiding the body, face, or entire self, slumped posture, etc.) | *Personal.* Alerts self of diminished global identity in the eyes of others; motivates attempts to reestablish positive global identity *Social.* Regulates individual action and construction of identity in terms of socially acceptable standards of worth and value. |

1998; Roseman, Spindel, & Jose, 1991; Scherer, 1997; Smith & Ellsworth, 1985, 1987; Weiner, 1985). A different body of research indicates the ways in which cognitive engagement or disengagement in relation to stressful events modulates physiological and affective responses (Averill, Malmstrom, Koriat, & Lazarus, 1972; Koriat, Melman, Averill, & Lazarus, 1972). The influence of affective state on appraisal and cognitive processes has ample empirical support as well.

Isen (1990) has demonstrated that the presence of positive affect can facilitate the process of remembering positive information, enhance problem solving, and generally promote flexibility, breadth, and creativity in an individual's attempt to organize information. Negative affect (e.g. sadness), on the other hand, appears to restrict attention and cognitive organization to the local demands of a given task (see also Forgas, 1991).

As appraisals shape and modify existing affect, affective systems provide simultaneous and continuous feedback to appraisal systems, functioning to amplify and select for conscious awareness and further action some of the very appraisals that helped initiate affective reactions in the first place (Brown, 1994; Brown & Kozak, 1998; M. D. Lewis, 1997; Mascolo & Harkins, 1998). As appraisals are selected, they continue to evolve, producing further affective changes that bias and continue to organize appraisal and activity (M. D. Lewis, 1995; M. D. Lewis & Douglas, 1998). Thus affect and appraisal mutually regulate each other in real time. As a result, it is not helpful to privilege either affect or appraisal as primary aspects of the emotion process.

## Affect-Action Relations

Not only do affective processes organize event appraisals, but they also activate and organize emotion-typical classes of action tendencies; and action tendencies in turn feed back to affective states. Some theorists have speculated that action tendencies are a major source of the "affective feel" of emotional experiences themselves (see Frijda & Mesquita, 1998, although Frijda rejects the notion of emotion-typical qualia). A variety of studies have supported the proposition that reports of different emotions are associated with universal and emotion-typical patterns of involuntary facial expressions (Ekman, 1989; Ekman & Friesen, 1971). More recent research has suggested that different basic emotional states may also be associated with different contours of vocal and postural activity (Banse & Scherer, 1996; Fernald, 1993; Mumme, Fernald, & Herrera, 1996; Wallbott, 1998). Further, different affective experiences are associated with the production of broad classes of instrumental action. Commonly accepted examples of emotion-typical instrumental action tendencies are displayed in Table 20.1.

A large body of research supports the contention that moods and emotional states bias behavioral dispositions. For example, research demonstrates the ways in which moods bias individuals toward or away from a variety of different behaviors, including helping and cooperation (Salovey, Mayer, & Rosenhan, 1991), self-destruction (Leith & Baumeister, 1996), polite conversation (Forgas, 1997, 1999), parenting (Holden, Coleman, & Schmidt, 1995; Jouriles & O'Leary, 1990), and behavior in a variety of other social domains and interpersonal contexts (Forgas & Fiedler, 1996; Hertel, 1999; Munz & Fallert, 1998). In an intriguing study that demonstrates how subtle differences in individual emotions bias behavior, deRivera and his colleagues induced states of elation and gladness by manipulating whether people were successful in attaining an unrealistic "wished for" outcome or a more realistic "hoped for" goal (de Rivera, Possell, Verette, & Weiner,

1989). Persons who reported elation indicated feeling "higher off the ground" and made more exaggerated judgments of the length of a line than did persons made to feel glad. Such findings indicate how differences in affective states can transform a person's bodily sense and behavioral disposition.

The relation between affect and action tendencies is not unidirectional. Action tendencies provide feedback that amplifies and modulates affective states and feeling tone (Fischer et al., 1990). In a variety of studies, individuals who have been instructed to produce emotion-typical facial configurations report enhanced experiences of those emotions (Hess, Kappas, McHugo, Lanzetta, & Kleck, 1992; Laird, 1984; Tourangeau & Ellsworth, 1979). These studies provide support for a weak version of the facial feedback hypothesis (Laird, 1984; Matsumoto, 1987; Tourangeau & Ellsworth, 1979). Feedback from emotion-typical facial activity can intensify or precipitate mild experiences of individual emotions but is not a necessary or sufficient precondition for emotional experience (Cacioppo et al., 1998). There is also evidence that emotion movements and postures can induce mild experiences of individual emotions as well (Cacioppo, Priester, & Berntson, 1993; Cacioppo et al., 1998; Riskind, 1984).

## Appraisal-Action Relations

Appraisal and overt action processes also mutually regulate each other. Specifically, motive-relevant appraisals specify the goals that guide and direct overt action, consistent with control theory approaches to action (Carver & Scheier, 1981; Mascolo, Fischer, & Neimeyer, 1999; Miller, Galanter, & Pribram, 1960; Powers, 1973). Conversely, overt actions result in environmental changes that provide feedback about the fate of a person's goals, motives, and concerns. Appraisals thus continuously monitor the extent to which goals, motives, and concerns have been met. In this way, overt actions are deployed and revised until appraisal-relevant goals are either met or abandoned. Changes in the goals and concerns implicated in event appraisals prompt the deployment of new action tendencies.

Both appraisals and affective processes organize the production of overt action. However, with psychological development, appraisals become mediated by increasingly sophisticated systems of personal, social, and cultural meaning. Whereas affective processes bias actions in terms of broad behavioral preferences, appraisals draw on a dynamic knowledge base to guide action in ways that are sensitive to the demands of particular social contexts. With development, individuals draw on knowledge that supports the construction of increasingly sophisticated event interpretations (Fischer et al., 1990: Mascolo & Griffin, 1998; Sroufe, 1996), strategies to advance one's goals and concerns in social contexts (Saarni, 1984), and rules for appropriate emotional communication (Barrett & Nelson-Goens, 1997), display (Averill, 1982; Saarni, 1984, 1990), and even feeling (Briggs, 1970; Hochschild, 1979).

## Social Sensitivity and Coregulation

Thus far, we have discussed the coregulation of components of the emotion process as they occur within individuals, but emotional episodes are coregulated between, as well as within, people. Just as component systems adjust to each other within persons, they also continuously adjust themselves to inputs and meanings that arise between individuals. The coregulation of emotion between persons is represented in terms of the double arrows between interacting individuals in Figure 20.1. In social interaction, an individual's appraisal-affect-action systems change continuously as they adjust to each other, as well as to the ongoing and anticipated actions of a social partner. In face-to-face interaction of mother and child, for example, a mother's continuous changes in facial and vocal activities directly influence her infant's ongoing and subsequent facial actions (Fogel et al., 1992; Trevarthen, 1984).

Fogel and his colleagues have investigated how different types of social interactions modulate emotional facial acts, with subtle differences emerging from social coregulation. In one study, specific types of smiles occurred for different types of play interactions between parents and their 12-month-olds (Dickson, Fogel, & Messinger, 1998). The researchers differentiated between *basic* (lip corners raised), *play* (corners of lips raised/jaw drops), and *Duchenne* (lip corners and cheeks raised) expressions. Basic smiles were most strongly associated with book reading, Duchenne smiles with vocal play, and play smiles with physical play. Infant laughter also differs in form and function in different social contexts (Dickson, Walker, & Fogel, 1997; Nwokah, Davies, Islam, Hsu, & Fogel, 1993; Nwokah, Hsu, Dobrowolska, & Fogel, 1994). The continuously evolving actions of coparticipants in interactions constitute an actual part of the emotion process. Emotion processes are not encased within individuals but adjust continuously to each other, between as well as within people.

## Self-Organization of Dynamic Emotion Families

Within a given sociocultural context, emotional states and experiences emerge through the mutual regulation of component systems both within and between individuals, with no single component system being primary. Emotional episodes self-organize through mutual regulation of component systems, both in development and in real time in particular contexts (Fischer et al., 1990; Fogel, 1993; M. D. Lewis, 1995; M. D. Lewis & Granic, 2000; Mascolo et

al., 2000; Thelen, 1990). The concept of self-organization stipulates that there is no single plan that directs the formation of any particular emotional reaction but that biology and culture constrain and shape the coactions of components systems over time to take specific shapes (Barrett & Campos, 1987; Fischer, Wang, Kennedy, & Cheng, 1998; Fogel et al., 1992; Mascolo et al., 2000).

In theory, the number of particular ways that component systems can combine to produce different emotional states is extremely large, but when component systems mutually regulate each other, they reduce the degrees of freedom that other component systems have to operate (Camras, 1992; Fogel, 1993). Emotions thus tend to settle into a finite number of fairly stable patterns, syndromes, or families. Emotions within a given category or family (e.g., anger, love, shame) bear a family resemblance (Rosch, 1978; Russell, 1991) to each other. That is, emotions fit into a given family not because they share characteristics with all members of the family but because they share them with category prototypes. For example, in American English, the words *sorry, distress, loneliness,* and *disheartenment* are all members of the sadness family, sharing some characteristics with the prototype of sadness and also differing in some characteristics.

Shaver, Wu, and Schwartz (1992) attempted to gain an understanding of how people organize emotions into families between and within different cultures. In so doing, they asked people in the United States and China to list as many different types of emotions as they could. One group of participants in each culture rated each of the many resulting terms to determine which words were seen as actual examples of emotions. A second group sorted the highly rated words into categories on the basis of how they go together. Figure 20.2 depicts the results of a hierarchical cluster analysis of the emotion terms for each culture.

As indicated in Figure 20.2, the American and Chinese structures show both commonality and important differences. Emotion families that bear the same meanings in both cultures are indicated with dark lines; emotion families that differ between cultures are marked with dotted lines. At the superordinate level of the hierarchy, both American and Chinese participants distinguished positive from negative emotions. Moving down the hierarchy, American and Chinese participants grouped emotion terms into basic level families, including anger, sadness, fear, and happiness. At the basic level of categorization, American participants differentiated five emotion families, with three negative (anger, sadness, and fear) and two positive (love and happiness). At the subordinate level, each family was composed of a number of different subcategories of emotion. In the Chinese data, shame emerged as a sixth basic family, subsuming such emotions as shame and guilt/regret, but shame did not emerge as a basic-level emotion family for American participants. In addition, for

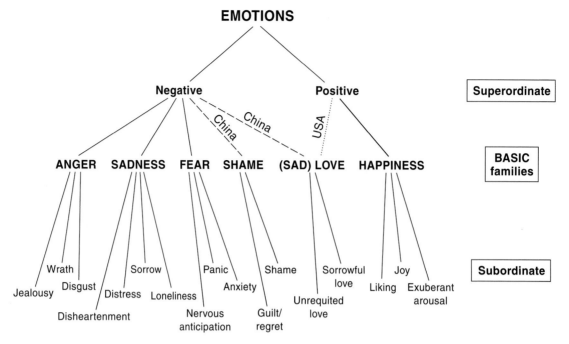

Figure 20.2 Cluster analysis of basic emotion families in Chinese and English. Note: The subordinate families are from the Chinese study. From Shaver, Wu, and Schwartz (1992).

the Chinese, love was viewed as a negative rather than a positive emotion family, "sad love," which included such subordinate emotions as unrequited love and sorrowful love. Thus, Chinese participants differentiated one positive emotion family (happiness) and five negative ones.

The negativity of love in the Chinese emotion taxonomy makes sense culturally. In traditional China, marriages have been arranged by parents. A marriage is seen not only as a marriage between two people but also as a joining of two extended families. Romantic love takes on secondary importance and is viewed as a disruptive emotion, with the potential to precipitate conflict between children and parents (Potter, 1988). It has the potential to break down the proper respect and deference that sons are traditionally expected to show their fathers, who have a position of authority and relative emotional distance (Ho, 1996; Potter, 1988; Russell & Yik, 1996; Wu, 1996; Wu & Tseng, 1985). This negative prototype does not mean that romantic love is absent, only that it is devalued (Jankowiak, 1993; Russell & Yik, 1996).

An even more important difference concerns the emotion of shame. Among the Chinese, shame is a hypercognized emotion, whereas it appears to be hypocognized among Americans (Levy, 1984; Marsella, 1980; Russell & Yik, 1996; Shaver et al., 1992; Wang & Leichtman, 2000). Unlike American children, Chinese children use the term *shame* as one of their first emotion words early in development. In contrast, American children produce words for all the emotion categories except shame (love, happiness,

anger, fear, and sadness, as well as the dimension of good/ bad; Bretherton & Beeghly, 1982; Dunn, Bretherton, and Munn, 1987; Fischer et al., 1990).

Wang, Li, and Fischer (2000) used methods similar to those of Shaver et al., (1987) to analyze the structure of the shame lexicon among mainland Chinese adults living in the United States and Canada (Wang, 1994). Eighty-three shame-related words were culled from the *Modern Chinese Dictionary* (Commercial Press, 1978). Ten Chinese adults examined these words and added additional terms, producing a total of 144 shame-related words. An additional sample of twenty Chinese adults rated each of these words on the extent to which each was representative of the emotion of shame. On the basis of these ratings, 31 words were eliminated, resulting in a total of 113 target words. Finally, 52 Chinese adults sorted these words into categories on the basis of similarities in their meanings. A hierarchical cluster analysis of the resulting sortings produced the organization depicted in Figure 20.3. Six basic shame families emerged from the sortings at three hierarchical levels (Fischer et al., 1998). At the superordinate level, Chinese adults discriminated between shame states and reactions. At the basic level of the hierarchy, there are three emotion families indicative of shame state, self-focus, and three indicative of reaction to shame, other-focus. As indicated in Figure 20.3, each of these basic families subsumes a series of lower level subordinate families as well. Because of the weak differentiation of shame in English, the Chinese elaboration of shame is informative.

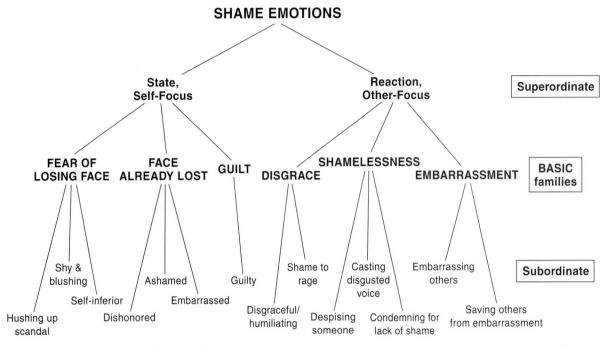

Figure 20.3 Cluster analysis of Chinese shame families. From Wang, Li, and Fischer (2000).

The three shame-state-self families are fear of losing face, face already lost, and guilt, with the first two dividing into a series of subordinate categories. The largest family, *fear of losing face*, subsumes subordinate categories that indicate physiological and psychological reactions prior to losing face, such as blushing, feeling inferior, and hushing up a scandal. The second family, *face already lost*, represents a person's feelings after he or she has lost face, as indicated by subcategories dishonored, ashamed, and embarrassed. Ashamed includes terms that reflect mild to extremely painful shame. Dishonor contains items such as dishonor on one's face and no place to hide from one's shame. The embarrassed subcategory reflects milder versions of shame-related emotion. The third basic category, guilt, indicates feelings of remorse or regret for shameful or inappropriate actions. Guilt subsumes no subordinate categories and is thus less differentiated than other shame-related families.

The three shame-reaction-other families consist of disgrace, shamelessness, and embarrassment, each of which divides into two or three subordinate categories. *Disgrace* refers to both loss of face and moral failure in others, which subsumes disgraceful-humiliating (public debasement) and shame to rage (intense shame producing intense anger at being shamed). *Shamelessness* is the second largest category of shame-related words. It is divided into three subordinate categories that indicate different ways of condemning others in shame. The first subcategory involves despising a shamed person (hate, disrespect). The second, casting disgusted voice, refers to ways of com-

municating with a shamed person, which include vocal and facial acts marking the other's behavior as shameful or disgusting. The final subcategory consists of condemning for lack of shame, which refers to ways of condemning others for their shamelessness. In China, shamelessness is even worse than being ashamed, as it connotes a lack of connection to the social values and moral systems that organize shame. The final basic category is *embarrassment*, which subsumes ways of embarrassing others and strategies to save others from embarrassment.

Shame is present in both English-language and Chinese cultures. However, in contrast to English, the organization of shame-related concepts in Chinese is extremely rich. Although it may be possible to make similar shame-related discriminations in all cultures, shame-related states and practices are relatively impoverished in English-language cultures and apparently in many other Western cultures (Shaver, Wu, & Schwartz, 1992). This difference reflects the comparatively central role that shame plays in regulating self and social behavior in China and the richly textured distinctions that Chinese people make to conceptualize, communicate, and socialize shame in self and others.

## Culture and the Dynamic Construction of Pride, Shame, and Guilt

What accounts for the similarities and differences in the cultural organization of emotion in the United States and

China? Cultures are constituted in part by socially shared meaning systems that mediate ways of interpreting one's social world (Geertz, 1973; Shweder & LeVine, 1984). As children construct and internalize cultural values, meanings, and beliefs in ontogenesis, cultural meanings transform the ways in which they appraise motive-relevant aspects of their environments and regulate emotional conduct. Emotions undergo successive transformation as they are shaped toward culturally defined ideals and endpoints. To the extent that different cultures are organized around different motive-relevant values and beliefs, emotions will develop along different pathways en route to different culturally valued endpoints. To illustrate, we examine cultural similarities and differences in the dynamic development of pride and shame in the United States and China. In so doing, we first examine the overarching individualist and Confucian belief systems that continue to frame understandings of persons, social relations, and moral values in the United States and China, respectively. Thereafter, we examine similarities and differences in the organization of some of the self-evaluative emotions (pride, shame, and guilt) that arise under American individualism and Chinese Confucianism. Finally, we chart the ways in which pride- and shame-related states take different pathways as they develop toward different culturally valued endpoints.

## Individualist and Confucian Cultural Frameworks

American individualism is founded on the primacy of individuals in personal, social, moral, and civic relations. American individualism values freedom to pursue personal happiness, equality before God and the law, and individual choice in matters of social relations. In this way, Americans can be said to construct selves that are relatively bounded and separate from others (Bellah, Madsen, Sullivan, Swidler, & Tipton, 1985; Dumont, 1992; Johnson, 1985; Markus & Kitayama, 1991; Sampson, 1994). At least in the Anglo middle class of American culture, individuals tend to make relatively clear distinctions about what to consider *me* and *mine* as opposed to *you* and *yours*. These individualist beliefs are organized around a morality based on principles of individual rights, justice, and equality (Kohlberg, 1981). Persons possess universal inalienable rights. Social relations are based on freely negotiated contracts and agreements. Although individualist systems demand that individuals refrain from actions that bring harm to others, there are no superogatory moral obligations to sacrifice the self on the behalf of others (Miller & Sperry, 1987). With exceptions (such as relationships to one's children), individuals are not constrained strongly by a priori obligations of duty, loyalty, or service to others, whether those others include one's spouse or extended family, employer, or nation. These beliefs follow from the

priority placed on both freedom to pursue individual happiness and freedom from arbitrary constraint (Locke, 1964/1975; Mill, 1859/1986).

Consistent with these beliefs, Americans place considerable value on individuality (Bellah et al., 1985; Johnson, 1985), independence (Emerson, 1941/1990; Raeff, 1998), and personal achievement (Maehr & Nicholls, 1980; McClelland, 1961). Persons are seen as unique individuals and are encouraged to express their personal feelings and desires and to develop their particular talents. Children are socialized to depend on themselves rather than on others in performing any given task. In consonance with these beliefs, Americans place considerable importance on self-esteem (Hewitt, 1997; Mecca, Smelser, & Vasconcellos, 1989), which is seen as both a determinant and product of personal achievement. Many Americans believe that in order to succeed, individuals must believe in their abilities (e.g., have self-confidence) and develop positive self-esteem. Because of the importance placed on self-esteem, Americans praise their children's successes and protect them from shame. In this way, personal achievement is outcome, rather than process, oriented. That is, the main focus of achievement activity is on producing specific outcomes rather than on the process of learning, developing, or achieving per se (Hong, Chiu, Dweck, Line, & Wan, 1999; Kamins & Dweck, 1999). As such, although effort and hard work are valued (e.g., the Protestant work ethic), they are seen as means to reaching desired ends rather than as valuable in themselves. Perhaps because of the value placed on demonstrating one's uniqueness, individuals often attribute their successes and failures to individual ability rather than to effort or hard work (Dweck & Leggett, 1988; Nicholls, 1976).

The situation is quite different in many Asian cultures. For example, Chinese Confucian conceptions of self and social life are organized around the idea of self-perfection as a relational process (Tu, 1985). This notion is embodied by the dual assumptions that (1) individuals develop through a lifelong process of self-cultivation and (2) the self is a nexus of social relationships (Tu, 1979, 1985). With regard to the first assumption, Confucianism maintains that individual development consists of a lifelong process of self-cultivation and self-perfection, sometimes called the Way (Tu, 1979). Through this process, one literally learns to become human. Confucianism specifies a series of ultimate life goals (Tu, 1979; Wu, 1996; Yu, 1996). These include *ren* (benevolence), *yi* (righteousness), and *li* (ritual propriety). Of these, *ren* is the most important, as it specifies the fundamental quality of being human. From this view, self-cultivation is a lifelong process of cultivating a moral and spiritual character—to become the most benevolent, sincere, and humane person possible.

There are several important implications of the cultivation of *ren*. First, self-cultivation refers to a lifelong process rather than a search for a fixed and attainable outcome. In this sense, the cultivation of *ren* is never complete. Any concrete achievement in life is seen as but a single step or milestone in a long, long process of learning to become *ren*. As such, particular developmental outcomes are secondary to the Way. Second, the search for *ren* involves a highly disciplined search for the good life, which cannot be reached without sustained effort and lifelong devotion. The search for *ren* is similar to the process of becoming a mathematician (or any other type of learned scholar). Although a rudimentary sense of numeracy may exist from the start, one cannot become a great mathematician without conscious effort and cultivation. In this way, effort functions as the primary tool in developing *ren* because it puts desire into action (Lee, 1996; Li, 1997, in press; Tu, 1979). Today the notion of continuous self-perfection through hard work continues to be a primary value of Chinese people (Li, in press).

However, self-cultivation is not an individualist process. *Ren*, the fundamental human quality of benevolence, is an inherently social and moral value. To become sincerely benevolent and humane requires that one put others first. This is a reflection of the primacy that Chinese Confucianism places on social harmony within hierarchy. In Confucianism, individuals are not isolated units; they are born into a web of social relationships that are organized in terms of a richly ordered hierarchy. As such, one is inherently connected to others as part of a hierarchically structured whole. One cultivates the self through relationships with others. Development is a lifelong process involving an "ever increasing awareness of the presence of the other in one's self-cultivation" (Tu, 1985, p. 232). As further articulated by Tu, "A Confucian self devoid of human-relatedness has little meaningful content of its own. . . . A Confucian man's self-awareness of being a son, a brother, a husband, or a father dominates his awareness of himself as a self-reliant and independent person" (p. 233). To become a harmonious being within the social hierarchy, self-cultivation occurs as one willingly learns to suppress one's own desires and define oneself in terms of the needs and wishes of others within the family and broader society. To maintain social harmony, it is necessary to praise others and efface the self in social relations (Bond, Leung, & Wan, 1982; Chen, 1993; Gao, Ting-Toomey, & Gudykunst, 1996; Stipek, 1999).

The social process of self-cultivation begins in the family. The indigenous concept of filial piety (*xiao qin*; Ho, 1986, 1996; Tu, 1985; Yu, 1996) is central to Chinese self and socialization. Yang (1988, 1996) has demonstrated that the traditional value of filial piety continues to be represented in Chinese culture today. Filial piety refers to the strict moral obligations that exist between children and parents. Filial piety establishes the absolute authority of parents over children and brings with it reciprocal obligations of parents to children. It specifies standards for how children relate to their parents and other family members, living or deceased. It specifies how they are to honor and respect their parents and family name (especially in the traditionally sacrosanct father-son relationship), to provide for them in old age, and to perform ceremonial rituals of worship. According to the *Book of Rites* (see Wu & Lai, 1992), a son demonstrates his filial piety in three ways: by honoring his father, by not disgracing him, and by caring for him in old age. It is difficult to overestimate the importance and scope of filial piety in shaping Chinese selves.

> If a man in his own house and privacy be not grave, he is not filial; if in serving his ruler he be not loyal, he is not filial; if in discharging the duties of office he be not serious, he is not filial; if with friends he be not sincere, he is not filial; if on the field of battle he be not brave, he is not filial. If he fail in these five things, the evil [of the disgrace] will reflect on his parents. Dare he but be serious? (Tu, 1985, pp. 237–238)

It is important to note that although filial piety is often understood in terms of obligations of children to parents, it is fully mutual and reciprocal. Parents have a duty to sacrifice for and support their children throughout their lifespan. It is the parental commitment to children that provides the basis for children's filial devotion (*xiao*) in the first place.

The Classic of Filial Piety is defined as "raising one's reputation in order to exalt one's parents" (cited in Yu, 1996), a definition that accentuates the importance of maintaining face and familial honor (Cocroft & Ting-Toomey, 1994; Gabrenya & Hwang, 1996). Hu (1944) proposed two basic aspects of face in Chinese society and social relations. *Lian* refers to an individual's moral character in the eyes of others, and it develops as one exhibits faithful compliance to moral, ritual, and social norms. To say that a person *bu yao lian* ("doesn't want face") indicates that the person is "shameless" or "immoral"; it is one of the worst insults that can be cast against a person. In China, the second aspect of face is *mianzi*, referring to one's reputation or social prestige. *Mianzi* is earned through success in life, attaining a high or respected social position. To say that a person *mei you mianzi* means that one is not deserving of honor or respect. Although still insulting, it is less harsh than being characterized as "shameless" (lacking *lian*). According to Hu (1944), although Westerners have a concept of "face" similar to *mianzi* (i.e. "social prestige"), it does not have the strong moral implications of the concept of *lian*. Face is a driving force in social relations among the Chinese, and failures to show *lian* or *mianzi* bring dishonor, disgrace, and shame to one's family, self, and other significant relationships (*guanxi*; Gabrenya & Hwang, 1996).

To promote the cultivation of *ren*, self-effacement, and

self-harmonization with others, Chinese parents adopt relatively strict socialization processes. Although efforts to socialize children begin soon after they begin to talk and walk, strict discipline increases precipitously at the "age of reason" (*dongshi*, around 5 years of age). A central value is affective control: Children are taught to control their impulses and not to reveal their thoughts and feelings. Violence is strictly forbidden and is met with severe consequences. Socialization may involve corporal punishment, which becomes unnecessary as soon as children are able to cease prohibited actions on demand (Ho, 1986; Wu, 1996). To promote filial piety, proper behavior, benevolence, and love of learning, parents draw on a variety of shaming techniques. If, for example, a child were to show inadequate learning in school, a parent might say, "Shame on you!," "You didn't practice hard enough!," "Everyone will laugh at you!," "I have no face with your teachers!," or "You show no filial piety!" Thus the use of shaming techniques and the creation of strong emotional bonds promote the self-cultivation of relational selves (Wu, 1996; Wu & Tseng, 1985).

### Cultural Organization of Self-Evaluative Emotions

Social, self-evaluative emotions exist across cultures, but their specific forms are strongly shaped by cultures (Fischer & Tangney, 1995). Figure 20.4 outlines the organization of social self-evaluative emotions within the contexts of American individualism and Chinese Confucianism. Whereas Americans tend to make sharp distinctions between the moral and the conventional (Turiel, 1983), under Confucianism all domains of human action are seen as having a strong moral component (Tu, 1979). For example, under American individualism, achievement is an important social value, but it is not considered a moral imperative or obligation. In contrast, under Confucianism obligations to family and social groups, to life-long learning and self-cultivation, and to physical/sexual/civic mores are all connected as part of the larger system of explicitly moral obligations to harmonize oneself with others (Tu, 1979, 1985).

### American Individualism: Separation of Achievement and Morality

Two separate routes to the experience of self-evaluative emotions within American individualism are social achievement (Atkinson, 1957; Maehr, 1974; Weiner, 1985) and moral conduct (Barrett, Zahn-Waxler, & Cole, 1993; Hoffman, 1982). Within achievement domains, if people succeed at an important task, they may become proud of the self's ability or accomplishment. Pride is a manifestation of self-esteem and is acceptable as celebration and sharing of one's worthy self and accomplishments with others. Pride becomes negative when taken to the extreme, evolving into hubris (M. Lewis, 1996). Conversely, upon failing in an achievement domain, people may become ashamed of their lack of ability (Stipek et al., 1993). In individualism, shame can arise from an uncontrollable flaw in the self, which is damaging to self-esteem (Lewis, 1996). As a result, shame engenders hiding, social with-

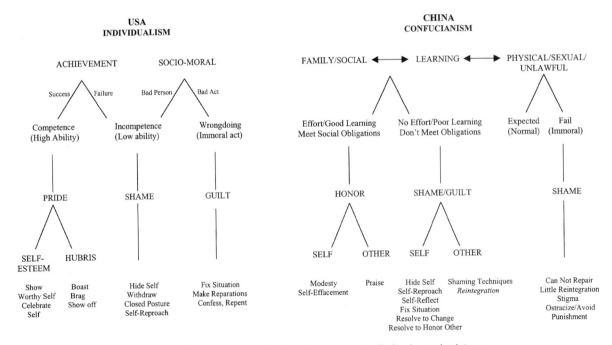

Figure 20.4 Cultural organization of pride, shame, and guilt in the United States and China.

drawal, and self-reproach (H. B. Lewis, 1971; M. Lewis, 1996; Tangney, Burggraf, & Wagner, 1995),

A second pathway to self-evaluative emotion under individualism is through moral violations. When people violate a moral norm (e.g., harm another person, violate their rights), they may experience guilt, shame, or both, depending on their appraisal of the situation. If they focus on their responsibility for an immoral outcome, they experience guilt and attempt to fix the situation, make reparations, or confess (Hoffman, 1992; Mascolo & Fischer, 1995). If instead they view themselves from the eyes of another and see themselves as an immoral, bad, or evil person, they experience shame (Barrett, Zahn-Waxler, & Cole, 1993; Lindsay-Hartz, de Rivera, & Mascolo, 1995). In this way, in individualist systems guilt functions primarily as a moral emotion, whereas shame can function as either a moral emotion or an emotion of social evaluation.

### Chinese Confucianism: Morality and Self-Harmonization

The situation is quite different under Confucianism. Instead of making a sharp distinction between the social evaluative and the moral, Confucianism treats social/familial obligations, learning, and physical/sexual mores as all primarily *moral* concerns (Li, 1997, in press; Tu, 1985; Yu, 1996). Because of the value placed on harmony within hierarchy in Chinese society (Gabreyna & Hwang, 1996), both the feeling of and enactment of pride are explicitly discouraged (Stipek, 1999). If one meets one's social and familial obligations, one brings honor to the family, not pride to oneself. Similarly, in light of the Confucian ideal that individuals are not viewed as isolated from their social relations, an individual's worthy accomplishments are not attributed exclusively to the self. Instead, they are seen as products of one's relationships with family and other social groups with whom individuals identify and from whom they gain their support (Li, 1997, in press). As such, a person who has produced a worthy outcome brings honor not primarily on the self but instead to his or her family and other significant social groups. Thus, when a person performs a worthy action, the appropriate response is not self-celebration but instead modesty, self-effacement, and praise for the other (Bond, Leung, & Wan, 1982; Gao, Ting-Toomey, & Gudykunst, 1996; Li, 1997, in press; Stipek, 1999).

The practice of modesty and self-effacement can be illustrated through an analysis of Chinese politeness strategies. In an analysis of Chinese and American responses to social compliments, Chen (1993) reported that Americans used four basic politeness strategies: accepting (39%), returning (19%), deflecting (30%), and rejecting (13%) compliments. In contrast, Chinese respondents showed three basic strategies but used primarily one rejecting (96%), in contrast to thanking and denigrating the

self (3%) and accepting the compliment (1%). For example, in response to a compliment such as "You look so nice!" a Chinese individual might say, "No, I know I don't look nice. In fact, you're the one that looks better," or perhaps, "No. Don't say that. I'm embarrassed" (Chen, 1993, pp. 72–73). Chen interpreted these results in terms of Leech's (1983) agreement and modesty maxims of conversation. Americans generally attempt to maximize agreement between interlocutors, whereas Chinese seek primarily to promote modesty in the self and praise for the other. Similarly, in a study on Chinese conceptions of learning, Li (1997) reported that Chinese people were more likely to report modesty and calmness from learning well rather than happiness or pride.

This practice cannot simply be viewed as a kind of "false modesty" or impression management. Markus and Kitayama (1991) studied the role of culture in the organization of emotional experiences and found that although both Japanese and American participants discriminated between socially engaged versus socially disengaged feelings, the affective valence of their reactions differed greatly (see also Kitayama, Markus, & Matsumoto, 1995). Socially engaged positive feelings include being together (feelings of closeness, friendliness, respect), whereas socially disengaged positive emotions cast individuals apart from each other (feelings of pride, superiority, being on top of the world). For Japanese in contrast to Americans, ratings of socially engaged emotions were more strongly correlated with general positive emotions (e.g., feeling happy, relaxed, calm, or elated; Kitayama, Markus, & Kurowkawa, 2000). Conversely, ratings of positive disengaged emotions were more strongly correlated with general positive feelings for Americans than for Japanese. That is, "feeling good" is strongly related to feelings of social engagement among the Japanese and to feelings of pride and superiority among Americans. Markus and Kitayama argue that individual attributes are important dimensions of self to Americans, but maintaining harmonious relationships is more central to Japanese sense of self. They suggest that the motivation for self-effacement among the Japanese is neither false modesty, lack of self-esteem, nor impression management, but *self-harmonization*—the desire to maintain a conception of self as part of a harmonious relationship with the other. We suggest that Chinese self-effacement similarly reflects genuine self-harmonization rather than false modesty.

In contrast to occasions for honor, if one does not meet one's social obligations, one brings dishonor to the family and experiences shame or guilt on the self. Because Chinese shame incorporates a moral dimension of obligation to others, shame and guilt are not as differentiated among the Chinese as among Americans. Chinese shame/guilt is not a discrete state but comprises a melding of elements of both shame and guilt. In this affective state, people are aware of both having committed a moral wrong and having brought dishonor on others. As such, shame/guilt brings about not only self-recrimination, a tendency to hide the self, and so forth, but also a resolve to change the self in order to restore honor to the other (fix the situation). Moreover, this resolve is enacted through deeds and not simply through words (Li, 1997, in press). In shame/guilt, people may neither confess nor even seek verbal forgiveness but do need to cultivate the self through correct action to assuage shame or guilt.

When people have failed to meet their obligations and duties, others will use shaming techniques (as described previously), but these techniques usually proceed under the presupposition of *reintegration* (Braithwaite, 1989). The shamed party is aware that, following the establishment of correct behavior, all will be forgiven, and he or she will be accepted back into the family or community. This is reflected in the Chinese aphorism, "Gold can't be exchanged for a returned soul." It is through reintegration that shaming and shame/guilt can function to effectively regulate social behavior. Reintegration reflects the role of the parent (and society) in filial piety: Although the child has the obligation to honor the parent, the parent has the reciprocal obligation to support the child in his or her attempt to cultivate the self.

An important exception to the rule of reintegrative shaming involves transgressions against important sexual, physical, or civic codes. Although Chinese parents are generally strict in their discipline practices (Ho, 1986; Wu, 1996), sanctions by parents and the larger society for major violations of the law and sexual mores are severe. For example, Vagg (1998) pointed out limits to reintegrative shaming in China, reporting evidence that for children labeled as delinquent in Hong Kong, negative sanctions are swift, severe, and stigmatizing (such as immediate expulsion from school and prosecution, rather than a warning, on the first criminal offense). Being cast as a "delinquent" in Hong Kong carries a substantial stigma with little opportunity for reintegration into the community. Such punitive and ostracizing practices reflect stigmatizing shame in response to transgressions of moral standards that are considered inviolable.

In summary, there appear to be at least two routes to shame and guilt in China. In the primary route, the affect regulates social conduct in daily social interactions, particularly within families and close social contexts, in order ultimately to integrate individuals back into society. In contrast, deintegrative shaming (Braithwaite, 1989) stigmatizes those who have acted beyond the pale by transgressing societal laws and cultural taboos, and it functions as a strong warning for others who might act similarly. Perhaps the former, more reintegrative mode of shaming is central to Chinese society, whereas Americans tend to conceptualize shame more unidimensionally with the latter, more stigmatizing version. This interpretation may help explain why Americans tend to protect their children from shame and avoid the use of shaming techniques in socialization (Massaro, 1997).

## Pathways in the Development of Self-Evaluative Emotions in the United States and China

How do self-evaluative emotions develop in directions defined by different cultural ideals? In this section, we examine similarities and differences in the development of pride- and shame-related emotions in the United States and China. Drawing on available evidence, we use dynamic skill theory as a framework to analyze the ways in which self-evaluative emotions develop along different pathways in these two countries.

### Dynamic Skill Theory as a Framework for Analyzing Pathways in Emotional Development

Dynamic skill theory provides a set of conceptual and methodological tools for predicting and assessing transformations in dynamic structures of action, thought, and feeling. The central unit in dynamic skill theory is the skill—a capacity to organize actions, thoughts, and feelings within a given context for a specific goal or task. For predicting developmental pathways, dynamic skill theory defines a developmental scale and a series of rules and methods for using it to analyze developing actions, thoughts, and feelings. The scale consists of 13 developmental levels in the capacity to organize skills, which are grouped into four tiers from birth through adulthood. In the first tier, reflexes consist of innate action elements, such as looking at an object placed in front of the face, and come under control initially at around 1 month of age. In the second tier, beginning around 4 months of age, children gain the capacity to coordinate systems of action elements (reflexes) into sensorimotor actions, which consist of flexible and controlled actions (relatively independent of postural constraints) on objects, such as controlled tracking of an object moving in front of the infant. In the third tier, beginning around 18 to 24 months of age, children begin to coordinate multiple sensorimotor systems into concrete representations. Using representations, a child can make one action sequence evoke or stand for an absent action or meaning, such as using the movement of a doll to stand for and evoke the action of walking. Finally, in the fourth tier, beginning around 10 to 11 years of age, children begin to construct abstractions consisting of generalized and intangible meaning structures, such as abstract and generalized representations of self, pride, and shame.

Within each tier, skills pass through four levels (single sets, mappings, systems, and systems of systems). Through a careful analysis of the ways in which specific sets of skill elements are coordinated within any given task and social context, skill theory allows fine-grained specification of an indefinite number of intermediate steps between any two consecutive levels. Each tier, level, and step in development emerges gradually as a result of the hierarchical coordination and differentiation of lower level skills into higher order structures within a given context. Unlike stages in theories such as Piaget's, developing structures do not reflect generic levels of competence; instead, skills develop within particular tasks, conceptual and emotional domains, and social contexts. The level of skill evinced by a particular child in any given context at a specific moment varies as a function of a wide variety of variables. For example, an individual's level of skill can vary as a result of the amount of support provided by the social context. Studies demonstrate, for example, that children function at higher levels in contexts that provide high social support for complex activity than in contexts that provide less social support (Fischer, Rotenberg, Bullock, & Raya, 1993; Fogel, 1993; Rogoff, 1993; Vygotsky, 1978). Similarly, an individual's skill level varies as a function of the task being performed, the conceptual or emotional domain in question, the temperament or affective state of the individual, and a suite of additional variables.

There are two important implications of these principles. First, it is not helpful to locate the developmental level of a person's skills at a single point on a ladder; instead, a person's skills occupy a *range* of different possible points within a given developmental pathway. Second, as illustrated in Figure 20.5, development is like a *web*, not a ladder (Bidell & Fischer, 1992; Fischer & Bidell, 1998). Whereas a ladder represents development in terms of a single unidirectional sequence of steps, a web represents development in terms of alternative and interconnected

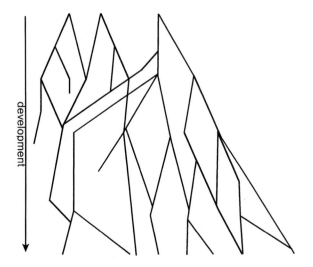

Figure 20.5 Web metaphor for developmental pathways. Adapted from Fischer and Bidell (1998).

pathways, each with potentially different starting and ending points. For example, skills for constructing pride-relevant appraisals and actions may develop along different pathways than skills for constructing shame-relevant appraisals. Similarly, for any given skill domain (such as shame or pride), different individuals may take different pathways in the development of the same skill domain. Factors that mediate these differences include temperament, personal history, culture, and a range of other processes. In what follows, we use dynamic skill theory to analyze alternative pathways in development of pride- and shame-relevant emotions that result from different cultural beliefs, values, and practices.

### Pathways in the Development of Emotional Reactions to Accomplishment

Whereas accomplishment in the United States typically leads to the experience of pride, the parallel emotions among the Chinese might be described as self-harmonization or social honor. Alternative developmental pathways in the development of pride and self-harmonization or social honor are depicted in Table 20.2. It is likely that both cultural pathways build on the biologically canalized capacity for experiencing joy in the context of self-produced outcomes. Such reactions can be observed as early as 6 weeks of age. For example, Watson and Ramey (1972) demonstrated that within days of exposure to mobiles activated by subtle head movements, 8-week-old infants smiled as their actions resulted in movements of the mobiles. In terms of dynamic skill theory, such reactions are mediated by the capacity of young infants to construct reflex mappings—the coordination of two simple reflexes or action elements. In this case, an infant is able to experience pleasure on actively coordinating moving his or her head with seeing a resulting effect (the shaking mobile). Beyond this point, the American and Chinese emotional pathways begin to diverge, with biases toward one pattern or the other. In the United States, pride undergoes development in the direction of increasingly complex representations of the self as competent, valuable, or capable of producing socially worthy outcomes. American parents often direct children's attention to themselves and their own worthy accomplishments. Parents encourage children to feel good about their own achievements and about their role in bringing about valued outcomes. Of course, some of these patterns occur in Chinese families, too, but the bias is toward the alternative pathway of self-harmonization.

Throughout the first year of life, American children are able to detect increasingly complex action-outcome contingencies. For example, at Step P2, with the onset of sensorimotor systems around 11 to 13 months of age, infants experience *joy over complex action-outcome contingencies* that involve a sensorimotor awareness of the evalua-

Table 20.2. Development of Pride (U.S.) and Self-Harmonization/Social Honor (China)

| Pride (United States) | | Self-Harmonization/Social Honor (China) | |
|---|---|---|---|
| Step and Description | Developmental Level and Appraisal Skill Structure | Step and Description | Developmental Level and Appraisal Skill Structure |

**Pride (United States)**

**P2: Joy over complex action-outcome contingency including other's evaluation**

Child connects action(s) to a shared goal-related positive outcome (e.g., throwing a block) and is aware of parent's smile and positive vocalizations (11–13 months)

*Sm3: Sensoriotor systems*

```
 grasp        let go           see smile
 ACT    <->   GOAL       <->   MOM
 move arm     see block fly    hear voice
```

**P3: Joy/pride in self as agent of outcome**

Child carries out action with goal-directed positive results and attributes outcome to the self. A child may throw a ball and notice the parent's smile, voice, statements, and gestures (applause, "good throw!"). Child makes appraisals, e.g., "I throw!" Action tendency includes self-celebration: child looks at other, smiles, and evaluates self positively (e.g., claps, says "I did it!") (18–24 months)

*Sm4/Rp1: Single representations*

```
 grasp        let go          seen
 ACT    <->   GOAL      <->   MOM
 move arm     see ball fly    heard
     <=>                                    ≡  [ SELF
 own body     "I"             "I"               result + ]
 SEE    <->   SAY       <->   HEAR
 act          "good"          "act"  "good"
```

**P4: Pride in self as competent agent**

Child carries out action with positive goal-related results that are evaluated as special, attributes result to self, and labels it using evaluative category. For example, child may throw a ball and make an appraisal category, e.g., "I throw good!" On success, parent evaluates child verbally and in gesture, smiles; praises child with exaggerated voice. Child's celebratory action tendency includes smile, social referencing, positive self-evaluation, expanding posture (2½–3 yrs).

*Sm4/Rp1: Single representations*

```
 grasp        let go          seen
 ACT    <->   GOAL      <->   MOM
 move arm     see ball fly    heard
     <=>                                    ≡  [ SELF
 own body     "I"             "I"               good ]
 SEE    <->   SAY       <->   HEAR
 outcome      "good"          "good"
```

**Self-Harmonization/Social Honor (China)**

**S/H2: Joy over action-outcome sequence involving other's goal and evaluation**

Child performs action to conform to parent's explicitly induced goal (e.g., give food to Grandma) and connects outcome to parent smile and vocalizations (11–13 months)

```
 let go       give candy      see smile
 ACT    <->   M's GOAL  <->   MOM
 move arm     G'ma eat        hear voice
```

**S/H3: Joy/pride in self as agent of socially induced outcome**

Child carries out action that conforms to parent's explicitly stated goal, connects outcome to parental evaluation and attributes it to the self. Child makes appraisal, e.g., "I give to Grandma!" Action tendency includes self-evaluation ("I did it!"). Parent and Grandma give modest noneffusive praise to the child; relatives offer exuberant praise.

```
 let go       give candy      seen
 ACT    <->   M's GOAL  <->   MOM
 move arm     G'ma eat        heard
     <=>                                    ≡  [ SELF
 own body     "I"             "I"               result + ]
 SEE    <->   SAY       <->   HEAR
 act          "act"           "act"
```

**S/H4: Quiet pride in meeting other's expectations**

Child carries out action to conform to parent's goal and connects outcome and parent's modest evaluation of child's ongoing effort and attributes the outcome to the self. Child makes appraisal, e.g., "I am doing o.k." Relatives praise child effusively ("Wonderful!"), but parent provides modest praise ("She sings hai-hao"), effaces outcome to relatives ("No, she just barely finished!"), and tells child to play down her accomplishment ("hai-hao").

```
 grasp        give candy      smile
 ACT    <->   M's GOAL  <->   MOM
 move arm     G'ma eat        "hai-hao"
     <=>                                    ≡  [ SELF
 own body     "I"             me                keep going ]
 SEE    <->   SAY       <->   ACT
 outcome      "act"           no talk
```

## P5: Pride over comparative performance

Child judges her performance in a valued area as better than or as good as another's. A child may throw a ball farther than or as far as a valued other. Child makes appraisal, e.g., "I can throw farther than [other child]!" Child celebrates self (3½ to 4 years).

## Rp2: Representational mappings

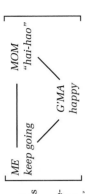

## P6: Proud of concrete valued trait

Child compares concrete performances in several contexts and coordinates them into a concrete trait that earns social approval of others. For example, child compares her positive performance in field hockey and soccer and connects this to positive evaluations by others. Child celebrates self (6–7 years).

## Rp3: Representational Systems

## P7: Pride in generalized personality characteristic

Person judges himself or herself to have two or more concrete traits that are valued by others, generalizes across these traits to characterize the self's identity positively. For example, adolescent may be aware of social approval earned by performing well in sports and academics. Child abstracts across traits and concludes, "I am a competent person" or something similar (10–12 years).

## Rp4/Ab1: Single abstractions

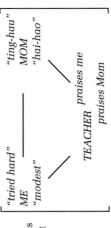

## S/H5: Modesty in accomplishment

Child carries out parent's goal for Grandma (e.g., sings song learned in school), attributes result to self but is aware of discrepancy between Grandma's praise and parent's effacement. Child makes appraisal, e.g., "I sang well for Grandma but must stay quiet."

## S/H6: Concrete self-effacing social honor.

Child is aware that teacher praises both self and mother for child's effortful learning. Given his awareness of need for piety (*ting-hau*) and that his parent approves of his learning but expects more (*hai-hao*), child is modest (quiet). Child makes appraisal, e.g., "My learning has brought praise to mother. She is pleased, but I must keep learning and be modest." This is supported by teacher's actual praising of mother and self and by mom's self-effacing comments about child.

## S/H7: Generalized self-effacing social honor

Child is aware that through her positive effort she has brought honor to her parents and/or family. Aware of the support she has received in making her accomplishment, she shows modesty and revolves to keep trying hard in school. Child's appraisal is socially supported by multiple other's explicit praise of mother and self and by parent's self-effacing comments about child.

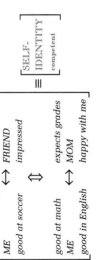

(continued)

391

Table 20.2. Development of Pride (U.S.) and Self-Harmonization/Social Honor (China) (continued)

| Pride (United States) | | Self-Harmonization/Social Honor (China) | |
|---|---|---|---|
| Step and Description | Developmental Level and Appraisal Skill Structure | Step and Description | Developmental Level and Appraisal Skill Structure |
| **P8: Pride in general characteristic of other person with identity related to one's own** | **Ab2: Abstract mappings** | **S/H8: Self-harmonizing social honor** | |
| Person judges another person of an identity similar to his or her own to have a desirable characteristic and relates own identity to that attribute. A person may judge someone else to be especially competent (e.g., singing). Linking his own ethnic identity to that of the other, he might say "I've never had such pride in seeing this [name of race] woman stand up there with this great royal dignity and sing!" (15+ yrs) | SELF-IDENTITY — OTHER IDENTITY  racial/ethnic   competent | Child is aware that his generalized positive efforts have brought honor to his family, attributes the outcome to his family, and effaces the self's contribution to the outcome. An adolescent makes an appraisal, e.g., "My family is honored even though I am unworthy of your praise." | SELF — FAMILY  keep trying to   bring   honor |

*Note:* Step numbers indicate both sequence of skills and parallel structure across domains in Tables 20.2 and 20.3. Steps 1, 9, and 10 are included only in Table 20.3, although similar steps could be described for Table 20.2.

In skill structures, brackets mark a single skill structure. Each capitalized word or phrase designates a main skill component, and each lowercased word or phrase below or above a capitalized one designates a subset of the main component. Plain letters indicate sensorimotor actions, italic letters representations, and outline letters abstractions. Lines connecting sets designate relations forming a mapping, single-line arrows relations forming a system, and double-line arrows relations forming a system of systems.

tions of others.(See Table 20.3 for an example of Step 1.) At this step, a child coordinates grasping and arm movements to achieve the goal of throwing an object and seeing and hearing the verbal and gestural praise of others. Upon success, children at this age often smile and reference their parent (Mascolo & Fischer, 1995). At Step P3, with the emergence of single representations at around 20 months of age, children develop a more sophisticated sense of *joy/pride in self as an agent of outcomes*. This step corresponds with the development of the onset of strong self-recognition and the ability to represent simple outcome standards (Pipp, Fischer, & Jennings, 1987). At this step, a child represents herself as an agent who caused an outcome and so can make appraisals such as "I did it!" or a nonverbal equivalent. Children's emotional reactions to self-caused actions change around this age. H. Heckhausen (1987) and J. Heckhausen (1988) have reported that beginning around 14 to 20 months, children stop and notice results of their acts. Lutkenhaus (1984) suggests that this occurs when children focus on outcomes per se rather than on the flow of activity. Kagan (1981) reported that smiles on completion of goal-directed acts increased between 20 and 24 months, around the same time children show full self-recognition (Bertenthal & Fischer, 1978; M. Lewis & Brooks-Gunn, 1978; Pipp, Fischer, & Jennings, 1987) and distress after inability to imitate modeled acts.

Beginning around 2½ years of age, as children gain the capacity to construct increasingly complex single representations, *pride in self as a competent agent* (Step P4) begins to emerge. At this step, a child not only constructs an awareness that he or she performed an outcome but also that the outcome is valued and/or that the self is competent (e.g. "I'm good at it!"). Several studies suggest that between about 2½ and 3 years of age, children begin to evaluate themselves positively in the context of achievement. M. Lewis, Alessandri, and Sullivan (1992) reported such a reaction in 3-year-olds in basketball tossing and drawing tasks. Halisch and Halisch (1980, as cited in H. Heckhausen, 1984) reported pride-like reactions in 2½-year-olds in a ring-stacking task. Only indirect evidence suggests that such reactions are mediated by a sense of competence (Geppert & Kuster, 1983). At Step P5, *pride over comparative performance*, which emerges with the onset of representational mappings around 3½ years of age, a child compares her or his performance with that of others in a given context. Such comparisons can take place in a variety of contexts, including competition (winning or losing in a competitive task or game) or identification (comparing one's performance with that of a valued other). In studies that employ competitive ring stacking, for example, Stipek, Recchia, and McClintic (1992) reported that, although children older than 32 months smiled more after winning than losing at competitive ring stacking, only 3½-year-olds appreciated competition, as shown by pausing, slowing down, or stopping after losing.

There are fewer empirical studies related to the development of pride in middle childhood and adolescence. With the onset of representational systems, children can control the relation between two representational mappings. At Step P6, using representational systems, a child coordinates multiple representations of successful outcomes and parental positive evaluations of those outcomes to feel *proud of a valued concrete trait*. For example, generalizing across different contexts, a child constructs an appraisal such as "Mom and Dad are happy with me because I do well at soccer and baseball. I'm good at sports!" With the onset of single abstractions at around 10 to 11 years of age, children construct abstractions for generalized and intangible aspects of their valued self-identity, such as feeling *pride in generalized personality characteristics* (Step P7). Generalizing across multiple positively evaluated concrete outcomes in sports and academics, a young adolescent makes the generalized appraisal that "I'm a competent person!"

Pride-related appraisals continue to develop within the tier of abstractions and well into adulthood (Fischer, Yan, & Stewart, in press). For example, consider the actual experience of Todd Duncan, an African American who retrospectively expressed his pride on having seen African American soprano Marian Anderson sing at the Lincoln Memorial after she was denied the opportunity to sing at Constitution Hall in 1939. "My feelings were so deep. . . . It was the same feeling I had . . . when we heard that 'I Have a Dream' speech. Number one, I never have been so proud to be an American. Number two, I've never been so proud to be an American Negro. Number three, I've never had such pride in seeing this Negro woman stand up there with this great royal dignity and sing" (James, 1991). At the very least, as indicated in Step P8, this self-reflective appraisal operates at the level of abstract mappings, which allow coordination of the relation between two abstractions. In identifying with Ms. Anderson and her achievement, Mr. Duncan related his own generalized racial identity to the symbolic significance of Ms. Anderson's performance for the status of African Americans in American society.

Emotional reactions to accomplishment among the Chinese follow a different pathway that is consistent with a Confucian cultural framework. With development, accomplishment-related appraisals increasingly incorporate representations of the impact of one's positive actions on the other. Whereas steps in the development of American pride are often analyzed most effectively for dyads, self-harmonization and social honor develop among the Chinese within triadic and larger interactions involving the child, a parent, and other relatives or members of significant social groups. When a child performs an action that meets social obligations and expectations, parents will acknowledge the success, but without the effusive praise that is often exhibited by American parents (H. Heckhausen, 1987; Mascolo & Harkins, 1998; Reissland, 1994). In addition, parents generally make self-effacing comments to others about the child and his or her accomplishment (e.g., "She just barely made it through the song!" "He did all right, but he needs to practice more"). In a display of social honor, relatives and guests who observe the child's worthy behavior will offer effusive praise of both the child and the parent. In this way, the discrepancy between a parent's child-effacing remarks and a third party's effusive praise sets the stage for the development of a child's proclivity to honor others in modest self-harmonization in contexts involving the self's accomplishments.

This socialization process begins in the first years of life. Step S/H2, *joy over action-outcome sequence*, is similar to pride in American children. However, instead of praising a child-chosen goal, parents often induce children to perform social goals chosen by parents by, for example, beginning to socialize sharing in the first year. A parent might coax her child, for example, to share candy with Grandma. To encourage success, a parent will praise the child, albeit with less effusiveness than American parents. Using complex sensorimotor systems, a 12-month-old coordinates reaching and opening the hand to yield the candy and connects these actions to the mother's ongoing request and to her subsequent smile and praise. Thus richly textured social interactions orient children's actions and feelings toward others even in infancy.

Step S/H3, *joy/pride in self as agent of socially induced outcomes*, is also comparable to pride among American children at this level, except that a child represents his or her role in complying with a parental request (e.g., share candy with Grandma) instead of a personally chosen goal. In this way, at the level of single representations, a Chinese child might make an appraisal such as "I give candy to Grandma" or "I did what Momma wanted." Again, a parent would likely acknowledge the outcome ("that's nice" or "good job") but without effusive affect. Step S/H4, *quiet pride in meeting others' expectations*, begins to diverge from pride among American children. It is customary in Chinese culture for children to display skills that they learn in school to relatives and guests. Within such a context, Chinese families begin the process of triangulating the child's accomplishments, social praise, and child effacement. On demonstrating a worthy skill (such as singing a song learned in school), a relative might offer effusive praise to both child and parent. The parent will acknowledge the child's accomplishment by saying *hai-hao* (meaning "okay" or something similar), which recognizes the positive outcome but implies that the child should continue his positive efforts and play down his accomplishment. Moreover, the parent effaces the child in front of the relative ("He did all right, but he has to learn the song better!"). As a result, children construct appraisals such as, "I have to keep going," which reflect an incipient sense that one has succeeded but must continue to work hard and improve; and they begin to show restraint in exhibiting self-celebratory actions on success.

With development, children differentiate further the need for modesty in accomplishment. At Step S/H5, *modesty in accomplishment*, they use representational mappings to coordinate a triangulated representation of the social meanings of success. For example, a child represents the relations among her mother's effacement (*hai-hao*), a relative's praise of the self, and the child's own need to continue to work hard to bring about positive outcomes. A child might make an appraisal such as, "Mom's friend is happy with my singing, but Mom wants me to keep working hard." In so doing, the child is beginning to represent the need for modesty and continued effort in the context of concrete positive outcomes. At Step S/H6, *concrete self-effacing social honor*, these appraisal elements become more explicit and intercoordinated. At this level, a child represents the complex relations between (1) his mother's expectations of piety (*ting-hua*, which means "listen to my words") and continued hard work (*hai-hao*), (2) his teachers' praiseful honoring of mother and self, and (3) his own need to continue to be modest (quiet) and to try hard in learning. To highlight the role of multiple others in the child's experience, we have represented this level in terms of a compounded representational system, which is more complex (and would develop later) than the corresponding structure provided for American pride at this level.

The final steps represent continued development of social honor. At Step S/H7, a young adolescent begins to coordinate two representational systems into a single abstraction of *self-effacing social honor*. At this level, a young adolescent enacts modesty in bestowing honor on his parents. Such an appraisal is reflected in a child's ability to connect different aspects of his positive effort to his mother's desire for continued hard work, as well as to others' praise for his parents and self. In so doing, a child makes an abstract appraisal such as, "My achievement can't be apart from my parents" (Li, 1997, in press) or "I have brought honor to my parents." Finally, at Step S/H8 and the level of abstract mappings, *self-harmonizing social honor*, an older adolescent or young adult begins to further differentiate her role in bestowing honor to her family—for example, making an abstract appraisal such as, "I must continue to show positive effort in all that I do in order to bring *mianzi* (social honor) and *lian* (moral adulation) to my family/school/country."

## Development of Chinese Shame/Guilt

Our developmental analysis of shame and guilt begins with the important differences between China and the United States in the organization, function, and socialization of shame. First, shame and shaming play central roles in Chinese socialization, whereas American parents often work to protect their children from shame. Second, shame among the Chinese arises when individuals have violated their duties and obligations in the eyes of significant others. As such, shame is often mixed with guilt, and we refer to this as shame/guilt (Li, 1997, in press; Wang, 1994). Third, whereas shame in the United States carries stigmatizing connotations, shame/guilt among the Chinese offers the promise of reintegration into the family or community following reestablishment of appropriate behavior. As such, shame is not primarily a threat to self-esteem: instead, it is a vehicle for social cohesion and the development of self. For these reasons, shame develops along different pathways in China and in the United States.

Table 20.3 provides a description of developmental changes in the organization and socialization of Chinese shame/guilt. We suggest that important precursors to shame (in both the United States and China) occur within the first year of life in the form of *affective misattunements* (Step S/G1) between infants and caregivers (Nathanson, 1987; Schore, 1998; Tomkins, 1962). Over the first months of life, infants and their caregivers develop increasingly sophisticated ways of anticipating and coregulating each other's actions and emotions (Trevarthen, 1993; Trevarthen & Hubley, 1978). Disruptions of such mutually established affective routines and expectations can result in negative emotions in the infant (Tronick, 1989). For example, using sensorimotor mappings, a child coordinates two actions into a single skill (such as looking at mother for a smile and seeing her frown). In the context of a simple social game such as peekaboo, an infant who has come to expect a smile from her caregiver may react with distress and gaze aversion if her turn in the game were met with a frown or some other negative emotional expression. Although some theorists suggest that such infant experiences reflect shame per se, we find that young infants are not yet able to construct reflective representations of self in the eyes of others. Such emotional reactions are best interpreted as early precursors of shame.

At Step S/G2, using sensorimotor systems, a child responds with *early social distress* in interpersonal contexts that involve negative caregiver reactions to violations of explicit requests. For example, a parent might respond to a child who refused to share her candy with Grandma by saying with a sad voice and expression, "Aiya, Lin won't share her candy," or "I have a child who won't share with Grandma." At the level of sensorimotor systems, a child connects seeing and hearing his mother's voice and facial expressions to his unwillingness to extend his hand and give grandma some candy. At this level, a child deflects his gaze away from others in social distress. Step S/G3, *self-conscious social distress*, arises at the level of single representations (18 to 24 months of age). At this step, a child attributes responsibility to the self-as-agent for an act that brings about explicit social disapproval. For example, alternating looking at mother and grandma, a child con-

nects his mother's coaxing and her negative reactions to his awareness that he continues to grasp his candy, constructing a single self-conscious appraisal such as, "I no give to Grandma" or "Mommy mad I no give to Grandma." Given his self-conscious awareness of his mother's negative reaction, at this level, a child may perform a variety of shame- and guilt-relevant behaviors, including gaze aversion, hiding, crying, displays of distress, or complying with the request at hand (sharing the candy).

Step S/G4, *shame over negative characterization of social self*, arises with the capacity to construct more complex single representations. At this step, a child attributes responsibility to self for performing or failing to perform a wanted action and also represents the value of such an act by using a single concrete social category. For example, a parent of a child who fails to share with Grandma might respond with "Be filially pious with grandma!" or "People will laugh at you if you don't share!" or "I am a mother of a child who is *buguai*." (*Buguai* can be translated as "not cute," a term similar to "naughty" that conveys mild to moderate disapproval.) These shaming statements function to orient the child's attention to the nature of the child's concrete social obligations to others and the evaluations that others will make of both the self *and the mother* if the child does not comply. Using a complex single representation, a child begins to represent the socially oriented evaluative aspects of his or her action, making an appraisal such as, "Grandma thinks I am *buguai*" or "Auntie will laugh at me." Because the child is able to represent the self in terms of violations of concrete social and moral standards, this step reflects a transition to a state we would call shame/guilt per se rather than simply social distress.

With development, awareness of how one's actions affect the social evaluation (face) of significant others is increasingly represented in children's shame/guilt experiences. At Step S/G5, using representational mappings, a child forms a more differentiated awareness of the relation between the self's action and the other's social evaluation (*differentiated social shame*). For example, a child who is unable to remember a song that she was asked to sing in front of guests can not only use social standards to evaluate the self but can also represent the concrete social implications of her actions for her mother. For example, a child constructs a representation that "I made Mother embarrassed because I didn't try hard enough on the song."

At this point, a triangulation of evaluation similar to that encountered in the development of self-harmonization begins to occur. When a child is asked to demonstrate her learning to others, a parent might first communicate the importance of correct performance to the child ("Be sure to sing 'twinkle, twinkle,' not 'tinkle tinkle' "). If the child shows poor learning, parents will efface the child's performance in front of both the child and the relative ("Lin didn't practice hard enough to learn

Table 20.3. Development of Chinese Shame/Guilt

| Level of Emotional Experience | Appraisal Skill Structure | Emotional Actions | Role of Other in Coregulation of Emotion | Sample Episode |
|---|---|---|---|---|
| **S/G1: Affective misattunement** | **Level Sm2: Sensorimotor mappings** | | | |
| Distress over inability to maintain expected emotional exchange with caregiver (7–9 months). | $$\left[\text{LOOK} \underline{\quad\quad} \begin{array}{l}\text{GOAL +}\\ \text{see smile}\end{array}\right]$$ mother | Gaze aversion | Parent does not engage child in expected facial exchange. She may exhibit neutral or negative facial or vocal expressions. | Infant directs gaze to parent, who, distracted for whatever reason, fails to provide wanted or expected emotional display. |
| **S/G2: Early social distress** | **Level Sm3: Sensorimotor Systems** | | | |
| Distress over caregiver's negative emotional reaction to child's unwillingness to perform a requested social act (12–13 months). | $$\left[\begin{array}{l}\text{look mom, Gra'ma} \\ \text{ACT} \\ \text{no give candy}\end{array} \longleftrightarrow \begin{array}{l}\text{hear coax} \\ \text{MOTHER} \\ \text{see head shake, frown}\end{array}\right]$$ | Gaze aversion | Caregiver alternates her attention between Grandma and child. To Grandma, with an embarrassed smile, she says "*Aiya*, Jin won't share her candy!" With a frown, she shakes her head sadly and says to child, "I have a child who won't share with Grandma!" | To encourage respect to elders, caregiver tries to coax unwilling infant to share her candy with her grandma. Caregiver's coaxing directs child's attention to her failure to give up candy. Caregiver's words, emotion, and vocal tone convey disapproval; child looks away. |
| **S/G3: Self-conscious social distress** | **Level Sm4/Rp1: Single representations** | | | |
| Child attributes responsibility to self for action (or failure to act) that brings about affective disapproval by others. Child makes appraisal, e.g., "Me no give candy" or "Mom unhappy with me" (18–24 months). | $$\left[\begin{array}{l}\text{look mother} \\ \text{ACT} \longleftrightarrow \begin{array}{l}\text{head shake, frown} \\ \text{MOTHER} \\ \text{hear coax}\end{array} \\ \text{look Grandma} \\ \\ \Updownarrow \\ \\ \text{grasp candy} \\ \text{ACT} \longleftrightarrow \begin{array}{l}\text{says 'me no share'} \\ \text{MOTHER} \\ \text{'aiya, my child is..'}\end{array} \\ \text{see own hands}\end{array}\right] \equiv \left[\begin{array}{l}ME \\ no\ give\ to \\ Gra'ma\end{array}\right]$$ | Gaze aversion; look down; run and hide; cry; distressed or anxious face | Caregiver responds much as above, but begins to describe child in terms of evaluative social categories, e.g., she says to Grandma in a self-effacing way: "*Aiya*, I am a mother of a child who is *buguai* (naughty)." Though child does not fully understand such terms, they orient her to social values of respect and duty, which develop later. | Same as above, but child is able to represent himself as a causal agent who fails to give candy to grandma as requested, or who makes mom unhappy, or something similar. Child is aware of other's negative evaluations but does not yet represent self or self's actions in terms of inner standards or concrete social categories. |

396

## Level Sm4/Rp1: Single representations

**S/G4: Shame over negative characterization of social self**

Child sees self through eyes of others and views self in terms of an unwanted social category (e.g., buguai). Child makes appraisal, e.g., "Me buguai" or "Me buguai for not giving candy" (2½–3 years)

```
 look mom        say 'have filial piety'
 ACT    ←→  MOTHER
 look Gra'ma     say 'embarrassed'
              ⇔                           ≡   ⎡ G'MA/ME  ⎤
 grasp candy     say 'me buguai'              ⎢  thinks...⎥
 ACT    ←→  GRANDMA                           ⎣  buguai   ⎦
 see own hands   head shake, etc.
```

Look down or away; remain quiet; run and hide; cry; distressed or anxious face

Caregiver invokes cultural value of filial piety to coax child to share candy with grandma ("Have filial piety with Grandma!") Caregiver makes increasingly strong evaluative discriminations in child's behavior ("I am embarrassed in front of grandma when you don't share!").

Same as above, although now child begins to represent self in terms of concrete evaluative standards and categories. The child's shameful self is defined in terms of a representation that incorporates both self and other, e.g., how grandma feels and categorizes self (buguai).

## Level Rp2: Representational mappings

**S/G5: Differentiated social shame**

Child understands the causal relation between her mother's embarrassed reaction. Child can make an appraisal, e.g., "I embarrassed mother because I didn't try hard enough." (3½–4 years)

```
 ⎡ ME                MOTHER              ⎤
 ⎢ didn't try hard ── embarrass in front ⎥
 ⎣ to learn song      of guest           ⎦
```

Look down or away; remain quiet; run and hide; cry

Caregiver has child sing for guests, stressing the import of performing well: "Sing 'twinkle twinkle,' not 'tinkle tinkle' ..." When child sings poorly, caregiver says to guest, "She didn't practice hard." The guest offers self-effacing praise: "No, she did better than my child would!"

Chinese parents typically have children demonstrate skill from school to relatives or guests. A caregiver may ask the child to sing a newly learned song. At this level, the child is aware that his poor learning causes embarrassment in the mother, who is self-effacing with relatives and guests.

**S/G6: Social comparative shame**

Child engages in social comparison of concrete acts. Child feels shame when she realizes that her friend's drawing is better than her own; mother states that her child did not practice as hard as friend. Child makes an appraisal, e.g., "Mother is embarrassed that Lin can draw better than me" (3½–5 years).

```
 ⎡ ME              FRIEND       ⎤
 ⎢ poor drawing    good drawing ⎥
 ⎢        \       /             ⎥
 ⎢        MOTHER                ⎥
 ⎣    "friend tried harder!"    ⎦
```

Look down; cry; say "her drawing is nice but mine isn't"; run and hide; remain quiet and withdrawn

Mother may say "Of course Lin made a nicer picture! She practiced hard!" Mother may say to friend's parent, "My child didn't practice enough." Friend's parent would say in self-effacing way, "No, she did a fine job!"

A child and his friend are drawing pictures with their parents present. Friend draws a picture that is better than self's. Child is able to compare the value of his drawing to the friend's. Parent states that friend practiced more than her child. Child is ashamed of poor comparative learning in mother's eyes.

*(continued)*

Table 20.3. Development of Chinese Shame/Guilt (continued)

| Level of Emotional Experience | Appraisal Skill Structure | Emotional Actions | Role of Other in Coregulation of Emotion | Sample Episode |
|---|---|---|---|---|
| **S/G7: Concrete internalized social shame** <br><br> Viewing the self through the eyes of the mother, a child realizes he exhibits a negative moral quality (disobedience), which causes embarrassment to the parent. Child appraises: "Mother is embarrassed and upset with me because I don't practice like she wants me to." (6–7 yrs). | **Level Rp3: Representational systems** <br><br> "disobedient son" ↔ upset with me <br> ME _MOTHER_ <br> should have embarrassed in <br> practiced harder front of teacher | Look down or away; remain quiet; hide, cry; resolve to fix situation; effort —to improve skill and uphold concrete standards of obedience; works to please parents | While "scratching her face with her finger in shame," a caregiver says to child, "Shame on you! You did not practice enough! I feel embarrassed when your teacher comes!" "If you don't study, people will laugh!" Such statements are typically made in front of both child and others and are accompanied by strong affect. | With the onset of the "age of reason," children are held to stringent moral standards (filial piety, hard work in learning). With poor learning, parents communicate embarrassment. At this level, a child can represent relations of his actual and ideal levels of effort in school with his parent's expectations and emotions. |
| **S/G8: Generalized dishonor** <br><br> An adolescent can construct single abstractions of aspects of his moral character in the eyes of his parents. In realizing that his poor learning and lack of filial piety prompt lack of face in his parents, the child can make an abstract appraisal, e.g., "I brought dishonor upon my self and my parents" (10–12 years) | **Level Rp4/Ab1: Single abstractions** <br><br> not a pious son upset with me <br> ME ↔ _MOTHER_ <br> poor learning no face when <br> teacher comes <br> ⇕ you have no <br> hao-xue-xin <br> 'worthless person' _FATHER_ <br> ME ↔ no face with <br> no practice Grandpa <br><br> SELF/ <br> PARENTS ≡ dishonorable <br> son | Looks down; quiet; resolves to cultivate self by upholding filial piety and hao-xue-xin; self-cultivation is not valued through verbalization but instead through changed action | In light of poor learning in school, both parents communicate their displeasure and "sense of shame" over the child's lack of hao-xue-xin and filial piety | Given poor learning in school and actual/anticipated feedback from both mother and father, the adolescent generalizes across multiple actual and anticipated interactions with significant others to construct an abstract sense of shame over "having no hao-xue-xin," "having no filial piety," and/or bringing dishonor to parents. |

ployment, or nation—for example, if a national athletic team were to lose at an international competition. At this level, a member of the losing team represents the ways the team's failure to gain *mianzi* (social prestige, in light of the team's failure to achieve a high level of performance in the eyes of the public) and *lian* (everyday moral duty, as indicated by failing to play honorably or prepare hard enough) brings dishonor to family and nation as a whole. Such shameful experiences might involve affect-laden public declarations of shame, public apologies, public weeping, and both public and private declarations of one's intention to change one's unworthy actions and identity (such as writing letters to family, public officials, etc.).

Appraisals that mediate shame/guilt are organized around one's role in bringing dishonor to significant others and social groups. Developmental transformations in shame/guilt are defined by the increasing participation of duty to others in defining the self. Chinese parents and socialization agents use shaming techniques to promote the development of shame/guilt. Although such techniques induce shame, they do so with the promise of social reintegration on reestablishment of correct behavior and with the presupposition that parents will support attempts to cultivate the self. This reintegration implication stands in contrast to the sense of shame as normally understood in the United States, which is organized around awareness of the self's unwanted identity as seen through the eyes of others. In the United States, shame is often seen as a stigmatizing emotion that is debilitating to an individual's self-esteem. However, with the exception of shaming that results from civic or sexual violations, debilitating shame is not the usual case among the Chinese. In Chinese cultures, persons are socialized to harmonize the self with others and to assume their proper role within the hierarchies of family and society (Ho, 1996; Wu, 1996). The establishment of a worthy independent self is not a primary concern. As such, self-esteem is not a salient motivational issue (Hewitt, 1997). One is not so much motivated to "feel good about one's independent self" as one is to harmonize one's self with others (see Kitayama et al., 1995; Markus & Kitayama, 1991). As such, shame/guilt functions to regulate social action and bring about social cohesion without serious threats to individual "self-esteem."

## Toward an Integrative Account of Emotional Development

We have examined pathways in the development of pride- and shame-related emotions in the United States and China, focusing mainly on changes in appraisal and action components of these states. Our analysis illustrates how components of emotions come together to produce similarities and differences in the ways that systems interact to produce different dynamic emotional pathways in development. It demonstrates how to use a dynamic component systems approach to analyze specific developmental pathways.

What are the appropriate roles of appraisal, action, and phenomenal experience in a theory of emotional development? How can we understand the contributions of culture, social interaction, individual activity, and biology to the development of emotions? Although we have focused on the roles of appraisal, action, and culture in emotion, our approach to emotional development cannot be regarded as either a cognitive or a cultural one. Instead, in a dynamic component systems approach, no single component system is primary in the constitution of an emotional state. Emotional states are defined in terms of the coordination of appraisal, affect, and action systems as they mutually regulate each other both within and between persons. Emotional experiences self-organize into a series of different, relatively stable forms that nonetheless exhibit a large number of dynamic variations. It follows that there is no single or fixed plan for the organization of any given class of emotion but that there are modal patterns or prototypes (attractors in dynamic systems terms) that define common patterns. Emotions are constituted by processes that occur among component systems rather than as a function of any particular component system itself.

Emotions undergo developmental transformations as a result of interactions that occur among component systems that operate at a variety of hierarchical levels. At the level of the individual experience and activity, emotions consist of appraisal-affect-action coordinations. Simultaneously, emotions are embodied in a series of relatively distinct and biologically canalized emotion systems in the brain and viscera. At the level of social interaction, emotions are jointly constructed as individuals adjust their component systems to the ongoing and anticipated actions of their social partners. At the level of culture, emotions are transformed by cultural meanings, values, and practices that frame, constrain, and help organize the lower order biological, individual, and dyadic activity. Thus emotions develop as a result of interactions that occur between and among biological, personal, and sociocultural systems instead of as a result of any one of these categories of processes in isolation.

For example, the developmental pathways for pride and shame build on partially distinct biological systems, presumably behavioral approach systems for pride and behavioral avoidance systems for shame (Gray, 1994). At the same time, the development and functioning of biological systems themselves are not sufficient to account for the emotional changes that we described. At the level of individual activity and experience, pride and shame are organized psychologically by the need to construct a worthy sense of self within one's local social and cultural group.

The self-representations that mediate such experiences are not constructed by isolated individuals but by people in social interactions that vary as a function of social context and culture. For example, in American dyads, pride experiences develop as socialization agents praise children's accomplishments; shame experiences develop in social contexts in which children are made aware of their flawed identities. In contrast, in China, modest self-harmonization develops as parents efface their children's accomplishments while relatives and other significant others praise them; shame is a normative emotion that develops as parents use explicit shaming techniques to socialize filial piety in children. Variations in the social interactions are embedded in larger cultural meaning systems, including American individualism and Chinese Confucianism.

Although we have highlighted the contributions of culture to the development of emotion, it follows from a dynamic component systems view that individuals are not simply subject to their social and cultural contexts. We are active participants in the process of our own emotional development (Fischer & Bidell, 1998; Mascolo et al., 1997). There are bound to be differences between individuals, even within cultures, in the pathways that emotions take in their development. Our pathways merely represent predicted general trends across the two cultures and should not be taken as a precise account of development for all people in the United States and China. Although the foregoing analysis is predicated on the notion that meaningful cultural differences exist between the two countries, neither culture is monolithic. Collectivist concerns and modes of relating often occur in Western society, and individualist concerns occur in Chinese culture (see Raeff, 1998). For example, shame-based codes and honor moralities have figured prominently in American culture and history, with prominent examples in the South (Cohen, Vandello, & Rantilla, 1998), under colonial Puritanism (Hawthorne, 1840/1994), and in the eighteenth-century practice of dueling (such as the fatal duel between political leaders Alexander Hamilton and Aaron Burr). Conversely, Chinese individuals are capable of experiencing typically Western emotions such as pride and guilt, and they practice nonintegrative shaming in response to legal violations and sexual taboos (Vagg, 1998). More individualist emotions may be increasing in modern China, as they have in the modern United States.

Dynamic component systems theory offers an integrative approach for understanding emotion and its development. Like differential emotions theory (Ackerman, Abe, & Izard, 1998; Izard, 1991) and other biologically oriented approaches (Panksepp, Knutson, & Pruitt, 1998), it supports the usefulness of analyzing distinct yet interacting affective and cognitive subsystems. Emotions cannot be understood in terms of any given component system in isolation without violating key concepts of the theory:

First, emotions consist of intentional states—that is, emotions are *about* something (Solomon, 1976)—and, therefore, appraisal processes are an important element not simply in the generation of intentions but also in their very constitution (Solomon, 1997). Second, although differential emotions theory maintains that distinct affective and cognitive systems interact, their interaction is limited to invariant feelings that become attached to changing cognitive structures (Ackerman, Abe, & Izard, 1998). The concept of mutual regulation of component systems implies that affect, appraisal, and other systems modulate each other. Affect does not simply organize appraisal; appraisal also organizes affect. Within any given category of emotions, subtle differences in appraisal and action promote subtle differences in feeling tone and phenomenal experience, so that, for example, American pride "feels" different from Chinese self-harmonization.

A dynamic component systems approach draws on appraisal (Lazarus, 1991; Roseman, 1984) and functionalist approaches to emotion as well (Barrett, 1998; Campos, 1994; Frijda & Mesquita, 1998). It embraces the idea that emotional experiences consist of multicomponent processes, and it extends functionalist approaches by invoking dynamic concepts such as self-organization and mutual regulation to explain the processes by which emotional syndromes arise and take shape (see Camras, 1992). Further, unlike some versions of functionalist theory (Barrett, 1998), this view embraces the analysis of developmental transformations or levels in the organization of emotional experiences (see also Sroufe, 1996).

Finally, a dynamic component systems approach draws on social process (Fogel et al., 1992; Dickson, Fogel, & Messinger, 1998) and social constructionist models (Harré, 1996; Lutz, 1988) of emotion. Like social process theory, this approach holds that any emotional experience arises on-line in coregulated interactions that occur between people. Like social constructionist approaches, it maintains that as children develop the capacity to represent and reconstruct cultural meanings from their social interactions, their appraisals and actions that compose emotional experiences undergo developmental change. With increased development, emotional experiences develop in the direction of culturally valued ideals. However, unlike social constructionist approaches, emotional experiences cannot be seen as only social or cultural constructions. Emotional experience emerges not only as a product of processes that occur between people but also as a result of coactions that occur within individuals, including biologically canalized emotion systems.

From a dynamic component systems view, it is a mistake to view biology and culture as independent forces. Instead, they work together and are inseparable as causal processes in emotional development (Fischer & Bidell, 1998; Fischer et al., 1998; Mascolo et al., 1997). Only by building frameworks and methods that include the multiple processes which produce emotions and emotional development can scientists go beyond simplistic approaches to build a deep understanding of human activity and experience.

## NOTE

1. The concept of emotional state reflects a "third person" perspective on an individual's emotion. That is, it refers to the patterning of those motive-relevant physiological, psychological, and interpersonal changes that are observable (such as statements, facial expressions, actions) or potentially observable (as with instruments to record physiological changes) to others, independent of whether they are accessible by the emoting individual him- or herself. The concept of emotional experience reflects a first-person point of view—the subjective or phenomenal aspects of component systems as they function in the context of a motive-relevant event (see Kagan, 1994; Mascolo & Harkins, 1998).

## REFERENCES

Ackerman, B. P., Abe, J. A. A., & Izard, C. E. (1998). Differential emotions theory and emotional development: Mindful of modularity. In M. F. Mascolo & S. Griffin (Eds.), *What develops in emotional development?* (pp. 85–106). New York: Plenum.

Atkinson, J. W. (1957). Motivational determinants of risk-taking behavior. *Psychological Review, 64*, 359–363.

Averill, J. R. (1982). *Anger and aggression: An essay on emotion.* New York: Springer-Verlag.

Averill, J. R., Malmstrom, E. J., Koriat, A., & Lazarus, R. S. (1972). Habituation to complex emotional stimuli. *Journal of Abnormal Psychology, 80*, 20–28.

Banse, R., & Scherer, K. R. (1996). Acoustic profiles in vocal emotion expression. *Journal of Personality and Social Psychology, 70*, 614–636.

Barrett, K. C. (1998). A functionalist perspective to the development of emotions. In M. F. Mascolo & S. Griffin (Eds.), *What develops in emotional development?* (pp. 109–133). New York: Plenum.

Barrett, K. C., & Campos, J. J. (1987). Perspectives on emotional development: 2. A functional approach to emotions. In J. D. Osofsky (Ed.), *Handbook of infant development* (2nd ed., pp. 555–578). New York: Wiley.

Barrett, K. C., & Nelson-Goens, G. (1997). Emotion communication and the development of the social emotions. In K. C. Barrett (Ed.), *New directions for child development. Vol. 77. The communication of emotion: Current research from diverse perspectives* (pp. 69–88). San Francisco, CA: Jossey-Bass.

Barrett, K. C., Zahn-Waxler, C., & Cole, P. A. (1993). Avoiders vs. amenders: Implications for the investigation of guilt and shame during toddlerhood? *Cognition and Emotion, 7*, 481–505.

Bell, M. A., & Fox, N. A. (1994). Brain development over the first year of life: Relations between electroencephalographic frequency and coherence and cognitive and affective behaviors. In G. Dawson & K. W. Fischer (Eds.), *Human behavior and the developing brain* (pp. 314–345). New York: Guilford Press.

Bellah, R. N., Madsen, R., Sullivan, W. M., Swidler, A., & Tipton, S. M. (1985). *Habits of the heart.* New York: Harper & Row.

Bertenthal, B. L., & Fischer, K. W. (1978). Development of self-recognition in the infant. *Developmental Psychology, 14*, 44–50.

Bidell, T., & Fischer, K. W. (1992). Beyond the stage debate: Action, structure, and variability in Piagetian theory and research. In R. J. Sternberg & C. A. Berg (Eds.), *Intellectual development* (pp. 100–140). New York: Cambridge University Press.

Bidell, T. R., & Fischer, K. W. (1997). Between nature and nurture: The role of human agency in the epigenesis of intelligence. In R. Sternberg & E. Grigorenko (Eds.), *Intelligence: Heredity and environment* (pp. 193–242). New York: Cambridge University Press.

Bond, M. H., Leung, K., & Wan, K.-C. (1982). The social impact of self-effacing attributions: The Chinese case. *Journal of Social Psychology, 118*, 157–166.

Braithwaite, J. (1989). *Crime, shame and reintegration.* Cambridge, England: Cambridge University Press.

Brentano, F. (1874). *Psychology from an empirical standpoint.* London: Routledge & Kegan Paul.

Bretherton, I., & Beeghly, M. (1982). Talking about internal states: The acquisition of an explicit theory of mind. *Developmental Psychology, 18*, 906–921.

Briggs, J. (1970). *Never in anger.* Cambridge, MA: Harvard University Press.

Brown, T. (1994). Affective dimensions of meaning. In W. T. Overton & D. S. Palermo (Eds.), *The nature and ontogenesis of meaning* (pp. 167–190). Hillsdale, NJ: Erlbaum.

Brown, T., & Kozak, A. (1998). Emotion and the possibility of psychologists entering into heaven. In M. F. Mascolo & S. Griffin (Eds.), *What develops in emotional development?* (pp. 135–155). New York: Plenum.

Cacioppo, J. T., Berntson, G. G., Klein, D. J., & Poehlmann, K. M. (1998). Psychophysiology of emotion across the life span. In K. W. Schaie & M. P. Lawton (Eds.), *Annual review of gerontology and geriatrics: Vol. 17. Focus on emotion and adult development* (pp. 27–74). New York: Springer.

Cacioppo, J. T., Priester, J. R. & Berntson, G. G. (1993). Rudimentary determinants of attitude: 2. Arm flexion and extension have differential effects on attitudes. *Journal of Personality and Social Psychology, 65*, 5–17.

Campos, J. J. (1994, Spring). The new functionalism in emotion. *SRCD Newsletter*, 1–14.

Camras, L. A. (1992). Expressive development and basic emotions. *Cognition and Emotion, 6*, 269–283.

Carver, M., & Scheier, C. (1981). *Attention and self-regulation.* New York: Springer-Verlag.

Chen, R. (1993). Responding to compliments: A contrastive study of politeness strategies between American English and Chinese speakers. *Journal of Pragmatics, 20*, 49–75.

Cheng, C.-L. (1998). *Constructing self-representations through social comparison in peer relations: The development of Taiwanese grade-school children.* Unpublished doctoral dissertation, Harvard Graduate School of Education, Harvard University.

Cocroft, B.-A., K., & Ting-Toomey, S. (1994). Facework in Japan and the United States. *International Journal of Intercultural Relations, 18*, 469–506.

Cohen, D., Vandello, J., & Rantilla, A. K. (1998). The sacred and the social: Cultures of honor and violence. In P. Gilbert & B. Andrews (Eds.), *Shame: Interpersonal behavior, psychopathology, and culture* (pp. 261–282). New York: Oxford University Press.

Davidson, R. J. (1992). Emotion and affective style: Hemispheric substrates. *Psychological Science, 3,* 39–43.

Davidson, R. J. (1994). Complexities in the search for emotion-specific physiology. In P. Ekman & R. J. Davidson (Eds.), *The nature of emotion* (pp. 237–247). New York: Oxford University Press.

Dawson, G. (1994). Frontal electroencephalographic correlates of individual differences in emotion expression in infants: A brain systems perspective on emotion. In N. Fox (Ed.), *Monographs of the Society for Research in Child Development: Vol. 59. The development of emotion regulation: Biological and behavioral considerations* (2–3, Serial No. 240); pp. 135–151.

de Rivera, J. (1981). The structure of anger. In J. H. de Rivera (Ed.), *Conceptual encounter* (pp. 35–82). Washington, DC: University Press of America.

de Rivera, J., Possell, L., Verette, J. A., & Weiner, B. (1989). Distinguishing elation, gladness and joy. *Journal of Personality and Social Psychology, 57,* 1015–1023.

Dickson, K. L., Fogel, A., & Messinger, D. (1998). The development of emotion from a social process view. In M. F. Mascolo & S. Griffin (Eds.), *What develops in emotional development?* (pp. 253–271). New York: Plenum.

Dickson, K. L., Walker, H., & Fogel, A. (1997). The relationship between smile type and play type during parent-infant play. *Developmental Psychology, 33,* 925–933.

Dumont, L. (1992). *Essays on individualism.* Chicago: University of Chicago Press.

Dunn, J., Bretherton, I., & Munn, P. (1987). Conversations about feeling states between mothers and their young children. *Developmental Psychology, 23,* 132–139.

Dweck, C. S., & Leggett, E. L. (1988). A social-cognitive approach to motivation and personality. *Psychological Review, 95,* 256–273.

Ekman, P. (1989). The argument and evidence about universals in facial expressions of emotion. In H. Wagner & A. Manstead (Eds.), *Handbook of social psychophysiology* (pp. 143–164). Chichester, England: Wiley.

Ekman, P., & Friesen, W. V. (1971). Constants across cultures in the face and emotion. *Journal of Personality and Social Psychology, 17,* 124–129.

Ekman, P., Levenson, R. W., & Friesen, W. V. (1983). Autonomic nervous system activity distinguishes between emotions. *Science, 221,* 1208–1210.

Emerson, R. W. (1990). *Selected essays, lectures, and poems.* New York: Bantam Books. (Original work published 1841)

Fernald, A. (1993). Approval and disapproval: Infant responsiveness to vocal affect in familiar and unfamiliar languages. *Child Development, 64,* 657–674.

Fischer, K. W. (1980). A theory of cognitive development: The control and construction of hierarchies of skills. *Psychological Review, 87,* 447–531.

Fischer, K. W., & Bidell, T. (1998). Dynamic development of psychological structures in action and thought. In W. Damon (Series Ed.), E. R. Lerner (Vol. Ed.), *Handbook of Child Psychology: Vol 1* (5th ed., pp. 467–561). *Theory.* New York: Wiley.

Fischer, K. W., Rotenberg, E. J., Bullock, D. H., & Raya, P. (1993). The dynamics of competence: How context contributes directly to skill. In R. Wozniak & K. W. Fischer (Eds.), *Development in context: Acting and thinking in specific environments* (pp. 93–117). Hillsdale, NJ: Erlbaum.

Fischer, K. W., Shaver, P. R., & Carnochan, P. (1990). How emotions develop and how they organize development. *Cognition and Emotion, 4,* 81–128.

Fischer, K. W., & Tangney, J. P. (1995). Self-conscious emotions and the affect revolution: Framework and overview. In J. P. Tangney & K. W. Fischer (Eds.), *Self-conscious emotions: Shame, guilt, embarrassment and pride* (pp. 3–22). New York: Guilford Press.

Fischer, K. W., Wang, L., Kennedy, B., & Cheng, C. (1998). Culture and biology in emotional development. In D. Sharma & K. W. Fischer (Eds.), *New directions for child development: Vol. 81. Socioemotional development across cultures* (pp. 21–48). San Francisco: Jossey-Bass.

Fischer, K. W., Yan, Z., & Stewart, J. (in press). Cognitive development in adulthood: Dynamics of variation and consolidation. In J. Valsiner & K. Connolly (Eds.), *Handbook of developmental psychology.* Thousand Oaks, CA: Sage.

Fogel, A. (1993). *Developing through relationships.* Chicago: University of Chicago Press.

Fogel, A., Nwokah, E., Dedo, J. Y., Messinger, D., Dickson, K. L., Matusov, E., & Holt, S. A. (1992). Social process theory of emotion: A dynamic systems perspective. *Social Development, 1,* 122–142.

Forgas, J. P. (Ed.) (1991). *Emotion and social judgments.* Oxford, England: Pergamon.

Forgas, J. P. (1997). Asking nicely? The effects of mood on responding to more or less polite requests. *Personality and Social Psychology Bulletin, 24,* 173–185.

Forgas, J. P. (1999). On feeling good and being rude: Affective influences on language use and request formulations. *Journal of Personality and Social Psychology, 76,* 928–939.

Forgas, J. P., & Fiedler, K. (1996). Us and them: Mood effects on intergroup discrimination. *Journal of Personality and Social Psychology, 70,* 28–40.

Fox, N. (1994). Dynamic cerebral processes underlying emotion regulation. In N. Fox (Ed.), *Monographs of the Society for Research in Child Development: Vol. 59. The development of emotion regulation: Biological and behavioral considerations* (2–3, Serial No. 240; pp. 152–166).

Frijda, N. (1986). *The emotions.* New York: Cambridge University Press.

Frijda, N., & Mesquita, B. (1998). The analysis of emotions: Dimensions of variation. In M. F. Mascolo & S. Griffin (Eds.), *What develops in emotional development?* (pp. 273–295). New York: Plenum.

Gabrenya, W. K., Jr., & Hwang, K. K. (1996). Chinese social interaction: Harmony and hierarchy on the good earth. In M. H. Bond (Ed.), *The handbook of Chinese psychology* (pp. 309–321). Hong Kong: Oxford University Press.

Gao, G., Ting-Toomey, S., & Gudykunst, W. (1996). Chinese communication processes. In M. H. Bond (Ed.), *The handbook of Chinese psychology* (pp. 280–293). Hong Kong: Oxford University Press.

Geertz, C. (1973). *The interpretation of cultures.* New York: Basic Books.

Geppert, U., & Kuster, U. (1983). The emergence of "Wanting to do it oneself": A precursor to achievement motivation. *International Journal of Behavioral Development, 3,* 355–369.

Gottlieb, G. (1997). *Synthesizing nature-nurture.* Mahwah, NJ: Erlbaum.

Gray, J. A. (1990). Brain systems that mediate both emotions and cognitions. In J. A. Gray (Ed.), *Psychobiolog-*

*ical aspects of relationships between emotion and cognition* (pp. 269–288). Hillsdale, NJ: Erlbaum.

Gray, J. A. (1994). The neuropsychology of emotions: Framework for a taxonomy of psychiatric disorders. In S. H. M. van Goozen, N. E. Van de Poll, & J. A. Sergeant (Eds.), *Emotions: Essays on emotion theory* (pp. 29–59). Hillsdale, NJ: Erlbaum.

Gray, J. A., Feldon, J., Rawlins, J. N. P., Hemsley, D. R., & Smith, A. D. (1991). The neuropsychology of schizophrenia. *Behavioral and Brain Sciences, 14*, 1–20.

Harré, R. (Ed.). (1996). *The social construction of emotions.* Cambridge, England: Blackwell.

Hawthorne, N. (1994). *The scarlet letter* New York: Dover. (Original work published 1850)

Heckhausen, H. (1984). Emergent achievement behavior: Some early developments. In J. Nicholls (Ed.), *Advances in motivation and achievement: Vol 3. The development of achievement motivation* (pp. 1–32). Greenwich, CT: JAI Press.

Heckhausen, H. (1987). Emotional components of action: Their ontogeny as reflected in achievement behavior. In D. Gorlitz & J. F. Wohlwill (Eds.), *Curiosity, imagination and play: On the development of spontaneous cognitive and motivational processes* (pp. 326–348). Hillsdale, NJ: Erlbaum.

Heckhausen, J. (1988). Becoming aware of one's competence in the second year: Developmental progression within the mother-child dyad. *International Journal of Behavioral Development, 3*, 305–326.

Hertel, G. (1999). Mood effects in social dilemmas: What we know so far. In M. Foddy & M. Smithsom (Eds.), *Resolving social dilemmas: Dynamic, structural, and intergroup aspects* (pp. 227–243). Philadelphia, PA: Taylor & Francis.

Hess, U., Kappas, A., McHugo, G. J., Lanzetta, J. T., & Kleck, R. E. (1992). The facilitative effect of facial expression on the self-generation of emotion. *International Journal of Psychophysiology, 12*, 251–265.

Hewitt, J. P. (1997). *The myth of self-esteem.* New York: St. Martin's Press.

Ho, D. Y. F. (1986). Chinese patterns of socialization: A critical review. In M. H. Bond (Ed.), *The psychology of the Chinese people* (pp. 1–37). Hong Kong: Oxford University Press.

Ho, D. Y. F. (1996). Filial piety and its psychological consequences. In M. H. Bond (Ed.), *The handbook of Chinese psychology* (pp. 155–165). Hong Kong: Oxford University Press.

Hochschild, A. (1979). Emotion work, feeling rules, and social structure. *American Journal of Sociology, 85*, 551–575.

Hoffman, M. (1982). Development of prosocial motivation: Empathy and guilt. In N. Eisenberg (Ed.), *The development of prosocial behavior* (pp. 281–313). New York: Academic Press.

Holden, G. W., Coleman, S. M., & Schmidt, K. L. (1995). Why 3-year-old children get spanked: Parent and child determinants as reported by college-educated mothers. *Merrill Palmer Quarterly, 41*, 431–452.

Hong, Y. Y., Chiu, C. Y., Dweck, C. S., Line, D. M. S., & Wan, W. (1999). Implicit theories, attributions, and coping: A meaning system approach. *Journal of Personality and Social Psychology, 77*, 588–599.

Hu, H. C. (1944). The Chinese concept of "face." *American Anthropologist, 46*, 45–64.

Isen, A. (1990). The influence of positive and negative af-fect on cognitive organization: Some implications for development. In N. L. Stein, B. Leventhal, & T. Trabasso (Eds.), *Psychological and biological approaches to emotion* (pp. 75–94). Hillsdale, NJ: Erlbaum.

Izard, C. (1991). *The psychology of emotions.* New York: Plenum.

James, D. (Producer). (1991). *Marian Anderson* [Film]. Washington, DC: WETA Public Television.

Jankowiak, W. R. (1993). *Sex, death, and hierarchy in a Chinese city: An anthropological account.* New York: Columbia University Press.

Johnson, F. (1985). The Western concept of self. In A. J. Marsella, G. DeVos, & F. L. K. Hsu (Eds.), *Culture and self* (pp. 91–138). New York: Tavistock.

Jouriles, E. N., & O'Leary, K. D. (1990). Influences of parental mood on parent behavior. In E. A. Blechman (Ed.), *Emotions and the family: For better or for worse* (pp. 181–199). Hillsdale, NJ: Erlbaum.

Kagan, J. (1981). *The second year: The emergence of self-awareness.* Cambridge, MA: Harvard University Press.

Kagan, J. (1984). *The nature of the child.* New York: Basic Books.

Kagan, J. (1994). On the nature of emotion. In N. Fox (Ed.) *Monographs of the Society for Research in Child Development: Vol. 59. The development of emotion regulation: Biological and behavioral considerations* (2–3, Serial No. 240; pp. 7–24).

Kamins, M. L., & Dweck, C. S. (1999). Person versus process praise and criticism: Implications for contingent self-worth and coping. *Developmental Psychology, 35*, 835–847.

Kitayama, S., Markus, H. R., & Kurokawa, M. (2000). Culture, emotion, and well-being: Good feelings in Japan and the United States. *Cognition & Emotion, 14*, 93–124.

Kitayama, S., Markus, H. R., & Matsumoto, H. (1995). Culture, self and emotion: A cultural perspective on self-conscious emotions. In J. Tangney & K. W. Fischer (Eds.), *Self-conscious emotions: The psychology of shame, guilt, embarrassment, and pride* (pp. 439–464). New York: Guilford Press.

Kohlberg, L. (1981). *Essays on moral development: The philosophy of moral development (Vol. 1).* San Francisco: Harper & Row.

Koriat, A., Melman, R., Averill, J. R., & Lazarus, R. S. (1972). The self-control of emotional reactions to a stressful film. *Journal of Personality, 40*, 601–619.

Laird, J. (1984). The real role of facial response in the experience of emotion: A reply to Tourangeau and Ellsworth, and others. *Journal of Personality and Social Psychology, 47*, 909–917.

Lazarus, R. S. (1991). *Emotion and adaptation.* New York: Oxford University Press.

Lazarus, R. S. (1999). *Stress and emotion: A new synthesis.* New York: Springer.

LeDoux, J. E. (1994). Emotion-specific physiological activity: Don't forget about CNS physiology. In P. Ekman & R. J. Davidson (Eds.), *The nature of emotion* (pp. 248–251). New York: Oxford University Press.

Lee, W. O. (1996). The cultural context for Chinese learners: Conceptions of learning in the Confucian tradition. In D. A. Watkins & J. B. Biggs (Eds.), *The Chinese learner* (pp. 45–67). Hong Kong: Comparative Education Research Centre (CERC) and The Australian Council for Educational Research (ACER).

Leech, G. N. (1983). *Principles of pragmatics*. London: Longman.

Leith, K. P., & Baumeister, R., F. (1996). Why do bad moods increase self-defeating behavior? Emotion, risk-taking, and self-regulation. *Journal of Personality and Social Psychology, 71*, 1250–1267.

Levenson, R. W., Carstensen, L. L., Friesen, W. V., & Ekman, P. (1991). Emotion, physiology and expression in old age. *Psychology and Aging, 6*, 28–35.

Levenson, R. W., Ekman, P., & Friesen, W. V. (1990). Voluntary facial action generates emotion-specific autonomic nervous system activity. *Psychophysiology, 6*, 28–35.

Levy, R. I. (1984). The emotions in comparative perspective. In K. R. Scherer & P. Ekman (Eds.), *Approaches to emotion* (pp. 397–412). Hillsdale, NJ: Erlbaum.

Lewis, H. B. (1971). *Shame and guilt in neurosis*. New York: International Universities Press.

Lewis, M. (1996). *Shame*. New York: Basic Books.

Lewis, M. (1998). The structure of emotional experience. In M. F. Mascolo & S. Griffin (Eds.), *What develops in emotional development?* (pp. 29–50). New York: Plenum.

Lewis, M., Alessandri, S., & Sullivan, M. W. (1992). Differences in shame and pride as a function of children's gender and task difficulty. *Child Development, 63*, 630–638.

Lewis, M., & Brooks-Gunn, J. (1979). *Social cognition and the acquisition of self*. New York: Plenum.

Lewis, M., Sullivan M. W., & Michalson, L. (1984). The cognition-emotion fugue. In C. E. Izard, J. Kagan, & R. B. Zajonc (Eds.), *Emotions, cognition and behavior* (pp. 264–288). New York: Cambridge University Press.

Lewis, M. D. (1995). Cognition-emotion feedback and the self-organization of developmental paths. *Human Development, 38*, 71–102.

Lewis, M. D. (1997). Personality self-organization: Cascading constraints on cognition-emotion interaction. In A. Fogel, M. C. Lyra, & J. Valsiner (Eds.), *Dynamics and indeterminism in developmental and social processes*. Mahwah, NJ: Erlbaum.

Lewis, M. D., & Douglas, L. (1998). A dynamic systems approach to cognition-emotion interactions in development. In M. F. Mascolo & S. Griffin (Eds.), *What develops in emotional development?* (pp. 159–188). New York: Plenum.

Lewis, M. D., & Granic, I. (Eds.). (2000). *Emotions, self-organization, and development*. New York: Cambridge University Press.

Li, J. (1997). *The Chinese "heart and mind for wanting to learn" (hao-xue-xin): A culturally based learning model*. Unpublished doctoral dissertation. Harvard University.

Li, J. (in press). A cultural model of learning: Chinese "heart and mind for wanting to learn." *Journal of Cross-Cultural Psychology*.

Lindsay-Hartz, J., de Rivera, J., & Mascolo, M. F. (1995). Guilt and shame and their effects on motivation. In K. W. Fischer & J. P. Tangney (Eds.), *Self-conscious emotions: Shame, guilt, embarrassment and pride* (pp. 274–300). New York: Guilford Press.

Locke, J. (1975). *The second treatise of government*. Indianapolis, IN: Bobbs-Merrill. (Original work published 1764)

Lutkenhaus, P. (1984). Pleasure derived from mastery in three-year-olds: Its function for persistence and the influence of maternal behavior. *International Journal of Behavioral Development, 7*, 343–358.

Lutz, C. (1988). *Unnatural emotions*. Chicago: University of Chicago Press.

Maehr, M. L. (1974). Culture and achievement motivation. *American Psychologist, 29*, 887–896.

Maehr, M. L., & Nicholls, J. G. (1980). Culture and achievement motivation: A second look. In N. Warren (Ed.), *Studies in cross-cultural psychology* (pp. 221–267). New York: Academic Press.

Mandler, G. (1984). *Mind and body*. New York: Norton.

Marcel, A. J. (1983). Conscious and unconscious perception: Experiments on visual masking and word recognition. *Cognitive Psychology, 15*, 197–237.

Marsella, A. J. (1980). Depressive experience and disorder across cultures. In H. C. Triandis & J. G. Draguns (Eds.), *Handbook of cross-cultural psychology: Vol. 6. Psychopathology* (pp. 237–289). Boston: Allyn & Bacon.

Markus, H. R., & Kitayama, S. (1991). Culture and the self: Implications for cognition, emotion, and motivation. *Psychological Review, 98*, 224–253.

Mascolo, M. F., & Fischer, K. W. (1995). Developmental transformations in appraisals for pride, shame and guilt. In J. Tangney & K. W. Fischer (Eds.), *Self-conscious emotions: The psychology of shame, guilt, embarrassment and pride* (pp. 64–113). New York: Guilford Press.

Mascolo, M. F., & Fischer, K. W. (1998). The development of self through the coordination of component systems. In M. Ferrari & R. Sternberg (Eds.), *Self-awareness: Its nature and development* (pp. 332–384). New York: Guilford Press.

Mascolo, M. F., Fischer, K. W., & Neimeyer, R. A. (1999). The dynamic co-development of intentionality, self and social relations. In J. Brandstadter & R. M. Lerner (Eds.), *Action and development: Origins and functions of intentional self-development* (pp. 133–166). Thousand Oaks, CA: Sage.

Mascolo, M. F., & Griffin, S. (Eds.). (1998). *What develops in emotional development?* New York: Plenum.

Mascolo, M. F., & Harkins, D. (1998). Toward a component systems model of emotional development. In M. F. Mascolo & S. Griffin (Eds.), *What develops in emotional development?* (pp. 189–217). New York: Plenum.

Mascolo, M. F., Harkins, D., & Harakal, T. (2000). The dynamic construction of emotion: Varieties in anger. In M. Lewis & I. Grinka (Eds.), *Emotion, self-organization and development* (pp. 125–152). New York: Cambridge University Press.

Mascolo, M. F., Li, J., Fink, R., & Fischer, K. W. (in press). Pathways to excellence: Value presuppositions and the development of academic and affective skills in educational contexts. In M. Ferrari (Ed.), *The pursuit of excellence in education*. Mahwah, NJ: Erlbaum.

Mascolo, M. F., Pollack, R., & Fischer, K. W. (1997). Keeping the constructor in development: An epigenetic systems approach. *Journal of Constructivist Psychology, 10*, 27–51.

Massaro, T. M. (1997). The meanings of shame: Implications for legal reform. *Psychology, Public Policy, and Law, 3*, 645–704.

Matsumoto, D. (1987). The role of facial response in the experience of emotion: More methodological problems and a meta-analysis. *Journal of Personality and Social Psychology, 53*, 769–774.

McClelland, D. (1961). *The achieving society.* Princeton, NJ: Van Nostrand.

Mecca, A. M., Smelser, N. J., & Vasconcellos, J. (Eds.) (1989). *The social importance of self-esteem.* Berkeley: University of California Press.

Mikula, G., Scherer, K. R., & Athenstaedt, U. (1998). The role of injustice in the elicitation of differential emotional reactions. *Personality and Social Psychology Bulletin, 24,* 769–783.

Mill, J. S. (1986). *On liberty.* Buffalo, NY: Prometheus Books. (Original work published 1859)

Miller, G. A., Galanter, E., & Pribram, K. H. (1960). *Plans and the structure of behavior.* New York: Holt, Rinehart & Winston.

Miller, P., & Sperry, S. (1987). The socialization of anger and aggression. *Merrill Palmer Quarterly, 33,* 1–31.

Mumme, D. L., Fernald, A., & Herrera, C. (1996). Infants' responses to facial and vocal emotional signals in a social referencing paradigm. *Child Development, 67,* 3219–3237.

Munz, D. C., & Fallert, A. L. (1998). Does classroom setting moderate the relationship between student mood and teaching evaluations? *Journal of Social Behavior and Personality, 13,* 23–32.

Nathanson, D. (1987). *The many faces of shame.* New York: Guilford Press.

Nicholls, J. G. (1976). Effort is virtuous, but it's better to have ability: Evaluative responses to perceptions of effort and ability. *Journal of Research in Personality, 10,* 306–315.

Nwokah, E., Davies, P., Islam, A., Hsu, H., & Fogel, A. (1993). Vocal affect in three-year olds: A quantitative acoustic analysis of child laughter. *Acoustical Society of America, 94,* 3076–3090.

Nwokah, E., Hsu, H., Dobrowolska, O., & Fogel, A. (1994). The development of laughter in mother-infant communication: Timing patterns and temporal sequences. *Infant Behavior and Development, 16,* 23–25.

Panksepp, J. (1998). *Affective neuroscience: The foundations of human and animal emotions.* New York: Oxford University Press.

Panksepp, J., Knutson, B., & Pruitt, D. L. (1998). Toward a neuroscience of emotion: The epigenetic foundations of emotional development. In M. F. Mascolo & S. Griffin (Eds.), *What develops in emotional development?* (pp. 53–83). New York: Plenum.

Parkinson, B. (1999). Relations and dissociations between appraisal and emotion ratings of reasonable and unreasonable anger and guilt. *Cognition and Emotion, 13,* 347–385.

Pipp, S., Fischer, K. W., & Jennings, S. (1987). Acquisition of self and mother knowledge in infancy. *Developmental Psychology, 23,* 86–96.

Potter, S. H. (1988) The cultural construction of emotion in rural Chinese social life. *Ethos, 16,* 181–208.

Powers, W. T. (1973). *Behavior: The control of perception.* Chicago, IL: Aldine.

Raeff, C. (1998). Individuals in relationships: Cultural values, children's social interactions, and the development of an American individualist self. *Developmental Review, 17,* 205–238.

Reissland, N. (1994). The socialization of pride in young children. *International Journal of Behavioral Development, 17,* 541–552.

Riskind, J. H. (1984). They stoop to conquer: Guiding and self-regulatory functions of physical posture after success and failure. *Journal of Personality and Social Psychology, 47,* 479–493.

Robinson, M. D. (1998) Running from William James' bear: A review of preattentive mechanisms and their contributions to emotional experience. *Cognition and Emotion, 12,* 667–696.

Rogoff, B. (1993). Children's guided participation and participatory appropriation in sociocultural activity. In R. H. Wozniak & K. W. Fischer (Eds.), *Development in context: Acting and thinking in specific environments* (pp. 121–153). Hillsdale, NJ: Erlbaum.

Rosch, E. (1978). Principles of categorization. In E. Rosch (Ed.), *Cognition and categorization* (pp. 28–49). Hillsdale, NJ: Erlbaum.

Roseman, I. J. (1984). Cognitive determinants of emotions: A structural theory. In P. Shaver (Ed.), *Review of Personality and Social Psychology* (Vol. 5, pp. 11–36). Beverly Hills, CA: Sage.

Roseman, I. J. (1991). Appraisal determinants of discrete emotions. *Cognition and Emotion, 5,* 161–200.

Roseman, I. J., Antoniou, A. A., & Jose, P. E. (1996). Appraisal determinants of emotions: Constructing a more accurate and comprehensive theory. *Cognition and Emotion, 10,* 241–277.

Roseman, I. J., Spindel, M. S., & Jose, P. E. (1990). Appraisals of emotion-eliciting events: Testing a theory of discrete emotions. *Journal of Personality and Social Psychology, 59,* 899–915.

Russell, J. A. (1991). In defense of a prototype approach to emotion concepts. *Journal of Personality and Social Psychology, 60,* 37–47.

Russell, J. A., & Yik, M. S. M. (1996). Emotion among the Chinese. In M. H. Bond (Ed.), *The handbook of Chinese psychology* (pp. 166–188). Hong Kong: Oxford University Press.

Saarni, C. (1984). An observational study of children's attempts to monitor their expressive behavior. *Child Development, 55,* 1504–1513.

Saarni, C. (1990). Emotional competence: How emotions and relationships become integrated. In R. A. Thompson & A. Ross (Eds.), *Nebraska Symposium on Motivation: Vol. 36. Socioemotional development.* (pp. 115–182). Lincoln: University of Nebraska Press.

Salovey, P., Mayer, J. D., & Rosenhan, D. L. (1991). Mood and helping: Mood as a motivator of helping and helping as a regulator of mood. In M. S. Clark (Ed.), *Review of personality and social psychology: Vol. 12. Prosocial behavior* (pp. 215–237). Newbury Park, CA: Sage.

Sampson, E. E. (1994). *Celebrating the other: A dialogical account of human nature.* Boulder, CO: Westview Press.

Schachter, S., & Singer, J. (1962). Cognitive, social and physiological determinants of emotional state. *Psychological Review, 69,* 370–399.

Scherer, K. (1994). Toward a concept of "modal emotions." In P. Ekman & R. J. Davidson (Eds.), *The nature of emotion* (pp. 25–31). New York: Oxford University Press.

Scherer, K. (1997). Profiles of emotion-antecedent appraisal: Testing theoretical predictions across cultures. *Cognition and Emotion, 11,* 113–150.

Schore, A. (1998). Early shame experiences and infant brain development. In P. Gilbert & B. Andrews (Eds.), *Shame: Interpersonal behavior, psychopathology, and culture* (pp. 57–77). New York: Oxford University Press.

Searle, J. R. (1980). *Intentionality*. Cambridge, England: Cambridge University Press.

Shaver, P., Schwartz, J., Kirson, D., & O'Connor, C. (1987). Emotion knowledge: Further exploration of a prototype approach. *Journal of Personality and Social Psychology, 52*, 1061–1086.

Shaver, P. R., Wu, S., & Schwartz, J. C. (1992). Cross-cultural similarities and differences in emotion and its representation: A prototype approach. In M. S. Clark (Ed.), *Review of personality and social psychology* (Vol. 13). Thousand Oaks, CA: Sage.

Shweder, R., & LeVine, R. A. (Eds.). (1984). *Culture theory*. New York: Cambridge University Press.

Smith, C. A., & Ellsworth, P. C. (1985). Patterns of cognitive appraisal in emotion. *Journal of Personality and Social Psychology, 48*, 813–838.

Smith, C. A., & Ellsworth, P. C. (1987). Patterns of appraisal and emotion related to taking an exam. *Journal of Personality and Social Psychology, 52*, 475–488.

Smith, C. A., & Lazarus, R. S. (1990). Emotion and adaptation. In L. A. Pervin (Ed.), *Handbook of Personality: Theory and research* (pp. 609–637). New York: Guilford Press.

Solomon, R. (1976). *The passions*. New York: Doubleday.

Solomon, R. (1980). Emotions and choice. In A. O. Rorty (Ed.), *Explaining emotions*. Berkeley: University of California Press.

Solomon, R. (1997). Beyond ontology: Ideation, phenomenology and the cross cultural study of emotion. *Journal for the Theory of Social Behavior, 27*, 289–303.

Sroufe, L. A. (1996). *Emotional development*. New York: Cambridge.

Stipek, D. (1995). The development of pride and shame in toddlers. In J. P. Tangney & K. W. Fischer (Eds.), *Self-conscious emotions: Shame, guilt, embarrassment and pride* (pp. 237–252). New York: Guilford Press.

Stipek, D. (1999). Differences between Americans and Chinese in the circumstances evoking pride, shame, and guilt. *Journal of Cross-Cultural Psychology, 29*, 616–629.

Stipek, D. J., Recchia, S., & McClintic, S. (1992). Self-evaluation in young children. *Monographs of the Society for Research in Child Development, 57* (1, Serial No. 226).

Tangney, J. P., Burggraf, S. A., & Wagner, P. E. (1995). Shame-proneness, guilt-proneness, and psychological symptoms. In J. P. Tangney & K. W. Fischer (Eds.), *Self-conscious emotions: Shame, guilt, embarrassment and pride* (pp. 343–367). New York: Guilford Press.

Thelen, E. (1990). Dynamic systems and the generation of individual differences. In J. Colombo & J. Fagen (Eds.), *Individual differences in infancy: Reliability, stability, prediction* (pp. 19–43). Hillsdale, NJ: Erlbaum.

Tomkins, S. S. (1962). *Affect, imagery, consciousness: Vol. 1. The positive affects*. New York: Springer.

Tourangeau, R., & Ellsworth, P. C. (1979). The role of facial response in the experience of emotion. *Journal of Personality and Social Psychology, 37*, 1519–1531.

Trevarthen, C. (1984). Emotions as regulators of contact and relationships with persons. In P. Ekman & K. Scherer (Eds.), *Approaches to emotion* (pp. 129–162). Hillsdale, NJ: Erlbaum.

Trevarthen, C. (1993). The self born in intersubjectivity: The psychology of an infant communicating. In U. Neisser (Ed.), *Emory Symposia in Cognition: Vol. 5. The perceived self: Ecological and interpersonal sources of self-knowledge* (pp. 121–173). New York: Cambridge University Press.

Trevarthen, C., & Hubley, P. (1978). Secondary intersubjectivity: Confidence, confiding and acts of meaning in the first year. In A. Lock (Ed.), *Action, gesture and symbol: The emergence of language* (pp. 183–227). New York: Academic Press.

Tronick, E. Z. (1989). Emotions and emotional communication in infants. *American Psychologist, 44*, 112–119.

Tu, W. M. (1979). *Humanity and self-cultivation: Essays in Confucian thought*. Berkeley, CA: Asian Humanities Press.

Tu, W. M. (1985). Selfhood and otherness in Confucian thought. In A. J. Marsella, G. DeVos, & F. L. K. Hsu (Eds.), *Culture and self: Asian and Western perspectives* (pp. 231–251). New York: Tavistock.

Turiel, E. (1983). *The development of social knowledge: Morality and convention*. Cambridge, England: Cambridge University Press.

Vagg, J. (1998). Delinquency and shame. *British Journal of Criminology, 38*, 247–264.

Vygotsky, L. (1978). *Mind in society*. Cambridge, MA: Harvard University Press.

Walbott, H. G. (1998). Bodily expression of emotion. *European Journal of Social Psychology, 28*, 879–896.

Wang, L. (1994). Analysis of Chinese shame structure. Cambridge, MA: Harvard University, Cognitive Development Laboratory Report.

Wang, L., Li, J., & Fischer, K. W. (2000). The organization of shame words in Chinese (Rep. No.). Cambridge, MA: Harvard University, Cognitive Development Laboratory.

Wang, Q., & Leichtman, M. D. (2000). Same beginnings, different stories: A comparison of American and Chinese children's narratives. *Child Development, 71*, 1329–1346.

Watson, J. S., & Ramey, C. T. (1972). Reactions to response-contingent stimulation in early infancy. *Merrill-Palmer Quarterly, 18*, 219–227.

Weiner, B. (1985). An attributional theory of achievement motivation and emotion. *Psychological Review, 92*, 548–573.

Wu, D. Y. H. (1996). Chinese childhood socialization. In M. H. Bond (Ed.), *The handbook of Chinese psychology* (pp. 143–154). Hong Kong: Oxford University Press.

Wu, D. Y. H., & Tseng, W. S. (1985). Introduction: The characteristics of Chinese culture. In W. S. Tseng & D. Y. H. Wu (Eds.), *Chinese culture and mental health* (pp. 3–13). New York: Academic Press.

Wu, S.-P., & Lai, C.-Y. (1992). *Complete text of the Four Books and Five Classics in modern Chinese*. Beijing: International Culture Press.

Yang, K. S. (Ed.) (1988). *Chinese people's psychology* [Chinese]. Taipei: Gwei Gwan Tu Shu.

Yang, K. S. (1996). Psychological transformation of the Chinese people as a result of societal modernization. In M. H. Bond (Ed.), *The handbook of Chinese psychology* (pp. 479–498). Hong Kong: Oxford University Press.

Yu, A. B. (1996). Ultimate life concerns, self, and Chinese achievement motivation. In M. H. Bond (Ed.), *The handbook of Chinese psychology* (pp. 227–246). Hong Kong: Oxford University Press.

# IV

## Expression of Emotion

# 21

## INTRODUCTION: EXPRESSION OF EMOTION

Dacher Keltner and Paul Ekman

If Charles Darwin were alive today, he would certainly have been pleased, and probably blushed, to witness the empirical and theoretical developments that his 1872 book, *Expression of Emotion in Man and Animals*, generated. The first four chapters in this part pay homage to Darwin, reviewing literature on how emotion is expressed in the face (Keltner, Ekman, Gonzaga, & Beer), by voice (Scherer, Johnstone, & Klasmeyer), and in language (Reilly & Seibert) in humans, as well as in displays across various nonhuman species (Snowdon). These four chapters generally suggest, with the occasional qualifications that empirical study inevitably requires, that select emotions are communicated in distinct facial and vocal displays and in language, and that this is so across different cultures and in different species.

The last two chapters of this part broaden the meaning of emotional expression and ask how emotion is expressed in different art forms, a question that dates back to Aristotle, and certainly earlier. Gabrielsson and Juslin apply methods used in the study of facial expression and voice (i.e., encoding and decoding studies) to address whether and how emotion is communicated in music. Oatley explores the thesis that emotion, and especially misunderstood emotion, inspires expression in pictorial arts, architecture, and literature.

Much in these chapters would likely have been familiar to Darwin—in particular the interest in the evolutionary history of expression, culture and universality, the biological roots of expression, and the focus on discrete emotions. At the same time, the chapters consistently reveal

how scholars are taking the study of expression in striking new directions. Scholars are exploring how emotion is communicated in new modalities (language, odor, music). They are exploring relations between expression and central nervous system activity. Careful, observational research is revealing new functions of emotion (e.g., see Snowdon on how expression regulates reproductive physiology). And there are now systematic studies of how emotion varies according to culture, personality, and development.

In this chapter, we bring together the convergent insights offered by the different authors of this part. We summarize where the field stands on many of the questions that Darwin posed (e.g., How is emotion is expressed? Are these expressions universal?). At the same time, we highlight new developments in the field and suggest directions for future research.

### Expression of Emotion

The field of emotional expression looked very different 20 years ago. Most of the literature focused on the face, and most of the research was judgment studies of a limited set of emotions. There was little examination of how emotion is expressed in the voice, body, or language. Scholars in the nonhuman literature were reluctant to ascribe emotion to displays of nonhuman species.

The chapters in this part reveal how fast and far the field has moved in the past 20 years. Although many central questions are the same (How is emotion expressed? How are expressions perceived?), the extensions and discoveries are remarkable. The review of Keltner, Ekman, Gonzaga, and Beer indicates that select emotions have distinct facial expressions. Scherer, Johnstone, and Klasmeyer reveal that this is also true in the study of vocal expression. Snowdon's review suggests that many human displays of emotion have parallels in nonhuman species (and many displays of nonhumans point to interesting candidates in humans, as we detail later).

These findings are not likely to surprise the longstanding student of expression. In other ways, however, the chapters in this part reveal how much more complex the field's view of expression is than it was 20 years ago. For example, one widespread critique of the literature on expression is that researchers have focused on a limited set of emotions. The empirical studies have emphasized anger, contempt, disgust, fear, happiness, sadness, or surprise, but most theorists and lay people recognize many more states as emotions. The chapters here suggest that more emotions may be expressed than previously thought (and taxonomies that are based on expression may need revision). Chapter 22's review of recent studies indicates that love, sympathy, amusement, and embarrassment may have distinct nonverbal displays that satisfy the criteria used to establish other displays. Snowdon's chapter suggests that there may be more signals of positive emotion than have been assumed, and this is an immensely important possibility—namely, that in nonhuman primates there are coos and girns related to affiliative contact, copulation calls, and food calls, all of which may have counterparts in humans.

Another widespread critique of the literature on expression is that research has tended to focus on prototypical displays of emotion (and many call into question the ecological validity of these displays). Less systematic attention, this critique continues, has been given to the variants of expression within any category. The view of expression represented by the authors in this part is more complex. They argue that each emotion is likely to be expressed by an array of related displays. Thus, Scherer notes that there are different vocal signals for the same emotion. Reilly and Seibert say that there are many kinds of facial displays and linguistic devices likely to signal emotion in the course of speech. And Gabrielsson and Juslin argue that the different acoustic cues of emotion in music are likely to have probabilistic relations to emotion. A major task for future research is to ascertain the different expressions for each emotion, and the extent to which different expressions (or components) covary with emotion.

More generally, the chapters in this part indicate that emotions are expressed in multiple channels, including the face and voice, and through words, prosody, and grammatical devices. Snowdon reviews fascinating studies indicating that certain affective states—for example, those related to sexual desire—may be communicated in odors in other species, for theoretically interesting reasons. Almost no work has been done on odors and emotional expression in humans.

The multiple modalities of emotional expression raise several fascinating issues. Little is known about how these different signals interact, and Reilly and Seibert offer provocative ideas on how language and facial expression gradually dovetail in their functions with development. The different signals most certainly vary in their time courses, which raises interesting questions about the boundaries of any particular emotional episode (e.g., certain signals will last longer than others). It is also likely, as Scherer, Johnstone, and Klasmeyer suggest, that the different emotions may be more reliably signaled in one modality than in another (e.g., disgust is reliably signaled in the face but not in the voice).

Finally, the chapters by Gabrielsson and Juslin and by Oatley ask why art is expressive of emotion. Music, it appears, conveys emotion with many of the same cues as does the human voice. In judgment studies, observers are just as accurate in identifying the emotional expression of music as they are in judging the human voice. Oatley considers how certain emotional experiences—namely, misunderstood emotions—propel artists to express emotion in the artistic flights of their imagination. This sort of speculation may inform research on why people enjoy art and why they engage in artistic acts. Continued focus on the connections between emotional experience and the arts is likely to yield illuminating insights into the nature of expression, the nature of art, and why we express emotions in the first place.

## The Perception of Emotional Expression

Judgment studies of expression, perhaps the most widely used method in the literature on expression, have addressed whether people across cultures agree in their judgments of different emotional expressions. These studies do indicate that there is agreement across cultures in judgments of the expression of emotion in the face, voice, and music. This appears to be true when different response formats are used, contrary to recent critiques, and when respondents offer answers of their own choosing rather than based on experimenters' terms.

More recent studies highlighted in the chapters of this part reveal how much more complex is the perception of expression than simply labeling an individual's behavior with an emotion term. Social observers make a variety of inferences from a single facial expression. For example, chapter 22 reveals that from fleeting facial expressions observers make inferences about intention, personality, and social relationship, and about objects in the environment. More systematic treatment of these sorts of issues is needed to explore how social observers make inferences about traits from the expression of brief states, and whether they are accurate in these inferences.

Several articles suggest that expressions of emotion evoke emotion in observers. Given what is known about how emotional experience shapes social judgment (chapter 30, this volume), it is clear that evoked emotions are likely to play an important role in the judgment of emotional expression. Little is known about this possibility.

The aforementioned comments raise perhaps a more intriguing question: How do we perceive expressions of emotion? The chapters in this section offer different answers to this difficult question. Some authors contend that the perception of emotion is located in certain central nervous system structures, and that this localization may even be modality and emotion-specific (Keltner, Ekman, Gonzaga, & Beer; Scherer, Johnstone, & Klasmeyer; Snowdon). This kind of research may eventually illuminate the complex and dynamic process by which observers perceive expressions and infer meaning from expressive behavior.

Other authors address the units of meaning that facial expressions convey. Certain studies of the face indicate that the perception of facial expression is categorical rather than dimensional (Keltner, Ekman, Gonzaga, & Beer). Scherer, Johnstone, and Klasmeyer, and Gabrielsson and Juslin, on the other hand, identify how perceptions of voice and music center on basic dimensions of meaning. Integrating the discrete and dimensional perspectives as they apply to the perception of expression remains one of the central questions in the field.

In reading these chapters one is struck by how actively social observers perceive the expression of emotion, and how relatively little is known about this process. Oatley asks how it is that individuals perceive emotion in pictorial art and literature, and provides theoretical guidance for answering the questions raised in this section. He suggests that, when reading of a literary character's expression of emotion, readers experience emotion via mental simulation processes. That is, they imagine how they themselves would feel in such a context. This may be true of the different arts that express emotion discussed in this part, and for the perception of emotion in everyday interactions as well.

## Expression in Culture and Context

A long-standing tension in the study of expression centers on the extent to which emotional expression varies according to social context and culture. The chapters in this part clearly move beyond simple assertions that expression is culturally constructed or universal. One is struck by the variety of ways in which context shapes emotional expression. Several authors (e.g., Scherer, Johnstone, &

Klasmeyer; Snowdon) reveal how basic features of the physical context (e.g., the distance between individuals, ambient noise) dictate the nature and selection of signals. More social features of social situations also shape emotional expression, including the familiarity of individuals as well as their status relations (Keltner, Ekman, Gonzaga, & Beer; Snowdon). And culture clearly shapes how emotion is expressed (for example, in music see Gabrielsson & Juslin) and how it is interpreted (Keltner, Ekman, Gonzaga, & Beer).

The influence of context on emotional expression and perception remains a line of inquiry rich with intellectual promise. This research will be promoted by characterizations of emotional expression that allow for variability within an emotion category, as evident in these chapters. The study of culture, context, and expression will progress with greater attention paid to recent advances in the study of culture and context (see chapter 46, this volume).

## Individual Variation in Expression

The field of affective science has seen great progress in delineating what emotions are, which sets the stage for researchers to ask how individuals vary in emotional expression (e.g., see chapter 34, this volume). Several authors turn their attention to individual variation in emotional expression, with provocative results. It does appear that individuals vary, according to their personality, in how they express emotion in the face and voice. The same is true for emotional disorders such as depression, which have certain emotional signals. Given the central role expression plays in social life, individual variation in expression is likely to have important social outcomes and contribute to the cumulative consequences of temperament, personality, and emotional disorders.

## Theoretical Developments

The chapters in this part highlight how the study of expression is intertwined with theoretical advances in the field of emotion. Studies of expression are germane to discrete and dimensional approaches to emotion, to questions of how emotion is universal and how it is culturally variable, and to individual differences in emotion.

Snowdon's chapter on the differing theoretical approaches to animal display highlights an interesting theoretical trend in the study of expression that prompts our final comment. According to Snowdon, a first approach holds that displays are reliable readouts of internal feeling and intended action. A second holds that displays are deceitful and designed to manipulate. A third holds that displays are dynamic processes that manage relations. One dramatic illustration Snowdon cites in developing this third view is the literature on display and the regulation of reproductive behavior. Various calls and odors regulate ovulation and sexual readiness.

This regulatory view of expression, with certain precedent in Darwin and those who followed Darwin, has emerged in the study of human emotion as well. The approach assumes that emotions regulate important interactions in relationships (e.g., attachment, flirtation) as they unfold, and the view generates several more immediate empirical questions. Researchers should systematically look at the observers' responses to others' expressions of emotion, to identify how those responses result in coordinated interactions between the individuals who express emotions and the individuals who perceive them. Sequences of expressions between individuals may be the more appropriate unit of analysis. More generally, this suggests that the field may benefit by returning to the study of expression in natural contexts.

## Concluding Thoughts

The study of expression has made great progress, as evident in the chapters of this part. Those in the field know a great deal about how emotions are expressed, how they are perceived, and how these processes vary across cultures and individuals. Yet the study of expression is really still in a nascent state and awaits basic research on the issues that have been identified (e.g., there are very few cross-cultural studies of how emotion is expressed in any modality) and on additional matters that await discovery.

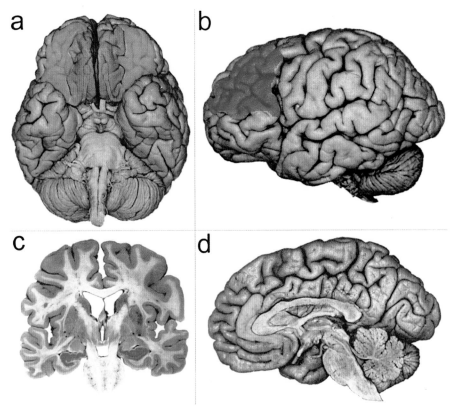

Figure 2.1 Key brain regions involved in affect and mood disorders. (A) Orbital prefrontal cortex (green) and the ventromedial prefrontal cortex (red). (B) Dorsolateral prefrontal cortex (blue). (C) Hippocampus (purple) and amygdala (orange). (D) Anterior cingulate cortex (yellow).

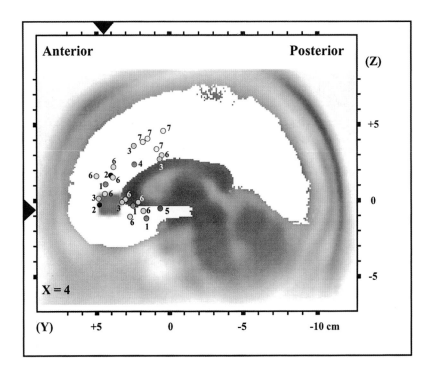

Figure 2.2 Summary of functional brain imaging studies of anterior cingulate cortex (ACC) involvement in depression as well as during various cognitive and affective task manipulations. Foci of ACC activation or deactivation were registered to a common stereotaxic brain atlas (Talairach & Tournoux, 1988) and plotted on a sagittal brain slice (anterior part of the head to the left). The large red area and the black triangles show the location of the ACC cluster found to be associated with degree of treatment response in our previous EEG study (Pizzagalli et al., 2001). The studies of depressed subjects showed pretreatment hyperactivity among patients who responded to treatment (1); posttreatment decreased activity in responders (2); hypoactivity in depressed subjects (3); increased activity with remission of depression (4); decreased activity with remission of depression (5). Studies involving emotional (6) and cognitive (7) tasks in nonpsychiatric subjects are also reported. Coordinates in mm (Talairach & Tournoux, 1988), origin at anterior commissure; (X)=left(–) to right(+); (Y)=posterior(–) to anterior(+); (Z)=inferior(–) to superior(+). Adapted from Pizzagalli et al. (2001).

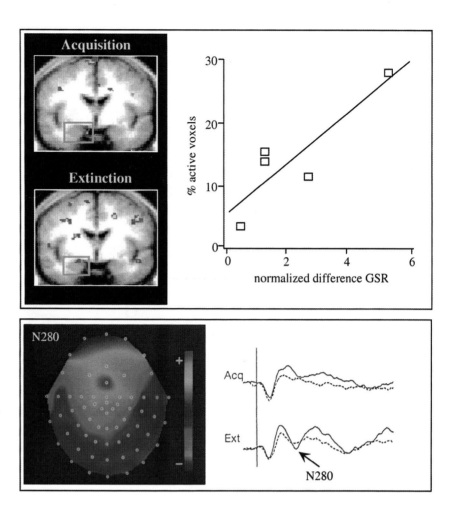

Figure 4.7 Mapping conditioned-related changes in the amygdala and prefrontal cortex of normal human subjects. *Top panel*: Hemodynamic changes in the amygdala (green box) during the early stages of fear acquisition and extinction is revealed by event-related functional magnetic resonance imaging (fMRI). The fMRI signal represents significant increases in CS-evoked responses relative to a control cue that was unpaired with a shock US. The hemodynamic activity decreased over additional training trials (data not shown). The degree to which the amygdala was engaged during acquisition significantly correlated with behavioral measures of conditioned fear in individual subjects (shown at right). GSR = galvanic skin response. Adapted from LaBar et al. (1998). *Bottom panel*: Conditioned-induced changes in event-related potential (ERP) activity measured at the scalp. Extinction (Ext) was characterized by an N280-P440 potential that was larger following paired CS-US training (solid line) than in pseudoconditioned controls (dashed line). The N280 component of this potential had a maximal scalp distribution over the prefrontal cortex (shown in purple at left). This potential may index extinction-specific learning, as it was not found during acquisition training (Acq). Vertical line indicates onset of the CS. Adapted from LaBar (1996).

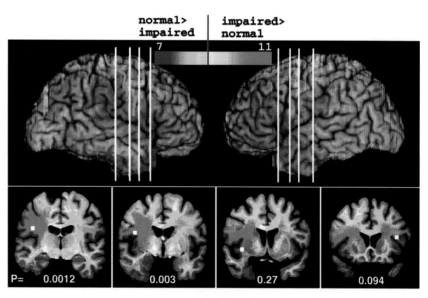

Figure 5.1 Distribution of lesions as a function of mean performance in recognizing emotion from faces in 108 subjects. Color codes the difference in density of lesions between those subjects with the lowest scores and those with the highest scores. Red regions correspond to locations where lesions resulted in normal performance more often than not. P-values indicating statistical significance are shown for voxels in 4 regions (white squares), on coronal cuts (bottom) that correspond to the white lines in the 3-D reconstructions (top). These p-values were calculated by resampling methods and corrected for multiple comparisons. Figure from Adolphs et al. (2000), copyright Society for Neuroscience.

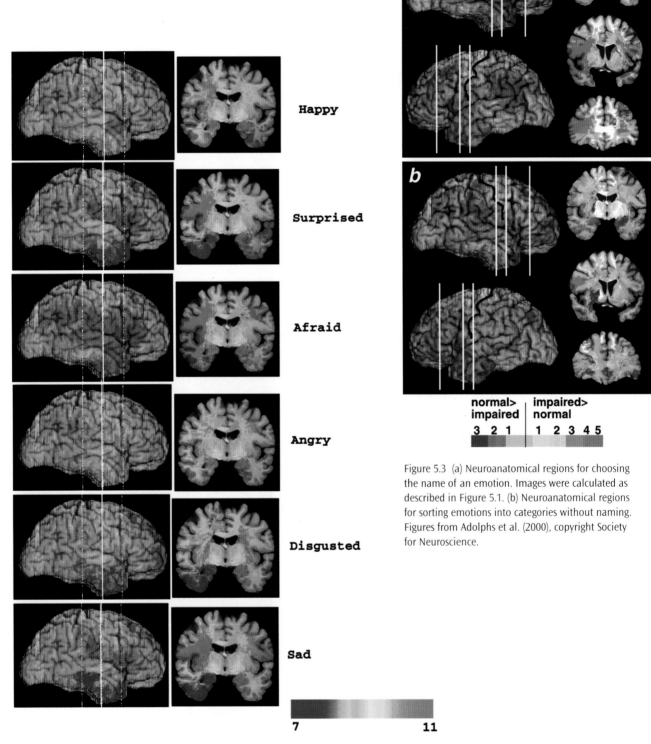

Happy

Surprised

Afraid

Angry

Disgusted

Sad

**normal> impaired**    **impaired> normal**

3 2 1 | 1 2 3 4 5

Figure 5.3 (a) Neuroanatomical regions for choosing the name of an emotion. Images were calculated as described in Figure 5.1. (b) Neuroanatomical regions for sorting emotions into categories without naming. Figures from Adolphs et al. (2000), copyright Society for Neuroscience.

7                    11

Figure 5.2 Recognition of different basic emotions draws upon overlapping but partially separable regions. Difference overlap images were calculated as described in Figure 5.1 for each of the 6 basic emotions in the same sample of 108 subjects. See Figure 5.1 caption for details. Data from Adolphs et al. (2000).

Figure 5.4 Recognition of emotion from prosody. MAP-3 images are shown in which the color at each voxel represents the difference in the overlaps of lesions from those subjects with performances in the bottom half of the distribution, compared to those subjects with performances in the top half (cf. Figure 5.1 for details on the general method). The scale at the bottom shows how color corresponds to number of subjects: blue colors correspond to a larger number of lesions from subjects with performances in the top half. The dependent measure was the mean emotion recognition from prosody. From Adolphs, Tranel, and Damasio (in press).

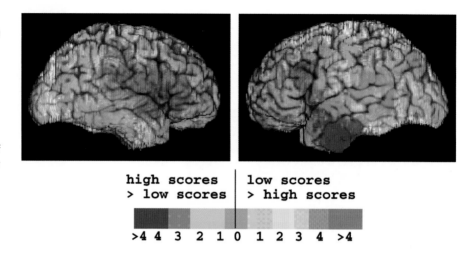

Figure 5.5 Comparisons between recognition of emotion from prosody and from facial expressions in 46 subjects who participated in rating both classes of stimuli. All data used were average correlation scores across all stimuli. MAP-3 images are shown in which color corresponds to the number of subjects with lesions at a given location, as indicated on the respective color scales. In all cases, the dependent measure was the mean correlation score across all stimuli. (a) Data from prosody and from facial expressions. Color represents the difference between the number of lesions from subjects in the top 50% compared to those in the bottom 50%. (b) Direct comparisons using within-subject difference scores. For clarity, only the overlaps of subjects in the bottom half of a distribution are shown. *Top panel*: Overlaps of subjects who were in the bottom partitions both for faces and for prosody (N = 13); red regions indicate lesions from the greatest number of subjects who were impaired in recognizing emotion from both faces and prosody. *Middle and bottom panels*: Overlaps of lesions from all subjects in the bottom partition (N = 23) for the derived difference in rank-orders of performances on prosody and on faces, showing differential performances in recognizing emotion from these two classes of stimuli. From Adolphs, Tranel, and Damasio (in press).

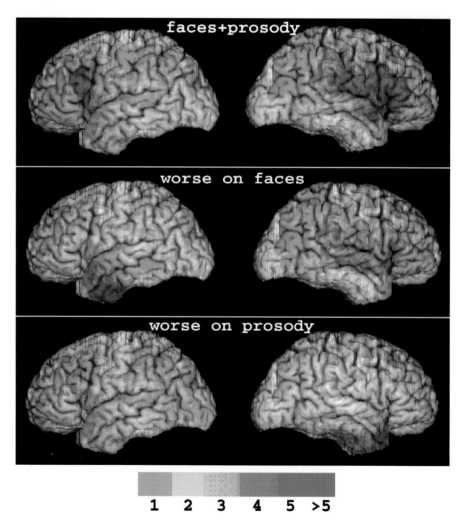

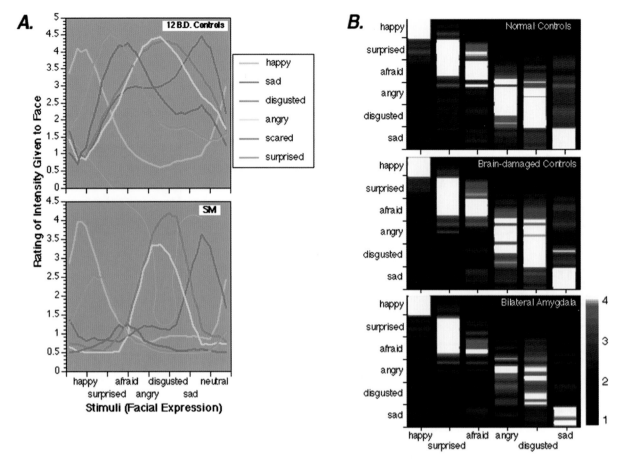

Figure 5.9  Recognition of facial emotion following bilateral amygdala damage. (a) Impaired recognition of fear in facial expressions in SM. Twelve brain-damaged control subjects (without damage to amygdala) and subject SM were shown 39 facial expressions of emotion from Ekman & Friesen, 1976, and asked to rate the 39 faces with respect to the intensity of one of the six basic emotions displayed (happiness, surprise, fear, anger, disgust, and sadness) on a scale of 0 (not at all showing this emotion) to 5 (most intense rating possible for this emotion). These data are shown for SM (bottom) and 12 brain-damaged controls (top), with the ratings that subjects gave to the 39 faces depicted by colored lines. Each differently colored line corresponds to subjects' ratings on one of the six different emotions. The stimuli (39 facial expressions) are ordered along the x-axis by their judged similarity (more similar emotional expressions are adjacent on the x-axis while dissimilar ones are farther apart); the order of the stimuli on the x-axis corresponds to the order obtained by proceeding clockwise around a circumplex model of emotion (Adolphs et al., 1995). Modified from Adolphs, Tranel, et al., 1995; copyright Society for Neuroscience, 1995. (b) Impaired recognition of emotions from facial expressions in subjects with bilateral amygdala damage. Raw rating scores of facial expressions of emotion are shown from eight subjects with bilateral amygdala damage (from Adolphs, Tranel, et al., 1999). The emotional stimuli (36 faces; 6 each of each of the 6 basic emotions indicated) are ordered on the y-axis according to their perceived similarity (stimuli perceived to be similar [e.g., happy and surprised faces] are adjacent; stimuli perceived to be dissimilar [e.g., happy and sad faces] are distant; cf. Adolphs, Tranel, et al., 1995). The six emotion labels on which subjects rated the faces are displayed on the x-axis. Grayscale brightness codes the mean rating given to each face by a group of subjects, as indicated in the scale. A darker line indicates a lower mean rating than a brighter line for a given face, and a thin bright line for a given emotion category would indicate that few stimuli of that emotion received a high rating, whereas a thick bright line would indicate that many or all stimuli within that emotion category received high ratings. Because very few mean ratings were <1 or >4, we truncated the graphs outside these values. Data from subjects with bilateral amygdala damage indicate abnormally low ratings of negative emotions (thinner bright bands across any horizontal position corresponding to an expression of a negative emotion). From Adolphs, Tranel, et al. (1999); copyright Elsevier Science Publishers, 1999.

A.

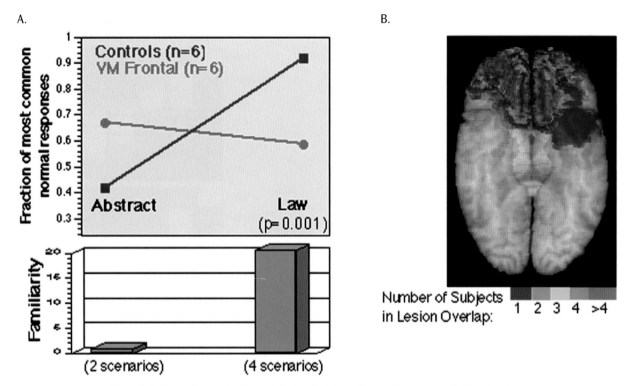

B.

Number of Subjects in Lesion Overlap: 1 2 3 4 >4

Figure 5.12 Reasoning on the Wason Selection Task by subjects with ventromedial frontal lobe lesions. (a) While subjects with VM frontal lesions gave the logically correct answer more often than did control subjects when reasoning about scenarios where the subject matter was logical and abstract (e.g., "If a student got an 'A' grade, then his card must be marked with the numeral 3"), they gave the logically correct answer less often than controls when the subject matter concerned familiar social situations, specifically social laws (e.g., "If you are drinking a beer, then you must be over the age of 18"). These findings support the idea that, in normal subjects, the VM frontal cortices may be part of a system that facilitates correct reasoning about social matters. The results were especially striking, since the scenarios on which the subjects with VM frontal damage fail are in fact the ones that are normally the easiest, and the most familiar, to reason about. When subjects were asked to indicate how familiar they found each of the scenarios, both VM frontal and normal control subjects judged the social laws to be much more familiar than the abstract scenarios (bar graph at bottom). (b) Volumetric overlap image of the lesions of all subjects with VM frontal lobe damage. Color codes the number of subjects who have a lesion at a given anatomical location, rendered onto a ventral view of the human brain. The anatomical sites shared in common by all subjects in the group were in the ventromedial frontal cortex, bilaterally. From Adolphs (1999c); copyright Elsevier Science Publishers.

**Difference map (ERP peak at 312 ms):
Pleasant - Neutral**

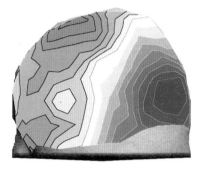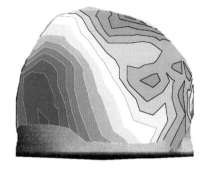

**Difference map (ERP peak at 312 ms):
Unpleasant - Neutral**

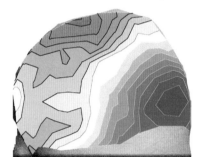

3.6
μV
-3.6

Figure 10.7 Topography of event-related-potential difference maps calculated by subtracting affective (pleasant and unpleasant) from neutral images. Voltages were interpolated to the scalp surface using spherical splines and back-projected to a model head. Contour lines were spaced every 0.4 μV.

Sagittal

Coronal

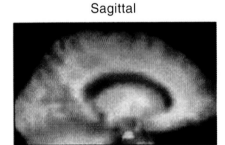

Transverse

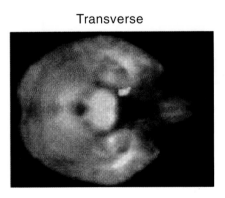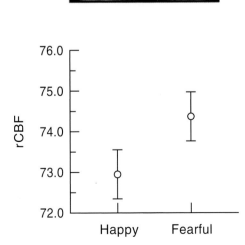

Figure 50.2 Left amygdala activation while viewing fearful versus happy faces. Statistical parametric map (SPM) of mean cerebral activation in five participants viewing fearful versus happy faces in a $H_2^{15}O$ PET facial emotion evaluation study. Views are orthogonal slices through the point of maximal activation in the left amygdala at Talairach coordinates (−18 −6 −16). The graph in the lower right shows (mean ± 2 standard errors) normalized CBF values ($p < 0.002$). From Morris et al. (1996), with permission from *Nature*, copyright 1996.

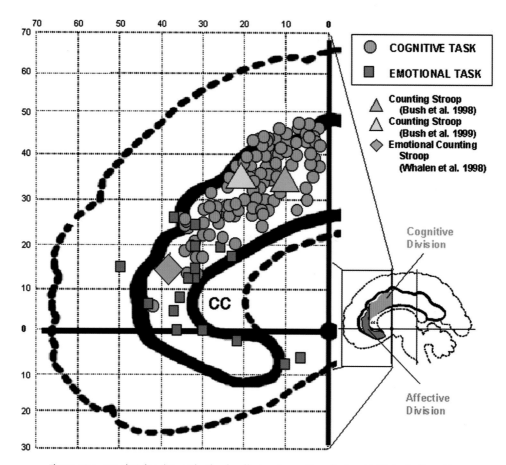

Figure 50.4 Anterior cingulate activation in affect and cognition studies. Multiple studies with varying affective and cognitive paradigms have demonstrated anterior cingulate activation. The ventral portion may be referred to as the affective division (ACad) and the dorsal portion as the cognitive division (ACcd). However, such differential roles for these two subregions are not uniformly present in studies. Additional studies implicating these regions are described in the text and outlined in tables 50.2, 50.3, and 50.4. From Bush et al. (2000), copyright 2000, with permission from Elsevier Science.

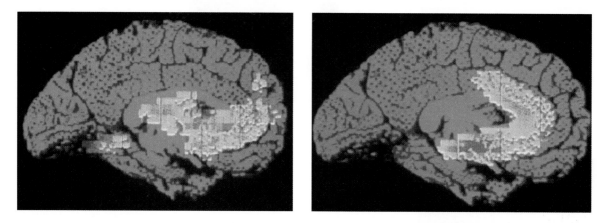

Figure 50.5 Overlapping anterior paralimbic activation with neuropsychologically and pharmacologically induced acute affective changes in healthy volunteers. Images are statistical parametric maps (SPMs) of cerebral blood flow activation rendered on the mesial aspect of the left hemisphere. *Left*: Regions activated during transient self-induced sadness in 11 healthy women (George et al., 1995). *Right*: Regions activated during acute intravenous procaine-induced affective symptoms in 32 healthy volunteers (Ketter et al., 1996). Note the overlap of anterior paralimbic activation patterns with these two different methods of inducing affective changes. Reproduced with permission from Ketter, George, Kimbrell, Benson, & Post (1996).

# 22

# FACIAL EXPRESSION OF EMOTION

Dacher Keltner, Paul Ekman, Gian C. Gonzaga, and Jennifer Beer

The study of facial expression of emotion has long been the focus of theoretical controversy and empirical research (e.g., Allport, 1924; Birdwhistell, 1963; Coleman, 1949; Darwin, 1872/1998; Ekman, 1973, 1994; Fridlund, 1991; Hunt, 1941; Landis, 1924; Mead, 1975; Munn, 1940; Osgood, 1966; Russell, 1994; Schlosberg, 1954; Woodworth, 1938). In studies of facial expression, researchers have addressed how emotions develop, to what extent the information they convey is best captured verbally by discrete categories or scalar dimensions, whether emotions have distinct biological substrates, and the extent to which facial expressions of emotion are universal and how they vary across cultures. In this chapter, we first briefly review the history of the study of facial expression, highlighting the ebb and flow of theory on the aforementioned issues. We then review evidence relevant to three long-standing questions in the field: Are facial expressions accurate indicators of emotion? In which respects are facial expressions of emotion universal and in which ways are they culturally specific? And are the states signaled or represented by facial expressions of emotion best viewed as discrete systems or dimension-based entities? We conclude by highlighting more recent developments in the study of facial expression, focusing on how facial expressions shape social interaction and how individual variations in facial expression relate to personality and psychopathology.

## History of the Study of Facial Expression of Emotion

The contemporary study of facial expression was profoundly shaped by Darwin's *Expression of Emotions in Man and Animals* (1872/1998). In this book, Darwin described distinct facial expressions of different emotions, thus setting the stage for discrete theories of emotion (e.g., Ekman, 1993). He also described the likely meaning of individual muscle actions (e.g., the furrowed brow), an intellectual foray that in part inspired componential theories of facial expression (Smith & Scott, 1997). He described similarities between human expressions and those of other species—an emphasis that guides research to this day (see chapter 24, this volume). And he argued that facial expressions were universal, and even obtained data from informants in different countries and within England, and analyzed observers' responses to different expressions. Although Darwin's influence is clear today, it would be almost 100 years before psychologists would conduct research to explore Darwin's insights.

For several decades, views of facial expression alternative to those advocated by Darwin prevailed. Floyd Allport (1924) proposed an alternative to Darwin's account of universality: species constant learning. Other early theorists focused on the structure of the language used to describe the information conveyed by facial expressions of emotion. Woodworth (1938) proposed a set of six emotion categories to bring order to the variety of responses observers gave when judging the emotion shown in expressions. Schlosberg (1954) proposed three dimensions that underlie categorical judgments. In an influential review, Bruner and Tagiuri (1954) concluded that facial expression did not provide much accurate information, and the study of facial expression was dormant.

Beginning in the early 1960s, three developments provided impetus for a renaissance of interest in facial expression. First, Plutchik (1962) and Tomkins (1962, 1963) offered evolutionary accounts of facial expression of emotion. Second, independently conducted cross-cultural studies by Ekman and his collaborators and by Izard strongly suggested universality in interpreting facial expressions of emotion (Ekman & Friesen, 1971; Ekman, Sorenson, & Friesen, 1969; Izard, 1977). These findings countered prevailing ideas of cultural relativism, and directed researchers to consider the functions facial expressions serve. Finally, researchers developed anatomically based coding systems to measure facial expression (Ekman & Friesen, 1978; Izard, 1977). These systems avoided the problems associated with relying on observers' inferences about emotion based on expressive behavior, and were less intrusive and more comprehensive than EMG methods of measuring facial activity (see Ekman & Rosenberg, 1997, for a sample of diverse studies measuring facial activity).

These conceptual and methodological advances have inspired vast literatures on facial expression (for reviews, see Ekman & Oster, 1979; Keltner & Kring, 1998). This evidence allows us to arrive at more informed positions regarding long-standing questions about facial expression. The first that we address in this review may be the most basic question in the literature: Are facial expressions reliable indicators of emotion?

## Facial Expressions as Accurate Indicators of Emotion

Do facial expressions convey information about emotion? Research on facial expression has seen the pendulum swing between polar responses to this question. Until the late 1960s it was widely assumed that facial expressions were not systematically associated with specific events or subjective experience, and as a consequence conveyed little information to others. In supporting this claim, researchers noted numerous instances in which facial expression did not correspond to the emotional meaning of preceding events. Individuals smiled at the decapitation of a rat (Landis, 1924) or at the news of their husband's death (for review of this position, see Ekman, 1973). Facial expressions were assumed to be like the phonemes of a language: the units of communication were attached to

specific events and experiences in context- and culture-specific ways.

The writings of Tomkins, Ekman, and Izard pointed to a different hypothesis. They argued that humans have evolved distinct facial expressions that accompany the experience of emotion and convey that experience to others. The benefits of having reliable expressions of emotion are numerous: Most generally, facial expressions coordinate interactions between individuals as they respond to the challenges (e.g., threats, injustice) and opportunities (e.g., formation of bonds, pursuit of resources) in their social environment. As we shall see, this view prevailed for several decades, but has more recently been challenged by advocates of the view that emotions may not necessarily be marked by distinct and recognizable facial expressions (e.g., Fernandez-Dols & Ruiz-Belda, 1997; Fridlund, 1991; and see reply to these challenges in Ekman, 1999).

These contrasting positions can be assessed by addressing the extent to which, if at all, facial expressions relate to other markers of emotion, including emotion-related experience, physiology, appraisal, or action tendencies. Researchers have approached this question from different theoretical perspectives. Discrete emotion theorists have looked at how prototypical facial displays of emotion relate to different indices of emotion. This view has guided much of the research that we review here. Componential theorists (e.g., Ortony & Turner, 1990; Smith & Scott, 1997) have looked at how components of facial expressions (e.g., the furrowed brow or pressed lips) relate to components of emotional response (e.g., specific appraisals). These perspectives work at different yet complementary levels of analysis. The studies they have inspired suggest that facial expression is not a noisy system but instead provides information about an individual's emotion.

## Correspondence Between Facial Expressions and the Experience of Emotion

The most concerted attempt to link facial expression to emotion has focused on self-reports of subjective emotion. This kind of study must overcome numerous difficulties (Davidson, Ekman, Saron, Senulis, & Friesen, 1990; Rosenberg & Ekman, 1994). Emotion must be reliably elicited and measured. The measurement of subjective emotion should occur in temporal proximity to the occurrence of facial expression. Researchers should compare the subjective correlates of closely related facial expressions (e.g., anger and disgust). And numerous methodological practices that increase the strength of potential correlations between facial expression and self-reported emotion, such as within-subjects design, should be considered (e.g., Ruch, 1995).

Notwithstanding these difficulties, several relevant studies have now documented consistent relations between facial expression and other markers of emotion. An early review of 11 studies of contrasting methods indicated that the effect size of the relation between facial expression and experience was small to moderate, but consistently significant across studies (Matsumoto, 1987). Studies using precise facial coding systems have consistently found relations between facial expression and reports about the subjective experience of emotion. In one study, subjects' facial expressions of disgust and smiling in response to viewing evocative films correlated with subsequent self-reports of emotion (Ekman, Friesen, & Ancoli, 1980). Duchenne smiles, which involve the raising of the cheeks, but not non-Duchenne smiles, have been shown to relate to the experience of positive emotion in young and old adults (e.g., Frank, Ekman, & Friesen, 1993; Hess, Banse, & Kappas, 1995; Keltner & Bonanno, 1997; Smith, 1995). The unique facial actions of embarrassment and amusement (e.g., gaze aversion and smile controls versus the open-mouthed smile) related in distinct ways to self-reports of these emotions (Keltner, 1995). Spontaneous laughter and smiling were found to have some distinct experiential correlates (Keltner & Bonanno, 1997). Reviews of the humor and laughter literature find that the intensity of laughter or smiling correlates between .3 and .4 with self-reports of the funniness of the humorous stimuli (McGhee, 1977; Ruch, 1995). There are certain emotions for which the jury is still out, such as fear and sadness. Nevertheless, relevant studies consistently indicate that facial expressions relate to the experience of emotion. These findings are all the more impressive when one considers the logical upper limits of the strength of correlations between measures coming from such different sources and the limitations in the adequacy of attempts to report in words on subjective experiences.

## Correspondence Between Facial Expression and Other Markers of Emotion

Other studies, fewer in number, have ascertained whether facial expressions of emotion relate to other markers of emotion. Select studies suggest that different facial expressions are associated with different autonomic responses; thus, following instructions to voluntarily contract the facial muscles into configurations theoretically presumed to characterize anger, fear, disgust, and sadness produce different patterns of autonomic activity (Ekman, Levenson, & Friesen, 1983; chapter 11, this volume; Levenson, Ekman, & Friesen, 1990). For example, the anger configuration triggers elevated heart rate and increased blood flow to the periphery; posing disgust triggers reduced heart rate. Of course, these findings pose the question of whether spontaneous expressions of emotion will likewise relate to distinct autonomic responses. Some evidence suggests the answer may be affirmative. Anger displays have been shown to relate to the incidence of ischemia in patients with coronary artery disease (see

Rosenberg et al., 1998). The oblique eyebrows and pressed lips of sympathy correlated with reduced heart rate, whereas prior wince of pain related to elevated heart rate (Eisenberg et al., 1989).

Still other studies have linked facial expression to other components of emotional response, including emotion-specific central nervous system activity, environmental events, and cognitive appraisals. Spontaneous Duchenne smiles have been shown to relate to left anterior activity (e.g., Davidson et al., 1990; Ekman, Davidson, & Friesen, 1990), whether someone is truthfully or dishonestly describing positive feelings (Ekman, Friesen & O'Sullivan, 1988), to whether an infant is approached by its mother or a stranger (Davidson & Fox, 1989), and whether patients are improving as a result of treatment (Ekman, Matsumoto, & Friesen, 1997). Other evidence suggests that patients with right-hemisphere damage are impaired in the production of facial expressions of emotion, particularly for positive emotion (Borod, Koff, Lorch, & Nicholas, 1986). Smith has shown that individuals imagining situations high in perceived obstacles to goals were more likely to show furrowed eyebrows (Smith, 1989; Smith & Scott, 1997). A recent study found that bereaved adults' facial expressions of anger and sadness while discussing their deceased spouses tended to co-occur with distinct appraisal themes (justice and loss) coded from participants' spontaneous discourse (Bonanno & Keltner, 2000). And one study suggests that facial expressions may be associated with specific patterns of thought: Posing facial expressions of anger was associated with the tendency to attribute social events to others' actions, whereas posing facial sadness was associated with the tendency to attribute the same events to situational causes (Keltner, Ellsworth, & Edwards, 1993).

This literature lends support to the general position that facial expressions relate to the different responses that are part of the "emotion package." For advocates of the discrete perspective, it is clear that more basic research is needed on the many states considered to be discrete emotions (e.g., there is little evidence linking facial expressions of sadness to distinct markers of emotion). It will also be important to link spontaneous facial expressions (many critical studies have focused on posed expressions) and responses other than self-report. For advocates of the componential view of facial expression, the charge is quite similar, although even more pronounced: Researchers need to document, as Smith has done, whether the different components of emotion relate in systematic ways to different facial actions.

## Challenges to the View That Facial Expressions Communicate Information About Emotion

Several theorists have recently challenged the view that facial expression conveys information about emotion (e.g.,

Fernandez-Dols & Ruiz-Belda, 1997). These challenges center on two widespread assumptions. The first is that facial expressions correlate with emotional experience. For example, Fridlund has argued that facial expressions (or displays) evolved to signal social intentions rather than private feeling. In fact, Fridlund argues, it may often be advantageous to deceive others about one's emotions, and to signal intentions without experiencing emotion.

Before turning to Fridlund's empirical evidence, it is important to remember that there is a vast repertoire of facial actions (e.g., eyebrow flashes, referential displays, back channel responses) that do not necessarily relate to emotion (e.g., Bavelas & Chovil, 1997; Ekman, 1979). There are certain to be facial actions, as Fridlund contends, that convey information in the absence of emotional experience. It is also likely that emotional experience is associated with social intentions (Frijda, 1986), and some have even argued that social intentions are more credible when accompanied by emotional experience (e.g., see Frank, 1988).

In several empirical studies, Fridlund has addressed whether facial expressions vary more as a function of social audience (which heightens the need to convey social intentions) or of private experience. In these studies, participants are led to experience an emotion (through imagery or by watching an evocative videotape) when they are alone, with others, or when imagining others are present (Fridlund, 1991; Fridlund, Kenworthy, & Jaffey, 1992). Facial expression is measured with EMG. These studies have shown that: (1) participants' self-reports of happiness do not correlate with measures of smiling behavior; and (2) greater smiling is observed when participants are in more social situations (and by implication, disposed to signal social intentions). Other authors have similarly observed that facial expression appears to be more tailored to the communicative demands than to the hedonic implications of the context. Kraut and Johnston (1979) found that participants smiled more when: (1) facing their friends after bowling a strike as opposed to when facing the pins just after having bowled the strike; (2) at a hockey game when engaged with their friends rather than when their team did well; and (3) talking to someone in the rain, rather than when alone in the sunshine. In a similar vein, during the awards ceremony, Olympic gold medal winners smiled more when interacting with others than when standing on the podium (Fernandez-Dolz & Ruiz-Belda, 1995).

Although provocative, these studies suffer from certain limitations. In the Fridlund studies, Duchenne or enjoyment smiles (which involve the *orbicularis oculi* muscle and are associated with pleasure) were not differentiated from non-Duchenne or polite smiles (for distinctions, see Frank, Ekman, & Friesen, 1993; Keltner & Bonanno, 1997). One might have observed robust correlations between Duchenne smiles and self-reports of happiness, but not for the non-Duchenne smiles. Measures of emotional experience were not gathered in the studies of bowlers, hockey fans, and gold medal winners, so we simply cannot make inferences about the emotional meaning of the events (e.g., gold medal winners may have been more awestruck, grateful, or wistful than happy while on the podium). These studies also suffer from a theoretical dualism that opposes emotion to communication, and fails to consider the evolutionary view that since emotions evolved to deal with the most important social interactions (mating, dealing with competitors, child care, etc.), we should expect emotions to be highly evident in social situations. Although these studies inspired a literature on the influences of social context upon facial expression, which we review later, they appear to do little to undermine the notion that facial expressions of emotion are reliably associated with specific emotional experiences.

A second challenge has centered on whether prototypical facial expressions of emotion are associated with theoretically relevant events. There is a good deal of research identifying the prototypical elicitors of emotion (e.g., Lazarus, 1991; Shaver, Schwartz, Kirson, & O'Connor, 1987), and one would certainly expect from the writings of Ekman, Izard, and others that facial expressions of emotion would follow prototypical elicitors of emotion (e.g., injustice, loss, violations of bodily integrity, rewards). The evidence for these claims is less substantial than one would imagine, in large part due to the difficulty of finding elicitors that will evoke the same relatively pure emotional state in most people. It is known that Duchenne smiles are associated with positive events, such as positive film clips and the approach from intimate others (see Keltner & Ekman, 1996, for review). Failure tends to produce shame-related gaze aversion and head movements down (Keltner & Harker, 1998). And in one study of bereaved participants, the dominant facial response to discussions of their deceased partner was sadness (Bonanno & Keltner, 1997). Clearly, more systematic work is needed to link specific events to distinct facial expressions of emotion. This work must avoid assuming that events will be appraised in the same way by all people. Progress will be made when, instead of trying to link emotions to events, emotions are linked to appraisals of events.

Others have taken a more critical view on this issue, suggesting that the prototypical facial expressions are not associated with prototypical elicitors of emotion. In extending this critique to theorizing about the development of facial expression, Camras has made two important observations (Camras, Lambrecht, & Michel, 1996). First, in experimental contexts in which one would expect infants and young children to show surprise (such as violations of object permanence), they in fact do not. Second, children often show facial expressions of surprise in rather unexpected contexts, as when they reach for desirable objects.

### Future Issues

The evidence suggests that there are links between facial expressions and emotional experience, physiology, and certain elicitors. Certain individual facial actions also seem to be associated with theoretically relevant appraisal themes. We have noted that the evidence is still incomplete, and there remain facial expressions and individual facial actions in need of study, as well as different markers of emotion. As the field progresses, we will move beyond more simple questions, such as whether facial expression is an indicator of emotion, to more nuanced questions. Are there indeed prototypical and less prototypical facial expressions of emotion, as evident in differing degrees of association with other markers of emotion? Are there indeed "reliable muscle" actions for each category of emotion, which are most strongly associated with the different markers of emotion (e.g., Ekman, 1993)? And how do the different facial actions within an emotion category relate to different markers of emotion? Answers to these questions may lead to a productive rapprochement between the discrete and componential views of facial expression.

### University and Cultural Variation in Facial Expressions of Emotion

Whether or not people of different cultures express emotion similarly is of central importance to those who believe that facial expressions evolved and are part of universal human nature (see Brown, 1991; Ekman, 1973). This sort of evidence is just as vital to those who study how emotions are shaped by cultural values and practices.

The search for universals in facial expression has a long and storied history (Darwin, 1872/1998; Ekman, 1973, 1998). Consistent with his zeitgeist, Darwin believed that facial expressions of emotion were universal, and distributed questionnaires to missionaries in different parts of the world, querying whether their observations led them to conclude that people in those faraway cultures expressed emotion in similar ways (Darwin, 1872/1998). No informant described a facial expression that was not identifiable from his Victorian perspective (although these informants may simply not have noticed, remembered, or been able to describe facial expressions that differed from their conceptions of emotion or facial expression).

A universalist view of facial expression, however, would be short-lived. In the 1930s, 40s, and 50s, social scientists, most notably Klineberg (1940), La Barre (1947), and Birdwhistell (1970), claimed that people in different cultures express emotions differently in the face. Their claims were based on faulty observational research, imprecise definitions of facial expressions, and failures by most to consider the role of display rules governing the expression of emotion. Nevertheless, they guided an initial wave of research on cultural specificity in the interpretation of emotion (reviewed in Ekman, 1973). Since then, numerous studies have been conducted, addressing whether individuals from different cultures: (1) show similar facial expressions when experiencing similar emotions and (2) judge facial expressions in similar ways. These studies suggest pretty strongly that facial expressions of emotion, at least in the eye of the beholder, are universal. This literature just as clearly hints at ways in which the meaning of facial expressions of emotion may vary across cultures in systematic ways.

### Universality of Facial Behavior

Perhaps most striking in the literature on facial expression is the paucity of evidence concerning whether, across cultures, individuals show similar facial expressions when experiencing emotion. The methodological difficulties of this work are obvious, as noted in a previous section. Cross-cultural studies of actual emotional behavior require cross-cultural equivalence in the meaning of emotional stimuli and the relative absence of the influence of culturally based display rules (Ekman, 1973).

A first study documented that when videotaped without awareness, Japanese and American students showed remarkably similar negative facial expressions while viewing a stress-inducing film (Ekman, 1973). More recently, it was found that 5- and 12-month-old Japanese and American infants responded with similar facial, postural, and vocal expressions of anger in response to a nonpainful arm restraint (Camras, Oster, Campos, Miyake, & Bradshaw, 1992). Ethological research, although not having safeguards against a single observer's possible bias, has shown that people in different cultures display similar facial expressions, such as laughter, embarrassment, or anger, during play, flirtation, or fighting (e.g., Eibl-Eibesfeldt, 1989). Clearly, more basic research documenting the nature of facial expression in different emotional contexts, when subjects are appraising events in a similar fashion, is sorely needed.

In other studies, like those Darwin himself conducted, researchers have gathered people's descriptions of facial expressions associated with different emotions. Although self-reports of behavior are clearly subject to a variety of biases, this evidence could be used to address the universality of facial expression. For example, across cultures people are in high agreement that embarrassment is expressed in a nervous smile and gaze aversion (reviewed in Keltner & Buswell, 1997). Other studies that have systematically gathered individuals' descriptions of expressive behavior across cultures (e.g., Scherer & Wallbott, 1994) could be similarly synthesized.

Finally, one study has examined the relations between facial expression and other markers of emotion across cultures. In this study, participants in the United States and the Minangkabau—a matrilineal, Muslim culture in Indonesia—configured their faces into the expressions of different emotions, during which time their autonomic physiology was recorded (Levenson, Ekman, Heider, & Friesen, 1992). Importantly, deliberately making the same set of facial movements produced similar autonomic responses in the two cultures, in the case of anger, disgust, and fear, pointing to universal links between facial action and emotion-specific autonomic physiology.

## Universality in Judgments of Facial Expressions of Emotion

Beginning with Ekman's initial work with the preliterate, isolated Fore of New Guinea, and Izard's work with a number of literate cultures, judgment studies have addressed whether people who speak different languages and adhere to different values and beliefs interpret facial expressions of emotion in similar ways (for reviews, see Ekman, 1998; Izard, 1977; Russell, 1994). Conducted in dozens of cultures, these studies have typically presented participants with photographs of prototypical facial expressions of emotion and asked them to label the expressions with a word from a list of emotion terms. These studies reveal that across cultures people judge facial expressions of emotion with levels of agreement that exceed chance, typically achieving agreement rates between 60 and 80% (when chance levels vary between 17 and 50%). These results have led theorists of differing theoretical persuasions to conclude that people across cultures judge facial expressions of anger, contempt, disgust, fear, sadness, and surprise in similar ways (Ekman, 1994; Haidt & Keltner, 1999; Russell, 1994).

These widely cited judgment studies have been critiqued in several ways (Fridlund, 1991; Russell, 1994). A first critique pertains to the fact that researchers provided the terms with which participants labeled the facial expressions. Perhaps if asked to label the facial expressions in their own words, members of different cultures would not agree, and in fact would choose different terms that reflect culture-specific concepts. A recent study in the United States and rural India (Haidt & Keltner, 1999), however, suggests otherwise. In this study, participants were allowed to label photos of 14 different expressions in their own words. Individuals from the United States and India spontaneously used similar concepts in labeling facial expressions of anger, disgust, fear, happiness, sadness, surprise, and embarrassment (see also Izard, 1977).

The forced choice, within-subject methods of these studies have been critiqued (e.g., Fridlund, 1992a; Russell, 1994; see responses of Ekman, 1994; Izard, 1994). Specifically, it has been argued that the forced-choice format may inflate artifactual agreement across cultures in the interpretation of facial expression. Recent work strongly suggests that this is not the case (Frank, in press). Specifically, in these studies participants were presented with the usual facial expressions and terms, but they were also given options such as "none of the above" or they were given additional response options. These techniques reduced the forced-choice nature of the judgment task, but they did not reduce agreement in judging facial expression. Also, Rosenberg and Ekman (1994) found that free-response formats produced the same results as fixed-response formats for judgments of facial expressions of anger, fear, disgust, sadness, surprise, and happiness.

Another critique of traditional judgment studies is that they used posed rather than spontaneous facial expressions of emotion as stimuli. The posed stimuli, furthermore, were prototypical displays of emotion (although theoretically derived). Perhaps observers would agree less in judging spontaneous displays of naturally occurring emotion. A recent study, however, suggests that observers are just as adept at judging spontaneous displays of emotion (Keltner, 1995). In that study (Study 5), observers were quite accurate in judging the spontaneous displays of amusement (i.e, laughter), anger, disgust, embarrassment, and shame (see Study 5; Keltner, 1995). The dynamic cues that accompany spontaneous facial expressions (e.g., movements of the head and eyes) may actually enhance agreement in judging some facial expressions.

These more recent studies suggest that the universality thesis stands the test of time and scientific challenge. The universality of facial expression, it is important to note, by no means implies universality in other components of emotion. Facial expressions of emotion may be the most universal of the different facets of emotion because of their central role in meeting different social problems that have been observed in different cultures, such as forming attachments, negotiating status, or apologizing for transgressions (Ekman, 1992a; Keltner & Kring, 1998). Other facets of emotion, such as the descriptions people give to the private feeling of emotion, may demonstrate more cultural variation.

## Cultural- and Context-Related Variation in Facial Expression

The universality thesis holds that across cultures humans have evolved similar facial expressions of emotion and tendencies to interpret those facial expressions. An alternative to this view holds that facial expressions are shaped by cultural values and concepts regarding emotion (e.g., Gordon, 1989). Members of different cultures learn to express emotions in different ways, and interpret those expressions through the lens of their cultures. There are at least two variants of this constructivist analysis.

The stronger version holds that there will be great cross-cultural variation in facial expression. A review of the ethnographic literature would evince numerous observations that are consistent with this thesis. The Utku of the Arctic were claimed never to express anger in the face (Briggs, 1960). In many cultures laughter is pervasive at funerals (Bonanno & Kaltmann, 1999). Given the ambiguity of terms like "laughter," these claims are problematic. Later we assess the current state of knowledge about how facial expression varies across culture.

A weaker version of social constructivism holds that the same stimulus will produce different facial expressions depending on the nature of the social context—for example, whether one is of low or high status or among familiar others or strangers. This sort of evidence does not challenge universalist claims, for features of the social context guide emotion-eliciting appraisals and display rules in ways that may be quite similar across cultures. Later we review how facial expression does vary according to social context.

## Culture and Context and Facial Expression

Only a few studies have examined whether members of different cultures vary in their expressive behavior. Members of different cultures are likely to vary in the latency of their facial expressions of emotion; for example, American infants responded with anger more quickly than Japanese infants (Camras et al., 1992). Cultures may also differ in the range of expressions used to convey a particular emotion. For example, although individuals from India and the United States agreed in their interpretation of a prototypical embarrassment display, only individuals from India indicated that a tongue bite expression—a Southeast Asian display of self-conscious emotion—expressed embarrassment (Haidt & Keltner, 1999). Cultures may vary most in the meaning of these iconic displays of emotion (see Ekman & Friesen, 1982, for related discussion on cultural variation in emblems). And in still the only study to show the operation of different display rules in different cultures, Ekman (1973) showed cultural differences in the control of facial expression. When an authority figure was present, Japanese individuals more than Americans masked negative emotional expressions in response to watching an unpleasant film, with a smile, although they had shown nearly identical facial expressions when watching such films alone.

The studies of how social context shapes facial expression are more numerous and converge on certain conclusions. First, facial expressions appear to be more intense, or mark emotion more reliably, when among familiar others as opposed to strangers. For example, observers were better able to judge the emotions (Wagner & Smith, 1991) or content of stimuli (Buck, Losow, Murphy, & Costanzo, 1992) from observations of the expressive behavior of women who had been exposed to evocative stimuli in the presence of friends as opposed to strangers. In another study, being in the presence of a friend enhanced the expressive behavior of female participants as they viewed films of slapstick comedy (Hess et al., 1995).

Social status also influences the quality and coherence of emotional expression. Thus, in a study of teasing interactions, low-status members were more likely to display embarrassment and fear, whereas high-status members were more likely to display anger and contempt (Keltner, Young, Heerey, Oemig, & Monarch, 1998). Hecht and La France and colleagues have shown that high-power individuals are more likely to show Duchenne smiles associated with pleasure, whereas low-power individuals were more likely to show non-Duchenne, polite smiles (Hecht & LaFrance, 1998). Perhaps more important, high-power individuals' self-reports of pleasure were significantly correlated with their Duchenne smiles, whereas this correlation was not significant for the low-power participants.

## Culture and Context in the Interpretation of Facial Expression

There is quite a rich literature indicating how members of different cultures interpret facial expressions through the epistemological lens of culture. First, individuals from different cultures differ in the emotional intensity that they attribute to facial expressions of emotion (Matsumoto & Ekman, 1989). In a first study to address this issue, Japanese participants attributed more intense emotion than Americans to all facial expressions of emotion posed by Caucasian and Japanese individuals, except expressions of disgust (Matsumoto & Ekman, 1989). Interestingly, members of the two cultures differed in which facial expression they judged to be expressing the most intense emotion: For the Japanese participants, it was the disgust expression; for the American participants, it was the happiness and anger expressions. In recent work, Matsumoto and colleagues have explored how culturally relevant variables, such as power distance and individualism, account for cultural differences in the intensity of emotion attributed to facial expression (e.g., Matsumoto & Kudoh, 1993).

Second, individuals from different cultures vary in the inferences they draw from facial expressions of emotion. For example, American, as compared to Japanese, college students were more likely to infer that an individual displaying a Duchenne smile was highly sociable (Matsumoto & Kudoh, 1993), consistent with the tendency for Americans to make dispositional inferences from social behavior. One might also expect cultures that somaticize emotional experience (e.g., Russell, 1991b) to be more likely to infer somatic responses associated with facial expressions. Other such cross-cultural predictions could be derived from the literature on emotion and culture (e.g., Frijda & Mesquita, 1992; Markus & Kitayama, 1991; Mesquita & Frijda, 1992).

Third, recent studies lend credence to ethnographic examples that strikingly different events elicit similar facial expression in different cultures. For example, in one study it was found that Japanese students indicated that it was more appropriate to show negative facial expressions to outgroup members (Matsumoto, 1990). American students, in contrast, indicated that it was more appropriate to display negative emotion to ingroup members. People from India were more likely to mention affiliation in explaining photographs of a Duchenne smile, whereas Americans were more likely to mention individual achievement (Haidt & Keltner, 1999), consistent with claims about independent and interdependent cultures (Markus & Kitayama, 1991).

### Future Issues

The field has made progress in addressing the extent to which facial expressions are universal and how they vary across cultures. People from radically different cultures appear to categorize a limited set of facial expressions in fairly similar ways. But members of different cultures vary in the inferences they draw from facial expression, and this issue is ripe for theoretical expansion. Once again there is a striking shortage of evidence concerning how individuals from different cultures vary, and how they are similar, in their actual facial expression.

## Dimensions or Discrete Emotions

A central question in the field of emotion is whether emotions are better thought of as discrete systems or interrelated entities that differ along global dimensions, such as valence, activity, or approach and withdrawal (Ekman, Friesen, & Ellsworth, 1982; Lang, 1995; Russell, 1997; Schlosberg, 1954). Most discrete emotion theorists take an evolutionary approach and posit that each discrete emotion has a different adaptive function that should be served by fundamentally distinct responses. A dimensional approach argues that emotions are not discrete and separate, but better measured and conceptualized as differing only in degree on one or another dimension (usually, two or three dimensions are invoked to explain similarities and differences in emotion). The dimensional perspective is more common among those who view emotions as being socially learned and culturally variable. It is also more common among those who focus on verbal representation of emotion, while the categorical approach is more popular among those focused on emotional responses or physiology. Four recent developments in the study of facial expression suggest that facial expressions are fruitfully thought of as discrete systems.

### Categorical Judgment Studies

Categorical judgment studies have addressed whether the perception of facial expressions of emotion is categorical or dimension based (e.g., Etcoff & Magee, 1992). Studies of the categorical perception of colors and sounds find that within-category distinctions are more difficult to make than between-category discriminations (reviewed in Etcoff & Magee, 1992). On the boundary of two categories, accuracy in discrimination rises. In the studies of the perception of facial expression, continua of facial expressions were computer generated, with each continuum defined by two endpoints that were prototypical facial expressions of emotion (e.g., anger and fear). The remaining stimuli between the endpoints included facial expressions that varied by equal physical differences. For all possible pairs within a continuum, participants were presented with two target stimuli and then a third stimuli that was identical to one of the first two stimuli, and asked to indicate which stimulus the third stimulus resembled.

If facial expressions are perceived categorically, one would expect discriminations between faces within a category to be less accurate than between pairs of faces between categories that differed by an equal physical amounts (i.e., a categorical boundary effect). Indeed, the evidence using computer-generated drawings of facial expressions (Etcoff & Magee, 1992) as well as computer-morphed photographs of facial expressions of emotion (Young et al., in press) has yielded boundary effects. There appear to be discrete boundaries between the facial expressions of emotion, much as there are perceived boundaries between different hues or sounds.

### Neuropsychological Evidence: fMRI, Lesion, and Disease Studies

Studies of the central nervous system correlates of facial expressions also bear upon the dimensionality versus discrete issue. Dimensional theorists have proposed that valence is primary in determining the perception of facial expression (e.g., Russell, 1997), implying that the same brain region might primarily be involved in the perception of different facial expressions of negative emotion. Similarly, other theorists have proposed that emotional face processing, regardless of valence, is localized to particular brain regions. For example, the right hemisphere has often been implicated in emotional face processing (Adolphs, Damasio, Tranel, Cooper, & Damasio, 2000; Borod, 1992; Ross, 1981). However, evidence for this position has been equivocal. Some studies have found that individuals are better at perceiving emotional faces presented in their left hemifield (controlled by the right hemisphere) and that patients with right-hemisphere damage are impaired at identifying negative emotional expressions (e.g., Borod, 1992; Borod et al., 1986). In contrast, other studies have shown that patients with left-hemisphere damage, in comparison to patients with right-hemisphere damage and normal controls, show selective impairments for perceiving emotional expression (e.g., Young, Newcombe, de Haan, Small, & Hay, 1993).

Another putative area for generalized emotional face processing is the orbitofrontal cortex (e.g., Hornak, Rolls, & Wade, 1996; Rolls, 2000). Two sources of evidence support this position. First, patient research has found that orbitofrontal damage is associated with impairment for identifying emotional expressions (Hornak et al., 1996). Other clinical populations that implicate the frontal cortex show impairment on emotional face perception, such as patients with autism (Celani, Battacchi, & Arcidiacano, 1999) and frontotemporal dementia (Lavenu, Pasquier, Lebert, Petit, & Van der Linden, 1999). Second, a PET study has found that the orbitofrontal cortex (BA 47) activates in response to emotional faces in comparison to neutral faces (Sprengelmeyer, Rausch, Eysel, & Przuntek, 1998).

Discrete theorists have argued that the experience and perception of different facial expressions of emotion involve distinct central nervous system regions (e.g., Ekman, 1992a; Izard, 1993). Two kinds of evidence suggest that distinct brain regions activate in the process of perceiving different negative emotions.

First, one class of studies has presented photographs of facial expressions of emotion and, typically with the use of fMRI or PET, ascertained that the perception of different facial expressions elicits activity in different brain regions when compared to neutral faces. The perception of fearful facial expressions activates regions in the left amygdala (Breiter et al., 1996; Phillips et al., 1997), even when the presentation of fearful facial expressions is masked by the presentation of an immediately ensuing neutral expression (Whalen et al., 1998). The perception of sad faces activates the left amygdala and right temporal lobe, whereas the perception of anger faces activates the right orbitofrontal cortex and cingulate cortex (Blair, Morris, Frith, Perrett, & Dolan, 1998; Sprengelmeyer et al., 1998). The perception of disgust faces activates the basal ganglia, anterior insula, and frontal lobes (Phillips et al., 1997; Sprengelmeyer et al., 1998).

Second, disease and lesion studies indicate that the perception of different emotions is associated with different brain regions. Specifically, bilateral lesions to the amygdala impair the ability to recognize fearful facial expressions and vocalizations but not the ability to recognize facial expressions of sadness, disgust, or happiness (Adolphs, Tranel, Damasio, & Damasio, 1994, 1995; Adolphs et al., 1999; Broks et al., 1998; Calder et al., 1996; Sprengelmeyer et al., 1999; Young, Hellawell, van de Wal, & Johnson, 1996). Individuals suffering from Huntington's disease, which affects the basal ganglia, were unable to recognize disgust expressions accurately but were accurate in judging facial expressions of other negative emotions (Sprengelmeyer et al., 1996). Even carriers of Huntington's disease were unable to recognize facial expressions of disgust (Gray, Young, Barker, Curtis, & Gibson, 1997).

These findings suggest that perception of emotional facial expressions may be associated both with general emotional processing activity (i.e., in the orbitofrontal cortex) and with activity in emotion-specific substrates. It may be that perception of emotional facial expression takes place in two or more steps. For example, specific brain areas may be involved in identifying particular emotional expressions, whereas the orbitofrontal cortex may be involved in higher order processing such as integrating facial expression information with contextual information (Sprengelmeyer et al., 1998). Future brain imaging research concerning the perception of emotional facial expression might provide a stronger test of the discrete versus dimension question by using a different study design and analysis approach. Event-related fMRI studies, in which participants are required to judge emotional expression (i.e., not gender) and in which comparisons are made between two different emotional conditions, will provide a more direct test of areas responsive to particular emotional expressions (see Blair et al., 1998; Morris et al., 1996).

Whereas these previous studies have established that the perception of different facial expressions activates different brain regions, less is known about whether the display of different facial expressions activates different brain regions. Work in progress studying multiple emotions using brain imaging techniques should provide important findings relevant to this matter (Davidson et al., 1990; Ekman, Davidson, & Friesen, 1990). Studies that have measured event-related potentials on the scalp have found that anger, happy, and fear faces elicit different event-related potentials in children as young as 7 months old (Nelson & de Haan, 1997; Pollak, Cichetti, Klorman, & Brumaghim, 1997). Finally, preliminary evidence indicates that the stimulation of a specific brain region produces laughter (Fried, Wilson, MacDonald, & Behnke, 1998). It should be noted that whereas dimensional theorists have also claimed that distinctions among negative emotions follow from higher order, effortful inferences (Russell, 1997), the perception of some negative facial expressions of emotion activates the amygdala, which is associated with relatively automatic information processing (LeDoux, 1996).

## Facial Expressions of Emotion and Autonomic Physiology

Discrete theorists have proposed that different emotions, and by implication different facial expressions, are linked to relatively distinct patterns of autonomic nervous system activity. Dimensional theorists, on the other hand, expect the major dimensions of emotion meaning, most notably valence and arousal, to organize the connections between facial expression and autonomic physiology (for relevant arguments, see Levenson et al., 1990).

Several kinds of studies have examined the autonomic patterns associated with different facial expressions. In the directed facial action (DFA) studies, participants were asked to follow instructions to contract specific facial muscles to produce configurations that resemble prototypical facial expressions of emotion (e.g., Ekman et al., 1983; Levenson et al., 1990). Participants' autonomic physiology was recorded as they held the prototypical facial expressions of emotion. Although methodological problems of these studies have been noted (e.g., Cacioppo, Klein, Berntson, & Hatfield, 1993), the studies indicate that facial configurations of negative emotion produce distinctions in autonomic activity. Specifically, anger, fear, and sadness all produced greater heart rate deceleration than disgust, and anger produced greater finger temperature than fear, indicative of increased vasodilation and increased blood flow to peripheral muscles (Ekman et al., 1983). These autonomic distinctions among negative emotions have been replicated across populations (Levenson et al., 1990), in young and elderly participants (Levenson, Carstensen, Friesen, & Ekman, 1991), in different cultures (Levenson et al., 1992), and in a relived emotion task (Levenson et al., 1991). A simple valence account has trouble explaining these autonomic distinctions among the facial expressions of different negative emotions.

Other studies have linked spontaneous facial expressions of emotion to distinct autonomic responses. The oblique eyebrows and concerned gaze of sympathy were associated with heart rate deceleration, whereas the facial display of distress was associated with increased heart rate (Eisenberg et al., 1989). The elevated heart rate and respiratory response of laughter appears to be different from the autonomic responses associated with facial expressions of other emotions (Ruch, 1993). Embarrassment, which has its own distinct display, is likely associated with the blush, which differs from the autonomic responses of other emotions (Shearn, Bergman, Hill, Abel, & Hinds, 1990).

## Facial Expressions and Evoked Responses in Others

Consistent with the view that facial expressions evolved to elicit distinct behaviors in conspecifics (Darwin, 1872/1998; Hauser, 1996), recent evidence indicates that facial expressions evoke fairly specific responses in observers (for reviews, see Dimberg & Ohman, 1996; Keltner & Kring, 1998). Facial expressions of anger, even when presented below the observer's conscious awareness, evoked fear-related facial and autonomic responses that were distinct from the responses evoked by smiles (Esteves, Dimberg, & Ohman, 1994). Facial expressions of distress have been shown to evoke sympathy (Eisenberg et al., 1989), and em-

barrassment and shame displays evoke amusement and sympathy, respectively (Keltner, Young, & Buswell, 1997). Facial expressions of different negative emotions evoke different emotions in observers, which fits a discrete approach to emotion more closely than a dimensional one.

## Reconciliation of Discrete and Dimensional Perspectives

We have reviewed evidence that indicates that facial expressions are perceived categorically and linked to distinct brain regions, autonomic activity, and evoked responses in others. Although this evidence lends credence to the discrete accounts of emotion, we believe that dimensional approaches are useful in many ways. For example, the discrete perspectives may best apply to the current, momentary experience of emotion; dimensional accounts may be most productively applied to emotional experience aggregated across time, and to the study of moods. It is also possible to reconcile these two approaches. For example, although the differences between emotions may seem to be categorical in nature, the differences within a category of emotion—say, between the varieties of anger—may be productively accounted for by dimensions such as intensity and unpleasantness (Ekman, 1992a; Ekman et al., 1982).

## What Are the Distinct Facial Expressions of Emotion?

The preceding review raises a more general question: What are the distinct facial expressions of emotion? The literature has almost exclusively focused on seven emotions: anger, disgust, fear, happiness, sadness, surprise, and contempt, the most contested of the expressions (Ekman, O'Sullivan, & Matsumoto, 1991; Matsumoto, 1992; Russell, 1991a). This same list of emotions replicates (with slight variations) in analyses of the structure of emotion lexicon, both in the United States (e.g., Shaver et al., 1987) and other cultures (Romney, Moore, & Rusch, 1997), and also in studies of other response channels, such as the voice (chapter 28, this volume), suggesting that this parsing of emotions is valid across methods, and not as culturally biased as some have argued (Wierzbicka, 1990).

Researchers are now examining other facial expressions of emotion by additionally studying the temporal dynamics of expression, and attending to gaze, head, and postural activity. Thus, encoding studies linking expressive behavior to emotional experience have documented distinct expressions for embarrassment and shame (Keltner, 1995; Keltner & Buswell, 1997; Keltner & Harker, 1998), sympathy (Eisenberg et al., 1989), and love (Gonzaga, Keltner, Londahl, & Smith, 2001), as well as different experiential correlates of laughter and smiling (Keltner & Bonanno, 1997). Ensuing judgment studies have found that posed displays of embarrassment, shame, amusement (laughter), and sympathy do reliably convey information about emotion but not to the same extent as the displays of the traditionally studied emotions (Haidt & Keltner, 1999; Keltner & Buswell, 1996). It should be noted that the seven emotions have what Ekman has called "snapshot" qualities in that a single moment in time at the apex of the expression is sufficient, while these other emotions require a flow of movement over time (Ekman, 1993). Finally, research has focused on the blush (Leary, Britt, Cutlip, & Templeton, 1992; Shearn et al., 1990) and the iconic tongue protrusion (Haidt & Keltner, 1999), both of which convey emotion.

## Facial Expression, Social Interaction, and Individual Differences

The empirical study of facial expression has long been guided by two tendencies. The first is to study facial expressions of the individual in isolation (and how that expressive behavior relates to experience, physiology, and so on), thus neglecting how facial expressions affect others (although see Dimberg & Ohman, 1996; Keltner & Kring, 1998). The second tendency has been to focus on what is prototypical and universal in facial expression rather than how it varies across individuals. Researchers have begun to move beyond these approaches to examine systematically how facial expressions shape interactions and vary according to individuals.

### Facial Expression and Social Interaction

It is widely assumed that facial expressions of emotion help contribute to more complex social interactions, from flirtation rituals to collective responses to threats (e.g., Ekman, 1992a; Eibl-Eibesfeldt, 1989; Frijda & Mesquita, 1994; Keltner & Haidt, 1999; Keltner & Kring, 1998; Lutz & White, 1986). This claim is consistent with the general assumption that the communicative behavior of sender and receiver co-evolved in reciprocal fashion (Eibl-Eibesfeldt, 1989; Hauser, 1996). From this perspective, one individual's emotional expression serves as a "social affordance" that evokes "prepared" responses in others (e.g., Ohman & Dimberg, 1978). The empirical literature suggests that facial expressions shape social interactions in at least three ways.

First, facial expressions of emotion provide observers with a rich source of information about the sender. As we have seen, facial expressions of emotion signal the sender's emotional state to receivers in brief yet fairly reliable fashion (Ekman, 1984, 1992a, 1993). Observers tend to make more complex inferences based on the observation of facial expressions. Thus, select studies indicate that emotional

displays also communicate the sender's social intentions—for example, whether to strike or flee, offer comfort or play (e.g., Fridlund, 1992; Haidt & Keltner, 1999). Facial expressions of emotion signal characteristics of the sender and receiver's relationship, including the extent to which it is defined by dominance and affiliation. For example, displays of anger communicate the sender's relative dominance (Knutson, 1996), whereas displays of embarrassment communicate the sender's relative submissiveness and inclination to affiliate (Keltner, 1995). Finally, facial expressions convey important information about objects and events in the environment. For example, observer monkeys who viewed model monkeys' fearful, avoidant behavior, including their facial displays, in response to snakes or toy snakes, rapidly acquire the model monkeys' fear of the real and toy snakes, even after just one observation of the model monkey (e.g., Mineka, Davidson, Cook, & Keir, 1984; Mineka & Cook, 1993). In humans, studies show that social referencing—parents' facial and vocal displays of positive emotion or fear—will determine whether their infants will walk across a visual cliff (Sorce, Emde, Campos, & Klinnert, 1985) or play in a novel context or respond to a stranger with positive emotion (Klinnert, Emde, Butterfield, & Campos, 1986; Walden & Ogan, 1988).

Second, facial expressions of emotion also evoke emotions in others. Thus, Ohman and Dimberg have documented how displays of anger evoke fear in observers, even when the faces were "masked" by a neutral face presented immediately following the presentation of the anger face, and presumably not consciously represented by the observer (reviewed in Dimberg & Ohman, 1996). Overt displays of distress, including facial displays, evoke concern and overt attempts to help beginning as early as 8 months (Zahn-Waxler, Radke-Yarrow, Wagner, & Chapman, 1992), and in adults, a pattern of sympathy-related expressive and physiological response predicts helping behavior (Eisenberg et al., 1989). Facial expressions of embarrassment evoke amusement and sympathy, which produce increased liking of the individual and, when relevant, more forgiveness (reviewed in Keltner & Buswell, 1997).

Finally, facial expressions of emotion provide incentives for others' social behavior (e.g., Klinnert et al., 1986). Displays of positive emotion by both parents and children reward desired behaviors (e.g., Tronick, 1989). For instance, as infants carry out intentional behaviors with the assistance of their parents—for example, when reaching for an object—they will smile when their parents engage in behavior that facilitates their own goal-directed behavior, and show signs of distress when the parents do not act in such fashion (Tronick, 1989). Other studies have shown that parents use positive emotional displays to direct the attention of their infants (Cohn & Tronick, 1987). In this same vein, parental laughter may facilitate learning by rewarding appropriate behavior in infants and children (Rothbart, 1973). Laughs occur almost exclusively at the end of the utterance (Provine, 1993), which may serve as a reward for preceding social behavior.

This sort of research strongly reveals how facial expressions are more than just markers of internal states. And they are more than simply signals divorced from internal states (e.g., Fridlund, 1992a). Instead, these findings support the view that facial expressions evolved to provide information to others about what the person showing the expression is preparing to do next, and this signal is likely to influence the perceiver's behavior (for further explanation of this view, see Eibl-Eibesfeldt, 1989; Ekman, 1999). This research suggests that humans have evolved systematic responses to each other's emotions (e.g., sympathy in response to distress; fear in response to anger). It is these coordinated emotional responses between sender and receiver that may prove to be the appropriate unit of analysis for those interested in understanding how facial expressions shape social interactions and relationships.

## Individual Differences in Facial Expressions of Emotion

Notwithstanding the conceptual and methodological promises of studying individual differences in facial expressions (Keltner, 1996), it is only recently that this issue has attracted the attention of empirical researchers. We trace this oversight to two historical trends. First, the early researchers of expressive behavior, such as Wolff (1943), focused on individual differences in a variety of expressive behaviors, such as gait, signature, or posture, but they did not consider facial expression. The study of the face may have been tainted by the pitfalls and ill repute of the study of physiognomy (Ekman, 1978). Second, early researchers have concentrated on universal, prototypical facial expressions, thus ignoring individual variation in facial expression.

Recent studies, however, have begun to illuminate how personality traits and psychological disorders relate to facial expressions of emotion (for reviews, see Keltner, 1996; Keltner & Kring, 1998). This literature is motivated by the idea that individual differences in emotion are central to the structure, process, and development of personality traits (e.g., Malatesta, 1990; Moskowitz & Cote, 1995; Pervin, 1993) and psychological disorders (e.g., Kring & Bachorowski, 1999). The accompanying empirical literature is in its nascent state, but is already beginning to shed light on important questions in the study of personality and psychopathology.

### The Structure and Organization of Traits and Disorders

At the most descriptive level, studies of facial expression can illuminate the structure of personality traits and emo-

tional disorders and how they differ from one another. For example, the finding that extraversion and neuroticism relate to facial expressions and self-reports of positive and negative emotion, respectively (Keltner, 1996; Larsen & Ketelaar, 1991; Watson & Clark, 1992), suggests that these two traits have an emotional core. In the realm of emotional disorder, internalizing and externalizing disorders overlap a great deal in terms of subjective dysphoria and distress, yet one study of adolescent males found externalizers to be particularly prone to express anger and internalizers fear (Keltner, Moffitt, & Stouthamer-Loeber, 1995). Here, the study of facial expression points to important distinctions among disorders that might be masked with the use of other methods, such as self-report.

In other studies, researchers have begun to examine the organization of emotion within particular traits and disorders. This research moves beyond simply characterizing the emotional profile of one particular trait or disorder, and starts to reveal the extent to which different processes (e.g., expressive behavior, subjective experience, physiological response) are organized within individuals. The most well-developed product of this line of inquiry is the literature on schizophrenia. Schizophrenic patients have been found to be less facially expressive than nonpatients in response to emotional films (Berenbaum & Oltmanns, 1992; Kring, Kerr, Smith, & Neale, 1993; Kring & Neale, 1996; Mattes, Schneider, Heimann, & Birbaumer, 1995), cartoons (Dworkin, Clark, Amador, & Gorman, 1996), and during social interactions (Krause, Steimer, Sanger-Alt, & Wagner, 1989; Mattes et al., 1995), but report experiencing *the same* or greater amount of emotion and exhibit the same or greater amount of skin conductance reactivity as nonpatients (Kring & Neale, 1996). Importantly, this research not only shows that schizophrenics display a disjunction between expression and experience; it also dispels certain misconceptions about the emotional nature of certain disorders—for example, that schizophrenics experience flat affect—that prevailed until researchers began to look at the face.

### Facial Expression as an Interface Between Individual Difference and the Social Environment

A central insight in recent years in the study of individual differences is that people select and create social environments that call forth and reinforce their underlying traits and dispositions (Caspi & Bem, 1990; Scarr & McCartney, 1983). For example, hostile children tend to have a pattern of hostile intimate relations and work interactions (e.g., Caspi, Elder, & Bem, 1987) that is certain to enhance the consistency and stability of their hostility. This line of thought raises the question of how internal traits (or disorders) shape the environment. One obvious possibility is facial expression.

More specifically, guided by what is known about facial expression and social interaction (see preceding section), research can begin to document how traits and disorders relate to specific styles of interaction and relationships, thus producing and perpetuating those individual differences (Keltner & Kring, 1998). For example, in one recent study it was found that women who expressed more positive emotion in college yearbook photos were more likely to enter into satisfying marriages several years later and become more competent, less prone to negative emotion, and more satisfied with their lives (Harker & Keltner, 2001). One inference from these findings is that the tendency to express positive emotion in the face (and other channels as well) creates more harmonious social relationships, which in turn fosters personal growth and well-being. Turning to the study of emotional disorders, it has been documented that depressed patients exhibit limited facial expressions, particularly expressions of positive emotions (Berenbaum & Oltmanns, 1992; Ekman & Friesen, 1974; Ekman et al., 1997; Jones & Pansa, 1979; Ulrich & Harms, 1985; Waxer, 1974). Again, one might expect this expressive tendency to have pronounced effects upon the quality of social interactions and relationships, which in turn would turn increase the likelihood of prolonged and severe depression.

### Charting the Development of Personality and Psychopathology

One of the great advantages of the study of facial expression is that it can be gathered unobtrusively from the first to the last moment of life. This gives researchers the great opportunity to chart the development of different traits and disorders in ways that are not possible with self-report methods. For example, it is known that infants vary in their expressive behavior starting as early as 7 months (Izard, Hembree, & Huebner, 1987). Linking these sorts of findings to the later development of personality traits has the promise of illuminating the rudiments of personality, and how it develops. To the extent that certain disorders have characteristic patterns of facial expression, researchers might improve early diagnosis and intervention. For similar reasons, facial expression can be used as a measure of progress in response to treatment (e.g., Ekman et al., 1997) and trauma, such as the loss of a spouse (Bonanno & Keltner, 1997).

### Conclusions

In this review we have drawn upon classic and contemporary studies of facial expression to address three abiding questions. Is facial expression an accurate indicator of emotion? How are facial expressions universal and how do they vary across cultures? Are facial expressions of emotion best thought of as discrete systems or entities that vary along global dimensions? We have also looked at emergent studies examining how facial expression shapes social interaction, and how individuals vary in their facial expressions of emotion. Given the breadth of issues covered in the study of facial expression, we inevitably could not review important research on facial feedback (Matsumoto, 1987) and the development of facial expression (Abe & Izard, 1999; Izard et al., 1987; Lewis, 2000).

Once largely ignored, the study of facial expression is now at the center of the emergent field of affective science. The study of facial expression will continue to be germane to basic questions about emotion, culture, and communication. The topic of facial expression will present continued opportunities for the study of emotion-relevant experience and autonomic and central nervous system physiology. Finally, the study of facial expression will continue to allow researchers to seek answers to fundamental questions about human nature.

### REFERENCES

Abe, J. A., & Izard, C. E. (1999). The developmental functions of emotions: An analysis in terms of differential emotions theory. *Cognition and Emotion, 13*, 523–549.

Adolphs, R., Damasio, H., Tranel, D., Cooper, G., & Damasio, A. (2000). A role for somatosensory cortices in the visual recognition of emotion as revealed by three-dimensional lesion mapping. *Journal of Neuroscience, 20*, 2683–2690.

Adolphs, R., Tranel, D., Damasio, H., & Damasio, A. R. (1994). Impaired recognition of emotion in facial expression following bilateral damage to the human amygdala. *Nature, 372*, 669–672.

Adolphs, R., Tranel, D., Damasio, H., & Damasio, A. R. (1995). Fear and the human amygdala. *Journal of Neuroscience, 15*, 5879–5891.

Adolphs, R., Tranel, D., Hamann, S., Young, A. W., Calder, A. J., Phelps, E. A., Anderson, A., Lee, G. P., & Damasio, A. R. (1999). Recognition of facial emotion in nine individuals with bilateral amygdala damage. *Neuropsychologia, 37*, 1111–1117.

Allport, F. H. (1924). *Social psychology*. Boston: Houghton Mifflin.

Bartlett, M. S., Hager, J. C., Ekman, P., & Sejnowksi, T. J. (1998). *Measuring facial expression by computer image analysis*. Manuscript submitted for publication.

Bavelas, J. B., & Chovil, N. (1997). Faces in dialogue. In J. A. Russell & J. M. Fernandez-Dols (Eds.), *The psychology of facial expression* (pp. 334–346). New York: Cambridge University Press.

Berenbaum, H., & Oltmanns, T. F. (1992). Emotional experience and expression in schizophrenia and depression. *Journal of Abnormal Psychology, 101*, 37–44.

Birdwhistell, R. L. (1963). The kinesic level in the investigation of the emotions. In P. H. Knapp (Ed.), *Expression of emotions in man* (Pt. II, pp. 123–139). New York: International Universities Press.

Birdwhistell, R. L. (1970). *Kinesics and context*. Philadelphia: University of Pennsylvania Press.

Blair, R. J. R., Morris, J. S., Frith, C. D., Perrett, D. I., &

Dolan, R. J. (1998). *Differential neural responses to sad and angry faces: Involvement of the amygdala and orbitofrontal cortex.* Manuscript submitted for review.

Bonanno, G. A., & Kaltman, S. (1999). Toward an integrative perspective on bereavement. *Psychological Bulletin, 125,* 760–776.

Bonanno, G. A., & Keltner, D. (1997). Facial expressions of emotion and the course of conjugal bereavement. *Journal of Abnormal Psychology, 106,* 126–137.

Bonanno, G. A., & Keltner, D. (2000). *Coherence between discrete facial expressions of emotion and core relational appraisal themes in bereavement narratives.* Manuscript submitted for publication.

Borod, J. C. (1992). Interhemispheric and intrahemispheric control of emotion: A focus on unilateral brain damage. *Journal of Consulting and Clinical Psychology, 60,* 339–348.

Borod, J. C., Koff, E., Lorch, M. P., & Nicholas, M. (1986). The expression and perception of facial emotion in brain-damaged patients. *Neuropsychologia, 24,* 169–180.

Breiter, H. C., Etcoff, N. L., Whalen, P. J., Kennedy, W. A., Rauch, S. L., Buckner, R. L., Strauss, M. M., Hyman, S. E., & Rosen, B. R. (1996). Response and habituation of the human amygdala during visual processing of facial expression. *Neuron, 17,* 875–887.

Briggs, J. L. (1960). *Never in anger: Portrait of an Eskimo family.* Cambridge, MA: Harvard University Press.

Broks, P., Young, A. W., Maratos, E. J., Coffey, P. J., Calder, A. J., Isaac, C. I., Mayes, A. R., Hodges, J. R., Montaldi, D., Cezayirli, E., Roberts, N., & Hadley, D. (1998). Face processing impairments after encephalitis: Amygdala damage and recognition of fear. *Neuropsychologia, 36,* 59–70.

Brow, D. E. (1991). *Human universals.* New York: McGraw-Hill.

Bruner, J. S., & Tagiuri, R. (1954). The perception of people. In G. Lindzey (Ed.), *Handbook of social psychology* (Vol. 2, pp. 634–654). Reading, MA: Addison Wesley.

Buck, R., Losow, J. I., Murphy, M. M., & Costanzo, R. (1992). Social facilitation and inhibition of emotional expression and communication. *Journal of Personality and Social Psychology, 63,* 962–968.

Cacioppo, J. T., Klein, D. J., Berntson, G. G., & Hatfield, E. (1993). The psychophysiology of emotion. In M. Lewis & J. M. Haviland (Eds.), *The handbook of emotions* (pp. 119–142). New York: Guilford Press.

Calder, A. J., Young, A. W., Rowland, D., Perrett, D. I., Hodges, J. R., & Etcoff, N. L. (1996). Facial emotion recognition after bilateral amygdala damage: Differentially severe impairment of fear. *Cognitive Neuropsychology, 13,* 699–745.

Camras, L. A., Lambrecht, L., & Michel, G. F. (1996). Infant "surprise" expressions as coordinative motor structures. *Journal of Nonverbal Behavior, 20,* 183–195.

Camras, L. A., Oster, H., Campos, J. J., Miyake, K., & Bradshaw, D. (1992). Japanese and American infants' responses to arm restraints. *Developmental Psychology, 28,* 578–583.

Capps, L., Yirmiya, N., & Sigman, M. (1992). Understanding of simple and complex emotions in non-retarded children with autism. *Journal of Child Psychology and Psychiatry, 33,* 1169–1182.

Caspi, A., & Bem, D. J. (1990). Personality continuity and change across the life course. In L. A. Pervin (Ed.), *Handbook of personality: Theory and research* (pp. 549–575). New York: Guilford Press.

Caspi, A., Elder, G., & Bem, D. J. (1987). Moving against the world: Life-course patterns of explosive children. *Developmental Psychology, 23,* 308–313.

Celani, G., Battacchi, M. W., & Arcidiacano, L. (1999). The understanding of the emotional meaning of facial expression in people with autism. *Journal of Autism and Developmental Disorders, 29,* 57–66.

Cohn, J. F., & Tronick, E. Z. (1987). Mother infant face-to-fact interaction: The sequence of dyadic states at 3, 6, and 9 months. *Developmental Psychology, 23,* 68–77.

Coleman, J. C. (1949). Facial expression of emotion. *Psychological Monograph, 63,* Whole No. 296.

Darwin, C. (1872/1998). *The expression of emotions in man and animals* (3rd ed.). New York: Oxford University Press.

Davidson, R. J. (1993). Parsing affective space: Perspectives from neuropsychology and psychophysiology. *Neuropsychology, 7,* 464–475.

Davidson, R. J., Ekman, P., Saron, C., Senulis, J., & Friesen, W. J. (1990). Emotional expression and brain physiology. I: Approach/withdrawal and cerebral asymmetry. *Journal of Personality and Social Psychology, 58,* 330–341.

Davidson, R. J., & Fox, N. A. (1989). Frontal brain asymmetry predicts infant's response to maternal separation. *Journal of Abnormal Psychology, 98,* 127–131.

Dimberg, U., & Ohman, A. (1996). Behold the wrath: Psychophysiological responses to facial stimuli. *Motivation and Emotion, 20,* 149–182.

Dworkin, R., Clark, S. C., Amador, X. F., & Gorman, J. M. (1996). Does affective blunting in schizophrenia reflect affective deficit or neuromotor dysfunction? *Schizophrenia Research 20,* 301–306.

Eibl-Eibesfeldt, I. (1989). *Human ethology.* New York: Aldine de Gruyter Press.

Eisenberg, N., Fabes, R. A., Miller, P. A., Fultz, J., Shell, R., Mathy, R. M., & Reno, R. R. (1989). Relation of sympathy and distress to prosocial behavior. A multimethod study. *Journal of Personality and Social Psychology, 57,* 55–66.

Ekman, P. (1973). Cross-cultural studies of facial expression. In P. Ekman (Ed.), *Darwin and facial expression: A century of research in review* (pp. 169–222). New York: Academic Press.

Ekman, P. (1978). Facial signs: Facts, fantasies, and possibilities. In T. Sebeok (Ed.), *Sight, sound, and sense* (pp. 124–156). Bloomington, IN: Indiana University Press.

Ekman, P. (1979). About brows: Emotional and conversational signals. In M. von Cranach, K. Foppa, W. Lepenies, & D. Ploog (Eds.), *Human ethology* (pp. 169–248). New York: Cambridge University Press.

Ekman, P. (1984). Expression and the nature of emotion. In K. Scherer & P. Ekman (Eds.), *Approaches to emotion* (pp. 319–344). Hillsdale, NJ: Lawrence Erlbaum.

Ekman, P. (1992a). An argument for basic emotions. *Cognition and Emotion, 6,* 169–200.

Ekman, P. (1992b). *Telling lies: Clues to deceit in the marketplace, marriage, and politics* (2nd ed.). New York: Norton.

Ekman, P. (1993). Facial expression and emotion. *American Psychologist, 48,* 384–392.

Ekman, P. (1994). Strong evidence for universals in facial

expressions: A reply to Russell's mistaken critique. *Psychological Bulletin, 115,* 268–287.

Ekman, P. (1998). Introduction. In C. Darwin, *Expression of emotion in man and animals.* New York: Oxford University Press.

Ekman, P. (1999). Basic emotions. In T. Dalgleish & M. J. Power (Eds.), *Handbook of cognition and emotion.* Chichester, England: Wiley.

Ekman, P., & Davidson, R. J. (1993). Voluntary smiling changes regional brain activity. *Psychological Science, 4,* 342–345.

Ekman, P., Davidson, R. J., & Friesen, W. V. (1990). The Duchenne smile: Emotional expression and brain physiology. II. *Journal of Personality and Social Psychology, 58,* 342–353.

Ekman, P., & Friesen, W. V. (1971). Constants across cultures in the face and emotion. *Journal of Personality and Social Psychology, 17,* 124–129.

Ekman, P., & Friesen, W. V. (1974). Nonverbal behavior and psychopathology. In R. J. Friedman & M. M. Katz (Eds.), *The psychology of depression: Contemporary theory and research.* Washington, DC: Wiley.

Ekman, P., & Friesen, W. V. (1978). *Facial action coding system: A technique for the measurement of facial movement.* Palo Alto, CA: Consulting Psychologists Press.

Ekman, P., & Friesen, W. V. (1982). Felt, false, and miserable smiles. *Journal of Nonverbal Behavior, 6,* 238–252.

Ekman, P., Friesen, W. V., & Ancoli, S. (1980). Facial signs of emotional experience. *Journal of Personality and Social Psychology, 39,* 1125–1134.

Ekman, P., Friesen, W. V., & Ellsworth, P. C. (1982). *Emotion in the human face.* Cambridge, England: Cambridge University Press.

Ekman, P., Friesen, W. V., & O'Sullivan, M. (1988). Smiles when lying. *Journal of Personality and Social Psychology, 54,* 414–420.

Ekman, P., Friesen, W. V., O'Sullivan, M., & Scherer, K. (1980). Relative importance of face, body, and voice in judgments of personality and affect. *Journal of Personality and Social Psychology, 38,* 270–277.

Ekman, P., Huang, T. S., Sejnowski, T. J., & Hager, J. C. (1993). Final report to NSF of the planning workshop on Facial Expression Understanding, July 30 to August 1, 1992. Washington, DC.

Ekman, P., Levenson, R. W., & Friesen W. V. (1983). Autonomic nervous system activity distinguishes among emotions. *Science, 221,* 1208–1210.

Ekman, P., Matsumoto, D., & Friesen, W. V. (1997). Facial expression in affective disorders. In P. Ekman & E. L. Rosenberg (Eds.), *What the face reveals* (pp. 331–341). New York: Oxford University Press.

Ekman, P., & Oster, H. (1979). Facial expression of emotion. *Annual Review of Psychology, 30,* 527–554.

Ekman, P., O'Sullivan, M., & Matsumoto, D. (1991). Contradictions in the study of contempt: What's it all about? *Motivation and Emotion, 15,* 293–296.

Ekman, P., & Rosenberg, E. L. (1997). *What the face reveals.* New York: Oxford University Press.

Ekman, P., Sorenson, E. R., & Friesen, W. V. (1969). Pancultural elements in facial displays of emotions. *Science, 164,* 86–88.

Esteves, F., Dimberg, U., & Ohman, A. (1994). Automatically elicited fear: Conditioned skin conductance responses to masked facial expressions. *Cognition and Emotion, 8,* 393–413.

Etcoff, N. L., & Magee, J. J. (1992). Categorical perception of facial expressions. *Cognition, 44,* 227–240.

Fernandez-Dols, J. M., & Ruiz-Belda, M. A. (1995). Are smiles a sign of happiness? Gold medal winners at the Olympic Games. *Journal of Personality and Social Psychology, 69,* 1113–1119.

Fernandez-Dols, J. M., & Ruiz-Belda, M. A. (1997). Spontaneous facial behavior during intense emotional episodes: Artistic truth and optical truth. In J. A. Russell & J. M. Fernandez-Dols (Eds.), *The psychology of facial expression* (pp. 255–294). Cambridge, England: Cambridge University Press.

Frank, M., Ekman, P., & Friesen, W. V. (1993). Behavioral markers and recognizability of the smile of enjoyment. *Journal of Personality and Social Psychology, 64,* 83–93.

Frank, M., & Stennett, J. (2001). The forced-choice paradigm and the perception of facial expressions of emotion. *Journal of Personality and Social Psychology, 80,* 75–85.

Frank, R. H. (1988). *Passions within reason.* New York: Norton.

Fridlund, A. J. (1991). Sociality of solitary smiling: Potentiation by and implicit audience. *Journal of Personality and Social Psychology, 60,* 229–240.

Fridlund, A. J. (1992). The behavioral ecology and sociality of human faces. *Review of Personality and Social Psychology, 13,* 90–121.

Fridlund, A. J. (1992). Audience effects in affective imagery: Replication and extension to dysphoric imagery. *Journal of Nonverbal Behavior, 16,* 191–212.

Fried, I., Wilson, C. L., MacDonald, K. A., & Behnke, E. J. (1998). Electric current stimulates laughter. *Nature, 391,* 650.

Frijda, N. H. (1986). *The emotions.* Cambridge: Cambridge University Press.

Frijda, N. H., & Mesquita, B. (1992). Emotions: Nature or culture? *Nederlands Tijdschrift voor de Psychologie en haar Grensgebieden, 47,* 3–14.

Gonzaga, G. C., Keltner, D., Londahl, E. A., & Smith, M. (2001). Love and the commitment problem in romantic relation and friendship. *Journal of Personality and Social Psychology, 81,* 247–262.

Gordon, S. L. (1989). The socialization of children's emotions: Emotional culture, competence, and exposure. In C. Saarni & P. L. Harris (Eds.), *Children's understanding of emotion* (pp. 319–349). New York: Cambridge University Press.

Gray, J. M., Young, A. W., Barker, W. A., Curtis, A., Gibson, D. (1997). Impaired recognition of disgust in Huntington's disease gene carriers. *Brain, 120,* 2029–2038.

Gross, J. J., & John, O. P. (1997). Revealing feelings: Facets of emotional expressivity in self-reports, peer ratings, and behavior. *Journal of Personality and Social Psychology, 72,* 435–448.

Haidt, J., & Keltner, D. (1999). Culture and facial expression: Open ended methods find more faces and a gradient of universality. *Cognition and Emotion, 13,* 225–266.

Hauser, M. D. (1996). *The evolution of communication.* Cambridge, MA: MIT Press.

Harker, L., & Keltner, D. (2001). Expressions of positive emotion in women's college yearbook pictures and their relationship to personality and life outcomes across adulthood. *Journal of Personality and Social Psychology, 80,* 112–124.

Hecht, M. A., & LaFrance, M. (1998). License or obligation to smile: The effect of power and sex on amount and type of smiling. *Personality and Social Psychology Bulletin, 24,* 1332–1342.

Hess, U., Banse, R., & Kappas, A. (1995). The intensity of facial expression is determined by underlying affective states and social situations. *Journal of Personality and Social Psychology, 69,* 280–288.

Hornak, J., Rolls, E. T., & Wade, D. (1996). Face and voice expression identification in patients' emotional and behavioral changes following ventral frontal lobe damage. *Neuropsychologia, 34,* 247–261.

Hunt, W. A. (1941). Recent developments in the field of emotions. *Psychological Bulletin, 38,* 249–276.

Izard, C. E. (1971). *The face of emotion.* New York: Appleton-Century-Crofts.

Izard, C. E. (1977). *Human emotions.* New York: Plenum.

Izard, C. E. (1993). Four systems of emotion activation: Cognitive and non-cognitive processes. *Psychological Review, 100,* 68–90.

Izard, C. E. (1994). Innate and universal facial expressions: Evidence from developmental and cross-cultural research. *Psychological Bulletin, 115,* 288–299.

Izard, C. E., Hembree, E. A., & Huebner, R. R. (1987). Infants' emotional expressions to acute pain: Developmental change and stability of individual differences. *Developmental Psychology, 23,* 105–113.

Jones, I. H., & Pansa, M. (1979). Some nonverbal aspects of depression and schizophrenia occurring during the interview. *Journal of Nervous and Mental Disease, 167,* 402–409.

Kagan, J., Reznik, J. S., & Snidman, N. (1988). Biological bases of childhood shyness, *Science, 240,* 167–171.

Keltner, D. (1995). The signs of appeasement: Evidence for the distinct displays of embarrassment, amusement, and shame. *Journal of Personality and Social Psychology, 68,* 441–454.

Keltner, D. (1996). Facial expressions of emotion and personality. In C. Malatesta-Magai and S. H. McFadden (Eds.), *Handbook of emotion, aging, and the lifecourse* (pp. 385–402). New York: Academic Press.

Keltner, D., & Bonanno, G. A. (1997). A study of laughter and dissociation: The distinct correlates of laughter and smiling during bereavement. *Journal of Personality and Social Psychology, 73,* 687–702.

Keltner, D., & Buswell, B. N. (1996). Evidence for the distinctness of embarrassment, shame, and guilt: A study of recalled antecedents and facial expressions of emotion. *Cognition and Emotion, 10,* 155–171.

Keltner, D., & Buswell, B. N. (1997). Embarrassment: Its distinct form and appeasement functions. *Psychological Bulletin, 122,* 250–270.

Keltner, D., & Ekman, P. (1996). Affective intensity and emotional experience. *Cognition and Emotion, 10,* 323–328.

Keltner, D., Ellsworth, P. C., & Edwards, K. (1993). Beyond simple pessimism: Effects of sadness and anger on social perception. *Journal of Personality and Social Psychology, 64,* 740–752.

Keltner, D., & Haidt, J. (1999). Social functions of emotions at four levels of analysis. *Cognition and Emotion, 13,* 505–521.

Keltner, D., & Harker, L. A. (1998). The forms and functions of the nonverbal display of shame. In P. Gilbert & B. Andrews (Eds.), *Interpersonal approaches to shame* (pp. 78–98). Oxford, England: Oxford University Press.

Keltner, D., & Kring, A. (1998). Emotion, social function, and psychopathology. *General Psychological Review, 2,* 320–342.

Keltner, D., Moffitt, T., & Stouthamer-Loeber, M. (1995). Facial expressions of emotion and psychopathology in adolescent boys. *Journal of Abnormal Psychology, 104,* 644–652.

Keltner, D., Young, R., & Buswell, B. N. (1997). Appeasement in human emotion, personality, and social practice. *Aggressive Behavior, 23,* 359–374.

Keltner, D., Young, R. C., Heerey, E. A., Oemig, C., & Monarch, N. D. (1998). Teasing in hierarchical and intimate relations. *Journal of Personality and Social Psychology, 75,* 1231–1247.

Klineberg, O. (1940). *Social psychology.* New York: Henry Holt.

Klinnert, M. D., Emde, R. N., Butterfield, P., & Campos, J. J. (1986). Social referencing: The infant's use of emotional signals from a friendly adult with mother present. *Developmental Psychology, 22,* 427–432.

Knutson, B. (1996). Facial expressions of emotion influence interpersonal trait inferences. *Journal of Nonverbal Behavior, 20,* 165–182.

Krause, R., Steimer, E., Sanger-Alt, C., & Wagner, G. (1989). Facial expressions of schizophrenic patients and their interaction partners. *Psychiatry, 52,* 1–12.

Kraut, R. E., & Johnston, R. E. (1979). Social and emotional messages of smiling: An ethological approach. *Journal of Personality and Social Psychology, 37,* 1539–1553.

Kring, A. M., & Bachorowski, J.-A. (1999). Emotions and psychopathology. *Cognition and Emotion, 13,* 575–599.

Kring, A. M., Kerr, S. L, Smith, D. A., & Neale, J. M. (1993). Flat affect in schizophrenia does not reflect diminished subjective experience of emotion. *Journal of Abnormal Psychology, 102,* 507–517.

Kring, A. M., & Neale, J. M. (1996). Do schizophrenics show a disjunctive relationship among expressive, experiential, and psychophysiological components of emotion? *Journal of Abnormal Psychology, 105,* 249–257.

La Barre, W. (1947). The cultural basis for emotions and gestures. *Journal of Personality, 16,* 49–68.

Landis, C. (1924). Studies of emotional reactions. II. General behavior and facial expression. *Journal of Comparative Psychology, 4,* 447–509.

Lang, P. J. (1995). The emotion probe: Studies of motivation and attention. *American Psychologist, 50,* 372–385.

Larsen, R. J., & Diener, E. (1987). Affect intensity as an individual difference characteristic: A review. *Journal of Research in Personality, 21,* 1–39.

Larsen, R. J., & Ketelaar, T. (1991). Personality and susceptibility to positive and negative emotional states. *Journal of Personality and Social Psychology, 61,* 132–140.

Lavenu, I., Pasquier, F., Lebert, F., Petit, H., & Van der Linden, M. (1999). Perception of emotion in frontotemporal dementia and alzheimer's disease. *Alzheimer Disease and Associated Disorders, 13,* 96–101.

Lazarus, R. S. (1991). *Emotion and adaptation.* New York: Oxford University Press.

Leary, M. R., Britt, T. W., Cutlip, W. D. II, & Templeton, J. L. (1992). Social blushing. *Psychological Bulletin, 112,* 446–460.

LeDoux, J. E. (1996). *The emotional brain: The mysterious underpinnings of emotional life.* New York: Simon & Schuster.

Levenson, R. W., Carstensen, L. L., Friesen, W. V., & Ekman, P. (1991). Emotion, physiology, and expression in old age. *Psychology and Aging, 6*, 28–35.

Levenson, R. W., Ekman, P., & Friesen, W. V. (1990). Voluntary facial action generates emotion-specific autonomic nervous system activity. *Psychophysiology, 27*, 363–384.

Levenson, R. W., Ekman, P., Heider, K., & Friesen, W. V. (1992). Emotion and autonomic nervous system activity in the Minangkabau of West Sumatra. *Journal of Personality and Social Psychology, 62*, 972–988.

Levenson, R. W., & Gottman, J. M. (1983). Marital interaction: Physiological linkage and affective exchange. *Journal of Personality and Social Psychology, 45*, 587–597.

Lewis, M. (2000). Toward a development of psychopathology: Models, definitions, and prediction. In A. J. Sameroff & M. Lewis (Eds.), *Handbook of developmental psychopathology.* New York: Kluwer Academic/Plenum Publishers.

Lutz, C., & White, G. M. (1986). The anthropology of emotions. *Annual Review of Anthropology, 15*, 405–436.

Malatesta, C. Z. (1990). The role of emotions in the development and organization of personality. In R. A. Thompson (Ed.), *Nebraska Symposium on Motivation: Vol. 36, Socioemotional Development* (pp. 1–56). Lincoln: University of Nebraska Press.

Markus, H. R., & Kitayama, S. (1991). Culture and the self: Implications for cognition, emotion, and motivation. *Psychological Review, 98*, 224–253.

Matsumoto, D. (1987). The role of facial response in the experience of emotion: More methodological problems and a meta-analysis. *Journal of Personality and Social Psychology, 52*, 769–774.

Matsumoto, D. (1990). Cultural similarities and differences in display rules. *Motivation and Emotion, 14*, 195–214.

Matsumoto, D. (1992). More evidence for the universality of a contempt expression. *Motivation and Emotion, 16*, 363–368.

Matsumoto, D., & Ekman, P. (1989). American-Japanese cultural differences in intensity ratings of facial expressions of emotion. *Motivation and Emotion, 13*, 143–157.

Matsumoto, D., & Kudoh, T. (1993). American-Japanese cultural differences in attributions of personality based on smiles. *Journal of Nonverbal Behavior, 17*, 231–243.

Mattes, R. M., Schneider, F., Heimann, H., & Birbaumer, N. (1995). Reduced emotional response of schizophrenic patients in remission during social interaction. *Schizophrenia Research, 17*, 249–255.

McGhee, P. E. (1977). Children's humour: A review of current research trends. In A. J. Chapman & H. C. Foot (Eds.), *It's a funny thing, humour* (pp. 199–209). Oxford: Pergamon.

Mead, M. (1975). Darwin and facial expression. *Journal of Communication, 25*, 209–213.

Mesquita, B., & Frijda, N. (1992). Cultural variations in emotions: A review. *Psychological Bulletin, 122*, 179–204.

Mineka, S., & Cook, M. (1993). Mechanisms involved in the observational conditioning of fear. *Journal of Experimental Psychology, 122*, 23–38.

Mineka, S., Davidson, M., Cook, M., & Keir, R. (1984). Observational conditioning of snake fear in rhesus monkeys. *Journal of Abnormal Psychology, 93*, 355–372.

Morris, J. S., Frith, C. D., Perrett, D. I., Rowland, D., Young, A. W., Calder, A. J., & Dolan, R. J. (1996). A differential neural response in the human amygdala to fearful and happy facial expressions. *Nature, 383*, 812–815.

Moskowitz, D. S., & Coté, S. (1995). Do interpersonal traits predict affect? A comparison of three models. *Journal of Personality and Social Psychology, 69*, 915–924.

Munn, N. L. (1940). The effect of knowledge of the situation upon judgment of emotion from facial expressions. *Journal of Abnormal and Social Psychology, 35*, 324–338.

Nelson, C. A., & de Haan, M. (1997). In J. A. Russell & J. M. Fernandez-Dols (Eds.), *The psychology of facial expression* (pp. 176–204). Cambridge, England: Cambridge University Press.

Ohman, A., & Dimberg, U. (1978). Facial expressions as conditioned stimuli for electrodermal responses: A case of "preparedness"? *Journal of Personality and Social Psychology, 36*, 1251–1258.

Ortony, A., & Turner, T. J. (1990). What's basic about basic emotions? *Psychological Review, 97*, 315–331.

Osgood, C. E. (1966). Dimensionality of the semantic space for communication via facial expressions. *Scandinavian Journal of Psychology, 7*, 1–30.

Patrick, C. (1994). Emotion and psychopathology: Startling new insights. *Psychophysiology, 31*, 319–330.

Pervin, L. (1993). Affect and personality. In M. Lewis & J. Haviland (Eds.), *The handbook of emotions* (pp. 301–312). New York: Guilford Press.

Phillips, M. L., Young, A. W., Senior, C., Brammer, M., Andrew, C., Calder, A. J., Bullmore, E. T., Perrett, D. I., Rowland, D., Williams, S. C. R., Gray, J. A., & David, A. S. (1997). A specific neural substrate for perceiving facial expressions of disgust. *Nature, 389*, 495–498.

Plutchik, R. (1962). *The emotions: Facts, theories, and a new model.* New York: Random House.

Plutchik, R. (1980). *Emotion: A psychoevolutionary synthesis.* New York: Harper & Row.

Pollack, S. D., Cicchetti, D., Klorman, R., & Brumaghim, J. T. (1997). Cognitive brain event-related potentials and emotion processing in maltreated children. *Child Development, 68*, 773–787.

Provine, R. R. (1993). Laughter punctuates speech: Linguistic, social and gender contexts of laughter. *Ethology, 95*, 291–298.

Rolls, E. T. (2000). The orbitofrontal cortex and reward. *Cerebral Cortex, 10*, 284–294.

Romney, A. K., Moore, C. C., & Rusch, C. D. (1997). Cultural universals: Measuring the semantic structure of emotion terms in English and Japanese. *Proceedings of the National Academy of Sciences of the USA, 94*, 5489–5494.

Rosenberg, E. L., & Ekman, P. (1994). Coherence between expressive and experiential systems in emotion. *Cognition and Emotion, 8*, 201–229.

Rosenberg, E. L., Ekman, P., Jiang, W., Buyback, M., Coleman, R. E., Hanson, M., O'Connor, C., Waugh, R., & Blumenthal, J. (1998). *Facial expressions of emotion predict myocardial ischemia.* Manuscript under review.

Ross, E. D. (1981). The aprosodias. *Archives of Neurology, 38*, 561–569.

Rothbart, M. (1973). Laughter in young children. *Psychological Bulletin, 80*, 247–256.

Ruch, W., (1993). Exhilaration and humor. In M. Lewis & J. M. Haviland (Eds.), *The handbook of emotion* (pp. 605–616). New York: Guilford Press.

Ruch, W. (1995). Will the real relationship between facial expression and affective experience please stand up: The case of exhilaration. *Cognition and Emotion, 9*, 33–58.

Russell, J. A. (1991a). The contempt expression and the relativity thesis. *Motivation and Emotion, 15*, 149–168.

Russell, J. A. (1991b). Culture and categorization of emotion. *Psychological Bulletin, 110* (3), 426–450.

Russell, J. A. (1994). Is there universal recognition of emotion from facial expression? A review of cross-cultural studies. *Psychological Bulletin, 115*, 102–141.

Russell, J. A. (1997). Reading emotions from and into faces: Resurrecting a dimensional-contextual perspective. In J. A. Russell & J. M. Fernandez-Dols (Eds.), *The psychology of facial expression* (pp. 295–320). Cambridge, England: Cambridge University Press.

Scarr, S., & McCartney, K. (1983). How people make their own environments: A theory of genotype → environmental effects. *Child Development, 54*, 424–435.

Scherer, K. R., & Wallbott, H. B. (1994). Evidence for universality and cultural variation of differential emotion response patterning. *Journal of Personality and Social Psychology, 66*, 310–328.

Schlosberg, H. (1954). Three dimensions of emotion. *Psychological Review, 61*, 81–88.

Shaver, P., Schwartz, J., Kirson, D., & O'Connor, C. (1987). Emotion knowledge: Further exploration of a prototype approach. *Journal of Personality and Social Psychology, 52*, 1061–1086.

Shearn, D., Bergman, E., Hill, K., Abel, A., & Hinds, L. (1990). Facial coloration and temperature responses in blushing. *Psychophysiology, 27*, 687–693.

Smith, C. A. (1989). Dimensions of appraisal and physiological response in emotion. *Journal of Personality and Social Psychology, 56*, 339–353.

Smith, C. A., & Scott, H. S. (1997). A componential approach to the meaning of facial expression. In J. A. Russell & J. M. Fernandez-Dols (Eds.), *The psychology of facial expression* (pp. 229–254). Cambridge, England: Cambridge University Press.

Smith, M. C. (1995). Facial expression in mild dementia of the Alzheimer type. *Behavioural Neurology, 8*, 149–156.

Sorce, J. F., Emde, R. N., Campos, J. J., & Klinnert, M. D. (1985). Maternal emotional signaling: Its effect on the visual cliff behavior of 1-year-olds. *Developmental Psychology, 21*, 195–200.

Sprengelmeyer, R., Rausch, M., Eysel, U. T., & Przuntek, H. (1998). Neural structures associated with recognition of facial expressions of basic emotions. *Proceedings of the Royal Society of London, 265*, 1927–1931.

Sprengelmeyer, R., Young, A. W., Calder, A. J., Karnat, A., Lange, H., Homberg, V., Perrett, D. I., & Rowland, D. (1996). Loss of disgust: Perceptions of faces and emotions in Huntington's disease. *Brain, 119*, 1647–1665.

Sprengelmeyer, R., Young, A. W., Schroedor, U., Grossenbacher, P. G., Federlein, J., Buettner, T., & Przuntek, H. (1999). Knowing no fear. *Proceedings of the Royal Society Biological Sciences Series B, 266*, 2451–2456.

Tomkins, S. S. (1962). *Affect, imagery, consciousness. Vol. 1: The positive affects.* New York: Springer.

Tomkins, S. S. (1963). *Affect, imagery, consciousness. Vol. 2: The negative affects.* New York: Springer.

Tomkins, S. S., & McCarter, R. (1964). What and where are the primary affects? Some evidence for a theory. *Perceptual and Motor Skills, 18*, 119–158.

Tronick, E. Z. (1989). Emotions and emotional communication in infants. *American Psychologist, 44*, 112–119.

Ulrich, G., & Harms, K. (1985). A video analysis of the nonverbal behavior of depressed patients and their relation to anxiety and depressive disorders. *Journal of Affective Disorders, 9*, 63–67.

Wagner, H. L., & Smith, J. (1991). Facial expressions in the presence of friends and strangers. *Journal of Nonverbal Behavior, 15*, 201–214.

Walden, T. A., & Ogan, T. A. (1988). The development of social referencing. *Child Development, 59*, 1230–1240.

Watson, D., & Clark, L. A. (1992). On traits and temperament: General and specific factors of emotional experience and their relation to the five factor model. *Journal of Personality, 60*, 441–476.

Waxer, P. H. (1974). Nonverbal cues for depression. *Journal of Abnormal Psychology, 83*, 319–322.

Whalen, P. J., Rauch, S. L., Etcoff, N. L., McInerney, S. C., Lee, M. B., & Jenike, M. A. (1998). Masked presentations of emotional facial expressions modulate amygdala activity without explicit knowledge. *Journal of Neuroscience, 18*, 411–418.

Wierzbicka, A. (Ed.). (1990). Special issue on the semantics of emotion. *Australian Journal of Linguistics, 10*, 2.

Wolff, W. (1943). *The expression of personality: Experimental depth psychology.* New York: Harper Brothers.

Woodworth, R. S. (1938). *Experimental psychology.* New York: Henry Holt.

Young, A. W., Hellawell, D. J., Van de Wal, C., & Johnson, M. (1996). Facial expression processing after amygdalotomy. *Neuropsychologia, 34*, 31–39.

Young, A. W., Newcombe, F., de Haan, E. H. F., Small, M., & Hay, D. C. (1993). Face perception after brain injury. *Brain, 116*, 941–959.

Young, A. W., Rowland, D., Calder, A. J., Etcoff, N. L., Seth, A., & Perrett, D. I. (in press). Facial expression megamix: Tests of dimensional and category accounts of emotion recognition. *Cognition.*

Zahn-Waxler, C., Radke-Yarrow, M., Wagner, E., & Chapman, M. (1992). Development of concern for others. *Developmental Psychology, 28*, 126–136.

Zajonc, R. B. (1985). Emotion and facial efference: A theory reclaimed. *Science, 228*, 15–21.

# 23

# VOCAL EXPRESSION OF EMOTION

Klaus R. Scherer, Tom Johnstone,
and Gundrun Klasmeyer

This chapter reviews theoretical models and empirical evidence on the effects of emotion on vocalization, in particular on human speech. Of all expressive manifestations of emotional arousal, vocalization represents the most phylogenetically continuous modality. The neural control structures, the voice production mechanisms, and the characteristics of vocal emotion signals are comparable across many species of mammals, including humans (Hauser, 1996; Marler & Tenaza, 1977; Morton, 1977; Scherer, 1985; see chapter 24, this volume). In consequence, the study of emotional vocalization constitutes a prime tool to investigate the relationships between the physiological production of affect vocalization and its use as a signal in social interaction and communication. The basis for the following discussion is a modified version of the Brunswikian lens model (Figure 23.1; see also Kappas, Hess, & Scherer, 1991; Scherer, 1978, 1982). This model allows one to clearly distinguish between the *expression* (or encoding) of emotion on the sender side, the *transmission* of the sound, and the *impression* (or decoding) on the receiver side, resulting in emotion inference or attribution. Consequently, the model encourages research on the complete process of emotion communication by (1) determining which distal characteristics of the sound wave emerging from the mouth of an affectively aroused speaker (i.e., the acoustic parameters) are produced by the underlying emotion, (2) determining how these cues are transmitted from sender to receiver through the vocal-acoustic-auditory channel, and (3) determining how these proximal

cues (the representation of the distal voice characteristics in the sensorium and the central nervous system) are used by the receiver to infer the emotion of the sender. As will be shown, most research in this area has focused either on encoding or decoding. Our aim in organizing the chapter by a model that charts the entire process is to encourage future research to attend to all of these aspects and their interrelationships.

## Encoding: Expression of Emotion in Voice and Speech

The first step described by the Brunswikian lens model is the encoding of emotion in the acoustic properties of the speech signal, through a selective modification of speech production. It has been suggested that the vocal characteristics of emotional utterances are determined by both push and pull effects (Scherer, 1985, 1994). *Push effects* refer to the direct effects of the physiological changes characterizing many emotional responses on the voice and speech production system (see Scherer, 1989). *Pull effects* reflect the fact that vocalization is, as is other expressive behavior, often closely monitored and regulated (or sometimes even expressly produced) for strategic reasons. When pull effects operate, voice production targets are determined, at least in part, by normatively proscribed or conventionalized acoustical signal patterns (see also Caffi & Janney, 1994). In this chapter we will mostly focus on

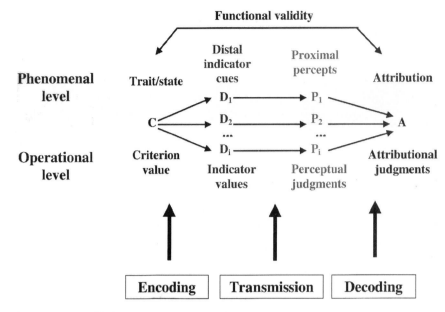

**Figure 23.1** Modified form of the Brunswikian lens model applied to the process of the vocal communication of emotion. Adapted from Scherer (1982).

push effects, although pull effects will be mentioned in places.

### Theoretical Predictions of Competing Emotion Models

Much of the work in this area has been atheoretical, searching to empirically determine which changes in voice and speech production, and which corresponding patterns of acoustic parameters, will be produced by inductions of stress or specific emotions in the speaker. As one might expect, this approach entails the problem of making sense of a multitude of different, often non-replicated results. In particular, it has been difficult to determine which type of emotional state has been induced in a study and to decide whether it can be reasonably compared with similarly labeled states in other studies. It can be shown (see Banse & Scherer, 1996; Scherer, 1986) that the term *anger* may cover anything from a mild irritation produced by a manipulation of experimenter rudeness to violent rage, as portrayed by an actor. In consequence, recent work has attempted to ground research on theoretical models of vocalization changes in emotion and to examine concrete predictions. In what follows we review the respective predictions of three major theoretical traditions: arousal theories, discrete emotion theories, and appraisal theories (see Scherer, 2000a, and the introduction to this volume).

### Arousal Theories

Proponents of this approach have generally neglected vocal behavior. For example, arousal models of emotion

(e.g., Duffy, 1962; Thayer, 1989) have focused on predicting physiological response in the autonomic nervous system (ANS), not being much concerned with vocal or facial expression. These models suggest that emotions are mostly differentiated along a continuum from low to high sympathetic activation (often linked to an active-passive dimension in terms of the corresponding feeling states). Even though these theorists have not produced explicit predictions of vocal expression patterns, it is relatively straightforward to extrapolate the vocal characteristics to be expected for certain emotions on the basis of the physiological predictions for sympathetic arousal (e.g., deeper and faster respiration, increased cardiovascular activity, increased muscle tension). The corresponding acoustical effects are increases in central tendency and range of fundamental frequency (F0) and intensity, as well as an increase in harmonic energy and in the rate of articulation. In consequence, if arousal models of emotion explain emotion differentiation with a sufficient degree of accuracy, one would expect vocal parameters that are directly tied to sympathetic arousal to provide an exhaustive set of predictors for the vocal patterning of different affect states. It has indeed long been presumed that vocal expression mostly, if not exclusively, indicates the arousal component of emotion, being unable to convey differences in valence or qualitative differences between emotion categories (see Banse & Scherer, 1996; Scherer, 1979, 1986, for a more detailed discussion).

One-dimensional arousal theories are less popular today, even though in many studies on vocal expression of emotion, and especially of stress, they seem to still implicitly determine the interpretation of the data by researchers.

Most modern dimensional researchers combine the arousal or activity dimension with the valence or pleasantness dimension (Lang, Greenwald, Bradley, & Hamm, 1994; Russell, 1980). As was the case of earlier arousal theorists, these modern dimensionalists have unfortunately not made any direct predictions about vocal expression (but see Bachorowski, 1999; Bachorowski & Owren, 1995, for a recent dimensional approach on vocal expression).

## Discrete Emotion Theories

After the waning of the popularity of arousal models in the 1960s, discrete emotion models, as suggested by Tomkins (1962, 1984) and popularized by Ekman (1972, 1992) and Izard (1971, 1977), dominated the field of emotion (as well as the textbooks). Following Darwin's (1872/1998) pioneering effort to define a limited number of basic emotions, Tomkins suggested that specific response patterns for these fundamental, discrete emotions were produced by innate neuromotor programs. While Tomkins, just as Darwin, insisted on the importance of specific vocal expressions for basic emotions, he did not develop specific hypotheses, contrary to the facial expression modality for which he, and in particular his followers, Ekman, Friesen, and Izard developed very elaborate predictions of facial patterning (as based on the presumed action of neuromotor programs; Ekman & Friesen, 1978; Izard, 1971). In consequence, it is difficult to extrapolate the predictions that discrete-emotion theorists might make for the vocal expression of these basic emotions. However, given the underlying philosophy of this approach, it seems reasonable to assume that discrete-emotion theorists would postulate clearly distinct and highly emotion-specific patterns of vocal parameter configurations, completely predictable on the basis of the type of emotion a particular token is expected to exemplify.

## Appraisal Theories

The most recent type of emotion models is represented by appraisal theories that assume that emotion differentiation is determined by the outcomes of event evaluation processes as based on a set of appraisal criteria (see chapter 29, this volume; Scherer, 1999a; Scherer, Schorr, & Johnstone, 2001). Many of these theorists assume that the efferent response patterns (including physiological changes and facial/vocal expression) are produced by specific appraisal results and serve as adaptive responses to the need for information processing and action tendencies (Scherer, 1984, 1992; Smith & Ellsworth, 1985). For example, Smith (1989) showed a correlation between the appraisal of goal obstructiveness and innervation of the corrugator muscle. Thus, while subscribing, like discrete-emotion theorists, to the assumption that emotion-specific patterning constitutes an adaptive response, appraisal theorists do not assume unitary mechanisms, such as neuromotor programs, for a small number of "basic" emotions. Rather, they propose that the specificity in the patterning can be best predicted as the cumulative result of the adaptive changes produced by a specific appraisal profile (see Scherer, 1986, 1992, 2000b, 2001; Smith & Scott, 1997, for detailed reviews of this hypothetical patterning mechanism).

On the basis of these assumptions, Scherer (1986) has produced an extensive set of predictions concerning the physiological changes and the ensuing consequences for the voice production mechanism that can be expected for *appraisal results on specific dimensions* (based on functional considerations). The complexity of these predictions does not allow us to present them in detail here. Briefly put, the justification for the predictions rests in using the assumed functional consequence of a particular appraisal result to predict the pattern of peripheral physiological arousal. Then, the effects of the respective physiological pattern on the voice production process are estimated and the acoustic concomitants are inferred. For example, appraisal of goal obstructiveness requires strong action (e.g., fighting), which should lead to high sympathetic arousal with the consequent changes for respiration and muscle tension, and thereby changes in phonation (higher F0, different glottal pulse shape producing energy changes in the spectrum). Similarly, it is predicted that an appraisal of high coping potential (e.g., power to deal with an obstacle) will lead to orofacial changes evolutionarily linked to biting behavior. The configuration of the vocal tract produced by this setting will privilege certain filter characteristics of the vocal tract (see Ladefoged, 1975; Scherer, 1982) and will thus affect energy distribution in the spectrum. Based on a theoretical analysis of emotion-specific appraisal profiles, Scherer (1986) has proposed a number of detailed hypotheses concerning the vocal parameter configurations to be expected for a number of *specific modal emotions*. The interested reader is invited to read further details of the underlying model and the predictions it generates in Scherer (1986) or Johnstone, van Reekum, and Scherer (2001).

In what follows, we review the empirical evidence available to date with respect to the predictions emanating from these three theoretical traditions. Specifically, three questions are addressed: (1) Is the notion of sympathetic arousal sufficient to describe vocal emotion expression differentiation (as would be held by arousal models)? (2) Is there evidence for highly prototypical vocal parameter configurations that might be produced by invariable neuromotor programs (as held by discrete emotion theorists)? (3) What is the evidence for the more molecular predictions from appraisal theory, either for the effects of results on specific appraisal dimensions or for the combined predictions for modal emotions? Sympathetic arousal theories imply that emotion-specific variance in the acoustic properties of speech are explainable in terms of a single arousal factor, and that emotions that are qualitatively different but similar with respect to sympathetic arousal (e.g., rage and elation) are vocally indistinguishable. Both discrete-emotion theories and appraisal theories posit the existence of more specific vocal expressions. Proponents of discrete-emotion theories would predict that specific vocal patterns would be found in well-defined clusters, each corresponding to a different discrete emotion. In contrast, appraisal theories suggest the existence of a highly differentiated set of vocal profiles, since the change in outcome of any single appraisal check is expected to result in changes to vocal production. In consequence, even for emotional states that are labeled with the same word, one may find somewhat varying vocal patterns, depending, for example, on the degree of goal obstruction or whether a reaction is considered to be urgent.

### Evidence from Empirical Research

The empirical studies conducted over the last six decades can be classified into three major categories, based on the criterion of the type of speech material used: natural vocal expression, induced emotional expression, and simulated emotional expression (see also Campbell, 2000).

Studies using *natural vocal expression* have made use of recorded material that was taped during naturally occurring emotional states of various sorts, such as dangerous flight situations for pilots, journalists reporting emotion-eliciting events, affectively loaded therapy sessions, and so on (see Table 7 in Scherer, 1986, for details on earlier studies; see also Bachorowski, 1999; Frick, 1985; Murray & Arnott, 1993). In recent years, affectively toned speech samples recorded off the air (e.g., from TV game or reality shows) have been used (Douglas-Cowie, Cowie, & Schröder, 2000; Roach, Stibbard, Osborne, Arnfield, & Setter, 1998). While the use of naturally occurring voice changes in emotionally charged situations has the obvious advantage of high ecological validity, there are serious drawbacks. In many cases, only brief voice samples for a very small number of speakers, often suffering from bad recording quality, are available. Furthermore, it is not always obvious which emotion the speakers have really experienced in the situation. While researchers using this type of material often infer emotional quality on the basis of the type of situation, appraisal theorists point out that the same event may provoke very different emotions in different individuals and insist on the need to study the subjective appraisal of each individual, even in apparently similar predicaments (see Roseman & Smith, 2001; chapter 29, this volume). In addition, it is possible that there are strong effects of self-presentation or display rules, especially for material recorded from TV shows, that may render the ecological validity of such material suspect.

In a number of experimental studies, vocal expression during *induced emotions* has been studied (again, more detailed information can be found in Table 7 in Scherer, 1986; see also Bachorowski, 1999; Frick, 1985; Murray & Arnott, 1993; for empirical research using these types of vocal emotional expression, see Bachorowski & Owren, 1995; Johnstone, 2001; Kappas, 1997; Karlsson et al., 2000; Scherer, Johnstone, Klasmeyer, & Bänziger, 2000; Tolkmitt & Scherer, 1986). The induction procedures have varied from study to study, including stress induction (e.g., difficult tasks to be completed under time pressure), presentation of emotion-inducing films or slides, imagery methods, or computer games. While the experimentally controlled induction procedures allow the production of comparable voice samples for all participants, these procedures often produce only relatively weak affect. Furthermore, in spite of using the same procedure for all participants, it is not certain, as mentioned just above, that the same affective states are produced in all individuals, given individual differences in event appraisal (see chapter 29, this volume).

By far the largest number of studies in this area have made use of *simulated vocal expressions* as produced by professional or lay actors (again see Table 7 in Scherer, 1986, for details on earlier studies; see also Bachorowski, 1999; Frick, 1985; Murray & Arnott, 1993; for empirical research using these types of vocal emotional expression see Banse & Scherer, 1996; Juslin & Laukka, 2001; Klasmeyer, 1999; Paeschke, Kienast, & Sendlmeier, 1999; Tischer, 1993; Wallbott & Scherer, 1986). While studies using simulated vocal portrayal of emotions can be expected to yield much more intense, prototypical expressions than either induced states or natural emotions that can be publicly observed (Scherer, 1986, p. 159), there is a danger that actors overemphasize relatively obvious cues and miss more subtle ones that might appear in natural expression of emotion (Scherer, 1986, p. 144). Clearly, such simulated speech samples reflect not only the push effects of emotion on the voice but also sociocultural norms that provide the actor with a target vocal pattern that pulls the voice in a particular direction. However, there is reason to believe (see Johnstone & Scherer, 2000; Scherer, 1986) that such vocal expressions still strongly resemble purely push-related vocal expressions of emotion: If the two were to diverge too much, the acted version would lose its credibility (as may sometimes be the case with bad actors). Yet it cannot be excluded that actors use conventionalized stereotypes of vocal expression (possibly in part dictated by specific acting schools) that allow them to differentially communicate the intended emotions in a way that corresponds only partly to natural expression.

### Classification and Measurement of Vocal Parameters

In this section, we discuss the nature of the vocal parameters that have served as indicators of emotional change and that will be used to summarize the findings. As in many other areas of psychological functioning, it is difficult to observe the mechanisms that underlie the effect of emotional arousal on voice and speech. The mental processes involved in speech production, including the planning of motor commands, can hardly be accessed at all. Using appropriate instruments, one can measure movements of the articulators (e.g., lips, tongue) or the behavior of the voice source (e.g., the vibrations of the vocal folds). But apart from the fact that specialized instruments such as flow masks, laryngographs, palatographs, or articulographs are rarely available to researchers interested in the vocal expression of emotions, there is another problem: If we subject a speaker to this type of intrusive measurement in order to study articulation or voice source dynamics, we can hardly expect him or her to produce natural emotional speech. This is why analysis of acoustic parameters of the speech signal resulting from the production process, which can be simply recorded with a microphone, has been the method of choice for researchers in this area, using analog measurement devices in the earlier periods and digital speech analysis procedures in recent years (see Ladefoged, 1975, for a general introduction to these measures; more technical treatment of these issues is provided in O'Shaughnessy, 2000; Rosen & Howell, 1991).

Historically, acoustic signal dimensions such as duration, amplitude (intensity), fundamental frequency of vocal fold vibration (F0), and energy distribution in the frequency spectrum were the first parameters to be objectively measured. They are relatively easy to define and can be measured fairly automatically. In contrast, parameters requiring more or less extensive phonetic interpretation often lack consensual definition and cannot easily be measured automatically. It so happens that the rather straightforward, automatically analyzable parameters are mostly indicative of arousal, making it necessary to employ more complex, derived parameters if one wants to go beyond the arousal dimension. As shown later, a large number of different acoustic parameters can be currently obtained by appropriate digital analysis of recorded speech. Table 23.1 summarizes the acoustic-phonetic and psychoacoustic parameters described throughout the chapter.

In order to interpret the acoustic parameters in a theoretical context, we need to define the acoustic parameters in terms of the physiology of speech production and the hypothesized links with physiological response patterns found for different emotions (see Scherer, 1986). While there is no one-to-one relationship, links with the underlying speech production mechanisms can be shown for many acoustic-phonetic parameters. Traditionally, the speech production process is classified into respiration, phonation, and articulation. In terms of acoustics, the effects of articulator positions and movements in the vocal tract can be regarded as a filter with time-varying filter characteristics applied to the (also time-varying) source

signal produced by respiration and phonation (Fant, 1960; see also Ladefoged, 1975; O'Shaughnessy, 2000). Therefore, it would be useful to obtain separate indicators for source and filter characteristics. Unfortunately, it is not a trivial task to distinguish clearly between the influence of articulation and the characteristics of the source signal in acoustic analyses of recorded speech signals. A further analytical subdivision between the acoustic effects of respiration and phonation as determinants of the source signal is even more difficult (see Sundberg, 1994, for details). This is why acoustic models often regard respiration and phonation as just one component of the speech production process.

Voice source parameters can be classified into *general voice quality* variables (such as type of phonation; Laver, 1980), which more or less reflect a generalized "tension state" of specific muscles in the larynx, and *prosodic* parameters that reflect voluntary, dynamic changes in the tension of specific larynx muscles during speech production (giving rise to intonation that has both syntactic and pragmatic functions). Scherer (1986) hypothesized that the general tension state of larynx muscles is affected directly by the outcomes of event evaluation and thus by the resulting emotional response characteristics. These tension states are assumed to appear independently of the subject's decision whether to speak or not. If speech is produced, dynamic changes in specific larynx muscles are superimposed on the general tension states.

Articulation parameters can be classified into those that are mandatory for the production of intelligible speech (e.g., those that determine formant positions) and those that might reflect extralinguistic factors such as facial expressions (e.g., Massaro, 2000; Ohala, 1980; de Gelder & Vroomen, 2000). Such detailed interpretations require a great deal of phonetic knowledge or make assumptions about the speech production process. A complicating factor is the nature of individual speaker characteristics, such as those related to form, size, and mass of vocal organs and their state of health, as well as to personal habits concerning their use (which Laver, 1991, distinguishes as "vocal equipment" and "vocal settings").

A further factor that renders the investigation of acoustic parameters so complicated is the fact that speech signals are transient signals: All parameters change constantly over time. In earlier studies on vocal expression, time-varying parameter values within the utterance were often aggregated into means and variability coefficients, but there is increasing evidence that these statistical descriptions of time series are not sufficient to understand the process of emotional expression in speech. More or less static parameters describing general voice quality, for example, can be measured more reliably in individual phonemes such as the open-vowel / a /, than in long-term average measurements because for these segments the vocal tract is open and articulatory effects have less effect

Table 23.1. Overview of Major Acoustic-Phonetic and Psychoacoustic Parameters

### 1. Acoustic-phonetic parameters

| | |
|---|---|
| Speech rate | Number of speech segments per time unit |
| F0 | Fundamental frequency (vibration rate of vocal folds) |
| F0 perturbation | Slight variations of duration of glottal cycle |
| F0 contour | Fundamental frequency values plotted over time (intonation or "speech melody") |
| Intensity | Average squared amplitude within a predefined time segment ("energy") |
| Spectral energy distribution | Relative amount of energy within predefined frequency bands |
| Spectral slope | Linear regression of energy distribution in the frequency band above 1 kHz |
| Laryngalization | Sudden change of oscillation mode of vocal folds (usually to double glottal cycle duration) |
| Tremor | Regular modulation of glottal cycle duration |
| Jitter | Regular or irregular variation of glottal cycle duration |
| Shimmer | Regular or irregular variation of amplitude maxima in subsequent glottal cycles |
| HNR | ("Harmonic-to-noise-ratio") Ratio between harmonic and aperiodic signal energy |
| GNE | "Glottal-noise-excitation," a measure of hoarseness |
| Inverse filtered glottal pulse | Transglottal airflow estimated by inverse filtering techniques |
| Formant | (Time-varying) resonance of vocal tract (significant energy concentration in the spectrum) |
| F1 | First formant—important for vowel identification |
| F2 | Second formant—important for vowel identification |
| Formant bandwidth | Width of the spectral band containing significant formant energy (− 3 dB threshold) |
| Formant precision | Degree to which formant frequencies attain values prescribed by phonological system of a language |

### 2. Psychoacoustic parameters

| | |
|---|---|
| Perceived loudness | Calculated from weighted energy distributions in specific frequency bands |
| Perceived pitch | Calculated from the F0 contour taking into consideration the linear and differential glissando-threshold |
| Perceived rhythm | Rhythmic events calculated from the perceived loudness contour |

*Note*: In many cases, these parameters are aggregated over segments of speech by using measures of central tendency and distribution statistics such as mode, mean, median, variance, standard deviation, and upper or lower 5(1)% of the distribution.

on the voice source signal. To extract dynamic features from time contours of acoustic parameters, such as F0 contours or formants, for example, it is helpful to modify measured contours into simplified, but functionally equivalent forms. Unfortunately, even among linguists and phoneticians there is little agreement on how to stylize F0 contours and how to separate meaningful from irrelevant information (see Mertens, Beaugendre, & d'Alessandro, 1997).

## Summary of the Empirical Results

Table 23.2 provides an overview of the major effects of emotion on vocal expression that have been empirically identified. Column 1 lists the acoustic parameters generally used to measure the effects of emotion, annotated with comments. Columns 2 to 7 summarize the research results of the effects of arousal, happiness, anger, sadness, fear, and boredom on the respective acoustic parameters. The entries in the table refer to differences on the respective parameter compared to "normal" speech. In order to maximize the number of studies upon which to base the inference, we list only the emotions that have been most frequently studied in this field. Other emotions such as pride, jealousy, love, and humor (laughter) have been studied considerably less frequently. In consequence, the evidence so far is extremely sparse and in urgent need of replication. Given the number of studies, the manifold differences in emotions studied and acoustic parameters measured, as well as inconsistencies in the data, it is impossible to document in detail how the entries in Table 23.2 have been excerpted from the literature. The authors

Table 23.2. Synthetic Review of the Empirical Findings Concerning the Effect of Emotion on Vocal Parameters

| Acoustic Parameters | Arousal/Stress | Happiness/ Elation | Anger/Rage | Sadness | Fear/Panic | Boredom |
|---|---|---|---|---|---|---|
| **Speech Rate and Fluency** | | | | | | |
| Number of syllables per second | > | >= | <> | < | > | < |
| Syllable duration | < | <= | <> | > | < | > |
| Duration of accented vowels | >= | >= | > | >= | < | >= |
| Number and duration of pauses | < | < | < | > | <> | > |
| Relative duration of voiced segments | | | > | | <> | |
| Relative duration of unvoiced segments | | | < | | <> | |
| **Voice Source—F0 and Prosody** | | | | | | |
| F0 mean[3] | > | > | > | < | > | <= |
| F0: 5th percentile[3] | > | > | = | <= | > | <= |
| F0 deviation[3] | > | > | > | < | > | < |
| F0 range[3] | > | > | > | < | <> | <= |
| Frequency of accented syllables | > | >= | > | < | | |
| Gradient of F0 rising and falling[3,6] | > | > | > | < | <> | <= |
| F0 final fall: range and gradient[3,4,7] | > | > | > | < | <> | <= |
| **Voice Source—Vocal Effort and Type of Phonation** | | | | | | |
| Intensity (dB) mean[5] | > | >= | > | <= | | <= |
| Intensity (dB) deviation[5] | > | > | > | < | | < |
| Gradient of intensity rising and falling[2] | > | >= | > | < | | <= |
| Relative spectral energy in higher bands[1] | > | > | > | < | <> | <= |
| Spectral slope[1] | < | < | < | > | <> | > |
| Laryngealization | | = | = | > | > | = |
| Jitter[3] | | >= | >= | | > | = |
| Shimmer[3] | | >= | >= | | > | = |
| Harmonics/Noise Ratio[1,3] | | > | > | < | < | <= |
| **Articulation—Speed and Precision** | | | | | | |
| Formants—precision of location | ? | = | > | < | <= | <= |
| Formant bandwidth | < | | < | > | | >= |

*Notes:*
1. depends on phoneme combinations, articulation precision or tension of the vocal tract
2. depends on prosodic features like accent realization, rhythm, etc.
3. depends on speaker-specific factors like age, gender, health, etc.
4. depends on sentence mode
5. depends on microphone distance and amplification
6. for accented segments
7. for final portion of sentences
In specific phonemes, < "smaller," "lower," "slower," "less," "flatter," or "narrower"; = equal to "neutral"; > "bigger," "higher," "faster," "more," "steeper," or "broader"; <= smaller or equal, >=bigger or equal; <> both smaller and bigger have been reported

have used their best judgment in synthesizing the emerging pattern of data from the studies cited earlier. It should be noted that for some of the more rarely measured acoustic parameters the table entry is based on only very few studies, and in some cases a single one. In consequence, Table 23.2 should be viewed as a set of empirical expectations rather than an authoritative summary of established results.

It is impossible to summarize or synthesize the mass of findings presented in Table 23.2. However, we will try to draw some preliminary conclusions with respect to how well the evidence available so far supports the three theoretical models outlined at the beginning. In order to do so, we will review the three questions posed earlier.

*1. Are sympathetic effects sufficient to describe the vocal emotion expression differentiation that has been empirically observed?* Based on the results reviewed, there can be no doubt that vocal parameters are very powerful indicators of physiological arousal (as stated in prior reviews by Frick, 1985; Murray & Arnott, 1993; Pittam &

Scherer, 1993; Scherer, 1979, 1986). High-stress or high mental workload conditions have generally been found to lead to raised values of F0, greater intensity, and faster speech rate than low-stress situations. Similarly, compared with neutral speech, vocal expressions of high-arousal emotions such as anger, fear, and elation have been measured as having high mean F0, high F0 variability, high intensity, and increased speaking rate. Conversely, sad and bored vocal expressions have been found to have low F0, low F0 variability, low intensity, and decreased speaking rate. On the basis of such combined results, it is evident that where there has been considerable consistency in the findings, it has usually been related to arousal, regardless of the specific quality of the emotion under investigation.

However, while there has never been any doubt as to the important role of arousal, there is debate as to whether sympathetic arousal is sufficient to account for the vocal differentiation of emotion, as unidimensional arousal theories of emotion would hold. Scherer and his collaborators (Banse & Scherer, 1996; Johnstone, Van Reeckum, & Scherer, 2001; Scherer, 1986) argue that while only very few studies of induced or real emotional speech identified acoustic patterns that could unambiguously differentiate the major non-arousal dimensions of emotion such as valence and control, there are good reasons for favoring a more differentiated model of emotional expression. Although comparisons between fairly extreme emotions, such as elation, rage, or fear on the one hand and sadness or boredom on the other, reflect mainly the effects of arousal, less extreme forms such as happiness, irritation, anxiety, and disappointment do not show such a consistent relationship with arousal. For example, anxious speech is often low in intensity and irritated speech has been found to be low in F0. The fact that these emotions can still be accurately perceived by listeners (as will be discussed in the section on decoding studies) implies that some aspects of the acoustic signal other than those related to arousal serve as a marker for the emotion. Since most studies have limited themselves to measuring those acoustic parameters that have a clear physiological connection with arousal, such as F0 and intensity, it is not surprising that nonarousal markers of emotion in speech have not been consistently identified so far.

Table 23.2 also provides evidence that certain emotions are accompanied by specific types of phonation (Klasmeyer & Sendlmeier, 1997), which cannot be explained by simple arousal models. For example—voicing irregularities that appear when the speaker is almost weeping or retching, or voice breaks, found for panic fear—are never found in angry utterances even when produced with extreme arousal. From these observations one may conclude that some parameters, such as voicing irregularities, can be best explained by emotion-specific innervation of the muscles in the larynx.

In addition to voice source parameters, the effect of emotion on articulation patterns (apart from elaboration or reduction phenomena) is difficult to explain with simple arousal models. These effects are likely to be emotion-specific rather than arousal-related. This is clearly seen in the effects of facial expression on acoustic parameters. For example, both the specific actions of the m. zygomaticus in smiling and the m. orbicularis oris in anger expression affect the energy distribution in the spectrum. While the respective contribution of phonetic-linguistic and emotional factors to the joint determination of vowel formant frequencies and bandwidth is difficult to assess given major differences in articulation patterns between individuals and dialectal forms, this group of parameters seems highly promising for future research.

Perhaps the most compelling evidence so far for the existence of acoustic profiles that distinguish not only between high and low arousal but also between different emotions with comparable levels of arousal comes from a recent study by Banse and Scherer (1996), in which 14 emotions were expressed (in two nonsense sentences) by 12 professional theater actors using a scenario-based Stanislaski technique. Acoustic analyses revealed quite specific acoustic profiles for a number of emotions. Emotions such as rage, panic, and elation, all high in arousal, had distinct acoustic profiles (as summarized by Johnstone & Scherer, 2000, table 3). When the acoustic parameters were used in discriminant analysis to classify each spoken token, the classification accuracies were well above chance levels for all emotions and corresponded closely to the classification accuracies of human judges as well as showing similar patterns of confusions.

*2. Is there evidence for highly prototypical vocal parameter configurations that might be produced by invariable neuromotor programs as postulated by discrete emotion theories?* While the evidence is certainly consistent with this position, the strength and prototypicality of the patterning that would be required to confirm the existence of neuromotor programs has not been found so far. On the contrary, as already shown, there are important differences in vocal patterning between members of the same emotion family. For example, as shown by Banse and Scherer (1996), "hot anger" is characterized by a strong increase in F0 and F0 variability, fast speech rate, and a strong increase in high frequency energy, but this is not true for "cold anger" (which seems to be encoded through subtler cues, possibly including intonation). This suggests that there are many factors contributing to the production of the vocal expression of a particular emotional state. Further research will need to identify these factors and explain their interactions. Unfortunately, discrete-emotion theorists have not, so far, specified concrete hypotheses for vocal patterning that could serve as guidance for a comparative test of different theoretical predictions.

*3. What is the evidence for the more molecular predic-*

*tions from appraisal theory, either for the effects of results on specific appraisal dimensions, or for the combined predictions for modal emotions?* Appraisal theory predictions for vocal patterning are relatively recent (Scherer, 1986) and consequently, there is little experimental evidence to date. However, the study by Banse and Scherer (1996) aimed at a systematic test of the respective predictions made for modal emotions. Johnstone, van Reekum, and Scherer (2001) have summarized the results in a table reproduced here (see Table 23.3). While many of the predictions were supported by the data, there were also a number of marked discrepancies. Similar results have been found in a more recent test of Scherer's predictions by Juslin and Laukka (2001). As pointed out by Johnstone, van Reekum, and Scherer, it is difficult to identify the source of such discrepancies because the predictions reflect the composite of a number of individual appraisal predictions. Although it is possible to speculate about the effects of individual appraisals by looking at differences between emotion pairs on a single appraisal dimension, it is obvious that such speculation needs to be backed up by direct empirical testing.

The predictions tested in the study by Banse and Scherer (1996) concerned the combined predictions, based on complete appraisal profiles for modal emotions (Scherer, 1994). What is needed to confirm the general approach is experimental confirmation for specific effects of individual appraisal predictions. This has been attempted in more recent research, using computer games and tasks to induce emotional vocal responses (Johnstone, 1996, 2001; Kappas, 1997). The computer games and tasks were manipulated so as to provoke specific appraisal outcomes that were theorized by Scherer (1986) to lead to specific vocal changes. For example, one such game included characters that either hindered or helped the player through situations that were accompanied by pleasant or unpleasant sounds. Such a game was designed to manipulate the player's appraisals of goal conduciveness and intrinsic pleasantness, respectively. During the gameplay, players were requested to say standard phrases, which were recorded for later acoustical analysis. The results showed that the acoustic patterns of induced vocal changes could not be explained by a single arousal dimension, since the pattern of changes across acoustic parameters was different for different manipulations. For example, Johnstone (2001) found that varying the intrinsic pleasantness of an event caused changes to spectral energy distribution, but not to overall energy, F0 level, or fluency. In contrast, changes to the conduciveness of an event produced changes to the latter set of variables, but not to spectral energy distribution. Although a single-dimension arousal model could be modified to fit such data (for example, by positing different non-monotonic relationships between arousal and individual acoustical parameters), a more parsimonious explanation is that emotional changes to the voice reflect two or more dimensions, presumably reflecting two or more underlying mechanisms.

## Summary of the Evidence on the Vocal Patterning of Emotion

This review of the pertinent research results does confirm the important role of arousal but strongly argues against the claim that a unidimensional arousal theory can account for the data in a satisfactory manner. While the data are consistent with discrete-emotion theories, there is little evidence so far that favors the more constraining predictions concerning prototypical patterns for a limited number of "basic" emotions over the more molecular predictions of appraisal theory. Similarly, the partial support for the appraisal-theory generated predictions in the work by Banse and Scherer (1996), Johnstone (1996, 2001), and Juslin and Laukka (2001) is also consistent with the assumption made by discrete-emotion theories that there are qualitative differences between emotions. In addition, they do not contradict dimensional theories, since psychophysiological arousal and subjective valence of emotional experience are components of both discrete and appraisal models. Although it is difficult to differentially test the theoretical views, it would seem desirable to abandon the atheoretical stance that has characterized this field and to plan and conduct further studies in this area with more

Table 23.3. Predicted and Measured Standardized Vocal Parameters for 12 Emotions as Reported by Banse and Scherer (1996)

| | Contempt | Boredom | Happiness | Anxiety | Shame | Sadness | Disgust | Cold Anger | Despair | Hot Anger | Panic | Elation |
|---|---|---|---|---|---|---|---|---|---|---|---|---|
| F0 | **0−** | − | − | **+−** | **+−** | 00 | **+0** | 00 | ++ | **0+** | ++ | ++ |
| Energy | **+−** | 0− | − | ?0 | ?− | − | **+−** | ++ | ++ | ++ | ++ | ++ |
| LF energy | **−0** | 0+ | ++ | **−+** | −0 | **0+** | −0 | − | − | − | −0 | 00 |
| Duration | ?0 | ?+ | **+−** | ?− | ?0 | ++ | ?0 | ?0 | **−0** | − | − | − |

*Note:* LF energy = Low frequency energy. In each cell, the first symbol represents the predicted value, the second symbol represents the measured value. −, 0, + : low, medium, high values, respectively. Symbols in bold indicate a significant difference between the predicted and measured values. ? indicates that no prediction was made. From Johnstone, van Reekum, & Scherer (2001), copyright © Oxford University Press, Inc. Used by permission of Oxford University Press, Inc.

explicit attempts at theory-driven investigation. This would not only allow a critical examination of conflicting predictions made by competing theories but also an accumulation of empirical findings to a systematic framework. Recent efforts in this direction have been made for facial expression of emotion (e.g., Wehrle, Kaiser, Schmidt, & Scherer, 2000), with mixed success. As mentioned at the start of this section, there are, in principle, some opposing claims made by discrete-emotion theories and appraisal theories that could be empirically tested. Given a large database of emotional speech recordings, it might be possible to use cluster analysis and factor analytic techniques to determine whether the acoustic characteristics of emotional speech are characterized by a small number of concentrated vocal prototypes, or by a more diffuse arrangement explainable by a number of dimensions corresponding to different appraisals. In addition, it might be that more neuroscientifically oriented research, as will be discussed later in the chapter, ultimately will indicate which of the theories presented earlier is better able to predict and explain the vocal patterning of emotional expression.

## Transmission of Voice Sounds and Perception by the Listener

One of the important features of the Brunswikian lens model is the consideration given to the transmission of the distal signals from the sender to the receiver/listener who perceives these signals as subjective, proximal cues. The Brunswikian lens model is useful to model these processes on a theoretical level. It can also be used for quantitative modeling (e.g., using path analysis or structural models; e.g., Scherer, 1978) for subsets of variables that are linked by linear functions. In modeling the transmission part of the model, two major aspects need to be taken into account: (1) the transmission of sound through space and (2) the transform functions in perception, as determined by the nature of human hearing mechanisms. These effects, which are highly nonlinear and thus require more complex statistical approaches, will be briefly described.

1. The transmission of sound through space (and consequently the nature of the cues that reach the listener's ear) is influenced by many environmental factors, including the distance between sender and receiver and the presence of other sounds and background noise. A consideration of such factors is important in understanding the physiological mechanisms that underlie both the expression and perception of emotional speech. If, for example, speech has to carry over a long distance to reach a listener, the mode of production will be different than that used for close-range communication. In particular, the speaker needs to produce more intense speech, requiring more vocal effort. However, the result of greater vocal effort is not simply an increase in intensity; a large number of acoustic characteristics related to voice production at the larynx will also be affected. In addition, articulation has to be rather precise in order to avoid misunderstanding, particularly since other nonverbal cues that normally support the verbal message, such as lip movements, gestures, eye contact, or facial expression, may not be be visible, or only marginally so. Thus, the need to communicate over a long distance will impose constraints on the use of certain vocal features for emotional expression. The absence of a number of nonvocal cues that accompany the affective vocal signal when the listener is close to the speaker but cannot be used at a distance will affect the characteristics of emotional vocal expression. For example, the effects of facial expression and gestures, especially head movements or body movements toward or away from the listener, on the intensity and spectral distribution of the acoustic signal (see Laver, 1991) may become increasingly smaller with increasing distance.

The importance of factors affecting the transmission of emotional vocal expressions between sender and receiver is twofold. First, transmission constrains the way the voice can be used for emotional signaling, possibly influencing the vocal expression of some emotions more than others. Second, if vocal communication evolved largely as part of an emotional signaling system, it is likely that the mechanisms that underlie vocal production and perception evolved in such a way as to exploit such constraints. A greater understanding of the transmission stage of the Brunswikian lens model is thus likely to lead to insights about the design and functioning of vocal production and perception systems.

2. The proximal cues available to the listener are determined by the transform functions for auditory stimuli that are built into the human hearing system. Psychoacoustic research has demonstrated that the perceptual representation of sounds does not correspond in a one-to-one fashion to the sound's objectively measured acoustic properties. For example, the perceived loudness of voiced speech signals correlates more strongly with the amplitude of a few harmonics or even a single harmonic than with its overall intensity (Gramming & Sundberg, 1988; Titze, 1992). Furthermore, listeners apparently use their knowledge about the specific spectral distribution of harmonics and noise in loud and soft voices to decide the vocal effort with which a voice was produced. This judgment is still reasonably correct when both loud and soft voices are presented at the same perceived loudness level, with the soft voice having more than six times higher overall intensity than the loud voice (Klasmeyer, 1999, p. 112).

Psychoacoustic effects also play a role in the perception of F0 contours. F0 movements have to cross the glissando threshold before they can be perceived as melodic movements (see d'Allessandro & Mertens, 1995). The glissando threshold for a uniform F0 change with constant slope is frequency dependent (about 0.16 times the square of F0 in synthetic stimuli and even higher in fluent speech), but changes in the slope (differential glissando threshold) are perceived more easily. If F0 does not change monotonically but oscillates regularly or irregularly around a fixed or slowly varying value, these changes are perceived as voice quality effects (tremor, jitter) rather than melodic movements.

Furthermore, F0 can influence the perceived duration of a spoken utterance. Higher F0 or an F0 rise at the end of an utterance is perceived as a faster speaking rate (Kohler, 1995). Spectral changes in fluent speech, which are caused either by fast articulatory movements or rapid F0 changes or both, result in a decrease of perceived phoneme duration, speech rate, and utterance duration (Klasmeyer, 1999, p. 49). There is only a weak correlation between physical signal duration and perceived duration of fluent speech segments. This also applies to perceived rhythm. Rhythm perception is based on the subsequence of accented syllables. But while time intervals between accented syllables in fluent speech might vary a great deal, the rhythm is generally perceived as being much more regular (Allen, 1975; Fraisse, 1963; Jakobson, Fant, & Halle, 1951). Speech rate and rhythm are used in synchronizing speaker and listener (Byers, 1976; Condon, 1986). This explains why the perceptual "equalization" of durations serves an important function in communication situations and why listeners are not very good at judging objective durations in fluent speech in a very precise manner.

All of these psychoacoustic properties affect which acoustic characteristics of emotional speech are likely to be the most perceptually salient. For example, if just a few harmonics of voiced speech determine its perceived loudness, these harmonics are likely to be particularly salient for the perception of emotions such as rage and elation. Similarly, the influence of F0 on perceived duration and speech rate implies that F0 will be an important perceptual cue for expressions of emotions such as anxiety and fear, which are perceived as involving more rapid speech.

The role of voice sound transmission and the transform functions specific to the human hearing system have been rarely studied in this area of research, mostly because researchers have focused exclusively on either encoding or decoding studies, rarely taking the complete vocal communication process into account. This is regrettable for theoretical reasons but also because we may have missed parameters that can be useful to differentiate the vocal expression of different emotions. For example, if one assumes that vocal emotion expressions need to be very distinctive to listeners because of their communicative function, it may pay to transform the objective signal characteristics into their perceptual counterparts using known psychoacoustic functions (e.g., perceived loudness, perceived pitch, perceived rhythm, or Bark bands in spectral analysis; see Zwicker, 1982).

## Decoding: Listener Inference of Emotion from Voice and Speech

The large majority of studies in the area of the vocal communication of emotion have focused on the decoding or inference part of the Brunswikian lens model. Generally, the portrayal paradigm has been used, that is, asking actors to act out or simulate a number of different emotions, generally with standard content utterances. Groups of lay judges are then requested to infer the emotions portrayed in a series of vocal stimuli, mostly on rating sheets with preestablished lists of emotion labels. The data analysis consists of the computation of the percentage of stimuli per emotion that were correctly recognized, which is then compared with the percentage of responses that would be expected to be correct on the basis of chance guessing. In some studies, confusion matrices are reported showing the patterns of errors.

### Empirical Evidence

The question of whether judges can recognize emotion solely on the basis of vocal cues has interested psychologists and psychiatrists from the beginning of the 20th century and was especially popular between 1950 and 1980 (see Scherer, 1979). As is generally the case in this research, a number of different emotions were vocally portrayed by professional or lay actors (using nonsense syllables or standard speech samples) and judges were asked to identify the emotion expressed. A review of approximately 30 of these early studies in which normal voice portrayals were used (excluding studies with pathological voice samples and filtered speech) yielded an average accuracy percentage of about 60%, or about five times higher than what would be expected by chance (Scherer, 1989). Since many of these early studies often used very short voice samples and included rarely studied emotions such as pride or jealousy (as compared to "basic" emotions such as anger, joy, sadness, or fear), this level of accuracy is quite remarkable. More recent studies reported similar levels of average recognition accuracy across different emotions. Van Bezooijen (1984) reports a mean accuracy of 65% for voice samples of disgust, surprise, shame, interest, joy, fear, sadness, and anger. Scherer, Banse, Wallbott, and Goldbeck (1991), who studied fear, joy, sadness, anger, and disgust as portrayed by professional radio actors, reported a mean accuracy of 56% across a variety of different types of listener and age groups.

Many of these studies can be criticized for using only a relatively small number of emotions, with often only one positive exemplar, thus constituting *discrimination* studies (deciding between alternatives) rather than *recognition* studies (recognizing a particular category in its own right). Therefore, it has been suggested to correct the accuracy

Table 23.4. Accuracy (%) of Facial and Vocal Emotion Recognition in Studies in Western and Non-Western Countries

|  | Neutral | Anger | Fear | Joy | Sadness | Disgust | Surprise | Mean |
|---|---|---|---|---|---|---|---|---|
| Facial/Western (20) |  | 78 | 77 | 95 | 79 | 80 | 88 | 78 |
| Vocal/Recent Western (11) | 74 | 77 | 61 | 57 | 71 | 31 |  | 62 |
| Facial/Non-Western (11) |  | 59 | 62 | 88 | 74 | 67 | 77 | 65 |
| Vocal/Non-Western (1) | 70 | 64 | 38 | 28 | 58 |  |  | 52 |

Note: Empty cells indicate that the respective emotions have not been studied in these regions. Numbers in parentheses in column 1 indicate the number of countries studied.

*Source*: From Scherer (1999b).

coefficients for guessing by taking the number of given alternatives and the response distribution in the margins into account (Wagner, 1993). However, it is difficult to determine the appropriate procedure for such a correction, each method having a different type of drawback (Banse & Scherer, 1996). Alternatively, one can compute different comparison levels for chance guessing of different emotions. For facial expression, Ekman (1994) has suggested using different levels of chance accuracy for positive and negative emotions, given their differential frequency in the stimulus material. While this may be useful for facial expression where the *m. zygomaticus* action is often a giveaway for positive emotions, it may be less adequate for vocal expression studies since exuberant joy or elation shares many vocal characteristics with anger (see Banse & Scherer, 1996; Scherer et al., 1991).

In addition, none of these studies took into account that there are often different instantiations or variants of specific emotions, such as hot and cold anger, which can be seen as different members of the same family of emotions (see also Ekman, 1992). These variants may have rather different vocal characteristics, a fact which could explain some of the lack of replication observed in the literature (see Scherer, 1986). To deal with this problem, Banse and Scherer (1996) used a large stimulus set, consisting of 14 emotions (in several cases, two members of the same emotion family were used) portrayed by 12 professional theater actors. The average accuracy level was found to be 48% (as compared to 7% expected by chance if all 14 categories were weighted equally). If, in an attempt to compare the data to earlier studies, one computes the agreement *between families* only for those emotions where there were two variants (yielding 10 categories) the accuracy percentage increases to 55% (as compared to 10% expected by chance). In reviewing the evidence from the studies to date, one can conclude that the recognition of emotion from standardized voice samples, using actor portrayals, attains between 55% and 65% accuracy, about five to six times higher than what would be expected by chance.

This figure is about 15% lower than what has been found for the recognition of facially expressed emotions (see Ekman, 1994). The difference is mostly due to facial expressions of joy and disgust being recognized with close to 100% accuracy, based on facial actions that are highly specific for these emotions (smiling for joy and nose wrinkling for disgust; see Ekman & Friesen, 1978). Table 23.4 shows a comparison of accuracy figures for vocal and facial portrayal recognition obtained in a set of studies having examined a comparable range of emotions in both modalities (the data in this table are based on reviews by Ekman, 1994, for facial expression, and Scherer, Banse, & Wallbott, 2001, for vocal expression). The table shows that the figure for average percent accuracy hides some rather large differences between emotions. Sadness and anger are generally best recognized vocally, followed by fear. Joy has rather mixed accuracy percentages in different studies, possibly due to differences with respect to quiet happiness versus elated joy being portrayed by the actors. Vocal disgust portrayals are recognized very badly, often barely above chance level. Johnstone and Scherer (2000) discuss a number of potential explanations of these differences, based on the evolutionary pressure toward accurate vocal communication for different emotions. For example, there is clear adaptive advantage in being able to warn (in fear) or threaten (in anger) others in an unambiguous fashion over large distances, something for which vocal expression is ideally suited. In contrast, warning others of rotten food (as in disgust) may be most functional to conspecifics eating at the same place as the signaler, in which case facial expression may be more appropriate.

These differences in the vocal communication functions of different emotions underline the need to analyze the recognizability of these emotions separately. In addition, confusion matrices should be reported regularly, as errors are not randomly distributed and as the patterns of misidentification provide important information on the judgment process. Banse and Scherer (1996), analyzing the confusion patterns in their recognition data in great detail, showed that while disgust portrayals are generally confused with almost all other negative emotions, there are more specific patterns for the other emotions. As one might expect, there are many errors between members of the same emotion family (for example, hot anger is confused consistently only with cold anger and contempt). Other frequent errors occur between emotions with similar valence (for example, interest is confused more often with pride and happiness than with the other 11 emotions taken together). Johnstone and Scherer (2000) argue that rather than considering confusions as errors, they should be interpreted as indicators of the similarity or proximity between emotion categories, taking into account quality, intensity, and valence. Emotions that are similar on one or more of these dimensions are obviously easier to confuse. An additional complication is due to individual differences in the use of emotion labels.

The analysis of confusion patterns is particularly important in cross-cultural studies of vocal emotion recognition. While such data are still rare in this area (especially compared with the abundance of cross-cultural studies on facial expression), there is some evidence (see Frick, 1985; van Bezooijen, Otto, & Heenan, 1983) that vocal expressions by members of one culture, for at least some emotions, are universally recognized by members of other cultures. Recently, Scherer, Banse, and Wallbott (2001) reported the findings of a series of cross-cultural studies including eight European and one Asian country. Vocal emotion portrayals (joy, anger, fear, sadness, neutral) by professional German radio actors were used. Local collaborators recruited college students to listen to these samples in small groups (using identical equipment in all countries) and to judge the intended emotions in a standardized rating procedure. The data show an overall accuracy percentage of 66% across all emotions and countries, with a high of 74% in Germany and a low of 52% in Indonesia. Joy was inferred with much lower accuracy (42%) than the other emotions (around 70%). Generally, accuracy decreased with increasing language dissimilarity from German in spite of the use of language-free speech samples (which suggests that portrayals may be characterized by culture and language-specific paralinguistic patterns that influence the decoding process). However, one of the striking results was that the patterns of confusion were similar across all countries, including Indonesia. This was interpreted as evidence for the existence of universal inference rules from vocal characteristics to specific emotions across cultures.

### Identifying the Acoustic Cues Used in Emotion Inference from Voice

In order to understand the nature of such universal inference rules, it is important to identify the acoustic cues perceived and used by listeners in the process of attributing emotion to a speaker. While the issue of the accuracy of recognition has dominated this field so far, a more comprehensive process model (like the Brunswikian lens model described earlier) requires detailed study of the vocal cues that are attended to in voice perception and how they are interpreted with respect to the underlying emotional state. We review studies in which attempts were made to systematically isolate or measure specific acoustic cues in order to determine their role in the inference process used by judges trying to identify the emotion expressed in a series of voice samples. The purpose of this type of research is to identify the vocal characteristics that judges use to identify the expressed emotion.

Johnstone and Scherer (2000) provide a detailed overview of the different research strategies that have been used to determine the role of various acoustic cues in the judgment process. One of the most frequently used techniques is the isolation of specific acoustic cues, such as pitch or rhythm, via filtering, masking, or speech synthesis or resynthesis. Scherer, Feldstein, Bond, and Rosenthal (1985) and Friend and Farrar (1994) have compared different masking techniques (filtering, randomized splicing, playing backwards, pitch inversion, and tone-silence coding). Each of these techniques removes and/or preserves different combinations of acoustic characteristics of a vocal expression. Speech intelligibility is removed by all of these procedures, allowing the use of natural speech from "real-life" rather than artificially posed emotions. For example, Scherer, Ladd, and Silverman (1984) used a corpus of affectively laden utterances produced by civil servants interacting with citizens to determine which acoustic cues are used by listeners to infer speaker emotion and attitude. One of the interesting findings was that politeness, as a speaker attitude, was still recognizable in the most severely masked speech samples.

Researchers in this area have been very interested in methods that allow a rigorously experimental approach in which acoustic variables are systematically varied to determine their effects, in isolation and in interaction, on listener judgment of emotional and attitudinal speaker state. Acoustic *synthesis* methods have been used early on to study the impressions produced by different acoustic variables (see Lieberman & Michaels, 1962; Scherer & Oshinsky, 1977), allowing researchers to determine the effects of parameters such as amplitude variation, pitch level, contour and variation, tempo, envelope, harmonic richness, tonality, and rhythm on emotion attributions. The development of easily available speech resynthesis techniques in the 1970s made it possible to take neutral natural voices and systematically change different cues via digital manipulation of the sound waves. In a number of studies by Scherer and his collaborators, F0 level, contour variability and range, intensity, duration, and accent structure of real utterances have been systematically manipulated in order to observe the effect of listener attributions of emotion and speaker attitude (Ladd, Silverman, Tolkmitt, Bergmann, & Scherer, 1985; Tolkmitt, Bergmann, Goldbeck, & Scherer, 1988). With the availability and quality of synthesis and resynthesis methods having greatly increased in recent years, it is not surprising that a fairly large number of such studies have been reported. Recent progress in speech technology has multiplied the tools available for a systematic, experimental study of vocal cue use in emotion attribution (see Abadjieva, Murray & Arnott, 1995; Burkhardt & Sendlmeier, 2000; Cahn, 1990; Carlson, Granström, & Nord, 1992; Granström, 1992; Heuft, Portele, & Rauth, 1996; Mozziconacci, 1995; Murray & Arnott; 1995; see also the special issue of the journal *Speech Communication*, 2002).

Apart from masking or resynthesis methods, it is possible to use *acoustic analyses* and/or voice experts to measure the acoustic and/or phonatory-articulatory characteristics of vocal emotion portrayals (acted or natural), and to correlate these with the listeners' judgments of underlying emotion or attitude of the speaker. Several studies of this type have yielded information concerning the vocal characteristics that determine judges' inference (van Bezooijen, 1984; Scherer et al., 1991; Wallbott & Scherer, 1986). The extensive data in the study conducted by Banse and Scherer (1996) statistically regressed the judges' emotion inferences on the various acoustic variables that had been obtained by digital speech analysis in order to determine which acoustic characteristics best predict the judges' attributions.

The highly significant results showed that a sizable proportion of the variance was explained by a set of about 9 to 10 variables, including mean F0, standard deviation of F0, mean energy, duration of voiced periods, proportion of energy up to 1000 Hz, and energy drop-off in the spectrum. For hot anger 36% of the variance could be explained by this set of variables; for the majority of the remaining emotion categories, 10 to 25% of the variance could be accounted for. To infer hot anger, judges used the cues of high F0 and strong F0 variation as well as a strong difference between energy in the lower and higher frequency bands. Examples for other cue-inference associations are low intensity = sadness; F0 increase, low F0 variability, and low intensity = anxiety; low F0, low intensity, and slow speech rate = boredom. Banse and Scherer (1996) also compared the performance of human judges to statistical classification algorithms such as discriminant analysis and jackknifing in order to determine whether the acoustic measures correlated with listener judgments do indeed allow the discrimination of the emotions used. They found that the discrimination rates were similar for human judges and statistical algorithms. Unexpectedly, they also found a high degree of correspondence between the confusion matrices, suggesting that the human inference rules mirror the underlying patterns of association between acoustic parameters and emotion class (as portrayed by actors).

While the analysis of the correspondence between human judgment and statistical classification algorithms is interesting, it does not replace an analysis based on the Brunswikian lens model, using path analysis or structural modeling. This kind of analysis would allow us to determine which distal vocal cues characterize specific emotions, how these cues are transmitted and proximally represented in listeners, and which patterns of inferences are based on those cues. Unfortunately, no comprehensive Brunswikian analysis of the vocal emotion communication process has yet been published.

## Neglected Issues

While the empirical research on the recognition of emotion from vocal expression has yielded interesting results, some aspects of the process have been neglected. One intriguing issue concerns the dimensions of affect that listeners tend to infer from the voice under natural conditions. In most studies, listener-judges are asked to identify discrete emotions, generally by checking one of several categories provided by the researcher, thus being forced to infer a category (see the controversy between Ekman, 1994, and Russell, 1994). In normal social interaction, this might not be the case. Listeners might tend to use the vocal characteristics to infer arousal of the speaker, an action tendency of the speaker (e.g., impending aggression), or the speaker's appraisal of an event (e.g., perceived urgency of action).

The issue of what is being expressed by emotional expression has been hotly debated. Thus, Fridlund (1994) has proposed that facial expressions do not express emotions but must be considered as social signals. However, researchers in the area of emotional expression, starting with Darwin, have always recognized that one of the essential functions of emotional expression is the social signaling of the expressor's reaction and action tendency (see Scherer, 1984, 1985). As suggested by Bühler (1934; see Scherer, 1988), all signs, including emotional expressions, have representation (meaning), symptom (expression), and appeal (social signaling) functions at the same time. What is more interesting than a sterile debate about what is being expressed is the issue of what is being inferred by listeners in particular contexts. Future research in this area may find this a rewarding question to ask.

## Selected Topics of Major Research Interest

We next deal with a number of special issues that show that the study of vocal emotion expression is even more complex than what has been intimated previously. These complexities are mostly due to the fact that we generally express emotion when we produce *speech*. Linguistic and expressive cues are intimately intertwined. This is particularly clear for prosody, which plays a major role in both language and expression. Another interesting issue is provided by tone languages that use F0, normally a mainstay for expression, for semantic purposes.

### The Role of Prosody

In the section on the encoding of emotion in the voice, it was noted that few vocal characteristics had been identified that successfully differentiated emotions of similar arousal. Prosody or intonation, which is often considered a prime carrier of such affective information, has been almost completely neglected by researchers in this area (with a few notable exceptions, e.g., Fonagy, 1981; Fonagy & Madgics, 1963, Ladd et al., 1985; Paeschke, Kienast, & Sendlmeier, 1999; Scherer et al., 1984). One of the reasons for this neglect is the lack of a consensual definition of "intonational form" (see, for example, Beckman, 1995; Ladd, 1995; Möbius, 1995), specifying how intonation should be empirically measured.

Scherer et al. (1984) suggested two general principles underlying the coding of emotional information in speech, covariation and configuration. The *covariation principle* assumes a continuous but not necessarily linear relationship between some aspect of the emotional response and a particular acoustic variable. Thus, if F0 is directly related to physiological arousal, F0 will be higher in rage as compared to mild irritation. Such continuous relationships can be assessed by standard statistical covariance measures.

In contrast, almost all linguistic descriptions assume that intonation involves a number of categorical distinctions, analogous to contrasts between segmental phonemes or between grammatical categories. In consequence, the *configuration principle* implies that the specific affective meaning conveyed by an utterance is actively inferred by the listener based on the total configuration of the linguistic choices in the context, based on phonological categories such as "falling intonation contour." In consequence, statistical assessment of the affective coding based on the configuration principle requires combinatorial analysis of category variables rather than scalar covariance.

Voice quality is generally coded according to the covariation principle and phonemic structure according to the configuration principle. The central acoustic variable that underlies intonation—F0—may be coded according to both types of principles, depending on specific features of its dynamic change over time. For example, *final pitch movements* are coded by the configuration principle: final-rise versus final-fall patterns of F0 in themselves do not carry emotional meanings, but they are linked to sentence modes such as question versus non-question. However, it can be shown that context, such as type of sentence, affects interpretation. While a falling intonation contour is judged as neutral in a WH-question, it is judged as aggressive or challenging in a yes/no question (Scherer et al., 1984). In contrast, F0 range shows a covariance relationship with attitudinal and affective information (Ladd et al., 1985). Further evidence for covariance coding of F0 has been found in other studies as well. For example, newborn infants (who do not know about phonological categories) are able to decode simple emotional meanings from intonation patterns (Papousek, 1994).

Ladd et al. (1985) suggested that *overall F0 range and voice quality* might reflect arousal, while differences of *prosodic contour type* signal differences of more cognitively based speaker attitudes. Alternatively, it could be hypothesized that continuous variables are linked to push effects (externalization of internal states), while configurations of category variables are more likely to be linked to pull effects (specific normative models for affect signals or display). More empirical data are required to test these assumptions experimentally.

In the last two decades a few studies of emotion effects on prosody were conducted using either analysis of emotional speech material or digital resynthesis to test the perceived effect of specific modifications. For example, Ladd et al. (1985) in a perception study systematically manipulated F0 range and contour to investigate the effects on emotion inference. To prepare the stimuli, a linguistic theory of intonation was first used to identify relative peaks on accented syllables (Garding & Bruce, 1981; Ladd, 1983; Liberman & Pierrehumbert, 1984). Then a logarithmic model was used to manipulate F0 range and F0 contour (uptrend vs. downtrend) by shifting relative F0 peaks in the accented syllables while preserving the declination line. These resynthesized stimuli were presented to listeners who were asked to judge the emotional message conveyed in the different representations of the sentence. The results showed strong main effects for these vocal cue manipulations: Wide F0 range and uptrend F0 contours were seen as signals of arousal, annoyance, and involvement. Narrow F0 range was seen as a sign of sadness or of absence of specific speaker attitudes. Uptrend contours also signaled greater emphasis, stronger contradiction, and less cooperativeness. Of all variables studied, F0 range had the most powerful effect on judgments. Relatively few effects due to interactions between the manipulated variables were found. This implies that the synthesized variables independently influenced judges' ratings. Only very minor effects for speaker and utterance content were found, indicating that the results are likely to generalize over different speakers and utterances. In subsequent perception studies of a similar nature (Goldbeck, Tolkmitt, & Scherer, 1988; Ladd, Scherer, & Silverman, 1986) modifications of mean F0, F0 perturbation, average intensity, "uptrend" versus "downtrend" contours, accent height in sentence-final (second) accent position, relative height of subsequent local maxima in the F0 contour, and durations of accented syllable were manipulated. The results showed that emotion inferences are systematically related to changes in these parameters.

Analysis studies, assessing prosodic features in natural or simulated speech material (Klasmeyer, 1999; Paeschke et al., 1999), have mainly focused on (1) frequency (expressed in percentage) of unstressed, weakly stressed, moderately stressed, and heavily stressed segments (as based on auditory impression (of lay or expert judges); (2)

FO stylizations (composition of straight, rising, and falling lines), particularly the frequency (%) and the gradients of rise/straight/fall segments; (3) FO contours (on the basis of a complete phrase expressed in stylized syllables steps, identifying the location of FO maxima and main stresses); (4) FO contours on syllable basis comparing relative locations of local FO maxima; and (5) microprosody (e.g., intonation changes in small segments).

## Evidence from Prosody for the Predictions of the Three Emotion Theories

All emotional information with respect to prosody should be coded exclusively in average FO and the variability of contours if arousal accounted for all emotion-caused vocal differentiation. However, Table 23.2 provides some evidence that specific prosodic patterns can be used to code discrete emotional meanings or appraisal results of specific situations. For example, in monosyllabic utterances, FO maxima seem to appear earlier in the case of happiness and later in the case of anger expressions (Klasmeyer, 1999). Thus, the limited evidence to date (as well as persuasive case studies, e.g., Fonagy, 1983) point to the existence of prosodic patterns that can differentiate emotional states in a qualitative fashion. As mentioned above, it would seem that discrete-emotion theorists should postulate a relatively small number of standard patterns (although there my be blends) for basic emotions. So far, there is limited evidence for such a restricted number, even within any one language. Given the interaction between emotion-generated prosodic changes and language- or dialect-specfic prosodic features, it seems unlikely that emotion-specific prosodic patterns for the standard basic emotions will be found. Appraisal theories do not introduce such constrained predictions. However, few concrete predictions for prosodic effects of individual appraisal checks have so far been ventured, let alone tested. More than in most other areas described in this chapter, further research on emotion effects on prosody is urgently needed.

## Choice of Intonational Models

This future work will have to develop prosody or intonation *models* that reduce the more or less continuous variety of possible intonation realizations to a limited number of more or less well-defined categories and link these to emotional variations. Unfortunately, a large number of rather different intonation models are proposed currently, and there is no established procedure for comparative evaluation, providing clear criteria for preferring one model over another.

Linguists classify intonation models into two major categories: (1) *hierarchically organized models* that interpret FO contours as a complex pattern resulting from the superposition of several components. For example, FO curves can be considered as the superposition of relatively fast pitch movements on a slowly falling FO line, the declination line or "baseline." Models of this type are called two-component models of intonation. One component represents the global aspect of the pitch curve, the declination line and relative pitch level; the other component represents pitch-movement variations and is related to pitch range; (2) *accent models* that interpret FO as a sequence of phonologically distinctive tones or categorically different pitch accents that are locally determined and do not interact. This type of intonation model considers FO targets rather than pitch movements. This is a matter of lively debate, too technical to be reproduced. As always, each model has both advantages and disadvantages for the purpose at hand.

## The Study of Tone Languages

The issues concerning prosody that have been discussed are intimately tied with the role of FO in intonation as part of Western languages. This makes it difficult to examine the effects of psychobiological push and sociolinguistic pull factors on this fundamental aspect of emotional vocalization. For this reason, it is interesting to study non-Western languages in which FO has yet another function, that of semantic differentiation. Tone languages, which are common in parts of East Asia and Africa, are those that use pitch variation to convey lexical information, as opposed to most Indo-European languages that do not. For example, in Thai, there are five contrastive tones used to distinguish among different syllables otherwise consisting of the same sequence of consonants and vowels. Because pitch is the principal carrier of prosody, including affective prosody, a potential conflict between prosodic and tonal-lexical information exists in tone languages. One might expect that the use of pitch to convey affective information is restricted in tone languages since pitch is already being used for lexical purposes. Giving credence to this hypothesis, some research has shown less use of short-term changes in fundamental frequency to express emotion in tone languages (Ross, Edmondson, & Seibert, 1986). In their research, Ross et al. performed acoustic analyses of a standard sentence spoken with happy, sad, angry, surprised, and neutral affective prosody by five speakers each of Mandarin, Taiwanese, Thai, and American English. They discovered that for all of the tone languages, the use of FO variation and FO slope to express affect was reduced compared to American English. In the three tone languages, the shape of the intonation contours of affective utterances differed less from neutral utterances than was the case for American English. It seems that the use of a particular acoustic feature (in this case, FO) in spoken language can constrain its use for the communication of emotion. It remains an open question whether this constraint reduces the ability to prosodically express affect in tone languages. One possibility is that parameters other than F0, such as intensity or speech rate, are used more in tone languages than in non-tone languages to compensate for reduced availability of F0. Ross et al., however, found no systematic differences between American English and the three tone languages for other measured parameters, such as intensity and rate of speech.

One might also argue that the lexical use of tones might render the language more susceptible to interference from expressed affect. Indeed, if one accepts that the effects of emotion on vocal production are due at least in part to involuntary physiological changes, for example, to the respiratory and laryngeal musculature, one might expect the expression of emotion in tone languages to interfere with lexical coding. Such interference would be manifest in increased speech comprehension errors by listeners to affective speech in tone languages. To our knowledge, no research has directly addressed this question.

## Neuropsychological Approaches to the Study of Vocal Communication

Neuropsychology, in particular the study of specific communicative deficits resulting from localized damage to the brain, provides evidence directly pertinent to questions of how the brain processes affective information in voice and speech. We will briefly point to the comparative perspective in neuropsychological assessment of vocalization since there is much to suggest that the characteristics of affective speech in humans reflect a phylogenetically continuous evolution of the affect system, including vocal affect (Hauser, 1996; Robinson, 1972; Scherer, 1985; see chapter 24, this volume). The assumption that the human emotion system is the result of continuous modification of and addition to a more primitive, phylogenetically older emotion system forms the basis of many modern emotion theories (LeDoux, 1996; Panksepp, 1998). It follows from such an assumption that similarities will exist between human affective signaling and signaling observed in other animals, particularly those phylogenetically close to humans. Furthermore, because other animals lack spoken language and, to a certain extent, the explicit cognitive abilities of humans (which are presumably responsible for many of the pull effects on affective speech), the study of these animals should lead to insights into the way in which emotion directly affects vocal production.

Jürgens (1979, 1988, 1994) has suggested that the functional evolution of vocalization is reflected in three hierarchically organized neural systems, the second of which—consisting of the mid-brain periaqueductal gray, parts of the limbic system including the hypothalamus, midline thalamus, amygdala and septum, and the anterior cingulate cortex—is also central to the generation and regulation of emotion. This system is thought to be responsible for the initiation of vocalization and selection from a number of different vocal patterns, presumably as part of an emotional signaling system making up part of a more general emotion response system. Consistent with the ideas of Jürgens, the "polyvagal theory of emotion" proposed by Porges (1997) posits a special role of the ventral vagal complex, which includes both somatic and visceral efferent neural fibers of the cranial nerves, in both the rapid regulation of metabolism to meet environmental challenges and the production of emotional expressions, including vocalizations. Organized neural structures have also been identified in the midbrain periaqueductal gray (PAG) that are involved in differentiated emotional responses and are also fundamental to the control of respiratory and laryngeal functioning during vocal production (Bandler & Shipley, 1994; Davis, Zhang, Winkworth & Bandler, 1996). In work with cats, stimulation of such PAG nuclei leads to specific types of hissing, mewing, or howling vocal patterns, depending on exactly which parts of the PAG are stimulated. When these results are integrated, a picture develops of an emotional expression system that makes up part of a more general emotional response system, in which specific brain stem nuclei, activated via pathways from the limbic system, coordinate the activation of groups of laryngeal and respiratory muscles leading to specific vocal patterns. Although such a signaling system seems to support the theory of emotion-specific, motor-expressive programs as posited by Ekman (1992) and Izard (1971), it remains to be seen if such neural mechanisms are organized around specific emotions or around appraisals, as suggested by Scherer (1986) and other appraisal theorists (see Smith & Scott, 1997). The extent to which such mechanisms are the exclusive result of automatic processing or might (particularly in humans) also be engaged in a controlled manner remains unclear. Furthermore, whether the neural mechanisms underlying animal vocalizations, which resemble most closely human affect bursts (see Scherer, 1994), are also responsible for the prosodic modification of speech, remains unanswered.

In the case of the human brain, it has long been generally accepted that processing of segmental, linguistic and grammatical speech information is concentrated in specialized centers in the left hemisphere. The most well-researched left-hemisphere speech centers are the left inferior frontal area (Broca's area) and the left temporo-parieto-occipital area (Wernicke's area), lesions on which lead to fluency and syntactic, and comprehension and lexical deficits, respectively. Due largely to a relative dearth of research, no such consensus exists for the localization (if it indeed exists) of nonlinguistic processing of affective information in speech. Hughlings-Jackson (1915) observed that patients with severe linguistic deficits due to brain damage still had the ability to communicate emotions through voice, and he suggested that such functions might be subserved by the right hemisphere. It was not until the 1970s that neurological evidence of a right-hemisphere specialization for affective speech comprehension was forthcoming (Heilman, Scholes, & Watson, 1975; Tucker, Watson, & Heilman, 1977). Since then, a number of studies comparing listeners with unilateral right-hemisphere brain damage (RHD) to listeners with left-hemisphere damage (LHD) have reported a deficit in the perception of affective prosody in RHD listeners (e.g., Bowers, Coslett, Bauer, Speedie, & Heilman, 1987; Heilman, Bowers, Speedie, & Coslett, 1984, Peper & Irle, 1997; Ross, 1981).

Not all studies support such a right-hemisphere lateralization for decoding emotional prosody, however, with several reporting similar performance by patients with right-hemisphere damage to those with left-hemisphere damage (e.g., Cancelliere & Kertesz, 1990; Tompkins & Flowers, 1985). Based on a detailed analysis of how the prosodic acoustic parameters were used by RHD and LHD patients in classifying (and misclassifying) emotional speech stimuli, Van Lancker and Sidtis (1992) suggested that the appearance of a right-hemisphere specialization for affective prosody might be the result of a more general hemispheric specialization for processing certain types of acoustic information. According to this view, disruption in RHD patients of processing of pitch level and variability, which are known to be major carriers of emotion information in speech (Banse & Scherer, 1996; Scherer, 1986), leads to deficient decoding of affective prosody. This explanation fits well with studies that have shown a right-hemisphere specialization for the processing of analog information—in particular, continuously changing acoustic parameters such as fundamental frequency and spectral energy distribution—in contrast to left-hemisphere specialization for the processing of categorical and temporal information (Fitch, Miller, & Tallal, 1997; Robin, Tranel, & Damasio, 1990). A corollary of this hypothesis is that types of information other than emotion that are conveyed in an analog manner, such as speaker identity, should also be decoded predominantly in the right hemisphere. Van Lancker, Kreiman, and Cummings (1989) found such a lateralization in the recognition of familiar voices but not in the discrimination between unfamiliar voices. The explanation given for these and similar results with other types of stimuli was that a right-hemisphere specialization exists for the processing of personally relevant and familiar information (Van Lancker, 1991). This position contradicts the theory that hemispheric lateralization reflects prosodic structure rather than affective content (see also Baum & Pell, 1999).

The lack of consistent neuropsychological findings regarding the localization of the perception of affective and nonaffective prosody is probably due in part to the variability in lesion size and location in brain-damaged patients. Lesions not only commonly span multiple cortical regions but also include subcortical areas, making it difficult to determine precisely which areas are implicated in prosodic processing. Lesion studies can also be criticized on the grounds that they do not directly address questions concerning the mental processes of healthy, non-brain-damaged individuals. Functional brain imaging techniques present an alternative method, allowing greater spatial and temporal isolation of functionally implicated brain regions, as well as an examination of prosodic processing in non-brain-damaged listeners.

To date, only a small number of prosodic imaging studies have been reported. In a recent positron emission tomography (PET) study, George et al. (1996) reported greater right prefrontal activity during processing of the emotional prosody than during processing of the emotional propositional content of spoken sentences. Pihan, Altenmüller, and Ackermann (1997) reported a right-hemisphere lateralization in DC components of the scalp electroencephalography (EEG) signal for the perception of both temporal (accented syllable duration) and frequency (F0 range) mediated emotional prosody. Imaizumi, Mori, Kiritani, Hosoi, and Tonoike (1998), using magnetoencephalography (MEG), found evidence supporting the existence of prosody-specific right-hemisphere processing, as well as the involvement of certain left hemisphere centers in both linguistic and prosodic processing. In a separate study, Imaizumi et al. (1997) found that regional cerebral blood flow, as measured by PET, indicated that a number of areas of both cerebral hemispheres were differentially involved in the identification of speaker versus the identification of emotion in spoken words. This latter study hints that some of the contradictory results obtained in lesion studies of the localization of affective and nonaffective prosodic perception might be resolved with techniques that have more precise spatial resolution, such as PET and functional magnetic resonance imaging (fMRI). Of these two techniques, fMRI has the advantage of allowing the functional image to be accurately overlaid upon a concurrently acquired structural image of the brain. FMRI is also noninvasive, in that no radioactive tracers are injected into the subject's body.

In summary, there is little consensus as to the extent and functional significance of the localization of decoding of affective and nonaffective prosody in speech. Certain researchers claim a special link between decoding of affect and hemispheric specialization (e.g., Ross, Homan, & Buck, 1994), while others propose that perception of prosody is a more multifaceted process that depends both on the structure of the parts of the speech signal being processed, as well as the information contained therein (Van Lancker, 1991).

## Applied Research: Vocal Indicators of Affective Disturbance and Therapy Outcomes

The analysis of vocal emotion expression is used increasingly in applied settings, including health psychology, consumer psychology, speech technology, media psychology, and many other areas in which speech plays a major role in daily life. Since it would be impossible to cover the entire gamut of applications in the context of this chapter, we are focusing one specific area: clinical psychology and psychiatry.

The study of the nonlinguistic aspects of speech, such as the vocal expression and perception of emotion, is directly pertinent to a number of applied issues in clinical domains. Clinical psychologists and psychiatrists have long used the tone of voice of a patient as a valuable indicator of the patient's mental state, but have had to rely on subjective and intuitive assessments rather than objective measures of the patient's vocal characteristics. Attempts were made to use acoustic measures of voice and speech measurement as early as the beginning of the 20th century in order to evaluate the diagnostic value of vocalization for the study of depression (Isserlin, 1925; Scripture, 1921; Zwirner, 1930). Following these pioneers, there have been many efforts to investigate this issue empirically (see reviews in Darby, 1981; Maser, 1987).

One of the clinical syndromes that has been most frequently studied with respect to vocal characteristics is depression, often using speech rate and F0 as indices. Normally, rate of speech tends to slow down in sad or depressed states, and this is indeed what is found in virtually all of the studies on emotion encoding (portrayals by actors or laymen; see Pittam & Scherer, 1993, for a review). Furthermore, in studies in which depressed states are induced experimentally, rate or tempo of speech goes down (e.g., Natale, 1977). Empirically, reduced rate or tempo of spontaneous speech in depression is a frequently reported finding and seems to be a stable phenomenon (see review by Siegman, 1987). On the whole, there is rather good evidence that patients in acute and severe depressive states are likely to speak more slowly and with longer pauses. Therefore, an increase in speech tempo and shortening of pauses may well indicate therapeutic success or remission from a depressive state. What is less clear is the mechanism that underlies this phenomenon.

With respect to F0, most studies have reported a rather low mean F0 for depressives in relation to normals, or decreased F0 in an acute state of depression, although there are reports of an increase in F0 with the severity of depression (see review in Scherer, 1987). The opposite pattern was found in studies on vocal changes following therapy. Most studies have found a decrease in F0 after therapy or during positive mood states (only one study suggested an increase in F0 and no significant effects were found in two other studies (see review in Scherer, 1987). The apparent discrepancy in the results may be explained at least in part by the fact that in most studies no clear distinction between manic and depressed states seems to have been made.

In a large-scale longitudinal study of depressive disorders, Ellgring and Scherer (1996) showed, as predicted, that an increase in speech rate and a decrease in pause duration are powerful indicators of mood improvement in the course of therapy (remission from depressive state). For F0, there were interesting sex differences. In female but not in male patients, a decrease in minimum fundamental frequency of the voice predicted mood improvement. The authors suggest that these differences may be due to differences in the emotions underlying depression. There are some indications that these could consist of suppressed anger in men and resignation in women. These and other data show the great promise of using vocal analysis as unobtrusive markers of affective change in patients suffering from emotional disorders.

## Conclusions

In closing, we want to reiterate the need for a more comprehensive model as a grounding for research on the process of the vocal communication of emotion, such as the Brunswikian lens model according to which this chapter was structured. As mentioned repeatedly, most studies have focused on only one aspect of the total process, generally encoding or decoding.

As has become abundantly clear in reviewing the evidence to date, such a one-sided approach implies the danger of neglecting the important interactions between expression and impression. Future theorizing and research may profit from modeling the vocal communication process in its complete form. This may help to better understand the recursive relationships between push and pull effects in encoding and decoding. For animal communication, Leyhausen (1967) has provided a powerful demonstration of how the reception requirements of the receiver (pull effects) can shape the expression of the sender (push effects). Similarly, the fact that objective signal characteristics are transformed by the hearing mechanism of the receiver requires one to study the complete process of encoding of speaker states in distal form, transmission of the signal, and perception and interpretation by the receiver.

Many of the inconsistencies in the findings in the literature to date might be interpretable upon having access to the missing pieces of the puzzle. In addition, studying vocal parameters that are based on perceptual cues rather than objective acoustic-phonetic signals, as has been the case in research in the past, may also help to better understand the process of emotion inference from the voice, including individual, group, and cultural differences.

Apart from studying the vocal communication process as a whole, it may also be time to drop the assumption of separate linguistic and nonlinguistic channels, together with the hermetic separation of the respective research traditions. As we have shown, there is much evidence that a large part of emotion signaling in voice and speech is dually coded, in both linguistic and nonlinguistic features. Thus, a rapprochement between researchers interested in expression and those interested in language (see chapter 27, this volume) is highly desirable, as is a more intensive interaction between researchers studying vocal and facial expression, two research areas that have had little contact so far, even though they have a common origin in the underlying emotion and are often interpreted as a Gestalt by the perceiver. The evolution of an affective science may help to create a context for theory and research that will encourage such a rapprochement.

## REFERENCES

Abadjieva, E., Murray, I. R., & Arnott, J. L. (1995). Applying analysis of human emotional speech to enhance synthetic speech. *Proceedings Eurospeech, 95,* 909–912.

Allen, G. D. (1975). Speech rhythm: Its relation to performance universals & articulatory timing. *Journal of Phonetics, 3,* 75–86.

Bachorowski, J. A. (1999). Vocal expression and perception of emotion. *Current Directions in Psychological Science, 8*(2), 53–57.

Bachorowski, J. A., & Owren, M. J. (1995). Vocal expression of emotion: Acoustic properties of speech are associated with emotional intensity and context. *Psychological Science, 6*(4), 219–224.

Bandler, R., & Shipley, M. T. (1994). Columnar organization in the mid-brain periaqueductal gray: Modules for emotional expression? *Trends in Neuroscience, 17,* 379–389.

Banse, R., & Scherer, K. (1996). Acoustic profiles in vocal emotion expression. *Journal of Personality and Social Psychology, 70*(3), 614–636.

Baum, S. R., & Pell, M. D. (1999). The neural bases of prosody: Insights from lesion studies and neuroimaging. *Aphasiology, 13*(8), 581–608.

Beckman, M. E. (1995). Local shapes and global trends. *Proceedings XIIIth ICPhS, 95,* Stockholm, Sweden, Vol. 2, pp. 100–108.

Bowers, D., Coslett, H. B., Bauer, R. M., Speedie, L. J., & Heilman, K. M. (1987). Comprehension of emotional prosody following unilateral hemispheric lesions: Processing defect versus distraction defect. *Neuropsychologia, 25,* 317–328.

Burkhardt, F., & Sendlmeier, W. F. (2000). Verification of acoustical correlates of emotional speech using formant-synthesis. In *Proceedings of the ISCA Workshop on Speech and Emotion,* Newcastle, Northern Ireland, September 5–7, 2000. Raleigh, NC: International Society for Computers and Their Applications.

Bühler, K. (1934). *Sprachtheorie* [Theory of speech]. Jena: Fischer (new ed. 1984).

Byers, P. (1976). Biological rhythms as information channels in interpersonal communication behavior. In P. P. G. Bateson & P. H. Klopfer (Eds.), *Perspectives in ethology,* Vol. 2 (pp. 135–164). New York: Plenum.

Caffi, C., & Janney, R. W. (1994). Toward a pragmatics of emotive communication. *Journal of Pragmatics, 22,* 325–373.

Cahn, J. (1990). The generation of affect in synthesised speech. *Journal of the American Voice I/O Society, 8,* 1–19.

Campbell, N. (2000). Databases of emotional speech. In *Proceedings of the ISCA Workshop on Speech and Emotion,* Newcastle, Northern Ireland, September 5–7, 2000, 114–121. Raleigh, NC: International Society for Computers and Their Applications.

Carlson, R., Granström, B., & Nord, L. (1992). Experiments with emotive speech—acted utterances and synthesized replicas. *Proceedings ICSLP, 92*(1), 671–674.

Cancelliere, A., & Kertesz, A. (1990). Lesion localization in acquired deficits of emotional expression and comprehension. *Brain and Cognition, 13,* 133–147.

Condon, W. S. (1986). Communication: Rhythm and structure. In J. Evans & M. Clynes (Eds.). *Rhythm in psychological, linguistic, and musical processes* (pp. 55–77). Springfield, IL: Charles C. Thomas.

d'Alessandro, C., & Mertens, P. (1995). Automatic pitch contour stylization using a model of tonal perception. *Computer Speech and Language, 9,* 257–288.

Darby, J. K. (Ed.) (1981). *Speech evaluation in psychiatry.* New York: Grune & Stratton.

Darwin, C. (1872/1978). *The expression of emotions in man and animals* (3rd ed.). P. Ekman (Ed.). London: HarperCollins.

Davis, P. J., Zhang, S. P., Winkworth, A., & Bandler, R. (1996). Neural control of vocalization: Respiratory and emotional influences. *Journal of Voice, 10,* 23–38.

de Gelder, B., & Vroomen, J. (2000). Bimodal emotion perception: Integration across separate modalities, cross-modal perceptual grouping or perception of multimodal events? *Cognition and Emotion, 14,* 321–324.

Douglas-Cowie, E., Cowie, R., & Schröder, M. (2000). A new emotion database: Considerations, sources and scope. In *Proceedings of the ISCA Workshop on Speech and Emotion,* Newcastle, Northern Ireland, September 5–7, 2000. Raleigh, NC: International Society for Computers and Their Applications.

Duffy, E. (1962). *Activation and behavior.* New York: Wiley.

Ekman, P. (1972). Universals and cultural differences in facial expression of emotion. In J. R. Cole (Ed.), *Nebraska Symposium on Motivation* (pp. 207–283). Lincoln: University of Nebraska Press.

Ekman, P. (1992). An argument for basic emotions. *Cognition and Emotion, 6*(3/4), 169–200.

Ekman, P. (1994). Strong evidence for universals in facial expressions: A reply to Russell's mistaken critique. *Psychological Bulletin, 115,* 268–287.

Ekman, P., & Friesen, W. V. (1978). *The Facial Action Coding System: A technique for the measurement of facial movement.* Palo Alto, CA: Consulting Psychologists Press.

Ellgring, H., & Scherer, K. R. (1996). Vocal indicators of mood change in depression. *Journal of Nonverbal Behavior, 20,* 83–110.

Fant, G. M. (1960). *Acoustic theory of speech production.* The Hague: Mouton.

Fitch, R. H., Miller, S., & Tallal, P. (1997). Neurobiology of speech perception. *Annual Review of Neuroscience, 20,* 331–353.

Fonagy, I. (1981). Emotions, voice and music. In J. Sundberg (Ed.). *Research aspects on singing* (pp. 51–79). Stockholm: Royal Swedish Academy of Music; Paris: Payot.

Fonagy, I. (1983). *La vive voix [The speaking voice]*. Paris: Payot.

Fonagy, I., & Magdics, K. (1963). Emotional patterns in intonation and music. *Zeitschrift für Phonetik, 16*, 293–326.

Fraisse, P. (1963). *The psychology of time*, New York: Harper & Row.

Frick, R. W. (1985). Communicating emotion: The role of prosodic features. *Psychological Bulletin, 97*, 412–429.

Fridlund, A. J. (1994). *Human facial expression: An evolutionary view*. New York: Academic Press.

Friend, M., & Farrar, M. J. (1994). A comparison of content-masking procedures for obtaining judgments of discrete affective states. *Journal of the Acoustical Society of America, 96*(3), 1283–1290.

Garding, E., & Bruce, G. (1981). A presentation of the Lund model for Swedish intonation. In T. Fretheim (Ed.), *Nordic prosody II* (pp. 33–39). Trondheim: TAPIR.

George, M. S., Parekh, P. I., Rosinsky, N., Ketter, T. A., Kimbrell, T. A., Heilman, K. M., Herscovitch, P., & Post, R. M. (1996). Understanding emotional prosody activates right hemisphere regions. *Archives of Neurology, 53*, 665–70.

Goldbeck, T., Tolkmitt, F., & Scherer, K. R. (1988). Experimental studies on vocal communication. In K. R. Scherer (Ed.), *Facets of emotion* (pp. 119–138). Hillsdale, NJ: Erlbaum.

Gramming, P., & Sundberg, J. (1988). Spectrum factors relevant to phonetogram measurement, *Journal of the Acoustical Society of America, 83*, 2352–2360.

Granström, B. (1992). The use of speech synthesis in exploring different speaking styles. *Speech Communication, 11*, 347–355.

Hauser, M. D. (1996). *The evolution of communication*. Cambridge, MA: MIT Press.

Heilman, K. M., Bowers, D., Speedie, L., & Coslett, H. B. (1984). Comprehension of affective and nonaffective prosody. *Neurology, 34*, 917–921.

Heilman, K. M., Scholes, R., & Watson, R. T. (1975). Auditory affective agnosia: Disturbed comprehension of affective speech. *Journal of Neurology, Neurosurgery and Psychiatry, 38*, 69–72.

Heuft, B., Portele, T., & Rauth, M. (1996). Emotions in time domain synthesis. *Proceedings ICSLP 96*(3), 1974–1977.

Hughlings-Jackson, J. (1915). On affections of speech from diseases of the brain. *Brain, 38*, 106–174.

Imaizumi, S., Mori, K., Kiritani, S., Hosoi, H., & Tonoike, M. (1998). Task-dependent laterality for cue decoding during spoken language processing. *NeuroReport, 9*, 899–903.

Imaizumi, S., Mori, K., Kiritani, S., Kawashima, R., Sugiura, M., Fukuda, H., Itoh, K., Kato, T., Nakamura, A., Hatano, K., Kojima, S., & Nakamura, K. (1997). Vocal identification of speaker and emotion activates different brain regions. *NeuroReport, 8*, 2809–2812.

Isserlin, M. (1925). Psychologisch-phonetische Untersuchungen. II. Mitteilung. (Psychological-phonetic studies. 2nd communication). *Zeitschrift für die Gesamte Neurologie und Psychiatrie, 94*, 437–448.

Izard, C. E. (1971). *The face of emotion*. New York: Appleton-Century-Crofts.

Izard, C. E. (1977). *Human emotions*. New York: Plenum.

Jakobson, R., Fant, C., & Halle, M. (1951). *Preliminaries to speech analysis*. Cambridge, MA: MIT Press.

Johnstone, T. (1996). Emotional speech elicited using computer games. *Proceedings ICSLP 96*(3), 1985–1988.

Johnstone, T. (2001). *The communication of affect through modulation of non-verbal vocal parameters*. Ph.D. Thesis. University of Western Australia.

Johnstone, T., & Scherer, K. R. (2000). Vocal communication of emotion. In M. Lewis & J. Haviland (Eds.). *Handbook of emotion* (2nd ed.) (pp. 220–235) New York: Guilford Press.

Johnstone, T., van Reekum, C. M., & Scherer, K. R. (2001). Vocal correlates of appraisal processes. In K. R. Scherer, A. Schorr, & T. Johnstone (Eds.). *Appraisal processes in emotion: Theory, methods, research* (pp. 271–284). New York: Oxford University Press.

Jürgens, U. (1979). Vocalization as an emotional indicator. A neuroethological study in the squirrel monkey. *Behaviour, 69*, 88–117.

Jürgens, U. (1988). Central control of monkey calls. In D. Todt, P. Goedeking, & D. Symmes (Eds.). *Primate vocal communication* (pp. 162–170). Berlin: Springer.

Jürgens, U. (1994). The role of the periaqueductal grey in vocal behaviour. *Behavioural Brain Research, 62*, 107–117.

Juslin, P. N., & Laukka, P. (2001). Impact of intended emotion intensity on cue utilization and decoding accuracy in vocal expression of emotion. *Emotion, 1*(4), 381–412.

Kappas, A. (1997). His master's voice: Acoustic analysis of spontaneous vocalizations in an ongoing active coping task. *Psychophysiology, 34*, S5. (abstract)

Kappas, A., Hess, U., & Scherer, K. R. (1991). Voice and emotion. In B. Rimé & R. S. Feldman (Eds.), *Fundamentals of nonverbal behaviour* (pp. 200–238) New York: Cambridge University Press.

Karlsson, I., Banziger, T., Dankovicova, J., Johnstone, T., Lindberg, J., Melin, H., Nolan, F., & Scherer, K. (2000). Speaker verification with elicited speaking styles in the VeriVox project. *Speech Communication, 31*(2–3), 121–129.

Klasmeyer, G. (1999). Akustische Korrelate des stimmlich emotionalen Ausdrucks in der Lautsprache [Acoustical correlates of emotional expression in voice.]. In H.-W. Wodarz, G. Heike, P. Janota, & M. Mangold (Eds.), *Forum Phoneticum, 67* (pp. 1–238). Frankfurt am Main: Hector.

Klasmeyer, G., & Sendlmeier, W. F. (1997). The classification of different phonation types in emotional and neutral speech. *Forensic Linguistics, 4*, 104–124.

Klasmeyer, G., & Sendlmeier, W. F. (1999). Voice and emotional states. In R. Kent & M. Ball (Eds.), *Voice quality measurement* (pp. 339–359). San Diego, CA: Singular Publishing Group.

Kohler, K. J. (1995). *Einführung in die Phonetik des Deutschen* [Introduction to the phonetics of German] (2nd ed.). Berlin: Erich Schmidt.

Ladefoged P. (1975). *A course in phonetics*. New York: Harcourt Brace Jovanovich.

Ladd, D. R. (1983). Phonological features of intonational peaks, *Language, 59*, 721–759.

Ladd, D. R. (1995). Linear and overlay descriptions: An autosegmental-metrical middle-way. *Proceedings XIIIth ICPhS 95*, Stockholm, Sweden, 2, 116–123.

Ladd, D. R., Silverman, K. E. A., Tolkmitt, F., Bergmann, G., & Scherer, K. R. (1985). Evidence for the independent function of intonation contour type, voice quality, and F0 range in signaling speaker affect. *Journal of the Acoustical Society of America, 78*, 435–444.

Ladd, D. R., Scherer, K. R., & Silverman, K. E. A. (1986).

An integrated approach to studying intonation and attitude. In C. Johns-Lewis (Ed.), *Intonation in discourse* (pp. 125–138). London: Croom Helm.

Laver, J. (1980). *The phonetic description of voice quality.* Cambridge: Cambridge University Press.

Laver, J. (1991). *The gift of speech.* Edinburgh: Edinburgh University Press.

LeDoux, J. (1996). *The emotional brain: The mysterious underpinnings of emotional life.* New York: Simon & Schuster.

Leyhausen, P. (1967). Biologie von Ausdruck und Eindruck (Teil 1). [The biology of expression and impression. Part 1]. *Psychologische Forschung, 31,* 113–176.

Liberman, M., & Pierrehumbert, J. (1984). Intonational invariance under changes in pitch range and length. In M. Aronoff & R. Oehrle (Eds.). *Language sound structures* (pp. 157–233). Cambridge, MA: MIT Press.

Lieberman, P., & Michaels, S. B. (1962). Some aspects of fundamental frequency and envelope amplitude as related to the emotional content of speech. *Journal of the Acoustical Society of America, 34,* 922–927.

Marler, P., & Tenaza, R. (1977). Signaling behavior of apes with special reference to vocalization. In T. A. Sebeok (Ed.), *How animals communicate* (pp. 965–1033). Bloomington: Indiana University Press.

Maser, J. D. (Ed.). (1987). *Depression and expressive behavior.* Hillsdale, NJ: Erlbaum.

Massaro, D. W. (2000). Multimodal emotional perception: Analogous to speech processes. In *Proceedings of the ISCA Workshop on Speech and Emotion,* Newcastle, Northern Ireland, September 5–7, 2000, 114–121.

Mertens, P., Beaugendre, F., & d'Alessandro, C. (1997). Comparing approaches to pitch contour stylization for speech synthesis. In J. P. H. van Santen, R. W. Sproat, J. P. Olive, & J. Hirschberg (Eds), *Progress in speech synthesis* (pp. 347–363). New York: Springer.

Möbius, B. (1995). Components of a quantitative model of German intonation, *Proceedings XIIIth ICPhS 95,* Stockholm, Sweden, 2, 108–117.

Morton, E. S. (1977). On the occurrence and significance of motivational-structural rules in some bird and mammal sounds. *American Naturalist, 111,* 855–869.

Mozziconacci, S. J. L. (1995). Pitch variations and emotions in speech. *Proceedings XIIIth ICPhS 95,* Stockholm, Sweden, 1, 178–181.

Murray, I. R., & Arnott, J. L. (1993). Toward a simulation of emotion in synthetic speech: A review of the literature on human vocal emotion. *Journal of the Acoustical Society of America, 93,* 1097–1108.

Murray, I. R., & Arnott, J. L. (1995). Implementation and testing of a system for producing emotion-by-rule in synthetic speech. *Speech Communication, 16,* 369–390.

Natale, M. (1977). Effects of induced elation-depression on speech in the initial interview. *Journal of Consulting and Clinical Psychology, 45,* 45–52.

Ohala, J. J. (1980). The acoustic origin of the smile. *Journal of the Acoustic Society of America, 68,* 33 (Abstract).

O'Shaughnessy, D. (2000). *Speech communication: Human and machine.* New York: IEEE Press.

Paeschke, A., Kienast, M., & Sendlmeier, W. F. (1999). F0-Contours in emotional speech, *Proceedings ICPhS 99,* San Francisco, Vol. 2, 929–933.

Panksepp, J. (1998). *Affective neuroscience: The foundations of human and animal emotions.* New York: Oxford University Press.

Papousek, M. (1994). *Vom Schrei zum ersten Wort: Anfänge der Sprachentwicklung in der vorsprachlichen Kommunikation* [From the infant cry to the first word: The bases of speech development in preverbal communication.] Bern: Hans Huber.

Peper, M., & Irle, E. (1997). Categorical and dimensional decoding of emotional intonations in patients with focal brain lesions. *Brain and Language, 57,* 233–264.

Pihan, H., Altenmüller, E., & Ackermann, H. (1997). The cortical processing of perceived emotion: A DC-potential study on affective speech prosody. *Neuro-Report, 8,* 623–627.

Pittam, J., & Scherer, K. R. (1993). Vocal expression and communication of emotion. In M. Lewis & J. M. Haviland (Eds.), *Handbook of emotions* (pp. 185–198). New York: Guilford Press.

Porges, S. W. (1997). Emotion: An evolutionary by-product of the neural regulation of the autonomic nervous system. *Annals of the New York Academy of Sciences, 807,* 62–77.

Roach, P., Stibbard, R., Osborne, J., Arnfield, S., & Setter, J. (1998). Transcription of prosodic and paralinguistic features of emotional speech. *Journal of the International Phonetic Association, 28,* 83–94.

Robin, D. A., Tranel, D., & Damasio, H. (1990). Auditory perception of temporal and spectral events in patients with focal left and right cerebral lesions. *Brain and Language, 39,* 539–555.

Robinson, B. W. (1972). Anatomical and physiological contrasts between human and other primate vocalizations. In S. L. Washburn & P. Dolhinow (Eds.), *Perspectives on human evolution* (pp. 438–443). New York: Holt, Rinehart & Winston.

Roseman, I., & Smith, C. (2001). Appraisal theory: Overview, assumptions, varieties, controversies. In K. R. Scherer, A. Schorr, & T. Johnstone (Eds.). *Appraisal processes in emotion: Theory, methods, research* (pp. 3–19). New York: Oxford University Press.

Rosen, S., & Howell, P. (1991). *Signals and systems for speech and hearing.* New York: Harcourt Brace Jovanovich.

Ross, E. D. (1981). The aprosodias: Functional-anatomical organization of the affective components of language in the right hemisphere. *Archives of Neurology, 38,* 561–569.

Ross, E. D., Edmondson, J. A., & Seibert, G. B. (1986). The effect of affect on various acoustic measures of prosody in tone and non-tone languages: A comparison based on computer analysis of voice. *Journal of Phonetics, 14,* 283–302.

Ross, E. D., Homan, R. W., & Buck, R. (1994). Differential hemispheric lateralization of primary and social emotions: Implications for developing a comprehensive neurology for emotions, repression, and the subconscious. *Neuropsychiatry, Neuropsychology, and Behavioral Neurology, 7,* 1–19.

Russell, J. A. (1980). A circumplex model of affect. *Journal of Personality and Social Psychology, 39,* 1161–1178.

Russell, J. A. (1994). Is there universal recognition of emotion from facial expression? A review of the cross-cultural studies. *Psychological Bulletin, 115,* 102–141.

Scherer, K. R. (1978). Personality inference from voice quality: The loud voice of extroversion. *European Journal of Social Psychology, 8,* 467–487.

Scherer, K. R. (1979). Non-linguistic indicators of emotion

and psychopathology. In C. E. Izard (Ed.), *Emotions in personality and psychopathology* (pp. 495–529). New York: Plenum.

Scherer, K. R. (1982). Methods of research on vocal communication: Paradigms and parameters. In K. R. Scherer & P. Ekman (Eds.), *Handbook of methods in nonverbal behavior research* (pp. 136–198). New York: Cambridge University Press.

Scherer, K. R. (1984). On the nature and function of emotion: A component process approach. In K. R. Scherer & P. Ekman (Eds.), *Approaches to emotion* (pp. 293–318). Hillsdale, NJ: Erlbaum.

Scherer, K. R. (1985). Vocal affect signaling: A comparative approach. In J. Rosenblatt, C. Beer, M. Busnel, & P. J. B. Slater (Eds.), *Advances in the study of behavior* (pp. 189–244). New York: Academic Press.

Scherer, K. R. (1986). Vocal affect expression: A review and a model for future research. *Psychological Bulletin, 99*(2), 143–165.

Scherer, K. R. (1987). Vocal assessment of affective disorders. In J. D. Maser (Ed.), *Depression and expressive behavior* (pp. 57–82). Hillsdale, NJ: Erlbaum.

Scherer, K. R. (1988). On the symbolic functions of vocal affect expression. *Journal of Language and Social Psychology, 7*, 79–100.

Scherer, K. R. (1989). Vocal correlates of emotion. In H. Wagner & A. Manstead (Eds.), *Handbook of psychophysiology: Emotion and social behavior* (pp. 165–197). London: Wiley.

Scherer, K. R. (1992). What does facial expression express? In K. Strongman (Ed.), *International review of studies on emotion* (Vol. 2, pp. 139–165). Chichester, England: Wiley.

Scherer, K. R. (1994). Affect bursts. In S. H. M. van Goozen, N. E. van de Poll, & J. A. Sergeant (Eds.), *Emotions: Essays on emotion theory* (pp. 161–196). Hillsdale, NJ: Erlbaum.

Scherer, K. R. (1999a). Appraisal theories. In T. Dalgleish & M. Power (Eds.), *Handbook of cognition and emotion* (pp. 637–663). Chichester, England: John Wiley.

Scherer, K. R. (1999b). Universality of emotional expression. In D. Levinson, J. Ponzetti, & P. Jorgenson (Eds.), *Encyclopedia of human emotions* (pp. 669–674). New York: Macmillan.

Scherer, K. R. (2000a). Psychological models of emotion. In J. Borod (Ed.), *The neuropsychology of emotion* (pp. 137–162). New York: Oxford University Press.

Scherer, K. R. (2000b). Emotions as episodes of subsystem synchronization driven by nonlinear appraisal processes. In M. Lewis & I. Granic (Eds.), *Emotion, development, and self-organization* (pp. 70–99). New York/Cambridge: Cambridge University Press.

Scherer, K. R. (2001). Appraisal considered as a process of multi-level sequential checking. In K. R. Scherer, A. Schorr, & T. Johnstone (Eds.). *Appraisal processes in emotion: Theory, methods, research* (pp. 92–120). New York: Oxford University Press.

Scherer, K. R., Banse, R., & Wallbott, H. G. (2001). Emotion inferences from vocal expression correlate across languages and cultures. *Journal of Cross-Cultural Psychology, 32*(1), 76–92.

Scherer, K. R., Banse, R., Wallbott, H. G., & Goldbeck, T. (1991). Vocal cues in emotion encoding and decoding. *Motivation and Emotion, 15*, 123–148.

Scherer, K. R., Feldstein, S., Bond, R. N., & Rosenthal, R. (1985). Vocal cues to deception: A comparative channel approach. *Journal of Psycholinguistic Research, 14*, 409–425.

Scherer, K. R., Johnstone, T., Klasmeyer, G., & Bänziger, T. (2000). Can automatic speaker verification be improved by training the algorithms of emotional speech? *Proceedings ICSLP2000*, Beijing, China.

Scherer, K. R., Ladd, D. R., & Silverman, K. E. A. (1984). Vocal cues to speaker affect: Testing two models. *Journal of the Acoustical Society of America, 76*, 1346–1356.

Scherer, K. R., & Oshinsky, J. S. (1977). Cue utilization in emotion attribution from auditory stimuli. *Motivation and Emotion, 1*, 331–346.

Scherer, K. R., Schorr, A., & Johnstone, T. (Eds.). (2001). *Appraisal processes in emotion: Theory, methods, research*. New York: Oxford University Press.

Scripture, E. W. (1921). A study of emotions by speech transcription. *Vox, 31*, 179–183.

Siegman, A. W. (1987). The pacing of speech in depression. In J. D. Maser (Ed.), *Depression and expressive behavior* (pp. 83–102). Hillsdale, NJ: Erlbaum.

Smith, C. A. (1989). Dimensions of appraisal and physiological response in emotion. *Journal of Personality and Social Psychology, 56*, 339–353.

Smith, C. A., & Ellsworth, P. C. (1985). Patterns of cognitive appraisal in emotion. *Journal of Personality and Social Psychology, 48*, 813–838.

Smith, C. A., & Scott, H. S. (1997). A componential approach to the meaning of facial expressions. In J. A. Russell & J. M. Fernández-Dols (Eds.), *The psychology of facial expression* (pp. 229–254). Cambridge: Cambridge University Press.

Sundberg, J. (1987). *The science of the singing voice.* DeKalb, IL: Northern Illinois University Press.

Sundberg, J. (1994). *Vocal fold vibration patterns and phonatory modes.* STL-QPRS 2–3, KTH Stockholm, Sweden, 69–80.

Thayer, R. E. (1989). *The biopsychology of mood and arousal.* New York: Oxford University Press.

Tischer, B. (1993). *Die vokale Kommunikation von Gefühlen.* [The vocal communication of emotions]. Weinheim: Psychologie-Verlags-Union.

Titze, I. (1992). Acoustic interpretation of the voice range profile (Phonetogram). *Speech Hearing Research, 35*, 21–34.

Tolkmitt, F., Bergmann, G., Goldbeck, T., & Scherer, K. R. (1988). Experimental studies on vocal communication. In K. R. Scherer (Ed.), *Facets of emotion: Recent research* (pp. 119–138). Hillsdale, NJ: Erlbaum.

Tolkmitt, F. J., & Scherer, K. R. (1986). Effects of experimentally induced stress on vocal parameters. *Journal of Experimental Psychology: Human Perception and Performance, 12*, 302–313.

Tompkins, C. A., & Flowers, C. R. (1985). Perception of emotional intonation by brain damaged adults: The influence of task processing levels. *Journal of Speech and Hearing Research, 28*, 527–583.

Tomkins, S. S. (1962). *Affect, imagery, consciousness. Vol. 1. The positive affects.* New York: Springer.

Tomkins, S. S. (1984). Affect theory. In K. R. Scherer & P. Ekman (Eds.), *Approaches to emotion* (pp. 163–196). Hillsdale, NJ: Erlbaum.

Tucker, D. M., Watson, R. T., & Heilman, K. M. (1977). Discrimination and evocation of affectively intoned speech in patients with right parietal disease. *Neurology, 27*, 947–950.

van Bezooijen, R. (1984). *The characteristics and recognizability of vocal expression of emotions*. Dordrecht, The Netherlands: Foris.

van Bezooijen, R., Otto, S., & Heenan, T. A. (1983). Recognition of vocal expressions of emotions: A three-nation study to identify universal characteristics. *Journal of Cross-Cultural Psychology, 14*, 387–406.

Van Lancker, D. (1991). Personal relevance and the human right hemisphere. *Brain and Cognition, 17*, 64–92.

Van Lancker, D., Kreiman, J., & Cummings, J. (1989). Voice perception deficits: Neuroanatomical correlates of phonagnosia. *Journal of Clinical and Experimental Neuropsychology, 11*, 665–674.

Van Lancker, D., & Sidtis, J. J. (1992). The identification of affective-prosodic stimuli by left- and right-hemisphere-damaged subjects: All errors are not created equal. *Journal of Speech and Hearing Research, 35*, 963–970.

Wagner, H. L. (1993). On measuring performance in category judgment studies on nonverbal behavior. *Journal of Nonverbal Behavior, 17*(1), 3–28.

Wallbott, H. G., & Scherer, K. R. (1986). Cues and channels in emotion recognition. *Journal of Personality and Social Psychology, 51*, 690–699.

Wehrle, T., Kaiser, S., Schmidt, S., & Scherer, K. R. (2000). Studying dynamic models of facial expression of emotion using synthetic animated faces. *Journal of Personality and Social Psychology, 78*(1), 105–119.

Zwicker, E. (1982). *Psychoacoustics*. New York: Springer.

Zwirner, E. (1930). Beitrag zur Sprache des Depressiven. [Contribution on the speech of depressives.] *Phonometrie III. Spezielle Anwendungen I.*, 171–187. Basel: Karger.

# 24

# EXPRESSION OF EMOTION
# IN NONHUMAN ANIMALS

Charles T. Snowdon

Darwin's *The Expression of Emotions in Man and Animals* (1872/1998) was the first book to provide explicit links between how human and nonhuman animals express emotions, and it serves as a model for the study of emotional expression today. Darwin's main focus was with the visual display of emotion. Although Darwin wrote briefly about vocalizations in nonhuman animals, it was much easier in his time to record and analyze facial expressions through drawings and the emerging new medium of photography. In the middle of the 20th century, the development of tape-recording equipment, coupled with technology originally developed for speech recognition, provided a means for accurate recording, description, and analysis of vocalizations. The last 50 years of experimental research on animal communication have been dominated by studies on vocal communication. With the recent advent of digital photography and editing systems, there has been an increased interest in the experimental study of visual signals.

Darwin introduced his volume with three general principles of emotional expression that have formed the theoretical basis of current research. The first principle of "serviceable associated habits" provides that under certain mental (emotional) states various complex actions relieve or gratify sensations and desires, and that through repeated association, these actions might be found in circumstances where they might not be directly useful or they might be brought under voluntary control.

Several suggestions follow from this principle. First,

emotional expressions might be developed from normal physiological reactions to various internal or external stimuli. Thus the rapid expulsion of air and vocalization ("ooof") that automatically results when we are hit in the stomach might become associated with other painful stimuli that do not result in a rapid expulsion of air. The resulting vocalization becomes an expression of pain experienced anywhere, and might even be used in anticipation of a painful stimulus to inhibit the infliction of pain by someone else. The conversion of an initial physiological reaction into a signal that represents an emotional state more directly is called *ritualization* by ethologists (Smith, 1977). Through progressive association, the physiological signal becomes more stereotyped in form, generalized to a broader array of contexts and universally used within a species.

The fact that many signals are thought to have developed through ritualization of initial physiological reactions should not lead us to conclude that all apparent signals have been adapted for communication. Recently, Blumberg and Alberts (1997) have pointed out several examples of apparent signals that probably do not serve a communicative function to the producer of the signal. Thus, the frequency of the buzzing of wing flapping in bees is directly related to the body temperature of the bee, but probably serves no communication function. The frequency of rattling of a rattlesnake is well above the range of rattlesnakes' auditory sensitivity, but ground squirrels can use the frequency of the rattle to estimate the size of the snake and how active it is (Swaisgood, Rowe, & Owings, 1999). Thus the rattling of a snake provides no information to other snakes but can be used by potential prey to influence their evasive actions. Newborn rodents emit ultrasonic vocalizations when separated from their nest, and these have been interpreted as "distress" vocalizations. Mothers retrieve infants that produce these calls, lending support to the interpretation of a "distress" function. However, Blumberg and Alberts (1997) found that isolated rat pups metabolized brown adipose tissue when cold, that this led in turn to an increased oxygen consumption that led to a change in respiration to constrict the larynx, which delays expiration and allows more time for gas exchange in the lungs. This laryngeal constriction produces ultrasonic sounds. Are the sounds produced by infant rats "distress" signals? Blumberg and Alberts suggest that they are not "distress" calls, but rather the natural physiological reactions of a cold rat pup activating metabolism of brown adipose tissue. What do the signals convey to mothers who retrieve pups that vocalize? The sounds may only convey information that a pup is cold and in need of being warmed. Whether these ultrasonic signals might be converted to "distress" calls would depend on finding an experimental situation that involved a warm rat pup and showing that similar ultrasonic vocalizations were produced. To show that a "distress" meaning was conveyed to a mother rat, one would need to observe mothers responding flexibly to pups, not simply providing the calling pup with warmth. As one reads about affective expression, one should be a healthy skeptic.

The second of Darwin's principles is antithesis. Emotions that are opposites are expressed through opposite body actions or postures. An aggressive dog stands tall with head, ears, and tail in the air and hair erected, and a submissive dog slouches down, lowering its tail and ears and sleeking its fur. Ekman (in Darwin 1872/1998, pp. 63–64) comments that, in humans, smiles contrast with each of the facial expressions related to negative emotional states. In nonhuman primates a clear contrast can be seen in facial expressions relating to fear and anger. Figure 24.1 (from Chevalier-Skolnikoff, 1973) shows facial expressions of fear and threat in stumptail macaques. From the neutral face in the upper left-hand corner to the confident threat in the upper right-hand corner the ears are brought forward, the mouth is opened in a circular shape without teeth showing, the hair on the head is erected, and the eyes stare directly at the target. In contrast, moving from the neutral face to extreme fear in the lower left-hand corner the hair remains smooth, the ears remain back, the eyes are averted, and the mouth is opened wide with teeth showing. The lower right-hand corner displays the combination of facial features that occur when the monkey displays high fear and threat combined.

A similar pattern has been proposed by Morton for vo-

cal signals related to threat and fear. Figure 24.2 provides a schematic diagram. In this case the neutral call is shown in the lower left-hand corner. With increasing aggression moving toward the lower right-hand corner, calls become increasingly lower in pitch and are more broadband (covering a larger frequency range, or a growl or bark). With increasing fear, moving toward the upper left-hand corner, calls become higher pitched with pure tones (a shrill whistle-like sound). As with the diagram of facial expressions, features of both fear and aggression can be combined into a blended vocalization. This system is meant to be dynamic, and Owings and Morton (1998, p. 124) provide an example of how vocal structure changes within an individual during a fight with another animal.

Implicit in both models of facial expression and vocal structure is that these principles will be valid across a wide range of species. Darwin explicitly noted that dogs and cats have different postures for fear and aggression, yet in each species, fear and aggression are expressed with opposite postures. Although the specific details of emotional-structural rules might vary between species, the ideas developed from Darwin's principle of antithesis lead to testable hypotheses about which forms of expression relate to which emotions.

Darwin's third principle is of the direct action of the excited nervous system on emotional expression. Strong feelings or sensations arouse neural activity that has direct effects on autonomic and motor function. Changes in activation of facial muscles or of blood flow can lead to changes associated with different emotional states. As noted in Darwin's first principle, this activity can be conditioned to other contexts or stimuli. Thus, the conditioning of emotional responses to specific contexts, events, or specific individuals could be a developmental component of communication. Today there is considerable interest in the ontogeny of communication (see Hauser, 1996; Snowdon & Hausberger, 1997), and one of the major issues is the degree to which early learning is important in shaping emotional expression. There is considerable contemporary interest in the neural and hormonal mechanisms underlying communication, another offshoot of Darwin's third principle.

One final contribution of Darwin was to treat emotional expression in both human and nonhuman animals. Although he clearly recognized species-specific means of emotional expression, he provided several examples of apparent parallels in both vocal and visual signals between human and nonhuman animals. Although generalizations among species must be done with caution, Darwin raised the possibility that an understanding of human emotional expression would emerge from understanding the cause and function of related expressions in animals. As we will see later, some studies of communication in animals are motivated by a desire to understand the origins of human

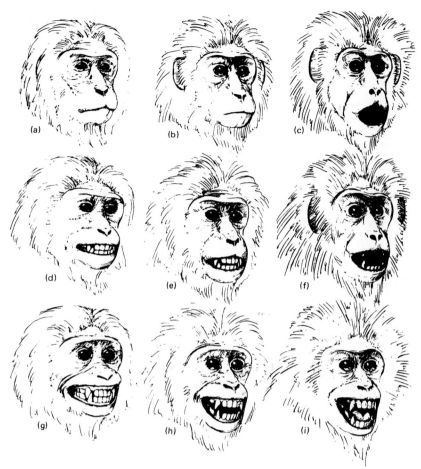

Figure 24.1 Facial expressions of stumptail macaques showing variation from neutral face (upper left, a) toward confident threat (upper right, c) and extreme fear (lower left, g). The lower right-hand corner (i) depicts an intense blend of fear and threat. From Chevalier-Skolnikoff (1973). Reprinted by permission of the author. Drawing by Eric Stoelting.

communication, and many of the results of animal studies may lead to new understandings of human emotional expression.

An effect of the cognitive revolution within psychology during the past 40 years was to produce an interest in the cognitive aspects of animal communication to the neglect of the emotional aspects of communication: Do animals display evidence of mental processes in communication? Do they have the equivalent of words? Is communication automatic and reflexive or can animals adjust communication signals for different recipients and different contexts? Thus, beginning in the early 1980s there were several studies describing referential communication in monkeys, ground squirrels, and birds, and several sarcastic comments about the conservative scientists of the "Groans of Pain" (GOP) school of animal communication unwilling to accept that animals might think (e.g., Griffin, 1985). Vervets, small monkeys from the African savannah,

face a variety of predatory threats and have developed an elaborate system of predator alarm calls, one form specific to aerial predators like eagles, another specific to snakes, and a third specific to leopards. Elegant field experiments involving playbacks of the calls alone in the absence of predators have shown that the monkeys react to vocalizations as if the predator is actually present (Seyfarth, Cheney, & Marler, 1980) and react to each type of call as a separate semantic category (Cheney & Seyfarth, 1988). Further studies have shown that ground squirrels have separate calls for aerial versus ground predators (Leger & Owings, 1978; Owings & Virginia, 1978). However, upon closer examination it appeared that ground squirrels, unlike vervets, were responding emotionally according to the degree of threat posed by each type of predator. If a terrestrial predator had approached close to a ground squirrel without being noticed, the squirrel gave the "aerial" alarm call. If a hawk was flying in a distance and not hunting,

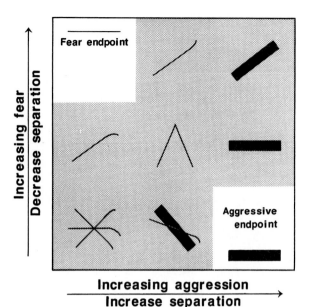

Figure 24.2 Motivational-structural rules for vocalizations going from a neutral state at the lower left-hand corner toward intense fear in the upper right-hand corner, intense aggression in the lower right-hand corners, and a blend of fear and aggression in the upper right-hand corner. Thick lines represent noisy vocalizations and thin lines represent pure tones. The relative vertical location indicates pitch. From Owings & Morton (1998). Reprinted by permission of the authors and Cambridge University Press.

the squirrels would give the "terrestrial" alarm call. For ground squirrels the apparent referential communication was, in fact, an emotional system that for the most part correlated with different predator types (Owings & Hennessey, 1984).

The other main class of referential signals is food-associated vocalizations. A variety of animals, from chickens to tamarin monkeys to macaques to chimpanzees, produce specific calls when they encounter food. Although other group members respond to these calls by approaching the location of the food, the type of call given, the rate of calling, or whether calling occurs at all is related to both the quality of food (toque macaques, Dittus, 1984; chickens, Marler, Dufty, & Pickert, 1986; cotton-top tamarins, Elowson, Tannenbaum, & Snowdon, 1991; rhesus macaques, Hauser & Marler, 1993a) and to the quantity of food (chimpanzees, Hauser, Teixidor, Fields, & Flaherty, 1993; Hauser & Wrangham, 1987). Thus, although the receiver may understand that food has been located, the communicator may simply be communicating its affective state.

In every case of referential signaling discovered to date, whether alarm calls or food calls (or agonistic screams, Gouzoules, Gouzoules, & Marler, 1984; intergroup "wrr" calls, Hauser, 1989) there is always an affective compo-

nent of the call. There are few, if any, affect-free communication signals among animals.

## Conceptual and Organizing Principles

Before reviewing the types of affective communication found in nonhuman animals, we need to examine two basic questions concerning affective communication. First, why should an organism communicate about its emotional state? What are the benefits of communication? Second, what are the environmental or ecological factors that constrain how communication occurs?

### Why Communicate About Emotions?

Production of a signal, whether visual, auditory, or olfactory, is associated with a cost. Some signals consume considerable amounts of energy—the dawn song of birds, the howling of howler monkeys, the songs of gibbons. Other signals are incompatible with other activities—gesturing or holding a specific posture might prevent an organism from looking for food, caring for infants, being vigilant against predators. Still other signals are highly conspicuous, attracting attention not only of conspecifics but also of potential predators. The potential costs of signaling suggest that there must be corresponding or greater benefits to be gained by expressing emotions than in not expressing them. Understanding the functional significance of affective signaling has consumed the energies of quite a few researchers. Three general theories have emerged.

The information perspective argues that animals benefit through honest communication about their internal states (Smith, 1977). An animal that expresses anger or aggression might minimize the possibility of attack if others can "read" the expression and avoid the angry or aggressive animal. Similarly, a fearful or submissive expression might inhibit another animal from attacking or threatening further. An animal that has a "good" experience—finding an unusually good source of food or a potential mate interested in copulation—might give a food or copulation call. The animal that first sees a predator gives an alarm call that warns others to take cover. The problem with each of these examples is that if one accepts that natural selection operates at the level of individuals, some of these "informational" signals do not seem adaptive. What advantage does one gain by calling attention of other group members to a potential predator by putting oneself at risk? What does an organism gain by calling the attention of other group members who are potential competitors to food or mates? An animal that communicates fear or submissiveness may simply encourage others to be even more aggressive. Some solutions to this dilemma have been proposed. If there is reciprocity, then if A signals about food or a predator today, it might benefit from B's providing similar signals in the future, despite the risks of predation or losing full access to food. But reciprocity is open to cheating. B could simply never reciprocate and continue to freeload on A's signals. With respect to aggressive and submissive signals, it can be argued that although the overall levels of physical aggression and potential wounding might be decreased, the unit of benefit is the dyad or group, not the individual.

A second approach has viewed affective communication as manipulative. Rather than providing honest information about affect, animals are said to use signals to manipulate the behavior of others (Krebs & Dawkins, 1984). From this perspective communication must benefit the producer and not the recipient of a signal. Thus a male might make himself look or sound bigger and thus more aggressive by fluffing his fur or feathers or using low-pitched growl vocalizations. A male that can exaggerate his aggressive potential will not only intimidate rivals without having to fight as often, he might also secure more matings with females who are tricked by the apparent aggressive potential of the male. The animal that discovers food should inhibit the expression of positive emotions unless there is more than enough to share with others. A dominant male might vocalize during copulation to signal others to stay away, but a subordinate animal would be silent during copulation. In each of these cases the communicator must increase its own self-interest by communicating.

Alarm calls create particular problems for both informational and manipulation perspectives. Two explanations have been proposed for producing alarm calls. In some cases giving the alarm call does increase the risk of predation, but in this case alarms are given only when several close relatives are nearby (Sherman, 1977). If the caller risks its life but at the benefit of saving close relatives, then alarm calling is adaptive to the caller. Other cases of alarm calling have suggested that the calls let predators know they have been detected and thus predation risk might actually be reduced for the animal that calls (Zuberbuhler, Jenny, & Bshary, 1999).

The difficulty with the manipulation theory is that it takes the perspective only of the communicator, and one should expect countermeasures from the recipients being manipulated. Thus, there is evidence that rhesus monkeys that fail to give food calls are "punished" by other group members if they are found with food (Hauser & Marler, 1993b), but, interestingly, lone males not part of a social group do not receive aggression if they fail to call. Animals that attempt to communicate deceptively about aggressive ability should be detected as recipients develop ways of evaluating the communicator.

The most recent view of affective communication is a management/assessment perspective (Owings & Morton, 1998), which is distinguished from the manipulation approach by its focus on the interests and interactions of both communicator and recipient. Animals use affective signals to manage the behavior of their companions, but they also continually assess and respond to the behavior of others. This has led to a much more dynamic approach to communication that focuses on a continuously changing interaction between individuals, where the roles of sender and receiver are rapidly interchangeable over an interaction. As examples, the calls of a Carolina wren varied over the course of a fight with a neighbor as a function of whether the bird was being aggressive or receiving aggression from its opponent (Owings & Morton, 1998, p. 124). Subadult common marmosets in the midst of aggressive defense of territory boundaries frequently pause and copulate with an animal from the adjacent group and then begin fighting again (Lazaro-Perea, 2001). The patterns of copulation predicted which animals would form new groups several months later (Lazaro-Perea, Harrison, Arajau, Arruda, & Snowdon, 2000) and suggested that one function of aggressive behavior during territory encounters is to allow animals to assess future breeding opportunities.

In an example of between-species assessment, California ground squirrels will kick dirt at rattlesnakes to provoke rattling. Adult ground squirrels are immune to rattlesnake venom but their infants are not. By provoking the rattlesnake, the squirrels can assess the size and temperature of the snake (Swaisgood et al., 1999) and thus determine how much risk the snake poses to the infants.

Young pygmy marmosets engage in long vocal bouts similar to the babbling of human infants (Elowson, Snowdon, & Lazaro-Perea, 1998a, 1998b), but adults occasionally produce babbling bouts as well when they are attacked by other marmosets. It is common to find submissive or fearful expressions mimicking actions in infants, as though displaying infantile behavior is an effective means to manage aggressive behavior.

The management/assessment perspective suggests several new ideas. First, it focuses on affective communication as a dynamic, interactive process, not a set of static expressions. Second, it focuses on both sender and receiver and attempts to consider how each might benefit from the interaction. Third, it suggests that individuals frequently probe the affective state of their companions. The implication is that individuals are constantly checking out the state of their companions, either to gain information for modifying current behavior or for making predictions about future behavior. The idea that individuals benefit by deliberately and continually probing the affective state of companions has intriguing implications for the study of human affective behavior.

## Ecological Constraints on Communication

Although emotional signals are thought to arise from physical and physiological reactions that become ritualized into formal signals, the signals are shaped by ecological factors that make different forms of signals effective for different species depending on the habitats in which they live and the distances over which signals must be transmitted to be effective. There are four basic principles:

1. Communication should not increase predation risk.
2. Different environments provide different amounts and types of noise, and effective signals maximize the ratio of signal to noise.
3. Signals effective over long distances require different structures from those effective over short distances.
4. The potential for signal complexity increases the subtleties of what can be communicated.

Communication is always a compromise between providing signals to other group members and avoiding predation risk. Several different strategies have been documented. One solution is to communicate using a channel that a predator cannot easily perceive. Thus, the pygmy marmoset, the world's smallest monkey, utilizes high-frequency calls that are above the optimal hearing range of most predatory birds, their major daytime threat (Snowdon & Hodun, 1981). Furthermore, pygmy marmosets use calls with few cues to sound localization when they are close to other group members, adding additional sound localization cues (that might also benefit predators) only when they are far from other group members (Snowdon & Hodun, 1981). Many small birds have alarm calls that are high pitched and have ambiguous cues for sound localization (Marler, 1955), presumably making it difficult for predators to detect them. Both songbirds and marmosets use highly distinctive and easily located calls when rallying other group members to mob or attack a threatening animal. Many animals are visually camouflaged but have color patches under the wings or can make brief conspicuous movements as signals (Hailman, 1977). Olfactory communication provides the greatest protection from predation since a signal can be deposited separate from the animal that produced it, yet be effective for hours or days afterwards.

Different types of habitats provide constraints on communication. Visual signals are not very effective for an organism that is primarily active at night. Similarly, birds and mammals living in forested habitats cannot use visual signals over a range of distances, and animals living in obscured conditions, such as murky streams or in chronically foggy conditions, will not make much use of visual signals. In these environments, auditory and olfactory signaling will be more effective.

Darkness, trees, and murky waters are not the only sources of noise that impede effective signaling. Other species constitute an important source of noise. For pygmy marmosets, another advantage of using high-frequency sounds is to avoid the "jamming" produced by ambient noise. Most of the calls of pygmy marmosets are above 8 kHz and two studies of ambient noise (one in Ecuador—de la Torre & Snowdon, in press; another in Peru—Snowdon & Hodun, 1981) found that most of the calls of birds and insects, as well as human-produced noises, were below 8 kHz. Thus, the pygmy marmosets use a frequency window that has little competing noise. Similar frequency windows have been described for mangabeys in East Africa (Waser & Brown, 1986) and for birds in Panama (Morton, 1975). However, the high-frequency range used by pygmy marmosets is associated with a cost in terms of long-distance communication. In a heavily forested environment, sounds become distorted by being absorbed and reflected from vegetation. This distortion is more severe for high frequencies (which have shorter wavelengths that are more easily absorbed or reflected). A second form of distortion is reverberation, which also results from sound reflection and distorts the temporal patterns of signals. Recently, de la Torre and Snowdon (in press) have shown that both frequency and temporal information are distorted in the high-frequency calls of pygmy marmosets so that the most common calls have become extremely distorted and have minimal audibility at 40 meters, severely limiting the distance over which marmosets can communicate effectively.

These results suggest that different types of signals are useful for different distances. As a general rule, the lower the frequency of a vocalization, the greater the distance it travels. This is most obvious in the recent discovery that elephants use infrasound (calls below the range of human hearing) that can travel for long distances with minimal distortion. Playback studies show that these signals can function to coordinate group movement over distances of several kilometers (Payne, Langbauer, & Thomas, 1986). Temperature gradients between the atmosphere and the ground are greatest at dawn, creating a large amplification of sound at dawn (Waser & Waser, 1977). Many territorial birds and monkeys give territorial calls most frequently at dawn.

Visual signals also are affected by distance between communicator and recipient. With increasing distance, even in an open habitat, atmospheric effects will make colors less saturated and contrasts between visual features less sharp. Movements or gestures made at greater distances need to be larger in order to be perceived within the limits of visual acuity (Hailman, 1977). Olfactory signals face the greatest constraints of distance, being dependent on passive transmission by wind to be carried away from the source. In general, small molecular weight odors will be more volatile than larger molecules. Olfactory communication frequently involves specific marking sites that are visited by several different individuals (e.g., Brashears & Arcese, 1999).

With both visual and vocal signals it is easy to imagine

a great variety of possible signals that can communicate subtle differences in affective states. Different muscles can be contracted with differing intensities. Hair or feathers can be raised or lowered to different degrees. An enormous variety of gestures are possible and most can be produced in a graded fashion. Vocal signals can be described in terms of three simple parameters: frequency, time, and amplitude. But these three parameters can be combined to produce infinite gradation and variation in signal structure. The potential for a highly complex, graded communication system is much greater for visual and auditory signals than for olfactory signals, where usually only a limited number of scent-producing glands are known.

Thus, the particular modality used for emotional communication and the specific form of signal structure within a modality will vary from species to species, according to when and where they are active. Factors such as predator deterrence, structure of habitat, time of day, and location of potential recipients can all affect the choice of which signal will be most effective. Finally, redundancy, where different forms of expression are produced at the same time (visual expression coupled with a vocalization or a vocalization coupled with an odor) might be more effective in certain conditions to ensure that the recipient will attend to the signal. We should not be surprised to see similar affective states expressed in multiple forms.

Although visual signals of emotion were the focus of Darwin's book and are still the most studied forms of emotional expression in humans, one value of studying a variety of nonhuman animals is to emphasize the diversity of modalities of affective communication available (such as olfactory signals that have received little attention in human studies). Some of the ecological constraints reviewed here might suggest ideas for new research on humans: How do we change affective signals as our recipients change in distance from us? What strategies do we use to overcome environmental noise? Do we change how we communicate emotionally in different environments?

## Types of Affective Signals

Smith (1977) provided a catalogue of the different messages of animal signals that are listed in Table 24.1 under three general classes: behavioral messages, modifiers, and identifiers. The majority of the behavioral messages listed can be inferentially linked to affective states, such as aggression, fear, affiliation, sex, and ambivalence, with only a few types of messages not directly related to some affective state. These messages can be modified to indicate the intensity or probability of the likely behavior, and coincident with an affective message and an intensity or probability modifier is information about the individual, sex, or species producing the signal. In addition some signals

Table 24.1. Messages of Animal Signals

### Behavioral Messages

Interactional behavior (type of interaction unspecified)
Attack
Escape
Copulation
Affiliative
Indecisiveness
Locomotion
Site specific (staying at current location)
Seeking (attempting to perform another behavior such as affiliation or escape)
Receptive (to interaction from others)
Attentive (vigilant, monitoring)

### Modifiers

Probability
Intensity
Stability
Direction

### Identifiers

Population (individual, group, species)
Physiological state (maturity, sex, estrous)
Relationship (pair bond, family, parent-infant)
Location

*Source*: Modified from Smith (1977).

provide specific information about physiological state or relationship. I provide some selective examples of affective signals from each of the main modalities—visual, vocal, and olfactory. Because the main focus of this book is on human affective processes, I review mainly research on nonhuman primates so that I can draw parallels, when possible, with similar signals used by humans.

## Visual Signaling

The earliest studies on visual expression of emotion derived from Darwin's work and have sought to find similarities between human and other primate species. Here I review literature primarily on chimpanzees and macaques, the species that have been studied most intensively.

Chevalier-Skolnikoff (1973) reviewed the facial expressions of stumptail macaques, chimpanzees, and humans, finding several parallels: a confident threat in macaques consisted of eyes wide open, with direct eye contact, brows raised and lowered, ears forward, and jaws slightly open but covering the teeth. In chimpanzees as well, the confident threat includes a direct stare with relaxed or closed jaw and teeth covered. Human anger is characterized by direct gaze with eye contact, brows lowered and pulled together, with jaws either clenched or moderately open showing teeth.

Fearful macaques avoid gaze with brows raised, ears back, and jaws closed or slightly opened showing teeth. In chimpanzees, fear is expressed by slightly open jaws revealing teeth (the silent, bared-teeth display), and in humans eyes are open with lower lids tense, brows are raised and drawn together, jaws open with lips slightly retracted.

Play is characterized in macaques as eyelids being slightly to extremely lowered, brows raised with forehead retracted, ears back, and jaws open wide with teeth showing. The chimpanzee play face likewise has a moderate to open jaw, lips retracted but relaxed, covering the upper teeth while showing the lower teeth, while playful humans display wrinkling of skin at the corner of the eyes and the jaws moderately to widely open, exposing the teeth. In both chimpanzees and humans the play face is often accompanied by rapid inhalation and exhalation, described as laughter for humans.

In affiliative interactions not involving play, macaques have lowered brows, ears back with jaws opening and closing, and tongue protruded and retracted in rhythm with the jaw movement. Lips are often extended to form a pucker and an unvoiced smacking sound is made. In chimpanzees, jaws are open with lips extended, or when more fear is associated with affiliation the jaws open and close with teeth clicking together.

Van Hooff (1972) was intrigued by both the similarities and differences among species in the silent bared-teeth display used by some macaques as a submissive or fearful signal and its resemblance to smiling in humans. In chimpanzees, van Hooff found two forms of the bared-teeth display: the horizontal bared-teeth display, which matched the submissive context in which it was found in macaques, and the open-mouth bared-teeth display, which was associated with affiliative contexts, like the human smile. The relaxed open-mouth display is found in playful situations in macaques, chimpanzees, and humans; and in both chimpanzees and humans, it is accompanied by laughter. Van Hooff (1972) argued that the relaxed open-mouth face was a common expression of playfulness or happiness across monkeys, apes, and humans, but that the smile is derived from a submissive face in macaques that in chimpanzees diverged into two forms—one indicating submission, the other indicating affiliation.

Preuschoft (1995) completed a comparative study of five species of macaques and found considerable diversity in the silent bared-teeth display that van Hooff found to be similar to a smile. In rhesus macaques and longtailed macaques, the silent bared-teeth display was clearly associated with submissiveness, given by the subordinate toward a more dominant animal. In Barbary macaques the silent bared-teeth display is generally used in submissive contexts but also includes aspects of affiliation, with close physical contact between animals often following the dis-

play. In lion-tailed and Tonkean macaques, the same facial expression is used solely in affiliative contexts, without any connotations of submissiveness. The patterns of usage of the silent bared-teeth display do not conform to the phylogenetic relationships among macaque species, but, Preuschoft argues, the submissive use of the silent bared-teeth display, or smile, was found in species with strict dominance hierarchies where status or position matters greatly, whereas the function more akin to human smiling appears in those macaques species with more relaxed or egalitarian relationships.

Lip smacking and teeth chattering are used by some species as signals of submission, whereas in other species, the same signals used in affiliative contexts. Van Hooff cites evidence that in some human cultures rhythmic tongue protrusion is used in courtship, and we have observed rapid tongue flicking in marmosets and tamarins both as part of courtship and during aggression.

Andrew (1963) describes a disgust reaction of lip retraction, strong expiration, tongue protrusion, and head shaking evoked by strong negative stimulation of the mouth and esophagus. We have been studying whether cotton-top tamarins can communicate to each other about the quality of food (Boe & Snowdon, unpublished data). We adulterate a highly preferred food (tuna) with invisible white pepper and present it to a group. Only a third of the animals even sample the tuna, and of those who sample the tuna, only a third of those ever approach the tuna on successive trials. The monkeys that sample the food produce a variety of facial expressions including frowns, head shakes, tongue protrusions, chin rubbing, and scratching at the mouth or face. The other group members appear to attend to these facial cues and avoid approaching the tuna. The production of a disgust reaction serves as a social cue that keeps other group members away.

Yawning is a common facial expression in humans that occurs in bored or sleepy people, frequently at the transition between waking and sleep. It is a highly contagious behavior that according to Provine (1996) has no known function. Many monkeys also display yawns and many of these occur in the same context of transition from sleep to waking as human yawns (Deputte, 1994). However, there is a second context of yawning accounting for about 10% of yawns, especially common among adult male monkeys. Deputte (1994) observed social yawns in the contexts of conflict, courtship, infant care, and social contact. This type of yawning is influenced by testosterone levels, and administration of antiandrogens, such as flutamide, inhibit yawning (Deputte, Johnson, Hempel, & Scheffler, 1994). Since a yawn allows a male to display his canine teeth, it has been thought that yawning might be a threat display, but the multiple contexts described by Deputte (1994) suggest that the yawns communicate tenseness, anxiety, or uneasiness instead of aggression.

Many studies have examined the response of primates

to visual signals for a variety of reasons: to determine the role of early social experience in responding to signals; to understand whether animals classify signals in the same way as human observers, and to discover the function of signals by observing what response signals evoke in animals under controlled conditions. Infant rhesus macaques reared in social isolation displayed disturbance behavior when exposed to pictures of threatening monkeys (Sackett, 1966). Boysen and Berntson (1989) recorded cardiac responses from a chimpanzee during exposure to photographs of an aggressive chimpanzee, a friendly companion animal, and an unfamiliar animal. There was a defensive (acceleration) response to the picture of the aggressive animal, an orienting (deceleration) response to the unfamiliar animal, and no reaction to the friendly, familiar companion. These studies suggest that perception of visual signals can induce emotional responses.

Recent studies have used operant methods to study perception of faces. Parr, Hopkins, and deWaal (1998) used a matching to sample task with chimpanzees using five species-typical facial expressions (bared-teeth display, hoot-face, relaxed-lip face, relaxed open-mouth face, and scream face). The photographs used were of unfamiliar chimpanzees so that the participants would be responding based on the facial expressions alone and not on prior social experience with the individuals whose faces were shown. One expression was shown as the sample and the participants then observed two different photographs and had to select the one that matched the expression of the sample. All of the expressions except the relaxed-lip face were discriminated at above chance levels, three of them after only two presentations of the stimulus set. Facial expressions that were more similar in number of shared features were harder to discriminate than expressions that were more distinct. In another study Parr, Dove, and Hopkins (1998) found that chimpanzees showed an inversion effect (upside-down faces were harder to discriminate than those in normal orientation) for chimpanzee and human faces, but not for capuchin monkey faces. The presence of an inversion effect has been evoked as a marker of species-specific face processing mechanisms in humans. Chimpanzees appear to share the inversion effect for faces with humans.

Can monkeys discriminate affective expressions in human faces? Kanazawa (1998) presented Japanese monkeys and human participants with a human sad and happy face. He morphed the features of the two faces graphically to create a neutral face and then added to this neutral face various features of the happy or sad faces: eyebrows, eyes, mouth, or cheeks. Both monkeys and humans used similar cues to distinguish the happy face, using cheeks more than other cues. On the other hand, human participants used both eyebrows and cheeks to detect the sad face whereas macaques used only the cheeks and did not attend to eyebrows. While one cannot know whether macaques found the sad human face to be "sad" or the happy face to be "happy," the overall similarity of cues used by both macaques and human to discriminate between faces suggests similar perceptual processes.

Two sets of studies have examined the communication of fear through visual signals in monkeys. Miller and colleagues (Miller, 1971; Miller, Banks, & Ogawa, 1963; Miller, Caul, & Mirsky, 1967) developed a cooperative conditioning task where one monkey was presented with a visual stimulus that predicted the onset of shock. A video camera was trained on the communicator monkey and projected an image of its face to a monitor observed by a responder monkey several rooms away. The responder monkey had a bar to press, and if it pressed the bar quickly enough, it would avoid shock for both monkeys. Mean response latency was less than 2 seconds. Miller and colleagues then filmed the expressions of the communicator monkeys and found that the films were also effective, although the response latency was now between 3 and 4 seconds. By observing which films were most effective, Miller found that the critical behavior involved repeated glances toward the signal with a final turning away. Normally reared monkeys were equally effective as communicators or responders, although isolate-reared monkeys were effective only as communicators and not as responders (see "Developmental Processes" in this chapter).

Using a very different paradigm, Mineka and Cook (1988) studied captive-born rhesus monkeys presented with a snake. They found little evidence of snake fear, but if these same monkeys watched a wild-born monkey react fearfully to a snake, they developed a snake fear after a single 15- to 20-minute trial. Subsequently, naive monkeys could acquire a snake fear by simply watching a videotape of a wild monkey reacting to a snake. Mineka and Cook did not attempt to determine which aspects of the wild monkey's behavior were most effective in training, but both studies show that visual signals are highly effective in transmitting fear.

## Vocal Signaling

Extensive work has been carried out on vocal communication in a wide range of species, and entire books have been published, many focusing on only one group of animals such as birds. I briefly review material on affective communication in birds, mainly providing references to more comprehensive sources and then focus attention on three species or groups of nonhuman primates that best illustrate the variety of studies on affective communication.

### Bird Vocalizations

Bird song has received the greatest attention among vocal signals, with several recent books providing extensive reviews of the structure, function, evolution, ontogeny, and mechanisms of production and perception (e.g., Catchpole & Slater, 1995; Kroodsma & Miller, 1996; Snowdon & Hausberger, 1997). Bird song is generally given by males in temperate-zone climates and functions to attract mates and repel other males. In the tropics, both sexes often sing duets, which appear to function in the same way: to attract opposite-sex mates and repel same-sex intruders. Some have argued that duets also function to maintain pair bonds between mated animals (Farabaugh, 1982), but others maintain that duets primarily serve the interests of each sex (Levin, 1996a, 1996b). Birds produce many other vocalizations in addition to song, but these other vocalizations have not received the intensive study that bird song has received. Among affective vocalizations are alarm and mobbing calls. Alarm calls fit the pattern of fear vocalizations (see Figure 24.2), being high-pitched, un-modulated calls without abrupt onset or offset amplitude modulations, making the calls difficult for a predator to detect (Marler, 1955). In contrast, mobbing vocalizations that attract other birds to attack a predator cover a broad frequency range and have abrupt onset and offset, providing cues for localizing the caller so that others can join in the attack, and with both calls there is convergence across several unrelated species (Marler, 1955).

## Primate Vocalizations

There have been extensive descriptions of vocalizations in nonhuman primates, and here we focus on the affective signals of squirrel monkeys and cotton-top tamarins that have the most complete descriptions, as well as the affective signals in a variety of macaque species.

### Squirrel Monkeys

There are several descriptive catalogues of vocalizations of squirrel monkeys—small monkeys from Central and South America—but Jurgens (1979, 1982) has completed the most interesting experimental analysis for understanding affective content. Jurgens and Ploog (1970) determined the neural sites from which each type of vocalization could be elicited. Jurgens (1979, 1982) then implanted electrodes at each site and arranged for monkeys to control the stimulation of these sites. Using a two-compartment apparatus, a monkey could enter one compartment to receive stimulation and the other to terminate stimulation. By stimulating the brain areas that elicit each vocal type separately, Jurgens could determine the hedonic quality associated with each vocal type. He could then determine which calls correlated with positive affect during brain stimulation, which were neutral, and which were associated with negative affect.

He examined 16 vocalizations that were organized into five broad categories based on structural similarities (Fig-ure 24.3). Within each of these categories, calls were graded from highly aversive to aversive to neutral. Only one of the 16 calls was clearly associated with positive affect. Based on behavioral observations of when the calls were given spontaneously in social interactions, each of the five categories had a different function: One consisted of threat or aggressive calls, the second of protest or defensive calls, the third of alarm or warning calls, the fourth of social contact calls, used by animals separated from partners or the group to regain contact, and the fifth used in affiliative behavior. In this last category was the only call type associated with positive self-stimulation, and this call is used most often in affiliative relationships between pairs of females that have strong affiliative bonds, almost as a friendship call (Smith, Newman, & Symmes, 1982). The most aversive calls in this category are those used to attract other group members to mob a threatening stimulus. Calls with neutral or positive valence with respect to brain stimulation were associated with more relaxed, calm, and affiliative behavior, whereas calls of greatest intensity were associated with highly negative responses to brain elicitation of the calls. In accordance with the motivational structural rules illustrated in Figure 24.2, threat or aggressive calls became lower in frequency with more noisy components with greater motivational intensity and aversiveness, and fearful calls increased in pitch and frequency range with increased motivational intensity. So far this is the only study that has correlated the structure and contextual use of different calls with the degree of aversion or pleasure the calls elicit in the animal producing the call.

### Cotton-Top Tamarins

The cotton-top tamarin is even smaller than the squirrel monkey. It is a cooperatively breeding species found only in northern Colombia. It has one of the most complex vocal repertoires of any primate with 35 different vocal types identified (Cleveland & Snowdon, 1982). There are calls that match each of the five functional dimensions that Jurgens identified for squirrel monkeys, though the structural relationships between calls with similar functions are not nearly as neat as with squirrel monkeys. There are at least three variants of a long whistle-like call: One variant is used in territory defense in response to hearing the approach of another group; a second variant is used within groups and is given in choruses during times of mild alarm or tension, as well as by animals that are separated from their mate or group; and the third variant is used by immature animals and combines other elements of the vocal repertoire. Playbacks of the territorial form of long call elicit high levels of arousal, counter-calling, and scent marking (Snowdon, Cleveland, & French, 1983). In contrast when mates are separated from each other for brief periods of time, they exchange the second form of long

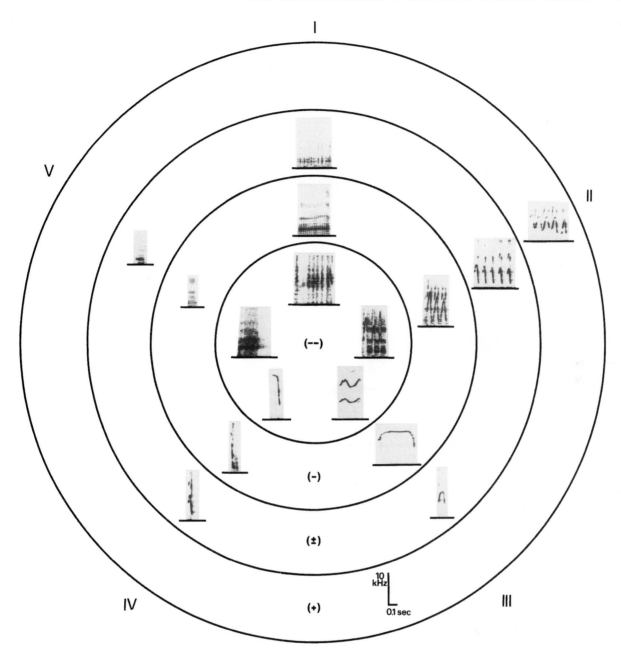

Figure 24.3 Vocalization system of the squirrel monkey based on self-stimulation re-
sults: (– – = highly aversive, – = moderately aversive, ± = neutral, + = positive).
Category I Threat and aggression, Category II Confirming social bonds, Category III Con-
tact-seeking-flight, Category IV Warning or Alarm, Category V Fear and Defensiveness.
From Jurgens (1982). Reprinted by permission of the author and Cambridge University
Press.

call continuously, stopping when they are reunited (Porter, 1994). When tamarin pairs are reunited, not only do
they stop giving long calls but they also increase rates of
grooming, proximity, and copulation. We have also observed long calls produced at high rates for two or three
days after the death of a mate.

Another complex of calls used by cotton-top tamarins
are short (< 100 ms), frequency-modulated, chirp-like

calls. Eight different variants have been identified that can
be separated from each other based on duration, presence,
or absence of an initial frequency upsweep; amount of frequency change; and peak frequency (Figure 24.4). The different chirp calls are each used in different contexts: One
is a mobbing call, another serves as an alarm call, one is
used as a threat toward conspecific intruders, two are used
only during feeding, another used for maintaining contact

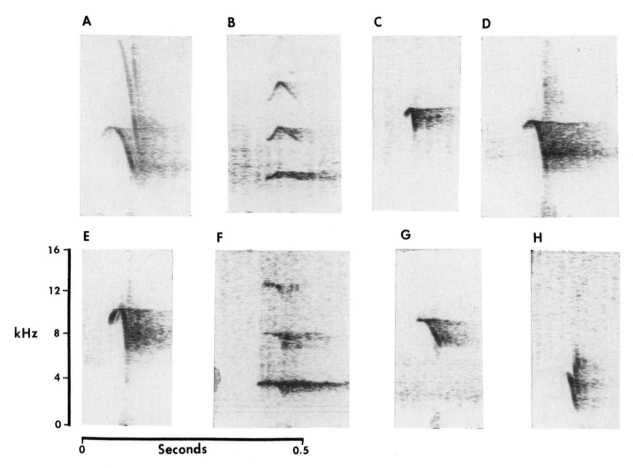

Figure 24.4 Distinctive features analysis of cotton-top tamarin chirps. Type A: Mobbing context; Type B: Investigation context; Types C and D: Feeding context; Type E: Alarm context; Type F: Aggressive context; Type G: Social contact; Type H: Mild alarm context. From Snowdon (1982). Reprinted by permission of Cambridge University Press.

as group members move around. We have created experimental procedures that reliably elicit each of these chirp types (Castro & Snowdon, 2000), and playback studies of some of the calls show that tamarins reliably distinguish between even the most similar of these variants (Bauers & Snowdon, 1990). This call system is unusual because structurally very similar calls appear to be used with very different affective states.

One other interesting facet of cotton-top tamarin calls is that some call types are combined to form a simple syntax. One sequence used in encounters with an unfamiliar group involves the combination of the threat call used primarily by males with the type of threat call primarily used by females. These combined calls are given equally often by both sexes at the peak of aggressive activity in a territorial encounter (McConnell & Snowdon, 1986). A second sequence is observed after animals have been alarmed and are beginning to become active again. In this case the combined call is an alarm call coupled with a contact call and seems to serve as an "all-clear" signal (Cleveland & Snow-

don, 1982). Thus the syntactical combinations observed represent either the intensification of arousal or the combination of two competing affective states.

### Macaques

Rhesus macaques are the most utilized in research, and they and their close relatives (other macaques and baboons) have been well studied with respect to vocal communication. Rowell and Hinde (1962) provided the first vocal repertoire of any monkey species. Green (1975) provided a complete repertoire of the Japanese macaque. One of the important results of Green's study was the discovery that the "coo" vocalization of Japanese macaques had seven distinct variations that were correlated with different social contexts. Coos could be differentiated by pitch, duration, the location of peak frequency within the call, and whether frequency modulation was smooth or had several inflection points. The contexts of calls ranged from calls used by dominants toward subordinates and subordinates toward dominants, by estrous females, by infants alone or infants seeking mothers, and by separated males. Although Green saw the coos as representing a continuum of arousal, one can also provide different affective labels for the calls: desire for contact, mild fear, mild threat, sexual arousal, and so on.

Two of the forms of coos have been extensively studied in perceptual studies and have close structural and functional parallels with similar calls in other macaque species. The Smooth Early High coo has a continuous frequency envelope and reaches its peak frequency early in the call. It is used by young infants alone, but not seeking contact, and by older animals moving away from the group. The Smooth Late High coo, which reaches its peak frequency late in the call, is given by infants seeking contact with mothers and by subordinates toward dominant animals. Lillehei and Snowdon (1978), studying infant stumptail macaques, found similar coo vocalizations used by infants alone and in seeking contact with mothers. In operant studies where monkeys were rewarded for discriminating between Smooth Early High and Smooth Late High coos, adult Japanese macaques learned the discrimination much faster than other species of monkey (Zoloth et al., 1979), and they demonstrated a right ear advantage for this discrimination (Petersen, Beecher, Zoloth, Moody, & Stebbins, 1978) compared with other species, suggesting both a species-specific specialization and left-hemisphere processing of these calls.

Coo vocalizations have often been used as response measures in studies of infant separation and accompanying distress. Levine, Weiner, Coe, Bayart, and Hayashi (1987) found that coo vocalizations were given frequently by infants separated from their mothers, and Bayart, Hayashi, Faull, Barchas, and Levine (1990) described two different forms of coo vocalizations, one given by infants out of visual and auditory contact of their mothers, and the other given when infants could see or hear their mothers. Measures of cortisol were higher in infants completely isolated from their mothers and overall coo rates were lower, suggesting that coo production might be mitigating the stress response rather than serving as an index of stress. Kalin, Shelton, and Snowdon (1992, 1993) provided further evidence that coo vocalizations are a form of affiliative communication. In the first experiment infants were separated from their mother and then reunited with the mother, placed with an unfamiliar male, or kept an additional time period alone. Infants produced coos at high rates when alone or when placed with a male, but ceased cooing when reunited with mothers. A different vocalization, a girn, similar to a cat's purring, was observed in infants reunited with their mothers and in the initial minutes of being placed with the male. However, girn rate rapidly decreased when the males rejected or ignored the infants. Both girns and coos were produced at high rates

by infants during the separation phase when they could see their mothers, but vocalization rates were low when infants were not in visual or auditory contact with mothers.

A second experiment examined reunion with mothers or unfamiliar males as a function of whether the mothers and males were awake or anesthetized. Infants produced high rates of coos when placed with an anesthetized mother, but girn rates were the same to both awake and anesthetized mothers. Infants gave frequent coos in the presence of males and produced more girns with either anesthetized or awake mothers than to males. Coos and girns appear to reflect different levels of affiliative motivation. Coos are used at greater distances to signal affiliative motivation but when the affiliative response has not been received. Girns are used at close distances most often during the time that contact affiliation is being provided. Girns might serve to reinforce affiliative behavior, much as a cat's purring reinforces contact with their human companions. These two different forms of affiliative vocalizations provide a dynamic index of the affiliative interactions an infant is seeking and whether it is receiving affiliative behavior.

The girns are very soft vocalizations that had not been recorded from infants prior to Kalin et al. (1992, 1993). However, analogous vocalizations are used by adult macaques of various species. Rowell and Hinde (1962) described girns in adult rhesus macaques when they approach each other for grooming, huddling, or sleeping together. Green (1975) described a call in Japanese macaque adults that is structurally similar to the girn of infant rhesus macaques, used in submissive contexts by females approaching a dominant. Blount (1985) found girns in Japanese macaques were used by subordinate females approaching a dominant and also by adult females approaching a mother with a new infant. Bauers (1993) described a structurally quite different call: the staccato grunt, used by stumptail macaque females approaching a mother and infant. Common to all of these uses is an animal seeking affiliation with another of higher status, whether a mother or more dominant animal.

Another vocalization, first described by Dittus (1984) for toque macaques in Sri Lanka, is a food call. Toque macaques give this call when they discover a source of ripe fruit, and all group members join the caller to feed. Although 97% of the time these calls are given, there is an association with the discovery of a fruiting tree, the other 3% of cases are also interesting. Monkeys would give the same call at the end of the dry season when the first clouds appeared to signal the onset of monsoon rains and also at the end of the monsoon with the first sunny day. This suggests that the "food" calls may communicate elation or joy not just about food. Elowson et al. (1991), analyzing food calls in adult cotton-top tamarins, found a correlation between an individual's rate of calling and its preference ranking of different foods, and Hauser and Wrangham (1987) and Hauser et al. (1993) found that chimpanzee food calls were correlated with the amount of food available, suggesting an affective component to food calls.

Copulation calls are given by chimpanzees and many macaques and baboons. In chimpanzees males give soft, short panting calls whereas females give long, loud screams; in rhesus macaques male copulation calls are a series of short, pulsed, frequency-modulated screams (Hauser, 1996). The function of these calls has been the source of controversy. Females might call to synchronize orgasm with the male (Hamilton & Arrowood, 1978), to announce their reproductive state, to announce the presence of a male consort and reduce harassment (O'Connell & Colishaw, 1994), to promote male-male competition (O'Connell & Colishaw, 1994), or as honest signals advertising mate quality (Hauser, 1996). Polygynous species use copulation calls much more than monogamous species do, suggesting a role in mate choice or competition. O'Connell and Colishaw (1994) found that female chacma baboons called most during the peak of estrus and the longest calls were associated with matings associated with ejaculation. Although O'Connell and Colishaw seek a functional explanation, the calls might be a by-product of sexual arousal and the stimulation of copulation. Semple (1998) used playbacks of female copulation calls in Barbary macaques and found that all males oriented toward the calls but only dominant males approached the speaker. When females were present, they received mating significantly sooner after playback of copulation calls than after a control playback, suggesting that copulation calls might make females more attractive, especially to higher ranking males. In rhesus macaques, males produce copulation calls, and Hauser (1996) suggests that calling males receive more aggression from other males, but also achieve more successful matings than noncalling males. Thus, copulation calls might also make males more attractive to females.

The majority of vocalizations among primates, both the species reviewed here and other species, are used to communicate about "negative" affect: states such as fear, anxiety, anger, threat in response to predators, to competing conspecifics, to the loss of social support or contact, or anxiety about how another animal might react. There appear to be relatively few calls that relate to positive affective states. The food calls described previously, and the one call type found by Jurgens to be associated with a positive self-stimulation site, the twitter, used between individual squirrel monkeys that have a strong positive relationship, are among the few positive calls. Even the girn vocalizations of macaques, while having a positive effect on recipients, still are given by individuals that are anxious or insecure. Why are there so few signals of positive affect?

## Parallels with Human Vocalizations

As with facial expressions, there is interest in finding whether there are parallels between vocal signals in nonhuman animals and in humans. Because great apes tend to vocalize infrequently compared with humans and with other primate species, and because the vocal production structures of many nonhuman animals appear very different from human speech, it is not as easy to find parallels. However, at least three phenomena display interesting parallels between human and animal vocal communication: crying, "motherese," and babbling. In each case there are close parallels between the structure and function of these calls in both human and nonhuman animals.

Crying consists of a long series of short units ranging from 0.4–0.9 s duration with short silent intervals in between. The typical cry has 50–70 utterances per minute with a rising, then falling frequency in each acoustic unit. Crying is given by infants that are hungry, cold, wet, but most commonly, alone, and caretakers respond rapidly to cries with attention and contact (Bell & Ainsworth, 1972). Newman (1985) has argued that infant separation calls in a wide range of species have characteristics similar to human infant cries. The coo vocalizations of macaques, described previously, are tonal with a rising and falling pitch and a duration of 0.5–0.9 s. As we have seen, the coos continue until the infant is reunited with its mother. Similarly structured calls are seen throughout the entire range of primates, from prosimian lemurs in Madagascar to squirrel monkeys, marmosets, and tamarins in South America, to vervet monkeys in Eastern Africa, to mountain gorillas (Fossey, 1972). The structure of individual notes varies greatly between species, with the duration of the notes and frequency patterns providing information about species, subspecies, and even individual identity. These calls are often the loudest vocalizations given by infants and, as with human infants, the variability of call structure increases with increasing time of crying. Newman (1985) argues that crying is a phylogenetically ancient vocal pattern to communicate infant distress.

"Motherese" is the use of specific forms of vocalizations to communicate with infants, generally involving speech given at a higher fundamental frequency and with more emphatic intonation contours than would be used in normal speech (Fernald, 1992). Fernald has studied parents representing six different language/dialect groupings and finds consistency across all six. Furthermore, she reports that across all these groups the same patterns are used in similar contexts. Thus, approval vocalizations have a pattern of a gently rising and then falling intonation ("What a GOOD boy!"—with the capitalized word representing a higher pitched word). Prohibition vocalizations consist of brief, staccato sounds ("No! No! No!"). Attention sounds are a sequence of phrases starting at a low pitch and rising in frequency ("Come HERE, Look at THIS"), and Comfort vocalizations involve a gentle decrease in intonation contour ("CALM down").

In completely independent research, McConnell and Baylis (1985) studied the sounds used by shepherds to control border collies. A series of upwardly rising whistles or calls (like the Attention contours) were used to arouse a dog and get it moving, a long whistle slowly decreasing in pitch (like the Comfort contours) were used to slow the dog down, and a series of sharp staccato sounds (like the Prohibition contours) were used to stop the dog's action. In subsequent research McConnell (1990) trained one group of naive puppies to come with the short staccato calls and to stay with the long descending call, and another group was trained with the opposite conditions (to come to the long descending call and stay to the short repeated calls). The four short notes were much more effective in training puppies to approach than was one long note (Figure 24.5). McConnell (1991) also recorded the sounds that people from a variety of linguistic groups used for controlling animals ranging from dogs, to cats, to horses and found a nearly universal pattern of calls used for arousal, for calming, and for stopping activity. The use of similar call structure to manipulate the behavior of our pets, working animals, and children suggests that "motherese" is based on evolutionarily conservative structures of calls and speech that allow us to change the behavior (and the affective state) of others.

Even more remarkable than the use of vocalizations to manipulate the affective state of others are recent studies on using vocalizations to modify one's own internal state. Cheng (1986) found that female ring doves have to hear coo vocalizations in order to ovulate. Further study (Cheng, 1992) showed that female doves responded most, in terms of ovulation, to hearing their own vocalizations compared with hearing coos of males, of other females, or hearing no coos. Recently Cheng, Peng, and Johnson (1998) demonstrated single neurons in the anterior hypothalamus of doves that responded most to a female's own coos. By collecting portal blood from the pituitary gland at the same time, Cheng et al. (1998) were able to show that a female's anterior hypothalamic response to her own coos led directly to increases in the pituitary release of luteinizing hormone, critical for ovulation.

Babbling is a characteristic of the development of human speech (Oller, 2000). Locke (1993) listed seven characteristics of human infant babbling: (1) Babbling is universal and frequent regardless of cultural environment; (2) babbling is rhythmic and repetitive; (3) babbling begins early in life; (4) babbling comprises a subset of the phonetic units of adult speech; (5) babbling has well-formed

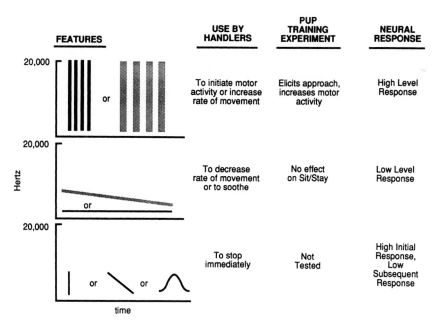

Figure 24.5 Consistent use of pitch contours in signals used by professional animal handlers across several languages, showing arousal or activation signals (top), Slowing or Soothing signals (middle), and Stop signals (bottom). These parallel closely the intonation contours used in talking with children in similar contexts (Fernald, 1992). The Pup Training Response indicates how pups, which had never heard human sounds, responded in an experimental test of these signals. Neural Responses are the hypothesized responses to each kind of signal. From McConnell (1991). Reprinted with permission from Plenum Press.

units with the structure of adult speech; (6) babbling lacks apparent meaning with respect to how babbling sounds relate to sounds in adult speech; and (7) babbling shapes the child-caregiver bond. A model of babbling in nonhuman animals has been suggested in the subsong and plastic song that precede adult song in songbirds (Marler, 1970). But most singing birds are males, subsong and plastic song appear relatively late in development (puberty), and song represents only one of several vocalizations used by birds.

Pygmy marmoset infants engage in long, complex bouts of vocal behavior beginning within two or three weeks after birth, and we have found clear parallels between this complex vocal behavior in pygmy marmosets (Elowson et al., 1998a, 1998b) and the characteristics of human babbling described by Locke (1993). All infants produce babbling at an early age, and there is frequent repetition and rhythmicity characteristic of reduplicative babbling. Infant marmosets produce about 60% of the vocalizations of the adult repertoire, and 90% of the individual calls analyzed were identical or similar in structure to adult calls suggestive of canonical babbling (Oller, 2000). The calls are produced in a seemingly random fashion with aggressive calls juxtaposed with affiliative and fearful calls. Babbling occurs at a much higher rate during social interactions than when infant marmosets are alone, suggesting this complex behavior is not crying or distress vocalizations but functions to promote affiliation. We have found that infants who babble more in early infancy produce more well-formed, adultlike calls at 5 months of age than those who babble less. As infants develop, babbling is used instrumentally, in situations of conflict or aggression to communicate submissiveness (Snowdon & Elowson, in press). Thus marmoset babbling begins as a seemingly random production of calls that include the full range of affective vocalizations of adults, but the effect of babbling is to increase social interaction between infants and caregivers. As infants mature and become independent, they begin to use babbling instrumentally to signal submission and reduce aggression directed toward them.

## Chemical Signals

Chemical signals are poorly perceived by humans and thus we often ignore the possibility of affective communication through chemical signals. Yet many species, including primates, have well-developed scent glands and specific behavior patterns for depositing scent secretions. In addition, it is possible for chemical signals to be produced through less specialized means such as through urine or sweat gland excretions. For example, a recent study reports that the axillary (underarm) secretions from donor women can alter the menstrual patterns of recipient women (Stern & McClintock, 1998). Among primates, spe-

cialized scent glands are more common in prosimians and in New World monkeys than in Old World monkeys and apes. There is evidence of a specialized accessory olfactory system that appears especially important in olfactory communication—the vomeronasal organ—in many of these monkeys (Epple, 1985). Whether Old World monkeys and apes have functioning vomeronasal organs is a matter of some dispute (Epple, 1985). Scent glands tend to be located in the anogential and superpubic regions, suggesting a connection with reproductive function. In addition, sternal glands are common, and in prosimians glands can be found at the wrist and forearm (Epple, 1985).

As with visual and vocal signals, chemical signals provide information about species, subspecies, sex, reproductive condition, and individual identity. Four general affective functions have been identified in chemical signals: fear or alarm, aggression or threat, reproduction or sexual receptivity, and affiliation.

As an example of a fear signal, von Frisch (1941) described an alarm chemical produced in fish skin that acted to keep other fish away from an injured fish. Carr, Martorano, and Kames (1970) showed that mice spent more time investigating the odors of mice who were winners in previous fights compared to losers, and investigated more the odors of nonstressed mice than those of mice that had received several shocks. Subsequently Rottman and Snowdon (1972) found that mice preferred the odors of normal mice compared with the odors of mice that had been injected with a small amount of hypertonic saline. The preference was abolished after destruction of the nasal mucosa, showing that this response was a true olfactory effect. Rottman and Snowdon (1972) also studied developmental influences on the alarm response. Mice reared in social isolation were as effective as group-reared mice in producing an avoidance response in other mice, but these isolate-reared mice were not able to display differential responses to odors of alarmed versus calm mice. Social experience appeared important in developing appropriate responses to alarm odors.

Many animals scent-mark to indicate territory boundaries and increase rates of scent marking in response to intruders. Oribi, a small antelope from Africa, produces dung piles at the edge of territories that are maintained by males, who are territorial, but not by females (Brashears & Arcese, 1999). In intruder studies with cotton-top tamarins, French and Snowdon (1981) found that females scent-marked extensively using the suprapubic gland in response to both male and female intruders. In this species males do not have well-developed scent glands and males displayed aggressive behavior rather than scent-marking toward intruders. Scent-marking behavior in females increases in response to vocal contact with unfamiliar groups (McConnell & Snowdon, 1986), as well as to presentation of odors from an unfamiliar female (Washabaugh

& Snowdon, 1998). Both pygmy marmosets and common marmosets have an unusual threat behavior where they turn their backs toward their targets, lift their tails, and expose their genitals. While this "mooning" display clearly has visual components, the main scent organs are presented as well, and recipients frequently approach and sniff the genitals while giving submissive calls (Epple, 1985). Studies of wild common marmosets observe high rates of scent-marking during territorial encounters between adjacent groups (Lazaro-Perea, Snowdon, & Arruda, 1999). Both sexes and adults and subadults participate in scent-marking.

As noted before, the close association of major scent glands with the anogenital region of many primates suggests a sexual or reproductive function. In a wide range of species males frequently sniff or lick the genital areas of females. Even in species without specialized scent glands, one frequently observes licking or sniffing of urine or vaginal secretions. In cotton-top tamarins, there is no evidence of changes in scent-marking behavior or olfactory investigation that is related to the female ovulatory cycle, and there are no changes in genital size or coloration related to ovulation nor any external signs of menstruation. For a long time tamarins were thought to be concealed ovulators. However, using a behavioral bioassay, Ziegler et al. (1993) collected daily anogenital scent secretions from an ovulating female and presented the odors to pairs where the female was pregnant and therefore not ovulating. Males showed increased rates of erection and of mounting their own mates on days when the donor female was ovulating. Ziegler et al. (1993) inferred that there were qualitative changes in odors over the cycle that allowed males to detect ovulation.

In addition to providing information about the timing of ovulation (and likely receptivity for sexual behavior), chemical signals have been involved in regulating reproductive physiology. In mice, odors from an adult male presented to young females leads to puberty acceleration whereas odors from reproducing females delay the onset of puberty (Vandenbergh, 1983). Odors from novel males can disrupt pregnancy in females (Marchlewska-Koj, 1983). In cooperatively breeding tamarins, odors from the reproductive female help to suppress ovulation in subordinate females. When daughters are removed from their family group and paired with a novel male, they ovulate very quickly. However, if maternal odors are transferred to the daughters' cages, ovulation and conception are delayed significantly (Savage, Ziegler & Snowdon, 1988, for cotton-top tamarins; Epple & Katz, 1984, for saddleback tamarins).

Several species use chemical signals in parent-offspring interactions. In the California mouse, the parental care behavior of the father is influenced by the presence of urinary odors from his mate (Gubernick, 1990). Without the continuous stimulation of maternal odors, the male quickly loses parental behavior. Odors are often used in attachment between parent and young. In squirrel monkeys, infants showed preference for their own mothers when given a choice, but when the mothers were anesthetized and odors washed off, the infants no longer showed a preference (Kaplan, Cubicotti, & Redican, 1977). Cebul, Alveario, and Epple (1978) showed that hand-reared common marmosets and saddleback tamarins preferred pieces of cloth that contained the odors of the woman who had hand-reared them to cloth containing odors of other women. These results suggest that chemical signals might be important for recognition of parents and offspring and for the maintenance of affiliative interactions.

## Neural Mechanisms

Several studies have used either stimulation or lesioning methods to determine the neural locus for the production of primate vocalizations. Two species have received most attention: squirrel monkeys (Ploog, 1981) and rhesus macaques (Robinson, 1967; Sutton, 1979). Studies of both species have shown that calls can be elicited through stimulation in a variety of subcortical areas, especially in the limbic system, but no effects of cortical stimulation on vocal production have been observed. If most or all vocalizations are primarily affective, this is to be expected. However, there have been no studies on the vervet monkey where the strongest evidence for referential communication has been found. Jurgens and Mueller-Preuss (1977) found that many of the areas in squirrel monkeys that elicited vocalizations projected to the anterior cingulate area, and they hypothesized that this area was the final common center for vocal production. Subsequently, Jurgens and Pratt (1979) demonstrated projections from the anterior cingulate to the motor nuclei controlling the larynx. In rhesus macaques, Sutton, Larson, and Lindeman (1974) and Aitken (1981) found that anterior cingulate lesions disrupted call structure for both conditioned and spontaneous vocalizations but did not disrupt social behavior. Lesions in cortical areas thought to be similar to Broca's and Wernicke's area had no effect on vocal production. The cerebellum is also involved in phonatory control of vocal production, coordinating laryngeal and respiratory movements during vocalization (Larson, Sutton, & Lindeman, 1978).

Although all of the studies on vocal production have failed to find any cortical control, there is evidence of cortical involvement in vocal perception. As noted before, Petersen et al. (1978) found that Japanese macaques displayed a right-ear advantage in discriminating between species-typical calls, whereas other species discriminating the same calls did not show lateralization. Newman (1979), reviewing auditory processing of vocalizations, reports that many neurons in the superior temporal cortex responded to vocalizations, but that most neurons responded to a broad range of calls. Only rarely were cells found that responded to a unique call type. Two studies have reported labile responses of single neurons to vocal input (Manley & Mueller-Preuss, 1979; Glass & Wollberg, 1979). Recordings of up to 5 hours of a single neuron indicated changing responsiveness to vocal signals. Lability was greater in secondary than in primary auditory cortex. Lesioning studies (Ploog, 1981) failed to show specific effects in auditory cortex on conditioned discrimination of vocalizations in squirrel monkeys, but Heffner and Heffner (1984) found that lesions of the left auditory cortex impaired discrimination of Early Smooth High and Late Smooth High coos in Japanese macaques, and bilateral auditory cortex lesions abolished discrimination ability. Rauschecker, Tian, and Hauser (1995) have found single cells in the area surrounding primary cortex that respond to complex sounds, including calls from the vocal repertoire. Thus, cortical processes are clearly involved in perception of species-typical calls in macaques.

Recent studies of the neural mechanisms involved in facial recognition suggest close parallels between monkeys and humans. Brothers, Ring, and Kling (1990) showed that neurons in the medial amygdala respond to features of facial expressions, and Morris et al. (1996), using PET studies in humans, reported a greater response to fearful faces than to happy faces in the amygdala. Hasselmo, Rolls, and Baylis (1989) and Perrett and Mistlin (1990) have found single neurons in the temporal visual cortex of macaques that respond to different facial expressions and to different individual monkeys with the neurons specific to emotional expression found in the superior temporal sulcus and those responding to individual faces in the inferior temporal gyrus. Using a combination of behavioral testing and CAT scans and magnetic resonance imaging of brain-damaged patients, Adolphs, Damasio, Tranel, and Damasio (1996) found that all subjects recognized happy expressions, but those with damage to the right inferior parietal cortex and right mesial anterior intercalcine cortex had impairments in recognizing sad and fearful expressions. Interestingly, patients with left-hemisphere damage to the same area showed no impairment in recognition of facial expressions. The close convergence of brain areas that respond to facial expression in humans and nonhuman primates further supports the evolutionary parallels in these expressions described previously.

## Developmental Processes

How does affective communication develop within an organism? There are three conceptually separate aspects to communication, each of which might have separate developmental processes: production, usage, and appropriate responses to signals from others. In a recent review of the development of communication in nonhuman primates, Seyfarth and Cheney (1997) argued that most vocal production occurred with no modification during development or that calls were broadly adultlike with some modification during development. There is no evidence of infant vocalizations that have no resemblance to adult calls, nor is there evidence that primates can learn new or arbitrary calls. Vocal usage is broadly adultlike in infancy with some modification during development, whereas making appropriate responses to the calls of others requires extensive experience during development.

In contrast with bird song, where social isolation has devastating effects on the production of song, social isolation in monkeys has produced only minor effects on vocal production. Thus Newman and Symmes (1974) found only minor abnormalities in the coo vocalizations of isolate-reared rhesus macaques, and squirrel monkeys reared in social isolation produce a normal adult repertoire (Winter, Handley, Ploog, & Schott, 1973). Socially isolated squirrel monkeys even produced appropriate alarm calls on their first exposure to a natural predator (Herzog & Hopf, 1984). Wild vervet monkey infants appear able to produce each of the appropriate predator alarm calls, although they overgeneralize and give "eagle" alarms to falling leaves, snake alarms to sinuous branches on the ground, and so forth (Seyfarth & Cheney, 1986).

Seyfarth and Cheney (1997) have cross-fostered Japanese macaque infants to rhesus macaque mothers and vice versa, and found that each species retained its own vocal repertoire. Thus, cross-fostered macaque infants did not learn the vocalizations of their foster mothers. Furthermore, in contexts where Japanese and rhesus macaques have distinctly different vocalizations, each cross-fostered infant used its species-typical vocalization. However, the cross-fostered animals responded to the calls of their foster mothers, and the foster mothers responded to the calls of their foster infants, suggesting that responses to the calls of other species can be learned. There is other evidence of cross-species learning: Hauser (1988) describes how vervet monkeys learn to respond to alarm calls provided by superb starlings, with infants in groups with frequent associations with starlings reacting more strongly and at an earlier age to starling calls than infants in groups with infrequent associations with starlings. Oba and Masataka (1996) have described cross-species responses to alarm calls in two species of lemurs.

Data from other communication modalities support this view. The studies of Miller (1971; Miller et al., 1967) using the cooperative conditioning task described previously found that isolate-reared rhesus monkeys communicated fear effectively when presented with an aversive conditioning stimulus, but they were unable to use the facial expression of other monkeys to make an appropriate response. Rottman and Snowdon (1972) found that isolate-reared mice were as effective as socially reared mice in producing an alarm odor, but they were unable to respond as normally reared mice when presented with the odor.

Most data support the idea that the production of affective signals is subject to only minor modification, whereas animals can readily learn to respond to affective signals of other species, and animals deprived of normal social experience during development have difficulty in responding appropriately to affective signals produced by other animals.

However, although there is no evidence for nonhuman primates learning completely novel affective signals, there are modifications that occur in response to social changes. In pygmy marmosets, trill vocalizations are used extensively to maintain affiliative contact between members of the group that in the wild often forage out of sight of each other. Marmosets change the structure of these affiliative trills in response to social change. A newly formed pair adjusts the structure of their individual trills to converge with the structure of their mate (Snowdon & Elowson, 1999). As described previously, pygmy marmoset infants produce complex strings of vocalizations that we have termed babbling (Elowson et al., 1998a). In infants these calls lead to increased social interactions with other group members. By month 5, the infants are independent and feed on their own. At this age if they compete with adults for access to food or water, they often receive aggression and respond by babbling. By month 6 many of the infants use babbling instrumentally, giving it before approaching food or water and avoiding aggression, suggesting that they have learned to use babbling as a means of minimizing aggression. We have recently found that several vocalizations recorded from two populations of wild pygmy marmosets in Ecuador separated by 120 kilometers have different structure, providing the first suggestion of "dialects" in monkeys (de la Torre & Snowdon, unpublished observation).

Cotton-top tamarins have two vocalizations used in feeding contexts (Elowson et al., 1991), but juvenile and subadult tamarins produce highly variable forms of these calls. To our surprise there was no evidence of improving call production with age (Roush & Snowdon, 1994). But in these cooperatively breeding monkeys where only the adult pair reproduces, perhaps it is important for subordinate animals to communicate their status clearly. We predicted that subordinate subadults would quickly show adult vocal structures when their social status was changed by being removed from the natal family and mated. This is exactly what happened (Roush & Snowdon, 1999). Newly paired monkeys quickly adopted adult forms of food calls within a few weeks.

It is not always true that monkeys are able to produce all adult calls at birth and that there is little role for experience in the appropriate use of calls. Castro and Snowdon (2000) found that infant cotton-top tamarins do not produce all of the eight types of chirps found in adult tamarins. Instead they found that infants used a generic "prototype" chirp in each of the situations in which adults used specific forms of chirps. By the end of 5 months when infants were independent of adults, they still rarely produced or used in appropriate contexts the forms of chirps used by adults. However, in parallel to what is known of human language development, infant tamarins appeared to comprehend vocalizations before they used them appropriately. Infants were attracted to the food calls given by an adult male who would share food with them, and they inhibited their own vocalizations after hearing threat or alarm calls from adults.

Although the general pattern of vocal development proposed by Seyfarth and Cheney (1997) holds across a wide range of primate species and appears to account for some findings in visual and chemical communication as well, there are some interesting exceptions. As a rule, if the function of affective communication is to provide recipients with an accurate representation of the communicator's internal state, then we should expect little plasticity in the production and usage of calls. At the same time we can expect that it will be important to read signals accurately from a variety of sources—group members, strangers of the same species and of other species—so plasticity in the development of responding to signals might be useful.

## Summary

In recent years studies of animal communication have focused extensively on the cognitive components of communication, frequently to the detriment of understanding the affective aspects of communication. Yet there is abundant evidence that nonhuman species communicate about a variety of affective states: affiliation, aggression, fear, sexual motivation, elation, food quality and quantity; and even in those examples where there is clear evidence for symbolic or referential communication, one finds affective components as well.

Although Darwin and subsequent researchers of human emotional expression have focused extensively of facial expressions, a review of nonhuman communication illustrates that affective communication occurs in a variety of modalities. The modalities used are a function of the habitat and social structure in which animals live. Thus, arboreal monkeys living in dense forest are more likely to use vocal and chemical signals than visual signals, whereas animals living in more open areas will make greater use of visual signals.

Darwin's principle of antithesis applies quite well to comparing fear versus threat communication in both visual and vocal modalities for many species, although there are other species that don't exactly fit this model. The majority of signals used seem to communicate about negative affect—fear, threat, anxiety—although a few affiliative signals communicate sexual arousal, the discovery of a high-quality food, or are used specifically between two individuals that have a special relationship: mothers and infants, females in female-bonded social groups, or pairs in monogamous species.

Many of the vocal and visual signals discussed here have some parallels with human affective communication. Smiles appear to have derived from an initial submissive response that has developed into a friendly signal in species with relaxed dominance orders; and laughter, yawning, and tongue showing appear in similar contexts in human and nonhuman primates. There is evidence that the structure of vocal signals can directly influence behavior and affective state in other organisms, both human infants and our pets. The crying and babbling of human infants have parallels in some nonhuman primates. We as yet have less evidence for parallels in chemical signals; however, recent evidence of pheromonal modification of the menstrual cycle in women suggests that we have much to learn about the potential for chemical communication of affect in humans. I have tried to develop some basic principles of signal structure related to function, so that we can start to develop new hypotheses about affective communication based on what we know about emotional expression in animals.

Several areas suggest exciting future research directions. With improved computer graphics systems, we can now develop sophisticated experimental methods to learn more about the function of visual communication and the important aspects used for perception of affective state. The argument that all referential signals made by nonhuman animals have an affective component suggests that studies of human speech should attend more to the paralinguistic cues associated with speech that might provide affective cues. The development of a management/assessment approach that suggests communication as an interactive, dynamic process, where the response of organism A to the signals of organism B leads B to alter its subsequent behavior, hints at the importance of looking more closely at dynamic affective changes during human social interactions. It is my impression that most research on both humans and non-humans has focused on the production or perception of an expression by a single individual, and that we rarely examine interactive processes. Finally, the development of functional imaging technology not only opens up new research areas for understanding emotional expression and perception in humans, but we can begin to learn about neural mechanisms underlying affective expression in nonhumans. Already my colleagues and I are able to present chemical signals to awake common marmosets undergoing fMRI to learn about the neural responses to these affective signals (Ferris et al., 2001).

## NOTE

Preparation of the chapter and my own research have been supported by USPHS Grants MH 29775 and MH 00177. I thank A. Margaret Elowson, Rebecca S. Roush, Cristina Lazaro-Perea, Carla Boe, and Kate Washabaugh for their collaboration and Dacher Keltner for critical feedback.

## REFERENCES

Adolphs, R., Damasio, H., Tranel, D., & Damasio, A. R. (1996). Cortical systems of the recognition of emotion in facial expressions. *Journal of Neuroscience, 16,* 7678–7687.

Aitken, P. G. (1981). Cortical control of conditioned and spontaneous vocal behavior in rhesus monkeys, *Brain and Language, 13,* 171–184.

Andrew, R. J. (1963). The origin and evolution of the calls and facial expressions of the primates. *Behaviour, 20,* 1–109.

Bauers, K. A. (1993). A functional study of staccato grunt vocalizations in the stumptailed macaque (*Macaca arctoides*). *Ethology, 94,* 147–161.

Bauers, K. A., & Snowdon, C. T. (1990). Discrimination of chirp vocalizations in the cotton-top tamarin. *American Journal of Primatology, 21,* 53–60.

Bayart, F., Hayashi, K. T., Faull, K. F., Barchas, J. D., & Levine, S. (1990). Influence of maternal proximity on behavioral and physiological responses to separation in infant rhesus monkeys (*Macaca mulatta*). *Behavioral Neuroscience, 104,* 98–107.

Bell, S. M., & Ainsworth, M. D. (1972). Infant crying and maternal responsiveness. *Child Development, 43,* 1171–1190.

Blount, B. G. (1985). "Girney" vocalizations among Japanese macaque females: Context and function. *Primates, 26,* 424–435.

Blumberg, M. S., & Alberts, J. R. (1997). Incidental emissions, fortuitous effects and the origins of communication. In D. H. Owings, M. D. Beecher, & N. S. Thompson (Eds.), *Perspectives in ethology, Volume 12, Communication* (pp. 225–249). New York: Plenum.

Boysen, S. T., & Berntson, G. G. (1989). Conspecific recognition in the chimpanzee (*Pan troglodytes*): Cardiac responses to significant others. *Journal of Comparative Psychology, 103,* 215–220.

Brashears, J., & Arcese, P. (1999). Scent marking in a territorial African antelope: I. The maintenance of borders between male oribi. *Animal Behaviour, 57,* 1–10.

Brothers, L., Ring, B., & Kling. A. (1990). Response of neurons in the macaque amygdala to complex social stimuli. *Behavioural Brain Research, 41,* 199–213.

Carr, W. J., Martorano, R. D., & Kames, L. (1970). Responses of mice to odors associated with stress. *Journal of Comparative and Physiological Psychology, 71,* 223–228.

Castro, N. A., & Snowdon, C. T. (2000). Development of vocal responses in infant cotton-top tamarins. *Behaviour, 137,* 629–646.

Catchpole, C. K., & Slater, P. J. B. S. (1995). *Bird song: Biological themes and variations.* Cambridge, England: Cambridge University Press.

Cebul, M. S., Alveario, M. C., & Epple, G. (1978). Odor recognition and attachment in infant marmosets. In H. Rothe, H.-J. Wolters & J. P. Hearn (Eds.), *Biology and behaviour of marmosets* (pp. 141–146). Gottingen, Germany: Eigenverlag Rothe.

Cheney, D. L., & Seyfarth, R. M. (1988). Assessment of meaning and the detection of unreliable signal by vervet monkeys. *Animal Behaviour, 36*, 477–486.

Cheng, M.-F. (1986). Female cooing promotes ovarian development in ring doves. *Physiology and Behavior, 37*, 371–374.

Cheng, M.-F. (1992). For whom do female doves coo? A case for the role of vocal self-stimulation. *Animal Behaviour, 43*, 1035–1044.

Cheng, M.-F., Peng, J. P., & Johnson, P. (1998). Hypothalamic neurons preferentially respond to female nest coo stimulation: Demonstration of direct acoustic stimulation on luteinizing hormone release. *Journal of Neuroscience, 18*, 5477–5489.

Chevalier-Skolnikoff, S. (1973). Facial expression of emotion in nonhuman primates. In P. Ekman (Ed.), *Darwin and facial expression* (pp. 11–89). New York: Academic Press.

Cleveland, J., & Snowdon, C. T. (1982). The complex vocal repertoire of the adult cotton-top tamarin (*Saguinus oedipus*). *Zeitschrift fur Tierpsychologie, 58*, 231–270.

Darwin, C. (1872/1998). *The expression of the emotions in man and animals*. Definitive edition with commentary by Paul Ekman. New York: Oxford University Press.

de la Torre, S., & Snowdon, C. T. (in press). Environmental correlates of vocal communication of wild pygmy marmosets (*Cebuella pygmaea*). *Animal Behaviour*.

Deputte, B. L. (1994). Ethological study of yawning in primates: I. Quantitative analysis and study of causation in two species of Old World monkeys (*Cercocebus albigena* and *Macaca fascicularis*). *Ethology, 98*, 221–245.

Deputte, B. L., Johnson, J., Hempel, M., & Scheffler, G. (1994). Behavioral effects of an anti-androgen on adult male rhesus macaques (*Macaca mulatta*). *Hormones and Behavior, 28*, 155–164.

Dittus, W. P. J. (1984). Toque macaque food calls: Semantic communication concerning food distribution in the environment. *Animal Behaviour, 32*, 470–477.

Elowson, A. M., Snowdon, C. T., & Lazaro-Perea, C. (1998a). Infant "babbling" in a nonhuman primate: Complex vocal sequences with repeated call types. *Behaviour, 135*, 643–664.

Elowson, A. M., Snowdon, C. T., & Lazaro-Perea, C. (1998b). "Babbling" and social context in infant monkeys: Parallels to human infants. *Trends in Cognitive Science, 2*, 31–37.

Elowson, A. M., Tannenbaum,. P. L., & Snowdon, C. T. (1991). Food-associated calls correlate with food preferences in cotton-top tamarins. *Animal Behaviour, 42*, 931–937.

Epple, G. (1985). Chemical signals. In G. Mitchell & J. Erwin (Eds.), *Comparative primate biology, Volume 2A* (pp. 531–580). New York: Alan R. Liss.

Epple, G., & Katz, Y. (1984). Social influences on estrogen secretion and ovarian cyclicity in the saddle-back tamarin (*Saguinus fuscicollis*). *American Journal of Primatology, 6*, 215–227.

Farabaugh, S. M. (1982). The ecological and social significance of duetting. In D. E. Kroodsman & E. H. Miller. *Acoustic communication in birds: II. Song learning and its consequences* (pp. 85–124). New York: Academic Press.

Fernald, A. (1992). Human maternal vocalizations to infants as biologically-relevant signals: An evolutionary perspective. In J. H. Barkow, L. Cosmides, & J. Tooby (Eds.), *The adapted mind: Evolutionary psychology and the generation of culture* (pp. 391–428). New York: Oxford University Press.

Ferris, C. F., Snowdon, C. T., King, J. A., Duong, T., Ziegler, T. E., Ugurbic, K., Ludwig, R., Schultz-Darkon, N. J., Wu, Z., Olson, D. P., Sullivan, J. B., Tannenbaum, P. L., & Vaughn, J. T. (2001). Functional imaging of brain activity in conscious monkeys responding to seriously arousing cues. *NeuroReport, 12*, 2231–2236.

Fossey, D. (1972). Vocalizations of the mountain gorilla (*Gorilla gorilla berengei*). *Animal Behaviour, 20*, 36–53.

French, J. A., & Snowdon, C. T. (1981). Sexual dimorphism in response to unfamiliar intruders in the tamarin (*Saguinus oedipus*). *Animal Behaviour, 29*, 822–829.

Glass, I., & Wollberg, Z. (1979). Lability in the response of cells in the auditory cortex of squirrel monkeys to species-specific vocalizations. *Experimental Brain Research, 34*, 489–498.

Gouzoules, S., Gouzoules, H., & Marler, P. (1984). Rhesus monkey (*Macaca mulatta*) screams: Representational signaling in recruitment of agonistic aid. *Animal Behaviour, 32*, 182–193.

Green, S. (1975). Variation of vocal pattern with social situation in the Japanese monkey (*Macaca fuscata*): A field study. In L. A. Rosenblum (Ed.), *Primate behavior: Developments in field and laboratory research, Volume 4* (pp. 1–102). New York: Academic Press.

Griffin, D. R. (1985). Animal consciousness. *Neuroscience and Biobehavioral Reviews, 9*, 615–622.

Gubernick, D. J. (1990). A maternal chemosignal maintains paternal behaviour in the biparental California mouse. *Animal Behaviour, 39*, 936–942.

Hailman, J. P. (1977). *Optical signals*. Bloomington: Indiana University Press.

Hamilton, W. J., III, & Arrowood, P. C. (1978). Copulatory vocalizations of chacma baboons (*Papio urinus*), gibbons (*Hylobates hoolock*) and humans. *Science, 200*, 1405–1409.

Hasselmo, M. E., Rolls, E. T., & Baylis, G. C. (1989). The role of expression and identity in the face-selective responses of neurons in the temporal visual cortex of the monkey. *Behavioural Brain Research, 32*, 203–218.

Hauser, M. D. (1988). How vervet monkeys learn to recognize starling alarm calls: The role of experience. *Behaviour, 105*, 187–201.

Hauser, M. D. (1989). Ontogenetic changes in the comprehension and production of vervet monkey (*Cercopithecus aethiops*) vocalizations. *Journal of Comparative Psychology, 103*, 149–158.

Hauser, M. D. (1996). *The evolution of communication*. Cambridge, MA: MIT Press.

Hauser, M. D., & Marler, P. (1993a). Food-associated calls in rhesus macaques (*Macaca mulatta*): I. Socioecological factors. *Behavioral Ecology, 4*, 194–205.

Hauser, M. D., & Marler, P. (1993b). Food-associated calls in rhesus macaques (*Macaca mulatta*): II. Costs and benefits of call production and suppression. *Behavioral Ecology, 4*, 206–212.

Hauser, M. D., Teixidor, P., Fields, L., & Flaherty, M. (1993). Food-elicited calls in chimpanzees: Effects of food quantity and divisibility. *Animal Behaviour, 45*, 817–819.

Hauser, M. D., & Wrangham, R. W. (1987). Manipulation of food calls in captive chimpanzees. *Folia Primatologica, 48*, 207–210.

Heffner, H. E., & Heffner, R. S. (1984). Temporal lobe lesions and perception of species-specific vocalizations by macaques. *Science, 226,* 75–76.

Herzog, M., & Hopf, S. (1984). Behavioral responses to species-specific warning calls in infant squirrel monkeys reared in social isolation. *American Journal of Primatology, 7,* 99–106.

Jurgens, U. (1979). Vocalization as an emotional indicator. A neuroethological study in the squirrel monkey. *Behaviour, 69,* 88–117.

Jurgens, U. (1982). A neuroethological approach to the classification of vocalization in the squirrel monkey. In C. T. Snowdon, C. H. Brown, & M. R. Petersen (Eds.), *Primate communication* (pp. 50–62). New York: Cambridge University Press.

Jurgens, U., & Mueller-Preuss, P. (1977). Convergent projections of different limbic vocalization areas in the squirrel monkey. *Experimental Brain Research, 29,* 75–83.

Jurgens, U., & Ploog, D. (1970). Cerebral representation of vocalization in the squirrel monkey. *Experimental Brain Research, 10,* 532–554.

Jurgens, U., & Pratt, R. (1979). The cingulate vocalization pathway in the squirrel monkey. *Experimental Brain Research, 34,* 499–510.

Kalin, N. H., Shelton, S. E., & Snowdon, C. T. (1992). Affiliative vocalizations in infant rhesus macaques (*Macaca mulatta*). *Journal of Comparative Psychology, 106,* 254–261.

Kalin, N. H., Shelton, S. E., & Snowdon, C. T. (1993). Social factors regulating security and fear in rhesus monkeys. *Depression, 1,* 137–142.

Kanazawa, S. (1998). What facial part is important for Japanese monkey (*Macca fuscata*) in recognition of smiling and sad faces of humans (*Homo sapiens*)? *Journal of Comparative Psychology, 112,* 363–370.

Kaplan, J., Cubicotti, D. D. III, & Redican, W. K. (1977). Olfactory recognition of squirrel monkey mothers by their infants. *Developmental Psychobiology, 10,* 447–453.

Krebs, J. R., & Dawkins, R. (1984). Animal signals: Mind reading and manipulation. In J. R. Krebs & N. B. Davies (Eds.), *Behavioural ecology: An evolutionary approach* (pp. 380–402). Sunderland, MA: Sinauer Associates.

Kroodsma, D. E., & Miller, E. H. (1996). *Ecology and evolution of acoustic behavior in birds.* Ithaca, NY: Cornell University Press.

Larson, C. R., Sutton, D., & Lindeman, R. (1978). Cerebellar regulation of phonation in rhesus monkey (*Macaca mulatta*). *Experimental Brain Research, 33,* 1–18.

Lazaro-Perea, C. (2001). Inter-group interactions in wild common marmosets (*Callithrix tacchus*): Territorial defense and assessment of neighbours. *Animal Behaviour, 62,* 11–21.

Lazaro-Perea, C. M., Harrison, R., Arajao, A., Arruda, F., & Snowdon, C. T. (2000). Behavioral and demographic changes following loss of the breeding female in wild common marmosets. *Behavioral Ecology and Sociobiology, 48,* 137–146.

Lazaro-Perea, C., Snowdon, C. T., & Arruda, M. F. (1999). Scent-marking behavior in wild groups of common marmosets (*Callithrix jacchus*). *Behavioral Ecology and Sociobiology, 46,* 313–324.

Leger, D. W., & Owings, D. H. (1978). Responses to alarm calls by California ground squirrels: Effects of call structure and maternal status. *Behavioral Ecology and Sociobiology, 3,* 177–186.

Levin, R. (1996a). Song behaviour and reproductive strategies in a duetting wren, *Thryothorus nigricapillus.* I. Removal experiments. *Animal Behaviour, 52,* 1093–1106.

Levin, R. (1996b). Song behaviour and reproductive strategies in a duetting wren, *Thryothorus nigricapillus.* II. Playback experiments. *Animal Behaviour, 52,* 1107–1117.

Levine, S., Weiner, S. G., Coe, C. L., Bayart, F. E. S., & Hayashi, K. T. (1987). Primate vocalization: A psychobiological approach. *Child Development, 58,* 1408–1419.

Lillehei, R. A., & Snowdon, C. T. (1978). Individual and situational differences in the vocalizations of young stump-trail macaques (*Macaca arctoides*). *Behaviour, 65,* 270–281.

Locke, J. L. (1993). *The child's path to spoken language.* Cambridge, MA: Harvard University Press.

Manley, J. A., & Mueller-Preuss, P. (1978). Response variability of auditory cortex cells in the squirrel monkey to constant acoustic stimuli. *Experimental Brain Research, 32,* 171–180.

Marchlewska-Koj, A. (1983). Pregnancy blocking by pheromones. J. G. Vandenbergh (Ed.), *Pheromones and reproduction in mammals* (pp. 151–174). New York: Academic Press.

Marler, P. (1955). Characteristics of some animal calls. *Nature, 176,* 6–8.

Marler, P. (1970). Birdsong and human speech: Could there be parallels? *American Scientist, 58,* 669–673.

Marler, P., Dufty, A., & Pickert, R. (1986). Vocal communication in the domestic chicken: Does a sender communicate information about the quality of a food referent to the receiver? *Animal Behaviour, 34,* 188–193.

McConnell, P. B. (1990). Acoustic structure and receiver response in domestic dogs, *Canis familiaris. Animal Behaviour, 39,* 897–904.

McConnell, P. B. (1991). Lessons from animal trainers: The effect of acoustic structure on an animal's response. In P. Bateson & P. Klopfer (Eds.), *Perspectives in ethology volume* (pp. 165–187). New York: Plenum.

McConnell, P. B., & Baylis, J. R. (1985). Interspecific communication in cooperative herding: Acoustic and visual signals from human shepherds and herding dogs. *Zeitschrift fur Tierpsychologie, 67,* 302–328.

McConnell, P. B., & Snowdon, C. T. (1986). Vocal interactions between unfamiliar groups of captive cotton top tamarins. *Behaviour, 97,* 273–296.

Miller, R. E. (1971). Experimental studies of communication in the monkey. In L. A. Rosenblum (Ed.), *Primate behavior: Developments in field and laboratory research,* Vol. 2 (pp. 139–175). New York: Academic Press.

Miller, R. E., Banks, J., & Ogawa, N. (1963). The role of facial expression in "cooperative-avoidance" conditioning in monkeys. *Journal of Abnormal and Social Psychology, 67,* 24–30.

Miller, R. E., Caul, W. F., & Mirsky, I. A. (1967). The communication of affects between feral and socially-isolated monkeys. *Journal of Personality and Social Psychology, 7,* 231–239.

Mineka, S., & Cook, M. (1988). Social learning and the acquisition of snake fear in monkeys. In T. R. Zentall & B. G. Galef Jr. (Eds.), *Social learning: Psychological and biological perspectives* (pp. 51–73). Hillsdale, NJ: Erlbaum.

Morris, J. S., Frith, C. D., Perrett, D. I., Rowland, D., Young, A. W., Calder, A. J., & Dolan, R. J. (1996). A differential neural response in the human amygdala to fearful and happy facial expressions. *Nature, 383,* 812–815.

Morton, E. S. (1975). Ecological sources of selection on avian sounds. *American Naturalist, 109,* 17–34.

Newman, J. D. (1979). Central nervous system processing of sounds in primates. In H. D. Steklis & M. J. Raleigh (Eds.), *Neurobiology of social communication in primates* (pp. 69–109). New York: Academic Press.

Newman, J. D. (1985). The infant cry of monkeys: An evolutionary perspective. In B. M. Lester & Z. Boukydis (Eds.), *Infant crying* (pp. 307–323). New York: Plenum.

Newman, J. D., & Symmes, D. (1974). Vocal pathology in socially-deprived monkeys. *Developmental Psychobiology, 7,* 351–358.

Oba, R., & Masataka, N. (1996). Interspecific responses of ringtailed lemurs to playback of antipredator alarm calls given by Verraux's sifakas. *Ethology, 102,* 441–453.

O'Connell, S. M., & Colishaw, G. (1994). Infanticide avoidance, sperm competition and male choice: The function of copulation calls in female baboons. *Animal Behaviour, 48,* 687–694.

Oller, D. K. (2000). *The emergence of the speech capacity.* Mahwah, NJ: Erlbaum.

Owings, D. H., & Hennessey, D. F. (1984). The importance of variation in sciurid visual and vocal communication. In J. H. Murie & G. H. Michener (Eds.), *The biology of ground-dwelling squirrels: Annual cycles, behavioral ecology and sociality* (pp. 169–200). Lincoln: University of Nebraska Press.

Owings, D. H., & Morton, E. S. (1998). *Animal vocal communication: A new approach.* Cambridge, England: Cambridge University Press.

Owings, D. H., & Virginia, R. A. (1978). Alarm calls of California ground squirrels (*Spermophilis beechyi*). *Zeitschrift fur Tierpsychologie, 46,* 58–78.

Parr, L. A., Dove, T., & Hopkins, W. D. (1998). Why faces may be special: Evidence of the inversion effect in chimpanzees. *Journal of Cognitive Neuroscience, 10,* 615–622.

Parr, L. A., Hopkins, W. D., & de Waal, F. B. M. (1998). The perception of facial expressions by chimpanzees (*Pan troglodytes*). *Evolution of Communication, 2,* 1–23.

Payne, K., Langbauer, W. R., & Thomas, E. (1986). Infrasonic calls of the Asian elephant (*Elephas maximus*). *Behavioral Ecology and Sociobiology, 18,* 297–301.

Perrett, D. I., & Mistlin, A. J. (1990). Perception of facial characteristics by monkeys. In W. C. Stebbins & M. A. Berkley (Eds.), *Comparative perception: Complex signals* (pp. 187–215). New York: Wiley.

Petersen, M., Beecher, M., Zoloth, S., Moody, D., & Stebbins, W. (1978). Neural lateralization of species-specific vocalizations by Japanese macaques (*Macaca fuscata*). *Science, 202,* 324–327.

Ploog, D. (1981). Neurobiology of primate audio-vocal behavior. *Brain Research Reviews, 3,* 35–61.

Porter, T. A. (1994). *The development and maintenance of heterosexual pair associations in cotton-top tamarins (Saguinus oedipus oedipus).* Unpublished Ph.D. dissertation, University of Wisconsin, Madison.

Preuschoft, S. (1995). *"Laughter" and "smiling" in macaques. An evolutionary perspective.* Ph.D. dissertation, University of Utrecht, Netherlands.

Provine, R. R. (1996). Contagious yawning and laughter: Significance for sensory feature detection, motor pattern generation, imitation and the evolution of social behavior. In B. G. Galef & T. R. Zentall, *Social learning in animals: The roots of culture* (pp. 179–208). San Diego, CA: Academic Press.

Rauschecker, J. P., Tian, B., & Hauser, M. D. (1995). Processing of complex sounds in the macaque nonprimary auditory cortex. *Science, 268,* 111–114.

Robinson, B. W. (1967). Vocalizations evoked from forebrain in *Macaca mulatta. Physiology and Behavior, 2,* 345–354.

Rottman, S. J., & Snowdon, C. T. (1972). Demonstration and analysis of an alarm pheromone in mice. *Journal of Comparative and Physiological Psychology, 81,* 483–490.

Roush, R. S., & Snowdon, C. T. (1994). Ontogeny of food-associated calls in cotton-top tamarins. *Animal Behaviour, 47,* 263–273.

Roush, R. S., & Snowdon, C. T. (1999). The effects of social status on food-associated calling behavior in captive cotton-top tamarins. *Animal Behaviour, 58,* 1299–1305.

Rowell, T. E., & Hinde, R. A. (1962). Vocal communication by the rhesus monkey (*Macaca mulatta*). *Proceedings of the Zoological Society of London, 138,* 279–294.

Sackett, G. S. (1966). Monkeys reared in social isolation with pictures as visual stimuli: Evidence for an innate releasing mechanism. *Science, 154,* 1468–1473.

Savage, A., Ziegler, T. E., & Snowdon, C. T. (1988). Sociosexual development, pairbond formation and mechanisms of fertility suppression in female cotton-top tamarins (*Saguinus oedipus oedipus*). *American Journal of Primatology, 14,* 345–359.

Semple, S. (1998). The function of Barbary macaque copulation calls. *Proceedings of the Royal Society of London, B, 265,* 287–291.

Seyfarth, R. M., & Cheney, D. L. (1986). Vocal development in vervet monkeys. *Animal Behaviour, 34,* 1640–1658.

Seyfarth, R. M., & Cheney, D. L. (1997). Some general features of vocal development in nonhuman primates. In C. T. Snowdon & M. Hausberger (Eds.), *Social influences on vocal development* (pp. 249–273). Cambridge, England: Cambridge University Press.

Seyfarth, R. M., Cheney, D. L., & Marler, P. (1980). Monkey responses to three different alarm calls: Evidence of predator classification and semantic communication. *Science, 210,* 801–803.

Sherman, P. W. (1977). Nepotism and the evolution of alarm calls. *Science, 197,* 1246–1253.

Smith, H. J., Newman, J. D., & Symmes, D. (1982). Vocal concomitants of affiliative behavior in squirrel monkeys. In C. T. Snowdon, C. H. Brown, & M. R. Petersen (Eds.), *Primate communication* (pp. 30–49). New York: Cambridge University Press.

Smith, W. J. (1977). *The behavior of communicating: An ethnological approach.* Cambridge, MA: Harvard University Press.

Snowdon, C. T., Cleveland, J., & French, J. A. (1983). Responses to context- and individual-specific cues in cotton-top tamarin long calls. *Animal Behaviour, 31,* 92–101.

Snowdon, C. T., & Elowson, A. M. (1999). Pygmy marmosets modify vocal structure when paired. *Ethology, 105,* 893–908.

Snowdon, C. T., & Elowson, A. M. (in press). "Babbling" in pygmy marmosets: Development after infancy. *Behaviour.*

Snowdon, C. T., & Hausberger, M. (1997). *Social influences on vocal development.* Cambridge, England: Cambridge University Press.

Snowdon, C. T., & Hodun, A. (1981). Acoustic adaptations in pygmy marmoset contact calls: Locational cues vary with distance between conspecifics. *Behavioral Ecology and Sociobiology, 9,* 295–300.

Stern, K., & McClintock, M. K. (1998). Regulation of ovulation by human pheromones. *Nature, 392,* 177–179.

Sutton, D. (1979). Mechanisms underlying vocal control in nonhuman primates. In H. D. Steklis & M. J. Raleigh (Eds.), *Neurobiology of social communication in primates* (pp. 45–67). New York: Academic Press.

Sutton, D., Larson, C. R., & Lindeman, R. C. (1974). Neocortical and limbic lesion effects on primate phonation. *Brain Research, 71,* 61–75.

Swaisgood, R., Rowe, M. P., & Owings, D. H. (1999). Assessment of rattlesnake dangerousness by California ground squirrels: Exploitation of cues from rattling sounds. *Animal Behaviour, 57,* 1301–1310.

Vandenbergh, J. G. (1983). Pheromonal regulation of puberty. J. G. Vandenbergh (Ed.), *Pheromones and reproduction in mammals* (pp. 95–112). New York: Academic Press.

Van Hooff, J. A. R. A. M. (1972). A comparative approach to the phylogeny of laughter and smiling. In R. A. Hinde (Ed.), *Non-verbal communication* (pp. 209–241). Cambridge, England: Cambridge University Press.

Von Frisch, K. (1941). Uber einen Schreckstoff der Fischhaut und seine biologisches Bedeutung [Concerning an alarm substance in fish and its biological significance.]. *Zeitschrift fur Vergleichende Physiologie, 29,* 46–145.

Waser, P. M., & Brown, C. H. (1986). Habitat acoustics and primate communication. *American Journal of Primatology, 10,* 135–154.

Waser, P. M., & Waser, M. S. (1977). Experimental studies of primate vocalization: Specializations for long-distance propagation. *Zeitschrift fur Tierpsychologie, 43,* 239–263.

Washabaugh, K., & Snowdon, C. T. (1998). Chemical communication of reproductive status in female cotton-top tamarins *(Saguinus o. oedipus). American Journal of Primatology, 45,* 337–349.

Winter, P., Handley, P., Ploog, D., & Schott, D. (1973). Ontogeny of squirrel monkey calls under normal conditions and under acoustic isolation. *Behaviour, 47,* 230–239.

Ziegler, T. E., Epple, G., Snowdon, C. T., Porter, T. A., Belcher, A., & Kuederling, I. (1993). Detection of the chemical signals of ovulation in the cotton-top tamarin, *Saguinus oedipus. Animal Behaviour, 45,* 313–322.

Zoloth, S. R., Petersen, M. R., Beecher, M. D., Green, S., Marler, P., Moody, D. B., & Stebbins, W. (1979). Species-specific perceptual processing of vocal sounds by Old World monkeys. *Science, 204,* 870–873.

Zuberbuhler, K, Jenny, D., & Bshary, R. (1999). The predator deterrence function of primate alarm calls. *Ethology, 105,* 477–490.

# 25

# CREATIVE EXPRESSION AND COMMUNICATION OF EMOTIONS IN THE VISUAL AND NARRATIVE ARTS

Keith Oatley

## Historical Perspective on Theories of Emotion in Art

Art is social communication. Although one can imagine a lover improvising a poem privately into her lover's ear, for the most part art is expressed in the form of objects that endure through time, and travel beyond the immediate. In this way, the emotions expressed in art can be thought of as extensions of the ephemeral and local expressions discussed elsewhere in this volume.

This chapter is based on the movement of romanticism, by which emotions came into primacy in art and politics. Think of the Western history of ideas as having various phases: pre-classical, Greek, Roman, medieval. The modern period in Western history, which follows the medieval, began around 1400 with the start of Renaissance. Until the introduction of the printing press, around 1450, almost no one could read or write. With printing there occurred a great burgeoning of education and literacy. European life came to be dominated by commercial cities like Venice, London, and Amsterdam. World exploration and communication began. The Renaissance in art, architecture, and literature, as well as the beginnings of science, transformed the intellectual life of Europe and started to transform everyday life. About 1750, there began the era of romanticism, felt first in literary arts and politics. Scientific interest in emotions can be dated to more than a hundred years later, to Darwin's book of 1872, *The Expression of the Emotions*.

Romanticism started, let us say, when Jean-Jacques Rousseau, citizen of Geneva—he who coined that ringing phrase "Man is born free and is everywhere in chains"—came first to public notice with an essay that won a prize. In this essay he argued that the natural is far to be preferred to the artificialities of civilization, which promote inequality and idleness. He wrote: "Human nature was [in former times] basically no better than it is now, but men found security in being able to discern each other's feelings and intentions, and this advantage . . . spared them many vices" (1750, p. 208). So, the romantic movement, as well as giving primacy to the emotions, was associated with the betterment of humanity. Its mood was responsible for the slogan of the French Revolution, "Liberty, Equality and Fraternity." Liberty was freedom from political repression and, as we might now say, from repression of emotions. It was freedom to create one's own life. (Its modern versions are ideas of being oneself, even of being what one really wants to be.) Earlier, the American Revolution, influenced by these same currents, led to the Declaration of Independence, drafted by Thomas Jefferson, which includes the pursuit of an emotional state among human rights: "We hold these truths to be self-evident, that all men are created equal, that they are endowed by their Creator with certain inalienable Rights, that among these are Life, Liberty and the pursuit of Happiness."

Jefferson and his contemporaries, as true romantics, believed that feeling (sensibility, sympathy) would be the basis for a new kind of democracy in America: As God has made people sociable, he has endowed them with benev-olent feelings toward each other that enable this sociabil-ity to occur without imposition by a state (Wood, 1999). At this time, also, was founded modern selfhood. We mod-erns think of ourselves as creating our own identities, of being, as it were, artists of ourselves rather than accepting identities from societal conventions. We think, too, of cre-ating relationships with spouses and children based pri-marily on affection. It is not that affection was absent from the family before 1750; it is, rather, that only subsequently did it come to be seen as the evident key to selfhood or to happiness (Taylor, 1989).

The core of Rousseau's romanticism was this: to find the good we look inward. We listen to the voice of our nature; we attune ourselves to it by emotion. Rousseau wrote polemics, books on education in the natural way, novels, and, of course, his own *Confessions*. The artist be-came an ideal of what a person could be: attuned to his or her own feelings and able to express them creatively.

The next prominent romantic literary figure after Rous-seau was Johann von Goethe (1774), who wrote a semi-autobiographical novel, *The Sorrows of Young Werther*. Werther, a sensitive young man, is an artist. He goes to live in a small town, which he describes as "disagreeable," but with "an inexpressible natural beauty all around." He feels awkward and is rejected by society in the small town. He falls in love with Charlotte, although she is engaged to another man. Enlivened at first, but then feeling intensely the hopelessness of his situation, he commits suicide. The book is full of subtle explorations of emotion. A cult grew up around it. There were Werther songs, Werther poems, imitations, and references of all kinds. It seems to have been the beginning of a craze to dress in the fashion of fictional characters. Young men wore Werther outfits—blue frock coats and buff waistcoats. The book was even said to have spawned an epidemic of suicides around Eu-rope. Here was expression of art based on emotion, accom-panied by its public reception as people were emotionally drawn to imitate in creating their own identities.

Romantic artists were interested in nature, in dreams, in travel to foreign places, and in yearnings for the infinite. As Drabble (1985) has it, "The stylistic keynote of Roman-ticism is intensity, and its watchword, is 'Imagination' " (pp. 842–843). Here, for instance, is the opening of a ro-mantic poem, characteristic in its preoccupations and imagery, written by Samuel Taylor Coleridge, in 1797 (Raine, 1957, pp. 87–89):

> In Xanadu did Kubla Khan
> A stately pleasure-dome decree:
> Where Alph, the sacred river, ran
> Through caverns measureless to man
>     Down to a sunless sea.

Coleridge later explained how the poem was written. He was staying in a lonely farmhouse in a wild part of England called Exmoore. He was unwell and had been prescribed an "anodyne." He wrote that he began to read a travel book, about Kubla Khan building a palace. He fell asleep, and a dream came to him full of vivid images to-gether with their corresponding verbal expressions. When he awoke he had a distinct recollection of the whole. He began to write, but after 54 lines, a person from Porlock came on business and kept him for more than an hour. When Coleridge returned to his room, he wrote that apart from a dim recollection of the vision, all the rest had passed away, "like the images on the surface of a stream into which a stone has been cast."

The ideas behind both the fragment and the longings implied by the story of its production were in the air. Buildings such as the stately pleasure dome in Xanadu would be habitations, not just for the body but also for the imagination. Romanticism was not accomplished by a group who explored a specific idea, as did the impres-sionist painters. It was a cultural shift. So let me postpone a definition, and give more of a sense of it by examples of two actual buildings of the era.

If you visit the south of England and drive east from Chichester, you may notice, just before Worthing, close to the road on the right-hand side, a large house that was built around 1790 by Biagio Rebecca for Sir Bysshe Shel-ley, grandfather of the poet. It is called Castle Goring. The entrance side, which faces the road, is Gothic, the style that would become the great favorite of the Victorians. This façade is flint and stone, with castellations, towers, and the pointed arches characteristic of European building of later medieval times. As Ian Nairn (Nairn & Pevsner, 1965) points out, "The details themselves are unexpected so early, including dogtooth and chevron ornament" (p. 126). The aspect is medieval, very castlelike. The emo-tions it induces are those induced by real medieval castles. One tiptoes toward it in somewhat apprehensive awe.

When I lived 10 miles from here, the house looked abandoned so that one could peer through cracks in the shutters of its windows and walk around to the back, where one saw an astonishing transformation. On the gar-den side the house is classical—that other form that would become a favorite of 19th-century building. From this side the house is a spacious villa in the style of Palladio, the great Renaissance architect who studied Greek and Roman buildings, and gave us their patterns and harmonies. From this side the building has the proportions of a Greek tem-ple. One sees a pediment, Ionic pilasters, and a ramped staircase to a balconied entrance—all elegant and elo-quent. Even the materials change, to expensive white stone. Here the mood is quite different from that of the front; here is serenity, order, the sense of everything in harmony.

As Nairn remarks, "There could not be a more telling illustration of the exact moment at which architecture be-came a matter of styles" (p. 126). Nor was this sensibility confined to Europe. Thomas Jefferson, having visited Roman buildings in Europe, and after his work in drafting the Declaration of Independence, built his home, Monticello, in Virginia, with its classical Greek portico and its Roman dome, and he used a Roman temple as the design for the Virginia Capitol at this same time.

Continue along the road from Castle Goring and you come to Brighton, a seaside resort town. Here, at much the same time as grandfather Shelley and Thomas Jefferson were building their homes, the prince regent (subsequently King George IV) decreed that a palace be built, so that he could be close to his mistress, Mrs. Fitzherbert. The palace, or Royal Pavilion as it is known, was completed by the prince's architect, John Nash. It is Muslim-Indian style on the outside, resplendent with onion domes and minarets. Inside the style is mainly Chinese. The whole is ostentatiously evocative of the exotic East. It is not easy to imagine such a building in India; it remains one of the most extraordinary in England. One might think that this is the "stately pleasure dome" of Coleridge's poem.

At the time of such architectural expressions, there was the sense that art should be concerned not just with aristocratic life. Indeed, attuned to Rousseau, many artists and thinkers held a profound distrust of the artificialities of civilization. As with other movements in art, romanticism was heralded by manifestos, the most famous of which in English was by Wordsworth in the preface to the second (1802) edition of his *Lyrical Ballads*, a collection of poems by Coleridge and him.

Low and rustic life was generally chosen [as subjects for the poems], because in that condition the essential passions of the heart find a better soil in which they can attain their maturity, are under less restraint, and speak a plainer and more emphatic language. (p. 597)

A bit further on, Wordsworth explicitly describes his theory of poetic composition:

Poetry is the spontaneous overflow of powerful feelings: it takes its origin from emotion recollected in tranquility: the emotion is contemplated till by a species of reaction the tranquility disappears, and an emotion, kindred to that which was before the subject of contemplation, is gradually produced and does itself actually exist in the mind. (p. 611)

### Theories of the Reader and Spectator in Art

Most Western theories of art start with Aristotle and his book *Poetics*. Poetics means the art of making, and the central term in Aristotle's book is *mimesis*. Let us here take this as meaning a relation between the work of art and the world; it is usually translated as "imitation." Aristotle insisted that art criticism and psychology were intimately connected. So, as well as criticism, Aristotle gave hints to writers and also discussed the emotions of the audience in tragic drama: pity for the characters on whom the tragedy has fallen, and fear for themselves.

In medieval times, a painter, sculptor, or maker of stained-glass windows was not so much concerned with the relation of his product to the world or with the psychology of the spectator. Instead, the concern was to offer memorable images (in the time before printed Bibles) for the spectator's construction of a proper sense of self in relation to God.

Let us date the Renaissance from around 1400, when the Byzantine scholar Manuel Chrysoloras began to teach ancient Greek in Florence (Holmes, 1996), to 1616, when Shakespeare died after his 20 years of writing, directing, acting, and co-ownership of a theatrical company and theater in London. The principal concern of visual and literary artists of the Renaissance was with rhetorical issues: how the artist addresses an audience. The relation between the artist and members of the public remains a central one in art, and it is a central concern in this chapter.

In the visual arts, the Renaissance concept was followed by the rococo idea that art should be suggestive of action the viewer might complete (suggestiveness, here, has some of its modern connotations). In our time, the mode of suggesting an action to be completed by the audience has been taken over by the images and words of advertising.

Romantic views are concerned more with the artist, and tend to be more solipsistic than those of the Renaissance. They allow the idea that expressing emotion is good in itself. From here it is not a long step to the idea that any emotion is as good to express as any other: prejudiced contempt as well as affection. It has led to a politics of identity that can be full of inspiring emotion, but can also be murderous to outgroups. It has led, too, not just to painting, music, or literature but also to molding people to the individual will. As Isaiah Berlin (1990) wrote, with examples such as Napoleon and Hitler in mind:

As the artist blends colours and the composer sounds, so the political demiurge imposes his will on his raw material—average, ungifted human beings, largely unconscious of the possibilities dormant within them—and shapes them into a splendid work of art—a state or army, or some great political, military, religious, juridical structure. This may entail suffering: but like discords in music it is indispensable to the harmony and effect of the whole. The victims of these great creative operations must take comfort, and indeed be exalted, by the consciousness that they are thereby lifted to

a height which their own lower natures could
never by themselves have achieved. (pp. 193–194)

And, as Berlin had commented a few pages earlier, the
romantic theory of identity would often accomplish what
Renaissance humanism had never postulated: "The division of mankind into two groups—men proper, and some
other, lower, order of beings, inferior races, inferior cultures, nations or classes condemned by history" (pp. 179–
180). Those who were to take their identity from such
movements were, needless to say, the group of "men
proper." The others, consigned to lower orders, suffered
results of which, in the 20th century, we became all too
aware.

There have been smaller scale artistic movements in
the last 250 years. At the beginning of the 20th century,
artistic modernism sought, in something of the same mood
as psychoanalysis, to recover meanings from fragments of
perception and memory. In the visual arts one thinks of
Picasso and Bracque, and their experiments of cubism, to
depict parts from which wholes can be constructed by the
viewer. In architecture, one thinks of the Bauhaus and Le
Corbusier. In fiction, one thinks of Marcel Proust, James
Joyce, and Virginia Woolf, replacing unifying plots with
invitations to readers to enter the inwardness of protagonists and to generate their own constructions of the stream
of mental life. Following modernism we have had postmodernism, with its kaleidoscopes of styles and its undermining of unified meanings.

Urban life today is more saturated with art than life
of any previous period. Almost every manufactured object was first drawn by someone who attended art
school. In almost every context, from T-shirt to television screen, from billboard to book cover, are advertisements visual and verbal, produced by visual artists and
writers. These sights and sounds add to the serried rush
of products and sensations with which we are surrounded, giving humans the sense of being particles in
this manufactured universe of multivarious sensory
availability. This is a world in which we choose what to
consume, and the making of such choices becomes an
important part of our identity.

Even with such conditions, and despite postmodernism, we are, at the beginning of the third millennium, still
very much within the romantic era. We still create our
identities in the romantic fashion. Art is still thought of,
not as contrived but as inspired, not as influenced by convention but by style, not as preoccupied by the relationship with its public, except insofar as the public should
be numerous and in this respect becomes part of the artist's work. This is the public you see as the camera cuts
from the ecstatic lead singer in the rock band to pan
around an auditorium of young people moving mimeti-
cally to the music's rhythms.

## The Role of Reader or Spectator in Romantic Theory

Romantic theory is strong on the activity of the artist but
weak on the role of the spectator or reader, but romantic
theorists do have a saving proposal. They cast spectators
or readers as themselves artists. People who read, see, or
hear the work of art enter states of mind similar to that of
the artist, and re-create the emotion and its exploration in
themselves. In this view, the only difference between the
creator of art and its audience is that the artist starts the
exploration, but both artist and audience enter it. Here, for
instance, are the intimate words of that most romantic of
romantic poets, John Keats (1795–1821), in a letter of 1818
to John Taylor: "Poetry should surprise by a fine excess
and not by Singularity—it should strike the Reader as a
wording of his own highest thoughts, and appear almost
a Remembrance" (1816–1820, p. 46). So romanticism allows that reader and spectator are not passive. As Barthes
(1975) argued, they actively construct their version of the
work. Both branches of art theory—creation and appreciation—are brought together. Appreciation is a form of expression: creation of a version of the work for which the
artist gives clues and directions.

## Art as the Creative Expression of Emotion

Perhaps the best exposition of the theory of art in relation
to emotion is Collingwood's (1938) *Principles of Art*. First
consider three activities that Collingwood says are not art.

*Art is not craft.* Craft is based on technique, for fabri-
cating a chair, a type font, a musical instrument, a psychological experiment. To practice a craft one has to learn
a great deal, often by apprenticeship. Although there are
artistic aspects to most crafts, and craft aspects to most
arts, a craft as such is based on an idea of the finished
product. There will be a plan, which may include a blue-
print, model, or drawing for how to accomplish an end.
The craft is judged by how good the end result is. What,
then, under a craft conception, would be the result of a
piece of art? A certain state of emotion in the audience? If
so, art would be merely entertainment (see later).

*Art is not magic.* We are accustomed to seeing magic
as an activity that occurs in societies different from our
own. It has sometimes been seen as pre-science, or pseu-
doscience. But, Collingwood argues, it is neither. It is a
form of pseudo art, related to craft, in which the intended
result is the arousal of particular emotions in the minds
of the receivers. Like craft, magic is socially important. In
modern life, advertisers are our principal magicians. They
arouse such emotions as envy and acquisitiveness, and
their activities, we are told, oil the economic wheels of
society. But if art proper were merely to induce certain
emotions in others, how could we (to use a more modern

example than Collingwood's) distinguish it from recreational drugs that induce emotions without bother, and that the consumer society makes available?

*Art is not amusement.* Entertainment or amusement, like craft and magic, is important in society. It occurs, however, not in the world of practical affairs, as does craft and magic, but in worlds set aside. Collingwood defines an amusement as "a device for the discharge of emotions in such a way as they shall not interfere with practical life" (p. 78). It is an escape, a pastime. Television has become our principal vehicle of entertaining escape. As shown by Kubey and Csikszentmihalyi (1990), the main effect of television is to induce in its watchers mildly, though not strongly, pleasant emotions that do indeed pass the time somewhat like a guided daydream.

Art proper, says Collingwood, is quite different. Imagine a man, as follows:

> At first he is conscious of having an emotion, but not conscious of what this emotion is. All he is conscious of is a perturbation or excitement, which he feels going on within him, but of whose nature he is ignorant. While in this state, all he can say about his emotion is: "I feel . . . I don't know how I feel." From this helpless and oppressed condition he extricates himself by doing something which we call expressing himself. This is an activity which has something to do with the thing we call language: he expresses himself by speaking. It also has something to with consciousness: the emotion expressed is the emotion of whose nature the person who feels it is no longer unconscious. (pp. 109–110)

This is the artist. The kind of expression that Collingwood sees at the center of art is neither universal nor general, and has nothing to do with the expressions of which Darwin (1872) wrote, which Collingwood calls symptoms of emotions. Neither does it have much to do with naming an emotion—"Oh, I feel angry." An artistic expression occurs as a person explains to him or herself the meaning of an emotion, in its particularity, in a language of words, painting, music. It is about the aspects of emotions that perturb and seem to impel us, although they are not yet understood. Collingwood gives an example within these terms—T. S. Eliot's (1922) *The Waste Land*, an elegiac meditation on the decay of our civilization, seen by many as the most important poem of the 20th century.

The romantic expressivist idea, which Collingwood expounds, is that our natural emotions and sentiments are latent. It is only in expressing them that they take shape. Percy Bysshe Shelley (1840, grandson of the owner of the stylish two-sided house, Castle Goring) put the idea like this: the poet "strips the veil of familiarity from the world"

(p. 332). And because each of us is different—so the argument goes—we should all explore the emotions that the artist in each of us discovers via music, image, or symbol.

## Mental Schemas: Sites of Imagination

We need next an account of what we mean by the languages of art, and by imagination. The important piece of psychological theory here is Bartlett's (1932) theory of mental schemas as the means for understanding anything at all. In either visual or verbal modalities, we assimilate events in the outside world to the schemas of what we know; at the same time (in Piaget & Inhelder's, 1969, terminology) the schemas (our implicit theories) may accommodate—that is, change. A work of art, then, is an expressed piece of thinking in response to an emotional challenge, a work of the imagination, a schematic construction, an accommodation, of the meaning of inchoate emotions.

Ernst Gombrich (1960), in a book that is widely regarded as the most important yet written on the psychology of the visual arts, has shown how in these arts expressions consist of visual schemas plus their arrangements and thoughtful modifications: schemas plus imaginative elaborations. Artists' emotions prompt learning, exploration, change. And as J. J. Gibson (1950) said, "The progress of learning is from indefinite to definite" (p. 222). This occurs with emotions and, in the experience that people interested in painting often describe, with learning to experience the world differently as a result of seeing the works of a painter. So rather than thinking that art imitates nature, nature comes to imitate art. Gombrich (1960, p. 324) quotes Oscar Wilde as saying, "There was no fog in London before Whistler painted it."

Since the work of Arnheim (1971) we have become used to the idea of visual thinking, but can the visual be a language of emotional expression? Some painters of the romantic period shared the idea of Wordsworth and other poets, of nature not just as a book to be read but as a window through which to experience the awe of the infinite. At the same time there is sufficient visual art in the world's museums that indicate preoccupations that are not especially emotional. There are, however, some statements by artists about what they are doing that fit the story I am giving. For instance, the following is quoted by Averill, Stanat, and More (1998, p. 160): The artist Ben Shahn painted a picture of a flame-headed beast bending over four children and said of the artist's motivation, "It is not your purpose to tell about a fire, not to describe a fire. Not at all; what you want to formulate is the terror, the heart-shaking fear."

To summarize, the romantic conception is the idea that art proper is the creative (imaginative) expression and exploration of emotions. This need not mean that this is all that goes on in art; rather, it means that to understand art, at least in modern terms, we need to see this expression as central.

## Theories of Art and the Psychology of Art

### Romanticism's Relations with the Psychology of Emotions

It is helpful to use the time spectrum of emotions offered by Oatley and Jenkins (1996) and distinguish emotions at the shorter end that last for a few seconds, like facial expressions, from those at the longer end. Brief facial expressions have been objects of scientific interest since Darwin's (1872) book, and are reviewed in chapter 22 of this volume. Darwin studied paintings and sculptures in preparation for his 1872 book, and he declared that, with a few exceptions, he did not profit thereby. He concluded that strong contractions of facial muscles were antipathetic to beauty, which he took to be the object of art.

There has been interest in brief facial, and accompanying bodily, gestures of emotion in painting—for instance, in the later work of Goya, in the Prado museum in Madrid. Observe the anguished faces in *Pilgrimage to San Isodore*, of 1820–1821, and the cruel anger on the face of *Saturn* of 1821–1823 (see, e.g., Rapelli, 1999). These works are already expressionist in style and prefigure the most famous of expressionist paintings, Edvard Munch's *Scream* of 1893 (see, e.g., Brettell, 1999). What is expressed in expressionism, of course, is intense emotion. During the romantic period, one sees the older theory of physiognomy—that the face reveals personality—coming to be accompanied by an interest in the fleeting moment of an emotional expression or gesture.

In literary art, fleeting expressions have been depicted to signify moments of interpersonal significance. George Eliot published *Middlemarch* (1871–1872) at the same time as Darwin was writing his book *Expression*, to explore how emotion worked in relations among people. I have annotated depictions of emotion in this novel. Of expressions there are at least 1, and typically more than 10, in each of its 87 chapters. Many expressions in *Middlemarch* are visual: a blush, a pallor, a smile. Some are acoustic: "a deep tone of indignation" (p. 293). In *Best Laid Schemes* (1992), I offered some analysis of emotions in chapter 29 of *Middlemarch*. Here are some more. I count 17 portrayals of emotional expression in this eight-page chapter, which starts with the narrator reflecting on the experience of the elderly scholar, Casaubon, then moves to an externally observed scene between him and his wife, Dorothea (the book's chief protagonist). Two letters have arrived, one addressed to her and one addressed to Casaubon, to which he takes objection. He says she may read the letter that came to him, if she wishes. Here is a typical piece of Eliot's depiction of emotional expression: "Dorothea left Ladislaw's two letters unread on her husband's writing table and went to her own place, the scorn and indignation within her rejecting the reading of these letters just as we should hurl away trash towards which we seem to have been suspected of mean cupidity" (p. 317).

This expression is in not doing something that the other had offered. Eliot mentions emotions no more often than, say, Charles Dickens. I have annotated and counted comparable numbers of emotional expressions in Dickens's *Hard Times*. But Dickens has a behaviorist stance and is typically more vague about emotions than Eliot, who was the first novelist to depict fully the inner life and set it in relation with the outer. More often than Dickens, she portrays the interpersonal accomplishments of emotions. We can note, too, that following Dickens and Eliot came the cinema, in which verbal depictions are replaced by moving pictures of emotional expressions. Not only do actors express each emotion of the script, but emotions are induced in the audience, so that the cinema becomes what Tan (1996) has called "an emotion machine."

As we move along the time spectrum from emotions that last a few seconds, we come to those that last hours or days, that we experience in ourselves and remember. Psychologists have asked people to record them in structured diaries. Such emotions are almost always confided to relatives and friends (Rimé, 1995), and they are of the same kind as many of those depicted in novels. Dorothea's anger, in the passage described previously, as well as having its outer expressions, is of this kind. So is Alexey Karenin's jealous possessiveness in *Anna Karenina* (Tolstoy, 1877, part 3, chapter 13) after his wife admits her affair with Vronsky. So is the delight of Clarissa Dalloway, on the opening page of *Mrs. Dalloway* (Woolf, 1925), as she remembers incidents of youthful friendship.

Rosenberg and Ekman (1994) have shown that, when people watch film clips, there is a moderate amount of coherence between their facial expressions of emotion and their self-reports. Some coherence has also been found in married people who engage in conversation on conflictual subjects while having indicators of emotion monitored physiologically: by facial expression, by analysis of what is said, and then later by self-report as they watch the videos of their interactions (Gottman & Levenson, 1992). We can see Gottman and Levenson's work on relating what is expressed interpersonally to the inward emotions of their participants as the empirical exploration of George Eliot's relating of outer and inner worlds in *Middlemarch*.

A second link can be made between the emotions studied by psychologists and those expressed by artists. Oatley and Duncan (1992) found that the proportion of everyday emotion incidents recorded in structured diaries that had some aspect that the participants did not understand varied between 5% and 25% in different samples. According to Oatley and Johnson-Laird (1987), whose theory is close to other cognitive theories in the area, such as that of Frijda (1986), an emotion with only its biological base may not be completely understandable. It has an inchoate quality. It is a readiness, a tendency. But it is on the foundation of such unarticulated emotions that culture and individuality build more specific understandings. In this sense, art provides examples and understandings of the emotions that are most important to us, and which therefore demand the most effort to understand.

To extend the theory, emotions occur in relation to what is important to us, to our concerns (Frijda, 1986). They occur with the vicissitudes of life, at junctures where our plans have not gone as expected, where no craft, technique, or magic is adequate. Psychologists Averill and Nunley (1992) have shown that emotions often demand a creative response, and are themselves spurs to creativity. This idea links to the romantic notion that our emotions become known only through expression. Because our more important emotions are guides that relate events to our concerns, and because they occur when aspects of these concerns are not fully understood, a creative response is needed. Art is the creative activity of expressing, and thereby understanding, such emotions in their depth and particularity.

## Romanticism's Relations to Psychological Theories of Artistic Expression

Next, I discuss three influential viewpoints in which emotion has played a role, and show their relation to the romantic view. All are concerned with a theme of the previous section: the relation of the outer to the inner world. All place emotions centrally in the psychology of art. In these approaches, expression may be thought of as an emotional state within a person that is manifested in outer behavior, from where it may be picked up by the attentive spectator.

### Lipps's Idea of Empathy

Lipps wrote around 1900; the central term in his work is *Einfühlung*, translated as "empathy" or "feeling into" (e.g., Lipps, 1962). He argued that spectators, or readers, feel into works of art or, putting it the other way round, that works of art are those cultural objects that lend themselves to this principle. The principle seems straightforward when applied to novels or films based on human action (Tan, 1996). Painting, sculpture, and architecture present more of a challenge. Here the argument is that people tend to feel into even inanimate objects in an empathetic way. We feel the weight of the roof bearing down on the heads of the caryatids in the Erechtheion on the Acropolis of Athens. We soar toward the heavens in the vaulted space of a great cathedral. Kreitler and Kreitler (1972) report an

experiment they did on this issue. Two researchers unobtrusively observed 90 randomly selected visitors to an exhibition of sculpture, choosing 15 visitors who viewed each of six figural sculptures. They used a notation system to document all the spectators' bodily movements, and found that 84% of the spectators "displayed overt imitatory movements during their inspection of the statues" (p. 275).

The idea of empathy links the creative impulse of the visual artist, responding to the aspect of the world on which he or she is working, to the response of the observer. It has implications for recent psychological understandings. We know from the work of Melzoff and Moore (1977) that human beings have a tendency to imitate. Melzoff has shown that even in their first day of life, babies will stick their tongues out at adults who stick their tongues out at them. Imitation is a still mysterious psychological phenomenon. You observe an action, the output of a motor program. Then you assemble a motor program that will generate a comparable action by yourself! Anyone who has written a computer program to accomplish anything at all will realize how remarkable this is. Hatfield, Cacioppo, and Rapson (1994) have discussed the issue in terms of emotional contagion, and Donald (1991) has called this "mimetic" ability, and he proposes that it is one of the great building blocks of the human mind.

The facial feedback hypothesis of emotions is that performing an action characteristic of an emotion engenders that emotion. Experimental work such as that of Strack, Martin, and Stepper (1988) has tended to confirm it. Melzoff (1993) has therefore proposed that imitating an emotional expression or gesture is the basis for empathy, since it gives the imitator feedback from the motor processes that will in turn produce corresponding emotions in that person.

### Arnheim and Gestalt Approaches

The core of Arnheim's theory was not very different from that of Lipps, except that for him and other Gestalt psychologists all perception was based on neurological processes within that have similar structural relations to those of objects that are being perceived. The visual cortex represents a pattern in the outside world by means of a spatial pattern within that is isomorphic with it, and this representation is subject to spatial forces that tend to organize it into what Gestaltists called "good forms." So a not very well drawn circle comes nonetheless be seen as circular because of such organizing inner forces. As far as expression goes, Arnheim (1949) proposed that:

> The way a person keeps his lips closed or raises his voice or strokes a child's head is said to contain factors whose meaning can be understood directly through mere inspection. . . . They are also

found in such "projective" material as the stirring red of a woman's favorite dress or the "emotional" quality of the music she prefers. In addition, inanimate objects are said to convey direct expression. The aggressive stroke of lightning or the soothing rhythm of rain. . . . (p. 264)

Since the advent of the movies, the use of such devices has become commonplace in conveying emotional tone. Gestalt psychologists argued that just as there are brain patterns that convey the underlying qualities of shapes and sound patterns, so the human mind resonates with dynamic qualities of gestures and movements. Arnheim offers the results of a preliminary experiment with five student dancers, asked to improvise dances to express three themes: sadness, strength, and night. Sadness was in all five dancers expressed as slow, mostly round, small, enclosed, indefinite, and passive movements. Strength was expressed as very different kinds of movements: large, straight, precise, active. Again, according to more modern evidence and theorizing, we could argue that these effects may be based on innate mimetic abilities that are part of our human inheritance.

### Freud's Psychoanalytic Approach

From early in his psychoanalytic work Freud wrote about the literary and visual arts. According to these ideas, art is a forum less distressing than neurotic symptoms, more public than dreams, and more substantial than jokes, but serving some of the same purposes of expressing aspects of inner emotional conflicts in disguised forms that allow some satisfaction of expression while avoiding censure. Freud's (1904) early paper on identification with characters on the stage is typical:

> Being present as an interested spectator at a spectacle or play does for adults what play does for children. . . . The spectator is a person who experiences too little, who feels that he is a "poor wretch for whom nothing of importance can happen," who has long been obliged to damp down, or rather displace, his ambition to stand in his own person at the hub of world affairs; he longs to feel and to act and to arrange things according to his desires—in short, to be a hero. And the playwright and actor enable him to do this by allowing him *to identify himself* with a hero. (pp. 121–122)

Identification, with or without a psychoanalytic flavor, has achieved an important place in understanding literary experience. It is, for instance, a typical ingredient of reading, which can be measured using Miall and Kuiken's (1995) Literary Reading Questionnaire. In this context one may also remark that without the psychoanalytic idea of emotional preoccupation, or something like it, explaining why artists apply themselves so diligently to the expression of their art would be far more difficult.

### Aesthetics, Appraisal, and Emotional Attractiveness

By far the largest amount of empirical work in the psychology of art has been in measuring responses to art. The argument is that the aesthetic sense is an emotional preference, a liking for something, such as beauty. Empirical aesthetics is as old as experimental psychology; the best introduction is Kreitler and Kreitler (1972). The most substantial empirical program in the area in recent times has been that of Berlyne (e.g., 1965), who argued that aesthetic preference is driven by curiosity. He proposed a set of what he called collative properties of visual and acoustic patterns, such as complexity, heterogeneity, and symmetry. His program included verbal responses to patterns and artworks, measures of physiological arousal, and behavioral measures such as the time a subject would spend to explore a pattern or painting. Berlyne's conclusions include the idea that people seek out patterns they judge to be beautiful and that lack properties that are too confusing, as measured by sharp arousal. People also show exploratory curiosity when they encounter novel, ambiguous, problem-raising, or otherwise conflict-arousing patterns. Interest, then, can involve a balance between properties that are harmonious (with each other and with the self) and those that are challenging.

The emotional processes identified by Berlyne in the 1960s were characteristic of that time: curiosity and arousal. Research on emotions is, however, now dominated by the cognitive-psychological idea of appraisal, introduced by Arnold and Gasson (1954; see part V of this handbook). It has shifted approaches to psychological aesthetics. Appraisal is an evaluation, sometimes unconscious and sometimes simple, that prompts an emotion. It relates an external object or event to something internal, such as a concern, a goal, an aspiration. One of the benefits of the shift is that it provides for understanding the engagement with art by the spectator and reader.

This idea of appraisal is present in literary criticism: T. S. Eliot (1919) introduced the term *objective correlative* to mean "a set of objects, a situation, a chain of events, which shall be the formula of that *particular* emotion" (p. 107).

How, then, should we understand aesthetic preferences? About 5 million years ago, our ancestors separated from the ancestors of chimpanzees. Our ancestors moved from the rain forest to the savannahs of East Africa. According to Orians and Heerwagen (1992), human genes still bias us toward aesthetic preference for the savannah. They found that American children, full of human genes but not yet full of cultural constructions on the genetic foundations, were shown photos of different habitats including forest and savannah, and they preferred savannah to other landscape types, even though they had never visited one. We inherit genetically based appraisal patterns that afford these preferences, which we experience as beauty.

As our ancestors moved nomadically about the savannah, they came to prefer areas that promised food and water. They also liked to be able to look out in order to spot predators or potentially hostile hominid groups, and to have areas that provided shade as well as refuge from such threats. They came to like, in the terms of Appleton (1975), who studied landscape painting to discern such preferences, "prospect" and "refuge." Neither Appleton nor Orians mentions it, but there is a connection here to Bowlby's (1971) influential theory of anxiety-based attachment of infant to mother. As Bowlby made clear, the first purpose of attachment is to protect the infant from harm. The second is to provide a secure base for exploration. Our ancestors were knowledge gatherers and knowledge users (Kaplan, 1992). We find flowers beautiful; they are signs of fertile soils. We like pathlike features that hint at mysterious features, but ones that seem accessible. We became attracted to landscapes that promise fruitful exploration from secure bases. Here, it is argued, are seeds of human exploratory curiosity and the interests of the romantics in the natural, sensed within by attunement to feelings, and sensed without in flowers, landscapes, and paintings of them. Here is the link to the psychological aesthetics of Berlyne (1965) in which the arousal of curiosity is an important component.

Here, too, is a link to the idea of living close to nature, or in such a way as to blend in with it. We know the magnificent settings of much classical Greek architecture: the Acropolis in Athens high on a hill so the Parthenon can be seen from afar, but not too high that it cannot be approached; the siting of the theater of Taormina in Sicily to offer spectators a view of the still active volcano of Mount Etna behind the performance. The idea that building and setting should blend was revived in the Renaissance, but perhaps its fullest expression was achieved by the English landscape gardeners of the early romantic period. These include "Capability" Brown, whose works included laying out most of the park and creating the lake at Blenheim. Such landscaped parks included vistas, lakes, streams, trees, and pathways leading to interesting places, all close to an imposing house, the safe refuge. Despite the expense of this kind of gardening—diverting rivers, replanting trees, and moving thousands of tons of earth—and in contrast to formal gardens such as those of Versailles, all was to look natural. The garden then becomes not merely a place to walk in but also a habitation for the soul, mediated by the emotions: here a serene vista, here a reflection in a lake to mirror our mental reflections, there a tomb to induce melancholy, there a ruin to remind us of life's transience. The interest in gardening to create

nourishment for our emotions has continued in the garden plots of millions of householders.

A general framework of aesthetics in relation to emotions that takes account of such matters has been provided by Averill et al. (1998). They argue that there are several biobehavioral systems, which induce attraction to certain features of the environment because of their importance for these systems. The systems are mating behavior (otherwise known as sex), attachment, aggression, avoidance of harm, foraging, and exploration. For each one, certain appraisal patterns are attractive, either because they have been genetically programmed or because of association. These patterns invite the person toward enacting the behavior in question. Moreover, as ethologists have shown, it is not the actual mate, attachment partner, predator, or piece of food that has the effects. Such effects are triggered easily by highly schematic patterns. Thus, in 1939, Tinbergen and Kuenen showed that fledgling birds would open their beaks not just to their actual parents bringing food but also to schematic cardboard cutouts of adult birds (see Tinbergen, 1951). Schematic patterns work also for humans. Show a babyface pattern—large rounded head, prominent eyes, protruding cheeks (a pattern known as *das Kinderschema*, baby schema)—to a large audience, and there is a good chance of hearing that reassuring maternal sound "aaaah." Similarly, the nubile young women whose photographs fill the pages of magazines on the upper racks of newsagents are almost as schematic and tend to elicit another kind of response. Certain kinds of art are designed only to activate species-specific schemas of attraction and, as Winston (1992) has argued, this kind of art is called sentimental.

Inner schemas, as described by Bartlett, are thus activated by corresponding external appraisal patterns, which can themselves be quite schematic. Genetically based inner schemas are start-up structures, which are elaborated by culture and by the individual in the course of a lifetime. The attractiveness of woman may be a human male universal; the attractiveness of Marilyn Monroe is a product of the 20th century.

## Schema Theory and the Relations of Artist to Spectator or Reader

How can we treat the communicative issues of the visual and narrative arts together? Here is a suggestion.

In the visual arts we stand outside the artwork. Artist and spectator are both affected by its appraisal patterns/objective correlatives. We assimilate it to our schemas, and these afford arousal and pleasure (Russell, 1980). We are also affected, as Cupchik and Winston (1992) point out, by art that is more challenging, not easily assimilated to existing schemas. The challenge is perhaps linked to the behavioral system of exploration, with its emotional mode of curiosity. Artwork of the challenging kind requires schemas to accommodate; it prompts us to learn. It took time, for instance, for Parisians to accept impressionism. But challenge has its pleasures: of expanding one's mind. As Kaplan (1992) explains, we are drawn to what is too complex for our understanding, and also to mystery, the seeming invitation to what may lie just round the corner. Peterson (1999), in his psychological study of mythology, puts it that we are forever on a tantalizing boundary between the safe and the frightening unknown. Exploration is what tames the unknown; curiosity is its emotional driver. Assimilation and accommodation, derived respectively from the schematically attractive and the not-yet-understood, are always in tension. Art, with its basis of schema plus elaboration, is often the exploration of such tension. The image of the relation of artist and spectator in visual art such as painting, therefore, is of artist and spectator standing shoulder to shoulder, looking at (say) a painting and, by means of schema-based processes, at the world of nature and the world of society.

In architecture, by contrast, the artist creates a new piece of the physical world—the home, the town hall, the office building. We can be drawn toward buildings, much as we are drawn toward a landscape. But now there is something not shared by paintings: Buildings fairly invite us to enter them. The walls of buildings do not just hold up the roof. They offer, as Goffman (1959) proposed, partitioned spaces in which we humans meet and give performances of ourselves. So there are areas for intimate meetings (the bedroom) and more public meetings (the living room). There are front-stage areas and back-stage areas. In Castle Goring, the Gothic-classical house of Shelley's grandfather, the dual styles of the outside continue within. You can look along corridors that flank the central circular hall toward the garden side, and see elegant ovals framed in parabolic arches. Look back toward the Gothic entrance and you see a ceiling with Gothic rib-vaulting. Here was a grand and stylish setting for aristocratic house parties: designed to impress, and to prompt emotions of admiration.

Narrative art allows comparable analyses. Some literature is labeled as sentimental, designed to elicit easily triggered responses. Much so-called genre fiction is of this kind. Collingwood would call it magic. The thriller, for instance, is designed to elicit fear, which will at last be reassuringly relieved (Vorderer, 1996). The romance novel is designed to take readers for a ride on wish-fulfilling fantasies of the ideal sexual partner. We have ready schemas to assimilate such patterns. But, as with visual art, some fiction is designed to challenge schemas. This has become almost a game: One person announces some schematic principle; writers then defy it. Aristotle (c. 330 B.C.) says a story has a beginning, middle, and end; Edgar Allan Poe in his story "The Cask of Amontillado" (1846) defies this prescription by offering a story with no beginning, not much middle, and only really an end, which is nonetheless emotionally chilling. With narrative there is also something else: in the edifices of fiction readers meet mentally with people they would never have met in their ordinary lives (Booth, 1983; Oatley, 1999a). When one picks up a novel or goes to the theater, one passes Alice-like through a looking glass, not just into a building but also into a whole world of the story. In the meetings that occur are possibilities of all the emotions of relationship, with characters or narrator. Because these are the reader's emotions, the reader constructs, just as the writer does, a world of expanding meaning to explore and explain these emotions.

## The Romantic View as a Psychological Hypothesis

In the history of art, romanticism was and continues to be a movement. In science, we could see it as a hypothesis with several tenets that go like this. Art is interpersonal communication by means of cultural objects, a creative (or imaginative) expression in various media such as music, paint, stone, or words. It typically has the object of exploring not just properties of the outer world (such as its beauty) but also the emotions that prompted the creation. Although emotions of everyday life prompt ephemeral responses, emotion-prompted artistic objects last for extended periods and/or reach an extended public who may explore the emotional experiences that arise from them in ways that are comparable to those of the artist. An aspect of the romantic hypothesis is that just as emotions often occur suddenly and unexpectedly, art typically comes to the artistic genius, an emotionally sensitive person, in a moment of inspiration.

The question arises as to how to explore this hypothesis. To do so, we should relax Collingwood's criteria and regard art as including creativity, but not necessarily as excluding craft, entertainment, and social magic. Although the relation of emotions to art is universally recognized, and includes the notion that aesthetics are emotion-based preferences, and although empirical study of the arts is extensive, empirical exploration of emotional issues within it is patchy. In this section I mention five methods that have been used to explore the creativity of art in relation to the romantic hypothesis.

The first method is psycho-biography together with study of the genesis of particular works of art. One tenet of the romantic hypothesis that has been tested is the idea of inspiration and its related idea of the genius to whom the inspiration occurs. In 1877 the American painter James McNeill Whistler had exhibited paintings that he called "nocturnes," and he priced each at 200 guineas. Though these paintings are now seen as extraordinarily beautiful, the art critic John Ruskin, an arbiter of Victorian taste, wrote, "I never expected to hear a coxcomb ask two hundred guineas for flinging a pot of paint in the public's face." Whistler sued him for libel. In the case, when it was put to Whistler: "For two days' labour you ask two hundred guineas?" he replied: "No, I ask it for the knowledge of a lifetime" (Gombrich, 1972b, p. 423). As every biographer of an artist has shown, what "knowledge of a lifetime" means is the artist devoting him or herself ceaselessly to his or her chosen art form over a long period.

Many studies have now shown that expertise in any field needs the devotion of at least 10,000 hours to the domain of interest (Chi, Glaser, & Farr, 1988). This works out as 3 hours a day for 10 years, or 10 hours a day for 3 years, and it is not just a matter of putting in the time. The time must be spent in the creative solution of problems in the domain. This is just as true of artistic expression of emotions as it is for other kinds of creativity. Gardner (e.g., 1997) has brought biographical study of exceptional people, including artists, strongly into psychology and derived some important principles. Among these are that in the apprenticeship to one's art, one of the most important principles is learning to learn from failures, of both technical and emotional kinds.

Nor does any single work spring fully formed into the mind, as Coleridge encouraged people to think in his 1816 account of the composition of *Kubla Khan* (discussed earlier). Coleridge's account of his poem appearing in a dream became famous in literary studies and in the psychology of creativity (e.g., Perkins, 1981). Coleridge was interested in dreams. His account was published 20 years after the poem's composition in 1797. An undated, but more recently discovered account in Coleridge's handwriting shows striking differences: in this other account the "anodyne" was two grains of opium taken to treat dysentery, and instead of a dream the idea came in a "reverie"—that is, while awake (Schneider, 1953). Opium was the albatross of Coleridge's poem, "The Rime of the Ancient Mariner," enormously destructive to him in the latter part of his life. Moreover, another version of "Kubla Khan" exists, and the published version seems to be the later one, making the handwritten version a draft.

I have argued here that the principal difference between art and facial or vocal emotional expression is that art has external form and persists in time. Thus the artist can indeed revise and improve the work. He or she alternates roles of creator and audience. Typical is Jane Austen, who put at least some of her novels through several drafts. *Pride and Prejudice* is the novel in which Austen (1813) developed her distinctive ironic voice of narration, which Harding (1940) called "regulated hatred" of the conditions of middle-class women of her time. Only with the invention of such a style could she have produced the best opening sentence of any novel in English: "It is a truth universally acknowledged, that a single man in possession

of a good fortune, must be in want of a wife." Her family remembers earlier versions of the novel, previously called *First Impressions*, as letters between characters, a form typical of the late 18th century, which could not have lent itself to the effects she achieved in *Pride and Prejudice*.

So there are two circles of iteration. The outer circle is of experimentation in the domain: learning from others (see Weisberg, 1986; Gardner, 1997), trial, error, and the feedback of interested friends, and from oneself in the role of reader or spectator. Tomalin (1997) describes this experimentation as starting for Jane Austen at age 12, when she began reading drafts of her writing to her large, literary-minded, family. A number of her juvenilia survive, and they let us see how she compiled the "knowledge of a lifetime" of which Whistler spoke. The inner circle is of iteration on any particular work, such as the drafts of *Pride and Prejudice*. Some writers, perhaps most famously Keats, have been able to write at breathless speed. Evidence for this is that Keats's first mature poem, the sonnet "On First Looking into Chapman's Homer," was written in a very short time to express the excitement of discovery. What seems to be his original manuscript exists with the sonnet rhyming scheme sketched in the margin, and just one word changed. Keats is thought to have composed it mentally in the early hours of the morning on his way home after reading Chapman's translation of Homer with a friend (Motion, 1998). At this time, just before his 21st birthday, Keats had been writing poetry for only 3 years, and had been experimenting with the sonnet form for just a few months. The norm is a long period of experiment and reconceptualization on any single work, which tends to include sketches, drafts, and redrafts. There are 15 extant versions of the opening scene of Tolstoy's *War and Peace* (Feuer, 1996).

The same principle holds for painting. In January 1937, the Spanish government in exile commissioned Picasso to make a mural for their pavilion at the World's Fair in Paris, where he was living. Aided by Picasso's habit of numbering and dating all his work, we have a record of the creation of that mural. On April 26, a large force of fascist Junkers and Heinkel bombers bombed the Basque civilian town of Guernica, with 10,000 population, and reduced it to flames and rubble, while Heinkel fighters strafed people trying to escape into the fields. Five days later Picasso started sketches for his mural. If *The Waste Land* is the 20th century's great poem, then *Guernica* is its great painting: an expression of the anguish of the murderous proclivity we humans have for annihilating members of other groups. Arnheim (1971) traces the genesis of the whole work and shows all 45 of the sketches made over 5 weeks of preparation, as well as seven photographs of the mural in progress.

Iteration in outer and inner circles is more typical than flashes of inspiration, and the idea of genius is more a mark of social respect than a descriptive concept. For all artists who have been studied in detail, compelling emotional attachment has been found—an obsessive interest in the work that we might properly call being in love with it.

A second method is systematic interviews with artists and other creative people. Csikszentmihalyi (1996) and his students interviewed 91 exceptional individuals, including artists. He ended with recommendations that include the idea that to become truly creative one should undertake self-monitoring to discover what one loves and hates in one's life, and concentrate on what one loves.

A third method is to ask people to think aloud while performing a task. This method was used by Catherine Patrick (1937) with 50 visual artists and 50 nonartists asked to draw in response to a poem. (This repeated a similar study by Patrick, on poets writing in response to a picture.) Before the age of the tape recorder, she took shorthand of her subjects thinking aloud. Most of her analysis is of stages of composition, and she confirms in her 100 subjects the conclusion that I drew earlier: that externalization allows revision. Recent research on thinking aloud makes it clear that experts in literature (those who have put in the 10,000 hours or so in the domain of interest) have more elaborate and useful schemas than beginners, which inform them as to what kinds of features to concentrate on in order to make sense of, for instance, a 17th-century poem (e.g., Peskin, 1998). They also have ways of comprehending wholes and their internal structure, rather than proceeding phrase by phrase (Graves & Frederickson, 1995). Since reading in an aspect of writing, such studies contribute to our understanding of expression. Ghent (1989) had three pianists, one international performer and two university piano students, think aloud while preparing a piece that was a transcription of Balinese gamelan music, which was unfamiliar to them. The expert found this an emotionally taxing task. He treated the problem in terms of a number of nonobvious goals: He was anxious about the problem as a whole, about creating finger movements like the xylophone-type instruments of the original music, and about not going cognitively so fast that what he called his "kinaesthetic" learning could not keep up. The task he set himself was to go beyond the safely comfortable, to transform his current knowledge, to accommodate his existing schemas. By contrast, one of the students simply assimilated the piece to what he already knew—French impressionist music—and was happy not to extend himself. His performance was judged by an ethnomusicologist to sound like Western music. Though this example is musical, the conclusion is general. Transformation of knowledge rather than reproduction of knowledge is, as argued by Ribot (1906), close to the heart of creativity.

A fourth method is experimentation. Lundholm (1921) had eight people who were not artists draw lines to express emotional adjectives. *Exciting, furious,* and *powerful* all prompted the drawing of straight lines with angles between them. *Sad, lazy,* and *merry* gave rise to curved lines. Eindhoven and Vinacke (1952) asked 13 artists and 14 nonartists to create a picture in response to a poem, within one to four laboratory sessions. Their activities were categorized and timed. The researchers studied the materials produced, and found artists experimented more than the nonartists and displayed a wider range of methods.

A fifth method is content analysis. One of the most interesting studies of this kind is by Haviland (1984), who studied Virginia Woolf's writings from childhood, adolescence, and adulthood. She found that specific emotions, and the juxtaposition of the ecstatic and despairing, as well as emotional themes to which Woolf had a lifelong attachment such as loss and the need for control, were formed into a fairly well-defined schema that informed her fiction.

There is a growing body of literature in which creativity in the arts, using such methods, is treated alongside creativity in other areas (e.g., Perkins, 1981). Emphasis in this field is mostly on whether there are or are not stages of creative work (preparation, incubation, insight or illumination, verification-plus-revision). It would, however, not be difficult for researchers to add affective considerations, as has Gruber (1995) in his studies of the creativity of Darwin and Piaget.

Overall, empirical work on creativity, using various methods, has replaced the romantic idea of inspiration with the idea of people who have a strong attachment to their work that can best be described as emotional, who invest huge amounts of time to create elaborate schemas, within which they can be creative in a chosen domain. This research confirms what Martha Graham said: "The difference between the artist and the non-artist is not the greater capacity for feeling. The secret is that the artist can objectify, can make apparent the feelings we all have" (Gardner, 1993, p. 298). This research contradicts, also, Collingworth's dismissive attitude toward craft. Technical aspects tend to preoccupy artists more than emotional issues, perhaps because of the need to objectify. To be truly creative, not just for oneself but for a sophisticated audience, one must know a domain deeply and move beyond the known. When the medium is mastered, emotional issues do arise: They include the emotional courage to transform one's knowledge, to extend oneself beyond one's limits, and insofar as one's goals are emotional, to tackle them in hitherto unexplored ways.

As well as the interest of this empirical work on art, there is a deeper issue. If art is (or includes) the expression (objectification) not just of specific emotions but also of a family of emotional concerns—preoccupations with identity, attachment to unique individuals who may be lost, the destructive repercussions of revenge, the understanding of others and their emotional idiosyncracies, the relation of humankind to the accidents of life—then as psychologists we do not want merely to test the underlying hypothesis as to whether art expresses emotions. Instead, we should take seriously what Isadora Duncan said: "If I could say it, I wouldn't have to dance it (Gardner, 1982, p. 90).

Thus, as well as conducting empirical studies of the emotions of art, we need to consider the enduring objects of art as valuable in our explorations of emotions. Linguistics uses oral and written utterances to understand syntax, semantics, and pragmatics. Researchers on emotions have the world of visual art and literature by which we can begin to understand the deeper human emotional concerns. To see art in this way means attuning oneself to the voices and the emotions within works of art. Such a program would have the additional effect of bringing psychology close to art criticism, as it was for Aristotle. In the last part of this chapter, therefore, I offer a preliminary approach to such a program, by considering the emotional implications of specific works of painting, architecture, and fiction, together with empirical analysis.

## Three Art Forms: Painting, Architecture, Fiction

### Painting

The earliest paintings of humankind that we know are at Chauvet, in France, estimated by carbon dating of charcoal used in them to be some 31,000 years old. The Chauvet cave, found in 1994 (*www.culture.fr/culture/arcnat/chauvet/en/recherche.htm*), is one of a substantial number of caves in France and Spain found since four teenagers in 1940 rediscovered the caves at Lascaux (Bataille, 1955). In every discussion of cave paintings, at least one speculation about their significance is necessary. We read of sympathetic magic to aid the hunt, we read dark hints of religious rituals. Visual art is widespread in human cultures around the world; some is frightening, much of it is strikingly beautiful. Although we can speculate, often we do not know what emotions prompted the artist, or what the emotions might have been among the art's intended recipients. What we can say is that at Chauvet the majority of the pictures (62%) are of frightening animals such as mammoths, rhinoceroses, lions, and bears. From the bones recovered from living sites, we know these were not animals used for food at that time.

In visual art, the romantic period started in England at the end of the 18th century with William Blake's visionary engravings that accompany his poetry, and with the great age of landscape painting begun by J. M. W. Turner—see, for instance, Turner's series of landscapes from his six visits to Rousseau's homeland, Switzerland (Russell & Wil-

ton, 1976), and John Constable's scenes of rustic life and landscape in East Anglia, England. Landscape painting of this period is covered by Appleton (1975), who drew from his study of it the themes of refuge and prospect. In France the acknowledged leader of romantic painters, reacting against the classicism of Jacques David and his followers, was Eugène Delacroix, whose themes were similar to those of romantic poets and included revolutionary political scenes. At least some of the ideals of romanticism were held in common among visual, literary, and musical artists in the 19th century.

I will first consider a painting from an earlier period, the high Renaissance, for which we have an idea of what the artist intended in relation to the emotions because we know of his plans. This painter is Sandro Botticelli (1444–1510), born in Florence, the youngest son of a tanner. His biography appears in Vasari's (1568) unique work, *The Lives of the Artists*. The painting is one of Botticelli's two most famous: *The Primavera* (Spring), at present in the Ufizzi in Florence, which depicts Venus, Flora, and some other figures. Reproductions of this and others of his paintings can be seen in many books (e.g., Ettlinger & Ettlinger, 1976). Research on the symbolism of *The Primavera* has been done by Gombrich (1972a), and it is upon that research I draw.

*The Primavera* was conceived and painted about 1477–1478 in partnership with Marsilio Ficino, the leading literary figure in Florence at the time, who had translated and introduced Greek classics into Italian culture. Ficino was employed by Florence's powerful Medici banking family, as tutor of the adolescent Lorenzo di Pierfrancesco de' Medici. Ficino arranged for Botticelli, to whom the Medici family was patron, to paint a picture for the young Lorenzo's villa, and he wrote a long letter to Lorenzo that Gombrich argues accompanied the painting, and that explains its significance:

> The astrologers have it that he is the happiest man for whom Fate has so disposed the heavenly signs that Luna [the moon] is in no bad aspect to Mars and Saturn, that furthermore she is in favourable aspect to Sol [the sun] and Jupiter, Mercury and Venus. . . . We must not look for these matters outside ourselves, for all the heavens are within us and the fiery vigour in us testifies to our heavenly origin. . . . Onward then, great minded youth . . . dispose your own heavens. (Gombrich, 1972a, p. 41)

And Ficino describes how the young man should arrange the different aspects of his personality within his own self, his Luna (the soul) in relation to Sol (God), Jupiter (justice), Mars, and so forth. Finally, he says, and this is the subject of the painting, he should fix the eye of his soul

on Venus herself, that is to say on Humanity . . . a
nymph of excellent comeliness born of heaven and
more than others beloved of God all highest. Her
soul and mind are Love and Charity . . . if you
were to unite with her in wedlock and claim her
as yours she would make all your years sweet and
make you the father of fine children. (p. 42)

With the revolutionary daring of the Renaissance, the
amoral Greco-Roman lust-goddess Venus has become love
and charity (humanity), the key to a worthwhile life. The
ancient gods and astrological influences mingle with ideas
of the Jewish-Christian God and of the idea that became
powerful at that time, and has remained with us since, that
beauty (comeliness) offers a glimpse of truth. Most important of all is the idea of the soul in charge of its own des-
tiny. Botticelli's picture, which he had discussed with Ficino, shows Venus with head slightly inclined. On her left
are the three Graces and Mercury. On her right is Flora
strewing flowers and a nymph (probably a different aspect
of Venus) being pursued by the wind. The other famous
painting by Botticelli from this same period had a similar
theme: Venus standing in a conch-shell, rising from the
waves. Botticelli painted this for the same villa of the
young Lorenzo de' Medici.

Here, then, is art with the conscious intention to be
beautiful, to attract and to engage the mind of the beholder
in contemplation of its subject matter. Here, moreover, is
art with an explicit program of exhorting the viewer to
dispose his own emotions—love, anger, and so forth—in
relation to each other in order to live a good life, a theme
as significant today as 500 years ago. In this pre-romantic
work the emphasis is not on the emotions or creativity of
the artist, but on the relationship of care and tutelage between the creators of the work—Botticelli and Ficino—
and its recipient, a young man at the threshold of adult
sexuality, and on the emotions of this young man.

I now move forward nearly 400 years to an impressionist painter and engraver. About the emotions in her pictures, we can only guess. But because she is chronologi-
cally close to us, we have a good chance of guessing
correctly. The artist is Mary Cassatt (1844–1926), who
along with Whistler and Winslow Homer, is among the
most important of American painters.

Cassatt was from a close and well-to-do family (Love,
1980). After art school in Philadelphia, she lived in France
and began exhibiting with the impressionists in 1879, the
only American to be a full member of the impressionist
group. Her work includes oils, pastels, and a set of prints
of great beauty and technical inventiveness (Mathews &
Shapiro, 1989). She had close relationships, especially
with her mother and a circle of women in the art world.
She had somewhat less close relationships with men, who
included the irascible Edgar Degas, her principal artistic

influence. The question of whether Cassatt had sexual relationships with anyone is a subject for speculation. She
is one of those artists of the 19th century for whom ideas
of romanticism—autonomy, equality, life in art—came
into being among womankind as well as mankind.

Cassatt had no children, and there is not much indication that she wanted any. Her selfhood was in her art.
But she introduced into painting the subject of being with
children, being with other women in conversation, going
on family outings. A recurrent subject in her work is a
middle-class mother, sometimes looking meditatively into
the middle distance, and in her lap a naked child. The
topic of mother and child was not new: The subject of
Mary with the naked baby Jesus is one of the most frequent
of later medieval and Renaissance painting. But there the
treatment was intended for contemplation, internalization,
reflection (themes for which Botticelli's *Primavera* was a
secularized version). With Cassatt the subject matter
changes utterly. It becomes the intense relationship of love
between woman and infant. Frequently this is caught in a
gesture of the most ephemeral kind. In one pastel picture,
for instance (*Baby's First Caress*, ca. 1890, in the New Brit-
ain Museum of American Art in Connecticut, color reproductions in Love, 1980, plate 11; and in Mathews & Shapiro, 1989, p. 139), the baby, perhaps a 1-year-old, looks
toward the mother, reaches with one hand up to her face,
covers her mouth, and pushes into her cheek slightly with
a little finger. The mother receives it, knowing the child
is comfortable in her containing arms and wants to touch
her face, even though the gesture is not comfortable for
her. The baby cannot achieve the caress that will—if all
goes well—be the gentler touch of a more mature love.
Here we glimpse not just the nursery but also the nursery
of Western middle-class culture, in which family and emotional relationships with children have come, through the
changes wrought in the years since Rousseau, to the center
of our modern identity (Taylor, 1989).

Cassatt depicted a world of women and expresses its
emotions (men are largely absent). Within that world she
chose to concentrate on motherhood. In her pictures are
the intimacy and informality learned from Degas, along
with his idea of portraying, not the poses of previous art,
but "the more subtle emotions characteristic of modern
life" (Reff, 1976, p. 147). Cassatt's pictures are scenes of
affection in which typically there is also conflict, such as
the mother with her baby shoving at her face. They are
scenes of women's negotiations of the emotions. Naked
toddlers, in the proper romantic fashion—unclothed, un-
fettered, natural—begin to discover their power, in scenes
of cultural embryology, that Dinnerstein (1976) would
later discuss in terms of that wonderful title: *The Rocking
of the Cradle and the Ruling of the World*.

I discussed work on empirical aesthetics previously.
Let me here give a coda: Cupchik and Winston (1992) have

argued that some artworks (among which one could name Cassatt's pictures) prompt viewers to reflect on the meaning of emotions depicted and elicited by them, and to think about the works interpretively. Thus, psychologist Cupchik and sculptor Shereck (1998) had visitors to a gallery view four of Shereck's sculptures that were groups of two or three figures, with strong emotional themes including childbirth and domination of one person by another. Viewers' responses were predominantly emotional at first. On a second viewing intellectual interpretive activity predominated. The study of responses to visual art parallels the growing interest in reader-response studies of literature. Emotional responses have been demonstrated, but a comprehensive account of the relations between emotions and personally meaningful interpretive activity of viewers has yet to be fully developed.

## Architecture

Towns and cities began to be built some 10,000 years ago. Their archeology is the record of that enormous social revolution from groups of seminomadic gatherer-scavenger-hunters to groups who live in fixed habitations. Now, rather than living almost exclusively with a small group of people we know well, we, astonishingly, live in cities alongside others whom we do not know at all.

I have already discussed some of the ideas and effects of the romantic movement in architecture (the coming of consciously constructed styles, the coming of landscape gardening). In this section, I concentrate on the time of the advent of new materials, when mass transit and then the automobile threatened to make the city center obsolete, and when the electric elevator made possible the skyscraper. I concentrate, moreover, on two architects, both of whom had enormous influence.

Frank Lloyd Wright (1867–1959) is by general consent America's greatest architect (Smith, 1998). Although he designed projects of every kind, it is houses such as those he designed for himself that epitomize his architecture. Here is an excerpt from his son John's description of the family house at Oak Park, Illinois, built in 1889–1890.

> Amid patriarch trees on the low-rolling land . . .
> Frank Lloyd Wright conceived something new in
> the building of his time. . . . Horizontal lines,
> double-leveled rooms of one and two stories, scattered vases filled with leaves and wild flowers,
> massive fireplaces seemed to be everywhere.
> (Wright, 1994, p. 15)

Ideally, Wright's family houses were set on their own pieces of land and became part of the natural environment that the land afforded. They were large and light but intimate; their windows afforded prospect. They were marked by horizontals that reflected the spaciousness of American life and landscape. Their extended roof overhangs imitated the effects of shading trees. Like the houses of the other great innovative architect of the period, Charles Rennie Macintosh, who worked in Scotland, exterior and interior design were integrated: Chairs, tables, interior spaces, and motifs combined elegant geometry with stems, leaves, flowers, and lots of wood.

Wright's accomplishment was to provide settings for the family, often in suburbia, that were functional for the new kind of middle-class nuclear families—mother, father, and two, three, or four children—which came into being at the beginning of the 20th century. These families had appliances and automobiles rather than servants and horses. They lived perhaps with a grandmother but seldom with a large extended family. The houses had kitchens in which a homemaker could prepare food, playrooms for the children, dining rooms in which the rituals of family meals could be enacted, living rooms for the family symbolically to gather round the hearth. At the same time they reflected artistic movements of the time and drew on the beauty of nature. It was in such settings that modern, well-to-do Americans would find their versions of the individuality and selfhood that Rousseau had foreseen a century and a half earlier. Here is the refuge of which Appleton wrote, evolved over 10,000 years. Here is the house that will be home, or that will disappoint.

"The house is a machine for living in." So announced Le Corbusier (1923, p. 4). He was born in Switzerland in 1887, just as Wright was beginning his work. He moved to France and founded what is known as the "international" style of architecture. Influenced by cubism, he was a painter and visionary. With facile and glittering penmanship, working in blocks and spaces, he was thought of as the Picasso of architecture. He was also a writer of grace and persuasiveness. If you want a vision from the perspective of 1923 on the new world of skyscrapers, automobiles, and airplanes, with its flowing functional lines of mass construction—the urban world we now inhabit—you could do no better than to read his writings. His idea that was so influential was called "Radiant City," introduced in the 1920s. The plan was for a dream city designed to retain the high population densities of urban living by means of 24 skyscrapers, and at the same time to designate 95% of the space as recreational parkland. Here is what he wrote:

> Suppose we are entering the city by way of the
> Great Park. Our fast car takes the special elevated
> motor track between the majestic skyscrapers: as
> we approach nearer, there is seen the repetition
> against the sky of the twenty-four sky-scrapers; to
> our left and right on the outskirts of each particular area are the municipal and administrative pub-

lic buildings; and enclosing the space are the museums and university buildings. The whole city is a park. (Jacobs, 1961, p. 31)

Notice the romantic ideal of nature as parkland. Notice the continuation of landscape gardening from the late 18th century, but now for the masses rather than for a few aristocrats. Notice the plan, which comes from inside the artist's head to outside in the world. Notice, too, the progressive cause: Cities of the older kind were seen as overcrowded, dirty, and diseased. As Le Corbusier said, with sweeping gesture, "Cafes and places for recreation would no longer be that fungus which eats up the pavements of Paris; they would be transferred to the flat roofs" (Le Corbusier, 1923, p. 60). And so with everything that would disrupt the elegant line or interfere with the sculptured parkland or impede the flow of traffic.

> ARCHITECTURE is a thing of art, a phenomenon of the emotions, lying outside questions of construction and beyond them. The purpose of construction is TO MAKE THINGS HOLD TOGETHER; of architecture TO MOVE US. Architectural emotion exists when the work rings within us in tune with a universe whose laws we obey, recognize and respect. (Le Corbusier, 1923, p. 19)

This quotation could have come from Jefferson, thinking of his design for the Virginia State Capitol. Le Corbusier's ideas were eagerly adopted by city planners and architects. Here are the words of an important American architect, Philip Johnson:

> We really believed, in a quasi religious sense, in the perfectibility of human nature, in the role of architecture as a weapon of social reform . . . the coming Utopia when everyone would live in cheap prefabricated flat-roofed multiple dwellings—heaven on earth. (Coleman, 1985, p. 3)

The dream was of abolishing slums and squalor, of providing ordinary people with affordable housing, with plumbing and sanitation, set among parklike areas in which sports and recreation would be on everyone's doorsteps. Radiant City is not without appeal. I recently visited Canberra, the capital of Australia, a completely planned and beautiful city, built with modern materials and situated in parkland around a lake. One glides in from the airport in a fast car, as Le Corbusier imagined. Here are the administrative buildings, here the museums, here the university, and there, zoned away from the public buildings, are the residential areas.

The important empirical investigations of emotional effects of architecture are rather different from those on aesthetics. They began to be made on the new town planning that flourished in the United States before World War II, and in Europe after it. The studies began because something went wrong with Le Corbusier's Radiant City. Oscar Newman (1972) and Jane Jacobs (1961) in New York and other American cities, and Alice Coleman (1985) in England, showed that what may be fine for offices and administrative buildings was not so good for most ordinary people. Architectural dream and built reality did not match. Town planners pulled down houses. They rehoused people. They had a theory of a romantic kind. Or, rather, it was not so much that they had a theory as they were in the grip of one. What is more, they had the political power to act on it, to become artists of the new city spaces of our time.

Newman (1972) studied all the public housing projects in New York City, which included 4,000 apartment buildings. He chose as a test measure the levels of crime and vandalism associated with each one. He was able to do this because New York had a special housing police force, 1,600 strong, that kept excellent records of what crimes occurred and exactly where—a light smashed in the ground floor lobby of such and such a building. His aim was to correlate the occurrence of vandalism and crime with design features of the buildings. He identified three main features. First, anonymity: Though impressive from the windows of a fast car, the high-rise apartment building is typically impersonal. Communities fail to develop and criminals can walk in and out of them, secure in the knowledge that they will not be confronted. Anonymity increased as more people used the same entrance, and increased too with the number of stories in a building. Second, lack of surveillance: Newman found that crime increased with the number of spaces, such as interior corridors, that were not observable from the windows of any apartment or from the street. Also, entrances that were set back were vulnerable. This principle that surveillance makes a difference to crime fits directly with the work of Orians and his colleagues (discussed previously) on the importance of being able to look out and survey what is happening outside. It is likely that our triumph over animal predators (cf. the Chauvet cave paintings) has been fundamentally important to human psychology (Ehrenreich, 1997). Braudel (1979) has shown how cities solved problems of defending against dangerous animals (though wolves survive in nursery stories). What Radiant City made worse was the potential for attack by human predators. Third, as exits multiplied (several external doors to a building, alternative access to elevators), so did crime: Criminals were more successful if they had many escape routes. People were frightened to live in such buildings, and frightened to step outside them.

Community was the issue that Jacobs (1961) studied in her book *The Death and Life of Great American Cities.* She found that zoning areas as industrial, commercial, or residential has been the death of huge amounts of American city space. Nonresidential zones, when not in use, are deserted by ordinary people but inhabited by human predators. By contrast, in city areas with mixed use and with a continuous life on the streets—markets, shops, apartments, commercial buildings—people keep an eye on things. Communities form, which opportunistic criminals cannot easily penetrate.

The most thorough empirical investigation of such effects has been by Coleman (1985), who studied local authority (public) housing in England, mostly in London: 4,099 apartment buildings and 4,172 houses and converted houses. Coleman's team used six measures: (1) litter, including decaying and uncollected garbage; (2) urine; (3) feces; (4) graffiti; (5) damage by vandalism; and (6) the number of children who had been taken into care (that is, who were removed from their families by the social services department of the local authority because of the parents' inability to care for them or to control them). Coleman's team correlated these measures with features of building design. Measures (1) to (5) signal emotions of disdainful neglect—opposites of the loving concern people lavish on their gardens and the interiors of their homes. Measure (6) is a sign of deeper emotional disintegration.

Coleman found that in London, Radiant City had been little short of a disaster. Houses were consistently better than apartment blocks on all measures of socioemotional well-being. As Coleman writes, in houses: "Litter is less common, graffiti extremely rare, and excrement virtually unheard of. Vandal damage may occur where houses are adjacent to flats [apartment buildings], but children are taken into care much less often" (pp. 170–171). She confirmed that the features discovered by Newman were associated with high scores on social disintegration: large size of blocks, anonymity, lack of surveillance, and other comparable features. She found also that as the social disintegration score for buildings increased so did the frequency of crime, including burglary, theft, criminal damage, and bodily harm. She concludes that no more high-rise apartment blocks should be built as public housing.

Whereas in painting and sculpture, meetings of artist with spectator can take their course, with architecture the roles of artist and what computer people call the "end user" are more peremptory. Though romanticism offered the idea of art as moving us emotionally, it also offered the idea of individuality and choice, which in the public housing movement was disregarded. New materials and new artistic ideas are not all. From the archeology and history of earlier periods we have building designs that we can infer from their longevity have provided settings in which human well-being can grow. We should learn from this history.

## Fiction as Mental Simulation

The telling of stories occurs in all societies, and one might imagine that it is almost as old as human conversation, from which it no doubt grew. Narrative, as Bruner (1986) has argued, is the distinctive mental mode by which we understand human action. The invention of the Greek amphitheater, capable of seating almost the whole of the local community, afforded public forums for fiction. The invention of writing and then of printing ensured that stories could be given more or less permanent form and distributed to people everywhere. With the invention of film and television, fiction reaches even more people in even more everywheres.

Theater was discussed by Aristotle (c. 330 B.C.) in a book that combines literary criticism and psychology. It introduced the idea of narrative art as *mimesis*. The novel is almost as old as Greek theater, though with perhaps more demotic roots (Doody, 1997). It is the form that, in the 250 years of romanticism, has been at the center of discussions of literary art. This period has seen the Western world's great novelists, who include Jane Austen, Herman Melville, Gustave Flaubert, George Eliot, Leo Tolstoy, James Joyce, Virginia Woolf, and Franz Kafka. Perhaps the best treatment of romanticism within literary criticism is by Abrams (1953).

Narrative is that mode of speech, writing, and understanding in which a protagonist with a goal acts upon it and thereby encounters vicissitudes. Fictional narrative, such as the novel, gives priority to the emotions that the protagonist experiences as a result of the vicissitudes, as well as to the emotions of the reader.

Fiction, as I have argued (Oatley, 1999b), is not the opposite of fact. It is a type of simulation that runs not on computers but on minds or, as Robert Louis Stevenson (1888) said, it is a kind of imaginative dream. These ideas of simulation or dream offer far better understandings of Aristotle's concept of *mimesis* than more usual translations, such as "imitation." In a literary simulation, we insert ourselves into the goal-plan-action-event-emotion structures of fictional characters. In this we do not simply interpret; we enact the story, we give an inner performance of it. By so doing we bring these characters into being, within the fictional worlds they inhabit. We accomplish this feat by emotional identification with a protagonist and by sympathetic emotions for story characters.

Computer simulations are nowadays used to understand the effects of multiple processes that interact with each other. For instance, current predictions about global warming are based on computer simulations. The social doings of ourselves and others are the most interesting of all matters to us. These, too, involve multiple processes that interact in complex and not quite predictable ways, so that they need simulations for understanding; the simulations that we prefer run not on computers but on minds.

Playgoers enter specially designed buildings to experience drama. And for a novel to come alive, to afford meetings with fictional characters, it is as if the reader, too, enters a building. Goffman (1961) has shown how entering any social interaction has some such properties: It is like passing through a semipermeable membrane into a distinctive world within. The membrane allows persons in, and it contains the transformations of self into enactments that occur inside. As readers or audience members start to run the simulation and create the performance of the piece of fiction, they take on new aspects of self, as they identify with, experience sympathy for, and have their memories resonate with what goes on in the fiction.

Emotions of assimilation to schemas, and accommodation of these schemas discussed in relation to visual art, can occur, but they are accompanied by other modes of emotional experience distinctive to fictional narrative. Emotions of these kinds fall out readily from the theory of simulation (Oatley, 1994). They are of three main kinds.

## Emotions of Identification

Oatley and Gholamain (1997) proposed that part of the mind on which the reader (or audience) runs the simulation of a novel, play, or film is the planning processor. Ordinarily, we use it in conjunction with our mental models of the world to assemble actions into plans to attain goals—for instance, to book a ticket and take a train journey. By contrast, in reading a story, the plot takes over the planning processor. We tend to identify with a protagonist, adopt his or her goals, take on his or her plans. We then experience emotions as events, and outcomes of actions are evaluated in relation to the protagonist's goals. But here is the extraordinary feature: Although the goals and plans are simulated, the emotions are not. They are the reader's own.

## Emotions of Sympathy

For the emotions of sympathy, the writer offers appraisal patterns (as T. S. Eliot would say, objective correlatives). A reader knows how these patterns would affect story characters, and therefore feels sympathetic emotions toward these characters. This kind of effect is especially clear in film, but occurs also in novels and plays (Tan, 1996).

## Emotional Memories

Emotions also derive from the author's prompting autobiographical memories in the reader or audience member who becomes attuned to a narrative. A loss in a piece of fiction, for instance, will tend consciously or unconsciously to elicit memories of our own losses. So as Scheff (1979) points out, when we cry at the fate of Romeo and Juliet, we are crying not for them but over losses of our own, which continue to affect us.

Let me now discuss three pieces of recent fiction.

The short story "Brokeback Mountain" by Annie Proulx (1999) is of two men who are members of that fabled class of Americans, cowboys, but neither sentimentalized nor gun toting. Their life is physically hard, and they are lonely. Their speech is limited not by the laconic conventionalities of the Hollywood tough guy; they have little education and not much skill with words. They solve their loneliness by beginning a sexual relationship when sleeping out on a bare mountain as they tend their cattle. The relationship is barely acknowledged by them at first. Then it comes to become more central, competing with marriage, competing too with their own prejudices against exactly the kind of relationship they are conducting. Toward the end of the story, one of the men is killed, battered to death, probably with a tire iron, probably because someone in the community suspects him of homosexuality.

*Titanic* is a film by James Cameron (1997), which won Oscars for best film and best director. It is a story of a working-class boy (an artist, as it happens) and a rich girl, on the voyage of *Titanic* from Southampton to New York in 1911. They fall in love, and this is stuff of the most usual kind. What makes the film unusual is its mythlike treatment of the idea that in a love relationship not only can a lover wake a person as from a kind of sleep, but that something of a loved one becomes part of the self. When that person dies he (or she) continues to live on in the other—not just as a memory, but as part of the self. Just as we pass parts of our physical selves forward in time, joining these parts (sperm and ova) with those of a partner, so we pass parts of our psychological selves forward to become part of the personality of another.

At the beginning of the novel *The Reader*, by Bernard Schlink (1997), the narrator, an adolescent boy in Germany, falls in love with an older woman, whom he discovers is a tram conductor. As the woman introduces him to the world of sexuality, he reads novels to her. Later he becomes a lawyer, and at the Nuremberg trials recognizes her as a defendant. She has been in the SS and is responsible for burning a large number of Jewish people locked in a church. The shock at the center of the novel is the discovery that the woman is illiterate; the reading of novels was her entry into the larger world of culture.

These three pieces of fiction explore the problematic of love. In Western society love is regarded as the most important of our emotions, the one that gives meaning to life. At the same time it is full of paradox, which presses its issues beyond the border of our understanding. Narrative fiction, in the form of simulation, gives us the opportunity to explore these issues. Emotions give priority to our concerns. In "Brokeback Mountain," this priority at first displaces the protagonists' own feelings about themselves; then comes into tragic conflict with society. In *Titanic*, tragedy works in the other direction: The individuality that we think is ours is extended as the protagonists become part of each other, even with the fact of death. In *The Reader*, we confront a horrifying fact of the 20th century: that we humans can fall eagerly in love with political systems dedicated to the annihilation of huge numbers of our own species; here too the prioritization given by emotions can displace all other considerations.

So, in the age of romanticism that, with the shift from external constraints to inward sources of our actions—the age which gave rise to Nietzsche's (1882) parable in which a madman goes into the marketplace looking for God, and is laughed at because God is dead and we have killed him—narrative fiction becomes one of the means by which the ethical issues of being responsive to our emotions can be explored. This is not a simple matter, not just getting in touch with one's feelings. Modern individuality had better not just be the unthinking expression of any emotion.

As to the empirical investigation of literature, a number of studies have shown that readers become emotionally engaged with stories. In questionnaire responses, children as young as 12, as well as adults, have reported a variety of emotional experiences from reading (Van den Oetelaar, Tellegen, & Wober, 1997). Larsen and Seilman (1988) introduced a method whereby a reader marked the margin of a story whenever a memory was triggered. This has been extended by having readers mark M's in the margin when memories occur, and E's when emotions are elicited. High school students reading literary short stories recorded in this way a mean of about four memories and five emotions per 4,000-word story (Oatley, 1996); using this method, it was found that many of the memories that occur when reading have emotional content. When people read narrative poetry such as Coleridge's "The Rime of the Ancient Mariner," Sikora, Miall, and Kuiken (1998) found that literary language aroused affect and that, as it did so, it prompted an enactment by the reader in which his or her mind resonated with that of the author (as Keats supposed) in reflection on existential issues. Next empirical steps in investigating the emotions of reading literary fiction or poetry might be to see whether they are associated with insights.

As one passes through the semipermeable membrane and enters the architectural interior of the story world, one performs one's own enactment of the story. In this interior space, the self can take on new forms and change, in its meetings with others. This change occurs as one both experiences emotions and reflects upon them in the contexts provided by the story. Here, then, is the potential for insight. As George Eliot—that greatest explorer of emotions in the novel—put it:

> The greatest benefit we owe to the artist, whether painter, poet or novelist, is the extension of our sympathies. Appeals founded on generalizations and statistics require a sympathy ready-made, a moral sentiment already in activity; but a picture of human life such as a great artist can give, surprises even the trivial and the selfish into that attention to what is apart from themselves, which may be called the raw material of moral sentiment.
> . . . Art is the nearest thing to life; it is a mode of amplifying experience and extending our contact with our fellow-men beyond the bounds of our personal lot. (Pinney, 1963, p. 270)

## NOTE

I gratefully acknowledge a grant from the Social Sciences and Humanities Research Council of Canada, and I also thank Kathleen Jenkins and Gerald Cupchik, who read an earlier draft of this chapter and advised me on it.

## REFERENCES

Abrams, M. H. (1953). *The mirror and the lamp: Romantic theory and the critical tradition.* Oxford, England: Oxford University Press.

Appleton, J. (1975). *The experience of landscape.* Chichester, England: Wiley.

Aristotle (1970). *Poetics* (G. E. Else, Trans.). Ann Arbor: University of Michigan Press. (Original work c. 330 B.C.).

Arnheim, R. (1949). The Gestalt theory of expression. *Psychological Review, 56,* 156–171.

Arnheim, R. (1962). *Picasso's Guernica: The genesis of a painting.* Berkeley: University of California Press.

Arnheim, R. (1971). *Visual thinking.* Berkeley: University of California Press.

Arnold, M. B., & Gasson, J. A. (1954). Feelings and emotions as dynamic factors in personality integration. In M. B. Arnold & J. A. Gasson (Eds.), *The human person* (pp. 294–313). New York: Ronald.

Austen, J. (1813/1906). *Pride and prejudice.* London: Dent.

Averill, J. R., Stanat, P., & More, T. (1998). Aesthetics and environment. *Review of General Psychology, 2,* 153–174.

Averill, J. R., & Nunley, E. P. (1992). *Voyages of the heart: Living an emotionally creative life.* New York: Free Press.

Barthes, R. (1975). *S/Z* (R. Miller, Trans.). London: Cape.

Bartlett, F. C. (1932). *Remembering: A study in experimental and social psychology.* Cambridge, England: Cambridge University Press.

Bataille, G. (1955). *Lascaux, or the birth of art.* Lausanne, Switzerland: Skira.

Berlin, I. (1990). *The crooked timber of humanity.* London: Murray.

Berlyne, D. E. (1965). Measures of aesthetic preference.

*Science de l'Art, 3*, 9–23. Reprinted in J. Hogg (Ed.), *Psychology and the visual arts* (pp. 129–145). Harmondsworth, England: Penguin, 1969.

Booth, W. C. (1983). *The rhetoric of fiction.* Chicago: University of Chicago Press.

Bowlby, J. (1971). *Attachment and loss, Volume 1. Attachment.* London: Hogarth Press.

Braudel, F. (1979). *Civilization and capitalism, 15th to 18th Century, Vol 1. The structures of everyday life: The limits of the possible* (M. Kochan & S. Reynolds, Trans.) London: Fontana.

Brettell, R. R. (1999). *Modern art 1851–1929: Capitalism and representation.* Oxford: Oxford University Press.

Bruner, J. (1986). *Actual minds, possible worlds.* Cambridge, MA: Harvard University Press.

Cameron, J. (1997). *Titanic* (film). Los Angeles: Paramount Pictures.

Chi, M. T. H., Glaser, R., & Farr, M. J. (1988). *The nature of expertise.* Hillsdale, NJ: Erlbaum.

Coleman, A. (1985). *Utopia on trial: Vision and reality in planned housing.* London: Hilary Shipman.

Collingwood, R. G. (1938). *The principles of art.* Oxford, England: Oxford University Press.

Csikszentmihalyi, M. (1996). *Creativity: Flow and the psychology of discovery and invention.* New York: HarperCollins.

Cupchik, G. (1994). Emotion in aesthetics: Reactive and reflective models. *Poetics, 23*, 177–188.

Cupchik, G. C., & Shereck, L. (1998). Generating and receiving contextualized interpretations of figural sculptures. *Empirical Studies of the Arts, 16*, 179–191.

Cupchik, G., & Winston, A. (1992). Reflection and reaction: A dual process analysis of emotional responses to art. In L. Y. Dorfman, D. A. Leontiev, V. M. Petrov, & V. A. Sozinov (Eds.), *Emotion and art: Problems, approaches, explorations* (pp. 65–77). Perm, Russia: Perm Institute for Arts and Culture.

Darwin, C. (1872/1998). *The expression of the emotions in man and animals (new edition with commentaries by P. Ekman).* New York: Oxford University Press.

Dickens, C. (1854/1969). *Hard times.* London: Penguin.

Dinnerstein, D. (1976). *The rocking of the cradle and the ruling of the world.* New York: Harper & Row.

Donald, M. (1991). *Origins of the modern mind.* Cambridge, MA: Harvard University Press.

Doody, M. A. (1997). *The true story of the novel.* London: HarperCollins.

Drabble, M. (Ed.) (1985). *The Oxford companion to English literature.* Oxford, England: Oxford University Press.

Ehrenreich, B. (1997). *Blood rites: Origins and history of the passions of war.* New York: Holt.

Eindhoven, J. E., & Vinacke, W. E. (1952). Creative processes in painting. *Journal of General Psychology, 47*, 139–164.

Eliot, G. (1965). *Middlemarch.* Baltimore: Penguin. (Original work published 1871)

Eliot, T. S. (1919/1953). Hamlet. In J. Hayward (Ed.), *T. S. Eliot: Selected prose* (pp. 104–109). Harmondsworth: Penguin.

Eliot, T. S. (1922). *The waste land.* London: Faber.

Ettlinger, L. D., & Ettlinger, H. S. (1976). *Botticelli.* London: Thames and Hudson.

Feuer, K. B. (1996). *Tolstoy and the genesis of War and Peace.* Ithaca, NY: Cornell University Press.

Freud, S. (1904/1985). Psychopathic characters on the stage. In A. Dickson (Ed.), *Pelican Freud Library, 14: Art and literature* (pp. 119–127). London: Penguin.

Frijda, N. H. (1986). *The emotions.* Cambridge, England: Cambridge University Press.

Gardner, H. (1982). *Art, mind, and brain: A cognitive approach to creativity.* New York: Basic Books.

Gardner, H. (1993). *Creating minds: An anatomy of creativity seen through the lives of Freud, Einstein, Picasso, Stravinsky, Eliot, Graham, and Gandhi.* New York: Basic Books.

Gardner, H. (1997). *Extraordinary minds: Portraits of exceptional individuals and an examination of our extraordinariness.* New York: Basic Books.

Ghent, P. R. (1989). *Expert learning in music.* MA thesis, University of Toronto.

Gibson, J. J. (1950). *The perception of the visual world.* Boston: Houghton Mifflin.

Goethe, J. W. v. (1774/1989). *The sorrows of young Werther* (M. Hulse, Trans.). London: Penguin.

Goffman, E. (1959). *The presentation of self in everyday life.* New York: Doubleday.

Goffman, E. (1961). *Encounters: Two studies in the sociology of interaction.* Indianapolis, IN: Bobbs-Merrill.

Gombrich, E. H. (1960). *Art and illusion.* London: Phaidon.

Gombrich, E. H. (1972a). Botticelli's mythologies: A study in the neo-Platonic symbolism of his circle. In E. H. Gombrich (Ed.), *Symbolic images: Studies in the art of the Renaissance.* London: Phaidon.

Gombrich, E. H. (1972b). *The story of art* (12th ed.). London: Phaidon.

Gottman, J. M., & Levenson, R. W. (1992). Marital processes predictive of later dissolution: Behavior, physiology and health. *Journal of Personality and Social Psychology, 63*, 221–233.

Graves, B., & Frederickson, C. H. (1995). A cognitive study of literary expertise. In R. J. Kreuz & M. S. MacNealy (Eds.), *Empirical approaches to literature and aesthetics* (pp. 397–416). Norwood, NJ: Ablex.

Gruber, H. (1995). Insight and affect in the history of science. In R. J. Sternberg & J. E. Davidson (Eds.), *The nature of insight* (pp. 397–431). Cambridge, MA: MIT Press.

Harding, D. W. (1940). Regulated hatred: An aspect of the work of Jane Austen. *Scrutiny, 8*, 346–362.

Hatfield, E., Cacioppo, J. T., & Rapson, R. L. (1994). *Emotional contagion.* New York: Cambridge University Press.

Haviland, J. M. (1984). Thinking and feeling in Woolf's writing: From childhood to adulthood. In C. E. Izard, J. Kagan, & R. B. Zajonc (Eds.), *Emotions, cognition, and behavior* (pp. 515–546). Cambridge, England: Cambridge University Press.

Holmes, G. (1996). *Renaissance.* London: Weidenfeld & Nicholson.

Jacobs, J. (1961). *The death and life of great American cities: The failure of town planning.* New York: Random House.

Kaplan, S. (1992). Environmental preference in a knowledge-seeking, knowledge-using organism. In J. H. Barkow, L. Cosmides, & J. Tooby (Eds.), *The adapted mind* (pp. 581–598). New York: Oxford University Press.

Keats, J. (1816–1820/1966). *Selected poems and letters of Keats* (R. Gittings, Ed.). London: Heineman.

Kreitler, H., & Kreitler, S. (1972). *Psychology and the arts.* Durham, NC: Duke University Press.

Kubey, R., & Csikszentmihalyi, M. (1990). *Television and the quality of life: How viewing shapes everyday experience.* Hillsdale, NJ: Erlbaum.

Larsen, S. F., & Seilman, U. (1988). Personal meanings while reading literature. *Text, 8,* 411–429.

Le Corbusier (1923/1986). *Towards a new architecture* (F. Etchells, Trans.). New York: Dover.

Lipps, T. (1962). Empathy, inner imitation, and sense feeling. In M. Rader (Ed.), *A modern book on esthetics: An anthology* (3rd ed., pp. 374–382). New York: Holt Rinehart & Winston.

Love, R. H. (1980). *Cassatt: The independent.* Chicago: Milton H. Kreines.

Lundholm, H. (1921). The affective tone of lines. *Psychological Review, 28,* 43–60.

Mathews, N. M., & Shapiro, B. S. (1989). *Mary Cassatt: The color prints.* New York: Abrams.

Melzoff, A. N. (1993). The centrality of motor coordination and proprioception in social and cognitive development: From shared actions to shared minds. In G. J. P. Savelsbergh (Ed.), *The development of coordination in infancy* (pp. 463–496). Amsterdam: Elsevier.

Melzoff, A. N., & Moore, M. K. (1977). Imitation of facial and manual gestures by human neonates. *Science, 198,* 75–78.

Miall, D. S., & Kuiken, D. (1995). Aspects of literary response: A new questionnaire. *Research in the Teaching of English, 29,* 37–58.

Motion, A. (1998). *Keats.* New York: Farrar, Strauss & Giroux.

Nairn, I., & Pevsner, N. (1965). *The buildings of England: Sussex.* Harmondsworth, England: Penguin.

Newman, O. (1972). *Defensible space.* New York: Macmillan.

Nietzsche, F. (1882/1974). *The gay science* (W. Kaufman, Trans.). New York: Random House.

Oatley, K. (1992). *Best laid schemes: The psychology of emotions.* New York: Cambridge University Press.

Oatley, K. (1994). A taxonomy of the emotions of literary response and a theory of identification in fictional narrative. *Poetics, 23,* 53–74.

Oatley, K. (1996). Emotions, rationality, and informal reasoning. In J. V. Oakhill & A. Garnham (Eds.), *Mental models in cognitive science* (pp. 175–196). Hove, England: Psychology Press.

Oatley, K. (1999a). Meetings of minds. *Poetics, 26,* 439–454.

Oatley, K. (1999b). Why fiction may be twice as true as fact: Fiction as cognitive and emotional simulation. *Review of General Psychology, 3,* 101–117.

Oatley, K., & Duncan, E. (1992). Incidents of emotion in daily life. In K. T. Strongman (Ed.), *International Review of Studies on Emotion* (pp. 250–293). Chichester, England: John Wiley.

Oatley, K., & Gholamain, M. (1997). Emotions and identification: Connections between readers and fiction. In M. Hjort & S. Laver (Eds.), *Emotion and the arts* (pp. 163–281). New York: Oxford University Press.

Oatley, K., & Jenkins, J. M. (1996). *Understanding emotions.* Oxford, England: Blackwell.

Oatley, K., & Johnson-Laird, P. N. (1987). Towards a cognitive theory of emotions. *Cognition and Emotion, 1,* 29–50.

Orians, G. H., & Heerwagen, J. H. (1992). Evolved responses to landscapes. In J. H. Barkow, L. Cosmides, & J. Tooby (Eds.), *The adapted mind* (pp. 555–579). New York: Oxford University Press.

Patrick, C. (1937). Creative thought in artists. *Journal of Psychology, 4,* 35–73.

Perkins, D. N. (1981). *The mind's best work.* Cambridge, MA: Harvard University Press.

Peskin, J. (1998). Constructing meaning when reading poetry: An expert-novice study. *Cognition and Instruction, 16,* 235–263.

Peterson, J. (1999). *Maps of meaning.* New York: Routledge.

Piaget, J., & Inhelder, B. (1969). *The psychology of the child.* London: Routledge and Kegan Paul.

Pinney, T. (1963). *Essays of George Eliot.* New York: Columbia University Press.

Poe, E. A. (1846). The cask of Amontillado. In D. Galloway (Ed.), *Edgar Allan Poe: Selected writings.* Harmondsworth, England: Penguin, 1967.

Proulx, A. (1999). *Close range: Wyoming stories.* New York: Scribner.

Raine, K. (Ed.). (1957). *Coleridge: Poems and prose.* Harmondsworth, England: Penguin.

Rapelli, P. (1999). *Goya* (E. Foa, Trans.). New York: Dorling-Kindersley.

Reff, T. (1976). *Degas: The artist's mind.* New York: Metropolitan Museum of Art.

Ribot, T. A. (1906). *Essay on the creative imagination,* (A. Baron, Trans.). Chicago: Open Court.

Rimé, B. (1995). The social sharing of emotion as a source for the social knowledge of emotion. In J. Russell, J.-M. Fernandez-Dols, A. S. R. Manstead, & J. Wellenkamp (Eds.), *Everyday conceptions of emotions: An introduction to the psychology, anthropology, and linguistics of emotion.* NATO ASI Series D 81 (pp. 475–489). Dordrecht, Netherlands: Kluwer.

Rosenberg, E. L., & Ekman, P. (1994). Coherence between expressive and experiential systems in emotion. *Cognition and Emotion, 8,* 201–229.

Rousseau, J.-J. (1750/1975). Discourse on the question: "Has the restoration of the arts and sciences been conductive to the purification of morals?" In *The essential Rousseau* (pp. 203–230). New York: Penguin-New American Library.

Russell, J., & Wilton, A. (1976). *Turner in Switzerland.* Zurich: De Clivo.

Russell, J. A. (1980). A circumflex model of affect. *Journal of Personality and Social Psychology, 39,* 1161–1178.

Scheff, T. J. (1979). *Catharsis in healing, ritual, and drama.* Berkeley: University of California Press.

Schlink, B. (1997). *The reader.* London: Random House.

Schneider, E. (1953). *Coleridge, opium, and Kubla Khan.* Chicago: Chicago University Press.

Shelley, P. B. (1840). A defence of poetry. In C. Norman (Ed.), *Poets on poetry* (pp. 180–211). New York: Free Press.

Sikora, S., Miall, D. S., & Kuiken, D. (1998). Enactment versus interpretation: A phenomenological study of readers' responses to Coleridge's "The rime of the ancient mariner." *Sixth Biennial Conference of the International Society for the Empirical Study of Literature.* Utrecht, The Netherlands.

Smith, K. (1998). *Frank Lloyd Wright: America's master architect.* New York: Abbeville.

Stevenson, R. L. (1888/1992). A chapter on dreams. *Scribner's Magazine, January.* Reprinted in C. Harman (Ed.),

*R. L. Stevenson Essays and Poems* (pp. 189–199). London: Dent Everyman's Library.

Strack, F., Martin, L. L., & Stepper, S. (1988). Inhibiting and facilitating conditions of the human smile: A nonobtrusive test of the facial feedback hypothesis. *Journal of Personality and Social Psychology, 54,* 768–777.

Tan, E. S. (1996). *Emotion and the structure of film: Film as an emotion machine.* Mahwah, NJ: Erlbaum.

Taylor, C. (1989). *Sources of the self: The making of the modern identity.* Cambridge, MA: Harvard University Press.

Tinbergen, N. (1951). *The study of instinct.* Oxford, England: Oxford University Press.

Tolstoy, L. (1877). *Anna Karenina* (C. Garnett, Trans.). London: Heineman.

Tomalin, C. (1997). *Jane Austen: A life.* London: Viking Penguin.

Van den Oetelaar, S., Tellegen, S., & Wober, M. (1997). Affective response to reading: A comparison of reading in the United Kingdom and the Netherlands. In S. Tötösy de Zepetnek & I. Sywenky (Eds.), *The systemic and empirical approach to literature and culture as theory and application* (pp. 505–513). Siegen: LUMIS.

Vasari, G. (1568/1965). *The lives of the artists* (G. Bull, Trans.). Harmondsworth, England: Penguin.

Vorderer, P. (1996). Towards a psychological theory of suspense. In P. Vorderer, H. J. Wulff, & M. Friedrichsen (Eds.), *Suspense: Conceptualizations, theoretical analyses, and empirical explorations* (pp. 233–254). Mahwah, NJ: Erlbaum.

Weisberg, R. W. (1986). *Creativity: Genius and other myths.* New York: Freeman.

Winston, A. S. (1992). Sweetness and light: Psychological aesthetics and sentimental art. In G. C. Cupchik & J. László (Eds.), *Emerging visions of the aesthetic process* (pp. 118–136). New York: Cambridge University Press.

Wood, G. S. (1999). The American love boat: Review of Andrew Burstein's *Sentimental democracy: The evolution of America's self image. New York Review of Books, 46,* October 7, 40–42.

Woolf, V. (1925). *Mrs Dalloway.* London: Hogarth Press.

Wordsworth, W. (1802/1984). Preface to *Lyrical Ballads.* In S. Gill (Ed.), *William Wordsworth* (pp. 595–615). Oxford, England: Oxford University Press.

Wright, J. L. (1994). *My father who is on earth.* Carbondale, IL: Southern Illinois University Press.

# 26

# EMOTIONAL EXPRESSION IN MUSIC

Alf Gabrielsson and Patrik N. Juslin

Pieces of music are dynamic events in time—not static, visible, or tangible as are pieces of pictorial and sculptural art. In the latter, perceived color, light, surface structure, and other properties cannot be separated from the objects themselves. Sounds, tones, and music may likewise be perceived as belonging to objects (e.g., instruments, performers), but they may also be attended to as such—as "pure events"—without any consideration of their origin or belonging (Scruton, 1997; Zuckerkandl, 1956). Music often seems abstract and ineffable, inaccessible to description by ordinary language, or only hinted at by means of similes or metaphors.

While most pictorial art depicts phenomena visible in nature, music rarely depicts in that sense, except in a few examples of program music (Davies, 1994, chap. 2). Nor can music be regarded as a language because its elements (e.g., tones, chords) do not have fixed dictionary meaning, as elements in language usually have (Davies, 1994, chap. 1; Hermerén, 1986; Langer, 1957, p. 228; Scruton, 1997, chap. 7). On the contrary, musical elements are ambiguous; they mean different things in different contexts.

So what, then, can music do? Richard Wagner, who wrote both libretto and music for his operas, declared that music begins where language comes to an end, and that music is the language of passion (Benestad, 1978). Langer (1957) claimed that music "can *reveal* the nature of feelings with a detail and truth that language cannot approach" (p. 235), and Cooke (1959) maintained that music is not apt to expression of ideas or abstract concepts but is the expression of emotion. Sounds, it seems, may ex-

press and arouse emotions more readily than visual stimuli. People who have become deaf as adults experience "a consequent draining of feeling from the world about them" (Brown, 1981, p. 240). Before the advent of sound film, a pianist was hired to strengthen the expression of what happened on the screen, and nowadays music is routinely used to generate or amplify emotional expression in plays, films, videos, television programs, and so forth (Cohen, 2001).

Before proceeding further, it is necessary to refer to a distinction between, on the one hand, a listener's perception of expression in the music—to perceive an expression of, say, sadness without being affected oneself—and, on the other hand, a listener's response to the music—to feel sad. This distinction is not always observed, neither in theoretical treatises nor in empirical investigations (and in reality the border between the two alternatives is somewhat blurred). In the following, however, we focus mainly on perceived emotional expression. (For discussions of emotional reactions to music, see Gabrielsson, 2001; Scherer & Zentner, 2001; Sloboda & Juslin, 2001.)

Expressive qualities of Western music have been discussed by philosophers, music theorists, and others ever since antiquity, and many opinions have been issued concerning what can be expressed in music. We first take a look at some of these ideas as they relate to emotion. Then, we review empirical investigations on emotional expression in music. Finally, we discuss methodological and theoretical issues and consider implications for future research.

503

## Historical and Theoretical Perspectives

### Music as Mirror of Human Character

During antiquity, philosophers believed that music, like other art forms, was a kind of *mimesis*—that is, imitation of nature—in this case an imitation of human character or states of mind.[1] It was also assumed that what was expressed in music would be automatically imitated by the listener (Allesch, 1987; Grout & Palisca, 1996; Scruton, 1997). Plato (427–347 B.C.) and Aristotle (384–322 B.C.) therefore advised on which modes, instruments, and rhythms ought to be used to educate young people to become good citizens, as well as to bring balance and calm, arouse enthusiasm or excitement, and so on. For instance, Plato thought that the Dorian mode embodied male determination, which he regarded as a political ideal.[2]

The Greeks also realized that the expressive qualities of music could be used for therapeutic purposes. In their view, man's natural and ideal state was one of perfect harmony, order, and health. Unfavorable states of the mind could be relieved and harmony and order reestablished by means of appropriate music, either by using music of a different emotional character from that of the upset state of mind or by deliberately driving unwanted feelings into extreme states to be discharged, thus achieving *catharsis*—the purification of the mind. Both principles can still be found in different forms of music therapy (Pratt & Jones, 1987; Spintge & Droh, 1987).

### Music in Support of Text

During most of the Middle Ages, music in the Roman Catholic church served to express and strengthen Christian faith as couched in the holy texts. Music had little aesthetic value in itself. Still, Saint Augustine (354–430) was well aware of the expressive powers of music and described in his *Confessiones* (cited in Lippman, 1986, pp. 28–29) how he vacillated between the temptation of merely enjoying the beautiful melodies themselves, forgetting the text, and his insight that faith was actually favored by having the texts performed with such beautiful melodies. Using music in the service of Christian religion has been, and still is, an important part of Western music history.

The idea of music as the "obedient daughter" of the text was also characteristic of Italian monody around 1600 (i.e., monophonic singing with a simple chord accompaniment). Vincenzo Galilei (1520–1591), father of Galileo, advised composers to study how prominent actors used their voices in order to express various affects. Singing, he argued, should imitate the characteristics of emotional speech.

At this time, the earliest operas were composed in Italy,

and opera successively became the most large-scale attempt to combine music and text (also dance, acting, scenography) to describe and express a vast range of human feelings, passions, and characters. Furthermore, it is about this time that various expression marks began to appear in composers' scores, such as *forte* and *piano* for dynamics, *allegro* and *adagio* for tempo. The number of expression marks successively increased during the following centuries to constitute hundreds. To mention but a few, in alphabetical order: *affettuoso* (with warmth), *amoroso* (with love), *burlesco* (burlesque), *capriccioso* (capricious), *dolce* (sweet), and *espressivo* (expressive).

Music's dependence on words became most obvious during the 17th and 18th centuries. In his influential treatise *Der vollkommene Capellmeister* (1739; see also Lippman, 1986), Johann Mattheson (1681–1764) presented a plan for musical composition in direct connection to basic concepts in rhetorics. So-called rhetorical figures were used in music to illustrate or emphasize words or ideas in the text. For instance, ascending stepwise movement could be used to express raising in a literal sense or in a transferred sense (e.g., resurrection); sequences of short notes could express rapidity such as in flight; chromatic falling melody could express suffering and sadness; falling melodies with inserted pauses, sighs, pain and exhaustion. There are long lists of musical-rhetoric figures (Benestad, 1978; "Rhetoric and music" in Sadie, 1980; Unger, 1979).

The *Doctrine of the Affections* (German, *Affektenlehre*) meant that music, predominantly vocal music, should express affects in the sense of idealized emotional states and have listeners feel these states (Buelow, 1983). It was assumed that every affect had its particular character expressible in music. Mattheson described some 30 affects (translated into English in Buelow, 1983, pp. 404–406), but concrete musical means to represent them were suggested only for a few—for example, large intervals to represent joy, small intervals to represent sadness, ascending motion for pride but descending motion for humility, and disordered sequences of notes for despair.

### Music as Independent Expressive Art

During the latter half of the 18th century, the *Doctrine of the Affections* was successively abandoned in favor of an *Empfindungsästhetik*, the possibility and freedom to use whatever means fantasy and intuition may suggest to express subjective feelings in music—a parallel to *Sturm und Drang* in the literature of that time. Important precursors were composers Johann Joachim Quantz (1752) and Carl Philipp Emanuel Bach (1753, 1762). The mimesis principle, central in art ever since antiquity, was questioned (Lippman, 1986, parts 6–7), and music came to be ascribed an independent position as expressive art with powers to affect listeners. From the late 18th century, instrumental music came to dominate vocal music and was often considered as the only genuine type of music, independent of words. Nineteenth-century musical romanticism emphasized the subjective and emotional in music. The composer was regarded as a divinely gifted genius, who followed solely his own inspiration, capable of insights into areas inaccessible to the common human being—the Infinite, the Eternal, the Transcendental.

### Absolute Music and Program Music

Music was also used to refer to various extra-musical phenomena in so-called program music. It could mean only occasional imitations of natural sounds—as bird song and a thunder storm in Beethoven's *Pastoral Symphony*—or refer to a complete story as in *Symphonie Fantastique* by Hector Berlioz (1803–1869), in which he intended to describe an artist's passionate and unhappy love of a woman. However, composers were aware of music's limited possibilities to represent events or ideas, and rather referred to the feelings associated with the program. Berlioz declared that he did not try to depict abstract ideas or moral qualities but only passions and impressions (Benestad, 1978, p. 233).

The famous Viennese music critic Eduard Hanslick considered program music and the claim that music should describe emotions as a threat to music's autonomy. He instead argued for what is usually called absolute or pure music—that is, instrumental music that is self-contained, not referring to anything outside itself. In his book *Vom musikalisch Schönen* (1854/1989), Hanslick claimed that *"Der Inhalt der Musik sind tönend bewegte Formen"* (p. 59)—that is, the contents of music are "sounding forms in motion" (Langer, 1953, p. 107), or "forms moved through sounding" or "forms moved through tones" (Scruton, 1997, p. 353). With regard to feelings, Hanslick argued that music can never describe the feelings per se, only their dynamic properties. It may reproduce the motion associated with physical events according to its momentum: rapid, slow, strong, soft, rising, or falling. But, emphasized Hanslick, motion is only a concomitant of feeling, not the feeling itself. That we perceive motion qualities—walking, dancing, rocking, swinging, driving forward, accelerating, retarding, etc.—in music is a generally accepted idea (for a review, see Shove & Repp, 1995), and motion qualities have emotional connotations: "motion is heard in music, and that motion presents emotion characteristics much as do the movements giving a person her bearing or gait" (Davies, 1994, p. 229; see also Gabrielsson, 1988). Hanslick's ideas still continue to elicit much discussion (Budd, 1985, chap. 2; Davies, 1994, p. 152, p. 202 onwards, p. 283; Kivy, 1990, pp. 184–189; Scruton, 1997, p. 165, pp. 348–350, 353–354; Tarasti, 1994, p. 30).

The work of composer Igor Stravinsky (1882–1971) is often mentioned as representative of absolute music. Stravinsky declared that "music, by its very nature, is essentially powerless to *express* anything at all, whether a feeling, an attitude of mind, a psychological mood, a phenomenon of nature etc. . . . *Expression* has never been an inherent property of music. . . . If, as is nearly always the case, music appears to express something, this is only an illusion. . . . It is simply an additional attribute that . . . we have lent it, thrust upon it, as a label, a convention" (cited in Fisk, 1997, pp. 280–281). Later he modified this statement but still held that "music expresses itself" (Fisk, 1997, p. 281).

In discussing these questions, Meyer (1956) made a distinction between "absolutists" and "referentialists." The former claim that the meaning of music is intramusical (embodied meaning) and music refers only to itself, whereas the latter claim that music receives meaning by referring to extramusical phenomena (designative meaning). Meyer emphasized, however, that these alternatives are not mutually exclusive but may coexist in the same piece of music.

### Modern Theories of Emotional Expression in Music

#### Cooke's Theory

The most pronounced spokesman for music as expression of emotion is probably the musicologist Deryck Cooke. In his book *The Language of Music* (1959), Cooke claimed that music considered as expression has three separate aspects: (1) an *architectural* aspect typified by contrapuntal works (e.g., a fugue) appealing to us by the beauty of pure form; (2) a *pictorial* aspect in a few works containing imitation of natural sounds (e.g., bird song); and a (3) *literary* aspect "found . . . in most Western music written between 1400 and the present day, since music is, properly speaking, a language of emotions, akin to speech. The appeal of this music is directly to the emotions and, to be fully appreciated, should be responded to in this way" (pp. 32–33).

Following a discussion of the emotional expression of different musical elements, Cooke identified, using an impressive number of examples from the late Middle Ages until our own time, 16 so-called basic terms of musical vocabulary, and he suggested the emotional expression connected with each of them. They were described in terms of sequences as, for example, "Ascending 1-(2)-3-(4)-5 (Major)" designating an ascending major triad (1-3-5, with possible insertions of the intervening notes, 2 or 4), said to express "an outgoing, active, assertion of joy" (p. 115). Its counterpart in minor was characterized as "expressive of an outgoing feeling of pain—an assertion of sorrow, a complaint, a protest against misfortune" (p. 122). Cooke went on to show how the short basic terms could also be traced in extended musical themes and even in the structure and emotional expression of separate movements and complete works. (Empirical tests of Cooke's theory are discussed in the next major section of this chapter.)

### Langer's Theory

Unlike Cooke, philosopher Susanne Langer claimed that music has no literal meaning apart from some onomatopoetic themes. The elements in music—tones, chords, rhythms, and so forth—do not carry fixed lexical meaning as do words in language. In her books *Philosophy in a New Key* (1957) and *Feeling and Form* (1953), she developed a theory of symbols in reason, rite, and art. Langer made a distinction between what she called *discursive* symbolism and *presentational* symbolism. Language is an example of discursive symbolism, in which the symbols have fixed meanings. Music, in contrast, is an example of a presentational symbolism—that is, an open ("unconsummated") symbol, where the meaning of various symbolic elements can be understood "only through the meaning of the whole, through their relations within the total structure" (1957, p. 97).

According to Langer, the composer's general knowledge about feelings receives a symbolic expression in music. "A composer . . . articulates subtle complexes of feeling that language cannot even name; he knows the forms of emotions and can handle them, 'compose' them" (1957, p. 222), and "Because the forms of human feeling are much more congruent with musical forms than with forms of language, music can *reveal* the nature of feelings with a detail and truth that language cannot approach" (1957, p. 235). Music expresses the dynamic forms of feelings, not their content; as earlier formulated by Pratt (1931, p. 191), the auditory structures in music "*sound* the way moods *feel*." This comes close to Hanslick's opinion, and Langer agreed with his description of music as sounding forms in motion. "Such motion is the essence of music: a motion of forms that are not visible, but are given to the ear instead of the eye" (1953, p. 107). Langer did not go into much musical detail, but she approvingly referred to an investigation by Huber (1923; see also "Emotional Expression and Musical Structure," in the next section of this chapter) on expression in short pitch patterns as evidence for how many factors in musical structure can have expressive functions.

The basic thrust of Langer's theory is that there is an *isomorphism* between the structure of feelings and the structure of music. Formal characteristics that may be similar in music and human feeling include "patterns of motion and rest, of tension and release, of agreement and disagreement, preparation, fulfillment, excitation, sudden change, etc." (1957, p. 228). Langer's ideas are intuitively appealing, but one problem with the theory is to provide a specification of the structure of feelings and how this should be measured, without which her hypothesis has little explanatory force. Therefore, there are no direct attempts to test her theory empirically. However, Langer's theory is still often discussed and criticized (cf. Budd, 1985, chap. 6; Davies, 1994, p. 123 onward; Scruton, 1997, p. 166; Tarasti, 1994, p. 12).

### Clynes's Theory

Clynes (1973, 1977, 1980) has argued for the existence of biologically preprogrammed spatiotemporal patterns, or *essentic forms*, for the communication of emotions. Each essentic form, Clynes claims, can be expressed by any of a number of output modalities (e.g., gesture, facial expression, tone of voice, a dance step, or a musical phrase), as long as the dynamic pattern is preserved. Clynes's theory is reminiscent of the seminal work by Tomkins (1962), who postulated the existence of biologically based "affect programs," stored in subcortical areas of the brain and associated with specific nonverbal expressions of a set of "basic" emotions. Clynes went further in that he specified the exact spatiotemporal patterns used in such emotional communication. For the measurement of these patterns he created a particular device—the *sentograph*—that allows the recording of both vertical and horizontal pressure exerted by a finger upon a small disk placed on a small box. Participants are asked to express specific emotions by pressing this disk—literally *ex-pressing* the emotion. Clynes claims that there is a high degree of concordance of such expressive patterns for particular emotions (e.g., joy, grief, anger, hate, reverence, love, sex) both within and across participants from different cultures; see figures and discussion in Clynes (1977, 1980) and Clynes and Nettheim (1982).

Clynes suggested using the sentograph to study emotional expression in music by having listeners pressing the disk in accordance with the flow of musical events. This should serve to uncover the essentic forms hypothesized for different emotions. He further proposed transforming pressure patterns into melodic contours for different emotions—for instance, a melody descending by semitone steps for expression of grief (Clynes & Nettheim, 1982, p. 73); this reminds of an earlier rhetorical figure for sadness (see earlier "Music in Support of Text"). (For attempts to test Clynes's theory, see "Clynes's Theory" in next major section of this chapter.)

## Emotional Expression in Performance

While most discussions of emotional expression in music concern variables in the musical structure specified by the musical notation (e.g., pitch, mode, melody, harmony), the influence of variables in the performance (e.g., articulation, timing, intonation) has so far received less attention.

But the same notated structure can be performed in a number of different ways, and the way it is performed may influence the listener's impression of the music in profound ways. Moreover, the mechanisms underlying emotional expression via performance might be different from those underlying emotional expression via composed structure. Therefore, it makes sense to consider performance separately.

The only elaborated theoretical framework focusing specifically on performance aspects has been presented by Juslin (1997a, 2001a, 2001b). He recommended that researchers adopt a *functionalist perspective* on communication of emotion via music performance. This involves the integration of ideas from research on emotion and nonverbal communication with Brunswik's (1956) lens model.

### Origin of the Code

As we shall see later in this chapter, performers can communicate specific emotions to their listeners. What is it that makes this possible? According to the functionalist perspective, the answer to this question lies in considering the *functions* that communication of emotions has served, and continues to serve, in social interaction. Emotional communication via acoustic signals did not begin when humans invented the first musical instrument. Humans have always communicated emotions via the voice (see chapter 28, this volume) and many animals communicate emotions via acoustic signals as well (see chapter 24, this volume). Although music performance may be a relatively recent addition to the human behavior repertoire, it seems plausible that how performers communicate emotions is *constrained* by psychological mechanisms for acoustic communication shaped by evolution (Juslin, 1997a).

Accordingly, Juslin (2001a) argues that cue utilization in emotional expression via music performance reflects a compromise between two factors. The first factor reflects innate "brain programs" for vocal expression of emotion (e.g., Jürgens & von Cramon, 1982; Ploog, 1986). It is hypothesized that performers can communicate emotions to listeners by using the same code as is used in vocal expression of emotion. The notion that there is an intimate relationship between music and the human voice has a long history (von Helmholtz, 1863/1954; Rousseau, 1761/1986; cf. Scherer, 1995), but this link is not sufficient to explain *all* aspects of music's expressiveness (Budd, 1985, chap. 7). Thus, it would seem that the hypothesis needs to be constrained in order to have any explanatory force (e.g., Juslin, 1999). More specifically, the parallels between vocal expression and music may apply only to those aspects of the music that are typically under the performer's control (e.g., tempo, sound level, timbre), and not to the other aspects of the musical structure (e.g., harmonic progression, tonality). Juslin also suggests that encoding and decoding of emotion from acoustic signals proceed in

terms of a small number of "basic" emotion categories (e.g., Izard, 1977; Oatley, 1992), which provide decoders with maximum information and discriminability (cf. Ross & Spalding, 1994). In this context, it is hypothesized that basic emotions (1) have distinct functions, (2) are found in all cultures, (3) are experienced as unique feeling states, (4) appear early in human development, (5) are associated with distinct neurological substrates, (6) can be inferred in other primates, and (7) have distinct expressions (see Oatley, 1992; Panksepp, 1998; Plutchik, 1994).

The second factor governing emotional expression in performance is *social learning*, or specific memories. This is a life-long process that begins with the interaction between mother and infant. When mothers talk to their infants—for example, if they want to calm an infant—they reduce the speed and intensity of their speech and talk with slowly falling pitch contours. If mothers want to express disapproval toward some unfavorable activity, they use brief, sharp, and staccato-like contours (Papoušek, 1996). Certain aspects of emotional expression in performance (e.g., the cues not shared with vocal expression) may be completely determined by cultural influence. Others, although based on innate mechanisms, are later modulated by experience. This factor can explain individual differences among performers and listeners. However, Juslin assumes that the first factor—the innate vocal code—has the greatest impact on performers' expression of emotion.

This assumption leads to a number of testable predictions: for example, that (1) there are parallels between vocal expression of emotion and expression of emotion via performance, (2) basic emotions are easier to communicate than other emotions, (3) decoding of emotions from performance is fast, (4) there is cross-cultural similarity and accuracy in emotional expression in performance, (5) decoding of emotions from performance develops early, and (6) decoding of emotions from performance is largely independent of musical training (see "Emotional Expression in Performance," in the next major section of this chapter).

### Description of the Code: The Lens Model

Juslin (1995) suggested that we should use Brunswik's (1956) lens model to illustrate how a performer *encodes* a certain emotion by means of a large number of *probabilistic* (i.e., uncertain) albeit partly *redundant* cues in the performance (e.g., articulation). The emotional expression is *decoded* by the listener, who uses the same cues to judge the intended emotional expression. Intercorrelations among the cues reflect both how sounds are produced on musical instruments (e.g., a harder string attack may produce a tone that is both louder and has sharper timbre) and how performers employ the cues to express emotions. To explain the success (or failure) of the communicative process, one needs to describe the performer's cue utilization (relationships between performer intention and cues), as well as the listener's cue utilization (relationships between cues and listener judgment). For reliable communication to occur, the performer's cue utilization must be as similar as possible to the listeners' cue utilization. However, because the cues are intercorrelated, many different cue utilization strategies may lead to a similar level of communication accuracy (Juslin, 2000).

### Summary of Modern Theories

The theories just discussed show both similarities and differences along a number of dimensions. First, they all agree in assuming a consistent relationship of some kind between musical structure and emotional expression. However, whereas Langer holds that music can symbolize only the general *form* of feelings, Cooke, Clynes, and Juslin assume that music can express particular emotions. The latter three theories agree in that they assume that there are specific patterns of musical factors that correspond to specific emotions, an idea that was expressed already in ancient Greece and later in the *Doctrine of Affections*, discussed earlier. All four theories differ with respect to scope: Langer is concerned with music in general; Cooke primarily with melodic factors; Clynes with patterns of pitch, loudness, and duration; and Juslin solely with factors in the performance (e.g., timing). The theories also differ regarding the specificity with which they describe the emotions associated with different musical factors: Langer is fairly unspecific, Clynes and Juslin consider broad emotion categories (e.g., joy, sadness), and Cooke provides elaborate descriptions (e.g., "an outgoing, active, assertion of joy"). The nature of the relationships between musical factors and specific emotions is most deterministic in Cooke's theory, fairly deterministic in Clynes's theory, but probabilistic in Juslin's theory.

### Review of Empirical Research

#### Emotional Expression and Musical Structure

Empirical research on emotional expression in music started in the late 19th century, but it was not until the 1930s that studies became more frequent. Usually, the purpose was to investigate listener agreement on perceived emotional expression, or to investigate what factors in the musical structure, as provided in musical notation, influenced perceived expression. Subjects listened to selected pieces of music or other tonal stimuli and reported perceived emotional expression by means of either (1) free phenomenological descriptions; (2) choice among descriptive terms, adjectives or nouns, provided by the investigator; or (3) ratings of how well such descriptive terms applied to the music in question. Techniques for contin-

uous or nonverbal recording of perceived expression have recently been developed as well. Characteristics of most studies with regard to stimuli, subjects, response type, and descriptive attributes are given in Table 26.1.

The studies reviewed in this section feature a broad range of affective terms. There is a growing consensus among emotion researchers that terms like *affect, emotion,* and *mood* should be differentiated from one another (e.g., Batson, Shaw, & Oleson, 1992; Ekman & Davidson, 1994, chap. 2). However, music researchers have tended to use these terms interchangeably, and in the following review we simply use the same terms as were used by the authors themselves.

#### Listener Agreement

A crucial question concerns whether listeners agree on which emotions are expressed in music. Results depend to a large extent on the methods used. When listeners were asked to provide their own free descriptions of what the music expressed, a variety of emotions were reported with considerable interindividual variability, as in the earliest reports by Gilman (1891, 1892) and Downey (1897). Downey noted great differences in the extent to which individuals received definite impressions, and that good agreement may exist regarding the broad emotional quality but less regarding nuances or variants of this quality. Large interindividual variation in perceived expression was also found by Huber (1923), who asked musically trained listeners to freely describe their impressions of short pitch patterns—only two or three tones. He classified their reports into (1) mood impressions; (2) impressions of human character described in emotional terms; (3) emotionally colored announcements (e.g., request, reproach, complaint); (4) impressions of movement (e.g., rising, falling) or of activity; and (5) various inner images (e.g., landscape).

Later researchers, instead of using free reports, compiled a list of descriptive terms—adjectives or nouns—and asked listeners to choose those terms that were appropriate for the music in question. Rigg (1937a) used this method as well as free reports and found that in some cases the supposed emotion was not frequently in the free description but more frequently chosen when presented among the emotion terms. Thus the two methods gave somewhat different results. Free descriptions are rare in later studies but may have a certain revival (e.g., Imberty, 1979; Juslin, 1997c; Osborne, 1989).

Gundlach (1935), Hampton (1945), Capurso (1952), and Sopchak (1955) had listeners choose among descriptive terms (see Table 26.1) and determined which of them were chosen by at least 50% (in Gundlach, 45%) of the listeners for one or more of the musical pieces used. Best agreement was found for various expressions of positive emotions (e.g., gay, glad, happy, joyful, brilliant, triumphant), neg-

Table 26.1 Music Stimuli, Subjects, Response Types, and Descriptive Attributes in Empirical Studies of Expression in Music (FA = factor analysis, MDS = multidimensional scaling, CA = cluster analysis, MRA = multiple regression analysis)

| Author | Stimuli | Subjects | Response Type | Descriptive Attributes |
|---|---|---|---|---|
| Gilman 1891, 1892 | 11 classical pieces | 28 musical amateurs | Free reports (answers to questions) | Various: happiness, sadness, peace, fear, pain, desire, religious sentiment, yearning, active and passive moods |
| Downey 1897 | 6 classical pieces | 22 non musicians | Free reports | Various: happiness, sadness, religious devotion, grief, hope |
| Huber 1923 | Pitch patterns, 2–3 tones | 6–12 musicians | Free reports | Moods, characters, announcements, motion, various inner images |
| Sherman 1928 | Single tones performed by singer | 30 psychology students | Free reports | 14–18 emotions: e.g., sorrow, anger-hate, fear-pain, surprise |
| Heinlein 1928 | Triads, major/minor | 30 mixed | Either of → | Happy/joyful, melancholy/sad |
| Gundlach 1932 | 334 Indian songs in scores | | Analysis of scores | Songs for love, healing, war |
| Gundlach 1935 | 40 classical pieces, phrases | 112 students | Choice, any number out of 17 terms → | Brilliant, animated, uneasy, tranquil, dignified, triumphant, exalted, glad, somber, melancholy, mournful, delicate, whimsical, flippant, sentimental, awkward, and grotesque |
| Hevner 1935a | 10 classical pieces, manipulated in mode | 205 students | Choice, any number out of → | 14 adjective clusters (later reduced to 8 clusters, see Figure 26.4) |
| Hevner 1936 | 26 classical, pieces, manipulated in rhythm, melodic line, harmony | 450 students, most of them musically untrained | Choice, any number out of → | 8 adjective clusters, see Figure 26.4 |
| Hevner 1937 | 21 pieces, most classical, some specially composed, manipulated in tempo and pitch level | 222 students | Choice, any number out of → | 8 adjective clusters, see Figure 26.4 |
| Rigg 1937a | 20 phrases, classical and composed | 100 students | Free reports + choice, one of → | (Mainly) joy, lamentation, hopeful longing, sorrowful longing, love |
| Rigg 1939 | 5 composed phrases systematically manipulated | 105 + 99 male students | Choice, one of → | (Mainly) pleasant/happy (e.g., joy, hopeful longing, love), serious/sad (e.g., lamentation, sorrowful longing) |
| Rigg 1940a | 5 phrases, same as Rigg 1939, varied in pitch level and tonality | 84 psychology students | Choice, one of → | (Mainly) pleasant/happy (e.g., joy, hopeful longing, love), serious/sad (e.g., lamentation, sorrowful longing) |
| Rigg 1940b | 5 phrases, same as Rigg 1939, varied in tempo | 88 psychology students | Choice, one of → | (Mainly) pleasant/happy (e.g., joy, hopeful longing, love), serious/sad (e.g., lamentation, sorrowful longing) |
| Campbell 1942 | 7 classical pieces, 7 folk songs | 40 seniors and freshmen | Choice, one of → | Gaiety, joy, yearning, sorrow, calm, assertion, tenderness |
| Watson 1942 | 30 classical pieces | 100 listeners at each of six age levels + 20 musical experts | First and second choice among → | Happy, mischievous, amusing, very happy, exciting, very exciting, dignified, kingly, peaceful, serious, pleading, sad, tragic, mysterious, unclassified |

*(continued)*

Table 26.1 *(continued)*

| Author | Stimuli | Subjects | Response Type | Descriptive Attributes |
|---|---|---|---|---|
| Hampton 1945 | 10 classical pieces | 58 female students | Choice, any number of 30 terms → | Rage, pity, determination, hate, despair, joy, terror, love, disgust, fear, surprise, grief, suspense, longing, resignation, sadness, devotion, horror, contempt, triumph, praise, defiance, agony, and seven others |
| Capurso 1952 | 105 classical pieces | 1075 students | Choice, one of → | 6 categories: (a) happy, gay, triumphant; (b) agitated, restless; (c) nostalgic, soothing, relaxing; (d) prayerful, reverent; (e) sad, grieving, lonely; (f) eerie, weird, grotesque |
| Farnsworth 1954 | 56 classical excerpts | 200 students | Choice, any number of adjectives → | 8 adjective clusters, see Figure 26.4 |
| Sopchak 1955 | 5 classical pieces, 7 popular with lyrics, 3 folk tunes with Russian lyrics | 553 sophomore students | Choice, any number of 12 terms → | Sorrow, joy, calm, yearning, love, eroticism, jealousy, wonder, solemnity, cruelty, rage/anger, assertion |
| Kleinen 1968 | 35 classical pieces, 5 popular pieces | 114 with varying musical knowledge → <br> 7 music experts → | 55 bipolar scales + FA → <br><br> 21 musicotechnical scales | 5 factors: Heiterkeit-Ernst; Robustheit-Zartheit; Kosmos-Chaos; Phantasie-Einfallslosigkeit; Gefuhi-Geist |
| Wedin 1969 | 18 classical and 2 jazz pieces | 100 psychology students, 100 music students | 40 adjective rating scales + factor analysis (FA) | 3 factors: tension/energy-relaxation; gaiety-gloom, solemnity |
| Wedin 1972a | 18 classical, 2 jazz, and 2 popular pieces | 26 music students | 40 adjective rating scales + factor analysis (FA) | 3 factors: tension/energy-relaxation, gaiety-gloom, solemnity-triviality |
| Wedin 1972b | 18 classical and 2 jazz pieces | 49 students | Choice of 40 adjectives + multidimensional scaling (MDS) | 3 dimensions: tension/energy-relaxation; gaiety-gloom; solemnity |
| Wedin 1972c | 40 classical, jazz, popular | 100 psychology students → <br> 15 music experts | Choice of adjectives + MDS → Ratings on 13 musicotechnical scales | 3 dimensions: intensity-softness; pleasantness-unpleasantness; solemnity-triviality |
| Gabrielsson 1973 | 20 pieces of dance music | 23 musicians + 24 nonmusicians | 80 adjective rating scales + FA | 5 factors: vital/gay-dull; simplicity-complexity; excited/intense-calm/soft; knocking/hard-rocking/soft; solemn-swinging |
| Batel 1976 | 30 classical | 52 music students | 55 adjective rating scales + cluster analysis | 7 clusters: Ordnung; Prägnanz; Temperament; Erregung; Fremdartigkeit; Ruhe; Empfindung |
| Kotlyar & Morozov 1976 | 50 renditions of a vocal phrase | 10 opera singers, 10 musically trained listeners | Forced choice → + performance measurements | Anger, fear, joy, sorrow + neutral |
| Hare 1977 | 16 classical excerpts | Students and music students | Similarity ratings + MDS, adjective ratings + FA | 3 dimensions: tempo/playfulness; potency; musical period |

Table 26.1 *(continued)*

| Author | Stimuli | Subjects | Response Type | Descriptive Attributes |
|---|---|---|---|---|
| Scherer & Oshinsky 1977 | Synthesized 8-tone sequences, systematically varied | 48 psychology students | Ratings on 3 bipolar scales → + choice of any number of 7 emotions → | Pleasantness-unpleasantness; activity-passivity; potency-weakness Anger, fear, boredom, surprise, happiness, sadness, disgust |
| Imberty 1979 | 16 pieces by Debussy, 16 by Brahms | 80 + 80 nonmusicians | Free choice of any suitable adjectives + correspondence analysis | 3 dimensions: Schèmes de tension et de détente; Schèmes des résonance émotionelles; Représentations iconiques et cinétiques |
| Brown 1981 | 12 + 12 classical pieces | Nonmusicians, instrumentalists and 19th century knowledgeables | Arrange 12 pieces into 6 pairs = expressive categories → and into 6 variants of sadness expression → | (A) Elegiac, gentle sorrow; (B) raptuous, luminous; (C) tender, hushed; (D) rustic, good-humor; (E) spring morning buoyancy; (F) boisterous, rude, heavy; (A) funereal, strong but sorrowful; (B) sadness tinged with romantic mystery; (C) wistful, delicately regretful; (D) depression, the "pits"; (E) poignant, plaintive; (F) relaxed, somber, reflective |
| Nielzén & Cesarec 1981 | 13 specially composed pieces | 50 nonmusicians | 20 bipolar scales + FA → | 3 factors: tension-relaxation; gaiety-gloom; attraction-repulsion |
| Nielzén & Cesarec 1982 | 13 specially composed + 13 classical pieces | 75 students → 8 music experts → | 12 bipolar scales + FA → 9 musicotechnical scales + FA → | 3 factors: tension-relaxation; gaiety-gloom; attraction-repulsion 3 factors: simple-sophisticated; vivid-placid; dark-light |
| Nielsen 1983, 1987 | Haydn: *London Symphony*, R. Strauss: *Also sprach Zarathustra* | 11 musicians, 12 high school students | Continuous recording of perceived tension in music | Tension |
| Asmus 1985 | 3 pieces, popular, classical | 2,057 students | 99 adjective rating scales + FA | 9 factors: evil, sensual, potency, humour, pastoral, longing, depression, sedative, activity |
| Crowder 1985 | Sinewave triads, major, minor | 24 young adults | Choice of major or minor, happy or sad | Major-happy, minor-sad |
| Senju & Ohgushi 1987 | 10 performances of Mendelsohn's *Violin Concerto* | 1 performer, 16 musically trained listeners | Ratings on semantic differential scales → + MDS | Weak, powerful, bright, sad, sophisticated, beautiful, dreamy, fashionable, simple, deep |
| Cunningham & Sterling 1988 | 30 classical pieces | 112 children, ages 4, 5, 6 (18, 24) | Forced choice → | Happy, sad, angry, afraid |
| Dolgin & Adelson 1990 | 16 specially composed melodies | 128 children, ages 4, 7, 9 + 100 students | Forced choice of drawings of faces → | Happy, sad, angry, frightened |
| Kastner & Crowder 1990 | 12 short passages, major/minor | 38 children, 3–12 years | Choice, one of four faces → | Happy, contented, sad, angry |
| Asada & Ohgushi 1991 | Ravel's *Bolero* | 13 music students | Ratings on 25 bipolar scales + MDS → | 2 dimensions: energetic/powerful-gentle/soft; comic/coquetttish-serious/reserved |

*(continued)*

Table 26.1 *(continued)*

| Author | Stimuli | Subjects | Response Type | Descriptive Attributes |
|---|---|---|---|---|
| Namba, Kuwano, Hatoh, & Kato 1991 | 18 performances of Mussorgsky's *Pictures at an Exhibition* | 44 female and 454 male students | Continuous choice among 15 adjectives during music → | Triumphant, magnificent, stirring, powerful, mild, quiet, leisurely, pastoral, calm, sorrowful, lonely, depressed, brilliant, delicate, smooth |
| Crowder, Reznick, & Rosenkrantz 1991 | Major and minor chord, consonant and dissonant chord | 14 infants, 6 months | Head-turning, direction of gaze | Happy, sad (inferred from responses) |
| Terwogt & van Grinsven 1991 | 8 short classical musical extracts | 64 children, ages 5, 10; 32 adults | Forced choice of drawings of faces | Happy, angry, fearful, sad |
| Thompson & Robitaille 1992 | Specially composed pieces | 14 moderately trained in music | Ratings on 6 emotion scales → | Joy, sorrow, excitement, dullness, anger, peace |
| Behrens & Green 1993 | 24 improvisations on violin, trumpet, timpani + vocals | 8 performers, 58 students | Ratings on 3 scales → | Angry, sad, scared |
| Giomo 1993 | 12 short classical compositions | 173 children, ages 5 and 9 | Ratings, semantic differential → | Softness/intensity, unpleasantness/pleasantness, triviality/solemnity |
| Kratus 1993 | 30 excerpts from Bach's *Goldberg Variations* on piano | 658 children, ages 6–12 | Forced choice of facial drawings → | Happy vs. sad (1st measure) Excited vs. calm (2nd measure) |
| Madsen & Fredrickson 1993 | Haydn (same as Nielsen 1983) | 40 musicians, 32 nonmusicians | Continuous recording of perceived tension | Tension |
| Baroni & Finarelli 1994 | 3 phrases from 3 operas | 3 singers + 3 actors | Performance measurements | Serene and joyful, sad and depressed, aggressive |
| Robazza, Macaluso, & D'Urso 1994 | 8 classical pieces (piano) | 40 adults, 40 children | Forced choice → | Anger, happiness, sadness, fear |
| Gabrielsson & Lindström 1995 | 20 synthesizer and sentograph performances of 2 popular pieces | 4 performers, 110 listeners: students, teachers and musicians | Forced choice → + performance measurements | Angry, happy, sad, soft/tender, solemn, indifferent |
| Siegwart & Scherer 1995 | 10, from 5 official recordings of opera performances | 5 opera singers, 11 musically trained listeners | Ratings of → + performance measurements | Madness, sadness, tender passion, fear of death, overall preference |
| Sundberg, Iwarsson, & Hagegård 1995 | 15 excerpts, folk tunes, classical, opera | 1 opera singer, 11 musically trained listeners | Forced choice → + performance measurements | Angry, happy, loving, sad, scared, secure |
| Gabrielsson & Juslin 1996 | Performances of 4 pieces (popular, folk, composed) on flute, violin, guitar, & singing voice | 9 performers, 93 university students | Ratings on 7 scales → + performance measurements | Angry, happy, sad, fearful, tender, solemn, expressive |
| Gregory, Worrall, & Sarge 1996 | 8 tunes, major/minor | 40 3–4-year olds, 28 7–8-year olds | Choice between two faces → | Happiness, sadness |
| Krumhansl 1996 | Mozart *Piano Sonata*, original and manipulated | 15 + 24, varying musical experience | Continuous recording of → | Segmentation, tension |
| Ohgushi & Hattori 1996a | *Vocalise* by Fauré | 10 music students | Ratings of → | Anger, fear, joy, sorrow |
| Ohgushi & Hattori 1996b | *Vocalise* by Fauré | 3 female singers | Performance measurements | Anger, fear, joy, sorrow + neutral |

Table 26.1 *(continued)*

| Author | Stimuli | Subjects | Response Type | Descriptive Attributes |
|---|---|---|---|---|
| Rapoport 1996 | 60 opera arias and lieder from official recordings | 7 professional singers | Performance measurements | Neutral-soft, calm, expressive, short, transitional-multistage, intermediate, excited, virtuoso |
| Krumhansl & Lynn Schenk 1997 | Mozart minuet + choreographed dance | 27 university students | Continuous recording of → | Segmentation, tension, new ideas, expressed emotion |
| Krumhansl 1997 | 6 classical pieces | 40 university students | Continuous recording of → + physiological measurements | Sadness, happiness, fear, tension |
| Fredrickson 1997 | Haydn (same as Nielsen 1983) | 112 school-age students | Continuous recordings of → | Tension |
| Madsen 1997 | 2 classical pieces | 50 + 48 students | Continuous recording of → | Valence (happiness-sadness) and Arousal (activeness-passiveness) |
| Juslin 1997a | 15 performances on electric guitar of a jazz piece | 3 performers, 24 university students | Ratings on 4 scales → + performance measurements | Anger, happiness, sadness, fear |
| Juslin 1997b | 108 synthesized and systematically varied performances + 10 performances of folk tune | 54 university students | Ratings on 6 scales → (MRA + CA) + forced choice → | Anger, happiness, sadness, fear, tenderness, expressiveness<br>Anger, happiness, sadness, fear, tenderness, expressiveness |
| Juslin 1997c | 10 synthesized and live performances of folk tune | 27 university students, musically trained | Free labeling + forced choice → (first and second choice) | Anger, happiness, sadness, fear, tenderness |
| Lindström 1997 | "Frère Jacques" manipulated in rhythm, melodic contour, & direction | 19 psychology students | Ratings on 6 bipolar scales → | Happy-sad, angry-tender, expressive-unexpressive, stable-unstable, simple-complex, tense-relaxed |
| Adachi & Trehub 1998 | Children's songs | 160 children, 4–12 years old (final sample) | Performance measurements + observer coding | Happy, sad |
| Peretz, Gagnon, & Bouchard 1998, Exp 2 | 32 synthesized classical pieces manipulated in tempo and mode | Brain-injured subject and normal subjects | Ratings of → | Happiness, sadness |
| Watt & Ash 1998 | 24 short excerpts, classical, popular | Undergraduate students | Forced choice in 14 dichotomies referring to → | People traits, people states, movement, terms rarely applied to people |
| Balkwill & Thompson 1999 | 12 performances of Hindustani ragas | 30 listeners | Forced choice → | Anger, joy, sadness, peace |
| Juslin & Madison 1999 | 120 performances (piano) of 2 pieces; folk tune, jazz (elimination of cues) | 20 university students | Ratings on 4 scales → (MRA) + performance measurements | Anger, happiness, sadness, fear |
| Schubert 1999a, b | 4 classical pieces | 25 musicians, 42 nonmusicians | Continuous recording of → | Valence (happiness-sadness) and Arousal (activeness-sleepiness) |

*(continued)*

513

Table 26.1 *(continued)*

| Author | Stimuli | Subjects | Response Type | Descriptive Attributes |
|---|---|---|---|---|
| Juslin 2000 | 72 performances on electric guitar of 3 pieces; folk, jazz | 30 students, some musically trained | Ratings on 4 scales → (MRA) + performance measurements | Anger, happiness, sadness, fear |
| Juslin & Laukka 2000 | 240 performances of 3 pieces (jazz, folk, popular) on electric guitar | 8 performers, 50 students | Ratings on 4 scales → (MRA) + performance measurements | Anger, happiness, sadness, fear |
| Laukka & Gabrielsson 2000 | 42 performances on drums of swing, beat, and waltz | 2 professional drummers, 13 students | Ratings on 7 scales → + performance measurements | Angry, fearful, happy, sad, solemn, tender, no expression |
| Bresin & Friberg (2000) | 14 synthesized performances of 2 pieces; classical and children's song | 20 listeners, some musically trained | Forced choice → | Anger, fear, happiness, sadness, solemnity, tenderness, no expression |

ative emotions (e.g., grief, melancholy, mournful, sadness, sorrow, despair), high arousal (e.g., agitated, angry, restless, rage, uneasy, violent), low arousal (e.g., gentle, relaxing, soothing, tranquil), and various other feelings such as love, yearning, nostalgia, sentimentality, prayerfulness, reverence, delicateness, assertiveness, determination, dignity, solemnity, eeriness, weirdness, and grotesqueness. Terms not reaching 50% agreement were (in alphabetical order) cruelty, devotion, disgust, eroticism, flippancy, hate, horror, irritation, jealousy, pity, whimsy, and worship.

Brown (1981) studied listeners' ability to recognize similar emotional expression in pieces from different styles and genres in classical music. He chose 12 musical excerpts and asked listeners to order them into six pairs according to six different emotional categories (see Table 26.1). In another task, listeners instead had to identify six pairs out of 12 other musical excerpts representing "twelve variations on sadness"—that is, within the same broad emotion category. While listeners were fairly successful in the first task, they were not so in the second task, until Brown supplied his own descriptions of the six sadness categories (see Table 26.1); however, nonmusicians were still unsuccessful. Brown thus concluded that if the different expressions are not too similar (as in the first task), synonymous pairs in expression can be identified even by persons not highly knowledgeable about classical music. However, with pieces as close in expression as in the variations on sadness, "the agreement on synonymous pairs can only be achieved by listeners highly conversant with the traditions involved" (p. 264).

Watt and Ash (1998) found higher intersubject agreement in choice of descriptive terms that can refer to "people traits" or states—male/female, young/old, good/evil,

joyful/sad, angry/pleased, gentle/violent—than for other terms (e.g., prickly). On the basis of this result they hypothesized that "the action of music is to mimic a person" (p. 49). This is reminiscent of the notion that listeners perceive music as a "virtual persona" (e.g., Levinson, 1996).

Studies in this section have provided examples of both good and poor listener agreement. Good agreement may exist regarding a basic emotional quality but less regarding nuances or variants of this quality (Brown, 1981; Downey, 1897; cf. also Campbell, 1942); appreciation of nuances may require good knowledge of the musical style (Brown, 1981). Of course, results may depend on the selection of music and on the response method (cf. Rigg, 1937a). Gender of the listener, on the other hand, did not seem to be important (e.g., Sopchak, 1955).

### Accuracy

Accuracy refers to listeners' "correct" recognition of emotional expression according to some independent criterion (e.g., composer's intention, expert judgment). Rigg (1937a) used short phrases supposed to express joy, lamentation, longing, and love. The expression of joy was correctly recognized by the listeners, but the recognition of the other expressions was far less accurate. Campbell (1942) selected pieces to represent seven emotions (see Table 26.1). The subjects were asked to associate each piece with one of the seven emotions. Agreement among listeners and agreement with Campbell's emotion designations were very high for gaiety, joy, and assertion; lower but still well above chance level for calm, sorrow, tenderness, and yearning. Yearning could be confused with sorrow, calm, and tenderness; and calm with tenderness and sorrow. Different amounts of musical training gave no difference in results. Watson (1942), using musical experts' judgments as criterion for the intended expression in selected pieces of music, found that even children in 6th and 8th grades showed good (>50%) agreement with the criterion, best for expressions such as mischievous, happy, exciting, kingly, dignified, and sad. Results were worse for expressions such as pleading, tragic, and mysterious, for which 50% agreement was not reached until respondents were the age of college students. The ability to discriminate musical expressions had no relation to general intelligence, only low correlations with scores on the Seashore Measures of Musical Talents (Seashore, Lewis, & Saetveit, 1939/1960), and no relation to musical training except at higher age levels. Robazza, Macaluso, and D'Urso (1994) asked adults and children (9–10 years) to decode the expression of eight pieces of classical piano music (selected by music experts to express anger, happiness, sadness, and fear) by means of forced choice. The results showed high overall accuracy for happiness and sadness (about 75% correct), but lower accuracy for anger (28%) and fear (39%). There were no differences between listeners with regard to musical experience or gender. In a study by Thompson and Robitaille (1992), listeners moderately trained in music were able to recognize expressions of joy, sorrow, excitement, anger, and dullness in melodies specially composed to carry these expressions; partial confusion occurred between expressions for peace and sorrow.

A special case of musical communication concerns program music (see earlier, "Absolute Music"), which aims at describing events or situations as well as associated emotions. If listeners do not know the intended program, they are usually unable to provide a "correct" description of events or situations, but they are somewhat better at perceiving the intended emotional expression (Batel, 1976; Brown, 1981; Downey, 1897; Foros, 1975; Hampton, 1945; Osborne, 1989; Rigg, 1937b; Weld, 1912); Osborne's study provided the most positive outcome.

Taken together, these studies indicate good recognition of intended emotional expressions for positive emotions (gaiety, happiness, joy, mischievous), negative emotions (sadness, sorrow; anger-hate; dullness), high arousal (excitement), low arousal (calm), tenderness, and dignity. Confusions may occur—for instance, yearning may be confused with sorrow, calm, and tenderness; calm with tenderness and sorrow; and peace with sorrow.

## Fundamental Dimensions in Emotional Expression

Following the introduction of the semantic differential technique (Osgood, Suci, & Tannenbaum, 1957) and the development of efficient computer programs for multivariate statistical techniques—factor analysis, cluster analysis, correspondence analysis, multidimensional scaling—investigators, rather than asking for listeners' choices

among ready-made clusters of descriptive terms, now gathered a large number of descriptive terms, asked listeners to provide numerical ratings of them, and then let multivariate analysis of the ratings show what terms belonged together. Rating scales were either bipolar—such as happy versus sad, excited versus calm—as in the semantic differential technique, or unipolar in cases where exact opposites were hard to find.

Despite large variation regarding musical stimuli, descriptive terms, and number and type of subjects, several studies using factor analysis (mostly), correspondence analysis (Imberty, 1979), or multidimensional scaling resulted in two common fundamental dimensions. One reflected positive versus negative emotions: "Heiterkeit–Ernst" (cheerful–serious; Kleinen, 1968; see Figure 26.1); gaiety–gloom (Wedin, 1969, 1972b; see Figure 26.2; Nielzén & Cesarec, 1981); pleasantness–unpleasantness (Wedin, 1972c); vital, gay, playful versus dull, restrained, and hesitating (Gabrielsson, 1973, experiments 4–5); and "Les schèmes de résonances émotionelles" (positive vs. negative emotions; Imberty, 1979).

Another dimension mainly reflected arousal or potency, or both: "Robustheit–Zartheit" (strong/powerful–soft/tender; Kleinen, 1968); tension/energy (e.g., tense vs. relaxed, vehement vs. mild, aggressive vs. gentle; Wedin, 1969, 1972b); intensity–softness (Wedin, 1972c); aggressive, excited, intense vs. calm and soft (Gabrielsson, 1973); tension–relaxation (Nielzén & Cesarec, 1981); and "Les schèmes de tension et de détente" (tension vs. relaxation; Imberty, 1979).

Thus, there is a good agreement on these emotion dimensions in several studies. The configuration of descriptive terms within the two-dimensional plane may be strikingly similar, as seen in a comparison of Figures 26.1 and 26.2 (and slight rotation of the axes may increase the similarity further). Note that most expressions studied so far belong to only two of the quadrants, which are opposite each other. This might reflect the choice of musical stimuli and descriptive terms in the studies.

Dimensions similar to those just mentioned also appeared in other studies: tempo/playfulness and potency (Hare, 1977); humor (amused, playful), depression (sad, gloomy), evil (anger, hate), activity (determined, vigorous), pastoral (calm, relaxed), sedative (serene, tranquil), potency (heroic, majestic), all in Asmus (1985); "temperament" (merry, playful), "Erregung" (excited, dramatic), "Ruhe" (calm, tired) in Batel (1976, cluster analysis); and a dimension extending from gentle and soft to energetic and powerful, reflecting the successive *crescendo* in Ravel's *Bolero* (Asada & Ohgushi, 1991). Solemnity–triviality may be an additional, independent dimension (Wedin, 1969, 1972a, 1972b, 1972c).

Although not present among the descriptors used in Figures 26.1 and 26.2, other feelings—love, tenderness, nostalgic, sentimental, prayerful, reverent, delicate, asser-

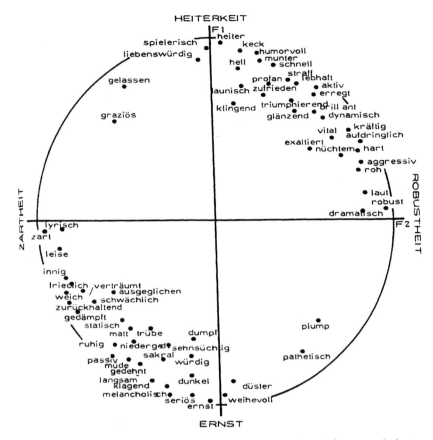

Figure 26.1 The first two dimensions obtained in Kleinen's (1968) factor analysis. Reproduced by permission of the author.

tion, determination, eerie, weird, and grotesque—could be placed within the two-dimensional plane. Some confusions among expressions—for instance, yearning confused with sorrow or calm, calm or peace with sorrow—seem understandable from their positions close to each other in Figures 26.1 and 26.2.

### Continuous Recording

As emotional expression may vary during a piece of music, researchers have recently devised procedures for continuous recording of perceived expression. Nielsen (1983, 1987) pioneered this work having listeners—one group of musically experienced listeners and another group of young nonmusical students—continuously press a pair of tongs in proportion to perceived tension in the music (the more tension, the harder press, and vice versa), when listening to the first movement of Haydn's *London Symphony* and to the initial part of Richard Strauss's *Also Sprach Zarathustra*. The pressures were transformed to electric voltage and registered on a polygraph. The visible result was thus waves of tension and relaxation, such as in Figure 26.3, which shows these waves for the Haydn movement, averaged across the musically experienced listeners. In the exposition of the movement, there were

waves of tension with periods of relaxation in between; in the development there was a practically continuous increase of tension up to its end, after which the pattern from the exposition returned in the repetition. The average curve of the inexperienced group looked similar to this already in their first listening, and the similarity increased in a second listening.

Nielsen's results have been replicated by Madsen and Fredrickson (1993), using another response device (CRDI, Continuous Response Digital Interface). Fredrickson (1997) found high correlation between young students' (grades 2, 5, 8, and 11/12) continuous ratings of perceived tension in the Haydn movement. Krumhansl (1996) had listeners adjust a slider at the center of the computer screen to indicate variations in tension in Mozart's Piano Sonata K. 282, and to indicate experienced expression of happiness, sadness, fear, and tension in six excerpts of classical music (Krumhansl, 1997). Krumhansl and Lynn Schenk (1997) studied relationships between dance and music by asking students to use a foot-switch to indicate the amount of tension in dance performance to a Mozart minuet.

Namba, Kuwano, Hatoh, and Kato (1991) assigned a separate key on a computer keyboard to each of 15 adjectives (see Table 26.1). While listening to Mussorgsky's *Pic-*

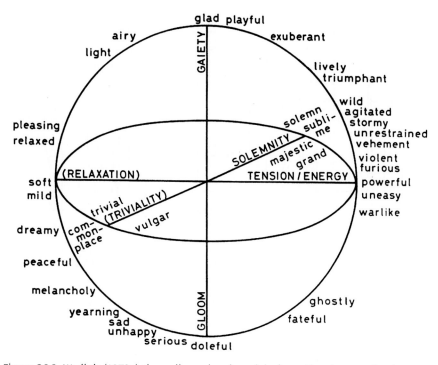

Figure 26.2 Wedin's (1972a) three-dimensional model of emotional expression in music. Reproduced by permission of the author.

*tures at an Exhibition*, the subjects successively pressed the different keys according to how well the respective adjectives described the perceived expression. Schubert (1999a, 1999b), in connection to results from multivariate analyses, had his subjects successively move the computer cursor to various positions in a two-dimensional emotion space with two main axes—valence (horizontal) and arousal (vertical)—according to perceived expression. The subjects' responses to four pieces of classical instrumental music were studied in relation to variations of various factors in the musical structure using time series and regression analyses. A similar device for continuous recording of emotional responses to music was developed by Madsen (1997). For a more extensive review of continuous response methodology, see Schubert (2001).

### Determinants of Perceived Expression

Which factors in the musical structure influence the perceived emotional expression? This question has been investigated using both experimental and post hoc analyses.

*Experimental approaches.* Hevner introduced experimental manipulation using short pieces of tonal music. Besides the original version of a piece, she created a variant differing in mode (Hevner 1935a), melodic direction, harmony, and rhythm (Hevner, 1936), tempo, and pitch level (Hevner, 1937). By manipulating one variable at a time while keeping all others constant, researchers could ascribe any difference in listeners' judgments of the respec-

tive two versions of a piece to the manipulated variable. Response variables were eight clusters of descriptive terms in a circular configuration, an "adjective circle" (see Figure 26.4). This has an obvious, although not perfect, similarity to the results from later multivariate analyses (cf. Figures 26.1 and 26.2): the vertical axis (cluster 6 vs. cluster 2) corresponds to gaiety versus gloom. The horizontal axis (cluster 8 to cluster 4) has a certain similarity with tension/energy versus relaxation, and the similarity seems even greater if one considers clusters 7 and 8 together (this would correspond to tension/energy) versus clusters 3 and 4 together (relaxation). Although Farnsworth (1954) slightly modified Hevner's clusters and abandoned the circular representation, Hevner's adjective circle has appeared again in later investigations (e.g., Batel, 1976; Gregory & Varney, 1996).

In Hevner's studies, listeners (usually hundreds of students) were instructed to mark as many of the terms in the adjective circle as they found appropriate for the music in question. Variables with largest effects on their choice turned out to be tempo and mode, followed by pitch level, harmony, and rhythm, whereas melodic direction had little, if any, effect. Fast tempos elicited judgments in the happy-gay and exciting-restless clusters (clusters 6–7), and to a lesser extent in vigorous and graceful clusters (clusters 8 and 5), slow tempos in the dignified, sad, sentimental-tender, and calm-serene clusters (clusters 1–4). Major mode was associated with happiness, gaiety, playfulness, and sprightliness (clusters 5–6), minor mode with sadness, sentimental, yearning, and tender effects (clusters 2–3).

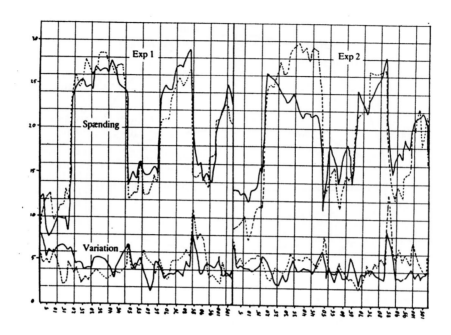

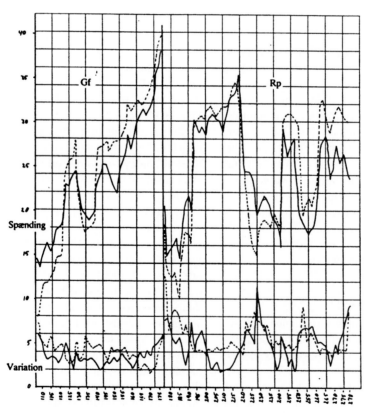

Figure 26.3 Tension curves from listeners' continuous rating of tension in Haydn's *London Symphony*, first movement, from Nielsen (1983) (spænding = tension, Exp = exposition, Gf = development, Rp = recapitulation, horizontal axis shows bar numbers, vertical axis shows exerted hand pressure, bold curve = first listening, dotted curve = second listening). Reproduced by permission of the author and Akademisk Forlag, Copenhagen.

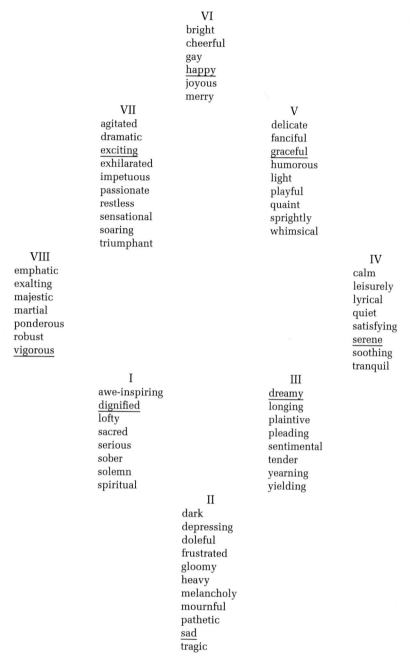

Figure 26.4 Hevner's adjective circle. Adjectives within each cluster appear in alphabetical order. Adjectives used by Hevner (1936, 1937) to represent the respective clusters are underlined. Adapted from Farnsworth (1954).

Higher pitch level had greatest effect on the sprightly-humorous cluster (cluster 5), lower pitch level on the sad, vigorous-majestic, and dignified-serious qualities (clusters 2, 8, and 1). Simple harmonies were characterized as happy, graceful, serene, and sentimental (clusters 6, 5, 4, 3), complex dissonant harmonies as exciting and to some extent both sad and vigorous (clusters 7, 2, 8). Flowing rhythm was light, happy, graceful, and sentimental (clusters 5, 6, 3), firm rhythm dignified (cluster 1). These results were largely independent of musical training and of scores

on the Seashore Measures of Musical Talents (Seashore et al., 1939/1960).

Hevner (1935b) emphasized the necessity of using pieces with similar emotional expression throughout the piece. If the piece contains different expressions in different parts, the resulting judgments may look very peculiar, even contradictory. She further warned against drawing too far-reaching conclusions from these data, pointing out their possible dependency on the selected pieces, difficulties in constructing adequate examples, and, above all, the fact that emotional expression usually results from several musical factors in complex interplay.

Experimental manipulation was also applied by Rigg (1939), who composed and manipulated five four-bar phrases regarding tempo, mode, articulation (legato, staccato), pitch level, loudness, rhythm (iambic, trochaic), and certain intervals; further transposed the same phrases up or down (Rigg, 1940a); and had the same five phrases played by a pianist at six different tempos (Rigg, 1940b; Rigg, 1964, provided a useful review of his work as well as that of Gundlach, Hevner, and Watson). Scherer and Oshinsky (1977) synthesized eight-tone sequences that were manipulated in two levels concerning amplitude variation, pitch level, pitch contour, pitch variation, tempo, envelope, and filtration cut-off level. Multiple regression analysis was used to estimate the predictive strength of each acoustic parameter on each response dimension (see Table 26.1). Juslin (1997b, experiment 2) used synthesized versions of "Nobody Knows," manipulating tempo (slow, medium, fast), sound level (low, medium, high), frequency spectrum (soft, bright, sharp), articulation (legato, staccato), and tone attack (slow, fast). Students rated these versions on six adjective scales: happy, sad, angry, fearful, tender, and expressive. Multiple regression analyses showed that the variance accounted for ($R^2$) by the manipulated factors was typically 0.78–0.88. Lindström (1997) similarly used synthesis to manipulate rhythm, melodic contour, and melodic direction in different versions of "Frère Jacques" and asked listeners to rate them on six bipolar scales (e.g., happy-sad, angry-tender, tense-relaxed). The results revealed complex interactions among the manipulated factors in their effects on listeners' ratings. Peretz, Gagnon, and Bouchard (1998, experiment 2) manipulated tempo and mode in synthesized versions of 32 excerpts of classical music and found that both factors affected both normal listeners' and a brain-injured listener's perception of happiness and sadness in similar ways.

Thompson and Robitaille (1992) asked five composers to compose short melodies to express joy, sorrow, excitement, dullness, anger, and peace. Listeners successfully recognized most of these expressions (see "Accuracy," earlier). Joyful melodies were strongly tonal and rhythmically varied. Sad melodies were slow with implied minor or chromatic harmony. Melodies for excitement were fast and contained intervallic leaps and high pitches. Dull melodies were tonal in stepwise motion. Angry melodies were rhythmically complex and with implied chromatic harmony or atonality. Melodies for peacefulness were tonal, slow, and often involved stepwise motion leading to melodic leaps.

*Post Hoc Analyses.* Variables in the musical structure related to perceived expressions have been studied post hoc using the score of the music (e.g., Gundlach, 1935; Krumhansl, 1996, 1997; Nielsen, 1983), using the score to construct indices for formal complexity and dynamism (Imberty, 1979), or using musical experts as judges (Kleinen, 1968; Watson, 1942; Wedin, 1972c). For instance, Wedin (1972c) had musical experts rate various musico-technical aspects of the pieces used, and their relations to the emotion dimensions were investigated by multiple regression analysis. Intensity–softness was most affected by articulation (staccato–legato) and intensity (forte–piano); the combination of staccato and forte expressed activity and energy, whereas legato and piano made the character soft. In the pleasantness–unpleasantness or gaiety–gloom dimension, the pleasant–glad pole was determined by consonance, fluent and fast rhythm, major mode, and high pitch; the opposite pole was determined by dissonance, firm and slow rhythm, minor mode, and low pitch. Solemnity was achieved by low pitch, slow tempo, and forte.

*Summary of Results.* Results from these studies are summarized in Table 26.2 in terms of how the most common emotions are related to variables in musical structure as studied by different investigators. Every expressed emotion is related to a large number of structural variables, whose relative importance may be roughly proportional to the number of investigators cited for each structural factor; for some emotions (boredom, disgust, surprise) studied by a single investigator, factors are listed in importance according to the respective author. Tempo, mode, consonance-dissonance, loudness, and pitch recur for most emotions, whereas factors related to melody, rhythm, timbre, articulation, and envelope appear less regularly. Various examples of how emotions have been expressed in classical music using these means can be found in de la Motte-Haber (1996, pp. 72–77).

The combination of positive valence and high arousal is associated with fast tempo, high loudness, high pitch level, large pitch variation, staccato articulation, bright or sharp timbre, and sharp envelopes, while the two dimensions may differ with regard to mode (positive valence rather in major mode, high arousal may be in either mode), in harmony (positive valence apt to consonance and simple harmony, high arousal may be dissonant and contain more complex harmony), rhythm (positive valence fluent rhythm, high arousal more complex rhythm), and formal complexity (positive valence less complex than high arousal). The combination of negative valence and low arousal is associated with slow tempo, soft loudness, low pitch level, small pitch variation, legato articulation, dark timbre, and round envelopes, while the two dimensions may differ with regard to mode (negative valence usually in minor mode, low arousal may be in either mode), harmony (negative valence more dissonant than low arousal), and formal complexity (negative valence more complex than low arousal).

With regard to mode, the common association between

Table 26.2 Summary of Determinants of Perceived Emotional Expression in Music

*Note.* Authors' names are abbreviated to the initial two letters of the (first) author, publication year to the two last digits (e.g., He36 = Hevner, 1936). References within parentheses refer to performance studies (Round envelope = slow tone attack/slow decay, sharp envelope = fast tone attack/fast decay).

| Emotion | Related variables in musical structure |
|---|---|
| Happiness, Joy, Gaiety | **Fast tempo** Gu35, He37, Ri40b Wa42, Ri64, Kl68, Mo68, We72c, Ga73, Sc77, Ni82, Th92, Ju97b, Kr97, Pe98, (Ba94), (Ga/Li95), (Ga96), (Ju97a), (Ad98), (Ju99), (Ba99), (Ju00), (Ju/La00), (La00)<br>**Moderate tempo variation** (Ga/Li95), (Ju99)<br>**Major mode** He36, Ri39, Kl68, We72c, Sc77, Cr85, Kr97, Pe98<br>**Consonance** He36, Ri39, Wa42, We72c<br>**High loudness** Ri39, Ni82, (Ko76), (Ga/Li95), (Su95), (Ga96), (Oh96b), (Ju97a), (Ad98), (Ju99), (Ju00, (Ju/La00)<br>**Small loudness variation** Wa42, Sc77, (Ju99)<br>**High pitch** He37, Ri40a, Kl68, We72c, (Ad98)<br>**Large pitch variation/pitch range** Gu35, Sc77, (Ba99)<br>**Ascending melody** Ge95, **rising intonation** (Ra 96)<br>**Rhythm: regular** Gu35, Wa42, **varied** Th92, **fluent** He36, We72c<br>**Staccato articulation** Ri39, Ni82, Ju97b, (Ga/Li95), (Ga96), (Ra96), (Ju99), (Ju00)<br>**Large articulation variation** (Ju99), (Ju00), (Ju/La00)<br>**Many harmonics/bright timbre** (Ga96), (Ju/La00)<br>**Sharp envelope** Sc77, (Ko76), (Ga96)<br>**Moderate timing variation** (Ga96), (Ju/La00)<br>**Sharpened contrasts between long and short notes** (Ga96), (La00)<br>**Low formal complexity and average dynamism** Im79 |
| Sadness/Gloom | **Slow tempo** He37, Ri40b, Wa42, Ri64, Kl68, Be72, We72c, Sc77, Ni82, Th92, Ju97b, Kr97, Pe98, (Ko76), (Ba94), (Ga96), (Oh96b), (Ju97a), (Ad98), (Ju99), (Ba99), (Ju00), (Ju/La00), (La00)<br>**Minor mode** He36, Ri39, Ri64, Kl68, We72c, Cr85, Kr97, Pe98<br>**Dissonance** He36, Wa42, Ri64, We72c<br>**Soft loudness** Gu35, Ju97b, (Ko76), (Ba94), (Ga96), (Oh96b), (Ju97a), (Ad98), (Ju99), (Ju00), (Ju/La00), (La00)<br>**Loudness variation: small** Wa42, **moderate** (Ju99)<br>**Low pitch** Gu35, He37, Ri40a, Wa42, Ri64, We72c, Sc77, (Ad98)<br>**Narrow pitch range** Gu35, (Ba99)<br>**Descending melody/pitch contour** Sc77, Ge95<br>**Firm rhythm** He36, We72c<br>**Legato articulation** Ri39, Ju97b, (Ga96), (Ju97a), (Ju99), (Ju00), (Ju/La00)<br>**Little articulation variation** (Ju99), (Ju00), (Ju/La00)<br>**Few harmonics/soft timbre** Sc77, Ju97b, (Ju00), (Ju/La00)<br>**Round envelope** Sc77, Ju97b, (Ko76), (Ga96)<br>**Large timing variation** (Ga96), (Ju/La00)<br>**Softened contrasts between long and short notes** (Ga96), (La00)<br>**Slow vibrato** (Ga96), (Ko00)<br>**High formal complexity combined with low dynamism** Im79 |
| Activity/Energy/ Excitement | **Fast tempo** Gu35, He37, Ri40b, Wa42, Ri64, Sc77, Th92<br>**Dissonance** He36, Ri39, Wa42, Ri64<br>**High loudness** Wa42, Ri64, We72c<br>**Small loudness variation** Sc77<br>**Pitch: high** Wa42, Sc77, **low** He37, Ri40a<br>**Large pitch variation** Sc77<br>**Intervallic leaps** Th92<br>**Staccato articulation** Ri39, We72c<br>**Many harmonics** Sc77<br>**Sharp envelope** Sc77<br>**Large vibrato extent** (Wa32), (Ra96) |
| Potency | **Fast tempo** Sc77<br>**High loudness** Kl68<br>**High pitch** Sc77<br>**Rising pitch contour** Sc77<br>**Many harmonics** Sc77<br>**Round envelope** Sc77 |

Table 26.2 *(continued)*

| Emotion | Related variables in musical structure |
|---|---|
| Tension | **Dissonance** Ni82a, Ni83<br>**High sound level, dynamics** Ni83, Kr96<br>**Ascending melody** Ni83, Kr96<br>**Increased note density** Ni83, Kr96<br>**Harmonic complexity** Ni83<br>**Rhythmic complexity** Ni82, Ni83<br>**Lack of melody** Ni82<br>**Various formal properties** Ni83, Kr96 |
| Relaxation/Calm/<br>Softness/Peace | **Slow tempo** Gu35, He37, Ri64, (Ba99)<br>**Consonance** He36, Ri64, Li97<br>**Soft loudness** Wa42, K168, We72c<br>**Pitch: high** He37, **low** Gu35<br>**Narrow pitch range** Gu35, (Ba99)<br>**Rhythm: regular** Wa42, **flowing** He36<br>**Legato articulation** We72c<br>**Small vibrato extent** (Wa32), (Ra96)<br>**Low formal complexity** Ni83 |
| Solemnity/Dignity | **Slow tempo** Gu35, He37, Ri40b, Ri64, We72c, (Ga/Li95), (Ga96)<br>**Mode: major** Ri39, **minor** He36<br>**Consonance** He36, Ri39, Wa42, Ri64<br>**Loudness: high** We72c, **moderate or high** (Ga/Li95), (Ga96)<br>**Few loudness changes** Wa42<br>**Low pitch** He37, Ri40a, We72c<br>**Narrow melodic range** Gu35<br>**Rhythm: regular** Wa42, Ri64, **firm** He36<br>**Legato articulation** Ri39, (Ga/Li95)<br>**Sharp envelope** (Ga96)<br>**Small timing variation** (Ga96) |
| Anger | **Fast tempo** Sc77, Ju97b, (Ko76), (Ba94), (Ga/Li95), (Su95), (Ga96), (Oh96b), (Ju97a), (Ju99), (Ju00), (Ju/La00), (La00)<br>**Minor mode** Sc77<br>**Dissonance** Li97<br>**High loudness** Ju97b, (Ko76), (Ba94), (Ga/Li95), (Su95), (Ga96), (Oh96b), (Ra96), (Ju97a), (Ju99), (Ju00), (Ju/La00), (La00)<br>**Little loudness variation** (Ju99)<br>**Pitch: high** Sc77<br>**Small pitch variation** Sc77<br>**Ascending pitch contour** Sc77<br>**Complex rhythm** Th92<br>**Articulation: staccato** Ju97b, (Ga/Li95), (Ga96), (Ju99), **legato** (Ju97a), (Ju00)<br>**Moderate articulation variation** (Ju99), (Ju00)<br>**Many harmonics/sharp timbre** Sc77, Ju97b, (Ga96), (Ju00), (Ju/La00)<br>**Sharp envelope** Ju97b, (Ko76), (Ga96)<br>**Small timing variation** (Ju/La00)<br>**Sharpened contrasts between long and short notes** (Ga96)<br>**Large vibrato extent** (Me32), (Ko00)<br>**High complexity combined with high dynamism** Im79 |
| Fear | **Tempo: fast** Sc77, (Ko76), (Oh96b), (Ju99), (La00), **slow** (Ju97a), (Ju00)<br>**Large tempo variation** (Ga96), (Ju99), (La00)<br>**Dissonance** Kr97<br>**Loudness: soft** Ju97b, (Ko76), (Ga96), (Ju97a), (Ju00), (Ju/La00), (La00), **moderate** (Oh96b)<br>**Large loudness variation** Sc77, (Ga96), (Ju99)<br>**Rapid loudness changes** Kr97<br>**Pitch: high level, ascending contour, small variation** Sc77<br>**Large pitch contrasts** Kr97<br>**Staccato articulation** Ju97b, (Ga96), (Ju97a), (Ju/La00)<br>**Large articulation variation** (Ju99), (Ju/La00)<br>**Harmonics: many** Sc77, **few** (Ju00), (Ju/La00)<br>**Large timing variation** (Ga96), (Ju/La00), (La00)<br>**Envelope: round** Sc77, Ju97b, **sharp** (Ko76)<br>**Vibrato: irregular** (Ra96), (Ga96), **fast** (Ko00) |

Table 26.2  *(continued)*

| Emotion | Related variables in musical structure |
|---|---|
| Tenderness/Love | **Tempo: slow** Ju97b, (Ga/Li95), (Su95), (Ga96), **moderate** (La00)<br>**Soft loudness** Ju97b, (Ga/Li95), (Su95), (Ga96), (La00)<br>**Rising intonation** (Ra96)<br>**Little loudness variation** (Ga/Li95)<br>**Legato articulation** Ju97b, (Ga/Li95), (Ga96)<br>**Round envelope** Ju97b (Ga96)<br>**Few harmonics/soft timbre** Ju97b (Ga96)<br>**Large timing variation** (Ga96)<br>**Softened contrasts between long and short notes** (Ga/Li95), (Ga96) |
| Boredom | **Slow tempo, low pitch level, few harmonics, descending pitch contour, round envelope, small pitch variation** Sc77 |
| Disgust | **Many harmonics, small pitch variation, round envelope, slow tempo** Sc77 |
| Surprise | **Fast tempo, high pitch level, ascending pitch contour, sharp envelope, many harmonics, large pitch variation** Sc77 |

major mode and happiness and between minor mode and sadness was questioned by Heinlein (1928). Listening to isolated major and minor chords, his subjects gave many "erroneous" responses—that is, sad-type responses to major chords and happy-type responses to minor chords (cf. discussion in Crowder, 1984). He also found that loud chords and chords at high pitch level evoked more happy-type responses than soft chords and chords at low pitch level, irrespective of mode. However, Crowder (1985) found the conventional major-happy and minor-sad associations in young adults who listened to sine-wave triads, and these associations appeared in many of the investigations using real music (Table 26.2). See also children's responses in the section on "Developmental Studies."

This summary should preferably be supplemented by the review in Gabrielsson and Lindström (2001), which summarizes the same results but in terms of the effects each structural factor has on respective emotion judgment. It also points out several gaps and uncertainties in research so far, especially regarding the effects of timbre, intervals, melody, rhythm, harmony, and properties of musical form. The most obvious gap concerns potential interactions between different factors. It has been repeatedly emphasized (e.g., Hevner, 1935b, 1937; Rigg, 1964) that no factor works in isolation; its effects are highly dependent on what other factors and levels are present in the actual context. Despite these problems, the findings clearly support the general assumption made in most theories of expression in music—namely, that specific patterns of musical factors correspond to specific emotions.

### Tests of Theories

*Cooke's Theory.* Some attempts have been made to test the validity of Cooke's (1959) theory. As explained in the section "Modern Theories of Emotional Expression in Music," Cooke postulated 16 so-called basic terms, each as-

sociated with a particular emotional expression. Gabriel (1978) generated the 16 basic terms using sinusoidals, constant tempo, and uniform rhythm. Students listened to these "reduced" basic terms and were given a response sheet with Cooke's description of each term. Their task was to rate the agreement between each basic term and the description on a five-point scale (5 = perfect match, 1 = no match at all). In one condition the description of each term was according to Cooke, but in another condition Cooke's descriptions were distributed randomly across the basic terms. It turned out that the mean agreement ratings were about the same under both conditions, thus failing to support Cooke's theory. However, this experiment has, in turn, been discussed and criticized regarding the choice of sinusoidal stimuli, the lack of musical context, and the use of musically untrained listeners (Cazden, 1979; Gabriel, 1979; Hampson, 2000; Kaminska & Woolf, 2000; Nettheim, 1979; Sloboda, 1985, pp. 60–64).

Hampson (2000) and Kaminska and Woolf (2000) again tried to test the validity of Cooke's theory. Hampson used selected pieces of 19th-century piano music (e.g., by Chopin, Schumann), thus real music, featuring nine of Cooke's basic terms. Musically experienced listeners rated on a five-point scale how well Cooke's descriptions matched their own perception of the emotion in the respective piece. Kaminska and Woolf first reduced Cooke's 16 basic terms to four bipolar dimensions (joy–sorrow, assertiveness–submissiveness, finality–continuation, outburst–constancy) and then had nonmusicians listen to the basic terms using sampled piano sound and keeping tempo, volume, and articulation constant (similar to Gabriel's approach). The listeners' task was to rate each basic term on each of the four bipolar scales. Although these two studies used different stimuli and procedures, both revealed that the different melodic lines in Cooke's basic terms carry different emotional meanings, but not in the precise way claimed by Cooke. Only one of Cooke's statements was confirmed, namely, the association of major and minor mode to positive and negative emotion, respectively, already known from other research.

However, the effect of "melodic line" on emotional expression cannot be separated from other factors because melody always implies some kind of rhythm (even if tones have equal duration), further a certain tempo, loudness, timbre, articulation, and so on. Variables in the musical structure may interact in many different ways (Gabrielsson & Lindström, 2001; Hevner, 1935b, 1937; Rigg, 1964), and their relative importance may therefore vary with different contexts.

*Clynes's Theory.* Clynes's suggestion to use the sentograph to study emotional expression in music was followed up in his own studies. This gave some indications of pressure patterns (e.g., for joy, sex), similar to those he had obtained without music, in listeners' sentograph responses to the pulse in pieces of ethnic and rock music (Clynes & Walker, 1982, pp. 202–207; see also examples in Gabrielsson, 1993, p. 107).

Independent attempts to test Clynes's theory about specific spatiotemporal patterns (sentograms) for different emotions have yielded mixed results. Asked to match a randomized list of the emotion labels (i.e., anger, love, sex, hate, joy, reverence) with the corresponding sentograms presented in graphic illustrations, subjects showed poor matching accuracy—barely above chance (Gorman & Crain, 1974). Trussoni, O'Malley, and Barton (1988) and Nettelbeck, Henderson, and Willson (1989) asked participants to produce sentograms for eight emotions, and examined their similarity to the spatiotemporal curves suggested by Clynes (1973). In both studies, the results were mainly negative. Trussoni et al. (1988), for instance, noted "the definite absence of a significant correlation between our sentograms and those of Clynes" (p. 423). However, Hama and Tsuda (1990) provided some support for the theory: Sentograms produced in response to a sad face lasted longer than those to an angry face, and sentograms produced in response to an angry face exhibited higher pressure than sentograms to faces representing joy, sorrow, or no emotion.

A more important test of Clynes's theory for our present purposes would involve the use of sounds shaped by the production of pressure patterns. Nettelbeck et al. (1989) used such "sentic" sound material from the soundsheet included in Clynes (1982) to replicate a study by Clynes and Nettheim (1982). Only three of the six sound stimuli (i.e., joy, anger, grief) were decoded with a fair degree of accuracy. Nettelbeck and associates therefore concluded that "Clynes and Nettheim's (1982) results are properly regarded as artefactual" (p. 36).

Some support for Clynes's theory was found by de Vries (1991), who asked 30 subjects to listen to 10 pieces of music and push the disk on a sentograph at the metrical accents of the music, "the way you do when tapping along with a piece of music" (p. 48). After compensating for individual differences in exerted force and calculating values for five parameters of the sentograms, de Vries found that sentograms were different for different pieces, and that there were similarities between the sentograms for pieces with a certain emotional expression (anger, grief, joy, love) and Clynes's sentograms for the corresponding emotions. Some (less formalized) evidence in the same direction was found in musicians' performances on the sentograph (without sound) of the same piece of music with different emotional expressions; the resulting pressure patterns showed some similarities with Clynes's sentograms for the corresponding emotions (Gabrielsson & Lindström, 1995). In sum, it seems that further research is needed to fully evaluate Clynes's theory.

### Developmental Studies

Children's perception of emotional expression has been investigated in a number of recent studies (e.g., Cunningham & Sterling, 1988; Dolgin & Adelson, 1990; Giomo, 1993; Kratus, 1993; Terwogt & van Grinsven, 1991). Children of varying age—from 4 to 12 years across these investigations—were asked to indicate which emotion they perceived in the music. The youngest children usually answered by choosing among faces with different emotional expressions. Older children could choose among verbal alternatives, and responses by adolescents or adults were used as reference. The music was mostly classical music or specially composed pieces (Dolgin & Adelson, 1990). Emotions to choose among were usually limited to happiness, sadness, anger, and fear (also "excited" and "calm" in Kratus, 1993). Even the youngest children were able to recognize these emotions with fair accuracy. However, most studies indicated better recognition with increasing age and better recognition of happiness and sadness than of anger and fear; the latter two may be confused (also seen in Robazza et al., 1994). Girls achieved better recognition than boys, generally or for some emotions, in most studies, but Dolgin and Adelson (1990) and Kratus (1993) found no consistent gender difference. There were certain differences in the results between the different studies, which may be due to differences in the type of music, instruments, and procedures used.

Do children associate major mode with happiness and minor mode with sadness? Infants (6 months old) showed no difference in their preference for a major or minor chord, but preference for a consonant chord over a dissonant chord (Crowder, Reznick, & Rosenkrantz, 1991). Children from preschool and elementary school associated major melodies to positive emotions (happy, contented) and minor melodies to negative emotions (sad, angry), not perfect but significantly different from what would happen on chance basis (Kastner & Crowder, 1990). Gregory, Worrall, and Sarge (1996), too, found the happy–major and sad–minor association for older children (7–8 years) but not for 3- to 4-year-olds. Thus, the conventional happy–major and sad–minor associations are found in older children, whereas the results for younger children are still inconclusive.

### Cross-Cultural Studies

There are only a few cross-cultural studies. Gundlach (1932) collected and analyzed transcriptions of 334 songs from different North American Indian tribes, including healing songs, love songs, and war songs. He then attempted to find similarities between European art music, Indian songs, and European folk songs (Gundlach, 1935, p. 637). Comparisons were hard to do, but some similarities were suggested. For example, high pitch used to characterize animated and glad feelings in European music occurred in Indian songs for happy love, and slow tempo used to express melancholy or mourning in European music occurred for sad love in Indian songs.

Morey (1940) played recordings of European art music, selected to express fear, reverence, rage, love, and no particular emotion, to 20 native West Africans, asking them about the activities and emotional expression suggested to them by these pieces. Nine of them left without answering, and the answers given by the remaining listeners showed little, if any, correspondence to the hypothesized expressions.

Kleinen (1994) had German and Chinese students judge the expression in two European (Mozart, Brahms) and two Chinese folklore pieces of music, using 11 scales referring to emotion (e.g., cheerful), motion, and structure (e.g., order). The results showed commonalities as well as marked differences between the two subject groups; differences were most obvious in aesthetic evaluation.

Gregory and Varney (1996) asked English and Indian students (living in England) to listen to Western classical, classical Indian, and New Age pieces of music and check one or more adjective groups with regard to emotional expression. There was an overall good agreement between the two subject groups, but also significant differences in perceived expression of many pieces.

Hoshino (1996) studied perceived expression of Japanese musical modes and Western major and minor modes using color associations and verbal associations as responses from different groups of Japanese subjects. While major and minor modes were perceived as contrasting in emotional character, the Japanese modes had weaker effects, which was related to the fact that traditional Japanese music does not primarily aim at expressing emotion but rather at describing the beauty and harmony of nature.

### Emotional Expression in Performance

As should be evident from the review so far, studies of emotional expression have almost exclusively been concerned with the impact of particular pieces of music, whereas they have ignored the impact of specific performances. However, the performance of a piece of music is also important in shaping the emotional expression. By performing the music in a certain way, a performer may intend to make fully manifest a quality of emotion that he or she considers to be important for the piece in question. Throughout history, there has been plenty of anecdotal evidence about the extraordinary expressive skills of particular performers. Empirical research on emotional expression in performance, however, is a fairly recent phenomenon.

Most studies have used the following paradigm. Professional performers are asked to play or sing brief melodies to express different emotions chosen by the researcher. The performances are recorded, and then judged by listeners to see whether they can infer the intended expressions. Each performance is also analyzed to study what means the performer used to accomplish each emotional expression. The assumption is that because the melody remains the same in the different versions, whatever effects appear in listeners' judgments or in acoustic measures should primarily be the result of the performer's expressive intention.

There are now about 30 studies of emotional expression in performance. They cover a wide range of musical styles, including opera (e.g., "Ardi gli incensi" from *Lucia di Lammermoor*; Siegwart & Scherer, 1995), classical music (*Violin Concerto* by Mendelsohn; Senju & Ohgushi, 1987), folk music ("Greensleeves"; Juslin, 2000), jazz (e.g., "When the Saints"; Juslin, 1997a), and popular tunes ("Happy Birthday"; Gabrielsson & Lindström, 1995). The emotions investigated have usually included happiness, sadness, anger, fear, solemnity, and love/tenderness. A variety of musical instruments have also been included, such as the flute, violin, clarinet, electric guitar, piano, trumpet, drums, synthesizer, and singing voice.

### Communication Accuracy

The primary question facing researchers was whether performers could communicate emotions to listeners at all. In what is probably the first study, Kotlyar and Morozov (1976) asked 10 opera singers to sing phrases from various pieces of music in such a way that they would convey joy, anger, sorrow, and fear to listeners. Then, 10 musically trained listeners were asked to judge the emotional expression of each performance. The results showed that listeners were highly successful at decoding the intended expression. Since then, many studies have confirmed that professional music performers are able to communicate specific emotions to listeners (e.g., Baroni & Finarelli, 1994; Behrens & Green, 1993; Gabrielsson, 1994, 1995; Gabrielsson & Juslin, 1996; Gabrielsson & Lindström, 1995; Juslin, 1997a, 1997b, 1997c, 2000; Juslin & Madison, 1999; Ohgushi & Hattori, 1996a; Sundberg, Iwarsson, & Hagegård, 1995). Listeners are even able to decode certain emotions with better than chance accuracy from single voice tones (Konishi, Imaizumi, & Niimi, 2000; Sherman, 1928). However, many studies have also revealed marked individual differences in encoding and decoding accuracy, consistent with the findings from studies of other nonverbal communication channels (Buck, 1984; Wallbott & Scherer, 1986).

Few studies have yet reported decoding accuracy in a manner that makes more precise estimates possible. However, Juslin (1997b) used a forced-choice format in order to make the results comparable to the results from studies of vocal expression. He found that decoding accuracy was 75% correct, or about four times higher than what would be expected by chance alone. This suggests that, at least under certain circumstances, the accuracy of communication of emotion via musical performance may approach the accuracy of facial or vocal expression (see chapter 22, this volume; chapter 28, this volume).

One objection to this finding might be that the accuracy of the communicative process is boosted because of the response format used. In most studies, listeners made their judgments by means of forced choice or adjective ratings—methods that offer only a limited number of response options. To address this problem, Juslin (1997c) investigated the generalizability of decoding accuracy across response formats by means of a *parallel enrichment procedure* (Rosenthal, 1982)—that is, quantitative data from forced-choice judgments of performances were augmented by qualitative data from free labeling of the same stimuli. The two methods converged on the conclusions that (1) communication was reliable regardless of the response format and (2) what could be communicated reliably were the basic-level emotion categories, but not specific nuances within these categories (cf. Brown, 1981; Campbell, 1942; Downey, 1897).

## Code Usage

The early studies were mainly concerned with exploring whether performers are able to communicate emotions to their listeners at all. However, if we want to study communication as a process, we need also to consider its mechanisms, particularly the code used by performers and listeners. Accordingly, researchers have tried to describe the means by which performers express specific emotions

(e.g., Gabrielsson & Juslin, 1996; Gabrielsson & Lindström, 1995; Juslin, 1997a, 2000; Juslin & Laukka, 2000; Juslin & Madison, 1999; Kotlyar & Morozov, 1976; Ohgushi & Hattori, 1996b; Rapoport, 1996).

One important finding from this research is that the performer's expressive intention affects almost every aspect of the performance. That is, emotional expression in performance seems to involve a whole set of *cues* (pieces of information) that are used by performers and listeners. Most of these cues are included in Table 26.2: tempo, sound level, timing, articulation, timbre, vibrato, intonation, attacks, and decays. Thus, for example, expressions of sadness are associated with slow tempo, low sound level, legato articulation, slow tone attacks, and "soft" timbre (i.e., little high-frequency energy in the spectrum), whereas expressions of anger are associated with fast tempo, high sound level, staccato articulation, fast tone attacks, and "sharp" timbre (i.e., much high-frequency energy in the spectrum). Of course, the number of cues available depends on the specific instrument used (for a more extensive review, see Juslin, 2001a).

Performance analyses have shown that performers can use a number of cues to express specific emotions. However, these analyses do not show that listeners actually *use* the same cues in their judgments. To test the validity of hypotheses derived from performance studies, it is necessary to carry out listening experiments with synthesized and systematically varied performances (Gabrielsson, 1985). Such listening experiments have confirmed that listeners make the same associations between cues and emotions as performers do (see Bresin & Friberg, 2000; Juslin, 1997b; Juslin, Friberg, & Bresin, in press).

## Tests of Predictions: The Functionalist Perspective

In this section, we summarize evidence with regard to the theoretical predictions of the functionalist perspective (see "Emotional Expression in Performance," earlier in chapter). One major prediction of this approach is that there should be similarities regarding the acoustic cues used to communicate emotions in vocal expression and music performance, because it is assumed that performers use the same code as is used in vocal expression. Juslin (1999) conducted a review of a large number of studies from both domains. This review revealed numerous similarities in code usage. For instance, anger is expressed by means of increased speed, intensity, and high-frequency spectral energy in both vocal expression and music performance.

One assumption of the functionalist perspective is that decoding of vocal expression of emotion (and hence also expression in performance) is done largely in terms of a set of basic emotion categories. Support for this view comes from evidence of categorical perception of vocal expression of emotion (de Gelder & Vroomen, 1996). Thus, another prediction of the functionalist perspective is that basic emotions should be easier to communicate than other emotions in music performances. Indeed, a survey of the literature suggests that commonly suggested basic emotions, such as sadness, anger, and happiness, are easier to communicate than other states, such as solemnity, tenderness, and dreaminess (Gabrielsson & Juslin, 1996; Gabrielsson & Lindström, 1995; Senju & Ohgushi, 1987).

The functionalist perspective holds that the vocal code on which performers base their communication of emotions is innate. Accordingly, it is predicted that there should be cross-cultural similarities in how performers employ cues in the performance to express emotions. While no study thus far has (explicitly) aimed to address this issue, there is evidence of cross-cultural similarities in performers' utilization of cues from investigations in India (Balkwill & Thompson, 1999), Russia (Kotlyar & Morozov, 1976), Italy (Baroni & Finarelli, 1994), Japan (Ohgushi & Hattori, 1996), and Sweden (Juslin, 2000). These studies indicate that cues, such as tempo, sound level, and timbre, are used in a similar manner in different cultures. However, when it comes to cross-cultural studies that involve other musical variables, such as harmony, there are usually larger differences.

One further prediction of the functionalist perspective is that the ability to decode basic emotions from performance should be present early in development. Although there are no developmental studies that focus specifically on children's perception of emotional expression in performance, there are studies that suggest that young children are able to decode basic emotions in pieces of music (see "Developmental Studies"). Considering that these studies involved *both* performance variables (e.g., tempo, articulation, timbre) and composed structure (e.g., harmonic progression, tonality), it seems plausible that young children are able to decode emotional expression from performance variables as such. Studies of children's ability to encode emotions in music are complicated by the fact that very young children may not be able to play an instrument. However, Adachi and Trehub (1998) found that children 4–12 years old were able to use cues to express emotions in singing. For instance, they used fast tempo and high intensity in happy expressions, whereas they used slow tempo and low intensity in sadness expressions.

There are also a number of predictions that derive from the conceptualization of the communicative process in terms of a Brunswikian lens model. For instance, the prediction that cues are only probabilistically related to performers' expressive intentions and listeners' judgments is supported by evidence in Juslin (1997a, 1997b, 2000) and Juslin and Madison (1999). It has further been shown that there are moderate intercorrelations between the cues (Juslin, 2000; see also Kratus, 1993). Finally, there is evidence from an experiment that used systematic manipulation of synthesized performances that performance cues contrib-

ute in an additive fashion to listeners' judgments (Juslin, 1997b). All this supports a conceptualization of the communicative process in terms of a Brunswikian lens model.

Performance studies have shown that the cue utilization is inconsistent both across and within performers (Juslin, 2000). Similarly, listening tests have shown that the cue utilization is inconsistent both across and within listeners (Juslin & Madison, 1999). This really presents something of a puzzle: How can the communicative process be accurate if the cue utilization is inconsistent? This apparent paradox can be explained by the lens model: Because cues are intercorrelated (and hence partly redundant), many different cue utilization strategies can lead to a similar level of accuracy (cf. Dawes & Corrigan, 1974). Indeed, a study by Juslin (2000) has shown that two performers can reach a similar level of communication accuracy despite differences in their cue utilization (for further discussion, see Juslin & Persson, in press).

## Discussion

### Methodological Issues

#### Selection of Stimuli

Ideally, the music stimuli should be a broad and representative sample from the universe of music, which is, of course, infinite. The number of musical pieces included in the investigations varies from 2 to 40, and the total number in all investigations together is still less than 1,000. Moreover, most of these are either very short pieces or excerpts from longer pieces, sometimes only a single phrase. The large majority belong to Western tonal music, and mostly art music (for discussions of popular music, see, e.g., Frith, 1996; Tagg, 1979). Representativity is thus so far very limited, in terms of both number of pieces and musical genres. The rationale for the selection of stimuli is sometimes explained, sometimes not. A certain arbitrariness is almost certainly present depending on the researcher's musical knowledge and preferences, and on practical and economical matters. An advantage of using music unknown to the listeners is that it does not prejudice their judgments due to common or private associations and memories.

The short duration of most music stimuli is usually motivated by the need to have stimuli with homogeneous expression, so as to optimize the conditions for consistency in the listener's judgments. Brief stimuli also make it easier to investigate which musical factors influence the perceived expression. On the other hand, brief stimuli mean a limitation in ecological validity. With recent proposals for continuous recording of perceived expression there are now possibilities for studying how expression varies in extended pieces of music.

## Response Formats

Listeners' descriptions of perceived expression in music are usually obtained by verbal responses. Nonverbal responses, such as drawings (Francès, 1988; Smith & Williams, 1999), finger pressure on a sentograph (Clynes & Walker, 1982), pressing a pair of tongs (Nielsen, 1983), moving a slider (Krumhansl, 1996) or a computer mouse (Schubert, 1999a), and the like, have rarely been used so far and may be difficult to interpret. Moreover, language is still used to define which aspect the listener should attend to (e.g., tension).

There are several problems with verbal responses. The meanings of words differ among people, investigators as well as subjects. Verbal labels attached to clusters or dimensions of emotional expression vary among researchers, a problem further aggravated when terms have to be translated into another language. The selection of descriptive terms is crucial. Some investigators rely on descriptors used in earlier studies; others collect a large number of descriptors from various sources and have them rated for suitability to describe expression in music (e.g., Schubert, 1999a; Terwogt & van Grinsven, 1991), keeping those that are highest rated. There is no generally agreed classification of emotions, or emotion words, to rely upon (Plutchik, 1994).

Verbal methods appear in many variants: forced choice between two descriptive terms; choice of any number of a given set of descriptive terms; numerical ratings using bipolar or unipolar scales; or free phenomenological description. Using choice or ratings of given descriptors allows the investigator to study just those descriptors that he or she considers relevant, and data can usually be suitably analyzed by common statistical methods. However, the given descriptors may not be the ones that the listener finds most adequate or that he or she would focus on in free phenomenological description. The latter are harder to analyze and to present in a condensed way; it may be necessary to present them in extenso to fully apprehend the contents. Which response format should be used must be considered in relation to the questions under scrutiny, the music used, the type of listeners, and so on. Using forced choice among a few alternative descriptors may indicate high agreement among listeners; however, with free descriptions by the same listeners agreement may be lower (e.g., Rigg, 1937a; see also Watt & Ash, 1998, p. 39). Expression in music should preferably be studied in a multimethod approach (cf. Juslin, 1997c).

Finally, it may be questioned whether it it is possible to describe all subtleties in music by words. Many would probably agree with Gilman's (1892, p. 72) statement that "what music expresses is literally *unutterable*." So far, the terminology developed in research for describing expression in music seems meager and void of nuances in relation to what sensitive listeners perceive. Even world-renowned authors complain about the elusiveness of music to verbal expression. In a way, music begins where language ends.

## Emotions Expressed in Music

A great variety of emotion descriptors have been used in the investigations reviewed (Table 26.1). Reliable recognition of intended emotions or high interindividual agreement on expressed emotion has been reported for many of them. Among so-called basic emotions, results are most convincing concerning happiness/gaiety/joy and sadness/gloom. Anger and fear have been little investigated except in performance studies, in which they are usually recognized well, but disgust has rarely appeared. The concept of basic emotions and other influences from emotion psychology in general have come into studies of musical expression quite recently and then mainly in studies of performance. Rather, in the bulk of investigations, the emotions considered have been chosen relying on statements by philosophers, music theorists, suggestions from earlier studies on expression, and, not the least, on folk psychology and personal experiences. All together the emotion descriptors used in these investigations are counted in hundreds.

The most far-reaching attempts to achieve reduction and order among these myriad terms are studies involving multivariate analysis techniques—factor analysis, cluster analysis, correspondence analysis, multidimensional scaling. Together these investigations suggest a valence dimension (gaiety–gloom, positive vs. negative feelings) and an arousal dimension (tension/energy–relaxation), in agreement with the results from studies in the emotion domain (Russell, 1980). The status of the potency dimension must be left open, because the reviewed studies do not provide unequivocal results to confirm its existence. There is perhaps another dimension called solemnity versus triviality (e.g., Wedin, 1972c). In Hevner's adjective clock this might correspond to an axis from cluster 1 (including solemn) to cluster 5 (fanciful, playful, whimsical; see Figure 26.4). Wedin (1972c) pointed out that solemnity–triviality may reflect a stylistic dimension, solemnity used to characterize certain kinds of art music but rarely applicable to popular music.

Some basic emotions, such as anger and fear, do not appear at all in Hevner's adjective circle and hardly in the dimensional studies, which may reflect both that these emotions are relatively little expressed in classical music and that studies on emotional expression in music have had little contact with emotion psychology in general (and vice versa). Moreover, most descriptive terms in Kleinen's and Wedin's representations (Figures 26.1 and 26.2) belong to the upper-right and lower-left quadrants, whereas there are few terms in the remaining quadrants. However, in Russell's (1980) model, emotions appear about equally in all quadrants. This may again reflect that certain emotions are more likely to be expressed in music than others (which does not mean that the latter cannot be expressed by musical means).

Many of music's most expressive qualities relate to changes over time, which makes possible expression of, say, shifting emotions, blending emotions, or conflicting emotions. Such changes involve elusive qualities that are best described in dynamic terms, such as growth, decay, tension and release, crescendo–diminuendo, and accelerando–ritardando. They recall what Stern (1985) termed "vitality affects," which seem intuitively appealing in the study of musical expression (e.g., Sloboda & Juslin, 2001). Phenomena like these are little investigated in research so far; the closest examples are studies on tension and release by means of continuous recording. Continuous recording of listeners' judgments seems a necessary prerequisite to study these phenomena.

Many studies indicate little or no difference in results between musically experienced and musically inexperienced subjects (e.g., Campbell, 1942; Gabrielsson, 1973; Hevner, 1936; Juslin, 1997a; Rigg, 1937b; Robazza et al., 1994; Wedin, 1969). However, Brown (1981) concluded that with pieces that are close in expression, agreement could only be achieved by highly trained listeners; if the expressions are not too similar, agreement may be reached also by musically untrained persons. Developmental studies indicate that even very young children are able to recognize basic emotions expressed in music, happiness and sadness earlier than anger and fear. Finally, gender differences have been reported in a number of studies (e.g., Cunningham & Sterling, 1988; Dolgin & Adelson, 1990; Gabrielsson & Juslin, 1996; Giomo, 1993; Juslin, 1997c).

## Conclusions and Directions for Future Research

We believe that the present review allows us to draw some tentative conclusions. The majority of empirical studies have investigated whether listeners agree in their descriptions of expression in music, and what musical characteristics correlate with listeners' judgments of expression. The results suggest that agreement about a perceived expression varies greatly depending on a number of factors (e.g., the piece of music, the musical genre, the response format, the type of listener). There is generally greater agreement or accuracy with regard to the expression of emotions than with regard to the expression of other aspects (e.g., in program music). Also, many studies suggest that there is good agreement among listeners regarding the broad emotional category expressed in music, but less agreement regarding the nuances or variants within this category. Attempts to reduce perceived emotions in pieces

of music to a small number of main dimensions have yielded dimensions corresponding to those discovered in other domains of emotion research, as well as some dimensions that may be more typical of music. It is quite obvious, however, that these dimensions cannot capture all the nuances that we can perceive in music.

There are several areas of musical expression that are not treated in this chapter: expression in film music (Cohen, 2001; Vol. 13 of *Psychomusicology*, 1994), music in advertising (e.g., North & Hargreaves, 1997), music therapy (e.g., Pratt & Jones, 1987 for historical account; Bonny & Savary, 1990, and Wigram, Saperston, & West, 1995, for contemporary examples). Works in musical aesthetics (e.g., Budd, 1985; Davies, 1994; Kivy, 1990; Scruton, 1997) or musical semiotics (e.g., Tarasti, 1994) have been only cursorily referred to. There is little, if any, reference to empirical studies in these works. Similarly, it is rare to find references to works in musical aesthetics or musical semiotics in empirical music psychology. We believe that much can be gained from the cross-fertilization of all these different domains.

The musical means that can be used to express various emotions constitute practically all variables in musical structure and performance, including several interactions, as evident in Table 26.2 (see also Gabrielsson & Lindström, 2001; Juslin, 2001a). Previous studies have focused mainly on rather simple physical variables (e.g., tempo, loudness, pitch), whereas much remains to be done concerning the effects of more specific rhythmic, melodic, and harmonic features, as well as various aspects of musical form. The possibilities afforded by sound synthesis have rendered systematic manipulation of such musical factors quite feasible.

One problem in previous research is that representativity has been limited, in terms of both the number of pieces and the number of musical genres studied. Future research should encompass a wider range of musical genres. Furthermore, cross-cultural research is badly needed because only through such research is it possible to determine whether there are universal relationships between musical factors and emotional expression.

Finally, much of the empirical work is characterized by a lack of theories. This has probably impeded the progress in this field. That musical training is not required to perceive emotional expression in music suggests that more general mechanisms of emotion perception are involved. Brain imaging techniques, such as PET and fMRI, might help to discriminate among different theoretical accounts of the mechanisms underlying emotional expression in music. Only recently have music researchers turned to emotion psychology for theoretical guidance. However, we believe that a closer alliance between music researchers and emotion researchers affords the royal road to progress in the field of musical expression.[3]

## NOTES

1. Unless otherwise stated, the text in this section is mainly based on Benestad (1978), Lippman (1986, 1988, 1990), and on articles in the *New Grove Dictionary of Music and Musicians* (Sadie, 1980): Aesthetics of music, Affections, Empfindsamkeit, Expression, Figures, Greece, Hermeneutics, Programme music, Rhetoric and music, Romantic, Tempo and expression marks. Further theories on musical expression developed within musicology are reviewed by de la Motte-Haber (1996, pp. 25–79). A historical account of performance practices used to enhance emotional expression is given by Hudson (1994).

2. For an explanation of various modes in ancient Greek music, see article "Greece" in Sadie (1980).

3. The writing of this chapter was supported by The Bank of Sweden Tercentenary Foundation.

## REFERENCES

Adachi, M., & Trehub, S. E. (1998). Children's expression of emotion in song. *Psychology of Music, 26,* 133–153.

Allesch, C. G. (1987). *Geschichte der psychologischen Ästhetik* [History of psychological aesthetics]. Göttingen: Hogrefe.

Asada, M., & Ohgushi, K. (1991). Perceptual analyses of Ravel's Bolero. *Music Perception, 8,* 241–250.

Asmus, E. P. (1985). The development of a multidimensional instrument for the measurement of affective responses to music. *Psychology of Music, 13,* 19–30.

Bach, C. P. E. (1753, 1762). *Versuch über die wahre Art, das Clavier zu spielen.* (Facsimile edition 1957, Breitkopf & Härtel, Leipzig.)

Balkwill, L-L., & Thompson, W. F. (1999). A cross-cultural investigation of the perception of emotion in music: Psychophysical and cultural cues. *Music Perception, 17,* 43–64.

Baroni, M., & Finarelli, L. (1994). Emotions in spoken language and vocal music. In I. Deliège (Ed.), *Proceedings of the Third International Conference for Music Perception and Cognition* (pp. 343–345). University of Liége, Liége, Belgium.

Batel, G. (1976). *Komponenten musikalischen Erlebens.* Göttingen, Germany: Göttinger Musikwissenschaftlicher Arbeiten.

Batson, C. D., Shaw, L. L., & Oleson, K. C. (1992). Differentiating affect, mood, and emotion: Toward functionally based conceptual distinctions. In M. S. Clark (Ed.), *Review of personality and social psychology: Emotion* (pp. 294–326). Newbury Park, CA: Sage.

Behne, K. E. (1972). *Der Einfluss des Tempos auf die Beurteilung von Musik.* Köln, Germany: Arno Volk Verlag.

Behrens, G. A., & Green, S. B. (1993). The ability to identify emotional content of solo improvisations performed vocally and on three different instruments. *Psychology of Music, 21,* 20–33.

Benestad, F. (1978). *Musik och tanke. Huvudlinjer i musikestetikens historia från antiken till vår egen tid [Music and thought. Main lines in the history of musical aesthetics from antiquity to our time].* Stockholm: Rabén & Sjögren.

Bonny, H. L., & Savary, L. M. (1990). *Music and your mind* (Rev. ed.). Barrytown, NY: Station Hill Press.

Bresin, R., & Friberg, A. (2000). Emotional coloring of computer-controlled music performance. *Computer Music Journal, 24,* 44–62.

Brown, R. (1981). Music and language. In *Documentary report of the Ann Arbor symposium. National symposium on the applications of psychology to the teaching and learning of music* (pp. 233–265). Reston, VA: Music Educators National Conference.

Brunswik, E. (1956). *Perception and the representative design of psychological experiments.* Berkeley: University of California Press.

Buck, R. (1984). *The communication of emotion.* New York: Guilford Press.

Budd, M. (1985). *Music and the emotions. The philosophical theories.* London: Routledge.

Buelow, G. J. (1983). Johann Mattheson and the invention of the Affektenlehre. In G. J. Buelow & H. J. Marx (Eds.), *New Mattheson studies* (pp. 393–407). Cambridge, England: Cambridge University Press.

Campbell, I. G. (1942). Basal emotional patterns expressible in music. *American Journal of Psychology, 55,* 1–17.

Capurso, A. (1952). The Capurso study. In A. Capurso, V. R. Fisichelli, L. Gilman, E. A. Gutheil, J. T. Wright, & F. Paperte (Eds.), *Music and your emotions* (pp. 56–86). New York: Liveright.

Cazden, N. (1979). Can verbal meanings inhere in fragments of melody? *Psychology of Music, 7,* 34–38.

Clynes, M. (1973). Sentics: Biocybernetics of emotion communication. *Annals of the New York Academy of Sciences, 220,* 55–131.

Clynes, M. (1977). *Sentics: The touch of emotions.* New York: Anchor Press/Doubleday.

Clynes, M. (1980). The communication of emotion: Theory of sentics. In R. Plutchik & H. Kellerman (Eds.), *Emotion: Theory, research, and experience. Vol. 1: Theories of emotion* (pp. 271–301). New York: Academic Press.

Clynes, M. (Ed.). (1982). *Music, mind, and brain: The neuropsychology of music.* New York: Plenum.

Clynes, M., & Nettheim, N. (1982). The living quality of music: Neurobiologic basis of communicated feeling. In M. Clynes (Ed.), *Music, mind, and brain: The neuropsychology of music* (pp. 47–82). New York: Plenum.

Clynes, M., & Walker, J. (1982). Neurobiologic functions of rhythm, time, and pulse in music. In M. Clynes (Ed.), *Music, mind, and brain: The neuropsychology of music* (pp. 171–216). New York: Plenum.

Cohen, A. (2001). Music as a source of emotion in film. In P. N. Juslin & J. A. Sloboda (Eds.), *Music and emotion: Theory and research* (pp. 249–272). New York: Oxford University Press.

Cooke, D. (1959). *The language of music.* London: Oxford University Press.

Crowder, R. G. (1984). Perception of the major/minor distinction: I. Historical and theoretical foundations. *Psychomusicology, 4,* 3–12.

Crowder, R. G. (1985). Perception of the major/minor distinction: III. Hedonic, musical, and affective discriminations. *Bulletin of the Psychonomic Society, 23,* 314–316.

Crowder, R. G., Reznick, J. S., & Rosenkrantz, S. L. (1991). Perception of the major/minor distinction: V. Preferences among infants. *Bulletin of the Psychonomic Society, 29,* 187–188.

Cunningham, J. G., & Sterling, R. S. (1988). Developmental changes in the understanding of affective meaning in music. *Motivation and Emotion, 12,* 399–413.

Davies, S. (1994). *Musical meaning and expression.* Ithaca, NY: Cornell University Press.

Dawes, R. M., & Corrigan, B. (1974). Linear models in decision making. *Psychological Bulletin, 81*, 95–106.

De Gelder, B., & Vroomen, J. (1996). Categorical perception of emotional speech. *Journal of the Acoustical Society of America, 100*, 2818.

Dolgin, K., & Adelson, E. (1990). Age changes in the ability to interpret affect in sung and instrumentally-presented melodies. *Psychology of Music, 18*, 87–98.

Downey, J. E. (1897). A musical experiment. *American Journal of Psychology, 9*, 63–69.

Ekman, P. (1992). An argument for basic emotions. *Cognition and Emotion, 6*, 169–200.

Ekman, P., & Davidson, R. J. (Eds.). (1994). *The nature of emotion*. New York: Oxford University Press.

Farnsworth, P. R. (1954). A study of the Hevner adjective list. *Journal of Aesthetics and Art Criticism, 13*, 97–103.

Fisk, J. (Ed.). (1997). *Composers on music. Eight centuries of writings* (2nd ed.). Boston: Northeastern University Press.

Foros, P. B. (1975). Hva er musikalsk kommunikasjon? [What is musical communication?] In J. P. Jensen & M. Poulsen (Eds.), *Musikopleven og musikformidling [Experience and communication of music]* (pp. 178–203). Copenhagen: Akademisk Vorlag.

Francès, R. (1988). *The perception of music*. Hillsdale, NJ: Erlbaum. (French original: *La perception de la musique*, 1958. Paris: Libraire Philosophique J. Vrin.)

Fredrickson, W. E. (1997). Elementary, middle, and high school student perceptions of tension in music. *Journal of Research in Music Education, 45*, 626–635.

Frith, S. (1996). *Performing rites. On the value of popular music rites*. Cambridge, MA: Harvard University Press.

Gabriel, C. (1978). An experimental study of Deryck Cooke's theory of music and meaning. *Psychology of Music, 6*, 13–20.

Gabriel, C. (1979). A note on comments by Nettheim and Cazden. *Psychology of Music, 7*, 39–40.

Gabrielsson, A. (1973). Adjective ratings and dimension analysis of auditory rhythm patterns. *Scandinavian Journal of Psychology, 14*, 244–260.

Gabrielsson, A. (1985). Interplay between analysis and synthesis in studies of music performance and music experience. *Music Perception, 3*, 59–86.

Gabrielsson, A. (1988). Timing in music performance and its relations to music experience. In J. A. Sloboda (Ed.), *Generative processes in music: The psychology of performance, improvisation, and composition* (pp. 27–51). Oxford, England: Clarendon Press.

Gabrielsson, A. (1993). The complexities of rhythm. In T. J. Tighe & W. J. Dowling (Eds.), *Psychology and music. The understanding of melody and rhythm* (pp. 93–120). Hillsdale, NJ: Erlbaum.

Gabrielsson, A. (1994). Intention and emotional expression in music performance. In A. Friberg, J. Iwarsson, E. Jansson, & J. Sundberg (Eds.), *Proceedings of the Stockholm Music Acoustics Conference 1993* (pp. 108–111). Stockholm: Publications issued by the Royal Swedish Academy of Music, No. 79.

Gabrielsson, A. (1995). Expressive intention and performance. In R. Steinberg (Ed.), *Music and the mind machine* (pp. 35–47). Heidelberg, Germany: Springer.

Gabrielsson, A. (2001). Emotions in strong experiences with music. In P. N. Juslin & J. A. Sloboda (Eds.), *Music and emotion: Theory and research* (pp. 431–449). New York: Oxford University Press.

Gabrielsson, A., & Juslin, P. N. (1996). Emotional expression in music performance: Between the performer's intention and the listener's experience. *Psychology of Music, 24*, 68–91.

Gabrielsson, A., & Lindström, E. (1995). Emotional expression in synthesizer and sentograph performance. *Psychomusicology, 14*, 94–116.

Gabrielsson, A., & Lindström, E. (2001). The influence of musical structure on emotional expression. In P. N. Juslin & J. A. Sloboda (Eds.), *Music and emotion: Theory and research* (pp. 223–248). New York: Oxford University Press.

Gilman, B. I. (1891). Report on an experimental test of musical expressiveness. *American Journal of Psychology, 4*, 558–576.

Gilman, B. I. (1892). Report of an experimental test of musical expressiveness (continued). *American Journal of Psychology, 5*, 42–73.

Giomo, C. J. (1993). An experimental study of children's sensitivity to mood in music. *Psychology of Music, 21*, 141–162.

Gorman, B. S., & Crain, W. C. (1974). Decoding of "sentograms." *Perceptual and Motor Skills, 39*, 784–786.

Gregory, A. H., & Varney, N. (1996). Cross-cultural comparisons in the affective response to music. *Psychology of Music, 24*, 47–52.

Gregory, A. H., Worrall, L., & Sarge, A. (1996). The development of emotional responses to music in young children. *Motivation and Emotion, 20*, 341–348.

Grout, D. J., & Palisca, C. V. (1996). *A history of Western music* (5th ed.). New York: Norton.

Gundlach, R. H. (1932). A quantitative analysis of Indian music. *American Journal of Psychology, 44*, 133–145.

Gundlach, R. H. (1935). Factors determining the characterization of musical phrases. *American Journal of Psychology, 47*, 624–644.

Hama, H., & Tsuda, K. (1990). Finger pressure waveforms measured on Clynes' sentograph distinguish among emotions. *Perceptual and Motor Skills, 70*, 371–376.

Hampson, P. (2000). A naturalistic empirical investigation of Deryck Cooke's theory of music and meaning. In C. Woods, G. Luck, R. Brochard, F. Seldon, & J. A. Sloboda (Eds.), *Proceedings of the Sixth International Conference on Music Perception and Cognition* (CD-ROM). University of Keele, UK.

Hampton, P. J. (1945). The emotional element in music. *Journal of General Psychology, 33*, 237–250.

Hanslick, E. (1854/1989). *Vom musikalisch Schönen* (21st ed.). English translation, *The beautiful in music* (New York: Liberal Arts Press, 1957) or *On the musically beautiful* (Indianapolis: Hackett, 1986).

Hare, F. G. (1977). Dimensions of music perception. *Scientific Aesthetics, 1*, 271–288.

Heinlein, C. P. (1928). The affective character of the major and minor modes in music. *Journal of Comparative Psychology, 8*, 101–142.

von Helmholtz, H. L. F. (1863/1954). *On the sensations of tone as a physiological basis for the theory of music*. New York: Dover.

Hermerén, G. (1986). Musik som språk [Music as language]. *Swedish Journal of Musicology, 68*, 7–16.

Hevner, K. (1935a). The affective character of the major and minor modes in music. *American Journal of Psychology, 47*, 103–118.

Hevner, K. (1935b). Expression in music: A discussion of experimental studies and theories. *Psychological Review, 47*, 186–204.

Hevner, K. (1936). Experimental studies of the elements of expression in music. *American Journal of Psychology, 48*, 246–268.

Hevner, K. (1937). The affective value of pitch and tempo in music. *American Journal of Psychology, 49*, 621–630.

Hoshino, E. (1996). The feeling of musical mode and its emotional character in a melody. *Psychology of Music, 24*, 29–46.

Huber, K. (1923). *Der Ausdruck musikalischer Elementarmotive*. Leipzig: Johann Ambrosius Barth.

Hudson, R. (1994). *Stolen time. The history of tempo rubato*. Oxford, England: Clarendon Press.

Imberty, M. (1979). *Entendre la musique*. Paris: Dunod.

Izard, C. E. (1977). *The emotions*. New York: Plenum.

Jürgens, U., & von Cramon, D. (1982). On the role of the anterior cingulate cortex in phonation: A case report. *Brain and Language, 15*, 234–248.

Juslin, P. N. (1995). Emotional communication in music viewed through a Brunswikian lens. In G. Kleinen (Ed.), *Musical expression. Proceedings of the Conference of ESCOM and DGM 1995* (pp. 21–25). University of Bremen, Bremen, Germany.

Juslin, P. N. (1997a). Emotional communication in music performance: A functionalist perspective and some data. *Music Perception, 14*, 383–418.

Juslin, P. N. (1997b). Perceived emotional expression in synthesized performances of a short melody: Capturing the listener's judgment policy. *Musicae Scientiae, 1*, 225–256.

Juslin, P. N. (1997c). Can results from studies of perceived expression in musical performances be generalized across response formats? *Psychomusicology, 16*, 77–101.

Juslin, P. N. (1999). *Communication of emotion in vocal expression and music performance: Different channels, same code?* Manuscript submitted for publication.

Juslin, P. N. (2000). Cue utilization in communication of emotion in music performance: Relating performance to perception. *Journal of Experimental Psychology: Human Perception and Performance, 26*, 1797–1813.

Juslin, P. N. (2001a). Communicating emotion in music performance: A review and a theoretical framework. In P. N. Juslin & J. A. Sloboda (Eds.), *Music and emotion: Theory and research* (pp. 309–337). New York: Oxford University Press.

Juslin, P. N. (2001b). A Brunswikian approach to emotional communication in music performance. In K. R. Hammond & T. R. Stewart (Eds.), *The essential Brunswik: Beginnings, explications, applications* (pp. 426–430). New York: Oxford University Press.

Juslin, P. N., Friberg, A., & Bresin, R. (in press). Toward a computational model of expression in music performance: The GERM model. *Musicae Scientiae*.

Juslin, P. N., & Laukka, P. (2000). Improving emotional communication in music performance through cognitive feedback. *Musicae Scientiae, 4*, 151–183.

Juslin, P. N., & Madison, G. (1999). The role of timing patterns in recognition of emotional expression from musical performance. *Music Perception, 17*, 197–221.

Juslin, P. N., & Persson, R. S. (in press). Emotional communication. In R. Parncutt & G. E. McPherson (Eds.), *The science and psychology of music performance: Creative strategies for teaching and learning*. New York: Oxford University Press.

Juslin, P. N., & Sloboda, J. A. (Eds.). (2001). *Music and emotion: Theory and research*. New York: Oxford University Press.

Kaminska, Z., & Woolf, J. (2000). Melodic line and emotion: Cooke's theory revisited. *Psychology of Music, 28*, 133–153.

Kastner, M. P., & Crowder, R. G. (1990). Perception of the major/minor distinction: IV. Emotional connotations in young children. *Music Perception, 8*, 189–202.

Kivy, P. (1990). *Music alone: Philosophical reflections on the purely musical experience*. Ithaca, NY: Cornell University Press.

Kleinen, G. (1968). *Experimentelle Studien zum musikalischen Ausdruck*. Hamburg, Germany: Universität Hamburg.

Kleinen, G. (1994). Musikalischer Ausdruck und ästhetische Wertung als interkulturelle Qualität und Differenz. *Musikpsychologie. Jahrbuch der Deutschen Gesellschaft für Musikpsychologie, 11*, 76–101.

Konishi, T., Imaizumi, S., & Niimi, S. (2000). Vibrato and emotion in singing voice (abstract). In C. Woods, G. Luck, R. Brochard, F. Seddon, & J. A. Sloboda (Eds.), *Proceedings of the Sixth International Conference on Music Perception and Cognition, August 2000*. (CD-rom). University of Keele, UK.

Kotlyar, G. M., & Morozov, V. P. (1976). Acoustic correlates of the emotional content of vocalized speech. *Soviet Physics. Acoustics, 22*, 370–376.

Kratus, J. (1993). A developmental study of children's interpretation of emotion in music. *Psychology of Music, 21*, 3–19.

Krumhansl, C. L. (1996). A perceptual analysis of Mozart's Piano Sonata K. 282: Segmentation, tension, and musical ideas. *Music Perception, 13*, 401–432.

Krumhansl, C. L. (1997). An exploratory study of musical emotions and psychophysiology. *Canadian Journal of Experimental Psychology, 51*, 336–352.

Krumhansl, C. L., & Lynn Schenk, D. (1997). Can dance reflect the structural and expressive qualities of music? A perceptual experiment on Balanchine's choreography of Mozart's Divertimento No. 15. *Musicae Scientiae, 1*, 63–85.

Langer, S. K. (1953). *Feeling and form*. London: Routledge.

Langer, S. K. (1957). *Philosophy in a new key* (3rd ed.). Cambridge, MA: Harvard University Press.

Laukka, P., & Gabrielsson, A. (2000). Emotional expression in drumming performance. *Psychology of Music, 28*, 181–189.

Levinson, J. (1996). *The pleasures of aesthetics*. Ithaca, NY: Cornell University Press.

Lindström, E. (1997). Impact of melodic structure on emotional expression. In A. Gabrielsson (Ed.), *Proceedings of the Third Triennial ESCOM Conference, Uppsala, June 1997* (pp. 292–297). Uppsala University, Uppsala, Sweden.

Lippman, E. A. (Ed.). (1986). *Musical aesthetics: A historical reader. Volume 1: From Antiquity to the eighteenth century*. New York: Pendragon Press.

Lippman, E. A. (Ed.). (1988). *Musical aesthetics: A historical reader. Volume 2: The nineteenth century*. Stuyvesant, NY: Pendragon Press.

Lippman, E. A. (Ed.). (1990). *Musical aesthetics: A historical reader. Volume 3: The twentieth century*. Stuyvesant, NY: Pendragon Press.

Madsen, C. K. (1997). Emotional responses to music. *Psychomusicology, 16*, 59–67.

Madsen, C. K., & Fredrickson, W. E. (1993). The experience of musical tension: A replication of Nielsen's research using the continuous response digital interface. *Journal of Music Therapy, 30*, 46–63.

Mattheson, J. (1739). *Der vollhommene Capellmeister.* (Facsimile edition 1954, Bärenreiter Verlag, Kassel, Germany, and Basel.)

Metfessel, M. (1932). The vibrato in artistic voices. In C. E. Seashore (Ed.), *University of Iowa studies in the psychology of music. Vol. I: The vibrato* (pp. 14–117). Iowa City: University of Iowa.

Meyer, L. B. (1956). *Emotion and meaning in music.* Chicago: University of Chicago Press.

Morey, R. (1940). Upset in emotions. *Journal of Social Psychology, 12*, 333–356.

de la Motte-Haber, H. (1968). *Ein Beitrag zur Klassifikation musikalischer Rhythmen.* Köln, Germany: Arno Volk Verlag.

de la Motte-Haber, H. (1996). *Handbuch der Musikpsychologie* (2nd ed.). Laaber: Laaber Verlag.

Namba, S., Kuwano, S., Hatoh, T., & Kato, M. (1991). Assessment of musical performance by using the method of continuous judgment by selected description. *Music Perception, 8*, 251–276.

Nettelbeck, T., Henderson, C., & Willson, R. (1989). Communicating emotion through sound: An evaluation of Clynes' theory of sentics. *Australian Journal of Psychology, 41*, 25–36.

Nettheim, N. (1979). Comment on a paper by Gabriel on Cooke's theory. *Psychology of Music, 7*, 32–33.

Nielsen, F. V. (1983). *Oplevelse av musikalsk spænding [Experience of musical tension].* Copenhagen: Akademisk Forlag. (Includes summary in English.)

Nielsen, F. V. (1987). Musical "tension" and related concepts. In T. A. Sebeok & J. Umiker-Sebeok (Eds.), *The semiotic web '86. An international yearbook* (pp. 491–513). Berlin: Mouton de Gruyter.

Nielzén, S., & Cesarec, Z. (1981). On the perception of emotional meaning in music. *Psychology of Music, 9*, 17–31.

Nielzén, S., & Cesarec, Z. (1982). Emotional experience of music as a function of musical structure. *Psychology of Music, 10*, 7–17.

North, A., & Hargreaves, D. J. (1997). Music and consumer behaviour. In D. J. Hargreaves & A. C. North (Eds.), *The social psychology of music* (pp. 268–289). Oxford: Oxford University Press.

Oatley, K. (1992). *Best laid schemes. The psychology of emotions.* Cambridge, MA: Harvard University Press.

Ohgushi, K., & Hattori, M. (1996a). Emotional communication in performance of vocal music. In B. Pennycook & E. Costa-Giomi (Eds.), *Proceedings of the Fourth International Conference on Music Perception and Cognition* (pp. 269–274). McGill University, Montreal, Canada.

Ohgushi, K., & Hattori, M. (1996b). *Acoustic correlates of the emotional expression in vocal performance.* Paper presented at the Third Joint Meeting of the Acoustical Society of America and the Acoustical Society of Japan, Honolulu, Hawaii, 2–6 December.

Osborne, J. W. (1989). A phenomenological investigation of the musical representation of extra-musical ideas. *Journal of Phenomenological Psychology, 20*, 151–175.

Osgood, C. E., Suci, G. J., & Tannenbaum, P. H. (1957). *The measurement of meaning.* Urbana, IL: University of Illinois Press.

Panksepp, J. (1998). *Affective neuroscience: The foundations of human and animal emotions.* New York: Oxford University Press.

Papoušek, M. (1996). Intuitive parenting: A hidden source of musical stimulation in infancy. In I. Deliège & J. A. Sloboda (Eds.), *Musical beginnings: Origins and development of musical competence* (pp. 89–112). Oxford, England: Oxford University Press.

Peretz, I., Gagnon, L., & Bouchard, B. (1998). Music and emotion: Perceptual determinants, immediacy, and isolation after brain damage. *Cognition, 68*, 111–141.

Ploog, D. (1986). Biological foundations of the vocal expressions of emotions. In R. Plutchik & H. Kellerman (Eds.), *Emotion: Theory, research, and experience. Volume 3: Biological foundations of emotion* (pp. 173–197). New York: Academic Press.

Plutchik, R. (1994). *The psychology and biology of emotion.* New York: HarperCollins.

Pratt, C. (1931). *The meaning of music: A study in psychological aesthetics.* New York: McGraw-Hill.

Pratt, R. R., & Jones, R. W. (1987). Music and medicine: A partnership in history. In R. Spintge & R. Droh (Eds.), *Music in medicine* (pp. 377–388). Berlin: Springer-Verlag.

Quantz, J. J. (1752). *Versuch einer Anweisung die Flöte traversiere zu spielen.* (Revised new printing with comments by Arnold Schering, 1926, C. P. Kahnt, Leipzig.)

Rapoport, E. (1996). Emotional expression code in opera and lied singing. *Journal of New Music Research, 25*, 109–149.

Rigg, M. G. (1937a). Musical expression: An investigation of the theories of Erich Sorantin. *Journal of Experimental Psychology, 21*, 442–455.

Rigg, M. G. (1937b). An experiment to determine how accurately college students can interpret the intended meanings of musical compositions. *Journal of Experimental Psychology, 21*, 223–229.

Rigg, M. G. (1939). What features of a musical phrase have emotional suggestiveness? *Publications of the Social Science Research Council of the Oklahoma Agricultural and Mechanical College, No. 1.*

Rigg, M. G. (1940a). The effect of register and tonality upon musical mood. *Journal of Musicology, 2*, 49–61.

Rigg, M. G. (1940b). Speed as a determiner of musical mood. *Journal of Experimental Psychology, 27*, 566–571.

Rigg, M. G. (1964). The mood effects of music: A comparison of data from four investigators. *Journal of Psychology, 58*, 427–438.

Robazza, C., Macaluso, C., & D'Urso, V. (1994). Emotional reactions to music by gender, age, and expertise. *Perceptual and Motor Skills, 79*, 939–944.

Rosenthal, R. (1982). Judgment studies. In K. R. Scherer, & P. Ekman (Eds.), *Handbook of methods in nonverbal behavior research* (pp. 287–361). Cambridge: Cambridge University Press.

Ross, B. H., & Spalding, T. L. (1994). Concepts and categories. In R. J. Sternberg (Ed.), *Thinking and problem solving* (2nd ed., pp. 119–150). New York: Academic Press.

Rousseau, J. J. (1761/1986). Essay on the origin of languages. In J. H. Moran & A. Gode (Eds.), *On the origin of language: Two essays* (pp. 5–74). Chicago: University of Chicago Press.

Russell, J. A. (1980). A circumplex model of affect. *Journal of Personality and Social Psychology, 39*, 1161–1178.

Sadie, S. (Ed.). (1980). *The new Grove dictionary of music and musicians* (6th ed.). London: Macmillan.

Scherer, K. R. (1995). Expression of emotion in voice and music. *Journal of Voice, 9,* 235–248.

Scherer, K. R., & Oshinsky, J. S. (1977). Cue utilization in emotion attribution from auditory stimuli. *Motivation and Emotion, 1,* 331–346.

Scherer, K. R., & Zentner, M. R. (2001). The emotional effects of music: Production rules. In P. N. Juslin & J. A. Sloboda (Eds.), *Music and emotion: Theory and research* (pp. 361–392). New York: Oxford University Press.

Schubert, E. (1999a). *Measurement and time series analysis of emotion in music.* Unpublished doctoral dissertation. University of South Wales, Sydney, Australia.

Schubert, E. (1999b). Measuring emotion continuously: Validity and reliability of the two-dimensional emotion-space. *Australian Journal of Psychology, 51,* 154–165.

Schubert, E. (2001). Continuous measurement of self-report emotional response to music. In P. N. Juslin & J. A. Sloboda (Eds.), *Music and emotion: Theory and research* (pp. 393–414). New York: Oxford University Press.

Scruton, R. (1997). *The aesthetics of music.* Oxford, England: Oxford University Press.

Seashore, C. E., Lewis, D., & Saetveit, J. (1939/1960). *Seashore measures of musical talents.* New York: Psychological Corporation.

Senju, M., & Ohgushi, K. (1987). How are the player's ideas conveyed to the audience? *Music Perception, 4,* 311–324.

Sherman, M. (1928). Emotional character of the singing voice. *Journal of Experimental Psychology, 11,* 495–497.

Shove, P., & Repp, B. H. (1995). Musical motion and performance: Theoretical and empirical perspectives. In J. Rink (Ed.), *The practice of performance. Studies in musical interpretation* (pp. 55–83). Cambridge, England: Cambridge University Press.

Siegwart, H., & Scherer, K. R. (1995). Acoustic concomitants of emotional expression in operatic singing: The case of Lucia in Ardi gli incensi. *Journal of Voice, 9,* 249–260.

Sloboda, J. A. (1985). *The musical mind: The cognitive psychology of music.* Oxford: Oxford University Press.

Sloboda, J. A., & Juslin, P. N. (2001). Psychological perspectives on music and emotion. In P. N. Juslin & J. A. Sloboda (Eds.), *Music and emotion: Theory and research* (pp. 71–104). New York: Oxford University Press.

Smith, L. D., & Williams, R. N. (1999). Children's artistic responses to musical intervals. *American Journal of Psychology, 112,* 383–410.

Sopchak, A. L. (1955). Individual differences in responses to different types of music in relation to sex, mood, and other variables. *Psychological Monographs: General and Applied, 69,* 1–20.

Spintge, R., & Droh, R. (Eds.). (1987). *Musik in der Medizin* [Music in medicine]. Berlin: Springer-Verlag.

Stern, D. N. (1985). *The interpersonal world of the infant.* New York: Basic Books.

Sundberg, J., Iwarsson, J., & Hagegård, H. (1995). A singer's expression of emotions in sung performance. In O. Fujimura & M. Hirano (Eds.), *Vocal fold physiology: Voice quality control* (pp. 217–229). San Diego, CA: Singular Press.

Tagg, P. (1979). Kojak—50 seconds of television music. Towards the analysis of affect in popular music. *Studies from Gothenburg University, Department of Musicology, No. 2.* Gothenburg, Sweden: Department of Musicology.

Tarasti, E. (1994). *A theory of musical semiotics.* Indianapolis: Indiana University Press.

Terwogt, M. M., & van Grinsven, F. (1991). Musical expression of mood states. *Psychology of Music, 19,* 99–109.

Thompson, W. F., & Robitaille, B. (1992). Can composers express emotions through music? *Empirical Studies of the Arts, 10,* 79–89.

Tomkins, S. S. (1962). *Affect, imagery, and consciousness: The positive affects.* New York: Springer.

Trussoni, S. J., O'Malley, A., & Barton, A. (1988). Human emotion communication by touch: A modified replication of an experiment by Manfred Clynes. *Perceptual and Motor Skills, 66,* 419–424.

Unger, H. H. (1979). *Die Beziehungen zwischen Musik und Rhetorik im 16–18. Jahrhundert.* Hildesheim, Germany: Georg Olms Verlag.

de Vries, B. (1991). Assessment of the affective response to music with Clynes's sentograph. *Psychology of Music, 19,* 46–64.

Wagner, A. H. (1932). Remedial and artistic development of the vibrato. In C. E. Seashore (Ed.), *University of Iowa studies in the psychology of music. Vol. I: The vibrato* (pp. 166–212). Iowa City: University of Iowa.

Wallbott, H. G., & Scherer, K. R. (1986). Cues and channels in emotion recognition. *Journal of Personality and Social Psychology, 51,* 690–699.

Watson, K. B. (1942). The nature and measurement of musical meanings. *Psychological Monographs, 54,* 1–43.

Watt, R. J., & Ash, R. L. (1998). A psychological investigation of meaning in music. *Musicae Scientiae, 2,* 33–53.

Wedin, L. (1969). Dimension analysis of emotional expression in music. *Swedish Journal of Musicology, 51,* 119–140.

Wedin, L. (1972a). Evaluation of a three-dimensional model of emotional expression in music. *Reports from the Psychological Laboratories, University of Stockholm, No. 349.* Stockholm, Sweden: Department of Psychology.

Wedin, L. (1972b). Multidimensional scaling of emotional expression in music. *Swedish Journal of Musicology, 54,* 1–17.

Wedin, L. (1972c). Multidimensional study of perceptual-emotional qualities in music. *Scandinavian Journal of Psychology, 13,* 241–257.

Weld, H. P. (1912), An experimental study of musical enjoyment. *American Journal of Psychology, 23,* 245–308.

Wigram, T., Saperston, B., & West, R. (Eds.). (1995). *The art and science of music therapy: A handbook.* Chur, Switzerland: Harwood Academic Publishers.

Zuckerkandl, V. (1956). *Sound and symbol.* Princeton, NJ: Princeton University Press.

# 27

# LANGUAGE AND EMOTION

Judy Reilly and Laura Seibert

For centuries, philosophers have been concerned with the two basic human systems involved in communication: language and emotion. The first reported experiment on language was conducted in the 7th century B.C. by the Egyptian King Psammetichus. He reputedly left two infants in an isolated mountain hideaway as a means to discover the "original" language of humans. Somewhat later, in the 4th century B.C., in the dialogue *Cratylus*, Plato wrote on the nature of reference and the origins of words. With respect to emotion, in modern times, Darwin has made the most impact and is cited in virtually every study of emotion. However, we have records from the Greeks discussing emotion and temperament and the role of the bodily humors in mediating emotions. Thus, from the oldest available records, language and emotion have been central themes in human behavior. What is most striking, however, is that these two literatures, which are both vast and voluminous, rarely refer to one another. These nonintersecting paths continue to this day, with linguists rarely referring to emotion and the influences it may have on language, and psychologists working in the area of emotions rarely considering language and how these systems intersect. Nonetheless, these two systems are concurrently involved in daily interactions of members of all cultures: In natural discourse, any linguistic utterance is produced and interpreted in an emotional context. Moreover, specific utterances convey emotion and are interpreted as emotionally significant. A spoken utterance can incorporate emotional information *paralinguistically*, using facial expression, vocal prosody, and gesture, as in, "JOHN!" (walking toward the person, arms outstretched, smiling). Or similar emotional information can be *lexically encoded* within the actual words of the sentence, as in "John, I am *so very happy* to see you again." Finally, speakers and writers have a vast repertoire of linguistic devices to convey subtle attitudinal information to "color" their utterances, and these can reflect emotional stance. For example, minimal modifications of the verb of the simple declarative sentence "I eat squid" can indicate a broad spectrum of personal preferences: I adore eating squid; I'll eat squid; I might eat squid; I could eat squid; I don't eat squid; I never eat squid; to I detest eating squid.

In this chapter, we examine some of the different relationships of language and emotion by focusing on their expression, and the integration of their co-expression from primarily a developmental perspective. In cultures all over the world, infants begin to produce their first words around their first birthday, yet they are already skilled affective communicators. One question that arises is the role affective expression plays in language acquisition. One possibility, reflecting a modular viewpoint, is that the systems develop orthogonally to one another; a second option, from a broader cognitive perspective is that the two communicative systems are linked. As such, emotional communication could serve as a bridge to the subsequently developing linguistic system, or both might reflect a more general symbolic system which later differentiates into these two distinct systems (as the adult neurological data indicate). Although our focus is developmental, we will first present a brief overview of several aspects of the adult model—that is, a variety of contexts in which adults integrate emotional and spoken linguistic expression—and then we consider the emergence and development of these relationships in toddlers and young children. By looking at how the relations between linguistic and emotional expression emerge and develop, we can better understand the components and organization of each communicative system individually, their developing intersections, and their seams and boundaries. Much of what we know about language and its intersection with emotion as in, for example, emotional prosody, stems from the vast body of research on spoken language. Spoken languages are expressed in the vocal channel and perceived by the auditory channel; and the oral/aural modalities impose certain contraints on the signal and its transmission. Unlike spoken languages, signed languages are conveyed in the gestural modality and perceived visually. Thus, as a means to identify those aspects of expressive development which are a product of the channel, or modality, in which the language is conveyed (e.g., oral/aural), and to distinguish them from those features which are universal, we will discuss both adult and developmental data from native Deaf adult signers and Deaf children of Deaf parents acquiring American Sign Language (ASL) as their first language. Past work on signed and spoken languages and their acquisition suggests that within the adult systems (spoken and signed language) the basic parameters are comparable; however, the forms will reflect the modality in which the languages are conveyed (oral/aural versus visual/gestural) and the conventions of use will differ from culture to culture, for example, hearing/deaf. With respect to development, we expect that the milestones for children acquiring English and ASL will be similar; these developing systems will reflect similar basic patterns regardless of the modality in which language and emotion are conveyed. However, similar to adults, the modality will play a role in how components are manifest. Overall, comparing the expressive behavior of these populations will provide a unique perspective on the development of the functional relations between language and emotion. Finally, we close the chapter with a lifespan perspective.

Before we begin, a brief discussion of what we mean by *language* and *emotion* is in order. Given the broad range of contexts in which these concepts have been discussed, any attempt at a comprehensive definition would be difficult. Thus, a general characterization of some of their essential features will suffice. For language, this includes (1) semanticity—the units of language convey meaning through their conventional association with referents; (2) arbitrariness—there is no necessary, intrinsic relationship between any unit of language and the nature of its referent; (3) displacement—language can communicate information about events that are distant in space or time from the moment of communication; (4) productivity—using the finite number of units of meaning in a given language, there is an infinite variety of meanings that can be expressed by using them in different combinations; and (5) traditional transmission—there is a necessary role of teaching and learning in the transmission of a given language from one generation to the next (Crystal, 1987). Language is *not* modality-specific—that is, it can be fully represented in spoken, written, and gestured (i.e., signed) forms.

Characterization of the essential features of emotion is also necessarily diverse. Phenomenologically, we know an emotion as a transient state in which we are permeated by a distinct feeling, which can vary in intensity and accompany physiological and behavioral changes. Yet emotions are not merely subjective experiences; they have a variety of functional roles. These include readying for action through recruitment and coordination of diverse physiological mechanisms, shaping attention and perception, facilitating memory, conforming behavior to goal-directed activities, adapting to changing social demands, influencing others' behavior, and aiding decision making, among others (Panksepp, 1998). Furthermore, the underlying organization of emotions has long been a matter of discussion and controversy, which we will not enter here as it is the focus of other chapters in this volume. Also, emotions are ultimately the inward and outward manifestation of neural processes, and the nature of these processes is covered elsewhere in this volume. Finally, our concern in this chapter is with emotion as it is expressed through different channels, facial expression, vocal and visual prosody as they co-occur with language, and as is it expressed within the linguistic system itself. We will not address the nature of the relationship between the inner experience of emotions and their outer expression, but rather focus on the production and, to some degree, the perception of expressed emotion and how it intersects with linguistic expression.

"Language" and "emotion" are often referenced by an assortment of related terms, and their meanings vary across the literature. Our use of these terms is as follows: "Linguistic" is understood as the adjectival equivalent of "language," and as such is not modality-specific—for example, language can be signed or spoken. "Nonlinguistic" communication is understood to include all other communication forms that are not linguistic. These forms include facial expression, prosody, and gesture (among others). As these forms of expression are often used concurrently with language, we also refer to them as "paralinguistic" communicative behaviors. Finally, "affective" is used here as synonymous with "emotional."

## Linguistic and Emotional Expression in Adults

### Linguistic Systems

#### Spoken Language

While the important defining features of language were discussed above, spoken language deserves some special attention here.

Spoken language, or speech, refers specifically to language produced through the oral channel and understood through the auditory channel. These two channels impose unique characteristics upon the linguistic signal passing through them. More commonly recognized characteristics include (1) broadcast transmission—the speech signal can be heard by any listener within earshot; (2) rapid fading—the speech signal is transient, so its reception is limited in time; and (3) specialization—the speech signal serves no other function besides communication (Crystal, 1987). Other distinctions of spoken language become apparent only when compared to sign language. Speech is expressed entirely through one channel, the oral channel and is received through the auditory channel. Sign, in contrast, utilizes multiple channels: the hands, the face, head, shoulders and body for production, and the visual channel for reception. Thus, signed languages can be characterized as visual/gestural whereas speech is oral/aural. Speech is almost entirely linear, or serial; units of meaning occur in sequence over a duration of time. Sign, on the other hand, communicates meaning in a more parallel fashion, with its simultaneous use of multiple channels. Spoken language can only encode the perspective of one subject at a time (e.g., "John gave Mary a ring and she was extremely pleased"). Sign language can encode several perspectives simultaneously; for example,

_____smile
RING RSj: iGIVEj

He gave her the ring and she was pleased.

(With respect to transcription conventions, glosses for manual signs are written in CAPS; the non-manual signal is denoted by a line over the manually signed utterance; the length of the line depicts the scope and duration of the non-manual behavior; these signals are labeled at the end of the line. Subscripts denote established loci in space and RS ["role shift"] indicates a shift in body position.)

These contrasts serve to illustrate some ways in which language is shaped by the modality through which it is transmitted. This is important to understand as we discuss below how emotion is expressed through different language modalities (i.e., speech versus sign), so one can dis-

tinguish differences attributable to the different channels themselves versus the potentially different relationships between each language modality and the underlying emotional system.

#### Signed Language: American Sign Language

American Sign Language is the predominant language of the Deaf community in the United States; because more is known about ASL and our experience is predominantly with this signed language, the sections on sign language focus on work conducted with ASL. However, the growing body of research on other signed languages suggests that the patterns found in ASL are consonant with those found in signed languages around the world. ASL is an independent linguistic system, not derived from any spoken language. Moreover, it exhibits both the grammatical complexity and the organizational principles common to the spoken languages of the world (Poizner, Klima, & Bellugi, 1987). For example, similar to Navajo and Turkish, ASL is morphologically complex and has been compared in typology to polysynthetic spoken languages (Bellugi & Klima, 1982). Some aspects of the language are, however, unique to its modality. Not so constrained by the general linearity of the aural/oral modality, signed languages are organized with co-occurring features or "layers." These are evident at all levels of the grammar: phonology, morphology, and syntax. For example, ASL relies on a multilayered organization in which the verb stem (e.g., LOOK-AT) and its aspectual and inflectional markers (e.g., habitual and distributive), all co-occur in space. (See Klima & Bellugi, 1979, for a comprehensive discussion.) Thus, ASL makes extensive use of co-occurring grammatical devices. Non-manual behaviors are another aspect of ASL which can be considered multilayered. While the most obvious articulators are the hands, much syntactic and lexical information is encoded on the face (Baker-Shenk, 1983; Baker & Cokely, 1980; Baker & Padden, 1978; Corina, Bellugi, & Reilly, 1999; Liddell, 1978, 1980) as is evaluative information in discourse (Emmorey & Reilly, 1997; Reilly, in press; Reilly McIntire, & Anderson, 1994). Shifts in eye gaze serve both pronominal and discourse functions (e.g., Bahan and Supalla, 1995) and changes in body position can mark discourse and syntactic information (Loew, Kegl, Poizner, 1997; also see Engberg-Pedersen, 1993, 1995, for a discussion of similar behaviors in Danish Sign Language; and Rossini, Reilly, Fabretti, & Volterra, 1998, for an initial investigation of nonmanual behaviors in narratives in Italian Sign Language). In contrast to the predominantly linear nature of spoken languages, in signed languages several channels (eye gaze, hands, faces, and torso) cooperate to convey the linguistic signal, and specific constellations of facial behaviors are the required morphological markers for both a set of adverbials and certain grammatical structures—for example, topics, conditionals, relative clauses, and questions (Anderson & Reilly, 1997, 1999; Baker & Padden, 1978; Baker-Shenk, 1983; Coulter, 1980; Liddell, 1978, 1986; Reilly & McIntire, 1991; Reilly, McIntire, & Bellugi, 1986/1990, 1991).

## Nonlinguistic Emotional Expression

### Prosody in Spoken Language

Prosody includes stress, intonation, loudness, pitch, juncture, and rate of speech. It is a suprasegmental feature of speech, in that it extends beyond the most basic linguistic unit, the phoneme, to complement syllables, words, phrases, or sentences. Any spoken utterance necessarily includes prosody; it is the acoustic means of conveying the speech signal, and in this sense, co-occurs with the lexically conveyed message. Though it is distinguished by some researchers from other, strictly paralinguistic aspects of speech, which include voice tension, quality, and qualification (Crystal, 1987), we will adopt the wider convention of understanding prosody to encompass all of these speech features. Prosody can serve purely linguistic functions, disambiguating word classes (e.g., nouns and verbs—"CONduct" versus "conDUCT") and syntactic structures (e.g., "The man and woman wearing red are my parents" versus "The man . . . and woman wearing red . . . are my parents"). Prosodic features also can distinguish sentence types ("He resigned?" versus "He resigned"), and clarify meaning ("He FELL?" versus "HE fell?"). In tone languages, such as Mandarin Chinese and most sub-Saharan African languages, the use of different intonation contours over single lexical items is a primary way to distinguish meaning. For example, in Mandarin Chinese, "ma" with a high-flat intonation contour means "mother," but with a low falling, then rising intonation contour means "horse." Prosody can also convey dialectical and idiosyncratic information (e.g., the sentence final pitch rise in the so-called valley-girl speak). Finally, of primary interest in this chapter, prosody can convey emotional and attitudinal information (e.g., "I'd love to help" can mean both its literal translation and its opposite, depending on its prosodic features).

Because affective prosody is discussed in greater detail elsewhere in this volume (chapter 23), only a brief overview of our current understanding of prosody is presented here. The manner in which affective prosody is encoded and expressed is influenced by a combination of internal and external factors (Scherer, 1985, 1994). Internal influences include the direct, physiological effects of the speaker's emotional state on his prosody, whereas external influences include the modifications of prosody that may occur as a consequence of the speaker's sociolinguistic context. Research into the internal influences, using acoustic and phonetic analyses of natural, induced, or simulated emotional prosody, clearly suggests prosody at minimum expresses speaker arousal (e.g., Murray & Arnott, 1993; Scherer, 1979, 1986). For example, expressions of emotion characterized by high sympathetic arousal (e.g., anger) have been associated with higher mean fundamental frequency ($F_O$), greater $F_O$ variability, greater intensity, and faster speaking rate (Frick, 1985; Murray & Arnott, 1993; Pittam & Scherer, 1993). There is a good deal of evidence pointing to further differentiation of prosodic emotion beyond the arousal dimension, though the degree to which prosody reflects discrete emotions or, alternatively, specific appraisals, is not yet clear. External influences on affective prosody include effects of linguistic, cultural, situational, psychological, and idiosyncratic factors on prosodic expression. For example, the intonation of the simplified speech directed to very young children (so-called motherese) has been documented to vary across cultures (Bohannon & Warren-Leubecker, 1988), yet it is unlikely these differences always reflect actual differences in the degree of interest or affection felt by the mothers. Empirical study specifically targeting external influences on affective prosody, however, is wanting, perhaps stalled by unknowns about the more primary, internal influences.

The manner in which affective prosody is perceived and leads to an emotion attribution by the receiver/listener is influenced by a number of factors. First, there is a physical modification of the acoustic signal between the speaker's lips and listener's ears. Then there is the sensory reception and perceptual processing of that signal by the listener which, as the psychophysical literature attests, does not necessarily correlate well with the external stimulus. Finally, an attribution of emotion is made. The accuracy of these attributions is considerably above chance, fueling a search for attribution universals (see chapter 23, this volume). Studies of emotion attribution using synthesized speech samples have found a number of acoustic and phonetic variables that influence judgments, such as $F_O$ range and $F_O$ rising or falling trend across the utterance. Sociocultural and psychological factors also appear to influence which emotion is perceived/attributed given certain prosodic cues. For example, whether the identically intoned exclamation, "I can't believe it!", is attributed to the elation or horror of the speaker (in the absence of facial or gestural cues) may depend upon the psychological context in which the utterance is heard—say, the positive context of a hospital nursery versus the negative context of the emergency room.

### Prosody in Signed Languages

Compared to research with spoken languages, prosody in signed languages represents a new and circumscribed field. Nonetheless, the underlying parameters that are modified in signing to convey emotional information appear to be comparable to those identified in spoken language.

Casting about for what might constitute prosody in signed languages, one finds that movement is a likely candidate. There is no question that movement of the hands is a critical feature of signed languages. In addition to handshape, location, and orientation, movement is one of the basic parameters of any manual sign (Stokoe, 1960) and has been given serious consideration in the context of the "visual" phonology of ASL (e.g., Stokoe, 1960; Coulter, 1993; Corina & Sandler, 1993; Liddell, 1995). As such, similar to vocal prosody and spoken language, any signed utterance has, by definition, a movement component. Attention has recently been devoted to patterns of movement shape and speed, as well as pauses, that might constitute the elements of linguistic prosody and the suprasegmentals for sign. (For a discussion of what might *represent* phonological stress and intonation in signed languages, see Wilbur, 1997, 2000; Boyes-Braem, 1999.) At the morphological level, movement patterns play a critical role, especially with predicates (see Klima & Bellugi, 1979, for discussion of verb morphology; Newport & Supalla, 1980, for noun verb distinctions). However, little was known regarding the elements of visual affective prosody—that is, how emotion might be conveyed through manual signing. Looking at this issue, we found consistency across signers in producing sentences with specific emotional meaning (Reilly, McIntire, & Seago, 1992). Sentences of neutral content signed with negative emotional prosody exhibited distinctive profiles: sad sentences were longer than neutral, and angry sentences were significantly shorter. By using a frame-by-frame analysis of the speed and the shape of the movement path of individual signs, we found that the two negative emotions (angry and sad) exhibited the most consistent differences, and they differed from each other on at least two parameters: sign duration and the shape of the sign's movement path.

In a complementary perceptual task, we asked deaf subjects to identify affective differences based solely on manual prosody, and all subjects were able to abstract emotional information from the manual signing alone (Reilly et al., 1992). Interestingly, errors occurred in both emotional valence and intensity, although more errors cluster along the dimension of intensity or arousal. For example, sad was often confused with neutral, and angry and surprise were more often confused with happy. Overall, we found subtle, yet consistent perceptible signing differences in the various affective conditions, and these are generally identifiable to native signers. These distinctions and patterns appear to be comparable to those identified in vocal affective prosody of spoken language (Scherer, 1986). In sum, for signed languages, modification of sign speed, duration, and the shape of the movement path are good candidates for conveying prosodic information.

## Facial Expression

Facial expression is another domain within nonlinguistic communication. Facial expressions include facial postures and movements that are purely reflexive (e.g., blinking to rapidly approaching objects), apparently emotional (e.g., eyes wide and mouth open, when surprised), and paralinguistic/communicative (e.g., a collusive wink or an affirmative head nod) (Fridlund, 1994). The latter type, expressions that accompany and supplement speech, are actually the most common (Ekman & Fridlund, 1987; Fridlund & Gilbert, 1985). Emotional facial displays in adults, on the other hand, have been empirically estimated to comprise about one-third of all facial displays (Ekman & Friesen, unpublished data). Much of the research into "emotional facial expressions" may well have included other paralinguistic displays, so important distinctions between the two types of facial behaviors may yet be unknown (Fridlund, 1994). Because the facial expression of emotion is reviewed in depth elsewhere in this volume (chapter 22), only a brief overview of our current understanding of affective facial expression is discussed here.

Evidence for universals in facial affect displays and attributions of emotion (Ekman, 1984, 1993; Ekman & Friesen, 1986) has supported a significant correspondence between specific emotions and specific facial expressions. Nevertheless, the question of the nature of the relationship between facial expressions and underlying emotional state is yet unresolved. Some theorists have more recently viewed facial expressions as fundamentally serving a functional role, namely, to signal one's intentions or elicit particular behaviors (e.g., Fridlund, 1994). Moreover, the underlying structure of emotions and how they are related to specific facial expressions is still under discussion. That is, are emotions discrete, and do they correspond to six or seven "basic" facial expressions as Ekman and his colleagues have suggested (Ekman, 1984, 1993; Ekman & Friesen, 1986)? Or do emotions, and their corresponding facial expressions, represent a continua of internal experiences, that may be better classified another way, such as along an approach-avoidance dimension (Davidson, 1988)? Another relevant aspect of facial expressions to consider is that their use is influenced by cultural and situational display rules (e.g., Goldschmidt, 1997), which further complicates interpretation of expression-emotion relationships. While display rules are well in place by adulthood, they are not yet part of an infant's knowledge base. As such, examining facial expressions in infants yields a clearer picture of the relationship between external expression and internal state, as we will discuss below.

## Facial Expression and Speech

In everyday life, we most frequently display and perceive dynamic, emotional facial expressions in our face-to-face dialogues. The ubiquity of conversation in day-to-day social interactions suggests the importance of examining the relationship between facial expressions and speech as they co-occur. Yet, to date, very little work has been done in this area. One early study did begin to address how these two signals intersect in natural discourse. Ekman (1979) found a consistent use of furrowed brows co-occuring with WH-questions (What is your name?) and raised brows with yes-no questions (Do you like chocolate?). More recently, comprehensive studies of facial expression during spontaneous conversation (Bavelas & Chovil, 1997; Chovil, 1989, 1991/1992) have revealed a number of interesting findings. Paramount among these is that facial expressions can serve not only to reflect the underlying emotional experience of a speaker but also to symbolize different meanings to both the speaker and the listener in dialogue. Oftentimes, the meaning symbolized is the emotional reaction of an individual who is being discussed. For example, one teenager relaying to another her father's attempts to rein in her social life may insert in her explanation a mock reproduction of her father's command, "You are not going out tonight!" As she says this, she may furrow her brow and narrow her eyes, portraying her father in a stern mood; in this case, the face and prosody reflect *his* rather than her emotions.

The meaning symbolized by facial expressions is not restricted to depictions of others' emotions, however. Chovil (1989) videotaped 12 conversational dyads (4 male, 4 female, and 4 mixed pairs) as they discussed three topics preselected to elicit a good range of discussion, and categorized the array of facial expressions shown by both the speaker and listener. No a priori categorization scheme was imposed; rather, the analysis approach in reviewing the videos was "both inductive and functional . . . (Chovil) asked: What is this display doing at this point in the conversation? How is it conveying meaning in the context in which it occurs?" (Bavelas & Chovil, 1997, p. 341). Facial movements that were involved in noncommunicative activities (e.g., blinking, swallowing, biting or licking the lips) and smiles (due to their sheer frequency) were set aside from the classification scheme. The result was a taxonomy of meaningful facial expressions comprising three linguistic function categories, and numerous subcategories. An independent scorer of a large sample of the video data yielded reliabilities of 82% to 97%.

Chovil found the most prevalent type of meaningful facial expression was a semantic display by the speaker. These are facial expressions that add meaning pertaining to the speaker's narrative. For example, "the speaker raised her eyebrows and one side of her upper lip and then squinted her eyes to illustrate her personal distaste, while saying, 'I hate, I hate desserts with alcohol in them' " (Bavelas & Chovil, 1997, p. 341; Chovil 1991/1992, p. 180). Not all semantic displays provide information redundant with the linguistic message, however. An example of a nonredundant facial display is, "(A participant said) 'That was only a couple of days ago but ah [pause]' (Chovil 1991/1992, p. 186). During the pause, the speaker pushed out his bottom lip and raised his eyebrows, as if to say, 'That's about it; the rest doesn't matter.' Based on the words alone, we would expect the speaker to continue, but his face conveyed that he was finished" (Bavelas & Chovil, 1997, pp. 342–343). Speakers also used facial expressions to symbolize syntactic markers. These were typically eyebrow movements, which usually served to emphasize a word or entire phrase. For example, as one participant recounted how her father rescued her as a child from falling off a barn roof, she "marked her Dad's yelling, 'Hang on! Hang on!', by raising her eyebrows precisely over that phrase" (Bavelas & Chovil, 1997, p. 343). Chovil found that listeners also display facial expressions in response to another's narrative. The most common of these were "back channel" expressions, such as "turning the corners of the lips down in appreciation of something serious, pressing the lips together in concern or suspense, closing the eyes briefly ('I don't want to see this'), and raising the brows in alarm or disbelief" (Bavelas & Chovil, 1997). Another type of listener facial expression was "motor mimicry," the portrayal of a reaction that would be appropriate for the situation the speaker is describing; for example, the wince a listener might make upon hearing of another's experience of pain. The listener does not obviously experience that pain vicariously, but rather appears to be signifying a message to the effect of, "I feel your pain."

In sum, facial expressions co-occur with speech and serve several functions: They can express the current emotions of the speaker himself, or the emotions of the subjects being discussed; they can provide semantic cues that may or may not be redundant with the linguistic message they accompany; they may also serve as syntactic markers, to help clarify a spoken utterance; and finally, facial expressions are used in communication not only by the speaker, but also the listener. Listeners provide feedback of various sorts to show their attention and emotional reaction to the speaker's utterances. This variety of roles for facial expressions underscores their communicative function, especially for conveying emotional information.

## Facial Expression in ASL

Similar to other signed languages of the world, facial expression in ASL serves multiple functions. Not only is it used for emotional purposes, as with spoken language, but certain specific configurations of facial behaviors also are the grammatical markers for a host of lexical, adverbial, and syntactic structures—for example, conditional sentences, relative clauses, and WH-questions. In addition, emotional facial expression comes under linguistic constraints in discourse and narratives. We will discuss these aspects of grammatical and emotional facial expression in ASL below in the developmental section of this chapter.

## The Lexical Encoding of Emotion

### Spoken Language

In the sections above, we have introduced how emotion is conveyed paralinguistically, both vocally and via facial expression, and how these behaviors co-occur and might modify the emotional significance of the utterance. Another venue for integrating emotion and language is within the linguistic code itself. This area has received the most attention from psychologists in the form of studying the lexicon for emotions. Findings of apparent universals in the display and recognition of emotional facial expressions led to the proposal that there is a set of discrete, basic human emotions denoted by the words *happiness, anger, fear, surprise, disgust,* and *shame* (Ekman, 1980, 1989; Izard, 1971, 1977). Such proposals prompted a search for universals in the emotion lexicon itself. For example, in the landmark study by Shaver, Schwartz, Kirson, and O'Connor (1987), subjects rated several hundred English emotion words on a Likert-type scale according to how well each word named an emotion. Of these several hundred words, those with high emotion prototypicality ratings were retained. Then a hierarchical cluster analysis was conducted, grouping the words into 25 clusters of similar emotion words. These emotion prototype categories have held up in studies of other languages as well (Church, Katigbak, Reyes, & Jensen, 1998; Hupka, Lenton, & Hutchison, 1999; Romney, Moore, & Rusch, 1997; Shaver, Wu, & Schwartz, 1992). Hupka, Lenton, and Hutchinson (1999) examined dictionaries of 64 representative languages of the roughly 6,000 languages of the world for evidence of similar emotion categories to those found in English by Shaver et al. (1987). One-third of the languages that they surveyed had words for all 25 of Shaver et al.'s (1987) categories, and all of the languages they studied had words for at least 15 of these categories. Furthermore, Hupka et al. (1999) found evidence of a fairly uniform developmental sequence of labeling emotion categories across languages, akin to the cross-cultural color-naming findings of Berlin & Kay (1969). Evidence of cross-linguistic universals in the lexical encoding of emotion has been cited as possible support for universals in underlying emotional experience (Johnson-Laird & Oatley, 1989), corroborating the evidence from facial and prosodic channels. However, the reality of lexical cross-linguistic

similarities in the encoding of emotion is not undisputed (e.g., see review by Russell, 1991; Wierzbicka, 1991, 1992, 1994).

Objections have been raised on several grounds, including the lack of isomorphism among many emotion concepts across languages, the use of grammatical categories in some languages to further differentiate emotion terms in ways not recognized in other languages, the extreme differences in size of different languages' emotion lexicons, and, more generally, the implication that these differences indicate cultures have vastly different perspectives on emotional experiences (Wierzbicka, 1994). An in-depth analysis of the evidence on either side of this issue is beyond our scope here. In sum, at issue is the relationship of language to emotion—whether the parsings of language reflect universal distinctions in underlying emotional experience or varying cultural constructions of emotions. This controversy parallels some of the questions that characterize the study of nonlinguistic expressions of emotion, as discussed above. This "nature versus nurture" debate pervades all discussions of the relationships between language—and, indeed, all forms of communication—and emotional experience.

Beyond the more direct encoding of emotion in language via emotion words themselves, speakers and signers have access to a wide variety of linguistic markers to convey subtle modulations of attitude or stance. Scholars of rhetoric have long considered the role of stance in spoken and written communication. For example, Biber and Finegan (1989) constructed a list of more than 100 lexical means of indicating differential attitudes in English. One discourse context in which personal stance plays a critical role is in narratives. This was first noted by Labov and Waletzky (1967), who introduced the evaluative function as a crucial aspect of any successful narrative. From their perspective, the *evaluative* function of the narrative is represented by those components that give meaning to the series of events in the story: "The evaluation of a narrative is defined by us as that part of the narrative which reveals the attitude of the narrator towards the narrative by emphasizing the relative importance of some narrative units as compared to others" (1967, p. 37). This information can be conveyed/packaged in several ways: *lexically,* for example, by using intensifiers (so, very, really), modals (would, might, will) or hedges (maybe, possibly), and affective predicates (love, despise, delight, cry, laugh) to reflect speaker attitude; and *syntactically,* where information can be backgrounded in a subordinate clause. In languages with a richer inflectional system, such as Russian or Italian, many of these attitudinal and emotional shades of meaning can be expressed *morphologically* with a suffix; in Italian, a boy is *un ragazzo,* a nasty boy is *un ragazzaccio,* a little boy is *un ragazzino,* and a nasty little boy is *un ragazzinaccio.*

Signed Language

Similar to spoken languages, emotional and attitudinal information can be conveyed lexically in ASL. Manual signs for emotions (e.g., *HAPPY, GUILTY, SAD, DISTRESSED* as well as degree of certainty (e.g., *TRUE, CAN, POSSIBLE, MAYBE, DOUBT*) are all available to signers. Moreover, subtle modulations of sign movement signal morphological distinctions such as inceptive (*She got sick*) versus habitual (*She's always sick*, as in being a hypochondriac). In addition, because signed languages recruit multiple channels—for example, hands, head, eye gaze, shoulders and face—signers have multiple avenues through which to convey evaluative information, and manual signs are just one venue. For example, "direct speech" or direct quotes in signed discourse are signaled by a break in eye contact with the addressee, and a shift in eye gaze, head position, and facial expression, as well as a slight body shift from narrator position to "take the role" of the character. Thus, quotes, which are extremely common in narrative discourse, are a rich context for examining the interplay of emotional and linguistic expression. Below we will discuss in detail how signers use eye gaze and emotional facial expression as linguistic devices to identify the character who is signing as well as to convey the attitude and emotions of that particular character in the narrative.

## Neurological Foundations

A discussion of the relationship between language and emotion would not be complete without an examination of their neural substrates, and, in fact, this is one of the few ways these two functional domains have been compared in the literature. The logic is typically that evidence of their distinct neural substrates is the capstone of proof of their functional independence. The evidence of their different neural foundations is clear, however, as emotional linguistic and nonlinguistic communication co-occur in time and are often congruent, at some level they may well share a common neural orchestration. That is, while much emphasis has been placed on the dissociation between the neurological bases of language and emotion, little attention has been paid to their points of neurological integration.

A presentation of the neural bases of emotion is well covered in other chapters within this volume. Briefly, it appears the experience of emotion is generated subcortically (e.g., via the basal ganglia and/or limbic system) and can be influenced by various regions of the neocortex (Panksepp, 1998), especially the prefrontal cortex (Le-Doux, 1995).

The neural substrates for spoken language in the adult brain are better understood than for most other functions. The dominant (usually, left) cerebral hemisphere appears to be the primary locus of control for the "classic" language components—phonology, morphology and syntax; for both spoken and signed languages (Poizner, Klima, & Bellugi, 1987). Comprehension has been associated with the left superior temporal lobe, and production with the left posterior frontal lobe. A role for the dominant thalamus has also been suggested (Nadeau & Crosson, 1997). A significant role of the nondominant (usually, right) hemisphere has been found for select linguistic functions as well, including comprehending and structuring narratives and discourse, drawing inferences, interpreting nonliteral uses of language (e.g., idioms, metaphors, irony), and fulfilling certain pragmatic functions (Joanette, Goulet, & Hannequin, 1990; Gardner, Brownell, Wapner, & Michelow, 1983).

The question of whether the linguistic communication of emotion is subserved by the same neural substrates as linguistic communication in general has received limited attention. A review of the available literature (Borod, Bloom, & Santschi-Haywood, 1998) reveals somewhat different findings according to whether normal or brain-damaged individuals were studied. Studies of the perception of lexical aspects of emotion in normal individuals have typically used single-word presentations in lateralization paradigms, e.g., by comparing the speed and accuracy with which emotional versus nonemotional words are recognized in each visual field in a lexical decision task. Such studies have variously found a superior role of the right hemisphere (RH) in perceiving emotion words (Brody, Goodman, Halm, Krinzman, & Sebrechts, 1987; Bryden & Ley, 1983; Graves, Landis, & Goodglass, 1981), a valence effect with differential hemispheric performance (Richards, French, & Dowd, 1995; Van Strien & Heijt, 1995; Van Strien & Morpugo, 1992; Wexler, Schwartz, Warrenburg, Servis, & Tarlatzis, 1986; Zieher & Zenhausern, 1984), and no hemispheric specialization for emotionality on lexical processing whatsoever (Eviatar & Zaidel, 1991; Strauss, 1983). The valence findings suggest that the RH mediates negative lexical emotion, whereas the LH mediates positive lexical emotion. Studies of the perception of lexical emotion in brain-damaged individuals which have used both single words and sentences, have been less equivocal. Several have supported a RH specialization, though others have found no hemispheric effects. Borod et al. (1998) suggest interpretation of the latter studies should take into account their methodological limitations, specifically, their failure to include nonemotional, lexical stimuli for controls. Studies of the linguistic expression of emotion in brain-damaged patients, e.g., using tasks eliciting spontaneous discourse on emotionally laden scenes, have usually found impairments in right-hemispheric–damaged patients, relative to left-hemisphere–damaged patients and controls (Bloom, Borod, Obler, & Koff, 1990; Borod, Koff, Lorch, & Nicholas, 1985). However, as these tasks demand comprehension of the emotional content of the scene, one must be cautious in inferring an expressive impairment (Myers, 1994). In sum, the literature suggests greater involvement of the RH in the processing of lexical emotion. That this finding is more consistent among brain-damaged than normal individuals may be due at least in part to methodological constraints in isolating emotional from nonemotional processing in normal individuals (Borod et al., 1998). Hence, the linguistic communication of emotion appears to involve somewhat different neural substrates than nonemotional linguistic communication.

The neural substrates for nonlinguistic communication (i.e., prosody, facial expression, and gesture) have been studied almost exclusively in relation to emotional expression. Most of the research to date has focused on affective facial expression and affective prosody; studies of the neural bases of emotional gesture are virtually non-existent. Thirty years of research have implicated a superior role of the right hemisphere in emotional facial expression and prosody, though the unanimity of these findings varies according to several variables. Borod (1993) has integrated this extensive literature by outlining a four-component approach to emotional processing: processing mode (comprehension, expression, and experience), communication channel (facial, prosodic, and lexical), emotional dimensions (e.g., valence), and discrete emotions (e.g., joy, fear). This approach recognizes the fact that the neurological bases of emotional expression, nonlinguistic or linguistic, may vary significantly according to these parameters.

Now that we have a perspective on some of the tools that adults can recruit to express emotion and how they intersect with language, we are ready to examine how these functional relations develop in childhood. In the adult system, the components generally function in an integrated fashion. By looking at the components as they are acquired and how these relations develop in infancy and childhood, we garner clues to the underlying organization of the adult system. Thus, as is the case with developmental studies overall, they aid our understanding not only of childhood and development, but they also represent a unique window into the adult model.

## The Developmental Picture

For most of the 20th century, behaviorism and the powerful role of the environment held center stage in child psychology. However, in the mid-1960s to early 1970s, two sets of work were published that dramatically changed the field of developmental psychology: Chomsky's work in the mid-1960s on language (1965) and independent studies by Ekman (1972) and Izard (1971) on the universality of specific emotional facial expressions. Ironically, these studies were of adult behavior and rarely,

if ever, even mentioned children. Nonetheless, their joint proposals of the universality of these systems spurred a keen interest in both emotional development and language acquisition as venues for identifying aspects and parameters of these communicative systems that might be innate. Thus, over the last 30 years, we have accrued a substantial body of literature in these domains and below we present brief sketches of the development of both emotion expression and of language.

### The Emergence of Emotional Communication

#### Emotional Facial Expression in Hearing and Deaf Children

Searching for the earliest indices of potentially innate behaviors, researchers studying infants have concentrated on the child's ability to produce certain facial expressions and to use them to express and to interpret different emotional states. In these cases, facial expression is used as an index to overall affective development (see Campos, Barrett, Lamb, Goldsmith, & Stenberg, 1983; Camras, Malatesta, & Izard, 1991; Nelson, 1987; Nelson & deHaan, 1997). Researchers have found that, at birth, facial muscle contractions configure in specific patterns that respect the basic emotional expressions (Oster, 1978). And within hours of birth, babies produce distinctive facial expressions in response to different flavors (sugar, quinine, and citric acid; Steiner, 1973). During a child's first year, affective facial expression becomes a significant communicative channel (e.g. Stern, 1977), and early on, infants use particular facial configurations to convey specific affective states. For example, 7-month-olds furrow their brows in anger in response to physical restraint or to the experimenter's withdrawal of a cookie (Stenberg, Campos, & Emde, 1983). From studies by Stenberg and Campos (1990), we know that infants show a fearful face in the visual cliff experiment at about 7 months. Studies investigating other affective dimensions have found that babies reliably respond with a surprise expression (raised brows and widened eyes) when faced with unexpected consequences—for example, a disappearing toy (Hiatt, Campos, & Emde, 1979). These same investigators have also shown that infants of 10 to 12 months reliably smile in positive interactive routines—for example, peek-a-boo. Babies appear to use faces to interpret affective states as well: by 10 to 12 months of age, social referencing develops and infants seek out emotional information from their caregivers and can use it to guide their own behavior (Klinnert, Campos, Sorce, Emde, & Svejda, 1983). Deaf infants growing up with sign language appear to follow a similar developmental pattern (Reilly, McIntire, & Bellugi, 1986/1990; Marschark, 1993). Thus, infants are fluent affective communicators, consistently using specific facial configurations both to express and to interpret emotional information.

## Development of Emotional Vocalization

From the moment of birth, infants use the vocal channel to express distress and displeasure. And a crying infant also has a characteristic cry face (e.g., Izard, Hembree, & Huebner, 1987). However, systematic studies on the nature of infant prelinguistic emotional vocalizations are rare. In contrast to the study of infant facial expressions, study of the parameters that characterize infant vocalizations is complicated by the absence of a clear homology in adults (Scherer, 1982). That is, many of the parameters used to characterize emotional prosody in adults are highly related to the articulation of speech sounds. Even the apparently more objective approach of performing acoustic analyses of infant vocalizations is not without its pitfalls, as the convention for reading spectrograms is largely influenced by the analysis of speech, and the data are not easily quantified in general (Scherer, 1982). Infant vocalizations differ from those of adults not only because of infants' prelinguistic status (with its nonspeech phonatory and articulatory processes) but also because of morphological differences between the infant and adult vocal tracts. The infant oral cavity is almost totally filled by the tongue, and the larynx is higher in the neck, leaving little distance between the oral and nasal cavities. This difference, in combination with a reduced capability to alter the shape of the vocal tract, produces vocalizations closer to the sounds of nonhuman primates than to human speech (Lieberman, Harris, Wolff, & Russell, 1971).

While our present understanding of infant emotional vocalizations remains limited, much work has been done demonstrating infants' sensitivity to adult prosody. Very young infants, for example, have been shown to prefer the voice of their mother over that of a stranger (DeCasper & Fifer, 1980; Mehler & Bertoncini, 1979; Mills & Melhuish, 1974). Five-month-old infants respond differently to the approving or prohibiting tone of infant-directed speech (Fernald, 1993). Seven-month-old infants have demonstrated the capacity to discriminate acoustic signals according to their fundamental frequency and their harmonic structure (Clarkson, Clifton, & Perris, 1988), and at 8½ months, infants show early regulation of their behavior based on vocalizations expressing happiness or fear (Svejda, 1981). Reflecting their limited receptive language competence and reliance on affective communication, babies at 9 months of age may regulate their behavior according to maternal prosody, even when it conflicts with lexical content (Lawrence, 1993). Somewhat later, at 15 to 16 months of age, as toddlers' receptive vocabulary increases, they are more likely to behave according to their mother's lexical, rather than prosodic, cues when these cues conflict (Friend, 2000). In sum, by their first birthdays, infants are using both facial expression and vocal prosody to convey and interpret affective information.

## Early Language Development: Spoken and Signed

Overall, researchers have found that Deaf children of Deaf parents acquiring ASL follow a similar developmental trajectory and respect the same principles of language acquisition as do children learning spoken languages (Bellugi & Klima, 1982; Newport & Meier, 1986; Petitto, 1988; Petitto & Marentette, 1991; Reilly, McIntire, & Bellugi, 1990a 1990b, 1991; Reilly & McIntire, 1991; Casselli & Volterra, 1990; Volterra & Iverson, 1995; Reilly, 2000; and see Meier, 1991, for reviews). Babbling occurs in both modalities; both signed and spoken babbling emerges at about 6 months of age (Stark, 1979; Petitto & Marentette, 1991) and we see evidence of language comprehension by 9 to 10 months of age. However, it is not until near the end of the child's first year that productive language emerges and children produce their first words (Fenson et al., 1993; also see Meier & Newport, 1990, for an extensive discussion of a possible sign advantage in the acquisition of first signs or words). At about 20 to 24 months, both Deaf and hearing children begin to combine two signs or words into sentences to convey a basic and limited set of semantic relationships (Brown, 1973; Newport & Ashbrook, 1977; Volterra & Iverson, 1995). After age 2 sentences become longer, and children grapple with the morphology of their respective languages (Bellugi & Klima, 1982; Reilly et al., 1990a, 1990b, 1991; Reilly & McIntire, 1991; Fenson et al., 1993; Caselli & Casadio, 1995). (See Brown, 1973, for a detailed discussion of these developments in English and the volumes edited by Slobin [e.g., 1985] for developmental chronicles of a wide range of languages.) By about 3 years, children are using complex sentences—conditionals, topics, relative clauses and subordinate adverbial clauses (ASL: Reilly et al., 1990a, 1990b, 1991; Reilly, 2000; Emmorey & Reilly, 1998; Lillo-Martin, 1999. English: Limber, 1973; Reilly, 1983, 1986; Bowerman, 1979). As in the acquisition of any language, spoken or signed, the grammar of the language (and its modality) influences the particular sequence and timing of the acquisition of individual language structures (see Slobin, 1982, 1985). An example of a sign-specific structure meeting these criteria is grammatical facial expression, which we discuss below. Overall, however, by their fifth year, children all over the world are well on their way toward mastering the vast majority of the basic grammatical structures of their language.

## The Representation of Emotion in Toddlers and Preschoolers

One of the very early intersections of language and emotion in which there is a substantial literature is in children's acquisition of emotional words. Developmentalists have seen these early labels as evidence of children's developing representations of emotions. These include labeling one's own state as well as inferring emotions in others. Beginning as early as 18–20 months of age children begin to use internal state words and signs, (e.g., *mad, happy*, or *sad*) to refer to their own emotional state (Bretherton & Beeghly, 1982; Bretherton, McNew, & Beeghly-Smith, 1981; Reilly et al., 1986/1990). In the second year of life, we also see the beginnings of empathy and prosocial behaviors (Radke-Yarrow, Zahn-Wexler, & Chapman, 1983), and at about 2;6, children attribute internal states to others (Bretherton & Beeghly, 1982; Dunn, Bretherton, & Munn, 1987; Brown & Dunn, 1991; Reilly et al., 1986/1990). Further, Smiley (1987) has found that even at this young age, children are beginning to infer motivations for people's emotional responses and to infer emotions in others. Additional studies confirm that 3-year-olds can provide motivations and causes for emotional responses (Stein & Levine, 1987). Finally by 3;6, they can distinguish and label mad, happy, and sad facial expressions. Scared and surprised are correctly identified by the majority of children by 4 (Smiley & Huttenlocher, 1989) and they can attribute these emotions to others (Reilly et al., 1986/1990; Reilly, 2000). In sum, by age 4, children's cognitive representation of emotion—their use of emotional terms, their understanding of causes of emotional responses, and their ability to attribute emotions to others—is rather sophisticated.

In the previous sections, we have tried to present brief overviews of the emergence and development of emotion, language, and emotion representation. We are now ready to examine in detail two different contexts in which language and emotion play significant roles: the acquisition of grammatical facial expression in ASL, exemplifying the bifurcation of emotion and language, and the developing evaluative function in narratives where emotion and language are integrated. Both these venues will inform our understanding of the development of different aspects of the relations of emotion and language.

# The Acquisition of Grammatical Facial Expression in ASL: The Divergence of Language and Emotion

## Emotion and Grammar on the Face

From the brief sketches presented above, we can see that as children's first productive vocabulary appears at around 12 months of age, they are already quite sophisticated emotional communicators. As language emerges, one challenge they face is to integrate these two communicative systems: emotional expression and language. The acquisition of signed languages offers a unique perspective on this developmental transition because facial expression serves both emotional and grammatical roles. This multifunctionality of similar facial expressions poses an interesting developmental problem: How do Deaf infants, acquiring ASL as their first language, make the transition from using facial expression to convey and interpret emotion (similar to hearing infants) to acquiring ASL and also using facial expression as part of the nonmanual grammar? One obvious route to the acquisition of grammatical facial signals would be for the child to extend and generalize prelinguistic communicative abilities to appropriate linguistic contexts. This would imply one global system of communication that serves linguistic, communicative, and affective functions. Alternatively, children might "ignore" the similarities in the signals and treat the grammatical facial signals as a separate system—as linguistic information to be analyzed independently. In sum, because facial expression and other nonmanual behaviors are multifunctional in ASL, serving affective, communicative, and linguistic purposes, their development provides a superb context to address issues bearing on the relationship of language to other symbolic and cognitive systems, specifically, the relation of prelinguistic and affective communicative behaviors to the development of language.

In the following sections we present data from some of our studies over the last 15 years on the emergence of grammatical facial behaviors in American Sign Language to illustrate how Deaf children make this transition. However, before we look at development, it would be helpful to know something about the adult system.

## Facial Morphology

Similar to other signed languages, in the ASL nonmanual grammar, specific constellations of facial behaviors serve as the obligatory morphological marking for a variety of linguistic structures, and these facial behaviors co-occur with the manual string over which they have scope. Grammatical facial signals in ASL play three different roles:

1. Lexical

        _____th
    LATE      NOT YET

2. Adverbial
   2A) BOY WRITE LETTER
   "The boy is writing/wrote a letter"

        _____mm
   2B) BOY WRITE LETTER
   "The boy writes/wrote letters regularly or easily"

        _____th
   2C) BOY WRITE LETTER
   "The boy writes/wrote letters carelessly"

3. Syntactic
        _____cond.
   EAT BUG, # SICK YOU
   "If you eat a bug, you get sick"

Again, with respect to transcription conventions, the non-manual signal is denoted by a line over the manually signed utterance (which is in CAPS); the length of the line depicts the scope and duration of the nonmanual behavior; these signals are labeled at the end of the line.

Grammatical facial behaviors in ASL often constitute the sole morphological signal for a particular linguistic structure, as in conditionals. If the utterance in example 3 is produced without the conditional, nonmanual marker, rather than being interpreted as the antecedent and consequent clauses of a conditional sentence, the utterance is merely two simple declarative statements. Thus, in this instance, the nonmanual signal *is* the conditional marker.

Although the facial morphology uses the same muscles as those that are recruited for affective expression, their timing, scope, and context often differ. Whereas affective facial expression can be used independently of language—for example, we might smile in response to a toddler's first steps—grammatical facial behaviors invariably co-occur with a manually signed utterance. Second, the timing of grammatical facial expression is linguistically constrained. It begins milliseconds before the initiation of the manual string over which it has scope, and immediately attains apex intensity that is maintained until the termination of the manual string. In contrast, emotional facial expression is variable in intensity, and its timing is inconsistent and inconstant. These patterns are graphically contrasted below:

4.   Grammatical facial expression

```
        _____
       /           \
    BOY WRITE LETTER
```

5.   Affective facial expression

```
      _____
     /                \
  MY CAT BORN[+] BABY {excitedly} "My cat had
```

kittens!"

## Baby Faces in ASL

Our initial studies chronicling the acquisition of grammatical facial expression began with the single sign productions of Deaf toddlers (Reilly, McIntire, & Bellugi, 1986/1990). Focusing on early multichannel productions—constructions that included both a manual sign and a co-occurring facial behavior—we found that initially, before age 2 years, these single-sign productions were acquired as whole unanalyzed chunks or gestalts, similar to the early unanalyzed phrases of hearing children (e.g., MacWhinney, 1978). For example, when toddlers signed *HAPPY* or *SAD*, the manual sign was accompanied by the appropriate emotional facial expression; when they asked *WHAT?* they generally furrowed their brows in puzzlement. In these cases, the utterances often involved facial behaviors that were emotional and/or communicative. At

about 2 to 2½ years of age, as children begin producing sentences, however, we found that the facial behaviors that we had previously witnessed were often missing from these same signs or structures. The very same children were fluently using manual signs and manually signed grammatical constructions that required grammatical facial expressions—for example WH-questions—however, their faces were often blank (Reilly & McIntire 1991).

The developmental profile for WH-questions can serve as an illustration. Data on the adult model come from Baker-Shenk's dissertation (1983) in which she used FACS (Facial Action Coding System; Ekman & Friesen, 1978) to analyze WH-questions. Her analyses demonstrate that for adults, WH-sign questions in ASL include a WH-sign (e.g., WHAT, HOW, WHERE, etc.) as well as a furrowed brow and head tilt; these nonmanual behaviors begin immediately before the manually signed string and have scope over the entire WH-question, as in the following:

```
    _____ 4+57 [brow furrow+head for-
  WHERE SHOE WHERE            ward]
```

(On the non-manual line, numbers reflect specific muscle contractions, called Action Units; from FACS; Ekman & Friesen, 1978).

Developmentally, children's questions before the age of 2 or so frequently were accompanied by aspects of the adult nonmanual behavior. However, the timing, scope, and individual components often did not match the adults':

6.  Corinne (1;6)
```
    _____ 4 [brow furrow]
    "WHAT"
```

7.  Corinne (1;9)
```
    _____ 51<>52[headshake]
    WHERE MELON
    "Where's the melon?"
```

By age 2 to 2½ years, the children's productive discourse included frequent manually signed questions; however, their faces were neutral and they omitted the obligatory nonmanual behaviors:

8.  Kate (2;3) WHERE "WHAT"
             "Where is it?"

It is not until after age 4 that children accompany the manually signed WH-questions with the required facial behaviors, and when they do, the facial behaviors first have scope only over the Wh-signs, rather than the entire WH-question.

Interestingly, this same developmental sequence recurs in linguistic structures that are signaled both manually and nonmanually, regardless of whether the grammatical structure had a similar communicative correlate or was unique to ASL. For example, grammatical negation in ASL can be signaled lexically with such negative signs as *CANT* or *NOT*, and by a grammatical headshake that is strikingly similar to the communicative headshake used by deaf and hearing people to signal negation. In contrast, the nonmanual adverbials, such as *mm* or *th* which respectively mean *easily* or *regularly* and *carelessly* and similar to the negative head-shake, co-occur with manually signed predicates, have no affective or communicative correlate; they are unique to ASL. We see similar developmental patterns in these two types of adverbial structures. That is, similar to WH-questions, for both very early adverbials and negation, we have examples of toddlers producing single manual signs with what appeared to be an appropriate nonmanual facial behavior, as in the following early productions:

9.  Kate: (1;8) _____neg headshake
    STINKY
    "[It's] not stinky."
10. Kate (2;3) _____mm (protruding lips and
    VACATION   raised chin boss)

Months later, similar constructions were signaled solely on the hands. Whether the structure had a comparable communicative counterpart—for example, the headshake for negation—or was exclusively a linguistic structure of ASL was not a factor; the developmental pattern was the same. These data suggest that at the single-sign stage children recruit affective/communicative facial expression to accompany their single-sign utterances. Then, as syntax emerges and the child is producing multisigned utterances, there is a reanalysis of the facial behaviors and their relation to language. In sum, once children are producing sentences, they are not able to directly generalize their affective and communicative abilities to the appropriate linguistic context.

In each of our developmental investigations, which include grammatical structures varying in complexity from single lexical items—for example, emotion signs (Reilly et al, 1990b), negation (Anderson & Reilly, 1997)—to adverbials (Anderson & Reilly, 1999) and clausal structures—for example, conditionals (Reilly et al., 1990a) and WH-questions (Reilly & McIntire, 1991)—after 24 to 30 months, the same developmental pattern occurred: Children ignored the nonmanual signals and produced only the manually signed string. It is only after children demonstrate fluency with the manual structure that they begin to incorporate the nonmanual behaviors. Further, rather than as a whole, these emerge componentially (for a discussion and more examples, see Reilly et al., 1991).

If we view these data as an index of the relation of language and affect, they suggest that initially, during the very early stages of language acquisition, both language

and emotional expression have access to a general, underlying symbolic function. Children at the one-sign stage draw on early affective and communicative abilities collaboratively with their first signs. However, as language emerges, especially as syntax develops, and the child begins to combine signs, there is a bifurcation of systems such that language and emotion unfold as independently organized and differentially mediated systems, each following its own developmental path. Finally, returning to the two alternatives proposed above, it is clear that affective/communicative information does *not* just generalize to the appropriate linguistic context. Once children were combining signs into sentences, they were unable to exploit their affective/communicative abilities for linguistic purposes. Nonmanual morphology, regardless of whether it is isomorphic with a an affective or communicative behavior, is independently acquired in a linguistically constrained and patterned way.

## Narratives: A Context for the Integration of Language and Emotion

Constructing a narrative requires tying together and giving meaning to a set of otherwise disconnected events, and narrators rely on affective expression as a primary means of expressing the relational significance of narrative events (Labov & Waletzky, 1967). These authors characterized a narrative as a sequence of temporally related clauses, and they also identified the referential and evaluative functions of narrative. They consider the *referential* to include information about the characters and events; it is what moves the story forward—the plot. In contrast, the *evaluative* aspect of narratives gives sense to the story, revealing the narrator's attitude or emotional stance to the referential components. An additional social function of evaluation is to engage and maintain the audience's attention.

In this section, our goal is to chronicle the changing nature of evaluation from the earliest stories of preschoolers to those of adults. Given the strong affective component of evaluation, tracing its development in narratives provides an informative context to examine the integration of linguistic and emotional expression. We begin with a brief discussion of our own work, as well as that of colleagues, on the development of evaluation in spoken English narratives. As a cross-linguistic, cross-modal study, we then consider aspects of the nature and development of the evaluative function in signed narratives.

### Evaluation in Narratives

As noted previously, the evaluative elements are those aspects of story telling that convey the significance of certain referential events in the narrative; they give the story meaning by transmitting the personal significance of particular aspects of the story. Whereas Labov and Waletzky initially focused on evaluative clauses and mentioned lexical evaluation (e.g., Labov, 1984), Peterson and McCabe (1983) noted that children sprinkled evaluative devices through-out clauses employing both lexical and phonological means. Thus, evaluative information can be conveyed/packaged in several ways: *lexically*, for example, by using intensifiers, modals, or hedges to reflect speaker attitude, that is, lexical stance markers, as noted before; *syntactically*, as in relative clauses, which commonly function as asides to comment on a person's behavior/ character (*You know, that one who will do anything to win*); and *paralinguistically*, by emotional facial expression, gesture, and affective prosody that can effectively convey narrator attitude or reflect the inferred emotions of a character. When evaluation is linguistically conveyed, it constitutes part of the body of the story proper. However, when evaluation is paralinguistically conveyed, via facial expression or prosody, it can co-occur with the referential aspects of the story. Since the seminal article of Labov and Waletzsky in 1967, researchers have considered aspects of evaluation in adult texts (e.g., Biber & Finegan, 1989; Labov, 1984) and from a developmental perspective (e.g., Bamberg & Damrad-Frye, 1991; Bamberg & Reilly, 1996; Berman, 1993, 1997; Berman & Reilly, 1995; Peterson & McCabe, 1983; Reilly, 1992; Reilly, Klima, & Bellugi, 1990), and the topic has been extensively revisited in the recent tribute to Labov that appeared in 1997 (Bamberg, 1997). Before presenting the developmental data, we present a brief summary of the adults' evaluation.

## Affective Expression in Adult Narratives: English and ASL

Previous studies of narratives from English-speaking adults found that linguistic evaluation (e.g., emotional words, casuals, negatives, mental verbs, intensifiers) clusters at two points in the story—immediately before the story conflict and at its resolution (Bamberg & Damrad-Frye, 1991; Bamberg & Reilly, 1996), emphasizing the significance of these events to the narrative as a whole. To assess other modes of conveying evaluation, we collected adult narratives to examine their use of paralinguistic expression (e.g., affective prosody and stress). In contrast to the distinct clusters of lexical evaluation, there was wide variability in both the frequency and distribution of paralinguistic expression in these English stories. Overall, the use of affective prosody by hearing adults is idiosyncratic (Provine & Reilly, 1992).

Complementing the English data, we also collected narratives from Deaf adults. Unlike Bamberg's hearing subjects, in these stories, lexical evaluative devices did not cluster at the conflict and resolution of the story. Instead, at these same critical narrative junctures, Deaf adults used more paralinguistic devices, especially prosodic changes: modified sign location, and modification of the shape or size of the movement path, or of the sign speed; Deaf adults also used more cohesion devices at these same critical narrative junctures (McIntire & Reilly, 1996). In sum, both Deaf and hearing parents use evaluation to signal the same structurally relevant episodes; it is the systems and devices they employ that differ. With this brief overview of evaluation in the adult stories, and the rather striking differences in the means recruited to convey evaluation in signed and spoken stories, we are now ready to address how children acquire these narrative skills.

## The Developmental Story of Evaluation

### Lexicalization of Evaluation in Spoken English

Intrigued by the question of how children integrate emotion and language we collected spoken narratives of children telling Mercer Mayer's (1979) *Frog, Where Are You?* (Reilly, 1992). Our focus was in how children learn "to tell a *good* story"—that is, how the narrator attributes meaning through evaluative devices, specifically through emotional expression. Eliciting narratives from preschool and school-aged English-speaking children, we coded for both structural coherence and types and tokens of the following evaluative devices. First, *characterization or quoted speech*: The child speaks for one of the characters—for example, "He said, 'Froggie, come back again.' " Second, *evaluative comments*: When the child infers the emotions of the characters using labels for emotional states and behaviors—for example, "an' when he woke up he was very sad" or "he was crying." Other examples include the evaluation of an action or a character (from the point of view of the narrator)—for example, "He was a nasty owl." Mental verbs reflecting cognitive processes of characters are also included in this category—for example, "He was wondering where that frog had gone." Third, *facial expressions*: for example, smile, frown. Fourth, *gestures*: those that appear to be related to a particular utterance—for example, covering the head to demonstrate hiding from the (apparently) attacking owl. Fifth, *prosodic features*: pitch, length, volume, and voice quality; "He said, "((*Fro:ggie*, come back again/))" ((high)).[1] Sixth, *lexical/phonological stress*: "He said, 'Froggie#(.) come back again.' "

In line with previous studies (e.g., Appleby, 1978; Bamberg 1987; Peterson & MaCabe, 1983; Berman & Slobin, 1994) we found that even though the 3- and 4-year-old children had some idea of a story, their narratives were structurally impoverished and tended to be interactive dialogues. With respect to evaluation, however, we found that the group of 3- and 4-year-olds used very little facial expression, but made extensive use of affective prosody, and that stress, vowel lengthening, and changing intonation contours occurred frequently. Overall their stories had a slightly breathless quality and were characterized by a sing-song intonation pattern in which prosodic contours did not map onto the adult syntactically motivated forms. In contrast, the stories of the older children, 7- and 8-year-olds, were structurally more complete, However, they used almost *no* paralinguistic evaluation, resulting in affectively rather flat and stereotypical narratives. Interestingly, Berman (1988) also noted this same stereotypicality in stories from school-aged Hebrew-speaking children. Reilly noted in the original study (1992) that early reliance on affective prosody may "serve to help propel the child through the process of telling the story, or . . . it may also serve as a type of global genre marking indicating that the child is participating in the very activity of storytelling. Given the structural immaturity of the preschoolers' stories, we suggest that they are using their well developed affective expressive abilities as a means to 'glue' their stories together" (p. 375). To give a flavor for this striking difference in narrative quality, in these examples a preschooler and then a 7-year-old describe an episode from *Frog, Where Are You?*

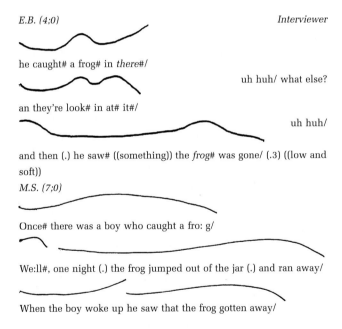

E.B. (4;0)                                          Interviewer

he caught# a frog# in *there*#/

                                         uh huh/ what else?

an they're look# in at# it#/

                                                uh huh/

and then (.) he saw# ((something)) the *frog*# was gone/ (.3) ((low and soft))

M.S. (7;0)

Once# there was a boy who caught a fro: g/

We:ll#, one night (.) the frog jumped out of the jar (.) and ran away/

When the boy woke up he saw that the frog gotten away/

To test whether the decline in affective expression stemmed from school conventions or was truly developmental, we asked 7- and 8-year-olds and then 10- and 11-year-olds first to tell the frog story to an adult and then to a 3-year-old, and we asked them to make it "really interesting." Overall, the narratives from the 7/8 group were just as flat as in the first study regardless of their audience. However, the 10- and 11-year-old children incorporated significantly more evaluation than the younger group us-

ing both linguistic and paralinguistic —for example, affective prosody and proxemics (for example, leaning toward the younger child devices; Reilly, 1992). These data confirmed our original hypothesis that the declining use of affective prosody in the school-aged stories was not due just to "schooling," but appeared to reflect a broader developmental trend in learning to tell a good story.

Concurrently, Bamberg and Damrad-Frye (1991) had been examining the development of lexical evaluation, also using "frog stories." Their framework included (1) *frames of mind*, including two categories, emotional labels and mental verbs; (2) *causal signs*, which explain a character's motivation; (3) *hedges*, which suggest that a narrator is making judgments about the likelihood of an event's occurrence; (4) *negatives*, which can maintain a storyline by referring to a goal that is not yet attained or convey that an event is contrary to expectations; and (5) *character speech*, both direct and indirect discourse attributed to characters in the story. These authors found that the 5-year-olds made few references to "frames of mind." However, there was a clear increase in the amount of lexical evaluation from ages 5 to 9 with a subsequent twofold increase in the adult stories. In the children's stories, they found that evaluation reflected local events in the narrative whereas adults also used global level evaluation. Integrating their findings, Bamberg and Reilly (1996) proposed a transition from paralinguistic to linguistically conveyed evaluation, that is, a lexicalization of affective expression that appears to occur during the early school years. At this developmental point, lexical evaluation is used primarily at the local level of the narrative. Subsequently, at about ages 10–11, the two communicative channels are reunited, and the older children are using both paralinguistic and lexically conveyed evaluation in a smoothly integrated manner.

## Lexicalization of Evaluation in ASL

If our proposal that paralinguistic expression functions as a support system and stepping stone into the lexicalized expression of evaluation is valid, we should see a similar pattern of development in the signed narratives of Deaf children. Our adult studies show that Deaf adults rely on paralinguistic devices to convey the evaluative aspects of the narrative, specifically affective prosody and emotional facial expression[2] (McIntire & Reilly, 1996; Provine & Reilly, 1992), and this contrasts markedly with hearing parents who rely more heavily on linguistically encoded evaluation. These differences in the adult models reflect the organization and rhetorical choices available in these two languages. Given the nature and style of evaluation in the ASL stories, one might predict that Deaf children would initially rely heavily on paralinguistic devices, especially prosody, in their storytelling and *would continue to do so during the school age period.* Or, as noted above, we might predict that Deaf children would follow their hearing peers and that initially, they would use a great deal of prosodic affect, which would decline substantially during elementary school.

To address this question, we collected narratives signed by 25 Deaf children (ages 3:4 to 7:10) whose first language is American Sign Language. Similar to our coding for spoken English, the types of linguistically encoded evaluation included manual signs in the following categories: (1) *frames of mind,* which included two categories: emotional labels, *ANGRY, EXCITED, LONELY, SORRY,* and mental verbs, e.g., *REALIZE, WORRY, IDEA, DREAM, THINK;* (2) *causal signs,* which suggested that the storyteller was making a judgment about the motivation for an event or a character's behavior, e.g., *BECAUSE, WHY, HOW;* (3) *Hedges,* which reflect the degree of certainty, e.g., *SEEMS, LOOK-LIKE, HOW;* (4) *negative* qualifiers, e.g., *CANNOT, NO, NOT YET, NONE.* To code the expression of affective prosody in the children's narratives, two Deaf signers independently tallied all signs in their stories that deviated in location, or speed, or size or shape of movement path from "normal" signing in that particular syntactic context.

Just like their hearing peers, deaf preschoolers made extensive use of affective prosody and included very little lexically encoded evaluation in their narratives. The frequency of tokens of lexical evaluation increased through this age span, and by age 6, children included all four categories of lexical evaluation in their stories. However, the use of *paralinguistic* expression, especially prosodic modifications, showed a marked decline. The signed stories of the 7-year-old Deaf children were as affectively bland as those of their hearing counterparts.

In sum, both Deaf and hearing preschoolers rely heavily upon paralinguistically conveyed affect, specifically affective prosody, and they use little lexically encoded evaluation. Then at about age 5 to 6, there is a significant drop in the use of vocal prosody (in English) and visual prosody (in ASL), as children make a transition to a lexical strategy for evaluation. Increasingly different types as well as tokens of evaluation emerge over the school years. By age 7, for both groups of children, paralinguistic affective expression declines significantly, and evaluation is expressed almost entirely lexically. Hence, in spite of the differing adult models, the developmental profile is the same, regardless of language, and regardless of the modality in which the language is conveyed.

What do these data mean in the broader context of the relation between emotional and linguistic expression? The preschool children's stories incorporate both emotional and linguistic information, thus recruiting both systems. The school-aged children appear to have incorporated the emotional/affective information into the linguistic system and although structurally and lexically richer, their stories are affectively quite flat. This pattern might be viewed as

a linearization as language subsumes and lexicalizes emotional expression. Then, the 10-year-olds begin to recruit paralinguistic devices, and language and emotional expression are reintegrated. This same transition is evidenced in the signed stories. What is perhaps most striking, overall, is that in spite of the differences in language, language organization and modality, Deaf children acquiring ASL and hearing children acquiring English reflect common strategies and developmental milestones in the integration of linguistic and affective expression.

## Bringing Emotional Facial Expression into the Service of Language

In our narrative studies above, we focused on affective prosody and the changing nature of evaluation in narratives. But we also looked at the use of emotional facial expression in narratives. The very first point to note is that for hearing children, both the preschoolers and the school-aged children, facial expression co-occurring with language is exceedingly rare (Reilly, 1992). It is clear that in this task, vocal prosody is overwhelmingly the preferred channel for conveying emotional information. However, in the stories of Deaf signing children and adults, facial expression is frequently recruited. In fact, in ASL affective facial expression plays a critical role in narratives and discourse in signaling point of view. In spoken English narratives, point of view—that is, speaking for a character, can be signaled by labeling, pronominal shifts or sometimes by a distinctive voice quality, and as Chovil (1991/1992) has shown, facial expression can also be recruited. In American Sign Language, in addition to manual linguistic means, for example, pointing at and naming characters in space, point of view is also obligatorily signaled by body shifts and the use of affective facial expression. Perspective marking has been commonly known in the literature as "role shift" (e.g., Padden, 1986; Smith, Lentz, & Mikos, 1988). Role shift recruits emotional facial expression (which can function to reflect the character's emotion) to linguistically delineate the scope of direct quote or reported action. As such, the acquisition of role or referential shift provides an additional perspective on how emotional expression comes to serve language.

Briefly, we looked at the stories from six Deaf mothers and 28 Deaf children (ages 3;0–7;5) telling the Three Bears, as this story has many opportunities for direct quotes. Adults signal point of view through both linguistic and affective means. When viewed in real time, the nonmanual behaviors signaling direct quote appear to emerge as a whole; however, frame-by-frame viewing reveals a pattern of sequential events: To produce a direct quote, and to signal that they are "taking on the perspective" of that character (referential shift), adults frequently label the character first, e.g., *MOTHER.* Accompanying this sign, the signer maintains eye contact with the addressee (in the

<pre>
_____topic                                                              _surprise  _____pouting
       +K                                                                           _____distress
_____                _____-K
BABY BEAR    LOOK-AT   LETS-SEE MY Cl: C HEY GONE SOUP Cl:1  SOMEONE FINISH EAT ALL
</pre>
Baby Bear looked at his soup, "Let's see my bowl.  Hey, my soup's gone! Someone ate it all up!"

(+K = eye contact with Addressee; -K = signals a gaze shift averting gaze from Addressee.)

Figure 27.1

role as narrator) and often raises brows to signal topic; he may also point to the already established locus in the signing space. Then, to signal that the quote is beginning, as the signer lowers his brows, he breaks eye gaze with the addressee, shifts head and often body position (taking on the stance of the character in contrast with that of the narrator), and assumes the facial expression of that character's emotional response to the current situation. Finally, the character's utterance is signed manually; this manual string which may span multiple clauses, dictates the scope of the accompanying nonmanual behaviors (gaze, head position, and facial expression). See Figure 27.1.

Across the adult instances of perspective shift, eye gaze and head behaviors are consistent with respect to timing and quality; they constitute the required grammatical markers to signal a change in perspective or "role shift." Body shift is less consistent and appears be a supplementary device. With respect to the accompanying affective facial expression, individual signers use appropriate, affective expressions (different configurations of facial muscles) for the characters in the story. However, individual signers may convey different emotions in the same episode. For example, when the baby bear discovers his cereal is gone, some signers convey surprise and others sadness or distress, or both, as in the example above. The overall scope of the facial behaviors remains constant and is limited by the quoted utterance. In these instances, affect is truly working in the service of language.

Looking at the children's narratives, gaze shifts are the first nonmanual aspect to be mastered. When signing for a character, facial expression is also used by all age groups. For the 3-year-olds emotional facial expression appears some of the time. However, it is not until age 6 and 7 that children use it consistently and differentially for individual quotes, as do adults. In sum, preschoolers' facial expressions for characters differ from the adult model on three counts: (1) they are not precisely timed to the manual utterances of the character; (2) the same facial expression may be used continuously for utterances from different characters; and (3) its occurrence is erratic.

Lexically, we found that all the 5-year-olds used the manual sign SAY to introduce direct quotes. However, it occurred in only a handful of instances in the stories from any other age group. Because this lexical marker does not occur in the adult stories and rarely, if at all, at the other ages, we suggest that the use of SAY reflects a linguistic reorganization: direct quotes are introduced lexically before the nonmanual behaviors are linguistically integrated with the manually signed quote. Specifically, younger children (3- and 4-year-olds) have considerable difficulty with the timing and use of character facial expression; although frequent, emotional facial expression is used fairly randomly. SAY is an alternative means to signal a direct quote and similar to the acquisition of other multichannel structures, this particular lexical item signals a significant development in the process of reanalyzing early affective and communicative behaviors for new linguistic purposes. Finally, in the acquisition of point of view, we have seen the early recruitment of affective facial expression and its transition to a linguistically constrained behavior. As we have seen repeatedly, the port of entry or bridge strategy was once again a linear, lexical manual sign. This recurrent pattern—first relying on affective means, then moving onto a manual lexical strategy, and finally, integrating both channels such that the facial behaviors are now under linguistic control—appears across structures, from single lexical items to phrasal, clausal, and now discourse level structures. These data provide strong evidence that the child's prelinguistic emotional abilities are not directly accessible to the linguistic system, even when they continue to convey affective information.

## Putting All the Pieces Together

If we ask adults to identify their primary communicative system, their answer is generally, "Why, language, of course!" However, as we have seen from the preceding sections, emotional information either colors or is included in the utterance proper. In the first section of this chapter, we saw how, under normal circumstances, the linguistic and nonlinguistic systems are smoothly integrated in adults. In the developmental section of this chapter, we then considered how the expression of these two systems comes to be the integrated product evidenced in adults. In this final section, we look across the lifespan to see how these systems interact within that integrated picture. For, as we will see, the integration of the communication channels does not merely yield their additive product. Rather, when the channels are integrated they appear to interact, such that some assume a more prominent role in the communication of emotion than the others. Next we examine what is known of this interaction as it occurs in both the production and reception of emotional communication.

## Channel Preferences for the Expression of Emotion

Recently we were interested in the channels that infants used to display positive and negative emotions (Bellama, Wallace, Relin, & Reilly, 1999). Using the Infant Laboratory Assessment Battery (Lab-TAB; Goldsmith & Rothbart, 1992) to elicit emotional responses, we tested 14 normally developing infants longitudinally at three different ages: 6 months, 12 months, and 24 months. Our goal was to examine emotional expression across the facial and vocal channels in order to determine if there is a preference for the expression of particular emotions and whether or not the emergence of language has an impact on the channel of expression. We found that for negative emotions, infants whimper and cry and use the characteristic cry face at all three data points. In contrast, to convey positive emotion, the face—that is, smiling—is the predominant channel across this entire age span. Interestingly, in addition to the face, in the oldest group, positive vocalizations were used significantly more than in the youngest group. It appears then, as productive language emerges, children are beginning to rely more heavily on the vocal channel to express positive emotion. Our findings suggest that the development of this new communicative system, language, also affects how children express emotion. These findings foreshadow our narrative studies which found that by ages three to four years, hearing children have a strong preference for prosody over facial expression for the expression of emotion in their story telling.

## Adult Channel Preferences for Emotional Expression

Unlike infants and children, normally functioning adults have access to both language and nonlinguistic forms of communication, and they typically integrate these systems both receptively and productively. However, it is clear that there are personal and contextual differences in expression. What are the decisive factors mediating how the communication "workload" is shared between the linguistic and nonlinguistic channels, specifically in the expression of emotion? For example, do we funnel most of our emotion through one channel, while some emotion merely "leaks out" through the other? There are surprisingly few studies on adults that specifically address this question. The most relevant, available literature may be that concerning contextual influences—cultural, psychological, and situational influences—on communication,

formalized as display rules (see, e.g., the compilation edited by Guerrero, DeVito, & Hecht, 1999). Display rules are implicit, learned guidelines that dictate how emotions are to be expressed appropriately according to one's culture, on both a broad scale—for example, ethnic-geographic culture—and on more local scales—for example, gender, sexual orientation, religious affiliation. Display rules also operate within cultures, dictating appropriate emotional expression in different situations (e.g., a party versus a funeral) and psychological contexts (e.g., one is in an authoritative versus subordinate role). From this research, inferences can be drawn about the relative weight accorded one channel over another in any given context. In some contexts it may be more appropriate to express distress via linguistic, rather than nonlinguistic, means. A professional who just receives word of his termination may accept this mandate with resignation or defiance, but regardless, carefully chosen words are the expectation, not crying or yelling. In other situations, emotional expression via nonlinguistic channels may be the expectation. For example, a woman's sincerity is likely to be doubted if, upon receiving a marriage proposal, she says, "I would be so wonderfully joyous to marry you," in a monotone voice and with an "expressionless" face. One tentative answer as to how the various channels share the workload in communicating emotion, thus, appears to be, "It depends." Thus, the display rule research suggests the way each channel should be used (or not used) to convey emotion depends upon the various contexts in which the communication occurs. So, in adults, the interaction between the linguistic and nonlinguistic channels in emotional communication is influenced by culturally specific display rules, although biological factors play a role as well. In fact, it is possible that one channel *universally* predominates the expression of emotion under some circumstances. Perhaps the nonlinguistic channels of facial and prosodic expression are more "closely tied" to the neural substrates for emotion and/or are under less volitional control under some circumstances. There is a growing literature that describes the language breakdown that can occur under conditions of "stress" (for a review, see Dick, Bates, Wulfeck, Utman, Dronkers, & Gernsbacher, 2001). This research suggests we have limited capacity cognitive processors, and when under sufficient cognitive load, aspects of language (e.g., grammar) can become impaired. Whether high emotional arousal also impacts these cognitive processors has yet to be directly investigated, though everyday intuition (e.g., that one can be "stunned speechless") suggests this question is worth pursuing.

## When Information across Channels Conflicts: The Developmental Picture

Several studies of infants who have been presented with conflicting messages demonstrate that prosodic intonation initially holds sway (Fernald, 1993; Lawrence, 1993; Friend, 2000). As language emerges, both receptively and productively, experimental studies have found a shifting preference, such that toddlers, at least by 18 months, and children appear to favor lexical cues to emotion over non-linguistic cues when these conflict (Bugental, Kaswan, & Love, 1970; Friend, 2000; Friend & Bryant, 2000; Lawrence, 1993; Reilly & Muzekari, 1986). This lexical bias decreases with development, and there is also notable individual variability in this bias at each age. Friend and Bryant (2000) found a lexical bias in 67%, 55%, and 11% of their 4-, 7-, and 10-year-old samples, respectively; the other children at each age level demonstrated a prosody bias. This lexical bias appears due at least in part to a relatively poorer ability to integrate and identify prosodic emotion. For example, judgments of emotion by seven and eleven-year-old children showed greater disagreement when based solely on prosodic, as opposed to uniquely lexical, information (Friend & Bryant, 2000). However, it is not that poorer acumen in judging prosodic emotion leads children to discount this information source altogether when presented with concurrent emotional language. Rather, they appear to apply a weighted averaging strategy, attending to both prosodic and lexical cues, but weighting the latter more heavily (Friend & Bryant, 2000).

In addition, Bugental and colleagues found that children were less influenced than adults by a facial expression (a smile) when it conflicted with the words and tone of voice (Bugental et al., 1970). In contrast, the majority of later childhood and adult years, as we saw in the narrative data, are characterized by greater attention to, the perhaps subtler, paralinguistic cues, and critically, the ability to integrate multiple sources of information, even when the information from the diverse channels conflicts. Interestingly, however, in aging adults, we see a movement back toward a lexical bias. Using stimulus utterances in which the linguistic and nonlinguistic affect were discrepant, Marquardt and colleagues (Marquardt, Harris, Sherrard, & Cannito, 1999) found that, with advancing age, judgments of speaker emotion are increasingly based on linguistic, rather than nonlinguistic, cues. Further, this age effect holds more strongly for males than females (Marquardt et al., 1999). So, as with the expression of emotion through the various channels, the perception of emotion tends to be based more upon one channel over another, in any given instance. Developmental factors play a crucial role in determining *which* channel holds sway.

## How Adults Respond to Conflicting Emotional Information

Given that adults are putatively skilled in the interpretation of facial expression, prosody, and language, the degree to which we favor some channels over others in mak-ing attributions of emotion becomes important. That is, as listeners/observers in social exchanges, do we tend to direct our attention to the message from one channel more than another? This question has been approached in a variety of ways. Numerous studies have compared observers' judgments of emotion when presented with information from only one or the various combinations of channels. Others have examined which channel's message is best remembered or acted upon when the information provided by the channels conflicts. The majority of these studies revealed that, when information is consistent in all channels, facial expressions yield more accurate judgments and higher interobserver agreement than speech content or prosody alone (Noller, 1985). Some discrepant reports have been made. For example, in a review, Scherer reported that comprehension of emotions from prosodic information is as good or better than that from facial expressions (1989; but see chapter 23, this volume). Note that many of these studies apparently assume the channel leading to greater accuracy is the channel most relied upon in judging emotion. A number of studies have found the weight accorded one channel over another is dependent upon the social context (Ekman, Friesen, O' Sullivan, & Scherer, 1980), the degree of consistency across channels (Hess, Kappas, & Scherer, 1988), and intimacy of the communication (Hess & Kappas, 1985). Hence, as with the production data, there does appear to be a channel bias in adults as they perceive emotional messages from linguistic and nonlinguistic channels; whether physiological state is implicated in these biases has not yet been addressed.

## A Last Word

In this chapter, we have discussed the nature of the linguistic and nonlinguistic communication forms, as well as how they independently express emotion. We have also reviewed how linguistic and nonlinguistic emotional expressions co-occur: Prosody and facial expression accompany and complement language, whether spoken or signed. Finally, we have looked at how some of these relationships develop in both hearing children acquiring English and Deaf children acquiring American Sign Language. One recurrent theme is how little we know about how adults or children integrate these two systems in a fine-grained way. As we outlined above, the integration of these systems as they communicate emotion is not simply an additive process. Rather, these systems interact in a dynamic way, according to both specific (i.e., contextual) and potentially universal (i.e., developmental and biological) factors. Research into the nature of these interactions is scant, at present. And so, in closing, we encourage linguists and psychologists to work together to elucidate how we integrate these two systems that represent human communication.

## NOTES

1. Transcription conventions for prosodic elements in spoken narratives include the following:
   ((double parentheses reflect scope, quality is specified at utterance end)),
   : = lengthened vowel, and
   *italics* = increased volume
   # = stress on the preceding syllable
   Intonation or pitch contour is reflected by a superscript line above the utterance.

2. One frequent context for affective facial expression in narratives is in direct discourse or reported action which are sometimes referred to as 'role shift' which is presented below. For more detailed discussions of these phenomena, see Engberg-Pedersen, 1995; Emmorey and Reilly, 1997; Reilly, 1999.

## REFERENCES

Anderson, D. S., & Reilly, J. S. (1997). The puzzle of negation: How children move from communicative to grammatical negation in ASL. *Applied Psycholinguistics, 18,* 411–429.

Anderson, D. & Reilly, J. S. (1999). PAH! The acquisition of non-manual adverbials in ASL. *Sign Language and Linguistics, 1*(2), 115–142.

Appleby, A. (1978). *The child's concept of story.* Chicago: University of Chicago Press.

Bahan, B., & Supalla, S. (1995). Line segmentation and narrative structure: A study of eyegaze behavior in American Sign Language. In K. Emmorey & J. Reilly (Eds.), *Language, gesture and space* (pp. 171–191). Norwood, NJ: Erlbaum.

Baker, C., & Cokely, D. (1980). *American Sign Language: A teacher's resource text on grammar and culture.* Silver Spring, MD: T. J. Publishers.

Baker, C., & Padden, C. (1978). Focusing on the nonmanual components of American Sign Language. In P. Siple (Ed.), *Understanding language through sign language research* (pp. 27–57). New York: Academic Press.

Baker-Shenk, C. (1983). *A microanalysis of the non-manual components of questions in American Sign Language.* Unpublished Ph.D. dissertation, University of California, Berkeley.

Bamberg, M. (1987). *The acquisition of narratives.* Berlin: Mouton de Gruyter.

Bamberg, M. (Ed.) (1997). *Journal of Narrative and Life History,* Special Issue: *Oral versions of personal experience: Three decades of narrative analysis, 7,* 1–4.

Bamberg, M. & Damrad-Frye, R. (1991). On the ability to provide evaluative comments: Further explorations of children's narrative competencies. *Journal of Child Language, 18,* 689–710.

Bamberg, M., & Reilly, J. S. (1996). Emotion, narrative and affect. In D. I. Slobin, J. Gerhardt, A. Kyratzis, & J. Guo (Eds.), *Social interaction, social context and language: Essays in honor of Susan Ervin-Tripp* (pp. 329–341). Norwood, NJ: Erlbaum.

Bavelas, J., & Chovil, N. (1997). Faces in dialogue. In J. A. Russell, J. M. Fernandez-Dols, et al. (Eds.), *The psychology of facial expression* (pp. 334–346). New York: Cambridge University Press.

Bellama, D., Wallace, S., Relin, M., & Reilly, J. (1999, April) *The development of differential use of emotional channels of expression in infancy.* Poster presented at the Society for Research in Child Development biennial meeting, Albuquerque, New Mexico.

Bellugi, U., & Klima, E. S. (1982). The acquisition of three morphological systems in American Sign Language. *Papers and Reports on Child Language Development, 21,* 1–35.

Berlin, B., & Kay, P. (1969). *Basic color terms.* Berkeley: University of California Press.

Berman, R. (1988). On the ability to relate events in narrative. *Discourse Processes, 11,* 469–497.

Berman, R. (1993). The development of language use: Expressing perspectives on a scene. In E. Dromi (Ed.), *Language and cognition: A developmental perspective* (pp. 172–201). Norwood, NJ: Ablex.

Berman, R. (1997). Narrative competence and storytelling performance: How children tell stories from different perspectives and in different contexts. *Journal of Narrative and Life History, 7,* 235–244.

Berman, R., & Reilly, J. (1995). *Evaluative elements in narratives.* Paper presented at the meeting of the Stanford Child Language Conference, Stanford, CA.

Berman, R., & Slobin, D. (1994). *Relating events in narrative: A crosslinguistic developmental study.* Hillsdale, NJ: Erlbaum.

Biber, D., & Finegan, E. (1989). Styles of stance in English: Lexical and grammatical marking of evidentiality and affect. *Text, 9,* 93–124.

Bloom, R., Borod, J., Obler, L., & Koff, E. A. (1990). Preliminary characterization of lexical emotional expression in right and left brain-damaged patients. *International Journal of Neuroscience, 55,* 71–80.

Bohannon, J. N., & Warren-Leubecker, A. (1988). Recent developments in child-directed speech: You've come a long way, Baby-Talk. *Language Science, 10*(1), 89–110.

Borod, J. (1993). Cerebral mechanisms of facial, prosodic, and lexical emotional expression: A review of neuropsychological studies and methodological issues. *Neuropsychology, 7,* 445–463.

Borod, J. C., Bloom, R. L., & Santschi-Haywood, C. (1998). Verbal aspects of emotional communication. In M. Beeman & C. Chiarello (Eds.), *Right hemisphere language comprehension: Perspectives from cognitive neuroscience* (pp. 285–307). Mahwah, NJ: Erlbaum.

Borod, J., Koff, E., Lorch, M., & Nicholas, M. (1985). Channels of emotional communication in patients with unilateral brain damage. *Archives of Neurology, 42,* 345–348.

Bowerman, M. (1979). The acquisition of complex sentences. In P. Fletcher & M. Garman (Eds.), *Language acquisition: Studies in first language development.* New York: Cambridge University Press.

Boyes-Braem, P. (1999). Rhythmic temporal patterns in the signing of deaf early and late learners of Swiss German Sign Language. *Language and Speech, 42,* 177–208.

Bretherton, I., & Beeghly, M. (1982). Talking about internal states: The acquisition of an explicit theory of mind. *Developmental Psychology, 18,* 906–921.

Bretherton, I., McNew, S., & Beeghly-Smith, M. (1981). Early person knowledge as expressed in gestural and verbal communication: When do infants acquire a "theory of mind"? In M. E. Lamb & L. R. Sherrod (Eds.), *Infant and social cognition: Empirical and theoretical considerations.* Hillsdale, NJ: Erlbaum.

Brody, N., Goodman, S., Halm, E., Krinzman, S., & Sebrechts, M. (1987). Lateralized affective priming of lateralized affectively valued target words. *Neuropsychologia, 25,* 935–946.

Brown, R. (1973). *A first language.* Cambridge, MA.: Harvard University Press.

Brown, J. R., & Dunn, J. (1991). 'You can cry, mum': The social and developmental implications of talk about internal states. *British Journal of Developmental Psychology, 9,* 237–256.

Bryden, M., & Ley, R. (1983). Right-hemispheric involvement in the perception and expression of emotion in normal humans. In K. Heilman & P. Satz (Eds.), *Neuropsychology of human emotion* (pp. 6–44). New York: Guilford Press.

Bugental, D. E., Kaswan, J. W., & Love, L. R. (1970). Perception of contradictory meanings conveyed by verbal and nonverbal channels. *Journal of Personality and Social Psychology, 16,* 647–655.

Campos, J., Barrett, K. C., Lamb, M. E., Goldsmith, H., & Stenberg, C. (1983). Socioemotional development. In M. M. Haith & J. J. Campos (Eds.), *Handbook of child psychology, Vol. 2: Infancy and developmental psychobiology.* New York: Wiley.

Camras, L. A., Malatesta, C., & Izard, C. E. (1991). The development of facial expressions in infancy. In R. S. Feldman & B. Rime (Eds.), *Fundamentals of nonverbal behavior* (pp. 73–105). Cambridge: Cambridge University Press.

Caselli, M. C., & Casadio, P. (1995). *Il primo vocabolario del bambino: Guida all'uso del questionario MacArthur per la valutazione della comunicazione e del linguaggio nei primi anni di vita [The child's first vocabulary: User's guide to the MacArthur questionnaire for the evaluation of language and communication in the first years of life].* Milan: FrancoAngeli.

Caselli, M. C., & Volterra, V. (1990). From communication to language in hearing and deaf children. In V. Volterra & C. J. Erting (Eds.), *From gesture to language in hearing and deaf children* (pp. 263–277). Berlin: Springer-Verlag.

Chomsky, N. (1965). *Aspects of the theory of syntax.* Cambridge, MA: MIT Press.

Chovil, N. (1989). *Communicative functions of facial displays in conversation.* Unpublished doctoral dissertation, University of Victoria, B.C., Canada.

Chovil, N. (1991/1992). Discourse-oriented facial displays in conversation. *Research on Language and Social Interaction, 25,* 163–194.

Church, A. T., Katigbak, M. S., Reyes, J. A. S., & Jensen, S. M. (1998). Language and organisation of Filipino emotion concepts: Comparing emotion concepts and dimensions across cultures. *Cognition and Emotion, 12,* 63–92.

Clarkson, M. G., Clifton, R. K., & Perris, E. E. (1988). Infant timbre perception: Discrimination of spectral envelopes. *Perception and Psychophysics, 43*(1), 15–20.

Corina, D., Bellugi, U., & Reilly, J. (1999). Neuropsychological studies of linguistic and affective facial expressions in Deaf signers. *Special Issue on Prosody in Spoken and Signed Languages. Language and Speech, 42,* 307–332.

Corina, D., & Sandler, W. (1993). On the nature of phonological structure in sign language. *Phonology, 10,* 165–207.

Coulter, G. (1980). *American Sign Language typology.* Unpublished Ph.D. dissertation. University of California, San Diego.

Coulter, G. (1993). *Phonetics and phonology: Current issues in ASL phonology.* San Diego, CA: Academic.

Crystal, D. (1987). *The Cambridge Encyclopedia of Language* (pp. 396–397). Cambridge: Cambridge University Press.

Davidson, R. J. (1988). Theoretical issues in the psychophysiology of emotion (structured panel discussion). *Psychophysiology, 25,* 422 (abstract).

DeCasper, A. J., & Fifer, W. P. (1980). Of human bonding: Newborns prefer their mothers' voices. *Science, 208,* 1174–1176.

Dick, F., Bates, E., Wulfeck, B., Utman, J., Dronkers, N., & Gernsbacher, M. (2001). Language deficits, localization, and grammar: Evidence for a distributive model of language breakdown in aphasic patients and neurologically intact individuals. *Psychological Review, 108*(4), 759–788.

Dunn, J., Bretherton, I., & Munn, P. (1987). Conversations about feeling states between mothers and their young children. *Developmental Psychology, 23*(1), 132–139.

Ekman, P. (1972). Universals and cultural differences in facial expression of emotion. In J. Cole (Ed.), *Nebraska symposium on motivation, 1971* (pp. 207–283). Lincoln: University of Nebraska Press.

Ekman, P. (1979). About brows: Emotional and conversational signals. In J. Aschoof, M. von Cranach, K. Foppa, W. Lepenies, & D. Ploog (Eds.), *Human ethology* (pp. 169–202). Cambridge: Cambridge University Press.

Ekman, P. (1980). *The face of man: Expressions of universal emotions in a New Guinea village.* New York: Garland.

Ekman, P. (1984). Expression and the nature of emotion. In K. R. Scherer & P. Ekman (Eds.), *Approaches to emotion* (pp. 319–343). Hillsdale, NJ: Erlbaum.

Ekman, P. (1989). The argument and evidence about universals in facial expressions of emotion. In H. Wagner & A. Manstead (Eds.), *Handbook of social psychophysiology* (pp. 43–164). New York: Wiley.

Ekman, P. (1993). Facial expression and emotion. *American Psychologist, 48*(4), 384–392.

Ekman, P., & Fridlund, A. J. (1987). Assessment of facial behavior in affective disorders. In J. D. Maser (Ed.), *Depression and expressive behavior.* Hillsdale, NJ: Erlbaum.

Ekman, P., & Friesen, W. (1978). *Facial action coding system.* Palo Alto: Consulting Psychologists Press.

Ekman, P., & Friesen, W. V. (1986). A new pan-cultural facial expression of emotion. *Motivation and Emotion, 10,* 159–168.

Ekman, P., Friesen, W. V., & Ancoli, S. (1980). Facial signs of emotional experience. *Journal of Personality and Social Psychology, 39,* 1125–1134.

Ekman, P., Friesen, W. V., O'Sullivan, M., & Scherer, K. (1980). Relative importance of face, body, and speech in judgments of personality and affect. *Journal of Personality and Social Psychology, 38,* 270–277.

Emmorey, K., & Reilly, J. (1997, April). *The development of quotation and depicted action: Conveying perspective in ASL.* Paper presented at the Child Language Research Forum, Stanford University.

Emmorey, K., & Reilly, J. (1998). The development of quotation and reported action: Conveying perspective in ASL. In E. Clark (Ed.), *Proceedings of the Stanford child language forum.* Stanford, CA: CSLI.

Engberg-Pedersen, E. (1993). *Space in Danish sign language.* SIGNUM-Verlag: Hamburg, Germany.

Engberg-Pedersen, E. (1995). Point of view expressed through shifters. In K. Emmorey & J. Reilly (Eds.), *Language, gesture and space.* Norwood, NJ: Erlbaum.

Eviatar, Z., & Zaidel, E. (1991). The effects of word length and emotionality on hemispheric contributions to lexical decision. *Neuropsychologia, 29,* 415–428.

Fenson, L., Dale, P. S., Reznick, S., Thal, D., Bates, E., Hartung, J. P., Pethick, S., & Reilly, J. S. (1993). *MacArthur communicative development inventories user's guide and technical manual.* San Diego, CA: Singular Publishing Group.

Fernald, A. (1993). Approval and disapproval: Infant responsiveness to vocal affect in familiar and unfamiliar languages. *Child Development, 64* (3), 657–674.

Frick, R. W. (1985). Communicating emotion: The role of prosodic features. *Psychological Bulletin, 97,* 412–429.

Fridlund, A. (1994). *Human facial expression: An evolutionary view.* San Diego, CA: Academic Press.

Fridlund, A. J., & Gilbert, A. N. (1985). Emotions and facial expressions. *Science, 230,* 607–608.

Friend, M. (2000). Developmental changes in sensitivity to vocal paralanguage. *Developmental Science, 3,* 148–162.

Friend, M., & Bryant, J. B. (2000). A developmental lexical bias in the interpretation of discrepant messages. *Merrill-Palmer Quarterly, 46,* 140–167.

Gardner, H., Brownell, H., Wapner, W., & Michelow, D. (1983). Missing the point: The role of the right hemisphere in the processing of complex linguistic materials. In E. Perceman (Ed.), *Cognitive processing in the right hemisphere.* New York: Academic Press.

Goldschmidt, W. (1997). Nonverbal communication and culture. In U. Segerstrale & P. Molnar (Eds.), *Nonverbal communication: Where nature meets culture* (pp. 229–243). Mahwah, NJ: Erlbaum.

Goldsmith, H., & Rothbart, M. (1992). *The laboratory temperament assessment battery.* Unpublished technical manual. University of Oregon.

Graves, R., Landis, T., & Goodglass, H. (1981). Laterality and sex differences for visual recognition of emotional and nonemotional words. *Neuropsychologia, 19,* 95–102.

Guerrero, L., DeVito, J., & Hecht, M. (Eds.). (1999). *The nonverbal communication reader: Classic and contemporary readings* (2nd ed.). Prospect Heights, IL: Waveland Press.

Hess, U., & Kappas, A. (1985). *Decoding discrepant information in facial and vocal communication channels, with regard to contextual effects.* Paper presented at the Second European Conference on Facial Measurement, Saarbrucken, Germany.

Hess, U., Kappas, A., & Scherer, K. R. (1988). Multichannel communication of emotion: Synthetic signal production. In K. R. Scherer (Ed.), *Facets of emotion: Recent research* (pp. 161–182). Hillsdale, NJ: Erlbaum.

Hiatt, S., Campos, J., & Emde, R. (1979). Facial patterning and infant emotional expression: Happiness, surprise, and fear. *Child Development, 50,* 1020–1035.

Hupka, R. M., Lenton, A. P., & Hutchison, K. A. (1999). Universal development of emotion categories in natural language. *Journal of Personality and Social Psychology, 77,* 247–278.

Izard, C. (1971). *The face of emotion.* New York: Appleton-Century-Crofts.

Izard, C. (1977). *Human emotion.* New York: Plenum Press.

Izard, C. E., Hembree, E. A., & Huebner, R. R. (1987). Infants' emotion expressions to acute pain: Developmental change and stability of individual differences. *Developmental Psychology, 23,* 105–113.

Joanette, Y., Goulet, P., & Hannequin, D. (1990). *Right hemisphere and verbal communication.* New York: Springer-Verlag.

Johnson-Laird, P. N., & Oatley, K. (1989). The language of emotions: An analysis of a semantic field. *Cognition and Emotion, 3,* 81–123.

Klima, E., & Bellugi, U. (1979). *The signs of language.* Cambridge, MA: Harvard University Press.

Klinnert, M., Campos, J., Sorce, J., Emde, R., & Svejda, M. (1983). Emotions and behavior regulators: Social referencing in infancy. In R. Plutchnik & H. Kellerman (Eds.), *Emotions in early development, vol. 2: The emotions.* New York: Academic Press.

Labov, W. (1984). Intensity. In D. Schiffin (Ed.), *Meaning, form and use in context: Linguistic applications* (pp. 43–70). Washington, DC: Georgetown University Press.

Labov, W., & Waletzky, J. (1967). Narrative analysis: Oral versions of personal experience. In J. Helm (Ed.), *Essays on the verbal and visual arts.* Seattle: University of Washington Press.

Lawrence, L. L. (1993). *When prosody and semantics conflict: Infants' developing sensitivity to discrepancies between tone of voice and verbal content.* Paper presented at the biennial meeting of the Society for Research in Child Development, New Orleans, LA.

LeDoux, J. E. (1995). Emotion: Clues from the brain. *Annual Review of Psychology, 46,* 209–235.

Liddell, S. (1978). Nonmanual signals and relative clauses in American Sign Language. In P. Siple (Ed.), *Understanding language through sign language research* (pp. 59–90). New York: Academic Press.

Liddell, S. (1980). *American Sign Language syntax.* The Hague: Mouton.

Liddell, S. (1986). Head thrust in ASL conditional marking. *Sign Language Studies, 52,* 243–262.

Liddell, S. (1995). Real, surrogate, and token space: Grammatical consequences in ASL. In K. Emmorey & J. Reilly (Eds.), *Language, gesture, and space* (pp. 19–41). Norwood, NJ: Erlbaum.

Lieberman, P., Harris, K. S., Wolff, P., & Russell, L. H. (1971). Newborn infant cry and nonhuman primate vocalization. *Journal of Speech and Hearing Research, 14,* 718–727.

Lillo-Martin, D. (1999). Modality effects and modularity in language acquisition: The acquisition of American Sign Language. In W. C. Ritchie & T. K. Bhatia (Eds.), *Handbook of language acquisition* (pp. 531–567). San Diego, CA: Academic Press.

Limber, J. (1973). The genesis of complex sentences. In T. E. Moore (Ed.), *Cognitive development and the acquisition of language* (pp. 169–182). New York: Academic Press.

Loew, R. C., Kegl, J. A., & Poizner, H. (1997). Fractionation of the components of role play in a right-hemispheric lesioned signer. *Aphasiology, 11,* 263–281.

MacWhinney, B. (1978). Processing a first language: The acquisition of morphophonology. *Monographs of the Society for Research in Child Development, 43*(1–2) (Serial number: 174).

Marquardt, T. P., Harris, L., Sherrard, K., & Cannito, M. (1999). *Age and gender effects in the identification of affective messages.* Manuscript submitted for publication.

Marschark, M. (1993). *Psychological development of deaf children.* New York: Oxford University Press.

Mayer, M. (1979). *Frog Where Are You?* New York: Dial Press.

McIntire, M. L., & Reilly, J. S. (1996). Searching for frogs in the narrative stream: A cross-linguistic and cross-modal study of maternal narratives. *Journal of Narrative and Life History, 6,* 65–86.

Mehler, J., & Bertoncini, J. (1979). Infants' perception of speech and other acoustic stimuli. In J. Morton & J. Marshall (Eds.), *Structure and processes. Psycholinguistic series 2.* London: Elek Science Books.

Meier, R. P. (1991). Language acquisition by deaf children. *American Scientist, 79,* 60–70.

Meier, R., & Newport, E. L. (1990). Out of the hands of babes: On a possible sign advantage in language acquisition. *Language, 66,* 1–23.

Mills, M., & Melhuish, E. (1974). Recognition of mother's voice in early infancy. *Nature, 252,* 123–124.

Murray, I. R., & Arnott, J. L. (1993). Toward a simulation of emotion in synthetic speech: A review of the literature on human vocal emotion. *Journal of the Acoustical Society of America, 93,* 1097–1108.

Nadeau, S., & Crosson, B. (1997). Subcortical aphasia. *Brain and Language, 58,* 355–402.

Nelson, C. A. (1987). The recognition of facial expressions in the first two years of life: Mechanisms of development. *Child Development, 58,* 890–909.

Nelson, C. A., & deHaan, M. (1997). A neuro-behavioral approach to the recognition of facial expressions in infancy. In J. A. Russell & J. M. Fernández-Dols (Eds.), *The psychology of facial expression.* Cambridge: Cambridge University Press.

Newport, E. L., & Ashbrook, E. (1977). The emergence of semantic relations in American Sign Language. *Papers and Reports on Child Language Development, 13,* 16–21.

Newport, E. L., & Meier, R. (1986). Acquisition of American Sign Language. In D. Slobin (Ed.), *The cross-linguistic study of language acquisition.* Hillsdale, NJ: Erlbaum.

Newport, E. L., & Supalla, T. (1980). The structuring of language: Clues from the acquisition of signed and spoken language. In U. Bellugi & M. Studdert-Kennedy (Eds.), *Signed and spoken language: Biological constraints on linguistic form.* Dahlem Konferenzen, Weinheim: Verlag Chemie.

Noller, P. (1985). Video primacy—A further look. *Journal of Nonverbal Behavior, 9,* 28–47.

Oster, H. (1978). Facial expression and affect development. In M. Lewis & L. Rosenblum (Eds.), *The development of affect.* New York: Plenum.

Padden, C. 1986. Verbs and role-shifting in ASL. In C. Padden (Ed.), *Proceedings of the Fourth National Symposium on Sign Language Research and Teaching.* Silver Spring, MD: National Association of the Deaf.

Panksepp, J. (1998). *Affective neuroscience: The foundations of human and animal emotions.* New York: Oxford University Press.

Peterson, C., & McCabe, A. (1983). *Developmental psycholinguistics: Three ways of looking at a child's narrative.* New York: Plenum Press.

Petitto, L. A. (1988). "Language" in the prelinguistic child. In F. S. Kessel (Ed.), *The development of language and language researchers* (pp. 187–221). Hillsdale, NJ: Erlbaum.

Petitto, L. A., & Marentette, P. F. (1991). Babbling in the manual mode: Evidence for ontogeny of language. *Science, 251,* 1493–1496.

Pittam, J., & Scherer, K. R. (1993). Vocal expression and communication of emotion. In M. Lewis & J. M. Haviland (Eds.), *Handbook of emotions* (pp. 185–198). New York: Guilford.

Poizner, H., Klima, E. S., & Bellugi, U. (1987). *What the hands reveal about the brain.* Cambridge, MA: MIT Press.

Provine, K., & Reilly, J. (1992, October). *The expression of affect in signed and spoken stories.* Paper presented at the Fourth Annual Meeting of the American Psychological Society, San Diego, CA.

Radke-Yarrow, M., Zahn-Waxler, C., & Chapman, M. (1983). Children's prosocial dispositions and behavior. In P. H. Mussen (Ed.), *Handbook of child psychology, Vol. 4: Socialization, personality and social development* (pp. 469–545). New York: Wiley.

Reilly, J. S. (1983). What are conditionals for? *Papers and Reports in Child Language Development, 22.*

Reilly, J. S. (1986). The acquisition of temporals and conditionals. In E. C. Traugott, A. Termeulen, J. S. Reilly, & C. A. Ferguson (Eds.), *On conditionals.* Cambridge: Cambridge University Press.

Reilly, J. (1992). How to tell a good story: The intersection of language and affect in children's narratives. *Journal of Narrative and Life History, 2,* 355–377.

Reilly, J. (2001). Bringing affective expression into the service of language: Acquiring perspective marking in narratives. In K. Emmorey & H. Lane (Eds.), *The signs of language revisited: An anthology in honor of Ursula Bellugi and Edward Klima.* Mahwah, NJ: Erlbaum.

Reilly, J. (in press). From affect to language: A cross-linguistic study of the development of evaluation in narratives. In L. Verhoeven & S. Stromqvist (Eds.), *Narrative development in a multilingual context.*

Reilly, J., Klima, E. S., & Bellugi, U. (1990). Once more with feeling: Affect and language in children from atypical populations. *Development and Psychopathology, 2,* 367–392.

Reilly, J. S., & McIntire, M. L. (1991). Where shoe: The acquisition of wh-questions in ASL. *Papers and Reports in Child Language Development* (pp. 104–111). Stanford University, Department of Linguistics.

Reilly, J., McIntire, M. L., & Anderson, D. (1994, November). *Look who's talking! Point of view and character reference in mothers' and children's ASL narratives.* Paper presented at the Boston Child Language Conference, Boston, MA.

Reilly, J., McIntire, M., & Bellugi, U. (1986/1990). FACES: The relationship between language and affect. In V. Volterra & C. Erting (Eds.), *From gesture to language in hearing and deaf children.* New York: Springer-Verlag.

Reilly, J., McIntire, M. L., & Bellugi, U. (1990a). Conditionals in American Sign Language: Grammaticized facial expressions. *Applied Psycholinguistics, 11* (4), 369–92.

Reilly, J. S., McIntire, M. L., & Bellugi, U. (1990b). Faces: The relationship of language and affect. In V. Volterra & C. Erting (Eds.), *From gesture to language in hearing and deaf children.* New York: Springer-Verlag.

Reilly, J., McIntire, M., & Bellugi, U. (1991). BABYFACE: A new perspective on universals in language acquisition. In P. Siple (Ed.), *Theoretical issues in sign language research: Psycholinguistics.* Chicago: University of Chicago Press.

Reilly, J. S., McIntire, M. L., & Seago, H. (1992). Affective prosody in American Sign Language. *Sign Language Studies, 75,* 113–128.

Reilly, S. S., & Muzekari, L. H. (1986). Effects of emotional illness and age upon the resolution of discrepant messages. *Perceptual and Motor Skills, 62,* 823–829.

Richards, A., French, C., & Dowd, R. (1995). Hemisphere asymmetry and the processing of emotional words in anxiety. *Neuropsychologia, 33,* 835–841.

Romney, A. K., Moore, C. C., & Rusch, C. D. (1997). Cultural universals: Measuring the semantic structure of emotion terms in English and Japanese. *Proceedings of the National Academy of Sciences, USA, 94,* 5489–5494.

Rossini, P., Reilly, J., Fabretti, D., & Volterra, V. (1998). *Non-manual behaviors in Italian Sign Language.* Paper presented at the Italian Sign Language Conference, Genoa.

Russell, J. A. (1991). Culture and the categorization of emotions. *Psychological Bulletin, 110,* 426–450.

Scherer, K. R. (1979). Non-linguistic indicators of emotion and psychopathology. In C. E. Izard (Ed.), *Emotions in personality and psychopathology* (pp. 495–529). New York: Plenum Press.

Scherer, K. R. (1982). The assessment of vocal expression in infants and children. In C. E. Izard (Ed.) *Measuring emotions in infants and children.* (pp. 127–163). New York: Cambridge University Press.

Scherer, K. R. (1985). Vocal affect signalling: A comparative approach. In J. Rosenblatt, C. Beer, M. Busnel, & P. J. B. Slater (Eds.), *Advances in the study of behavior* (pp. 189–244). New York: Academic Press.

Scherer, K. R. (1986). Vocal affect expression: A review and a model for future research. *Psychological Bulletin, 99* (2), 143–165.

Scherer, K. R. (1989). Vocal correlates of emotion. In H. Wagner & A. Manstead (Eds.), *Handbook of psychophysiology: Emotion and social behavior* (pp. 165–197). London: Wiley.

Scherer, K. R. (1994). Affect bursts. In S. H. M. van Goozen, N. E. van de Poll, & J. A. Sergeant (Eds.), *Emotions: Essays on emotion theory* (pp. 161–196). Hillsdale, NJ: Erlbaum.

Shaver, P., Schwartz, J., Kirson, D., & O'Connor, C. (1987). Emotion knowledge: Further exploration of a prototype approach. *Journal of Personality and Social Psychology, 52* (6), 1061–1086.

Shaver, P. R., Wu, S., & Schwartz, J. C. (1992). Cross-cultural similarities and differences in emotion and its representation: A prototype approach. In M. S. Clark (Ed.), *Review of personality and social psychology: Volume 13. Emotion* (pp. 175–212). Newbury Park, CA: Sage.

Slobin, D. I. (1982). Universal and particular in the acquisition of language. In E. Wanner & L. R. Gleitman (Eds.), *Language acquisition: The state of the art.* Cambridge: Cambridge University Press.

Slobin, D. I. (Ed.). (1985). *The crosslinguistic study of language acquisition, Vol. 1: The data.* Hillsdale, NJ: Erlbaum.

Smiley, P. (1987). *The development of a concept of person: The young child's view of the other in action and in interaction.* Unpublished doctoral dissertation, University of Chicago.

Smiley, P., & Huttenlocher, J. (1989). Young children's acquisition of emotion concepts. In C. Saarni & P. Harris (Eds.), *Children's understanding of emotion.* New York: Cambridge University Press.

Smith, C., Lentz, E., & Mikos, K. (1988). *Signing naturally: Teacher's curriculum guide.* Berkeley, CA: Dawn Sign Press.

Stein, N. L., & Levine, L. J. (1987). Thinking about feelings: The development and organization of emotion knowledge. In R. E. Snow & M. Farr (Eds.), *Aptitude, learning, and instruction, Vol. 3: Cognition, conation, and affect.* Hillsdale, NJ: Erlbaum.

Steiner, J. E. (1973). The human gustofacial response. In J. F. Bosma (Ed.), *Fourth symposium on oral sensation and perception.* Rockville, MD: United States Department of Health, Education and Welfare.

Stenberg, C. R., & Campos, J. J. (1990). The development of anger expressions in infancy. In N. L. Stein, B. Leventhal, & T. Trabasso (Eds.), *Psychological and biological approaches to emotion* (pp. 247–282). Hillsdale, NJ: Erlbaum.

Stenberg, C., Campos, J., & Emde, R. (1983). The facial expression of anger in seven-month-old infants. *Child Development, 54,* 178–184.

Stern, D. (1977). *The first relationship.* Cambridge, MA: Harvard University Press.

Stokoe, W. (1960). Sign language structure: An outline of the visual communication systems of the American Deaf. *Studies in Linguistics, Occasional papers, 8.* Silver Spring, MD: Linstok Press.

Strauss, E. (1983). Perception of emotional words. *Neuropsychologia, 21,* 99–103.

Svejda, M. J. (1981). The development of infant sensitivity to affective messages in the mother's voice. *Dissertation Abstracts International, 42*(11), 4623B.

Van Strien, J. W., & Heijt, R. (1995). Altered visual field asymmetries for letter naming and letter matching as a result of concurrent presentation of threatening and nonthreatening words. *Brain and Cognition, 29,* 187–203.

Van Strien, J. W., & Morpugo, M. (1992). Opposite hemispheric activation as a result of emotionally threatening and non-threatening words. *Neuropsychologia, 30,* 845–848.

Volterra, V., & Iverson, J. (1995). When do modality factors affect the colors of language acquisition? In K. Emmorey & J. S. Reilly (Eds.), *Language, gesture, and space.* Hillsdale, NJ: Erlbaum.

Wexler, B. E., Schwartz, G., Warrenburg, S., Servis, M., & Tarlatzis, I. (1986). Effects of emotion on perceptual asymmetry: Interactions with personality. *Neuropsychologia, 24,* 699–710.

Wierzbicka, A. (1991). *Cross-cultural pragmatics: The semantics of human interaction.* Berlin: Mouton de Gruyter.

Wierzbicka, A. (1992). Talking about emotions: Semantics, culture and cognition. *Cognition and Emotion, 6,* 285–319.

Wierzbicka, A. (1994). Emotion, language, & cultural scripts. In S. Kitayama & H. R. Markus (Eds.), *Emotion and culture: Empirical studies of mutual influence* (pp. 133–196). Washington, DC: American Psychological Association.

Wilbur, R. (1997, June). *Stress in ASL: What we know, how we know it, and typological implications thereof.* Paper presented at Prosody and Intonation in Signed and Spoken Languages, Haifa.

Wilbur, R. B. (2000). Phonological and prosodic layering of non-manuals in American Sign Language. In K. Emmorey & H. Lane (Eds.), *The signs of language revisited:* *An anthology to honor Ursula Bellugi and Edward Klima* (pp. 215–243). Mahwah, NJ: Erlbaum.

Zieher, W., & Zenhausern, R. (1984). *Hemispheric asymmetries in the cognitive and affective processing of emotional words and faces.* Paper presented at the meeting of the International Neuropsychological Society, Houston, TX.

# V

## Cognitive Components of Emotion

# 28

## INTRODUCTION: COGNITIVE COMPONENTS OF EMOTION

Klaus R. Scherer

Cognition is often seen as an antagonist to emotion, as emotion is seen as an impediment to the proper functioning of the pinnacle of cognition—rational thought. This widely shared assumption is the result of a philosophical debate about the roles of passion and reason in human nature that goes back to Plato. In arguing for a tripartite structure of the soul, Plato created the concepts of "cognition," "emotion," and "conation" (motivation), and placed them in partial opposition to each other. While this doctrine has had many critics, including Plato's own pupil Aristotle, it has, reinforced by the philosophical notion of indivisible human faculties (Mendelsohn, Kant; see Hilgard, 1980), profoundly affected modern psychology. The latest consequence of Plato's doctrine has been a debate on how much cognition is required for emotion, if any (see final statements of the two major protagonists in this debate; Lazarus, 1999b; Zajonc, 2000). While there are good reasons to believe that this particular issue is largely used based on semantic quibbles concerning the definition of cognition (Leventhal & Scherer, 1987), the impact it has had is indicative of the difficulties scientists face in coming to grips with the interaction between these two fundamental aspects of human functioning. Therefore, this section of the *Handbook*, presenting current views as well as empirical evidence on the role of cognition in affective science (and the role of emotion in cognitive science) takes on special significance. As the contributions in this section illustrate, the Zeitgeist seems to be dominated by efforts to integrate rather than oppose cognition and emo-

tion. As shown by the research efforts reported in these chapters, there is an increasing tendency to study the *interaction* between cognition and emotion in trying to understand fundamental aspects of memory, inference, judgment, decision making, and problem solving, on the one hand, and social and emotional behavior, on the other.

In this introduction, the following issues, running through much of the discussions in the chapters of this section, will be reviewed briefly: (1) the cognitive factors eliciting and differentiating emotions, (2) the effects of affective states and traits on cognitive processes, (3) the perception and cognition of affect, (4) the recursive processes between cognition and emotion, and (5) affective components in "frozen" cognitive structures such as language.

### Cognitive Factors Eliciting and Differentiating Emotions

For Aristotle, the issue of which emotion is elicited in a particular situation did not need much discussion. From his writings (e.g., his *Ethica Nicomachea*; Aristotle, 1941) one can assume that he thought that it was through the appropriate evaluation of an event, for example interpreting the utterance of another person as an insult, that the required emotion—that is, anger—would result. Similarly, most philosophers working during the past two millennia implicitly assumed that it was an evaluation of an event or situation in the light of a person's interests that would

563

lawfully call forth the appropriate emotion. Thus, Spinoza, Descartes, and Hume have developed catalogs of the meaning structures of events that are likely to produce specific emotions (Gardiner, Clark-Metcalf, & Beebe-Center, 1937/1980). Even William James, who made the radical proposal that emotion *is* the perception of bodily symptoms upon encountering a certain event (like a bear trotting out of the woods), never doubted that it is "the overriding idea of the significance of the event" (James, 1894, p. 518) that produces the specific bodily symptoms in the first place (see Scherer, 2000, p. 171). Modern psychologists have had more difficulties in acknowledging this simple fact. It seemed too trivial. Thus, the "nontrivial" Schachter-Singer theory of emotion that dominated the textbooks until very recently claimed that the type of emotion a person will feel depended on the interpretation of social cues available in the situation (assuming that the person experiences a feeling of general arousal that cannot be reasonably explained; see Scherer, 2000).

It was the pioneering work of Magda Arnold (1960) and Richard Lazarus (1966) that reasserted the central role of *appraisal* in eliciting and differentiating emotional reactions. Based on this tradition, vigorous research activity, generally based on *appraisal theories of emotion*, has sprung up, attempting to theoretically refine and empirically buttress the longstanding assumption that emotions are based on subjective evaluations of the significance of events to the well-being of the person concerned (see Scherer, Schorr, & Johnstone, 2001). Ellsworth and Scherer, in their contribution in this part, outline the fundamental assumptions and the current status of these theories and the research efforts that have been generated by it. The fundamental tenet of appraisal theory is that people evaluate events in terms of the perceived relevance for their current needs and goals, including considerations of their ability to cope with consequences and the compatibility of the underlying actions with social norms and self-ideals.

Appraisal theories have been criticized for being too "cognitivistic"—in other words, for placing too much emphasis on elaborate cognitive computations (see, for example, Berkowitz, 1994; Frijda & Zeelenberg, 2001). Many of the critics claim that emotions can be elicited by much simpler types of sensations that are generally unconscious (e.g., familiarity, memory associations, pain). Appraisal theorists have countered this criticism by arguing that the evaluation of the significance of an event can occur on very low levels of processing, including highly automatic, unconscious appraisals (Leventhal & Scherer, 1987; Teasdale, 1999; van Reekum & Scherer, 1997), although there is debate, even within this tradition, about how many different processes can be usefully subsumed under the term *appraisal* (see Scherer, 2001b, for a review of the issues).

However, apart from the terminological issues, it is of great importance to determine the mechanisms underlying these evaluation processes. Öhman and his colleagues (Öhman, 1997, 1999; Öhman, Flykt, & Lundqvist, 2000) argue that there are a certain number of stimuli for which we have an evolutionarily prepared appraisal pattern. This position argues that images of snakes and spiders, for example, provide innate signals of danger and are thus processed automatically and very rapidly. One of the most basic forms of bestowing emotion-elicitation power to an object or event is classic conditioning—that is, pairing the respective stimulus with other stimuli that have universal biological significance such as pain- or pleasure-inducing stimuli, like preferred food (see also chapter 13, this volume). LeDoux (1998, 2000) has used this fundamental psychobiological mechanism to study primitive fear responses in rats, demonstrating the dual nature of the neural pathways involved (see also chapter 4, this volume). It is to be expected that conditioning plays a major role in human emotions, and it is thus not surprising that several learning theorists have attempted to describe these mechanisms theoretically in their accounts of emotion (see overview of learning theories of emotion in Strongman, 1986). However, given the victory of cognitivism over behaviorism, conditioning explanations of emotion elicitation have not been popular in recent years. The related notion of associationism has had a similar fate, although there are recent "neo-associationist" accounts of emotional phenomena (Berkowitz, 2001).

Appraisal theorists have acknowledged that many emotional phenomena cannot appropriately be explained by the notion of significance evaluation. This is true, for example, for memory associations and emotional reactions to music (see Ellsworth, 1994). It is a well-known phenomenon that a sudden thought of events or persons one has encountered in the past can trigger complex emotional states. While in some cases this emotion may mirror the state one experienced in the original situation (e.g., sadness because of the loss of a loved one), this is not always the case. In some cases, the current context or salient values may produce different and potentially more complex emotional states—for example, regret. It is possible that in such cases appraisal mechanisms do play a role—for example, in evaluating past opportunities in the light of current goals or values. So far, the mechanisms underlying the production of emotion through memory associations and the interaction between recall and current evaluation have been rarely studied, constituting an important area for further study on the role of cognition in emotion elicitation. With respect to music, one can identify a number of potential *routes* for emotion elicitation through exposure to musical stimuli. These include peripheral routes, such as the external coupling of internal oscillators through strong musical rhythms, and central routes involving cognitive processing, including appraisal (see Scherer & Zentner, 2001, for a review).

Another research tradition that has been centrally concerned with the role of cognition in eliciting emotion is motivated by an interest in understanding the pathology of emotion—affective disturbance. Many clinical psychologists confronted with affective disorders have focused on the role of cognitive processing in attempting to understand the etiology of clinical syndromes and in developing appropriate therapeutic intervention methods. Whereas appraisal theorists, who have been generally trained as social psychologists, have concentrated on conceptually identifying the *content* of the appraisals that would produce specific emotions to the detriment of the *process* (but see Leventhal & Scherer, 1987; Smith & Kirby, 2001; Scherer, 2001a), the clinical approach has focused on the structures and processes involved in eliciting emotions. One tradition that has been particularly influential in this domain is based on the work of a British group of clinical psychologists advocating an *information processing approach* to affective illness. This tradition is reviewed by Dalgleish in this part. The pioneers of this approach, strongly influenced by Broadbent (1971), started from the notion of a hierarchically organized modular information-processing system. Adopting the idea of automatic vs. controlled processing, they have oriented their research around the issue of attention deployment as one of the major indicators of resource allocation in cognitive processing and thus a potential predictor of various emotional disturbances. For example, anxiety disorders are seen as characterized by an unconscious processing bias for threatening stimuli; see Mathews & MacLeod, 1994; Teasdale, 1997; Williams, Watts, MacLeod, & Matthews, 1988). In addition to outlining basic assumptions and representative research of an information processing approach to emotion elicitation, Dalgleish describes a number of theories exemplifying this approach.

## Effects of Affective States on Cognitive Processes

In the 1950s a group of cognitive psychologists set out to demonstrate that perception was far from being the passive reception process as it had been treated in theory and research by earlier scholars. Using a number of ingenious experimental designs, these researchers demonstrated rather striking effects of motivation and affect on perception and cognition. They called their approach a "new look in perception" (Bruner & Postman, 1947; Erdelyi, 1974). Unfortunately, their example, while being widely cited in social psychology at the time, did not have a lasting impact on the study of cognition. In fact, as the cognitive revolution swept through psychology and the behavioral and neurosciences generally, motivational and affective factors were largely ignored, if not systematically neglected. This glaring neglect of the role of affect in perception and cognition eventually prompted a reaction

from inside cognitive science, with prominent researchers suggesting to turn from an exclusive concern with "cold" cognition to an investigation of "hot" cognition (see, for example, contributions in Schank & Langer, 1994, and editors' introduction in Nunez & Freeman, 2000). Importantly, the influential handbook *The Cognitive Neurosciences* (Gazzaniga, 1995) included chapters on emotion, stress, and affective disorder, signaling a significant change in the definition of the field.

But even during the heyday of "cognitivism," a number of research traditions outside mainstream cognitive science contributed to the study of the role of affect in cognition. Thus, the effect of emotion on memory (and vice versa) has been the object of much interest (see the fascinating early account by Rapoport, 1971, or the interest in the "flashbulb memory," Brown & Kulik, 1977; Conway, 1995; Schooler & Eich, 2000), even though much of it received little attention from mainstream cognitivists. Given this longstanding preoccupation with affective elements in memory, it is not surprising that it has been research and theory on memory that has heralded the reawakening of interest in affective phenomena by cognitive scientists. Since then, a large number of scholars have demonstrated the multiple ways in which affect can be expected to influence storage in and retrieval of significant events from memory.

In their chapter in this part, Ochsner and Schacter review the major strands of these research traditions and synthesize the underlying processes in an overarching "social-cognitive-neuroscience approach." By looking across many levels, including the social level of experience and behavior, the cognitive level of information processing, and the neural level of brain systems and mechanisms, they provide a comprehensive account of how emotional experiences are stored in and retrieved from memory. Ochsner and Schacter first discuss the systems for the construction of memory and emotion separately, highlighting in particular the important distinction between controlled and automatic processes in both of these domains (see also chapter 6, this volume). They then review the various ways in which emotion guides the encoding and storage of information, such as the sensitization for affectively charged stimuli, the recruitment of attention, the role of affectively charged schemata, and the cognitive rehearsal that follows many emotional events and serves to consolidate memory traces. The final section in Ochsner and Schacter's chapter describes the way in which emotion influences and guides, often also biases, retrieval. The chapter also covers the state of the art on neural mechanisms for encoding, storing, and retrieving emotional information.

As one might have expected from the impact of the "new look" approach on social psychology, research on social cognition never completely abandoned studying the role of motivational and emotional factors in cognitive processes, particularly in the context of person and event perception and social judgment. However, it has only been in more recent years that some of the leading social cognition researchers have turned their attention to effects of mood on a variety of cognitive processes and on the intriguing mechanism of implicit processing through affective priming (Fazio, 2001; Klauer, 1998). This literature, mostly but not exclusively based in social psychology, is reviewed in the chapter by Forgas in this part. After a brief survey of the role of affect in the organization of attitudes, including the historically important psychodynamic and associationist views as well as the contemporary cognitive approaches, Forgas reviews three major theoretical approaches that differ with respect to their accounts of the underlying mechanism of the effect, in particular memory-based mechanisms (e.g., mood congruence), inferential mechanisms (e.g., extrapolating from one's current feeling state), or processing consequences of affect (e.g., the effect of mood on cognitive processing style). In a critical survey of the empirical evidence available, Forgas examines the relative merits of the respective theoretical positions and proposes an integrative approach in the form of an Affect Infusion model. The most prominent finding in this research tradition is that the infusion of affect is most effective for complex or "deep" cognitive processing.

In the area of judgment and decision making, a new impetus for giving a bigger role to motivational and affective factors has been provided by the ingenious experiments by Tversky and Kahneman (see Kahneman & Tversky, 2000). In their chapter in this part, Loewenstein and Lerner introduce this tradition and review the current state of the literature. Analyzing the decision process in detail, the authors outline the effects of *expected* emotions (the emotion one expects to feel upon experiencing the outcome of the decision) and of *immediate* emotions (emotions one feels during the decision-making process). With respect to the effect of expected emotions, Loewenstein and Lerner provide a detailed account of the progress decision researchers have made in modeling the complex factors involved in estimating one's emotional reactions to future outcomes (including the capacity to consider situational change, implications for competence assessment, and uncertainty and time delay). At the same time, researchers in this domain now have a much better understanding of forecasting errors and of systematic biases in predicting one's future emotions. As Loewenstein and Lerner's review shows, research on the effects of immediate emotions (elicited by the anticipation of decision outcomes or due to incidental factors) on decision making has mushroomed in the past decade. They systematically review both direct effects (action tendencies primed by specific emotions or general valence and intensity effects) and indirect effects (e.g., changes in the prediction of consequences or changes in the quality of processing). Most im-

portant, Loewenstein and Lerner conclude their contribution with a balanced evaluation of the advantages and disadvantages of the effects that expected and immediate emotions can have on the decision process. They argue against both a simplistic rational choice model (affect-free decision making) and a "gut feeling" model that advocates abandoning the quest for systematic evaluation of consequences altogether. Rather, the authors suggest an approach to evaluating the role of affect in decision making that carefully weighs the potential benefits (e.g., prioritizing processing goals, providing important intangible information in holistic form) and the potential pitfalls (e.g., systematic processing biases).

This concludes the brief review of the issues discussed in the chapters contained in this part. Clearly, the areas treated here cannot entirely cover the territory of cognition in the affective sciences.

## Perception and Cognition of Affective Processes

Apart from the fact that cognition triggers affect and that affect, in turn, has a powerful influence on cognitive processes, affective science needs to address the issue of perceiving and cognizing affective processes in oneself and others. Self-perception has played an important role in major theories of emotion, particularly in the peripheralist views advocated by James-Lange and Schachter (see Scherer, 2000, for a historical overview), and is of central significance for the phenomena of emotion control and regulation (see Gross, 1999).

One of the most important components of emotion is subjective experience or feeling (see introductory chapter to this volume). It can be argued (Scherer, 2001a) that conscious feeling consists of the self-perception of the integrated representation of the changes in all other emotion components (appraisal, physiology, motor expression, motivation). Given the overwhelming importance of this component, it is surprising that the conceptual sophistication and the empirical evidence with respect to feeling lag far behind other areas of emotion psychology. One obvious problem is the terminological confusion due to the frequent tendency to use the terms "emotion" and "feeling" as synonyms (in fact, it can be argued, that this misunderstanding is the basis of one of the major debates in the history of the affective science—the controversy between James and Cannon; see Scherer, 2000, p. 171). Another fundamental problem is the fact that, so far, our only window on this component of emotion is verbal self-report, an access that is far from providing a royal road to this type of subjective experience.

It is surprising, for example, that despite the fact that participants in psychological experiments are routinely asked to rate the intensity (and sometimes the duration) of the emotions they report, we know very little indeed about the self-perception processes whereby these judgments of intensity and duration are generated. It is only recently that researchers have started to investigate the role of peak experiences and durations of episodes for the integration of overall intensity of affect, with the results so far suggesting that peak and end intensities of affective episodes have the strongest effect on overall intensity judgments (e.g., Kahneman, 1999). Similarly, while appraisal researchers have attempted, with reasonable success, to predict the qualitative differentiation on the basis of event evaluation results, little effort has been spent on predicting the intensity or the duration of the experience from appraisal results (but see Frijda, Ortony, Sonnemans, & Clore, 1992; Ortony, Clore, & Collins, 1988; Sonnemans & Frijda, 1994).

The approaches reviewed so far have all focused on subjective experience or appraisal as reported verbally. However, as William James and Carl Lange correctly pointed out (assuming that they meant "feeling" when they wrote "emotion"), the subjective experience of emotion also depends on the self-perception of emotion-induced changes in the other components, such as changes in the autonomous and somatic nervous systems. Again, in view of the central importance of these phenomena, we know little about the underlying processes. The self-perception of various physiological changes has been studied using the term *interoception* (Dworkin, 2000; Vaitl, 1996), but the available empirical evidence is far from conclusive. One of the major issues of debate is the apparent dissociation between objective physiological indicators and subjective reports of affective experience (e.g., Myrtek & Brügner, 1996), which might well be due to the fact that only relatively weak affective experiences, for which one might expect little synchronization of the different emotion components (see Scherer, 2001a) have been studied so far.

As mentioned above, the self-perception of one's affective state lies at the root of any attempt to regulate or control the type or intensity of the felt affect. Most researchers interested in regulation, starting with Wundt (1900), have suggested that there are internal (self image) and external (social norms) standards that prescribe the suppression or modification of a specific emotion, either in terms of its outward expression (e.g., in the form of display rules; Ekman, 1972), or in terms of the experience of the emotion as a whole (e.g., feeling rules; Hochschild, 1983). One can assume that there is a constant interaction between psychobiological *push* effects, which prepare the organism for adaptation, and *pull* effects, which move expression and feeling closer to standards or models imposed by self concept or salient social reference groups (see Scherer, 2000). Presumably, we constantly monitor the type and intensity of affective experiences against such external and internal standards in order to engage in appropriate regulation or control efforts (see also part IV, this volume).

## Recursive Processes Between Cognition and Emotion

So far, only unidirectional effects have been described—cognitive appraisal processes producing emotion, emotion affecting cognition in the form of judgment and decision making, and emotion being perceived and cognitively represented. However, one of the most intriguing aspects of the cognition-emotion interaction is the recursive chaining that can be shown to exist between these influence processes. Figure 28.1 shows a simple illustration of these recursive effects.

There are two major sources of recursive effects. One is the feedback from the pattern of emotional reaction in the different response modalities on the ongoing appraisal process (arrow 1 in Figure 28.1). This effect has been theoretically postulated by a number of appraisal theorists, but it has rarely been studied empirically (but see Keltner, Ellsworth, & Edwards, 1993) nor have there been more detailed accounts of the underlying mechanisms. Obviously, this feedback loop must be centrally involved in any regulation attempts, on both a conscious and an unconscious level (see Gross, 1999). For example, an attempt at reducing the intensity of an emotional experience via re-appraisal (i.e., problem-focused coping) necessarily implies some kind of representation of the emotional response patterns and its regulatory impact on the ongoing appraisal processes. A central question in this context concerns the way in which such feedback information is integrated into the evaluation process. One possibility is that it directly affects a particular appraisal criterion. For example, becoming aware of being frightened might further reduce one's perceived coping potential or power in the face of a threatening event. Another possibility is that the self-perception of one's emotional reaction constitutes

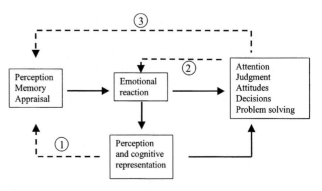

Fig. 28.1 Recursive effects between cognition and emotion.

a new event to be appraised in its own right. This may be the case in social situations in which emotional expression is subject to social control. Thus, I may perceive a joyful reaction to hearing good news from an interaction partner as inappropriate (in the sense of internal or external standards) to a situational context (e.g., a funeral).

A second source of recursive effects is the impact of decisions or behaviors that have been determined by specific emotional reactions both on the emotion itself (especially the component of subjective experience or feeling; arrow 2) and on the ongoing appraisal processes, arrow 3). Thus, starting to flee from a dangerous situation may, at least initially, increase my feelings of fear and may also affect the evaluation of central appraisal characteristics (such as power or coping potential). While the contributions in this section mention the possibility of such feedback effects in various places (see also Lewis, 1996), it will require much more ambitious efforts to explore the general issue of recursiveness and its link to emotion regulation in greater detail. This is undoubtedly one of the most promising areas for future development in theory and research.

## Affective Components in "Frozen" Cognitive Structures

One of the cognitive issues in the affective sciences that is rather underrepresented in this part, reflecting a general neglect in research activity, concerns what one might call affective components or features in "frozen" cognitive structures such as language and other symbol systems (as distinct from the role of affect in actual speech, covered in detail in chapter 27, this volume). A prime example is the structure of the affect lexicon in a particular language and the semantic fields established by emotion terms. The affect lexicon represents the way in which a particular culture or language community conceptualizes affective phenomena and their role in social interaction and communication. Work in linguistic anthropology has provided very important insights into the different ways in which emotional phenomena can be categorized and labeled and thereby become more or less available for conscious reflection and verbal communication (Heider, 1991; Wierzbicka, 1999; Lutz, 1988a). Of particular interest in this context is Levy's (1984) suggestion to link such features to a process of hypo- and hypercognition of certain types of affect in a culture or society (probably strongly linked to prevailing cultural value systems; see Shweder, 1993). One of the pitfalls of this kind of analysis is the tendency to interpret the presence or absence of specific labels in terms of the existence of or the capacity to experience a particular emotion. Thus, Briggs's (1970) observation of the absence of specific anger terms in the Inuit language has often been interpreted as the absence of anger in that

society (see also Lutz, 1988b). Future work in this area will have to distinguish carefully between appraisal processes and response patterning, on the one hand, and the categorization, labeling, and communication of emotional states, on the other. While the latter are clearly influenced by the semantics of the affect lexicon and possibly other, pragmatic factors, the former are not, or at least to a much lesser degree. A more satisfactory theoretical analysis of the relationships between the psychobiological emotion processes as linked to preverbal, and largely unconscious appraisal, resulting in neurophysiological changes and nonverbal expression, and the conscious activity of categorizing, labeling, and communicating the resulting subjective experience constitutes one of the major tasks for affective scientists in the near future.

The affective aspects of language (highlighted by early anthropological linguists and psychologists of language; e.g., Brown, 1958; Osgood & Sebeok, 1954; Sapir, 1921) in general deserve more interest from affective scientists. For example, one of the intriguing aspects of affective connotations of words is that they tend to be more or less aligned with the general dimensions of affective feeling, as first suggested by Wundt (1905). The work by Osgood and his collaborators (Osgood, May, & Miron, 1975) has shown that the valence and activation dimensions are universal. Modern dimensional theories of affect (Russell, 1980; Watson & Tellegen, 1985) have produced much evidence for the power of these fundamental dimensions of affective experience. One of the challenging issues is to provide a more satisfactory theoretical analysis of the links between the dimensions that seem to be underlying both affective experience and frozen cognitive structures, such as the lexicon or other symbolic systems (such as icons of facial expression, for example).

In general, language is an area of study that holds great promise for cognitive approaches to the affective sciences. At one extreme are interjections or affect bursts that, in the words of Wundt (1900) have been domesticated into language and its phonetic and conceptual system (see Scherer, 1994). At the other extreme one finds a large number of highly elaborate emotion metaphors (as highlighted in the work of Lakoff & Kövecses, 1987 and Kövecses, 2000).

Another frozen symbol system with great importance for the affective sciences is music, often even called the "language of the emotions" (e.g., Cooke, 1959). There is strong evidence that listeners will very reliably ascribe emotional meaning to certain types of music and often claim to actually experience the respective emotional states (see contributions in Juslin & Sloboda, 2001). One of the most influential theories of emotional effects of music has been Meyer's (1956) analysis of the affective reactions to the violation or confirmation of expectations with respect to the unfolding of musical structure in the course of the execution of a piece of music. In this vein, an important area of empirical work in music psychology is concerned with the temporal variation in perceived affective tension as related to local variations in musical structure (Krumhansl, 1997; see also chapter 26, this volume).

As in the performing arts, in the visual arts, painting, sculpture, and architecture, there has been a longstanding interest in the affect-eliciting effects of the symbol systems. Again, it has been typically assumed that such effects are mediated by cognitive factors, often, as in music, linked to expectancy violation and variability (Berlyne, 1960). Emotional reactions such as admiration or revelry have generally been attributed to the perception of beauty, which is often linked to the evenness or balance of proportions or the inherent quality of colors. Given our general lack of understanding of the esthetic emotions, this area certainly deserves increased attention in future affective science research (see Cupchik & Laszlo, 1992).

## REFERENCES

Aristotle. (1941). Ethica Nicomachea. In R. McKeon (Ed.), *The basic works of Aristotle*. New York: Random House.

Arnold, M. B. (1960). *Emotion and personality. Vol. 1: Psychological aspects*. New York: Columbia University Press.

Berkowitz, L. (1994). Is something missing: Some observations prompted by the cognitive-neoassociationist view of anger and emotional aggression. In L. R. Huesmann (Ed.), *Aggressive behavior: Current perspectives* (pp. 35–57). New York: Plenum Press.

Berkowitz, L. (2001). On the formation and regulation of anger and aggression: A cognitive-neoassociationistic analysis. In W. G. Parrott (Ed), *Emotions in social psychology: Essential readings* (pp. 325–336). Philadelphia: Psychology Press/Taylor & Francis.

Berlyne, D. E. (1960). *Conflict, arousal and curiosity*. New York: McGraw-Hill.

Briggs, J. L. (1970). *Never in anger: Portrait of an eskimo family*. Cambridge, MA: Harvard University Press.

Broadbent, D. E. (1971). *Decision and stress*. London: Academic Press.

Brown, R. (1958). *Words and things*. Glencoe, IL: Free Press.

Brown, R., & Kulik, J. (1977). Flashbulb memories. *Cognition, 5*(1), 73–99.

Bruner, J. S., & Postman, L. (1947). Emotional selectivity in perception and reaction. *Journal of Personality, 16*, 69–77.

Conway, M. A. (1995). *Flashbulb memories*. Hillsdale, NJ: Lawrence Erlbaum.

Cooke, D. (1959). *The language of music*. London: Oxford University Press.

Cupchik, G. C., & Laszlo, J. (Eds.). (1992). *Emerging visions of the aesthetic process: Psychology, semiology, and philosophy*. New York: Cambridge University Press.

Dworkin, B. R. (2000). Interoception. In J. T. Cacioppo & L. G. Tassinary (Eds.), *Handbook of psychophysiology, 2nd ed.* (pp. 482–506). New York: Cambridge University Press.

Ekman, P. (1972). Universals and cultural differences in facial expression of emotion. In J. R. Cole (Ed.), *Nebraska Symposium on Motivation* (pp. 207–283). Lincoln: University of Nebraska Press.

Ellsworth, P. C. (1994). Sense, culture, and sensibility. In H. R. Markus & S. Kitayama (Eds.), *Emotion and culture: Empirical studies of mutual influence* (pp. 23–50). Washington, DC: American Psychological Association.

Erdelyi, M. H. (1974). A new look at the new look: Perceptual defense and vigilance. *Psychological Review, 81*(1), 1–25.

Fazio, R. H. (2001). On the automatic activation of associated evaluations: An overview. *Cognition and Emotion, 15*(2), 115–141.

Frijda, N. H., Ortony, A., Sonnemans, J., & Clore, G. L. (1992). The complexity of intensity: Issues concerning the structure of emotion intensity. In M. S. Clark (Ed.), *Emotion: Review of personality and social psychology, No. 13* (pp. 60–89). Newbury Park, CA: Sage Publications.

Frijda, N. H., & Zeelenberg, M. (2001). Appraisal: What is the dependent? In K. R. Scherer, A. Schorr, & T. Johnstone (Eds.), *Appraisal processes in emotion: Theory, methods, research* (pp. 141–151). New York: Oxford University Press.

Gardiner, H. M., Clark-Metcalf, R. C., & Beebe-Center, J. G. (1937). *Feeling and emotion: A history of theories*. New York: American Book (reprinted 1980).

Gazzaniga, M. S. (Ed.) (1995). *The cognitive neurosciences*. Cambridge, MA: MIT Press.

Gross, J. J. (1999). Emotion regulation: Past, present, future. *Cognition and Emotion, 13*(5), 551–573.

Heider, K. G. (1991). *Landscapes of emotion: Mapping three cultures of emotion in Indonesia*. New York: Cambridge University Press.

Hilgard, E. R. (1980). The trilogy of mind: Cognition, affection, and conation. *Journal of the History of the Behavioral Sciences, 16*, 107–117.

Hochschild, A. R. (1983). *The managed heart: The commercialization of human feeling*. Berkeley: University of California Press.

James, W. (1894). The physical basis of emotion. *Psychological Review, 1*, 516–529.

Juslin, P. N. & Sloboda, J. A. (Eds.) (2001). *Music and emotion: Theory and research*. Oxford: Oxford University Press.

Kahneman, D. (1999). Objective happiness. In D. Kahneman & E. Diener (Eds.), *Well being: The foundations of hedonic psychology* (pp. 3–25). New York: Russell Sage Foundation.

Kahneman, D., & Tversky, A. (Eds.). (2000). *Choices, values, and frames*. New York: Cambridge University Press.

Keltner, D., Ellsworth, P. C., & Edwards, K. (1993). Beyond simple pessimism: Effects of sadness and anger on social perception. *Journal of Personality and Social Psychology, 64*(5), 740–752.

Klauer, K. C. (1998). Affective priming. In W. Stroebe & M. Hewstone (Eds.), *European Review of Social Psychology, Vol. 8* (pp. 67–103). New York: John Wiley.

Kövecses, Z. (2000). *Metaphor and emotion: Language, culture, and body in human feeling*. New York: Cambridge University Press.

Krumhansl, C. L. (1997). An exploratory study of musical emotions and psychophysiology. *Canadian Journal of Experimental Psychology, 51*(4), 336–352.

Lakoff, G., & Kövecses, Z. (1987). *Women, fire, and dan-*

*gerous things: What categories reveal about the mind.* Chicago: University of Chicago Press.

Lazarus, R. S. (1966). *Psychological stress and the coping process.* New York: McGraw-Hill.

Lazarus, R. S. (1999a). *Stress and emotion: A new synthesis.* New York: Springer.

Lazarus, R. S. (1999b). The cognition-emotion debate: A bit of history. In T. Dalgleish & M. J. Power (Eds.), *Handbook of cognition and emotion* (pp. 3–19). Chichester, England: John Wiley.

LeDoux, J. (1998). Fear and the brain: Where have we been, and where are we going? *Biological Psychiatry, 44*(12), 1229–1238.

LeDoux, J. (2000). Cognitive-emotional interactions: Listen to the brain. In R. D. Lane & L. Nadel (Eds), *Cognitive neuroscience of emotion. Series in affective science* (pp. 129–155). New York: Oxford University Press.

Leventhal, H., & Scherer, K. R. (1987). The relationship of emotion to cognition: A functional approach to a semantic controversy. *Cognition and Emotion, 1,* 3–28.

Levy, R. I. (1984). The emotions in comparative perspective. In K. R. Scherer & P. Ekman (Eds.), *Approaches to emotion* (pp. 397–410). Hillsdale, NJ: Lawrence Erlbaum.

Lewis, M. D. (1996). Self-organising cognitive appraisals. *Cognition and Emotion, 10*(1), 1–25.

Lutz, C. (1988a). Ethnographic perspectives on the emotion lexicon. In V. Hamilton, G. H. Bower, & N. H. Frijda (Eds.), *Cognitive perspectives on emotion and motivation. NATO ASI series D: Behavioral and social sciences, Vol. 44* (pp. 399–419). Dordrecht, Netherlands: Kluwer.

Lutz, C. A. (1988b). *Unnatural emotions: Everyday sentiments on a Micronesian atoll and their challenge to Western theory.* Chicago: University of Chicago Press.

MacLeod, C., & Mathews, A. M. (1991). Cognitive-experimental approaches to the emotional disorders. In P. R. Martin (Ed.), *Handbook of behavior therapy and psychological science: An integrative approach.* Pergamon general psychology series, Vol. 164 (pp. 116–150). Elmsford, NY: Pergamon Press.

Mathews, A., & MacLeod, C. (1994). Cognitive approaches to emotion and emotional disorders. *Annual Review of Psychology, 45,* 25–50.

Meyer, L. B. (1956). *Emotion and meaning in music.* Chicago: University of Chicago Press.

Myrtek, M., & Bruegner, G. (1996). Perception of emotions in everyday life: Studies with patients and normals. *Biological Psychology, 42*(1–2), 147–164.

Nunez, R., & Freeman, W. J. (Eds.). (2000). *Reclaiming cognition: The primacy of action, intention and emotion.* Thorverton, England: Imprint Academic.

Öhman, A. (1997). As fast as the blink of an eye: Evolutionary preparedness for preattentive processing of threat. In P. J. Lang & R. F. Simons (Eds.), *Attention and orienting: Sensory and motivational processes* (pp. 165–184). Mahwah, NJ: Lawrence Erlbaum.

Öhman, A. (1999). Distinguishing unconscious from conscious emotional processes: Methodological considerations and theoretical implications. In T. Dalgleish & M. J. Power (Eds.), *Handbook of cognition and emotion* (pp. 321–352). Chichester, England: John Wiley.

Öhman, A., Flykt, A., & Lundqvist, D. (2000). Unconscious emotion: Evolutionary perspectives, psychophysiological data and neuropsychological mechanisms. In R. D. Lane & L. Nadel (Eds.), *Cognitive neuroscience of emotion. Series in affective science* (pp. 296–327). New York: Oxford University Press.

Ortony, A., Clore, G. L., & Collins, A. (1988). *The cognitive structure of emotions.* New York: Cambridge University Press.

Osgood, C. E., May, W. H., & Miron, M. S. (1975). *Cross-cultural universals of affective meaning.* Urbana, IL: University of Illinois Press.

Osgood, C. E., & Sebeok, T. A. (Eds.). (1954). Psycholinguistics: A survey of theory and research problems. *Supplement to the International Journal of American Linguistics,* 1954, 20.

Rapaport, D. (1971). *Emotions and memory.* New York: International Universities Press.

Russell, J. A. (1980). A circumplex model of affect. *Journal of Personality and Social Psychology, 39,* 1161–1178.

Sapir, E. (1921). *Language.* New York: Harcourt, Brace, & World.

Schank, R. C., & Langer, E. (Eds.). (1994). *Beliefs, reasoning, and decision making: Psychologic in honor of Bob Abelson.* Hillsdale, NJ: Lawrence Erlbaum.

Scherer, K. R. (1994). Affect bursts. In S. van Goozen, N. E. van de Poll, & J. A. Sergeant (Eds.), *Emotions: Essays on emotion theory* (pp. 161–196). Hillsdale, NJ: Lawrence Erlbaum.

Scherer, K. R. (1999). Appraisal theories. In T. Dalgleish, & M. Power (Eds.), *Handbook of cognition and emotion* (pp. 637–663). Chichester: John Wiley.

Scherer, K. R. (2000). Emotion. In M. Hewstone & W. Stroebe (Eds.), *Introduction to social psychology: A European perspective* (3rd. ed., pp. 151–191). Oxford: Blackwell.

Scherer, K. R. (2001a). Appraisal considered as a process of multi-level sequential checking. In K. R. Scherer, A. Schorr, & T. Johnstone (Eds.), *Appraisal processes in emotion: Theory, methods, research* (pp. 92–120). New York: Oxford University Press.

Scherer, K. R. (2001b). The nature and study of appraisal: A review of the issues. In K. R. Scherer, A. Schorr, & T. Johnstone (Eds.), *Appraisal processes in emotion: Theory methods, research* (pp. 369–391). New York: Oxford University Press.

Scherer, K. R., Schorr, A., & Johnstone, T. (Eds.). (2001). *Appraisal processes in emotion: Theory, methods, research.* New York: Oxford University Press.

Scherer, K. R. & Zentner, K. R. (2001). The expression of emotion in music. In P. N. Juslin & J. A. Sloboda (Eds.), *Music and emotion* (pp. 361–392). Oxford: Oxford University Press.

Schooler, J. W., & Eich, E. (2000). Memory for emotional events. In E. Tulving & F. I. M. Craik (Eds.), *The Oxford handbook of memory* (pp. 379–392). New York: Oxford University Press.

Shweder, R. A. (1993). The cultural psychology of the emotions. In M. Lewis & J. M. Haviland (Eds.), *Handbook of emotions* (pp. 417–431). New York: Guilford Press.

Smith, C. A., & Kirby, L. D. (2001). Affect and cognitive appraisal processes. In J. P. Forgas (Ed.), *Handbook of affect and social cognition* (pp. 75–92). Mahwah, NJ: Lawrence Erlbaum.

Sonnemans, J., & Frijda, N. H. (1994). The structure of subjective emotional intensity. *Cognition and Emotion, 8*(4), 329–350.

Strongman, K. T. (1986). *The psychology of emotion.* Chichester: Wiley (3rd ed.; Orig. 1973).

Teasdale, J. D. (1997). The relationship between cognition and emotion: The mind-in-place in mood disorders. In D. M. Clark & C. G. Fairburn (Eds), *Science and practice of cognitive behavior therapy* (pp. 67–93). New York: Oxford University Press.

Teasdale, J. D. (1999). Multi-level theories of cognition-emotion relations. In T. Dalgleish & M. J. Power (Eds), *Handbook of cognition and emotion* (pp. 665–681). Chichester, England: John Wiley.

Vaitl, D. (1996). Interoception. *Biological Psychology, 42(1–2),* 1–27.

van Reekum, C. M., & Scherer, K. R. (1997). Levels of processing for emotion-antecedent appraisal. In G. Matthews (Ed.), *Cognitive science perspectives on personality and emotion* (pp. 259–300). Amsterdam: Elsevier Science.

Watson, D., & Tellegen, A. (1985). Toward a consensual structure of mood. *Psychological Bulletin, 98*(2), 219–235.

Wierzbicka, A. (1999). *Emotions across languages and cultures: Diversity and universals.* New York: Cambridge University Press.

Williams, J. M. G., Watts, F. N., MacLeod, C., & Mathews, A. (1988). *Cognitive psychology and emotional disorders.* New York: John Wiley. (Reprinted 1990).

Wundt, W. (1900). *Völkerpsychologie. Eine Untersuchung der Entwicklungsgesetze von Sprache, Mythos und Sitte. Band I. Die Sprache.* [Psychology of cultures: A study of the developmental laws of language, myth, and customs. Vol. 1. Language]. Leipzig: Kröner.

Wundt, W. (1905). *Grundzüge der physiologischen Psychologie* (5th ed., orig. ed. 1874). [Fundamentals of physiological psychology] Leipzig: Engelmann.

Zajonc, R. B. (2000). Feeling and thinking: Closing the debate over the independence of affect. In J. P. Forgas (Ed), *Feeling and thinking: The role of affect in social cognition.* Studies in emotion and social interaction, second series (pp. 31–58). New York: Cambridge University Press.

# 29

# APPRAISAL PROCESSES IN EMOTION

Phoebe C. Ellsworth and Klaus R. Scherer

## The Nature of the Appraisal Process

Usually, people's emotions arise from their perceptions of their circumstances—immediate, imagined, or remembered. This idea has been implicit in many philosophical treatments of emotions (e.g., in Aristotle, Spinoza, and even Descartes and James; see Ellsworth 1994a; Gardiner, Clark-Metcalf, & Beebe-Centa, 1980; Scherer, 2000) and explicit in some (e.g., Hume and Hobbes), and it is the central emphasis of current appraisal theories of emotion. Thinking and feeling are inextricably interrelated most of the time: Certain ways of interpreting one's environment are inherently emotional, few thoughts are entirely free of feelings, and emotions influence thinking. Reason and passion are not independent domains, or are rarely so. Of course there are exceptions: Brain stimulation, hormones, and drugs can produce emotions without external environmental circumstances, just as they can produce sensations, cognitions, and ideas without external environmental circumstances (Penfield, 1975). The fact that exceptions exist does not mean that there is no rule. The general rule suggested by appraisal theorists is that emotions consist of patterns of perception, or rather interpretation, and their correlates in the central and peripheral nervous systems (see Ellsworth, 1994c; Roseman & Smith, 2001; Scherer, 2001a, 2001b).

A further assumption is that emotions are fundamentally adaptive, rather than maladaptive. In order to survive, an organism cannot simply understand its situation; it has to be motivated to do something about it. Many spe-

cies have solved this problem with a mechanism that triggers fixed action patterns in response to appropriate stimuli. Emotions provide a more flexible alternative. They imply action tendencies (Frijda, 1986) without complete rigidity. Lower organisms respond to stimulus patterns with behavior. Emotions, although they still motivate behavior, "decouple" it from the perception of the stimulus so that reconsideration is possible (Scherer, 1984). Fear creates a tendency to flee, but a person may quickly realize that the threat is directed at someone else (reinterpretation of the event) or that an aggressive stance will intimidate the attacker (reinterpretation of response alternatives). Emotions allow flexibility both in event interpretation and in response choice. Emotions, from this point of view, represent an important evolutionary alternative. The phylogenetic expansion of the cerebral cortex enabled an increasing variety of interpretations, emotions, and behavioral options (see Hebb, 1949).

### History

Although some features of appraisal theory were foreshadowed in early work (e.g., Leeper, 1948; see also Reisenzein & Schönpflug, 1992), current versions of the theory trace their roots to the work of Magda Arnold (1960), who first used the term *appraisal*, in the sense of direct, immediate, and intuitive evaluations, to account for qualitative distinctions among emotions. She argued that organisms constantly evaluate the relevance of environmental changes for their own well-being, checking whether significant stimuli are present or absent, beneficial or harmful, and easy or difficult to approach or avoid. These appraisals result in action tendencies, which are experienced as emotions. The most influential early appraisal theorist was Richard Lazarus (1966), who distinguished between "primary appraisals" of the implications of a situation for one's well-being and "secondary appraisals" of one's ability to cope with the situation. Although not all current appraisal theories maintain this distinction, two of Lazarus's other ideas are common to almost all current theories. First, he argued that because the human mind is capable of making subtle distinctions that allow for enormous variability in interpretation of the environment, human emotions themselves are characterized by enormous variability and subtle distinctions. Thus, initially, his appraisal theory rejected the idea that there is a limited number of categorically distinct basic emotions (although more recently he has claimed a limited number of "relational themes" somewhat reminiscent of discrete emotions; see Lazarus, 1991). Second, he proposed that the experience of emotion is a continuous process: The "same" event (including one's own reaction to the event) can be reappraised, so that the initial emotional response changes over time. This idea of emotion as process is widely shared among current appraisal theorists.

In the 1980s, the appraisal approach was "discovered" by a number of different researchers, largely working independently of each other, and became a major theoretical perspective in the study of emotion. The basic idea is that "emotional experience . . . is experience of the situation" (Frijda, 1986, p. 193) as interpreted by the organism. The emotions people feel are predictable from their appraisal of their circumstances (and, conversely, their interpretation of the situation is predictable on the basis of their emotional reactions). Each of the theorists went further and proposed a specific set of appraisals that would be particularly important in differentiating one emotion from another (De Rivera, 1977; Frijda, 1986; Oatley & Johnson-Laird, 1987; Ortony, Clore, & Collins, 1988; Roseman, 1984, 2001; Scherer, 1982, 1984, 1986a, 2001a; Smith & Ellsworth, 1985; Smith & Kirby, 2001; Solomon, 1976; Stein & Levine, 1987; Weiner, 1982, 1986). A more extensive description of the history of the appraisal approach can be found in Schorr (2001).

### Basic Assumptions

Again, the basic premise of appraisal theories is that the organism's evaluation of its circumstances (current or remembered or imagined) plays a crucial role in the elicitation and differentiation of its emotions. Theorists differ somewhat on the appraisals they believe to be most important, but in general, the similarities among them are more striking than the differences. Table 29.1 shows some of the central dimensions proposed by four of the theorists of the 1980s. Novelty, intrinsic pleasantness, certainty or predictability, goal significance, agency, coping potential, and compatibility with social or personal standards are all commonly suggested dimensions. Some theorists include more, some fewer; and there are different arrangements of superordinate and subordinate appraisals. Some theorists have been primarily concerned with causation and agency (Abelson, 1983; Weiner, 1982), focusing on a somewhat more limited domain of emotions but sharing general agreement with other theorists within that domain. Others have proposed overarching themes related to centrally important universal goals, such as attachment or autonomy (Oatley & Johnson-Laird, 1987; Smith & Lazarus, 1993; Stein & Levine, 1987), adding a superordinate classification to the appraisal dimensions. Nonetheless, substantial consensus exists among the theorists in their descriptions of the appraisal dimensions and in their assumptions about the appraisal process during a particular emotional episode.

Table 29.1 Comparative overview of major appraisal dimensions as postulated by different theorists

|  | Frijda (1986) | Roseman (1984) | Scherer (1984) | Smith/Ellsworth (1985) |
|---|---|---|---|---|
|  | Change |  | Novelty<br>suddenness<br>familiarity | Attentional activity |
| Novelty | Familiarity |  |  |  |
| Valence | Valence |  | Intrinsic pleasantness | Pleasantness |
|  | Focality | Appetitive/aversive motives | Goal significance<br>concern relevance | Importance |
| Goals/needs | Certainty | Certainty | outcome probability | Certainty |
| Agency | Intent/Self-other | Agency | cause: agent<br>cause: motive | Human agency |
| Norms/values | Value relevance |  | Compatibility with standards<br>external<br>internal | Legitimacy |

The idea of emotions as processes is central to most appraisal theories and is one of the ideas that most clearly distinguishes them from more structural theories (see Roseman & Smith, 2001). The idea that appraisals occur sequentially and that the nature of the emotional experience changes each time a new appraisal is added was first explicitly proposed by Scherer (1984) but is compatible with several appraisal theories. Generally, the first appraisal in the sequence is that of novelty—something in the environment (physical, social, or mental) changes, and the organism's attention is attracted. An orienting response may occur, and the organism is in a state of readiness for further emotional responding (Ellsworth, 1994c; Kagan, 1991). If whatever attracted the organism's attention cannot be disregarded as irrelevant to its well-being, further appraisal will take place. Very often the next step is a sense of intrinsic pleasantness or unpleasantness (Zajonc, 1980), often occurring so quickly that it is subjectively indistinguishable from the experience of attention. Especially when the valence is negative, further appraisals ensue, and the emotional experience changes from "feeling good" or "feeling bad" to some more differentiated state. Is this important to me (concern relevance)? Do I understand what's going on (certainty, predictability)? Is something impeding my progress toward a goal? Facilitating it (goal conduciveness)? What caused this to happen (agency)? Can this be controlled (controllability)? By me (power)? Has a social norm been broken (compatibility with standards)? By whom? By me? Different combinations of answers to these questions characterize different emotions. Of course, the person does not actually pose such a series of questions each time he or she appraises an event; appraisal is not an internal dialogue (see Kappas, 2001). How conscious the person is of the separate appraisals is a matter of debate. However, theorists generally assume that appraisals are often automatic and unconscious.

Whether the appraisals always occur in the same sequence (Scherer, 1984) or whether variable sequences are common is also a matter of debate, as is the issue of whether all of the appraisals must always occur. It should be noted that the assumption of sequential changes in appraisal results does not contradict the assumption of parallel information processing (see Scherer, 1999b, 2000a, 2001a).

Appraisal theories contrast sharply with categorical theories of emotions that posit a limited number of qualitatively distinct basic emotions, such as fear, anger, and sorrow. As originally proposed by Tomkins (1962, 1963, 1984), Ekman (1972), and Izard (1977), these theories suggested that each of these basic emotions is produced by an innate hardwired neuromotor program with characteristic neurophysiological, expressive, and subjective components. More recent versions have loosened up the model somewhat, to better capture the variety and subtlety

of human emotional life, and now speak of "families" of emotions (Ekman, 1992). Appraisal theories postulate that emotions are composed of simpler but still meaningful elements, elements that correspond to the appraisals and their correlates. It implies that emotional experience is typically a process that changes over the course of an episode, sometimes very rapidly, sometimes more gradually—in line with additions and revisions in the appraisals. It implies a potentially infinite range of emotional experience, with intermediate or transitional states between the named categories of emotions; with vacillation between emotions that corresponds to uncertain or vacillating appraisals; with transitions between emotions that correlate with changes in specifiable appraisals; and with episodic, individual, and cultural variability within a given emotion, such as anger, depending on variations in the person's appraisal and reappraisal of the circumstances.[1]

Appraisal theories can also be distinguished from dimensional theories of emotion. These theories, which have existed in various forms for a century, generally focus on sensations, subjective experience, or, in philosophical parlance, on *qualia*. They postulate that emotions can be classified along certain underlying dimensions such as pleasantness, excitement, and tension (Wundt, 1874/1902), suggesting that each emotion occupies a unique region in this multidimensional space. The number of dimensions proposed varies, with most versions including only two—pleasantness and activation (Bradley & Lang, 1994; Plutchik, 1980; Russell, 1980; Schlosberg, 1952)—or three—pleasantness, activation, and some other (Osgood, 1966; Osgood, May, & Mirou, 1975; Wundt, 1874/1902). Unlike categorical theories, dimensional theories can account for an infinite number of emotional states and provide a basis for discussing similarities and differences among emotions, albeit typically only with respect to their valence and activation.

Appraisal theories attempt not only to describe but also to explain emotions: The appraisal process is a link between the organism and the situation that produces the emotion. Emotions are adaptive responses to the world, not simply abstract sensations, as dimensional theories seem to imply. Appraisal theorists would argue that fear and anger cannot be distinguished simply on the basis of differences in levels of activation and pleasantness.[2] In order to differentiate qualitatively different emotions, we need to know more about how the organism interprets its situation.

## How Appraisals Work

The initial work of the appraisal theorists demonstrated that the general framework was heuristic and promising, as were the specific appraisals identified, at least as a starting point. The approach has generated a considerable amount of research and even more discussion. Many issues remain unresolved, and new issues have been identified both by critics and by appraisal theorists themselves as the theories evolve.

Should appraisals be considered as antecedents (or even *causes*) of emotion, or should they be thought of as components of emotion? The sequencing of the emotional process has been a central issue for emotions theorists since William James (1884) upset received opinion by proposing that bodily responses preceded subjective feelings, and it was brought back to prominence when Zajonc (1980) again upset received opinion by proposing that subjective feelings preceded interpretations. With respect to appraisal theory, a simplistic view would seem to imply that the appraisals are clearly separable *antecedents* of emotion, that is, that the organism first evaluates the environment and then feels the appropriate emotion.[3]

An alternative view, held by many appraisal theorists, is that appraisals are components of emotions—that the subjective experience of fear, for example, is the feeling of high attention, negative valence, high uncertainty about what is happening or one's ability to cope with it, and so on (in addition to the physiological and motor reactions elicited by these appraisals).[4] Of course, when all the requisite appraisals occur, what the person feels is fear, not a collection of identifiable elements (see also the discussion in Kappas, 2001). This perspective is compatible with the idea of emotions as continuous processes, changing as appraisals are added or revised. When the first appraisal, typically the appraisal of novelty, is made, there are changes in the central and peripheral nervous system, in action tendencies (e.g., the ongoing action is interrupted), and in the organism's subjective feeling. With appraisals of valence, certainty, goal relevance, agency, and the other appraisals, new changes occur in all of these systems. Whereas the appraisals-as-antecedents point of view encourages the idea of a clear boundary between cognition and emotion or reason and passion, the appraisals-as-components view dissolves the boundary and renders meaningless a dichotomy which many theorists have considered dubious and even dangerous.

As soon as the initial appraisal is made, the organism is in a sense "emotional," compared with what it was before, although it is not experiencing any of the full-fledged basic emotions described by folk and category theories; the nature of this emotionality is highly fluid, constantly changing as appraisals are added and revised. Much of the writing and research on appraisal theory has explored the appraisal combinations that correspond to categories of emotion in an attempt to show that these categories have distinct profiles of appraisals. When the profile resulting from the appraisal process corresponds to a specific emotion category, the person feels "fear" or "anger" or "shame." But it does not follow that the person feels nothing at all *until* the full complement of appraisals is in place. The view that appraisals are components of emotion allows for *emotionality*, if not any named emotion, from the very beginning of the process.

The appraisals-as-components point of view also challenges the definition of individual emotions as bounded categories. Rather than a single emotion of anger, there can be many varieties of "almost-anger" and many nuances of the anger experience. If someone else causes something negative—but not *very* negative—to happen to me, I may feel irritation. If my sense of control is very high, and I feel that the person has broken a social or moral norm I care about, I may feel a rather pleasurable righteous indignation. If intensity is very high, and I am losing control, I may feel a desperate rage. Appraisal theories, like dimensional theories, are compatible with the idea of an infinite range of emotional states.

Empirical tests of the cause versus component versions of appraisal theories are more difficult than might be imagined and may inevitably be inconclusive because so much hinges on one's definition of "emotion" (see Scherer, 2000b, for more detail on definitional issues). The changes that accompany the novelty appraisal have already been well documented (Posner, 1992; Posner & Petersen, 1990), for example, but whether they correspond to *emotional* changes depends on how the theorist chooses to define emotion. Various theorists have attempted to resolve this problem by suggesting terms such as *preappraisals* (Lazarus & Smith, 1988) and *protoemotions* (Elster, 1999), but new semantic dichotomies are unlikely to be useful for empirical research unless they include clear operational definitions (which has not been the case so far).

The idea that a person who has made some but not all of the appraisals typically found in traditional categories of emotions is already "emotional" may also be useful in extending the theory to cover emotional states such as moods, which have generally been considered as different from emotions. Moods have valence; they may involve a sense of control or lack of it; but they lack novelty, agency, and other appraisals. In many circumstances all of the appraisals are made very quickly, and the person experiences the sudden onset of a very specific emotion. However, if one allows for the possibility that some appraisals are not made or remain ambiguous for longer periods of time, so that the person would admit to feeling "emotional" but would be unable to come up with a label more specific than "good," "bad," or "upset," then the range of appraisal theory is potentially expansible to include other feelings typically designated "borderline" or "nonemotional."

The idea of emotions as processes that develop over time also liberates the theory in directions that may succeed better than other theories in capturing some of the complexities of human emotion (Ellsworth, 1991). First, the person's initial emotional response to the situation may provoke behavior that changes the situation, so that reappraisal is inevitable. Second, the person's emotional response to the situation also becomes a part of the situation; it too can be appraised and can result in further emotions. If my initial angry response strikes me as excessive, I may feel that I have been unjust and feel ashamed of my anger (Ellsworth, 1994b; Elster, 1999). Finally, emotions can bias further cognitions by facilitating the corresponding appraisals, so that an angry person is more likely to see other people as causal agents of new events (Keltner, Ellsworth, & Edwards, 1993), and a happy person is more likely to see favorable outcomes as likely (Johnson & Tversky, 1983).

## Major Dimensions of Appraisal: Theory and Evidence

The central feature of an appraisal perspective on the elicitation and differentiation of emotion is the assumption that organisms constantly evaluate stimuli and events for their significance for the individual. This significance is operationally defined by a number of dimensions or criteria which constitute the meaning structure in which the evaluation takes place.

In this section, these dimensions are explored, with appropriate reference to the pertinent empirical evidence. Considerable emphasis is placed on the idea that appraisals can occur at several levels of processing. In 1987 Leventhal and Scherer proposed the idea that appraisals can occur at three different levels, specifically the sensorimotor, the schematic, and the conceptual level, and that processes occurring at different levels can interact: Subcortical processes can stimulate cortical involvement and vice-versa (Leventhal & Scherer, 1987; see also van Reekum & Scherer, 1997; Teasdale, 1999, for a review, and chapter 33, this volume). Related ideas have been proposed by Teasdale and Barnard (1993), Öhman (1987), Johnson and Multhaup (1992), and Logan (1988).

### Basic Stimulus Characteristics: Novelty, Pleasantness

The most basic dimensions of stimulus events to be coded in perception are the novelty (with respect to the level of habituation) and the intrinsic pleasantness or valence of a stimulus. These dimensions are often coded at a very low level of processing, often in a highly automatic fashion. Some theorists object to the use of terms such as *evaluation* or *appraisal* for this kind of low-level information processing, insisting that these terms imply some higher, "properly cognitive" operation (see Scherer, 2001b; Schorr, 2001, for current and historical aspects of this ongoing debate). Because these dimensions are evolutionarily important and fundamental to the experience of emotion, and because they can be processed on different levels of cognitive functioning, they are included in this chapter.

### Novelty

Because environments are not stable and changes may imply dangers (such as the appearance of predators) organisms need to be sensitive to novelty. A novel stimulus draws attention and mobilizes processing resources to determine whether ongoing activity can be continued or whether further processing and possibly adaptive action are required. It is thus to be expected that even at a very primitive level of sensory-motor processing, sudden and intense stimuli are registered as novel and deserving of attention. The literature on attention (Bargh, 1984; Parasuraman, 1983; Posner, 1992) and on the orienting reflex (Barry, 1996; Graham, 1979; Kimmel, van Olst, & Orlebeke, 1979; Siddle & Lipp, 1997; Sokolov, 1963; Turpin, Schaefer, & Boucsein, 1999) has demonstrated the existence of such primitive detection mechanisms and explored the nature of the neurophysiological changes induced by novelty detection. The studies in this area suggest a large number of factors (involving both stimulus characteristics, such as timing and intensity, and the prior state of the organism, such as arousal level) that affect novelty detection.

Beyond this most primitive level, the criteria for novelty detection may vary greatly for different species, different individuals, and different situations and may depend on motivational state, prior experience with a stimulus (e.g. habituation), or expectation. For example, whereas an amoeba might be able to detect only whether the temperature of the water is changing or not, humans can detect novelty on a number of dimensions. On the schematic level of processing, the detection of *familiarity* could be generated by the presence (and the well formedness) of stored schemata that match the input. On the conceptual level, an evaluation of the lawfulness or regularity of occurrence of certain stimuli or events can yield estimates of *probability* and *predictability*. Potentially, any improbable or unpredicted event (including the absence of predicted ones) requires the organism's attention to determine its potential consequences. Novel events may signal unusual dangers or opportunities. Novelty detection is directly concerned with "predictability" of stimuli or outcomes as used in the extensive literature on control of stimulation (see Miller, 1981; Mineka & Henderson, 1985), as it operates on the expectedness of stimulation, which would seem to be largely determined by predictability.

In summary, novelty detection in its various forms can be considered as a gateway to the emotion system. Emotions are relevance detectors (Frijda, 1986), and attention is the first step in the evaluation of the pertinence of an event for the organism. There is also an important recursive aspect: Attention to an event is important for the elicitation of emotion; conversely, emotion leads to further deployment of attention (see also the work on the relationship between orientation and vigilance; Posner, 1992).

## Valence/Intrinsic Pleasantness

Whereas novelty detection alerts the organism to potentially significant stimuli and motivates the search for appropriate information from the environment and from memory, the sense of intrinsic pleasantness or valence determines the fundamental reaction or response of the organism—liking or attraction, which encourages approach, versus dislike or aversion, which leads to withdrawal or avoidance (Schneirla, 1959). Pleasure and pain are so basic to many affective responses that emotion is often equated with the positive or negative reaction toward a stimulus. Even though the concept of pleasure is as old as the philosophical inquiry into human nature, and even though concepts of pleasurable rewards and reinforcement are the cornerstones of many influential psychological theories, we are still far from understanding which features of stimuli produce liking, pleasure, or preference on the one hand or dislike, aversion, or distress on the other hand.

One of the earliest efforts to specify the nature of hedonic tone was Wundt's (1874/1902) association of feelings of pleasantness and unpleasantness with different stimulus intensities. Berlyne (1960) formalized this assumption as an inverted U-shaped curve, with hedonic tone becoming more positive with the increase of stimulus intensity up to a maximum and then becoming negative as intensity increases further. From a comparative perspective, Schneirla (1959) made similar observations on approach-withdrawal processes in animal behavior, showing that low stimulus intensities tend to elicit and maintain approach responses, whereas high stimulus intensities tend to produce adjustment responses and withdrawal. In a similar vein, Tomkins (1962, 1963, 1984) hypothesized that the differential elicitation of various positive or negative emotions depends on the "density of neural firing" and argued that positive emotions are characterized by a decrease of the gradient of stimulation. Although there has been some empirical support for this general idea, many studies have shown that other stimulus characteristics, such as complexity, need to be taken into account (see Berlyne & Madsen, 1973, for an overview of different perspectives). Frequency of exposure also seems to increase intrinsic pleasantness evaluation, as shown by extensive research by Zajonc and his collaborators (Murphy, Monahan, & Zajonc, 1995; Zajonc, 1980; Zajonc & Markus, 1984).

In addition to general characteristics of stimuli such as intensity or complexity, it is likely that particular kinds of stimuli are evaluated as intrinsically pleasant or unpleasant by innate detection mechanisms. Comparative and developmental work suggests that this may be true for a number of different stimuli. For example, it has been shown that many animals, including humans, have an apparently hardwired preference for sweet and an aversion for bitter tastes (Chiva, 1985; Pfaffman, 1960, 1978; Rozin, 1996; Rozin & Fallon, 1987; Steiner, 1979). Similar results have been found for different odors (Engen, Lipsitt, & Kaye, 1963; Soussignan, Schaal, Marlier, & Jiang, 1997). Some facial features and expressions also seem to be intrinsically valenced (Vinter, Lanares, & Mounoud, 1985), possibly serving as simple "innate releasing mechanisms" for approach or avoidance responses (Eibl-Eibesfeldt, 1979; Hinde, 1974). Whereas some of these evaluation patterns might well be universal and even phylogenetically continuous, others are likely to be species specific. All of the foregoing examples share the characteristic of being very potent intrinsic elicitors; that is, the criteria utilized in the organism's intrinsic pleasantness detection are probably innate rather than acquired.

The intrinsic pleasantness appraisals described so far are likely to be processed almost exclusively at hardwired, sensorimotor levels. However, humans and many animals also have differential preferences that are not based on innate evaluation processes. As the huge literature on learning and conditioning shows, nothing seems to be easier than to acquire a like or a dislike for various things, even things that may never have been encountered before (through generalization, for example). Both the schematic level of processing (e.g., conditioning) and the conceptual level (e.g., judgment of anticipated or derived pleasantness) are likely to be involved. The detection of intrinsic pleasantness must include the evaluation of input in terms of learned preferences or aversions—a process which may produce different results for each individual organism. Obviously, one would expect very powerful cultural differences in this respect, as illustrated, for example, by food preferences (Rozin, 1996, 1999)

It is important to note that the intrinsic pleasantness or unpleasantness detected is mostly a characteristic of the stimulus. Even though the preference may have been acquired and processing may depend on sensory organ specificities or memory or both, it is independent of the momentary state of the organism. In contrast, the positive evaluation of stimuli that help us to reach goals or satisfy needs depends on the significance of the stimulus for the organism's current motivations (see the next subsection).

A special type of valence detection may underlie what is commonly called the *esthetic emotions*, that is, preferences or aversions with respect to music or art. Rozin (1999) suggests that although the hedonic evaluation underlying reactions to esthetically salient stimuli are different from normal pleasure and pain, they involve the same neurobiological system.

## Motivational Bases: Needs, Goals, Values

The appraisal of motivational relevance is essential because it determines to what extent a stimulus or situation furthers or endangers an organism's survival and adaptation to a given environment, the satisfaction of its needs, and the attainment of its goals. Some theorists even restrict the term *emotion* to reactions to goal-relevant events. In the original formulation of appraisal by Arnold (1960) and Lazarus (1966), the implications of the event for the well-being of the organism took center stage, involving "primary appraisals," according to Lazarus (see also Lazarus, 1999). This dimension also occupies a central position in all subsequent appraisal theories, albeit under somewhat different labels. Thus Roseman (1984, 2001) suggests the term *motive consistency* (distinguishing between aversive and appetitive motives), Smith and Ellsworth (1985) used *importance* and *perceived obstacle*, and Scherer (1982, 1984, 2001a) proposes *concern relevance* and *goal/need conduciveness* (Table 29.1 provides a comparative listing of some of the central terms used by major appraisal theorists).

This brief review of terminology suggests that there are at least three questions involved in the appraisal of motivational relevance: (1) Is the event pertinent at all? (2) If so, what are the motives or goals concerned? (3) Are the consequences of the event consistent or inconsistent with the respective motivational state or conducive or obstructive to reaching a goal or satisfying a need?

1. Most appraisal theorists (except Roseman) explicitly postulate that the organism evaluates the general motivational relevance or pertinence of an event on a separate dimension (Frijda, 1986, talks of *focality* for different concerns), presumably before determining its consistency or conduciveness. This seems reasonable with respect to both attention deployment and cognitive economy (e.g., the possibility of lower level processing). Individuals may have schemata that quickly dismiss entire classes of stimuli or events as being unworthy of further processing, based on built-in detection mechanisms (cf. the discussion on the "significance" of stimuli eliciting the orienting response; Bernstein, 1981; Öhman, 1987) or prior learning. Although this notion of *rapid relevance detection* seems reasonable at a high level of abstraction, it is difficult to conceive of the underlying mechanism, particularly if one wants to go beyond a simple binary relevant-nonrelevant distinction and determine the focality of an event or its position in the goal hierarchy, thus determining the importance of the specific goal affected by an event (see Scherer, 2001b). Relevance as a continuous dimension from low to high may depend on the number of goals or needs affected, their relative priority in the hierarchy, or

both. For example, an event is much more relevant if it threatens one's livelihood or even one's survival than if it merely endangers one's need for peace and quiet.

Given the major importance of the appraisal of goal relevance for all ensuing appraisal processes, we need a much more sophisticated account of how motivational information is processed than is available so far. Unfortunately, although the phenomena of motivation and goal-directed behavior are central to behavioral science, we still have little concrete understanding of how the relevance of events to motives, needs, concerns, or goals is likely to be computed. Even the terminology is confusing; there is no consensus on the distinctions among such terms as *drive, need, instinct, motive, concern,* or *goal,* many of which cannot be used because they are burdened with connotations that stem from outdated theories (see Austin & Vancouver, 1996). There is also wide variation in theorists' conceptions of the nature of motivational goals. Some psychologists use the term *goal* as a general motivational construct, without implying awareness or conscious planning, whereas others presume goals to be conceptually represented end states.

In this section we use the term *goals* broadly so as to include basic needs (Maslow, 1962; Murray, 1938; Scott, 1958). In line with a long tradition of theorizing in psychology, we suggest that organisms have hierarchies of goals and needs that they try to satisfy (whether they know it or not, whether motivated by their own free will and decision or by "ultimative" factors related to natural selection). Given this broad conceptualization, we include goals as disparate as the goal of survival (which is obviously very basic in the hierarchy), the goal of maintaining positive social relationships, the goal of enjoying pleasurable experiences, and even the goal of crossing the street to buy a newspaper. It would be impossible even for simple organisms to check the relevance of an event for all possible goals and needs. Consequently, one must assume that the goal and need significance evaluation is based on those goals and needs that are high in priority at the moment. This notion seems well established in the literature on motive hierarchies and goal-directed behavior. As an emotional episode unfolds, the accessibility and priority of various goals may change, although some of the central goals and needs, such as survival and bodily integrity, probably have a stable position near the top of the hierarchy and will almost always assume priority when threatened.

The concept of goal conduciveness, so plausible and apparently simple, raises tricky issues of the relationships between conscious and unconscious goals, between idiosyncratic and universal goals and needs, and between current and latent goals, as well as a host of other distinctions that are beyond the scope of this chapter. The use of a term such as *relational theme,* which has been suggested by Lazarus and his collaborators (Lazarus, 1991; Smith & Lazarus, 1993) as the central motivational underpinning and differentiator of emotions, does not help to disentangle the manifold components of the underlying motivational constructs (see Parkinson, 2001).

2. Some appraisal theorists believe specification of the nature of the motives concerned is essential for predicting the ensuing emotion. Thus, Roseman (1984, 2001) uses the distinction between appetitive and aversive motives to make the distinction between relief (an aversive stimulation stops) and frustration (an appetitive stimulation stops). Furthermore, although any interruption of a goal-directed act or the thwarting of a need may result in frustration, the particular emotional state elicited may be determined by the nature of the motive concerned.[5] In general, it may be reasonable to expect that cross-cultural differences in appraisal and consequent emotional reactions are largely determined by differences in the nature of goals and goal hierarchies in different cultures (Mesquita, Frijda, & Scherer, 1997; Rozin, Lowery, Imada, & Haidt, 1999).

3. Many appraisal theorists believe that the single most important evaluation dimension is the conduciveness of a stimulus event to goal attainment or need satisfaction (see Scherer, 1999b). Acts or events can satisfy goals or needs or can make progress toward satisfaction. Events can also obstruct goal attainment by putting satisfaction out of reach, creating delays, or requiring additional effort (see Srull & Wyer, 1986, for a detailed analysis of these different types of obstruction). This is the classic case of "frustration," the blocking of a goal-directed behavior sequence. Obviously, both goal facilitation and goal interference can vary in strength.

Although this appraisal sounds straightforward, many problems emerge when we attempt to analyze the mechanism in detail. One problem is that the consequences of an event may be conducive for one goal and obstructive for another. If both goals are relatively important for the individual, goal or motive conflict may ensue, giving rise to ambiguous emotions, mixed emotions, or emotional conflict (Weigert, 1991). Furthermore, assuming that the conduciveness dimension is continuous, as previously implied, it remains to be specified how the degree of conduciveness is computed, for example, taking into account the importance (or focality) of the goals or values concerned, their position on the goal gradient, the expectedness of the outcome, the timing of gratifications or punishments, and so forth. It is unclear whether complex events are generally perceived in terms of a bottom-line value on the goal conduciveness dimension, or whether vacillation and ambiguity are common.

There is much debate about whether it is necessary to distinguish the intrinsic-pleasantness appraisal from the goal/need-conduciveness appraisal because both seem so intimately related to positive versus negative emotional experience (Frijda & Zelenberg, 2001). We consider *intrin-*

*sic* pleasantness to be independent of the motivational state of the organism, whereas motivational state is the decisive element in goal conduciveness. The difference is obvious in cases in which an inherently pleasant stimulus blocks goal achievement in a particular situation (such as the sitcom stereotype of the sexy girlfriend turning up at an inopportune moment or the sound of one's favorite music when one is trying to concentrate on a difficult task). Heroin addiction can destroy the possibility of achieving *any* major life goals, yet few present or former users would deny that the injections are intensely pleasurable (Berridge, 1999). Furthermore, whereas intrinsic-pleasantness detection provides the organism with *general* guidance on whether or not a stimulus should be approached or avoided, the goal/need-conduciveness evaluation provides the organism with information about *specific* adaptational responses or adjustments (see Scherer, 1988, 2001b).

In addition to the central dimensions of relevance and conduciveness, appraisal theorists have suggested a number of further dimensions related to the motivational domain. One dimension concerns the *probability* or *certainty* of the goal-relevant outcomes. Because it is often not the event itself but the outcome that matters to the individual, the likelihood or certainty of possible effects needs to be assessed. This is of particular importance in cases in which both the probability of the event occurring and its consequences are in doubt, as in the case of the *prospective* emotions, for example, hope and fear. But even when an event has already happened, the future consequences for the individual may be uncertain. For example, if a student fails an exam, some of the potential outcomes, such as the reaction of the parents, can only be assessed in a probabilistic fashion.

*Urgency* is another suggested dimension in the motivational domain (Frijda, 1986; Scherer, 1984, 2001a). The need for action is particularly urgent when high-priority goals or needs are in immediate danger, when it is likely that delay will make matters worse, or both. Urgency is also evaluated on a continuous scale: The more important the goals or needs and the greater the time pressure, the more urgent immediate action becomes. Urgency depends not only on the significance of an event but also on temporal contingencies and thus requires rather sophisticated contingency assessments and probability estimates.

The importance of motivational factors is related to the important adaptational function of emotion: to facilitate appropriate responses to environmental stimuli of major significance for survival and well-being. Unlike the automatism of simple reflexes, emotions provide a latency time for reevaluation of the stimulus and selection of the most promising response (see Scherer, 1984). Because the behavioral response is not automatically triggered, a risk exists that the organism will not respond at all, for example, because of indecision or intervening events. The safeguard in the emotion system against this happening is that appraisal is repeated continuously as long as the stimulus is present, physically or in active mental representation. Thus the appraisal that one's goals are threatened provides a continuous warning signal until the appraisal changes, either because the organism acts on the stimulus (e.g., removing an obstacle by subduing an opponent) and thus gets closer to the original goal, or because it reassesses the priority of goals (the literature on reactions to frustration is instructive here; see Cofer & Appley, 1964), or because it reinterprets the stimulus. Until one of these resolutions is accomplished, the stimulus event continues to engage the emotional response system.

In spite of the importance accorded to motivational antecedents of emotion, goals may not be a necessary antecedent. For example, it is not clear whether we need goals or needs to account for vicarious emotions such as pity for someone's plight, the delight of watching a kitten play, or laughing with others at a joke. Of course, one can always postulate underlying motives, such as a "need to feel with others," but that becomes dangerously close to a tautological proposal of new needs for anything not yet accounted for by other "basic" needs (a procedure which led to the demise of McDougall's instinct theory; Krantz, Hall, & Allen, 1969). Similarly, esthetic emotions, such as the emotions produced by music or art, are not easily interpretable with respect to goal conduciveness.

## Power and Coping

One of Lazarus's (1966) pioneering contributions was his insistence that emotion and stress depend not only on the evaluation of a situation's significance for our well-being (primary appraisal) but also on our assessment of our ability to deal with the situation (secondary appraisal). Appraisal is proactive, going beyond the immediate situation and assessing the probability of possible outcomes by taking into account the ability to change the situation and its consequences. The ability to cope with a stimulus event can be seen as the ability to free the emotion system from being controlled by this particular event or to reestablish a new equilibrium. This does not imply that the organism is necessarily able to reach its original goals; it may modify them, postpone them, or give them up altogether. The major function of the power or coping appraisal is to determine the appropriate response to an event, given the nature of the event and the resources at one's disposal. For example, in the case of a threat by a predator, the power or coping appraisal evokes flight if the organism is weak or powerless or fight if there is a likely chance of winning.

In evaluating one's power to deal with an event and its consequences, it is useful to know what caused the event. This is why some (but not all) appraisal theorists subsume the dimension of causation or responsibility (postulated by all appraisal theorists) under the general heading of power and control assessment. Weiner's (1985) attribution theory of emotion, developed to account for attribution in an achievement context, suggests that success and failure experiences (in addition to generating "primitive" positive and negative affect) generate distinct emotions depending on the result of causal attribution. Weiner suggested three fundamental dimensions that underlie causal attribution: (1) internal (to self) versus external (to others), (2) controllable versus uncontrollable outcomes, and (3) stable (e.g., dispositional) versus unstable (e.g., event dependent).

Like Weiner, all appraisal theorists postulate a dimension called *agency, responsibility*, or *causation* (see Table 29.1), reflecting the determination of the agent (oneself, someone else, or circumstances) and the cause (e.g., intention, chance) of the event. The attribution of agency has been shown to be particularly important in distinguishing among the negative emotions of anger (other agency), guilt (self-agency), and sorrow (circumstance agency; Ellsworth & Smith, 1988a). Several theorists postulate that, at least in the case of an animate agent, causal appraisal will include an inference about motive or intention (Michotte, 1950). Clearly, it makes a difference if someone steps on your foot by design or by mistake.

The attribution of casual agency, whether or not it is accurate, influences the organism's appraisal of its ability to deal with the event and its consequences. This dimension, postulated by all appraisal theorists, is often linked to the general notion of *controllability* or *coping ability* (see Table 29.1). Scherer (1984, 1988) has suggested distinctions among control, power, and adjustment capacity as separate aspects of coping ability. Control relates to the assessment of how well an event or its outcomes can be influenced or controlled by people, animals, or human artifacts. For example, while the behavior of a friend or the direction of an automobile is generally controllable, the weather or the incidence of a genetic disorder is usually not. Control is not the same as predictability, although it often implies predictability, particularly as far as offset of a stimulus is concerned (see Mineka & Henderson, 1985, pp. 508–509, for a detailed discussion of this point).

If the situation is controllable, the outcome depends on one's own power to exert control or to recruit others to help. Here, the organism evaluates the resources at its disposal for changing contingencies and outcomes according to its interests. Sources of power might be physical strength, money, knowledge, or social attractiveness, among others (see French & Raven, 1959). In the case of an obstructive event brought about by a conspecific aggressor or a predator, the comparison between the organism's estimate of its own power and the agent's perceived power is likely to decide between anger and fear and thus between fight and flight. In many aggressive encounters the organism vacillates between fight and flight. This may reflect the constantly changing outcomes of these power comparisons, for example, as affected by the distance from the adversary and the reactions of other group members.

The independence of control and power needs to be strongly emphasized, since these two criteria are not always clearly distinguished in the literature, where "controllability" often seems to imply both aspects (see discussions in Garber & Seligman, 1980; Miller, 1981; Öhman, 1987). Control here refers exclusively to the perception that the course of events can be influenced. Power, on the other hand, refers to the perception that the course of events can be influenced by *oneself*, possibly with the help of others. A similar distinction has been suggested by Bandura (1977) in contrasting outcome expectation (contingency between response and outcome) and efficacy expectation (assumption that one's own response can produce the desired outcome). The important work by Bandura and his associates (1977, 1982; Bandura, Reese, & Adams, 1982) on self-efficacy illustrates how the individual's appraisal of his or her power can be empirically measured and manipulated.

Finally, the adjustment evaluation concerns the organism's potential to adapt to changing conditions in the environment. This is particularly important if the control and power appraisals suggest that it is not possible for the organism to change the outcome of an event. Here, the possibility of changing goals or reducing their priority and the cost of doing this is established. Lazarus (1991) refers to this aspect of coping ability as "emotion-focused coping potential."

## Social Dimensions: Identity, Norms, Values, Justice

For the most part, the appraisals discussed so far are within the capability of many species, at least in a rudimentary fashion. This is why we have generally used the term *organism* in this chapter. Furthermore, they all concern motives, often with respect to rather basic concerns, that can exist without a social context (i.e., cases in which the attribution of agency and intentionality to another human being is an exception). If appraisal theory included only these dimensions, the criticism that it neglects the social dimension of appraisal and emotion (Kappas, 1996; Manstead & Fischer, 2001; Parkinson, 1997, 1999, 2001) might be justified. However, from its origin appraisal theory has recognized the important role of the social context of appraisal, particularly with respect to norms, values, and justice on the one hand and the self and its social identity on the other.

The underlying idea is that in socially living species it is important for an organism to take into account the reactions of other group members. Social organization depends on shared rules (norms) concerning status hierarchies, prerogatives, and acceptable and unacceptable behaviors. Such norms are sustained by appropriate emotional reactions of group members to behavior that violates norms, as well as to conforming behavior. The most severe sanction, short of actual aggression, a group can use on a norm violator is emotional avoidance, that is, excluding the individual and thus depriving him or her of the positive emotional atmosphere of group contact. Therefore, evaluating the social consequences of a particular action is an important step before finalizing the evaluation process and deciding on appropriate behavioral responses.

In consequence, several appraisal theorists have suggested dimensions such as *legitimacy, value relevance*, or *compatibility with external standards* (see Table 29.1), which are used to evaluate the compatibility of an action with the perceived norms of a salient reference group (discrepancy results, for example, in states that one could label *righteous rejection* when evaluating another person or *shame* when one's own behavior is evaluated). Anger often results when behaviors of others are judged to be in violation of social norms or salient values. In consequence, the appraisal on this "moral" dimension is a powerful factor in socialization and the maintenance of social order.

A particularly important dimension in this respect is the evaluation of *deservedness* or *justice*. Work by Mikula and his associates (Mikula, Petri, & Tanzer, 1990; Mikula, Scherer, & Athenstaedt, 1998) has shown that perceived injustice can provoke and increase the intensity of a number of different emotions, anger in particular. Appraisal theorists vacillate on whether to postulate justice or equity as a separate dimension, given their powerful effects, or to subsume them under a general dimension of moral and normative standards (see Scherer, 2001a).

Another eminently social aspect of the appraisal process is the evaluation of one's behavior with reference to the self-ideal, one's salient social identity or self-concept. This dimension, like the social-moral dimension described previously, is central for the genesis of the so-called self-reflexive emotions (see Tangney & Fischer, 1995). The individual consistently evaluates the extent to which an action falls short of or exceeds internal standards such as one's personal self-ideal (desirable attributes) or internalized moral code (obligatory conduct). Although these internal standards generally echo sociocultural values or moral standards, they can sometimes be at variance with cultural or group norms, particularly in the case of conflicting role demands or incompatibility between the norms or demands of several reference groups or persons. Discrepancy with the internal standards might lead to states often referred to as *contempt* in judging the behavior of others and as *guilt feelings* in the case of one's own behavior. Exceeding internal or external standards may produce *pride*. Markus and Kitayama (1991) have highlighted the central role of the self-concept and its cultural variation in these processes.

## Other Suggested Dimensions

The dimensions outlined herein are common to virtually all currently active appraisal theories and can be considered as the backbone of the appraisal system. Obviously, human beings evaluate events and their consequences on many other dimensions (see Frijda, 1986; Frijda, Kuipers, & ter Schure, 1989; Manstead & Fischer, 2001; Parkinson, 2001; and Reisenzein & Spielhofer, 1994, for some examples). We have described how the appraisal of control can be further refined into dimensions of controllability, power, and adjustment, and finer distinctions can undoubtedly be made for other appraisals as well. Clearly, the more dimensions one includes in trying to account for emotion differentiation, the more emotions can be explained, in an ever more subtle fashion. One drawback is a serious loss of parsimony (see Scherer, 1997a). More important, highly nuanced systems are likely to lack generality, because different individuals and cultures may elaborate the appraisal-emotion repertoire in different directions, and certain situations may also call for an elaboration of appraisals that is irrelevant to other situations.

## Predictions and Efferent Effects of Appraisal (Including Recursiveness)

As outlined previously, appraisal theorists assume that the type of emotion elicited by an event can be reliably predicted if one knows how the individual has appraised the event. The result of this appraisal process can be represented as a profile of evaluation outcomes on the basic appraisal dimensions. Several appraisal theorists have ventured theoretical predictions about the necessary and sufficient profiles for some of the basic emotions. Table 29.2 shows an illustration of this approach in the form of a simplified, generic prediction table. One relatively straightforward way to test such predictions is to ask people to recall situations in which they experienced specific emotions and to then describe the way in which they had appraised the situation, using questionnaires based on the dimensions of hypothesized appraisal (Ellsworth & Smith, 1988a, 1988b; Fitness & Fletcher, 1993; Folkman & Lazarus, 1988; Frijda, Kuipers, & ter Schure, 1989; Gehm & Scherer, 1988; Mauro, Sato, & Tucker, 1992; Reisenzein & Hofmann, 1993; Reisenzein & Spielhofer, 1994; Roseman, Antoniou, & Jose, 1996; Roseman, Spindel, & Jose, 1990; Scherer, 1993b, 1997a; Smith & Ellsworth, 1985; Smith, Haynes, Lazarus, & Pope, 1993; Tesser, 1990).

Another method is to use naturally occurring events, such as examinations, or to induce emotions experimentally and obtain verbal reports on the appraisal processes (Folkman & Lazarus, 1985; Scherer & Ceschi, 1997; Smith, 1989; Smith & Ellsworth, 1987). Or the researcher can systematically construct scenarios that correspond to the theoretically postulated appraisal profiles and ask people which emotion they would feel if they were to find themselves in that situation (Borg, Staufenbiel, & Scherer, 1988; McGraw, 1987; Roseman, 1984; Russel & McAuley, 1986; Smith, Haynes, Lazarus, & Pope, 1993; Smith & Lazarus, 1993; Stipek, Weiner, & Li, 1989; Weiner, Amirkhan, Folkes, & Verette, 1987; Weiner, Graham, & Chandler, 1982; Weiner, Russell, & Lerman, 1979). Research using all of these methods has generally supported the theoretical predictions of appraisal theorists. Using methods of regression or discriminant analysis, the set of predictor dimensions outlined here generates correct classifications for about 40–50% of the emotions studied.

The fact that often the same respondents report on both the emotions they experienced and their appraisals of the situation raises concerns of circular or tautological reasoning (Matsumoto, 1995; Parkinson, 1997, 2001). This problem is somewhat less worrisome in studies that use systematically constructed, and thus manipulated, scenarios or vignettes. However, this method may be criticized for the hypothetical or inferential nature of the emotional experiences: Responses could be more representative of social stereotypes than of actual appraisal-emotion relationships. For this reason, several appraisal theorists have attempted to predict the relation between appraisals and other indications of emotion, such as motor expression or physiological responses. These predictions are based on functional considerations, hypothesizing that appraisal outcomes should produce appropriate adaptive reactions in these modalities. For example, Scherer, in his component process theory, has suggested that each individual outcome of a stimulus evaluation check (his term for appraisal) directly affects other organismic subsystems (e.g., the somatic and autonomic nervous systems) and has presented detailed prediction tables for the effects of appraisal outcomes on facial and vocal expression, physiological responses, and behavior tendencies (Scherer, 1984, 1986a, 1987a, 1992). Smith and Ellsworth (1985) and Frijda (1986) have suggested similar links between appraisal outcomes and response patterns. Smith (1989), using electromyography (EMG) measurement, showed a significant correlation between the appraisal of anticipated effort and corrugator activity. Frijda (1986, 1987) has demonstrated associations between appraisals and action tendencies (Frijda, Kuipers, & ter Schure, 1989). In a more theoretical vein, Ortony and Turner (1990) and Roseman (2001) also argue that appraisal categories correspond to specific response patterns. Some of these predictions have been confirmed in empirical studies of vocal expression

Table 29.2  Examples of Theoretically Postulated Appraisal Profiles for Different Emotions

| Appraisal Criteria | Joy/Happiness | Anger/Rage | Fear/Panic | Sadness |
|---|---|---|---|---|
| Novelty | high | high | high | low |
| Intrinsic pleasantness | high | open | low | open |
| Goal significance | | | | |
|   Outcome probability/certainty | high | very high | high | very high |
|   Conduciveness/consistency | conducive | obstructive | obstructive | obstructive |
|   Urgency | low | high | very high | low |
| Coping Potential | | | | |
|   Agency/responsibility | self/other | other | other/nature | open |
|   Control | high | high | open | very low |
|   Power | high | high | very low | very low |
|   Adjustment | high | high | low | medium |
| Compatibility with standards/ value relevance/legitimacy | high | low | open | open |

(Banse & Scherer, 1996; Kappas, Pecchinenda, & Bherer, 1999), facial expression (Smith, 1989; Wehrle, Kaiser, Schmidt, & Scherer, 2000), and physiological responses (Banse, Etter, van Reekum, & Scherer, 1996; Kirby & Smith, 1996; Pecchinenda & Kappas, 1998; Pecchinenda & Smith, 1996; van Reekum et al., submitted).

## Comparative, Developmental, and Cultural Aspects of Appraisal

### Phylogenetic and Ontogenetic Development

Appraisal theorists explicitly claim that the differentiation of emotion is dependent on the evaluation processes described previously. This assumption has important consequences for three interesting issues: (1) the nature of emotion in different species of animals, (2) emotional development in human infants and children, and (3) cultural similarities and differences in emotion. Specifically, it implies that the complexity of the emotional reactions, and thus the emotional experience available to an organism, must be bounded by the sophistication of the cognitive abilities available to the organism. In a similar vein, Hebb (1949) very early argued for the existence of a positive correlation across species between cognitive sophistication and emotional differentiation, leading one to predict that the variety and differentiation of an organism's emotions depend on its phylogenetic or maturational stage.

So far, little attention has been paid to the comparative study of emotion in animals and humans. However, many of the emotion theorists who adopt a psychobiological approach (e.g., LeDoux, 1996; Panksepp, 1998; Plutchik, 1980; see also chapter 7, this volume), as well as proponents of evolutionary psychology (e.g., Tooby & Cosmides, 1990), suggest that there is phylogenetic continuity of emotion across species, by both homology and analogy. There is some evidence for such continuity in patterns of

facial and vocal expression (Chevalier-Skolnikoff, 1973; Hauser, 1996; Redican, 1982; Scherer, 1985; Van Hooff, 1972). In consequence, it seems entirely reasonable to consider the application of the notion of appraisal to the study of animal emotions and to use similar hypotheses to predict modal patterns of reaction or individual differences in response to similar situations (e.g., the position of an animal in the status hierarchy should confer higher coping potential). Obviously, nonverbal techniques of assessing appraisal (discussed later in the chapter) will be required to study such predictions empirically.

With respect to ontogenesis, Scherer (1984) has suggested that a child's capacity for differentiated emotional reactions should depend on his or her current stage of cognitive maturation, which limits the complexity of available appraisal processes. In recent years, several cognitive developmental theorists have suggested that cognitive and emotional maturation go hand in hand and may be mutually dependent (Case, 1991; Case, Hayward, Lewis, & Hurst, 1988; Fischer, Shaver, & Carnochan, 1990; Mascolo & Fischer, 1995; Sroufe, 1996). Many of these suggestions are highly commensurate with appraisal theory. Based on empirical observations of the onset of different emotions in children, Scherer (1982) has made specific predictions concerning the links between the age of onset of the emotions in infants and children (as inferred from studies in this area, particularly those using facial expressions) and the cognitive capacity of the child, suggesting that the cognitively more complex dimensions will need to be evaluated only for emotions that are observed fairly late in development (see Scherer, Zentner, & Stern, 2001, for an attempt to empirically test this notion). It should be noted, however, that appraisal can occur at several levels of processing (Leventhal & Scherer, 1987; Teasdale, 1999; van Reekum & Scherer, 1997; see also chapter 33, this volume) and that infants and young children may rely to a large extent on the sensorimotor or schematic levels rather than the conceptual level of appraisal.

## Individual Differences

Appraisal theorists claim that appraisal involves people's subjective perception of events rather than their objective characteristics and that the resulting emotion is determined by this subjective interpretation. The empirical confirmation of this underlying assumption would require a systematic assessment of individual differences in appraising similar events and the differences observed in the resulting emotions. However, so far there has been little research to identify the *stable* individual traits that might predispose persons to show systematic appraisal tendencies or even biases in the appraisal process.

On a theoretical level, van Reekum and Scherer (1997) have reviewed some of the individual difference factors that are likely to systematically affect appraisal. They suggest that appraisal may differ among individuals with respect to process characteristics such as speed, thoroughness, or completeness, degree of cognitive effort, or the relative complexity of the analysis, that is, gross versus more fine-grained appraisal. Further individual differences could exist for vigilance, that is, the detection of events that are marginally pertinent to an individual, the nature of the attention deployment strategies used, and the differential use of levels of processing. These authors further suggest that there may exist appraisal biases with respect to content, such as slow habituation and lack of inhibition in evaluating novelty, differences in the tuning of valence detectors for the evaluation of intrinsic pleasantness, and differences in the intensity of motivational striving that affect the evaluation of goal conduciveness, as well as differential ability to evaluate consequences of and establish links between events, resulting either in overassimilation and overgeneralization or in lack of concern or caring (e.g., the frontal lobe lesion syndromes described by Damasio, 1994). Personality traits such as optimism-pessimism, external-internal control, self-assurance, or self-efficacy may also play an important role, particularly for the appraisal of coping potential. As to the evaluation of individual and social standards, systematic differences can be expected for moral and ethical norms. As potential sources for individual differences in appraisal tendencies, Van Reekum and Scherer (1997) identify predispositions such as innate characteristics of the central nervous system (CNS) and/or autonomic nervous system (ANS), cognitive styles (e.g., holistic vs. analytic processing, field dependence, cognitive complexity, need for cognition, disposition to engage in effortful cognitive processing), and personality traits (e.g., extroversion, repression-sensitization, neuroticism, rigidity, dysphoria, worrying, sensation-seeking, or openness).

It can be expected that individuals who differ on these dimensions are likely to evaluate events differently and consequently to experience different emotions. While most of these differences may produce emotional reactions that remain within the limits of what is considered as appropriate, some individual differences or appraisal biases may be associated with affective disturbance. Scherer (1987b) suggested that different types of emotional disorders can be categorized on the basis of appraisal malfunctioning. While appraisal is subjective and may vary from individual to individual, it must bear a reasonable relationship to the objective situation (e.g., through reality testing) and to the coping potential that is within the individual's means. Violation of these appraisal reality constraints, as one might call them, will lead to abnormal or disordered emotion. For example, Scherer (1987a) proposed that one particular form of depression, helplessness, might be partly due to a consistent underestimation of one's coping potential. Similar descriptions for potential appraisal biases characterizing different types of affective disturbances can be easily derived (see Alloy & Abramson, 1979; Beck, 1967; Kaiser & Scherer, 1997; Roseman & Kaiser, 2001; Scherer, 1987a; Seligman, 1975). Whether these are mainly symptoms or have a part in the etiology of the disease remains to be established by future research.

## Cultural Differences

According to appraisal theories, emotions and appraisals of events are likely to be culturally variable, but the relationship between appraisals and emotions is culturally general, perhaps even universal. This is the hypothesis of universal contingencies (Ellsworth, 1994b; Scherer, 1997a, 1997b): If people from different cultures appraise a situation in the same way, they will experience the same emotion. If they experience a different emotion, it is because they have appraised the situation differently. What is universal is the link between appraisal patterns and emotions—the if-then contingency. For example, appraisal theories predict that people everywhere will feel angry when they believe that another person has harmed them, though their beliefs about the kinds of harm that can be caused by other people, and even their definitions of "harm" may vary. Goals, values, and tastes can vary enormously across cultures, creating manifest and important differences in the *content* of emotional experience. According to appraisal theories the *process* remains the same: The appraisal of *goal conduciveness* has the same emotional consequences across cultures, regardless of cultural differences in the definition of what's worth striving for.

The universal contingency hypothesis does not imply universality of either the events that elicit emotions or of the emotions themselves. In some cultures the sight of a woman wearing shorts may elicit revulsion; in others, revulsion may be elicited by the sight of a woman being whipped because she is wearing shorts. Certain combinations of appraisals may be common in some cultures, rare in others, and perhaps even absent in some, and the corresponding emotion will likewise be common, rare, or absent in those cultures. For example, in the United States, positive valence and a sense of high personal agency tend to co-occur, so that pride and a sense of high self-esteem are common (Kitayama, Markus, Matsumoto, & Norasakkunkit, 1997), whereas in other cultures agency attributions may generally be more mixed or ambiguous (cf. Matsumoto, Kudoh, Scherer, & Wallbott, 1988), so that unadulterated personal pride is less common. It is appraisal-emotion association that is assumed to be universal.

The hypothesis of universal contingency has received support from a number of cross-cultural studies, although so far there is not much research. Typically respondents are asked to remember times when they experienced particular emotions, and then to answer questions about how they appraised these emotional situations (Frijda, Markam, Sato, & Wiers, 1995; Haidt, Koller, & Dias, 1993; Mauro, Sato, & Tucker, 1992; Mesquita & Ellsworth, 2001; Roseman, Dhawan, Rettek, Naidu, & Thapa, 1995; Scherer, 1997a, 1997b). The research generally supports the hypothesis of universal contingency. Scherer (1997b) found that joy, fear, anger, sadness, disgust, shame, and guilt were characterized by similar appraisal patterns in 37 countries. Joyful situations were appraised as pleasant, expected, self-esteem enhancing, and requiring no action; fear situations were unpleasant, obstructing goals, and hard to cope with; anger situations were unpleasant, unexpected, obstructing goals, unfair, and caused by other people.

In general, the evidence supports the hypothesis of a cross-culturally similar experiential core of "equivalent" emotions, characterized by similar appraisals, but most researchers have also found cultural differences in the appraisal-emotion relationship. Scherer (1997b) found that people in African countries appraised negative emotions as more immoral, unfair, and externally caused, whereas those in Latin American countries appraised events leading to emotional situations as less immoral than respondents in other parts of the world. Mauro et al. (1992) found that the United States and three Asian cultures differed from each other in perceptions of the contributions made by effort, control, and responsibility to emotions (see also Roseman, Dhawan, Retteck, Naidu, & Thapa, 1995). Markus and Kitayama (1991) proposed that "interpersonal engagement" was an important appraisal dimension in Japan, although absent from (Western) appraisal theories.

These cultural differences remain largely unexplained (and unreplicated) so far. Appraisal theory is not a theory about cultural differences, and so explanations must come from collaboration with cultural experts. There are several possibilities, all interesting: Cultural differences may be due to the absence of an appraisal dimension proposed by the theorists, or to the existence of additional culture-specific appraisal dimensions, or to the presence or absence of certain combinations of appraisals in the same multidimensional space, or to all three. Some emotions

may be considered desirable or unacceptable in some cultures, so that their experience always involves a set of secondary appraisals and emotions that increase the complexity of the experience; the same may be true of some appraisals, for example, personal responsibility (Mesquita & Ellsworth, 2001). At the moment, there are many more questions than answers, and the role of culture in appraisal is a provocative area for future research.

## Problems (Real and Imaginary)

Appraisal theories have developed over the years. Both their possibilities and their problems are now more apparent. As they have become more widely known, they have inevitably become more widely criticized. Some of these criticisms reflect a misunderstanding of the theories, and we will deal with these first before going on to the more difficult problems.

### Appraisal Theories Are Too Cold, Cognitive, Conscious, and Slow

The most frequent criticism in the literature is that the emotion process as described by appraisal theories is too cold, cognitive, conscious, and slow. Some critics accuse appraisal theories of equating emotional experience with conscious, cortical, deliberate thought: The appraisal researchers "assume that the kind of information that subjects use when they reflect back on an emotional experience is the same kind of information that the brain uses in creating that experience" (LeDoux, 1996, p. 52). At times these critics claim that appraisal theorists maintain that people are conscious not only of the appraisal process but also of the *basis* of the appraisal. At times they claim that appraisal theorists believe that emotions are nothing but collections of beliefs.

Appraisal theorists saw themselves as adding cognitions to the emotional mix, not as replacing the other, generally accepted components. They do not see their theories as incompatible with subcortical processing, autonomic responses, expressive responses, or action tendencies. Their goal was to bring the eliciting circumstances into the picture, and their assumption was that the emotional meaning of circumstances is inevitably mediated by the perceiver's interpretation of those circumstances.

In retrospect, the use of the term *cognitive* in some of the early publications of the appraisal theorists (Lazarus, Averill, & Opton, 1970; Roseman, 1984; Smith & Ellsworth, 1985) may have created a misleading impression, suggesting that the appraisals were verbal, propositional, conscious, or deliberate. The term *cognitive* was probably chosen by researchers in the 1980s partly to differentiate themselves from a concurrent proposal that emotional differentiation was produced by feedback from the facial muscles (Izard, 1971; Laird, 1974; Tomkins, 1962) and partly in response to Zajonc's claim that affective responses to a stimulus precede cognitive evaluations of the stimulus (Zajonc, 1980; Zajonc & Markus, 1984).

Even a cursory examination of the actual appraisals common to appraisal theories makes it clear that they are not all cold, logical, verbalized cognitive evaluations. The very first appraisal, in most theories, is attention or novelty. Something changes in the environment, and the organism notices and orients toward the novel stimulus. This is not a cold verbal evaluation that "there is something new out there." It involves subcortical and cortical processing (Posner, 1992; Posner & Petersen, 1990), autonomic changes (e.g., slowed heartbeat), a change in facial expression—often to one of watchful anticipation—and an action tendency (orienting response). In many situations it occurs nearly simultaneously with another appraisal—intrinsic pleasantness, valence, or, in Zajonc's terms (1980), "preference." In some situations, such as the subliminal stimulus presentations used by Zajonc, valence may be elicited without attention. Valence may also be accompanied by subcortical (and often but not necessarily cortical) changes, autonomic changes, changes in facial muscle movements, and action tendencies (approach or avoidance). Again, there is no requirement in appraisal theory that the person should say, "I think this is a good thing."

Thus appraisals are not cold, and appraisal theories do not claim that emotions are nothing more than a combination of cognitions, because the appraisals themselves have physiological and experiential correlates which are also part of the emotional experience. They are not cognitive if the term *cognitive* is taken to imply propositional representation or deliberation. Appraisals may take this form, but they may also occur subcortically and automatically, as described previously.

Finally, the appraisal need not be conscious or felt as a separate phenomenon. It is important here to distinguish several types of consciousness, which have often been confused in the literature. First, Zajonc (1980), for example, argued that one could have an affective response without recognizing the *stimulus*, without consciousness of the stimulus object. Appraisal theories do not require that a stimulus must be recognized before an emotional response can occur or before a simple appraisal of pleasantness can be made, as in Zajonc's research.

Second, a person might be aware or unaware of the *separate appraisals*. If a person interrupts us, or cuts ahead in line, or speeds by us to take the last parking space in the lot, our attention is engaged, and we appraise the situation as unpleasant, our efforts to reach our goal thwarted, and the other person as responsible. These appraisals seem to occur automatically and are not experienced separately as appraisals: What we experience is *anger*. Emotion is defined by appraisal theorists as a combination of appraisals (and their correlates), but that does not mean that it is *experienced* as a combination of appraisals. In the usual situation, as Frijda argued in 1986, "One knows, generally, that one has an emotion; one does not always know why, and what exactly makes one have it; and if one does know, it is a construction, a hypothesis, like those one makes about the emotion of someone else" (1986, p. 464). Sometimes, for example in slow-developing or ambiguous situations, one may be aware of the separate appraisals, but awareness is not a necessary feature of the theory.

Most appraisal theorists would probably agree with Frijda that "one knows, generally, that one has an *emotion*," and they have reserved the vexing question of unconscious emotions for future exploration. Although many appraisal theorists may in fact be agnostic on the question of unconscious emotions, their initial goal was to account for the person's subjective experience of emotion at the time it is felt.

It should be clear by now that even though a fully developed emotion may involve a dozen or more appraisals and subappraisals, the process need not be a slow, sequential series of interpretations, each completed before the next begins, and in fact it very rarely is. Scherer (1999a) refers to this criticism as reflecting a "cranking-cogwheel" picture of appraisal and points out that "given the massively parallel architecture of cognitive appraisal, the entire process can take milliseconds," particularly in familiar situations such as that of the inconsiderate boor who steals your speaking time, place in line, or parking space. Many emotional situations involve familiar scripts and may elicit bundles of interrelated appraisals. The first time a person ever cut ahead of you in line, the appraisal process probably took longer.

### The Theory and the Method

Many of the criticisms of appraisal theories may reflect a fundamental confusion between the theory itself and the methods used to test it. Even now, and especially in the initial empirical research on appraisal theory, most of the studies involved verbal reports of remembered emotional experiences (Folkman & Lazarus, 1988; Frijda, Kuipers, & ter Schure, 1989; Gehm & Scherer, 1988; Smith & Ellsworth, 1985). The initial goal of the appraisal theorists was to discover whether combinations of a limited number of different appraisals would be sufficient to differentiate among a much larger number of emotions—whether different emotions were characterized by distinctive appraisal profiles. In order to study all of the proposed appraisal dimensions at once, so that their large number of combinations could be compared, verbal measures seemed like the only choice at the time. Although some appraisals, such as attention and valence, might be measurable nonverbally, others, such as the perception of responsibility or conformity with social norms, do not yet have recognized nonverbal correlates, and it seemed important to use the same method to measure all of the appraisals. The choice of this method did *not* rest on the assumption that the appraisals were verbalized or even verbalizable at the time of the original emotion but on the failure to come up with any other method that might provide an efficient test of such complicated models.

Nonetheless, the heavy reliance on verbal techniques seems to have misled some scholars about the nature of the theory itself. LeDoux, for example, begins by criticizing appraisal theories for "bas[ing] their understanding of appraisal processes largely on self-reports" (1996, p. 52) and, by degrees, comes to the conclusion that "appraisal theories did not quite get it right, as they required that the appraisal mechanism get all involved in introspectively accessible levels of higher cognition from the start" (1996, p. 64). The weaknesses of the method are genuine weaknesses, but they should not lead to the conclusion that there are analogous weaknesses in the theory. Historically, theories of emotion have often been far more subtle and complex than the methods available to test them.

Still, as a method, self-report has obvious drawbacks, and its prevalence in the study of appraisal and emotion has generated substantial criticism, both from critics of appraisal theories and from appraisal theorists themselves (Frijda, 1993; Lazarus, 1995; Parkinson, 1996; Parkinson & Manstead, 1992, 1993). Empirical tests of appraisal theories have not always relied on verbal reports of recalled memories (see the later discussion of alternative methods). However, many of the other methods also require conscious inferences about the appraisal-emotion relationship—participants either begin with the emotions and are asked about the corresponding appraisals or are given the appraisals and asked about the corresponding emotions. Verbal questions tell the participant what the investigator cares about and thus may encourage socially desirable, "rational," or "normal" answers (Aronson, Ellsworth, Carlsmith, & Gonzales, 1990; Schwarz, Groves, & Schuman, 1998). Verbal questions about *why* the person felt a particular emotion may ask for information about processes that the person cannot access, prompting the person to rely on "common knowledge" to generate a plausible answer on the spot (Nisbett & Wilson, 1977). Appraisal theorists rarely ask participants simply to explain why they felt the emotion (as Nisbett and Wilson did in several of their studies); instead they ask more specific questions: "Was it good or bad?" "To what extent was it caused by something you did?" These specific questions have the advantage of drawing people away from cultural stereotypes; however, they have the corresponding disadvantage of drawing them toward the hypotheses of the appraisal theorists. It is important to point out, however, that in the early studies the participants' responses sometimes did not correspond to the theorists' expectations, and the

theories were revised (Smith & Ellsworth, 1985). Also, the appraisal dimensions generated by participants who were simply asked to describe emotions were somewhat different (and possibly more reflective of cultural stereotypes) than the dimensions generated by participants who were asked to remember an actual emotional experience (Ellsworth & Smith, unpublished ms., 1986).

Finally, there *have* been a few studies in which the measures are nonverbal. Smith (1989) showed that appraisals of effort corresponded to responses of the corrugator muscle, and he and his colleagues have made progress in linking other appraisals to facial, vocal, and physiological responses (Kappas, Pecchinenda, & Bherer, 1999; Kirby & Smith, 1996; Pecchinenda & Kappas, 1998; Pecchinenda & Smith, 1996). Scherer has explored links between appraisals and both vocal (Banse & Scherer, 1996) and facial (Wehrle, Kaiser, Schmidt, & Scherer, 2000) expression, and both Kappas and Scherer and their colleagues, manipulating appraisals by varying the events in computer games, have measured a variety of physiological, facial, and vocal responses, in addition to verbal descriptions (Banse, Etter, van Reekum, & Scherer, 1996; Kaiser & Wehrle, 1996; Kappas & Pecchinenda, 1999; van Reekum et al., 2001; van Reekum, Johnstone, & Scherer, 1997). Kubzansky and Ellsworth (1999) used speech hesitations as an indicator of uncertainty.

It is obvious that exclusive reliance on self-report measures leaves many questions unanswered, including the fundamental question of whether the reports reflect the actual experience or a later reconstruction. The addition of nonverbal measures is an important step, and one that should be encouraged and expanded. The substitution of nonverbal for verbal measures, however, is not advisable, as nonverbal measures raise different problems. First, diagnostic nonverbal indicators of specific emotions are rare and, except for facial muscle movements (the nonverbal indicator most subject to conscious control; Ekman, 1984), capable of far less subtle variation than language. Diagnostic nonverbal indicators of appraisals are even less common, and for some appraisals, such as attributions of agency or perceptions of compatibility with social norms, none have even been suggested. Second, many nonverbal measures, especially behavioral measures, have multiple meanings, and thus the evidence they provide for the existence of a corresponding appraisal is typically suggestive rather than definitive. Checking a 6 on a 7-point scale of uncertainty has more face validity than a sudden increase in speech hesitations; thus, although the use of novel nonverbal methods has obvious benefits for the theory as a whole, it may lessen the persuasiveness of any particular study.

In the future the development of new methods and the use of multiple methods (not necessarily in every study but in the field as a whole) are centrally important (see Scherer, 1993a). We should recognize, however, that the value of any given method may not be the same for all appraisals: Attention, for example, may be better assessed nonverbally than verbally, whereas attributions of agency may be more reliably assessed with verbal measures. There is no reason to assume that the same measures will work equally well for all appraisals.

## Theoretical Issues

Although appraisal theory has been doing rather well in explaining many aspects of emotion, there are some phenomena that may challenge its generality. First, many people report feeling emotions in response to instrumental music, a problem discussed by Ellsworth (1994c) and one which leads Elster to conclude that "it strains belief to argue that the feeling . . . simply *is* the pleasurable perception of arousal, action tendency, etc." (1999, p. 28); instead there is a unique emotional *quale* or "feel" which is more than, or different from, the sum of its parts. Elster adduces brain stimulation and chemical inductions as additional evidence, but these are less problematical, as brain stimulation and chemical inductions can induce all manner of mental phenomena, perhaps by mimicking the central nervous system correlates of the naturally induced versions. Visual images, auditory perceptions, and memories can all be stimulated artificially and do not lead us to doubt our usual theories of information processing in these systems. Music is different, because there *is* an external stimulus, and, aside from novelty and valence, the usual appraisal dimensions do not seem relevant. Novelty and valence are relevant, but they are insufficient to account for the complex emotions many people feel when they listen to music (Budd, 1995). Perhaps musical rhythms and phrases create physiological responses that mimic the physiological and noncognitive aspects of appraisals and emotions, so that, by association, the emotion itself is elicited. In any case, neither appraisal theory nor any other current emotion theory can easily accommodate emotional responses to music (see Scherer & Zentner, 2001, for different *production rules*).

Although there has been little research on Solomon's (1980) opponent process theory of emotion in recent years, strong evidence for this theory would also be troublesome for appraisal theorists. According to Solomon's theory, the termination of one emotion triggers the opposite emotion automatically, without new appraisals. The rebound is more than a homeostatic return to baseline: It is an actual stimulus for a different emotion, and the rebound emotion becomes greater after many trials. There is very little controlled laboratory research on this phenomenon in humans, especially research that rules out reappraisals (but see Mauro, 1988), but if the phenomenon proves to be robust, it poses a challenge to appraisal theories.

There are also emotions, or emotion-like phenomena, that have been avoided by appraisal theories (and by most

of the rival theories). Love and desire are conspicuous examples. *Love* is usually set aside as a term that embraces too many different feelings—love of a parent for a child, a child for a parent, a lover for a lover, an unrequited lover for a lover, an owner for a pet, a patriot for a country. But this dismissal is not entirely satisfactory, as most theories of emotion, including appraisal theories, do not deal with *any* of the varieties of love. Desire also has many emotion-like qualities and has often been set aside as some lower drive, like hunger. But research by Robinson and Berridge (1993) on addiction suggests that "wanting" is not the same as "liking" (or valence), that a stimulus can demand attention and exert a powerful attraction without being seen as positive (Robinson & Berridge, 1993). Appraisal theories which make a distinction between intrinsic pleasantness and goal conduciveness may hold promise for dealing with the emotions involved in addictive cravings; but Robinson and Berridge (1993) argue that in some cases neither intrinsic pleasantness nor goal conduciveness exists, yet still the addict desperately craves the experience. It would be easy to simply dismiss addictions as "beyond the scope of the theory," but to do so would also be somewhat evasive and artificial. It would be preferable to at least consider these emotions as special cases, involving special appraisal dimensions or relations.

Another problem is that appraisal theories do not match intuitions. Folk theories generally favor the categorical point of view. Fear, anger, and grief are categories that come naturally to people and that seem to have considerable cross-cultural generality (Russell, 1991; Shaver, Wu, & Schwartz, 1992). In experiments, results often show stronger effects for emotion ratings than for appraisal ratings (Tiedens, Ellsworth, & Mesquita, 2000). Of course the mismatch between folk theories and scientific theories is no reason to reject the scientific theories. Black, white, and red are also categories that come naturally to people and that have enormous cross-cultural generality (Berlin & Kay, 1969), but we do not feel that this challenges the scientific view that brightness and wavelength are continuous or that the rods and the cones make different appraisals of light. Still, the fact that, among the infinity of emotions conceivable by appraisal theories, certain ones seem much more salient and available than others and that there is even some cross-cultural generality (although also considerable variability) in these, raises interesting questions. What role does language play? That is, are nameable emotions experienced more commonly than unnamed states? More cross-cultural work on emotions in relation to local emotion words is needed. Do certain appraisals tend to occur together, independent of language? For example, can we imagine positive valence combined with many goal obstacles? Yes—for example, the hour before an important test or contest—but it is rare. Can we imagine a great and certain loss, like the death of a loved one, combined with a high sense of power? Even less likely. Although appraisal theories generally envision a vast multidimensional space in which an infinity of named and unnamed emotional states exists, there still may be magnetic regions in this space, perhaps named regions, that attract ambiguous emotions and are salient in folk psychology (cf. Lewis & Granic, 1999).

Finally, the idea that appraisals can occur at different levels, from the sensorimotor to the conceptual, raises as many questions as it answers, forcing us to attend to the relationships among processes at these different levels. If valence can be registered unconsciously, how does that process relate to the conscious perception of valence? Is it the same process, but communicated to the cortex, and, if so, why is it sometimes communicated and sometimes not? Is it a different process, and, if so, what is the relationship between processes? The same questions could be asked about other appraisals, and indeed about the combinations of appraisals we label "emotions." How do "learned" emotions, such as disgust at the thought of eating pork, come to trigger apparently "innate" mechanisms, such as nausea? These problems are not fatal flaws. They are, however frustrating, opportunities, because they force as to consider new questions, questions that would have been harder to formulate before appraisal theory, questions that will push our thoughts in new directions.

## Summary and Outlook

This chapter has provided a general overview of the way in which appraisal theorists attempt to explain the elicitation and differentiation of emotion processes and of the problems encountered by this approach. We have given preference to the treatment of conceptual issues that may be of interest to researchers in the affective sciences rather than discussing the empirical data generated by this vigorous research tradition. This information can be found in the comprehensive volume edited by Scherer, Schoor, and Johnstone (2001), which surveys theories, methods, and, in particular, empirical findings, with contributions by most major appraisal theorists.

Judging by the achievements in its brief history as a testable theory rather than a philosophical presupposition, appraisal theory has been quite successful. It has succeeded in raising hard questions which had hitherto been ignored or muddled, and that is one of the hallmarks of a useful theory. One of its advantages, apart from a strong convergence of opinion between different theorists, is its capacity to synthesize theoretical input from many areas of psychology—cognitive psychology, neurophysiological social psychology, social psychology—so that emotion can be considered as the truly interdisciplinary phenomenon it is. Another advantage is its capacity to generate empirical research, both inside and outside of the laboratory. Chances are, then, that this tradition of work can usefully

contribute to further theorizing and research in the affective sciences.

## NOTES

1. Scherer (1984) has argued that we can feel as many different emotions as there are reliably differentiated appraisal outcomes. He proposes to call the emotions for which cultures provide distinctive labels in their respective languages *modal* emotions (Scherer, 1994), suggesting that the underlying appraisal profiles occur disproportionally frequently.

2. This does not exclude the possibility of mapping a more complex emotion categorization onto a simpler two-dimensional space with respect to one of the components of emotion, subjective experience, or feeling (see Scherer, 2001a).

3. This is the view that is generally attributed to appraisal theory by its critics, and appraisal theorists have been criticized for failing to demonstrate experimentally that appraisals play a *causal* role in generating emotions.

4. Scherer (1984) has suggested viewing feelings as a monitoring instance that reflects the appraisal process and the reactions produced by its results.

5. For example, in summarizing the findings on emotion-eliciting situations from a study of emotional experience in several European countries, Scherer (1986b) distinguished three major types of motives or concerns: person concerns (survival, bodily integrity, fulfillment of basic needs, self-esteem), relationship concerns (establishment, continued existence and intactness of relationships, cohesiveness within social groups), and social-order concerns (sense of orderliness and predictability in the social environment, including phenomena such as fairness and appropriateness). The findings showed that the different emotions were not evenly distributed across these three classes of basic concerns. Person concerns, such as physical welfare and self-esteem, produce mainly joy and fear, depending on whether the goals concerned have been attained. Relationship needs lead to joy or sadness experiences, depending on how well things go in the relationship or group. Social-order concerns are often at the root of anger emotions, particularly in cases in which the social order is disrupted by inappropriate, norm-violating, or unjust behavior (see Kulik & Brown, 1979, for an experimental demonstration).

## REFERENCES

Abelson, R. P. (1983). Whatever became of consistency theory? *Personality and Social Psychology Bulletin, 9*, 37–54.

Alloy, L. B., & Abramson, L. Y. (1979). Judgment of contingency in depressed and nondepressed students: Sadder but wiser? *Journal of Experimental Psychology: General, 108*, 441–485.

Arnold, M. B. (1960). *Emotion and personality: Vol. 1. Psychological aspects.* New York: Columbia University Press.

Aronson, E., Ellsworth, P. C., Carlsmith, J. M., & Gonzales, M. H. (1990). *Methods of research in social psychology* (2nd ed.). New York: McGraw-Hill.

Austin, J. T., & Vancouver, J. B. (1996). Goal constructs in psychology: Structure, process, and content. *Psychological Bulletin, 120*(3), 338–375.

Bandura, A. (1977). Self-efficacy: Toward a unifying theory of behavioral change. *Psychological Review, 84,* 191–215.

Bandura, A. (1982). Self-efficacy mechanisms in human agency. *American Psychologist, 37,* 122–147.

Bandura, A., Reese, L., & Adams, N. E. (1982). Microanalysis of action and fear arousal as a function of differential levels of perceived self-efficacy. *Journal of Personality and Social Psychology, 43,* 5–21.

Banse, R., Etter, A., Van Reekum, C., & Scherer, K. R. (1996, October). Psychophysiological responses to emotion-antecedent appraisal of critical events in a computer game. Poster presented at the annual meeting of the Society for Psychophysiological Research, Vancouver, Canada.

Banse, R., & Scherer, K. R. (1996). Acoustic profiles in vocal emotion expression. *Journal of Personality and Social Psychology, 70*(3), 614–636.

Bargh, J. A. (1984). Automatic and conscious processing of social information. In R. S. Wyer, Jr., & T. K. Srull (Eds.), *Handbook of social cognition* (Vol. 3, pp. 1–44). Hillsdale, NJ: Erlbaum.

Barry, R. J. (1996). Preliminary process theory: Towards an integrated account of the psychophysiology of cognitive processes. *Acta Neurobiologiae Experimentalis, 56*(1), 469–484.

Beck, A. T. (1967). *Depression: Clinical, experimental and theoretical aspects.* New York: Harper & Row.

Berlin, B. O., & Kay, P. D. (1969) *Basic color terms.* Berkeley: University of California Press.

Berlyne, D. E. (1960). *Conflict, arousal and curiosity.* New York: McGraw-Hill.

Berlyne, D. E., & Madsen, K. B. (1973). *Pleasure, reward, and preference. Their nature, determinants and role in behavior.* New York: Academic Press.

Bernstein, A. S. (1981). The orienting response and stimulus significance: Further comments. *Biological Psychology, 12,* 171–185.

Berridge, K. C. (1999). Pleasure, pain, desire, and dread: Hidden core processes of emotion. In D. Kahneman, E. Diener, & N. Schwarz (Eds.), *Well-being: The foundations of hedonic psychology* (pp. 525–557). New York: Russell Sage Foundation.

Borg, I., Staufenbiel, T., & Scherer, K. R. (1988). On the symbolic basis of shame. In K. R. Scherer (Ed.), *Facets of emotion: Recent research* (pp. 79–98). Hillsdale, NJ: Erlbaum.

Bradley, M. M., & Lang, P. J. (1994). Measuring emotion: The Self-Assessment Manikin and the semantic differential. *Journal of Behavior Therapy and Experimental Psychiatry, 25*(1), 49–59.

Budd, M. (1995). *Values of art.* London: Allen Lane.

Case, R. (1991). *The mind's staircase.* Hillsdale, NJ: Erlbaum.

Case, R., Hayward, S., Lewis, M., & Hurst, P. (1988). Toward a neo-Piagetian theory of cognitive and emotional development. *Developmental Review, 8,* 1–51.

Chevalier-Skolnikoff, S. (1973). Facial expressions of emotions in non-human primates. In P. Ekman (Ed.), *Darwin and facial expression: A century of research in review.* New York: Academic Press.

Cofer, C. N., & Appley, M. H. (1964). *Motivation: Theory and research.* New York: Wiley.

Damasio, A. R. (1994). *Descartes' error: Emotion, reason, and the human brain.* New York: Avon Books.

De Rivera, J. (1977). A structural theory of the emotions. *Psychological Issues, 10* (4, Monograph No. 40).

Eibl-Eibesfeldt, I. (1979). Human ethology: Concepts and implications for the sciences of man. *Behavioral and Brain Sciences, 2,* 1–57.

Ekman, P. (1972). Universals and cultural differences in facial expressions of emotions. In J. Cole (Ed.), *Nebraska Symposium on Motivation* (pp. 207–283). Lincoln: University of Nebraska Press.

Ekman, P. (1984). Expression and the nature of emotion. In K. R. Scherer & P. Ekman (Eds.), *Approaches to emotion* (pp. 319–344). Hillsdale, NJ: Erlbaum.

Ekman, P. (1992). An argument for basic emotions. *Cognition and Emotion, 6*(3–4), 169–200.

Ellsworth, P. C. (1991). Some implications of cognitive appraisal theories of emotion. In K. Strongman (Ed.), *International review of studies on emotion* (pp. 143–161). New York: Wiley.

Ellsworth, P. C. (1994a). William James and emotion: Is a century of fame worth a century of misunderstanding? *Psychological Review, 101,* 222–229.

Ellsworth, P. C. (1994b). Sense, culture and sensibility. In S. Kitayama & M. R. Markus (Eds.), *Emotion and culture: Empirical studies of mutual influence* (pp. 23–50). Washington, DC: American Psychological Association.

Ellsworth, P. C. (1994c). Levels of thought and levels of emotion. In P. Ekman, & R. J. Davidson (Eds.), *The nature of emotion: Fundamental questions* (pp. 192–196). New York: Oxford University Press.

Ellsworth, P. C. (1997, April). Chinese and American emotional responses to basic social situations. Paper presented at the Fifth Geneva Emotion Week, Geneva, Switzerland.

Ellsworth, P. C., & Smith, C. A. (1986). Models and memories of emotion: A comparison of their associated appraisals and facial expressions. Unpublished manuscript, University of Michigan.

Ellsworth, P. C., & Smith, C. A. (1988a). Shades of joy: Patterns of appraisal differentiating pleasant emotions. *Cognition and Emotion, 2,* 301–331.

Ellsworth, P. C., & Smith, C. A. (1988b). From appraisal to emotion: Differences among unpleasant feelings. *Motivation and Emotion, 12,* 271–302.

Elster, J. (1999). *Strong feelings.* Cambridge, MA: MIT Press.

Engen, T., Lipsitt, L. P., & Kaye, H. (1963). Olfactory responses and adaptation in the human neonate. *Journal of Comparative and Physiological Psychology, 56,* 73–77.

Fischer, K. W., Shaver, P. R., & Carnochan, P. (1990). How emotions develop and how they organise development. *Cognition and Emotion, 4*(2), 81–127.

Fitness, J., & Fletcher, G. J. O. (1993). Love, hate, anger, and jealousy in close relationships: A prototype and cognitive appraisal analysis. *Journal of Personality and Social Psychology, 65,* 942–958.

Folkman, S., & Lazarus, R. S. (1985). If it changes it must be a process: Study of emotion and coping during three stages of a college examination. *Journal of Personality and Social Psychology, 48,* 150–170.

Folkman, S., & Lazarus, R. S. (1988). Coping as a mediator of emotion. *Journal of Personality and Social Psychology, 54,* 466–475.

French, J. R. P., Jr., & Raven, B. H. (1959). The bases of social power. In D. Cartwright (Ed.), *Studies in social power* (pp. 150–167). Ann Arbor: University of Michigan Press.

Frijda, N. H. (1986). *The emotions.* Cambridge, England: Cambridge University Press.

Frijda, N. H. (1987). Emotion, cognitive structure, and action tendency. *Cognition and Emotion, 1*, 115–143.

Frijda, N. H. (1993). The place of appraisal in emotion. *Cognition and Emotion, 7*, 357–387.

Frijda, N. H., Kuipers, P., & ter Schure, E. (1989). Relations among emotion, appraisal, and emotional action readiness. *Journal of Personality and Social Psychology, 57*, 212–228.

Frijda, N. H., Markam, S., Sato, K., & Wiers, R. (1995). Emotions and emotion words. In J. A. Russell, A. S. R. Manstead, J. C. Wellenkamp, & J. M. Fernandez-Dols (Eds.), *Everyday conception of emotions* (pp. 121–143). Dordrecht, The Netherlands: Kluwer Academic.

Frijda, N. H., & Zelenberg, M. (2001). Appraisal: What is the dependent? In K. R. Scherer, A. Schorr, & T. Johnstone (Eds.), *Appraisal processes in emotion: Theory, methods, research* (pp. 141–155). New York: Oxford University Press.

Garber, J., & Seligman, M. E. P. (Eds.). (1980). *Human helplessness: Theory and applications.* New York: Academic Press.

Gardiner, H. M., Clark-Metcalf, R. C., & Beebe-Center, J. G. (1980). *Feeling and emotion: A history of theories.* New York: American Book (Original work published 1937).

Gehm, T. L., & Scherer, K. R. (1988). Relating situation evaluation to emotion differentiation: Nonmetric analysis of cross-cultural questionnaire data. In K. R. Scherer (Ed.), *Facets of emotion: Recent research* (pp. 61–78). Hillsdale, NJ: Erlbaum.

Graham, F. K. (1979). Distinguishing among orienting, defense and startle reflexes. In H. D. Kimmel, E. H. van Olst, & J. F. Orlebeke (Eds.), *The orienting reflex in humans* (pp. 137–167). Hillsdale, NJ: Erlbaum.

Graham, F. K., & Clifton, R. K. (1966). Heart rate as a component of the orienting response. *Psychological Bulletin, 65*, 305–320.

Haidt, J., Koller, S. H., & Dias, M. G. (1993). Affect, culture and morality, or is it wrong to eat your dog? *Journal of Personality and Social Psychology, 65*, 613–628.

Hauser, M. D. (1996). *The evolution of communication.* Cambridge, MA: MIT Press.

Hebb, D. O. (1949). *The organization of behavior.* New York: Wiley.

Hinde, R. A. (1974). *Biological bases of human social behaviour.* New York: McGraw-Hill.

Izard, C. E. (1971). *The face of emotion.* New York: Appleton-Century-Crofts.

Izard, C. E. (1977). *Human emotions.* New York: Plenum.

James, W. (1884). What is an emotion? *Mind, 9*, 188–205.

Johnson, E. J., & Tversky, A. (1983). Affect, generalization, and the perception of risk. *Journal of Personality and Social Psychology, 45*, 20–31.

Johnson, M. K., & Multhaup, K. S. (1992). Emotion and MEM. In S. A. Christianson (Ed.), *The handbook of emotion and memory: Research and theory* (pp. 33–66). Hillsdale, NJ: Erlbaum.

Kagan, J. (1991). A conceptual analysis of the affects. *Journal of the American Psychoanalytic Association, 39* (Suppl.), 109–129.

Kaiser, S., & Scherer, K. R. (1997). Models of "normal" emotions applied to facial and vocal expressions in clinical disorders. In W. F. Flack, Jr. & J. D. Laird (Eds.), *Emotions in psychopathology* (pp. 81–98). New York: Oxford University Press.

Kaiser, S., & Wehrle, T. (1996). Situated emotional problem solving in interactive computer games. In N. H.

Frijda (Ed.), *Proceedings of the Eighth Conference of the International Society for Research on Emotions* Storrs, CT: International Society for Research on Emotions.

Kappas, A. (1996). The sociality of appraisals: Impact of social situations on the evaluation of emotion antecedent events and physiological and expressive reactions. In N. H. Frijda (Ed.), *Proceedings of the Ninth Conference of the International Society for Research on Emotions* (pp. 116–120). Toronto, Ontario, Canada: International Society for Research on Emotions.

Kappas, A. (2001). A metaphor is a metaphor is a metaphor: Exorcising the homunculus from appraisal theory. In K. R. Scherer, A. Schorr, & T. Johnstone (Eds.), *Appraisal processes in emotion: Theory, methods, research* (pp. 157–172). New York: Oxford University Press.

Kappas, A., & Pecchinenda, A. (1999). Don't wait for the monsters to get you: A videogame task to manipulate appraisal in real time. *Cognition and Emotion, 13*, 119–124.

Kappas, A., Pecchinenda, A., & Bherer, F. (1999). The wizard of Oz: Appraisals and emotions in a voice-controlled video game. *Psychophysiology, 36*, S65.

Keltner, D., Ellsworth, P. C., & Edwards, K. (1993) Beyond simple pessimism: Effects of sadness and anger on social perception. *Journal of Personality and Social Psychology, 64*, 740–752.

Kimmel, H. D., van Olst, E. H., & Orlebeke, J. F. (Eds.). (1979). *The orienting reflex in humans.* Hillsdale, NJ: Erlbaum.

Kirby, L. D., & Smith, C. A. (1996). Freaking, quitting, and staying engaged: Patterns of psychophysiological response to stress. In N. H. Frijda (Ed.), *Proceedings of the Ninth Conference of the International Society for Research on Emotions* (pp. 359–363). Toronto, Ontario, Canada: International Society for Research on Emotions.

Kitayama, S., Markus, H. R., Matsumoto, H., & Norasakkunkit, V. (1997). Individual and collective processes in the construction of the self: Self-enhancement in the United States and self-criticism in Japan. *Journal of Personality and Social Psychology, 72*, 1245–1267.

Krantz, D. L., Hall, R., & Allen, D. (1969). William McDougall and the problem of purpose. *Journal of the History of the Behavioral Sciences, 5*(1), 25–38.

Kubzansky, L., & Ellsworth, P. C. (1999). *Emotions in action: The role of appraisals and emotions in performance.* Unpublished manuscript.

Kulik, J. A., & Brown, R. (1979). Frustration, attribution of blame and aggression. *Journal of Experimental Social Psychology, 15*, 183–194.

Laird, J. D. (1974). Self-attribution of emotion: The effect of expressive behavior on the quality of emotional experience. *Journal of Personality and Social Psychology, 29*, 475–486.

Lang, P. J. (1984). Cognition in emotion: Concept and action. In C. E. Izard, J. Kagan, & R. B. Zajonc (Eds.), *Emotions, cognition, and behavior* (pp. 192–226). Cambridge, England: Cambridge University Press.

Lazarus, R. S. (1966). *Psychological stress and the coping process.* New York: McGraw-Hill.

Lazarus, R. S. (1991). *Emotion and adaptation.* New York: Oxford University Press.

Lazarus, R. S. (1995). Vexing research problems inherent in cognitive-mediational theories of emotion and some solutions. *Psychological Inquiry, 6*, 183–196.

Lazarus, R. S. (1999). Appraisal, relational meaning, and emotion. In T. Dalgleish & M. Power (Eds.), *Handbook of cognition and emotion* (pp. 3–19). Chichester, England: Wiley.

Lazarus, R. S., Averill, J. R., & Opton, E. M., Jr. (1970). Towards a cognitive theory of emotion. In M. B. Arnold (Ed.), *Feeling and emotion: The Loyola Symposium.* (pp. 207–232). New York: Academic Press.

Lazarus, R. S., & Smith, C. A. (1988). Knowledge and appraisal in the cognition-emotion relationship. *Cognition and Emotion, 2,* 281–300.

LeDoux, J. E. (1996). *The emotional brain.* New York: Simon & Schuster.

Leeper, R. W. (1948). A motivational theory of emotion to replace "emotion as disorganized response." *Psychological Review, 55,* 5–21.

Leventhal, H., & Scherer, K. R. (1987). The relationship of emotion to cognition: A functional approach to a semantic controversy. *Cognition and Emotion, 1,* 3–28.

Lewis, M. D., & Granic, I. (1999) Self-organization of cognition-emotion interactions. In T. Dalgleish & M. Power (Eds.), *Handbook of cognition and emotion* (pp. 783–801). Chichester, England: Wiley.

Logan, G. D. (1988). Toward an instance theory of automatization. *Psychological Review, 95,* 492–527.

Manstead, A., & Fischer, A. (2001). Social and cultural dimensions of appraisal. In K. R. Scherer, A. Schorr, & T. Johnstone (Eds.), *Appraisal processes in emotion: Theory, methods, research* (pp. 221–232). New York: Oxford University Press.

Markus, H. R., & Kitayama, S. (1991). Culture and the self: Implications for cognition, emotion, and motivation. *Psychological Review, 98,* 224–253.

Mascolo, M. F., & Fischer, K. W. (1995). Developmental transformations in appraisals for pride, shame, and guilt. In J. P. Tangney & K. W. Fischer (Eds.), *Self-conscious emotions: The psychology of shame, guilt, embarrassment, and pride* (pp. 64–113). New York: Guilford Press.

Maslow, A. (1962). *Toward a psychology of being.* Princeton, NJ: Van Nostrand.

Matsumoto, D. (1995). Lazarus's vexing research problems are even more vexing than he thinks. *Psychological Inquiry, 6,* 228–230.

Matsumoto, D., Kudoh, T., Scherer, K., & Wallbott, H. (1988). Antecedents of and reactions to emotions in the United States and Japan. *Journal of Cross-Cultural Psychology, 19,* 267–286.

Mauro, R. (1988). Opponent process in human emotions? An experimental investigation of hedonic contrast and affective interaction. *Motivation and Emotion, 12,* 333–351.

Mauro, R., Sato, K., & Tucker, J. (1992). The role of appraisal in human emotions: A cross-cultural study. *Journal of Personality and Social Psychology, 62,* 301–317.

McAuley, E., & Duncan, T. E. (1990). Cognitive appraisal and affective reactions following physical achievement outcomes. *Journal of Sport and Exercise Psychology, 12,* 415–426.

McGraw, K. M., (1987). Guilt following transgression: An attribution of responsibility approach. *Journal of Personality and Social Psychology, 53,* 247–256.

Mesquita, B. (in press) *Cultural variations in emotions: A comparative study of Dutch, Surinamese, and Turkish people in the Netherlands.* New York: Oxford University Press.

Mesquita, B., & Ellsworth, P. C. 2001. The role of culture in appraisal. In K. R. Scherer, A. Schorr, & T. Johnstone (Eds.), *Appraisal processes in emotion: Theory, methods, research* (pp. 233–248). New York: Oxford University Press.

Mesquita, B., Frijda, N. H., & Scherer, K. R. (1997). Culture and emotion. In J. E. Berry, P. B. Dasen, & T. S. Saraswathi (Eds.), *Handbook of cross-cultural psychology: Vol. 2. Basic processes and developmental psychology* (pp. 255–297). Boston: Allyn & Bacon.

Michotte, A. E. (1950). The emotions as functional connections. In M. Reymert (Ed.), *Feelings and emotions* (pp. 114–126). New York: McGraw-Hill.

Mikula, G., Petri, B., & Tanzer, N. K. (1990). What people regard as unjust: Types and structures of everyday experiences of injustice. *European Journal of Social Psychology, 20* (2), 133–149.

Mikula, G., Scherer, K. R., & Athenstaedt, U. (1998). The role of injustice in the elicitation of differential emotional reactions. *Personality and Social Psychology Bulletin, 24* (7), 769–783.

Miller, S. M. (1981). Predictability and human stress: Toward a clarification of evidence and theory. In L. Berkowitz (Ed.), *Advances in experimental social psychology* (Vol. 14, pp. 203–256). New York: Academic Press.

Mineka, S., & Henderson, R. W. (1985). Controllability and predictability in acquired motivation. *Annual Review of Psychology, 36,* 495–529.

Murphy, S. T., Monahan, J. L., & Zajonc, R. B. (1995). Additivity of nonconscious affect: Combined effects of priming and exposure. *Journal of Personality and Social Psychology, 69,* 589–602.

Murray, H. A. (1938). *Explorations in personality: A clinical and experimental study of fifty men of college age.* New York: Oxford University Press.

Nisbett, R. E., & Wilson, T. D. (1977). Telling more than we can know: Verbal reports on mental processes. *Psychological Review, 84,* 231–259.

Oatley, K., & Johnson-Laird, P. N. (1987). Towards a cognitive theory of emotions. *Cognition and Emotion, 1,* 29–50.

Öhman, A. (1987). The psychophysiology of emotion: An evolutionary-cognitive perspective. In P. K. Adeles, J. R. Jennings, & M. G. H. Coles (Eds.), *Advances in psychophysiology* (Vol. 2). Greenwich, CT: JAI Press.

Ortony, A., Clore, G. L., & Collins, A. (1988). *The cognitive structure of emotions.* New York: Cambridge University Press.

Ortony, A., & Turner, T. (1990). What's basic about basic emotions? *Psychological Review, 97,* 315–331.

Osgood, C. E. (1966). Dimensionality of the semantic space for communication via facial expressions. *Scandinavian Journal of Psychology, 7,* 1–30.

Osgood, C. E., May, W. H., & Miron, M. S. (1975). *Cross-cultural universals of effective meaning.* Urbana: University of Illinois Press.

Panksepp, J. (1998). *Affective neuroscience: The foundations of human and animal emotions.* New York: Oxford University Press.

Parasuraman, R. (1983). *Varieties of attention.* New York: Wiley.

Parkinson, B. (1996). Emotions are social. *British Journal of Psychology, 87,* 663–683.

Parkinson, B. (1997). Untangling the appraisal-emotion connection. *Personality and Social Psychology Review, 1,* 62–79.

Parkinson, B. (2001). Putting appraisal into context: Towards a pragmatic theory of emotional function. In K. R. Scherer, A. Schorr, & T. Johnstone (Eds.), *Appraisal processes in emotion: Theory, methods, research* (pp. 173–186). New York: Oxford University Press.

Parkinson, B., & Manstead, A. S. R. (1992). Appraisal as a cause of emotion. *Review of Personality and Social Psychology, 13*, 122–149.

Parkinson, B., & Manstead, A. S. R. (1993). Making sense of emotions in stories and social life. *Cognition and Emotion, 7*, 295–323.

Pecchinenda, A., & Kappas, A. (1998). Impact of competitive and collaborative instructions on appraisals and physiological activity during dyadic interactions in a video game. *Psychophysiology, 35*, S65.

Pecchinenda, A., Kappas, A., & Smith, C. A. (1997). Effects of difficulty and ability in a dual-task video game paradigm on attention, physiological responses, performance, and emotion-related appraisal. *Psychophysiology, 34*, S70.

Pecchinenda, A., & Smith, C. A. (1996). The affective significance of skin conductance activity during a difficult problem-solving task. *Cognition and Emotion, 10*, 481–503.

Penfield, W. (1975). *The mystery of the mind.* Princeton, NJ: Princeton University Press.

Pfaffman, C. (1960). The pleasure of sensation. *Psychological Review, 67*, 253–268.

Pfaffman, C. (1978). The vertebrate phylogeny, neural code and integrative processes of taste. In E. C. Carterette & M. P. Friedman (Eds.), *Handbook of perception* (pp. 51–124). New York: Academic Press.

Plutchik, R. (1980). *Emotion: A psychobioevolutionary synthesis.* New York: Harper & Row.

Posner, M. I. (1992). Attention as a cognitive and neural system. *Current Directions in Psychological Science, 1*, 11–14.

Posner, M. I., & Petersen, S. E. (1990). The attention system of the human brain. *Annual Review of Neuroscience, 13*, 25–42.

Redican, W. K. (1982). An evolutionary perspective on human facial displays. In P. Ekman (Ed.), *Emotion in the human face* (2nd ed., pp. 212–280). New York: Cambridge University Press.

Reisenzein, R., & Hofmann, T. (1993). Discriminating emotions from appraisal-relevant situational information: Baseline data for structural models of cognitive appraisals. *Cognition and Emotion, 7*, 271–294.

Reisenzein, R., & Schönpflug, W. (1992). Stumpf's cognitive-evaluative theory of emotion. *American Psychologist, 47*, 34–45.

Reisenzein, R., & Spielhofer, C. (1994). Subjectively salient dimensions of emotional appraisal. *Motivation and Emotion, 18*, 31–77.

Robinson, T. E., & Berridge, K. C. (1993). The neural basis of drug craving: An incentive-sensitization theory of addiction. *Brain Research Reviews, 18*, 247–291.

Roseman, I. J. (1984). Cognitive determinants of emotion: A structural theory. In P. Shaver (Ed.), *Review of personality and social psychology* (Vol. 5, pp. 11–36). Beverly Hills, CA: Sage.

Roseman, I. J. (1991). Appraisal determinants of discrete emotions. *Cognition and Emotion, 5*, 161–200.

Roseman, I. J. 2001. Proposals for an integrated appraisal theory. In K. R. Scherer, A. Schorr, & T. Johnstone (Eds.), *Appraisal processes in emotion: Theory, methods, research* (pp. 68–91). New York: Oxford University Press.

Roseman, I. J., Antoniou, A. A., & Jose, P. E. (1996). Appraisal determinants of emotions: Constructing a more accurate and comprehensive theory. *Cognition and Emotion, 10*, 241–277.

Roseman, I. J., Dhawan, N., Rettek, S. I., Naidu, R. K., & Thapa, K. (1995). Cultural differences and cross-cultural similarities in appraisals and emotional responses. *Journal of Cross-Cultural Psychology, 26*, 23–48.

Roseman, I. J., & Kaiser, S. (2001). Pathological appraisal processes. In K. R. Scherer, A. Schorr, & T. Johnstone (Eds.), *Appraisal processes in emotion: Theory, methods, research* (pp. 249–267). New York: Oxford University Press.

Roseman, I. J., & Smith, C. A. 2001. Appraisal theory: Overview, assumptions, varieties, controversies. In K. R. Scherer, A. Schorr, & T. Johnstone (Eds.), *Appraisal processes in emotion: Theory, methods, research* (pp. 3–19). New York: Oxford University Press.

Roseman, I. J., Spindel, M. S., & Jose, P. E. (1990). Appraisal of emotion-eliciting events: Testing a theory of discrete emotions. *Journal of Personality and Social Psychology, 59*, 899–915.

Rozin, P. (1996). Towards a psychology of food and eating: From motivation to module to model to marker, morality, meaning, and metaphor. *Current Directions in Psychological Science, 5* (1), 18–24.

Rozin, P. (1999). Preadaptation and the puzzles and properties of pleasure. In D. Kahneman, E. Diener, & N. Schwarz (Eds.), *Well-being: The foundations of hedonic psychology* (pp. 109–133). New York: Russell Sage Foundation.

Rozin, P., & Fallon, A. (1987). A perspective on disgust. *Psychological Review, 94*, 23–41.

Rozin, P., Lowery, L., Imada, S., & Haidt, J. (1999). The CAD triad hypothesis: A mapping between three moral emotions (Contempt, Anger, Disgust) and three moral codes (Community, Autonomy, Divinity). *Journal of Personality and Social Psychology, 76*, 574–586.

Ruch, T. C. (1979). Neurophysiology of emotion, affect and species-specific behavior. In W. H. Howell & J. F. Fulton (Eds.), *Physiology and biophysics: The brain and neural function* (pp. 671–722). Philadelphia: Saunders.

Russel, D., & McAuley, E. (1986). Causal attributions, causal dimensions, and affective reactions to success and failure. *Journal of Personality and Social Psychology, 50*, 1174–1185.

Russell, J. A. (1980). A circumplex model of affect. *Journal of Personality and Social Psychology, 39*, 1161–1178.

Russell, J. A. (1991). Culture and the categorization of emotions. *Psychological Bulletin, 110*, 426–450.

Scherer, K. R. (1982). Emotion as a process: Function, origin, and regulation. *Social Science Information, 21*, 555–570.

Scherer, K. R. (1984). On the nature and function of emotion: A component process approach. In K. R. Scherer & P. Ekman (Eds.), *Approaches to emotion* (pp. 293–318). Hillsdale, NJ: Erlbaum.

Scherer, K. R. (1985). Vocal affect signalling: A comparative approach. In J. Rosenblatt, C. Beer, M.-C. Busnel, & P. J. B. Slater (Eds.), *Advances in the study of behavior* (Vol. 15, pp. 189–244). New York: Academic Press.

Scherer, K. R. (1986a). Vocal affect expression: A review

and a model for future research. *Psychological Bulletin, 99,* 143–165.

Scherer, K. R. (1986b). Emotion experiences across European cultures: A summary statement. In K. R. Scherer, H. G. Wallbott, & A. B. Summerfield (Eds.), *Experiencing emotion: A cross-cultural study* (pp. 173–190). Cambridge, England: Cambridge University Press.

Scherer, K. R. (1987a). Toward a dynamic theory of emotion: The component process model of affective states. *Geneva Studies in Emotion and Communication, 1,* 1–98. Retrievable from http://www.unige.ch/fapse/emotion/genstudies/genstudies.html.

Scherer, K. R. (1987b). Vocal assessment of affective disorders. In J. D. Maser (Ed.), *Depression and expressive behavior* (pp. 57–82). Hillsdale, NJ: Erlbaum.

Scherer, K. R. (1988). Criteria for emotion-antecedent appraisal: A review. In V. Hamilton, G. H. Bower, & N. H. Frijda (Eds.), *Cognitive perspectives on emotion and motivation* (pp. 89–126). Dordrecht, The Netherlands: Nijhoff.

Scherer, K. R. (1992). What does facial expression express? In K. Strongman (Ed.), *International review of studies on emotion* (Vol. 2, pp. 139–165). Chichester, England: Wiley.

Scherer, K. R. (1993a). Neuroscience projections to current debates in emotion psychology. *Cognition and Emotion, 7,* 1–41.

Scherer, K. R. (1993b). Studying the emotion-antecedent appraisal process: An expert system approach. *Cognition and Emotion, 7,* 325–355.

Scherer, K. R. (1994). Toward a concept of "modal emotions." In P. Ekman & R. J. Davidson (Eds.), *The nature of emotion: Fundamental questions* (pp. 25–31). New York: Oxford University Press.

Scherer, K. R. (1997a). Profiles of emotion-antecedent appraisal: Testing theoretical predictions across cultures. *Cognition and Emotion, 11,* 113–150.

Scherer, K. R. (1997b). The role of culture in emotion-antecedent appraisal. *Journal of Personality and Social Psychology, 73,* 902–922.

Scherer, K. R. (1999a). Appraisal theories. In T. Dalgleish & M. Power (Eds.), *Handbook of cognition and emotion* (pp. 637–663). Chichester, England: Wiley.

Scherer, K. R. (1999b). On the sequential nature of appraisal processes: Indirect evidence from a recognition task. *Cognition and Emotion, 13*(6), 763–793.

Scherer, K. R. (2000a). Emotions as episodes of subsystem synchronization driven by nonlinear appraisal processes. In M. Lewis & I. Granic (Eds.), *Emotion, development, and self-organization* (pp. 70–99). New York: Cambridge University Press.

Scherer, K. R. (2000b). Psychological models of emotion. In J. Borod (Ed.), *The neuropsychology of emotion* (pp. 137–162). Oxford: Oxford University Press.

Scherer, K. R. (2000c). Emotion. In M. Hewstone & W. Stroebe (Eds.). *Introduction to social psychology: A European perspective* (3rd ed., pp. 151–191). Oxford: Blackwell.

Scherer, K. R. (2001a). Appraisal considered as a process of multi-level sequential checking. In K. R. Scherer, A. Schorr, & T. Johnstone (Eds.), *Appraisal processes in emotion: Theory, methods, research* (pp. 92–120). New York: Oxford University Press.

Scherer, K. R. (2001b). The nature and study of appraisal: A review of the issues. In K. R. Scherer, A. Schorr, & T. Johnstone (Eds.), *Appraisal processes in emotion: The-*

*ory, methods, research* (pp. 369–391). New York: Oxford University Press.

Scherer, K. R., & Ceschi, G. (1997). Lost luggage emotion: A field study of emotion-antecedent appraisal. *Motivation and Emotion, 21,* 211–235.

Scherer, K. R., Schorr, A., & Johnstone, T. (Eds.). (2001). *Appraisal processes in emotion: Theory, methods, research.* New York: Oxford University Press.

Scherer, K. R., & Zentner, K. R. (2001). The expression of emotion in music. In J. Sloboda & P. Juslin (Eds.), *Music and emotion* (pp. 361–392). Oxford, England: Oxford University Press.

Scherer, K. R., Zentner, M. R., & Stern, D. (2001). *The development of emotion-constituent appraisal: A study of infants' expressive behavior following violation of expectancies.* Manuscript submitted for publication.

Schlosberg, H. (1952). The description of facial expressions in terms of two dimensions. *Journal of Experimental Psychology, 44,* 229–237.

Schneirla, T. C. (1959). An evolutionary and developmental theory of biphasic processes underlying approach and withdrawal. In M. R. Jones (Ed.), *Nebraska Symposium on Motivation: Vol. 7* (pp. 1–42). Lincoln: University of Nebraska Press.

Schorr, A. (2001). Appraisal: The evolution of an idea. In K. R. Scherer, A. Schorr, & T. Johnstone (Eds.), *Appraisal processes in emotion: Theory, methods, research* (pp. 20–34). New York: Oxford University Press.

Schwarz, N., Groves, R. M., & Schuman, H. (1998). Survey methods. In D. T. Gilbert, S. T. Fiske, & G. Lindzey (Eds.), *The handbook of social psychology* (4th ed., pp. 143–179). Boston, MA: McGraw-Hill.

Scott, J. P. (1958). *Animal behavior.* Chicago: University of Chicago Press.

Seligman, M. E. P. (1975). *Helplessness: On depression, development and death.* San Francisco: Freeman.

Shaver, P. R., Wu, S., & Schwartz, J. C. (1992). Cross-cultural similarities and differences in emotion and its representation. In M. S. Clark (Ed.), *Emotion: Review of personality and social psychology* (pp. 175–213). Newbury Park, CA: Sage.

Siddle, D. A. T., & Lipp, O. V. (1997). Orienting, habituation, and information processing: The effects of omission, the role of expectancy, and the problem of dishabituation. In P. J. Lang, R. F. Simons, & M. Balaban (Eds.), *Attention and orienting: Sensory and motivational processes* (pp. 23–40). Mahwah, NJ: Erlbaum.

Smith, C. A. (1989). Dimensions of appraisal and physiological response in emotion. *Journal of Personality and Social Psychology, 56,* 339–353.

Smith, C. A., & Ellsworth, P. C. (1985). Patterns of cognitive appraisal in emotion. *Journal of Personality and Social Psychology, 48,* 813–838.

Smith, C. A., & Ellsworth, P. C. (1987). Patterns of appraisal and emotion related to taking an exam. *Journal of Personality and Social Psychology, 52,* 475–488.

Smith, C. A., Haynes, K. N., Lazarus, R. S., & Pope, L. K. (1993). In search of the "hot" cognitions: Attributions, appraisals, and their relation to emotion. *Journal of Personality and Social Psychology, 65,* 916–929.

Smith, C. A., & Kirby, L. D. (2001). Breaking the tautology: Toward delivering on the promise of appraisal theory. In K. R. Scherer, A. Schorr, & T. Johnstone (Eds.), *Appraisal processes in emotion: Theory, methods, research* (pp. 121–138). New York: Oxford University Press.

Smith, C. A., & Lazarus, R. S. (1993). Appraisal components, core relational themes, and the emotions. *Cognition and Emotion, 7*, 233–269.

Sokolov, J. N. (1963). *Perception and the conditioned reflex.* Oxford, England: Pergamon.

Solomon, R. C. (1976). *The passions: The myth and nature of human emotion.* Garden City, NY: Doubleday.

Solomon, R. L. (1980). The opponent-process theory of acquired motivation: The costs of pleasure and the benefits of pain. *American Psychologist, 35*, 691–712.

Soussignan, R., Schaal, B., Marlier, L., & Jiang, T. (1997). Facial and autonomic responses to biological and artificial olfactory stimuli in human neonates: Re-examining early hedonic discrimination of odors. *Physiology and Behavior, 62*(4), 745–758.

Sroufe, L. A. (1996). *Emotional development: The organization of emotional life in the early years.* Cambridge, England: Cambridge University Press.

Srull, T. S., & Wyer, R. S., Jr. (1986). The role of chronic and temporary goals in social information processing. In R. M. Sorrentino & E. T. Higgins (Eds.), *Handbook of motivation and cognition* (pp. 503–549). New York: Wiley.

Stein, N. L., & Levine, L. J. (1987). Thinking about feelings: The development and organization of emotional knowledge. In R. E. Snow & M. Farr (Eds.), *Aptitude, learning, and instruction: Cognition, conation and affect* (Vol. 3, pp. 165–198). Hillsdale, NJ: Erlbaum.

Steiner, J. E. (1979). Human facial expressions in response to taste and smell stimulation. In H. W. Reese & L. P. Lipsitt (Eds.), *Advances in child development and behavior* (Vol. 13, pp. 257–295). New York: Academic Press.

Stipek, D., Weiner, B., & Li, K. (1989). Testing some attribution-emotion relations in the People's Republic of China. *Journal of Personality and Social Psychology, 56*(1), 109–116.

Tangney, J. P., & Fischer, K. W. (Eds.). (1995). *Self-conscious emotions: The psychology of shame, guilt, embarrassment, and pride.* New York: Guilford Press.

Teasdale, J. D. (1999). Multi-level theories of cognition-emotion relations. In T. Dalgleish & M. J. Power (Eds.), *Handbook of cognition and emotion* (pp. 665–681). Chichester, England: Wiley.

Teasdale, J. D., & Barnard, P. J. (1993). *Affect, cognition, and change: Remodelling depressive thought.* Hove, England: Erlbaum.

Tesser, A. (1990). Smith and Ellsworth's appraisal model of emotion: A replication, extension, and test. *Personality and Social Psychology Bulletin, 16*, 210–223.

Tiedens, L. Z., Ellsworth, P. C., & Mesquita, B. (2000). Sentimental stereotypes: Emotional expectancies for high- and low-status group members. *Personality and Social Psychology Bulletin, 26*, 560–574.

Tomkins, S. S. (1962). *Affect, imagery, consciousness: Vol. 1. The positive affects.* New York: Springer.

Tomkins, S. S. (1963). *Affect, imagery, consciousness: Vol. 2. The negative affects.* New York: Springer.

Tomkins, S. S. (1984). Affect theory. In K. R. Scherer & P. Ekman (Eds.), *Approaches to emotion* (pp. 163–196). Hillsdale, NJ: Erlbaum.

Tooby, J., & Cosmides, L. (1990). The past explains the present: Emotional adaptations and the structure of ancestral environments. *Ethology and Sociobiology, 11*(4–5), 375–424.

Turpin, G., Schaefer, F., & Boucsein, W. (1999). Effects of stimulus intensity, rise time, and duration on autonomic and behavioral responding: Implications for the differentiation of orienting, startle, and defense responses. *Psychophysiology, 36*(4), 453–463.

van Hooff, J. A. R. A. M. (1972). A comparative approach to the phylogeny of laughter and smiling. In R. A. Hinde (Ed.), *Non-verbal communication* (pp. 209–237). Cambridge, England: Cambridge University Press.

van Reekum, C. M., Banse, R., Johnstone, T., Scherer, K. R., Etter, A., & Wehrle, T. (2001). Psychophysiological responses to emotion-antecedent appraisal in a computer game. Manuscript submitted for publication.

van Reekum, C. M., Johnstone, T., & Scherer, K. R. (1997, May). Multimodal measurement of emotion induced by the manipulation of appraisals in a computer game. Paper presented at the European Congress of Psychophysiology, Konstanz, Germany.

van Reekum, C. M., & Scherer, K. R. (1997). Levels of processing for emotion-antecedent appraisal. In G. Matthews (Ed.), *Cognitive science perspectives on personality and emotion* (pp. 259–300). Amsterdam: Elsevier Science.

Vinter, A., Lanares, J., & Mounoud, P. (1985). Development of face perception. *Semiotic Inquiry, 3*, 240–258.

Wehrle, T., Kaiser, S., Schmidt, S., & Scherer, K. R. (2000). Studying dynamic models of facial expression of emotion using synthetic animated faces. *Journal of Personality and Social Psychology, 78*(1), 105–119.

Weigert, A. J. (1991). *Mixed emotions: Certain steps toNward understanding ambivalence.* Albany: State University of New York Press.

Weiner, B. (1982). The emotional consequences of causal attributions. In M. S. Clark & S. T. Fiske (Eds.), *Affect and cognition* (pp. 185–209). Hillsdale, NJ: Erlbaum.

Weiner, B. (1986). *An attributional theory of motivation and emotion.* New York: Springer.

Weiner, B., Amirkhan, J., Folkes, V. S., & Verette, J. A. (1987). An attributional analysis of excuse giving: Studies of a naive theory of emotion. *Journal of Personality and Social Psychology, 52*, 316–324.

Weiner, B., Graham, S., & Chandler, C. (1982). Pity, anger, and guilt: An attributional analysis. *Personality and Social Psychology Bulletin, 8*, 226–232.

Weiner, B., Russel, D., & Lerman, D. (1979). The cognition-emotion process in achievement-related contexts. *Journal of Personality and Social Psychology, 37*, 1211–1220.

Wundt, W. (1902). *Grundzüge der physiologischen Psychologie: Vol. 2.* [Fundamentals of physiological psychology] (5th ed., orig. ed. 1874). Leipzig: Wilhelm Engelmann.

Zajonc, R. B. (1980). Thinking and feeling: Preferences need no inferences. *American Psychologist, 35*, 151–175.

Zajonc, R. B., & Markus, H. (1984). Affect and cognition: The hard interface. In C. E. Izard, J. Kagan, & R. B. Zajonc (Eds.), *Emotions, cognition, and behavior* (pp. 73–102). Cambridge: Cambridge University Press.

# 30

## AFFECTIVE INFLUENCES ON ATTITUDES AND JUDGMENTS

Joseph P. Forgas

Writers, artists, and laypersons have always been fascinated by the subtle influence of feelings on attitudes and behavior. This question has also occupied the minds of such classic philosophers as Plato, Aristotle, Epicurus, Descartes, Pascal, Kant, and others. Many of these theorists saw affect as a potentially dangerous, invasive force that tends to subvert rational judgment and attitudes, an idea that was to reemerge in Freud's psychodynamic theories early this century. However, during the past few decades important advances in neuroanatomy, psychophysiology, and social cognition research produced a radically different view. Rather than viewing affect as a dangerous and disruptive influence on our attitudes and judgments, recent evidence suggests that affect is often a useful and even essential component of adaptive responding to social situations (Adolphs & Damasio, 2001; Damasio, 1994; Ito & Cacioppo, 2001).

The research I review here shows that affective states have a powerful influence on the way we perceive and respond to social situations. Most of the time these influences are adaptive and helpful in guiding attitudes and judgments (Clore, Schwarz, & Conway, 1994; Forgas, 1995a, 2000; Zajonc, 2000). The past two decades saw something like an "affective revolution" in psychological research. Indeed, one could argue that most of what is known about the influence of affect on attitudes and judgments has been discovered since the early 1980s. One of the key objectives of contemporary research and of this

chapter in particular is to explore how, when, and why affective states will influence attitudes and judgments. In a broader sense, my aim is thus to make a contribution to the age-old quest to understand the relationship between the rational and the emotional aspects of human nature (Hilgard, 1980; see also chapter 31, this volume).

Affect has a particularly important influence on people's attitudes and judgments, two constructs that most directly touch on how we respond to social stimuli. The concept of attitudes has long been considered as one of the "most distinctive and indispensable" concepts in social psychology (Allport, 1954, p. 43), and its importance to understanding human social behavior remains undiminished to this day (Eagly & Chaiken, 1993). Terms such as *attitude* and *judgment* appear to be closely related, in the sense that judgments involve the on-line, immediate, and dynamic evaluation of social stimuli, whereas attitude refers to more enduring, stable, and crystallized responses to the social world. Most attitudes have their origin in social judgments, and social judgments in turn are frequently influenced by preexisting attitudes.

No doubt the enduring importance of the attitude concept is at least partly due to its ability to capture the complex, multidimensional character of the way human beings respond to their social environment. The term *attitude* was first introduced into empirical social research by Thomas and Znaniecki (1928), who relied on this concept to analyze the changing patterns of cultural adaptation manifested by Polish emigrants to the United States. Contemporary theories see attitudes as an individual rather than a cultural construct, comprising distinct cognitive, affective, and conative (behavioral) components (Eagly & Chaiken, 1993). Affect thus always constituted a critical part of the attitude concept. Surprisingly, despite the voluminous research on attitudes over several decades, relatively little work has been done on the dynamic role that affective states and moods play in the way attitudes are generated, maintained, cognitively represented, organized, and expressed in social situations.

This chapter seeks to provide an integrative review of recent work on the role of affect in the organization and functioning of attitudes and the role of affect in social and interpersonal judgments. First, a brief overview of the early history of research on this area is presented, followed by a theoretical summary of some of the more influential contemporary cognitive explanations for affective influences on attitudes and judgments. I then review a number of substantive areas in which affective influences on attitudes and judgments have been studied, such as the role of affect in self-related attitudes and judgments, interpersonal judgments, stereotyping and prejudice, and attitude change processes. The final section of the chapter presents some evidence for the behavioral consequences of affective influences on attitudes, and an integrative theory linking affect to attitudes and judgments is outlined. In particular, evidence for the critical role of different information processing strategies in mediating the influence of affect on attitudes and judgments is discussed.

## Philosophical and Psychological Antecedents

It is interesting that even though affect has always been recognized as a critical part of attitudes and judgments, empirical research on its functions was rare until quite recently. How can we explain this surprising neglect? Historians of psychology such as Hilgard (1980) suggested that one reason for the relative absence of research on affect until recently may be the traditional assumption of psychology that different components of the human mind, such as affect, cognition, and conation, can and should be studied in separation from each other as independent, isolated entities. Neither the earlier behaviorist approach nor the more recent cognitive paradigm has assigned much importance to the study of affective phenomena. As a result, affect has remained the most "neglected" member of the trilogy of mind, at least until recently (Hilgard, 1980).

Radical behaviorism explicitly excluded the study of mental phenomena such as affect from the legitimate subject matter of psychology. Emotion, if considered at all, was manipulated through such crude devices as the delivery of electric shocks and food or drink deprivation. I can still recall an early demonstration study in my undergraduate days when we spent an afternoon assessing "emotionality" in the rat. Emotionality was operationalized in terms of the number of fecal boli the wretched creature produced as it scurried around its cage trying to avoid receiving electric shocks. Not surprisingly, behaviorist research contributed relatively little to our understanding of the role of affect in social attitudes and judgments. The emerging cognitive paradigm in the 1960s produced little improvement. Most information processing theories, until quite recently, assumed that the proper objective of cognitive research was to study cold, affectless mentation. Affect, if considered at all, was seen as a source of noise and disruption. The idea that affect is an integral and often adaptive part of how information about the social world is processed was not seriously entertained until the early 1980s (Bower, 1981; Scherer, 1984; Zajonc, 1980).

## The Primacy of Affect as a Feature of Attitudes and Judgments

Research on attitudes and judgments is one of the areas in psychology in which the traditional attempt to separate affect, cognition, and conation is most problematic. Although attitude theories clearly recognize that affect is a key component of attitude, there has been disproportionate preoccupation with the study of the cognitive and conative components to the relative neglect of affective features (Eagly & Chaiken, 1993). Similarly, research on social judgments has traditionally emphasized the rational, logical processes involved in combining external stimulus information with internal knowledge structures in producing a response (Wyer & Srull, 1989). Just how important is affect as a component of, and as a determinant of, attitudes and judgments?

In an influential article, Zajonc (1980) argued that affective reactions often constitute the primary and determining response to social stimuli. Recently, Zajonc (2000) reviewed recent evidence and concluded that affect indeed functions as an independent, primary, and often dominant force in determining people's responses to social situations. There are a variety of studies that can be construed as supporting such a conclusion. It appears that people may readily acquire an affective response toward stimuli even though they have no awareness of having encountered it before (Zajonc, 1980, 2000). These affective reactions can be extremely enduring and may influence subsequent attitudes and behaviors directly even in the absence of any associated memory or beliefs (Zajonc, 2000). This evidence suggests that affect may be seen as not just one of the three components of attitudes—and a relatively neglected one at that—but as the major driving force behind many responses to social stimuli and perhaps the primary dimension of all interpersonal behavior (Zajonc, 1980). This view is also supported by evidence indicating that affective dimensions play a key role in determining our implicit cognitive representations about the social world.

## Affect and the Organization of Attitudes

Affect also plays a crucial role in how people organize their social experiences and how they cognitively represent their attitudes and judgments about them. The ability to symbolically represent and categorize social events lies at the heart of orderly social behavior (Mead, 1934). Affective reactions seem to play a key role in how attitudes toward and implicit cognitive representations about common, recurring social experiences are organized (Forgas, 1979). Affective reactions such as feelings of anxiety, confidence, intimacy, pleasure, or discomfort seem to be critical in defining the implicit structure and complexity of people's cognitive representations about social encounters. Surprisingly, the descriptive, denotative features of these events play comparatively little role in mental representations.

More recently, Niedenthal and Halberstadt (2000) showed in a series of ingenious experiments that "stimuli can cohere as a category even when they have nothing in common other than the emotional responses they elicit" (p. 381). Findings such as these indicate that affect is indeed a primary dimension of social attitudes and judgments as suggested by Zajonc (1980, 2000). Nor are these results entirely unexpected. Twenty-five years ago researchers such as Pervin (1976) argued that "what is striking is the extent to which situations are described in terms of affects (e.g. threatening, warm, interesting, dull, tense, calm, rejecting) and organized in terms of similarity of affects aroused by them" (p. 471). Thus affective characteristics—how we feel about various people, events, and social experiences—play a predominant role in people's cognitive representations of their attitudes and judgments.

In addition to influencing how attitudes are organized and represented, affect also has a more dynamic role in the formation of social judgments. A number of early studies confirmed that experiencing a positive and negative affect has an affect-congruent influence on subsequent attitudes and judgments. Thus feeling good should make our attitudes and judgments more positive, and feeling bad should somehow "infuse" our evaluation of social stimuli in a negative direction. Such affect infusion effects were initially explained in terms of either psychodynamic or associationist principles.

## The Psychodynamic View of Affect, Attitudes, and Judgments

Freud's psychodynamic speculations played a key role in highlighting the relationship between affect and mental representations such as attitudes and judgments. Psychoanalytic theories suggested that affect has a dynamic, invasive quality and can "take over" attitudes and judgments unless adequate psychological resources are deployed to control these impulses. In an interesting early study, Feshbach and Singer (1957) tested the psychoanalytic prediction that attempts to suppress affect should increase the "pressure" for affect to infuse unrelated attitudes and judgments. They induced fear in their participants through electric shocks and then instructed some of them to suppress their fear. Fearful participants' attitudes toward another person were significantly influenced by this manipulation—they were more likely to see "another person as fearful and anxious" (p. 286). Further, this effect was increased when participants were trying to suppress their fear. Feshbach and Singer (1957) explained this in terms of the infusion of temporary affect into an unrelated attitude; they argued that "suppression of fear facilitates the tendency to project fear onto another social object" (p. 286).

## The Associationist View of Affect, Attitudes, and Judgments

Conditioning and associationist theories provide an alternative account for the infusion of affect into attitudes and judgments. Although radical behaviorism denied the value of studying internal constructs such as affect and attitudes, associationist theories nevertheless had an important influence on subsequent research. Watson's "little Albert" studies were among the first to show that attitudes toward a previously neutral stimulus, such as a furry rabbit, can be rapidly influenced by associating fear-arousing stimuli, such as a loud noise, with the attitude object. According to Watson, all our complex affective reactions acquired throughout life—and thus all our attitudes and judgments—are influenced by such a pattern of complex and cumulative associations. This principle was perhaps first demonstrated some 60 years ago in an intriguing experiment by Razran (1940). Razran (1940) found that people who were made to feel bad or good (being exposed to highly aversive smells or receiving a free lunch) spontaneously reported significantly more negative or positive attitudes toward persuasive messages presented to them.

The conditioning approach to understanding affective influences on attitudes and judgments was later used by Byrne and Clore (1970) and Clore and Byrne (1974) to explain the role of affect in interpersonal attitudes. These researchers argued that affective states triggered by unrelated events can also influence attitudes and responses to other people. Thus aversive environments (the unconditioned stimuli) should produce a negative affective reaction (the unconditioned response). When people encounter a neutral attitude object (such as another person or partner, the conditioned stimulus) in this setting, the affective reaction elicited by the environment should become readily associated with this new target and should influence attitudes and evaluations (a conditioned response). In other words, simple temporal and spatial contiguity is enough to link an independently elicited affective state and an incidentally encountered stimulus or person. Several studies demonstrated just such a conditioning effect (Gouaux, 1971; Gouaux & Summers, 1973; Griffitt, 1970). In recent years, Berkowitz and his colleagues (Berkowitz, Jaffee, Jo, & Troccoli, 2000) have reached back to early associationist theories and proposed a neoassociationist account of affective influences on attitudes and judgments.

## Contemporary Cognitive Approaches Linking Affect to Attitudes and Judgments

There is little doubt that positive or negative affective states often infuse people's thoughts and attitudes, as several of the early experiments just reviewed showed. What are the psychological mechanisms that make such affect infusion possible? Neither the psychoanalytic nor the associationist explanations offer a convincing theory of just how and why these effects occur. In contrast, contemporary cognitive theories offer a more finely grained explanation for the observed infusion of affect into thinking and judgments based on information processing mechanisms. Two kinds of cognitive theories have been proposed to explain these informational effects: *memory-based* accounts (e.g., the affect priming model; see Bower & Forgas, 2001) and *inferential* models (e.g., the affect-as-information model; see Clore et al., 1994). In addition, several theories also emphasize the influence of affect on how social information is *processed*. I review these three theoretical frameworks in this section.

### Memory-Based Mechanisms

Several social cognitive theories suggest that affect may infuse judgments and attitudes through its influence on the memory structures people use when constructively interpreting social information (see also chapter 32, this volume, on this topic). For example, Wyer and Srull's (1989) "storage bin" model suggests that recently activated concepts are more accessible because such concepts are returned to the top of mental "storage bins" and subsequent sequential search for interpretive information is more likely to access the same concepts again. To the extent that affect involves the active use of positively or negatively valenced mental concepts, this could account for the more affect-congruent attitudes and judgments often reported by happy or sad people. Another memory-based account was put forward by Isen (1984), who suggested that the pref-

erential use of affectively primed information may be responsible for the mood-congruent judgmental effects demonstrated in her studies.

This principle was outlined in the associative network model proposed by Bower (1981). Bower's model suggests that the links between affect and thinking are neither motivationally based as psychodynamic theories suggest, nor are they the result of merely incidental, blind associations, as conditioning theories imply. Instead, Bower (1981) proposed that affect, cognition, and attitudes are integrally linked within an associative network of mental representations. An affective state should thus selectively and automatically prime associated thoughts and representations that are more likely to be used in constructive cognitive tasks. We may define as "constructive" those cognitive tasks that involve the active elaboration and transformation of the available stimulus information, require the activation and use of previous knowledge structures, and result in the creation of new knowledge from the combination of stored information and new stimulus details. Constructive processing differs from merely reconstructive thinking when existing information is used without active elaboration.

Despite strong evidence for mood-congruent effects in early studies (Bower, 1981; Clark & Isen, 1982; Fiedler & Stroehm, 1986; Forgas & Bower, 1987; Isen, 1984, 1987), subsequent research showed that affect priming and, indeed, all affect congruity phenomena are subject to important boundary conditions (Eich & Macauley, 2000; Forgas, 1995a). It appears that affect congruence in attitudes, judgments, memories, and thoughts is not an invariable and universal phenomenon. In a series of ingenious experiments exploring mood effects on memory, Eric Eich and his collaborators (for a review, see Eich & Macauley, 2000) showed that mood-state dependence in memory is more likely to occur in circumstances in which the affective state induced is strong, salient, and self-relevant. Further, these effects are stronger when the social task involves the active generation and elaboration of information rather than the simple reproduction of stimulus details. It is probably for this reason that mood-state dependence has been difficult to demonstrate with abstract and uninvolving stimulus materials, such as the word lists typically preferred by cognitive researchers (Eich & Macauley, 2000). In contrast, mood effects on memory, attitudes, and judgments are reliably found in social cognitive experiments in which the stimulus information to be recalled and judged is complex, realistic, and involving (Forgas, 1994; Forgas & Bower, 1987; Sedikides, 1995).

In his insightful review of this literature, Fiedler (1991) made a somewhat similar point. He distinguished between constructive and reconstructive cognitive processes and argued that affect congruence in attitudes and judgments should be found only when a task requires open, constructive elaboration of the available stimulus details and the combination of new information with stored knowledge structures. According to Fiedler (1991, 2000), whether such constructive processing occurs when producing an attitude or a judgment also depends on the kind of dependent measures used. Some tasks that require simply recognizing a stimulus or retrieving a prestructured response involve no constructive thinking. As there is little opportunity to use affectively primed information in such tasks, they should show little affect congruence. Thus recognition memory is typically far less influenced by a person's affective state than is recall memory. In a similar way, attitude and judgmental responses that require the mere retrieval of a prestructured response should be similarly impervious to mood effects (Forgas, 1995a).

To summarize, affect priming occurs when an existing affective state preferentially activates and facilitates the use of affect-consistent information from memory in a constructive cognitive task. The consequence of affect priming is affect infusion—that is, a marked tendency for judgments, memories, thoughts, and behaviors to become more mood congruent. However, for affective states to have a mood-congruent influence on attitudes and judgments, it is also necessary for people to adopt an open, elaborate information processing strategy that facilitates the incidental use of affectively primed memories and information (Fiedler, 1991, 2000; Forgas, 1995a; Sedikides, 1995). Thus the nature and extent of affective influences on attitudes and judgments should largely depend on the kind of information processing strategy people employ in a particular situation. There is now much empirical evidence for this prediction, and recent integrative theories of affective influences on attitudes and judgments, reviewed at the end of this chapter, explicitly emphasize the key role of information processing strategies in moderating affect congruence (e.g., the affect infusion model; Forgas, 1995a).

### Inferential Mechanisms

An alternative inferential theory capable of explaining some affective influences on attitudes and judgments was proposed by Schwarz and Clore (1983). These authors argued that "rather than computing a judgment on the basis of recalled features of a target, individuals may . . . ask themselves: 'How do I feel about it?' [and] in doing so, they may mistake feelings due to a pre-existing state as a reaction to the target" (Schwarz, 1990, p. 529). This "how-do-I-feel-about-it" heuristic assumes that affective states influence attitudes and judgments mainly because of an inferential error: People misread their prevailing affective states as due to an attitude target they are trying to respond to.

The origins of this theory that links affect to attitudes and judgments can be traced to at least three different research traditions in the past. First, the predictions and methods of affect-as-information theory are often indistinguishable from the earlier conditioning research reported by Clore and Byrne (1974). In both cases, an incidental association between separately elicited affect and exposure to a new judgmental or attitude object is responsible for the affect-congruent outcome. Whereas the associationist account emphasized blind temporal and spatial contingencies in linking affect to attitudes and judgments, the affect-as-information model—rather less parsimoniously—posits an internal inferential process as mediating the same effect (cf. Berkowitz et al., 2000). The second background for the affect-as-information model can be found in extensive research on misattribution and self-attribution processes. According to this view, people may have no privileged direct access to the real reasons for their evaluative reactions, and they often infer their judgments and attitudes on the basis of salient but irrelevant available cues—in this case, their prevailing affective states. Based on prior research on misattribution phenomena, the affect-as-information theory also predicts that once an affective state is already attributed to a prior cause, it can no longer be "misattributed" to a judgmental target and should thus have no further judgmental consequences. The third line of work that shows a distinct affinity with the affect-as-information model is research on judgmental heuristics. According to the affect-as-information model, temporary affective states function as a heuristic cue in informing people's attitudes and judgments.

Again, these effects are not universal. Typically, people seem to rely only on their affective state as a heuristic cue to infer an attitude or judgment in specific circumstances. This most likely occurs when they are unfamiliar with the attitude object, they have no prior evaluations to fall back on, their personal involvement is low, and they have insufficient cognitive resources to compute a more thorough response. For example, the pivotal experiment by Schwarz and Clore (1983), often cited in support of this model, involved telephoning respondents and asking them unexpected and unfamiliar questions. In this situation they presumably had little personal involvement in responding to a stranger and had little motivation, time, or cognitive resources to engage in extensive processing to produce a response (for a similar critique of this approach, see chapter 29, this volume). Relying on their prevailing mood as a shortcut to infer a response appears a reasonable strategy in such circumstances. Other studies also found significant affect infusion into social attitudes in similar circumstances. For example, in one study we asked almost 1,000 people who were feeling good or bad after seeing happy or sad films to complete an attitude survey after leaving the movie theater (Forgas & Moylan, 1987). As they presumably had little time and little capacity to engage in elaborate processing before producing a response, they may well have relied on their temporary affect as a heuristic cue to infer a reaction.

We need to consider several issues when critically evaluating this theory. Schwarz and Clore (1983, 1988; Clore et al., 1994) argue that their model is falsifiable because it predicts the *absence* of affect congruence in attitudes and judgments whenever the affective state has already been attributed. Several experiments found that calling people's attention to the source of their affect can indeed reduce or even eliminate affect congruence (Berkowitz et al., 2000; Clore et al., 1994; Schwarz & Clore, 1983, 1988). However, there are two serious problems with the falsifiability argument. The first one is logical: The fact that an effect can be eliminated by additional manipulations (such as calling participants' attention to the correct source of their affect) cannot be construed as evidence for how the effect occurs when this manipulation is absent. Indeed, in a series of experiments Berkowitz et al. (2000) showed that affect congruence in judgments due to affect-priming mechanisms can similarly be reversed by instructing participants to focus on their internal states. Further, affect congruence in attitudes and judgments is not always eliminated when people know the correct source of their moods. The overwhelming majority of experiments that demonstrated affect congruence used mood manipulations (such as the Velten method, Velten, 1968; false feedback on performance, or recalling autobiographical events) in which judges must have been acutely aware of the correct source of their moods—yet affect-congruent effects were nevertheless observed. In a further criticism of the affect-as-information model, Martin (2000) argued that the informational value of affective states for attitudes and judgments is not permanent and given but is essentially configural and depends on the particular situational context. Thus a positive mood may inform us that a positive response is appropriate (if the setting happens to be a cabaret), but the same mood may send exactly the opposite informational signal in a different setting (such as a funeral).

Another conceptual problem with the affect-as-information model is that it essentially assumes that people will rely only on their affective states when forming a judgment or an attitude. The model has little to say about how other cues, such as the available external stimulus information, and internal knowledge structures are combined in producing a response. In that sense, this is really a theory of nonjudgment or aborted judgment rather than a theory of judgment. Several critics of the model, such as Abele and Petzold (1994), also argue that experienced affect is just one among many information inputs that must be integrated in order to produce an attitude or a judgment. A somewhat similar point is made by Martin (2000), who argued that one cannot simply assume that the informational value of an affective state is simply determined by its valence. Rather, identical affective reactions can give rise to very different judgments and attitudes, depending on the situational context that qualifies the meaning of the affective state. On balance, it now appears that

most realistic attitudes and judgments that require some degree of elaboration and processing are more likely to be influenced by affect due to the affect-priming rather than the affect-as-information mechanisms. Affect priming involves the activation and preferential use of affect-related information and can thus account for the various degrees of affect congruence observed in realistic tasks when more extensive processing is used.

## The Processing Consequences of Affect

Affect can influence not only the content of people's attitudes and judgments but also the way they go about computing their responses. The memory-based and inferential theories reviewed herein both focus on the cognitive mechanisms responsible for the informational role of affect. In addition to such informational effects (influencing *what* people think), affect may also influence the *process* of cognition, that is, *how* people think about and evaluate social information when they formulate their judgments and attitudes (Clark & Isen, 1982; Fiedler & Forgas, 1988; Forgas, 2000).

Since the early 1980s, there is strong cumulative evidence that positive and negative affect have very different consequences for social information processing. People experiencing positive affect appear to employ less effortful and more superficial processing strategies, reach decisions more quickly, use less information, avoid demanding, systematic thinking, and are more confident about their decisions. In contrast, negative affect seemed to trigger a more effortful, systematic, analytic, and vigilant processing style (Clark & Isen, 1982; Isen, 1984, 1987; Mackie & Worth, 1989; Schwarz, 1990). More recent studies, however, also showed that positive affect can also produce distinct processing advantages. Happy people are more likely to adopt more creative, open, and inclusive thinking styles, use broader categories, and show greater mental flexibility, and they can perform more effectively on secondary tasks (Bless, 2000; Fiedler, 2000, Hertel & Fiedler, 1994; Isen & Daubman, 1984). How can we explain the role of affect in producing such processing differences?

One early idea was that affect influences information processing because emotional experiences take up scarce processing capacity. Ellis and his colleagues suggested, for example, that depressed mood and negative affect directly influence the way attentional resources are allocated and reduce the processing capacity and attention available to cognitive tasks (Ellis & Ashbrook, 1988). In contrast, Isen (1984) and Mackie and Worth (1989) proposed that it is positive affect that reduces information processing capacity. These authors found that the more superficial processing produced by happy mood when computing judgments can be reversed if extra processing resources, such as time, become available. However, as the processing consequences of affect are clearly asymmetrical—positive and negative affect clearly promote very different thinking styles—it is unlikely that the explanations put forward by Ellis and Ashbrook (1988) and Mackie and Worth (1989) could both be correct. It remains unclear whether cognitive capacity plays an important role in mediating affective influences on information processing.

An alternative explanation emphasizes the motivational consequences of positive and negative affect. According to some versions of this view (Clark & Isen, 1982; Isen, 1984, 1987), people experiencing positive mood may try to maintain this pleasant state by refraining from any effortful activity—such as elaborate information processing—that might interfere with their mood. In contrast, negative affect should motivate people to engage in vigilant, effortful processing as an adaptive response to improve an aversive state. In contrast with this affect maintenance–affect repair hypothesis, others, such as Schwarz (1990), offer a slightly different "cognitive tuning" account. Schwarz (1990) argued that positive and negative affect have a signaling or tuning function and that their role is to automatically inform the person of whether a relaxed, effort-minimizing (in positive affect) or a vigilant, effortful (negative affect) processing style is appropriate. These ideas are of course rather similar to earlier evolutionary ideas about the adaptive functions of affect.

One problem with these explanations is that they assume that the main consequence of positive and negative affect is an increase or decrease in the effort, vigilance, and elaborateness of information processing. More recently, theorists such as Bless (2000) and Fiedler (2000; Fiedler & Bless, in press) put forward a rather different view. According to them, the fundamental evolutionary significance of positive and negative affective states is not simply to influence processing effort but to trigger equally effortful, but fundamentally different, processing styles. Thus positive affect generally promotes a more assimilative, schema-based, top-down processing style, in which preexisting ideas, attitudes, and representations dominate information processing. In contrast, negative affect produces a more accommodative, bottom-up, and externally focused processing strategy in which attention to situational information drives thinking (Bless, 2000; Fiedler 2000; Higgins, 2001). These processing strategies can produce very different judgmental outcomes (Forgas, 1998c), yet they can both be vigilant and effortful.

## The Empirical Evidence

As the previous discussion suggests, there are good theoretical reasons to assume that affect plays a significant and interactive role in influencing attitudes and judgments. Affective states can determine how we represent the social world and organize our attitudes toward various social objects; affect can also influence our thoughts, memories, and responses to social stimuli, as well as the information processing styles we adopt. In this section, I review a number of empirical studies that illustrate the multiple roles of affect in attitudes, judgments, social thinking, and behavior. The review focuses on several substantive areas in which the role of affect on attitudes and judgments has been recently demonstrated, including (1) affective influences on attitudes and judgments about the self, (2) affect and person perception judgments, (3) affect and stereotyping, prejudice, and intergroup attitudes, (4) the role of affect in attitude change and persuasion, and (5) the applied implications of this work for areas such as health-related judgments.

## Affective Influences on Attitudes and Judgments About the Self

Affective states seem to have a particularly strong influence on self-related attitudes and judgments (Sedikides, 1995). Most of the research suggests a fundamental affect-congruent pattern: Positive affect improves, and negative affect impairs, the valence of self-conceptions (Abele-Brehm & Hermer, 1993; Nasby, 1994, 1996). For example, when students were asked to make judgments about their success or failure on a recent exam, induced positive or negative mood had a significant mood-congruent influence. Those in a negative mood blamed themselves more when failing and took less credit for their successes, whereas those in a positive mood claimed credit for success but refused to accept responsibility for their failures (Forgas, Bower, & Moylan, 1990). However, more recent studies indicate a somewhat more complex picture, suggesting that affect congruence in self-related thinking is subject to a number of boundary conditions.

### Task Effects

The nature of the judgmental task appears to significantly moderate mood effects on self-judgments, according to studies by Nasby (1994). In this study, participants were induced into a happy, neutral, or sad mood through the Velten (1968) procedure and were then asked to make affirmative (yes) or nonaffirmative (no) judgments about how a series of trait adjectives applied to them. Later, their recall memory for the trait adjectives rated was tested. Happy persons remembered more positive and sad persons remembered more negative self-traits, but only when prior ratings required an affirmative format. This result seems to be due to the different processing strategies that affirmative and nonaffirmative trait judgments require. Rejecting a trait as not applicable to the self may be a short and direct process that requires little elaborate processing. Affectively primed information is thus less likely to be incidentally used. In contrast, deciding whether a trait applies to the self (an affirmative judgment) invites more elaborate thinking, and it is in the course of such elaborate processing that affect is most likely to have an impact on how the information is interpreted and integrated into the existing self-concept.

### Central Versus Peripheral Self-Judgments

Mood effects on self-judgments also seem to depend on which aspect of the self is being judged. It appears that central and peripheral self-conceptions may be differentially sensitive to affect infusion (Sedikides, 1995). Compared with peripheral self-conceptions, central self-conceptions are more diagnostic and certain and contain more detailed autobiographical knowledge. Central self-conceptions are closer to what a person believes is his or her "true" self and are affirmed more strongly than peripheral ones (Markus, 1977; Pelham, 1991; Sedikides, 1995; Sedikides & Strube, 1997; Swann, 1990). Because central self-conceptions are well rehearsed and stable, judgments about the "central" self require less on-line elaboration, and there should be less scope for affect to infuse these judgments. This "differential sensitivity" hypothesis was tested in an elegant series of experiments by Sedikides (1995). Participants were put into a happy, neutral, or sad mood using a guided imagery mood induction, and then they rated themselves on a number of behaviors related to their central and peripheral traits, as assessed previously. Affect had no influence on judgments related to central traits but had a significant mood-congruent influence on judgments related to peripheral traits. Later experiments showed that reduced certainty and the more extensive, elaborate processing required to make judgments about peripheral traits were responsible for the greater influence of affect on these responses (Sedikides, 1995, Exps. 2 and 3). The process mediation of this effect was further confirmed when it was found, paradoxically, that encouraging people to think more extensively about peripheral self-conceptions further increased the influence of mood on these judgments.

### The Role of Self-Esteem

A number of individual-difference variables or traits such as self-esteem may also mediate mood effects on self-judgments (Baumeister, 1993, 1998; Rusting, 1998, 2001). Persons with low self-esteem generally have less certain and stable self-conceptions (Campbell et al., 1996; Kernis & Waschull, 1996). Affect may thus have a greater influence on the self-judgments and attitudes of individuals with low rather than high self-esteem. This prediction was tested in a study by Brown and Mankowski (1993), who used the Velten (1968) procedure or music to induce good or bad mood and asked participants to rate themselves on a number of adjectives. Induced mood had a significant mood-congruent influence on the self-judgments of persons with low self-esteem, but had a much less clear-cut effect on self-rating by individuals with high self-esteem.

Another series of experiments by Smith and Petty (1995) confirmed the role of self-esteem in mediating mood effects on self-related judgments. These authors induced happy and sad mood in participants with high and low self-esteem, who were then asked to report on three memories from their school years. Mood had a significant influence on the quantity and quality of responses by the low- but not by the high-self-esteem group. It seems that people with high self-esteem have a more certain and stable self-concept and seem to respond to self-related questions by directly accessing this stable knowledge, a process that does not allow the incidental infusion of affect into judgments. People with low self-esteem in turn may engage in more open and elaborate processing when thinking about themselves, and their current mood may thus influence the outcome (Sedikides, 1995). Affect intensity may be another individual-difference moderator of mood-congruency effects (Larsen & Diener, 1987). Recent work suggests that mood-congruency effects may indeed be stronger among participants with high affect intensity (Haddock, Zanna, & Esses, 1994) and among people who score higher on measures that assess openness to feelings as a personality trait (Ciarrochi & Forgas, 2001).

### Motivational Effects

Affect infusion is not the only possible consequence of mood on self-judgments. Sometimes the opposite, affect-incongruent outcome may occur. Cervone, Kopp, Schaumann, and Scott (1994) induced either a sad or a neutral mood. Next, participants either evaluated their own *performance* on a task or indicated the minimum *standard* of performance that they would have to attain in order to be satisfied with themselves. Performance ratings showed a clear mood-congruent pattern: Sad participants expressed lower evaluations of the same level of performance than neutral participants. However, mood had the opposite effect on performance standards: Sad participants now expressed higher personal standards than neutral-mood participants. One explanation for this interesting finding is that negative mood may have primed more negative performance expectations in both groups. When the question asked for performance standards, however, those in a negative mood may have nominated higher expected standards as a defensive strategy to justify their expected failure, in a process somewhat similar to self-handicapping attributions.

The likely moderating influence of such motivated judgmental strategies on mood effects on self-judgments is further illustrated in an experiment by Sedikides (1994). In this study, participants were induced to feel good, neutral, or bad using guided-imagery procedures and were then asked to write an extended series of self-descriptive statements. Early responses showed a clear mood-congruent effect. Sad-mood participants described themselves in more negative, and happy participants in more positive, terms than did controls. However, with the passage of time, negative self-judgments were spontaneously reversed, suggesting something like a spontaneous, automatic mood-management strategy. This "mood management" hypothesis was further investigated in a recent series of experiments (Forgas, Ciarrochi, & Moylan, in press). We found that negative mood effects on self-descriptions were spontaneously reversed over time. These motivated mood-management processes seem to be closely linked to individual differences such as self-esteem. People who scored high on self-esteem were able to spontaneously eliminate the negativity of their self-judgments very rapidly, whereas individuals with low self-esteem continued to persevere with negative self-descriptions to the end of the task.

### Positive Affect as a Resource in Processing Self-Relevant Information

Affect also has a further important influence on self-related attitudes and judgments. Positive mood may serve as a resource that allows people to overcome defensiveness and deal with potentially threatening information about themselves (Trope, Ferguson, & Ragunanthan, 2001). The decision to accept negative feedback involves powerful motivational conflicts and requires a trade-off between immediate emotional cost and long-term information gain (Trope, 1986). In two studies, Trope and Neter (1994) found that mood influences the relative weight people assign to the emotional costs versus the informational benefits of receiving negative feedback. Those in a positive mood were more likely to voluntarily expose themselves to threatening but diagnostic information. It seems that positive mood functioned as a buffer, enabling people to handle the affective costs of receiving negative information. Further studies by Trope and Pomerantz (1998) and by Aspinwall (1998; Reed & Aspinwall, 1998) also showed that positive mood plays an important role in facilitating the process of acquiring self-knowledge.

The mood-as-a-resource hypothesis suggests that positive mood allows people to focus on diagnostic negative information. However, this effect is not unconditional. It is important for the negative feedback to be seen as useful before people will willingly undergo the emotional cost of acquiring it (Trope & Gervey, 1998). These effects may have important applied consequences. Raghunathan and Trope (1999) evaluated the mood-as-a-resource hypothesis in the processing of health-related persuasive messages. They found that people in a positive mood not only selectively sought but also processed in greater detail and remembered better negatively valenced arguments about health risks.

In summary, the evidence thus suggests a complex picture; affect seems to have a strong mood-congruent influence on many self-related attitudes and judgments, but only when some degree of open and constructive processing is required and there are no motivational forces to override affect congruence. Low self-esteem, judgments related to peripheral rather than central self-conceptions, and ratings that require elaborate rather than simple processing all seem to promote affect infusion into self-judgments. In addition to its dynamic influence on self-judgments, affect also seems to play an important role in the structure and organization of the self-concept (Niedenthal & Halberstadt, 2000). One indicative example comes from the work of DeSteno and Salovey (1997). These investigators found that neutral-mood participants structured their self-conceptions around the descriptive dimensions of achievement and affiliation. However, participants who experienced positive or negative affect organized their self-conceptions in terms of the positive or negative valence of their self-representations. In other words, affect may also function as a key organizing dimension of the self, likely to reduce the complexity of self-conceptions and structure of the self-concept whenever intense affective states are experienced.

## Affective Influences on Attitudes and Judgments About Others

Human beings are an extremely gregarious species. Responding to and developing an attitude toward others in our social environment is perhaps the most ubiquitous and important social cognitive task we undertake in everyday life. Several of the early experiments based on psychoanalytic or conditioning theories by Feshbach and Singer (1957), Clore and Byrne (1974), Griffitt (1970), and others investigated the role that temporary affect plays in judgments and attitudes of others. These studies typically found that those in a positive mood formed more lenient, positive judgments and that those feeling bad were more negative and critical in their attitudes toward others. More recently, the boundary conditions and the cognitive mechanisms responsible for these effects received growing attention.

### Affect and Behavior Interpretation

Perhaps the most fundamental judgment we make about others in everyday life arises from observing ongoing social behaviors and developing an evaluation and attitude based on what we see. In terms of memory-based theories of affect infusion, there should be some affect infusion into such judgments due to greater availability and use of affectively primed information when interpreting ambiguous observed behaviors. This prediction was first tested by inducing happy or sad affect in participants, who were then shown a videotape of their own social interactions with a partner from the previous day (Forgas, Bower, & Krantz, 1984). Participants were asked to make a series of rapid, on-line judgments evaluating their own observed behaviors, as well as those of their partners. There was a significant affective influence on these judgments. Happy people identified significantly more positive, skilled behaviors and fewer negative, unskilled behaviors both in themselves and in their partners than did sad people. In contrast, observers who received no mood manipulation showed no such differences. These results establish that affect can have a fundamental influence on how observed interpersonal behaviors are interpreted and judged, even when objective, videotaped evidence is readily available.

These effects seem to occur because affect priming influences the kinds of interpretations, constructs, and associations that people rely on as they form attitudes about intrinsically complex and indeterminate social behaviors. For example, the same smile that may be seen as "friendly" in a good mood could be judged as "awkward" or "condescending" when the observer is experiencing negative affect. Talking about a recent vacation may be seen as "poised" by a person in good mood but might appear "boring" when the observer is in a bad mood. Later experiments showed that these affect infusion effects persevere even when people are asked to form attitudes and make judgments about familiar and well-known others, such as their intimate partners (Forgas, 1995a).

## The Role of Processing Strategies

Memory mechanisms and affect priming appear to be largely responsible for these affect infusion effects, according to compelling evidence in the form of reaction times and recall rates that have been provided by further experiments. Happy or sad people were asked to form attitudes and make judgments about target persons described in terms of a number of positive and negative qualities on a computer screen (Forgas & Bower, 1987). Happy judges formed more positive attitudes and judgments, and sad judges did the opposite. The most interesting finding was that affect significantly influenced processing times. Generally, people spent longer reading and thinking about affect-congruent information, but they were faster in producing an affect-congruent judgment. These processing differences are consistent with affect-priming theories. When *learning* new information, affect priming produces a richer activated knowledge base and thus increases the time it takes to link new information to this more elaborate memory structure. In contrast, when *producing* affect-congruent attitudes or judgments, the task takes less time because the relevant response is already primed by the affective state. These results support memory-based theories and suggest that affective states can infuse social attitudes and judgments because of the disproportionate influence of affectively primed information in the way social stimuli are learned, interpreted, and remembered.

### When More Thinking Increases Affect Infusion: A Paradoxical Effect

Surprisingly, several experiments show that the more people need to think in order to compute an attitude, the greater the likelihood that affectively primed thoughts and associations will influence their judgments. These studies manipulated the complexity of the information processing task in order to create more or less demand for extensive, elaborate processing styles (Forgas, 1993, 1994, 1995b). When people have to form a judgment about a complex, ambiguous, or indeterminate person, couple, or event, they will need to engage in more constructive processing and rely more on their stored knowledge about the world to make sense of these stimuli. Affectively primed associations should thus have a greater chance to infuse the outcome. In some experiments (Forgas, 1993, 1995b), happy or sad participants were asked to form impressions about couples who were either highly typical and well matched or were atypical and badly matched in terms of physical attractiveness. Happy participants formed more positive, lenient, and generous attitudes than did sad participants. However, these mood effects were far greater when the couples were unusual and badly matched and thus required more extensive processing.

The same kind of result could also be obtained using verbal descriptions of more or less typical, unusual people as stimuli (Forgas, 1992b). Once again, there was a highly significant mood effect that was much more pronounced when participants judged complex, atypical target persons. An analysis of processing latencies and recall memory confirmed that judgments of more atypical persons took longer to process, and there was correspondingly greater affect infusion into these elaborate judgments. Do these affect infusion effects also occur in realistic interpersonal judgments? In several experiments, the effects of mood on judgments about real-life interpersonal relationships were investigated (Forgas, 1994). Partners in long-term intimate relationships also made more mood-congruent judgments, and these mood effects were greater when the events judged were more complex and serious and thus required more elaborate, constructive processing. These experiments provide strong evidence for the process sensitivity of affect infusion into social judgments and attitudes. Even judgments about highly familiar people are more prone to affect infusion when a more substantive processing strategy is used.

## Affective Influences on Stereotyping, Prejudice, and Intergroup Attitudes

It has long been assumed that affect also plays a key role in intergroup attitudes and judgments. Early theories based on the frustration-aggression hypothesis and psychoanalytic notions of projection and displacement suggested that aversive affective states may directly produce more negative responses to disliked groups. More recently, Bodenhausen (1993, 2001) proposed that in order to understand the multifaceted relationship between affect and intergroup judgments, we need to distinguish between affective states that are long term or short term and that are either directly elicited by the out-group or are caused by incidental factors.

### Long-Term Links Between Affect and Intergroup Attitudes

Most early research on affect and intergroup attitudes was descriptive and sought to analyze the affective content of intergroup attitudes (for reviews, see Cooper, 1959; Haddock, Zanna, & Esses, 1993; Stangor, Sullivan, & Ford, 1991). Several theorists suggested that conditioning processes play a major role in explaining how long-term negative affect comes to be associated with particular out-groups (Gaertner & Dovidio, 1986; Katz, 1976). We know that positive and negative affect can be readily induced as a result of conditioning and that evaluative reactions to individuals and groups can be influenced by these states through conditioning processes (Clore & Byrne, 1974; Griffitt, 1970; Zanna, Kiesler, & Pilkonis, 1970). Such chronic cultural conditioning—regularly encountering and associating certain groups with positive or negative affective states—can account for the ease with which culturally devalued groups can so readily elicit negative emotions such as anger, disgust, and resentment.

Most of the early evidence that linked affect and intergroup attitudes was correlational, and until recently there was little research on the cognitive processes that link affect and groups. Some theorists, such as Fiske and Pavelchak (1986), proposed that it is "affective tags" linked to group representations that trigger an emotional response. More recently, general memory-based and inferential theories were developed to link affect and intergroup judgments. It appears that affective biases on intergroup responses tend to be greater when people are unaware of their feelings, are not motivated or lack the cognitive resources to control their biases or both, and have relatively little information about the target group (Bodenhausen & Moreno, 2001).

### Short-Term Affective Influences

In addition to long-term associations between affect and responses to out-groups, affect can also influence immediate, on-the-spot reactions to out-group members. Early research on this issue was dominated by the so-called contact hypothesis (Allport, 1954; Amir, 1969; Brewer & Miller, 1996). It was assumed that increased contact with out-group members may reduce aversive feelings and improve intergroup relations (see Stephan & Stephan, 1996). In particular, contact episodes that generate positive feelings—such as successful cooperation—are likely to be especially effective (Jones, 1997).

Alternatively, positive affect may also promote more inclusive cognitive categorizations of social stimuli such as groups, thus reducing intergroup distinctions (Dovidio, Gaertner, Isen, Rust, & Guerra, 1998; Isen, Niedenthal, & Cantor, 1992). Several theories of affect and cognition suggest that positive mood tends to increase the schema-driven, top-down processing of social information (Bless, 2000; Fiedler, 2000). However, whether this effect is beneficial depends on whether the categories activated are group categories or superordinate categories. According to some recent experimental studies, when group membership is of low relevance, positive mood may well facilitate the use of in-group verses out-group categories, and intergroup discrimination may be increased rather than reduced as a result (Forgas & Fiedler, 1996).

Other studies also investigated the consequences of temporary *negative* affect on intergroup attitudes. After all, contact with an out-group may often produce feelings of anxiety, uncertainty, and insecurity (Stephan & Stephan, 1985). The experience of anxiety, for example, may reduce information processing capacity and amplify reliance on stereotypes, producing a tendency to see all out-group members in stereotypic ways, irrespective of individual differences between them (Wilder & Shapiro, 1989). In recent experiments we also found that trait anxiety significantly moderates the influence of negative mood on intergroup judgments (Ciarrochi & Forgas, 1999). Low-trait-anxious whites in the United States reacted more negatively to a threatening black out-group when experiencing negative affect. Surprisingly, high-trait-anxious individuals showed the opposite pattern: They went out of their way to control their negative tendencies when feeling bad and produced more positive judgments. It appears that low-trait-anxious people processed automatically and allowed affect to influence their judgments, whereas high trait anxiety combined with aversive mood triggered a more controlled, motivated processing strategy designed to eliminate socially undesirable intergroup judgments.

### Experimental Studies of Affect and Intergroup Attitudes

In recent years, a number of experimental studies investigated the consequences of manipulated affect on intergroup attitudes and judgments. Based on early notions derived from the frustration-aggression hypothesis and psychoanalytic theories, it was initially expected that negative affective states might generally increase intergroup discrimination and prejudice. However, these effects turned out to be considerably more complex. For one thing, it appears that not all negative affective states have the same effects. For example, sadness, anger, and anxiety can have quite different consequences for intergroup attitudes, with sadness reducing, but anger and anxiety increasing, reliance on stereotyped attitudes (Bodenhausen, Sheppard, & Kramer, 1994; Keltner, Ellsworth, & Edwards, 1993; Raghunathan & Pham, 1999).

Experimental research on responding to an out-group has typically been based on stereotyping theories. Although the term *stereotyping* remains somewhat ill defined, it seems to involve at least four distinct cognitive operations (Gilbert & Hixon, 1991): assigning the target to a category (*category identification*), accessing the features of the category (*stereotype activation*), interpreting the target in terms of the activated features (*stereotype application*), and correcting for inappropriate stereotyping (*stereotype correction*). Affect may influence intergroup responses at each of the four stages of the stereotyping process. For example, as we have seen, positive affect often promotes a schema-driven, top-down information processing strategy (Bless, 2000). This strategy may facilitate reliance on group stereotypes when responding to others as long as there are no other demands for more elaborate processing (Forgas & Fiedler, 1996, Exp. 1). On the other hand, Dovidio, Gaertner, Isen, and Lowrance (1995) found that positive affect facilitated the use of more inclusive, superordinate categories; this strategy may come to reduce intergroup discrimination (Dovidio et al., 1998). It seems that much depends on the level of inclusiveness of the activated category, which is likely to be influenced by a number of variables in addition to mood, such as the personal relevance of the judgment (Forgas & Fiedler, 1996).

Once assigned to a category, affect may also influence the amount of stereotyped information people access. If processing resources are limited due to time pressure, distraction, or other interference, fewer stereotyped details are likely to be retrieved (Gilbert & Hixon, 1991). Past work suggests that both negative affect (Ellis & Ashbrook, 1988) and positive affect (Mackie & Worth, 1989) can increase reliance on prior knowledge such as stereotypes. Given the highly prepared and automatic activation of stereotyped knowledge, however, it seems unlikely that affect should have a major influence on the amount of stereotyped knowledge activated, and there is little unequivocal evidence for affective influences on stereotype activation. Once activated, stereotyped knowledge is likely to guide attitudes and judgments in a number of ways (Bodenhausen & Macrae, 1998). In the simplest instance, stereotypic beliefs can be directly used as the basis for a judgment, in essence functioning as a heuristic cue that eliminates the need for further processing. For example, when allocating rewards to members of in-groups and out-groups, positive mood increased reliance on simple group

stereotype information (Forgas & Fiedler, 1996). More commonly, activated stereotypes provide just an initial, heuristic influence on judgments that may be supplemented by other information (Chaiken & Maheswaran, 1994; Duncan, 1976; for a recent review, see Bodenhausen, Macrae, & Sherman, 1999).

Affect is thus likely to influence intergroup judgments both by influencing the information processing strategies used and by influencing the way additional information is selected and used. As positive moods often facilitate top-down, schematic processing (Bless, 2000; Fiedler, 2000), happy persons may produce less accurate social judgments (Forgas, 1998c; Sinclair & Mark, 1995) and are more likely to rely on stereotype information than neutral or sad persons (Abele, Gendolla, & Petzold, 1998; Bless, Schwarz, & Wieland, 1996; Bodenhausen, Kramer, & Süsser, 1994; Park & Banaji, 1999). However, negative affective states other than sadness, such as anger or anxiety, may also increase reliance on stereotyping, according to evidence from several experiments (e.g., Bodenhausen et al., 1994). In addition to such processing effects associated with mood, affective states may also have informational effects, simply facilitating the use of mood-congruent knowledge in stereotype judgments. For example, Esses and Zanna (1995) found in several studies that negative moods increased the tendency to form negative judgments about ethnic minorities.

The final attitude or judgment may further be influenced by people's motivated tendency to correct what they perceive as undesirable or socially unacceptable judgments (Bodenhausen, Macrae, & Milne, 1998). This tendency may involve a genuine attempt to correct for affective biases by either abandoning or recomputing an unacceptable judgment (Strack, 1992). Affect can influence stereotype correction processes in several ways. There is some evidence that negative affect generally facilitates a more cautious, defensive interpersonal style (Forgas, 1999a, 1999b). Consistent with this notion, sad persons seem to be more likely to engage in stereotype correction (Lambert, Khan, Lickel, & Fricke, 1997). Other negative affective states such as guilt also produce a motivated tendency to reduce or eliminate stereotyping, especially among otherwise low-prejudiced persons (Devine & Monteith, 1993). It almost appears as if negative affect sometimes functioned as a warning signal, indicating the need for a motivated reassessment of potentially prejudiced responses (Monteith, 1993). We have found that this "alerting" effect of negative mood is particularly strong for individuals who are habitually anxious and score high on trait anxiety (Ciarrochi & Forgas, 1999).

It appears then that affect plays a complex and multiple role in intergroup judgments, prejudice, and stereotyping, potentially influencing every stage of the stereotyping process. Most of these effects can be understood in terms of the informational and processing consequences of affect discussed previously. However, contextual and situational factors also play a critical role in mediating these effects (Martin, 2000). For example, the quality of the particular affective state, whether it was directly elicited by the outgroup, and individual differences such as trait anxiety all seem to influence when and how affect will have an impact on intergroup judgments. A comprehensive explanation of these effects will require an integrative model, an issue that I return to in the final section of this chapter.

## The Role of Affect in Persuasion and Attitude Change

Affect plays an important role in persuasion and attitude change, as several recent reviews indicate (Petty, DeSteno, & Rucker, 2001). Students of rhetoric and persuasion have long assumed that the ability to induce an emotional response in an audience is an important prerequisite for effective communication. Experimental studies also showed that induced positive affect promotes a positive response to persuasive messages (McGuire, 1985; Petty, Gleicher, & Baker, 1991; Razran, 1940), although this effect is also subject to important limitations (Bless, Bohner, Schwarz, & Strack, 1990; Mackie & Worth, 1989; Wegener, Petty, & Smith, 1995). Several theories of the persuasion process (Cacioppo, 1986) also suggest that how one responds to a persuasive message depends on the particular information processing strategy adopted. Further, affect may influence both the content of thinking and the process of thinking as people process persuasive messages. These effects will also depend on whether the affective reaction is directly elicited by the attitude object (such as a fear-arousing message about AIDS) or is produced incidentally by an unrelated event.

Extensive research and meta-analyses of the effectiveness of fear-arousing messages in promoting attitude change suggest that increasing fear produces increased persuasion (Boster & Mongeau, 1984). However, this effect is undermined when fear triggers a defensive, self-protective reaction or a level of anxiety and arousal that is distracting (Ditto & Lopez, 1992; Janis & Feshbach, 1953). In fact, fear seems most effective when the audience believes that following the message is effective in avoiding negative consequences (Petty et al., 2001).

### Mood Affects Responding to Persuasion

Affective influences on reactions to persuasion largely depend on what kind of information processing strategies people use when dealing with the message (Petty et al., 1991, 2001). When people pay little attention to the message and rely on simplistic, heuristic processing (peripheral route processing), affect often functions as a heuristic cue and produces a mood-congruent response to the message. This may occur because of simple conditioning

mechanisms (Clore & Byrne, 1974 ; Griffitt, 1970; Razran, 1940). A similar affect-attitude link can also be explained in terms of the direct "how do I feel about it?" heuristic suggested by Schwarz and Clore (1983). For example, Sinclair, Mark, and Clore (1994) showed that college students were significantly more likely to agree with persuasive messages advocating comprehensive exams when they were interviewed on a pleasant, sunny day rather than an unpleasant, rainy day. Such direct effects of mood on responses are particularly likely when people are not able or willing to engage in detailed processing.

In an interesting study that illustrates the process sensitivity of mood effects on persuasion, Petty, Schumann, Richman, and Strathman (1993) asked participants to view mood-arousing films that contained ads for a pen. Some participants' involvement was increased by allowing them to choose a pen after viewing the ads. Positive mood generally improved responses to the ads; this effect occurred due to direct, heuristic processing when involvement was low. However, in the high-involvement condition (when choosing a pen to keep was an option), the effect was linked to a different mechanism, involving more affect-congruent thoughts primed by the mood induction. In general, affect will selectively prime mood-congruent thoughts and will influence responses to persuasion when people adopt a systematic, central-route strategy when thinking about a persuasive message. Some individuals, such as people who score high on need for cognition (Cacioppo & Petty, 1982), may be habitually inclined to think systematically and elaborately and may thus be more open to affect infusion effects when responding to persuasive arguments.

The way the persuasive message is framed may also moderate the consequences of affect, as shown in an interesting study by Wegener, Petty, and Klein (1994). When persuasive arguments emphasized positive outcomes, happy mood produced more favorable responses. When the arguments pointed to the negative consequences of failing to follow the recommended course, it was sad mood that produced more favorable responses. It seems as if good mood selectively primed positive ideas that helped persuasion only when thinking about positive outcomes was helpful. When thinking about negative outcomes most helped persuasion, it was bad mood that was more effective. These mood effects were present only for judges high in need for cognition, consistent with the view that it was the elaborate, effortful processing of the persuasive message and the greater use of mood-congruent ideas that was responsible for this outcome.

### The Processing Consequences of Affect

As we have seen previously, positive and negative affect typically promote very different information processing strategies. People in a positive mood may process persuasive messages more superficially and may respond to both low- and high-quality messages the same way. Sad persons, in contrast, seem to be more persuaded by high-quality messages, consistent with their preference for a more externally focused and bottom-up information processing style (Bless et al., 1990). However, as we have also seen previously, the processing consequences of affective states may be modified as a result of additional motivational effects. The most obvious of these is that, all things being equal, people will prefer to think and behave in ways that prolong positive affective states and improve negative ones (Clark & Isen, 1982). In an ingenious study, Wegener et al. (1995) manipulated such motivational effects on the processing of persuasive messages by telling people in happy or neutral moods that the persuasive message they would read tended to make people either happy or sad. When happy individuals believed that the message would make them sad, they did not process the message extensively and were equally influenced by high- and low-quality messages. However, when they thought the message would keep them happy, they engaged in more elaborate, systematic processing and showed differential persuasion in response to strong and weak arguments. Results such as these show that the processing consequences of affect may be readily modified by motivational influences. The flexible correction model (FCM) proposed by Petty and Wegener (1993; Wegener & Petty, 1997) seeks to explain the circumstances in which such motivated corrections are likely to occur.

## Affect and Dissonance-Induced Attitude Change

As Festinger (1957) proposed many years ago, and as dozens of experiments now show, the experience of dissonance between our attitudes and behaviors is one of the most potent mechanisms that produce attitude change (Cooper & Fazio, 1984; Harmon-Jones, 2001; Zanna & Cooper, 1974). As the experience of dissonance clearly involves feelings of arousal and negative affect, affective states are heavily implicated in this attitude change mechanism as well. Cognitive dissonance produces negative affect because discrepancy among cognitions undermines our clear and certain knowledge about the world and thus our ability to engage in effective action (Harmon-Jones, 1999, 2001; Harmon-Jones, Brehm, Greenberg, Simon, & Nelson, 1996). This view is based on Darwin's (1872/1965) evolutionary ideas about affect and on functionalist theories of emotion, in particular (Frijda, 1986; Izard, 1977), that predict that emotions have adaptive functions and trigger responses that have survival value.

However, some revisions of dissonance theory maintain that the experience of cognitive discrepancy is neither necessary nor sufficient to produce dissonance. Rather, it is only when consequences are "real" and there is an experience of personal responsibility for producing negative

consequences that motivated attitude change is triggered (Cooper & Fazio, 1984). In several experiments that contradict this view, Harmon-Jones et al. (1996) found that dissonance and attitude change also occurred when the actor's action had no real consequences. These experiments suggest that cognitive dissonance alone can directly cause negative affect even when the situation does not involve any aversive consequences. This finding seems consistent with other evidence from research on emotional appraisal, in which imagined consequences appear sufficient to produce a reaction (Scherer, 1999; see also chapter 29, this volume). It also appears that self-esteem may moderate affective responses to cognitive discrepancy, as people high in self-esteem seem generally better able to handle negative affective states (Forgas et al., 2000; Harmon-Jones, 2001). Qualitatively different dissonance experiences also seem to trigger qualitatively different affective reactions. Belief disconfirmation is more likely to produce anxiety, whereas postdecisional dissonance is more likely to induce regret. This is also consistent with self-discrepancy theory that specifically predicts that different kinds of self-discrepancies evoke qualitatively distinct affective reactions (Higgins, 1989, 2001; see also chapter 31, this volume).

Some experiments suggest a direct relationship between discrepancy-produced negative affect and subsequent attitude change (Zanna & Cooper, 1974). Others, however, failed to find such a link (Elliot & Devine, 1994; Higgins, Rhodewalt, & Zanna, 1979). Measures of arousal also failed to show a direct link between electrodermal activity and attitude change (Elkin & Leippe, 1986; Harmon-Jones et al., 1996; Losch & Cacioppo, 1990). Harmon-Jones (2001) suggested that these findings may be inconclusive because the attitudes measured are very resistant to change. Further, as affect intensity increases, controlled processing may take over, and discrepancy reduction may not occur. Other studies also support the idea that once attention is directed at an affective state, its influence on cognition and behavior is often reduced (Berkowitz et al., 2000). The availability of alternative attributions for aversive affect may also reduce subsequent attitude change (Losch & Cacioppo, 1990). Other studies suggest that positive affect decreases, and negative affect increases, dissonance reduction and attitude change even if the source of affect is unrelated (Kidd & Berkowitz, 1976; Rhodewalt & Comer, 1979). Once consonance is restored, affective state also tends to improve (Burris, Harmon-Jones, & Tarpley, 1997; Elliot & Devine, 1994). In conclusion, affective states seem to play an important role in attitude change, influencing both the way people respond to persuasive messages and the way they resolve attitude-behavior discrepancies. However, much work remains to be done in discovering the precise cognitive mechanisms responsible for these effects.

## Affect, Attitudes, and Behavior

One of the perennial questions in attitude research concerns the links between attitudes and behavior. Although it is frequently claimed that attitudes can predict behavior, in practice these links can be quite tenuous (Eagly & Chaiken, 1993). In this section, I discuss some experiments that speak to a related question: If affect can influence attitudes and judgments, as we have seen in previous experiments, will it also influence subsequent social behaviors? Most interpersonal behaviors necessarily require people to engage in substantive, generative information processing, as they need to evaluate and plan their behaviors in inherently complex and uncertain social situations (Heider, 1958). To the extent that affective states may influence attitudes, thinking, and judgments, they should also have a corresponding effect on subsequent social behaviors that are the outcome of elaborate, constructive thinking. Positive affect should thus prime positive information and produce more confident, friendly, and cooperative "approach" attitudes and behaviors, whereas negative affect should prime negative memories and produce avoidant, defensive, or unfriendly attitudes and behaviors. This possibility was evaluated in a series of more recent studies.

### Affect Infusion and Responding to Interpersonal Situations

One field study investigated affective influences on attitudes toward, and responses to, a person who unexpectedly approached participants with an impromptu request (Forgas, 1998b). The scene of the study was a university library. Affect was induced by leaving folders containing pretested pictures (or text) designed to induce positive or negative mood on some unoccupied library desks, with an instruction, "Please open and consider this." Students occupying the desks were surreptitiously observed to ensure that they fully exposed themselves to the mood induction. Soon afterward, they were approached by another student (in fact, a confederate) and received an unexpected polite or impolite request for several sheets of paper needed to complete an essay. Their responses were noted, and a short time later they were asked to complete a brief questionnaire assessing their attitudes toward and evaluation of the request and the requester.

There was a clear mood-congruent pattern in attitudes and responses to the requester. Negative mood resulted in a more critical, negative attitude to the request and the requester and less compliance than did positive mood. In an interesting pattern, these mood effects were greater when the request was impolite rather than polite, presumably because impolite, unconventional requests are likely to require more elaborate and substantive processing. This explanation was supported by evidence for better recall

memory for these messages. More routine, polite, and conventional requests, on the other hand, were processed less substantively, were less influenced by mood, and were also remembered less accurately later on. These results confirm that affect infusion can have a significant effect on determining attitudes and behavioral responses to people encountered in realistic everyday situations.

### Affective Influences on Strategic Communication

Requesting is a strategic interpersonal task that is characterized by psychological ambiguity and conflict and that requires open, elaborate processing to produce just the right degree of directness and politeness. Positive mood should prime a more confident, direct requesting style, and negative mood should lead to more cautious, polite requests (Forgas, 1999a). Further, these mood effects on requesting seem to be much stronger when the request situation was more demanding and difficult and required more extensive, substantive processing to evaluate.

Are these affect infusion effects into interpersonal attitudes and behavior also likely to occur in real-life interpersonal situations? In order to establish the external validity of this phenomenon, an unobtrusive experiment was carried out (Forgas, 1999b, Exp. 2). Affect was induced by asking participants to view happy or sad films. Next, in an apparently impromptu development, the experimenter casually asked participants to get a file from a neighboring office while the next experiment was set up. All participants agreed. In fact, their actual words used in requesting the file were recorded by a concealed tape recorder in the neighboring office, and their requests were subsequently analyzed for politeness and other qualities. Results showed a strong affective influence on these naturally produced requests. Negative mood resulted in more polite, indirect, friendly, and elaborate forms of request. Positive mood in turn produced less polite, more direct, and less elaborate requests. Affective state also influenced the latency of the request: Those in a negative mood were more hesitant and delayed making their requests much longer than did control or happy persons. Recall memory for the exact words used showed that recall accuracy—used here as an index of elaborate processing—was positively and significantly related to the degree of affect infusion. This result confirms that affect infusion into attitudes and behaviors should be greater when more elaborate, substantive processing is required to produce a strategic response in realistic social situations.

### Affect, Attitudes, and Strategic Negotiation

Affective states should play a particularly important role in elaborately planned interpersonal encounters, such as attitudes toward future bargaining partners and the planning and performance of complex negotiating encounters

(Forgas, 1998a). In a series of studies, positive mood produced more positive and optimistic attitudes about the interaction partners and the task and led to more ambitious negotiating goals and the formulation of more optimistic, cooperative, and integrative negotiating strategies. These findings suggest that even slight changes in affective state due to an unrelated prior event can influence the attitudes people develop to novel social situations, the goals they set for themselves, and the way they ultimately behave in strategic interpersonal encounters.

Why do these effects occur? When people face an uncertain and unpredictable social encounter, such as a negotiating task, they need to rely on open, constructive processing in order to formulate new attitudes, thoughts, and plans to guide their interpersonal behaviors. In other words, they must go beyond the information given and rely on their available thoughts and memories to construct a response. Affect can selectively prime more affect-congruent thoughts and associations, and these ideas should ultimately influence the formulation of attitudes, plans, and behaviors. Overall, these results establish that affect has a significant influence not only on attitudes and judgments but also on people's interpretation of social situations and their subsequent interpersonal behaviors. These findings also show that affective influences on social behaviors are highly process dependent: Affect infusion is increased or reduced depending on just how much open, constructive processing is required to deal with a more or less demanding interpersonal task.

### Some Applied Consequences: Affect and Health-Related Attitudes and Judgments

The role of affect in health-related attitudes, judgments, and behaviors has received intense attention (Salovey, Detweiler, Steward, & Bedell, 2001). Positive or negative affective states may promote healthy or unhealthy perceptions, judgments, and attitudes and may ultimately also influence physical well-being. Numerous studies found a clear correlation between good moods and subjective health outcomes. Other experiments suggest that happy moods reduce the incidence of reported physical symptoms and promote more positive, optimistic attitudes and beliefs about health-related issues (Salovey & Birnbaum, 1989).

It is hardly surprising that ill health is typically associated with more negative moods, thoughts, and judgments. The more interesting question is whether there is a reverse effect: Can induced mood have a causal influence on reported health symptoms and attitudes? Several studies suggest that the answer is likely to be "yes." Individuals who experience negative moods report more and more severe physical symptoms, and these findings appear to be quite robust (Abele & Hermer, 1993; Croyle & Uretsky, 1987). Salovey and Birnbaum (1989) found that sick students who were suffering from cold or flu reported symptoms of differing intensity depending on their induced mood. Sad participants reported nearly twice as many aches and pains as those made to feel happy, even though there were no differences between the two groups before the mood induction.

Affect also influences attitudes and beliefs about one's ability to manage one's health. Mood effects on health-related self-efficacy are an important predictor of actual health behaviors such as engaging in safe sex, smoking cessation, and adopting a healthy diet (Salovey, Rothman, & Rodin, 1998). Happy persons typically judge themselves as more able to carry out such health-promoting behaviors (Salovey & Birnbaum, 1989) and tend to form more optimistic estimates of the likelihood of future positive and negative events (Forgas & Moylan, 1987; Mayer, Gaschke, Braverman, & Evans, 1992; Mayer & Volanth, 1985).

Although the effects of affect on health-related attitudes and judgments appear robust and reliable, the psychological mechanisms responsible for these effects are not yet fully understood. One possibility is that affective states may directly influence the immune system and susceptibility to disease. Interestingly, these effects tend to be stronger when participants are instructed to express rather than repress their moods (Labott & Martin, 1990). Individual difference variables such as optimism, affect intensity, anxiety, hope, and affect regulation skills appear to mediate many of these effects (Salovey et al., 2001). Optimism, for example, can have a direct effect not only on health-related attitudes but also on immune system functioning. Hope also seems to be linked to having a larger number of and more adaptive ideas and attitudes about how to take care of oneself when sick (Snyder, 1994). It appears, then, that affect has a highly important influence on attitudes, judgments, and behaviors related to health and illness. However, these effects are subject to quite complex mediating influences that involve a range of variables, such as immune system responses, personality characteristics, and social relationships (Salovey et al., 2001).

### Toward a Theoretical Integration: The Affect Infusion Model

As this necessarily brief review of the evidence shows, affective states have a powerful and multifaceted influence on the way people perceive, interpret, and represent social information and the way they formulate attitudes and judgments. Two major kinds of influences have been identified: informational effects, in which affect informs the content of attitudes and judgments, and processing effects, in which affect influences how people deal with social information. It is also clear, however, that affective influences on attitudes and judgments are highly context specific. A comprehensive explanation of these effects needs to specify the circumstances that promote or inhibit affect congruence and should also define the conditions that lead to affect priming, or the affect-as-information mechanisms.

A recent integrative theory, the affect infusion model (AIM; Forgas, 1995a), sought to accomplish this task by predicting that affect infusion should only occur in circumstances that promote an open, constructive processing style (Fiedler, 1991; Forgas, 1992b, 1995b). Constructive processing involves the active elaboration of the available stimulus details and the use of memory-based information in this process. The AIM thus assumes that (1) the extent and nature of affect infusion should be dependent on the kind of processing strategy that is used and (2) that all things being equal, people should use the least effortful and simplest processing strategy capable of producing a response. As this model has been adequately described elsewhere, only a brief overview is included here (Forgas, 1992a, 1995a).

The AIM identifies four alternative processing strategies: *direct access, motivated, heuristic,* and *substantive* processing. The first two of these strategies, direct access and motivated processing, involve highly targeted and predetermined patterns of information search and selection, strategies that limit the scope for incidental affect infusion. These four strategies differ in terms of two basic dimensions: the degree of *effort* exerted in seeking a solution and the degree of *openness* and constructiveness of the information search strategy. The combination of these two processing features, quantity (effort) and quality (openness), produces four distinct processing styles: *substantive processing* (high effort/open, constructive), *motivated processing* (high effort/closed), *heuristic processing* (low effort/open, constructive), and *direct access processing* (low effort/closed). According to the model, mood congruence and affect infusion are most likely when constructive processing, such as substantive or heuristic processing, is used. In contrast, affect is unlikely to affect the outcome of closed, merely reconstructive tasks that involve motivated or direct access processing (see also Fiedler, 1990, 1991).

The *direct access strategy* involves the direct retrieval of a preexisting response and is most likely to occur when the task is highly familiar and when no strong cognitive, affective, situational, or motivational cues call for more elaborate processing. For example, if somebody asks you to make an evaluative judgment about a very well-known political leader, a previously computed and stored response can be readily retrieved, as this topic has been extensively thought about in the past. People possess a rich store of such preformed attitudes and judgments. As such, standard responses—such as judging central features of our self-concept (Sedikides, 1995)—require no constructive processing, and affect infusion should not occur. The *motivated processing strategy* involves highly selective and targeted thinking that is dominated by a particular motivational objective. This strategy also precludes open information search and should be impervious to affect infusion (Clark & Isen, 1982). For example, if in a job interview you are asked about your attitude toward the company you want to join, the response will be dominated by the motivation to produce an acceptable response. Open, constructive processing is inhibited, and affect infusion is unlikely to occur. However, the consequences of motivated processing may be more complex and, depending on the particular processing goal, may also produce a reversal of affect infusion effects (Berkowitz et al., 2000; Forgas, 1991; Forgas & Fiedler, 1996). Recent theories, such as as Martin's (2000) configural model, go some way toward accounting for these context-specific influences.

The remaining two processing strategies, *heuristic* and *substantive* processing, require more constructive and open-ended information search strategies and thus facilitate affect infusion. *Heuristic processing* is most likely when the task is simple, familiar, and of little personal relevance, when cognitive capacity is limited, and when there are no motivational or situational pressures for more detailed processing. This is the kind of superficial, quick processing people are likely to adopt when they are asked to respond to unexpected questions in a telephone survey (Schwarz & Clore, 1983) or are asked to reply to a street survey (Forgas & Moylan, 1987). Heuristic processing can lead to affect infusion as long as people rely on affect as a simple inferential cue and adopt the "how do I feel about it" heuristics to produce a response (Clore et al., 1994; Schwarz & Clore, 1988). When simpler processing strategies such as direct access, motivated, or heuristic processing prove inadequate, people will actually need to engage in *substantive processing* to fully deal with a social situation. Substantive processing requires individuals to select, encode, and interpret novel information and to relate this information to their preexisting memory-based knowledge structures in order to compute and produce a response. This is the kind of strategy people might employ when thinking about interpersonal conflicts or trying to decide how to make a problematic request (Forgas, 1994, 1999a, 1999b).

Substantive processing should be adopted when the task is in some ways demanding, atypical, complex, novel, or personally relevant; when there are no direct access responses available; when there are no clear motivational goals to guide processing; and when there are adequate time and other processing resources available to engage in elaborate processing. Substantive processing is an inherently open and constructive strategy, and affect may selectively prime access to, and facilitate the use of, related thoughts, ideas, memories, and interpretations. The AIM makes the interesting and counterintuitive prediction that affect infusion (and mood congruence) should be increased when more extensive and elaborate processing is required to deal with a more complex, demanding, or novel task. Such a pattern has now been confirmed in several of the experiments reviewed herein (Fiedler & Stroehm, 1986; Forgas, 1992b, 1993, 1995b, 1998a, 1998b; Forgas & Bower, 1987; Sedikides, 1995).

The AIM also specifies a range of contextual variables related to the *task*, the *person*, and the *situation* that jointly influence processing choices. For example, greater task familiarity, complexity, and typicality should recruit more substantive processing. Personal characteristics that influence processing style include motivation, cognitive capacity, and personality traits such as self-esteem (see also Rusting, 1998, 2001), as well as the affective state itself. Situational features that have an impact on processing style include social norms, public scrutiny, and social influence by others (e.g., Forgas, 1990). An important feature of the AIM is that it recognizes that affect itself can also influence processing choices. As we have seen before (e.g., Bless, 2000; Fiedler, 2000), positive affect typically generates a more top-down, schema-driven processing style in cases in which internal, existing knowledge dominates and new stimulus information is assimilated to what is already known. In contrast, negative affect often triggers more piecemeal, bottom-up processing strategies in cases in which attention is focused on the outside world and attention to external details dominates over existing stored knowledge. The key prediction of the AIM is the *absence* of affect infusion when direct access or motivated processing is used and the *presence* of affect infusion during heuristic and substantive processing. The implications of this model have now been supported in a number of the experiments considered here.

## Summary

The evidence reviewed in this chapter shows that mild everyday affective states can have a highly significant influence on the way people perceive and interpret social situations and the attitudes they form. Not surprisingly, affective reactions to social events can also play a critical role in how attitudes and social information are cognitively represented and categorized (Forgas, 1979; Niedenthal & Halberstadt, 2000). Further, several of the experiments discussed here show that different information processing strategies play a key role in explaining these effects. The multiprocess affect infusion model (Forgas, 1995a) in particular offers a simple and parsimonious explanation of when, how, and why affect infusion into attitudes and judgments is likely to occur. A number of studies found support for the counterintuitive prediction

derived from the AIM that more extensive, substantive processing enhances mood congruity effects (Forgas, 1992b, 1994, 1995b; Nasby, 1994, 1996; Sedikides, 1995).

These affect infusion effects influence not only attitudes and judgments but also both simple and complex interpersonal behaviors. Several of the experiments described here found that affect can influence the monitoring and interpretation of observed encounters, the formulation of and responses to requests, and the planning and execution of strategic negotiations (Forgas, 1998a, 1998b, 1999a, 1999b). In contrast, affect infusion is absent whenever a social cognitive task could be performed using a simple, well-rehearsed direct access strategy or a highly motivated strategy. In these conditions, there is little need and little opportunity for incidentally primed mood-congruent information to infuse information processing (Fiedler, 1991; Forgas, 1995a). Several of these experiments also demonstrated that affect infusion occurs not only in the laboratory but also in many real-life situations. Even such highly involved and complex tasks as forming attitudes and dealing with intimate relationship conflicts can be subject to a mood-congruent bias (Forgas, 1994).

In summary, this chapter emphasized the closely interactive relationship between affective states and different information processing strategies as the key to understanding affective influences on attitudes, judgments, social cognition, and interpersonal behavior. The affect infusion model offers a multiprocess explanation of the conditions likely to facilitate or inhibit affect infusion effects. Obviously a great deal more research is needed before we can fully understand the multiple influences that affect has on attitudes, judgments, and interpersonal behavior. Hopefully, this paper will stimulate further interest in this fascinating and rapidly developing area of inquiry.

## NOTE

This work was supported by a Special Investigator award from the Australian Research Council, and the Research Prize by the Alexander von Humboldt Foundation to Joseph P. Forgas. The contribution of Joseph Ciarrochi, Stephanie Moylan, Patrick Vargas, and Joan Webb to this project is gratefully acknowledged. Please address all correspondence in connection with this paper to Joseph P. Forgas at the School of Psychology, University of New South Wales, Sydney 2052, Australia; e-mail *jp.forgas@unsw.edu.au.* For further information on this research project, see also website at *www.psy.unsw.edu.au/~users/JForgas/jforgas.htm.*

## References

Abele, A., Gendolla, G. H. E., & Petzold, P. (1998). Positive mood and in-group–out-group differentiation in a minimal group setting. *Personality and Social Psychology Bulletin, 24,* 1343–1357.

Abele, A., & Hermer, P. (1993). Mood influences on health-related judgments: Appraisal of own health versus appraisal of unhealthy behaviours. *European Journal of Social Psychology, 23*, 613–625.

Abele, A., & Petzold, P. (1994). How does mood operate in an impression formation task? An information integration approach. *European Journal of Social Psychology, 24*, 173–188.

Adolphs, R., & Damasio, A. (2001). The interaction of affect and cognition: A neurobiological perspective. In J. P. Forgas (Ed.), *The handbook of affect and social cognition* (pp. 27–49). Mahwah, NJ: Erlbaum.

Allport, G. W. (1954). *The nature of prejudice.* Reading, MA: Addison-Wesley.

Amir, Y. (1969). Contact hypothesis in ethnic relations. *Psychological Bulletin, 71*, 319–342.

Aspinwall, L. G. (1998). Rethinking the role of positive affect in self-regulation. *Motivation and Emotion, 22*, 1–32.

Baumeister, R. F. (1993). *Self-esteem: The puzzle of low self-regard.* New York: Plenum.

Baumeister, R. F. (1998). The self. In D. T. Gilbert, S. T. Fiske, & G. Lindzey (Eds.), *The handbook of social psychology* (pp. 680–740). New York: Oxford University Press.

Berkowitz, L., Jaffee, S., Jo, E., & Troccoli, B. T. (2000). On the correction of feeling-induced judgmental biases. In J. P. Forgas (Ed.), *Feeling and thinking: The role of affect in social cognition* (pp. 131–152). New York: Cambridge University Press.

Bless, H. (2000). The interplay of affect and cognition: The mediating role of general knowledge structures. In J. P. Forgas (Ed.), *Feeling and thinking: The role of affect in social cognition* (pp. 201–222). New York: Cambridge University Press.

Bless, H., Bohner, G., Schwarz, N., & Strack, F. (1990). Mood and persuasion: A cognitive response analysis. *Personality and Social Psychology Bulletin, 16*, 331–345.

Bless, H., Schwarz, N., & Wieland, R. (1996). Mood and the impact of category membership and individuating information. *European Journal of Social Psychology, 26*, 935–959.

Bodenhausen, G. V. (1993). Emotions, arousal, and stereotypic judgments: A heuristic model of affect and stereotyping. In D. M. Mackie & D. L. Hamilton (Eds.), *Affect, cognition, and stereotyping* (pp. 13–37). San Diego, CA: Academic Press.

Bodenhausen, G. V., Kramer, G. P., & Süsser, K. (1994). Happiness and stereotypic thinking in social judgment. *Journal of Personality and Social Psychology, 66*, 621–632.

Bodenhausen, G. V., & Macrae, C. N. (1998). Stereotype activation and inhibition. In R. S. Wyer, Jr. (Ed.), *Stereotype activation and inhibition: Advances in social cognition* (Vol. 11, pp. 1–52). Mahwah, NJ: Erlbaum.

Bodenhausen, G. V., Macrae, C. N., & Milne, A. B. (1998). Disregarding social stereotypes: Implications for memory, judgment, and behavior. In J. M. Golding & C. M. MacLeod (Eds.), *Intentional forgetting: Interdisciplinary approaches* (pp. 349–368). Mahwah, NJ: Erlbaum.

Bodenhausen, G. V., Macrae, C. N., & Sherman, J. W. (1999). On the dialectics of discrimination: Dual processes in social stereotyping. In S. Chaiken & Y. Trope (Eds.), *Dual-process theories in social psychology* (pp. 271–290). New York: Guilford Press.

Bodenhausen, G. V., & Moreno, K. N. (2001). How do I feel about them? The role of affective reactions in intergroup perception. In H. Bless & J. P. Forgas (Eds.), *The role of subjective states in social cognition and behavior* (pp. 319–343). Philadelphia: Psychology Press.

Bodenhausen, G. V., Mussweiler, T., Gabriel, S., & Moreno, K. N. (in press). Affective influences on stereotyping and intergroup relations. In J. P. Forgas (Ed.), *Handbook of affect and social cognition.* Mahwah, NJ: Erlbaum.

Bodenhausen, G. V., Sheppard, L. A., & Kramer, G. P. (1994). Negative affect and social judgment: The differential impact of anger and sadness. *European Journal of Social Psychology, 24*, 45–62.

Boster, F. J., & Mongeau, P. (1984). Fear-arousing persuasive messages. In R. N. Bostrom (Ed.), *Communication yearbook* (Vol. 8, pp. 330–375). Beverly Hills, CA: Sage.

Bower, G. H. (1981). Mood and memory. *American Psychologist, 36*, 129–148.

Bower, G. H., & Forgas, J. P. (2001). Mood and social memory. In J. P. Forgas (Ed.), *Handbook of affect and social cognition* (pp. 95–120). Mahwah, NJ: Erlbaum.

Brewer, M. B., & Miller, N. (1996). *Intergroup relations.* Pacific Grove, CA: Brooks/Cole.

Brown, J. D., & Mankowski, T. A. (1993). Self-esteem, mood, and self-evaluation: Changes in the mood and the way you see you. *Journal of Personality and Social Psychology, 64*, 421–430.

Burris, C. T., Harmon-Jones, E., & Tarpley, W. R. (1997). "By faith alone": Religious agitation and cognitive dissonance. *Basic and Applied Social Psychology, 19*, 17–31.

Byrne, D., & Clore, G. L. (1970). A reinforcement model of evaluation responses. *Personality: An International Journal, 1*, 103–128.

Cacioppo, J. T., & Petty, R. E. (1982). The need for cognition. *Journal of Personality and Social Psychology, 42*, 116–131.

Campbell, J. D., Trapnell, P. D., Heine, S. J., Katz, I. M., Lavallee, L. F., & Lehman, D. R. (1996). Self-concept clarity: Measurement, personality correlates, and cultural boundaries. *Journal of Personality and Social Psychology, 70*, 141–156.

Cervone, D., Kopp, D. A., Schaumann, L., & Scott, W. D. (1994). Mood, self-efficacy, and performance standards: Lower moods induce higher standards for performance. *Journal of Personality and Social Psychology, 67*, 499–512.

Chaiken, S., & Maheswaran, D. (1994). Heuristic processing can bias systematic processing: Effects of source credibility, argument ambiguity, and task importance on attitude judgment. *Journal of Personality and Social Psychology, 66*, 460–473.

Ciarrochi, J. V., & Forgas, J. P. (1999). On being tense yet tolerant: The paradoxical effects of trait anxiety and aversive mood on intergroup judgments. *Group Dynamics: Theory, Research and Practice, 3*, 227–238.

Ciarrochi, J. V., & Forgas, J. P. (2000) The pleasure of possessions: Affect and consumer judgments. *European Journal of Social Psychology, 30*, 631–649.

Clark, M. S., & Isen, A. M. (1982). Towards understanding the relationship between feeling states and social behavior. In A. H. Hastorf & A. M. Isen (Eds.), *Cognitive social psychology* (pp. 73–108). New York: Elsevier–North Holland.

Clore, G. L., & Byrne, D. (1974). The reinforcement affect model of attraction. In T. L. Huston (Ed.), *Foundations of interpersonal attraction* (pp. 143–170). New York: Academic Press.

Clore, G. L., Gasper, K., & Garvin, E. (2001). Affect as information. In J. P. Forgas (Ed.), *Handbook of affect and social cognition* (pp. 121–144). Mahwah, NJ: Erlbaum.

Clore, G. L. Schwarz, N., & Conway, M. (1994). Affective causes and consequences of social information processing. In R. S. Wyer & T. K. Srull (Eds.), *Handbook of social cognition* (2nd ed.). Hillsdale, NJ: Erlbaum.

Cooper, J., & Fazio, R. H. (1984). A new look at dissonance theory. In L. Berkowitz (Ed.), *Advances in experimental social psychology* (Vol. 17, pp. 229–266). San Diego, CA: Academic Press.

Cooper, J. B. (1959). Emotion in prejudice. *Science, 130,* 314–318.

Croyle, R. T., & Uretsky, M. D. (1987). Effects of mood on self-appraisal of health status. *Health Psychology, 6,* 239–253.

Damasio, A. R. (1994). *Descartes' error.* New York: Grosset Putnam.

Darwin, C. (1965). *The expression of emotions in man and animals.* Chicago: University of Chicago Press. (Original work published in 1872)

DeSteno, D. A., & Salovey, P. (1997). The effects of mood on the structure of the self-concept. *Cognition and Emotion, 11,* 351–372.

Devine, P. G., & Monteith, M. J. (1993). The role of discrepancy-associated affect in prejudice reduction. In D. M. Mackie & D. L. Hamilton (Eds.), *Affect, cognition, and stereotyping: Interactive processes in group perception* (pp. 317–344). San Diego, CA: Academic Press.

Ditto, P. H., & Lopez, D. F. (1992). Motivated skepticism: Use of differential decision criteria for preferred and nonpreferred conclusions. *Journal of Personality and Social Psychology, 63,* 568–584.

Dovidio, J. F., Gaertner, S. L., Isen, A. M., & Lowrance, R. (1995). Group representations and intergroup bias: Positive affect, similarity, and group size. *Personality and Social Psychology Bulletin, 18,* 856–865.

Dovidio, J. F., Gaertner, S. L., Isen, A. M., Rust, M., & Guerra, P. (1998). Positive affect, cognition, and the reduction of intergroup bias. In C. Sedikides, J. Schopler, & C. A. Insko (Eds.), *Intergroup cognition and intergroup behavior* (pp. 337–366). Mahwah, NJ: Erlbaum.

Duncan, B. L. (1976). Differential social perception and attribution of intergroup violence: Testing the lower limits of stereotyping of blacks. *Journal of Personality and Social Psychology, 34,* 590–598.

Eagly, A. H., & Chaiken, S. (1993). *The psychology of attitudes.* New York: Harcourt Brace Jovanovich.

Eich, E., & Macauley, D. (2000). Fundamental factors in mood-dependent memory. In J. P. Forgas (Ed.), *Feeling and thinking: The role of affect in social cognition* (pp. 109–130). New York: Cambridge University Press.

Elkin, R. A., & Leippe, M. R. (1986). Physiological arousal, dissonance, and attitude change: Evidence for a dissonance-arousal link and a "don't remind me" effect. *Journal of Personality and Social Psychology, 51,* 55–65.

Elliot, A. J., & Devine, P. G. (1994). On the motivation nature of cognitive dissonance: Dissonance as psychological discomfort. *Journal of Personality and Social Psychology, 67,* 382–394.

Ellis, H. C., & Ashbrook, T. W. (1988). Resource allocation model of the effects of depressed mood state on memory. In K. Fiedler & J. P. Forgas (Eds.), *Affect, cognition*

*and social behaviour* (pp. 25–43). Toronto, Ontario, Canada: Hogrefe.

Esses, V. M., & Zanna, M. P. (1995). Mood and the expression of ethnic stereotypes. *Journal of Personality and Social Psychology, 69,* 1052–1068.

Feshbach, S., & Singer, R. D. (1957). The effects of fear arousal and suppression of fear upon social perception. *Journal of Abnormal and Social Psychology, 55,* 283–288.

Festinger, L. (1957). *A theory of cognitive dissonance.* Palo Alto, CA: Stanford University Press.

Fiedler, K. (1990). Mood-dependent selectivity in social cognition. In W. Stroebe & M. Hewstone (Eds.), *European review of social psychology* (Vol. 1, pp. 1–32). New York: Wiley.

Fiedler, K. (1991). On the task, the measures and the mood in research on affect and social cognition. In J. P. Forgas (Ed.), *Emotion and social judgments* (pp. 83–104). Oxford, England: Pergamon.

Fiedler, K. (2000). Towards an integrative account of affect and cognition phenomena using the BIAS computer algorithm. In J. P. Forgas (Ed.), *Feeling and thinking: The role of affect in social cognition.* New York: Cambridge University Press.

Fiedler, K., & Bless, H. (in press). In N. Frijda, A. Manstead, & S. Bem (Eds.), *The influence of emotions on beliefs.* Cambridge University.

Fiedler, K., & Forgas, J. P. (Eds.), (1988). *Affect, cognition, and social behavior: New evidence and integrative attempts* (pp. 44–62). Toronto, Ontario, Canada: Hogrefe.

Fiedler, K., & Stroehm, W. (1986). What kind of mood influences what kind of memory: The role of arousal and information structure. *Memory and Cognition, 14,* 181–188.

Fiske, S. T., & Pavelchak, M. A. (1986). Category-based versus piecemeal-based affective responses: Developments in schema-triggered affect. In R. M. Sorrentino & E. T. Higgins (Eds.), *Handbook of motivation and cognition* (Vol. 1, pp. 167–203). New York: Guilford Press.

Forgas, J. P. (1979). *Social episodes: The study of interaction routines.* London: Academic Press.

Forgas, J. P. (1990). Affective influences on individual and group judgments. *European Journal of Social Psychology, 20,* 441–453.

Forgas, J. P. (1991). Mood effects on partner choice: Role of affect in social decisions. *Journal of Personality and Social Psychology, 61,* 708–720.

Forgas, J. P. (1992a). Affect in social judgments and decisions: A multi-process model. In M. Zanna (Ed.) *Advances in experimental social psychology* (Vol. 25, pp. 227–275). New York: Academic Press.

Forgas, J. P. (1992b). On bad mood and peculiar people: Affect and person typicality in impression formation. *Journal of Personality and Social Psychology, 62,* 863–875.

Forgas, J. P. (1993). On making sense of odd couples: Mood effects on the perception of mismatched relationships. *Personality and Social Psychology Bulletin, 19,* 59–71.

Forgas, J. P. (1994). Sad and guilty? Affective influences on the explanation of conflict episodes. *Journal of Personality and Social Psychology, 66,* 56–68.

Forgas, J. P. (1995a). Mood and judgment: The affect infusion model (AIM). *Psychological Bulletin, 117*(1), 39–66.

Forgas, J. P. (1995b). Strange couples: Mood effects on judgments and memory about prototypical and atypical targets. *Personality and Social Psychology Bulletin, 21*, 747–765.

Forgas, J. P. (1998a). On feeling good and getting your way: Mood effects on negotiation strategies and outcomes. *Journal of Personality and Social Psychology, 74*, 565–577.

Forgas, J. P. (1998b). Asking nicely? Mood effects on responding to more or less polite requests. *Personality and Social Psychology Bulletin, 24*, 173–185.

Forgas, J. P. (1998c). Happy and mistaken? Mood effects on the fundamental attribution error. *Journal of Personality and Social Psychology, 75*, 318–331.

Forgas, J. P. (1999a). On feeling good and being rude: Affective influences on language use and request formulations. *Journal of Personality and Social Psychology, 76*, 928–939.

Forgas, J. P. (1999b). Feeling and speaking: Mood effects on verbal communication strategies. *Personality and Social Psychology Bulletin, 25*, 850–863.

Forgas, J. P. (Ed.). (2000). *Feeling and thinking: The role of affect in social cognition*. New York: Cambridge University Press.

Forgas, J. P., & Bower, G. H. (1987). Mood effects on person perception judgments. *Journal of Personality and Social Psychology, 53*, 53–60.

Forgas, J. P., Bower, G. H., & Krantz, S. (1984). The influence of mood on perceptions of social interactions. *Journal of Experimental Social Psychology, 20*, 497–513.

Forgas, J. P., Bower, G. H., & Moylan, S. J. (1990). Praise or blame? Affective influences on attributions for achievement. *Journal of Personality and Social Psychology, 59*, 809–818.

Forgas, J. P., Ciarrochi, J. V., & Moylan, S. J. (2000). Subjective experience and mood regulation: The role of information processing strategies. In H. Bless & J. P. Forgas (Eds.), *The message within: The role of subjective experience in social cognition* (pp. 179–202). Philadelphia: Psychology Press.

Forgas, J. P., & Fiedler, K. (1996). Us and them: Mood effects on intergroup discrimination. *Journal of Personality and Social Psychology, 70*, 36–52.

Forgas, J. P., & Moylan, S. J. (1987). After the movies: The effects of transient mood states on social judgments. *Personality and Social Psychology Bulletin, 13*, 478–489.

Frijda, N. (1986). *The emotions*. Cambridge, England: Cambridge University Press.

Gaertner, S. L., & Dovidio, J. F. (1986). The aversive form of racism. In J. F. Dovidio & S. L. Gaertner (Eds.), *Prejudice, discrimination, and racism* (pp. 91–125). San Diego, CA: Academic Press.

Gilbert, D. T., & Hixon, J. G. (1991). The trouble of thinking: Activation and application of stereotypic beliefs. *Journal of Personality and Social Psychology, 60*, 509–517.

Gouaux, C. (1971). Induced affective states and interpersonal attraction. *Journal of Personality and Social Psychology, 20*, 37–43.

Gouaux, C., & Summers, K. (1973). Interpersonal attraction as a function of affective states and affective change. *Journal of Research in Personality, 7*, 254–260.

Griffitt, W. (1970). Environmental effects on interpersonal behavior: Ambient effective temperature and attraction. *Journal of Personality and Social Psychology, 15*, 240–244.

Haddock, G., Zanna, M. P., & Esses, V. M. (1993). Assessing the structure of prejudicial attitudes: The case of attitudes toward homosexuals. *Journal of Personality and Social Psychology, 65*, 1105–1118.

Haddock, G., Zanna, M. P., & Esses, V. (1994). Mood and the expression of intergroup attitudes: The moderating role of affect intensity. *European Journal of Social Psychology, 24*, 189–205.

Harmon-Jones, E. (1999). Toward an understanding of the motivation underlying dissonance effects: Is the production of aversive consequences necessary? In E. Harmon-Jones & J. Mills, *Cognitive dissonance: Progress on a pivotal theory in social psychology* (pp. 71–99). Washington, DC: American Psychological Association.

Harmon-Jones, E. (2001). The role of affect in cognitive dissonance processes. In J. P. Forgas (Ed.). *The handbook of affect and social cognition* (pp. 237–255). Mahwah, NJ: Erlbaum.

Harmon-Jones, E., Brehm, J. W., Greenberg, J., Simon, L., & Nelson, D. E. (1996). Evidence that the production of aversive consequences is not necessary to create cognitive dissonance. *Journal of Personality and Social Psychology, 70*, 5–16.

Heider, F. (1958). *The psychology of interpersonal relations*. New York: Wiley.

Hertel, G., & Fiedler, K. (1994). Affective and cognitive influences in a social dilemma game. *European Journal of Social Psychology, 24*, 131–145.

Higgins, E. T. (1989). Self-discrepancy theory: What patterns of self-beliefs cause people to suffer? In L. Berkowitz (Ed.), *Advances in Experimental Social Psychology, 22*, 93–136.

Higgins, E. T. (2001). Promotion and prevention experiences: Relating emotions to non-emotional motivational states. In J. P. Forgas (Ed.), *Handbook of affect and social cognition* (pp. 186–211). Mahwah, NJ: Erlbaum.

Higgins, E. T., Rhodewalt, F., & Zanna, M. P. (1979). Dissonance motivation: Its nature, persistence, and reinstatement. *Journal of Experimental Social Psychology, 15*, 16–34.

Hilgard, E. R. (1980). The trilogy of mind: Cognition, affection, and conation. *Journal of the History of the Behavioral Sciences, 16*, 107–117.

Isen, A. M. (1984). Towards understanding the role of affect in cognition. In R. S. Wyer & T. K. Srull (Eds.), *Handbook of social cognition* (Vol. 3, pp. 179–236). Hillsdale, NJ: Erlbaum.

Isen, A. M. (1987). Positive affect, cognitive processes and social behaviour. In L. Berkowitz (Ed.), *Advances in experimental social psychology* (Vol. 20, pp. 203–253). New York: Academic Press.

Isen, A. M., & Daubman, K. A. (1984). The influence of affect on categorization. *Journal of Personality and Social Psychology, 47*, 1206–1217.

Isen, A. M., Niedenthal, P., & Cantor, N. (1992). An influence of positive affect on social categorization. *Motivation and Emotion, 16*, 65–78.

Ito, T., & Cacioppo, J. (2001). Affect and attitudes: A social neuroscience approach. In J. P. Forgas (Ed.), *Handbook of affect and social cognition* (pp. 50–74). Mahwah, NJ: Erlbaum.

Izard, C. E. (1977). *Human emotions*. New York: Plenum.

Janis, I. L., & Feshbach, S. (1953). Effects of fear-arousing communications. *Journal of Abnormal and Social Psychology, 48,* 78–92.

Jones, J. M. (1997). *Prejudice and racism* (2nd ed.). New York: McGraw-Hill.

Katz, P. A. (1976). The acquisition of racial attitudes in children. In P. A. Katz (Ed.), *Towards the elimination of racism.* Elmsford, NY: Pergamon Press.

Keltner, D., Ellsworth, P. C., & Edwards, K. (1993). Beyond simple pessimism: Effects of sadness and anger on social judgment. *Journal of Personality and Social Psychology, 64,* 740–752.

Kernis, M. H., & Waschull, S. B. (1996). The interactive roles of stability and level of self-esteem: Research and theory. In M. P. Zanna (Ed.), *Advances in experimental social psychology, 27,* 93–141.

Kidd, R. F., & Berkowitz, L. (1976). Effect of dissonance arousal on helpfulness. *Journal of Personality and Social Psychology, 33,* 613–622.

Labott, S. M., & Martin, R. B. (1990). Emotional coping, age, and physical disorder. *Behavioral Medicine, 16,* 53–61.

Lambert, A. J., Khan, S. R., Lickel, B. A., & Fricke, K. (1997). Mood and the correction of positive versus negative stereotypes. *Journal of Personality and Social Psychology, 72,* 1002–1016.

Larsen, R. J., & Diener, E. (1987). Affect intensity as an individual difference characteristic: A review. *Journal of Research in Personality, 21,* 1–39.

Losch, M. E., & Cacioppo, J. T. (1990). Cognitive dissonance may enhance sympathetic tonus, but attitudes are changed to reduce negative affect rather than arousal. *Journal of Experimental Social Psychology, 26,* 289–304.

Mackie, D. M., & Worth, L. T. (1989). Processing deficits and the mediation of positive affect in persuasion. *Journal of Personality and Social Psychology, 57,* 27–40.

Markus, H. (1977). Self-schemata and processing information about the self. *Journal of Personality and Social Psychology, 35,* 63–78.

Martin, L. (2000). Moods don't convey information: Moods in context do. In J. P. Forgas (Ed.), *Feeling and thinking: The role of affect in social cognition* (pp. 153–177). New York: Cambridge University Press.

Mayer, J. D., Gaschke, Y. N., Braverman, D. L., & Evans, T. W. (1992). Mood-congruent judgment is a general effect. *Journal of Personality and Social Psychology, 63,* 119–132.

Mayer, J. D., & Volanth, A. J. (1985). Cognitive involvement in the emotional response system. *Motivation and Emotion, 9,* 261–275.

McGuire, W. J. (1985). Attitudes and attitude change. In G. Lindzey & E. Aronson (Eds.), *Handbook of social psychology* (3rd ed., Vol 2, pp. 233–346). New York: Random House.

Mead, G. H. (1934). *Mind, self and society.* Chicago: University of Chicago Press.

Monteith, M. J. (1993). Self-regulation of prejudiced responses: Implications for progress in prejudice-reduction efforts. *Journal of Personality and Social Psychology, 65,* 469–485.

Moreno, K. M., & Bodenhausen, G. V. (1999). *Intergroup affect and social judgment.* Manuscript in preparation.

Nasby, W. (1994). Moderators of mood-congruent encoding: Self-/other-reference and affirmative/nonaffirmative judgement. *Cognition and Emotion, 8,* 259–278.

Nasby, W. (1996). Moderators of mood-congruent encod-

ing and judgment: Evidence that elated and depressed moods implicate distinct processes. *Cognition and Emotion, 10,* 361–377.

Niedenthal, P., & Halberstadt, J. (2000). Grounding categories in emotional response. In J. P. Forgas (Ed.), *Feeling and thinking: The role of affect in social cognition* (pp. 357–386). New York: Cambridge University Press.

Park, J., & Banaji, M. R. (1999). *Mood and heuristics: The influence of happy and sad states on sensitivity and bias in stereotyping.* Manuscript submitted for publication.

Pelham, B. W. (1991). On confidence and consequences: The certainty and importance of self-knowledge. *Journal of Personality and Social Psychology, 60,* 518–530.

Pervin, L. A. (1976). A free-response description approach to the analysis of person-situation interaction. *Journal of Personality and Social Psychology, 34,* 465–474.

Petty, R. E., & Cacioppo, J. T. (1986). The elaboration likelihood model of persuasion. In L. Berkowitz (Ed.), *Advances in experimental social psychology* (Vol. 19, pp. 123–205). New York: Academic Press.

Petty, R. E., DeSteno, D., & Rucker, D. (2001). The role of affect in attitude change. In J. P. Forgas (Ed.), *The handbook of affect and social cognition* (pp. 212–236). Mahwah, NJ: Erlbaum.

Petty, R. E., Gleicher, F., & Baker, S. M. (1991). Multiple roles for affect in persuasion. In J. P. Forgas (Ed.), *Emotion and social judgments* (pp. 181–200). Oxford, England: Pergamon Press.

Petty, R. E., Schumann, D. W., Richman, S. A., & Strathman, A. J. (1993). Positive mood and persuasion: Different roles for affect under high- and low-elaboration conditions. *Journal of Personality and Social Psychology, 64,* 5–20.

Petty, R. E., & Wegener, D. T. (1993). Flexible correction processes in social judgment: Correcting for context-induced contrast. *Journal of Experimental Social Psychology, 29,* 137–165.

Raghunathan, R., & Pham, M. T. (1999). All negative moods are not equal: Motivational influences of anxiety and sadness on decision making. *Organizational Behavior and Human Decision Processes, 79,* 56–77.

Raghunathan, R., & Trope, Y. (1999). Mood-as-a-resource in processing persuasive messages. Unpublished manuscript.

Razran, G. H. S. (1940). Conditioned response changes in rating and appraising sociopolitical slogans. *Psychological Bulletin, 37,* 481.

Reed, M. B., & Aspinwall, L. G. (1998). Self-affirmation reduces biased processing of health-risk information. *Motivation and Emotion, 22,* 99–132.

Rhodewalt, F., & Comer, R. (1979). Induced-compliance attitude change: Once more with feeling. *Journal of Experimental Social Psychology, 15,* 35–47.

Rusting, C. (2001). Personality as a mediator of affective influences on social cognition. In J. P. Forgas (Ed.), *Handbook of affect and social cognition* (pp. 371–391). Mahwah, NJ: Erlbaum.

Rusting, C. L. (1998). Personality, mood, and cognitive processing of emotional information: Three conceptual frameworks. *Psychological Bulletin, 124*(2), 165–196.

Salovey, P., & Birnbaum, D. (1989). Influence of mood on health-relevant cognitions. *Journal of Personality and Social Psychology, 57,* 539–551.

Salovey, P., Detweiler, J. B., Steward, W. T., & Bedell, B. T. (2001). Affect and health-relevant cognition. In J. Forgas (Ed.), *Handbook of affect and social cognition* (pp. 344–370). Mahwah, NJ: Erlbaum.

Salovey, P., Rothman, A. J., & Rodin, J. (1998). Health behavior. In D. T. Gilbert, S. T. Fiske, & G. Lindzey (Eds.), *The handbook of social psychology* (4th ed., Vol. 2, pp. 633–683). New York: McGraw-Hill.

Scherer, K. R. (1984). On the nature and function of emotion: A component process approach. In K. R. Scherer & P. Ekman (Eds.), *Approaches to emotion* (pp. 293–318). Hillsdale, NJ: Erlbaum.

Scherer, K. R. (1999). Appraisal theory. In T. Dalgleish & M. Power (Eds), *Handbook of cognition and emotion*. Chichester, England: Wiley.

Schwarz, N. (1990). Feelings as information: Informational and motivational functions of affective states. In E. T. Higgins & R. Sorrentino (Eds.), *Handbook of motivation and cognition: Foundations of social behaviour* (Vol. 2, pp. 527–561). New York: Guilford Press.

Schwarz, N., & Clore, G. L. (1983). Mood, misattribution and judgments of well being: Informative and directive functions of affective states. *Journal of Personality and Social Psychology, 45*, 513–523.

Schwarz, N., & Clore, G. L. (1988). How do I feel about it? The informative function of affective states. In K. Fiedler & J. P. Forgas (Eds.), *Affect, cognition, and social behavior* (pp. 44–62). Toronto, Ontario, Canada: Hogrefe.

Sedikides, C. (1994). Incongruent effects of sad mood on self-conception valence: It's a matter of time. *European Journal of Social Psychology, 24*, 161–172.

Sedikides, C. (1995). Central and peripheral self-conceptions are differentially influenced by mood: Tests of the differential sensitivity hypothesis. *Journal of Personality and Social Psychology, 69*(4), 759–777.

Sedikides, C., & Strube, M. J. (1997). Self-evaluation: To thine own self be good, to thine own self be sure, to thine own self be true, and to thine own self be better. In M. P. Zanna (Ed.), *Advances in experimental social psychology* (Vol. 29, pp. 209–270). New York: Academic Press.

Sinclair, R. C., & Mark, M. M. (1995). The effects of mood state on judgmental accuracy: Processing strategy as a mechanism. *Cognition and Emotion, 9*, 417–438.

Sinclair, R. C., Mark, M. M., & Clore, G. L. (1994). Mood related persuasion depends on (mis)attributions. *Social Cognition, 12*, 309–326.

Smith, S. M., & Petty, R. E. (1995). Personality moderators of mood congruency effects on cognition: The role of self-esteem and negative mood regulation. *Journal of Personality and Social Psychology, 68*, 1092–1107.

Snyder, C. R. (1994). *The psychology of hope: You can get there from here.* New York: Free Press.

Stangor, C., Sullivan, L. A., & Ford, T. E. (1991). Affective and cognitive determinants of prejudice. *Social Cognition, 9*, 359–380.

Stephan, W. G., & Stephan, C. W. (1985). Intergroup anxiety. *Journal of Social Issues, 41*(3), 157–175.

Stephan, W. G., & Stephan, C. W. (1996). *Intergroup relations.* Boulder, CO: Westview Press.

Strack, F. (1992). The different routes to social judgments: Experiential versus informational strategies. In L. L. Martin & A. Tesser (Eds.), *The construction of social judgments* (pp. 249–275). Hillsdale, NJ: Erlbaum.

Swann, W. B., Jr. (1990). To be adored or to be known? The interplay of self-enhancement and self-verification.

In E. T. Higgins & R. M. Sorrentino (Eds.), *Handbook of motivation and cognition: Foundations of social behavior* (Vol. 2, pp. 408–448). New York: Guilford Press.

Thomas, W. I., & Znaniecki, F. (1928). *The Polish peasant in Europe and America.* Boston: Badger.

Trope, Y. (1986). Self-enhancement and self-assessment in achievement behavior. In R. M. Sorrentino & E. T. Higgins (Eds.), *Handbook of motivation and cognition: Foundations of social behavior* (Vol. 2). New York: Guilford Press.

Trope, Y., Ferguson, M., & Raghunanthan, R. (2001). Mood as a resource in processing self-relevant information. In J. P. Forgas (Ed.), *Handbook of affect and social cognition* (pp. 256–274). Mahwah, NJ: Erlbaum.

Trope, Y., & Gervey, B. (1998). Resolving conflicts among self-evaluative motives. Paper presented at the annual convention of Workshop of Achievement and Task Motivation, Thessaloniki, Greece.

Trope, Y., & Neter, E. (1994). Reconciling competing motives in self-evaluation: The role of self-control in feedback seeking. *Journal of Personality and Social Psychology, 66*, 646–657.

Trope, Y., & Pomerantz, E. M. (1998). Resolving conflicts among self-evaluative motives: Positive experiences as a resource for overcoming defensiveness. *Motivation and Emotion, 22*, 53–72.

Velten, E. (1968). A laboratory task for induction of mood states. *Advances in Behavior Research and Therapy, 6*, 473–482.

Wegener, D. T., & Petty, R. E. (1997). The flexible correction model: The role of naïve theories of bias in bias correction. In M. P. Zanna (Ed.), *Advances in experimental social psychology* (Vol. 29, pp. 141–208). New York: Academic Press.

Wegener, D. T., Petty, R. E., & Klein, D. J. (1994). Effects of mood on high elaboration attitude change: The mediating role of likelihood judgments. *European Journal of Social Psychology, 24*, 25–43.

Wegener, D. T., Petty, R. E., & Smith, S. M. (1995). Positive mood can increase or decrease message scrutiny: The hedonic contingency view of mood and message processing. *Journal of Personality and Social Psychology, 69*, 5–15.

Wilder, D. A., & Shapiro, P. N. (1989). Role of competition-induced anxiety in limiting the beneficial impact of positive behavior by an outgroup member. *Journal of Personality and Social Psychology, 56*, 60–69.

Wyer, R. S., & Srull, T. K. (1989). *Memory and cognition in its social context.* Hillsdale, NJ: Erlbaum.

Zajonc, R. B. (1980). Feeling and thinking: Preferences need no inferences. *American Psychologist, 35*, 151–175.

Zajonc, R. B. (2000). Feeling and thinking: Closing the debate over the independence of affect. In J. P. Forgas (Ed.), *Feeling and thinking: The role of affect in social cognition* (pp. 31–58). New York: Cambridge University Press.

Zanna, M. P., & Cooper, J. (1974). Dissonance and the pill: An attribution approach to studying the arousal properties of dissonance. *Journal of Personality and Social Psychology, 29*, 703–709.

Zanna, M. P., Kiesler, C. A., & Pilkonis, P. A. (1970). Positive and negative attitudinal affect established by classical conditioning. *Journal of Personality and Social Psychology, 14*, 321–328.

# 31

# THE ROLE OF AFFECT IN DECISION MAKING

George Loewenstein and Jennifer S. Lerner

Until recently, emotions attracted little attention from decision researchers. Decision making was viewed as a cognitive process—a matter of estimating which of various alternative actions would yield the most positive consequences.[1] Decision makers were assumed to evaluate the potential consequences of their decisions dispassionately and to choose actions that maximized the "utility" of those consequences. Once chosen, it was assumed that the utility-maximizing course of action would be implemented automatically.

The critiques of traditional decision theory that emerged in the late 1960s under the heading of "behavioral decision theory" largely adhered to this cognitive perspective. The main thrust of behavioral decision theory has been to identify (1) cognitive errors that people make when they judge the likelihood of future consequences and (2) simplifying heuristics that people use to cope with the complexity of decision making (e.g., Tversky & Kahneman, 1974). The boom in decision research associated with the emergence of behavioral decision theory, then, largely ignored the role played by emotions in decision making.

The last several years, however, have witnessed a burst of interest in the role of emotions in decision making. Research conducted within the last decade has shown that (1) even incidental affect—affect that is unrelated to the decision at hand—can have a significant impact on judgment and choice (for reviews, see Clore, 1992; Forgas, 1995; Isen, 1993; Lerner & Keltner, 2000; Schwarz, 1990), that (2) emotional deficits, whether innate (Damasio, 1994)

or experimentally induced (Wilson et al., 1993), can degrade the quality of decision making, and that (3) incorporating affect in models of decision making can greatly increase their explanatory power (Lopes, 1987; Lopes & Oden, 1998; Mellers, Schwartz, Ho, & Ritov, 1997). Thus, contemporary decision research is characterized by an intense focus on emotion.

Our goal in this chapter is to highlight and organize these new emotion-related developments in decision research. We organize our review around a general theoretical framework for understanding the different ways in which emotions enter into decision making. Such a framework, we hope, can facilitate integration of the wide-ranging findings that have emerged from recent research and shed new light on several central topics in decision theory, such as how people deal with outcomes that are uncertain and how they discount delayed costs and benefits.

The proposed framework helps to address not only descriptive issues but also normative ones. Throughout recorded human intellectual history there has been active debate about the nature of the role of emotions or "passions" in human behavior, with the dominant view being that passions are a negative force in human behavior (for discussion, see Elster, 1999; Hirschman, 1977; Solomon, 1993; Zajonc, 1998). By contrast, some of the latest research has been characterized by a new appreciation of the positive functions served by emotions (e.g., Damasio, 1994; Frank, 1988, 1992; Isen, 1993).[2] By clarifying some of the different ways in which emotion enters into decision making, our framework sheds light on both the functions and the pitfalls of emotional influences on decision making. Emotions clearly do serve essential functions in decision making, but they are also a potential source of biased judgment and reckless action (see Averill, 1983; Berkowitz, 1990; Tangney, Hill-Barlow, et al., 1996; Tangney, Wagner, et al., 1996).

## Two Types of Affective Influences

To understand the different roles played by emotions in decision making, one needs to distinguish two different ways in which emotions enter into decision making. These two influences are depicted in Figure 31.1.

The first influence—of *expected emotions*—consists of predictions about the emotional consequences of decision outcomes. Dominant models of decision making, such as the expected utility model, assume that people attempt to predict the emotional consequences associated with alternative courses of action and then select actions that maximize positive emotions and minimize negative emotions. This influence of expected emotions on decision making is depicted in Figure 31.1 by line *a*, running from the expected emotions produced by the consequences of a decision to the decision itself. As an example, consider an investor's choice of whether to move some of her savings into a risky high-tech stock fund. In making this decision, the investor might attempt to predict the probabilities of different outcomes, such as losing or gaining different amounts of money (line *e*, stemming from the decision to its expected consequences) and how she would feel under the various scenarios she can envision (line *f*, running from consequences to feelings). For example, she might muse, "If I invest in the high-tech fund and it happens to take a dive at this moment, I'll feel regret about having transferred the funds." The desire to avoid experiencing regret might then dissuade her from transferring the funds (line *a*). Note that the expected emotions are not experienced as emotions per se at the time of decision making; rather, as the label suggests, they are expectations about emotions that will be experienced in the future. The first section of this chapter focuses on expected emotions.

The second kind of affective influence on decision making, discussed in the second section, consists of *immediate emotions* that are experienced at the time of decision making. Immediate emotions influence decision making in two qualitatively distinct ways: (1) They can exert a *direct* impact, as depicted in Figure 31.1 by line *d*, and (2) they can exert an *indirect* impact, by altering the decision maker's expectations of the probability (line *h*) or desirability (line *i*) of future consequences or by changing the way that these consequences (objective and emotional) are processed.[3] Both direct and indirect impacts of im-

mediate emotions can be illustrated by the example of the conflicted investor. As an example of a direct impact, the prospective investor might experience immediate anxiety at the prospect of shifting savings to the high-tech fund. This anxiety might then deter her from investing in the risky stock. As an example of an indirect influence, her preexisting good mood when she is making her decision may make her feel more optimistic about the prospects of the fund, about her ability to shrug off regret if the fund were to drop in value, or about the gratifying uses to which any profits could be put. All of these influences might encourage her to "throw caution to the wind."

As the investing example illustrates, immediate emotions reflect the combined effects of emotions that arise from contemplating the consequences of the decision itself—what we call *anticipatory influences*—as well as emotions that arise from factors unrelated to the decision, which we call *incidental influences*.[4] Anticipatory influences are depicted in Figure 31.1 by lines *b* and *c*, running from expected consequences and expected emotions to immediate emotions. Returning to the conflicted investor, the act of thinking about the objective or subjective consequences of investing or not investing in the fund could induce anxiety. Note, however, that anticipatory influences are not simply a shrunken version of the emotions that will be experienced in the future once the fund has either gained or lost in value but are qualitatively different. In general, because immediate emotions depend on a variety of factors that have little or no influence on expected emotions, the immediate emotions associated with thinking about the consequences of a decision will differ in intensity and quality from the emotion experienced when the consequence occurs. Because the nature of these anticipatory emotions and their determinants are different from the nature and determinants of expected emotions, anticipatory emotions often propel behavior in directions that are very different from those that arise from a contemplation of expected consequences and their associated emotions (for applications of this point to decision making under risk, see Loewenstein, Weber, Hsee, & Welch, 2001). For example, many people experience intense fear when they think about flying in airplanes, even though they recognize that the risks are minuscule. At the opposite extreme, the same person who is afraid of flying may experience no fear about driving but recognize that the objective risks of driving are far greater.

Incidental influences on immediate emotions are depicted by line *g* in Figure 31.1. Recall that incidental influences are emotional influences that do not result from consideration of the decision(s) at hand. Such influences could include the individual's immediate environment or chronic dispositional affect. As suggested, if the weather is warm and sunny, the conflicted investor might experience incidental happiness at the time she contemplates

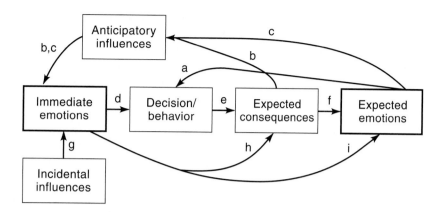

Figure 31.1 Determinants and consequences of immediate and expected emotions.

her choice. Note that incidental influences, by their very definition, are unrelated to the expected emotional consequences of the decision and are thus especially likely to produce divergences between immediate and expected emotions.

Emotions can enter into decision making in other ways that are not depicted in Figure 31.1 and which we do not discuss in any detail. For example, decisions that are difficult to make, perhaps because they involve "taboo" trade-offs such as lives against money, can evoke negative emotions (Luce, 1998; Luce, Bettman, & Payne, 1997; Luce, Payne, & Bettman, 1999), which can influence decision makers' choice processes or even cause them to avoid the decision altogether.

The remainder of the chapter is organized as follows. The first section reviews research on expected emotions. We begin by discussing some of the unrealistic assumptions that decision theorists sometimes make about the emotional consequences of decision making. Next, we review different attempts to increase the realism with which expected emotions are modeled, focusing on two important generic categories of decision making: decision making under risk and intertemporal choice. Finally, we review research on "affective forecasting," which documents systematic errors people make when predicting the emotional consequences of their own decisions.

The second section reviews research on the effects of immediate emotions on decision making. We first discuss the different routes, both direct and indirect, by which immediate emotions influence decision making. Next, we discuss the determinants of immediate emotions, focusing in turn on anticipatory and incidental influences. Of special concern is the question of why immediate emotions often propel decision makers in directions that are different from those that would be dictated by a contemplation of expected emotions. We end the section with a discussion of the conditions under which immediate emotions do and do not affect decision making.

We conclude the chapter with a discussion of the benefits and pitfalls of emotional influences on decision making. This discussion draws explicitly on our theoretical framework and its differentiation between expected and immediate emotions. Expected emotions clearly play an essential role in decision making; indeed, most theories of decision making assume that they are all that matter. However, two major factors limit the efficacy of decision making based on expected emotions: the fact that people systematically mispredict their own affective reactions to the outcomes of their own decisions and the fact that expected emotions leave out "gut" considerations that are important to people. The strength of immediate emotions is that they provide such amorphous, but often important, inputs into decision making. The pitfall of immediate emotions is that they often crowd out considerations of expected emotions altogether and cause people to make decisions that ignore or underweight important future consequences. Both types of emotions, therefore, are essential to decision making, but the wrong mix in the wrong situation can be destructive.

## Expected Emotions

Descriptive and prescriptive theories of decision making, to the degree that they incorporate emotions at all, typically assume that expected emotions are the only emotions that matter. Decision making is viewed as consequentialist in character; people are assumed to choose options that they expect will maximize the net balance of positive to negative emotions (e.g., "I'll be happier if I choose a red car instead of yellow car"). Many theories are quite naive, however, in the implicit or explicit assumptions they make about the determinants of emotion or in the way that they are taken into account by decision makers. In this section, we enumerate some of these unrealistic assumptions about emotions and the efforts that have been made to develop theoretical models that incorporate more realistic assumptions.

## Consequentialist Decision Theories and Their Assumptions

Even when decision theorists do not deliberately make any assumptions about emotions, their theoretical models inevitably incorporate implicit assumptions. Models of decision making, such as the expected utility model, that continue to be widely employed in research and applied in practical settings assume that all people care about are the concrete, absolute outcomes of their decisions. In contrast, modern cognitive-appraisal theories of emotion capture the insight that the emotions associated with outcomes depend not only on the specific outcomes that are experienced but also on a host of other characteristics, such as whether those outcomes were expected or unexpected and whether they were caused by situational or individual factors (Lazarus, 1991; Ortony, Clore, & Collins, 1988; Roseman, 1984; Scherer, 1999; Smith & Ellsworth, 1985; Weiner, 1986).[5]

This next section reviews efforts by decision researchers to develop more descriptively realistic models of the role of expected emotions in decision making. To make sense of these efforts, some background on consequentialist models of decision making is essential. Consequentialist models of decision making address two major problems, each of which has spawned a large amount of research. The first problem, which is addressed by models of *decision making under risk*, is how to choose among outcomes that may not happen—that is, that are probabilistic. If people choose options so as to produce maximally desirable consequences, they must evaluate not only the desirability of different outcomes but also their likelihood of occurring, and they must integrate these likelihoods into their decision-making calculus in some fashion. The second problem, which is addressed by models of *intertemporal choice*, is how to make decisions involving consequences that extend over different points in time.

## Decision Making Under Risk

For centuries, the dominant theoretical model for dealing with uncertainty was the expected utility model (EU). EU remains in widespread use despite ample evidence of its limitations (for recent reviews of EU's limitations, see Camerer, 1992; Harless & Camerer, 1994). EU assumes that people choose between alternative courses of action by assessing the desirability or "utility" of each action's possible outcomes and weighting those utilities by their probability of occurring. The normative status of EU was enhanced by the demonstration by von Neumann & Morgenstern (1944) that the model could be derived from a fairly compelling set of choice *axioms*. These axioms are

primitive, and seemingly sensible, assumptions about decision making, such as that people should obey transitivity—if they prefer gamble A over B and B over C, then they should prefer A over C. However, descriptive research has identified a number of expected utility *anomalies*—patterns of behavior that contradict the axioms and therefore violate the predictions of the model (Kahneman & Tversky, 1979; Tversky & Kahneman, 1984). Many of these anomalies can be attributed to the model's unrealistic assumptions about emotions. Next we review several of these assumptions and efforts to update them.

### First Innovation: Relaxing the Assumption of Asset Integration

Perhaps the single most important theoretical advance in modeling decision making under uncertainty has been the abandonment of the assumption of "asset integration." EU, as it was originally proposed, assumes that what people care about—what makes them happy or sad—is their overall situation after consequences occur. However, as first pointed out by Markowitz (1952) and developed further by Kahneman and Tversky (see also Kahneman & Tversky, 1979; Tversky & Kahneman, 1992), when people evaluate the possible consequences of gambles, they do not think in terms of the final levels of wealth associated with different outcomes but in terms of incremental gains and losses.

To illustrate this modification, consider an individual's choice of whether to accept or reject a gamble that offers a 50% chance of winning $200 and a 50% chance of losing $100. If the individual currently possesses $100,000 in wealth, then EU assumes that she views this choice as one between the utility of a sure level of wealth of $100,000 or a 50% chance of experiencing the utility associated with $99,900 and a 50% chance of experiencing the utility of $100,200. Markowitz (1952) pointed out, however, that most people would not view the gamble in these terms but would instead perceive the choice as one between the utility of gaining and losing nothing and a 50-50 chance of gaining $200 or losing $100. If the individual gambled and ended up $100 poorer, she might *want* to react joyfully by thinking, "I feel great because I have $99,900," but the reality is that she would more likely lament having lost $100. Incorporating the assumption that people choose between risky prospects based on their anticipated feelings toward gains and losses (as opposed to final asset positions) is a major step in the direction of realism about emotions and has wide-ranging implications for decision making (Tversky & Kahneman, 1984; Yates, Yaniv, & Smith, 1991).

Other recent models of decision making under uncertainty not only relax the assumption of asset integration but also explicitly account for the fact that individuals care about emotional attributes of choice alternatives. In contrast to the expected utility model and its variants, which assume that people evaluate gambles in terms of probabilities and utilities of their outcomes, Lopes and colleagues (Lopes, 1987; Lopes & Oden, 1998) argue that risky decision making is a function of two dimensions: security/potential and aspiration level. Security/potential is a dispositional variable that is closely related to risk aversion. Security-minded individuals, according to the theory, focus on the worst outcome of a gamble, whereas potential-minded individuals focus on the best. Aspiration level is a situational variable that reflects the opportunities at hand, as well as the constraints imposed by the environment (e.g., the decision maker's need to earn a certain amount). Initial tests of this model do suggest that some people focus on best outcomes and others focus on worst outcomes. However, the exact role that affect plays in these effects remains to be specified.

## Second Innovation: Pleasure and Pain from Counterfactual Comparisons

A second line of efforts to modify EU in the direction of greater emotional realism responds to the observation that people often compare the consequences of their decisions to what could have happened under different circumstances, which results in "counterfactual emotions" (see Mellers et al., 1997). Two important counterfactual emotions are disappointment and elation, both of which stem from a comparison of what happens against what was expected to happen. Winning nothing from a gamble is likely to feel worse if the alternative was to win $1,000 than if it was to win $100 and worse if there was a 99% chance of winning the $1,000 than if there was only a 1% chance of winning the $1,000. These types of emotional reactions are incorporated into a number of different "disappointment theories" of decision making under risk (Bell, 1982; Gul, 1991; Loomes & Sugden, 1986).

A particularly striking example of the role of counterfactual thoughts in shaping emotion comes from research on Olympic medalists in the 1992 games. Medvec, Madley, and Gilovich (1995) found that bronze medalists, on average, displayed more positive affect when receiving their medals than did silver medalists. To explain these findings, Medvec and Savitsky (1997) proposed that just making a cutoff, as in the case of bronze medalists, elicits downward counterfactual comparisons ("I might have not won any award"). By contrast, just missing a cutoff, as in the case of silver medalists, elicits upward counterfactual comparisons ("I might have won the gold"). Thus, counterfactual thoughts can reverse the expected relationship between objective achievement and subjective satisfaction.

Other theories incorporate a different counterfactual emotion—regret—which results from a comparison between the outcome one experiences as a consequence of

a decision and the outcome one would have experienced if one had chosen differently. Early versions of regret theory (Loomes & Sugden, 1982) predicted that decision makers' desire to minimize feelings of regret could lead to suboptimal decision outcomes, such as *violations of transitivity* and *violations of dominance* (if A offers higher probabilities of superior outcomes than B, then it should be chosen; Bell, 1982; Loomes, Starmer, & Sugden, 1992). But empirical tests have, at best, provided mixed support for either regret or disappointment theories. Robust and systematic effects of regret have mainly been observed in conditions that make the possibility of regret highly salient to decision makers (Zeelenberg & Beattie, 1997; Zeelenberg, Beattie, van der Plight, & de Vries, 1996).

The mixed support for early regret and disappointment theories may be surprising to those who have experienced the intensity of these emotions. However, note that for regret or disappointment to influence decision making, it is not sufficient that it *occurs*. Although regret and disappointment may be experienced intensely *after* the consequences of one's actions are experienced, to influence decision making they must be anticipated at the moment of decision and taken into account. Moreover, even if people do anticipate experiencing regret or disappointment, they might believe it is not sensible to take these emotions into account and hence might try to prevent them from influencing their decisions.[6] Thus, for example, it seems unlikely that the Olympic athletes studied by Medvec et al. (1995) trained any less hard (or harder!) because they imagined themselves not being happy if they won a silver medal; they probably were not aware of the effect and would not consider it relevant to their decision making if they had been.

Another possible reason for the mixed empirical support for regret theories may be that they are misspecified. The original regret theories (Bell, 1982; Loomes & Sugden, 1982, 1987) assumed that the intensity of experienced regret depends on a simple comparison of the outcome one experiences against the outcome one would have experienced if one had made a different choice. Consider, for example, the choice between gambles A and B represented in the table below, in which the payoffs depend on the roll of a die. The theory assumed that if an individual chose gamble B and rolled a 4 (giving her a payoff of $10), she would experience a level of regret that depended only on the comparison of $10 (what she received) to $20 (what she would have received if she had chosen A).

| Choice | roll 1, 2, or 3 | roll 4 | roll 5 or 6 |
| --- | --- | --- | --- |
| A | $10 | $20 | $0 |
| B | $20 | $10 | $0 |

This assumption is probably unrealistic. Sugden (1986), for example, questions whether it is regret that people really care about (and avoid) or whether it is *recrimination*—

regret accompanied by the feeling that one should have known better. Given that gamble B is obviously the right choice, Sugden would predict that the individual would feel much less bad if, having chosen B, she rolled a 4 than if, having chosen A, she rolled a 1, 2 or 3. In naturalistic settings, especially given the operation of hindsight (Fischhoff, 1975), recrimination may be particularly intense because, after the fact, people will almost always be able to find clues that they believe should have been evident beforehand about which decision would provide the best payoff.

Overcoming the mixed support of early regret theories, a recent series of studies explicitly built in the assumption that people care not only about the relative outcomes of a decision but also about what the chosen outcome implies for their own self-evaluation as a competent, intelligent person (see Josephs, Larrick, Steele, & Nisbett, 1992; Larrick, 1993). Specifically, these researchers hypothesize that a motive to protect self-esteem from the threat of regret about a particular choice will influence the choice, especially if the decision maker will receive feedback about the results of forgone alternatives. Several studies support this view. For example, Larrick and Boles (1995) compared two employment negotiation situations, one in which coming to agreement on salary precluded recruits from receiving other salary offers (limited regret potential), the other in which other salary offers might still be received even after agreement had been reached (maximal regret potential). Results revealed that recruits were willing to settle for less money when reaching agreement would preclude receiving feedback. According to the researchers, the motivation to avoid experiencing regret (in this case, if a better offer came through) can have a strong influence on decision making.

Mellers, Schwartz, Ho, and Ritov (1997) have also proposed a new theory that incorporates counterfactual emotion and that appears to have greater explanatory power than the early regret theories. The theory assumes that the feelings associated with the resolution of uncertainty depend not only on the outcome one would have experienced had one made a different choice (as in regret theories) and on the a priori probability of experiencing a better or worse outcome (as in disappointment theories) but also on the *surprise* that one experiences. Mellers et al.'s theory can therefore be viewed as a synthesis of disappointment and regret theories that also incorporates the idea that people respond with greater emotional intensity to outcomes that are surprising—that is, unexpected.

### Third Innovation: Nonlinear Probability Weighting

A third significant theoretical breakthrough in modeling decision making under risk has come from the recognition that the weight that people place on the various potential consequences of a decision is not directly proportional to

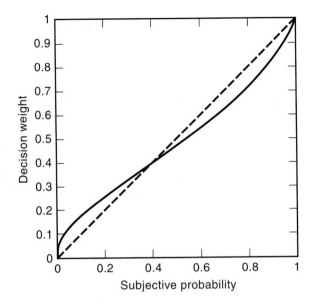

Figure 31.2 Probability weighting function.

the probability of the consequence occurring. Whereas EU assumes that people weight uncertain outcomes according to their raw probability of occurring, numerous studies have shown that a nonlinear probability weighting function best describes behavior (see, e.g., Edwards, 1953, 1954; Kahneman & Tversky, 1979; Quiggin, 1982). Figure 31.2 illustrates a probability weighting function that is broadly consistent with observed decision-making behavior. The function incorporates three primary assumptions: (1) that people overweight small probabilities, (2) that they are insensitive to variations of probability in the midrange, and (3) that they underweight moderate and high probabilities (Prelec, 1998). The impact of the first and third of these features can be glimpsed in parimutuel betting (e.g., on horses or dogs): Because people overweight small probabilities, long shots (which have a small probability of winning) tend to be favored by amateur bettors (and hence provide substandard returns). Because they underweight moderate and high probabilities, strongly favored entrants (which have a high probability of winning) tend to be undervalued (Hausch, Lo, & Ziemba, 1994; Thaler & Ziemba, 1988). (In the second section, which focuses on immediate emotion, we elaborate on the possible role played by immediate emotions in probability weighting.)

### Intertemporal Choice

Recall that the second major problem that confronts consequentialist models of decision making is how to evaluate consequences of decisions that are delayed in time—that is, decisions that involve a temporal dimension. The discounted utility model (DU) is the dominant model of decision making that specifies how decision makers deal with delayed outcomes (see Loewenstein, 1992). DU is closely parallel to EU in structure and underlying assumptions. Like EU, DU has been axiomatically derived (Koopmans, 1960), and a series of DU anomalies have been identified that call into question the descriptive realism of the axioms (Loewenstein & Prelec, 1992).

## First Innovation: Hyperbolic Discounting

The discounted utility model assumes that people treat future flows of utility in much the same way that financiers treat money flows—that they *discount* them at a fixed discount rate according to when they will be experienced. Most models of intertemporal choice assume that people generally place less weight on outcomes that are delayed, referred to as "positive time discounting." Discounting at a fixed rate means that a given time delay leads to the same discounting regardless of when it occurs. Thus delaying delivery of an object by 1 month leads, according to DU, to the same degree of time discounting, whether the delay makes the difference between experiencing the outcome in 1 month rather than immediately or in 24 months rather than 23 months. There is, however, overwhelming evidence that people (as well as other animals) do not discount the future in this fashion (Kirby & Hernstein, 1995; Rachlin & Raineri, 1992; Vuchinich & Simpson, 1998). Rather, people care more about the same time delay if it occurs earlier than if it occurs later. This general pattern, which has been labeled "hyperbolic time discounting" (Ainslie, 1975), has profound implications for behavior. Most important, hyperbolic time discounting can produce a pattern of behavior that is commonly referred to as "impulsivity." People are farsighted toward future decisions; they choose options that give substantial weight to long-term costs and benefits. However, when making decisions with immediate consequences, they will tend to be much more shortsighted and to place disproportionate weight on immediate costs and benefits.

Although hyperbolic time discounting is well documented, it has significant limitations as an explanation for impulsivity (see Loewenstein, 1996). First, it does not explain why certain types of consumption are commonly associated with impulsivity whereas others are not. People commonly display impulsive behavior when they are hungry, thirsty, sexually aroused, or in elevated emotional states such as anger or fear. When not in one of these states, people often make relatively evenhanded trade-offs between immediate and delayed gratifications. The hyperbolic discounting perspective has difficulty accounting for such situation- and reward-specific variations in impulsivity. Second, the hyperbolic discounting perspective cannot explain why many situational features other than time delay—for example, physical proximity and sensory contact with a desired object—are commonly associated with impulsive behavior (Hoch & Loewenstein, 1991). For example, pet shops rely on the emotions elicited by physical contact with a cute animal to produce impulse acquisitions by people whose homes are not set up for a pet.

As the foregoing discussion suggests, an additional factor that may be operating in these situations is the impact of immediate emotions. Many emotional states, as well as physical drives such as hunger and sexual desire, are powerfully influenced by temporal and other forms of proximity. Neurochemical research on animals shows that the expectation of an imminent reward produces an aversive dopaminic state in the brain that is analogous to the impact of food expectation on hunger (Gratton & Wise, 1994). That is, the mere expectation of an imminent reward seems to trigger appetitive mechanisms at the most basic level of the brain's reward system. Short time delays, however, are only one factor that can produce such a visceral response. Other forms of proximity, such as physical closeness or sensory contact (the sight, smell, sound, or feeling of a desired object), can elicit visceral cravings and alter one's course of action (Rolls, 1999). In addition, dispositional affect may serve to amplify or attenuate these effects. Ability to delay gratification varies across individuals (Mischel, Shoda, & Peake, 1988), as does susceptibility to experiencing positive versus negative affective states (Larsen & Ketelaar, 1989).

The case of hyperbolic discounting, therefore, illustrates the difficulty of separating out the influence of expected and immediate emotions. In this case, an innovation in modeling expected emotions—the assumption that people discount delayed costs and benefits hyperbolically—may represent an attempt to deal with effects that are at least partially produced by immediate emotions.

## Second Innovation: Affective Forecasting

An important complication that affects intertemporal decision making is the fact that tastes often change with the passage of time. Changes in tastes can result from a multitude of factors: fluctuations in bodily states such as hunger and satiation; habit formation as a result of past consumption; and maturation as a function of aging and life experiences. Normative models of decision making assume that the only tastes that are relevant to decision making are those that prevail at the time at which the consequences of decisions are experienced. However, considerable research on "affective forecasting" finds that people make systematic errors in predicting their own future tastes (for a review of these errors, see Loewenstein & Schkade, 1999; for a formal model of these errors and discussion of their consequences for economic behavior, see Loewenstein, O'Donoghue, & Rabin, 2000).

Two sources of misprediction errors identified in the literature are (1) people's underappreciation of their own powers of adaptation to both favorable and unfavorable events (see Gilbert, Pinel, Wilson, Blumberg, & Wheatley, 1998; Loewenstein & Frederick, 1997) and (2) the tendency to exaggerate the hedonic impact of any event on which one's attention is focused (Wilson, Wheatley, Meyers, Gilbert, & Axsom, 2000). Numerous studies have obtained results that are consistent with one or both of these effects. Schkade and Kahneman (1998), for example, found that students at Midwestern universities thought they would be happier in California, and students at California universities believed they would be less happy in the Midwest, despite no significant difference between the two groups in mean levels of self-reported well-being.[7] Loewenstein and Frederick (1997) found that, across a wide range of changes in objective circumstances, people expected future changes to affect their overall well-being much more than they believed that matched changes in the past had actually affected their well-being; they seemed to recognize that they had adapted to change that took place in the past but not to realize that they would adapt to similar change in the future. An especially interesting example of failure to predict adaptation involved reactions to tenure decisions among university faculty. Gilbert et al. (1998) studied assistant professors' forecasts of how they would feel at various points in time after their tenure decisions and compared these forecasts to the self-reported well-being of others whose tenure decisions had been made in the past. Current assistant professors predicted that they would be much happier during the first 5 years after a positive decision and much less happy after a negative decision, but recognized that the impact of the tenure decision would be minimal 5 years later. In fact, both groups converged to baseline levels of happiness shortly after the decision. All of these findings, as well as many others, could be attributed to either a focusing illusion (when people exaggerate the impact on well-being of specific narrow changes in their circumstances) or to underprediction of adaptation (when people underappreciate the degree to which they will get used to the changes).

### Synthesis of Expected Emotions

Decision researchers are becoming increasingly sophisticated when it comes to modeling people's emotional reactions to the consequences of their own decisions. Major advances include recognizing that people (1) respond emotionally to relative changes in their situations rather than to the absolute consequences of their decisions, (2) compare what happened against counterfactual scenarios and derive utility not only from concrete outcomes but also from what the outcomes imply for one's competence, and (3) discount outcomes for uncertainty and time delay in a fashion that is different from that specified by standard models. All of these advances have important consequences for decision making, and incorporating these insights into models of decision making increases the models' explanatory power.

As researchers are becoming more sophisticated in modeling people's emotional reactions to outcomes, they are also becoming aware of limitations in people's ability to predict their own hedonic reactions to events. Such mispredictions may constitute a major source of suboptimality in decision making. Many, if not most, of the consequences of decisions occur in the future, when the emotions an individual experiences may be different from those that prevailed when the decision was made. Optimal decision making involves making decisions that will result in positive emotions at the time at which the consequences of the decision will actually be experienced. But the different types of forecasting errors just discussed suggest that people are often systematically biased when it comes to predicting those emotions.

## Immediate Emotion

Recall that emotions enter into decision making not only as future anticipated consequences (i.e., expected emotions) but also as feelings experienced at the moment of decision making. Such immediate emotions often drive behavior in directions that are different from those dictated by a consequentialist evaluation of future consequences. This section provides an overview of the ways in which immediate emotions enter into decision making. First, we discuss relevant research on the mechanisms, both direct and indirect, through which affect influences decision making. Next, we discuss two types of influences on immediate emotions—anticipatory influences and incidental influences—and identify their respective determinants.

### Direct and Indirect Influences of Immediate Affect

Immediate emotions influence decision making via two routes, which we refer to as *direct* and *indirect*.[8] Indirect effects are those that are mediated by (1) changes in expected emotions (immediate emotions influence people's expectations of the emotions they will experience in the future, which affects the decisions they make) or (2) changes in the quality and/or quantity of information processing. Direct effects are those that are *not* mediated by changes in expected emotions or in cognitive processing.

#### Direct Effects of Immediate Affect

Emotions and moods can exert a direct impact on behavior, as illustrated by line *d* in Figure 31.1 (running from immediate emotions to decisions/behavior), even without altering the decision maker's perceptions of decision attributes (e.g., probabilities and outcome values). The nature of such influences depends critically on the intensity of the experienced emotions (see Loewenstein, 1996).

*Low and Moderate Levels of Intensity.* At low and moderate levels of affect intensity, immediate emotions appear to play a largely "advisory" role. A number of theories posit that emotions carry information that people use as an input into the decisions they face (e.g., Damasio, 1994; Slovic, Finucane, Peters, & MacGregor, in press). Affect-as-information theory represents the most well-developed of these approaches (Clore, 1992; Schwarz, 1990; Schwarz & Clore, 1983). According to the affect-as-information hypothesis, when making evaluative judgments, people ask themselves, "How do I feel about it?" and then use their present feelings to form the judgment. Applied to decision making, if present feelings happen to be positive, then the decision maker's evaluations of specific options are likely to be relatively positive, and vice versa for negative feelings (see Clore, 1992; Clore, Schwarz, & Conway, 1994; Schwarz, 1990; Schwarz & Clore, 1983, 1996).

Immediate affect does not appear to influence all types of decisions, but only those for which affect is relevant (e.g. Schwarz, 1990; Wilson, Dunn, Kraft, & Lisle, 1989). For example, a decision about which movie to see renders your present feelings highly relevant (see Pham, 1998). Other decisions, such as whether to run an analysis of variance or a regression on your data, do not render feelings particularly relevant. Feelings are less relevant to the statistical decision in part because expected consequences are not affectively charged (for most researchers) and in part because other considerations dominate. In support of the latter idea, feelings have been shown to influence evaluations of unfamiliar, but not familiar, consumer products (Srull, 1983, 1984). Presumably, consumers have specific factual knowledge about the familiar products, which renders them less vulnerable to affective influences.

The importance of relevance can be seen not only in studies that compare different types of decisions but also in studies that manipulate the perceived relevance of emotions to a particular decision. For example, one study found that participants' immediate emotions influenced their decisions about whether to attend a movie, but only when instructions emphasized the subjective benefits they might get from relaxing at the movie and not when instructions emphasized the instrumental benefits one might get from seeing the movie (in this case, qualifying for a subsequent study that would pay $4.00; Pham, 1998). Other studies have shown that encouraging participants to attribute their present feelings to judgment-irrelevant situational factors reliably reduces the tendency for situational affect to inform judgment (Keltner, Locke, & Audrain, 1993; Schwarz & Clore, 1983). For example, although reading a sad story can temporarily reduce estimates of life satisfaction, having participants focus on the causes of their present sad feelings before rating life satisfaction reduces this effect (Keltner, Locke, & Audrain, 1993).

Certain kinds of accountability manipulations that encourage individuals to carefully scrutinize the relevance of any cues used in forming an opinion also attenuate the impact of immediate emotions on judgment and choice (Lerner & Tetlock, 1999). For example, the tendency for incidental anger to increase punitiveness in unrelated legal cases was attenuated by accountability (Lerner, Goldberg, & Tetlock, 1998). But highlighting the irrelevance of specific affective reactions is not a simple matter. Given that cognitive and affective pathways overlap considerably (Panksepp, 1998), it is often difficult to discern whether one's present feelings are reactions to a judgment/decision target or simply incidental feelings carried over from other events. People are usually completely unaware that emotion activated in one situation has influenced their judgment in another situation (Johnson & Tversky, 1983; Lerner et al., 1998; Wilson & Brekke, 1996). Even if people do become aware of undesirable influences on their judgments and choices, they may have difficulty discounting those influences without over- or undercompensating (see Strack, 1992; Wegener & Petty, 1997; Zillmann, 1971). Moreover, efforts to suppress the emotional experience itself meet with limited success and sometimes have the unintended effect of increasing underlying sympathetic nervous system arousal (Gross & Levenson, 1993).

To recap, these types of "advisory" influences are *weak* in the sense that they can be altered by the relatively simple manipulations just discussed (see Forgas, 1995, and chapter 30, this volume, for a review of conditions that limit the potential for affect to infuse judgment). Aside from problems of over- and undercorrection, increasing decision makers' level of vigilance is often sufficient to attenuate the impact of weak-to-moderate immediate emotions.[9]

*Higher Levels of Intensity.* As emotions intensify, they exert an ever-increasing influence on behavior. Indeed, at sufficient levels of intensity, emotions can overwhelm cognitive processing and deliberative decision making altogether. Under the influence of intense emotions, people often report themselves as being (or having been) "out of control" or "acting against their own self-interest" (Baumeister, Heatherton, & Tice, 1994; Bazerman, Tenbrunsel, & Wade-Benzoni, 1998; Hoch & Loewenstein, 1991; Loewenstein, 1996). The overriding of cognition by intense emotions is perhaps best illustrated in the clinical literature by cases of patients with affective disorders such as agoraphobia who are typically well aware that there is little or nothing to fear in the situations they find so difficult (Barlow, 1988, p. 13) but are helpless to act on that awareness. (Human-subjects committees rarely, if ever, allow researchers to induce intense emotion, so such research on nonclinical populations is scant.) As Rolls (1999, p. 282) writes,

> Emotions often seem very intense in humans, indeed sometimes so intense that they produce behaviour which does not seem to be adaptive, such as fainting instead of producing an active escape response, or freezing instead of avoiding, or vacillating endlessly about emotional situations and decisions, or falling hopelessly in love even when it can be predicted to be without hope or to bring ruin. The puzzle is not only that the emotion is so intense, but also that even with our rational, reasoning, capacities, humans still find themselves in these situations, and may find it difficult to produce reasonable and effective behaviour for resolving the situation.

Such divergences between emotional reactions and cognitive evaluations arise, Rolls argues, because "in humans, the reward and punishment systems may operate implicitly in comparable ways to those in other animals. But in addition to this, humans have the explicit system (closely related to consciousness) which enables us consciously to look and predict many steps ahead" (1999, p. 282). Expressed in our terminology, immediate and expected emotions often propel behavior in different directions.

The direct impact of immediate emotions depends not only on their intensity but also on their qualitative character. Specific emotions carry specific "action tendencies" (Frijda, 1986; Frijda & Mesquita, 1994) or implicit goals that, all things being equal, signal the most evolutionarily adaptive response. In this view, emotions save cognitive processing by triggering time-tested responses to universal experiences (such as loss, injustice, and threat). For example, anger triggers aggression, and fear triggers flight. Lazarus (1991) has argued that each emotion is associated with a *core-relational theme*—"the central relational harm or benefit in adaptational encounters that underlies each specific kind of emotion" (p. 121). According to Lazarus, when a person appraises a given situation, whatever emotion happens to be active can produce an action impulse that is consistent with the core-relational theme of the emotion.

The action tendency produced by an emotion appears to linger for some period if it is not discharged—that is, if an emotion-relieving action is not taken. The result can be that the implicit emotion goals (or *appraisal tendencies*) from one situation imbue judgments in unrelated situations (see Keltner, Ellsworth, & Edwards, 1993; Lerner & Keltner, 2000, 2001; Raghunathan & Pham, 1999). Scholars as far back as Aristotle (1962) have described the perils of emotional carryover. Recent studies highlight ways of deactivating the carryover. For example, a study of anger and punitive judgments found that the attainment of emotion-

specific goals moderated the effects of emotion on judgment (Goldberg, Lerner, & Tetlock, 1999). Participants viewed a film clip of an anger-inducing crime in which a violent perpetrator was said either to have been punished or to have evaded punishment because of a legal technicality. In an ostensibly separate study, participants then read fictional legal cases and specified what they viewed as appropriate punishment for the defendants. In both conditions, participants reported equivalent levels of anger in response to the crime. However, it was only in the condition in which the perpetrator evaded punishment that participants' anger led to increased punitive judgments in unrelated legal cases. If the perpetrator had been appropriately punished and the goal of anger served, participants' anger did not lead to elevated punitive judgments.

As reviewed earlier, affect-as-information theory also highlights a reliable way to attenuate direct emotional carryover. Specifically, encouraging decision makers to attribute the incidental emotion to a judgment-irrelevant source reliably reduces emotional carryover (Schwarz & Clore, 1983) unless the incidental emotion happens to match the chronic disposition of the decision maker. Gasper and Clore (1998) have shown, for example, that dispositionally anxious individuals rely on incidental feelings of state anxiety to inform subsequent judgments, even if the anxious individuals have attributed their incidental state anxiety to a judgment-irrelevant source.

### Indirect Effects of Immediate Affect

Emotions exert not only a direct influence on behavior but also an indirect influence via their impact on judgments of expected consequences and emotional reactions to them, as well as the quality and quantity of information processing.

*Indirect Effects on Expected Values.* A number of studies have found that immediate emotions influence people's judgments of the probability of positive and negative outcomes (line *h* in Figure 31.1). A well-replicated finding is that people in good moods make optimistic judgments and choices and people in bad moods make pessimistic judgments and choices (see Bower, 1981, 1991; Isen, Shalker, Clark, & Karp, 1978; Johnson & Tversky, 1983; Kavanagh & Bower, 1985; Mayer, Gaschke, Braverman, & Evans, 1992; Mayer & Hanson, 1995; Schwarz & Clore, 1983; Wright & Bower, 1992). For example, a pivotal set of studies found that people who read happy newspaper articles subsequently made more optimistic judgments about risk than people who read sad articles (Johnson & Tversky, 1983).[10]

Immediate emotions influence people's perceptions not only of the likelihood of different outcomes but also of how they will feel about those outcomes. Loewenstein and colleagues find that when people attempt to predict their own future feelings and behavior, they tend to "project" their current feelings onto the future (see Loewenstein et al., 2000; Loewenstein, Prelec, & Shatto, 1996). When people are in a "cold" state—for example, not hungry, angry, sexually aroused, and so forth—they underappreciate what it will feel like to be in a hot state in the future and how such a state will affect their behavior. They make an analogous mistake when in a hot state and predicting how they will feel or behave when the heat dissipates—that is, when they are in a cold state. Such "hot/cold empathy gaps" occur not only prospectively, when people predict their own future feelings and behavior, but also retrospectively (as in the infamous "morning after" syndrome in which a cold morning self struggles to make sense of a hot past self's evening escapades; Loewenstein, 1996; Loewenstein & Schkade, 1999) and interpersonally, whereby people have difficulty predicting the behavior of others who are in a different visceral state than themselves (VanBoven, Dunning, & Loewenstein, 2000; VanBoven, Loewenstein, Welch, & Dunning, 2001).

Visceral states for which hot/cold empathy gaps have been documented include hunger (Read & van Leeuwen, 1998), curiosity (Loewenstein et al., 1996), anxiety (Sieff, Dawes, & Loewenstein, 1999), pain (Read & Loewenstein, 1999), sexual arousal (Loewenstein, Nagin, & Paternoster, 1997), and embarrassment (VanBoven et al., 2001). In the study of sexual arousal, for example, the researchers found that male youths who were exposed to sexually arousing materials reported substantially higher likelihoods of behaving aggressively in a hypothetical date scenario than did youths who were not exposed to arousing materials (Loewenstein et al., 1997).

*Indirect Effects on the Nature of Processing.* Immediate emotions can systematically bias the interpretation of decision-relevant cues such that decision makers selectively attend to, encode, and retrieve emotion-relevant information (see Bower, 1981, 1991; Niedenthal & Kitayama, 1994; Niedenthal & Setterlund, 1994). Some studies of selective processing suggest that emotional valence (positivity vs. negativity) determines the nature of subsequent information processing (see Forgas, 1989, 1995; Forgas & Moylan, 1991). For example, a host of studies find that, whereas negative emotions narrow attentional focus, positive emotions broaden attentional focus (Basso, Schefft, Ris, & Dember, 1996; Conway & Giannopoulos, 1993; Derryberry & Tucker, 1994; Isen, 1999; Kienen, 1987). In one illustrative study in which participants were supposed to choose a team partner, participants in negative moods were more goal directed than participants in positive moods. Not only did the former spend more time considering interpersonal aspects of potential partners, but they also remembered more negative features of potential partners than did participants in positive moods

(Forgas, 1991). Participants in positive moods, by contrast, reached decisions rapidly, with fewer repetitions, and were not as focused on particular attributes. Other studies on selective information processing suggest that incidental emotions exert an emotion-specific, rather than global, valence effect (see Niedenthal, Halberstadt, & Innes-Ker, 1999).

*Indirect Effects on Depth of Processing.* Several emotion theorists have posited that negative emotions trigger more systematic processing than positive emotions (see Schwarz, 1990; Schwarz & Bless, 1991). One possible explanation is that emotions serve an adaptive function by signaling situations that demand increased attention. Whereas happy feelings signal that "all is well," negative feelings alert the body to the fact that a problem needs attention.[11] In line with these predictions, several studies find that dysphoric mood is associated with vigilant, ruminative thought (Lyubomirsky & Nolen-Hoeksema, 1995; Nolen-Hoeksema & Morrow, 1993), whereas happiness is associated with relatively heuristic processing (Bodenhausen, Kramer, & Süsser, 1994; Forgas, 1998). Forgas (1998) found, for example, that happy participants were more likely to demonstrate a correspondence bias, over-attributing behavior to individual characteristics rather than to situational influences. Similarly, Bodenhausen and colleagues (1994) found that happiness increased reliance on use of stereotypes, which indicates categorical rather than piecemeal processing.

More recent studies have suggested a refinement of the original hypothesis that happiness decreases processing motivations. Bless and colleagues (1996) found that although happy moods increased and sad moods decreased reliance on general knowledge structures, happiness did not lower cognitive performance across the board. In fact, happy participants outperformed sad ones when they performed a secondary task in addition to the primary task, but only when the amount of script-inconsistent information in the primary task was small. This pattern of findings indicates higher reliance on general knowledge structures under happy rather than sad moods, but not a general reduction in processing motivation. Other refinements that have been proposed examine the effect of arousal level, in addition to affect valence (Bodenhausen, 1993).

Other recent studies suggest that specific emotions, rather than emotional valence, drive depth-of-processing effects. For example, Tiedens and Linton (2001) have shown in a series of studies that, whereas emotions characterized by a sense of certainty (e.g., contentment and anger) lead decision makers to rely on heuristic cues, emotions characterized by uncertainty (e.g., worry and surprise) lead decision makers to scrutinize information carefully. In their work, the appraisal dimension of certainty carries considerably more explanatory power than does the valence dimension. Along the same lines, Bodenhausen, Sheppard, and Kramer (1994) found that, although sadness and anger share the same (negative) valence, anger triggered heuristic decision processes and sadness did not.

## Determinants of Immediate Emotions

The immediate emotions experienced by a decision maker reflect the combined effect of two factors: *anticipatory influences*, which stem from thinking about the future consequences of the decision at hand, and *incidental influences*, which encompass all factors that are unrelated to future consequences of one's decisions. Here it may be useful to contrast these influences with expected emotions. Whereas expected emotions fundamentally consist of cognitions (about future affect or utility), immediate emotions consist of present feelings that happen to influence decisions. In the case of anticipatory influences, the present feelings stem from anticipated choices or utilities. In the case of incidental influences, the present feelings stem from factors unrelated to the decision at hand that nevertheless influence decision making.

### Anticipatory Influences

Thinking about the future consequences of one's decisions has some predictable effects on immediate (on-line) emotions. Thinking about negative consequences generally produces negative affect. Thinking about positive consequences generally produces positive affect, although it can produce frustration if the decision maker becomes impatient for the consequences to occur. Moreover, the intensity of experienced affect is generally monotonically related to the hedonic significance of the consequences themselves; outcomes that will cause a lot of pleasure or pain when they occur typically lead to commensurately intense anticipatory emotions. All of these response patterns produce a rough parallelism between the nature and intensity of anticipatory emotions and the anticipated consequences that produce them.

As noted in the introduction, however, the immediate emotions that result from anticipation often propel behavior in different directions from those dictated by a contemplation of expected emotions (Loewenstein, Weber, Hsee, & Welch, 2001). To understand why, one needs to examine the specific determinants of anticipatory emotions and how they differ from the determinants of expected emotions.

*Differential Sensitivity to Probabilities.* In the expected utility model (which incorporates expected affect), the value of an uncertain prospect is the sum of the products of outcome utilities and their probabilities of occurring. Thus probabilities and payoffs are on an equal footing when it comes to determining the value of a gamble. The same is not true for anticipatory emotional reactions to uncertain prospects. Psychophysiological studies of anxiety indicate that probabilities play a relatively subordinate role in determining emotional reactions. In a typical experiment, animal or human participants experience "countdown" periods of established length, at the end of which they receive, with some probability, a painful electric shock of varying intensity. A common finding from these studies is that physiological responses to the impending shock are correlated with the intensity of the anticipated shock but not with probability, except in the extreme case in which there is a zero probability of a shock (e.g. Monat, Averill, & Lazarus, 1972). Anticipation of a shock is sufficient to arouse participants, but the likelihood of being shocked has little impact on the level of arousal.

One potential explanation for the lack of responsiveness to probability may be that anticipatory emotions arise as a reaction to mental images of a decision's outcomes (Damasio, 1994). Such images are discrete and not much affected by probabilities; one's mental image of what it would be like to experience a crash landing on an airplane, for example, is likely to be about the same regardless of whether there is a 1 in 10 million chance of crashing or a 1 in 10,000 chance of crashing. One's mental image of a crash landing, however, is likely to be very different from one's mental image of a safe landing. Consistent with this interpretation, one study of risk perceptions found virtually a complete dissociation between intellectual judgments of risk and emotional reactions to the same risks (Sjoeberg, 1998). Other studies have found that the technique of capturing one's "mental image" of an object is an especially useful tool for predicting subsequent evaluations of that object (see Peters & Slovic, 1996, 2000; Sjoeberg, 1998; Slovic et al., in press; Slovic, Flynn, & Layman, 1991). For example, MacGregor, Slovic, Dreman, and Berry (1999) found that affective imagery, elicited by word associations, predicted preferences for investing in new companies in the stock market. Affective images were also useful predictors of such varied outcomes as preferences for visiting certain cities (Slovic, Layman, et al., 1991) and adolescents' decisions to take part in health-threatening and health-enhancing behaviors (Benthin et al., 1995). Moreover, people who are able to generate more vivid mental imagery experience certain kinds of emotions more intensely. Thus, vivid imagers, as compared with those who do not form vivid images, salivate significantly more while thinking about their favorite food (White, 1978), become more sexually aroused in structured fantasy exercises (Smith & Over, 1987), and have greater ability to voluntarily increase their heart rate using visual imagery (Carroll, Baker, & Preston, 1979).

The lack of a linear relationship between the probability that an outcome will occur and the emotions associated with anticipating the outcome may help to explain the phenomena discussed earlier in this chapter in the subsection on nonlinear probability weighting. The idea that people's affective reactions to an outcome depend on the nature of the outcome but much less on its probability can help to explain the overweighting of small probabilities and insensitivity to variations in probability in the mid-region of the scale. It can also help to explain the recent finding that probability weighting depends on the emotional impact of the associated outcomes (Rottenstreich & Hsee, 2000). In one study, participants were asked to indicate a cash certainty equivalent for avoiding an undesirable outcome that occurred with different levels of probability. The undesirable outcome was either a loss of $20 (a relatively pallid outcome) or a brief but painful electric shock (a more emotional/visceral outcome). When the outcome was pallid (losing $20), the participants were quite sensitive to probability variations: The median certainty equivalent changed from $1 (for $p = .01$) to $18 (for $p = .99$). However, when the outcome evoked emotion (receiving an electric shock), participants were extremely insensitive to probability variations: The median certainty equivalent changed only from $7 (for $p = .01$) to $10 (for $p = .99$). In other words, when probability increased by a factor of 99 (from 1% to 99%), the certainty equivalent increased by less than a factor of 1.5 (from $7 to $10). The probability weighting function is flatter (i.e., more overweighting of small probabilities) for vivid outcomes that evoke emotions than for pallid outcomes.

Vividness effects can also help to explain other curious findings in the decision-making literature. For example, Johnson and Tversky (1983) found that people were willing to pay more for airline travel insurance covering death from "terrorist acts" (a highly imaginable event) than death from "all possible causes" (which, of course, implicitly subsumes terrorist acts, in addition to a range of other causes, but does not bring spontaneous mental images to mind). It is also well established that people place greater importance on identifiable victims than statistical victims, which could be explained by the fact that identifiable victims produce more vivid imagery (see Schelling, 1984).

*Time Interval Between a Decision and Its Consequences.* Another factor that affects immediate emotions differently from expected emotions and that can therefore cause the two influences on decision making to diverge is the time interval between a decision and its consequences. As an event approaches in time, anticipatory emotions such as fear and excitement tend to intensify, even when evaluations of the event's probability or likely severity remain constant (Loewenstein, 1987; Roth, Breivik, Jorgensen, & Hofmann, 1996). For example, when research participants are told that they will receive an electric shock at a specific point in time, heart rate, galvanic skin conductance, and self-reported anxiety all increase as that moment approaches in time (Breznitz, 1971; Monat, 1976).

The intensification of immediate emotions as decision consequences become imminent may contribute to the well-known phenomenon of "chickening out," as illustrated by two studies reported by VanBoven et al. (2001). In one study, participants were offered a payment of $1 in exchange for telling a joke in front of a class the following week. When the appointed time arrived, students who had agreed to tell the joke and those who had declined to do so were given the opportunity to change their minds. As predicted, there was substantial chickening out. Sixty-seven percent of those who initially volunteered to tell a joke (6 out of 9) decided not to do so when the time came, but none of those who had initially declined the offer (0 out of 49) changed their minds and decided to tell a joke at the last minute ($p < .01$). Moreover, these changes were not accompanied by predictive changes in the students' self-reported perceived probability or severity of possible negative consequences. In a second study, the researchers manipulated affect by having half of the students view a fear-inducing film clip just before they decided whether to tell a joke in front of the class one week later in exchange for payment. As predicted, students who watched the film clip were significantly less likely to volunteer to tell the joke as compared with those who did not view the film. The tendency to chicken out is probably augmented, in many situations, by the tendency, demonstrated in research by Liberman and Trope (1998), for people to place greater weight on practical considerations relative to more vague dimensions of desirability as the moment of taking an action draws near.

*Perceived Control.* Another dimension that distinguishes hedonic expectations from anticipatory emotions is control (see Johnson & Tversky, 1984). Whereas perceptions of control are orthogonal to the normative determinants of expected emotions (i.e., probability and value), they are critical determinants of anticipatory emotion. Seligman and Maier (1967), for example, showed that dogs who were given shocks that they could terminate by making body motions got fewer ulcers than "yoked" dogs who received identical, but uncontrollable, sequences of shock. More recently, in an experiment with humans, Sanderson, Rapee, and Barlow (1988) administered a known panic-provoking agent (5.5% carbon dioxide, CD) to panic-prone patients. Half of the participants were told that they could reduce the concentration of CD by turning a dial when a light was illuminated. Although they did not actually take advantage of the opportunity to turn the dial (which was inoperative), this group reported fewer and less severe panic symptoms, had fewer catastrophic thoughts, and reported less distress.

*Evolutionary Preparedness.* Many animals, including humans, seem to be evolutionarily prepared to experience a fear reaction to certain types of stimuli. For example, cage-reared mice exhibit a powerful fear reaction to the smell of cat fur, even when they have never been exposed to a cat previously (Panksepp, 1998). There has been no demonstration that cognitive evaluations of probabilities or outcome values—that is, expected emotions—are linked to such evolutionary preparedness except insofar as expected emotions are influenced by immediate emotions (which themselves depend on preparedness). To the degree that emotional reactions to risks depend on evolutionary programming whereas cognitive evaluations do not, evolutionary preparedness can constitute a source of divergence between anticipatory and expected emotional influences on behavior.[12]

*Synthesis.* To recap, although anticipatory affect and expected affect both share the same decision target, their determinants are quite different. First, unlike expected emotions, anticipatory emotional responses to future events seem to be relatively insensitive to probabilities. Second, anticipatory affective responses are especially sensitive to the timing and vividness of outcomes in ways that expected emotions are not. Third, anticipatory affective responses depend on the individual's control over the environment, even if such control does not affect probabilities and outcomes. Finally, animals, including people, seem to be evolutionarily prepared to fear certain types of objects and experiences and not others. These differences should not be surprising. Whereas expected affect is fundamentally a *cognition* (about future utilities), anticipatory affect is fundamentally an *emotion* (about future utilities). As such, they should proceed along distinct neural pathways, and they should also have different potential to shape behavior (for elaboration, see Panksepp, 1998).

### Incidental Influences

The immediate emotions that people experience when making a decision are influenced not only by contemplating the decision itself but also by other factors that are incidental to—that is, unrelated to—the decision (Bodenhausen, 1993). Because incidental emotions do not arise from considering the consequences of decisions, their influence on decision making is typically considered nonnormative. Many effects of incidental emotions have already been discussed in the previous sections on direct and indirect influences. It is useful here, however, to briefly review two (nonindependent) sources of incidental affect: dispositional (trait) affect and situational affect.

*Dispositional Affect.* Dispositional affect can be an important source of immediate emotion. Whereas situational affect involves a transient reaction to specific events (see the following subsection), dispositional affect represents a tendency to react in a particular affective way to a variety of events across time and situations (Frijda, 1994; Lazarus,

1994). Recent research points to systematic links between specific emotion dispositions and specific judgment and choice propensities. Lerner and Keltner (2000, 2001) hypothesized and found that fearful individuals made relatively pessimistic risk assessments and risk-averse choices but that angry individuals made optimistic judgments and risk-seeking choices. Moreover, the judgments and choices of angry individuals more closely resembled those of happy individuals than those of fearful individuals—a counterintuitive pattern that was predicted based on the fact that happiness and anger are both associated with cognitive appraisals of certainty and control. Fear, by contrast, is associated with appraisals of uncertainty and lack of individual control (Smith & Ellsworth, 1985). Specific emotion dispositions, it appears, activate specific "appraisal tendencies" that guide the perception of judgments and choices.

Dispositional and state affect may influence decision making in an interactive fashion. Recently, it has been argued that dispositional affect moderates the influence of state affect on judgment by providing a schema through which events are interpreted (Gasper & Clore, 1998; Magai & McFadden, 1995). In support of this view, Gasper and Clore (1998) found that when dispositional affect matched state affect, state affect exerted a stronger influence on judgment; when it did not match, state affect exerted a weaker influence. Similarly, the origins of dispositional affect may interact recursively with cognitive aspects of decision making.

*Situational (State) Affect.* Lingering (incidental) moods and emotions contribute to situational affect. Research on anger, for example, reveals that even when the object of a subsequent decision bears no relation to the source of one's anger, anger still increases tendencies to overlook mitigating details before attributing blame, to perceive ambiguous behavior as hostile, to discount the role of uncontrollable factors when attributing causality, and to punish others for their mistakes (Goldberg et al., 1999; Keltner, Ellsworth, & Edwards, 1993; Lemerise & Dodge, 1993; Lerner et al., 1998; Quigley & Tedeschi, 1996). The specific influence of such incidental emotions appears to depend not only on the valence of the emotion (i.e., positive or negative) but also on the specific nature of the emotion. For example, consistent with dispositional-affect findings reported previously, Lerner and Keltner (2000, 2001) found that incidental (experimentally manipulated) state fear and anger had opposing effects on risk perception, even though the risks evaluated had no normative relation to the source of participants' emotions. People induced to feel anger perceived far less risk than did people induced to feel fear, and appraisals of control mediated this emotion-judgment pattern. Specific-emotion effects have also been observed for other negative emotions, such as sadness and anxiety. Raghunathan and Pham (1999) contrasted the effects of incidental state anxiety and incidental state sadness, both on gambling decisions and on job-selection decisions. Drawing on the core themes and appraisal patterns associated with these emotions (see Lazarus, 1991; Roseman, 1984; Smith & Ellsworth, 1985), they hypothesized that sadness would trigger the implicit goal of replacing loss, whereas fear would trigger the implicit goal of reducing uncertainty. As predicted, the emotional carryover effects were consistent with the underlying appraisal themes of each emotion. Across both of these outcome domains, incidental sadness increased tendencies to favor high-risk–high-reward options. Incidental anxiety, in contrast, increased tendencies to favor low-risk–low-reward options.

The preceding evidence pertains to full-blown induced emotions. It is important to note, however, that even minimal sensory cues can contribute to situational affect and influence subsequent decision making. As any magazine reader knows, advertisers bank on eliciting this kind of incidental affect. Although empirical work on this topic has been less than abundant, several good studies attest to the fact that sights, scents, and sounds do influence affect and decision making. For example, Baron (1997) found that passersby in a shopping mall were significantly more likely to help in response to requests from a confederate when the request was made in the presence of pleasant ambient odors than in the absence of such odors. Researchers have documented numerous other effects of odor on cognitive processes (see Engen, 1991), driving behavior (Baron & Kalsher, 1998), and task performance (Baron & Thomley, 1994). Similarly, other environmental factors, such as crowding, sights, and sounds, can all instigate incidental affect (Gifford, 1987).

### Synthesis of Immediate Emotions

Immediate emotions can have both direct and indirect effects on decision making. Direct effects include action tendencies associated with specific emotions, as well as general valence effects in which decision makers select relatively more optimistic courses of action when in a good mood than when in a bad one. At lower levels of intensity, people seem to be able to overcome the influence of immediate emotions when they deem those emotions to be irrelevant to a decision at hand. At higher levels of intensity, emotions progressively assume control of behavior. Indirect effects include changes in the prediction of consequences, selective processing of information, and changes in the quality and depth of processing.

Immediate emotions are the joint product of two types of inputs. *Anticipatory influences* stem from contemplation of the consequences of the decision at hand. *Incidental influences* reflect any factors that influence immediate emotions that are unrelated to the decision. For reasons that we have specified in this section, each of these influ-

ences can cause immediate emotions to propel behavior in directions different from those dictated by a consideration of expected emotions.

## Benefits and Pitfalls of Expected and Immediate Emotions

Throughout most of recorded human intellectual history, emotions have been viewed in largely negative terms—as an unruly and unpredictable corrupting influence. Accounts of human behavior, from the ancient Greeks to Enlightenment philosophers, focused mainly on the role played by emotions in self-control problems—on the propensity for emotions to override reason, deliberation, or self-interest. This negative view of emotions is evident not only in philosophical discussions throughout recorded intellectual history, but also in literature, and even in the modern legal system (in which "crimes of passion" are treated differently because the perpetrator is viewed as being "out of control").

Recently, however, emotions have begun to enjoy a significant rehabilitation. Rather than ignoring emotions altogether or focusing exclusively on their hypothesized role in producing self-destructive behavior, recent influential research on emotion highlights both (1) the essential functions served by emotions in coordinating cognition and behavior and (2) the detrimental consequences associated with ignoring emotions. This rehabilitation of emotions finds expression not only in the work of academics but also in the popular literature, as evidenced by such best sellers as *Emotional Intelligence: Why It Can Matter More Than IQ* (Goleman, 1995) and *The Gift of Fear: Survival Signals That Protect Us From Violence* (DeBecker, 1997).

As is usually the case in such matters, both perspectives have some validity. Emotions *do* often impel people in directions that are not commensurate with self-interest. But emotions also serve essential functions. Our distinction between expected and immediate emotions can shed light on these two effects.

The benefits and pitfalls of expected and immediate emotions are summarized in Table 31.1. The main benefit of expected emotions is that they take explicit account of the consequences of a decision. Maximizing the positivity of expected emotions is widely seen as a normatively compelling criterion for decision making and forms the basis of most theories of "rational choice." But decision making on the basis of expected emotions is beneficial only to the extent that two conditions are met. First, expected emotions must encompass all the factors that decision makers care about. Second, the expectations themselves must be accurate.

On the first condition, evidence that expected emotions *do not* capture everything people care about comes from research, which shows that blocked access to one's im-

Table 31.1 Benefits and Pitfalls of Expected and Immediate Affect

|  | Expected Affect | Immediate Affect |
|---|---|---|
| Definition | Predictions about how one will feel if certain decision outcomes occur | Affect experienced at the time of making a decision (produced by anticipatory or incidental factors) |
| Time when affect occurs | Future: when decision outcomes are experienced | Present: at time of decision |
| Potential benefits associated with incorporating affect | Determination of optimal course of action to maximize long-term well-being | Prioritizing information processing and introducing important, but intangible, considerations |
| Potential pitfalls associated with incorporating affect | When expectations are biased (e.g., forecasting errors), decision making will be commensurately biased | Can propel behavior in directions that are counter to self-interest |

mediate emotions degrades the quality of decision making. A clever set of studies has shown that introspecting about one's reasons for preferring a particular choice object—hence deflecting attention from one's feelings—reduces the quality of decision making (see Wilson et al., 1993; Wilson & Schooler, 1991). In one study (Wilson, Kraft, & Dunn, 1989), research participants rated the quality of several strawberry jams, and half were asked to give reasons for liking or disliking the jams. The ratings of those who were not asked to provide reasons for their tastes correlated strongly with the jam ratings given by experts, but the ratings of those who did give reasons showed absolutely no relationship to the expert ratings. In an even more compelling study, college students selected their favorite poster from among a set (see Wilson et al., 1993). Students asked to provide reasons why they liked or disliked the posters ended up, on average, less happy with their choice of poster and less likely to keep it on display in their dorm rooms than were those who were not asked to provide reasons. Apparently, analyzing reasons "cognitivizes" one's preferences and makes salient certain features about the target that may not have anything to do with why we liked or disliked it in the first place.

A fundamentally similar point about the importance of immediate emotions for decision quality comes from neuroscientific studies. Damasio, Bechara, and colleagues (Bechara, Damasio, Damasio, & Anderson, 1994; Bechara, Damasio, Damasio, & Lee, 1999; Damasio, 1994) show that individuals with minimal cognitive, but major emotional, deficits have difficulty making decisions and, when they do, often make poor decisions. In one study that compared normal participants with neurologically impaired participants, the impaired participants repeatedly chose a high-risk option until they went bankrupt. Moreover, physiological measures taken during the task suggested that they did so because they lacked the necessary "somatic markers"—affective signals through which decision makers would normally encode the consequences of alternative courses of action. Although the impaired participants technically knew that certain options were risky, they apparently failed to experience the fear that would normally be associated with repeatedly choosing those high-risk options. These studies, and the studies by Wilson and colleagues (Wilson et al., 1989; Wilson, Kraft, & Dunn, 1989; Wilson & Schooler, 1991), converge on the common conclusion that immediate affect constitutes an important input into decision making. If expected emotions captured everything that people care about, then the absence of immediate emotional influences would not degrade decisions as much as it does.

The second condition necessary for expected emotions to be beneficial is that predictions regarding future emotions must be accurate. Earlier in the chapter, we reviewed some of the large number of recent studies that document pervasive and systematic biases in people's predictions of their own future emotions. Such biases in the prediction of future emotional states can have diverse negative consequences for decision making. For example, the hot-cold empathy gap suggests that nonaddicts, or addicts who are not currently craving drugs, will underpredict the force of future drug craving (see Loewenstein, 1999). This may explain why only 15% of high school students who were occasional smokers (less than one cigarette per day) predicted that they might be smoking in 5 years when in fact 43% were still smoking 5 years later (Slovic, 2000). The hot-cold empathy gap can also shed light on the differences between healthy and sick persons' attitudes toward "heroic measures" to extend the lives of terminally ill individuals. Many healthy Americans state that they do not want to die in a nursing home or hospital or, worse yet, an intensive care unit, but 90% of dying patients, most of whom die in acute care hospitals, view favorably the care they receive. In one study

(Slevin, Plant, Lynch, Drinkwater, & Gregory, 1988), different groups of respondents were asked whether they would accept a grueling course of chemotherapy if it would extend their lives by 3 months. No radiotherapists and only 6% of oncologists and 10% of healthy people said that they would accept the chemotherapy; but 42% of current cancer patients say they would. The premise of advanced directives, such as living wills, is that people can predict what they will want at a time when they cannot express their wishes. Results such as these cast doubt on this assumption (see Coppola et al., 1999; Druley et al., 1993).

We conclude, therefore, that neither of the two conditions for expected emotions is completely met. Expected emotions do not capture all the factors that decision makers care about, and decision makers predict such emotions in a biased fashion.

But if expected emotions do not capture everything, what is it that immediate emotions contribute? First, as postulated early on by Simon (1967), emotions direct attention to important events. Viewing the central nervous system as a serial information processor, Simon argued that emotions serve as "cognitive interrupts" that tell us what's important, thus facilitating prioritization of processing resources (see the section on indirect effects of immediate affect). Emotions thus enable intrapersonal adaptive responses to changing environments (Ekman & Davidson, 1994; Frijda, 1986; Nesse, 1990; Robert & Carnevale, 1997; Rolls, 1999).[13]

Second, emotions provide useful information about the desirability of different courses of action, a function highlighted by a number of other new theories (Brehm, 1999; Frank, 1992; Frijda, 1988; Johnson-Laird & Oatley, 1992; Keltner & Kring, 1998; Lerner & Keltner, 2000; Levenson, 1994; Panksepp, 1998; Slovic et al., in press), including Damasio's (1994) "somatic marker hypothesis." Note that this benefit is the mirror image of one of the major limitations of expected emotions—that they don't incorporate all considerations that are important to people. Immediate emotions may incorporate factors such as moral or aesthetic values that people have difficulty articulating and which, perhaps as a result, tend to receive little weight in deliberative decision making.

Third, immediate emotions often provide the motivation necessary to implement chosen courses of action (Frijda, 1986, 1988; Frijda & Mesquita, 1994; Keltner & Gross, 1999). In conventional decision theory, behavior is viewed as a matter of simply choosing an appropriate course of action. Once chosen, it is implicitly assumed that the action will automatically be executed. As a large literature on self-control reveals, however, there is often a big difference between *knowing* what's best and *doing* what's best (Baumeister et al., 1994; Loewenstein, 1996; Metcalfe & Mischel, 1999; Mischel, Cantor, & Feldman, 1996; Schelling, 1978).

Although immediate emotions provide useful information about the best course of action, as well as the impetus to execute it, their historically negative reputation has some empirical grounding. A tendency to override deliberations—to cause people to behave self-destructively—has been well documented (Loewenstein, 1996; Loewenstein et al., 2001). Immediate emotions can exert such influences on decision making for three reasons.

First, there may be a mismatch between the evolutionary adaptiveness of emotions and current decision-making environments. Emotions, like other visceral influences, have evolved to motivate people to perform certain kinds of typically adaptive behaviors (Nesse, 1990). Hunger provides a motive for eating, sex for copulation; and specific emotions likewise are programmed to produce specific actions. However, all of these functions evolved during a time when people were not faced with the range of temptations that are currently available—for example, abundant high-fat foods, pornography, and pleasure-producing drugs. Although we may realize, at times, that some of these temptations are not good for us, the motivational function of emotions can operate largely independent of higher level cognitive functioning and can overwhelm our cognitive evaluations of self-interest.

Second, as discussed in the second section of the chapter, immediate emotions are responsive to a wide range of factors, such as vividness and the proximity of consequences, that are difficult to justify as normative guides to behavior. As a result, anticipatory influences sometimes drive immediate emotions, and hence behavior, in directions that are opposed to those dictated by a dispassionate appraisal of consequences. For example, as discussed earlier, many people are afraid of flying but not of driving, even though they recognize that driving is far more dangerous. The influence of incidental emotions—emotions elicited by factors unrelated to a decision—is particularly difficult to so justify.

Third, as discussed in the section on indirect effects, immediate emotions can distort people's evaluations of the probability and value of different possible consequences of a decision, thus distorting the influence of expected emotions. Sometimes distortions arise from direct influences of immediate emotions (e.g. Goldberg et al., 1999; Lerner et al., 1998; Lerner & Keltner, 2000, 2001; Loewenstein, 1996; Loewenstein et al., 2001; Schwarz, 1990; Schwarz & Clore, 1983). Other times they arise from indirect influences, such as when specific emotions trigger the over- or underscrutinization of information (e.g., Bless et al., 1996; Bodenhausen, Sheppard, & Kramer, 1994; Bodenhausen, Kramer, & Süsser, 1994; Nolen-Hoeksema & Morrow, 1993; Nolen-Hoeksema, Morrow, & Fredrickson, 1993; Tiedens & Linton, in press).

The benefits and pitfalls of expected and immediate emotions are very nearly mirror images of one another. The main benefit of expected emotions is that they provide a guide to behavior that takes account of the long-term consequences of one's actions. The main pitfalls are that such long-term consequences are not the only things that people care about and that people make systematic errors when it comes to predicting those consequences. The main benefit of immediate emotions is that they provide information to decision makers about intangible but important values that are not captured by expected emotions. The main pitfalls of immediate emotions are that they can drive people to take actions that run contrary to their long-term actions and can distort people's evaluations of expected emotions.

## Summary

In this chapter we have sought to draw attention to some of the complexities in the ways that emotions enter into decision making. Conventional theories of decision making include only expected emotions. This approach has been enriched by recent efforts to elucidate the nature and determinants of the emotions that decision makers are assumed to anticipate experiencing (and thus take into account when making decisions). However, it neglects to take account of the important influence of immediate emotions—emotions experienced at the time of decision making. Immediate emotions can influence decisions indirectly by altering the decision maker's perceptions of probabilities or outcomes or by altering the quality and quantity of processing of decision-relevant cues. They can also affect behavior directly. As the intensity of immediate emotions intensifies, they progressively take control of decision making and override rational decision making.

Beyond simply pointing out the complex ways in which emotions influence decision making, our investigation of the role of emotions in decision making also draws attention to two fundamental limitations of the decision-making perspective. First, not all behavior should be treated as the product of decisions. Affect does serve as an input into decision making, as highlighted by many recent theoretical perspectives, but it also, in some cases, exerts direct effects that circumvent decision making altogether. Second, no simple dichotomy between good and bad influences of affect can be drawn. We have seen that the traditional view ("all affect is irrational") is not tenable. The absence or suppression of affect can lead decisions astray, and the presence of affect can guide behavior in adaptive ways, such as by regulating processing strategies. We have also seen that a simple dichotomy between beneficial expected affect and destructive immediate affect does not do justice to the benefits and pitfalls of each of these influences. Both the traditional view that one should suppress or disregard emotions and the modern, more benign, view that emotions are crucial guides to behavior capture important aspects of reality. Both imme-diate affect *and* expected affect are crucial for normal functioning but are also potential sources of bias. Expected affect can lead to decision errors because people are prone to systematic errors in predicting how they will feel in the future. Immediate emotions can produce decision errors for reasons that were understood by the ancient Greeks; they can distort people's judgments of self-interest. Even when people have a realistic understanding of their own self-interest, immediate emotions can cause people to "lose control" of their own behavior. But these potential biases should be weighed against the essential functions they serve, such as prioritizing processing goals and introducing important, but intangible, "gut" feelings. Any comprehensive understanding of decision making or of the limits of the decision-making perspective must come to terms with these diverse, sometimes conflicting, and sometimes complementary functions of expected and immediate emotions.

## NOTES

We thank Gerald Clore, Barbara Mellers, and Klaus Scherer for helpful comments and Rosa Stipanovic for assistance in preparing the manuscript. We are also grateful for financial support during preparation of this work. Loewenstein received support from the Center for the Study of Human Dimensions of Global Change at Carnegie Mellon University (NSF Grant SBR-9521914). Lerner received support from a postdoctoral fellowship at UCLA (NIH Grant MH15750), a grant from the Fetzer Institute, and a Carnegie Mellon Faculty Development Grant.

1. For a notable exception, see Janis and Mann (1977).

2. An appreciation for the positive functions is not entirely new in behavioral science. Darwin (1872/1998) was one of the first to hypothesize the adaptive mechanisms through which emotion might guide human behavior.

3. Forgas's affect infusion model (1995) proposes a similar set of processes with respect to social judgment.

4. See Bodenhausen (1993) for the original use of this term.

5. For thorough discussion of cognitive-appraisal theories of emotion, we refer the interested reader to chapter 29 in this volume.

For judgment and decision-making research that explicitly draws on cognitive-appraisal theories of emotion, see Lerner and Keltner, 2000, in press; Tiedens & Linton, in press.

6. Alternatively, people may exaggerate the amount of regret they will experience and hence overweight considerations of regret in decision making.

7. An alternative interpretation is that students in California have a higher threshold for classifying themselves as happy than students in the Midwest. More generally, many findings in the well-being literature may be open to reinterpretation when one considers problems of numerical anchors, defensive response tendencies, and specifying the underlying parameters involved in global assessments of well-being.

8. This distinction is largely consistent with Forgas's (1995) affect infusion model, which specifies that one's present feelings can influence judgment via two routes: affect priming (indirect route) and affect-as-information

(direct route). Our framework elaborates on this idea by specifying how different processes interact with different kinds of emotional inputs and the consequences of those interactions for decision making.

9. It would be critical, of course, for manipulations that increase processing vigilance to occur *prior* to exposure to information about the decision. People have trouble retroactively correcting for faulty encoding of information (Lerner & Tetlock, 1999).

10. When it comes to *behavior*, however, Isen and colleagues (Isen, Nygren, & Ashby, 1988) have observed a rather different pattern. Because positive-affect individuals want to protect their positive state, they are less inclined to risk meaningful loss than are controls.

11. This pattern would also be consistent with hypotheses about affective motivations. Whereas negative moods trigger a "mood repair" goal of focusing on problems, positive moods trigger a "mood maintenance" goal of not paying too much attention to details (Isen & Geva, 1987; Isen et al., 1988).

12. Even when there is not such *direct* fear programming, evolutionary programming can take more subtle forms. For example, it appears that animals are biologically "prepared" to become fear-conditioned to certain objects—such as snakes, spiders, water, and enclosed spaces—but not to others; not all stimuli have the same capacity to become conditioned aversive stimuli (see Ohman, 1993, 1994). It also appears that fear conditioning can occur vicariously—by an animal observing a fear reaction by another animal—and that such vicarious conditioning also exhibits the phenomenon of preparedness (e.g., Cook & Mineka, 1990; Mineka & Cook, 1993).

13. Theorists have also proposed that emotions serve *interpersonal functions*. For example, they help humans to respond quickly to specific problems and opportunities in the social environment, including forming attachments, resolving injustices, negotiating hierarchies, and adhering to social norms (Barrett & Campos, 1987; Ekman, 1992; Frank, 1988; Keltner & Ekman, 2000; Keltner & Kring, 1998; Lutz & White, 1986; Nesse, 1990; Schwarz, 1990). Emotions enable such responses by providing information about ongoing social relations (Nesse, 1990). For example, emotional communication in the voice, face, and posture signals socially relevant information to individuals in interactions about their own, and their interaction partners', emotions, intentions, attitudes, and orientations to the relationship (Buck, 1984; Ekman, 1984; Keltner, 1995).

## REFERENCES

Ainslie, G. (1975). Specious reward: A behavioral theory of impulsiveness and impulse control. *Psychological Bulletin, 82*(4), 463–496.

Aristotle. (1962). *Nicomachean ethics.* Indianapolis: Bobbs-Merrill.

Averill, J. R. (1983). Studies on anger and aggression. *American Psychologist, 38,* 1145–1160.

Barlow, D. H. (1988). *Anxiety and its disorders: The nature and treatment of anxiety and panic.* New York: Guilford Press.

Baron, R. A. (1997). The sweet smell of . . . helping. *Journal of Personality and Social Psychology, 23,* 498–503.

Baron, R. A., & Kalsher, M. J. (1998). Effects of a pleasant ambient fragrance on simulated driving performance: The sweet smell of . . . safety? *Environment and Behavior, 30*(4), 535–552.

Baron, R. A., & Thomley, J. (1994). A whiff of reality: Positive affect as a potential mediator of the effects of pleasant fragrances on task performance and helping. *Environment and Behavior, 26* (6), 766–784.

Barrett, K. C., & Campos, J. J. (1987). Perspectives on emotional development: II. A functionalist approach to emotions. In J. D. Osofsky (Ed.), *Handbook of infant development* (2nd ed., pp. 555–578). New York: Wiley.

Basso, M. R., Schefft, B. K., Ris, M. D., & Dember, W. N. (1996). Mood and global-local visual processing. *Journal of the International Neuropsychological Society, 2*(3), 249–255.

Baumeister, R. F., Heatherton, T. F., & Tice, D. M. (1994). *Losing control: How and why people fail at self-regulation.* San Diego: Academic Press.

Bazerman, M. H., Tenbrunsel, A. E., & Wade-Benzoni, K. A. (1998). Negotiating with yourself and losing: Understanding and managing conflicting internal preferences. *Academy of Management Review, 23,* 225–241.

Bechara, A., Damasio, A. R., Damasio, H., & Anderson, S. W. (1994). Insensitivity to future consequences following damage to human prefrontal cortex. *Cognition, 50*(1–3), 7–15.

Bechara, A., Damasio, H., Damasio, A. R., & Lee, G. P. (1999). Different contributions of the human amygdala and ventromedial prefrontal cortex to decision-making. *Journal of Neuroscience, 19*(13), 5473–5481.

Bell, D. (1982). Regret in decision making under uncertainty. *Operations Research, 30,* 961–981.

Benthin, A., Slovic, P., Moran, P., Severson, H., Mertz, C. K., & Gerrard, M. (1995). Adolescent health-threatening and health-enhancing behaviors: A study of word association and imagery. *Journal of Adolescent Health, 17,* 143–152.

Berkowitz, L. (1990). On the formation and regulation of anger and aggression: A cognitive-neoassociationistic analysis. *American Psychologist, 45*(4), 494–503.

Bless, H., Clore, G. L., Schwarz, N., Golisano, V., Rabe, C., & Wök, M. (1996). Mood and the use of scripts: Does a happy mood really lead to mindlessness? *Journal of Personality and Social Psychology, 71*(4), 665–679.

Bodenhausen, G., Sheppard, L., & Kramer, G. (1994). Negative affect and social judgment: The different impact of anger and sadness. *European Journal of Social Psychology, 24,* 45–62.

Bodenhausen, G. V. (1993). Emotions, arousal, and stereotypic judgments: A heuristic model of affect and stereotyping. In D. M. Mackie & D. L. Hamilton (Eds.), *Affect, cognition, and stereotyping: Interactive processes in group perception* (pp. 13–37). San Diego, CA: Academic Press.

Bodenhausen, G. V., Kramer, G. P., & Süsser, K. (1994). Happiness and stereotypic thinking in social judgment. *Journal of Personality and Social Psychology, 66,* 621–632.

Bower, G. H. (1981). Mood and memory. *American Psychologist, 36,* 129–148.

Bower, G. H. (1991). Mood congruity of social judgment. In J. Forgas (Ed.), *Emotion and social judgment* (pp. 31–54). Oxford, England: Pergamon Press.

Brehm, J. W. (1999). The intensity of emotion. *Personality and Social Psychology Review, 3,* 2–22.

Breznitz, S. (1971). A study of worrying. *British Journal of Social and Clinical Psychology, 10*(3), 271–279.

Buck, R. (1984). *The communication of emotion.* New York: Guilford Press.

Camerer, C. F. (1992). Recent tests of generalizations of expected utility theory. In W. Edwards (Ed.), *Studies in risk and uncertainty*: No. 3. *Utility theories: Measurements and applications* (pp. 207–251). Norwell, MA: Kluwer Academic.

Carroll, D., Baker, J., & Preston, M. (1979). Individual differences in visual imaging and the voluntary control of heart rate. *British Journal of Psychology, 70*(1), 39–49.

Clore, G. L. (1992). Cognitive phenomenology: Feelings and the construction of judgment. In L. L. Martin & A. Tesser (Eds.), *The construction of social judgments* (pp. 133–163). Hillsdale, NJ: Erlbaum.

Clore, G. L., Schwarz, N., & Conway, M. (1994). Affective causes and consequences of social information processing. In R. S. Wyer, Jr., & T. K. Srull (Eds.), *Handbook of social cognition* (2nd ed., Vol. 1, pp. 323–417). Hillsdale, NJ: Erlbaum.

Conway, M., & Giannopoulos, C. (1993). Dysphoria and decision making: Limited information use for evaluations of multiattribute targets. *Journal of Personality and Social Psychology, 64*, 613–623.

Cook, M., & Mineka, S. (1990). Selective associations in the observational conditioning of fear in Rhesus monkeys. *Journal of Experimental Psychology: Animal Behavior Processes, 16*, 372–389.

Coppola, K. M., Bookwala, J., Ditto, P. H., Lockhart, L. K., Danks, J. H., & Smucker, W. D. (1999). Elderly adults' preferences for life-sustaining treatments: The role of impairment, prognosis, and pain. *Death Studies, 23*(7), 617–634.

Damasio, A. R. (1994). *Descartes' error: Emotion, reason, and the human brain*. New York: Putnam.

Darwin, C. (1998). *The expression of the emotions in man and animals* (3rd ed.). New York: Oxford University Press. (Original work published 1872)

DeBecker, G. (1997). *The gift of fear: Survival signals that protect us from violence*. Boston: Little, Brown.

Derryberry, D., & Tucker, D. M. (1994). Motivating the focus of attention. In P. Niedenthal & S. Kitayama (Eds.), *The heart's eye: Emotional influences in perception and attention* (pp. 167–196). San Diego, CA: Academic Press.

Druley, J. A., Ditto, P. H., Moore, K. A., Danks, J. H., Townsend, A., & Smucher, W. D., et al. (1993). Physicians' predictions of elderly outpatients' preferences for life-sustaining treatment. *Journal of Family Practice, 37*(5), 469–475.

Edwards, W. (1953). Experiments on economic decision-making in gambling situations. *Econometrica, 21*, 349–350.

Edwards, W. (1954). The theory of decision making. *Psychological Bulletin, 51*, 380–417.

Ekman, P. (1984). Expression and the nature of emotion. In K. Scherer & P. Ekman (Eds.), *Approaches to emotion* (pp. 319–344). Hillsdale, NJ: Erlbaum.

Ekman, P. (1992). Are there basic emotions? *Psychological Review, 99*(3), 550–553.

Ekman, P., & Davidson, R. J. (Eds.). (1994). *The nature of emotion: Fundamental questions*. New York: Oxford University Press.

Elster, J. (1999). *Alchemies of the mind: Rationality and the emotions*. Cambridge, England: Cambridge University Press.

Engen, T. (1991). *Odor sensation and memory*. New York: Praeger.

Fischhoff, B. (1975). Hindsight is not equal to foresight: The effect of outcome knowledge on judgment under uncertainty. *Journal of Experimental Psychology: Human Perception and Performance, 1*(3), 288–299.

Fishbein, M., & Ajzen, I. (1975). *Belief, attitude, intention, and behavior: An introduction to theory and research*. Reading, MA: Addison-Wesley.

Forgas, J. P. (1989). Mood effects on decision making strategies. *Australian Journal of Psychology, 41*(2), 197–214.

Forgas, J. P. (1991). Affective influences on partner choice: Role of mood in social decisions. *Journal of Personality and Social Psychology, 61*, 708–720.

Forgas, J. P. (1995). Mood and judgment: The affect infusion model (AIM). *Psychological Bulletin, 117*, 39–66.

Forgas, J. P. (1998). On being happy and mistaken: Mood effects on the fundamental attribution error. *Journal of Personality and Social Psychology, 75*, 318–331.

Forgas, J. P., & Moylan, S. J. (1991). Affective influences on stereotype judgements. *Cognition and Emotion, 5*, 379–395.

Frank, R. (1988). *Passions within reason: The strategic role of the emotions*. New York: Norton.

Frank, R. H. (1992). The role of moral sentiments in the theory of intertemporal choice. In G. Loewenstein & J. Elster (Eds.), *Choice over time* (pp. 265–284). New York: Russell Sage Foundation.

Frijda, N. (1988). The laws of emotion. *American Psychologist, 43*, 349–358.

Frijda, N. H. (1986). *The emotions*. Cambridge, England: Cambridge University Press.

Frijda, N. H. (1994). Varieties of affect: Emotions and episodes, moods, and sentiments. In P. Ekman & R. Davidson (Eds.), *The nature of emotion: Fundamental questions* (pp. 59–67). New York: Oxford University Press.

Frijda, N. H., & Mesquita, B. (1994). The social roles and functions of emotions. In S. Kitayama & H. R. Markus (Eds.), *Emotion and culture: Empirical studies of mutual influence* (pp. 51–87). Washington, DC: American Psychological Association.

Gasper, K., & Clore, G. L. (1998). The persistent use of negative affect by anxious individuals to estimate risk. *Journal of Personality and Social Psychology, 74*(5), 1350–1363.

Gifford, R. (1987). *Environmental psychology: Principles and practice*. Needham Heights, MA: Allyn & Bacon.

Gilbert, D. T., Pinel, E. C., Wilson, T. D., Blumberg, S. J., & Wheatley, T. P. (1998). Immune neglect: A source of durability bias in affective forecasting. *Journal of Personality and Social Psychology, 75*(3), 617–638.

Goldberg, J. H., Lerner, J. S., & Tetlock, P. E. (1999). Rage and reason: The psychology of the intuitive prosecutor. *European Journal of Social Psychology, 29*, 781–795.

Goleman, D. (1995). *Emotional intelligence: Why it can matter more than IQ*. New York: Bantam Books.

Gratton, A., & Wise, R. A. (1994). Drug- and behavior-associated changes in dopamine-related electrochemical signals during intravenous cocaine self-administration in rats. *Journal of Neuroscience, 14*(7), 4130–4146.

Gross, J. J., & Levenson, R. W. (1993). Emotional suppression: Physiology, self-report, and expressive behavior. *Journal of Personality and Social Psychology, 64*(6), 970–986.

Gul, F. (1991, May 3). A theory of disappointment aversion. *Econometrica, 59*(3), 667–686.

Harless, D. W., & Camerer, C. F. (1994, November 6). The

predictive utility of generalized expected utility theories. *Econometrica, 62*(16), 1251–1289.

Hausch, D. B., Lo, V. S. Y., & Ziemba, W. T. (1994). Introduction to utility preferences of racetrack bettors. In D. B. Hausch, V. S. Y. Lo, & W. T. Ziemba (Eds.), *Efficiency of racetrack betting markets* (pp. 39–40). San Diego, CA: Academic Press.

Hirschman, A. O. (1977). *The passions and the interests: Political arguments for capitalism before its triumph.* Princeton, NJ: Princeton University Press.

Hoch, S. J., & Loewenstein, G. F. (1991). Time-inconsistent preferences and consumer self-control. *Journal of Consumer Research, 17*(4), 492–507.

Isen, A. M. (1993). Positive affect and decision making. In M. Lewis & J. M. Haviland (Eds.), *Handbook of emotions* (pp. 261–277). New York: Guilford Press.

Isen, A. M. (1999). Positive affect. In T. Dalgleish & M. J. Power (Eds.), *Handbook of cognition and emotion* (pp. 521–539). Chichester, England: Wiley.

Isen, A. M., & Geva, N. (1987). The influence of positive affect on acceptable level of risk: The person with a large canoe has a large worry. *Organizational Behavior and Human Decision Processes, 39*(2), 145–154.

Isen, A. M., Nygren, T. E., & Ashby, F. G. (1988). Influence of positive affect on the subjective utility of gains and losses: It is just not worth the risk. *Journal of Personality and Social Psychology, 55*(5), 710–717.

Isen, A. M., Shalker, T. E., Clark, M., & Karp, L. (1978). Affect, accessibility of material in memory, and behavior: A cognitive loop? *Journal of Personality and Social Psychology, 36*(1), 1–12.

Janis, I. L., & Mann, L. (1977). *Decision making: A psychological analysis of conflict, choice, and commitment.* New York: Free Press.

Johnson, E. J., & Tversky, A. (1983). Affect, generalization, and the perception of risk. *Journal of Personality and Social Psychology, 45*, 20–31.

Johnson, E. J., & Tversky, A. (1984). Representations of perceptions of risks. *Journal of Experimental Psychology: General, 113*(1), 55–70.

Johnson-Laird, P. N., & Oatley, K. (1992). Basic emotions, rationality, and folk theory. *Cognition and Emotion, 6*, 201–223.

Josephs, R. A., Larrick, R. P., Steele, C. M., & Nisbett, R. E. (1992). Protecting the self from the negative consequences of risky decisions. *Journal of Personality and Social Psychology, 62*(1), 26–37.

Kahneman, D., & Tversky, A. (1979). Prospect theory. *Econometrica, 47*, 263–292.

Kavanagh, D. J., & Bower, G. H. (1985). Mood and self-efficacy: Impact of joy and sadness on perceived capabilities. *Cognitive Therapy and Research, 9*, 507–525.

Keltner, D. (1995). Signs of appeasement: Evidence for the distinct displays of embarrassment, amusement, and shame. *Journal of Personality and Social Psychology, 68*, 441–454.

Keltner, D., & Ekman, P. (2000). Facial expressions of emotion. In J. Haviland-Jones & M. Lewis (Eds.), *Handbook of emotion* (2nd ed.). New York: Guilford Press.

Keltner, D., Ellsworth, P. C., & Edwards, K. (1993). Beyond simple pessimism: Effects of sadness and anger on social perception. *Journal of Personality and Social Psychology, 64*, 740–752.

Keltner, D., & Gross, J. J. (1999). Functional accounts of emotions. *Cognition and Emotion, 13*(5), 467–480.

Keltner, D., & Kring, A. (1998). Emotion, social function,

and psychopathology [Special issue: New direcitons in research on emotion]. *Review of General Psychology, 2*(3).

Keltner, D., Locke, K. D., & Audrain, P. C. (1993). The influence of attributions on the relevance of negative feelings to personal satisfaction. *Personality and Social Psychology Bulletin, 19*(1), 21–29.

Kienen, G. (1987). Decision making under stress: Scanning of alternatives under controllable and uncontrollable threats. *Journal of Personality and Social Psychology, 52*, 639–644.

Kirby, K. N., & Hernstein, R. J. (1995). Preference reversals due to myopic discounting of delayed reward. *Psychological Science, 6*(2), 83–89.

Koopmans, T. C. (1960). Stationary ordinal utility and impatience. *Econometrica, 28*, 287–309.

Larrick, R. P. (1993). Motivational factors in decision theories: The role of self-protection. *Psychological Bulletin, 113*(3), 440–450.

Larrick, R. P., & Boles, T. L. (1995). Avoiding regret in decisions with feedback: A negotiation example. *Organizational Behavior and Human Decision Processes, 63*(1), 87–97.

Larsen, R. J., & Ketelaar, T. (1989). Extraversion, neuroticism and susceptibility to positive and negative mood induction procedures. *Personality and Individual Differences, 10*, 1221–1228.

Lazarus, R. (1994). The stable and the unstable in emotion. In P. Ekman & R. Davidson (Eds.), *The nature of emotion: Fundamental questions* (pp. 79–85). New York: Oxford University Press.

Lazarus, R. S. (1991). *Emotion and adaptation.* New York: Oxford University Press.

Lemerise, E. A., & Dodge, K. A. (1993). The development of anger and hostile interactions. In M. Lewis & J. M. Haviland (Eds.), *Handbook of emotions* (pp. 537–546). New York: Guilford Press.

Lerner, J. S., Goldberg, J. H., & Tetlock, P. E. (1998). Sober second thought: The effects of accountability, anger and authoritarianism on attributions of responsibility. *Personality and Social Psychology Bulletin, 24*, 563–574.

Lerner, J. S., & Keltner, D. (2000). Beyond valence: Toward a model of emotion-specific influences on judgment and choice. *Cognition and Emotion, 14*(4), 473–493.

Lerner, J. S., & Keltner, D. (2001). Fear, anger, and risk. *Journal of Personality and Social Psychology, 81*, 146–159.

Lerner, J. S., & Tetlock, P. E. (1999). Accounting for the effects of accountability. *Psychological Bulletin, 125*(2), 255–275.

Levenson, R. (1994). Human emotion: A functional view. In P. Ekman & R. J. Davidson (Eds.), *The nature of emotion* (pp. 123–126). New York: Oxford University Press.

Liberman, N., & Trope, Y. (1998). The role of feasibility and desirability considerations in near and distant future decisions: A test of temporal construal theory. *Journal of Personality and Social Psychology, 75*(1), 5–18.

Loewenstein, G. (1987). Anticipation and the valuation of delayed consumption. *Economic Journal, 97*(387), 666–684.

Loewenstein, G. (1992). The fall and rise of psychological explanations in the economics of intertemporal choice. In G. Loewenstein & J. Elster (Eds.), *Choice over time* (pp. 3–34). New York: Russell Sage Foundation.

Loewenstein, G. (1996). Out of control: Visceral influences

on behavior. *Organizational Behavior and Human Decision Processes, 65*, 272–292.

Loewenstein, G. (1999). A visceral account of addiction. In J. Elster & O.-J. Skog (Eds.), *Getting hooked: Rationality and addiction* (pp. 235–264). Cambridge, England: Cambridge University Press.

Loewenstein, G., & Frederick, S. (1997). Predicting reactions to environmental change. In M. H. Bazerman & D. M. Messick (Eds.), *Environment, ethics, and behavior: The psychology of environmental valuation and degradation* (pp. 52–72). San Francisco: New Lexington Press/Jossey-Bass.

Loewenstein, G., Nagin, D., & Paternoster, R. (1997). The effect of sexual arousal on expectations of sexual forcefulness. *Journal of Research in Crime and Delinquency, 34*(4), 443–473.

Loewenstein, G., O'Donoghue, T., & Rabin, M. (2000). Projection bias in the prediction of future utility.

Loewenstein, G., & Prelec, D. (1992). Anomalies in intertemporal choice: Evidence and an interpretation. *Quarterly Journal of Economics.* 573–597.

Loewenstein, G., Prelec, D., & Shatto, C. (1996). Hot/cold empathy gaps and the underprediction of curiosity.

Loewenstein, G., & Schkade, D. (1999). Wouldn't it be nice? Predicting future feelings. In D. Kahneman & E. Diener (Eds.), *Well-being: The foundations of hedonic psychology* (pp. 85–105). New York: Russell Sage Foundation.

Loewenstein, G. F., Weber, E. U., Hsee, C. K., & Welch, E. (2001). Risk as feelings. *Psychological Bulletin, 127*, 267–286.

Loomes, G., Starmer, C., & Sugden, R. (1992). Are preferences monotonic? Testing some predictions of regret theory. *Economica, 59*(233), 17–33.

Loomes, G., & Sugden, R. (1982). Regret theory: An alternative theory of rational choice under uncertainty. *Economic Journal, 92*, 805–824.

Loomes, G., & Sugden, R. (1986). Disappointment and dynamic consistency in choice under uncertainty. *Review of Economic Studies, 53*(2), 271–282.

Loomes, G., & Sugden, R. (1987). Some implications of more general form of regret theory. *Journal of Economic Theory, 41*(2), 270–287.

Lopes, L. L. (1987). Between hope and fear: The psychology of risk. In B. Leonard (Ed.), *Advances in experimental social psychology* (Vol. 20, pp. 255–295). San Diego, CA: Academic Press.

Lopes, L. L., & Oden, G. C. (1998, November). *The role of aspiration level in risky choice: A comparison of cumulative prospect theory and SP/A theory.* Paper presented at the Society for Judgment and Decision Making, Dallas, TX.

Luce, M. F. (1998). Choosing to avoid: Coping with negatively emotion-laden consumer decisions. *Journal of Consumer Research, 24*(4), 409–433.

Luce, M. F., Bettman, J. R., & Payne, J. W. (1997). Choice processing in emotionally difficult decisions. *Journal of Experimental Psychology: Learning, Memory, and Cognition, 23*(2), 384–405.

Luce, M. F., Payne, J. W., & Bettman, J. R. (1999). Emotional trade-off difficulty and choice. *Journal of Marketing Research, 36*(2), 143–159.

Lutz, C., & White, G. M. (1986). The anthropology of emotions. *Annual Review of Anthropology, 15*, 405–436.

Lyubomirsky, S., & Nolen-Hoeksema, S. (1995). Effects of self-focused rumination on negative thinking and interpersonal problem solving. *Journal of Personality and Social Psychology, 69*(1), 176–190.

MacGregor, D. G., Slovic, P., Dreman, D., & Berry, M. (1999). *Imagery, affect, and financial judgment* (Article 99-3). Eugene, OR: Decision Research.

Magai, C., & McFadden, S. H. (1995). *The role of emotions in social and personality development: History, theory, and research.* New York: Plenum.

Markowitz, H. (1952). The utility of wealth. *Journal of Political Economy, 60*, 151–158.

Mayer, J. D., Gaschke, Y. N., Braverman, D. L., & Evans, T. W. (1992). Mood-congruent judgment is a general effect. *Journal of Personality and Social Psychology, 63*, 119–132.

Mayer, J. D., & Hanson, E. (1995). Mood-congruent judgment over time. *Personality and Social Psychology Bulletin, 21*, 237–244.

Medvec, V. H., Madley, S. F., & Gilovich, T. (1995). When less is more: Counterfactual thinking and satisfaction among Olympic medalists. *Journal of Personality and Social Psychology, 69*(4), 603–610.

Medvec, V. H., & Savitsky, K. (1997). When doing better means feeling worse: The effects of categorical cutoff points on counterfactual thinking and satisfaction. *Journal of Personality and Social Psychology, 72*(6), 1284–1296.

Mellers, B. A., Schwartz, A., Ho, K., & Ritov, I. (1997). Decision affect theory: Emotional reactions to the outcomes of risky options. *Psychological Science, 8*(6), 423–429.

Metcalfe, J., & Mischel, W. (1999). A hot/cool-system analysis of delay of gratification: Dynamics of willpower. *Psychological Review, 106*(1), 3–19.

Mineka, S., & Cook, M. (1993). Mechanisms involved in the observational conditioning of fear. *Journal of Experimental Psychology: General, 122*, 23–38.

Mischel, W., Cantor, N., & Feldman, S. (1996). Principles of self-regulation: The nature of willpower and self-control. In E. T. Higgins & A. W. Kruglanski (Eds.), *Social psychology: Handbook of basic principles* (pp. 329–360). New York: Guilford Press.

Mischel, W., Shoda, Y., & Peake, P. K. (1988). The nature of adolescent competencies predicted by preschool delay of gratification. *Journal of Personality and Social Psychology, 54*(4), 687–696.

Monat, A. (1976). Temporal uncertainty, anticipation time, and cognitive coping under threat. *Journal of Human Stress, 2*, 32–43.

Monat, A., Averill, J. R., & Lazarus, R. S. (1972). Anticipatory stress and coping reactions under various conditions of uncertainty. *Journal of Personality and Social Psychology, 24*, 237–253.

Nesse, R. M. (1990). Evolutionary explanations of emotions. *Human Nature, 1*(3), 261–289.

Niedenthal, P. M., Halberstadt, J. B., & Innes-Ker, A. H. (1999). Emotional response categorization. *Psychological Review*, 337–361.

Niedenthal, P. M., & Kitayama, S. (Eds.). (1994). *The heart's eye: Emotional influences in perception and attention.* San Diego, CA: Academic Press.

Niedenthal, P. M., & Setterlund, M. B. (1994). Emotion congruence in perception. *Personality and Social Psychology Bulletin, 20*, 401–411.

Nolen-Hoeksema, S., & Morrow, J. (1993). Effects of rumination and distraction on naturally occurring depressed mood. *Cognition and Emotion, 7*(6), 561–570.

Nolen-Hoeksema, S., Morrow, J., & Fredrickson, B. L. (1993). Response styles and the duration of episodes of depressed mood. *Journal of Abnormal Psychology, 102*(1), 20–28.

Ohman, A. (1993). Fear and anxiety as emotional phenomena: Clinical phenomenology, evolutionary perspectives, and information-processing mechanisms. In M. Lewis & J. M. Haviland (Eds.), *Handbook of emotions* (pp. 511–536). New York: Guilford Press.

Ohman, A. (1994). The psychophysiology of emotion: Evolutionary and non-conscious origins. *International perspectives on psychological science: Vol. 2: The state of the art* (pp. 197–227). Hillsdale, NJ: Erlbaum.

Ortony, A., Clore, G. L., & Collins, A. (1988). *The cognitive structure of emotions.* New York: Cambridge University Press.

Panksepp, J. (1998). *Affective neuroscience.* New York: Oxford University Press.

Peters, E., & Slovic, P. (1996). The role of affect and worldviews as orienting dispositions in the perception and acceptance of nuclear power. *Journal of Applied Social Psychology, 26,* 1427–1453.

Peters, E., & Slovic, P. (2000). The springs of action: Affective and analytical information processing in choice. *Personality and Social Psychology Bulletin, 26*(12), 1465–1475.

Pham, M. T. (1998). Representativeness, relevance, and the use of feelings in decision making. *Journal of Consumer Research, 25*(2), 144–159.

Prelec, D. (1998). The probability weighting function. *Econometrica, 66,* 497–527.

Quiggin, J. (1982). A theory of anticipated utility. *Journal of Economic Behavior and Organization, 3*(4), 323–343.

Quigley, B. M., & Tedeschi, J. T. (1996). Mediating effects of blame attributions on feelings of anger. *Personality and Social Psychology Bulletin, 22,* 1280–1288.

Rachlin, H., & Raineri, A. (1992). Irrationality, impulsiveness, and selfishness as discount reversal effects. In G. Loewenstein & J. Elster (Eds.), *Choice over time* (pp. 93–118). New York: Russell Sage Foundation.

Raghunathan, R., & Pham, M. T. (1999). All negative moods are not equal: Motivational influences of anxiety and sadness on decision making. *Organizational Behavior and Human Decision Processes, 79*(1), 56–77.

Read, D., & Loewenstein, G. (1999). Enduring pain for money: Decisions based on the perception and memory of pain. *Journal of Behavioral Decision Making, 12*(1), 1–17.

Read, D., & van Leeuwen, B. (1998). Predicting hunger: The effects of appetite and delay on choice. *Organizational Behavior and Human Decision Processes, 76*(2), 189–205.

Robert, C., & Carnevale, P. J. (1997). Group choice in ultimatum bargaining. *Organizational Behavior and Human Decision Processes, 72*(2), 256–279.

Rolls, E. T. (1999). *The brain and emotion.* New York: Oxford University Press.

Roseman, I. J. (1984). Cognitive determinants of emotion: A structural theory. *Review of Personality and Social Psychology, 5,* 11–36.

Roth, W. T., Breivik, G., Jorgensen, P. E., & Hofmann, S. (1996). Activation in novice and expert parachutists while jumping. *Psychophysiology, 33,* 63–72.

Rottenstreich, Y., & Hsee, C. K. (2000). Money, kisses and electric shocks: On the affective psychology of probability weighting. (Working paper). Chicago: University of Chicago.

Sanderson, W. C., Rapee, R. M., & Barlow, D. H. (1988). Panic induction via inhalation of 5.5% $CO_2$ enriched air: A single subject analysis of psychological and physiological effects. *Behaviour Research and Therapy, 26*(4), 333–335.

Schelling, T. C. (1978). Egonomics, or the art of self-management. *American Economic Review, 68* (2), 290–294.

Schelling, T. C. (1984). The life you save may be your own. In T. C. Schelling, *Choice and consequence.* Cambridge, MA: Harvard University Press.

Scherer, K. R. (1999). Appraisal theory. In T. Dalgleish & M. J. Power (Eds.), *Handbook of cognition and emotion* (pp. 637–663). Chichester, England: Wiley.

Schkade, D. A., & Kahneman, D. (1998). Does living in California make people happy? A focusing illusion in judgments of life satisfaction. *Psychological Science, 9*(5), 340–346.

Schwarz, N. (1990). Feelings as information: Informational and motivational functions of affective states. In E. T. Higgins & R. M. Sorrentino (Eds.), *Handbook of motivation and cognition: Foundations of social behavior* (Vol. 2, pp. 527–561). New York: Guilford Press.

Schwarz, N., & Bless, H. (1991). Happy and mindless, but sad and smart? The impact of affective states on analytic reasoning. In P. F. Joseph (Ed.), *Emotion and social judgments: International series in experimental social psychology* (pp. 55–71). Oxford, England: Pergamon Press.

Schwarz, N., & Clore, G. (1996). Feelings and phenomenal experiences. In E. T. Higgins & A. W. Kruglanski (Eds.), *Social psychology: Handbook of basic principles* (pp. 433–465). New York: Guilford Press.

Schwarz, N., & Clore, G. L. (1983). Mood, misattribution and judgments of well-being: Informative and directive functions of affective states. *Journal of Personality and Social Psychology, 45,* 513–523.

Seligman, M. E., & Maier, S. F. (1967). Failure to escape traumatic shock. *Journal of Experimental Psychology, 74*(1), 1–9.

Sieff, E. M., Dawes, R. M., & Loewenstein, G. (1999). Anticipated versus actual reaction to HIV test results. *American Journal of Psychology, 112* (2), 297–311.

Simon, H. A. (1967). Motivational and emotional controls of cognition. *Psychological Review, 74* (1), 29–39.

Sjoeberg, L. (1998). Worry and risk perception. *Risk Analysis, 18* (1), 85–93.

Slevin, M. L., Plant, H., Lynch, D., Drinkwater, J., & Gregory, W. M. (1988). Who should measure quality of life, the doctor or patient? *British Journal of Cancer, 57,* 109–112.

Slovic, P. (2000). What does it mean to know a cumulative risk? Adolescents' perceptions of short-term and long-term consequences of smoking. *Journal of Behavioral Decision Making, 13* (2), 259–266, 273–276.

Slovic, P., Finucane, M., Peters, E., & MacGregor, D. (in press). The affect heuristic. In T. Gilovich, D. Griffin, & D. Kahneman (Eds.), *Heuristics and biases.* New York: Cambridge University Press.

Slovic, P., Flynn, J. H., & Layman, M. (1991). Perceived risk, trust, and the politics of nuclear waste. *Science, 254,* 1603–1607.

Slovic, P., Layman, M., Kraus, N., Flynn, J., Chalmers, J., & Gesell, G. (1991). Perceived risk, stigma, and potential economic impacts of a high-level nuclear waste repository in Nevada. *Risk Analysis, 11*, 683–696.

Smith, C. A., & Ellsworth, P. C. (1985). Patterns of cognitive appraisal in emotion. *Journal of Personality and Social Psychology, 48*, 813–838.

Smith, D., & Over, R. (1987). Male sexual arousal as a function of the content and the vividness of erotic fantasy. *Psychophysiology, 24*(3), 334–339.

Solomon, R. C. (1993). *The passions.* Indianapolis: Hackett.

Srull, T. K. (1983). Affect and memory: The impact of affective reactions in advertising on the representation of product information in memory. In R. Bagozzi & A. Tybout (Eds.), *Advances in consumer research* (Vol. 10, pp. 324–328). Ann Arbor, MI: Association for Consumer Research.

Srull, T. K. (1984). The effects of subjective affective states on memory and judgment. In T. Kinnear (Ed.), *Advances in consumer research* (Vol. 11, pp. 530–533). Provo, UT: Association for Consumer Research.

Strack, F. (1992). The different routes to social judgments: Experiential versus informational strategies. In L. Martin & A. Tesser (Eds.), *The construction of social judgment* (pp. 249–275). Hillsdale, NJ: Erlbaum.

Sugden, R. (1986). Regret, recrimination and rationality. In L. E. Daboni, A. E. Montesano, & M. Lines (Eds.), *Theory and Decision Library Series: Vol. 47. Recent developments in the foundations of utility and risk theory* (pp. 67–80). Dordrecht: Reidel.

Tangney, J. P., Hill-Barlow, D., Wagner, P. E., Marschall, D. E., Borenstein, S. K., Sanftner, J., Mohr, T., & Gramzow, R. (1996). Assessing individual differences in constructive versus destructive responses to anger across the lifespan. *Journal of Personality and Social Psychology, 70* (4), 780–796.

Tangney, J. P., Wagner, P. E., Hill-Barlow, D., Marschall, D. E., & Gramzow, R. (1996). Relation of shame and guilt to constructive versus destructive responses to anger across the lifespan. *Journal of Personality and Social Psychology, 70* (4), 797–809.

Thaler, R. H., & Ziemba, W. T. (1988). Parimutuel betting markets: Racetracks and lotteries. *Journal of Economic Perspectives, 2* (2), 161–174.

Tiedens, L. Z., & Linton, S. (2001). Judgment under emotional certainty and uncertainty: The effects of specific emotions on information processing. *Journal of Personality and Social Psychology, 81*(6), 973–988.

Tversky, A., & Kahneman, D. (1974). Judgment under uncertainty: Heuristics and biases. *Science, 185*), 1124–1131.

Tversky, A., & Kahneman, D. (1984). Choices, values, frames. *American Psychologist, 39*, 341–350.

Tversky, A., & Kahneman, D. (1992). Advances in prospect theory: Cumulative representation of uncertainty. *Journal of Risk and Uncertainty, 5*, 297–323.

VanBoven, L., Dunning, D., & Loewenstein, G. (2000). Egocentric empathy gaps between owners and buyers. *Journal of Personality and Social Psychology, 79*, 66–76.

VanBoven, L., Loewenstein, G., Welch, E., & Dunning, D. (2001). The illusion of courage: Underestimating social-risk aversion in self and others. (Working paper). Carnegie Mellon University, Department of Social and Decision Sciences.

von Neumann, J., & Morgenstern, O. (1944). *Theory of games and economic behavior.* New York: Wiley.

Vuchinich, R. E., & Simpson, C. A. (1998). Hyperbolic temporal discounting in social drinkers and problem drinkers. *Experimental and Clinical Psychopharmacology, 6* (3), 292–305.

Wegener, D., & Petty, R. (1997). The flexible correction model: The role of naive theories of bias in bias correction. *Advances in Experimental Social Psychology, 29*, 141–208.

Weiner, B. (1986). Attribution, emotion, and action. In R. M. Sorrentino & E. T. Higgins (Eds.), *Handbook of motivation and cognition: Foundations of social behavior* (pp. 281–312). New York: Guilford Press.

White, K. D. (1978). Salivation: The significance of imagery in its voluntary control. *Psychophysiology, 15*, 196–203.

Wilson, T. D., & Brekke, N. (1996). Mental contamination and mental correction: Unwanted influences on judgments and evaluations. *Psychological Bulletin, 116* (1), 117–142.

Wilson, T. D., Dunn, D. S., Kraft, D., & Lisle, D. J. (1989). Introspection, attitude change, and attitude-behavior consistency: The disruptive effects of explaining why we feel the way we do. In L. Berkowitz (Ed.), *Advances in experimental social psychology* (Vol. 22, pp. 287–343). San Diego, CA: Academic Press.

Wilson, T. D., Kraft, D., & Dunn, D. S. (1989). The disruptive effects of explaining attitudes: The moderating effect of knowledge about the attitude object. *Journal of Experimental Social Psychology, 25*, 379–400.

Wilson, T. D., Lisle, D. J., Schooler, J. W., Hodges, S. D., Klaaren, K. J., & LaFleur, S. J. (1993). Introspecting about reasons can reduce post-choice satisfaction. *Personality and Social Psychology Bulletin, 19*, 331–339.

Wilson, T. D., & Schooler, J. W. (1991). Thinking too much: Introspection can reduce the quality of preferences and decisions. *Journal of Personality and Social Psychology, 60*, 181–192.

Wilson, T. D., Wheatley, T., Meyers, J., Gilbert, D. T., & Axsom, D. (2000). Focalism: A source of durability bias in affective forecasting. *Journal of Personality and Social Psychology, 78*, 821–836.

Wright, W. F., & Bower, G. H. (1992). Mood effects on subjective probability assessment. *Organizational Behavior and Human Decision Processes, 52*, 276–291.

Yates, J. F., Yaniv, I., & Smith, J. K. (1991). Measures of discrimination skill in probabilistic judgment. *Psychological Bulletin, 110*, 611–617.

Zajonc, R. (1998). Emotions. In D. Gilbert, S. Fiske, & G. Lindzey (Eds.), *Handbook of social psychology* (Vol. 1, pp. 591–632). New York: Oxford University Press.

Zeelenberg, M., & Beattie, J. (1997). Consequences of regret aversion: 2. Additional evidence for effects of feedback on decision making. *Organizational Behavior and Human Decision Processes, 72*(1), 63–78.

Zeelenberg, M., Beattie, J., van der Plight, J., & de Vries, N. K. (1996). Consequences of regret aversion: Effects of expected feedback on risky decision making. *Organizational Behavior and Human Decision Processes, 65* (2), 148–158.

Zillmann, D. (1971). Excitation transfer in communication-mediated aggressive behavior. *Journal of Experimental Social Psychology, 7* (4), 419–434.

# 32

# REMEMBERING EMOTIONAL EVENTS: A SOCIAL COGNITIVE NEUROSCIENCE APPROACH

Kevin N. Ochsner and Daniel L. Schacter

How we respond emotionally to the peaks and valleys of life reveals much about who we are now, who we have been, and has implications for who we could be in the future. The question of how we remember these emotional events is thus of central importance to understanding human experience, and is the subject of this chapter. In addressing this question, our goals are to understand the specific neurocognitive mechanisms that preserve records of significant experiences, the motivational and contextual factors that influence their operation, and what their interaction tells us about the relationship between memory and emotion more generally.

We begin with a brief historical sketch of previous approaches to emotion and memory and then move to our own multileveled social cognitive neuroscience approach. We then apply this approach to understanding how the emotional nature of an event influences the encoding, storage, and retrieval of information about it. We conclude with suggestions for ways in which a social cognitive neuroscience approach can guide future research.

## Perspectives on the Emotional Past

Most investigations of emotion and memory have begun with the same question: How do we remember emotionally evocative events? But investigators have framed this question differently and, as a result, have reached different conclusions. Three approaches have dominated past

research, and the strengths and weaknesses of each are rooted in the ways in which their questions have been posed.

### Indelible or Reconstructed?

Debate over whether emotional memories, and especially traumatic ones, are remembered poorly or well has a long history and is central to current discussion about the recovery of supposedly repressed memories of sexual and physical abuse during childhood (for discussion, see Conway, 1997; Loftus & Ketcham, 1994; Schacter, 1996). The question of whether emotion improves or impairs memory often is framed in terms of the question of whether emotional memories are indelible or reconstructed. Debate concerning this issue has played out in three different arenas.

#### Repression: Fact or Fiction?

First, some have argued that memories of especially aversive experiences may be temporarily lost—driven out of consciousness by repressive mechanisms that seek to protect the psyche from the harmful consequences of thinking about them. Yet if recovered at some later time, such memories are held to be highly accurate (e.g., van der Kolk & Fisler, 1995). This account seems to turn on the truth of a traditional metaphor for memory as a library in which are stored volumes of experience that contain verbatim records of events that can be retrieved later (Conway, 1997). On this account, repressed memories of emotional experiences are simply volumes that have been lost due to operation of a repressive process but that can later be found and reread in their entirety. As argued by various investigators (cf. Lindsay & Read, 1994; Loftus, 1993; Schacter, 1996; Schacter, Koutstaal, & Norman, 1996), this account is problematic because (1) traumatic memories are typically difficult to forget, even when one wants to do so (e.g., Wenzlaff et al., 1993; for review, see Schacter, 1996), and (2) false memories for various kinds of information, including personal life events, can be generated, sometimes with relative ease (e.g., Hyman, Husband, & Billings, 1995; Loftus & Pickrell, 1995; Roediger & McDermott, 1995; Schacter, Verfaellie, & Pradere, 1996).

### Fading Flashbulbs

Second, investigators studying "flashbulb" memories also have argued that special mechanisms may promote the indelible recording of traces of emotional events (e.g., Brown & Kulik, 1977). However, this view has been abandoned in light of a growing body of evidence demonstrating that so-called flashbulb memories are far from photographic recordings and in fact are subject to some of the same kinds of distortions as is recall of more generic personal experiences (Brewer, 1992; Neisser & Harsch, 1992).

It is worth noting that conclusions about the putative indelibility of flashbulb memories may depend on the kind of mnemonic information that is assessed. On the one hand, people do not often forget *that* an emotional event has occurred, and they tend to recall accurately the themes and action sequences central to an event's emotional significance (Heuer & Reisberg, 1992). On the other hand, emotional experiences involve substantial evaluation of, and inferences about, one's own and others' motivations and intentions (Lazarus, 1991; Stein, Wade, & Liwag, 1997); current goals and desires can distort perception and memory for these aspects of emotional situations during both encoding and retrieval. Thus memories for the broad "objective facts" of an event may be less subject to distortion than are one's subjective interpretations of its personal and emotional significance (Johnson & Sherman, 1990).

### Focus on Fear

The third arena in which the indelibility issue has emerged involves fear conditioning in rats. Fear responses to conditioned stimuli appear to remain indefinitely intact when brain areas responsible for extinguishing them are damaged (LeDoux, 1995). Recent accounts of the forgetting of conditioned responses have suggested that past conditioned associations are not lost but that their expression is inhibited by the learning of new responses that preempt expression of old behavioral patterns (Bouton, 1994).

Although it may be true that some traces of fearful events are relatively long-lasting and enduring, it is important to note that the findings that support this conclusion come primarily from indirect tests of behavior in animals. In contrast, reconstruction and distortion is common when memory for emotional experiences is examined using explicit tests in humans (e.g., Eich, Reeves, Jaeger, & Graff-Radford, 1985; Levine, 1997; Ochsner & Schacter, 2000). It appears that whether one reaches the conclusion that emotional memories are indelible or reconstructed may depend on the kinds of data under consideration. Although these traces are reflexively expressible on indirect tests of behavior, they may be of a different type than those used when we consciously reflect on emotional experiences.

### Emotion Is in the Details

A closely related debate concerns whether memory for emotional events accurately preserves records of only central details or of both central and peripheral details (e.g., Christianson & Loftus, 1991). The majority of studies indicate that central details are most accurately recalled because emotional events activate goals that favor evaluation of the personal meaning of potentially significant stimuli during both encoding and retrieval. During the initial appraisal and encoding of an emotional event, it is important to understand which characteristics of external stimuli are related to internal feeling states. For example, when walking alone at night along a deserted street, it would be more important to draw inferences about the possible intentions of the person walking toward you and to determine whether the object in his hands is a weapon than it would be to notice the color of his hat, shoes, or coat (Lazarus, 1991; Stein et al., 1997). Similar goals at memory retrieval may further focus attention on central information and can lead to biases in the way in which events are recalled. The key point is that the kind of information that is recalled most accurately depends on where attention is directed and which emotion appraisal scripts are activated (Levine, 1997).

A methodological shortcoming of some of the foregoing research involves a failure to independently verify the affective qualities of experimental stimuli. Because the extent to which to-be-remembered stimuli elicit affect is not known, when a given type of detail is remembered poorly we cannot be sure why this has occurred: It could be because that kind of detail is not remembered well, or it could be that the stimuli were not arousing enough to lead participants to more deeply encode them.

### Quantity Versus Quality

A third long-running debate in the emotion and memory literature concerns what aspect of emotion—arousal (quantity of emotion) or valence (the positive or negative quality of emotion)—most critically determines how emotion influences memory. Early theorists postulated that people preferentially encode and recall positive experiences because reflecting on negative ones is too painful (see Bradley, 1994, and Matlin & Stang, 1978, for review). More recently, the focus has shifted toward comparing memory for negative, often highly aversive, events with memory for more mundane experiences. Some of this research has found aversive memories to be less accurate, as when encoding is disrupted by extremes of emotion produced by highly traumatic experiences (Kihlstrom, 1998; Schacter, 1996), whereas other research has concluded that these memories are more accurate, as in the case of flashbulb memories or studies of fear conditioning (Brewer, 1992; Brown & Kulik, 1977; LeDoux et al., 1989). We considered some of the problems with interpreting this research in the preceding sections.

The relationship of arousal to memory has been thought to depend on exactly how arousing an experience is, with moderate amounts of arousal producing the most accurate memory, and either too little or too much arousal causing memory impairments (see Revelle & Loftus, 1992, for review). Support for this proposal in human studies has been somewhat shaky (Christianson, 1992) but is strongly supported by studies in animals showing a dose-dependent relationship between memory for stressful events and release of arousal-related neurotransmitters (e.g., McGaugh, 1995).

In most studies aversive or positive events have also been highly arousing, and it is natural to ask how each factor influences memory independently. Unfortunately, however, it has been difficult to tease apart the independent effects of arousal and valence because the two variables seldom have been manipulated systematically within a single experiment. This is partly attributable to the fact that, in recent years, the memory and emotion literature has been concerned primarily with understanding memory for traumatic events such as abuse that are both highly arousing and extremely negative. It also may be due to the fact that negative affect can be more easily and reliably elicited than positive affect.

Nevertheless, two studies have compared memory for positive and negative information that varied in degree of associated arousal. Both found that it is the quantity of arousal, not the quality of valence, that predicts memory performance. In a study of autobiographical memory, Reisberg, Heuer, McLean, and O'Shaughnessy (1988) found that retrospective reports of arousal predicted ratings of vividness, independent of the valence ascribed to an event. In a study of recognition and recall for carefully validated emotionally evocative pictures, Bradley, Greenwald, Petry, and Lang (1992) found that participants' ratings of arousal predicted memory accuracy in the same way for both positive and negative images.

It is possible that these studies did not find that va-

lence influenced memory because they used quantitative dependent measures that are insensitive to qualitative variations in the experience of recollection. The conscious experience of emotion differs as a function of which emotion is being aroused, and thus we would expect recollection of emotional events to reflect this qualitative difference in experiential awareness. In a series of studies, we (Ochsner, 2000) used the *remember/know* procedure (Tulving, 1983) to measure conscious recollective experience of positive, neutral, and negative photos (Lang et al., 1993) that varied in degree of arousal and complexity of visual detail. In this method participants are asked to classify items presented on a recognition memory test as either new (the item was not seen during a prior study phase), as "known" (the item evokes a sense of familiarity and the participant is sure it was seen previously, but no specific details come to mind about its prior occurrence), or as "remembered" (the item evokes a detailed sense of recollective re-experiencing of the prior study episode replete with sensory, affective, or semantic details). Previous research has shown that *remember* responses are sensitive to how distinctively an item has been encoded, whereas *know* responses are sensitive to the factors that influence general familiarity (Rajaram & Roediger, 1997). Highly distinctive items possess a greater number of unique attributes, may be more deeply encoded, and may elicit a greater number of cognitive and affective appraisals than less distinctive items (Hunt & McDaniel, 1993; Ochsner, 2000). As discussed later, affective stimuli possess more attributes than neutral ones and tend to capture and hold our attention. On this basis we reasoned that affective stimuli will be encoded more distinctively than neutral stimuli and hence should be "remembered" more often. In addition, we reasoned that because encoding biases may operate more strongly, or even preferentially, for negative information (e.g., Pratto & John, 1991), negative photos would be encoded more distinctively and should tend to elicit more "remember" responses than positive photos. Under a variety of encoding conditions, we found clear and consistent support for both hypotheses (Ochsner 2000): Independent of the effects of arousal, both negative and positive stimuli were remembered more often than neutral ones, which is consistent with the idea that affective events are encoded distinctively. In addition, negative photographs tended to be remembered more often than positive photos, whereas positive photographs tended to be known more often than negative ones. This is consistent with the idea that negative events are encoded distinctively. In addition, negative photographs tended to be *remembered* more often than positive photos, whereas positive photographs tended to known more often than negative ones. This is consistent with the idea that negative events are encoded more distinctively than positive ones and so are re-experienced differently during recollection.

## The Social Cognitive Neuroscience Approach

Past research on memory and emotion has failed to develop an overarching theoretical approach that specifies what emotion is, how emotional information is processed, and how we would expect it to influence memory mechanisms. Studies have been concerned more with providing an explanation for a particular phenomenon than with developing an integrated theoretical approach.

In contrast, the present approach combines theories of memory and emotion drawn from social psychology and cognitive neuroscience to provide an account of how we remember affecting experiences (Ochsner & Lieberman, 2001). Our account cuts across many levels, ranging from the social level of experience and behavior, to the cognitive level of information processing, down to the neural level of brain systems and mechanisms. We call this type of analysis the social cognitive neuroscience (SCN) approach to denote its emphasis on integrating data and theory across these three broadly defined levels of analysis (Lieberman, 2000; Lieberman, Ochsner, Gilbert, & Schacter, 2001; Ochsner & Feldman Barrett, 2001; Ochsner & Lieberman, 2001; Ochsner & Schacter, 2000; cf. Ochsner & Kosslyn, 1999). Owing somewhat to the relative novelty of our approach, the account of emotion and memory we derive is less than a comprehensive theory that explains all emotion and memory phenomena, but more than a distillation of recent research. It is an attempt to draw principled conclusions about the way in which emotional events are remembered that draw on and make sense of data at the social, cognitive, and neural levels (Ochsner & Lieberman, 2001).

From an SCN perspective, the answer to the question of how emotional events are remembered is that it depends on the goals one has in encoding, storing, and retrieving information. It should be noted that the term *goal* is shorthand for a variety of motivational processes that may influence memory. Goals may be conscious or unconscious, and may range from relatively basic biological needs (such as eating food or avoiding pain) and impulses (such as sexual desire) to more complex strivings that drive us to protect our self-esteem or attain professional success. The relationship of events to goals in turn determines both the nature of our initial emotional response to the event and how cognitive processes will be deployed in the service of remembering it. This means that memory is inherently constructive and that questions about the absolute strength or quality of one type of remembered information are ill posed. Answering a question about the absolute accuracy of memory depends on specifying exactly what it means to say that a memory is more or less accurate, and it may be difficult to agree on criteria that

apply to all conditions equally well. Furthermore, Tulving (1983) has suggested that the absolute strength of a memory can never be determined because expression of stored information is strongly determined by situational and strategic factors. Instead of asking whether memory is good or bad, research should focus on elucidating the factors that determine which aspects of emotional episodes will be remembered accurately, when this will occur, and what mechanisms mediate these effects. Our analyses are motivated by exactly this kind of approach, and we begin with a brief overview of current theories of memory and emotion to serve as the backdrop against which we discuss studies of their relationship in later sections.

### Systems for the Construction of Memory

Memory is not a copy or reproduction of past experiences, but instead involves a complex construction that draws on various kinds of information. Schacter, Norman, and Koutstaal (1998) have recently proposed a "constructive memory framework" that summarizes some of the major encoding and retrieval processes that underlie such constructions. In this framework, representations of new experiences are viewed as patterns of features. Constituent features of a memory representation are distributed widely across different parts of the brain; no single location contains a complete record of the trace or engram of a specific experience (Damasio, 1989; Squire, 1992). Retrieval of a past experience involves a process of "pattern completion" (McClelland, McNaughton, & O'Reilly, 1995). Subsets of the features that comprise a particular past experience are reactivated by a retrieval cue, and activation spreads to the remaining features.

To produce mainly accurate representations of past experience, a memory system that operates in such a manner must solve a number of problems. At the encoding stage, features must be linked together to form a bound or "coherent" representation (Moscovitch, 1994). A closely related encoding process, sometimes referred to as pattern separation (McClelland et al., 1995), is required to keep bound episodes separate from one another in memory. If episodes overlap extensively with one another, individuals may recall what is common to many episodes but fail to remember distinctive particulars that distinguish one episode from another (e.g., Schacter, Israel, & Racine, 1999).

Similar kinds of problems arise when retrieving information from memory. Because retrieval cues can potentially match stored experiences other than the sought-after episode, the rememberer may form a more refined description of the characteristics of the episode to be retrieved (Burgess & Shallice, 1996), referred to as a process of "focusing" (Norman & Schacter, 1996). When the pattern completion process produces a match, the rememberer must decide whether the retrieved information constitutes a specific memory of a particular experience or a generic image. The rememberer now needs to consider the diagnostic value of perceptual vividness, semantic detail, and other kinds of information that can help to specify the origin of the retrieved pattern (Johnson, Hashtroudi, & Lindsay, 1993; Schacter & Wagner, 1999).

## Controlling Encoding and Retrieval

A variety of brain regions have been linked to these and related aspects of constructive memory functions (see Schacter et al., 1998). However, two regions are particularly relevant to memory construction: the medial temporal region and the prefrontal cortex. The medial temporal region has long been associated with memory functions, because damage to this region produces a severe impairment of memory for recent experiences (Squire, 1992). Recent neuroimaging data indicate that the medial temporal area is involved in encoding novel events into memory (e.g., Stern et al., 1996; for review, see Schacter & Wagner, 1999). Indeed, a consensus account has begun to emerge regarding how exactly the medial temporal region implements feature binding and pattern separation (e.g., McClelland et al., 1995; see Schacter et al., 1998, for a summary).

The medial temporal region also contributes to pattern completion at retrieval (cf. McClelland et al., 1995; Moscovitch, 1994). Although the neuroimaging data on medial temporal contributions to such retrieval are not entirely clear-cut—many studies have failed to observe medial temporal activity during retrieval—several brain imaging studies have implicated the medial temporal area in the successful recollection of recently acquired information (Nyberg, Cabeza, & Tulving, 1996; Schacter, Alpert, Savage, Rauch, & Albert, 1996; Squire et al., 1992; for review, see Schacter & Wagner, 1999).

The prefrontal cortex has also been implicated in both encoding and retrieval processes. On the encoding side, specific regions within the prefrontal cortex play an important role in elaborative encoding activities that relate incoming information to previous experiences (for recent studies, see Brewer, Zhao, Glover, & Gabrieli, 1998; Wagner et al., 1998). Numerous neuroimaging studies have also documented prefrontal activity during episodic retrieval, especially in the right hemisphere (for reviews, see Buckner, 1996; Nyberg, Cabeza, & Tulving, 1996). Although the exact nature of the functions indexed by these activations remains to be determined, they appear to tap effortful aspects of retrieval (Schacter, Alpert et al., 1996) related to focusing or entering the "retrieval mode" (Nyberg et al., 1995) and also to postretrieval monitoring and criterion setting (Rugg et al., 1997; Schacter, Buckner, Koutstaal, Dale, & Rosen, 1997).

## Automatic or Implicit Processes

Whereas the constructive memory framework focuses on conscious, explicit, or episodic memory for specific past experiences, other memory systems are involved in nonconscious or implicit forms of memory (for reviews, see Schacter, Chiu, & Ochsner, 1993; Schacter, Wagner, & Buckner, 2001; Squire, 1992). Consider briefly two such systems: the perceptual representation system (PRS) and procedural memory.

According to Schacter (1994) and Tulving and Schacter (1990), the PRS plays an important role in the identification of words and objects on the basis of their form and structure. PRS operates at a "presemantic" level and is not involved in representing associative or conceptual information (which is the province of yet another system, semantic memory; see Tulving, 1983). Schacter (1994) has distinguished among three major PRS subsystems: a visual word form subsystem that handles information concerning physical and orthographic features; an auditory word form system that handles phonological and acoustic information; and a structural description subsystem that handles information about the relations between parts of an object that specify its global form and structure.

The PRS appears to play a prominent role in the phenomenon known as priming, which has been studied intensively during the past decade. Priming refers to changes in one's ability to identify a word or an object from reduced perceptual cues as a consequence of a recent exposure to it (Tulving & Schacter, 1990). Priming appears to operate nonconsciously, in the sense that people can exhibit effects of priming under conditions in which they lack explicit memory for having studied a word or object (for reviews, see Roediger & McDermott, 1993; Schacter et al., 1993). Further, patients with amnesic syndromes that result from damage to the medial temporal lobes—patients who have great difficulties explicitly remembering recent experiences—exhibit intact priming across a wide variety of tasks, materials, and situations (for review, see Schacter & Buckner, 1998; Squire, 1992). These findings indicate that priming does not depend on the medial temporal structures that mediate explicit remembering. Recent neuroimaging studies of priming suggest that regions of extrastriate visual cortex play a key role (see Schacter & Buckner, 1998, for review). Changes in the PRS that arise as a consequence of analyzing perceptual features, words, or objects likely constitute the basis of many kinds of priming.

Procedural memory refers to the acquisition of skills and habits: "knowing how" rather than "knowing that." Procedural memories are acquired gradually over time through repetitive practice. Studies of amnesic patients have revealed that even patients with a profound inability to explicitly remember past experiences can gradually acquire new perceptual, motor, and cognitive skills (e.g., Cohen & Squire, 1980), habits that are involved in classification and categorization (e.g., Knowlton & Squire, 1993), and implicit knowledge of sequences (Nissen & Bullemer, 1987) or grammatical rules (Knowlton, Ramus, & Squire, 1992). These results show clearly that the acquisition of procedural knowledge does not depend on the medial temporal lobe structures that are damaged in amnesic patients. In contrast, patients with Huntington's disease, who are characterized by damage to the basal ganglia, have difficulties acquiring new motor and cognitive skills despite relatively intact explicit memory—the exact opposite of the pattern exhibited by amnesic patients (e.g., Salmon & Butters, 1995; see Lieberman, 2000, for review). Recent neuroimaging evidence also implicates the basal ganglia, as well as motor cortex, in procedural learning (e.g., Karni et al., 1995; Petersen, van Mier, Fiez, & Raichle, 1998).

Ultimately, the construction of memories depends on interactions among networks that involve multiple brain regions. The exact nature of the operations performed by the constituent regions remains to be specified, and we are just beginning to explore interactions among them.

## Systems for the Construction of Emotion

As was the case for memory, emotion depends on multiple systems, each dedicated to processing a specific type of information. In general, emotion systems are concerned with determining whether stimuli are significant to current or long-term goals and guiding action and thought accordingly. An emotional response is generated by the pattern of activity across these systems and may include physiological, behavioral, experiential, and cognitive components (Lazarus, 1991). The process of determining the significance of a stimulus often is called *appraisal*, and may involve separate processes that organize perception of and responses to emotional stimuli (van Reekum & Scherer, 1997). Various theorists have argued that appraisals involve the interaction of two kinds of processes: those that quickly and automatically evaluate the valence of a stimulus and can promote appropriate behavior without need of conscious processing and those that operate consciously and deliberately to control, modify, or initiate ongoing emotional responses (Damasio, 1994; LeDoux, 1995; Leventhal & Scherer, 1987; Ochsner & Feldman Barrett, 2001; Ohman, 1988). Although our understanding of emotion systems is still in its infancy, at present it is useful to broadly organize them along the continuum between automatic and controlled processing to better understand their contributions to the appraisal process (Ochsner & Feldmann Barrett, 2001; Ohman, 1988; van Reekum & Scherer, 1997; see also Dalgliesh, chap. 33, this volume).

### Systems for Automatic Emotion Processing

At least two different systems for encoding emotional information can be activated automatically. The information stored in these systems is the knowledge base that guides emotional responses. The most well-studied system involves the amygdala, which receives both coarse sensory input from the thalamus and highly processed information about the identity and appearance of objects from higher cortical centers (Aggleton et al., 2000). Lesion studies in rats and primates, as well as neuroimaging and neuropsychological studies in humans, indicate that the fast subcortical route enables the amygdala to code the potential threat value of stimuli (such as shocks, aversive noises, or fear faces) without conscious awareness (Anderson & Phelps, 2001; Davis, 1997; LeDoux, 1995; Morris, Ohman, & Dolan, 1999; Ochsner & Feldman Barrett, 2001; Whalen, 1998; Whalen et al., 1998). The registration of potential threats promotes the fast linkage of orienting, arousal, and fear responses to coarse representations of these eliciting stimuli (Davis, 1998). The cortical route may supplement this first-pass analysis with information about the precise characteristics of threatening stimuli that differentiate them from nonthreatening ones (Davis, 1997; LeDoux, 2000).

A second system involves the basal ganglia and is important for coding behavioral and cognitive sequences that have become habitual over time. The basal ganglia can be activated automatically by positive or rewarding stimuli, including subliminally presented positive faces (Morris et al., 1996) and cocaine (London et al., 1990). Stimuli that consistently have been reinforced over time promote release of the neurotransmitter dopamine, which stamps in learning of responses to those stimuli (Lieberman, 2000; Schulz, Apicella, Romo, & Scarnati, 1995).

### Systems for Controlled Emotion Processing

Three systems are essential for the regulation and monitoring of affective reactions to internal and external stimuli. The first depends upon areas of the ventral medial and orbital frontal cortices and is used to represent the current motivational value of an external stimulus and use it to guide behavior. Neuroimaging studies show activation of these areas by perceived or imagined positive and negative stimuli (e.g., Rauch et al., 1997; Rolls, 1999; Shin et al., 1997) and damage to these areas impairs ability to use affect to guide decision making (Bechara et al., 1995, 1996; Damasio, 1994), the ability to change behavior toward stimuli with learned affective value (Rolls, 1999), and may cause general disinhibition and socially inappropriate affect and behavior (Rolls, 1999). A second system depends upon the anterior cingulate cortex and is used to monitor the extent to which the current motivational state deviates from one that is desired (Ochsner & Feldman-Barrett,

2001; Ochsner, Kosslyn et al., 2001; cf. Botvinick et al., 1999; Posner & DiGirolamo, 1998). This function is important for many behaviors, and activation of regions of cingulate cortex has been associated with many phenomena including mental imagery (Kosslyn, Alpert et al., 1993), working memory (Petit et al., 1998), divided attention (Corbetta et al, 1991) and attention to emotion (Lane, Fink et al., 1997), hypothesis generation (Elliott & Dolan, 1998), the experience of pain (e.g. Talbot, Marrett et al., 1991), and the detection and correction of errors (Botvinick, 1999; Carter et al., 1998). The third structure is the lateral prefrontal cortex. In general, this brain region is important for working memory and implementing cognitive control (Knight et al., 1999; Miller & Cohen, 2001). Recent work suggests lateral prefrontal cortex may play a special role in emotion regulation: Ochsner, Bunge et al. (2001) used functional neuroimaging to compare brain activation when participants either let themselves respond naturally to aversive images or interpreted (or reappraised) these images in unemotional terms. They found that reappraisal activated regions of lateral prefrontal cortex and deactivated regions of the ventromedial prefrontal cortex and amygdala. These results are important because they suggest that exerting cognitive control over emotion can influence both automatic (amygdala) and controlled (ventromedial prefrontal cortex) emotion processing systems (cf. Hariri, Bookheimer, & Mazziotta, 2000).

## Emotion Guides the Encoding and Storage of Information

Our emotional responses signal the occurrence of events and stimuli of particular significance to both short- and long-term goals (Lazarus, 1991). In general, these responses serve to protect the self from harm and help us to regulate current mood and behavior (Lazarus, 1991). Emotions thus motivate us to attend to, appraise, reappraise, and organize our understanding of the personally significant stimuli that aroused our feelings (cf. Dalgleish, this volume). The consequence of this added attention and consideration is that we tend to remember affectively charged events differently than we remember mundane ones. This interaction between emotion and encoding has been studied primarily in four domains: the way in which threatening stimuli automatically grab attention, how emotion regulation strategies influence attention and impact on memory, how existing emotion knowledge (in the form of schemas) guides encoding of information, and post-event rehearsal of affective events.

### Detecting Threats, Attention, and Weapon Focus

Quite often, the activation of an emotional response is automatic, as strongly valenced stimuli are classified as positive or negative. In the emotional Stroop task, for exam-

ple, it takes more time to name the color in which words with strong personal significance are printed than it takes to name the print color of neutral words (MacLeod, 1992; Mineka & Nugent, 1995; Williams et al., 1990). This effect seems most pronounced for aversive words (e.g., Pratto & John, 1991), and so long as these words have immediate affective significance, they can capture our attention and interfere with our ability to do other things (Matthews, Mogg, Kentish, & Eysenck, 1995).

The attention-grabbing power of affective and especially threatening stimuli on memory has been demonstrated in studies of a phenomenon known as "weapon focus." This term refers to the tendency of threatening stimuli to dominate initial perception and subsequent memory of stressful events. A classic demonstration of this effect was provided by Loftus and Burns (1982), who asked participants to watch a videotape of a staged bank robbery in which the escaping robbers either did or did not shoot a small boy in the face. Viewing the gunshot impaired memory for immediately preceding events while preserving vivid recall of the shot itself (see also Loftus, Loftus, & Messo, 1987). The apparent automaticity of this effect is underscored in a study by Christianson, Loftus, Hoffmann, and Loftus (1991). Using very brief stimulus presentations or eye-tracking records, they equated viewing time for emotional and neutral slides and found that memory for the emotional stimuli was consistently more accurate.

In some cases, unexpected and incongruent, but non-threatening, stimuli (such as a banana held by bank robber) also may grab attention and be better remembered (Pickel, 1998). Such stimuli are not directly threatening, however, and it is likely that incongruent and affective stimuli are remembered well for different reasons. This was demonstrated by a recent functional neuroimaging study that related memory to patterns of neural activation during encoding of bizarre and affective stimuli matched for their degree of interest (Hamann et al., 1999). Although both affective and bizarre stimuli were recalled better than neutral stimuli, only for affective stimuli was amygdala activity at encoding correlated with subsequent memory (see also Cahill et al., 1996).

### Attention and Emotion Regulation

Although the emotional content of stimuli may automatically grab hold of our attention, we can consciously redirect it to change our response to an event before, during, or after it has occurred. Such attempts at active emotion regulation can change the way in which we encode events and, therefore, how we remember them later on (Gross, 1998). One commonly used regulatory strategy entails suppressing the expression of emotional behavior (e.g., keeping a neutral facial expression or tone of voice so that others do not know that one is unhappy). Although expression suppression may be successful, it takes a physiological toll (Gross & Levenson, 1993) and impairs memory accuracy, possibly by diverting attention from external events to the internal regulatory process (Richards & Gross, 1999). Suppressing one's experience also may impair memory, but by reducing the detail with which events are recollected (Ochsner, 2000). Another commonly used regulatory strategy is to try to forget negative events after they have ended. Studies of intentional or directed forgetting using emotionally evocative words suggest that this strategy can be successful for normal individuals (depending on how and how much one tries to forget; for discussion, see Koutstaal & Schacter, 1997) but may be more difficult for some patients with emotional disorders (McNally, Metzger, Lasko, Clancy, & Pitman, 1998; Wilhelm, McNally, Baer & Florin, 1996). Suppression of visual images may be more difficult, however. Ochsner and Sanchez (2001) found that, whereas neutral photos could be intentionally forgotten, both negative and positive photos resisted attempts to forget them. Although the mechanisms which underlie intentional forgetting are not yet completely understood, they seem to involve restricting attention during exposure to information in anticipation that one may want to forget it, as well as diminishing postevent attention to and rehearsal of target events (Koutstaal & Schacter, 1997).

### Schemas and Thematic Detail

The affective significance of a stimulus is not always immediately apparent, and in these cases we rely on knowledge of similar situations to guide a search for disambiguating cues. The emotion knowledge we draw upon may be organized in the form of schemas or scripts that specify the origins, sequelae, and meaning of our emotional responses (Lazarus, 1991). For example, when you return home after a long day at work, your spouse's furrowed brow and sharply inflected voice could indicate either unhappiness with you or the experience of a frustrating day. As is the case for understanding most emotions, it is relevant to find out whether your spouse intended to express himself or herself in this way and what might be motivating his or her actions (Lazarus, 1991; Stein, Wade, & Liwag, 1997). To determine which scenario is correct, one can search for relevant emotion knowledge in associative or episodic memory (e.g., whenever I am late, my spouse is upset) or in the environment (e.g., my spouse had a big presentation today and it might have gone badly).

The use of schematic emotion knowledge during encoding suggests that we will remember information central to and congruent with the schema for a particular kind of emotional experience. Numerous studies have demonstrated better recall for so-called central than peripheral details, including enhanced memory for the actions and weapons, rather than appearance, of attackers (Burke,

Heuer, & Reisberg, 1992; Christianson & Loftus, 1987; Clifford & Scott, 1978; Yuille & Cutshall, 1986). The particular kind of information central to the schema depends on the emotion (Levine & Burgess, 1997; Stein et al., 1997), and there is good evidence that schemas help us draw inferences pertaining to causality and intention during the encoding of an emotional event and cause us to misremember these inferences as facts later on (Heuer & Reisberg, 1990).

Self-schemas represent the positive or negative views we have of ourselves, and also may direct us to attend to and encode different aspects of positive or negative events. Which aspects we encode depends upon the nature of our self-schema. The majority of individuals have a positive self-schema, which means that positive information may be elaborated more fully with respect to their existing self-views. As a consequence they may recall and recognize positive self-descriptive words more accurately than neutral and negative words (e.g., Denny & Hunt, 1992; Mogg et al., 1987). By contrast, individuals with negative self-concepts and self-schemas might be more likely to encode and elaborate negative as opposed to positive self-relevant information. This has been shown for depressed patients, who tend to recall or recognize negative depression-related words more accurately than other word types (e.g., Watkins, Mathews, Williamson, & Fuller, 1992). Because their self-schemas focus attention on elaborating internal sensations and thoughts that are consistent with their negative self-view, depressives tend to miss the details of their life experiences and recall episodes in an overly general way (Williams & Dritschel, 1988). Attention to schema-congruent information does not always lead to better memory, however, and in some cases our goal may be *not* to remember what we have experienced. This is the pattern shown by patients with generalized anxiety disorder who sometimes exhibit impaired recall of anxiety-relevant words (Mineka & Nugent, 1995).

### Postevent Rehearsal, Consolidation, and Reminiscence

The emotions we experience in response to significant events may reveal to us what we consider important, what we want, and why we want it (Ross & Conway, 1986; Singer & Salovey, 1996). Whether personal or public, emotional events tend to retain their significance for long periods of time and are recounted and rehearsed more often than neutral ones (Neisser & Harsch, 1992; Schacter, 1996), and the amount of rehearsal is generally associated with increased subsequent memory (Cohen, Conway, & Maylor, 1994; Conway & Bekerian, 1988; Rubin & Kozin, 1984; see, however, Christianson & Loftus, 1990; Pillemer, 1984). Negative events are hard to ignore and may be more important to revisit because they may signal threats that could continue in the future (Skowronski & Carlston,

1989); diary studies have shown that people tend to rehearse unpleasant experiences more than pleasant ones and, as a result, may tend to overestimate the frequency with which they occurred (Thomas & Diener, 1995).

Although memory for arousing events ultimately surpasses memory for neutral events, initially it may actually be worse (Revelle & Loftus, 1992). The initial decline and subsequent improvement in memory for arousing events is called the "reminiscence effect," and it has been demonstrated with both words (Bradley & Baddeley, 1990; Kleinsmith & Kaplan, 1963) and pictures (Kaplan & Kaplan, 1969). The effect is somewhat small and variable (Burke et al., 1992; Corteen, 1969) but is reliable (Park & Banaji, 1996) and may depend on as yet unclear particulars of the paired-associate paradigm most commonly used to study it.

Theoretical accounts of the reminiscence effect have appealed to various kinds of consolidation mechanisms that take more time to integrate emotional events into existing knowledge structures. Revelle and Loftus (1992) suggested that because we extract more information per unit time from emotional than from neutral experiences (Christianson et al., 1991), it may be difficult to access that information initially. The amygdala, which is essential for detecting preattentive threats, seems to be the essential mediator of this consolidation. LaBar and Phelps (1998) found that reminiscence is eliminated by damage to the temporal lobe that includes the amygdala.

### Neural Mechanisms for Encoding and Storing Emotional Information

The systems responsible for encoding and storing specifically affective information include the systems for automatic emotion processing reviewed herein. The system involving the amygdala is best understood. Lesion research in rats (e.g., LeDoux et al., 1989) and lesion (e.g., LaBar LeDoux, Spencer, & Phelps, 1995) and neuroimaging studies with humans (e.g., LaBar et al., 1998) indicate that the amygdala is essential for coding conditioned associations between stimuli and visceral responses. Encoding of emotional information depends on the release of norepinephrine (NE), and drugs that block NE release in animals and humans eliminate the memory advantage for arousing stimuli (Cahill, Prins, Weber, & McGaugh, 1994; McGaugh & Cahill, 1997). The amygdala also modulates consolidation of episodic and semantic information by the hippocampus and related structures: Enhanced recall of the aversive portions of a story is associated with amygdala activity during encoding (Cahill et al., 1996) and is eliminated by amygdala lesions (Markowitsch, Calabrese et al., 1994). Although the majority of studies in humans suggest that the amygdala plays a special role in the detection of threat and memory for aversive stimuli (Ochsner & Feldman-Barrett, 2001), this may be because only a single

study has examined memory for positive, as well as negative, information. Hamann et al. (1999) found that recall of both positive and negative photos was correlated with amygdala activity at encoding, which fits with animal studies that show that amygdala lesions block learning of associations between stimuli and appetitive, as well as aversive, visceral states (Holland & Gallagher, 1999).

It is possible that the amygdala's role in emotional memory is to help consolidate the storage of events to the extent that they are arousing, irrespective of their valence, and that the effects of valence on memory are mediated by schematic knowledge stored in associative memory. In keeping with this notion, amygdala lesions eliminate the memory advantage for emotional stimuli only on episodic memory tasks in which the valence or emotional theme of stimuli could not be used to help organize encoding of them (Phelps & Anderson, 1997).

Processing and storing information about appetitive states that involve moving closer to a goal state or stimulus, regardless of whether that stimulus is exclusively positive, seems to be the job of the basal ganglia. In some studies, basal ganglia activation has been observed during the recall of positive, but not negative, personal experiences (Lane, Reiman, Bradley, et al., 1997) and in others during recall of sad, but not happy, ones (Lane, Reiman, Ahern, & Schwartz, 1997). Animal work has indicated that the basal ganglia are important for potentiating and reinforcing conditioned associations between stimuli and appetitive reinforcers, such as food and sex; future neuroimaging research may explicate a similar role for the basal ganglia in humans.

## Emotion Influences and Guides Retrieval

Although the product of the encoding process forms the foundation for our recollections, why and how we pull up a record of a past emotional experience is as important a determinant of what we remember as is why and how we initially encoded certain aspects of it. Indeed, retrieval of emotional information does not take place in a vacuum, and it can be influenced strongly by the context in which we recall, and the goals that motivate the search for, remembered information.

### Cues That Confound

The first step of the retrieval process involves the activation of stored memory traces by cues that either are self-generated (in the case of recall) or are provided in the retrieval environment (in the case of recognition). Following the classic work of Semon (1909/1923; Schacter, 2001), Tulving (1983) theorized that the conscious product of this process is not a pure representation of activated memory traces but a synergistic combination of cue and trace together. Thus retrieval cues themselves may be incorporated into our conscious recollections. As discussed earlier, unless we have reason to believe the information that comes to mind is incorrect, the second stage of retrieval that allows for monitoring and correction of the memory search may not proceed (Norman & Schacter, 1996).

Affective cues can powerfully bias memory in this way. In some cases, these cues may be internal states. Thus Eich et al. (1985) found that for chronic pain patients, recall of past levels of pain were systematically biased upward or downward in the direction of the level of pain currently being experienced. Interestingly, only if current pain is emotionally evocative does it distort memory for past pain, indicating that it is the emotional, not the physical, state that provides the cues that bias memory (Eich, Rachman, & Lopatka, 1990). These cues also may involve more complex patterns of emotional appraisal. During the 1992 presidential campaign, Levine (1997) studied the supporters of former presidential candidate Ross Perot after he had reentered the race in October to determine how well they could remember their feelings about his withdrawal from the race in July. In general, past feelings were recalled as being more consistent with current feelings than they actually were. For example, if an individual was excited about Perot's return in October but had been upset about his departure in July, he or she recalled having been more hopeful for his return than he or she actually was. The specific direction and kind of bias depended on the specific emotions experienced and were recalled accurately (or were overestimated) only if current feelings had remained constant. Bias also may be caused by external cues, as shown by Ochsner, Schacter, and Edwards (1997), who found that when asked to recall the pleasant or unpleasant tone of voice in which a person had spoken earlier, recall was biased in the direction of affect present in a photo of that person used as a retrieval cue.

Although numerous factors likely influence the degree of bias caused by a retrieval cue, such as the relative perceptual dominance of one type of cue over another (Ochsner et al., 1997) and the relative specificity of the cue and completeness of the memory trace (Norman & Schacter, 1996), this important topic has been little studied for emotional memories (for discussion of retrieval bias in other domains, see Schacter, 1999).

## Schemas: The Goals, the Biases, and the Unknown

The second stage of the retrieval process involves evaluating the information brought to awareness by the retrieval cues. When recalling emotional events, our schematic emotion knowledge can guide this process in at least three primary ways: by setting the goals which initiate memory search, by setting the criteria against which past experiences are judged desirable or accurate, and by guiding conscious or nonconscious inferences that fill in missing or unknown information that was not encoded initially. Because of their close interdependence on a shared pool of knowledge, each of these schematic influences often occurs in combination with at least one of the others. In each of the examples that follow, although we highlight only one kind of influence for purposes of illustration, more than one kind may be present.

### Self- and Mood-Regulatory Goals

Our self-knowledge may act as a chronic goal that guides retrieval of past experiences to confirm or create a compatible self-image in the present (Ochsner & Schacter, 2000; Ross, 1986). For most individuals, this means maintaining a positive self-view (Taylor, 1989) that can guide us, for example, to remember past faults and foibles, such as poor grades (Bahrick, Hall, & Berger, 1996) or unsuccessful gambling ventures (Frank & Gilovich, 1989), either as less common or as more positive than they actually were (Conway & Ross, 1984). Similarly, married men might protect themselves from feeling responsible about marital decline by misremembering early marital life in less rosy terms (Holmberg & Holmes, 1994, as cited in Levine, 1997). As discussed earlier, depressives may recall experiences as more negative than they actually were, which reinforces their negative self-view (Nolen-Hoeksema, 1991).

Higgins (Higgins & Tykocinski, 1992) has suggested that there may be two ways in which we maintain our self-views: We either focus on attaining our ideals or on avoiding the consequences of failing to fulfill our duties and responsibilities. He has found that each type of individual will tend to recall different kinds of information: An ideal focus leads one to recall more positive information, whereas a duty focus (or ought-focus, as he calls it) leads one to recall more negative information (Higgins & Tykocinski, 1992; see also Singer, 1990).

Retrieval of emotional experiences also may be used to regulate our present mood. Just as we want to maintain a positive self-concept, most of the time we want to feel good and will recall positive life events when feeling bad. Thus Josephson, Singer, and Salovey (1994, as cited in Singer & Salovey, 1996) found that, although negative memories were initially brought to mind by a sad film, participants tended to then recall positive experiences, and most were consciously attempting to change their mood by doing so. The tendency to recall positive memories in response to negative moods may be more pronounced in individuals with high self-esteem (Smith & Petty, 1995) or who exhibit a repressive coping style (Boden & Baumeister, 1997), although they may have different reasons for exhibiting this tendency. Individuals with high self-esteem may acknowledge that they felt bad, whereas repressors may not. As a consequence, individuals with high self-esteem may learn that they can successfully cope with negative affect, whereas repressors fail to learn that they can adapt and may continue to avoid situations in which negative affect may be evoked (McFarland & Buehler, 1997). It is important to note that in some cases recall of negative experiences may be desirable, such as when we want to dampen a playful mood to focus on work or other tasks (Parrot & Sabini, 1990).

## Criterion Setting and Reevaluation

When deciding what to search for in memory and deciding whether what we have recalled is accurate, our judgments may be informed by cultural and personal theories about how feelings and attitudes rise or fall over time (Ross, 1989). In some cases, these theories are implicit and guide the assumptions we make without our being aware that our recollections are being biased. For example, women tend to recall past menstrual cycles as being more painful then they actually were, which fits with popular notions that anxiety increases just before menstruation begins but contrasts with empirical research that indicates that this increase in anxiety may not occur (McFarland, Ross, & DeCourville, 1989; Ross & Buehler, 1994).

In other cases, our theories may be more explicit and can be used to control the impact that past events have on us in the present. Of particular importance are theories one holds about the need to revisit past experiences, because the nature of these theories determines whether or not we learn from them. For example, one could believe that reliving past pain begets more pain in the present, and research does suggest that recollecting unpleasant experiences can depress mood and may bring other, like experiences to mind, especially if the experiences are traumatic (Bower & Forgas, 2000; Strack, Schwarz, & Gschneidinger, 1985). One might hold this belief because a particularly extreme past experience has changed the way in which one evaluates the quality of present experiences. Lottery winners, for example, take less pleasure in normal everyday activities, presumably because they fail to match the pleasure of their win (Brickman, Coates, & Janoff-Bulman, 1978). Similarly, paraplegics also may enjoy the present less than they did before their life-changing event because they remember life before the accident as having been better than it is now. Belief that the past produces pain that cannot be controlled or diminished may foster avoidance and fear of new painful experiences, as well as a repressive coping style that has adverse health consequences.

However, if one believes that the causes of past tragedies or joys can be understood and controlled, then past pains can be recollected much more positively (Janoff-Bulman, 1992). For individuals with this belief, recollection serves to restructure beliefs about the past and the ability to cope in the future, thereby fostering a sense of learning and growth by allowing people to feel that they have gained control over the factors that influence their happiness (Janoff-Bulman, 1992; Folkman & Lazarus, 1984).

For example, when recounting traumatic experiences, understanding and expressing one's feelings and their sources can have salutary effects on mental and physical health (Pennebaker, 1997). Studies of the way in which we recall pain also illustrate this point nicely: Sometimes recalling pain as less severe than it was can make people feel more hopeful and in control, as is the case for mothers recollecting the pain of childbirth (Norvell, Gaston-Johansson, & Fridh, 1987); but sometimes recollecting pain as more severe can serve the same end, as shown by people with high dental anxiety who recall more pain than they actually reported experiencing following a trip to the dentist (Kent, 1985). In the long term, our tendencies to construe and re-recollect events positively or negatively can determine our overall level of happiness (Seidlitz & Diener, 1993; Suh, Diener, & Fujita, 1996).

Our goals in remembering past events and our ability to learn from them may be different depending on how long ago they occurred. Strack et al. (1985) suggested that recent events may indicate how able we are to cope with stresses and enjoy successes and can shift mood in a direction congruent with the emotion recalled. In contrast, we may recall long-distant events when we want to make inferences about how we have developed over time. Thus remembering an argument with one's father could make us nostalgic and wistful if the argument took place during childhood but upset and angry if it took place only a few days ago (Strack et al., 1985).

## Filling in for What Is Unknown

Another reason that schematic emotion knowledge can influence memory for past events is that our initial affective responses to them may not have been well encoded in the first place. If our initial feelings are not easily recoverable because they were not well stored, then schematic knowledge may be used to fill in what is missing.

For example, information about the duration of events is one attribute that seems to be poorly encoded, and we use memory of the intensity of the experience to draw inferences about it. Thus, when asked to rate the likability of a film, our judgments are based on its content and not its duration (Fredrickson & Kahneman, 1993), and estimates of the duration of violent scenes increase as a function of the intensity of our emotional reactions to them (Loftus et al., 1987). We may focus on intensity and neglect duration to such an extent that we prefer a longer lasting, but less painful, experience to a shorter but more painful one (Varey & Kahneman, 1992).

### Altered States of Awareness

A final way in which emotion may influence retrieval is by influencing the subjective state of awareness accompanying recollection of past events. In general, as compared to neutral events, emotional events tend to be subjectively re-experienced in a way that seems to more closely approximate our original experience of them. The effects of emotion on awareness may stem from the fact that affecting stimuli activate physiological responses that can add heat and color to our initial experiences and our memories of them. The sense of subjective re-experiencing has been studied in at least three different ways.

The first involves simply asking people to rate the vividness with which they recall past personal experiences. Numerous studies have shown that recollections of significant, affecting, or consequential events are rated as more vivid than neutral events (e.g., Conway & Bekerian, 1988; Christianson & Loftus, 1990). Vividness ratings are ambiguous, however, with respect to the basis on which they are made (see Ochsner & Schacter, 2000, for discussion), and a second—more direct—method for assessing states of awareness employs the *remember/know* method of Tulving (1983), Gardiner, and others (e.g., Gardiner & Java, 1993). As discussed earlier, this method asks participants to indicate whether their recall or recognition of an event is accompanied by a detailed sense of re-experiencing an event (in which case, a *remember* response would be made), or whether it simply seems familiar (in which case, a *know* response is made). Ochsner (in press) found that emotionally arousing and especially negative photos were more likely to be remembered than neutral ones, and also found that this effect did not require one to explicitly appraise the emotionality of the images when they first were seen. The final way in which awareness has been assessed has to do with our subjective point of view when visualizing past experiences. Events can be re-viewed in the mind's eye either from one's original first-person, or *field*, perspective or from a detached, third-person *observer* perspective in which the rememberer sees herself as part of the memory. Focusing on recovering past feelings makes us more likely to see events unfold from a *field* perspective (Robinson & Swanson, 1993).

### Neural Systems for Retrieving Emotional Information

Retrieval of emotional memories seems to involve most of the systems used for retrieval in general (reviewed in the section titled "Systems for the Construction of Memory"), in combination with the systems used for controlled, and to a lesser extent automatic, emotion processing. In this section we focus on the contributions of those structures involved in emotion.

The two automatic emotion systems that encode and store information about the link between conditioned stimuli or behaviors and visceral states are involved in retrieval of those links. For example, studies of fear conditioning have shown that expression of conditioned fear responses is eliminated if the amygdala is lesioned after training has been completed (LeDoux, 1995). Similarly, posttraining lesions of the basal ganglia can disrupt expression of well-learned sequences of rewarded behavior, including grooming (Berridge & Whishaw, 1992). Although amygdala activity at encoding may be correlated with memory for episodic and associative information (e.g., Cahill et al., 1996; Hamann et al., 1999), presumably because it is helping to consolidate storage of it, the amygdala does not seem to be so important for the retrieval of declarative emotion knowledge. The dissociability of conditioned and episodic emotional knowledge also has been shown in studies that compare amnesiacs who cannot remember a fear-conditioning procedure even though they show conditioned fear responses and patients with amygdala lesions who remember the procedure but acquired no conditioned associations (e.g., Bechara, Tranel, Damasio, & Adolphs, 1995).

Although it is likely that the basal ganglia also do not participate in the retrieval of associative or episodic emotion knowledge, the requisite studies have not yet been performed. One study did show basal ganglia activation during retrieval of positive memories (Lane, Reiman, Bradley, et al., 1997), but it is not clear whether the activation was due to retrieval of information or to the experience of positive affect per se. This interpretive problem is quite general and affects other studies of the retrieval of emotional memories: It is seldom clear whether activation or the failure to find activation of a putative emotion area means that it is or is not involved in retrieval or experience (e.g., George, Ketter, Parekh, & Horwitz, 1995).

Areas involved in controlled emotion processing are important for mediating retrieval of emotional information. For example, the orbital and ventral medial prefrontal regions seem to be essential for gating the expression of learned conditioned behaviors. Lesions to these areas in rats, monkeys, or humans will cause perseverative responding to stimuli that are no longer being reinforced (Bechara, Damasio, Tranel, & Damasio, 1996, 1997; Rolls, 1999; Stuss, Eskes, & Foster, 1994). An inability to inhibit previously learned responses following medial prefrontal damage also can slow extinction of conditioned fear responses (Morgan & LeDoux, 1995).

Retrieval of emotional memories also may activate more strongly systems that are used to retrieve information more generally. Shin et al. (1997) asked normals and patients with posttraumatic stress disorder to generate from memory mental images of either combat-related or neutral scenes that they had studied earlier. Areas of visual cortex thought to be the "mental screen" on which images are viewed were activated more strongly by the combat scenes. It is possible that this pattern of heightened activity is the neural signature of the vividness and experiential detail that characterizes emotional recollection.

## Summary

It is a truism in science that all else being equal, theories that can account for the largest body of data possible are most robust, generalizable, and desirable. For the past century, researchers in cognitive neuroscience and social psychology have conducted studies of phenomena related to emotion and memory. Social psychological theories have emphasized the individualized nature of the emotion process and how goals influence what we recollect and how accurately we do so. Cognitive neuroscientists, following in the footsteps of the cognitive psychologists who preceded them, have related the accuracy of emotional memory to the functional specialization of neural systems. Current theories account only for the data obtained within the confines of one discipline or the other, but not both.

We believe that the time is right to put the methods, data, and theories of these two disciplines together to construct theories of emotion and memory that make contact with data at many levels of analysis. This is the essence of the social cognitive neuroscience approach that has guided this chapter, and it has led to some general conclusions that integrate insights from social psychological and cognitive neuroscientific research. The first is that emotion and memory are inherently constructive, goal-directed, and individual; the second is that each depends on a set of separate but interacting neural systems, each dedicated to processing a specific type of information; the third and last is that many emotion and memory phenomena can be seen as arising from the interaction of those systems that operate automatically and those that operate under conscious control. This means that the content of recollection depends on the goals that guide encoding and recollection, the nature of the emotion involved, and the neural systems that are activated.

Although it is clear that what we recollect depends on why we are trying to remember, at present our knowledge of how neural systems mediate this process is much murkier. In general, future research should continue to apply a social cognitive neuroscience approach to explore how and why the activity of different neural systems is influenced by different encoding and retrieval goals and how

these systems are involved in either the encoding, storage, or retrieval and reexperiencing of episodes past.

## REFERENCES

Aggleton, J. (Ed.). (2000). *The amygdala: A functional analysis.* New York: Guilford Press.

Anderson, A. K., & Phelps, E. A. (2001). Lesions of the human amygdala impair enhanced perception of emotionally salient events. *Nature, 411,* 305–309.

Bahrick, H. P., Hall, L. K., & Berger, S. A. (1996). Accuracy and distortion in memory for high-school grades. *Psychological Science, 7,* 265–271.

Bechara, A., Damasio, H., Damasio, A. R., & Lee, G. P. (1999). Different contributions of the human amygdala and ventromedial prefrontal cortex to decision-making. *Journal of Neuroscience, 19,* 5473–5481.

Bechara, A., Damasio, H., Tranel, D., & Damasio, A. R. (1996). Failure to respond autonomically to anticipated future outcomes following damage to prefrontal cortex. *Cerebral Cortex, 6,* 215–225.

Bechara, A., Tranel, D., Damasio, H., & Adolphs, R. (1995). Double dissociation of conditioning and declarative knowledge relative to the amygdala and hippocampus in humans. *Science, 269,* 1115–1118.

Berridge, K. C., & Whishaw, I. Q. (1992). Cortex, striatum and cerebellum: Control of serial order in a grooming sequence. *Experimental Brain Research, 90,* 275–290.

Boden, J. M., & Baumeister, R. F. (1997). Repressive coping: Distraction using pleasant thoughts and memories. *Journal of Personality and Social Psychology, 73,* 45–62.

Botvinick, M. M., Braver, T. S., Carter, C. S., Barch, D. M., & Cohen, J. D. (1999). Evaluating the demand for control: Anterior cingulate cortex and cross-talk monitoring. (Tech. Rep.). Pittsburgh, PA: Carnegie-Mellon University.

Bouton, M. E. (1994). Context, ambiguity, and classical conditioning. *Current Directions in Psychological Science, 3*(2), 49–53.

Bower, G. H., & Forgas, J. P. (2000). Affect, memory, and social cognition. In E. E. Eich (Ed.), *Cognition and emotion.* New York: Oxford University Press.

Bradley, B. P., & Baddeley, A. D. (1990). Emotional factors in forgetting. *Psychological Medicine, 20,* 351–355.

Bradley, M. M. (1994). Emotional memory: A dimensional analysis. In S. H. M. v. Goozen, N. E. V. d. Poll, & J. A. Sergeant (Eds.), *Emotions: Essays on emotion theory* (pp. 97–134). Hillsdale, NJ: Erlbaum.

Bradley, M. M., Greenwald, M. K., Petry, M. C., & Lang, P. J. (1992). Remembering pictures: Pleasure and arousal in memory. *Journal of Experimental Psychology: Learning, Memory, and Cognition, 18,* 379–390.

Brewer, J. B., Zhao, Z., Glover, G. H., & Gabrieli, J. D. E. (1998). Making memories: Brain activity that predicts whether visual experiences will be remembered or forgotten. *Science, 281,* 1185–1187.

Brewer, W. F. (1992). The theoretical and empirical status of flashbulb memory hypothesis. In E. Winograd & U. Neisser (Eds.), *Affect and accuracy in recall: Studies of "flashbulb" memories* (pp. 274–305). New York: Cambridge University Press.

Brickman, P., Coates, D., & Janoff-Bulman, R. (1978). Lottery winners and accident victims: Is happiness relative? *Journal of Personality and Social Psychology, 36*(8), 917–927.

Brown, R., & Kulik, J. (1977). Flashbulb memories. *Cognition, 5,* 73–99.

Buckner, R. L. (1996). Beyond HERA: Contributions of specific prefrontal brain areas to long-term memory retrieval. *Psychonomic Bulletin and Review, 3,* 149–158.

Bunge, S. A., Ochsner, K. N., Desmond, J. E., Glover, G. H., & Gabrieli, J. D. E. (2001). Prefrontal regions involved in keeping information in and out of mind. *Brain, 124,* 2074–2086.

Burgess, P. W., & Shallice, T. (1996). Confabulation and the control of recollection. *Memory, 4,* 359–411.

Burke, A., Heuer, F., & Reisberg, D. (1992). Remembering emotional events. *Memory and Cognition, 20,* 277–290.

Cahill, L., Haier, R. J., Fallon, J., Alkire, M., Tang, C., Keator, D., Wu, J., & McGaugh, J. L. (1996). Amygdala activity at encoding correlated with long-term, free recall of emotional information. *Proceedings of the National Academy of Sciences, 93,* 8016–8021.

Cahill, L., Prins, B., Weber, M., & McGaugh, J. L. (1994). b-Adrenergic activation and memory for emotional events. *Nature, 371,* 702–704.

Carter, C. S., Braver, T. S., Barch, D. M., Botvinick, M. M., Noll, D., & Cohen, J. D. (1998). Anterior cingulate cortex, error detection, and the online monitoring of performance. *Science, 280,* 747–749.

Christianson, S.-Å. (1992). Emotional stress and eyewitness memory: A critical review. *Psychological Bulletin, 112,* 284–309.

Christianson, S.-Å., & Loftus, E. F. (1987). Memory for traumatic events. *Applied Cognitive Psychology, 1,* 225–239.

Christianson, S.-Å., & Loftus, E. F. (1990). Some characteristics of people's traumatic memories. *Bulletin of the Psychonomic Society, 28,* 195–198.

Christianson, S.-Å., & Loftus, E. (1991). Remembering emotional events: The fate of detailed information. *Cognition and Emotion, 5,* 81–108.

Christianson, S.-Å., Loftus, E. F., Hoffmann, H., & Loftus, G. R. (1991). Eye fixations and memory for emotional events. *Journal of Experimental Psychology: Learning, Memory, and Cognition, 17,* 693–701.

Clifford, B. R., & Scott, J. (1978). Individual and situational factors in eyewitness testimony. *Journal of Applied Psychology, 63,* 352–359.

Cohen, G., Conway, M. A., & Maylor, E. A. (1994). Flashbulb memories in older adults. *Psychology and Aging, 9,* 454–463.

Cohen, N. J., & Squire, L. R. (1980). Preserved learning and retention of pattern analyzing skill in amnesics: Dissociation of knowing how and knowing that. *Science, 210,* 207–210.

Conway, M., & Ross, M. (1984). Getting what you want by revising what you had. *Journal of Personality and Social Psychology, 47,* 738–748.

Conway, M. A. (1997). *Recovered and false memories.* Oxford, England: Oxford University Press.

Conway, M. A., & Bekerian, D. A. (1988). Characteristics of vivid memories. In M. M. Grunebeg, P. Morris, & R. N. Sykes (Eds.), *Practical aspects of memory: Current research and issues* (Vol. 1, pp. 519–524). Chichester, England: Wiley.

Corbetta, M., Miezin, F. M., Dobmeyer, S., Shulman, G. L., & Petersen, S. E. (1991). Selective and divided attention during visual discriminations of shape, color, and speed: Functional anatomy by positron emission tomography. *Journal of Neuroscience, 11* (8), 2383–2402.

Corteen, R. S. (1969). Skin conductance changes and word recall. *British Journal of Psychology, 60,* 81–84.

Damasio, A. R. (1989). Time-locked multiregional retroactivation: A systems-level proposal for the neural substrates of recall and recognition. *Cognition, 33,* 25–62.

Damasio, A. R. (1994). *Descartes' error: Emotion, reason, and the human brain.* New York: Putnam.

Davis, M. (1997). Neurobiology of fear responses: The role of the amygdala. *Journal of Neuropsychiatry and Clinical Neurosciences, 9,* 382–402.

Davis, M. (1998). Are different parts of the extended amygdala involved in fear versus anxiety? *Biological Psychiatry, 44,* 1239–1247.

Denny, E. B., & Hunt, R. R. (1992). Affective valence and memory in depression. *Journal of Abnormal Psychology, 101,* 575–580.

Eich, E., Rachman, S., & Lopatka, C. (1990). Affect, pain, and autobiographical memory. *Journal of Abnormal Psychology, 99,* 174–178.

Eich, E., Reeves, J. L., Jaeger, B., & Graff-Radford, S. B. (1985). Memory for pain: Relation between past and present pain intensity. *Pain, 23,* 375–380.

Elliott, R., & Dolan, R. J. (1998). Activation of different anterior cingulate foci in association with hypothesis testing and response selection. *Neuroimage, 8,* 17–29.

Folkman, S., & Lazarus, R. (1984). Personal control and stress and coping processes: A theoretical analysis. *Journal of Personality and Social Psychology, 46,* 839–852.

Frank, M. G., & Gilovich, T. (1989). Effect of memory perspective on retrospective causal attributions. *Journal of Personality and Social Psychology, 57,* 399–403.

Fredrickson, B. L., & Kahneman, D. (1993). Duration neglect in retrospective evaluations of affective episodes. *Journal of Personality and Social Psychology, 65* (1), 45–55.

Gardiner, J. M., & Java, R. I. (1993). Recognising and remembering. In A. F. Collins, S. E. Gathercole, M. A. Conway, & P. E. Morris (Eds.), *Theories of memory* (pp. 163–188). Hove, England: Erlbaum.

George, M. S., Ketter, T. A., Parekh, P. I., & Horwitz, B. (1995). Brain activity during transient sadness and happiness in healthy women. *American Journal of Psychiatry, 152,* 341–351.

Gross, J. J. (1998). Antecedent- and response-focused emotion regulation: Divergent consequences for experience, expression, and physiology. *Journal of Personality and Social Psychology, 74,* 224–237.

Gross, J. J., & Levenson, R. W. (1993). Emotional suppression: Physiology, self-report, and expressive behavior. *Journal of Personality and Social Psychology, 106,* 970–986.

Hariri, A. R., Bookheimer, S. Y., & Mazziotta, J. C. (2000). Modulating emotional responses: Effects of a neocortical network on the limbic system. *Neuroreport, 11,* 43–48.

Hamann, S. B., Ely, T. D., Grafton, S. T., & Kilts, C. D. (1999). Amygdala activity related to enhanced memory for pleasant and aversive stimuli. *Nature Neuroscience, 2,* 289–293.

Heuer, F., & Reisberg, D. (1992). Vivid memories of emotional events: The accuracy of remembered minutiae. *Memory and Cognition, 18,* 496–506.

Higgins, E. T., & Tykocinski, O. (1992). Self-discrepancies and biographical memory: Personality and cognition at the level of psychological situation. *Personality and Social Psychology Bulletin, 18*, 527–535.

Holland, P. C., & Gallagher, M. (1999). Amygdala circuitry in attentional and representational processes. *Trends in Cognitive Sciences, 3*(2), 65–73.

Hunt, R. R., & McDaniel, M. A. (1993). The enigma of organization and distinctiveness. *Journal of Memory and Language, 32*, 421–445.

Hyman, I. E., Husband, T. H., & Billings, F. J. (1995). False memories of childhood experiences. *Applied Cognitive Psychology, 9*, 181–197.

Janoff-Bulman, R. (1992). *Shattered assumptions: Towards a new psychology of trauma*. New York: Free Press.

Johnson, M. K., Hashtroudi, S., & Lindsay, D. S. (1993). Source monitoring. *Psychological Bulletin, 114*, 3–28.

Johnson, M. K., & Sherman, S. J. (1990). Constructing and reconstructing the past and future in the present. In E. T. Higgins & R. M. Sorrentino (Eds.), *Handbook of motivation and cognition: Volume 2. Foundations of social behavior*. New York: Guilford Press.

Kaplan, R., & Kaplan, S. (1969). The arousal-retention interval revisited: The effects of some procedural changes. *Psychonomic Science, 15*, 84–85.

Karni, A., Meyer, G., Jezzard, P., Adams, M. M., Turner, R., & Ungerleider, L. G. (1995). Functional MRI evidence for adult motor cortex plasticity during motor skill learning. *Nature, 377*, 155–158.

Kent, G. (1985). Memory of dental pain. *Pain, 21*, 187–194.

Kleinsmith, L. J., & Kaplan, S. (1963). Paired-associate learning as a function of arousal and interpolated interval. *Journal of Experimental Psychology, 65*, 190–193.

Knight, R. T., Staines, W. R., Swick, D., & Chao, L. L. (1999). Prefrontal cortex regulates inhibition and excitation in distributed neural networks. *Acta Psychologica, 101*, 159–178.

Knowlton, B. J., Ramus, S. J., & Squire, L. R. (1992). Intact artificial grammar learning in amnesia: Dissociation of classification learning and explicit memory for specific instances. *Psychological Science, 3*, 172–179.

Knowlton, B. J., & Squire, L. R. (1993). The learning of categories: Parallel brain systems for item memory and category level knowledge. *Science, 262*, 1747–1749.

Koutstaal, W., & Schacter, D. L. (1997). Intentional forgetting and voluntary thought suppression: Two potential methods for coping with childhood trauma. In L. H. Dickstein, M. B. Riba, & J. M. Oldham (Eds.), *Annual Review of Psychiatry* (Vol. 16). Washington, DC: American Psychiatric Press.

LaBar, K. S., Gatenby, J. C., Gore, J. C., LeDoux, J. E., & Phelps, E. A. (1998). Human amygdala activation during conditioned fear acquisition and extinction: A mixed-trial fMRI study. *Neuron, 20*, 937–945.

LaBar, K. S., LeDoux, J. E., Spencer, D. D., & Phelps, E. A. (1995). Impaired fear conditioning following unilateral temporal lobectomy in humans. *Journal of Neuroscience, 15*, 6846–6855.

LaBar, K. S., & Phelps, E. A. (1998). Arousal-mediated memory consolidation. *Psychological Science, 9*, 490–493.

Lane, R. D., Fink, G. R., Chau, P. M.-L., & Dolan, R. J. (1997). Neural activation during selective attention to subjective emotional responses. *Neuroreport, 8*, 3969–3972.

Lane, R. D., Reiman, E. M., Ahern, G. L., & Schwartz, G. E. (1997). Neuroanatomical correlates of happiness, sadness, and disgust. *American Journal of Psychiatry, 154*, 926–933.

Lane, R. D., Reiman, E. M., Bradley, M. M., Lang, P. J., Ahern, G. L., Davidson, R. J., & Schwartz, G. E. (1997). Neuroanatomical correlates of pleasant and unpleasant emotion. *Neuropsychologia, 35*, 1437–1444.

Lang, P. J., Greenwald, M. K., Bradley, M. M., & Hamm, A. O. (1993). Looking at pictures: Affective, facial, visceral, and behavioral reactions. *Psychophysiology, 30*(3), 261–273.

Lazarus, R. S. (1991). *Emotion and adaptation*. New York: Oxford University Press.

LeDoux, J. E. (1995). Emotion: Clues from the brain. *Annual Review of Psychology, 46*, 209–235.

LeDoux, J. E. (2000). Emotion circuits in the brain. *Annual Review of Neuroscience, 23*, 155–184.

LeDoux, J. E., Romanski, L., & Xagoraris, A. (1989). Indelibility of subcortical emotional memories. *Journal of Cognitive Neuroscience, 1*, 238–243.

Leventhal, H., & Scherer, K. (1987). The relationship of emotion to cognition: A functional approach to a semantic controversy. *Cognition and Emotion, 1*, 3–28.

Levine, L. J. (1997). Reconstructing memory for emotions. *Journal of Experimental Psychology: General, 126*, 165–177.

Levine, L. J., & Burgess, S. L. (1997). Beyond general arousal: Effects of specific emotions on memory. *Social Cognition, 15*, 157–181.

Lieberman, M. D. (in press). Intuition: A social cognitive neuroscience approach. *Psychological Bulletin*.

Lieberman, M. D., Ochsner, K. N., Gilbert, D. T., & Schacter, D. L. (2001). Do amnesics exhibit cognitive dissonance reduction? The role of explicit memory and attention in attitude change. *Psychological Science, 12*, 135–140.

Lindsay, D. S., & Read, J. D. (1994). Psychotherapy and memories of childhood sexual abuse: A cognitive perspective. *Applied Cognitive Psychology, 8*, 281–338.

Loftus, E. F. (1993). The reality of repressed memories. *American Psychologist, 48*, 518–537.

Loftus, E. F., & Burns, T. (1982). Mental shock can produce retrograde amnesia. *Memory and Cognition, 10*, 318–323.

Loftus, E. F., & Ketcham, K. (1994). *The myth of repressed memory: False memories and allegations of sexual abuse*. New York: St. Martin's Press.

Loftus, E. F., Loftus, G., & Messo, J. (1987). Some facts about "weapon focus." *Law and Human Behavior, 11*, 55–62.

Loftus, E. F., & Pickrell, J. E. (1995). The formation of false memories. *Psychiatric Annals, 25*, 720–725.

London, E. D., Broussolle, E. P., Links, J. M., Wong, D. F., Cascella, N. G., Dannals, R. F., Sano, M., Herning, R., Snyder, F. R., Rippetoe, L. R., Toung, T. J., Jaffe, J. H., & Wagner, H. N. (1990). Morphine-induced metabolism changes in human brain: Studies with positron emission tomography and [fluorine 18] fluorodeoxyglucose. *Archives of General Psychiatry, 47*, 73–81.

Markowitsch, H. J., Calabrese, P., Würker, M., Durwen, H. F., Kessler, J., Babinsky, R., Brechtelsbauer, D., Heuser, L., & Gehlen, W. (1994). The amygdala's contribution to memory—a study on two patients with Urbach-Wiethe disease. *Neuroreport, 5,* 1349–1352.

Mathews, A., Mogg, K., Kentish, J., & Eysenck, M. (1995). Effect of psychological treatment on cognitive bias in generalized anxiety disorder. *Behaviour Research and Therapy, 33,* 293–303.

Matlin, M. W., & Stang, D. J. (1978). *The Pollyanna principle.* Cambridge, MA: Schenkman.

McClelland, J. L., McNaughton, B. L., & O'Reilly, R. C. (1995). Why there are complementary learning systems in the hippocampus and neocortex: Insights from the successes and failures of connectionist models of learning and memory. *Psychological Review, 102,* 419–457.

McFarland, C., & Buehler, R. (1997). Negative affective states and the motivated retrieval of positive life events: The role of affect acknowledgement. *Journal of Personality and Social Psychology, 73,* 200–214.

McFarland, C., Ross, M., & DeCourville, N. (1989). Women's theories of menstruation and biases in recall of menstrual symptoms. *Journal of Personality and Social Psychology, 57,* 522–531.

McGaugh, J. L. (1995). Emotional activation, neuromodulatory systems and memory. In D. L. Schacter (Ed.), *Memory distortion: How minds, brains, and societies reconstruct the past* (pp. 255–273). Cambridge, MA: Harvard University Press.

McGaugh, J. L., & Cahill, L. (1997). Interaction of neuromodulatory systems in modulating memory storage. *Behavioural Brain Research, 83,* 31–38.

McNally, R. J., Metzger, L. J., Lasko, N. B., Clancy, S. A., & Pitman, R. K. (1998). Directed forgetting of trauma cues in adult survivors of childhood sexual abuse with and without posttraumatic stress disorder. *Journal of Abnormal Psychology, 107,* 596–601.

Miller, E. K., & Cohen, J. D. (2001). An integrative theory of prefrontal cortex function. *Annual Review of Neuroscience, 24,* 67–202.

Mineka, S., & Nugent, K. (1995). Mood-congruent memory biases in anxiety and depression. In D. L. Schacter, J. T. Coyle, G. D. Fischbach, M.-M. Mesulam, & L. E. Sullivan (Eds.), *Memory distortion: How minds, brains, and societies reconstruct the past* (pp. 173–196). Cambridge, MA: Harvard University Press.

Mogg, K., Mathews, A., & Weinman, J. (1987). Memory bias in clinical anxiety. *Journal of Abnormal Psychology, 96,* 94–98.

Morgan, M. A., & LeDoux, J. E. (1995). Differential contribution of dorsal and ventral medial prefrontal cortex to the acquisition and extinction of conditioned fear in rats. *Behavioral Neuroscience, 109*(4), 681–688.

Morris, J. S., Frith, C. D., Perrett, D. I., Rowland, D., Young, A. W., Calder, A. J., & Dolan, R. J. (1996). A differential neural response in the human amygdala to fearful and happy facial expressions. *Nature, 383,* 812–815.

Morris, J. S., Ohman, A., & Dolan, R. J. (1999). A subcortical pathway to the right amygdala mediating "unseen" fear. *Proceedings of the National Academy of Sciences, 96,* 1680–1685.

Moscovitch, M. (1994). Memory and working-with-memory: Evaluation of a component process model and comparisons with other models. In D. L. Schacter & E. Tulving (Eds.), *Memory systems 1994* (pp. 269–310). Cambridge, MA: MIT Press.

Neisser, U., & Harsch, N. (1992). Phantom flashbulbs: False recollections of hearing the news about Challenger. In E. Winograd & U. Neisser (Eds.), *Affect and accuracy in recall: Studies of "flashbulb memories"* (pp. 9–31). Cambridge, England: Cambridge University Press.

Nissen, M. J., & Bullemer, P. (1987). Attentional requirements of learning: Evidence from performance measures. *Cognitive Psychology, 19,* 1–32.

Nolen-Hoeksema, S. (1991). Responses to depression and their effects on the duration of depressive episodes. *Journal of Abnormal Psychology, 100,* 569–582.

Norman, K. A., & Schacter, D. L. (1996). Implicit memory, explicit memory, and false recognition: A cognitive neuroscience perspective. In L. M. Reder (Ed.), *Implicit memory and metacognition.* (pp. 00–00). Hillsdale, NJ: Erlbaum.

Norvell, K. T., Gaston-Johansson, F., & Fridh, G. (1987). Remembrance of labor pain: How valid are retrospective pain measurements? *Pain, 31,* 77–86.

Nyberg, L., Cabeza, R., & Tulving, E. (1996). PET studies of encoding and retrieval: The HERA model. *Psychonomic Bulletin and Review, 3,* 135–148.

Nyberg, L., Tulving, E., Habib, R., Nilsson, L.-G., Kapur, S., Houle, S., Cabeza, R., & McIntosh, A. R. (1995). Functional brain maps of retrieval mode and recovery of episodic information. *Neuroreport, 6,* 249–252.

Ochsner, K. N. (2000). Are affective events richly recollected or simply familiar? The experience and process of recognizing feelings past. *Journal of Experimental Psychology: General, 129,* 242–261.

Ochsner, K. N., Bunge, S. A., Gross, J. J., & Gabrieli, J. D. E. (2001, April). *Rethinking feelings: Exploring the neurocognitive bases of emotion control.* Paper presented at UCLA conference on social cognitive neuroscience, Los Angeles, CA.

Ochsner, K. N., & Feldman-Barrett, L. (2001). In T. Mayne & G. Bonnano (Eds.), *Emotion: Current issues and future directions.* New York: Guilford Press.

Ochsner, K. N., & Kosslyn, S. M. (1999). The cognitive neuroscience approach. In D. E. Rumelhart & B. Martin-Bly (Eds.), *Handbook of cognition and perception* (Vol. 10). San Diego: Academic Press.

Ochsner, K. N., Kosslyn, S. M., Cosgrove, G. R., Price, B., Cassem, N., Nierenberg, A., & Rauch, S. (2001). Deficits in visual cognition and attention following bilateral anterior cingulotomy. *Neuropsychologia, 39,* 219–230.

Ochsner, K. N., & Lieberman, M. D. (2001). The emergence of social cognitive neuroscience. *American Psychologist, 56,* 717–734.

Ochsner, K. N., & Sanchez, H. (2001). *The relation between the regulation and recollection of affective experience.* Unpublished manuscript.

Ochsner, K. N., & Schacter, D. L. (2000). A social cognitive neuroscience approach to emotion and memory. In J. C. Borod (Ed.), *The neuropsychology of emotion* (pp. 163–193). New York: Oxford University Press.

Ochsner, K. N., Schacter, D. L., & Edwards, K. (1997). Illusory recall of vocal affect. *Memory, 5,* 433–455.

Ohman, A. (1988). Preattention processes in the generation of emotions. In V. Hamilton, G. H. Bower, & N. H. Frijda (Eds.), *Cognitive perspectives on emotion and motivation* (Vol. 44, pp. 127–143).

Park, J., & Banaji, M. (1996, May). *The effect of arousal and retention delay on memory: A meta-analysis.* Paper presented at the annual convention of the American Psychological Society, San Francisco.

Parrott, W. G., & Sabini, J. (1990). Mood and memory under natural conditions: Evidence for mood incongruent recall. *Journal of Personality and Social Psychology, 59*, 321–336.

Pennebaker, J. W. (1997). Writing about emotional experiences as a therapeutic process. *Psychological Science, 8*, 162–166.

Petersen, S. E., van Mier, H., Fiez, J. A., & Raichle, M. E. (1998). The effects of practice on the functional anatomy of task performance. *Proceedings of the National Academy of Science, 95*, 853–860.

Petit, L., Courtney, S. M., Ungerleider, L. G., & Haxby, J. V. (1998). Sustained activity in the medial wall during working memory delays. *Journal of Neuroscience, 1822*, 9429–9437.

Phelps, E. A., & Anderson, A. K. (1997). Emotional memory: What does the amygdala do? *Current Biology, 7*(5), R311–314.

Pickel, K. L. (1998). Unusualness and threat as possible causes of "weapon focus." *Memory, 6*, 277–295.

Pillemer, D. B. (1984). Flashbulb memories of the assassination attempt on President Reagan. *Cognition, 16*, 63–80.

Posner, M. I., & DiGirolamo, G. J. (1998). Executive attention: Conflict, target detection, and cognitive control. In R. Parasuraman (Ed.), *The attentive brain* (pp. 401–423). Cambridge, MA: MIT Press.

Pratto, F., & John, O. P. (1991). Automatic vigilance: The attention-grabbing power of negative social information. *Journal of Personality and Social Psychology, 61*, 380–391.

Rajaram, S. (1993). Remembering and knowing: Two means of access to the personal past. *Memory and Cognition, 21*, 89–102.

Rauch, S. L., Savage, C. R., Alpert, N. M., Fischman, A. J., & Jenike, M. A. (1997). The functional neuroanatomy of anxiety: A study of three disorders using positron emission tomography and symptom provocation. *Biological Psychiatry, 426*, 446–452.

Reisberg, D., Heuer, F., McLean, J., & O'Shaughnessy, M. (1988). The quantity, not the quality, of affect predicts memory vividness. *Bulletin of the Psychonomic Society, 26*, 100–103.

Revelle, W., & Loftus, D. A. (1992). The implications of arousal effects for the study of affect and memory. In S.-Å. Christianson (Ed.), *The handbook of emotion and memory: Research and theory* (pp. 113–149). Hillsdale, NJ: Erlbaum.

Richards, J. M., & Gross, J. J. (1999). Composure at any cost? The cognitive consequences of emotion suppression. *Personality and Social Psychology Bulletin, 25*, 1033–1044.

Robinson, J. A., & Swanson, K. L. (1993). Field and observer modes of remembering. *Memory, 1*, 169–184.

Roediger, H. L., III & McDermott, K. B. (1993). Implicit memory in normal human subjects. In H. Spinnler & F. Boller (Eds.), *Handbook of neuropsychology* (Vol. 8, pp. 63–131). Amsterdam: Elsevier.

Roediger, H. L., III & McDermott, K. B. (1995). Creating false memories: Remembering words not presented in lists. *Journal of Experimental Psychology: Learning, Memory, and Cognition, 21*, 803–814.

Rolls, E. T. (1999). *The brain and emotion*. New York: Oxford University Press.

Ross, M. (1989). Relation of implicit theories to the construction of personal histories. *Psychological Review, 96*, 341–357.

Ross, M., & Buehler, R. (1994). Creative remembering. In U. Neisser & R. Fivush (Eds.), *The remembering self: Construction and accuracy in the self-narrative* (Vol. 6, pp. 205–235). New York: Cambridge University Press.

Ross, M., & Conway, M. (1986). Remembering one's own past: The construction of personal histories. In R. M. Sorrentino & E. T. Higgins (Eds.), *Handbook of motivation and cognition: Foundations of social behavior* (pp. 122–144). New York: Guilford Press.

Rubin, D. C., & Kozin, M. (1984). Vivid memories. *Cognition, 16*, 81–95.

Rugg, M. D., Fletcher, P. C., Frith, C. D., Frackowiak, R. S. J., & Dolan, R. J. (1996). Differential activation of the prefrontal cortex in successful and unsuccessful memory retrieval. *Brain, 119*, 2073–2083.

Rugg, M. D., Fletcher, P. C., Frith, C. D., Frackowiak, R. S. J., & Dolan, R. J. (1997). Brain regions supporting intentional and incidental memory: A PET study. *NeuroReport, 8*, 1283–1287.

Salmon, D. P., & Butters, N. (1995). Neurobiology of skill and habit learning. *Current Opinion in Neurobiology, 5*, 184–190.

Schacter, D. L. (1994). Priming and multiple memory systems: Perceptual mechanisms of implicit memory. In D. L. Schacter & E. Tulving (Eds.), *Memory systems 1994* (pp. 244–256). Cambridge, MA: MIT Press.

Schacter, D. L. (1996). *Searching for memory: The brain, the mind, and the past*. New York: Basic Books.

Schacter, D. L. (1999). The seven sins of memory: Insights from psychology and cognitive neuroscience. *American Psychologist, 54*(3), 182–203.

Schacter, D. L. (2001). *Stranger behind the engram: Theories of memory and the psychology of science*. Hillsdale, NJ: Erlbaum.

Schacter, D. L., Alpert, N. M., Savage, C. R., Rauch, S. L., & Albert, M. S. (1996). Conscious recollection and the human hippocampal formation: Evidence from positron emission tomography. *Proceedings of the National Academy of Sciences, 93*, 321–325.

Schacter, D. L., & Buckner, R. L. (1998). Priming and the brain. *Neuron, 20*, 185–195.

Schacter, D. L., Buckner, R. L., Koutstaal, W., Dale, A. M., & Rosen, B. R. (1997). Late onset of anterior prefrontal activity during retrieval of veridical and illusory memories: An event-related fMRI study. *NeuroImage, 6*, 259–269.

Schacter, D. L., Chiu, C. Y. P., & Ochsner, K. N. (1993). Implicit memory: A selective review. *Annual Review of Neuroscience, 16*, 159–182.

Schacter, D. L., Israel, L., & Racine, C. (1999). Suppressing false recognition in younger and older adults: The distinctiveness heuristic. *Journal of Memory and Language, 40*, 1–24.

Schacter, D. L., Koutstaal, W., & Norman, K. A. (1996). Can cognitive neuroscience illuminate the nature of traumatic childhood memories? *Current Opinion in Neurobiology, 6*, 207–214.

Schacter, D. L., Norman, K. A., & Koutstaal, W. (1998). The cognitive neuroscience of constructive memory. *Annual Review of Psychology, 49*, 289–318.

Schacter, D. L., Verfaellie, M., & Pradere, D. (1996). The neuropsychology of memory illusions: False recall and recognition in amnesic patients. *Journal of Memory and Language, 35,* 319–334.

Schacter, D. L., & Wagner, A. D. (1999). Medial temporal lobe activations in fMRI and PET studies of episodic encoding and retrieval. *Hippocampus, 9,* 7–24.

Schacter, D. L., Wagner, A. D., & Buckner, R. L. (2001). Memory systems of 1999. In E. Tulving & F. I. M. Craik (Eds.), *Handbook of memory.* New York: Oxford University Press.

Schultz, W., Apicella, P., Romo, R., & Scarnati, E. (1995). Context-dependent activity in primate striatum reflecting past and future behavioral events. In J. C. Houk & J. L. Davis (Eds.), *Models of information processing in the basal ganglia: Computational neuroscience* (pp. 11–27). Cambridge, MA: MIT Press.

Seidlitz, L., & Diener, E. (1993). Memory for positive versus negative life events: Theories for the differences between happy and unhappy persons. *Journal of Personality and Social Psychology, 64,* 654–663.

Semon, R. (1923). *Mnemic psychology.* London: George Allen & Unwin. (Original work published 1909)

Shin, L. M., Kosslyn, S. M., McNally, R. J., Alpert, N. M., Metzger, L. J., Lasko, N. B., Orr, S. P., & Pitman, R. K. (1997). Visual imagery and perception in posttraumatic stress disorder: A positron emission tomographic investigation. *Archives of General Psychiatry, 543,* 233–241.

Singer, J. A. (1990). Affective responses to autobiographical memories and their relationship to long-term goals. *Journal of Personality, 58,* 535–563.

Singer, J. A., & Salovey, P. (1996). Motivated memory: Self-defining memories, goals, and affect regulation. In L. L. Martin & A. Tesser (Eds.), *Striving and feeling: Interactions among goals, affect, and self-regulation* (pp. 229–250). Mahwah, NJ: Erlbaum.

Skowronski, J. J., & Carlston, D. E. (1989). Negativity and extremity biases in impression formation: A review of explanations. *Psychological Bulletin, 105,* 131–142.

Smith, S. S., & Petty, S. M. (1995). Personality moderators of mood congruency effects on cognition: The role of self-esteem and negative mood regulation. *Journal of Personality and Social Psychology, 68,* 1092–1107.

Squire, L. R. (1992). Memory and the hippocampus: A synthesis from findings with rats, monkeys, and humans. *Psychological Review, 99,* 195–231.

Squire, L. R., Ojemann, J. G., Miezin, F. M., Petersen, S. E., Videen, T. O., & Raichle, M. E. (1992). Activation of the hippocampus in normal humans: A functional anatomical study of memory. *Proceedings of the National Academy of Sciences, 89,* 1837–1841.

Stein, N. L., Wade, E., & Liwag, M. D. (1997). A theoretical approach to understanding and remembering emotional events. In N. L. Stein, P. A. Ornstein, B. Tversky, & C. Brainerd (Eds.), *Memory for emotional and everyday events* (pp. 15–47). Mahwah, NJ: Erlbaum.

Stern, C. E., Corkin, S., Gonzalez, R. G., Guimaraes, A. R., Baker, J. R., Jennings, P. J., Carr, C. A., Sugiura, R. M., Vedantham, V., & Rosen, B. R. (1996). The hippocampal formation participates in novel picture encoding: Evidence from functional magnetic resonance imaging. *Proceedings of the National Academy of Sciences, 93,* 8660–8665.

Strack, F., Schwarz, N., & Gschneidinger, E. (1985). Hap-

piness and reminiscing: The role of time perspective, affect, and mode of thinking. *Journal of Personality and Social Psychology, 49,* 1460–1469.

Stuss, D. T., Eskes, G. A., & Foster, J. K. (1994). Experimental neuropsychological studies of frontal lobe functions. In F. Boller & J. Grafman (Eds.), *Handbook of neuropsychology.* Amsterdam: Elsevier.

Suh, E., Diener, E., & Fujita, F. (1996). Events and subjective well-being: Only recent events matter. *Journal of Personality and Social Psychology, 70,* 1091–1102.

Talbot, J. D., Marrett, S., Evans, A. C., Meyer, E., Bushnell, M. C., & Duncan, G. H. (1991). Multiple representations of pain in human cerebral cortex. *Science, 251,* 1355–1358.

Taylor, S. (1989). *Positive illusions: Creative self-deception and the healthy mind.* New York: Basic Books.

Thomas, D. L., & Diener, E. (1990). Memory accuracy in the recall of emotions. *Journal of Personality and Social Psychology, 59,* 291–297.

Tulving, E. (1983). *Elements of episodic memory.* Oxford, England: Clarendon Press.

Tulving, E., & Schacter, D. L. (1990). Priming and human memory systems. *Science, 247,* 301–306.

van der Kolk, B. A., & Fisler, R. (1995). Dissociation and the fragmentary nature of traumatic memories: Overview and exploratory study. *Journal of Traumatic Stress, 8,* 505–525.

van Reekum, C. M., & Scherer, K. R. (1997). Levels of processing in emotion antecedent appraisal. In G. Matthews (Ed.), *Cognitive science perspectives on personality and emotion* (pp. 259–300). Amsterdam: Elsevier Science.

Varey, C. A., & Kahneman, D. (1992). Experiences extended across time: Evaluation of moments and episodes. *Journal of Behavioral Decision Making, 5,* 169–185.

Wagner, A. D., Schacter, D. L., Rotte, M., Koutstaal, W., Maril, A., Dale, A. M., Rosen, B. R., & Buckner, R. L. (1998). Building memories: Remembering and forgetting of verbal experiences as predicted by brain activity. *Science, 281,* 1188–1191.

Watkins, P. C., Matthews, A., Williamson, D. A., & Fuller, R. D. (1992). Mood congruent memory in depression: Emotional priming or elaboration. *Journal of Abnormal Psychology, 101,* 581–586.

Whalen, P. J., Rauch, S. L., Etcoff, N. L., McInerney, S. C., Lee, M. B., & Jenike, M. A. (1998). Masked presentations of emotional facial expressions modulate amygdala activity without explicit knowledge. *Journal of Neuroscience, 18*(1), 411–418.

Wilhelm, S., McNally, R. J., Baer, L., & Florin, I. (1996). Directed forgetting in obsessive-compulsive disorder. *Behaviour Research and Therapy, 34,* 633–641.

Williams, J. M., & Dritschel, B. H. (1988). Emotional disturbance and the specificity of autobiographical memory. *Cognition and Emotion, 2,* 221–234.

Williams, J. M. G., Watts, F. N., MacLeod, C., & Matthews, A. (1990). *Cognitive psychology and emotional disorders.* Chichester, England: Wiley.

Yuille, J. C., & Cutshall, J. L. (1986). A case study of eyewitness memory of a crime. *Journal of Applied Psychology, 71,* 291–301.

# 33

# INFORMATION PROCESSING APPROACHES TO EMOTION

Tim Dalgleish

## What Is the Information Processing Approach to Emotion?

Psychological theorists typically draw on widely agreed-on sets of assumptions and concepts when constructing models of psychological processes. The range of assumptions and concepts places parameters on the type of model that is generated and constitutes the scientific paradigm within which modeling occurs (Kuhn, 1962). Of course, a paradigm in psychology is neither true nor false. Rather, its worth to the discipline is a function of how fertile the paradigm is for the generation of models and of programs of empirical research to test those models.

Within the broad area of cognitive psychology, the dominant paradigm is the information processing approach. Information processing psychologists conceptualize the mind as a multipurpose processing system. Mental representations, which relate to or designate structures outside themselves and ultimately relate to things in the external world, are acted on in the system by various cognitive processes (Johnson-Laird, 1993). These processes manipulate and transform the representations and give rise to the range of psychological phenomena. Different types of information processing theory instantiate mental representations within different types of cognitive architecture, such as localized or distributed connectionist systems (e.g., McClelland, 1995) or symbol processing systems (e.g., Anderson, 1992).

The information processing paradigm had its genesis in the 1940s and 1950s and gathered considerable momentum from the publication of seminal texts such as Broadbent's book, *Perception and Communication* (1958) and Neisser's *Cognitive Psychology* (1967). Development of the paradigm in psychology has also paralleled the development of computer science, and the existence of commonalities in the information processes that are employed by computers and the mind is a strong theme that permeates recent developments in psychology (see Johnson-Laird, 1993, for a discussion).

At the end of the 20th century, there was a consensus in cognitive psychology that the information processing paradigm is an appropriate and informative way to study human cognition. The enduring popularity of the information processing approach is largely a result of its successful instantiation in a range of models that cover the waterfront of cognitive psychology. The paradigm has been successfully applied to such cognitive processes as basic vision, higher level vision, attention, memory, spoken and written language, judgment, reasoning, and higher level thought (see Eysenck & Keane, 1995, for a broad introduction to cognitive psychology across these different domains). Information processing theories have been informed by a wealth of empirical data and, in turn, have generated a host of testable predictions. This is not to say that the information processing approach is without its critics (e.g., Shotter, 1991). However, much of this criticism is directed either at the inability of the computer metaphor to account for social and historical contextual influences in psychology or at particular symbolic instantiations of cognitive processes rather than at the conceptual core of the information processing approach as a paradigm for intraindividual cognitive processing, as presented herein.

The stock of the information processing paradigm has remained high because, along with its theoretical and empirical utility, it offers a level of psychological analysis that complements both "lower level" neurobiological and "higher level" social-cognitive approaches in psychology. Indeed, the information processing movement has gained considerable impetus from the advent and development of cognitive neuroscience due to the high degree of congruence between proposed information processing systems and identifiable brain regions.

Despite this widespread application of information processing models and theories within the range of domains of interest of cognitive psychology, information processing theorists have been relatively slow in turning their attentions to the domain of emotion. Despite the success of cognitive therapy from the early 1970s onward (e.g., Beck, 1970), cognition and emotion as a rigorous empirical and theoretical discipline only emerged in the early 1980s (see Dalgleish & Power, 1999a; Williams, Watts, MacLeod, & Mathews, 1997, for reviews).

In what ways can the information processing paradigm inform us about emotions and emotional disorders? In empirical terms, there are three ways in which the interaction of emotion and the cognitive processing of information have traditionally been investigated (Williams et al., 1997). First, there is the study of the cognitive processing of emotional information (that is, information that is either semantically related to emotions themselves or to events or stimuli that are associated with the experience of emotional states), as compared with the processing of affectively neutral information that is the mainstay of cognitive psychology experiments. Second, there is the investigation of information processing in healthy individuals who are in an emotional state or who have traitlike characteristics focused on one emotion or another. Third, there is the investigation of individuals who meet criteria for a diagnosis of an emotional disorder such as major depression. All three of these domains of cognition and emotion research now have a burgeoning theoretical and empirical base (see Dalgleish & Power, 1999a).

The structure of this chapter is as follows. First I introduce four of the central concepts that have historically characterized the information processing paradigm and illustrate them with brief examples from both mainstream cognitive psychology and the cognition and emotion literature. This section is not intended to be exhaustive; rather, it is designed to illustrate the emergence and evolution of the key information processing concepts that prototypically define the paradigm and how they have been

applied in the emotion domain. Second, I discuss a number of theories of emotion and emotional disorders in the information processing tradition in order to illustrate the development and increasing sophistication of information processing approaches to emotion. Inevitably, the coverage of theoretical models is far from exhaustive. Third, in a summary section I endeavor to evaluate briefly the overall contribution of the information processing paradigm to our understanding of emotion and emotional disorder in the context of other paradigms in the field.

## Some Central Concepts of the Information Processing Paradigm

### Selectivity of Processing and Limited Cognitive Resources

The information processing approach assumes that there is competition within the processing system between streams of information. This is a function of capacity or resource limitations within the system. In other words, if the system has only so many resources and the demands on the system outweigh those resources, then competition for resources is inevitable. This competition in turn leads to selection, a process commonly referred to as selective attention. A host of theories exist about the nature of selective attention (see Johnston & Dark, 1986, for a review). Two important theoretical commonalities in the extensive literature on selective attention merit highlighting. The first is that selectivity can be governed by the characteristics of the information that is selected, for example, its saliency with respect to the organism. The second is that the attentional system can be primed in various ways to select information from particular modalities, stimulus domains, semantic categories, or temporal-spatial domains. So, for example, a fast-moving object in the visual field may always attract selective attentional resources. Similarly, for an individual who has been presented with task instructions to visually search for red letters, a red letter in the visual field will attract attentional resources (cf. Treisman & Gelade, 1980).

These two aspects of selective attention are reflected in the theoretical developments in the area. A distinction has traditionally been made between two types of theory. First, there are theories that have viewed attention as merely a description of patterns of primed processing advantages in the system for particular patterns of input (e.g., Johnston & Dark, 1986). Second, there are theories that construe selective attention as an active cause of differential processing (e.g., Marcel, 1983). As with many theories within the information processing paradigm, recent approaches have synthesized these cause-and-consequence accounts (e.g., Duncan & Humphreys, 1989) and put forward models in which priming of information domains occurs but in which a degree of intentional control over such patterns of priming is also possible.

As mentioned previously, the notion of selectivity arises because the information processing paradigm assumes that cognitive systems have a capacity limitation. In other words, mental resources for the performance of cognitive operations are limited. When those resources are fully deployed, then extra task demands will result in detriments in task performance as selection within the system becomes manifest. For example, in an early study, Allport, Antonis, and Reynolds (1972) asked participants to repeat back prose passages that they were hearing in one ear while at the same time trying to learn lists of words that they were hearing in their other ear. Allport et al. found that the addition of the prose task reduced to chance levels the participants' ability to recognize the words that they had been trying to learn. The implication of these data is that those components of the cognitive system that are involved in processing and remembering streams of auditory information are capacity limited, and if demands on the system are increased, then levels of performance will be accordingly impaired (see Allport, 1993, for a critical review of this research on dual-task performance).

During the historical development of the information processing approach, there have been various theoretical conceptualizations of the idea of limited cognitive capacity. An early version was the proposal of a single reservoir of cognitive resources that could be drawn on by the whole gamut of cognitive processes (e.g., Johnston & Heinz, 1978). However, this idea proved to be inconsistent with findings that indicated that interference between tasks, as demonstrated by the Allport et al. (1972) study, has as much to do with task *similarity* as it does with task *difficulty* (e.g., McLeod, 1977). This type of finding led to the development of architecturally driven accounts of capacity limitation (e.g., Fodor, 1983) that propose that the cognitive system can be conceptualized as a set of relatively autonomous modules (see below), each with its own separate capacity limits. Consequently, interference is low between tasks that utilize different modules and high between tasks that utilize the same modules.

More recently, a rapprochement has emerged between single, central-capacity accounts and completely modular approaches in the form of compromise positions that involve hierarchical cognitive organization (e.g., Baddeley, 1986). Some form of central processor is at the top of the hierarchy, and this is involved in the coordination and control of a number of specific subsystems that operate in relative autonomy. So, for example, Baddeley's model of working memory (Baddeley, 1986) posits a central processor, the central executive, which provides generic processing resources and exerts executive control over modular subsidiary processors. These include the articulatory loop, which holds phonological information in short-term memory, and the visuo-spatial scratch pad, which holds visuo-spatial information in short-term memory. Both of these subsidiary systems are capacity limited with respect to the particular domains of information that they serve.

These twin notions of limited capacity and, consequently, some form of selectivity of processing have provided a framework for understanding how individuals in emotional states exhibit systematic biases in various cognitive domains in favor of information that corresponds to those emotional states. Similar effects are present in those with traitlike emotional dispositions and those with emotional disorders (see Williams et al., 1997, for a comprehensive review). The argument is that in a cognitive system with limited resources, priority will be afforded to information that potentially has immediate and important consequences for the organism, and such information will be selectively processed. Emotional states and traits are seen as setting conditions for designating the sorts of information that are likely to be important. So, for example, an anxious mood is likely to be associated with a context of danger—something that potentially has immediate consequences for the organism. It is therefore adaptive if anxiety sets the system up such that the cognitive resources available are selectively allocated, even more than they are normally, to the processing of danger-related information.

This selectivity of processing associated with emotion can be demonstrated empirically. For example, Teasdale and Fogarty (1979) showed that participants who had received an elation mood induction were significantly faster to recall positive autobiographical memories than negative memories, with the reverse being true of individuals who had received a depression mood induction. That is, there was selective mnemonic processing of mood-congruent material (see also chapter 32, this volume).

Selective processing of emotion-related information has also been demonstrated frequently with groups of clinical participants. For example, Taghavi, Neshat-Doost, Moradi, Yule, and Dalgleish (1999) tested groups of children and adolescents with a diagnosis of generalized anxiety disorder and matched controls on a visual attention task (adapted from MacLeod, Mathews, & Tata, 1986). Participants had to respond as fast as possible when a dot appeared on the screen. In half of the trials, the location of the dot corresponded to the prior location of a threatening word, and in the other half of the trials the threat word was in a different prior spatial location to the subsequent dot. The results revealed that the anxious participants were faster to respond to the dot when it replaced a threat word and slower when the threat word had been in a different spatial location, compared with the performance of controls. Similar effects are reported in adults (e.g., MacLeod et al., 1986). These findings appear to illustrate selective attention to threat words in anxious individuals such that stimuli appearing in the same location as the threat are also selectively processed.

Selectivity of processing is also evident in the interpretation of ambiguous emotional and nonemotional information. For example, Mathews, Richards, and Eysenck (1989) asked clinically anxious individuals to write down homophones that were read out to them in a list. Homophones are words with two meanings and spellings but with only one sound (e.g., *dye, die*). In the Mathews et al. (1989) study, all of the homophones had both a neutral and a threat meaning (balanced for frequency dominance across the two meaning types). The data revealed that the clinically anxious participants were more likely to write down the threat meaning of the homophone than the neutral meaning, relative to the controls. This indicates that anxiety is associated with a tendency to resolve ambiguity in favor of threat, though it is unclear from these data whether the participants were aware of both meanings of the homophone or not. There is a wealth of research in this tradition that reveals emotion-related selectivity of processing in most cognitive domains, including perception, attention, memory, judgment, thinking, and reasoning (see Williams et al., 1997, and chapter 30, this volume).

In addition to *selectivity* of processing of this kind, it seems clear that, in information processing terms, cognition-emotion processes are affected by limitations in *capacity*. For example, Wegner, Erber, and Zanakos (1993) asked participants to write down a sad autobiographical narrative but encouraged them to try to suppress the sad mood that would normally be generated. Under normal conditions, participants were able to successfully suppress mood. However, when controlled processing resources were utilized in a secondary mental load task (remembering numbers), the ability to suppress mood was reversed, and there was an ironic elevation of mood. These data indicate the importance of limited-capacity controlled processing resources in the mental control of mood.

In addition, it seems that emotions themselves place a resource demand on the system. For example, a common way in which individuals deal with unwanted emotions is to "keep busy." That is, they channel limited-capacity resources into nonemotional activities by way of distraction. The rationale here is that the generation of negative emotions is to a degree resource dependent, and, therefore, by recruiting those resources for a nonemotional task, the negative affect will subside. Indeed, such distraction is a common technique in the clinical treatment of emotional disorders (Beck, 1970). Clients are encouraged to rapidly process large amounts of affectively neutral information, for example, by describing to themselves quickly and in detail the contents of a room.

Individuals suffering from emotional disorders frequently report being overwhelmed by negative thoughts and emotions. Correspondingly, they also find it difficult to carry out neutral tasks effectively (see Ellis & Moore, 1999, for a review). Again, a conceptualization in terms of cognitive capacity would propose that limited resources are being utilized in the processing both of information about negative emotional events and also of negative emotions. Consequently, nonemotional task performance that is resource dependent becomes impaired.

## Modularity

As noted previously, there has historically been a tension in the information processing literature between those theorists who advocate a single, central, limited-capacity processor that places the final constraints on how much processing can occur at a given time and other theorists who propose that the cognitive system is modular—in other words, that it consists of numerous, relatively independent subsystems or modules, each of which has its own limited capacity (Fodor, 1983). At the present time, most theoreticians would advocate some level of modularity within the cognitive system. This weighting of opinion in favor of a modularized mind is largely the result of findings from cognitive neuropsychology, in which a wealth of case studies seem to indicate that the brain itself is organized in a modular fashion. For example, Ellis and Young's (1988) model of reading involves separable or modularized reading routes. One of these routes involves visual recognition of familiar words that are stored in a lexicon. In contrast, another route involves conversion of spellings into sounds, and it is proposed that this route is used for unfamiliar and irregular words.

Support for the modular independence of these two routes is provided by patients with so-called phonological dyslexia. For example, Beauvois and Derousne (1979) describe a patient, RG, who, when presented with lists of words and nonwords, was able to read 100% of the real words successfully but only 10% of the nonwords. The argument is that, for RG, the visual input lexicon is intact, and therefore there is little or no difficulty in pronouncing familiar words. In contrast, however, damage to the separate spelling-to-sound conversion (grapheme-phoneme conversion) route means that he or she finds it very difficult to pronounce nonwords.

The current consensus within information processing models is that the set of modularized subsystems is hierarchically organized such that higher level processes can determine the long-term goals of the system and delegate appropriate short-term goals to lower levels of the system (e.g., Baddeley, 1986; Shallice, 1994). So, for example, in a complex task such as playing tennis, higher level processes will determine overall goals such as the strategy for the game, thus setting subgoals for playing particular points or serving in a particular fashion. At the next level of control, even shorter term goals will be involved in the control of individual shots, and these in turn determine the plans for motor programs to execute those shots.

The relationship of modularity to emotion is a complex one (see below) and unambiguous empirical illustrations are not readily available. However, the concept of modularity is addressed to some extent in a series of studies by Marcia Johnson and her colleagues (see Johnson & Multhaup, 1992, for a summary) that tested predictions derived from their multiple entry modular memory system (MEMS). In brief, this theory proposes four modularized memory subsystems that interact in the processing of information. Two of the subsystems are *perceptual*, for engaging in and recording perceptual activities, and two are *reflective*, for engaging in and recording self-generated activities such as planning, speculating, imagining, and so on. Johnson and colleagues set out to illustrate how the perceptual and reflective modules deal with different aspects of emotional information by examining the performance of patients with amnesia on two tasks: one involving mostly perceptual aspects of a situation (the melodies task) and the other involving mostly reflective aspects (the good guy–bad guy task; Johnson & Multhaup, 1992).

In the melodies task, participants listened to recordings of unfamiliar melodies. Participants were then asked to rate their preferences for the melodies that they had heard and also for a set of new, filler melodies that they had never heard. Preference ratings are normally higher for previously exposed information (the mere exposure effect), and the prediction was that amnesic patients would be no different from controls in preferring previously heard melodies because perceptual acquisition of affect should be unimpaired in amnesia. The results were consistent with predictions and revealed normal preference ratings in the amnesiacs. Johnson and Multhaup (1992) take this as support for the idea that affective encoding of *perceptual attributes* of stimuli is preserved in amnesia.

In the good guy–bad guy task, participants were shown matched photographs of two men. They were then presented with brief biographies of the men that indicated that one of them was a "good guy" and one of them was a "bad guy." They then rated the men on various personal attributes. The results revealed that the amnesic patients were less affected by the biographical information than the controls in that, although their ratings of the two men did change from baseline, the extent to which they rated them as "good" and "bad" was attenuated relative to the control group. Similarly, although the control participants' impressions of the two men remained firmly "good" and "bad," the amnesiacs tended to rate the two men as more and more similar over time. Johnson and Multhaup (1992) argue that these results from the good guy–bad guy study indicate that, when *reflective processes* are required for the processing of affective information, acquisition of that information is impaired in amnesia despite these processes appearing to be intact for more perceptual affective attributes, as demonstrated by the results of the melodies study.

Overall, these data are taken as support for the idea that different modularized subsystems are involved in the processing of different aspects of affective information, as indicated by the fact that these different systems can be differentially impaired by organic brain problems.

## Simultaneous Processing of Information at Different Levels of Analysis

A fundamental theme in the type of modularized information processing approaches that we have been discussing is the idea that the same internal or external event can be simultaneously processed by a number of different modules or levels within the system. A good example of this comes from psycholinguistics, in which there is a wealth of evidence for the simultaneous processing of phonological (sound) information and semantic information in reading. For example, Baron (1973) asked participants to decide whether written phrases were meaningful. He discovered that the sounds of words influenced performance such that participants, when reading, had particular difficulty in rejecting phrases such as "tie the not." These data seem to indicate that visual and phonological analyses were both occurring within a similar time frame.

An early distinction in the development of the idea of simultaneous processing by different parts of the cognitive system was that between automatic and strategic (or controlled) processes (Shiffrin & Schneider, 1977). Automatic processes are viewed as those that are not strategically modifiable, that involve sequences of information processing that are executed in an invariant manner, that have little or no requirement for limited-capacity resources, and that rely on relatively permanent sets of associative connections. Strategic or controlled processes, on the other hand, are temporary and variable sequences of processes under the control of volitional attentional effort on the part of the participant and are thus highly constrained by capacity limitations.

This simple twofold distinction was further developed by Norman and Shallice (1986), who identified three levels of functioning: (1) fully automatic processing; (2) deliberate control by a supervisory attentional system (as described previously); and (3) partially automatic processing in which contention schedule takes place within the cognitive system without deliberate direction or conscious control. One theoretical consequence of the postulated concepts of both strategic and partially automatic cognitive processes is that the same cognitive task may be performed in different ways by different individuals or by the same individual on different occasions. This flexibility of the cognitive system is now identified as one of its defining features (Pressley, 1994).

A good clinical example of simultaneous processing at

different levels within the system is that of simple phobias. Phobias are fear reactions to specifically identifiable stimuli that the person is able to rationalize as not being objectively fear inducing. So, for example, a spider phobic would feel very afraid in the presence of a small spider but would, in principle, be able to recognize that the fear was inappropriate and disproportional. Similar dissociations between conscious appraisals of the emotionality of particular stimuli and the affect that those stimuli generate are also a characteristic of other emotional disorders, such as obsessive-compulsive disorder (OCD), in which sufferers are able to acknowledge that their concerns that, for example, they may be contaminated and therefore need to wash are unrealistic and "irrational."

A more empirical demonstration in the cognition and emotion domain of processing at different levels of the system is provided by Richards and French's (1992) study on the interpretation of ambiguity. Richards and French presented high- and low-anxious participants with homographs (words with one spelling but different meanings, e.g., *club*). Each homograph had a threat-related and a neutral meaning. The homographs were used as primes for targets related to one of the two meanings (e.g., *club-smash*), and the interval between the homograph and the target was varied. The results revealed that at short homograph-target intervals (500 msec), high- and low-anxious participants processed targets relating to either meaning of the homograph equally quickly, suggesting that both meanings were automatically activated to the same extent. However, by 750 msec, the high-trait-anxious participants were processing targets relating to the threat meaning of the homograph more quickly than the controls. Based on previous research in this area (e.g., Neely, 1977), these data can be taken to imply a relatively fast automatic process, in which both meanings of an ambiguous stimulus are activated, complemented by a slower, more controlled process, in which meanings more relevant to the individual's ongoing concerns and mood state are selectively processed.

## Top-Down Versus Bottom-Up Processing

A final important distinction that is made in the information processing literature is between bottom-up, or predominantly stimulus driven, processing and top-down, or predominantly conceptually driven, processing. Bottom-up processing is more strongly affected directly by patterns of stimulus input. In contrast, top-down processing is principally affected by what an individual brings to the processing situation, for example, expectations determined by the context of the situation. It is generally agreed that most cognitive activity involves both types of processing in combination. A good, clear example of this is visual object perception. Most theories of higher level vi-

sion, for example, Kosslyn, Flynn, Amsterdam, and Wang (1990), propose that basic stimulus-driven analysis of the visual field is combined with representations of the visual properties of objects and that these two streams of information can be integrated in a bottom-up and top-down manner to lead to successful object perception.

Top-down processing is not limited to visual perception. A cyclical relationship between bottom-up and top-down processing has been proposed for the range of cognitive abilities. It is generally agreed that most top-down processing requires the existence of complex higher order knowledge structures. In cognitive psychology, concepts such as schemas (e.g., Bartlett, 1932), scripts (Schank & Abelson, 1977), frames (Minsky, 1975), mental models (Johnson-Laird, 1983), and thematic abstraction units (Dyer, 1983) are all concerned with the representation of knowledge at higher levels. These knowledge structures contain large amounts of default information that is prototypically true but that is also capable of modification and tuning by the demands of a particular processing situation. Such structures operate by exerting top-down constraints on the way information is processed at lower levels of the system.

In information processing terms, research of the kind that was presented earlier in support of selective biases in the processing of emotion-related information in individuals (e.g., Taghavi et al., 1999; Teasdale & Fogarty, 1979) has also been seen as evidence for a role of emotions, moods, traits, and emotional disorders as top-down influences on a range of cognitive activities. For example, in Taghavi et al.'s (1999) attentional probe experiment described earlier, it can be argued that, the presence of an anxiety disorder and consequently a chronic anxious mood had a top-down influence on selective visual attention such that areas of the visual field that contained information congruent with that mood (that is, threat words) were selectively processed.

Perhaps an even more powerful demonstration of top-down influences comes from research that shows that selective processing of emotional information can be a function of current concerns. For example, MacLeod and Mathews (1988), again using the dot-probe task, found no difference between high- and low-trait-anxious students in their attentional bias for negative exam-related words when tested some months before an examination. However, when tested again immediately prior to the exam, the high-trait-anxious students showed increased vigilance for negative exam-related information.

The proposal that emotions and emotional disorders act as broad top-down influences on a range of cognitive processes has been a widely endorsed theoretical concept in the cognition and emotion literature. However, this kind of approach begs the question as to what emotions are within the system and how they themselves might be conceptualized within an information processing model. The fact that emotion processing seems to require cognitive resources (as discussed previously) underlines the importance of developing information processing models of emotions themselves, in addition to models that explicate the influence of emotions on other sets of processes.

## Information Processing Theories of Emotion

In the preceding sections, I have discussed a number of core concepts within the information processing paradigm. The picture that I have tried to paint is that information processing theories consist of mental processing systems that comprise a set of hierarchically organized modules, with each module having some limitations of capacity but also some process specificity. All but the simplest task performance involves configurations of processing modules acting together, with simultaneous processing of different aspects of the information array in the different modules. The control hierarchy in a particular modular configuration is determined by combinations of bottom-up and top-down processes (e.g., Barnard, 1985). Finally, the degree of overall volitional control varies from entirely strategically controlled cognitive processing through to fully automatic processing consisting of invariant sequences of processes.

Within the framework of this type of model, what is the best way of theoretically conceptualizing emotions in information processing terms and accounting for the various data presented in the first part of the chapter? Are emotions separate levels or modules within the system that influence the performance and configuration of other levels and modules? Do they represent particular configurations of the system? Are emotions best viewed as strategic, partially automatic, or controlled processes? What is the relationship, in information processing terms, between emotion and emotional disorder?

In this section I consider a number of information processing theories of emotion and emotional disorder that have endeavored to provide answers to these questions. Three theories have been selected to illustrate the evolution of theory in the information processing paradigm, from single-level associative models (e.g., Bower, 1981) through more complex appraisal-driven explanations (e.g., Oatley & Johnson-Laird, 1987) to multilevel models that combine associative and appraisal-driven elements (e.g., Power & Dalgleish, 1997). Although the list of theories presented is clearly not exhaustive, it hopefully serves to illustrate the range of different modeling techniques that have been used within the information processing paradigm, and brief discussions of theories that bear some family resemblance to the three that have been selected are included to provide some sense of the broader theoretical canvas.

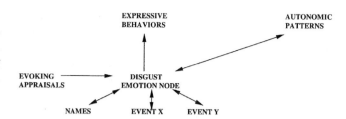

Figure 33.1 Schematic of Bower's associative network theory of emotion illustrating the disgust node.

### Bower's Network Theory

An early influential information processing theory of emotion is Bower's network theory (Bower, 1981; Bower & Cohen, 1982). Bower proposed that concepts, events, and emotions can all be represented as nodes within a representational network (see Figure 33.1).

Activation across the network depends on a number of factors, which include the proximity of nodes to each other, the strength of the initial activation, and the time lapse since activation. In the example shown (see Figure 33.1), the disgust emotion node possesses a variety of types of links, such as links to phenomenological and physiological characteristics, linguistic labels, and disgust-related events and memories.

Activation of any one of the nodes in the network shown in Figure 33.1 may therefore spread to adjoining nodes; for example, if an individual experiences something "disgusting," the experience could activate the disgust node and spread to a range of adjoining nodes, even activating previous events in which the individual experienced disgust and activating innate and learned expressive and autonomic patterns.

Bower's network theory initially gave rise to a great deal of supportive evidence based primarily on the effects of the temporary induction of happy or sad moods in normal individuals. Bower (1981) reported data that showed that mood induction led to mood-state-dependent memory and that it influenced a range of processes, including free association, reported fantasies, social judgments about other people, and perceptual categorization. For example, in a typical experiment, Bower (1981) induced sad or happy moods in a group of hypnotizable participants and then asked the participants to recall childhood incidents. The results showed that when the participants were in a happy mood, they recalled significantly more pleasant events from childhood, but when they were in a sad mood, they recalled significantly more unpleasant events. On the assumption, therefore, that the participants were in a matching mood at the time of the experience of the events (that is, a happy mood for a pleasant event and a sad mood for an unpleasant event), this study can be interpreted as evidence for mood-state-dependent memory. Similar explanations can be put forward for the data from the experiments by Teasdale and Fogarty (1979) and Taghavi et al. (1999), described previously.

As data testing Bower's original network theory accumulated, it became apparent that there were a number of empirical and theoretical problems. To give just one example, the theory makes the broad prediction that each mood state should be associated with a range of perceptual, attentional, and mnemonic biases. However, it became clear that different types of biases tend to be associated with different mood states; as Williams et al. (1997) have summarized, the evidence to some degree suggests that anxiety is primarily associated with attention-related biases, as in the Taghavi et al. (1999) experiment described previously, whereas depressed mood may be more associated with memory-related biases (e.g., Clark & Teasdale, 1982). Indeed, in the Taghavi et al. (1999) study, children and adolescents with mixed anxiety and depression did not show an attentional bias for threat, and this is also true of children, adolescents, and adults with a diagnosis of depression (MacLeod et al., 1986; Neshat-Doost, Moradi, Taghavi, Yule, & Dalgleish, 2000).

Bower's network approach to modeling emotions instantiates in a particular cognitive architecture a number of the core concepts of the information processing paradigm that were discussed earlier. Selectivity of processing is a function of patterns of activation within the network. Consequently, anxious mood is associated with selective processing of threat because the anxiety node spreads activation to threat-related representations. In this way, emotions exert a top-down influence on processing within the system. However, as already noted, in processing terms there is no distinction between different emotions within this model in that they all affect the range of cognitive processes in a similar way. A further consequence of the network architecture is that it is clear that simultaneous processing of different aspects of the same information array can take place merely as a function of appropriate activation spread within the network. However, it is not immediately clear how more sophisticated distinctions, such as those between automatic, partially automatic, and strategically controlled processes, might operate (Norman & Shallice, 1986).

Within Bower's network model, each emotion is represented by a node, and to this extent the system exhibits modularity. This modularity, however, does not explicitly extend to other cognitive processes, such as attention and memory, that emerge from an undifferentiated network. The modularity of emotions on offer here is of a very simple form in that the emotion nodes are not unpacked in any way and activation of the node is synonymous with having the emotion.

Bower's theory is principally concerned with modeling the way emotion interacts with cognitive processing. It provides no more than a very simple analysis of the generation of emotions; that is, they occur when the emotion node is activated. To this extent it is difficult to see immediately how the concept of limited-capacity cognitive resources can be instantiated in the model. One possibility is that there is a finite amount of activation within the system and that activation of an emotion-related network precludes activation of parts of the system involved in non-affect-related processing. However, this is not explicit in the model.

More recent associative network approaches acknowledge the limitations of the original Bower model and argue that the kind of affect infusion processes predicted by the associative approach occur only in certain contexts (Fiedler, 1991)—specifically, those processes that allow the generative use of previously stored and affectively primed information such as open-ended thinking and problem solving. Consequently, more recent models, such as Forgas's affect infusion model (AIM; Forgas, 1995), outline important boundary conditions for the application of associative network processing and illustrate how such processing can integrate with other processing approaches such as the use of heuristics. For a discussion of these approaches and of the future of network theories in cognition and emotion, see Forgas (1999).

## Oatley and Johnson-Laird's Theory

Oatley and Johnson-Laird's (1987) theory of emotions is designed to complement a fully modularized, hierarchically organized information processing model of mind (Johnson-Laird, 1983), as I broadly implied in the first part of this chapter. Processing within the system is driven by goals. Within such a system, goals are symbolic representations of states of the environment that the system is trying to achieve. Goal achievement occurs through the execution of plans—sequences of transformations of represented information within the system.

Oatley and Johnson-Laird (1987) propose that, in such a cognitive system engaged in multiple goals and plans, there have to be mechanisms by which priority can be assigned, because not all active goals and plans can be pursued at once. They argue that one of the important roles for emotion, therefore, is to provide a possible mechanism by which such priorities can be assigned or altered. This echoes the contention scheduling role proposed for partially automatic processes by Norman and Shallice (1986).

In the Oatley and Johnson-Laird (1987) theory, emotions operate by the propagation within the system of "emotion signals." Emotion signals work by configuring the cognitive system in particular ways (modes) so as to respond optimally to the setting circumstances that generated the signal. Emotion signals are conceptualized as originating at junctures in plans as a function of obstacles to the attainment of important goals. Emotion signals are seen as being devoid of symbolic content in that they do not refer to the semantic attributes of the precipitating stimulus. They are therefore seen as operating purely causally. Full emotional experience is seen as being a function of the operation of an emotion signal accompanied by propositional signals within the system that ascribe a meaning to the emotion mode, thereby allowing the possibility of strategically driven, intentional processing.

Oatley and Johnson-Laird (1987) propose a set of at least five basic emotions that form the foundation for their theory. They base this foundation on evidence from, for example, studies of the facial expression of emotion (e.g., Ekman, 1992), studies of emotional development, and so on. In addition, Johnson-Laird and Oatley (1989) carried out a linguistic analysis of emotion terms in which the basic emotions were treated as unanalyzable semantic primitives which, in combination with other factors, can lead to more complex emotions (see also Ortony, Clore, & Collins, 1988, for an alternative approach to such linguistic analysis). The five basic emotions that Oatley and Johnson-Laird derive from these different types of study are happiness, sadness, fear, anger, and disgust; thus, other emotions are considered to be derived from one of these basic emotions through the inclusion of additional information that relates the basic emotion, for example, to the self or to some sociocontextual element such as a significant other.

Oatley and Johnson-Laird (1987) propose that each of the five basic emotions is linked to a particular key juncture in goals and plans. Happiness is linked to progress being made toward a goal; sadness is linked to the failure or loss of a goal; anger results when a goal or plan is blocked or frustrated; anxiety results from the general goal of self-preservation being threatened; and disgust is considered to result from the violation of a gustatory goal, either literally (e.g., in response to tastes or smells) or metaphorically (e.g., in response to individuals or ideas).

Oatley and Johnson-Laird's (1987) theory of emotion is strongly in the information processing tradition. Emotions are seen as partially automatic processes that reconfigure a modularized, hierarchically controlled cognitive system in a top-down manner. The ways in which the system is reconfigured determine the selectivity of processing and differ across basic emotions. Basic emotional reconfiguration of the system can be modified and tuned by strategically driven processes, and the same information array can thereby be simultaneously processed in different ways. Although not explicit in the model, it seems plausible that the generation of emotion signals, requiring as it does analysis of incoming information with respect to ongoing goals and plans, is resource dependent.

Oatley and Johnson-Laird's (1987) model of emotions is essentially an appraisal-based model in that information is evaluated or appraised with respect to particular goals

and plans that the organism is currently pursuing and in that the results of this appraisal have implications for the generation of emotion. This approach currently has considerable currency within the cognition and emotion literature and is critically reviewed by Scherer (1999) and Ellsworth and Scherer (chapter 29, this volume).

### The SPAARS Model

The SPAARS (schematic, propositional, analogical, and associative representational systems) model (Power & Dalgleish, 1997) of emotion and emotional disorder is in the same broad tradition as that of Oatley and Johnson-Laird (1987) in that it proposes a modularized cognitive system which operates as a function of the pursuit of goals and plans.

SPAARS is a multilevel model (see also Johnson & Multhaup, 1992; Teasdale & Barnard, 1993, for similar models) that comprises four levels or formats of representation of information (see Figure 33.2). The *analogical* representational system stores information and memories in analogical form. This information includes visual, olfactory, auditory, gustatory, body state, and proprioceptive "images" that are either episodic or semantic; that is, they are either memories of specific events or fragments of events from an individual's life or they are active representations of the properties of objects, smells, sounds, and so forth, in the world.

*Propositional* representations within SPAARS are encodings of verbal information. They represent beliefs, ideas, objects, and concepts and the relations between them in a form that is not specific to any language. Propositions refer to thoughts and beliefs that can be expressed in natural language without any corresponding loss of meaning or content.

The *schematic model* level represents higher order ideational content which cannot readily be expressed in nat-

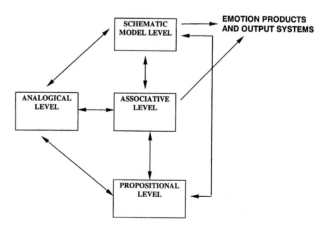

Figure 33.2 The SPAARS model of emotion and emotional disorder. From Power and Dalgleish (1997), reprinted with permission of Psychology Press.

ural language, for instance, models of the self, the world, and others that are so important in understanding emotion and emotional disorder. So, for example, a schematic model of the world as a safe place is likely to contain more complexity than is captured by a simple propositional level statement such as "the world is safe"; rather, a model of the world as safe incorporates all aspects of what the concept of safety means to the individual and is a guiding construct for the way information is processed and organized within the system.

The configuration of schematic models within SPAARS is seen to be what provides individuals with their sense of self and of reality and meaning. The proposal is that the self has structure and the world has coherence because of the way they are modeled within this highest level of meaning.

Events and interpretations of events are appraised at the schematic model level of meaning with respect to the individual's active goal structure, and this appraisal can lead to the generation of emotions in a similar way to that described by Oatley and Johnson-Laird (1987; see also chapter 29, this volume). In this analysis, appraisal is shorthand for the construction of a schematic model that represents the implications of any incoming information for the individual's valued goals. In the schematic model system, for each emotion there are several levels of appraisal which increase in sophistication. For example, a more sophisticated appraisal for anger, over and above the appraisal of a goal blocked by a recognizable agent, would involve some attribution of blame or intent on the part of that agent. The more sophisticated the appraisal components involved, it is suggested, the more processing resources they take up within SPAARS.

Once generated, emotions are conceptualized within the SPAARS model as acting so as to reconfigure the system in a top-down fashion in order to deal with the appraised obstacle to goal achievement. Different emotions are a function of different patterns of appraisal in a similar way to that proposed by Oatley and Johnson-Laird (1987).

In addition to the partially automatic generation of emotion via the schematic model level within SPAARS, a completely automatic route to emotion is also proposed. Automatized emotion generation occurs via the *associative* level of representation and requires no concurrent access to the schematic model level of representation, as outlined herein.

Essentially, then, automatized emotions are generated in a way that does not involve appraisal with respect to the individual's goals at the time of the event's occurrence; rather, automatically generated emotions are a learned function of the individual's emotional responses in the past. This automatized emotional reaction is akin to what Logan (1988) has called "single step direct-access retrieval of past solutions from memory." It is conceived of as a relatively inflexible and unmodifiable process once acti-

vated. Within SPAARS, it is proposed that the generation of emotions can become automatized in two ways: (1) through repetition of the event-emotion relationship; or (2) when the event is biologically "prepared" in some way, as, for example, in specific animal phobias (Seligman, 1971).

The SPAARS model was conceived as a way of conceptualizing both emotions and emotional disorders. To illustrate this, it is useful to consider the case of two anxiety disorders: simple phobias and panic disorder. Phobias are fear reactions to specifically identifiable stimuli that the person is able to rationalize as not being objectively fear inducing. I discussed phobias earlier as an illustration of the simultaneous processing of information at different levels of the system. Within SPAARS, phobias would be conceptualized as comprising automatic fear reactions, generated via the associative level of representation, in tandem with the appraisal that the situation is *not* currently threatening to active goals at the schematic model level of representation.

Panic disorder is characterized by the experience of attacks of extremely high levels of physiological anxiety, usually accompanied by thoughts about losing control, not coping, having a heart attack, dying, and so on (Clark, 1986). In contrast to phobic reactions, the fear generated in a panic situation often seems syntonic with the contents of the person's thoughts.

Within SPAARS, the fear reactions during a panic attack are conceptualized as consisting of a combination of automatic fear reactions generated by the associative level of representation and appraisal-driven fear reactions generated via the schematic level of representation. A possible course of events for a panic attack, according to SPAARS, might be as follows: (1) Some (incidental) change in bodily state is appraised at the schematic level as an indication that something is wrong with the person, and fear is generated (Clark, 1986). (2) This schematic model level of appraisal leads to the generation of negative thoughts, represented at the propositional level, that focus on the negative attributes of the experience that the person is having (e.g., "I am having a heart attack"). (3) The discrepancy between thought content, represented at the propositional level, and active goals is appraised as threatening at the schematic model level and leads to further generation of fear. (4) The bodily sensations accompanying the generation of fear are appraised as further indications that something is wrong, leading to further appraisal-driven generation of fear. Thus, according to SPAARS, the individual experiencing a panic attack is a victim of two vicious circles (based on Clark, 1986) of processing revolving through the schematic model level of representation.

In addition, it is proposed in SPAARS that in panic disorder a number of the aforementioned processes can become automatized such that the individual is also the victim of automatic fear reactions generated in response to particular bodily sensations, propositional contents, or both. This process can contribute to panic attacks "out of the blue" and also to nocturnal panic attacks, triggered by bodily changes during sleep.

The SPAARS model instantiates the majority of the core concepts of the information processing paradigm. In conception, it is similar to the model of Oatley and Johnson-Laird (1987). The principal differences are: the proposal of more than one route to the generation of emotions; the more explicit description of the modular subsystems involved in cognition and emotion, thus making SPAARS a truly multilevel approach; and the emphasis on modeling emotional disorder, as well as normal emotions.

The SPAARS model falls within the category of multilevel theories of emotion (see Teasdale, 1999, for a review). Other, similar approaches include the MEMs model (Johnson & Multhaup, 1992) discussed earlier, interacting cognitive subsystems (Teasdale & Barnard, 1993), and the multilevel appraisal model of Leventhal and Scherer (1987). All of these theories share the common assumption that different levels of the cognitive system vary in their relationship to emotion, with some levels being directly involved in the generation of emotion and others being relatively insulated from this process. This greater involvement of emotion within some levels compared to others allows the models to explain, as in the example of phobic reactions discussed previously, how information relating to emotional events can be processed in both a "cool," factual way, with no ensuing emotion generation, and a "hot," emotional way. Such dissociations are clearly difficult for single-level approaches such as associative network theory to deal with. A further advantage of multilevel approaches is that they are more similar to both psychological theories in mainstream cognitive psychology (e.g., Shallice, 1988) and neurobiological models of emotion (e.g. LeDoux, 1995) than are single-level approaches—qualities that are important if we are going to successfully integrate theoretical explanations across different levels and domains of analysis (Dalgleish & Power, 1999b). There is not space here to do justice to a comparison of the strengths and weaknesses of the various multilevel models; however, see Teasdale (1999) for a critical review.

## Summary

According to the information processing framework, mental experience and activity are mediated by the amount of limited-capacity processing resources available and by the priorities of various selective processes that allocate these resources. Processing will be affected by the structure, efficiency, and hierarchical relationship of the various stages and modules that analyze the flow of information and will be constrained by the range of active and available higher order representations (such as schemas) that exert top-down control over more basic processes such as perception, attention, and memory.

This chapter has reviewed a number of these central tenets of the information processing approach in psychology and has illustrated them with reference to empirical examples from the literature in both cognitive psychology and cognition and emotion. Various theories within the cognition and emotion field have also been discussed. The proposed role of emotions within the system, according to these theories, and their relative strengths and weaknesses with respect to the core aspects of the information processing approach have been reviewed.

The information processing approach to psychology offers a number of potential advantages for modeling emotion and emotion-related processes. First, there is a rich potential for modeling individual differences. The organization of the overall control structure within the system and the goals and subgoals established at each level of the system will vary across individuals (Williams et al., 1997). Similarly, the degree to which various processes and routines, including emotion generation itself, have become automatized will be idiosyncratic. This flexibility allows the possibility of developing models that can provide accounts not only of individual variations in cognition-emotion processing but also of emotional disorders. Furthermore, the same framework has the potential to model nonemotional aspects of cognitive processing, consequently providing much-needed theoretical links between mainstream cognitive science and the affective sciences.

The second potential advantage of the information processing approach is that it provides connective tissue between social-cognitive accounts of emotions (see part VII of this volume) and neuroscience accounts (see part I). Multirepresentational information processing models of cognition-emotion relations such as the SPAARS approach, interacting cognitive subsystems (Teasdale & Barnard, 1993) and MEMs (Johnson & Multhaup, 1992) lend themselves to integration with neuroscience accounts that refer to multiple routes to emotion and multiple systems involved in emotional regulation (e.g., LeDoux, 1995). Similarly, those same models make extensive reference to appraisal processes, attributions, schemes, complex emotions, theory of mind issues, and so on, that characterize the social-cognitive literature on emotions.

Finally, the information processing approach is closely allied to the experimental methodologies of cognitive psychology. Such methods complement the self-report methodologies of social cognition and the techniques used in neuroscience research, such as neuroimaging. Consequently, the information processing approach can be usefully conceptualized as one of a number of important and complementary levels of analysis of emotion, ranging from the molecular biological to the cross-cultural.

## REFERENCES

Allport, A. (1993). Attention and control: Have we been asking the wrong questions? A critical review of twenty-five years. In D. E. Meyer & E. S. Kornblum (Eds.), *Attention and performance* (Vol. 14). London: MIT Press.

Allport, D. A., Antonis, B., & Reynolds, P. (1972). On the division of attention: A disproof of the single channel hypothesis. *Quarterly Journal of Experimental Psychology, 24*, 225–235.

Anderson, M. (1992). *Intelligence and development: A cognitive theory.* Oxford, England: Blackwell.

Baddeley, A. (1986). *Working memory.* Oxford, England: Oxford University Press.

Barnard, P. J. (1985). Interacting cognitive subsystems: A psycholinguistic approach to short-term memory. In A. Ellis (Ed.), *Progress in psychology of language* (Vol. 2). London: Erlbaum.

Baron, J. (1973). Phonemic stage not necessary for reading. *Quarterly Journal of Experimental Psychology, 25*, 241–246.

Bartlett, F. C. (1932). *Remembering: A study in experimental and social psychology.* Cambridge, England: Cambridge University Press.

Beauvois, M.-F., & Derousne, J. (1979). Phonological alexia: Three dissociations. *Journal of Neurology, Neurosurgery and Psychiatry, 42*, 1115–1124.

Beck, A. T. (1970). Cognitive therapy: Nature and relation to behaviour therapy. *Behaviour Therapy, 1*, 184–200.

Bower, G. H. (1981). Mood and memory. *American Psychologist, 36*, 129–148.

Bower, G. H., & Cohen, P. R. (1982). Emotional influences on memory and thinking: Data and theory. In S. Fiske & M. Clark (Eds.), *Affect and cognition,* Hillsdale, NJ: Erlbaum.

Broadbent, D. E. (1958). *Perception and communication.* New York: Pergamon Press.

Clark, D. M. (1986). A cognitive approach to panic. *Behaviour Research and Therapy, 24*, 461–470.

Clark, D. M., & Teasdale, J. D. (1982). Diurnal variation in clinical depression and accessibility of memories of positive and negative experiences. *Journal of Abnormal Psychology, 91*, 87–95.

Dalgleish, T., & Power, M. (Eds). (1999a). *Handbook of cognition and emotion.* Chichester, England: Wiley.

Dalgleish, T., & Power, M. (1999b). Cognition and emotion: Future directions In T. Dalgleish & M. Power (Eds.), *Handbook of cognition and emotion.* Chichester, England: Wiley.

Duncan, J., & Humphreys, G. W. (1989). Visual search and stimulus similarity. *Psychological Review, 96*, 433–458.

Dyer, M. G. (1983). *In-depth understanding: A model of integrative processing for narrative comprehension.* Cambridge, MA: MIT Press.

Ekman, P. (1992). An argument for basic emotions. *Cognition and Emotion, 6*, 169–200.

Ellis, A. W., & Young, A. W. (1988). *Human cognitive neuropsychology.* London: Erlbaum.

Ellis, H. C., & Moore, B. A. (1999). Mood and memory. In T. Dalgleish & M. Powers (Eds.), *Handbook of cognition and emotion* (pp. 193–210). Chichester, England: Wiley.

Eysenck, M. W., & Keane, M. T. (1995). *Cognitive psychology: A student's handbook* (3rd ed.). Hove, England: Psychology Press.

Fiedler, K. (1991). On the task, the measures and the mood in research on affect and social cognition. In J. P. Forgas (Ed.), *Emotion and social judgements.* Oxford, England: Pergamon Press.

Fodor, J. A. (1983). *The modularity of mind: An essay on faculty psychology.* Cambridge, MA: MIT Press.

Forgas, J. P. (1995). Mood and judgement: The affect infusion model (AIM). *Psychological Bulletin, 117*, 1–28.

Forgas, J. P. (1999). Network theories and beyond. In T. Dalgleish & M. Power (Eds.), *Handbook of cognition and emotion.* Chichester, England: Wiley.

Johnson, M. K., & Multhaup, K. S. (Eds.). (1992). *Emotion and MEM.* Hillsdale, NJ: Erlbaum.

Johnson-Laird, P. N. (1983). *Mental models: Towards a cognitive science of language, inference and consciousness.* Cambridge, England: Cambridge University Press.

Johnson-Laird, P. N. (1993). *The computer and the mind* (2nd ed.). London: Fontana.

Johnson-Laird, P. N., & Oatley, K. (1989). The language of emotions: An analysis of a semantic field. *Cognition and Emotion, 3*, 81–123.

Johnston, W. A., & Dark, V. J. (1986). Selective attention. *Annual Review of Psychology, 37*, 43–75.

Johnston, W. A., & Heinz, S. P. (1978). Flexibility and capacity demands of attention. *Journal of Experimental Psychology: General, 107*, 420–435.

Kosslyn, S. M., Flynn, R. A., Amsterdam, J. B., & Wang, G. (1990). Components of high-level vision: A cognitive neuroscience analysis and accounts of neurological syndromes. *Cognition, 34*, 203–277.

Kuhn, T. S. (1962). *The structure of scientific revolutions.* Chicago: University of Chicago Press.

LeDoux, J. E. (1995). Emotion: Clues from the brain. *Annual Review of Psychology, 46*, 209–235.

Leventhal, H., & Scherer, K. R. (1987). The relationship of emotion to cognition: A functional approach to a semantic controversy. *Cognition and Emotion, 1*, 3–28.

Logan, G. D. (1988). Toward an instance theory of automatisation. *Psychological Review, 95*, 492–527.

MacLeod, C., & Mathews, A. (1988). Anxiety and the allocation of attention to threat. *Quarterly Journal of Experimental Psychology: Human Experimental Psychology, 38*, 659–670.

MacLeod, C., Mathews, A., & Tata, P. (1986). Attentional bias in emotional disorders. *Journal of Abnormal Psychology, 95*, 15–20.

Marcel, A. J. (1983). Conscious and unconscious perception: An approach to the relations between phenomenal experience and perceptual processes. *Cognitive Psychology, 15*, 238–300.

Mathews, A., Richards, A., & Eysenck, M. W. (1989). Interpretation of homophones related to threat in anxiety states. *Journal of Abnormal Psychology, 98*, 31–34.

McClelland, J. L. (1995). A connectionist perspective on knowledge and development. In T. J. Simon & G. S. Halford (Eds.), *Developing cognitive competence: New approaches to process modelling.* Hillsdale, NJ.: Erlbaum.

McLeod, P. (1977). A dual task response modality effect: Support for multi-processor models of attention. *Quarterly Journal of Experimental Psychology, 29*, 651–667.

Minsky, M. (1975). A framework for representing knowledge. In P. H. Winston (Ed.), *The psychology of computer vision.* New York: McGraw-Hill.

Neely, J. R. (1977). Semantic priming and retrieval from

lexical memory: Roles of spreading activation and limited-capacity attention. *Journal of Experimental Psychology: General, 106*, 226–254.

Neisser, U. (1967). *Cognitive psychology*. New York: Appleton-Century-Crofts.

Neshat-Doost, H., Moradi, A., Taghavi, R., Yule, W., & Dalgleish, T. (2000). Lack of attentional bias for emotional information in clinically depressed children and adolescents on the dot probe task. *Journal of Child Psychology and Psychiatry, 41*, 363–368.

Norman, D. A., & Shallice, T. (1986). Attention to action: Willed and automatic control of behaviour. In R. J. Davidson, G. E. Schwartz, & D. Shapiro (Eds.), *The design of everyday things*. New York: Doubleday.

Oatley, K., & Johnson-Laird, P. N. (1987). Towards a cognitive theory of emotions. *Cognition and Emotion, 1*, 29–50.

Ortony, A., Clore, G. L., & Collins, A. (1988). *The cognitive structure of emotions*. New York: Cambridge University Press.

Power, M. J., & Dalgleish, T. (1997). *Cognitive and emotion: From order to disorder*. Hove, England: Psychology Press.

Pressley, M. (1994). Embracing the complexity of individual differences in cognition: Studying good information processing and how it might develop. *Learning and Individual Difference, 6*, 259–284.

Richards, A., & French, C. C. (1992). An anxiety-related bias in semantic activation when processing threat/neutral homographs. *Quarterly Journal of Experimental Psychology, 45A*, 503–525.

Schank, R. C., & Abelson, R. P. (1977). *Scripts, plans, goals, and understanding*. Hillsdale, NJ: Erlbaum.

Scherer, K. R. (1999) Appraisal theory. In T. Dalgleish & M. Power (Eds.), *Handbook of cognition and emotion*. Chichester, England: Wiley.

Seligman, M. (1971). Phobias and preparedness. *Behavior Therapy, 2*, 307–320.

Shallice, T. (1994). Multiple levels of control processes. In C. Umilta & M. Moscovitch (Eds.), *Attention and performance: Vol. 15: Conscious and nonconscious information processing* (pp. 395–420). Cambridge, MA: Bradford.

Shiffrin, R. M., & Schneider, W. (1977). Controlled and automatic human information processing: 2. Perceptual learning, automatic attending, and a general theory. *Psychological Review, 84*, 127–190.

Shotter, J. (1991). The rhetorical-responsive nature of mind: A social constructionist account. In A. Still & A. Costall (Eds.), *Against cognitivism: Alternative foundations for cognitive psychology*. Hemel Hempstead, England: Harvester Wheatsheaf.

Taghavi, R., Neshat-Doost, H. T., Moradi, A. R., Yule, W., & Dalgleish, T. (1999). Biases in visual attention in children and adolescents with clinical anxiety and mixed depression-anxiety disorder. *Journal of Abnormal Child Psychology, 27*, 215–223.

Teasdale, J. (1999). Multi-level theories of cognition and emotion relations. In T. Dalgleish & M. Power (Eds.), *Handbook of cognition and emotion*. Chichester, England: Wiley.

Teasdale, J., & Barnard, P. (1993). *Affect, cognition and change*. Hove, England: Erlbaum.

Teasdale, J. D., & Fogarty, S. J. (1979). Differential effects of induced mood on retrieval of pleasant and unpleasant events from episodic memory. *Journal of Abnormal Psychology, 88*, 248–257.

Treisman, A. M., & Gelade, G. (1980). A feature integration theory of attention. *Cognitive Psychology, 12*, 97–136.

Wegner, D. M., Erber, R., & Zanakos, S. (1993). Ironic processes in the mental control of mood and mood-related thought. *Journal of Personality and Social Psychology, 65*, 1093–1104.

Williams, J. M. G., Watts, F. N., MacLeod, C., & Mathews, A. (1997). *Cognitive psychology and emotional disorders* (2nd ed.). Chichester, England: Wiley.

# VI

## Personality

# 34

# INTRODUCTION: PERSONALITY

H. Hill Goldsmith and Richard J. Davidson

Personality is one of broadest and thus hardest to delineate subareas of psychological science. Investigators who employ a traitlike approach to individual differences in the domains of psychophysiology, psychometrics, clinical disorders, social relations, and development might define themselves as personality psychologists, or at least might have done so at some stages of the development of the field of psychology. Thus, the boundaries for the content of this part of the *Handbook* are somewhat arbitrary and much that might qualify as personality research in a broad sense appears in virtually every other section of this *Handbook*.

In this part, we have included three chapters that represent important trends in personality research—trends that we expect will help define the intersection of personality and affective science during the coming years. On the other hand, some areas where personality research and the study of affect intersect have been treated extensively in prior literature, and we judged it unnecessary to recount the issues within this *Handbook*.

Historically, several fundamental issues required resolution before traditional trait-oriented personality research meaningfully integrated emotion concepts. One such issue was whether emotion had an organizing role for behavior or instead functioned more as a factor that interrupted ongoing behavior. It is easy to say that emotion plays both roles, but the organizing role is the one that would seem crucial for personality development and functioning. Over the first part of the past half-century, the view that emotion was an organizer of behavior had only a few advocates,

exemplified by the seminal perspective of Leeper (1948). Several influential theorists emphasized the disruptive nature of emotion (Arnold, 1960; Simon, 1967), and it was only in the 1980s that the organizational role began to dominate thinking in the area (e.g., Lazarus, 1991).

Several contemporary theorists, including Goldsmith and Campos (1982) and Clark and Watson (1999), view the emotional aspects of personality as temperament. This view reflects Allport's (1937) definition of temperament: "Temperament refers to the characteristic phenomena of an individual's emotional nature, including his susceptibility to emotional stimulation, his customary strength and speed of response, the quality of his prevailing mood, and all peculiarities of fluctuation and intensity in mood" (p. 54). Thus, emotion sometimes enters into the study of personality via temperament and then interacts with attitudes, self-concepts, contextual influences, and other factors in personality functioning. This tradition is represented in several chapters in part III, "Genetics and Development."

Another prominent affect-related issue in personality research is the distinction between "trait" and "state." Emotional phenomena have been considered part of the state domain, and thus systematically excluded from the trait domain—for instance, in the research underlying the Five Factor approach to personality by Tupes and Christol (1961) and others. The investigation of "state" features of personality has proceeded relatively independently of the study of trait features, and this work is not covered extensively in this *Handbook*. Watson's (2001) recent monograph on the dispositional nature of mood reviews much of the relevant literature.

Substantial effort has been devoted to the study of the psychological structure of the meaning of emotion words. When these words are used to describe the self, researchers hope to discover the psychological structure of consciously experienced emotional states. Research in this tradition has a long tradition (Block, 1957; Goldberg, 1982). Study participants are typically asked to judge—among other attributes—the similarity of words such as *daring, defiant, delighted, demanding, depressed, disagreeable, disappointed, discouraged, disgusted,* and so on, or to rate how well such terms describe the self or others. In delineating the words that qualify for such studies, a basic finding is that more emotion terms exist to describe hedonically negative than positive emotion phenomena, at least in English. (Thus, the shape of the affective semantic space in English might be more like a pear, with a broad negative pole and a narrower positive one.) When a large corpus of emotion words is analyzed, a structure of the semantic "affective space" emerges from factor analysis or multidimensional scaling, although the best way to describe this space has been a long-running controversy (e.g., Shaver, Schwartz, Kirson, & O'Connor, 1987). This space has often been depicted as a circumplex (Lorr & McNair, 1965; Russell, 1980), which can be generated by two underlying dimensions. The most widely accepted two-dimensional account of the semantic affective space entails nearly orthogonal positive affect and negative affect factors, each ranging from highly activated to nonactivated (Watson & Tellegen, 1985). The most popular instrument based on this conceptualization is the PANAS (Positive Affect Negative Affect Scale; Watson & Tellegen, 1985). An alternative two-dimensional structure includes a bipolar pleasure dimension and an activation dimension (Feldman Barrett & Russell, 1999). One proposal for integrating these alternatives is a three-level hierarchy with a broad bipolar happiness versus unhappiness at the top, the relatively independent positive affect and negative affect dimensions at an intermediate level, and the discrete emotions at the base (Tellegen, Watson, & Clark, 1999).

A related issue that concerns personality researchers is how to characterize affective phenomena: as traits, as moods, or as emotional responses (Davidson & Ekman, 1994). An embedded controversy within this issue is whether a dimensional versus a discrete affect approach better captures the structure of affective phenomena. Emotional responses are most often treated as discrete phenomena (Ekman, 1992). Moods are characterized both dimensionally and categorically, and a widely accepted taxonomy of affective traits that differs from the emotional response and mood taxonomies is lacking. The discrete affect approach tends to draw much more fully from sources other than the language of emotion, and it seems clear that these other sources (behavior, physiology) are

necessary to resolve this issue, as well as to place personality research more generally on the cutting edge of advances in affective science.

A few other issues that are not covered substantially in this part deserve mention owing to their importance for personality research on affect. One of these issues is the role of culture on emotional expression and understanding (Kitayama & Markus, 1994); see part VIII for coverage of cultural issues. Another is the interface of personality, psychopathology, and affect. Chapters elsewhere in the *Handbook* by Newman, by Mineka, and by Kagan all consider the interface of these three concepts. A third perspective not well covered in this part is the neo-Pavlovian perspective on affect and personality (e.g., Nebylitsyn, 1972; Rusalov, 1989; Teplov, 1964). Basic concepts of affect and activity from the neo-Pavlovian perspective are not isomorphic with Western concepts, but several researchers have sought to interpret neo-Pavlovian concepts to Western researchers; Strelau (1998) has probably offered the most compelling synthetic perspective. An issue emphasized in the neo-Pavlovian tradition is the role of individual differences in certain parameters of central nervous system function and their import for personality processes. Modern approaches to individual differences in brain function and their relevance to emotion-related personality characteristics are covered in some of the chapters in part I of the *Handbook* on neuroscience. Finally, the issue of emotional regulation, featured in other sections of the *Handbook*, has also become central in the personality sphere (Larsen, 2000).

Despite the diversity of the methodological approaches described in this part, one approach that is not treated fully deserves emphasis here. The motivating idea of this approach is that assessing individuals' emotional experience and moods "on-line" in natural contexts will be uniquely revealing of its nature. Early exemplars of the approach (e.g., Zevon & Tellegen, 1982) used adjective checklists completed after blocks of a few hours. Subjects completed these checklists once or more per day for periods of weeks or months; thus, each person was the subject of an idiographic analysis of daily mood. This methodology probably entailed some recall and reconstruction of the mood. With the advent of pagers and other technology, the investigator can assume much more control over the timing of sampling and approach more closely the on-line ideal. This experience-sampling methodology has wide-ranging applications in testing theories of personality functioning (Diener, Larsen, Levine, & Emmons, 1985; Kahneman, 1999).

## The Chapters of This Part

The part opens with Derryberry and Reed's summary of significant theoretical work integrating individual differences in emotional reactivity with contemporary understandings of cognitive science. Their work is informed by an unusually deep understanding of cognitive processes. Derryberry and Reed emphasize that cognitive processes (e.g., attentional and perceptual processes) that regulate, and otherwise interact with, affective processes in the brain can be the source of individual differences in behavior that we typically view as "emotional." Thus, a small number of emotion systems in the brain, as postulated by, for example, Gray and Panksepp (references in the chapter), can generate the wide range of human emotions. This chapter also emphasizes that the cognition-emotion relationship is bidirectional; emotional activity often precedes cognitive processing. One of their conclusions is worth quoting as a preview of the chapter: "Emotional processing is thus highly distributed and interactive, with individual differences arising at many locations within the processing system. This complexity makes it difficult to isolate a single source of individual differences. [But] . . . easy to appreciate the diversity and subtlety of these differences." The chapter offers a systematic treatment of the evidence for perceptual (both external and internal inputs) and conceptual (appraisals of both the importance of input and the ability to cope the associated events) influences on emotion. In doing so, it incorporates much of the best work from social cognitive and clinical approaches. The chapter concludes with a consideration of emotional influences that motivate cognitive information processing. Among other processes, they consider emotional effects on activation and attentional processing, incorporating cognitive processes elucidated by G. Bower and M. Posner (references in the chapter). This chapter is unusual in its treatment of cognition and affect while maintaining a focus on individual differences and adaptation throughout.

The second chapter in this part, by Krohne, treats individual differences in emotionality from several perspectives. It recognizes that much research in the area is largely descriptive and provides an overview of major concepts intended to reflect differences in emotional reactivity. European approaches are well represented in this overview, and physiological sources of individuality are also included. The chapter offers an important argument that structural considerations (often linked to trait concepts) and processing considerations (sometimes linked to situational demands) are not fundamentally in opposition, but that global and uncontextualized trait concepts (e.g., neuroticism) require revision to incorporate goals, self-regulatory competencies, and other cognitive-affective units. Theoretical positions of Mischel, Lazarus, and Scherer (see chapter for references) are described and evaluated, along with the author's own theory of coping. The latter theory distinguishes vigilant (approach-oriented) and avoidant coping processes and views them as dispositional preferences related to personality. Empir-

ical evidence reviewed at the end of the chapter supports this theoretical approach.

The final chapter in this part, by Carstensen and colleagues, argues that affect is at the core of personality traits throughout the life span. Additionally, changes in responses to emotion-eliciting events and in the types of such events typically encountered—that is, change in emotional experiences—account for age differences in personality over the life span. These authors point out the "fundamental disconnect" between the literature on infant and childhood emotion and its regulation and the literature on personality in adulthood and old age. Then, the chapter exemplifies how such connections can and should be made, enriching both literatures. This chapter has a remarkable range, encompassing temperament, attachment, emotional regulation and understanding, and the development of autobiographical memory during early development (and echoing themes treated in part III of the Handbook). Its major focus is on adulthood, where evidence is presented that emotions become more salient for older adults, and that older adults not only tend to maintain intact emotional functioning but actually regulate emotions better than younger individuals. The chapter also conveys some findings using experience-sampling methodology, an innovative approach improved by recent technology (e.g., pagers) that allows a dense sampling of interpretations of individuals' emotional states during daily activities. In its concluding pages, the chapter treats the authors' own "socioemotional selectivity" theory, the literature on well-being in later life, the role of context in affective experience, and the implications of emotional processing for mental and physical health.

One of the important conclusions about the topic of personality and emotion is that individual differences in parameters of emotional reactivity and affective style are now being addressed in all of the various subareas within the affective sciences. Every section of this Handbook contains chapters that make some reference to individual differences. In some sense, one of the key goals of personality research—to underscore the importance of individual differences—is being realized in a major way in the affective sciences since work on individual differences has infused virtually every major research tradition and approach in the study of emotion. In this sense, research on individual differences is less likely to be segregated as a separate area but rather is becoming an important component of all other topics within the affective sciences.

## REFERENCES

Allport, G. W. (1937). *Personality: A psychological interpretation*. New York: Henry Holt.

Arnold, M. B. (1960). *Emotion and personality* (Vols. 1 and 2). New York: Columbia University Press.

Block, J. (1957). Studies in the phenomenology of emotion. *Journal of Abnormal and Social Psychology, 54,* 358–363.

Bruer, J. T. (1999). *The myth of the first three years.* New York: Free Press.

Clark, L. A., & Watson, D. (1999). Temperament: A new paradigm for trait psychology. In L. A. Pervin & O. P. John (Eds.), *Handbook of personality: Theory and research* (2nd ed.; pp. 399–423). New York: Guilford Press.

Davidson, R. J., & Ekman, P. (Eds.). (1994). *Questions about emotion.* New York: Oxford University Press.

Diener, E., Larsen, R. J., Levine, S., & Emmons, R. A. (1985). Intensity and frequency: Dimensions underlying positive and negative affect. *Journal of Personality and Social Psychology, 48,* 1253–1265.

Ekman, P. (1992). An argument for basic emotions. *Cognition and Emotion, 6,* 169–200.

Feldman Barrett, L., & Russell, J. A. (1999). The structure of current affect: Controversies and emerging consensus. *Current Directions in Psychological Science, 8,* 10–14.

Goldberg, L. R. (1982). From Ace to zombie: Some explorations in the language of personality. In C. D. Spielberger & J. N. Butcher (Eds.), *Advances in personality assessment* (Vol 1, pp. 203–234). Hilldale, NJ: Erlbaum.

Goldsmith, H. H., & Campos, J. J. (1982). Toward a theory of infant temperament. In R. N. Emde & R. J. Harmon (Eds.), *The development of attachment and affiliative systems* (pp. 161–193). New York: Plenum Press.

Kahneman, D. (1999). Objective happiness. In E. Kahneman, E. Diener, & N. Schwartz. (Eds.), *Well-being: The foundations of hedonic psychology* (pp. 3–25). New York: Russell Sage Foundation.

Kitayama, S., & Markus, H. R. (1994). *Emotion and culture: Empirical studies of mutual influence.* Washington, DC: American Psychological Association.

Larsen, R. J. (2000). Toward a science of mood regulation. *Psychological Inquiry, 11,* 129–141.

Lazarus, R. S. (1991). *Emotion and adaptation.* New York: Oxford University Press.

Leeper, R. W. (1948). A motivational theory of emotion to replace "emotion as disorganized response." *Psychological Review, 55,* 5–21.

Lorr, M., & McNair, D. M. (1965). Expansion of the interpersonal behavior circle. *Journal of Personality and Social Psychology, 2,* 823–830.

Nebylitsyn, V. D. (1972). *Fundamental properties of the human nervous system.* New York: Plenum Press.

Rusalov, V. M. (1989). Object-related and communicative aspects of human temperament: A new questionnaire of the structure of temperament. *Personality and Individual Differences, 10,* 817–827.

Russell, J. A. (1980). A circumplex model of affect. *Journal of Personality and Social Psychology, 39,* 1161–1178.

Shaver, P., Schwartz, J., Kirson, D., & O'Connor, C. (1987). Emotion knowledge: Further exploration of a prototype approach. *Journal of Personality and Social Psychology, 52,* 1061–1086.

Simon, H. A. (1967). Motivational and emotional controls of cognition. *Psychological Review, 74,* 29–39.

Strelau, J. (1998). *Temperament: A psychological perspective.* New York: Plenum Press.

Tellegen, A., Watson, D., & Clark, L. A. (1999). On the dimensional and hierarchical structure of affect. *Psychological Science, 10,* 297–303.

Teplov, B. M. (1964). Problems in the study of general types of higher nervous activity in man and animals. In J. A. Gray (Ed.), *Pavlov's typology: Recent theoretical and experimental developments from the laboratory of B. M. Teplov* (pp. 3–153). Oxford, England: Pergamon Press.

Tupes, E. C., & Christal, R. E. (1961). *Recurrent personality factors based on trait ratings.* USAF ASD Technical Report, No. 61–97.

Watson. D. (2001). *Mood and temperament.* New York: Guilford Press.

Watson, D., & Tellegen, A. (1985). Toward a consensual structure of mood. *Psychological Bulletin, 98,* 219–235.

Zevon, M. A., & Tellegen, A. (1982). The structure of mood change: An idiographic/nomothetic analysis. *Journal of Personality and Social Psychology, 43,* 111–122.

# 35

## INFORMATION PROCESSING APPROACHES TO INDIVIDUAL DIFFERENCES IN EMOTIONAL REACTIVITY

Douglas Derryberry and Marjorie A. Reed

Individual differences in emotional reactivity are commonly approached from two contrasting perspectives. Cognitive approaches emphasize the perceptual and conceptual processes thought to cause emotion, while temperament approaches are more concerned with emotional and arousal processes. Although these approaches have developed independently, they are complementary in that they adopt different levels of analysis and focus on different processes. This makes it possible to employ a broader framework and an intermediate level of analysis to integrate the two approaches. This chapter employs current models of information processing as such a comprehensive and integrative framework.

Information-processing approaches have several advantages. Regarding the levels of analysis, temperament models tend to view individual differences from a bottom-up perspective grounded in physiological processes. In contrast, cognitive approaches adopt a top-down approach that emphasizes higher level conceptual processing. Fortunately, information-processing models provide an intermediate-level language that can accommodate processing expressed in terms of both interacting neural systems and abstract conceptual structures. Regarding the different processes, cognitive models focus on the perceptual and conceptual processes, whereas temperament models emphasize emotional, arousal, and response processes. Modern information-processing models are based

on extensive study of many aspects of human performance, ranging from the earliest perception to the latest response. This provides the flexibility to incorporate emotion-related factors at all phases of processing. Finally, information-processing approaches provide detailed models of certain crucial processes, such as attention, that tend to be neglected in most temperament and cognitive approaches. In short, information processing provides a framework for enriching as well as integrating the major approaches to emotional reactivity.

In this chapter we take a broad view of information-processing approaches to emotional reactivity. We work within the framework of a general processing system, schematically illustrated in Figure 35.1. At the center of the network are pathways devoted to different emotions. Many temperament models assume that individual differences in the reactivity of these "emotional systems" are pivotal to personality and clinical problems. As illustrated on the diagram's left side, the emotional systems receive perceptual inputs conveying exteroceptive and interoceptive information, as well as conceptual input concerned with appraising the information's significance and with developing coping options. Most cognitive theorists focus on the perceptual, and in particular conceptual, inputs as the primary source of individual differences. Upon activation, the emotional systems feed back to activate the perceptual and conceptual processors. As illustrated on

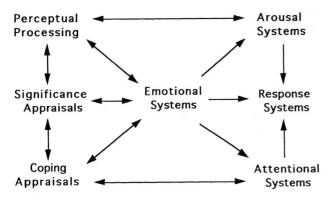

Figure 35.1 Schematic diagram illustrating the inputs (left side) and outputs (right side) of the central emotional systems. Developing emotional activity is influenced by converging perceptual and conceptual information relevant to the situation's significance and the individual's coping potential. Activated emotional systems influence developing perceptual and conceptual activity by direct connections, by regulating responses that generate interoceptive information, and by regulating attentional and arousal systems that modulate perceptual and conceptual pathways. The diagram does not illustrate the following connections: (1) direct connections from the perceptual and conceptual appraisals to the arousal, response, and attentional systems; (2) direct connections from arousal, response, and attentional systems to all perceptual and conceptual processes.

the diagram's right side, the emotional systems adjust arousal, attentional, and response mechanisms, which feed back to modulate the entire range of perceptual and conceptual processing. Recent findings suggest that individual differences in processes such as arousal and attention may further shape emotional reactivity. A major goal of this chapter is to demonstrate that individual differences can be expressed at multiple levels within this processing system.

We begin with individual differences arising from the emotional systems, followed by their perceptual and conceptual inputs. We end by considering the outputs of the emotional systems and, in particular, the ways in which emotion influences cognition. The general model is highly interactive, with cognitive and emotional processes shaping one another in multiple ways. Although Figure 35.1 may suggest a sequence of successive stages, the processing within and between "stages" is parallel and temporally overlapping, with multiple perceptual, conceptual, and response pathways functioning simultaneously. The figure may also suggest one-directional flows of information between stages, but as will be seen, top-down influences from later to earlier stages must also be considered. Due to this complexity, we tend to emphasize the various types of emotion-relevant information processed within each stage, making rather limited references to the underlying computations. An emphasis on informational content pro-

vides a useful view of the richness and uniqueness of individual variability. At the process level, we describe the extensive "automaticity" involved within the system, but at the same time, we emphasize the multiple regulatory processes that serve to constrain and guide this reactivity. It is hoped that this will provide a better appreciation of the processing system as a whole as it relates to an individual's functioning personality.

## Emotional Systems

The emotional systems emphasized in temperament approaches are most often viewed as an interface between perceptual/cognitive and response stages. In anatomical terms, perceptual and cognitive information from the cortex activates emotional circuits within the limbic system, which in turn regulate response, arousal, and attentional processes within the brainstem (Derryberry & Tucker, 1992). Emotional circuits are often viewed as "motivational" systems in the sense that they respond to significant cortical input by organizing an adaptive response pattern (across response, arousal, and attentional subsystems) designed to deal with the significant situation. This response pattern generates the interoceptive information involved in emotional feelings, but it is the adaptive, organizing, and regulatory (i.e., motivational) nature of these systems that is fundamental to their role in information processing.

Most temperament approaches focus on individual differences in the reactivity of the emotional systems as pivotal to personality. Reactivity refers to the sensitivity and responsivity of the circuits to incoming information, and can be conceptualized in terms of the response's threshold, peak intensity, rise time, and recovery time. It is usually assumed that reactivity varies continuously across individuals for distinct emotional systems. The resulting dimensions of emotional reactivity are thought to be fundamental to the broad (extraversion, neuroticism, etc.) and specific (anxiety, impulsivity, etc.) dimensions of personality. Individuals at the extremes of the dimensions, either high or low in reactivity, are most vulnerable to clinical problems.

The greatest challenge facing temperament approaches is that of identifying the fundamental emotional systems. So far, there is a general consensus supporting at least three such systems. The first is a positive or appetitive system related to approach behavior. The positive system has been described as an approach system (Davidson, 1994; Sutton & Davidson, 1997), a behavioral activation system (BAS; Gray, 1987a, 1987c; Gray & McNaughton, 1996), a behavioral facilitation system (Depue & Collins, 1999; Depue & Iacono, 1989), and a seeking or exploratory/foraging system (Panksepp, 1986, 1998). The positive system is often viewed as responding to conditioned perceptual information signaling reward and nonpunishment to generate approach behavior accompanied by emotional states of hope and relief (Depue & Iacono, 1989; Gray, 1987a). Depue and Iacono (1989) suggest that the appetitive system also promotes irritative aggression when goals are blocked, and Panksepp (1986) proposes that the system can also be engaged by regulatory imbalances (e.g., hunger) to facilitate search behavior and a state of "desire." Davidson's (1994) "approach system" generates "pre-goal attainment" positive affects such as eagerness and enthusiasm, as the goal is represented in working memory. Depue and Collins (1999) emphasize the processing involved in identifying the most rewarding or intense incentive within an environmental context.

Individual differences in the positive system are commonly linked to the personality dimension of extraversion, with positive emotionality increasing as one moves from introverts to extraverts (Larsen & Ketelaar, 1989; Watson & Clark, 1992). However, others propose that its reactivity underlies an "impulsivity dimension" that increases from the stable introvert to the neurotic extravert within Eysenck's two-dimensional space (Gray, 1987b; Wallace, Newman, & Bachorowski, 1991). Clinical problems may arise from either an overreactive or an underreactive positive system. Overreactivity has been related to manic and impulsive disorders (e.g., conduct problems, secondary psychopathy), whereas an underreactive system may promote depression (Fowles, 1994; Gray, 1994).

A second emotional system involves negative emotions related to fear and anxiety. Examples include Gray's (Gray, 1982; Gray & McNaughton, 1996) behavioral inhibition system, Panksepp's (1986, 1998) fear system, Gilbert and Trower's (1990) defense system, and Davidson's (Davidson, 1994; Sutton & Davidson, 1997) withdrawal system. Panksepp's and Davidson's models focus on general avoidance behavior related to fear. Gray's approach emphasizes anticipatory anxiety, with the behavioral inhibition system (BIS) producing inhibition to signals of punishment (anxiety), signals of nonreward (frustration), and novelty (anxiety). In a recent extension, Gray and McNaughton (1996) propose that the BIS is particularly involved in resolving conflicts in contexts eliciting competing approach and avoidance tendencies, a process referred to by Blanchard and Blanchard (1988) as risk assessment. Examples include social contexts that offer possible rejection as well as acceptance, and achievement contexts that offer failure as well as success.

Regarding individual differences, some view anxiety as a component of more general negative emotionality, which is usually equated with the dimension of neuroticism (Larsen & Ketelaar, 1989; Watson & Clark, 1992). Alternatively, Gray views BIS variability as underlying an anxiety dimension that runs from the stable extravert to the neurotic introvert (Gray, 1982; Wallace et al., 1991). In the clinical domain, an overreactive anxiety system is assumed to pro-

mote a general predisposition for various anxiety disorders, including generalized anxiety disorder, phobias, and obsessive-compulsive disorder. Owing to its crucial inhibitory function, an underreactive anxiety system may contribute to various disinhibitory or impulsive disorders, including conduct problems and primary psychopathy (Barlow, Chorpita, & Turovsky, 1996; Fowles, 1994; Gray, 1994).

A third emotional system promotes more primitive forms of defensive behavior. Gray has described a "fight/flight" system that responds to unconditioned punishment to produce escape behaviors and defensive aggression. Similar circuits have been described as a "rage" system by Panksepp (1986, 1998). Physiological evidence suggests that the flight and fight circuits are distinct (Bandler & Keay, 1996; Risold, Canteras, & Swanson, 1994), and thus it may prove useful to view this circuitry in terms of separate fear and anger systems. In any event, Gray has viewed the fight/flight system as related to the psychoticism dimension of Eysenck's three-factor model. Approaches emphasizing "negative emotionality" would view the fear and anger produced by this system as combining with anxiety to increase neuroticism. It is also possible that the anger/defensive-aggressive functions of the system may contribute to the "hostile" pole of the agreeableness dimension found in five-factor models. If the fear and anger circuits are viewed as separable, people with highly reactive fear circuits may be vulnerable to panic attacks (Gray & McNaughton, 1996), while those with highly reactive anger circuits may be prone to "anger attacks" (Barlow et al., 1996).

A final and less researched emotional system (or set of systems) involves affiliative, nurturant, and affectionate behaviors. MacDonald (1992, 1995) describes an affectional system, which is viewed as a specialized social reward system that evolved to facilitate close family relationships. By promoting feelings of warmth, the system supports feelings of empathy, identification with the parents, and the adoption of parental values. Along related lines, Panksepp (1986) suggests that social cohesion is supported by a separation distress-panic system. This system responds to the loss of social support by mobilizing separation distress behaviors and sets the stage for intense reward and bonding when the caregiver returns. Individual differences in these systems should contribute to the agreeableness dimension, with increasing warmth, trust, and empathy evident as one moves from the hostile pole to the agreeable pole. In the clinical domain, an underreactive affectional system may contribute to the alienated, cold, and callous characteristics of some psychopaths, whereas an overreactive system may promote problems involving separation anxiety and dependency.

From a information-processing perspective, the emotional systems can be viewed as relatively independent circuits that function in a parallel way to detect and respond to specific forms of information. At the same time, these parallel systems are likely to interact and influence one another. In some cases, multiple systems may become simultaneously active, resulting in a blend of emotions. For example, Panksepp (1998) suggests that defensive aggression results from activation of the fear and rage systems. In other cases, it is likely that an activated system will suppress activity in other systems. Gray has suggested that anxiety-related circuits inhibit appetitive circuits under threatening conditions, thereby protecting the individual from inadvertent approach. When exerted across long periods of time, such inhibition may be one of the factors contributing to the reduced positive affect and approach behavior often seen in depression (Fowles, 1988, 1994). Inhibitory connections also help explain a variety of "rebound" phenomena seen in emotions. A rapid offset of intense activity within anxiety circuits may release the reward system from inhibition, resulting in an opponent state of relief or elation (Grossberg & Gutowski, 1987). Similarly, Panksepp (1998) has suggested that a suppression of activity within the appetitive seeking system may disinhibit the rage system, leading to feelings of anger and frustration when positive expectations are not fulfilled. While the above examples involve inhibitory interactions, it is also likely that emotional systems may at times excite or recruit one another, forming "coalitions" to deal with a crucial situation (Gallistel, 1980). Given threatening circumstances, for example, anxiety-related systems may recruit other systems involved in finding and approaching safety or relief. The two systems could then work in parallel to promote effective avoidance of danger and approach of safety.

Models emphasizing individual differences in such basic emotional systems provide a powerful approach to individual differences, particularly when multiple systems are viewed in relation to major personality dimensions. They also provide useful perspectives on clinical problems, not only in the simple examples mentioned above but also in cases involving comorbid disorders (e.g., anxious depression). In addition, they fit well within a developmental perspective, for the systems begin to function early in life and can be studied longitudinally in relation to developing cognition. Finally, emotional systems fit well within an information-processing approach. As described in later sections, their inputs are fairly well described, and their outputs involve typical processes such as arousal, attention, and response selection.

As noted above, however, a major challenge facing temperament models is that of identifying the set of major emotional systems. Some cognitive theorists have argued that as few as two systems (positive and negative) are necessary (Ortony & Turner, 1990), whereas some evolutionary approaches suggest that many highly specific systems are available (e.g., Cosmides & Tooby, 1987). As will become clearer in later sections, this is a crucial issue because the four or five systems described above cannot easily account for the range of human emotions, which includes many complex states such as guilt, shame, gratitude, admiration, and so on. Future discoveries of additional systems or subsystems may help in this respect, but it may also turn out that a relatively small set of emotional systems depends on cognition to provide differentiated emotional states.

Perhaps the most fundamental issue involving emotional systems concerns their functional relation to other information-processing systems within the brain. The dominant paradigm in psychology views emotion as a result of cognitive processing: Incoming information is processed through perceptual and conceptual stages, and as a result of such appraisal, an emotional response is activated. Emotion then functions as an early stage of response processing, biasing peripheral motor, autonomic, and endocrine activity in terms of the cognitive appraisal. It is worth noting that some cognitive theorists suggest doing away with an emotional stage altogether, simply allowing appraisal processes to directly bias responses (Frijda, 1986; Ortony & Turner, 1990). In contrast, others have argued that emotional systems function as command or executive systems (e.g., Panksepp, 1992). Emotional systems are viewed as working concurrently to monitor the importance of incoming perceptual and conceptual information. If significant input is detected, the activated emotional system assumes a control function: Peripheral response systems are organized to prepare adaptive responses, and at same time, central networks are modulated so as to prepare adaptive perceptual and conceptual processing (Derryberry & Tucker, 1992). In terms of information-processing stages, emotional systems would form the basis of a central decision/executive stage that exerted a top-down bias upon earlier cognitive processing and a feed-forward influence on subsequent response stages.

Other chapters in this volume discuss these issues in greater detail. Our approach, in its emphasis on individual differences and information processing, may provide some clarification. As will be seen in the next sections, emotional reactivity depends not only on the emotional systems but also on information arising from perceptual and conceptual pathways. However, emotional activity often precedes cognitive processing, allowing emotion-related states of arousal and attention to influence conceptual processing. Emotional processing is thus highly distributed and interactive, with individual differences arising at many locations within the processing system. This complexity makes it difficult to isolate a single source of individual differences. But, on the other hand, it makes it easy to appreciate the diversity and subtlety of these differences.

## Perceptual Influences on Emotion

A wide range of perceptual information, both exteroceptive and interoceptive, is involved in eliciting emotion. Some of these inputs have direct projections to the emotional systems that allow them to bypass or at least precede more extensive cognitive processing. Such direct connections are supported by anatomical and physiological data indicating that perceptual circuits within the brain stem, thalamus, and cortex project directly upon emotional circuits of the limbic system (Derryberry & Tucker, 1992; LeDoux, 1996). They are also consistent with psychological data demonstrating relatively automatic processing of emotional information prior to or in the absence of high-level cognition (e.g., Bargh, Litt, Pratto, & Spielman, 1988; Zajonc, 1980).

### Exteroceptive Information

A useful general approach to the exteroceptive stimulus properties important to emotion was first formulated by Berlyne (1960, 1971). *Psychophysical* stimulus properties refer to the physical characteristics of the stimulation, such as its intensity, rate, size, and complexity. *Collative* properties refers to the information's degree of match or mismatch with existing perceptual models, giving rise to perceptual experiences that are familiar and expected as opposed to surprising, incongruous, novel, and so on. *Ecological* properties of the stimulus refer to its relevance to ongoing motivational needs, such as the smell of food or the sight of a predator. Berlyne further proposed that as these perceptual properties increase, the reticular activating system increases the individual's level of arousal. In turn, the perceptually generated arousal impacts two basic emotional systems. As arousal increases from low to moderate levels, a "reward system" becomes progressively activated, resulting in an increase in positive affect that peaks at moderate levels of stimulation or arousal. As arousal increases from moderate to high levels, as might occur in very intense or novel environments, an aversion system is progressively engaged, leading to an increase in negative affect. By summing the activity within the reward and aversion systems, Berlyne was able to produce the famous curvilinear function relating affect to stimulation: Positive affect peaks at a moderate or "optimal" level of stimulation, and fades into negative affect at low and high levels of stimulation.

While Berlyne extended this model to study aesthetics and humor, it was Eysenck (1967) who applied it to individual differences. Eysenck proposed that differences in extraversion are based on reactivity of the reticular activating system. Introverts are assumed to have a more highly reactive reticular system than extraverts, and are thus more sensitive to the arousing effects of perceptual information (i.e., its intensity, rate, unexpectedness, and so on). Such greater arousability causes introverts to attain their optimal level of stimulation at lower levels than extraverts do. Given their low optimal levels, introverts tend to avoid more intense and novel sources of information, and actively seek out less stimulating information. In contrast, extraverts' higher optimal levels motivate them to seek out more stimulating environments and avoid those featuring less intense and familiar information. Although much behavioral evidence is consistent with Eysenck's model, more recent approaches have moved toward more specific and multidimensional views of "arousal." Nevertheless, the evidence relating psychophysical, collative, and ecological stimulus properties to extraversion remains strong, which suggests that their influence may not require mediation by a general arousal mechanism.

A more detailed model emphasizing perceptual information has been developed by Gray. As mentioned above, Gray's model emphasizes unconditioned pain and nonreward inputs to the fight/flight system, conditioned reward and nonpunishment inputs to the behavioral activation system, and conditioned punishment, conditioned nonreward, and novel inputs to the behavioral inhibition system. Presumably, these systems have evolved to respond differently to distinct perceptual inputs. For example, the fight/flight system generates different defensive behaviors depending on the proximity or immediacy of a punishing signal. If a prey animal observes a distant predator, it may respond by directed escape in an opposite or safe direction. If the predator is closer, a freezing response may be elicited. If the predator is even closer and no escape route is available, explosive escape or defensive aggression may occur. If the predator is making physical contact and the prey is injured, then a form of tonic immobility (playing dead) may prove adaptive (Barlow et al., 1996; Blanchard & Blanchard, 1988; Gray & McNaughton, 1996). Even with relatively primitive emotions, sophisticated perceptual processing is required in recognizing the threat and computing spatial and temporal relations.

Although models such as Gray's emphasize perceptual inputs, the actual source of individual differences lies in their target emotional systems. Presumably, a strong anxiety system facilitates classically conditioned connections involving anxiety-relevant information. It is also possible, however, that individual differences arise from perceptual systems themselves. Marks and Neese (1994) examined anxious symptoms from an evolutionary perspective and suggest a variety of perceptual inputs that would have been adaptive in promoting fear. These include snakes, spiders, heights, storms, thunder, lightning, darkness, blood, strangers, social scrutiny, separation, and leaving the home range. While variability in the target anxiety system may promote a general vulnerability to such stimuli, variability in the perceptual processes themselves may be required to explain the variety of anxious symptoms across individuals.

At this point, it is unclear whether genetic differences in perceptual processors promote distinct anxious symptoms. A clear alternative is that the perceptual systems are tuned through experience, with various forms of learning selectively stabilizing perceptual inputs to emotional systems. In the case of social fears, for example, Ohman has found superior classical conditioning for slides of angry as compared to happy or neutral facial stimuli. Such effects appear rather automatic, elicited even when the angry conditioned stimulus is presented subliminally (Ohman, 1993; Ohman & Soares, 1993). These findings are consistent with an evolutionary preparedness to acquire anxiety to angry, critical, or rejecting facial stimuli. Mineka and Zinbarg (1996) note that a large proportion of people with social phobias report that their fears are directly related to some earlier traumatic experience. Even if no trauma occurs, some children may acquire anxiety through observational learning (e.g., observing a parent's anxiety in social contexts). This research underscores the possibility that anxious reactions may develop in some individuals with initially weak anxiety-related emotional systems. Provided that the relevant experiences and learning occur, the perceptual systems may enhance the emotional systems' reactivity.

### Interoceptive Information

In addition to external perceptual inputs, interoceptive information from the body may often initiate emotional reactions. Animal research suggests that while superficial pain elicits flight and defensive aggression, deep pain (somatic and visceral) gives rise to a quiescent state involving a decreased responsivity. This reaction is similar to those following injury or social defeat and perhaps to human depression (Bandler & Keay, 1996; Bandler & Shipley, 1994).

It is also likely that interoceptive information related to energy states has an emotional impact. A multidimensional approach by Thayer (1989) has identified two primary energy states—energetic arousal and tense arousal. These energy states align fairly well with hedonic states of positive affect and negative affect, respectively. Additional evidence can be found in the positive states arising from the use of stimulant drugs, such as those that facilitate dopamine, as well as the close relation between low energy and depressed states. Although it is not yet possible to describe the peripheral sources of energy information, likely candidates are peripheral autonomic (e.g., sympathetic) and endocrine (e.g., cortisol) events (Dienstbier, 1989).

Other interoceptive inputs relevant to emotion arise from the digestive, cardiovascular, respiratory, and vestibular systems. Digestive sensations of nausea appear closely related to disgust. Sensations from the cardiovascular (e.g., palpitations), respiratory (e.g., suffocation), and vestibular (e.g., dizziness) systems have been viewed as setting off alarm reactions related to panic disorder and agoraphobia (Ehlers & Breuer, 1992; Kenardy, Evans, & Oei, 1992; Klein, 1993; Ohman, 1993). Barlow (Antony & Barlow, 1996; Barlow et al., 1996) has suggested that uncued panic attacks may function as false alarms, which, in the absence of salient external cues, may become conditioned to internal body cues. Such interoceptive conditioning allows for apparently spontaneous panic attacks, triggered by conditioned bodily stimuli such as an increasing heart rate.

Additional interoceptive contributions may involve generalized sensations related to fear and anxiety. McNally (1996) points out that individuals differ not only in their susceptibility to anxious emotions but also in their fear of the associated anxious feelings. Such "fear of fear" likely depends on the person's belief that the experienced anxious symptoms are harmful and thus extends beyond simple perception. Nevertheless, it provides a useful approach to individual differences. Zinbarg, Barlow, and Brown (1997) found McNally's measure, the Anxiety Sensitivity Index, to have a hierarchical structure with three lower order factors: physical concerns (e.g., "It scares me when my heart beats rapidly"); social concerns (e.g., "It is important for me not to appear nervous"); and mental incapacitation concerns (e.g., "When I'm nervous, I worry that I am mentally ill"). Patients suffering from panic disorder were particularly high in physical concerns, social phobics were high in social concerns, and those with generalized anxiety disorder tended to be high on all three factors. Patients with simple phobias were lower than the other groups on all three factors.

In summary, a wide range of perceptual information, both exteroceptive and interoceptive, is involved in eliciting emotion. In terms of individual differences, it is not yet clear whether the primary source of perceptual differences arises from the perceptual systems or from the emotional systems with which they interact. Even if it were the emotional systems, this would in no way diminish the importance of perceptual processes. Exteroceptive and interoceptive processes provide direct access to each person's phenomenal experience, which is essential to understanding individual differences. But at the same time, it is necessary to move beyond perception and consider differences arising from conceptual processing. While perception may initiate activity within an emotional system, it is typically followed by conceptual thought that may amplify or attenuate the developing emotion. We turn next to these conceptual processes.

## Conceptual Influences on Emotion

In many instances emotional relevance is not fully revealed through perceptual processing and must be extracted through further conceptual processing. This can be done through the activation and manipulation of conceptual representations of objects, actions, and events. Many cognitive theorists argue that conceptual processing provides distinct patterns of appraisals that initiate distinct emotions. Individual differences thus arise from different pattern of "emotion-antecedent" appraisals.

Following Lazarus's original insights, we approach conceptual processing in terms of two general forms of appraisals. The processing involved in primary appraisals assesses the importance of perceptual input, whereas secondary appraisals assess the person's capacity to cope with the important events (Lazarus & Folkman, 1984). These general appraisal categories consist of a number of more specific appraisals, allowing for many sources of individual differences. Although we will not be able to do justice to the many cognitive models, other chapters in this volume provide more detailed accounts.

Unfortunately, most models have paid limited attention to the underlying processing mechanisms that generate appraisals. It is therefore worthwhile to briefly consider some potential mechanisms. Perhaps the most utilized mechanism is that of spreading activation, a subthreshold spread of excitation from an activated to related concepts. Spreading activation is usually viewed as an "automatic" process that is difficult to control and often occurs outside of awareness. For example, perceptual pain may activate the concept of disease, which in turn may instantly spread activation to concepts of doctors, hospitals, and so on. Individual differences related to spreading activation will depend in large part upon the learned, structural associations among concepts.

Given a pattern of activated concepts, additional processing operations may be brought into play. The most important from an information processing perspective is that of attention. We discuss attention in more detail later, but in general, it refers to a selective, limited-capacity "facilitation" of the most important information. Closely related to attention is a mechanism of inhibition, which suppresses activated concepts in order to reduce interference with other functions (e.g., awareness, working memory). A more general mechanism involves the "integration" of activated concepts into propositions (e.g., "the pain is a bruise" versus "the pain is a tumor"). Although automatic processing may play a role, evidence suggests that attentional facilitation and inhibition may be crucial to integrating concepts (e.g., Keele & Neill, 1978). A final mechanism relevant to appraisals is a comparison process through which a proposition ("I am shy") is compared to a standard ("I should be outgoing").

## Primary Appraisals

Primary appraisals are concerned with assessing the general importance of incoming or activated information. An initial form appraises "novelty" in terms of more specific appraisals such as *suddenness, familiarity*, and *predictability* (Scherer, 1984, 1993; van Reekum & Scherer, 1997), *change* and *familiarity* (Frijda, 1986), and *unexpectedness* (Ortony, Clore, & Collins, 1988). Novelty may be extracted through perceptual processing, as described above in the models of Berlyne and Gray. However, more subtle forms of novelty arise from mismatches between existing and new propositions and expectancies. While theorists such as Gray would argue that even conceptual novelty would depend on the reactivity of the BIS, cognitive and appraisal models would emphasize learning and cognitive structures as crucial to individual differences in appraising novelty. For example, some anxious people may avoid certain situations, leading to limited or inaccurate expectancies. Their limited conceptual framework may render them more vulnerable to certain unexpected events, and perhaps less sensitive to more subtle forms of novelty.

Another basic form of appraisal focuses on *intrinsic pleasantness* (Scherer, 1984, 1993; van Reekum & Scherer, 1997), *valence* (Frijda, 1986), or *appealingness* (Ortony et al., 1988). Emotional systems such as Gray's BAS or BIS may extract rewards and punishments from simple perceptual inputs (e.g., of a smile or frown), but more abstract processing is often required to evaluate outcomes in complex domains such as achievement, morality, and social behavior. From a cognitive perspective, individual differences may arise from conceptual frameworks that form distinct propositions by integrating abstract concepts such as good-bad and success-failure with various objects, events, and actions.

A third general category of appraisal involves the relevance of the perceptual input to one's needs and goals. These appraisals have been approached in terms of more specific appraisals of *concern relevance, outcome probability, expectation, goal conduciveness*, and *urgency* (Scherer, 1984, 1993); *focality, certainty, presence, open-closed*, and *urgency* (Frijda, 1986); and *likelihood, prospect realization, desirability*, and *proximity* (Ortony et al., 1988). Such appraisals fit well with the notion of emotional systems, for this is precisely the type of information that such systems are designed to respond to. Appetitive and defensive systems may respond to perceptual goals such as food and dangerous objects, but also to more abstract goals related to self, achievement, social, religious, and other needs. While the simpler perceptual processing may generate emotions such as hope, frustration, fear, and relief, conceptual appraisals would lead to more subtle and differentiated versions of these states in which factors such as the outcome probability (likelihood) and urgency are taken into account. Individual differences may arise in many ways, including the strength of the underlying need and consequent goal, the computations involved in estimating a probable outcome, the breadth of factors that are taken into account, their weighting, appraised urgency, and so on (van Reekum & Scherer, 1997). To give an example, some anxious students may respond to an upcoming exam with the simple appraisal "the exam is dangerous," while others may limit their anxiety through appraisals such as "the exam is dangerous but it will probably not be difficult and it is not imminent."

A related form of goal appraisal involves comparisons of the self to a standard. Higgins (1987, 1991) proposed that the "actual self" is compared to two standards: the ideal self and the ought self. Development of the ideal self is thought to be promoted when caregivers emphasize the potential rewards inherent in the child's accomplishments. The ideal self then orients the person to maximize the rewards (i.e., attaining the standard) that generate "cheerful" emotions (e.g., joy) and to minimize the nonrewards (i.e., falling short of the standard) that generate "dejected" emotions (e.g., depression; Higgins, 1996 1997). In contrast, the ought self is facilitated when caregivers emphasize the potential punishments that arise from failures to carry out duties and obligations. The ought self orients the person to minimize punishing outcomes that cause "agitated" emotions (e.g., anxiety) and to maximize nonpunishing outcomes that elicit "quiescent" emotions (e.g., relief).

Individual differences could arise from the content of the actual self, the ideal self, and the ought self, and from the importance assigned to various aspects of these selves. Structural differences are also relevant, such as the distinction between compartmentalized and integrative self organizations (Showers, 1995; Showers & Kling, 1996). In addition, Higgins (1997) suggests that individual variability depends on the person's regulatory focus—that is, whether the underlying motivation favors a "positive outcome focus" (reward and nonreward) or a "negative outcome focus" (e.g., punishment and nonpunishment). It is interesting that Higgins's cognitive approach arrives at eliciting conditions and emotions similar to those emphasized in temperament models such as Gray's. The main difference is that Higgins relates reward and nonreward to a positive outcome focus (e.g., the ideal self) and punishment and nonpunishment to a negative outcome focus (e.g., the ought self), whereas Gray relates reward and nonpunishment to the BAS and punishment and nonreward to the BIS. Although this is a crucial difference, the general convergence of these two approaches again suggests an underlying compatibility of cognitive and temperament approaches.

Conceptual processing also allows for more complex comparisons involving highly abstract representations and standards. In a model of social anxiety, Rapee and Heimberg (1997) suggest that in social situations individuals form an "external self representation" of their appearance and behavior as they think it is seen by others. They also construct a performance standard that they expect the other person(s) to utilize. The external representation is then compared to the performance standard, with discrepancies generating increasing expectancies of a negative evaluation by the other, and thus increasing social anxiety. In this model, individual differences could arise from the external self representation and/or the expected performance standard. Those with relatively negative external representations and high performance standards would be most vulnerable to social anxiety. In addition, Rapee and Heimberg point out that this is a highly demanding form of processing, requiring shifts of attention among one's own behavior, its appearance to the other, the other's performance standard, and the other's reactions.

Beyond comparisons to standards, much theorizing has emphasized the attributions aimed at explaining the causes of positive and negative outcomes. These approaches suggest that individual differences in emotion arise from distinct attributional or "explanatory" styles. Best known is the relationship between depression and a pessimistic style involving internal, stable, and global attributions for failure. Depressed people tend to blame themselves for failure, to view this as a stable shortcoming, and to view it as a global reflection of their character rather than a specific behavioral shortcoming. The tendency to make internal, stable, and global attributions is also evident in trait anxious and clinically anxious persons, which fits with the common comorbidity of anxiety and depression (Mineka, Pury, & Luten, 1995). Tangney (1995) has found different attributional patterns for the self-conscious emotions of shame and guilt. Guilt tends to involve internal, unstable, and specific behavior. In contrast, shame involves more external, stable, and global attributions, leading to a global view of the self as lacking. Weiner (1991) has examined attributions underlying perceived responsibility. When a person's negative actions are attributed to an internal cause, viewing his or her behavior as something that was controllable can lead to anger, but viewing it as uncontrollable can lead to pity.

## Secondary Appraisals

The second general category of appraisals is the secondary appraisals of one's capacity to cope effectively in the significant situation. Secondary appraisals are difficult to separate from primary appraisals, for the two often involve similar information and interact with one another. As described below, however, coping appraisals are more concerned with evaluating response options than stimuli and may involve more attention and less automatic processing.

In evaluating response options, it is crucial that an appropriate object is available in relation to which the response can be directed. Relevant object information can arise from the goal-significance appraisals described above, especially those aspects appraising goal conduciveness (Scherer, 1993). Given appetitive needs, relevant objects include not only the rewarding object (to be approached) but also the potentially frustrating obstacles (to be avoided). Given defensive needs, relevant stimuli include the sources of safety or relief as well as the threatening object itself. To cope with a dangerous predator, for example, the prey animal needs a source of safety (e.g., an escape route, a nearby tree) toward which to direct its escape response.

Beck and Clark (1997) describe a model of anxiety in which an initial stage of threat appraisal proceeds relatively automatically and can lead to problems such as automatic negative thoughts, selective abstraction (i.e., overemphasizing danger), and catastrophizing (e.g., imagining the worst possible outcome). A subsequent stage, concerned with evaluating coping resources and finding safety, involves processing that is more controlled, reflective, and slower. Safety may often be found through perceptual processing of reassuring or relieving objects. At a conceptual level, certain safe propositions may attenuate anxiety by compensating for threatening propositions (e.g., "I'm bad at math but good at history"). Across longer time frames, much worrisome thought can be viewed as an attempt to find a safe solution to a dangerous problem. In general, individual differences may arise from the balance between threat and safety signals. An overemphasis on threat at the expense of safety may lead to accelerating anxiety and poorly focused coping responses. An overemphasis on safety may alleviate the anxiety, but with limited coping responses (e.g., premature avoidance, dependency on others; Derryberry & Reed, 1996).

Beyond safety-related information, adequate coping requires the selection of an effective response or strategy. As mentioned earlier, temperament approaches suggest that emotional systems may potentiate a number of response options. Cognitive approaches place more emphasis on existing associations between response options and perceptual/conceptual information. This allows a wide range of individual differences arising from various perceptual-response and conceptual-response associations. In addition, individuals may differ in the strengths of these associations. Previous experience may render some responses more "dominant" than others, and thus more likely to be initiated without adequate evaluation. Prepotent response pathways may contribute to the impulsive approach behaviors seen in some extraverts (Newman, 1987; Newman, Wallace, Schmitt, & Arnett, 1997; Wallace et al., 1991) and the premature avoidance seen in some anxious people. In other instances, certain response options may be weak, leaving the person with a relative lack of choices. Shy people may have difficulty in social settings because they lack experience in telling stories, telling jokes, being assertive, and so on.

Also important to secondary appraisal are evaluations of the response options' effectiveness. Appraisal theorists have long emphasized the extent to which the situation is construed as modifiable and subject to potential *control* by the individual (Frijda, 1986; Mineka & Zinbarg, 1996; Scherer, 1984, 1993). Controllability in part depends on the availability of safety-type signals and attributions related to locus of control and stability of the situation (Wiener, 1991). In addition, people may differ in terms of their certainty regarding these causal explanations. Those with high "causal uncertainty" are likely to view situations as uncontrollable, which exacerbates their helplessness expectancies and vulnerability to depression (Edwards & Weary, 1998). Even if the situation is viewed as controllable, the individual must also appraise his or her *power* to actually modify it (Frijda, 1986; Scherer, 1984, 1993). Such appraisals will depend in part on previous outcomes with specific response options, as might be reflected in individual differences in "self-efficacy" (Bandura, 1997). But in addition, people may differ in terms of the assessed difficulty of modifying the situation, the assessed effort required to make the response, and one's current level of energy available for making the effort (Dienstbier, 1989).

A final category of coping appraisals concerns the compatibility of response options with one's own and others' standards (e.g., Scherer, 1984, 1993). Even if a response is potent enough to alter the situation, it may be selected against if it violates these standards. Thus, individual differences may arise from the self standards, such as Higgins's ideal and ought selves, or from perceived standards of others. To return to Rapee and Heimberg's (1997) account of social anxiety, shy people may have difficulty selecting a response because they view the other as having high performance standards (e.g., "I could say this but it wouldn't be witty enough").

While the appraisal approaches identify many potential sources of individuality, their emphasis on automatic processing leads to a relative neglect of attentional processing. An exception can be found in Matthews's research and theorizing (Matthews, 1997; Wells & Matthews, 1994). Matthews employs a processing architecture similar to that of Shallice's supervisory attentional system (Stuss, Shallice, Alexander, & Picton, 1995). Lower level systems carry out relatively automatic exteroceptive, interoceptive, and conceptual processing. A higher level, limited-capacity "executive" system monitors and regulates lower level processing. Matthews suggests that a "self-referent executive function (SREF)" may often become active within the limited capacity system. Based on self-relevant knowledge structures, this executive function serves to appraise lower level output and initiate strategies aimed at reducing self discrepancies and threats to the self. Many of these strategies (e.g., monitoring lower level outputs, worrying, planning active coping) demand a great deal of attention, which reduces attention available for other supervisory functions. In stressful social situations, for example, the self-focused attention may limit the person's ability to monitor and respond to important aspects of the social interaction, leading to increased feelings of inadequacy and anxiety. In assessing coping options, the individual may be forced to rely on less demanding and preferred coping strategies (e.g., diverting attention away from the threat) rather than more effective strategies requiring greater attention (e.g., cognitive reappraisal). Regarding individual differences, Matthews suggests that the content of the underlying self-relevant knowledge may be crucial. Individuals with predominantly negative self concepts, such as those high in neuroticism and trait anxiety, would be most vulnerable to the maladaptive SREF activity described above. As discussed in later sections, individual differences in attentional efficiency may also be important (Wells & Matthews, 1994).

To summarize, the appraisal models suggest that multiple computations related to the event itself (its novelty, pleasantness, goal significance, relations to standards, and causality) and to response options (target availability, response availability, response effectiveness, response compatibility) modify the nature of the developing emotion. It is assumed that different patterns of appraisals underlie the range of human emotions. Such approaches provide a fertile ground for studying individual differences, especially in regard to phenomenal experiences of the self and others.

It can also be seen that the appraisal approaches present problems for models emphasizing relatively simple emotional systems. In particular, the many appraisal processes allow for a differentiation of emotion that goes well beyond the systems related to simple appetitive and defensive needs. Some cognitive theorists even argue that basic emotion systems are unnecessary, for the appraisal computations can directly regulate peripheral response systems to generate different emotions (Frijda, 1986; Ortony & Turner, 1990). If emotion systems are required, it remains necessary to predict that more specific systems, capable of producing different emotions such as anxiety, guilt, and shame, will be discovered in the future. Alternatively, it will be necessary to account for how a relatively general system, such as that underlying anxiety, can accommodate different appraisal patterns to produce guilt and shame, as well as the different forms of anxiety.

On the other hand, models emphasizing emotion systems also point out the limitations of appraisal models. The difficulty here is that most appraisal models view appraisals as emotion-antecedent and emotion-causal. However, as discussed above under perceptual processing, emotional processes can be activated by a discrete input prior to conceptual processing. Moreover, emotional processing will often precede conceptual processing in the case of extended emotions or moods. In terms of personality, where activity within emotion systems can be viewed as more or less chronic, some theorists might argue that emotional activity almost always precedes appraisals.

Furthermore, both physiological and psychological evidence suggests that emotional systems serve motivational functions—that is, they are designed to react to significant input by facilitating the most adaptive coupling of sensory information to response pathways. The most effective way of doing this would be to regulate perceptual and conceptual pathways as well as peripheral response systems. From a motivational perspective, the interesting question becomes: How might emotional processes influence perception and appraisals?

## Emotional Influences on Perception and Cognition

In the remainder of this chapter, we examine four mechanisms through which activated emotions influence perceptual and conceptual processes. We consider individual differences arising from (1) automatic activation, (2) response-related interoceptive information, (3) arousal, and (4) attention.

### Automatic Activation

A common mechanism through which emotion might influence perceptual and conceptual processing involves direct and spreading forms of activation. Relevant pathways in Figure 35.1 involve direct projections from the emotional systems to the processing systems on the diagram's left side. Such a mechanism has been proposed to explain mood congruency effects—that is, facilitated retrieval or positive and negative information given positive and negative moods, respectively. As described by Bower (1981), an activated emotion node spreads subthreshold excitation to related conceptual nodes, making these nodes more easily retrieved. Spreading activation is often viewed as a relatively automatic and unconscious process that may bias appraisals in a manner that is congruent with the ongoing emotional state.

Activation mechanisms are also helpful in explaining the escalation and persistence of emotional states. In depression, for example, initial activation of depression-related concepts feeds back to deepen the depression, which in turn feeds back to activate depressed content, and so on. In a recent connectionist approach, Siegle and Ingram (1997) have demonstrated that reciprocal excitatory connections between semantic and affective levels can be used to model coping styles in depression. Ruminative coping may result from cyclic semantic-emotional reverberations focused on a specific event (e.g., a loss), whereas distractive coping may involve a weakening of this excitatory loop.

Automatic activation can also be viewed as an adaptive function that helps the person resolve the motivational state. Deutsch (1960) originally suggested that appetitive need states (e.g., hunger) function by activating goal representations (e.g., food), which in turn spread activation to related environmental objects. Because the activation pattern dissipates as it spreads out from the goal, the resulting activation gradient can be used as a map to navigate toward the goal.

A similar mechanism might be used during defensive states such as anxiety to rapidly prime relevant information (e.g., threat and safety). At the same time, automatic activation could prime the response options relevant to secondary appraisals. Defensive states may potentiate a set of response options, such as freezing, fleeing, fighting, or playing dead. Primed perceptual information (e.g., the predator's proximity, available escape routes) would then release the most appropriate of the primed responses (e.g., Gallistel, 1980; Tinbergen, 1951).

In this fear-related example, automatic processes could instantly prepare almost all relevant information channels, including those concerned with the threat, safety, and response options. This would be highly efficient in that its automaticity would require little attention, allowing attention to serve other coordinative functions. However, the automaticity might also lead to impulsive and inflexible processing that is difficult to control through voluntary means. In any event, individual differences could arise from the variable connections between the emotional system and threat-, safety-, and response-related processors, as well as from the strength or automaticity of these connections. In contrast to the cognitive approaches, these connections would in large part depend on the reactivity of the underlying emotion system. Emotional reactivity would influence the degree of activation in these connections, as well as attention to them (see below), which together would serve to stabilize the relevant pathways. Through learning, the anxious child would tend to form relatively automatic connections.

### Interoceptive Information

A second mechanism through which emotional activity might influence cognition involves interoceptive information. The underlying idea is that different emotions generate different muscular, autonomic, and endocrine responses, which in turn give rise to distinct interoceptive patterns. This interoceptive background may directly bias perception and cognition, or may be used as another source of information taken into account during the appraisal process (Schwarz, 1990). For example, the positive or negative affect related to an ongoing emotion might become integrated with the affect elicited by a specific object, leading to a congruent bias in appraisals such as "intrinsic pleasantness" and "goal conduciveness." Forgas's

(1995) "affect infusion model" proposes that people vulnerable to negative affect, such as neurotics, are likely to have their judgments biased in a mood-congruent direction toward threat appraisals. In neurotics and anxious people, strong negative affect may draw attention toward the self, in this way biasing attributions favoring internal over external causes (Dienstbier, 1984; Hass & Eisenstadt, 1991).

While the above examples emphasize biasing effects, hedonic information may often be adaptive in guiding appraisals related to response and strategy selection. Damasio (1994) has proposed that emotion-related interoceptive information functions as "somatic markers" to assist in decision making and planning. Positive and negative markers serve to enhance attention to relevant information and assign an initial affective value that may immediately facilitate or disrupt a developing decision process. Similarly, we have suggested that, with experience, interoceptive representations become associated with conceptual and response representations, such that concepts and responses are associated with feelings of pain, reward, relief, and so on. The distribution of positive and negative valences across such representations allows them to function as "affective maps," guiding appraisal toward more positive outcomes. For example, responses associated with relief or reward will be selected over those associated with pain or frustration (Derryberry & Reed, 1994b, 1996). Finally, interoceptive information concerning the body's energy status should be important in power and controllability appraisals. Low energy may promote appraisals that a response will be ineffective and the situation is uncontrollable (Dienstbier, 1989), resulting in depressed helplessness in severe instances.

Individual differences owing to interoceptive content could arise from the strength of the peripheral emotional reactions, or from the resolution of the perceptual systems that process the input. People who pay attention to bodily input might be expected to develop more articulated interoceptive representations. Also important will be the connectivity and automaticity between the interoceptive representations and their associated conceptual and response components. In appraising the effectiveness of coping options, for example, if the available options are linked more strongly to reward than frustration, individuals may persist in their efforts to cope. But if the links favor frustration, the person may tend to give up.

### Arousal

A third mechanism involves emotional effects on central arousal. Arousal is usually viewed as a relatively general modulation of the processing system, such as might be promoted through reticular projections to the cortex. Although initially viewed as a unitary process, arousal is now known to arise from multiple subsystems that exert distinct neuromodulatory effects on distinct (but overlapping) cortical regions. The arousal systems are differentially recruited during emotional states, allowing different patterns of arousal or "readiness" to be imposed upon the cortex. Interesting in this respect is Oatley and Johnson-Laird's (1987) proposal that emotions function to "reorganize" the processing system in a manner conducive to the needs and priorities of the particular emotion. For example, Mathews (1990) suggests that anxiety assigns priority to processes involved in detecting and acting upon danger, with a corresponding reduction in resources available for other tasks. Sadness serves to motivate a search for new plans and goals, and thus assigns priority to the elaborative processes that facilitate memory retrieval.

In a more specific model, Tucker and his colleagues have suggested that emotional states related to anxiety-relaxation and elation-depression recruit dopaminergic and noradrenergic arousal systems (Tucker & Derryberry, 1992; Tucker & Williamson, 1984). During elation, a noradrenergic facilitation promotes a state of "phasic arousal" that biases processing in favor of novel content. This produces an expansive processing state. An extreme example would include the manic's thought, involving remote propositions with little integration among them. Less extreme examples can be found in heuristic and remote processing found following positive mood inductions (e.g., Isen, 1990). During anxiety, a dopaminergic facilitation produces a state of "tonic activation" in which processing is biased in favor of redundant information. This leads to a narrow processing style that favors the tightly connected and sequenced responses useful in threatening situations. An extreme example would be paranoid thought, where a subset of propositions may be tied intricately together and focused strongly upon the self, but with a neglect of the general context. Less extreme examples can be seen in the narrow perceptual and conceptual processing of trait anxious persons (Derryberry & Reed, 1998; Mikulincer, Kedem, & Paz, 1990). In general, the focused mode of processing is common in anxious individuals, while the expansive mode is most closely related to extraversion.

Other researchers have approached arousal as a variable "resource" required by different cognitive processes. According to Eysenck's (1967) "general arousal" model, the relatively low arousal of extraverts might impair performance across a range of tasks, especially when the task is relatively unarousing. Revelle (1989) provided evidence that such an arousal-based performance decrement is tied to the impulsivity rather than sociability component of extraversion, and is most influential in tasks requiring sustained information transfer (e.g., vigilance tasks) rather than short-term memory. In more recent work Matthews (1997) suggests that differences in arousal and information-processing architecture provide extraverts with sets

of skills (i.e., a cognitive patterning) that allow them to adapt to and to seek out high-information environments. For example, the abilities to effectively divide attention, to rapidly retrieve information from memory, and to hold information in working memory help extraverts adapt to social and other high-information environments. In introverts, abilities to maintain vigilance and show strategic caution give rise to skills compatible with solitary, reflective behaviors. Although the source of these cognitive patterns remains unclear, they are generally compatible with the patterns of reticular projections upon the cortex. Interesting in this respect are Matthews's findings that self-reported "energetic arousal" correlates positively with extraversion, appraisals of challenge and control, and active coping, but negatively with neuroticism, threat appraisals, and emotion-focused and avoidant coping. In performance studies, subjective energy enhances performance on tasks that are simple and attentionally demanding, especially dual tasks compared to single tasks. Matthews (1997) suggests that energy may act through dopaminergic projections that facilitate frontal attentional mechanisms. Recruitment of this energetic arousal/attentional mechanism during stressful states is one of several mechanisms allowing extraverts to adapt to high-information environments.

### Attention

The work of Tucker and Matthews points to the importance of the fourth mechanism, attention. As mentioned above, attention is often viewed as a separate mechanism involved in the facilitation and inhibition of information. While various arousal systems regulate relatively general functions, attention operates in a more limited and specific manner on the most important sources of information. Although highly specific effects can also be achieved through automatic activation, automatic effects tend to be very rapid, primarily excitatory, and unlimited in capacity. In contrast, attentional influences tend to be slower, involve inhibition as well as excitation, and are limited in their focus. Moreover, automatic effects are relatively involuntary, inflexible, and unrelated to consciousness, whereas attention can be voluntary, flexible, and closely related to consciousness. Attention also seems crucial to stabilizing important processing pathways, thereby promoting automaticity through learning. Assuming that emotional systems are designed to promote adaptive processing, it makes sense that they should have access to the most flexible and voluntary regulatory systems, especially those involved in learning.

Considerable evidence supports such a relationship, with trait- and clinically anxious individuals showing attentional biases favoring threat (e.g., MacLeod & Matthews, 1988; Williams, Mathews, & MacLeod, 1996). Although threat-related biases are important in understanding many aspects of anxious thought, it is likely that attention influences processing in many complex ways. As mentioned earlier, much processing required in primary and secondary appraisal is highly sophisticated (e.g., Rapee & Heimberg, 1997; Wells & Matthews, 1994) and cannot always be accomplished through automatic processes. This makes it necessary to consider the possibility that individual differences in the attention processes themselves may be particularly important. If attention is a primary mechanism through which emotional systems carry out their adaptive functions, then the efficiency of these functions should depend on the efficiency of the individual's attention.

To consider efficiency, it is worth distinguishing two attentional systems investigated by Posner and his colleagues (Posner & Petersen, 1990; Posner & Raichle, 1994; Posner & Rothbart, 1998). The posterior attentional system is a relatively reactive system that orients attention from one spatial location to another. The orienting system consists of interacting subsystems that perform three component operations: Attention must first disengage from its current location, move to the new location, and then engage the new location. Our findings suggest that emotional and personality effects occur after attention has moved to and engaged a significant stimulus. Once the stimulus is engaged, the engagement appears to deepen, leading to delays in disengaging and shifting away. Thus, neurotic introverts and anxious individuals are slow to disengage from threatening locations, while neurotic extraverts are slow to shift from rewarding locations (Derryberry & Reed, 1994a, 1997).

It should be emphasized that some attentional biases may be relatively reactive, occurring with little voluntary control. Although they may help the person deal with the threat, their inflexibility may also lead to problems. Some anxious persons may have difficulty in disengaging from a threat, leading to an imbalance in the processing of threat and safety relevant to many appraisal processes. In other cases, some individuals may develop a reflexive strategy of disengaging threatening objects or concepts. The avoidant strategy may reduce anxiety, but limit the person's opportunities to learn more effective coping (Derryberry & Rothbart, 1997).

Posner's second system, the anterior attentional system, provides more voluntary and flexible control. This executive system is located in midfrontal regions where it receives extensive inputs from emotional, perceptual, conceptual, response, and arousal systems. Based on this input, the anterior system provides voluntary control across the course of processing. It regulates the posterior orienting system, thereby providing more flexible control over incoming perceptual content. When conceptual content is activated, the anterior system inhibits dominant conceptual associations, allowing control over highly automatized primary appraisals. It also inhibits dominant response tendencies, allowing more flexible assessment of coping options during secondary appraisal. In addition, anterior facilitation of short-term memory allows more flexible significance appraisals and planning of coping options. Finally, the anterior system is involved in detecting errors, allowing for corrections of responses and plans that go wrong (Posner & DiGirolamo, 1998; Posner & Raichle, 1994).

Rothbart and Posner have proposed that the anterior system underlies an individual difference dimension of "effortful control" (Rothbart, Derryberry, & Posner, 1994; Rothbart, Posner, & Boylan, 1990). Effortful control is usually measured by parents' report of the child's ability to focus attention and to inhibit responses. Factor analytic studies indicate that effortful control forms a factor that is separable from factors of positive emotionality and negative emotionality. High effortful control should allow extraverted individuals to constrain some aspects of positive emotionality, leading to less impulsivity, more delay of gratification, and resistance to temptation. Similarly, high effortful control should allow anxious individuals to constrain reactive components of anxiety, such as enhanced attention to threat and avoidant response tendencies. These predictions are generally supported by development studies relating effortful control to impulsivity, aggression, and conscience (Kochanska, 1995; Kochanska, Murray, Jacques, Koenig, & Vandegeest, 1996; Rothbart, Ahadi, & Hershey, 1994; Rothbart, Derryberry, & Hershey, 2000).

Our research has recently focused on the attentional aspects of adults' effortful control through a self-report measure of attentional control. Attentional control assesses capacities to focus attention, to shift attention between tasks, and to flexibly control thought. An initial series of studies examined the anterior attentional function of inhibiting dominant response tendencies. Although anxious subjects with low attentional control showed strong dominant responses, anxious subjects with high attentional control were able to suppress the prepotent response tendencies (Derryberry & Reed, 2001). A second study examined the anterior function of regulating the posterior attentional systems orienting. Subjects were engaged in a game, where spatial cues reflexively drew their attention to "threatening" (where points would probably be lost) or "safe" (where points would probably not be lost) locations. Anxious subjects with poor attentional control showed a bias favoring the threatening locations, and were delayed in shifting from a threatening to a safe situation. In contrast, anxious subjects with good control were better able to shift from the threatening to the safe location. Such an ability to disengage from threat and take advantage of safety may allow some individuals to constrain anxiety and cope more effectively (Derryberry & Reed, in press).

In general, attentional or effortful control may influence appraisals in many ways. Anxious individuals with poor control may have difficulty disengaging from threat and suppressing dominant response tendencies. In addition, these people may be particularly vulnerable to automatic activation effects leading to appraisals that overestimate threat and underestimate coping potential. In contrast, those with good control can inhibit inappropriate responses and disengage from threat to take advantage of safety information. If it turns out that the anterior system also inhibits dominant conceptual associations, those with good control may be able to voluntarily constrain the maladaptive "automatic" processing described above. Given an anticipated threat, for example, they may be able to constrain the spread of activation in a way that balances the weighting of threat and safety and thus arrives at more realistic primary and secondary appraisals. Even if a failure occurs, good attentional control should allow the person to suppress the activation of negative aspects of the self, and perhaps compensate by facilitating a positive aspect. If attentional control is diminished, as may occur following prolonged stress or effort, then the person may become vulnerable to the reactive and often maladaptive processing related to emotional responses and appraisals. In most instances, it is not simply automatic appraisals that are involved in emotion, but also the person's capacity to voluntarily regulate appraisals.

## Conclusions

We began this chapter with the notion that an information-processing approach provides an integrative framework for linking physiological/temperament and cognitive approaches to personality. What we are most impressed with in closing is the richness of individual differences that such an approach reveals. Emotionality depends on the central emotion systems, their many perceptual inputs, and the many conceptual processes devoted to primary and secondary appraisals. In addition, individual differences arise from the output functions of emotional systems, including response-generated interoceptive information, direct activation of cognitive content, the general modulation of cognitive organization through arousal, and the more specific regulation of content through attention. Given the richness of these sources, it is easy to appreciate the diversity of human emotionality.

However, this complexity can become overwhelming, and thus an integrative framework is strongly desired. Although we have been unable to touch on it in this chapter, a developmental perspective may prove particularly useful. From a cognitive perspective, Matthews (1997) has provided a model in which the individual's pattern of cognitive skill allows him or her to adapt to, to seek out, and to learn from certain environments. As a result of numerous interactions with those environments, the child's belief systems, coping strategies, and emotional tendencies become increasingly organized. From an emotional perspective, several authors have proposed that early activity within emotional systems will control the arousal and attentional mechanisms that selectively stabilize the child's developing beliefs and appraisals. Across time, information-processing systems become tuned to the specific needs and goals of the underlying emotional systems, as if the processing system self-organizes around the central emotional systems (Depue & Collins, 1999; Derryberry & Reed, 1994b, 1996; Tucker, 1992).

As for the information-processing approach, its greatest value at this point is that of providing a broad integrative framework that can link and incorporate the processes emphasized in emotional and cognitive approaches. Such a framework provides a comprehensive view of personality, arising from a highly distributed, interactive, and essentially adaptive processing system. It provides a view of the importance of cognitive differences in computing the detailed information required by emotional processes, and the importance of emotional differences in motivating the cognitive processes. Finally, it provides a clearer view of our tendencies to react to the world in automatic ways and, at the same time, our capacity to bring this reactivity under voluntary control.

## REFERENCES

Antony, M. M., & Barlow, D. H. (1996). Emotion theory as a framework for explaining panic attacks and panic disorder. In R. M. Rapee (Ed.), *Current controversies in the anxiety disorders* (pp. 55–76). New York: Guilford Press.

Bandler, R., & Keay, K. A. (1996). Columnar organization in the midbrain periaqueductal gray and the integration of emotional expression. In G. Holstege, R. Bandler, & C. B. Saper (Eds.), *Progress in brain research, Volume 107. The emotional motor system* (pp. 285–300). Amsterdam: Elsevier.

Bandler, R., & Shipley, M. T. (1994). Columnar organization in the midbrain periaqueductal gray: Modules for emotional expression? *Trends in Neurosciences, 17*, 379–389.

Bandura, A. (1997). *Self-efficacy: The exercise of control.* New York: W. H. Freeman.

Bargh, J. A., Litt, J. E., Pratto, F., & Spielman, L. A. (1988). On the preconscious evaluation of social stimuli. In K. McConkey & A. Bennet (Eds.), *Proceedings of the XXIV International Congress of Psychology (Vol. 3)* (pp. 1–57). Amsterdam: Elsevier/North Holland.

Barlow, D. H., Chorpita, B. F., & Turovsky, J. (1996). Fear, panic, anxiety, and disorders of emotion. In D. A. Hope (Ed.), *Nebraska symposium on motivation, Vol. 43: Perspectives on anxiety, panic, and fear* (pp. 251–328). Lincoln: University of Nebraska Press.

Beck, A. T., & Clark, D. A. (1997). An information processing model of anxiety: Automatic and strategic processes. *Behavioural Research and Therapy, 35*, 49–58.

Berlyne, D. E. (1960). *Conflict, arousal, and curiosity.* New York: McGraw-Hill.

Berlyne, D. E. (1971). *Aesthetics and psychobiology.* New York: Appleton-Century-Crofts.

Blanchard, D. C., & Blanchard, R. J. (1988). Ethoexperimental approaches to the biology of emotion. *Annual Review of Psychology, 39*, 43–68.

Bower, G. H. (1981). Mood and memory. *American Psychologist, 36*, 129–148.

Cosmides, L., & Tooby, J. (1987). From evolution to behavior: Evolutionary psychology as the missing link. In J. Dupre (Ed.), *The latest on the best: Essays on evolution and optimality* (pp. 277–306). Cambridge, MA: MIT Press.

Damasio, A. R. (1994). *Descartes' error: Emotion, reason, and the human brain.* New York: Putnam.

Davidson, R. J. (1994). Assymetry, affect, psychopathology, and plasticity. *Development and Psychopathology, 6*, 741–758.

Depue, R. A., & Collins, P. F. (1999). Neurobiology of the structure of personality: Dopamine, facilitation of incentive motivation, and extraversion. *Behavioral and Brain Sciences, 22*, 491–555.

Depue, R. A., & Iacono, W. G. (1989). Neurobehavioral aspects of affective disorders. *Annual Review of Psychology, 40*, 457–492.

Derryberry, D., & Reed, M. A. (1994a). Temperament and attention: Orienting toward and away from positive and negative signals. *Journal of Personality and Social Psychology, 66*, 1128–1139.

Derryberry, D., & Reed, M. A. (1994b). Temperament and the self-organization of personality. *Development and Psychopathology, 6*, 653–676.

Derryberry, D., & Reed, M. A. (1996). Regulatory processes and the development of cognitive representations. *Development and Psychopathology, 8*, 215–234.

Derryberry, D., & Reed, M. A. (1997). Motivational and attentional components of personality. In G. Matthews (Ed.), *Cognitive science perspectives on personality and emotion* (pp. 443–473). Amsterdam: Elsevier.

Derryberry, D., & Reed, M. A. (1998). Anxiety and attentional focusing: Trait, state and hemispheric influences. *Personality and Individual Differences, 25*, 745–761.

Derryberry, D., & Reed, M. A. (2001). *Attentional control, trait anxiety, and the regulation of irrelevant response information.* Manuscript submitted for publication.

Derryberry, D., & Reed, M. A. (in press). Anxiety-related attentional biases and their regulation by attentional control. *Journal of Abnormal Psychology.*

Derryberry, D., & Rothbart, M. K. (1997). Reactive and effortful processes in the organization of temperament. *Development and Psychopathology, 9*, 633–652.

Derryberry, D., & Tucker, D. M. (1992). Neural mechanisms of emotion. *Journal of Consulting and Clinical Psychology, 60*, 329–338.

Deutsch, J. A. (1960). *The structural basis of behavior.* Chicago: University of Chicago Press.

Dienstbier, R. A. (1984). The role of emotion in moral socialization. In C. E. Izard, J. Kagan, & R. B. Zajonc (Eds.), *Emotions, cognition, and behavior* (pp. 484–514). Cambridge: Cambridge University Press.

Dienstbier, R. A. (1989). Arousal and physiological toughness: Implications for mental and physical health. *Psychological Review, 96*, 84–100.

Edwards, J. A., & Weary, G. (1998). Antecedents of causal uncertainty and perceived control: A prospective study. *European Journal of Personality, 12*, 135–148.

Ehlers, A., & Breuer, P. (1992). Increased cardiac awareness in panic disorder. *Journal of Abnormal Psychology, 101*, 371–382.

Eysenck, H. J. (1967). *The biological basis of personality.* Springfield, IL: Thomas.

Forgas, J. P. (1995). Mood and judgement: The affect infusion model (AIM). *Psychological Bulletin, 21*, 747–765.

Fowles, D. C. (1988). Psychophysiology and psychopathology: A motivational approach. *Psychophysiology, 25*, 373–392.

Fowles, D. C. (1994). A motivational theory of psychopathology. In W. G. Spaulding (Ed.), *Nebraska symposium on motivation, Vol. 41: Integrative views of motivation, cognition, and emotion* (pp. 181–238). Lincoln: University of Nebraska Press.

Frijda, N. H. (1986). *The emotions.* Cambridge: Cambridge University Press.

Gallistel, C. R. (1980). *The organization of action: A new synthesis.* Hillsdale, NJ: Erlbaum.

Gilbert, P., & Trower, P. (1990). The evolution and manifestation of social anxiety. In W. R. Crozier (Ed.), *Shyness and embarrassment: Perspectives from social psychology* (pp. 144–177). Cambridge: Cambridge University Press.

Gray, J. A. (1982). *The neuropsychology of anxiety.* London: Oxford University Press.

Gray, J. A. (1987a). Perspectives on anxiety and impulsivity: A commentary. *Journal of Research in Personality, 21*, 493–509.

Gray, J. A. (1987b). *The psychology of fear and stress* (2nd ed.). New York: McGraw-Hill.

Gray, J. A. (1994). Framework for a taxonomy of psychiatric disorder. In S. H. M. van Goozen, N. E. Van de Poll, & J. A. Sergeant (Eds.), *Emotions: Essays on emotion theory* (pp. 29–60). Hillsdale, NJ: Erlbaum.

Gray, J. A., & McNaughton, N. (1996). The neuropsychology of anxiety: Reprise. In D. A. Hope (Ed.), *Nebraska symposium on motivation, Vol. 43: Perspectives on anxiety, panic, and fear* (pp. 61–134). Lincoln: University of Nebraska Press.

Grossberg, S., & Gutowski, W. E. (1987). Neural dynamics of decision making under risk: Affective balance and cognitive-emotional interactions. *Psychological Review, 94*, 300–318.

Hass, G. R., & Eisenstadt, D. (1991). The effects of self-focused attention on perspective-taking and anxiety. In R. Schwarzer & R. A. Wicklund (Eds.), *Anxiety and self-focused attention* (pp. 55–66). London: Harwood Academic Publishers.

Higgins, E. T. (1987). Self-discrepancy: A theory relating self and affect. *Psychological Review, 94*, 319–340.

Higgins, E. T. (1991). Development of self-regulatory and self-evaluative processes: Costs, benefits, and tradeoffs. In M. R. Gunnar & L. A. Sroufe (Eds.), *Self processes and development: The Minnesota Symposia on Child Development, Volume 23.* Hillsdale, NJ: Erlbaum.

Higgins, E. T. (1996). Ideals, oughts, and regulatory focus: Affect and motivation from distinct pains and pleasures. In P. M. Gollwitzer & J. A. Bargh (Eds.), *The psychology of action: Linking cognition and motivation to behavior* (pp. 91–114). New York: Guilford Press.

Higgins, E. T. (1997). Beyond pleasure and pain. *American Psychologist, 52*, 1280–1300.

Isen, A. M. (1990). The influence of positive and negative affect on cognitive organization: Some implications for development. In N. Stein, B. Leventhal, & T. Trabasso (Eds.), *Psychological and biological approaches to emotion* (pp. 75–94). Hillsdale, NJ: Erlbaum.

Keele, S. W., & Neill, W. T. (1978). Mechanisms of attention. In E. L. Carterette & M. P. Friedman (Eds.), *Handbook of perception* (Vol. 9; pp. 3–47). New York: Academic Press.

Kenardy, J., Evans, L., & Oei, T. (1992). The latent structure of anxiety symptoms in anxiety disorders. *American Journal of Psychiatry, 149,* 1058–1061.

Klein, D. F. (1993). False suffocation alarms, spontaneous panics, and related conditions. *Archives of General Psychiatry, 50,* 306–317.

Kochanska, G. (1995). Children's temperament, mothers' discipline, and security of attachment: Multiple pathways to emerging internalization. *Child Development, 66,* 597–615.

Kochanska, G., Murray, K., Jacques, T. Y., Koenig, A. L., & Vandegeest, K. A. (1996). Inhibitory control in young children and its role in emerging internalization. *Child Development, 67,* 490–507.

Larsen, R. J., & Ketelaar, T. (1989). Extraversion, neuroticism and susceptibility to positive and negative mood induction procedures. *Personality and Individual Differences, 10,* 1221–1228.

Lazarus, R. S., & Folkman, S. (1984). *Stress, appraisal and coping.* New York: Springer.

LeDoux, J. (1996). *The emotional brain.* New York: Simon & Schuster.

MacDonald, K. (1992). Warmth as a developmental contruct: An evolutionary analysis. *Child Development, 63,* 753–773.

MacDonald, K. (1995). Evolution, the Five-Factor Model, and levels of personality. *Journal of Personality, 63,* 525–567.

MacLeod, C., & Mathews, A. (1988). Anxiety and the allocation of attention to threat. *Quarterly Journal of Experimental Psychology, 40,* 653–670.

Marks, I. M., & Neese, R. M. (1994). Fear and fitness: An evolutionary analysis of anxiety disorders. *Ethology and Sociobiology, 15,* 247–261.

Mathews, A. (1990). Why worry? The cognitive function of anxiety. *Behavioral Research and Therapy, 28,* 455–468.

Matthews, G. (1997). Extraversion, emotion and performance: A cognitive-adaptive model. In G. Matthews (Ed.), *Cognitive science perspectives on personality and emotion* (pp. 399–442). Amsterdam: Elsevier.

McNally, R. J. (1996). Anxiety sensitivity is distinguishable from trait anxiety. In R. M. Rapee (Ed.), *Current controversies in the anxiety disorders* (pp. 214–227). New York: Guilford Press.

Mikulincer, M., Kedem, P., & Paz, D. (1990). Anxiety and categorization-1. The structure and boundaries of mental categories. *Personality and Individual Differences, 11,* 805–814.

Mineka, S., Pury, C. L., & Luten, A. G. (1995). Explanatory style in anxiety and depression. In G. M. Buchanan & M. E. P. Seligman (Eds.), *Explanatory style* (pp. 135–158). Hillsdale, NJ: Erlbaum.

Mineka, S., & Zinbarg, R. (1996). Conditioning and ethological models of anxiety disorders: Stress-in-dynamic context anxiety models. In D. A. Hope (Ed.), *Nebraska symposium on motivation, Vol. 43: Perspectives on anxiety, panic, and fear* (pp. 133–210). Lincoln: University of Nebraska Press.

Newman, J. P. (1987). Reaction to punishment in extraverts and psychopaths: Implications for the impulsive behavior of disinhibited individuals. *Journal of Research in Personality, 21,* 464–480.

Newman, J. P., Wallace, J. F., Schmitt, W. A., & Arnett, P. A. (1997). Behavioral inhibition system functioning in anxious, impulsive and psychopathic individuals. *Personality and Individual Differences, 23,* 583–592.

Oatley, K., & Johnson-Laird, P. (1987). Towards a cognitive theory of emotions. *Cognition and Emotion, 1,* 29–50.

Ohman, A. (1993). Fear and anxiety as emotional phenomena: Clinical phenomenology, evolutionary perspectives, and information-processing mechanisms. In M. Lewis & J. M. Haviland (Eds.), *Handbook of emotions* (pp. 511–536). New York: Guilford Press.

Ohman, A., & Soares, J. J. F. (1993). On the automatic nature of phobic fear: Conditioned electrodermal responses to masked fear-relevant stimuli. *Journal of Abnormal Psychology, 102,* 121–132.

Ortony, A., Clore, G. L., & Collins, A. (1988). *The cognitive structure of emotions.* Cambridge, England: Cambridge University Press.

Ortony, A., & Turner, T. J. (1990). What's basic about basic emotions? *Psychological Review, 97,* 315–331.

Panksepp, J. (1986). The anatomy of emotions. In R. Plutchik & H. Kellerman (Eds.), *Emotion: Theory, research and experience. Vol. 3: Biological foundations of emotions* (pp. 91–124). San Diego, CA: Academic Press.

Panksepp, J. (1992). A critical role for "affective neuroscience" in resolving what is basic about basic emotions. *Psych. Rev., 99,* 554–560.

Panksepp, J. (1998). *Affective neuroscience.* New York: Oxford University Press.

Posner, M. I., & DiGirolamo, G. J. (1998). Executive attention: Conflict, target detection and cognitive control. In R. Parasuraman (Ed.), *The attentive brain* (pp. 401–423). Cambridge, MA: MIT Press.

Posner, M. I., & Petersen, S. E. (1990). The attention system of the human brain. *Annual Review of Neuroscience, 13,* 25–42.

Posner, M. I., & Raichle, M. E. (1994). *Images of mind.* New York: Scientific American Library.

Posner, M. I., & Rothbart, M. K. (1998). Attention, self-regulation and consciousness. *Philosophical Transactions of the Royal Society of London B, 353,* 1915–1927.

Rapee, R. M., & Heimberg, R. G. (1997). A cognitive-behavioral model of anxiety in social phobia. *Behavior Research and Therapy, 35,* 741–756.

Revelle, W. (1989). Personality, motivation, and cognitive performance. In R. Kanfer, P. L. Ackerman, & R. Cudeck (Eds.), *Abilities, motivation, and methodology: The Minnesota symposium on learning and individual differences* (pp. 297–342). Hillsdale, NJ: Erlbaum.

Risold, P. Y., Canteras, N. S., & Swanson, L. W. (1994). Organization of projections from the anterior hypothalamic nucleus: A phaseolus vulgaris-leucoagglutinin study in the rat. *Journal of Comparative Neurology, 348,* 1–40.

Rothbart, M. K., Ahadi, S. A., & Hershey, K. L. (1994). Temperament and social behavior in childhood. *Merrill-Palmer Quarterly, 40,* 21–39.

Rothbart, M. K., Derryberry, D., & Hershey, K. (2000). Stability of temperament in childhood: Laboratory infant assessment to parent report at seven years. In V. J. Molfese & D. L. Molfese (Eds.), *Temperament and development across the lifespan* (pp. 85–120). Mahwah, NJ: Erlbaum.

Rothbart, M. K., Derryberry, D., & Posner, M. I. (1994). A

psychobiological approach to the development of temperament. In J. E. Bates & T. D. Wachs (Eds.), *Temperament: Individual differences at the interface of biology and behavior* (pp. 83–116). Washington, DC: American Psychological Association.

Rothbart, M. K., Posner, M. I., & Boylan, A. (1990). Regulatory mechanisms in infant development. In J. T. Enns (Ed.), *The development of attention: Research and theory* (pp. 47–66). New York: Elsevier Science.

Scherer, K. R. (1984). On the nature and function of emotion: A component process approach. In K. R. Scherer & P. Ekman (Eds.), *Approaches to emotion* (pp. 293–318). Hillsdale, NJ: Erlbaum.

Scherer, K. R. (1993). Studying the emotion-antecedent appraisal process: An expert system approach. *Cognition and Emotion, 7*, 325–355.

Schwarz, N. (1990). Feelings as information: Informational and motivational functions of affective states. In E. T. Higgins & R. M. Sorrentino (Eds.), *Handbook of motivation and cognition: Foundations of social behavior,* (Vol. 2; pp. 527–561). New York: Guilford Press.

Showers, C. J. (1995). The evaluative organization of self-knowledge: Origins, processes, and implications for self-esteem. In M. H. Kernis (Ed.), *Efficacy, agency, and self-esteem* (pp. 101–120). New York: Plenum.

Showers, C. J., & Kling, K. C. (1996). The organization of self-knowledge: Implications for mood regulation. In L. L. Martin & A. Tesser (Eds.), *Striving and feeling: Interactions among goals, affect, and self regulation* (pp. 151–174). Mahwah, NJ: Erlbaum.

Siegle, G. J., & Ingram, R. E. (1997). Modeling individual differences in negative information processing biases. In G. Matthews (Ed.), *Cognitive science perspectives on personality and emotion* (pp. 301–354). Amsterdam: Elsevier.

Stuss, D. T., Shallice, T., Alexander, M. P., & Picton, T. W. (1995). A multidisciplinary approach to anterior attentional functions. In J. Grafman, K. J. Holyoak, & F. Boller (Eds.), *Annals of the New York Academy of Sciences, Volume 769. Structure and functions of the human prefrontal cortex*. New York: New York Academy of Sciences.

Sutton, S. K., & Davidson, R. J. (1997). Prefrontal brain asymmetry: A biological substrate of the behavioral approach and inhibition systems. *Psychological Science, 8*, 204–210.

Tangney, J. P. (1995). Shame and guilt in interpersonal relationships. In J. P. Tangney & K. W. Fisher (Eds.), *Self-conscious emotions: The psychology of shame, guilt, embarrassment, and pride* (pp. 114–139). New York: Guilford Press.

Thayer, R. E. (1989). *The biopsychology of mood and arousal*. New York: Oxford University Press.

Tinbergen, N. (1951). *The study of instinct*. Oxford: Oxford University Press.

Tucker, D. M. (1992). Developing emotions and cortical networks. In M. Gunnar & C. A. Nelson (Eds.), *Minnesota symposium on child psychology. Vol. 24: Developmental behavioral neuroscience* (pp. 75–128). Hillsdale, NJ: Erlbaum.

Tucker, D. M., & Derryberry, D. (1992). Motivated attention: Anxiety and the frontal executive mechanisms. *Neuropsychiatry, Neuropsychology, and Behavioral Neurology, 5*, 233–252.

Tucker, D. M., & Williamson, P. A. (1984). Asymmetric neural control systems in human self-regulation. *Psychological Review, 91*, 185–215.

van Reekum, C. M., & Scherer, K. R. (1997). Levels of processing in emotion-antecedent appraisal. In G. Matthews (Ed.), *Cognitive science perspectives on personality and emotion* (pp. 259–300). Amsterdam: Elsevier.

Wallace, J. F., Newman, J. P., & Bachorowski, J. (1991). Failures of response modulation: Impulsive behavior in anxious and impulsive individuals. *Journal of Research in Personality, 25*, 23–44.

Watson, D., & Clark, L. A. (1992). On traits and temperament: General and specific factors of emotional experience and their relation to the five-factor model. *Journal of Personality, 60*, 441–476.

Weiner, B. (1991). On perceiving the other as responsible. In R. A. Dienstbier (Ed.), *Nebraska symposium on motivation, 1990* (pp. 165–198). Lincoln: University of Nebraska Press.

Wells, A., & Matthews, G. (1994). *Attention and emotion: A clinical perspective*. Hillsdale, NJ: Erlbaum.

Williams, J. M. G., Mathews, A., & MacLeod, C. (1996). The emotional stroop task and psychopathology. *Psychological Bulletin, 120*, 3–24.

Zajonc, R. C. (1980). Feeling and thinking: Preferences need no inferences. *American Psychologist, 35*, 151–175.

Zinbarg, R. E., Barlow, D. H., & Brown, T. A. (1997). Hierarchical structure and general factor saturation of the Anxiety Sensitivity Index: Evidence and implications. *Psychological Assessment, 9*, 277–284.

# 36

# INDIVIDUAL DIFFERENCES IN EMOTIONAL REACTIONS AND COPING

Heinz W. Krohne

Researchers in the emotions domain have always been concerned with individual differences in emotional reactions. Early in antiquity, the Greek physician Hippocrates developed the idea that chemical processes in the body (described by so-called body fluids or "humores") lead to the manifestation of four temperaments—phlegmatic, sanguine, choleric, and melancholic. These temperaments, in turn, should form the person-specific basis for emotional reactions. These speculations not only influenced poetry, philosophy, and medicine of later centuries but also had an impact on early modern psychology theories. Wundt (1903) turned the temperament typology into a dimensional system. He suggested one can differentiate among individuals by the speed and intensity of their emotional arousal. By combining two levels of each dimension (slow/fast and weak/strong), he created a system of person-specific emotional reaction tendencies that closely corresponded to the four temperaments of Hippocrates. (Cholerics, for example, should be characterized by fast and strong emotional arousal, while phlegmatics are described by the opposite pattern.) In a more modern approach, H. J. Eysenck (1981) explicitly related his central personality dimensions extraversion-introversion and emotional stability-lability (or neuroticism) to Wundt's reformulation of the antique model of temperaments.

Although modern physiology, endocrinology, and personality psychology view these temperamental approaches as inappropriate simplifications, there is no doubt that the speed, intensity, duration, and—very likely—quality of elicited emotions depend to a great degree on certain person-specific characteristics (cf. Frijda, 1986; Pervin, 1993). In the following sections I will present a number of these relationships.

In analyzing individual differences in emotional reactions, two perspectives can be differentiated. The *descriptive* perspective concentrates on the registration of individual differences in emotional reactions and tests these differences for transtemporal and cross-situational consistency. Thus, stable individual-specific emotional reaction patterns are the personality variables under study (cf. Fahrenberg, 1986). The *explicative* perspective, on the other hand, searches for person-specific determinants of certain emotional reactions, such as anxiety, anger, or sadness.

Research on individual differences in emotional reactions (descriptive perspective) and on individual differences in the determinants of these reactions (explicative perspective) form no dichotomy but a continuum of approaches with an increasingly stronger foundation in elaborated psychological (especially personality) concepts. Thus, early approaches—for example, Lacey's work on individual-specific response patterns (Lacey, 1950; for more details see next section)—concentrated on individual differences in comparatively stable constellations of certain physiological reactions without proposing explanations of these differences in terms of personality concepts. More recent approaches in this domain, however—such as emotional expressivity (cf. Gross & John, 1997) or subjective-autonomic response dissociation (cf. Newton & Contrada, 1992)—are clearly more theory based. The explicative perspective, on the other hand, shows a strong and explicit theory orientation. Since these approaches view personality variables as determinants (or co-determinants) of emotional processes, they attempt to derive hypotheses from elaborated personality concepts that predict these processes and to test these hypotheses in theory-based experiments.

I start the analysis with an overview about descriptive concepts of individual differences. Three groups of approaches are distinguished: first, variables that focus on comparatively stable differences in biological reactions such as, for example, frontal brain asymmetry; second, models that concentrate on the description of differences in psychological responding, for example, emotional expressivity; and, finally, an approach that brings together both groups within the concept of subjective-autonomic response dissociation.

I then change the perspective and present a selection of explicative approaches. I first discuss two seemingly contradictory concepts: *traits* (or personality structure) and *process*. We will see that this controversy is a pseudo-issue that can be settled by linking stable personality dispositions to contextually sensitive processing dynamics. Based on Mischel and Shoda's (1995) cognitive-affective personality system, three units especially relevant to explaining individual differences in emotional reactions and coping are discussed: appraisals, self-regulatory strategies, and goals. I conclude the chapter with a presentation of a recently proposed coping theory, the model of coping modes. This model attempts to integrate these units into a theory of processing aversive emotion-related information.

## The Descriptive Perspective

The constructs to be presented in this rubric make up a rather heterogeneous group. Some are narrow with regard to explaining variance in observable data (such as circadian rhythm); others are empirically related to a multitude of experiential and behavioral dimensions (such as, symptom reporting). Some are directly expressing individual differences in emotionality (such as, at the biological level, frontal brain asymmetry or, at the subjective-experiential level, negative and positive affectivity), whereas other constructs are related to individual differences in emotionality only indirectly, through variables that contribute to emotional experience such as activation level, perception of visceral activity, or reporting of bodily symptoms. Finally, some concepts are descriptive in the strict sense specified above (e.g., individual-specific re-

sponse patterns); others (e.g., negative and positive affectivity or emotional expressivity) are intimately related to other personality constructs, thus demonstrating considerable explicative power. These latter constructs, in fact, bridge the gap between the descriptive and the explicative perspectives.

### Biological Approaches

#### Individual-Specific Response Patterns

The autonomic response pattern observed in a given moment is the result of simultaneous sympathetic and parasympathetic activity. Based on early speculations by Eppinger and Hess (1910), Wenger (1941) introduced the concept of *autonomic balance*. He assumed that individuals tend to differ in habitual dominance of one of these autonomic systems (cf. Wenger & Cullen, 1972). While most persons should exhibit a habitual balance between sympathetic and parasympathetic activity, some individuals are supposed to characteristically show an autonomic imbalance—that is, either a sympathetic or a parasympathetic dominance. This imbalance is supposed to relate to differences in experiencing negative or positive emotions.

Empirical support for this hypothesis, however, is almost nonexistent (for a critical reexamination, see Myrtek, 1980). If at all, stable individual differences may be observed at the level of specific physiological reactions. With respect to this idea, Malmo and Shagass (1949; Malmo, Shagass, & Davis, 1950) introduced the concept of *symptom specificity*. The authors had observed that during a stressful situation patients showed the strongest reactions in the specific physiological subsystem that was associated with their psychosomatic complaints. For example, patients with heart disease showed elevated heart rates, whereas patients suffering from headaches displayed higher electromyogram (EMG) readings of their neck muscles.

The principle of individual-specific response patterns can be conceptualized as an extension of the concept of symptom specificity to the normal population. It is based on the observation that indicators of activation of different physiological subsystems often show low correlations across individuals and situations (Fahrenberg, 1986). These findings are compatible with the assumption of a selective activation of specific subsystems in different persons. In a series of pioneer studies, Lacey (1950; Lacey, Bateman, & Van Lehn, 1953) showed that individuals tend to respond with maximal activation in the same physiological function to a variety of stress situations. According to these findings, Foerster, Schneider, and Walschburger (1983, p. 2) defined individual-specific response (ISR) as the "habitual disposition of an individual to exhibit a similar response pattern (so-called *reaction stereotyping*) to various stimuli or situations. The ISR *type* refers to the habitual disposition of an individual to exhibit a *particular* response pattern, such as maximal response in a specific subsystem."

An analysis of ISR patterns obviously requires an advanced research methodology with multivariable and multisituational designs. Foerster et al. (1983) conducted a study with a large sample of participants in which seven physiological variables (skin conductance, heart rate, finger pulse, EMG, eye blink frequency, EEG, respiration) were monitored during four stress conditions (mental arithmetic, free speech, cold-pressor test, and blood-taking). Their main finding was that about one-fourth of the variance in a three-factorial ANOVA design (participants, situations, variables) may be considered as ISR patterns. Fahrenberg, Foerster, Schneider, Müller, and Myrtek (1986) examined whether ISR patterns derived from laboratory sessions could also be found in field settings. Their participants completed six laboratory tasks (mental arithmetic, relaxation, reaction time task, free speech, cold pressor, and 100 Watt exercise) and four tasks outside the laboratory (relaxation, approaching the stadium, relaxation in the stadium, and 1000-m run) while their heart rate and respiratory rate were measured. The authors found cross-situational consistent and stable ISR patterns in more participants than it would be expected by chance.

Concerning temporal stability, Foerster et al. (1983) demonstrated in a repeated measurement design (three tests in weekly intervals) that ISR patterns proved to be stable over 2 weeks. Foerster (1985) investigated the long-term stability of ISR patterns over an extended period of time: 25% of the participants showed a stable pattern over 2 months, and 14% were stable when tested again after 1 year. Marwitz and Stemmler (1998) reviewed 15 studies and concluded that approximately 30% of the participants (magnitude estimates varied from 22 to 43% between studies) tend to display an ISR pattern and one-half of these individuals (i.e., 15% of the total sample) show the same ISR pattern at intervals up to a few months.

Marwitz and Stemmler (1998) argue that the view that mere constitutional factors contribute to habitual differences in physiological responses might be too simple. Instead, they propose a revised ISR model that also takes situational and psychological factors into account. They point out that situations vary along a strong-weak dimension: Strong situations (e.g., a red traffic light) are characterized by high situational constraints and few behavioral options that allow only little variability between individuals. Weak situations, in contrast, are characterized by few situational constraints and many behavioral options and, thus, leave room for different motivational and cognitive processes. Marwitz and Stemmler reason that when two dissimilar strong conditions are presented, weak ISR is to be expected because of large situational

effects, whereas two weak conditions should result in comparatively high ISR magnitudes. Regarding psychological variables, they suggest that situation perception and appraisals are most important. These appraisals might depend on the person's goals, intentions, needs, etc. (cf. Lazarus, 1991; see also the section on "Goals and Emotions"). The authors predict that appraisals that make the psychological meaning of the situations more similar will lead to larger ISR magnitudes because situations appraised as similar result in more similar physiological responses (Stemmler, 1997). Indeed, Marwitz and Stemmler found in their study that trait anxiety (operationalized by the combination of high scores in neuroticism and low scores in extraversion) was associated with larger ISR magnitudes.

All in all, the ISR approach seems to be a promising research strategy in the field of peripheral psychophysiology, an area where different activation indexes often show low intercorrelations (Fahrenberg, 1986). Relatively stable and cross-situational consistent ISR patterns, at least in some participants, reflect the meaningfulness of this concept as an individual difference variable related to emotional reactions. On the other hand, as pointed out by Marwitz and Stemmler (1998), stability coefficients are far from being perfect. Thus, this research approach could benefit from taking situational and psychological factors into account.

Furthermore, ISR patterns might be important not only in differential psychophysiology but also in research that aims at clarifying the origins and courses of psychosomatic disorders. Strong and consistent individual-specific responses to a variety of different stimuli might lead to malfunctions of the respective physiological system that shows maximal responses. Studies conducted by Fredrikson et al. (1985) and Fahrenberg, Foerster, and Wilmers (1995), which showed that borderline hypertensives more often displayed an ISR with maximal responses in systolic blood pressure, point in this direction. The best way to prove the usefulness of the ISR concept in psychosomatic research would be prospective research. In a first step the individual's respective maximal response system would be identified in the laboratory. In a longitudinal design, it could then be analyzed whether participants develop a disease located in their "preferred" response system. Finally, if this relationship is established, specific prevention programs should be developed.

## Frontal Brain Asymmetry

Based on clinical observations that unilateral left- and right-sided lesions produce different emotional reactions in patients (cf. Tucker, 1981), researchers tried to identify the underlying biological substrata of individual differences in affective reactivity. Evidence has accumulated that activation of the left anterior hemisphere is associated with positive emotions, and activation of the right anterior hemisphere with negative emotions (Davidson, 1992). Davidson (1984) postulated that the fundamental basis of this anterior asymmetry is approach/withdrawal. It was proposed that the left frontal region is a major brain site within a brain circuit mediating approach-related behavior and that the right anterior hemisphere plays a major role in a withdrawal-related brain cycle. It was hypothesized that this differential asymmetric activation of the frontal region would be associated with affective style because positive and negative emotions involve approach and withdrawal behavior, respectively. Affective style may be separated into different features such as threshold for reactivity, peak amplitude of response, rise time to peak, and recovery time (Davidson, 1998a).

In an ambitious research program it was shown that EEG measures of frontal activation were indeed related to several variables in the affective domain (overview in Davidson, 1998a). In sum, four areas of investigation can be distinguished: (1) differential reactivity to experimental emotion induction, (2) differences in dispositional affect measures, (3) association with affective disorders, and (4) psychometric properties (internal consistency and stability) of the indexes.

Concerning *affective responses to experimental emotion induction*, Tomarken, Davidson, and Henriques (1990) showed that greater relative right-sided frontal activation at rest was related to more intense negative affect in response to negative film clips. This finding was extended by a study that analyzed affective reactions to positive and negative films 3 weeks after an initial EEG session. For participants with stable frontal asymmetry across the 3-week period, greater left frontal activation was associated with more positive affect during positive films while greater right frontal activation correlated with more intense reports of negative affect in response to negative films (Wheeler, Davidson, & Tomarken, 1993).

Employing the trait version of the Positive and Negative Affect Schedule (PANAS; Watson, Clark, & Tellegen, 1988) as a measure of *dispositional affectivity*, Tomarken, Davidson, Wheeler, and Doss (1992) showed that left-frontally activated participants reported more positive affectivity and less negative affectivity than individuals with right frontal activation. Sutton and Davidson (1997) examined the association of measures of prefrontal asymmetry with scores on the Behavioral Inhibition and Activation Scales (BIS/BAS scales; Carver & White, 1994), a trait measure more closely related to approach and avoidance than the PANAS. It was found that left-sided (as compared to right-sided) prefrontal activation was related to relative more BAS to BIS activity in the self-report domain. This association was even stronger than the one reported above for the PANAS.

If individuals display different susceptibility for positive and negative emotional states (as indexed by EEG measures of frontal asymmetry), then it might be possible to identify specific *vulnerabilities for emotion-related disorders* (cf. Tucker, 1981). Thus, chronically elevated reactivity to negative stimuli and/or diminished reactivity to positive stimuli might be an antecedent or concomitant of affective disorders. Indeed, Henriques and Davidson (1991) reported that depressive patients displayed left frontal hypoactivation. This pattern is regarded as neural correlate of the diminished capacity for positive emotional states, loss of interest, and decline in goal-related motivation and behavior (Davidson, 1998a). On the other hand, there is accumulating evidence that anxiety is associated with right frontal hyperactivation (Heller, 1993; Heller & Nitschke, 1998).

A study conducted by Tomarken, Davidson, Wheeler, and Kinney (1992) examined if indexes of anterior EEG asymmetry display the kind of *psychometric properties* that would be expected of an individual difference measure. The authors recorded baseline brain activity during two sessions separated by 3 weeks and computed coefficient alpha for the different derived measures. All values exceeded .85, thus showing good internal consistency for resting alpha asymmetry. Test-retest stability was acceptable with intraclass correlations ranging from .65 to .75 (depending on sites and methods). Thus, measures of anterior EEG asymmetry can be regarded as a trait-like index.

These findings highlight the possibility to relate theoretical concepts in the intersection of emotion, personality, and clinical psychology to neuropsychological structures and mechanisms. Results in the four areas of research described above show that a reliable and stable EEG measure of frontal asymmetry is related to reactions to affective stimuli, emotional disorders, and personality dimensions (but see also Davidson, 1998b, for a critical discussion of some negative findings). Together with the elaboration of underlying theoretical concepts this approach might profit from the further development and refinement of advanced neuroimaging methods like functional magnetic resonance imaging (fMRI) and positron emission tomography (PET) to gain a better understanding of temporal and structural mechanisms involved in individual differences in central emotional processing.

## Circadian Rhythm

The measurement of physiological, biochemical, and psychological variables at different times of day indicates individual differences in course and variability of these parameters. *Circadian rhythm* refers to the characteristic curve that describes the course of these variables within a 24-hour cycle (Kerkhof, 1985). The shape of this curve depends on the sleep-wake cycle and on specific activation patterns as determined, for example, by work schedules.

To assess individual differences in the sleep-wake cycle and to examine the preferred time of day for mental and physical performance, Horne and Östberg (1976) devised a self-report instrument. This scale allows the separation of so-called morning-type (M-type) and evening-type (E-type) individuals as extremes of the distribution; most people are classified as intermediate type (I-type). Validation studies of this concept revealed differences between M-types and E-types in several psychophysiological variables on early or late times of the day. The general trend reported in these studies is that M-types show higher activation levels as indexed by these variables in the morning than in the evening, whereas E-types displayed the opposite pattern (overview in Kerkhof, 1985).

Nebel et al. (1996) related the circadian variation of cardiovascular stress levels and reactivity to individual differences in M-E-type in both healthy and coronary artery disease participants and found significant interactions between circadian type and time of day on physiological variables. In both populations M-types exhibited higher levels of cardiovascular activity (heart rate, blood pressure) in the morning, whereas E-types reached their individual peak in the evening. Other studies examined the association between M-E-type and early-morning salivary cortisol levels (Bailey & Heitkemper, 1991) as well as sleep phases and brain potentials (Kerkhof & Lancel, 1991).

Aside from these biological variables, circadian type is also related to differential peaks in reaction times: M-types react faster in the morning and E-types faster in the evening (Kerkhof, 1985). Furthermore, Fahrenberg, Brügner, Foerster, and Käppler (1999) showed that M-E-type was related to diurnal change in working memory performance: Morning types showed a better performance index at earlier times of the day. In contrast, E-types reached their peak performance later in the day. Cofer et al. (1999) reported that M-E-type was related to ease of rising, level of tiredness, and conflict with parents over daily routines in retrospective reports of college students. Although sleep-wake patterns exhibit a strong genetic component (Hur, Bouchard, & Lykken, 1998, estimated that genetic variability accounted for about 54% of the total variance in morningness-eveningness), nonshared environmental influences such as activities with peers, as well as school and work schedules, also have an important influence on M-E-type. Specific relevance of the M-E-type distinction lies in its application to factors associated with working times (especially shift work). If (some) individuals do have biological "preferences" (as indexed by psychophysiological variables and performance measures), it would be useful to identify these persons and to match their working environment with the optimal level of their sleep-wake cycle (Khaleque, 1999; Nachreiner, 1998).

The relationship of M-E-type to arousal-related personality dimensions such as extroversion-introversion seems to be rather low. There is a weak trend that morningness and extraversion are negatively correlated—that is, greater scores on extraversion scales correspond with a greater tendency to eveningness (Tankova, Adan, & Buela-Casal, 1994). This effect may be interpreted as reflecting an indirect relationship because both variables have an influence on sleep-wake behavior: Bedtimes are not only determined by an endogenous clock but also by psychosocial influences. Habitual differences in sleep times and patterns could have a masking effect upon other circadian rhythms. It is assumed that the extroversion-introversion dimension has its impact on diurnal patterns through these differences in sleeptimes (Kerkhof, 1985).

## Subjective and Behavioral Approaches

### Interoception

The field of interoception or visceral perception is concerned with the perception of internal bodily changes like heartbeat, blood pressure, or signals of the gastrointestinal system (Vaitl, 1996). The importance of the perception of these changes—in particular autonomic activity—for the generation of emotions is put forward in prominent theories such as those formulated by James (1884), Cannon (1927), and Schachter and Singer (1962).

A great variety of research paradigms have been developed to measure the ability to accurately detect or estimate physiological activity in the body (overviews in Hodapp & Knoll, 1993; Jones, 1994). In general, two different approaches can be distinguished. The first approach examines detection ability in laboratory settings and aims at measuring pure perceptions of autonomic activity by controlling for all environmental or situational factors. Experiments of this tradition often use signal-detection methodologies that require participants to identify the correct pattern of their autonomic activity over several trials while they sit quietly in sound-attenuated chambers. The second approach, which is less controlled and more naturalistic, requires participants to report their autonomic activity repeatedly in their natural environment (e.g., at their home or at work) or after performing physically or emotionally demanding tasks in the laboratory. The latter approach allows participants to rely on internal and external cues when estimating autonomic activity, whereas the former approach solely relies on internal cues. In addition, two types of accuracy have been distinguished (cf. Pennebaker & Watson, 1988): *Level accuracy* describes the overall discrepancy between average estimated autonomic activity and mean actual levels; *covariation accuracy* refers to the degree to which fluctuations of estimated autonomic responding covary with actual fluctuations (see also Kohlmann, 1993b).

The ability to accurately perceive bodily processes has been related, among others, to gender, hemispheric lateralization, and attentional style.

In general, interoceptive accuracy is lowest when signal-detection paradigms are employed, slightly better in self-report studies after performing certain tasks in the laboratory, and best in natural settings. Obviously, accuracy increases with the availability of external cues. *Gender differences* are manifested in the same sequence (cf. Roberts & Pennebaker, 1995). In signal-detection studies, male participants are generally more accurate than women in perceiving autonomic activity, especially heartbeat. This difference becomes weaker in more naturalistic self-report laboratory studies with some, albeit limited external information, and disappears in field studies—that is, when external cues are fully available (see also Kohlmann, 1993b). This relationship suggests that women rely more on external cues when assessing their bodily state, whereas men use internal as well as external cues.

In a naturalistic laboratory setting relying on self-report, Kohlmann (1993b) assessed level accuracy and covariation accuracy in blood pressure estimation in response to certain tasks and rest periods. He observed, first, that women tend to rely more on external cues than men; second, men and women were equal in covariation accuracy, but, third, that marked gender differences exist for level accuracy. Women overestimated their systolic blood pressure in response to cognitive tasks (e.g., mental arithmetic), whereas men underestimated their blood pressure in response to a rest period. Kohlmann assumes that self-concepts about abilities might be a crucial moderating variable that, however, needs further investigation.

Another variable of relevance, possibly related to gender differences, is *hemispheric lateralization.* Presumably, the right hemisphere is particularly involved in the processing of emotional stimuli (cf. Kinsbourne & Bemporad, 1984; Safer, 1981). It has been found that right-hemisphere activation and preference (as tested by lateral eye movements) are associated with better heartbeat detection ability in signal detection paradigms (e.g., Davidson, Horowitz, Schwartz, & Goodman, 1981; Hantas, Katkin, & Reed, 1984; Katkin, Cestaro, & Weitkunat, 1991; Montgomery & Jones, 1984).

Two findings might relate hemispheric lateralization to the gender differences in the ability to perceive bodily states reported above (cf. Roberts & Pennebaker, 1995; Safer, 1981): Men show greater right-hemisphere lateralization for a number of domains than women, and women are generally less lateralized than men. Roberts and Pennebaker assume that men's greater right-hemisphere dominance provides an advantage when the estimation of bodily states solely rests on the accurate processing of internal cues, as is the case in signal-detection designs.

A further important individual difference variable in interoception research is *attentional style* (cf. Cioffi, 1991). As will be elaborated in the section on individual differences in coping, some individuals, called vigilants (cf.

Krohne, 1989, 1993a, 1993b), have a tendency to focus on—in particular unpleasant—emotional states, while other individuals, designated as cognitive avoiders, distract their attention away from (internal and external) emotional cues. This basic definition of attentional styles leads to the hypothesis that vigilant orientation is positively associated with better interoception and, consequently, better access to one's feeling states (see McFarland & Buehler, 1997). In contrast, avoidant attentional orientation should be negatively correlated with interoceptive performance.

Empirical support for this hypothesis, however, seems to be mixed. Kohlmann (1993b) found level accuracy in blood pressure estimation to be unrelated to vigilant or avoidant styles. However, for individuals high in cognitive avoidance, the percentage of variance in blood pressure estimation accounted for by external (i.e., situational) cues was significantly higher than for low avoiders. Kohlmann related this finding to Pennebaker's (1989) concept of "low-level thinking." This type of thinking can be observed during stressful encounters and is characterized by a narrow perspective, a lack of self-reflection, and a low awareness of feeling states. By adopting this strategy, the individual effectively blocks the processing of emotional information.

Hodapp and Knoll (1993) report a finding that only at first glance seems to contradict the results reported by Kohlmann. The authors observed that good heartbeat perception as assessed with a signal detection procedure is associated with lower emotionality (i.e., affect intensity and anxiety), lower vigilance, and higher cognitive avoidance. This pattern seems to contradict the idea that vigilance leads to better and cognitive avoidance to poorer interoceptive performance. It fits, however, rather nicely into Pennebaker's concept of low-level thinking and even better into Cioffi's (1991) cognitive-perceptual model of somatic interpretation. Following Leventhal's notion that monitoring of internal states works to the extent that sensation-distress associations are disrupted (cf. Leventhal & Everhart, 1979), Cioffi views sensory attention to internal physical sensations as a distraction strategy that works at the expense of any higher order interpretation of this event. As the individual processes this internal information, fixed attentional capacity may allow the processing of little else. "Thus sensory monitoring may 'work' because of what it avoids or replaces" (Cioffi, 1991, p. 34).

## Symptom Reporting

Experimental studies on individual-specific response (ISR) patterns described above revealed individual differences in physiological reactions to various situations. Pennebaker (1982) analyzed whether one could find similar individual differences on the subjective-experiential level.

Two main questions are to be answered: Do specific associations between perceived autonomic arousal (i.e., physical sensations) and reported emotions exist? Do people consistently differ in their perceptions or reports of physical sensations and symptoms, respectively?

To analyze *associations of physical sensations with reported emotions*, Pennebaker (1982) asked participants to complete a symptom-emotion checklist on a variety of occasions. A few symptoms were indeed related to specific feeling states in most participants—for example, feeling "tense" was associated with the symptoms of "trembling" or "tense muscles." On the other hand, there were huge individual differences in the magnitude and direction of the association between emotions and physical sensations. Similar findings were reported in a study by Pennebaker, Gonder-Frederick, Stewart, Elfman, and Skelton (1982). The authors analyzed associations between changes in blood pressure and the reporting of symptoms during several laboratory tasks. A between-subject analysis revealed no significant association between blood pressure and any symptom. However, in a within-subject analysis (correlating the symptoms with blood pressure across 40 observations for each participant individually), 23 of the 30 participants had at least one significant association and 13 had at least one correlation that exceeded $r = .70$. Type of association, however, differed between participants. For example, for one person the symptoms of pounding heart, heavy breathing, and tense stomach correlated highly with blood pressure, whereas for another only the perception of sweaty hands was significantly related to blood pressure. In addition, within-subject factor analysis of the symptom reports yielded one factor that reflected the within-subject correlations of symptoms with blood pressure for the majority of participants. The composition of this symptom factor was, of course, different for each individual. Analogous results were reported for field studies with blood pressure and blood glucose level as physiological variables (Pennebaker, 1982; see also Pennebaker, 2000, for a most recent review).

A number of studies demonstrated that *individuals consistently differ in the extent to which they report physical symptoms* (cf. Leventhal, 1986). Kroenke and Spitzer (1998) assessed the effect of gender on the reporting of 13 common physical symptoms. After adjusting for depressive and anxiety disorders as well as age, race, education, and medical comorbidity, the authors registered that women had significantly higher reporting scores for 10 of 13 symptoms. Although depressive and anxiety disorders were the strongest correlates of symptom reporting, gender had an independent effect and was the most important demographic predictor of symptom reporting. In a study relating dispositional coping to symptom reporting, Kohlmann and Krohne (1991) found that vigilance was significantly associated with high scores on a symptom-emotion

checklist to be completed five times per day on 7 consecutive days.

Pennebaker conceptualized symptom reporting as a stable unidimensional construct. This variable, which can be assessed by means of the Pennebaker Inventory of Limbic Languidness (PILL; Pennebaker, 1982), is internally consistent, meaning that a person reporting any symptom is likely to report others. Watson and Pennebaker (1989, 1991) postulated that the dispositional basis of symptom reporting is negative affectivity (NA): "NA reflects pervasive individual differences in negative emotionality and self-concept: High-NA individuals tend to be distressed and upset and have a negative view of self" (Watson & Clark, 1984, p. 465). A commonly used instrument for measuring affectivity is the Positive and Negative Affect Schedule (PANAS; Watson et al., 1988). Watson and Pennebaker (1989, 1991) presented data sets that showed a strong correlation between the PANAS NA subscale and PILL scores ($r$'s between .40 and .50). The authors argue that individuals high in NA are more likely than low-NA persons to attend to or to complain about physical sensations and symptoms. Consequently, NA is more strongly related to the reporting of symptoms than to objective indicators of health.

## Negative and Positive Affectivity

There is strong agreement that the constructs negative affectivity, trait anxiety, and neuroticism form one fundamental part, beside extraversion-introversion, of any personality taxonomy (cf. Revelle, 1995). These constructs are not identical but closely related. *Negative affectivity* (NA) is the most general concept. The negative emotional states experienced by persons high in NA include the anxiety-related feelings of nervousness, tension, and worry, but also such states as anger, guilt, self-dissatisfaction, and sadness. NA is viewed as a very pervasive personality disposition that manifests itself even in the absences of overt stressors. "NA . . . emphasizes how people feel about themselves and their world rather than how effectively they may actually handle themselves in the world" (Watson & Clark, 1984, p. 466).

The NA components nervousness, tensions, and worry indicate a substantial overlap between the negative affectivity disposition and trait anxiety. A major difference between both constructs, however, is that anxiety is conceived as being largely reactive in nature, whereas negative affectivity is viewed as a pervasive disposition not necessarily dependent for its manifestation on the confrontation with a "negative" situation. In line with this differentiation, *trait anxiety* is defined as the intraindividually stable but interindividually varying tendency to appraise situations as threatening and to react to these situations with an elevated state of anxiety (cf. Krohne, 1996a; Spielberger, 1972).

Watson and Clark view NA as being unrelated to the experience of positive affects (PA). Empirical support for this (somewhat counterintuitive) conception of affective experience comes from results obtained with the PANAS. This inventory generally produces largely independent scores for positive (PA) and negative affect (NA). This two-dimensional conception has been challenged, however, by several authors (see Egloff, Tausch, Kohlmann, & Krohne, 1995; Feldman Barrett & Russell, 1998; Green, Goldman, & Salovey, 1993; Russell & Feldman Barrett, 1999). Egloff et al., for example, pointed out that the PA subscale of the PANAS is largely defined by items that describe states of positive activation (e.g., active, strong, attentive), whereas items referring to a positive but less active state (e.g., happy, content, at ease) are not included in the PANAS (see also Larsen & Diener, 1992). Egloff et al. (1995) constructed two different measures to assess PA, one to measure the activation component (including items such as active, attentive, inspired), the other to measure the (non-active) pleasantness component of PA (e.g., happy, content, at ease). They obtained a correlation of $r = .45$ between PA-activation and PA-pleasantness. More interestingly, however, PA-activation and NA were indeed unrelated ($r = -.07$), while PA-pleasantness and NA exhibited a highly negative correlation ($r = -.58$). The authors concluded that it was the activation bias of the PANAS that resulted in the frequently observed independence of the PA and NA scales (see also Feldman Barrett & Russell, 1998, for similar conclusions).

## Emotional Expressivity

Individuals express the emotions they feel through their verbal and nonverbal behavior. The most prominent *nonverbal* communication channel of feeling states is the human face. To quantify facial expressive behavior, Ekman and Friesen (1978) developed the anatomically based Facial Action Coding System (FACS), which specifies 44 distinct facial movements ("action units"). Aside from facial expressions, changes in motor activity of the body are another sign of how someone feels (e.g., sitting upright in pride; Stepper & Strack, 1993). Concerning *verbal* behavior, the most obvious information about how people feel is what they say (e.g., "I feel anxious"). The PANAS described above is currently the most widely used instrument for assessing self-reported emotional states. While the original scale (Watson et al., 1988) primarily aimed at independently measuring the two broad emotion categories of positive and negative affect, the expanded form (PANAS-X; Watson & Clark, 1994) allows a more fine-grained analysis of different positive (e.g., joviality, serenity) and negative (e.g., fear, sadness, guilt) emotional

states. Further scales used to assess verbal reports of emotional experience are the Multiple Affect Adjective Check List (MAACL; Zuckerman & Lubin, 1965), the Profile of Mood States (POMS; McNair, Lorr, & Droppleman, 1971), and the Differential Emotions Scale (DES; Izard, 1991).

Individual differences in emotional expressivity have always been an interesting topic for personality psychologists (see Allport & Vernon, 1933, for an early approach). Differences between persons in the communication of affect via nonverbal expressions may be located at both the sender and the receiver side of an affect-related message. Buck (1984; Buck, Miller, & Caul, 1974; Buck, Savin, Miller, & Caul, 1972) developed an experimental paradigm to study individual differences in sending and receiving accuracy. A participant serving as sender was shown a series of emotion-eliciting slides. After a short period of time, the participant had to describe his or her emotional response. Unknown to the sender, his or her face was televised (without audio) to a receiver who had to rate the sender's emotional state and the category of the slide (e.g., sad, fear-arousing).

Two groups of findings seem to be most important. First, female senders displayed greater facial responsiveness to the induced emotion than male senders (i.e., they showed more accurate communication of emotions), but were not more accurate than males as observers. The finding that women are more emotionally expressive than men was replicated in several studies (e.g., Kring & Gordon, 1998). Second, participants who were the most expressive facially were least responsive physiologically (especially concerning skin conductance responses). Buck (1984) related this well-documented finding (see, e.g., Notarius & Levenson, 1979) to the internalizer-externalizer distinction first proposed by Jones (1935): A person high in overt emotional expression and low in skin conductance responding is described as an externalizer, whereas the internalizer shows the opposite pattern. I will resume this concept of a dissociation between different emotion channels when I discuss subjective-autonomic response dissociation.

Gross and John (1997, p. 435) defined emotional expressivity as "behavioral (e.g., facial, postural) changes that typically accompany an emotion, such as smiling, frowning, crying, or storming out of the room." Thus, this definition is not limited to a specific channel of expression or to a specific emotion. According to their model of emotion, individual differences in emotional expressivity can arise at several stages of the emotion process: at the input level, at the appraisal level, at the response tendency level, and at the output filter (i.e., at the translation of response tendencies into behavior).

In contrast to unidimensional conceptions of emotional expressivity (see Friedman, Prince, Riggio, & DiMatteo, 1980; Kring, Smith, & Neale, 1994), Gross and John (1997) found in their factor analyses three correlated facets of expressivity: impulse strength, negative expressivity, and positive expressivity. While the first facet measures the general strength of the emotion-response tendencies, the expressivity facets refer to the subsequent modulation of the activated response tendencies. Negative (positive) expressivity represents the degree to which negative (positive) emotional response tendencies are expressed behaviorally. All three facets correlated with one another in the $r = .50$ range. Consequently, Gross and John suggested a hierarchical model with a general expressivity factor as the superordinate dimension.

Validation studies showed positive correlations of peer- and self-ratings in expressivity. Furthermore the expressivity questionnaire differentially predicted expressive behavior: Positive expressivity predicted amusement expressions (e.g., smiling) but not sadness expressions to a positive film, and negative expressivity was associated with sadness expressions (e.g., crying) but not with amusement expressions to a negative film. Impulse strength showed a moderate positive correlation with both negative and positive expressive behavior. These associations held even when controlling for subjective experience and physiological responding (Gross & John, 1997).

Recently, Gross and John (1998) conducted a factor analysis of six expressivity scales and introduced a revised and expanded structural model of emotional expressivity with general expressivity at the top, core emotional expressivity at the second level, and positive expressivity, negative expressivity, and impulse strength at the bottom of the hierarchy. Expressive confidence (e.g., "I would probably make a good actor") and masking ("I'm not always the person I appear to be") formed two further facets at the second level. Women scored higher than men on all three core expressivity components, whereas men scored higher on masking. Although this is a promising approach to emotional expressivity in the self-report domain, future research is warranted to clarify the structure of these dimensions. Furthermore, validation studies with criterion measures that are more ecologically valid than film clips are needed to substantiate the value of this construct.

## Subjective-Autonomic Response Dissociation

When relying on different parameters as indicators of emotional arousal, the following restrictions have to be taken into account. Each parameter is subject to specific physiological and psychological regulations (Leventhal, 1991). These regulatory processes may have different temporal extensions and are determined by different factors, including personality dispositions. It is therefore highly unlikely that an individual will exhibit parallel courses of these parameters during an emotion-inducing situation.

Even if we observe parallel changes in the data aggregated across a subject sample, this does not necessarily imply that these parameters are correlated. In fact, correlations among emotion variables from different domains are generally rather low (cf. Krohne, 1996a). Low correlations, however, do not necessarily indicate a lack of validity of one or the other assessment procedure. They only demonstrate that no parameter (e.g., self-reported arousal) can be substituted by another parameter (e.g., variables from the autonomic nervous system). Each parameter must be interpreted with respect to the specific emotion-inducing situation (for example, controllable vs. uncontrollable situations; Frankenhaeuser, 1986), the time point of assessment (e.g., preparation for an emotional confrontation, confrontation, or postconfrontation), and relevant personality dispositions (cf. Lazarus, 1966). The idea that the single parameters of emotional arousal are subject to situation- and person-specific regulatory processes is fundamental to the concept of subjective-autonomic response dissociation.

With respect to personality, a number of studies demonstrated that the dimension *cognitive avoidance* is related to a so-called subjective-autonomic response dissociation. (For a more detailed conceptualization of cognitive avoidance, see the section on individual differences in coping.) In general, individuals high in cognitive avoidance report relatively low levels of subjective distress but at the same time exhibit considerable elevations in physiological arousal in response to a stressful encounter (cf. Kohlmann, 1993a, 1997, for overviews).

The dissociation of subjective and autonomic stress responses among avoidant individuals was first discussed by Lazarus (1966) and first systematically investigated in a reanalysis of experiments conducted by Lazarus and co-workers (cf. Weinstein, Averill, Opton, & Lazarus, 1968). Recognizing the above-mentioned lack of covariation in subjective and autonomic responses, Lazarus stated that "when a person says he does not feel anxious or disturbed but shows a marked physiological-stress reaction, we learn something different about the ongoing psychological processes . . . than if he reports marked anxiety along with concordant physiological responses. In the former instance, we might speak of social pressures or defensive efforts . . . different ways of coping with threat are associated with different autonomic as well as behavioral patterns of reaction" (Lazarus, 1966, pp. 387–388, 390). In accordance with this assumption, Weinstein et al. (1968) demonstrated relatively greater autonomic (heart rate, skin conductance) than subjective (self-reported anxiety) stress reactions in avoidant as compared to nonavoidant individuals (as assessed by the Repression-Sensitization Scale; Byrne, 1961). Similar results have been reported, among others, by Weinberger, Schwartz, and Davidson (1979); Asendorpf and Scherer (1983), and Kiecolt-Glaser and

Greenberg (1983). These studies identified avoidant individuals (called "repressers") by low scores in trait anxiety and high scores in social desirability.

Gudjonsson (1981) reversed this individual difference paradigm by trying to predict scores on personality scales from discrepancies between self-reports of distress and relative changes in autonomic responses (skin conductance). Participants were asked ego-threatening questions such as "Did you ever steal things?" and rated their distress on a visual analogue scale. In addition, electrodermal responses were recorded for each question. Avoidant individuals (repressers) were defined by low scores in subjective distress and high autonomic responding, while the opposite configuration made up the group of vigilant persons (sensitizers). In accordance with the results reported above, avoidant individuals had significantly higher scores in social desirability and on a lie scale, and lower scores in neuroticism than participants with other patterns of subjective and physiological data.

Some authors applied the discrepancy paradigm to the prediction of health-related variables. Comparing malignant melanoma patients to matched cardiovascular disease patients and disease-free controls, Kneier and Temoshok (1984) identified avoidant and vigilant individuals with a procedure very similar to the one described in the Gudjonsson study. The authors observed that the melanoma group was significantly more avoidant, as defined by the discrepancy score, while the cardiovascular disease patients were the least avoidant (or most vigilant). In a longitudinal study with conjugally bereaved participants, Bonanno, Keltner, Holen, and Horowitz (1995) defined "emotionally avoidant" individuals by a negative verbal-autonomic response dissociation (low self-rated negative emotion coupled with heightened cardiovascular activity) measured during an interview 6 months after a conjugal loss. While emotional avoidance was correlated positively with high levels of somatic symptoms 6 months after loss, this relationship reversed by 14 months. In addition, negative dissociation scores at 6 months were associated with minimal grief symptoms after 14 months.

More recent studies on subjective-autonomic response dissociation have considered situational variables as possible moderators of the relationship between avoidant-vigilant personality styles and subjective/objective stress reactions (cf. Kohlmann, 1997; Newton & Contrada, 1992). One important variable seems to be the presence of evaluative cues. It has been shown that these cues heighten public self-awareness and thereby increase the salience of social standards (Carver & Scheier, 1981). Newton and Contrada (1992) conceptualized dispositional avoidance (or repression) as an emotion-focused coping style in which emotional responses are regulated by self-appraisals involving social evaluative standards. The authors conducted a study in which participants gave a self-disclosure speech (about the most undesirable aspect of their personality) under conditions in which social evaluative concerns were minimized (private condition) or maximized by leading participants to believe they were being observed (public condition). In accordance with expectations, Newton and Contrada observed that repressers (defined by low self-reported anxiety and high social desirability) exhibited heart rate elevations that were greater in magnitude than their self-reported negative affect, but only in the public condition. Individuals high in anxiety and low in social desirability (so-called high-anxious persons) in both conditions showed the opposite pattern of subjective-autonomic dissociation—that is self-reported distress exceeded cardiac response. Individuals low in both anxiety and social desirability (low-anxious persons) showed little responsivity in either channel and, consequently, no dissociation.

In explaining these contrasting subjective-autonomic response dissociations in individuals with opposing patterns of anxiety and social desirability scores, Newton and Contrada proposed a self-regulatory theory in which differences in self-concept in the domain of emotionality predispose these two groups of individuals to engage in contrasting, emotion-focused coping strategies. Kohlmann (1993a), however, carefully reanalyzed a number of studies on the relationship between coping dispositions and response dissociation and concluded that discrepancy between subjective and objective measures of arousal can be mostly reduced to two main effects: an effect of (trait) anxiety on self-reported distress and an effect of social desirability on autonomic arousal. While the anxiety-distress effect is self-evident, Kohlmann assumes for social desirability that this personality disposition leads to intensified effort and engagement, especially if social standards are salient. This engagement, in turn, is associated with the investment of energy when solving a concomitant task (such as delivering a speech). Thus, Kohlmann reasons that "discrepancies" are simply the result of two main effects on two different classes of variables.

Although this critique does not apply to every experiment in this field (Kohlmann, 1997, himself reported data displaying a "true" discrepancy effect), it certainly points to a number of shortcomings to be eliminated in future research on individual differences in subjective-autonomic response dissociation. First, when multiple-variable approaches are employed in determining certain personality styles, independent effects for each variable on discrepancy scores together with interactive effects have to be determined. Second, before calculating discrepancy scores it has to be determined whether each variable entering the score is independently affected by the personality variables. Third, more attention should be paid to the specific autonomic variable that will most likely be influenced by (coping-related) regulatory processes. Candidates for this analysis are indicators of beta-adrenergic activation (increases in heart rate and systolic blood pressure; see, e.g., Kohlmann, Weidner, & Messina, 1996). Fourth, research is needed that systematically varies situations according to parameters relevant to processes of self-regulation and, thus, registers situational influence on the relationship between personality and response dissociation.

## The Explicative Perspective

### Personality Dispositions and Processing Dynamics

About two decades ago, a controversy evolved concerning the usefulness of the trait (or disposition) concept for predicting an individual's actual behavior and emotional reactions. An illustration of this controversy can be found in research on stress. The main objection against a trait-centered approach in this field, which has been put forward in particular by Richard Lazarus and colleagues (Folkman & Lazarus, 1985; Lazarus, 1990, 1993; Lazarus & Folkman, 1984, 1987), points to the variability in behavior observed for the majority of individuals in stressful or emotion-inducing situations. Lazarus characterized this intraindividual variability in behavior as a process, and contrasted this process with structure, which in his opinion refers to stable factors such as personality traits. Because these traits are assumed to be intraindividually invariable, or *static*, Lazarus and colleagues argued that "structural approaches cannot reveal changes in stress-related phenomena" (Folkman & Lazarus, 1985, p. 228). Lazarus therefore called for a shift away from trait concepts as the focal points in the analysis of stress, emotions, and coping, and, instead, for an emphasis on the contingencies of situational demands and specific behavior patterns (cf. Lazarus, 1990, 1993; Lazarus & Folkman, 1987).

Several authors have argued against this view and suggested reconsidering the potential of the personality concept for clarifying phenomena of coping and emotions (cf. Ben-Porath & Tellegen, 1990; Costa & McCrae, 1990; Krohne, 1986, 1990, 1993b; Larsen, 1989; Watson, 1990). Krohne (1993b, p. 20) presented a number of points demonstrating that an antagonism between personality trait or structure and the concept of process (i.e., changes in emotional and coping behavior during a stressful encounter) does not exist:

1. The terms *process* and *structure* represent different conceptual levels. Process refers to a stream of *observed* events, while structure describes the regularity that one might *infer* from such an observation and the constellation of assumed mechanisms

that affect this process. Structure, regularity, and mechanisms make up the concept of system.

2. Change and stability are not opposing concepts because *stable* is not the same as *static*. Static, in fact, means "no change." Changes, however, can be stable or unstable. *Instability* refers to a system's inability to put a boundary on its states along the time course of an encounter. This instability frequently indicates the imminent breakdown of a system (Ashby, 1956). *Stability of change* (cf. Herrmann, 1973), on the other hand, implies that a process is—of course only to a certain degree—replicable. These stable changes, however, can only be identified if the crucial effect mechanisms that this process is based on have been previously identified. Consequently, Mischel and Shoda (1998, p. 242) reversed the Folkman and Lazarus (1985) statement "if it changes, it must be a process" into "if it is a processing system, then it must respond to changing conditions." Empirical evidence for this stability of change has been obtained, for example, in the frequency and regularity of daily mood changes over time when individuals are assessed repeatedly (cf. Larsen, 1987, 1989; Larsen & Kasimatis, 1990).

3. Effect mechanisms are identified by using both methods of induction and deduction (see also Mischel & Shoda, 1998). First, a fine-grained analysis of a stream of events is applied. This *inductive* analysis aims at obtaining evidence for a transtemporal or cross-situational consistency in this stream (cf. Laux & Weber, 1987), and, thus, at generating ideas about possible effect mechanisms. Regularity (or stability) in this stream may then be detected by *deduction*—that is, by applying specific theoretical concepts to the behavioral analysis (cf. Herrmann, 1973).

This stability-of-change conception moves away from global and uncontextualized trait concepts (such as, e.g., anxiety, neuroticism, or optimism) and toward building a theory of processing dynamics that mirrors the complexity of human cognitive operations and behavioral expressions. Most of these approaches draw on models of information processing (cf. Krohne, 1993b; Mischel & Shoda, 1995) and are associated with a shift in focus. The focus now is not primarily on how much of a particular unit a person has, but more on "how the units relate to each other within that person, forming a unique network of interconnections that functions as an organized whole" (Mischel & Shoda, 1998, p. 237).

In searching for central elements of this network, Mischel and Shoda (1995) have proposed five units (called mediators) that form the core of their cognitive-affective personality system (CAPS): (1) encodings, (2) expectancies and beliefs, (3) affect, (4) goals and values, and (5) self-regulatory plans and competencies. Karoly (1999) has recently questioned the notion that each of these five units should be afforded equivalent explanatory status. He points out that these units differ in their complexity, cognitive accessibility, temporal extendedness, and dependence on intellect. He contends, instead, that goals and self-regulation are at the core of the personality network and that the other elements should be regarded as subsidiary. I basically agree with Karoly's notion, with the exception of encodings (or appraisal tendencies), which I view as another fundamental processing unit.

In the remaining part of this section, I first consider the role of the mediating personality units appraisals, emotion regulation (as a special case of self-regulation), and goals as constructs related to individual differences in emotional reactions. I then present the concept of coping, together with a recently proposed personality-oriented theory that attempts to integrate these mediating units into a dynamic model of processing aversive information.

### Appraisals and Emotion Generation

The concept of appraisal, introduced into emotion research by Arnold (1960) and elaborated with respect to stress and anxiety processes by Lazarus (1966; Lazarus & Launier, 1978), and to emotion generation in general by Frijda (1986, 1993), Lazarus (1991), and Scherer (1984, 1993), is a key factor for understanding the personality-emotion relationship. (For a review of different approaches, see Scherer, 1988.) This concept is based on the idea that emotional processes are dependent on expectancies that persons manifest with regard to the outcome of a specific episode. This concept is necessary to explain individual differences in quality, intensity, and duration of an elicited emotion in environments that are objectively equal for different individuals (e.g., a classroom test). It is generally assumed that the resulting emotional state is generated, maintained, and eventually altered by a specific pattern of appraisals. These appraisals, in turn, are determined by a number of situational and personal factors. The most important factors on the personality side are motivational dispositions, goals, values, and generalized (self-efficacy and outcome) expectancies. In this section I will concentrate on two prominent approaches: first, the Lazarus conception of appraisal (Lazarus, 1991); and second, Scherer's "stimulus evaluation check" model (Scherer, 1984).

In his monograph on emotion and adaptation, Lazarus (1991) has developed a comprehensive emotion theory that distinguishes two basic forms of appraisal—primary and secondary appraisal (see also Lazarus, 1966). These forms have different sources of information. *Primary appraisal* concerns whether something of relevance to the individual's well-being occurs, whereas *secondary appraisal* concerns coping options.

Within *primary appraisal*, three components are distinguished: goal relevance, goal congruence, and type of ego-involvement. *Goal relevance* designates the extent to which an encounter refers to issues about which the person cares. *Goal congruence* describes the extent to which an episode proceeds in accordance with personal goals. *Type of ego-involvement* refers to a number of (rather fuzzy) aspects of personal commitment such as self-esteem, moral values, ego-ideal, or ego-identity.

Likewise, three *secondary appraisal* components are distinguished: blame or credit, coping potential, and future expectations. *Blame or credit* is the result of an individual's appraisal of who is responsible for a certain outcome. *Coping potential* refers to a person's evaluation of the prospects for generating certain (cognitive or behavioral) operations that will positively influence a personally relevant encounter. *Future expectations* describes the appraisal of the further course of an encounter with respect to goal congruence or incongruence.

Lazarus distinguishes 15 basic emotions. The emergence of each emotion is the consequence of a specific pattern of these components of primary and secondary appraisal. At a more molar level, these specific appraisal patterns are described as "core relational themes." The core relational theme of anxiety, for example, is the confrontation with uncertainty and existential threat. At a more molecular level, the anxiety theme is based on the following pattern of primary and secondary appraisals: There must be some goal relevance to the encounter; furthermore, goal incongruence is high—that is, personal goals are thwarted; finally, ego involvement concentrates on the protection of personal meaning or ego-identity against existential threats.

Based on his component process theory of emotions, Scherer (1984) postulates that appraisal criteria (called stimulus evaluation checks, or SEC) occur in an invariant sequence. This notion is based on phylogenetic, ontogenetic, and microgenetic considerations. It is assumed that the organism continuously performs evaluations to gain updated information about changes in the external world and the internal state (e.g., current needs, goals, regulatory options). This SEC sequence frequently progresses in a loop—that is, the sequence may be resumed several times. It is therefore expected that the sequential SECs occur in very rapid succession, which implies that the different steps are not necessarily present in awareness. The assumptions of continuous operation and rapid succession may explain sudden changes in emotional reactions and coping behavior frequently observed during an emotion-inducing episode.

The SEC model defines a sequence of five main appraisal categories: novelty, intrinsic pleasantness, goal significance, coping potential, and compatibility standards. Each category is specified by a number of subcategories that are the true appraisal units. For novelty, for example, these categories are suddenness, familiarity, and predictability. The specific patterns resulting from the different appraisals along these categories are supposed to differentiate among 14 basic emotions (cf. Scherer, 1988). For each emotion, however, only a limited number of categories is relevant. For anxiety, for example, the following SEC sequence is postulated: a low degree of suddenness; the event is significant with respect to the individual's goals and needs; probability and urgency of goal attainment are medium. With respect to coping potential, the event is first appraised as being caused by other persons or natural circumstances; the individual then expects to possess only a low coping potential; and, finally, the individual assumes to exhibit a certain (medium) adjustment potential.

Although there is a high degree of convergence of these two approaches, some differences are striking. The first difference concerns the complexity of the appraisal categories. The Lazarus categories are markedly more complex than Scherer's categories. This implies that Scherer's system may also be employed for the analysis of laboratory stressors (and probably has been developed for this purpose), while the categories defined by Lazarus seem to be more relevant for real-life encounters.

The second difference is related to the role of personality variables as determinants of appraisals and, hence, emotional reactions. The Lazarus theory emphasizes the importance of personality concepts, such as personal goals, self-esteem, ego-ideal, or self-efficacy expectancies concerning coping, in the process of emotion generation. In contrast, Scherer, though not neglecting individual differences altogether, is clearly more concerned with the general determinants of appraisal and emotion generation.

A third difference refers to the assumed sequence of appraisals. Scherer proposes an invariant sequence, whereas Lazarus argues that different sequences are possible. (Under certain circumstances, primary appraisal, for example, may even follow secondary appraisal.) Unfortunately, Lazarus fails to specify the situational and personal conditions that lead to a specific sequence of appraisals. In addition, definition of categories is so fuzzy that it is sometimes difficult to assign a specific appraisal to a certain category. What is, for example, the precise difference between goal incongruence (personal goals are thwarted) and threats to ego-identity?

Although both researchers accept that appraisal processes may be automatic (leading to unconscious appraisals) or controlled (resulting in conscious awareness of the appraisal outcome), the study of appraisal processes almost exclusively relies on verbal reports, thus implicitly assuming that all appraisal outcomes are conscious. What is needed are assessment techniques that do not depend on self-report. These techniques may include neuropsychological strategies (cf., e.g., LeDoux, 1996) as well as

"classical" psychological data sources (e.g., reaction times, memory data, or ratings; cf. Hock, Krohne, & Kaiser, 1996).

## Mechanisms and Processes of Emotion Regulation

The topic of emotion regulation has been of interest since Freud (1923/1961) began to examine the relationship between the control of affective impulses and psychic health. Emotional regulation can be defined as the process by which activation in one domain serves to influence (stabilize, attenuate, or enhance) activation in another domain (see Dodge, 1989). More specifically, Gross (1998, p. 275) pointed out that emotion regulation involves changes in "the latency, rise time, magnitude, duration, and offset of responses in behavioral, experiential, or physiological domains."

Thompson (1994) listed neurophysiological responses, the cognitive processes of attention, information processing, and encoding of internal cues, as well as behavioral mechanisms such as regulating the demands of familiar settings or response selection as areas of emotion regulation (see also Walden & Smith, 1997). Similarly, Gross (1998) distinguished five sets of emotion regulatory processes: situation selection, situation modification, attention deployment, cognitive change, and response modulation. A major problem of research in this field, however, concerns the lack of a precise distinction between these processes and several processes involved in the complex episode of an unfolding emotion, such as appraisal (see Lazarus, 1991), coping, or the experience (and reporting) of an emotional state. Consequently, Kagan (1994) has argued that it is not yet possible to separately measure the intensity of the experienced emotion and the process of regulating that emotion. Similarly, Gross (1998, p. 286) concluded that "disentangling emotion generative and emotion regulatory processes represents a tremendous challenge." In this section I will concentrate on the analysis of the two central cognitive mechanisms of emotional regulation: attention deployment—that is, the regulation of emotions by shifting attentional focus; and regulating emotions by generating emotion-congruent or -incongruent cognitions. These processes may be automatic (not requiring central capacity) or strategic (requiring the allocation of cognitive effort; see Kanfer & Karoly, 1982; Morris & Reilly, 1987).

### Attention Deployment

Research has shown that emotional processes may exert an important influence on the course of information processing. In particular, emotional states may recruit attentional mechanisms to regulate perceptual and conceptual processes (for an overview, see Blaney, 1986; Derryberry

& Tucker, 1994). Several theories about emotion-related phenomena have concentrated on changes in attentional focus after induction of emotional states. Tomkins (1962, 1963), for example, proposed that positive emotions result in an increased tendency to engage in social interaction and to focus attention on other persons, while negative emotions direct attention to the self and to internally generated cues (for experimental tests of this hypothesis, see Cunningham, 1988; Sedikides, 1992). Izard (1991), on the other hand, theorizes that only negative emotions such as guilt or shame result in self-focused attention, while the negative emotional states of fear or anger increase the tendency to attend to cues in the environment. Salovey (1992, p. 699) contrasted three hypotheses concerning the influences of positive and negative emotional states (especially happiness and sadness):

1. *Positive as well as negative emotional states attenuate self-focus.* This prediction is derived from Schachter's hypothesis that emotions are experienced as unspecific arousal states that are appraised more specifically only after an externally oriented search for causes of that arousal (Schachter, 1964; Schachter & Singer, 1962).
2. *Only negative emotions induce self-focus.* This prediction is based on substantial clinical evidence indicating that negative emotional states (in particular depression) are associated with increased self-awareness and self-focus of attention (Ellis, 1991; Ingram, 1990).
3. *Both positive and negative emotional states induce self-focus.* Wood and colleagues, for example, proposed that both types of emotional states are caused by unexpected events which result in a multitude of self-related cognitions (Wood, Saltzberg, & Goldsamt, 1990; Wood, Saltzberg, Neale, Stone, & Rachmiel, 1990; see also Salovey & Rodin, 1985, for a similar hypothesis). Furthermore, emotions are associated with autonomic arousal that generates self-relevant, attention-demanding cues (see also Wegner & Giuliano, 1980). Finally, following Carver and Scheier's (1981) model of self-regulation, Wood and colleagues assume that emotions initiate self-regulatory processes that require increased self-focused attention for their adequate execution.

If one considers shifting attentional focus as a powerful (strategic) mechanism of emotion regulation, a fourth hypothesis can be derived: *individuals in a negative mood state attempt to reduce that state through an external focus of attention.* Corresponding with this prediction, Nix, Watson, Pyszczynski, and Greenberg (1995), for example, reported that tension and depressive mood may be reduced through an external attentional focus. Similarly, Bryant and Zillmann (1984) found that watching a humorous TV program reduces feelings of anger and hostility.

## Generating Emotion-Congruent or Emotion-Incongruent Cognitions

A further way of regulating unadaptive emotional states, closely related to shifting attentional focus, may be generating and processing certain types of thoughts or memories (cf. Parrott, 1993). Bower's network theory of affect (Bower, 1981, 1992) provides a useful theoretical framework to study the relationship between emotional states and cognitive processes involved in emotion regulation. A core hypothesis of this theory is that mood states lead directly to mood-congruency effects. Applied to emotion regulation, this general assumption contains a more specific prediction (cf. Bower & Mayer, 1991): individuals' thoughts, free associations, and judgments are thematically congruent with their current emotional state. This mood-congruency effect is the result of an automatic process.

Evidence for mood-congruency effects is mixed, however (reviews in Isen, 1984; Power & Dalgleish, 1997; Rusting, 1998; Singer & Salovey, 1988; Teasdale & Barnard, 1993; Wells & Matthews, 1994). Isen, for example, found that good moods reliably produce mood-congruency effects, while bad moods frequently failed to do so. Singer and Salovey (1988) assume that one reason for these inconsistent findings is the neglect of motivational processes by the network theory of affect.

These motivational processes are addressed in the cognitive loop hypothesis introduced by Isen and colleagues (cf. Isen, Shalker, Clark, & Karp, 1978). Following the accessibility concept (Tulving & Pearlstone, 1966), this hypothesis starts by making similar predictions as the network theory. The concept of cognitive loop refers to the automatic accessibility of emotionally valenced cognitive structures. Isen et al. suggest that thoughts associated with a positive or negative mood might cue other valence-congruent material in memory, making this material more accessible. This accessed material may then prolong positive or negative thoughts and associations by keeping them in mind, which then should prolong the respective mood state (Isen, 1987).

Basically, this cognitive loop could occur for positive as well as negative mood states. However, by stating that maintaining a negative mood is probably not a goal for most people and that they therefore try to counter this process and change the undesired state, this approach integrates automatic mood-maintenance with strategic (i.e., motivationally determined) mood-modificatory variables. The motivation to change an unpleasant emotional state and to employ certain regulatory strategies implies that negative emotion states are generally less extended (i.e., the cognitive loop is shorter) than positive states. Consequently, positive and negative emotional states are structurally different and have asymmetric effects (cf. Isen, 1985). For most people positive material is better integrated and more extensive in memory than negative material, which allows a positive emotion to cue a wider range of associations than a negative emotion.

The cognitive loop hypothesis marks the transition from automatic (effortless) to strategic (resource-dependent) processes of emotion regulation. Automatic is the generation of mood-congruent cognitions. Isen and colleagues, however, assume that this automatic process is restricted to the "positive" cognitive loop (cf. Isen et al., 1978). For negative emotional states, the first automatic mood-congruency phase should be soon replaced in most people by a subsequent strategic mood-incongruency phase called "mood repair" (cf. Clark & Isen, 1982). This mood repair should be facilitated by the comparatively low integration of negative material in the memory of most people.

### Individual Differences in Emotion Regulation

Although the hypotheses presented so far assumed that people may differ with respect to their (strategic) emotion regulation, none of these approaches *explicitly* considered individual differences as moderators of the influence of emotional arousal on cognitive change and attention deployment (see also Rusting, 1998, for a similar conclusion). Investigations on self-esteem and (trait) depression, however, demonstrated the importance of individual differences as moderators of the emotion-cognition relationship. For example, individuals high in self-esteem recalled positively valenced material after induction of a negative mood state (mood-incongruent recall), while persons low in self-esteem exhibited mood-congruent recall (Dodgson & Wood, 1998; Smith & Petty, 1995; see also Rusting, 1998, for a more general review). Similarly, Josephson, Singer, and Salovey (1996) induced a sad mood and observed that individuals who after mood induction followed a first negative memory with a second positive one (mood repair) scored lower in trait depression than participants who recalled two consecutive negative memories. In addition, Rusting (1999) found that extraversion and positive affectivity were related to retrieval of positive memories, while neuroticism and negative affectivity were related to retrieval of negative memories. Finally, Pyszczynski and Greenberg (1985, 1987) observed that depressive individuals tend to increase their self-focus after failure but not after success, whereas the opposite strategy is employed by nondepressives.

While dimensions such as depression, positive affectiv-

ity, or self-esteem represent affect-laden personality variables, the comparatively new construct of emotional intelligence (EI; cf. Mayer & Salovey, 1997) refers to *skills* in dealing with emotions in oneself and others. EI can be defined as the ability to identify one's feelings and the feelings of others, to regulate these feelings, and to use the information provided by feelings to initiate adaptive behavior (see Mayer & Salovey, 1995; Salovey, Hsee, & Mayer, 1993). Following Salovey, Mayer, and colleagues, EI encompasses the dimensions of "clarity of emotional perception," "strategies of emotion regulation," "attention to emotions," and "attitudes about emotions" (for measurement of the different aspects of EI, see Mayer, Caruso, & Salovey, 1999). Of specific interest to our topic are, of course, strategies of emotion regulation. Applied to the skills perspective taken by EI research, this concept can be defined as a person's efficacy in constructing and regulating certain emotional states, in particular stabilizing a desired state or modifying a state appraised as inappropriate (e.g., by employing repair strategies).

Further personality variables related to emotion regulation are coping styles. Among these the avoidant style (cf. Davis, 1990; Krohne, 1989, 1993a, 1993b; Roth & Cohen, 1986; Weinberger, 1990) may be an important moderator of the mood-cognition relationship. Boden and Baumeister (1997), for example, presented an unpleasant (disgusting) film to their participants and were able to observe mood-incongruency effects (recall of happy memories, spontaneous generation of pleasant thoughts) in individuals with an avoidant coping style. In contrast, nonavoiders displayed mood-congruency effects. I will resume this topic when I address individual differences in coping.

### Goals and Emotions

"Goals are the core of personality" (Karoly, 1999, p. 267). They define the transsituational and transtemporal relevance of certain settings; serve as links to other constructs such as roles, self-concept, or expectancies; provide an anchor for planful thinking; define the nature of adjustment and change; and influence emotion-related appraisal processes (cf. Karoly, 1999; Lazarus, 1991).

In general, three types of factors are seen as determinants of goal setting (cf. Markus & Wurf, 1987): expectations (e.g., self-efficacy expectations; Bandura, 1986), affective factors (needs, motives, or values), and desired self-conceptions (for example, being a high-achieving person). Researchers in this field (cf. Karoly, 1999) have emphasized that personality might best be studied if less attention is paid to what people are actually doing and more to the process of goal setting and its determinants—that is, to what people are trying to do. Consequently, the adaptiveness of certain regulatory operations may best be evaluated by taking individual goals and their determinants into account. I will exemplify this idea by relating possible individual motives to the employment of certain strategies of emotion regulation.

When I introduced the concept of mood repair, I pointed out that individuals are motivated to employ strategies that help terminate an aversive emotional experience—for example, summoning thoughts incongruent with this state (cf. Isen, 1985; Singer & Salovey, 1988). Correspondingly, one would expect that people are motivated to maintain a happy mood. However, this goal setting may not apply to every person and every situation (cf. Erber, 1996). Parrott (1993) listed a number of motives for the two counterintuitive regulations of inhibiting positive emotional states and maintaining negative ones: to promote focused, analytical problem solving; to motivate oneself to work hard, to sustain a perspective needed at a later time; to avoid distraction and to improve concentration; to protect oneself against future disappointment. In accordance with this reasoning, Levine and Burgess (1997), for example, found that negative emotions facilitate the processing of functional information (see also Parrott & Sabini, 1990). These types of goal setting depend on situational constraints as well as on personal dispositions (e.g., motives, tolerance for aversive emotional states).

## Coping: An Integrative Concept

### Definitions and Conceptions

The concept of coping is intimately related to the term *stress*. Although there is still little agreement on the definition of stress, the majority of more recent approaches tend to view stress as a special class of emotional reactions. Scherer (1986), for example, defines stress as a class of emotional reactions that are specified by "changes in various subsystem states that maintain a disequilibrium for a long period of time without returning to baseline or without the establishment of a new equilibrium at a different level" (p. 176). Coping is then defined as "cognitive and behavioral efforts to manage specific external or internal demands (and conflicts between them) that are appraised as taxing or exceeding the resources of the person" (Lazarus, 1991, p. 112). This definition contains the following implications (cf. Krohne, 1986):

1. Coping responses are not classified according to their effects (e.g., reality-distorting vs. reality-adapted), but according to certain characteristics of the coping process.
2. This process encompasses behavioral as well as cognitive reactions.
3. It is common to stress-inducing situations that they can be met (if at all) only by intensified effort. Consequently, all automatic adaptations to stress

do not belong to the rubric of coping (cf. Lazarus & Folkman, 1984).

4. Coping responses can be distinguished by their focus on different elements of the situation. They can aim at external elements, either attempting to passively avoid the situation or to actively change it. Lazarus (1991) has called this function problem-focused coping. Responses can also relate to internal elements, aiming to change the way in which the stressful situation-person relationship is attended to or interpreted. Lazarus called this function cognitive coping. A subclass of these responses specifically aims to decrease negative emotion experience and is therefore called emotion-focused coping. Recently, Hock et al. (1996) described another class of cognitive coping responses that do not directly aim at reducing negative emotions. Rather, these cognitive responses involve the avoidance or reduction of the uncertainty inherent in most stressful transactions. In relating to the Lazarus terminology, the authors called this additional function uncertainty-focused coping.

Although this definition overlaps with conceptions of emotion regulation as presented above, coping and emotion regulation are by no means redundant. The following differences are especially important (see also Gross, 1998):

1. In general, by examining specific emotions, researchers make more fine-grained distinctions among the regulatory processes than are possible within the broader coping concept.
2. While emotion-focused coping concentrates on the aspect of decreasing a negative emotion experience, emotion regulation research emphasizes that both positive and negative emotions may be regulated, and that regulation may involve attenuation as well as enhancement or stabilization of emotional states.
3. Coping, in contrast, also includes actions that do not target emotions and are taken to achieve nonemotional goals.
4. While coping always refers to strategic processes (requiring effort), emotion regulation includes processes that may vary on the automatic-strategic dimension.

Approaches that conceptualize different forms of coping may be classified according to two independent aspects: (1) trait-oriented versus state-oriented, and (2) microanalytic versus macroanalytic (cf. Krohne, 1996b). Trait-oriented and state-oriented research strategies have different objectives. The trait-oriented strategy aims at an early identification of those persons whose coping repertoire is inadequate for the demands of a specific stressful encounter, for example, surgery, exams, or athletic competitions. An early identification of persons with inadequate coping will offer the opportunity for establishing a successful primary prevention program. State-oriented approaches have a more general objective. They investigate the relationship between coping strategies applied by an individual and emotional reactions accompanying and following certain coping acts, self-reported or objectively registered coping efficiency, and more long-term outcome variables such as performance or health status. This approach intends to lay the foundation for a general modificatory program to improve coping competence.

Microanalytic conceptions study a large number of specific coping strategies, as exemplified in the Ways of Coping Checklist (Folkman & Lazarus, 1985) or the COPE (Carver, Scheier, & Weintraub, 1989). Macroanalytic approaches operate at a higher level of aggregation, thus concentrating on more fundamental coping constructs, such as repression-sensitization (Byrne, 1964) or vigilance and cognitive avoidance (Krohne, 1993a, 1993b; Roth & Cohen, 1986). The micro-macro distinction is important for the assignment of single coping strategies (e.g., attentional diversion) to larger coping categories (e.g., cognitive avoidance), as well as for the problem of transsituational consistency or variability of certain strategies applied by an individual. The more microanalytic the distinction among coping strategies, the more likely it is to observe transsituational variability among these strategies. The model of coping modes (MCM; Krohne, 1993b) to be presented next combines a trait-oriented with a macroanalytic strategy.

### Individual Differences in Coping: Vigilance and Cognitive Avoidance

After a period of criticism of personality-oriented research on coping with stress, the recent years have seen renewed interest in personality models of coping (see Endler & Parker, 1994; Krohne, 1989, 1993a, 1996a; Krohne & Egloff, in press; Miller, 1987, 1996; Singer, 1990). Most of these personality-oriented approaches have established two constructs central to investigating coping with stress: *vigilance*, or the orientation toward threatening aspects of a stressor, and *cognitive avoidance*, or averting attention away from the stressor (see Krohne, 1989, 1993b; Roth & Cohen, 1986; Suls & Fletcher, 1985). Approaches corresponding to these constructs are the earlier repression-sensitization dimension (Byrne, 1964; Eriksen, 1952) or the more recent conceptions of monitoring/blunting (Miller, 1980, 1987) and attention/rejection (Mullen & Suls, 1982). With regard to the relationships between these two constructs, Byrne's approach specified a unidimensional, bipolar structure, while Miller, as well as Mullen and Suls, left this question open. Krohne (1989, 1993b), on the other hand, developed a coping theory, the model of coping

modes, that explicitly postulates an independent variation of the vigilance and cognitive avoidance dimensions.

The model of coping modes (MCM) deals with processes of attention orientation and, as a consequence of those processes, with emotional and behavioral regulation under stressful conditions. The two fundamental constructs of vigilance and cognitive avoidance have been elaborated to describe these processes. Both constructs describe actual stress-related operations as well as interindividual differences regarding the disposition to frequently employ one or the other group of coping strategies. Concerning the dispositional (trait) level, it is posited that vigilance and cognitive avoidance are dimensions that vary independently of each other. The specific configuration of an individual's standing on both dimensions (e.g., high vigilance and low cognitive avoidance) is called *coping mode*.

The MCM extends beyond similar personality-oriented coping models (e.g., Byrne, 1964; Miller, 1980; for an overview, see Roth & Cohen, 1986) in that it relates the (descriptive) constructs vigilance and cognitive avoidance to an explicative basis (cf. Krohne, 1993b). According to a number of theoretical approaches and empirical findings (see Epstein, 1972; Krohne, 1996a, for overviews), most confrontations with anxiety-evoking situations are characterized by two general aspects: the presence of aversive stimuli (Epstein: "primary overstimulation") and a high degree of ambiguity (Epstein: "cognitive incongruity"). The experiential counterparts of these features, which are conceived as basic ingredients of emerging anxiety states, are an increased emotional arousal (caused by the presence of aversive stimuli) and an elevated state of uncertainty (resulting from situational ambiguity).

These two reactions are viewed as elementary feeling states that could lead, however, to more complex anxiety reactions. Thus, "elementary" uncertainty, manifesting itself in questions such as "What does it mean?" may lead to a more complex reaction that can be described as apprehension toward being surprised by negative developments in the situation ("negative surprise"; Krohne, 1989). Other researchers (e.g., Breznitz, 1984) designated similar reactions as "fear of danger." On the other hand, the perception of arousal when confronted with aversive stimuli could lead to the expectation of a further increase in emotionality that might not be controllable as it arises. This type of reaction has been called "fear of anxiety" (Reiss, 1987; see also the more recent concept of "anxiety sensitivity"; Taylor, 1999). The MCM further postulates that the intensified experience of uncertainty should release behavioral impulses characteristic of vigilance. In contrast, the self-perception or anticipation of intense arousal should initiate the tendency to avoid threat-related cues. This conception of attention orientation as resulting from elementary feeling states requires a process view of cognitive coping. Consequently, following developments in

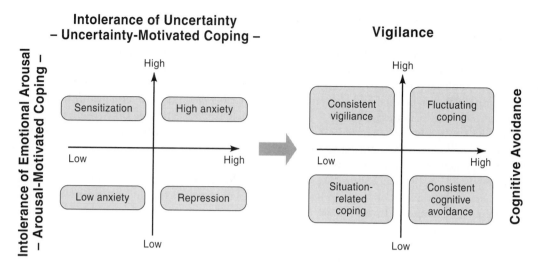

Figure 36.1 The model of coping modes.

research on perceptual defense (cf. Erdelyi, 1974; Krohne, 1978), the MCM conceptualizes allocation of attention as a two-stage process: After a (perhaps only rudimentary) identification of threat, attention is either turned toward (vigilance) or away (avoidance) from such stimuli.

These two coping processes are conceptually linked to personality by the hypothesis that the dispositional preference for vigilant or avoidant coping strategies reflects individual differences in the susceptibility to uncertainty or emotional arousal (cf. Figure 36.1). The MCM postulates that individuals who are dispositionally high in vigilance are especially susceptible to the uncertainty experienced in most aversive encounters. In order to reduce this state, vigilant persons intensify their intake and processing of threat-related information, even if this would imply a simultaneous increase in emotional arousal. In terms of the recent personality-oriented approaches on goal setting and self-regulation described above (cf. Karoly, 1999; Metcalfe & Mischel, 1999; Mischel & Shoda, 1995), the primary self-regulatory goal of vigilant persons is not to dampen their arousal but to reduce their threat-related uncertainty (danger control; see also Breznitz, 1984; Leventhal, 1970). Their coping behavior thus follows a plan that is aimed at minimizing the probability of unanticipated occurrence of aversive events and at construing a detailed schema of the to-be-expected encounter. Consequently, this type of coping behavior is supposed to be *uncertainty-motivated*.

Individuals who are high in cognitive avoidance are supposed to be especially affected by states of stress-induced emotional (somatic) arousal. In order to reduce this aversive state or to prevent a further strong and eventually uncontrollable increase in arousal, they turn their attention away from (internal or external) threat-related cues. Cognitively avoidant coping strategies thus primarily aim at shielding the person from high states of emo-

tional arousal. The goal of this process is anxiety control, and the behavior is called *arousal-motivated*.

Since the MCM conceives dispositional vigilance and cognitive avoidance as independent personality dimensions, four groups, called *coping modes*, can be identified on the basis of a median split of the respective scores:

1. Individuals with the configuration of high intolerance of uncertainty and low intolerance of arousal are especially affected by the ambiguity inherent in threatening situations. They direct their attention to threat-related information and, thus, manifest comparatively consistent vigilant coping. Following the traditional terminology (cf. Krohne, 1986, 1989), individuals of this mode are called *sensitizers*.

2. Persons with the opposite pattern—that is, high intolerance of arousal and low intolerance of uncertainty—are especially stressed by the emotional arousal induced by the perception of aversive cues. They cope with this state by turning away from such cues, thereby inhibiting the further processing of threat-related information (consistent cognitive avoidance). They can tolerate the subsequent increase in uncertainty, because this state is not particularly stressful for them. Individuals of this mode are called *repressers*.

3. Individuals who are characterized by a low intolerance of both factors can withstand both uncertainty and arousal relatively well. Because of their high tolerance for uncertainty and emotional arousal, they can pursue a certain strategy long enough to determine its effectiveness. They therefore possess a comparatively large repertoire of coping strategies (including instrumental strategies), and are able to flexibly adapt their coping

behavior to the demands of different types of stressful situations. Such (low-anxious) individuals are called *nondefensives*. (It should be pointed out, however, that extremely low scores on both dimensions could also indicate a lack of sensitivity to uncertainty and emotional arousal and, perhaps, a general deficit in coping resources.)

4. Individuals who are highly intolerant of both aspects of stressful encounters feel threatened by the lack of valid expectations as well the emotional arousal triggered by aversive cues. Since they cannot defend themselves against both types of threat at the same time (i.e., attend to threat-related information and disregard this information), they experience a typical approach-avoidance conflict: When they attempt to reduce the uncertainty that they experience as stressful by increased preoccupation with the stressor, they simultaneously heighten their emotional arousal to a level exceeding their threshold of tolerance. If they turn away from the stressor to reduce this state of arousal, then their uncertainty will increase, together with the stress resulting from it. Thus, these individuals should be unable to wait and see if a certain coping strategy has been effective. As a result, these persons are assumed to exhibit less efficient coping that is characterized by acts of only short duration and by generally fluctuating (or erratic) behavior that mainly relies on cognitive (vigilant and avoidant) strategies. Consequently, individuals of this mode are designated as *high-anxious* or *unsuccessful copers*.

Individual differences on the dimensions vigilance and cognitive avoidance are assessed by the Mainz Coping Inventory (MCI; Krohne, 1989; Krohne & Egloff, in press; Krohne, Egloff, et al., 2000). The MCI is a stimulus-response inventory that describes four ego-threatening (e.g., important exams) and four physically threatening scenarios (e.g., visiting the dentist) of varying controllability and predictability. Depending on the purpose of the investigation (such as coping with an important exam or with aversive medical procedures), only scenarios that involve ego-threat (subtest MCI-E) or physical threat (subtest MCI-P) are administered. Descriptions of five vigilance (e.g., information search) and five cognitive avoidance (e.g., attentional diversion) reactions are assigned to each scenario. Participants indicate on a true-false scale which of the coping reactions listed they generally employ in a given situation. The answers are summed up separately with regard to vigilance and cognitive avoidance items across the four scenarios of one subtest, thus yielding four scores of dispositional coping: vigilance in the subtests ego-threat (VIG-E) or physical threat (VIG-P), and cognitive avoidance in both subtests (CAV-E and CAV-P). Detailed

information on statistical characteristics and psychometric properties of the scales is presented in Krohne and Egloff (in press); Krohne, Schmukle, Burns, and Spielberger (2001); and Krohne et al. (2000).

Predictions derived from the MCM have been tested in a number of studies (overviews in Krohne, 1993a, 1993b, 1996a, 1996b; Krohne, Hock, & Kohlmann, 1992). Only a few findings, particularly those including behavioral measures, will be summarized in the final part of this section.

Krohne and Hock (1993) found that cognitive avoidance functions as a moderator between state anxiety and recognition of emotional material: for persons high in cognitive avoidance, state anxiety was positively correlated with later recognition of success items (solved anagrams), whereas for individuals low in avoidance anxiety was negatively associated with the recognition of unsolved anagrams. Obviously, as anxiety rises avoiders recognize positive material increasingly well, thus trying to regulate their negative affect (see also Boden & Baumeister, 1997, for findings confirming this relationship). Krohne, Pieper, Knoll, and Breimer (2002) investigated repressive emotion regulation more directly by applying a thought-listing technique (see Amsel & Fichten, 1990) in an emotional situation. The authors elicited positive and negative emotional states by exposing participants to the experience of success or failure and assessed cognitions immediately following this procedure. They observed that high avoiders increased and low avoiders decreased the number of neutral thoughts after failure. In accordance with the mood-repair hypothesis it is generally assumed that repressers cope with exposure to negative experiences by accessing positive thoughts (cf. Boden & Baumeister, 1997). The finding of Krohne et al. (2002) does not support this assumption. The problem with replacing negative cognitions when feeling bad by positive ones is that this strategy still allows affective material to enter consciousness. In fact, retrieving happy memories when feeling bad could make one feel even worse. A strategy for circumventing this hazard is to temporarily exclude emotional material entirely and to only register neutral facts. This pattern corresponds to Freud's (1926/1959) definition of isolation as a central repressive defense mechanism.

Closely related to isolation is an effect called "repressive emotional discreteness" (cf. Hansen & Hansen, 1988): In an emotion-inducing situation, only repressers' nondominant emotions are less intense compared to nonrepressers, whereas the dominant emotion is of equal intensity in both coping groups. Egloff and Krohne (1996) investigated the influence of coping modes on this effect and were able to demonstrate that repressers, compared to nonrepressers, reported the same amount of guilt, which was the dominant emotion after failure, but showed lower fear, sadness, and hostility. No differences were observed for positive emotions after success, indicating that re-

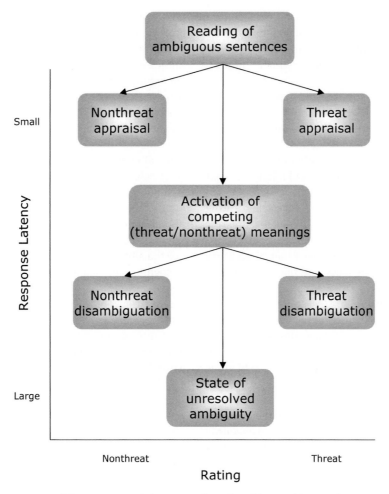

Figure 36.2  Possible outcomes of the processing of ambiguous (threatening/nonthreatening) sentences. Adapted from Hock et al. (1996).

pressive discreteness is restricted to negative emotional states.

Hock et al. (1996) examined relationships between MCI dimensions and the processing of ambiguous (threatening/nonthreatening) stimuli by employing an experimental design modeled after previous work of Eysenck, Mogg, May, Richards, and Mathews (1991). First, a rating task was conducted that provided indicators of the initial processing of ambiguous items. During this task, a series of threat-related ambiguous sentences was auditorily presented (e.g., "In the middle of the flight the captain suddenly addresses the passengers"). The participants had to rate each sentence in terms of its affective valence on a scale ranging from very pleasant to very unpleasant while their response latencies were being measured. Following this rating task, a recognition memory task was carried out, in which the participants had to judge disambiguated (threatening and nonthreatening) variants of the original sentences according to their similarity to one of the sentences presented during the rating task (e.g., "In the middle of the flight it is announced that an engine has broken down" / "In the

middle of the flight the meteorological data are announced"). This procedure yielded measures of individuals' memory for threatening and nonthreatening meanings of the ambiguous sentences.

The assessment of different types of processing outcomes was based on a classification, in which valence ratings and corresponding response latencies obtained in the first task were considered jointly (cf. Figure 36.2). In the case of immediate threat or nonthreat interpretations, the assignment of a rating category to an item should be relatively easy for the individual. As a consequence, the response latency should be small, with the pleasant-unpleasant score reflecting the interpretation reached by the individual. These types of processing outcomes were called (threat or nonthreat) appraisals to emphasize their fast and immediate nature (Scherer, 1984). However, if two or more competing meanings are activated that substantially differ in their affective valence, the individual should have difficulties in assigning one rating category to the item. In a number of cases, a more thorough analysis of the item content may finally lead to a disambiguation in terms of a dominant threatening or a dominant non-threatening meaning, reflected in moderately delayed ratings. As a third type of outcome, extremely delayed intermediate ratings were considered, which indicate ambiguity-unresolved states.

Consistent with hypotheses derived from the MCM, compared to nonvigilants vigilant individuals produced more threat interpretations (i.e., fast threat-related ratings as well as delayed threat disambiguations). The number of threat disambiguations was especially high for sensitizers. Unexpectedly, repressers also showed a large number of delayed responses. These responses, however, were associated with an intermediate valence rating, indicating unresolved ambiguity. The similarity between repressers and sensitizers with respect to the number of delayed responses to ambiguous stimuli indicates that at an early processing stage both groups recognize the simultaneous presence of threatening and nonthreatening implications of ambiguous event descriptions. This similarity, however, did not become apparent in the subsequent recognition memory test. Instead, vigilants (sensitizers and high-anxious individuals) showed a retrieval bias which favored the threatening meanings of the ambiguous sentences, whereas nonvigilants (repressers and nondefensives) manifested a retrieval bias which favored the potential nonthreatening implications of those sentences. One reason for this repressive discontinuity between encoding and retrieval of threat-related information could be that the threatening meaning activated during encoding decreases more rapidly over time in accessibility than the nonthreatening meaning. Consequently, an event which repressers initially coded multiply ends up as a mere non-threat memory.

A second study (Hock & Krohne, 2001) specifically addressed the question of whether repressers' and sensitizers' processing of ambiguous information actually leads to a comparatively distinct representation of only one meaning alternative or whether the memory representations reflect the recognition of an item's ambiguity at encoding. By additionally introducing ambiguous variants of the original sentences in the recognition memory task the authors obtained separate measures of memory for threatening, nonthreatening, and ambiguous features of the original sentences. This extension allowed the separation of the relative balance in the activation of threatening and nonthreatening meanings during recognition from the strength of ambiguous elements' representation in memory. This separation should clarify whether repressers' ability to identify ambiguity during stimulus presentation (cf. Hock et al., 1996) is also reflected in their memory for the scenarios presented. In addition, the separation should help to identify the basis of sensitizers' distress when confronted with ambiguity.

Results of this second study demonstrated that in their similarity ratings sensitizers endorsed the unambiguously threatening more frequently than the unambiguously neutral variants of the ambiguous original sentences, whereas repressers exhibited the opposite pattern. These findings indicated that for sensitizers the threatening features of ambiguous stimuli were well represented in memory, whereas repressers only had a weak memory of these aspects. This conclusion was supported by an inspection of the reaction times during recognition. Sensitizers were very fast in endorsing threatening variants as compared to neutral ones, whereas repressers rejected these sentences. This relationship points to an easy accessibility of the respective memory representation and, consequently, to a high subjective certainty in sensitizers when judging threatening stimuli.

When analyzing recognition scores and reaction times for the ambiguous variants, repressers exhibited a superior recognition of ambiguous variants of the original scenarios combined with a marked delay in delivering their similarity ratings. In line with the repressive discontinuity hypothesis (cf. Krohne, 1978, 1993b), the authors assumed that during the rating task repressers first recognize both threatening and nonthreatening meanings of ambiguous stimuli, and then reject the unambiguously threatening implication of this information. During recognition, this threatening implication, which has been activated only for a short time during the rating task, is still accessible but difficult to retrieve. This configuration resulted in the comparatively fast rejection of unambiguously threatening variants. The ambiguous variants of the original stimuli, however, contain the nonthreatening meaning favored by repressers as well as the threatening implication that is still accessible during recognition. As a consequence, repressers should find it comparatively difficult to make a fast decision for these items.

In sum, repressive discontinuity means that repressers are characterized by two—in part antagonistically operating—processing characteristics: first, an early-stage attentional focus on threat-related stimuli; and second, an only superficial further processing of the meaning and implications of these stimuli. This notion revises the traditional definition of repressers (cf. Byrne, 1964) as being hyposensitive to threat. At an early stage of processing they are, in fact, very sensitive to these aspects. Inhibition of threat only starts at a later stage of processing.

The second question was concerned with the basis of sensitizers' frequently observed negative evaluation of ambiguous information (see, e.g., Hock et al., 1996). Two alternatives seem plausible: Sensitizers experience ambiguous situations as unpleasant because ambiguity blocks their intention to construe a detailed schema of the to-be-expected encounter. An ambiguous situation, however, may also cause apprehension in sensitizers because they are inclined to over-accentuate its threatening (relative to its nonthreatening) meaning. The MCM predicts that sensitizers react negatively only to those ambiguous stimuli that contain a potentially threatful meaning. Results clearly support this hypothesis. During recognition, sensitizers were very fast in endorsing the threatening variants and in rejecting the ambiguous variants of the original scenarios. Obviously, they accentuate the threatful stimulus aspects during encoding (and likely neglect the more neutral ones). Consequently, threatening meanings of ambiguous information are well represented in the sensitizer's memory, whereas the ambiguity of the original stimulus only has a weak representation.

## Conclusion

This chapter has presented different personality concepts related to emotional reactions and coping with aversiveness. Two perspectives have been distinguished. Under the rubric of descriptive perspective, approaches have been discussed that are centered around the registration of (transtemporally and transsituationally comparatively consistent) individual differences in emotional responding or in reactions (such as symptom reporting) closely related to emotional experience. Although these approaches have been designated as descriptive, most of them nevertheless yield explicative power. Some of these concepts play an increasingly important role in clarifying the origin and course of physical diseases or affective disorders. Examples are the relationship of individual-specific response patterns to psychosomatic disorders, (repressive) subjective-autonomic response dissociation to cancer, and frontal brain asymmetry or negative affectivity to affective disorders. In addition, for a number of biological approaches subsumed under this perspective we expect a rapid theoretical elaboration as refinement of the assessment procedures (such as PET) progresses.

Concerning the explicative perspective, the global and relatively context-free trait concepts—such as anxiety, neuroticism, depression, extraversion, or optimism—that have dominated this field for decades are clearly in need of a major overhaul. In fact, global concepts—for example, trait anxiety—may be better described by a network of cognitive-affective units as proposed by Mischel and Shoda (1995). Three of these units stand out as being especially fertile in explaining individual differences in emotional reactions and self-regulatory processes: appraisals, strategies of self-regulation, and goals (including motives and values). The model of coping modes presented in the final section of this chapter might serve as an example of this reconceptualization.

## NOTES

I thank Boris Egloff and Elizabeth Ray-Schröder for helpful comments on an earlier version of this chapter.

## REFERENCES

Allport, G. W., & Vernon, P. E. (1933). *Studies in expressive movement*. New York: Macmillan.

Amsel, R., & Fichten, C. S. (1990). Ratio versus frequency scores: Focus of attention and the balance between positive and negative thoughts. *Cognitive Therapy and Research, 14*, 257–277.

Arnold, M. B. (1960). *Emotion and personality* (2 vols.). New York: Columbia University Press.

Asendorpf, J. B., & Scherer, K. R. (1983). The discrepant repressor: Differentiation between low anxiety, high anxiety, and repression of anxiety by autonomic-facial-verbal patterns of behavior. *Journal of Personality and Social Psychology, 45*, 1334–1346.

Ashby, W. R. (1956). *An introduction to cybernetics*. London: Chapman & Hall.

Bailey, S. L., & Heitkemper, M. M. (1991). Morningness-eveningness and early morning salivary cortisol levels. *Biological Psychology, 32*, 181–192.

Bandura, A. (1986). *Social foundations of thought and action. A social cognitive theory*. Englewood Cliffs, NJ: Prentice Hall.

Ben-Porath, Y. S., & Tellegen, A. (1990). A place for traits in stress research. *Psychological Inquiry, 1*, 14–17.

Blaney, P. H. (1986). Affect and memory: A review. *Psychological Bulletin, 99*, 229–246.

Boden, J. M., & Baumeister, R. F. (1997). Repressive coping: Distraction using pleasant thoughts and memories. *Journal of Personality and Social Psychology, 73*, 45–62.

Bonanno, G. A., Keltner, D., Holen, A., & Horowitz, M. J. (1995). When avoiding unpleasant emotions might not be such a bad thing: Verbal-autonomic response dissociation and midlife conjugal bereavement. *Journal of Personality and Social Psychology, 69*, 975–989.

Bower, G. H. (1981). Mood and memory. *American Psychologist, 36*, 129–148.

Bower, G. H. (1992). How might emotions affect learning? In S.-A. Christianson (Ed.), *The handbook of emotion and memory. Research and theory* (pp. 3–31). Hillsdale, NJ: Erlbaum.

Bower, G. H., & Mayer, J. D. (1991). In search for mood-dependent retrieval. In D. Kuiken (Ed.), *Mood and memory. Theory, research, and applications* (pp. 133–168). Newbury Park, CA: Sage Publications.

Breznitz, S. (1984). *Cry wolf: The psychology of false alarms*. Hillsdale, NJ: Erlbaum.

Bryant, J., & Zillmann, D. (1984). Using television to alleviate boredom and stress: Selective exposure as a function of induced emotional states. *Journal of Broadcasting, 28*, 1–20.

Buck, R. (1984). *The communication of emotion*. New York: Guilford Press.

Buck, R., Miller, R. E., & Caul, W. F. (1974). Sex, personality, and physiological variables in the communication of affect via facial expression. *Journal of Personality and Social Psychology, 30*, 587–596.

Buck, R., Savin, V. J., Miller, R. E., & Caul, W. F. (1972). Communication of affect through facial expressions in humans. *Journal of Personality and Social Psychology, 28*, 362–371.

Byrne, D. (1961). The repression-sensitization scale: Rationale, reliability, and validity. *Journal of Personality, 29*, 334–349.

Byrne, D. (1964). Repression-sensitization as a dimension

of personality. In B. A. Maher (Ed.), *Progress in experimental personality research* (Vol. 1, pp. 169–220). New York: Academic Press.

Cannon, W. B. (1927). The James-Lange theory of emotions: A critical examination and an alternative theory. *American Journal of Psychology, 39,* 106–124.

Carver, C. S., & Scheier, M. F. (1981). *Attention and self-regulation: A control-theory approach to human behavior.* New York: Springer.

Carver, C. S., Scheier, M. F., & Weintraub, J. G. (1989). Assessing coping strategies: A theoretically based approach. *Journal of Personality and Social Psychology, 56,* 267–283.

Carver, C. S., & White, T. L. (1994). Behavioral inhibition, behavioral activation, and affective responses to impending reward and punishment: The BIS/BAS scales. *Journal of Personality and Social Psychology, 67,* 319–333.

Cioffi, D. (1991). Beyond attentional strategies: A cognitive-perceptual model of somatic interpretation. *Psychological Bulletin, 109,* 25–41.

Clark, M. S., & Isen, A. M. (1982). Toward understanding the relationship between feeling states and social behavior. In A. H. Hastorf & A. M. Isen (Eds.), *Cognitive social psychology* (pp. 73–108). New York: Elsevier.

Cofer, L. F., Grice, J. W., Sethre-Hofstad, L., Radi, C. J., Zimmermann, L. K., Palmer-Seal, D., & Santa-Maria, G. (1999). Developmental perspectives on morningness-eveningness and social interactions. *Human Development, 42,* 169–198.

Costa, P. T., & McCrae, R. R. (1990). Personality: Another "hidden factor" in stress research. *Psychological Inquiry, 1,* 22–24.

Cunningham, M. R. (1988). What do you do when you're happy or blue? Mood, expectancies, and behavioral interest. *Motivation and Emotion, 12,* 309–331.

Davidson, R. J. (1984). Hemispheric asymmetries and emotion. In K. R. Scherer & P. Ekman (Eds.), *Approaches to emotion* (pp. 30–57). Hillsdale, NJ: Erlbaum.

Davidson, R. J. (1992). Emotion and affective style: Hemispheric substrates. *Psychological Science, 3,* 39–43.

Davidson, R. J. (1998a). Affective style and affective disorders: Perspectives from affective neuroscience. *Cognition and Emotion, 12,* 307–330.

Davidson, R. J. (1998b). Anterior electrophysiological asymmetries, emotion, and depression: Conceptual and methodological conundrums. *Psychophysiology, 35,* 607–614.

Davidson, R. J., Horowitz, M. E., Schwartz, G. E., & Goodman, D. M. (1981). Lateral differences in the latency between finger tapping and the heart beat. *Psychophysiology, 18,* 36–41.

Davis, P. J. (1990). Repression and the inaccessibility of emotional memories. In J. L. Singer (Ed.), *Repression and dissociation* (pp. 387–403). Chicago: University of Chicago Press.

Derryberry, D., & Tucker, D. M. (1994). Motivating the focus of attention. In P. M. Niedenthal & S. Kitayama (Eds.), *The heart's eye. Emotional influences in perception and attention* (pp. 167–196). New York: Academic Press.

Dodge, K. A. (1989). Coordinating responses to aversive stimuli: Introduction to a special section on the development of emotion regulation. *Developmental Psychology, 25,* 339–342.

Dodgson, P. G., & Wood, J. V. (1998). Self-esteem and the cognitive accessibility of strengths and weaknesses after failure. *Journal of Personality and Social Psychology, 75,* 178–197.

Egloff, B., & Krohne, H. W. (1996). Repressive emotional discreteness after failure. *Journal of Personality and Social Psychology, 70,* 1318–1326.

Egloff, B., Tausch, A., Kohlmann, C.-W., & Krohne, H. W. (1995). Relationships between time of day, day of the week, and positive mood: Exploring the role of the mood measure. *Motivation and Emotion, 19,* 99–110.

Ekman, P., & Friesen, W. V. (1978). *The facial action coding system.* Palo Alto, CA: Consulting Psychologists Press.

Ellis, H. C. (1991). Focused attention and depressive deficits in memory. *Journal of Experimental Psychology: General, 120,* 310–312.

Endler, N. S., & Parker, J. D. A. (1994). Assessment of multidimensional coping: Task, emotion, and avoidance strategies. *Psychological Assessment, 6,* 50–60.

Eppinger, H., & Hess, L. (1910). *Die Vagotonie.* Berlin: Hirschwald.

Epstein, S. (1972). The nature of anxiety with emphasis upon its relationship to expectancy. In C. D. Spielberger (Ed.), *Anxiety: Current trends in theory and research* (Vol. 2, pp. 291–337). New York: Academic Press.

Erber, R. (1996). The self-regulation of moods. In L. L. Martin & A. Tesser (Eds.), *Striving and feeling. Interactions among goals, affect, and self-regulation* (pp. 251–275). Mahwah, NJ: Erlbaum.

Erdelyi, M. H. (1974). A new look at the New Look: Perceptual defense and vigilance. *Psychological Review, 81,* 1–25.

Eriksen, C. W. (1952). Defense against ego-threat in memory and perception. *Journal of Abnormal and Social Psychology, 47,* 230–235.

Eysenck, H. J. (1981). General features of the model. In H. J. Eysenck (Ed.), *A model for personality* (pp. 1–37). Berlin: Springer.

Eysenck, M. W., Mogg, K., May, J., Richards, A., & Mathews, A. (1991). Bias in interpretation of ambiguous sentences related to threat in anxiety. *Journal of Abnormal Psychology, 100,* 144–150.

Fahrenberg, J. (1986). Psychophysiological individuality: A pattern analytic approach to personality research and psychosomatic medicine. *Advances in Behaviour Research and Therapy, 8,* 43–100.

Fahrenberg, J., Brügner, G., Foerster, F., & Käppler, C. (1999). Ambulatory assessment of diurnal changes with a hand-held computer: Mood, attention, and morningness-eveningness. *Personality and Individual Differences, 26,* 641–656.

Fahrenberg, J., Foerster, F., Schneider, H.-J., Müller, W., & Myrtek, M. (1986). Predictability of individual differences in activation processes in a field setting based on laboratory measures. *Psychophysiology, 23,* 323–333.

Fahrenberg, J., Foerster, F., & Wilmers, F. (1995). Is elevated blood pressure level associated with higher cardiovascular responsiveness in laboratory tasks and with response specificity? *Psychophysiology, 32,* 81–91.

Feldman Barrett, L., & Russell, J. A. (1998). Independence and bipolarity in the structure of current affect. *Journal of Personality and Social Psychology, 74,* 967–984.

Foerster, F. (1985). Psychophysiological response specificities: A replication over a 12-month period. *Biological Psychology, 21,* 169–182.

Foerster, F., Schneider, H. J., & Walschburger, P. (1983). The differentiation of individual-specific, stimulus-specific, and motivation-specific response patterns in activation processes: An inquiry investigating their stability and possible importance in psychophysiology. *Biological Psychology, 17*, 1–26.

Folkman, S., & Lazarus, R. S. (1985). If it changes it must be a process: Study of emotion and coping during three stages of a college examination. *Journal of Personality and Social Psychology, 48*, 150–170.

Frankenhaeuser, M. (1986). A psychobiological framework for research on human stress and coping. In M. H. Appley & R. Trumbull (Eds.), *Dynamics of stress. Physiological, psychological, and social perspectives* (pp. 101–116). New York: Plenum.

Fredrikson, M., Danielssons, T., Engel, B. T., Frisk-Holmberg, M., Ström, G., & Sundin, Ö. (1985). Autonomic nervous system function and essential hypertension: Individual response specificity with and without beta-adrenergic blockade. *Psychophysiology, 22*, 167–174.

Freud, S. (1926/1959). Inhibitions, symptoms and anxiety. In J. Strachey (Ed. and Trans.), *The standard edition of the complete psychological works of Sigmund Freud* (Vol. 20, pp. 77–175). London: Hogarth. (Original work published in 1926)

Freud, S. (1923/1961). The ego and the id. In J. Strachey (Ed. and Trans.), *The standard edition of the complete psychological works of Sigmund Freud* (Vol. 19, pp. 3–66). London: Hogarth. (Original work published in 1923)

Friedman, H. S., Prince, L. M., Riggio, R. E., & DiMatteo, M. R. (1980). Understanding and assessing nonverbal expressiveness. The affective communication test. *Journal of Personality and Social Psychology, 39*, 333–351.

Frijda, N. H. (1986). *The emotions.* New York: Cambridge University Press.

Frijda, N. H. (1993). The place of appraisal in emotion. *Cognition and Emotion, 7*, 357–387.

Green, D. P., Goldman, S. L., & Salovey, P. (1993). Measurement error masks bipolarity in affect ratings. *Journal of Personality and Social Psychology, 64*, 1029–1041.

Gross, J. J. (1998). The emerging field of emotion regulation: An integrative review. *Review of General Psychology, 2*, 271–299.

Gross, J. J., & John, O. P. (1997). Revealing feelings: Facets in emotional expressivity in self-reports, peer ratings, and behavior. *Journal of Personality and Social Psychology, 72*, 435–448.

Gross, J. J., & John, O. P. (1998). Mapping the domain of expressivity: Multimethod evidence for a hierarchical model. *Journal of Personality and Social Psychology, 74*, 170–191.

Gudjonsson, G. H. (1981). Self-reported emotional disturbance and its relation to electrodermal reactivity, defensiveness and trait anxiety. *Personality and Individual Differences, 2*, 47–52.

Hansen, R. D., & Hansen, C. H. (1988). Repression of emotionally tagged memories: The architecture of less complex emotions. *Journal of Personality and Social Psychology, 55*, 811–818.

Hantas, M., Katkin, E. S., & Reed, S. D. (1984). Heartbeat discrimination training and cerebral lateralization. *Psychophysiology, 21*, 274–278.

Heller, W. (1993). Neuropsychological mechanisms of individual differences in emotion, personality, and arousal. *Neuropsychology, 7*, 476–489.

Heller, W., & Nitschke, J. B. (1998). The puzzle of regional brain activity in depression and anxiety: The importance of subtypes and comorbidity. *Cognition and Emotion, 12*, 421–447.

Henriques, J. B., & Davidson, R. J. (1991). Left frontal hypoactivation in depression. *Journal of Abnormal Psychology, 100*, 535–545.

Herrmann, T. (1973). *Persönlichkeitsmerkmale: Bestimmung und Verwendung in der psychologischen Wissenschaft.* Stuttgart: Kohlhammer.

Hock, M., & Krohne, H. W. (2001). *Coping with threat and memory for ambiguous information.* Manuscript submitted for publication.

Hock, M., Krohne, H. W., & Kaiser, J. (1996). Coping dispositions and the processing of ambiguous stimuli. *Journal of Personality and Social Psychology, 70*, 1052–1066.

Hodapp, V., & Knoll, J. F. (1993). Heartbeat perception, coping, and emotion. In H. W. Krohne (Ed.), *Attention and avoidance. Strategies in coping with aversiveness* (pp. 191–211). Seattle: Hogrefe & Huber.

Horne, J. A., & Östberg, O. (1976). A self-assessment questionnaire to determine morningness-eveningness in human circadian rhythms. *International Journal of Chronobiology, 4*, 97–110.

Hur, Y.-M., Bouchard, T. J. Jr., & Lykken, D. T. (1998). Genetic and environmental influence on morningness-eveningness. *Personality and Individual Differences, 25*, 917–925.

Ingram, R. E. (1990). Attentional nonspecificity in depressive and generalized anxious affective states. *Cognitive Therapy and Research, 14*, 25–35.

Isen, A. M. (1984). Toward understanding the role of affect in cognition. In R. S. Wyer & T. K. Srull (Eds.), *Handbook of social cognition* (Vol. 3, pp. 179–236). Hillsdale, NJ: Erlbaum.

Isen, A. M. (1985). Asymmetry of happiness and sadness in effects on memory in normal college students: Comment on Hasher, Rose, Zacks, Sanft, and Doren. *Journal of Experimental Psychology: General, 114*, 388–391.

Isen, A. M. (1987). Positive affect, cognitive processes, and social behavior. In L. Berkowitz (Ed.), *Advances in experimental social psychology* (Vol. 20, pp. 203–253). New York: Academic Press.

Isen, A. M., Shalker, T. E., Clark, M. S., & Karp, L. (1978). Affect accessibility of material in memory and behavior: A cognitive loop? *Journal of Personality and Social Psychology, 36*, 1–12.

Izard, C. E. (1991). *The psychology of emotions.* New York: Plenum.

James, W. (1884). What is an emotion? *Mind, 9*, 188–205.

Jones, G. E. (1994). Perception of visceral sensations: A review of recent findings, methodologies, and future directions. In J. R. Jennings, P. K. Ackles, & M. G. H. Coles (Eds.), *Advances in psychophysiology: A research annual* (Vol. 5, pp. 55–191). London: Kingsley.

Jones, H. E. (1935). The galvanic skin reflex as related to overt emotional expression. *American Journal of Psychology, 47*, 241–251.

Josephson, B. R., Singer, J. A., & Salovey, P. (1996). Mood modulation and memory: Repairing sad moods with happy memories. *Cognition and Emotion, 10*, 437–444.

Kagan, J. (1994). On the nature of emotion. In N. A. Fox (Ed.), The development of emotion regulation. Biological and behavioral considerations (pp. 7–24). *Monographs of the Society for Research in Child Development, 59*, (2–3, Serial No. 240).

Kanfer, F. H., & Karoly, P. (1982). The psychology of self-management: Abiding issues and tentative directions. In P. Karoly & F. H. Kanfer (Eds.), *Self-management and behavior change from theory to practice* (pp. 571–599). Elmsford, NY: Pergamon.

Karoly, P. (1999). A goal systems self-regulatory perspective on personality, psychopathology, and change. *Review of General Psychology, 3*, 264–291.

Katkin, E. S., Cestaro, V. L., & Weitkunat, R. (1991). Individual differences in cortical evoked potentials as a function of heartbeat detection ability. *International Journal of Neuroscience, 61*, 269–276.

Kerkhof, G. A. (1985). Inter-individual differences in the human circadian system: A review. *Biological Psychology, 20*, 83–112.

Kerkhof, G. A., & Lancel, M. (1991). EEG slow wave activity, REM sleep, and rectal temperature during night and day sleep in morning-type and evening-type subjects. *Psychophysiology, 28*, 678–688.

Khaleque, A. (1999). Sleep deficiency and quality of life of shift workers. *Social Indicators Research, 46*, 181–189.

Kiecolt-Glaser, J. K., & Greenberg, B. (1983). On the use of physiological measures in assertion research. *Journal of Behavioral Assessment, 5*, 97–109.

Kinsbourne, M., & Bemporad, B. (1984). Lateralization of emotions: A model and the evidence. In N. A. Fox & R. J. Davidson (Eds.), *The psychobiology of affective development* (pp. 259–291). Hillsdale, NJ: Erlbaum.

Kneier, A. W., & Temoshok, L. (1984). Repressive coping reactions in patients with malignant melanoma as compared to cardiovascular disease patients. *Journal of Psychosomatic Research, 28*, 145–155.

Kohlmann, C.-W. (1993a). Development of the repression-sensitization construct: With special reference to the discrepancy between subjective and physiological stress reactions. In U. Hentschel, G. Smith, W. Ehlers, & J. G. Draguns (Eds.), *The concept of defense mechanisms in contemporary psychology: Theoretical, research, and clinical perspectives* (pp. 184–204). New York: Springer-Verlag.

Kohlmann, C.-W. (1993b). Strategies in blood pressure estimation: The role of vigilance, cognitive avoidance, and gender. In H. W. Krohne (Ed.), *Attention and avoidance. Strategies in coping with aversiveness* (pp. 213–238). Seattle: Hogrefe & Huber.

Kohlmann, C.-W. (1997). *Persönlichkeit und Emotionsregulation: Defensive Bewältigung von Angst und Streß.* Bern: Huber.

Kohlmann, C.-W., & Krohne, H. W. (1991, July). *The coping dispositions vigilance and cognitive avoidance: Associations with symptom reporting.* Paper presented at the 6th annual meeting of the International Society for Research on Emotions, Saarbrücken, Germany.

Kohlmann, C.-W., Weidner, G., & Messina, C. (1996). Avoidant coping style and verbal-cardiovascular response dissociation. *Psychology and Health, 11*, 371–384.

Kring, A. M., & Gordon, A. H. (1998). Sex differences in emotion: Expression, experience, and physiology. *Journal of Personality and Social Psychology, 74*, 686–703.

Kring, A. M., Smith, D. A., & Neale, J. M. (1994). Individual differences in dispositional expressiveness: Development and validation of the Emotional Expressivity scale. *Journal of Personality and Social Psychology, 66*, 934–949.

Kroenke, K., & Spitzer, R. L. (1998). Gender differences in the reporting of physical and somatoform symptoms. *Psychosomatic Medicine, 60*, 150–155.

Krohne, H. W. (1978). Individual differences in coping with stress and anxiety. In C. D. Spielberger & I. G. Sarason (Eds.), *Stress and anxiety* (Vol. 5, pp. 233–260). Washington, DC: Hemisphere.

Krohne, H. W. (1986). Coping with stress: Dispositions, strategies, and the problem of measurement. In M. H. Appley & R. Trumbull (Eds.), *Dynamics of stress. Physiological, psychological, and social perspectives* (pp. 207–232). New York: Plenum.

Krohne, H. W. (1989). The concept of coping modes: Relating cognitive person variables to actual coping behavior. *Advances in Behaviour Research and Therapy, 11*, 235–248.

Krohne, H. W. (1990). Personality as a mediator between objective events and their subjective representation. *Psychological Inquiry, 1*, 26–29.

Krohne, H. W. (Ed.). (1993a). *Attention and avoidance. Strategies in coping with aversiveness.* Seattle: Hogrefe & Huber.

Krohne, H. W. (1993b). Vigilance and cognitive avoidance as concepts in coping research. In H. W. Krohne (Ed.), *Attention and avoidance. Strategies in coping with aversiveness* (pp. 19–50). Seattle: Hogrefe & Huber.

Krohne, H. W. (1996a). *Angst und Angstbewältigung.* Stuttgart: Kohlhammer.

Krohne, H. W. (1996b). Individual differences in coping. In M. Zeidner & N. S. Endler (Eds.), *Handbook of coping: Theory, research, applications* (pp. 381–409). New York: John Wiley.

Krohne, H. W., & Egloff, B. (in press). Vigilant and avoidant coping. Theory and measurement. In C. D. Spielberger & I. G. Sarason (Eds.), *Stress and emotion* (Vol. 17). Washington, DC: Taylor & Francis.

Krohne, H. W., Egloff, B., Varner, L. J., Burns, L. R., Weidner, G., & Ellis, H. C. (2000). The assessment of dispositional vigilance and cognitive avoidance: Factorial structure, psychometric properties, and validity of the Mainz Coping Inventory. *Cognitive Therapy and Research, 24*, 297–311.

Krohne, H. W., & Hock, M. (1993). Coping dispositions, actual anxiety, and the incidental learning of success- and failure-related stimuli. *Personality and Individual Differences, 15*, 33–41.

Krohne, H. W., Hock, M., & Kohlmann, C.-W. (1992). Coping dispositions, uncertainty, and emotional arousal. In K. T. Strongman (Ed.), *International review of studies on emotion* (Vol. 2, pp. 73–95). Chichester, England: Wiley.

Krohne, H. W., Pieper, M., Knoll, N., & Breimer, N. (2002). The cognitive regulation of emotions: The role of success versus failure experience and coping dispositions. *Cognition and Emotion, 16*, 217–243.

Krohne, H. W., Schmukle, S. C., Burns, L. R., Egloff, B., & Spielberger, C. D. (2001). The measurement of coping in achievement situations: An international comparison. *Personality and Individual Differences, 30*, 1225–1243.

Lacey, J. I. (1950). Individual differences in somatic response patterns. *Journal of Comparative and Physiological Psychology, 43*, 338–350.

Lacey, J. I., Bateman, D. E., & Van Lehn, R. (1953). Autonomic response specificity: An experimental study. *Psychosomatic Medicine, 15*, 8–21.

Larsen, R. J. (1987). The stability of mood variability: A spectral analytic approach to daily mood assessments. *Journal of Personality and Social Psychology, 52*, 1195–1204.

Larsen, R. J. (1989). A process approach to personality psychology: Utilizing time as a facet of data. In D. Buss & N. Cantor (Eds.), *Personality psychology: Recent trends and emerging directions* (pp. 177–193). New York: Springer-Verlag.

Larsen, R. J., & Diener, E. (1992). Promises and problems with the circumplex model of emotions. In M. S. Clark (Ed.), *Review of personality and social psychology: Volume 13. Emotion* (pp. 25–59). Newbury Park, CA: Sage Publications.

Larsen, R. J., & Kasimatis, M. (1990). Day-to-day physical symptoms: Individual differences in the occurrence, duration, and emotional concomitants of minor daily illnesses. *Journal of Personality, 59*, 387–424.

Laux, L., & Weber, H. (1987). Person-centred coping research. *European Journal of Personality, 1*, 193–214.

Lazarus, R. S. (1966). *Psychological stress and the coping process.* New York: McGraw-Hill.

Lazarus, R. S. (1990). Theory-based stress measurement. *Psychological Inquiry, 1*, 3–13.

Lazarus, R. S. (1991). *Emotion and adaptation.* New York: Oxford University Press.

Lazarus, R. S. (1993). Coping theory and research: Past, present, and future. *Psychosomatic Medicine, 55*, 234–247.

Lazarus, R. S., & Folkman, S. (1984). Coping and adaptation. In W. D. Gentry (Ed.), *The handbook of behavioral medicine* (pp. 282–325). New York: Guilford Press.

Lazarus, R. S., & Folkman, S. (1987). Transactional theory and research on emotions and coping. *European Journal of Personality, 1*, 141–169.

Lazarus, R. S., & Launier, R. (1978). Stress-related transactions between person and environment. In L. A. Pervin & M. Lewis (Eds.), *Perspectives in interactional psychology* (pp. 287–327). New York: Plenum.

LeDoux, J. E. (1996). *The emotional brain: The mysterious underpinnings of emotional life.* New York: Touchstone.

Leventhal, H. (1970). Findings and theory in the study of fear communications. In L. Berkowitz (Ed.), *Advances in experimental social psychology* (Vol. 5, pp. 119–186). New York: Academic Press.

Leventhal, H. (1986). Symptom reporting: A focus on process. In S. McHugh & T. M. Vallis (Eds.), *Illness behavior. A multidisciplinary model* (pp. 219–237). New York: Plenum.

Leventhal, H. (1991). Emotion: Prospects for conceptual and empirical development. In R. G. Lister & H. J. Weingartner (Eds.), *Perspectives on cognitive neuroscience* (pp. 325–348). Oxford, England: Oxford University Press.

Leventhal, H., & Everhart, D. (1979). Emotion, pain, and physical illness. In C. E. Izard (Ed.), *Emotions in personality and psychopathology* (pp. 263–299). New York: Plenum.

Levine, L. J., & Burgess, S. L. (1997). Beyond general arousal. Effects of specific emotions on memory. *Social Cognition, 15*, 157–181.

Malmo, R. B., & Shagass, C. (1949). Physiologic study of symptom mechanisms in psychiatric patients under stress. *Psychosomatic Medicine, 11*, 25–29.

Malmo, R. B., Shagass, C., & Davis, F. H. (1950). Symptom specificity and bodily reactions during psychiatric interview. *Psychosomatic Medicine, 12*, 362–376.

Markus, H. R., & Wurf, E. (1987). The dynamic self-concept: A social psychological perspective. *Annual Review of Psychology, 38*, 299–337.

Marwitz, M., & Stemmler, G. (1998). On the status of individual response specificity. *Psychophysiology, 35*, 1–15.

Mayer, J. D., Caruso, D. R., & Salovey, P. (1999). Emotional intelligence meets traditional standards for an intelligence. *Intelligence, 27*, 267–298.

Mayer, J. D., & Salovey, P. (1995). Emotional intelligence and the construction and regulation of feelings. *Applied and Preventive Psychology, 4*, 197–208.

Mayer, J. D., & Salovey, P. (1997). What is emotional intelligence? In P. Salovey & D. J. Sluyter (Eds.), *Emotional development and emotional intelligence* (pp. 3–31). New York: Basic Books.

McFarland, C., & Buehler, R. (1997). Negative affective states and the motivated retrieval of positive life events: The role of affect acknowledgment. *Journal of Personality and Social Psychology, 73*, 200–214.

McNair, D. M., Lorr, M., & Droppleman, L. F. (1971). *Manual: Profile of mood states.* San Diego, CA: Educational and Industrial Testing Services.

Metcalfe, J., & Mischel, W. (1999). A hot/cool-system analysis of delay of gratification: Dynamics of willpower. *Psychological Review, 106*, 3–19.

Miller, S. M. (1980). When is little information a dangerous thing? Coping with stressful events by monitoring versus blunting. In S. Levine & H. Ursin (Eds.), *Health and coping* (pp. 145–169). New York: Plenum.

Miller, S. M. (1987). Monitoring and blunting: Validation of a questionnaire to assess styles of information seeking under threat. *Journal of Personality and Social Psychology, 52*, 345–353.

Miller, S. M. (1996). Monitoring and blunting of threatening information: Cognitive interference and facilitation in the coping process. In I. G. Sarason, G. R. Pierce, & B. R. Sarason (Eds.), *Cognitive interference: Theories, methods, and findings* (pp. 175–190). Mahwah, NJ: Erlbaum.

Mischel, W., & Shoda, Y. (1995). A cognitive-affective system theory of personality: Reconceptualizing situations, dispositions, dynamics, and invariance in personality structure. *Psychological Review, 102*, 248–268.

Mischel, W., & Shoda, Y. (1998). Reconciling processing dynamics and personality dispositions. *Annual Review of Psychology, 49*, 229–258.

Montgomery, W. A., & Jones, G. E. (1984). Laterality, emotionality, and heartbeat perception. *Psychophysiology, 21*, 459–465.

Morris, W. N., & Reilly, N. P. (1987). Toward the self-regulation of mood: Theory and research. *Motivation and Emotion, 11*, 215–249.

Mullen, B., & Suls, J. (1982). The effectiveness of attention and rejection as coping styles: A meta-analysis of temporal differences. *Journal of Psychosomatic Research, 26*, 43–49.

Myrtek, M. (1980). *Psychophysiologische Konstitutionsforschung. Ein Beitrag zur Psychosomatik.* Göttingen: Hogrefe.

Nachreiner, F. (1998). Individual and social determinants

of shiftwork tolerance. *Scandinavian Journal of Work, Environment and Health, 24*, 35–42.

Nebel, L. E., Howell, R. H., Krantz, D. S., Falconer, J. J., Gottdiener, J. S., & Gabbay, F. H. (1996). The circadian variation of cardiovascular stress levels and reactivity: Relationship to individual differences in morningness eveningness. *Psychophysiology, 33*, 273–281.

Newton, T. L., & Contrada, R. J. (1992). Repressive coping and verbal-autonomic response dissociation: The influence of social context. *Journal of Personality and Social Psychology, 62*, 159–167.

Nix, G., Watson, C., Pyszczynski, T., & Greenberg, J. (1995). Reducing depressive affect through external focus of attention. *Journal of Social and Clinical Psychology, 14*, 36–52.

Notarius, C. I., & Levenson, R. W. (1979). Expressive tendencies and physiological responses to stress. *Journal of Personality and Social Psychology, 37*, 1204–1210.

Parrott, W. G. (1993). Beyond hedonism: Motives for inhibiting good moods and for maintaining bad moods. In D. W. Wegner & J. W. Pennebaker (Eds.), *Handbook of mental control* (pp. 278–305). Englewood Cliffs, NJ: Prentice Hall.

Parrott, W. G., & Sabini, J. (1990). Mood and memory under natural conditions: Evidence for mood incongruent recall. *Journal of Personality and Social Psychology, 59*, 321–336.

Pennebaker, J. W. (1982). *The psychology of physical symptoms*. New York: Springer.

Pennebaker, J. W. (1989). Stream of consciousness and stress: Levels of thinking. In J. S. Uleman & J. A. Bargh (Eds.), *Unintended thought* (pp. 327–350). New York: Guilford Press.

Pennebaker, J. W. (2000). Psychological factors influencing the reporting of physical symptoms. In A. A. Stone, J. S. Turkkan, C. A. Bachrach, I. B. Jobe, H. S. Kurtzman, & V. S. Cain (Eds.), *The science of self-report: Implications for research and practice* (pp. 299–315). Mahwah, NJ: Erlbaum.

Pennebaker, J. W., Gonder-Frederick, L., Stewart, H., Elfman, L., & Skelton, J. A. (1982). Physical symptoms associated with blood pressure. *Psychophysiology, 19*, 201–210.

Pennebaker, J. W., & Watson, D. (1988). Blood pressure estimation and beliefs among normotensives and hypertensives. *Health Psychology, 7*, 309–328.

Pervin, L. A. (1993). Affect and personality. In M. Lewis & J. M. Haviland (Eds.), *Handbook of emotions* (pp. 301–311). New York: Guilford Press.

Power, M., & Dalgleish, T. (1997). *Cognition and emotion. From order to disorder*. Hove, England: Psychology Press.

Pyszczynski, T., & Greenberg, J. (1985). Depression and preferences for self-focusing stimuli after success and failure. *Journal of Personality and Social Psychology, 49*, 1066–1075.

Pyszczynski, T., & Greenberg, J. (1987). Self-regulatory perseveration and the depressive self-focusing style: A self-awareness theory of reactive depression. *Psychological Bulletin, 102*, 122–138.

Reiss, S. (1987). Theoretical perspectives on the fear of anxiety. *Clinical Psychology Review, 7*, 585–596.

Revelle, W. (1995). Personality processes. *Annual Review of Psychology, 46*, 295–328.

Roberts, T.-A., & Pennebaker, J. W. (1995). Gender differences in perceiving internal state: Toward a his-and-hers model of perceptual cue use. In M. P. Zanna (Ed.), *Advances in experimental social psychology* (pp. 143–175). San Diego, CA: Academic Press.

Roth, S., & Cohen, L. J. (1986). Approach, avoidance, and coping with stress. *American Psychologist, 41*, 813–819.

Russell, J. A., & Feldman Barrett, L. (1999). Core affect, prototypical emotional episodes, and other things called emotion: Dissecting the elephant. *Journal of Personality and Social Psychology, 76*, 805–819.

Rusting, C. L. (1998). Personality, mood, and cognitive processing of emotional information: Three conceptual frameworks. *Psychological Bulletin, 124*, 165–196.

Rusting, C. L. (1999). Interactive effects of personality and mood on emotion-congruent memory and judgment. *Journal of Personality and Social Psychology, 77*, 1073–1086.

Safer, M. A. (1981). Sex and hemisphere differences in access to codes for processing emotional expressions and faces. *Journal of Experimental Psychology: General, 110*, 86–100.

Salovey, P. (1992). Mood-induced self-focused attention. *Journal of Personality and Social Psychology, 62*, 699–707.

Salovey, P., Hsee, C. K., & Mayer, J. D. (1993). Emotional intelligence and the self-regulation of affect. In D. M. Wegner & J. W. Pennebaker (Eds.), *Handbook of mental control* (pp. 258–277). Englewood Cliffs, NJ: Prentice Hall.

Salovey, P., & Rodin, J. (1985). Cognitions about the self: Connecting feeling states to social behavior. In P. Shaver (Ed.), *Review of personality and social psychology* (Vol. 6, pp. 143–166). Beverly Hills, CA: Sage Publications.

Schachter, S. (1964). The interaction of cognitive and physiological determinants of emotional states. In L. Berkowitz (Ed.), *Advances in experimental social psychology* (Vol. 1, pp. 49–80). San Diego, CA: Academic Press.

Schachter, S., & Singer, J. E. (1962). Cognitive, social, and physiological determinants of emotional state. *Psychological Review, 69*, 379–399.

Scherer, K. R. (1984). On the nature and function of emotion: A component process approach. In K. R. Scherer & P. Ekman (Eds.), *Approaches to emotion* (pp. 293–318). Hillsdale, NJ: Erlbaum.

Scherer, K. R. (1986). Voice, stress, and emotion. In M. H. Appley & R. Trumbull (Eds.), *Dynamics of stress. Physiological, psychological, and social perspectives* (pp. 157–179). New York: Plenum.

Scherer, K. R. (1988). Criteria for emotion-antecedent appraisals: A review. In V. Hamilton, G. H. Bower, & N. H. Frijda (Eds.), *Cognitive perspectives on emotion and motivation* (pp. 89–126). Dordrecht, The Netherlands: Nijhoff.

Scherer, K. R. (1993). Studying the emotion-antecedent appraisal process: An expert system approach. *Cognition and Emotion, 7*, 325–355.

Sedikides, C. (1992). Mood as a determinant of attentional focus. *Cognition and Emotion, 6*, 129–148.

Singer, J. A., & Salovey, P. (1988). Mood and memory: Evaluating the network theory of affect. *Clinical Psychology Review, 8*, 211–251.

Singer, J. L. (Ed.). (1990). *Repression and dissociation. Implications for personality theory, psychopathology, and health*. Chicago: University of Chicago Press.

Smith, S. M., & Petty, R. P. (1995). Personality moderators of mood congruency effects on cognition: The role of self-esteem and negative mood regulation. *Journal of Personality and Social Psychology, 68,* 1092–1107.

Spielberger, C. D. (1972). Anxiety as an emotional state. In C. D. Spielberger (Ed.), *Anxiety: Current trends in theory and research* (Vol. 1, pp. 23–49). New York: Academic Press.

Stemmler, G. (1997). Selective activation of traits: Boundary conditions for the activation of anger. *Personality and Individual Differences, 22,* 213–233.

Stepper, S., & Strack, F. (1993). Proprioceptive determinants of emotional and nonemotional feelings. *Journal of Personality and Social Psychology, 64,* 211–220.

Suls, J., & Fletcher, B. (1985). The relative efficacy of avoidant and non-avoidant coping strategies: A meta-analysis. *Health Psychology, 4,* 249–288.

Sutton, S. K., & Davidson, R. J. (1997). Prefrontal brain asymmetry: A biological substrate of the behavioral approach and inhibition systems. *Psychological Science, 8,* 204–210.

Tankova, I., Adan, A., & Buela-Casal, G. (1994). Circadian typology and individual differences. A review. *Personality and Individual Differences, 16,* 671–684.

Taylor, S. (Ed.). (1999). *Anxiety sensitivity. Theory, research, and treatment of the fear of anxiety.* Mahwah, NJ: Erlbaum.

Teasdale, J. D., & Barnard, P. J. (1993). *Affect, cognition, and change. Re-modeling depressive thought.* Hove, England: Erlbaum.

Thompson, R. A. (1994). Emotion regulation: A theme in search of definition. In N. A. Fox (Ed.), The development of emotion regulation. Biological and behavioral considerations (pp. 25–52). *Monographs of the Society for Research in Child Development, 59* (2–3, Serial No. 240).

Tomarken, A. J., Davidson, R. J., & Henriques, J. B. (1990). Resting frontal brain asymmetry predicts affective responses to films. *Journal of Personality and Social Psychology, 59,* 791–801.

Tomarken, A. J., Davidson, R. J., Wheeler, R. E., & Doss, R. C. (1992). Individual differences in anterior brain asymmetry and fundamental dimensions of emotion. *Journal of Personality and Social Psychology, 62,* 676–687.

Tomarken, A. J., Davidson, R. J., Wheeler, R. E., & Kinney, L. (1992). Psychometric properties of resting anterior EEG asymmetry: Temporal stability and internal consistency. *Psychophysiology, 29,* 576–592.

Tomkins, S. S. (1962). *Affect, imagery, and consciousness, Vol. 1: The positive affects.* New York: Springer.

Tomkins, S. S. (1963). *Affect, imagery, and consciousness, Vol. 2: The negative affects.* New York: Springer.

Tucker, D. M. (1981). Lateral brain function, emotion, and conceptualization. *Psychological Bulletin, 89,* 19–46.

Tulving, E., & Pearlstone, Z. (1966). Availability versus accessibility of information in memory for words. *Journal of Verbal Learning and Verbal Behavior, 5,* 381–391.

Vaitl, D. (1996). Interoception. *Biological Psychology, 42,* 1–27.

Walden, T. A., & Smith, M. C. (1997). Emotion regulation. *Motivation and Emotion, 21,* 7–25.

Watson, D. (1990). On the dispositional nature of stress measures: Stable and nonspecific influences on self-reported hassles. *Psychological Inquiry, 1,* 34–37.

Watson, D., & Clark, L. A. (1984). Negative affectivity: The disposition to experience aversive emotional states. *Psychological Bulletin, 96,* 465–490.

Watson, D., & Clark, L. A. (1994). *PANAS-X. Manual for the Positive and Negative Affect Schedule—Expanded Form.* Iowa City: University of Iowa Press.

Watson, D., Clark, L. A., & Tellegen, A. (1988). Development and validation of brief measures of positive and negative affect: The PANAS scales. *Journal of Personality and Social Psychology, 54,* 1063–1070.

Watson, D., & Pennebaker, J. W. (1989). Health complaints, stress, and distress: Exploring the central role of negative affectivity. *Psychological Review, 96,* 234–254.

Watson, D., & Pennebaker, J. W. (1991). Situational, dispositional, and genetic bases of symptom reporting. In J. A. Skelton & R. T. Croyle (Eds.), *Mental representation in health and illness* (pp. 60–84). New York: Springer-Verlag.

Wegner, D. M., & Giuliano, T. (1980). Arousal-induced attention to self. *Journal of Personality and Social Psychology, 38,* 719–726.

Weinberger, D. A. (1990). The construct validity of the repressive coping style. In J. L. Singer (Ed.), *Repression and dissociation. Implications for personality theory, psychopathology, and health* (pp. 337–386). Chicago: University of Chicago Press.

Weinberger, D. A., Schwartz, G. E., & Davidson, R. J. (1979). Low-anxious, high-anxious, and repressive coping styles: Psychometric patterns and behavioral and physiological responses to stress. *Journal of Abnormal Psychology, 88,* 369–380.

Weinstein, J., Averill, J. R., Opton, E. M., & Lazarus, R. S. (1968). Defensive style and discrepancy between self-report and physiological indexes of stress. *Journal of Personality and Social Psychology, 10,* 406–413.

Wells, A., & Matthews, G. (1994). *Attention and emotion. A clinical perspective.* Hove, England: Erlbaum.

Wenger, M. A. (1941). The measurement of individual differences in autonomic balance. *Psychosomatic Medicine, 3,* 427–434.

Wenger, M. A., & Cullen, T. D. (1972). Studies of autonomic balance in children and adults. In N. S. Greenfield & R. A. Sternbach (Eds.), *Handbook of psychophysiology* (pp. 535–569). New York: Holt, Rinehart and Winston.

Wheeler, R. E., Davidson, R. J., & Tomarken, A. J. (1993). Frontal brain asymmetry and emotional affectivity: A biological substrate of affective style. *Psychophysiology, 30,* 82–89.

Wood, J. V., Saltzberg, J. A., & Goldsamt, L. A. (1990). Does affect induce self-focused attention? *Journal of Personality and Social Psychology, 58,* 899–908.

Wood, J. V., Saltzberg, J. A., Neale, J. M., Stone, A. A., & Rachmiel, T. B. (1990). Self-focused attention, coping responses, and distressed mood in everyday life. *Journal of Personality and Social Psychology, 58,* 1027–1036.

Wundt, W. (1903). *Grundzüge der physiologischen Psychologie, Vol. 3* (5th ed.). Leipzig: Engelmann.

Zuckerman, M., & Lubin, B. (1965). *Manual for the multiple affect adjective check list.* San Diego, CA: Educational and Industrial Testing Service.

# 37

# EMOTION AND LIFE-SPAN PERSONALITY DEVELOPMENT

Laura L. Carstensen, Susan T. Charles,
Derek M. Isaacowitz, and Quinn Kennedy

The field of personality development aims to understand how individuals acquire distinctive ways of being in the world. In this chapter, we adopt an agentic model of personality in which temperamental inheritance, exposure to different types of environments, acquired beliefs and expectations, and, most important, the interplay among these factors lead to characteristic styles of behaving (Bandura, 1997). Unlike typological or trait approaches to personality in which emotion is either largely ignored, or even designated as more or less salient to particular characteristics—such as the association of happiness with extraversion or anger with choleric tendencies—the approach we take assumes that emotional experience, expression, and regulation are far more broadly and more fundamentally related to personality development. The emotions people come to feel when they encounter challenges and the effectiveness with which they learn to regulate their emotions are the cardinal components of personality development (see Rothbart & Derryberry, 1981).

Indeed, we contend that a model of personality development in which emotion is core provides the most parsimonious framework for understanding and predicting individual differences in behavior, thinking, and feeling in day-to-day life. Emotions are not simply related to personality. Emotions are the essence of personality.

At the most basic level, emotions direct attention and subsequently orient people toward and away from various environmental stimuli (Zajonc, 1997). Individual differences in the propensity to experience specific emotions not only influence the psychological and biological reactivity of the person in the moment but come to influence conscious choices about preferred environments and behavioral styles and influence the social partners to which people are drawn. Because emotion is a central feature of all self-referent phenomena (Izard, 1977; Izard & Ackerman, 1998), as the self develops it comes to proactively mediate environmental input through the schematic processing of experience, activation of motivation, and the regulation of emotion (Bandura, 1989, 1999). That is, personality ultimately reflects individual adaptations to the social and physical conditions within which it develops. Adaptations always involve emotion. The most interesting questions about personality development concern how complex and persistent styles of living in the world evolve out of dynamic and reciprocal relations among what are, in all likelihood, rudimentary differences in biologically based affective tendencies and the social and cultural world. The overarching aim of this chapter is to review evidence for emotion-related processes in life-span personality development. In doing so, we offer a conceptual framework that presumes that inherited emotional tendencies in infancy contribute to a constellation of factors that influence persistent and patterned styles of engagement in the world. We begin by describing both cross-sectional and longitudinal evidence for genetic influence on temperament and suggest that emotional predispositions, not "personalities," are what gets inherited. We then present evidence for the social modification of these qualities during the early years of life. Precisely because emotional responsiveness and reactivity are socially modifiable, we believe that this model helps to explain why evidence for both heritability and environmental influence is abundant in the literature on personality. Rather than be pitted against one another, as genetic and social perspectives too often are, we argue that the most intriguing and important questions in personality development consider the interaction of the two.

Next, we overview evidence for the stability of personality in adulthood and old age and argue, as has Izard (1977), that specific traits are, at their core, emotion based. Later in the chapter we consider theories about life-span development and emotion, and we suggest ways in which changes in emotion regulation and emotion experience alter goal-directed behavior in adulthood. Finally, we examine the relationships among emotion, coping, and mental and physical heath. We conclude that a sophisticated understanding of the bidirectional influence of environment and basic biological processes on emotion holds great promise for both theory and application in the area of personality development across the life span.

## Personality: Origins and Development Across the Life Span

Virtually all parents of more than one child believe ardently in a genetic basis for individual differences. Some babies are easy to soothe, others difficult. Some babies are immediately social, others are more watchful and pensive. Some babies are active whereas others are more subdued. Differences among infants are evident so shortly after birth that one can easily wonder if personality really develops

or if it simply unfolds, genetically preprogrammed from the start. Despite subjective feelings that this may be the case, it is scientifically implausible. There are no known or suspected genetic mechanisms by which situated interactional styles, such as whether one laughs at a joke at a party or feels shy in front of an audience, are determined by single or multiple genes.

Nevertheless, much light has been shed on the heritability of personality in the past two decades and it is clear that genes do play a role even in complex behavior conceptualized as personality. Perhaps more striking, however, is that the same body of research underscores vast flexibility in human behavior. Recent assertions that the environment, particularly parental behavior (e.g., Harris, 1998), has little influence on children are based mostly on misinterpretations of the meaning of heritability coefficients. Estimates based on such mathematical computations suggest that shared environments are less influential than nonshared environments (Goldsmith, 1993). However, rather than implying that environments do not matter, they suggest instead that some of the obvious, and often crude, ways scientists have thought environment mattered are incorrect (see Turkheimer, 2000, for an excellent review on the meaning of behavioral genetic studies; Turkheimer & Waldron, 2000).

What does behavior genetics literature suggest? A large number of studies—focused on research participants spanning infancy to old age—have been conducted during the 1980s and 1990s that link genetic inheritance to emotion-relevant behaviors. Studies of children ranging from 6 months to 2 years of age find moderate heritability coefficients for measures of temperament, mood, emotional intensity, and distractibility (Cyphers, Phillips, Fulker, & Mrazek, 1990; Matheny, Wachs, Ludwig, & Phillips, 1995). Studies of preadolescent children ranging from a little under 2 to a little over 9 years old also find evidence for moderate heritability of emotionality, activity, sociability, impulsivity, fearfulness, and emotion regulation (Buss & Plomin, 1975; Goldsmith, Buss, & Lemery, 1997; Goldsmith & Gottesman, 1981; Plomin, 1976; Plomin & Rowe, 1977). Twin studies yield consistent findings, also suggesting moderate heritability for temperament.

Moreover, there is considerable evidence that basic individual differences in temperamental variables are reasonably stable and coherent. Although researchers differ in the behaviors and constructs viewed as temperament, there is considerable overlap among them and virtually all include some measure of negative and positive emotionality. Rothbart (1986) operationalizes temperament by activity level, smiling and laughter, fear, distress (or frustration), soothability, and vocal activity. In the early 1960s, Thomas and Chess and their colleagues undertook a now classic study of infants' styles involving mood and emotional reactivity to their environments (e.g., Chess & Thomas, 1996; Thomas, Chess, Birch, Hertzig, & Korn, 1963) and showed that these styles persisted over the first few months of life. Later evidence suggested that early temperament predicts mood states even years later (Costa & McCrae, 1990).

More recently and armed with far more sophisticated research methods, Kagan and his colleagues have charted the developmental trajectories of behaviorally inhibited children. In an extensive research program, they have examined the behavioral and physiological correlates of people with two distinct temperamental qualities (e.g., Kagan, Reznick, & Gibbons, 1989; Kagan, Resnick, Snidman, Gibbons, & Johnson, 1988; Kagan, Snidman, Arcus, & Reznick, 1994). The first type—inhibited—includes people who are characterized as shy and affectively restrained; and the second type—uninhibited—includes people who are outgoing, spontaneous, and sociable. Although many people fall outside of these two categories, Kagan and his colleagues have focused primarily on children who display behavior that fits into one of the two categories.

This research team has followed infants and toddlers, classified as either inhibited or uninhibited based on behavioral responses to strangers and other unfamiliar stimuli, from as young as 21 months into their preteens (Kagan, Snidman, Zentner, & Peterson, 1999). They report that behavioral styles characterizing inhibited and uninhibited toddlers correlate highly with inhibited and uninhibited behavioral patterns later in childhood (Kagan et al., 1999). Another study found that children categorized as either inhibited or uninhibited when they were toddlers differed significantly from each other over 10 years later on self-report and parent ratings in terms of externalizing behavior (Schwartz, Snidman, & Kagan, 1996); toddlers in the inhibited group were much less likely to display externalizing behavior at age 13 than toddlers who were in the uninhibited group.

Further evidence suggests that behavior corresponding to these behavioral traits in the first 3 years of life correlate with traits in young adults, in some cases even predicting the professions people choose in adulthood. In one study, for example, adults who had been more reserved as children were more likely to hold jobs that were predictable and/or solitary, whereas more outgoing children developed into adults who were more likely to enter into occupations that included a high amount of risk taking or that were more entrepreneurial in nature (Kagan & Moss, 1962). Findings from an independent research group found that temper tantrums in children between the ages of 8 and 10 years predicted downward mobility and divorce for men and women in middle age (Caspi, Elder, & Bem, 1987).

Moreover, genetic influence on emotion-relevant behavior does not appear to diminish at more advanced ages despite the linear life-course increase in acquired and unique life experiences that theoretically could increase environmental variance. On the contrary, the majority of findings underscore great stability throughout adulthood (e.g., Costa, McCrae, & Arenberg, 1980; Gustavsson, Weinryb, Goransson, Pedersen, & Asberg, 1997). One study found that adults ranging from 27 to 80 years of age did not differ in heritability estimates (20 to 40%) for emotionality variables including distress, fear, and anger, nor on measures of sociability and activity (Plomin, Pedersen, McClearn, Nesselroade, & Bergeman, 1988). Comparing twin studies with adoption studies suggests that heritability may be somewhat overestimated in twin studies (Scarr, Webber, Weinberg, & Wittig, 1981), probably because the environments of identical twins are more similar than the environments of fraternal twins, and this greater environmental similarity for identical twins is misattributed to genetic variance.

Although behavioral genetic findings have been used to support the powerful role of genes in behavior, the fact remains that for most personality and temperament variables, the majority of the variance is explained by factors other than heritability. The strong role that nonshared environment plays may be best explained by the agentic capacity of human beings. By the age of 7 or so, children are able to reflect about themselves and show considerable insight into their personal qualities and preferences. Social cognitive theory of personality views individuals as agentic creatures who shape their own environments (Bandura, 1999). As people age, they come to have greater choice in the selection of environments and select environments that support self views. Caspi and Herbener (1990), for example, found that people tend to choose spouses similar to themselves, and further show that people who have spouses similar to themselves are less likely than people with dissimilar spouses to display personality change in adulthood. Throughout adulthood, people actively construct and hone social networks to meet social goals (Lang & Carstensen, 1994, in press), forming increasingly well-contoured social convoys that accompany them throughout life (Antiknock & Jackson, 1987; Lansford, Sherman, Aurora, & Antiknock, 1998). Thus, it may be that stability is maintained across the life course because people create environments that maintain stability.

To date, the pathways of genetic influence remain poorly specified, however, and there is growing evidence that interactive models are needed. Consider the following examples: Rowe, Woulbroun, and Gulley (1994) find that siblings have higher concordance on substance abuse than nonsiblings. However, they also find that this relationship is mediated by siblings having mutual friends. Siblings who share friends show greater concordance on substance abuse than siblings who do not share friends. Similarly, in a study of Finnish twins, Dick, Rose, Viken, and Kaprio (2000) find associations of age at menarche and alcohol abuse; however, the findings appear only in urban, not rural, settings. Simple interpretation of such findings could implicate genetics alone, but clearly the proximal causal mechanism is the interaction between the social situation and genetic effects.

Other studies have found long-term effects of childhood temperament on adult behaviors and personality ratings, but—like the Finnish twin studies examining age at menarche and alcohol abuse cited above (Dick et al., in press)—these patterns vary with cultural context. In a longitudinal study that examined mothers' shyness ratings of their 8- to 10-year-old boys and girls and the career and marital patterns of these children 35 years later, findings indicate that boys reared in Sweden who were classified as shy tended to marry later and have children later, similar to American boys (Kerr, Lambert, & Bem, 1996). Unlike American men, however, for whom shyness in childhood predicted less career success (Caspi, Elder, & Bern, 1988), Swedish men did not differ in their career attainment according to childhood shyness ratings. For girls, shyness also predicted later marriage and childbearing, but in Sweden it also predicted lower educational attainment. These findings suggest a complex interplay between biology and culture. There may be universals in emotional experience and personality structure, but the rules for displaying emotions may differ among cultures, as seen in the differences in Swedish and American children regarding the correlates of shyness. Additionally, the connection between personality and emotional expression may be different cross-culturally, a topic that will require further research.

We expect that a major barrier to understanding gene/environment interactions is rooted in the customary language and algorithms used in social science that support artificial delineations between biologically and socially acquired processes. Terms like *heritability coefficients* and reference to the "percent of variance" accounted for by either the environment or genetics tacitly give credence to the idea that environmental and biological influences can be cleanly separated. Without recognizing possible environmental influences and examining genetically related individuals who are both concordant and discordant for these influences, we cannot study these complex interactional relationships. Turkheimer (2000) writes that when we speak of personality, "Everything is interactive in the sense that no arrows proceed uninterrupted from cause to effect, any gene or environmental event produces an effect only by interacting with other genes and environments" (p. 161). Although in recent years substantial discussion has centered around whether biology or environment is most influential in personality development, we take the position that the nature of the interaction between the two is the more interesting and the more important puzzle social scientists must address.

If genes play a role in personality development, which behavior genetic studies suggest they do, what gets inherited? Demonstrating genetic patterns in a population is only a first step. The more penetrating questions concern the mechanisms of transmission. Kagan and colleagues have found physiological differences between children of very different temperaments (Kagan et al., 1999). Inhibited toddlers display greater sympathetic nervous system reactivity, including higher heart rates, larger pupil diameters, and higher levels of morning cortisol compared to uninhibited toddlers (Snidman, Kagan, Riordan, & Shannon, 1995). When these children reach 4½ years of age, the boys classified as highly reactive or inhibited have significantly higher resting heart rates than boys classified as low-reactive toddlers (although, interestingly, girls did not show these differences at follow-up; Kagan, 1997). These same groups of toddlers differ in morning cortisol levels that, some argue, may lead to enduring differences in amygdala functioning (Schmidt, Fox, Rubin, & Sternberg, 1997). The amygdala, cingulate, and septal nuclei are instrumental in behaviors that include wariness, fear, and selective attachments (e.g., Joseph, 1999). Therefore, higher cortisol levels as toddlers may lead to physiological changes that influence behavior at age 4, even if the higher morning cortisol levels are no longer present (Schmidt et al., 1997).

Recent research by Richard Davidson and his colleagues provides important evidence that not only do human infants come into the world biologically preprogrammed to experience emotions but also that individual differences are apparent. To briefly summarize, research based on functional neuroanatomy shows that neural circuits involved in emotion include not only well-established emotion centers such as the amygdala but also involve the prefrontal cortex, which allows for mental representations of emotional events (Davidson et al., 1998). In addition, evidence for hemispheric differentiation has accrued (Davidson & Hugdahl, 1995). Put simply, left hemispheric activation is involved with positive affect and approach behavior. Right hemispheric activation is involved in negative affect and withdrawal behavior. Perhaps most relevant to personality is intriguing evidence for individual differences in baseline activation of left and right hemispheres (Davidson & Fox, 1989), differences that are associated with dispositional moods, affective reactivity, and immune system functioning, a point to which we return in our discussion of personality and health (Davidson, 1992). Davidson relates that the same central circuitry mediates both the temperamental styles in children and the affective style—a traitlike stable pattern of behavior that is linked to personality—in adults (Davidson, 1992). Thus, Davidson has identified individual differences in neural functions, which are plausibly inherited and may underlie temperament.

## Environmental Influences—The Importance of Socialization

The body of research described in the previous section shows that temperamental "types" can be described by stable profiles that include observed behavior and physiological responsiveness. Although it importantly reveals the relevance of individual differences in reactivity and other temperamental qualities, it does not address the ways in which temperament is maintained and, importantly, fails to explain cases in which it is not. This latter point is critical. Although the correlations between physiological and behavioral correlates predicting later temperament and behavior are statistically significant, there is substantial variation in developmental trajectories. A considerable number—roughly 40% of shy toddlers—are no longer so by the time they enter preschool (Kagan et al., 1988). Thus, although in some people temperamental qualities present at birth are relatively enduring, in others, they are not (Kagan et al., 1994). If temperament is biologically based and inherited, how does change come about?

In a beautiful synthesis of the ways that temperamental qualities develop into personality, Rothbart and Ahadi (1994) argue that "temperamental characteristics are not static and unchanging but adapt to environmental demands" (p. 56). The ways in which situations and social partners respond to particular behaviors (irritability, smiling, etc.) feed back into a developing self system that subsequently filters new incoming information. Certain types of situations may be inherently distressing to individuals with low thresholds for stimulation, but as Bandura (1988) has shown repeatedly, when individuals believe that they can competently control their response to the situation, they are likely to behave effectively even in situations that are initially arousing. This experience feeds back into the self system and future episodes are subsequently approached differently. In other words, beliefs about whether one can exercise control over unwanted arousal play a central role in perpetuating the arousal. Approach and avoidance are conceptualized as self-regulatory processes that modify internal states. Whereas avoidant behavior relates directly to perceived coping inefficacy, successful approach behavior modifies self-relevant beliefs and associated responses in the future. Interviews with previously shy 7-year-olds (i.e., who had been classified as shy when they were toddlers but were no longer shy at age 7) suggest that parental caregiving behavior was critical in their change (Fox, Sobel, Calkins, & Cole, 1996). Many of these previously shy children reported that their parents had facilitated encounters with novel and mildly stressful events within safe environments, enabling them to overcome their fears. Caregivers also promote empathy in young children by helping them to understand the ef-

fects of their transgressions against others (Zahn-Waxler, Cole, & Barrett, 1991). Again, there is evidence for the interplay between temperament and the regulation of emotion, with children low in negative emotionality showing greater sympathy over time (Eisenberg, Fabes, Shepard, Murphy, et al., 1998).

Typically, the first and arguably the most important social context involves infants' relationships with their primary caregivers. The attachment process, originally described by Bowlby (1973) and elaborated by Ainsworth (Ainsworth, Blehar, Waters, & Wall, 1978), is widely accepted as a biologically based propensity for human infants to bond to attachment figures. The attachment process is guided by emotional exchanges between the infant and the caretaker. Within these relationships, reciprocal dyadic interactions with caregivers—in which infants' needs are (or are not) satisfied—establish in the infant an inner working model that subsequently influences how information is processed and emotions are regulated (Grossmann & Grossmann, 1990). The quality of this relationship differs substantially as a function of the sensitivity and responsiveness of the caregiver and the temperamental qualities of the infant. Successful attachment varies. Securely attached infants, for example, trust others, tolerate conflicting emotions, and evenly consider a full range of external causes for emotions; whereas insecurely attached infants attend to fractionated elements of emotions and selectively scan the environment for potential causes of emotions, accepting only those that are emotionally tolerable (Grossmann & Grossmann, 1990).

The attachment process appears to be a potent social mediator of temperamental qualities leading to rational emotional appraisal processes in healthy individuals or, alternatively, to distorted (neurotic) appraisal processes in unhealthy persons (Bowlby, 1973). Observational studies that follow children longitudinally suggest that there is considerable stability in attachment styles from infancy into the middle years (Grossmann & Grossmann, 1990) and that patterns of attachment replicate across cultures (VanIJzendoorn & Kroonenberg, 1988) and provide tentative (viz., retrospective) evidence that they persist into adulthood (Bartholomew, 1997).

Attachment, thus, is process by which children learn to regulate their emotions. As Rothbart (1994) has noted, "from the earliest days, emotion is regulated by others, and many of our emotions and cognitions about emotion [are] developmentally shaped in a social context" (p. 371). Initially, the emotional states of infants are regulated by caregivers. Crying infants may be held, rocked, or soothed with spoken words. From the first days of life, emotions are influenced by cultural rules—typically embodied in parents' reactions to emotions—that shape culturally appropriate expressions of emotions, such as under what circumstances the expression of anger is acceptable (Hochschild, 1979). And by actively referencing parental figures for emotional cues, infants learn how to react to potentially arousing situations, such as a stranger entering a room or hearing a sudden loud noise (Campos & Barrett, 1984)—reactions that are also culture bound. Children are also explicitly taught by their parents to avoid contact with certain play partners and not others as they observe varying emotional consequences (Thompson, 1990).

Children contribute to the relationship with their primary caregiver. Compliance with caregivers' requests and subsequent internalization of prohibitions requite the modulation of negative emotions (Kochanska, Tjebkes, & Forman, 1998; Kochanska, Coy, Tjebkes, & Husarek, 1998). Importantly, Kochanska (1997) shows that maternal styles interact with toddlers' temperament in the development of conscience. In fearful children, gentle discipline from the mother effectively socializes the child. However, among fearless children gentle discipline is ineffective; instead, positive responsiveness from the mother is required for socialization of conscience. Kochanska argues that the critical factor in the development of conscience is the way that the mother tailors her response to the child as a function of the child's temperament.

In fact, individual differences in the ways that—and the competence with which—children regulate emotions form the basis for many typological approaches to personality in childhood in which "undercontrolled" and "overcontrolled" are the primary distinctions (van Aken & Asendorf, 1996). The regulation of emotion is also inherently part of the development of conscience. Early on, children acquire the ability to soothe themselves. Very young children learn that their actions lead to differentiated emotional experience (Gross & Munoz, 1995). They learn that by shifting their gaze, or turning their heads toward rewarding objects and events and away from threatening ones, they can modify their emotion states (Derryberry & Rothbart, 1988; Lazarus, 1991). The ability to control their own negative emotions and to share their positive emotions allows children to influence the emotions of their social partners, and subsequently to meet their own emotional needs (Dunn, 1994). Longitudinal studies show that the acquisition of emotion regulation is clearly bidirectional, with parents and children influencing the other from early childhood to preadolescence (Eisenberg, Fabes, Shepard, Guthrie, et al., 1999).

In summary, evidence for coherent and reasonably stable temperamental dispositions from infancy through later childhood is considerable. Just as clear is evidence for the social modifiability of the expression and regulation of emotion associated with various temperamental styles. This relationship is not unidirectional, with parents shaping children's emotional styles. Rather, parents appear to be influenced by their children as well and—in good parenting, as Kochanska and her colleagues have shown—tailor their behaviors to their children's individual styles.

## Personality in Adulthood

Although a handful of studies showing continuities between child and adult personality have been published (e.g., Friedman, et al., 1995), such linkages are clearly understudied. Identifying potential continuities is made all the more difficult because of different research traditions adopted by students of child and adult personality. Whereas child developmentalists tend to focus on the acquisition of self-regulatory processes, the study of adult personality, at least for the past two decades, has been dominated by a taxonomic approach to personality. Although relationships among traits, temperaments, and emotions have been noted in the literature (e.g., Goldsmith, 1993; Izard, Libero, Putnam & Haynes, 1993)—for example, childhood temperaments have been shown to predict personality traits as much as 7 years later (Hagekull & Bohlin, 1998) and categorical formulations of temperament have been shown to map reasonably well onto "Big 5" factors of neuroticism, extraversion, openness to experience, agreeableness, and conscientiousness (Kagan, 1997)—there remains a fundamental disconnect between studies of self regulation in the early years and personality in adulthood and old age. Moreover, because traits are based on linguistic terms used in everyday language, they tend to be rather imprecise characterizations of individual differences in the experience and regulation of emotion. Thus, the broader literature on personality in adulthood connects only loosely with the literature on emotion.

In the model we have adopted throughout this chapter, the predilection to experience certain types of emotions, the intensity with which emotions are experienced, and the ability to regulate this experience form the core of personality. In this section, we first selectively review the personality literature, noting the relevance of emotional experience to traits, and then consider the literature that directly addresses life-span development in the domain of emotion. We argue that trait approaches, because they are, by definition, the most encompassing lexical terms that describe individual differences (John, 1990), will tend to find stability across adulthood, whereas a focus on emotion is more likely to reveal change.

Despite the incongruities noted above, research has shown that traits, particularly extraversion and neuroticism, are associated with affective experience in day-to-day life (Larsen & Ketelaar, 1989). In a landmark article by Costa and McCrae (1980), extraversion was shown to relate strongly to positive affect and neuroticism to negative affect, not only concordantly but 10 years later as well (Costa & McCrae, 1980). More recent work on well-being supports these relationships (see Diener, Suh, Lucas, & Smith, 1999). Indeed, McCrae and Costa (1994) argue that psychopathology, specifically major affective disorder, may result from a traitlike configuration of personality factors that place individuals at risk to experience chronic periods of negative affect. Research by Costa and McCrae shows definitively that whereas changes in personality, as operationalized by self-reported levels of five factors including neuroticism, extraversion, conscientiousness, agreeableness, and openness to experience, are evident into early adulthood (Costa & McCrae, 1988), personality stabilizes by roughly the age of 30 and only modest changes appear after that point. Thus, relationships between traits and affective states are clearly related. We differ from Costa and McCrae and other trait researchers, however, in the interpretation of these relationships. Whereas trait researchers interpret these patterns as reflections of the *influence of traits* on subjective well-being, we see traits as imperfect measures of affective states.

Although the general stance of trait researchers is that personality is cemented by the third decade of life, some recent evidence suggests that modest age differences appear consistently across samples drawn from countries representing diverse language groups, including Germany, Portugal, Israel, China, Korea, and Japan (McCrae & Costa, 1997). Middle-aged adults score somewhat higher on agreeableness and conscientiousness and somewhat lower on measures of neuroticism, extraversion, and openness than young adults (McCrae, et al., 1999). Using both American and Chinese samples, Yang, McCrae, and Costa (1998) administered the California Psychological Inventory (CPI) to adults of various ages. After deriving five personality factors from CPI scores, they found similar age patterns in both cultures: namely, agreeableness and conscientiousness are higher in older age groups, whereas neuroticism, extraversion, and openness are lower among older adults. Because different historical events have taken place in the various countries, Yang and colleagues contend that the similar age differences found across the countries indicate universal psychological-personality maturational processes. Because the five-factor model, particularly extraversion and neuroticism, are linked with emotion, change in emotional experience—in both the types of emotional events and the responses to emotional events—may be the core variable in explaining age differences in personality. Indeed, several theoretical models of personality contend that emotional experience plays an integral role in personality development across the life span. We argue below that these age differences are consistent with improved emotion regulation.

## Emotional Development Across the Life Span

Do emotions develop? To this point, we have considered the interactive role that emotion plays in personality development. A related point concerns emotional development. Emotions in and of themselves are vital to under-

standing human behavior. Emotions direct attention and motivate people throughout life (e.g., Carstensen, 1995; Izard, 1977); emotional experience is central to issues of quality of life and comprises measures of psychological well-being. Uncontrolled emotions can lead to destructive and dangerous rages or paralyzing depression. In this section, we review findings about emotion from childhood to old age, emphasizing recent research on the emotional experience of older adults.

### Emotional Understanding in Children

Stein and her colleagues (as summarized in Stein & Levine, 1999) have investigated the development of emotional understanding in young children. Working from a model in which emotions are experienced primarily in the context of changes that affect personally relevant goals, they have investigated the extent to which specific profiles of instigating events and appraisals are linked to specific reports of emotions among children of different ages and among adults. Affective responses to stimuli in the first 6 months of life are not considered emotional by this definition because at this time infants are unable to represent goal states or exhibit preferences. However, discrete emotions soon develop and infants begin to nonverbally monitor events in the world in terms of their own goals. Their program of research has focused on age 2.5–6 years, during which children are able to verbally report and discuss emotions. Several important findings have emerged from this research. First, almost all children were able to provide events that had initiated emotional responses of happiness, fear, anger, and sadness. Second there was some overlap in the initiators of the three negative emotions, suggesting an important role for appraisals in determining the link between event and emotions, even among young children. However, differential appraisals led to distinct emotional experiences; even sadness and anger could be differentiated based on the types of goal-outcome states revealed when the children were probed for the reasons for their emotional experience.

An interesting developmental difference has emerged from this program of research concerning appraisals that lead to anger (Levine, 1995; Stein & Levine, 1999). For 3-year-olds, anger appears to emerge from situations in which they feel that a goal has been blocked, but could still be accomplished. Sadness happens when it seems as though a goal cannot be accomplished. For them, the intentions of the person who has caused the goal to be blocked are irrelevant. In contrast, intentions become increasingly important in causing anger among older children (Stein & Levine, 1989). This illustrates how emotional understanding may have important links to cognitive development, especially the understanding of the links between goals and intentions.

In addition, Stein, Trabasso, and Liwag (1993) argue

that there is no perfect correspondence between stimuli and emotional responses, except in cases in which individuals have the same base of knowledge and same tendencies toward appraisals. This suggests, once again, that individual differences partially mediate the relationship between environmental stimuli and emotional experience.

## Emotion in Adults

Differential emotions theory (DET) posits that a small group of distinct emotions serves as fundamental motivators of human behavior (Dougherty, Abe, & Izard, 1996; Izard, 1977). Each independent emotion, including interest, joy, anger, sadness, fear, surprise, and disgust, motivates a unique subtype of personality and behavior and can be activated without cognitive evaluation. What is distinct about DET is that these emotions are considered to be the building blocks of personality processes. Rather than resulting from personality variables as in the work of McCrae and Costa, DET views emotions and personality as highly similar, but with the emotions motivating the specific personality traits. Personality development is seen to occur as people link emotions systems with cognition and behavior. With advancing age, the emotion-cognition-personality system appears to become more differentiated, with emotions becoming linked to an ever-increasing array of cognitions. Furthermore, DET researchers speculate that the development of cognitive capabilities leads to age-related changes in what brings about emotional experiences, giving the example of an actual experience and a memory for that experience ultimately having the same emotional impact. By early adulthood, emotions are clearly distinguished and understood. This model derives support from research by Gisela Labouvie-Vief and her colleagues, who find that whereas adolescents generally describe mood states in sensorimotor, concrete terms, adults more often describe their mood states acknowledging specific physical reactions and complex cognitive states (Labouvie-Vief, DeVoe, & Bulka, 1989). Between young and middle adulthood, emotional understanding continues to improve (Cornelius & Caspi, 1987), and some researchers argue that emotional understanding may peak in middle age (Labouvie-Vief et al., 1989).

A peak in emotional understanding in middle age, however, tacitly suggests emotional decline in old age. Indeed, early researchers posited that emotional experience dampened with age, bringing with it an emotional disengagement from the world (e.g., Cumming & Henry, 1961). However, recent work on emotion and aging suggests otherwise (see, for example, Carstensen & Charles, 1998; Carstensen, Pasupathi, Mayr, & Nesselroade, 2000). Evidence is converging around several critical points: (1) Intact emotional functioning is maintained well into old age; (2) emotions become more salient to people as they get older;

and (3) older people are better at emotional regulation than are younger people.

Addressing the first point, several studies have shown that older adults do not necessarily have less intense emotions and experience more negative affect. Malatesta and Kalnok (1984) found no differences between older adults compared to middle-aged and young adults in self-reports concerning the experience of negative affect. Another study by Cameron (1975) also revealed no significant age differences in those aged 4 to 90 for happy, sad, and neutral moods in four different situations—work, school, home, and leisure. Lawton and colleagues (Lawton, Kleban, Rajagopal, & Dean, 1992) found no age differences on any self-report aspect of affective experience, with the notable exception that older people reported lower levels of positive emotion in which arousal is core (e.g., excitement) than the younger people in the sample. More recent evidence suggests cross-sectional decreases in negative affect and increases in positive affect in middle age (Mroczek & Kolarz, 1998) and continued decrease in negative affect but also decreased positive affect in old and very old age (Isaacowitz & Smith, 2000; Smith, Fleeson, Geiselmann, Settersten, & Kunzmann, 1999).

There is little reliable evidence for age-related dampening of subjective emotional experience. One study that did find support for emotional dampening with age was conducted by Diener, Sandvik, and Larsen (1985). On retrospective self-report measures, younger adults reported higher intensities of both positive and negative emotions. The age differences, however, may be due to the sample or the methodology used; 41% of their total sample consisted of high school or college students. It is possible, then, that academic life is the explanatory variable rather than age. Another possible bias could be differences in memory of the intensity of the experience. Indeed, most evidence for the lack of age difference in emotional experience comes from self-reported measures. Recent evidence using an experience sampling approach to the study of affective experience across the adult life span has yielded evidence that emotional life becomes even better as people age and not less intense (Carstensen et al., 2000). Participants in this study, who ranged in age from 18 to 94, were paged at random times during the day for a period of 1 week; at each point, they would report on their current affective state. While no age differences were found in the intensity or frequency with which positive affect was reported or for the intensity of negative affect, older adults appeared to have less frequent episodes of negative affect than younger adults.

Findings from two studies using psychophysiological measurements suggest that older adults have lesser overall physiological arousal than younger adults when discussing emotional topics (Levenson, Carstensen, Friesen, & Ekman, 1991; Levenson, Carstensen, & Gottman, 1993) and argue that lesser physiological arousal may serendipitously hold benefits for emotion regulation (Carstensen, Graff, Levenson, & Gottman, 1996). That is, there may be less to control.

## Socioemotional Selectivity Theory

One life-span model directly relevant to emotional development across adult life span is socioemotional selectivity theory (Carstensen, 1993, 1995; Carstensen & Charles, 1998; Carstensen, Isaacowitz, & Charles, 1999). Emotions play a central role in this theory, although not as a function of age per se but rather in relation to people's sense of future time. When people perceive their futures as unlimited, they interact with people for many different reasons, including gaining novel information, which mostly involve banking resources for use in the future. In contrast, when time is perceived as relatively limited, emotional goals appear to be prioritized over informational ones. This has been demonstrated in several studies, some in which age has been used as a proxy for distance to endings (Fredrickson & Carstensen, 1990), and others in which age and time toward endings have been disentangled through the use of terminal groups such as HIV-positive men (Carstensen & Fredrickson, 1998).

When time is limited, emotions become more salient, and people prioritize emotions and focus their attention on regulating them effectively. Gross et al. (1997) review converging evidence from several studies that used self-report measures indicating that older adults feel more in control of their emotional life than do younger adults. But perhaps the best evidence that older people are expert emotion regulators is the maintenance and possible improvement of emotional experience that takes place with age despite the increasing ratio of losses to gains that people experience as they get older (Heckhausen, Dixon, & Baltes, 1989).

Recent evidence also indicates that, in addition to reporting better control over their emotional lives, older adults show a more differentiated pattern of emotional experiences than do younger adults (Carstensen et al., 2000). Using data from the experience sampling study described above, each of the individual participants' 35 affective reports (each containing information about 19 emotional states each time they were paged) were factor analyzed to determine how many factors adequately described each person's experience over the week. More factors were required to describe the affective experiences of older adults than of younger adults, suggesting that older adults experience a more differentiated set of emotions. Further analyses based on the same sample also indicate an increase in poignancy with age, in which older adults are more likely than younger adults to experience positive and negative emotions together at the same moment (Carstensen et al., 2000).

These results are consistent with socioemotional selec-

tivity theory's assertion that, when time is perceived as limited, emotions become central to cognition and behavior (see also Isaacowitz, Charles, & Carstensen, 2000). Advancing age is perhaps the most dramatic reminder that time is limited, and thus socioemotional selectivity theory can predict these age-related differences. Findings that older people focus more on emotions than do younger people (Carstensen & Turk-Charles, 1994) and experience a well-regulated and satisfying emotional life, in combination with studies linking time perspective, age, and emotions (see Carstensen et al., 1999, for a review), provide evidence for viewing emotional development in adulthood from the socioemotional selectivity theory framework.

## Emotion and the Self in Adult Development

Carol Ryff and her colleagues (1989, 1991; Schmutte & Ryff, 1997) have taken a differentiated approach to understanding emotions and well-being across the life span. Rather than calculating global positive and negative affect as indicators of psychological well-being, Ryff developed six well-being scales that combine different perspectives on positive experience, such as humanistic and idiographic conceptions (Ryff, 1989). The six dimensions that contribute to well-being are self-acceptance, environmental mastery, purpose in life, personal growth, positive relations with others, and autonomy. There are several important points about this formulation of psychological well-being. First, the dimensions appear to have differential relationships with age, with older adults scoring higher than younger adults on Environmental Mastery and Autonomy, but lower on Purpose in Life and Personal Growth (Ryff, 1995). Second, there appears to be an important life-span development trajectory concerning the relationship between people's conception of their present status and their ideal selves on these dimensions. Due primarily to lowered ideal selves, older people tend to have less distance between their actual and ideal selves than do younger adults (Ryff, 1991). Self-discrepancy theory (Higgins, 1987) would suggest that this should have important affective ramifications, and promote lower levels of negative affect and depression.

Ryff and colleagues have also used this conceptualization of psychological well-being in an attempt to disentangle the influence of personality on well-being (Schmutte & Ryff, 1997). Previous research on the relationship between personality and well-being has focused on affective measures of well-being that had substantial content overlap with the personality measures being used as predictors (e.g., Costa & McCrae, 1980), which is not surprising given the degree of overlap in the constructs. To remedy this situation, Schmutte and Ryff (1997) used FFM (five-factor model) personality factors to predict the six dimensions of psychological well-being, while further controlling for shared content and affect levels. Results indicated that links between personality and psychological well-being were attenuated, but in many cases remained even after these conservative control procedures. Furthermore, the six well-being dimensions showed differential relationships with the five personality traits.

## The Role of Emotion and Autobiographical Memory in Personality

It has been argued that by examining the links among emotion, memory, and goals, psychologists can better assess continuity of personality over the life span (Singer & Salovey, 1993). Several studies have shown mood-congruent information in which one's current mood affects the emotional valence of one's memory (Bower, 1981; Forgas, 1991). Mood-congruent recall is also found in more long-term moods: Nondepressed persons tend to remember a greater number of positively valenced events, while depressed persons tend to remember a greater number of negatively valenced events (Matt, Vazquez, & Campbell, 1992). This finding is enhanced when recalling personal information rather than information about others. Ample evidence indicates the role of emotion in autobiographical memory; together, emotion and autobiographical memory influence personality development.

The emotional and social aspect of recounting autobiographical memories is seen from the very beginning, when young children first learn to tell autobiographical stories. Work by Fivush and colleagues (Fivush, Haden, & Reese, 1996) has demonstrated that, when learning how to tell autobiographical stories, children are actually learning a form of communication and social interaction that can help develop, shape, maintain, and/or enhance relationships. The child learns that the sharing of a personal memory, rather than stating a general belief or feeling, signals emotionality and intimacy (Pillemer, 1998) Furthermore, the parental role in teaching autobiographical memory skills may have an impact on the child's later personality (Pillemer, 1998). Children whose parents encourage personal memory sharing, especially of emotional events, may see it as a desired way to receive and give love and caring. Indeed, marital satisfaction has been linked with the expressiveness of a spouse's memory sharing (Buehlman, Gottman, & Katz, 1992). Husbands who were not expressive in memory sharing at baseline were more likely to be separated or divorced 3 years later than those who were expressive. In this way, the interplay of emotion, telling of autobiographical memories, and early childhood relationships may influence personality development.

The function of emotion in autobiographical memory appears to change in adulthood in ways related to affective experience. Identity/problem solving is a frequent form of reminiscing across the life span, but more so in the first three decades of life. Another study found that middle-aged adults most frequently used a problem-solving form of reminiscing, whereas older adults more often used a "self satisfaction" form (Lieberman & Falk, 1971). This suggests that with age, personal memory sharing is done more so for its immediate emotional benefits than for future problem-solving potential. Research by Levine and Bluck (1997) also indicates that autobiographical memory varies with age. They examined experienced and remembered emotional intensity in response to a major public event: A major presidential candidate, Ross Perot, withdrew from the race. No age differences were found in the intensities of emotions reported by supporters of this candidate. Four months later, participants were asked to recall how sad, angry, and hopeful they had reported feeling in response to Perot's announcement and to describe their current political goals. An age x current political goal interaction was found; for those supporters who still wished that Perot had been elected, the intensity of recalled sadness decreased with age. According to Levine and Bluck, these older loyal Perot supporters used reappraisal when recalling their feeling of sadness in order to feel less negative about the event. This is consistent with other research that indicates that autobiographical memories are more likely to serve immediate emotional benefits for older adults than young adults (Lieberman & Falk, 1971). However, this explanation is only partially supported as no age differences were found for the intensities of recalled anger and hope.

In summary, the literature suggests that emotion in autobiographical memory influences personality development across the life course. Young children learn that it can be a way to enhance the social and emotional aspects of their personality by sharing their memories with others. As they age and become adults, autobiographical memory becomes a device for identity and problem solving. George Vaillant (1977, p. 197) wrote: "It is all too common for caterpillars to become butterflies and then to maintain that in their youth they had been little butterflies. Maturation makes liars of us all." We expect that in later life, autobiographical memory serves to benefit acceptance of the self in the moment.

## Theoretical Models of Personality Development Across the Life Span

In the past decade, substantial evidence has accrued suggesting changes in emotion, motivation, and self-regulation in adulthood. Once again, however, this body of literature is often disconnected from the literature on personality development. We argue that even traditional models of personality development, however, imply (if not state directly) that emotional change is inherent in personality development. In Erikson's stage model of development, for example, emotions are not specifically addressed, but they are part of the growth that occurs during and after each of his life stages. Magai and Hunziker (1993) argue that certain emotions emerge at each stage and the experience of dealing with these emotions fosters one's personality development. For example, they suggest that during the autonomy versus shame and doubt stage, an infant experiences varying degrees of self-confidence, rage, and shame. Thus, the interplay of psychosocial crises and the frequency and intensity of emotions that occur within a particular crisis constitute personality development.

Similarly, Tomkins's affect theory (1961, 1962) describes how different types of emotions lead to individual differences in personality. The theory posits that we develop "ideoaffective organizations" (Magai & Hunziker, 1993, p. 251) around certain emotions, which then shape our personality and our behavior. These organizations act as selective filters in evaluating the relevance of incoming information to one's emotional biases and influencing coping strategies. Although these organizations are influenced by the environment and thus subject to change, the theory does not discuss the mechanisms by which changes in ideoaffective organizations occur.

Magai and Hunziker (1993) offer a model that addresses how emotions influence individual differences. Their basic contention is that emotions influence personality development over the life span, particularly during transition stages. Their model begins with the assumption that one of the most fundamental aspects of personality organization revolves around the formation and emotional quality of early attachment relationships. They then use Erikson's life stages to illustrate their model. At each stage of development, the emotional by-products of the previous stage, the emotional aspects of the current stage, the type of attachment between a parent/caregiver and the child, the conflict management style of the parent, and the child's temperament interact together to influence the child's personality and life path.

## Personality, Emotion and Mental Health Across the Life Span

In this section, we consider the links between personality and emotion in a life-span framework and discuss the implications of the interplay between the two for the study of coping with stressful events, and with both mental and physical health.

### Emotion, Personality, and Coping

Emotion regulation is critical to coping processes, as the outcome of adjusting to negative life events is most often conceptualized in terms of psychological well-being and other aspects of self-regulation. One of the most notable ways that people differ is their ability to regulate their emotions, such that positive emotions are generated and negative emotions are quelled (Nolen-Hoeksema, 1998; Nolen-Hoeksema, Morrow, & Fredrickson, 1993).

In a review of how coping may change over the life course, Lazarus (1996) emphasizes the importance of focusing on the changing contexts of coping rather than orthogenetic factors that may have a developmental trajectory. He maintained that people use a wide range of coping styles, and that these coping styles vary according to the types of daily stressors people encounter. For example, in a study where he and his colleagues compared adults at ages 35–45 to those 65–74 years old, they found that the younger adults were predominantly working parents whose daily stressors revolved around these roles (Lazarus, 1996). In contrast, the older sample, consisting mostly of retired people whose children were grown and lived independently, discussed problems with their health and ability to carry out functional activities of daily life. Consistent with these stressors, younger adults rated their stressors as more controllable and used more problem-focused strategies than older adults. Lazarus maintains that rather than people changing their coping style based on a developmental process or a biological mechanism, differences might instead reflect having to cope with a different set of issues. Moreover, he adds that in many studies examining coping with the same problem, few age differences in fact exist, again underscoring the emphasis on context over development.

If development does influence coping to any extent, this development produces changes focused on cognitive reframing and emotional regulation. Cross-sectional studies document age differences representing either a developmental process or a cohort effect. One study tried to control the situation by examining the coping styles of younger and older adults who had the same type of chronic health problem (Felton & Revenson, 1987). Older adults engaged in less information seeking and emotional expression and were more likely to focus on interpersonal processes such as minimizing the threat of the disease (Folkman, Lazarus, Pimley, & Novacek, 1987). Other studies have found that older adults may report fewer coping responses, but that older and younger adults reported equal effectiveness for their coping styles (Meeks, Carstensen, Tamsky, & Wright, 1989; Sorkin, Rudy, Hanlon, & Turk, 1990). In addition, no studies examining the psychological well-being of adults have found age differences suggesting that older adults have decreased capabilities for regulating their emotions compared to younger adults.

The relationship between personality and life events has been expanded by work in behavior genetics. Using three of the five factors from the FFM, Saudino and colleagues (Saudino, Pedersen, Lichtenstein, McClearn, &

Plomin, 1997) investigated the relationship between personality and life events in a large sample of adult twin pairs raised together and apart. While uncontrollable events did not seem to contain any genetic component, other types of events (undesirable, desirable, and controllable) had a substantial genetic component for female twin pairs only. What is interesting, however, is that this genetic variation was entirely accounted for by personality factors. Openness to experience and extraversion appeared to be the most powerful mediators of the genetics–life-event relationship, whereas neuroticism was less important. The authors interpret these results as reflecting genotype-environment covariation effects, in which genetic dispositions influence the niche that people create for themselves and the ways in which other people react to them. The important message for the purpose of this chapter is that personality may influence affect not only directly but also via the life events a person experiences and reports. The relationship between life events and affect, while often weak, has nonetheless been amply demonstrated (see Thoits, 1983, for a review).

Affective experience also can be influenced through the way that one perceives, or cognitively frames, events. The argument could be made that individual difference variables have arisen primarily in the context of cognitive models of emotion, such as dispositional optimism (Scheier & Carver, 1985) and explanatory style (Peterson & Seligman, 1984)—traits that are highly stable and related to both concurrent and prospective affective outcomes. For example, Robinson-Whelen and colleagues investigated dispositional optimism and pessimism, or the tendency to hold generalized positive and negative expectations for the future, in middle-aged and older adults (Robinson-Whelen, Kim, MacCallum, & Kiecolt-Glaser, 1997). Using the Life Orientation Test (LOT; Scheier & Carver, 1985), these researchers found that optimism and pessimism were related strongly only among these participants facing the stressor of caregiving; more important, they found that pessimism as assessed by the LOT predicted anxiety and perceived stress over time, though not depressive symptomatology. In another study using the LOT, Bromberger and Matthews (1996) found that dispositional pessimism predicted which middle-aged women became depressed following menopause and which did not.

Similarly, research on the ways people explain causes for events that happen in their lives has been shown to predict depressive symptomatology in young adults and children, especially after actually facing stressful events (see, for example, Metalsky, Halberstadt, & Abramson, 1987; Peterson & Seligman, 1984). In these populations, a more pessimistic explanatory style involving making internal, stable, and global explanations for negative events has been linked with negative affect. While recent research has found that this pessimistic explanatory style may actually be adaptive in older adults facing life stres-

sors (Isaacowitz & Seligman, 2000), what is most relevant is that these habitual, personological variables have been shown to influence emotional experience and should therefore be included in any review of links between personality and emotion.

Furthermore, the study by Robinson-Whelen et al. (1997) found that, despite the relatively dispositional way in which the above cognitive variables have been conceptualized, they may also be subject to the impact of life events. In this study, those participants who were also caregivers showed less optimism and a trend toward higher pessimism. This illustrates the reciprocal relationship between dispositional-type person variables and life events in the prediction of emotional experience.

## Emotion, Personality, and Mental Health

Stable affective qualities have been used to develop theoretical models to predict predispositions to certain types of psychological disorders. Cloninger, Bayon, and Svrakic (1998) derived several different personality types based on temperament and character dimensions. The character dimensions consisted of self-directedness (responsible, goal-directed vs. insecure, inept); cooperativeness (helpful, empathic vs. hostile, aggressive), and self-transcendence (imaginative, unconventional vs. controlling, materialistic). Their model predicts that a melancholic type, who is low on all three dimensions, should experience a limited range of emotions, with a great deal of hostility and very little joy. Because of the combination of frequent experiences of negative emotions and negative or unhealthy personality characteristics, people of this type should have an increased risk for mood disorders. In contrast, a creative type, who scores high on all three dimensions, should frequently feel love, joy, and hope. Because of their particular combination of positive emotions and positive personality characteristics, creative types are expected to be at lower risk for mental disorder. Empirical studies supported some of the model's predictions. For example, melancholic types showed an increased risk for depression and attempted suicide.

Other research has found that personality traits linked to emotion can predict future mental health. In a longitudinal study, Levenson, Aldwin, Bosse, and Spiro (1988) examined the relationship among extraversion, emotionality, and mental health in older men. They found that emotionality, as measured by the EPI-Q (Floderus, 1974), predicted 23% of the variance in older men's mental health 10 years later. Those who reported high levels of emotionality at baseline had a greater number of mental health symptoms 10 years later. While extraversion was negatively correlated with mental health symptoms, it only accounted for 2% of the variance. However, these findings should be viewed tentatively, as this study did not include preexisting mental health data or a personality inventory at the same time of follow-up.

Some have argued that many psychopathologies are due in part to impairment of one or more components of emotional processing (Kring & Bachorowski, 1999). Based on a behavioral approach and withdrawal model (see Gray, 1987, for detailed description), in which positive emotions are connected with approach behavior and negative emotions with withdrawal, researchers demonstrate the centrality of emotional functioning in mental health. For example, psychopaths tend to have impairments with both approach and withdrawal behavior in response to positive and negative stimuli. They fail to differentiate between emotional and neutral words at both the behavioral and neurological levels (Williamson, Harpur, & Hare, 1991). This indicates that in daily life, they would react similarly to positive, negative, and neutral stimuli in the environment. In addition, psychopaths fail to show startle potentiation when exposed to aversive stimuli (Patrick, 1994; Patrick, Bradley, & Lang, 1993).

Schizophrenia is another disorder in which impairments of the emotional processing play a central role. Schizophrenia comprises several emotion-linked symptoms, such as emotional dullness in experience and expression, decline in interests, and inability to perceive emotional stimuli (Kring & Bachorowski, 1999). Some researchers propose that positive symptoms of schizophrenia, such as hallucinations and delusions, are due to overactivity of the behavioral approach system, whereas negative symptoms, such as flattened affect, are due to underactivity of the behavioral approach system (Earnst & Kring, 1999; Fowles, 1994). If this is indeed the case, then many of the symptoms of schizophrenia can be explained by impairments of the motivational system at the biological level.

Goodman and Gotlib (1999) have recently proposed a model to direct research on the transmission of depression from depressed mothers to their children. In this model, four possible mechanisms through which affective dysfunction can be transmitted intergenerationally are posited: heritability of depression, dysfunctional neurological mechanisms such as regulatory neuroendocrine functioning, exposure to maladaptive aspects of the depressed mother, and exposure to a stressful environment (which may be related to the mother's depression). Possible moderators of this relationship include factors related to the parenting style of the father, the timing and the course of the mother's depression, and characteristics of the child such as gender, temperament, and IQ. This model combines biological, personological, and life-stress type approaches to understand the apparent increased rates of depression among children of depressed mothers, and thus illustrates the reciprocal causation between personality and emotional experience that forms the framework for this chapter.

## Personality, Emotion, Physical Health, and Mortality

The idea that affective qualities such as temperament or affective traits like hostility may influence morbidity and mortality is not new, but it remains controversial. Some people critically reject the idea that psychological influences such as personality traits can interact with health status (Angell, 1985; Cassileth, 1985). They criticize the belief that emotional and mental states cause or contribute to health problems such as cancer for its lack of evidence (e.g., Cassileth, 1990). In addition, Cassileth (1985) found that once the disease process has been initiated, such as when people have unresectable cancer, psychosocial variables failed to predict life expectancy.

Other researchers maintain that psychological factors do play a role in disease susceptibility and even mortality. They support their assertions using findings from both animal studies (Sklar & Anisman, 1979; Visintainer, Volpicelli, & Seligman, 1982) and human studies (Irwin, Daniels, Bloom, Smith, & Weiner, 1987). Researchers using human samples have found that greater stress predicts immune system functioning and overall health among college students (see Cohen & Herbert, 1996), medical students (Glaser, Pearl, Kiecolt-Glaser, & Malarkey, 1994), and older adults (Kiecolt-Glaser, Glaser, Cacioppo, & MacCallum, 1997). Longitudinal studies have examined the relationship between health and psychological constructs such as pessimism, control, and emotional expression among samples of college students (Pennebaker, Colder, & Sharp, 1990) and older adults (Kamen-Siegel, Rodin, Seligman, & Dwyer, 1991; Langer & Rodin, 1976), and have found that greater pessimism and lower perceived control predict worse physical health. In addition, one longitudinal study found that high levels of pessimism and low levels of optimism expressed by men in their 20s predicted poorer physical health into middle and old age (Peterson, Seligman, & Valliant, 1988). Childhood personality variables predicted mortality after age 50 (Friedman, Tucker, Tomlinson-Keasey, Schwartz, Wingard, & Cirqui, 1993; Schwartz, 1993; Friedman, Tucker, Schwartz, Martin, Tomlinson-Keasey, Wingard, & Cirqui, 1995), such that those who were lower in conscientiousness were more likely to die, as well as those who scored higher on the measure of agreeableness. Although the personality factors studied by Friedman and his colleagues were not the sole cause of the mortality, their predictive power was as strong as biological factors including obesity, hypertension, and tobacco use.

For many researchers, the question is not whether or not psychological functioning has an influence of physical health, but what the mechanism is through which temperament, personality, and mood might exert its influence. One mechanism through which a patterned response may influence health is a predisposition to react strongly to emotional stimuli, causing a heightened physiological arousal. A person who scores high on scales of trait hostility, for example, shows greater physiological reactivity in reaction to a negative event than someone with a lower hostility score (Suarez, Kuhn, Schanberg, Williams, & Zimmermann, 1998). Because hostility is one of several measures that have been linked to the incidence of disease, this greater expressive reaction is one plausible pathway responsible for the relationship.

Health-related behavior is a second pathway wherein personality and affect may influence physical status. Conscientiousness may predispose people away from dangerous, impulsive behaviors, and agreeableness may lead people to engage in unhealthy but social behaviors, such as drinking alcohol, smoking, and eating to excess. However, although people who score high on agreeableness are more likely to smoke and report drinking more than people who score low on this measure, these health behaviors do not completely explain the relationship between agreeableness and longevity (Friedman et al., 1995). In addition, the likelihood of mortal accidents based on impulsive behavior would seem greater among those low in conscientiousness, but again this explanation does not explain the relationship between conscientiousness and mortality (Friedman et al., 1995).

A final possible reason that temperament and affective response might be linked to health status could be that similar genes are linked to both longevity and to low levels of hostility and depression and high levels of conscientiousness. Although this idea might be enticing (a body that is more physically adaptive would also be more psychologically adaptive), intuitively, the connection between greater longevity and low levels of agreeableness is difficult to explain. As we have noted above, there are no known mechanisms by which situated behavioral tendencies can be inherited and no obvious reason to expect that they are. Rather, we expect that there are few pure genetic effects that do not interact with the environment.

## Conclusion

Although early philosophers and scientists clearly saw emotion as the essential basis of personality (Kagan et al., 1994), during the past two decades the subfield of psychology that addresses personality and the subfield of psychology that addresses emotion have moved apart. We expect that the division was fueled by trait and genetic approaches to personality where the focus was often on taxonomies and inheritance rather than the underlying mechanisms that contribute to individual differences. In this chapter, we have adopted an agentic model of personality development, advocated by Albert Bandura (1999), in which temperamental styles, which are in all likelihood

biologically based tendencies to experience particular emotions, are shaped in social context. Although some researchers acknowledge associations between particular emotions and particular traits, we take a more extreme stand and argue that emotion is not simply related to personality; it is the very essence of personality. The emotions people feel when they encounter challenges and the effectiveness with which they learn to regulate their emotions are the cardinal components of personality development and form the basis for individual differences in persistent tendencies to behave, think, and feel in day-to-day life (see Rothbart & Derryberry, 1981).

Importantly, this approach to personality points to the need for a sophisticated integration of genetic inheritance and environmental influences that are mediated by self-regulation (e.g., Goodman & Gotlib, 1999). In this view, genes do not lead to sociopathy, but reflect parenting patterns that are inappropriate to the needs of a particular child. Substance abuse is not determined by genetics but by an environment that facilitates it. Genes do matter. Temperament matters. Environments matter as well. Attempts to separate the amounts each contributes miss the mark. Main effects are few and far between; interaction effects hold the answers to the puzzles of individual differences. An anxious infant who develops secure relationships with his or her caregivers, for example, comes to trust others, tolerate conflicting emotions, and consider multiple external causes for emotions. The same infant who fails to develop a secure relationship attends to fractionated elements of emotions and selectively scans the environment for potential causes of emotions, accepting only those that are emotionally tolerable (Grossmann & Grossmann, 1990). By early adulthood, the two scenarios have shaped two very different individuals. There is enormous human flexibility in the degree to which individuals can influence their own life trajectories. There is no question that a sophisticated understanding of the interplay will centrally feature emotion in personality development.

## REFERENCES

Ainsworth, M., Blehar, M. C., Waters, E., & Wall, S. (1978). *Patterns of attachment*. Hillsdale, NJ: Erlbaum.

Angell, M. (1985). Disease as a reflection of the psyche [editorial]. *New England Journal of Medicine, 312*, 1570–1572.

Antiknock, T. C., & Jackson, J. S. (1987). Social support, interpersonal efficacy, and health. In L. L. Carstensen & B. A. Edelstein (Eds.), *Handbook of clinical gerontology* (pp. 291–311). Elmsford, NY: Pergamon.

Bandura, A. (1986). *Social foundations of thought and action: A social cognitive theory*. Englewood Cliffs, NJ: Prentice Hall.

Bandura, A. (1988) Self-efficacy conception of anxiety. *Anxiety Research, 1*, 77–98.

Bandura, A. (1989). Self-regulation of motivation and action through internal standards and goal systems. In L.

Pervin (Ed.), *Goal concepts in personality and social psychology* (pp. 19–85). Hillsdale, NJ: Erlbaum.

Bandura, A. (1997). *Self-efficacy: The exercise of control.* New York: W. H. Freeman.

Bandura, A. (1999). Social cognitive theory of personality In L. Pervin & O. John (Eds.), *Handbook of personality* (2nd ed, pp. 154–196). New York: Guilford Press.

Bartholomew, K. (1997). Adult attachment processes: Individual and couple perspectives. *British Journal of Medical Psychology, 70,* 249–263.

Bower, G. (1981). Mood and memory. *American Psychologist, 36,* 129–148.

Bowlby, J. (1973). *Attachment and loss: Vol. 2. Separation.* London: Hogarth Press.

Bromberger, J. T., & Matthews, K. A. (1996). A longitudinal study of the effects of pessimism, trait anxiety, and life stress on depressive symptoms in middle-aged women. *Psychology and Aging, 11,* 207–213.

Buehlman, K. T., Gottman, J. M., & Katz, L. F. (1992). Special issue: Diversity in contemporary family psychology. *Journal of Family Psychology, 5,* 295–318.

Buss, A. H., & Plomin, R. (1975). *A temperament theory of personality development.* New York: Wiley-erscience.

Cameron, P. (1975). Mood as an indicant of happiness: Age, sex, social class, and situational differences. *Journal of Gerontology, 30,* 216–224.

Campos, J. J., & Barrett, K. C. (1984). Toward a new understanding of emotions and their development. In C. E. Izard, J. Kagan, & R. B. Zajonc (Eds.), *Emotions, cognition and behavior* (pp. 229–263). New York: Cambridge University Press.

Carstensen, L. L. (1993). Motivation for social contact across the life span: A theory of socioemotional selectivity. In J. Jacobs (Ed.), *Nebraska symposium on motivation: Vol. 40. Development perspectives on motivation* (pp. 209–254). Lincoln: University of Nebraska Press.

Carstensen, L. L. (1995). Evidence for a life-span theory of socioemotional selectivity. *Current Directions in Psychological Science, 4,* 151–156.

Carstensen, L. L., & Charles, S. T. (1998). Emotion in the second half of life. *Current Directions in Psychological Science, 7,* 144–149.

Carstensen, L. L., & Fredrickson, B. F. (1998). Influence of HIV status and age on cognitive representations of others. *Health Psychology, 17,* 494–503.

Carstensen, L. L., Graff, J., Levenson, R. W., & Gottman, J. M. (1996). Affect in intimate relationships: The developmental course of marriage. In C. Magai & S. H. McFadden (Eds), *Handbook of emotion, adult development, and aging* (pp. 227–247). San Diego: Academic Press.

Carstensen, L. L., Isaacowitz, D. M., & Charles, S. T. (1999). Taking time seriously: A theory of socioemotional selectivity. *American Psychologist, 54,* 165–181.

Carstensen, L. L., Pasupathi, M., Mayr, U, & Nesselroade, J. (2000). Emotion experience in everyday life across the adult life span. *Journal of Personality and Social Psychology, 79,* 644–655.

Carstensen, L. L., & Turk-Charles, S. (1994). The salience of emotion across the adult life span. *Psychology and Aging, 9,* 259–264.

Caspi, A., Elder, G. H., & Bem, D. J. (1988). Moving against the world: Life-course patterns of explosive children. *Developmental Psychology, 23,* 308–313.

Caspi, A., & Herbener, E. S. (1990). Continuity and change: Assortative marriage and the consistency of personality in adulthood. *Journal of Personality and Social Psychology, 58,* 250–258.

Cassileth, B. R. (1985). Psychosocial correlates of survival in advanced malignant disease? *New England Journal of Medicine, 312,* 1551–1555.

Cassileth, B. R. (1990). Mental health quackery in cancer treatment. Special issue: Unvalidated, fringe, and fraudulent treatment of mental disorders. *International Journal of Mental Health, 19,* 81–84.

Chess, S., & Thomas, A. (1996). *Temperament: Theory and practice.* New York: Brunner/Mazel.

Cloninger, C. R., Bayon, C., & Svrakic, D. M. (1998). Measurement of temperament and character in mood disorders: A model of fundamental states as personality types. *Journal of Affective Disorders, 51,* 21–32.

Cohen, S., & Herbert, T. B. (1996). Health psychology: Psychological factors and physical disease from the perspective of human psychoneuroimmunology. *Annual Review of Psychology, 47,* 113–142.

Conley, J. J. (1984). Longitudinal consistency of adult personality: Self-reported psychological characteristics across 45 years. *Journal of Personality and Social Psychology, 47,* 1325–1333.

Cornelius, S. W., & Caspi, A. (1987). Everyday problem solving in adulthood and old age. *Psychology and Aging, 2,* 144–153.

Costa, P. T., Jr., & McCrae, R. R. (1980). Influence of exraversion and neuroticism on subjective well-being. *Journal of Personality and Social Psychology, 38,* 668–678.

Costa, P. T., Jr., & McCrae, R. R. (1988). Personality in adulthood: A six-year longitudinal study of self-reports and spouse ratings on the NEO Personality Inventory. *Journal of Personality and Social Psychology, 54,* 853–863.

Costa, P. T., Jr., & McCrae, R. R. (1990). *Personality in adulthood.* New York: Guilford Press.

Costa, P. T., & McCrae, R. R. (1994). Depression as an enduring disposition. In L. S. Schneider, C. F. Reynolds, B. D. Lebowitz, & A. J. Friedhoff (Eds.), *Diagnosis and treatment of depression in late life: Results of the NIH consensus development conference* (pp. 155–167). Washington, DC: American Psychiatric Press.

Costa, P. T., McCrae, R. R., & Arenberg, D. (1980). Enduring dispositions in adult males. *Journal of Personality and Social Psychology, 38,* 793–800.

Costa, P. T., McCrae, R. R., & Siegler, I. C. (1999). Continuity and change over the adult life cycle: Personality and personality disorders. In C. R. Cloninger (Ed.), *Personality and psychopathology* (pp. 129–154). Washington, DC: American Psychiatric Press.

Cumming, E., & Henry, W. E. (1961). *Growing old: The process of disengagement.* New York: Basic Books.

Cyphers, L. H., Phillips, K., Fulker, D. W., & Mrazek, D. A. (1990). Twin temperament during the transition from infancy to early childhood. *Journal of the American Academy of Child and Adolescent Psychiatry, 29,* 392–397.

Davidson, R. J. (1992). Emotion and affective style: Hemispheric substrates. *Psychological Science, 3,* 39–43.

Davidson, R. J., Coe, C., Dolski, I., & Donzella, B. (1999). Individual differences in prefrontal activation asymmetry predict natural killer cell activity at rest and in response to challenge. *Brain, Behavior and Immunity, 13,* 93–108.

Davidson, R. J., & Fox, N. (1989). Frontal brain asymmetry predicts infants' response to maternal separation. *Journal of Abnormal Psychology, 98*, 127–131.

Davidson, R. J., & Hugdahl, K. (Eds). (1995). *Brain asymmetry.* Cambridge, MA: MIT Press.

Davidson, R. J., Irwin, W., Eisenberg, N., Fabes, R., Shepard, S., Murphy, B., Jones, S., & Guthrie, I. (1998). Contemporaneous and longitudinal prediction of children's sympathy from dispositional regulation and emotionality. *Developmental Psychology, 34*, 910–924.

Derryberry, D., & Rothbart, M. K. (1988). Arousal, affect, and attention as components of temperament. *Journal of Personality and Social Psychology, 55*, 958–966.

Dick, D. M., Rose, R. J., Viken, R. J., & Kaprio, J. (2000). Pubertal timing and substance use: Associations between and within families across late adolescence. *Developmental Psychology, 36*, 180–189.

Diener, E., Sandvik, E., & Larsen, R. J. (1985). Age and sex differences for emotional intensity. *Development Psychology, 21*, 542–546.

Diener, E., Suh, E. K., Lucas, R. E., & Smith, H. L. (1999). Subjective well-being: Three decades of progress. *Psychological Bulletin, 125*, 276–302.

Dougherty, L. M., Abe, J. A., & Izard, C. E. (1996). Differential emotions theory and emotional development in adulthood and later life. In C. Magai & S. H. McFadden (Eds.), *Handbook of emotion, adult development, and aging* (pp. 27–41). San Diego, CA: Academic Press.

Dunn, J. (1994). Experience and understanding of emotions, relationships, and membership in a particular culture. In P. Ekman & R. J. Davidson (Eds.), *The nature of emotions: Fundamental questions* (pp. 352–355). New York: Oxford University Press.

Earnst, K. S., & Kring, A. M. (1999). Emotional responding in deficit and non-deficit schizophrenia. *Psychiatry Research, 88*, 191–207.

Eisenberg, N., Fabes, R., Shepard, S., Guthrie, I., Murphy, B., & Reiser, M. (1999). Parental reactions to children's negative emotions: Longitudinal relations to quality of children's social functioning. *Child Development, 70*, 513–534.

Eisenberg, N., Fabes, R., Shepard, S., Murphy, B., Jones, S., & Guthrie, I. (1998). Contemporaneous and longitudinal prediction of children's sympathy from dispositional regulation and emotionality. *Developmental Psychology, 34*, 910–924.

Elder, G., & Conger, R. D. (2000). *Children of the land: Adversity and success in rural America.* Chicago: University of Chicago Press.

Felton, B. J., & Revenson, T. A. (1987). Age differences in coping with chronic illness. *Psychology and Aging, 2*, 164–170.

Fivush, R., Haden, C., & Reese, E. (1996). Remembering, recounting, and reminiscing: The development of autobiographical memory in social context. In D. C. Rubin (Ed.), *Remembering our past: Studies in autobiographical memory* (pp. 341–359). Cambridge, England: Cambridge University Press.

Floderus, B. (1974). Psycho-social factors in relation to coronary heart disease and associated risk factors [Special issue]. *Nordisk Hygienisk Tid Skrift Supplementum, 6.*

Folkman, S., Lazarus, R. S., Pimley, S., & Novacek, J. (1987). Age differences in stress and coping processes. *Psychology and Aging, 2*, 171–184.

Forgas, J. P. (1991). Affective influences on partner choice: Role of mood in social decisions. *Journal of Personality and Social Psychology, 61*, 708–720.

Fowles, D. C. (1992). Schizophrenia: Diathesis-stress revisited. *Annual Review of Psychology, 43*, 303–336.

Fowles, D. C. (1994). A motivational theory of psychopathology. In W. D. Spaulding (Ed.), *Integrative views of motivation, cognition, and emotion. Vol. 41 of the Nebraska Symposium on Motivation* (pp. 181–238). Lincoln: University of Nebraska Press.

Fox, N., Sobel, A., Calkins, S., & Cole, P. (1996). Inhibited children talk about themselves: Self-reflection on personality development and change in 7-year-olds. In M. Lewis & M. W. Sullivan (Eds.), *Emotional development in atypical children* (pp. 131–148). Mahwah, NJ: Erlbaum.

Fredrickson, B. F., & Carstensen, L. L. (1990). Choosing social partners: How old age and anticipated endings make us more selective. *Psychology and Aging, 5*, 335–347.

Friedman, H. S., Tucker, J. S., Tomlinson-Keasey, C., Schwartz, J. E., Wingard, D. L., & Cirqui, M. H. (1993). Does childhood personality predict longevity? *Journal of Personality and Social Psychology, 65*, 176–185.

Friedman, H. S., Tucker, J. S., Schwartz, J. E., Martin, L. R., Tomlinson-Keasey, C., Wingard, D. L., & Cirqui, M. H. (1995). Childhood conscientiousness and longevity: Health behaviors and cause of death. *Journal of Personality and Social Psychology, 68*, 696–703.

Glaser, R., Pearl, D. K., Kiecolt-Glaser, J. K., & Malarkey, W. B. (1994). Plasma cortisol levels and reactivation of latent Epstein-Barr virus in response to examination stress. *Psychoneuroendocrinology, 19*, 765–772.

Goldsmith, H. (1993). Nature-nurture issues in the behavioral genetic context: Overcoming barriers to communication. In R. Plomin & G. McClearn (Eds.), *Nature, nurture and psychology* (pp. 325–339). Washington, DC: American Psychological Association.

Goldsmith, H. H. (1993). Temperament: Variability in developing emotion systems. In M. L. J. Haviland (Ed.), *The handbook of emotions* (pp. 353–364). New York: Guilford Press.

Goldsmith, H. H., Buss, K. A., & Lemery, K. S. (1997). Toddler and childhood temperament: Expanded content, stronger genetic evidence, new evidence for the importance of environment. *Developmental Psychology, 33*, 891–905.

Goldsmith, H. H., & Gottesman, I. I. (1981). Origins of variation in behavioral style: A longitudinal study of temperament in young twins. *Child Development, 52*, 91–103.

Goodman, S. H., & Gotlib, I. H. (1999). Risk for psychopathology in the children of depressed mothers: A developmental model for understanding mechanisms of transmission. *Psychological Review, 156*, 458–490.

Gottesman, I. (1991). *Schizophrenia genesis: The origins of madness.* New York: W. H. Freeman.

Gray, J. A. (1987). *The psychology of fear and stress.* New York: McGraw-Hill.

Gross, J. J., Carstensen, L. L., Pasupathi, M., Tsai, J., Skorpen, C. G., & Hsu, A. Y. C. (1997). Emotion and aging: Experience, expression, and control. *Psychology and Aging, 12*, 590–599.

Gross, J. J., & Munoz, R. F. (1995). Emotion regulation and mental health. *Clinical Psychology: Science and Practice, 2*, 151–164.

Grossman, K. E., & Grossman, K. (1990). The wider concept of attachment in cross-cultural research. *Human Development, 33,* 31–47.

Gustavsson, J. P., Weinryb, R. M., Goransson, S., Pedersen, N. L., & Asberg, M. (1997). Stability and predictive ability of personality traits across 9 years. *Personality and Individual Differences, 22,* 783–791.

Haan, N., Millsap, R., & Hartka, E. (1986). As time goes by: Change and stability in personality over fifty years. *Psychology and Aging, 1,* 220–232.

Hagekull, B., & Bohlin, G. (1998). Preschool temperament and environmental factors related to the five-factor model of personality in middle childhood. *Merrill-Palmer Quarterly, 44,* 194–215.

Harris, J. R. (1998). *The nurture assumption: Why children turn out the way they do.* New York: Free Press.

Heckhausen, J., Dixon, R. A., & Baltes, P. B. (1989). Gains and losses in development throughout adulthood as perceived by different adult age groups. *Developmental Psychology, 25,* 109–121.

Helson, R., & Wink, P. (1992). Personality change in women from the early 40s to the early 50s. *Psychology and Aging, 7,* 46–55.

Higgins, E. T. (1987). Self-discrepancy: A theory relating self and affect. *Psychological Review, 94,* 319–340.

Hochschild, A. R. (1979). Emotion work, feeling rules and social structure. *American Journal of Sociology, 85,* 551–575.

Irwin, M., Daniels, E. T., Smith, T. L., & Weiner, H. (1987). Life events, depressive symptoms, and immune function. *American Journal of Psychiatry, 144,* 437–441.

Isaacowitz, D. M., Charles, S. T., & Carstensen, L. L. (2000). Emotion and cognition. In F. I. M. Craik & T. Salthouse (Eds.), *Handbook of aging and cognition* (2nd ed., pp. 593–631). Mahwah, NJ: Erlbaum.

Isaacowitz, D. M., & Seligman, M. E. P. (2001). Is pessimism a risk factor for depressive mood among community-dwelling older adults? *Behaviour Research and Therapy, 39,* 255–272.

Isaacowitz, D. M., & Smith, J. (2000). *Positive and negative affect in very old age.* Manuscript submitted for publication.

Izard, C. (1977). *Human emotions.* New York: Plenum Press.

Izard, C. (1992). Basic emotions, relations among emotions and emotion-cognition relations. *Psychological Review, 99,* 561–565.

Izard, C., & Ackerman, B. P. (1998). Emotions and self-concept across the life span. In K. W. Schaie & M. P. Lawton (Eds.), *Annual review of gerontology and geriatrics: Focus on emotion and adult development* (Vol. 17 pp. 1–26). New York: Springer.

Izard, C., Libero, D. Z., Putnam, P., & Haynes, O. (1993). Stability of emotion experiences and their relations to traits of personality. *Journal of Personality and Social Psychology, 64,* 847–860.

John, O. (1990). The big-five factor taxonomy: Dimensions of personality in the natural language and questionnaires. In L. A. Pervin (Ed.) *Handbook of personality: Theory and research* (pp. 66–100). New York: Guilford Press.

Joseph, R. (1999). Environmental influences on neural plasticity, the limbic system, emotional development and attachment: A review. *Child Psychiatry and Human Development, 29,* 189–208.

Kagan, J. (1997). Temperament and the reactions to unfamiliarity. *Child Development, 68,* 139–143.

Kagan, J., & Moss, H. A. (1962). *Birth to maturity: A study in psychological development.* New York: John Wiley.

Kagan, J., Reznick, J. S., & Gibbons, J. (1989). Inhibited and uninhibited types of children. *Child Development, 60,* 838–845.

Kagan, J., Reznick, J. S., Snidman, N., Gibbons, J., & Johnson, M. (1988). Childhood derivatives of inhibition and lack of inhibition to the unfamiliar. *Child Development, 59,* 1580–1589.

Kagan, J., Snidman, N., Arcus, D., & Reznick, J. S. (1994). *Galen's prophecy: Temperament in human nature.* New York: Basic Books.

Kagan, J., Snidman, N., Zentner, M., & Peterson, E. (1999). *Development and Psychopathology, 11,* 209–224.

Kamen-Siegel, L., Rodin, J., Seligman, M. E. P., & Dwyer, J. (1991). Explanatory style and cell-mediated immunity in elderly men and women. *Health Psychology, 10,* 229–235.

Kerr, M., Lambert, W. W., & Bem, D. J. (1996). Life course sequelae of childhood shyness in Sweden: Comparison with the United States. *Developmental Psychology, 32,* 1100–1105.

Kiecolt-Glaser, J. K., Glaser, R., Cacioppo, J. T., & MacCallum, R. C. (1997). Marital conflict in older adults: Endocrinological and immunological correlates. *Psychosomatic Medicine, 59,* 339–349.

Kochanska, G. (1997). Multiple pathways to conscience for children with different temperaments: From toddlerhood to age 5. *Developmental Psychology, 33,* 228–240.

Kochanska, G., Coy, K., Tjebkes, T., & Husarek, S. J. (1998). Individual differences in emotionality in infancy. *Child Development, 69,* 375–390.

Kochanska, G., Tjebkes, T. L., & Forman, D. R. (1998). Children's emerging regulation of conduct: Restraint, compliance, and internalization from infancy to the second year. *Child Development, 69,* 1378–1389.

Kring, A. M., & Bachorowski, J. (1999). Emotions and psychopathology. *Cognition and Emotion, 13,* 575–599.

Kuiper, N. A., & Derry, P. A. (1982). Depressed and nondepressed content self-reference in mild depressives. *Journal of Personality, 50,* 67–80.

Labouvie-Vief, G., DeVoe, M., & Bulka, D. (1989). Speaking about feelings: Conceptions of emotion across the life span. *Psychology and Aging, 4,* 425–437.

Labouvie-Vief, G., Diehl, M., Tarnowski, A., & Shen, J. (1997). Age differences in adult personality: Findings from the United States and China. *Journals of Gerontology, Series B: Psychological Sciences and Social Sciences, 55B,* 4–17.

Lang, F. R., & Carstensen, L. L. (1994). Close emotional relationships in late life: Further support for proactive aging in the social domain. *Psychology and Aging, 9,* 315–324.

Lang, F. R., & Cartensen, L. L. (in press). Time counts: Future time perspective, goals and social relationships. *Psychology and Aging.*

Langer, E. J., & Rodin, J. (1976). The effects of choice and enhanced personal responsibility for the aged: A field experiment in an institutional setting. *Journal of Personality and Social Psychology, 34,* 191–198.

Lansford, J. E., Sherman, A. M., Aurora, M., & Antonucci, T. C. (1998). Satisfaction with social networks: An examination of socioemotional selectivity theory across cohorts. *Psychology and Aging, 13,* 544–552.

Larsen, R. J., & Ketelaar, T. (1989). Extraversion, neuroticism and susceptibility to positive and negative mood induction procedures. *Personality and Individual Differences, 10* (12), 1221–1228.

Lawton, M. P., Kleban, M. H., Rajagopal, D., & Dean, J. (1992). Dimensions of affective experience in three groups. *Psychology and Aging, 7,* 171–184.

Lazarus, R. S. (1991). *Emotion and adaptation.* New York: Oxford University Press.

Lazarus, R. S. (1996). The role of coping in the emotions and how coping changes over the life course. In C. Magai & S. H. McFadden (Eds.), *Handbook of emotion, adult development, and aging* (pp. 289–306). San Diego: Academic Press.

Levenson, M. R., Aldwin, C. M., Bosse, R., & Spiro, A. (1988). Emotionality and mental health: Longitudinal findings from the normative aging study. *Journal of Abnormal Psychology, 97,* 94–96.

Levenson, R. W., Carstensen, L. L., Friesen, W., & Ekman, P. (1991). Emotion, physiology and expression in old age. *Psychology and Aging, 4,* 425–437.

Levenson, R. W., Carstensen, L. L., & Gottman, J. M. (1993). Long-term marriage: Age, gender, and satisfaction. *Psychology and Aging, 8,* 301–313.

Levine, L. J. (1995). Young children's understanding of the causes of anger and sadness. *Child Development, 66,* 697–709.

Levine, L. J., & Bluck, S. (1997). Experienced and remembered emotional intensity in older adults. *Psychology and Aging, 12,* 514–523.

Lieberman, M. A., & Falk, J. M. (1971). The remembered past as a source of data for research on the life cycle. *Human Development, 14*(2), 132–141.

Magai, C., & Hunziker, J. (1993). Tolstoy and the riddle of developmental transformation: A lifespan analysis of the role of emotions in personality development. In M. H. Lewis & J. M. Haviland (Eds.), *Handbook of emotions* (pp. 247–259). New York: Guildford Press.

Malatesta, C. Z. (1990). The role of emotions in the development and organization of personality. In R. A. Thompson (Ed.), *Nebraska symposium on motivation* (Vol. 36, *Socioemotional development,* pp. 1–56). Lincoln: University of Nebraska Press.

Malatesta, C. Z., & Kalnok, M. (1984). Emotional experience in younger and older adults. *Journal of Gerontology, 39,* 301–308.

Matheny, A. P., Wachs, T. D., Ludwig, J. L., & Phillips, K. (1995). Bringing order out of chaos: Psychometric characteristics of the confusion, hubbub, and order scale. *Journal of Applied Developmental Psychology, 16,* 429–444.

Matt, G. E., Vazquez, C., & Campbell, W. K. (1992). Mood-congruent recall of affectively toned stimuli: A meta-analytic review. *Clinical Psychology Review, 12,* 227–255.

McCrae, R. R., & Costa, P. T., Jr. (1994). The stability of personality: Observation and evaluations. *Current Directions in Psychological Science, 3,* 173–175.

McCrae, R. R., & Costa, P. T., Jr. (1997). Personality trait structure as a human universal. *American Psychologist, 52,* 509–516.

McCrae, R. R., Costa, P. T., Jr., de Lima, M. P., Simoes, A., Ostendorf, F., Angleitner, A., Marusic, I., Bratko, D., Caprara, G. V., Barbaranelli, C., Chae, J.-H., & Piedmont, R. L. (1999). Age differences in personality across the adult lifespan. *Developmental Psychology, 35,* 466–477.

Meeks, S., Carstensen, L. L., Tamsky, B., & Wright, T. L. (1989). Age differences in coping: Does less mean worse? *International Journal of Aging and Human Development, 28,* 127–140.

Metalsky. G. I., Halberstadt, L. J., & Abramson, L. Y. (1987). Vulnerability to depressive mood reactions: Toward a more powerful test of the diathesis-stress and causal mediation components of the reformulated theory of depression. *Journal of Personality and Social Psychology, 52,* 386–393.

Mischel, W. (1973). Toward a cognitive social learning reconceptulaization of personality. *Psychological Review, 80,* 252–283.

Mroczek, D. K., & Kolarz, C. M. (1998). The effect of age on positive and negative affect: A developmental perspective on happiness. *Journal of Personality and Social Psychology, 75,* 1333–1349.

Nolen-Hoeksema, S. (1998). The other end of the continuum: The costs of rumination. *Psychological Inquiry, 9,* 216–219.

Nolen-Hoeksema, S., Morrow, J., & Fredrickson, B. L. (1993). Response styles and the duration of episodes of depressed mood. *Journal of Abnormal Psychology, 102,* 20–28.

Patrick, C. J. (1994). Emotion and psychopathology: Startling new insights. *Psychophysiology, 31,* 319–330.

Patrick, C. J., Bradley, M. M., & Lang, P. J. (1993). Emotion in the criminal psychopathologies: Startle reflex modulation. *Journal of Abnormal Psychology, 102,* 82–92.

Pennebaker, J. W., Colder, M., & Sharp, L. K. (1990). Accelerating the coping process. *Journal of Personality and Social Psychology, 58,* 528–537.

Peterson, C., & Seligman, M. E. P. (1984). Causal explanations as a risk factor for depression: Theory and evidence. *Psychological Review, 91,* 347–374.

Peterson, C., Seligman, M. E. P., & Valliant, G. E. (1988). Pessimistic explanatory style is a risk factor for physical illness: A thirty-five-year longitudinal study. *Journal of Personality and Social Psychology, 55,* 23–27.

Pillemer, D. B. (1998). *Momentous events, vivid memories.* Cambridge, MA: Harvard University Press.

Plomin, R. (1976). A twin and family study of personality in young children. *Journal of Psychology, 94,* 233–235.

Plomin, R., Pedersen, N. L., McClearn, G. E., Nesselroade, J. R., & Bergeman, C. S. (1988). EAS temperaments during the last half of the life span: Twins reared apart and twins reared together. *Psychology and Aging, 3,* 43–50.

Plomin, R., & Rowe, D. C. (1977). A twin study of temperament in young children. *Journal of Psychology, 97,* 107–113.

Robinson-Whelen, S., Kim, C., MacCallum, R. C., & Kiecolt-Glaser, J. K. (1997). Distinguishing optimism from pessimism in older adults: Is it more important to be optimistic or not to be pessimistic? *Journal of Personality and Social Psychology, 73,* 1345–1353.

Rothbart, M. (1986). Longitudinal observation of infant temperament. *Developmental Psychology, 22,* 356–365.

Rothbart, M. (1994). Emotion development: Changes in reactivity and self-regulation. In P. Ekman & R. J. Davidson (Eds.), *The nature of emotions: Fundamental questions* (pp. 369–372). New York: Oxford University Press.

Rothbart, M., & Ahadi, S. A. (1994). Temperament and the development of personality. *Journal of Abnormal Psychology, 103,* 55–66.

Rothbart, M., & Derryberry, D. (1981). Development of individual differences in temperament. In M. E. Lamb & A. L. Brown (Eds.), *Advances in developmental psychology* (Vol. 1, pp. 37–86). Hillsdale, NJ: Erlbaum.

Rowe, D., Woulbroun, J. E., & Gulley, B. L. (1994). Peers and friends as nonshared environmental influences. In E. M. Hetherington & D. Reiss (Eds.), *Separate social worlds of siblings: The impact of nonshared environment on development* (pp. 159–173). Hillsdale, NJ: Erlbaum.

Ryff, C. D. (1989). In the eyes of the beholder: Views of psychological well-being among middle-aged and older adults. *Psychology and Aging, 4,* 195–210.

Ryff, C. D. (1991). Possible selves in adulthood and old age: A tale of shifting horizons. *Psychology and Aging, 6,* 286–295.

Ryff, C. D. (1995). Psychological well-being in adult life. *Current Directions in Psychological Science, 4,* 99–104.

Saudino, K. J., Pedersen, N. L., Lichtenstein, P., McClearn, G. E., & Plomin, R. (1997). Can personality explain genetic influences on life events? *Journal of Personality and Social Psychology, 72,* 196–206.

Scarr, S., Webber, P. L., Weinberg, R. A., & Wittig, M. A. (1981). Personality resemblance among adolescents and their parents in biologically related and adoptive families. *Journal of Personality and Social Psychology, 40,* 885–898.

Scheier, M. F., & Carver, C. S. (1985). Optimism, coping and health: Assessment and implications of generalized coping expectancies. *Health Psychology, 4,* 219–247.

Schmidt, L. A., Fox, N. A., Rubin, K. H., & Sternberg, E. M. (1997). Behavioral and neuroendocrine responses in shy children. *Developmental Psychobiology, 30,* 127–140.

Schmutte, P. S., & Ryff, C. D. (1997). Personality and well-being: Reexamining methods and meanings. *Journal of Personality and Social Psychology, 73,* 549–559.

Schwartz, C. E., Snidman, N., & Kagan, J. (1996). Early childhood temperament as a determinant of externalizing behavior in adolescence. *Development and Psychopathology, 8,* 527–537.

Singer, J. A., & Salovey, P. (1993). *The remembered self: Emotion and memory in personality.* New York: Free Press.

Sklar, L. S., & Anisman, H. (1979). Stress and coping factors influence tumor growth. *Science, 204,* 513–515.

Smith, J., Fleeson, W., Geiselmann, B., Settersten, R. A., Jr., & Kunzmann, U. (1999). Sources of well-being in very old age. In P. B. Baltes & K. U. Mayer (Eds.), *The Berlin aging study: Aging from 70 to 100* (pp. 450–471). Cambridge, England: Cambridge University Press.

Snidman, N., Kagan, J., Riordan, L., & Shannon, D. C. (1995). Cardiac function and behavioral reactivity during infancy. *Psychophysiology, 32,* 199–207.

Sorkin, B. A., Rudy, T. E., Hanlon, R. B., & Turk, D. C. (1990). Chronic pain in old and young patients: Differences appear less important than similarities. *Journals of Gerontology, 45,* 64–68.

Starratt, C., & Peterson, L. (1997). Personality and normal aging. In P. D. Nussbaum (Ed.), *Handbook of neuropsychology and aging* (pp. 15–31). New York: Plenum.

Stein, N. L., & Levine, L. J. (1989). The causal organization of emotional knowledge: A developmental study. *Cognition and Emotion, 3,* 343–378.

Stein, N. L., & Levine, L. J. (1999). The early emergence of emotional understanding and appraisal: Implication for theories of development. In T. Dagleish & M. J. Power (Eds.), *Handbook of cognition and emotion* (pp. 383–408). Chichester, England: John Wiley.

Stein, N. L., Trabasso, T., & Liwag, M. (1993). The representation and organization of emotional experience: Unfolding the emotion episode. In M. Lewis & J. M. Haviland (Eds.), *Handbook of emotions* (pp. 279–300). New York: Guilford Press.

Suarez, E. C., Kuhn, C. M., Schanberg, S. M., Williams, R. B., & Zimmermann, E. A. (1998). Neuroendocrine, cardiovascular, and emotional responses of hostile men: The role of interpersonal challenge. *Psychosomatic Medicine, 60,* 78–88.

Thoits, P. A. (1983). Multiple identities and psychological well-being: A reformulation and test of the social isolation hypothesis. *American Sociological Review, 48,* 174–187.

Thomas, A., Chess, S., Birch, H. G., Hertzig, M. E., & Korn, S. (1963). *Behavioral individuality in early childhood.* New York: New York University Press.

Thompson, R. (1990). Emotion and self-regulation. In *Nebraska Symposium on Motivation, 1988* (pp. 367–467). Lincoln: University of Nebraska Press.

Tomkins, S. (1961). *Affect, imagery, consciousness: Vol. 1. The positive affects.* New York: Springer.

Tomkins, S. (1962). *Affect, imagery, consciousness: Vol. 2. The negative affects.* New York: Springer.

Tsai, J., & Levenson, R. W. (1997). Cultural influences on emotional responding: Chinese American and European American dating couples during interpersonal conflict. *Journal of Cross-Cultural Psychology, 28,* 600–625.

Turkheimer, E. (2000). Three laws of behavior genetics and what they mean. *Current Directions in Psychological Science, 9,* 160–164.

Turkheimer, E., & Waldron, M. (2000). Nonshared environment: A theoretical, methodological and quantitative review. *Psychological Bulletin, 126,* 78–108.

Vaillant, G. E. (1977). *Adaptation to life.* Boston: Little, Brown.

Van Aken, M. A., & Asendorf, J. B. (1996). Continuity of prototypes of social competence and shyness over the life span and across life transitions. *Journal of Adult Development, 4,* 205–216.

VanIJzendoorn, M. H., & Kroonenberg, P. M. (1988). Cross-cultural patterns of attachment: A meta-analysis of the strange situation. *Child Development, 59,* 147–156.

Visintainer, M. A., Volpicelli, J. R., & Seligman, M. E. (1982). Tumor rejection in rats after inescapable or escapable shock. *Science, 216,* 437–439.

Webster, J. D. (1993). Construction and validation of the Reminiscence Functions Scale. *Journals of Gerontology, 48,* 256–262.

Williamson, S., Harpur, T. J., & Hare, R. D. (1991). Abnormal processing of emotional words by psychopaths. *Psychophysiology, 28,* 260–273.

Yang, J., McCrae, R. R., & Costa, P. T., Jr. (1998). Adult age differences in personality traits in the United States and the People's Republic of China. *Journals of Gerontology: Series B: Psychological Sciences and Social Sciences, 53B* (6), 375–383.

Zahn-Waxler, C., Cole, P. M., & Barrett, K. C. (1991). Guilt and empathy: Sex differences and implications for the development of depression. In J. Garber & K. A. Dodge (Eds.), *The development of emotion regulation and dysregulation* (pp. 243–272). New York: Cambridge University Press.

Zajonc, R. (1997). Emotions. In D. Gilbert, S. T. Fiske, & G. Lindzey (Eds.), *Handbook of social psychology* (4th ed., pp. 591–631). New York: McGraw-Hill.

# VII

## Emotion and Social Processes

# 38

## INTRODUCTION: EMOTION AND SOCIAL PROCESSES

Peter Salovey

To call this part in the *Handbook of Affective Sciences* "Emotion and Social Processes" is a bit misleading. The title implies that emotions as a phenomenon are distinct from social behavior but that the interested investigator can study the impact of affective processes on interpersonal interactions and vice versa. In fact, the emotions themselves *are* social processes. Emotions arise, in part, through interactions or anticipated interactions with others. They are part of the landscape of an organism's social environment.

### Emotions as Social Processes

As a scientist who asked why humans and other species express emotions in certain ways, Charles Darwin (1872/ 1998) can be seen as the first emotions theorist who offered a social explanation for the purpose of the affective system. His principle of serviceable habits articulated a view that emotional expressions reflect movements that were originally useful to our progenitors. These movements were often of a social nature—striking when angry, running away when fearful, mating when joyful, for example. Pairs of humans may bring their mouths together to kiss rather than share food, but in either case, associated emotions motivate distinctly social behaviors.

Moreover, the signaling system that many scholars believe to be part of the function of emotions is social by definition. Darwin himself (1872/1998) only hinted at this communicative function for emotional expression, although other scholars following in his tradition have ac-

corded it more importance. The idea is that, through facial expressions and bodily postures, humans and animals communicate to their conspecifics something important about impending social interactions. The baring of teeth in anger says, for instance, "See these fangs? If you continue to bother me, they could end up sunk into your flesh!" Although expressions may originate from physiological sensations and central nervous system (CNS) activity, that does not lessen their potentially important social function as communicative devices (see Ekman, 1998, for a fascinating personal account of the debate about expressions as reflecting internal changes in preparation for action, communication, or both). This essentially social nature of the emotional system is captured well by Ekman in his own influential theorizing about the functionality of emotion (e.g., the following passage from an imagined dialogue with anthropologist Gregory Bateson):

> [M]ost emotions have expressions which communicate to others. They inform us that something important is happening inside the person who shows the emotion. Those internal changes are preparing the person to deal quickly with an important event, most often *some interpersonal encounter* [italics added], in a way that has been adaptive in the past. (Ekman, 1998, p. 372)

Emotions theorists not working explicitly in a Darwinian framework also emphasize the inherently social nature of emotion. For example, Lazarus's (1991) appraisal-oriented conceptualization views emotions as the result of interactions with the (mostly social) environment. His theory centers on the delineation of person-environment relationships, the emotions they generate, and the cognitive representation of these expectations about social interactions in the form of core relational themes. These themes are defined as the central relational harm or benefit in social encounters that underlies each specific emotion. For example, a theme of wanting what someone has undergirds the emotion of envy, and resenting a third party for loss or threat to another's affection characterizes jealousy (see also Salovey & Rothman, 1991).

Affective scientists—using this term as broadly as possible—in fields other than psychology also represent emotions as largely social phenomena. In reviewing the philosophy of emotions, Solomon (2000) describes how Aristotle was particularly fond of placing the emotions in a social context, noting, for instance, that anger is always directed toward someone in particular, especially in response to a "slight" (Aristotle, 1941). Hume's enlightenment-era philosophy emphasized the importance of emotions aroused in reaction to the afflictions of others. Hume viewed sympathy as the foundation for morality and society (Hume, 1739/1988).

Anthropologists often describe the social construction of the meanings of the terms we use to speak about emotions. For instance, White (2000) notes that "any approach to emotional meaning that seeks to represent the common-sense (cultural) significance of ordinary emotion words and categories will need to take account of the actual discursive practices within which emotion talk (and, more generally, communicative action) occurs" (p. 42). And, of course, sociologists place emotions squarely in a social context, studying such issues as the following:

> the emotional foundation of social solidarity in groups . . . ; the determination of emotions by outcomes of social interaction; the normative regulation of emotional expression and the management of emotional deviance; the socialization of emotions through transfer of meaning to physiological experience; the linkage of emotion to socially derived conceptions of identity and the self; the variation in emotional experience according to categories of social organization such as social class, occupation, gender, race/ethnicity, and the like; and emotions in large-scale societal processes of stability and change. (Kemper, 2000, p. 45)

The sociologist asks the deceptively simple questions, "[W]hich emotions are likely to be expressed when and where, on what grounds and for what reasons, by what modes of expression, by whom?" (Kemper, 2000, p. 46), often focusing on issues of social power and status in order to address them. My point is a simple one: It is often

fruitful to study emotion in its social context, and there is a substantial tradition in several different disciplines of doing just this.

## Emotion and Three Potentially Social Processes

The close coupling of emotion and social processes is likely due to the three motivational goals served by the emotions: (1) adaptation, (2) social coordination, and (3) self-regulation (delineated elegantly by Buck, 1984). Adaptation refers to the adjustments that organisms must make in response to changes in environmental circumstances. Emotions are often triggered in response to such changes: A predator threatening one's survival may lead to fear, and competition for food when one is hungry may produce anger, for example. The physiological changes associated with these emotional states prepare the body for social actions that may be necessary in such circumstances, such as running away or fighting. Human infants may cry in distress when hungry to elicit feeding by a caretaker, a clear social interaction in response to an attempt to adjust to changes in the environment.

Many behaviors relevant to the survival of the individual and species require social coordination. The emotional system plays an important role in facilitating these interactions. Emotional reactions in response to the displays of others that then motivate behaviors relevant to social dominance or submission grease the wheels of social intercourse. Crying may elicit help from others in threatening situations; joy may motivate approach, friendship, and mating. The behavioral changes that follow when two angry dogs growl at each other allow both to survive another day. The same could be said for a parallel interaction between a department chairman and the dean of a college. Emotional expression allows for smoother social interaction in the long run by making the need for social coordination salient and by motivating appropriate restorative behaviors.

The subjective experiences associated with emotions can be thought of as a direct "readout" of motivational states into conscious experience (Buck, 1984, p. 32). This knowledge about the status of one's current relationship to the environment with respect to adaptation and homeostasis affords self-regulation. Social behaviors initiated in the service of self-regulation often are motivated by such feelings. My jealous feelings may signal that an important relationship is being threatened by a rival, motivating such self-regulatory behaviors as reaffirming the importance of the relationship, chasing away the rival, or repairing aspects of the relationship that have disintegrated (Salovey & Rodin, 1989). The subjective feelings associated with emotions of all kinds may signal the need for self-regulatory planning and action.

## Linking Mood and Action

So far, this discussion of emotion and social processes focuses mostly on social contexts that give rise to specific emotions and the behaviors that are then motivated in these contexts by these emotions. Another research tradition has explored the links between more transient mood states and social behavior. Unlike emotions, one is often unaware of the causes of moods, allowing higher order cognitive processes to intervene in the relationship between them and behavior. As such, the motivational implications of moods with respect to social processes are less stable than the influence of emotions. Although social behavior of one kind or another is often motivated by the arousal of mood states, uncovering the mechanisms by which affective arousal stimulates a particular behavioral response has been somewhat elusive.

Some years ago, we argued that moods serve to make salient to the persons experiencing them particular kinds of information about themselves, and it is these thoughts about the self that mediate the impact of mood on social behavior (Salovey & Rodin, 1985). An affectively charged experience changes the way in which an individual organizes information about and evaluates the self. The focus of attention shifts inward following the arousal of a mood state, and certain thoughts about oneself become differentially available (Salovey, 1992). These temporary changes in the way in which one thinks about oneself promote or inhibit different social behaviors, such as helping another person. Finally, these mood-induced social behaviors serve either to maintain positive affect and positive thoughts about oneself or to repair negative affect and negative self-relevant thoughts (Salovey & Rosenhan, 1989).

More recently, Gendolla (2000) has described the mood-behavior model (MBM), which proposes that moods influence social behavior through two processes: (1) informational effects on behavior-related judgments and appraisals that in turn motivate behavioral adjustments, and (2) directive effects on behavioral preferences and interests, usually in association with a hedonic motive (cf. Wyer & Carlston, 1979). Gendolla argues that the informational and directive impact of mood on social processes are conceptually independent, determined by different variables, and refer to different aspects of the motivation process and behavior itself. The informational effects of moods are most apparent when exploring the judgments and appraisals that guide behavior. These judgments might include thoughts about the effort necessary to carry out the behavior, how long one must perform it to reach a goal, or whether the performance itself is satisfactory (cf. Forgas, 1995; Martin, Ward, Achee, & Wyer, 1993; Schwarz & Clore, 1988). The directive effects of mood on behavior are most obvious when individuals choose their behaviors strategically in order to enhance or terminate a particular affective state (cf. Morris & Reilly, 1987; Wegener & Petty, 1994). For example, individuals experiencing happiness often express preferences for prosocial and recreational activities (Cunningham, 1988).

Cognitive models such as the two outlined here can be used to understand the relatively systematic effects of mood on social processes studied during the past two decades. For example, joyful moods tend to promote self-gratification, to make people more willing to initiate conversations, and to motivate expressions of liking for other people. These happy individuals are more likely to take risks, so long as these risks are not too great and do not threaten to endanger their pleasant feelings. Positive moods create a glow of goodwill that increases prosocial behaviors. On the other hand, sad moods often inhibit helping others, unless they are tinged with shame or guilt or the helping is clearly viewed as a way of terminating the unpleasant mood.

## The Chapters in This Part of the *Handbook*

The boundaries between this part of this volume, the two that preceded it, and the one following are, to some extent, arbitrary. Chapter 30, concerned with emotion and social judgment, in the cognitive components section, could have just as easily appeared in this one. Similarly, chapter 36 on coping, in the personality section, also would fit nicely with the chapters here. It is a bit difficult to define at what point social processes end and cultural processes begin, and so it is not surprising that there is a nice synergy between chapter 41 in this part and chapter 45 in part VIII.

The five chapters in this part of the volume can actually be divided into two groups. The first two chapters concern emotion and social cognition, and the remaining three deal with emotion and social behavior. All of the chapters represent topics in the mainstream of the field of social psychology—the self, persuasion, aggression, helping, and close relationships. All of these issues have been studied in their own right by investigators who would not consider themselves affect scientists. However, they are also areas of inquiry that have been fruitfully examined from a distinctly emotional point of view.

A concept of self is, in part, what separates humans from nearly every other animal species. As such, we should expect some distinctly human aspect to emotional experience. As Mark Leary describes in chapter 40, "The Role of Self-Reflection in the Generation and Regulation of Affective Experience," having a self permits humans to evoke emotions in themselves by imagining self-relevant events, to react emotionally to abstract and symbolic images of themselves in their own minds, to consciously contemplate the causes of their emotions, to experience emotions by thinking about how they are perceived by other people, and to deliberately try to regulate their emotions. As Leary argues, it would be difficult to imagine what the subjective experience of mood and emotion would be like without self-awareness.

In chapter 39, "Emotional Factors in Attitudes and Persuasion," Richard Petty, Leandre Fabrigar, and Duane Wegener examine the role of affect in the structure of attitudes and in attitude change. These topics have deep roots in psychological science: An affective component is what has often been considered defining in conceptualizing attitudes as distinct from other kinds of beliefs, and the role of emotions such as fear in persuasion situations is still debated in fields as diverse as health psychology and marketing science. In fact, in the early 1990s, a brief fad in consumer psychology concerned emotion-based marketing, with many advertisers using emotion-laden appeals—think of those spots for Kodak film depicting parents daydreaming about their daughter's wedding years ago or the telephone company urging us to reach out and touch someone—to compete for the attention of radio and television audiences. Such approaches may be effective in some contexts but not in others, and Petty and his colleagues discuss the situations in which individuals are likely to be influenced by aroused feelings or to actively try to correct for such influences. In exploring the multiple roles for mood and emotion in attitude formation and change, this chapter meshes with chapter 30.

Leonard Berkowitz's chapter, "Affect, Aggression, and Antisocial Behavior," marks the shift from social cognition to social behavior. He argues that strong negative affect produced by unpleasant experiences—from hot weather and foul odors to frustrations and social stresses—can generate an urge to attack a suitable target, what he terms "affective aggression." In Berkowitz's view, a decidedly unpleasant condition activates, automatically and with relatively little thought, two kinds of relatively primitive inclinations: one to escape from or avoid the aversive stimulus but also another to attack and destroy the aversive stimulus. He argues that aversive stimuli give rise not to "flight *or* fight" but to "flight *and* fight."

The remaining two chapters turn from negative social processes to more positive ones. In chapter 41, "Affect and Prosocial Responding," Nancy Eisenberg, Sandra Losoya, and Tracy Spinrad describe the affective antecedents and consequences of voluntary social behaviors intended to benefit others. Two related affective processes play important roles in prosocial behavior: dispositional empathy and transient moods and emotions. Empathy is the affective response that stems from the accurate apprehension or comprehension of another person's emotional states. It often turns into sympathy or personal distress. Sympathy generally motivates helping behavior, but personal distress, which can result from empathic overarousal, only does so when such helping can relieve one's aversive emotional state. As for more transient moods and emotions, the link to helping is more complex. Guilt, for example,

often motivates prosocial acts in children and adults as a way to expiate these troubling feelings. Shame, however, is more likely to have antisocial consequences, as it motivates a desire to hide or even to lash out in rage in order to restore a sense of self-competence. In general, research on prosocial behavior has been exemplary in making salient the importance of emotional development in undergirding social development and the socialization of desirable behavior.

Finally, Margaret Clark and Ian Brissette explore the role of emotion in two kinds of close relationships in chapter 43, "Two Types of Relationship Closeness and Their Influence on People's Emotional Lives." Experience sampling studies of the ebb and flow of human behavior suggest that emotions are most likely to be experienced and expressed in the context of relationships with other people. In interdependent relationships, two people have a substantial impact on each other's thoughts, feelings, and behaviors. In communal relationships, two people feel a responsibility for each other's welfare and actively try to promote the other's well-being. Not surprisingly, these two kinds of close relationships have different effects on a person's emotional life. Individuals in highly interdependent relationships experience strong emotions when expected routines are disrupted. Communal relationships are characterized by greater emotional disclosure and sharing on an ongoing basis; in communal relationships, expressions of emotion—even troubling emotions—are typically reacted to positively, whereas we generally avoid strangers or mere acquaintances who express negative feelings. Clark and Brissette make a strong case for the argument that some affective phenomena are simply not understandable if studied at the level of the individual. They argue instead that understanding relationships is central to understanding emotion.

The chapters in this part of the *Handbook* represent cutting-edge research in the social psychology of emotions. By studying the influence of affect on social cognition and social behavior, we learn more not only about the contextual influences on these social processes but also about moods and emotions themselves. The interface between affect and social processes is not a distinct boundary but, rather, a dynamic interaction.

## REFERENCES

Aristotle (1941). *The basic works of Aristotle* (R. McKeon, Ed.). New York: Random House.

Buck, R. (1984). *The communication of emotion.* New York: Guilford Press. Cunningham, M. R. (1988). What do you do when you're happy or blue? Mood, expectancies, and behavioral interest. *Motivation and Emotion, 12,* 309–331.

Darwin, C. (1998). *The expression of the emotions in man and animal* (3rd ed.). New York: Oxford University Press. (Original work published 1872)

Ekman, P. (1998). Afterword: Universality of emotional expression? A personal history of the dispute. In C. Darwin, *The expression of the emotions in man and animals* (3rd ed., pp. 363–393). New York: Oxford University Press.

Forgas, J. P. (1995). Mood and judgment: The affect infusion model (AIM). *Psychological Bulletin, 117,* 39–66.

Gendolla, G. H. E. (2000). On the impact of mood on behavior: An integrative theory and review. *Review of General Psychology, 4,* 378–408.

Hume, D. (1988). *A treatise on human nature* (L. A. Selby-Bigge, Ed.). Oxford, England: Oxford University Press. (Original work published 1739)

Kemper, T. D. (2000). Social models in the explanation of emotions. In M. Lewis & J. M. Haviland-Jones (Eds.), *Handbook of emotions* (2nd ed., pp. 45–58). New York: Guilford Press.

Lazarus, R. S. (1991). *Emotion and adaptation.* New York: Oxford University Press.

Martin, L. L., Ward, D. W., Achee, J. W., & Wyer, R. S. (1993). Mood as input: People have to interpret the motivational implications of their moods. *Journal of Personality and Social Psychology, 64,* 317–326.

Morris, W. N., & Reilly, N. P. (1987). Toward the self-regulation of mood: Theory and research. *Motivation and Emotion, 11,* 215–249.

Salovey, P. (1992). Mood-induced self-focused attention. *Journal of Personality and Social Psychology, 62,* 699–707.

Salovey, P., & Rodin, J. (1985). Cognitions about the self: Connecting feeling states to social behavior. *Review of Personality and Social Psychology, 6,* 143–166.

Salovey, P., & Rodin, J. (1989). Envy and jealousy in close relationships. *Review of Personality and Social Psychology, 10,* 221–246.

Salovey, P., & Rosenhan, D. L. (1989). Mood states and prosocial behavior. In H. Wagner & A. Manstead (Eds.), *Handbook of social psychophysiology* (pp. 371–391). Chichester, England: Wiley.

Salovey, P., & Rothman, A. J. (1991). Jealousy and envy: Self and society. In P. Salovey (Ed.), *The psychology of jealousy and envy* (pp. 271–286). New York: Guilford Press.

Schwarz, N., & Clore, G. L. (1988). How do I feel about it? The informative function of affective states. In K. Fiedler & J. P. Forgas (Eds.), *Affect, cognition, and social behavior* (pp. 44–62). Göttingen, Germany: Hogrefe.

Solomon, R. C. (2000). The philosophy of emotions. In M. Lewis & J. M. Haviland-Jones (Eds.), *Handbook of emotions* (2nd ed., pp. 3–15). New York: Guilford Press.

Wegener, D. T., & Petty, R. E. (1994). Mood management across affective states: The hedonic contingency hypothesis. *Journal of Personality and Social Psychology, 66,* 1034–1048.

White, G. M. (2000). Representing emotional meaning: Category, metaphor, schema, discourse. In M. Lewis & J. M. Haviland-Jones (Eds.), *Handbook of emotions* (2nd ed., pp. 30–44). New York: Guilford Press.

Wyer, R. S., & Carlston, D. (1979). *Social cognition, inference, and attribution.* Hillsdale, NJ: Erlbaum.

# 39

# EMOTIONAL FACTORS IN ATTITUDES AND PERSUASION

Richard E. Petty, Leandre R. Fabrigar,
and Duane T. Wegener

In this chapter we examine the role of emotional factors in attitudes and persuasion. Attitudes refer to people's global evaluations of any object, such as oneself, other people, possessions, issues, abstract concepts, and so forth. Thus a person's dislike of ice cream and favorable predisposition toward a political candidate are examples of attitudes. Persuasion is said to occur when a person's attitude changes. Change can refer to moving from no attitude to some attitude or from one attitude to another. Persuasion can be very explicit and blatant, such as when a person sets out to modify another's evaluation and provides a strong communication against the other's point of view, or it can be rather implicit and subtle, such as when a person's attitude changes simply because the attitude object (e.g., one's car) shifts from being associated with pleasant to unpleasant outcomes. Classic treatises on persuasion have held that understanding emotion is critical to understanding attitude change. For example, Aristotle's *Rhetoric* described how to make an audience feel specific emotions, such as anger or fear, and then how to use these emotions to influence the audience (see also Cicero, 55 B.C./1970). The importance of emotional factors was also recognized in some of the earliest contemporary work on attitudinal processes. We begin by discussing work on the structure of attitudes because it is in this work that emotional factors first received substantial attention as a theoretical construct. Then we turn to the role of affect in producing attitude change.

## Attitude Structure

Attitude structure refers to the underlying foundation, components, and organization of a person's evaluation. Probably the first major attitude structure theory to feature affect prominently was the tripartite theory of attitudes. According to advocates of this perspective (e.g., Insko & Schopler, 1967; Katz & Stotland, 1959; Rosenberg & Hovland, 1960; Smith, 1947), attitudes can be conceptualized as made up of three components: affective, cognitive, and behavioral. The affective component consists of positive and negative feelings associated with the attitude object. The cognitive component comprises beliefs about and perceptions of the attitude object. Finally, the behavioral component is made up of response tendencies and overt actions related to the attitude object.

Since its conception more than five decades ago, the tripartite theory has continued to guide research on attitude structure. One important difference between most contemporary theorists who use the tripartite theory (e.g., see Cacioppo, Petty, & Geen, 1989; Petty & Cacioppo, 1986a; Zajonc & Markus, 1982; Zanna & Rempel, 1988) and the original proponents has been in the way affect is defined. The earliest views conceptualized affect as relatively global and undifferentiated positive or negative evaluations associated with an attitude object without any clear distinction between the evaluative and the emotional dimensions of an attitude (e.g., Insko & Schopler, 1967; Katz & Stotland, 1959; Rosenberg & Hovland, 1960). Although some researchers have continued to follow the original conceptualization (e.g., Bagozzi & Burnkrant, 1979; Chaiken & Baldwin, 1981; Granberg & Brown, 1989; Norman, 1975), most investigators have come to view affect in a more differentiated fashion. That is, attitude-relevant affect is viewed as consisting of discrete and qualitatively distinct emotions (e.g., anger, sadness, joy) associated with an object (e.g., Abelson, Kinder, Peters & Fiske, 1982; Breckler, 1984; Breckler & Wiggins, 1989; Crites, Fabrigar, & Petty, 1994; Eagly, Mladinic, & Otto, 1994; Kothandapani, 1971; Ostrom, 1969; Stangor, Sullivan, & Ford, 1991). Thus this newer conceptualization more clearly distinguishes affect (emotion) from evaluation (attitudes).

A second major shift in more recent theorizing has been researchers' assumptions concerning the structural relations of affect and the other components of attitudes. In early discussions, an attitude was viewed as consisting of affect, cognition, and behavior. Thus, an attitude was not viewed as having an existence separable from its components. More recently, some theorists have argued that attitudes are distinct psychological entities that are related to but separable from the affect, cognition, and behavior relevant to the attitude object (Cacioppo et al., 1989; Crites et al., 1994; Zanna & Rempel, 1988). The newer perspectives conceptualize the attitude as the global or summary positive or negative evaluation of the object and postulate that this evaluation is stored separately from the affective, cognitive, and behavioral information on which the evaluation is based. In addition, these newer perspectives hold that attitudes can be based mostly on affect, cognition, behavioral experience, or some combination of the three.

As will become clear in this chapter, the literature that examines the role of affect in attitude structure reflects both continuity and change. In the sections that follow, we briefly review some of the major empirical questions addressed in this literature.

## Establishing the Affective, Cognitive, and Behavioral Bases of Attitudes

One of the first questions that attitude structure researchers grappled with was whether attitude-relevant affect, cognition, and behavior were in fact distinct constructs. Some of this research specifically tested the three-basis view of attitudes by measuring each of these bases and then assessing the extent to which these bases were correlated with one another (e.g., Bagozzi, 1978; Breckler, 1984; Kothandapani, 1971; Ostrom, 1969). These studies generally found that although the three bases were positively correlated with each other, they were in fact separable constructs.[1]

Other research focused more narrowly on establishing

that affect could be distinguished from cognition by examining the impact of these two constructs on global attitudes and social judgments. These studies demonstrated that in spite of a substantial positive association between attitude-relevant affect and cognition, both constructs typically exerted some independent influence. These findings have been obtained for attitudes and social judgments related to political candidates (Abelson et al., 1982; Granberg & Brown, 1989), social groups (Eagly et al., 1994; Haddock, Zanna, & Esses, 1993; Haddock, Zanna, & Esses, 1994; Stangor et al., 1991), social issues (Breckler & Wiggins, 1989; Crites et al., 1994; Eagly et al., 1994; Haddock & Zanna, 1998a), health behaviors (Breckler & Wiggins, 1989), drug use (Simons & Carey, 1998), and product advertisements (Batra & Ray, 1985, 1986). Thus, considerable empirical support has been obtained for the utility of differentiating between affect, cognition, and (to a lesser extent) the behavioral bases of attitudes.

Despite this evidence, the claim that attitudes are based on affect as well as cognition has not gone unchallenged (Fishbein & Middlestadt, 1995; Ottati, 1997). Critics of this literature have argued that attitudes are best conceptualized as entirely belief-based constructs and that past findings suggesting that attitudes might be partially based on affect have been a function of methodological limitations. Specifically, critics have argued that measures of cognition in past studies have often failed to include *all* relevant beliefs. Had such beliefs been measured, these researchers reason that the impact of affect on attitudes would not have been found. Although this argument is a reasonable criticism of some studies, it is not clear that it can plausibly account for all of the data. For instance, the measures used in some past studies have been very broad in content, and sometimes have been subjected to considerable pretesting (e.g., Breckler, 1984; Crites et al., 1994). Such procedures substantially reduce the likelihood that important beliefs have failed to be assessed. Second, some studies that demonstrate independent influence of affect, cognition, and behavior on attitudes have used open-ended measures of these constructs, thereby severely attenuating the risk of failing to include relevant items (e.g., Haddock et al., 1993, 1994). Thus, it seems difficult to fully attribute past results that show an independent effect for affect to methodological flaws.

## The Measurement of Attitude Bases

Given the substantial interest in examining affect and other attitude bases, it is not surprising that a number of studies have been devoted to the development of measures of the postulated bases of attitudes. Although some of this research has focused on assessing all three traditional bases (Haddock & Zanna, 1998b), most research has concentrated on the affective and cognitive bases (e.g., Batra &

Ahtola, 1990; Crites et al., 1994; Eagly et al., 1994). Two primary approaches have been used.

One approach uses rating scales to assess the different bases. For example, Crites et al. (1994) developed a set of general scales to assess the affective (e.g., how happy one feels in the presence of the object) and cognitive (e.g., how useful the object is perceived to be) bases of a wide variety of attitude objects. They found the affective and cognitive measures to have high and comparable levels of reliability across a range of different attitude objects (coefficients ranged from .77 to .96, with only one coefficient below .80). Factor analyses revealed that the measures strongly reflected the constructs they were intended to assess but were not substantially influenced by other constructs. Finally, the measures were shown to be successful in detecting experimental manipulations of the bases of attitudes (see also Fabrigar & Petty, 1999).

A different measurement approach was adopted by Eagly and colleagues (1994). They administered open-ended measures that asked respondents to list emotions (affect) or characteristics (cognition) associated with an attitude object. They then had participants rate the negativity or positivity of each characteristic and emotion on 7-point rating scales. They found that the affect and cognition scales that resulted from these two measures often produced satisfactory and comparable levels of reliability (coefficient ranged from .61 to .94). They also found these scales to be useful in predicting global evaluations.

Although both open- and closed-ended measures of affect and other bases have been widely used in research, some researchers have argued that open-ended approaches are superior to closed-ended methods (Eagly et al., 1994; Haddock & Zanna, 1998b; Ottati, 1997). For example, it is argued that respondents might use their attitudes as a basis for inferring how they should respond to rating-scale and checklist measures of affect and cognition and thus report emotions and beliefs that they do not really associate with the object. Although criticisms of rating scales have some merit, the claim of superiority of open-ended measures has been based largely on conceptual arguments rather than empirical tests. Direct empirical comparisons of these approaches have been lacking. In addition, closed-ended measures might also have some advantages. For instance, it is not clear whether respondents always have a sufficiently well-developed conceptualization of the construct of interest to report in an open-ended question only responses relevant to that construct. Because closed-ended measures explicitly define the appropriate domain of responses for participants, researchers can be sure that their measures include all the emotions and traits they wish to have considered and do not include responses that are inappropriate in light of their definitions of the constructs.

Given these issues, it is not clear whether one approach should be considered fundamentally superior. Each approach has potential advantages and disadvantages. Thus, either measurement procedure seems reasonable, but researchers should keep in mind the limitations of their measures and, when possible, include both types of measures.

## Consequences of Attitude Bases

Although a substantial amount of research has focused simply on establishing that attitudes can have distinct cognitive, affective, and behavioral bases, some research has also explored the consequences of these bases. Early discussions of attitude bases assumed that people had strong motivations to maintain consistency among the bases of their attitudes (e.g., Rosenberg, 1960). And, as noted earlier, research does suggest that attitude bases tend to be positively associated with one another. That is, if a person's attitude is supported by favorable cognitive content, it is likely to be supported by favorable affective and behavioral tendencies, as well. But attitude bases are not invariably consistent with each other (e.g., Chaiken, Pomerantz, & Giner-Sorolla, 1995). In fact, the contents of any *one* basis of attitudes are not necessarily consistent. That is, people can hold both positive and negative cognitions toward any one attitude object or can have both positive and negative emotions and behavioral tendencies, as well (see Bell, Esses, & Maio, 1996; Cacioppo & Berntson, 1994; Kaplan, 1972; Priester & Petty, 1996; Thompson, Zanna, & Griffin, 1995). As we discuss next, investigators have examined a number of the consequences of consistency or inconsistency of underlying bases of attitudes with the attitude or with each other.

### Attitude-Behavior Relations

The ability of attitudes to predict behavior is determined in part by whether the attitude is consistent with its cognitive and affective bases and whether these bases are consistent with each other.[2] For example, Strathman (1992) found that when attitude-affective and attitude-cognitive consistency were low, attitude-behavior consistency was low. Lavine, Thomsen, Zanna, and Borgida (1998) examined the impact of affective-cognitive consistency on the ability of attitude bases to predict global attitudes and behavior related to political candidates. They found that when affect and cognition were consistent with one another, both exerted comparable levels of influence on attitudes and behaviors. However, when these two bases were inconsistent with one another, affect was found to be more influential than cognition. What is less clear is exactly why affect was more influential than cognition when the two bases were inconsistent with one another (see Lavine et al., 1998, for further discussion) and whether this effect would generalize to other attitude objects.

Other researchers have adopted a somewhat different approach to understanding the role of consistency among attitude bases in attitude-behavior processes. Most notably, Millar and Tesser (1986, 1989; see also Millar & Millar, 1996, 1998) have postulated that variations in the consistency of attitude bases with the global attitude can moderate the type of behavior an attitude influences. Millar and Tesser proposed that behaviors can be divided into at least two categories: instrumental and consummatory. Instrumental behaviors are behaviors that are performed to accomplish a goal independent of the behavior itself. Consummatory behaviors, on the other hand, are behaviors that are performed because the behavior is intrinsically rewarding. Furthermore, Millar and Tesser argued that instrumental behaviors are primarily cognitively driven, whereas consummatory behaviors are primarily affectively driven. In a series of studies designed to test these ideas, the predicted attitude-basis type-of-behavior matching effects were found when the affective and cognitive bases of attitudes were inconsistent with one another (Millar & Millar, 1998; Millar & Tesser, 1989). When affective-cognitive consistency was high, both types of attitudes predicted both types of behaviors equally well.

## Attitude Persistence and Resistance

Some research has also examined the impact of attitude bases on the persistence and resistance of attitudes. For instance, Chaiken et al. (1995) examined how levels of both attitude-affective and attitude-cognitive consistency were related to the persistence of attitudes over time. They found that when both types of consistency were low, attitudes had little stability. However, when either type of consistency was high or both types were high, attitudes demonstrated much higher and comparable levels of stability over time. In another study, Chaiken et al. (1995) assessed participants' attitude-affective consistency and attitude-cognitive consistency, exposed them to attitude-relevant information, and then assessed memory for this information. They found that participants who were high in attitude-cognitive consistency tended to remember information incongruent with their attitudes better than information congruent with their attitudes, regardless of their level of attitude-affective consistency. However, participants low in attitude-cognitive consistency and high in attitude-affective consistency recalled congruent information better than incongruent information. Finally, people low in both types of consistency showed no memory bias. Chaiken et al. (1995) speculated that these results might indicate that people whose attitudes have a strong cognitive basis resist persuasion by actively processing incongruent information and attempting to refute it. This process would account for their superior recall of attitude-incongruent information over congruent information (see also Cacioppo & Petty, 1979). In contrast, peo-

ple whose attitudes are largely based on a strong affective foundation might use more passive resistance processes, such as avoiding incongruent information. Thus, this process would explain their superior recall of attitude-congruent information over incongruent information. Finally, participants who lack consistency of either type might have no meaningful attitude and would therefore not be predisposed to process information in a biased manner. Although these speculations are interesting and plausible, direct evidence in support of them has yet to be obtained.

Finally, some research has examined the role that the affective and cognitive bases of attitudes play in influencing people's evaluative responses to persuasive messages.[3] These studies have not examined levels of consistency between bases and attitudes but have instead typically examined the degree to which the overall valence of these bases influences the valence of evaluative responses to persuasive messages. For example, Breckler and Wiggins (1991) provided evidence suggesting that the valence of the affective basis of attitudes determined the valence of evaluative responses to persuasive messages such that there was a tendency for people to generate responses consistent with the affective (rather than the cognitive) basis of their attitudes. Batra and Ray (1985) obtained evidence that suggested that the cognitive basis of attitudes toward an advertisement was a stronger determinant of purchasing intentions than was the affective basis when involvement during the processing of the advertisement was high. In contrast, when involvement was low, the affective component appeared to be a stronger predictor of purchasing intentions than the cognitive component. Biek, Wood, and Chaiken (1996) examined the extent to which the affective basis of attitudes motivated people to process messages in a biased manner. They found that when people showed extensive negative affect related to AIDS risk and were very knowledgeable about AIDS, they generated evaluative responses to an AIDS-related message that tended to be consistent with their attitudes. However, if they lacked strong negative affect related to AIDS risk and/or lacked knowledge regarding AIDS, they did not process the message in a biased manner. Thus, the researchers speculated that negative affect provided the motivation to process information in a biased manner and that knowledge provided the ability to do so (Biek et al., 1996).

In considering the experiments on attitude bases and attitude change, some caution seems advisable, because the findings from these studies are often preliminary. Most of these effects have yet to be replicated, and the mechanisms that underlie them are not well understood. Another important caveat is that these studies have explored the role of attitude bases in responses to persuasive communications but have not considered the nature of the persuasive communications themselves. As we discuss in later sections, it is entirely possible that the manner in which attitude bases influence reactions to messages could be influenced by the extent to which a message is primarily affective or cognitive in content. Thus, it is not clear whether the results obtained in the studies just reviewed would have been the same had other messages that differed in their affective or cognitive content been used.

## Understanding the Role of Relevant Affect in Attitude Change

### Historical Foundations

Just as the affect construct has a long tradition in attitude structure research, so too has its importance been recognized in persuasion research. Probably the first use of the construct in this domain was as one of the primary categories (along with cognition) used to classify types of persuasive communications. That is, some persuasive communications induce some type of emotion or affective experience in the recipient. Perhaps the most studied type of message in this regard is the "fear appeal" (Rogers, 1983). Other messages, however, simply supply cold hard facts. The literature on affective versus cognitive (or emotional versus rational) appeals has a long intellectual tradition (Chen, 1933; Cronkhite, 1964; Hartman, 1936; Knepprath & Clevenger, 1965; Millar & Millar, 1990; Pallak, Murroni, & Koch, 1983; Rosselli, Skelly, & Mackie, 1995; Ruechelle, 1958; Weiss, 1960). McGuire (1969) traced the use of the affect-cognition distinction in persuasive communications to Aristotle's *Rhetoric*.

Early empirical research that examined the distinction between emotional and rational appeals addressed two questions. Some research simply explored the extent to which the content of persuasive appeals could be classified as affective or cognitive (Becker, 1963; Knepprath & Clevenger, 1965; Ruechelle, 1958)—similar to the research we described earlier looking at whether the content of one's attitude could be classified as affective or cognitive in nature. Other research focused on examining the relative impact of affective versus cognitive persuasive appeals on attitudes, behaviors, and memory (Chen, 1933; Eldersveld, 1956; Hartman, 1936; Knower, 1935; Matthews, 1947; Menefee & Granneberg, 1940; Weiss, 1960). Still other research examined whether the effectiveness of emotional versus rational appeals was mediated by affective or cognitive responses. It is to this research that we turn first.

### The Nature of Evaluative Responses and the Nature of Persuasive Communications

One line of research involving affect and attitude change that has evolved quite directly out of early research has been the literature exploring the processes by which affective and cognitive persuasive appeals influence attitudes. Whereas early researchers were interested primarily in classifying appeals or assessing the type of appeal that was most influential, contemporary research has investigated the processes by which these types of appeals change attitudes. For instance, Roselli et al. (1995) investigated the extent to which affective and cognitive persuasive appeals produce attitude change via affective and cognitive responses to the messages. Their analyses revealed that persuasion in response to cognitive-based arguments was mediated by cognitive responses to the message. In contrast, they found that persuasion in response to affective-based arguments was mediated by both cognitive and affective responses to the message.

Other research has simply examined the role of different types of evaluative responses in persuasion without specifically investigating differences in the affective-cognitive content of the messages. Zuwerink and Devine (1996) examined the role of affective and cognitive responses to a message in producing resistance to persuasion. They found that people who considered the message topic to be important were more resistant to an opposition message than those who considered the topic to be relatively unimportant. Additionally, they found that the impact of importance on resistance was mediated by message-inconsistent affective and cognitive responses generated in reaction to the message. That is, as importance increased, people generated more affective and cognitive responses that contradicted the message, and these responses in turn led to less attitude change (see also Munro & Ditto, 1997).

When we consider the various studies that have examined how affective and cognitive messages differ in the manner in which they change attitudes or the role of affective and cognitive responses in persuasion, reaching definitive conclusions is difficult. One problem is that the effects in these studies have seldom been replicated. When such effects have been replicated, they have often involved operationalizations of the key constructs that are very similar (e.g., effects have been demonstrated using a single attitude object). Thus the robustness and generality of many of these effects have yet to be established. Another limitation to many of these studies is that the effects observed in them often lack a compelling theoretical rationale, and explanations for them have often been ad hoc. Finally, these studies have seldom considered potential moderators. For example, one factor that might moderate the manner in which different types of persuasive appeals change attitudes or the extent to which cognitive and affective responses influence attitude change might be the nature of the premessage attitude. That is, the extent to which an attitude is based on either affect or cognition or both might well moderate the process by which persuasive appeals of different types change attitudes or the extent to which different types of evaluative responses are involved in attitude change. Such complexities have seldom been considered in these studies.

## Affective/Cognitive Bases and Susceptibility to Persuasion

Some researchers have begun to explore how the bases of attitudes and the nature of persuasive appeals might interact to influence attitude change. Specifically, researchers in this area have been interested in whether persuasive appeals that are primarily either affective or cognitive are more effective when they match or mismatch the basis of the attitude. Initial investigations produced apparently contradictory evidence, with some studies suggesting that persuasion was greatest when the nature of the appeal matched the basis of the attitude (Edwards, 1990; Edwards & von Hippel, 1995) and other studies indicating persuasion was greatest when the nature of the appeal mismatched the basis of the attitude (Millar & Millar, 1990).

However, limitations in methodology made interpretation of these findings difficult (see Fabrigar & Petty, 1999; Messé, Bodenhausen, & Nelson, 1995). For example, these studies lacked clear evidence that the affective and cognitive bases of attitudes and persuasive appeals had been manipulated successfully. Additionally, manipulations of affect and cognition often confounded these constructs with direct and indirect experience, thereby leading some researchers to question whether affect and cognition were actually responsible for past effects (Messé, Bodenhausen, & Nelson, 1995).

More recently, clearer evidence for matching effects has been reported (Fabrigar & Petty, 1999). In these experiments, affective-cognitive matching effects were shown to occur using manipulations of affect and cognition that were validated. Additionally, these experiments showed that such matching effects occur even when the direct-indirect experience distinction has been unconfounded from affect-cognition manipulations. Thus there is reasonably good evidence for matching effects. That is, attitudes based primarily on affect are more readily changed with affective appeals, whereas attitudes based primarily on cognition are more easily changed with cognitive appeals. The empirical status of affective-cognitive mismatching effects is less certain. Although some attempts have been made to establish the conditions under which matching and mismatching effects occur (e.g., Millar, 1992; Millar & Millar, 1993), no definitive evidence yet exists (see Fabrigar & Petty, 1999).

Nonetheless, it is possible to generate plausible predictions regarding conditions that might foster matching versus mismatching (see Edwards, 1990; Edwards & von Hippel, 1995; Fabrigar & Petty, 1999; Millar & Millar, 1990; Petty, Gleicher, & Baker, 1991). For instance, one possibility is that matching should occur when it is possible to

directly overwhelm the basis of the attitude. If so, matching effects should occur when the basis of an attitude is relatively weak, the persuasive appeal is particularly strong, or both. In contrast, if the basis of an attitude is extremely strong or the appeal is relatively weak, it is likely to be difficult to completely overwhelm the basis of an attitude with a persuasive appeal focused on that basis. Indeed, a strong attitude basis (whether affective or cognitive) might serve as a resource for counterarguing or resisting the appeal. In such cases, matching persuasion to bases could prove relatively ineffective. Thus it might be more promising to use a mismatched persuasive appeal that provides novel information that does not directly challenge the existing basis. This analysis presumes that people actively analyze the persuasive information presented. If this is not the case, then other possibilities emerge. For example, some people may have a default preference for experiential/emotional messages, and others have a default preference for rational/logical messages, based on chronic individual differences in the way they approach the world (Epstein & Rosemary, 1999).

## Fear Appeals

As we just demonstrated, a number of investigations have examined the conditions under which affective versus cognitive appeals will be more effective. The affective appeal that has been the most studied in the persuasion literature is the fear appeal, perhaps because of its great potential relevance to various important health issues (e.g., AIDS, drunken driving). When very strong negative consequences (e.g., death, serious illness) are implied if an advocacy is not adopted (e.g., using condoms), a fear appeal is being attempted.[4] Based on expectancy-value theories of attitudes (e.g., see Fishbein & Ajzen, 1975), it would appear that such appeals would be very effective, because they depict extremely negative consequences as being likely to occur unless the recipient agrees with the message. In fact, a meta-analysis of the fear-appeals literature indicated that, overall, increasing fear is associated with increased persuasion (Boster & Mongeau, 1984).

Yet fear appeals are not invariably found to be more effective. Notably, one of the earliest studies on fear appeals suggested that using fear was ineffective (Janis & Feshbach, 1953). A number of studies have pointed to several factors that work against the utility of fear appeals. First, even if people view the threatened negative consequence as horrific, they are often motivated by self-protection to minimize the likelihood that some frightening consequence might befall them (e.g., Ditto, Jemmott, & Darley, 1988; Ditto & Lopez, 1992). That is, they engage in "defensive processing." To the extent that this defensiveness can be minimized by encouraging objective processing, the effectiveness of a fear appeal can be increased (Keller & Block, 1995). Second, to the extent that the threat is so strong that it becomes physiologically arousing or distracting, message processing could be disrupted (Baron, Inman, Kao, & Logan, 1992; Jepson & Chaiken, 1990). Thus, persuasion would be reduced if the arguments were strong (because favorable thoughts would be disrupted) but persuasion could be increased if the arguments were weak (because counterarguments would be disrupted; Petty, Wells, & Brock, 1976). Fear is especially likely to reduce message processing if recipients are assured that the recommendations are effective and if processing might undermine this assurance (Gleicher & Petty, 1992).[5]

The dominant theoretical perspective in the literature on fear appeals is Rogers' (1975, 1983) protection motivation theory. Consistent with expectancy-value notions, this model holds that fear appeals will be effective to the extent that the message convinces the recipient that the postulated consequences are severe (i.e., very undesirable) and very likely to occur if the recommended action is not followed. Importantly, this theory also holds that effective fear messages should also convey that the negative consequences can be avoided if the recommended action is followed and that the recipient has the requisite skills to take the recommended action (see also Beck & Frankel, 1981; Sutton, 1982; Witte, 1992). Considerable evidence supports these predictions and has also shown that if people do not believe that they can cope effectively with the threat, then increasing threat tends to produce a boomerang effect, presumably as a consequence of attempting to restore control or reduce fear (e.g., Mulilis & Lippa, 1990; Rippetoe & Rogers, 1987; Rogers & Mewborn, 1976). In sum, fear seems to be effective when the fear enhances the realization that some negative consequences are severe and likely but can be overcome by following the recommendations. If fear is elicited in the absence of these cognitive processes, it is counterproductive.

## Understanding the Role of Incidental Affect in Attitude Change

As noted previously, the earliest research on the role of affect in persuasion investigated how affect that was part of the communication influenced attitudes. Another line of research with a somewhat more recent history has examined the extent to which affect that is extraneous or incidental to the communication influences attitudes. For example, if a person felt angry because of the television program that preceded a political advertisement and not because of the advertisement itself, what effect would this have on attitudes? The relatively recent multiprocess theories of persuasion (e.g., Chaiken, Liberman, & Eagly, 1989; Petty & Cacioppo, 1986b) offer a framework within which the varied effects of incidental affect can be under-

stood. In these frameworks, the focus is on the multiple processes by which affect helps or hinders persuasion.

### Elaboration Likelihood Model

Both the elaboration likelihood model (ELM; Petty & Cacioppo, 1981, 1986b; Petty & Wegener, 1999) and the heuristic-systematic model (HSM; Chaiken et al., 1989) dictate that attitude change occurs through different mechanisms, depending on the level of cognitive effort individuals allocate when considering persuasive appeals. Therefore, the manner in which affect has an impact on persuasion also varies as a function of individuals' levels of elaboration regarding the message at hand (Petty, Schumann, Richman, & Strathman, 1993). Within the ELM, persuasion variables are postulated to take on different roles at different levels of elaboration likelihood (Petty & Cacioppo, 1986b; Petty & Wegener, 1998; Petty, Wegener, Fabrigar, Priester, & Cacioppo, 1993). Specifically, when the elaboration likelihood is low (i.e., when people are unwilling or unable to scrutinize attitude-relevant information), variables such as a person's affective state have an impact on attitudes by the operation of relatively low-effort peripheral processes, such as forming a direct association between the feeling and attitude object (Zanna, Kiesler, & Pilkonis, 1970) or serving as part of a mood-based heuristic (e.g., "I feel good, so I must like it"; Chaiken, 1987). When the elaboration likelihood is high (i.e., when people are both willing and able to scrutinize attitude-relevant information), variables have an impact by influencing the type of reactions that people have to attitude-relevant information or by acting as items of attitude-relevant information (i.e., providing information central to the merits of the attitudinal position). Finally, when elaboration likelihood is neither so high that people are already thinking extensively about attitude-relevant information nor so low that people are avoiding extensive attitude-relevant thought, emotional states, like other variables, can influence the amount of scrutiny that people give to attitude-relevant information (Petty, Cacioppo, & Kasmer, 1988; Petty et al., 1991). With this framework in mind, we turn to the impact of emotional factors on attitudes across the elaboration continuum.

### Effects of Emotional Factors Under Low-Elaboration Conditions

Under conditions of low elaboration, when individuals lack the motivation or ability to process a persuasive message, affect has been shown to function as a peripheral cue and to influence attitudes in a manner consistent with its valence. Thus, incidental positive affect tends to lead to more positive attitudes toward an object, but incidental negative affect tends to elicit more negative attitudes.

Early demonstrations of the effects of incidental affect

under conditions of low elaboration can be found in the extensive research on evaluative classical conditioning (e.g., Janis, Kaye, & Kirschner, 1965; Staats & Staats, 1958). Conditioning is, by nature, a process of simple association rather than one that involves scrutiny of message-relevant information. A number of studies that use classical conditioning to study emotional input have demonstrated that emotions can influence attitudes by becoming directly associated with the attitude object. That is, repeatedly pairing an attitude object with stimuli that bring about positive feelings (e.g., delicious food; Razran, 1940) can lead to more positive attitudes toward the attitude object than pairing the same object with stimuli that produce negative reactions (e.g., electric shock; Zanna et al., 1970; see also Gouaux, 1971; Griffit, 1970). The accumulated studies on classical conditioning are quite consistent, and relatively recent research suggests that such conditioning effects are most likely when the likelihood of elaboration of the attitude object is low (Cacioppo, Marshall-Goodell, Tassinary, & Petty, 1992; Priester, Cacioppo, & Petty, 1996).

A second way in which emotions can influence attitudes under conditions of low elaboration is through the misattribution of one's emotional states to an attitude object (e.g., Zillmann, 1983). Rather than evaluating the merits of a message, an individual uses his or her emotional feeling as a simple cue to decide whether the message was good or bad (e.g., "if I'm feeling good, I must like or agree with the message"). Rather than being based on the merit of the message, an individual's attitude is based on the answer to the question, "How do I feel about it?" (Schwarz, 1990; Schwarz & Clore, 1983; Sinclair, Mark, & Clore, 1994; Srull, 1983). Incidental affect is especially likely to have these simple and direct cue effects when people are not inclined to be thinking about the message (see Petty et al., 1993).

### Effects of Emotional factors Under High-Elaboration Conditions

Incidental affect can also influence attitudes under high-elaboration conditions, but the process is different. In high elaboration contexts, people are carefully scrutinizing persuasive messages for merit. Emotional states themselves can also be scrutinized for their information value. Whereas under low elaboration, people might use their moods as an informative heuristic with relatively little thought ("if I feel good, I must like it"), under high elaboration, experienced emotions are subjected to greater scrutiny, and they can affect attitudes if they are seen as relevant to the attitude object under consideration. For example, if one's judgment concerns whether or not a person would make a suitable spouse, the feelings associated with the presence of that person are a central dimension of the

merits of that potential companion (Petty & Cacioppo, 1986a; Wegener & Petty, 1996).

In one recent empirical example, Martin, Abend, Sedikides, and Green (1997) presented people in either a happy or sad mood with either a happy or sad story. These individuals were asked to evaluate the story and their liking for it. In such a case (in which the "target" story was obviously meant to bring about a particular feeling), the mood people felt when reading the story was likely to be perceived as a central merit of the story. Consistent with this notion, research participants' evaluations of and liking for the target stories were highest when the mood before the story (and presumably during the story) matched rather than mismatched the intended effect of the story. For example, when the purpose of the target story was to make people feel sad and people did feel sad, the sad mood actually led to higher ratings of the story than did a happy mood.

Perhaps more often, when people are actively evaluating information about the target (i.e., when elaboration likelihood is high), mood can bias the interpretation of that information, especially if the information is ambiguous (Chaiken & Maheswaran, 1994; Petty et al., 1991). Forgas (1994) refers to this as an "affect infusion" effect. For example, positive moods might activate more positive interpretations of information than would negative moods (e.g., Bower, 1981; Bower & Forgas, 2001; Breckler & Wiggins, 1991; Isen, Shalker, Clark, & Karp, 1978). Regardless of whether one conceptualizes such activation in terms of associative networks (e.g., Anderson & Bower, 1973; Bower, 1981) or connectionist models (e.g., McClelland, Rumelhart, & Hinton, 1986; Smith, 1996), happy moods have often been found to make events or objects seem more desirable and/or more likely than the same events or objects appear when individuals are in sad or neutral moods (e.g., see Forgas & Moylan, 1987; Johnson & Tversky, 1983; Mayer, Gaschke, Braverman, & Evans, 1992). Recently, it has been shown that specific emotions have specific effects on the perceived likelihood of events, such that angry states make angering events seem more likely than sad ones but sad states make sad events seem more likely than angering ones (DeSteno, Petty, Wegener, & Rucker, 2000).

Explicit evidence of mood biasing information processing was obtained in several studies. For example, in the high-elaboration conditions of two experiments conducted by Petty et al. (1993) (i.e., when people were high in need for cognition or encountered information about a self-relevant product), the affect induced by an irrelevant context (e.g, a "happy" television program) influenced judgments of an attitude object (e.g., a product advertised during the program) by influencing the evaluative responses people had to the attitude object. That is, when effortful elaboration of judgment-relevant information was likely, positive affect produced greater positivity in thought content, which in turn influenced evaluations of the targets. When the likelihood of elaboration was low (i.e., when people were low in need for cognition or encountered information about a non–self-relevant product), incidental affect still influenced judgments of the attitude object, but did so without affecting the content of people's evaluative responses.[6]

It is also important to note that when affect biases processing, the emotional state does not invariably lead to affect-congruent biases in overall evaluation (Petty & Wegener, 1991; Wegener, Petty, & Klein, 1994). Using the expectancy (likelihood) × value (desirability) approach to attitude judgments (e.g., Fishbein & Ajzen, 1975), Wegener et al. (1994) found that differential framing of information about target actions led to different biasing effects of mood on assessments of those actions. Specifically, when the arguments in a persuasive message were framed to support the view that adopting the recommended position was likely to make good things happen, a happy mood was associated with more favorable views of the advocacy than a sad mood (cf. Weiss & Fine, 1956). However, when the arguments were framed such that failing to adopt the advocacy was likely to make bad things happen, a sad mood was associated with more favorable views of the advocacy than a happy mood. The reason for this was that a happy mood made the good things that would occur if the advocacy was adopted seem more likely, and the sad mood made the bad things that would occur if the advocacy was *not* adopted seem more likely. Consistent with the notion of this likelihood-desirability calculus being a relatively effortful activity, the likelihood mediation of mood effects on judgment took place only for people high in need for cognition. Of course, using this same likelihood-desirability view, one could also predict situations in which mood changes the perceived desirability of consequences of adopting the advocacy (thereby providing another means by which mood might bias the effortful assessment of the central merits of an advocacy; see Petty & Wegener, 1991, for additional discussion).

## Effects of Emotional Factors Under Moderate-Elaboration Conditions

As mentioned earlier, according to the multiprocess theories of persuasion, variables can influence persuasion in many ways. According to the ELM, sometimes a variable serves as a central merit of consideration, but at other times it influences persuasion by invoking a more peripheral process (e.g., is used as a heuristic). In addition, sometimes variables bias the thoughts that come to mind. Finally, variables can also determine, either in isolation or in concert with other variables, the extent of processing a persuasive appeal receives. Therefore, in instances in which the level of elaboration a message receives is not constrained by other variables to be high or low, an individual's affective state can push processing along the elaboration continuum in one direction or another.

### Positive Versus Negative Mood Effects

The majority of research on emotion and information processing in persuasion settings has documented a general pattern. Individuals experiencing a positive mood have typically been less likely to engage in careful processing of the specific information contained in a persuasive appeal than those experiencing a negative mood (Bless, Bohner, Schwarz, & Strack, 1990; Bohner, Crow, Erb, & Schwarz, 1992; Kuykendall & Keating, 1990; Mackie, Asuncion, & Rosselli, 1992; Mackie & Worth, 1989). For example, Bless et al. (1990) manipulated emotional state by asking participants to remember happy or sad experiences from their pasts. They were then presented with a message announcing a fee increase at their university that contained either strong or weak arguments. Under moderate-elaboration conditions, sad participants were more persuaded by strong than weak arguments, but happy participants were not, thereby indicating a relatively higher level of processing in sad than in happy conditions (Petty et al., 1976).

Currently, one of the most accepted theoretical explanations for the effects of affect on level of message elaboration is the feelings-as-information, or cognitive tuning, framework proposed by Schwarz, Clore, and colleagues (Schwarz, Bless, & Bohner, 1991; Schwarz & Clore, 1988). This theory holds that individuals' emotions serve as informational cues regarding the status of their environment. Specifically, negative affective states are theorized to inform individuals that their current environment is problematic, and, therefore, they engender a relatively high level of effortful processing that would be appropriate in dealing with such situations. Positive states are believed to signal that the current situation is safe and, therefore, does not require a high level of cognitive effort because everything is fine.

Although negative emotional states might indeed signal that the world is a problematic place and induce greater processing, emotional states can have other motivational consequences as well. For example, the hedonic contingency model (Wegener & Petty, 1994) begins with the fairly obvious assumption that people prefer to keep their positive emotional states but avoid their negative ones. The crux of the model hinges on the fact that as an individual's affective state becomes more and more positive, the actions in which he or she can engage that will maintain or further elevate the mood state become increasingly limited. However, when an individual is sad, the majority of actions in which he or she can engage will tend to elevate mood. Therefore, success in positive mood states (i.e., maintaining one's positive mood) is highly contingent on the consideration of the hedonic consequences of actions, because only a small proportion of possible actions will serve to maintain or elevate one's affective state further. However, negative mood states require less vigilance, because most activities will serve to reduce negative mood. Due to these contingencies, over time people become more sensitive to the hedonic consequences of their actions in positive rather than in negative emotional states.

In extending the hedonic contingency framework to the study of persuasion, Wegener, Petty, and Smith (1995) noted that the persuasive appeals used in past research that examined the effect of emotional states on information processing comprised largely negative content (e.g., tuition increases, acid rain). Consequently, the lack of effortful consideration of such messages by individuals experiencing a positive mood state might represent a mood-management strategy, as opposed to the utilization of a feelings-as-information motivational cue. Thinking about a tuition increase, after all, would likely not maintain an already pleasant affective state. Therefore, happy individuals should choose not to process the message in an effortful manner. Sad individuals, being less sensitive to hedonic contingencies, should devote more resources toward message processing.

The critical test for the hedonic contingency view involves the case in which effortful processing of a persuasive message could be considered a mood-enhancing endeavor. In such a situation, the hedonic contingency perspective predicts a relatively high level of effortful processing by happy people. To examine the hedonic contingency prediction, Wegener et al. (1995) conducted a study in which affective states (happy vs. sad), argument quality, and message valence were all varied. All participants read the same message, but it was introduced as being either one that tended to make people happy or as one that tended to make them sad when processed. In accord with the hedonic contingency predictions, Wegener et al. (1995) found that when the message was believed to cause sadness, happy people were not differentially persuaded by strong rather than weak arguments, but sad people were. When the message was believed to cause happiness, however, happy people were more influenced by argument quality than were sad people, indicating a relatively high level of information processing.

Although such findings might appear to contradict the feelings-as-information view, Schwarz and Clore (1996) have recently noted that attention to the hedonic qualities of activities may represent a rational mood-management strategy, but one that individuals have the luxury of engaging in only when they first appraise their current environment as nonproblematic through the use of a feelings-as-information process (i.e., "the world is fine, so I think I'll stay happy by processing this message"). Consequently, they have argued that the hedonic contingency

model does not stand in opposition to the feelings-as-information perspective but, rather, might be a secondary process that can further moderate the primary effect of positive mood (see Wegener et al., 1995).

## Cognitive Dissonance and Processing

One other process by which affective experience has been shown to influence the amount of issue-relevant thinking and attitude change is cognitive dissonance. As is well known, Festinger (1957) defined cognitive dissonance as a state in which two elements (i.e., cognitions, behaviors, etc.) are inconsistent. Such inconsistency is believed to be experienced as an aversive state by individuals and motivates actions aimed at reducing the dissonance. Decades of research have documented this phenomenon and the specific conditions under which it occurs (Cooper & Fazio, 1984). Most relevant to our concerns here are the affective consequences of dissonance and the effects of this affect on information processing and attitude change.

Work by Zanna and Cooper (1974) has clearly demonstrated that dissonance is experienced as an unpleasant affective state, much akin to tension. As Festinger (1957) noted, one way in which dissonance can be alleviated is through the changing of cognitions so that they no longer are discrepant. In support of this theory, much evidence had accumulated demonstrating that individuals' attitudes toward certain objects can change dramatically in response to dissonance manipulations that place their initial attitudes at odds with other thoughts or behaviors (for reviews, see Cooper & Fazio, 1984; Harmon-Jones & Mills, 1999). Consequently, cognitive dissonance can be understood to exert its influence on attitude change through a motivation to reduce the inconsistencies that are causing an aversive affective state. The mechanism by which dissonance produces attitude change involves effortful reconsideration of the attitude object and the generation of biased thoughts that render the attitude object more consistent with the other elements in the cognitive system.

## Corrections for Perceived Effects of Emotion

As noted earlier in this chapter, one of the most common effects of affect on attitudes is a mood-congruence or "assimilation" effect. That is, positive mood often leads to more favorable judgments or attitudes when compared with neutral or negative moods. As shown in the previous sections, there are a number of processes that can produce this congruent outcome. First, positive mood can lead to more favorable judgments because positive mood serves as a cue (or is used as a heuristic). Or positive mood can serve effectively as an argument that the object should be valued. Or positive mood can produce a favorable bias to the thoughts about the object. Positive mood can also lead to more favorable judgments when it increases processing of strong arguments or decreases processing of weak arguments. Although positive mood can sometimes lead to less favorable judgments under conditions described earlier (e.g., see Martin et al., 1997; Wegener et al., 1994), the affect-congruency effect is clearly the most common. Each of the types of processes described thus far naturally occurs when people are operating under their typical motivation to seek "correct" or reasonable views of an object (Petty & Cacioppo, 1986a). What happens, however, when people become aware of some unwanted (biasing) effect on their judgments or attitudes? It is here that the most consistent mood-incongruency effects have been found. That is, the most common settings in which mood-incongruency effects occur are those in which some biasing effect of mood is perceived and people attempt to correct for this bias.

Although correction processes have recently been studied in standard persuasion contexts (e.g., Petty, Wegener, & White, 1998), most of the mood-correction work to date has focused on ratings and evaluations of people in an impression formation paradigm. Similar to the typical persuasion paradigm in which people receive information about a product or proposed policy, the traditional impression formation setting provides raters with information about a novel person. After receiving this information, research participants are asked to rate the person either on a purely evaluative dimension (e.g., good-bad) or on trait dimensions that carry specific semantic information along with their evaluative implications (e.g., kind-unkind).

## The Flexible Correction Model

We organize the existing mood and correction work using the flexible correction model (FCM; Wegener & Petty, 1997). According to the FCM, corrections for one's mood and other potential biasing agents are generally guided by the naive theories (perceptions) of social perceivers regarding the effects of the biasing agent on assessments of targets. These theory-based corrections should be most likely to occur when people are motivated and able both to identify and correct for the perceived bias. Corrective efforts work to avoid or remove perceived biases, so corrections proceed in a direction opposite to the perceived bias and in a magnitude commensurate with the perceived magnitude of the bias. Finally, "corrected assessments" generally require greater mental effort than "uncorrected assessments" see Petty & Wegener, 1993; Wegener & Petty, 1997, 2001, for additional aspects of the model). In the FCM, both assimilation (mood congruence) and contrast (mood incongruence) could be either the "default" (uncorrected) outcome of some judgment process or the result

of effortful corrections, depending on the direction of the perceived bias associated with mood. Mood is believed by social perceivers to create mood-congruent judgments in many settings (e.g., see Isbell & Wyer, 1999; Petty & Wegener, 1993), and existing studies have generally studied mood-congruent "uncorrected" outcomes that are eliminated or reversed when corrections occur.

## Identification of Bias and Cognitive Ability

Although a variety of possibilities exist, the most common circumstances associated with corrections for mood have involved a high level of salience of the mood during or prior to exposure to the judgment target. That is, identification of mood as a potential "bias" has been crucial in determining when mood-congruent versus mood-incongruent outcomes occur. In one of the earliest studies that investigated correction for a highly salient feeling state, Berkowitz and Troccoli (1990) induced muscular discomfort in some participants (by having them either hold out their nondominant arm unsupported—high discomfort—or rest it on a table—low discomfort) while they listened to a tape-recorded statement by a target person. When the statement ended, the investigators had half of the participants rate their feelings in order to create high levels of attention to feelings. The other half of the participants were distracted by completing a word association task. After each of these manipulations, participants rated the target person. Participants who were distracted from their feelings prior to rating the target person showed the common affect-congruence (assimilation) effect. Participants whose attention had been drawn to the feelings, however, showed affect-incongruence (contrast) in their ratings. That is, not only were the effects of discomfort removed from ratings of the target, but the participants who had experienced discomfort actually rated the target more favorably than those who had not experienced discomfort (see also Berkowitz, Jaffee, Jo, & Troccoli, 2000).

A number of unique features of this procedure are relevant to whether or not correction would occur. Notably, participants completed a manipulation check on feelings after exposure to the target but before completing the target ratings. This would presumably make feelings extremely salient at the time of the target judgment. The distraction procedure was also unique. Not only did target judgments take place some time after exposure to the target but also any thoughtful cognitive processes were probably impossible during the word association task; so thoughtful corrections would be less likely when the cognitive load was present (see Martin, Seta, & Crelia, 1990). It is also possible that the distraction task itself made the possible effects of mood less salient. Each of these aspects of the procedure would hold important implications for target judgments (see Wegener, Dunn, & Tokusato, 2001, for additional discussion).

## Motivation

Motivation has also been shown to play a role in correction for mood. Consistent with the work on distraction, people low in need for cognition (i.e., people who do not enjoy effortful cognitive activities; Cacioppo & Petty, 1982b) have also been shown to be less likely to correct their judgments than people high in need for cognition, even when blatant biases are present (Martin et al., 1990). For example, in one study in which emotion was made salient to social perceivers, people low in need for cognition provided judgments of event likelihood that were both mood congruent and emotion specific (i.e., with sad events rated as more likely when people were sad rather than angry, and angering events rated as more likely when they were angry rather than sad). People high in need for cognition engaged in emotion-specific correction, however, showing the reverse pattern. That is, these individuals made judgments of *lower* likelihood for sad events when feeling sad rather than angry and for angering events when feeling angry rather than sad (DeSteno et al., 2000). It should be noted, however, that high levels of cognitive motivation (or cognitive effort per se) do not necessarily mean that corrections will occur. As shown by Petty et al. (1998), high levels of cognitive effort can also be given to uncorrected assessments of targets, and these uncorrected assessments can be further adjusted when biases are brought to the attention of social perceivers. Therefore, the blatant nature of the biases involved in the DeSteno et al. (2000) and Martin et al. (1990) research are presumably crucial for finding correction effects when motivation to think is high.

In addition to representing a general enjoyment of cognitive activities, correction-relevant motivation might also be more domain specific. As an example, consider research conducted by Isbell and Wyer (1999; see also Ottati & Isbell, 1996). In this research, people were given information about specific position statements made by a novel political candidate. The recipients of this information were identified as either strong or weak partisans (i.e., people with strong versus weak identification with a liberal or conservative ideology—but equal in political expertise) and were asked to read an article about the candidate in one of two ways. Those high in partisanship were presumably high in intrinsic motivation to process information about the candidates. Extrinsic motivation to process was also varied. That is, some participants were either told to focus on the format and structure of the article (low extrinsic motivation to process) or on evaluating the candidate and deciding whether or not to vote for him (high extrinsic motivation to process). The target article was presented just after participants completed an autobiographical-recall manipulation of happy versus sad events from their past (presumably making the source of current mood salient). Results showed that both intrinsic and extrinsic motivation were capable of inducing corrections. When weak partisans focused on structural features of the article (low intrinsic and low extrinsic motivation to process), the candidate was rated more favorably when encountered by happy than by sad social perceivers (assimilation). When either intrinsic or extrinsic motivation to process was high, however, mood-incongruent judgments occurred (contrast).

Therefore, the FCM perspective appears capable of organizing the existing research on corrections for mood. One direct, but unstudied, implication of the FCM framework would be that corrections for mood could sometimes make a bias worse in the same direction of the original bias. For example, if people hold a general naive theory that sad mood makes their judgments less favorable, they would tend to correct their judgments in a more favorable manner. If the effect of sad mood in a given context was actually to render judgments more favorable (such as when processing a negatively framed persuasive message in a sad mood; Wegener et al., 1994), a correction could exacerbate the bias by making judgments even more favorable. In addition to making negatively framed persuasive appeals more agreeable, sad mood has also made sad stories appear higher in quality (Martin et al., 1997). In addition, exposing people to extreme negative events (e.g., imagining the death of a friend) has been found to increase the positivity of judgments about one's own life (Dermer, Cohen, Jacobsen, & Anderson, 1979). To the extent that any or all of these have been "uncorrected" effects of mood, it seems quite possible that people could correct for such potential biases by making judgments even less rather than more congruent with mood and exacerbate the original bias (if the theory of bias is assimilative).

## Diversity of Theories on Affect and Judgment

As is evident in the organization of this chapter, researchers have identified a number of conceptually distinct ways in which feelings can influence evaluations of the objects and people in one's environment. We have relied primarily on two models, the ELM (Petty & Cacioppo, 1986b) and the FCM (Wegener & Petty, 1997), to account for the effects of emotion on judgment (see also Wegener & Petty, 2001). Here we briefly summarize these and other multiprocess perspectives that we mentioned earlier in this chapter to account for the impact of emotion on attitudes.

### Elaboration Likelihood and Flexible Correction Models

As described previously, the ELM includes a number of ways in which mood can influence attitudes and persuasion across the elaboration continuum. At low levels of elaboration, feelings can act as a cue—through processes such as classical conditioning or use of a "how do I feel about it?" heuristic. At high levels of elaboration, mood could bias processing of information (making certain interpretations of information more likely in some moods than in others, biasing assessments of likelihood or desirability of consequences) or, in certain circumstances, could serve as information (arguments) directly relevant to the merits of the attitude object. When elaboration likelihood is not constrained to be high or low, emotions can affect the amount of information processing activity that takes place. One of the most useful features of the ELM is its dissociation of process from outcome (Petty, 1997). That is, the processes by which emotions are postulated to affect attitudes and persuasion are independent of the outcomes produced by these processes. Thus the same attitudinal outcome (e.g., increased favorability in judgment in positive mood states) could come about for many reasons (i.e., mood acting as a cue or an argument, mood biasing processing or affecting amount of processing). Each of these "multiple roles" has been conceptualized as taking place when people are attempting to form and maintain reasonable views of the attitude object and are not concerned about bias (see Petty & Cacioppo, 1986a; Petty & Wegener, 1999, for additional discussion).

If the possibility of bias is salient (because the perceiver is chronically disposed toward such concerns or because the situation creates this salience), then attempts at bias correction (as described by the FCM) are more likely. If motivation and ability to identify and correct for perceived biases are sufficiently high, people might use their perceptions of the bias(es) at work for the given situation and target to attempt to avoid the perceived bias(es). As described previously, this could result in corrections of different magnitudes and in different directions if the perceptions of bias differ across people, targets, or situations (see Wegener & Petty, 1997, 2001; Wegener, Petty, & Dunn, 1998, for additional discussion). Like the ELM, in the FCM processes are dissociated from outcomes. Thus the same outcome could be an "uncorrected" effect of mood (e.g., increased favorability in judgment because positive mood serves as a cue) or could be the result of a correction (e.g., increased favorability in judgment because of a correction for an expected contrast effect of positive mood).

Importantly, the different processes hypothesized by the ELM and FCM can result in different consequences for the "outcome." For instance, outcomes resulting from considerable thought should be stronger (e.g., more stable, resistant, etc.) than outcomes resulting from little thought (see Petty, Haugtvedt, & Smith, 1995; Wegener & Petty, 1997). This is true whether the outcome is uncorrected or corrected.

## Affect Infusion

Although the ELM and FCM were developed as general models of attitudes (or social judgment more generally) and are capable of dealing with a variety of variables (including affect), some models have been developed explicitly to deal with the impact of emotion on judgments. Perhaps the most comprehensive of these affect and judgment models is Forgas's (1992a, 1995a) affect infusion model (AIM). According to the AIM, mood can influence judgments through either "heuristic" or "substantive" processing. That is, mood could be used as a cue (following basically the "how do I feel about it?" heuristic; Cacioppo & Petty, 1982a; Schwarz & Clore, 1983) or could influence thoughts that come to mind during more effortful scrutiny of the attitude object (largely via mood-congruent memory processes; e.g., see Forgas & Bower, 1987). In addition, Forgas postulates that mood can influence whether heuristic or substantive processing occurs, with positive mood leading to heuristic and negative mood to substantive processing. Therefore, AIM hypotheses are somewhat similar to the ELM's multiple-roles perspective on affect that we outlined earlier (e.g., see Petty et al., 1991, 1988). The AIM also states that affect is *unlikely* to influence judgment when people retrieve a previously stored judgment (termed *direct access*) and that influences of mood can be overridden by strong motivations to pursue a particular outcome (called *motivated processing*).

This proposed difference in effects of mood under substantive versus heuristic processing is one important point of departure between the AIM and the ELM views. In the AIM, although some affect infusion is expected with heuristic processing, the impact of affect on judgments is expected to be greater when substantive processing enables mood-congruent memory processes to dominate (Forgas, 1994). That is, the "longer judges spend in substantive processing, the greater the infusion of affect into their judgments" (Forgas, 1994, p. 20). However, the evidence on this point is equivocal. In studies purported to directly measure substantive processing via response latencies, typical targets (expected to receive heuristic processing; Forgas, 1995a) show less mood congruency in judgments than atypical targets, and typical targets are judged more quickly (with longer response latencies being associated with larger mood congruence in judgment; e.g., Forgas, 1992b; see Forgas, 1995b). This pattern might suggest that larger mood-congruency effects are associated with more substantive processing, but it need not. It also seems plausible that typical targets receive a prestored judgment, whereas atypical targets receive judgments based on a heuristic use of mood. Alternatively, one could think of typical targets as receiving a judgment based on the category or stereotype associated with the relevant prototype. If one thinks of this as being an alternative salient heuristic, then the latency data could be used to argue that prestored heuristics are used more quickly than "generative" heuristics such as mood. These data are interesting and might ultimately be consistent with the AIM perspective (or other theories), but they might have little to say about substantive processing per se.[7] According to the ELM, there is no reason to believe that a heuristic use of mood will generally lead to less, equal, or greater impact on judgments than biased processing or mood-as-argument processes. The reason is that the size of each effect depends on such things as the salience of other potential cues in the environment, the ambiguity versus clarity of target-relevant information, the availability of relevant nonmood information, and so forth (see Petty et al., 1993, for equal mood effects under high- and low-elaboration settings).

Theoretical differences between the AIM and ELM go beyond the size of affect infusion effects. For example, the models diverge in their predictions about when and how mood has its effects. In the AIM, both heuristic use of mood and effects of mood on amount of processing occur only if the judgment is important (if the judgment is unimportant, direct access of a prior evaluation occurs). For the ELM, heuristic and other "direct" influences of mood (e.g., classical conditioning) are more likely at low rather than high elaboration likelihood (i.e., low rather than high importance of the attitude object or judgment), and effects of mood on amount of processing are most likely when the elaboration likelihood is not constrained to be high or low. Although the AIM predicts decreased processing in happy moods, as noted previously, research has shown that happy moods can either increase or decrease processing of judgment-relevant information (see Wegener et al., 1995). Finally, the AIM, like the ELM, does not deal with possible corrections for perceived effects of mood (see Petty & Wegener, 1999, for additional comparison of the ELM and AIM).

### Affect-as-Information

Though not formulated as a "multiprocess" theory in the same way as the previous views, as noted earlier in this chapter, affect-as-information (AAI) has been used as an explanation for different types of mood effects. Growing out of initial studies on the role of affect in interpersonal attraction (e.g., see Clore & Byrne, 1974), early discussions of affect-as-information stressed the use of feelings as a direct informational influence on judgments, occurring especially when the judgment related closely to affective criteria (e.g., judgments of liking or satisfaction; Schwarz, 1990; Schwarz & Clore, 1983). Although the informative functions of specific emotions have been thought to be more restricted than those of general moods, informative functions of specific emotions have also been found recently (see DeSteno et al., 2000). Schwarz and his colleagues have expanded the initial AAI perspective to in-

clude not only direct influence of mood on judgment but also effects of mood on the amount of scrutiny of incoming information. That is, as noted previously, positive moods are thought to inform people that the environment is safe and that effortful thought about the environment is unnecessary. Negative moods are thought to inform people that the environment is problematic and that effortful thought about the environment is needed (e.g., Bless et al., 1990; Schwarz, 1990).

Since the early 1990s a number of variants on the basic AAI theme have been proposed. First, mood was said to provide input into information processing without holding any meaning in and of itself (Martin, Ward, Achee, & Wyer, 1993). That is, instead of positive (or negative) moods necessarily informing people of a safe (or problematic) environment, mood was viewed as meaning different things in different situations. Therefore, if people are given an explicit rule to engage in a task until they feel they have done enough, negative moods lead to greater effort in the task than positive moods (because people in negative moods don't feel as if they have done enough). But, if people are asked to engage in the task until they no longer enjoy the task, they expend more effort if they are in a positive rather than a negative mood (because people in positive moods feel that they are still enjoying the task; see Hirt, Melton, McDonald & Harackiewicz, 1996; Martin et al., 1993). In a recent variation of this view, Martin et al. (1997) noted that the meaning of mood for judgment can also be rather "configural" in that certain settings can lead negative moods to suggest positive judgments of the target (e.g., when the experience of sad mood suggests to people that a sad story was a "good" sad story; see earlier discussion of affect as an argument).

Recently, Bless and colleagues (1996) suggested that mood effects on information processing were not tied to motivation (as in Schwarz, 1990) or capacity differences (Mackie & Worth, 1989) across moods. Rather, positive moods were thought to lead to reliance on general knowledge, and this reliance on general knowledge was responsible for the judgment outcomes that look like simplified processing. Bless et al. (1996) argued for this point of view based on happy people "recognizing" script-consistent information as having been presented in a brief story more often than people in a sad or neutral mood (regardless of whether or not the consistent information had actually been presented). In addition, happy people performed better on a secondary task that was completed while they listened to the story. This perspective was viewed as consistent with previous theorizing in that mood-based "information" that the environment is safe allows one to rely on general knowledge, but mood-based "information" that the environment is problematic focuses people on the specifics of the situation.

In an integrative account, Wyer, Clore, and Isbell (1999) argued that all of the previously identified AAI effects exist. One difference is that Wyer et al. go beyond the "global knowledge" version of AAI postulated by Bless et al. (1996) and argue that mood informs people about *whatever* they are currently thinking about a target. That is, positive moods inform people that both their current way of processing target-relevant information *and* the output of that processing are appropriate. In contrast, negative moods inform people that both their current way of processing target-relevant information and the output of that processing are inappropriate. This apparently holds regardless of whether or not one's current view of the target (or method of processing information) focuses on global or specific pieces of information. In addition, Wyer et al. (1999) diverge from past AAI theorizing regarding corrections for the perceived impact of mood. The AAI research has almost exclusively discussed mood as being discounted when people are made aware of the true source of the mood (i.e., the mood is "set aside" and the judgment is constructed using alternative information; Schwarz, 1990). According to Wyer et al. (1999), this discounting would not occur if feelings were the primary criterion for judgment. In such circumstances, theory-based corrections (as postulated in the FCM) would occur.

Much of this more recent AAI conceptualization awaits direct empirical tests. The most important questions for this research to address would involve when each of the proposed effects of mood is most likely to occur. Although some interesting speculations are provided by Wyer et al. (1999), some of the existing data seem in conflict with respect to when and why various AAI effects occur. For example, Wyer et al. expect that people should use affect as a direct basis for judgments when a message is "attitude focused" (because the message relates relatively closely to feelings about the advocacy—attitudes are taken to closely reflect affect) but should not do so when a message is "belief focused" (because the message does not relate closely to feelings). Moreover, this is expected regardless of processing objectives at the time (Wyer et al., 1999). Yet mood has been found to influence both beliefs about the likelihood of events described in a message and evaluations of the message advocacy (e.g., Wegener et al., 1994). In addition, there are many examples of "attitude-based" messages that have failed to show the mood main effect that should occur when affect is used as a direct basis for judgments (e.g., see Schwarz, Bless, & Bohner, 1991).

Many of the traditional AAI effects hold a great deal in common with effects described earlier from the ELM and FCM perspective. For example, Wyer et al. (1999) hypothesize that need for cognition (NC; Cacioppo & Petty, 1982b) represents an individual difference in the likelihood of applying a "performance" versus "enjoyment" criterion for engaging in intellectual activity. This, they note, might be why positive affect increased persistence on a thought-generation task for people high in NC but decreased persistence on the task for people low in NC (see

Martin et al., 1993). Alternatively, if high-NC people enjoy but low-NC people dislike these types of activities, this result could simply be indicative of hedonic contingency–based mood management (with happy moods increasing engagement in enjoyable activities but decreasing engagement with disliked activities; Wegener et al., 1995). In addition, Wyer et al. (1999) adopt the same theory-based corrections hypothesized in the FCM to form part of their approach. Perhaps in some ways, the various AAI theories are cutting up the same research pie into slightly different pieces. However, as noted earlier, there also seem to be some ways in which existing attitude-change data provide some challenges for the version of the AAI view introduced by Wyer et al. (1999). This will be an easier determination to make as the newest revision of the AAI view receives more direct empirical scrutiny.

## Summary

In this chapter we review the numerous ways in which affect contributes to attitudes and persuasion. First, affect has long been recognized as one of the important and measurable bases of attitudes. That is, across a wide variety of attitude objects and issues, emotional factors have been shown to be highly predictive of people's evaluations, although some attitudes are more dependent on affect than others. In addition, whether or not attitudes are consistent with the affect underlying an object has important consequences. When the affect associated with an object is consistent with the overall attitude toward that object, the attitude is more stable and resistant to pressure and predicts behavior better than when the attitude is inconsistent with object-relevant affect.

Just as attitudes can vary in their affective basis, so too can persuasive messages rely or not rely on affect. Preliminary research has demonstrated that the use of emotional tactics in persuasive messages, such as in fear appeals, can be effective but depends on a number of other variables. Emotions can also influence attitude change, even if they stem from sources extraneous to the persuasive communication. The impact of such emotions is the result of a diversity of processes. That is, such emotions can influence attitudes by low-effort peripheral mechanisms (such as classical conditioning), can serve as items of issue-relevant information, can bias message processing, and can determine the extent of message scrutiny. Furthermore, considerable research suggests that people sometimes correct for an anticipated biasing effect of emotion on their judgments. These corrections can reverse the typical effect of the emotion if people overcorrect and have an appropriate theory about the direction of bias. In understanding the role of emotions on attitudes, we rely mostly on the elaboration likelihood and flexible correction models but note that the affect infusion model and the various affect-as-information models allow unique predictions as well.

## NOTES

1. In the early attitude structure literature, affect, cognition, and behavior were referred to as *components* of attitudes, thereby implying that the attitude was made up of these elements. In more recent literature, these constructs have often been referred to as *bases* of attitudes. This term is more in line with contemporary theorizing that conceptualizes the attitude as a construct that is derived from these bases but somewhat separate from them. Throughout this chapter, we use the term *bases* to reflect this more contemporary perspective.

2. It is worth noting that a number of studies of attitude-cognitive consistency (e.g., Chaiken & Baldwin, 1981; Norman, 1975; Rosenberg, 1968) were originally framed as studies of affective-cognitive consistency. As we stated earlier, much of the early research on attitude bases defined affect either implicitly or explicitly in terms of general evaluations. Not surprisingly, a number of studies on affective-cognitive consistency thus measured affect using global evaluative (i.e., attitude) measures. However, more contemporary treatments of attitude bases have defined affect in terms of distinct emotions. Because we adopt the latter definition of attitude-relevant affect, we consider past studies using general evaluative measures of affect as examinations of attitude-cognitive consistency (see also Chaiken et al., 1995).

3. In this section and subsequent sections, we use the term *evaluative responses* to refer to inferences, evaluations, and other content-relevant responses generated in reaction to a persuasive communication. Such responses have traditionally been referred to as *cognitive responses* (e.g., see Petty, Ostrom, & Brock, 1981). However, this term implies a somewhat more narrow construal of the construct than presumably intended. Specifically, this term has usually been defined quite broadly to include any sort of message-topic-relevant evaluative response in reaction to the message (e.g., "I hate the message") and has not been used to imply that the response is predominantly cognitive in nature. Thus we use the more generic term *evaluative response*. More recently, some researchers have begun to distinguish between evaluative responses that are primarily affective or cognitive in nature (e.g., Ickes, Robertson, Tooke, & Teng, 1986). When making such distinctions in this chapter, we use the terms *affective responses* and *cognitive responses* to designate that responses are predominantly affective or cognitive in nature.

4. In the literature on fear appeals, a number of operationalizations of fear are used. In some, the high-fear message may include a greater number of negative consequences or negative consequences of greater severity than those used in the low-fear message; or the same consequences may be implied but depicted more vividly or repeated more times in the high- than low-fear message. In still other studies, the same message is given, but recipient reactions are assessed to determine fear. Or combinations of these features may be used to create high- and low-fear messages. Because of this complexity and confounding, some fear studies are open to alternative (non–fear-based) interpretations regarding the effectiveness (or lack thereof) of the fear appeal.

5. Some have argued that fear has opposite effects on some of the underlying-processes of persuasion (e.g., reducing reception but enhancing yielding). If so, then an inverted-U relationship might be expected between fear and persuasion (e.g., Janis, 1967; McGuire, 1969, 1985). This has not generally been observed (Boster & Mongeau, 1984), but perhaps the high levels of fear needed to obtain it have not been present in the available research.

6. Of course, mood would be less likely to exert a biasing impact on processing if there were salient and competing biasing factors operating—such as a strong prior attitude—or if the judgment-relevant information was completely unambiguous (see also Forgas, 1994).

7. In some studies that include response latencies for judgments, some mood effects have also been observed on recall (e.g., Forgas, 1995b; Forgas & Bower, 1987). Unfortunately, it has often not been clear if these recall patterns are "mood congruent" (e.g., sad mood leads to better recall of information about atypical targets, but happy mood leads to better recall of typical targets; Forgas, 1995b). Furthermore, these recall patterns have not been tested as mediators of mood effects on judgment. Therefore, the meaning of the existing studies for the AIM is not clear. "Substantive" processing might or might not be involved in the mood-congruent judgments obtained, and mood effects on memory might or might not play a role in these mood-congruent judgments.

## REFERENCES

Abelson, R. P., Kinder, D. R., Peters, M. D., & Fiske, S. T. (1982). Affective and semantic components in political person perception. *Journal of Personality of Social Psychology, 42*, 619–630.

Anderson, J. R., & Bower, G. H. (1973). *Human associative memory*. Washington, DC: Winston.

Bagozzi, R. P. (1978). The construct validity of the affective, behavioral, and cognitive components of attitude by the analysis of covariance structures. *Multivariate Behavioral Research, 13*, 9–31.

Bagozzi, R. P., & Burnkrant, R. E. (1979). Attitude organization and the attitude-behavior relationship. *Journal of Personality and Social Psychology, 37*, 913–929.

Baron, R. S., Inman, M. L., Kao, C. F., & Logan, H. (1992). Negative emotion and superficial social processing. *Motivation and Emotion, 16*, 323–346.

Batra, R., & Ahtola, O. T. (1990). Measuring the hedonic and utilitarian sources of consumer attitudes. *Marketing Letters, 2*, 159–170.

Batra, R., & Ray, M. L. (1985). How advertising works at contact. In L. Alwitt & A. Mitchell (Eds.), *Psychological processes and advertising effects: Theory, research, and applications* (pp. 13–43). Hillsdale, NJ: Erlbaum.

Batra, R., & Ray, M. L. (1986). Affective responses mediating acceptance of advertising. *Journal of Consumer Research, 13*, 234–249.

Beck, K. H., & Frankel, A. (1981). A conceptualization of threat communications and protective health behavior. *Social Psychology Quarterly, 44*, 204–217.

Becker, S. L. (1963). Research on emotional and logical proofs. *Southern Speech Journal, 28*, 198–207.

Bell, D. W., Esses, V. M., & Maio, G. R. (1996). The utility of open-ended measures to assess intergroup ambivalence. *Canadian Journal of Behavioural Science, 28*, 12–18.

Berkowitz, L., Jaffee, S., Jo, E., & Troccoli, B. (2000). On the correction of possible feeling-induced judgmental biases. In J. P. Forgas (Ed.), *Feeling and thinking: The role of affect in social cognition* (pp. 131–152). New York: Cambridge University Press.

Berkowitz, L., & Troccoli, B. T. (1990). Feelings, direction of attention, and expressed evaluations of others. *Cognition and Emotion, 4*, 305–325.

Biek, M., Wood, W., & Chaiken, S. (1996). Working knowledge, cognitive processing, and attitudes: On the determinants of bias. *Personality and Social Psychology Bulletin, 22*, 547–556.

Bless, H., Bohner, G., Schwarz, N., & Strack, F. (1990). Mood and persuasion: A cognitive response analysis. *Personality and Social Psychology Bulletin, 16*, 331–345.

Bless, H., Clore, G. L., Schwarz, N., Golisano, V., Rabe, C., & Wölk, M. (1996). Mood and the use of scripts: Does being in a happy mood really lead to mindlessness? *Journal of Personality and Social Psychology, 71*, 665–679.

Bohner, G., Crow, K., Erb, H. P., & Schwarz, N. (1992). Affect and persuasion: Mood effects on the processing of message content and context cues and on subsequent behavior. *European Journal of Social Psychology, 22*, 511–530.

Boster, F. J., & Mongeau, P. (1984). Fear-arousing persuasive messages. In R. N. Bostrom (Ed.), *Communication yearbook* (Vol. 8, pp. 330–375). Beverly Hills, CA: Sage.

Bower, G. (1981). Mood and memory. *American Psychologist, 36*, 129–148.

Bower, G., & Forgas, J. (2001). Mood and social memory. In J. P. Forgas (Ed.), *Handbook of affect and social cognition* (pp. 95–120). Hillsdale, NJ: Erlbaum.

Breckler, S. J. (1984). Empirical validation of affect, behavior, and cognition as distinct components of attitude. *Journal of Personality and Social Psychology, 47*, 1191–1205.

Breckler, S. J., & Wiggins, E. C. (1989). Affect versus evaluation in the structure of attitudes. *Journal of Experimental Social Psychology, 25*, 253–271.

Breckler, S. J., & Wiggins, E. C. (1991). Cognitive responses in persuasion: Affective and evaluative determinants. *Journal of Experimental Social Psychology, 27*, 180–200.

Cacioppo, J. T., & Berntson, G. (1994). Relationship between attitudes and evaluative space: A critical review, with emphasis on the separability of positive and negative substrates. *Psychological Bulletin, 115*, 401–423.

Cacioppo, J. T., Marshall-Goodell, B. S., Tassinary, L. G., & Petty, R. E. (1992). Rudimentary determinants of attitudes: Classical conditioning is more effective when prior knowledge about the attitude stimulus is low than high. *Journal of Experimental Social Psychology, 28*, 207–233.

Cacioppo, J. T., & Petty, R. E. (1979). The effects of message repetition and position on cognitive responses, recall, and persuasion. *Journal of Personality and Social Psychology, 37*, 97–109.

Cacioppo, J. T., & Petty, R. E. (1982a). A biosocial model of attitude change. In J. T. Cacioppo & R. E. Petty (Eds.), *Perspectives in cardiovascular psychophysiology* (pp. 151–188). New York: Guilford Press.

Cacioppo, J. T., & Petty, R. E. (1982b). The need for cognition. *Journal of Personality and Social Psychology, 42*, 116–131.

Cacioppo, J. T., Petty, R. E., & Geen, T. R. (1989). Attitude structure and function: From the tripartite to the ho-

meostasis model of attitudes. In A. Pratkanis, S. J. Breckler, & A. G. Greenwald (Eds.), *Attitude structure and function* (pp. 275–309). Hillsdale, NJ: Erlbaum.

Chaiken, S. (1987). The heuristic model of persuasion. In M. P. Zanna, J. M. Olson, & C. P. Herman (Ed.), *Social influence: The Ontario symposium* (Vol. 5, pp. 3–39). Hillsdale, NJ: Erlbaum.

Chaiken, S., & Baldwin, M. W. (1981). Affective-cognitive consistency and the effect of salient behavioral information on self-perception of attitudes. *Journal of Personality and Social Psychology, 41*, 1–12.

Chaiken, S., Liberman, A., & Eagly, A. (1989). Heuristic and systematic information processing within and beyond the persuasion context. In J. S. Uleman & J. A. Bargh (Eds.), *Unintended thought: Limits of awareness, intention, and control* (pp. 212–252). New York: Guilford Press.

Chaiken, S., & Maheswaran, D. (1994). Heuristic processing can bias systematic processing: Effects of source credibility, argument ambiguity, and task importance on attitude judgment. *Journal of Personality and Social Psychology, 66*, 460–473.

Chaiken, S., Pomerantz, E. M., & Giner-Sorolla, R. (1995). Structural consistency and attitude strength. In R. E. Petty & J. A. Krosnick (Eds.), *Attitude strength: Antecedents and consequences* (pp. 387–412). Mahwah, NJ: Erlbaum.

Chen, W. K. (1933). The influence of oral propaganda material upon students' attitudes. *Archives of Psychology, 150*, 43.

Cicero, M. T. (55 B.C./1970). *De oratore* (J. S. Watson, Trans.). Carbondale, IL: Southern Illinois University Press.

Clore, G. L., & Byrne, D. (1974). A reinforcement affect model of attraction. In T. L. Huston (Ed.), *Foundations of interpersonal attraction* (pp. 143–170). New York: Academic Press.

Cooper, J., & Fazio, R. H. (1984). A new look at dissonance theory. In L. Berkowitz (Ed.), *Advances in experimental social psychology* (Vol. 17, pp. 229–266). San Diego, CA: Academic Press.

Crites, S. L. Jr., Fabrigar, L. R., & Petty, R. E. (1994). Measuring the affective and cognitive properties of attitudes: Conceptual and methodological issues. *Personality and Social Psychology Bulletin, 20*, 619–634.

Cronkhite, G. L. (1964). Logic, emotion, and the paradigm of persuasion. *Quarterly Journal of Speech, 50*, 13–18.

Dermer, M., Cohen, S., Jacobsen, E., & Anderson, E. A. (1979). Evaluative judgments of aspects of life as a function of vicarious exposure to emotional extremes. *Journal of Personality and Social Psychology, 37*, 247–260.

DeSteno, D., Petty, R. E., Wegener, D. T., & Rucker, D. D. (2000). Beyond valence in the perception of likelihood: The role of emotion specificity. *Journal of Personality and Social Psychology, 78*, 397–416.

Ditto, P. H. Jemmott, J. B., & Darley, J. M. (1988). Appraising the threat of illness: A mental representational approach. *Health Psychology, 7*, 183–201.

Ditto, P. H., & Lopez, D. F. (1992). Motivated skepticism: Use of differential decision criteria for preferred and nonpreferred conclusions. *Journal of Personality and Social Psychology, 63*, 568–584.

Eagly, A. H., Mladinic, A., & Otto, S. (1994). Cognitive and affective bases of attitudes toward social groups and social policies. *Journal of Experimental Social Psychology, 30,* 113–137.

Edwards, K. (1990). The interplay of affect and cognition in attitude formation and change. *Journal of Personality and Social Psychology, 59,* 202–216.

Edwards, K., & von Hippel, W. (1995). Hearts and minds: The priority of affective versus cognitive factors in person perception. *Personality and Social Psychology Bulletin, 21,* 996–1011.

Eldersveld, S. J. (1956). Experimental propaganda techniques and voting behavior. *American Political Science Review, 50,* 154–165.

Epstein, S., & Rosemary, P. (1999). Some basic issues regarding dual-process theories, from the perspective of cognitive-experiential self-theory. In S. Chaiken & Y. Trope (Eds.), *Dual-process theories in social psychology* (pp. 462–482). New York: Guilford Press.

Fabrigar, L. R., & Petty, R. E. (1999). The role of the affective and cognitive bases of attitudes in susceptibility to affectively and cognitively based persuasion. *Personality and Social Psychology Bulletin, 25,* 363–381.

Festinger, L. (1957). *A theory of cognitive dissonance.* Palo Alto, CA: Stanford University Press.

Fishbein, M., & Ajzen, I. (1975). *Belief, attitude, intention, and behavior: An introduction to theory and research.* Reading, MA: Addison-Wesley.

Fishbein, M., & Middlestadt, S. (1995). Noncognitive effects on attitude formation and change: Fact or artifact? *Journal of Consumer Psychology, 4,* 181–202.

Forgas, J. P. (1992a). Affect in social judgments and decisions: A multiprocess model. In M. Zanna (Ed.), *Advances in experimental social psychology* (Vol. 25, pp. 227–275). San Diego, CA: Academic Press.

Forgas, J. P. (1992b). On bad mood and peculiar people: Affect and person typicality in impression formation. *Journal of Personality and Social Psychology, 62,* 863–875.

Forgas, J. P. (1994). The role of emotion in social judgments: An introductory review and an affect infusion model (AIM). *European Journal of Social Psychology, 24,* 1–24.

Forgas, J. P. (1995a). Mood and judgment: The affect infusion model (AIM). *Psychological Bulletin, 117,* 39–66.

Forgas, J. P. (1995b). Strange couples: Mood effects on judgments and memory about prototypical and atypical relationships. *Personality and Social Psychology Bulletin, 21,* 747–765.

Forgas, J. P., & Bower, G. H. (1987). Mood effects on person perception judgments. *Journal of Personality and Social Psychology, 53,* 53–60.

Forgas, J. P., & Moylan, S. (1987). After the movies: Transient moods and social judgments. *Personality and Social Psychology Bulletin, 13,* 467–477.

Gleicher, F., & Petty, R. E. (1992). Expectations of reassurance influence the nature of fear-stimulated attitude change. *Journal of Experimental Social Psychology, 28,* 86–100.

Gouaux, C. (1971). Induced affective states and interpersonal attraction. *Journal of Personality and Social Psychology, 20,* 37–43.

Granberg, D., & Brown, T. A. (1989). On affect and cognition in politics. *Social Psychology Quarterly, 52,* 171–182.

Griffit, W. B. (1970). Environmental effects on interpersonal affective behavior: Ambient effective temperature and attraction. *Journal of Personality and Social Psychology, 15,* 240–244.

Haddock, G., & Zanna, M. P. (1998a). Assessing the impact of affective and cognitive information in predicting attitudes toward capital punishment. *Law and Human Behavior, 22,* 325–339.

Haddock, G., & Zanna, M. P. (1998b). On the use of open-ended measures to assess attitudinal components. *British Journal of Social Psychology, 37,* 129–149.

Haddock, G., & Zanna, M. P., & Esses, V. M. (1993). Assessing the structure of prejudicial attitudes: The case of attitudes toward homosexuals. *Journal of Personality and Social Psychology, 65,* 1105–1118.

Haddock, G., & Zanna, M. P., & Esses, V. M. (1994). The (limited) role of trait-laden stereotypes in predicting attitudes toward Native peoples. *British Journal of Social Psychology, 33,* 83–106.

Harmon-Jones, E., & Mills, J. (Eds.). (1999). *Cognitive dissonance: Progress on a pivotal theory in social psychology.* Washington, DC: American Psychological Association.

Hartman, G. W. (1936). A field experiment on the comparative effectiveness of "emotional" and "rational" political leaflets in determining election results. *Journal of Abnormal and Social Psychology, 31,* 99–114.

Hirt, E. R., Melton, R. J., McDonald, H. E., & Harackiewicz, J. M. (1996). Processing goals, task interest, and the mood-performance relationship: A mediational analysis. *Journal of Personality and Social Psychology, 71,* 245–261.

Ickes, W., Robertson, E., Tooke, W., & Teng, G. (1986). Naturalistic social cognition: Methodology, assessment, and validation. *Journal of Personality and Social Psychology, 51,* 66–82.

Insko, C. A., & Schopler, J. (1967). Triadic consistency: A statement of affective-cognitive-conative consistency. *Psychological Review, 74,* 361–376.

Isbell, L., & Wyer, R. S. (1999). Correcting for mood-induced bias in the evaluation of political candidates: The role of intrinsic and extrinsic motivation. *Personality and Social Psychology Bulletin, 25,* 237–249.

Isen, A. M., Shalker, T., Clark, M. S., & Karp, L. (1978). Affect, accessibility of material in memory, and behavior: A cognitive loop? *Journal of Personality and Social Psychology, 36,* 1–12.

Janis, I. L. (1967). Effects of fear arousal on attitude change: Recent developments in theory and experimental research. In L. Berkowitz (Ed.), *Advances in experimental social psychology* (Vol. 3, pp. 166–224). San Diego, CA: Academic Press.

Janis, I. L., & Feshbach, S. (1953). Effects of fear-arousing communications. *Journal of Abnormal and Social Psychology, 48,* 78–92.

Janis, I. L., Kaye, D., & Kirschner, P. (1965). Facilitating effects of "eating while reading" on responsiveness to persuasive communications. *Journal of Personality and Social Psychology, 1,* 181–186.

Jepson, C., & Chaiken, S. (1990). Chronic issue-specific fear inhibits systematic processing of persuasive communications. *Journal of Social Behavior and Personality, 5,* 61–84.

Johnson, E., & Tversky, A. (1983). Affect, generalization, and the perception of risk. *Journal of Personality and Social Psychology, 45,* 20–31.

Kaplan, K. J. (1972). On the ambivalence-indifference problem in attitude theory and measurement: A suggested modification of the semantic differential technique. *Psychological Review, 77,* 361–372.

Katz, D., & Stotland, E. (1959). A preliminary statement to a theory of attitude structure and change. In S. Koch (Ed.), *Psychology: A study of a science: Vol. 3. Formulations of the person and the social context* (pp. 423–475). New York: McGraw-Hill.

Keller, P. A., & Block, L. G. (1995). Increasing the persuasiveness of fear appeals: The effect of arousal and elaboration. *Journal of Consumer Research, 22,* 448–459.

Knepprath, E., & Clevenger, T., Jr. (1965). Reasoned discourse and motive appeals in selected political speeches. *Quarterly Journal of Speech, 51,* 152–156.

Knower, F. H. (1935). Experimental studies of change in attitude: I. A study of the effect of oral arguments on changes of attitudes. *Journal of Social Psychology, 6,* 315–347.

Kothandapani, V. (1971). Validation of feeling, belief, and intention to act as three components of attitude and their contribution to prediction of contraceptive behavior. *Journal of Personality and Social Psychology, 19,* 321–333.

Kuykendall, D., & Keating, J. (1990). Mood and persuasion: Evidence for the differential influence of positive and negative states. *Psychology and Marketing, 7,* 1–9.

Lavine, H., Thomsen, C. J., Zanna, M. P., & Borgida, E. (1998). On the primacy of affect in the determination of attitudes and behavior: The moderating role of affective-cognitive ambivalence. *Journal of Experimental Social Psychology, 34,* 398–421.

Mackie, D. M., Asuncion, A. G., & Rosselli, F. (1992). Impact of positive affect on persuasion processes. *Review of Personality and Social Psychology, 14,* 247–270.

Mackie, D. M., & Worth, L. T. (1989). Cognitive deficits and the mediation of positive affect in persuasion. *Journal of Personality and Social Psychology, 57,* 27–40.

Martin, L. L., Abend, T. A., Sedikides, C., & Green, J. (1997). How would I feel if . . . ? Mood as input to a role fulfillment evaluation process. *Journal of Personality and Social Psychology, 73,* 242–253.

Martin, L. L., Seta, J. J., & Crelia, R. A. (1990). Assimilation and contrast as a function of people's willingness and ability to expend effort in forming an impression. *Journal of Personality and Social Psychology, 59,* 27–37.

Martin, L. L., Ward, D. W., Achee, J. W., & Wyer, R. S. (1993). Mood as input: People have to interpret the motivational implications of their moods. *Journal of Personality and Social Psychology, 64,* 317–326.

Matthews, J. (1947). The effect of loaded language on audience comprehension of speeches. *Speech Monographs, 14,* 176–187.

Mayer, J., Gaschke, Y., Braverman, D., & Evans, T. (1992). Mood-congruent judgment is a general effect. *Journal of Personality and Social Psychology, 63,* 119–132.

McClelland, J. L., Rumelhart, D. E., & Hinton, G. E. (1986). The appeal of parallel distributed processing. In D. E. Rumelhart, J. L. McClelland, & The PDP Research Group (Eds.). *Parallel distributed processing* (Vol. 1, pp. 3–44). Cambridge, MA: MIT Press.

McGuire, W. J. (1969). The nature of attitudes and attitude change. In G. Lindzey & E. Aronson (Eds.), *The handbook of social psychology* (2nd ed., Vol. 3, pp. 136–314). Reading, MA: Addison-Wesley.

McGuire, W. J. (1985). Attitudes and attitude change. In G. Lindzey & E. Aronson (Eds.), *The handbook of social psychology* (3rd ed., Vol. 2, pp. 233–346). New York: Random House.

Menefee, S. C., & Granneberg, A. G. (1940). Propaganda and opinions on foreign policy. *Journal of Social Psychology, 11,* 393–404.

Messé, L. A., Bodenhausen, G. V., & Nelson, T. D. (1995). *Affect-cognition congruence and attitude change: A reexamination.* Paper presented at the annual convention of the American Psychological Society, New York.

Millar, M. G. (1992). Effects of experience on matched and mismatched arguments and attitudes. *Social Behavior and Personality, 20,* 47–56.

Millar, M. G., & Millar, K. U. (1990). Attitude change as a function of attitude type and argument type. *Journal of Personality and Social Psychology, 59,* 217–228.

Millar, M. G., & Millar, K. U. (1993). Changing breast self-examination attitudes: Influences of repression-sensitization and attitude-message match. *Journal of Research in Personality, 27,* 301–314.

Millar, M. G., & Millar, K. U. (1996). The effects of direct and indirect experience on affective and cognitive responses and the attitude-behavior relation. *Journal of Experimental Social Psychology, 32,* 561–579.

Millar, M. G., & Millar, K. U. (1998). The effects of prior experience and thought on the attitude-behavior relation. *Social Behavior and Personality, 26,* 105–114.

Millar, M. G., & Tesser, A. (1986). Effects of affective and cognitive focus on the attitude-behavior relation. *Journal of Personality and Social Psychology, 51,* 270–276.

Millar, M. G., & Tesser, A. (1989). The effects of affective-cognitive consistency and thought on the attitude-behavior relation. *Journal of Experimental Social Psychology, 25,* 189–202.

Mulilis, J., & Lippa, R. (1990). Behavioral change in earthquake preparedness due to negative threat appeals: A test of protection motivation theory. *Journal of Applied Social Psychology, 20,* 619–638.

Munro, G. D., & Ditto, P. H. (1997). Biased assimilation, attitude polarization, and affect in reactions to stereotype-relevant scientific information. *Personality and Social Psychology Bulletin, 23,* 636–653.

Norman, R. (1975). Affective-cognitive consistency, attitudes, conformity, and behavior. *Journal of Personality and Social Psychology, 32,* 83–91.

Ostrom, T. M. (1969). The relationship between the affective, behavioral and cognitive components of attitude. *Journal of Experimental Social Psychology, 5,* 12–30.

Ottati, V. C. (1997). When the survey question directs retrieval: Implications for assessing the cognitive and affective predictors of global evaluation. *European Journal of Social Psychology, 27,* 1–21.

Ottati, V. C., & Isbell, L. M. (1996). Effects of mood during exposure to target information on subsequently reported judgments: An on-line model of misattribution and correction. *Journal of Personality and Social Psychology, 71,* 39–53.

Pallak, S. R., Murroni, E., & Koch, J. (1983). Communicator attractiveness and expertise, emotional versus rational appeals, and persuasion: A heuristic versus systematic processing interpretation. *Social Cognition, 2,* 122–141.

Petty, R. E. (1997). The evolution of theory and research in social psychology: From single to multiple effect and process models. In C. McGarty & S. A. Haslam (Eds.), *The message of social psychology: Perspectives on mind in society* (pp. 268–290). Oxford, England: Blackwell.

Petty, R. E., & Cacioppo, J. T. (1981). *Attitudes and persuasion: Classic and contemporary approaches.* Dubuque, IA: Brown.

Petty, R. E., & Cacioppo, J. T. (1986a). *Communication and persuasion: Central and peripheral routes to attitude change.* New York: Springer-Verlag.

Petty, R. E., & Cacioppo, J. T. (1986b). The elaboration likelihood model of persuasion. In L. Berkowitz (Ed.), *Advances in experimental social psychology* (Vol. 19, pp. 123–205). New York: Academic Press.

Petty, R. E., & Cacioppo, J. T., & Kasmer, J. (1988). The role of affect in the elaboration likelihood model of persuasion. In L. Donohew, H. Sypher, & E. T. Higgins (Eds.), *Communication, social cognition, and affect* (pp. 117–146). Hillsdale, NJ: Erlbaum.

Petty, R. E., Gleicher, F., & Baker, S. M. (1991). Multiple roles for affect in persuasion. In J. Forgas (Ed.), *Emotion and social judgments* (pp. 181–200). New York: Pergamon Press.

Petty, R. E., Haugtvedt, C. P., & Smith, S. M. (1995). Elaboration as a determinant of attitude strength. In R. E. Petty & J. A. Krosnick (Eds.), *Attitude strength: Antecedents and consequences* (pp. 93–130). Mahwah, NJ: Erlbaum.

Petty, R. E., Ostrom, T. M., & Brock, T. C. (1981). *Cognitive responses in persuasion.* Hillsdale, NJ: Erlbaum.

Petty, R. E., Schumann, D. W., Richman, S. A., & Strathman, A. J. (1993). Positive mood and persuasion: Different roles for affect under high and low elaboration conditions. *Journal of Personality and Social Psychology, 64,* 5–20.

Petty, R. E., & Wegener, D. T. (1991). Thought systems, argument quality, and persuasion. In R. S. Wyer & T. K. Srull (Eds.), *Advances in social cognition* (Vol. 4, pp. 143–161). Hillsdale, NJ: Erlbaum.

Petty, R. E., & Wegener, D. T. (1993). Flexible correction processes in social judgment: Correcting for context-induced contrast. *Journal of Experimental Social Psychology, 29,* 137–165.

Petty, R. E., & Wegener, D. T. (1998). Attitude change: Multiple roles for persuasion variables. In D. T. Gilbert, S. T. Fiske, & G. Lindzey (Eds.), *The handbook of social psychology* (4th ed., Vol. 1, pp. 323–390). New York: McGraw-Hill.

Petty, R. E., & Wegener, D. T. (1999). The elaboration likelihood model: Current status and controversies. In S. Chaiken & Y. Trope (Eds.), *Dual-process theories in social psychology* (pp. 41–72). New York: Guilford Press.

Perry, R. E., Wegener, D. T., Fabrigar, L. R., Priester, J. R., & Cacioppo, J. T. (1993). Conceptual and methodological issues in the Elaboration Likelihood Model of persuasion: A reply to the Michigan State critics. *Communication Theory, 3,* 336–362.

Petty, R. E., Wegener, D. T., & White, P. (1998). Flexible correction processes in social judgment: Implications for persuasion. *Social Cognition, 16,* 93–113.

Petty, R. E., Wells, G. L., & Brock, T. C. (1976). Distraction can enhance or reduce yielding to propaganda: Thought disruption versus effort justification. *Journal of Personality and Social Psychology, 34,* 874–884.

Priester, J. R., Cacioppo, J. T., & Petty, R. E. (1996). The influence of motor processes on attitudes toward novel versus familiar semantic stimuli. *Personality and Social Psychology Bulletin, 22,* 442–447.

Priester, J. M., & Petty, R. E. (1996). The gradual threshold model of ambivalence: Relating the positive and nega-

tive bases of attitudes to subjective ambivalence. *Journal of Personality and Social Psychology, 71,* 431–449.

Razran, G. H. S. (1940). Conditioned response changes in rating and appraising sociopolitical slogans. *Psychological Bulletin, 37,* 481.

Rippetoe, P. A., & Rogers, R. W. (1987). Effects of components of protection-motivation theory on adaptive and maladaptive coping with a health threat. *Journal of Personality and Social Psychology, 52,* 596–604.

Rogers, R. W. (1975). A protection motivation theory of fear appeals and attitude change. *Journal of Psychology, 91,* 93–114.

Rogers, R. W. (1983). Cognitive and physiological processes in fear appeals and attitude change: A revised theory of protection motivation. In J. T. Cacioppo & R. E. Petty (Eds.), *Social psychophysiology: A sourcebook* (pp. 153–176). New York: Guilford Press.

Rogers, R. W., & Mewborn, C. R. (1976). Fear appeals and attitude change: Effects of a threat's noxiousness, probability of occurrence, and the efficacy of coping responses. *Journal of Personality and Social Psychology, 34,* 54–61.

Rosenberg, M. J. (1960). An analysis of affective-cognitive consistency. In M. Rosenberg, C. Hovland, W. McGuire, R. Abelson, & J. Brehm (Eds.), *Attitude organization and change* (pp. 15–64). New Haven, CT: Yale University Press.

Rosenberg, M. J. (1968). Hedonism, inauthenticity, and other goals toward expansion of consistency theory. In R. P. Abelson, E. Aronson, W. J. McGuire, T. M. Newcomb, M. J. Rosenberg, & P. H. Tannenbaum (Eds.), *Theories of cognitive consistency: A sourcebook* (pp. 73–111). Chicago: Rand McNally.

Rosenberg, M. J., & Hovland, C. I. (1960). Cognitive, affective, and behavioral components of attitudes. In C. I. Hovland & M. J. Rosenberg (Eds.), *Attitude organization and change: An analysis of consistency among attitude components* (pp. 1–14). New Haven, CT: Yale University Press.

Rosselli, F., Skelly, J. J., & Mackie, D. M. (1995). Processing rational and emotional messages: The cognitive and affective mediation of persuasion. *Journal of Experimental Social Psychology, 31,* 163–190.

Ruechelle, R. C. (1958). An experimental study of audience recognition of emotional and intellectual appeals in persuasion. *Speech Monographs, 25,* 49–58.

Schwarz, N. (1990). Feelings as information: Informational and motivational functions of affective states. In R. M. Sorrentino & E. T. Higgins (Eds.), *Handbook of motivation and cognition: Foundations of social behavior* (Vol. 2, pp. 527–561). New York: Guilford Press.

Schwarz, N., Bless, H., & Bohner, G. (1991). Mood and persuasion: Affective states influence the processing of persuasive communications. In M. P. Zanna (Ed.), *Advances in experimental social psychology* (Vol. 24, pp. 161–199). San Diego, CA: Academic Press.

Schwarz, N., & Clore, G. L. (1983). Mood, misattribution, and judgments of well-being: Informative and directive functions of affective states. *Journal of Personality and Social Psychology, 45,* 513–523.

Schwarz, N., & Clore, G. L. (1988). How do I feel about it? Informative functions of affective states. In K. Fiedler & J. Forgas (Eds.), *Affect, cognition, and social behavior* (pp. 44–62). Göttingen, Germany: Hogrefe.

Schwarz, N., & Clore, G. L. (1996). Feelings and phenomenal experiences. In E. T. Higgins & A. W. Kruglanski

(Eds.), *Social psychology: Handbook of basic principles* (pp. 433–465). New York: Guilford Press.

Simons, J., & Carey, K. B. (1998). A structural analysis of attitudes toward alcohol and marijuana use. *Personality and Social Psychology Bulletin, 24,* 727–735.

Sinclair, R. C., Mark, M. M., & Clore, G. L. (1994). Mood related persuasion depends on (mis)attributions. *Social Cognition, 12,* 309–326.

Smith, E. R. (1996). What do connectionism and social psychology offer each other? *Journal of Personality and Social Psychology, 70,* 893–912.

Smith, M. B. (1947). The personal setting of public opinions: A study of attitudes toward Russia. *Public Opinion Quarterly, 11,* 507–523.

Srull, T. K. (1983). The role of prior knowledge in the acquisition, retention, and use of new information. *Advances in Consumer Research, 10,* 572–576.

Staats, A. W., & Staats, C. K. (1958). Attitudes established by classical conditioning. *Journal of Abnormal and Social Psychology, 57,* 37–40.

Stangor, C., Sullivan, L. A., & Ford, T. E. (1991). Affective and cognitive determinants of prejudice. *Social Cognition, 9,* 359–380.

Strathman, A. J. (1992). *Investigation of the influence of need for cognition on attitude-behavior consistency.* Unpublished doctoral dissertation, Ohio State University.

Sutton, S. R. (1982). Fear-arousing communications: A critical examination of theory and research. In J. R. Eiser (Ed.), *Social psychology and behavioral medicine* (pp. 303–337). Chichester, England: Wiley.

Thompson, M. M., Zanna, M. P., & Griffin, D. W. (1995). Let's not be indifferent about attitudinal ambivalence. In R. E. Petty & J. A. Krosnick (Eds.), *Attitude strength: Antecedents and consequences* (pp. 361–386). Mahwah, NJ: Erlbaum.

Wegener, D. T., Dunn, M., & Tokusato, D. (2001). The flexible correction model: Phenomenology and the use of naive theories in avoiding or removing bias. In G. Moskowitz (Ed.), *Cognitive social psychology: On the tenure and future of social cognition* (pp. 277–290). Mahwah, NJ: Erlbaum.

Wegener, D. T., & Petty, R. E. (1994). Mood management across affective states: The hedonic contingency hypothesis. *Journal of Personality and Social Psychology, 66,* 1034–1048.

Wegener, D. T., & Petty, R. E. (1996). Effects of mood on persuasion processes: Enhancing, reducing, and biasing scrutiny of attitude-relevant information. In L. L. Martin & A. Tesser (Eds.), *Striving and feeling: Interactions among goals, affect, and self-regulation* (pp. 329–362). Mahwah, NJ: Erlbaum.

Wegener, D. T., & Petty, R. E. (1997). The flexible correction model: The role of naïve theories of bias in bias correction. In M. P. Zanna (Ed.), *Advances in experimental social psychology* (Vol. 29, pp. 141–208). New York: Academic Press.

Wegener, D. T., & Petty, R. E. (2001). Understanding effects of mood through the elaboration likelihood and flexible correction models. In L. L. Martin & G. L. Clore (Eds.), *Theories of mood and cognition: A user's guidebook* (pp. 177–210). Mahwah, NJ: Erlbaum.

Wegener, D. T., Petty, R. E., & Dunn, M. (1998). The metacognition of bias correction: Naive theories of bias and the flexible correction model. In V. Yzerbyt, G. Lories, & B. Dardenne (Eds.), *Metacognition: Cognitive and social dimensions* (pp. 202–227). London: Sage.

Wegener, D. T., Petty, R. E., & Klein, D. J. (1994). Effects of mood on high elaboration attitude change: The mediating role of likelihood judgments. *European Journal of Social Psychology, 24,* 25–43.

Wegener, D. T., Petty, R. E., & Smith, S. M. (1995). Positive mood can increase or decrease message scrutiny: The hedonic contingency view of mood and message processing. *Journal of Personality and Social Psychology, 69,* 5–15.

Weiss, W. (1960). Emotional arousal and attitude change. *Psychological Reports, 6,* 267–280.

Weiss, W., & Fine, B. J. (1956). The effect of induced aggressiveness on opinion change. *Journal of Abnormal and Social Psychology, 52,* 109–114.

Witte, K. (1992). Putting the fear back into fear appeals: The extended parallel process model. *Communication Monographs, 59,* 329–349.

Wyer, R. S., Clore, G. L., & Isbell, L. M. (1999). Affect and information processing. In M. P. Zanna (Ed.), *Advances in experimental social psychology* (Vol. 31, pp. 1–77). San Diego, CA: Academic Press.

Zajonc, R. B., & Markus, H. (1982). Affective and cognitive factors in preferences. *Journal of Consumer Research, 9,* 123–131.

Zanna, M. P., & Cooper, J. (1974). Dissonance and the pill: An attribution approach to studying the arousal properties of dissonance. *Journal of Personality and Social Psychology, 29,* 703–709.

Zanna, M. P., Kiesler, C. A., & Pilkonis, P. A. (1970). Positive and negative attitudinal affect established by classical conditioning. *Journal of Personality and Social Psychology, 14,* 321–328.

Zanna, M. P., & Rempel, J. K. (1988). Attitudes: A new look at an old concept. In D. Bar-Tal & A. W. Kruglanski (Eds.), *The social psychology of knowledge* (pp. 315–334). Cambridge, England: Cambridge University Press.

Zillmann, D. (1983). Transfer of excitation in emotional behavior. In J. T. Cacioppo & R. E. Petty (Eds.), *Social psychophysiology: A sourcebook* (pp. 153–176). New York: Guilford Press.

Zuwerink, J. R., & Devine, P. G. (1996). Attitude importance and resistance to persuasion: It's not just the thought that counts. *Journal of Personality and Social Psychology, 70,* 931–944.

# 40

# THE SELF AND EMOTION: THE ROLE OF SELF-REFLECTION IN THE GENERATION AND REGULATION OF AFFECTIVE EXPERIENCE

Mark R. Leary

The evolution of the human self constituted a quantum shift in mammalian psychology. Although some of our prehuman ancestors may have had rudimentary forms of self-awareness, much like modern chimpanzees and orangutans (Gallup & Suarez, 1986), the capacity to think about oneself in the complex, abstract, and symbolic ways that characterize modern human beings did not appear until relatively recently in the evolutionary past. Of course, no one knows precisely when the human ability for self-reflection first emerged, but evidence suggests that it could have been as recently as 40,000 years ago (Leary & Cottrell, 1999; for other views, see Jaynes, 1976; Sedikides & Skowronski, 1997).

The earliest human beings, who appeared about 100,000 years ago, left little evidence to suggest that they were self-aware (Mithen, 1996). Only between around 40,000 and 60,000 years ago does the archeological record begin to indicate that people were able to engage in the full range of behaviors that require self-awareness and self-focused thought. Whereas human culture—if it can be called that—prior to about 60,000 years ago consisted mostly of rough stone tools, after that time, we see indications that people could think of themselves in complex ways. For the first time, we find clear evidence of personal adornment (which requires one to imagine oneself from others' perspectives), anthropomorphism and totemism (which requires thinking of oneself as an animal and vice versa), boat making (which requires long-range planning),

and burials that include grave goods (indicating the ability to imagine oneself after death). Mithen (1996) discussed several cognitive changes that may have precipitated the "cultural big bang" that occurred between 40,000 and 60,000 years ago, but self-reflexive thinking seems to have been involved. All of these cultural advances required a sophisticated ability to imagine oneself in the future or to think about oneself from the perspectives of other people (Leary & Cottrell, 1999). After millions of years in which life forms on earth lacked self-awareness, creatures finally appeared who could take themselves as the objects of their own thoughts and think consciously about themselves.

The evolution of self-awareness had important implications for the emotional experiences of human beings. Of course, animals who lack the ability to self-reflect experience emotions, so a sense of self is clearly not necessary for emotional experience. Yet, as we will see, having a sense of self has important implications for the stimuli that trigger affective states, the kinds of emotions one experiences, and whether one can consciously regulate one's feelings.

## The Nature of the Self

"Self" has been a problematic construct in psychology, partly because of psychologists' traditional ambivalence about mentalistic terms and partly because of carelessness

773

and inconsistency in how the term has been used. The self was a central construct in the early days of behavioral science (see James, 1890), but with the advent of behaviorism, the concept of self fell out of favor, along with other hypothetical constructs that could not be observed and measured directly. Even so, during the middle part of the 20th century, the self maintained a foothold within personality psychology, in which it appeared in the writings of theorists from many theoretical orientations, including Allport, Murray, Adler, Sullivan, and Horney. The humanistic perspective in particular gave the self a prominent place, as reflected in the work of Rogers, Maslow, and Jourard.

During the 1970s, the self reemerged into mainstream psychology, riding on the wave of the cognitive revolution. The popularity and obvious usefulness of cognitive perspectives again made it fashionable to study mental processes, and so behavioral scientists no longer shied away from the self. Today, the self is an exceptionally popular topic, being studied by researchers in virtually every domain of psychology (for reviews, see Baumeister, 1998; Hoyle, Kernis, Leary, & Baldwin, 1999).

Many definitions of self have been offered over the years, differing in their emphasis and focus. For our purposes, the essence of the self involves the ability to take oneself as the object of one's own attention and thought. People may have beliefs and feelings about themselves (encompassing constructs such as identity, self-concept, self-schema, and self-esteem), but these cognitions and emotions are not the self per se. Rather, the self is the cognitive mechanism that permits self-reflexive thought.

Evidence suggests that most animals lack a self in that they do not have the ability to think consciously about themselves except in the most rudimentary ways. All organisms seem to have the ability to distinguish, at least phenomenologically, between themselves and the rest of the world (animals do not eat their own flesh, for example) and thus possess what has been called "subjective self-awareness." However, only a few animals—including chimpanzees, orangutans, and human beings—have a self that is sophisticated enough to permit self-recognition and self-referential behavior (Gallup & Suarez, 1986; Parker, Mitchell, & Boccia, 1994), and only human beings appear to be able to think about themselves in highly abstract and symbolic ways (thus, possessing what Sedikides & Skowronski, 1997, call "symbolic self-awareness").

Two aspects of symbolic self-awareness are particularly important to understanding the role of the self in emotional experience. First, having a self allows people to create a cognitive "analogue-I" (Jaynes, 1976) that they then use as a mental stand-in for themselves. Through the "eyes" of their analogue-I, they can imagine themselves in other situations, intentionally plan for the future, consider behavioral options, mentally rehearse future actions, ret-

rospectively imagine how events might have turned out differently, and even contemplate their mortality.

Second, an organism capable of symbolic self-awareness can create a mental representation of itself, thus allowing it to think about its own characteristics and behaviors. This representation may be visual (i.e., I can "see" myself in my own mind) or descriptive (i.e., I can define, label, and otherwise characterize myself). Furthermore, symbolic self-awareness allows animals with a self to evaluate these mental representations of themselves. Although all animals can assess the adequacy of their ongoing behavior in accomplishing goals, only animals with a self can step back and evaluate themselves and their behavior according to abstract standards, then react to the symbolic meaning of those self-evaluations.

Even for animals that have a self, however, that self is not always "turned on." People move in and out of self-awareness and spend much of their lives in a non–self-aware state (Carver & Scheier, 1985; Duval & Wicklund, 1972). In some situations, they think consciously about themselves—imagining what might happen to them, considering options and their implications, pondering their attributes and motives, evaluating themselves, and so on. In other situations, however, people are not self-aware but rather are focused on the external environment or, sometimes, on nothing at all. People often function quite well without self-awareness, easily engaging in habitual actions such as eating, walking, talking, driving, reading, singing, and making love without devoting conscious attention to themselves (although, of course, the self may be active during these activities).

## Emotion With and Without a Self

Animals clearly do not need a self in order to experience emotion. Although we cannot know for sure what animals feel, their behavior suggests that they experience a wide array of emotions, including fear, sadness, joy, and rage (Darwin, 1872/1998; Masson & McCarthy, 1995). The emotional reactions of animals that do not have a self (and, for that matter, the emotions of human beings when they are not self-aware) are controlled by two primary processes. First, many stimuli naturally and automatically evoke emotions. One obvious example involves stimuli that cause fear without learning or prior experience. Most species react naturally with fear to certain threat cues; for example, the silhouette of a hawk in flight elicits fear in ducks and the threat gesture of a dominant member of the group causes fear in monkeys. Human beings may also be innately prepared to experience fear in response to certain stimuli. For example, objects that "loom" appear to create fear automatically (particularly if they are perceived as approaching; Riskind, 1997), as does a sudden loss of physical support (as when one begins to fall or an elevator lurches suddenly).

Second, emotions may be conditioned to previously neutral stimuli through classical conditioning. For example, human and nonhuman animals may come to respond with negative emotions to an otherwise neutral stimulus that has been paired with aversive stimuli or to respond with positive emotions to a neutral stimulus that has been associated with rewarding events. (Watson's conditioning of Little Albert was an early demonstration of this effect.)

Both of these processes—involving species-specific behavior and classical conditioning, respectively—can occur without conscious self-awareness. However, the capacity for self-relevant thought renders an organism's emotional life far more extensive and complex than that of self-less animals. In the remainder of this chapter, we examine five ways in which the possession of a self affects emotional experience. Specifically, having a self permits people to (1) evoke emotions in themselves by imagining self-relevant events, (2) react emotionally to abstract and symbolic images of themselves in their own minds, (3) consciously contemplate the cause of their emotions, (4) experience emotions by thinking about how they are perceived by other people, and (5) deliberately regulate their emotional experience.

## Imagined Self-Relevant Events

Although we do not know for certain, it seems plausible that nonhuman animals may experience emotions in response to memories of past events. Darwin (1902) thought so, asking whether we can be sure "that an old dog with an excellent memory and some power of imagination, as shewn by his dreams, never reflects on his past pleasures in the chase?" (p. 118). Although animals without a self may experience emotions in response to spontaneous memories of actual events, they would presumably not react emotionally to thinking about what may befall them in the future nor to purely imagined experiences that have no basis in reality whatsoever. Without the ability to create the analogue-I in consciousness, they could not imagine themselves in situations that had not actually occurred. In contrast, people are quite good at evoking emotions in themselves simply by imaging themselves in various situations, and they may even work themselves into an emotional frenzy by doing so. The ability to self-reflect allows human beings to react emotionally to stimuli and events that exist only inside their own heads.

### Imagining Oneself

Many of people's emotional experiences occur not because anything has happened to them but because they imagine something happening. People can experience strong emotions by reliving real past experiences in their own minds, by anticipating things that may happen in the future, and even by imagining events that have neither happened in the past nor have much likelihood of happening later. The past, anticipated, and fantasized experiences of the analogue-I often have the emotional potency of real, ongoing events.

Although most emotions can be triggered purely by self-thoughts, fear is perhaps the most familiar. People regularly scare themselves by thinking about past, anticipated, or imagined threats to their well-being. Indeed, without a self that permits them to imagine what might or might not happen in the future, people would have no capacity for worry. Nonhuman animals may feel fear in the presence of real threats (or in the presence of stimuli that have become associated with threats), but one does not get the impression that they lie awake at night worrying about what might happen to them the day after tomorrow. All worry about future events is mediated by self-relevant thought and thus requires a self.

Such anticipation is sometimes adaptive in terms of preparing people to confront impending threats. Before danger arrives, people can take steps to avoid it, or, if avoidance is not possible, they may plan how to deal with it most effectively. Thus, in some cases, the self's ability to imagine the individual in potentially dangerous situations is undoubtedly beneficial. Even so, the human capacity to worry about things that have not yet happened—and, indeed, that may never come to pass—exacts a heavy emotional price (Roemer & Borkovec, 1993). Many—perhaps most—of the things that people worry about never materialize, and, even when they do, the anticipatory emotional distress does not necessarily help people prevent or dilute the threat through advance preparation. As Shakespeare noted in *Julius Caesar*, "Cowards die many times before their deaths/The valiant never taste of death but once." Each one of those imagined deaths of the analogue-I is nearly as traumatic as the real thing. Practicing psychologists and other mental health professionals owe a great deal of their business to the self's penchant for making up unpleasant stories about what might happen, sending anxious clients seeking professional relief from their anxiety.

Martin (1999) has raised the intriguing possibility that self-generated worry about the future became prevalent only with the emergence of agriculture around 10,000 years ago. Although people possessed the capacity for self-awareness before this time (Leary & Cottrell, 1999), the prevailing lifestyle of human beings prior to the advent of agriculture did not evoke a great deal of rumination about the future. During most of their evolution, human beings and their homonid ancestors lived in nomadic bands of hunter-gatherers. With no way to preserve or transport large amounts of food, they lived day to day and had little interest in accumulating either food or possessions. Furthermore, hunter-gatherers, then and now, live in an immediate-return environment in which they receive nearly continuous feedback indicating whether they are accomplishing important goals. They would search for food, and if they found some, they'd eat it soon afterward; if they didn't find food, they would keep looking. In either case, they had little doubt about whether or not they were accomplishing vital goals, and, because they had no long-term aspirations to succeed, achieve, accumulate, or otherwise improve their lot in life, our hunter-gatherer ancestors had little reason to imagine themselves in the future or to pursue long-range goals. Early human beings would certainly have experienced emotions in response to events that had immediate (or short-term) implications for their well-being, but they would not have been inclined to worry much about the distant future.

With the emergence of agriculture, however, people moved from an immediate-return environment to a delayed-return environment in which important outcomes, both good and bad, lay weeks or months in the future. People who rely on farming for sustenance think about the future a great deal. They must plan for planting, as well as for how the yield will be harvested and saved. Farmers cannot help but fret about the weather, pests, thieves, and whether crops will grow and then about protecting what is produced. And, as the growing season progresses, feedback regarding their progress toward these long-term goals is sporadic and uncertain. Furthermore, along with agriculture came sedentary communities and property ownership, prompting worries about protecting one's belongings, home, barns, and stored food. And, with the development of economic and social roles, people had to worry not only about their personal futures but also about the well-being of the other people on whom they depended. If Martin (1999) is correct, agriculture brought with it a new set of psychological stresses.

Modern industrialized societies are profoundly delayed-return environments. People spend much of their time planning, thinking about, and working toward future goals. Many such goals, such as one's paycheck, lie days or weeks ahead, whereas others (such as educational degrees and job promotions) may be years in the future. Furthermore, people rarely receive the kind of ongoing and immediate feedback that characterized the daily lives of prehistoric hunter-gatherers. As a result, much of our emotional lives deal with distal, often uncertain events rather than with immediate satisfactions and threats. Martin's (1999) analysis raises the possibility that anxiety is a much more pervasive problem in contemporary society than it was in prehistoric times because modern human beings spend much more of their time engaged in self-focused thought (mostly about the future) and thus experience a great deal of self-generated negative affect.

Although I have dealt in detail with only one emotion—anxiety—many other emotions are likewise caused by imagining oneself in various situations. We can create anger by imagining what people have done or might do to us, sadness by thinking about losses we have experienced (even in the very distant past), and happiness by thinking about past and future satisfactions (Davis, 1999; McIntosh & Martin, 1992).

When people imagine future emotion-producing situations, they often think about how they are likely to feel in them. Wilson and Klaaren (1992) reviewed evidence showing that people's affective expectations influence their subsequent emotional experiences. Expecting to feel a particular way in an upcoming situation may lead one to feel differently when the situation is actually encountered than if the person had started with different expectations (Wilson, Lisle, Kraft, & Wetzel, 1989). Again, these affective expectations involve imagining the reactions of the analogue-I. Without a self, people could not anticipate their emotional reactions.

## Imagining Significant Others

Many theorists have pointed out that a person's sense of identity involves not only the individual him- or herself but also other people and objects in whom the person is personally invested. James (1890) noted that a person's empirical self (i.e., identity) is the sum total of all that the individual can call his or hers—not only one's physical body but also one's house, spouse, children, friends, prized belongings, and accomplishments. To see that this is so, we need only observe the strength of people's emotional reactions to the fortunes of their possessions, reputations, families, and bank accounts.

Because people construe other individuals and even inanimate objects as aspects of their identities, imagining events that involve those self-relevant individuals or belongings can provoke emotions. Animals without a self may react emotionally to events that have direct implications for their offspring or territory, but we see little evidence that they mentally conjure up events that affect their extended sense of self. It seems doubtful, for example, that animals worry about the security of their nests or burrows while they are away from home or feel happy thinking about their "loved ones" when they are not physically present. In contrast, human beings regularly experience emotions thinking about these appendages of themselves.

Jealousy is a particularly potent emotional response that can be induced by imagining other people in whom one is invested. Jealousy arises when people believe that another person does not value his or her relationship with them as much as they desire because of the presence or intrusion of a third party (Leary, Koch, & Hechenbleikner, 2001). Nonhuman animals sometimes show a response that resembles jealousy but only in the immediate presence of the rival (Masson & McCarthy, 1995). Human beings, in contrast, suffer painful bouts of jealousy simply from imagining that the loved one's attention is being usurped by a rival (Salovey & Rodin, 1986), whether or not that fantasy has any basis in reality. Nonhuman animals often spar over mates but, again, I know of no case in which any other animal goes berserk from simply imagining its mate's dalliances.

In brief, the capacity for self-reflection allows human beings to experience emotions from imagined events that have personal implications. Although self-generated emotions are often unpleasant and sometimes maladaptive, they also can be beneficial. By using the analogue-I to anticipate what might happen and how they will feel, people can make more judicious decisions about what courses of action to take.

## Symbolic Threats to Desired Self-Images

Although not without controversy, the evidence suggests that human infants have no self (Kagan, 1998). Babies do not appear to begin to differentiate between themselves and other people until after 3 months, and until they do so, all of their emotions are reactions to physical stimuli, whether those are environmental stimuli or bodily sensations (Lewis & Brooks-Gunn, 1979). The self develops slowly during the first year and a half, so that by around 15–18 months, most children are capable of recognizing themselves in a mirror (Gallup & Suarez, 1986; Lewis, 1994). Equipped with the capacity for self-reflection, children then begin to construct ideas and images of themselves. By age 2, children can distinguish themselves from other people and realize that other people have perspectives and goals that differ from their own, and they become able to articulate their views of themselves, for example, accurately reporting whether they are a boy or a girl (Thompson, 1975). As the self becomes more sophisticated, children characterize themselves in increasingly complex and abstract ways in a developmental progression that continues into late adolescence (Crain, 1996).

Once people are able to think about themselves in abstract ways and to label, characterize, and evaluate themselves, they begin to react emotionally to this cognitive representation of themselves and to information that validates or threatens it. Psychologists have shown great interest in how people respond to threats to their self-identity or "ego" without stopping to realize how peculiar this reaction really is. To overdramatize only slightly, people develop conceptions of themselves that, when reduced to their essence, are little more than a particular pattern of electrochemical neuroactivity in the brain. Then events in the real world that are consistent or inconsistent with this particular pattern evoke strong emotional reactions,

even when those events have no real consequences for the individual's well-being. Events that affirm one's ego then create positive emotions, whereas ego-threatening events cause negative emotions. By virtue of having a self, people become emotionally invested in whether reality conforms to their view of themselves.

Three kinds of symbolic satisfactions and threats to people's self-construals have received the most attention from researchers. People respond emotionally to events that (1) support or threaten their positive images of themselves, (2) validate or disconfirm their current self-images, and (3) fulfill or violate their desires regarding the kind of person they want and do not want to be.

## Self-Enhancement

People prefer to evaluate themselves positively rather than negatively, and a great deal of theory and research has examined the ways in which people try to maintain an image in their own minds of being good and effective individuals (Baumeister, 1998; Greenwald, 1980; Hoyle et al., 1999). For our purposes, the important fact is that events that support a favorable view of oneself tend to create positive feelings (such as pride, happiness, and satisfaction), whereas events that contradict one's favorable self-view are associated with negative feelings (such as anxiety, despondency, frustration, shame, and even rage; e.g., Baumeister, Smart, & Boden, 1996; Dutton & Brown, 1997; Rhodewalt & Morf, 1998; Scheff & Retzinger, 1991). Many of people's most positive emotional reactions stem from events that enhance their positive image of themselves, and many of their most negative emotional reactions stem from events that call their positive self-image into question or, worse, incontrovertibly refute it.

As noted earlier, people's identities include not only themselves but also other people with whom they are somehow linked. One implication of this fact is that people sometimes feel good or bad because of the fortunes of other people with whom they are associated. One compelling example of this phenomenon involves the tendency for people to feel good when those with whom they are associated are successful but to feel bad when those with whom they are associated fail or are disgraced. Thus, for reasons that have little rational basis, people may be elated or devastated depending on whether their favorite sports team wins or loses (Cialdini et al., 1976). Presumably, the team has been incorporated into the person's identity, and thus the team's fortunes are treated as one's own. One exception to this general pattern occurs when another person's success reflects badly on the individual. For example, when a person with whom we are linked succeeds in a domain that is important to our own identity, their success may be perceived as threatening and generate negative emotions (Tesser, Millar, & Moore, 1988). Thus, people's reactions to another individual's fortunes are based on a complex set of inferences about their implications for their own perception and evaluation of themselves.

Theorists have generally assumed that people inherently desire to see themselves favorably and that events that have implications for people's self-esteem naturally evoke emotional reactions. However, sociometer theory (Leary & Baumeister, 2000; Leary & Downs, 1995) suggests that, rather than being merely a response to events that reflect on their private egos, people's affective reactions to self-enhancing and self-depreciating events serve an important interpersonal function. In particular, these feelings provide feedback to the individual regarding the degree to which he or she is being valued and accepted by other people. Events that threaten an individual's positive self-image generally cast the person in an undesirable light in other people's eyes as well, thereby undermining his or her relationships with them (Leary, Tambor, Terdal, & Downs, 1995). From this perspective, the feelings associated with self-esteem are part of a monitoring system that keeps the individual apprised of his or her relational value and that motivates behaviors to help the individual avoid social rejection. The negative emotions that arise from threats to people's egos are thus part of a warning system that promotes social acceptance (Kirkpatrick & Ellis, 2001; Leary, 1999). For example, guilt may serve as a warning that one has behaved in ways that may jeopardize one's relationships, and jealousy may alert people that their relationship with another person is being usurped by a rival (Leary et al., 2001).

### Self-Consistency

In addition to wanting to maintain a positive view of themselves, people desire to maintain a stable, consistent self-view as well. As a result, information that suggests that people are not actually who or what they think they are evokes negative feelings.

Cognitive dissonance theory was among the first perspectives to describe the emotional effects of having beliefs that are inconsistent with one another. Any pair of contradictory beliefs may potentially evoke the unpleasant affective state of dissonance (Festinger, 1957), but inconsistent beliefs involving aspects of oneself appear to be particularly unpleasant (Aronson, 1968). In fact, over the years, cognitive dissonance theory moved from being a theory about cognitive inconsistency per se to being a theory about how people react to disturbing incongruencies between their views of themselves and the knowledge that they have behaved in a foolish, irrational, or immoral fashion (see Steele & Liu, 1983). In fact, research suggests that many effects that were initially attributed to dissonance may not be due to cognitive inconsistency at all but rather to people's concerns that others are perceiving them as inconsistent, immoral, hypocritical, or otherwise socially

undesirable (Schlenker, Forsyth, Leary, & Miller, 1980). Thus, rather than reflecting an inherent need for internal consistency, many of the behavioral and emotional reactions studied by dissonance researchers may reflect people's concerns with how they are perceived and evaluated by others (Schlenker, 1982).

Swann and his colleagues have examined specifically how people respond to events that verify or disconfirm their private views of themselves (Swann, 1996). People tend to be troubled by information that discredits their existing self-perceptions, presumably because disconfirming information undermines their certainty in their beliefs about themselves and the world, thereby lowering their sense of predictability and control (Swann, Stein-Seroussi, & Giesler, 1992). Thus, receiving information that is inconsistent with one's self-concept is often distressing, even if it otherwise makes the person feel good because it reflects positively on him or her (Swann, Griffin, Predmore, & Gaines, 1987). Clearly, people's emotional reactions to events are moderated by the degree to which those events support or disconfirm their existing views of themselves.

### Self-Relevant Standards and Goals

A person's self-identity involves not only beliefs regarding who one is and what one is like, but also goals that reflect how the person would like to be (Emmons, 1986; Markus & Nurius, 1986; Palys & Little, 1983). These mental representations of desired future states serve as incentives that motivate action and as guides that channel behavior in particular directions. The capacity for self-reflexive thought again enters the picture as people compare themselves and their outcomes in life to these goals and standards and experience various emotions depending on whether or not their goals have been met. Progress toward one's goals evokes positive emotions, and lack of progress (and particularly movement away from those goals) evokes negative emotions (Higgins, 1987; Markus & Nurius, 1986; Ogilvie, 1987). Thus, emotions are experienced not just because the current state of affairs is favorable or unfavorable to one's well-being but also because the current state of affairs does or does not reflect movement toward one's identity-relevant goals and standards. As James (1890) observed in his inimitable way:

> So we have the paradox of a man shamed to death because he is only the second pugilist or the second oarsman in the world. That he is able to beat the whole population minus one is nothing; he has "pitted" himself to beat that one; and as long as he doesn't do that nothing else counts. (pp. 53–54)

In such cases, the person's reaction is clearly a function of the standards and goals he or she has set for him- or herself.

According to self-discrepancy theory (Higgins, 1987), the specific emotions that people experience when they fail to achieve their goals depend on the type of discrepancy involved. When people perceive a discrepancy between their actual and ideal selves (i.e., between how they think they are and how they would like to be), dejection-related emotions (such as disappointment, sadness, and depression) result. However, perceiving a discrepancy between one's actual and "ought" selves (i.e., between how they think they are and how they think they ought to be) leads to agitation-related emotions such as guilt, fear, and anxiety. Research has generally supported the notion that self-discrepancies produce emotion (e.g., Carver, Lawrence, & Scheier, 1999; Higgins, Bond, Klein, & Strauman, 1986; Higgins, Klein, & Strauman, 1985; Strauman & Higgins, 1987, 1988), although Tangney, Niedenthal, Covert, and Barlow (1998) failed to obtain the differential effects of actual-ideal versus actual-ought discrepancies predicted by self-discrepancy theory (see also Gralinski, Safyer, Hauser, & Allen, 1995). Furthermore, Carver et al. (1999) showed that discrepancies from one's feared self predict agitation-related emotions better than discrepancies from one's ought self, particularly when people think they are already fairly close to their feared selves (see also Ogilvie, 1987). Apparently, avoiding one's feared self takes precedence over attaining one's ought self. Although more work is needed to document the precise relationships between particular kinds of self-discrepancies and various emotions, there is little doubt that discrepancies between how people think they are and how they want and do not want to be cause negative emotions and lower subjective well-being (e.g., Fischer, Manstead, & Mosquera, 1999; Gralinski et al., 1995; Grimmell, 1998; Hart, Field, Garfinkle, & Singer, 1997; Ogilvie, 1987; Pavot, Fujita, & Diener, 1997; Sheeran, Abrams, & Orbell, 1995; Tangney et al., 1998).

People judge themselves not only in comparison with their goals and standards but also relative to other outcomes that might have occurred. The ability to manipulate the analogue-I in consciousness allows people to imagine themselves in alternative worlds and to consider how things might have turned out differently. Thus people may feel better or worse about their lot depending on whether the alternatives they imagine are better or worse than what actually transpired. Medvec, Madey, and Gilovich's (1995) research on the reactions of silver and bronze medal winners in the Olympics demonstrates this effect. Bronze-medal winners (i.e., third-place finishers) are actually happier than silver-medal winners (i.e., second-place finishers), presumably because bronze medalists compare finishing third with not getting a medal at all, whereas silver medalists compare their second-place finish with the imagined alternative of winning the gold. Differences in how they think about alternative outcomes lead to different emotional reactions.

For many self-evaluations—such as judgments of one's physical attractiveness, intelligence, popularity, and income—no objective standard for evaluation exists. As a result, people often judge themselves in such domains by comparing themselves with other people. Having a self allows people to compare their own attributes and accomplishments with those of others and to experience positive or negative affect depending on whether they compare favorably or unfavorably. Again, it is difficult to imagine a self-less animal feeling good or bad simply from comparing itself with other members of its flock, herd, pack, or troop.

Although theorists once assumed that downward social comparisons (comparing oneself with those who are worse off than oneself) generally lead to more positive emotions than upward social comparisons (comparing oneself with better-off others), research has shown that whether downward or upward comparisons lead to positive or negative affect depends on how the individual interprets the comparative information. When downward comparisons make them feel better or more fortunate than others, people feel good (Kleinke & Miller, 1998). However, when downward social comparisons raise the specter that one might also fare poorly (as when a newly diagnosed cancer patient compares him- or herself with a patient in later stages of the illness), downward comparisons lead to negative affect (Buunk, Collins, Taylor, Van Y Peren, & Dakof, 1990; Hemphill & Lehman, 1991; Van der Zee, Oldersma, Buunk, & Bos, 1998). Similarly, comparing oneself with outstanding role models leads to positive affect if the superstar's accomplishments seem attainable but to negative affect when they are not (Lockwood & Kunda, 1997). The effects of upward and downward social comparison are quite complex and, further, are moderated by several individual difference variables, including self-esteem, mood, neuroticism, and optimism (Aspinwall & Taylor, 1993; Hemphill & Lehman, 1991; Lyubomirsky & Ross, 1997; Van der Zee et al., 1998).

## Self-Attributions

People often analyze their emotional experiences, trying to understand both why particular situations evoked certain emotions (e.g., Why did I lose my temper?) and why emotion-inducing events occurred in the first place (e.g., Why was I passed over for the promotion?). Since Schachter and Singer's (1962) initial demonstration that people's interpretations of arousing events affect the nature of their specific emotional experiences, research has shown that attributions have a strong effect on emotion (although Schachter and Singer's precise experiments have been difficult to replicate; Maslach, 1979). The same event can evoke drastically different emotions depending on the person's attributions for the event, attributions that involve self-focused thought.

Weiner (1985) offered the most complete theory that describes the relationship between patterns of attributions and specific emotions. From his perspective, emotional responses to positive and negative events depend on three aspects of the attributions that people make—causal locus (whether the cause of the event was internal or external to the individual), stability (whether the cause is short-lived or long-lasting), and controllability (whether the cause is under the individual's control). For example, attributing a failure to one's lack of effort (an internal, unstable, controllable cause) should produce shame or guilt, whereas attributing the same failure to sabotage by another person (an external, stable, uncontrollable cause) should produce anger. Research has supported some, though not all, aspects of Weiner's theory (Russell & McAuley, 1986; Weiner, Russell, & Lerman, 1978, 1979). Smith, Haynes, Lazarus, and Pope (1993) extended the attributional perspective by showing that the effects of attributions on emotion are mediated by people's appraisals of the implications of those attributions for their well-being.

In a somewhat different approach to the relationship between attribution and emotion, Janoff-Bulman (1979) distinguished between two kinds of self-attributions that have different implications for people's emotional reactions to negative events. Following a failure, trauma, or other aversive event, people may engage in "behavioral self-blame" in which they attribute the event to a behavioral mistake or miscalculation on their part, or they may engage in "characterological self-blame" in which they attribute the event to a relatively unchangeable aspect of themselves. Characterological self-blame for negative events is associated with depression, presumably because attributing negative events to unchangeable aspects of oneself induces a sense of helplessness (Anderson, Miller, Riger, Dill, & Sedikides, 1994; Janoff-Bulman, 1979; Rotenberg, Kim, & Herman-Stahl, 1998). Importantly, people differ in the degree to which they tend to make characterological attributions for events in their lives, thereby predisposing them to particular patterns of emotions. For example, people who characteristically attribute failure to dispositional variables, such as their lack of ability, are particularly prone to be depressed, lonely, and shy (Anderson & Arnoult, 1985; Anderson, Horowitz, & French, 1983).

People make attributions not only for the events that cause emotions but also for their reactions to those events. That is, they ask not only why the event occurred but also why they reacted to it as they did. Imagine two individuals who have experienced identical emotional reactions to the same traumatic situation. One individual views his or her reaction as a normal response to such an experience, but the other person thinks that his or her reaction reflects an inability to cope. The second individual's interpretation of the emotion may fuel other reactions, such as frustration (What's wrong with me that I can't cope?) or shame (I'm a loser who's incapable of dealing with life). Under certain circumstances, people's attributions may intensify or prolong their emotional experiences, as when people make a characterological attribution for being anxious, thereby leading them to worry about their "problem" and fueling even more anxiety (Storms & McCaul, 1976). Although the effects of people's attributions on their emotional experiences received considerable attention in the 1970s and 1980s (see Leary & Miller, 1986; Storms & McCaul, 1976; Valins & Nisbett, 1972; Zillmann, 1978), interest waned during the 1990s. Given the theoretical and clinical importance of the effects of self-attributions on emotion, the topic deserves renewed attention.

## Reflected Appraisals

For reasons that are not entirely clear, the capacity to think consciously about oneself goes hand in hand with the ability to think about what other people are thinking. In young children, the ability to imagine other people's perspectives emerges at about the same time as self-awareness (Lempers, Flavell, & Flavell, 1977). The same pattern is seen in nonhuman animals; animals with self-awareness appear to be able to take others' perspectives, whereas those who show no evidence of self-awareness appear unable to do so (Gallup & Suarez, 1986).

Certain emotions arise from thinking about what other people are thinking or feeling. For example, empathic emotional responses occur when people identify with another individual's experience. We feel distressed because someone we love is upset but happy when we know that they are content. Without an ability to put ourselves in the other person's shoes and imagine the world from their perspective, these kinds of reactions would not be possible. It is informative that true prosocial behavior, which requires that one infer the needs of another person, also appears at about the same time as self-awareness (Hoffman, 1975; Lewis & Brooks-Gunn, 1979; Zahn-Waxler, Radke-Yarrow, & King, 1979; see also Eisenberg, Losoya, & Spinrad, chapter 41, this volume).

Some emotions—such as fear, anger, joy, sadness, disgust, and surprise—can be observed within the first few weeks or months of life (Lazarus, 1991; Lewis, 1994). However, other emotions—such as social anxiety, embarrassment, shame, envy, pride, and guilt—do not appear until later (Lewis, 1994; Miller, 1996). The reason is that these so-called self-conscious emotions require people to think about what other people are thinking and specifically to think about what other people are thinking about them. They can even carry these cognitive activities through another iteration or two, imagining what other people are thinking about what they are thinking about what the other people might be thinking about them.

When people think about how they are being perceived and evaluated by other people, these "reflected appraisals" can elicit a variety of emotions.

For example, people experience social anxiety when they think that they are unable to make the impressions on other individuals that they desire to make (Schlenker & Leary, 1982). Because many valued outcomes in life are contingent on being perceived by other people in particular ways, people are often interested in conveying certain impressions of themselves to others. When people are motivated to make a particular impression on other people but think that they will not successfully do so, they experience social anxiety (Leary & Kowalski, 1995). Thus, when an actor on stage, an adolescent on a first date, or a job applicant in an interview feels nervous, their anxiety is mediated by their self-relevant thoughts about others' perceptions and evaluations of them.

Likewise, people become embarrassed when they believe that other people have formed undesired impressions of them (Miller, 1996). Given that embarrassment requires that one take the perspective of others and imagine the impressions others have formed of oneself, it is not surprising that the first signs of embarrassment emerge developmentally at about the same time as self-awareness (Lewis, 1994; Lewis & Brooks-Gunn, 1979). Similarly, people experience hurt feelings when they think that other people do not sufficiently value having a relationship with them (Leary, Springer, Negel, Ansell, & Evans, 1998). Thus the capacity for hurt feelings also depends on the ability to infer how others feel about oneself.

Guilt and shame also involve concerns about other people's evaluations, but they differ from social anxiety, embarrassment, and hurt feelings in that they can be caused either by reflected appraisals or by one's self-appraisal. Although people will not feel socially anxious, embarrassed, or hurt simply from evaluating themselves unfavorably, they may feel guilty or ashamed about actions to which only they are privy. At the same time, knowing that other people regard their behavior or character unfavorably can also lead people to feel guilty or ashamed, sometimes even if the person him- or herself believes that he or she did nothing wrong. A full discussion of the complexities of guilt and shame would take us far afield, but the central point is that both emotions are mediated by self-thought (Tangney & Salovey, 1999).

The emotions that people experience in response to the real or imagined evaluations of other people typically involve an acute feeling of self-consciousness. People who feel socially anxious, embarrassed, guilty, or ashamed feel conspicuous, ruminate over their real or perceived misdeeds, and agonize over others' evaluations of them. People who are experiencing such states think a great deal about themselves and their social plight, as well as about what other people might be thinking about them.

Although I have focused on negative emotional reactions to reflected appraisals, people may also experience positive emotions from imagining other people's reactions to them. For example, people may feel pride when they think others admire them and joy when they think that others love them deeply. In both cases, people may experience these emotions even in the absence of explicit indications of admiration or love. Simply imagining others' positive reactions is sufficient to evoke such feelings.

## Self-Regulation of Emotions

Thus far, I have focused on how the ability to think consciously about oneself influences the factors that elicit emotions and the nature of the emotions that people experience. To conclude this chapter, I turn to the fact that possession of a self allows people to modify their own emotional experiences. People may wish to control how they feel not just because they prefer pleasant emotions over unpleasant ones but also because they view some emotions as more socially appropriate or morally correct than others or because they think that certain emotions will help them to achieve their goals (Wegner & Wenzlaff, 1996). Self-less animals, including human infants, can influence their emotional states by changing their behavior (for example, by avoiding feared stimuli and approaching rewarding ones), but only animals with a self may regulate their emotions by deliberately controlling how they think about themselves and their experiences (see Eisenberg & Fabes, 1992, and Bridges & Grolnick, 1995, for discussions of how emotional self-regulation develops in humans). People can regulate their emotions in many ways, but I discuss just three—predictive control, social comparison, and attenuating self-awareness.

### Predictive Control

People's emotional reactions to events depend in part on what they expect to happen. For example, negative outcomes that are expected may evoke less distress than those that take one by surprise. Similarly, events that fail to occur as anticipated may evoke strong reactions, whereas the same nonevents would evoke no reaction whatsoever had they not been expected.

A self is not needed for the formation of expectations, nor for organisms to react emotionally to fulfilled and unfulfilled expectancies. Nonhuman animals clearly form expectancies that events will occur and react emotionally when those expectations are violated. (For example, the family pet may become distressed when daily routines are disrupted.) However, the ability to self-reflect allows people to exert deliberate "predictive control" (Rothbaum, Weisz, & Snyder, 1982), in which they strategically tell themselves what to expect in an effort to influence their feelings about upcoming events.

We are all familiar with people using positive self-talk to allay their anxiety about upcoming events. By telling themselves that things will turn out all right, people can sometimes influence how they feel. Ironically, people may also try to regulate their emotions through negative self-talk. By lowering their expectations, reflecting on possible negative outcomes, and telling themselves that the worst is likely to happen, people try to prepare themselves for failures, bad news, disappointments, and other aversive events, and thereby soften the blow that such events would otherwise deal. For people who use this strategy regularly (i.e., defensive pessimists), anticipating negative outcomes appears to lower anxiety. In fact, preventing defensive pessimists from ruminating about upcoming stressful events increases their negative affect. However, for people who generally avoid thinking about impending negative events, thinking about the bad things around the corner only makes them feel worse (Norem & Illingworth, 1993). Thus, defensive pessimism appears to be a useful means of emotional self-regulation for some people but not for others.

### Social Comparison

I noted earlier that people's emotions are affected by how they compare themselves with others. In light of this fact, people may regulate their emotional reactions through their choices of comparisons (Wills, 1981). Sometimes people seek downward comparisons to feel better about themselves by contrast, but in other cases, they seek upward comparisons because those who are faring better than they are offer inspiration or hope. Although people sometimes select comparison targets who will provide the most accurate indication of their own attributes, their selections often appear designed to promote positive feelings (Buunk et al., 1990; Hemphill & Lehman, 1991; Van der Zee et al., 1998; Wood, Taylor, & Lichtman, 1985).

### Attenuating Self-Awareness

Although self-reflection prolongs and intensifies negative emotional states (Broderick, 1998; Duval & Wicklund, 1972; Hertel, 1998; Scheier, 1976), people find it very difficult to stop ruminating about unpleasant events. In fact, trying not to think about disturbing thoughts actually increases their frequency (for a review, see Wegner & Wenzlaff, 1996), so that trying to control one's feelings sometimes leads to a mood that is the opposite of the one intended (Wegner, Erber, & Zanakos, 1993). Because people find it difficult to stop thinking about themselves by force of will, they sometimes try instead to impede the self's ability to function and thereby eliminate their unpleasant feelings. To the extent that self-reflection is needed to experience the emotions we have discussed, rendering oneself unable to process information in a self-relevant fashion may provide relief from emotional distress.

Distraction is perhaps the most common way in which people attenuate self-awareness. People report that they watch television, socialize, read, engage in hobbies, and exercise to "take their mind off" unpleasant events, and these kinds of distracting activities do, in fact, reduce negative feelings (Tice & Baumeister, 1993; Wenzlaff, Wegner, & Roper, 1988; Zillmann, 1988). Although the effects of distraction on emotion may be mediated by a number of processes, the attenuation of self-awareness is likely involved. Not only does ruminating over one's experiences help to maintain one's emotional reactions to them, but self-awareness also appears to intensify affective states. For example, Scheier (1976) showed that self-attention increased subjective feelings of anger among participants who had been led to become angry, and Scheier and Carver (1977) were able to intensify participants' reports of depression, elation, attraction, and revulsion through increasing their self-attention. Thus, anything that takes one's attention away from one's self and lowers self-awareness should mute emotional reactions.

Baumeister (1991) has described many of the maladaptive ways in which people try to "escape" the self. For example, part of the appeal of alcohol and certain other psychoactive drugs lies in the fact that they interfere with self-awareness. Research has shown that alcohol reduces self-attention (Hull, 1981; Hull, Levenson, Young, & Sher, 1983) and that people use alcohol for precisely that purpose (Hull & Young, 1983; Hull, Young, & Jouriles, 1986). When thinking about oneself leads to unpleasant emotions, alcohol helps to reduce self-focused thought. Binge eating may serve the same purpose; the process of binging and purging appears to narrow people's focus and reduce self-attention (Heatherton & Baumeister, 1991). Masochism, which has baffled psychologists for over a century because it seems to be counter to hedonism, may likewise provide relief from aversive self-awareness (Baumeister, 1988, 1991). Finally, suicide may be the ultimate means to escape the aversive emotions that self-attention can bring (Baumeister, 1990).

Not all of the ways that people try to escape self-awareness are deleterious. For example, there is a long tradition, extending far back into ancient times, of using meditation to quiet one's internal dialogue. Although meditative practices, such as yoga and zazen, are often promoted within spiritual or mystical traditions, their primary function is simply to reduce the amount of time that the practitioner engages in self-reflection. By taming what Hindus call the "chattering monkey mind," people are less likely to respond emotionally to events that are self-mediated and thus to feel more composed and relaxed.

## Summary

My focus in this chapter is on the ways in which the human ability to self-reflect affects emotional experience. As I have shown, possessing a self allows people to experience emotions from imagining self-relevant events, to react to representations of themselves in their own minds, to think about the causes of emotion-eliciting events and their reactions to them, to respond to how they are perceived by other people, and to regulate their emotional experiences. By virtue of having a self, human beings live in a much different emotional world than other animals do. Indeed, it is difficult to imagine what subjective experience would be like without self-awareness, the analogue-I, and the internal self-talk that underlie so much human emotion.

Although my focus is on the implications of the self for emotion, I should note that affective experiences can affect the nature and operation of the self. For example, emotions can affect people's self-perceptions, sense of self-efficacy, and ability to self-regulate (DeSteno & Salovey, 1997; Leith & Baumeister, 1996; Wright & Mischel, 1982). Emotional experiences also influence where people focus their attention (Green & Sedikides, 1999; Salovey, 1992; Wood, Saltzberg, & Goldsamt, 1990) and how they make decisions (Gray, 1999; Trope & Pomerantz, 1998). Thus, not only is the self intimately involved in the generation and regulation of emotion but emotions also reciprocally affect the self.

The idea that the self is involved in emotion is by no means new. Even before Aristotle provided the earliest systematic discussion of emotions in Western philosophy, Guatama ("the Buddha") identified the self as the source of emotion. The Buddha taught that human unhappiness arises from the self's tendency to evaluate events in terms of the individual's own egoistic desires and that the way to avoid negative emotions is to recognize that the self is a mental construction and not the final arbiter of the events that happen in the world (Easwaran, 1985). The Greek philosopher Epictetus echoed much the same notion a few centuries later when he observed that people are not disturbed by things, but rather by their view of them. It took behavioral researchers some time to begin to explore the details of these ancient insights, but in a relatively short amount of time, they have produced a rich body of knowledge dealing with the role of the self in emotional experience.

## REFERENCES

Anderson, C. A., & Arnoult, L. H. (1985). Attributional style and everyday problems in living: Depression, loneliness, and shyness. *Social Cognition, 3,* 16–35.

Anderson, C. A., Horowitz, L. M., & French, R. (1983). Attributional style of lonely and depressed people. *Journal of Personality and Social Psychology, 45,* 127–136.

Anderson, C. A., Miller, R. S., Riger, A. L., Dill, J. C., & Sedikides, C. (1994). Behavioral and characterological attributional styles as predictors of depression and loneliness: Review, refinement, and test. *Journal of Personality and Social Psychology, 66,* 549–558.

Aronson, E. (1968). Dissonance theory: Progress and problems. In R. P. Abelson, E. Aronson, W. J. McGuire, T. M. Newcomb, M. J. Rosenberg, & P. H. Tannenbaum (Eds.), *Theories of cognitive consistency: A sourcebook* (pp. 5–27). Chicago: Rand McNally.

Aspinwall, L. G., & Taylor, S. E. (1993). Effects of social comparison direction, threat, and self-esteem on affect, self-evaluation, and expected success. *Journal of Personality and Social Psychology, 64,* 708–722.

Baumeister, R. F. (1988). Masochism as escape from self. *Journal of Sex Research, 25,* 28–59.

Baumeister, R. F. (1990). Suicide as escape from self. *Psychological Review, 97,* 90–113.

Baumeister, R. F. (1991). *Escaping the self.* New York: Basic Books.

Baumeister, R. F. (1998). The self. In D. T. Gilbert, S. T. Fiske, & G. Lindzey (Eds.), *Handbook of social psychology* (4th ed., Vol. 2, pp. 680–740). Boston, MA: McGraw-Hill.

Baumeister, R. F., Smart, L., & Boden, J. M. (1996). Relation of threatened egotism to violence and aggression: The dark side of high self-esteem. *Psychological Review, 103,* 5–33.

Bridges, L. J., & Grolnick, W. S. (1995). The development of emotional self-regulation in infancy and early childhood. In N. Eisenberg (Ed.), *Social development* (pp. 185–211). Thousand Oaks, CA: Sage.

Broderick, P. C. (1998). Early adolescent gender differences in the use of rumination and distracting coping strategies. *Journal of Early Adolescence, 18,* 173–191.

Buunk, B. P., Collins, R. L., Taylor, S. E., VanYperen, N. W., & Dakof, G. A. (1990). The affective consequences of social comparison: Either direction has its ups and downs. *Journal of Personality and Social Psychology, 59,* 1238–1249.

Carver, C. S., Lawrence, J. W., & Scheier, M. F. (1999). Self-discrepancies and affect: Incorporating the role of feared selves. *Personality and Social Psychology Bulletin, 25,* 783–792.

Carver, C. S., & Scheier, M. F. (1985). *Attention and self-regulation: A control-theory approach to human behavior.* New York: Springer-Verlag.

Cialdini, R. B., Borden, R. J., Thorne, A., Walker, M. R., Freeman, S., & Sloan, L. R. (1976). Basking in reflected glory: Three (football) field studies. *Journal of Personality and Social Psychology, 34,* 366–375.

Crain, R. M. (1996). The influence of age, race, and gender on child and adolescent multidimensional self-concept. In B. A. Bracken (Ed.), *Handbook of self-concept: Developmental, social, and clinical considerations* (pp. 395–420). New York: Wiley.

Darwin, C. (1902). *The descent of man.* New York: Collier.

Darwin, C. (1998). *The expression of the emotions in man and animals.* New York: Oxford University Press. (Original work published 1872)

Davis, P. (1999). Gender differences in autobiographical memory for childhood emotional experiences. *Journal of Personality and Social Psychology, 76,* 498–510.

DeSteno, D. A., & Salovey, P. (1997). The effects of mood

on the structure of the self-concept. *Cognition and Emotion, 11*, 351–372.

Dutton, K. A., & Brown, J. D. (1997). Global self-esteem and specific self-views as determinants of people's reactions to success and failure. *Journal of Personality and Social Psychology, 73*, 139–148.

Duval, S., & Wicklund, R. A. (1972). *A theory of objective self-awareness.* New York: Academic Press.

Easwaran, E. (Trans.). (1985). *The Dhammapada.* Tomales, CA: Nilgiri Press.

Eisenberg, N., & Fabes, R. A. (1992). Emotion, regulation, and the development of social competence. In M. S. Clark (Ed.) *Review of personality and social psychology: Vol. 14. Emotion and social behavior* (pp. 119–150). Newbury Park, CA: Sage.

Emmons, R. A. (1986). Personal strivings: An approach to personality and subjective well-being. *Journal of Personality and Social Psychology, 51*, 1058–1068.

Festinger, L. (1957). *A theory of cognitive dissonance.* Stanford, CA: Stanford University Press.

Fischer, A. H., Manstead, A. S. R., & Mosquera, P. M. R. (1999). The role of honour-related vs. individualistic values in conceptualising pride, shame, and anger: Spanish and Dutch cultural prototypes. *Cognition and Emotion, 13*, 149–179.

Gallup, G. G., Jr., & Suarez, S. D. (1986). Self-awareness and the emergence of mind in humans and other primates. In J. Suls & A. G. Greenwald (Eds.), *Psychological perspectives on the self* (Vol. 3, pp. 3–26). Hillsdale, NJ: Erlbaum.

Gralinski, J. H., Safyer, A. W., Hauser, S. T., & Allen, J. P. (1995). Self-cognitions and expressed negative emotions during midadolescence: Contributions to young adult psychological adjustment. *Development and Psychopathology, 7*, 193–216.

Gray, J. R. (1999). A bias toward short-term thinking in threat-related negative emotional states. *Personality and Social Psychology Bulletin, 25*, 65–75.

Green, J. D., & Sedikides, C. (1999). Affect and self-focused attention revisited: The role of affect orientation. *Personality and Social Psychology Bulletin, 25*, 104–119.

Greenwald, A. G. (1980). The totalitarian ego: Fabrication and revision of personal history. *American Psychologist, 35*, 603–613.

Grimmell, D. (1998). Effects of gender-role discrepancy on depressed mood. *Sex Roles, 39*, 203–214.

Hart, D., Field, N. P., Garfinkle, J. R., & Singer, J. L. (1997). Representations of self and other: A semantic space model. *Journal of Personality, 65*, 77–105.

Heatherton, T. F., & Baumeister, R. F. (1991). Binge eating as escape from self-awareness. *Psychological Bulletin, 110*, 86–108.

Hemphill, K. J., & Lehman, D. R. (1991). Social comparisons and their affective consequences: The importance of comparison dimension and individual difference variables. *Journal of Social and Clinical Psychology, 10*, 372–394.

Hertel, P. T. (1998). Relation between rumination and impaired memory in dysphoric moods. *Journal of Abnormal Psychology, 107*, 166–172.

Higgins, E. T. (1987). Self-discrepancy: A theory relating self and affect. *Psychological Review, 94*, 319–340.

Higgins, E. T., Bond, R. N., Klein, R., & Strauman, T. (1986). Self-discrepancies and emotional vulnerability: How magnitude, accessibility, and type of discrepancy

influence affect. *Journal of Personality and Social Psychology, 51*, 5–15.

Higgins, E. T., Klein, R., & Strauman, T. (1985). Self-concept discrepancy theory: A psychological model for distinguishing among different aspects of depression and anxiety. *Social Cognition, 3*, 51–76.

Hoffman, M. L. (1975). Developmental synthesis of affect and cognition and its implications for altruistic motivation. *Developmental Psychology, 11*, 607–622.

Hoyle, R. H., Kernis, M. H., Leary, M. R., & Baldwin, M. W. (1999). *Selfhood: Identity, esteem, regulation.* Boulder, CO: Westview Press.

Hull, J. G. (1981). A self-awareness model of the causes and effects of alcohol consumption. *Journal of Abnormal Psychology, 90*, 586–600.

Hull, J. G., Levenson, R. W., Young, R. D., & Sher, K. J. (1983). Self-awareness-reducing effects of alcohol consumption. *Journal of Personality and Social Psychology, 44*, 461–473.

Hull, J. G., & Young, R. D. (1983). Self-consciousness, self-esteem, and success-failure as determinants of alcohol consumption in male social drinkers. *Journal of Personality and Social Psychology, 44*, 1097–1109.

Hull, J. G., Young, R. D., & Jouriles, E. (1986). Applications of the self-awareness model of alcohol consumption: Predicting patterns of use and abuse. *Journal of Personality and Social Psychology, 51*, 790–796.

James, W. (1890). *The principles of psychology.* New York: Holt, Rinehart, & Winston.

Janoff-Bulman, R. (1979). Characterological versus behavioral self-blame: Inquiries into depression and rape. *Journal of Personality and Social Psychology, 37*, 1798–1809.

Jaynes, J. (1976). *The origin of consciousness in the breakdown of the bicameral mind.* Boston: Houghton Mifflin.

Kagan, J. (1998). Is there a self in infancy? In M. Ferrari & R. J. Sternberg (Eds.), *Self-awareness: Its nature and development* (pp. 137–147). New York: Guilford Press.

Kirkpatrick, L. A., & Ellis, B. J. (2001). Evolutionary perspectives on self-evaluation and self-esteem. In M. Clark & G. Fletcher (Eds.), *Blackwell handbook of social psychology: Interpersonal processes* (pp. 411–436). Oxford, England: Blackwell.

Kleinke, C. L., & Miller, W. F. (1998). How comparing oneself favorably with others relates to well-being. *Journal of Social and Clinical Psychology, 17*, 107–123.

Lazarus, R. S. (1991). *Emotion and adaptation.* New York: Oxford University Press.

Leary, M. R. (1999). The social and psychological importance of self-esteem. In R. M. Kowalski & M. R. Leary (Eds.), *The social psychology of emotional and behavioral problems: Interfaces of social and clinical psychology* (pp. 197–221). Washington, DC: American Psychological Association.

Leary, M. R., & Baumeister, R. F. (2000). The nature and function of self-esteem: Sociometer theory. In M. Zanna (Ed.), *Advances in experimental social psychology* (pp. 1–62). San Diego, CA: Academic Press.

Leary, M. R., & Cottrell, C. A. (1999). Evolution of the self, the need to belong, and life in a delayed-return environment. *Psychological Inquiry, 10*, 229–232.

Leary, M. R., & Downs, D. L. (1995). Interpersonal functions of the self-esteem motive: The self-esteem system as a sociometer. In M. Kernis (Ed.), *Efficacy, agency, and self-esteem* (pp. 123–144). New York: Plenum.

Leary, M. R., Koch, E. J., & Hechenbleikner, N. R. (2001). Emotional responses to interpersonal rejection. In M. R. Leary (Ed.), *Interpersonal rejection* (pp. 145–166). New York: Oxford University Press.

Leary, M. R., & Kowalski, R. M. (1995). *Social anxiety.* New York: Guilford.

Leary, M. R., & Miller, R. S. (1986). *Social psychology and dysfunctional behavior.* New York: Springer-Verlag.

Leary, M. R., Springer, C., Negel, L., Ansell, E., & Evans, K. (1998). The causes, phenomenology, and consequences of hurt feelings. *Journal of Personality and Social Psychology, 74,* 1225–1237.

Leary, M. R., Tambor, E. S., Terdal, S. K., & Downs, D. L. (1995). Self-esteem as an interpersonal monitor: The sociometer hypothesis. *Journal of Personality and Social Psychology, 68,* 518–530.

Leith, K. P., & Baumeister, R. F. (1996). Why do bad moods increase self-defeating behavior? Emotion, risk-taking, and self-regulation. *Journal of Personality and Social Psychology, 71,* 1250–1267.

Lempers, J. D., Flavell, E. R., & Flavell, J. H. (1977). The development in very young children of tacit knowledge concerning visual perception. *Genetic Psychology Monographs, 95,* 3–53.

Lewis, M. (1994). Myself and me. In S. T. Parker, R. W. Mitchell, & M. L. Boccia (Eds.), *Self-awareness in animals and humans* (pp. 20–34). Cambridge, England: Cambridge University Press.

Lewis, M., & Brooks-Gunn, J. (1979). *Social cognition and the acquisition of self.* New York: Plenum.

Lockwood, P., & Kunda, Z. (1997). Superstars and me: Predicting the impact of role models on the self. *Journal of Personality and Social Psychology, 73,* 91–103.

Lyubomirsky, S., & Ross, L. (1997). Hedonic consequences of social comparison: A contrast of happy and unhappy people. *Journal of Personality and Social Psychology, 73,* 1141–1157.

Markus, H., & Nurius, P. (1986). Possible selves. *American Psychologist, 41,* 954–969.

Martin, L. (1999). I-D compensation theory: Some implications of trying to satisfy immediate-return needs in a delayed-return culture. *Psychological Inquiry, 10,* 195–208.

Maslach, C. (1979). Negative emotional biasing of unexplained arousal. *Journal of Personality and Social Psychology, 37,* 953–969.

Masson, J. M., & McCarthy, S. (1995). *When elephants weep: The emotional lives of animals.* New York: Delta.

McIntosh, W. D., & Martin, L. L. (1992). The cybernetics of happiness: The relation of goal attainment, rumination, and affect. In M. S. Clark (Ed.), *Emotion and social behavior* (pp. 222–246). Newbury Park, CA: Sage.

Medvec, V. H., Madey, S. E., & Gilovich, T. (1995). When less is more: Counterfactual thinking and satisfaction among Olympic medalists. *Journal of Personality and Social Psychology, 69,* 603–610.

Miller, R. S. (1996). *Embarrassment: Poise and peril in everyday life.* New York: Guilford Press.

Mithen, S. (1996). *The prehistory of the human mind.* London: Thames & Hudson.

Norem, J. K., & Illingworth, K. S. S. (1993). Strategy-dependent effects of reflecting on self and tasks: Some implications of optimism and defensive pessimism. *Journal of Personality and Social Psychology, 65,* 822–835.

Ogilvie, D. M. (1987). The undesired self: A neglected variable in personality research. *Journal of Personality and Social Psychology, 52,* 379–385.

Palys, T. S., & Little, B. R. (1983). Perceived life satisfaction and the organization of personal project systems. *Journal of Personality and Social Psychology, 44,* 1221–1230.

Parker, S. T., Mitchell, R. W., & Boccia, M. L. (1994). *Self-awareness in animals and humans,* Cambridge, England: Cambridge University Press.

Pavot, W., Fujita, F., & Diener, E. (1997). The relation between self-aspect congruence, personality, and subjective well-being. *Personality and Individual Differences, 22,* 183–191.

Rhodewalt, F., & Morf, C. C. (1998). On self-aggrandizement and anger: A temporal analysis of narcissism and affective reactions to success and failure. *Journal of Personality and Social Psychology, 74,* 672–685.

Riskind, J. H. (1997). Looming vulnerability to threat: A cognitive paradigm for anxiety. *Behavior Research and Therapy, 35,* 685–702.

Roemer, L., & Borkovec, T. D. (1993). Worry: Unwanted cognitive activity that controls unwanted somatic experience. In D. M. Wegner & J. W. Pennebaker (Eds.), *Handbook of mental control* (pp. 220–238). Englewood Cliffs, NJ: Prentice Hall.

Rotenberg, K. J., Kim, L. S., & Herman-Stahl, M. (1998). The role of primary and secondary appraisals in the negative emotions and psychological maladjustment of children of divorce. *Journal of Divorce and Remarriage, 29,* 43–66.

Rothbaum, F., Weisz, J. R., & Snyder, S. S. (1982). Changing the world and changing the self. A two-process model of perceived control. *Journal of Personality and Social Psychology, 42,* 5–37.

Russell, D., & McAuley, E. (1986). Causal attributions, causal dimensions, and affective reactions to success and failure. *Journal of Personality and Social Psychology, 50,* 1174–1185.

Salovey, P. (1992). Mood-induced self-focused attention. *Journal of Personality and Social Psychology, 62,* 699–707.

Salovey, P., & Rodin, J. (1986). The differentiation of social-comparison and romantic jealousy. *Journal of Personality and Social Psychology, 50,* 1100–1111.

Schachter, S., & Singer, J. E. (1962). Cognitive, social, and physiological determinants of emotional state. *Psychological Review, 69,* 379–399.

Scheff, T. J., & Retzinger, S. M. (1991). *Emotions and violence: Shame and rage in destructive conflicts.* Lexington, MA: Lexington Books.

Scheier, M. F. (1976). Self-awareness, self-consciousness, and angry aggression. *Journal of Personality, 44,* 627–644.

Scheier, M. F., & Carver, C. S. (1977). Self-focused attention and the experience of emotion: Attraction, repulsion, elation, and depression. *Journal of Personality and Social Psychology, 35,* 625–636.

Schlenker, B. R. (1982). Translating actions into attitudes: An identity-analytic approach to the explanation of social conduct. In L. Berkowitz (Ed.), *Advances in experimental social psychology* (Vol. 15). New York: Academic Press.

Schlenker, B. R., Forsyth, D. R., Leary, M. R., & Miller, R. S. (1980). A self-presentational analysis of the effects of incentives on attitude change following counterattitudinal behavior. *Journal of Personality and Social Psychology, 39,* 553–577.

Schlenker, B. R., & Leary, M. R. (1982). Social anxiety and self-presentation: A conceptualization and model. *Psychological Bulletin, 92,* 641–669.

Sedikides, C., & Skowronski, J. J. (1997). The symbolic self in evolutionary context. *Personality and Social Psychology Review, 1,* 80–102.

Sheeran, P., Abrams, D., & Orbell, S. (1995). Unemployment, self-esteem, and depression: A social comparison theory approach. *Basic and Applied Social Psychology, 17,* 65–82.

Smith, C. A., Haynes, K. N., Lazarus, R. S., & Pope, L. K. (1993). In search of the "hot" cognitions: Attributions, appraisals, and their relation to emotion. *Journal of Personality and Social Psychology, 65,* 916–929.

Steele, C. M., & Liu, T. J. (1983). Dissonance processes as self-affirmation *Journal of Personality and Social Psychology, 45,* 5–19.

Storms, M. D., & McCaul, K. D. (1976). Attribution processes and emotional exacerbation of dysfunctional behavior. In J. H. Harvey, W. J. Ickes, & R. F. Kidd (Eds.), *New directions in attribution research* (Vol. 1, pp. 143–164). Hillsdale, NJ: Erlbaum.

Strauman, T. J., & Higgins, E. T. (1987). Automatic activation of self-discrepancies and emotional syndromes: When cognitive structures influence affect. *Journal of Personality and Social Psychology, 53,* 1004–1014.

Strauman, T. J., & Higgins, E. T. (1988). Self-discrepancies as predictors of vulnerability to distinct syndromes of chronic emotional distress. *Journal of Personality, 56,* 685–707.

Swann, W. B., Jr. (1996). *Self-traps: The elusive quest for higher self-esteem.* New York: Freeman.

Swann, W. B., Jr., Griffin, J. J., Predmore, S. C., & Gaines, B. (1987). The cognitive-affective crossfire: When self-consistency confronts self-enhancement. *Journal of Personality and Social Psychology, 52,* 881–889.

Swann, W. B., Jr., Stein-Seroussi, A., & Giesler, R. B. (1992). Why people self-verify. *Journal of Personality and Social Psychology, 62,* 392–401.

Tangney, J. P., Niedenthal, P. M., Covert, M. V., & Barlow, D. H. (1998). Are shame and guilt related to distinct self-discrepancies? A test of Higgins's (1987) hypotheses. *Journal of Personality and Social Psychology, 75,* 256–268.

Tangney, J. P., & Salovey, P. (1999). Problematic social emotions: Shame, guilt, jealousy, and envy. In R. M. Kowalski & M. R. Leary (Eds.). *The social psychology of emotional and behavioral problems* (pp. 167–195). Washington, DC: American Psychological Association.

Tesser, A., Millar, M., & Moore, J. (1988). Some affective consequences of social comparison and reflective processes: The pain and pleasure of being close. *Journal of Personality and Social Psychology, 54,* 49–61.

Thompson, S. K. (1975). Gender labels and early sex role development. *Child Development, 46,* 339–347.

Tice, D. M., & Baumeister, R. F. (1993). Controlling anger: Self-induced emotion change. In D. M. Wegner & J. W. Pennebaker (Eds.), *Handbook of mental control* (pp. 393–409). Englewood Cliffs, NJ: Prentice Hall.

Trope, Y., & Pomerantz, E. M. (1998). Resolving conflicts among self-evaluative motives: Positive experiences as a resource for overcoming defensiveness. *Motivation and Emotion, 22,* 53–72.

Valins, S., & Nisbett, R. E. (1972). Attribution processes in the development and treatment of emotional disorders. In E. E. Jones, D. E. Kanouse, H. H. Kelley, R. E. Nisbett, S. Valins, & B. Weiner (Eds.), *Attribution: Perceiving the causes of behavior* (pp. 137–150). Morristown, NJ: General Learning Press.

Van der Zee, K., Oldersma, F., Buunk, B. P., & Bos, D. (1998). Social comparison preferences among cancer patients as related to neuroticism and social comparison orientation. *Journal of Personality and Social Psychology, 75,* 801–810.

Wegner, D. M., Erber, R., & Zanakos, S. (1993). Ironic processes in the mental control of mood and mood-related thought. *Journal of Personality and Social Psychology, 65,* 1093–1104.

Wegner, D. M., & Wenzlaff, R. M. (1996). Mental control. In E. T. Higgins & A. W. Kruglanski (Eds.), *Social psychology: Handbook of basic principles* (pp. 466–492). New York: Guilford Press.

Weiner, B. (1985). An attributional theory of achievement motivation and emotion. *Psychological Review, 92,* 548–573.

Weiner, B., Russell, D., & Lerman, D. (1978). Affective consequences of causal ascriptions. In J. H. Harvey, W. J. Ickes, & R. F. Kidd (Eds.) *New directions in attribution research* (Vol. 2, pp. 59–90). Hillsdale, NJ: Erlbaum.

Weiner, B., Russell, D., & Lerman, D. (1979). The cognition-emotion process in achievement-related contexts. *Journal of Personality and Social Psychology, 37,* 1211–1220.

Wenzlaff, R. M., Wegner, D. M., & Roper, D. W. (1988). Depression and mental control: The resurgence of unwanted negative thoughts. *Journal of Personality and Social Psychology, 55,* 882–892.

Wills, T. A. (1981). Downward social comparison principles in social psychology. *Psychological Bulletin, 90,* 245–271.

Wilson, T. D., & Klaaren, K. J. (1992). "Expectation whirls me round": The role of affective expectations in affective experience. In M. S. Clark (Ed.), *Emotion and social behavior* (pp. 1–31). Newbury Park, CA: Sage.

Wilson, T. D., Lisle, D. J., Kraft, D., & Wetzel, C. G. (1989). Preferences as expectation-driven influences: Effects of affective expectations on affective experience. *Journal of Personality and Social Psychology, 56,* 519–530.

Wood, J. V., Saltzberg, J. A., & Goldsamt, L. A. (1990). Does affect induce self-focused attention? *Journal of Personality and Social Psychology, 58,* 899–908.

Wood, J. V., Taylor, S. E., & Lichtman, R. R. (1985). Social comparison and adjustment to breast cancer. *Journal of Personality and Social Psychology, 49,* 1169–1183.

Wright, J., & Mischel, W. (1982). Influence of affect on cognitive social learning person variables. *Journal of Personality and Social Psychology, 43,* 901–914.

Zahn-Waxler, C., Radke-Yarrow, M., & King, R. A. (1979). Child rearing and children's prosocial initiations toward victims of distress. *Child Development, 50,* 319–330.

Zillmann, D. (1978). Attribution and misattribution of excitatory reactions. In J. H. Harvey, W. J. Ickes, & R. F. Kidd (Eds.), *New directions in attribution research* (Vol. 2, pp. 335–368). Hillsdale, NJ: Erlbaum.

Zillmann, D. (1988). Mood management: Using entertainment to full advantage. In L. Donohew, H. E. Sypher, & E. T. Higgins (Eds.), *Communication, social cognition, and affect* (pp. 147–171). Hillsdale, NJ: Erlbaum.

# 41

# AFFECT AND PROSOCIAL RESPONDING

Nancy Eisenberg, Sandra Losoya,
and Tracy Spinrad

Prosocial behavior, defined as voluntary behavior intended to benefit another (Eisenberg & Fabes, 1998), has
been a topic of psychological interest for some time but
especially since the late 1960s. Much of the work on this
topic has pertained to the role of sociocognitive skills,
situational and socialization influences in the development or maintenance of prosocial behavior (Dovidio,
1984; Eisenberg, 1986; Eisenberg & Fabes, 1998; Krebs &
Miller, 1985; Radke-Yarrow, Zahn-Waxler, & Chapman,
1983). However, unlike in the study of moral judgment
(Kohlberg, 1969, 1984), emotion also has played an important role in theory and research on prosocial behavior.

The role of emotion in prosocial behavior has been
considered primarily in theory and research pertaining
to two types of potential motivators: empathy and mood.
Affectively based empathy has been viewed as the basis
for much prosocial behavior for decades (e.g., Feshbach,
1978; Hoffman, 1975). Thus, researchers have investigated the role of empathy-related responses both in the
development of prosocial responding and in individual
differences in prosocial behavior. In contrast, temporary
positive and negative mood states have been examined
primarily as situational factors that affect the likelihood
of individuals performing prosocial behaviors. These
bodies of work are reviewed in this chapter, as well as
work linking self-conscious emotions and dispositional
emotionality to empathy-related and prosocial responding.

## Definitional Issues

As defined herein, prosocial behavior is mute about an
actor's motivation for assisting. Yet psychologists generally have been interested in the motives behind prosocial
actions. Helping behavior motivated by self-interest usually is valued less than helping motivated by moral values
or concern for another.

Based on this interest in motivation, altruism has been
differentiated from other types of prosocial behaviors. *Altruism* often is defined as intrinsically motivated, voluntary behaviors intended to benefit others—prosocial behaviors motivated by internal motives, such as concern for
others or internalized values, goals, and self-rewards,
rather than by the expectation of concrete or social rewards (Eisenberg & Fabes, 1998). There is disagreement in
regard to whether even altruism actually is motivated by
self-rewards or whether altruism can be motivated by
moral values (Batson, 1991; Batson, 1998; Cialdini,
Brown, Lewis, Luce, & Neuberg, 1997), but these issues
are not central to the focus of this chapter and are not
discussed further.

Eisenberg and colleagues (Eisenberg, Shea, Carlo, &
Knight, 1991), like Hoffman (1975), Feshbach (1978), and
Batson (1991, 1998), believe empathy involves emotion,
as well as cognition (e.g., identification of emotion states,
perspective taking). Similar to Hoffman (1982), Eisenberg
has defined *empathy* as an affective response that stems

from the apprehension or comprehension of another's emotional state or condition and that is identical or very similar to what the other person is feeling or would be expected to feel. However, Eisenberg has suggested that empathy often turns into either sympathy or personal distress or both. *Sympathy* is defined as an affective response that consists of feelings of sorrow or concern for a distressed or needy other. People who experience sympathy do not feel the same emotion as the other person; rather, they feel other-oriented concern (perhaps after or in combination with experiencing empathy). Sympathy can stem from cognitive perspective taking or accessing stored cognitions related to another person's emotional state or condition (e.g., what it is like to have a friend die), as well as from empathy. Sympathy (or sometimes empathy) is considered to be an important motivation for altruistic behavior.

In contrast to sympathy, *personal distress* is defined as a self-focused, aversive emotional reaction to the vicarious experiencing of another's emotions. Thus it involves feelings such as anxiety or discomfort (Batson, 1991). Eisenberg et al. (1991) argued that personal distress, like sympathy, can stem from empathy or from cognitive processes. The distinction between sympathy and personal distress is critical when considering the role of emotion in prosocial behavior. Batson (1991) hypothesized that sympathy (labeled *empathy* by Batson), but not personal distress, is associated with altruistic behavior. When individuals experience sympathy, they are motivated by their other-oriented concern to alleviate the other's distress or need, as long as the cost of helping is not overly high. In contrast, personal distress involves the egoistic motivation of alleviating oneself of distress or discomfort. Thus, Batson hypothesized that people experiencing personal distress will help primarily when they cannot escape from the distressed person easily (and without sanctions) and when helping is the easiest way to reduce one's own aversive emotional state. If escape is easy, people experiencing personal distress are expected to avoid the needy or distressed individual rather than assist.

Given the central role of empathy-related responding in prosocial behavior, much of this chapter concerns empathy-related responding. First, we consider the development of empathy and prosocial behavior. Next we summarize research on the relation of empathy-related responding to individual differences in prosocial behavior. The role of self-conscious emotions (e.g., guilt) in prosocial behavior is considered next, followed by an examination of research on the role of emotionality and regulation in empathy-related responding (situational and dispositional) and prosocial behavior. Finally, we survey theory and findings on the relation of positive and negative mood states to prosocial responding.

## Empathy-Related Responding and Prosocial Behavior

### The Development of Empathy and Its Role in the Emergence of Prosocial Behavior

Contrary to the Piagetian notion that young children are egocentric, many researchers now share the view that rudimentary empathic responding can be observed at an early age. The growth of prosocial behavior is strongly linked to the development of empathy, as altruistic behaviors in early childhood are thought to be motivated primarily by an emotional reaction to another's distress (Hoffman, 1982).

The emergence of empathy and prosocial behaviors occurs during the second year of life and is accompanied by developments in infants' self-awareness and self-other differentiation. Hoffman (1982, 1984) proposed a theoretical model to delineate the processes involved in the development of empathy and prosocial behavior and the role of empathy in children's prosocial behavior. He described a series of four phases that underlie the development of empathy, guilt, and prosocial behavior. This developmental framework outlines the shift with age from self-concern in response to others' distress to empathic concern for others that results in other-oriented prosocial behavior.

Hoffman asserted that in newborns and infants, rudimentary empathic responses are manifested as "global empathy." This stage is defined by a period in which the infant does not differentiate between the self and other (at least in regard to internal states) and in which infants experience self-distress in response to others' distress. The newborn's reactive or contagious crying in response to the sound of someone else's cry is viewed as a simple form of global empathy (or as a precursor of global empathy).

According to Hoffman, around the second year of life, the period of "egocentric empathy" emerges. Although many researchers believe that infants begin to differentiate the self from others during the first year of life (Harter, 1998), young toddlers probably do not distinguish clearly between their own and another's internal states. As toddlers become capable of differentiating the emotional responses of the self from those of others, they can experience empathic concern for another, rather than seeking comfort for themselves. Toddlers in this stage can voluntarily make efforts to comfort another person, but prosocial action is likely to involve the toddlers giving the other person what they themselves find comforting. For example, in response to a distressed adult, the toddler may fetch his or her own teddy bear to comfort the adult. Although this stage is labeled as egocentric, it differs from empathy in the previous stage and should not be considered purely egocentric, as toddlers are responding with appropriate empathic affect.

The period of empathy for another's feelings emerges with the development of rudimentary role-taking abilities as early as 2 to 3 years of age. According to Hoffman (1982), this stage marks the period in which children are increasingly aware of other people's feelings and that others' perspectives may differ from their own. Thus, prosocial actions reflect an awareness of the other person's needs (versus the egocentric empathy of the previous stage). Moreover, with the development of language, children begin to empathize and sympathize with a wider range of emotions.

Hoffman (1982) suggested that, with further cognitive development, children begin to exhibit the ability to experience empathic responses even when the other person is not physically present. By late childhood, children can empathize with another person's general condition or plight. Further, children eventually understand the plight of an entire group or class of people (e.g., the poor) and may respond empathically.

Thus Hoffman (1982) proposed that with increasing cognitive maturation, children are better able to respond with concern for others' distress. There is some support for Hoffman's theory. As suggested by Hoffman, there is evidence of "global empathy" in newborns and young infants. Newborns have been found to cry in response to the cries of other infants (Sagi & Hoffman, 1976; Simner, 1971), suggesting that infants are biologically predisposed to experience a rudimentary form of empathy. However, reactive crying is not found in all infants or situations (Hay, Nash, & Pederson, 1981; Martin & Clark, 1982), and it is unclear if it reflects primitive empathy, a conditioned response, or emotional contagion (R. Thompson, 1987).

Six-month-old infants' reactions to others' distress tend to take the form of seeking comfort for themselves or merely exhibiting interest (e.g., Hay et al., 1981). However, by 9 months of age, it is clear that infants are responsive to the emotional signals of at least some people. For instance, in a study in which mothers expressed sadness, their 9-month-old infants were found to display more negative emotional expressions than they did when their mothers expressed joy. The infants tended then to avert their gaze away from their mothers. On the other hand, the infants expressed more joy during a condition in which mothers' expressions of joy were induced (Termine & Izard, 1988).

Research on social referencing provides evidence that infants not only are responsive to others' emotional signals but also make use of others' emotional displays to alter their own behavior. In these procedures, infants are confronted with an ambiguous situation and with their caregivers' reactions to the situation. The infants' behavior is then observed. For example, 1-year-old infants avoided crossing an apparent drop-off on the visual cliff (Campos, Barrett, Lamb, Goldsmith, & Sternberg, 1983; Sorce, Emde, Campos & Klinnert, 1985) and were less likely to approach unusual toys (Gunnar & Stone, 1984; Klinnert, 1984) when their mothers displayed negative affect toward the cliff or toys. On the other hand, when mothers displayed positive emotional signals, infants were willing to cross the apparent drop-off and were more likely to approach an unusual toy. Thus, infants appear to be sensitive to others' nonverbal expressions from an early age.

Consistent with Hoffman's theory, between 12 and 18 months of age, toddlers clearly react to others' negative emotions and sometimes exhibit prosocial behavior in response to another's distress. Zahn-Waxler, Radke-Yarrow, and their colleagues (1982; Zahn-Waxler, Radke-Yarrow, Wagner, & Chapman, 1992) found that toddlers often react to others' negative emotions with orienting responses and distress reactions. However, between 12 and 18 months, toddlers also sometimes displayed concerned attention and help giving (including positive contact, verbal reassurance, prosocial acts), and self-oriented distress reactions decreased (see also Kaneko & Hamazaki, 1987). Moreover, observations of young children's responses to their siblings' distress indicate that toddlers recognize others' distress and are capable of responding with attempts to comfort (Dunn, 1988).

As proposed by Hoffman (1982), young children's prosocial behaviors also have been associated with indices of cognitive maturation. Toddlers who display evidence of self-recognition (indicating a clear self-other distinction) tend to be relatively empathic and likely to display prosocial behaviors (Bischof-Kohler, 1991; Johnson, 1982; Zahn-Waxler et al., 1992). Further, children's hypothesis testing in response to witnessing another's distress (an indication of perspective taking) was positively related to children's prosocial behaviors at ages 2 and 4 to 5 (Zahn-Waxler et. al., 1995; Zahn-Waxler, Robinson, & Emde, 1992).

With increasing age, preschoolers are more likely to respond to others' distress with empathy and prosocial behaviors. Phinney, Fesbach, and Farver (1986), for example, found that preschoolers' empathic reactions to crying peers were relatively infrequent; however, older preschoolers responded more empathically than did younger preschoolers. In addition, children report more empathy with increasing age in the preschool and elementary school years (Eisenberg & Fabes, 1998; Lennon & Eisenberg, 1987; Strayer, 1993).

Fabes and Eisenberg (1996; Eisenberg & Fabes, 1998) conducted a meta-analysis of 179 studies and confirmed this developmental trend. Older children exhibited more prosocial behavior than did younger children. However, effect sizes for age differences varied depending on the study qualities (e.g., method, type of design, type of prosocial behavior). For example, effect sizes were greater when the prosocial-behavior variable was giving instrumental help in two age-group comparisons (childhood vs. preschool and early childhood vs. later childhood comparisons) but were lower for comparisons of older children (adolescence vs. childhood and early adolescence vs. later adolescence comparisons). In addition, larger effect sizes were found when researchers used observational or self-report measures than other-report measures when comparing preschool and childhood age groups, but not older groups. Moreover, there were higher effect sizes in studies with experimental/structured than with naturalistic/correlational methods. In addition, empathy increased with age, at least for observational and self-report measures of empathy-related responding. Thus, although the age differences identified were complex, it appears that empathy and prosocial actions increase as children get older.

## The Relation of Empathy-Related Responding to Prosocial Behavior

As was noted previously, empathy-related responding, especially sympathy, is believed to motivate much prosocial behavior. In general, empirical evidence exists of a positive association between empathy-related responding and prosocial behavior, although results have varied with the measure of empathy-related responding (Eisenberg & Miller, 1987).

In many studies, measures of global or undifferentiated empathy-like responses have been used. However, as noted earlier, sympathy and personal distress are expected to be differentially related to helping behavior. In fact, in studies in which sympathy and personal distress have been differentiated, the pattern of findings has been relatively systematic.

Consistent relations of empathy-related responding to prosocial behavior have been obtained most often when empathy has been assessed within a single context, with the beneficiary of assistance being the same person or group as the target of empathy. Assessments of empathy-related responding usually have consisted of people's self-reported, facial, and physiological responses to empathy-inducing media (i.e., audiotaped or film clips of distressed others) or to distressed or needy confederates. Measures of prosocial behavior directed toward the object of participants' vicarious responses often have taken the forms of reported or enacted generosity, helpfulness, and volunteerism (Batson, 1991; Eisenberg & Fabes, 1990). However, some researchers have examined the relationship of situational empathy-related responding to dispositional prosocial behavior (often assessed with self-or other-reports) or to prosocial behavior in other contexts (e.g., Eisenberg et al., 1990; see Eisenberg & Fabes, 1998).

In studies in which situational self-report measures of empathy or sympathy were collected, relationships with prosocial behavior often have not been significant for younger children (see Eisenberg & Fabes, 1990; Eisenberg et al., 1989; Eisenberg et al., 1990), whereas situational self-reports usually have predicted prosocial behavior in the expected manner reasonably well for adults (Batson, 1991, 1998; Eisenberg & Fabes, 1998; Eisenberg & Miller, 1987). Children's reports of positive affect to empathy-inducing films occasionally have been negatively related to prosocial behavior, and their reports of negative emotionality, including sympathy and personal distress, occasionally predict helping among school-aged children (e.g., Fabes, Eisenberg, & Miller, 1990).

In studies with adults, especially those involving less extreme empathy-inducing situations, reports of both distress and sympathy sometimes have been positively associated with prosocial behavior (Carlo, Eisenberg, Troyer, Switzer, & Speer, 1991). This pattern of findings may have occurred because in some situations adults' reports on the adjectives selected to reflect personal distress could tap sympathy as well as personal distress (i.e., the adjectives do not clearly differentiate between the two types of response; Batson et al., 1988).

Most studies that contain facial and gestural measures have been conducted with children. The number of significant findings has differed across studies; however, very few findings are contrary to predictions, and only infrequently have researchers obtained no significant findings. For example, Zahn-Waxler and her colleagues found that 1- to 2-year-olds who displayed high levels of facial empathic concern also were high on prosocial behavior in response to distressed others (Zahn-Waxler, Radke-Yarrow, et al., 1992; Zahn-Waxler, Robinson, & Emde, 1992). Moreover, toddlers' self-distress in response to another's emotion (indicative of personal distress) was negatively correlated with toddlers' prosocial behaviors when they were bystanders to the other person's distress (although this correlation was positive when the other's distress was caused by the child, perhaps because self-distress reflected guilt; Zahn-Waxler, Radke-Yarrow, et al., 1992).

Facial reactions to empathy-inducing films usually have been obtained in studies with preschoolers and school-aged children. In these studies, concerned attention and/or sadness generally have been positively related to prosocial behavior, whereas distressed facial expressions have been negatively correlated (Fabes et al., 1994; Miller, Eisenberg, Fabes, & Shell, 1996; see also Eisenberg & Fabes, 1990, 1998). In addition, facial markers of situational facial sadness or concerned attention to an empathy-inducing film have been related to spontaneous real-life prosocial behavior in other contexts (Eisenberg et al., 1990; Eisenberg, McCreath, & Ahn, 1988) and occasionally to teachers' reports of children's dispositional prosocial behavior (findings are quite weak for parents' or peers' reports of prosocial behavior; Holmgren, Eisenberg, & Fabes, 1998; Roberts & Strayer, 1996).

In some studies, facial personal distress has been positively related to preschoolers' compliant (i.e, requested) prosocial behaviors but not to spontaneously emitted prosocial behavior (Eisenberg et al., 1990; Eisenberg, Mc-Creath & Ahn, 1988). The former type of prosocial behavior appears to reflect low assertiveness rather than other-oriented concern and generally has been measured in actual interactions with peers who were not the target of the children's empathy-related responding. These findings support the view that children experiencing personal distress reactions may engage in prosocial behaviors in situations in which it is difficult to escape contact with peers who request prosocial behavior. Other data suggest that children prone to personal distress are low in social skills and may become targets of peer requests for objects and assistance (Eisenberg & Fabes, 1992; Eisenberg et al., 1990).

Few researchers have examined the relationships of facial markers of adults' empathy-related responding to prosocial behavior. In one study in which adults and children viewed an empathy-inducing videotape, facial sadness was positively related to adults' prosocial behavior (Eisenberg, Fabes, et al., 1989). However, sometimes adults exhibit so little facial responding that it is difficult to use facial reactions as measures of empathy-related reactions (Eisenberg, Fabes, Schaller, Miller, et al., 1991).

Researchers also have examined the relation of prosocial behavior to physiological measures of heart rate (HR) and skin conductance (SC). Typically, children's or adults' physiological reactions to empathy-inducing films have been measured, and subsequently they have had opportunities to assist individuals in the film (or people in the same situation). Heart rate deceleration, a measure that has been associated with the intake of information and an outward focus of attention in psychophysiological studies of arousal (Cacioppo & Sandman, 1978; Lacey, Kagan, Lacey, & Moss, 1963), has been viewed as a marker of sympathy when assessed during an evocative portion of the film and generally has been positively related to prosocial behavior. In contrast, heart rate acceleration, a response that has been associated with anxiety, distress, and active coping (Cacioppo & Sandman, 1978; Lazarus, 1974), generally has been associated with low prosocial behavior (Eisenberg & Fabes, 1990; Eisenberg et al., 1990; Fabes et al., 1994; see also Eisenberg & Fabes, 1998). Although not all findings have been consistent and a few have contradicted the general pattern of findings (e.g., Eisenberg, Fabes, Karbon, Murphy, Carlo, & Wosinski, 1996), the overall pattern is fairly clear. In one study, high mean HR in response to empathy-inducing stimuli was positively related to higher prosocial behavior; however, HR deceleration during the saddest portion of an empathy-inducing film also predicted a variety of measures of prosocial behavior (Zahn-

Waxler, Cole, Welsh, & Fox, 1995). Thus, HR deceleration in response to the clearest depictions of sadness or distress may be a better predictor of prosocial behavior than is overall level of HR in response to evocative films. Moreover, HR acceleration is likely to be positively related to helping if it is measured as the individual is preparing to stand up and assist another person (Gaertner & Dovidio, 1977) because preparation for physical mobilization and actual mobilization increase HR.

In a couple of studies, Fabes and Eisenberg have found evidence that higher SC is associated with lower helpfulness in an experimental setting or as reported by mothers (Fabes, Eisenberg & Eisenbud, 1993; Fabes et al., 1994). In contrast, Zahn-Waxler et al. (1995) obtained no relationship between SC in response to a sad stimulus and children's responding to others' distress. Thus more research is needed to verify whether SC predicts low prosocial responding.

In a number of studies, *dispositional* empathy-related responding, assessed with self-reports and other-reports, has been the index of empathy-related responding. In general, dispositional measures of sympathy have been positively related to prosocial behavior, whereas personal distress occasionally has been negatively related to prosocial behavior (more so in adults; Carlo, Eisenberg, & Knight, 1992; Eisenberg et al., 1999; Estrada, 1995; Strayer & Roberts, 1989; see also Davis, 1994; Eisenberg & Miller, 1987; Eisenberg & Fabes, 1998). Sometimes dispositional measures of empathy-related responding have contained items that tap empathy and sympathy, as well as personal distress, which could undermine the pattern of relationships in some studies for some age groups (see Eisenberg & Miller, 1987).

Taken together, these findings provide support for the notion that there are clear and relatively consistent relationships between empathy-related responding and prosocial behaviors. Nonetheless, it should be recognized that most work on the relationship between markers of empathy-related responding and prosocial behaviors has been conducted in the United States. It is possible that empathy-related responses (and/or measures thereof) vary across cultures as a function of factors such as cultural emphasis on an other-orientation (and differences in who is considered part of the in-group and worthy of empathy/ sympathy) or on masking of emotion. In one cross-cultural study, German and Japanese kindergarten girls' responses to an adult's distress were observed. Sympathetic responses and prosocial behaviors were positively related for both German and Japanese girls. There was a negative relation between distress and prosocial behavior for the German girls but not for the Japanese girls (Trommsdorff, 1995). It is unclear why the latter finding occurred; perhaps Japanese children are less overwhelmed by their distress than are German girls because they receive more comfort and support when distressed. Dispositional measures of empathy or sympathy also have been associated with prosocial behavior in Japan (Ando, 1987; Asakawa, Iwawaki, Mondori, & Minami, 1987). Thus, it is likely that the relationship between empathy-related responding and prosocial behavior is found in a number of countries and cultures.

## The Role of Moral Emotions in Prosocial Behavior

Self-conscious emotions, like empathy-related responding, have been linked to the development and performance of prosocial behaviors. Recently investigators have differentiated between guilt and shame and have proposed that these emotions have distinct relations to prosocial outcomes. Both emotions can be experienced as a result of a transgression or a violation of a moral standard (Linsay-Hartz, 1984; Tangney, 1996); however, these emotions purportedly differ in the degree of focus on the self (Lewis, 1971; Tangney, 1990, 1991, 1998). Shame has been defined as a feeling involving a negative evaluation of the entire self. Thus shame is associated with painful feelings of low worth and powerlessness. Guilt, on the other hand, entails a negative evaluation of a particular behavior, not the individual's identity or sense of self. However, the degree to which these two emotions actually are distinct is unclear (e.g., Ferguson, Stegge, Miller, & Olsen, 1999), and part of the differences may reflect how they are operationalized in research.

Shame and guilt begin to emerge during the second year of life and are connected with advances such as development of self-awareness and the internalization of standards (Hoffman, 1982; Lewis, 1992; Lewis, Sullivan, Stanger, & Weiss, 1989). In regard to shame, children as young as 2 years of age exhibit shamelike behaviors in reaction to achievement failures (Stipek, Recchia, & McClintic, 1992). Moreover, there is evidence that 3-year-olds are more likely to exhibit shame reactions when failing at an easy task than at a difficult task, indicating that young children's shame reactions are associated with an understanding of standards and ideals (Lewis, Alessandri & Sullivan, 1992; Stipek et al., 1992).

In discussing the development of guilt, Hoffman (1982) proposed that guilt is dependent on feelings of empathy toward another and an awareness of being the cause of the other's distress. According to Hoffman (1982), guilt, like empathy, emerges with changes in cognitive development. Early signs of guilt cannot occur until the individual has a cognitive awareness of the self as distinct from others. Further, when the child develops an awareness of the causal effects of his or her actions, true interpersonal guilt can be observed. With age, when children are able to differentiate between one's own and another's internal states, they can experience guilt over another's hurt feelings. Fi-

nally, in late childhood or adolescence, the individual can begin to feel guilt over action or inaction beyond the immediate situation (e.g., imagining the harmful effects of one's behavior on a victim, including over time.)

Consistent with Hoffman's proposal, signs of guilt or conscience have been observed in young toddlers (Barrett, 1995; Cole, Barrett, & Zahn-Waxler, 1992; Kochanska, 1993; Kochanska, Casey, & Fukumoto, 1995; Zahn-Waxler et al., 1983; Zahn-Waxler & Kochanksa, 1990). There is evidence that some 2-year-olds try to repair the situation when they have hurt others or caused harm (Cole et al., 1992; Zahn-Waxler, Radke-Yarrow, et al., 1992). Guilt reactions in response to distress to others caused by the child tend to increase with age (R. Thompson & Hoffman, 1980; Zahn-Waxler & Robinson, 1995).

Although shame and guilt may have similar developmental trajectories, they are believed to be differentially linked to moral behavior, empathy, and prosocial behavior. Many view guilt as the more "moral" emotion (Barrett & Campos, 1987; Baumeister Stillwell, & Heatherton, 1994; Lewis, 1971; Tangney, 1998). Normal guilt (rather than pathological guilt) is believed to be associated with reparation and is viewed as motivating people to apologize, seek forgiveness for wrongdoing, or make reparations (Hoffman, 1982, 1984; Linsay-Hartz, 1984). Shame, on the other hand, is thought to motivate an avoidance response or even rage, and shame experiences have been described as feeling the need to hide or escape the situation (Linsay-Hartz, 1984; Tangney, 1998).

Shame and guilt have been distinguished in research with young children, as well as adults. In work with 2-year-olds, children were presented with the experimenter's "favorite doll," which broke when the experimenter left the room. Children responded in either one of two ways. Some children, labeled "Amenders," demonstrated behaviors consistent with a guilt response, as they confessed that the doll had broken and tried to repair the situation. Other children were labeled "Avoiders"; they demonstrated behavior consistent with shame reactions. They did not confess that the doll had broken, and they tried to avoid the experimenter (Barrett, Zahn-Waxler & Cole, 1993).

Some researchers have used the term "conscience" in describing children's reactions to wrongdoings—reactions that seem to reflect, in part, guilt. Kochanska and her colleagues found that components of conscience (that were highly suggestive of guilt) were associated with a low frequency of children's transgressions (touching a forbidden object) in 26- to 41-month-old children. In addition, toddlers' sensitivity to violations of standards (i.e., flawed objects) was related to their attempts to repair situations or apologize after mishaps with an experimenter (Kochanska et al., 1995). Further, Ferguson, Stegge, and Damhuis (1991) found that 8- to 11-year-olds believed that guilty feelings, much more than feelings of shame, were associated with a sense of regret and an urge to make reparations.

Guilt appears to be related to prosocial behavior, even in young children. In one study, children's attributions of guilt when discussing simple stories about suffering individuals were strongly linked to helping among preschool through sixth-grade children, supporting the notion that children who have the disposition to feel responsibility for others' distress are more likely to help in situations that call for it (Chapman, Zahn-Waxler, Cooperman, & Iannotti, 1987). Children and adolescents also sometimes report that feelings of guilt are important determinants of prosocial behavior (Eisenberg-Berg, 1979; Karylowski, 1982; R. Thompson & Hoffman, 1980), and the degree to which adolescents describe guilt as a motivator of prosocial behavior (in studies of prosocial moral reasoning) increases with age (Eisenberg, Carlo, Murphy, & Van Court, 1995).

In laboratory studies with adults, people who have accidentally harmed others (e.g., broken a valued object), in comparison with those who have done no harm, are more likely to help the injured party (e.g., Freedman, 1970; Wallace & Sadalla, 1966). Such helping may be due to guilt, although it also could be due to the desire to look or feel better (i.e., alleviate the negative mood that guilt produces; Cialdini, Kenrick, & Baumann, 1982).

Consistent with Hoffman's (1982) theorizing, guilt appears to be linked not only with prosocial behavior but also with empathy. R. Thompson and Hoffman (1980) tested the effects of an empathy induction on guilt arousal in children and found that children who were asked to consider the victim's feelings after wrongdoing (i.e., to empathize or take another's perspective) exhibited more intense guilt than those who were not. In a study of adults, guilt was positively associated with adults' self-reported, other-oriented empathic responsiveness to others, whereas shame was negatively associated, especially when guilt was statistically controlled for. Shame was positively correlated with personal distress reactions (i.e., aversive, self-focused reactions to others in need or distress; Tangney, 1991). When people provided autobiographical accounts of shame and guilt experiences, they conveyed more empathy in guilt than in shame descriptions, although this association was somewhat stronger among adults than among children (Tangney, Marschall, Rosenberg, Barlow, & Wagner, 1996). Nonetheless, because shame and guilt are substantially correlated in much of this research and because these analyses often were part correlations controlling for one another, it is likely that the distinction between guilt and shame and how they relate to empathy are not quite as clear-cut as these findings suggest. Moreover, measures that tap more global and chronic guilt tend to be positively associated with children's and adults' ex-

ternalizing problem behavior (Ferguson & Stegge, 1998; Ferguson, Stegge, Miller, & Olsen, 1999). It is possible that these measures of chronic guilt assess a different form of guilt than some other measures (i.e, anxiety-based guilt as opposed to empathy-based guilt) or that extremely low or high levels of guilt do not foster moral behavior.

## The Role of Emotionality and Regulation in Empathy-Related Responding and Prosocial Behavior

### Emotion and the Experience of Situational Empathy-related Responding

The findings summarized herein provide substantial support for the assertion that sympathy and personal distress are distinct emotional reactions linked to different motivational states (i.e., altruistic and egoistic motivation, respectively). An important question is why sympathy often is associated with other-oriented motivation, whereas personal distress is associated with egoistic motivation.

Before sympathy and personal distress were consistently differentiated in the research, Hoffman (1982) suggested that overarousal due to empathy results in a self-focus. Consistent with this view, Eisenberg, Fabes, Murphy, et al. (1994; also see Eisenberg & Fabes, 1992) hypothesized that feelings of personal distress often stem from empathic overarousal in situations involving another's negative emotion. When others' emotions evoke too much empathic negative emotion, the resultant emotional arousal is aversive and thus results in a focus on one's own emotional state.

Some empirical findings are consistent with the view that empathic overarousal results in self-focused personal distress. First, in some experimental studies, negative emotional arousal has been associated with a focus on the self (e.g., Wood, Saltzberg, & Goldsamt, 1990; Wood, Saltzberg, Neale, Stone, & Rachmiel, 1990). There also is evidence that people, especially girls and women, sometimes verbally report more distress when in situations designed to elicit distress rather than sympathy (Eisenberg, Fabes, et al., 1988; Eisenberg, Schaller, et al., 1988). In addition, people exhibit higher skin conductance and heart rate acceleration in situations likely to elicit an emotion akin to personal distress (in contrast to sympathy or baseline responding; Eisenberg, Fabes, et al., 1988; Eisenberg, Fabes, Schaller, Carlo, & Miller, 1991; Eisenberg, Fabes, Schaller, Miller, et al., 1991; Eisenberg, Schaller, et al., 1988). Further, distressed or fearful facial reactions sometimes have been shown to be higher in experimental contexts expected to induce reactions akin to personal distress than in neutral or sympathy-inducing contexts (e.g., Eisenberg, Fabes, et al., 1988; Eisenberg, Fabes, Schaller, Carlo, &

Miller, 1991; compare with Eisenberg, Schaller, et al., 1988).

Eisenberg, Fabes, Murphy, et al. (1994) further argued that people who can maintain their vicarious emotional arousal at a moderate but nonaversive level would be expected to experience sympathy. The type of evidence just cited generally is consistent with this view. Specifically, skin conductance and heart rate are lower when people are viewing sympathy-inducing rather than distress-inducing films (Eisenberg, Fabes, et al., 1988; Eisenberg, Fabes, Schaller, Miller, et al., 1991; Eisenberg, Fabes, Schaller, Miller, & Carlo, 1991) or are talking about sympathy-inducing events versus distressing events (Eisenberg, Schaller, et al., 1988). Moreover, facial concerned attention and sadness in response to empathy-inducing stimuli—emotional reactions reported to reflect less arousal than distress (e.g., Shaver, Schwartz, Kirson, & O'Connor, 1987)—tend to be associated with situational sympathy in children (Eisenberg, Fabes, et al., 1988; Eisenberg, Fabes, Schaller, Carlo, & Miller, 1991; Eisenberg, Schaller, et al., 1988). Further, according to teacher ratings, low and moderate levels of children's emotional intensity but not high emotional intensity have been associated with young children's concerned facial responses to an empathy-inducing film (Eisenberg & Fabes, 1995).

Thus, there is initial evidence that personal distress is associated with higher levels of negative emotion arousal than is sympathy. The notion that level of vicarious emotional arousal affects empathy-related responding is important because it provides a basis for making predictions about individual differences linked to sympathetic and prosocial responding.

## The Role of Dispositional Emotionality and Regulation in Empathy-Related Responding and Prosocial Behavior

If personal distress is associated with empathic overarousal, whereas sympathy is an outcome of a moderate and optimal level of empathic arousal, dispositional differences in emotionality and regulatory capacities would be expected to influence individual differences in trait sympathy and personal distress.

In regard to emotion, both the dispositional tendency to experience emotions intensely and the ease with which individuals respond intensely are likely to contribute to the degree to which children become emotionally aroused in a given empathy-inducing context. These aspects of temperament and personality have a constitutional basis (Plomin & Stocker, 1989; Rothbart & Bates, 1998) and may account for part of the genetic contribution to empathy (Zahn-Waxler, Robinson, & Emde, 1992). Of course, it is likely that environmental factors also influence the quantity or quality of individual differences in emotionality

(Belsky, Fish, & Isabella, 1991; Goldsmith, Buss, & Lemery, 1997).

Eisenberg and Fabes (Eisenberg, Fabes, Murphy, et al., 1994; Eisenberg, Fabes, Murphy, et al. 1996) hypothesized that individuals who are high in *emotional intensity* should be especially prone to personal distress. Sympathy also was hypothesized to be linked to relatively high emotional intensity, especially on measures of emotional intensity that reflect intensity of a range of emotions (positive as well as negative). However, individuals prone to intense emotions were hypothesized to experience sympathy only if they also are well regulated. A predisposition to experience *negative* emotions frequently (but not necessarily intensely) was hypothesized to predict primarily personal distress, although the degree of prediction might be expected to vary with the type of negative emotion. For example, people prone to anger and frustration or anxiety would be expected to be prone to personal distress (Eisenberg & Fabes, 1992; Eisenberg, Fabes, Guthrie, & Reiser, 2000). In contrast, people prone to nonhostile and less arousing negative emotions (such as sadness) might be prone to sympathy as well as personal distress.

In regard to regulation, modulation of both internal emotional states or processes (i.e., emotional regulation) and emotion-related behavior is hypothesized to be relevant to empathy-related responding. Emotion regulation includes neurophysiological regulation and control of attentional processes (e.g., the ability to voluntarily shift and focus attention), as well as coping by modifying one's cognitive interpretation of emotionally arousing events and information (Eisenberg, Fabes, Guthrie, & Reiser, 2000; R. Thompson, 1994). The abilities to shift and focus attention have been related to the management of negative emotion (Buss & Goldsmith, 1998; Derryberry & Rothbart, 1988; Eisenberg, Fabes, Nyman, Bernzweig, & Pinuelas, 1994; Rothbart, Ziaie, & O'Boyle, 1992; Rusting & Nolen-Hoeksema, 1998; also see Kochanska, Coy, Tjebkes, & Husarek, 1998). In addition, the capacity to regulate emotion-related behavior is likely to contribute to sympathy, especially when combined with the ability to regulate attention. If people can manage their behavior when emotionally aroused, they are likely to be able to cope with negative emotion in constructive ways (e.g., by inhibiting anger rather than aggressing). Moreover, due to repeated experiences of success in dealing with situations involving negative emotion, regulated people may be less likely than unregulated peers to become threatened and over-aroused in contexts involving negative emotion.

In summarizing relevant empirical findings, we focus primarily on the data pertaining to dispositional emotionality and discuss regulation only in regard to its interaction with dispositional emotionality in predicting empathy-related responding (see Eisenberg, Wentzel, & Harris, 1998, for a broader review). Findings on the relationship between empathy-related responding and emotionality differ for the index of emotionality and the age of the study participants; moreover, age and type of measure are confounded. Measures of adults' dispositional emotionality generally have been self-reported, although other reports (e.g., from friends) sometimes have been obtained. Measures of children's dispositional emotional responding usually have consisted of other reports (from teachers and parents), although self-reports also have been obtained occasionally. People probably are better able to assess relatively covert emotions such as sadness or anxiety in themselves than in others simply by viewing them. Moreover, adults' reports of children's negative emotionality often may inordinately reflect externalizing emotions, such as anger and frustration, rather than internalizing emotions, such as sadness and anxiety, simply because the former are associated with more salient problem behavior, especially in the school context (Eisenberg, Fabes, Nyman, et al., 1994). Thus, it is likely that adults' reports of children's negative emotions reflect somewhat more externalizing emotions than do self-reports of adults' own emotions.

These differences in measures of emotionality may underlie the differences found in the relationship of emotionality to empathy-related responding in adults and children. Personal distress consistently has been positively correlated with adults' self-reported dispositional frequency and intensity of negative emotions (Eisenberg, Fabes, Murphy, et al., 1994; Eisenberg & Okun, 1996). Findings for sympathy are less consistent. In one study, Carlo, Eisenberg, Troyer, Switzer, and Speer (1991) found that dispositional personal distress, but not sympathy, grouped in a factor analysis with a measure of high emotional intensity. However, other findings suggest a positive association between emotional intensity and adults' sympathy (Eisenberg, Fabes, Murphy, et al., 1996; Eisenberg & Okun, 1996; Larsen, Diener, & Cropanzano, 1987; Okun, Shepard, & Eisenberg, 2000).

The tendency to experience negative emotions frequently tends to be somewhat less strongly positively associated with sympathy than with personal distress (Davis, 1983), although dispositional sadness correlates as strongly with sympathy as with personal distress (Eisenberg, Fabes, Murphy, et al., 1994). For example, Eisenberg, Fabes, Murphy, et al. (1994) found that self-reported dispositional negative emotionality (frequency of negative emotions) was somewhat more strongly related to adults' self-reported dispositional personal distress than to sympathy; moreover, personal distress but not sympathy was related to reports by friends of participants' dispositional negative emotionality. Thus, to some degree, negative emotionality has been linked to both adults' self-reported dispositional sympathy and personal distress, although the association may be somewhat stronger or more consistent for personal distress.

Among children, general emotional intensity (i.e., intensity of emotionality on items in which valence of emotion was not specifically positive or negative) has not been consistently correlated with dispositional sympathy (Eisenberg, Fabes, Murphy, et al., 1996; Eisenberg, Fabes, Shepard, et al., 1998; Guthrie et al., 1997; Murphy, Shepard, Eisenberg, Fabes, & Guthrie 1999). Moreover, dispositional and situational negative emotionality sometimes have been positively related to measures of empathy (rather than of clear sympathy), especially in young children (e.g., Robinson, Zahn-Waxler, & Emde, 1994; Rothbart, Ahadi, & Hershey, 1994; Saklofske & Eysenck, 1983; see also Eisenberg & Fabes, 1998). In contrast, researchers often have found a negative association between adults' reports of frequency and intensity of children's negative emotionality and children's dispositional sympathy (Eisenberg, Fabes, Murphy et al., 1996; Eisenberg et al., 1998; Murphy et al., 1999), as well as situational concern (Eisenberg & Fabes, 1995). Moreover, Eisenberg, Fabes, Murphy et al. (1996) found that boys prone to high physiological arousal in response to a distressing film clip were low on dispositional sympathy. Thus, children prone to negative emotions appear to be low in situational and dispositional sympathy, and there is some, albeit very limited, evidence that children's personal distress is associated with their tendency to experience negative emotions intensely.

Relations between prosocial behavior and measures of children's emotionality generally are consistent with the findings for sympathy. Children prone to negative emotions, including anger, fear, sadness, and anxiety, tend to be relatively low in prosocial behavior (Denham, 1986; Eisenberg, Fabes, Karbon, Murphy, Wosinski, et al., 1996; Tremblay, Vitaro, Gagnon, Piche, & Royer, 1992; see also Eisenberg & Fabes, 1998). Conversely, children who are emotionally positive in general tend to be relatively high in prosocial behavior as well as empathy/sympathy (Denham, 1986; Eisenberg, Cameron, Tryon, & Dodez, 1981; Eisenberg, Fabes, Murphy, et al., 1996; Strayer, 1980; see Eisenberg & Fabes, 1998).

Of most interest are interaction effects between dispositional emotionality and regulation. As mentioned previously, Eisenberg, Fabes, and colleagues hypothesized that people prone to intense and frequent negative emotions are especially likely to experience personal distress if they also are unregulated (Eisenberg, Fabes, Murphy, et al., 1994). In contrast, people who are optimally regulated would be expected to more readily experience sympathy than personal distress, even if they are prone to intense emotions, because they are able to effectively modulate their vicarious negative emotion. Some findings support this prediction or at least indicate that there are interaction effects, although relevant tests of the hypothesis are few and the data are not highly consistent.

In studies with adults, the predicted interactions have not been found (Eisenberg, Fabes, Murphy, et al., 1994;

Eisenberg & Okun, 1996; Okun et al., 2000). However, in a study of the elderly in which most of the study participants were women, an interaction was found for women between dispositional negative emotional intensity and regulation (a composite of emotional and behavioral regulation) when predicting personal distress. Personal distress decreased with increasing regulation for women at all levels of negative emotional intensity, but particularly for women who were low or average in negative emotional intensity. Thus, the relationship between regulation and personal distress was especially stronger for women who were not prone to intense negative emotions. Older women who were high in negative emotional intensity appeared more likely than their peers to be overwhelmed by vicariously induced negative emotion, even if they were high in regulation, although even this group of women showed a significant drop in personal distress as a function of increasing regulation. Perhaps elderly people have more difficulty than younger individuals modulating intense negative emotion and often are not successful.

In research with children, Eisenberg and colleagues obtained evidence of the predicted moderational effects. In a study of 6- to 8-year-olds, an interaction was found between general emotional intensity and regulation when predicting teacher-reported child sympathy (Eisenberg, Fabes, Murphy, et al., 1996). Children rated low in regulation were low in sympathy regardless of their general emotional intensity. However, for children who were moderate or relatively high in regulation, sympathy increased with greater general emotional intensity. Thus, children who were likely to be emotionally intense were sympathetic if they were at least moderately well regulated. Two years later, dispositional sympathy was predicted by a similar interaction between behavioral regulation and general emotional intensity, albeit only in boys. Sympathy increased with greater regulation in boys who were moderate or high in general emotional intensity. Boys low in general emotional intensity were relatively low in sympathy regardless of regulation, perhaps because they were unlikely to experience vicarious emotion.

In addition, at the follow-up, children low in both general emotional intensity and attention focusing were low in sympathy, whereas those low in general emotional intensity but high in attention focusing were relatively high in sympathy. Sympathy did not change as a function of level of attention focusing for children who were average or high in general emotional intensity. Thus, attention focusing was associated with sympathy in children who were relatively low in general emotional intensity. In children who are not predisposed to experience emotions with much intensity, the tendency to focus attention on external events may enhance their sympathy by increasing the intake of information about others and, consequently, cognitive perspective taking (Eisenberg, Fabes, Shepard, et al., 1998).

In another study of elementary schoolchildren, dispositional emotionality and regulation interacted when predicting dispositional prosocial behavior (nominations by peers). For girls, high regulation was associated with high levels of prosocial behavior regardless of negative emotionality. However, for girls who were moderate or low in regulation, prosocial nominations decreased as a function of increased negative emotionality. For boys, low regulation was associated with low levels of prosocial nominations regardless of level of negative emotion, whereas prosocial nominations decreased with increases of negative emotionality for boys who were moderate or high in regulation. Girls in this study were high in attentional regulation, so it is possible that highly regulated girls were able to modulate very high levels of negative emotion. In contrast, boys low in regulation may have been so low that they had difficulty regulating their emotion even if they were not prone to negative emotionality (Eisenberg, Fabes, Karbon, Murphy, Wosinski, et al., 1996).

In summary, it appears that children's sympathy is predicted by a combination of individual differences in emotionality and regulation. This pattern of findings supports the view that sympathy is an outcome of an optimal level of vicarious emotional arousal. For children prone to intense positive and negative emotions, regulation is important for modulating the effects of that emotional reactivity. For children who are not emotional, the ability to focus attention may enhance the likelihood of children attending to others' needs.

## The Relationship of Mood to Prosocial Behavior

Emotional states that are transient and not specifically vicariously induced, such as positive and negative moods, also have been associated with prosocial behavior. Positive mood, experimentally induced through procedures such as receiving money or gifts, scoring well on exams or games, or recalling happy events, generally has been found to increase prosocial behavior in both children and adults (Carlson, Charlin, & Miller, 1988; Isen, Clark, & Schwartz, 1976; Isen & Levin, 1972). For instance, children induced to feel happy share more of their experimental winnings with classmates than do those induced to feel sad or neutral (Rosenhan, Underwood, & Moore, 1974), and adults induced to feel positive through a success-versus-failure manipulation show increases in helpfulness (Isen, 1970; Rosenhan, 1972).

Although positive mood has been found to increase prosocial behavior in general, certain factors associated with the specific helping task or situation may counteract the altruistic tendencies evoked by positive mood. For instance, some studies have shown that positive mood-related helping decreases when the helping task is thought to be unpleasant (Forest, Clark, Mills, & Isen, 1979; Isen & Levin, 1972). The thought of engaging in an unpleasant helping task may elicit negative emotions such as anxiety or disgust. Thus, any inclination toward positive mood-related helping may be diminished because the positive mood is overridden by emotions that inhibit prosocial behavior or that produce responses incompatible with helping (Cialdini & Fultz, 1990). Positive mood also is unlikely to increase prosocial behavior when the helping task is extraordinarily effortful (Carlson et al., 1988) or when participants (i.e., children) are placed in competitive situations and the recipient of benevolence is a potential competitor (McGuire & Thomas, 1975).

Researchers have offered several explanations for the association between positive mood and prosocial behavior. Some investigators have suggested that positive mood motivates helping because it increases memories of previous positive helping experiences, gives people a feeling of having an emotional advantage and a sense of greater social responsiveness, or increases positive perceptions of humanity (i.e., increased liking of other individuals). Happy people may remember how good it felt to help others, may feel emotionally prepared to help someone they perceive as less fortunate, or may feel it is their social responsibility to do so (Cialdini, Kenrick, & Baumann, 1982; Clark & Isen, 1982; Isen, Shalker, Clark, & Karp, 1978; Rosenhan, Salovey, Karylowski, & Hargis, 1981). Others propose that engaging in helping behavior, which has been shown to be a rewarding, mood-elevating experience (Millar, Millar, & Tesser, 1988; Weiss, Boyer, Lombardo, & Stitch, 1973), simply may be a mood-maintenance activity (Carlson et al., 1988). That is, those in a good mood may seek activities that preserve or continue the positive tone of their emotional experience. Evidence to support this idea has been found in a study of mood management in which a major consideration of those in a good (vs. sad or neutral) mood was the hedonic qualities (consequences) associated with potentially engaging in activities (Wegener & Petty, 1994). Thus, it appears that positive mood-related helping may occur as a "concomitant of good mood" (Cialdini et al., 1982) or as a sustainer of positive mood when the helping task or helping in general is perceived as inherently rewarding (Carlson et al., 1988).

In contrast to the relatively consistent positive association found between positive mood and helping, the effect of negative moods on benevolence is less consistent (see Carlson & Miller, 1987; Eisenberg, 1991). In studies with adults, increased willingness to help has been found in people induced to feel sad or downhearted (Cialdini et al., 1982). However, in studies with children, the relationship is more complicated. In some studies, children who have been induced to feel a negative mood tend to help or share less than individuals in happy or neutral moods (Barnett, King, & Howard, 1979; Isen, Horn, & Rosenhan, 1973).

However, other researchers have found the opposite or no effect, especially when the negative mood induced involves empathy (Eisenberg & Miller, 1987; Rosenhan et al., 1974).

Theorists have proposed a number of explanations for the relationship between negative mood and helping, some of which have been hotly debated (Carlson & Miller, 1987; Cialdini & Fultz, 1990; Miller & Carlson, 1990). For instance, Cialdini and his colleagues proposed a negative-state relief model in which negative mood is thought to be accompanied by the desire to reduce negative feelings by engaging in mood-elevating activities (Cialdini, Brown, Lewis, Luce, & Neuberg, 1997; Cialdini, Darby, & Vincent, 1973). According to this theory, helpfulness has acquired its mood-elevating status through socialization processes designed to inculcate individuals with socially valued behaviors (Cialdini, Baumann, & Kenrick, 1981). Children induced to feel a negative mood who have not yet learned that helping is associated with social rewards would thus be unlikely to help (unless there are rewards or approval for doing so), whereas prosocial behavior is more likely among older children and adults who have fully internalized social norms related to helpfulness and to whom helping is self-reinforcing. Evidence to support this hypothesis has been found in studies with both children and adults (Barnett et al., 1979; Cialdini & Kenrick, 1976; see also Cialdini et al., 1981), although in one meta-analysis, the negative state relief model generally was not supported (Carlson & Miller, 1987).

Another explanation of the relationship of negative mood to prosocial behavior emphasizes one's inward versus outward focus of attention. The attentional focus model proposes that those who are induced to feel bad by focusing on the negative aspects of another's desperate plight tend to be more helpful or generous than those instructed to focus on themselves (Rosenhan, Salovey, Karylowski, & Hargis, 1981; see also W. Thompson, Cowan, & Rosenhan, 1980, for a similar study with adults). In a meta-analysis, Carlson and Miller (1987) obtained modest support for this explanation.

Other explanations of the effect of negative mood on helping take into account factors such as one's sense of social responsibility to others and issues related to living up to an ideal standard (Wicklund, 1975). Carlson and Miller (1987) found considerable support for this view in their meta-analytic review.

An area of research that has contributed to our understanding of mood states and prosocial or moral behavior is the work on affect and attribution theory. Some researchers have proposed that the influence of an emotion on judgments of others' needs or behavior corresponds to the appraisals associated with that emotion. To illustrate, sadness has been associated with the perception that events and circumstances are uncontrollable, whereas the experience of anger is associated with the perception that someone else is to blame for one's own misfortune. When investigators have manipulated the experience of anger, they have found that adults in an angry mood attribute poor outcomes to individuals rather than to situational factors (Keltner, Ellsworth, & Edwards, 1993) and are punitive toward defendants in fictional negligence cases (Lerner, Goldberg, & Tetlock, 1998). Thus, people in an angry mood probably are less likely to assist another person, unless the potential helper's anger is due to the perception that the potential recipient has been treated unjustly (Hoffman, 1987). Moreover, there is evidence that feelings of sympathy or anger mediate the relationship between appraisals of the reason for another's need (e.g., whether it is due to factors under voluntary control) and the degree of helping given to that person (Weiner, 1995).

## Summary

Dispositional and temporary affectivity play a multifaceted role in prosocial responding, including empathy-related responding and prosocial behavior. In addition, morally relevant emotions such as guilt (as well as empathy-related responding) appear to contribute to prosocial behavior. Thus, an understanding of emotion is central to theory and empirical research on prosocial development and behavior. If one views prosocial behavior and empathy/sympathy as components of socially competent behavior, it also is clear that emotion is fundamental to the development of quality of social functioning more generally (e.g., Eisenberg, Fabes, Guthrie, & Reiser, 2000; Saarni et al., 1998). Thus theory and research on the role of emotion in adjustment and quality of social functioning has much to contribute to an understanding of a more broadly defined role of emotion in positive development.

In addition, the research on empathy highlights the role of individual differences in the ability to regulate emotion and emotion-related behavior in the quality of people's social functioning. Well-regulated people are more likely than less-regulated people to be at an advantage in regard to managing not only their own directly experienced emotion but also their vicariously induced emotion. Because affect plays such a major role in interpersonal interactions and communication, processes related to the modulation of emotional arousal must contribute substantially to social and emotional competence. Thus, it is important to understand and learn more about how individuals express and cope with their own negative emotions, as well as how they respond to others' emotion and experiences.

### NOTE

This research was supported by grants from the National Institute of Mental Health (1 RO1 HH55052) to Nancy Eisenberg and Richard Fabes and a Research Scientist Award from the National Institute of Mental Health (KO5 M801321) to Nancy Eisenberg. Correspondence concerning this article should be addressed to the first author at Department of Psychology, Arizona State University, Tempe, AZ 8587-1104.

## REFERENCES

Ando, K. (1987, July). *The development of empathy in prosocial behavior*. Paper presented at the International Society for the Study of Behavioral Development, Tokyo.

Asakawa, K., Iwawaki, S., Mondori, Y., & Minami, H. (1987, July). *Altruism in school and empathy: A developmental study of Japanese pupils*. Paper presented at the International Society for the Study of Behavioral Development, Tokyo.

Barnett, M. A., King, L. M., & Howard, J. L. (1979). Inducing affect about self and other: Effects on generosity in children. *Developmental Psychology, 15*, 164–167.

Barrett, K. C. (1995). A functionalist approach to shame and guilt. In J. P. Tangney & K. W. Fischer (Eds.) *Self-conscious emotions: The psychology of shame, guilt, embarrassment, and pride* (pp. 25–63). New York: Guilford Press.

Barrett, K. C., & Campos, J. J. (1987). Perspectives on emotional development: II. A functionalist approach to emotions. In J. Osofsky (Ed.), *Handbook of infant development* (2nd ed., pp. 555–578). New York: Wiley.

Barrett, K. C., Zahn-Waxler, C., & Cole, P. M. (1993). Avoiders vs. amenders: Implications for the investigation of guilt and shame during toddlerhood? *Cognition and Emotion, 7*, 481–505.

Batson, C. D. (1991). *The altruism question: Toward a social-psychological answer*. Hillsdale, NJ: Erlbaum.

Batson, C. D. (1998). Altruism and prosocial behavior. In D. T. Gilbert, S. T. Fiske, & G. Lindzey (Eds.), *The handbook of social psychology* (Vol. 2, pp. 282–316). Boston, MA: McGraw-Hill.

Batson, C. D., Dyck, J. L., Brandt, J. R., Batson, J. G., Powell, A. L., McMaster, M. R., & Griffitt, C. (1988). Five studies testing two new egotistic alternatives to the empathy-altruism hypothesis. *Journal of Personality and Social Psychology, 55*, 52–77.

Baumeister, R. F., Stillwell, A. M., & Heatherton, T. F. (1994). Guilt: An interpersonal approach. *Psychological Bulletin, 115*, 243–267.

Belsky, J., Fish, M., & Isabella, R. (1991). Continuity and discontinuity in infant negative and positive emotionality: Family antecedents and attachment consequences. *Development Psychology, 27*, 421–431.

Bischof-Kohler, D. (1991). The development of empathy in infants. In M. E. Lamb & H. Keller (Eds.), *Infant development: Perspectives from German-speaking countries* (pp. 245–273). Hillsdale, NJ: Erlbaum.

Buss, K. A., & Goldsmith, H. H. (1998). Fear and anger regulation in infancy: Effects on the temporal dynamics of affective expression. *Child Development, 69*, 359–374.

Cacioppo, J. T., & Sandman, C. A. (1978). Psychological differentiation of sensory and cognitive tasks as a function of warning processing demands and reported unpleasantness. *Biological Psychology, 6*, 181–192.

Campos, J. J., Barrett, K. C., Lamb, M. E., Goldsmith, H. H., & Sternberg, C. (1983). Socio-emotional development. In P. H. Mussen (Ed.), *Handbook of child psychology* (4th ed., pp. 783–915). New York: Wiley.

Carlo, G., Eisenberg, N., & Knight, G. P. (1992). An objective measure of adolescents' prosocial moral reasoning. *Journal of Research on Adolescence, 2,* 331–349.

Carlo, G., Eisenberg, N., Troyer, D., Switzer, G., & Speer, A. L. (1991). The altruistic personality: In what contexts is it apparent? *Journal of Personality and Social Psychology, 61,* 450–458.

Carlson, M., Charlin, V., & Miller, N. (1988). Positive mood and helping behavior: A test of six hypotheses. *Journal of Personality and Social Psychology, 55,* 211–229.

Carlson, M., & Miller, N. (1987). Explanation of the relation between negative mood and helping. *Psychological Bulletin, 102,* 91–108.

Chapman, M., Zahn-Waxler, C., Cooperman, G., & Lannotti, R. (1987). Empathy and responsibility in the motivation of children's helping. *Developmental Psychology, 23,* 140–145.

Cialdini, R. B., Baumann, D. J., & Kenrick, D. T. (1981). Insights from sadness: A three-step model of the development of altruism as hedonism. *Developmental Review, 1,* 207–223.

Cialdini, R. B., Brown, S. L., Lewis, B. P., Luce, C., & Neuberg, S. L. (1997). Reinterpreting the empathy-altruism relationship: When one into one equals oneness. *Personality and Social Psychology, 73,* 481–494.

Cialdini, R. B., Darby, B. L., & Vincent, J. E. (1973). Transgression and altruism: A case for hedonism. *Journal of Experimental Social Psychology, 9,* 502–516.

Cialdini, R. B., & Fultz, J. (1990). Interpreting the negative mood-helping literature via "mega"-analysis: A contrary view. *Psychological Bulletin, 107,* 210–214.

Cialdini, R. B., & Kenrick, D. T. (1976). Altruism as hedonism: A social development perspective on the relationship of negative mood state and helping. *Journal of Personality and Social Psychology, 34,* 907–914

Cialdini, R. B., Kenrick, D. T., & Baumann, D. J. (1982). Effects of mood on prosocial behavior in children and adults. In N. Eisenberg (Ed.), *The development of prosocial behavior* (pp. 339–359). New York: Academic Press.

Clark, M. S., & Isen, A. M. (1982). Toward understanding the relationship between feeling states and social behavior. In A. Hastorf & A. M. Isen (Eds.), *Cognitive social psychology* (pp. 73–108). New York: Elsevier.

Cole, P. M., Barrett, K. C., & Zahn-Waxler, C. (1992). Emotion displays in two-year-olds during mishaps. *Child Development, 63,* 314–324.

Davis, M. H. (1983). Measuring individual differences in empathy: Evidence for a multidimensional approach. *Journal of Personality and Social Psychology, 44,* 113–126.

Davis, M. H. (1994). *Empathy: A social psychological approach.* Madison, WI: Brown & Benchmark.

Denham, S. A. (1986). Social cognition, prosocial behavior, and emotion in preschoolers: Contextual validation. *Child Development, 57,* 194–201.

Derryberry, D., & Rothbart, M. K. (1988). Arousal, affect, and attention as components of temperament. *Journal of Personality and Social Psychology, 55,* 958–966.

Dovidio, J. F. (1984). Helping behavior and altruism: An empirical and conceptual overview. In L. Berkowitz (Ed.), *Advances in experimental social psychology* (Vol. 17, pp. 361–427). New York: Academic Press.

Dunn, J. (1988). *The beginnings of social understanding.* Oxford, England: Blackwell.

Eisenberg, N. (1986). *Altruistic emotion, cognition, and behavior.* Hillsdale, NJ: Erlbaum.

Eisenberg, N. (1991). Meta-analytic contributions to the literature on prosocial behavior. *Personality and Social Psychology Bulletin, 17,* 273–282.

Eisenberg, N., Cameron, E., Tryon, K., & Dodez, R. (1981). Socialization of prosocial behavior in the preschool classroom. *Developmental Psychology, 17,* 773–782.

Eisenberg, N., Carlo, G., Murphy, B., & Van Court, P. (1995). Prosocial development in late adolescence: A longitudinal study. *Child Development, 66,* 1179–1197.

Eisenberg, N., & Fabes, R. A. (1990). Empathy: Conceptualization, measurement, and relation to prosocial behavior. *Motivation and Emotion, 14,* 131–149.

Eisenberg, N., & Fabes, R. A. (1992). Emotion, regulation, and the development of social competence. In M. S. Clark (Ed.), *Review of personality and social psychology: Vol. 14. Emotion and social behavior* (pp. 119–150). Newbury Park, CA: Sage.

Eisenberg, N., & Fabes, R. A. (1995). The relation of young children's vicarious emotional responding to social competence, regulation, and emotionality. *Cognition and Emotion, 9,* 203–229.

Eisenberg, N., & Fabes, R. A. (1998). Prosocial development. In W. Damon (Series Ed.) & N. Eisenberg (Vol. Ed.). *Handbook of child psychology: Vol. 3. Social, emotional and personality development* (pp. 701–778). New York: Wiley.

Eisenberg, N., Fabes, R. A., Bustamante, D., Mathy, R. M., Miller, P., & Lindholm, E. (1988). Differentiation of vicariously induced emotional reactions in children. *Developmental Psychology, 24,* 237–246.

Eisenberg, N., Fabes, R. A., Guthrie, I. K., & Reiser, M. (2000). Dispositional emotionality and regulation: Their role in predicting quality of social functioning. *Journal of Personality and Social Psychology, 78,* 136–157.

Eisenberg, N., Fabes, R. A., Karbon, M., Murphy, B. C., Carlo, G., & Wosinski, M. (1996). Relations of school children's comforting behavior to empathy-related reactions and shyness. *Social Development, 5,* 330–351.

Eisenberg, N., Fabes, R. A., Karbon, M., Murphy, B. C., Wosinski, M., Polazzi, L., Carlo, G., & Juhnke, C. (1996). The relations of children's dispositional prosocial behavior to emotionality, regulation, and social functioning. *Child Development, 67,* 974–992.

Eisenberg, N., Fabes, R. A., Miller, P. A., Fultz, J., Mathy, R. M., Shell, R., & Reno, R. R. (1989). The relations of sympathy and personal distress to prosocial behavior: A multimethod study. *Journal of Personality and Social Psychology, 57,* 55–66.

Eisenberg, N., Fabes, R. A., Miller, P. A., Shell, C., Shea, R., & May-Plumlee, T. (1990). Preschoolers' vicarious emotional responding and their situational and dispositional prosocial behavior. *Merrill-Palmer Quarterly, 36,* 507–529.

Eisenberg, N., Fabes, R. A., Murphy, B., Karbon, M., Maszk, P., Smith, M., O'Boyle, C., & Suh, K. (1994). The relations of emotionality and regulation to dispositional and situational empathy-related responding. *Journal of Personality and Social Psychology, 66,* 776–797.

Eisenberg, N., Fabes, R. A., Murphy, B., Karbon, M., Smith, M., & Maszk, P. (1996). The relations of children's dispositional empathy-related responding to their emotionality, regulation, and social functioning. *Developmental Psychology, 32*, 195–209.

Eisenberg, N., Fabes, R. A., Nyman, M., Bernzweig, J., & Pinuelas, A. (1994). The relations of emotionality and regulation to children's anger-related reactions. *Child Development, 65*, 109–128.

Eisenberg, N., Fabes, R. A., Schaller, M., Carlo, G., & Miller, P. A. (1991). The relations of parental characteristics and practices to children's vicarious emotional responding. *Child Development, 62*, 1393–1408.

Eisenberg, N., Fabes, R. A., Schaller, M., Miller, P. A., Carlo, G., Poulin, R., Shea, C., & Shell, R. (1991). Personality and socialization correlates of vicarious emotional responding. *Journal of Personality and Social Psychology, 61*, 459–471.

Eisenberg, N., Fabes, R. A., Shepard, S. A., Murphy, B. C., Jones, J., & Guthrie, I. K. (1998). Contemporaneous and longitudinal prediction of children's sympathy from dispositional regulation and emotionality. *Developmental Psychology, 34*, 910–924.

Eisenberg, N., Guthrie, I. K., Murphy, B. C., Shepard, S. A., Cumberland, A., & Carlo, G. (1999). Consistency and development of prosocial dispositions: A longitudinal study. *Child Development, 70*, 1360–1372.

Eisenberg, N., McCreath, H., & Ahn, R. (1988). Vicarious emotional responsiveness and prosocial behavior: Their interrelations in young children. *Personality and Social Psychology Bulletin, 14*, 298–311.

Eisenberg, N., & Miller, P. (1987). The relation of empathy to prosocial and related behaviors. *Psychological Bulletin, 101*, 91–119.

Eisenberg, N., & Okun, M. A. (1996). The relations of dispositional regulation and emotionality to elders' empathy-related responding and affect while volunteering. *Journal of Personality, 64*, 157–183.

Eisenberg, N., Schaller, M., Fabes, R. A., Bustamante, D., Mathy, R., Shell, R., & Rhodes, K. (1988). The differentiation of personal distress and sympathy in children and adults. *Developmental Psychology, 24*, 766–775.

Eisenberg, N., Shea, C., Carlo, G., & Knight, G. (1991). Empathy-related responding and cognition: A "chicken and the egg" dilemma. In W. Kurtines & J. Gewirtz (Eds.), *Handbook of moral behavior and development. Vol. 2, Research* (pp. 63–88). Hillsdale, NJ: Erlbaum.

Eisenberg, N., Wentzel, M., & Harris, J. D. (1998). The role of emotionality and regulation in empathy-related responding. *School Psychology Review, 27*, 506–521.

Eisenberg-Berg, N. (1979). Development of children's prosocial moral judgment. *Developmental Psychology, 15*, 128–137.

Estrada, P. (1995). Adolescents' self-reports of prosocial responses to friends and acquaintances: The role of sympathy-related cognitive, affective, and motivational processes. *Journal of Research on Adolescence, 5*, 173–200.

Fabes, R. A., & Eisenberg, N. (1996). *An examination of age and sex differences in prosocial behavior and empathy*. Unpublished manuscript.

Fabes, R. A., Eisenberg, N., & Eisenbud, L. (1993). Behavioral and physiological correlates of children's reactions to others' distress. *Developmental Psychology, 29*, 655–663.

Fabes, R. A., Eisenberg, N., Karbon, M., Bernzweig, J., Speer, A. L., & Carlo, G. (1994). Socialization of children's vicarious emotional responding and prosocial behavior: Relations with mothers' perceptions of children's emotional reactivity. *Developmental Psychology, 30*, 44–55.

Fabes, R. A., Eisenberg, N., & Miller, P. (1990). Maternal correlates of children's vicarious emotional responsiveness. *Developmental Psychology, 26*, 639–648.

Ferguson, T., & Stegge, H. (1998). Measuring guilt in children: A rose by any other name still has thorns. In J. Bybee (Ed.), *Guilt and children* (pp. 19–74). San Diego, CA: Academic Press.

Ferguson, T. J., Stegge, H., & Damhuis, I. (1991). Children's understanding of guilt and shame. *Child Development, 62*, 827–839.

Ferguson, T. J., Stegge, H., Miller, E. R., & Olsen, M. E. (1999). Guilt, shame, and symptoms in children. *Developmental Psychology, 35*, 347–357.

Feshbach, N. D. (1978). Studies of empathic behavior in children. In B. A. Maher (Ed.), *Progress in experimental personality research* (Vol. 8, pp. 1–47). New York: Academic Press.

Forest, P., Clark, M., Mills, J., & Isen, A. M. (1979). Helping as a function of feeling state and nature of the helping behavior. *Motivation and Emotion, 3*, 161–169.

Freedman, J. L. (1970). Transgression, compliance and guilt. In J. R. Macaulay & L. Berkowitz (Eds.), *Altruism and helping behavior* (pp. 155–161). New York: Academic Press.

Gaertner, S. L., & Dovidio, J. F. (1977). The subtlety of white racism, arousal, and helping behavior. *Journal of Personality and Social Psychology, 35*, 691–707.

Goldsmith, H. H., Buss, K. A., & Lemery, K. S. (1997). Toddler and childhood temperament: Expanded content, stronger genetic evidence, new evidence for the importance of environment. *Developmental Psychology, 33*, 891–905.

Gunnar, M. R., & Stone, C. (1984). The effects of positive maternal affect on infant responses to pleasant, ambiguous, and fear-provoking toys. *Child Development, 55*, 1231–1236.

Guthrie, I. K., Eisenberg, N., Fabes, R. A., Murphy, B. C., Holmgren, R., Mazsk, P., & Suh, K. (1997). The relations of regulation and emotionality to children's situational empathy-related responding. *Motivation and Emotion, 21*, 87–108.

Harter, S. (1998). The development of self-representations. In W. Damon (Series Ed.), & N. Eisenberg (Vol. Ed.), *Handbook of child psychology: Vol. 3. Social, emotional and personality development* (pp. 553–617). New York: Wiley.

Hay, D. F., Nash, A., & Pederson, J. (1981). Responses of six-month-olds to the distress of their peers. *Child Development, 52*, 1071–1075.

Hoffman, M. L. (1975). Developmental synthesis of affect and cognition and its implications for altruistic motivation. *Developmental Psychology, 11*, 607–622.

Hoffman, M. L. (1982). Development of prosocial motivation: Empathy and guilt. In N. Eisenberg (Ed.), *The development of prosocial behavior* (pp. 281–313). New York: Academic Press.

Hoffman, M. L. (1984). Interaction of affect and cognition in empathy. In C. E. Izard, J. Kagan, & R. B. Zajonc (Eds.), *Emotions, cognition, and behavior*. London, England: Cambridge University Press.

Hoffman, M. L. (1987). The contribution of empathy to justice and moral judgment. In N. Eisenberg & J. Strayer (Eds.), *Empathy and its development* (pp. 47–80). Cambridge: Cambridge University Press.

Holmgren, R. A., Eisenberg, N., & Fabes, R. A. (1998). The relations of children's situational empathy-related emotions to dispositional prosocial behavior. *International Journal of Behavioral Development, 22*, 169–193.

Isen, A. M. (1970). Success, failure, and reaction to others: The warm glow of success. *Journal of Personality and Social Psychology, 15*, 294–301.

Isen, A. M., Clark, M., & Schwartz, M. F. (1976). Duration of the effects of good mood on helping: "Footprints in the sands of time." *Journal of Personality and Social Psychology, 34*, 385–393.

Isen, A. M., Horn, N., & Rosenhan, D. L. (1973). Effects of success and failure on children's generosity. *Journal of Personality and Social Psychology, 27*, 239–247.

Isen, A. M., & Levin, P. F. (1972). Effect of feeling good on helping: Cookies and kindness. *Journal of Personality and Social Psychology, 21*, 384–388.

Isen, A. M., Shalker, T., Clark, M., & Karp, L. (1978). Affect, accessibility of material in memory, and behavior: A cognitive loop? *Journal of Personality and Social Psychology, 36*, 1–12.

Johnson, D. B. (1982) Altruistic behavior and the development of self in infants. *Merrill-Palmer Quarterly, 28*, 379–388.

Kaneko, R., & Hamazaki, T. (1987). Prosocial behavior manifestations of young children in an orphanage. *Psychologia, 30*, 235–242.

Karylowski, J. (1982). Doing good to feel good v. doing good to make others feel good: Some child-rearing antecedents. *School Psychology International, 3*, 149–156.

Keltner, D., Ellsworth, P. C., & Edwards, K. (1993). Beyond simple pessimism: Effects of sadness and anger on social perception. *Journal of Personality and Social Psychology, 64*, 740–752.

Klinnert, M. D. (1984). The regulation of infant behavior by maternal facial expression. *Infant Behavior and Development, 7*, 447–465.

Kochanska, G. (1993). Toward a synthesis of parental socialization and child temperament in early development of conscience. *Child Development, 64*, 325–347.

Kochanska, G., Casey, R. J., & Fukumoto, A. (1995). Toddlers' sensitivity to standard violations. *Child Development, 66*, 643–656.

Kochanska, G., Coy, K. C., Tjebkes, T. L., & Husarek, S. J. (1998). Individual differences in emotionality in infancy. *Child Development, 64*, 375–390.

Kohlberg, L. (1969). Stage and sequence: The cognitive-developmental approach to socialization. In D. A. Goslin (Ed.), *Handbook of socialization theory and research* (pp. 325–480). New York: Rand McNally.

Kohlberg, L. (1984). *Essays on moral development: Vol. 2. The psychology of moral development*. San Francisco, CA: Harper & Row.

Krebs, D. L., & Miller, D. T. (1985). Altruism and aggression. In G. Lindzey & E. Aronson (Eds.), *Handbook of social psychology* (3rd ed., Vol. 2, pp. 1–71). New York: Random House.

Lacey, J. I., Kagan, J., Lacey, B. C., & Moss, H. A. (1963). The visceral level: Situational determinants and behavioral correlates of autonomic response patterns. In P. H. Knapp (Ed.), *Expression of emotions in man* (pp. 161–196). New York: International Universities Press.

Larsen, R. J., Diener, E., & Cropanzano, R. A. (1987). Cognitive operations associated with individual differences in affect intensity. *Journal of Personality and Social Psychology, 53*, 767–774.

Lazarus, R. S. (1974). A cognitively oriented psychologist looks at biofeedback. *American Psychologist, 30*, 553–561.

Lennon, R., & Eisenberg, N. (1987). Gender and age differences in empathy and sympathy. In N. Eisenberg & J. Strayer (Eds.), *Empathy and its development* (pp. 195–217). Cambridge, England: Cambridge University Press.

Lerner, J. S., Goldberg, J. H., & Tetlock, P. E. (1998). Sober second thought: The effects of accountability, anger, and authoritarianism on attributions of responsibility. *Personality and Social Psychology Bulletin, 24*, 563–574.

Lewis, H. B. (1971). *Shame and guilt in neurosis*. New York: International Universities Press.

Lewis, M. (1992). *Shame, the exposed self*. New York: Free Press

Lewis, M., Alessandri, S., & Sullivan, M. W. (1992). Differences in shame and pride as a function of children's gender and task difficulty. *Child Development, 63*, 630–638.

Lewis, M., Sullivan, M., Stanger, C., & Weiss, M. (1989). Self development and self-conscious emotions. *Child Development, 60*, 146–156.

Linsay-Hartz, J. (1984). Contrasting experiences of shame and guilt. *American Behavioral Scientist, 27*, 689–704.

Martin, G. B., Clark, R. D., III. (1982). Distress crying in neonates: Species and peer specificity. *Developmental Psychology, 18*, 3–9.

McGuire, J. M., & Thomas, M. H. (1975). Effects of sex, competence, and competition on sharing behavior in children. *Journal of Personality and Social Psychology, 32*, 490–494.

Millar, M., Millar, K., & Tesser, A. (1988). The effects of helping and focus attention on mood states. *Personality and Social Psychology Bulletin, 14*, 536–543.

Miller, N., & Carlson, M. (1990). Valid theory-testing meta-analyses further question the negative state relief model of helping. *Psychological Bulletin, 107*, 215–225.

Miller, P. A., Eisenberg, N., Fabes, R. A., & Shell, R. (1996). Relations of moral reasoning and vicarious emotion to young children's prosocial behavior toward peers and adults. *Developmental Psychology, 32*, 210–219.

Murphy, B. C., Shepard, S. A., Eisenberg, N., Fabes, R. A., & Guthrie, I. K. (1999). Contemporaneous and longitudinal relations of young adolescents' dispositional sympathy to their emotionality, regulation, and social functioning. *Journal of Early Adolescence, 19*, 66–97.

Okun, M. A., Shepard, S. A., & Eisenberg, N. (2000). The relations of emotionality and regulation to dispositional empathy-related responding among volunteers-in-training. *Personality and Individual Differences, 28*, 367–382.

Phinney, J., Fesbach, N., & Farver, J. (1986). Preschool children's responses to peer crying. *Early Childhood Research Quarterly, 1*, 207–219.

Plomin, R., & Stocker, C. (1989). Behavioral genetics and emotionality. In J. S. Reznick (Ed.), *Perspectives on behavioral inhibition* (pp. 219–240). Chicago: Chicago University Press.

Radke-Yarrow, M., Zahn-Waxler, C., & Chapman, M. (1983). Prosocial dispositions and behavior. In P. Mussen (Ed.), *Handbook of child psychology: Vol. 4. Socialization, personality, and social development* (pp. 469–545). New York: Wiley.

Roberts, W., & Strayer, J. (1996). Empathy, emotional expressiveness, and prosocial behavior. *Child Development, 67,* 449–470.

Robinson, J. L., Zahn-Waxler, C., & Emde, R. N. (1994). Patterns of development in early empathic behavior: Environmental and child constitutional influences. *Social Development, 3,* 125–145.

Rosenhan, D. L. (1972). Learning theory and prosocial behavior. *Journal of Social Issues, 28,* 151–164.

Rosenhan, D. L., Salovey, P., Karylowski, J., & Hargis, K. (1981). Emotion and altruism. In J. P. Rushton & R. M. Sorrentino (Eds.), *Altruism and helping behavior* (pp. 233–248). Hillsdale, NJ: Erlbaum.

Rosenhan, D. L., Underwood, B., & Moore, B. (1974). Affect moderates self-gratification and altruism. *Journal of Personality and Social Psychology, 30,* 546–552.

Rothbart, M. K., Ahadi, S. A., & Hershey, K. L. (1994). Temperament and social behavior in childhood. *Merrill-Palmer Quarterly, 40,* 21–39.

Rothbart, M. K., & Bates, J. E. (1998). Temperament. In W. Damon (Series Ed.) & N. Eisenberg (Vol. Ed.), *Handbook of child psychology: Vol. 3. Social, emotional, and personality development* (pp. 105–176). New York: Wiley.

Rothbart, M. K., Ziaie, H., & O'Boyle, C. G. (1992). Self-regulation and emotion in infancy. *New Directions in Child Development, 55,* 7–23.

Rusting, C. L., & Nolen-Hoeksema, S. (1998). Regulating responses to anger: Effects of rumination and distraction on angry mood. *Journal of Personality and Social Psychology, 74,* 790–803.

Saarni, C., Mumme, D. L., & Campos, J. J. (1998). Emotional development: Action, communication, and understanding. In W. Damon (Series Ed.) and N. Eisenberg (Vol. Ed.), *Social, emotional, and personality development. Vol. 3. Handbook of child psychology* (pp. 237–309). New York: Wiley.

Sagi, A., & Hoffman, M. L. (1976). Empathic distress in the newborn. *Developmental Psychology, 12,* 175–176.

Saklofske, D. H. & Eysenck, S. B. G. (1983). Impulsiveness and venturesomeness in Canadian children. *Psychological Reports, 52,* 147–152.

Shaver, P., Schwartz, J., Kirson, D., & O'Connor, C. (1987). Emotion knowledge: Further exploration of a prototype approach. *Journal of Personality and Social Psychology, 52,* 1061–1086.

Simner, M. L. (1971). Newborns' responses to the cry of another infant. *Developmental Psychology, 5,* 136–150.

Sorce, J. F., Emde, R. N., Campos, J. J., & Klinnert, M. D. (1985). Maternal emotional signaling: Its effect on the visual cliff behavior of 1-year-olds. *Developmental Psychology, 21,* 195–200.

Stipek, D., Recchia, S., & McClintic, S. (1992). Self evaluation in young children. *Monographs of the Society for Research in Child Development, 57* (1, Serial No. 226).

Strayer, J. (1980). A naturalistic study of empathic behaviors and their relation to affective states and perspective-taking skills in preschool children. *Child Development, 51,* 815–822.

Strayer, J. (1993). Children's concordant emotions and cognitions in response to observed emotions. *Child Development, 64,* 188–201.

Strayer, J., & Roberts, W. (1989). Children's empathy and role taking: Child and parental factors, and relations to prosocial behavior. *Journal of Applied Developmental Psychology, 10,* 227–239.

Tangney, J. P. (1990). Assessing individual differences in proneness to shame and guilt: Development of the Self-Conscious Affect and Attribution Inventory. *Journal of Personality and Social Psychology, 59,* 102–111.

Tangney, J. P. (1991). Moral affect: The good, the bad, and the ugly. *Journal of Personality and Social Psychology, 61,* 598–607.

Tangney, J. P. (1996). Conceptual and methodological issues in the assessment of shame and guilt. *Behavioral Research Therapy, 34,* 741–754.

Tangney, J. P. (1998). How does guilt differ from shame? In J. Bybee (Ed.), *Guilt and children* (pp. 1–17). San Diego, CA: Academic Press.

Tangney, J. P., Marschall, D., Rosenberg, K., Barlow., D. H., & Wagner, P. (1996). *Children's and adults' autobiographical accounts of shame, guilt, and pride experiences: An analysis of situational factors and interpersonal concerns.* Unpublished manuscript, George Mason University.

Termine, N. T., & Izard, C. E. (1988). Infants' responses to their mothers' expressions of joy and sadness. *Developmental Psychology, 24,* 223–229.

Thompson, R. A. (1987). Empathy and emotional understanding: The early development of empathy. In N. Eisenberg & J. Strayer (Eds.), *Empathy and its development* (pp. 119–145). Cambridge, England: Cambridge University Press.

Thompson, R. A. (1994). Emotional regulation: A theme in search of definition. *Child Development Monographs, 59,* 25–52.

Thompson, R. A., & Hoffman, M. L. (1980). Empathy and the development of guilt in children. *Developmental Psychology, 16,* 155–156.

Thompson, W., Cowan, C., & Rosenhan, D. (1980). Focus of attention mediates the impact of negative affect on altruism. *Journal of Personality and Social Psychology, 38,* 291–300.

Tremblay, R. E., Vitaro, F., Gagnon, C., Piche, C., & Royer, N. (1992). A prosocial scale for the preschool behaviour questionnaire: Concurrent and predictive correlates. *International Journal of Behavioral Development, 15,* 227–245.

Trommsdorff, G. (1995). Person-context relations as developmental conditions for empathy and prosocial action: A cross-cultural analysis. In T. A. Kindermann & J. Valsiner (Eds.), *Development of person-context relations* (pp. 189–208). Hillsdale, NJ: Erlbaum.

Wallace, J., & Sadalla, E. (1966). Behavioral consequences of transgression: 1. The effects of social recognition. *Journal of Experimental Research in Personality, 1,* 187–194.

Wegener, D. T., & Petty, R. E. (1994). Mood management across affective states: The hedonic contingency hypothesis. *Journal of Personality and Social Psychology, 66,* 1034–1048.

Weiner, B. (1995). *Judgments of responsibility: A foundation for a theory of social conduct.* New York: Guilford Press.

Weiss, R., Boyer, J., Lombardo, J., & Stitch, M. (1973). Altruistic drive and altruistic reinforcement. *Journal of Personality and Social Psychology, 25,* 390–400.

Wicklund, R. A. (1975). Objective self-awareness. In L. Berkowitz (Ed.), *Advances in experimental social psychology* (Vol. 8, pp. 233–275). New York: Academic Press.

Wood, J. V., Saltzberg, J. A., & Goldsamt, L. A. (1990). Does affect induce self-focused attention? *Journal of Personality and Social Psychology, 58,* 899–908.

Wood, J. V., Saltzberg, J. A., Neale, J. N., Stone, A. A., & Rachmiel, T. B. (1990). Self-focused attention, coping responses, and distressed mood in everyday life. *Journal of Personality and Social Psychology, 58,* 1027–1036.

Zahn-Waxler, C., Cole, P. M., Welsh, J. D., & Fox, N. A. (1995). Psychophysiological correlates of empathy and prosocial behaviors in preschool children with problem behaviors. *Developmental Psychopathology, 7,* 27–48.

Zahn-Waxler, C., Friedman, S. L., & Cummings, E. M. (1983). Children's emotions and behaviors in response to infants' cries. *Child Development, 54,* 1522–1528.

Zahn-Waxler, C., & Kochanska, G. (1990). The origins of guilt. In R. Thompson (Ed.), *Nebraska symposium on motivation: Socioemotional development* (pp. 183–258). Lincoln: University of Nebraska Press.

Zahn-Waxler, C., & Radke-Yarrow, M. (1982). The development of altruism: Alternative research strategies. In N. Eisenberg (Ed.), *The development of prosocial behavior* (pp. 109–137). New York: Academic Press.

Zahn-Waxler, C., Radke-Yarrow, M., Wagner, E., & Chapman, M. (1992). Development of concern for others. *Developmental Psychology, 28,* 126–136.

Zahn-Waxler, C. & Robinson, J. (1995). Empathy and guilt: Early origins of feelings of responsibility. In J. P. Tangney & K. W. Fischer (Eds.), *Self-conscious emotions: The psychology of shame, guilt, embarrassment, and pride* (pp. 143–173). New York: Guilford Press.

Zahn-Waxler, C., Robinson, J. L., & Emde, R. N. (1992). The development of empathy in twins. *Developmental Psychology, 28,* 1038–1047.

# 42

# AFFECT, AGGRESSION, AND ANTISOCIAL BEHAVIOR

Leonard Berkowitz

Before embarking on this examination of the influence of feelings on antisocial behavior, I must spell out what this concept *antisocial behavior* refers to as far as this chapter is concerned. The term is employed frequently in psychology and psychiatry (although not in sociology), but it does not always have the same specific meaning and/or involve exactly the same issues. Sometimes it refers, relatively narrowly, only to behavior. However, most discussions involving this notion—usually those focused on persistent patterns of conduct—often have a broader meaning in mind, one that has to do with both actions and personality characteristics.

Farrington (1997) has highlighted this latter, broader usage. He noted that definitions and measurements of the "antisocial syndrome" typically encompass both a wide variety of behaviors—ranging from those that are illegal (such as violent offenses and drug use) to those that deviate from conventional norms but are not criminal (such as sexual promiscuity and repeated lying)—and also such personality features as impulsiveness, selfishness, and aggressiveness. This wide-ranging conception is certainly warranted for many purposes; research has repeatedly demonstrated that the people who frequently engage in antisocial behaviors tend to have the particular personality qualities just listed (e.g., Farrington, 1982; Robins & Price, 1991). Nevertheless, this chapter concentrates only on actions, not on personality dispositions, because I am concerned primarily with situational influences on what people are apt to do.

Furthermore, the behaviors of interest here are more

than violations of traditional rules of conduct. I deal mainly with those counternormative actions that harm others directly—primarily acts of aggression—and do not take up other antisocial behaviors, such as imbibing alcohol or abusing drugs, that lack this feature. The injury can be inflicted in many different ways, of course—through burglary, embezzlement, the sale of drugs, partner battering, child abuse, barroom brawls, and so on—but in order to keep the literature review within manageable limits, I combine these various behaviors conceptually into one broad class.

There is some empirical justification for such a general notion of antisocial behavior, at least when dealing with relatively long-lasting individual differences. Investigations of troublesome adolescents have found that these youths often can be grouped meaningfully into just a few categories. Some researchers have even proposed that this typology is unidimensional (see Berkowitz, 2000a; Loeber & Schmaling, 1985; Patterson, Reid, & Dishion, 1992). As one example, the Loeber and Schmaling (1985) analysis of 22 studies of school-age children indicated that the youngsters' antisocial behaviors could be ordered along a "covert-overt" continuum. The covert end of this dimension consists of such actions as stealing, fire setting, and alcohol and drug use, whereas the other extreme comprises more overt behaviors, such as attacking others and fighting.[1] Disobedience is located between these opposing poles. If results such as these can be generalized to the varieties of antisocial conduct displayed by people across the social spectrum, these counternormative actions can be located along a bipolar dimension, with strong attacks on others as its most extreme form. For this reason, as well as in the interests of brevity, this chapter emphasizes aggression as the prime example of antisocial conduct.[2]

I must also clarify what I mean here by *affect* and *feelings*. As these words are used in this chapter, they refer to a conscious affective state, not to a belief, attitude, or preference. This conscious experience can arise in any number of ways. It might grow out of a specific event or might be produced by a vague condition; and, moreover, those who experience the affect may or may not be aware of what generated the feeling. Just what effect the feeling has on the person may well vary with its perceived cause, but much of the following discussion does not address this particular consideration. Also, even though people can discriminate among a great number of feelings—sadness, elation, disgust, contentment, fear, nausea, among many others—these affective states can be grouped in terms of their hedonic valence, whether they are experienced as pleasant or unpleasant. By and large, then, this chapter disregards the differences among the various affective states and concentrates on the role of negative, unpleasant affect in promoting antisocial behavior.

Because of the concern with affect and affective aggression, it is also important to recognize at the outset the distinction many psychologists draw between hostile and instrumental aggression (Feshbach, 1964; also see Berkowitz, 1993a). Both forms of aggression seek the injury or even the destruction of the target, but I and others call the assault *instrumental* aggression when the chief aim of the behavior is the attainment of some goal other than injuring the target, such as the restoration of wounded self-esteem, the approval of one's peers, monetary gain, or the elimination of an unpleasant state of affairs. In the case of *hostile* aggression, on the other hand, the main objective of the action is to injure the victim, regardless of what other purposes might also be served. This attack can vary in the extent to which it is consciously controlled. Sometimes it is carried out in a cold and deliberate manner, impelled by the anticipated pleasure of seeing the victim in pain. Even those who aren't sadists may at times engage in a calculated campaign designed to hurt an enemy, verbally if not physically, simply because they want this person to suffer. But the hostile aggression can also be instigated by an internal excitation in a relatively uncontrolled outburst. We all know of people who have lost their temper in an argument and lashed out at their antagonists, not thinking of the possible future consequences but only seeking to injure (or maybe even to destroy) the offender. Many instances of domestic violence and barroom brawls are of this nature. Another example is displaced aggression, in which the provoked persons strike at a substitute target because the perceived provocateur is either unavailable or too dangerous to attack (Berkowitz, 1993a; Miller, 1948). Policemen called to intercede in a domestic quarrel are sometimes also the victims of displaced aggression. As the couple fight, one or the other of them might well strike out in fury at an innocent bystander who gets in the way. This happens often enough so that, at least a generation ago, about 20% of the policemen killed in the line of duty died in trying to break up a domestic fight (Goode, 1969).

In all of the cases just mentioned, the emotionally impelled—or affective—aggression grew out of some provocation, an insult or other affront. This chapter extends the range of conditions that can also evoke affective aggression. It holds that (1) a surprisingly great variety of unpleasant states of affairs can activate an instigation to aggression and (2) it is the intense negative affect produced by the aversive conditions that generates the aggressive urge.

## Do Feelings Have a Role in Antisocial Behavior?

Although psychologists as a group are prepared to assume that emotional factors play a significant part in quite a few antisocial actions, the leading sociological and criminological theories of crime causation say little explicitly about affective influences. Virtually every behavior, including aggression, is for them instrumental in nature. The conceptions that follow the "rational choice" and/or "control" perspectives typically share this view. Like most analytic schemes in the social sciences, they contend that people choose (consciously or unconsciously) to behave as they do. And so, as they see it, offenders decide to carry out a socially undesirable action because of their belief that the payoff will outweigh the possible costs. Unlike a number of psychological formulations, however, they give little weight to feelings in the decisions that are made or to the possibility of affective (hostile) aggression.[3] Because this chapter is primarily concerned with the role of affect, it is worth contrasting this instrumental (or rationalistic, nonaffectively oriented) approach to antisocial behavior with the theme advanced in this chapter: Feelings matter.

Wilson and Herrnstein's (1985) analysis of criminal behavior is a good example of a nonaffectively oriented formulation. Its basic position is that miscreants do not anticipate sufficiently negative consequences for their counternormative behavior. Many wrongdoers are impulsive, Wilson and Herrnstein held, but only in the sense that they place greater emphasis on immediate rather than distant outcomes. In this view, crimes of passion are "no more irresistible than cheating on one's income tax . . . [and] could have been suppressed by a greater or more certain penalty" (p. 56).

A number of objections to the adoption of gun controls also take this general stance. Contending that few, if any, murders are impulsive actions impelled by intense rage,

Wolfgang (1958) argued that few killings "due to shooting could be avoided merely if a firearm were not immediately present. . . . The offender would select some other weapon to achieve the same destructive goal" (p. 83). In their questioning of the efficacy of gun-control legislation, Wright, Rossi, and Daly (1983) also maintained that there are not many impulsive homicides. They cited a study of domestic murders in Kansas City that indicated that "no fewer than 85% of all homicides involving family members had been preceded at some point in the past by some other violent incident sufficiently serious that the police were called in" (p. 193). This shows, they maintained, that the killings were typically "the culminating event in a pattern of interpersonal abuse, hatred, and violence that stretches well back into the histories of the parties involved" (p. 193). In other words, for Wright, Rossi, and Daly (1983), a woman who shoots her husband after years of frequent abuse presumably does so because she had intended to kill him sooner or later, and she acts deliberately when a suitable opportunity presents itself.

This is not to say that all sociologically oriented criminologists deny the occurrence of relatively thoughtless violent actions. Several criminological theorists recognize the possibility of such impulsive behavior by explicitly differentiating between instrumental and more expressive (i.e., affectively evoked hostile) aggressive behaviors. Block's (1977) examination of Chicago homicides is illustrative. For him, many robberies are deliberate in that the victim and the offender both act to maximize their benefits and minimize their costs in a dangerous situation. But in addition, Block held, in agreement with Feshbach's (1964) conception of hostile aggression, that there can also be an impulsive expressive aggression in which "there is no weighing of costs and benefits, only the desire to injure or kill" (p. 9). He argued that this can happen during a robbery. The criminal might initially want only to take his victim's money. But then some external influence—a perceived threat, the victim's defiance—might suddenly excite the robber's existing tension state even further. If he has a gun in his hand, he shoots. Block also suggested that a good many violent assaults can be impulsive/expressive acts of aggression.

This chapter argues that these relatively thoughtless and unplanned attacks are apt to arise under intense negative feelings and can thus be termed instances of affective aggression. Other forms of affective aggression can exist as well, and affective influences can do more than promote impulsive assaults, as I discuss later. My basic thesis is that, in all of these cases, strong negative affect produced by an unpleasant experience had generated an urge to attack a suitable target.

The following two sections offer evidence in support of this general proposition. I first look at investigations that inquire into the consequences of physically unpleasant environmental conditions, such as hot weather, noise, and foul odors; then, in the next section, I consider the impact of occurrences that are more psychologically aversive: frustrations and social stresses. In all of these cases, I am concerned with aggressive reactions to the negative events, but I refer more specifically to criminal violence in cases in which relevant studies are available. The chapter concludes with a discussion of some theoretical models that have been developed to account for the relationship between negative affect and the instigation to aggression. In this review I concentrate on the relatively automatic and nonthoughtful processes that can influence affective aggression, largely because these processes have not received much attention in contemporary analyses of antisocial aggression, neither in social psychology nor in sociology and criminology. This is not to say, of course, that cognition should be disregarded in accounts of emotionally impelled violence; it obviously can play a very important part in determining how people respond to unpleasant events. However, at the risk of being unduly one-sided, and because cognitive influences have been discussed in detail elsewhere (see Anderson & Anderson, 1998; Dodge, 1993; Huesmann, 1998; Liau, Barriga, & Gibbs, 1998), relatively little is said about these influences in this chapter.

## Environmental Stimulation to Affective Aggression

Quite a few investigations have now demonstrated that exposure to decidedly unpleasant physical stimuli increases the chances of aggressive behavior. In some respects this has long been recognized in social psychology. Writing more than a quarter of a century ago, Baron, Byrne, and Griffitt (1974) suggested that "environmental variables that produce negatively toned affective responses will, under certain circumstances, lead to increased negativity in interpersonal behaviors" (p. 525). But whereas most studies of that period focused on attitudinal reactions to negative events, I go somewhat further here. Along with several other writers, I propose that the "negatively toned affect" will evoke a number of negative reactions, including an instigation to aggression.

### Physical Pain

Physical pain obviously is almost always aversive, and physical pain often instigates aggressive inclinations. I offer a few observations about this effect in order to show how general this pain-elicited aggression is, even though we have little direct evidence that physical pain can be a stimulus to criminal offenses.

Research with nonhumans provides the best known demonstrations of aggression spurred by physical pain. A good number of animal experiments (see Berkowitz, 1983; Hutchinson, 1983; Ulrich, 1966) have shown that when two animals cooped together in a small chamber receive noxious stimuli (such as physical blows or electric shocks), they frequently begin to fight. Prior learning is not necessary for this to occur. Aversively stimulated animals can become aggressive even when they had not previously learned that their attacks could terminate the unpleasant occurrence. Nor is the pain-instigated aggression only a defensive reaction aimed merely at the elimination or lessening of the aversive stimulation. The assault can also be offensive in nature, an attempt to injure the intended target (see Berkowitz, 1993a). However, all this does not mean that the aggression is inevitable; many afflicted animals prefer to avoid or escape from the aversive situation rather than attack an available target (Hutchinson, 1983). Nevertheless, the studies also indicate that the pained animals are especially likely to assault a target when they do not know how to get away from the pain source. I discuss this further later in the chapter.

Medical and psychological reports of the behavior of humans experiencing physical pain suggest that these findings are not necessarily limited to the lower animal species. For example, people suffering from the intense pain caused by severe headaches or from a lasting injury to their spinal cords are frequently angry and/or hostile (Berkowitz, 1993b). Summarizing their observations of patients suffering from frequent bouts of pain, Fernandez and Turk (1995) maintained that anger is a "feature of chronic pain" and that "anger stands out as one of the most salient emotional correlates of pain" (p. 165).

### Effects of Unpleasant Temperatures

Obviously, some environmental conditions can be decidedly uncomfortable without arousing clear physical pain. One of these is unpleasant weather, especially high ambient temperatures. Space does not permit an exceedingly detailed and comprehensive review of all the relevant studies (see Anderson, 1989; Anderson & Anderson, 1998; Cohn & Rotton, 1997, for helpful surveys), and I touch on only some of the main issues in these investigations.

I note at the outset, however, that one question that arises in these studies has to do with just what the shape of the relation is between the temperature level and the subsequent aggressive urge. On the basis of their research, Baron and Bell (1976; also see Baron & Richardson, 1994; Bell, 1992; Bell & Baron, 1976) argued for an inverted-U relationship. They said the instigation to aggression strengthens only up to a point as the felt displeasure grows. Beyond this level, the affected people presumably become more concerned with escaping from the unpleasant situation than with attacking the target, because they now want primarily to reduce their negative affect. Anderson (1989; Anderson & Anderson, 1998; Anderson & DeNeve, 1992) disputed this idea, favoring the existence of a linear temperature-aggression relation.

Two kinds of archival studies inquire into the effects of unpleasant temperature. Some compare geographic areas having different climates, and others look at changes in violence rates within one or more regions as the weather changes over time. Taking up the first of these approaches, social scientists have long noted that, in a number of countries, violent crime rates tend to be higher in warmer than in cooler regions. As an example, in his survey of the early research on this topic, Anderson (1989; Anderson & Anderson, 1998) cited Lombroso's research that indicated that in England, France, and Italy the rates of violent offenses were greater in the southern than in the northern latitudes of the countries. Pointing out that "latitude is essentially a proxy measure of average temperature" (Anderson & Anderson, 1998, p. 264), Anderson then added to these early observations by citing more recent studies showing essentially the same kind of south-north differences. His own sophisticated analysis of area differences within the United States demonstrated that cities with the hottest weather typically had the highest violence rates, even when their social and economic characteristics were partialled out (Anderson & Anderson, 1998). Whatever effect an area's economic level may have on the residents' proclivity to violence, its average temperature level is a significant influence.[4]

The relatively high homicide rate in the southern United States is a good example of such a regional effect on violence. Over the generations, more murders and assaults have been committed in the southern states, controlling for population size, than in the northern parts of the country. Several theories have been offered to account for this high level of violence (see Messner & Hawley, 1989; Nisbett & Cohen, 1996), but perhaps the best known of these assigns the blame to a prevailing *culture of honor* in the South. In the version advanced by Nisbett and Cohen (1996), Southerners do not have a general proclivity to violence. Instead, men, especially white males, growing up in this area have learned that they must redress a perceived threat to their honor by attacking the offender. They presumably are ready to see such threats, are strongly angered when they do detect the insult, and believe they have to resort to violence in order to protect their image as tough and able to protect themselves and their possessions. Although Nisbett and Cohen (1996) provided a substantial body of evidence consistent with their thesis, Anderson and Anderson (1996, 1998) argued that regional temperature is a better predictor of the South's high violence rates than is its "culture of honor." When they analyzed data from 260 standard metropolitan areas in the United States for 1980, they found that the average heat in an area significantly predicted its overall violence rate and the rate at which whites were arrested for violent crimes, even when the area's "southernness"[5] and other demographic and economic characteristics were held constant. Indeed, in these data, when temperature and other social and economic variables were controlled, the area's "southernness" was no longer related to its violence level (see Anderson & Anderson, 1998). The researchers concluded that whatever influence the southerners' culture of honor had on their response to affronts was only indirect; they presumably developed and maintained their violence-encouraging attitudes and values largely because of the region's hot weather (1998).[6]

The second archival approach investigates changes in violence rates over time periods that differ in temperature.[7] The Anderson and Anderson (see, e.g., 1998) survey of relevant studies that employ this methodology again points to the violence-increasing effect of high temperatures. Although there are some ambiguities and even differences of opinion (see Bell, 1992; Cohn & Rotton, 1997), the research here generally indicates that murders and violent assaults, but not property crimes, are most frequent during the hottest weather. Not surprisingly, then, these violent crimes are at their peak during the summer months (see Anderson, 1989; Anderson & Anderson, 1998; Cohn & Rotton, 1997).

Of course, this time effect can be interpreted in a number of ways. Some writers (e.g., Cohen & Felson, 1979; Felson, 1994) prefer to view the differences in violence rates from one period to another in terms of what activities are customarily carried out at these times. According to this *routine-activity* theorizing, work, school, family, or social schedules sometimes make certain kinds of activities obligatory and restrain people's interactions with others. On other occasions, though, people have greater discretion as to just what they can do. The routine-activity proponents hold that it is at these freer times, away from work or home and the scrutiny of restraining agents, that violence is most likely to arise. Typically these constraint-free occasions occur more often when the weather is warm, the argument goes, and as a consequence, there are more interpersonal encounters and a greater chance of open conflict in these hotter periods. It may be these relatively frequent interchanges, then, rather than the unpleasant heat that is responsible for the increased aggression.

We obviously have to recognize the significance of these frequent encounters on the hotter days, as I note later, and Anderson and Anderson (1998) did not care to dismiss this routine-activity interpretation outright. Nonetheless, they pointed to yet another study whose findings seem to counter this alternative explanation. Michael and Zumpe (1986) ascertained the number of crisis calls made to various women's shelters in five locations by battered women seeking help. The data from any one location covered at least 2 consecutive years. In the investigators' view, the routine-activity thesis expects wife battering to decrease in the warmer weather because the couple members

are routinely more apt to go their separate ways outside the home during this time of year and thus are less likely to come into conflict. Contrary to this expectation, however, the women's calls were most frequent in the hottest months. Michael and Zumpe also reported that the peak number of abuse calls occurred about 40 days earlier in Atlanta and Texas than in Oregon and California, corresponding, of course, to the earlier rise in temperatures in the more southern regions. Anderson and Anderson (1998) concluded that "These data do not rule out the possibility that some type of routine activity effect also occurs independently of temperature, but they do show that the routine activity theory . . . [in itself] cannot account for the summer increase in wife battering" (p. 276).

Still, other research shows that it is important to consider the likelihood and nature of interpersonal encounters when explaining the relationship between temperature and violent offenses. Cohn and Rotton (1997) investigated the variables that predicted the number of calls that were made to the Minneapolis police to report assaults in 1987 and 1988. The temperature during the 3-hour periods they utilized proved to be a relatively unimportant predictor of the violence measure in comparison with time of day and day of week.

Nevertheless, temperature itself seemed to have some effect. Most important for this chapter, Cohn and Rotton (1997) found that their data supported *both* the linear and curvilinear expectations. Temperature was linearly related to the assault measure early in the morning and from 6 P.M. to midnight, but there was a curvilinear relationship during the late afternoon and early evening. Although we do not know just what types of people were involved in the reported abuses, many of the early-morning and nighttime conflicts could have been between domestic partners. The hotter it was, apparently, the greater was the likelihood that one or both of the couple members would become antagonistic to the other person close by and start a fight. In the late afternoon and early evening, on the other hand, people presumably could cope with the heat in several ways as the temperature climbed, such as with a cooling drink or by escaping into an air-conditioned bar, restaurant, or movie. The setting they were in and the activities they carried out at this time evidently were not conducive to the development of hostile interchanges. Whatever had happened, however, the results point to the importance of situational variables in displays of affective aggression. The afflicted persons might well have an instigation to aggression, but if they are engaged in distracting activities, if there is no suitable target nearby, and/or if their inhibitions against aggression are fairly strong because of the presence of nearby aggression-restraining people, their urge will not become manifest in open behavior.

The Cohn and Rotton (1997) findings regarding the effects of cold weather also highlight the role of the social context in determining what actions are undertaken in aversive conditions. Whereas the present analysis of affective aggression contends that virtually any decidedly aversive condition, including unpleasant cold, should produce an urge to aggression, Cohn and Rotton (1997) indicated that there were actually relatively few reported assaults on the coldest days. Nevertheless, because we do have evidence of aversively generated aggressive inclinations under cold temperatures, as is shown later, it could be, as Cohn and Rotton (1997) recognized, that people in the everyday world can more easily protect themselves from cold than from hot weather.[8]

What about laboratory experiments in which the ambient temperature is deliberately manipulated? The findings here, overall, seem quite inconsistent (see Anderson & Anderson, 1998). Nonetheless, we can make some sense of the results by recognizing that, for all of the control that laboratory studies exert over many extraneous variables, the outcome of an experiment can still be affected by various artifacts, such as the participants' social concerns.

Following up on earlier experiments (e.g., Griffitt, 1970) that demonstrated that people in a hot room are all too apt to judge others in a hostile manner, Baron (see Baron & Bell, 1976; Baron & Richardson, 1994; Bell & Baron, 1976) carried out the first laboratory studies of the effect of heat on aggressive behavior. He had initially believed that high ambient temperature would promote open assaults only when other influences operating at that time had activated aggressive inclinations. And so, in the study by Baron and Bell (1975), the researchers thought that the participants confined to an unpleasantly hot room would display strong aggression only if they were already disposed to be aggressive because they had just been provoked or had seen someone else attack a target or both. However, the experimental results not only failed to support this particular expectation but also pointed to the curvilinear relationship between negative affect and aggression. The participants who had been exposed to both negative treatments—by having been insulted by the experimenter's accomplice and by being in an uncomfortably hot room at the time—rated themselves as more uncomfortable than any of their other counterparts in the study. Nevertheless, when they had an opportunity to punish the accomplice with electric shocks, they delivered *less* punishment than the other men in the equally hot room who had not been provoked beforehand. Putting these findings together with the results of other experiments (e.g., Bell & Baron, 1976), Baron and his associates concluded that only those who experienced moderately negative affect had become aggressive; the persons exposed to the most aversive conditions, and who thus felt very bad, were more intent on escaping from the extremely unpleasant situation than on attacking the target.

My own interpretation of these results is somewhat different. Whereas Baron (see Baron & Richardson, 1994) regards escape inclinations as being incompatible with ag-

gressive tendencies, so that the afflicted persons want *either* to "flee" *or* to "fight," in my view (Berkowitz, 1983, 1993a) both inclinations can exist together. People can want to escape from the aversive setting at the same time that they have an urge to attack the perceived source of their discomfort. Situational, prior-learning, and genetic factors presumably determine which of these behavioral tendencies is dominant on any one occasion. Of course, on any given occasion one or the other inclination may be dominant, in control of the person's behavior, and so it might appear that the individual is oriented *either* to fight *or* flight. However, and this is my point, both tendencies actually can be activated at the same time even though this is not always apparent.[9] The "cornered rat" phenomenon is a good illustration of this. An animal or human might prefer to escape from some threat or disturbance, but he or she could still become aggressive if escape is not possible. From my perspective, then, the decidedly unhappy men in the Bell and Baron experiment (who had been insulted by the accomplice and were in the hot room) had presumably developed both a desire to get away from the unpleasant situation and an aggressive urge. Being well socialized, their escape inclination might have been fairly strong; thus they may have decided they would look better to the watching psychologist if they restrained themselves somewhat and did not punish the offender as much as they wanted. Put simply, I am saying that people experiencing strong negative affect can become highly aggressive, as the archival studies just reviewed indicate, or they may inhibit their violent urge if they believe it is to their benefit to do so.

Anderson's research also suggests that the display of open aggression can be inhibited by social considerations. His experiments (e.g., Anderson, Anderson, & Deuser, 1996) repeatedly showed that an unpleasant temperature (cold or hot) produced stronger negative affect, angry feelings, and hostile attitudes and cognitions than did more comfortable ambient temperatures. But these reactions were not always accompanied by strong attacks on an available target. Another study (see Anderson & Anderson, 1998) is a good case in point. According to the participants' self-ratings in this experiment, those put to work in either an uncomfortably cold or uncomfortably hot laboratory room were angrier and had more hostile attitudes than their counterparts exposed to more moderate temperatures. When all the participants were placed in an ambiguous and slightly unpleasant interaction with a supposed competitor, the people in the uncomfortable room (either too cold or too hot) were more punitive to this other person than were those in the moderate temperature settings—but this was true only the first time they could administer punishment, not on the later occasions.[10] Presumably they were aggressively inclined, but they may have attacked their competitors more or less impulsively at first, then decided it was best to restrain themselves.

Whatever happened in this experiment by the Anderson team, research reported by Berkowitz, Cochran, and Embree (1981) shows that an aversive temperature can indeed create an urge to aggression. In this latter case, though, the aversive situation was produced by physically painful cold water rather than by an unpleasant ambient temperature. The female university students in the two studies conducted by these investigators kept one hand in water that was either very cold or at a more comfortable room temperature as they evaluated a fellow student's solutions to several assigned problems. They could provide these assessments by giving their peer either rewards (nickels) or punishments (noise blasts). Cutting across the water-temperature variation, half of the participants were told that any punishment they delivered was likely to hurt the other person, whereas the remaining women were informed that these punishments would be helpful because they would motivate the problem solver to do better.

The results in both studies indicated that the participants were generally reluctant to punish the other person, especially when their hand was immersed in the more comfortable water. However, those exposed to the painfully cold water were somewhat more willing to hurt the problem solver—but primarily when they believed their punishments would hurt this person. Apparently because the great discomfort they were experiencing had activated an urge to do injury, the people told they could hurt the problem solver seemed to have taken advantage of this opportunity by giving their peer the most punishments and fewest rewards.[11]

### Other Unpleasant Environmental Stimulation

Although less frequently investigated than temperature variations, other aversive environmental conditions have also been found to promote aggressive reactions. We should not be surprised at some of these conditions. As a notable example, surely many of us recognize how we have been annoyed at times by loud noises. Donnerstein and Wilson (1976) extended this observation by showing that loud noise is not only disturbing but also can intensify angered persons' attacks on those who had provoked them (although in this study the intense noise did not heighten the strength of the nonangered participants' aggression toward another nearby individual). Then, too, supporting the Glass and Singer (1972) demonstration that it is the uncontrollability of the noise that is especially bothersome, Donnerstein and Wilson (1976) reported that when previously angered people believed they had control over the noxious noise bombarding them, the adverse impact of the noise on them was substantially reduced.

Unpleasant atmospheric pollution can also promote hostility. After Rotton and his associates (Rotton, Barry, Frey, & Soler, 1978) first found that people exposed to foul odors expressed stronger dislike for others not sharing their discomfort,[12] a later experiment (Rotton, Frey, Barry, Milligan, & Fitzpatrick, 1979) investigated the effects of odors that varied in their unpleasantness on physical aggression. Like the Donnerstein and Wilson (1976) results, the outcome indicated that the moderately noxious stimulation led to intensified punishment given by angered persons to their antagonist. But interestingly, the Rotton et al. (1979) findings also pointed to the curvilinear relationship between displeasure and aggression postulated by Baron and his colleagues (see Baron & Richardson, 1994). Only the angry persons in the moderately smelly room were significantly more aggressive than the other insulted people breathing the more normal air; those afflicted by an extremely bad odor were no more punitive than the controls under the normal air condition, perhaps because they were preoccupied with their desire to escape from the very malodorous situation. But at any rate, because air pollution is often bothersome, at least moderate levels of this nuisance can promote aggression. Relatively high levels of atmospheric ozone apparently can also be disturbing, and so, in an extension of Rotton's earlier research, an archival study done in Dayton, Ohio, by Rotton and Frey (1985) found that those periods in which high levels of ozone were recorded were the times in which the greatest number of instances of domestic violence were reported.

Those of us who do not use tobacco also know how irritating other people's cigarette smoke can be. Not surprisingly, then, two experiments (Jones & Bogat, 1978; Zillmann, Baron, & Tamborini, 1981) showed that people's hostility toward another person was greater when the air was heavy with secondary cigarette smoke than when there was no tobacco odor. Moreover, unlike the Donnerstein and Wilson (1976) and Rotton et al. (1979) studies just mentioned, in these experiments the aversive stimulation (cigarette smoke) led to greater aggression even when the participants had not been provoked beforehand. Zillmann and his colleagues (1981) went further than this in their investigation of the effect of secondary cigarette smoke. They found that the people exposed to the tobacco-laden air were more hostile to a nearby individual even when this person was not responsible for the smoke.[13]

### Social Stresses and Frustrations

Although few theorists in the social sciences have discussed the possible role of physically unpleasant conditions in antisocial behavior, a good number of them have proposed that harsh social situations, especially frustrations, are major contributors to criminal activities. Sociologists and criminologists often speak of these frustrations as *social strains* and refer to *strain theories* of crime causation, whereas psychologists typically employ the term *frustration* much more explicitly and at times trace their thinking to the *frustration-aggression hypothesis* advanced by Dollard, Doob, Miller, Mowrer, and Sears (1939) more than three generations ago. But whatever words are used in these analyses, I propose that they can be greatly enriched and extended by an explicit recognition of the central role of negative affect in antisocial behavior.

## The Original Strain and Frustration-Aggression Formulations

Those who couch their analyses in strain terms (e.g., Cloward & Ohlin, 1960; Merton, 1957) typically maintain that social structural factors, such as the stratification system, effectively prevent segments of the population from attaining the economic and social goals society has taught them to seek. People in the groups that experience the strain of this frustrating disjunction between means and goals may then turn to crime. As Merton (1957) observed, "a cardinal American virtue, 'ambition,' promotes a cardinal American vice, 'deviant behavior' " (as cited in Wilson & Herrnstein, 1985, p. 215).

The Dollard et al. (1939) conception of a link between frustrations and aggression is altogether consistent with strain theory even with its very different terminology. The central proposition in this analysis maintains that every frustration, defined as an obstacle to the attainment of an expected gratification (rather than as an emotional reaction to some thwarting), generates an instigation to hostile aggression, an urge to harm someone, principally but not only the perceived source of the goal blocking. This theory, it should be noted, did not regard all privations as frustrations. Even though Dollard and his colleagues did not use the words *hope* and *expectations*, their reasoning essentially held that people are frustrated, and thus become aggressively inclined, only if they had been hopeful—had been anticipating the pleasures to be derived from reaching a particular goal—and not merely because they lack the good things in life that others enjoy.

The frustration-aggression theorists also discussed, among other things, how the possibility of punishment for aggression would affect the probability of an overt assault and the nature of the target that is attacked. In this latter connection, Dollard et al. (1939) reasoned that the strongest urge is to strike at the perceived source of the frustration, but they also proposed that the threat of punishment could lead to displaced aggression in which the assault is directed at substitute targets. Miller (1948) later spelled out in more detail the processes affecting this displacement. In his model the strength of the frustrated individual's attack on any particular available target is not an outgrowth of calculated, rationalistic decision making but instead is a function of the intensity of the instigation to aggression, the strength of the inclination to avoid engaging in aggression, and also the degree of association between the perceived source of the frustration and the given target.

Although the 1939 frustration-aggression formulation is much more detailed and microanalytic than strain theory, the two are fundamentally in agreement in tracing much antisocial conduct to socially produced thwartings. However, the Dollard team's conception went somewhat further than strain theory in its tacit emphasis on the importance of dashed hopes in the genesis of socially disapproved behavior. In this regard, the frustration-aggression theory shares the position taken by a number of other social science analyses, holding that many social disorders are rooted in the resentment generated by a failure to meet rising expectations. Davies' (1962) classic theory of revolutions is an example of such a formulation. He argued that the American, French, and Russian revolutions did not grow out of severe, prolonged hardships. Instead, Davies said, in each of these cases the established order was overthrown when a sudden, sharp socioeconomic decline abruptly thwarted the expectations that had developed over a number of years of improving conditions. Studies of the black men who participated in the widespread urban riots in the United States in the 1960s also suggest that this social unrest was prompted in part by the gap between their rising expectations and what they were able to achieve. According to Caplan's (1970) survey of this research, a disproportionately high fraction of the rioters were better educated than many of the other members of the African-American communities rather than being the most deprived persons at the bottom of the socioeconomic ladder. These relatively educated men could have come to expect many of the good things in life enjoyed by other Americans and may well have been frustrated at their inability to fulfill these hopes.[14]

Both strain theory and the frustration-aggression model have been criticized as seriously incomplete or even incorrect. Thus one objection to strain theory (e.g., Vold & Bernard, 1986) faults the easy assumption made by quite a few of the theory's adherents that poverty in itself is the major spur to crime and delinquency (also see Wilson & Herrnstein, 1985). And then, too, critics of the Dollard et al. (1939) frustration theory (see Berkowitz, 1989, 1993a, for a summary of their views) frequently have insisted on a number of limiting conditions, such as that the thwartings must be regarded as improper or ego threatening or both if they are to generate an aggressive urge and that, even then, aggression would not be displayed unless the frustrated persons had learned earlier that this behavior would pay off for them.

Although it is now clear that the strain and frustration-aggression analyses are by no means complete accounts of all antisocial behavior, this does not mean that these theories have no utility at all. Research results have been published that are consistent with strain and frustration conceptions by showing that barriers to economic success can have criminogenic effects over a substantial sample of people, even if there are a good number of individual exceptions (e.g., Anderson, 1989;[15] Browning, Thornberry, & Porter, 1999; Farrington, 1993).

In general, though, it seems fair to say that the strongest results in accordance with strain and frustration-aggression theorizing appear when the people involved have fairly definite economic goals that they are unable to satisfy. A well-known study that illustrates this point was reported by Hovland and Sears (1940). Employing aggregate data from the U.S. South at a time when cotton was that region's economic mainstay, these investigators showed that, up until the 1930s, sudden drops in the market value of cotton were often accompanied by an increased number of lynchings of blacks in that part of the country. A later reanalysis of the Hovland-Sears data (Hepworth & West, 1988), using a more sophisticated statistical procedure, essentially corroborated the earlier results, although a more recent study (Green, Glaser, & Rich, 1998) indicates that the relationship between economic fluctuations and the lynching of blacks was significant only up to 1930 but not through the Great Depression. At least for that time period, then, the unexpected loss of income apparently had generated an instigation to aggression which was then directed against blacks believed to have violated community norms. It is important to recognize, though, that the frustration-engendered instigation to aggression was readily translated into the antiblack violence because the lynch mobs' beliefs and social norms justified the hanging of blacks who had supposedly committed a serious offense, because their restraints against aggression were relatively weak at the time, and because a suitable target was available for them.[16]

In another possible example, Devine, Sheley, and Smith (1988) found that increases in unemployment in the United States between 1948 and 1985 were associated with jumps in homicide rates, perhaps because the sudden joblessness thwarted the economic expectations built up when work was available. And then, too, when Blau and Blau (1982) analyzed the 1970 murder and assault rates in the 125 largest metropolitan areas of the United States, they saw that the highest rates of criminal violence occurred in those areas having the greatest socioeconomic inequalities. In this case the area residents may have raised their economic aspirations because of the attainments of their relatively well-off neighbors and then were disturbed by their inability to fulfill these increased desires.

Turning to research that specifically addresses the idea of a linkage between frustrations and aggression, the accumulating body of evidence (summarized in Berkowitz, 1989, 1993a) indicates that even legitimate and/or non–ego-threatening frustrations can produce aggressive reactions at times. In one of these supporting investigations, Geen (1968) showed that socially legitimate frustrations

can spur young adults to increased aggressiveness even when the target is not responsible for their inability to reach the goal. The aggressive urge generated by a socially proper and/or nonthreatening frustration is often weaker than that produced by an improper and/or ego-threatening barrier to goal attainment, but it could still be there. Several investigators (Lewis, 1993; Stenberg, Campos, & Emde, 1983) have even reported that very young human infants become angry (as indicated by their facial expressions) when they are deliberately frustrated. Lewis (1993) contends that anger is an unlearned reaction to the frustration of a goal-directed action. In his research he conditioned 2- to 8-month-old infants to pull one of their arms in order to see a picture of a baby's smiling face. An extinction phase was then established in which the arm pull no longer revealed the happy picture. Analysis of the infants' facial expressions demonstrated that the great majority of them displayed anger during this extinction period, whereas little anger was shown in the training phase. Furthermore, this pattern held for the 8-week-old as well as for the 8-month-old, babies, long before they have an opportunity to learn that their anger display will be rewarded. We apparently are "preprogrammed" to react to a frustration with an instigation to aggression, although, of course, learning that an aggressive response will be beneficial can heighten the probability that an assault will be made, whereas anticipated negative consequences will lower this likelihood (Berkowitz, 1993a).

## Revising the Original Formulations

Despite the supporting evidence, for me and several other researchers a major problem with both the original strain and frustration-aggression formulations is not that they are too general in their aspirations but that, as they were initially conceived, they were too narrowly focused. Agnew (1992), a sociologist, has proposed a general strain theory that goes well beyond Merton's initial analysis.[17] He maintains that strains can be generated by the failure to achieve any objective, social as well as economic—parental approval, popularity with one's peers, academic or sexual success, and so on—and even by negative experiences, such as the termination of a romantic relationship, the death of a loved one, academic failure, and peer rejection. Agnew also emphasized that the goals sought have to be important and/or the negative experiences fairly strong if there is to be a significant strain. Such a strain produces negative emotions, and these can lead to delinquency and aggression. It is possible to interpret the tragic shootings at Columbine High School in Colorado in April 1999 in these terms. The violence was evidently spurred, at least in part, by the offenders' anger at being rejected by many of their classmates.

In a very similar vein, I have proposed (Berkowitz, 1989, 1993a) a modification of the original frustration-aggression thesis that broadens its scope and makes it entirely commensurate with general strain theory. This revision says it is the negative affect produced by frustrations, and not the mere inability to achieve an anticipated goal, that generates the urge to aggression. Any aversive occurrence can initiate aggression, not just unexpected barriers to goal attainment, but only to the degree that the event is decidedly unpleasant to those affected. And so, contrary to the usual appraisal-attributional theories that maintain that another person's action will generate anger and aggression only to the degree that it is appraised as morally unjustified, blameworthy, or both (e.g., Averill, 1982; Clore, Ortony, Dienes, & Fujita, 1993; Weiner, Graham, & Chandler, 1982), this formulation holds that thwarted people can experience anger and become aggressively inclined even when they regard the barrier to their goal attainment as morally proper—as long as the incident generates a decided displeasure. Dill and Anderson (1995) have provided supporting evidence. In their investigation the experimenter imposed either an unjustifiable or justifiable difficulty on the participants seeking to carry out their assignment. The people exposed to the unjustifiable impediment then expressed the greatest hostility to the experimenter, but even those given the justifiable difficulty were more hostile than the nonfrustrated control group. Even the presumably proper barrier to goal attainment apparently was unpleasant enough in this situation to generate aggressive tendencies. From this perspective (see Berkowitz, 1993a), unjustified frustrations usually produce a stronger aggressive reaction than socially warranted thwartings, primarily because the former are typically more unpleasant.

This line of thought readily explains why antisocial aggression is most clearly seen, in accordance with strain and frustration-aggression theorizing, when the people involved are unable to reach their expected goals. Barriers that prevent us from enjoying our hoped-for pleasures are obviously likely to generate a fairly strong displeasure, whereas expected privations might only produce a somewhat weaker resentment. Because the intensity of the resulting aggressive urge is proportional to the intensity of the negative affect, privations are therefore apt to produce weaker aggressive reactions than are the unexpected thwartings. But nonetheless, as this formulation holds, even privations can give rise to antisocial conduct. Continuing poverty can promote delinquency and crime (Anderson, 1987; Browning et al., 1999; Farrington, 1993). Keep in mind, though, that the aversive occurrence generates an *instigation*, not necessarily overt behavior. A good many intervening factors can influence the extent to which the negative-affect-produced aggressive urge is manifested in an open assault on an available target, and I discuss this later in the chapter.

For now, though, let us look at more evidence that indicates that psychologically unpleasant situations can give rise to overt aggression. An experiment by Passman and Mulhern (1977) is relevant. The mothers in this study worked on an assigned task at the same time that they monitored their children's performances on a puzzle. The experimenters deliberately placed some of the women under a high degree of stress as they worked by confusing them as to what the requirements were, whereas other women were clearly told how to carry out their job so that they were under low stress. The highly stressed mothers were more punitive to their youngsters when they saw a mistake made than were their counterparts, who were more comfortable in their assigned work. The stresses encountered in the everyday world can lead to more naturalistic aggression as well. Straus (1980) and his colleagues asked the men and women in their nationally representative U.S. sample to indicate whether they had experienced each of 18 stressful life events—such as "troubles with other people at work," "the death of someone close," "a move to a different neighborhood or town," and a family member with a health or behavior problem. Whether the respondents were male or female, the greater the number of stressors they reported experiencing during the past year, the more likely they were also to say they had abused their children. Stresses confronting a nation as a whole can also promote violence. Research in Israel (Landau & Pfeffermann, 1988; Landau & Raveh, 1987) found that highly salient threats to that country's security predicted a rise in homicide rates and that various stress indices for the years between 1950 and 1981, including rapid growths in population and high inflation and unemployment, were also positively correlated with that nation's homicide rate in this period.

## Theories About Negative Affect-Produced Aggression

The two most detailed social psychological analyses of how negative affect can give rise to aggression were published by Anderson and his associates (e.g., Anderson & Anderson, 1998; Anderson, Anderson, & Deuser, 1996; Anderson, Anderson, Dill, & Deuser, 1998; Anderson, Deuser, & DeNeve, 1995) and by Berkowitz (1983, 1989, 1993a, 1998). These two formulations have many similarities, but they are also different in important respects.

### The Anderson Group's Cognitive Model

Calling their conception the *general affective aggression model*, Anderson and his colleagues have now extended their formulation to cover the many factors that can govern the display of affective aggression, including personality characteristics, physical exercise, and the presence of aggression-related cues. However, because here I am

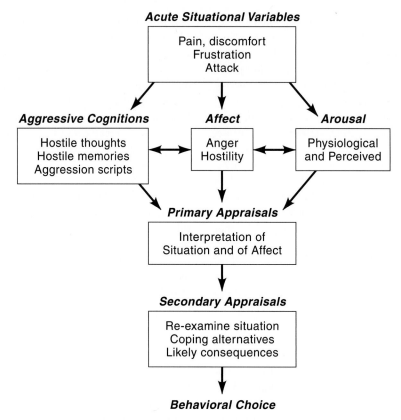

**Figure 42.1** Anderson's general model of affective aggression. Adapted from Anderson, Deuser, and DeNeve (1995).

concerned primarily with situational influences, I summarize a somewhat briefer earlier version (Anderson, Deuser, & DeNeve, 1995), outlined in Figure 42.1, that focuses on reactions to aversive events. This theory states, as the Anderson group has repeatedly demonstrated, that a decidedly unpleasant occurrence (here termed an "acute situational variable") has cognitive, affective, and arousal effects.[18] What is especially important about these three response systems, as far as Anderson and colleagues are concerned, is that each of them influences "the interpretation and understanding of incoming information" (Anderson et al., 1995, p. 436). If the incoming information is ambiguous so that it could be understood in various ways, this initial primary appraisal quickly and automatically shapes the affected persons' interpretation of what is happening in such a way that they are apt to believe the others around them are unfriendly and maybe even intend to do them harm. In addition, whatever uncertain feelings they might be experiencing at this time could be understood as anger. Then, if time permits and there are no conflicting situational demands, a secondary appraisal arises in which additional information is considered. The affected persons might now reinterpret what had happened before, and even if they do not, they might think about how they should cope with the situation before them and what might be the consequences of the possible courses of ac-

tion. Guided by these appraisals, the Anderson model emphasizes, they then decide what to do and act accordingly.

### Berkowitz's Cognitive-Neoassociationistic Model

My own theoretical analysis, which I call a *cognitive-neoassociationistic model*, also posits a sequence of responses to the aversive event. However, unlike the Anderson formulation, this conception explicitly holds that the initial reaction is largely governed by associative processes. Cognitions then become more important later. Basically, as can be seen in Figure 42.2, I propose that decidedly unpleasant conditions tend to activate, automatically and with relatively little thought, at least two sets of "primitive" inclinations: one to escape from or avoid the aversive stimulation and also another to attack and even destroy the source of this stimulation.[19] In other words, the aversive state of affairs presumably gives rise to several inclinations, including *both* flight *and* fight tendencies. Genetic factors, prior learning, and situational influences all enter to determine the relative strengths of these various reactions.

Also important here is that both the flight and fight tendencies should be regarded as syndromes, networks of associatively linked physiological, motoric, and cognitive components. The activated flight-associated syndrome is

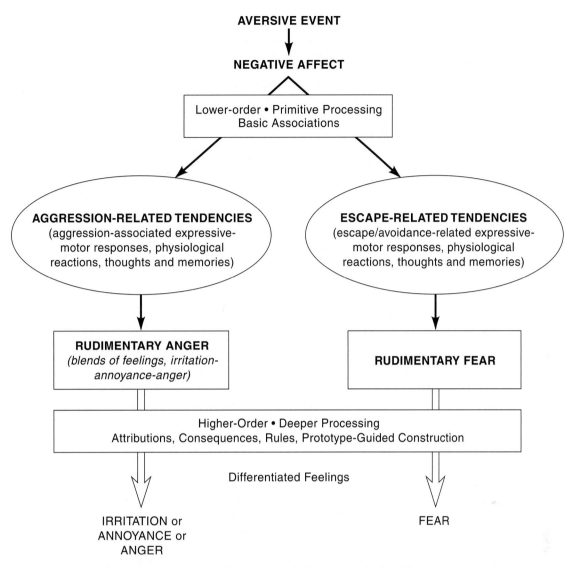

Figure 42.2  A cognitive-neoassociationistic conception of anger.

consciously experienced as *fear*, whereas the activated fight-linked syndrome (or network) is felt (i.e., perceived) as *annoyance* or *irritation* (at relatively weak levels) or *anger* (at more intense levels). Because this model views the syndromes as associatively linked networks, it maintains that the activation of any particular syndrome component will also tend to bring the other parts of the network into operation. Thus, more than the formulations that rest exclusively on cognitive concepts, this theory can accommodate the research that shows that the display of the facial expressions and bodily postures characteristic of a given affective state, such as anger, can generate the feelings typical of this state (DuClos et al., 1989).

My model differs from the Anderson et al. (1995) formulation primarily through its emphasis on these first, relatively automatic and noncognitively mediated reactions to the experienced negative affect. Suggestive evidence consistent with my position was obtained in an experi-

ment on displaced aggression conducted by Pedersen, Gonzales, and Miller (1999). After the participants in one condition were intentionally provoked by the experimenter, some of them were mildly annoyed by the investigator's confederate, posing as a fellow participant. Although the other participants who had not been previously provoked by the experimenter did not react especially negatively to the confederate's mild annoyance, those who had been exposed earlier to the experimenter's unpleasant treatment of them responded with some hostility to the confederate's "triggering" annoyance by evaluating him relatively unfavorably. What is significant is that the participants' hostility toward the annoying confederate was more strongly determined by the intensity of their negative feelings at that time than by their appraisal of how fair and reasonable the confederate's behavior toward them had been.

All this does not mean, of course, that appraisals do

not have any influence at all on the affected persons' subsequent hostility. The cognitive-neoassociationistic model proposes that the initial, fairly primitive reactions can be modified and even substantially altered by cognitive processes introduced after the first affective responses occur. It is in this second phase that appraisals, attributions, and the like can control the reactions to the aversive event. As the Anderson model posits, the affected persons think more about what had happened, consider what might have been the other people's motives and what had caused the event to occur, and what could be the appropriate ways of acting under the circumstances. The present perspective emphasizes, nevertheless, that active information processing is required to bring these modifiers into operation so that particular appraisals and attributions are not necessary to produce the primitive experiences of fear and anger and even the open display of fear and affective aggression. People can become angry and assault someone impulsively without the intervention of the complicated thought processes postulated by appraisal and attribution theorizing (see Berkowitz, 1993a, b). As a matter of fact, I suggest that people exposed to decidedly unpleasant stressful conditions sometimes blame a salient available target for their troubles because of the hostile thoughts and angry feelings that had been generated within them; their attributions might then be the result rather than the cause of their affective reactions. At least two studies have obtained findings consistent with such a possibility. In one, when Quigley and Tedeschi (1996) analyzed their respondents' self-reported angry incidents, they concluded that anger can lead to blame rather than being a consequence of blame. Earlier, Keltner, Ellsworth, and Edwards (1993) induced angry or sad feelings in their participants by, among other things, varying their bodily movements, and they showed that the people in the angry condition were more apt to blame others for mishaps that occurred.

### Does the Aversive Event Automatically Activate an Impulse to Aggression?

Cognitively oriented emotion theorists such as Anderson and his colleagues typically contend that emotions influence behavior mainly by affecting cognitive mechanisms—including attention, judgment, decision making, and memory—rather than by directly priming a class of behaviors. By contrast, other researchers, most notably Frijda (e.g., Frijda, Kuipers, & ter Schure, 1989), hold that this priming does occur in many emotional states. According to Frijda, an emotionally relevant appraisal elicits not only specific physiological and experiential reactions but also a particular action readiness, a "readiness to engage in or disengage from interaction with some goal object in some particular fashion" (Frijda et al., 1989, p. 213). Although the term *readiness* here might be taken

as referring only to a latent disposition, for Frijda the notion also involves active motor responses. Thus, whereas in his research (e.g., Frijda et al., 1989) Frijda typically assessed action readiness by asking the participants what they wanted to do when they were in particular emotional states, he at times indicated that these wants can also involve "impulses" and involuntary skeletal muscular reactions.

For me, however, the phrase *action readiness* does not adequately characterize the impulses activated by the aversive event. The cognitive-neoassociationistic model maintains that the affective syndromes put into operation include action programs, motor reactions oriented toward the aims of a target's injury (in the case of the aggression-related syndrome) and/or escape from the noxious situation (the fear-related syndrome). More than having a mere "readiness," the persons in whom the aggression-associated affective network is strongly activated presumably have a strong urge to attack, even to hurt, someone, especially (but not only) the perceived source of the noxious event.

Spielberger's (personal communication, 1996) factor analysis of responses to his latest questionnaire assessing individual differences in experienced anger testifies to such an aggressive urge. He found three intercorrelated clusters, one dealing with angry feelings (composed of items such as "I am furious"), one with a felt pressure to verbal expression (items such as "I feel like screaming"), and the third reflecting an urge to physical aggression (items such as "I feel like kicking somebody"). As the cognitive-neoassociationistic model says, angry feelings are paralleled by aggression-related motor impulses. Furthermore, these impulses could have the aim of doing injury. Izard (1991) thought this was so when he spoke of anger being accompanied by "an impulse to strike out, to attack the [perceived] source of the anger" (p. 241). Roseman, Wiest, and Swartz (1994) obtained evidence of this desire to hurt someone when they asked their respondents to indicate what they felt like doing when they were angry. Many of these people answered that in such a state they characteristically thought "how unfair something was." But more important, quite a few of them also said that they felt "like hitting someone" and that they wanted "to hurt someone." The experimental results published by Berkowitz, Cochran, and Embree (1981), cited earlier, also point to such an aggressive goal. In their two studies the participants (women) were most apt to punish a peer when (1) they were exposed to presumably legitimate but physically painful stimulation, and (2) they had been told that their punishment would hurt, rather than help, the target. It is as if these suffering and angry persons were most likely to act on their aggressive urges when they believed they had an opportunity to reach their goal of inflicting hurt.

## Inhibiting the Activated Affective Aggression

The activation of the affective aggression syndrome obviously does not mean that there necessarily will be an open display of aggression, because various influences may operate to keep the aggressive reactions from becoming manifest. For one thing, because of the person's genetic background, prior learning history, and/or the presence of situational influences, the aversive stimulation might evoke stronger flight-related than aggression-related reactions. I discuss here only the last mentioned of these factors, situationally induced restraints, because of space limitations.

### Threat of Punishment

Common sense and everyday experience quickly point to the most obvious situational factor: threat of punishment. Unless people are exceedingly strongly instigated to attack their tormentors, the possibility that they will suffer severe consequences for such an assault may well keep them from aggressing openly (although they might displace their hostility onto a safer target). Years of research (summarized in Berkowitz, 1993a) tell us more about the effectiveness of punishment as a disciplinary technique. By and large, this research indicates, punishment works best when it is: (1) severe; (2) delivered quickly, before the individual whose behavior is to be disciplined can enjoy the benefits of his or her disapproved conduct; and (3) administered consistently and with certainty. One might ask, however, whether these findings, mostly obtained from laboratory experiments, can be extended to our criminal justice system. Under what conditions is punishment most effective in controlling antisocial behavior?

The National Academy of Sciences commissioned a review of studies that investigated the effectiveness of various types of judicial sentences for crimes (see Berkowitz, 1993a). This review is suggestive. According to the review, the certainty of punishment (condition 3) is much more important than the severity of the sentence (condition 1) in deterring criminal behavior. The greater the probability that criminals will be apprehended and punished, the more likely it is that they will refrain from criminal conduct. This matter of punishment certainty can help explain why capital punishment does little to deter many murders. If we compare the homicide rates in regions (U.S. states or entire countries) that execute convicted killers with the rates in demographically matched regions (states or countries) that do not carry out capital punishment, we generally find little evidence that many would-be murderers are restrained by the threat of execution (see Berkowitz, 1993a). One possible reason for the ineffectiveness of this ultimate penalty is that the punishment is by

no means certain. Some murderers do get away with their crimes. Only about 70% of the homicides that have received police attention in recent years have resulted in arrests, and only about 7 in 10 of these cases led to convictions (see Berkowitz, 1993a).

But capital punishment may also not deter many murders because a substantial fraction of these killings are emotionally charged and highly impulsive in nature. Most homicides grow out of conflicts between people who know each other (although there has been an increase in the proportion of cases in which a stranger is slain). The persons involved in these conflicts are apt to be highly enraged at the time they assault their antagonist (Berkowitz, 1993a). If so, furiously intent on inflicting pain, they might not think of the possible long-term consequences of their violence—the possibility of punishment is not apparent to them at that time—and they strike at their victim more or less impulsively with whatever weapon is available to them.

### Cognitions That Promote and/or Control Affective Aggression

As I noted earlier, this discussion concentrates on the part played by stressful circumstances in activating aggressive motor impulses, largely because this type of phenomenon has received relatively little attention in current discussions of aggression and antisocial behavior. However, as both my cognitive-neoassociationistic formulation and, even more so, Anderson's analysis of affective aggression recognize, there can be no doubt that cognitive processes have a major role in governing just what behavior is exhibited in response to the negative affect (e.g., see Anderson & Anderson, 1998; Huesmann, 1998). But what is especially important to emphasize in this chapter is that the unpleasant feelings can also have a considerable impact on these cognitive processes: The negative affect can determine what matters are given attention, how they are interpreted and understood, what aspects of the past are remembered, and also how the primed aggressive ideas and impulses might be regulated.

### Affective Influences on Attention

It is now widely recognized that strong emotional excitation tends to reduce the range of cues to which one pays attention. Highly aroused people are thus apt to focus on the main features of the situation that confronts them to the neglect of matters that are relatively peripheral for them at that time (see, for example, Christianson, 1992). Faced with a threat or disturbance, their attention narrows to concentrate on the perceived source of this problem, and less salient details are ignored, even though these details might well be exceedingly important in the long run.

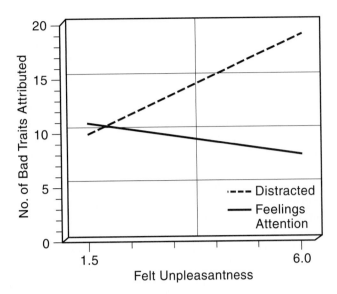

Figure 42.3 Relationships between negative affect and negative judgments as a function of attention direction.

More than this, though, there is also a good chance that their negative feelings will bias what aspects of the surrounding environment command their notice. Studies of mood effects have repeatedly demonstrated a mood-congruence bias in attention (Berkowitz, 2000b; Bower, 1992): Unpleasant feelings promote the quick recognition of negative details, anxiety leads to the ready detection of threatening stimuli, and, according to Cohen, Eckhardt, & Schagat, (1998), angry people are fast to attend to anger-related cues in the situation before them (particularly if they have hostile dispositions). With these affect-induced influences, those persons who are angered by a decidedly aversive event might well focus their attention narrowly on those they blame for the unpleasant occurrence and be quick to pick up information they regard as congruent with their angry mood. Concentrating their attention on the wrongdoer, they might then totally disregard other considerations, such as the possibility of being punished for aggression, and therefore fail to restrain their activated aggressive urges.

But the attentional focus might also lead to greater self-control and a reduced likelihood of open aggression—under some conditions. A series of experiments carried out in my laboratory (Berkowitz, 1993a; Berkowitz & Troccoli, 1990) suggests that this kind of regulation could happen when people become highly aware of their aroused feelings and think this arousal might influence them to act in socially improper or inappropriate ways.

Two experiments by Berkowitz and Troccoli (1990) point to some such process at work. Comparable results were obtained in both studies, but I summarize here only the second experiment. The male undergraduates were given a physical activity to carry out that was decidedly uncomfortable in half of the cases and affectively neutral

for the other men. Half of the participants in each of these conditions were then distracted with an irrelevant assignment, whereas the remaining participants were led to be highly attentive to their moods by a request to rate their feelings on a series of items. Immediately after this, all of the participants listened to a brief autobiographical statement supposedly made by a fellow student and gave their impressions of this individual's personality.

A multiple regression analysis was then carried out to test whether the experimental variations interacted with the participants' self-rated discomfort in predicting how many bad qualities the men assigned to the target person. Figure 42.3 shows that such a significant interaction was obtained. As the figure indicates, when the participants' attention was turned away from themselves, the worse they felt, the more unfavorable their impression of the target was. By contrast, those who were highly aware of their discomfort seemed to "lean over backward" in their judgments; the greater their felt displeasure, the *fewer* was the number of bad qualities they attributed to the target. Presumably wanting to be "fair" and "objective" in their assessment, they apparently sought to minimize the possible distorting influence of their mood, and they overcorrected for this possible source of bias.

All in all, the attention to feelings in these studies apparently gave rise to a relatively careful consideration of what was socially appropriate under the given circumstances and, consequently, produced a heightened self-restraint. However, as was implied before, attention to one's feelings probably will not always have such an effect. The target person in these experiments clearly was not the source of the participants' displeasure, and wanting to be fair and proper, they realized they should not blame their distress on this other individual. But on the other hand, under different circumstances those who are highly aware of themselves and their bad feelings conceivably might become even more hostile toward an available target—when (1) it is not clear to them that this person is not responsible for their distress and (2) they are not motivated to be fair and socially proper in their judgments and actions.

### Anger-Lessening Interventions

Psychologists have now clearly documented that the appraisal of a negative event as a deliberate and malicious injustice heightens the likelihood that anger and aggression will result (e.g., Averill, 1982; Roseman et al., 1994; also see Berkowitz, 1999) and also that anger, once created, often leads to the same kind of appraisal of a disturbing incident (e.g., Anderson & Anderson, 1998; Keltner et al., 1993). Many interventions designed to lower people's proclivity to anger and violence therefore attempt to achieve this end by reducing their readiness to interpret negative occurrences as intentional affronts.

Tafrate's (1995) meta-analytic review of studies that assess the effectiveness of treatments for anger disorders indicates that cognitively oriented therapies that seek to alter persons' thoughts and interpretations and even the statements they make to themselves when they are provoked can be quite successful in decreasing the likelihood of anger arousal. However, Tafrate (1995) also shows that a variety of procedures besides appraisal modification can also contribute to this anger reduction, such as relaxation procedures aimed at training persons to lower their physiological/motoric arousal by relaxing when they encounter disturbing incidents and systematic desensitization that seeks to extinguish the anger-aggression reactions automatically elicited by provocative situations (also see Deffenbacher, 1995).

## Summary

This brief overview of some of the ways in which cognitive processes can influence affective aggression obviously does not indicate that, for me, cognitions have only a minimal role in the determination and regulation of emotional reactions. Indeed, I term the theoretical framework that guides this discussion a "cognitive-neoassociationistic" perspective because I believe an adequate account of affective aggression must employ both cognitive and associationistic ideas. But whether the concepts employed in such an analysis derive from a cognitive or an associationistic tradition, in my view it is also necessary to recognize the great degree to which the various components of the affective aggression syndrome operate in a largely automatic manner. Affectively aroused persons do not always decide what they should feel, think, and do. Their negative, agitated feelings can be a direct spur to aggression-related motor reactions, as well as to the associatively linked thoughts that facilitate these responses.

## NOTES

1. As Liau, Barriga, and Gibbs (1998) have commented, this distinction between overt and covert behavior is similar to the difference Quay (1987) drew between undersocialized and socialized delinquent behavior. Overt aggression is a main feature of undersocialized delinquency, along with disobedience and destructive behavior, whereas socialized aggression involves less overt aggression and includes such actions as stealing, truancy, and drug use.

2. A number of researchers contend that aggressive behavior and the violation of conventional rules are governed by different beliefs and values, so that the factors that influence one of these transgressions do not necessarily affect the other. According to an investigation reported by Crane-Ross, Tisak, and Tisak (1998), self-report measures of aggression and violation of conventional rules "are related but separate constructs" (p. 361). Still, in this study some of the beliefs held by highly aggressive youths,

such as the belief that aggression was legitimate behavior, predicted convention-violating behavior. For them, if aggression was acceptable, so was the violation of many conventional norms.

3. Rational choice theories are coming under increasing attack in several social sciences. For example, as Peter Salovey pointed out in a personal communication to me, Green and Shapiro (1994) criticized the application of this approach in political science, holding that there is no good basis for the claim that rational choice theory has led to notable achievements in a number of areas in political science. Also testifying to this growing disenchantment with rational choice theorizing, the *Economist* magazine, in its December 18, 1999, issue, observed that "Economists are starting to abandon their assumption that humans behave rationally, and instead are finally coming to grips with the crazy, mixed up creatures we really are" (p. 63).

4. The summary given here generally follows Anderson's (1989; Anderson & Anderson, 1998) basic argument. It should be noted, however, that Bell (1992) and Rotton (see especially Cohn & Rotton, 1997) have raised important objections to aspects of the Anderson analysis. Bell (1992) argued that the evidence for the temperature-aggression relationship is more inconsistent than is indicated in this survey. For his part, among other things, Rotton (1993) has shown that some kinds of violent crimes, such as murders, are more apt to be correlated with high temperatures than are other violent crimes, such as rapes. He has also wondered at times whether the temperature index favored by Anderson—the number of hot days—is as good a measure as average temperature. However, this chapter assumes the basic validity of Anderson's thesis (although with some qualifications), and I attempt to reconcile the conflicting views.

5. A standard metropolitan area's "southernness" was based on an index that comprised the area's "south" or "north" location according to the U.S. Census, the percentage of the people in the area who had migrated from the old South, and the percentage of voters in the area who had voted for George Wallace in the 1968 presidential election (see Anderson & Anderson, 1998).

6. Rotton's (1993) analysis of Anderson's data indicated that latitude was related to the violence measure even when the climate measure was partialled out. This suggested to Rotton that there was a cultural influence on the South's high violence rate.

7. A variation on this theme identifies a number of violent events and then determines what the temperature was at the time of these occurrences. A good example is the Carlsmith and Anderson (1979) investigation of the impact of hot weather on the urban riots of the late 1960s and early 1970s. On reanalyzing the data studied by Baron and Ransberger (see Baron & Richardson, 1994), Carlsmith and Anderson concluded that the likelihood of a riot occurring in those turbulent times was a monotonic function of the temperature in the city.

8. Using the routine-activities perspective, Cohn and Rotton (in press) also noted that people are apt to remain at home for longer intervals when the outside temperature is low rather than normal or relatively high, so that they are more likely to be constrained by the aggression-inhibiting persons nearby and by their home-based activities. Interestingly, in this later study, also based on their statistical analysis of crimes in Minneapolis, Cohn and Rotton (1999) reported that weather variables had a significant but weaker relationship with property crimes than

with violent crimes. They proposed that weather affected property crimes mainly by influencing people's routine activities—primarily the routine activities taking them away from home—whereas psychological variables, such as negative affect, as well as routine activities, contributed to the violent crimes.

9. Essentially this idea underlies Neal Miller's (1948) classic stimulus-response analysis of aggression displacement. Extrapolating from animal experiments, Miller proposed that approach and avoidance inclinations can operate together and that the strength of each tendency varies with the degree of association between an available target and the aggression-provoking agent.

10. Anderson and Anderson (1998) reported that temperature had no reliable effect on the intensity of the punishment delivered to the competitor when this other person had been *clearly* antagonistic or nonantagonistic to the participant. In these cases, the authors suggested, there might have been "ceiling" or "floor" effects that limited the participants' punitiveness.

11. Anderson et al. (1998) have pointed to another factor that can influence the pain-aggression relationship. In accordance with their general model of affective aggression, they demonstrated that people with relatively highly aggressive personalities are especially apt to have aggressive thoughts when they are in physical pain. Nonetheless, even those who were low in trait hostility had more aggressive thoughts when they were in pain than when they were free of pain.

12. In another variation of their experiment, the investigators found that the people exposed to the foul odor actually became friendlier to a stranger supposedly also sharing their unpleasant experience.

13. This finding is conceptually similar to the results reported by Riordan and Tedeschi (1983). In this experiment also, people exposed to a disturbance (in this case the threat of coming electric shocks) became more hostile to an innocent bystander nearby.

14. Interestingly, Caplan's (1970) survey noted that the rioters seemed to be more sensitive to their socioeconomic position in comparison with other blacks rather than with whites.

15. In Anderson's (1989) study, as a case in point, he found a significantly positive relation between the poverty rate in a sample of 260 U.S. metropolitan areas and the areas' rates of violent crimes even after the influence of many other social variables had been statistically controlled.

16. Findings obtained by other social scientists have not consistently supported the Hovland and Sears (1940) results (see Green, Glaser, & Rich, 1998, for a review of the relevant research). The time-series analysis by Green et al. (1998) of the relationship between the economic fluctuations and lynching of blacks, which found that this relationship was significant only for the period 1882–1930, not for the longer time through the Great Depression, indicates that social conditions can affect the extent to which economic frustrations promote antisocial aggression. When these authors extended their investigation to other sections of the country and to contemporary hate crimes against other minority groups, such as gay bashing, they did not see a relationship between macroeconomic changes and their crime measures. The authors suggested "that the predictive force of macroeconomic fluctuation is undermined by the rapid rate of decay in the frustration-bred aggressive impulse and the absence of prominent political actors affixing economic blame on target groups" (1998, p. 82).

17. Mawson (1987) has a somewhat similar conception.

18. It is worth noting that although the early version of the Anderson model summarized here talks about both *hostility* and *anger* as affective states, later studies refer only to *hostile affect*, a term evidently synonymous with *anger*.

19. Parkinson and Totterdell (1999) have recently advanced a classification of affect-regulation strategies that suggests a more complete list of alternative responses to the aversive event.

## REFERENCES

Agnew, R. (1992). Foundation for a general strain theory of crime and delinquency. *Criminology, 30,* 47–87.

Anderson, C. A. (1989). Temperature and aggression: Ubiquitous effects of heat on occurrence of human violence. *Psychological Bulletin, 106,* 74–96.

Anderson, C. A., & Anderson, K. B. (1996). Violent crime rate studies in philosophical context: A destructive testing approach to heat and southern culture of violence effects. *Journal of Personality and Social Psychology, 70,* 740–756.

Anderson, C. A., & Anderson, K. B. (1998). Temperature and aggression: Paradox, controversy, and a (fairly) clear picture. In R. G. Geen & E. Donnerstein (Eds.), *Human aggression: Theories, research, and implications for social policy* (pp. 247–298). San Diego, CA: Academic Press.

Anderson, C. A., Anderson, K. B., & Deuser, W. E. (1996). Examining an affective aggression framework: Weapon and temperature effects on aggressive thoughts, affect, and attitudes. *Personality and Social Psychology Bulletin, 22,* 366–376.

Anderson, C. A., & DeNeve, K. M. (1992). Temperature, aggression, and the negative affect escape model. *Psychological Bulletin, 111,* 347–351.

Anderson, C. A., Deuser, W. E., & DeNeve, K. M. (1995). Hot temperatures, hostile affect, hostile cognition, and arousal: Tests of a general model of affective aggression. *Personality and Social Psychology Bulletin, 21,* 434–448.

Anderson, K. B., Anderson, C. A., Dill, K. E., & Deuser, W. E. (1998). The interactive relations between trait hostility, pain, and aggressive thoughts. *Aggressive Behavior, 24,* 161–171.

Averill, J. R. (1982). *Anger and aggression: An essay on emotion.* New York: Springer-Verlag.

Baron, R. A., & Bell, P. A. (1975). Aggression and heat: Mediating effects of prior provocation and exposure to an aggressive model. *Journal of Personality and Social Psychology, 31,* 825–832.

Baron, R. A., & Bell, P. A. (1976). Aggression and heat: The influence of ambient temperature, negative affect, and a cooling drink on physical aggression. *Journal of Personality and Social Psychology, 33,* 245–255.

Baron, R. A., Byrne, D., & Griffitt, W. (1974). *Social psychology.* Boston: Allyn & Bacon.

Baron, R. A., & Richardson, D. R. (1994). *Human aggression* (2nd ed.). New York: Plenum.

Bell, P. A. (1992). In defense of the negative affect escape model of heat and aggression. *Psychological Bulletin, 111,* 342–346.

Bell, P. A., & Baron, R. A. (1976). Aggression and heat: The mediating role of negative affect. *Journal of Applied Social Psychology, 6*, 18–30.

Berkowitz, L. (1983). Aversively stimulated aggression: Some parallels and differences in research with animals and humans. *American Psychologist, 38*, 1135–1144.

Berkowitz, L. (1989). The frustration-aggression hypothesis: Examination and reformulation. *Psychological Bulletin, 106*, 59–73.

Berkowitz, L. (1993a). *Aggression: Its causes, consequences, and control.* New York: McGraw-Hill.

Berkowitz, L. (1993b). Pain and aggression: Some findings and implications. *Motivation and Emotion, 17*, 277–293.

Berkowitz, L. (1998). Affective aggression: The role of stress, pain, and negative affect. In R. G. Geen & E. Donnerstein (Eds.), *Human aggression: Theories, research, and implications for social policy* (pp. 49–72). San Diego, CA: Academic Press.

Berkowitz, L. (1999). Anger. In T. Dalgleish & M. Power (Eds.), *Handbook of cognition and emotion* (pp. 411–428). Chichester, England: Wiley.

Berkowitz, L. (2000a). Antisocial behavior. In A. E. Kazdin (Ed.), *Encyclopedia of psychology*, Vol. 1. Washington, DC, and New York: American Psychological Association and Oxford University Press.

Berkowitz, L. (2000b). *Feelings: Causes and consequences of positive and negative feelings.* New York: Cambridge University Press.

Berkowitz, L., Cochran, S., & Embree, M. (1981). Physical pain and the goal of aversively stimulated aggression. *Journal of Personality and Social Psychology, 40*, 687–700.

Berkowitz, L., & Troccoli, B. T. (1990). Feelings, direction of attention, and expressed evaluations of others. *Cognition and Emotion, 4*, 305–325.

Blau, J. R., & Blau, P. M. (1982). The cost of inequality: Metropolitan structure and violent crime. *American Sociological Review, 47*, 114–129.

Block, R. (1977). *Violent crime.* Lexington, MA: Lexington Press and D. C. Heath.

Bower, G. H. (1992). How might emotions affect learning? In S.-A. Christianson (Ed.), *Handbook of emotion and memory: Research and theory* (pp. 3–33). Hillsdale, NJ: Erlbaum.

Browning, K., Thornberry, T. P., & Porter, P. K. (1999). Highlights of findings from the Rochester Youth Development Study. *Office of Juvenile Justice and Delinquency Prevention Fact Sheet.* Washington, DC: Office of Juvenile Justice and Delinquency Prevention.

Caplan, N. (1970). The new ghetto man: A review of recent empirical studies. *Journal of Social Issues, 26*, 59–73.

Carlsmith, J. M., & Anderson, C. A. (1979). Ambient temperature and the occurrence of collective violence: A new analysis. *Journal of Personality and Social Psychology, 37*, 337–344.

Christianson, S.-A. (1992). Emotional stress and eyewitness memory: A critical review. *Psychological Bulletin, 112*, 284–309.

Clore, G. L., Ortony, A., Dienes, B., & Fujita, F. (1993). Where does anger dwell? In R. S. Wyer, Jr., & T. K. Srull (Eds.), *Advances in social cognition* (Vol. 6, pp. 57–87). Hillsdale, NJ: Erlbaum.

Cloward, R. A., & Ohlin, L. E. (1960). *Delinquency and opportunity: A theory of delinquent gangs.* Glencoe, IL: Free Press.

Cohen, D. J., Eckhardt, C. I., & Schagat, K. D. (1998). Attention allocation and habituation to anger-related stimuli during a visual search task. *Aggressive Behavior, 24*, 399–409.

Cohen, L. E., & Felson, M. (1979). Social change and crime rate trends: A routine activity approach. *American Sociological Review, 44*, 588–608.

Cohn, E. G., & Rotton, J. (1997). Assault as a function of time and temperature: A moderator-variable time-series analysis. *Journal of Personality and Social Psychology, 72*, 1322–1334.

Cohn, E. G., & Rotton, J. (in press). Weather, seasonal trends, and property crimes in Minneapolis, 1987–1988: A moderator-variable time-series analysis of routine activities. *Journal of Environmental Psychology.*

Crane-Ross, D., Tisak, M. S., & Tisak, J. (1998). Aggression and conventional rule violation among adolescents: Social reasoning predictors of social behavior. *Aggressive Behavior, 24*, 347–365.

Davies, J. C. (1962). Toward a theory of revolution. *American Sociological Review, 27*, 5–19.

Deffenbacher, J. L. (1995). Ideal treatment package for adults with anger disorders. In H. Kassinove (Ed.), *Anger disorders* (pp. 151–172). Washington, DC: Taylor & Francis.

Devine, J. A., Sheley, J. F., & Smith, M. D. (1988). Macroeconomic and social-control policy influences on crime rate changes, 1948–1985. *American Sociological Review, 53*, 407–420.

Dill, J. C., & Anderson, C. A. (1995). Effects of frustration justification on hostile aggression. *Aggressive Behavior, 21*, 359–369.

Dodge, K. A. (1993). Social-cognitive mechanisms in the development of conduct disorder and depression. *Annual Review of Psychology, 44*, 559–584.

Dollard, J., Doob, L., Miller, N., Mowrer, O., & Sears, R. (1939). *Frustration and aggression.* New Haven, CT: Yale University Press.

Donnerstein, E., & Wilson, D. W. (1976). Effects of noise and perceived control on ongoing and subsequent aggressive behavior. *Journal of Personality and Social Psychology, 34*, 774–781.

DuClos, S. E., Laird, J. D., Schneider, E., Sexter, M., Stern, L., & Van Lighten, O. (1989). Emotion-specific effects of facial expressions and postures on emotional experience. *Journal of Personality and Social Psychology, 57*, 100–108.

Farrington, D. P. (1982). Longitudinal analyses of criminal violence. In M. E. Wolfgang & N. A. Weiner (Eds.), *Criminal violence* (pp. 171–200). Beverly Hills, CA: Sage.

Farrington, D. P. (1993). Childhood origins of teenage antisocial behavior and adult social dysfunction. *Journal of the Royal Society of Medicine, 86*, 13–17.

Farrington, D. P. (1997, June). *Advancing knowledge about the early prevention of adult antisocial behavior.* Paper presented at the meeting of the High Security Psychiatric Services Board, London.

Felson, M. (1994). *Crime and everyday life: Insight and implications for society.* Thousand Oaks, CA: Pine Forge.

Fernandez, E., & Turk, D. C. (1995). The scope and significance of anger in the experience of chronic pain. *Pain, 61*, 165–175.

Feshbach, S. (1964). The function of aggression and the regulation of aggressive drive. *Psychological Review, 71*, 257–272.

Frijda, N. H., Kuipers, P., & ter Schure, E. (1989). Relations among emotion, appraisal, and emotional action readiness. *Journal of Personality and Social Psychology, 57*, 212–228.

Geen, R. G. (1968). Effects of frustration, attack, and prior training in aggressiveness upon aggressive behavior. *Journal of Personality and Social Behavior, 9*, 316–321.

Glass, D., & Singer, J. (1972). *Urban stress.* New York: Academic Press.

Goode, W. (1969). Violence among intimates. In D. J. Mulvihill, M. M. Tumin, & L. A. Curtis (Eds.), *Crimes of violence* (Vol. 13, pp. 941–977). Washington, DC: U.S. Government Printing Office.

Green, D. P., Glaser, J., & Rich, A. (1998). From lynching to gay bashing: The elusive connection between economic conditions and hate crime. *Journal of Personality and Social Psychology, 75*, 82–92.

Green, D. P., & Shapiro, I. (1994). *Pathologies of rational choice theory: A critique of applications in political science.* New Haven, CT: Yale University Press.

Griffitt, W. (1970). Environmental effects on interpersonal affective behavior: Ambient effective temperature and attraction. *Journal of Personality and Social Psychology, 15*, 240–244.

Hepworth, J. T., & West, S. G. (1988). Lynchings and the economy: A time-series reanalysis of Hovland and Sears (1940). *Journal of Personality and Social Psychology, 55*, 239–247.

Hovland, C. I., & Sears, R. R. (1940). Minor studies of aggression: VI. Correlation of lynchings with economic indices. *Journal of Psychology, 9*, 301–310.

Huesmann, L. R. (1998). The role of social information processing and cognitive schema in the acquisition and maintenance of habitual aggressive behavior. In R. G. Geen & E. Donnerstein (Eds.), *Human aggression: Theories, research, and implications for social policy* (pp. 73–109). San Diego, CA: Academic Press.

Hutchinson, R. R. (1983). The pain-aggression relationship and its expression in naturalistic settings. *Aggressive Behavior, 9*, 229–242.

Izard, C. E. (1991). *The psychology of emotions.* New York: Plenum.

Jones, J. W., & Bogat, G. A. (1978). Air pollution and human aggression. *Psychological Reports, 43*, 721–722.

Keltner, D., Ellsworth, P. C., & Edwards, K. (1993). Beyond simple pessimism: Effects of sadness and anger on social perception. *Journal of Personality and Social Psychology, 64*, 740–752.

Landau, S. F., & Pfeffermann, D. (1988). A time series analysis of violent crime and its relation to prolonged states of warfare: The Israeli case. *Criminology, 26*, 489–504.

Landau, S. F., & Raveh, A. (1987). Stress factors, social support, and violence in Israeli society: A quantitative analysis. *Aggressive Behavior, 13*, 67–85.

Lewis, M. (1993). The development of anger and rage. In R. A. Glick & S. P. Roose (Eds.), *Rage, power, and aggression* (pp. 148–168). New Haven, CT: Yale University Press.

Liau, A. K., Barriga, A. Q., & Gibbs, J. C. (1998). Relations between self-serving cognitive distortions and overt vs covert antisocial behavior in adolescents. *Aggressive Behavior, 24*, 335–346.

Loeber, R., & Schmaling, K. B. (1985). Empirical evidence for overt and covert patterns of antisocial conduct problems: A meta-analysis. *Journal of Abnormal Child Psychology, 13*, 337–353.

Mawson, A. R. (1987). *Transient criminology: A model of stress-induced crime.* New York: Praeger.

Merton, R. K. (1957). Social structure and anomie. In R. K. Merton (Ed.), *Social theory and social structure* (Rev. ed.). Glencoe, IL: Free Press.

Messner, S. F., & Hawley, F. F. (1989). The southern violence construct: A review of arguments, evidence, and normative context. *Justice Quarterly, 6*, 481–511.

Michael, R. P., & Zumpe, D. (1986). An annual rhythm in the battering of women. *American Journal of Psychiatry, 143*, 637–640.

Miller, N. E. (1948). Theory and experiment relating psychoanalytic displacement to stimulus-response generalization. *Journal of Abnormal and Social Psychology, 43*, 155–178.

Nisbett, R. E., & Cohen, D. (1996). *Culture of honor: The psychology of violence in the South.* Boulder, CO: Westview Press.

Parkinson, B., & Totterdell, P. (1999). Classifying affect-regulation strategies. *Cognition and Emotion, 13*, 277–303.

Passman, R. H., & Mulhern, R. K., Jr. (1977). Maternal punitiveness as affected by situational stress: An experimental analogue of child abuse. *Journal of Abnormal Psychology, 86*, 565–569.

Patterson, G. R., Reid, J. B., & Dishion, T. J. (1992). *Antisocial boys: A social interactional approach.* Eugene, OR: Castalia.

Pedersen, W. C., Gonzales, C., & Miller, N. (1999). The moderating effect of trivial triggering provocation on displaced aggression. Unpublished manuscript. Los Angeles: University of Southern California.

Quay, H. C. (1987). Patterns of delinquent behavior. In H. C. Quay (Ed.), *Handbook of juvenile delinquency.* New York: Wiley.

Quigley, B. M., & Tedeschi, J. T. (1996). Mediating effects of blame attributions on feelings of anger. *Personality and Social Psychology Bulletin, 22*, 1280–1288.

Riordan, C., & Tedeschi, J. T. (1983). Attraction in aversive environments: Some evidence for classical conditioning and negative reinforcement. *Journal of Personality and Social Psychology, 44*, 683–692.

Robins, L. N., & Price, R. K. (1991). Adult disorders predicted by childhood conduct problems: Results from the NIMH Epidemiological Catchment Area project. *Psychiatry, 54*, 116–132.

Roseman, I. J., Wiest, C., & Swartz, T. S. (1994). Phenomenology, behaviors, and goals differentiate discrete emotions. *Journal of Personality and Social Psychology, 67*, 206–221.

Rotton, J. (1993). Geophysical variables and behavior: Ubiquitous errors: A reanalysis of Anderson's (1987) "Temperature and aggression." *Psychological Reports, 73*, 259–271.

Rotton, J., Barry, T., Frey, J., & Soler, E. (1978). Air pollution and interpersonal attraction. *Journal of Applied Social Psychology, 8*, 57–71.

Rotton, J., & Frey, J. (1985). Air pollution, weather, and violent crimes: Concomitant time-series analysis of archival data. *Journal of Personality and Social Psychology, 49*, 1207–1220.

Rotton, J., Frey, J., Barry, T., Milligan, M., & Fitzpatrick,

M. (1979). The air pollution experience and physical aggression. *Journal of Applied Social Psychology, 9,* 397–412.

Stenberg, C. R., Campos, J. J., & Emde, R. N. (1983). The facial expression of anger in seven-month-old infants. *Child Development, 54,* 178–184.

Straus, M. A. (1980). Stress and child abuse. In H. Kempe & R. E. Helfer (Eds.), *Stress and child abuse* (3rd ed). Chicago: University of Chicago Press.

Tafrate, R. C. (1995). Evaluation of treatment strategies for adult anger disorders. In H. Kassinove (Ed.), *Anger disorders: Definition, diagnosis, and treatment* (pp. 109–129). Washington, DC: Taylor & Francis.

Ulrich, R. E. (1966). Pain as a cause of aggression. *American Zoologist, 6,* 643–662.

Vold, G., & Bernard, T. (1986). *Theoretical criminology* (3rd ed.). New York: Oxford University Press.

Weiner, B., Graham, S., & Chandler, C. (1982). Pity, anger, and guilt: An attributional analysis. *Personality and Social Psychology Bulletin, 8,* 226–232.

Wilson, J. Q., & Herrnstein, R. J. (1985). *Crime and human nature.* New York: Simon & Schuster.

Wolfgang, M. E. (1958). *Patterns in criminal homicide.* Philadelphia: University of Pennsylvania Press.

Wright, J. D., Rossi, P. H., & Daly, K. (1983). *Under the gun: Weapons, crime, and violence.* New York: Aldine.

Zillmann, D., Baron, R. A., & Tamborini, R. (1981). Social costs of smoking: Effects of tobacco smoke on hostile behavior. *Journal of Applied Social Psychology, 11,* 548–561.

# 43

# TWO TYPES OF RELATIONSHIP CLOSENESS AND THEIR INFLUENCE ON PEOPLE'S EMOTIONAL LIVES

Margaret S. Clark and Ian Brissette

To date, psychologists' efforts to understand emotion have focused almost entirely on processes that occur within a single individual. In this chapter we break with that *intra*personal tradition and discuss emotion from an *inter*personal perspective. After all, emotion appears to be most often experienced and expressed within the context of interpersonal relationships (Csikszentmihalyi & Larson, 1984; DeRivera, 1984; Larson, Csikszentmihalyi, & Graef, 1982; Scherer, Wallbott, & Summerfield, 1986; Schwartz & Shaver, 1987; Trevarthen, 1984). There must be something about interpersonal relationships that accounts for this.

What are we to make of the fact that emotion occurs most frequently in the context of our interpersonal relationships? Perhaps the answer is simple. Perhaps other people's actions (more often than other factors) produce our emotions by facilitating attainment of our goals or by impeding attainment of them. A person might throw a rock at us, endangering our safety and eliciting our anger. Alternatively, a person might give us some money, facilitating our ability to purchase something we have been wanting and eliciting happiness. If so, perhaps the processes through which other people elicit our emotions are no different from the processes through which inanimate objects elicit our emotions. For instance, a rock might slide from a hillside and hit us, making us angry. A slot machine may spew out coins, making us happy. Emotion may be more frequent within relationships than outside relationships only because people more frequently facilitate or impede our goals than do inanimate entities. If,

indeed, the processes through which other people elicit emotions are not so different from the ways in which non-interpersonal events elicit emotions, then there would seem to be nothing special, theoretically, that relationship researchers could contribute to understanding people's emotional lives.

We do believe that other people facilitating or impeding our goals is a large part of why emotion is more frequently experienced within than outside relationships. However, we also firmly believe that relationship researchers *do* have some special knowledge that will prove very useful to emotion researchers in their efforts to understand people's day-to-day emotional lives. Relationship context *does* make a difference. Winning a gift certificate to a good bookstore in a raffle may elicit moderate happiness. It facilitates your goal of getting a particular book. But what if another person gives you that certificate as a gift? Will you always feel moderately happy? No. Your emotional reactions will depend on who gives it to you. If it comes from your mother (who routinely gives you lots of gifts), you may feel mildly happy. If it comes from your brother (who has never given you a gift in the past and with whom you would love to have a better relationship), you may feel much happier. And what of expressing emotions? Imagine you lose a job and feel depressed. Will you express your depression? It depends. Again relationship context matters. If you are still at work, you will probably remain rather stoic, expressing little emotion. You may continue to suppress expressions of sadness or distress on the way home on the bus. However, once in your home with your spouse, you may express considerable distress.

Just what is it about relationship context that does matter? Recent work on relationships suggests that two conceptually distinct dimensions of relationships, each of which might be thought of as a type of closeness, matter. One is *relationship interdependence*. The other is the *communal strength of the relationship*. We discuss both in this chapter. Our goal is to demonstrate that taking both dimensions into account will help us to understand people's emotional lives.

The first type of closeness, how interdependent two people are, is not something that we have personally investigated. It has been discussed by relationship researchers such as Berscheid, Kelley, and their colleagues (Kelley et al., 1983). Interdependence is considered by many to be what determines whether a relationship exists. Two people are interdependent (and have a relationship) if each has an impact on the other. Just how interdependent two people are refers to the degree to which two people in a relationship influence each other's thoughts, feelings, and behaviors. Interdependence is greater the more frequently each person's thoughts, feelings, and/or behaviors influence the other's thoughts, feelings, and/or behaviors. It also is greater the more diverse the effects each has on the other are. Finally, it is greater the stronger and more long-lasting the impact of one person's thoughts, feelings, and behavior are on the other person (Berscheid, Snyder, & Omoto, 1989). Berscheid (1981, 1983, 1991; Berscheid & Ammazzalorso, 2000) has discussed the ways in which the degree of interdependence between two people (which she refers to as *relationship closeness* but which we call the *degree of relationship interdependence* in this chapter, to distinguish it from the other type of closeness that we also discuss) influences people's emotional lives. We review her theory and the empirical evidence that supports it. Her argument is that the greater the interdependence of a relationship, the greater the potential for emotional experience in that relationship.

The second, conceptually distinct type of closeness has been discussed by Clark and Mills (1979, 1993; Mills & Clark, 1982). It refers to the degree to which two people in a relationship feel a responsibility for one another's welfare and, therefore, benefit the other in order to promote the other's welfare. As this type of closeness increases, the costs (in time, effort, money, and sacrifice) that each person is willing to incur to benefit the other increase. Recently Clark, Fitness, and Brissette (2001) have discussed the ways in which this sort of closeness (which we call the *communal strength of relationships*) influences people's emotional lives. We review our theory and the empirical evidence that supports it. We argue that the greater the communal strength of a relationship, the greater the expression of emotion will be in that relationship (and, to

some extent, the greater the experience of emotion in that relationship as well.)

Both types of closeness deal with the very structure of the relationship in question. Moreover, both are closely tied to how people meet their daily goals and, indeed, what those goals are. However, they are conceptually independent. One can easily imagine two highly interdependent people who care little about one another's welfare. Business rivals provide an example of this sort of relationship. Their thoughts, feelings, and actions may influence one another every day in diverse and strong ways. At the same time, they may feel little, if any, responsibility for one another's welfare. So, too, is it easy to imagine two people who are very concerned with one another's welfare but who, on a day-to-day basis, have little interdependence. Two men who grew up as best friends may each be living highly successful, busy lives on opposite sides of the country and have little concrete need for one another's help. Perhaps they keep in touch only with an occasional note or call. Yet they may still consider themselves to be best friends, feel great affection for one another, and, most important for our argument, have great concerns and feelings of obligation for one another's welfare. Should one really need the other, a phone call would result in that other immediately flying there and attending to the situation. Their day-to-day interdependence is very low, yet their feelings of obligation for one another and their willingness to incur costs and sacrifices to benefit one another should need arise on either part are high. Of course, empirically, these two types of closeness often may be related. Great feelings of responsibility for one another's welfare (closeness in the sense of communal strength) would seem to lead, quite naturally, to greater interdependence in most circumstances. Actively attending and responding to one another's welfare day to day involves people having considerable impact on one another.

In this chapter we discuss how these two conceptually distinct types of interpersonal closeness can and do influence people's emotional lives. Afterward, we comment briefly on how they may come together to influence actual, ongoing relationships and the role that individual differences may place in the processes we discuss.

## How Interdependence Influences Our Emotional Lives

### Degree of Interdependence and People's Emotional Lives

Berscheid, along with many other relationship researchers, defines a relationship as the interaction that takes place between two people (Kelley et al., 1983). If each person's thoughts, feelings, and/or behavior are influenced by the other person's thoughts, feelings, and/or behaviors, then a relationship exists. Their lives are interdependent. According to Berscheid and her colleagues, the closeness of the relationship has to do with how much interdependence exists. The degree of interdependence can be assessed in four ways—how frequent, how diverse, and how strong the effects two people have on each other are, as well as how long the mutual effects have been going on. If two members of a relationship spend a lot of time together and have many effects on each other each and every day, they are more interdependent than are two members of a relationship who see each other once a month. Next, consider diversity of effects. If each member of the relationship can influence where the other lives, what the other eats, the other's self-esteem, the other's choice of a career, and the other's physical fitness, they are more interdependent than if they can influence only each other's career-related choices. Finally, consider the strength of effects. If each member of the relationship has the capability of producing a big or a long-lasting impact on the other person's thoughts, feelings, and behaviors, then the relationship is more interdependent than if that is not the case.

According to Berscheid's analysis, whether or not a relationship exists and whether it is highly interdependent are conceptually independent of whether the sorts of effects each person has on the other are positive or negative. If each person has an influence on the other, there is a relationship. If the influences are frequent, diverse, and strong, it is a highly interdependent relationship (or a close relationship), according to Berscheid.

Now, what does this all have to do with emotion? A great deal, according to Berscheid. If we are in a highly interdependent relationship, we have many expectations regarding our partner's behaviors. Moreover, our own behaviors are very dependent on our partner's fulfilling our expectations. It is this dependency (or this kind of closeness) that provides the grist for emotional experiences.

Autonomic arousal, Berscheid argues, together with a valence determined by what is going on in one's environment, is integral to what many emotion theorists (e.g., James, 1884; Mandler, 1997; Schachter & Singer, 1962) and everyday folk consider an emotion to be. In addition, Berscheid points out, Mandler has set forth a theory of emotion that starts out with the assumption that, as a result of evolutionary forces, people have an innate capacity to detect whether their world is the "same" or "different" from what it was before. In other words, we have evolved so as to be able to detect discrepancies between what we expect our environment to be like and how we currently perceive it. If our environment is different, the difference is a cue that it is potentially dangerous and that we must take action to protect ourselves or, alternatively, that we should take advantage of new opportunities that have presented themselves. If the environment is different (a discrepancy has been detected), then we feel aroused, and we evaluate

our current situation. This allows us to take actions necessary either to avoid danger or to take advantage of new opportunities that have presented themselves. In either case, we experience emotion.

In Mandler's theoretical framework (1975), the interruption of an organized behavior sequence or high-order plan is a sufficient and possibly necessary condition for the experience of autonomic arousal. It is because individuals in highly interdependent relationships, by definition, have lasting, multiple, strong, and diverse effects on each other's organized behavior sequences and goals, says Berscheid, that the potential for the experience of emotion is greater in such relationships than in less interdependent relationships. In less interdependent relationships our own behavior sequences and expectancies are independent of the other person's behavior. Thus opportunities for one person to disrupt the other and produce disruption and subsequent emotion are fewer. This is why Berscheid sees highly interdependent relationships as more emotionally fertile than less interdependent relationships. Of course, it must be kept in mind that emotion may not be experienced in highly interdependent relationships so long as both partners behave as expected. It is when they do not that arousal is experienced and that emotion will abound.

How intense or long-lasting the emotion will be depends on the extent of the disruption and how easily the disrupted partner can fall back into a well-practiced, routine pattern of behavior. If the disruption within the relationship is quickly resolved, or if a person can turn to another partner and, with that new partner, follow a routine pattern of behavior, then emotions will be short-lived. Otherwise, they will persist. For instance, if a person expects to play her weekly tennis game with her husband and he fails to show up at the appointed time, negative emotion is likely. If he appears within a few minutes, the negative emotion is likely to dissipate. If not, it will continue unless the disruption in the routine can be quickly resolved in a different fashion. For instance, if a friend just happens to stop by seeking a partner and takes the husband's place, the negative emotion should drop. Fitting well with Berscheid's ideas in this regard is some research by Thoits (1983) that reveals that possessing multiple behavior patterns to "fall into," as indicated by the number of available roles, is associated with lower levels of psychological distress.

## High Interdependence and Disruption of the Relationship

Two studies conducted specifically to test Berscheid's emotion-in-relationships model (ERM) have provided results that support the model. One study was reported by Simpson (1987) and one by Attridge (1995, as cited in Berscheid & Ammazzalorso, 2000). We first consider the Simpson (1987) research. Simpson conducted a longitudinal survey of 234 college undergraduates (126 women and 108 men) who were dating someone. At the start of the study, he measured a number of aspects of their relationships: how satisfied they were with aspects of the relationships (e.g., finances, partner's physical attractiveness, similarity of attitudes and values, the other's ability to be kind and understanding, similarity of activity interests, personality, social status, intimacy, and sexual attractiveness), their closeness in interdependence terms (using an inventory created by Berscheid et al., 1989), the length of the relationship, whether they were sexually involved, the quality of their best alternative dating partner, the ease with which they thought they could find an alternative dating partner, and, finally, whether the relationship was exclusive. Three months later he recontacted the original participants. Ninety-four of these participants reported having broken up with their dating partners. For those who had broken up, he assessed the intensity and duration of emotional distress with six questions (e.g. "How upset were you immediately after the breakup?" "How long did it take you to make an emotional adjustment after the breakup?"). He combined these into a single index of emotional distress upon breakup.

Five factors significantly predicted relationship stability—satisfaction, length of the relationship, sexual nature of the relationship, exclusivity of the relationship, and sexual orientation restricted to the relationship. In contrast to this, and pertinent to this chapter, a different set of three variables predicted emotional distress upon breakup. Specifically, those individuals who experienced the most distress had been more interdependent (closer, in Berscheid's terms) with their partner, had dated that partner for a longer period of time, and believed they could not find a suitable alternative easily. Strikingly, reported satisfaction with the relationship did not relate to later distress on breakup. This is, of course, just what Berscheid's theory predicts. She argues that it is the disruption of the routines that characterize highly interdependent relationships that presages emotion. Moreover, this emotion should be more long-lasting and intense if a substitute partner cannot be found with whom one can reestablish one's prior routines. Relationships that were highly satisfying will not elicit much emotion on breakup if those involved led quite independent lives (e.g., had separate jobs, separate sets of friends, separate routines on the weekend). Moreover, even relationships that might be described as highly *unsatisfying* (e.g., perhaps because conflict was routine) may elicit a great deal of emotion on breakup because those routines have been disrupted.

Next, consider the more recent Attridge study. Attridge (1995, as cited in Berscheid & Ammazzalorso, 2000) began her research with 86 women who were in serious dating relationships of about 1½ years in duration. Forty-two of these women experienced separation from their dating partners because those partners chose to participate in a

study-abroad program. The remaining 44 women did not experience such a separation. All women filled out a series of measures at three times, which, for the women with partners studying abroad, occurred prior to, during, and following separation. At the first and third assessments, participants filled out a measure of interdependence (Berscheid Relationship Closeness Inventory, RCI; Berscheid et al., 1989), a measure of the length of the relationship, and a measure of satisfaction (Hendrick, 1988). They also filled out a five-item measure of the degree to which the partner's absence would lead to a disruption of the woman's everyday activities and routines and of her likelihood of finding a substitute partner during the separation.

Attridge assessed emotion by giving participants a list of positive and negative emotions and asking them to indicate the frequency with which they felt each emotion toward their partners during the prior week. As would be expected from the theory, neither the degree of interdependence (closeness) nor the index of disruption that would be caused by separation led, by itself, to emotional experience. Rather, just as expected from the theory, they interacted with the event of separation to produce the experience of emotion. Specifically, Attridge found that emotions characterized by high arousal (fear, jealousy, passion, and joy) were positively and significantly associated with greater interdependence during separations but not when partners were together. (The same effects were not observed for milder feeling states characterized by less arousal, for instance, feeling content or lonely.)

## How Communal Relationships Influence Our Emotional Lives

### Mutual Feelings of Responsibility and People's Emotional Lives

High interdependence with another person constitutes one type of closeness, but sometimes people use the term *close* to mean something conceptually distinct. They use it to refer to two people caring deeply about each other's welfare and being willing to incur considerable costs to meet each other's needs if and when such needs arise. This kind of closeness is what Clark, Mills, and their colleagues have referred to as having a strong, communal relationship (Mills & Clark, 1982; Clark & Mills, 1993). A husband and wife who are very responsive to each other's needs on a day-to-day basis may have both this kind of closeness (a strong communal relationship) and closeness in the Berscheid et al. (1989) sense of interdependence. A parent and his or her adult child, living on opposite sides of the country, may also feel such a sense of caring and concern (a strong communal relationship) while simultaneously not experiencing closeness in the sense in which

Berscheid et al. (1989) refer to closeness. This may occur so long as both individuals are doing well and have minimal needs that are being met by others with whom they may also have communal relationships.

Recently, we (Clark & Brissette, 2000; Clark, Fitness, & Brissette, 2001) have argued that closeness in the sense of high communal strength should also have profound effects on people's emotional lives, albeit for conceptually distinct reasons from those discussed by Berscheid. Our arguments are based on some simple assumptions. First, many emotions, such as distress and fear, function to communicate our own needs not only to ourselves (Frijda, 1993; Mandler, 1975, 1997; Simon, 1967) but also to others in our social environment (Fridlund, 1991; Jones, Collins, & Hong, 1991; Levenson, 1994; Miller & Leary, 1992). Such communication allows others to recognize our needs and allows us to mobilize external resources (Buck, 1984, 1998; Scott, 1958, 1980). A good example is an infant's cries of distress, alerting the mother that the infant has a need (for food, comfort, soothing) and bringing the mother to the infant, thereby allowing the infant's needs to be met.

The second assumption is that certain emotions, for instance, guilt, empathic sadness, and empathic happiness, communicate both to ourselves and to others the extent to which we care about the needs of others. The experience of these emotions serves this communication function to ourselves. The expression of these emotions serves to communicate our caring to our partners.

The third and final assumption is that our relationships can be distinguished from one another based on the degree of responsibility that we feel for one another's needs. Sometimes we feel very little responsibility for another's needs. Such is typically the case with strangers. Sometimes we feel a moderate amount of responsibility, as with casual friends, and sometimes we feel a great deal of responsibility, as with a child or a spouse.

Putting these assumptions together leads us to some specific hypotheses. First, to the extent to which we believe others are concerned with our welfare and will attempt to meet our needs (and not to harm us), we will express more emotion, because our emotions convey information about our needs (or lack thereof) to those caring others. For instance, when we are with caring others, we should express more sadness when experiencing a loss, more fear when facing something that worries us, and more anger when we believe we have been treated unjustly. Our partner can then help us cope with our losses, anxieties, and perceived injustices. We should also express more happiness when having accomplished something or when something that was wrong has been righted. Our partner can then share or even enhance our happiness.

In mutual, strong communal relationships, both members ought to express more emotion. Moreover, to the extent to which expression of emotion encourages the experience of emotion (cf. Laird, 1974; Laird & Bresler, 1992; Riskind, 1984; Riskind & Gotay, 1982), we may experience more emotion in such relationships as well. In the case of empathic emotions (e.g., guilt, empathic fear, sadness, or happiness), our theoretical position leads directly to the prediction that more emotion will be experienced, as well as expressed, because we care about the other's welfare. In a sense, their fear is our fear; their sadness or happiness is our sadness or happiness. If we neglect their needs, we have violated a special obligation and desire to meet their needs, and we ought to feel guilty.

The more communal the relationship, the more we should express emotions such as fear, sadness, and happiness and experience and express emotions such as guilt and empathic sadness and happiness. Furthermore, once these emotions are expressed, our partners ought to react to them more positively. Such positive reactions should include such things as listening carefully and sympathetically to our emotional expressions, providing help in the case of our negative emotion, sharing positive emotions, and welcoming our empathic sadness as well as guilt.

## Expressing More Emotion in Communal Relationships

Several studies provide evidence that emotions are expressed more often in communal than in other relationships. First, in a study reported by Clark and Taraban (1991, Study 2), same-sex friends were told they would be having a discussion with their own friend or with a member of a different friendship pair with whom they were not previously acquainted. They then rank ordered a list of potential discussion topics in terms of their preferences for the discussion. Some of the topics required discussion of emotion (e.g., times you have felt serene, your fears, things that make you sad, things that make you angry, and what makes you happy); the rest did not. All five emotional topics received higher rankings when participants expected to engage in the discussion with their friends than when they expected to engage in the discussion with a stranger. Four of the differences were statistically significant; one was marginally significant.

The Clark and Taraban (1991, Study 2) research demonstrates a greater willingness to discuss emotion in friendships (typically mutual communal relationships in which members feel responsible for one another's needs) than in relationships with strangers (typically noncommunal relationships in which benefits, if they must be given or received, are given or received on an exchange basis). However, relationships are not simply qualitatively communal or noncommunal in nature. As Mills and Clark (1982; Clark & Mills, 1993) point out, there is a quantitative dimension to communal relationships as well—a dimension they refer to as the *communal strength* of the relationship. People feel different degrees of responsibility toward the various people with whom they have communal relationships. Most people have very weak communal relationships with many other people—even with strangers. For instance, most of us would give directions to a stranger without expecting anything in return. We have stronger communal relationships with such people as friends and cousins. We do such things as treat them to lunch, send cards, and listen to their troubles. We have even stronger communal relationships with people such as parents, spouses, and our children, often going to great costs to benefit them. The concept of communal relationship strength is important in this chapter because the stronger the communal relationship, the more willing participants in that relationship should be to express emotion, and the more empathic emotion and guilt should be felt within that relationship.

A recent questionnaire study we have conducted provides evidence that more emotions are indeed expressed as communal relationships grow stronger. We began by defining a communal relationship for our 42 participants. We told them a communal relationship is one in which a person responds to his or her partner's needs without requiring or expecting repayments, without carefully keeping track of who has contributed what to whom, but keeping track of what his or her partner's needs are. Then participants rated their relationships with the following people—strangers, their mothers, casual friends, sisters or brothers, their bosses, their professors, neighbors, close friends, co-members of a team, classmates, their cousins, members of their church or temple, their priests, ministers, or rabbis, fellow employees, their fathers, members of a club, and roommates—in terms of how communal those relationships were (from −4, indicating "not at all communal," to +4, indicating "very strongly communal"). Next, on a separate sheet they rated their willingness to express happiness, contentment, hurt, sadness, anger, disgust, guilt, and fear to each of these people. They did this for each emotion, once assuming the partner caused it, and again assuming someone or something else caused it. Each rating was made on a scale from −3 (indicating likely suppression of the emotion) to +3 (indicating likely expression of the emotion.)

The results were clear. All 16 within-subject correlations between each participant's rating of how communal a relationship was and his or her rated willingness to express a particular emotion (both when caused by the partner and when caused by someone or something else) were positive. Fourteen of the 16 ratings reached traditional levels of significance. (The exceptions to the positive correlations reaching significance occurred with expressing anger and disgust caused by the partner to that partner. These exceptions may be easily understood by considering that people in mutual communal relationships not only wish their partner to be concerned with their own needs but also care about the partner's feelings. Thus they

may be reluctant to express their own feelings of anger and disgust when caused by the partner lest they distress that partner.)

Others also have reported evidence consistent with the idea that the more communal a relationship is, the more emotion will be expressed within the context of that relationship. For example, Barrett, Robin, Pietromonaco, and Eyssell (1998) had college students keep diaries of their experiences of happiness, sadness, nervousness, surprise, anger, embarrassment, and shame for 7 days. They also had participants rate the closeness of their ongoing relationships with the other people on whom they reported (and we argue that most people interpret the term *closeness*, when undefined, in terms of mutual caring or a communal relationship). They found that the intensity of people's emotions and the degree to which they expressed those emotions was positively and significantly associated with the rated closeness of their relationship with the partner in question. Moreover, Fitness (2000) found that 83% of people who reported experiencing anger at work also reported having expressed those feelings to close friends and/or family members (which are typically strong communal relationships), not only to "let off steam" but also to seek reassurance.

### Positive Reactions to Expressions of Emotion in Communal Relationships

Our position suggests not only that people will express more emotion to the extent to which they have a communal relationship with another, but also that such expressions of emotion will be reacted to positively. Empirical evidence for this position exists. Clark and Taraban (1991, Study 1), for instance, manipulated people's desire for a communal or a noncommunal relationship with another. They did this by having an attractive other indicate availability and desire for a relationship such as a friendship with the participant or a lack of availability and desire for such a relationship with the participant. Then all participants read a background introductory questionnaire supposedly filled out by this other person. On the questionnaire the other person either expressed no emotion or expressed irritability, sadness, or happiness. Finally, participants rated their liking for the other person. The results clearly supported the prediction that emotion would be reacted to more positively the more communal in nature the relationship. Specifically, when no emotion was expressed, liking ratings in the communal and in the noncommunal condition were identical. However, when *any* emotion was expressed, liking was greater in the communal than in the noncommunal condition, suggesting that expression of emotion is reacted to more positively the more a communal relationship is desired.

A second study that supports the idea that expressions of emotion are reacted to more positively when communal rather than noncommunal relationships are desired has been reported by Clark, Ouellette, Powell, & Milberg (1987, Study 2). All participants were relatively new college students who believed that they and an attractive, friendly other were involved in an investigation of how moods influence creativity. During the course of the session, half of the participants—the majority of whom presumably were anxious to form new friendships and romantic relationships—found out that the other participant was also interested in forming new communal relationships (communal condition). The remaining half discovered instead that the other was a busy, married student (noncommunal condition). Crossed with this relationship manipulation was a manipulation of sad feelings on the part of the other person, with sadness being either conveyed or not conveyed through the other's facial expression, together with self-ratings of mood on a questionnaire that the true participant was allowed to see. During the course of the study a low-pressure opportunity to voluntarily help the participant occurred, and the crucial measure was how long (if at all) the participant spent helping the other. As expected, participants helped significantly longer in the communal conditions. More important to our argument is the fact that participants in the communal conditions (but not those in the noncommunal conditions) helped significantly more when the other was sad than when the other was not sad. In other words, another's expression of negative emotion elicited only prosocial responses in the communal conditions.

We suspect that expressions of emotions such as sadness often may lead people to avoid others in noncommunal contexts. The expression of such emotions may be seen as putting undue pressure on people to respond prosocially in a situation in which they do not feel obligated and in which they do not desire to help the other. In the Clark et al. (1987) study, however, the levels of helping in the noncommunal conditions were so low to begin with that a "floor effect" on the measure of helping effectively precluded the possibility of observing such a drop.

### Expressing Emotion in Response to a Partner's Needs in Communal Relationships

Most communal relationships are mutual. Not only do we assume that the other cares about our needs (which is why we may selectively express emotion to the other), but we also care about our partner's needs and feel we should respond to those needs on a communal basis. Sometimes, in asymmetric communal relationships, we feel more responsibility for the welfare of the other than we expect the other to feel for us (e.g., between parents and young children). Feelings of responsibility for the other's welfare have clear implications for both expressing emotions experienced in response to the other's needs (e.g., guilt, em-

pathic sadness, and empathic happiness) and for experiencing these emotions in the first place.

First consider experiencing emotions. One example of an emotion we may feel in response to another person's needs is empathic sadness for a loss our partner has experienced. According to our analysis, when a relationship partner has experienced a loss, one should feel more empathic sadness the more communal in nature the relationship. Batson, Duncan, Ackerman, Buckley, and Birch (1981) conducted a study that provides evidence for this. They manipulated the similarity that college women felt to another college woman by providing feedback that the other woman had answered a personal profile form and interest inventory either in much the same way as had the participant (high similarity) or in quite a discrepant manner (low similarity). Later on, the participants in the high-similarity condition reported not only feeling more similar but also, importantly, valuing the other's welfare more. Later participants discovered that the other person was needy and the experimenter measured the extent to which those participants felt sympathy, compassion, soft-heartedness, and tenderness toward the other. Those in the high-similarity condition reported not only feeling especially concerned about the other's welfare but also experiencing more empathic compassion than did those in the low-similarity condition.

Next, consider evidence that empathic happiness, too, is experienced more frequently within the context of relationships in which we feel responsible for our partner's needs than in other relationships. Williamson and Clark (1989, Study 3; 1992) report two studies in which they examined links between the expectation or desire for a communal relationship and changes in a helper's feeling from before to after helping another person. They compared those changes with changes in moods over a comparable time period in which no help was provided to the other. Changes in both positive and negative moods were assessed. In both studies, helping was associated with increases in positive moods and decreases in negative moods *only if* participants had been led to desire and expect a communal relationship with the other person. When no such relationship was expected, moods did not improve. Moreover, in the 1992 study, half the participants who had helped were led to believe that they had freely chosen to help, whereas half were led to believe that they were required to help. The improvements in mood when a communal, but not when an exchange, relationship was desired occurred whether or not the participant had freely chosen to help. This suggests that the fact that the needy other was benefited in the communal conditions was the key to the improvement in mood rather than the improvement being dependent on the helper seeing himself or herself as a good person for having chosen to help. (Interestingly, choosing to help in the exchange conditions actually led to deteriorations in moods—quite a different effect from empathic happiness!)

Finally, consider guilt. Guilt implies that one feels bad about having neglected or harmed one's relationship partner in some way. Our theoretical position suggests that this too should be an emotion that is experienced primarily within the context of communal relationships. Moreover, given the same neglectful or harmful act, more guilt ought to be experienced the stronger the communal relationship is.

Empirical work by Baumeister, Stillwell, and Heatherton (1994, 1995) supports these predictions. These researchers had participants recall and write about two situations in which they had angered another person. The participants described the background of the incident, the incident itself, and the consequences of the incident. One of the two descriptions was to be of an incident after which the student had felt bad or had suffered from a feeling of having done something wrong. The other was to be of an incident after which the participant had not felt bad or suffered from a feeling of having done something wrong. The stories were later coded in terms of "whether the victim was depicted as someone with whom the subject had a communal relationship (defined as involving norms of mutual concern for each other's welfare, such as in family or romantic relationship" or not; Baumeister et al., 1995, p. 181). The finding of importance to this chapter is that incidents chosen to exemplify times at which the participants had felt bad or suffered from feelings of having done something wrong (i.e., felt guilty) were significantly more likely to have taken place in the context of a communal relationship than were the incidents chosen to exemplify times participants did not feel bad or suffer from a feeling of having done something wrong.

Interestingly, and fitting well with the evidence just cited, quite a number of studies reveal that people infer that they care about another person's welfare if they feel good when the other's needs are met and bad when the other's needs are not met or the other is harmed (Aderman, Brehm, & Katz, 1974; Batson, Turk, Shaw, & Klein, 1995; Mills, Jellison, & Kennedy, 1976; Zillmann & Cantor, 1977).

### Expressing More Empathic Emotion When Another Has a Need the More Communal the Relationship

According to our analysis, we should experience more guilt, empathic compassion, and empathic happiness within the context of a relationship in which we feel responsible for a partner's needs, and we should express these emotions more often. Experiencing these emotions communicates to the self that one cares about the other. Expressing these emotions communicates to one's partner

that one cares about him or her. In this regard it is interesting to note that Baumeister et al. (1995) found that guilt was not only experienced more often in the context of communal relationships but was also expressed more often within these relationships. Of course people may express more guilt in communal relationships simply because they experience more guilt in such relationships. However, our own study (described previously) also yields evidence for people being more willing to express guilt the more communal the relationship—evidence unconfounded by the experience of guilt. In this study, we asked people to report on how communal a number of their relationships were. Then we asked them how willing they would be to express guilt that they felt in each of those relationships. Participants indicated that they would be far less willing to express guilt to those with whom they had weak communal relationships (e.g. strangers, coworkers, neighbors, professors, and classmates) than they would be to express guilt to those with whom they had stronger communal relationships (e.g. roommates, siblings, close friends, mothers, and fathers).

### Influences of Interdependence, Communal Norms, and Individual Differences on People's Lives

The overall focus of this chapter has been on how two qualities of interpersonal relationships—the degree of interdependence in the relationship and the extent to which the relationship is communal in nature—are likely to influence people's emotional experience and expression. These are conceptually distinct qualities of relationships. That is why we have discussed them independently. Yet it is also interesting to speculate on how these two aspects of relationships might combine with one another to influence people's emotional lives in their friendships, romantic relationships, and business relationships. It is also interesting to speculate on how what we have said in this chapter may relate to some individual-difference work in the emotion area. We briefly do so in this section.

### Strong Communal Ties and Emotions in Friendships, Romantic Relationships, and Family Relationships

Few people would disagree with the claim that the experience and expression of emotion tends to be higher in people's friendships, romantic relationships, and family relationships than in other relationships. The conceptual analyses presented in this chapter offer two explanations for this. First, our culture dictates that friendships, romantic relationships, and family relationships ought to be strong, mutual, and communal relationships (Grote & Clark, 1998). That is, people are expected to be very responsive to one another's needs in such relationships. As we argue here, to adequately follow this rule we should be willing to express our feelings to the other because those feelings convey our need states and allow our partners to respond to those states. To suppress our feelings would hinder the ability of the other to help us. Moreover, expressing our feelings may heighten the experience of those feelings (Laird, 1974; Laird & Bresler, 1992). So, too, should we experience and express more emotion in response to our partners' needs because we care about those needs and because we wish to communicate the caring to our partners.

Beyond this, the communal nature of friendships, romantic relationships, and family relationships ought to lead to considerable interdependence between partners. The more routinely a person turns to his or her partner for help and is helped, the more interdependent the relationship becomes. As Berscheid and her colleagues point out, with interdependence comes great potential for emotional experience, both good and bad. Because it is hard to imagine members of any highly interdependent pair being perfectly predictable, we would suspect that the potential for disruptions in routines to elicit arousal and emotion quite often becomes a reality in strong, communal relationships. Thus we suspect that the communal nature of many friendships, romantic relationships, and family relationships results in great emotional experience and expression for the reasons that we have pointed out here and in other recent papers (Clark & Brissette, 2000; Clark, Fitness, & Brissette, in press) and for the reasons that Berscheid and her colleagues have pointed out in their work (Berscheid, 1981, 1983, 1991; Berscheid & Ammazzalorso, 2000).

## High Interdependence in Business Settings

Whereas expressions of emotions tend to run high in our friendships, romantic relationships, and family relationships, by contrast, workplaces seem relatively emotionally quiescent. Expressing a great deal of emotion in such settings is not considered appropriate (cf. Hoover-Dempsey, Plas, & Strudler-Wallston, 1986).

Is the reason that emotion is not experienced in such settings? We do not think so. People's work is important to them, and interdependence is often high in the workplace. Bosses rely on personnel to get work done so they can proceed with their own work; clerical personnel rely on bosses to provide enough lead time to get that work done. People share space, equipment, and support personnel so that, even when they are supposedly working independently, there is much potential for them to influence each other positively and negatively. We are sure that people's interdependent routines often are disrupted and that emotions often result. However, it is simultaneously the case that people in work settings typically do not have strong communal relationships with one another. It is for this reason, we suspect, that workplaces tend, on the surface, to be more tranquil emotionally than personal relationships. Emotions exist because of interdependence and interruptions in routines, but they are often not expressed due to the low communal strength of the relationships. Work situations in which emotions run high but in which expression is low may be particularly toxic to the people involved.

It may also be these sorts of work situations that lead workers to take emotions home and express them there. Sometimes this may be done in a manner appropriate to communal relationships at home (as in seeking solace from one's spouse for things that have gone wrong at the office), but sometimes this may be done inappropriately—such as the angry worker who takes that anger out on his or her spouse and children (Bolger, DeLongis, Kessler, & Wethington, 1989). Such inappropriate expression of emotions at home may disrupt routines there as well, heightening emotion in that setting.

In any case, our general point in discussing how the variables of relationship interdependence and communal relationship may add together to influence emotion (in intimate relationships) or interact to help us to understand when emotion may be experienced but not expressed (in business settings) is to make clear the value of taking these constructs into account in striving to understand people's emotional lives. The structure of relationships matters.

## Taking Individual Differences into Account

We argue that relationships such as friendships, romantic relationships, and family relationships tend to be emotionally alive because they tend to be characterized by high interdependence and strong communal ties. So, too, have we speculated that business relationships generally seem more emotionally calm because, although some may be characterized by high interdependence, most tend to be characterized by weak communal ties. However, we hasten to add that these generalizations—particularly for friendships, romantic relationships, and family relationships—are likely to be compromised by individual differences in people's abilities and motivations to follow communal norms. Whereas most people will say that a communal norm is ideal for their friendships and romantic and family relationships, people also seem to vary a great deal in terms of their motivations and abilities to live up to such a norm (Clark & Brissette, 2000). Some people doubt that friends, spouses, and family members will "be there" for them should they need help, or they may doubt that they themselves are worthy of help. As a result, even in these normatively communal relationships, such people may be reluctant to express emotion that conveys their needs (Feeney, 1995, 1999; Feeney, Noller, & Roberts,

1998) and to seek help when it is needed (Simpson, Rholes, & Nelligan, 1992.) They may behave in friendships and in romantic and family relationships much like most people operate within more formal settings—keeping their emotions to themselves and not responding positively to others' expressions of emotions. In other words, although they may believe that such relationships should be communal in nature, they may not treat them as such when it comes to expressing emotions (and seeking help) and to reacting to their partner's needs emotionally (and providing support). It may turn out that it is the experience of great interdependence in such relationships, combined with disruptions that cause negative emotions which cannot be readily expressed, that can make even personal relationships a toxic environment for such people.

## Summary

We began this chapter with the assertion that recent research by relationship researchers could contribute to an understanding of people's emotional lives. In particular, we argued that two different types of relationship closeness—the degree of interdependence between two people and the felt communal obligations between two people—ought to have an impact on people's emotional lives. Relationship interdependence ought to influence the potential for and the frequency of emotional experience in relationships. An individual's belief that the other feels a communal obligation toward him or her ought to influence his or her willingness to express emotion to that other. In addition, to the extent to which expression and suppression of emotion influence actual experience of emotion, belief in the other's communal feelings should influence emotional experience as well. Finally, one's own feelings of communal obligation toward the other ought to influence both the experience and expression of guilt and empathic emotions.

Both the degree of interdependence in a relationship and the communal strength of a relationship are qualities inherent in relationships, not in individuals. These qualities, which, we argue, are central to determining the shape our emotional lives take, simply cannot be understood independently of relationships. The fact that both have clear implications for emotional life is the reason we believe that understanding relationships is central to understanding emotion.

We conclude by returning to some examples, presented at the beginning of this chapter, in which relationship context makes a difference to people's emotional lives. Here we explain them in terms of the theoretical ideas discussed in this chapter. Why do we feel happier when receiving a gift certificate from a brother who has never given us a gift than when receiving one from a mother who always gives us gifts? Berscheid and her colleagues would

say that the unexpected gift from the brother is more of a surprise; it disrupts interpersonal routines more (Berscheid & Ammazzalorso, 2001). Thus it is associated with greater arousal. This arousal, combined with the interpretation that it is due to a good thing that facilitates one's goals, will likely produce greater happiness. In contrast, the gift from one's mother is expected. Although it will be interpreted positively, it produces little arousal and therefore only mild positive emotion. From our communal relationship perspective we might add that the gift from the brother is a particularly valued sign of the beginning and strengthening of a communal relationship, whereas the gift from the mother is merely a sign that the established communal relationship is continuing. The explanations are not in conflict. Both may contribute to the effect.

Turning to our other example, why does a person not express distress over the loss of his or her job while still at work and on the bus ride home but then express a great deal of emotion once home? We would say that our relationships with people at work and with the strangers on the bus were not communal ones. Those people are not responsible for our needs. Thus emotion is supressed in those contexts. The relationship with a spouse is a strong communal one. Our spouses are supposed to respond to our needs. Thus emotion is expressed (and perhaps even exaggerated a bit). Berscheid and her colleagues might add that the shock of hearing of the job loss is also likely to disrupt the interpersonal routines at home, producing arousal and intensifying emotion further. Again the two explanations are not in conflict. Both may contribute to the effect.

## NOTE

Preparation of this chapter was facilitated by NSF Grant No. SBR9630898 and NIH Grant No. T3219953.

## REFERENCES

Aderman, D., Brehm, S. S., & Katz, L. B. (1974). Empathic observation of an innocent victim: The just world revisited. *Journal of Personality and Social Psychology, 29,* 342–347.

Arnsten, A. F. T. (1998). The biology of being frazzled. *Science, 280,* 1711–1712.

Barrett, L. F., Robin, L., Pietromonaco, P. R., & Eyssell, K. M. (1998). Are women the "more emotional" sex? Evidence from emotional experiences in social context. *Cognition and Emotion, 12,* 555–578.

Batson, C. D., Duncan, B. D., Ackerman, P., Buckley, T. & Birch, K. (1981). Is empathic emotion a source of altruistic motivation? *Journal of Personality and Social Psychology, 40,* 290–302.

Batson, C. D., Turk, C. L., Shaw, L. L., & Klein, T. R. (1995). Information function of empathic emotion: Learning that we value the other's welfare. *Journal of Personality and Social Psychology, 40,* 290–302.

Baumeister, R. F., Stillwell, A. M., & Heatherton, T. F.

(1994). Guilt: An interpersonal approach. *Psychological Bulletin, 115,* 243–267.

Berscheid, E. (1981). Attraction and emotion in interpersonal relations. In M. S. Clark & S. T. Fiske (Eds.), *Affect and cognition: The seventeenth annual Carnegie symposium on cognition* (pp. 37–54). Hillsdale, NJ: Erlbaum.

Berscheid, E. (1983). Emotion. In H. H. Kelley, E. Berscheid, A. Christensen, J. H. Harvey, T. L. Huston, J. Levinger, E. McClintock, L. A. Peplau, & D. R. Peterson, *Close relationships* (pp. 110–168). New York: Freeman.

Berscheid, E. (1991). The emotion-in-relationships model: Reflections and update. In W. Kessen & A. Ortony (Eds.), *Memories, thoughts, and emotions: Essays in honor of George Mandler.* Hillsdale, NJ: Erlbaum.

Berscheid, E., & Ammazzalorso, H. (2001). Emotional experience in close relationships. In M. Hewstone & M. Brewer (Series Eds.) & G. Fletcher & M. S. Clark (Vol. Eds.), *Blackwell handbook of social psychology: Vol. 2. Interpersonal processes* (pp. 308–330). Oxford, England: Blackwell.

Berscheid, E., Gangestad, S. W., & Kulakowski, D. (1984). Emotion in close relationships: Implications for relationship counseling. In S. D. Brown & R. W. Lent (Eds.), *Handbook of counseling psychology* (pp. 435–476). New York: Wiley.

Berscheid, E., Snyder, M., & Omoto, A. (1989). The Relationship Closeness Inventory: Assessing the closeness of interpersonal relationships. *Journal of Personality and Social Psychology, 57,* 792–807.

Bolger, N., DeLongis, A., Kessler, R. C., & Wethington, E. (1989). The contagion of stress across multiple roles. *Journal of Marriage and the Family, 51,* 175–183.

Buck, R. (1984). *The communication of emotion.* New York: Guilford Press.

Buck, R. (1989). Emotional communication in personal relationships: A developmental-interactionist view. In C. Hendrick (Ed.), *Review of personality and social psychology: Vol. 10. Close relationships* (pp. 144–163). Beverly Hills, CA: Sage.

Clark, M. S., & Brissette, I. (2000). Relationship beliefs and emotion: Reciprocal effects. In N. Frijda, A. Manstead. & G. Semin (Eds.), *Emotions and beliefs: How feelings influence thoughts* (pp. 212–240). Cambridge: Cambridge University Press.

Clark, M. S., Fitness, J., & Brissette, I. (2001). Understanding people's perceptions of relationships is crucial to understanding their emotional lives. In G. J. O. Fletcher & M. S. Clark (Eds.), *Blackwell handbook of social psychology: Interpersonal processes.* Oxford, England: Blackwell.

Clark, M. S., & Mills, J. (1979). Interpersonal attraction in exchange and communal relationships. *Journal of Personality and Social Psychology, 36,* 1–12.

Clark, M. S., & Mills, J. (1993). The difference between communal and exchange relationships: What it is and is not. *Personality and Social Psychology Bulletin, 19,* 684–691.

Clark, M. S., Mills, J., & Corcoran, D. (1989). Keeping track of needs and inputs of friends and strangers. *Personality and Social Psychology Bulletin, 15,* 533–542.

Clark, M. S., Mills, J., & Powell, M. (1986). Keeping track of needs in two types of relationships. *Journal of Personality and Social Psychology, 51,* 333–338.

Clark, M. S., Ouellette, R., Powell, M., & Milberg, S. (1987). Recipient's mood, relationship type, and help-

ing. *Journal of Personality and Social Psychology, 53,* 94–103.

Clark, M. S., & Taraban, C. B. (1991). Reactions to and willingness to express emotion in two types of relationships. *Journal of Experimental Social Psychology, 27,* 324–336.

Csikszentmihalyi, M., & Larson, R. (1984). *Being adolescent: Conflict and growth in teenage years.* New York: Basic Books.

DeRivera, J. (1984). The structure of emotional relationships. In P. Shaver (Ed.), *Review of personality and social psychology: Emotions, relationships, and health* (pp. 116–145). Beverly Hills, CA: Sage.

Feeney, J. A. (1995). Adult attachment and emotional control. *Personal Relationships, 2,* 143–159.

Feeney, J. A. (1999). Adult attachment, emotional control, and marital satisfaction. *Personal Relationships, 6,* 169–185.

Feeney, J. A., Noller, P., & Roberts, N. (1998). Emotion, attachment, and satisfaction in close relationships. In P. A. Andersen & L. K. Guerrero (Eds.), *The handbook of communication and emotion* (pp. 473–505). San Diego, CA: Academic Press.

Fitness, J. (2000). Anger in the workplace: An emotion script approach to anger episodes between workers and their superiors, co-workers, and subordinates. *Journal of Organizational Behavior, 21,* 147–162.

Fridlund, A. J. (1991). Sociality of solitary smiling: Potentiation by an implicit audience. *Journal of Personality and Social Psychology, 60,* 229–240.

Frijda, N. H. (1993). Moods, emotion episodes, and emotions. In M. Lewis & J. M. Haviland (Eds.), *Handbook of emotions* (pp. 381–404). New York: Guilford Press.

Grote, N. K., & Clark, M. S. (1998). Distributive justice norms and family work: What is perceived as ideal, what is applied, and what predicts perceived fairness? *Social Justice Research, 11,* 243–269.

Hendrick, S. S. (1988). A generic measure of relationship satisfaction. *Journal of Marriage and the Family, 50,* 93–98.

Hoover-Dempsey, K. V., Plas, J. M., & Strudler-Wallston, B. (1986). Tears and weeping among professional women: In search of new understanding. *Psychology of Women Quarterly, 10,* 19–34.

James, W. (1884). What is an emotion? *Mind, 9,* 188–205.

Jones, S. S., Collins, K., & Hong, H. (1991). An audience effect on smile production in 10-month-old infants. *Psychological Science, 2,* 45–49.

Kelley, H. H., Berscheid, E., Christensen, A., Harvey, J. H., Huston, T. L., Levinger, G., McClintock, E., Peplau, L. A., & Peterson, D. R. (1983). *Close relationships.* New York: Freeman.

Laird, J. D. (1974). Self-attribution of emotion: The effects of expressive behavior on the quality of emotional experience. *Journal of Personality and Social Psychology, 33,* 475–486.

Laird, J. D., & Bresler, C. (1992). The process of emotional experience: A self-perception theory. In M. S. Clark (Ed.), *Emotion.* Newbury Park, CA: Sage.

Larson, R. M., Csikszentmihalyi, M., & Graef, R. (1982). Time alone in daily experience: Loneliness or renewal? In L. A. Peplau & D. Perlman (Eds.), *Loneliness: A sourcebook of current theory, research and therapy.* New York: Wiley-Interscience.

Levenson, R. W. (1994). Human emotion: A functional view. In P. Ekman & R. J. Davidson (Eds.), *The nature of emotion: Fundamental questions* (pp. 123–126). New York: Oxford University Press.

Mandler, G. (1975). *Mind and emotion*. New York: Wiley.

Mandler, G. (1997). *Human nature explored*. New York: Oxford University Press.

Miller, R. S., & Leary, M. R. (1992). Social sources and interactive functions of emotion: The case of embarrassment. In M. S. Clark (Ed.), *Emotion and social behavior* (pp. 202–221). Newbury Park, CA: Sage.

Mills, J., & Clark, M. S. (1982). Exchange and communal relationships. In L. Wheeler (Ed.), *Review of personality and social psychology* (Vol. 3, pp. 121–144). Beverly Hills, CA: Sage.

Mills, J., Jellison, J. M., & Kennedy, J. (1976). Attribution of attitudes from feelings: Effect of positive or negative feelings when the attitude object is benefited or harmed. In J. Harvey, W. Ickes, & R. Kidd (Eds.), *New directions in attribution research* (Vol. 1, pp. 271–289). Hillsdale, NJ: Erlbaum.

Riskind, J. H. (1984). They stoop to conquer: Guiding and self-regulatory functions of physical posture after success and failure. *Journal of Personality and Social Psychology, 47*, 479–492.

Riskind, J. H., & Gotay, C. C. (1982). Physical posture: Could it have regulatory or feedback effects on motivation and emotion? *Motivation and Emotion, 6*, 273–298.

Schachter, S., & Singer, J. E. (1962). Cognitive, social and physiological determinants of emotional state. *Psychological Review, 69*, 379–399.

Scherer, K. R., Wallbott, H. G., & Summerfield, A. B. (Eds.). (1986). *Experiencing emotion: A cross-cultural study*. Cambridge, England: Cambridge University press.

Schwartz, J. C., & Shaver, P. R. (1987). Emotion and emotion knowledge in interpersonal relationships. In W. Jones & D. Perlman (Eds.), *Advances in personal relationships*. Greenwich, CT: JAI Press.

Scott, J. P. (1958). *Animal behavior*. Chicago: University of Chicago Press.

Scott, J. P. (1980). The function of emotions in behavioral systems: A systems theory analysis. In R. Plutchik & H. Kellerman (Eds.), *Emotion: Theory, research, and experience: Vol. 1. Theories of emotion* (pp. 35–56). New York: Academic Press.

Simon, H. A. (1967). Motivational and emotional controls of cognition. *Psychological Review, 74*, 29–39.

Simpson, J. (1987). The dissolution of romantic relationships: Factors involved in relationship stability and emotional distress. *Journal of Personality and Social Psychology, 53*, 683–692.

Simpson, J. A., Rholes, W. S., & Nelligan, J. S. (1992). Support seeking and support giving within couples in an anxiety-provoking situation: The role of attachment styles. *Journal of Personality and Social Psychology, 62*, 434–446.

Thoits, P. A. (1983). Multiple identities and psychological well-being: A reformulation of the social isolation hypothesis. *American Sociological Review, 48*, 174–187.

Trevarthen, C. (1984). Emotions in infancy: Regulators of contact and relationships with persons. In K. Scherer & P. Ekman (Eds.), *Approaches to emotion*. Hillsdale, NJ: Erlbaum.

Williamson, G. M., & Clark, M. S. (1989). Providing help and desired relationship type as determinants of changes in moods and self-evaluations. *Journal of Personality and Social Psychology, 56*, 722–734.

Williamson, G. M., & Clark, M. S. (1992). Impact of desired relationship type on affective reactions to choosing and being required to help. *Personality and Social Psychology Bulletin, 18*, 10–18.

Zillmann, D., & Cantor, J. R. (1977). Affective responses to the emotions of a protagonist. *Journal of Experimental Social Psychology, 13*, 155–165.

# VIII

Evolutionary and Cultural Perspectives on Affect

# 44

## INTRODUCTION: EVOLUTIONARY AND CULTURAL PERSPECTIVES ON AFFECT

Paul Rozin

### The Domain and Definition of Affect

Affect is important, understudied, and hard to define. There has been a recent burst of interest in psychology in this area, as evidenced by this volume. In this section of the book, we merge the study of affect, substantially ignored by most of psychology during the twentieth century, with two perspectives, the evolutionary and cultural, which were also substantially ignored by psychology during the past century. As there has been a burst of interest in affect, so has there been in both evolutionary and cultural psychology in the past decade or so. So in this section of this volume, we experience the excitement of a new problem of interest, from two new perspectives. Because all this is very new, there are more questions than answers. Of course, concern about affect and emotion, and in particular their evolution, did not originate in recent times. Perhaps the greatest book that deals with these fundamental issues, Darwin's *The Expression of the Emotions in Man and Animals* (1872/1998), was written in 1872. P. T. Young (1959) also mounted an excellent experimental research program devoted to understanding the role of affect in animal function in the mid-twentieth century. However, in the context of behaviorism, it was more or less ignored and was not integrated into developing experimental psychology.

On the surface, combining cultural and evolutionary approaches in one section may seem arbitrary. However, these two approaches have two things in common from the viewpoint of psychology. First, each brings the perspective of another discipline to bear on problems of psychological interest. Second, cultures evolve, so concepts from biological evolution such as variation, selection, and adaptation can be applied. Furthermore, many of the problems of scanty evidence that result from the fragmentary state of evidence of past lives that complicate evolutionary and adaptive accounts in biological evolution are more tractable in the case of cultural evolution. In the past thousands of years, cultures have obligingly left a substantial record of artifacts, particularly writing, that tell us about how things were.

Psychology, like all scholarly endeavors, is subject to fads. Technological or conceptual breakthroughs, persuasive leaders, and a host of other factors create high concentrations of effort in certain areas, whereas others languish. This may well be a good model for progress. The possibilities of phenomena to study in psychology are almost limitless, and just as the visual system selects and focuses from the bewildering array of events that impinge on the retina, so we must select and focus on some of the possibilities. We must hope that our judgment causes the most productive and representative phenomena to fall in our "research fovea." Just as affect, evolution, and culture have been outside of the mainstream of psychology for long, within the modern study of affect, some subareas have been relatively ignored. The great focus in the resurgence of affect has been the study of emotion, one manifestation of affect, with some emotions, particularly sadness, anger, and fear, privileged over others. Note that the following three chapters in this section are about emotion, as are almost all of the chapters in this book. The evolutionary approach causes us to attend more than others, perhaps, to the most fundamental of affects, pleasure and pain, along with issues such as liking and wanting, or craving (discussed rather sparingly in this volume and in the literature on affect but treated in sophisticated detail in the work of Berridge, 1999). The cultural and cultural evolutionary approaches bring to the fore issues of values and morality, which play a central role in two of the chapters in this section although they remain in the background in most of the rest of this volume.

Although there are clear reasons, as stated previously, to combine cultural and evolutionary approaches, there is one major difference in the approaches that a reader must realize in order to assimilate the material that follows in this section. Evolutionary explanation is inherently about time. The question asked is, How did the phenomena under study get to be the way they are? To distinguish this question from the parallel one asked by the developmental approach, the evolutionary approach limits itself to causes that occur prior to fertilization. Thus the question is really, How did the zygote get to be, and to what extent (presumably, the extent of genetic determination of the phenomena) does that account for the phenomenon? A natural sequel to evolutionary explanation is adaptive explanation, which essentially looks forward rather than backward in time. It asks, What is the function (adaptive value) of the phenomenon under study? (See Rozin & Schull, 1988, for a fuller discussion of these types of explanations.) There are a number of types of answers to this question, including: (1) designation of the current biological or cultural advantage that the characteristic in question bestows on its possessor; (2) designation of some aspect of the ancestral environment within which the characteristic has an adaptive function; or (3) suggestion that the adaptive value of the trait cannot be identified in either the current or ancestral environment. The latter indicates that the feature in question is a "neutral" trait or that it has a complex and subtle linkage to other adaptive traits.

Cultural explanation, in contrast to evolutionary-adaptive explanation, refers to a level of analysis rather than a time period (Rozin & Schull, 1988). Phenomena can be accounted for at various levels of organization: thus carrying out a ritual such as the standard greeting of a stranger in any culture can be explained as a motor sequence, in stimulus-response terms, or as enacting of a cultural norm. These are not conflicting accounts, but rather accounts that differ in level of discourse. The cultural level of discourse has not generally been favored in psychology, though of course it is explicit in the Freudian superego and implicit in much of social psychology. Thus, in impression management, psychological analysis often takes for granted the cultural values that determine the type of impression one would like to present. The point is that cultural accounts typically supplement or enrich, rather than contradict, accounts at the level of individual behavior and that all levels-of-analysis accounts of an ongoing behavior (in terms of immediate causes and consequences) are orthogonal to, rather than in opposition to, evolutionary-adaptive accounts. Similarly, accounts of how a cultural norm or schema works are orthogonal to how the norm came to be.

In this chapter, I set the stage for a cultural, evolutionary, and, most particularly, cultural-evolutionary approach by considering some fundamental questions: What is affect? What is the relation between the on-line experience, memory, and anticipation of affect? Why does affect exist? Why is the negative-positive dimension primary in affect? Why does negative valence usually dominate positive valence? Why are the elicitors of affect so elaborated in humans and so modulated by culture? What are the processes, in an evolutionary framework, by which cultures have transformed affect—most particularly, emotions?

## What Is Affect?

I consider affect to cover the set of all valenced mental states, along with their associated physiological representations and behaviors. I consider valence to be positive or negative. A positive state is one that we seek or try to maintain or enhance, and a negative state is one that we seek to reduce, eliminate, or avoid.

The power of affect and valence is captured by Jeremy Bentham (1789/1948): "Nature has placed mankind under the governance of two sovereign masters, *pain* and *pleasure*. It is for them alone to point out what we ought to do, as well as to determine what we shall do. . . . They govern us in all we do, in all we say, in all we think" (p. 1).

An alternative framing of affect can privilege the behavioral side and define it in terms of approach and avoidance (Davidson, Ekman, Saron, Senvlis, & Friesen, 1990; Schneirla, 1959). This view has much appeal, as it is behavior that ultimately determines fitness. Practically, the major distinction between a "positive-negative" and "approach-withdrawal" framework is their different categorizations of the important emotion of anger, which is usually approach and negative in valence. One shortcoming of an approach-withdrawal scheme is that it oversimplifies the options available to an animal or human: freezing in fright or being paralyzed in ecstasy are clearly valenced activities, not well signatured by the approach-withdrawal dichotomy.

Formulated in this broad way, I propose the following taxonomy of affect.

## Direct Sensory Links

### External

Some affective responses seem to be directly produced by certain types of stimuli that impinge on the body surface and by the receptors that have access to it. These rather simple sensory inputs do not necessarily seem to involve the action of appraisal that identifies emotion. Normally, the affective consequences of such stimuli are described as *pleasure* and *pain*. It is presumably the lack of appraisal and the often long duration of these inputs that disqualifies them as emotions, though there are very characteristic facial expressions associated with pain. As noted by both Sherrington (1906) and Troland (1928), certain sensory modalities, those in which the actual, material aspect of the stimulus object contacts the body (the "contact" senses), tend to have inherently valenced inputs. Troland included the chemical senses (taste and smell) and visceral sensitivity; I am inclined to include most of the input from the skin senses as well. Troland used the terms *beneceptive* (beneficial) and *nociceptive* (harmful) to describe the valenced systems, in contrast to vision, audition, and some forms of touch, which he classified as *neutroceptive*, that is, more informative than directly evaluative.

Of particular relevance to psychology and to evolution and culture are those special points on the body at which there is a breach, or aperture, connecting the inside and the outside. Most of these apertures—in particular, those involved in ingestion/breathing, excretion, and sexual activity—produce inputs of particular salience, which are eminently valenced. They are vulnerable points in the body, places at which the sheath of skin that separates self from other is broken, and hence at which the self-other physical boundary is blurred. The mouth and vagina are particularly inclined, at least in humans, to assign high valence to the various contacts or intrusions that they encounter (Rozin, Nemeroff, Horowitz, Gordon, & Voet, 1995). Because these are the two loci in the body through which physical material from the outside world has access to the body (the nostrils are actually a third, but the salience of material transfer is much lower), and given both the basic risks and benefits of traffic in these two apertures, it is not surprising that they should be heavily valenced.

### Internal

Sensory inputs from within the body can be, and have been, classified by Troland's system as either neutroceptive (e.g., proprioceptive information) or nociceptive. Examples of the latter include visceral pain and the motivation-specific negative inputs associated with hun-

ger, thirst, lack of oxygen, and the need to empty the bladder or the colon. It is to be noted (see Rozin, 1999, for more detail) that virtually all valenced internal sensory inputs are negative: "this can be interpreted to mean that for the body interior the normal state is neutral and only malfunction is signaled. From the perspective of the body interior, 'no news is good news'" (Rozin, 1999 p. 110). In dealing with the external environment, there are events to approach and events to avoid. In the internal environment, action is only requisite if something is wrong.

## Appraised Inputs

### Emotion

There is no need to define the term *emotion* in a book about emotion that already contains many definitions. Suffice it to say that in contrast to simple, direct affect, it involves a rather complex attribution or appraisal process and, in contrast to moods, is of rather short duration. Emotions typically have an expressive component.

### Aesthetic and Mastery Pleasure

Aesthetic and mastery pleasures are relatively ignored in the field, but they are common and distinctively human experiences. They figure prominently in Duncker's (1941) taxonomy of affect (reviewed in Rozin, 1999). Aesthetic pleasures are distinguished by the complexity of the inputs and/or the amount of experience and education that is needed to appreciate them. No animal has ever been made to like Mozart's music, whereas few humans, properly exposed, can resist it. Mastery pleasures may well have animal parallels and serve the purpose of motivating accomplishment of difficult-to-attain goals.

In both aesthetic and mastery affect, the pleasure itself seems rather elemental, having much in common with sensory pleasures. But the elicitors are vastly more complex, and unlike the direct pleasures, these pleasures do not emanate from a specific location on or in the body. Unlike emotions, aesthetic and mastery pleasures are not reliably associated with expressions.

## Nonsensory Affect of Long Duration: Moods

Finally, and discussed only briefly in this section of the volume, are the moods, dispositions which change only slowly, over minutes, hours, or days. The moods most commonly studied are sadness (depression) and happiness. They are similar in important ways to basic motivations such as hunger.

Each of the types of affect designated exists in three temporal frames: on-line (experienced), remembered, and anticipated. These temporal frames will be considered in the next section of this chapter.

In general, the direct sensory types of affect are more similar between humans and animals, more likely to have innate linkages, and less likely to vary across culture. As appraisal becomes more important, so do culture and context. But this is not so simple; the "sensory," direct positive affect of a luscious piece of chocolate can turn negative when we discover that there is a fly in it. The pleasant sensation of genital stroking can become unpleasant when we discover that it is being accomplished by an unsavory person. And a sharp pain on one's earlobe may turn to pleasure in the context of sexual activity, when delivered as a bite by one's romantic partner.

## What Is the Relationship Between the On-line Experience, Memory, and Anticipation of Affect?

The study of affect has focused almost entirely on "affect in the moment"; the on-line experience, expressive and other behaviors, and physiological responses. But an affective episode exists in an important sense in memory and anticipation as well (Elster & Loewenstein, 1992; Kahneman, Wakker, & Sarin, 1997; see also chapter 31 in this volume). A visit to the dentist may involve a few seconds of sharp pain, a rather trivial amount of experienced displeasure. But the affective import of the visit is much greater than that. There are the many times the reluctant patient anticipates the visit with its impending pain and the many times that the patient is reminded of the pain experience after the visit. Daniel Kahneman and his colleagues (Fredrickson & Kahneman, 1993; Kahneman et al., 1997) and George Loewenstein (Loewenstein & Schkade, 1999; chapter 31, this volume) have recently opened up this important area.

The focus of most of Kahneman's empirical work has been on pain, but it applies as well to pleasure, mood, and some emotional and aesthetic experiences. The study of the relationship among experienced, anticipated, and remembered affect is of central importance for an evolutionary-adaptive perspective on affect, and for any other perspective as well. It is the memory of an affect-laden experience that determines future behavior with respect to that experience, not the experience itself. It is one's memory for how much one enjoyed a product in the past, not the actual enjoyment in the past, that determines whether we will buy the product again. Insofar as affective experiences are "consulted" to determine present action, the central issue is not experienced affect but rather remembered affect. Kahneman and colleagues (Kahneman, Fredrickson, Schreiber, & Redelmeier, 1993; Kahneman et al, 1997; see important extensions and elaborations of these findings by Ariely, 1998) have made a very impor-

tant beginning in exploring this area. Perhaps the most robust finding is that under many circumstances, remembered affect is dominated by change; steady states are not remembered in terms of their duration. This duration neglect means that both long episodes and short but steadily valenced episodes are remembered as roughly equivalent. In terms of adaptation, this fits in with the fact that it is changes that we respond to, not only on-line but also in our memory representations. Kahneman and colleagues (Ariely, 1998; Kahneman et al., 1993) have also reported results from the pain domain that suggest that the peak and termination of pain episodes disproportionately determine the quality of memory.

On the anticipation side, the major finding is that people are quite poor at predicting their own affective trajectories; that is, they are inaccurate at determining whether continued experience with a valenced object (e.g., a food) will lead to enhanced liking, enhanced disliking, or no change (Kahneman & Snell, 1992). Over a wide range of decisions involving tastes, health, alternative purchases, and other domains, anticipated preferences are often biased or distorted representations of actual future preferences (Gilbert, Pinel, Wilson, Blumberg, & Wheatley, 1998; Loewenstein & Schkade, 1999).

These issues bear on animals as well as humans, but they have very special relevance to humans because of the way that humans rehearse past experiences and play out future experiences in their minds. One can reasonably claim that most of the "affect" experienced by a human is of either the remembered or the anticipated variety.

## Why Does Affect Exist? The Adaptive Value of Affect

On the surface, it is easy to account, in an adaptive sense, for the existence of pleasure and pain. Organisms learn to continue or obtain that which produces pleasure and to terminate or avoid that which produces pain. The basic motivational systems, involving optimal temperatures, nutrition, oxygen, and successful sex, are nicely tied to pleasure in the achievement of and pain or distress in the absence of life-promoting states. For the domains of temperature and food, Michel Cabanac (1971, 1985) has shown that pleasure decreases with departure from ideal physiological values, a phenomenon he calls "alliesthesia." These valenced events can contribute to plasticity by functioning as the unconditioned stimuli in Pavlovian paradigms or the rewards in instrumental learning.

One of the features of pleasure and pain is their system-wide nature; for humans they are powerful, riveting mental experiences, and for many animals they seem to capture the focus or direction of behavior. This feature raises a problem that is illustrated by a well-documented but little known contrast in food aversion learning. If ingestion of a food, by rats, humans, or other animals, is followed by nausea, that food comes to be disliked. That is, there is an affective change in reaction to the food, such that the food itself elicits the type of negative response that innately distasteful entities elicit (Garcia, Hankins, & Rusiniak, 1974; Rozin & Kalat, 1971). This type of response includes facial and bodily behaviors, such as gaping and face wiping, that serve to rid the organism of the stimulus (Grill & Norgren, 1978). However, if the same food is followed by electric shock rather than nausea in rats, or perhaps by a respiratory allergic response or lower gut cramps in humans, the food comes to be avoided but does not acquire negative affective properties. This contrast between nausea and shock or lower gastrointestinal events has been documented in rats using facial responses (Parker, 1982; Pelchat, Grill, Rozin, & Jacobs, 1983), and in humans using self-report (Pelchat & Rozin, 1982). Thus nausea produces an affective change in the evaluation of the object, a dislike, and shock produces an avoidance without such a change. Now why should there be such a difference? In both cases, the behavioral result of avoidance or rejection is the same. Why have two different mechanisms, what we have called distaste (with nausea) and danger (with shock) (Rozin & Fallon, 1980)? I don't know the answer, but I believe that that answer may partly account for why we have affect, at least in the sense of a system-wide conscious entity.

If the aim is to produce rejection and avoidance, there are adequate instrumental and Pavlovian routes to this end without involving an affective state or change in affect. The law of effect would function well to keep us away from the dangerous things and near the beneficial things. This could all be done mechanically, computationally, the way we would program it in a robot. So why do we have affect, whether pleasure or pain, fear or joy? Why is there a "qualia" associated with emotions? Following are some possible accounts (see Rozin, 1999, for a more complete discussion).

First, even if pleasure is an epiphenomenon, some noncausal readout of the integrated utility function, it may be a powerful and useful indicator of the nature of that function.

Second, pleasure as a mental event may function in the mental calculus of choice and decision making. Because humans plan for their futures and use their pasts as a guide to their futures, the instantiation of a salient, integrative representation of past and future experiences, that is, a remembered or anticipated and integrated hedonic value, may be a convenient shorthand for decision making on-line (Kahneman et al., 1997). The integrated affective memory or anticipation may be just what is needed to make sensible decisions. If this is so, then there is substantial adaptive value in our mental representation of remembered and anticipated pleasure (utility).

Third, and related to the second reason, there are many

shortcomings of purely conscious, rational choices. They are time-consuming and sometimes incorrect. Implicit knowledge, such as sensitivity to probabilities of events, has evolved to a high degree in nonhuman animals. It is typically not available to consciousness, hence to rational consideration, and is frequently represented affectively. The dominant verbal mode of encoding in humans is not capable of representing all of our experience; hence rational decision making may downgrade such important knowledge. There is considerable evidence that pure rational approaches to decision making have shortcomings and that affect is often a guide to adaptive decisions (e.g., Damasio, 1994; chapter 31, this volume). Furthermore, affective disorders have been linked to deficits in decision making (Damasio, 1994). Frank (1988; chapter 47, this volume) illustrates convincingly how emotions can promote social harmony, acting to discourage some disruptive "rational" strategies such as deceit and contributing to the importance of reputation. In other words, there may be wisdom in affectively based tendencies or dispositions.

Haidt (2001; chapter 45, this volume) argues persuasively that moral emotions typically precede and guide "rational" moral judgment, rather than the other way around. Loewenstein and Lerner (chapter 31, this volume) systematically explore ways in which affect can improve or degrade the adaptive value of decisions, sometimes promoting long-term over short-term interests (as in some manifestations of anticipated regret), and sometimes the reverse.

Fourth, as system-wide experiences, that is, occupants of consciousness, hedonic experiences allow for translation into system-wide responses. In this sense, the general representation of a hedonic state might function the way epinephrine functions as a hormone; it allows for a system-wide activation. That is, the reason we have epinephrine as a system-wide hormone, as well as the parallel locally acting norepinephrine transmitter, is that the former activates the whole system in one orchestrated response.

Fifth, another evolutionary perspective derives affect from the adaptive value of communicating one's intentions (Fridlund, 1994; Smith, 1965). Pain, mood, and emotions, all present in animals, are indicative of particular behavioral dispositions. The conveyance of information to conspecifics about likely actions has clear adaptive value. However, even if this account is at least partly correct, it still does not explain the experience of affect as opposed to the signals and behavioral dispositions that accompany these experiences.

It is also possible that affect is a by-product of the competition of different systems for control of the motor system; affect is a mode of attracting and maintaining conscious attention. Surely it is true that those things that create affect are significant in life on the whole. In the conscious calculus of choice, affect may be a useful summation of information and a way to categorize events and options; thus all of the things that elicit disgust become a useful category in navigating the world.

## Why Is the Negative-Positive Dimension Primary in Affect?

A wide variety of linguistic, literary, and psychological sources privilege the negative-positive dimension in describing human experience. The semantic differential technique reliably recovers the evaluative dimension as the principal factor in analysis of meaning cross-culturally (Osgood, May, & Miron, 1975). It seems very reasonable that negative (avoidance/withdrawal) and positive (approach) would constitute a dominant dimension, the core of motivation. In addition to pleasure and pain, moods and emotions are typically categorized in terms of positive and negative. Thus it is not surprising that Davidson (Davidson & Irwin, 1999) and others find that the human cerebral hemispheres also parse along the positive-negative dimension. The same negative-positive dimension permeates the literature on animal motivation. This all fits with the division of opportunities and events in the world into those that promote survival, those that are neutral, and those that decrease survival.

### One or Two Dimensions

In much of lay discourse and experimental psychology, at least in the English-speaking world, the pleasure dimension is taken for granted. People easily use the hedonic dimension (for example, multipoint scales anchored by *dislike extremely* and *like extremely* or *happy* and *sad*). However, these results indicate only that people are capable of combining or integrating experiences of varying hedonic qualities. There is abundant evidence that both people and animals can have simultaneous negative and positive hedonic experiences. The existence of negative and positive readouts in the two hemispheres allows for the possibility of independent readouts.

In 1925, Ruckmick argued in favor of separate negative and positive dimensions, noting that the pleasure–displeasure opposition is more logical than psychological. Hot and cold are opposites, but there is both physiological and psychological evidence that these two sensations are mediated by separate systems.

A term such as *bittersweet* applied to chocolate, the existence of "love-hate" relationships, and the simultaneous or near simultaneous facial and bodily expressions of pleasure and aversion in humans and laboratory rats (Berridge & Grill, 1983) argue for co-occurrence. These behaviors are more easily interpreted as due to a simultaneous activation of opposite affects. When increases in the magnitude of aversive responses are produced by increasing the bitterness of taste mixtures, there is not necessarily a reciprocal decrease in positive ingestive responses (Berridge & Grill, 1983). Furthermore, surprisingly to many, psychometric measures of positive and negative affect (as with the Positive Negative Affect Scale [PANAS]) are uncorrelated or almost uncorrelated over short or long periods (Diener & Emmons, 1985; Watson, Clark, & Tellegen, 1988). From an adaptive point of view, these separate registrations make sense, as there is certainly reason to distinguish between situations in which there are no important stimuli and others in which there are both strong positive and negative stimuli (see Cacioppo & Gardner, 1999, for a fuller discussion of this issue).

### Negativity Bias

In the broad domain of affect, a number of investigators, including Peeters (1971; Peeters & Czapinski, 1990) and Taylor (1994) have pointed out that negative events or states seem more powerful than positive states.

Recently, Baumeister, Bratslavsky, Finkenauer, and Vohs (2001) and Rozin and Royzman (2001) have reviewed a wide range of findings in psychology and related disciplines and concluded that under most circumstances, negative dominates positive. Rozin and Royzman (2001) have described this phenomenon as negativity bias. According to their analysis, negativity bias manifests itself in four different ways. First, negative potency, which has been the focus of most research and of the Baumeister et al. (2001) review, refers to the fact that when positive and negative events are equated on some type of objective scale (e.g., money), the negative event is psychologically more extreme than its objective positive equivalent. In some of its manifestations, this reaction has been described as loss aversion (Kahneman, Knetsch, & Thaler, 1991).

A second, very striking but less noticed, feature of negativity bias is negative dominance. When negative and positive events that are subjectively equated are combined, the outcome is usually negative. A third feature of negativity bias is negative gradient dominance; negative events grow more negative as temporal or spatial proximity increases faster than positive events become more positive (e.g., Brown, 1948). The evidence for this point is much less robust than the evidence for the first two features. The fourth aspect of negativity bias is greater negative differentiation. This differentiation is clearest in the emotions; there seem to be more negative than positive emotions by almost all counts (the exception being the emotional taxonomy deriving from the ancient Hindu *Natyasastra*, (Hejmadi, 1999; Hejmadi, Davidson, & Rozin, 2000).

Three of the four manifestations of negativity bias (the exception is negativity dominance) are clearly present in nonhuman animals. This broader phylogenetic base argues for some biologically important function for the bias.

There are four different accounts for negativity bias (reviewed in more detail in Rozin & Royzman, 2001).

The first is based on the fact that most events are positive (that is, they promote well-being) for most animals. Judged from this baseline (e.g., Parducci, 1995), and given that it is change that generally motivates organisms, negative events should be more attention grabbing and significant. Safe landings of airplanes are not news; airplane crashes are. The greater incidence of positive events is manifested for humans in the fact that there are positive biases in language, such that positive words tend to be the default words to describe valenced dimension (*goodness* covers the full range from good to bad, whereas *badness* extends only from "extremely bad" to "neutral") and that positive words tend to occur before negative words when they are conjoined (e.g., *good and bad*, rather than *bad and good*). These relations seem to occur across languages (Rozin, Berman, & Royzman, 1999).

Second, the most negative event with respect to survival is death, and there is no event that is as significant on the positive side. Thus a negative bias (particularly negative potency, but also negative gradient dominance) would be expected because of the asymmetry in the biological significance of negative and positive events.

Third, an organism typically faces more options in the face of a negative as opposed to a positive situation. Positive situations generally promote approach, whereas negative situations may promote withdrawal, freezing, or approach (e.g., attack). This asymmetry, perhaps, accounts for the greater differentiation of negative emotions. In addition, with respect to the moral emotions, as analyzed and listed by Haidt in chapter 45 in this volume, there are more than twice as many negative types as positive. And the number of moral emotions that may be considered positive in some sense, for example, compassion, but that are elicited by negative events is also much higher than the number that are elicited by positive events.

Fourth, in relation to negativity dominance, we (Rozin & Royzman, 2001) suggest that one reason it occurs is that negative events are more contagious. Just as germs are contagious and antibiotics are not, negative events have a way of contaminating basically positive situations. The effect is clearly illustrated in the psychology of contagion (Rozin & Nemeroff, 1990), by which brief contact with a cockroach (even if sterilized) ruins an otherwise delicious food, whereas nothing can contact a pile of cockroaches and make them edible.

## Why Are the Elicitors of Affect So Elaborated in Humans and So Modulated by Culture?

Human enculturation has drastically changed the human environment and the human mind. Humans grow up, to a large extent, in a world of cultural artifacts, a world that, unlike the natural world, contains many sharp angles, saturated colors, and high-velocity objects. In addition to the obvious quantum leap in communication ability produced by and perhaps related to language, we have the awareness of our continuity in the life course, that we have descendants and ancestors; the realization of death; an extraordinarily complex social world; and a set of institutions, including religion.

There are both culture-general (cultural universal) and culture-specific effects in the domain of affect. Most of the literature on culture and emotion concerns how cultures shape affect in culture-specific ways, and there is impressive evidence for this process, as documented by Mesquita in chapter 46 in this volume. However, the striking and important differences among cultures may cause us to ignore the universal or almost universal effects of culture on affect. All cultures have cuisines, music, some form of religion, moral systems, and moral emotions (see chapter 45, this volume). Culture-derived affects, such as shame, pride, contempt, and aesthetic pleasure, seem to be universal.

Many of the effects of culture on affect are indirect, in the sense that culture changes the world we live in, and hence they introduce new risks and benefits. Thus fear of guns or airplanes and love of music are both afforded by opportunities created by culture. The realization of the finality of death, a product of culture, produces yet another fear. Some combination of the enhanced cognitive processing ability of humans and the major changes humans have introduced into their world probably accounts for most of the blossoming of affect in humans.

### Culture and Direct Sensory Affect

In keeping with the broad range of affect that is the subject of this part, I consider first the fundamental sensory-based affects. It is probably true that the more complex and appraisal-related eliciting situations are, the more influence culture may have, as culture acts so powerfully on appraisals. Yet there are many ways in which culture acts on the experience of pleasure and pain. Most striking is the fact that it is very common, perhaps universal, that some innately negative stimuli become positive under the influence of culture. Painful massages, bitter foods, thrill experiences, irritating and spoiled foods can all undergo this effect. Consider the liking for the innately negative irritation produced by chili pepper (Rozin, 1990). So far as we know, the oral irritation produced by chili peppers is innately aversive, at least to humans and other mammals. It is probably a form of plant defense. Yet perhaps 2 billion humans eat chili pepper daily and like the very same burn that is innately aversive. We aren't certain how this hedonic change occurs, but it certainly involves culture in a number of ways. First, at a minimum, a period of exposure is needed to allow for the operation of whatever process converts dislikes into likes. Cultural traditions program this exposure; in their absence, after one unpleasant encounter with chili, a child would never try it again. Second, as one effect of repeated exposure, and in accordance with my benign-masochism account for eating chili pepper (Rozin, 1990), the pleasure of the burn derives from the discovery that it is painful but harmless. This puts chili pepper in the same category as roller coaster riding and watching sad or horror movies. This uniquely human pleasure, flirting with danger or harm in a context in which one knows one is safe, seems to be a universal and unique feature of human cultures. Third, it is very likely that the social situation of the meal, in which the young child experiences parents and older siblings eating and enjoying chili pepper, plays an important role in fostering liking. This is a direct socialization influence. To my knowledge, hedonic reversal of innately negative responses is either uniquely human, or almost so.

Most addictive substances have negative sensory properties and often negative effects on first administration. It is sociocultural forces that induce second and further samplings that lead to addiction—both because of social pressure and because others tell us that we will come to like the substance and that the negative consequences of withdrawal can be countered by additional doses. It is much more difficult to establish addictive cycles in animals, without these social links, than in humans.

More generally, even simple sensory affect, such as genital sensations or the odor of decay, can, by virtue of context, come to be interpreted as positive or negative. For the genital sensation, it has to do with the human source of the stimulation; for the decay odor, whether it is perceived as coming from cheese or body waste products.

The importance of direct sensory affect varies across time and place. Many of the philosophies from the Far East and South Asia hold that sensory pleasure is not very important and that happiness or fulfillment comes from rising above it. For example, one of the sayings in the *Dhammapada*, the Buddhist prayer book, is "From pleasure comes grief, from pleasure comes fear; he who is free from pleasure neither sorrows nor fears" (Babbitt, 1936, p. 34). Although it is clear that for Americans doing what is pleasant is a major part of living a successful life, this seems to be less the case for, among others, Hindus in India. Pleasure seems less important and duty and tradition more important in daily Hindu life. For example, in a questionnaire given to college students in both the United States and India, 34% of Indian participants and only 12% of Americans agreed with the statement, "Whether or not an outcome of an action will be pleasant or unpleasant for me is not an important consideration." On the other hand, in evaluating the statement, "Do your duty above all else," 86% of Hindu Indians expressed agreement, in contrast to 45% of Americans (Rozin, 2000).

## Culture and Temporal Frames of Affect

Although it has not been systematically studied, it is likely that there are major cultural differences in the relative emphasis on remembered, experienced, and anticipated affect. For example, feelings of guilt and regret are no doubt influenced by cultural views about the responsibility one has for one's actions.

## Culture and Emotion

Mesquita (chapter 46, this volume) notes that both cultural schema and cultural practices provide a context and a direction for affect. Mesquita covers the various components of emotion—appraisal, action readiness, behavior/expression, and regulation—and documents the ways in which culture modifies what she recognizes as a core of emotions and emotion components that may be biologically determined and shared with other animals. She emphasizes and documents the breadth of influence of culture. However, it may be that some components of emotion are more malleable than others, in general and with respect to culture. I suspect that, for the domain of emotion, cultural influences have least effect on what Ekman (1992) calls the emotion programs (expressions, behavioral tendencies, physiological manifestations) and most effect on the areas of appraisal and regulation: appraisal because this is the principal locus at which meaning and context enter into affect; and regulation because it involves conscious intervention and hence can be more influenced by acquired values and beliefs.

Research in cultural psychology in the past two decades has identified some basic themes that represent cultural differences, including the interdependent versus the dependent self, the degree of personal agency and amount of control that individuals have over their lives and actions, the domains of moral concern, the importance of social hierarchy, and the degree of expression of emotions (see chapter 46, this volume; also Markus & Kitayama, 1991; Mesquita & Frijda, 1992; Shweder, 1991; Shweder, Much, Mahapatra, & Park, 1997). These themes vary in salience and polarity (e.g., interdependent-dependent) across cultures and affect both the quality and frequency of reported emotions in Japan and the United States: The most commonly reported emotions in the United States are joy (22%) and stress (13%), whereas in Japan they are security/contentment (14%), joy (14%), and resignation (13%) (Mesquita & Karasawa, 2000). As Mesquita points out, the cultural manifestations are complex and subtle, such that an emotion that is important in a particular culture may occur infrequently because either its expression is suppressed or situations that elicit it are avoided. Other important themes mentioned by Mesquita include the emphasis on restoring balance in Japan versus changing the world in the West; the emphasis on shame in cultures of honor; and the suppression of the expression of happiness in some cultures because it calls attention to the self.

There has been a particular interest in demonstrating emotions that are qualitatively distinct and specific to particular cultures or groups of cultures, such as *lajya* (related to shame) in Hindu South Asia and *amae* (related to dependence) in Japan. Such examples are important to illustrate the malleability of emotions and the ways in which cultures differ in terms of important themes. However, they are a lesser force in the shaping of emotion by culture. Most cultural effects involve more subtle modulation of a more universal set of emotions and the general expansion, across culture, of the domains of concern and, hence, elicitors of emotion.

Consider an example of one way in which culture can affect the contextualization of emotion. Shweder (personal communication, 1985) asked Brahmins in India and some Americans to consider three emotions (shame [*lajya*], happiness, and anger) and to select from the three the two that belong best together. He reported informally that Americans reliably separated out happiness, using a negative-positive distinction. However, his Brahmin participants chose anger as the unique emotion, on the grounds that shame and happiness are socially constructive and anger is socially disruptive. We have confirmed this finding using college students in the United States and India; whereas virtually all Americans chose happiness as the singleton, almost half of the Indian participants chose anger (Rozin, 2000). There are two implications of these results. One is that different cultures may parse emotions differently. The second is that, although there is a large cultural difference here, members of each culture can readily understand the alternative principles of parsing (valence and social constructiveness). It is primarily a matter of which categorization is more salient, or, as I have described it, a difference in the default dimensions in different cultures (Rozin, 2000).

## Culture and the Positive/Negative Balance

Cultures may differ in the balance between positive and negative affects. One of the manifestations of negativity bias is the greater differentiation of negative emotions. Thus most Western taxonomies of "basic" emotions, from James and Darwin on, designate one positive emotion (joy/happiness) and three to five negative emotions (most commonly anger, disgust, fear, and sadness). However, the Hindu *Natya Sastra* and its later elaboration (Hejmadi, 1999) designates 10 basic emotions, with only 4 clearly negative (anger, disgust, fear, and sadness) and at least 4 clearly positive (amusement, awe, heroism, and love). Furthermore, the remaining two, *lajya* (shame) and peace, in the Hindu context, could well be classified as positive. The clear classification of shame as negative in the West contrasts with its mixed valence categorization in Hindu

India. The greater differentiation on the positive side does not, in itself, speak to the frequency of positive emotions, but it does suggest that there may be different positive-negative balances, perhaps related to some of the major cultural themes discussed previously.

There is also a possibility of cultural differences in the relations between positive and negative emotions. Thus, whereas the frequency of positive and negative emotions are negatively correlated in Americans, they are positively correlated in the Japanese (Kitayama, Markus, & Kurokawa, 2000). Evidence from the work of Mesquita, Kitayama and Markus, and their collaborators suggests that the socially engaged dimension is more important in Japan than is valence, and the shame classification study in India and the United States, referred to previously, supports the same idea.

Looking at the contrast between humans and other animals, one of the most striking differences is the high frequency of moral emotions in humans (Haidt, 2001; see also chapter 45, this volume) as opposed to their virtual absence in animals. These emotions are notably much more common in the case of moral violations (negative) than of positive (morally uplifting) elicitors.

In the domain of liking and disliking, there is a striking human-animal distinction that has been rarely noted. Acquired likes, including preferences and values, seem to be much more common and robust in humans. To function well in a cultural context, humans have to learn a wide range of behaviors, values, and beliefs. A well-enculturated person likes what his or her culture values and dislikes what the culture shuns. Such a solution reduces conflict, allowing more time and energy for other life and social functions, and is more efficient than a purely instrumental reaction to cultural values. Cultural values imply many positive, as well as negative, feelings. I have suggested elsewhere (Rozin, 1982) that these demands may account for the fact that humans have a strong proclivity to develop very strong, lifelong likings for all kinds of objects and activities, such as specific foods, pets, particular principles and institutions, and hobbies. This may be a hedonic adaptation to culture; such strong acquired likes are very uncommon, so far as we know, in nonhuman animals.

## The Aesthetic and Mastery Domains

There is every reason to believe that something like an affective response to mastery is present in some nonhumans and is universal in humans. It is probably principally the *range* of mastery situations that is expanded. For the case of aesthetic affect, the situation is entirely different. There is no clear precedent for such reactions in nonhumans, whereas again, they seem universal in humans. Music, for example, is a human universal without any parallel in animals. Although there are major cultural differences in the types of experiences that produce aesthetic responses, the most remarkable fact is that such experiences exist.

Aesthetic affect may be described as an emotion, given its typical short time course and expressive characteristics. It is some form of pleasure, but unlike the sensory pleasures, it is not localizable; the pleasure of mousse comes from the mouth, but the pleasure of Mozart comes from the mind, certainly not the ear. Aesthetic emotions clearly involve high-level appraisals; perhaps we understand these best in music. Meyer (1956) explains the emotional experience of music as a set of learned (style-based) expectations, perhaps a touch of mastery emotion, punctuated by constrained violations of these expectations (somewhat along the line of some theories of humor). Narmour (1991) adds to this formulation the idea that we have innate expectations of sequence and that musical styles build around these, disconfirming them in specific ways. These accounts offer a possible explanation for the adaptive value of music and perhaps other aesthetic emotions. It is reasonable to assume that many animals, certainly including primates, are built with a mastery motivation/emotion system. One thing that engages it is the comprehension of previously baffling complexity. It is possible that the aesthetic emotions derive from comprehension of certain types of human-created complexity that we call art.

### The Moral Domain

It is in the moral and aesthetic domains that we see the greatest flowering of human affect. Morality is a pervasive aspect of human life that is affectively expressed principally in the domain of emotion. It is no accident that both chapters 47 and 45 in this volume, one with an adaptive orientation and the other with a cultural orientation, center on moral emotions. As Frank (1988; chapter 47, this volume) notes, emotions serve to keep us honest, to indicate our unfaithfulness, and as commitment devices that work for both the self and the other. Haidt (chapter 45, this volume) develops a taxonomy into which he fits nine moral emotions: other condemning (contempt, anger, disgust), self-condemning (shame, embarrassment, guilt), other suffering (compassion), and other praising (gratitude and elevation). Haidt puts order into a whole range of emotions and appropriately subsumes at least part of nine emotions under the moral rubric. He argues, along with Frank, that moral emotions are far from epiphenomena, that they are at the core of moral judgment and actions, functioning as causes (Haidt, in press, 2001).

### What Are the Processes by Which Cultures Have Transformed Emotions?

Compared with other primates, humans live in very high densities, in a world of artifacts that includes complex in-

stitutions and that requires incorporation of a wide set of rules and values. The world of "what matters" is much larger, including such things as the fate of one's nation or the preservation of the natural world (Asch, 1952). On the other hand, issues of hierarchy, deference, and memories for past encounters with individuals are surely part of the primate heritage.

At least superficially, the world of human affect has some new entries: aesthetic emotions; pleasure derived from innately negative experiences; and specific emotions, such as pride, embarrassment, shame, guilt, contempt, awe, and elevation (Haidt, in press). In other cases, there seem to be qualitative changes in the "basic emotions" that we share with other primates, that lead to sadness or anger about the plight of refugees 6,000 miles away, fear of global warming, disgust at child abuse by parents, or happiness about the prospects for peace in the Middle East. It is of evolutionary significance that indications of the presence of something like morality, bereavement, and understandings of complex social relations have been described in nonhuman primates (Cheney & Seyfarth, 1990; de Waal, 1996). However, it would seem that aesthetic, moral, and other such experiences are a major part of life only for humans.

My position is that for the basic and some other emotions, the major changes that have resulted from the development of culture have to do with appraisals—the widening range of eliciters and meanings that they induce. The output systems of expression, physiological response, and behaviors seem relatively unchanged. Significant differences exist across cultures in the output systems (Mesquita, chapter 46, this volume; Mesquita & Frijda, 1992; Scherer & Wallbott, 1994). As Mesquita notes in chapter 46, substantial developments of conscious/intentional modulation of emotion also occur at all levels, from avoiding eliciters to reinterpreting them to inhibiting behaviors, expressions, and physiological responses. The high level of emotion modulation in humans is important and may be an outcome of cognitive developments, the development of consciousness, and planning abilities. It is not discussed further here but is treated fully in chapter 46.

There are two general types of evolutionary accounts for the explosion of types of affect in humans. These accounts can refer to either biological or cultural evolution. One is that genuine new affect systems arise in humans. This position implies that distinctive expressions and behaviors come into play, that is, that there are new "Ekman emotion programs" (Ekman, 1992). This may well have happened, but it is worth noting that one reason the basic emotions keep reappearing in discussions of emotion is that they have distinctive expressions and that these tend to be lacking for the more elaborated human emotions. However, there may be some truly unique human emotions. Haidt's (in press; chapter 45, this volume) description of elevation, an emotion resulting from observing a morally admirable act in another, and one which has no clear expressive component, may be one such unique emotion.

A second account proposes that most human changes result from expansion of preexisting systems. In some cases, this would qualify as preadaptation (Bock, 1959; Mayr, 1960) or as exaptation (Gould & Vrba, 1982). Either process involves use of an existing system for a new purpose; preadaptation presumes that the existing system already had another adaptive value, and exaptation does not make this assumption. I propose that most of the major human innovations in the domain of affect involve preadaptations, in which additional, much elaborated meaning/appraisal systems are attached to emotion programs that already exist in nonhumans. In some cases, such as anger and fear, the systems are salient in many nonhuman animals. In others, such as shame and pride, the systems are not salient in most mammals and appear principally in nonhuman primates, in a form less common and distinct than they do in humans.

A clear example of preadaptation involves the human mouth. The mouth evolved for food and fluid intake (and for respiratory exchange). The tongue and teeth, in humans and other mammals, serve this purpose admirably. However, in human evolution, the mouth was co-opted as part of the language articulatory system, and the teeth, tongue, and oral cavity acquired vital linguistic functions in addition to their food processing functions. Hence, in later human evolution, properties of the mouth and pharynx have been shaped by natural selection to improve language functions.

Our analysis of disgust (Rozin, Haidt, McCauley, & Imada, 1997; see also chapter 45, this volume), exemplifies the preadaptive account, in which new elicitors and meanings become attached to an older emotion program. We suggest that disgust began, both phylogenetically and ontogenetically, as part of a food rejection system. In cultural evolution and development, the expressive and output side of this system remained more or less constant. But the elicitors and accompanying meanings and appraisals expanded, depending on the culture and historical time, to include reminders of our animal nature (such as gore and death), contact with most other human beings, and certain types of moral offenses.

In cultural evolution, the range of elicitors that engage a basic biological system can be extended through socialization. The same preadaptive type of process occurs in development: Systems may appear early in development in narrow domains, and the domains in which they are applied may become broader over development. In part, this is what Piaget (1955) meant by *décalage* and by the transition from domain-bound concrete operations to more domain-free formal operations. This type of developmental sequence can be described as increased accessibility (Rozin, 1976). For disgust, it implies the progressive engagement of the basic disgust emotion program for distasteful foods, foods objectionable because of their nature or origin, reminders of animal nature, contact with strangers, and last, perhaps, certain moral offenses.

As indicated by Haidt (chapter 45, this volume), Fessler's (in press) formulation of shame and protoshame and Keltner's (1995) linking of appeasement to embarrassment establish the same type of preadaptive accounts of elaborated human emotions. Frank's (1988; chapter 47, this volume) account of the functions of emotion, related to expanded concerns about deception and reputation in humans, may also fall under the rubric of preadaptation.

I have argued, along the same lines, that the wide range of human pleasures and pains, including aesthetic pleasures, derives its basic experiential character from the fundamental life-protecting inputs from the skin surface and apertures (Rozin, 1999). That is, at some point in the final common path of experience, the pleasures of genital touch, chocolate, and Mozart may converge on a basic positive/approach system, which imparts a particular general positive experience. Presumably, context, such as the localization of skin sensations or the memory of the music, allows us to attribute the pleasure to its source and perhaps in this action changes the experience itself.

A major feature of the evolution of the brain is encephalization—increased participation, control, or modulation by higher (ultimately, cortical) centers (Jerison, 1977). Encephalization occurs within the context of hierarchical organization, in which lower centers remain essentially intact (Hughlings Jackson, 1958). This feature of biological evolution may be mirrored in cultural evolution, as affects organized at lower brain levels come to be influenced by cultural values, largely through expansion of appraisals and elicitors, superimposed on emotion programs organized at subcortical levels.

In short, the great cognitive expansion of the world of humans and the world of artifacts it has created may have capitalized on a rather conservative preexisting affect system, allowing us to experience pleasure from Mozart, fear of death and atomic weapons, anger at the immoral acts of others, disgust at loss of purity, shame at a poor performance, and pride at the success of our favorite football team.

## NOTE

The preparation of this chapter was supported by research funds from the Edmund J. and Louise W. Kahn Faculty Excellence Chair in Psychology at the University of Pennsylvania.

## REFERENCES

Ariely, D. (1998). Combining experiences over time: The effects of duration, intensity changes and on-line measurements on retrospective pain evaluations. *Journal of Behavioral Decision Making, 11*, 19–45.

Asch, S. (1952). *Social psychology.* New York: Prentice Hall.

Babbitt, I. (Trans.). (1936). *The Dhammapada.* New York: New Directions.

Baumeister, R., Bratslavsky, E., Finkenauer, C. & Vohs, K. (2001). Bad is stronger than good. *Review of General Psychology, 5,* 323–370.

Bentham, J. (1948). *Principles of morals and legislation.* New York: Hafner. (Original work published 1789)

Berridge, K. C. (1999). Pleasure, pain, desire, and dread: Hidden core processes of emotion. In D. Kahneman, E. Diener, & N. Schwarz (Eds.), *Well-being: The foundations of hedonic psychology* (pp. 525–557). New York: Russell Sage Foundation.

Berridge, K. C., & Grill, H. J. (1983). Alternating ingestive and aversive consummatory responses suggest a two-dimensional analysis of palatability in rats. *Behavioral Neuroscience, 97,* 221–231.

Bock, W. J. (1959). Preadaptation and multiple evolutionary pathways. *Evolution, 13,* 194–211.

Brown, J. S. (1948). Gradients of approach and avoidance responses and their relation to level of motivation. *Journal of Comparative and Physiological Psychology, 41,* 450–465.

Cabanac, M. (1971). Physiological role of pleasure. *Science, 173,* 1103–1107.

Cabanac, M. (1985). Preferring for pleasure. *American Journal of Clinical Nutrition, 42,* 1151–1155.

Cacioppo, J. T., & Gardner, W. L. (1999). Emotion. *Annual Review of Psychology, 50,* 191–214.

Cheney, D. L., & Seyfarth, R. M. (1990). *How monkeys see the world.* Chicago: University of Chicago Press.

Damasio, A. R. (1994). *Descartes' error: Emotion, reason, and the human brain.* New York: Putnam.

Darwin, C. (1998). *The expression of the emotions in man and animals.* New York: Oxford University Press. (Original work published 1872).

Davidson, R. J., Ekman, P., Saron, C., Senulis, J., & Friesen, W. V. (1990). Approach/withdrawal and cerebral asymmetry: Emotional expression and brain physiology: I. *Journal of Personality and Social Psychology, 58,* 330–341.

Davidson, R. J., & Irwin, W. (1999). The functional neuroanatomy of emotion and affective style. *Trends in Cognitive Science, 3,* 11–21.

de Waal, F. (1996). *Good natured: The origins of right and wrong in humans and other animals.* Cambridge, MA: Harvard University Press.

Diener, E., & Emmons, R. A. (1985). The independence of positive and negative affect. *Journal of Personality and Social Psychology, 47,* 1105–1117.

Duncker, K. (1941). On pleasure, emotion, and striving. *Philosophy and Phenomenological Research, 1,* 391–430.

Ekman, P. (1992). An argument for basic emotions. *Cognition and Emotion, 6,* 169–200.

Elster, J., & Loewenstein, G. (1992). Utility from memory and anticipation. In G. Loewenstein & J. Elster (Eds.), *Choice over time* (pp. 213–234). New York: Russell Sage Foundation.

Fessler, D. T. (in press). Towards an understanding of the universality of second order emotions. In A. Hinton (Ed.), *Beyond nature or nurture: Biocultural approaches to the emotions.* Cambridge, England: Cambridge University Press.

Frank, R. (1988). *Passions within reason.* New York: Norton.

Fredrickson, B. L., & Kahneman, D. (1993). Duration neglect in retrospective evaluation of affective episodes. *Journal of Personality and Social Psychology, 65,* 45–55.

Fridlund, A. J. (1994). *Human facial expression: An evolutionary view.* San Diego, CA: Academic Press.

Garcia, J., Hankins, W. G., & Rusiniak, K. W. (1974). Behavioral regulation of the *milieu interne* in man and rat. *Science, 185,* 824–831.

Gilbert, D. T., Pinel, E. C., Wilson, T. D., Blumberg, S. J., & Wheatley, T. P. (1998). Immune neglect: A source of durability bias in affective forecasting. *Journal of Personality and Social Psychology, 75* (3), 617–638.

Gould, S. J., & Vrba, E. S. (1982). Exaptation: A missing term in the science of form. *Paleobiology, 8,* 4–15.

Grill, H. J., & Norgren, R. (1978). The taste reactivity test: I. Oro-facial responses to gustatory stimuli in neurologically normal rats. *Brain Research, 143,* 263–279.

Haidt, J. (in press). Elevation and the positive psychology of morality. In C. L. M. Keyes & J. Haidt (Eds.), *Flourishing: Positive psychology and the life well-lived.* Washington, DC: American Psychological Association.

Haidt, J. (2001). The emotional dog and its rational tail: A social intuitionist approach to moral judgment. *Psychological Review.*

Hejmadi, A. (1999). Classical Hindu Indian emotion theory: Implications for interdisciplinary and cross-cultural research. Manuscript submitted for publication.

Hejmadi, A., Davidson, R., & Rozin, P. (2000). Exploring Hindu Indian emotion expressions: Evidence for accurate recognition by Americans and Indians. *Psychological Science, 11,* 183–187.

Hughlings Jackson, J. (Ed.). (1958). *Selected writings of John Hughlings Jackson (Vols. 1 & 2).* London: Staples Press.

Jerison, H. J. (1977). The theory of encephalization. *Annals of the New York Academy of Sciences, 299,* 146–160.

Kahneman, D., Fredrickson, B. L., Schreiber, C. A., & Redelmeier, D. A. (1993). When more pain is preferred to less: Adding a better end. *Psychological Science, 4,* 401–405.

Kahneman, D., Knetsch, J. L., & Thaler, R. H. (1991). The endowment effect, loss aversion, and status quo bias. *Journal of Economic Perspectives, 5,* 193–206.

Kahneman, D., & Snell, J. (1992). Predicting a change in taste: Do people know what they will like? *Journal of Behavioral Decision Making, 5,* 187–200.

Kahneman, D., Wakker, P. P., & Sarin, R. (1997). Back to Bentham? Explorations of experienced utility. *Quarterly Journal of Economics, 112,* 375–405.

Keltner, D. (1995). Signs of appeasement: Evidence for the distinct displays of embarrassment, amusement, and shame. *Journal of Personality and Social Psychology, 68,* 441–454.

Kitayama, S., Markus, H. R., & Kurokawa, M. (2000). Culture, emotion, and well-being: Good feelings in Japan and the United States. *Cognition and Emotion, 14*(1), 93–124.

Loewenstein, G., & Schkade, D. (1999). Wouldn't it be nice? Predicting future feelings. In D. Kahneman, E. Diener, & N. Schwarz (Eds.), *Well-being: The foundations of hedonic psychology* (pp. 85–105). New York: Russell Sage Foundation.

Markus, H. R., & Kitayama, S. (1991). Culture and the self: Implications for cognition, emotion and motivation. *Psychological Review, 98,* 224–253.

Mayr, E. (1960). The emergence of evolutionary novelties.

In S. Tax (Ed.), *Evolution after Darwin: Vol. 1. The evolution of life* (pp. 349–380). Chicago: University of Chicago Press.

Mesquita, B., & Frijda, N. H. (1992). Cultural variations in emotions: A review. *Psychological Bulletin, 112,* 179–204.

Mesquita, B., & Karasawa, M. (2000). *Emotion words: The difference between prototypical concepts and daily experiences.* Unpublished manuscript.

Meyer, L. (1956). *Emotion and meaning in music.* Chicago: University of Chicago Press.

Narmour, E. (1991). The top-down and bottom-up systems of musical implication: Building on Meyer's theory of emotional syntax. *Music Perception, 9,* 1–26.

Osgood, C. E., May, W. H., & Miron, M. S. (1975). *Cross-cultural universals of affective meaning.* Urbana: University of Illinois Press.

Parducci, A. (1995). *Happiness, pleasure, and judgment: The contextual theory and its applications.* Mahwah, NJ: Erlbaum.

Parker, L. A. (1982). Nonconsummatory and consummatory behavioral CRs elicited by lithium- and amphetamine-paired flavors. *Learning and Motivation, 13,* 281–303.

Peeters, G. (1971). The positive-negative asymmetry: On cognitive consistency and positivity bias. *European Journal of Social Psychology, 1,* 455–474.

Peeters, G., & Czapinski, J. (1990). Positive-negative asymmetry in evaluations: The distinction between affective and informational effects. In W. Stroebe & M. Hewstone (Eds.), *European Review of Social Psychology* (Vol. 1, pp. 33–60). New York: Wiley.

Pelchat, M. L., & Rozin, P. (1982). The special role of nausea in the acquisition of food dislikes by humans. *Appetite, 3,* 341–351.

Pelchat, M. L., Grill, H. J., Rozin, P., & Jacobs, J. (1983). Quality of acquired responses to tastes by *Rattus norvegicus* depends on type of associated discomfort. *Journal of Comparative Psychology, 97,* 140–153.

Piaget, J. (1955). Les stades du developpement intellectuel de l'enfant et de l'adolescent. In P. Osterrieth, P. Piaget, R. Saussure, J. Tanner, H. Wallon, R. Zazzo, B. Inhelder, & A. Roy (Eds.), *Le probleme des stades en psychologie de l'enfant* (pp. 33–113). Paris: Presses Universitaires.

Rozin, P. (1976). The evolution of intelligence and access to the cognitive unconscious. In J. A. Sprague & A. N. Epstein (Eds.), *Progress in psychobiology and physiological psychology* (Vol. 6, pp. 245–280). New York: Academic Press.

Rozin, P. (1982). Human food selection: The interaction of biology, culture and individual experience. In L. M. Barker (Ed.), *The psychobiology of human food selection* (pp. 225–254.) Westport, CT: AVI.

Rozin, P. (1990). Getting to like the burn of chili pepper: Biological, psychological and cultural perspectives. In B. G. Green, J. R. Mason, & M. L. Kare (Eds.), *Chemical irritation in the nose and mouth* (pp. 231–269). New York: Dekker.

Rozin, P. (1999). Preadaptation and the puzzles and properties of pleasure. In D. Kahneman, E. Diener, & N. Schwarz (Eds.), *Well-being: The foundations of hedonic psychology* (pp. 109–133). New York: Russell Sage.

Rozin, P. (2000). *Five principles relating cultural differences to individual differences.* Unpublished manuscript.

Rozin, P., Berman, L., & Royzman, E. (1999). Negativity and positivity biases across 17 natural languages. Unpublished manuscript.

Rozin, P., & Fallon, A. E. (1980). Psychological categorization of foods and non-foods: A preliminary taxonomy of food rejections. *Appetite, 1,* 193–201.

Rozin, P., Haidt, J., McCauley, C. R., & Imada, S. (1997). The cultural evolution of disgust. In H. M. Macbeth (Ed.), *Food preferences and taste: Continuity and change* (pp. 65–82). Oxford, England: Berghahn.

Rozin, P., & Kalat, J. W. (1971). Specific hungers and poison avoidance as adaptive specializations of learning. *Psychological Review, 78,* 459–486.

Rozin, P., & Nemeroff, C. J. (1990). The laws of sympathetic magic: A psychological analysis of similarity and contagion. In J. Stigler, G. Herdt, & R. A. Shweder (Eds.), *Cultural psychology: Essays on comparative human development* (pp. 205–232). Cambridge, England: Cambridge University Press.

Rozin, P., Nemeroff, C., Horowitz, M., Gordon, B., & Voet, W. (1995). The borders of the self: Contamination sensitivity and potency of the mouth, other apertures, and body parts. *Journal of Research in Personality, 29,* 318–340.

Rozin, P., & Royzman, E. (2001). Negativity bias, negativity dominance, and contagion. *Personality and Social Psychology Review.*

Rozin, P., & Schull, J. (1988). The adaptive-evolutionary point of view in experimental psychology. In R. C. Atkinson, R. J. Herrnstein, G. Lindzey, & R. D. Luce (Eds.), *Handbook of experimental psychology* (pp. 503–546). New York: Wiley-Interscience.

Ruckmick, C. A. (1925). The psychology of pleasantness. *Psychological Review, 32,* 362–383.

Scherer, K. R., & Wallbott, H. G. (1994). Evidence for universality and cultural variation of differential emotion response patterning. *Journal of Personality and Social Psychology, 66,* 310–328.

Schneirla, T. C. (1959). An evolutionary and developmental theory of biphasic processes underlying approach and withdrawal. *Nebraska Symposium on Motivation* (pp. 1–42). Lincoln: University of Nebraska Press.

Sherrington, C. (1906). *The integrative action of the nervous system.* London: Constable.

Shweder, R. A. (1991). *Thinking through cultures.* Cambridge, MA: Harvard University Press.

Shweder, R. A., Much, N. C., Mahapatra. M., & Park, L. (1997). The "big three" of morality (autonomy, community, divinity) and the "big three" explanations of suffering. In A. Brandt & P. Rozin (Eds.), *Morality and health* (pp. 119–169). New York: Routledge.

Smith, W. J. (1965). *The behavior of communicating.* Cambridge, MA: Harvard University Press.

Taylor. S. E. (1991). Asymmetrical effects of positive and negative events: The mobilization-minimization hypothesis. *Psychological Bulletin, 110,* 67–85.

Troland, L. T. (1928). *The fundamentals of human motivation.* New York: Van Nostrand.

Watson, D., Clark, L. A., & Tellegen, A. (1988). Development and validation of brief measures of positive and negative affect: The PANAS Scale. *Journal of Personality and Social Psychology, 54,* 1063–1070.

Young, P. T. (1959). The role of affective processes in learning and motivation. *Psychological Review, 66,* 104–125.

# 45

## THE MORAL EMOTIONS

Jonathan Haidt

Morality dignifies and elevates. When Adam and Eve ate the forbidden fruit, God said "Behold, the man is become as one of us, to know good and evil" (Gen. 3:22). In many of the world's religious traditions, the good go up, to heaven or a higher rebirth, and the bad go down, to hell or a lower rebirth. Even among secular people, moral motives are spoken of as the "highest" and "noblest" motives, whereas greed and lust are regarded as "baser" or "lower" instincts. Morality is therefore like the temple on the hill of human nature: It is our most sacred attribute, a trait that is often said to separate us from other animals and bring us closer to God.

For 2,400 years, the temple has been occupied by the high priests of reason. Plato (4th century B.C./1949) presented a model of a divided self in which reason, firmly ensconced in the head, rules over the passions, which rumble around in the chest and stomach (*Timaeus*, 69). Aristotle had a similar conception of reason as the wise master and emotion as the foolish slave: "anger seems to listen to reason, but to hear wrong, like hasty servants, who run off before they have heard everything their master tells them, and fail to do what they were ordered, or like dogs, which bark as soon as there is a knock without waiting to see if the visitor is a friend" (*Ethics*, 1962, 1149a). Throughout the long history of moral philosophy, the focus has generally been on moral reasoning, whereas the moral emotions have been regarded with some suspicion (Solomon, 1993).

Even when moral psychology finally separated itself from moral philosophy and began to make its own empir-

ical contributions, it invested almost all of its capital in the study of moral reasoning. Piaget (1932/1965) studied the child's developing understanding of fairness and rules. Kohlberg (1969; Kohlberg, Levine, & Hewer, 1983) built on Piaget to provide both a measurement tool and a conceptual framework for the study of moral reasoning, and the field grew rapidly. Kohlberg's work was an important part of the cognitive revolution, demonstrating that morality, like language, could be studied as a system of transformations of underlying cognitive constructs.

Yet as the cognitive revolution matured, researchers recognized the growing need for a parallel "affect revolution" (Tomkins, 1981). Table 45.1 shows that this revolution has indeed taken place, for the moral emotions have been growth stocks in the 1980s and 1990s. Although the number of journal articles on morality and moral reasoning rose in the 1980s and then began to decline in the 1990s, the number of articles on emotion in general, and on the moral emotions in particular, has increased greatly. Table 45.1 shows that the "old academy" stocks of empathy and guilt, which were the most widely studied moral emotions in the 1970s, have not grown in the 1990s, whereas the "new academy" stocks of anger, shame, and disgust have racked up impressive gains in scholarship. As research on the moral emotions has broadened beyond empathy and guilt, a new appreciation has arisen of what they as a group can do. A few theorists have even begun to claim that the emotions are in fact in charge of the temple of morality and that moral reasoning is really just a servant masquerading as the high priest (Haidt, 2001;

852

Table 45.1. Journal Articles in PsycINFO on Selected Emotions and Topics

| Emotion | 1975–1979 | 1985–1989 | 1995–1999 | % Increase |
|---|---|---|---|---|
| Disgust | 0 | 10 | 36 | infinite |
| Shame | 18 | 70 | 173 | 860 |
| Anger | 105 | 309 | 525 | 400 |
| Contempt | 1 | 9 | 4 | 300 |
| Embarrassment | 10 | 31 | 22 | 120 |
| Empathy or sympathy | 195 | 285 | 303 | 55 |
| Guilt | 158 | 240 | 199 | 26 |
| Moral Emotion Index[a] | 487 | 954 | 1262 | 159 |
| *Emotion* or *emotions*[b] | 211 | 933 | 1300 | 516 |
| *Moral* or *morality*[b] | 505 | 739 | 698 | 38 |
| *Moral reasoning*[b] | 54 | 110 | 81 | 50 |
| Fear[c] | 535 | 815 | 983 | 83 |

*Note.* The count was limited to journal articles that contained the word(s) in the left-hand column either in the key-phrase field or in the title of the article. Sorted by declining % increase from the late 1970s to the late 1990s.

[a]Moral Emotion Index refers to the simple sum of the seven moral emotions listed.

[b]These three terms are included to show that research on the emotions has increased greatly, whereas research on morality and moral reasoning has grown more slowly and has declined since the 1980s.

[c]Research on fear, a nonmoral emotion, has grown more slowly than has research on most of the moral emotions.

Wilson, 1993). This chapter is a report from the hill, including a census of the moral emotions and a discussion of the ways in which moral emotions and moral reasoning work together in the creation of human morality.

## What Is a Moral Emotion?

How can we identify the subset of emotions that should be called moral emotions? One approach would be first to define morality and then to say that the moral emotions are the emotions that respond to moral violations or that motivate moral behavior. Attempts to define morality have long been made by philosophers, who have generally taken one of two approaches (Gewirth, 1984). The first approach is to specify the formal conditions that make a statement a moral statement (e.g., that it is prescriptive, that it is universalizable, and that it overrides nonmoral concerns, such as expedience; Hare, 1981). The second approach is to specify the material conditions of a moral issue, for example, that moral rules and judgments "must bear on the interest or welfare either of society as a whole or at least of persons other than the judge or agent" (Gewirth, 1984, p. 978). This second approach is more promising for psychological work, for it does not tie morality to language, thereby allowing discussions of the origins of the moral emotions in prelinguistic animals and children. The second approach suggests a preliminary definition of the moral emotions as *those emotions that are linked to the interests or welfare either of society as a whole or at least of persons other than the judge or agent.*

In other words, all emotions are responses to perceived changes, threats, or opportunities in the world, but in most cases it is the *self* whose interests are directly affected by these events. It is presumably because quick and reliable emotional responses were adaptive to individuals that emotions evolved in the first place (Lazarus, 1991a; Plutchik, 1980). The puzzle of the moral emotions is that *Homo sapiens,* far more than any other animal, appears to devote a considerable portion of its emotional life to reacting to social events that do not directly affect the self. The main goal of this chapter is to classify and describe these emotions that go beyond the direct interests of the self.

### The Two Prototypical Features of a Moral Emotion

Emotions are often analyzed into component features, such as an eliciting event, a facial expression, a physiological change, a phenomenological experience, and a motivation or action tendency (Frijda, 1986; Russell, 1991a; Scherer, 1984; Shweder, 1994). Two of these components are useful for identifying the moral emotions, for they are easily linked to the interests of society or of other people: elicitors[1] and action tendencies.

#### Disinterested Elicitors

Some emotions, such as fear and happiness, occur primarily when good or bad things happen to the self. They can also occur when good or bad things happen to another person, but such reactions seem to require the self to be related to the other (as when one is happy for a friend's success) or to identify temporarily with the other (as when one fears for the protagonist in a movie). Other emotions can be triggered easily and frequently even when the self has no stake in the triggering event. Simply reading about an injustice or seeing a photograph of a suffering child can trigger anger or sympathy. Anger may be most frequently triggered by perceived injustices against the self, and sympathy may be most strongly felt for one's kin, but the point here is that some emotions are easily triggered by triumphs, tragedies, and transgressions that do not directly touch the self, whereas other emotions are not. The more an emotion tends to be triggered by such disinterested elicitors, the more it can be considered a prototypical moral emotion.

### Prosocial Action Tendencies

Emotions generally motivate some sort of action as a response to the eliciting event. The action is often not taken, but the emotion puts the person into a motivational and cognitive state in which there is an increased tendency to engage in certain goal-related actions (e.g., revenge, affiliation, comforting, etc). These action tendencies (Frijda, 1986) can be ranked by the degree to which they either benefit others or else uphold or benefit the social order.

Crossing these two criteria creates a two-dimensional space (Figure 45.1) in which the $x$ axis shows the degree to which an emotion can be elicited by situations that do not directly harm or benefit the self and the $y$ axis shows the degree to which an emotion's action tendencies are prosocial. The most prototypical moral emotions (elevation, compassion, anger, and guilt) are shown in the upper right corner. The placement of emotions in Figure 45.1 is highly speculative, and each reader may favor a different arrangement. For now Figure 45.1 is simply meant to illustrate that there is no neat division between the moral emotions and the nonmoral emotions. Each emotion and

its many variants can partake to a greater or lesser degree in each of the two features that make an emotion a moral emotion. Anger, for example, is shown in the upper right corner because in its "best case" scenario it can be felt in disinterested situations, with highly prosocial action tendencies. In other cases, however (e.g., violent rage triggered by sexual frustration), anger could be placed in the lower left, with highly self-interested appraisals and antisocial action tendencies.

### Selfish Genes and Moral Emotions

It is important to note at the outset that all of the moral emotions are likely to have *indirect* benefits to the self. Many writers, beginning with Darwin (1874/1998), have wondered how the competition of natural selection could create altruistic individuals. Many of the current answers to this question draw on game theory (Maynard Smith & Price, 1973) and on Trivers's (1971) ideas about the role of emotions in reciprocal altruism. The general point of these theories is that the emotions act as "commitment devices" (Frank, 1988) that force individuals to follow strategies in repeated-play games that are good for them in the long run, even if they appear nonoptimal at any given moment (see also Ridley, 1996; Sober & Wilson, 1998).

So when deciding where in Figure 45.1 to place an emotion, it is not relevant that the emotion confers long-term benefits on its bearers. A more relevant heuristic is to imagine a perfectly selfish creature, the mythical *Homo economicus*,[2] who cares only about her own well-being and who cooperates with others only to the extent that she expects a positive net payoff from the transaction. *Homo*

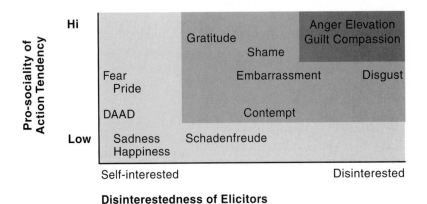

Figure 45.1 The moral emotions, plotted by the two criteria that make an emotion a moral emotion. *Note*: Moral emotionhood is a matter of degree. More prototypical moral emotions are near the upper right corner. The placement of each emotion is highly speculative, and many alternate arrangements could be justified. Each emotion has many forms or subtypes, for example, righteous indignation for anger; only the most moral subtype of each emotion is shown. DAAD = distress at another's distress.

*economicus* may experience negative affect when some resource is taken away from her, but she would retaliate only if she thought that the benefits of retaliation outweighed the costs. And she would have no affective reactions when good or bad things happened to other people. An alternative definition of the moral emotions can therefore be stated as *the difference between the emotional life of Homo sapiens and the emotional life of Homo economicus* (or of a psychopath, whom *Homo economicus* resembles; Cleckley, 1955).

### Emotion Families

There has been heated debate about whether there is a set of "basic" emotions (Ekman, 1992a, 1994a; Izard, 1977; Tomkins, 1962, 1963) or whether emotions should be thought of as scripts or sets of components that can be mixed and matched, allowing for a very large number of possible emotions (Russell, 1991a; Shweder, 1994; Wierzbicka, 1992). However, even those who argue for a small set of basic emotions acknowledge that each emotion comes in many different types or variants. Ekman (1992) calls the set of all such variants on a basic theme an emotion "family." For example, indignation, irritation, and rage are not identical in their eliciting conditions, action tendencies, or facial expressions, but they are somewhat similar, just as siblings are both similar and different in their physical appearance. In this chapter, therefore, I adopt the emotion family perspective but take it one step further by discussing extended families, such as the traditional Indian family. In a traditional Indian joint-family household, several brothers and their wives and children live together, often with each subfamily in an adjoining hut, within a single compound.

Using the Indian joint family as a metaphor for emotion families, the principal moral emotions can be divided into two large and two small joint families. The large families are the "other-condemning" family, in which the three brothers are contempt, anger, and disgust (and their many children, such as indignation and loathing), and the "self-conscious" family (shame, embarrassment, and guilt; see Rozin, Lowery, Imada, & Haidt, 1999, for an earlier discussion of these two families). I call the two smaller families the "other-suffering" family (compassion) and the "other-praising" family (gratitude and elevation). The rest of this chapter presents brief biographies of these four families. The biographies are highly abridged, focusing on the eliciting conditions and action tendencies that make each emotion a moral emotion.

An important theme of this chapter is that most of the emotions reviewed have cognitively simpler forms or precursors that can be seen in infants and in other animals. In most cases these simple forms do not qualify as moral emotions. I suggest that one reason that the moral emotions have not been given their due in research on moral-

ity is that the overzealous pursuit of parsimony has led many researchers to focus on the simplest forms of each emotion rather than on the more complex variants on which human morality depends.

A second theme of this chapter is that the moral emotions are simultaneously panhuman products of evolution and cultural scripts that are shaped by local values and meanings. The four joint families of emotion can be found in all cultures, but differences in some of the components of emotional experience lead to slightly different sets of children inhabiting the corresponding households in different cultures (Ellsworth, 1994; Mesquita, Frijda, & Scherer, 1997; Shweder & Haidt, 2000).

A third theme of this chapter is that there is more to morality than altruism and niceness. Emotions that motivate helping behavior are easy to label as moral emotions, but emotions that lead to ostracism, shaming, and murderous vengeance are no less a part of our moral nature. The human social world is a miraculous and tenuous coconstruction of its participants, and any emotion that leads people to care about that world and to support, enforce, or improve its integrity should be considered a moral emotion, even when the actions taken are not "nice."

## The Other-Condemning Emotions: Contempt, Anger, and Disgust

Evolutionary theorists who have searched for the origins of human morality have generally found its source in the dynamics and difficulties of reciprocal altruism (de Waal, 1982; Frank, 1988; Ridley & Dawkins, 1981; Trivers, 1971). Many social species, from vampire bats to chimpanzees, have figured out the "trick" of playing tit for tat within dyads, such that cooperating pairs end up reaping more benefits than either member would on its own (Axelrod, 1984; Wilkinson, 1984). Reciprocal altruism can work, however, only as a two-edged sword: Individuals must be built with a motivation to cooperate with those who have cooperated in the past, but they must also be built with a motivation to avoid or to actively punish those who have tried to cheat or exploit them (Trivers, 1971).

Most social animals, however, are doomed to size up interaction partners by themselves. If vampire bat A fails to share a blood meal with vampire bat B, after bat B shared with bat A, bat B does not go around to bats C, D, and E to warn them away from future interactions with bat A. Among human beings, however, this is exactly what happens. Language and highly developed social-cognitive abilities allow human beings to keep track of the reputations of hundreds of individuals (Dunbar, 1996). In endless hours of gossip, people work together to catch cheaters, liars, hypocrites, and others who are trying to fake the appearance of being reliable interaction partners. Human beings, then, live in a rich moral world of reputations and third-party concerns. We care what people do to each other, and we readily develop negative feelings toward individuals with whom we have never interacted. It is these negative feelings about the actions or character of others that unites the "other-condemning" emotions of contempt, anger, and disgust.

### Anger

Anger is perhaps the most underappreciated moral emotion. A search of PsycINFO shows that anger is usually thought of as an *immoral* emotion. Titles such as "Anger: The hidden destroyer" and "Controlling competitive anger among male soccer players" make anger sound like a dark primal urge that must be suppressed by cultural and educational forces. But for every spectacular display of angry violence, there are many more mundane cases of people indignantly standing up for what is right or angrily demanding justice for themselves or others (Tavris, 1982).

#### Elicitors

The reason anger has such a bad reputation may be that it can be seen clearly in rats, dogs, toddlers, and other creatures without a well-developed moral life. In such cognitively simple creatures, anger is generally said to be a response to goal blockage and frustration (Berkowitz & Heimer, 1989; Dollard & Miller, 1950; Stein, Trabasso, & Liwag, 1993). But there are other elicitors that lead to more recognizably moral responses. Aristotle (1941) linked anger with honor. He defined anger as "an impulse, accompanied by pain, to a conspicuous revenge for a conspicuous slight directed without justification towards what concerns oneself or toward what concerns one's friends" (*Rhetoric*, Bk 2, Ch.2). Note that anger is not just a response to insults, in which case it would be just a guardian of self-esteem. Anger is a response to *unjustified* insults, and anger can be triggered on behalf of one's friends, as well as oneself.

Empirical studies support and extend Aristotle's claims. In one of the first such studies, Stanley Hall (1898) collected detailed questionnaires from more than 2,000 people about their actual experiences of anger. Although his corpus included many cases of goal blockage and frustration, even these cases generally included an appraisal that somebody else had done something for which they had no justification or right. For example, a 20-year-old woman said:

> The chief causes are contradiction, especially if I
> am right; slights, especially to my parents or
> friends even more than myself; to have my veracity
> questioned; the sight of my older brother smoking

> when we are poor; injustice, dislike, or hate from
> those who fear to speak right out; being tired and
> out of sorts, etc . . . Injustice is the worst and its ef-
> fects last longest. (Hall, 1898, p. 538)

*Homo economicus* could never have given such a list. Similar findings emerge from studies by Baumeister, Stillwell, and Wotman (1990), Izard (1977), and Shaver, Schwartz, Kirson, and O'Connor (1987). All three studies collected open-ended descriptions of angry episodes and found that themes of frustration and goal blockage mixed with more moral concerns about being betrayed, insulted, and treated unfairly. Similarly, Scherer (1997) found that descriptions of angry episodes in a large cross-cultural study were rated by participants as eliciting the highest appraisals of unfairness and immorality, even higher than the appraisals of goal obstruction and unpleasantness.

#### Action Tendencies

The second part of Aristotle's definition of anger adds that anger "must always be attended by a certain pleasure—that which arises from the expectation of revenge (*Rhetoric*, Bk 2, Ch. 2)." More recent studies confirm that anger generally involves a motivation to attack, humiliate, or otherwise get back at the person who is perceived as acting unfairly or immorally (Izard, 1977; Shaver et al., 1987). The fact that anger often involves a motivation for revenge has been noted in a great many cultures (Nisbett & Cohen, 1996), some of which elevate blood feuds into a major cultural activity (Boehm, 1999; Frijda, 1994). Of course there are cultures and religions that exhort people to forswear revenge: "for it is written, vengeance is Mine; I will repay, saith the Lord" (Rom. 12:19). However, the mere fact that such exhortations must be frequently made testifies to the widespread human desire for revenge. Furthermore, it is rarely noted that the New Testament tries to sell its appeal by recasting kindness as vengeance. The next line in Romans is: "Therefore if thine enemy hunger, feed him; if he thirst, give him drink: *for in so doing thou shalt heap coals of fire on his head* [italics added]."

The action tendency of anger may appear at first glance to be both selfish and antisocial, and in many cases it is. But the motivation to redress injustices can also be felt strongly in third-party situations, in which the self has no stake. Racism, oppression, exploitation, and ethnic cleansing can all lead people with no ties to the victimized group to demand retaliatory or compensatory action. Even fictional accounts of injustice can lead to a desire for revenge. Haidt and Sabini (2000) showed clips from Hollywood films that portrayed injustice and then asked participants to rate a variety of alternative endings. Results showed that participants were unsatisfied by endings in which the victim found growth and fulfillment by accepting the loss and forgiving the transgressor. Participants were instead most satisfied by endings in which the perpetrator suffered, knew that the suffering was repayment for the transgression, suffered in a way that matched the initial transgression, and, if possible, suffered in a way that involved public humiliation.

### Disgust

The second brother in the other-condemning joint family is disgust. Like anger, disgust has both simpler and more complex forms, which must be distinguished to fully appreciate its moral nature.

#### Elicitors

Disgust is a response both to physical objects and to social violations. Thus Darwin offered this two-part definition: Disgust "refers to something revolting, primarily in relation to the sense of taste, as actually perceived or vividly imagined; and secondarily to anything which causes a similar feeling, through the sense of smell, touch, and even of eyesight" (1872/1965, p. 234). Similarly Lazarus (1991b) resorted to metaphor to unite the physical and social aspects of disgust: "taking in or standing too close to—metaphorically speaking—an indigestible object or idea" (p. 826). These and other definitions (Angyal, 1941; Ekman & Friesen, 1975; Rozin & Fallon, 1987; Tomkins, 1963; Wierzbicka, 1992) focus on the mouth and revulsion toward physical objects and then suggest that some class of nonphysical objects can cause a similar feeling of revulsion. But it turns out that this class is extraordinarily heterogeneous, ranging from incest to amputation to hypocrisy. How can we make sense of this class of elicitors and distinguish it from the larger class of "all disliked things"?

Rozin, Haidt, and McCauley (1993, 2000) offer an answer. They argue that disgust grew out of a distaste response found in other animals, which was then shaped by evolution to become a more generalized guardian of the mouth. Disgust rejects foods not principally for their sensory properties but for their ideational properties (e.g., the source of the food or its contact history). This food-related "core disgust" appears to be only a bit player in Western morality, showing up, for example, as a support of moral vegetarianism but not health vegetarianism (Rozin, Markwith, & Stoess, 1997). However, core disgust was well suited as a preadaptation (Mayr, 1960) for a more general rejection system, easily extended to a variety of bodily actions and issues. This expanded disgust can most succinctly be described as a "guardian of the temple of the body" (Haidt, Rozin, McCauley, & Imada, 1997, p. 114), for it is triggered by people who violate local cultural rules for how to use their bodies, particularly in domains of sex, drugs, and body modification (Haidt & Hersh, 2001; MacCoun, 1998). A general principle that guides this ex-

pansion in many cultures seems to be that disgust helps to draw lines that separate a group from groups or individuals that are thought to be below one's own group. Thus caste boundaries in India and racial segregation in the American South followed a disgust-like logic, in which the bodily activities of lower-status groups (eating, bathing, excreting, and even drinking from water fountains) had to be kept separate from those of the higher-status groups, lest the higher-status groups become contaminated. Rozin et al. (1993) refer to disgust at contact with people whose mere physical presence is thought to be contaminating as "interpersonal disgust."

But the expansion of disgust elicitors did not stop there. In many cultures and languages, the words and facial expressions used to express disgust toward rotting meat or feces are also used to condemn social transgressions that do not involve the body in any physically disgusting way (Haidt et al., 1997). Miller (1997) nominates the vices of hypocrisy, betrayal, cruelty, and fawning as the principal vices that elicit disgust, rather than anger or hatred. Survey evidence supports Miller's list of disgusting vices (Haidt, McCauley, & Rozin, 1994; Rozin, Lowery, & Ebert, 1994) but also suggests that the expansion of disgust into the sociomoral domain involves different issues in different cultures (Haidt et al., 1997). For Westerners, at least, sociomoral disgust can be described most succinctly as the guardian of the lower boundary of the category of humanity. People who "de-grade" themselves, or who in extreme cases blur the boundary between humanity and animality, elicit disgust in others. Disgust is a one-way border guard, however; it is triggered by people moving down, not by animals moving up (e.g., by a chimpanzee using sign language or by a dog wearing human clothing).

#### Action Tendencies

As the eliciters of disgust expanded from core disgust through sociomoral disgust, the action tendencies of disgust appear to have undergone much less change. All forms of disgust include a motivation to avoid, expel, or otherwise break off contact with the offending entity, often coupled to a motivation to wash, purify, or otherwise remove residues of any physical contact that was made with the entity (Rozin & Fallon, 1987; Rozin et al., 1993). This motivation is clearly adaptive when dealing with potentially lethal bacterial contamination of potential foods, but it appears to have made the transition into our moral and symbolic life with surprisingly little change. Thus people want nothing to do with the clothing or other possessions of evil people, such as a sweater worn by Adolph Hitler (Rozin, Markwith, & McCauley, 1994). Furthermore, the moral taint left in physical objects is almost impossible to remove. A sweater worn by a hated person cannot be rendered wearable by washing in hot water, or even by unravelling it and reknitting it (Nemeroff & Rozin, 1994). Even books that present socially disgusting ideas are treated as a contagious threat, often labeled as "filth," banned from libraries, and, in extreme cases, burned.

The action tendency of disgust is often prosocial. By ostracizing those who trigger moral disgust, people in a society set up a reward-and-punishment structure that acts as a strong deterrent to culturally inappropriate behaviors, particularly those involving the body. This disgust-based moral order may be disturbing to some people, particularly to political liberals and libertarians (Miller, 1997), who want to carve out a large protected zone of private behavior. Disgust has an unfortunate habit of bringing condemnation down on people for what they *are*, not just for what they *do*. Indeed, disgust is a major factor in the condemnation of homosexuals (Haidt & Hersh, 2001). But as stated previously, morality is not just about being nice. Attempts to ostracize and exclude homosexuals from schools, neighborhoods, and jobs may be immoral by the standards of most readers of this chapter, but it must be acknowledged that these attempts are often morally motivated—that is, they are attempts to impose, defend, or rectify a particular (conservative) moral order against perceived threats (Hunter, 1991; Lakoff, 1996).

### Contempt

Contempt is the middle brother of the other-condemning family. It falls so squarely in between anger and disgust that it is sometimes said to be a blend of the two (Plutchik, 1980), or else it is folded into the anger family (Lazarus, 1991a). Ekman and Friesen (1975) originally considered contempt to be a variant of disgust, but they elevated it to the status of a "basic" emotion in the 1980s, based on findings that the contempt expression is widely and reliably recognized and is distinguished both from anger and from disgust (Ekman & Friesen, 1986; Ekman & Heider, 1988). This finding has been challenged, because in several studies the contempt expression has been labeled not as contempt but as disgust (Russell, 1991b). However, the most recent studies find that the source of these conflicting findings appears to be that English speakers simply do not know the meaning of the word "contempt." Studies conducted in non-English-speaking nations find high rates of "correct" labeling (Haidt & Keltner, 1999; Matsumoto, 1992; Rozin et al., 1999), and studies that have asked English speakers to match the contempt expression to a story (Rosenberg & Ekman, 1995) or to make up their own potential elicitor (Haidt & Keltner, 1999) find that contempt performs about as well as the other "basic" emotions.

### Elicitors

Almost all writers who discuss the causes of contempt agree that it involves looking down on someone and feel-

ing morally superior (Ekman, 1994b; Izard, 1977). But if research on the facial expression of contempt is excluded, almost no other empirical research on contempt exists (see Table 45.1). Perhaps the most perceptive discussion of contempt comes from Miller (1997), who draws out the subtle ways in which contempt functions to mark out and maintain distinctions of rank and prestige. In hierarchical societies, contempt toward those beneath the self is a kind of cool indifference, a statement that the other is not even worthy of strong feelings such as anger. In more egalitarian societies, however, contempt is more often elicited by the perception that another person does not measure up, either to the position that he occupies or to the level of prestige that he claims for himself. Miller points out that in democratic societies it becomes common to feel "upward contempt," that is, the contempt of workers for bosses, of the working class for the upper class, and of nonelites for self-proclaimed elites of all sorts.

### Action Tendencies

Little has been written about the action tendency of contempt. Contempt is often said to be a "cool" emotion, relative to the heat of anger or the visceral power of disgust (Darwin, 1872/1965; Izard, 1977). Contempt motivates neither attack nor withdrawal; rather, it seems to cause social-cognitive changes such that the object of contempt will be treated with less warmth, respect, and consideration in future interactions (Oatley & Johnson-Laird, 1996). Contempt paints its victims as buffoons worthy of mockery or as nonpersons worthy of complete disregard. It therefore weakens other moral emotions, such as compassion.

### The Moral Importance of the Other-Condemning Emotions

The CAD-triad hypothesis (Rozin et al., 1999) proposes that the emotions of contempt, anger, and disgust (CAD) are responses to violations of Shweder's three moral codes—called, respectively, the ethics of community, autonomy, and divinity (Shweder, Much, Mahapatra, & Park, 1997). Rozin et al. (1999) found that American and Japanese participants consistently paired contempt (the word and the facial expression) with moral violations involving disrespect and violations of duty or hierarchy (the ethics of community); they paired anger with violations of rights and fairness (ethics of autonomy); and they paired disgust with violations of physical purity, such as food and sex taboos (ethics of divinity). Contempt, anger, and disgust therefore act as guardians of different portions of the moral order. People are exquisitely sensitive to the propriety of the actions of others, even when those actions do not affect themselves. Anger and disgust can be felt strongly toward people in third-party situations, so they are listed in

Figure 45.1 as involving (at least potentially) disinterested elicitors. Contempt can be felt in third-party situations, but because it is generally tied to the relative positions of the self and the object of contempt, strong contempt probably requires a larger dose of self-relevance.

As guardians of the moral order, all three emotions motivate people to change their relationships with moral violators. But only anger motivates direct action to repair the moral order and to make violators mend their ways. Anger thus can be considered the most prototypical moral emotion of the three (at least for Western cultures), followed by disgust, and lastly by contempt.

## The Self-Conscious Emotions: Shame, Embarrassment, and Guilt

Once people (or earlier hominids) began reacting with contempt, anger, and disgust to social violations, it became adaptive for individuals to monitor and constrain their own behavior. People have a strong need to belong to groups (Baumeister & Leary, 1995), and the self-conscious emotions seem designed to help people navigate the complexities of fitting into groups without triggering the contempt, anger, and disgust of others.

There is, however, an important ambiguity about how many members there are in the family. Most Western researchers list shame, embarrassment, and guilt as the principal self-conscious emotions, along with pride as a positive opposite of shame (M. Lewis, 1993; Tangney & Fischer, 1995). Yet anthropologists generally report that non-Western cultures see things differently. Most Asian cultures do not distinguish lexically[3] between shame and embarrassment; rather, in these cultures a single culturally central emotion combines what appear to be shame and embarrassment, along with shyness, modesty, and social fear (Abu-Lughod, 1986; Fessler, 1999; Heider, 1991; Levy, 1973; Menon & Shweder, 1994; Russell, 1991a). And in some non-Western cultures it has been suggested that guilt does not even exist or at least that it is culturally unelaborated or "hypocognated," whereas shame/embarrassment is highly elaborated or "hypercognated" (Benedict, 1946; Levy, 1973).

This cultural difference makes sense once it is realized that the self-conscious emotions depend critically on two of the most culturally variable aspects of social life: whether the self is construed as independent or as interdependent (Markus & Kitayama, 1991; see also Triandis, Bontempo, Villareal, Asai, & Lucca, 1988) and whether the social structure is hierarchical or egalitarian (Boehm, 1999). In this chapter I treat shame and embarrassment as discrete emotions but suggest that the discreteness of shame and embarrassment is itself culturally variable. In cultures with an interdependent construal of the self and a hierarchical social structure, embarrassment and shame

merge together into a single emotion of tremendous moral importance, whereas in cultures that are egalitarian and that have an independent construal of the self, embarrassment splits off from shame as a less prototypical moral emotion.

### Shame and Embarrassment

As with disgust, the key to understanding the moral nature of shame is to recognize that it has a phylogenetically older and simpler version. Fessler (in press) found that his informants in Dusun Baguk, Indonesia, used the word *malu* to describe two different sorts of shamelike experiences. Most cases involved the kinds of violations of norms that Westerners would recognize as shameful, but the remainder involved simply being in the presence of a high-ranking person. Almost every analysis of shamelike emotions within hierarchical societies reports a similar phenomenon (see especially *lajya* in Orissa, India; Menon & Shweder, 1994, and *hasham* among the Bedouins of Egypt; Abu-Lughod, 1986). Fessler further points out that displays of shame and of pride in Dusun Baguk, as in the West, are exact opposites of each other and are very similar to widespread mammalian displays of submission and dominance (eye contact avoided vs. sought; apparent body size decreased vs. increased; social interaction avoided vs. sought). Fessler therefore argues that there are two major forms of shame: a simpler "protoshame" that is caused simply by being in the presence of one's superiors in a dominance hierarchy and a more cognitively complex form of shame that is triggered by violating a norm and knowing that someone else knows about the violation. Just as sociomoral disgust involves expanding the elicitors of core disgust while keeping the output of the system relatively constant, shame appears to involve a similar expansion of protoshame.

Fessler's (1999) description of protoshame closely matches Keltner's analysis of embarrassment (Keltner, 1995; Keltner & Buswell, 1997). Keltner finds numerous similarities between human embarrassment and nonhuman appeasement displays. The expression of embarrassment includes all of the physical signs Fessler describes for protoshame, plus a few that may be unique to embarrassment, such as a face touch and a nervous or "silly" smile. Embarrassment is clearly related to hierarchical interactions: It is felt most easily when one is around people of higher status, and it is less likely to be experienced when one is around people of lower status (Keltner, Young, Oemig, Heerey, Monarch, 1998; Miller, 1996; see also Frijda & Mesquita, 1994, on shyness).

Putting Fessler's and Keltner's research together, the following argument can be made. There appears to be a panhuman emotional sensitivity to behaving properly and presenting the proper "face" (Goffman, 1967), particularly when in the presence of higher ranking or prestigious members of one's group. In most human cultures the proper presentation of the self is a profoundly moral enterprise, in which one shows respect for authority and for the group. The failure to be vigilant about one's presentation brings shame and dishonor to the self and to one's (interdependent) kin and marks one both as a poor partner for future interactions and as an appropriate target for contempt, disgust, and ostracism. In such a society, the elicitors of protoshame readily expand to include failures to follow all cultural norms, not just norms about hierarchical interaction. There is no clear separation between moral norms and social conventions (Shweder, Mahapatra, & Miller, 1987). In such a society shame (as *malu, lajya, hasham,* etc.) becomes the central emotion of moral regulation, and protoshame is a variant of it that is triggered by simply being in the presence of a superior.

In modern Western societies, however, the expansion of protoshame may follow a different path. Protoshame still begins as a regulator of how one should *act*, but it then expands to take on broader issues about how one should *be*. Westerners are charged with the task of creating a strong, competent, and virtuous "true self" or "core self," a self that is defined not by its relationships to others but by its contrasts with others. Thus, for Westerners, pride is generally thought to be a pleasurable emotion resulting from actions that indicate that the self is indeed good, competent, and virtuous (Lazarus, 1991a; M. Lewis, 1993), whereas shame is said to be a painful emotion that results from actions that reveal the self to be flawed or defective (H. Lewis, 1971).

Given this Western emphasis on the virtues of the true self, it makes sense that Westerners experience shame and embarrassment as very different emotions. Western societies partially separate the moral order (issues of harm, rights, and justice) from the social order (issues of nonmoral social convention, such as choices of clothing, food, and hygiene; Turiel, 1983). Embarrassment is often reported to be felt when one violates social conventions, whereas shame is more typically elicited by one's own perceived violation of a moral norm (Keltner & Buswell, 1996; Tangney, Miller, Flicker, & Barlow, 1996). Embarrassment, therefore, does not cut so deeply. If a Westerner violates a social convention or botches a social presentation, it says little about his or her true self. Embarrassment episodes can therefore be quite lighthearted, with the embarrassed person smiling and witnesses laughing (Keltner & Buswell, 1997). To a Westerner, however, shame always hurts, for it draws attention to a defect in the true self. (For more on cultural variations in shame and embarrassment, see Fischer, Manstead, & Mosquera, 1999; Haidt & Keltner, 1999; Kitayama, Markus, & Matsumoto, 1995; Triandis, 1994; see also chapter 46, this volume.)

## Eliciters

To summarize: In Western cultures, shame is elicited by the appraisal that there is something wrong or defective with one's core self, generally due to a failure to measure up to standards of morality, aesthetics, or competence (Babcock & Sabini, 1990; Keltner & Buswell, 1996; H. Lewis, 1971; M. Lewis, 1993; Tangney et al., 1996). Embarrassment, in contrast, is said to be elicited by appraisals that one's social identity or persona within an interaction is damaged or threatened, most commonly because one has violated a social-conventional rule but also at times because of events beyond one's control (Goffman, 1959; Keltner & Buswell, 1997; Miller, 1996; Silver, Sabini, & Parrott, 1987). In many non-Western societies, however, any appraisal that one has violated cultural standards of behavior in front of other people or that one is at high risk of such violations (as when one is around one's superiors) triggers a self-conscious emotion that combines shame and embarrassment.

## Action Tendencies

Because of their common origin in submissive behavior, shame and embarrassment have some common features in their action tendencies. They both lead people to reduce their social presence, creating a motivation to hide, withdraw, or disappear, and making movement and speech more difficult and less likely (Asendorpf, 1990; Keltner & Buswell, 1997; M. Lewis, 1993; Miller, 1996). Such changes inhibit assertive behavior and signal that the individual recognizes that a violation has occurred, thereby reducing the likelihood of attack or further punishment from dominant others. Little has been written about the unique action tendencies of shame and embarrassment, because empirical efforts to distinguish the two emotions have primarily found differences in appraisals, phenomenology, and facial and bodily expressions (Keltner & Buswell, 1997; Tangney et al, 1996). However, the principal difference seems to be that shame involves a darker and more painful urge to withdraw, which can even motivate suicide (Durkheim, 1951; Mokros, 1995). Because Westerners tend to feel embarrassment in less serious situations, in which repair and restoration of face are usually possible, embarrassment seems to cause a milder and less painful urge to withdraw. Attempts at reparation are common, although they are complicated by the flustering and confusion that embarrassment causes (Keltner & Buswell, 1997).

## Guilt

Guilt is often confused with shame by native speakers of English, but the two emotions appear to grow out of different psychological systems. Whereas the elicitors and displays of shame clearly link it to hierarchical interactions, the elicitors and action tendencies of guilt suggest that it grows out of communal relationships and the attachment system (Baumeister, Stillwell, & Heatherton, 1994; Tangney, 1991).

### Elicitors

As the traditionally central moral emotion, guilt was said to be caused by the violation of moral rules and imperatives (Freud, 1930/1961; Lazarus, 1991), particularly if those violations caused harm or suffering to others (Hoffman, 1982a). But Baumeister, Stillwell, and Heatherton's (1994) review and reinterpretation of the voluminous literature on guilt allows even greater specificity: Guilt feelings occur overwhelmingly in the context of communal relationships (Clark & Mills, 1979; Fiske, 1991) in which one believes one has caused harm, loss, or distress to a relationship partner. Guilt is not just triggered by the appraisal that one has caused harm; it is triggered most powerfully if one's harmful action also creates a threat to one's communion with or relatedness to the victim. Guilt can be triggered in properly socialized adults even by the appraisal that one has harmed a stranger, but guilt reactions appear to be stronger and far more common in close relationships than in distant ones (Baumeister et al., 1994).

Guilt is generally distinguished from shame by its specificity. In guilt situations one appraises one's *action* as bad, not one's entire self (M. Lewis, 1993). Self-report studies of guilt invariably turn up a small number of cases of solitary guilt that do not involve relationship partners, such as guilt over breaking one's diet or masturbating, but to the extent that these feelings involve more than simple regret, they appear to be examples of shame mislabeled as guilt.

### Action Tendencies

Guilt has generally been seen as a good or prototypical moral emotion because it motivates one to help one's victim or otherwise to make up for one's transgression (Hoffman, 1982b; H. Lewis, 1971; M. Lewis, 1993). Baumeister et al. (1994) conclude that guilt motivates people to treat their relationship partners well. Inducing guilt in one's partners is therefore a common and effective strategy people use when they feel neglected or mistreated in a valued relationship. Psychoanalysts have long maintained that guilt also creates a desire for punishment or suffering (Freud, 1930/1961), but empirical research offers little support for this claim (Baumeister et al., 1994). Rather, guilt motivates people to apologize and to confess, not as a way to debase themselves but as a way to restore or improve their relationships.

## The Moral Importance of the Self-Conscious Emotions

Psychologists and educators have long recognized the moral importance of guilt; they have had more ambivalent feelings about shame, the "ugly" moral emotion (Tangney, 1991); and they have generally dismissed embarrassment as a nonmoral emotion based in part on the fact that it is a response to nonmoral violations. But by the criteria used in this chapter, all three emotions are important moral emotions, because their action tendencies generally make people conform to rules and uphold the social order. All three are therefore placed in the upper half of Figure 45.1. Guilt deserves the highest placement on the y axis as it is the only one of the three that motivates direct helping behavior; but shame and embarrassment are probably even more important in daily life, because they are potentially at work in all public interactions. The placement of the three emotions on the x axis of Figure 45.1 is more problematic. If the criterion of "disinterestedness" is the capacity to feel the emotion in situations that do not involve the self, then the self-conscious emotions fare poorly, as they are almost always about the self's relations to others. But if the alternative criterion is used (the difference between the emotional life of Homo sapiens and the emotional life of *Homo economicus*), then the self-conscious emotions earn a place nearer to the right side of Figure 45.1. A purely self-interested creature would find reasons to restrain his behavior in cases in which norm violations would lead to punishment, but he would not feel guilt over harms that only he knew about or shame over the discovery of his own moral depravity, or even embarrassment at being caught in a lie. Indeed, the complete lack of shame, embarrassment, and guilt is one of the most salient hallmarks of the psychopath, along with the absence of sympathy (Cleckley, 1955).

## The Other-Suffering Family

The oldest of the old academy moral emotions is sympathy, which was said to be the foundation of morality by Adam Smith (1759/1976), David Hume (1739/1969), and even Jean Piaget (1932/1965). All of these writers saw it as a basic fact about human nature that people feel bad when others suffer and are sometimes moved by these feelings to help. Research on children shows that emotional reactions to the suffering of others emerge clearly in the 1st year of life, and that during the 2nd year these concerns begin to motivate attempts to help the sufferer (Harris, 1989; Zahn-Waxler, Radke-Yarrow, & King, 1979). Research on other primates demonstrates that a sensitivity to the suffering of others is not just a part of human nature, it is in some form a part of chimpanzee and bonobo nature as well (de Waal, 1996).

How many emotions are part of this other-suffering family? The research literature supports a distinction between only two major constructs: distress at another's distress (DAAD) and sympathy/compassion. DAAD, as its name implies, refers to the tendency for individuals to become distressed when they see or hear other individuals emit signs of distress (Batson & Shaw, 1991; Cialdini, 1991). It is present in newborn infants, who are more upset by the sounds of another infant crying than they are by equally loud non-crying sounds (Sagi & Hoffman, 1976). It is at work in studies of helping behavior, in which some people exposed to a suffering victim will take steps to escape from the victim (Cialdini et al., 1987). But DAAD is not truly an emotion. It does not have a distinctive physiology, facial expression, or action tendency, other than the general characteristics of distress (e.g., a motivation to escape the source of the distress). It should rather be thought of as an affective precursor of sympathy/compassion (Hoffman, 1982a), in the same way that distaste is an affective precursor of disgust without being an emotion itself.

The real emotion in this family is generally called "empathy" (Hoffman, 1982a). Yet empathy is in some ways an inappropriate word. It was coined by Titchener in 1909 as a translation of the German word *einfuhlung*, which had been used in perceptual contexts to refer to the process of seeing an event from the inside (Batson & Shaw, 1991). Empathy researchers continue this emphasis on general perspective taking, defining empathy as "an emotional response that stems from another's emotional state or condition and is congruent with the other's emotional state or condition" (Eisenberg, Shea, Carlo, & Knight, 1991, p. 65). Defined in this way, empathy is not an emotion at all; it is a tendency or an ability to feel whatever another person is feeling, including happiness, anger, or boredom. Some researchers have therefore tried to resurrect the older term *sympathy*, defining it as a vicarious emotional reaction that is "based on the apprehension of another's emotional state or situation, which involves feelings of sorrow or concern for the other" (Eisenberg et al., 1991, p. 65). But even the word *sympathy*, as it is defined in English-language dictionaries, refers to the tendency of two things to move together, "an inclination to think or feel alike" (*Webster's Third New International Dictionary*). A more appropriate word may therefore be *compassion*, which Lazarus (1991b) describes as "being moved by another's suffering," and which *Webster's* defines as "deep feeling for and understanding of misery or suffering and the concomitant desire to promote its alleviation."

### Elicitors

Compassion is elicited by the perception of suffering or sorrow in another person. Compassion appears to grow out of the mammalian attachment system, in which it has obvious benefits as a mediator of altruism toward kin (Hoffman, 1982b). People can feel compassion for total strangers, and that is why compassion is shown on the far right of Figure 45.1; however, compassion is most strongly and readily felt for one's kin and for others with whom one has a close, communal relationship (Batson & Shaw, 1991).

### Action Tendencies

Compassion makes people want to help, comfort, or otherwise alleviate the suffering of the other (Batson, O'Quinn, Fulty, Vanderplass, & Isen, 1983; Batson & Shaw, 1991; Eisenberg et al., 1989; Hoffman, 1982b). Compassion is linked to guilt conceptually (Baumeister et al., 1994; Hoffman, 1982a) and empirically. People who are more prone to feel other people's pain are more prone to feel guilt but are less prone to feel shame (Tangney, 1991). Because compassion has such a directly prosocial action tendency, it is shown at the top of Figure 45.1.

## The Other-Praising Family

All of the emotions discussed so far have been responses to bad deeds done by others or by the self or responses to bad things experienced by others. But there is also a brighter side to the moral emotions: People are emotionally sensitive to good deeds and moral exemplars. As the movement for "positive psychology" (Seligman & Czikszentmihalyi, 1999) gathers force, the study of these positive moral emotions is an exciting new frontier of research.

Positive emotions are different from negative emotions. Negative emotions behave like red-alert buttons, focusing attention on a problem and setting in motion a corrective procedure. But positive emotions generally arise in safer situations in which direct and focused action is not called for. Fredrickson (1998) has therefore proposed a "broaden and build" model in which the purpose of positive emotions is to broaden a person's "momentary thought-action repertoire." This broadening counteracts the narrowing effect that negative emotions typically have, and it makes a person more open to new ideas, new relationships, and new possibilities. Positive emotions help people to "be here now" (Dass, 1971). Positive emotions encourage people to build social bonds, practice skills, and make improvements in themselves that may pay off in the future, when the environment becomes more demanding (Fredrickson, 1998).

How many positive moral emotions are there? Ekman's (1994a) long list of 17 potentially basic emotions includes the positive emotions of amusement, awe, contentment, excitement, interest, pride in achievement, relief, and sensory pleasure. Of these emotions, only awe and pride in achievement appear to meet even one of the two criteria for moral emotionhood used in this chapter (i.e., disinterested elicitors, prosocial action tendencies). Pride was discussed briefly, as a self-conscious emotion and as the ultimate self-praising emotion. Awe that is produced by exemplary human virtue is discussed later, along with elevation. The only other positive moral emotion that has been mentioned by several theorists is gratitude (Lazarus, 1991b; Trivers, 1971). There may well be other positive moral emotions that Western emotion theorists have missed, but for now the emotions of elevation and gratitude can be thought of as two brothers in a joint family of positive emotions that are produced by the good or virtuous actions of other people. To maintain parallelism with the naming of the self-conscious and other-condemning families, this family might tentatively be called the "other-praising" family.

## Gratitude

Very little empirical research has been done on gratitude. A scan of the PsycINFO database shows only 47 articles in which *gratitude* appears in the title or key phrase. The majority of these articles are unpublished dissertations, or else they stem from Klein's (1957) psychoanalytic theories about the infant's gratitude for the mother's breast. Theorizing from an evolutionary perspective suggests that gratitude is part of the emotional mechanism of reciprocal altruism, encouraging individuals to repay benefactors, just as anger motivates individuals to punish cheaters (Trivers, 1971). More recent thinking within positive psychology has argued that gratitude is an important human strength and that feelings of gratitude contribute to personal well-being, civic engagement, and spiritual satisfaction (Emmons & Crumpler, 2000; Emmons & Shelton, 2002). A recent review article (McCullough, Kilpatrick, Emmons, & Larson, 2001) has rounded up all available research on gratitude and concluded that gratitude is indeed an important moral emotion, functioning both as a response to moral behavior and as a motivator of moral behavior.

### Elicitors

Gratitude is defined as "the state of being grateful; warm and friendly feeling toward a benefactor prompting one to repay a favor" (*Webster's Third*). The few empirical studies that have been done on gratitude confirm that it is indeed triggered by the perception that another person has done a good deed for the self, intentionally and voluntarily (Tesser, Gatewood, & Driver, 1968; Weiner & Graham, 1989). McCullough et al. (2001) propose that gratitude functions as a "moral barometer," sensitive to events in which another person provides benefits to the self, although they note that the feeling of gratitude is always

pleasant, whereas the feeling of indebtedness is often unpleasant.

### Action Tendency

McCullough et al. (2001) propose that gratitude functions as a moral motive in that it makes people act more prosocially, although their review found no empirical evidence that gratitude causes people to help anyone beyond their direct benefactors. In one of the earliest and largest studies of gratitude, Baumgarten-Tramer (1938) asked 2,000 Swiss children to state their greatest wish and then to say how they would feel and react toward a person who granted them their wish. The results mirror *Webster's* definition, showing friendliness toward the benefactor and a tendency to express thanks and to try to return a similar favor. However, public expressions of gratitude should not automatically be taken to indicate real feelings of gratitude; sometimes, like expressions of modesty, they are superficial concessions to self-presentational norms (Baumeister & Ilko, 1995).

## Awe and Elevation

Even less empirical research has been done on awe than on gratitude—only 11 articles in PsycINFO have *awe* in the title or key phrase. Lazarus (1991a) says that awe is an ambiguous state which can often be a negative experience, blending fright and amazement. Frijda (1986) discusses wonder rather than awe, which he links to surprise and amazement and interprets as a passive, receptive mode of attention in the presence of something unexpected. A recent questionnaire study of the causes and consequences of awe (Shin, Keltner, Shiota, & Haidt, in preparation) finds that awe is elicited by a heterogeneous set of experiences, the largest of which are experiences of natural beauty, artistic beauty, and exemplary or exceptional human actions or abilities. Awe appears to be elicited by exposure to certain kinds of beauty and perfection. As for its action tendencies, Shin et al. (in preparation) find, consistent with Frijda's description of wonder, that awe seems to make people stop, admire, and open their hearts and minds. It may be for this reason that awe is so often discussed in a religious context as the proper and desirable response to the presence of God (James, 1902/1961). This sort of awe may qualify as a moral emotion in a devoutly religious culture, and the design of many religious spaces can be seen as an attempt to produce or amplify awe experience, which in turn should make people more receptive to the teachings they hear.

There is, however, one emotional experience related to awe that qualifies as a moral emotion according to the two criteria of this chapter: elevation (Haidt, 2000; in press). Many people report being deeply moved simply by hearing stories about acts of kindness and charity. Haidt, Algoe, Meijer, and Tam (2002) set out to investigate this emotional state by collecting narratives of such experiences and by inducing it in the lab with videos about moral exemplars. They found that these emotional experiences have most of the hallmarks of a basic emotion, with the exception of a distinctive facial expression. Elevation appears to be caused by seeing manifestations of humanity's higher or better nature; it triggers a distinctive feeling in the chest of warmth and expansion; it causes a desire to become a better person oneself; and it seems to open one's heart, not only to the person who triggered the feeling but also to other people. In all of its components, elevation appears to be the opposite of social disgust. Whereas social disgust is caused by seeing people blur the lower boundary between humans and nonhumans, elevation is caused by seeing people blur the upper boundary between humans and God (i.e., saints or people who act like saints). Whereas disgust makes people close off and avoid contact, elevation makes people open up and seek contact. Whereas disgust creates negative contamination (Nemeroff & Rozin, 1994), elevation creates positive contamination (e.g., people want to touch living saints or, in some cultures, to collect the hair, clothing, or bones of dead saints).

### Elicitors

Elevation is elicited by moral beauty, just as social disgust is elicited by moral depravity. Acts of charity, kindness, loyalty, and self-sacrifice seem to be powerful elicitors, but more work is needed on the degree to which displays of different virtues produce the same feeling or slightly different feelings.

### Action Tendency

Like gratitude, elevation makes a person feel warmth and affection toward the person who elicited the emotion. But unlike gratitude, elevation seems to create a more generalized desire to become a better person oneself and to follow the example of the moral exemplar. People who experience elevation are more likely to want to help other people, to give money to charity, and to list prosocial actions when asked to write about their life goals (Haidt et al., 2002). Elevation therefore fits well with Fredrickson's (1998) "broaden and build" model. It opens people up to new possibilities for action and thought, making them more receptive to the lessons of a moral exemplar. This opening process may explain why narratives of the lives of saints and religious leaders (e.g., Buddha, Jesus, Mother Teresa) so often include accounts of people who, on meeting the holy person, dropped their previous lives and even their previous names and became reborn on the spot into a new, more altruistic and less materialistic identity. Elevation may function as a kind of "moral reset button" in the human mind. Moral exemplars can push this reset button in others, creating a virtuous ripple effect (Haidt, 2000).

## The Moral Nature of the Other-Praising Family

Elevation and gratitude directly motivate prosocial behavior and are therefore placed along the top of Figure 45.1. The eliciting situations of gratitude are more self-interested, involving paying back one's *own* debts, so gratitude is shown in the left half of the figure. But the elicitors of elevation are perfectly disinterested. It is a remarkable and encouraging fact about human beings that simply hearing about a good deed, done by a stranger for another stranger, can profoundly affect us. Elevation therefore is, arguably, the most prototypical moral emotion of all.

Far more work needs to be done on the other-praising emotions. Fredrickson (1998) points out that the positive emotions are generally less discrete than the negative emotions and therefore harder to divide up into families. I have assumed in this chapter that elevation is closely related to awe, being perhaps awe that is inspired by moral perfection. But the exact relationship will only be known as research on the positive emotions spreads out beyond the well-established fields of love and happiness and takes on such emotional states as awe, admiration, elevation, respect, and gratitude.

## Other Moral Emotions

Other emotions, of course, play a role in human moral life. I have argued in this chapter that moral emotionhood is a matter of degree and that any emotion is a moral emotion to the extent that it has disinterested elicitors and prosocial action tendencies. Almost any emotion can meet at least one of these criteria at least some of the time. Fear, for example, can be an important cause of law-abiding or norm-respecting behavior. However the elicitors of fear generally trigger concerns about the self (or the self's closest kin). Likewise *schadenfreude*, the joy that is elicited by the misfortunes of others, contains an important moral component in that it is strongest when the person brought down was thought unworthy of her previous high status (Portmann, 2000). However, *schadenfreude* appears to involve no prosocial action tendency. Fear and *schadenfreude* are therefore marginal or nonprototypical moral emotions, and they are shown along the left and bottom margins, respectively, of Figure 45.1.

A more difficult question is the emotion of love. Love certainly distinguishes Homo sapiens from Homo economicus; love can lead people to do enormously prosocial and self-sacrificial acts; and at least one form of love—agape—is defined as a selfless and unconditional form of love. Agape love is a central emotion in the ethical systems of many religions (Templeton, 1999). However, psychological work on agape love has treated it primarily as a trait, a "love style" (Lee, 1973) used by some people in their romantic relationships. More work is needed to determine whether agape love as an emotional *experience* can be triggered in social situations with prosocial results.

A third consideration when searching for moral emotions is that cultural variation in both emotions and in moral systems can create local moral emotions, or locally moralized emotions. For example, the *Natyasastra*, a Hindu treatise on drama and the emotions from the second century A.D., discusses the emotion of *sama*, glossed in translation as "serenity/calmness" (Masson & Patwardhan, 1970). Many Westerners may recognize that such an affective state, sometimes obtained through meditation, has benefits for mental health. But in the context of Hindu beliefs about transcendence and the importance of nonattachment, *sama* becomes an important moral emotion. The action tendency of *sama*, which is, paradoxically, inaction and detachment, is good not only for one's own spiritual advancement but also for the health of the cosmos (Shweder & Haidt, 2000). The selection and placement of emotions in Figure 45.1 must therefore be seen as the best guess of a Western emotion researcher, speculating about his own culture. The mapping of moral emotions in other cultures would be somewhat different.

## Emotion Versus Reason: Who's in Charge?

Ever since Plato crowned reason as the king of the soul and ruler of the passions, there have been occasional voices of protest. David Hume's voice has been the loudest, with his famous claim that "reason is, and ought only to be the slave of the passions, and can never pretend to any other office than to serve and obey them" (1739/1969, p. 462). In psychology, Hume's emotivism found a rare but ready ally in Freud (1900/1976), who said that the ego is a servant of the id and that reasoning is often just rationalization. As psychology moved into the cognitive revolution, however, the study of morality became increasingly limited to the study of moral reasoning, based on Piagetian ideas about cognitive development (Kohlberg, 1969; Piaget, 1932/1965).

The balance of power began to change dramatically in the 1980s. Research on moral reasoning reached its quantitative peak (see Table 45.1), but it began losing some of its energy and focus as Kohlberg's theory became more complicated and as his critics grew louder (see Kohlberg, Levine, & Hewer, 1983). At the same time, however, research on the moral emotions grew rapidly, and the "toolbox" of emotions expanded to include emotions other than guilt and empathy/sympathy (see Table 45.1). As re-

searchers began to chronicle the early and dramatic emergence of the moral emotions in children (Harris, 1989) and the early affective responses children have to the violation of standards (Kagan, 1981), the weapons became available to wage what might be called the "moral-emotional correction" (*revolution* would be too strong a word). Jerome Kagan was one of its first leaders. In *The Nature of the Child* (1984), he proposed that "beneath the extraordinary variety of surface behavior and consciously articulated ideals, there is a set of emotional states that form the bases for a limited number of universal moral categories that transcend time and locality" (p. 118). Kagan thought that these emotional reactions are the driving force of moral judgment and that moral reasoning is often just post hoc rationalization. "Because humans prefer—or demand, as some psychologists would say—a reason for holding a standard, they invent the arguments that rationalists regard as essential" (Kagan, 1984, p. 122).

Kagan's arguments were extended by theorists in a variety of fields. The economist Robert Frank (1988) showed that the moral emotions serve as "commitment devices," which allow people to work together in the face of temptations to defect, while simultaneously signaling to others that they can be counted on in future interactions not to defect. The philosopher Allan Gibbard (1990) argued that the moral emotions are adaptive syndromes shaped by evolution to make people liable to "normative governance," that is, the pull of rules and moral discourse. The sociologist James Q. Wilson (1993) revived Hume's arguments about the "moral sense" and grounded them firmly in a review of findings from across the behavioral sciences.

By the early 1990s social psychologists began taking part in the moral-emotional correction. Major review articles on shame (Tangney et al., 1996), guilt (Baumeister et al., 1994), embarrassment (Keltner & Buswell, 1997), and disgust (Rozin et al., 1993) stressed the moral functions of these emotions and the ways in which they work together to structure social interactions (for a review, see Keltner & Haidt, 1999). At the same time, social psychologists began rediscovering the importance of automaticity in mental life and questioning the causal efficacy of consciously reportable reasoning (Bargh, 1994; Wegner & Bargh, 1998), a view that harkens back to Nisbett and Wilson (1977). These converging trends made it possible to ask in the 1990s: Could moral reasoning be an epiphenomenon? Could human morality really be run by the moral emotions, while moral reasoning struts about pretending to be in control?

I have recently argued for this "Wizard of Oz" scenario. Drawing on research in primatology, neurology, anthropology, and psychology I suggested that moral judgment involves quick gut feelings, or affectively laden intuitions, which then trigger moral reasoning as an ex post facto social product. This "social intuitionist" model of moral judgment says that people do indeed engage in moral reasoning, but they do so to persuade others, not to figure things out for themselves. This model reverses the Platonic ordering of the psyche, placing the emotions firmly in control of the temple of morality, whereas reason is demoted to the status of not-so-humble servant.[4]

## Summary

Whether the moral emotions are ultimately shown to be the servants, masters, or equal partners of moral reasoning, it is clear that they do a tremendous amount of work in the creation and daily functioning of human morality. The capacity to feel contempt, anger, disgust, shame, embarrassment, guilt, compassion, gratitude, and elevation may or may not separate humans neatly from other animals, but it certainly separates us from *Homo economicus*. Morality dignifies and elevates because it ties us all to something greater than ourselves: each other.

## NOTES

I thank Paul Rozin for helpful comments and editorial guidance. Preparation of this chapter was supported by the National Institute on Drug Abuse, grant #1-RO3-DA12606-01. Correspondence concerning this article should be addressed to Jonathan Haidt, Department of Psychology, University of Virginia, P.O. Box 400400, Charlottesville, VA 22904-4400. Electronic mail may be sent to *haidt@virginia.edu*.

1. Emotion theorists often distinguish between specific antecedent events and the highly abstract appraisals of those events for a person's well-being, such as "novelty" or "goal blockage" (Scherer, 1984; Smith & Ellsworth, 1985). The word *elicitor* was chosen as a way of obtaining an intermediate level of abstraction. It should be taken to refer to a class of events in the world, as perceived and understood by a person, that generally triggers a particular emotional response. Examples of elicitors include being insulted or seeing an act of generosity. This usage is similar to what Mesquita and Frijda (1992) call *event coding*.

2. "Economic (hu)man," a perfectly rational calculator of expected costs and benefits for the self.

3. Differences in emotion lexicons are not in themselves reliable guides to differences in emotional experience (Haidt & Keltner, 1999; Mesquita & Frijda, 1992). However, ethnographic accounts (e.g., Abu-Lughod, 1986) strongly suggest that there are real differences in the experience of the self-conscious emotions.

4. The model does allow reason to play a casual role in moral judgment under limited circumstances, such as when intuitions conflict or are so weak that they are easily overridden. Furthermore, the model discusses cultural variation in the relations between reasoning and intuition (which includes the moral emotions). In highly educated subcultures, such as those of academics, members are immersed in a culture of reasoning and reason giving, and they may at times reason their way to a judgment that conflicts with their initial intuition.

## REFERENCES

Abu-Lughod, L. (1986). *Veiled sentiments*. Berkeley: University of California Press.

Angyal, A. (1941). Disgust and related aversions. *Journal of Abnormal and Social Psychology, 36*, 393–412.

Aristotle (1941). *The basic works of Aristotle* (R. McKeon, Trans. and Ed.). New York: Random House. (Original work published 4th century B.C.)

Aristotle (1962). *Nichomachean ethics* (Martin Oswald, Trans.). Indianapolis, IN: Bobbs-Merrill.

Asendorpf, J. (1990). The expression of shyness and embarrassment. In W. R. Crozier (Ed.), *Shyness and embarrassment: Perspectives from social psychology* (pp. 87–118). Cambridge, England: Cambridge University Press.

Axelrod, R. (1984). *The evolution of cooperation*. New York: Basic Books.

Babcock, M., & Sabini, J. (1990). On differentiating embarrassment from shame. *European Journal of Social Psychology, 20*, 151–169.

Bargh, J. (1994). The four horsemen of automaticity: Awareness, efficiency, intention, and control in social cognition. In J. R. S. Wyer & T. K. Srull (Eds.), *Handbook of social cognition* (2nd ed., pp. 1–40). Hillsdale, NJ: Erlbaum.

Batson, C. D., O'Quinn, K., Fulty, J., Vanderplass, M., & Isen, A. M. (1983). Influence of self-reported distress and empathy on egoistic versus altruistic motivation to help. *Journal of Personality and Social Psychology, 45*, 706–718.

Batson, C. D., & Shaw, L. L. (1991). Evidence for altruism: Toward a pluralism of prosocial motives. *Psychological Inquiry, 2*, 107–122.

Baumeister, R. F., & Ilko, S. (1995). Shallow gratitude: Public and private acknowledgment of external help in accounts of success. *Basic and Applied Psychology, 16*, 191–209.

Baumeister, R. F., & Leary, M. R. (1995). The need to belong: Desire for interpersonal attachments as a fundamental human motivation. *Psychological Bulletin, 117*, 497–529.

Baumeister, R. F., Stillwell, A., & Wotman, S. R. (1990). Victim and perpetrator accounts of interpersonal conflict: Autobiographical narratives about anger. *Journal of Personality and Social Psychology, 59*, 994–1005.

Baumeister, R. F., Stillwell, A. M., & Heatherton, T. F. (1994). Guilt: An interpersonal approach. *Psychological Bulletin, 115*, 243–267.

Baumgarten-Tramer, F. (1938). "Gratefulness" in children and young people. *Journal of Genetic Psychology, 53*, 53–66.

Benedict, R. (1946). *The chrysanthemum and the sword*. Boston: Houghton Mifflin.

Berkowitz, L., & Heimer, K. (1989). On the construction of the anger experience: Aversive events and negative priming in the formation of feelings. In L. Berkowitz (Ed.), *Advances in experimental social psychology* (Vol. 22, pp. 1–37). New York: Academic Press.

Boehm, C. (1999). *Hierarchy in the forest: The evolution of egalitarian behavior*. Cambridge, MA: Harvard University Press.

Cialdini, R., Schaller, M., Houlihan, D., Arps, K., Fultz, J., & Beaman, A. (1987). Empathy based helping: Is it selflessly or selfishly motivated? *Journal of Personality and Social Psychology, 52*, 749–758.

Cialdini, R. B. (1991). Altruism or egoism? That is (still) the question. *Psychological Inquiry, 2*, 124–126.

Clark, M. S., & Mills, J. (1979). Interpersonal attraction in exchange and communal relationships. *Journal of Personality and Social Psychology, 37*, 12–24.

Cleckley, H. (1955). *The mask of sanity.* St. Louis, MO: Mosby.

Darwin, C. (1998). *The descent of man.* Amherst, NY: Prometheus Books. (Original work published 1874)

Darwin, C. (1965). *The expression of the emotions in man and animals.* Chicago: University of Chicago Press. (Original work published 1872)

Dass, R. (1971). *Be here now.* New York: Crown.

de Waal, F. (1982). *Chimpanzee politics.* New York: Harper & Row.

de Waal, F. (1996). *Good natured: The origins of right and wrong in humans and other animals.* Cambridge, MA: Harvard University Press.

Dollard, J., & Miller, N. E. (1950). *Personality and psychotherapy.* New York: McGraw-Hill.

Dunbar, R. (1996). *Grooming, gossip, and the evolution of language.* Cambridge, MA: Harvard University Press.

Durkheim, E. (1951). *Suicide* (J. A. Spalding & G. Simpson, Trans.). New York: Free Press. (Original work published 1897)

Eisenberg, N., Fabes, R. A., Miller, P. A., Fultz, J., Shell, R., Mathy, R. M., & Reno, R. R. (1989). Relation of sympathy and distress to prosocial behavior: A multimethod study. *Journal of Personality and Social Psychology, 57*, 55–66.

Eisenberg, N., Shea, C. L., Carlo, G., & Knight, G. P. (1991). Empathy-related responding and cognition: A "chicken and the egg" dilemma. In W. M. Kurtines & J. L. Gewirtz (Eds.), *Handbook of moral behavior and development: Vol. 1. Theory* (pp. 63–88). Hillsdale, NJ: Erlbaum.

Ekman, P. (1992a). Are there basic emotions? *Psychological Review, 99*, 550–553.

Ekman, P. (1992b). An argument for basic emotions. *Cognition and Emotion, 6*, 169–200.

Ekman, P. (1994a). All emotions are basic. In P. Ekman & R. J. Davidson (Eds.), *The nature of emotion: Fundamental questions* (pp. 15–19). New York: Oxford University Press.

Ekman, P. (1994b). Antecedent events and emotion metaphors. In P. Ekman & R. J. Davidson (Eds.), *The nature of emotion: Fundamental questions* (pp. 146–149). New York: Oxford University Press.

Ekman, P., & Friesen, W. V. (1975). *Unmasking the face.* Englewood Cliffs, NJ: Prentice Hall.

Ekman, P., & Friesen, W. V. (1986). A new pan-cultural facial expression of emotion. *Motivation and Emotion, 10*, 159–168.

Ekman, P., & Heider, K. (1988). The universality of a contempt expression: A replication. *Motivation and Emotion, 12*, 303–308.

Ellsworth, P. C. (1994). Sense, culture, and sensibility. In S. Kitayama & H. R. Markus (Eds.), *Emotion and culture: Empirical studies of mutual influence* (pp. 23–50). Washington, DC: American Psychological Association.

Emmons, R. A., & Crumpler, C. A. (2000). Gratitude as a human strength: Appraising the evidence. *Journal of Social and Clinical Psychology, 19*, 56–69.

Emmons, R. A., & Shelton, C. M. (2002). Gratitude and the science of positive psychology. In C. R. Snyder & S. J. Lopez (Eds.), *The handbook of positive psychology.* New York: Oxford University Press.

Fessler, D. T. (1999). Toward an understanding of the universality of second order emotions. In A. Hinton (Ed.), *Beyond nature or nurture: Biocultural approaches to the emotions* (pp. 75–116). Cambridge, England: Cambridge University Press.

Fischer, A. H., Manstead, A. S. R., & Mosquera, P. M. R. (1999). The role of honour-related vs. individualistic values in conceptualising pride, shame, and anger: Spanish and Dutch cultural prototypes. *Cognition and Emotion, 13*, 149–179.

Fiske, A. P. (1991). *Structures of social life.* New York: Free Press.

Frank, R. (1988). *Passions within reason: The strategic role of the emotions.* New York: Norton.

Fredrickson, B. L. (1998). What good are positive emotions? *Review of General Psychology, 2*, 300–319.

Freud, S. (1961). Civilization and its discontents. In J. Strachey (Ed. and Trans.), *The standard edition of the complete psychological works of Sigmund Freud* (Vols. 4–5). New York: Norton. (Original work published 1930)

Freud, S. (1976). *The interpretation of dreams.* In J. Strachey (Ed. and Trans.), *The standard edition of the complete psychological works of Sigmund Freud* (Vols. 4–5). New York: Norton. (Original work published 1900)

Frijda, N. (1986). *The emotions.* Cambridge, England: Cambridge University Press.

Frijda, N. H. (1994). The lex talionis: On vengeance. In S. H. M. v. Goozen, N. E. v. d. Poll, & J. A. Sargeant (Eds.), *Emotions: Essays on emotion theory* (pp. 263–289). Hillsdale, NJ: Erlbaum.

Frijda, N. H., & Mesquita, B. (1994). The social roles and functions of emotions. In S. Kitayama & H. Marcus (Eds.), *Emotion and culture: Empirical studies of mutual influence* (pp. 51–87). Washington, DC: American Psychological Association.

Gewirth, A. (1984). Ethics. In the *Encyclopedia Brittanica 15th Edition* (Vol. 6, pp. 976–998). Chicago: Encyclopedia Brittanica.

Gibbard, A. (1990). *Wise choices, apt feelings.* Cambridge, MA: Harvard University Press.

Goffman, E. (1959). *The presentation of self in everyday life.* Garden City, NY: Doubleday.

Goffman, E. (1967). *Interaction ritual: Essays on face-to-face behavior.* Garden City, NY: Anchor.

Haidt, J. (2000). The positive emotion of elevation. *Prevention and Treatment.* http://journals.apa.org/prevention/volume3/pre003003c.html

Haidt, J. (2001). The emotional dog and its rational tail: A social intuitionist approach to moral judgment. *Psychological Review, 108*, 814–834.

Haidt, J. (in press). Elevation and the positive psychology of morality. In C. L. M. Keyes & J. Haidt (Eds.), *Flourishing: The positive person and the well lived life.* Washington, DC: American, Psychological Association Press.

Haidt, J., Algoe, S., Meijer, Z., & Tam, A. (2002). *The elevation-altruism hypothesis: Evidence for a new prosocial emotion.* Unpublished manuscript, University of Virginia.

Haidt, J., & Hersh, M. (2001). Sexual morality: The cultures and reasons of liberals and conservatives. *Journal of Applied Social Psychology, 31*, 191–221.

Haidt, J., & Keltner, D. (1999). Culture and facial expression: Open-ended methods find more faces and a gradient of recognition. *Cognition and Emotion, 13*, 225–266.

Haidt, J., McCauley, C., & Rozin, P. (1994). Individual differences in sensitivity to disgust: A scale sampling seven domains of disgust elicitors. *Personality and Individual Differences, 16,* 701–713.

Haidt, J., Rozin, P., McCauley, C. R., & Imada, S. (1997). Body, psyche, and culture: The relationship between disgust and morality. *Psychology and Developing Societies, 9,* 107–131.

Haidt, J., & Sabini, J. (2000). *What exactly makes revenge sweet?* Unpublished manuscript, University of Virginia.

Hall, G. S. (1898). A study of anger. *The American Journal of Psychology, 10,* 516–591.

Hare, R. M. (1981). *Moral thinking: Its levels, method, and point.* Oxford, England: Oxford University Press.

Harris, P. L. (1989). *Children and emotion.* Oxford, England: Basil Blackwell.

Heider, K. G. (1991). *Landscapes of emotion: Mapping three cultures of emotion in Indonesia.* Cambridge, England: Cambridge University Press.

Hoffman, M. L. (1982a). Affect and moral development. In D. Ciccetti & P. Hesse (Eds.), *New directions for child development: Vol. 16. Emotional development* (pp. 83–103). San Francisco: Jossey-Bass.

Hoffman, M. L. (1982b). Development of prosocial motivation: Empathy and guilt. In N. Eisenberg (Ed.), *The development of prosocial behavior* (pp. 218–231). New York: Academic Press.

Hume, D. (1969). *A treatise of human nature.* London: Penguin. (Original work published 1739–1740)

Hunter, J. D. (1991). *Culture wars: The struggle to define America.* New York: Basic Books.

Izard, C. E. (1971). *The face of emotion.* New York: Appleton-Century-Crofts.

Izard, C. E. (1977). *Human emotions.* New York: Plenum Press.

James, W. (1961). *The varieties of religious experience.* New York: Macmillan. (Original work published 1902)

Kagan, J. (1981). *The second year.* Cambridge, MA: Harvard University Press.

Kagan, J. (1984). *The nature of the child.* New York: Basic Books.

Keltner, D. (1995). Signs of appeasement: Evidence for the distinct displays of embarrassment, amusement, and shame. *Journal of Personality and Social Psychology, 68,* 441–454.

Keltner, D., & Buswell, B. N. (1996). Evidence for the distinctness of embarrassment, shame, and guilt: A study of recalled antecedents and facial expressions of emotion. *Cognition and Emotion, 10,* 155–171.

Keltner, D., & Buswell, B. N. (1997). Embarrassment: Its distinct form and appeasement functions. *Psychological Bulletin, 122,* 250–270.

Keltner, D., & Haidt, J. (1999). The social functions of emotions at four levels of analysis. *Cognition and Emotion, 13,* 505–521.

Keltner, D., Young, R. C., Oemig, C., Heerey, E. A., & Monarch, N. D. (1998). Teasing in hierarchical and intimate relations. *Journal of Personality and Social Psychology, 75,* 1231–1247.

Kitayama, S., Markus, H. R., & Matsumoto, H. (1995). Culture, self, and emotion: A cross-cultural perspective on "self-conscious" emotions. In J. P. Tangney & K. W. Fischer (Eds.), *Self-conscious emotions* (pp. 439–464). New York: Guilford Press.

Klein, M. (1957). *Envy and gratitude: A study of unconscious sources.* New York: Basic Books.

Kohlberg, L. (1969). Stage and sequence: The cognitive-developmental approach to socialization. In D. A. Goslin (Ed.), *Handbook of socialization theory and research* (pp. 347–480). Chicago: Rand McNally.

Kohlberg, L., Levine, C., & Hewer, A. (1983). *Moral stages: A current formulation and a response to critics.* Basel, Switzerland: Karger.

Lakoff, G. (1996). *Moral politics: What conservatives know that liberals don't.* Chicago: University of Chicago Press.

Lazarus, R. S. (1991a). *Emotion and adaptation.* New York: Oxford University Press.

Lazarus, R. S. (1991b). Progress on a cognitive-motivational-relational theory of emotion. *American Psychologist, 46,* 819–834.

Lee, J. A. (1973). *Colors of love.* Toronto: New Press.

Levy, R. I. (1973). *Tahitians.* Chicago: University of Chicago Press.

Lewis, H. B. (1971). *Shame and guilt in neurosis.* New York: International Universities Press.

Lewis, M. (1993). Self-conscious emotions: Embarrassment, pride, shame, and guilt. In M. Lewis & J. Haviland (Eds.), *Handbook of emotions* (pp. 563–573). New York: Guilford Press.

MacCoun, R. J. (1998). Toward a psychology of harm reduction. *American Psychologist, 53,* 1199–1208.

Markus, H. R., & Kitayama, S. (1991). Culture and the self: Implications for cognition, emotion, and motivation. *Psychological Review, 98,* 224–253.

Masson, J. L., & Patwardhan, M. V. (1970). *Aesthetic rapture: The Rasadhyaya of the Natyasastra.* Poona, India: Deccan College.

Matsumoto, D. (1992). More evidence for the universality of a contempt expression. *Motivation and Emotion, 16,* 363–368.

Maynard Smith, J., & Price, G. R. (1973). The logic of animal conflict. *Nature, 246,* 15–18.

Mayr, E. (1960). The emergence of evolutionary novelties. In S. Tax (Ed.), *Evolution after Darwin: Vol. 1. The evolution of life* (pp. 349–380). Chicago: University of Chicago Press.

McCullough, M. E., Kilpatrick, S. D., Emmons, R. A., & Larson, D. B. (2001). Is gratitude a moral affect? *Psychological Bulletin, 127,* 249–266.

Menon, U., & Shweder, R. A. (1994). Kali's tongue: Cultural psychology, cultural consensus and the meaning of "shame" in Orissa, India. In H. Markus & S. Kitayama (Eds.), *Emotion and culture: Empirical studies of mutual influence* (pp. 241–284). Washington, DC: American Psychological Association.

Mesquita, B., & Frijda, N. (1992). Cultural variations in emotions: A review. *Psychological Bulletin, 112,* 179–204.

Mesquita, B., Frijda, N. H., & Scherer, K. R. (1997). Culture and emotion. In P. R. Dasen & T. S. Saraswathi (Eds.), *Handbook of cross-cultural psychology: Vol. 2. Basic processes and human development* (pp. 255–297). Boston: Allyn & Bacon.

Miller, R. S. (1996). *Embarrassment: Poise and peril in everyday life.* New York: Guilford Press.

Miller, W. I. (1997). *The anatomy of disgust.* Cambridge, MA: Harvard University Press.

Mokros, H. B. (1995). Suicide and shame. *American Behavioral Scientist, 38,* 1091–1103.

Nemeroff, C., & Rozin, P. (1994). The contagion concept in adult thinking in the United States: Transmission of germs and of interpersonal influence. *Ethos, 22,* 158–186.

Nisbett, R. E., & Cohen, D. (1996). *Culture of honor: The psychology of violence in the South.* Boulder, CO: Westview Press.

Nisbett, R. E., & Wilson, T. D. (1977). Telling more than we can know: Verbal reports on mental processes. *Psychological Review, 84,* 231–259.

Oatley, K., & Johnson-Laird, P. N. (1995). The communicative theory of emotions: Empirical tests, mental models, and implications for social interaction. In L. L. Martin & A. Tesser (Eds.), *Striving and feeling: Interactions among goals, affect, and emotion.* Mahwah, NJ: Erlbaum.

Piaget, J. (1965). *The moral judgment of the child* (M. Gabain, Trans.). New York: Free Press. (Original work published 1932)

Plato (1949). *Timaeus* (Benjamin Jowett, Trans.) Indianapolis: Bobbs-Merrill.

Plutchik, R. (1980). *Emotion: A psychoevolutionary synthesis.* New York: Harper & Row.

Portmann, J. (2000). *When bad things happen to other people.* New York: Routledge.

Ridley, M. (1996). *The origins of virtue.* Harmondsworth, England: Penguin.

Ridley, M., & Dawkins, R. (1981). The natural selection of altruism. In P. Rushton & R. Sorrentino (Eds.), *Altruism and helping behavior.* Hillsdale, NJ: Erlbaum.

Rosenberg, E., & Ekman, P. (1995). Conceptual and methodological issues in the judgment of facial expressions of emotion. *Motivation and Emotion, 19,* 111–138.

Rozin, P., & Fallon, A. (1987). A perspective on disgust. *Psychological Review, 94,* 23–41.

Rozin, P., Haidt, J., & McCauley, C. (1993). Disgust. In M. Lewis & J. Haviland (Eds.), *Handbook of emotions* (pp. 575–594). New York: Guilford Press.

Rozin, P., Haidt, J., & McCauley, C. R. (2000). Disgust. In M. Lewis & J. Haviland (Eds.), *Handbook of emotions* (2nd ed., pp. 637–653). New York: Guilford Press.

Rozin, P., Lowery, L., & Ebert, R. (1994). Varieties of disgust faces and the structure of disgust. *Journal of Personality and Social Psychology, 66,* 870–881.

Rozin, P., Lowery, L., Imada, S., & Haidt, J. (1999). The CAD triad hypothesis: A mapping between three moral emotions (contempt, anger, disgust) and three moral codes (community, autonomy, divinity). *Journal of Personality and Social Psychology, 76*(4), 574–586.

Rozin, P., Markwith, M., & McCauley, C. R. (1994). The nature of aversion to indirect contacts with other persons: AIDS aversion as a composite of aversion to strangers, infection, moral taint, and misfortune. *Journal of Abnormal Psychology, 103,* 495–504.

Rozin, P., Markwith, M., & Stoess, C. (1997). Moralization and becoming a vegetarian: The transformation of preferences into values and the recruitment of disgust. *Psychological Science, 8,* 67–73.

Russell, J. A. (1991a). Culture and the categorization of emotions. *Psychological Bulletin, 110,* 426–450.

Russell, J. A. (1991b). Negative results on a reported facial expression of contempt. *Motivation and Emotion, 15,* 281–291.

Sagi, A., & Hoffman, M. L. (1976). Empathetic distress in the newborn. *Development Psychology, 12,* 175–176.

Scherer, K. R. (1984). On the nature and function of emotion: A component process approach. In K. R. Scherer & P. Ekman (Eds.), *Approaches to emotion* (pp. 293–317). Hillsdale, NJ: Erlbaum.

Scherer, K. R. (1997). The role of culture in emotion-antecedent appraisal. *Journal of Personality and Social Psychology, 73,* 902–922.

Seligman, M., & Czikszentmihalyi, M. (1999). Positive psychology: An introduction. *American Psychologist, 55,* 5–14.

Shaver, P., Schwartz, J., Kirson, D., & O'Connor, C. (1987). Emotion knowledge: Further exploration of a prototype approach. *Journal of Personality and Social Psychology, 52,* 1061–1086.

Shin, M., Keltner, D., Shiota, L., & Haidt, J. (in preparation). The causes and consequences of awe. Manuscript in preparation.

Shweder, R. A. (1994). "You're not sick, you're just in love": Emotion as an interpretive system. In P. Ekman & R. J. Davidson (Eds.), *The nature of emotion: Fundamental questions* (pp. 32–44). New York: Oxford University Press.

Shweder, R. A., & Haidt, J. (2000). The cultural psychology of the emotions: Ancient and new. In M. Lewis & J. Haviland (Eds.), *Handbook of emotions* (2nd ed., pp. 397–414). New York: Guilford Press.

Shweder, R. A., Mahapatra, M., & Miller, J. (1987). Culture and moral development. In J. Kagan & S. Lamb (Eds.), *The emergence of morality in young children* (pp. 1–83). Chicago: University of Chicago Press.

Shweder, R. A., Much, N. C., Mahapatra, M., & Park, L. (1997). The "big three" of morality (autonomy, community, and divinity), and the "big three" explanations of suffering. In A. Brandt & P. Rozin (Eds.), *Morality and health* (pp. 119–169). New York: Routledge.

Silver, M., Sabini, J., & Parrott, J. (1987). Embarrassment: A dramaturgic account. *Journal for the Theory of Social Behavior, 17,* 47–61.

Smith, A. (1976). *The theory of moral sentiments.* Oxford, England: Oxford University Press. (Original work published 1759)

Smith, C., & Ellsworth, P. (1985). Patterns of cognitive appraisal in emotion. *Journal of Personality and Social Psychology, 48,* 813–838.

Sober, E., & Wilson, D. S. (1998). *Unto others: The evolution and psychology of unselfish behavior.* Cambridge, MA: Harvard University Press.

Solomon, R. C. (1993). The philosophy of emotions. In M. Lewis & J. Haviland (Eds.), *Handbook of emotions* (pp. 3–15). New York: Guilford Press.

Stein, N. L., Trabasso, T., & Liwag, M. (1993). The representation and organization of emotional experience: Unfolding the emotion episode. In M. Lewis & J. Haviland (Eds.), *Handbook of emotions* (pp. 279–300). New York: Guilford Press.

Tangney, J. P. (1991). Moral affect: The good, the bad, and the ugly. *Journal of Personality and Social Psychology, 61,* 598–607.

Tangney, J. P., & Fischer, K. W. (Eds.). (1995). *Self-conscious emotions: The psychology of shame, guilt, embarrassment, and pride.* New York: Guilford Press.

Tangney, J. P., Miller, R. S., Flicker, L., & Barlow, D. H. (1996). Are shame, guilt and embarrassment distinct emotions? *Journal of Personality and Social Psychology, 70,* 1256–1269.

Tavris, C. (1982). *Anger: The misunderstood emotion.* New York: Simon & Schuster.

Templeton, J. M. (1999). *Agape love: A tradition found in eight world religions.* Philadelphia: Templeton Foundation Press.

Tesser, A., Gatewood, R., & Driver, M. (1968). Some determinants of gratitude. *Journal of Personality and Social Psychology, 9*, 233–236.

Tomkins, S. (1962). *Affect, imagery, consciousness: Vol. 1. The positive affects.* New York: Springer.

Tomkins, S. (1963). *Affect, imagery, consciousness: Vol. 2. The negative affects.* New York: Springer.

Tomkins, S. S. (1981). The quest for primary motives: Biography and autobiography of an idea. *Journal of Personality and Social Psychology, 14*, 306–329.

Triandis, H. (1994). Major cultural syndromes and emotion. In S. Kitayama & H. R. Markus (Eds.), *Emotion and culture: Empirical studies of mutual influence* (pp. 285–306). Washington, DC: American Psychological Association.

Triandis, H., Bontempo, R., Villareal, M., Asai, M., & Lucca, N. (1988). Individualism and collectivism: Cross-cultural perspectives on self-ingroup relationships. *Journal of Personality and Social Psychology, 54*, 323–338.

Trivers, R. L. (1971). The evolution of reciprocal altruism. *Quarterly Review of Biology, 46*, 35–57.

Turiel, E. (1983). *The development of social knowledge: Morality and convention.* Cambridge, England: Cambridge University Press.

Wegner, D., & Bargh, J. (1998). Control and automaticity in social life. In D. T. Gilbert, S. T. Fiske, & G. Lindzey (Eds.), *Handbook of social psychology* (4th ed., pp. 446–496). New York: McGraw-Hill.

Weiner, B., & Graham, S. (1989). Understanding the motivational role of affect: Lifespan research from an attributional perspective. *Cognition and Emotion, 3*, 401–419.

Wierzbicka, A. (1992). *Semantics, culture, and cognition.* New York: Oxford University Press.

Wilkinson, G. S. (1984). Reciprocal food sharing in the vampire bat. *Nature, 308*, 181–184.

Wilson, J. Q. (1993). *The moral sense.* New York: Free Press.

Zahn-Waxler, C., Radke-Yarrow, M., & King, R. (1979). Child rearing and children's prosocial initiations toward victims of distress. *Child Development, 50*, 319–330.

# 46

# EMOTIONS AS DYNAMIC CULTURAL PHENOMENA

Batja Mesquita

## Cultural Differences Conceptualized

Following Darwin's work on emotional expression, many psychologists set out to demonstrate the features of emotions that are universal. Cross-cultural research has suggested universality of a number of facial, vocal, and bodily expressions, antecedent events, appraisals, action readiness modes, and physiological changes associated with certain emotions (for reviews of this evidence, see Mesquita & Frijda, 1992; Mesquita, Frijda, & Scherer, 1997). The evidence for universal constituents of emotions is convincing.

But does this evidence mean that the emotional experience of people in different cultures is similar? In this chapter I suggest that this is not the case: Emotional experience greatly varies across cultures. I argue that cultural models are necessary to understand and predict these variations.

## Cultural Models as Organizing Principles of Emotional Practice

The central purpose of this chapter is to suggest that emotional experience is to be understood and predicted from cultural models. Cultural models are at one and the same time forms of knowledge and social practices (Moscovici, 1988). Cultural models are like schemas: They can be flexibly applied to the context. Somewhat different properties of the schema will emerge depending on their relevance to the situation at hand. Cultural models importantly con-

stitute a person's reality, because they focus attention, they guide perception, they lend meaning, and they imbue emotional value. A cultural model is decisive in what your world is like (Bruner, 1986) and reflects the cultural "answers" to existential questions, such as the real, the good, the self, the group, and so forth (D'Andrade, 1984; D'Andrade & Strauss, 1992; Holland & Quinn, 1987).

In a middle-class American context an important aspect of the cultural model is to gain success through one's own contributions. Through individual hard work, people can be successful; this will boast their self-esteem, a central concern in America, and it will make them happy, the most desirable emotion in an American context (e.g., D'Andrade, 1984; Heine, Lehman, Markus, & Kitayama, 1999). Success is good, happiness is good, and high self-esteem is good, and those goals need to be fostered and if necessary protected from group pressure. In fact, the very choice of the groups that one is part of should be made to serve individual success and happiness (Triandis, 1995). The promotion of happiness and the fostering of situations which afford happiness are important themes in America.

In contrast, in many Mediterranean cultures, honor is central to the cultural model (Bourdieu, 1966; Peristiany, 1966; Pitt-Rivers, 1966). In these cultures the cultural models emphasize maintaining one's social status and respect (i.e., one's position in the society) rather than the gain of individual success. One's honor is in great part determined by the honor of close family members. Therefore, the self includes the in-group. What counts is others' view of a person, rather than that person's self-esteem. In cultures of honor, it is very important to persistently and continuously avoid shame or embarrassment situations, in which other people can make negative judgments about you.

Self-esteem in an American context and honor in a Mediterranean context are central in discourse but also in the ways life is organized. American parents and schools are motivated by a concern to boost and protect the self-esteem of their youth (Stigler & Perry, 1990; Miller, Fung, & Mintz, 1990b), whereas the Awlad 'Ali and many other Mediterranean cultures try to protect their honor through institutionalized sex segregation that prevents women from being shamed in encounters with men, who are seen as naturally more honorable (Abu-Lughod, 1986). Life is lived according to cultural models.

Importantly, no two individuals in a culture will engage the model in exactly the same way. Therefore, a focus on cultural models does not mean that people in a given context are homogeneous clones of one another (Markus, Mullaly, & Kitayama, 1997). As is the case with schemas, an individual's particular representations of the model are specific to his or her specific experiences in that culture. What is critical, though, is that the world—the ways in which things are done in the culture—still powerfully reflects the dominant cultural models (Shweder, 1991, 1999). Those models set the reality boundaries within which self, relationships, and goals are defined, formed, and promoted (Bruner, 1986).

### Emotions

This chapter adopts a componential approach to emotions. In this approach, emotions consist of combinations of emotion components (e.g., Frijda, 1986; Lang, 1988; Oatley & Johnson-Laird, 1987; Scherer, 1984). The components involve the antecedent event, the appraisal, action readiness, ANS activity, expression, instrumental behavior, and conscious regulation (Frijda, 1986).

The central idea in the componential approach is that different emotion components do not automatically follow from each other. Each has its particular determinants, in addition to the occurrence of an emotionally charged event. The components tend to influence, but not fully determine, each other. The implication is that each of these components can cross-culturally vary independently from each other (Mesquita et al., 1997).

This is not to say that the different components are completely independent of each other or that all patterns of emotion components are equally likely to occur. It is plausible, for instance, that major appraisal outcomes and major interaction patterns, although not invariably linked, maintain a nonarbitrary coherence. Cross-culturally, the realization that another person intentionally inflicts harm will lead to a readiness to change the relationship with the other person (rather than be exuberant, for example). There are logical constraints to the combinations of appraisals and action readiness to be found. Certain patterns are more likely to occur than are others. It should be emphasized, though, that the level of association between different components is an empirical question. There is no basis for making a priori assumptions about the existence of homogeneous, integral mechanisms of emotions (Mesquita et al., 1997).

Within each component, different responses are available. For example, within the component of appraisal, one can appraise an event as pleasant, as one's own responsibility, and so forth. And within the component of facial expression, one can smile, frown, and so forth. The available responses within each emotion component have been called "emotion potential" (Mesquita et al., 1997; Scherer, 1999). Some of these responses are demonstrably hardwired, but others may be socially learned.

In each emotion instance, out of the emotion potential some responses are "activated," whereas most others remain inactive or unused (Lang, 1988; Mesquita & Frijda, 1992). Response activation refers to a largely automatic process rather than to conscious decision making. Activation is assumed when only one response is actualized amidst a larger availability of options. The resultant emotional responses—the activation outcomes—can be called "emotion practice." In addition to the initial activation of responses, effortful regulation also determines the occurrence of emotional responses. This type of regulation is a conscious adjustment or replacement of initial responses in order to render them more consistent with desirable outcomes and it thus also affects emotional practice.

Thus emotional potential consists of the responses that are available to the individual in principle, whereas emotional practices are the combined responses that actually or typically occur in specific contexts. It is argued that emotional practice, rather than emotional potential, is experientially close (cf. Averill, 1982; Oatley, 1993; Parkinson, 1995).

Emotional experience is thus constituted by awareness of activation outcomes across components. There is some discussion in the literature as to whether "feeling qualia" are separate from emotions (Oatley & Johnson-Laird, 1987; Zajonc, 1984, 2000) or whether emotional experience *is* the awareness of specific responses in other components of the emotion (Frijda, 1987; Oatley & Johnson-Laird, 1989). There is no cross-cultural evidence that addresses this issue. Therefore, I capitalize on the consensus among componential approaches that the awareness of all emotional responses importantly, if not exclusively, constitutes emotional experience (Frijda, 1986). Emotional experience is thus a matter of practice rather than potential. The potential constrains emotional experience but does not constitute it.

## Emotional Practice

Cultural differences in emotional experience are thus expected to derive from differences in emotional practice: the responses that actually or typically occur in specific contexts. Emotional practice can be described (1) for each of the components of emotions separately or (2) at the levels of patterns of responses. At the *within-component level*, emotional practice refers to the likelihood of occurrence of particular responses. Cultural differences in the likelihood of occurrence may be conceptualized as differences in response activation and are likely due to differences in the responses that are "chronically accessible" (Higgins, 1989). The accessibility of certain responses will increase when those responses are either importantly promoting the cultural model or importantly incongruent with it. Accessibility of desirable responses will increase the likelihood that they will become materialized, and accessibility of undesirable ones will promote their suppression (Strack, Schwarz, Bless, & Kuebler, 1993). One class of responses are regulatory responses: the tendency to inhibit or strengthen other responses. Cultural models may focus in different degrees on certain components rather than others. Thus, for example, whereas some cultures promote a certain type of initial appraisals, others may emphasize certain forms of regulation.

At the *level of patterning*, emotional practice refers to the probability of associations between certain responses and thus the frequency of certain emotional patterns (or "emotions"). Emotional practices in this sense may thus exceed the level of the individual emotion, reflecting the emotion patterns that occur with particularly high or low frequency in a culture. Differences in the rate of certain emotions can be an aggregate result of cultural differences in response activation, but alternatively they may be connected to culture-specific distributions of emotional contexts. There may be cross-cultural differences in the prevalence of certain contexts that elicit emotions, affording or adding to the relatively low or high occurrence of those emotions. The prevalence of emotional contexts may be structurally determined; that is, the societal organization may promote certain contexts and limit others. Alternatively, the prevalence of certain contexts may differ because individuals tend to seek or create them or, to the contrary, avoid exposure to them.

Central to this chapter is the proposition that emotional practices are better understood and predicted at every level if we have knowledge of the context of the cultural models within which they occur. Thus consideration of cultural models makes the differences in emotional responses less random, more predictable, and more coherent. The role of cultural models becomes particularly clear when we look at all aspects and levels of

Table 46.1 Cultural Models as Organizing Principles of Emotional Practice

| Process | Emerging Quality of the Emotional Practice |
|---|---|
| ***Response Activation*** | |
| • Activation of appraisal | *High* frequency of appraisals *consistent* with cultural model <br> *Low* frequency of appraisals *inconsistent* with cultural model |
| • Activation of action readiness | *High* frequency of action readiness modes *consistent* with cultural model <br> *Low* frequency of action readiness modes *inconsistent* with cultural model |
| • Activation of expression and behavior | *High* frequency of expressions and behaviors *consistent* with cultural model <br> *Low* frequency of expressions and behaviors *inconsistent* with cultural model |
| • Activation of regulatory processes | *High* frequency of regulatory processes (inhibition, amplification) that are model consistent and produce model-consistent emotional elements |
| ***Emotional Patterning*** | |
| • Cultural focality of emotions | *High* frequency of emotions (i.e., patterns of responses) that are *consistent* with cultural model <br> *Low* frequency of emotions that are *inconsistent* with cultural model |
| • Ecologies of contexts | *High* frequency of contexts that afford and promote emotions which are *consistent* with cultural model <br> *Low* frequency of contexts that afford and promote emotions which are *inconsistent* with cultural model |
| • Diversity of cultural goals for emotions | Cultural emphasis on *initial response activation* when cultural models are univocal <br> Cultural emphasis on *effortful regulation* when cultural models involve various goals |

emotional practices at the same time (see Table 46.1). The same cultural models can often be recognized as organizing principles of emotion practices across the board. There is redundancy in the cultural shaping of emotions (Levy, 1978) such that cultural models shape emotion practices into congruence at many different loci in many different ways. This chapter illustrates the organizing role of cultural models at different levels of emotional practice.

## Cultural Differences in Emotional Practice: Within Components

Cultural differences in response activation amount to different emotion practices. These differences in response activation can be assumed on the basis of differences in the mere frequencies of responses. However, they can be established with more confidence when responses that are inconsistent with a given cultural model have a low rate of occurrence or when responses that are consistent have a high rate of occurrence. Therefore, prediction and interpretation of differences in responses activation are facilitated by interpretation of the emotional phenomena within the cultural model in which they occur.

### Appraisal

The ways in which people appraise a situation are assumed to constitute the emotional experience to an important degree (Mesquita & Ellsworth, 2001). The appraisal that the situation is positively relevant to the self, for example, will be associated with positive emotions, whereas perceived negative relevance to the self will be related to the experience of negative emotions. Appraisals are also assumed to further differentiate between emotions (e.g., Frijda, Kuipers & Terschure, 1989; Lazarus, 1991), for example, by attributing responsibility to the self, to a particular other, or to nobody in particular (this dimension is called *agency*). One of the likely correlates of the attribution of responsibility to a specific agent—be it another person or the self—is that specific people can be influenced or controlled in ways that fate or the world in general cannot. Attribution of responsibility means that positive outcomes can be achieved once more and negative outcomes can be avoided (Weiner, 1982). It affords active and instrumental ways of coping and is therefore likely to make for a substantially different emotional experience.

Agency is thus an important dimension in differentiating between different types of emotional experience; moreover, it is a dimension on which cultural models appear to differ. A key aspect of Western cultural models, American in particular, is success through independent, personal accomplishment (Markus & Kitayama, 1991). Claiming responsibility and a personal sense of control are at the center of what it is to be a person in this culture. The cultural model would thus predict that Westerners find responsibility a relevant appraisal dimension in many situations and that they strive for a state of responsibility and control.

In contrast, East Asian cultural models stress fate, the multidetermination of events, and the interdependence of an individual and his or her (social) environment (Fiske, Kitayama, Markus, & Nisbett, 1998; Heine et al., 1999; Nisbett, Peng, Choi, & Norenzayan, 2001). Personal agency

has very limited applicability in these models. Rather, Japanese people should be expected to explain the occurrence of emotional situations by fate and by the combination of many circumstances together.

Many African cultures emphasize the connectedness of human and supernatural forces (Markus et al., 1997; Mbiti, 1970). Attribution of agency to ancestors and spirits—both good and evil—is common. Ancestors are thought to keep the clan together, and thus they punish behavior that threatens the unity or the order of the clan. The punishment is not necessarily directed at the individual in transgression but may hit all those who are connected to him or her. Evil spirits tend to cause an individual to suffer illness, adversity, or bad fate (e.g., Lienhardt, 1961). Other people who hold a grudge against the individual invoke evil spirits. Agency is thus an extremely relevant dimension, attributed to other people, ancestors, and supernatural forces.

Causal explanations in the social world thus vary largely between cultures. These differences in cultural models have been reflected by cultural differences in agency appraisal: the dimensions of responsibility and control. The data on this dimension of cultural variation come from a limited number of questionnaire studies. Participants in most of these studies were asked to remember an instance of a given emotion, to describe the situation, and then to rate the situation on a number of appraisal scales that are provided by the researchers (Mesquita & Ellsworth, in press).[1]

In an early study, Matsumoto, Kudoh, Scherer, and Wallbott (1988), comparing Japanese and American students, found that Japanese students judged the dimension of responsibility to be inapplicable to emotional situations more often than did American students. Thus, when asked to report their appraisals for emotions such as anger and sadness, many Japanese respondents felt that responsibility was not a relevant question to be asked, possibly because of the idea that situations are constituted by the combination of many factors together. Consistently, Mauro, Sato, and Tucker (1992), studying emotional appraisal in students from the United States, the People's Republic of China, Hong Kong, and Japan, found the dimensions of control and responsibility to be two of three dimensions for which substantial cross-cultural differences were observed. In this study the differences in appraisal meant that similar emotions loaded in cross-culturally different ways on these dimensions. Mauro et al. (1992) reported the appraisal patterns neither by cultural group nor by emotion by cultural group. Congruence coefficients between the culture-specific models of appraisal suggested that the principal component solutions of Japan and the People's Republic of China on the one hand and the United States on the other are least congruent for effort and control dimensions. Consistently, in Scherer's study among students from 37 different countries, agency emerged as one of the three appraisal dimensions that differed across six geopolitical regions: northern and central Europe, Mediterranean countries, Anglo-American New World countries, Latin American, Asian, and African countries (Scherer, 1997a, 1997b). Agency was coded as *self, close persons, other persons,* or *impersonal* agency and roughly corresponded to Mauro et al.'s (1992) dimensions of responsibility and control. In this study, however, the African participants attributed negative emotional situations more to external causes than students from any of the other regions did. For example, African participants rated sad situations as significantly more externally caused than did participants from any of the other geopolitical regions. This finding may reflect an African cultural model in which losses and misfortune are due to spirits' attacks and other people's black spells. Asian students in Scherer's study did not differ from students from the other continents, but this result is hard to interpret because the variance between different Asian countries was high.

Cultural differences in the American and African perceptions of agency are not very well captured by the appraisal research. The cultural models of these cultures suggest some additional categories of appraisal that would tailor the African cultural models better. Thus, as Shweder (1991) suggested, supernatural agents are seen in many cultures as significant players in daily life, and they might elicit emotions that are not well captured by the traditional agency distinctions of "someone else" or "no one."

Despite the insensitivity of measurements, the cultural differences found in agency appraisals are consistent with documented cultural models of causality in the social domain. There is reason to assume that differences in agency appraisals have important correlates in the course and experience of emotions. Thus interpreting misfortune as the outcome of other people's negligence, as the outcome of other people's spells, or as the outcome of fate is likely to have important implications for the subsequent action readiness, the physiological preparation of action, and the behavior itself, and thus for emotional experience. Such consequences of the differences in appraisal have yet to be addressed in empirical research.

The results from a recent experience-sampling study that monitored the daily emotions of 50 Japanese and 50 American students throughout a week offered some initial evidence that the relevance of agency appraisals might in fact be different cross-culturally. For American students, "personal control" was a good predictor of pleasantness, whereas for Japanese students pleasantness was much less related to personal control (Mesquita & Karasawa, in press). Overall, Americans thus not only have a higher tendency to appraise emotional situations as being under control but also have more positive emotions when they do so than Japanese people.

Fairness is another dimension on which cultures appear to differ, and one that may relate to the same differences in cultural models as the agency appraisals. The relevance of fairness seems to be higher if events are perceived to result from some agent's intentional behavior. Therefore, to the extent that cultures frame events as intentional rather than as, for instance, the result of fate, fairness should be expected to be central. In his large-scale study, Scherer found that respondents from the African continent tended to appraise negative situations as more unfair than respondents from the other geopolitical regions did (Scherer, 1997b). Scherer, Wallbott, Matsumoto, and Kudoh (1988), comparing antecedents reported by American and Western European respondents with those reported by Japanese respondents, found that injustice was much less commonly quoted as an antecedent of anger by the Japanese than by the Western groups (4% vs. 21%). Mesquita and Karasawa (2001) found that Americans appraised the daily emotional events in their life on the average as more fair than the Japanese did. Moreover, fairness had a higher correlation with pleasantness in the American than in the Japanese group, suggesting that fairness was more decisive for emotional experience in Americans than in Japanese people. A similar pattern of results emerges for fairness as for agency. Despite the huge differences between the North American and the African cultural models, personal agency *and* fairness appear to be more important in these cultures than in the East Asian ones, the Japanese in particular.

Another domain of appraisal on which cultures may differ is that of morality. Shweder, Much, Mahapatra, and Park (1997) proposed three ethics that are differently represented across cultures. Immorality in the ethics of autonomy would be an infraction of individual rights and freedom (e.g., the right to physical integrity). Immorality in the ethics of community would consist of a violation of the hierarchy or of duties. Finally, immorality in the ethics of divinity would have to do with disrespect for the divine (sin) and degradation. There is some evidence that immorality in each of these different domains is paired to a different class of emotions: Anger is associated with violations of autonomy, contempt with violations of community, and disgust with violations of divinity (Rozin, Lowery, Imada & Haidt, 1999; see also chapter 45, this volume). It is not completely clear how appraisals would mediate this process. One way of conceptualizing the process would be to see immorality as increasingly nonnegotiable for the three types of ethics, from "unfair" (autonomy) to "disrespectful" (community) to "sinful" (divinity), and therefore as associated with emotions that are decreasingly under voluntary control: anger, contempt, and disgust. If all domains of ethics would be represented, so would all instantiations of the appraisal of immorality, whereas a relative underrepresentation of one domain would mean a lower frequency of this type of immorality appraisal. The relative insignificance of fairness appraisals in our Japanese respondents (Mesquita & Karasawa, 2001) may thus reflect the lesser place that autonomy ethics have in that culture. It is clear that the cross-cultural appraisal literature has failed to capture these rich distinctions in morality appraisals. In the most comprehensive cross-cultural study of appraisal, Scherer (1997b) operationalized immorality by asking to what extent the behavior central in the emotional situation would be "judged as *improper* or *immoral* by your acquaintances" (p. 124). It is unclear what kinds of immorality would be captured by this question or if particular types of morality would be excluded. His finding that African respondents identified more immorality in emotional situations and that South American respondents identified less than the other geopolitical regions is therefore hard to interpret.

Many non-Western cultural models appear to be centered on the maintenance of relationships. Therefore, one would expect that one of the salient dimensions of appraisal in those cultures is that of interpersonal engagement. For example, Kitayama and Markus found that adding Japanese emotion terms "that presuppose the presence of others" (Kitayama & Markus, 1990, cited in Markus & Kitayama, 1991, p. 238) to a standard sample of emotions resulted in an appraisal dimension of interpersonal engagement, with ego-focused emotions such as pride and anger at one pole and other-focused emotions, such as shame and the Japanese sense of *fureai* (feeling of connection with someone), at the other pole. Similarly, Kitayama, Markus, and Kurokawa (2000) found that frequencies of Japanese emotions were best explained by whether they were interpersonally engaged or not, regardless of their valence. Interpersonal engagement may be an appraisal dimension across cultures, but its salience appears to differ considerably (Mesquita & Ellsworth, 2001). The extent to which cultural models focus on harmony in the relationship is likely to form the basis of the activation of this appraisal.

In sum, cultural differences have been found in the appraisal practices of agency, fairness, and interpersonal engagement that can be related to corresponding differences in cultural models. Moreover, morality appraisals may be hypothesized to correspond with different ethics. Cultural models of the causes of behavior, personhood, and of the constitution of the good make it possible to understand and predict the cultural differences in appraisal practices and, to some extent, to see them in connection. An emphasis on cultural models may also suggest the inclusion of culture-specific or non-Western categories of appraisal that have only recently started to be considered in some studies (Mesquita, 2001; Mesquita & Karasawa, 2001). One challenge to appraisal research will thus be to include dimensions of appraisal as they appear relevant (and sometimes *most* relevant) to non-Western cultures.

A more radical challenge is that the concept of appraisal may itself be a Western invention, reflecting the importance that Western cultural models lend to intrapersonal, subjective meanings (Kitayama & Masuda, 1994). In cultures that do not place as much emphasis on subjectivity and on the individual as the generator of meaning, the process of meaning making may be perceived—and perhaps also attained—in different ways. The meanings of situations may be socially negotiated and thus perceived not to exist in separation from the individual, or they may be socially scripted and thus interpreted as a fixed feature of a particular type of situation (Mesquita, 2001). Future cross-studies may, therefore, want to take the concept of appraisals one step beyond Western ideology and replace it by a component that reflects meaning making, whether projected and experienced in the social situation or, alternatively, in the "head" of an individual. There is no empirical research as yet that has tried to capture this "different" type of meaning making and its relationship with emotion.

## Action Readiness

Emotions involve an urgent priority for one kind of action; this aspect of emotion is called *action readiness* (Arnold, 1960; Frijda, 1986). Action readiness has been defined as the readiness to change the relationship between the self and the environment. In many cases, action readiness reflects a "relational intent" (Frijda & Mesquita, 1994, p. 56). Definitions of self and of others, as well as the schemas and goals for relationships, are to a large extent implicated by cultural models. Therefore, cultural models are likely to penetrate the relational aims—the end goals—that form the core of action readiness. Action readiness has been operationalized at a more concrete level as the preferred means to achieve end goals. For example, one action readiness mode would be "a tendency to physical aggression," which is certainly more specific than the relational goal of subjecting another person to one's will. The preferred means will be shaped by cultural models as well, as the efficient ways to attain certain end goals will vary according to their meaning and fit into cultural practices. The literature on action readiness is sparse, but it does offer some support for the fit of action readiness with cultural models.

Frijda, Markam, Sato, & Wiers (1995) compared the action readiness modes reported by Dutch, Indonesian, and Japanese participants. The participants were asked to recall an experience of a given emotion. Respondents from the different cultural groups rated these self-reported instances of emotions with regard to the same 36 action readiness items. Nineteen stimulus emotions were used in the study. The words had proven to be among the most frequent in recall studies done with Dutch and Indonesian respondents. The Japanese words were translations of those concepts.

Each respondent provided action readiness ratings for several emotions—the number of emotions per respondent also varied by cultural group—so that the observations for different emotions were not independent. As an exploration of the data, factor analyses of the 36 action readiness items were conducted for each culture separately. Those analyses suggested that 5 (of the 6 to 9) factors in each of the three cultural groups were similar: moving away, moving toward, moving against, wanting help, and submitting. The factors can be interpreted as the relational aims of the action readiness. The study thus suggests a number of goals that are universally available. However, the relative importance of those goals differed. *Moving away* and *moving against* explained more variance in emotion words in the Dutch group than in either of the other groups, and *moving toward* and *submitting* explained more variance in the Indonesian and Japanese groups than in the Dutch. *Wanting help*, furthermore, explained more variance in emotions in the Indonesian than in either of the other two groups. Clearly, cultural differences existed with regard to the relevance of those behavioral goals for the differentiation of emotions.

Although it is possible that any differences in action readiness stem from differences in the meaning of the stimulus words that were used, this is not likely. Cultural models of the three groups offer plausible explanations for the variations in action readiness across cultures. The Dutch cultural model of seeking to be independent, if necessary through opposition (as a way of expressing oneself; Stephenson, 1989; Van der Horst, 1996), may explain the significance of action readiness modes that have just that goal: moving away and moving against. On the other hand, the two East Asian cultures appear to promote goals of relational harmony, either by reducing social distance or by fitting in and making oneself acceptable to the other person (Markus et al., 1997); hence the relative importance of moving toward and submitting as behavioral goals. It should be noted that the rigor of this study is wanting.

The same study also provides evidence for cross-cultural differences in the prevalent means used to achieve these behavioral goals. It proved impossible to construct a common factor structure for the three groups, despite the similarities that could be observed between the factor solutions in each culture (Frijda et al., 1995). The authors suggest as a reason that the specific modes of behavior that loaded onto the factors in each culture was different. For example, the behavioral goal of submission was instantiated by *comply, depend,* and *apathy* in the Dutch group. In the Indonesian group it was instantiated by those same three action readiness modes plus modes that reflected a lack of control over one's actions (*inhibited, helpless, blocked,* and, negatively, *in command*). In

Japan, submission was formed by action readiness modes of dependence (*depend* and *comply*), of lack of control (*blocked, helpless*), and of social engagement (*make up for it, tenderness*). The specific action readiness modes that are adopted to strive for the overarching behavioral goal—submission in this case—appear to be cross-culturally different, consistent with cultural models. In interdependent cultures, not being in control may be a sufficient condition for others to take the lead. Therefore, to feel blocked or helpless may automatically mean to submit. Furthermore, consistent with the Japanese model of relationship (e.g., Lebra, 1994), social engagement in Japan may in fact mean being able and willing to yield to other people.

Similarly, in comparative work with Dutch, Surinamese, and Turkish respondents in the Netherlands, I found that aggressive goals tend to be sought after in ways that make sense within the unique cultural models (Mesquita, 1993). For example, Surinamese and Turkish respondents reported a higher tendency to show indifference in situations in which they had been harmed by another person. The high value attached to relatedness in those cultures, as compared with the Dutch, turns indifference—the denial of engagement—into an effective act of aggression.

Recently, we interviewed 40 European Americans, 20 Mexicans living in the United States, and 40 Japanese respondents. Respondents were selected both from community and college student samples (Mesquita, Karasawa, Haire, & Izumi, in preparation). In the interviews, each respondent reported three different emotional situations from their own pasts: one in which they had experienced "offense," one of "pride" (a situation in which they felt extremely valued or important), and one of "humiliation" (a situation in which they felt very small or humiliated). For each situation the respondents were asked to report if they had felt like doing or not doing something in particular. The three cultural groups reported very different patterns of action readiness.

Generally, the Japanese responses were most distinct. Many respondents in this group said they did not understand the question, and the most frequent response to it was that there had been nothing they had wanted to do. Across the different situations, the Japanese—males and females alike—focused on coming to terms with the emotional situations rather than on changing anything in the environment or their relationship with the environment. The goal seemed to be to restore internal balance rather than to establish any external goal (cf. Heine et al., 1999) This trend is consistent with the well-documented Japanese preference for secondary control, as opposed to primary control strategies prevalent in Western cultures (Morling & Kitayama, 1999; Weisz, Rothbaum, & Blackburn, 1984). "In primary control, individuals enhance their rewards by influencing existing realities. . . . In secondary control, individuals enhance their rewards by accommodating to existing realities and maximizing satisfaction or goodness of fit with things as they are" (Weisz et al., 1984, p. 955). The tendency may also fit in with the focal Japanese cultural goals of harmony with the environment and mental balance (Heine et al., 1999).

The pattern of action readiness in the Mexican group was clearly penetrated by a concern with relatedness (Sanchez-Burks, Nisbett, & Ybarra, 2000), specifically with the honor and coherence of the family (Condon, 1985). In the "pride" situation, Mexicans reported the tendency to be closer; for example, "I felt like hugging them all at once" (Mexican woman) or "to be near my family, to be with them" (Mexican man). In the negative situations, many Mexicans reported a readiness for action that would hurt the offender by severing the relationship (withdrawing, leaving) or by aggression (hit and curse), but they also wanted to protect the honor of their families: "I tried to avoid a bad situation for my family" (Mexican man).

Finally, action readiness in the American group reinforced the separateness and individuality of the person. In the pride situations, American participants reported being thankful (a state that emphasizes the separateness of two individuals, as well as the exchange relation between them) and getting further involved in the gratifying activity. In the negative situations, the most common response was a tendency for verbal or physical aggression. In readiness for aggression, the emphasis was on venting the emotion and thereby on expressing one's individuality (Lutz, 1988; Markus & Kitayama, 1991) rather than on hurting the offender, as appeared to be the main purpose of the Mexican respondents.

Cultural models thus appear helpful in interpreting cultural differences in the activation of action readiness responses. The research in this domain is very scarce and not very rigid methodologically. The study of cultural differences in action readiness would be facilitated by starting from distinct cultural models. These models should help to predict cultural differences with regard to both the general goals of action readiness and the specific behaviors that are put forward to instantiate these goals.

### Expression and Behavior

Cultural differences in the frequencies of certain types of expressions and behaviors tend to reflect differences in cultural models as well. High-frequency responses correspond with or fulfill cultural goals, whereas low-frequency responses are contrary to certain cultural goals. Therefore, cultural models may be thought of as influencing the relative salience of different behavioral options.

Several studies suggest an East Asian focus on composed emotional behavior. For example, Japanese respondents reported many fewer hand and arm gestures and less whole body activity than did Americans in situations of anger, sadness, fear, and happiness (Scherer et al., 1988). The cultures did not differ in reported control of these emotions. The lower frequency of active nonverbal behaviors among the Japanese may thus be considered a result of a lower level of initially generated activity rather than a result of post hoc regulation.

These self-report data converge with actual measurements of general somatic behavior. Tsai and Levenson (1997) found that Chinese American couples who discussed a conflict area in their relationship displayed less general somatic activity than did European American couples. General somatic activity—the amount of movement in any direction—was one of the few physical response measures on which the two cultural groups differed.

Generally, expansive behavior such as general somatic activity may be taken to signal that the individual is occupying space in the relationship. Personal expansion seems to contrast with the relational objective of fitting into the relationship that has been reported for many East Asian cultures. A concern with relational harmony may make somatic activity undesired, because it is indicative of personal expansiveness rather than adjustment. There is some indication that the expression of happiness, another expansive behavior, is rare in cultures that place an emphasis on harmony in relationships (Lutz, 1987). Happiness expressions are seen as potentially disruptive because they may painfully contrast with the emotional state of others, or because they may be seen to indicate the plausibility of an individual challenging social obligations and evading responsibilities (Lutz, 1987; Karasawa, personal communication, August 1999).

Ethnographic work suggests that culture-specific behaviors sometimes emerge as a compromise between relational goals and conflicting emotional goals. Behavioral models that serve the emotional goals without being disruptive of the cultural ideals of self and relationship tend to be favored (Mesquita & Frijda, 1992). For example, the Balinese reaction to frightening events—falling asleep—can be understood as a culture-specific instantiation of the general emotional goal of fear—avoidance (Bateson & Mead, 1942). Falling asleep satisfies—at least subjectively—the goal of reducing one's exposure to the threat while avoiding the emotional disruption that other fear responses are felt to cause. Therefore, falling asleep can be considered an effective cultural compromise between the cultural model of emotions and relationships and the emotional goal of avoidance.

Similarly, *satru* is the Javanese compromise between social harmony and hostility. The Javanese ideal of social harmony, *rukun* (H. Geertz, 1961), requires the concealment of all dissonant aspects. Sometimes this concealment is reached through *satru*, an institutionalized pattern of avoidance in which the individuals in conflict refuse to speak or interact with one another. *Satru* "is an excellent mechanism for the adjustment of hostility in a society that plays down violence and the expression of real feelings, since it allows for the avoidance of an outbreak of rage while still permitting significant expression of it" (Geertz, 1961, pp. 117–118).

Cultural models may specify the context of expression, as is the case for rituals. The whole purpose of ritual may be to channel emotional expression in ways that are compatible with cultural models. For example, the Philippine Ilongot appeared to use the ritual of head-hunting to divert in-group aggression and maintain their cohesive group life. The Ilongot concept of *liget* stands for our notions of passion, energy, and anger simultaneously (Rosaldo, 1980). When one or more Ilongot men had heavy feelings of *liget*, they went out to head-hunt. The preparations for the killing led one's *liget* to a climax and focused it on the specific goal of head-hunting. After the beheading, the Ilongot men returned home, purged of violence. Men and women celebrated the overcoming of *liget* by singing. Ilongot head-hunting may be seen as a socially provided and effective way of anger, or *liget*, expression. The Ilongot believed that *liget*, focused in this manner, is productive, whereas unfocused *liget* causes chaos and disturbs social life. The Ilongot were probably right about the usefulness of head-hunting. By carefully shifting the direction of the aggression to far outside the group and creating community spirit, the ritual manages to master and take advantage of the individual's *liget*.

Cultural models of self and relationship thus imbue certain behaviors with valence. Aggression and happy expansiveness may universally emphasize individuality and self-other boundaries, but this is consistent with some cultural models—and thus good—and inconsistent with others—and therefore bad. The culture-specific valence of certain behaviors may affect their rate of occurrence. Some cultures provide behavioral models that compromise between emotional intentions and cultural goals of self and relationships and thus create an outlet for action readiness that is not quite so offensive to the cultural goals. Finally, cultures may create specific contexts for emotional behavior. Even in those contexts, the requirement is often that emotion be expressed in prescribed and culturally modeled ways.

It should be no surprise that cultural models affect emotional expression and behavior, as the primary function of both is communication. These communications together likely help to constitute the very cultural models that shaped and restrained them.

### Regulation of Emotions

Effortful regulation of responses, the regulation that people are aware of in some sense, does not necessarily pertain only to behavioral or expressive responses. Regulation of emotions also happens through such acts as changing the circumstances, changing one's focus of attention, changing one's appraisal, or changing one's subjective feelings (Frijda, 1986).

Often regulation has as its explicit purpose to align emotional responses with the cultural models of self and emotion. For example, relational harmony is a cornerstone of many Southeast Asian cultural models. Emotional control and the avoidance of anger and other strong emotions are tools to achieve this harmony. Some cultures appear to achieve equanimity (see the later subsection titled "Prevalence of emotions") and therefore seldom control their feelings in any effortful ways. Yet many other cultures, such as the Balinese, the Javanese, and the Torajan (all living in different parts of Indonesia; C. Geertz, 1960; H. Geertz, 1961; Hollan, 1988, 1992), seem to do "emotion work": They actively manage inner feelings (Hochschild, 1983). H. Geertz (1974) notes that the "quietness and calmness" of the Javanese "give an appearance of passivity, which is, however, illusory. Their poise and control are not relaxed, but vigilant; they always seem to be on their guard" (1974, p. 250). Therefore, Balinese, Javanese, and Torajan all appear to be active regulators of their emotional states.

Hollan (1988, 1992) described in some detail the emotion work in which the Torajan (South Sulawesi, Indonesia) engage to inhibit the experience and expression of "hot emotions" (anger, frustration, intense grief, drunkenness, and possession). The Torajan believe that hot emotions

> violate traditional forms of behavior, are formally prohibited, and may be punished by ancestors and spirits with visitations of illness and misfortune, including death, [that] prolonged emotional distress is thought to lead to more severe physical and mental disorders . . . ,[that] the diminution or loss of consciousness and awareness that accompany such states may lead one to commit the sorts of shameful or offensive acts which in turn may cause others to become emotionally upset and revengeful, [and thus] that hot, choked emotions may spread from person to person and so eventually come to jeopardize or destroy a community's unity, cohesion, and solidarity. (Hollan, 1992, p. 47)

These negative consequences highly motivate the Torajan to avoid or suppress hot feelings, primarily by changing the focus of their attention away from the troubling circumstances. They do this either by reminding themselves of the dangers of hot or choked emotions or by consciously suppressing the troubling thoughts or feelings.

The other Torajan strategy of emotion work has to do with the regulation of appraisal itself. "Goal relevance" (Frijda, 1986; Smith & Ellsworth, 1985) is reduced by reminding or convincing oneself that the gods and ancestors will assure that people end up getting what they deserve, good or bad. "The view that supernatural beings will 'exchange' or 'repay' unexpected or unjustified deprivations is quite strong" (Hollan, 1992, p. 50). The idea of which the Torajan are trying to convince themselves is thus that in the long run the current hassles will not affect their well-being.

Consistently, Hochshild's (1983) work on American emotion regulation in job contexts suggested regulation of the appraisal as well. Flight attendants—who strived for total agreeableness—were trained to adopt several strategies to avoid anger, of which the first two had to do with their shifting of attention and their regulation of appraisal. The first strategy flight attendants were taught was "to focus on what the *other* person might be thinking and feeling: imagine a reason that excuses his or her behavior" (Hochschild, 1983, p. 113). The second one was to reduce goal relevance by imagining that one can escape. For example, counting off the minutes until landing. Clearly, emotion work is used across cultures to align the emotional behavior and feelings with the behavior models required in the cultural context. In many cultural contexts, this alignment does not feel automatic and is mediated by a conscious effort to refocus attention and adjust appraisals.

Regulation may also take place in the expression and behavior aspect of the emotion. In some cases, regulation becomes clear from explicitly stated *display rules* (Ekman, Friesen, & Ellsworth, 1982). Display rules appear to fit in with cultural models. The Ifaluk (who live on a Pacific atoll) center their lives around harmony. The Ifaluk concept of harmony stresses that everyone keeps their proper place. The emotion of happiness is seen as threatening to harmony because it makes the elated person unreliable and likely not to attend to his or her business. Regulation of expression appears to be one of the means to prevent this socially disruptive state from coming to the surface. Lutz (1987) reported that she was reprimanded for smiling at a little Ifaluk girl who displayed happiness. She was told to be justifiably angry (*song*) at the girl instead. Regulation of happy expressions is thus part of the Ifaluk repertoire for living the cultural model.

In some ways American display rules are opposite to those of the Ifaluk (Wierzbicka, 1994), and so is the cultural model (D'Andrade, 1987; Markus, 1999; Markus & Kitayama, 1994). Cheerfulness is encouraged by American culture. "The norm in question can be presented as follows: 'It is good if people think that I feel something good all the time. I want people to think this.' What can I do to comply with the above norm? I can, of course, smile" (Wierzbicka, 1994, p. 179). It may be suggested that the American display rule of cheerfulness fits and expresses the cultural ideal of being self-sufficient, autonomous, and prepared to undertake the unusual—all cultural goals that are in stark opposition with the Ifaluk cultural model of restrained dutifulness.

The need for regulation also becomes clear from the projected ease with which certain emotions would be expressed. Negative emotions are potentially disturbing to the collectivist goal of harmony (Matsumoto, 1989; Stephan, Stephan, & Cabezas de Vargas, 1996; Stephan, Stephan, Saito, & Barnett, 1998). People in collectivist cultures can be predicted to feel uncomfortable with the expression of negative emotions. On the other hand, the discontent and disapproval expressed by many negative emotions may not be as disturbing in an individualist context, as the expression of individuality and dissent does not to the same extent violate cultural expectations (Matsumoto, 1989). The Stephans and their colleagues (Stephan et al., 1996; Stephan et al., 1998) studied how comfortable individualist American students expected to be expressing their emotions as compared with collectivist Costa Rican and Japanese students. Overall, American students expected to feel more comfortable expressing their emotions than either Costa Rican or Japanese students did. The differences in projected ease of expression were most pronounced for the negative emotions. Whereas the overall comfort of expression was no different in the Costa Rican than in the American group, differences in comfort were found for the negative emotions. In the Japan–United States comparison, a country-by-valence interaction was found, indicating that the difference in comfort of expression between pleasant and unpleasant emotions was larger in Japan than in the United States. The research failed to show a relation between measured individualism-collectivism and the comfort of expression. This may be due to problems with the measurement of collectivism and individualism (Peng, Nisbett, & Wong, 1997). The measurement of the constructs, rather than the constructs themselves, may therefore be problematic in the explanation of cultural differences in comfort of expression.

Cole and Tamang (1998) found evidence for the masking of emotions among one of the two cultural groups of Nepali children that they studied (the other group is discussed in the following section). The Chhetri-Brahmins, a group that practices Hinduism, emphasize spiritual purity, social order, and disciplined action. "The caste system is the social instantiation of these beliefs. Social behavior is organized around avoidance of spiritual pollution. . . . The emphasis is on highly disciplined control of self, of differences between self and others [the caste system], and of emotional self-control" (Cole & Tamang, 1998, p. 641). Consistent with the Chhetri-Brahmin emphasis on self-control, children from this group indicated that they would mask their emotions. The children were presented with six stories (e.g., about peer aggression toward the child) that together constituted the Challenging Situation Task (CST). For each story, children selected one of five emotions—happy, angry, sad, scared, and just okay—that they would feel. In four of the six situations the modal response of the Chhetri-Brahmin children was "angry." The children were then asked if they would want the other person in the situation to know that they felt this particular emotion. About 50–70% of the children reported that they would mask the emotion. A group of Chhetri-Brahmin mothers were asked if they felt they had taught their children how to manage their emotions, and the majority of mothers (about 70%) answered this question affirmatively. Therefore, willful regulation may be willfully induced by mothers.

Regulation in one of the components may have impact on the responses that are activated in one or more other components. For example, Richards and Gross (1999) found in female American undergraduate students that suppression affected incidental memory for what happened during suppression and that it increased cardiovascular activation. Therefore, regulation in one component may automatically influence some other components. Cross-cultural evidence is lacking.

The literature suggests that effortful regulation is responsible for at least some of the cultural differences in emotions. Hypotheses about the conditions under which the alignment of emotions with cultural models tends to be achieved by effortful regulation versus initial response activation is discussed later. It is important to note that conscious regulation is not restricted to the expression of emotion but is also applied to attention, appraisal, and feeling as well. Often the cultural goals explicitly motivate this regulation.

## Differences in Emotional Patterning

Emotional practices are more than the frequency of single responses and even more than the combined profiles of frequent and infrequent responses that characterize emotional practices. Emotional practices are what has been referred to as *ethos* (Schieffelin, 1985) or emotional style (Middleton, 1989):

> Ethos refers to the dominant emotional emphases, attitudes, and modes of expression of a culture as a whole. . . . The concept of ethos has generally been used as a descriptive ethnographic characterization. However, to the extent that individuals regularly exhibit attitudes and moods characterized by the ethos, that ethos can be considered expressively normative. That is, it is culturally expected that a person feel a certain way and adopt a certain affective posture and expressive style in relation to particular events . . . A culture's ethos is thus not only a characterization of a style of feeling and behavior but also a model for it. (Schieffelin, 1985, pp. 172–173)

Schieffelin acknowledges that "the problem is how these broad cultural emphases are to be related to the details of cultural behavior and individual experience" (1985, pp. 172–173).

The ethos, or the resultant cultural pattern of emotions, is more than the single response tendencies, described previously, added on to each other. Even if those response tendencies for the individual components of emotion are framed by cultural models of emotions, they do not quite capture the different gestalts that emotional lives in different cultures may take on. In the discussion that follows, several features of emotional lives are distinguished that further add to the gestalt. The distinctions are conceptual and not necessarily empirical. First, cultural differences in the experience of emotion generally, as well as in the most common or most focal emotions, are discussed. The influence of the cultural organization of life and of the frequencies of certain kinds of contexts on landscapes of emotion are addressed next. Finally, I discuss the effects of culturally different kinds of social regulation for the alignment of emotions to the cultural model.

## Prevalence of Emotions

Differences in the prevalent emotions tend to be predictable from cultural models. Kitayama et al. (2000) hypothesized that the frequent emotions in American and Japanese students differed as a function of cultural models or of the culturally sanctioned concerns of the self. The American imperative of the self is to be independent. The central concern is to discover and confirm the desirable attributes of the self, because these allow one to be self-sufficient (Markus & Kitayama, 1991). The Japanese imperative of the self, on the other hand, is to fit in and adjust oneself to the interpersonal context. These goals allow one to maintain mutually engaging social relationships. Americans were predicted to have a greater frequency of positive emotions than negative emotions. Japanese were predicted to have a greater tendency to enhance and augment the experience of engaging emotions regardless of whether these emotions are negative or positive.

In both cultures, respondents rated how often they experienced each of a list of emotions (*never to always*). Correlations were computed among the frequency ratings across respondents. The correlation matrix was submitted to a multidimensional scaling analysis showing that the first two underlying dimensions of the emotions in each culture could be interpreted as *pleasant-unpleasant* and *engaged-disengaged*. Consistent with their search for good self-characteristics, Americans reported a much higher frequency of positive than negative emotions. The frequencies of positive and negative emotions did not differ in the Japanese group. As the Japanese concern for harmony would suggest, Japanese reported a greater frequency of experiencing interpersonally engaged emotions than disengaged emotions, regardless of the valence of these emotions. The American practice of emotions centered on valence. Valence explained a sizable part of the variance in emotions for American respondents (70% for men, 38% for women). In contrast, Japanese emotions are centered on interpersonal engagement, which accounted for most of the variance in emotions in this group (29% for Japanese men, 52% for Japanese women).

As gender differences in interdependence in the United States would predict (Cross & Madson, 1997), the interpersonal engagement dimension explained some variance in emotions for American women (29%) and much less for American men (8%). In Japan, pleasantness explained variance for neither men (1%) nor women (0%).

Finally, pleasant and unpleasant experiences were negatively correlated in the United States sample. One interpretation of this finding is that it reflects the American objective to maximize positive feelings and minimize negative feelings. In contrast, positive and negative feelings were positively correlated in the Japanese group, meaning that the de-emphasizing of positive feelings in this group coincided with de-emphasizing negative feelings (Kitayama et al., 2000). This finding may indicate that balance rather than pleasantness is sought after in the Japanese group and that some people—the ones who are able to regulate both positive and negative emotions—are better at it than others (Kitayama & Markus, 1999).

The cultural goal of balance in the Japanese was also illustrated by the daily emotions of Japanese and American students (Mesquita & Karasawa, 2000). Four times a day for about a week, respondents reported the last emotion they had experienced in the preceding 3 hours. Emotions were categorized. The most common categories of emotions reported by American students were joy (22%) and stress/anxiety (13%). Most common among the Japanese students were security/contentment (14%), joy (14%), and resignation (13%). Americans' daily emotions thus reflected personal expansion and control and/or feelings of the challenge thereof, whereas two of the most common categories of Japanese emotions reflected balance and fit with the environment. Another way of interpreting the same data is that the prevalent emotion category in each group represented the dominant cultural model of coping with the environment: changing the environment and imposing one's will on it in the American context and adjusting to and harmonizing with it in the Japanese context (Morling & Kitayama, 1999; Weisz et al., 1984).

Finally, there are several indications that good feelings are closely tied with the models (Markus & Kitayama, 1994). Kitayama et al. (2000) found that general positive feelings had different correlates in the American and the Japanese groups. In Japan, general positive feelings (e.g. calm, relaxed) were most closely associated with engaged positive emotions (being interdependent). In contrast, pos-

itive feelings in the United States were most closely associated with interpersonally disengaged emotions (being interdependent). Similarly, Mesquita and Karasawa (2001) found that pleasantness in Japan was predicted by concerns of interdependence (e.g., interpersonal distance), whereas pleasantness in the United States was best predicted by concerns of independence (e.g., personal control). In other words, fulfillment of the culturally dominant concerns makes for pleasantness; obstruction of those concerns makes for unpleasantness. When one assumes that the meaning of the situation becomes an important part of the emotional experience, these different correlates should turn the experience of pleasantness into a different one.

## Initial Feelings or Effortful Regulation

To what extent, then, are the differences in emotional practices a result of effortful regulation of expression or a result of the different occurrence of emotions? Both seem to occur; it is impossible at this point to establish at what rate. However, the dominance of these different cultural strategies seems to vary across cultures. The best example of this difference is provided by the study that compared emotional responses of two groups of Nepali children and their mothers: the Chhetri-Brahmin and the Tamang (Cole & Tamang, 1998). As discussed, the Chhetri-Brahmin children, coming from a hierarchically organized culture, responded to several challenging situations with anger, and then reported as a majority that they would mask that emotion. The Tamang children—whose cultural values are egalitarian and communal—reported that they would feel "just okay" in each of the challenging situations. Accordingly, the Tamang children did not feel the need for response regulation.

Whereas Chhetri-Brahmin mothers felt that they taught their children to manage their emotions, Tamang mothers did not recognize this influence on their children's emotion management. The Chhetri-Brahmin mothers reported that they told their angry preschool children how to behave. In contrast, the majority of Tamang mothers reported they would try to make their children happy, to cajole them and give them good food. The Tamang children were thus consistently distracted in bad situations, which may have changed their appraisals of such negative situations in a positive direction. In other words, Chhetri-Brahmin mothers explicitly taught their children to change emotional display, whereas Tamang mothers implicitly taught their children to feel different in situations that would otherwise have elicited negative emotions. The mother's behavior may have been one of the cultural ways to promote the tendencies of effortful regulation versus those of implicit activation of appraisals.

At this point we can only guess at the conditions for one versus the other cultural mechanism. One hypothesis is that univocal cultural models are better suited for concern regulation than are ambivalent cultural models. For example, there appears to be a difference between cultures in which anger seems to be relatively absent—Tahitians (Levy, 1973), Utku Inuits (Briggs, 1970), and the Nepali Tamang (Cole & Tamang, 1998)—and those in which anger is explicitly regulated—the Balinese (C. Geertz, 1984), the Javanese (H. Geertz, 1974), the Torajan (Holland, 1988, 1992), and the Nepali Chhetri-Brahmin (Cole & Tamang, 1998). The former class of cultures has egalitarian relationships between the members, whereas the latter cultures are hierarchical and thus foster striving. Both groups of cultures stress harmony. In the egalitarian societies, such as the Tahitians, anger does not seem to be a "problem—it does not often manifest itself in socially disruptive behavior nor in somatic or psychological symptoms at the individual level—and the active suppression of hostility is largely unnecessary" (Levy, 1978, p. 233). On the other hand:

> when a society establishes distinctions of social rank, and in fact demands a certain degree of striving simply to protect one's position in the hierarchy from encroachment, clashes of interest and wills are inevitable. Yet a commitment to social harmony and mutual aid means that these conflicts and the interpersonal hostility that they engender cannot be openly expressed. . . . Conscious strategies are likely to be one of the complex of controls that regulate hostility and aggression in societies where competition is to some extent inescapable and the environment is experienced as frustrating. (Hollan, 1988, pp. 67–68)

Egalitarian cultures may thus afford harmony, whereas hierarchical societies may rather foster the appearance of harmony.

Other cultural dimensions also may influence the dominance of initial response activation versus effortful regulation. Bernstein (1974, cited in Hochschild, 1983) described lower-class families as having a more positional control system and middle-class families as having a more personal control system. Positional control bases authority on impersonally assigned status, whereas personal control systems focus on the feelings of parent and child. The "personal" child is persuaded to do what the parents want, whereas "positional" children are more likely to be told what to do. Middle-class children are thus made to feel that their own feelings are important and, in addition, that those feelings need to be controlled. When children behave inappropriately, the appeal made to middle-class children is to change their feelings ("don't be angry"), whereas the appeal made to working-class children will merely concern emotional expression ("don't yell"). It is possible that a socialization history that focuses on internal feelings will more readily affect the initial activation of emotional responses than will an emphasis on correct display. Middle-class and working-class families can be seen to represent different cultural environments.

Even if we adhere to a definition of culture as associated with different geographic areas, a dimension of outward versus inward orientation may be relevant. For example, some cultures appear to be centered on the concept of "honor"—an individual's reputation in the perception of others (e.g., Blok, 1980; Abu-Lughod, 1986)—whereas others are strongly focused on self-esteem (Kitayama, Markus, Matsumoto, & Norasakkunit, 1997). The concern for external manifestations is dominant in honor cultures, whereas the management of internal feelings is likely to prevail in self-esteem cultures.

The different loci of emphasis—external manifestations versus internal cues—may also be reflected in the criteria for selection of emotion words. *Hasham* among the 'Awlad Ali (roughly translated as *shame*) is recognized when the behaviors characteristic of *hasham*, namely deferent behaviors, are displayed—regardless of the simultaneous presence of the involuntary subjective response (Abu-Lughod, 1986). Similarly, *shing*—the Surinamese counterpart of shame—is defined by the condition of compromised pride, often in the absence of shame feelings (Mesquita, in preparation). Different cues may be used to establish whether something is an emotion in general. Minangkabau men did not recognize their physiological and facial responses as emotions if they were all by themselves, whereas American respondents would (Levenson, Ekman, Heider, & Friesen, 1992). The social context was a defining characteristic of an emotion for the Minangkabau, but not for Americans. Therefore, cultures appear to differ with respect to the primary criteria for establishing an emotion or specific emotions. Some cultures recognize emotions on the basis of circumstances and behaviors (e.g., Abu-Lughod, 1986; Lutz, 1986), and others predominantly on the basis of feelings or action readiness (Frijda, Kuipers, & Terschure, 1989; Kitayama et al., 2000).

### Focality of Emotions

The frequency of occurrence is only one way in which emotions can be culturally significant. Emotions may be very rare and yet play a central role in the emotional practice of a culture. This is the case in which the avoidance of emotions is a focal cultural concern. According to Briggs (1970), the Utku Inuits consider angry thoughts and acts as dangerous. It is felt that angry people are always likely to lose control. Angry people might ultimately be very destructive and commit murder, and angry people are thus frightening. Anger appears to be extremely important in the Utku culture. Everybody knows what anger elicitors are and avoids them. Furthermore, any sign of anger is met with disapproval, shame, or fear. Anger situations are constantly avoided. We have called anger in this case a focal—but infrequent—emotion (Mesquita et al., 1997).

In many cultures, avoiding emotions that signal the loss of honor or dignity is a focal concern. *Hasham* among the Awlad 'Ali Bedouins (Abu-Lughod, 1986), *haji* among the Japanese (Lebra, 1983), and *lek* among the Balinese (C. Geertz, 1973; Keeler, 1983) are examples of emotions that are persistently avoided. Emotional practices in these relevant cultures focus on the avoidance of situations that might give rise to loss of dignity or honor. Furthermore, even the slightest threat to dignity or honor will elicit the emotions that signal loss of honor or dignity. People have extended expertise on the situations associated with loss of honor and thus can recognize many different situations as relevant to this concern (Frijda & Mesquita, 1994). Social life is geared toward the prevention of honor or dignity loss. For instance, among the Awlad 'Ali, sex segregation and the practice of veiling reduce the likelihood of women losing their honor in confrontation with men, who would make them look humble by definition (Abu-Lughod, 1986). In Bali the loss of dignity is avoided by strict observance of the rules of decorum. Balinese role playing reduces the possibility of a faux pas (C. Geertz, 1973). Therefore, these are more or less formalized cultural strategies to prevent focal emotions—emotions that conflict with the cultural models—from arising. Depending on the effort that is experienced in maintaining these strategies, as well as the individual behaviors that support them, they can be conceived of as initial response tendencies or effortful regulation. Usually they seem to consist of a mix of the two.

Low visibility of emotions may lead to behavior that is consistent with the cultural model as well. Western cultures that value the independence and autonomy of the individual underemphasize emotions of dependence and submission, as each person should be independent from his or her social environment. From a Western point of view, a person's motivation should be guided by internal motives rather than by the structural qualities of the social environment (Markus & Kitayama, 1991). Consistently, shame—the awareness that one may be judged (negatively) by other people—has been characterized as a "low visibility" emotion in the West (Scheff, 1988, p. 400). People in Western cultures tend to be leery of shame and to conceal it (Goffman, 1967). The sociocultural consequence of the Western attitude toward shame is that there are fewer social scripts that guide recognition, avoidance, and expression of shame. Therefore, Western cultures do not make use of shame as a social regulator as much as do cultures that emphasize the importance of being judged by others, for instance, cultures of honor. Shyness, an emotion that emphasizes social distinctiveness, appears to be frowned on in cultures that deny or condemn social distinctions such as class and gender and to be prevalent in cultures that value such distinctions as important (Frijda & Mesquita, 1994; Gomperts, 1992; Shweder, 1994).

Levy (1973) proposed the distinction between *hypercognized* and *hypocognized* emotions, with hypercognition being similar to the concept of "focality" proposed here: "I have suggested that some sets of feelings are 'hypercognated,' controlled so to speak, by discrimination, and others are 'hypocognated' and controlled by cultural invisibility or at least by difficulty of access to communication" (Levy, 1973, p. 324). Like focality, the distinction between hyper- and hypocognition highlights the fact that the frequency of emotions is not the only criterion of the cultural significance of emotions. The term "focal emotions" is preferred here, as hyper- and hypocognition suggest an exclusive role for cultural representations in controlling emotions. Although formal cultural representations clearly affect emotion practices, they are only some of the ways in which cultural models constitute the focality of emotions. Furthermore, the suggestion that the number of emotion concepts would contribute to hypercognition (Levy, 1984, p. 219), with larger numbers indicating more hypercognition, appears to be contradicted by the facts. Focal emotions are in many cases expressed by one word that covers a wide range of connected emotional states. For example, the focal emotions *hasham* (among the Awlad 'Ali; Abu-Lughod, 1986), *liget* (among the Ilongot; Rosaldo, 1980), and *lek* (among the Balinese; C. Geertz, 1973; Keeler, 1983), all represented by only one word, each have several Western counterparts. Relevance to the one focal concern seems to *unify* different shades of emotion into one concept. Focality of emotions thus does not imply that words are more discriminatory but may, to the contrary, result in a more inclusive concept. By using one concept for a range of different (emotional) response patterns, one recognizes a similar concern across different experiences. The relevance of an emotional episode for the focal cultural concern is the criterion for selection of this broadly used word.

Cultural models thus seem to highlight certain emotional concerns. These focal concerns give rise to the high frequency of concern-consistent emotions and to the active avoidance of concern-inconsistent ones. There appear to be cultural differences in the propensity to either approach the good or avoid the bad, including good and bad emotions. Some cultures, such as middle-class American culture, are geared toward the search for happiness (Bellah, Madsen, Sullivan, Swidler, & Tipton, 1985), whereas others, such as the Awlad 'Ali (Abu-Lughod, 1986), focus on avoidance of the negative, that is, shame.

### Ecologies of Contexts

Rituals may serve to make powerful emotional experiences consistent with the cultural model. As Mauss put it, "On the whole the *feeling* [italics added] is not excluded but implied by the descriptions of facts and juridical ritual themes" (1921, p. 433). The ritual provides an interpretation of the events and affords and sometimes requires certain ways of feeling and responding.

In "the walk to Emmaus," Anglo American males living in Arizona retreat for a long weekend to contemplate their religious beliefs (Blackwell, 1991). The retreat models the emotions of its participants in a ritual way. The retreat is presented as a "once-in-a-lifetime experience" in which the participants "will study, discuss, and experience God's grace" (Blackwell, 1991, p. 436). They are asked to "put aside mistrust, to withhold judgment until the facts are in. . . . The men are asked to submit themselves to the spirit of self-surrender" (p. 436). In this way, the participants, who come from a nonritualistic white Anglo-Saxon background, are seduced into yielding to the ritual.

Three events are created in the context of the ritual. At three different times during the weekend each participant gets a bag of letters from friends and family members that was collected by the organizers of the retreat. The letters contain many words of love and appreciation and are labeled as "sacrificial love." The second event is a surprise welcome in the sanctuary by a large group of people (organizers and former participants of the retreat who sponsored the current participants) who are holding lighted candles up for them. The participants are then led into a "healing service" during which they whisper confessions in the spiritual leader's ear. Others in the group pray for them. The weekend is concluded by an address in which the men are told that they have experienced "a miracle: a group of dedicated men getting together and working very hard for others . . . [and] that the life of a Christian has to be achieved in concert with others" (p. 440). Opportunities for emotionality are provided, not only by creating these events but also by (1) the modeling of emotional and physical closeness by the leaders, (2) persuading the participants to overcome their resistance and embarrassment, thereby giving room to emotion and emotional expression, and (3) giving ample opportunity for self-disclosure, which focuses the men on their own feelings.

The walk to Emmaus thus affords emotions, both by creating the events and by offering representations of those events that justify and reify the men's feelings. The walk to Emmaus also provides a social environment that models behavior, explicit feeling, and display rules. All those characteristics helped to render emotionally constrained Anglo men emotional and socially involved in the course of only one weekend. "The male expression of emotion constitutes the behavior by which the Emmaus community defines itself. It is a behavior which the ritual arouses and on which the ritual focuses, constructing common representations" (Blackwell, 1991, p. 50).

Just like other rituals, the Emmaus retreat serves as a useful metaphor for the influence of cultural contexts. First, cultural practices create opportunities to feel (and express) certain emotions, most notably the emotions that fit the cultural model. Second, cultural models provide shared representations of the events that occur. And finally, the cultural context—including other people's expectations and reactions—reinforce certain model-consistent feelings and expressions.

Just like rituals, cultural models provide opportunity for certain types of individual feelings and behaviors by affording the contexts in which they can occur. For example, Americans promote happiness by creating and promoting many contexts in which happiness is likely to occur. They praise, compliment, and encourage each other, give awards and trophies for all varieties and levels of accomplishment, avoid being critical or inattentive, and generally foster a positive and optimistic view of themselves (D'Andrade, 1987). Similarly, cultures that devalue anger tend to reduce the contexts in which anger is likely to emerge (Briggs, 1970; Heelas, 1983; Levy, 1973). In those cultures, thwarting and frustrating acts are nearly absent.

That cultural models foster model-consistent situations was confirmed by a comparative study on emotions by Kitayama, Markus, Matsumoto, and Norasakkunkit (1997). Japanese and American students rated success and failure situations that were previously generated by different groups of Americans and Japanese. The prevalent situations in each culture could be constructed as relevant for the cultural self-goals. The "American" situations were recognized as more self-enhancing by both groups of respondents, and the "Japanese" situations were found more conducive to self-criticism (Kitayama et al., 1997). Thus types of situations that were most prevalent, as perceived by respondents in both cultures, were different across cultures. This suggests a different ecology of contexts.

The prevalent cultural contexts seem to provide the best opportunities for the culturally valued tendencies of both self-enhancement and self-criticism. The American goal is to maintain and enhance a positive evaluation of the self, as positive self-esteem is conditional to healthy independence. American respondents generated situations that were recognized by both Japanese and American raters to meet this goal. On the other hand, the Japanese cultural system tends to emphasize the importance of maintaining, affirming, and becoming part of social relationships. In order to be and stay a good member of the social unit, one has to constantly reflect on and improve one's shortcomings. Self-criticism is, therefore, essential (Karasawa, 2001; Lewis, 1995).

In a way comparable to rituals, cultural models also provide ways of interpretation and response that are model consistent and often shared. In the study by Kitayama et al. (1997), individuals in each culture appeared to benefit from the culturally provided opportunities. Americans judged that their self-esteem would increase more in success situations than it would decrease in the failure situations. By contrast, the Japanese students judged that their self-esteem would decrease more in the failure situations than it would increase in the success situations (Kitayama et al., 1997). Situations provided by the culture itself were particularly powerful in eliciting the desired psychological tendencies. The tendency of Americans to appraise situations as self-enhancing was particularly strong for situations that were generated by Americans. On the other hand, the tendency of the Japanese to self-criticism was particularly strong for situations that were generated by Japanese. Thus interpretations consistent with the cultural model were most strongly suggested by culturally generated contexts.

A similar interaction between types of situations and the resulting emotions was found in a diary study that compared Italians and Canadians (Grazzani-Gavazzi & Oatley, 1999). Italians were considered interdependent and Canadians independent in orientation. Emotions were conceived of as signals that some plans or goals went wrong—signals of a so-called error. The diary focused on such errors in relation to a plan agreed on with another person. Consistent with the different cultural orientations, Italians found such errors more important to relationships than did the Canadians, whereas the Canadians reported that the errors were more important to the plan itself than did the Italians. Italians may have focused more on the prevention of social errors and Canadians on the prevention of task-related errors, because there was a trend for Italians to report fewer errors in social meetings and more errors in work and other tasks than did Canadians. Therefore, the errors most *inconsistent* with the cultural concerns appeared to be best avoided.

As would be expected, Italians reported more interdependent emotions, such as sorrow, in response to error, whereas Canadians reported more independent emotions, such as anger. In general, errors in social meetings—that were most negatively relevant to interdependent concerns—were slightly more associated with sorrow than errors in work and other tasks (the difference was marginal). This may suggest that Italians tried to avoid negative interdependent emotions—the ones most inconsistent with their cultural model—by the relative avoidance of errors in social meetings.

Another way in which cultural models seem to operate as rituals is that the direct cultural context, the others involved in the situation, afford and encourage culturally appropriate responses as well. Others may actively sustain certain emotions and emotional displays. A Torajan, for instance, will avoid an angry person in order to facilitate the process of self-control and to not further frustrate him or her (Holland, 1992). Tamang mothers respond to their children's anger displays by soothing them and trying to make them feel okay (Cole & Tamang, 1998). Kipsigis mothers refrain from spontaneously comforting a crying child, and when the child turns to the mother, they try to quickly distract him or her; in doing so, crying is discouraged (Harkness & Super, 1985). Within the United States, children's attachment style has been associated with the history of how the parent has responded to the expressions of emotions (Cassidy, 1994). Securely attached children, for example, show a broad range of emotions because the parent has been responsive to all their emotional experiences. Thus the social environment may suggest what emotions and emotional expressions are acceptable in certain contexts, and it may do so according to its cultural model.

In one experiment, German and Japanese 2-year-olds were observed as they interacted in the presence of their mothers with an unknown adult playmate (Friedlmeier & Trommsdorff, 1999). The playmate became visibly distressed after breaking the arm of a doll. The children's subsequent emotional reactions were observed, as were the interactions between children and their mothers. Whereas most children in both groups sought support from the mother and the majority of mothers responded in a contingent way (i.e., tailored to the needs of the child), the effects of maternal behavior were cross-culturally different. In the German group, contingent maternal behavior tended to change the child's reaction of distress into a state of relaxation. In contrast, contingent maternal behavior left the distressed Japanese children tense. The authors interpret these results as "culture-specific interpersonal cycles" (Friedlmeier & Trommsdorff, 1999, p. 707). Whereas the German mothers reassured their children:

> Japanese mothers pursue[d] the child-rearing goal that the child feels one with the other person in an in-group situation. In this sense the child is expected to feel the pain and sadness of the playmate and consequently react in an emotional way . . . To the extent that the child turns to the mother for support in this situation, the mother's reaction is ambiguous. On the one hand, she calms the child, and on the other hand, she makes the child more tense, because the mother represents the agent who most emphasizes the importance of empathy. (Friedlmeier & Trommsdorff, 1999, p. 707).

How Japanese mothers emphasize the need for empathy in this particular interaction was not measured in this study, but the emotional effects this presumed emphasis has on the child is indeed suggestive of differences in social regulation.

In sum, cultural models appear to create and promote "good" contexts, meaning contexts that afford "good" emotions or help to inhibit and avoid "bad" ones. The good contexts of a particular culture appear to be particularly well suited for people from that culture: Cultures produce contexts with a maximal impact on the good emotions of their members. Conversely, individuals may be said to have the psychological tendencies that are particularly well tailored to contexts provided by their own cultures. Others that are part of the immediate social context guide the individual's emotional responses in direct ways that have yet to be studied carefully.

## Summary

There are important cultural differences in emotions that can be predicted and understood, but more importantly connected to each other, in the light of cultural models. Cultural differences have been identified in the initial response tendencies of appraisal, of action readiness, and of expression and instrumental behavior, but also in regulation strategies. Furthermore, the ecologies of emotions and contexts, as well as their mutual reinforcement, were suggested to be different across cultures. At all those levels, cultural models appear to shape and afford emotional practices, and there is thus a redundancy in the ways in which cultures control emotional practices. It was hypothesized that cultural models may favor some ways of emotional control over others and that even the prevalence of control strategies may be a function of the cultural model.

Represented at these multiple levels, the influence of cultural models goes beyond providing content to an otherwise static and universal emotion process. Rather, cultural models affect the very processes of emotions themselves: The response selection at the levels of different components, the relative priorities of initial response selection and effortful regulation, the sensitivity to certain contexts, and the goals and plans that are entailed by the emotions, as well as the likely means to achieve them, are all guided and afforded by cultural models. The very course of emotions—the ways in which the potential of emotions is realized—appears to differ as a function of cultural models. Culture is, therefore, not spoiling or distracting from the basic theory of emotions, as has long been assumed. Rather, it should be considered a necessary aspect of emotion theory. Basically, emotions are cultural, even though that is not the only thing they are.

### NOTE

1. Naturally, the general challenge to studies with this methodology is that we cannot rule out the possibility that the results reflect post hoc explanations of emotions rather than automatic processes at the initial stages of emotions. Future research will have to establish whether the results can be replicated even with more implicit measures of appraisal.

### REFERENCES

Abu-Lughod, L. (1986). *Veiled sentiments*. Berkeley: University of California Press.

Arnold, M. B. (1960). *Emotion and personality* (Vols. 1 & 2). New York: Columbia University Press.

Averill, J. R. (1982). *Anger and emotion: An essay on emotion*. New York: Springer.

Bateson, G., & Mead, M. (1942). *Balinese character*. New York: Academy of Sciences.

Bellah, R. N., Madsen, R., Sullivan, W. M., Swidler, A., & Tipton, S. M. (1985). *Habits of the heart: Individualism and commitment in American life*. Berkeley: University of California Press.

Blackwell, J. (1991). The walk to Emmaus: Culture, feeling, and emotion. *Ethos, 19*, 432–452.

Blok, A. (1980, June). Eer en de fysieke persoon [Honor and the physical person]. *Tijdschrift voor Sociale Geschiedenis*, 211–230.

Bourdieu, P. (1966). The sentiment of honour in Kabyle society. In J. G. Peristiany (Ed.), *Honour and shame: The values of Mediterranean society* (pp. 191–242). Chicago: University of Chicago Press.

Briggs, J. L. (1970). *Never in anger: Portrait of an Eskimo family*. Cambridge, MA: Harvard University Press.

Bruner, J. (1986). *Actual minds, possible worlds*. New York: Plenum Press.

Cassidy, J. (1994). Emotion regulation: Influences of attachment relationships. In N. A. Fox (Ed.), The development of emotion regulation. *Monographs of the Society for Research in Child Development, 59* (2–3, Serial No. 240, pp. 228–249).

Cole, P. M., & Tamang, B. L. (1998). Nepali children's ideas about emotional displays in hypothetical challenges. *Developmental Psychology, 34*(4), 640–646.

Condon, J. C. (1985). *Good neighbors: Communicating with the Mexicans*. Yarmouth, ME: Intercultural Press.

Cross, S. E., & Madson, L. (1997). Models of the self: Self-construals and gender. *Psychological Bulletin, 122*(1), 5–37.

D'Andrade, R. (1987). A folk model of the mind. In D. Holland & N. Quinn (Eds.), *Cultural models in language and thought* (pp. 112–149). Cambridge, England: Cambridge University Press.

D'Andrade, R., & Strauss, C. (1992). *Human motives and cultural models*. Cambridge, England: Cambridge University Press.

D'Andrade, R. G. (1984). Cultural meaning systems. In R. A. Shweder & R. LeVine (Eds.), *Culture theory: Essays on the social origins of mind, self, and emotions* (pp. 88–123). Chicago: University of Chicago Press.

Ekman, P., Friesen, W. V., & Ellsworth, P. (1982). What are the similarities and differences in facial behavior across cultures? In P. Ekman (Ed.), *Emotion in the human face* (pp. 128–146). Cambridge, England: Cambridge University Press.

Fiske, A. P., Kitayama, S., Markus, H. R., & Nisbett, R. E. (1998). The cultural matrix of social psychology. In D. T. Gilbert & S. T. Fiske (Eds.), *The handbook of social psychology* (4th ed., Vol. 2, pp. 915–981). Boston, MA: McGraw-Hill.

Friedlmeier, W., & Trommsdorff, G. (1999). A cross-cultural comparison between German and Japanese toddlers. *Journal of Cross-Cultural Psychology, 30*(6), 684–711.

Frijda, N. H. (1986). *The emotions*. Cambridge, England: Cambridge University Press.

Frijda, N. H. (1987). Emotions, cognitive structure, and action tendency. *Cognition and Emotion, 1*(2), 115–143.

Frijda, N. H., Kuipers, P., & Terschure, E. (1989). Relations among emotion, appraisal, and emotion action readiness. *Journal of Personality and Social Psychology, 57*(2), 212–228.

Frijda, N. H., Markam, S., Sato, K., & Wiers, R. (1995). Emotions and emotion words. In J. A. Russell, A. S. R. Manstead, J. C. Wellenkamp, & J. M. Fernandez-Dols (Eds.), *Everyday conceptions of emotion: An introduction to the psychology, anthropology and linguistics of emotion* (pp. 121–143). Dordrecht, Germany: Kluwer.

Frijda, N. H., & Mesquita, B. (1994). The social roles and functions. In S. Kitayama & H. Markus (Eds.), *Emotion and culture: Empirical studies of mutual influence* (pp. 51–88). Washington, DC: American Psychological Association.

Geertz, C. (1960). *The religion of Java.* Chicago: University of Chicago Press.

Geertz, C. (1973). Deep play: Notes on the Balinese cockfight. In C. Geertz (Ed.), *The interpretation of cultures* (pp. 412–453). New York: Basic Books.

Geertz, C. (1984). From the native's point of view: On the nature of anthropological understanding. In R. A. Shweder & R. A. LeVine (Eds.), *Culture theory: Essays on mind, self, and emotion* (pp. 123–136). Cambridge: Cambridge University Press.

Geertz, H. (1961). *The Javanese family.* New York: Free Press.

Geertz, H. (1974). The vocabulary of emotion. In R. A. Levine (Ed.), *Culture and personality* (pp. 249–264). New York: Basic Books.

Goffman, E. (1967). *Interaction ritual: Essays on face-to-face behavior.* New York: Pantheon Books.

Gomperts, W. (1992). *The opkomst van de sociale phobie* [The rise of social phobias]. Amsterdam: Bert Bakker.

Grazzani-Gavazzi, I., & Oatley, K. (1999). The experience of emotions of interdependence and independence following interpersonal errors in Italy and anglophone Canada. *Cognition and Emotion, 13*(1), 49–63.

Harkness, S., & Super, C. M. (1985). Child-environment interactions in the socialization of affect. In M. Lewis & C. Saarni (Eds.), *The socialization of emotions* (pp. 21–36). New York: Plenum Press.

Heelas, P. (1983). Indigenous representatives of the emotions: The Chewong. *Journal of the Anthropological Society of Oxford, 14*(1), 87–103.

Heine, S. H., Lehman, D. R., Markus, H. R., & Kitayama, S. (1999). Is there a universal need for positive self-regard? *Psychological Review, 106*(4), 766–794.

Higgins, E. (1989). Knowledge accessibility and activation: Subjectivity and suffering from unconscious sources. In J. S. Uleman & J. A. Bargh (Eds.), *Unintended thought* (pp. 75–123). New York: Guilford Press.

Hochschild, A. R. (1983). *The managed heart: Commercialization of human feeling.* Berkeley: University of California Press.

Hollan, D. (1988). Staying "cool" in Torja: Informal strategies for the management of anger and hostility in a nonviolent society. *Ethos, 161,* 52–72.

Hollan, D. (1992). Emotion work and the value of emotional equanimity among the Toraja. *Ethnology, 3,* 45–56.

Hollan, D., & Quinn, N. (1987) *Cultural models in language and thought.* Cambridge, England: Cambridge University Press.

Johnson-Laird, P. N., & Oatley, K. (1989). The language of emotions: An analysis of a semantic field. *Cognition-and-Emotion, 3*(2), 81–123.

Karasawa, M. (2001). Nihonnjinni okeru jitano ninnshiki: Jikohihan baiasuto tasyakouyou baiasu [A Japanese mode of self-making: Self criticism and other enhancement]. *Japanese Journal of Psychology, 72,* 198–209.

Keeler, W. (1983). Shame and stage fright in Java. *Ethos, 11,* 152–165.

Kitayama, S., & Markus, M. R. (1994). *Emotion and culture: Empirical studies of mutual influence.* Washington, DC: American Psychological Association.

Kitayama, S., & Markus, H. R. (1999). Yin and yang of the Japanese self: The cultural psychology of personality coherence. In D. Cervone & Y. Shoda (Eds.), *The coherence of personality: Social cognitive basis of personality consistency, variability, and organization* (pp. 242–302). New York: Guilford Press.

Kitayama, S., & Markus, H. R. (2000). The pursuit of happiness and the realization of sympathy: Cultural patterns of self, social relations, and well-being. In E. Diener & E. Suh (Eds.), *Subjective well-being across cultures* (pp. 113–161). Cambridge, MA: MIT Press.

Kitayama, S., Markus, H. R., & Kurokawa, M. (2000). Culture, emotion, and well-being: Good feelings in Japan and the United States. *Cognition and Emotion, 14*(1), 93–124.

Kitayama, S., Matsumoto, D., Markus, H. R., & Norasakkunkit, V. (1997). Individual and collective processes in the construction of the self: Self-enhancement in the US and self-criticism in Japan. *Journal of Personality and Social Psychology, 72,* 1245–1267.

Kitayama, S., & Masuda, T. (1994). Re-appraising cognitive appraisal from a cultural perspective. *Psychological Inquiry, 6,* 217–223.

Lang, P. J. (1988). What are the data of emotion? In V. Hamilton, G. H. Bower, & N. Frijda (Eds.), *Cognitive perspectives on emotion and motivation* (NATO ASI, Series D, Vol. 44, pp. 173–191). Dordrecht, The Netherlands: Kluwer.

Lazarus, R. S. (1991). *Emotion and adaptation.* New York: Oxford University Press.

Lebra, T. S. (1983). Shame and guilt: A psychological view of the Japanese self. *Ethos, 11,* 192–209.

Lebra, T. S. (1994). Mother and child in Japanese socialization: A Japan-U.S. comparison. In P. Greenfield & R. R. Cocking (Eds.), *Cross-cultural roots of minority child development* (pp. 259–274). Hillsdale, NJ: Erlbaum.

Levenson, R. W., Ekman, P., Heider, K., & Friesen, W. V. (1992). Emotion and autonomic nervous system activity in the Minangkabau of West Sumatra. *Journal of Personality and Social Psychology, 62,* 972–988.

Levy, R. I. (1973). *Tahitians: Mind and experience in the Society Islands.* Chicago: University of Chicago Press.

Levy, R. I. (1978). Tahitian gentleness and redundant controls. In A. Montagu (Ed.), *Learning non-aggression* (pp. 222–235). Oxford, England: Oxford University Press.

Levy, R. I. (1984). Emotion, knowing, and culture. In R. A. Shweder & R. A. LeVine (Eds.), *Culture theory: Essays on mind, self, and emotion* (pp. 214–237). Cambridge, England: Cambridge University Press.

Lewis, C. C. (1995) *Educating hearts and minds.* New York: Cambridge University Press.

Lienhardt, G. (1961). *Divinity and experience.* London: Oxford University Press.

Lutz, C. (1986). The domain of emotion words on Ifaluk. In R. M. Harré (Ed.), *The social construction of emotions* (pp. 267–288). Oxford, England: Blackwell.

Lutz, C. (1987). Goals, events and understanding in Ifaluk

emotion theory. In N. Quinn & D. Holland (Eds.), *Cultural models in language and thought* (pp. 290–312). Cambridge, England: Cambridge University Press.

Lutz, C. (1988). *Unnatural emotions: Everyday sentiments on a Micronesian atoll and their challenge to Western theory.* Chicago: University of Chicago Press.

Markus, H. R. (1999, April) American well-being: A comparison of college vs. high school educated Americans. Paper presented at the Symposium for Culture, Mind and Behavior, Winston-Salem, NC.

Markus, H. R., & Kitayama, S. (1991). Culture and the self: Implications for cognition, emotion, and motivation. *Psychological Review, 98,* 224–253.

Markus, H. R., & Kitayama, S. (1994). The cultural construction of self and emotion: Implications for social behavior. In S. Kitayama & H. R. Markus (Eds.), *Emotion and culture: Empirical studies of mutual influence* (pp. 89–130). Washington, DC: American Psychological Association.

Markus, H. R., Mullaly, P. R., & Kitayama, S. (1997). Selfways: Diversity in modes of cultural participation. In U. Neisser & D. Jopling (Eds.), *The conceptual self in context* (pp. 13–60). New York: Cambridge University Press.

Matsumoto, D. (1989). Cultural influences on the perception of emotion. *Journal of Cross-Cultural Psychology, 20,* 298–318.

Matsumoto, D., Kudoh, T., Scherer, K., & Wallbott, H. (1988). Antecedents of and reactions to emotions in the United States and Japan. *Journal of Cross-Cultural Psychology, 19,* 267–286.

Mauro, R., Sato, K. & Tucker, J. (1992). The role of appraisal in human emotions: A cross-cultural study. *Journal of Personality and Social Psychology, 62,* 301–317.

Mauss, M. (1921). L' expression oblogatoire des emotions [The obligatory expression of emotions]. *Journal de Psychologie, 18,* 425–434.

Mbiti, J. (1970). *African religions and philosophy.* Garden City, NY: Doubleday.

Mesquita, B. (1993). Unpublished Ph.D. thesis, University of Amsterdam, Amsterdam. *Cultural variations in emotions: A comparative study of Dutch, Surinamese, and Turkish people in the Netherlands.*

Mesquita, B. (2001). Emotions in collectivist and individualist contexts. *Journal of Personality and Social Psychology, 80,* 68–74.

Mesquita, B., & Ellsworth, P. (2001). The role of culture in appraisal. In K. R. Scherer & A. Schorr (Eds.), *Appraisal processes in emotion: Theory, methods, research* (pp. 233–248). New York: Oxford University Press.

Mesquita, B., & Frijda, N. H. (1992). Cultural variations in emotions: A review. *Psychological Bulletin, 112,* 179–204.

Mesquita, B., Frijda, N. H., & Scherer, K. R. (1997). Culture and emotion. In P. Dasen & T. S. Saraswathi (Eds.), *Handbook of cross-cultural psychology* (Vol. 2, pp. 255–297). Boston: Allyn & Bacon.

Mesquita, B., & Karasawa, M. (2001). Different emotional lives. *Cognition and Emotion.*

Mesquita, B., & Karasawa, M. (2000). Emotion words: The difference between prototypical concepts and daily experiences. Unpublished manuscript.

Mesquita, B., Karasawa, M., Haire, A., & Izumi, K. The goal of emotion across cultures: Action readiness. Manuscript in preparation.

Middleton, D. R. (1989). Emotional style: The cultural ordering of emotions. *Ethos, 17,* 187–201.

Miller, P. J., Fung, H., & Mintz, J. (1996). Self-construction through narrative practices: A Chinese and American comparison of early socialization. *Ethos, 24*(2), 237–280.

Morling, B., & Kitayama, S. (1999, August). Cultural differences in influencing the environment and adjusting to the environment: Are there independent and collective styles of control? Paper presented at the conference of the Asian Association of Social Psychology, Taipei, Taiwan.

Moscovici, S. (1988). Notes toward a description of social representation. *European Journal of Social Psychology, 18*(3), 211–250.

Nisbett, R. E., Peng, K., Choi, I., & Norenzayan, A. (2001). Culture and systems of thought: Holistic vs. analytic cognition. *Psychological Review, 108,* 291–310.

Oatley, K. (1993). Social construction in emotions. In M. Lewis & J. M. Haviland (Eds.), *Handbook of emotions* (pp. 341–352). New York: Guilford Press.

Oatley, K., & Johnson-Laird, P. N. (1987). Towards a cognitive theory of emotions. *Cognition and Emotion, 1*(1), 29–50.

Parkinson, B. (1995). *Ideas and realities of emotion.* London: Routledge.

Peng, K., Nisbett, R. E., & Wong, N. Y. C. (1997). Validity problems comparing values across cultures and possible solutions. *Psychological Methods, 2,* 329–344.

Peristiany, J. G. (1966). Honour and shame in a Cypriot highland. In J. G. Peristiany (Ed.), *Honour and shame: The values of Mediterranean society* (pp. 171–190). Chicago: University of Chicago Press.

Pitt-Rivers, J. (1966). Honour and social status. In J. G. Peristiany (Ed.), *Honour and shame: The values of Mediterranean society* (pp. 19–78). Chicago: University of Chicago Press.

Richards, J. M., & Gross, J. J. (1999). Composure at any cost? The cognitive consequences of emotion suppression. *Personality and Social Psychology Bulletin, 25*(8), 1033–1044.

Rosaldo, M. Z. (1980). *Knowledge and passion: Ilongot notions of self and social life.* Cambridge, England: Cambridge University Press.

Rozin, P., Lowery, L., Imada, S., & Haidt, J. (1999). The CAD triad hypothesis: A mapping between three moral emotions (contempt, anger, disgust) and three moral codes (community, autonomy, divinity). *Journal of Personality and Social Psychology, 76*(4), 574–586.

Sanchez-Burks, J., Nisbett, R. E., & Ybarra, O. (2000). Cultural styles, relational schemas, and prejudice against out-groups. *Journal of Personality and Social Psychology, 79,* 174–189.

Scheff, T. J. (1988). Shame and conformity: The deference-emotion system. *American Sociological Review, 53,* 115–135.

Scherer, K. (1984). Emotion as a multicomponent process: A model and some cross-cultural data. In P. Shaver (Ed.), *Review of personality and social psychology* (Vol. 5, pp. 37–63). Beverly Hills, CA: Sage.

Scherer, K. (1997a). Profiles of emotion-antecedent appraisal: Testing theoretical predictions across cultures. *Cognition and Emotion, 11,* 113–150.

Scherer, K. (1997b). The role of culture in emotion-antecedent appraisal. *Journal of Personality and Social Psychology, 73,* 902–922.

Scherer, K. (1999). Cross-cultural patterns. In D. Levinson, J. J. Ponzetti, & P. F. Jorgensen (Eds.), *Encyclopedia of human emotions* (Vol. 1, pp. 147–156). New York: Macmillan.

Scherer, K. R., Wallbott, H. G., Matsumoto, D., & Kudoh, T. (1988). Emotional experience in cultural context: A comparison between Europe, Japan, and the United States. In K. R. Scherer (Ed.), *Faces of emotions* (pp. 5–30). Hillsdale, NJ: Erlbaum.

Schieffelin, E. L. (1985). Anger, grief, and shame: Toward a Kaluli ethnopsychology. In G. M. White & J. Kirkpatrick (Eds.), *Person, self and experience: Exploring Pacific ethnopsychologies* (pp. 169–182). Berkeley: University of California Press.

Shweder, R. A. (1991). *Thinking through cultures.* Cambridge, MA: Harvard University Press.

Shweder, R. A. (1994). "You're not sick, you're just in love": Emotion as an interpretive system. In P. Ekman & R. J. Davidson (Eds.), *The nature of emotion: Fundamental questions* (pp. 32–44). New York: Oxford University Press.

Shweder, R. A. (1999). Why cultural psychology? *Ethos, 27*(1), 62–73.

Shweder, R. A., Much, N. C., Mahapatra, M., & Park, L. (1997). The "big three" of morality (autonomy, community, and divinity), and the "big three" explanations of suffering. In A. Brandt & P. Rozin (Eds.), *Morality and health* (pp. 119–169). New York: Routledge.

Smith, C. A., & Ellsworth, P. C. (1985). Patterns of cognitive appraisal in emotion. *Journal of Personality and Social Psychology, 48,* 813–838.

Stephan, C. W., Stephan, W. G., Saito, I., & Barnett, S. M. (1998). Emotional expression in Japan and the United States: The nonmonolithic nature of individualism and collectivism. *Journal of Cross-Cultural Psychology, 29*(6), 728–748.

Stephan, G. S., Stephan, C. W., & De Vargas, M. (1996). Emotional expression in Costa Rica and the United States. *Journal of Cross-Cultural Psychology, 27*(2), 147–160.

Stephan, W. G., Stephan, C. W., & Cabezas de Vargas, M. (1996). Emotional expression in Costa Rica and the United States. *Journal of Cross-Cultural Psychology, 27,* 147–160.

Stephenson, P. H. (1989). Going to McDonald's in Leiden: Reflections on the concept of self and society in the Netherlands. *Ethos, 17*(2), 226–247.

Stigler, J. W., & Perry, M. (1990). Mathematics learning in Japanese, Chinese, and American classrooms. In J. W. Stigler, R. A. Shweder, & G. Herdt (Eds.), *Cultural psychology: Essays on comparative human development* (pp. 328–353). Cambridge, England: Cambridge University Press.

Strack, F., Schwarz, N., Bless, H., & Kuebler, A. (1993). Awareness of the influence as a determinant of assimilation versus contrast. *European Journal of Social Psychology, 23*(1), 53–62.

Triandis, H. C. (1995). *Individualism and collectivism.* Boulder, CO: Westview Press.

Tsai, J. L., & Levenson, R. W. (1997). Cultural influences on emotional responding: Chinese American and European American dating couples during interpersonal conflict. *Journal of Cross-Cultural Psychology, 28*(5), 600–625.

Van Der Horst, H. (1996). *The low sky: Understanding the Dutch: The book that makes the Netherlands familiar.* Schiedam, The Netherlands: Scriptum Books.

Weiner, B. (1982). The emotional consequences of causal ascriptions. In M. S. Clark & S. T. Fiske (Eds.), *Affect and cognition* (pp. 185–210). Hillsdale, NJ: Erlbaum.

Weisz, J. R., Rothbaum, F. M., & Blackburn, T. C. (1984). Standing out and standing in: The psychology of control in America and Japan. *American Psychologist, 39,* 955–969.

Wierzbicka, A. (1994). Emotion, language, and "cultural scripts." In S. Kitayama & H. R. Markus (Eds.), *Emotion and culture: Empirical studies of mutual influence* (pp. 133–196). Washington, DC: American Psychological Association.

Zajonc, R. B. (1984). On the primacy of affect. *American Psychologist, 39*(2), 117–123.

Zajonc, R. B. (2000). Feeling and thinking. In J. P. Forgas (Ed.), *Feeling and thinking: The role of affect in social cognition* (pp. 31–58). New York: Cambridge University Press.

# 47

## ADAPTIVE RATIONALITY AND THE MORAL EMOTIONS

Robert H. Frank

Although they have been the subject of intense discussion for literally thousands of years, the terms *rationality* and *morality* remain shrouded in ambiguity. My goal in this chapter is to identify some of the sources of this ambiguity and to describe a conceptual framework that reduces it somewhat by taking account of the strategic role of moral emotions in social interaction. This same framework, however, suggests that ambiguity cannot be fully purged from the concepts of rationality and morality.

### Sources of Ambiguity

There are many conceptions of rationality, each with its own strengths and weaknesses. Much of the ambiguity concerning rationality stems from the simple fact that no single conception has managed to prevail over its competitors. I illustrate by considering two specific conceptions, the present-aim standard and the self-interest standard.

The present-aim standard holds that a person is rational if she or he is efficient in the pursuit of whatever objectives she or he happens to hold at the moment of action (Parfit, 1984). This standard makes no attempt to evaluate the objectives themselves. Its appealing feature is that it enables us to accommodate the plurality of goals that most people actually hold.

But this virtue turns out also to be a handicap, for it keeps the present-aim model from making many testable predictions about behavior. Thus, for example, virtually any bizarre behavior can be "explained" after the fact simply by assuming that the individual had a sufficiently strong taste for it. I call this the "crankcase-oil problem": If someone drinks a gallon of used crankcase oil from his car, then writhes in agony and dies, a present-aim theorist has a ready explanation: The man must have *really* liked crankcase oil.

The self-interest conception of rationality avoids this problem by committing itself to a specific assumption about preferences: It holds that a person is rational if he or she is efficient in the pursuit of self-interested objectives. Of course, the modifier "self-interest" is itself ambiguous. Some writers interpret it to mean only the acquisition of material wealth; others interpret it more broadly, embracing not only wealth but also aesthetic pleasures and various other less materialistic concerns. But in all cases, the self-interest model excludes concerns about honor, duty, the welfare of the poor, and other manifestly "unselfish" motives.

Quite apart from the fact that self-interest is an important human motive, a clear attraction of the self-interest model is that it facilitates testable predictions about behavior. Given the opportunities a self-interested person faces in any given situation, the model predicts what he or she will do. Moreover, the model's predictions are often remarkably accurate. Its proponents have demonstrated its capacity to explain behavior across an impressive spectrum of domains.

The self-interest model's shortcoming is that a great deal of human behavior appears flatly inconsistent with it. People give anonymously to charity, they tip in restaurants out of town, they vote in presidential elections, they help strangers in distress, and in countless other ways they appear to subordinate narrow self-interest to the pursuit of other goals. The self-interest model is simple and elegant. Unfortunately, it is also often wrong.

With the obvious deficiencies and strengths of each standard of rationality in view, it is hardly a puzzle that multiple, conflicting standards continue to be widely used. This would be confusing enough even if scholars were always clear about which standard they had in mind. In practice, however, the problem is compounded by the fact that scholars rarely acknowledge that there are competing standards of rationality.

There are perhaps even more conceptions of morality than of rationality, but for purposes of this discussion I focus on a feature that is common in many conceptions, namely, the subordination of one's own narrow interests to the interests of a broader community. The narrow self-interest standard of rationality is incompatible with morality thus conceived. The present-aim standard, by contrast, allows this conception of morality, but only in the case in which someone happens to have a taste for behaving morally. For someone who lacks that taste, the present-aim model joins the self-interest model in denying the compatibility of rationality and morality.

No matter how rationality and morality are defined, both concepts have considerable motivational force. People want to think of themselves as moral, and they also want to think of themselves as rational. When our behavior is characterized by others as immoral or irrational, we usually respond in one of two ways: by changing our behavior or by changing our beliefs about rationality and morality. Instances of moral behaviors being adopted to win approval from others are familiar. (Less common are cases in which people choose immoral behaviors to bolster their sense of rationality. I discuss evidence of such responses in the last section of this chapter.)

The second response—changing beliefs to accommodate behavior—is called "dissonance reduction" by psychologists, and it, too, is common. People who focus on advancing their own narrow interests tend to be drawn to beliefs about morality that stress the social gains that often spring from self-interested behavior. Mother Teresa and others whose behavior is more attuned to community interests are more likely to hold moral beliefs that emphasize the need for self-restraint.

With these brief remarks, I have tried to illustrate why confusion and ambiguity might be equilibrium properties of the concepts of rationality and morality. In the next section, I discuss a third standard of rationality—which I call adaptive rationality—that promises to narrow the scope of this ambiguity. Adaptive rationality incorporates the most attractive features of both the self-interest and present-aim standards of rationality and at the same time sheds some of the worst deficiencies of each. In the process, it also helps to limit some of the conflicts between morality and other conceptions of rationality. But it also makes clear that some conflicts are unavoidable.

## Adaptive Rationality

Rationality—in both the self-interest and present-aim conceptions—involves the choice of efficient means to achieve given ends. Adaptive rationality retains the requirement that people be efficient in their choice of means. But unlike the other conceptions, which take goals as given, adaptive rationality regards goals themselves as objects of choice and, as such, subject to a similar efficiency requirement.

Now, the idea of subjecting an individual's goals to an efficiency test may strike many readers as odd. Ever since Bentham, who insisted that a taste for poetry was no better than a taste for pushpins, the rational choice tradition has emphasized that individual preferences are beyond scrutiny. By what standard could we possibly evaluate an individual's choice of goals?

One way to approach this question is to investigate preferences in an evolutionary context. Darwin's theory of natural selection, enriched to allow for the influence of cultural and other environmental forces during development, is the only theory that provides a coherent account of how the components of human motivation were forged. In this framework, the design criterion for a preference is the same as for an arm or a leg or an eye: To what extent does it assist the individual in the struggle to acquire the resources required for survival and reproduction? If it works better than the available alternatives, selection pressure will favor it. Otherwise, selection pressure will work against it.

At first glance, this theoretical structure might seem to throw its weight squarely behind the self-interest conception of rationality. Indeed, if natural selection favors the traits and behaviors that maximize individual reproductive fitness, and if we define behaviors that enhance personal fitness as selfish, then self-interest becomes the only viable human motive by definition. This tautology was a central message of much of the sociobiological literature of the 1970s and 1980s.

On a closer look, however, the issues are not so simple. For there are many situations in which individuals whose only goal is self-interest are likely to be especially bad at acquiring and holding resources. Thomas Schelling (1960) provides a vivid illustration with his account of a kidnapper who gets cold feet and wants to set his victim free but fears that if he does so, the victim will go to the police. The victim promises to remain silent. The problem, however, is that both he and the kidnapper know that it will not be in the victim's narrow self-interest to keep this promise once he is free. And so the kidnapper reluctantly concludes that he must kill his victim.

Suppose, however, that the victim was not a narrowly self-interested person but rather a person of honor. If this fact could somehow be communicated to the kidnapper, their problem would be solved. The kidnapper could set the victim free, secure in the knowledge that even though it would then be in the victim's interests to go to the police, he would not want to do so.

Schelling's kidnapper and victim faced a "commitment problem," a situation in which they have an incentive to commit themselves to behave in a way that will later seem contrary to self-interest. Such problems are a common feature of social life. Consider, for example, the farmer who is trying to deter a transient thief from stealing his ox. Suppose this farmer is known to be a narrowly self-interested rational person. If the thief knows that the farmer's cost of pursuing him exceeds the value of the ox, he can then steal the ox with impunity. But suppose that the farmer also cares about not being victimized, quite independently of the effect of victimization on his wealth. If he holds this goal with sufficient force, and if the potential thief knows this, the ox will no longer be such an inviting target.

The one-shot prisoner's dilemma is another example of a commitment problem. If both players cooperate, each does better than if both defect, and yet each individual gets a higher payoff by defecting no matter which strategy the other player chooses. Both players thus have a clear incentive to commit themselves to cooperate. Yet a mere promise issued by a narrowly self-interested person clearly will not suffice, for his partner knows he will have no incentive to keep this promise. If both players know one another to be honest, however, both could reap the gains of cooperation.

In all of these examples, note that merely having the relevant preferences or goals is by itself insufficient to solve the problem. It is also necessary that the presence of these goals be discernible by outsiders. Someone with a predisposition to cooperate in the one-shot prisoner's dilemma, for instance, is in fact at a disadvantage unless others can identify that predisposition in him and he can identify similar predispositions in others.

Can the moral sentiments and other psychological forces that often drive people to ignore narrow self-interest be reliably discerned by outsiders? In a recent study, Frank, Gilovich, and Regan (1993a) found that participants were surprisingly accurate at predicting who would cooperate and who would defect in one-shot prisoner's dilemmas played with near strangers.

In our study, the base rate of cooperation was 73.7%, the base rate of defection only 26.3%. A random prediction of cooperation would thus have been accurate 73.7% of the time, a random prediction of defection accurate only 26.3% of the time. The actual accuracy rates for these two kinds of prediction were 80.7% and 56.8%, respectively. The likelihood of such high accuracy rates occurring by chance is less than 1 in 1,000.

Participants in this experiment were strangers at the outset and were able to interact with one another for only 30 minutes before making their predictions. It is plausible to suppose that predictions would be considerably more accurate for people who have known each other for a long time. For example, consider a thought experiment based on the following scenario:

> An individual has a gallon jug of unwanted pesticide. To protect the environment, the law requires that unused pesticide be turned in to a government disposal facility located 30 minutes' drive from her home. She knows, however, that she could simply pour the pesticide down her basement drain with no chance of being caught and punished. She also knows that her one gallon of pesticide, by itself, will cause only negligible harm if disposed of in this fashion.

Now the thought experiment: Can you think of anyone who you feel certain would dispose of the pesticide properly? Most people generally respond affirmatively, and usually they have in mind someone they have known for a long time. If you answer yes, then you, too, accept the central premise of the adaptive rationality account—namely, that it is possible to identify non–self-interested motives in at least some other people.

The presence of such motives, coupled with the ability of outsiders to discern them, makes it possible to solve commitment problems of the sort previously discussed. Knowing this, even a rational, self-interested individual would have every reason to choose preferences that were not narrowly self-interested. Of course, people do not choose their preferences in any literal sense. The point is that if moral sentiments can be reliably discerned by others, then the complex interaction of genes and culture that yields human preferences can sustain preferences that lead people to subordinate narrow self-interest in the pursuit of other goals.

## An Equilibrium Mix of Motives

It might seem that if moral sentiments help solve important commitment problems, then evolutionary forces would assure that everyone have a full measure of these sentiments. But a closer look at the interplay between selfish and altruistic motives suggests that this is unlikely to be the case. Imagine, for example, an environment populated by two types of people, cooperators and defectors.

And suppose that people earn their livelihood by interacting in pairs and that the commitment problem they confront is the one-shot prisoner's dilemma.

If cooperators and defectors were perfectly indistinguishable, interactions would occur on a random basis and the average payoff would always be larger for the defectors (owing to the dominance of defection in all prisoner's dilemmas). In evolutionary models, the rule governing population dynamics is that each type reproduces in proportion to its material payoff relative to other types. This implies that if the two types were indistinguishable, the eventual result would be extinction for the cooperators. In highly simplified form, this is the Darwinian story that inclines many social scientists to believe that self-interest is the only important human motive.

But now suppose that cooperators were distinguishable at a glance from the defectors. Then interaction would no longer take place on a random basis. Rather, the cooperators would pair off systematically with one another to reap the benefits of mutual cooperation. Defectors would be left to interact with one another and would receive the lower payoff associated with these pairings. The eventual result this time is that the defectors would be driven to extinction.

Neither of these two polar cases seems descriptive of actual populations, which typically contain a mix of cooperators and defectors. Such a mixed population is precisely the result we get if we make one small modification to the original story. Again suppose that cooperators are observably different from defectors but that some effort is required to make the distinction. If the population initially consisted almost entirely of cooperators, it would not pay to expend this effort because one would be overwhelmingly likely to achieve a high payoff merely by interacting at random with another person. In such an environment, cooperators would cease to be vigilant in their choice of trading partners. Defectors would then find a ready pool of victims, and their resulting higher payoffs would cause their share of the total population to grow.

As defectors became more numerous, however, it would begin to pay for cooperators to exercise greater vigilance in their choice of partners. With sufficiently many defectors in the population, cooperators would be vigilant in the extreme, and we would again see pairings among like types only. That, in turn, would cause the prevalence of altruists to grow. At some point, a stable balance would be struck in which cooperators were just vigilant enough to prevent further encroachment by defectors. The average payoff to the two types would be the same, and their population shares would remain constant. There would be, in other words, a stable niche for each type.

Ecological models like the one sketched here can also be offered in support of a more nuanced portrait of individual human motivation. For example, rather than starting with a population in which people are exclusively one type or the other, we might begin with individuals with some mix of different motives. Such models would lead us to expect an equilibrium in which each individual experiences both selfish and altruistic motives to varying degrees.

But although the details of the story may differ according to the particular model chosen, ecological models as a group have an important feature in common: Each stresses that we should not expect a world populated exclusively by the *Homo economicus* caricature that populates conventional rational choice models. Such creatures may survive at the margins in environments in which monitoring costs make it too expensive to ferret them out. But they hardly represent a sensible basis on which to ground a universal science of human behavior.

The adaptive rationality framework provides theoretical underpinning for a remarkably commonsensical portrait of human nature. It tells us that people are driven by a combination of selfish and altruistic motives, just as experience seems to suggest. The mix of motives is highly variable across individuals, yet polar cases are by no means common.

The adaptive rationality approach also retains the most important strengths of both the present-aim and self-interest conceptions of rationality while eliminating the most glaring weaknesses of each. For example, like the present-aim standard, it permits the incorporation of a broad repertoire of human objectives. But unlike the present-aim standard, it does not give investigators a free hand to assume any objective that might prove convenient in a given context. Under the adaptive rationality standard, a goal can be included only if it can be shown that persons who hold that goal are not handicapped in their efforts to acquire and hold resources. Like the self-interest standard, the adaptive rationality standard makes a commitment to a given repertoire of tastes and is thus equally able to generate refutable hypotheses about behavior. But because the repertoire of tastes it includes is broader than that of the self-interest model, the adaptive rationality model can accommodate a much larger suite of behaviors than can the self-interest model.

Another advantage of the adaptive rationality model is that it narrows the range of inconsistency between rationality and morality. By accommodating preferences for moral behavior, it is like the present-aim standard in saying that morality and rationality are often consistent. At the same time, it preserves the possibility of a distinction between the two concepts. Not everyone need have moral preferences under the adaptive rationality standard, and, indeed, if people's preferences are costly to discern, there will almost certainly be at least some individuals whose preferences are not moral. The real departure of the adaptive rationality standard on this dimension is from the self-interest standard, which holds that rationality and morality are never compatible.

## Links to Other Work

The adaptive rationality model is an evolutionary game theoretic model of the kind described by Brian Skyrms (1998a). Also in keeping with the class of models that Skyrms discusses, it is a model in which cooperation evolves through correlated pairings. The key to the evolution of cooperation in these models is that cooperators interact with one another with a frequency higher than their share of the total population. Without this property, defection remains the only evolutionarily stable strategy.

There are numerous other antecedents and close relatives of the adaptive rationality model in the literature. The concept of commitment problems traces to Thomas Schelling's 1960 book, *The Strategy of Conflict*. Schelling (1978) went on to suggest that emotions might help solve commitment problems. George Akerlof (1983) published an elaboration of this idea. Amartya Sen (1985) acknowledged the benefits of non–self-interested behavior, and David Gauthier's book, *Morals by Agreement* (1985), described how behavioral predispositions might solve various commitment problems. Jack Hirshleifer (1987) also explored these issues. I investigated the equilibrium properties of the model under imperfect signaling (Frank, 1987).

All of these works assume that the relevant behavioral predispositions can somehow be made known to outsiders, if only with some uncertainty. My 1988 book, *Passions Within Reason*, focuses on the problem of mimicry and tries to spell out how information about behavioral predispositions can be credibly transmitted in environments in which individuals have strong incentives to misrepresent themselves.

## Adaptive Rationality and Voodoo Causation

The adaptive rationality model also sheds light on the problem of "voodoo causation" that arises in models with correlated pairings. Skyrms (1998b) describes this problem, although not by that name. Max and Moritz must play a one-shot prisoner's dilemma with each other, and each believes, correctly, that their probabilities of choosing the same strategy are highly correlated. Should knowledge of this correlation change the attractiveness, in purely material terms, of cooperating? Under conventional expected utility models, the answer is no, for the correlations do not change the fact that defection is a dominant strategy. Even though their modes of play are correlated, neither player's play has any causal influence on the other's. Choosing to cooperate in the belief that this will make one's partner more likely to cooperate is thus to believe in "voodoo causation."

Yet something strikingly akin to voodoo causation

emerges from a more complete account of the dynamics of interaction under adaptive rationality. When behavioral predispositions cannot be observed with certainty, cooperative individuals must decide whether to interact with a given partner on the basis of an estimate of the probability that that partner is also a cooperator. These estimates will depend on information specific to the individual partner and also on the perceived base rate of cooperators in the population of interacting individuals. A cooperator will thus be more likely to interact with a given partner when that base rate is high than when it is low.

Now suppose that a defector experiences an epiphany and decides to become a cooperator. By so doing, he increases the base rate of cooperators in the interacting population. This, in turn, raises all other cooperators' estimates of the likelihood that a given potential partner is a cooperator. Some cooperators whose initial pessimistic estimates kept them on the sidelines will now be moved to join the interacting population, raising the base rate of cooperators in that population still further. When and if a new equilibrium is reached, it will be one in which there is a larger—possibly substantially larger—share of cooperators in the interacting population.

Through its effect on others' estimates of the likelihood of cooperation, then, an individual's decision to cooperate in a one-shot prisoner's dilemma may indeed cause others also to cooperate. Of course, there will be no causal effect on his or her own partner in the first venture, so in this sense the traditional model's position on voodoo causation is sustained. Yet a person's initial decision to cooperate may nonetheless be said to have caused an increase in cooperation in subsequent encounters.

## Do Conceptions of Rationality and Morality Matter?

Are conceptions of rationality and morality of concern only to social scientists, philosophers, and other academics, or do they have implications for behavior in the broader community? Given the apparent motivational force of these ideas, the different conceptions may indeed give rise to different behavior.

In the behavioral sciences, the core theoretical paradigm in economics is the one most closely identified with the self-interest conception of rationality. If beliefs mold behavior, economists should then be more likely than others to behave opportunistically in social dilemmas. In a recent study, Frank, Gilovich, and Regan (1993b) found preliminary evidence for this hypothesis. Consider, for example, the free-rider hypothesis of the self-interest model, which says that in large populations, people will not make voluntary contributions in support of public goods. We found that academic economists were more than twice as likely as the members of any other discipline we surveyed to report that they give no money at all to any private charity. We also found that economics majors were more than twice as likely as nonmajors to defect when playing one-shot prisoner's dilemmas with strangers. This difference was not merely a reflection of the fact that people who chose to major in economics were more opportunistic to begin with. We found, for example, that the difference in defection rates grew larger the longer a student had studied economics. Questionnaire responses also indicated that freshmen in their first microeconomics course were more likely at the end of the term to expect opportunistic behavior from others than they were at the beginning. On the strength of these findings, Frank, Gilovich, and Regan (1993b) tentatively concluded that conceptions of rationality do indeed appear to mold behavior.

## Summary

Conceptions of rationality and morality have important practical consequences. The functional role of human drives of a narrow biological sort and, more broadly, of preferences and belief systems is to motivate suites of adaptive behaviors. People can exercise at least a limited range of choice about which goals to pursue or which belief systems to adopt. In purely pragmatic terms, the adaptive rationality standard has much to commend it over the self-interest and present-aim standards of rationality.

Unlike the present-aim standard, it does not leave investigators vulnerable to the crankcase-oil objection. On the contrary, it provides us with a disciplined framework for evaluating whether a given preference or goal is a proper basis for explaining a behavior: If the preference or goal promotes, or at least does not hamper, the individual's ability to acquire and hold resources, it may be included; otherwise, not.

Another advantage is that, by showing that the willingness to put community interests ahead of one's own interests can often help a person solve commitment problems, the adaptive rationality standard helps establish that morality—defined as a willingness to put community interests ahead of one's own at least some of the time—is not only consistent with individual survival but often even conducive to it. People want to think of themselves as rational, and they also want to think of themselves as moral. Under the self-interest standard of rationality, the only way this can be accomplished is by adopting what amount

to bizarre conceptions of either interest or morality. By contrast, the adaptive rationality standard makes clear that morality is not only consistent with rationality but, under some conditions, even required by it.

At the same time, the adaptive rationality standard does not encourage the naive view that community interests and individual interests are always one and the same. On the contrary, it stresses that there will always be at least some tension between these two levels in environments in which individual predispositions are costly to assess. Thus, although the adaptive rationality standard is in several respects a step forward from the present-aim and self-interest standards, it also makes clear that rationality and morality are concepts that inescapably entail at least some ambiguity.

## REFERENCES

Akerlof, G. (1983, March). Loyalty filters. *American Economic Review, 73*, 54–63.

Frank, R. H. (1987, September). If *Homo economicus* could choose his own utility function, would he want one with a conscience? *American Economic Review, 77*, 593–604.

Frank, R. H. (1988). *Passions within reason*, New York: Norton.

Frank, R. H., Gilovich, T., & Regan, D. (1993a). The evolution of one-shot cooperation. *Ethology and Sociobiology, 14*, 247–256.

Frank, R. H., Gilovich, T., & Regan, D. (1993b). Does studying economics inhibit cooperation? *Journal of Economic Perspectives, 7*, 159–171.

Gauthier, D. (1985). *Morals by agreement*. Oxford, England: Clarendon.

Hirshleifer, J. (1987). On the emotions as guarantors of threats and promises. In J. Dupre (Ed.), *The latest on the best: Essays in evolution and optimality* (pp. 307–326). Cambridge, MA: MIT Press.

Parfit, D. (1984). *Reasons and persons*. Oxford, England: Clarendon.

Schelling, T. (1960). *The strategy of conflict*. Cambridge, MA: Harvard University Press.

Schelling, T. (1978). Altruism, meanness, and other potentially strategic behaviors. *American Economic Review, 68*, 229–230.

Sen, A. K. (1985). Goals, commitment, and identity. *Journal of Law, Economics, and Organization, 1*, 341–355.

Skyrms, B. (1998a). Mutal aid: Darwin meets *The logic of decision*: Correlation in evolutionary game theory. In P. Danielson (Ed.), *Modeling rationality, morality, and evolution* (pp. 379–407). New York: Oxford University Press.

Skyrms, B. (1998b). Subjunctive conditionals and revealed preference. *Philosophy of Science, 65*, 545–574.

# IX

## Emotion and Psychopathology

# 48

# INTRODUCTION:
# EMOTION AND PSYCHOPATHOLOGY

Robert M. Post

Given the complexity and exquisite regulation of emotion described in previous chapters, it is not surprising that emotional dysfunction lies at the core of a variety of psychopathological conditions. The syndromes of emotional dysregulation lie on a continuum of temporal characteristics, ranging from seconds/minutes (panic attacks) to hours/days (borderline personality disorder) to weeks/months (unipolar and bipolar illness) to years/lifetime (schizophrenia and autism).

The panic/anxiety disorders are characterized by paroxysmal episodes of panic, sometimes superimposed on more chronic components of dysphoria, agoraphobia, and depression.

The marked mood lability of borderline personality disorder and its interdigitation with posttraumatic stress disorder (PTSD) syndromes are typified by extremely rapid and major mood shifts. Included in this phasic dysregulation are prominent components of anxiety, depression, proneness to substance abuse, and chaotic experience of the self and relationships to others.

The unipolar and bipolar affective disorders range from chronic dysthymia to irregular bursts of recurrent brief depression to minor and major depression to these conditions in the context of hypomania (bipolar II) and full-blown mania (bipolar I). This range of depressive and manic mood disorders is common in the general population and most typical of psychopathologies involving dysfunction of emotional regulation.

The schizophrenias are more commonly associated with a persistent disconnection of affect from its appropriate context, and thus they present with prominent autistic components. In childhood autism itself there is an early and chronic breakdown of emotional communication that often involves an absence of normal language and affective responsiveness to others. Given this range of type and temporal dissimilarities among the major psychopathological syndromes of emotion, we chose to highlight in this part several of the more prominent syndromes and components that bridge diagnostic categories

Although each of the chapters has a separate focus, it is worth emphasizing the constant interaction and interplay of cognition, emotion, and neurobiology that is important not only for understanding the psychological and neurobiological substrates of affective dysregulation but also for approaches to therapeutics that can also involve each of three domains (affective, cognitive, and somatic) as primary targets.

Joseph Newman and Amanda Lorenz (Chapter 49) introduce the part with a focus on self-regulation, which is particularly important not only to the borderline personality syndromes but also to the primary affective and autistic spectrum disorders. It is appropriate to link emotion and self because each would appear to represent a higher order concept, perhaps emanating from the convergence of multiple secondary and tertiary association pathways of the brain. Just as objects in the environment are "synthesized" by a variety of pathways that carry information on and encompass their shape, movement, color, and context, the emotional meaning of objects appears to be a supraordinate integration of all of these characteristics in the context of a developing history of experiences with its affective and emotional valences and labels. The self is a more complex object (abstraction) that is differentiated from other individuals in the environment, and it too is likely to represent an even higher order concept of integrating past experiences, associated learning and memory, and sense of anticipation of the future. Newman and Lorenz lay out the concept of emotion and self-regulation as a three-part interrelationship encompassing: (1) affective, (2) cognitive, and (3) somatic processes and their bidirectional interaction.

The contribution of both internal and external components of emotional representation and regulation appears to be a central theme in viewing emotions from the opposing positions of Walter Cannon and Phillip Bard, James Lang, and others discussed in previous chapters. In the pathological disorders of language we recognize sensory (or agnosic) components dependent on Wernicke's area in the brain, as well as expressive (or apraxic) components dependent on Broca's area. The primary affective disorders are also characterized by dysfunctions in both input and output domains. We are used to thinking of only the expressive components (manifested in the dramatic tearfulness and self-abnegation of depression and the euphoric grandiosity of mania), but there is increasing awareness of the affective agnosias that also accompany these syndromes.

A distorted view of the emotional self is characteristic in depression and mania, along with an inability to accurately describe emotions internally and externally. Patients with both unipolar and bipolar depression have deficits, for example, in the external recognition of facial emotional expression, an ability that depends in part on structures in the amygdala and prefrontal cortex.

In addition, an internal affective agnosia appears to exist because, particularly with bipolar depressed patients, rather marked alterations in mood are often misperceived or completely denied. For instance, a severely depressed patient who has been virtually speechless and immobile may begin to show increased sociability, appetite and sleep, and increases in activity, animation, and relatedness to others (that are readily perceived by others and that might reflect as much as a 50% improvement on the Hamilton Depression Rating Scale), but this improvement is dismissed by the patient with the view that he or she remains just as depressed as ever. That is, the bipolar patient often tends to see his or her depressed mood as an all-or-none phenomenon, with some of the intermediate gradations either not perceived at all or viewed as irrelevant.

It is thus of considerable interest that two of the structures in the brain most intimately associated with mood and cognition, that is, the amygdala and hippocampus,

respectively, both show a convergent neuroanatomy wherein inputs from the internal milieu and the external world converge on the same neural elements. For example, this occurs in the hippocampal dendrites of the CA1 subfield, where information from the external world enters in the perforant pathway, which synapses on the lateral third of the dendritic tree. Information from the internal milieu enters through the comissural pathway, which synapses on the inner third of the dendritic tree. Thus dysregulation of hippocampal pyramidal cell integration and firing could account for not only dysfunction of each one of these pathways but also their ability to be discriminated. In auditory hallucinations, for example, there may be a misperception of what sounds are emanating from the outside or are generated from within. Similarly, such confusion of internal and external reality seems to apply to visual hallucinations as well.

A convergence of information from affective recognition of the outside world is conveyed from a variety of cortical areas to the basolateral nucleus of the amygdala via the external capsule. At the same time, information from the internal milieu also arrives from the basal and mediobasal nuclei onto the same amygdala neurons of the basolateral nucleus, with further convergence of information from basolateral and lateral to the output system of the amygdala in the central nucleus. Thus, again, dysfunction of a single neuronal substrate could lead not only to a variety of types of affective dysregulation but also to components of emotional agnosia and emotional apraxia based on misinterpretation of signals from the internal and external milieus. Moreover, because stimulation or lesion of the corticomedial versus basolateral parts of the amygdala may result in opposite effects on behavioral, autonomic, and endocrine function, one could conceive how the relative balance of dysfunction within a single structure such as the amygdala could become manifest in the opposite extremes of mania and depression.

The imaging reviews of the mood induction paradigms and alterations of unipolar and bipolar affective illness by Terence Ketter et al. (Chapter 50) and of the anxiety disorders by Scott Rauch (Chapter 51) emphasize the themes of regional specificity of function of Hughlings Jackson, the more nonspecific brain mass concepts of Karl Lashley, and the neuroplasticity of learning and memory circuits and cell assemblies of Karl Pribram and Donald Hebb. One can only marvel at the data illustrated by Ketter and colleagues and by Rauch and many others in the field who are now able to see evidence of reliable alterations in function in both global areas of cortex and discrete areas such as a single amygdala. That we can begin to dissect brain function and dysfunction at this level of microanatomy is truly one of the remarkable accomplishments of the late twentieth century. One must also be impressed with findings that show that very diverse syndromes of affective dysregulation appear to involve many of the same structures of the frontal lobe, cingulate gyrus, amygdala, and hippocampus.

The enormous plasticity of the brain must also give us pause in ascribing any specific pathological affective syndrome to a given neurochemical or anatomical system. Initial processes of learning that involve *representational memory* may depend on the integrity of the amygdala, the hippocampus, and related structures of the medial and lateral temporal lobe. However, with forms of repeated learning involving *habit memory*, other neural systems appear more critically involved, including the striatum and perhaps cerebellar circuits. Thus, although the hippocampus is crucially involved in some encoding components of learning and memory, the site of memory storage, or the engram, likely resides elsewhere in the cortex, and it may even migrate neuroanatomically over time.

Similarly, with a variety of types of affective learning, the amygdala or the bed nucleus of the stria terminalis (BNST) may be a crucial initial modulatory pathway, but many aspects of affective modulation may proceed in its absence, as affective and emotional engrams are coded elsewhere. In this regard, one must wonder about the various stages in the evolution and resolution of the PTSD syndromes that are evident on a neuropsychological basis: Are they, too, mediated by changing and evolving neuroanatomical and neurochemical substrates? Such a view, if proven correct, would obviously have important implications for therapeutics as well. Does affective memory separate into representative versus habit types and accordingly become more or less amenable to conscious control?

Sue Mineka and her associates (Chapter 52) emphasize the cognitive biases that appear inextricably interwoven into the syndromes of human emotional pathology. Monkeys and dogs seem to have a full range of affective expression, but the ability of humans to generate language and higher concept formation adds a new level of cognitive appraisal, anticipation, and readiness for future action and planning that is uniquely human.

In this regard it becomes crucial to recognize the cognitive and contextual elements of affective experience. The familiar anecdote of differential emotional reactivity depending on the context in which one sees a lion is worth repeating. If one is at the zoo, viewing a lion may be associated with curiosity, pleasure, and a sense of aesthetic beauty, whereas a similar close encounter in the wild (without the safety of heavy steel bars) might engender a sense of panic and terror. In a parallel fashion, the physical act of sexual intercourse can be associated with love and the highest levels of ecstatic experience in the conjugal relationship, or with the most profound sense of dread, violation, and catastrophe in the context of a forced encounter.

Thus the appreciation of the cognitive and contextual

components of a situation may be overwhelming determinants of affective reaction and responsivity. At the same time, internal affective responses may enormously color cognitive interpretation, and each may have dramatic impacts on neurochemical and physiological underpinnings and concomitants of such experiences. The biochemistry and behavior of learned helplessness will not occur if an animal has control over the stress and the ability to cope with it. In turn, the neurobiological predispositions and vulnerabilities, both of the hereditary genetic and experiential sort, may exert major effects on the affective and cognitive worlds and their appreciation and interpretation. Each of these three interacting domains involving the affective, cognitive, and somatic realms is the basis of different respective treatment approaches.

The importance of the cognitive components of the pathological syndromes of affect is crystallized in the therapeutic approaches that have been engendered and targeted to specific cognitive distortions in different psychopathological syndromes. Thus, we have (1) cognitive-behavioral therapies for the panic and affective disorders and obsessive-compulsive disorder (OCD) and emerging cognitive-behavioral approaches to the thought disorders and hallucinatory experiences of schizophrenia; (2) therapeutic approaches to depression that are more focused on the affective elements of communication and interpersonal interaction; and (3) therapeutic approaches targeted at neurobiological substrates of depression, using drugs to ameliorate the underlying abnormalities found in a variety of neurochemical and endocrinological systems. Even the physiological components of psychopathology are now becoming more specifically targeted. For example, whereas electroconvulsive therapy (ECT), by necessity, required the induction of a generalized seizure, a more focal probe of the brain is possible with electroacupuncture, repeated transcranial magnetic stimulation (rTMS) of the brain, and even a more invasive procedure, such as the implantation of a vagus nerve stimulator (VNS).

In each of these three domains (affective, cognitive, and somatic), we are targeting either putative pathological or adaptive deficits and excesses in a given chemical system or a more complex pathway of neural circuit excitability. Thus there are exogenous attempts at better modulating endogenous chemicals and physiological processes whose levels of regulation are deficient. In this regard, it is crucial to identify which of the abnormalities is related to the primary pathology of a given affective syndrome versus those that are compensatory and adaptive mechanisms.

We might try to suppress the excess or replace the deficient chemical if it is involved in the primary pathology of the mood or anxiety experience or, conversely, to enhance or augment compensatory mechanisms once they are so identified. It is perhaps this balance of primary/pathological processes with secondary/compensatory processes that occur at the level of gene expression that may help determine periods of relative wellness (euthymia) versus periods of affective and anxiety dysfunction in the recurrent anxiety and affective disorders (Post & Weiss, 1996). It would also appear that each of the therapeutic approaches to the affective disorders that focus on the cognitive, affective, or somatic domains can thus target either the pathological mechanisms for suppression or the compensatory mechanisms for enhancement.

Perhaps the most effective strategies for dealing with the recurrent primary affective disorders are treatments that address all the elements involved: interpersonal social support for better coping and stress reduction, cognitive therapy to decrease distortions, dynamic and behavioral approaches to affect modulation, and medication and somatic treatment for neurochemical and neuroanatomical abnormalities.

Because of limitation of space and focus, we have chosen to present and discuss only the syndrome of autism itself, not the multiplicity of schizophrenic syndromes that are characterized by a vast array of emotion dysfunctions that include a prominent component of autism in many of the most seriously disturbed individuals. Thomas Insel (Chapter 53) focuses on the neurochemical and neuroanatomical substrates putatively involved in social affiliation as a potential entrée to better understanding the full range of autistic syndromes. This would appear to be a particularly informative approach—using animal models to explore normal and pathological components of social affiliation—because so little of the pathological anatomy of the human clinical syndromes of autism has as yet been revealed.

Whereas the affective and anxiety disorders appear to be predominantly syndromes of affect and anxiety dysregulation, autism appears to represent a more fundamental deficit or dysfunctional disorder. Given the profound language, cognitive, and emotional-affiliative dysfunctions, it would appear that there is a basic flaw in the neurochemical and anatomical substrates that are crucial for the normal development of these functions. The anxiety and affective disorders appear more akin to broken bones or damaged peripheral nerves that can regrow and heal themselves, whereas the autistic syndromes appear more akin to congenital malformations or pathway misalignment that results in the more permanent and intractable deficits associated with an affective cerebral palsy. In cerebral palsy, one strives for significant rehabilitation, but full repair of the dysfunction is not currently possible.

Blindness or paralysis of a given limb reflects an underlying severe dysfunction of the specific anatomical pathways involved. In the autistic syndromes, we presume that there are similar major abnormalities and anomalies in areas of the brain crucially involved in language and emotion communication that leave the autistic individual at such a haunting level of isolation. In the classic studies of Hubel and Wiesel (Hubel & Wiesel, 1979), deprivation of visual sensory input to one eye for increasing periods of time resulted in a range of deficits, from transient dysfunction associated with loss of normal physiology and biochemistry to complete and irreversible blindness of the deprived eye, associated with compensatory anatomical mechanisms that mediate vision in the functioning eye (i.e., increased width of the ocular dominance columns in the visual cortex). In a parallel fashion, we know that the emotional deprivation of the orphanages of the late 19th and early 20th centuries described by Emde, Polak, and Spitz (1965) and by Kaler and Freeman (1994), and in more recent observations of Romanian orphanages, can also result in long-lasting, if not permanent, deficits in emotional and communicative abilities, with associated decrements in structure and function observed with brain imaging (Chugani, Sundram, Behen, Lee, & Moore, 1999). In the absence of evidence of catastrophic emotional neglect or trauma in the classic autistic syndromes, we must look to endogenous aberrations in the neural circuitry crucial for this magnitude of communication deficit among mammals

As such, the work with animal models of emotional deprivation, enrichment, and trauma that is described elsewhere in this volume promises to help identify the crucial circuits potentially involved in emotional deficits and dysfunction and lead to a new realm of theoretical and practical therapeutic possibilities. The past decade has brought unequivocal evidence for the efficacy of serotonin-selective compounds on at least some components of the autistic syndrome. The pioneering studies conducted and reviewed by Insel and others should rapidly translate into therapeutic advances toward this most crippling disorder of human emotional capacity.

The neurochemical review by Steven Garlow and Charles Nemeroff (Chapter 54) shows how we have progressed from measuring the global irrigation and sewage pathways of the brain by assessing cerebrospinal fluid, blood, and urine amines and metabolites to measuring a more precise regional neurobiology based on modern brain imaging technologies and assessment of a variety of discrete chemicals in the brains of autopsied patients.

It is an act of faith to hope that understanding the pathological anatomy of these alterations will ultimately lead to a new era of therapeutics. There is already preliminary evidence that substance P antagonists may have antidepressant effects, and there are many pharmaceutical firms racing to provide corticotropin-releasing factor (CRF) antagonists for therapeutic studies in the affective and anxiety disorders. Similarly, one might envision somatostatin and thyrotropin-releasing hormone (TRH) replacement techniques as potentially helpful in the mood and anxiety disorders as well.

Thus the chapters in this part should begin to form an outline of several of the emotional psychopathologies and their underlying neural substrates in animals and man as a prelude to better therapeutic interventions in each of the syndromes discussed. The disorders of emotion can leave a devastating toll in suffering and mortality. Twenty-five percent of women and 12% of men in the United States will suffer a bout of major depression. The incidence of panic disorder is as high as 6%, and that of PTSD is 4–8%. Schizophrenia occurs in 1% of the population and bipolar illness in another 1–3%. One in 1,000 newborns develops autism. The cohort effect described by Gershon, Hamovit, Guroff, and Nurnberger (1987) and Weissman and Boyd (1984) reveals an increased incidence and earlier onset of both unipolar depression and bipolar illness in every successive birth cohort in the United States born since World War I, suggesting that these prototypical types of emotional psychopathology are, if anything, on the rise. Thus, exploring and revealing processes that contribute to psychopathology, as well as to health and normal human emotional development, will have a great impact on clinical therapeutics and, ultimately, on the health of a vast segment of the world's population.

## REFERENCES

Chugani, D. C., Sundram, B. S., Behen, M., Lee, M. L., & Moore, G. J. (1999). Evidence of altered energy metabolism in autistic children. *Progress in Neuropsychopharmacology and Biological Psychiatry, 23,* 635–641.

Emde, R. N., Polak, P. R., & Spitz, R. A. (1965). Anaclitic depression in an infant raised in an institution. *Journal of the American Academy of Child and Adolescent Psychiatry, 4,* 545–553.

Gershon, E. S., Hamovit, J. H., Guroff, J. J., & Nurnberger, J. I. (1987) Birth-cohort changes in manic and depressive disorders in relatives of bipolar and schizoaffective patients. *Archives of General Psychiatry, 44,* 314–319.

Hubel, D. H., & Wiesel, T. N. (1979) Brain mechanisms of vision. *Scientific American, 241,* 150–162.

Kaler, S. R., & Freeman, B. J. (1994) Analysis of environmental deprivation: Cognitive and social development in Romanian orphans. *Journal of Child Psychology and Psychiatry and Allied Disciplines, 35,* 769–781.

Post, R. M., & Weiss, S. R. B. (1996). A speculative model of affective illness cyclicity based on patterns of drug tolerance observed in amygdala-kindled seizures. *Molecular Neurobiology, 13,* 33–60.

Weissman, M. M., & Boyd, J. H. (1984). The epidemiology of affective disorders. In R. M. Post & J. C. Ballenger (Eds.), *Neurobiology of mood disorders* (pp. 60–75). Baltimore: Williams & Wilkins.

# 49

# RESPONSE MODULATION AND EMOTION PROCESSING: IMPLICATIONS FOR PSYCHOPATHY AND OTHER DYSREGULATORY PSYCHOPATHOLOGY

Joseph P. Newman and Amanda R. Lorenz

Regardless of its specific etiology, most psychopathology involves maladaptive responses to environmental circumstances. Thus, to the extent that a primary function of emotions is to facilitate appropriate responses to environmental circumstances, psychopathology is likely to reflect an emotion processing deficit. Emotion, however, is an exceedingly broad construct that promotes adjustment by coordinating numerous biopsychological systems, spanning motivation, memory, attention, cognition, and learning. Given this broad view, the emotion deficits associated with psychopathology may reflect a similarly diverse array of biopsychological dysfunctions, including difficulty coordinating the various aspects of emotion processing. Rather than review the myriad possibilities regarding emotion processing deficits in psychopathology, we have elected to focus on a specific biopsychological process, *response modulation*, which we believe is fundamental to emotion processing but which, to date, has been underutilized by emotion theorists and psychopathologists.

More specifically, the purpose of this chapter is to clarify the extent to which deficient response modulation may short-circuit adaptive emotion processing, interfere with self-regulation, and culminate in psychopathology. Toward this end, we (1) briefly review the construct of response modulation, (2) outline a model of emotion processing that highlights the importance of response modulation, and (3) examine the role of response modu-

lation and emotion processing in moderating the self-regulation of behavior. Next, we illustrate the potential importance of response modulation for emotion processing and psychopathology, using psychopathy as a case example. Psychopaths are infamous for their profound emotion and self-regulatory deficits which, we argue, reflect a primary deficit in response modulation. Finally, we broaden our analysis of the relation between response modulation and psychopathology by considering how intense emotion responses may short-circuit adaptive emotion processing and, thus, contribute to the development and maintenance of dysregulatory psychopathology.

## Evolution of the Response Modulation Concept

The term *response modulation* derives from the literature on limbic system dysfunction in animals (e.g., Gray, 1987; McCleary, 1966) and involves suspending a dominant response set (i.e., ongoing approach behavior) in reaction to negative and/or unexpected events (e.g., punishment, frustrative nonreward, contingency reversals, and novel stimuli). Using the literature on limbic system dysfunction as a model, Gorenstein and Newman (1980) proposed that deficient response modulation may help to explain the behavior control problems that characterize psychopathy and other "syndromes of disinhibition," including attention deficit disorder, early-onset alcoholism, somatization disorder, and impulsivity. Given a deficit in response modulation, individuals are less likely to suspend approach behavior (i.e., pause), evaluate their response strategies (i.e., reflect), and learn from corrective feedback (Newman, 1987).

Subsequent elaborations and extensions of this model have served to broaden its scope and are particularly relevant to this chapter. Based on a series of studies that highlight the information processing consequences of deficient response modulation, Patterson and Newman (1993) translated the response modulation concept into cognitive/attentional terms. According to the revised definition, response modulation involves "temporary suspension of a dominant response set and a brief concurrent shift of attention from the organization and implementation of goal-directed responding to its evaluation" (p. 717). Individuals who show response modulation deficits not only fail to interrupt maladaptive approach behavior but are also less likely to process an array of secondary information or contextual cues that might otherwise influence ongoing, goal-directed behavior (e.g., Newman, Schmitt, & Voss, 1997; Wallace, Vitale, & Newman, 1999).

Research from our laboratory also suggests that there are separate pathways to deficient response modulation (Newman & Wallace, 1993a). Some individuals appear to be characterized by an intrinsic and cross-situation deficiency in response modulation that is manifested whenever they are engaged in the active organization and implementation of goal-directed behavior (see Bernstein, Newman, Wallace, & Luh, 2000; Newman, 1998). However, the response modulation deficits of other individuals occur when emotionally significant cues engender high levels of nonspecific arousal,[2] which, in turn, serve to increase the speed, force, and attentional focus with which dominant responses are implemented (Wallace, Bachorowski, & Newman, 1991; Wallace & Newman, 1997). Regardless of the pathway, individuals with response modulation deficits are inclined to emit dominant responses without adequate consideration of secondary/contextual information. The response modulation deficits of the latter type, however, are relatively specific to circumstances that generate high levels of nonspecific arousal (cf. Easterbrook, 1959).

In summary, response modulation involves suspending a dominant response set to accommodate peripheral or contextual information. Though early research focused on the implications of response modulation deficits for regulating maladaptive approach behavior, more recent investigations have focused on automatic shifts of attention and the way in which deficient response modulation short-circuits the processing of contextual information that would otherwise inform (i.e., provide perspective on) ongoing behavior. This extension, involving the relatively automatic accommodation of contextual cues, supplies a fundamental link between response modulation and emotion processing.

## Emotion Processing: A Context for Interpreting and Responding to Environmental Stimuli

Given the importance and multidimensional nature of emotion experience, it is not surprising to find diverse views regarding its definition, functions, necessary and sufficient conditions, relation to other biopsychological processes, and regulation (see Ekman & Davidson, 1994). In this section, we discuss our working assumptions about emotion processing for the purposes of clarifying the associations between response modulation and emotion processing.

Specifically, we assume that (1) emotion processing is an associative process that leads to the formation of associative networks; (2) the type and intensity of emotion processing elicited by a stimulus develops with experience; (3) emotion processing involves a cascade of physiological and psychological reactions that exists on a continuum from highly automatic and basic emotions to relatively well-elaborated and complex emotions; (4) the course of emotion processing and resulting associative networks may be altered by cognitive appraisals that affect the array of associations activated and by the use of controlled processing, which allows a person to coordinate more automatic processes; and (5) although emotions generally facilitate quick and relatively automatic responses to environmental stimuli, they may also enhance deliberate decision making and self-regulation (e.g., as when controlled processing of emotional reactions is used to select appropriate interpretations and responses).

Adopting an associational perspective (Bower, 1981; Lang, 1979; Leventhal & Scherer, 1987), we assume that stimuli come to elicit the physiological, attentional, and behavioral responses with which they have been paired. When a person encounters a novel stimulus, the stimulus tends to elicit an orienting response that involves known physiological, attentional, and behavioral consequences (Graham, 1979). Moreover, he or she will typically evaluate the stimulus to determine whether it is positive or negative or merits further investigation. In addition, he or she will likely approach a positive stimulus and withdraw from (or attack) a negative stimulus. When the same or related stimuli are next encountered, his or her associative network will be activated and will automatically "reactivate" these physiological and psychological reactions. In this manner, the associative network provides a context for rapidly interpreting and reacting to internal thoughts and external events.

In the previous example, we noted that the associative

networks, which shape emotion experience, include both physiological and psychological reactions. With regard to the physiological aspect of emotions, Levenson (1994) proposed that "emotions rapidly organize the responses of different biological systems, including facial expression, muscular tonus, voice, autonomic nervous system activity, and endocrine activity to produce a bodily milieu that is optimal for effective response" (p. 123). In addressing the psychological aspect of emotion processing, he observed that emotions alter attention, shift certain behaviors upward in response hierarchies, and activate relevant associative networks in memory. These reactions, in turn, play a major role in shaping a person's response to emotion eliciting situations (Levenson, 1994).

Although some emotion responses may occur in the absence of prior learning, we assume that associative networks develop and evolve as a person experiences diverse physiological and psychological reactions with repeated exposure to a stimulus context. Thus the structure of the associative network varies as a function of the person's learning. For example, riding a roller coaster may initially cause a child to become scared, anxious, and terrified. However, realizing that he or she survived and will not likely die from riding a roller coaster, he or she may experience subsequent roller coaster rides as more exhilarating and exciting. Alternatively, as a friendship evolves from a set of hopeful expectations through the development of trust and affection to extensive interdependence, the associative network activated by the friend will become more extensive and likely grow in affective complexity. Other reactions may not develop in complexity with experience but, instead, grow even more automatic as the person exhibits the same brief and powerfully organized reaction time and again. For example, a spider may routinely elicit a strong negative reaction and behavioral avoidance in a person with a spider phobia. Thus, depending on events and the individual's construal of these events, his or her associative networks and associated emotion responses may develop in a particular direction (e.g., from fear to enjoyment), may become more extensive, differentiated, and complex (e.g., a friendship), or may become increasingly rapid and automatic (e.g., phobic avoidance).

We also assume that the quality of a person's emotion processing plays a fundamental role in determining how experiences are processed and, thus, the evolution and structure of associative networks. In this regard, we find Klaus Scherer's (1982, 1994) stimulus-evaluation-check model to provide a useful framework for conceptualizing how a person's reaction to a stimulus context develops with experience. According to Scherer, emotion acts as an interface, mediating between environmental input and behavioral output. When working well, emotions facilitate the generation and implementation of adaptive responses.

These functions are facilitated by a five-stage process of stimulus evaluation. At Stage 1, stimuli are evaluated for novelty and unexpectedness, with consequences for the direction of attention. At Stage 2, the inherent pleasantness-unpleasantness of a stimulus is evaluated, which, in turn, causes a person to experience pleasure or distress. At Stage 3, stimuli are evaluated for their goal relevance, which confers motivational significance to a situation. At Stages 4 and 5, people evaluate the availability of responses for achieving their ends in light of the current circumstances (i.e., degree of control) and consider how their actions, along with their anticipated consequences, relate to social norms and various aspects of self-concept.

From our perspective, Scherer's model serves to clarify the evolving and reciprocal interaction between emotion and cognitive processing. We assume that cognitive appraisals both (1) develop in response to and (2) serve to shape emotion processing in a manner that is substantially the same as other physiological and psychological reactions engendered by potentially significant stimuli. However, because they are more amenable to controlled (i.e., attention-regulated) processing, we believe that cognitive appraisals play a particularly potent role in directing emotion processing. Thus, with increasing stages of cognitive appraisal, emotion processing becomes less automatic (i.e., determined by the stimulus per se), and its associations are increasingly influenced by controlled processing (i.e., directed attention). In other words, a person's emotion experience may be significantly altered by his or her allocation of attention and controlled processing resources.

To this point, we have proposed that emotion processing is determined by the relatively automatic activation of associative networks that develop with experience. Moreover, cognitive appraisals are instrumental in determining the pattern of automatic associations that is elicited by a stimulus and may themselves become relatively automatic. Nevertheless, emotions also play a crucial role in signaling the need for more deliberate information processing. At such times, emotion processing may shift from relatively automatic to controlled processing so that judicious decisions may be made. According to Schneider, Dumais, and Shiffrin (1984), automatic processing involves a "fast, parallel, fairly effortless process that is not limited by short-term memory (STM) capacity, is not under direct subject control, and is responsible for the performance of well-developed skilled behaviors" (p. 1). This type of process is "activated automatically without the necessity of active control or attention by the subject" (Schneider & Shiffrin, 1977, p. 2). By contrast, controlled information processing involves "a slow, generally serial, effortful, capacity-limited, subject-regulated processing mode that must be used to deal with novel or inconsistent information" (Schneider et al., 1984, p. 2). With controlled processing, an individual can deliberately focus on a particular set of associations and use attention to guide emotion processing.

An example of this transition might involve the consequences of tasting a novel but ultimately disgusting food at a dinner party. The fundamental and relatively automatic response would involve spitting out the disgusting substance. This reaction requires little or no controlled processing. However, because the stimulus is encountered in the context of a dinner party, one's automatic reaction is likely to be evaluated and replaced by a more socially acceptable reaction. The reason is that the social context will have primed (i.e., automatically activated) a set of acceptable and unacceptable behaviors that will, under most circumstances, influence a person's reaction. The force of such influences is likely to reflect equally automatic emotion responses, which accrue as a person anticipates the reactions of other guests to his or her behavior. In the end, one's conflicting urges to spit and to avoid potential embarrassment might prime thoughts about privacy and rest rooms, which, in turn, might attract controlled processing and yield an acceptable solution to the problem. This example illustrates how adaptive emotion processing often involves shifting attention among multiple automatic associations and then allocating controlled processing resources to particular associations for the purposes of identifying adaptive responses.

The preceding characterization of emotion processing as facilitating deliberate responding may appear paradoxical. As noted by Scherer (1994), it seems paradoxical to propose that emotions engender a pause and time to reflect before acting, because strong emotions typically result in rapid action. After proposing that emotion is also a "relevance detector" that may be expected to reflect the importance or urgency of an event, Scherer concluded that "the inverse relationship between the intensity of an emotion and the length of the latency time is actually one of the most powerful design features of the emotion mechanism" (p. 129). When intensity is very high, as in emergency situations, "the organism cannot afford the luxury of repeated evaluations" and thus reverts to the "wisdom of the body" (p. 129). Similarly, Levenson (1994) described "short-circuiting cognitive processing" as a primary function of emotion. "In situations where hesitation could have the most dire consequences, emotion functions to set aside cognitive processing that is too cumbersome, too obsessive, too self-indulgent, and ultimately, too likely to be inconclusive" (p. 124).

To function adaptively in mediating between environmental input and behavioral output, emotions need to vary widely in time course and complexity to accommodate the extraordinary range of environment-behavior interactions that require mediation. Emotion reactions subserve split-second reactions, as well as momentous decisions. When necessary, people can respond to a stimulus based on its apparent valence in a reflexive or highly automatized manner. However, given time, people are inclined to consider more aspects of a stimulus context, engage in more levels of analysis, and consider a wider range of potential responses. Though the more reflective response has the obvious advantages of employing higher level cognitive processing, critical evaluation, and response choice, many situations require more rapid action. By this reckoning, the function of emotion is best served by reactions that match the nature of an eliciting stimulus.

In this regard, Scherer (1994) has proposed that emotions serve to "decouple stimulus and response" and may "interpose a response latency between stimulus and response."[3] This decoupling allows for a high degree of flexibility in responding to diverse situations. Although it may be bypassed in emergency situations, "the latency time can be used to analyze and evaluate the stimulus event as well as one's repertoire of reactions or coping alternatives more thoroughly. On the basis of this additional information, the response can be modified appropriately" (p. 128). Thus adaptive responding often involves making use of this capacity in order to pause and reflect on one's cognitive and affective associations.

## The Association Between Response Modulation and Emotion Processing

The preceding discussion of response latency and pausing to evaluate one's responses clarifies the fundamental association between response modulation and emotion processing. The process of response modulation involves the automatic redirection of attention and facilitates the shift from automatic to controlled processing (see Wallace, Schmitt, Vitale, & Newman, 2000). Despite its rudimentary nature, involving a brief and relatively automatic shift of attention, response modulation enables individuals to (1) use their active attention to consider diverse aspects of a stimulus array, including associations derived from past experience, and (2) use their controlled processing resources to elaborate, evaluate, and utilize contextual information, thus improving the quality of their stimulus analysis and behavioral responses. Referring to the orienting response concept employed by psychophysiologists (e.g., Graham, 1979), Patterson and Newman (1993) noted that certain stimuli elicit an "automatic call for processing" and that the response modulation variable refers to a person's tendency and/or ability "to answer the call." To the extent that individuals answer the call for processing (i.e., switch their focus of attention), they are able to analyze the meaning of a stimulus and purposely use that information to improve the quality of their responses. In the absence of response modulation, people are less able to shift attention and thus to utilize contextual cues, past experience, and controlled processing resources to refine responding. According to our view that emotion processing requires the use of contextual information (i.e., associative networks), a deficit in response modulation would dramatically diminish the quality of emotion processing.

## Response Modulation, Emotion Processing, and Psychopathology

Our goal in this section is to clarify how individual differences in response modulation and emotion processing contribute to the development and maintenance of psychopathology. Toward this end, we discuss the importance of response modulation and emotion processing for regulating one's behavioral and affective responses. Individuals may be at high risk for developing psychopathology due to a variety of biological, psychological, and social factors. However, people are also equipped with a remarkable capacity for coping, problem solving, and adjustment. Thus people should be able to identify problematic responses, analyze them, and generate solutions. In other words, people can use controlled processing to check and revise maladaptive thinking and behavior. Given the capacity to correct problematic behavior, the existence of persistent psychopathology suggests a failure of self-regulation.

According to Kanfer and Gaelick (1986), self-regulation involves the *deliberate* monitoring, evaluating, and, if needed, correction of behavioral responses. By definition, self-regulation is mediated by controlled processing (Kanfer & Gaelick, 1986). The literature on self-regulation is concerned primarily with using self-regulation to treat maladaptive behaviors within a therapeutic context. The goal of such interventions is to "deautomatize" maladaptive behaviors and "reautomatize" more adaptive ones. Regardless of the factors that produced the psychopathology, the expectation is that people can learn to alter maladaptive reactions by evaluating and replacing them. Similar formulations have been proposed for cognitive and emotion regulation (Beck, 1976; Ellis & Harper, 1975; Gross & Munoz, 1995)

In spite of the sizable literature on self-regulation as a therapeutic technique, researchers have rarely considered the implications of self-regulation for the development and maintenance of psychopathology. Nevertheless, the self-regulation model provides a compelling perspective on psychopathology that, moreover, serves to clarify the contribution of deficient response modulation and emotion processing to psychopathology. Although it is natural to focus on the controlled processing resources that mediate self-regulation, the shift to controlled processing and self-regulation is typically initiated by emotion cues and requires response modulation (Newman, 1998).

Although we recognize that it is possible for self-regulation to be initiated deliberately, as it is in the therapeutic context, we believe that such behavior is relatively uncommon. Examples of deliberately initiated self-regulation would include monitoring one's smoking for the purpose of altering a bad habit or monitoring one's verbal behavior to make a good impression during a job interview. More commonly, however, self-regulation is initiated in response to motivationally or emotionally significant stimuli, which generate an automatic call for processing by virtue of their significance. For example, in response to a parent's glare, an unanticipated disappointment, or even a surprising compliment, an automatic call for processing is likely to initiate self-regulatory processing. Thus the initiation of self-regulation will typically depend on relatively automatic shifts of attention, and failures of self-regulation will often reflect situation-specific deficits in shifting attention to utilize such peripheral cues (i.e., response modulation).

In our view, response modulation, emotion processing, and self-regulation are closely related processes which, when combined, constitute a highly effective system for interacting with the environment. When operating effectively, the system reacts to potentially significant events by interrupting ongoing processing and redirecting attention to potentially relevant stimuli in the environment and/or to potentially relevant details of their primed associations. Depending on the products (i.e., results) of this automatic processing, certain cues may come to command controlled processing and thus allow a person to coordinate affective and cognitive processing to achieve effective self-regulation.

A deficit in response modulation would significantly alter the automatic and controlled processing of motivationally significant events and hamper self-regulatory processing. Under such circumstances, people would consider fewer aspects of a situation and would respond based on the unchecked affective, cognitive, and behavioral products of automatic processing. Many psychologists have written about the importance of using controlled processing resources to "check" and, if necessary, correct the products of automatic processing (e.g., Gilbert, 1989). Although a person's automatic responses are typically appropriate, it is essential to regulate one's behavior when circumstances elicit maladaptive automatic responses (Hollon & Garber, 1990). In the absence of effective self-regulation, maladaptive reactions continue and, with repetition, may become highly automatic. Depending on the severity of the problem behavior and subsequent efforts to alter it, such reactions may culminate in a diagnosis of psychopathology.

For instance, after disciplining a child and observing the child's emotional distress, a father may recognize that his style of parenting has become overly harsh and potentially destructive. With such awareness, this father may deliberately engage in self-regulation during subsequent interactions with his child so that the unacceptable behavior is "deautomatized" and replaced with a more appropriate response. Unfortunately, a deficit in response modulation tends to interfere with the ability to recognize problems (i.e., emotion processing), as well as with subsequent efforts to monitor, evaluate, and correct the behavior (i.e., self-regulation). Thus, in addition to increasing a person's risk for developing unchecked, maladaptive responses, deficient response modulation contributes to the maintenance of psychopathology by hampering the controlled evaluation and correction of maladaptive habits.

To this point, we have emphasized the fact that a deficit in response modulation may short-circuit emotion processing, but the relationship between response modulation and emotion processing appears to be reciprocal. Just as deficient response modulation may curtail emotion processing, an unusually intense emotion response may preclude effective response modulation. That is, in a manner analogous to the "short-circuiting" of emotion processing described by Levenson (1994), we have proposed that intense emotions create a sense of urgency (i.e., arousal) which, in turn, leads a person to focus narrowly on specific, emotion-related cues and/or products of automatic processing (Wallace et al., 1991). This intense focus, in turn, hampers response modulation and, by extension, results in the relatively automatic expression of unchecked behavior patterns (i.e., a breakdown in self-regulation; Wallace & Newman, 1997). For example, if a father's anger is sufficiently intense, he may lack the ability to pause and consider other interpretations of or reactions to his child's behavior (see Berkowitz, 1993).[4]

To the extent that we regard deficient self-regulation as a proximal and sufficient cause of psychopathology, this analysis suggests two major pathways to the development and maintenance of psychopathology. The first concerns a general deficiency in response modulation that curtails emotion processing and hampers self-regulation. The second involves an emotion-mediated disruption of response modulation that precludes adaptive self-regulation in response to situations that have acquired intense emotional significance. In the following sections, we review research on psychopathic and emotionally reactive individuals, respectively, to elucidate these pathways.

## Pathway 1: The Emotion Processing Deficits of Psychopathic Individuals

A wealth of clinical and laboratory evidence attests to the deficient emotion processing of psychopathic individuals. In this section, we review evidence demonstrating that psychopaths' emotion processing deficits may be explained by a deficiency in response modulation. More-

over, we argue that deficient response modulation provides a more comprehensive explanation of the existing evidence than alternative explanations that involve a diminished capacity for fear or negative affect.

### Clinical Descriptions of Psychopathic Behavior

In his classic book, *The Mask of Sanity*, Hervey Cleckley (1976) used his extensive clinical experience and acumen to set out the construct of psychopathy. Cleckley viewed psychopathy as a profound failure of adjustment that could not be attributed to inadequate intelligence, psychotic-like thought disorder, or excessive neurotic anxiety. In contrast to the American Psychiatric Association's (1994) diagnosis of antisocial personality disorder, which identifies a rigid and maladaptive antisocial adjustment, Cleckley's syndrome highlights dysfunctional psychological processes such as "poverty in major affective reactions," "poor judgement and failure to learn by experience," "pathologic egocentricity," and "failure to follow any life plan" (p. 224). Cleckley described psychopathic individuals as lacking the essential capacity for maintaining normal adjustment rather than being driven to antisocial behavior.

Concerning psychopaths' emotion deficits, Cleckley (1976) wrote: "My concept of the psychopath's functioning postulates a selective defect or elimination which prevents important components of normal experience from being integrated into the whole human reaction, particularly an elimination or attenuation of those strong affective components that ordinarily arise in major personal and social issues" (p. 374). Though he emphasized emotion deficits in his description of the syndrome, Cleckley also highlighted an emotion paradox (see Lorenz & Newman, 2001). He wrote: "All judgments of value and emotional appraisals are sane and appropriate when the psychopath is tested in verbal examinations" (p. 369) and that "only when the subject sets out to conduct his life can we get evidence of how little his good theoretical understanding means to him. . . . What we take as evidence of his sanity will not significantly or consistently influence his behavior" (p. 385).

Given his emphasis on emotion deficits, it is noteworthy that Cleckley's characterization of psychopaths' core dysfunction posits a more general defect in semantic processing that prevents them from appreciating the meaning of their actions. "In attempting to account for the abnormal behavior observed in the psychopath, we have found useful the hypothesis that he has a serious and subtle abnormality or defect at deep levels disturbing the integration and normal appreciation of experience and resulting in a pathology that might, in analogy with Henry Head's classification of the aphasias, be described as semantic" (p. 388). Also highlighting a more general, integrative deficit that hampers their judgment and affective processing,

Shapiro (1965) proposed that psychopaths do not lack pertinent information or knowledge, "but rather the active, searching attention and organizing process that normally puts such information to use" (p. 149). This failure to consider the ramifications of one's behavior was amusingly portrayed by an escaped convict who was using a charity scheme to support himself until he made an appearance on national television to promote his cause (Hare, 1970). Such clinical observations regarding the psychopath's failure to integrate a variety of important information are at least as consistent with a deficit in response modulation as they are with an incapacity for affective experience.

## Laboratory Evidence

Next, we review evidence from four domains of psychopathy research: passive avoidance learning, emotion facilitation of lexical decisions, psychophysiological reactivity to emotion stimuli, and affect-mediated startle modulation. In addition to demonstrating emotion deficits, the results suggest that psychopaths' deficiency in emotion processing is (1) restricted to the relatively automatic, as opposed to deliberate, use of contextual emotion cues and (2) matched by comparable problems in the relatively automatic processing of affectively neutral contextual cues. The purpose of this review is to demonstrate that the psychopath's emotion processing deficits may be accurately and usefully understood as a consequence of deficient response modulation and thus to demonstrate that response modulation may play a crucial role in mediating emotion processing.

### Passive Avoidance: Using Emotion Cues to Inhibit Punished Responses

In what is arguably the most influential study on psychopathy, Lykken (1957) examined the extent to which psychopaths' putative fear deficit would interfere with learning to inhibit punished responses (i.e., passive avoidance learning). Participants were instructed to learn a sequence of responses to work their way through a mental maze. Superimposed on this primary task was a "latent" shock contingency that involved learning to inhibit particular responses at each step of the maze. Although participants were obviously aware that shock electrodes had been attached, they were apparently provided with a cover story rather than with explicit instructions concerning the punishment contingency. Lykken (1995) stated that the rationale for this deception was that if the contingency had been explicit, participants would have been motivated by external factors to master the contingency. By contrast, learning a latent contingency would likely reflect intrinsic motivation. As predicted, psychopaths demonstrated little to no learning of the passive avoidance contingency and made significantly more shocked errors than controls.

Lykken's (1957) findings (see also Schmauk, 1970) are typically interpreted as evidence that psychopaths are characterized by a fundamental emotion deficit (i.e., lack of fear) that undermines passive avoidance learning (e.g., Lykken, 1995). However, an equally plausible interpretation is that psychopaths have difficulty learning latent contingencies which, by definition, are peripheral to participants' primary task and focus of attention. If, as predicted by the response modulation hypothesis, psychopaths are less likely to shift attention from a primary task to process peripheral cues, then their poor learning of the latent avoidance contingency may reflect attentional, as opposed to purely emotional, limitations.

To the extent that deficient response modulation is primarily responsible for psychopaths' passive avoidance deficits, their avoidance deficits should be specific to conditions involving relatively automatic shifts of attention and should disappear if the avoidance contingency becomes the focus of primary attention. To test this hypothesis, Newman and Kosson (1986) assessed passive avoidance learning under two sets of experimental conditions. Both conditions featured 10 blocks of trials that involved the consecutive presentation of 8 two-digit numbers on a computer monitor. Participants were instructed to learn, by trial and error, which numbers required them to respond and which required response inhibition (see Figure 49.1).

In the first condition, participants earned monetary rewards for responding to a set of arbitrarily designated "good numbers" and lost money for responding to "bad numbers." The second (punishment-only) condition involved the same discrimination task, but participants lost money if they failed to respond to good numbers, as well as for responding to bad numbers. Even though the passive avoidance contingency was identical in both conditions,

| | | CONDITION | |
|---|---|---|---|
| STIMULUS | RESPONSE | REW PUN | PUN ONLY |
| S+ | YES | WIN | --- |
| | NO | --- | LOSE |
| S− | YES | LOSE | LOSE |
| | NO | --- | --- |

Figure 49.1 Representation of the response contingencies for the reward-punishment and punishment-only conditions of the passive avoidance task used by Newman and Kosson (1986).

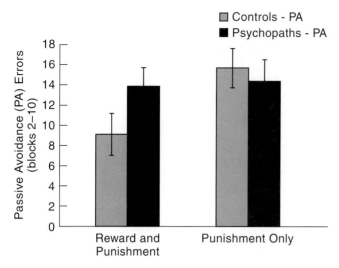

Figure 49.2 Number of passive avoidance errors committed by psychopaths and controls in reward-punishment and punishment-only conditions of the Newman and Kosson (1986) study.

it was less salient and thus more dependent on response modulation in the former, the reward-punishment, condition than in the latter, the punishment-only, condition. Whereas participants focus initially on responding for reward and then shift attention to process punishment feedback in the reward-punishment condition, avoiding punishment is participants' primary focus of attention from the outset of the punishment-only condition. As predicted, psychopaths exhibited a passive avoidance deficit in the reward-punishment condition, but they performed at least as well as controls when avoiding punishment was their only task (i.e., their dominant response set; see figure 49.2).

Inadequate attention to latent avoidance contingencies also provides a compelling explanation for psychopaths' insensitivity to punishment, and consequent self-regulatory deficits, in laboratory gambling tasks. In 1978, Siegel demonstrated that psychopaths persist in "betting" on playing cards even when the probability of losing exceeds that of winning. After playing a deck of 40 cards involving 100% reward, participants were allowed to play as many cards as they wished from nine other decks that ranged from 0% to 90% reward with a complementary percentage of punishment. Although floor and ceiling effects appeared to prevent group differences from reaching statistical significance at the extreme percentages, psychopaths played more cards than controls on all decks. Although their performance suggested that psychopaths were less accurate in perceiving the diverse probabilities of rewards and punishments, a direct test of this possibility indicated otherwise. During play with the 30% and 70% decks, Siegel interrupted his participants and asked them to estimate the likelihood that the next card would

be a winner. Psychopaths and controls were equally adept at judging the probabilities under these circumstances.

Following Siegel (1978), Newman, Patterson, and Kosson (1987) developed a computerized card-playing task with one deck of 100 cards. Participants won 5 cents for playing a face card (jack, queen, king, or ace) and lost 5 cents for playing a number card. The probability of reward was 90% for the first block of 10 cards, 80% for the second block of cards, 70% for the third block of cards, and so on until the last block of cards, which were all losers. Thus the probability of punishment increased from 10% to 100% as the task progressed. Participants were told that they could not "pass" cards but that they could quit the game whenever they wanted to by pressing a second button. The dependent measure was the number of cards played before quitting the game. As predicted, psychopaths played significantly more cards and lost significantly more money than controls (see also Fisher & Blair, 1998; O'Brien, Frick, & Lyman, 1994; Shapiro, Quay, Hogan, & Schwartz, 1988; see Figure 49.3).

Our interpretation of these findings is that the psychopaths' deficiency in response modulation interfered with their ability to monitor, evaluate, and alter their maladaptive response strategy (i.e., self-regulation). To evaluate this interpretation, another condition was employed that forced participants to wait for 5 seconds, while a cumulative record of their response feedback was displayed, be-

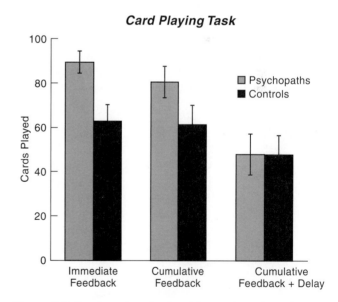

Figure 49.3 Number of cards played by psychopaths and controls in the card-playing task (Newman, Patterson, & Kosson, 1987). Immediate feedback involved monetary feedback only; cumulative feedback involved monetary feedback plus a cumulative visual representation of the cards played; and cumulative feedback + delay involved monetary, cumulative feedback, and a 5-second delay between presentation of the feedback and the next opportunity to play a card.

fore allowing them to play the next card. The purpose of this manipulation was to obviate the need for response modulation by forcing participants to stop and reflect on the changing contingencies. Under these conditions, psychopaths and controls played the same number of cards and earned comparable amounts of money. Given access to the same information, psychopaths and controls appeared to weigh the information similarly and make the same decisions.

To this point, the evidence suggests that psychopaths' deficiencies in using punishment cues to facilitate self-regulation is specific to conditions that require response modulation, but the studies cited here did not directly measure the association between response modulation and passive avoidance. Toward this end, Newman, Patterson, Howland, and Nichols (1990)[5] modified the reward-punishment version of the passive avoidance task used by Newman and Kosson (1986; see Figure 49.1) to provide an estimate of response modulation. Specifically, whenever a participant responded to a stimulus number, the computer display, including the stimulus number and response feedback, remained on until participants gave responses that advanced them to the next trial. By comparing response times following punishment to response times following reward, it was possible to estimate the extent to which participants paused or suspended a dominant response set for reward to process negative feedback. Consistent with predictions, psychopaths paused approximately half as long as controls following negative feedback, and, across groups, pausing predicted participants' ability to use punishment cues to inhibit punished responses (see Figures 49.4, 49.5, 49.6). Thus the results of this study lend credence to our proposal that deficient response modulation hampers the psychopath's use of punishment cues to regulate ongoing, goal-directed behavior.

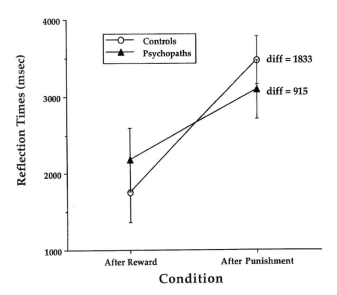

Figure 49.5 Amount of time (in msec) that low-anxious psychopaths and controls paused following presentation of correct (i.e., after reward) and incorrect (i.e., after punishment) response feedback in the passive avoidance task. From Newman, Patterson, Howland, and Nichols (1990), copyright 1990, with permission from Elsevier Science.

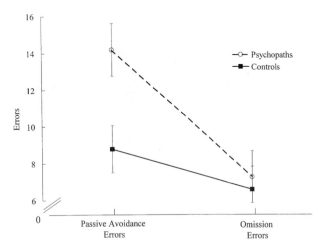

Figure 49.4 Passive avoidance and omission errors committed by low-anxious psychopaths and controls. From Newman, Patterson, Howland, and Nichols (1990), copyright 1990, with permission from Elsevier Science.

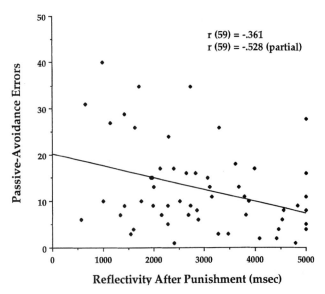

Figure 49.6 Relation between pausing (i.e., reflectivity) after punishment feedback and learning (i.e., passive avoidance errors). Each block dot represents one participant. The partial correlation refers to the association between pausing and learning after removing the variance associated with pausing after reward and provides a better estimate of response modulation. Data are from Newman, Patterson, Howland, and Nichols (1990).

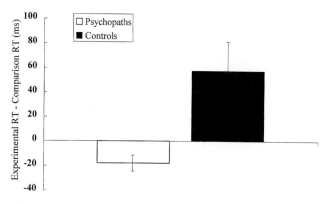

Figure 49.7 Amount of interference (reaction time [RT] to incongruent trials − RT to neutral trials) shown by low-anxious psychopaths and controls in the picture-word task employed by Newman, Schmitt, and Voss (1997) (measured in msec).

We have proposed that the poor passive avoidance learning of psychopathic individuals reflects a fundamental deficiency in response modulation as opposed to a primary deficit in capacity for negative affect. If we are correct, then psychopaths should display deficits in processing affectively neutral contextual cues, as well as contextual emotion cues. To examine this prediction, we conducted a series of experiments using variations of the traditional Stroop paradigm. In one task, participants were instructed to press a button as quickly as possible to indicate whether two successively presented words (or pictures) on a computer screen were conceptually related or not. The first word (or picture) always appeared in conjunction with a picture (or word) that participants were instructed to ignore. Consistent with previous research (e.g., Gernsbacher & Faust, 1991), nonpsychopathic controls responded significantly more slowly when the to-be-ignored stimulus conflicted with their primary task. However, as shown in Figure 49.7, psychopaths were essentially unaffected by the incongruent contextual information (Newman, Schmitt, & Voss, 1997). These findings have been replicated using a noncomputerized picture-word Stroop task and another computerized task that required participants to name the color of rectangles containing incongruent color names (Schmitt & Newman, 2000). In each case, psychopaths were unaffected by incongruent contextual cues, which automatically interfered with the primary task performance of controls.

These findings demonstrate that psychopaths are characterized by an "insensitivity" to affectively neutral cues that parallels their insensitivity to emotion cues and provide empirical support for Shapiro's (1965) speculation that the cognition of psychopathic individuals "is characterized by an insufficiency of integrative processes that is comparable to the insufficiency of integrative processes on the affective side" (p. 299). Although a deficit in response modulation can account for psychopaths' insensi-

tivity to both types of contextual information, it is difficult to understand why psychopaths would be insensitive to affectively neutral cues if their core deficit is emotional. Thus these laboratory findings further suggest that the emotion deficits seen in psychopaths may reflect a more general information processing deficiency (Cleckley, 1976; Newman, 1998).

## Using Emotion Cues to Facilitate Word Recognition

Many researchers have assessed emotion processing in the context of passive avoidance learning because of its association with poorly regulated, antisocial behavior. To assess emotion utilization more directly, however, other investigators have examined psychopaths' ability to utilize emotion cues while performing a lexical decision task. In a lexical decision task, participants are instructed to identify strings of letters, as quickly and accurately as possible, as words or nonwords. Based on previous research demonstrating that emotion-related words are identified as words more quickly than affectively neutral words, Williamson, Harpur, and Hare (1991) predicted and found that psychopaths were significantly less affected by the affective quality of words than were controls (see also Day & Wong, 1996). We recently replicated and extended these results using a larger sample and several methodological refinements (Lorenz & Newman, 2001).

Psychopaths' deficits in emotion facilitation on the lexical decision task are especially relevant to the current discussion because the task is thought to measure the relatively automatic influence of associative processing. Whereas emotional cues appear to activate associative networks that aid performance in controls, such cues have little effect on the performance of psychopaths. This powerful evidence of deficient utilization of emotion in psychopaths provides another opportunity to ask whether their deficit reflects an attentional or purely emotional problem. To evaluate this question, Lorenz and Newman (2001) examined the extent to which affectively neutral contextual cues influenced the lexical decisions of both psychopaths and controls. Specifically, using the same task that had demonstrated group differences in emotion facilitation, we compared the extent to which high (versus low) word frequency facilitated participants' lexical decisions. Although the mechanisms that underlie such effects are not well understood, research shows that high-frequency words are identified more quickly than low-frequency words (Rajaram & Neely, 1992). Consistent with this finding, nonpsychopathic controls demonstrated significant frequency facilitation, as well as emotion facilitation. However, paralleling our results for emotion facilitation, differences in word frequency had significantly less effect on the lexical decisions of psychopaths relative to controls (see Figure 49.8). In light of the fact that high-

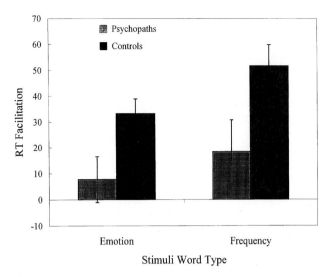

Figure 49.8 Amount of facilitation (RT to neutral words − RT to emotional [high-frequency] words) shown by low-anxious psychopaths and controls on the lexical decision task employed by Lorenz and Newman (2001) measured in msec.

and low-frequency words were matched on emotionality (i.e., arousal and valence), as well as other important characteristics, such findings suggest that psychopaths are deficient in both semantic and emotion processing (see also Hare, 1998). The lexical decision results are, therefore, consistent with our proposal that psychopaths are less likely to utilize the same associations that automatically influence the behavior of nonpsychopaths.

In addition to performing the lexical decision task, Williamson et al. (1991) asked their participants to appraise the affective valence of the words employed in their study. In contrast to their performance on the lexical decision task, the affective appraisals of psychopaths and controls were indistinguishable. This discrepancy between appraising and utilizing emotion cues was also replicated by Lorenz and Newman (2001), and similar findings have been reported by Patrick, Bradley, and Lang (1993) and by Blair (1999). Such findings show that psychopaths perform as well as controls when their primary task is evaluating affective stimuli (i.e., when the task depends on deliberate attention as opposed to response modulation).

Results from the lexical decision experiments complement previous behavioral evidence in demonstrating that psychopaths' inefficient use of emotion cues reflects a problem with attention rather than an emotion-specific deficit. When emotion processing involves deliberate attention, as it does in the word rating task and the punishment-only condition of the passive avoidance task, psychopaths perform as well as controls. However, when emotion processing depends on relatively automatic shifts of attention from a deliberate focus (i.e., primary task) to other, less salient, aspects of a stimulus array or associative network, then psychopaths are deficient. Moreover,

the reduced accessibility of such primed associations in psychopaths is not restricted to fear, negative affect, or even positive affect cues. Indeed, there is now considerable evidence that this processing anomaly extends to affectively neutral contextual cues. Deficient response modulation provides a relatively parsimonious explanation for all of these findings.

## Psychophysiological Responses to Emotion Stimuli

Further evidence for an emotion deficit comes from research using electrodermal activity (EDA) to assess emotion processing in psychopaths. These EDA studies have provided good support for the hypothesis that psychopaths display less anticipatory and conditioned arousal to threat cues than do controls (see Arnett, 1997; Fowles & Missel, 1994, Hare, 1978). For example, Hare (1965) examined EDA while participants watched numbers count up from 1 to 10. Participants were informed that they would receive a strong electric shock each time the number 8 appeared. Relative to nonpsychopathic controls, psychopaths displayed smaller electrodermal responses, and their increases in EDA occurred in closer proximity to the shock (i.e., to the number 7 rather than earlier numbers), indicating weaker anticipatory conditioning (see also Ogloff & Wong, 1990). More recently, Patrick, Cuthbert, and Lang (1994) demonstrated that psychopaths displayed less EDA than controls in response to tones that had been associated with fear images (e.g., "Taking a shower, alone in the house, I hear the sound of someone forcing the door, and I panic").

Because such findings are well replicated, they are generally regarded as providing strong and differential support for the low-fear hypothesis (e.g., Lykken, 1995). Although we recognize the merits of this view, we believe that there are important limitations in the evidence that preclude such strong conclusions. First, with few exceptions, investigators have failed to include appropriate control conditions. Without comparing participants' EDA to fear cues with their EDA to other, equally potent emotion cues, it is impossible to know whether psychopaths' deficient EDA reflects fear conditioning or some other process. In one of the few studies to include a positive affect control condition, Hare and Quinn (1971) found similarly deficient conditioning among psychopaths regardless of whether slides of nude females or electric shocks were the unconditioned stimuli. Although this difference failed to reach statistical significance in the positive condition, inspection of the data indicates that psychopaths were similarly hyperreactive to the stimuli paired with shocks and with nude females. That is, the difference in statistical significance appears to reflect the fact that controls reacted much more strongly to the stimuli associated with electric shocks. Despite consistent evidence regarding poor fear conditioning in psychopaths, it is not yet possible to evaluate whether this deficit reflects lack of capacity to experience fear or a more general deficit that impairs EDA conditioning.

A second reason to be cautious when interpreting the EDA findings is that psychopaths and controls typically display comparable emotional (EDA) responses when instructed to attend to emotion slides. For example, Patrick, Bradley, and Lang (1993) instructed participants to "view each slide for the entire time it appeared on the screen" (p. 85) and found comparable EDA and subjective ratings to both positive and negative emotional slides in psychopaths and in controls. Using the same procedure, Levenston, Patrick, Bradley, and Lang (2000) obtained the same result. Blair, Jones, Clark, & Smith (1997) compared the EDA of psychopaths and controls as they viewed threat, distress, and neutral slides and failed to find significant group differences in response to the threat slides. Because these studies all reported significant main effects, with participants displaying larger psychophysiological reactions to the affective slides than to the neutral slides, the lack of group differences in EDA is unlikely to reflect weak or inadequate emotion stimuli. In fact, both psychopaths and controls displayed significant increases in EDA to the negative slide stimuli. As the only exception to this pattern of results, psychopaths displayed significantly less EDA to the distress slides (e.g., crying child) than controls did, despite showing a significant increment in EDA relative to baseline (Blair et al., 1997). Paralleling the behavioral data, then, psychopaths and controls appear to display comparable EDA when their task involves deliberately attending to affective stimuli.

To our knowledge, the only study to evaluate EDA while manipulating psychopaths' dominant response set was conducted by Arnett, Smith, and Newman (1997). The study employed a continuous motor task in which one of five peripheral green lights was lit each time a participant pressed the center button. Participants were instructed to press the button corresponding to the peripheral green light as quickly as possible and then to press the center button again. In one (i.e., reward-punishment) condition, participants earned 5 cents each time they completed five presses within the allotted time. In the other (i.e., punishment-only) condition, rapid responding enabled participants to avoid losing 5 cents. After performing the task for 1 minute, a central red light was activated to indicate that the peripheral green lights could change from green to red between the time participants released the center button and pressed the peripheral button. If participants pressed the peripheral button in the presence of a peripheral red light, they lost 50 cents. This phase also lasted 1 minute, and the two phases were repeated four times.

In both conditions, then, the center red light indicated that task contingencies were changing and that participants would now have to inhibit specific responses to

avoid relatively large monetary punishments. When this passive avoidance contingency was superimposed on a response set for reward, there was a significant main effect, with psychopaths displaying less EDA than controls to the salient punishment cues. However, when the same contingency was superimposed on the active avoidance (i.e., punishment-only condition) task, which already involved a focus on avoiding money, psychopaths' EDA increased as much as controls'. Thus, paralleling the behavioral evidence, these results demonstrate that group differences in EDA appear to depend on participants' dominant response set. When psychopaths are instructed to attend to slides or are provided with punishment cues that are consistent with their dominant response set (i.e., avoiding punishment), then their EDA appears comparable to that of controls.

A third limitation of the EDA evidence that precludes strong conclusions is that, with rare exceptions, investigations of EDA in psychopathic and nonpsychopathic participants have failed to control for trait anxiety (see Arnett, 1997). Examination of anxiety is important because it has been found to moderate (i.e., interact with) psychopathy in determining both behavioral and psychophysiological responses to threat cues. For example, after using a pretreatment manipulation to establish the letter $Q$ as a cue for punishment, Newman, Wallace, Schmitt, and Arnett (1997) examined the extent to which presentation of this cue slowed responses to target letters during a subsequent block of trials. Even though the cue no longer predicted punishment, participants with high anxiety responded to targets more slowly on cue-present trials than on cue-absent trials than did low-anxious controls. When the task was administered to criminal offenders, the researchers obtained a significant main effect for psychopathy and a psychopathy-by-anxiety interaction. Consistent with a low-fear interpretation, controls displayed more response inhibition to the peripheral punishment cues than psychopaths did. However, this main effect was qualified by a significant interaction that indicated that the effect was specific to the high-anxious psychopaths and controls. Whereas high-anxious controls resembled high-anxious students in displaying increased response inhibition to the cues, high-anxious psychopaths responded more quickly in the presence of punishment cues. In contrast, the punishment cues had minimal impact on low-anxious participants regardless of psychopathy status. Such findings suggest that sensitivity to threat cues relates primarily to trait anxiety and that the contribution of psychopathy reflects some other process, perhaps attention related, that moderates the quality of an individual's response to threat cues.

The results of the Arnett et al. (1997) investigation described here demonstrate that psychopathy and anxiety may also interact to determine EDA in response to threat cues. Recall that this study assessed EDA in response to a central red light that signaled that participants might have to inhibit approach responses (or active avoidance responses in the punishment condition) to avoid relatively large (i.e., 50-cent) punishments. As already noted, the groups did not differ in the punishment-only condition, but there was a significant main effect for psychopathy in the reward-punishment condition. Furthermore, this main effect was qualified by a significant psychopathy-by-anxiety interaction. As shown in Figure 49.9, both the main effect and interaction were carried by the strong reaction of high-anxious nonpsychopaths. Whereas low-anxious psychopaths and controls displayed comparable skin conductance responses to the red lights, high-anxious controls displayed significantly greater skin conductance responses than high-anxious psychopaths.

The association between psychopathy and EDA in response to threat and other emotional cues is generally regarded as the most widely replicated and important finding in the field (Lykken, 1995). Moreover, such findings are the cornerstone of proposals that postulate that a fundamental emotion (i.e., fear) deficit underlies the syndrome of psychopathy. Although the poor-fear-conditioning finding is well replicated, it seems clear that there are inconsistencies and unresolved issues that need to be addressed before we can draw firm conclusions. If psychopaths lack the capacity for fear and negative affect, why do they display normal EDA while viewing emotional pictures (e.g., Patrick et al., 1993) and in response to informative punishment stimuli while working to avoid punishment (e.g., Arnett et al., 1997)? Furthermore, in the absence of evidence that psychopaths' weak EDA is specific to conditioned threat cues (i.e., that it does not apply to appetitive stimuli), there is little reason to attribute such findings to a diminished capacity for fear or negative affect as opposed to other factors that mediate conditioned electrodermal responses. Finally, the fact that psychopathy and anxiety interact to determine EDA in response to threat cues suggests that EDA reflects diverse psychological processes and that sensitivity to threat cues is not the only explanation for such evidence.

We have proposed that psychopathy is associated with an attentional (i.e., response modulation) deficit that impairs emotion processing. We believe that this explanation is no less consistent with the EDA evidence than is the low-fear hypothesis. Psychopaths display normal emotional responses when they are instructed to attend to emotion stimuli (e.g., pictures) and when emotion stimuli are relevant to their dominant response set (e.g., avoiding punishment). Conversely, they display emotion deficits (i.e., less EDA) when processing emotion stimuli that rely on the automatic activation of associative networks (i.e., conditioned stimuli). Moreover, an attentional explanation involving the automatic activation of associative networks would apply to positive, as well as aversive, conditioned stimuli and might clarify the meaning of the observed

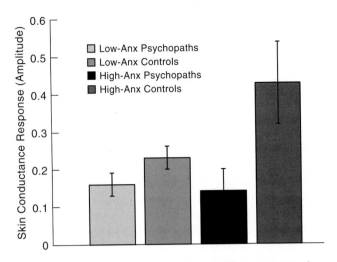

Figure 49.9 Skin conductance magnitude of responses to the central threat cue (i.e., red light) in the reward-punishment condition of the continuous motor task employed by Arnett, Smith and Newman (1997). *Anx* refers to level of anxiety (Welsh, 1956).

psychopathy-by-anxiety interactions. For instance, a person's level of anxiety may influence the meaning of threat cues, whereas his or her level of psychopathy may influence the degree to which the meaning is processed.

Although this characterization of the EDA evidence is generally consistent with the response modulation hypothesis, the requirement to shift attention is not manipulated and thus is not explicit in all paradigms that reveal group differences in EDA. For example, the count-up to shock/noise procedure (e.g., Hare, 1965) involves the central presentation of threat cues, and there are no explicit requirements to process additional information. Within the response modulation framework, then, it is not clear why the threat cues fail to elicit comparable EDA in psychopaths and controls.

Despite the absence of an explicit requirement to alter a dominant response set, we do not believe that the count-up to shock/noise findings are inconsistent with the response modulation hypothesis. In contrast to paradigms in which psychopaths display normal EDA, there is no explicit instruction or reason to process the conditioned threat cues in the quasi-conditioning (i.e., count-up) and other conditioning paradigms. Indeed, the stimuli used in such studies are intentionally selected to have no intrinsic meaning prior to conditioning. Thus processing the meaning or associative network primed by these stimuli typically relies on relatively automatic shifts of attention (i.e., the spontaneous activation and processing of relevant associations). If, as we have proposed, such automatic shifts of attention do not occur in psychopathic individuals, then they would be less affected by the meaning of such stimuli. Nevertheless, as already noted, psychopaths are capable of deliberately shifting attention and processing the meaning of such stimuli when there is a reason to do so.

Our use of response modulation in this analysis retains the key aspects of the response modulation concept that involves relatively automatic shifts of attention and a dominant response set. However, the attentional shift and dominant response set are not explicitly operationalized in the experimental context. Rather, they refer to a person's cognitive set. An automatic shift of attention refers to the person's ability to spontaneously activate and process a new (i.e., previously inactive) associative network in response to environmental stimuli. The dominant response set determines which environmental stimuli are deemed relevant and which dimensions of a stimulus context receive further processing. When the meaning and emotional significance of a stimulus is consistent with the dominant response set, they are processed, because no shift of attention is required. However, if the meaning of a stimulus requires the automatic activation and processing of an alternative associative network or set, then it is unlikely to influence the psychopath's behavior regardless of whether it is a central or peripheral aspect of the experimental context. This approach to defining central and peripheral stimuli (i.e., as related to the response/cognitive set) was also used in predicting and interpreting the results of the lexical decision task (e.g., Lorenz & Newman, 2001; Williamson et al., 1991). Despite the fact that letter strings were centrally presented in the absence of other explicit demands for attention, psychopaths were relatively unaffected by the affective connotations of the words, presumably because such effects require automatic shifts of attention.

Despite a long history of equating EDA with fear and anxiety, researchers are becoming increasingly aware that this view is excessively narrow and that EDA should not be regarded as synonymous with fear or negative affect (Damasio, 1994; Newman & Wallace, 1993b; Patrick & Lang, 1999). For instance, Patrick and Lang (1999, p. 214) note that:

> skin conductance is a nonspecific index of sympathetic arousal (Venables & Christie, 1973) that is subject to cortical influences (Tranel & Damasio, 1994) and which reflects negative affect only indirectly. Therefore, an alternative to the low fear interpretation of this diminished EDA is the notion that it reflects a deficit in the vigilance and higher associative processing normally evident during anticipation of an emotionally potent event (Miller, Curtin, & Patrick, 1997).

To the extent that EDA reflects a person's tendency to access conditioned associations or other meaningful, internal representations (see Damasio, 1994; Gorenstein, 1991), then it depends on relatively automatic shifts of attention (Newman, 1997). Thus group differences in EDA may often reflect the psychopath's failure to shift attention from environmentally presented cues for punishment to the associative networks that lend emotional support to these cues (see Shapiro, 1965). Although the processing of conditioned emotional stimuli and concomitant EDA appears to be relatively automatic (Öhman & Soares, 1994), a deficit in response modulation may, nevertheless, interfere with the processing of such associations and limit EDA. Though this proposal may be counterintuitive, it is no more so than evidence that shows that psychopaths are less influenced by the incongruity of peripheral stimuli in the Stroop-like tasks that automatically disrupts performance in controls (e.g., Newman et al., 1997).

In sum, we propose that psychopaths' weak EDA may, like other evidence that demonstrates deficient emotion processing in psychopaths, reflect an attentional problem that limits the effects of emotion cues rather than an incapacity for emotion experience. Proponents of the low-fear hypothesis (e.g., Lykken, 1995) have cited psychophysiological experts such as Fowles (e.g., 1980, 1987, 1988), who have interpreted the EDA data as evidence for a fundamental fear/anxiety (i.e., behavioral inhibition system; BIS) deficit in psychopaths. However, even Fowles has begun to endorse alternative explanations. In the conclusion of a recent paper, he writes, "Two perspectives in the recent literature raise the possibility that psychopaths suffer from a broader deficit than a weak BIS and that electrodermal hyporeactivity might relate to this broader deficit" (Fowles, 2000, p. 187). This revised view is highly compatible with the response modulation hypothesis and, in fact, is nearly indistinguishable from our earlier proposals (see Newman, 1997).

### Affect-Modulated Startle

The final line of research that we review involves the extent to which people's reactions to startle probes are modulated by the affective valence of pictures that they are viewing. Under normal circumstances, people exhibit larger startle responses to noise probes while viewing unpleasant slides and smaller startle responses while viewing pleasant slides relative to startle responses that occur during neutral slides. Psychopaths, however, do not display this linear trend (Patrick et al., 1993). Rather, they display larger startle responses during neutral slides than during the affectively valenced pictures (a quadratic trend). Based on the fact that psychopaths' startle responses during unpleasant slides were, contrary to the typical pattern, smaller than their responses during the neutral slides, Patrick (1994) interpreted these results as further evidence that psychopathy is associated with a reduced capacity to experience fear.

The Patrick et al. (1993) study represents an ingenious application of the startle-probe methodology, but it is not without important limitations. Specifically, (1) none of the group comparisons involving the startle responses of psychopaths and controls achieved statistical significance; (2) it was difficult to determine whether the groups differed more during neutral slides or during unpleasant slides; and (3) the authors did not distinguish between the groups' reactions during fear versus other negative-affect slides. In contrast to the basic analyses, subsequent analyses revealed significant differences in startle modulation for subgroups of prisoners with high and low scores on Factor 1 (i.e., callous, unemotional traits) of the Psychopathy Checklist—Revised (PCL-R; 1991).

A more recent paper by Levenston, Bradley, Lang, and Patrick (2000) addresses a number of the questions raised by the initial study. First, the study yielded significant group differences between psychopaths (preselected to have high scores on Factor 1) and controls. Similar to the initial findings, nonpsychopathic controls displayed the "normal" pattern of "startle inhibition for pleasant pictures and startle potentiation for unpleasant pictures," whereas psychopaths "showed an aberrant pattern of blink inhibition for both pleasant and unpleasant pictures in relation to neutral pictures" (p. 5). Interestingly, however, the predicted Group × Valence interaction was qualified by a significant three-way interaction involving probe time. Whereas "nonpsychopaths showed robust linear modulation (unpleasant greater than pleasant) at both the 800-ms and late-interval times," psychopaths "showed an emergent linear effect at the late times only" (pp. 5–6). As noted later, this finding raises the possibility that an attentional anomaly is responsible for psychopaths' unusual performance.

Levenston et al. (2000) also examined group differences for specific slide categories. Psychopaths displayed significantly less startle potentiation than controls during the mutilation, assault, threat, and thrill slides. The only slide category that did not differentiate the groups involved erotic scenes, which apparently elicited greater orienting and startle suppression in controls than the other slide categories did.

Although it is possible to reconcile these recent findings with the low-fear hypothesis (see Levenston et al., 2000), they may also be consistent with the proposed deficit in response modulation (i.e., attentional interpretation). To the extent that processing of affective stimuli is less automatic for psychopaths than for controls, as evidenced by their lack of emotion facilitation in lexical decision tasks, psychopaths may invest more attention and controlled processing resources to the processing of the affective (i.e., both pleasant and unpleasant) pictures. According to Bradley, Cuthbert, and Lang (1993), startle potentiation is inversely related to the amount of attention invested in a slide. Thus, to the extent that psychopaths invest more attention in the affective slides than in the neutral slides, it follows that their startle responses during

the neutral slides will be larger than during affective slides.

It seems clear that attention can moderate startle responses, as well as emotion. However, it is not clear why psychopaths invest more attention in the affective slides or withdraw attention from the unpleasant slides more slowly than controls do. One possibility concerns the speed of emotion processing. To the extent that psychopaths' reactions to the slide stimuli are less automatic and thus involve more effortful processing relative to controls, psychopaths would be slower to reach the stage of affective processing that involves affective valence (e.g., Stage 2 of Scherer's [1982] model). Consequently, the resulting inclination to approach (i.e., invest more attention) or avoid (withdraw attention) may be slower to develop in psychopaths. Interestingly, this is exactly what was found for both pleasant and unpleasant slides at the 800 ms probe time. Such findings appear to be more consistent with individual differences in processing efficiency than with a general incapacity to experience fear. Moreover, the former interpretation may help to explain lack of group differences on the other (self-report and psychophysiological) measures of emotion processing (see Levenston et al., 2000; Patrick et al., 1993).

This attentional perspective also raises questions about the validity of interpreting valence-specific findings in the startle paradigm. To the extent that an information processing deficit slows processing of the more complex, affect-ladened slides, the increased attention needed to process the slide would suppress startle responses during both positive and negative slides. However, because normal affect modulation for pleasant stimuli involves suppression, an information processing deficit that suppresses startle responses would be hard to distinguish from normal, positive modulation. Conversely, the same information processing deficit would result in a distinctive failure of negative modulation that would be difficult to distinguish from a deficit in processing negative affect. The reason is that, in the case of unpleasant slides, any attention-mediated suppression would be opposite in direction to the expected potentiation engendered by unpleasant slides.

Sutton, Vitale, and Newman (2001) recently reported a replication of Patrick et al.'s (1993) findings in incarcerated female offenders. Psychopaths and controls were assigned to groups using the standard cut-scores on the PCL-R and further subdivided according to scores on the Welsh anxiety scale. Noise probes were predicted either 2 or 4.5 seconds following slide onset. A four-way interaction indicated that probe time was a significant factor that moderated group differences in emotion-modulated startle. The key finding was that low-anxious psychopaths failed to display the typical linear trend at the 2 s probe time. Similar to Patrick et al.'s findings, this group displayed smaller startle responses during unpleasant pictures than

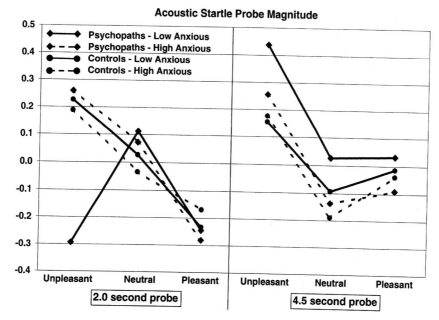

Figure 49.10 Magnitude of startle responses shown by subgroups of female prisoners to noise probes delivered 2 or 4.5 seconds following the onset of unpleasant, neutral, and pleasant pictures. From Sutton, Vitale, and Newman (2001).

during neutral pictures. However, this effect was limited to the early probe time, as in the Levenston et al. (2000) study. At the 4.5 s probe time, low-anxious psychopaths displayed significantly greater negative potentiation than they did for the 2 s probes and displayed as much or more negative potentiation than the other groups at the 4.5 s probe times. Such findings are difficult to reconcile with a low-fear interpretation because psychopaths demonstrate substantial sensitivity to unpleasant slides after 4.5 s. Nevertheless, these findings are compatible with an interpretation that involves information processing efficiency (see Figure 49.10).

Although the startle-modulation studies provide clear evidence of anomalous emotion processing in psychopaths, the results appear to parallel those from other paradigms and are thus amenable to similar interpretation. Specifically, psychopaths' anomalous emotion processing is not specific to threat cues but extends to the processing of positive (e.g., thrill), as well as negative, affect cues (Levenston et al., 2000; Lorenz & Newman, 2001; Williamson et al., 1991). Moreover, psychopaths display normal reactivity to a wide range of emotional cues, both positive and negative, when they are deliberately processing the cues and speed of processing is not an important factor.

## Implications of the Evidence for Psychopaths' Emotion Processing and Psychopathology

The preceding review of research on psychopathy provides clear evidence that psychopaths are deficient in response modulation, emotion processing, and self-

regulation. Moreover, we believe that the evidence supports our contention that psychopaths' deficient response modulation gives rise to their deficits in emotion processing and self-regulation. This view is based, in large part, on the pattern of results that indicates that (1) psychopaths are deficient in emotion processing when it relies on relatively automatic shifts of attention but perform like controls when they are deliberately attending to emotion cues and (2) psychopaths' deficient processing of contextual emotion cues is paralleled by their weak processing of affectively neutral contextual cues. Whereas these findings are consistent with the response modulation hypothesis, the pattern is both more specific and more general than would be expected if psychopathic behavior were due to a primary emotion deficit.

Having demonstrated that a deficit in response modulation may short-circuit emotion processing and self-regulation in the laboratory, we now turn our attention to the implications of psychopaths' deficient response modulation for their nonlaboratory behavior. Toward this end, we consider the consequences of deficient response modulation for emotion processing within the context of Scherer's (1982) model and use examples to illustrate how psychopaths' deficient response modulation may explain the core characteristics of psychopathy, including their deficient emotion responses.

We expect the emotion processing of psychopaths to be relatively normal, at least to a point, before initiating goal-directed behavior. Using Scherer's (1982) model as a framework, we assume that psychopaths would orient attention to novel cues (Stage 1), discern the potential pleasant or unpleasant implications of the information (Stage 2), and identify the motivational significance of the information (Stage 3). Thus, to at least some extent, psychopaths do engage in emotion processing and would be expected to form emotion-related associative networks. However, we believe that once a particular urge (i.e., response inclination) is activated, psychopaths' emotion processing would typically progress no further. That is, psychopaths would be unlikely to evaluate the adequacy of their anticipated response for achieving their ends (Stage 4) or to consider its consistency with personal/societal values (Stage 5).

Furthermore, once they are engaged in the active organization and implementation of goal-directed behavior, psychopaths' processing of additional, emotion-related information will typically not progress beyond Stage 1 of Scherer's model. Considering their level of emotion processing both during, and in the absence of, ongoing goal-directed behavior, it follows that psychopaths will typically respond to immediate incentives by initiating goal-directed behavior. However, their responses will generally reflect minimal consideration of contextual information, alternative response strategies, past experiences, or likely consequences. Moreover, once focused on their goal, psychopaths would have difficulty accommodating feedback from the environment, using associative networks to broaden their perspective, and modifying inappropriate response strategies.

Consider the example of date rape. After sharing a drink with Marie at a bar, Jess suggests that they go to his apartment. With regard to Jess's emotion processing, we assume that Marie has captured his attention (Stage 1), that he finds something about her appealing (Stage 2), and that he desires to have sex with her (Stage 3). Consequently, Jess acts on the first strategy that occurs to him, "let's go to my place." Once Jess focuses on the goal of sexual intercourse, the use of emotional or other contextual cues will require response modulation. Thus, even if Marie is uncomfortable with his advances and resists (or is married to his brother), Jess will be relatively unlikely to process and make use of these cues. Moreover, even if he happens to reflect on his behavior afterward, Jess's lack of awareness of Marie's distress and of his "decision" to commit rape will interfere with his perception of responsibility and ability to experience guilt or remorse (see also Shapiro, 1965).

The next example, involving a crime committed by one of our research participants, is somewhat more complex but illustrates how deficient response modulation may relate to the more general characteristics of the psychopathy syndrome. Harry was many months behind in his rent and had received several warnings from his landlord. Then, one day, the landlord came to Harry's apartment, insulted him, and told him that he would have to leave. At that point, Harry became angry, beat the landlord with a stick,

and tied him to a chair. Before leaving the apartment, Harry hurled a final threat: "I'm takin' the first bus to St. Louis and if you try to stop me I'll kill you."

Harry's behavior illustrates many of the hallmarks of psychopathy and deficient response modulation. First, though paying rent is generally a secondary concern, inability to make rent payments is generally sufficient to revise a person's priorities. Harry's failure to revise his priorities and address the problem (i.e., irresponsibility, failure to plan) set the stage for the conflict that led to his arrest. Second, ignoring for the moment ethical issues about paying or not paying rent, Harry could have left his apartment without assaulting his landlord. Instead, he committed an impulsive, violent act which reflected a total lack of problem-solving skills. Third, Harry's beating of and blaming his landlord illustrates the callousness and profound lack of perspective (e.g., empathy) that characterizes psychopathy. Harry reacted emotionally to the concrete threats and immediate insults of his landlord and, on that basis, felt that his actions were justified. However, because he did not consider other contextual information, Harry's behavior demonstrated a complete failure to appreciate his landlord's dilemma or his own contribution to the problem (i.e., shallow affect). Finally, in relating his escape plan to the landlord, Harry showed a remarkable lack of insight and poor judgment for a person of normal intelligence.

Harry's failure to achieve perspective in the heat of the moment fits our response modulation model, but if the problem is due to poor response modulation, why doesn't he feel remorse later and learn from his experience? Indeed, we have argued that psychopaths have the capacity to reflect on their behavior and draw appropriate inferences using effortful processing resources. We believe that the answer to this question is captured succinctly in the following quote: "I always know damn well I shouldn't do these things, that they're the same as what brought me to grief before. I haven't forgotten anything. It's just that when the time comes I don't think of anything else. I don't think of anything but what I want now" (Grant, 1977, p. 60). Even if psychopaths occasionally do think about the inappropriateness of their behavior and resolve to behave differently, their response modulation deficit would interfere with their ability to follow through. Then, to the extent that they fail to alter their behavior, psychopaths are left either to despise themselves or find some means of rationalizing their behavior.

The ability to reflect on one's behavior and draw appropriate inferences is also essential for most forms of psychotherapy in which a client and therapist collaborate to achieve insight and plan more adaptive response strategies. Despite the psychopath's capacity for insight, we believe that such learning will rarely result in stable behavior change. In order to achieve an adaptive, well-socialized adjustment, psychopaths would have to access this "contextual information" automatically in situations that elicit maladaptive, dominant responses. Unfortunately, doing so is largely incompatible with their response modulation deficit (see Wallace et al., 1999). Although we recognize the difficulties involved, we are hopeful that effective interventions for psychopathy may, nevertheless, be developed. Indeed, it is our hope that a detailed understanding of the psychopath's response modulation deficit will facilitate progress toward this goal.

In summary, as a result of their response modulation deficit and consequent short-circuiting of emotion processing, psychopaths are predisposed to engage in poorly considered, impulsive, and potentially callous behavior. Moreover, their relatively weak processing of corrective feedback diminishes the likelihood of their using controlled processing resources to rehearse and correct their maladaptive response inclinations. Finally, even when they do learn from experience, psychopaths' deficient response modulation typically interferes with their ability to put such knowledge to use.

## Pathway II: Emotion-Generated Problems Associated with Dysregulatory Psychopathology

In the previous section, we proposed that psychopathy reflects a general deficiency in response modulation that curtails emotion processing and hampers self-regulation. However, psychopathy is a relatively unique form of psychopathology that involves inadequate as opposed to excessive emotional conflicts. More commonly, psychopathology is associated with exaggerated or maladaptive reactions to intense emotion stimuli. Examples of such dysregulatory psychopathology (Wallace & Newman, 1997) include the "loss of control" drinking seen in some forms of alcoholism, the phobic avoidance seen in certain anxiety disorders, the excessive rumination on personal inadequacies manifested by some depressed individuals, and the self-destructive, poorly regulated behaviors (e.g., inappropriate spending, aggression, sexual behavior) seen in borderline personality disorder. In this section, we address the deficits in response modulation and self-regulation that occur in stimulus contexts that have acquired intense emotional significance.

Whereas psychopaths' emotion processing is limited by their failure to process contextual emotion cues, the problem in dysregulatory psychopathology is that emotion processing is short-circuited owing to the intensity of an emotional response. Recall that "the inverse relationship between the intensity of an emotion and the length of the latency time is actually one of the most powerful design features of the emotion mechanism" (Scherer, 1994, p. 129). Accordingly, when intensity is very high, as in emergency situations, "the organism cannot afford the lux-

ury of repeated evaluations" and thus reverts to the "wisdom of the body" (Scherer, 1994, p. 129). In dysregulatory psychopathology, people are especially sensitive to certain emotion cues, but their resulting sense of urgency causes them to consider a limited range of associations and to react with prepotent (i.e., dominant) responses (see Wallace & Newman, 1997).

To investigate this phenomenon, we typically select individuals with particular sensitivities (e.g., to physical or social threat cues) and then assess their behavioral and attentional regulation following motivational/emotional manipulations that do or do not prime their concerns. Although such manipulations often lead to improved performance owing to the motivational significance of emotion cues (Gray, 1987), we have demonstrated that they often impair performance when secondary or peripheral processing is needed to regulate ongoing behavior.

In a study designed to test these theoretical propositions, Wallace and Newman (1990) examined motor inhibition (i.e., self-regulation) under experimental conditions designed to match the emotional sensitivities of their research participants. According to Gray (1981), neurotic extraverts are hypersensitive to reward cues, whereas neurotic introverts are especially sensitive to punishment cues. These groups are typically defined using the Extraversion and Neuroticism scales of the Eysenck Personality Questionnaire (Eysenck & Eysenck, 1975). Whereas neurotic extraverts are identified with trait impulsivity and are usually compared with stable introverts (i.e., low-impulsive individuals), neurotic introverts are considered to be trait anxious and are usually compared with stable extraverts (low-anxious individuals). After instructing participants to trace a circle, we told them to "trace the circle again but, this time, trace the circle as slowly as possible" (Wallace & Newman, 1990, p. 00–00). Thus tracing was their dominant response and monitoring the speed of tracing was an explicit secondary consideration. As predicted by our theoretical framework, neurotic extraverts displayed the poorest inhibition in the reward condition, and neurotic introverts traced the fastest in the punishment condition (see also Bachorowski & Newman, 1985, 1990; Nichols & Newman, 1986; see Figure 49.11).

A constructive replication of this work was undertaken to examine the attentional consequences of engendering high nonspecific arousal by presenting emotionally significant stimuli to samples with more diverse sensitivities. Specifically, we (Newman et al., 1993) used a letter-number discrimination task in which a character string (i.e., five numbers or letters) appeared in the center of the computer monitor on 75% of the trials. On 25% of the trials, the string appeared unpredictably in one of the four corners. Participants were instructed to respond as quickly as possible by pressing one of the two buttons to indicate whether numbers or letters composed the character string. At the beginning of each trial, participants were presented

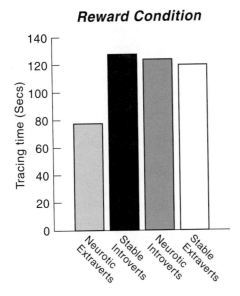

**Reward Condition**

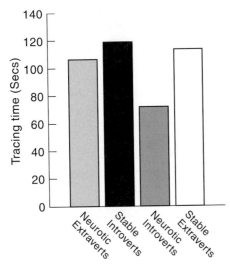

**Punishment Condition**

Figure 49.11 The effects of incentive condition on reward-sensitive (i.e., neurotic extraverts) and punishment-sensitive (i.e., neurotic introverts) participants relative to their respective control groups (i.e., stable introverts and stable extraverts) on speed of circle tracing following instructions to trace as slowly as possible. Data from Wallace and Newman (1990).

with a "ready stimulus" that was either a word with emotional significance or a neutral word. Based on the assumption that emotionally significant cues attract attention and hamper response modulation, we predicted that participants would respond more slowly to strings in the nondominant, peripheral locations on trials initiated by emotionally significant words as opposed to neutral words.

In one experiment, threat (e.g., accident) and safety words were presented to high- and low-anxious groups of participants. In another, weight- and body-shape-related

words (e.g., *scale*) were presented to women with and without eating disorders. In a third study, we identified specific "self-discrepancies" for each participant using the Selves questionnaire (Higgins, 1987) and then primed these self-discrepancies on a subset of trials. Results were consistent across all three experiments: There were no group differences in the speed with which participants correctly identified the string type when it was presented in the more common, central position, regardless of the ready stimulus. However, when trials were initiated by an emotionally significant cue, individuals with the specified sensitivity responded significantly more slowly to the peripheral strings relative to controls. These experiments show that priming an affectively significant concern may interfere with participants' ability to modulate a dominant response set (see Figure 49.12).

Following Gray (1981, 1987), we have proposed that motivationally significant cues increase arousal in proportion to their perceived significance and to the physiological reactivity of a person's "nonspecific arousal system." Reactivity of the nonspecific arousal system, in turn, relates to individual differences in Eysenck's (Eysenck &

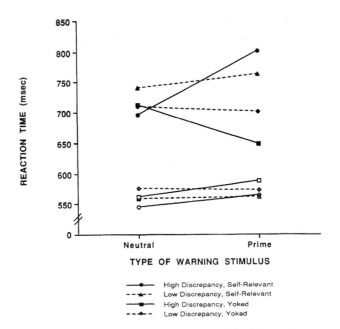

Figure 49.12 The effects of beginning a trial with a self-relevant warning stimulus on time to categorize character strings as numbers or letters when the strings occur in expected (open symbols) or unexpected (filled symbols) locations. Warning stimuli either were or were not self-relevant and were or were not selected to represent some participants' self-discrepancies. Self-discrepant words refer to traits that a person believes that he or she ought to have and ideally would like to have but does not. Self-relevant words relate to the participant's word ratings, whereas yoked words relate to the self-discrepancies of other participants and are therefore not self-relevant.

Eysenck, 1975) trait neuroticism. As nonspecific arousal increases, a person perceives an increasing sense of urgency that narrows the focus of attention, promotes the rapid selection and initiation of responses, and decreases behavioral flexibility (Wallace et al., 1991). High nonspecific arousal may reflect the intensity of environmental elicitors, temperament-related differences in emotional reactivity (neuroticism), or both. Moreover, because controlled attention follows automatic attention, controlled processing resources are disproportionately focused on the automatic products (i.e., results) of emotion processing and are less available for checking or regulating these automatic products. Consequently, prepotent, relatively automatic interpretations and responses are made without the benefit of effortful evaluation or regulation (Wallace & Newman, 1997). Though such reactions are typically appropriate, they are not always. To the extent that they are stable, inflexible, and maladaptive, such reactions may give rise to psychopathology.

Deficits in self-regulation that stem from hyperarousal may even involve diminished processing of peripheral punishment cues and thus resemble deficits seen in psychopaths. For instance, investigations of passive avoidance learning in neurotic extraverts have revealed results that closely resemble those obtained with psychopathic offenders. Specifically, under conditions involving monetary rewards and punishments, neurotic extraverts fail to pause following punishment feedback and display significantly more passive avoidance errors than controls (Patterson, Kosson, & Newman, 1987). Despite the similarity of these results to those obtained with psychopaths, the underlying process appears to be different (see Newman & Wallace, 1993). Whereas neurotic extraverts are hypersensitive to reward stimuli, this does not seem to be the case for psychopaths (Newman et al., 1990). Conversely, whereas psychopaths display response modulation deficits in affectively neutral contexts, the same does not appear to occur in neurotic extraverts (Newman & Wallace, 1993a).

## Summary and Implications for Dysregulatory Psychopathology

We have proposed that individuals with high levels of trait neuroticism (emotional reactivity) are prone to the development of dysregulatory psychopathology. More specifically, we hypothesized that their hyperreactivity to highly salient emotion cues results in a strong "call for processing" that they answer by allocating attention to the emotional cues and the automatic products of emotion processing (i.e., related associative networks). Moreover, their heightened reactivity results in high arousal, which increases the speed, force, and focus of subsequent behavior. Consequently, their reactions to emotional situations are initiated more rapidly, are more difficult to interrupt, and

occur with less attention to peripheral cues or other considerations (Wallace et al., 1991; Wallace & Newman, 1997). In addition, the strong call for processing commands a disproportionate amount of controlled processing resources, which, in turn, leaves relatively little capacity for self-regulation (which relies on controlled processing resources). The result is that neurotic individuals are prone to emit relatively automatic and frequently maladaptive responses that reflect a short-circuiting of normal emotional and self-regulatory processing. In other words, intense emotional reactions may interfere with the flexible allocation of attention (i.e., response modulation), impair self-regulation, and result in various forms of dysregulatory psychopathology.

In psychopathy, the response modulation deficits preclude the use of contextual emotion cues whenever attention is actively directed elsewhere. In contrast, the emotion processing of neurotic individuals is relatively normal owing to the acquired and highly situation-specific nature of their response modulation deficits. The importance of this distinction is that, relative to psychopaths, neurotic individuals have extensive practice in processing emotion material and thus have a better developed emotion structure. In terms of Scherer's (1982) model, the emotion processing of such individuals typically includes consideration of all five stages. As a result, their emotion processing normally transcends consideration of immediate goals and their likelihood of achieving them to include consideration of self-standards and societal reactions. Moreover, neurotic individuals are more likely to perceive connections between present and past circumstances, as well as the future implications of present events. Furthermore, they are likely to consider a variety of affectively related experiences, which influences their perspective on immediate circumstances. In light of their more elaborate emotion processing, we assume that the associative networks of neurotic individuals are also more extensive and interconnected than those of psychopathic individuals.

The heightened risk for psychopathology manifested by neurotic individuals (Trull & Sher, 1994) does not, in our opinion, reflect a general deficit in emotion processing. Rather, their hyperreactivity to emotional stimuli makes them vulnerable to the development of maladaptive perceptions and responses in particular emotion-related contexts. In most cases, their maladaptive behavior is acquired gradually as a result of an unfortunate person-by-situation interaction.

For example, after experiencing a panic attack in a university lecture hall, a student (Sally) may experience anxiety as she prepares to attend her next class in the same lecture hall. If Sally is hyperreactive to emotion cues, this experience will initiate a relatively strong call for processing and more extensive emotion processing. Such processing may include evaluating the threat, her ability to cope with the threat, and the personal and social implications of attending versus skipping her class. All things considered, she may decide to attend the class. However, as she approaches the classroom and her arousal increases, Sally may again experience a strong desire to avoid the class. Unfortunately, Sally's capacity for emotion processing at this point will be strongly influenced by her high level of nonspecific arousal. In particular, her attention will focus more sharply on her concern (fear) and dominant response (escape). In addition, her sense of urgency will promote the rapid selection and initiation of her dominant response. Moreover, these factors will simultaneously limit the accessibility of contextual cues and Sally's ability to directly use controlled processing resources to evaluate and correct her dominant response inclinations. Whereas a person with a less reactive, nonspecific arousal system might resist the urge, Sally's hyperreactivity is likely to short-circuit self-regulation and result in her skipping the class.

This example illustrates how hyperreactivity to emotion stimuli may interfere with making the most adaptive response in particular situations, but we believe that the development of maladaptive behavior in vulnerable individuals reflects maladaptive learning that develops gradually over time. To continue the example, owing to multiple sources of stress and arousal or other vulnerabilities, Sally may be unable to mobilize sufficient resources to fight her urge to avoid her lectures. With each lecture, Sally's struggle to regulate her behavior may become more short-lived as she accepts the inevitable result. Moreover, with each such experience her associative network will increasingly reflect her new response bias. In the end, skipping the class will become a dominant and relatively automatic response, and Sally's initial consideration of other factors and responses will be less well represented in her associative network.

Although Sally's problem—skipping her class—is likely to interfere with her performance in that class, it could remain a relatively circumscribed problem. However, if she now experiences a panic attack in another social context (e.g., a shopping mall), Sally's fears are likely to grow, and her dominant means of coping with such fears is already well established. Thus, in a manner analogous to the class experience, she is likely to struggle at first but to choose to avoid more and more places.

This example illustrates the development of dysregulatory psychopathology. When a person experiences intense emotions that limit other emotion and information processing, he or she responds on the basis of the most readily available considerations and coping responses. Although prepotent responses are often appropriate, they may also be maladaptive for any number of reasons. Quite commonly, it is simply the person's overreaction or harsh evaluation of his or her response that confers emotional significance to the situation. Regardless of the factors that confer the emotional significance, to the extent that the

circumstances are encountered repeatedly, that they elicit high arousal, and that they result in the same coping responses time after time, the sequence becomes increasingly automatic and alters the structure of a person's associative network. Relatedly, processing of alternative considerations and means of responding becomes increasingly difficult. Consequently, in the absence of concerted effort or outside intervention, such maladaptive reactions are likely to develop into psychopathology.

Once a maladaptive sequence reaches a certain level of automaticity, a number of factors serve to maintain the problem. First, by virtue of its automaticity, a person may have more difficulty monitoring the problem and, even if the problem does attract attention, alternative considerations and responses will have become relatively inaccessible. However, in contrast to psychopaths, neurotic individuals are predisposed to notice when their behavior violates a personal standard, owing to their reactivity to emotional events and tendency to answer emotion-related calls for processing. In addition to violating personal standards, maladaptive behaviors typically elicit unpleasant reactions from others and hamper social and occupational adjustment. Such sources of frustration and negative affect are potent stimuli for neurotic individuals and generally attract their attention. Thus neurotic individuals would seem to be well equipped to engage in constructive self-regulation and to modify their behavior.

Unfortunately, their tendency to react to emotion cues with excessive levels of nonspecific arousal also appears to disrupt adaptive self-regulation. The reason is that cues for self-regulation (e.g., self-discrepancies, frustration, negative feedback) increase arousal, as well as eliciting attention. Under normal circumstances, the arousal engendered by a call for processing facilitates reflectivity and the constructive redirection of attention (see Patterson & Newman, 1993). However, to the extent that a person's attempt to monitor, evaluate, and alter behavior directs attention to an associative network that involves a well-rehearsed, emotional sequence that reliably results in maladaptive behavior, it is unlikely to facilitate adaptive self-regulation. Ironically, such attempts to regulate behavior may only serve to increase arousal and trigger the prepotent, maladaptive response (see Wegner, 1994). Consistent with this speculation, several investigators have discussed how people's critical self-evaluations of their alcohol use may paradoxically disinhibit further abuse because using alcohol is their dominant means of coping with negative affect (Marlatt & Gordon, 1985; Tiffany, 1990; Wallace & Newman, 1997).

With regard to treating this type of dysregulation, we believe that the implications are more straightforward and the prospects for success much better than they are for psychopathy. We believe that, in dysregulatory psychopathology, high arousal comes to interfere with response modulation and thus constrains emotion processing and self-regulation, resulting in the development and maintenance of relatively automatic, maladaptive behavioral strategies. The formula for treating such dysfunctions would seem to require reversing this causal sequence. Specifically, using the therapeutic relationship to create a safe, supportive, relatively low-arousal environment, it should be possible to analyze problem situations and generate clear and specific strategies for behaving differently. Such strategies may be practiced initially in low-stress situations and then in more stressful ones. Optimally, the individual would then practice his or her alternative coping responses in the presence of the emotional circumstances that have routinely elicited his or her maladaptive behavior. With such practice, it should be possible to "deautomatize" maladaptive thoughts and behavior and "reautomatize" (e.g., Kanfer & Gaelick, 1986) more adaptive ones so that the relevant associative networks and emotion responses acquire a more adaptive structure. In contrast to psychopaths, whose intrinsic deficits in response modulation interfere with their ability to pause, reflect, and implement a therapeutic intervention, the prognosis for individuals with dysregulatory psychopathology is more optimistic owing to their ability to access and utilize therapy-related training.

## Summary

In this chapter, we have addressed the role of response modulation in coordinating the interaction of emotion and attention and the implications of this interaction for psychopathology. When people encounter motivationally or emotionally significant stimuli, they experience a call for processing. To the extent that people answer the call for processing, they (1) may use the resulting information to improve the quality of their immediate responses, (2) modify associative networks and thus the automatic associations that are primed on future occasions, and (3) are able to utilize existing associative networks to enhance perspective on present circumstances. Owing to its role in moderating emotion-attention interactions, response modulation exerts a major influence on a person's awareness of emotion stimuli, on his or her development of emotional reactions, and on his or her ability to utilize the results of emotion processing.

To illustrate how potential problems in response modulation and emotion processing may influence the development of psychopathology, we considered two disparate forms of psychopathology. The literature on psychopathy demonstrates (1) how a fundamental deficit in response modulation is sufficient to disrupt emotion processing and thus the self-regulation of behavior; (2) how a failure to pause and process emotion cues alters the development of associative networks, particularly in connection with emotion experiences that normally interrupt ongoing,

goal-directed behavior (i.e., behavioral inhibition in response to threat cues); and (3) how response modulation deficits interfere with a person's ability to utilize diverse internal representations (i.e., associative networks), which may deter them from integrating information from different time periods and diverse learning experiences and thus severely constrain the development of perspective (see also Newman, 1998; Shapiro, 1965). In our view, it is this difficulty utilizing past learning and other potentially important associations (e.g., personal resolutions) while engaged in goal-directed behavior that creates the greatest obstacle for anyone concerned with altering the psychopath's behavior.

Regarding the second pathway to psychopathology, we discussed how intense reactions to emotion stimuli may come to hamper response modulation and the regulation of maladaptive behavior. More specifically, we proposed that certain people are predisposed by temperament or experience to react with high arousal to particular emotion stimuli. This arousal, in turn, creates a sense of urgency and simultaneously narrows the focus of attention to specific, emotion-related environmental cues and internal associates, thus interfering with response modulation and normal information processing. Moreover, the person's narrow focus on emotion-eliciting cues serves to maintain his or her intense emotions and maladaptive coping strategies, resulting in the development of psychopathology. We do not believe that this form of psychopathology, in contrast to psychopathy, reflects a fundamental (i.e., primary) deficit in response modulation. Thus, we assume that affected individuals have a greater capacity for using specific environmental and/or internal cues to initiate self-regulation and are thus more amenable to therapeutic interventions designed to modify their emotion responses.

In conclusion, emotions play a major role in organizing responses to specific environmental circumstances. In addition to influencing immediate reactions to emotionally significant events, such reactions contribute to the development of associative networks, thus increasing or decreasing the likelihood that particular reactions will occur in the future. We have proposed that response modulation deficits alter immediate reactions to emotion stimuli and, by extension, that they may alter the development of associative networks. In our view, this framework clarifies the processes by which maladaptive attention-emotion interactions lead to the development and maintenance of psychopathology. To the extent that emotions fail to direct attention to significant stimuli and/or internal considerations, as occurs in psychopathy, people are less likely to process a variety of important information; their associative networks will fail to reflect such information; and thus their automatic reactions to such circumstances will be relatively unaffected by experience (i.e., learning). Moreover, to the extent that emotion stimuli produce high arousal and cause a person to focus attention narrowly on particular concerns and response inclinations, emotionally reactive individuals (e.g., neurotics) will also be at high risk for developing information processing deficiencies, selectively impoverished associative networks, and inflexible maladaptive response inclinations.

## NOTES

1. Preparation of this chapter was supported by a grant from the National Institute of Mental Health. We thank Chad Brinkley, Donal MacCoon, Kristi Hiatt, and Jennifer Vitale for their helpful comments on an earlier version of this chapter.

2. We use the term *nonspecific arousal* to refer to activity in Gray's (1981) nonspecific arousal system. Activity in the nonspecific arousal system increases in response to perceived threats and reward opportunities and acts to increase the intensity of approach- or avoidance-related behaviors.

3. Importantly, emotion-induced arousal may also facilitate dominant responses, as illustrated by the phenomenon of "drive summation" (see Gray, 1987, pp. 179–184).

4. Another possibility is that an individual's emotional response may be too weak to signal an effective "call for processing" and thus may hamper response modulation. We do not discuss this scenario in this chapter because (1) this possibility is thoroughly addressed by Lykken (1995) with regard to his low-fear hypothesis and (2) we are unaware of any evidence that provides differential support for this pathway (i.e., that cannot be explained by the response modulation hypothesis that is described in the next section of this chapter).

5. Although our lab's initial research on passive avoidance learning (i.e., Newman, Widom, & Newman, 1985) tested hypotheses by comparing low-anxious psychopaths and controls, we abandoned this strategy between 1986 and 1990 when we adopted Hare's (1980, 1991) Psychopathy Checklist (PCL) as our measure of psychopathy. Because Hare's checklist is relatively independent of anxiety, we assumed initially that it would not be important to stratify our sample using a measure of anxiety, However, with time it became apparent that a large percentage of individuals who met the checklist criteria for psychopathy had high levels of neurotic anxiety and performed differently than low-anxious psychopaths on laboratory tasks (see Newman & Brinkley, 1997; Schmitt & Newman, 1999). Thus, owing to our interest in studying Cleckley psychopaths, who are distinguished by their low neurotic anxiety, we returned to our focus on low-anxious psychopaths and controls beginning with this publication (Newman et al., 1990).

## REFERENCES

American Psychiatric Association. (1994). *Diagnostic and statistical manual of mental disorders, fourth edition.* Washington, DC: Author.

Arnett, P. A. (1997). Autonomic responsivity in psychopaths: A critical review and theoretical proposal. *Clinical Psychology Review, 17*(8), 903–936.

Arnett, P. A., Smith, S. S., & Newman, J. P. (1997). Approach and avoidance motivation in incarcerated psychopaths during passive avoidance. *Journal of Personality and Social Psychology, 72*, 1413–1428.

Bachorowski, J., & Newman, J. P. (1985). Motor inhibition and time interval estimation tasks as measures of impulsivity in adults. *Personality and Individual Differences, 6*, 133–136.

Bachorowski, J., & Newman, J. P. (1990). Impulsive motor behavior: Effects of personality and goal salience. *Journal of Personality and Social Psychology, 58*(3), 512–518.

Beck, A. T. (1976). *Cognitive therapy and the emotional disorders.* New York: International Universities Press.

Berkowitz, L. (1993). *Aggression: Its causes, consequences, and control.* New York, Washington, DC: McGraw-Hill.

Bernstein, A., Newman, J. P., Wallace, J. F., & Luh, K. E. (2000). Left-hemisphere activation and deficient response modulation in psychopaths, *Psychological Science, 11*(5), 414–418.

Blair, R. J. R., (1999). Responsiveness to distress cues in the child with psychopathic tendencies. *Personality and Individual Differences, 27*(1), 135–145.

Blair, R. J. R., Jones, R. L., Clark, F., & Smith, M. (1997). The psychopathic individual: A lack of responsiveness to distress cues? *Psychophysiology, 34*(2), 192–198.

Bower, G. H. (1981). Mood and memory. *American Psychologist, 36*(2), 129–148.

Bradley, M. M., Cuthbert, B. N., & Lang, P. J. (1993). Pictures as prepulse: Attention and emotion in startle modification. *Psychophysiology, 30*(5), 541–545.

Cleckley, H. (1976). *The mask of insanity* (5th ed.) St. Louis, MO: Mosby.

Damasio, A. R. (1994). *Descartes's error: Emotion, reason, and the human brain.* New York: Putnam.

Day, R., & Wong, S. (1996). Anomalous perceptual asymmetries for negative emotional stimuli in the psychopath. *Journal of Abnormal Psychology, 105*(4), 648–652.

Easterbrook, J. A. (1959). The effect of emotion on cue utilization and the organization of behavior. *Psychological Review, 66*, 183–201.

Ekman, P., & Davidson, R. J. (Eds.). (1994). *The nature of emotion: Fundamental questions.* New York: Oxford University Press.

Ellis, A., & Harper, R. A. (1975). *A new guide to rational living.* Englewood Cliffs, NJ: Prentice Hall.

Eysenck, H. J., & Eysenck. S. B. G. (1975). *Manual of the Eysenck Personality Questionnaire (Adult).* London: Hodder & Stoughton.

Fisher, L., & Blair, R. J. R. (1998). Cognitive impairment and its relationship to psychopathic tendencies in children with emotional and behavioral difficulties. *Journal of Abnormal Child Psychology, 26*(6), 511–519.

Fowles, D. C. (1980). The three arousal model: Implications of Gray's two-factor learning theory for heart rate, electrodermal activity, and psychopathy. *Psychophysiology, 17*, 87–104.

Fowles, D. C. (1987). Application of a behavioral theory of motivation to the concepts of anxiety and impulsivity. *Journal of Research in Personality, 21*, 417–435.

Fowles, D. C. (1988). Psychophysiology and psychopathology: A motivational approach. *Psychophysiology, 25*, 373–391.

Fowles, D. C. (2000). Electrodermal hyporeactivity and antisocial behavior: Does anxiety mediate the relationship? *Journal of Affective Disorders, 61*, 177–189.

Fowles, D. C., & Missel, K. (1994). Electrodermal hyporeactivity, motivation, and psychopathy: Theoretical issues. In D. Fowles, P. Sutker, & S. Goodman (Eds.),

*Progress in experimental personality and psychopathology research: Vol. 17. Psychopathy and antisocial personality: A developmental perspective* (pp. 263–284) New York: Springer.

Gernsbacher, M. A., & Faust, M. E. (1991). The mechanism of suppression: A component of general comprehension skill. *Journal of Experimental Psychology: Learning, Memory, and Cognition, 17*(2), 245–262.

Gilbert, D. T. (1989). Thinking lightly about others: Automatic components of the social inference process. In J. S. Uleman & J. A. Bargh (Eds.), *Unintended thought* (pp. 189–211). New York: Guilford Press.

Gorenstein, E. E. (1991). A cognitive perspective on antisocial personality. In P. A. Magaro (Ed.), *Annual review of psychopathology: Vol. 1. Cognitive bases of mental disorders* (pp. 100–133). Newbury Park, CA: Sage.

Gorenstein, E. E., & Newman, J. P. (1980). Disinhibitory psychopathology: A new perspective and a model for research. *Psychological Review, 87*, 301–315.

Graham, F. K. (1979). Distinguishing among orienting, defense, and startle reflexes. In H. D. Kimmel, E. H. van Oist, & J. F. Orlebke (Eds.), *The orienting reflex in humans* (pp. 137–167). Hillsdale, NJ: Erlbaum.

Grant, V. W. (1977). *The menacing stranger: A primer on the psychopath.* Oceanside, NY: Dabor Science.

Gray, J. A. (1981). A critique of Eysenck's theory of personality. In H. J. Eysenck (Ed.), *A model for personality* (pp. 246–276). New York: Springer-Verlag.

Gray, J. A. (1987). *The psychology of fear and stress.* New York: Cambridge University Press.

Gross, J. J., & Munoz, R. F. (1995). Emotion regulation and mental health. *Clinical Psychology: Science and Practice, 2*, 151–164.

Hare, R. D. (1965). Temporal gradient of fear arousal in psychopaths. *Journal of Abnormal Psychology, 70*, 442–445.

Hare, R. D. (1970). *Psychopathy: Theory and research.* New York: Wiley.

Hare, R. D. (1978). Psychopathy and electrodermal responses to nonsignal stimulation. *Biological Psychology, 6*(4), 237–246.

Hare, R. D. (1980). A research scale for the assessment of psychopathy in criminal populations. *Personality and Individual Differences, 1*, 111–119.

Hare, R. D. (1991). *The Hare Psychopathy Checklist-Revised.* Toronto: Multi-Health Systems.

Hare, R. D. (1998). Psychopathy, affect and behavior. In D. J. Cooke, R. D. Hare, & A. Forth (Eds.), *Psychopathy: Theory, research and implications for society* (pp. 81–104). The Netherlands: Kluwer Academic Publishers.

Hare, R. D., & Quinn, M. J. (1971). Psychopathy and autonomic conditioning. *Journal of Abnormal Psychology, 77*, 223–235.

Higgins, E. T. (1987). Self-discrepancy: A theory relating self and affect. *Psychological Review, 94*(3), 319–340.

Hollon, S. D., & Garber, J. (1990). Cognitive therapy for depression: A social cognitive perspective. *Personality and Social Psychology Bulletin, 16*, 58–73.

Kanfer, F. H., & Gaelick, L. (1986). Self-management methods. In F. H. Kanfer & A. P. Goldstein (Eds.), *Helping people change: A textbook of methods* (3rd ed.). Elmsford, NY: Pergamon Press.

Lang, P. J. (1979). A bio-informational theory of emotional imagery. *Psychophysiology, 16*, 495–512

Lang, P. J., Bradley, M. M., & Cuthbert, B. N. (1995). *International Affective Picture System (IAPS): Technical manual and affective ratings.* Gainesville: University of Florida, Center for Research in Psychophysiology.

Levenson, R. L. (1994). Human emotion: A functional view. In P. Ekman & R. J. Davidson (Eds.), *The nature of emotion: Fundamental questions.* New York: Oxford University Press.

Levenston, G. K., Bradley, M. M., Lang, P. J., & Patrick, C. J. (in press). Psychopathy and startle modulation during emotional picture processing: Reactions to victimization, explicit threat, thrill, and sex scenes. *Journal of Abnormal Psychology.*

Levenston, G. K., Patrick, C. J., Bradley, M. M., & Lang, P. J. (2000). The psychopath as observer: Emotion and attention in picture processing. *Journal of Abnormal Psychology, 109*, 373–385.

Leventhal, H., & Scherer, K. (1987). The relationship of emotion to cognition: A functional approach to a semantic controversy. *Cognition and Emotion, 1*, 3–28

Lorenz, A. R., & Newman, J. P. (2001). Deficient response modulation and emotion processing in psychopathic offenders: Results from a lexical decision task. Manuscript submitted for publication.

Lykken, D. T. (1957). A study of anxiety in the sociopathic personality. *Journal of Abnormal and Social Psychology, 55*, 6–10.

Lykken, D. T. (1995). *The antisocial personalities.* Hillsdale, NJ: Erlbaum.

Marlatt, G. A., & Gordon, J. R. (1985). *Relapse prevention: Maintenance strategies in the treatment of addictive behaviors.* New York: Guilford Press.

McCleary, R. A. (1966). Response-modulating function of the limbic system: Initiation and suppression. In E. Stellar & J. M. Sprague (Eds.), *Progress in psychopathology* (Vol. 1, pp. 209–271). New York: Plenum.

Miller, M. W., Curtin, J. J., & Patrick, C. J. (1999). A startle-probe methodology for investigating the effects of active avoidance on negative emotional reactivity. *Biological Psychology, 50*, 235–257.

Newman, J. P. (1987). Reaction to punishment in extraverts and psychopaths: Implications for the impulsive behavior of disinhibited individuals. *Journal of Research in Personality, 21*, 464–485.

Newman, J. P. (1997). Conceptual models of the nervous system: Implications for antisocial behavior. In D. M. Stoff, J. Breiling, & J. D. Maser (Eds.), *Handbook of antisocial behavior* (pp. 324–335). New York: Wiley.

Newman, J. P. (1998). Psychopathic behavior: An information processing perspective. In D. J. Cooke et al. (Eds.), *Psychopathy: Theory, research, and implications for society* (pp. 81–104). The Netherlands: Kluwer.

Newman, J. P., & Brinkley, C. A. (1997). Reconsidering the low-fear explanation for primary psychopathy. *Psychological Inquiry, 8*, 236–244.

Newman, J. P., & Kosson, D. S. (1986). Passive avoidance learning in psychopathic and non-psychopathic offenders. *Journal of Abnormal Psychology, 95*, 257–263.

Newman, J. P., Patterson, C. M., Howland, E. W., & Nichols, S. L. (1990). Passive avoidance in psychopaths: The effects of reward. *Personality and Individual Differences, 11*(11), 1101–1114.

Newman, J. P., Patterson, C. M., & Kosson, D. S. (1987). Response preservation in psychopaths. *Journal of Abnormal Psychology, 96*, 145–148.

Newman, J. P., & Schmitt, W. A., (1998). Passive avoidance

in psychopathic offenders: A replication and extension. *Journal of Abnormal Psychology, 107*(3), 527–532.

Newman, J. P., Schmitt, W. A., & Voss, V. (1997). The impact of motivationally neutral cues on psychopathic individuals: Assessing the generality of the response modulation hypothesis. *Journal of Abnormal Psychology, 106*(4), 563–575.

Newman, J. P., & Wallace, J. F. (1993a). Diverse pathways to deficient self-regulation: Implications for disinhibitory psychopathology in children. *Clinical Psychology Review, 13*, 690–720.

Newman, J. P., & Wallace, J. F. (1993b). Psychopathy and cognition. In P. C. Kendall & K. S. Dobson (Eds.), *Psychopathology and cognition* (pp. 293–349). New York: Academic Press.

Newman, J. P., Wallace, J. F., Schmitt, W. A., & Arnett, P. A. (1997). Behavioral inhibition system functioning in anxious, impulsive, and psychopathic individuals, *Personality and Individual Differences, 23*, 583–592.

Newman, J. P., Wallace, J. F., Strauman, T. J., Skolaski, R. L., Oreland, K. M., Mattek, P. W., Elder, K. A., & McNeely, J. (1993). Effects of motivationally significant stimuli on the regulation of dominant responses. *Journal of Personality and Social Psychology, 65*, 165–175.

Newman, J. P., Widom, C. S., & Nathan, S. (1985). Passive-avoidance in syndromes of disinhibition: Psychopathy and extraversion. *Journal of Personality and Social Psychology, 48*, 1316–1327.

Nichols, S. L., & Newman, J. P. (1986). Effects of punishment on response latency in extraverts. *Journal of Personality and Social Psychology, 50*, 624–630.

O'Brien, B. S., Frick, P. J., & Lyman, R. D. (1994). Reward dominance among children with disruptive behavior disorders. *Journal of Psychopathology and Behavioral Assessment, 16*(2), 131–145.

Obrist, P. A. (1976). The cardiovascular-behavioral interaction: As it appears today. *Psychophysiology, 13*, 95–107.

Ogloff, J. R., & Wong, S. (1990). Electrodermal and cardiovascular evidence of a coping response in psychopaths. *Criminal Justice and Behavior, 17*(2), 231–245.

Öhman, A., & Soares, J. J. F. (1994). "Unconscious anxiety": Phobic responses to masked stimuli. *Journal of Abnormal Psychology, 103*, 231–240.

Patrick, C. J. (1994). Emotion and psychopathy: Startling new insights. *Psychophysiology, 31*, 319–330.

Patrick, C. J., Bradley, M. M., & Lang, P. J. (1993). Emotion in the criminal psychopath: Startle reflex modulation. *Journal of Abnormal Psychology, 102*, 82–92.

Patrick, C. J., Cuthbert, & Lang, P. J. (1994). Emotion in the criminal psychopath: Fear image processing. *Journal of Abnormal Psychology, 103*(3), 523–534.

Patrick, C. J., & Lang, P. J. (1999). Psychopathic traits and intoxicated states: Affective concomitants and conceptual links. In M. Dawson & A. Schell (Eds.), *Startle modification: Implications for clinical science, cognitive, science, and neuroscience* (pp. 209–230). New York: Cambridge University Press.

Patterson, C. J., & Newman, J. P. (1993). Reflectivity and learning from aversive events: Toward a psychological mechanism for the syndromes of disinhibition. *Psychological Review, 100*, 716–736.

Patterson, C. M., Kosson, D. S., & Newman, J. P. (1987). Reaction to punishment, reflectivity, and passive avoidance learning in extraverts. *Journal of Personality and Social Psychology, 52*, 565–576.

Rajaram, S., & Neely, J. H. (1992). Dissociative masked repetition priming and word frequency effects in lexical decision and episodic recognition tasks. *Journal of Memory and Language, 31*(2), 152–182.

Scherer, K. R. (1994). Emotion as a process: Function, origin and regulation. *Social Science Information, 21*(4–5), 555–570.

Scherer, K. R. (1994). Emotion serves to decouple stimulus and response. In P. Ekman & R. J. Davidson (Eds.), *The nature of emotion: Fundamental questions*. New York: Oxford University Press.

Schmauk, F. J. (1970). Punishment, arousal, and avoidance learning in sociopaths. *Journal of Abnormal Psychology, 76*, 325–335.

Schmitt, W. A., Brinkley, C. A., & Newman, J. P. (1999). The application of Damasio's somatic marker hypothesis to psychopathic individuals: Risk-takers or risk averse? *Journal of Abnormal Psychology, 108*, 538–543.

Schmitt, W. A., & Newman, J. P. (1999). Are all psychopathic individuals low-anxious? *Journal of Abnormal Psychology, 108*, 353–358.

Schmitt, W. A., & Newman, J. P. (2000). *Psychopathy and the response modulation hypothesis: Conceptual replications using Stroop-like tasks.* Manuscript submitted for publication.

Schneider, W., Dumais, S. T., & Shiffrin, R. M. (1984). Automatic and control processing and attention. In R. Parasuraman & D. R. Davies (Eds.), *Varieties of attention* (pp. 1–27). New York: Academic Press.

Schneider, W., & Shiffrin, R. M. (1977). Controlled and automatic human information processing: I. Detection, search, and attention. *Psychological Review, 84*(1), 1–66.

Shapiro, D. (1965). *Neurotic styles*. New York: Basic Books.

Shapiro, S. K., Quay, H. C., Hogan, A. E., & Schwartz, K. P. (1988). Response perseveration and delayed responding in undersocialized aggressive conduct disorder. *Journal of Abnormal Psychology, 97*(3), 371–373.

Shiffrin, R. M., & Schneider, W. (1984). Automatic and controlled processing revisited. *Psychological Review, 91*(2), 269–276.

Siegel, R. A. (1978). Probability of punishment and suppression of behavior in psychopathic and nonpsychopathic offenders. *Journal of Abnormal Psychology, 87*, 514–522.

Sutton, S. K., Vitale, J. E., & Newman, J. P. (2001). *Emotional reactions to unpleasant pictures in female psychopaths.* Manuscript submitted for publication.

Tiffany, S. T. (1990). A cognitive model of drug urges and drug-use behavior: Role of automatic and nonautomatic processes. *Psychological Review, 97*, 147–168.

Tranel, D., & Damasio, H. (1994). Neuroanatomical correlates of electrodermal skin conductance responses. *Psychophysiology, 31*(5), 427–438.

Trull, T. J., & Sher, K. J. (1994). Relationship between the five-factor model of personality and Axis I disorders in a nonclinical sample. *Journal of Abnormal Psychology, 103*, 350–360.

Venables, P. H., & Christie, M. J. (1973). Mechanisms, instrumentation, scoring techniques, and quantification of responses. In W. F. Prokasy & D. C. Raskin (Eds.), *Electrodermal activity in psychological research* (pp. 1–124). New York: Wiley.

Wallace, J. F., Bachorowski, J., & Newman, J. P. (1991).

Failures of response modulation: Impulsive behavior in anxious and impulsive individuals. *Journal of Research in Personality, 25,* 23–44.

Wallace, J. F., & Newman, J. P. (1990). Differential effects of reward and punishment cues on response speed in anxious and impulsive individuals. *Personality and Individual Differences, 11,* 999–1009.

Wallace, J. F., & Newman, J. P. (1997). Neuroticism and the attentional mediation of dysregulatory psychopathology. *Cognitive Therapy and Research, 21*(2), 135–156.

Wallace, J. F., & Newman, J. P. (1998). Neuroticism and the facilitation of the automatic orienting of attention. *Personality and Individual Differences, 2*(2), 253–266.

Wallace, J. F., Schmitt, W. A., Vitale, J. E., & Newman, J. P. (2000). Information processing deficiencies and psychopathy: Implications for diagnosis and treatment. In C. Gacono (Ed.), *Clinical and forensic assessment of psychopathy: A practitioner's guide* (pp. 87–109). Mahwah, NJ: Erlbaum.

Wallace, J. F., Vitale, J. E., & Newman, J. P. (1999). Response modulation deficits: Implications for the diagnosis and treatment of psychopathy. *Journal of Cognitive Psychotherapy, 13,* 55–70.

Wegner, D. M. (1994). Ironic processes of mental control. *Psychological Review, 101*(1), 34–52.

Welsh, G. (1956). Factor dimensions A and R. In G. S. Welsh & W. G. Dahlstrom (Eds.), *Basic readings on the MMPI in psychology and medicine* (pp. 264–281). Minneapolis: University of Minnesota Press.

Williamson, S., Harpur, T. J., & Hare, R. D. (1991). Abnormal processing of affective words by psychopathic individuals. *Psychophysiology, 28*(3), 260–273.

# 50

# PHYSIOLOGICAL AND PHARMACOLOGICAL INDUCTION OF AFFECT

Terence A. Ketter, Po W. Wang,
Anna Lembke, and Nadia Sachs

Systematically provoking affects and studying the resulting phenomena is an important strategy in affective science. Such induction studies not only yield insights into mechanisms of feeling states experienced in health but also provide models for psychopathological states, which in some cases may differ clinically from healthy affects, primarily in duration, intensity, or reactivity. In this chapter we review physiological and pharmacological methods of inducing affects, with a focus on studies that combine these techniques with functional brain imaging to explore the cerebral processes that underlie affects.

## Emotions, Moods, and Temperaments

Affective processes are extremely complex and diverse. They vary in duration, frequency, quality, and intensity. One method of subtyping affects is by temporal domains, with emotions the briefest, moods intermediate, and temperaments the most sustained. These entities vary in several ways in addition to duration (Table 50.1). Thus emotions are brief (lasting seconds to minutes) experiences that are often intense, reactive to acute precipitants, and accompanied by autonomic arousal (increased heart rate and blood pressure), and they lead to actions. In contrast, moods are of longer duration (lasting hours to days) and somewhat less intense; they range from reactive to spontaneous, they may be accompanied by more subtle (hypothalamic-pituitary-adrenal axis dysregulation) arousal, and they tend to result in cognitions. Temperaments are the most sustained (lasting years to decades) and generally the least intense; they are largely constitutional but can occasionally be modified by persistent experiential factors, they generally lack autonomic features, and they yield integrative styles of interacting with the environment.

These temporal domains of affective experiences are related to one another; different temperaments yield predispositions to different moods, which in turn yield tendencies to varying emotions. Influences also exist in the opposite direction, with intense emotional experiences in rapid succession yielding particular moods and repeated or chronic moods on occasion resulting in temperamental shifts.

These domains may have different neurobiological substrates. Recent functional brain imaging evidence suggests that emotions may be mediated by phylogenetically older anterior paralimbic structures. Such structures have access to motor circuits and could thereby provide primitive, perceptually triggered, action-oriented affective processing. Moods may be related to more recent overlying prefrontal neocortical elements and could thus provide more refined, complexly (perceptual, mnemonic, cognitive) triggered, cognition-oriented affective processing. To date, there has been less exploration of the neuroanatomical substrates of temperament, but some studies have explored proposed brainstem-subcortical-cortical network

Table 50.1. Temporal Domains of Affects

|  | Emotions | Moods | Temperaments |
| --- | --- | --- | --- |
| Duration | Seconds to minutes | Hours to days Weeks to months* | Years to decades |
| Relative intensity | High | Intermediate | Low |
| Precipitants | Acute | Variable/absent | Genetic/chronic |
| Autonomic arousal | Acute, robust | Variable/subtle | Absent/subtle |
| Products | Actions | Cognitions | Cognitive-affective interactions |
| Possible neural substrates | Anterior limbic/ brainstem | Anterior cortical/ anterior limbic | Anterior cortical/ anterior limbic/ brainstem |

*in mood disorders

models. In this chapter we review how functional brain imaging research is proving useful in testing hypotheses regarding the neuroanatomical substrates of affects across these temporal domains.

## Neuroanatomical Substrates of Affective Processes

### Emotion and Mood

Emotions have evaluative, experiential, and expressive components, which are intimately related to one another. One can hardly evaluate a powerful affective stimulus without eliciting some feelings, which in turn tend to be expressed in some manner. Thus studies of emotion induction often involve all three components, despite variable efforts to restrict attention to a single facet.

Charles Darwin focused on expression of emotions, which he viewed as evolutionary vestiges. Thus he considered relationships between such expressions and social behaviors, with the brief consideration he gave neural substrates confined to vagal-mediated bidirectional communication between brain, heart, and gut (Darwin, 1872; Darwin, 1872/1998). William James emphasized relationships between emotions and somatic perception (James, 1884) and thus contended that there need not be any special brain centers for emotions: "Supposing the cortex to contain parts, liable to be excited by changes in each special sense-organ, in each portion of the skin, in each muscle, each joint, and each viscus, and to contain absolutely nothing else, we still have a scheme capable of representing the process of the emotions" (James, 1890). Carl G. Lange had similar views (Lange & James, 1922). The James-Lange theory was influential into the early part of the twentieth century, when it declined in the face of evidence from animal experiments by Walter Bradford Can-

non that affective responses were more rapid than visceral responses and persisted after disconnecting the brain from the viscera (Cannon, 1927; Cannon, 1929).

In contrast, John Hughlings Jackson proposed a more regional view suggesting that the right hemisphere was dominant for emotion. He extended Darwin's theories concerning evolution and hypothesized that failure of higher (more phylogenetically recent) structures to control lower (more primitive) structures could yield psychiatric disorders (Jackson, 1887). This view, in a more metaphorical form, was present in Sigmund Freud's theory that psychiatric disorders were due to the loss of the ability of higher functions (the ego) to manage internal conflicts between learned values (the superego) and primitive drives (the id; Freud, 1927). Psychoanalytic models remained influential for much of the twentieth century but gradually declined as psychopharmacology provided important new treatment options for psychiatric disorders and as advances in neuroscience methodology provided opportunities to directly test specific hypotheses regarding the neural substrates of affective experiences.

Deep midline cerebral structures have been suggested as mediators of affective experiences since the nineteenth century (for a review, see Mega, Cummings, Salloway, & Malloy, 1997). Broca defined the *great limbic lobe* as a midline cortical ring seen in mammals (Broca, 1878) and noted relationships between this set of structures and olfaction and the assessment of the affective significance of olfactory stimuli (Figure 50.1). Brown and Schäfer (1888) noted that bilateral temporal lobe resection yielded unusual tameness, decreased fear, and visual agnosia in rhesus monkeys. Fifty years later, Klüver and Bucy reported that in monkeys, bilateral temporal lobectomy yielded a syndrome (named after them) that included visual agnosia, dietary changes, coprophagia, excessive oral and other exploration, hypersexuality, and loss of emotional reactivity (Klüver & Bucy, 1939). Orbitofrontal and temporal pole lesions can cause some features of this syndrome. Although rare, the full syndrome can occur in humans after extensive bilateral temporal lobe damage (Marlowe, Mancall, & Thomas, 1975). More focal bilateral amygdala damage can yield inability to recognize fearful facial expressions (Adolphs, Tranel, Damasio, & Damasio, 1994).

Papez (1937) suggested corticothalamic mediation of emotion, and MacLean (1952) used the term *limbic system* to describe the limbic cortex and related structures. Alexander and colleagues described a series of basal ganglia-thalamocortical circuits (Alexander, Crutcher, & DeLong, 1990), including *limbic* and *lateral orbitofrontal circuits*, implicated in affective processes, and a *dorsolateral prefrontal circuit*, which may contribute to integration of such processes with higher cognitive functions. Dysfunction in these circuits may yield impaired thalamic gating or modulation of sensory or affective information, which in turn could allow such data to disrupt cognitive and

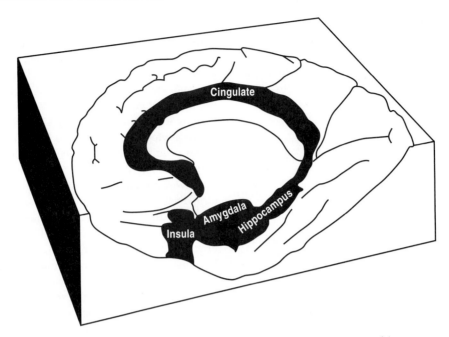

Figure 50.1 The Limbic Lobe (Limbic Cortex). Three-dimensional cartoon of human brain showing subdivisions of the limbic *lobe* (in black). The limbic *system* includes these cortical areas, as well as closely related brainstem structures. Anterior paralimbic and cortical structures are emerging as particularly important to emotional processes and disorders. From MacLean (1990), with permission from Kluwer Academic.

motor processes and thus contribute to the clinical profiles of mood disorders.

The valence model of affects assigns major roles in positive affect (approach behavior) and negative affect (withdrawal behavior) to the left and right fronto-temporal regions, respectively (Davidson, 1992). Electrophysiological studies suggested that state changes in emotion were related to shifts in anterior activation asymmetry which were superimposed on stable baseline (temperamental) differences. However, as noted subsequently, more recent functional brain imaging studies have had variable findings with respect to valence.

Clinical observations have related damage in prefrontal and anterior paralimbic structures to affective changes. The high prevalence of mood disorders in patients with stroke, Huntington's disease, Parkinson's disease, traumatic brain injury, epilepsy, multiple sclerosis, and brain tumors has yielded hypotheses about the neuroanatomy of mood disorders due to such conditions. Thus the risk of depression may be greater after anterior than posterior strokes and after left-hemisphere than right-hemisphere strokes, whereas the risk of mania may be greater after right-hemisphere than left-hemisphere strokes (Robinson, 1997; Starkstein & Robinson, 1989; Stern & Bachmann, 1991). However, not all clinical studies support this lateralization hypothesis (Fujikawa, Yamawaki, & Touhouda, 1995; Jampala & Abrams, 1983). Basal ganglia strokes may

be associated with secondary depression (Mendez, Adams, & Lewandowski, 1989). The profound basal ganglia damage noted in Huntington's disease and Parkinson's disease and the high prevalence of mood symptoms in these disorders also provide support for a role for basal ganglia dysfunction in secondary mood disorders (Caine & Shoulson, 1983; Folstein & Folstein, 1983; Horn, 1974; Mindham, 1970). With traumatic brain injury, left dorsolateral prefrontal and/or left basal ganglia lesions may increase the risk of depression (Federoff et al., 1992), whereas right temporal basal polar lesions may increase the risk of mania (Jorge et al., 1993). The risk of depression in patients with epilepsy may be greater with left than with right temporal lobe lesions (Altshuler, Devinsky, Post, & Theodore, 1990). Temporal (Honer, Hurwitz, Li, Palmer, & Paty, 1987) and left frontal lobe (George, Kellner, Bernstein, & Goust, 1994) lesions may also increase the risk of depression secondary to multiple sclerosis, although a recent study failed to replicate these findings (Moller, Wiedemann, Rohde, Backmund, & Sonntag, 1994). Finally, frontal lobe brain tumors may be associated with depression (Direkze, Bayliss, & Cutting, 1971; Kanakaratnam & Direkze, 1976).

## Temperament

Theories of temperament have existed since antiquity. In ancient Greece, humors or bodily fluids (blood, phlegm, black bile, yellow bile) were believed related to combinations of qualities (wet, dry, hot, cold) associated with elements (water, earth, fire, and air). Thus blood was hot and wet, black bile cold and dry, phlegm cold and wet, and yellow bile hot and dry. Galen (ca. 170 A.D.) suggested that excesses of individual humors were related to temperaments. Thus sanguine (happy) temperament was related to excessive hot wet blood, melancholic (sad) to excessive cold dry black bile, phlegmatic (calm) to excessive cold wet phlegm, and choleric (irritable) to excessive hot dry yellow bile. This theory was thus a two-dimensional (sanguine/melancholic and phlegmatic/choleric) model of temperament that persisted for centuries.

Hans Eysenck (1953) integrated clinical observations with earlier theories to initially develop two major dimensions of personality, namely introversion/extroversion and neuroticism/stability. These axes were diagonal to those of the classical formulation, so that sanguine temperament was viewed as extroverted and stable, melancholic as introverted and neurotic, phlegmatic as introverted and stable, and choleric as extraverted and neurotic.

Introverts tend to be reclusive, less socially active, quiet, reserved, and introspective and to prefer books to people, whereas extraverts are gregarious, socially active, cheerful, excitable, impulsive, and assertive. Eysenck proposed that introverts have more active, and extraverts less active, cortical activity/arousal, as regulated by ascending reticulocortical activating system (ARAS) pathways (Eysenck, 1967, 1986). In contrast, he suggested that neuroticism, or emotionality, was related to high levels of "visceral brain" (limbic; i.e., amygdala, hippocampus, cingulate, septum, and hypothalamus) activity. Eysenck later expanded his model with a third (psychoticism/normalcy) dimension, which ranged from clinically psychotic through antisocial through normal behavior.

Jeffrey Gray initially focused on behavioral inhibition and suggested that introverts had more active, and extraverts less active, reticulo-septal-hippocampal-orbitofrontal cortical pathways mediating behavioral inhibition (Gray, 1970, 1972). He later suggested a two-dimensional model, with axes diagonal to those in Eysenck's schema (Gray, 1987). Thus an anxiety (inhibition, avoidance) dimension ran from high anxiety (high neuroticism, high introversion, low psychoticism) to low anxiety (low neuroticism, low introversion, high psychoticism), and an orthogonal impulsivity (approach) dimension ran from high impulsivity (high neuroticism, low introversion, high psychoticism) to low impulsivity (low neuroticism, high introversion, low psychoticism).

Gray postulated that the anxiety (behavioral inhibition) system consisted of the aforementioned reticulo-septal-hippocampal-orbitofrontal network and that the impulsivity (approach) system consisted of dopaminergic reward circuitry that runs from brain stem (ventral tegmental area) to limbic and neocortical regions. He postulated that cortical arousal through the ARAS was related to the sum of behavioral inhibition and approach system activity and that introversion/extraversion was related to the balance of activities in these two circuits.

Most recently, C. Robert Cloninger (1987) devised a model in which three main dimensions of personality are functions of basal tone in distributed brain biochemical networks. Thus, novelty seeking, harm avoidance, and reward dependence are putatively related to dopamine, norepinephrine, and serotonin, respectively.

Hence, increasingly sophisticated models of the neural substrates of affects have evolved, incrementally implicating anterior paralimbic, prefrontal, and brain stem-subcortical-cortical networks as contributing importantly to emotions, moods, and temperaments, respectively. In the next section, we review functional brain imaging studies, which have explored relationships between affects and these putative neurobiological substrates.

## Functional Brain Imaging Studies of Emotions

Anterior paralimbic structures appear to contribute importantly to affective processing. Emerging evidence suggests differential roles for different anterior paralimbic structures. For example, the amygdala has become increasingly appreciated as playing an important role, primarily in emotion perception but also to some extent in emotional memory and emotional cognition (Davis, 1997; LeDoux, 1995; McGaugh, et al., 1993). In contrast, the anterior cingulate may contribute primarily to emotional memory and emotional cognition and, to a lesser extent, to emotional perception (Devinsky, Morrell, & Vogt, 1995; Vogt, Finch, & Olson, 1992). Indeed, subdivision of the anterior cingulate into a ventral affective division (ACad) and a dorsal cognitive division (ACcd) has been proposed (Bush et al., 2000).

In view of the brief (a few minutes) temporal domain of emotions, functional brain imaging studies of emotion have utilized techniques with compatible temporal resolutions. Thus investigators have primarily used xenon-133 gas ($^{133}$Xe) single photon emission computed tomography (SPECT), technetium-99m hexamethyl-propylene-amine-oxime ($^{99m}$Tc-HMPAO) SPECT, oxygen-15 water ($H_2^{15}O$) positron emission tomography (PET), and functional magnetic resonance imaging (fMRI). In contrast, fluorine-18 deoxyglucose ($^{18}$FDG) PET allows assessment of cerebral glucose metabolism (CMRglu), based on a 30-minute uptake time, and thus has temporal resolution more suited to studying mood and temperament rather than emotion.

$^{133}$Xe SPECT is an older technique, which allows evaluation of cerebral blood flow (CBF), but only in superficial (cortical) regions, and thus has the important limitation of not accessing deep structures such as the limbic system.

[99m]Tc-HMPAO SPECT and H$_2$[15]O PET can assess CBF throughout the brain, but, like [133]Xe SPECT, expose participants to ionizing radiation. In contrast, fMRI allows assessment of cerebral (presumably CBF) activations without radiation exposure and offers enhanced spatial and temporal resolution. However, the neurobiological meaning of the fMRI (compared with SPECT or PET) activation signal is less well established. H$_2$[15]O PET, in conjunction with arterial blood sampling, assesses quantitative (absolute) CBF, whereas other methods assess only semiquantitative (normalized) activation. Quantitative data offers an important advantage over semiquantitative data in situations in which there is a shift in global (whole brain) activity, such as with drug challenges or in certain psychiatric disorders.

In the following sections, we review studies of emotion evaluation and induction that use these functional brain imaging methods. We emphasize the emerging roles of the amygdala and anterior cingulate in emotion processing.

## Emotion Evaluation Studies

Limbic structures appear crucial in the evaluation of the affective salience of stimuli. Thus patients with bilateral amygdala lesions have difficulty in assessing facial emotion expression (Adolphs et al., 1994). Functional brain imaging studies indicate that evaluation of emotion content of facial expressions, and to a lesser extent other perceptual (but not lexical) stimuli, involves the amygdala (Table 50.2). The anterior cingulate appears to contribute to evaluation of emotion content of facial expressions and other perceptual and lexical stimuli.

It is important to distinguish between explicit and implicit modes of emotion evaluation. Explicit evaluation requires participants to interact in some predetermined way with emotion stimuli. For example, participants may be instructed to verbally identify, memorize, assign valence, or choose the stimulus from a group. Implicit evaluation consists of presenting emotional stimuli without explicitly instructing participants to perform an emotion evaluation task. Stimuli may be presented within the realm of conscious awareness (having declarative knowledge of stimulus exposure) or outside of conscious awareness, as in backward-masking studies.

In the next sections, we consider important differences in study designs in emotion evaluation studies of facial expressions and other perceptual, as well as lexical, stimuli. We provide an integrative overview of studies in the text and accompanying tables.

### Facial Emotion Evaluation Studies

Imaging studies of evaluation of the emotional content of facial expressions are important in view of the large body of literature that specifically examines evaluation of emo-

tion in the human face and studies in humans and monkeys that suggest that a specific set of inferior temporal lobe neurons processes facial emotion (Rolls, 1995). Multiple studies of facial emotion evaluation (Blair et al., 1999; Breiter et al., 1996; Morris, Friston, et al., 1998; Morris et al., 1996; Morris, Ohman, & Dolan, 1998; Morris, Ohman, & Dolan, 1999; Phillips et al., 1998; Phillips et al., 1997; Sprengelmeyer et al., 1998; Whalen, Rauch, et al., 1998) have used the Pictures of Facial Affect (PFA) stimuli (Ekman & Friesen, 1976), which depict several adults posing neutral and emotionally expressive facial expressions. In addition, some investigators have used a battery of pictures of actors with various facial expressions, developed at the University of Pennsylvania (Erwin et al., 1992).

An early H$_2$[15]O PET study was performed by Mark George and associates at the National Institute of Mental Health (NIMH). Nine healthy women, with a mean age of 38.4 years, matched two of three facial photographs at a time for happy, sad, or neutral emotional expressions. The results showed occipital, anterior temporal, and prefrontal, right greater than left, normalized CBF increases (George et al., 1993). These investigators used facial emotion expression pictures from the University of Pennsylvania battery. This study employed a brain atlas analysis in which a stereotactic transformation into the brain atlas of Talairach (Talairach & Tournoux, 1988) is followed by pixel-by-pixel parametric comparisons across conditions (Friston, Frith, Liddle, & Frackowiak, 1991). Emotion matching minus a facial identity matching control task yielded right ACcd and prefrontal and frontal cortices (inferior frontal gyrus), left greater than right CBF increases, but not preferential amygdalar activation. However, emotion matching minus a spatial matching control task comparison did reveal left anterior mesial temporal (amygdalar) activation (see table 50.2). The three emotional valences were combined within each scan, so that this study explored facial emotion matching in general without considering potential differences between specific emotions.

Subsequent studies tended to involve more implicit emotion evaluation designs, using either passive interactions with facial emotion stimuli or performance of non-emotion evaluation tasks such as gender discrimination. An fMRI study performed by Hans Breiter and associates used an exploratory brain atlas analysis in a first cohort of 10 healthy men with a mean age of 27.1 years, followed by a confirmatory region of interest (ROI) analysis in a second cohort of 8 healthy men with a mean age of 25.9 years (Breiter et al., 1996). Presentation (without an explicit task assigned) of fearful and happy PFA faces compared with neutral faces yielded left greater than right amygdalar and fusiform gyrus activation. The amygdala response showed rapid habituation, consistent with the notion that the amygdala is a rapid, early detector of emotionally valenced stimuli. The second cohort in this study

Table 50.2. Paralimbic Changes in Emotion Evaluation Studies

| Stimulus | Affect | Amygdala | Anterior cingulate Medial frontal gyrus Basal forebrain |
|---|---|---|---|
| **Facial Expressions** | | | |
| George et al., 1993 | Mixed | ↑ L | ↑ R ACcd |
| Breiter et al., 1996 | Fear | ↑ L>R | — |
| | Happy | ↑ L>R | — |
| Morris et al., 1996 | Fear | ↑ L | ↑ L ACcd |
| | Happy | — | — |
| Morris, Friston, et al., 1998 | Fear | ↑ L | ↑ LR ACcd |
| | Happy | — | — |
| Blair, Morris, Frith, Perrett, & Dolan, 1999 | Sad | ↑ L | ↑ LR ACcd |
| | Angry | — | ↑ LR ACcd |
| Phillips et al., 1997 | Fear | ↑ LR | — |
| | Disgust | — | ↑ LR MFG |
| Phillips et al., 1998 | Fear | ↑ L | ↑ LR MFG |
| | Disgust | ↑ R | — |
| Sprengelmeyer, Rausch, Eysel, & Przuntek, 1998 | Fear | — | — |
| | Disgust | — | — |
| Whalen, Rauch, et al., 1998a | Fear (masked) | ↑ LR | ↑ BF |
| | Happy (masked) | ↓ LR | ↑ BF |
| Morris, Ohman, & Dolan, 1998 | Angry (masked, conditioned) | ↑ R | — |
| | Angry (nonmasked, not conditioned) | ↑ L | — |
| Subtotal | | 9/10 | 7/10 |
| **Other Perceptual** | | | |
| George, Parekh, et al., 1996 | Mixed vocal | — | — |
| | | — | — |
| Phillips et al., 1998 | Fear vocal | ↑ R | ↑ R ACcd/MFG |
| | Disgust vocal | — | — |
| Maddock & Buonocore, 1997 | Threat vocal | — | — |
| | | — | — |
| Blood, Zatorre, Bermudez, & Evans, 1999 | Pleasant music | — | ↑ LR ACad |
| | Unpleasant music | — | ↓ LR ACad |
| Sobel et al., 1998 | Pleasant odors | — | — |
| | Unpleasant odors | — | — |
| Zald & Pardo, 1997 | Pleasant odors | — | — |
| | Unpleasant odors | ↑ LR | — |
| Zald, Lee, Fluegel, & Pardo, 1998 | Pleasant tastes | ↓ R | ↓ LR ACad |
| | Unpleasant tastes | ↑ R | ↑ LR ACad/ACcd |
| Subtotal | | 3/7 | 3/7 |
| **Lexical** | | | |
| Whalen, Bush, et al., 1998 | Negative distractor words | — | ↑ LR ACad |
| Beauregard et al., 1997 | Negative words | — | ↑ L ACad |
| Subtotal | | 0/2 | 2/2 |

L: left; R: right; ACad: (ventral) anterior cingulate affective division; ACcd: (dorsal) anterior cingulate cognitive division; MFG: medial frontal gyrus; BF: basal forebrain involved an ROI rather than the brain atlas analysis. The ROI approach has advantages over the brain atlas method, such as the ability to test a priori hypotheses, to limit the confound of multiple comparisons, and to avoid smoothing operations that tend to obscure changes in small structures such as the amygdala. However, for larger regions the brain atlas method is more sensitive, particularly if activated regions do not correspond directly to those specified in the ROI approach. Thus, in this study, the authors generated a (amygdala) hypothesis in the first cohort with a brain atlas analysis and confirmed it in the second cohort with an ROI analysis.

An $H_2^{15}O$ PET study performed by J. S. Morris and associates used a brain atlas analysis in four male and one female healthy volunteers with a mean age of 42.8 years (Morris et al., 1996). Left amygdalar and left ACcd activation occurred when participants were viewing fearful, but not happy, PFA faces (Figure 50.2). The degree of amygdala activation increased with the degree of fearfulness and decreased with the degree of happiness. These results suggest differential amygdalar responses for fear and happiness, in contrast with the more uniform response to varying emotions reported by Breiter and associates (Breiter et al., 1996).

Morris and colleagues also reported an $H_2^{15}O$ PET

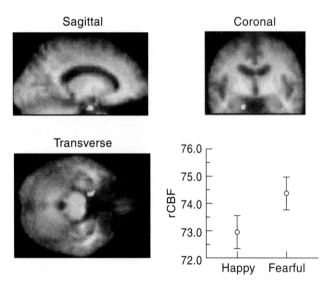

Figure 50.2 Left amygdala activation while viewing fearful versus happy faces. Statistical parametric map (SPM) of mean cerebral activation in five participants viewing fearful versus happy faces in a $H_2^{15}O$ PET facial emotion evaluation study. Views are orthogonal slices through the point of maximal activation in the left amygdala at Talairach coordinates (−18 −6 −16). The graph in the lower right shows (mean ± 2 standard errors) normalized CBF values ($p < 0.002$). From Morris et al. (1996), with permission from *Nature,* copyright 1996. (*See color insert.*)

study, using a brain atlas analysis, in four male and one female healthy volunteers with a mean age of 42.8 years, using a gender discrimination task to ensure that emotion processing was not dependent on volition or attention (Morris, Friston, et al., 1998). Thus indicating gender while viewing PFA faces with varying degrees of fearful (but not happy) expressions yielded left amygdala, left pulvinar, left anterior insula, and bilateral ACcd activation. The left lateralization was consistent with Breiter and colleagues' (1996) findings, and involvement of the anterior cingulate was similar to that observed by George and associates (1993).

These investigators reported a similar $H_2^{15}O$ PET study in thirteen healthy men with a mean age of 25.3 years, in which left amygdala and right inferior and middle temporal gyri responded to sad but not angry facial expressions and right orbitofrontal cortex responded to angry but not sad expressions (Blair et al., 1999). ACcd and right temporal pole responded to both sad and angry expressions.

An fMRI study using a brain atlas analysis, performed by M. L. Phillips and associates (Phillips et al., 1997) with five female and two male healthy volunteers with a mean age of 27 years, confirmed bilateral amygdalar activation on viewing fearful PFA faces but also found that disgust perception yielded anterior insular rather than amygdalar activation, supporting the notion that different brain regions mediate perception of different emotions. Anterior cingulate activation was absent. However, disgust, but not fear, perception yielded medial frontal gyrus activation. Phillips and colleagues (Phillips et al., 1998) replicated and extended these observations in an fMRI study of six healthy men with a mean age of 37 years, observing that fearful PFA facial expressions (and fearful vocal stimuli) activated amygdala, facial (but not vocal) expressions of disgust activated anterior insula and caudate-putamen, and all four stimuli (fear/disgust, faces/voices) yielded superior temporal gyrus activation (Phillips et al., 1998). Facial (but not vocal) expressions of disgust also activated right hippocampus/amygdala.

An fMRI study with similar design performed by Sprengelmeyer and associates (Sprengelmeyer et al., 1998) used a brain atlas analysis with four female and two male healthy volunteers with a mean age of 23.5 years and found that viewing fearful versus neutral PFA facial expressions increased right fusiform and left dorsolateral prefrontal (but not amygdala) activity. Viewing facial expressions of disgust, compared with viewing neutral facial expressions, activated right putamen and left insula. Similarly, angry versus neutral expressions activated right posterior cingulate and left medial temporal gyrus. Viewing expressions of all three emotions (fear, disgust, neutral) yielded inferior left frontal (Brodmann area 47) activation. Thus the authors suggested that fear, disgust, and anger recognition have separate neural substrates, with outputs that converge on overlapping frontal regions for further information processing (Sprengelmeyer et al., 1998). Although different with respect to details, this notion was consistent with the observations by Phillips and associates (1997, 1998) that there may be both affect-specific and affect-nonspecific neuroanatomical substrates to emotion evaluation. The 1998 Sprengelmeyer study is unique among the facial emotion evaluation studies reviewed in that it did *not* observe amygdala activation. The authors (Sprengelmeyer, 1998) speculated that rapid habituation of amygdala responses accounted for the absence of this expected finding.

Other studies have used masked facial expression presentations. An fMRI study by Paul Whalen and associates (Whalen, Rauch, et al., 1998) used a brain atlas analysis and studied eight healthy men with a mean age of 23.8 years. In contrast to viewing nonmasked (overt, 167 ms, consciously perceived) neutral PFA facial expressions, masked (covert, 33 ms, too fleeting to be consciously perceived) fearful facial expressions increased amygdalar activity and masked happy facial expressions decreased amygdalar activity. Both masked emotions yielded sublenticular substantia innominata (basal forebrain) activation (Whalen, Rauch, et al., 1998).

In an $H_2^{15}O$ PET study that used a brain atlas analysis with 10 healthy men with a mean age of 32.7 years, viewing masked, aversively conditioned (by white noise bursts), angry PFA facial expressions yielded right amygdalar activation, and viewing nonmasked, not aversively conditioned, angry facial expressions yielded left amygdalar activation (Morris, Ohman, & Dolan, 1998). The authors concluded that level of awareness of emotional stimuli affects laterality of amygdalar responses, potentially explaining varying results in prior studies. Thus, depending on the level of awareness at which emotional stimuli are processed, the same stimulus may activate different parts of the brain. In a similar $H_2^{15}O$ PET study (Morris et al., 1999) that used a brain atlas analysis with ten healthy men with a mean age of 32.7 years, viewing masked, aversively conditioned, fearful PFA facial expressions yielded increased right (but not left) amygdala, pulvinar, and superior colliculus connectivity and decreased right (but not left) amygdala, fusiform, and orbitofrontal connectivity. These results suggest that a right-sided midbrain-thalamo-amygdala pathway processes unseen visual stimuli in parallel with a cortical route for conscious identification (Morris et al., 1999).

Thus amygdala activation has been present in nine (Blair et al., 1999; Breiter et al., 1996; George et al., 1993; Morris, Friston, et al., 1998; Morris et al., 1996; Morris, Ohman, & Dolan, 1998; Phillips et al., 1997; Phillips et al., 1998; Whalen, Rauch, et al., 1998) and absent in only one (Sprengelmeyer et al., 1998) study of emotion evaluation of facial visual stimuli (Table 50.2). The amygdala finding appeared consistently, despite being performed at multiple centers, and despite implicit-explicit, conscious-subconscious, and aggregated-segregated emotion paradigm differences across studies. Amygdala activation was most consistently related to fear processing. There was modest evidence of left-sided laterality, but this was not consistently related to affective valence. Anterior cingulate–medial frontal gyrus–basal forebrain activation was noted in 7 out of 10 studies, with little evidence of valence or laterality effects.

### Other Perceptual Emotion Evaluation Studies

Auditory (Blood, Zatorre, Bermudez, & Evans, 1999; George, Parekh, et al., 1996; Maddock & Buonocore, 1997; Phillips et al., 1998; Stiller et al., 1997), olfactory (Sobel et al., 1998; Zald & Pardo, 1997), and gustatory (Zald et al., 1998) stimuli have been used to explore emotion evaluation.

In an $H_2^{15}O$ PET study (George, Parekh, et al., 1996) that used a brain atlas analysis with eight male and five female healthy volunteers with a mean age of 28.5 years, listening to and evaluating "happy," "sad," "angry," or "neutral" emotional inflection (prosody) of speech activated right frontal cortex, whereas listening to and evaluating emotional propositional content of speech increased left more than right prefrontal CBF. Amygdala and anterior cingulate were not activated. The four emotions were combined within each scan, so that this study explored emotional evaluation based on prosody compared with propositional content in general, without considering potential differences across specific emotions.

In an fMRI study that focused on the supratemporal plane, using a brain atlas analysis, with 20 healthy volunteers, detecting sad intonation (prosody) versus detecting phonemes did not reveal lateralization of primary auditory or anterior auditory association cortical activation (Stiller et al., 1997). However, the sample could be divided into 7 participants who showed left and 13 who showed right lateralized activations during detection of sad intonation (prosody).

A facial emotion evaluation fMRI study, previously described, also explored auditory stimuli with six healthy men with a mean age of 37 years. The study used an implicit emotional evaluation paradigm in which participants performed a gender discrimination task (Phillips et al., 1998). Listening to fearful vocal (and viewing fearful facial) expressions activated amygdala and superior temporal gyrus. Vocal (and facial) expressions of disgust also activated superior temporal gyrus, but vocal expressions of disgust failed to yield the insula and caudate-putamen activation seen with facial expressions of disgust. An fMRI study performed by Richard Maddock and Michael Buonocore (1997) using an ROI analysis with five male and five female healthy volunteers with a mean age of 38 years who listened to and evaluated threat-related versus neutral words yielded left posterior (especially retrosplenial) cingulate activation. Neutral words versus no words activated bilateral temporal and frontal regions, but not posterior cingulate.

An H$_2$$^{15}$O PET study was performed by Anne Blood and associates using a brain atlas analysis with five male and five female (ages not specified) healthy volunteers (Blood et al., 1999). Participants listened to six versions of a novel musical passage that varied systematically in degree of dissonance. Increasing unpleasantness (dissonance) was associated with activity in right parahippocampal gyrus and precuneus. In contrast, increasing pleasantness (consonance) was associated with activity in ACad, frontal pole, and orbitofrontal cortex. Amygdala activation was not observed in this study.

In an fMRI study using a brain atlas analysis (Sobel et al., 1998), seven female and six male healthy volunteers with a mean age of 28 years sniffed and evaluated the presence or absence of an odor. Aversive (decanoic acid) and nonaversive (vanillin) odorants activated anterolateral orbitofrontal cortex, whereas sniffing (in the absence of odorant or of instruction to evaluate for the presence of odor) activated posteromedial orbitofrontal, as well as piriform, cortex.

Another H$_2$$^{15}$O PET study (Zald & Pardo, 1997) used a brain atlas analysis with 12 healthy women ranging from 19 to 49 years of age. Strongly aversive odorants increased bilateral amygdala and left orbitofrontal normalized CBF, and less aversive odorants activated orbitofrontal, but not amygdalar, CBF, suggesting that stimulus intensity determines activation pattern, with more intense stimuli required to yield amygdala activation (Zald & Pardo, 1997). In another H$_2$$^{15}$O PET study (Zald et al., 1998) using a brain atlas analysis with nine healthy women with a mean age of 37 years, tasting aversive saline solution versus pure water increased right amygdala, left anterior orbitofrontal, medial thalamus, pregenual and dorsal anterior cingulate, and right hippocampus normalized CBF. In contrast, chocolate versus pure water decreased right amygdala, left orbitofrontal cortex, and pregenual cingulate CBF.

Thus amygdala activation was present in three (Phillips et al., 1998; Zald et al., 1998; Zald & Pardo, 1997) but absent in four (Blood et al., 1999; George, Parekh, et al., 1996; Maddock & Buonocore, 1997; Sobel et al., 1998) studies of emotion evaluation of other perceptual stimuli (Table 50.2). Anterior cingulate activation was seen in three out of seven studies. Stimulus modality, implicit-explicit, and aggregated-segregated paradigm differences could contribute to variation in findings. Hence some studies of emotional evaluation of other stimuli implicated anterior paralimbic regions, but studies are too few and too varied in design to provide definitive conclusions. However, cross-modality consistency may occur, as both

olfactory and gustatory aversive stimuli may increase amygdala and orbitofrontal activity.

## Lexical Emotion Evaluation Studies

Two imaging studies have explored emotional evaluation of lexical stimuli. An fMRI study by Whalen and colleagues (Whalen et al., 1998) used a brain atlas analysis with five male and four female healthy volunteers with a mean age of 24.2 years. Participants indicated by pressing a button the number of emotionally negative (distractor) or neutral words on a screen (the "Emotional Counting Stroop"). Negative versus neutral words yielded greater ACad activation (Table 50.2), Whalen et al., 1998). Both negative and neutral words, compared with a baseline fixation task, decreased ACad activity. The same participants, encountering numerical (rather than emotional) word distractors (the "counting Stroop") compared with neutral words, showed increased dorsal anterior cingulate ACcd and decreased ACad activity (Bush et al., 1998). The authors (Bush et al., 1998) noted that these observations were consistent with a spatial dissociation of anterior cingulate function based on the emotional content of stimuli.

Mario Beauregard and associates (Beauregard et al., 1997) performed an H$_2$$^{15}$O PET study using a brain atlas analysis with ten healthy men ranging from 18 to 28 years of age. Passively viewing words with high positive and negative emotional relevance (sex, murder, sadness), compared with viewing a plus sign, yielded anterior paralimbic (orbitofrontal, left inferior frontal, left middle frontal, left medial frontal, left anterior cingulate, left middle temporal), left caudate, left occipital, and cerebellar vermis, but not amygdala, activation.

Thus amygdala activation was absent but anterior cingulate activation present in these two studies (Beauregard et al., 1997; Whalen et al., 1998) of emotion evaluation of lexical stimuli (Table 50.2). Pictorial-lexical and aggregated-segregated emotion paradigm differences could contribute to this variation in findings. In particular, the relatively large cognitive compared with perceptual component of such tasks is consistent with the greater involvement of the anterior cingulate and amygdala in cognitive and perceptual aspects of emotion evaluation, respectively.

In summary, functional brain imaging studies of emotion evaluation thus far suggest a framework for how the brain perceives and processes emotional stimuli. The amygdala appears important in processing emotional stimuli, especially fear, and it was implicated most strongly in 9 out of 10 studies of facial emotion evaluation, present in 3 out of 7 studies of other perceptual stimuli, but absent in 2 studies of lexical emotion evaluation (Table 50.2). Anterior cingulate–medial frontal gyrus–basal forebrain were implicated in 7 out of 10 studies of facial emotion evaluation and present in 3 out of 7 studies of other perceptual stimuli, as well as in 2 studies of lexical emotion evaluation. For both amygdala and anterior cingulate, laterality effects were modest. In spite of the considerable variability in paradigms, these studies provide substantial support for amygdala involvement in emotion evaluation, particularly for fear, and for facial stimuli.

## Emotion Induction Studies

Limbic structures appear important not only in emotion evaluation but also in emotional experience. Physiological and pharmacological methods have been utilized to induce emotion. The former offer naturalistic approximations of spontaneous emotional reactions, which are useful in assessing the underlying neuroanatomy. The latter allow not only neuroanatomical but also biochemical probing of the neurobiological substrates of emotions. These methods, combined with functional brain imaging, have implicated anterior paralimbic structures as contributing importantly to emotional experiences. We consider studies of specific emotions, broadly dichotomized negative and positive emotions, and emotions in general.

## Physiological Emotion Induction Studies

Physiological methods of emotion induction employ cognitive, perceptual, and other somatic stimuli to yield affective responses. Cognitive methods include recalling or imagining emotionally salient events, attempting to solve demanding or even unsolvable problems, or punishment or reward or the anticipation thereof. Perceptual stimuli include visual, auditory, olfactory, gustatory, and somatosensory challenges intended to evoke specific emotions. For example, viewing emotionally charged still pictures, films, or facial expressions or experiencing music, odors, tastes, or somatosensory stimulation (mild electrical shocks, exercise, and hyperventilation) can induce emotional reactions. Stimuli can be presented with the primary intention of studying evaluation of emotion as discussed in the previous section, or of studying induction of emotion, as described in this section.

Brain imaging studies of physiological induction of emotion have shown regional specificity, consistently implicating anterior paralimbic structures and nearby cortical regions. However, the direction of change of activity in these structures has been variable, perhaps due to variation in the age and gender of participants, in methods and durations of inductions, in the particular emotions induced, in scanning methodology, and in data analysis methods. In addition, heterogeneity of cerebral organization across individuals may yield subgroups, which utilize different brain areas to induce affects, by employing different induction strategies or perhaps even when utilizing

similar strategies. The small sample sizes used in many studies may provide inadequate power to explore such heterogeneity or to detect changes, particularly in smaller structures.

In order to allow a detailed review, we focus on two classes of emotion induction studies. First, we consider studies of induction of negative and positive affect. Then, in view of relevance to valence issues and of potential relationships to moods and mood disorders, we focus on studies of sadness and happiness induction. Readers interested in induction of other specific emotions are referred to the extensive literature concerning anxiety and fear induction (Fischer, Wik, & Fredrikson, 1996; Fredrikson, Wik, Annas, Ericson, & Stone-Elander, 1995; Fredrikson, Wik, Fischer, & Andersson, 1995; Fredrikson et al., 1993; Gottschalk et al., 1991; Gottschalk et al., 1992; Gur et al., 1987; Kimbrell et al., 1999; LaBar, Gatenby, Gore, LeDoux, & Phelps, 1998; Maddock & Buonocore, 1997; Mountz et al., 1989; O'Carroll et al., 1993; Rauch, Savage, Alpert, Fischman, & Jenike, 1997; Rauch et al., 1995; Rauch et al., 1996; Reiman, Fusselman, Fox, & Raichle, 1989; Reiman, Raichle, & Robins, 1989; Schneider et al., 1999; Shin et al., 1997; Wik et al., 1993; Zohar et al., 1989) and to the more limited literature on anger induction (Dougherty et al., 1999; Kimbrell et al., 1999).

### Negative and Positive Affect Induction Studies.

Multiple studies have used still pictures from the International Affective Picture System (IAPS; Lang, Bradley, & Cuthbert, 1995) or similar stimuli to externally elicit affective responses (Table 50.3). Negative and high-arousal positive images from this instrument yield increases and decreases, respectively, in magnitude of eyeblink responses to an acoustic startle probe, offering objective evidence of the presence of physiological responses associated with negative and positive emotions (Lang, 1995; Sutton, Davidson, Donzella, Irwin, & Dottl, 1997).

William Irwin and associates (Irwin et al., 1996) performed an fMRI study using a brain atlas analysis confined to three contiguous 5-mm-thick coronal slices, with the middle slice centered on the amygdala, with three healthy women ranging from 18 to 32 years of age. Negative (mutilated faces), neutral (books), and moderately positive (sunsets) IAPS pictures were used to elicit affective responses. Participants viewed 11 alternating 6.6-s blocks of neutral and negative pictures, beginning and ending with neutral. Thus one 72.6-s trial featured six neutral blocks, lasting a total of 39.6 s, and five negative blocks, lasting a total of 33 s. Participants subsequently rated the affective valence of the pictures. Viewing negative (but not moderately positive), compared with neutral, pictures yielded bilateral amygdala activation.

Kevin LaBar and associates (LaBar, Gatenby, Gore, &

Table 50.3. Paralimbic Changes in Negative and Positive Affect Induction Studies

| Study | Negative Affect | | Positive Affect | |
|---|---|---|---|---|
| | Amygdala | Anterior cingulate Medial frontal gyrus | Amygdala | Anterior cingulate Medial frontal gyrus |
| Irwin et al., 1996 | ↑ LR | — | — | — |
| LaBar, Gatenby, Gore, & Phelps, 1998 | ↑ LR | — | ↑ LR | — |
| Irwin et al., 1997 | ↑ LR | — | — | — |
| Kalin et al., 1997 | ↑ LR | — | — | — |
| Lane et al., 1997 | ↑ L | ↑ LR MFG | — | ↑ LR MFG |
| Canli, Desmond, Zhao, Glover, & Gabrieli, 1998 | — | ↑ L ACad | — | ↑ LR ACcd |
| Kosslyn et al., 1996 | — | — | NA | NA |
| Paradiso et al., 1999 | ↑ L | ↓ LR ACcd | ↓ L entorhinal | — |
| Taylor et al., 1998 | ↑ L (encoding) —(recognition) | —(encoding) ↑ LR ACad (recog) | NA NA | NA NA |
| Teasdale et al., 1999 | — | ↑ R ACcd/MFG | — | ↑ R ACcd/MFG |
| Total | 7/10 | 5/10 | 1/8 | 3/8 |

NA: Not applicable

Phelps, 1998) subsequently used a similar design but included erotic pictures in the positive stimuli and included male, as well as female, participants. They found bilateral amygdala activation with negative and positive pictures versus neutral ones and with negative versus positive pictures.

Irwin et al. (1997) subsequently reported a replication, which imaged the entire brain, in a different, larger sample of five female and two male healthy volunteers. Negative (but not moderately positive) versus neutral still pictures once again yielded bilateral amygdala activation. Both negative and positive versus neutral still pictures yielded occipital-parietal and occipital-temporal activation.

In a subsequent fMRI study, Peter Lang and associates (Lang et al., 1998) explored occipital-parietal responses to viewing pleasant, neutral, or unpleasant IAPS pictures presented in eight 12-s picture presentation periods and 12-s interpicture intervals. Negative and positive, compared with neutral, pictures yielded occipital, right fusiform, and right parietal activation. In view of efferents from the amygdala to multiple levels of visual processing pathways (Amaral & Price, 1984; Amaral, Price, Pitkanen, & Carmichael, 1992; see Figure 50.3), the visual cortical activations observed in the latter two reports could be related to amygdala activation.

Kalin and colleagues (Kalin et al., 1997) reported pilot fMRI findings in two depressed patients and two healthy controls. Viewing negative compared with neutral IAPS pictures yielded amygdala (left in patients and bilateral in controls), parieto-occipital, and prefrontal activation. These effects were attenuated on repeat scanning 2 weeks later in the patients (who had recovered on venlafaxine),

as well as in controls. For both groups, viewing positive versus neutral pictures yielded occipito-cerebellar (but not amygdalo-frontal) activation, and on repeat scanning 2 weeks later, effects were attenuated in controls and enhanced in patients. Negative, compared with positive, pictures yielded greater volumes of activation in both groups at both sessions.

An $H_2^{15}O$ PET study was performed by Richard Lane and associates (Lane et al., 1997) using a brain atlas analysis with 12 healthy women ranging from 18 to 45 years old. Viewing unpleasant versus neutral or pleasant IAPS pictures increased left amygdalar, hippocampal and parahippocampal, and bilateral occipito-temporal and cerebellar normalized CBF. Unpleasant and pleasant, compared with neutral, pictures also increased medial prefrontal (Brodmann's area 9), thalamus, hypothalamus, and midbrain CBF. Pleasant versus neutral (but not unpleasant) pictures increased left head of caudate CBF (Lane et al., 1997).

In an fMRI study by Turhan Canli and associates (Canli et al., 1998) using a brain atlas analysis, 14 healthy women with a mean age of 25.6 years viewed positive (happy couples, puppies, deserts, sunsets) and negative (angry or crying faces, spiders, guns, cemetery) IAPS pictures. Each 34.5-s block included four pictures, each presented for 7.5 s, alternating with four interstimulus intervals, each lasting 1.125 s. Five alternating positive and negative blocks thus yielded a total scan time of 345 s. Viewing positive pictures resulted in left frontal and left temporal activation, whereas viewing negative pictures yielded right frontal and right gyrus rectus activation. Controlling for degree of emotional arousal, overall brain reactivity was lateral-

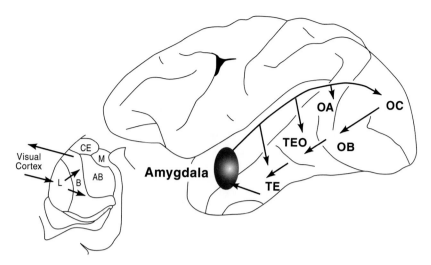

Figure 50.3 Amygdala connections with occipital and temporal visual regions. Visual information originates in primary visual cortex (OC). Increasingly complex information is processed in the temporal lobes (OA, OB, TEO, TE) and is relayed to the amygdala. This circuitry is consistent with the amygdala activation demonstrated in functional brain imaging studies of facial emotion evaluation. Also, efferents from the amygdala project back to all levels of visual processing. Reproduced with permission from Amaral et al. (1992).

ized toward the left hemisphere for positive pictures and toward the right hemisphere for negative pictures. No significant amygdalar activation was found for negative (or positive) stimuli, despite the putative role of the amygdala in evaluation of negatively valenced emotion.

Stephen Kosslyn and associates (Kosslyn et al., 1996) performed an H$_2$$^{15}$O PET study using a brain atlas analysis in which seven healthy men with a mean age of 50.0 years viewed or visualized (recalled) pictures of negative or neutral stimuli and then determined whether auditorily presented statements correctly described the stimuli. Visual stimuli included negative (baby with a tumor occluding one eye, bloody face, funeral) and neutral (truck, hikers, umbrella) pictures, from the IAPS and other sources. The negative images were, in the view of the authors, most likely to elicit disgust. Viewing negative versus neutral pictures and hearing related spoken words increased left middle frontal gyrus (area 46), left inferior frontal gyrus (area 47), left middle temporal gyrus, left angular gyrus, and left area 19 normalized CBF. Visualizing (recalling) negative versus neutral pictures from memory and hearing related spoken words increased medial occipital, anterior insula, and left middle frontal (areas 8 and 9) CBF. Both viewing and visualizing negative stimuli failed to significantly alter amygdala CBF. This finding could be explained by a habituation effect, as participants had exposure to the stimuli in practice trials prior to the actual test trails.

In an H$_2$$^{15}$O PET study by Sergio Paradiso and associates (Paradiso et al., 1999) using a brain atlas analysis with 10 female and 7 male healthy volunteers with a mean age

of 31.2 years, assigning valence to unpleasant versus pleasant IAPS pictures increased left amygdala, visual cortical, and cerebellar normalized CBF, and assigning valence to unpleasant versus neutral pictures increased nucleus accumbens, precuneus, and visual cortex and decreased ACcd CBF. Assigning valence to pleasant versus unpleasant pictures increased orbital, medial frontal, and dorsolateral prefrontal cortical CBF, and assigning valence to pleasant versus neutral pictures increased posterior cingulate, precuneus, and visual cortex and decreased left entorhinal CBF.

In an H$_2$$^{15}$O PET study performed by Stephan Taylor and associates (Taylor et al., 1998) using a brain atlas analysis with eight healthy women with a mean age of 27.9 years, viewing and encoding negative versus neutral (IAPS and the researchers' own) pictures for later recognition yielded increased left amygdala normalized CBF. The negative pictures were selected for elicitation of fear/disgust (facial mutilation/gunshot wounds, murder victims, dead bodies). The neutral pictures included people at rest, faces with neutral expressions, and benign scenes. Subsequent recognition of negative versus neutral pictures yielded ACad activation. Recognizing versus encoding negative pictures yielded ACcd, right middle frontal gyrus, and lingular gyrus activation. The lack of amygdala activation with recognition of negative compared with neutral pictures is consistent with the notion that amygdala responses can rapidly habituate.

John Teasdale and associates (Teasdale et al., 1999) performed an fMRI study using a brain atlas analysis with three male and three female healthy volunteers with a

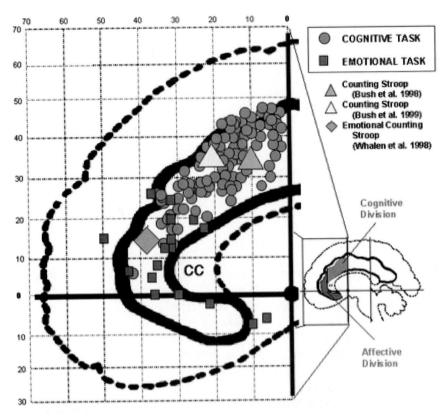

Figure 50.4 Anterior cingulate activation in affect and cognition studies. Multiple studies with varying affective and cognitive paradigms have demonstrated anterior cingulate activation. The ventral portion may be referred to as the affective division (ACad) and the dorsal portion as the cognitive division (ACcd). However, such differential roles for these two subregions are not uniformly present in studies. Additional studies implicating these regions are described in the text and outlined in tables 50.2, 50.3, and 50.4. From Bush et al. (2000), copyright 2000, with permission from Elsevier Science.

mean age of 29.8 years. Participants viewed (non-IAPS) pictures which in themselves did not evoke affect, along with either captions that, when matched with the content of the pictures, elicited negative or positive affect or control captions that were irrelevant to the content of the pictures and thus did not elicit affective responses. Images were presented for 9 s each, with a 1-s interpicture blank interval. Three images from one condition alternated with three from another condition in repeating 30-s cycles for 5 minutes. Concordant negative (but not irrelevant) captions yielded right ACcd/medial frontal gyrus, right middle frontal gyrus, and right thalamus activation. Concordant positive (but not negative) captions yielded insula, right inferior frontal gyrus, posterior cingulate, and left precuneus activation. Concordant positive, compared with concordant negative, captions yielded right ACcd/medial frontal gyrus, right precentral gyrus, and left caudate activation.

Thus Teasdale et al. (1999), in their discussion of this study, noted that their findings, along with those of other investigators (Lane, Reiman, Ahern, Schwartz, & David-

son, 1997; Lane, Reiman, et al., 1997; Reiman et al., 1997), suggested that ACcd/medial frontal gyrus activation occurred with affective induction independent of affective valence or induction stimulus (pictures, film clips, memories). Teasdale et al. (1999) suggested that ACcd/medial frontal gyrus activation could be related to processing of affect-related meanings derived from memory, which generate affect by cognitive processes (Figure 50.4). Amygdala activation did not occur in Teasdale et al.'s (1999) study, consistent with Reiman's suggestion (Reiman et al., 1997) that such activation is seen in response to perceptual rather than cognitive inductions. Thus Teasdale suggested two emotion generation circuits for responses to stimuli— a subcortical/perceptual pathway involving the amygdala for simple perceptual and associative inductions and a cortical/cognitive route involving the anterior cingulate for complex meaning and interpretation inductions.

Thus amygdala (most commonly bilateral) activation was present in 7 out of 10 negative but only 1 out of 8 positive affect induction studies (see table 50.3). Habituation effects could explain some negative findings. Anterior cingulate/medial frontal gyrus activation was seen in 5 out of 10 negative and 3 out of 8 positive affect induction studies. Taken together, these data suggest a role for the amygdala in affect processing. Affective valence appears more related to the presence (with negative affect) or absence (with positive affect), rather than the laterality, of amygdala activation. Valence appears to have less influence on anterior cingulate activation.

## Sadness and Happiness Affect Induction Studies

Transient sadness induction studies offer models of sadness as an emotion and, to a more limited extent, of the sad affect seen in depressive disorders. Table 50.4 summarizes the findings of such studies.

José Pardo and associates (Pardo et al., 1993) reported the first such functional brain imaging study, using PET and intravenous administration of $H_2^{15}O$ to explore transient sadness (3 minutes before scans and 2 minutes during scans). Dysphoria induced by recalling or imagining sad events with eyes closed was compared with a passive rest condition with eyes closed for four male and three female healthy volunteers with a mean age of 25.1 years. Using a 21-slice low-resolution (17 mm full width at half maximum) PET scanner and a brain atlas analysis, the researchers found normalized CBF increases in inferior frontal and orbitofrontal regions and a trend toward increases in medial frontal regions. Even this small sample suggested the possibility of a gender confound, as men had more confined left-sided activation and women more extensive bilateral activation, including the left insula. Changes were not observed in amygdala or anterior cingulate, perhaps due to the small size of such structures combined with small sample size and intergender variation, yielding inadequate statistical power.

Schneider, Gur, Jaggi, & Gur (1994) used inhalation of $^{133}$Xe SPECT to assess absolute cortical cerebral blood flow changes with transient (10 minute) sadness and happiness in five male and seven female healthy volunteers with a mean age of 21.7 years. This study involved an ROI analysis. For the affect inductions, participants looked at pictures from the University of Pennsylvania battery that showed actors with sad or happy facial expressions and used these, along with imagining or recalling sad or happy events, to induce sad or happy affect. The control conditions for these inductions were passive rest with eyes open and a gender-differentiation task. In the latter task participants looked at a mixed series of the same pictures of actors with sad and happy facial expressions used for the affect inductions and indicated the gender of the actors in the pictures. Widespread cortical CBF increased during sadness and decreased during happiness induction, relative to the nonactivated (resting) and activated (sex differentiation) nonemotional control conditions. For both sadness and happiness inductions, increased CBF was associated with stronger subjective affective experiences. There was only sparse evidence of regional specificity, with higher occipito-temporal CBF during sadness than happiness. In the frontal pole, left relative to right CBF was higher during sadness and lower during happiness induction. For sadness, but not happiness, induction, regional differences emerged among correlations between CBF and self-ratings, differences that were attributed to higher positive correlations between self-rated sadness and midtemporal, occipito-temporal, and postcentral CBF. Changes were not observed in deep structures such as the amygdala or anterior cingulate, due to the limitation of sensitivity of the $^{133}$Xe SPECT to superficial cortical structures. Also, the small sample size and intergender variation compromised statistical power.

Schneider et al. (1995) employed similar affect induction methods and different imaging technology in a subsequent $H_2^{15}O$ PET study of eleven male and five female healthy volunteers with a mean age of 23.5 years. This study utilized a high-resolution (6 mm full width at half maximum) 15-slice scanner and an ROI analysis. Mean absolute CBF for the entire brain varied only 1.4% across the four conditions, so that globally normalized CBF values were used for the regional analysis. In addition, an average of the rest and gender-discrimination conditions was used as the comparator for the affect inductions. The reciprocal CBF changes with sadness and happiness in the initial $^{133}$Xe SPECT study were replicated in subcortical but not in cortical regions. Thus, compared with the control condition, sadness yielded increased left amygdala and caudate and decreased mamillary body normalized CBF, whereas happiness was associated with the opposite changes in these structures. Left amygdala activation correlated with degree of negative affect. In addition, sadness yielded increased globus pallidus and thalamic and decreased right amygdala CBF. Happiness was associated with globus pallidus and thalamic CBF decreases on the right and increases on the left, as well as with posterior cingulate CBF increases. Also, correlations with affect were opposite for subcortical compared with frontal-temporal cortical regions. Schneider et al. (1995) stated that the latter finding suggested some reciprocity between subcortical and frontal-temporal regulation of emotional experience.

Grodd, Schneider, Klose, and Nägele (1995) employed modified methods and functional magnetic resonance imaging (fMRI) with an ROI analysis. This approach offers superior temporal and spatial resolution compared with PET but provides relative (globally normalized) rather than absolute CBF data. Viewing sad facial portraits and recalling sad life events, compared with viewing neutral facial portraits and making identity judgments, yielded increased left amygdala activity. Happiness induction failed to yield this effect.

Schneider et al. (1997) employed these methods and

Table 50.4 Paralimbic Changes in Sadness and Happiness Induction Studies

| Paradigm/Study | Sadness | | Happiness | |
|---|---|---|---|---|
| | Amygdala | Anterior cingulate Medial frontal gyrus Basal forebrain | Amygdala | Anterior cingulate Medial frontal gyrus Basal forebrain |
| **_Recall ± Faces_** | | | | |
| Pardo, Pardo, & Raichle, 1993 | — | — | NA | NA |
| Schneider et al., 1995 | ↑ L, ↓ R | — | ↓ L | — |
| Grodd, Schneider, Klose, & Nägele, 1995 | ↑ L | — | — | — |
| Schneider et al., 1997 | ↑ L | ↑ L ACcd | ↑ L | ↑ L ACcd |
| Schneider et al., 1998 | ↑ LR (Healthy) —(Schiz) | — | —(Healthy) —(Schiz) | — |
| Schneider, Hatbel, Kessler, Salloum, & Posse, 2000 | —(Women) ↑ R (Men) | — — | — — | — — |
| George et al., 1995 | — | ↑ LR ACad/MFG | — | — |
| George, Ketter, Parekh, Herscovitch, & Post, 1996 | — — | ↑ LR ACad, ACcd (Women) —(Men) | — — | ↑ L ACad (Women) ↑ R MFG (Men) |
| Gemar, Kapur, Segal, Brown, & Houle, 1996 | — | ↑ L MFG vs rest ↓ L MFG vs neutral | NA | NA |
| Mayberg et al., 1999 | — | ↑ LR ACad, ↓ L ACcd | NA | NA |
| Damasio et al., 1998 | ↑ L | — | — | — |
| Damasio et al., 1999 | — | ↑ R AC | — | ↑ BF |
| Lane, Reiman, Ahern, 1997 | — | ↑ LR MFG | — | ↑ LR MFG |
| Subtotal | 6/13 | 7/13 | 2/11 | 4/11 |
| **_Film Clips_** | | | | |
| Lane, Reiman, Ahern, 1997 | ↑ LR | ↑ LR MFG | ↑ L | ↑ LR MFG |
| Beauregard et al., 1998 | — | ↑ LR ACcd/MFG | NA | NA |
| Paradiso et al., 1997 | NA | NA | ↑ R entorhinal | ↓ L ACcd |
| **_Velten Statements_** | | | | |
| De Raedt, D'Haenen, Everaert, Cluydts, & Bossuyt, 1997 | —(Unmasked) ↑ LR (Masked) | — — | NA NA | NA NA |
| **_Script Generation_** | | | | |
| Partiot, Grafman, Sadato, Wachs, & Hallett, 1995 | — | ↑ L ACad/MFG | NA | NA |
| **_Multimodal*_** | | | | |
| Baker, Frith, & Dolan, 1997 | — | Attenuated LR ACcd verbal fluency activation | — | — |

*Velten + music + investigator interaction ± monetary gift, during verbal fluency/word repetition

fMRI with an ROI analysis in a study of seven male and five female healthy volunteers with a mean age of 29.7 years. This study used a single picture per activated condition, and a cognitive task (memorizing, in alphabetical order, first names of the same gender as the person in the picture, as well as surnames) was used in lieu of the gender-discrimination task used in prior studies. Participants commenced the tasks 1 minute before scanning and had a total of 3.5 minutes of scanning time for each condition. Signal intensity increased in the left amygdala and left ACcd with both sadness and happiness. Thus, although the left amygdala was again implicated, this study lacked the differential findings for sadness versus happiness seen in prior studies.

Schneider et al. (1998) reported an fMRI study with an ROI analysis with 13 male schizophrenia patients on antipsychotic medications with a mean age of 32.5 years and 13 healthy men on no medications with a mean age of 31.7 years. This study used a sex-discrimination control condition. Healthy controls had nonlateralized amygdala activation with sadness, but not happiness, induction. Schizophrenia patients did not show amygdala activation with sadness, despite negative affect ratings similar to those of controls, and did not show amygdala activation with happiness. The authors concluded that the blunted amygdala responses to sadness induction in schizophrenia patients compared with healthy controls were consistent with reports of impaired emotion processing in schizophrenia.

Schneider et al. (2000) reported an fMRI study with an ROI analysis with 13 female (with a mean age of 30.8 years) and 13 male (with a mean age of 31.7 years) healthy volunteers. Men, but not women, had right amygdala activation with sadness. Women, compared with men, had more widespread and less lateralized activation with sadness, which, consistent with earlier work (Pardo et al., 1993), suggested more focal processing of sadness in men. Taken together, the preceding five studies by Schneider and colleagues are noteworthy in view of the consistent and increasingly focal observations of functional amygdala changes with sadness and, to a lesser extent, happiness induction.

George et al. (1995) performed a transient (90-s) sadness and happiness induction $H_2^{15}O$ PET study with 11 healthy women with a mean age of 33.3 years. Like Pardo et al. (1993), these investigators used a brain atlas analysis. Participants viewed the same battery of faces that was used in the studies of Schneider and associates, but they uniformly invoked recall of sad events (without the alternative of imagining sad events, as in the previous studies) to induce sadness. Affect inductions lasted for 30 s before and 60 s during scans. The control condition was viewing pictures with affectively neutral facial expressions and recalling affectively neutral events. This study utilized a high-resolution (7 mm full width at half maximum) 15-slice scanner. Sadness, compared with neutral affect, induction was associated with increased normalized CBF in ACad and medial prefrontal, as well as other, anterior, paralimbic structures (Figure 50.5). Sadness, directly compared with happiness, induction was associated with similar anterior paralimbic CBF increases. Happiness compared with neutral affect induction was associated with midtemporal and right prefrontal CBF decreases. Thus sadness was associated with limbic and paralimbic activation and happiness with cortical deactivation. Amygdala CBF did not significantly change with happiness or sadness. There was evidence of attenuation of the sadness-induced CBF changes on the second sadness scan, with more variable repetition effects occurring with happiness induction.

In an extension of the preceding study, George, Ketter, et al. (1996) investigated 10 healthy women with a mean age of 34.5 years and 10 healthy men with a mean age of 35 years. As in the previous study, women showed widespread, primarily paralimbic, activation during transient sadness compared with neutral affect, including increased ACad, ACcd, left-sided medial, middle, and superior frontal gyrus, left insula, left thalamus, and basal ganglia and cerebellum normalized CBF. In contrast, men showed more focal left insula and right-sided posterior cingulate, caudate, and cuneus activation. Thus, for sad versus neutral affect, women showed significantly greater left middle frontal, right basal ganglia, and right brain stem activation. During transient happiness versus neutral affect, women showed left ACad and right caudate, men showed right medial frontal gyrus, left superior frontal gyrus, and basal ganglia activation, and women showed greater activation than men in left inferior frontal gyrus, left precentral gyrus, and right cerebellum. Transient sadness, compared with happiness, yielded results similar to the findings on sadness versus neutral affect. Again, amygdala CBF did not significantly change with happiness or sadness. The gender difference observations in this study were consistent with those in other studies (Pardo et al., 1993; Schneider et al., 2000), providing increasing support for the notion that women show more widespread cerebral activation with transient sadness than do men.

Michael Gemar and associates (Gemar et al., 1996) performed a transient (2-minute) sadness induction $H_2^{15}O$ PET study with 11 healthy men ranging from 23 to 34 years old. These investigators assessed normalized CBF changes, utilizing the same type of high-resolution scanner and brain atlas analysis as did George et al. (1995). However, the induction methods differed, relying on recall of sad events without the visual stimuli used in the studies of Schneider et al. (Grodd, 1995; Schneider, 1994, 1995, 1997, 1998, 2000) and George et al. (1995). In order to allow comparisons with prior studies, control conditions included both rest and a neutral affect induction. Sadness induction, compared with rest, yielded focal left-sided

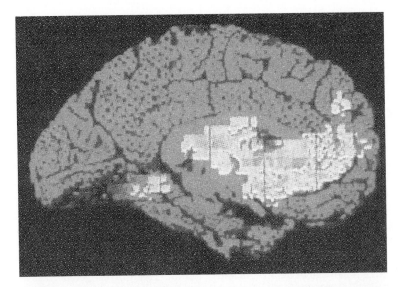

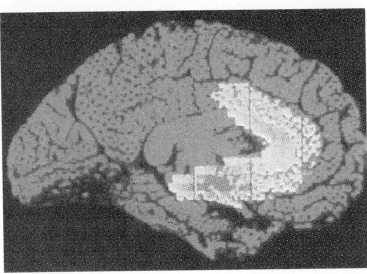

Figure 50.5 Overlapping anterior paralimbic activation with neuropsychologically and pharmacologically induced acute affective changes in healthy volunteers. Images are statistical parametric maps (SPMs) of cerebral blood flow activation rendered on the mesial aspect of the left hemisphere. *Top*: Regions activated during transient self-induced sadness in 11 healthy women (George et al., 1995). *Bottom*: Regions activated during acute intravenous procaine-induced affective symptoms in 32 healthy volunteers (Ketter et al., 1996). Note the overlap of anterior paralimbic activation patterns with these two different methods of inducing affective changes. Reproduced with permission from Ketter, George, Kimbrell, Benson, & Post (1996). (*See color insert.*)

prefrontal CBF increases, as previously reported by Pardo and associates (1993), albeit in regions that were more medial than those observed by Pardo et al. However, Gemar et al. (1996) also noted more prominent right-sided lateral prefrontal CBF decreases, in contrast to the inferior and orbitofrontal increases reported by Pardo et al. (1993). In contrast to the $H_2^{15}O$ PET study of Schneider et al. (1995), sadness induction, compared with rest, failed to yield changes in subcortical anterior paralimbic structures. Sadness versus neutral affect induction yielded left temporal

lobe CBF decreases which paralleled right temporal lobe decreases in the first study by George et al. (1995). However, Gemar et al. (1996) also reported left lateral and medial prefrontal CBF decreases, in contrast to the increases reported in these regions by George et al. (1995). Thus amygdala CBF did not change with sadness induction compared with either rest or neutral induction. Gemar et al. (1996) did not perform a happiness induction, so a direct sadness-versus-happiness comparison was not possible. Thus this study reported that transient sadness induction yielded CBF changes in regions which overlapped those reported in prior studies, but the directions of CBF changes partially agreed and partially disagreed with those in prior studies. The use of a small all-male sample may account for some of these differences.

In an $H_2^{15}O$ PET study performed by Helen Mayberg and associates (Mayberg et al., 1999), eight healthy women with a mean age of 36 years were scanned during 2 minutes of introspection (monitoring their mood state without rumination) with eyes closed, subsequent to a 10-minute period of inducing sad affect by recalling sad personal life events. The mean duration of attained sadness was 5 minutes. Participants in the sad state, compared with those in the rest condition, showed increased ventral limbic and paralimbic (ACad, ventral, mid- and posterior insula), as well as cerebellar vermis and right premotor, CBF; and decreased dorsal cortical (right dorsal prefrontal, left ACcd, posterior cingulate, and inferior parietal), as well as inferior frontal, and right inferior temporal normalized CBF. Of interest, $^{18}$FDG PET scans performed in depressed patients before and after recovery showed a similar pattern of increased ventral limbic and paralimbic metabolism and decreased dorsal cortical metabolism. There were inverse relationships between ACad and right dorsolateral prefrontal activity in both studies. Mayberg et al. (1999) noted that these observations were consistent with a cortico-limbic dysregulation model of sad/depressed affect. Neither study found changes in amygdala activity.

An $H_2^{15}O$ PET study was performed by Antonio Damasio and associates (Damasio et al., 1999) using a brain atlas analysis with 25 healthy volunteers ranging between 24 and 42 years of age. Participants signaled that the target affect had been attained prior to beginning scans. Sixteen participants who recalled sad rather than neutral life events showed increased hypothalamus, basal ganglia, anterior insula, ventromedial frontal, and right-sided anterior cingulate, thalamus, pons, and midbrain normalized CBF. Eight participants who recalled happy rather than neutral life events showed increased right-sided posterior cingulate and basal forebrain normalized CBF. Recalling fearful and angry life events also yielded increased right-sided pons and midbrain normalized CBF. Thus brain stem activation was associated with negative, but not positive, affect induction. All inductions failed to yield amygdala changes and tended to deactivate neocortex. However, in an earlier analysis of six participants, left amygdala activation was seen with sadness (Damasio et al., 1998).

Some investigators have used film clips to induce affect. An $H_2^{15}O$ PET study was performed by Lane, Reiman, Ahern, et al. (1997) using a brain atlas analysis with 12 healthy women with a mean age of 23.3 years. Sadness, happiness, disgust, and neutral affects were both invoked by recall of life events and induced by viewing evocative film clips. Recall of sad events activated medial frontal gyrus, thalamus, left insula, basal ganglia, hypothalamus, midbrain, and cerebellar normalized CBF. Recall of happy events activated medial frontal gyrus and thalamus and also increased temporal lobe CBF. Viewing sad film clips activated similar regions to those activated by sad recall but also increased amygdala and occipito-parieto-temporal CBF. Viewing happy film clips activated similar regions to those activated by happy recall but also increased left amygdala, ventral striatum, posterior cingulate, and occipito-parieto-temporal CBF. Sadness, for recall and film clips combined, was associated with increased middle frontal gyrus, thalamus, hypothalamus, occipito-parieto-temporal, basal ganglia, midbrain, and cerebellum CBF. Happiness, for recall and film clips combined, was associated with increased middle frontal gyrus, thalamus, hypothalamus, and occipito-parieto-temporal CBF. Happiness, compared with sadness, for recall and film clips combined, was associated with increased ACad and ventromesial frontal CBF. The authors suggested that ventromedial prefrontal cortex was differentially involved in positive and negative emotions (more activated in positive emotions).

Reiman et al. (1997) described differential effects of external (film clips) and internal (recall) induction of affect. Recall inductions for all emotions (sadness, happiness, and disgust) combined, compared with neutral affect, yielded medial frontal gyrus, anterior insula and possibly orbitofrontal, and anterior temporal activation. Film clip inductions for all emotions combined, compared with neutral affect, yielded medial frontal gyrus and thalamus, activation, as well as activation in the amygdala, hypothalamus, midbrain, occipito-parieto-temporal region, and cerebellum. Reiman et al. (1997) suggested that medial prefrontal and thalamus activation was related to emotional experience, independent of the particular emotion or the induction modality. They also suggested that occipito-temporo-parietal, lateral cerebellum, hypothalamus, and anterior temporal (including amygdala and hippocampus) activation was related to perception and processing of the external sensory stimuli.

Mario Beauregard and associates (Beauregard et al., 1998) performed an fMRI study using a brain atlas analysis with four female and three male patients with unipolar depression (two on selective serotonin reuptake inhibitors—SSRIs), who had a mean age of 42 years, and four female and three male healthy volunteers who had a mean age of 45 years. Participants viewed a 154-s neutral film clip depicting carpentry, rested with a blank screen for 32 s, and then viewed a 154-s film clip from a color feature film depicting the tragic death of a father in the presence of his young son that had been empirically validated to induce transient sadness (Gross & Levenson, 1995). In both depressed patients and healthy volunteers, sad versus neutral film clips produced increased medial, right inferior and right superior prefrontal, left cerebellar, and caudate activity. Depressed patients also showed increased left middle prefrontal, right ACcd, left midcingulate, right fornix, superior temporal, right fusiform, and left middle occipital activity. Healthy volunteers also showed increased right middle temporal, left superior parietal, left fusiform, left cuneus, left precuneus, and right middle occipital activity. Depressed patients had greater left medial prefrontal and right ACcd activation than healthy volunteers. Amygdala activation was not observed.

An $H_2^{15}O$ PET study (Paradiso et al., 1997), studied affect induction in six female and two male elderly healthy volunteers with a mean age of 62.6 years. Participants viewed 60-s soundless film clips selected from commercial movies to induce happiness (but not sadness), disgust, fear/disgust, or neutral affective response. Viewing happy versus neutral film clips yielded increased right entorhinal (adjacent to amygdala), calcarine, cuneus, fusiform, posterodorsal temporal, inferior parietal, superior temporal gyrus, and medial cerebellar normalized CBF. The authors suggested that the entorhinal activation was related to happy affect and the remainder of the pattern to recognition and memory components of viewing the film clips. Viewing happy, compared with neutral, film clips also produced decreased inferior medial and left orbital frontal, left inferior temporal, left ACcd and left posterior cingulate, precuneus and right lateral cerebellar CBF. However, Paradiso et al. (1997) viewed these changes as activations for neutral versus happy clips (rather than deactivations for happy versus neutral) and noted that this pattern overlapped that observed during "rest" in a prior study (Andreasen et al., 1995). Paradiso et al. (1997) also suggested that the differential medial thalamus activation seen in disgust induction versus neutral affect and the left orbitofrontal activation in fear/disgust versus neutral affect was consistent with regional specialization of emotion. They also suggested that other overlapping patterns of activation were related to visual processing and memory components of viewing the film clips.

Rudt De Raedt and associates (De Raedt et al., 1997) performed an affect induction study with a novel design. Cerebellar-normalized CBF was assessed by $^{99m}$Tc-HMPAO SPECT in fourteen healthy women with a mean age of 21.9 years. An ROI analysis was utilized. Overt depressive Velten statements (Velten, 1968) were presented for 3 minutes to induce sadness "within the realm of attention," and covert depressive Velten statements, masked by louder neutral Velten statements, were presented to induce sadness "out of the realm of attention." Overt neutral Velten statements were presented in the control condition. These two methods of sadness induction produced CBF effects in overlapping regions with commonalities and dissocia-

tions in directions of changes. Thus both methods yielded increased left and decreased right subcortical, and decreased right thalamic, normalized CBF but lacked regional cortical effects. Sadness within the realm of attention also yielded increased left hemisphere and left cortical CBF, whereas sadness out of the realm of attention had the opposite effects in these regions and increased hippocampal/amygdalar CBF.

Arnaud Partiot and associates (Partiot, Grafman, Sadato, Wachs, & Hallett, 1995) performed a study using another novel induction method. Sadness was induced by having participants imagine the sequence of events and feelings concerned with preparation and dressing to go to their mothers' funerals, and neutral affect was induced by having them imagine the sequence of events and feelings concerned with preparation and dressing before their mothers came over for dinner. Control conditions included generating words or identifying objects from categories of items ordinarily utilized in dressing and preparing to go out or have someone over for dinner. They studied normalized CBF in 12 healthy participants (gender not specified) ranging from 21 to 38 years old, with the same equipment and brain atlas analysis method used by George and associates. Sadness induction, compared with the pooled control conditions, yielded increased left ACad, left greater than right medial frontal, bilateral anterior middle temporal gyrus, and posterior cingulate CBF. Neutral affect induction, compared with the pooled control conditions, yielded increased left frontopolar, right superior frontal, bilateral middle frontal, right posterior temporal, right inferior parietal, and left precuneus CBF. Amygdala CBF did not change with affect induction, perhaps due to the large cognitive-lexical component of the induction.

Simon Baker and associates (Baker et al., 1997) reported an affect induction study with another distinctive design. Sad, happy, and neutral affects were induced in nine healthy men ranging from 18 to 35 years old by simultaneous affect-congruent Velten induction, music, and interpersonal interactions by the investigator with the participants. In addition, in the happiness induction, participants were presented with an unexpected monetary gift of 30 pounds. After 7.5 minutes of affect induction, $H_2^{15}O$ PET scans to assess globally normalized CBF were obtained while subjects performed verbal fluency and word repetition tasks. A brain atlas analysis method was used. Affect induction did not alter task performance. Effects related to sadness and happiness versus neutral affect induction had commonalities and dissociations. Thus both sadness and happiness were associated with increased left superior dorsolateral prefrontal, right lateral premotor, and bilateral lateral orbitofrontal CBF, with the latter region having more robust increases with happiness than with sadness. Also, both sadness and happiness decreased right caudate CBF. In addition, sadness was associated with increased posterior cingulate and supplementary motor area and with decreased rostral medial prefrontal and right dorsolateral prefrontal CBF. Happiness induction also produced increased left superior frontal, posterior hypothalamus, and midbrain CBF and decreased inferior/middle temporal and thalamic CBF. CBF responses to the verbal fluency versus the word repetition task were blunted in left prefrontal and premotor cortex and thalamus during sadness and happiness and in right ACcd during sadness (Figure 50.6). The pattern of blunting with sadness resembled the pattern of decreases seen in a prior sample of primarily unipolar depressed patients compared with healthy volunteers (Bench et al, 1992), suggesting that the sadness induction in healthy volunteers was affecting similar brain regions to those with disrupted function in depression patients. None of these comparisons revealed sadness or happiness induction effects on amygdala CBF, perhaps due to the somewhat long 7.5-minute duration, to the multimodal nature of the induction, or to the prominent lexical-cognitive components of the tasks.

In summary, studies of sadness and happiness induction have had variable findings (see Table 50.4). Restricting attention to studies that used recall (some of which also used faces), amygdala activations were seen in 6 out of 13 sadness but in only 2 out of 11 happiness studies. Anterior cingulate/medial frontal gyrus activations were seen in 7 out of 13 sadness but in only 4 out of 11 happiness studies. There was a tendency toward left-sided amygdala activation preponderance in sadness induction (four left, one bilateral, one right) and toward left-sided amygdala changes (one left increases, one left decreases)

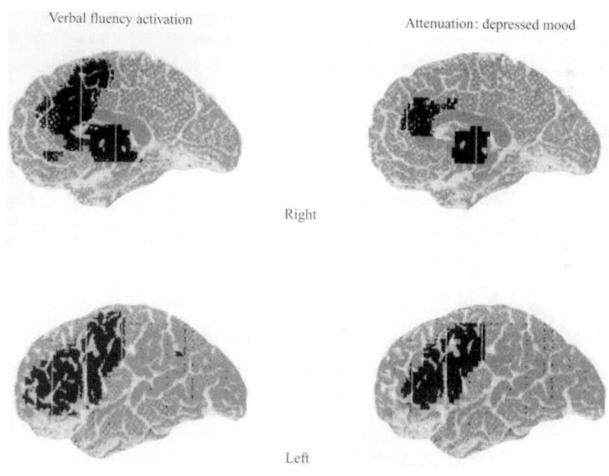

Verbal fluency activation

Attenuation: depressed mood

Right

Left

Figure 50.6 Blunted verbal fluency task-induced cerebral blood flow activation pattern with transient sadness induction in ten healthy men. Medial (*top*) and lateral (*bottom*) cortical rendering of regions with increased normalized cerebral blood flow during performance of a verbal fluency task versus a word repetition task after neutral affect (*left*) and transient sadness (*right*) induction. Performance of the tasks after transient sadness induction produced blunting of responses in brain regions overlapping those having decreased activity in depressed patients compared with healthy controls in prior studies. From Baker et al. (1997), with permission of Cambridge University Press.

in happiness induction. Thus affective valence appeared more related to the presence (negative affect, i.e., sadness) or absence (positive affect, i.e., happiness), rather than the laterality, of activation. Gender may be an important factor in sadness induction, with three studies (George et al., 1995; Pardo et al., 1993; Schneider et al., 2000) finding more widespread activation in women than in men.

## Pharmacological Emotion/Mood Induction Studies

Pharmacological methods of affect induction are diverse and complex. Different substances have varying dosage ranges, routes of administration, pharmacokinetics (rates of absorption, distribution, and excretion), and pharmacodynamics (effects at receptors). Dosage is important, as some drugs yield biphasic responses, with certain effects at lower doses and different (even opposite) effects at higher doses. Route of administration matters, as very rapid (e.g., intravenous) administration can provide high brain concentrations too quickly for cerebral homeostatic mechanisms to intervene. Duration of administration is a crucial factor. Some agents (such as benzodiazepines, alcohol, and drugs of abuse) have rapid-onset (within minutes) effects, which attenuate with ongoing exposure (tolerance) and may yield opposite effects with rapid discontinuation after chronic exposure (withdrawal). Other agents (such as antidepressants) have response latencies of days to weeks, may evidence consolidation of response over even longer periods, and may or may not yield withdrawal effects (depending on pharmacokinetics and pharmacodynamics) with rapid discontinuation. Depending on these factors, administration of medications may yield models of, or be used to treat disturbances of, both emotions and moods. In this section we provide an overview of studies of effects of pharmacological agents on brain activity, focusing primarily on commonly used agents (Table 50.5).

### Caffeine

Caffeine is the most widely consumed central nervous system stimulant. In four studies (Cameron, Modell, & Hariharan, 1990; Mathew, Barr, Weinman, 1983; Mathew & Wilson 1985a; Mathew & Wilson, 1990), acute (given just before imaging) caffeine yielded global CBF decreases without differences in regional CBF or clinical responses, across both healthy volunteers and anxiety-disorder patients. Also, in one study, caffeine use produced regional increases in lactate that were not related to clinical responses (Dager et al., 1999). These data are consistent with the notion that caffeine could increase global cerebral energy metabolism but also decrease global CBF, inducing relative brain hypoperfusion (Nehlig, Daval, & Debry, 1992).

### Ethanol

Ethanol is frequently used and abused in efforts to produce calmness, anxiolysis, and euphoria. Acute ethanol administration produced global/regional CBF increases in four studies (Mathew & Wilson, 1986; Sano et al., 1993; Schwartz et al., 1993; Tiihonen et al., 1994) and regional CBF increases and decreases in four studies (Boecker et al., 1996; Ingvar et al., 1998; Sano et al., 1993; Volkow et al., 1988). In contrast, ethanol decreased CMRglu in two studies (de Wit, Metz, Wagner, & Cooper, 1990; Volkow et al., 1990). Ethanol withdrawal may be associated with CBF decreases in mild to moderate cases (Tutus et al., 1998) and with increases in severe cases (Hemmingsen et al., 1988). Clinical and CBF effects of ethanol were blocked by naloxone (Tiihonen et al., 1994), but benzodiazepine receptor binding was not altered with acute ethanol or in ethanol-dependent participants (Farde et al., 1994).

Taken together, these data suggest that acute ethanol increases widespread (including frontal and temporal) CBF in the brief (few minutes) time frame of blood flow

Table 50.5. Cerebral Changes with Pharmacological Induction of Affect

| | CBF | CMRglu | Amygdala/Ref |
|---|---|---|---|
| Caffeine | ↓ global | — | |
| Ethanol | ↑↓ regional ↓ cerebellum | ↓ global | |
| Nicotine | ↑↓ regional | ↓ global | ↑ (Stein et al., 1998) |
| Marijuana (THC) | ↑ regional | ↑ regional | |
| Benzodiazepines | ↓ global | ↓ global | |
| Dextroamphetamine | ↑↓ regional | ↑↓ regional | ↑ (Trivedi et al., 1995) |
| Cocaine | ↑↓ regional | — | ↑↓ (Breiter et al., 1997) |
| Procaine | ↑↓ regional ↑ global | — | ↑↓ (Ketter, Andreason, et al., 1996) |

studies yet decreases widespread CMRglu in the more extended (30-minute) time frame of metabolism studies. Biphasic clinical effects of arousal/disinhibition at lower doses and sedation at higher doses may be accompanied by biphasic increases and decreases in cerebral activity. Acute ethanol appears to decrease cerebellar activity, consistent with its adverse effects on motor function. The clinical agitation seen in severe alcohol withdrawal appears to be accompanied by increased CBF.

## Nicotine

Nicotine is commonly used in efforts to provide calming or alerting effects. Cigarette smoking or nicotine use yielded CBF decreases in two studies (Cruickshank, Neil-Dwyer, Dorrance, Hayes, & Patel, 1989; Kimura, Matsumoto, Handa, Hashikawa, & Moriwaki, 1993), regional decreases and increases in one study (Ghatan et al., 1998), and increases in two studies (Nagata, Shinohara, Kanno, Hatazawa, & Domino, 1995; Stein et al., 1998). One of the latter was an fMRI study in which nicotine induced dose-dependent increases in amygdala, cingulate, nucleus accumbens, and frontal lobe activity, consistent with clinical arousing and reinforcing effects (Stein et al., 1998). Pilot data suggest that cigarette smoking may decrease CMRglu (London, 1995). Carbon-11 ($^{11}$C) nicotine binding is maximal in prefrontal and anterior paralimbic regions (Nyback et al., 1989).

## Marijuana

Marijuana produces euphoria and is the most commonly used illicit drug in the United States. Acute administration of the active ingredient of marijuana, delta 9-tetrahydrocannabinol (THC), has been used in brain imaging studies. THC yielded variable global effects (Volkow et al., 1991) but consistent regional CBF increases in five studies (Mathew et al., 1999; Mathew, Wilson, Coleman, Turkington, & DeGrado, 1997; Mathew, Wilson, Turkington, & Coleman, 1998; Volkow et al., 1991; Volkow et al., 1996). THC-induced cerebellar, frontal, and anterior paralimbic, CBF, and CMRglu changes may correlate with clinical responses. Heterogeneity in clinical responses may contribute to some of the observed variability in cerebral functional responses.

## Benzodiazepines

Benzodiazepines (BZs) are commonly used to control anxiety and insomnia and are also used during medical procedures to provide deep sedation as an alternative to general anesthesia. BZs consistently decreased CBF in five studies (Forster, Juge, & Morel, 1982; Mathew & Wilson, 1991; Matthew et al., 1995; Roy-Byrne et al., 1993; Veselis et al., 1997), and CMRglu in eight studies (de Wit, Metz, Wagner, & Cooper, 1991; Foster et al., 1987; Volkow, Wang, Begleiter, et al., 1995; Volkow, Wang, Hitzemann, et al., 1995; Volkow, Wang, Overall, et al., 1997; Wang et al., 1998; Wang, Volkow, Levy, et al., 1999; Wang et al., 1996). BZ-induced decreases in global cerebral activity are consistent with sedative effects, and decreases in cerebellar activity are consistent with adverse motor effects. BZ clinical and cerebral effects were reversed or partially reversed by benzodiazepine receptor blocker flumazenil (Matthew et al., 1995; Volkow, Wang, Hitzemann, et al., 1995), which on its own fails to alter cerebral activity (Wolf et al., 1990). Alcoholism patients and their relatives have blunted CMRglu responses to BZs (Volkow, Wang, Begleiter, et al., 1995; Volkow, Wang, Overall, et al., 1997). Anxiety disorder patients had prefrontal and anterior paralimbic BZ receptor binding, which was decreased in three studies (Kaschka, Feistel, & Ebert, 1995; Malizia et al., 1998; Schlegel et al., 1994) but increased in one study (Kuikka et al., 1995). The BZ receptor alterations in anxiety disorder patients are consistent with the vulnerability of these patients to anxiety states.

## Stimulants

Stimulants are commonly used and abused in efforts to increase alertness and energy and decrease appetite. Dextroamphetamine has variable effects on cerebral activity. Hence this stimulant produced cortical CBF decreases in three intravenous low dose (= 0.3 mg/kg) $^{133}$Xe SPECT studies with healthy volunteers and schizophrenia patients (Kahn, Prohovnik, Lucas, & Sackeim 1989; Mathew & Wilson, 1985b; Mathew & Wilson, 1989), but cortical and subcortical activity increases in an fMRI study of healthy volunteers and depression patients given an oral 0.4 mg/kg dose (Trivedi et al., 1995). This medication also yielded variable changes in task-induced CBF activations in two studies of healthy volunteers and schizophrenia patients given an oral 0.25 mg/kg dose (Daniel et al., 1991; Mattay et al., 1996). Dextroamphetamine caused CMRglu decreases in two studies in which an oral intermediate dose (0.5 mg/kg) was given to schizophrenia patients (Wolkin et al., 1987; Wolkin et al., 1994) and produced increases in one study in which an oral high dose (1.0 mg/kg) was given to healthy volunteers (Vollenweider, Maguire, Leenders, Mathys, & Angst, 1998). This stimulant also produced variable CMRglu changes in two studies in which an intravenous low dose (= 0.25 mg/kg) was given to healthy volunteers and ADHD patients (Ernst et al., 1997; Matochik et al., 1993) and produced no CMRglu change in a study of ADHD patients given an intravenous very low dose (0.15 mg/kg; Ernst et al., 1994).

Variability in findings could be due to differences in dextroamphetamine doses (0.15 to 1.0 mg/kg), administration routes (oral or intravenous), imaging modalities (SPECT, PET, or fMRI), acquisition times (seconds for fMRI, about 1 minute for CBF, or about 30 minutes for CMRglu), samples (healthy volunteers or patients with schizophrenia, ADHD, and depression), clinical responses, and activity during scanning (rest, simple auditory continuous performance task, more difficult cognitive tasks). Finally, general measures of cerebral activity such as CBF and CMRglu may lack sufficient biochemical sensitivity, as dextroamphetamine-induced release of endogenous striatal dopamine appeared related to affective responses to dextroamphetamine (Laruelle et al., 1995).

### Cocaine

Cocaine is a local anesthetic with euphoriant properties, which render it an important drug of abuse. Cocaine yielded CBF decreases in six studies (Gollub et al., 1998; Johnson et al., 1998; Kaufman et al., 1998; Li et al., 2000; Pearlson et al., 1993; Wallace et al., 1996), CBF increases in one study (Mathew et al., 1996), CBF increases and decreases in one study (Breiter et al., 1997), and CMRglu decreases in one study (London et al., 1990). Cocaine craving increased CBF (Maas et al., 1998) and CMRglu (Wang, Volkow, Fowler, et al., 1999). Cocaine-induced euphoria was associated with striatal DAT blockade in two studies (Malison et al., 1995; Volkow, Wang, Fischman, et al., 1997). Breiter and associates have noted heterogeneous amygdala responses to cocaine (Breiter et al., 1997).

### Procaine

The local anesthetic procaine (Novocain) has long been utilized as a dental anesthetic, but it has more recently been used as an affective probe. Procaine activates limbic structures in animals. In humans, acute intravenous procaine yields compelling emotional and psychosensory experiences and temporal lobe fast activity, both of which last a few minutes. Procaine lacks cardiac toxicity and abuse potential and is thus safer than cocaine. In addition, procaine-induced affective experiences have considerable interindividual variability, ranging from intensely positive (euphoria) to intensely negative (fear, panic). Hence, procaine-induced experiences can model both positive and negative emotions.

In an $H_2^{15}O$ study, Ketter, Andreason, et al. (1996) studied acute procaine's effects on CBF in relationship to clinical responses in 17 male and 15 female healthy volunteers with a mean age 30.1 years. Both brain atlas and ROI analyses were used. Procaine increased global and, to a greater extent, anterior paralimbic CBF (see figure 50.5). Participants with intense procaine-induced fear had greater increases in left amygdalar CBF than those with euphoria. Absolute and normalized left (but not right) amygdalar CBF changes tended to correlate positively with fear and negatively with euphoria intensity. Procaine-induced visual hallucinations appeared associated with greater global and occipital CBF increases. Absolute occipital CBF increases appeared to correlate positively with visual hallucination intensity. Thus procaine increased anterior paralimbic CBF, and different clinical responses appeared to be associated with different patterns of CBF changes. These findings were subsequently independently replicated (Servan-Schreiber, Perlstein, Cohen, & Mintun, 1998).

In summary, pharmacological emotion/mood induction studies have suggested variable cerebral effects across drugs, or even with the same drug across individuals. There are many potential sources for such variability, which may on occasion be advantageous. Indeed, in the case of procaine, variability in clinical responses was accompanied by systematic variability in cerebral responses.

## Functional Brain Imaging Studies of Moods

An extensive literature describes altered anterior paralimbic and prefrontal activity in patients with mood disorders (for a review, see Ketter, George, et al., 1996). As with emotions, both physiological and pharmacological methods have been utilized in mood induction studies. The former offer naturalistic approximations which are useful in assessing the underlying neuroanatomy of spontaneous moods. The latter allow more specific biochemical probing of the neurobiological substrates of moods. These affect-induction methods, combined with functional brain imaging, have implicated overlying prefrontal, as well as anterior, paralimbic structures as contributing importantly to moods.

Compared with emotion, relatively few studies have been done of induction of mood, perhaps due to the additional time and effort required. Utilizing cognitive methods to not only induce affective experiences but also maintain them long enough to be considered moods is time and effort intensive and requires well-motivated participants. Some of the emotion induction studies reviewed herein had durations that were intermediate between emotions (seconds to a few minutes) and moods and thus lasted 7.5 (Baker et al., 1997) to 10 (Mayberg et al., 1999) minutes. In view of evidence that raises the issue of rapid habituation of amygdala (and hence possibly other paralimbic) responses (Breiter et al., 1996), longer (more than 5 minutes) induction durations could account for some differences between findings of these studies and those of studies with briefer (less than 5 minutes) induction durations.

An $^{18}$FDG PET study performed by Larry Cahill and associates (Cahill et al., 1996) investigated normalized CMRglu in eight healthy men with a mean age of 21.1 years. This study involved a brain atlas analysis, but the authors focused on amygdala activity. Viewing negative (animal mutilation, violent crime eliciting primarily fear or disgust) versus neutral (court proceeding, stunt man performance, travelogue) 32-minute film clips failed to yield amygdala CMRglu changes. Also, affect ratings for both negative and neutral film clips failed to correlate with amygdala activity. However, free recall of negative (but not neutral) clips 3 weeks later correlated with right amygdala (and medial frontal gyrus) activity at the time of viewing. Cahill et al. (1996) also noted that free recall of negative and neutral clips 3 weeks later correlated with medial prefrontal and right superficial inferotemporal activity at the time of viewing. The authors concluded that the right amygdala and related basal forebrain regions may be important for encoding of emotional memories. The lack of limbic activation during encoding could be due to habituation or to the complex nature of the stimuli.

We have been studying the use of sad autobiographical memories to induce and maintain sustained sad affect (Ketter et al., 2000). In contrast to studies of transient sadness that lasts a few minutes and model sad emotion, our sustained sadness induction lasts 30 minutes and is intended to model sad mood. Participants recall a specific event from their past which triggered sad affect and to focus on the event to emulate the affect. Positive and Negative Affect Schedule (PANAS) sadness subscale ratings are obtained every 10 minutes to determine the degree of sadness induced. The cerebral concomitants of sad mood induction are assessed with PET and fluorine-18 deoxyglucose (FDG). Additional biochemical concomitants of sustained sadness are investigated with assays of blood from indwelling catheters for changes in plasma amino acids and hypothalamic-pituitary-adrenal and hypothalamic-pituitary-thyroid axis function. Thus far, we have studied 25 healthy controls, 25 bipolar disorder patients, and 5 (unipolar) major depression patients.

Preliminary results from this study indicate that the sustained-sadness technique is effective in inducing and maintaining sad affect for 30 minutes, without major attenuation of the effect with time. It is of interest that not only healthy controls but also depressed mood disorder patients have been able to effectively maintain sustained sad affect. Anterior paralimbic structures have shown the greatest regional changes, concordant with studies of transient sadness. However, the direction of change with sustained sadness differs. Thus we have noted decreases in glucose metabolism in these structures, with the most robust effects occurring in the left insula, which contrasts with reports of increases in overlapping areas with transient sadness, as described previously.

In mood disorders, acute somatic interventions which yield mood changes are accompanied by changes in cerebral activity. Sleep deprivation decreases cerebral metabolism and can yield brief (generally 1-day duration) antidepressant effects in some mood disorder patients (Wu et al., 1992). Responders, compared with nonresponders and healthy controls, have higher baseline ACad, medial

prefrontal cortex, and posterior subcallosal gyrus normalized CMRglu (Wu et al., 1999). Tryptophan depletion triggers depressive relapse in patients with serotonin reuptake inhibitor-induced remission of depressive symptoms. Patients prone to depletion-induced relapse have baseline increased prefrontal and limbic CMRglu, and with depletion-induced relapse they develop decreased middle frontal gyrus, thalamus, and orbitofrontal cortex CMRglu (Bremner et al., 1997).

Similarly, chronic interventions that allow relief of depressive symptoms are accompanied by alterations in cerebral (often anterior paralimbic and prefrontal) activity (Ketter, George, et al., 1996; Ketter et al., 1999). Of particular interest is the study by Mayberg and associates described previously, which notes the opposite nature of changes in cerebral activity with sadness induction, compared with relief of depression (Mayberg et al., 1999).

In summary, the literature relating moods to cerebral activity is dominated by investigations of patients with mood disorders compared with healthy controls. A smaller collection of studies describes cerebral changes with mood induction. However, studies within both of these subgroups of investigations implicate anterior paralimbic and prefrontal structures in mood and mood disorders.

## Functional Brain Imaging Studies of Temperaments

There are relatively few functional brain imaging studies of temperament. We focus on studies which have used the models of Eysenck and Cloninger. Space does not permit review of the related emerging literature that describes cerebral function in personality traits such as impulsivity (Siever et al., 1999), aggression (Goyer et al., 1994), violence (Volkow, Tancredi, et al., 1995), and detachment (Breier et al., 1998; Laakso et al., 2000); or disorders such as schizotypal (Buchsbaum, Trestman, et al., 1997; Buchsbaum, Yang, et al., 1997; Dickey et al., 1999; Dickey et al., 2000; Kwon et al., 1998; Raine, Sheard, Reynolds, & Lencz, 1992), borderline (de la Fuente et al., 1997; de la Fuente et al., 1994; Goyer et al., 1994; Lyoo, Han, & Cho, 1998), and antisocial (Intrator et al., 1997; Kuruoglu et al., 1996; Raine et al., 1994; Raine, Lencz, Bihrle, LaCasse, & Colletti, 2000) personality disorders.

An early [18]FDG PET study performed by R. J. Haier and associates (Haier, Sokolski, Katz, & Buchsbaum, 1987) used an ROI analysis and studied 18 patients with generalized anxiety disorder. Relationships were seen between absolute CMRglu and personality during continuous performance task but not during rest. Extraversion correlated positively with cortical (frontal, temporal) and right-sided limbic/subcortical (cingulate, hippocampal, parahippocampal, and basal ganglia) absolute CMRglu. Neuroticism had little correlation with either cortical or limbic/subcortical activity. Psychoticism correlated negatively with cortical (primarily occipital) and limbic/subcortical (cingulate and thalamic) absolute CMRglu. These observations were not consistent with Eysenck's predictions of lower cortical activity with extraversion (higher in introversion) and higher limbic/subcortical activity with neuroticism. This inconsistency could be due to the use of participants who had generalized anxiety disorder rather than healthy controls or to the nature of the continuous performance task.

Roy Mathew and associates (Mathew, Weinman, & Barr, 1984) reported a $^{133}$Xe SPECT study of 51 healthy women, with a mean age of 32 years, at rest with eyes closed, in which introverts had higher CBF than extraverts in all 16 cortical regions assessed. Introversion-extraversion (but not neuroticism) correlated modestly ($r = 0.24$ to $0.41$, $p = 0.04$ to $0.001$) with CBF in all regions, in agreement with Eysenck's model.

A subsequent $^{133}$Xe SPECT study was performed by Stenberg, Risberg, Warkentin, & Rosén (1990) with 18 healthy women and 19 healthy men with a mean age of 34 years. At rest with eyes closed, introverts, compared with extraverts, had higher bilateral temporal lobe CBF but lower left inferolateral prefrontal (Broca's area) CBF and failed to demonstrate the expected higher global cortical CBF. However, restricting the sample to women and covarying for age, or further restricting the sample to the 14 women under 50 years of age, with a mean age of 29 years, yielded trends ($r = 0.34$ and $0.33$, respectively) toward the expected higher global CBF in introverts. These data suggested that gender and age are important factors in the neurobiology of personality.

Debra Johnson and associates (Johnson et al., 1999) performed a resting H$_2$$^{15}$O PET study with a brain atlas analysis with 10 healthy men and 8 healthy women with a mean age of 28.9 years. Introversion correlated with higher frontal (including Broca's area), left mid-cingulate, right anterior temporal, right anterior insular, and anterior thalamic CBF. Extraversion correlated with higher ACad, left amygdalar, posterior temporal, right posterior insular, and posterior thalamic CBF. However, introversion had a nonsignificant negative correlation ($r = -0.21$, $p = 0.20$) with global CBF. Johnson et al. (1999) concluded that introversion was associated with increased anterior, and extraversion with increased posterior, CBF.

George and associates studied 13 healthy volunteers at rest with H$_2$$^{15}$O PET, and using a brain atlas analysis found that novelty-seeking tended to correlate positively ($r = .3$, $p < 0.07$) with left caudate and brain stem (areas with rich dopamine innervation) CBF, while harm-avoidance correlated positively ($r = .5$, $p < 0.01$) with brain stem and cerebellum CBF (George, Ketter, et al., 1994).

In a subsequent $^{18}$FDG PET study, George, Cloninger, et al. (1996) studied 31 healthy volunteers who were per-

forming an auditory continuous performance task. Using a brain atlas analysis, novelty seeking correlated positively ($p < 0.001$) with left caudate and mid-cingulate (areas with rich dopamine innervation) CMRglu and negatively with left medial prefrontal CMRglu. Harm avoidance correlated positively with left medial prefrontal CMRglu.

Menza, Mark, Burn, and Brooks (1995) studied nine Parkinson's disease patients with $^{18}$F-fluorodopa PET and found that novelty seeking was related to uptake in left caudate but not in other areas.

In summary, emerging data suggest relationships between brainstem-subcortical-cortical networks and temperament. Eysenck's hypotheses (1986) linking introversion with higher global cortical activity and neuroticism with higher limbic activity have not been consistently supported. However, other possible relationships have emerged, such as introversion being associated with higher anterior and extroversion with higher posterior cerebral activity. In contrast, preliminary imaging evidence supports Cloninger's (1987) more biochemically oriented tridimensional model of temperament. Thus three studies using different radiotracers detected relationships between novelty seeking and activity in the left caudate, an area rich in dopaminergic innervation, consistent with the notion that novelty seeking is related to dopaminergic function.

## Conclusion

Increasingly sophisticated models of the neurobiology of affective processes have evolved over the past century. Emotions, moods, and temperaments not only differ in temporal domains but also vary in phenomenology and putative neural substrates. Recently, functional brain imaging studies have allowed investigators to test hypotheses that relate affective processes to their putative substrates. Anterior paralimbic and prefrontal structures appear to contribute importantly to emotions and moods, respectively. Temperaments may be related to activity in brainstem-subcortical-cortical networks. Advances in imaging technology and paradigm design promise to help further advance our knowledge of the neurobiology of affective processes in health and in mood disorders.

## REFERENCES

Adolphs, R., Tranel, D., Damasio, H., & Damasio, A. (1994). Impaired recognition of emotion in facial expressions following bilateral damage to the human amygdala. *Nature, 372*, 669–672.

Alexander, G. E., Crutcher, M. D., DeLong, M. R. (1990). Basal ganglia-thalamocortical circuits: Parallel substrates for motor, oculomotor, prefrontal and limbic functions. *Progress in Brain Research, 85*, 119–146.

Altshuler, L. L. Devinsky, O., Post, R. M., & Theodore, W.

(1990). Depression, anxiety, and temporal lobe epilepsy: Laterality of focus and symptoms. *Archives of Neurology, 47,* 284–288.

Amaral, D. G., & Price, J. L. (1984). Amygdalo-cortical projections in the monkey (*Macaca fascicularis*). *Journal of Comparative Neurology, 230,* 465–496.

Amaral, D. G., Price, J. L., Pitkanen, A., & Carmichael, S. T. (1992). Anatomical organization of the primate amygdaloid complex. In J. P. Aggleton (Ed.), *The amygdala: Neurobiological aspects of emotion, memory, and mental dysfunction* (pp. 1–66). New York: Wiley-Liss.

Andreasen, N. C., O'Leary, D. S., Cizadlo, T., et al. (1995). Remembering the past: Two facets of episodic memory explored with positron emission tomography. *American Journal of Psychiatry, 152,* 1576–1585.

Baker, S. C., Frith, C. D., & Dolan, R. J. (1997). The interaction between mood and cognitive function studied with PET. *Psychological Medicine, 27,* 565–578.

Beauregard, M., Chertkow, H., Bub, D., Murtha, S., Dixon, R., & Evans, A. (1997). The neural substrate for concrete, abstract, and emotional word lexica: A positron emission tomography study. *Journal of Cognitive Neuroscience, 9,* 441–461.

Beauregard, M., Leroux, J. M., Bergman, S., et al. (1998). The functional neuroanatomy of major depression: An fMRI study using an emotional activation paradigm. *Neuroreport, 9,* 3253–3258.

Bench, C. J., Friston, K. J., Brown, R. G., Scott, L. C., Frackowiak, R. S., & Dolan, R. J. (1992). The anatomy of melancholia: Focal abnormalities of cerebral blood flow in major depression. *Psychological Medicine, 22,* 607–615.

Blair, R.J.R., Morris, J. S., Frith, C. D., Perrett, D. I., & Dolan, R. J. (1999). Dissociable neural responses to facial expressions of sadness and anger. *Brain, 122,* 883–893.

Blood, A. J., Zatorre, R. J., Bermudez, P., & Evans, A. C. (1999). Emotional responses to pleasant and unpleasant music correlate with activity in paralimbic brain regions. *Nature Neuroscience, 2,* 382–387.

Boecker, H., Wills, A. J., Ceballos-Baumann, A., et al. (1996). The effect of ethanol on alcohol-responsive essential tremor: A positron emission tomography study. *Annals of Neurology, 39,* 650–658.

Breier, A., Kestler, L., Adler, C., et al. (1998). Dopamine D2 receptor density and personal detachment in healthy subjects. *American Journal of Psychiatry, 155,* 1440–1442.

Breiter, H. C., Etcoff, N. L., Whalen, P. J., et al. (1996). Response and habituation of the human amygdala during visual processing of facial expression. *Neuron, 17,* 875–887.

Breiter, H. C., Gollub, R. L., Weisskoff, R. M., et al. (1997). Acute effects of cocaine on human brain activity and emotion. *Neuron, 19,* 591–611.

Bremner, J. D., Innis, R. B., Salomon, R. M., et al. (1997). Positron emission tomography measurement of cerebral metabolic correlates of tryptophan depletion-induced depressive relapse. *Archives of General Psychiatry, 54,* 364–374.

Broca, P. (1878). Anatomie comparée des circonvolutions cérébrales: Le grand lobe limbique et la scissure limbique dans la série des mammifères [Anatomic considerations of cerebral convolutions: The great limbic lobe and limbic sulci in a series of mammals]. *Rev Anthropol, 1*(Ser. 2): 385–498.

Brown, S., & Schäfer, E. A. (1888). An investigation into the functions of the occipital and temporal lobes of the monkey's brain. *Philosophical Transactions of the Royal Society of London, Series B, 179,* 303–327.

Buchsbaum, M. S., Trestman, R. L., Hazlett, E., et al. (1997). Regional cerebral blood flow during the Wisconsin Card Sort Test in schizotypal personality disorder. *Schizophrenia Research, 27,* 21–28.

Buchsbaum, M. S., Yang, S., Hazlett, E., et al. (1997). Ventricular volume and asymmetry in schizotypal personality disorder and schizophrenia assessed with magnetic resonance imaging. *Schizophrenia Research, 27,* 45–53.

Bush, G., Luu, P., & Posner, M. I. (2000). Cognitive and emotional influences in anterior cingulate cortex. *Trends in Cognitive Sciences, 4*(6), 215–222.

Bush, G., Whalen, P. J., Rosen, B. R., Jenike, M. A., McInerney, S. C., & Rauch, S. L. (1998). The counting Stroop: An interference task specialized for functional neuroimaging—validation study with functional MRI. *Human Brain Mapping, 6,* 270–282.

Cahill, L., Haier, R. J., Fallon, J., et al. (1996). Amygdala activity at encoding correlated with long-term, free recall of emotional information. *Proceedings of the National Academy of Science, , 93,* 8016–9021.

Caine, E. D., & Shoulson, I. (1983). Psychiatric syndromes in Huntington's disease. *American Journal of Psychiatry, 140,* 728–733.

Cameron, O. G., Modell, J. G., & Hariharan, M. (1990). Caffeine and human cerebral blood flow: A positron emission tomography study. *Life Sciences, 47,* 1141–1146.

Canli, T., Desmond, J. E., Zhao, Z., Glover, G., & Gabrieli, J. D. (1998). Hemispheric asymmetry for emotional stimuli detected with fMRI. *Neuroreport 9,* 3233–3239.

Cannon, W. B. (1927). The James-Lange theory of emotion: A critical examination and an alternative theory. *American Journal of Psychology, 39,* 106–124.

Cannon, W. B. (1929). *Bodily changes in pain, hunger, fear and rage* (2nd ed.). New York: Appleton.

Cloninger, C. R. (1987). A systematic method for clinical description and classification of personality variants. A proposal. *Archives of General Psychiatry, 44,* 573–588.

Cruickshank, J. M., Neil-Dwyer, G., Dorrance, D. E., Hayes, Y., & Patel, S. (1989). Acute effects of smoking on blood pressure and cerebral blood flow. *Journal of Human Hypertension, 3,* 443–449.

Dager, S. R., Layton, M. E., Strauss, W., et al. (1999). Human brain metabolic response to caffeine and the effects of tolerance. *American Journal of Psychiatry, 156,* 229–237.

Damasio, A. R., Grabowski, T. J., Bechara, A., Damasio, H., Ponto, L. L. B., & Hichwa, R. D. (1998). Neural correlates of the experience of emotion. *Society for Neuroscience Abstracts, 24,* 258.

Damasio, A. R., Grabowski, T. J., Bechara, A., et al., (1999, June). The contribution of subcortical nuclei to the processing of emotion and feeling. Abstract presented at the International Conference on Functional Mapping of the Human Brain, Düsseldorf, Germany, *NeuroImage, 9* (6, Pt. 2), S359.

Daniel, D. G., Weinberger, D. R., Jones, D. W., et al. (1991). The effect of amphetamine on regional cerebral blood flow during cognitive activation in schizophrenia. *Journal of Neuroscience, 11,* 1907–1917.

Darwin, C. (1872). *The expression of the emotions in man and animals.* London: Murray.

Darwin, C. (1998). *The expression of the emotions in man and animals* (3rd ed.). Oxford, England: Oxford University Press. (Original work published 1872)

Davidson, R. J. (1992). Anterior cerebral asymmetry and the nature of emotion. *Brain and Cognition, 20,* 125–151.

Davis, M. (1997). Neurobiology of fear responses: The role of the amygdala. *Journal of Neuropsychiatry and Clinical Neurosciences, 9,* 382–402.

De la Fuente, J. M., Goldman, S., Stanus, E., et al. (1997). Brain glucose metabolism in borderline personality disorder. *Journal of Psychiatric Research, 31,* 531–541.

De la Fuente, J. M., Lotstra, F., Goldman, S. et al. (1994). Temporal glucose metabolism in borderline personality disorder. *Journal of Psychiatric Research, 55,* 237–245.

De Raedt, R., D'Haenen, H., Everaert, H., Cluydts, R., & Bossuyt, A. (1997). Cerebral blood flow related to induction of a depressed mood within and out of the realm of attention in normal volunteers. *Journal of Psychiatry Research, 74,* 159–171.

Devinsky, O., Morrell, M. J., & Vogt, B. A. (1995). Contributions of anterior cingulate cortex to behaviour. *Brain, 118,* 279–306.

de Wit, H., Metz, J., Wagner, N., & Cooper, M. (1990). Behavioral and subjective effects of ethanol: Relationship to cerebral metabolism using PET. *Alcoholism, Clinical and Experimental Research, 14,* 482–489.

de Wit, H., Metz, J., Wagner, N., & Cooper, M. (1991). Effects of diazepam on cerebral metabolism and mood in normal volunteers. *Neuropsychopharmacology, 5,* 33–41.

Dickey, C. C., McCarley, R. W., Voglmaier, M. M., et al. (1999). Schizotypal personality disorder and MRI abnormalities of temporal lobe gray matter. *Biological Psychiatry, 45,* 1393–1402.

Dickey, C. C., Shenton, M. E., Hirayasu, Y., et al. (2000). Large CSF volume not attributable to ventricular volume in schizotypal personality disorder. *American Journal of Psychiatry, 157,* 48–54.

Direkze, M., Bayliss, S. G., & Cutting, J. C. (1971). Primary tumours of the frontal lobe. *British Journal of Clinical Practice, 25,* 207–213.

Dougherty, D. D., Shin, L. M., Alpert, N. M., et al. (1999). Anger in healthy men: A PET study using script-driven imagery. *Biological Psychiatry, 46,* 466–472.

Ekman, P., & Friesen, W. V. (1976). *Pictures of facial affect.* Palo Alto, CA: Consulting Psychologists Press.

Ernst, M., Zametkin, A. J., Matochik, J., et al. (1997). Intravenous dextroamphetamine and brain glucose metabolism. *Neuropsychopharmacology, 17,* 391–401.

Ernst, M., Zametkin, A. J., Matochik, J. A., Liebenauer, L., Fitzgerald, G. A., & Cohen, R. M. (1994). Effects of intravenous dextroamphetamine on brain metabolism in adults with attention-deficit hyperactivity disorder (ADHD): Preliminary findings. *Psychopharmacology Bulletin 30,* 219–225.

Erwin, R. J., Gur, R. C., Gur, R. E., Skolnick, B., Mawhinney-Hee, M., & Smailis, J. (1992). Facial emotion discrimination: I. Task construction and behavioral findings in normal subjects. *Psychiatry Research, 42,* 231–240.

Eysenck, H. J., (1953). *The structure of human personality.* London: Methuen.

Eysenck, H. J. (1967). *The biological basis of personality.* Springfield, IL: Thomas.

Eysenck, H. J. (1986). Psychophysiology and personality: Extraversion, neuroticism, and psychoticism. In A. Gale & J. A. Edwards (Eds.), *Physiological correlates of human behavior: Vol. 3. Individual differences and psychopathology* (pp. 13–30) Orlando, FL: Academic Press.

Farde, L., Pauli, S., Litton, J. E., Halldin, C., Neiman, J., & Sedvall, G. (1994). PET-determination of benzodiazepine receptor binding in studies on alcoholism. *EXS, 71,* 143–153.

Federoff, J. P., Starkstein, S. E., Forrester, A. W., et al. (1992). Depression in patients with acute traumatic brain injury. *American Journal of Psychiatry, 149,* 918–923.

Fischer, H., Wik, G., & Fredrikson, M. (1996). Functional neuroanatomy of robbery reexperience: Affective memories studied with PET. *Neuroreport, 7,* 2081–2086.

Folstein, S. E., Folstein, M. F. (1983). Psychiatric features of Huntington's disease: Recent approaches and findings. *Psychiatric Development, 1,* 193–205.

Forster, A., Juge, O., & Morel, D. (1982). Effects of midazolam on cerebral blood flow in human volunteers. *Anesthesiology, 56,* 453–455.

Foster, N. L., VanDerSpek, A. F., Aldrich, M. S., et al. (1987). The effect of diazepam sedation on cerebral glucose metabolism in Alzheimer's disease as measured using positron emission tomography. *Journal of Cerebral Blood Flow and Metabolism, 7,* 415–420.

Fredrikson, M., Wik, G., Annas, P., Ericson, K., & Stone-Elander, S. (1995). Functional neuroanatomy of visually elicited simple phobic fear: Additional data and theoretical analysis. *Psychophysiology, 32,* 43–48.

Fredrikson, M., Wik, G., Fischer, H., & Andersson, J. (1995). Affective and attentive neural networks in humans: A PET study of Pavlovian conditioning. *Neuroreport, 7,* 97–101.

Fredrikson, M., Wik, G., Greitz, T., et al. (1993). Regional cerebral blood flow during experimental phobic fear. *Psychophysiology, 30,* 126–130.

Freud, S. (1927). *The ego and the id.* London: Hogarth Press.

Friston, K. J., Frith, C. D., Liddle, P. F., & Frackowiak, R. S. (1991). Comparing functional (PET) images: The assessment of significant change. *Journal of Cerebral Blood Flow and Metabolism, 11,* 690–699.

Fujikawa, T., Yamawaki, S., & Touhouda, Y. (1995). Silent cerebral infarctions in patients with late-onset mania. *Stroke, 26,* 946–949.

Gemar, M. C., Kapur, S., Segal, Z. V., Brown, G. M., & Houle, S. (1996). Effects of self-generated sad mood on regional cerebral activity: A PET study in normal subjects. *Depression, 4,* 81–88.

George, M. S., Cloninger, C. R., Kimbrell, T. A., et al. (1996, December). *Toward the neurobiological basis of temperament: PET studies of Cloninger's tridimensional scale in healthy adults.* Paper presented at the Annual Meeting of the American College of Neuropsychopharmacology, San Juan, Puerto Rico.

George, M. S. Kellner, C. H., Bernstein, H., & Goust, J. M. (1994). A magnetic resonance imaging investigation into mood disorders in multiple sclerosis. *Journal of Nervous and Mental Disease, 182,* 410–412.

George, M. S. Ketter, T. A., Gill, D. S., et al. (1993). Brain regions involved in recognizing facial emotion or identity: An oxygen-15 PET study. *Journal of Neuropsychiatry and Clinical Neurosciences, 5,* 384–394.

George, M. S. Ketter, T. A., Parekh, P. I., Herscovitch, P., &

Post, R. M. (1996). Gender differences in regional cerebral blood flow during transient self-induced sadness or happiness. *Biological Psychiatry, 40*, 859–871.

George, M. S. Ketter, T. A., Parekh, P. I., et al. (1994, May). *Personality traits correlate with resting rCBF.* Paper presented at the annual meeting of the American Psychiatric Association, Philadelphia.

George, M. S. Ketter, T. A., Parekh, P. I., Horwitz, B., Herscovitch, P., & Post, R. M. (1995). Brain activity during transient sadness and happiness in healthy women. *American Journal of Psychiatry, 152*, 341–351.

George, M. S. Parekh, P. I., Rosinsky, N., et al. (1996). Understanding emotional prosody activates right hemisphere regions. *Archives of Neurology, 53*, 665–670.

Ghatan, P. H., Ingvar, M., Eriksson, L., et al. (1998). Cerebral effects of nicotine during cognition in smokers and non-smokers. *Psychopharmacology (Berlin) 136*, 179–189.

Gollub, R. L., Breiter, H. C. Kantor, H., et al. (1998). Cocaine decreases cortical cerebral blood flow but does not obscure regional activation in functional magnetic resonance imaging in human subjects. *Journal of Blood Flow and Metabolism, 18*, 724–734.

Gottschalk, L. A., Buchsbaum, M. S., Gillin, J. C., Wu, J., Reynolds, C. A., & Herrera, D. B. (1992). The effect of anxiety and hostility in silent mentation on localized cerebral glucose metabolism. *Comprehensive Psychiatry 33*, 52–59.

Gottschalk, L. A., Buchsbaum, M. S., Gillin, J. C., Wu, J. C., Reynolds, C. A., & Herrera, D. B. (1991). Anxiety levels in dreams: Relation to localized cerebral glucose metabolic rate. *Brain Research 538*, 107–110.

Goyer, P. F., Andreason, P. J., Semple, W. E., et al. (1994). Positron-emission tomography and personality disorders. *Neuropsychopharmacology, 10*, 21–28.

Gray, J. A. (1970). The psychophysiological basis of introversion-extraversion. *Behaviour Research Therapy, 8*, 249–266.

Gray, J. A. (1972). The psychophysiological basis of introversion-extraversion: A modifiction of Eysenck's theory. In V. D. Nebylitsyn & J. A. Gray (Eds.), *The biological bases of individual behavior* (pp. 182–205). New York: Academic Press.

Gray, J. A. (1987). The neuropsychology of emotion and personality. In S. M. Stahl, S. D. Iverson, & E. C. Goodman (Eds.), *Cognitive neurochemistry* (pp. 171–190). Oxford, England: Oxford University Press.

Grodd, W., Schneider, F., Klose, U., & Nägele, T. (1995). Functional magnetic resonance tomography of psychological functions exemplified by experimentally induced emotions. *Radiologe, 35*, 283–289.

Gross, J. J., & Levenson, R. W. (1995). Emotion elicitation using films. *Cognition and Emotion 9*, 87–108.

Gur, R. C., Gur, R. E., Resnick, S. M., Skolnick, B. E., Alavi, A., & Reivich, M. (1987). The effect of anxiety on cortical cerebral blood flow and metabolism. *Journal of Blood Flow and Metabolism, 7*, 173–177.

Haier, R. J., Sokolski, K., Katz, M., & Buchsbaum, M. S. (1987). The study of personality with positron emission tomography. In J. Strelau & H. J. Eysenck (Eds.), *Personality dimensions and arousal* (pp. 251–267). New York: Plenum.

Hemmingsen, R., Vorstrup, S., Clemmesen, L., et al. (1988). Cerebral blood flow during delirium tremens and related clinical states studied with xenon-133 inhalation tomography. *American Journal of Psychiatry*, 145, 1384–1390.

Honer, W. G., Hurwitz, T., Li, D. K. Palmer, M., & Paty, D. W. (1987). Temporal lobe involvement in multiple sclerosis patients with psychiatric disorders. *Archives of Neurology, 44*, 187–190.

Horn, S. (1974). Some psychological factors in Parkinsonism. *Journal of Neurology, Neurosurgery, and Psychiatry, 37*, 27–31.

Ingvar, M., Ghatan, P. H., Wirsen-Meurling, A., et al. (1998). Alcohol activates the cerebral reward system in man. *Journal of Studies on Alcohol, 59*, 258–269.

Intrator, J., Hare, R., Stritzke, P., et al. (1997). A brain imaging (single photon emission computerized tomography) study of semantic and affective processing in psychopaths. *Biological Psychiatry, 42*, 96–103.

Irwin, W., Davidson, R. J., Lowe, M. J., Mock, B. J., Sorenson, J. A., & Turski, P. A. (1996). Human amygdala activation detected with echo-planar functional magnetic resonance imaging. *Neuroreport, 7*, 1765–1769.

Irwin, W., Mock, B. J., Sutton, S. K. et al. (1997). Positive and negative affective responses: Neural circuitry revealed using functional magnetic resonance imaging. *Society of Neuroscience Abstracts, 23*, 1318.

Jackson, J. H. (1887). Remarks on evolution and dissolution of the nervous system. *Journal of Mental Science, 33*, 25–48.

James, W. (1884). What is an emotion? *Mind, 9*, 188–205.

James, W. (1890). *The principles of psychology* (Vol. 2, pp. 442–485). New York: Henry Holt.

Jampala, V. C., & Abrams, R. (1983). Mania secondary to left and right hemisphere damage. *American Journal of Psychiatry, 140*, 1197–1199.

Johnson, B., Lamki, L., Fang, B., et al. (1998). Demonstration of dose-dependent global and regional cocaine-induced reductions in brain blood flow using a novel approach to quantitative single photon emission computerized tomography. *Neuropsychopharmacology, 18*, 377–384.

Johnson, D. L., Wiebe, J. S., Gold, S. M., et al. (1999). Cerebral blood flow and personality: A positron emission tomography study. *American Journal of Psychiatry, 156*, 252–257.

Jorge, R. E., Robinson, R. G., Starkstein, S. E., Arndt, S. V., Forrester, A. W., & Geisler, F. H. (1993). Secondary mania following traumatic brain injury. *American Journal of Psychiatry, 150*, 916–921.

Kahn, D. A., Prohovnik, I., Lucas, L. R., & Sackeim, H. A. (1989). Dissociated effects of amphetamine on arousal and cortical blood flow in humans. *Biological Psychiatry, 25*, 755–767.

Kalin, N. H., Davidson, R. J., Irwin, W., et al. (1997). Functional magnetic resonance imaging studies of emotional processing in normal and depressed patients: Effects of venlafaxine. *Journal of Clinical Psychiatry, 58* (Suppl. 16), 32–39.

Kanakaratnam, G., & Direkze, M. (1976). Aspects of primary tumours of the frontal lobe. *British Journal of Clinical Practice, 30*, 220–221.

Kaschka, W., Feistel, H., & Ebert, D. (1995). Reduced benzodiazepine receptor binding in panic disorders measured by iomazenil SPECT. *Journal of Psychiatric Research, 29*, 427–434.

Kaufman, M. J., Levin, J. M., Maas, L. C., et al. (1998). Cocaine decreases relative cerebral blood volume in humans: A dynamic susceptibility contrast magnetic resonance imaging study. *Psychopharmacology (Berlin), 138,* 76–81.

Ketter, T. A., Andreason, P. J., George, M. S., et al. (1996). Anterior paralimbic mediation of procaine-induced emotional and psychosensory experiences. *Archives of General Psychiatry, 53,* 59–69.

Ketter, T. A., George, M. S., Kimbrell, T. A., Benson, B. E., & Post, R. M. (1996): Functional brain imaging, limbic function, and affective disorders. *Neuroscientist, 2,* 55–65.

Ketter, T. A., Kimbrell, T. A., George, M. S., et al. (1999). Baseline cerebral hypermetabolism associated with carbamazepine response, and hypometabolism with nimodipine response in mood disorders. *Biological Psychiatry, 46,* 1364–1374.

Ketter, T. A., Wang, P., Sachs, N., Rennicke, C. M., & Segall, G. M. (2000, September). *Differential anterior paralimbic metabolic decreases with sustained sadness and happiness in healthy volunteers.* Paper presented at the annual meeting of the American College of Neuropsychopharmacology, San Juan, Puerto Rico.

Kimbrell, T. A., George, M. S., Parekh, P. I., et al. (1999). Regional brain activity during transient self-induced anxiety and anger in healthy adults. *Biological Psychiatry, 46,* 454–465.

Kimura, K., Matsumoto, M., Handa, N., Hashikawa, K., & Moriwaki, H. (1993). Non-invasive assessment of acute effects of cigarette smoking on cerebral circulation. *Yakubutsu Seishin Kodo, 13,* 183–190.

Klüver, H., & Bucy, P. C. (1939). Preliminary analysis of functions of the temporal lobes in monkeys. *Archives of Neurologic Psychiatry, 42,* 979–1000.

Kosslyn, S. M., Shin, L. M., Thompson, W. L., et al. (1996). Neural effects of visualizing and perceiving aversive stimuli: A PET investigation. *Neuroreport, 7,* 1569–1576.

Kuikka, J. T., Pitkanen, A., Lepola, U., et al. (1995). Abnormal regional benzodiazepine receptor uptake in the prefrontal cortex in patients with panic disorder. *Nuclear Medicine Communications, 16,* 273–280.

Kuruoglu, A. C., Arikan, Z., Vural, G., Karatas, M., Arac, M., & Isik, E. (1996). Single photon emission computerised tomography in chronic alcoholism: Antisocial personality disorder may be associated with decreased frontal perfusion. *British Journal of Psychiatry, 169,* 348–354.

Kwon, J. S., Shenton, M. E., Hirayasu, Y., et al. (1998). MRI study of cavum septi pellucidi in schizophrenia, affective disorder, and schizotypal personality disorder. *American Journal of Psychiatry, 155,* 509–515.

Laakso, A., Vilkman, H., Kajander, J., et al. (2000). Prediction of detached personality in healthy subjects by low dopamine transporter binding. *American Journal of Psychiatry, 157,* 290–292.

LaBar, K. S., Gatenby, J. C. Gore, J. C., LeDoux, J. E., & Phelps, E. A. (1998). Human amygdala activation during conditioned fear acquisition and extinction: A mixed-trial fMRI study. *Neuron, 20,* 937–945.

LaBar, K. S., Gatenby, J. C., Gore, J. C., & Phelps, E. A. (1998). Role of the amygdala in emotional picture evaluation as revealed by fMRI. *Journal of Cognitive Neuroscience,* (Suppl.), S108.

Lane, R. D., Reiman, E. M., Ahern, G. L., Schwartz, G. E., & Davidson, R. J. (1997). Neuroanatomical correlates of happiness, sadness, and disgust. *American Journal of Psychiatry, 154,* 926–933.

Lane, R. D., Reiman, E. M., Bradley, M. M., et al. (1997). Neuroanatomical correlates of pleasant and unpleasant emotion. *Neuropsychologia, 35,* 1437–1444.

Lang, P. J. (1995). The emotion probe: Studies of motivation and attention. *American Psychologist, 50,* 372–385.

Lang, P. J., Bradley, M. M., & Cuthbert, B. N. (1995). *The International Affective Picture System (IAPS): Photographic slides.* Gainesville: University of Florida Press.

Lang, P. J., Bradley, M. M., Fitzsimmons, J. R., et al. (1998). Emotional arousal and activation of the visual cortex: An fMRI analysis. *Psychophysiology, 35,* 199–210.

Lange, C. G., & James W. (1922). *The emotions* (I. A. Haupt, Trans.). Baltimore: Williams & Wilkins.

Laruelle, M., Abi-Dargham, A., van Dyck, C. H., et al. (1995). SPECT imaging of striatal dopamine release after amphetamine challenge. *Journal of Nuclear Medicine, 36,* 1182–1190.

LeDoux, J. E. (1995). Emotion: Clues from the brain. *Annu Rev Psychol 46,* 209–235.

Li, S. J., Biswal, B., Li, Z., et al. (2000). Cocaine administration decreases functional connectivity in human primary visual and motor cortex as detected by functional MRI. *Magnetic Resonance Medicine, 43,* 45–51.

London, E. D. (1995). Mapping the cerebral metabolic response to nicotine. In E. F. Domino (Ed.), *Brain imaging of nicotine and tobacco smoking* (pp. 153–166). Ann Arbor, MI: NPP Books.

London, E. D., Cascella, N. G., Wong, D. F., et al. (1990). Cocaine-induced reduction of glucose utilization in human brain: A study using positron emission tomography and [fluorine 18]-fluorodeoxyglucose. *Archives of General Psychiatry, 47,* 567–574.

Lyoo, I. K., Han, M. H, & Cho, D. Y. (1998). A brain MRI study in subjects with borderline personality disorder. *Journal of Affective Disorders, 50,* 235–243.

Maas, L. C., Lukas, S. E., Kaufman, M. J., et al. (1998). Functional magnetic resonance imaging of human brain activation during cue-induced cocaine craving. *American Journal of Psychiatry, 155,* 124–126.

MacLean, P. D. (1952). Some psychiatric implications of physiological studies on the frontotemporal portion of limbic system (visceral brain). *Electroencephalography and Clinical Neurophysiology, 4,* 407–418.

MacLean, P. D. (1990). *The triune brain in evolution: Role in paleocerebral functions.* New York: Plenum.

Maddock, R. J., & Buonocore, M. H. (1997). Activation of left posterior cingulate gyrus by the auditory presentation of threat-related words: An fMRI study. *Psychiatry Research, 75,* 1–14.

Malison, R. T., Best, S. E., Wallace, E. A., et al. (1995). Euphorigenic doses of cocaine reduce [123I]beta-CIT SPECT measures of dopamine transporter availability in human cocaine addicts. *Psychopharmacology (Berlin), 122,* 358–362.

Malizia, A. L., Cunningham, V. J., Bell, C. J., Liddle, P. F., Jones, T., & Nutt, D. J. (1998). Decreased brain GABA(A)-benzodiazepine receptor binding in panic disorder: Preliminary results from a quantitative PET study. *Archives of General Psychiatry 55,* 715–720.

Marlowe, W. B., Mancall, E. L., & Thomas, J. J. (1975). Complete Kluver-Bucy syndrome in man. *Cortex, 11,* 53–59.

Mathew, R. J., Barr, D. L., & Weinman, M. L. (1983). Caffeine and cerebral blood flow. *British Journal of Psychiatry, 143,* 604–608.

Mathew, R. J., Weinman, M. L., & Barr, D. L. (1984). Personality and regional cerebral blood flow. *British Journal of Psychiatry, 144*, 529–532.

Mathew, R. J., & Wilson, W. H. (1985a). Caffeine consumption, withdrawal and cerebral blood flow. *Headache, 25*, 305–309.

Mathew, R. J., & Wilson, W. H. (1985b). Dextroamphetamine-induced changes in regional cerebral blood flow. *Psychopharmacology (Berlin), 87*, 298–302.

Mathew, R. J., & Wilson, W. H. (1986). Regional cerebral blood flow changes associated with ethanol intoxication. *Stroke, 17*, 1156–1159.

Mathew, R. J., & Wilson, W. H. (1989). Changes in cerebral blood flow and mental state after amphetamine challenge in schizophrenic patients. *Neuropsychobiology, 21*, 117–23.

Mathew, R. J., & Wilson, W. H. (1990). Behavioral and cerebrovascular effects of caffeine in patients with anxiety disorders. *Acta Psychiatria Scandinavica, 82*, 17–22.

Mathew, R. J., & Wilson, W. H., (1991). Evaluation of the effects of diazepam and an experimental anti-anxiety drug on regional cerebral blood flow. *Journal of Psychiatric Research, 40*, 125–34.

Mathew, R. J., Wilson, W. H., Chiu, N. Y., Turkington, T. G., Degrado, T. R., & Coleman, R. E. (1999). Regional cerebral blood flow and depersonalization after tetrahydrocannabinol administration. *Acta Psychiatria Scandinavica, 100*, 67–75.

Mathew, R. J., Wilson, W. H., Coleman, R. E., Turkington, T. G., & DeGrado, T. R. (1997). Marijuana intoxication and brain activation in marijuana smokers. *Life Sciences, 60*, 2075–2089.

Mathew, R. J., Wilson, W. H., Lowe, J. V., & Humphries, D. (1996). Acute changes in cranial blood flow after cocaine hydrochloride. *Biological Psychiatry 40*, 609–616.

Mathew, R. J., Wilson, W. H., Turkington, T. G., & Coleman, R. E. (1998). Cerebellar activity and disturbed time sense after THC. *Brain Research 797*, 183–189.

Matochik, J. A., Nordahl, T. E., & Gross, M., et al. (1993). Effects of acute stimulant medication on cerebral metabolism in adults with hyperactivity. *Neuropsychopharmacology, 8*, 377–386.

Mattay, V. S., Berman, K. F., Ostrem, J. L., et al. (1996). Dextroamphetamine enhances "neural network-specific" physiological signals: A positron-emission tomography rCBF study. *Journal of Neuroscience, 16*, 4816–4822.

Matthew, E., Andreason, P., Pettigrew, K., et al. (1995). Benzodiazepine receptors mediate regional blood flow changes in the living human brain. *Proceedings of the National Academy of Sciences USA, 92*, 2775–2779.

Mayberg, H. S., Liotti, M., Brannan, S. K., et al. (1999). Reciprocal limbic-cortical function and negative mood: Converging PET findings in depression and normal sadness. *American Journal of Psychiatry 156*, 675–682.

McGaugh, J. L., Introini-Collison, I. B., Cahill, L. F., et al. (1993). Neuromodulatory systems and memory storage: Role of the amygdala. *Behavioural Brain Research, 58*, 81–90.

Mega, M. S., Cummings, J. L., Salloway, S., & Malloy, P. (1997). The limbic system: An anatomic, phylogenetic, and clinical perspective. *Journal of Neuropsychiatry and Clinical Neurosciences 9*, 315–330.

Mendez, M. F., Adams, N. L., & Lewandowski, K. S. (1989). Neurobehavioral changes associated with caudate lesions. *Neurology, 39*, 349–354.

Menza, M. A., Mark, M. H., Burn, D. J., & Brooks, D. J. (1995). Personality correlates of [18F]dopa striatal uptake: Results of positron-emission tomography in Parkinson's disease. *Journal of Neuropsychiatry and Clinical Neurosciences, 7*, 176–179.

Mindham, R. H. (1970). Psychiatric symptoms in Parkinsonism. *Journal of Neurology, Neurosurgery, and Psychiatry, 33*, 188–91.

Moller, A., Wiedemann, G., Rohde, U., Backmund, H., & Sonntag, A. (1994). Correlates of cognitive impairment and depressive mood disorder in multiple sclerosis. *Acta Psychiatria Scandinavica 89*, 117–121.

Morris, J. S., Friston, K. J., Buchel, C., et al. (1998). A neuromodulatory role for the human amygdala in processing emotional facial expressions. *Brain, 121*, 47–57.

Morris, J. S., Frith, C. D., Perrett, D. I., et al. (1996). A differential neural response in the human amygdala to fearful and happy facial expressions. *Nature, 383*, 812–815.

Morris, J. S., Ohman, A., & Dolan, R. J. (1998). Conscious and unconscious emotional learning in the human amygdala. *Nature, 393*, 467–470.

Morris, J. S., Ohman, A., & Dolan, R. J. (1999). A subcortical pathway to the right amygdala mediating "unseen" fear. *Proceedings of the National Academy of Sciences USA, 96*, 1680–1685.

Mountz, J. M., Modell, J. G., Wilson, M. W., et al. (1989). Positron emission tomographic evaluation of cerebral blood flow during state anxiety in simple phobia. *Archives of General Psychiatry, 46*, 501–504.

Nagata, K., Shinohara, T., Kanno, I., Hatazawa, J., & Domino, E. F. (1995). Effects of tobacco cigarette smoking on cerebral blood flow in normal adults. In E. F. Domino (Ed.), *Brain imaging of nicotine and tobacco smoking* (pp. 95–108). Ann Arbor, MI: NPP Books.

Nehlig, A., Daval, J. L., & Debry, G. (1992). Caffeine and the central nervous system: Mechanisms of action, biochemical, metabolic and psychostimulant effects. *Brain Research Reviews 17*, 139–170.

Nyback, H., Nordberg, A., Langstrom, B., et al. (1989). Attempts to visualize nicotinic receptors in the brain of monkey and man by positron emission tomography. *Progress in Brain Research, 79*, 313–1319.

O'Carroll, R. E., Moffoot, A. P., Van Beck, M., et al. (1993). The effect of anxiety induction on the regional uptake of $^{99m}$Tc-exametazime in simple phobia as shown by single photon emission tomography (SPET). *Journal of Affective Disorders, 28*, 203–210.

Papez, J. W. (1937). A proposed mechanism of emotion. *Archives of Neurologic Psychiatry 38*, 725–743.

Paradiso, S., Johnson, D. L., Andreasen, N. C., et al. (1999). Cerebral blood flow changes associated with attribution of emotional valence to pleasant, unpleasant, and neutral visual stimuli in a PET study of normal subjects: *American Journal of Psychiatry 156*, 1618–1629.

Paradiso, S., Robinson, R. G. Andreasen, N. C., et al. (1997). Emotional activation of limbic circuitry in elderly normal subjects in a PET study. *American Journal of Psychiatry, 154*, 384–389.

Pardo, J. V., Pardo, P. J., & Raichle, M. E. (1993). Neural correlates of self-induced dysphoria. *American Journal of Psychiatry, 150*, 713–719.

Partiot, A., Grafman, J., Sadato, N., Wachs, J., & Hallett, M. (1995). Brain activation during the generation of non-emotional and emotional plans. *Neuroreport, 6,* 1397–1400.

Pearlson, G. D., Jeffery, P. J., Harris, G. J., Ross, C. A., Fischman, M. W., & Camargo, E. E. (1993). Correlation of acute cocaine-induced changes in local cerebral blood flow with subjective effects. *American Journal of Psychiatry, 150,* 495–497.

Phillips, M. L., Young, A. W., Scott, S. K., et al. (1998). Neural responses to facial and vocal expressions of fear and disgust. *Proceedings of the Royal Society of London, Series B, 265,* 1809–1817.

Phillips, M. L., Young, A. W., Senior, C., et al. (1997). A specific neural substrate for perceiving facial expressions of disgust. *Nature, 389,* 495–498.

Raine, A., Buchsbaum, M. S., Stanley, J., Lottenberg, S., Abel, L., & Stoddard, J. (1994). Selective reductions in prefrontal glucose metabolism in murderers. *Biological Psychiatry, 36,* 365–373.

Raine, A., Lencz, T., Bihrle, S., LaCasse, L., & Colletti, P. (2000). Reduced prefrontal gray matter volume and reduced autonomic activity in antisocial personality disorder. *Archives of General Psychiatry, 57,* 119–127.

Raine, A., Sheard, C., Reynolds, G. P., & Lencz, T. (1992). Pre-frontal structural and functional deficits associated with individual differences in schizotypal personality. *Schizophrenia Research, 7,* 237–247.

Rauch, S. L., Savage, C. R., Alpert, N. M., Fischman, A. J., & Jenike, M. A. (1997). The functional neuroanatomy of anxiety: A study of three disorders using positron emission tomography and symptom provocation. *Biological Psychiatry, 42,* 446–452.

Rauch, S. L., Savage, C. R., Alpert, N. M., et al. (1995). A positron emission tomographic study of simple phobic symptom provocation. *Archives of General Psychiatry, 52,* 20–28.

Rauch, S. L., van der Kolk, B. A., Fisler, R. E., et al. (1996). A symptom provocation study of posttraumatic stress disorder using positron emission tomography and script-driven imagery. *Archives of General Psychiatry, 53,* 380–387.

Reiman, E. M., Fusselman, M. J., Fox, P. T., & Raichle, M. E. (1989). Neuroanatomical correlates of anticipatory anxiety. *Science, 243,* 1071–1074.

Reiman, E. M., Lane, R. D., Ahern, G. L., et al. (1997). Neuroanatomical correlates of externally and internally generated human emotion. *American Journal of Psychiatry, 154,* 918–925.

Reiman, E. M., Raichle, M. E., & Robins, E. (1989). Involvement of the temporal poles in pathological and normal forms of anxiety. *Journal of Cerebral Blood Flow and Metabolism, 9,* S589.

Robinson, R. G. (1997). Neuropsychiatric consequences of stroke. *Annual Review of Medicine, 48,* 217–229.

Rolls, E. T. (1995). A theory of emotion and consciousness, and its application to understanding the neural basis of emotion. In M. S. Gazzaniga (Ed.). *The cognitive neurosciences* (pp. 1091–1106). Cambridge, MA: MIT Press.

Roy-Byrne, P., Fleishaker, J., Arnett, C., et al. (1993). Effects of acute and chronic alprazolam treatment on cerebral blood flow, memory, sedation, and plasma catecholamines. *Neuropsychopharmacology, 8,* 161–169.

Sano, M., Wendt, P. E., Wirsen, A., Stenberg, G. Risberg, J., & Ingvar, D. H. (1993). Acute effects of alcohol on regional cerebral blood flow in man. *Journal of Studies on Alcohol, 54,* 369–376.

Schlegel, S., Steinert, H., Bockisch, A., Hahn, K., Schloesser, R., & Benkert, O. (1994). Decreased benzodiazepine receptor binding in panic disorder measured by IOMAZENIL-SPECT: A preliminary report. *European Archives of Psychiatry and Clinical Neuroscience, 244,* 49–51.

Schneider, F., Grodd, W., Weiss, U., et al. (1997). Functional MRI reveals left amygdala activation during emotion. *Journal of Psychiatric Research, 76,* 75–82.

Schneider, F., Gur, R. C., Jaggi, J. L., & Gur, R. E. (1994). Differential effects of mood on cortical cerebral blood flow: A $^{133}$xenon clearance study. *Journal of Psychiatric Research, 52,* 215–236.

Schneider, F., Gur, R. E., Mozley, L. H., et al. (1995). Mood effects on limbic blood flow correlate with emotional self-rating: A PET study with oxygen-15 labeled water. *Journal of Psychiatric Research, 61,* 265–283.

Schneider, F., Hatbel, U., Kessler, C., Salloum, J. B., & Posse, S. (2000). Gender differences in regional cerebral activity during sadness. *Human Brain Mapping, 9,* 226–238.

Schneider, F., Weiss, U., Kessler, C., et al. (1999). Subcortical correlates of differential classical conditioning of aversive emotional reactions in social phobia. *Biological Psychiatry, 45,* 863–871.

Schneider, F., Weiss, U., Kessler, C., et al. (1998). Differential amygdala activation in schizophrenia during sadness. *Schizophrenia Research, 34,* 133–142.

Schwartz, J. A., Speed, N. M., Gross, M. D., et al. (1993). Acute effects of alcohol administration on regional cerebral blood flow: The role of acetate. *Alcoholism, Clinical and Experimental Research, 17,* 1119–1123.

Servan-Schreiber, D., Perlstein, W. M., Cohen, J. D., & Mintun, M. (1998). Selective pharmacological activation of limbic structures in human volunteers: a positron emission tomography study. *Journal of Neuropsychiatry and Clinical Neurosciences, 10,* 148–159.

Shin, L. M., Kosslyn, S. M., McNally, R. J., et al. (1997). Visual imagery and perception in posttraumatic stress disorder: A positron emission tomographic investigation. *Archives of General Psychiatry, 54,* 233–241.

Siever, L. J., Buchsbaum, M. S., New, A. S., et al. (1999). d,1-fenfluramine response in impulsive personality disorder assessed with [18F]fluorodeoxyglucose positron emission tomography. *Neuropsychopharmacology, 20,* 413–423.

Sobel, N., Prabhakaran, V., Desmond, J. E., et al. (1998). Sniffing and smelling: Separate subsystems in the human olfactory cortex. *Nature, 392,* 282–286.

Sprengelmeyer, R., Rausch, M., Eysel, U. T., & Przuntek, H. (1998). Neural structures associated with recognition of facial expressions of basic emotions. *Proceedings of the Royal Society of London, Series B, 265,* 1927–1931.

Starkstein, S. E., & Robinson, R. G., (1989). Affective disorders and cerebrovascular disease. *British Journal of Psychiatry, 154,* 170–182.

Stein, E. A., Pankiewicz, J., Harsch, H. H., et al. (1998). Nicotine-induced limbic cortical activation in the human brain: A functional MRI study. *American Journal of Psychiatry, 155,* 1009–1015.

Stenberg, G., Risberg, J., Warkentin, S., & Rosén, I. (1990) Regional patterns of cortical blood flow distinguish extraverts from introverts. *Personal and Individual Differences, 11,* 663–673.

Stern, R. A., & Bachmann, D. L. (1991). Depressive symptoms following stroke. *American Journal of Psychiatry, 148*, 351–356.

Stiller, D., Gaschler-Markefski, B., Baumgart, F., et al. (1997). Lateralized processing of speech prosodies in the temporal cortex: A 3-T functional magnetic resonance imaging study. *MAGMA, 5*, 275–284.

Sutton, S. K., Davidson, R. J., Donzella, B., Irwin, W., & Dottl, D. A., (1997). Manipulating affective state using extended picture presentations. *Psychophysiology, 34*, 217–226.

Talairach, J., & Tournoux, P. (1988). *Co-planar stereotaxic atlas of the human brain* (M. Rayport, Trans.). New York: Thieme Medical Publishers.

Taylor, S. F., Liberzon, I., Fig, L. M., Decker, L. R., Minoshima, S., & Koeppe, R. A. (1998). The effect of emotional content on visual recognition memory: A PET activation study. *Neuroimage, 8*, 188–197.

Teasdale, J. D., Howard, R. J., Cox, S. G., et al. (1999): Functional MRI study of the cognitive generation of affect. *American Journal of Psychiatry, 156*, 209–215.

Tiihonen, J., Kuikka, J., Hakola, P. et al. (1994). Acute ethanol-induced changes in cerebral blood flow. *American Journal of Psychiatry, 151*, 1505–1508.

Trivedi, M. H., Blackburn, T., Lewis, S., et al. (1995). Effects of amphetamine in major depressive disorder using functional MRI [Abstract]. *Biological Psychiatry, 37*(9), 657.

Tutus, A., Kugu, N., Sofuoglu, S., et al. (1998). Transient frontal hypoperfusion in Tc-99m hexamethylpropyleneamineoxime single photon emission computed tomography imaging during alcohol withdrawal. *Biological Psychiatry, 43*, 923–928.

Velten, E., Jr. (1968). A laboratory task for induction of mood states. *Behaviour Research and Therapy, 6*, 473–482.

Veselis, R. A., Reinsel, R. A., Beattie, B. J., et al. (1997). Midazolam changes cerebral blood flow in discrete brain regions: An H2(15)O positron emission tomography study. *Anesthesiology, 87*, 1106–1107.

Vogt, B. A., Finch, D. M., & Olson, C. R., (1992). Functional heterogeneity in cingulate cortex: The anterior executive and posterior evaluative regions. *Cerebral Cortex, 2*, 435–443.

Volkow, N. D., Gillespie, H., Mullani, N., et al. (1991). Cerebellar metabolic activation by delta-9-tetrahydrocannabinol in human brain: A study with positron emission tomography and 18F-2-fluoro-2-deoxyglucose. *Journal of Psychiatric Research, 40*, 69–78.

Volkow, N. D., Gillespie, H., Mullani, N., et al. (1996). Brain glucose metabolism in chronic marijuana users at baseline and during marijuana intoxication. *Journal of Psychiatric Research, 67*, 29–38.

Volkow, N. D., Hitzemann, R., Wolf, A. R., et al. (1990). Acute effects of ethanol on regional brain glucose metabolism and transport. *Journal of Psychiatric Research, 35*, 39–48.

Volkow, N. D., Mullani, N., Gould, L., et al. (1988). Effects of acute alcohol intoxication on cerebral blood flow measured with PET. *Journal of Psychiatric Research, 24*, 201–209.

Volkow, N. D., Tancredi, L. R., Grant, C., et al. (1995). Brain glucose metabolism in violent psychiatric patients: A preliminary study. *Journal of Psychiatric Research, 61*, 243–253.

Volkow, N. D., Wang, G. J., Begleiter, H., et al. (1995). Regional brain metabolic response to lorazepam in sub-

jects at risk for alcoholism. *Alcoholism, Clinical and Experimental Research, 19*, 510–516.

Volkow, N. D., Wang, G. J., Fischman, M. W., et al. (1997). Relationship between subjective effects of cocaine and dopamine transporter occupancy. *Nature, 386*, 827–830.

Volkow, N. D. Wang, G. J., Hitzemann, R., et al. (1995). Depression of thalamic metabolism by lorazepam is associated with sleepiness. *Neuropsychopharmacology, 12* 123–132.

Volkow, N. D. Wang, G. J., Overall, J. E., et al. (1997). Regional brain metabolic response to lorazepam in alcoholics during early and late alcohol detoxification. *Alcoholism, Clinical and Experimental Research, 21*, 1278–1284.

Vollenweider, F. X., Maguire, R. P., Leenders, K. L., Mathys, K., & Angst, J. (1998). Effects of high amphetamine dose on mood and cerebral glucose metabolism in normal volunteers using positron emission tomography (PET). *Journal of Psychiatric Research, 83*, 149–162.

Wallace, E. A., Wisniewski, G., Zubal, G., et al. (1996). Acute cocaine effects on absolute cerebral blood flow. *Psychopharmacology (Berlin), 128*, 17–20.

Wang, G. J., Volkow, N. D., Fowler, J. S., et al. (1999). Regional brain metabolic activation during craving elicited by recall of previous drug experiences. *Life Sciences, 64*, 775–784.

Wang, G. J., Volkow, N. D., Fowler, J. S., Hitzemann, R. J., Pappas, N. R., & Netusil, N. (1998). Evaluation of gender difference in regional brain metabolic responses to lorazepam. *Journal of Psychiatric Research, 82*, 37–46.

Wang, G. J., Volkow, N. D., Levy, A. V., et al. (1999). Measuring reproducibility of regional brain metabolic responses to lorazepam using statistical parametric maps. *Journal of Nuclear Medicine, 40*, 715–720.

Wang, G. J., Volkow, N. D., Overall, J., et al. (1996). Reproducibility of regional brain metabolic responses to lorazepam. *Journal of Nuclear Medicine, 37*, 1609–1613.

Whalen, P. J., Bush, G., McNally, R. J., et al. (1998). The emotional counting Stroop paradigm: A functional magnetic resonance imaging probe of the anterior cingulate affective division. *Biological Psychiatry 44*, 1219–1228.

Whalen, P. J., Rauch, S. L., Etcoff, N. L., McInerney, S. C., Lee, M. B., & Jenike, M. A., (1998). Masked presentations of emotional facial expressions modulate amygdala activity without explicit knowledge. *Journal of Neuroscience, 18*, 411–418.

Wik, G., Fredrikson, M., Ericson, K., Eriksson, L., Stone-Elander, S., & Greitz, T. (1993). A functional cerebral response to frightening visual stimulation. *Journal of Psychiatric Research, 50*, 15–24.

Wolf, J., Friberg, L., Jensen, J., Hansen, P. B. Andersen, A. R., Lassen, N. A. (1990). The effect of the benzodiazepine antagonist flumazenil on regional cerebral blood flow in human volunteers. *Acta Anaesthesiologica Scandinavica, 34*, 628–631.

Wolkin, A., Angrist, B., Wolf, A., et al. (1987). Effects of amphetamine on local cerebral metabolism in normal and schizophrenic subjects as determined by positron emission tomography. *Psychopharmacology (Berlin), 92*, 241–246.

Wolkin, A., Sanfilipo, M., Angrist, B., et al. (1994). Acute d-amphetamine challenge in schizophrenia: Effects on cerebral glucose utilization and clinical symptomatology. *Biological Psychiatry, 36,* 317–325.

Wu, J., Buchsbaum, M. S., Gillin, J. C., et al. (1999). Prediction of antidepressant effects of sleep deprivation by metabolic rates in the ventral anterior cingulate and medial prefrontal cortex. *American Journal of Psychiatry, 156,* 1149–1158.

Wu, J. C., Gillin, J. C., Buchsbaum, M. S., Hershey, T., Johnson, J. C., & Bunney, W. E. (1992). Effect of sleep deprivation on brain metabolism of depressed patients. *American Journal of Psychiatry, 149,* 538–543.

Zald, D. H., Lee, J. T., Fluegel, K. W., & Pardo, J. V. (1998). Aversive gustatory stimulation activates limbic circuits in humans. *Brain, 121,* 1143–1154.

Zald, D. H., & Pardo, J. V. (1997). Emotion, olfaction, and the human amygdala: Amygdala activation during aversive olfactory stimulation. *Proceedings of the National Academy of Sciences USA, 94,* 4119–4124.

Zohar, J., Insel, T. R., Berman, K. F., Foa, E. B., Hill, J. L., & Weinberger, D. R. (1989). Anxiety and cerebral blood flow during behavioral challenge: Dissociation of central from peripheral and subjective measures. *Archives of General Psychiatry 46,* 505–510.

# 51

# NEUROIMAGING AND THE NEUROBIOLOGY OF ANXIETY DISORDERS

Scott L. Rauch

Over the past decade, neuroimaging research has helped to advance neurobiological models of psychiatric disorders. In this chapter, I review neuroimaging research pertaining to anxiety disorders and interpret it in terms of neuroanatomical models of these diseases. Here the focus is on a subset of disorders for which neuroimaging data have provided a convergent series of results. This chapter necessarily extends previous reviews on the same and related topics (Rauch & Baxter, 1998; Rauch, Shin, et al., 1998; Rauch, Whalen, et al., 1998; Rauch, Shin, & Whalen, in press).

## Anxiety and the Anxiety Disorders

Anxiety and fear are normal human emotional states that serve an adaptive function. Anxiety disorders represent one category of psychiatric syndromes (*DSM-IV*; American Psychiatric Association, 1994) that are characterized by maladaptive anxiety symptoms. *Obsessive compulsive disorder (OCD)* is characterized by intrusive, unwanted thoughts (i.e., obsessions) and ritualized, repetitive behaviors (i.e., compulsions). In OCD, the obsessions are typically accompanied by anxiety that drives the compulsions; the compulsions are performed to neutralize the obsessions and attendant anxiety. *Posttraumatic stress disorder (PTSD)* is one of few psychiatric conditions for which the etiology is defined. In PTSD, individuals evolve a constellation of anxiety symptoms in the aftermath of an

emotionally traumatic event; the cardinal features of PTSD include reexperiencing phenomena (e.g., flashbacks), avoidance (e.g., avoiding situations that remind the individual of the traumatic event), and hyperarousal (e.g., exaggerated startle response). Phobias are characterized by reliable exaggerated anxiety responses to innocuous stimuli or situations. *Social phobia (SoP)* may entail phobic responses to a range of different social situations; *specific phobias (SpP)* may entail phobic responses to any of various particular stimuli or situations (e.g., small animals, heights, water, enclosed spaces, etc.). Finally, *panic disorder (PD)* is characterized by recurrent panic episodes, typically occurring spontaneously, without overt precipitants. Panic attacks entail a rapid escalation to extreme anxiety, accompanied by physical symptoms such as rapid breathing, palpitations, sweating, and dizziness, as well as emotional and cognitive symptoms, such as the feeling that something catastrophic is about to happen or that immediate escape is necessary. Individuals with panic disorder often develop avoidance of places or situations in which they believe panic attacks are more likely to occur or from which escape may be difficult (e.g., crowded or confined places).

Given that patients with anxiety disorders either suffer exaggerated fear responses to relatively innocuous stimuli (e.g., phobias) or spontaneous fear responses in the absence of true threat (e.g., panic disorder), it is important to consider the mediating neuroanatomy of normal threat assessment and the fear response. Contemporary models posit various patterns of dysfunction within these systems as candidate neural substrates for the various anxiety disorders.

## Neuroanatomy of Threat Assessment and Normal Fear

The limbic system plays an important role in mediating human emotion; anterior paralimbic cortex (i.e., posterior medial orbitofrontal, anterior temporal, anterior cingulate, and insular cortex) serves as a conduit for the flow of information between cortical regions that subserve higher level cognition, as well as sensory processing to deep limbic structures, such as the amygdala and hippocampus (Mesulam, 1985).

Modern models of threat assessment and the normal fear response have focused on the role of the amygdala (Aggleton, 1992; LeDoux, 1996). Briefly, the amygdala is located in the anterior portion of the medial temporal lobes and receives input regarding the environment directly, and thus rapidly, from the thalamus. The amygdala appears to serve several functions, including: (1) preliminary threat assessment; (2) preparing for fight or flight (via its ascending projections to motor areas and descending projections to brain stem nuclei that control autonomic responses); (3) facilitating the acquisition of more information (via its projections to sensory areas); and (4) enhancing arousal and plasticity (via projections to the basal forebrain, hippocampus, ventral striatum, and brain stem monoaminergic nuclei) so that the organism can learn from the current experience to optimally guide responses in future similar situations.

Conversely, several brain areas provide important feedback to the amygdala (Aggleton, 1992; LeDoux, 1996): (1) medial frontal cortex (presumably including anterior cingulate and orbitofrontal cortex) may provide critical "top-down" governance over the amygdala, enabling attenuation of the fear response once danger has passed or when the meaning of a potentially threatening stimulus has changed; (2) the hippocampus provides information about the context of a situation beyond the attributes of a specific cue (this may depend on information retrieved from explicit memory stores); (3) cortico-striato-thalamic circuits mediate "gating" at the level of the thalamus, thereby regulating the flow of incoming information that reaches the amygdala.

Finally, neuromodulators influence the activity within each of these various brain areas, as well as the interactions among the nodes of the entire system outlined previously. Ascending projections from the raphe nuclei (serotonin) and the locus ceruleus (norepinephrine), as well as widespread local GABAergic neurons, are perhaps most relevant to the physiology of anxiety (Charney, Bremner, & Redmond, 1995; Kent, Coplan, & Gorman, 1998; Salz-man, Miyawaki, le Bars, & Kerrihard, 1993). These transmitter systems likely serve as the principal substrates for contemporary anxiolytic medications, including serotonergic reuptake inhibitors, monoamine oxidase inhibitors, other antidepressant medications, and benzodiazepines.

## Neuroimaging Methods

Structural neuroimaging methods can be used to test hypotheses regarding abnormalities in the size or shape of particular brain elements. *Morphometric magnetic resonance imaging (mMRI)* represents the modern application of this approach, whereas early studies were performed using computed axial tomography. Contemporary mMRI typically entails semiautomated schemes for segmenting named brain structures so that corresponding volumes can be precisely calculated. Evolving methods in this field include strategies for parceling cortical territories, as well as subdividing subcortical nuclei.

Various experimental paradigms have been employed in conjunction with a range of functional neuroimaging modalities in efforts to delineate the pathophysiology of psychiatric disorders. In the studies subsequently reviewed, imaging methods include positron emission tomography (PET) with tracers that measure blood flow (e.g., oxygen-15-labeled carbon dioxide) or glucose metabolism (i.e., F-18-labeled fluorodeoxyglucose [FDG]), single photon emission tomography (SPECT) with tracers that measure correlates of blood flow (e.g., technetium-99-labeled hexamethyl propylene amine oxime [TcHMPAO]), and functional magnetic resonance imaging (fMRI) to measure blood-oxygenation-level-dependent (BOLD) signal changes. Each of these techniques yields maps that reflect regional brain activity.

Such brain activity profiles are sensitive to the state of the individual at the time of tracer distribution or image acquisition. Hence functional imaging paradigms can be categorized based on the type of state manipulations employed by the investigators and the principal statistical comparisons applied. In *neutral state* paradigms participants are studied during a nominal "resting" state or while performing a nonspecific continuous task. Thus between-group comparisons are made to test hypotheses regarding group differences in regional brain activity without particular attention to state variables. In *treatment* paradigms participants are scanned in the context of a treatment protocol. In pre- and post-treatment studies, participants are scanned both before and after a trial. Then within-group comparisons are made to test hypotheses regarding changes in brain activity profiles associated with symptomatic improvement. Alternatively, correlational analyses can be performed to identify pretreatment brain activity characteristics that predict good or poor treatment response. In *symptom provocation* paradigms participants are scanned during a symptomatic state (after symptoms were intentionally induced), as well as during control conditions. Within-group comparisons can be made to test hypotheses regarding the mediating anatomy of the symptomatic state; group-by-condition interactions can be sought to distinguish responses in patient versus control groups. Behavioral and/or pharmacological challenges can be used to induce symptoms. In some cases, when symptomatic states occur spontaneously, experiments are designed to capture these events without the need for provocation or induction per se. In *cognitive activation* paradigms participants are studied while performing specially designed cognitive/behavioral tasks. This approach is intended to increase sensitivity by employing tasks that specifically activate brain systems of interest. Again, group-by-condition interactions are sought to test the functional responsivity or integrity of specific brain systems in patients versus control participants.

Imaging studies of neurochemistry have employed PET and SPECT methods in conjunction with radiolabeled high affinity ligands. In this way, regional receptor number and/or affinity can be characterized in vivo (i.e., *receptor characterization studies*). Other approaches include the use of *magnetic resonance spectroscopy* (MRS) to measure the regional relative concentration of select "MRS-visible" compounds. For instance, MRS can be used to measure the compound N-acetyl aspartate (NAA), which is a purported marker of healthy neuronal density.

These various neuroimaging techniques should be viewed as complementary. In instances in which results from multiple studies converge, more cohesive and compelling models of pathophysiology have emerged.

## Obsessive Compulsive Disorder

### Cortico-Striatal Model of OCD

Briefly, the prevailing model of OCD focuses on corticostriato-thalamo-cortical circuitry (see Rauch, Whalen, et al., 1998, for review). One hypothesis suggests that primary pathology within the striatum (specifically, the caudate nucleus) leads to inefficient gating at the level of the thalamus, which results in hyperactivity within orbitofrontal cortex (corresponding to the intrusive thoughts) and hyperactivity within anterior cingulate cortex (corresponding to anxiety in a nonspecific manner). Further, by this model, compulsions are conceptualized as repetitive behaviors that are performed to recruit the inefficient striatum so as to ultimately achieve thalamic gating, and hence, neutralize the unwanted thoughts and anxiety.

### Structural Imaging Findings

Four mMRI studies of adult participants with OCD have been conducted using contemporary imaging methods.

Findings from three of these four investigations suggested volumetric abnormalities involving the caudate nucleus. However, the nature of the observed abnormalities has been inconsistent. Scarone et al. (1992) studied a mixed-gender cohort of 20 patients with OCD versus 16 matched controls and found increased right caudate volume in the OCD group. Robinson et al. (1995) studied a mixed-gender cohort of 26 patients with OCD versus 26 matched controls and found bilaterally decreased caudate volumes in the OCD group. Jenike et al. (1996) studied an all-female cohort of 10 patients with OCD versus matched controls and found trends toward a rightward shift in caudate volume ($p = .06$), as well as overall reduced caudate volume ($p = .10$), in the OCD group. Aylward et al. (1996) studied a mixed-gender cohort of 24 patients with OCD versus 21 matched controls and found no significant differences in striatal volumes.

Of note, Rosenberg et al. (1997) performed an analogous mMRI study in treatment-naive pediatric participants. In their analysis of mMRI data from 19 participants with OCD and 19 case-matched psychiatrically healthy comparison participants, Rosenberg and colleagues also found reduced striatal volumes. Moreover, in this study, striatal volume was inversely related to OCD symptom severity.

### Functional Imaging Findings

Neutral-state paradigms that employ PET and SPECT have most consistently indicated that patients with OCD exhibit increased regional brain activity within orbitofrontal and anterior cingulate cortex, in comparison with normal control participants (Baxter et al., 1987; Baxter et al., 1988; Machlin et al., 1991; Nordahl et al., 1989; Rubin et al., 1992; Swedo et al., 1989). Observed differences in regional activity within the caudate nucleus have been less consistent (Baxter et al., 1987; Rubin et al., 1992).

Pre- and posttreatment studies (Baxter et al., 1992; Benkelfat et al., 1990; Hoehn-Saric et al., 1991; Perani et al., 1995; Schwartz et al., 1996; Swedo et al., 1992) have likewise indicated attenuation of abnormal regional brain activity within orbitofrontal cortex, anterior cingulate cortex, and caudate nucleus associated with treatment. Moreover, similar changes have been observed for both pharmacological and behavioral therapies (e.g., Baxter et al., 1992; Schwartz et al., 1996).

Treatment studies using PET-FDG methods have also indicated that the magnitude of frontal activity prior to therapy predicts response. Specifically, Swedo et al. (1989) found that responders to clomipramine treatment had lower pretreatment regional cerebral metabolic rates for glucose (rCMRglc) in right orbitofrontal cortex and right anterior cingulate cortex than did nonresponders. Brody and colleagues (1998) found that pretreatment rCMRglc in left orbitofrontal cortex differentially predicted response to cognitive behavior therapy versus fluoxetine in patients with OCD (Brody et al., 1998). Lower pretreatment left orbitofrontal rCMRglc was significantly correlated with response to fluoxetine, but higher pretreatment left orbitofrontal rCMRglc was correlated with response to cognitive behavior therapy. Recently, Saxena and colleagues (1999) extended these findings by showing that lower pretreatment rCMRglc in bilateral orbitofrontal cortex was significantly correlated with better response to paroxetine. Taken together, these results suggest that OCD patients with particular patterns of brain metabolism may respond preferentially to specific types of treatment, with lower pretreatment activity in orbitofrontal cortex predicting better response to serotonergic reuptake inhibitors.

Symptom provocation studies employing PET (McGuire et al., 1994; Rauch et al., 1994), as well as functional MRI (Breiter et al., 1996) have also most consistently shown increased brain activity within anterior/lateral orbitofrontal cortex, anterior cingulate cortex, and caudate nucleus associated with the OCD symptomatic state. Qualitative comparisons with other anxiety disorders have emphasized the relative specificity of anterior/lateral orbitofrontal and caudate activation in OCD, whereas activation of posteromedial orbitofrontal and anterior cingulate cortex has been observed nonspecifically across other anxiety disorders and normal anxiety states (see Rauch & Baxter, 1998).

Two cognitive activation studies of OCD have been conducted (Rauch, Savage, Alpert, Dougherty, et al., 1997; Rauch, Whalen, et al., 2000) that employed an implicit (i.e., nonconscious) learning paradigm shown to reliably recruit striatum (Rauch, Savage, Brown, et al., 1995; Rauch, Whalen, et al., 1997). An initial study was performed using PET (Rauch, Savage, Alpert, et al., 1997), and then the findings were replicated using functional MRI (Rauch, Whalen, et al., 2000). In both studies, although patients with OCD exhibited normal performance on the learning task, brain activity profiles indicated that they failed to normally recruit striatum and instead activated medial temporal regions typically associated with conscious information processing.

### Imaging Studies of Neurochemistry

Several MRS studies have been performed to measure NAA concentrations in patients with OCD versus healthy comparison participants. Ebert and colleagues (1997) found that, in comparison with six healthy control participants, 12 OCD participants exhibited reduced relative NAA levels in right striatum, as well as anterior cingulate cortex. Similarly, Bartha and colleagues (1998) found reduced left striatal NAA concentrations in a cohort of 13 OCD patients versus an equal number of matched control participants. The findings of these MRS-NAA studies have been viewed as convergent with those from mMRI studies;

reduced NAA is likewise consistent with primary pathology within the striatum associated with subtle volumetric abnormalities or reduced indices of healthy neuronal density.

MRS has also been used to demonstrate elevated glutamatergic concentrations within the striatum of a child with OCD (Moore, MacMaster, Stewart, & Rosenberg, 1998). Interestingly, elevated striatal glutamate levels were attenuated toward normal following successful pharmacotherapy. Given that glutamate is the principal transmitter mediating frontostriatal communication, these findings are consistent with the prevailing neurocircuitry model of OCD. Specifically, orbitofrontal hyperactivity in OCD is apparently mirrored by elevated glutamate at the site of orbitofrontal ramifications in striatum. Further, as orbitofrontal hyperactivity is attenuated with successful treatment, so too is the elevated concentration of glutamate attenuated within the striatum.

Taken together, the neuroimaging data on OCD suggest dysregulation of activity within cortico-striato-thalamo-cortical circuitry; the orbitofrontal-caudate circuit is specifically implicated in OCD. In contrast, paralimbic cortex, including anterior cingulate cortex, has been conceptualized as mediating nonspecific aspects of the anxious state. Models that posit primary striatal pathology find support from mMRI studies showing reduced striatal volume, as well as MRS results of reduced striatal NAA, indicating decreased density of viable neurons in that region. Hyperactivity within orbitofrontal cortex is associated with the obsessional symptomatic state. Further, in normal participants, the performance of repetitive motor routines does facilitate striatal recruitment in the service of thalamic gating, whereas this pattern is not readily demonstrated in patients with OCD. These imaging data further support the working model of striatal pathology and striato-thalamic inefficiency, together with orbitofrontal hyperactivity. Perhaps of greatest clinical relevance, the magnitude of orbitofrontal hyperactivity in OCD predicts response to treatment, with less severe abnormalities heralding superior response to serotonergic medication.

## Posttraumatic Stress Disorder

### Amygdalocentric Model of PTSD

We have previously presented a neurocircuitry model of PTSD (Rauch, Shin, et al., 1998) that emphasizes the central role of the amygdala, as well as its interactions with the hippocampus, medial prefrontal cortex, and other heteromodal cortical areas purported to mediate higher cognitive functions. Briefly, this model hypothesizes hyperresponsivity within the amygdala to threat-related stimuli, with inadequate top-down governance over the amygdala by medial prefrontal cortex (specifically, the affective division of anterior cingulate cortex; see Whalen, Bush, et al., 1998) and the hippocampus. Amygdala hyperresponsivity mediates symptoms of hyperarousal and explains the indelible quality of the emotional memory for the traumatic event; inadequate influence by the anterior cingulate cortex underlies deficits of habituation; and decreased hippocampal function underlies deficits in identifying safe contexts, as well as accompanying explicit memory difficulties (see Bremner et al., 1995). Further, we propose that in threatening situations, patients with PTSD exhibit an exaggerated reallocation of resources toward regions that mediate fight-and-flight responses and away from widespread heteromodal cortical areas as a neural substrate for dissociation.

This model represents a final common pathophysiological pathway. Consequently, the pathogenesis of PTSD can be conceptualized as a fear-conditioning process that is superimposed over some diathesis, which could entail any combination of premorbid intrinsic amygdala hyperresponsivity, anterior cingulate deficiency, hippocampal deficiency, or exaggerated susceptibility to stress. In fact, current theories suggest that damage to or sensitization of this system is likely to be a consequence of prior exposure to stress. Further, chronic PTSD might involve progressive deterioration of function within this system.

## Structural Imaging Findings

Morphometric MRI studies of PTSD have focused on subtle between-group differences with respect to hippocampal volume. Bremner et al. (1995) studied 26 Vietnam combat veterans with PTSD and 22 civilian comparison participants. They found that right hippocampal volumes were 8% smaller in the PTSD group than in the control group, and this difference persisted when years of education and alcohol abuse were considered as covariates. Of note, the mean left hippocampal volume was also smaller (3.8%) for the PTSD group than for the control group, although this difference did not achieve statistical significance. In addition, the PTSD group exhibited poorer performance on a standard measure of verbal memory, and their percent retention scores on this test were directly correlated with right hippocampal volume (i.e., lower scores were associated with smaller right hippocampal volumes). Gurvits and colleagues (1996) studied three groups of participants using mMRI: 7 Vietnam combat veterans with PTSD, 7 Vietnam combat veterans without PTSD, and 8 nonveterans without PTSD. They found significantly smaller hippocampal volumes bilaterally for the PTSD group in comparison with both control cohorts. Furthermore, these findings survived adjustments for age, total brain volume, and lifetime alcohol consumption. Across the 14 veterans, total hippocampal volume was inversely correlated with both the extent of combat exposure and PTSD symptom severity; however, there was no sig-

nificant difference in hippocampal volume between the two control groups.

Morphometric MRI studies of PTSD resulting from childhood abuse indicated similar hippocampal volumetric differences. Bremner et al. (1997) conducted a study of 17 adult survivors of childhood sexual and/or physical abuse with PTSD and 21 comparison participants who reported no history of childhood abuse. They found 12% smaller left hippocampal volumes in the PTSD group than in the control group. Stein and colleagues (Stein et al., 1997) studied hippocampal volume in 21 adult survivors of childhood sexual abuse (most of whom had PTSD) and a comparison cohort of 21 adults who reported no childhood history of abuse. They found 5% smaller left hippocampal volumes in the abused cohort, and total hippocampal volume was smaller in abused participants with high PTSD symptom severity than in those with low PTSD symptom severity. Of note, left hippocampal volume was negatively correlated with dissociative symptoms but not significantly correlated with indices of memory function.

These mMRI findings provide initial support for the contention that PTSD is associated with reduced hippocampal size, which in turn is associated with cognitive deficits. Moreover, the findings indicate that although the extent of traumatic exposure might be related to hippocampal volume, it appears to be the presence of PTSD that distinguishes among the groups in this regard.

## Functional Imaging Findings

Semple and colleagues (Semple et al., 1993) reported results from a PET study that involved patients with combat-related PTSD and comorbid substance abuse versus normal control participants. Measurements of regional cerebral blood flow (rCBF) were made during three conditions: a nominal resting state, an auditory continuous performance task, and a word-generation task. Compared with the control group, the patient group exhibited greater rCBF during both task conditions within the orbitofrontal cortex. They also showed a trend toward lower left/right hippocampal rCBF ratios during the word-generation task.

Rauch et al. (1996) studied a mixed-gender cohort of participants with PTSD, using PET and a script-driven imagery method for inducing symptoms. For the provoked versus control contrasts, patients exhibited increased rCBF within the right orbitofrontal, insular, anterior temporal, and visual cortex, as well as the anterior cingulate cortex and the right amygdala. Decreases in rCBF were observed within the left inferior frontal (Broca's area) and left middle temporal cortex. Interpretations of this initial study, with regard to the pathophysiology of PTSD, were limited by the absence of a comparison group. For instance, Fischer, Wik, and Fredrikson (1996) studied normal participants who had been exposed to the emotional stress of an armed bank robbery without developing PTSD.

PET rCBF measurements were made during a provoked condition, while participants watched an actual security videotape of the robbery, and a control condition, while they watched a neutral videotape of park scenes. In the provoked versus control contrast, the researchers also found rCBF increases within the orbitofrontal and visual cortex, as well as the posterior cingulate cortex. Furthermore, rCBF decreases were noted in a variety of regions, including Broca's area. This suggested that both individuals with PTSD and psychiatrically healthy participants might show similar patterns of brain activity in response to reminders of emotionally traumatic events. More formal comparisons would be needed to identify between-group differences in brain activity.

Subsequently, using a similar paradigm, Shin and colleagues (Shin et al., 1999) studied female adult participants with childhood sexual abuse–related PTSD and matched trauma-exposed control participants without PTSD. Both the patient and control groups exhibited anterior paralimbic activation during the provoked condition. Most important, an assessment of group-by-condition interactions suggests that the control group manifested a significantly greater increase in rCBF within the anterior cingulate cortex than did the PTSD group, whereas the PTSD group showed significantly greater increases in rCBF within the anterior temporal and orbitofrontal cortex but significantly larger decreases in rCBF within anterior prefrontal areas. Bremner and colleagues (1999a) also used script-driven imagery in conjunction with PET to study rCBF patterns in female victims of childhood sexual abuse with and without PTSD. Consistent with the findings of Shin et al. (1999), Bremner, Narayan, et al. (1999) reported relatively attenuated recruitment of anterior cingulate cortex during the trauma-related condition. In addition, they found that the PTSD group was characterized by exaggerated rCBF decreases in subcallosal gyrus, right hippocampus, fusiform gyrus, supramarginal gyrus, and visual association cortex, as well as by exaggerated rCBF increases in the posterior cingulate, anterior prefrontal, and motor cortex.

Bremner, Staib, et al. (1999) studied responses to trauma-related pictures and sounds in Vietnam veterans with and without PTSD. They reported that, in response to reminders of traumatic events, the non-PTSD group exhibited attenuated anterior cingulate activation, as well as decreases in ventral prefrontal cortex, that were not seen in the non-PTSD group. Liberzon et al., (1999) used SPECT to study Vietnam veterans with and without PTSD, as well as a cohort of comparison participants without combat exposure. They contrasted the brain activation profiles associated with exposure to combat sounds versus white noise. All three groups exhibited activation in anterior cingulate and middle prefrontal gyrus, whereas only the PTSD group exhibited significant activation of the left amygdala/nucleus accumbens region.

Shin and colleagues (Shin et al., 1997) studied patients with combat-related PTSD and matched trauma-exposed control participants without PTSD in the context of a PET cognitive activation paradigm. Participants were required to make judgments about pictures from three categories: neutral, general negative, and combat related. The paradigm also entailed two types of tasks: one involved responding while actually seeing the pictures (perception), and another involved responding while recalling the pictures (imagery). The PTSD group showed several areas of significant rCBF change not seen in control participants: increased rCBF was found within the right amygdala and anterior cingulate cortex during combat imagery versus comparison conditions, and decreased rCBF was found within the left inferior frontal cortex (Broca's area) for the combat perception versus negative perception contrast. These findings closely paralleled results from the PTSD symptom provocation study of Rauch et al. (1996).

## Imaging Studies of Neurochemistry

Schuff and colleagues (Schuff et al., 1997) studied 7 veterans with PTSD and 7 nonveteran control participants. Although they found a nonsignificantly smaller (6%) right hippocampus in the PTSD group by mMRI, they found an 18% reduction in right hippocampal NAA by MRS.

Taken together, imaging data support the current neurocircuitry model of PTSD that emphasizes the functional relationship between a triad of brain structures: the amygdala, the hippocampus, and the medial prefrontal cortex. Morphometric MRI studies show decreased hippocampal volume, which is convergent with MRS findings of decreased NAA in the hippocampus. Functional studies indicate a rightward shift in hippocampal activity at rest. When exposed to reminders of traumatic events, patients appear to most consistently recruit anterior paralimbic regions, as well as the amygdala, while exhibiting decreased activity within other heteromodal cortical areas. In comparison with control participants, however, patients with PTSD exhibit anterior cingulate activation of diminished magnitude but exaggerated rCBF increases within other paralimbic regions, as well as the amygdala, and exaggerated decreases within widespread areas that are associated with higher cognitive functions, such as Broca's area.

## Social and Specific Phobias

### Neuroanatomical Models of Phobias

One possibility is that phobias are learned and hence reflect another example of fear conditioning to specific stimuli or situations. Alternatively, phobias may represent the product of dysregulated systems specific to archetypal varieties of potentially threatening stimuli or situations. For instance, if humans have evolved a neural network specifically designed to assess social cues for threatening content, another to assess threat from small animals, and so forth, these might represent the neural substrates for the pathophysiology that underlies phobias. At this juncture, there are no cohesive neuroanatomically based models for the phobias (see Fyer, 1998; Stein, 1998); rather, it is from further neuroimaging studies of the type described in this section that such models might arise.

## Structural Imaging Findings

Given the high prevalence of phobias and the relative ease with which medication-free phobic participants without significant comorbidities can be recruited, it is striking how few imaging studies have been conducted in this arena. In fact, I was unable to find a single quantitative structural brain imaging study that involved SpP subjects. Potts, Davidson, Krishnan, and Doraiswamy (1994) used mMRI to examine volumetric measures of total cerebrum, caudate, putamen, and thalamus in 22 SoP participants and an equal number of matched healthy control participants. No significant between-group differences were found in any of these regional brain volumes. Thus further morphometric brain imaging studies of the phobias are sorely needed.

## Functional Imaging Findings

Studies of SpP to date have principally employed PET symptom provocation paradigms. In an initial study by Mountz et al. (1989), small-animal phobics exhibited increased heart rates, respiratory rates, and subjective reports of anxiety during exposure to phobic stimuli; however, no changes in rCBF measurements were observed. The lack of findings may have been attributable to the data analytic methods applied.

Subsequently, Wik and colleagues (Wik et al., 1993) studied patients with snake phobias during exposure to videotapes of neutral, generally aversive, and snake-related scenes. During the phobic condition, they found significant increases in rCBF within the secondary visual cortex; rCBF decreases were noted within the prefrontal cortex, posterior cingulate cortex, anterior temporopolar cortex, and hippocampus. These findings were ostensibly replicated by the same laboratory in two subsequent studies, including an analogous study of spider phobia (Fredrickson et al., 1993; Fredrikson et al., 1995).

Rauch, Savage, Alpert, et al. (1995) conducted a PET study involving a cohort of participants with a variety of small-animal phobias and in vivo exposure to phobia-related and control stimuli. Of note, Rauch and colleagues measured rCBF while participants had their eyes closed whereas participants in previous studies of SpP were measured with eyes open. Rauch, Savage, Alpert, et al. (1995) found significant rCBF increases within multiple anterior paralimbic territories (i.e., right anterior cingulate, right anterior temporal pole, left posterior orbitofrontal cortex, and left insular cortex), left somatosensory cortex, and left thalamus. Dominant-sided somatosensory cortical activation was interpreted in the context of participants' reports that they engaged in tactile imagery, worrying that the phobic stimulus would come into bodily contact with them. This was conceptualized as analogous to visual cortical activation in previous SpP studies, in which exposures to phobic stimuli were mediated via the visual sensory modality.

Whereas a single neutral-state SPECT study of SoP participants and healthy controls found no significant between-group differences in rCBF (Stein & Leslie, 1996), more recent cognitive activation studies performed in conjunction with fMRI have yielded more informative results. Birbaumer et al. (1998) used fMRI to study 7 SoP participants versus 5 healthy controls while they were exposed either to slides of neutral human faces or to aversive odors. In comparison with the control group, the SoP group exhibited hyperresponsivity within the amygdala that was specific to the human face stimuli. In a follow-up study, Schneider et al. (1999) used fMRI to study 12 SoP participants versus an equal number of healthy control participants in the context of a classical conditioning paradigm; neutral faces were the conditioned stimuli and odors (negative odor, odorless air) served as the unconditioned stimuli. In response to conditioned stimuli associated with the negative odor, the SoP group displayed signal increases within amygdala and hippocampus, whereas healthy comparison participants displayed signal decreases in these same regions.

## Imaging Studies of Neurochemistry

Tiihonen et al. (1997) used SPECT and I-123-labeled-beta CIT to measure the density of dopamine reuptake sites in 11 SoP participants and 28 healthy comparison participants. They found significantly reduced striatal dopamine reuptake binding site density in the SoP versus the control group.

The body of imaging data on the phobias remains quite limited. Taken together, imaging findings in SpP suggest activation of anterior paralimbic regions, as well as sensory cortex, corresponding to stimulus inflow associated with a symptomatic state. Although such results are consistent with a hypersensitive system for assessment of or response to specific threat-related cues, they do not provide clear anatomical substrates for the pathophysiology of SpP. Studies of SoP indicate exaggerated responsivity of medial temporal lobe structures to human face stimuli, as well as an aberrant pattern of activity within medial temporal lobe structures during aversive conditioning with human face stimuli. This is consistent with a hypersensitive system for the assessment or assignment of threat to human faces as a neural substrate for the underpinnings of social anxiety in SoP. Moreover, the preliminary finding of dopamine receptor abnormalities in SoP is consistent with theories of dysregulated reward as a factor in social deficits (see Stein, 1998).

## Panic Disorder

### Neuroanatomical Models of Panic Disorder

Contemporary neurobiological models of PD have emphasized a wide range of disparate elements (see Coplan & Lydiard, 1998), including dysregulated ascending noradrenergic and/or serotonergic systems, aberrant responsivity to $CO_2$ at the level of brain stem (so-called false suffocation alarm), global cerebral abnormalities in lactate metabolism, and abnormalities in the interactions between hippocampus and amygdala. Whereas the behavioral sequelae of recurrent panic attacks, such as agoraphobic avoidance, can be readily explained based on learning theory and the fear-conditioning model, a satisfactory model of panic disorder must primarily explain the occurrence of spontaneous panic episodes.

One possibility is that a core physiological (i.e., normal) anxiety response, mediated by normal anxiety/fear circuitry, is recruited spontaneously as an aberrant event due to homeostatic deficits. This fits well with the suffocation-alarm model, as well as with theories regarding fundamental monoaminergic dysregulation. Another possibility is that panic attacks evolve in the context of what should be minor anxiety episodes because of failures in the systems responsible for limiting such normal responses; similar to the aforementioned model of PTSD, hippocampal deficits might underlie such a mechanism in the case of PD. Finally, we should consider that panic episodes described as spontaneous (i.e., without identifiable precipitants) could reflect anxiety responses to stimuli that are not processed at the conscious (i.e., explicit) level but that instead recruit anxiety circuitry without awareness (i.e., implicitly). This is an intriguing concept, as there is strong evidence that the amygdala can be recruited into action in the absence of awareness that a threat-related stimulus has been presented (e.g., see Whalen, Rauch, et al., 1998). By this model, PD might be characterized by fundamental amygdala hyperresponsivity to subtle environmental cues, triggering full-scale threat-related responses in the absence of conscious awareness.

### Structural Imaging Findings

Although I could find no quantitative mMRI studies of PD, Fontaine, Breton, Dery, Fontaine, and Elie (1990) pub-

lished a qualitative MRI study involving 31 consecutive patients with PD and 20 matched healthy control participants. They found a higher frequency of gross structural abnormalities in the PD group (40%) than in the control group (10%); in particular, the most striking focal findings in the PD group involved abnormal signal or asymmetric atrophy of the right temporal lobe. Formal quantitative mMRI studies of PD are sorely needed.

### Functional Imaging Findings

In an initial PET neutral-state study, Reiman et al. (1986) studied 16 patients with PD and 25 normal control participants. In the subset of patients who were vulnerable to lactate-induced panic ($N = 8$), the investigators found abnormally low left/right ratios of parahippocampal blood flow. DeCristofaro, Sessarego, Pupi, Biondi, and Faravelli (1993) used SPECT to measure rCBF at rest in 7 treatment-naive PD participants and 5 age-matched healthy controls. In comparison with the control group, PD participants exhibited elevated rCBF in left occipital cortex and reduced rCBF in the hippocampal area bilaterally.

Nordahl et al. (1990) used PET-FDG methods to measure rCMRglc in 12 patients with PD and 30 normal controls, while they engaged in an auditory continuous performance task. The investigators found that the PD group exhibited a lower left/right hippocampal ratio. Bisaga et al. (1998) used PET-FDG methods to study a cohort of 6 women with PD and an equal number of matched controls. In contrast to previous studies, the PD patients displayed elevated rCMRglc in the left hippocampus and parahippocampal area. The PD group was further characterized by reduced rCMRglc in right inferior parietal and right superior temporal regions.

Three symptom provocation studies of PD have been published, all of which employed pharmacological interventions. Stewart, Devous, Rush, Lane, and Bonte (1988) used the xenon inhalation method in conjunction with SPECT to measure CBF in superficial cortical areas during lactate-induced panic. Ten PD patients and 5 normal controls were studied during saline infusion and during sodium infusion; 6 of the PD participants and none of the controls experienced lactate-induced panic attacks during the study. Whereas both PD and control participants who failed to panic exhibited global cortical increases in CBF during lactate infusions, the PD participants who experienced lactate-induced panic attacks displayed global cortical decreases in CBF. Woods et al. (1988) employed SPECT and yohimbine infusions to study 6 patients with PD and an equal number of normal control participants. In the patient group, but not the control group, yohimbine administration induced increased anxiety and decreased rCBF in bilateral frontal cortex. In another report, Reiman et al. (1989) used PET methods to measure rCBF in 17 patients with PD and 15 normal control participants during lactate infusions. The 8 patients who suffered lactate-induced panic episodes exhibited rCBF increases in bilateral temporopolar cortex and bilateral insular cortex/claustrum/putamen. No such increases were observed in either the normal controls nor in the PD patients who did not experience lactate-induced panic. Of note, the temporopolar findings were subsequently questioned as possibly reflecting extracranial artifacts from muscular contractions (Drevets et al., 1992; Benkelfat et al., 1995).

Fischer, Andersson, Furmark, and Fredrikson (1998) published a PET case report illustrating the functional neuroimaging profile associated with a spontaneous panic attack. This example of symptom capture revealed decreased rCBF in right orbitofrontal, prelimbic (area 25), anterior cingulate, and anterior temporal cortex during the acute event.

Of relevance, Benkelfat and colleagues (1995) studied pharmacologically induced anxiety attacks in psychiatrically healthy participants. They used cholecystokinin tetrapeptide (CCK-4) infusions as the method for producing a reliable panic response; saline infusions were given during control conditions. Participants were also studied in an anticipatory anxiety condition during which they expected to receive CCK-4 but were actually injected with saline. The anticipatory anxiety condition was associated with rCBF increases within the left orbitofrontal cortex and cerebellum; the CCK-4 condition was associated with rCBF increases in anterior cingulate cortex, cerebellum, and a bilateral region spanning insula, claustrum, and amygdala. Signal increases were also observed in the vicinity of bilateral anterior temporal poles; however, these were attributed to artifacts from extracranial sources. Using similar methods, Javenmard and colleagues (1999) extended this work by sampling the induced panic episodes at two different time points (1st minute or 2nd minute after CCK-4 bolus injection). They found that the early phase was associated with rCBF increases within the hypothalamic region, the late phase was associated with rCBF increases in the claustrum-insular region, and both phases were associated with rCBF decreases in the medial frontal region. In contrast to results from their previous study (Benkelfat et al., 1995) an anticipatory anxiety condition was associated with rCBF increases in anterior cingulate cortex and decreases in visual cortical areas.

Nordahl and colleagues (1998) used PET-FDG methods to study imipramine-treated patients with panic disorder. With respect to rCMRglc, they found a rightward shift in symmetry within hippocampus and posterior inferior frontal cortex, similar to that which they had previously observed in nontreated patients with panic disorder (Nordahl et al., 1990). Further, in comparison with the untreated group, the imipramine-treated group exhibited rCMRglc decreases in posterior orbital frontal cortex. Nor-

dahl and colleagues (1998) noted that this difference bears resemblance to changes observed in OCD following successful treatment (e.g., Baxter et al., 1992).

## Imaging Studies of Neurochemistry

Dager and colleagues (1995) used MRS to measure brain lactate levels during hyperventilation in 7 treatment-responsive patients with PD and an equal number of healthy comparison participants. Although the two groups did not significantly differ with respect to brain lactate levels at rest, the PD group showed a significantly greater rise in brain lactate in response to the same level of hyperventilation. Of note, there were no significant between-group differences in blood lactate levels either before or after hyperventilation. The authors proposed that patients with PD might accrue higher levels of brain lactate during hyperventilation as a consequence of an exaggerated rCBF decrease in response to hypocapnia. In a follow-up study, Dager et al. (1999) used MRS to measure brain lactate levels during lactate infusions in 15 participants with PD and 10 healthy comparisons. The PD group exhibited a significantly greater brain lactate level during lactate infusion, consistent with the interpretation of reduced clearance, rather than higher production, of lactate in PD. Further, the absence of any particular regional distribution of this phenomenon suggests a global or widespread abnormality in cerebral vascular function in PD.

Kuikka et al. (1995) used SPECT in conjunction with I-123-labeled-iomazenil to measure benzodiazepine receptor uptake in 17 participants with PD and an equal number of matched healthy comparison participants. In comparison with the control group, the PD group exhibited a greater left/right ratio in benzodiazepine receptor uptake that was most prominent in the prefrontal cortex. Malizia et al. (1998) used PET and carbon-11-labeled flumazenil to conduct an analogous study in 7 patients with PD and 8 healthy comparison participants. They found that the PD group exhibited a global reduction in benzodiazepine binding that was most pronounced in the right orbitofrontal and right insular cortex.

Brandt et al. (1998) used SPECT and I-123-labeled iomazenil to measure benzodiazepine receptor density in 12 medication-naive PD participants and 9 matched healthy controls. The PD group exhibited significantly elevated benzodiazepine receptor binding within the right supraorbital frontal cortex, as well as a trend toward elevated binding in the right temporal cortex.

Taken together, the neuroimaging data on PD suggest abnormalities in hippocampal activity at rest; during a symptomatic state, patients exhibit activation of insular and motor striatal regions, as well as reduced activity in widespread cortical regions, including prefrontal cortex. MRS studies of brain lactate implicate a global phenomenon consistent with an exaggerated hemodynamic response to hypocapnea. Similarly, receptor binding studies suggest widespread abnormalities in the GABAergic/benzodiazepine system, which also appear to be most pronounced in insular and prefrontal regions; these findings must be interpreted with caution, appreciating that some abnormalities in receptor profiles can be a consequence of prior exposure to psychotropic medications. Consistent with prevailing neurobiological models of PD, it is possible that fundamental abnormalities in monoaminergic neurotransmitter systems that originate in the brainstem underlie the abnormalities of metabolism, hemodynamics, and chemistry found in widespread territories of cortex. Further, regional abnormalities within the medial temporal lobes provide some support for theories regarding hippocampal or amygdala dysfunction in PD.

## Summary and Future Directions

Contemporary neurobiological models of the anxiety disorders have been substantially shaped by data gleaned from neuroimaging studies. Interestingly, such findings have begun to delineate signature abnormalities of brain structure and/or function, perhaps foreshadowing a future diagnostic scheme in psychiatry that will be more firmly rooted in pathophysiology.

Neuroimaging studies of OCD have provided a great depth and breadth of convergent data, resulting in a relatively cohesive model that implicates cortico-striato-thalamo-cortical circuitry. These findings will help to focus future investigations within the orbitofrontal cortex and the striatum, as well as on the interactions among the nodes that make up this system. Theories about the neurobiology of PTSD have been informed to a large degree by animal studies of fear conditioning. Neuroimaging studies of PTSD have provided an initial means for testing such hypotheses in human participants. Thus far, there is considerable evidence to support prevailing models of PTSD that focus on the amygdala and its relationship with the hippocampus and medial prefrontal cortex. Neuroimaging research pertaining to the phobias is relatively limited thus far. For SpP preliminary evidence exists of increased activity within sensory pathways and anterior paralimbic regions, which might reflect a hypersensitivity within systems evolved for assessing specific archetypal classes of potentially threatening stimuli (e.g., animals, heights, etc.). For SoP, the preliminary evidence for increased responsivity of the amygdala to human face stimuli is likewise consistent with hypersensitivity within a specialized system to a discrete class of stimuli. Of course, this fits with the fundamental phenomenology of the phobias. Finally, in the case of PD, neuroimaging research has raised a wide range of possible neural substrates for the disease. Regional abnormalities within the temporal lobe

may reflect fundamental deficits in threat assessment similar to those found in SoP and PTSD. However, more global abnormalities in homeostatic mechanisms related to lactate metabolism and vascular responses to $CO_2$, as well as widespread abnormalities in benzodiazepine receptor binding, may prove specific to PD. These diffuse abnormalities may somehow mirror the phenomenon of spontaneously occurring fear responses in the absence of identifiable true-threat stimuli.

Although this brand of research has begun to identify characteristic imaging profiles that distinguish among anxiety disorders, it is clear that striking commonalities also exist. In fact, taken together, functional neuroimaging studies in normal participants and across anxiety disorders principally implicate anterior paralimbic cortex, sensory cortex, and deep brain structures, such as the amygdala, hippocampus, striatum, and brainstem nuclei, in the mediating neuroanatomy of anxiety states (see Benkelfat et al. 1995; Rauch, Savage, Alpert, Fischman, et al., 1997; Rauch, Shin, & Whalen, in press). It is also becoming clear that extreme states of anxiety or fear, such as that induced by recollection of a traumatic event, lead to a reallocation of resources away from territories that subserve higher cognitive functions. This likely occurs in the service of efficient fight-or-flight responses; it may be most adaptive for an organism to rapidly shift computational (and hence energy) resources toward limbic, paralimbic, sensory, and motor territories and away from other heteromodal cortical areas, because higher order mentation or speech are of lower priority in such situations. Interestingly, this same phenomenon of reduced rCBF within widespread heteromodal areas has now also been demonstrated for positively valenced sexual and competitive arousal conditions (Rauch et al., 1999). Thus this pattern is not limited to anxiety or negatively valenced high-arousal states.

This chapter also underscores the need for additional work in this field. In some instances, even initial studies are lacking, as evidenced by the dearth of mMRI data regarding PD and the phobias. In many cases, replication of prior work is needed to corroborate initial findings. Finally, extending our current knowledge should proceed along several dimensions. First, it is critical to appreciate the importance of integrating neuroimaging research with other modes of inquiry, perhaps especially from the disciplines of genetics and molecular biology, and particularly through complementary studies in animals. Second, within the neuroimaging domain, future studies should begin to include psychiatric comparison groups in addition to healthy control groups. This is necessary to establish the specificity of findings versus their generalizability across classes of psychopathology. Third, longitudinal studies and those that adopt a developmental perspective will be of tremendous value. For instance, the relationship between SoP and early temperament calls for studies that begin in childhood, as do OCD and related disorders that have their onset in youth. Also, questions about the diathesis for PTSD and how brain dysfunction evolves over the posttraumatic period can best be addressed via study designs that acquire data prior to trauma exposure and that follow participants over time. Fourth, new and emerging imaging techniques will doubtless provide enhanced capabilities for advancing our understanding of these diseases. For example, combining functional MRI methods with magnetoencephalography promises the capacity to image brain function with greater temporal and spatial resolution than previously possible. Similarly, as new radiolabeled receptor-specific ligands are developed as tracers for use with PET and SPECT, outstanding questions regarding in vivo neurochemistry and neuropharmacology can be addressed.

In summary, neuroimaging data have already been used to help fashion contemporary neurobiological models of the anxiety disorders. Convergent data have provided relatively well-developed and cohesive models of OCD and PTSD, whereas the data for phobias and PD do not yet provide as clear a picture. There is great excitement about the future of this field, which promises to help delineate the pathophysiology of anxiety disorders, as well as to influence the treatment of people who suffer from these illnesses.

## REFERENCES

Aggleton, J. P. (Ed.). (1992). *The amygdala: Neurobiological aspects of emotion memory and mental dysfunction*, New York: Wiley-Liss.

American Psychiatric Association. (1994) *Diagnostic and statistical manual of mental disorders* (4th ed.). Washington, DC: Author.

Aylward, E. H., Harris, G. J. Hoehn-Saric, R, et al. (1996). Normal caudate nucleus in obsessive-compulsive disorder assessed by quantitative neuroimaging. *Archives of General Psychiatry, 53*, 577–584.

Bartha, R., Stein, M. B., Williamson, P. C., et al. (1998). A short echo 1H spectroscopy and volumetric MRI study of the corpus striatum in patients with obsessive-compulsive disorder and comparison subjects. *American Journal of Psychiatry, 155*(11), 1584–1591.

Baxter, L., Schwartz, J., Mazziotta, J., et al. (1988). Cerebral glucose metabolic rates in nondepressed patients with obsessive-compulsive disorder. *American Journal of Psychiatry, 145*, 1560–1563.

Baxter, L. R., Phelps, M. E., Mazziotta, J. C., et al. (1987). Local cerebral glucose metabolic rates in obsessive compulsive disorder: A comparison with rates unipolar depression and in normal controls. *Archives of General Psychiatry, 44*, 211–218.

Baxter, L. R., Jr., Schwartz, J. M., Bergman, K. S., et al. (1992). Caudate glucose metabolic rate changes with both drug and behavior therapy for obsessive-compulsive disorder. *Archives of General Psychiatry, 49*, 681–689.

Benkelfat, C., Bradwejn, J., Meyer, E., et al. (1995). Functional neuroanatomy of CCK4-induced anxiety in normal healthy volunteers. *American Journal of Psychiatry, 152*, 1180–1184.

Benkelfat, C. Nordahl, T. E., Semple, W. E., et al. (1990). Local cerebral glucose metabolic rates in obsessive-compulsive disorder: Patients treated with clomipramine. *Archives of General Psychiatry, 47*, 840–848.

Birbaumer, N., Grodd, W., Diedrich, O., et al. (1998). fMRI reveals amygdala activation to human faces in social phobics. *Neuroreport 9*(6), 1223–1226.

Bisaga, A., Katz, J. L., Antonini, A. et al. (1998). Cerebral glucose metabolism in women with panic disorder. *American Journal of Psychiatry, 155*, 1178–1183.

Brandt, C. A., Meller, J., Keweloh, L., et al. (1998). Increased benzodiazepine receptor density in the prefrontal cortex in patients with panic disorder. *Journal of Neural Transmission, 105*, 1325–1333.

Breiter, H. C. Rauch, S. L., Kwong, K. K., et al. (1996). Functional magnetic resonance imaging of symptom provocation in obsessive compulsive disorder. *Archives of General Psychiatry, 53*, 595–606.

Bremner, J. D., Narayan, M., Staib, L. H., Southwick, S. M., McGlashum, T., & Charney, D. S. (1999). Neural correlates of memories of childhood sexual abuse in women with and without posttraumatic stress disorder. *American Journal of Psychiatry, 156*, 1787–1795.

Bremner, J. D., Randall, P., Scott, T. M., et al. (1995) MRI-based measurement of hippocampal volume in patients with combat-related posttraumatic stress disorder. *American Journal of Psychiatry, 152*, 973–981.

Bremner, J. D., Randall, P., Vermetten, E., et al. (1997). Magnetic resonance imaging-based measurement of hippocampal volume in posttraumatic stress disorder related to childhood physical and sexual abuse: A preliminary report. *Biological Psychiatry, 41*, 23–32.

Bremner, J. D., Staib, L. H., Kaloupek, D., et al. (1999). Neural correlates of exposure to traumatic pictures and sound in Vietnam combat veterans with and without posttraumatic stress disorder: A positron emission tomography study. *Biological Psychiatry, 45*, 806–816.

Brody, A. L., Saxena, S., Schwartz, J. M., et al. (1998). FDG-PET predictors of response to behavioral therapy versus pharmacotherapy in obsessive-compulsive disorder. *Psychiatry Research: Neuroimaging, 84*, 1–6.

Charney, D. S., Bremner, J. D., & Redmond, D. E. (1995). Noradrenergic neural substrates for anxiety and fear: Clinical associations based on pre-clinical research. In F. E. Bloom & D. J. Kupfer (Eds.), *Psychopharmacology: The fourth generation of progress* (pp. 387–396). New York: Raven Press.

Coplan, J. D., & Lydiard, R. B. (1998). Brain circuits in panic disorder. *Biological Psychiatry, 44*, 1264–1276.

Dager, S. R., Friedman, S. D., Heide, A., Layton, M. E., Richards, T., Artru, A., Strauss, W., Hayes, C., & Posse, S. (1999). Two-dimensional proton echo-planar spectroscopic imaging of brain metabolic changes during lactate-induced panic. *Archives of General Psychiatry, 56*, (1), 70–77.

Dager, S. R., Strauss, W. L., Marro, K. I., Richards, T. L., Metzger, G. D., & Artru, A. A. (1995). Proton magnetic resonance spectroscopy investigation of hyperventilation in subjects with panic disorder and comparison subjects. *American Journal of Psychiatry, 152*(5), 666–672.

De Cristofaro, M. T., Sessarego, A., Pupi, A., Biondi, F., & Faravelli, C. (1993). Brain perfusion abnormalities in drug-naive, lactate-sensitive panic patients: A SPECT study. *Biological Psychiatry, 33*(7) 505–512.

Drevets, W. C., Videen, T. O., MacLeod, A. K., et al. (1992).

PET images of blood flow changes during anxiety: A correction. *Science, 256,* 1696.

Ebert, D., Speck, O., Konig, A., Berger, M., Hennig, J., & Hohagen, F. (1997). ¹H-magnetic resonance spectroscopy in obsessive-compulsive disorder: Evidence for neuronal loss in the cingulate gyrus and the right striatum. *Psychiatry Research, 74*(3), 173–176.

Fischer, H., Andersson, J. L., Furmark, T., & Fredrikson, M. (1998). Brain correlates of an unexpected panic attack: A human positron emission tomographic study. *Neuroscience Letters, 251*(2), 137–140.

Fischer, H., Wik, G., & Fredrikson, M. (1996). Functional neuroanatomy of robbery re-experience: Affective memories studied with PET. *NeuroReport 7,* 2081–2086.

Fontaine, R., Breton, G., Dery, R., Fontaine, S., & Elie, R. (1990). Temporal lobe abnormalities in panic disorder: An MRI study. *Biological Psychiatry, 27*(3) 304–310.

Fredrikson, M., Wik, G., Annas, P., et al. (1995). Functional neuroanatomy of visually elicited simple phobic fear: Additional data and theoretical analysis. *Psychophysiology, 32,* 43–48.

Fredrikson, M., Wik, G., Greitz, T., et al. (1993). Regional cerebral blood flow during experimental fear. *Psychophysiology, 30,* 126–130.

Fyer, A. J. (1998). Current approaches to etiology and pathophysiology of specific phobia. *Biological Psychiatry, 44,* 1295–1304.

Gurvits, T. V., Shenton, M. E., Hokama, H., et al. (1996). Magnetic resonance imaging study of hippocampal volume in chronic, combat-related posttraumatic stress disorder. *Biological Psychiatry, 40,* 1091–1099.

Hoehn-Saric, R., Pearlson, G. D., Harris, G. J., et al. (1991). Effects of fluoxetine on regional cerebral blood flow in obsessive-compulsive patients. *American Journal of Psychiatry, 148,* 1243–1245.

Javanmard, M., Shlik, J., Kennedy, S. H., Vaccarino, F. J., Houle, S., & Bradwejn, J. (1999). Neuroanatomic correlates of CCK-4-induced panic attacks in healthy humans: A comparison of two time points. *Biological Psychiatry, 45*(7), 872–882.

Jenike, M. A., Breiter, H. C., Baer, L., et al. (1996). Cerebral structural abnormalities in obsessive-compulsive disorder: A quantitative morphometric magnetic resonance imaging study. *Archives of General Psychiatry, 53,* 625–632.

Kent, J. M., Coplan, J. D., & Gorman, J. M. (1998). Clinical utility of the selective serotonin reuptake inhibitors in the spectrum of anxiety. *Biological Psychiatry, 44,* 812–824.

Kuikka, J. T., Pitkanen, A., Lepola, U., et al. (1995). Abnormal regional benzodiazepine receptor uptake in the prefrontal cortex in patients with panic disorder. *Nuclear Medicine Communications, 16*(4), 273–280.

LeDoux, J. E. (1996). *The emotional brain.* New York: Simon & Schuster.

Liberzon, I., Taylor, S. E., Amdur, R., et al. (1999). Brain activation in PTSD in response to trauma-related stimuli. *Biological Psychiatry, 45,* 817–826.

Machlin, S. R., Harris, G. J., Pearlson, G. D., et al. (1991). Elevated medial-frontal cerebral blood flow in obsessive-compulsive patients: A SPECT study. *American Journal of Psychiatry, 148,* 1240–1242.

Malizia, A. L., Cunningham, V. J., Bell, C. J., Liddle, P. F., Jones, T., & Nutt, D. J. (1998). Decreased brain GABA(A)-benzodiazepine receptor binding in panic disorder: Preliminary results from a quantitative PET study. *Archives of General Psychiatry, 55,* 715–720.

McGuire, P. K., Bench C. J., Frith, C. D., et al. (1994). Functional anatomy of obsessive-compulsive phenomena. *British Journal of Psychiatry, 164,* 459–468.

Mesulam, M.-M. (1985). Patterns in behavioral neuroanatomy: Association areas, the limbic system, and hemispheric specialization. In M.-M. Mesulam (Ed.), *Principles of behavioral neurology* (pp. 1–70). Philadelphia: Davis.

Moore, G. J., MacMaster, F.P., Stewart, C., & Rosenberg, D. R. (1998). Case study: Caudate glutamatergic changes with paroxetine therapy for pediatric obsessive-compulsive disorder. *Journal of the American Academy of Child and Adolescent Psychiatry, 37*(6), 663–667.

Mountz, J. M., Modell, J. G., Wilson M. W., et al. (1989). Positron emission tomography evaluation of cerebral blood flow during state anxiety in simple phobia. *Archives of General Psychiatry, 46,* 501–504.

Nordahl, T. E., Benkelfat, C., Semple, W., et al. (1989). Cerebral glucose metabolic rates in obsessive-compulsive disorder. *Neuropsychopharmacology, 2,* 23–28.

Nordahl, T. E., Semple, W. E, Gross, M., et al. (1990). Cerebral glucose metabolic differences in patients with panic disorder. *Neuropsychopharmacology, 3,* 261–272.

Nordahl, T. E., Stein M. B., Benkelfat, C., et al. (1998). Regional cerebral metabolic asymmetries replicated in an independent group of patients with panic disorders. *Biological Psychiatry, 44*(10), 998–1006.

Perani, D., Colombo, C., Bressi, S., et al. (1995). FDG PET study in obsessive-compulsive disorder: A clinical metabolic correlation study after treatment. *British Journal of Psychiatry, 166,* 244–250.

Potts, N. L., Davidson, J. R., Krishnan, K. R., Doraiswamy, P. M. (1994). Magnetic resonance imaging in social phobia. *Psychiatry Research, 52*(1), 35–42.

Rauch, S. L., & Baxter, L. R. (1998). Neuroimaging of OCD and related disorders. In M. A., Jenike, L. Baer, & W. E. Minichiello (Eds.), *Obsessive-compulsive disorders: Theory and management* (pp. 289–317). Boston: Mosby.

Rauch, S. L., Jenike, M. A., Alpert, N. M., et al. (1994). Regional cerebral blood flow measured during symptom provocation in obsessive-compulsive disorder using ¹⁵O-labeled $CO_2$ and positron emission tomography. *Archives of General Psychiatry, 51,* 62–70.

Rauch, S. L., Savage, C. R., Alpert, N. M., et al. (1995). A positron emission tomographic study of simple phobic symptom provocation. *Archives of General Psychiatry, 52,* 20–28.

Rauch, S. L., Savage, C. R., Alpert, N. M., Dougherty, D., et al. (1997). Probing striatal function in obsessive compulsive disorder: A PET study of implicit sequence learning. *Journal of Neuropsychiatry and Clinical Neurosciences, 9,* 568–573.

Rauch, S. L., Savage, C. R., Alpert, N. M., Fischman, A. J., et al. (1997). The functional neuroanatomy of anxiety: A study of three disorders using PET and symptom provocation. *Biological Psychiatry, 42,* 446–452.

Rauch, S. L., Savage, C. R., Brown, H. D., et al. (1995). A PET investigation of implicit and explicit sequence learning. *Human Brain Mapping, 3,* 271–286.

Rauch, S. L., Shin, L. M., Dougherty, D., et al., (1999). Neural activation during sexual and competitive arousal in healthy men. *Psychiatry Research: Neuroimaging, 91,* 1–10.

Rauch, S. L., Shin, L. M., & Whalen, P. J. (in press). Functional neuroimaging and the neuroanatomy of anxiety disorders. *Psychiatric Annals.*

Rauch, S. L., Shin, L. M., Whalen, P. J., & Pitman, R. K. (1998). Neuroimaging and the neuroanatomy of PTSD. *CNS Spectrums, 3*(Suppl. 2), 30–41.

Rauch, S. L., van der Kolk, B. A., Fisler, R. E., et al. (1996). A symptom provocation study of posttraumatic stress disorder using positron emission tomography and script-driven imagery. *Archives of General Psychiatry, 53,* 380–387.

Rauch, S. L., Whalen, P. J., Curran, T., et al. (2000). Probing striato-thalamic function in OCD and TS using neuroimaging methods. In D. J. Cohen, C. Goetz, & J. Jankovic (Eds.). *Tourette syndrome and associated disorders* (pp. 207–224). Philadelphia: Lippincott, Williams & Wilkins.

Rauch, S. L., Whalen, P. J., Dougherty, D. D., & Jenike, M. A. (1998). Neurobiological models of obsessive compulsive disorders. In M. A. Jenike, L, Baer, & W. E. Minichiello, (Eds.). *Obsessive-compulsive disorders: Practical management* (pp. 222–253). Boston: Mosby.

Rauch, S. L., Whalen, P. J., Savage, C. R., et al. (1997). Striatal recruitment during an implicit sequence learning task as measured by functional magnetic resonance imaging. *Human Brain Mapping, 5,* 124–132.

Reiman, E. M., Raichle, M. E., Robins, E., et al. (1986). The application of positron emission tomography to the study of panic disorder. *American Journal of Psychiatry, 143,* 469–477.

Reiman, E. M., Raichle, M. E., Robins E., et al. (1989). Neuroanatomical correlates of a lactate-induced anxiety attack. *Archives of General Psychiatry, 46,* 493–500.

Robinson, D., Wu, H., Munne, R. A., et al. (1995). Reduced caudate nucleus volume in obsessive-compulsive disorder. *Archives of General Psychiatry, 52,* 393–398.

Rosenberg, D. R., Keshevan, M. S., O'Hearn K. M., et al. (1997). Frontostriatal measurement in treatment-naive children with obsessive-compulsive disorder. *Archives of General Psychiatry, 554,* 824–830.

Rubin R. T., Villaneuva-Myer, J., Ananth, J., et al. (1992). Regional xenon-133 cerebral blood flow and cerebral Technetium 99m HMPAO uptake in unmedicated patients with obsessive-compulsive disorder and matched normal control subjects. *Archives of General Psychiatry, 49,* 695–702.

Salzman, C., Miyawaki, E. K., le Bars, P., & Kerrihard, T. N. (1993). Neurobiologic basis of anxiety and its treatment. *Harvard Review of Psychiatry, 1,* 197–206.

Saxena, S., Brody, A. L., Maidment, K. M., et al. (1999). Localized orbitofrontal and subcortical metabolic changes and predictors of response to paroxetine treatment in obsessive-compulsive disorder. *Neuropsychopharmacology, 21,* 683–693.

Scarone, S., Colombo, C., Livian, S., et al. (1992). Increased right caudate nucleus size in obsessive compulsive disorder: Detection with magnetic resonance imaging. *Psychiatry Research: Neuroimaging, 45,* 115–121.

Schneider, F., Weiss, U., Kessler, C., et al. (1999). Subcortical correlates of differential classical conditioning of aversive emotional reactions in social phobia. *Biological Psychiatry, 45,* 863–871.

Schuff, N., Marmar, C. R. Weiss, D. S., et al. (1997). Reduced hippocampal volume and N-acetyl aspartate in posttraumatic stress disorder. In R. Yehuda & A. C. McFarlane (Eds.). *Annals of The New York Academy of Sciences: Vol 821. Psychobiology of Posttraumatic Stress Disorder* (pp. 516–520).

Schwartz, J. M., Stoessel, P. W., Baxter, L. R., et al. (1996). Systematic changes in cerebral glucose metabolic rate after successful behavior modification. *Archives of General Psychiatry, 53,* 109–113.

Semple, W. E., Goyer, P., McCormick, R., et al. (1993). Preliminary report: Brain blood flow using PET in patients with posttraumatic stress disorder and substance-abuse histories. *Biological Psychiatry, 34,* 115–118.

Shin, L. M., Kosslyn, S. M., McNally, R. J., et al. (1997). Visual imagery and perception in posttraumatic stress disorder: A positron emission tomographic investigation. *Archives of General Psychiatry, 54,* 233–241.

Shin, L. M., McNally, R. J., Kosslyn S. M., et al. (1999). Regional cerebral blood flow during script-driven imagery in childhood sexual abuse-related posttraumatic stress disorder: A PET investigation. *American Journal of Psychiatry, 156,* 575–584.

Stein, M. B. (1998). Neurobiological perspectives on social phobia: From affiliation to zoology. *Biological Psychiatry, 44,* 1277–1285.

Stein, M. B., Koverola, C., Hanna, C., et al. (1997). Hippocampal volume in women victimized by childhood sexual abuse. *Psychological Medicine, 27,* 951–960.

Stein M. B., & Leslie, W. D. (1996). A brain SPECT study of generalized social phobia. *Biological Psychiatry, 39,* 825–828.

Stewart, R. S., Devous, M. D., Sr., Rush, A. J., Lane, L., & Bonte, F. J. (1988). Cerebral blood flow changes during sodium-lactate-induced panic attacks. *American Journal of Psychiatry, 145*(4), 442–449.

Swedo, S. E., Pietrini, P., Leonard H. L., et al. (1992). Cerebral glucose metabolism in childhood-onset obsessive-compulsive disorder: Revisualization during pharmacotherapy. *Archives of General Psychiatry, 49,* 690–694.

Swedo, S. E., Shapiro, M. B., Grady, C. L., et al. (1989). Cerebral glucose metabolism in childhood-onset obsessive-compulsive disorder. *Archives of General Psychiatry, 46,* 518–523.

Tiihonen, J., Kuikka, J., Bergstrom, K., Lepola, U., Koponen, H., & Leinonen, E. (1997). Dopamine reuptake site densities in patients with social phobia. *American Journal of Psychiatry, 154*(2), 239–242.

Whalen, P. J., Bush, G., McNally, R. J., et al. (1998). The emotional counting Stroop paradigm: An fMRI probe of the anterior cingulate affective division. *Biological Psychiatry, 44,* 1219–1228.

Whalen, P. J., Rauch, S. L., Etcoff, N. L., McInerney, S., Lee, M. B., & Jenike M. A. (1998). Masked presentations of emotional facial expressions modulate amygdala activity without explicit knowledge. *Journal of Neuroscience, 18,* 411–418.

Wik, G., Fredrikson, M., Ericson, K., et al. (1993). A functional cerebral response to frightening visual stimulation. *Psychiatry Research: Neuroimaging, 50,* 15–24.

Woods, S. W., Koster, K., Krystal J. K., et al. (1988). Yohimbine alters regional cerebral blood flow in panic disorder. *Lancet, 2,* 678.

# 52

# COGNITIVE BIASES IN EMOTIONAL DISORDERS: INFORMATION PROCESSING AND SOCIAL-COGNITIVE PERSPECTIVES

Susan Mineka, Eshkol Rafaeli,
and Iftah Yovel

In the past several decades emotion and psychopathology researchers have devoted a great deal of attention to the study of emotions such as anxiety and depression as they are experienced in the normal range, as well as to their more extreme manifestations, seen in clinically significant emotional disorders such as anxiety and mood disorders. During this time research and theory from various perspectives have been converging on a consensus that views emotion and cognition as closely intertwined. The complex interplay between the two is still being unraveled and explored. Nonetheless, the field has reached a clear appreciation of a number of factors that play a part in this emotion-cognition interface—both for "normal" levels of these emotions and for maladaptive forms of these emotions seen in emotionally disordered individuals. These factors include the evolutionary forces that shaped the architecture of emotion systems at the species level, as well as the basic and social-cognitive learning processes that affect the ontogenesis and functioning of these emotion systems at the individual level.

Plutchik (1984) argued from a psychoevolutionary perspective that "cognitions have largely evolved in the service of emotions" (p. 209). According to Plutchik, the interaction of cognition with emotion allows our emotional behaviors to be adaptive responses to biologically significant events. In addition, Gray (1990) has also argued for a "genuine interweaving of emotional and cognitive processes in the workings of the brain" (p. 271). This related argument is that over the course of human evolution, human beings were selected for their ability to learn information about reinforcing events (predators, food, mates). Further, because reinforcers elicit primary emotions, cognitions (appraisals of reinforcing events) are linked to the experience of emotion. Finally, Gray (1990) also cites research which implicates the same neuroanatomical structures and systems in the brain as being involved in important emotion- and cognition-related functions (e.g., hippocampus and amygdala).

Recently, Cosmides and Tooby (2000) summarized the evolutionary view by noting that emotions serve as "superordinate programs," or modules of the mind, which are responsible for setting priorities. According to this model, when an emotion is elicited, it activates some subordinate mechanisms (e.g., attention, heuristic processing, or action-readiness programs) and deactivates others (e.g., higher level goals, systematic processing, digestion). In contrast to most other adaptations or modules (cf. Barkow, Cosmides, & Tooby, 1992), emotions are a "mode of operation for the entire psychological architecture": They are, in a sense, primary.

A fundamental theme of recent emotion research is that biased cognitive processes are central features of probably

976

all emotional disorders (as well as of normal, healthy emotional functioning). As we discuss in this chapter, these biases may have both a phylogenetic and an ontogenetic basis. Nowhere has the phylogenetic or evolutionary basis of biased cognitive processing been more evident than in human and nonhuman studies of fear and phobias, which have demonstrated that these emotions do not tend to occur to an arbitrary group of objects or situations associated with trauma. Instead, it appears that human and nonhuman primates have an evolutionarily based predisposition to acquire fears and phobias of certain objects or situations that may once have posed a threat to our early ancestors (e.g., Cook & Mineka, 1990, 1991; Öhman, Dimberg, & Öst, 1985; Öhman & Mineka, 2001; Seligman, 1971; see also chapter 14, this volume).

The thumbprint of evolutionary forces may also be evident in other examples of emotion-cognition interactions. In particular, much attention has been focused on how anxiety and depression may differentially affect cognitive processing of emotional (usually mood-congruent) material, possibly based on adaptive pressures that may have shaped the kinds of cognitive biases seen in these emotional disorders (e.g., Mathews, 1993; Mineka, 1992; Williams, Watts, MacLeod, & Mathews, 1988, 1997). Three kinds of mood-related cognitive biases have been examined: attentional biases, memory biases, and judgmental/interpretive biases. Underlying this work is the belief of some researchers that the neuronal or neuroanatomical architecture of emotion systems is, by design, responsible for the biases in cognitive processing (Cosmides & Tooby, 2000). We review the extant literature on information processing biases in anxiety and depression in the first half of this chapter.

Although it is not derived from an evolutionary framework, a complementary approach to cognition and emotion emphasizes the antecedence of biased cognition to emotion. This approach stems from two rich and interrelated traditions: social cognitive appraisal theories of stress and emotion (e.g., Lazarus, 1991) and cognitive-behavioral approaches to psychopathology (e.g., Beck, 1967, 1976). Often interrelated, these two traditions emphasize the centrality of the *subjective*, and often biased, interpretation of reality in the elicitation of normal and abnormal emotion. Within this complementary approach to the cognition-emotion interface, three domains of mood-related social-cognitive biases have been examined: self-related, other-related, and future-related cognitions. These three domains are reviewed in the second half of this chapter.

Rather than attempt to demarcate the boundary between the evolutionary ("primacy of emotion") and social-cognitive ("primacy of cognition") models, we treat them as complementary and at times overlapping. Separating the two is sometimes reminiscent of the debate between proponents of emotion primacy versus those of cognition primacy (cf. Lazarus, 1984; Zajonc, 1984; see also Scherer, 1999, for a recent integration). In many ways, that debate has been settled. One solution has been to elaborate on the term *cognition* to include both lower level (e.g., automatic attention or perception) and higher level (e.g., conscious appraisal) processes. Another solution has been to acknowledge the temporal fugue-like nature of cognition and emotion. As Lazarus (1999, p. 8) notes, "depending on where one begins one's entry into the flow [of emotion and cognition], which is arbitrary, any response can also be a stimulus." Thus, in both of the following sections and in the conclusion of this chapter, we discuss models of cognition in emotional disorders that fit within one and sometimes both of these emotion-cognition primacy frameworks.

## Information Processing Biases in Anxiety and Depression

### Attentional Biases

Because our cognitive resources are limited, we constantly need to make numerous decisions, many of which are automatic and unconscious, as to which of the infinite number of stimuli that surround us will be processed and which will be discarded. Mood-congruent attentional biases are said to occur when this rapid decision-making process is systematically influenced by the emotional meaning of stimuli. For example, when anxious individuals read the newspaper, their attention may frequently be drawn to articles with threatening content. Similarly, any small insect may quickly attract the attention of a person who has a spider phobia. During the past two decades, many studies have demonstrated that emotional disorders are indeed associated with mood-congruent attentional biases (for a comprehensive review, see Williams et al., 1997).

In this section we first consider the evidence for attentional biases in anxiety and the anxiety disorders and then in depression. We also consider the types of stimuli that produce these biases: Do mood-congruent attentional biases occur with any emotional material, or are they specific to negative or threatening stimuli? Does the material need to be specific to the person's concerns or specific diagnosis, or is a generally negative (or even positive) valence all that is necessary? Several other questions are also addressed: Are there particular stages in the information processing sequence in which the biases occur? Are these biases associated with certain stable traits, or with transient mood states, or with their interaction? First, however, we introduce the paradigms and techniques most frequently used to detect these biases in the laboratory.

In one paradigm, the visual dot probe, individuals with emotional disorders are expected to show both facilitated and disrupted performance in response to emotional stimuli (C. MacLeod, Mathews, & Tata, 1986). This obviates any interpretive problems that arise with some other paradigms in which bias is always indexed by disrupted performance with the emotional stimuli. In the dot-probe task, pairs of words appear simultaneously on a computer screen, one above the other. Participants are instructed to read aloud the top word and to detect as quickly as possible a small dot probe that occasionally replaces one of the words. MacLeod et al. (1986) found that relative to controls, clinically anxious participants were faster to detect the probe when it replaced a threat word rather than a neutral word. If, however, the probe replaced a neutral word that appeared together with a threat word, the performance of anxious participants was slower. Nonanxious participants tended to show an opposite bias. As MacLeod et al. (1986) emphasized, the dot-probe paradigm is an excellent way of examining attentional biases because it is unlikely that participants' responses to the probe are affected by any type of response bias. For example, in earlier paradigms, such as the perceptual defense method (e.g., Small & Robins, 1988), participants might simply have been reluctant to respond to emotionally charged material. Moreover, it has also been shown that the probe detection latency is a sensitive way of assessing visual attention (Navon & Margalit, 1983).

Despite the superiority of the dot-probe paradigm, many more studies have used the emotional Stroop test, in which the experimental stimuli are expected only to interfere with measured performance (i.e., never to facilitate it). In the Stroop task, participants are asked to name as quickly as possible the color of ink in which stimuli are printed, while ignoring any other aspects of these stimuli (e.g., their semantic meaning; Stroop, 1935; cf. C. MacLeod, 1991, for a review). In the classic version of this task, when the words are color names printed in an incongruent color of ink (e.g., the word "blue" printed in red ink), the response latency is considerably larger than to noncolor or meaningless words. Apparently, the to-be-ignored aspect of the stimulus (i.e., its semantic meaning) is salient enough to compete with its attended aspect, the color of the ink with which it is written, resulting in a strong interference effect (see C. M. MacLeod, 1991). In the emotional version of the Stroop test (e.g., Gotlib & McCann, 1984), certain types of participants (e.g., emotionally disordered patients) show longer color-naming latencies to experimental stimuli (such as emotion-related words) than to neutral nonemotional stimuli, whereas normals show comparable latencies to both types of stimuli. This result is presumed to demonstrate that the emotionally disordered patients are devoting a disproportionate amount of attention to the meaning of disorder-relevant emotional words relative to neutral words. The main advantages of this task are its rich cognitive background literature and ease of administration and the fact that it is

less susceptible to response-bias interpretations than earlier paradigms, such as perceptual defense, because participants are not asked to report the emotionally charged word. Nonetheless, some argue that the color-naming interference is actually not a completely pure measure of attentional bias, because the interference in this task may still be the result of processes that are related to the response rather than to the input stage of information processing (e.g., Mogg & Bradley, 1998; see also J. M. G. Williams, Mathews, & MacLeod, 1996, and J. M. G. Williams et al., 1997, for reviews of emotional Stroop studies).

## Attentional Biases in Anxiety and Anxiety Disorders

Attentional bias to threatening material has been shown to occur in a wide range of anxiety disorders, including generalized anxiety disorder (GAD; see, e.g., Mogg, Bradley, & Williams, 1995), panic disorder (e.g., Hope, Rapee, Heimberg, & Dombeck, 1990), posttraumatic stress disorder (PTSD; e.g., McNally, Kaspi, Riemann & Zeltin, 1990), social phobia (e.g., Hope et al., 1990), specific phobia (e.g., Kindt & Brosschot, 1999), and obsessive-compulsive disorder (OCD; e.g., Tata, Leibowitz, Prunty, Cameron, & Pickering, 1996). With subclinical anxious participants (i.e., normal individuals with high levels of trait anxiety), some studies have found attentional biases for negative stimuli (e.g., Bradley, Mogg, Falla, & Hamilton, 1998; Broadbent & Broadbent, 1988), but others have not (e.g., Martin, Williams, & Clark, 1991; Richards, French, Johnson, Naparstek, & Williams, 1992). The Martin et al. (1991) study used the emotional Stroop to compare patients diagnosed with GAD and high-trait-anxious individuals. Interestingly, although the two groups showed comparable levels of trait anxiety, only the patients were slower in color-naming threatening words than nonthreatening words. One possibility is that high-trait-anxious participants, in an attempt to follow the task's instructions, may use conscious strategies in order to override their tendency to be distracted by the threatening words (Mathews & MacLeod, 1994).

### Automatic Versus Strategic Biases?

If high-trait-anxious participants can use conscious strategies to overcome their attentional biases, are the attentional biases automatic or strategic (Bradley, Mogg, Millar, & White, 1995; Mogg, Bradley, & Williams, 1995; Mogg, Bradley, Williams, & Mathews, 1993)? In tasks such as the Stroop or the dot probe, when stimuli are presented subliminally, participants are not aware of the semantic content of the material to which they are exposed. Thus any bias that is detected under these conditions is presumably automatic because it takes place at a preconscious level of awareness that does not allow it to be affected by strategic or conscious efforts. In the more widely used supraliminal presentation mode, the exposure duration of stimuli is long enough so that participants are aware of their semantic content. Several studies have shown that GAD was associated with attentional bias to negative words that were presented either supraliminally (MacLeod et al., 1986; Mogg, Bradley, et al., 1993; Mogg, Bradley, & Williams, 1995) or subliminally, using both the emotional Stroop (Bradley, Mogg, Millar, & White, 1995; Mogg, Bradley, et al., 1993) and the dot-probe (Mogg, Bradley, & Williams, 1995) tasks.

However, studies of nonclinical high-trait-anxious individuals have sometimes shown that emotional Stroop interference occurs only with subliminal (not supraliminal) presentations, which do not allow participants to use strategies that are based on conscious examination of the stimuli (e.g., Bradley, Mogg, & Lee, 1997; Fox, 1996; Mogg, Kentish, & Bradley, 1993).[1] A clinical diagnosis is possibly associated with some kind of breakdown of cognitive controls such that strategic controls that might be used by high-trait-anxious participants to suppress any supraliminal bias cannot operate (Mathews & MacLeod, 1994). This might explain the fact that almost none of the published studies that used the supraliminal emotional Stroop task with diagnosed anxious patients yielded null results (Williams et al., 1997).

In yet other studies this preconscious attentional bias has been shown to serve as a vulnerability marker for more serious levels of clinical distress. For example, C. MacLeod and Hagan (1992) studied women undergoing a test for cervical cancer. The researchers administered the emotional Stroop task for threatening information to the women before they were given the test. For the half of the women who eventually received a diagnosis of cervical pathology, the interference index on the subliminal Stroop task was the best predictor of a dysphoric reaction to the diagnosis ($r = -.54$, $p < .05$). In a similar experiment, MacLeod and Ng (cited in C. MacLeod, 1999) also found that early measures of subliminal threat interference on the Stroop task predicted response to a different stressful life event. Specifically, the emotional Stroop was administered to Singaporean high school graduates several weeks prior to their departure to Australia to attend university. Threat interference was the best predictor of the amount of state anxiety experienced on arrival in Australia.

### The Emotionality and Specificity of Experimental Stimuli

Next we address issues that are related to characteristics of the stimuli that produce mood-congruent attentional biases. The question of emotionality is whether attentional bias is specific to negative or threatening stimuli or whether it can occur with any, even positive, emotional material (see Ruiz-Caballero & Bermudez, 1997, for a review). Some studies have shown interference effects for positive stimuli (e.g., Martin et al., 1991, Exp. 4; Riemann & McNally, 1995). In others (Cassiday, McNally, & Zeitlin, 1992; McNally, Riemann, Louro, Lukach, & Kim, 1992), positive stimuli produced some interference, but not as large in magnitude as that caused by threatening stimuli; thus the general emotionality hypothesis was only partially supported. For example, Cassiday et al. (1992) found that rape victims with PTSD showed greater interference for high-threat words (e.g., *rape, penis*) relative to positive (e.g., *love, friendship*) or moderate-threat (e.g., *crime, bruises*) words, although the interference effect for the two latter word types was also significant. (It is important to note, however, that in this study the highly threatening and positive words were not equated for salience.) In spite of these few studies that show interference with positive stimuli under some conditions, most studies that have used both negative and positive material as stimuli found interference effects only for the negative stimuli (e.g., Bryant & Harvey, 1995, in PTSD; McNally, Amir, et al., 1994, in panic disorder; Mogg, Bradley, et al., 1993, in GAD; see Ruiz-Caballero & Bermudez, 1997, for a review).

Several methodological issues have been suggested as possible explanations for the infrequent findings of attentional biases for positive stimuli, including, for example, whether the positive words are antonyms of anxiety-related words (and therefore strongly semantically related to these words; e.g., Mathews & Klug, 1993; Small & Robins, 1988). However, none of the factors studied can fully account for those few findings of attentional biases to positive stimuli. Thus the fact that most studies failed to show any interference effect for positive material indicates that emotion-related attentional biases are generally specific to threatening, negatively valenced stimuli

One very interesting study by Mathews and Klug (1993) used the emotional Stroop paradigm in order to examine both the emotionality and the specificity issues (i.e., do the biases occur only with stimuli directly related to the participant's worries and concerns?). The two groups in their study were a mixed diagnostic group of anxious patients and a group of controls, and the five sets of stimuli varied along the dimensions of valence (positive vs. negative) and relatedness to anxiety: negative and anxiety-related (e.g., *nervous, tense*), negative and anxiety-unrelated (e.g., *sin, negative*), positive and anxiety-related (e.g., *fearless, relaxed*), positive and anxiety-unrelated (*beauty, delightful*) and matched neutral words. The results showed that color-naming latencies in the anxious group were longer for both negative and positive anxiety-related words (but not for any of the anxiety-unrelated words) than for neutral words. The control participants' latencies did not vary significantly across the five word types. Thus in this study relatedness to anxiety and not simple emotionality or valence of the words was critical in explaining the anxious participants' patterns of interference. Unfortunately, most studies that used both positive and negative stimuli did not simultaneously address the issue of specificity as did Mathews and Klug (1993). It is therefore unclear if they too would have found Stroop interference for positive anxiety-relevant words.

Additional studies have examined the specificity issue independent of the emotionality issue. For example, Hope and colleagues (Hope et al., 1990), studying patients with social phobia and panic disorder, used the emotional Stroop to examine color-naming interference for both social- and physical-related threat words. As predicted by the specificity hypothesis, social phobics showed interference for social but not for physical threat words, and the reverse was true for the panic patients. Thus patients showed attentional biases only for disorder-relevant information. Similarly, Mathews and Sebastian (1993, Exp. 2) found that snake-avoidant participants showed more interference in the emotional Stroop for snake-relevant than for general threat words. Related studies found greater interference for words associated with combat for Vietnam veterans with PTSD (McNally et al., 1990), for contamination words in OCD patients (Tata et al., 1996), and for spider-related words in spider phobics (Watts, McKenna, Sharrock, & Trezise, 1986). Thus, across a wide range of anxiety disorders, semantic relatedness or specificity of experimental material to participants' disorders and concerns have been proven to be an important factor. Overall, combining the two issues of emotionality and specificity, it appears that emotionally disordered individuals generally tend to be particularly vigilant to materials that are related to both the content and the valence of their worries and concerns.

## Do Attentional Biases Occur in Recovered Patients?

Studies that assessed recovered anxiety-disordered patients have generally (but not always) found that an attentional bias which was present before treatment disappeared after successful treatment. This has been shown in GAD (e.g., Mathews, Mogg, Kentish, & Eysenck, 1995), OCD (Foa & McNally, 1986), spider phobia (Watts et al., 1986; although see also Thorpe & Salkovskis, 1997), and social phobia (Mattia, Heimberg, & Hope, 1993). For example, one study of GAD patients showed both subliminal and supraliminal Stroop interference for negative words relative to controls, but immediately after successful treatment and at 20-month follow-up interference in both conditions was gone (Mogg, Bradley, Millar, & White, 1995). In addition, the magnitude of decreased interference after treatment in the recovered patients correlated with reduced ratings of anxious thoughts. Similarly, using a supraliminal version of the dot-probe task, Mogg, Mathews, and Eysenck (1992) showed that GAD patients, but not

recovered patients, were faster to detect probes in the location of the threatening words.

## Are Attentional Biases State or Trait Effects or Do They Interact?

Another important issue concerning the nature of anxiety-related attentional biases is whether they are associated with trait (i.e., stable) or state (i.e., transient) aspects of emotions. Early studies that used questionnaires such as the State-Trait Anxiety Inventory (STAI; Spielberger, Gorsuch, & Lushene, 1970) yielded mixed results (e.g., Broadbent & Broadbent, 1988; Mathews & MacLeod, 1985; Mogg, Mathews, & Weinman, 1989). Perhaps more interesting questions are raised by studies that have manipulated state anxiety to determine how it interacts with trait anxiety. Different types of stressors have been used to manipulate anxiety, either by experimentally inducing it (e.g., giving participants unsolvable anagrams or placing their feared objects/situations in close proximity) or by tapping naturally occurring mood (e.g., testing before end-of-the-semester examinations). Three different kinds of stressors have been used: (1) acute stressors not directly relevant to the participants' concerns; (2) acute stressors that are directly and immediately relevant to the participants' concerns; and (3) more long-term naturally occurring stressors that are quite relevant to the participants' concerns.

Regarding acute stressors not directly relevant to participants' concerns, two studies manipulated state anxiety levels by giving high- and low-trait-anxious participants very difficult and unsolvable (high stress) or easy (low stress) anagrams to solve (Mogg, Mathews, Bird, & Macgregor-Morris, 1990). The emotional Stroop (Study 1) or the dot-probe task (Study 2) were administered after this mood induction procedure. Under high stress (and elevated state anxiety), both high- and low-trait-anxious groups showed color-naming interference and facilitated dot-probe detection for threatening words. Thus, with this kind of stressor, state and trait anxiety may operate independently.

Other studies used stress-induction manipulations which were acute but also more immediately and intensely related to participants' fears than was the stress in Mogg et al.'s (1990) study. In one such study, Mathews and Sebastian (1993, Exp. 1) used the presence of a snake in the testing room as a means of mood induction for students who were high and low on fear of snakes. To maintain high-state anxiety, students were told that after the Stroop task they would be asked to try to touch the snake. Results indicated that neither group showed color-naming interference for snake-related words relative to neutral categorized words. However, when the snake was not present (Mathews & Sebastian, 1993, Exp. 2), the anticipated color-naming interference for threatening stimuli in the snake-fearful group did occur. Another study replicated this suppression-of-interference effect in social phobics whose state anxiety was manipulated by telling them that they would have to give a speech that would be taped (Amir, McNally, Riemann, Burns et al., 1996). Thus J. M. G. Williams et al. (1996) suggested that, under stressful conditions in which the source of stress is obvious and immediately relevant to participants' concerns, anxious participants may increase their conscious efforts to avoid attending to the threatening words, thereby overriding their attentional bias.

Finally, a study that used a naturally occurring stress manipulation found an interesting interaction effect between trait and state anxiety (C. MacLeod & Rutherford, 1992). In this study, when levels of state anxiety were low (early in the semester), students both high and low in trait anxiety did not show color-naming interference for negative versus positive exam-related words presented subliminally. However, in the week prior to end-of-semester exams, when state anxiety levels were elevated for both groups, high-trait-anxious students did show an increased subliminal interference effect for threat words, whereas low-trait-anxiety students showed an opposite effect, a color-naming facilitation for negative words (i.e., avoidance of threat).[2] C. MacLeod and Mathews (1988) had found similar results using a supraliminal version of the dot-probe paradigm. In light of these findings, J. M. G. Williams and colleagues (1996, 1997) suggested that an interaction between trait and state anxiety tends to occur only in cases in which the heightened levels of state anxiety have "time to incubate" (e.g., when anticipating an exam; J. M. G. Williams et al., 1997, p. 98) and not when it is short-lived. Thus the nature of the mood manipulation must be taken into account when interpreting results of such studies.

In summary, accumulated findings from studies that used various methods of mood manipulations show that either or both trait and state anxiety, or the interaction between the two, may have an influence on the presence of anxiety-related attentional biases, although not in an easy, straightforward manner. With laboratory stressors not immediately related to participants' concerns, high experimental stress produces attentional biases in both high- and low-trait-anxious participants (Mogg et al., 1990). In contrast, when long-term naturally occurring stressors that are relevant to the participants' concerns are used, high trait anxiety interacts with high state anxiety to provide an increased interference effect for subliminally presented threat words (e.g., C. MacLeod & Rutherford, 1992; but see also C. MacLeod & Mathews, 1988, for similar effects with supraliminal conditions). By further contrast, when the nature of the stressor is immediately and imminently relevant to worries or fears of the participants being tested and participants are consciously aware of the content of the presented stimuli, high levels of state anxiety appear

to actually suppress the occurrence of attentional biases (e.g., Amir, McNally, Riemann, Burns, et al., 1996; Mathews & Sebastian, 1993; see also C. MacLeod & Rutherford's, 1992, supraliminal results with a long-term type of stressor). Thus, although the pattern is somewhat complex and there are issues that are yet unresolved (e.g., whether some of the findings are confined only to automatic versus strategic biases), the findings of these studies are actually reasonably consistent.

### Attentional Biases in Depression

In contrast to the relatively robust results that indicate the presence of an attentional bias in anxiety and anxiety disorders, evidence in support of a similar bias in depression is much less consistent. In an early study, Gotlib and McCann (1984) used the emotional Stroop and showed that mildly depressed (dysphoric) students were slower in naming the colors of negative words than of neutral or positive words. However, it should be noted that these dysphoric and nondysphoric students undoubtedly also differed on levels of anxiety, a difference which could account for the results. Moreover, results of later studies, some using clinically diagnosed participants, were quite inconsistent: Some failed to find evidence for an attentional bias in depression (e.g., Mogg, Bradley, et al., 1993), whereas others did find such evidence (e.g., Mogg, Bradley, & Williams, 1995; Segal, Gemar, Truchon, & Guirguis, 1995). When such biases have been found, they seem to disappear when the depression remits (e.g., Gotlib & Cane, 1987; Segal & Gemar, 1997).

Yet another pattern of bias was observed by Gotlib, McLachlan, and Katz (1988). In a study using a modified dot-probe task, mildly depressed individuals attended equally to positive and negative words (i.e., an even-handed bias), whereas nondepressed participants showed an attentional bias toward the positive stimuli. However, another study of subclinically anxious and depressed individuals that used a very similar paradigm indicated that anxiety might actually be responsible for this effect (Mogg et al., 1991). Further complicating the picture, a more recent study using the dot-probe paradigm found that depressed participants did show selective attention to socially threatening words, although only when the words were presented supraliminally (Mathews, Ridgeway, & Williamson, 1996). Thus the pattern of findings with depression is decidedly inconsistent, and most studies have not been able to rule out the possibility that the biases sometimes observed may be a function of the elevated anxiety seen in depressed patients.

### Automatic Versus Strategic Biases?

A number of studies that have examined the automatic versus strategic issue have reported mixed results. One such study found that only anxiety and not depression was associated with supraliminal biases (Mogg, Bradley, et al., 1993), whereas in another study (Mogg, Bradley, & Williams, 1995) both anxious and depressed groups, relative to controls, showed attentional biases toward the negative words that were presented supraliminally. Similarly, an even more recent study found that induced dysphoric mood resulted in supraliminal but not subliminal attentional bias using the dot-probe task (see also Mathews et al., 1996), whereas high trait anxiety was associated only with the subliminal bias (Bradley, Mogg, & Lee, 1997). Interestingly, when anxiety (GAD) was comorbid with depression, the depression seemed to eliminate the usually observed bias seen with anxiety in a subliminal condition (Bradley, Mogg, Millar, & White, 1995). Overall, although some studies have found evidence for an attentional bias in depression using supraliminal (but not subliminal) presentations, the results are not entirely consistent.

One plausible explanation for at least some of the inconsistencies in the literature discussed thus far on attentional biases in depression may be that measures of depression and anxiety tend to be poor at discriminating these two disorders (e.g., the very high correlations between measures such as the Beck Depression Inventory [BDI] and the Beck Anxiety Inventory [BAI]; Watson et al., 1995). Thus, as noted earlier, it is possible that many of the effects seen in depressed patients were actually due to their high anxiety levels. Moreover, it is important to note that this problem is not merely psychometric. Depression tends to co-occur with various anxiety disorders, and in general depressed patients show high levels of anxious symptomatology, but the reverse is not necessarily true (for a recent review of the comorbidity between anxiety and depression, see Mineka, Watson, & Clark, 1998). Although one study previously mentioned found that comorbid depression seems to suppress at least preconscious attentional biases in anxiety (Bradley et al., 1995), in general this complex issue is still far from being understood. What is it, for example, about depressive symptoms that sometimes seems to mask or suppress attentional biases for threat, despite the fact that depressed participants show as high or higher levels of anxious symptoms than anxious participants (e.g., Bradley, Mogg, Millar, & White, 1995; Mogg, Bradley, et al., 1993)?

### The Emotionality and Specificity of Experimental Stimuli

One study on the emotionality and specificity issue in depression found Stroop interference effects for all negative stimuli (whether related to participant's concerns or not), but interference did not occur with positive stimuli (Nunn, Mathews, & Trower, 1997). In an interesting study, Segal and colleagues (Segal et al., 1995) asked depressed

and nondepressed control participants to select self-descriptive negative and positive adjectives. Later, participants were tested using a version of the emotional Stroop in which (in order to activate their self-schemata) every word was primed by a positive (e.g., "able to feel close") or negative (e.g., "I often feel judged") short phrase that had been previously rated by the participants as self-descriptive or not. Results indicated that depressed participants showed longer color-naming latencies for self-descriptive negative words that were primed by negative self-phrases than for any other combination. In addition, the depressed group showed greater interference for all negative (even non–self-descriptive) than for positive words, whereas the nondepressed group did not show any interference effect whatsoever.

In summary, findings of attentional bias in depression are decidedly more mixed than in anxiety and the anxiety disorders. Using both Stroop interference and dot-probe paradigms, attentional bias has been observed in some studies but not others and observed quite clearly only with supraliminal presentations of negative words.

In summary, numerous studies in the past two decades using cognitive paradigms, such as the emotional Stroop and the dot probe, have shown that emotional disorders are often associated with attentional biases for mood-congruent material. It is well established that anxiety-disordered individuals show these biases, particularly to negatively valenced stimuli that are related to their fears and concerns. High-trait-anxious participants, with or without laboratory-induced state anxiety, clearly show attentional biases in some (but not in all) studies, with effects depending on a number of factors, such as the nature of the stressors and whether the task is subliminal or supraliminal. By contrast, the existence of these biases in depressed populations is not as clear. As is discussed later, a number of models have been recently suggested as possible frameworks for explanation of this pattern of mood-congruent attentional biases (e.g., Mogg & Bradley, 1998; J. M. G. Williams et al., 1997; see section on "Theories of Information Processing and the Emotional Disorders," this chapter).

### Memory Biases

Given that some attentional processing of material (however brief or cursory) generally must occur before the material can be remembered, one might expect that individuals who show attentional biases for emotion-relevant material might be likely to show especially good memory for the same kind of material. Moreover, the two most prominent theories of the effects of emotion on information processing—Bower's semantic associative network theory (e.g., 1981) and Beck's schema theory (e.g., 1967, 1976)—predict that both anxiety and depression should produce generally the same effects on attention and memory for emotion-relevant material. However, the picture that has emerged from research over the past 15 to 20 years is far more complicated.

*Mood-congruent memory* is said to occur when depressed or anxious individuals remember previously presented material better if that material is congruent with their mood or emotional state. Sometimes mood affects which material is encoded in the first place (mood-congruent processing), and sometimes it affects which material is retrieved (mood-congruent retrieval). Mood-congruent memory should not be confused with *mood-dependent memory*, in which any material (neutral or emotional) learned while in one mood is best recalled when in the same mood (see Ellis & Moore, 1999, for a discussion of these distinctions). For the present purposes we focus on mood-congruent memory, by which, typically, a depressed individual exposed to neutral, negative, and positive material would later remember more negative than neutral or positive material, whereas a nondepressed individual would often remember more positive than negative material.[3]

In this section we consider several different issues that have been studied in this area. The first issue is the type of memory being assessed. Until the past 15 to 20 years, most memory studies were of *explicit memory* (e.g., free recall, cued recall, or recognition), in which participants are instructed to consciously retrieve previously studied material through one of these methods. More recently attention has focused increasingly on *implicit memory* research, in which memory is assessed indirectly by, for example, comparing the performance of participants on various implicit tasks that involve either previously presented material or new material. Much of the renewed interest in this topic has stemmed from extensive research on amnesic patients who show severe deficits on explicit memory tests but relatively normal performance on tests of implicit memory (e.g., Roediger, 1990; Schacter, 1987). Paralleling this more recent focus on general implicit memory has been increased interest in mood-congruent implicit memory. In contrast to explicit memory tasks, performance on implicit memory tasks is not influenced by volitional strategies and is unconscious in nature (C. MacLeod & Rutherford, 1999). Evidence for mood-congruent implicit memory might give us one possible reason that negative memories so often come to mind in individuals with emotional disorders without their having made any attempt to retrieve those memories.

A second issue concerns whether any biases shown are vulnerability or state markers. That is, do they exist as vulnerability factors prior to and/or following a depressive episode? Finally, another issue in studies of autobiographical memory is whether differences in retrieval for positive versus negative memories are simply a function of possible real differences in past experiences, as opposed to current mood state.

## Depression

*Explicit Memory Biases with Experimentally Presented Material.* Mood-congruent memory studies in depression involve comparing depressed and nondepressed individuals on their memories for either autobiographical or experimentally presented material of several valences (usually negative with neutral and/or positive). With experimentally presented material, participants are usually asked to encode the material with a self-referential encoding task (e.g., asking the person to create a visual scene associating the presented word with him- or herself or to rate how well the word describes him or her). Researchers have generally found that clinically depressed patients show a bias to recall experimentally presented negative, especially self-referential, information. (This bias appears to be lower in magnitude when the material is not encoded in a self-referential manner, primarily because it is not as elaborately encoded in non–self-referential encoding tasks; see Teasdale & Barnard, 1993.) Nondepressed controls tend to favor recall of positive material. Dysphoric participants tend to show even-handed memory, recalling approximately equal amounts of negative and positive information (see J. M. G. Williams et al., 1997; see also Matt, Vacquez, & Campbell, 1992, for a meta-analysis.)

Next we turn to some of the more important parameters that influence mood-congruent memory biases in depression. Although this topic has not been as extensively studied for memory biases as for attentional biases, some studies have suggested that these explicit memory biases associated with depression seem to occur primarily with depression-relevant words (vs. threat words, for example; cf. Bellew & Hill, 1990; Bradley, Mogg, & Williams, 1994; Watkins, Mathews, Williamson, & Uller, 1992). Regarding the issue of whether such memory biases are a vulnerability factor or a state marker of depression, several studies have compared depressed, previously depressed, and normal control individuals to determine whether the bias remits following recovery. Although the results are not entirely consistent here, a number of studies have shown that these negative memory biases may not completely remit along with remission from depression. The lingering negative memory bias is especially evident when previously depressed individuals are given a negative mood induction (e.g., Bradley & Mathews, 1988; Gilboa & Gotlib, 1997; Hedlund & Rude, 1995; Teasdale & Dent, 1987). Several studies have also shown that individual differences in the tendency for negative memory biases may precede and predict onset of a depressive episode (e.g., Bellew & Hill, 1991) or susceptibility to a depressive mood induction procedure (Bellew & Hill, 1990). Such studies support the idea that negative memory biases may be an enduring marker of vulnerability to depression (at least when in a depressed mood), preceding its onset and lasting into recovery.

*Autobiographical Memory Biases.* Several different ways of studying autobiographical memory biases have been successfully employed in this literature. For example, some studies have examined the content of the autobiographically recalled memories to determine whether there are differences in the specificity versus overgenerality of the positive and negative memories recalled. Overgeneral memories do not include reference to specific times or places (e.g., responding with "whenever I played soccer" vs. "when I played soccer last Sunday" to the cue word "fun"; e.g., J. M. G. Williams et al., 1997). Several studies (e.g., Moffitt, Singer, Nelligan, Carlson, & Vyse, 1994; M. Williams & Scott, 1988) have found that depressed patients retrieve less specific (i.e., overgeneral) positive memories than nondepressed controls (and sometimes less specific negative memories, too; cf. Kuyken & Dalgleish, 1995; Moore, Watts, & Williams, 1988). Thus at present it is not entirely clear whether the depressive bias toward overgeneral memories is specific to positive or also includes negative memories.

Using a different method that is not focused on content differences, depressed and nondepressed participants are sometimes asked to retrieve specific autobiographical positive and/or negative memories to neutral cue words (or to retrieve autobiographical memories to positive and negative cue words). In these paradigms, the number of these recalled memories and the latency to recall them is recorded. Typically what is found is that depressed individuals, but not normal controls, take longer to recall positive memories (even to positive cue words). Moreover, some studies have also found that the more severe the depression, the more quickly the depressed patient retrieves an unpleasant memory (e.g., Lloyd & Lishman, 1975; see Healy & Williams, 1999, and J. M. G. Williams et al., 1997, for reviews).

Do these differences in autobiographical memories occur because depressed people have simply experienced more negative events than nondepressed people? To examine this question, several studies have tested participants on multiple occasions and in different affective states. If the "different experiences" hypothesis is correct, then people should show the same pattern of recall whether they are currently depressed or nondepressed. In one ingenious study, D. M. Clark and Teasdale (1982) recruited depressed patients who showed significant diurnal variation in mood and studied them at several different points in their day. As the participants' depression level increased, the probability of their recalling a negative autobiographical memory also increased (and decreased for positive memories). As they became less depressed, the opposite occurred; thus the different-experiences hypothesis was not supported. Rather, these results suggest that it is the current affective state that drives these biases. Other studies of normals with induced depressed or positive moods also show an effect of mood on autobiographical memory, even when past experience is clearly con-

trolled (e.g., Gilligan & Bower, 1984; Teasdale & Fogarty, 1979).

A third technique for studying a specific kind of autobiographical memory bias has also been developed in recent years. Brewin and colleagues, in a series of studies, have shown that depressed patients, such as those with PTSD, have a higher than expected level of *intrusive memories* for negative events. Intrusive memories are measured at the end of a detailed interview that assesses a series of stressful events that may have occurred in the patient's life. After these events have been recorded, patients are asked if they had noticed any of these stressful life events spontaneously coming to mind in the past week. "To qualify, memories had to consist of a visual image of a specific scene that had actually taken place. General thoughts or worries were not included" (Brewin, Reynolds, & Tata, 1999, p. 513). Intrusive memories occurred in depressed patients nearly as much as in PTSD patients, and there were no differences in attempts to avoid or suppress them. Differences did occur, however, in the typical content of the intrusive memories: family deaths, illness, and interpersonal events for depression patients versus personal assault or illness for PTSD patients (Reynolds & Brewin, 1999). In addition, for the depressed group a combined measure of the presence and extent of intrusive memories predicted depression levels 6 months later, even when controlling for Time 1 depression level.

Teasdale (1988) and others have argued that these memory biases for negative self-referential or autobiographical material, in combination with interpretive and judgmental biases (to be discussed briefly later), can be seen as creating what Teasdale calls a vicious cycle of depression. He argues that if one is already depressed and if his or her memory is biased to recall negative things that have happened, these biases help perpetuate the depression. Consistent with this idea are findings by Dent and Teasdale (1988). They found that, for depressed patients, the number of negative trait words the patients had previously rated as self-descriptive was highly correlated ($r = .8$) with the number of such words they recalled on an incidental recall task and that both of these predicted how depressed the patients would be five months later (even when controlling for initial depression). Indeed, this was the only predictor variable other than initial level of depression to predict depression significantly at this later point. Brittlebank, Scott, Williams, and Perrier (1993) also found that the extent of overgeneralization of their positive memories recalled in an autobiographical memory task in depressed inpatients at Time 1 was the single best predictor of depression three and seven months later.

*Implicit Memory.* Another issue in mood-congruent memory research is whether any such biases occur with implicit, as well as explicit, memory tasks. Implicit memory in depression is generally assessed by exposing depressed and nondepressed participants to negative and neutral information. Participants' memories are assessed indirectly in a later task by comparing their performance on that task with previously presented versus new information (the priming or implicit memory index). An implicit memory bias for negative information would result in a higher priming index for the depressed participants with previously presented negative words than with previously presented neutral words. The first three published studies with depressed patients on this topic found no significant evidence for an implicit mood-congruent memory bias (although all three replicated the standard explicit mood-congruency effects; Denny & Hunt, 1992; Hertel & Hardin, 1990; Watkins et al., 1992; see Roediger & McDermott, 1992, for a review and commentary).

However, in their commentary on several of these studies, Roediger and McDermott (1992) proposed that those studies were inconclusive regarding possible implicit memory biases because there had been a mismatch between the nature of the encoding task and the nature of the mood-congruent implicit memory task. The cognitive processes involved in such tasks can be either data-driven/perceptual (e.g., focusing on the physical characteristics of the word, such as the number of letters), or conceptual (e.g., elaborating or focusing on the meaning of the word). For memory in general, Roediger and colleagues have hypothesized and found that the greater the overlap between the processes used during the encoding and the memory tasks (e.g., perceptual-perceptual or conceptual-conceptual), the better the memory performance on a particular task (e.g., Roediger & Blaxton, 1987). Accordingly, Watkins, Vache, Verney, Muller, and Mathews (1996) used an implicit memory task that met these requirements (conceptually based encoding and memory tasks) and found the hypothesized mood-congruent implicit memory bias for depression-relevant words (and an opposite bias in controls, who showed more priming for positive words than for negative words). Moreover, four separate experiments using a different kind of conceptual implicit memory task (primed lexical decision; Bradley, Mogg, & Williams, 1994, 1995; Bradley, Mogg, & Millar, 1996) also found evidence for an implicit memory bias for negative words in dysphoric and clinically depressed patients, and the effects were clearly a function of their depression rather than of anxiety (see the next section; see also Ruiz-Caballero & Gonzalez, 1994). Mood-congruent implicit memory biases are of particular interest because they suggest one possible explanation for the fact that negative information so often enters the consciousness of depressed individuals without their making any conscious effort to recall it.

As this section indicates, there is a great deal of evidence for explicit memory biases for negative mood-congruent

information in depression, although the absolute magnitude of this bias is usually rather small; Matt et al., (1992) reported that clinically depressed participants tended to recall approximately 10% more negative than positive material. Nondepressed participants generally recall more positive than negative material (by about 8%). In autobiographical memory, it seems that the bias seen in depressed individuals most likely reflects current differences in emotional state rather than differences in experiences. Finally, at least six recent studies have also found good evidence for a mood-congruent implicit memory bias for negative information in depression.

### Anxiety and Anxiety Disorders

In contrast to the strong evidence for mood-congruent memory biases in depression, the research examining whether such biases for threatening information exist with anxiety and anxiety disorders is much more mixed. Very few studies claim to find evidence for explicit memory biases in anxiety, and results for implicit memory biases are somewhat inconsistent. The results for generalized or high trait anxiety are discussed separately from those in other anxiety disorders, as the emerging picture in the latter case is somewhat more complicated.

*Explicit Memory.* Most explicit memory studies on clinically anxious or high-trait-anxious participants have found no significant memory biases for threatening versus neutral information. Indeed, several have even found a trend toward the opposite bias (e.g., Mogg, Mathews, & Weinman, 1987). Most typical, however, are simply findings of no differences between groups on explicit recall (or recognition) of threatening versus neutral information (e.g., Bradley, Mogg, & Williams, 1995; Mathews, Mogg, May, & Eysenck, 1989; Mogg, 1988; Mogg et al., 1992; Nugent & Mineka, 1994). J. M. G. Williams et al. (1997) summarized this literature by noting that at the time of their review, only 5 out of 16 studies that examined explicit memory biases in high trait anxiety or GAD showed any evidence for such a bias; they further noted that of these five, the results of three provided only very weak support for such a bias (see also Becker, Roth, Andrich, & Margraf, 1999). Given the strong bias toward publishing positive rather than negative results, we are not confident that a reliable explicit memory bias in anxiety will be found. One possible explanation of such results, which we detail later, is that although highly anxious participants clearly show heightened vigilance for threat, once their attention is drawn to it, they may avoid further elaborative rehearsal that would be necessary to produce concomitant explicit memory biases (M. Williams et al., 1988; J. M. G. Williams et al., 1997).

*Autobiographical Memory.* Regarding autobiographical memory biases in anxiety, two studies, using paradigms similar to those used with depression, suggested that anxious participants may show superior autobiographical memory biases for threatening material (Burke & Mathews, 1992; Richards & Whittaker, 1990, using GAD patients and high-trait-anxious participants, respectively). However, one study of high-trait-anxious participants failed to replicate these results with a design that was in some ways superior to the other two (Levy & Mineka, 1998), leaving the status of an autobiographical memory bias in anxiety uncertain. Moreover, no studies to date have examined whether any such effects that may exist are due to differential experiences with threatening events or to differential encoding (by anxious participants) of more ambiguous events as highly threatening (see the subsequent section, "Judgmental or Interpretive Biases").

*Implicit Memory.* As in the studies of mood-congruent memory in depression, implicit memory in anxiety is generally assessed by exposing anxious and nonanxious participants to threatening and neutral words. Participants' memories are assessed indirectly in a later task by comparing their performance with threatening versus neutral words that are either new or previously presented (the priming or implicit memory index). Mathews, Mogg, May, & Eysenck (1989) first reported results that suggested that GAD patients may show a relative bias in implicit (but not explicit) memory for threatening information. Since then, however, the picture that has emerged is very mixed. On the one hand, one study did report a significant implicit memory bias in GAD patients using a perceptual identification task (C. MacLeod & McLaughlin, 1995), although the researchers did not rule out the possibility that depression could be mediating the bias (cf. Bradley et al., 1996). Moreover, Eysenck and Byrne (1994) also found such a bias in high-trait-anxious participants with an implicit memory task chosen to involve the same kind of processing at encoding and at the indirect memory test, although again whether this bias was due to depression rather than anxiety was unclear. On the other hand, Mathews himself reported a failure to replicate his earlier finding with GAD patients (Mathews et al., 1995); however, a slightly different paradigm was used that in retrospect might be less likely to result in such a bias (see Roediger & McDermott, 1992). In addition, Nugent and Mineka (1994) failed to find evidence in two studies for such a bias in high-trait-anxious individuals (whose levels of trait anxiety were comparable to those of the GAD patients in the Mathews, Mogg, May, & Eysenck 1989, study). Four subsequent studies also failed to produce such an effect in high-trait-anxious individuals, even when both conceptual encoding and implicit memory tasks were used (Mineka, 1997, unpublished data). Finally, perhaps

the single most important study in this area was conducted by Bradley et al. (1995). They compared the performance of GAD patients with that of depressed patients and normal controls on implicit and explicit memory tasks and found no evidence of either implicit or explicit memory biases in anxiety (although both biases were present in depression). Thus, although Williams et al. (1997) concluded that the bulk of the evidence supported the existence of implicit memory biases in anxiety, we differ in our conclusions and see the emerging picture as decidedly inconsistent.[4]

Overall, the pattern of largely negative findings for anxiety—using a range of paradigms—stands in rather striking contrast to the positive findings seen with depression. Especially important in this regard are studies such as that of Bradley, Mogg, and Williams (1995), which directly compared depressed and anxious participants using both depression- and anxiety-relevant words and both implicit and explicit memory tasks. Such studies are ideal because, when they reveal such biases in depression but not anxiety, we are quite certain that the paradigm is sensitive for demonstrating such differences. Nevertheless, more work is needed to try to determine whether there are particular conditions under which implicit memory biases in anxiety can be found reliable.

### Memory Biases in Other Anxiety Disorders

As noted earlier, the status of possible memory biases in other anxiety disorders is somewhat more complex than for general anxiety. Moreover, because fewer studies have been done, the degree of confidence that we can place in any conclusions we draw is somewhat lower. Additionally, many of the studies that claim to find such biases have either failed to or been unable to rule out the possibility that the biases seen could be a function of the clinical participants' elevated levels of depression rather than their anxiety.

*Specific Phobias.* Starting with specific phobias, Watts, Sharrock, and Trezise (1986) and Watts and Dalgleish (1991) found that spider phobics demonstrated poorer explicit memory for spiders than did controls (dead spiders were mounted on cards). However, Watts and Coyle (1993) did not replicate their earlier findings of inferior memory in spider phobics when spider words were used, but their results also lent only weak support to the idea of a memory bias for spider words. Moreover, Rusted and Dighton (1991) found that spider phobics showed enhanced recall for prose material related to spiders (e.g., a story about a visit to an old house with an empty garage and lots of cobwebs) but not involving direct reference to them. This seemingly opposite effect may have occurred because the spider phobics did not have to encode or recall details of spiders per se (as they did in the three Watts studies); phobics may be reluctant to respond with objects that they fear (see J. M. G. Williams et al., 1997). Finally, we found only one study that examined whether implicit memory biases occur in specific phobia. Using analogue participants who were fearful of insects, Harris, Adams, Menzies, and Hayes (1995) found evidence for an implicit bias (but no explicit bias) for insect pictures. Such findings obviously need to be replicated with real phobic participants, however, before much confidence can be placed in them.

*Social Phobia.* At least four studies have found no evidence that demonstrates an explicit memory bias in social phobia for threatening material (see Becker et al., 1999, for a review). One additional study using a very different paradigm did find evidence of a recognition bias for previously presented photographs of critical, relative to neutral, faces (Lundh & Öst, 1996), although this study suffers from several methodological limitations (cf. C. MacLeod, 1999). In another study, a subset of socially phobic participants (those with specific social fears) did show an implicit memory bias for socially threatening material (Lundh & Öst, 1997). Thus, although the number of studies is not yet large enough to be conclusive, the evidence suggests that mood-congruent memory biases in social phobia are certainly not robust.

*Obsessive-Compulsive Disorder.* One study that examined autobiographical memory in OCD found that OCD patients had overgeneralized memories in response to cue words but that the effects were not a function of OCD per se but rather of their comorbid diagnoses of depression (Wilhelm, McNally, Baer, & Florin, 1997). Another study found no evidence for either an implicit or explicit memory bias in OCD patients for OCD-relevant material compared with controls (Foa, Amir, Gershuny, Molnar, & Kozak, 1997).

*Posttraumatic Stress Disorder.* Only a few memory bias studies on PTSD exist, and they show somewhat mixed results. For example, one study that used a conceptual memory task found better implicit memory for combat-relevant sentences in PTSD patients (Amir, McNally, & Wiegartz, 1996), whereas another that used a perceptual memory task failed to find such an effect (McNally & Amir, 1996). These findings suggest the possibility that the type of memory task may influence the results, which would not be surprising given the points mentioned earlier by Roediger and McDermott (1992).

In studies of autobiographical memory, overgeneralized memories were found in several studies of PTSD patients (McNally, Litz, & Prassas, 1994; McNally, Lasko, Macklin, & Pitman, 1995). These studies also found evidence of a more traditional autobiographical memory bias for nega-

tive memories, although it is quite possible that this occurred simply because patients had experienced more negative events. Moreover, intrusive memories, such as were discussed previously with regard to depression, are of course a hallmark of PTSD but quite clearly must be a function of differential experiences (e.g., Reynolds & Brewin, 1999).

*Panic Disorder.* In contrast to studies of the anxiety disorders reviewed previously, the picture seems somewhat more consistent with panic disorder, suggesting that explicit memory biases for threat may be a special feature of this condition. However, questions about whether this bias is truly a function of panic disorder remain. Seven out of at least eight studies found some evidence of an explicit memory bias for threatening information in panic disorder (see C. MacLeod, 1999, for a review of seven of these; see also Becker et al., 1999). However, in one study the bias was found only in patients who showed laterality scores that favored left-hemisphere processing (Otto, McNally, Pollack, Chen, & Rosenbaum, 1994), and in another the authors showed that some of the results were due more to the high levels of depressive symptoms than anxiety symptoms seen in their panic-disordered patients (Becker et al., 1999). Several other of these studies also did not rule out the possibility that the bias could be a function of elevated depression levels. Thus, although explicit memory biases do seem to occur in panic disorder, the possibility remains that such biases may be due to elevated levels of depression.

Studies on implicit memory biases in panic disorder have been inconsistent. Two have claimed to find such a bias (Amir, McNally, Riemann, & Clements, 1996; Cloitre, Shear, Cancienne, & Zeitlin, 1994), but the former one found bias on only one of three dependent measures, and the latter used a somewhat unconventional implicit memory task. Moreover, two other studies failed to find such a bias (Becker, Rinck, & Margraf, 1994; Lundh & Öst, 1997).

Overall, the pattern of results regarding mood-congruent memory biases in the other anxiety disorders is somewhat inconsistent, with the most consistent evidence for explicit memory biases existing for panic disorder, although even in these cases it is not as yet entirely clear what role depression plays in mediating these biases. Some studies of some disorders have found evidence of an implicit memory bias, but many have not. Given the bias against publishing null results, one can only conclude that the evidence for such biases is rather inconsistent at the present time. Autobiographical memory biases have been studied extensively only for PTSD and have not ruled out the different-experience hypothesis to explain positive results. Overgeneralized autobiographical memory, however, does appear to occur in PTSD, and current speculations are that a style of overgeneralized memory (even for neutral events) may arise as a response to the experience of trauma (Healy & Williams, 1999; J. M. G. Williams et al., 1997).

## Judgmental or Interpretive Biases

Both anxiety and depression are associated with several forms of judgmental and interpretive biases. Some of the research on these biases involves subjective estimates of the probability of future events (positive and negative); other work involves sophisticated information processing paradigms to determine whether these disorders are associated with biased interpretations of ambiguity.

### Probability Judgments of Future Events

As reviewed by A. MacLeod (1999), numerous studies that have examined subjective probability judgments about future events have found that depressed and anxious individuals judge negative future events as more likely to happen to them than do controls. There is also a tendency for depressed (and perhaps anxious) individuals to show a reduced perceived likelihood of future positive events (although results here are less consistent). Unfortunately, it is impossible to determine in any absolute sense how realistic such biases may be, given that people vulnerable to depression are known actually to experience more stressful life events (e.g., Kendler, Neale, Kessler, Heath, & Eaves, 1993). MacLeod's own research supports the idea that heightened anticipation of future negative experiences is associated with the general factor of negative affect (nonspecific to both depression and anxiety), whereas the other general factor of low positive affect (specific to depression) is associated with the reduced anticipation of future positive experiences (e.g., A. MacLeod & Byrne, 1996). In addition to a biased forecast of future probabilities, anxious patients generate more numerous different negative (but not positive) future events that are going to happen to them, whereas depressed patients have difficulty generating different positive (but not negative) future events (A. MacLeod, Tata, Kentish, & Jacobsen, 1997). Additionally, Byrne and MacLeod (1997) found that anxious and anxious/depressed participants generated more explanations than did control participants for why future positive outcomes would not, and future negative outcomes would, happen.

A. MacLeod (1999) discusses evidence for mechanisms that possibly underlie these biased future-related cognitions. First, invoking Tversky and Kahneman's (1973) availability heuristic, he suggests that anxious and depressed individuals have easier access to negative (but not positive) memories or cognitive content. Second, invoking Kahneman and Tversky's (1982) simulation heuristic, MacLeod suggests that emotionally disordered individuals may differ in their simulation processes for future events. Specifically, this implies that an active process of deline-

ating the actual steps or subgoals that will precede a future event is at the root of the probability with which that event will be forecast. Given that anxious and depressed individuals can generate many reasons why negative events will, and positive events will not, happen to them, this may explain why they overestimate their occurrence.

### Interpretation of Ambiguity

In self-report studies, individuals with emotional disorders show a tendency to interpret ambiguous events negatively. For example, Butler and Mathews (1983) found that both depressed and anxious patients were more likely to interpret ambiguous scenarios in a threatening manner (e.g., "Suppose you wake with a start in the middle of the night thinking you heard a noise, but all is quiet. What do you suppose woke you up?"; J. M. G. Williams et al., 1997, p. 228). Similar findings were obtained with panic patients and agoraphobics (e.g., D. M. Clark, 1988; McNally & Foa, 1987).

Unfortunately, with self-report measures it is difficult to determine whether patients simply have a negative response bias, prompting investigators to use other less problematic paradigms. Nearly all of these studies have used anxious populations. Biased interpretations of ambiguity have been shown to occur both with ambiguous homophones (e.g., *die/dye, pain/pane*; Mathews, Richards, & Eysenck, 1989) and with ambiguous sentences (e.g., "the doctor examined Little Emma's growth" or "they discussed the priest's convictions"; e.g., Eysenck, Mogg, May, Richards, & Mathews, 1991).[5] One very elegant study involved a text comprehension paradigm (C. MacLeod & Cohen, 1993). Results clearly showed that these interpretive biases were occurring while the anxious individuals were reading the text (on-line) rather than afterward, in which case a memory bias could potentially have contributed to the effect in the Eysenck et al. (1991) study (see also Calvo, Eysenck, & Castillo, 1997; Calvo, Eysenck, & Estevaz, 1997).

These issues have not been studied in depression, except with self-report, for reasons that are unclear. In the only study we are aware of that examined interpretation of ambiguity with a priming methodology, Lawson and MacLeod (1999) found no evidence for such a bias in mildly depressed college students. However, such results clearly need to be replicated with clinically depressed samples to determine how reliable they are.

### Judgments of Covariation

Phobic fears also seem to be the basis for biased judgments of the covariation between feared stimuli and aversive outcomes. Tomarken, Mineka, and Cook (1989) exposed high or low snake-fearful participants to a series of slides of fear-relevant (snakes) and fear-irrelevant (flowers and mushrooms) stimuli, each of which was followed by an aversive or nonaversive outcome (shocks, tones, or nothing). Slide categories and outcomes were paired an equal number of times. Yet when asked to judge the probability that each slide category had been followed by each outcome type, high-fear participants dramatically overestimated the percentage of trials on which the fear-relevant stimuli had been followed by shock but were quite accurate in all other estimates; that is, only the co-occurrence of snakes and shocks was overestimated. A second study showed that it was the aversiveness of the shock rather than its greater salience per se that was responsible for this effect (Tomarken et al., 1989). Such biased judgments of the covariation between feared stimuli and aversive outcomes may well have the effect of promoting the maintenance or enhancement of fear. If one is already afraid of some object or situation and then overestimates the probability with which that object is paired with aversive events, fears should be maintained or exacerbated. Consistent with this, in one study participants who were treated for spider phobia as a group no longer showed this bias, but any residual bias they did show was predictive of return of fear 2 years later (de Jong, Merckelbach & Arntz, 1995).

In addition, several studies have extended the generality of the covariation-bias phenomenon by studying other categories of fear-relevant stimuli. For example, Pauli, Montoya, and Martz (1996) found that panic-prone individuals showed covariation bias for slides depicting fear-relevant situations, such as emergency situations and aversive outcomes. In addition, Pury and Mineka (1997) examined blood-injury fear-relevant stimuli (surgery slides or mutilation slides) compared with conceptually related fear-irrelevant stimuli and consistently found that participants overestimated the covariation between this class of fear-relevant stimuli and aversive outcomes (see Öhman & Mineka, 2001, for a comprehensive review).

As the preceding review suggests, a variety of different kinds of judgmental and interpretive biases have been shown to be associated with depression and various anxiety disorders. In all cases the biases lead emotionally disordered individuals to more negative conclusions about current ambiguous situations, to overestimates of the likelihood that bad things will happen in the presence of feared outcomes, and to overestimates of the probability of future negative events (and/or to underestimates of the probability of future good events). Thus it can be expected that each bias is likely to contribute to the maintenance of anxiety or depression.

## Theories of Information Processing and the Emotional Disorders

As has been noted, anxiety and depression appear to have somewhat different effects on cognitive processing of mood-congruent information. The evidence is quite strong that anxiety is associated with preconscious and conscious attentional bias for threatening cues and that depression is associated with a memory bias for negative self-referential information (although both seem to be associated with various judgmental and interpretive biases). Theories of the effects of emotion on cognition need to be able to account for this apparent dissociation between the most prominent mood-congruent biases for these two different emotional disorders (J. M. G. Williams et al., 1988, 1997). The two theories originally used to account for the relationship between emotion and cognition—Bower's (1981) semantic associative network model and Beck's (1967, 1976) schema model—predicted that evidence for both attentional and memory biases should be evident in both anxiety and depression. The reason is that in both of these models different emotions are all thought to have the effect of giving priority to mood-congruent information at each stage of the information processing continuum—from early perceptual detection to subsequent recall and judgment. Such models would also suggest that attentional and memory biases might well be closely related because a common mechanism was hypothesized to be responsible for each. Unfortunately, there has been very little research that examines both attentional and memory biases within the same individuals. Thus we do not know about their interrelationship within individuals. However, as already discussed, any close relationship may be unlikely given that anxiety seems to be much more closely related to attentional biases than is depression, and vice versa for memory biases.

Only in the past 15 years have models been developed that have begun to help us to understand these differential effects of anxiety and depression on attention versus memory (e.g., J. M. G. Williams et al., 1988, 1997). Although the framework of Williams and his colleagues does a better job of accounting for these differences, it still has some difficulties in accounting for certain results in this complex array of findings (e.g., Mineka & Nugent, 1995; Mineka & Zinbarg, 1998). The Williams et al. (1988, 1997) model draws on the distinction made by Graf and Mandler (1984) between the *activation* or *integration* of mental representations, which is a relatively automatic process, and the *elaboration* of mental representations, which is a more strategic process. According to Graf and Mandler, integration results when exposure to a stimulus automatically activates an associated schema, leading to a strengthening of the internal organization of the schema. Integration makes the activated schema and its components more readily accessible, facilitating perception of schema-congruent information and implicit memory performance. However, explicit memory requires more elaborative processing, and so integration does not necessarily facilitate explicit memory (e.g., recall or recognition). Elaboration involves developing and strengthening connections between the schema and other contextual cues at encoding and with other associated representations in memory; the effects of elaboration are reflected on tests of explicit memory.

Williams et al. (1988, 1997) also integrated the activation-elaboration distinction of Graf and Mandler (1984) with Oatley and Johnson-Laird's (1987) proposal that there may be unique modes of cognitive operation associated with the different primary emotions. They proposed that anxiety selectively activates mood-congruent (e.g., threatening) representations but reduces the tendency to elaborate mood-congruent representations (indeed, they hypothesize that anxiety leads to avoidance of elaboration in anxious individuals). This would account for the consistent pattern of preconscious (i.e., automatic) attentional biases for threatening material seen in anxiety patients and for the great paucity of findings on explicit memory biases for threatening material in anxiety. It would also predict findings of implicit mood-congruent biases in anxiety (e.g., C. MacLeod & McGlaughlin, 1995; Mathews, Mogg, et al., 1989) but has difficulty explaining the inconsistency of such results as those reviewed previously.

In contrast to anxiety, Williams et al. (1988, 1997) proposed that depression is characterized by a tendency to elaborate mood-congruent material to a disproportionate degree. This overelaboration of depression-relevant material would account for the consistent evidence seen in the depression literature for mood-congruent explicit memory biases (Matt et al., 1992). However, this elaboration does not stem from any special early activation of mood-congruent material, thus explaining early failures to find evidence for mood-congruent implicit memory biases (cf. Denny & Hunt, 1992; Watkins et al., 1992) and the relatively sparse and inconsistent evidence for attentional biases for negative information—especially at the preconscious or automatic level, when the biases for anxiety occur reliably. However, this proposal does not as easily explain why an implicit memory bias has recently been shown in at least four implicit memory studies of depressed individuals (Bradley et al., 1994, 1996; Bradley, Mogg, & Williams, 1995; Watkins et al., 1996).

The idea that anxiety is characterized by an early (and often automatic) selective attentional bias for threat and avoidance of more elaborative processing of this threat and that depression is associated with greater elaboration of and memory for depression-relevant information can be understood from the vantage point of psychoevolutionary theories of cognition and emotion (Cosmides & Tooby, in press; Mineka, 1992; Plutchik, 1984; J. M. G. Williams et al., 1988, 1997). According to these theories, cognition evolved as a means of shaping and regulating the adaptive function of emotions. Given that there were probably quite different pressures which shaped the evolution and development of anxiety and depression, it is not surprising that distinct modes of information processing would fa-

cilitate the function of different emotions (e.g., Mathews, 1993; Oatley & Johnson-Laird, 1987). For example, anxiety, like fear, would seem to require a cognitive system which could very quickly (and often automatically) scan for and perceive cues for danger, allowing for continuous monitoring of the environment for signals of potential threat. Depression, by contrast, involves reflective consideration of events that have led to failure and loss and would seem to require a cognitive system adept at remembering vital information concerning loss and failure to facilitate reflection on these important events. Thus anxiety as a forward-looking emotion may have evolved to be associated with attentional biases because such biases facilitate the very rapid detection of threat and its subsequent avoidance (Mathews, 1993). By contrast, depression as a more backward-looking emotion may be associated with memory biases, perhaps because, as Mathews (1993, p. 273) argued, "cognitive processes involved in the recall of past events and reflection on their meaning are more relevant to the function of sadness than are those involved in maintaining vigilance for possible future threat."

## Higher Level and Social Cognitive Biases in Depression and Anxiety

The information processing biases in attention, memory, and judgment may serve the adaptive function of the emotions themselves. However, another broad set of *higher level* cognitive processes also may play an important role in shaping our emotions and in one sense may even serve as gatekeepers for emotions. These processes, which include individuals' perceptions of themselves and their abilities, of significant others and social interactions, and of the future and what it holds for them, are essential to the understanding of depression and anxiety. In particular, these higher level and social-cognitive factors play a part in determining whether life events are perceived as personally relevant, significantly harmful, or reflective of loss and failure. As such, they may play a part in the instigation and maintenance of anxiety and depression.

In the next section, we address higher level and social-cognitive models of the emotional disorders. In doing so, we use two frameworks, one borrowed from Beck's (1967) seminal cognitive theory of depression and the other from the cognitive science distinction between declarative and procedural knowledge (cf. Smith, 1994). To date, the majority of social-cognitive research in psychopathology has addressed depression rather than anxiety disorders; this imbalance is evident in the following sections.

The primary framework for this section adopts Beck's (1967) notion of a negative cognitive triad. Based on clinical observations, Beck hypothesized that a depressive cognitive style is characterized by a negative view of the self, the environment, and the future and that this negative cognitive triad is the core proximal cause for depression. Beck's more general framework has generated abundant discussion, research, and a good deal of criticism, particularly for the causal aspects of the theory. In appropriating it here, we do not necessarily align ourselves with all aspects of Beck's theory, noting that several reviews (e.g., Haaga, Dyck, & Ernst, 1991) have uncovered serious problems with some of its definitions and hypotheses. However, there is strong evidence for the existence and descriptive value of the three components of the negative cognitive triad, which we believe serve as a useful heuristic organizational scheme. Specifically, social cognitive models can be classified as dealing with self-related, other-related, or future-related variables. This classification (with some acknowledged overlap between the classes) can aid researchers in recognizing present trends in the literature, as well as areas for future exploration.

A second, and very different, framework distinguishes between declarative and procedural features of cognition. Declarative features refer to the content and structure of stored knowledge, whereas procedural features refer to the processes, including attention and regulation, that are involved in the processing of information (Smith, 1994). This distinction between declarative and procedural knowledge has been used by social cognition personality researchers (e.g., Cantor & Kihlstrom, 1987; Kihlstrom & Klein, 1994). The terms *content* and *structure* (approximately equivalent to declarative features of cognition) and the term *processes* (approximately equivalent to procedural features of cognition) have also been used previously in classifying psychopathology research (e.g., Dobson & Kendall, 1993). Because it best fits in a review of psychopathology research, we use the distinction of content, structure, and process as a way to further subdivide each third of Beck's cognitive triad. In our review, we examine the current state of knowledge on each of these types of cognitive variables. In doing so, we try to clarify existing trends and to highlight promising areas for future investigation.

## Self-Related Cognition

The greatest amount of social-cognitive research regarding depression and anxiety focuses on various aspects of the self. A denigrating view of one's self, which is so common to negative affect, as well as a heightened attention to the self and an idiosyncratic organization of self-knowledge, may play roles as vulnerability, maintenance, and/or recovery factors in anxiety and depression. Particularly in depression, the role of self-cognition is so central that some have equated Beck's (1967) notion of a depressive schema with a depressive *self*-schema (cf. Shaw, 1985). In this section, we review the literature that explores the role of self-related cognitive content, structure, and processes in abnormal affect.

### Self-Related Content

Perhaps the most straightforward cognitive generalization about depression and anxiety is that individuals with these disorders hold idiosyncratic negative beliefs about themselves; that is, they view themselves more negatively than do normals. In this section, we discuss the evidence for this claim and review issues of measurement, mood-state dependence, content specificity, congruence effects, and the suggestion that mood disorders are characterized by an evenhanded, rather than a negative, outlook.

*The Nature of Self-Related Content.* Initially, investigators sought to examine negative self-related beliefs using self-report measures such as the Dysfunctional Attitudes Scale (DAS; Weissman & Beck, 1978) and the Automatic Thoughts Questionnaire (ATQ; Hollon & Kendall, 1980). Although these measures are consistently related to depressive symptoms, in the past several critics have suggested that such measures are more likely to detect symptoms or concomitants rather than vulnerability or maintenance factors for depression (e.g., Barnett & Gotlib, 1988; Haaga et al., 1991). This is consistent with findings that DAS scores decrease following remission from depression, even when the remission results from pharmacotherapy (e.g., Fava, Bless, Otto, Pava, & Rosenbaum, 1994). In addressing the possibility that a dysfunctional schema is only a concomitant of depressed mood, Persons and Miranda (1992) presented results consistent with a mood-state dependence model that posits that depressive cognitive schemata do evidence stability but, importantly, that they remain dormant unless activated by stress or negative mood. The combination of a stable (though dormant) chronic vulnerability and an eliciting event activates the depressive schema and serves as a proximal cause for depression (see also Zuroff, Blatt, Sanislow, Bondi, & Pilkonis, 1999, for further support of the idea that depressive schemata are mood-state dependent).

A different critique of work using the DAS is that self-report questionnaires that purport to tap depressive self-schemas actually use the cognitive "products" of the schema to infer its existence (e.g., Dobson & Kendall, 1993). Therefore, several investigators have utilized methodologies that go beyond self-report scales and, in doing so, have elaborated and clarified the term *depressive schema*. For example, using a self-referent encoding task, Derry and Kuiper compared depressed, psychiatric control, and nonpsychiatric control groups and found that the depressed group showed evenhanded recall (Derry & Kuiper, 1981) or superior recall (Kuiper & Derry, 1982) of depressive self-referential words, whereas both nondepressed groups had superior recall of neutral self-referential words. Thus, in refining the definition of an underlying depressive schema, Kuiper and Derry suggested that vulnerability to depression stems from holding a chronically accessible set of negative self-related information, the presence of which can be another measure of depressive schemas (see our earlier detailed discussion of memory biases).

As with the self-report measures (e.g., the DAS), it appears that the differences in the accessibility of self-related content between individuals with and without depression is mood dependent (e.g., Sutton, Teasdale, & Broadbent, 1988). Thus Persons and Miranda's (1992) analysis of mood-primed cognition is relevant here as well. For example, Gilboa and Gotlib (1997) compared nondysphoric individuals who were or were not previously dysphoric. Following a negative mood induction, the vulnerable individuals displayed higher incidental recall of negative words, a finding that is consistent with those of Persons and Miranda (1992).

In addition, Abramson, Alloy, and their colleagues (Alloy, Abramson, Murray, Whitehouse, & Hogan, 1997; McClain & Abramson, 1995) recently reported two studies that utilized a somewhat different methodology to assess the self-schemata of depressives. On a self-report task requiring me–not-me judgments, students at risk for depression endorsed more numerous negative traits. Importantly, an analysis of reaction times revealed that the at-risk participants endorsed negative items more rapidly, indicating increased accessibility. Moreover, scores on this judgment task interacted with relevant life stress to predict depression: Individuals with more negative self-schemata became more depressed when life stress was high. Thus, well-designed tasks do provide evidence for a diathesis role of negative self-content for depression. No similar studies on vulnerability to anxiety were located.

## The Specificity of Self-Related Content

Subsequent elaborations of Beck's (1967) cognitive model of depression built on observations that negative content also appeared to be present in anxiety (e.g., Beck & Emery, 1985) and in other forms of psychopathology. This led Beck and his colleagues to suggest a *content-specificity effect*, which applies to both depression and anxiety. The content-specificity approach posits that self-related information comprises two specific sets of cognitive beliefs for anxiety and depression, as well as a third general set shared by the two disorders (D. A. Clark, Beck, & Stewart, 1990). This view is quite consistent with L. A. Clark and Watson's (1991) tripartite model of affective disorders, which notes that high levels of negative affectivity are common to the two disorders, whereas specific symptom sets are also unique to each disorder (see also D. A. Clark, Steer, & Beck, 1994; Steer, Clark, Beck, & Ranieri, 1995).

Several investigations from other research groups have also supported the content-specificity hypothesis, although not all of these tested the existence of cognitions that are common to the two disorders. For example, Jolly and Dykman (1994) provided evidence for both the specific and the general components of this model in reporting that, although danger-related cognitions predicted anxiety and loss or failure cognitions predicted depression, a third group of cognitions seemed generally predictive of both sets of symptoms (see also Westra & Kuiper, 1997, and Woody, Taylor, McLean, & Koch, 1998, for related demonstrations). However, D. A. Clark and Steer's (1996) recent review suggests that loss and failure cognitions may show more specificity to depression than do harm and danger cognitions to anxiety.

In an extension of the content-specificity hypothesis, Beck (1983, 1987) elaborated on the idea that specific contents serve as vulnerability factors in depression (see Blatt & Zuroff, 1992, for a similar conceptualization that is rooted in a psychodynamic approach). Focusing on broad personality organization, Beck identified two possible "modes"—*sociotropy* and *autonomy*—which may place individuals at risk for depression. The sociotropic mode involves an overvaluation of relationships, including strong dependency and acceptance needs. The autonomous mode involves an overvaluation of personal achievement, strong independence, and a need for success. These modes are thought to precipitate a depressive reaction when the individual faces a congruent stressor: loss or rejection (for sociotropy) and failure (for autonomy). These predictions regarding specific personality vulnerability are most appropriately tested in prospective studies that examine whether individuals with either personality mode are more likely to become depressed (or to relapse following recovery) when a congruent stressor occurs. The findings of many such studies were summarized by Coyne and Whiffen (1995), who concluded that support for the congruency model is inconsistent. On the whole, it appears that autonomy or self-criticism (at least as assessed by current self-report instruments) is more consistently a marker of distress than a vulnerability to it (although see Segal, Shaw, Vella, & Katz, 1992). In contrast, dependency cognitions associated with sociotropic personalities received some support as both a marker of distress and a vulnerability for depression.

As noted by Beck (1996), loss, rejection, and failure may be particularly potent themes in depression because of their evolutionary significance. Other central themes or personality modes also related to various evolutionarily significant tasks may be active in anxiety disorders. One example already mentioned is the role of harm and danger themes in anxiety, particularly in GAD. In addition, Salkovskis (1999; see also Tallis, 1994) suggests that individuals with OCD struggle with a core theme of *personal responsibility* over possible harm or danger. Driven by this core theme, they tend to overvalue normally occurring intrusive thoughts, imbuing them with great significance.

Subsequently, they seem motivated to neutralize anxiety and guilt or blame by engaging in overt or covert acts (compulsions).

*Accuracy of Self-Content.* Are depressives negatively skewed in their cognitive content or do they simply have an evenhanded view of the world, free from the rosy tint of nondistressed individuals? A discussion of cognitive content in depression should clearly address this question, yet answering it is no small feat. Specifically, to examine the truth value of self-related depressive cognitions, investigators need to establish an objective reference with which depressive beliefs can be compared.

Some insight into the accuracy question comes from the literature on "depressive realism," which has focused more on judgmental processes than on cognitive content. The first demonstration of such a realism effect (Alloy & Abramson, 1979) was based on a contingency paradigm, in which students had to estimate their control over the onset of a light. Dysphoric students showed more accurate estimation, whereas nondepressed students displayed "illusions of control." In reviewing the inconsistent literature that ensued on this topic, Ackermann and DeRubeis (1991) argued that depressive realism may be limited to laboratory contingency situations. In other situations, such as in the assessment of both past and future life events, dysphoric or depressed individuals do display a pervasive negatively biased view (cf. Pacini, Muir, & Epstein, 1998, for a possible explanation of the limited occurrence of depressive realism in "trivial" situations). Nevertheless, the work on depressive realism has emphasized the fact that the "norm," or cognitive content of nondistressed individuals, may be equally or more biased in the other direction. Specifically, optimism, elevated self-esteem, and illusions of control characterize "normal" thinking (cf. Taylor & Brown, 1988).

### Self-Related Structure

Several authors have suggested that moods and mood disorders are associated with an idiosyncratic *structure* of self-knowledge, arguing that particular features of the organization of self-knowledge (e.g., differentiation, integration, complexity) influence mood above and beyond the influence of informational content. As a group, the contemporary models of self-structure have their roots in the early cognitive work of Kelly (1955), Zajonc (1960), and Block (1961). Adopting some of the terminology of these cognitive pioneers, the contemporary models seem to address two broad issues: the differentiation and the integration of the self-concept (cf. Campbell, Assanand, & DiPaula, 2000). Differentiation is the extent to which one's self-representation is multifaceted and contains several selves or roles. Integration is the extent to which these multiple facets are similar, clear, consistent, or overlapping.

*Differentiation Variables.* Do individuals with multiple selves, aspects, roles, or identities differ in their vulnerability to mood disorders? Several researchers have argued that maintaining a multifaceted view of oneself (i.e., high self-complexity) may serve as a buffer of negative life events. For example, Linville (1985) found that compared to normal students low on self-complexity, normal students high on self-complexity experienced less negative affect in response to failure and experienced more moderate fluctuations in their moods in a 2-week study using daily diaries. Brown and Rafaeli (2001) also found that more differentiated students, those who reported more numerous self-aspects, experienced fewer depressive symptoms in response to stress. However, a recent meta-analysis of the self-complexity literature (E. Rafaeli & Steinberg, in press) shows that low cognitive differentiation (i.e., low self-complexity) is at best a weak vulnerability for future depressive symptoms following stress. Moreover, the cross-sectional relationship in the absence of measured stress of high self-complexity with depression, negative mood, or poor well-being is slightly positive. Thus holding few cognitive self-aspects may act as a weak vulnerability factor in times of stress but may be a mildly adaptive strategy at other times. (For a discussion of self-complexity measurement, see E. Rafaeli-Mor, Gotlib, & Revelle, 1999).

Few of the studies on cognitive differentiation (and cognitive structure in general) have explored these effects in clinical samples. In the few studies that did, no relationship was obtained between differentiation (Linville's [1985] self-complexity index) and abnormal affect (cf. E. Rafaeli & Steinberg, in press). Moreover, one study found that clinically diagnosed depressives actually show a higher cognitive differentiation but only of negative information about themselves (Gara et al., 1993).

*Integration Variables.* Integration refers to the similarity or shared variance between pairs of self-aspects (e.g., Brown & Rafaeli, 2001; Donahue, Robins, Roberts, & John, 1993). Individuals who lack integration are those who view themselves as quite different in their various roles. Are consistency and overlap across different selves signs of positive well-being, protective factors against stress, or emotional liabilities? Most theorists view integration (i.e., consistency or coherence) as a marker of well-being (Campbell et al., 2000; Donahue et al., 1993). Low integration has been termed "fragmentation" by some and has been equated with a lack of identity or a poor articulation of the self. For example, Block (1961) found that individuals with "role stability" were less susceptible to anxiety and to other forms of maladjustment.

In contrast to these authors, Linville (1985, 1987) suggested that high overlap between different selves increases the risk of a spillover effect, a process of spreaded activation of affect in response to stress. Unfortunately, most self-complexity studies have used Linville's own measure, which has been found to reflect only the differentiation component of her model, not the integration component (E. Rafaeli-Mor et al., 1999). However, two studies using an appropriate integration index with normal participants demonstrated that overlap among self-aspects buffers the effects of severe stress but exacerbates the effects of minor hassles on depressive symptoms (Brown & Rafaeli, 2001; E. Rafaeli-Mor & Brown, 1997).

### Self-Related Cognitive Processes

We have reviewed several features of the content and the structure of self-knowledge in emotional disorders. Both of these classes of variables reflect *declarative knowledge*. However, there appear to be particular features of higher level cognitive *processes* focused on the self that are also related to disordered mood. This section covers two sets of processes: goal-directed cognition (self-regulatory processes) and self-focused attention.

*Self-Regulatory Processes.* Regulatory processes govern goal-directed behavior. These processes bring together cognition and motivation and play a major role in both normal and abnormal affect (Carver & Scheier, 1990). For example, certain features of motivation and of self-regulation are primary symptoms in both anxiety (e.g., the heightened goals of averting an impending disaster) and depression (e.g., the apathy and lack of motivation characteristic of individuals with major depression). Additionally, affective states are often a function of the subjective assessment of the status of one's goal pursuits (Emmons & Kaiser, 1996). In this section, we highlight some findings regarding mood, affect, and self-regulatory processes.

Most goal theories have at their base a cybernetic model of self-regulation. Goal-directed behavior is guided by a discrepancy-reduction process, a Test-Operate-Test-Exit (TOTE) cycle (e.g., Carver & Scheier's [1982] control theory). Individuals maintain a representation both of goals and of current states. In an iterative process, individuals compare (test) the current and strived-for states. They then operate on any discrepancy, attempting to reduce it. Finally, when the test reveals a sufficiently small discrepancy, individuals exit this feedback loop. Negative affect, depression, and anxiety can influence the inputs to this process (both the perceived "actual" state and the strived-for state) or the dynamics of the process itself. We address declarative parameters of goal systems (i.e., their content and structure) that have been related to mood disorders (see Austin & Vancouver, 1996, and Emmons, 1996, for recent reviews that examine the functioning of the self-

regulatory processes in these disorders, a topic not covered here.)

*Inputs to self-regulatory process: actual and strived-for states.* As discussed earlier, in the sections devoted to the content and structure of declarative self-knowledge, depressed and anxious individuals often hold a self-view (the "actual self") that is qualitatively different (e.g., more negative and less integrated) from that of nondisordered individuals. The actual self is one input into the regulatory process. We now elaborate on the second input, which are the strived-for states, goals, or standards.

Goals are often categorized by the type of motivation or need implicit in them. Recent work with nonclinical participants has revealed lawful cross-sectional and exacerbating relationships between different motivations or needs (e.g., intimacy, power, generativity) and affect (cf. Emmons, 1996). Goals can also be categorized using several theoretically based classification schemes. Deci and Ryan (1985) differentiated between different sources of goals. Using their scheme, Sheldon and Kasser (1995) found that holding extrinsic goals was associated with lower life satisfaction and less positive affect than was holding intrinsic ones. Similarly, individuals who hold "judgment/performance" goals (similar to extrinsic goals) are thought to respond to failure with hopelessness, whereas those who hold "development/mastery" goals (similar to intrinsic goals) respond with renewed effort (cf. Grant & Dweck, 1999). Grant and Dweck argue that this difference reflects an implicit theory regarding the malleability of personal abilities, traits, and characteristics. People who are implicit "entity theorists" (i.e., those who believe that abilities are set and traits are fixed) view their successes and failures as performance tests, and so each failure is a threat or a loss rather than a challenge. Such thoughts are pervasive in depressive and anxious states.

A widely used categorization scheme for goals is the model of Higgins and his colleagues, first known as self-discrepancy theory and later broadened into a discussion of regulatory foci (Higgins, 1999; Higgins, Bond, Klein, & Strauman, 1986). This model stems from the distinction of approach and avoidance systems, mediating pleasure and pain respectively. Individuals are seen to differ in their focus on each of these systems. Individuals with a *prevention* focus are those who are highly sensitive to the presence or absence of pain. Individuals with a *promotion* focus are highly sensitive to the presence or absence of pleasure. This differential sensitivity, along with strategic predilections to use approach behaviors or avoidance behaviors, are the main components of the regulatory foci.

Higgins's and others' distinction between approach and avoidance goals may be the most important contribution of goal theories to the study of emotional disorders. Both theoretically and empirically, approach goals have been related to behavioral activation and to positive affect, and avoidance goals have been related to behavioral inhibition and negative affect (Higgins, Shah, & Friedman, 1997). Emmons and Kaiser (1994, cited in Emmons, 1996) and Elliot, Sheldon, and Church (1997) found that a higher proportion of avoidance goals (and a lower proportion of approach goals) was associated with neuroticism, depression, anxiety, and decreased positive affect, both concurrently and over longer periods of time. This latter finding may mask the divergent roles of avoidance and approach goals (cf. Higgins, 1999) by combining them into a simple ratio index.

Regulatory foci provide a broad framework within which some more specific mechanisms operate. One central postulate is that people compare their actual selves to one of two self-guides: the "ideal" self and the "ought" self (Higgins et al., 1986). The ideal self is composed of characteristics that an individual desires to have. The ought self is composed of those characteristics which an individual (and very often significant others) believes he or she should have. Individuals vulnerable to depression or anxiety may have a particular regulatory focus, that is, chronic accessibility of a particular self-guide. When a self-guide is accessible and discrepant from the actual self, specific affect is generated. In an ought-actual discrepancy, these are agitation-related emotions (i.e., anxiety or high negative affect), whereas in an ideal-actual discrepancy, these are dejection-related emotions (i.e., low positive affect and depression).

Higgins's self-discrepancy model is unique among regulatory-process models in its clear clinical predictions and in the amount of empirical attention given to these predictions. Strauman and Higgins (1988) reported finding the expected predictive relationship between ideal-actual (I/A) discrepancies and dejection and between ought-actual (O/A) discrepancies and agitation 2 months later. In a cross-sectional study, Strauman (1989) found the greatest I/A discrepancies in a depressed group and the greatest O/A discrepancies in a socially phobic group, both when compared with each other and with a control group (see also Scott & O'Hara, 1993, for related results in diagnosed depressed and anxious students). In addition, Strauman (1989) found that when a particular discrepancy (I/A or O/A) was temporarily primed, the effect of the priming was strongest in the group that had the greater chronic accessibility to this discrepancy (i.e., depression and I/A, social phobia and O/A). Fairbrother and Moretti (1998) further found that depressives were higher on I/A discrepancies than remitted depressives, who were themselves higher than nondepressed controls. Finally, extending these findings to psychophysiological measures of emotional distress, Strauman, Lemieux, and Coe (1993) reported that priming anxious or dysphoric individuals with their own (but not with others') ought-self or ideal-self, respectively, leads to an increase in the stress hormone cortisol and a decrease in natural killer cell activity. Overall, given the high degree of overlap between depression

and anxiety (both being high in negative affectivity), the specificity of these results are as striking as those generally found for the basic cognitive biases in attention and memory, described earlier in this chapter.

Much of the research on goals and goal orientation has relied on self-reports (e.g., work by Emmons and others in which goals are inferred from an open-ended task in which participants list their current life goals). As with other self-report indices, the concern is raised that the predictor variable (in this case, regulatory focus) may simply be a symptom of the disorder rather than a causal construct. Recently, however, less transparent methods have also been used to operationalize goal orientation and self-discrepancies. For example, Higgins et al. (1997) operationalized regulatory focus using response latencies to measure accessibility of the self-guide. Results using more sophisticated methods like this have produced encouraging results.

*The structure of goals.* Individuals' goal systems differ not only in the content (identity) of the goals but also in their organization. Goal systems can be more or less integrated, conflicted, or defined; each of these dimensions is associated with differences in affect and affective symptomatology. For example, Emmons and King (1988, 1989) found that dissimilarity and inconsistency within goal systems (such as in approach-avoidance conflicts or other kinds of conflicting goals) were associated with negative affectivity and depressive symptoms, both concurrently and over time. One clue to the cause of this effect is that conflicting or ambivalent goals tend to promote less action and more rumination; thus they remain in focus but often are not reached. A preponderance of high-level goals that are vague and abstract in detail has also been found to be related to negative affect and anxiety (Emmons, 1992), perhaps because such high-level goals are more difficult to achieve and are associated with greater frustration (although with greater meaning, as well; e.g., Little, 1989). However, Pennebaker (1989) proposed that high-level thought is a consequence, not a cause, of negative affect. According to Pennebaker, distress leads to a change in thinking, from concrete levels to broad, abstract, and self-reflective thinking. Pennebaker suggested that one might view such high-level thought as repressive and avoidant and therefore as a (poor) defense against distress.

*Self-Focused Attention.* The process of attending to the self is embedded within a self-regulatory framework and is part of the comparison of the actual to the standard. Self-focused attention is both a state in which we all can be found at times and an individual difference variable that reflects the degree to which individuals tend to focus on themselves and their attributes. Pyszczynski and Greenberg (1987) suggested that depressives are high on the self-focus trait and attend particularly to negative aspects of themselves. Elaborating on this link, Ingram (1990) suggested that self-focused attention (particularly "self-absorption"—a more rigid and excessive type of self-focus) is related to a wide range of psychopathological conditions, including depression, anxiety, alcohol use, and other disorders.

More recently, a meta-analysis (N. Rafaeli-Mor, 1999; Mor & Winquist, 2001) systematically examined the relationship between self-focused attention and emotional distress. The overarching relationship of self-focus and negative affect was found to be moderately positive, but this relationship was qualified by several important caveats. The effects were strongest within clinical and subclinical ("analogue") populations relative to nonclinical samples. Consistent with Nolen-Hoeksema's (1991) response styles theory, studies that examined the ruminative type of self-focus, in which individuals focus on their depressed mood and its possible causes and consequences, revealed stronger associations of ruminative self-focus to negative affect than of nonruminative self-focus. As might be expected, studies that examined attentional focus on negative versus positive aspects of the self or focus on the self following a failure versus a success reported a stronger effect on negative affect (Mor & Winquist, 2001).

Private self-focus, which is defined as attention to internal experiences, such as thoughts or moods, has been differentiated from public self-focus, which is defined as attention to social or public aspects of one's self (such as one's appearance; e.g., Fenigstein, Scheier, & Buss, 1975). An interesting pattern revealed by Mor and Winquist's (2001) meta-analysis concerns the different relationships between depression versus anxiety and private versus public self-focus. Specifically, there are strong correlations of both public and, especially, private self-focus with depressive symptoms (with private self-focus having a significantly stronger effect over numerous replications). In contrast, only public self-focus was associated with anxious symptoms. Mor and Winquist (2001) suggest the possibility that Higgins's self-discrepancy theory (described earlier) may be useful in understanding these differential associations. Specifically, focus on public self-aspects is likely to activate "ought" discrepancies (by calling attention to the self as visible to others), perhaps leading to increased negative affect, which plays a part in both depression and anxiety. In contrast, focus on private self-aspects is likely to activate "ideal" discrepancies (by calling attention to the individual's wishes, plans, and goals), perhaps leading to decreased positive affect, a unique feature of depression (cf., L. A. Clark & Watson, 1991).

Finally, several self-focus researchers have examined the issue of causality or antecedence. Mor and Winquist's (2001) meta-analysis reviews evidence that self-focus can be either an antecedent, concomitant, or consequence of disordered affect. Thus self-focus and negative affect may display the fugue-like pattern we discussed in the over-

view with regard to cognition and emotion in general. Although both could be causes and consequences, their most prominent feature is the way they maintain each other in a cyclical pattern.

We have reviewed evidence for the negativity of cognitive self-related content, as well as evidence for some biases in the organization of this self-related information in emotional disorders. We have also reviewed two promising avenues of exploration into self-related cognitive processes and emotional disorders: goal-directed self-regulation and self-focused attention. It is important to note that much of this research has been limited to analogue populations; we hope this review will motivate psychopathology researchers to examine these models with appropriate clinical designs.

### Other-Related Cognition

Are the biases seen in emotionally disordered individuals in the content, structure, and processing of social-cognitive information limited to the self or do they also occur in the way these individuals process information about others? In answering these questions, we review studies that examine the way mood-disordered people view others, process information about others, and believe others perceive them.

#### Other-Related Content

Weary and Edwards (1994) reviewed the findings regarding person perception biases in depression and anxiety. For example, dysphoric individuals do not differ from normal controls in the accessibility of negative information about target others (e.g., Bargh & Tota, 1988). However, dysphorics do have an increased expectation of future negative events in the lives of hypothetical others, but not in the lives of actual people in the social environment (Pietromonaco & Markus, 1985).

Few studies have examined the social judgments of clinically depressed and anxious patients. Butler and Mathews (1983) found that patients with GAD did not hold biased negative expectations for other people but that patients with major depression did. Gara et al. (1993) reported that depressed individuals viewed significant others more negatively and less positively than did control participants. Additionally, within the depressed group, those with more severe symptoms had a less positive view of others (and of self). Finally, are biases in other-related cognition driven by the same biased content that drives self-related cognition? Andersen, Spielman, and Bargh (1992) provided evidence that they are not. Instead, other-related bias is likely to be driven by other-schemata or by future-schemata and not necessarily by the negative self-schema.

## Other-Related Attention

Dysphoric individuals also show an increased attention to social information (e.g., Weary, Marsh, & McCormick, 1994). Weary suggests that as a consequence of their feelings of lack of control, depressives pay increased attention to clues about causality in an attempt to regain control. Whether this quest for information is also typical of individuals with major depression or anxiety disorders is unclear. Indeed, it seems quite possible that at least for clinical depression, which is characterized by pervasive feelings of helplessness and hopelessness (discussed in a subsequent section), such attempts to regain a sense of control would be relinquished (Abramson, Metalsky, & Alloy, 1989; Alloy, Kelly, Mineka, & Clements, 1990).

## Interpersonal Cognitive Dynamics

Researchers who focus on interpersonal process in depression and anxiety have developed an interactional model that emphasizes the ways in which the motives and behaviors of depressed individuals maintain their disorder (e.g., Coyne, 1976; Joiner & Metalsky, 1995). These interpersonal processes involve cognition, in addition to motivation (e.g., self-verification needs; see Swann & Read, 1981) and behavioral skills (Coyne, 1976). A key cognitive factor in the interpersonal dynamics of individuals with mood disorders is their perception of others' criticism, and, more generally, others' perceived stance toward them. For example, Hooley and Teasdale (1989) found that in successfully treated unipolar depressed patients, the patients' perceptions of spouses' criticism was a strong predictor of 9-month relapse, above and beyond the actual criticism or the degree of marital distress. Indeed, perceived criticism has a powerful exacerbating effect on depression and other disorders (cf. Butzlaff & Hooley, 1998).

Any discussion of cognitive interpersonal dynamics must also mention attachment theory, which has become a prominent framework for understanding both normal and abnormal affective and interpersonal functioning. The theory suggests that insecurely attached children (e.g., Bowlby, 1980) and adults (e.g., Hazan & Shaver, 1987), are prone to anxiety and depression and hold chronically accessible "mental models" of significant others as rejecting and unavailable. Work by Baldwin and colleagues suggests that idiosyncratic cognitive representations (which include self- and other-schemata and an interpersonal script) underlie attachment styles; attachment "styles" are simply an aggregation of a person's chronically accessible "if-then" interpersonal contingencies (Baldwin, Fehr, Keedian, Seidel, & Thomson, 1993). For example, insecure participants who were primed with the sentence stem "if I trust my partner, then my partner will . . ." were quicker to recognize *hurt* (as opposed to *care*) as a word in a sub-sequent semantic judgment task (see also Baldwin & Sinclair, 1996). Combining experimental work on attachment with the issue of perceived criticism, Baldwin (e.g., Baldwin & Holmes, 1987; see Baldwin, 1999, for review) also demonstrated the self-evaluative impact of perceiving criticism. Individuals subliminally primed with the face or name of a critical other (e.g., a scowling picture of the pope for a sample of Catholic students) were more self-critical after a failure in a rigged task and overgeneralized their failure more than did those primed with a noncritical other.

In sum, cognitive biases in the perception of others, particularly the attention given to others' criticism, appear to play an important role in generating negative affect and harsh self-evaluations among depressed and anxious individuals. However, very little of this research has been done with clinical samples, and almost none at all has addressed anxiety disorders, although such research is clearly called for.

## Future-Related Cognition

A bleak and joyless future or a danger-fraught one seems to be the rule in the minds of individuals with emotional disorders. This phenomenon is the third component in Beck's (1967) negative cognitive triad. Idiosyncratic forecasts or anticipations of the future are a defining feature of anxiety disorders. The perception of the future also plays a major role in depression, although this disorder also has a retrospective focus on past loss or failure. Consequently, several social-cognitive models of these disorders emphasize the role of future-related cognitions, including hopelessness, helplessness, control, and efficacy expectancies.

We review here several of the approaches that address future-related cognitions. Given that self, world, and future (the three subsections of our social-cognitive discussion) are not truly distinct, some future-related topics (such as goal systems and judgmental biases) were discussed elsewhere, and constructs are included here which could themselves be located in other sections. The remaining material is divided into two subsections. The first is devoted to helplessness, hopelessness, and attributional style, which involve both cognitive content and processes. The second discusses related issues of self-efficacy and uncontrollability (cognitive contents).

## Hopelessness and Explanatory Style

The learned-helplessness theory of depression (Seligman, 1975), its reformulation (Abramson, Seligman, & Teasdale, 1978), and its direct descendent, the hopelessness theory of depression (Abramson et al., 1989), have made up one of the most influential strands of cognitive theories of psychopathology. In its current formulation, the hopelessness theory proposes an etiological vulnerability model for a particular subtype of depression, hopelessness depression. Hopelessness cognitions (i.e., the expectation that one has no control over what is going to happen and the absolute certainty that an important bad outcome will occur or that a highly desired good outcome will not occur) are hypothesized to be a proximal sufficient cause for this subtype of depression. In other words, once hopelessness cognitions about an important event occur, hopelessness depression is bound to follow.

Hopelessness cognitions may stem from several contributory factors, but the theory focuses on the operation of traitlike pessimistic attributions or explanations of particular negative life events. Specifically, people with a depressogenic explanatory style who experience negative life events are likely to make pessimistic attributions about the causes of those events, which can lead to hopelessness and then depression. The traitlike style involves attributing negative events to causes that are global (i.e., affect a broad range of life domains) and stable (i.e., are expected to wield their effect well into the future). In this theory, hopelessness depression is hypothesized to develop in individuals with a pessimistic attributional style who also experience negative life events *only* if they also respond to these events with feelings of hopelessness—the proximal sufficient cause of hopelessness depression.

Some support for this theory has been building for more than 20 years. First, ample research has documented that depressed (and sometimes anxious) individuals do tend to show a depressive explanatory style for negative events and often for positive events as well (i.e., attributing positive outcomes to specific and unstable factors; see Sweeney, Anderson, & Bailey, 1986, for an early meta-analysis; see also Barnett & Gotlib, 1988; Buchanan & Seligman, 1995; Joiner & Wagner, 1995, for reviews; see Mineka, Pury, & Luten, 1995, for a review with anxiety disorders). More important, however, for the past decade research has been examining hopelessness theory with prospective tests of the diathesis-stress component of the theory and for the mediational role of hopelessness. Several supportive studies with college students found that those with a pessimistic attributional style who also had low self-esteem and had experienced a negative life event were most likely to develop a depressed mood for several days, and hopelessness has at least partially mediated this effect (e.g., Metalsky & Joiner, 1992; Metalsky, Joiner, Hardin, & Abramson, 1993; but see Ralph & Mineka, 1998, for a somewhat different pattern of results). More important, a major longitudinal prospective study of students who are hypothesized to be at high risk for unipolar depression because of their pessimistic attributional style (and dysfunctional beliefs; cf. Beck, 1967) is currently under way. These students are being followed for 4 or more years to test major tenets of this theory. Only partial results have

been reported to date. These indicate that the high-risk group (especially those who ruminate about their negative thoughts and moods) was eight times more likely than the low-risk group to develop an episode of hopelessness depression in the first 2½-year period (41% vs. 5%); rates for a first onset of *DSM-III-R* major depression were 17% vs. 1%, respectively. Similar results were reported for increased recurrences in the high-risk group (Alloy et al., 1999). However, these results are still rather preliminary: Findings regarding whether stress interacts with negative cognitive styles and whether it does so in the way postulated by the theory (with hopelessness as a mediator) have not yet been reported. In addition, more work is needed on the validity of the hopelessness depression construct itself in that some have argued that evidence that it is a distinct subtype of depression is weak (e.g., Whisman & Pinto, 1997).

The hopelessness model of depression was extended in order to account for certain aspects of anxiety disorders, as well, especially for the patterns of overlap observed between anxiety and depressive disorders. Specifically, Alloy and Mineka and colleagues presented a helplessness-hopelessness theory that addresses many of the interrelationships between depression and anxiety disorders, especially their high comorbidity and sequential pattern (with anxiety more often preceding depression than the reverse; Alloy et al., 1990). In essence, this model presents an etiological route, leading from uncontrollable events to helplessness (sense of uncertain or certain inability to control important events) and sometimes further to hopelessness (expectations both of certain helplessness and of certainty of a negative outcome). In this model, the experience of uncontrollable events is seen as common to both depression and anxiety, instigating feelings of helplessness. Anxiety disorders are characterized by varying degrees of subjective probability of helplessness (ranging from uncertain to certain) with negative outcomes, whereas depression is marked by certain helplessness and hopelessness, that is, complete conviction that negative events will happen. Thus anxiety will often precede depression temporally (both within episodes and across the lifetime) and will sometimes occur without depressive symptoms (whereas the inverse is less common).

Another important feature of comorbidity is the higher comorbidity of certain anxiety disorders, as opposed to others, with depression. The helplessness-hopelessness model explains this by reference to the scope of helplessness and hopelessness in each disorder. Those anxiety disorders in which anxiety and helplessness are related to a narrow domain (e.g., in a specific phobia) will engender uncertain helplessness and primarily anxiety symptoms. When the helplessness is limited to one domain, comorbid depression is not likely to develop. In contrast, in the more severe (and pervasive) anxiety disorders (e.g., PTSD and OCD), the sense of helplessness becomes more certain and of a broader scope (including helplessness over OCD or PTSD symptoms themselves) and therefore more likely to give rise to comorbid depression. Full-blown hopelessness depression is hypothesized to set in when the person also becomes certain that negative outcomes will occur (i.e., hopelessness cognitions set in). Epidemiological studies are generally consistent with this pattern of differential comorbidity (cf. Mineka et al., 1998), although a great deal of work is needed to test more specific aspects of the theory.

### Self-Efficacy and Controllability Beliefs

A rich research tradition has documented the role of lack and loss of control in stress reactions, fear, anxiety, and depression (see Mineka & Hendersen, 1985; Mineka & Kelly, 1989, for reviews). The majority of this work has been concerned with the effects of prior experience with uncontrollable and/or unpredictable events on subsequent behavior, motivation, and learning. Early demonstrations of the deleterious effects of uncontrollable stress often used animal models of anxiety (e.g., Mineka, 1985; Mineka & Zinbarg, 1996; Mowrer & Viek, 1948) or depression (Overmier & Seligman, 1967; Seligman & Maier, 1967). The work led to the development of the learned-helplessness model of human depression, which later evolved into the helplessness-hopelessness theory reviewed here.

In the past three decades, much work has focused on trying to understand the cognitive processes that mediate the effects of unpredictable, uncontrollable stress. One way in which the view of control has expanded has been through increased attention to *perceived* control and prediction, particularly within self-efficacy theory. Self-efficacy theory emphasizes the importance of beliefs about control or about the capacity to carry out certain behaviors in pursuing (or avoiding) certain goals (Bandura, 1986). Two features distinguish this approach from the helplessness-hopelessness model. First, it distinguishes between two types of expectancies that play a part in producing action or emotion. *Outcome expectancies* are beliefs regarding the contingency of an outcome on a behavior; that is, the likelihood that an outcome will occur if the behavior is performed. *Self-efficacy expectancies* reflect the belief in one's capacity to carry out the behavior (regardless of the outcome expectancy). Second, self-efficacy researchers (e.g., Cervone, 1997; Cervone & Scott, 1995) emphasize the contextuality of efficacy beliefs, that is, efficacy beliefs can be task specific. And although they may generalize from one context to another, they do so through idiosyncratic networks of subjective similarities. For example, to be able to accurately predict the generalization of therapy gains from exposure treatment of one agoraphobic situation to another, the therapist needs to establish each individual's idiographic network of similarities between feared activities or contexts.

Self-efficacy theory and uncontrollability theories can be viewed as cognitive, future-related models of both anxiety (Bandura, 1988; Mineka & Kelly, 1989; Mineka & Zinbarg, 1996) and depression (Alloy et al, 1990; Bandura, 1986; Miller, 1979; Mineka et al., 1998). According to such models, each based on a substantial amount of research, individuals who believe they lack the ability to cope, behaviorally or cognitively, with a potential threat are prone to experience anxiety or depression. For example, in an elegant experiment on perceived control, Sanderson, Rapee, and Barlow (1989) exposed panic-disorder patients to 20 minutes of 5% carbon dioxide–enriched air. All patients were told that adjusting a dial would reduce the rate of infusion of $CO_2$, but only if a red light was on. For half the patients, the light was on for a prolonged time, and for the other half, it was never turned on. In reality, the dial had no effect on the inhaled air, but this did not matter, as neither group of patients attempted to adjust it. However, only 20% of the perceived-control group experienced a panic attack, compared with 80% of the no-perceived-control group (see also Glass, Reim, & Singer, 1971, for related results in normal participants).

As the Sanderson et al. (1989) study illustrates, controllability models suggest that anxiety and depression are affected by perceptions that extend beyond actual control of external events or consequences to also stress the importance of perceived ability to control or carry out behaviors and thoughts. In studies that have examined individual differences in perceived control (i.e., self-efficacy) in depression, for example, Kanfer and Zeiss (1983) found that depressed college students differed from nondepressed ones in their efficacy for interpersonal functioning, but not in their self-held standards for successful functioning. Bandura, Pastorelli, Barbaranelli, and Caprara (1999) also found that low self-efficacy for academic and social tasks contributed to concurrent and subsequent depression in children. Importantly, efficacy beliefs rather than actual performance predicted concurrent depression. In fact, current depression, along with problem behavior and academic achievement, mediated the effect of self-efficacy on future depression. Kavanagh and Wilson (1989) also reported that efficacy beliefs regarding emotional coping skills were related (above and beyond the skills themselves) to improvement in cognitive therapy. Low self-efficacy also predicted relapse within 12 months (see also Usaf & Kavanagh, 1990, for related results in cognitive therapy for depression). Finally, tying together both the hopelessness and the self-efficacy models, Houston (1995) found that the interaction of low efficacy beliefs and a pessimistic attributional style predicted depression after a failure manipulation. In a chronically medically ill sample, Shnek et al. (1997) found that both helplessness and low self-efficacy predicted depression after controlling for other confounding variables.

Self-efficacy deficits would lead to depression when the

particular behavior a person feels unable to perform involves avoiding loss or failure. In contrast, self-efficacy deficits would lead to anxiety when the particular behavior a person feels unable to complete involves harm avoidance. Thus Bandura (1986) posited that it is low self-efficacy, or a perceived inability to cope, that makes people anxious. Indeed, self-efficacy theory was associated primarily with anxiety, and particularly with phobic reactions, for many years. The literature on the role of self-efficacy in anxiety has been reviewed recently (e.g., S. L. Williams, 1995). In general, self-efficacy beliefs appear to play a role in coping behaviors, negative affect, and anxiety. For example, Valentiner, Telch, Petruzzi, and Bolte (1996) found that self-efficacy beliefs predicted both subjective and physiological measures of fear in claustrophobics, even when other expectancies (e.g., expected anxiety levels) were partialed out (see also Zane & Williams, 1993). It should also be noted, however, that studies of self-efficacy rarely employ measures of perceived control from the related learned helplessness tradition to determine the relative utility of the two approaches.

Overall, both depressed and anxious individuals appear to hold a negative view of the future and to make assessments of personal inability to control negative outcomes or affect positive ones. This view appears both when content (e.g., beliefs and thoughts about the future) is assessed and when on-line judgments are produced (see the previous section titled "Judgmental or Interpretive Biases"). To some degree, these beliefs may be malleable through modeling, exposure, or similar processes (Mineka & Thomas, 1999).

### Theories of Social Cognition and the Emotional Disorders

In this section, we reviewed the role of higher level social-cognitive structures and processes in the onset and maintenance of emotional disorders. Together, the various studies reviewed suggest a model of the social-cognitive personality of individuals susceptible to emotional distress and emotional disorders. To organize this section, we used Beck's (1967) negative cognitive triad framework, which posits the presence of unique self-, other-, and future-related cognitions. Indeed, we provided examples of cognitive biases that play a part in anxiety and depression within each of the triad's domains. In addition to Beck's framework, we characterized each of the studies reviewed here as reflective of either declarative cognition (i.e., content and structure) or procedural cognition (i.e., cognitive processes). By organizing the section according to these two frameworks, we intended to uncover gaps in the literature. Indeed, it is clear that certain areas (e.g., self-related cognitive content) have received extensive empirical attention but that other areas are relatively unexplored. Specifically, we located limited work on self-related processes (e.g., self-focused attention, goal-directed processes) and on self-related cognitive structures in clinical populations. Very little empirical attention has been given to other-related cognition in anxiety or depression. Finally, in each section, we have seen that depression has clearly received a far greater amount of attention than has anxiety and its disorders.

An additional challenge facing researchers who examine social-cognitive factors in anxiety and mood disorders is the need for greater methodological sophistication that will move the field beyond self-report methodology. Some of the areas reviewed here have already begun to incorporate more rigorous methods (e.g., the use by Kuiper and Derry [1982] of incidental recall in examining self-referential cognitive content or the use by Higgins and others of response latencies in examining regulatory foci). However, many of the somewhat tentative conclusions drawn here would be greatly strengthened by the adoption of additional experimental and measurement techniques that would obviate the possible confound inherent in self-reports.

As we noted earlier, biases in self-, other-, and future-related cognition are presumed to be learned. It is therefore not surprising that researchers who have identified these biases have gone on to develop cognitive interventions aimed at changing the cognitive schemata or altering the cognitive processes that play a part in psychopathology. Indeed, for more than 30 years, the social-cognitive approaches to psychopathology have given rise to a cognitive-learning model of psychotherapy (e.g., Beck, 1976). Application of these social-cognitive findings in the design of appropriate interventions is continuing. Recent developments include Seligman and colleagues' use of explanatory style training in the prevention of depression (e.g., Gillham, Reivich, Jaycox, & Seligman, 1995) and Strauman et al.'s self-system therapy program, which applies the findings on self-discrepancies to treatment of mood disorders. In addition to the inherent importance of such programs as effective interventions, they will provide important experimental information and will contribute to future understanding of the causal role of social-cognitive biases in depression and anxiety.

### Summary

In the previous sections, we have reviewed major parts of the literature that explores the interplay between cognition and emotional disorders. The purpose of this chapter is not so much to offer a unifying framework for this interplay as to provide an update of the fruitful and important avenues of research that have been used to explore it. By necessity, we could not explore each of the various studies in great depth. However, we did choose to bring together here a wide spectrum of cognitive variables, ranging from automatic, split-second biases in attention to idiosyncratic, longstanding, and often conscious expectancies and goals.

Both the basic cognitive biases and the higher level ones may precede, accompany, or result from emotional disorders. Nonetheless, we find two theoretical frameworks useful in understanding major portions of the broad set of findings. First, following a psychoevolutionary perspective (e.g., Gray, 1990; Plutchik, 1984), we believe emotion and emotional disorders have helped to organize certain aspects of lower level cognition. As such, somewhat distinct modes of information processing may have evolved to accompany anxiety versus depression. To a large degree, anxiety serves a future-oriented purpose of preparing for a possible upcoming dangerous situation. Therefore, a bias toward attending in a split-second, often automatic, fashion toward potentially threatening information may have been selected for. Depression, serving a past-oriented purpose, is accompanied by a bias toward great recall and elaborative processing of already-acquired information (cf. Mathews, 1993; J. M. G. Williams et al., 1988, 1997).

The second framework we employ is consistent with social-cognitive theories of emotion and psychopathology, as well as with appraisal models of stress, coping, and emotion. This framework highlights the role of higher level cognitive biases (i.e., the representation and processing of self-, other-, and future-related information) in the elicitation and maintenance of anxiety and depressive episodes. Specifically, these social-cognitive variables, such as attributional styles, self-focused attention, self-schemata, and future-event schemata, exert their influence by determining what aspects of a person's life are chronically salient, as well as which life events are appraised and how they are appraised (as moderate or severe, as self-relevant or irrelevant, etc.).

Although we have not attempted to provide a unified theoretical framework that could successfully merge the two already broad theoretical frameworks discussed here, we hope to have contributed to such future attempts by juxtaposing our discussion of low- and high-level cognitive biases in emotional disorders. Moreover, we firmly believe in the importance of further exploring both the information processing and the social-cognitive frameworks for understanding the vulnerability, maintenance, and treatment of emotional disorders. Such approaches are relatively unique in their ability to address psychological and phenomenological aspects of these all too prevalent psychopathological conditions.

## NOTES

1. However, not all studies of high-trait-anxious participants have failed to find threat interference with supraliminal presentations on the emotional Stroop task (e.g., Broadbent & Broadbent, 1988).

2. Interestingly, a different pattern of results was obtained in the supraliminal condition of the emotional Stroop in this study that used semester examinations as the stressor. Indeed, when the high-trait-anxious participants were aware of the semantic content of the presented stimuli, there was a suppression of the interference effect for exam-relevant words, as in the Mathews and Sebastian (1993) study with snake phobics who had a snake nearby. See Mogg, Kentish, and Bradley (1993) for somewhat related results.

3. It should be noted, however, that in naturally occurring anxiety and depression, these studies usually involve both mood-congruent encoding and retrieval given that both encoding and retrieval usually occur in one experimental session.

4. J. M. G. Williams et al. (1997) did not cite the Bradley et al. (1995) or the C. MacLeod and McLaughlin (1995) studies.

5. One potential problem in interpreting the results of this study is that it is impossible to know whether the anxious individuals interpreted the ambiguous sentence in a threatening manner as they heard it (an on-line bias) or whether the bias occurred at the time they were asked to recognize which of several disambiguated interpretations was the one they heard (in which case a memory bias could be what was being displayed).

## REFERENCES

Abramson, L. Y., Metalsky, G. I., & Alloy, L. B. (1989). Hopelessness depression: A theory-based subtype of depression. *Psychological Review, 96*, 358–372.

Abramson, L. Y., Seligman, M. E., & Teasdale, J. D. (1978). Learned helplessness in humans: Critique and reformulation. *Journal of Abnormal Psychology, 87*, 49–74.

Ackermann R., & DeRubeis, R. J. (1991). Is depressive realism real? *Clinical Psychology Review, 11*, 565–584.

Alloy, L. B., & Abramson, L. Y. (1979). Judgment of contingency in depressed and nondepressed students: Sadder but wiser? *Journal of Experimental Psychology: General, 108*, 441–485.

Alloy, L. B., Abramson, L. Y., Murray, L. A., Whitehouse, W. G., & Hogan, M. E. (1997). Self-referent information-processing in individuals at high and low cognitive risk for depression. *Cognition and Emotion, 11*, 539–568.

Alloy, L. B., Abramson, L. Y., Whitehouse, W. G., Hogan, M. E., Tashman, N. A., Steinberg, D. L., Rose, D. T., & Donovan, P. (1999). Depressogenic cognitive styles: Predictive validity, information processing and personality characteristics, and developmental origins. *Behaviour Research and Therapy, 37*, 503–531.

Alloy, L. B., Kelly, K. A., Mineka, S., & Clements, C. M. (1990). Comorbidity of anxiety and depressive disorders: A helplessness-hopelessness perspective. In J. D. Maser & C. R. Cloninger (Eds.), *Comorbidity of mood and anxiety disorders* (pp. 499–543). Washington, DC: American Psychiatric Press.

Amir, N., McNally, R. J., Riemann, B. C., Burns, J., Lorenz, M., & Mullen, J. T. (1996). Suppression of the emotional Stroop effect by increased anxiety in patients with social phobia. *Behaviour Research and Therapy, 34*, 945–948.

Amir, N., McNally, R. J., Riemann, B. C., & Clements, C. (1996). Implicit memory bias for threat in panic disorder: Application of the "white noise" paradigm. *Behaviour Research and Therapy, 34*, 157–162.

Amir, N., McNally, R. J., & Wiegartz, P. S. (1996). Implicit memory bias for threat in posttraumatic stress disorder. *Cognitive Therapy and Research, 20*, 625–635.

Andersen, S. M., Spielman, L. A., & Bargh, J. A. (1992). Future-event schemas and certainty about the future: Automaticity in depressives' future-event predictions. *Journal of Personality and Social Psychology, 63*, 711–723.

Austin, J. T., & Vancouver, J. B. (1996). Goal constructs in psychology: Structure, process, and content. *Psychological Bulletin, 120*, 338–375.

Baldwin, M. W. (1999). Relational schemas: Research into social-cognitive aspects of interpersonal experience. In D. Cervone & Y. Shoda (Eds.), *The coherence of personality: Social-cognitive bases of consistency, variability, and organization* (pp. 127–154). New York: Guilford Press.

Baldwin, M. W., Fehr, B., Keedian, E., Seidel, M., & Thomson, D. W. (1993). An exploration of the relational schemata underlying attachment styles: Self-report and lexical decision approaches. *Personality and Social Psychology Bulletin, 19*, 746–754.

Baldwin, M. W., & Holmes, J. G. (1987). Salient private audiences and awareness of the self. *Journal of Personality and Social Psychology, 53*, 1087–1098.

Baldwin, M. W., & Sinclair, L. (1996). Self-esteem and "if . . . then" contingencies of interpersonal acceptance. *Journal of Personality and Social Psychology, 71*, 1130–1141.

Bandura, A. (1986). *Social foundations of thought and action: A social-cognitive theory.* Englewood Cliffs, NJ: Prentice Hall.

Bandura, A. (1988). Self-efficacy conceptions of anxiety. *Anxiety Research, 1*, 77–98.

Bandura, A., Pastorelli, C., Barbaranelli, C., & Caprara, G. V. (1999). Self-efficacy pathways to childhood depression. *Journal of Personality and Social Psychology, 76*, 258–269.

Bargh, J. A., & Tota, M. E. (1988). Context-dependent automatic processing in depression: Accessibility of negative constructs with regard to self but not others. *Journal of Personality and Social Psychology, 54*, 925–939.

Barkow, J., Cosmides, L., & Tooby, J. (Eds.). (1992). *The adapted mind: Evolutionary psychology and the generation of culture.* New York: Oxford University Press.

Barnett, P. A., & Gotlib, I. H. (1988). Psychosocial functioning in depression: Distinguishing among antecedents, concomitants and consequences. *Psychological Bulletin, 104*, 97–126.

Beck, A. T. (1967). Depression: Clinical, experimental, and theoretical aspects. New York: Harper & Row.

Beck, A. T. (1976). *Cognitive therapy and the emotional disorders.* New York: International Universities Press.

Beck, A. T. (1983). Cognitive therapy and depression: New perspectives. In P. J. Clayton & J. E. Barrett, (Eds.), *Treatment of depression: Old controversies and new approaches* (pp. 265–289). New York: Raven.

Beck, A. T. (1987). Cognitive models of depression: *Journal of Cognitive Psychotherapy, 1*, 2–27.

Beck, A. T. (1996). Beyond belief: A theory of modes, personality, and psychopathology. In P. M. Salkovskis (Ed.), *Frontiers of cognitive therapy* (pp. 1–25). New York: Guilford Press.

Beck, A. T., & Emery, G. (1985). *Anxiety disorders and phobias: A cognitive perspective.* New York: Basic.

Becker, E. S., Rinck, M., & Margraf, J. (1994) Memory bias in panic disorder. *Journal of Abnormal Psychology, 103*. 396–399.

Becker, E. S., Roth, W. T., Andrich, M., & Margraf, J. (1999) Explicit memory in anxiety disorders. *Journal of Abnormal Psychology, 108*, 153–163.

Bellew, M., & Hill, B. (1990). Negative recall bias as a predictor of susceptibility to induced depressive mood. *Personality and Individual Differences, 11*, 471–480.

Bellew, M., & Hill, B. (1991). Schematic processing and the prediction of depression following childbirth. *Personality and Individual Differences, 12*, 943–949.

Blatt, S. J., & Zuroff, D. C. (1992). Interpersonal relatedness and self-definition: Two prototypes for depression. *Clinical Psychology Review, 12*, 527–562.

Block, J. (1961). Ego-identity, role variability, and adjustment. *Journal of Consulting and Clinical Psychology, 25*, 392–397.

Bower, G. H. (1981). Mood and memory. *American Psychologist, 36*, 129–148.

Bowlby, J. (1980). *Loss.* New York: Basic Books.

Bradley, B., & Mathews, A. (1988). Memory bias in recovered clinical depressives. *Cognition and Emotion, 2*, 235–246.

Bradley, B. P., Mogg, K., Falla, S. J., & Hamilton, L. R. (1998). Attentional bias for threatening facial expressions in anxiety: Manipulation of stimulus duration. *Cognition and Emotion, 12*(6), 737–753.

Bradley, B. P., Mogg, K., & Lee, S. C. (1997). Attentional biases for negative information in induced and naturally occuring dysphoria. *Behaviour Research and Therapy, 35*, 911–927.

Bradley, B. P., Mogg, K., & Millar, N. (1996). Implicit memory bias in clinical and non-clinical depression. *Behaviour Research and Therapy, 34*, 865–880.

Bradley, B. P., Mogg, K., Millar, N., & White, J. (1995). Selective processing of negative information: Effects of clinical anxiety, concurrent depression, and awareness. *Journal of Abnormal Psychology, 104*, 532–536.

Bradley, B. P., Mogg, K., & Williams, R. (1994) Implicit and explicit memory for emotional information in non-clinical subjects. *Behaviour Research and Therapy, 32*, 65–78.

Bradley, B. P., Mogg, K., & Williams, R. (1995) Implicit and explicit memory for emotion-congruent information in depression and anxiety. *Behaviour Research and Therapy, 33*, 755–770.

Brewin, C. R., Reynolds, M., & Tata, P. (1999) Autobiographical memory processes and the course of depression. *Journal of Abnormal Psychology, 108*, 511–517.

Brittlebank, A. D., Scott, J., Williams, J. M., & Perrier, I. N. (1993). Autobiographical memory in depression: State or trait marker? *British Journal of Psychiatry, 162*, 118–121.

Broadbent, D., & Broadbent, M. (1988). Anxiety and attentional bias: State and trait. *Cognition and Emotion, 2*(3), 165–183.

Brown, G. P., & Rafaeli, E. (2001). *Self-knowledge organization and vulnerability to dysphoria: Revisiting self-complexity.* Manuscript submitted for publication.

Bryant, R. A., & Harvey, A. G. (1995). Processing threatening information in posttraumatic stress disorder. *Journal of Abnormal Psychology, 104*, 537–541.

Buchanan, G. M., & Seligman, M. E. P. (Eds.). (1995). *Explanatory style.* Hillsdale, NJ: Erlbaum.

Burke, M., & Mathews, A. (1992). Autobiographical memory and clinical anxiety. *Cognition and Emotion, 6,* 23–35.

Butler, G., & Mathews, A. (1983). Cognitive processes in anxiety. *Advances in Behaviour Research and Therapy, 5,* 51–62.

Butzlaff, R. L., & Hooley, J. M. (1998). Expressed emotion and psychiatric relapse. *Archives of General Psychiatry, 55,* 547–552.

Byrne, A., & MacLeod, A. K. (1997). Attributions and accessibility of explanations for future events in anxiety and depression. *British Journal of Clinical Psychology, 36,* 505–520.

Calvo, M. G., Eysenck, M. W., & Castillo, M. D. (1997). Interpretive bias in test anxiety: The time course of predictive inference. *Cognition and Emotion, 11,* 43–63.

Calvo, M. G., Eysenck, M. W., & Estevaz, A. (1994). Ego-threat interpretative bias in test anxiety: On line inferences. *Cognition and Emotion, 2,* 127–146.

Campbell, J. D., Assanand, S., & DiPaula, A. (2000). Structural features of the self-concept and adjustment. In A. Tesser, R. Felson, & J. Suls (Eds.), *Perspectives on self and identity.* Washington, DC: APA.

Cantor, N., & Kihlstrom, J. F. (1987). *Personality and social intelligence.* Englewood Cliffs, NJ: Prentice Hall.

Carver, C. S., & Scheier, M. F. (1982). Control theory: A useful conceptual framework for personality/social, clinical, and health psychology. *Psychological Bulletin, 92,* 111–135.

Carver, C. S., & Scheier, M. F. (1990). Origins and functions of positive and negative affect: A control-process view. *Psychological Review, 97,* 19–35.

Cassiday, K. L., McNally, R. J., & Zeitlin, S. B. (1992). Cognitive processing of trauma cues in rape victims with post-traumatic stress disorder. *Cognitive Therapy and Research, 16,* 283–295.

Cervone, D. (1997). Social-cognitive mechanisms and personality coherence: Self-knowledge, situational beliefs, and cross-situational coherence in perceived self-efficacy. *Psychological Science, 8,* 43–50.

Cervone, D., & Scott, W. D. (1995). Self-efficacy theory of behavioral change: Foundations, conceptual issues, and therapeutic implications. In W. T. O'Donohue & L. Krasner (Eds.), *Theories of behavior therapy: Exploring behavior change* (pp. 349–383). Washington, DC: American Psychological Association.

Clark, D. A., Beck, A. T., & Stewart, B. L. (1990). Cognitive specificity and positive-negative affectivity. Complementary or contradictory views on anxiety and depression? *Journal of Abnormal Psychology, 99,* 148–155.

Clark, D. A., & Steer, R. A. (1996). Empirical status of the cognitive model of anxiety and depression. In P. M. Salkovskis (Ed.), *Frontiers of cognitive therapy* (pp. 75–96). New York: Guilford Press.

Clark, D. A., & Steer, R. A., & Beck, A. T. (1994). Common and specific dimensions of self-reported anxiety and depression: Implications for the cognitive and tripartite models. *Journal of Abnormal Psychology, 103,* 645–654.

Clark, D. M. (1988). A cognitive model of panic attacks. In S. Rachman & J. D. Maser (Eds.), *Panic: Psychological perspectives* (p. 71–89). Hillsdale, NJ: Erlbaum.

Clark, D. M., & Teasdale, J. D. (1982). Diurnal variation in clinical depression and accessibility of memories of positive and negative experiences. *Journal of Abnormal Psychology, 91,* 87–95.

Clark, L. A., & Watson, D. (1991). Tripartite model of anx-

iety and depression: Psychometric evidence and taxonomic implications. *Journal of Abnormal Psychology, 100,* 316–336.

Cloitre, M., Shear, M. K., Cancienne, J., & Zeitlin, S. B. (1994). Implicit and explicit memory for catastrophic associations to bodily sensation words in panic disorder. *Cognitive Therapy and Research, 18,* 225–240.

Cook, M., & Mineka, S. (1990). Selective associations in the observational conditioning of fear in monkeys. *Journal of Experimental Psychology: Animal Behavior Processes, 16,* 372–389.

Cook, M., & Mineka, S. (1991). Selective associations in the origins of phobic fears and their implications for behavior therapy. In P. Martin (Ed.), *Handbook of behavior therapy and psychological science: An integrative approach* (pp. 413–434). New York: Pergamon Press.

Cosmides, L., & Tooby, J. (2000). Evolutionary psychology and the emotions. In M. Lewis & J. M. Haviland-Jones (Eds.), *Handbook of emotions* (2nd ed.). New York: Guilford Press.

Coyne, J. C. (1976). Depression and the response of others. *Journal of Abnormal Psychology, 85,* 186–193.

Coyne, J. C., & Whiffen, V. E. (1995). Issues in personality as diathesis for depression: The case of sociotropy/dependency and autonomy/self-criticism. *Psychological Bulletin, 118,* 358–378.

Deci, E. L., & Ryan, R. M. (1985). The general causality orientations scale: Self-determination in personality. *Journal of Research in Personality, 19,* 109–134.

De Jong, P. J., Mercklebach, H., & Arntz, A. (1995). Covariation bias in phobic women: The relationship between a priori expectancy, on-line expectancy, autonomic responding, and a posteriori contingency judgment. *Journal of Abnormal Psychology, 104,* 55–62.

Denny, E., & Hunt, R. (1992). Affective valence and memory in depression: Dissociation of recall and fragment completion. *Journal of Abnormal Psychology, 101,* 575–582.

Dent, J., & Teasdale, J. (1988). Negative cognition and the persistence of depression. *Journal of Abnormal Psychology, 97,* 29–34.

Derry, P. A., & Kuiper, N. A. (1981). Schematic processing and self-reference in clinical depression. *Journal of Abnormal Psychology, 90,* 286–297.

Dobson, K. S., & Kendall, P. C. (1993). *Psychopathology and cognition.* San Diego, CA: Academic Press.

Donahue, E. M., Robins, R. W., Roberts, B. W., & John, O. P. (1993). The divided self: Concurrent and longitudinal effects of psychological adjustment and social roles on self-concept differentiation. *Journal of Personality and Social Psychology, 64,* 834–846.

Elliot, A. J., Sheldon, K. M., & Church, M. A. (1997). Avoidance personal goals and subjective well-being. *Personality and Social Psychology Bulletin, 23,* 915–927.

Ellis, H. C., & Moore, B. A. (1999). Mood and memory. In T. Dalgleish & M. Power (Eds.), *Handbook of cognition and emotion* (pp. 193–210). New York: Wiley.

Emmons, R. A. (1992). Abstract versus concrete goals: Personal striving level, physical illness, and psychological well-being. *Journal of Personality and Social Psychology, 62,* 292–300.

Emmons, R. A. (1996). Striving and feeling: Personal goals and subjective well-being. In P. M. Gollwitzer & J. A. Bargh (Eds.), *The psychology of action: Linking cogni-*

*tion and motivation to behavior* (pp. 313–337). New York: Guilford Press.

Emmons, R. A., & Kaiser, H. A. (1996). Goal orientation and emotional well-being: Linking goals and affect through the self. In L. L. Martin & A. Tesser (Eds.), *Striving and feeling: Interactions among goals, affect, and self-regulation* (pp. 79–98). Mahwah, NJ: Erlbaum.

Emmons, R. A., & King, L. A. (1988). Conflict among personal strivings: Immediate and long-term implications for psychological and physical well-being. *Journal of Personality and Social Psychology, 54,* 1040–1048.

Emmons, R. A., & King, L. A. (1989). Personal striving differentiation and affective reactivity. *Journal of Personality and Social Psychology, 56,* 478–484.

Eysenck, M., & Byrne, A. (1994). Implicit memory bias, explicit memory bias, and anxiety. *Cognition and Emotion, 8,* 415–431.

Eysenck, M. W., Mogg, K., May, J., Richards, A., & Mathews, A. (1991). Bias in interpretation of ambiguous sentences related to threat in anxiety. *Journal of Abnormal Psychology, 100,* 144–150.

Fairbrother, N., & Moretti, M. (1998). Sociotropy, autonomy, and self-discrepancy: Status in depressed, remitted depressed, and control participants. *Cognitive Therapy and Research, 22,* 279–297.

Fava, M., Bless, E., Otto, M. W., Pava, J. A., & Rosenbaum, J. F. (1994). Dysfunctional attitudes in major depression: Changes with pharmacotherapy. *Journal of Nervous and Mental Disease, 182,* 45–49.

Fenigstein, A., Scheier, M. F., & Buss, A. H. (1975). Public and private self-consciousness: Assessment and theory. *Journal of Consulting and Clinical Psychology, 43,* 522–527.

Foa, E., Amir, M., Gershuny, B., Molnar, C., & Kozak, M. (1997). Implicit and explicit memory in obsessive-compulsive disorder. *Journal of Anxiety Disorders, 11,* 119–129.

Foa, E., & McNally, R. J. (1986). Sensitivity to feared stimuli in obsessive-compulsives: A dichotic listening analysis. *Cognitive Therapy and Research, 10,* 477–485.

Fox, E. (1996). Selective processing of threatening words in anxiety: The role of awareness. *Cognition and Emotion, 10,* 449–480.

Gara, M. A., Woolfolk, R. L., Cohen, B. D., Goldston, R. B., Allen, L. A., & Novalany, J. (1993). Perception of self and other in major depression. *Journal of Abnormal Psychology, 102,* 93–100.

Gilboa, E., & Gotlib, I. H. (1997). Cognitive biases and affect persistence in previously dysphoric and never-dysphoric individuals. *Cognition and Emotion, 11,* 517–538.

Gillham, J. E., Reivich, K. J., Jaycox, L. H., & Seligman, M. E. P. (1995). Prevention of depressive symptoms in schoolchildren: Two-year follow-up. *Psychological Science, 6,* 343–351.

Gilligan, S. G., & Bower, G. H. (1984). Cognitive consequences of emotional arousal. In C. Izard, J. Kagan, & R. Zajonc (Eds.), *Emotions, cognitions and behavior.* New York: Cambridge University Press.

Glass, D. C., Reim, B., & Singer, J. E. (1971). Behavioral consequences of adaptation to controllable and uncontrollable noise. *Journal of Experimental Social Psychology, 7,* 244–257.

Gotlib, I. H., & Cane, D. B. (1987). Construct accessibility and clinical depression: A longitudinal investigation. *Journal of Abnormal Psychology, 96,* 199–204.

Gotlib, I. H., & McCann, C. D. (1984). Construct accessibility and depression: An examination of cognitive and affective factors. *Journal of Personality and Social Psychology, 47,* 427–439.

Gotlib, I. H., McLachlan, A. L., & Katz, A. N. (1988). Biases in visual attention in depressed and nondepressed individuals. *Cognition and Emotion, 2,* 185–200.

Graf, P., & Mandler, G. (1984). Activation makes words more accessible, but not necessarily more retrievable. *Journal of Verbal Learning and Verbal Behavior, 23,* 553–568.

Grant, H., & Dweck, C. S. (1999). A goal analysis of personality and personality coherence. In D. Cervone & Y. Shoda (Eds.), *The coherence of personality: Social-cognitive bases of consistency, variability, and organization* (pp. 345–371). New York: Guilford Press.

Gray, J. A. (1990). Brain systems that mediate both emotion and cognition. *Cognition and Emotion, 4,* 269–288.

Haaga, D. A., Dyck, M. J., & Ernst, D. (1991). Empirical status of cognitive theory of depression. *Psychological Bulletin, 110,* 215–236.

Harris, L. M., Adams, R. D., Menzies, R. G., & Hayes, B. K. (1995). Identification and memory for fear-relevant stimuli: Implicit memory performance of insect fearfuls favours fear-relevant pictures. *Australian Journal of Psychology, 47,* 105–109.

Hazan, C., & Shaver, P. (1987). Romantic love conceptualized as an attachment process. *Journal of Personality and Social Psychology, 52,* 511–524.

Healy, H., & Williams, J. M. G. (1999). Autobiographical memory. In T. Dalgleish & M. Power (Eds.), *Handbook of cognition and emotion* (pp. 229–242). New York: Wiley.

Hedlund, S., & Rude, S. (1995) Evidence of latent depressive schemas in formerly depressed individuals. *Journal of Abnormal Psychology, 104,* 517–525.

Hertel, P. T., & Hardin, T. S. (1990). Remembering with and without awareness in a depressed mood: Evidence of deficits in initiative. *Journal of Experimental Psychology: General, 119,* 45–59.

Higgins, E. T. (1999). Persons and situations: Unique explanatory principles or variability in general principles. In D. Cervone & Y. Shoda (Eds.), *The coherence of personality: Social-cognitive bases of consistency, variability, and organization* (pp. 61–93). New York: Guilford Press.

Higgins, E. T., Bond, R. N., Klein, R., & Strauman, T. (1986). Self-discrepancies and emotional vulnerability: How magnitude, accessibility, and type of discrepancy influence affect. *Journal of Personality and Social Psychology, 51,* 5–15.

Higgins, E. T., Shah, J., & Friedman, R. (1997). Emotional responses to goal attainment: Strength of regulatory focus as moderator. *Journal of Personality and Social Psychology, 72,* 515–525.

Hollon, S. D., & Kendall, P. C. (1980). Cognitive self-statements in depression: Development of an automatic thoughts questionnaire. *Cognitive Therapy and Research, 4,* 383–395.

Hooley, J. M., & Teasdale, J. D. (1989). Predictors of relapse in unipolar depressives: Expressed emotion, marital distress, and perceived criticism. *Journal of Abnormal Psychology, 98,* 229–235.

Hope, D. A., Rapee, R. M., Heimberg, R. G., & Dombeck, M. J. (1990). Representations of the self in social phobia: Vulnerability to social threat. *Cognitive Therapy and Research, 14,* 177–189.

Houston, D. M. (1995). Surviving a failure: Efficacy and a laboratory based test of the hopelessness model of depression. *European Journal of Social Psychology, 25,* 545–558.

Ingram, R. E. (1990). Self-focused attention in clinical disorders: Review and a conceptual model. *Psychological Bulletin, 107,* 156–176.

Joiner, T. E., & Metalsky, G. I. (1995) A prospective test of an integrative interpersonal theory of depression: A naturalistic study of college roommates. *Journal of Personality and Social Psychology, 69,* 778–788.

Joiner, T. E., & Wagner, K. D. (1995). Attribution style and depression in children and adolescents: A meta-analytic review. *Clinical Psychology Review, 15,* 777–798.

Jolly, J. D., & Dykman, R. A. (1994). Using self report data to differentiate anxious and depressive symptoms in adolescents: Cognitive content specificity and global distress? *Cognitive Therapy and Research, 18,* 25–37.

Kahneman, D., & Tversky, A. (1982). The simulation heuristic. In D. Kahneman, P. Slovic, & A. Tversky (Eds.), *Judgment under uncertainty: Heuristics and biases* (pp. 201–208). Cambridge, England: Cambridge University Press.

Kanfer, R., & Zeiss, A. M. (1983). Depression, interpersonal standard setting, and judgments of self-efficacy. *Journal of Abnormal Psychology, 92,* 319–329.

Kavanagh, D. J., & Wilson, P. H. (1989). Prediction of outcome with group cognitive therapy for depression. *Behaviour Research and Therapy, 27,* 333–343.

Kelly, G. A. (1955). *The psychology of personal constructs* (Vols. 1–2). New York: Norton.

Kendler, K., Neale, M. C., Kessler, R. C., Heath, A. C., & Eaves, L. J. (1993). A twin study of recent life events and difficulties. *Archives of General Psychiatry, 50,* 789–796.

Kihlstrom, J. F., & Klein, S. B. (1994). The self as a knowledge structure. In R. S. Wyer & T. K. Srull (Eds.), *Handbook of social cognition* (2nd ed., Vol. 1, pp. 153–208). Hillsdale, NJ: Erlbaum.

Kindt, M., & Brosschot, J. F. (1999). Cognitive bias in spider-phobic children: Comparison of a pictorial and a linguistic spider Stroop. *Journal of Psychopathology and Behavioral Assessment, 21,* 207–220.

Kuiper, N. A., &. Derry, P. A. (1982). Depressed and nondepressed content self-reference in mild depressives. *Journal of Personality, 50,* 67–80.

Kuyken, W., & Dalgleish, T. (1995). Autobiographical memory and depression. *British Journal of Clinical Psychology, 34,* 89–92.

Lawson, C., & MacLeod, C. (1999). Depression and the interpretation of ambiguity. *Behaviour Research and Therapy, 37,* 463–474.

Lazarus, R. S. (1984). On the primacy of cognition. *American Psychologist, 39,* 124–129.

Lazarus, R. S. (1991). *Emotion and adaptation.* New York: Oxford University Press.

Lazarus, R. S. (1999). The cognition-emotion debate: A bit of history. In T. Dalgleish & M. J. Power (Eds.), *Handbook of cognition and emotion* (pp. 637–664). Chichester, England: Wiley.

Levy, E., & Mineka, S. (1998). Anxiety and mood-congruent autobiographical memory: A conceptual failure to replicate. *Cognition and Emotion, 12,* 625–634.

Linville, P. W. (1985). Self-complexity and affective extremity: Don't put all of your eggs in one cognitive basket. *Social Cognition, 3,* 94–120.

Linville, P. W. (1987). Self-complexity as a cognitive buffer against stress-related illness and depression. *Journal of Personality and Social Psychology, 52,* 663–676.

Little, B. F. (1989). Personal projects analysis: Trivial pursuits, magnificant obsessions, and the search for coherence. In D. M. Buss & N. Cantor (Eds.), *Personality psychology: Recent trends and emerging directions* (pp. 15–31). New York: Springer-Verlag.

Lloyd, G., & Lishman, W. (1975). Effects of depression on the speed of recall of pleasant and unpleasant experiences. *Psychological Medicine, 5,* 173–180.

Lundh, L.-G., & Öst, L.-G. (1996). Recognition bias for critical faces in social anxiety. *Behaviour Research and Therapy, 34,* 787–794.

Lundh, L.-G., & Öst, L.-G. (1997) Explicit and implicit memory bias in social phobia: The role of diagnostic subtype. *Behaviour Research and Therapy, 35,* 305–317.

MacLeod, A. K. (1999). Prospective cognitions. In T. Dalgleish & M. J. Power (Eds.), *Handbook of cognition and emotion* (pp. 267–280). Chichester, England: Wiley.

MacLeod, A. K., & Byrne, A. (1996). Anxiety, depression and the anticipation of future positive and negative experiences. *Journal of Abnormal Psychology, 105,* 286–289.

MacLeod, A. K., Tata, P., Kentish, J., & Jacobsen, H. (1997), Retrospective and prospective cognitions in anxiety and depression. *Cognition and Emotion, 11,* 467–479.

MacLeod, C. (1999) Anxiety and anxiety disorders. In T. Dalgleish & M. Power (Eds.), *Handbook of cognition and emotion* (pp. 447–478). New York: Wiley.

MacLeod, C., & Cohen, I. (1993). Anxiety and the interpretation of ambiguity: A text comprehension study. *Journal of Abnormal Psychology, 102,* 238–247.

MacLeod, C., & Hagan, R. (1992). Individual differences in the selective processing of threatening information, and emotional responses to a stressful life event. *Behaviour Research and Therapy, 30,* 151–161.

MacLeod, C., & Mathews, A. (1988). Anxiety and the allocation of attention to threat. *Quarterly Journal of Experimental Psychology: A. Human Experimental Psychology, 40,* 653–670.

MacLeod, C., Mathews, A., & Tata, P. (1986). Attentional bias in emotional disorders. *Journal of Abnormal Psychology, 95,* 15–20.

MacLeod, C., & McgLaughlin, L. (1995). Implicit and explicit memory bias in anxiety: A conceptual replication. *Behaviour Research and Therapy, 33,* 1–14.

MacLeod, C., & Rutherford, E. M. (1992). Anxiety and the selective processing of emotional information: Mediating roles of awareness, trait and state variables, and personal relevance of stimulus materials. *Behaviour Research and Therapy, 30,* 479–491.

MacLeod, C., & Rutherford, E. M. (1999). Automatic and strategic cognitive biases in anxiety and depression. In K. Kirsner, C. Speelman, M. Mayberg, A. O'Brien-Malone, M. Anderson, & C. MacLeod (Eds.), *Implicit and explicit mental processes.* Mahwah, NJ: Erlbaum.

MacLeod, C. M. (1991). Half a century of research on the Stroop effect: An integrative review. *Psychological Bulletin, 109,* 163–203.

Martin, M., Williams, R. M., & Clark, D. M. (1991). Does anxiety lead to selective processing of threat-related information? *Behaviour Research and Therapy, 29,* 147–160.

Mathews, A. (1993). Anxiety and the processing of emotional information. In L. Chapman, J. Chapman, & D. Fowles (Eds.), *Models and methods of psychopathology: Progress in experimental personality and psychopathology research* (pp. 254–280). New York: Springer.

Mathews, A., & Klug, F. (1993). Emotionality and interference with color-naming in anxiety. *Behaviour Research and Therapy, 31,* 57–62.

Mathews, A., & MacLeod, C. (1985). Selective processing of threat cues in anxiety states. *Behaviour Research and Therapy, 23,* 563–569.

Mathews, A., & MacLeod, C. (1994). Cognitive approaches to emotion and emotional disorders. *Annual Review of Psychology, 45,* 25–50.

Mathews, A., Mogg, K., Kentish, J., & Eysenck, M. (1995). Effect of psychological treatment on cognitive bias in generalized anxiety disorder. *Behaviour Research and Therapy, 33,* 293–303.

Mathews, A., Mogg, K., May, J., & Eysenck, M. (1989). Implicit and explicit memory bias in anxiety. *Journal of Abnormal Psychology, 98,* 236–240.

Mathews, A., Richards, A., & Eysenck, M. (1989). Interpretation of homophones related to threat in anxiety states. *Journal of Abnormal Psychology, 98,* 31–34.

Mathews, A., Ridgeway, V., & Williamson, D. A. (1996). Evidence for attention to threatening stimuli in depression. *Behaviour Research and Therapy, 34,* 695–705.

Mathews, A. M., & Sebastian, S. (1993). Suppression of emotional Stroop effects by fear-arousal. *Cognition and Emotion, 7,* 517–530.

Matt, G., Vacquez, C., & Campbell, W. K. (1992) Mood-congruent recall of affectively toned stimuli: A meta-analytical review. *Clinical Psychology Review, 12,* 227–255.

Mattia, J. I., Heimberg, R. G., & Hope, D. A. (1993). The revised Stroop color-naming task in social phobics. *Behaviour Research and Therapy, 31,* 305–313.

McClain, L., & Abramson, L. Y. (1995). Self-schemas, stress, and depressed mood in college students. *Cognitive Therapy and Research, 19,* 419–432.

McNally, R. J., & Amir, N. (1996). Perceptual implicit memory for trauma-related information in post-traumatic stress disorder. *Cognition and Emotion, 10,* 551–556.

McNally, R. J., Amir, N., Louro, C. E., Lukach, B. M., Riemann, B. C., & Calamari, J. E. (1994). Cognitive processing of idiographic emotional information in panic disorder. *Behaviour Research and Therapy, 32,* 119–122.

McNally, R. J., & Foa, E. (1987). Cognition and agoraphobia: Bias in the interpretation of threat. *Cognitive Therapy and Research, 11,* 567–581.

McNally, R. J., Kaspi, S. P., Riemann, B. C., & Zeitlin, S. B. (1990). Selective processing of threat cues in post-traumatic stress disorder. *Journal of Abnormal Psychology, 99,* 398–402.

McNally, R. J., Lasko, N. B., Macklin, M., & Pitman, R. K. (1995). Autobiographical memory disturbance in combat-related posttraumatic stress disorder. *Behaviour Research and Therapy, 28,* 407–412.

McNally, R. J., Litz, B. T., & Prassas, A. (1994). Emotional priming of autobiographical memory in posttraumatic stress disorder. *Cognition and Emotion, 8,* 351–367.

McNally, R. J., Riemann, B. C., Louro, C. E., Lukach,

B. M., & Kim, E. (1992). Cognitive processing of emotional information in panic disorder. *Behaviour Research and Therapy, 30,* 143–149.

Metalsky, G. I., & Joiner, T. E. (1992). Vulnerability to depressive symptomatology: A prospective test of the diathesis-stress and causal mediation components of the hopelessness theory of depression. *Journal of Personality and Social Psychology, 63,* 667–675.

Metalsky, G. I., Joiner, T. E., Hardin, T. S., & Abramson, L. Y. (1993). Depressive reactions to failure in a naturalistic setting: A test of the hopelessness and self-esteem theories of depression. *Journal of Abnormal Psychology, 102,* 101–109.

Miller, S. M. (1979). Controllability and human stress: Method, evidence and theory. *Behaviour Research and Therapy, 17,* 287–304.

Mineka, S. (1985). Animal models of anxiety-based disorders: Their usefulness and limitations. In T. A. Hussain & J. D. Maser (Eds.), *Anxiety and the anxiety disorders* (pp. 199–244). Hillsdale, NJ: Erlbaum.

Mineka, S. (1992). Evolutionary memories, emotional processing and the emotional disorders. In D. Medin (Ed.), *The psychology of learning and motivation* (Vol. 28, pp. 161–206). New York: Academic Press.

Mineka, S. (1997). *Four failures to find implicit memory biases in high trait anxiety using conceptual and recall tasks.* Unpublished manuscript.

Mineka, S., & Hendersen, R. W. (1985). Controllability and predictability in acquired motivation. *Annual Review of Psychology, 36,* 495–529.

Mineka, S., & Kelly, K. A. (1989). The relationship between anxiety, lack of control, and loss of control. In A. Steptoe & A. Appels (Eds.), *Stress, personal control, and health* (pp. 163–191). Brussels, Belgium: Wiley.

Mineka, S., & Nugent, K. (1995). Mood-congruent memory biases in anxiety and depression. In D. Schacter (Ed.), *Memory distortion: How minds, brains, and societies reconstruct the past* (pp. 173–193). Cambridge, MA: Harvard University Press.

Mineka, S., Pury, C. L., & Luten, A. G. (1995). Explanatory style in anxiety and depression. In G. M. Buchanan & M. E. P. Seligman (Eds.), *Explanatory style* (pp. 135–158). Hillsdale, NJ: Erlbaum.

Mineka, S., & Thomas, C. (1999). Mechanisms of change in exposure therapy for anxiety disorders. In T. Dalgleish & M. J. Power (Eds.), *Handbook of cognition and emotion* (pp. 747–764). Chichester, England: Wiley.

Mineka, S., Watson, D., & Clark, L. A. (1998). Comorbidity of anxiety and unipolar mood disorders. *Annual Review of Psychology, 49,* 377–412.

Mineka, S., & Zinbarg, R. (1996). Conditioning and ethological models of anxiety disorders: Stress-in-dynamic-context anxiety models. In D. A. Hope (Ed.), *Nebraska Symposium on Motivation: Vol. 43. Perspectives on anxiety, panic, and fear: Current theory and research in motivation* (pp. 135–210). Lincoln, NE: University of Nebraska Press.

Mineka, S., & Zinbarg, R. (1998) Experimental approaches to understanding the mood and anxiety disorders. In J. Adair, D. Belanger, & K. Dion (Eds.) *Proceedings of the 26th International Congress of Psychology: Vol. 1. Advances in psychological science: Social, personal, and cultural aspects* (pp. 429–454). Hove, England: Psychology Press.

Moffitt, K. H., Singer, J. A., Nelligan, D. W., Carlson, M. A., & Vyse, S. A. (1994). Depression and memory narrative type. *Journal of Abnormal Psychology, 103,* 581–583.

Mogg, K. (1988). Processing of emotional information in clinical anxiety states. Unpublished doctoral dissertation. University of London.

Mogg, K., & Bradley, B. P. (1998). A cognitive-motivational analysis of anxiety. *Behaviour Research and Therapy, 36,* 809–848.

Mogg, K., Bradley, B. P., Millar, N., & White, J. (1995). A follow-up study of cognitive bias in generalized anxiety disorder. *Behaviour Research and Therapy, 33,* 927–935.

Mogg, K., Bradley, B. P., & Williams, R. (1995). Attentional bias in anxiety and depression: The role of awareness. *British Journal of Clinical Psychology, 34,* 17–36.

Mogg, K., Bradley, B. P., Williams, R., & Mathews, A. (1993). Subliminal processing of emotional information in anxiety and depression. *Journal of Abnormal Psychology, 102,* 304–311.

Mogg, K., Gardiner, J. M., Starron, S., & Golombok, S. (1992). Recollection experience and recognition memory for threat in clinical anxiety states. *Bulletin of the Psychonomic Society, 30,* 109–112.

Mogg, K., Kentish, J., & Bradley, B. P. (1993). Effects of anxiety and awareness on colour-identification latencies for emotional words. *Behaviour Research and Therapy, 31,* 559–567.

Mogg, K., Mathews, A., Bird, C., & Macgregor-Morris, R. (1990). Effects of stress and anxiety on the processing of threat stimuli. *Journal of Personality and Social Psychology, 59,* 1230–1237.

Mogg, K., Mathews, A., & Eysenck, M. (1992). Attentional bias to threat in clinical anxiety states. *Cognition and Emotion, 6,* 149–159.

Mogg, K., Mathews, A., May, J., Grove, M., Eysenck, M., & Weinman, J. (1991). Assessment of cognitive bias in anxiety and depression using a colour perception task. *Cognition and Emotion, 5,* 221–238.

Mogg, K., Mathews, A., & Weinman, J. (1987). Memory bias in clinical anxiety. *Journal of Abnormal Psychology, 96,* 94–98.

Mogg, K., Mathews, A., & Weinman, J. (1989). Selective processing of threat cues in anxiety states: A replication. *Behaviour Research and Therapy, 27,* 317–323.

Moore, R. G., Watts, F. N., & Williams, J. M. G. (1988). The specificity of personal memories in depression. *British Journal of Clinical Psychology, 27,* 275–276.

Mor, N., & Winquist, J. R. (2001). *Self-focused attention and negative affect: A comprehensive meta-analysis.* Manuscript submitted for publication.

Mowrer, O. H., & Viek, P. (1948). An experimental analogue of fear from a sense of helplessness. *Journal of Abnormal and Social Psychology, 43,* 193–200.

Navon, D., & Margalit, B. (1983). Allocation of attention according to informativeness in visual recognition. *Quarterly Journal of Experimental Psychology: A. Human Experimental Psychology, 35,* 497–512.

Nolen-Hoeksema, S. (1991). Responses to depression and their effects on the duration of depressive episodes. *Journal of Abnormal Psychology, 100,* 569–582.

Nugent, K., & Mineka, S. (1994). The effects of high and low trait anxiety on implicit and explicit memory tasks. *Cognition and Emotion, 8,* 147–163.

Nunn, J. D., Matthews, A., & Trower, P. (1997). Selective processing of concern-related information in depres-

sion. *British Journal of Clinical Psychology, 36,* 489–503.

Oatley, K., & Johnson-Laird, P. (1987). Towards a cognitive theory of emotions. *Cognition and Emotion, 1,* 29–50.

Öhman, A., Dimberg, U., & Öst, L.-G. (1985). Animal and social phobia: Biological constraints on learned fear responses. In S. Reiss & R. R. Bootzin (Eds.), *Theoretical issues in behavior therapy* (pp. 123–178). New York: Academic Press.

Öhman, A., & Mineka, S. (2001). Fears, phobias, and preparedness: Toward an evolved module of fear learning. *Psychological Review, 108,* 483–522.

Otto, M. W., McNally, R. J., Pollack, M. H., Chen, E., & Rosenbaum, J. F. (1994). Hemispheric laterality and memory bias for threat in anxiety disorder. *Journal of Abnormal Psychology, 103,* 828–831.

Overmier, J. B., & Seligman, M. E. (1967). Effects of inescapable shock upon subsequent escape and avoidance responding. *Journal of Comparative and Physiological Psychology, 63,* 28–33.

Pacini, R., Muir, F., & Epstein, S. (1998). Depressive realism from the perspective of cognitive-experiential self-theory. *Journal of Personality and Social Psychology, 74,* 1056–1068.

Pauli, P. P., Montoya, P., & Martz, G.-E. (1996). Covariation bias in panic-prone individuals. *Journal of Abnormal Psychology, 105,* 658–662.

Pennebaker, J. W. (1989). Stream of consciousness and stress: Levels of thinking. In J. S. Uleman & J. A. Bargh (Eds.), *Unintended thought* (pp. 327–350). New York: Guilford Press.

Persons, J. B., & Miranda, J. (1992). Cognitive theories of vulnerability to depression: Reconciling negative evidence. *Cognitive Therapy and Research, 16,* 485–502.

Pietromonaco, P. R., & Markus, H. (1985). The nature of negative thoughts in depression. *Journal of Personality and Social Psychology, 48,* 799–807.

Plutchik, R. (1984). Emotions: A general psychoevolutionary theory. In K. Scherer & P. Ekman (Eds.), *Approaches to emotion* (pp. 197–219). Hillsdale, NJ: Erlbaum.

Pury, C., & Mineka, S. (1997). Fear-relevant covariation bias for blood-injury-relevant stimuli and aversive outcomes. *Behaviour Research and Therapy, 35,* 35–47.

Pyszczynski, T., & Greenberg, J. (1987). Self-regulatory perseveration and the depressive self-focusing style: A self-awareness theory of reactive depression. *Psychological Bulletin, 102,* 122–138.

Rafaeli, E., & Steinberg, J. (in press). Self-complexity and well-being: A meta-analysis. *Personality and Social Psychology Review.*

Rafaeli-Mor, E., & Brown, G. P. (1997). *Reexamining self-complexity's role in buffering depression: An alternative measurement strategy.* Poster session presented at the European Conference on Psychological Assessment, Lisbon, Portugal.

Rafaeli-Mor, E., Gotlib, I. H., & Revelle, W. (1999). The meaning and measurement of self-complexity. *Personality and Individual Differences, 27,* 341–356.

Rafaeli-Mor, N. (1999, June). *Self-focused attention and negative affect: A comprehensive meta-analysis.* Poster session presented at the annual convention of the American Psychological Society, Denver, CO.

Ralph, J. A., & Mineka, S. (1998). Attributional style and self-esteem; The prediction of emotional distress following a midterm exam. *Journal of Abnormal Psychology, 107,* 203–215.

Reynolds, M., & Brewin, C. (1999). Intrusive memories in depression and posttraumatic stress disorder. *Behaviour Research and Therapy, 37*, 201–215.

Richards, A., French, C. C., Johnson, W., Naparstek, J., & Williams J. (1992). Effects of mood manipulation and anxiety on performance of an emotional Stroop task. *British Journal of Psychology, 83*, 479–491.

Richards, A., & Whittaker, T. (1990). Effects of anxiety and mood manipulation in autobiographical memory. *British Journal of Clinical Psychology, 29*, 145–154.

Riemann, B. C., & McNally, R. J. (1995). Cognitive processing of personally relevant information. *Cognition and Emotion, 9*(4), 325–340.

Roediger, H. L. (1990). Implicit memory: Retention without remembering. *American Psychologist, 45*, 1043–1056.

Roediger, H. L., & Blaxton, T. A. (1987). Retrieval modes produce dissociation in memory for surface information. In D. Gorfein & R. R. Hoffman (Eds.), *Memory and cognitive processes: The Ebbinghaus Centennial Conference.* Hillsdale, NJ: Erlbaum.

Roediger, H. L., & McDermott, K. (1992). Depression and implicit memory: A commentary. *Journal of Abnormal Psychology, 101*, 587–591.

Ruiz-Caballero, J. A., & Bermudez, J. (1997). Anxiety and attention: Is there an attentional bias for positive emotional stimuli? *Journal of General Psychology, 124*(2), 194–210.

Ruiz-Caballero, J., & Gonzalez, P. (1994). Implicit and explicit memory bias in depressed and nondepressed subjects. *Cognition and Emotion, 8*, 555–569.

Rusted, J. L., & Dighton, K. (1991). Selective processing of threat-related material by spider phobics in a prose recall task. *Cognition and Emotion, 5*, 123–132.

Salkovskis, P. M. (1999). Understanding and treating obsessive-compulsive disorder. *Behaviour Research and Therapy, 37*, S29–S52.

Sanderson, W. C., Rapee, R. M., & Barlow, D. H. (1989). The influence of an illusion of control on panic attacks induced via inhalation of 5.5% carbon dioxide-enriched air. *Archives of General Psychiatry, 46*, 157–162.

Schacter, D. L. (1987). Implicit memory: History and current status. *Journal of Experimental Psychology: Learning, Memory, and Cognition, 13*, 501–518.

Scherer, K. R. (1999). Appraisal theory. In T. Dalgleish & M. J. Power (Eds.), *Handbook of cognition and emotion* (pp. 637–664). Chichester, England: Wiley.

Scott, L., & O'Hara, M. W. (1993). Self-discrepancies in clinically anxious and depressed university students. *Journal of Abnormal Psychology, 102*, 282–287.

Segal, Z. V., & Gemar, M. (1997). Changes in cognitive organisation for negative self-referent material following cognitive behaviour therapy for depression: A primed Stroop study. *Cognition and Emotion, 11*, 501–516.

Segal, Z. V., Gemar, M., Truchon, C., & Guirguis, M. (1995). A priming methodology for studying self-representation in major depressive disorder. *Journal of Abnormal Psychology, 104*, 205–213.

Segal, Z. V., Shaw, B. F., Vella, D. D., & Katz, R. (1992). Cognitive and life stress predictors of relapse in remitted unipolar depressed patients: Test of the congruency hypothesis. *Journal of Abnormal Psychology, 101*, 26–36.

Seligman, M. E. P. (1971). Preparedness and phobias. *Behavior Therapy, 2*, 307–320.

Seligman, M. E. P. (1975). *Helplessness: On depression, development, and death.* San Francisco: Freeman.

Seligman, M. E. P., & Maier, S. F. (1967). Failure to escape traumatic shock. *Journal of Experimental Psychology, 74*, 1–9.

Shaw, B. F. (1985). Closing commentary: Social cognition and depression. *Social Cognition, 3*, 135–144.

Sheldon, K. M., & Kasser, T. (1995). Coherence and congruence: Two aspects of personality integration. *Journal of Personality and Social Psychology, 68*, 531–543.

Shnek, Z. M., Foley, F. W., LaRocca, N. G., Gordon, W. A., DeLuca, J., Schwartzman, H. G., Halper, J., Lennox, S., & Irvine, J. (1997). Helplessness, self-efficacy, cognitive distortions, and depression in multiple sclerosis and spinal cord injury. *Annals of Behavioral Medicine, 19*, 287–294.

Small, S. A., & Robins, C. J. (1988). The influence of induced depressed mood on visual recognition thresholds: Predictive ambiguity of associative network models of mood and cognition. *Cognitive Therapy and Research, 12*, 295–304.

Smith, E. R. (1994). Procedural knowledge and processing strategies in social cognition. In R. S. Wyer Jr., & T. K. Srull (Eds.), *Handbook of social cognition* (pp. 99–151). Hillsdale, NJ: Erlbaum.

Spielberger, C. D., Gorsuch, R. L., & Lushene, R. (1970). *Manual for the State-Trait Anxiety Inventory.* Palo Alto, CA: Consulting Psychologists Press.

Steer, R. A., Clark, D. A., Beck, A. T., & Ranieri, W. F. (1995). Common and specific dimensions of self-reported anxiety and depression: A replication. *Journal of Abnormal Psychology, 104*, 542–545.

Strauman, T. J. (1989). Self-discrepancies in clinical depression and social phobia: Cognitive structures that underlie emotional disorders? *Journal of Abnormal Psychology, 98*, 14–22.

Strauman, T. J., & Higgins, E. T. (1988). Self-discrepancies as predictors of vulnerability to distinct syndromes of chronic emotional distress. *Journal of Personality, 56*, 685–707.

Strauman, T. J., Lemieux, A. M., & Coe, C. L. (1993). Self-discrepancy and natural killer cell activity: Immunological consequences of negative self-evaluation. *Journal of Personality and Social Psychology, 64*, 1042–1052.

Stroop, J. R. (1935). Studies of interference in serial verbal reactions. *Journal of Experimental Psychology, 18*, 643–662.

Sutton, L. J., Teasdale, J. D., & Broadbent, D. E. (1988). Negative self-schema: The effects of induced depressed mood. *British Journal of Clinical Psychology, 27*, 188–190.

Swann, W. B., & Read, S. J. (1981). Self-verification processes: How we sustain our self-conceptions. *Journal of Experimental Social Psychology, 17*, 351–372.

Sweeney, P. D., Anderson, K., & Bailey, S. (1986). Attributional style in depression: A meta-analytic review. *Journal of Personality and Social Psychology, 50*, 974–991.

Tallis, F. (1994). Obsessions, responsibility and guilt: Two case reports suggesting a common and specific aetiology. *Behaviour Research and Therapy, 32*, 143–145.

Tata, P. R., Leibowitz, J. A., Prunty, M. J., Cameron, M., & Pickering A. D. (1996). Attentional bias in obsessive compulsive disorder. *Behaviour Research and Therapy, 34*, 53–60.

Taylor, S. E., & Brown, J. D. (1988). Illusion and well-being: A social psychological perspective on mental health. *Psychological Bulletin, 103*, 193–210.

Teasdale, J. D. (1988). Cognitive vulnerability to persistent depression. *Cognition and Emotion, 2*, 247–274.

Teasdale, J. D., & Barnard, P. J. (1993). *Affect, cognition and change: Re-modelling depressive thought.* Hillsdale, NJ: Erlbaum.

Teasdale, J. D., & Dent, J. (1987). Cognitive vulnerability to depression: An investigation of two hypotheses. *British Journal of Clinical Psychology, 26*, 113–126.

Teasdale, J. D., & Fogarty, S. (1979). Differential effects of induced mood on retrieval of pleasant and unpleasant events from episodic memory. *Journal of Abnormal Psychology, 88*, 248–257.

Thorpe, S. J., & Salkovskis, P. M. (1997). Information processing in spider phobics: The Stroop colour naming task may indicate strategic but not automatic attentional bias. *Behaviour Research and Therapy, 35*, 131–144.

Tomarken, A. J., Mineka, S., & Cook, M. (1989). Fear-relevant selective associations and covariation bias. *Journal of Abnormal Psychology, 98*, 381–394.

Tversky, A., & Kahneman, D. (1973). Availability: A heuristic for judging frequency and probability. *Cognitive Psychology, 5*, 207–232.

Usaf, S. O., & Kavanagh, D. J. (1990). Mechanisms of improvement in treatment for depression: Test of a self-efficacy and performance model. *Journal of Cognitive Psychotherapy, 4*, 51–70.

Valentiner, D. P., Telch, M. J., Petruzzi, D. C., & Bolte, M. C. (1996). Cognitive mechanisms in claustrophobia: An examination of Reiss and McNally's expectancy model and Bandura's self-efficacy theory. *Cognitive Therapy and Research, 20*, 593–612.

Watkins, P., Mathews, A., Williamson, D. A., & Uller, R. D. (1992). Mood-congruent memory in depression: Emotional priming or elaboration? *Journal of Abnormal Psychology, 101*, 581–586.

Watkins, P. C., Vache, K., Verney, S. P., Muller, S., & Mathews A. (1996). Unconscious mood-congruent memory bias in depression. *Journal of Abnormal Psychology, 105*, 34–41.

Watson, D., Weber, K., Assenheimer, J. S., Clark, L. A., Strauss, M. E., & McCormick, R. A. (1995). Testing a tripartite model: I. Evaluating the convergent and discriminant validity of anxiety and depression symptom scales. *Journal of Abnormal Psychology, 104*, 3–14.

Watts, F., & Coyle, K. (1993). Phobics show poor recall of anxiety words. *British Journal of Medical Psychology, 66*, 373–382.

Watts, F., & Dalgleish, T. (1991). Memory for phobia-related words in spider phobics. *Cognition and Emotion, 5*, 313–329.

Watts, F., Sharrock, R., & Trezise, L. (1986). Processing of phobic stimuli. *British Journal of Clinical Psychology, 25*, 253–261.

Watts, F. N., McKenna, F. P., Sharrock, R., & Trezise, L. (1986). Colour naming of phobia-related words. *British Journal of Psychology, 77*, 97–108.

Weary, G., & Edwards, J. A. (1994). Social cognition and clinical psychology: Anxiety, depression, and the processing of social information. In R. S. Wyer & T. K. Srull (Eds.), *Handbook of social cognition* (2nd ed., Vol. 1, pp. 289–338). Hillsdale, NJ: Erlbaum.

Weary, G., Marsh, K. L., & McCormick, L. (1994). Depression and social comparison motives. *European Journal of Social Psychology, 24*, 117–129.

Weissman, A. N., & Beck, A. T. (1978). *Development and validation of the Dysfunctional Attitudes Scale: A preliminary investigation.* Paper presented at the annual meeting of the Educational Research Association, Toronto, Ontario, Canada.

Westra, H. A., & Kuiper, N. A. (1997). Cognitive content specificity in selective attention across four domains of maladjustment. *Behaviour Research and Therapy, 35*, 349–365.

Whisman, M. A., & Pinto, A. (1997). Hopelessness depression in depressed inpatient adolescents. *Cognitive Therapy and Research, 21*, 345–358.

Wilhelm, S., McNally, R. J., Baer, L., & Florin, I. (1997). Autobiographical memory in obsessive-compulsive disorder. *British Journal of Clinical Psychology, 36*, 21–31.

Williams, J. M. G., Mathews, A., & MacLeod, C. (1996). The emotional Stroop task and psychopathology. *Psychological Bulletin, 120*(1), 3–24.

Williams, J. M. G., & Scott, J. (1988). Autobiographical memory in depression. *Psychological Medicine, 18*, 689–695.

Williams, J. M. G., Watts, F., MacLeod, C., & Mathews, A. (1988). *Cognitive psychology and the emotional disorders.* Chichester, England: Wiley.

Williams, J. M. G., Watts, F. N., MacLeod, C., & Mathews, A. (1997). *Cognitive psychology and emotional disorders* (2nd ed.). Chichester, England: Wiley.

Williams, S. L. (1995). Self-efficacy, anxiety, and phobic disorders. In J. E. Maddux (Ed.), *Self-efficacy, adaptation, and adjustment: Theory, research, and application* (pp. 69–107). New York: Plenum.

Woody, S. R., Taylor, S., McLean, P. D., & Koch, W. J. (1998). Cognitive specificity in panic and depression: Implications for comorbidity. *Cognitive Therapy and Research, 22*, 427–443.

Zajonc, R. B. (1960). The process of cognitive tuning in communication. *Journal of Abnormal and Social Psychology, 61*, 159–167.

Zajonc, R. B. (1984). On the primacy of affect. *American Psychologist, 39*, 117–123.

Zane, G., & Williams, S. L. (1993). Performance-related anxiety in agoraphobia: Treatment procedures and cognitive mechanisms of change. *Behavior Therapy, 24*, 625–643.

Zuroff, D. C., Blatt, S. J., Sanislow, C. A., Bondi, C. M., & Pilkonis, P. A. (1999). Vulnerability to depression: Reexamining state dependence and relative stability. *Journal of Abnormal Psychology, 108*, 76–89.

# 53

# THE NEUROBIOLOGY OF AFFILIATION: IMPLICATIONS FOR AUTISM

Thomas R. Insel

A decade from now, when we look back at the early years of affective neuroscience, we may wonder about our conspicuous preoccupation with "negative" emotions. Fear and anxiety, sadness and depression, anger and aggression have received considerable attention in the past few years. By contrast, the neurobiology of "positive" affects, such as joy, affiliation, and love, seem almost taboo subjects. No doubt our focus on negative emotions derives from a need to understand psychopathological states. Most major forms of psychopathology, such as the anxiety and affective disorders, involve an excess of one of the negative emotions. Recently, we have begun to appreciate that most mental disorders also involve a loss of positive affect, whether it is the anhedonia of major depressive disorder, the absence of affiliation in autism, or the negative symptoms of schizophrenia. An important first step toward accounting for the loss of positive affects will be to understand their normal expression. Clearly, joy is not just the absence of sadness, and love/affiliation is much more than the absence of hate or fear. Positive affects will undoubtedly have a circuitry and a neurochemistry that is unique from what we have already learned about fear, sadness, and anger. But how can we study these complex affects with the modern tools of neurobiology? In this chapter, I review one approach based on animal studies. This approach demonstrates that current molecular and cellular tools, when combined with comparative, ethologically relevant studies, can reveal some intriguing leads into the neural basis of affiliation in nonhuman animals.

*Affiliation* is an ethological term generally used to describe membership in a conspecific group. In fact, there are two quite different uses of the term *affiliation*. The first, relevant to all species, is sociality. Some highly affiliative species, including our own, cluster in flocks or herds in which group membership is essential for survival. Other, nonaffiliative species, such as orangutans or certain cats, are loners, living solitary lives except when mating or caring for young. A second use of the term *affiliation* describes specific aspects of behavior within a species. In this latter sense, affiliative behaviors include side-by-side or huddling behavior, parent-infant attachment, and pair bonding. Because these behaviors are most relevant to understanding the basis of the powerful human experiences of acceptance, attachment, and love, this chapter focuses on this second meaning of affiliation.

## Animal Models of Affiliation

We have no problem accepting the notion that nonhuman animals experience "negative" affects such fear, rage, and helplessness. For some reason, we are less able to accept that other species can also experience the "better angels of our nature." Indeed, as Frans de Waal has pointed out, we describe our own expressions of rage or lust as "bestial," but we fail to recognize that some of our most "humane" qualities are present in other species (de Waal, 1996). In fact, the ability to form attachments has an an-

Table 53.1.  Forms of Social Organization

| Feature | Monogamy | Polygamy/Promiscuity |
|---|---|---|
| Habitat | Shared nest and territory | Solitary nest, overlapping territories |
| Parental care | Biparental | Uniparental—usually maternal |
| Nest guarding | Frequent | Variable |
| Mating strategy | Pair bonding | Multiple mates |
| Prevalence | > 90% birds | > 90% mammals |

cient evolutionary heritage, with pair bonding and intense parental care evident in select species of fishes, amphibia, and reptiles (Rosenblatt & Snowdon, 1996). Birds are the ultimate example of affiliation, with nearly 90% of known species mating for life and demonstrating biparental (paternal and maternal) behaviors (Buntin, 1996).

One way to classify social organization borrows terms originally used to describe mating systems: *monogamy, polygamy, and promiscuity*. Although these labels, in a popular sense, define sexual behavior, they are used in an ethological sense to define social behavior (see Table 53.1). Monogamous species tend to be highly affiliative (highly social), and, most important for our purposes, they form lasting, selective attachments, which we call *pair bonds*. It is important to note that nearly all laboratory species that have been used for behavioral neuroscience, such as Norway rats, inbred mice, and rhesus monkeys, are promiscuous or polygamous; that is, they do not form selective, enduring bonds. With rare exceptions, parental or mating behavior does not involve the formation of a selective attachment, and separation in these species involves social, not individual, loss.

To study selective attachments, one must use nontraditional laboratory animals. Voles or microtine rodents have proven especially helpful. The prairie vole (*Microtus ochrogaster*) is a mouse-sized rodent which lives in burrows across the American midwest. Prairie voles are usually found in multigenerational family groups with a single breeding pair (Getz, Carter, & Garish, 1981; Getz & Hofman, 1986). They manifest the classic features of monogamy: A breeding pair shares the same nest and territory, where they are in frequent contact, males participate in parental care, and intruders of either sex are rejected. Following death of one of the pair, a new mate is accepted only about 20% of the time (the rate is approximately the same whether the male or the female is the survivor; Getz, McGuire, Pizzuto, Hoffman, & Frase, 1993). Prairie voles also demonstrate a curious pattern of reproductive development. Offspring remain sexually suppressed as long as they remain within the natal group. For females, puberty occurs not at a specific age but after exposure to a chemosignal in the urine of an unrelated male (Carter, Witt,

Schneider, Harris, & Volkening, 1987). Within 24 hours of exposure to this signal, the female becomes sexually receptive. She mates repeatedly with an unrelated male and, in the process, forms a selective and enduring preference or pair bond (Carter, DeVries, & Getz, 1995).

Two attributes of the prairie vole make this species particularly useful for neurobiological investigation. The first is that the highly developed social behaviors described in field studies are also manifest in the lab using either captive or lab-bred animals. In the lab, prairie voles appear highly affiliative, sitting side by side more than 50% of the time and attacking adult intruders (Carter et al. 1995; Shapiro & Dewsbury 1990). Both sexes display intense parental care (McGuire & Novak, 1984; Oliveras & Novak, 1986). Even neonatal prairie voles appear to crave social contact. During a brief social separation, 5-day-old prairie voles emit ultrasonic "distress" calls and secrete corticosterone (Shapiro & Insel, 1990).

Another advantage is that prairie voles offer the possibility of comparative studies. The closely related montane vole (*Microtus montanus*) looks remarkably similar to the prairie vole and shares many features of its nonsocial behaviors, but it differs consistently on measures of social behavior (Dewsbury, 1988; McGuire, 1986). Montane voles are generally found in isolated burrows (in high meadows in the Rockies), show little interest in social contact, and are clearly not monogamous (Jannett, 1980). Males show little if any parental care, and females frequently abandon their young between 8 and 14 days postpartum (Jannett, 1982). In laboratory studies, montane voles spend little time in side-by-side contact, even within the confines of a mouse cage (Shapiro & Dewsbury, 1990). Montane pups at Day 5 do not respond to social separation with either isolation calls or corticosterone release, although the pups give both responses to nonsocial stressors (Shapiro & Insel, 1990; see Table 53.2).

How can one measure attachment formation? Two simple laboratory measures have proven especially informative. In prairie voles, in the field, pair bonding occurs after mating. In the laboratory, the effect of mating can be demonstrated in a choice test, which assumes that formation

Table 53.2.  Behavioral Comparison of Prairie Voles and Montane Voles

| Feature | Prairie voles | Montane voles |
|---|---|---|
| Shared nest | Frequent | Infrequent |
| Maternal care | High | Low |
| Paternal care | High | Absent |
| Nest guarding | High | Absent |
| Side-by-side time | High | Low |
| Partner preference | Present | Absent |
| Separation distress | Present | Absent |

of a pair bond requires the formation of a preference for the mate over a stranger. Indeed, in tests of this assumption, prairie vole females reliably choose to sit next to their mates, whereas female montane voles are equally likely to sit with a novel male as with the male with whom they have mated (Figure 53.1). This "partner preference" is enduring and reciprocal. Prairie voles continue to show a preference for their mates even after weeks of separation, and this preference can be detected in both males and females (Insel, Preston, & Winslow, 1995; Insel & Hulihan, 1995; Figure 53.1). In addition, after mating, male prairie voles switch from being highly affiliative to highly aggressive toward conspecifics. The increase in aggression is in the service of guarding the nest and the mate (Insel et al., 1995). The male never attacks his mate. Mate guarding behavior is not observed in montane voles.

## Candidate Neural Systems

Given that voles provide a potential comparative model for understanding affiliative behavior, where do we begin to look for neurobiological differences? One approach is to define morphological differences between monogamous and polygamous species. This has been tried with mixed success (Shapiro, Leonard, Sessions, Dewsbury, & Insel, 1991). The problem is that even when we find an anatomical difference (and there is almost always some difference detectable in cross-species comparisons), we cannot prove that the neuroanatomical differences are important for the behavioral differences. At the level of chemical neuroanatomy, the species differences have been more profound, and the recent advent of transgenic techniques has provided an opportunity for rigorously linking differences in form to differences in function. The following summary describes our studies with oxytocin and vasopressin. Although there are many other neurotransmitters that might be described here, I focus on these two neuropeptides because they provide results that bridge molecular, cellular, and behavioral studies.

### Nonapeptides

Oxytocin (OT) and vasopressin (AVP) are closely related nine-amino-acid neuropeptides. They were among the first neuropeptides to be isolated and sequenced. Curiously, they are found exclusively in mammals (Gainer & Wray, 1994). OT mediates the prototypically mammalian function of milk ejection during lactation by binding to receptors in the cells that line the lactation ducts, causing these ducts to contract and expel milk. AVP, originally called antidiuretic hormone, has a classic role in the kidney, where it promotes reabsorption of water. Although the primary action of OT is in breast and AVP is in kidney, both

hormones are made in the hypothalamus, stored in the posterior pituitary, and released into the circulation following suckling (OT) or osmotic challenge (AVP). In most mammals that have been studied, both OT and AVP are released during labor to increase contractions via receptors in the uterus. Vagino-cervical stimulation is a potent releaser of both peptides, during either labor or copulation (Gainer & Wray, 1994).

OT and AVP cells in the hypothalamus of the brain appear to have two personalities. One group projects to the pituitary and is responsible for the actions of these hormones on peripheral organs. Another group of cells sends projections deep into the brain itself. The role of these brain-directed neuropeptide cells has been the subject of considerable investigation (de Wied, Diamant, & Fodor, 1993) The discovery of receptors for OT and AVP within the brain demonstrated that the brain is also a target organ for these hormones (Barberis & Tribollet, 1996). So what are OT and AVP doing in the brain?

### OT and Maternal Behavior

One possibility is that OT acts centrally to integrate maternal behavior, consistent with its role for parturition and lactation. This hypothesis was first tested by Cort Pedersen and coworkers more than 20 years ago in a classic experiment using laboratory rats (Pedersen, Ascher, Monroe, & Prange, 1982; Pedersen & Prange, 1979) For this experiment, the laboratory rat was an ideal subject because, unlike many mammals that are promiscuously maternal, female rats show little interest in pups until just prior to parturition. In the hours just prior to delivery, they exhibit a profound behavioral change. Rather than ignoring or avoiding pups, they build a nest, retrieve pups placed near the nest, exhibit crouching and grooming behavior toward the pups, and even defend the pups from an intruder at risk of personal injury. Pedersen administered OT to nonpregnant females and found that within 60 minutes they showed a full range of maternal behavior. Injections of several other neuropeptides had no such effect (AVP was a notable exception). For OT to induce maternal behavior, the females had to be primed with estrogen, and OT needed to be injected directly into the brain. Peripheral injections were ineffective, as OT does not cross the blood-brain barrier.

Perhaps more important than the effects of the hormone were the effects of treatments that inhibit OT action. Whether by lesion of OT cells, reductions of OT synthesis, or antagonists of OT binding, treatments that reduce OT in the brain inhibit the onset of maternal behavior (Insel, 1997) But the most important lesson from these studies was that none of these treatments was effective in females with established maternal behavior. OT is necessary for the onset, not the maintenance, of maternal behavior. The hormone appears critical for the transition from avoidance

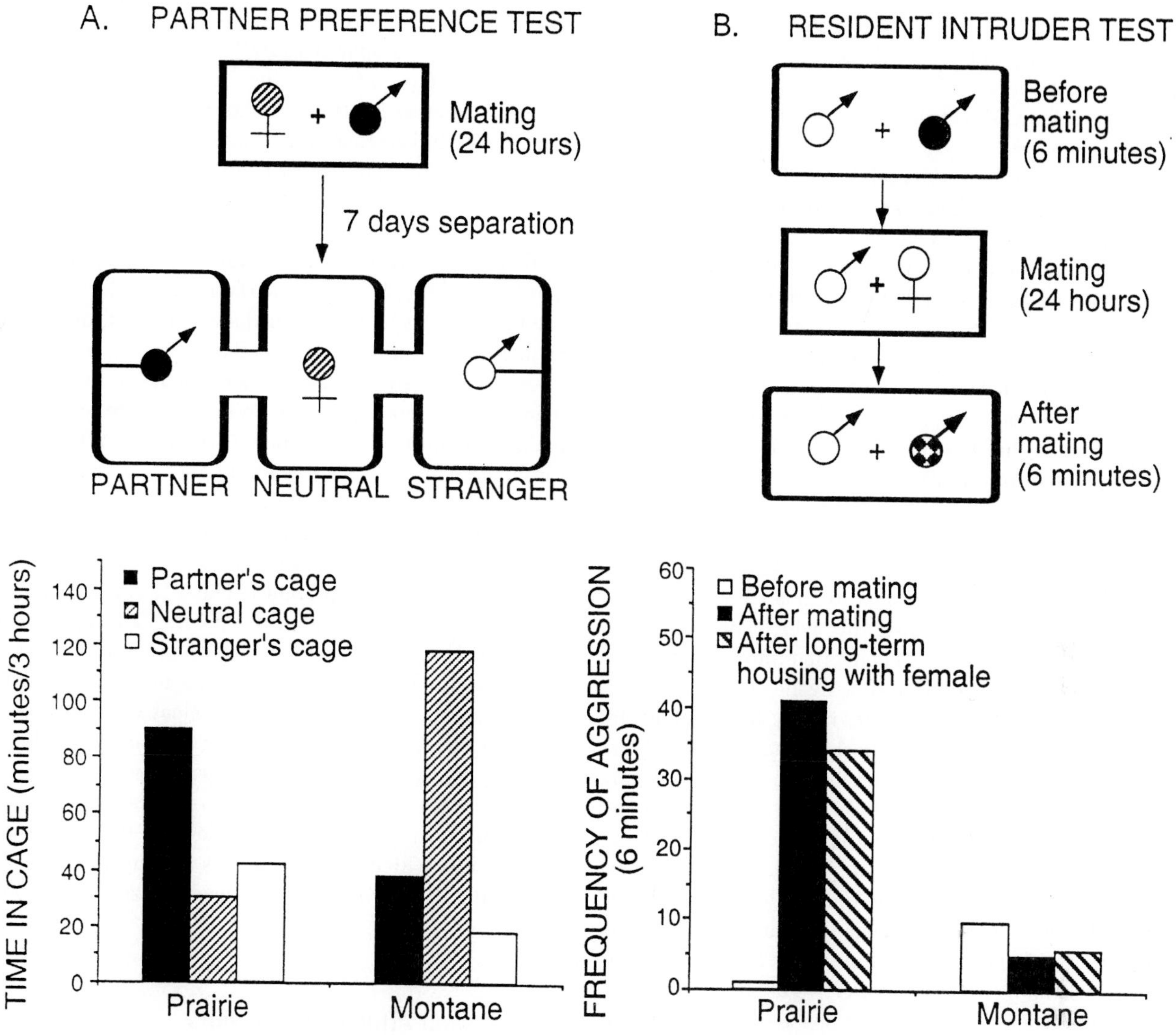

Figure 53.1 Behavioral measures of pair bonding include (A) partner preference test and (B) resident intruder test. In the partner preference test, the female is placed with a male for 24 hours, then tested for preference for original male (partner) or novel male (stranger). Males are tethered in respective cages, and the female, initially placed in a central cage (neutral) has free access to all three cages. In a 3-hour preference test, prairie voles (n = 10) spend more time in the partner's cage, and montane voles (n = 9) spend more time in the neutral cage. In the data shown, from Insel and Huli-han, 1995, females were separated from their mates for 7 days before partner preference testing. No species differences were apparent in mating behavior, and significant species differences in time with mate were evident immediately after mating. In (B), the resident intruder test is used as a measure of mate guarding. As a pretest, an intruder is placed for 6 minutes in male's home cage. Following 24 hours of mating, the experimental male receives a second intruder test with a new male. In the highly affiliative prairie vole (n = 9), the frequency of aggression is minimal before mating but increases almost fortyfold within 24 hours and is sustained for several months, as shown by testing after long-term housing with females (breeders). In montane voles (n = 7), mating has no apparent effect on intruder aggression. Data adapted from Win-slow, Hastings, Carter, Harbaugh, & Insel, 1993). Increased aggression in monogamous species probably represents defense of the mate (mate guarding), a key feature of pair bond formation. From Insel (1997). Reprinted with permission from American Psychiatric Association.

to approach of pups, that is, the initiation of maternal motivation. In a sense, then, OT is necessary for the affiliative aspects of maternal care.

We know that OT leads to milk ejection and parturition via muscle contraction, so how does this hormone work in the brain to induce maternal interest? We don't know the entire answer, but there are several relevant observations. As noted, the brain has receptors for OT. In the rat brain, these receptors are localized to a few key areas, and in some of these areas, the number of receptors increases markedly just prior to parturition or following estrogen treatment (Insel et al., 1997). One might expect that these areas are important for OT's effects on maternal behavior, but we still do not know the details. The important point to remember is that the regulation of OT effects may be more dependent on number of receptors than on peptide concentration and that the distribution of these receptors determines not only where OT acts but also what OT does within the brain. The extraordinary plasticity of these receptors and their responsiveness to gonadal steroids suggests a powerful mechanism by which physiological changes in estrogen might be converted into large, regionally specific changes in OT responsiveness.

Although the OT experiments in rats have helped to elucidate a mechanism for the onset of maternal behavior, the role of OT in other species is less clear. In sheep, which also show a rapid transition from avoidance to approach of offspring, OT has similar effects when administered centrally (Kendrick et al., 1997). However, mice engineered to lack OT show normal maternal interest in pups, although they fail to lactate (Nishimori et al., 1996) Unlike rats and sheep, these mice never avoid offspring, so there is no apparent need for OT to facilitate the onset of maternal behavior. In our own species, the role of OT for maternal behavior has not been studied. There is no simple way to increase or decrease central OT neurotransmission in the human brain because of the blood-brain barrier. However, based on the data from experiments in rats and sheep, one can conclude that a deficit of central OT neurotransmission could reduce maternal interest without altering labor or lactation.

## AVP and Social Memory

Central administration of AVP has been shown to influence the consolidation of social memory in rats (Dantzer, Bluthe, Koob, & Le Moal, 1987) The paradigm involves introducing a novel intruder into the cage of the test animal for 10 minutes. The test animal will investigate the novel intruder for several minutes. If the intruder is removed and then returned 30 or 60 minutes later, the test animal shows a clear reduction in investigation, presumably reflecting recognition of the intruder. If the interval from removal to reintroduction of the intruder is extended to 120 minutes, there is no reduction in investigation time;

the test animal treats the intruder as a novel stranger. Treating the test animal with AVP after the initial exposure extends the recognition of the intruder to at least 120 minutes, whereas treating with an AVP antagonist reduces the "recall" to less than 60 minutes. The stimulus for this "social memory" is not known, and the relationship of this memory to other forms of memory is not clear. Nevertheless, the effects of AVP are interesting because they are evident exclusively in males and appear androgen dependent (Bluthe, Schoenen, & Dantzer, 1990).

Other studies have described an important role for AVP in territorial behaviors such as flank marking in hamsters (Ferris, 1992; Ferris, Albers, Wesolowski, Goldman, & Leeman, 1984). Here again, the AVP effects are specific for males and androgen dependent. In addition, AVP has been implicated in male aggression in rats (Compaan, Buijs, Pool, de Ruiter, & Koolhaas, 1993).

AVP binds to four different receptors with markedly different distributions. The V1a receptor is found in brain, liver, and vascular membranes. The V1b (or V3) receptor is found primarily in the pituitary. The V2 receptor is the classic kidney receptor. Finally, AVP binds to the OT receptor, leading to the possibility that many apparent OT effects could be the result of AVP release. Unlike the OT receptor, the V1a receptor does not appear highly dependent on the concentration of estrogen or testosterone. Testosterone clearly influences AVP neurotransmission, but these effects appear mostly at the level of the synthesis of the peptide, which in some regions is sexually dimorphic (De Vries, Duetz, Buijs, Van Heerikhuize, & Vreeburg, 1986).

## OT, AVP and Affiliative Behaviors

### Pharmacological Studies

Given the evidence implicating OT in rat and sheep maternal behavior and AVP in social memory and territorial behavior, these neuropeptides are obvious candidates for the study of affiliation in voles. To determine if OT or AVP might be involved in the formation of a pair bond, we studied the role of these peptides in the mating-induced changes in partner preference and mate guarding in prairie voles.

As shown in Figure 53.2, OT (but not AVP) given centrally to females facilitates the development of a partner preference in the absence of mating (Insel & Hulihan, 1995; Williams, Insel, Harbaugh, & Carter, 1994). A selective OT antagonist given prior to mating blocks formation of the partner preference without interfering with mating (Insel & Hulihan, 1995). This effect appears specific: Neither cerebrospinal fluid (CSF) nor an AVP antagonist given in an identical fashion blocks partner preference formation. Presumably, the OT antagonist prevents the binding

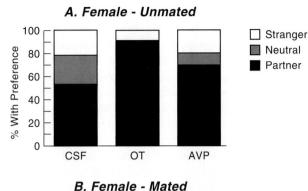

### A. Female - Unmated

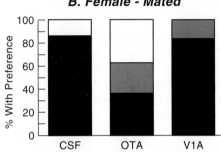

### B. Female - Mated

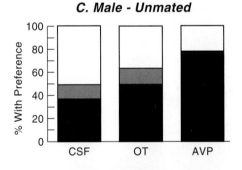

### C. Male - Unmated

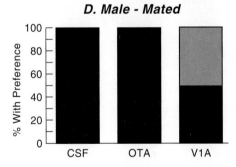

### D. Male - Mated

Figure 53.2 Oxytocin and vasopressin effects on pair bonding in prairie voles. Partner preference tests were used to determine if oxytocin or vasopressin was necessary or sufficient for pair-bond formation in a monogamous mammal. Peptides, selective antagonists (OTA and V1A), or cerebrospinal fluid (CSF) were administered by minipump into the lateral ventricle during social exposure. Data represent percentage of 3-hour test spent in partner's, stranger's, or neutral cage, as shown in figure 53.1. (A) If females were placed with a male for 6 hours but did not mate (females were ovariectomized), a partner preference was not observed unless oxytocin (0.5 ng/hr.) was administered icv. Females given an equal dose of vasopressin were not different from those treated with CSF. (B) In females allowed to mate for 14 hours, a partner preference develops (as expected from figure 53.1) with CSF icv injection. Females given a vasopressin antagonist (V1A, 5.0 ng icv) also show a significant partner preference. Females given an oxytocin antagonist (OTA, 5.0 ng icv) mated normally but failed to form a partner preference. Taken together, (A) and (B) suggest that oxytocin (released with mating) is sufficient and necessary for partner preference formation in the female prairie vole. The male shows an opposite pattern. In (C), neither CSF nor oxytocin (0.5 ng/hr.) supports partner preference formation in unmated males, but vasopressin (0.5ng/hr.) appears sufficient. In (D), when males have the opportunity to mate, the vasopressin antagonist (5.0ng icv), but not CSF or the oxytocin antagonist (5.0 ng icv), blocks partner preference formation. Thus, in contrast to females, for male prairie voles, vasopressin appears necessary and sufficient for partner preference formation. Data adapted with permission from Insel et al. (1995); Insel & Hulihan (1995). From Insel (1997). Reprinted with permission of American Psychiatric Association.

of OT to its receptor and thereby blocks the behavioral consequences of mating. These results suggest that OT released with mating is both necessary and sufficient for the formation of a pair bond in the female prairie vole. Essentially, female prairie voles given the OT antagonist resemble montane voles—they mate normally but show no lasting interest in their mates.

What about the male in this process? As noted, males show a partner preference and increased aggression or mate guarding after mating. Surprisingly, it is not OT but AVP that is critical for these effects (figure 53.2). An AVP

antagonist administered centrally to male prairie voles prior to mating blocks the development of a partner preference and precludes the increase in aggression toward an intruder (Winslow, Hastings, et al., 1993). As with females, the antagonist does not interfere with mating; rather, it appears to block the consequences of mating. An OT antagonist has no effect, suggesting that the AVP effects are specific. AVP may also be sufficient for male pair bonding. When males are not permitted to mate but are exposed to ovariectomized females, they fail to form a partner preference. However, when AVP is given centrally, in the absence of mating, males form a partner preference for the unreceptive female and will exhibit increased aggression toward an intruder (Winslow, Hastings, et al., 1993). OT given in the same fashion has no effect on these measures.

### Cellular Studies

Curiously, OT and AVP fail to induce pair bonding in the montane vole. Indeed, OT and AVP, even at high doses, have little effect on social behavior in montane voles (Winslow, Shapiro, Carter, & Insel, 1993). How can there be such a difference in the ways that the prairie vole and the montane vole brains respond to identical peptide exposure? There are various techniques to investigate the cellular mechanisms for these species differences in the behavioral response to OT. Immunocytochemical studies reveal only subtle species differences in OT and AVP cell bodies and fibers, consistent with the conclusion that peptide content (for both OT and AVP) is roughly similar in the two species (Wang, Zhou, Hulihan, & Insel, 1996). In contrast to the similarities in cell bodies and fibers, the species show markedly different patterns of receptor distribution for both OT (Insel and Shapiro, 1992) and AVP (Insel, Wang, & Ferris, 1994; see Figure 53.3).

Recent studies have demonstrated that the species differences in receptor binding maps can be replicated by maps of receptor mRNA expression (Young, Huot, Nilsen, Wang, & Insel, 1996; Young, Winslow, Nilsen, & Insel, 1997). In fact, there are virtually identical cDNAs in both species for the OT and V1a receptor—demonstrating that these species share the same receptors but differ in the regional expression of both receptors (Young et al., 1996; Young, Winslow, Nilsen, & Insel, 1997).

This species difference in regional receptor distribution indicates that different brain areas are responding to OT and AVP in prairie voles and montane voles. Thus the central effects of both neuropeptides should be quite different in the two species. For instance, in the prairie vole, OT receptors are found in brain regions associated with reward (nucleus accumbens and prelimbic cortex), suggesting that OT might have reinforcing properties selectively in this species. Recent evidence supports this mechanism, as an OT antagonist injected directly into the reward pathway is sufficient to prevent a partner preference (Young, Lim, Gingrich, & Insel, 2001). In the montane vole, which lacks receptors in this reward circuit, OT may be released with mating, but it would not confer reinforcing properties. Similarly, in the prairie vole but not the montane vole, the V1a receptor is found in the ventral pallidum, a region implicated in reinforcement. AVP release would therefore be expected to have markedly different cognitive effects in these two closely related species.

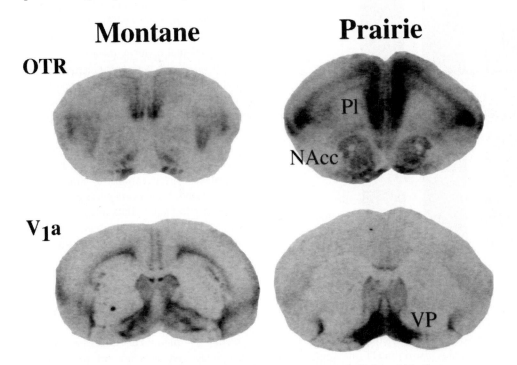

Figure 53.3 Receptor binding in prairie and montane voles. Radioligand binding was used to map OT and V1a receptors in prairie voles and montane voles. Dark areas represent specific binding of 125I-OTA (OTR) or 125I-linAVP (V1a) receptors. Note high density of OTR in prairie vole prelimbic cortex (Pl) and nucleus accumbens, regions with very low or undetectable OTR in the montane vole. V1a receptors are abundant in the ventral pallidum (VP) of the prairie vole but not of the montane vole.

Of course, such differences in chemical neuroanatomy may be unrelated to the patterns of social organization which first drew our attention to these animals. However, two observations suggest that the differences in receptor distribution may be related to the species differences in social behavior. First, other vole species (pine voles and meadow voles) selected for analogous differences in social organization (i.e., affiliative and monogamous vs. asocial and nonmonogamous) manifest similar differences in OT and AVP receptor distribution (Insel & Shapiro, 1992). Second, the findings with OT and AVP receptors appear relatively specific; the patterns of binding for mu opiate receptors and benzodiazepine receptors (two systems previously implicated in the mediation of social attachment) do not differ across the four vole species (Insel & Shapiro, 1992).

In summary, highly affiliative, monogamous voles show distinct patterns of OT and AVP receptor distribution in the brain, and both peptides appear to be important for pair-bond formation. It is remarkable that the two peptide systems have been adapted for different roles in male and female prairie voles. Apparently, pair bonding in male and female voles activates two different, albeit closely related, neural systems. The cellular mechanism for this gender difference is not yet clear. A sexual dimorphism has not been observed for either OT or V1a receptors in the prairie vole brain.

### Molecular Studies

As noted in the previous sections, the pattern of OT and V1a receptor binding in the brain is highly variable among species and appears to be critical for species differences in the response to both exogenous and endogenous OT and AVP. What is the mechanism for such a marked phylogenetic variation in receptor distribution? Genes can be thought of as two large packets of information. Best known is the coding region, which provides the information for building proteins via mRNA. A second region includes the sequences that flank the coding region and appear to regulate gene activation. For many genes, the DNA sequences located in the flanking region upstream from the coding region are responsible for conferring tissue-specific expression. This appears to be the case for the OTR gene. Mice genetically engineered to include the flanking region of the prairie vole OTR receptor gene express this transgene in several brain regions that express OTR in the prairie vole (Young, Winslow, Wang, et al., 1997). This finding suggests that species differences in this region of the gene could potentially account for species differences in expression pattern. Indeed, sequence analysis of this region of the OTR gene reveals several mutations that may result in different expression patterns among vole species.

Even more dramatic mutational events are evident in the V1a receptor promoter and appear to account for dif-

ferences in the regional distribution of AVP receptor expression and the behavioral responses to AVP. A transgenic mouse has been developed that has the prairie vole AVP V1a receptor gene (Young, Nilsen, Waymire, MacGregor, & Insel, 1999). Not only does this mouse show a prairie-vole–like pattern of V1a receptors in its brain, but like the prairie vole, when injected with AVP, this mouse shows a marked increase in social affiliation. These kinds of experiments help to define the molecular mechanisms by which species differ in their patterns of receptor distribution. Apparently the flanking regions of the OT and AVP receptor genes are "hypermutable"; that is, these are areas that are frequent targets for mutations. The recent data suggest that the hypermutable nature of these sequences contributes to the species-specific expression of these receptors and may therefore contribute to the evolution of species-typical behaviors such as monogamy or the capacity to form selective attachments (Figure 53.4). Of course, it is not yet clear which specific region is critical for pair-bond formation. The development of a viral vector that can deliver OT and V1a receptor genes selectively to neurons in a given brain region should help to define how an increase in receptors in the nucleus accumbens or the ventral pallidum can influence affiliation.

### Autism: A Disorder of Affiliative Behavior?

Autism is a poorly understood developmental disorder characterized by social impairment, disturbed or absent communication, and stereotyped behaviors. Fein has argued that the primary deficit is an absence of social interest (Fein, Pennington, Markowitz, Braverman, & Waterhouse, 1986). Although this point remains controversial, the deficits in social relationships in autism have been noted since its original description (Kanner, 1943). The etiology is unknown, but the evidence for a genetic cause for autism may be more powerful than for any other major psychiatric disorder (Bailey et al., 1995). We still lack an effective medical treatment for this disorder, although several drugs have been tried with occasional success (Bristol et al., 1996).

Given the evidence that OT and AVP are involved in affiliative behaviors in voles, we might consider these as potential candidates for the pathoetiology of autism. In fact, Modahl and colleagues (1998) reported that children with autism had a 50% decrease in circulating OT relative to age-matched controls. Others have reported that OT is markedly increased in the CSF of children with OCD (Leckman et al., 1994). Of course, given the rodent research, one would expect that the relevant variable would be the receptor, not the amount of neuropeptide in plasma or CSF. The receptors in the human brain have been mapped (Loup, Tribollet, Dubois-Dauphin, & Dreifuss, 1991; Loupe, Tribollet, Dubois-Dauphin, Pizzolato, & Dreifuss, 1989) but not compared in postmortem studies of

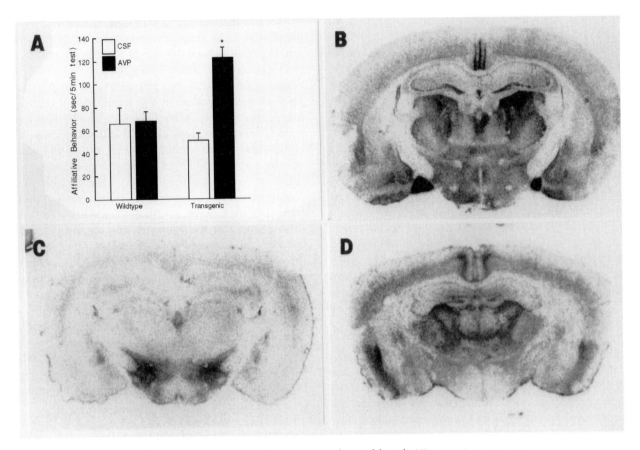

Figure 53.4 Transgenic study of V1a receptor. The prairie vole V1a receptor gene was inserted into the mouse genome. The resulting transgenic mice responded to AVP (1ng icv) with an increase in affiliative behavior (A), measured as time in contact with a novel ovariectomized female. These transgenic mice had an altered pattern of V1a receptor distribution in the brain (B) that differs markedly from the native pattern of the wild-type mice (C) and resembles the pattern observed in prairie voles (D). These kinds of studies move beyond correlational differences between form and function to test specific hypotheses by changing patterns of receptor expression and then observing differences in behavior. From Young et al. (1999), with permission of *Nature,* copyright 1999.

psychiatric groups. It is worth noting that the V2 receptor, in the same family as the V1a and OT receptors, is the prototype for polymorphisms with functional consequences. There have been more than 40 mutations reported in the V2 receptor, each of which causes diabetes insipidus (Merendino et al., 1993; Rosenthal, Siebold, & Antaramian, 1992; Seibold, Brabet, Rosenthal, & Birnbaumer, 1992). If the V1a or OT receptor had similar mutations, one might expect behavioral consequences. Preliminary studies have identified several polymorphisms in the flanking regions of the V1a and OT receptor genes, but their association with any form of psychopathology remains to be determined.

It is worth noting that even if by some remote chance a mutation in the OT or V1a receptor was shown to cause autism, this discovery would not suggest an obvious treatment. As we saw with the montane vole, even high doses of the neuropeptide administered centrally failed to increase affiliation because the receptors were not in the circuits important for social behavior. The transgenic approach cannot be used in humans, but the delivery of a healthy receptor to the appropriate circuit with viral vector technology might provide an effective gene therapy. Of course, this presumes that the receptor gene mutation is etiological, that we know the critical circuit, and that the vector can induce long-term expression.

## Summary

The neurobiological study of affiliation is still in its infancy. Studies described here are an example of how this field might develop using a comparative approach with species that differ behaviorally in both field and lab studies. Our studies have led to findings with oxytocin and vasopressin, but these are not the only neurotransmitters involved in affiliation, Indeed, as shown by the knockout studies, they may have no role in other species. Nevertheless, by studying the molecular and cellular mechanisms by which these neuropeptides influence complex behaviors, we can glean some fundamental principles about how other neuropeptides might influence positive affects, such as pair bonding. These principles can be summarized as follows: (1) variability in flanking regions of behaviorally relevant genes may be important for both species and individual differences in gene expression, (2) these differences can alter the neural patterns of receptor expression, and (3) changes in the location of receptors may completely alter the functional consequences of neuropeptide release. As we begin functional studies with the roughly 40,000 genes in the mammalian genome, there will be hundreds and potentially thousands that influence behavior. At most, oxytocin and vasopressin will fit into a complex cascade with some of these neurotransmitters that modulate emotion and behavior. The challenge will be to understand these cascades. Certainly, this is as important for the so-called positive affects, such as affiliation and joy, as for the negative affects, such as fear and aggression. Studies of all of these affects will be enhanced by using nontraditional laboratory animals with behaviorally distinct features sculpted by natural selection. Indeed, as Paul MacLean has noted (1989, personal communication), Nature has performed some of the best experiments for us—the challenge is to understand Her results.

## REFERENCES

Bailey, A., LeCouteur, A., Gottesman, I., Bolton, P., Simonoff, E., Yuzda, E., & Rutter, M. (1995). Autism as a strongly genetic disorder: Evidence from a British twin study. *Psychological Medicine, 25*, 63–78.

Barberis, C., & Tribollet, E. (1996). Vasopressin and oxytocin receptors in the central nervous system. *Critical Reviews in Neurobiology, 10*, 119–154.

Bluthe, R.-M., Schoenen, J., & Dantzer, R. (1990). Androgen-dependent vasopressinergic neurons are involved in social recognition in rats. *Brain Research, 519*, 150–157.

Bristol, M. M., Cohen, D. J., Costello, E. J., Denckla, M., Eckberg, T. J., Kallen, R., Kraemer, H. C., Lord, C., Maurer, R., McIlvane, W. J., Minshew, N., Sigman, M., & Spence, M. A. (1996). State of the science in autism: Report to the National Institutes of Health. *Journal of Autism and Developmental Disorders, 26*, 121–154.

Buntin, J. D. (1996). Neural and hormonal control of parental behavior in birds. In J. S. Rosenblatt & C. T. Snowdon (Eds.), *Parental care: Evolution, mechanisms, and adaptive significance* (Vol. 25, pp. 161–213). San Diego, CA: Academic Press.

Carter, C., DeVries, A., & Getz, L. (1995). Physiological substrates of mammalian monogamy: The prairie vole

model. *Neuroscience and Biobehavioral Reviews, 19*, 303–314.

Carter, C. S., Witt, D. M., Schneider, J., Harris, L., & Volkening, D. (1987). Male stimuli are necessary for female sexual behavior and uterine growth in prairie voles (*Microtus ochrogaster*). *Hormones and Behavior, 21*, 74–82.

Compaan, J. C., Buijs, R. M., Pool, C. W., de Ruiter, A. J. H., & Koolhaas, J. M. (1993). Differential lateral septal vasopressin in aggressive and nonaggressive mice. *Brain Research Bulletin, 30*, 1–6.

Dantzer, R., Bluthe, R., Koob, G., & Le Moal, M. (1987). Modulation of social memory in male rats by neurohypophyseal peptides. *Psychopharmacology 91*, 363–368.

De Vries, G. J., Duetz, W., Buijs, R. M., Van Heerikhuize, J., & Vreeburg, J. T. M. (1986). Effects of androgens and estrogens on the vasopressin and oxytocin innervation of the adult rat brain. *Br Res 399*, 296–302.

de Waal, F. (1996). *Good natured*. Cambridge, MA: Harvard University Press.

de Wied, D., Diamant, M., & Fodor, M. (1993). Central nervous system effects of the neurohypophyseal hormones and related peptides. *Frontiers in Neuroendocrinology. 14*, 251–302.

Dewsbury, D. A. (1988). The comparative psychology of monogamy. In D. W. Leger (Ed.), *Nebraska Symposium on Motivation: Vol. American zoology* (pp. 1–50). Lincoln: University of Nebraska Press.

Fein, D., Pennington, B., Markowitz, P., Braverman, M., & Waterhouse, L. (1986). Toward a neuropsychological model of infantile autism: Are the social deficits primary? *Journal of the American Academy of Child Psychiatry, 25*, 198–212.

Ferris, C. (1992). Role of vasopressin in aggressive and dominant/subordinate behaviors. In C. Pedersen, J. Caldwell, G. Jirikowski, & T. Insel (Eds.), *Oxytocin in maternal, sexual, and social behaviors* (Vol. 652, pp. 212–227). New York: New York Academy of Sciences Press.

Ferris, C. Albers, H., Wesolowski, S., Goldman, B., & Leeman, S. (1984). Vasopressin injected into the hypothalamus triggers a stereotypic behavior in Golden hamsters. *Science, 224*, 521–523.

Gainer, H., & Wray, S. (1994). Cellular and molecular biology of oxytocin and vasopressin. In E. Knobil & J. Neill (Eds.), *The physiology of reproduction* (2nd ed., Vol. 1, pp. 1099–1130). New York: Raven Press.

Getz, L., McGuire, B., Pizzuto, T., Hoffman, J., & Frase, B. (1993). Social organization of the prairie vole (*Microtus ochrogaster*). *Journal of Mammology, 74*, 44–58.

Getz, L. L., Carter, C. S., & Gavish, L. (1981). The mating system of the prairie vole *Microtus ochrogaster*: Field and laboratory evidence for pair bonding. *Behavioral Ecology and Sociobiology, 8*, 189–194.

Getz, L. L., & Hofman, J. E. (1986). Social organization in free living prairie voles, *Microtus ochrogaster*. *Behavioral Ecology and Sociobiology, 18*, 275–282.

Insel, T. R., & Hulihan, T. J. (1995). A gender specific mechanism for pair bonding: Oxytocin and partner preference formation in monogamous voles. *Behavioral Neuroscience, 109*, 782–789.

Insel, T. R., Preston, S., & Winslow, J. T. (1995). Mating in the monogamous male: Behavioral consequences. *Physiology and Behavior, 57*, 615–627.

Insel, T. R., & Shapiro, L. E. (1992). Oxytocin receptor distribution reflects social organization in monogamous and polygamous voles. *Proceedings of the National Academy of Sciences USA, 89,* 5981–5985.

Insel, T. R., Wang, Z., & Ferris, C. F. (1994). Patterns of brain vasopressin receptor distribution associated with social organization in microtine rodents. *Journal of Neuroscience, 14,* 5381–5392.

Insel, T. R. (1997). A neurobiological basis of social attachment. *American Journal of Psychiatry, 154* 726–735.

Jannett, F. J. (1980). Social dynamics in the montane vole *Microtus montanus* as a paradigm. *The Biologist, 62,* 3–19.

Jannett, F. (1982). The nesting patterns of adult voles (*Microtus montanus*) in field populations. *Journal of Mammology 63,* 495–498.

Kanner, L. (1943). Autistic disturbances of affective contact. *Nervous Child, 2,* 217–250.

Kendrick, K. M., Costa, A. P. C. D., Broad, K. D., Ohkura, S., Guevara, R., Levy, F., & Keverne, E. B. (1997). Neural control of maternal behavior and olfactory recognition of offspring. *Brain Research Bulletin, 44,* 383–395.

Leckman, J., Goodman, W., North, W., Chappell, P., Price, L., Pauls, D., Anderson, G., Riddle, M., McSwiggan-Hardin, M., & McDougle, C. (1994). Elevated cerebrospinal fluid levels of oxytocin in obsessive compulsive disorder: Comparison with Tourette's syndrome and healthy controls. *Archives of General Psychiatry 51,* 782–792.

Loup, F., Tribollet, E., Dubois-Dauphin, M., & Dreifuss, J. J. (1991). Localization of high-affinity binding sites for oxytocin and vasopressin in the human brain: An autoradiographic study. *Brain Research, 555,* 220–232.

Loup, F., Tribollet, E., Dubois-Dauphin, M., Pizzolato, G., & Dreifuss, J. J. (1989). Localization of oxytocin binding sites in the human brainstem and upper spinal cord: An autoradiographic study. *Brain Research, 500,* 223–230.

McGuire, B. (1986). Parental care and its relationship to social organization in the montane vole (*Microtus montanus*). *Journal of Mammology 67,* 305–311.

McGuire, B., & Novak, M. (1984). A comparison of maternal behavior in the meadow vole, prairie vole, and pine vole. *Animal Behavior, 32,* 1132–1141.

Merendino, J. J., Spiegel, A. M., Crawford, J. D., A-M OC, Brownstein, M. J., & Lolait, S. J. (1993). A mutation in the V2 vasopressin receptor gene in a kindred with X-linked nephrogenic diabetes insipidus. *New England Journal of Medicine, 328,* 1538–1541.

Modahl, C., Green, L., Fein, D., Morris, M., Waterhouse, L., Feinstein, C., & Levin, H. (1998). Plasma oxytocin levels in autistic children. *Biological Psychiatry, 432,* 270–277.

Nishimori, K., Young, L., Guo, Q., Wang, Z., Insel, T., & Matzuk, M. (1996). Oxytocin is required for nursing but is not essential for parturition or reproductive behavior. *Proceedings of the National Academy of Sciences USA, 93,* 777–783.

Oliveras, D., & Novak, M. (1986). A comparison of paternal behavior in the meadow vole, the pine vole, and the prairie vole. *Animal Behavior, 34,* 519–526.

Pedersen, C. A., Ascher, J. A., Monroe, Y. L., & Prange, A. J., Jr. (1982). Oxytocin induces maternal behaviour in virgin female rats. *Science, 216,* 648–649.

Pedersen, C. A., & Prange, A. J., Jr. (1979). Induction of maternal behaviour in virgin rats after intracerebro-

ventricular administration of oxytocin. *Proceedings of the National Academy of Sciences USA, 76,* 6661–6665.

Rosenblatt, J. S., & Snowdon, C. T. (1996). *Parental care: Evolution, mechanisms, and adaptive significance.* (Vol. 25) San Diego: Academic Press.

Rosenthal, W., Siebold, A., & Antaramian, A. (1992). Molecular identification of the gene responsible for nephrogenic congenital diabetes insipidus. *Nature, 359*; 233–235.

Seibold, A., Brabet, P., Rosenthal, W., & Birnbaumer, M. (1992). Structure and chromosomal localization of the human antidiuretic hormone receptor gene. *American Journal of Human Genetics, 51,* 1078–1083.

Shapiro, L. E., & Dewsbury, D. A. (1990). Differences in affiliative behavior, pair bonding, and vaginal cytology in two species of vole. *Journal of Comparative Psychology, 104,* 268–274.

Shapiro, L. E., & Insel, T. R. (1990). Infant's response to social separation reflects adult differences in affiliative behavior: A comparative developmental study in prairie and montane voles. *Developmental Psychobiology, 23,* 375–394.

Shapiro, L. E., Leonard, C. M., Sessions, C. E., Dewsbury, D. A., & Insel, T. R. (1991). Comparative neuroanatomy of the sexually dimorphic hypothalamus in monogamous and polygamous voles. *Brain Research, 541,* 232–240.

Wang, Z. X., Zhou, L., Hulihan, T. J., & Insel, T. R. (1996). Immunoreactivity of central vasopressin and oxytocin pathways in microtine rodents: A quantitative comparative study. *Journal of Comparative Neurology, 366,* 726–737.

Williams, J., Insel, T., Harbaugh, C., & Carter, C. (1994). Oxytocin administered centrally facilitates formation of a partner preference in female prairie voles (*Microtus orchrogaster*). *Journal of Neuroendocrinology, 6,* 247–250.

Winslow, J. T., Hastings, N., Carter, C. S., Harbaugh, C. R., & Insel, T. R. (1993). A role for central vasopressin in pair bonding in monogamous prairie voles. *Nature, 365*; 545–548.

Winslow, J. T., Shapiro, L. E., Carter, C. S., & Insel, T. R., (1993). Oxytocin and complex social behaviors: Species comparisons. *Psychopharmacology Bulletin, 29,* 409–414.

Young, L. J., Huot, B., Nilsen, R., Wang, Z., & Insel, T. R. (1996). Species differences in central oxytocin receptor gene expression: Comparative analysis of promoter sequences. *Journal of Neuroendocrinology, 8,* 777–783.

Young, L. J., Lim, M. M., Gingrich, B., & Insel, T. R. (2001). Cellular mechanisms of social attachment. *Hormones and Behavior, 40,* 133–139.

Young, L. J., Nilsen, R., Waymire, K., MacGregor, G., & Insel, T. (1999). Increased affiliative response to vasopressin in mice expressing the V1a receptor from a monogamous vole. *Nature, 400,* 766–768.

Young, L. J., Winslow, J. T., Nilsen, R., & Insel, T. R. (1997). Species differences in $V_1a$ receptor gene expression in monogamous and nonmonogamous voles: Behavioral consequences. *Behavioral Neuroscience, 111,* 599–605.

Young, L. J., Winslow, J. T., Wang, Z., Gingrich, B., Guo, Q., Matzuk, M. M., & Insel, T. R. (1997). Gene targeting approaches to neuroendocrinology: Oxytocin, maternal behavior, and affiliation. *Hormones and Behavior, 31,* 221–231.

# NEUROBIOLOGY OF DEPRESSIVE DISORDERS

Steven J. Garlow and Charles B. Nemeroff

*The deficiencies in our description would probably vanish if we were already in a position to replace the psychological terms with physiological or chemical ones. . . . [W]e may expect [physiology and chemistry] to give the most surprising information and we cannot guess what answers it will return in a few dozen years of questions we have put to it. They may be of a kind that will blow away the whole of our artificial structure of hypothesis.*

Sigmund Freud

The empirical study of mental illnesses, with the subsequent formulation of theories of pathophysiology, began in the latter part of the nineteenth and early twentieth centuries. The seminal work of Emil Kraepelin in carefully describing the different psychiatric syndromes and separating affective syndromes from psychotic disorders was initiated in this era. Kraepelin's distinction of affective syndromes from psychotic ones is generally considered the origin of scientific efforts to categorize psychiatric diseases and also represents the first step toward systematically studying their pathophysiology. During the first half of the twentieth century, in many countries, including the United States, the ideas and theories of Sigmund Freud superseded the empirical and biological description of psychiatric diseases pioneered by Kraepelin. Thus Freud's description of psychological processes in mental illness and his theories of the psychodynamic conflicts involved in the pathogenesis of psychiatric symptoms formed the dominant theoretical perspective in psychiatry through the early 1960s.

In the psychodynamic model proposed by Freud and his followers, mood and anxiety disorders are considered to be symptoms of unresolved unconscious conflicts and essentially psychological in nature. The neurobiological basis of these disorders was largely minimized or ignored in the psychodynamic model, though, as seen in the opening quotation, not by Freud himself. This is not to say that valuable ideas were not promulgated by psychodynamic theories. Of particular interest was Freud's focus on the significance of early life events in the pathophysiology of major mental illness. There is considerable ongoing research into the long-term neurobiological consequences of adverse events in early life as antecedents to the development of depressive disorders. In addition, a number of recent functional magnetic resonance imaging (fMRI) studies have convincingly demonstrated the existence of unconscious cognitive processes.

Renewed interest in the neurobiological basis of psychiatric diseases occurred in the mid-1950s. This renewed interest was stimulated by the identification of effective psychotherapeutic drugs, first chlorpromazine for the treatment of psychosis, followed later in the decade by the introduction of the tricyclic antidepressants (TCAs) and monoamine oxidase inhibitors (MAOIs) for the treatment of depression.

The confluence of several important observations led to the earliest modern theories of the pathogenesis of depression, which were focused on catecholamines, particularly norepinephrine (Bunney & Davis, 1965; Prange, 1964; Schildkraut,1965). One key observation in the development of the amine hypothesis of depression was the description of the in vitro action of imipramine. Imipramine, a TCA, was the first of this class to be identified as an effective antidepressant. A series of simple yet elegant experiments demonstrated that imipramine blocked the reuptake of norepinephrine (NE) into presynaptic neurons, and this action was hypothesized to be the basis of its antidepressant activity (Glowinski & Axelrod, 1966; Glowinski, Axelrod, Kopin, & Wurtman, 1964; Glowinski & Iverson, 1966; Glowinski, Snyder, & Axelrod, 1966). These observations led early researchers to focus on neuronal catecholamines in the pathogenesis of depression and contributed to the catecholamine hypothesis of depression, originally proposed by Schildkraut (1965). The role of catecholamines in the pathogenesis of depression continues to be the subject of intense research, and this neurotransmitter system continues to be the target of drug development efforts aimed at identifying new antidepressants.

One recurrent theme in the study of depression has been to base theories of pathophysiology on the observed actions of antidepressants. This is true for both catecholamines and indoleamines. A seminal role for serotonin in the pathophysiology of depression was originally suggested by the identification of antidepressants that acted on serotonergic neurons, including certain TCAs and trazodone, the first "atypical" antidepressant (Brogden, Heel, Speight, & Avery, 1981; Bryant & Ereshefsky, 1982; Silvestrini, 1986). This latter drug was shown to possess a pharmacological profile distinctly different from the TCAs or MAOIs, with pharmacodynamic activities on the serotonergic system that accounted for its antidepressant efficacy. The subsequent identification of highly selective serotonin reuptake inhibiting antidepressants (fluoxetine, sertraline, paroxetine, citalopram, and fluvoxamine) was also concordant with a role of serotonin-containing circuits in the pathophysiology of depression. Demonstration of serotonergic abnormalities in the central nervous system (CNS) and periphery directly implicated serotonin in the pathophysiology of depression, leading to the formulation of a "serotonin hypothesis" of depression. Other theories attempted to account for the changes observed in both NE and 5-hydroxytryptamine (5-HT) circuits in depression, such as the "permissive hypothesis" proposed by Prange (1964).

In the late 1950s and early 1960s, hypercortisolinemia was first described in depressed patients. This led to intensive scrutiny of the hypothalamic-pituitary-adrenal (HPA) axis in depression. A multitude of studies have shown that 40%–50% of patients with endogenous depression demonstrate resistance to dexamethasone-induced HPA axis suppression, in what has been termed the dexamethasone suppression test (DST; W. A. Brown, Johnston, & Mayfield, 1979; Carroll, 1982; Carroll & Davies, 1970). Research exploring the relationship between HPA axis function, early life stress, stress-responsiveness, and depression continues to the present day.

This brief historical account of the biological study of affective disorders over the past 40 years is intended to highlight the most important observations and theories of the pathogenesis of depression. Although considerably more information concerning the neurobiology of major depression is available today than was 40 years ago, the systems initially hypothesized to be central to the pathology of depression, namely the monoaminergic systems and the HPA axis, continue to be the principal foci of research. Despite the concerted research effort devoted to understanding the biology of major depression, the fundamental, root cause (or causes) of depression remains unknown.

## Methodological Considerations

The function of presynaptic neurons has been studied mainly by measuring the concentration of neurotransmitters and their metabolites in cerebrospinal fluid (CSF) and other bodily fluids. One assumption that underlies CSF studies is that the fluid is contiguous with the extraneuronal spaces in the brain, in particular with the synaptic cleft, so that the concentration of neurotransmitter in CSF reflects the concentration in the synapse. Results from this type of analysis are generally considered to reflect the activity state of the presynaptic neurons that release the transmitter or the "availability" of the particular neurotransmitter in the synapse. Neurotransmitters, receptors, transporters, and second messenger systems have all been measured in postmortem brain samples, typically from individuals who committed suicide, and compared with various nonpsychiatric control groups.

Another method used to study neurotransmitter systems in depression is neuroendocrine challenge assays, which utilize the so-called neuroendocrine window strategy. In these experiments, participants receive a pharmacological agent known to alter the secretion of anterior pituitary or target gland hormone via a particular neurotransmitter system. The secretory response to the challenge is thought to be correlated with the functional state of the particular transmitter system. Examples of this method are the fenfluramine challenge test, in which prolactin release in response to a dose of this 5-HT releasing agent is related to the state of the serotonergic system, or the clonidine challenge test, in which growth hormone release in response to this $\alpha_2$-agonist is related to the activity of noradrenergic neurons (Siever, Murphy, Slater, de la Vega, & Lipper, 1984; Siever, 1982).

Neurotransmitter depletion has also been used to assess the role of particular transmitters in the pathophysiology of depression and in the action of antidepressants. In these experiments, a neurotransmitter is depleted in participants either by dietary manipulation or pharmacological treatment. The impact of this depletion on mood (or anxiety) is then measured. With the development of positron emission tomography (PET) and other high-resolution neuroimaging techniques, studies previously only possible through postmortem analyses, such as neurotransmitter receptor or transporter binding assays, can now be performed in living participants. This will allow for the testing of hypotheses promulgated from postmortem or other types of studies directly in vivo.

A number of peripheral measures have been proposed as surrogates for their cognate systems in the CNS. The expression of neurotransmitter system components on blood cells has been posited to reflect these same systems in the CNS. In particular, platelets have been studied extensively in depression and other psychiatric disorders. The rationale for these studies includes the observation that megakaryocytes, the precursor cells from which platelets are shed, share embryological origins with 5-HT neurons and that platelets contain several serotonergic and adrenergic receptors, the serotonin transporter, and the inositol trisphosphate and adenylate cyclase second messenger systems. Platelets concentrate serotonin in and secrete serotonin from secretory granules that resemble synaptic vesicles (Da Prada, Cesura, Launay, & Richards, 1988; Stahl, 1977; Wirz-Justice, 1988). Blood lymphocytes and skin fibroblasts are other peripheral cells that have been utilized for the study of depression. Both of these cell types express a number of neurotransmitter receptors, glucocorticoid receptors, and second messenger systems. The neurotransmitter receptors expressed on peripheral cells are indeed identical to those expressed in the CNS. An assumption that underlies the study of peripheral cell types in depression is that these receptors are subjected to the same molecular regulation in the CNS and in the periphery.

There are a large number of reported observations in major depression that have either not been replicated at all or have been replicated only in a minority of studies. This could be due to a number of factors; most prominent is diagnostic heterogeneity. The diagnosis of major depression has evolved over the past 40 years, with progressively more precise definitions with each edition of the *Diagnostic and Statistical Manual of Mental Disorders (DSM; American Psychiatric Association, 1994)*. However, the interpretation of the *DSM* (and other) criteria for depression is, unfortunately, not universally standardized among all investigators and quite broad in disease severity. The result is that there is often significant heterogeneity between study cohorts. Other factors that also might contribute to the failure to replicate certain observations are the potential effects of previous treatments, the cumulative effect of the disease process itself, and methodological differences in the assays used and the handling of tissue samples. Given all of these potential confounds,

it is remarkable that changes in the serotonergic and noradrenergic systems have been so consistently documented in depressed patients, across many studies and by different investigators. This fact argues convincingly that these two systems play a central role in the pathophysiology of major depression.

## Neurotransmitter Systems

As neurotransmitter systems have been discovered and characterized, they have been assessed for a potential role in the pathophysiology of depressive disorders. Virtually all of the major neurotransmitter systems (serotonin, norepinephrine, dopamine, gamma aminobutyric acid [GABA], neuropeptides, etc.) have been scrutinized for a role in depressive disorders. Using a variety of multidisciplinary techniques, the noradrenergic and serotonergic systems have consistently been shown to be altered in major depression. Both of these systems appear to be central to the pathophysiology of depression, and one or the other or both appear to be involved in the mechanism of action of most antidepressants. Major depression is associated with alterations of the serotonergic and noradrenergic systems at both presynaptic and postsynaptic levels. There are many other interesting, yet less well-studied, findings in other neurotransmitter systems in depression that hint at the complexity and interrelatedness of these systems in the CNS and at the widespread impact that major depression has on the CNS.

### Norepinephrine

Three different types of observations led early investigators to focus on noradrenergic (NE) systems in major depression. Reserpine, a Rauwolfia alkaloid used to treat hypertension, was also noted to cause depressive symptoms in many patients. Reserpine depletes biogenic amines from cells in the CNS and periphery, a fact that accounts for its antihypertensive actions but that was also hypothesized to account for its depressogenic properties. A complementary observation that further implicated the NE system was the discovery of the antidepressant properties of monoamine oxidase inhibitors (MAOI). The antidepressant action of these agents was discovered serendipitously through reports of patients with tuberculosis who were being treated with iproniazid and who experienced significant mood improvement. Monoamine oxidase was known to degrade intraneuronal NE and other amines, so with the discovery that inhibitors of this enzymatic activity had antidepressant properties, it was a logical extension to focus on this neurotransmitter in the pathogenesis of depression. The final and perhaps most important observation was of the actions of imipramine, a tricyclic antidepressant. This compound was shown to block the uptake of [³H]-NE into neurons, a finding that directly implicated the availability or concentration of NE in the CNS in the pathophysiology of depression. All of these observations led to very intensive investigation of the biochemistry of catecholamine systems in general and the NE system in particular. The biosynthetic and degradative pathways were described in detail, and many aspects of the regulation of these pathways were investigated.

The original catecholamine hypothesis of affective disorders promulgated by Schildkraut (1965) 35 years ago was the natural extension of the previously described research. This theory proposed that depression was due to a relative deficiency of catecholamines, particularly NE, at important sites in the brain; mania was posited to be due to relative NE excess (Schildkraut, 1965). Considerable effort has been expended to test this and related hypotheses. Although NE and other catecholamines are undoubtedly involved in the pathophysiology of affective disorders, the catecholamine hypothesis as originally proposed is surely an oversimplification that has not been empirically validated.

Dopamine (DA), NE, and epinephrine are referred to as catecholamines because they contain the catechol ring structure or 1,2-dihydroxybenzene. They are all produced from the same biosynthetic pathway. The amino acid tyrosine is converted to L-dopa by tyrosine hydroxylase. L-dopa is converted to DA by aromatic amino acid decarboxylase. Norepinephrine is produced from DA by dopamine β-hydroxylase. Epinephrine results from the actions of phenylethanolamine-N-methyltransferase on NE. There are distinct neuronal groupings in the CNS that exclusively use each one of these transmitters.

The concentration of NE in CSF, serum, and urine is difficult to measure because the transmitter is rapidly catabolized, but the principal metabolite of NE, 3-methoxy-4-hydroxyphenylglycol (MHPG) is stable, and its concentration has been posited to be an accurate indicator of NE levels. This metabolite can be measured in urine, and approximately 20% of urinary MHPG is derived from the CNS pool (Potter, Karoum, & Linnoila, 1984). Measurement of urinary MHPG has been used extensively in efforts at validating the catecholamine hypothesis. The assumption is that changes in urinary levels of MHPG reflect changes in the level of activity of NE neurons in the CNS. In early reports, urinary levels of MHPG were found to be significantly lower in depressed patients than in control participants (Maas, Fawcett, & Dekirmenjian, 1972; Schildkraut, 1973). This finding has not, however, been consistently replicated, especially in patients with unipolar depression. In this patient group, urinary MHPG levels cover a wide range that overlaps with control values and are frequently not statistically different from control values, depending on the study (Schatzberg et al., 1982; Schildkraut et al., 1978).

Initial reports indicated that patients suffering from bipolar disorder had the lowest urinary MHPG values during the depressed phase of their illness, lower than those of patients with unipolar depression and of healthy controls. As the distinctions between bipolar types I and II have been realized, patients with Type I bipolar disorder have been reported to have the lowest urinary MHPG values during the depressed phase of their illness. Patients with Type II bipolar disorder have urinary MHPG values similar to those of patients with unipolar depression, values that, as a group, are higher than those of depressed patients with Type I bipolar disorder (Schatzberg et al., 1989). Some patients with unipolar depression also have low urinary MHPG values, similar to those of patients with Type I bipolar disorder. These patients may in fact have incipient Type I bipolar disorder but have simply not yet undergone their first manic episode. Preliminary data suggest that these patients are more likely to develop subsequent manic symptoms than are patients with unipolar depression and higher urinary MHPG concentrations.

One obvious prediction from the reports that patients with Type I bipolar disorder have the lowest concentrations of urinary MHPG during the depressed phase of their illness is that these same Type I patients would have increased levels of MHPG during the manic phase of the illness. This prediction has been confirmed in several studies. Bipolar patients in manic episodes have significantly higher plasma NE and epinephrine levels than they do when depressed or euthymic (Maj, Ariano, Arena, & Kemali, 1984). Others have reported that both urinary MHPG and CSF NE levels are significantly higher in manic patients than in depressed or control participants (Swann et al., 1987). This finding has been partially replicated in a report that documents increased plasma MHPG levels in manic patients when compared with bipolar depressives (Halaris, 1978). There is at least one report that lithium treatment reduces peripheral NE levels in patients with bipolar disorder. Interestingly, both lithium-responsive and lithium-nonresponsive patients exhibited similar reductions in peripheral NE levels (Swann et al., 1987).

Clearly, the measurement of NE and its metabolites in peripheral samples has been invaluable historically in developing the disease concept of major depression. However, given the wide variance in levels of serum NE and urinary MHPG in patients suffering from unipolar depression, the original hypothesis that depression results from a simple deficiency of NE has not been validated by these methods. One of the original goals of this research was to develop laboratory tests that would aid in diagnosing depression and predicting the treatment response. However, measurement of peripheral NE or MHPG concentrations has never been validated for such uses in clinical psychiatry. With the emergence of high-resolution functional neuroimaging methods with which to study catecholamine function in the CNS, the peripheral measurement of catecholamine function as an index of CNS function may now be obsolete (Schatzberg & Schildkraut, 1995).

The majority of noradrenergic cells in the CNS are located in the locus coeruleus (LC). Axons from LC neurons project diffusely throughout the CNS and are the major source of forebrain NE neurotransmission. Postmortem analysis of suicide victims reveals that the activity of tyrosine hydroxylase, the first enzyme in the catecholamine biosynthetic pathway, is increased in the LC of suicides compared with normal controls (Ordway, 1997). Specific psychiatric diagnoses were not reported in this particular study, but the author hypothesized that the upregulation of TH in suicide victims is indicative of a state of chronic stress or arousal. Another postmortem analysis of suicide victims found 23% fewer NE neurons in the LC of the suicides than in controls (Arango, Underwood, & Mann, 1996). In a subsequent study of 15 suicide victims who had been given an antemortem diagnosis of major depression, no differences were found in the number of LC cells between the suicides and controls, but the suicides had significantly fewer LC norepinephrine transporter (NET) sites than controls (Klimek et al., 1997). The authors speculated that this NET downregulation might be due to decreased synaptic concentrations of NE in the suicide victims. The results of these postmortem studies suggest that the NE system is dysfunctional in depressive disorders and suicide. Whether the changes observed in the LC are pathonomonic for depression has not yet been determined.

Even though the direct measurement of NE or MHPG has not yielded unequivocal evidence of catecholamine system dysfunction in depression, other experimental approaches suggest that the NE system plays a crucial role in the action of antidepressants. One such method is transient inhibition of tyrosine hydroxylase (TH) with alpha-methyl-para-tyrosine (AMPT). AMPT transiently inhibits TH activity, which in turn transiently depletes NE and other catecholamines. The effects of this neurotransmitter depletion on mood state are then typically quantified with standard symptom severity scales, such as the Hamilton Depression Rating Scale (HDRS). Administration of AMPT to normal healthy control participants with no history of depression does not produce symptoms of depression (Salomon, Miller, Krystal, Heninger, & Charney, 1997), just as a minority of patients became depressed after treatment with the monoamine depleting antihypertensive reserpine. Moreover, administration of AMPT to depressed patients before they receive antidepressant treatment does not cause worsening of core symptoms of depression but does cause worsening of some neurovegetative symptoms such as tiredness and anergia (Miller, Delgado, Salomon, Heninger, & Charney, 1996). These results are concordant with the view that NE depletion is not the fundamental cause of depression or depressive symptoms.

In contrast, depressed participants treated with anti-

depressants that are specific NE reuptake inhibitors (e.g., desipramine and mazindol) suffer a significant return of depressive symptoms when treated with AMPT (Miller, Delgado, Salomon, Berman, et al., 1996). Those patients treated with specific serotonin reuptake inhibitors (fluoxetine, sertraline) do not exhibit such a relapse when treated with AMPT. This finding implies that parallel treatment response pathways that involve either NE or 5-HT systems exist and that manipulation of one or the other system is often adequate to cause resolution of depression. In another pioneering study of medication-free, euthymic participants with a history of major depression, administration of AMPT caused a significant return of depressive symptoms (Berman et al., 1999). These results are interpreted as demonstrating a potential "trait" marker of vulnerability to depression. One particular shortcoming of this study is that the authors did not specify what types of treatments the depressed participants had received in the past or whether there was a correlation between response to specific types of antidepressants and NE depletion-induced relapse.

The results from the NE depletion studies have led to the formulation of a revised "catecholamine hypothesis of depression" (Heninger, Delgado, & Charney, 1996). In this revised hypothesis, the fundamental cause of depression is assumed to be in a nonmonoaminergic system, but clearly, integrity of the monoamine systems is essential for response to antidepressants. The implication is that "other" neurotransmitter systems are modulated by the monoamine systems and that treatment with antidepressants further modifies these "other" systems, the result being resolution of symptoms of depression.

Neurotransmission in the noradrenergic system is mediated by a number of different neurotransmitter receptors, grouped into classes known as $\alpha$ and $\beta$. The receptors are further divided into subtypes ($\alpha_1$, $\alpha_2$, etc.) by molecular sequence and evolutionary relatedness. The $\alpha_2$ and the $\beta$ adrenergic receptors have been the focus of considerable research into their putative roles in the biology of depression. The $\alpha_2$ adrenergic receptors are negatively coupled to adenylate cyclase (AC). Thus agonists of the $\alpha_2$ receptor result in inhibition of AC activity and decreased intracellular cAMP availability. There are both pre- and postsynaptic $\alpha_2$ receptors in the CNS, and there are $\alpha_2$ receptors on platelets. In contrast to the $\alpha_2$ receptors, the $\beta_1$ and $\beta_2$ adrenergic receptors are exclusively postsynaptic and are positively coupled to AC. Agonists acting on the $\beta$ receptors stimulate AC activity and cause an increase in the intracellular cAMP levels. There are $\beta$ receptors in the CNS, on circulating leukocytes, and on other peripheral cell types.

An increase in the density of $\alpha_2$ receptors on platelets has been repeatedly reported in drug-free patients with depression (Garcia-Sevilla, Padro, Giralt, Guimon, & Areso, 1990; Garcia-Sevilla, Udina, Fuster, Alvarez, & Casas, 1987; Halaris & Piletz, 1990). The exact opposite result, however—of decreased platelet $\alpha_2$ receptor $B_{max}$—has also been reported in a cohort of unmedicated depressives (Maes, Van Gastel, Delmeire, & Meltzer, 1999). There are also reports of increased $B_{max}$ of $\alpha_2$ receptors in postmortem brain tissue of patients who committed suicide (Meana, Barturen, & Garcia-Sevilla, 1992). In one report that specifically scrutinized $\alpha$-receptor subtypes in suicide victims, no differences were found in $B_{max}$ values for $\alpha_1$ receptors between suicides and controls. There was an increase in $B_{max}$ values for $\alpha_2$ receptors in the suicides, but not for the $\alpha_{2A}$ subtype (De Paermentier, Mauger, et al., 1997). In another study, the $B_{max}$ for the $\alpha_2$ receptor in the locus coeruleus was reported to be increased in suicide victims (Ordway, 1997). Clearly, the findings of increased $\alpha_2$-receptor density in depression have not been consistently replicated, and the cause of these discrepant findings remains obscure.

The clonidine challenge test is an indirect means of assessing the functional state of CNS $\alpha_2$ receptors (Siever et al., 1982). Clonidine is an $\alpha_2$ agonist that is a potent secretagogue for growth hormone (GH) release from the anterior pituitary gland, presumably through a postsynaptic mechanism. A blunted GH response to a clonidine test dose in depressed patients has been widely reported in several studies (Amsterdam, Maislin, Skolnick, Berwish, & Winokur, 1989; Siever, Uhde, Jimerson, et al., 1984). This blunted GH response has been reported in acutely symptomatic depressed patients, in patients successfully treated with antidepressants, and in remitted patients (Mitchell, Bearn, Corn, & Checkley, 1988; Siever et al., 1992). This suggests that the alteration in $\alpha_2$ receptor function revealed by the clonidine challenge test is a trait characteristic of some depressed patients.

Alteration of $\beta$-adrenergic receptor function has been postulated to contribute to the pathophysiology of depression. As with the $\alpha$-adrenergic receptors, the results with the $\beta$-receptors have been discrepant and difficult to replicate. There are reports of increased $B_{max}$ for the $\beta$-adrenergic receptor in postmortem brain tissue of suicide victims, but some reports are discordant (Crow et al., 1984; De Paermentier, Cheetham, Crompton, Katona, & Horton, 1990; Mann, Stanley, McBride, & McEwen, 1986). $\beta$-adrenoceptor binding has been measured in the pineal glands of suicide victims with a "firm" antemortem diagnosis of major depression. No differences were found in the numbers of $\beta$ receptors between the depressed participants and matched normal controls (De Paermentier, Lowther, Crompton, Katona, & Horton, 1997).

Similarly contradictory results have been reported for studies in which the $B_{max}$ for $\beta$ receptors on leukocytes was determined. There are both reports of decreased $B_{max}$ values for peripheral $\beta$ receptors in patients suffering from depression and studies that report no difference between depressed and healthy control participants (Extein, Tall-man, Smith, & Goodwin, 1979; Healy, Carney, O'Halloran, & Leonard, 1985). Certainly treatment with antidepressants can alter the $B_{max}$ of $\beta$ receptors, and much of the variability in these studies could be accounted for by differences in the type, duration, and intensity of antidepressant treatment (De Paermentier, Cheetham, Crompton, Katona, & Horton, 1991).

### Serotonin

Interest in the functioning of serotonergic neural circuits in mood disorders has grown since antidepressants believed to have primarily serotonergic mechanisms of action were identified. A large and concerted research effort has taken place over the past two decades that has focused on the serotonergic system in depression and other mood disorders. The results of this research effort clearly demonstrate dysfunction of the serotonergic system in both major depression and suicidal behavior. Evidence exists for dysfunction of the serotonergic system in depression at both presynaptic and postsynaptic levels. The "serotonin hypothesis" of depression is based on the results of this substantial research effort (Maes & Meltzer, 1995; Meltzer & Lowy, 1987). Whether serotonergic dysfunction is sufficient to cause depression or is merely a necessary risk factor remains unclear.

Serotonin is synthesized from the essential amino acid l-tryptophan (l-TRP). Tryptophan hydroxylase converts tryptophan to 5-hydroxytryptophan (5-HTP), which in turn is converted to serotonin (5-hydroxytryptamine, 5-HT) by L-aromatic amino acid decarboxylase. Extracellular serotonin is rapidly metabolized into 5-hydroxyindole acetic acid (5-HIAA), which is stable in bodily fluids. The concentration of 5-HIAA is often reported as a surrogate measure for serotonergic neuronal activity.

All of the serotonin in the CNS is synthesized in neurons of the raphé nuclei from l-TRP that crosses the blood-brain barrier (BBB). Peripherally synthesized serotonin in plasma does not enter the CNS. The intraneuronal concentration of l-TRP determines the amount of serotonin synthesized (Maes et al., 1990). Tryptophan crosses the BBB by a carrier-mediated transporter that also carries other large neutral and aromatic amino acids (phenylalanine, tyrosine, etc.) into the CNS; these other amino acids compete for this transport site. The plasma concentration of l-TRP (or the ratio of l-TRP to the other competing amino acids) ultimately determines the quantity of l-TRP that crosses the BBB and hence the amount of serotonin synthesized within the CNS.

The potential contribution that the availability of l-TRP in plasma plays in the pathophysiology of depression has been investigated with two main techniques: directly measuring plasma l-TRP concentrations and changing plasma l-TRP concentrations via dietary manipulation. There are reports that the plasma concentration of l-TRP is lower in patients with major depression than in healthy controls (Maes et al., 1990; Meltzer & Lowy, 1987). The cause of this is unclear, but it may be due to increased clearance of l-TRP via hepatic biotransformation. Peak plasma concentrations of l-TRP are lower in depressed patients than in controls after oral or intravenous l-TRP loading doses (Maes, De Ruyter, & Suy, 1987).

As noted previously, 5-HT produced in the CNS is directly dependent on the amount of tryptophan that crosses the BBB, and this amount is directly determined by the serum concentration of l-TRP. Therefore, it is possible to transiently deplete CNS serotonin by lowering the plasma l-TRP concentration. This effect has been demonstrated in a small cohort of healthy control participants, as well as in nonhuman primate studies. Dietary manipulation was used to lower plasma l-TRP concentrations, with the result being decreases in plasma and CSF l-TRP concentrations of 92% and 85%, respectively, and CSF 5-HIAA concentrations decreasing 31% (Carpenter el al., 1998). This is a direct demonstration that CNS serotonin can be transiently depleted by dietary manipulation of plasma tryptophan.

In normal control participants, lowering plasma l-TRP via dietary manipulation has been reported to transiently produce a depressed mood (Delgado, Charney, Price, Landis, & Henninger, 1990; Young, Smith, Pihl, & Ervin, 1985). The response to l-TRP depletion may be a trait vulnerability factor for depression. Depressed mood following l-TRP depletion occurs much more readily in participants who have first-degree relatives who suffer from depression than in those with no family history of depression (Benkelfat, Ellenbogen, Dean, Palmour, & Young, 1994; Ellenbogen, Young, Dean, Palmour, & Benkelfat, 1996).

The mood-altering effect of l-TRP depletion is more dramatically demonstrated in recently remitted depressed patients (Heninger, Delgado, Charney, Price, & Aghajanian, 1992; Smith, Fairburn, & Cowen, 1997). These patients display a remarkably rapid return of depressed mood and cognitive and neurovegetative symptoms of depression. Patients treated with selective serotonin reuptake inhibitors (SSRIs) are much more sensitive to this manipulation than are patients treated with antidepressants that act primarily on NE systems (Delgado et al., 1999). PET analysis of cerebral metabolism has been used to study the CNS consequences of l-TRP depletion in vivo. Depressed patients successfully treated with SSRIs who suffer a depressive relapse in response to l-TRP depletion demonstrate decreased cerebral glucose utilization in dorsolateral prefrontal cortex, thalamus, and orbitofrontal cortex (Bremner, Innis, et al., 1997). Those patients who do not relapse in response to l-TRP depletion do not exhibit these alterations in cerebral metabolism. This response is believed to identify either those brain regions that participate in the production of depressive symptoms

or the sites of action of SSRIs or both. Interestingly, untreated depressed patients do not worsen in symptom severity response to l-TRP depletion (Delgado el al., 1994). Patients with seasonal affective disorder who have been successfully treated with light therapy suffer depressive relapse when subjected to l-TRP depletion (Lam et al., 1996), but recently remitted bipolar manic patients do not (Cassidy, Murry, & Carrol, 1998).

There are, however, discrepant reports in which l-TRP depletion produced no alteration in the mood state of remitted depressives. The failure to replicate this finding may be due to differences in treatment modality, severity of depression, suicidal ideation, or duration and intensity of treatment. In at least one such study, patients who were considered at risk for suicide or self-destructive behavior were excluded (Leyton, Young, & Benkelfat, 1997). Depressed patients who had been successfully treated with antidepressants to complete euthymia, for whom antidepressants were discontinued, were more resistant to the effects of l-TRP depletion than recently remitted patients (Leyton, Young, Blier, et al., 1997). A similar lack of effect of l-TRP depletion has been reported for patients specifically treated with SSRIs who were fully remitted (Moore et al., 1998). In this study, the participants were still being treated with an SSRI at the time of the depletion protocol. This lack of effect clearly implicates duration of treatment and remission as relevant parameters in interpreting the results of l-TRP depletion studies. Depressed participants successfully treated with electroconvulsive therapy (ECT) have been reported to remain in remission when subjected to l-TRP depletion (Cassidy, Murry, Weiner, & Carroll, 1997).

This concatenation of data, taken together, suggests that l-TRP availability may be decreased in some depressed patients, leading to decreased serotonin synthesis in the CNS. Moreover, the availability of l-TRP and hence serotonin in the CNS may play a critical role in the response to antidepressants, in particular the SSRIs.

Synaptic activity of serotonergic neurons has been frequently estimated by measuring the serotonin metabolite 5-HIAA in CSF. Although consistent evidence for serotonergic hypofunction in depression has not emerged from these studies, the most reproducible finding is one in patients who attempted or committed suicide—a finding of reduced CSF 5-HIAA concentrations, which is presumably a measure of reduced CNS serotonergic function. The finding of low CSF 5-HIAA concentrations is particularly robust in patients who used violent means to commit suicide (Asberg, Traskman, & Thoren, 1976; Gibbons & Davis, 1986; Roy, DeJong, & Linnoila, 1989), independent of psychiatric diagnosis (Traskman, Asberg, Bertilsson, & Sjostrand, 1981; Van Praag, 1982). Other reports (Virkkunen et al., 1994, 1995, 1996) link low CSF 5-HIAA concentrations with poor impulse control in violent criminal offenders and arsonists. In all of these patient samples, the strongest relationship appears to be between low CSF 5-HIAA concentrations and violent, impulsive behavior. This behavioral spectrum is quite distinct from the constellation of symptoms that constitute major depression, but it does appear to intersect with the depressive syndromes. One current hypothesis is that depression in combination with low CNS serotonin availability, as demonstrated by low CSF 5-HIAA concentrations, is a prominent risk factor for impulsive and highly lethal suicide attempts.

Additional evidence for dysfunction of serotonergic neurons in major depression has been provided by results from a number of neuroendocrine challenge paradigms. Tryptophan depletion has been shown to decrease serotonergic transmission, and tryptophan loading to increase serotonergic transmission. Intravenous infusion of tryptophan causes an acute increase in serotonergic transmission that is associated with an increase in serum prolactin concentration (Price, Charney, Delgado, & Heninger, 1991). Depressed patients demonstrate a blunted prolactin response to tryptophan infusion when compared with control participants (Price et al., 1991; Cappiello et al., 1996). This effect is interpreted as a defect in the integrity of serotonergic neurotransmission in major depression.

The appetite suppressant fenfluramine causes a rapid release of serotonin from presynaptic neurons, which also is associated with increased plasma prolactin levels. A blunted prolactin response to fenfluramine challenge has been repeatedly documented in depressives compared with controls (Malone et al., 1993; Mitchell & Smythe, 1990; O'Keane & Dinan, 1991; Shapira, Cohen, Newman, & Lerer, 1993). Studies disagree as to whether the blunted prolactin response normalizes with treatment and syndrome resolution (Malone et al., 1993; Shapira, Cohen, Newman, & Lerer, 1993). One study reports that the prolactin response to fenfluramine challenge remains blunted, even when the participants were in full remission for at least 1 year (Flory, Mann, Manuck, & Muldoon, 1998). This finding suggests that there is a persistent change in the serotonergic system that may be a trait marker of vulnerability for depression. A novel variation of the fenfluramine challenge test uses PET scanning to measure cerebral glucose utilization instead of prolactin release in response to the fenfluramine dose (Mann et al., 1996). Consistent with the results obtained with serum prolactin measurements, depressed participants displayed reduced cerebral glucose utilization in response to fenfluramine. Interestingly, prolactin responses to fenfluramine challenge are also blunted in actively manic bipolar patients (Thakore, O'Keane, & Dinan, 1996). This finding has been interpreted as indicative of a general serotonergic dysfunction in mood disorders, both for bipolar and unipolar disorders.

Another neuroendocrine challenge assay used to assess CNS serotonergic activity uses sumatriptan as the challenge agent. This anti-migraine compound is an agonist at the 5-HT$_{1D}$ serotonin receptor. This receptor is the nerve terminal autoreceptor on serotonergic neurons. Sumatriptan administration results in an increase in plasma growth hormone (GH) levels. The GH response to sumatriptan in depressed participants is blunted compared with normal controls or bipolar manic participants (Cleare, Murray, Sherwood, & O'Keane, 1998; Yatham, Zis, Lam, Tam, & Shiah, 1997). This finding provides further evidence of presynaptic serotonergic dysfunction in depression, either at the level of the 5-HT$_{1D}$ receptor, its effector coupling pathway, or the cellular response machinery.

The serotonin transporter (SERT) is a member of the 12-transmembrane family of transport molecules. In the CNS, the SERT appears to be expressed exclusively on serotonergic neurons. Serotonergic neurotransmission is terminated by the SERT, which clears 5-HT from the synapse by pumping it back into the presynaptic terminal. The SERT is also expressed on platelets, where it concentrates serotonin from plasma and eventually into secretory granules. The SERT is the site of action of many antidepressants, which act as antagonists of its reuptake action. Because the SERT is the site of action of so many different antidepressants and controls the amount of 5-HT available in the synapse, it has been hypothesized as a possible molecular substrate for the pathology of depression.

Regulation of the SERT on platelets has been hypothesized to mirror the biology of the molecule in the CNS. The SERT is transcribed from a single copy gene, and therefore the transporters expressed on platelets and in the CNS are identical (Lesch, Wolozin, Murphy, & Riederer, 1993). The underlying hypothesis is that the expression of the SERT in the CNS and in the periphery is subject to the same molecular regulation; hence, differences in SERT function on platelets of depressives should mirror similar changes in the CNS. The SERT has been studied on platelets of depressed patients, in postmortem brain tissue of patients suffering from depression at the time of death, and more recently with PET imaging with SERT-specific ligands.

The concentration of the SERT on platelets has been measured with either [³H]-imipramine binding (Briley, Langer, Raisman, Sechter, & Zarifian, 1980a; Briley, Langer, Raisman, Sechter, & Zarifian, 1980b; Nemeroff, Knight, et al., 1988) or [³H]-paroxetine binding (Nemeroff, Knight, Franks, Craighead, & Krishnan, 1994). Although some discrepant reports have failed to detect differences in the B$_{max}$ for the platelet SERT between depressives and controls, the vast majority of these studies report a decrease in the platelet SERT B$_{max}$ in major depression. A comprehensive meta-analysis of the worldwide platelet [³H]-imipramine binding data identified approximately 70 independent studies that included data on approximately 1900 depressed participants and slightly fewer controls (Ellis & Salmond, 1994). The meta-analysis revealed that the lower $B_{max}$ value for platelet [³H]-imipramine binding is a highly significant finding in major depression. This has been reported to be a state marker for depression because the $B_{max}$ tends to normalize with successful treatment. The biological underpinning of the decreased platelet SERT $B_{max}$ value in depression remains obscure. It is not clear whether the regulation of the SERT on platelets is related to the regulation of the SERT in the CNS, nor is it certain that the decreased platelet $B_{max}$ value in major depression mimics or mirrors any alteration in SERT levels in the CNS. One possible interpretation is that the alterations in platelet biology in depression, including the decreased SERT $B_{max}$, are reflections of systematic neuroendocrine or neuroimmune dysfunction, independent of changes that occur in the CNS.

The SERT has been measured in postmortem brain tissue of suicide victims. These studies are not nearly as consistent as the platelet studies, with some reporting decreased $B_{max}$ for the SERT in the frontal cortices of suicide victims compared with controls and others reporting no such differences (Gross-Isseroff, Israeli, & Biegon, 1989; Lawrence et al., 1990; Leake, Fairbairn, McKeith, & Ferrier, 1991; Perry et al., 1983). In one study, radioligand autoradiography and in situ hybridization histochemistry was used to examine the numbers and distribution of the SERT from eight depressed suicide victims (Little et al., 1997). No differences in the numbers or distribution of the SERT were detected, nor were there differences in the amount of SERT mRNA in the cells of the raphé nuclei from the suicide victims. These results would suggest that changes in the expression or distribution of the SERT in the CNS are not central to the pathophysiology of major depression.

Recently PET and SPECT ligands relatively specific for the SERT have become available and have been used to interrogate the SERT in living participants with major depression. In one study, drug-free depressives were compared with healthy controls using the SERT ligand [¹²³I]-β-CIT, imaged with SPECT (Malison et al., 1998). This study revealed a significant difference between the depressives and the controls, with the depressed participants exhibiting reduced SERT binding in the raphé nuclei. This finding is interpreted as indicating fewer SERT sites in the brainstems of the depressed participants. Interestingly, there were no differences in platelet [³H]-paroxetine binding between the depressed and control groups, suggesting that central and peripheral regulation of the SERT may in fact be different. Clearly these studies need to be repeated, with larger groups of participants, multiple investigators, and more specific ligands before any definitive conclusions can be drawn.

A bi-allelic genetic polymorphism has been described in the promoter of the SERT gene (Heils et al., 1996). The two alleles are known as short (S) and long (L), with the L form being more transcriptionally active than the S

form. Differences in promoter strength could be one molecular mechanism that cause differences in the SERT $B_{max}$. Whether or not this promoter polymorphism plays a role in the pathophysiology of depression is not known. There has been a genetic association reported between the S allele and measures of anxiety, as revealed by psychometric tests (Lesch et al., 1996). These data suggest that differences in the strength of the SERT promoter can contribute to the development of anxiety symptoms. Association and linkage studies have produced contradictory results, with some reporting an overrepresentation of the S allele in depressives and others finding no association between SERT promoter alleles and depression. Whether or not the different promoter alleles contribute to the pathogenesis of major depression is not at all clear based on the contradictory reports of genetic association.

There are at least 14 distinct serotonin receptors (Glennon & Dukat, 1995; Saxena, 1995). The advent of low-stringency polymerase chain reaction (PCR) cloning strategies has revealed the existence of a large number of previously unknown and unpredicted serotonin receptors. The receptors are grouped into families based on their molecular structure, which also determines their other characteristics, such as ligand affinities, second messenger coupling, and so forth. The serotonin receptors are grouped into seven different families. The 5-HT$_3$ receptor is a ligand-gated ion channel, and all of the others are seven-transmembrane, G-protein coupled receptors. Prior to the discovery of the "new" serotonin receptors, the 5-HT$_{1A}$ and 5-HT$_{2A}$ receptors were the subject of the majority of serotonin receptor research in depression. The contribution of the newly discovered serotonin receptors to the pathophysiology of depression or the action of antidepressants has yet to be determined.

The 5-HT$_{2A}$ receptor is positively coupled to phospholipase C and the mobilization of intracellular $Ca^{++}$, whereas the 5-HT$_{1A}$ receptor is negatively coupled to adenylate cyclase (AC) activity. The 5-HT$_{1A}$ and 5-HT$_{2A}$ receptors are postsynaptic in location, though the 5-HT$_{1A}$ receptor is the predominant serotonin receptor on the serotonergic perikarya in the raphé nucleus. The 5-HT$_{1A}$ autoreceptor controls the firing rate of the serotonergic neurons, and agonist binding to this receptor causes a decrease in the firing rate of these neurons. The 5-HT$_{2A}$ receptor is located on a number of different cell types in the CNS, on platelets, smooth muscle cells, cells in the immune system, skin fibroblasts, and a number of other peripheral cell types. The 5-HT$_{1A}$ receptor is found predominantly in the CNS but also on lymphocytes in the periphery.

The platelet 5-HT$_{2A}$ receptor has been the focus of considerable scrutiny in depression, with at least 12 independent publications reporting the $B_{max}$ for the platelet 5-HT$_{2A}$ receptor in major depression (Arora & Meltzer, 1989a, 1993; Biegon, Essar, et al., 1990; Biegon, Grinspoon, et al.,

1990; Biegon et al., 1987; Cowen, Charig, Frasier, & Elliot, 1987; Hrdina, Bakish, Chudzik, Ravindran, & Lapierre, 1995; Mann et al., 1992; McBride et al., 1994; Pandey et al., 1995; Pandey, Pandey, Janicak, Marks, & Davis, 1990; Sheline, Bargett, Jackson, Newcomer, & Csernansky, 1995). One of these studies reported no difference between depressives and controls. The others all report a significant increase in the $B_{max}$ for the platelet 5-HT$_{2A}$ receptor for depressed or suicidal patients. Several of the studies reported that the increased $B_{max}$ is related to suicidality, whereas others suggested that the increased $B_{max}$ is related to the syndromal diagnosis of depression. Initially the increased $B_{max}$ was considered a state marker of depression because the $B_{max}$ was reported to normalize with recovery from depression. One group has now, however, reported that the increased $B_{max}$ does not normalize with successful treatment, raising the question as to whether this increase may be a trait marker for vulnerability to depression (Bakish, Cavazzoni, Chudzik, Ravindran, & Hrdina, 1997). Several other studies have inferred changes in the $B_{max}$ for the platelet 5-HT$_{2A}$ receptor by a number of secondary measures, including platelet shape change, PI hydrolysis, and Ca$^{++}$ mobilization. All of these responses are mediated by the 5-HT$_{2A}$ receptor, and all are enhanced in major depression.

There are at least 10 publications in which the $B_{max}$ for the 5-HT$_{2A}$ receptor has been measured in the CNS of suicide victims (Arango et al., 1990; Arora & Meltzer, 1989b; Cheetham, Crompton, Katona, & Horton, 1988; Crow et al., 1984; Hrdina, Demeter, Vu, Sotonyi, & Palkovits, 1993; Lowther, Paermentier, Crompton, Katona, & Horton, 1994; Mann et al., 1986; McKeith et al., 1987; Owen et al., 1986; Stanley & Mann, 1983). The results from these analyses are considerably more variable than those of the platelet studies. Approximately half of the publications report an increase in the $B_{max}$ for the 5-HT$_{2A}$ receptor in the brains of suicide victims, and the other half report no difference. As in the other postmortem studies, the variability in these results could be due to a number of technical and artifactual factors. Based on postmortem analysis, it is not clear whether the $B_{max}$ for the 5-HT$_{2A}$ receptor is altered in the CNS of depressed individuals.

The development of 5-HT$_{2A}$ specific PET ligands has allowed this receptor to be studied in vivo. There are two such studies that use [$^{18}$F]-setoperone to visualize the 5-HT$_{2A}$ receptor in depressed participants. One study compared 14 depressives with 19 healthy controls and found no differences in ligand binding between the depressives and controls (Meyer et al., 1999). This work attempted to study the 5-HT$_{2A}$ receptor in depression, isolated from suicidality by excluding participants with a history of suicide attempt within 5 years of the study. This depressed, but not suicidal, population showed no evidence of changes in numbers of 5-HT$_{2A}$ receptors in depression. In a study

that used [$^{18}$F]-altanserin to image the 5-HT$_{2A}$ receptor, a different result was obtained (Biver et al., 1997). In this study, 8 drug-free depressives were compared with 22 healthy controls, and there was a significant reduction in 5-HT$_{2A}$ signal in the right posterolateral orbitofrontal cortex and anterior cingulate cortex of the depressives compared with the controls. Clearly these studies need to be repeated with much larger cohorts of patients and standardized methods, ligands, and so forth. The exclusion of potentially suicidal participants from the first study cited could contribute to the discrepant findings between the studies.

Similarly contradictory results have been reported for PET-mediated 5-HT$_{2A}$ imaging of the response to antidepressant treatment. In a study that used the TCA clomipramine to treat depressed patients, there was a significant reduction in cortical 5-HT$_{2A}$ binding density, as revealed by [$^{18}$F]-setoperone labeling (Attar-Levy et al., 1999). These authors reported no relationship between measures of depression severity and the intensity of labeling of the 5-HT$_{2A}$ receptor in the treated group. A similar result was reported in a study of 10 depressed patients treated with desipramine (Yatham et al., 1999). In this study, 8 of 10 of the patients exhibited a significant antidepressant response, as revealed by a 50% reduction in the HDRS. All of the patients demonstrated a reduction in [$^{18}$F]-setoperone labeling bilaterally throughout the cortex regardless of antidepressant response. However, as in the previous study, there was no relationship between measures of depression severity and change in 5-HT$_{2A}$ labeling. The opposite result has also been reported (Massou et al., 1997). In this study, 6 depressed patients treated with SSRIs showed an increase in cortical [$^{18}$F]-setoperone labeling compared with untreated depressives. Clearly, no conclusions can be drawn from these results about the regulation of the 5-HT$_{2A}$ receptor in depression or in response to antidepressant treatment. Larger, standardized studies will have to be conducted to clarify this situation.

The 5-HT$_{1A}$ receptor is the somatodendritic autoreceptor on the serotonergic neurons. This receptor controls the rate of firing of the serotonergic neurons and hence the availability of serotonin in the synapse. Changes in the numbers or responsiveness of the 5-HT$_{1A}$ receptor might be expected to change the firing rate of the serotonergic neurons, which in turn could lead to symptoms of depression. Drugs that are agonists for this receptor and increase the firing rate of the neurons would be predicted to be antidepressants. There is at least one report of increased $B_{max}$ of the 5-HT$_{1A}$ receptor in the frontal cortex of patients who committed suicide via nonviolent means versus those who used violent means or nonsuicidal controls (Matsubara, Arora, & Meltzer, 1991). Discordant reports have also appeared (Cheetham, Crompton, Katona, & Horton, 1990). In one postmortem study of suicide victims with a "firm" retrospective diagnosis of depression, no differences in 5-HT$_{1A}$ B$_{max}$ were detected in all brain regions analyzed, and there was no relationship between B$_{max}$ and method of suicide or antidepressant exposure (Lowther et al., 1997). Again, these postmortem studies are subject to all of the potential "nuisance confounds" mentioned previously, including variable antemortem treatment, postmortem processing, and low participant number.

There is considerable evidence for dysfunction of the serotonergic system in major depression. Although one specific pathological change that causes depression has not been found, multiple alterations throughout the serotonergic system, both pre- and postsynaptic, have been reported. Many different antidepressants have pharmacodynamic targets in the serotonergic system, and many if not most act in part through serotonergic circuits. Antidepressants cause widespread adaptive changes in the serotonergic systems of both experimental animals and human participants.

Future research into the function of 5-HT systems will surely address the molecular mechanisms that result in the observed changes in depression and in response to antidepressants. The role that the "new" serotonin receptors play in the pathophysiology of depression and/or in the mechanism of action of antidepressants has yet to be determined. The advent of improved functional neuroimaging and improved ligands specific to key components of the serotonergic system will allow the direct study of this system in depressed patients before, during, and after treatment.

### Dopamine

Historically, dopamine (DA) has not received the attention that 5-HT and NE circuits have in theories of the pathophysiology of depression. The DA systems were largely considered to have little or no importance in the biology of depression, with the exception of a seminal role in producing psychotic symptoms in delusional depressives. Clearly its major role has traditionally been viewed in the biology of schizophrenia. There is evidence of DA dysfunction in depression, and some antidepressants may act through a dopaminergic mechanism (Wilner, 1995). Several lines of evidence are consistent with a role for DA systems in the pathophysiology of depression, including evidence of altered DA function in depressed patients, pathological mood symptoms in patients suffering from other diseases that affect DA systems (principally Parkinson's disease), and the effects on mood of psychopharmacological agents that alter DA neurotransmission.

Like the other monoamine neurotransmitters, DA neurotransmission is estimated by measuring its major metabolite, homovanillic acid (HVA), in bodily fluids. The concentration of HVA is directly related to the extracellular concentration of DA, and therefore the concentration of HVA is thought to represent differences in activity of presynaptic DA neurons. Several studies have reported decreased CSF HVA levels in depressed patients, as well as in depressed participants who attempted suicide (R. G. Brown & Gershon, 1993; Reddy, Khanna, Subash, Channabasavanna, & Sridhara Rama Rao, 1992; Roy, Karoum, & Pollack, 1992; Roy et al., 1985). Remarkably, the exact opposite result has also been reported in a study of 24 depressives compared with 10 controls (Gjerris, Werdelin, Rafaelson, Alling, & Christensen, 1987). In this study, the depressives showed higher CSF DA levels and no differences in CSF HVA, NE, or MHPG. The cause of this discrepancy is unclear, but the majority of published data support the notion of decreased CSF HVA concentrations in depression.

Although low CSF HVA levels have been reported in major depression, this same finding has also been reported in both Parkinson's disease and Alzheimer's disease (Van Praag, Korf, Lakke, & Schut, 1975; Wolfe et al.,1990). There are also reports of increased CSF HVA in agitated patients and in manic patients (Willner, 1983). These findings suggest that CSF HVA level and hence DA neurotransmission may be a marker for psychomotor activity more than for mood state.

Dopamine metabolites are detectable in urine and have been measured in cohorts of depressives compared with various control groups. In one study of 28 depressed participants and 25 controls, the urinary concentration of DOPAC, another DA metabolite, was significantly lower in the depressives than controls (Roy, Pickar, Douillet, Karoum, & Linnoila, 1986). In another study in which the 24-hour urinary excretion of a number of DA metabolites was measured, patients with depression and a suicide attempt had lower DA metabolite concentrations than did patients with depression and no suicidality (Roy et al., 1992). In a 5-year follow-up, the relationship between suicide attempt and urinary HVA persisted, with those patients who attempted suicide in the follow-up period having significantly lower urinary HVA than those who did not.

Another line of evidence that supports a role for DA system dysfunction in depressive syndromes is suggested by the mood symptoms that commonly occur in patients with Parkinson's disease. Patients with Parkinson's disease often have prominent symptoms of depression that frequently precede the development of the physical manifestations of the disorder (Van Praag et al., 1975; Guze & Barrio, 1991). As many as 50% of Parkinson's patients experience depression that does not appear to be related to the severity of disability resulting from the disease itself (Murray, 1996). Treatment of Parkinson's disease patients with L-dopa is often associated with antidepressant effects that can precede the improvement in the physical symptoms of the disease (Murphy, 1972). These observations support the interpretation that the depressed mood that occurs in Parkinson's disease is the result of decreased DA availability. Whether this interpretation is generalizable to depression that occurs independent of Parkinson's disease is not known.

Increased DA neurotransmission has been hypothesized to be central to the production of psychotic symptoms in schizophrenia, in stimulant-induced psychoses, and in major depression with psychoses. Patients with psychotic depression have increased serum levels of DA and HVA compared with patients with nonpsychotic depression (Devanand, Bowers, Hoffman, & Nelson, 1985; Schatzberg, Rothschild, Langlais, Bird, & Cole, 1985). Some data suggest that the increased levels of glucocorticoids routinely observed in psychotic depression may underlie the increased DA activity (Rothschild et al., 1984). This possibility has led to the hypothesis that increased glucocorticoid secretion in depressed patients produces increased DA neurotransmission, which in turn leads to the development of psychotic symptoms (Schatzberg et al., 1985).

Another potential measure of presynaptic DA function is the number and distribution of DA transporters. This transporter is structurally related to the 5-HT and NE transporters and serves the same role on DA neurons, namely of terminating synaptic neurotransmission by pumping DA back into the presynaptic neuron. Two different postmortem studies have examined the density of DA transporters in the CNS of suicide victims (Allard & Norlen, 1997; Bowden et al., 1997). These studies used different ligands to label the DA transporter. In neither study was there any difference in $B_{max}$ for the DA transporter in the suicide victims compared with the controls. There also was no association between transporter $B_{max}$ and method of suicide or previous treatment with antidepressants.

Functional neuroimaging data suggest that there are regional changes in the numbers of DA receptors in major depression. Two different studies have used the D2/3 receptor ligand [123I]-IBZM and SPECT imaging to measure DA receptors in depressed participants in vivo (D'haenen & Bossuyt, 1994; Shah, Ogilvie, Goodwin, & Ebmeier, 1997). Both studies report an increase in [123I]-IBZM signal in the striatum of depressives compared with controls. One of these studies localized the increased signal to the right striatum (Shah et al., 1997). These results are interpretable as indicating upregulation of D2 DA receptors in the striatum in patients with major depression. This finding is consistent with the notion of decreased DA transmission in depression with concomitant upregulation of postsynaptic receptors.

Neuroendocrine challenge data are also suggestive of DA dysfunction in depression. Apomorphine is an agonist at multiple DA receptors and causes increased secretion of growth hormone (GH) through a postsynaptic mecha-

nism. Some studies report a blunted GH response to apomorphine challenge in major depression (Pichot, Ansseau, Gonzalez Moreno, Hansenne, & von Frenckell, 1992; Pichot, Hansenne, Gonzalez Moreno, & Ansseau, 1995). Results from this paradigm in actively manic patients were equivocal and did not directly support the hypothesis of excessive DA activity in mania (Ansseau et al., 1987). The GH response to apomorphine does not differ between participants with panic disorder and controls, again pointing to some role for DA dysfunction in depressive disorders.

The actions of a number of different drugs suggest that potentiating dopamine transmission can relieve depressive symptoms. The psychostimulants d-amphetamine and methylphenidate increase DA release, with resultant increased energy, activation, and elevated mood. Although these drugs cause transient mood elevations in depressed and euthymic individuals (Jacobs & Silverstone, 1988; Little, 1988), they are ineffective as antidepressants, at least as monotherapy. They may be effective as adjuncts to SSRIs and other antidepressants in nonresponders (Fawcett & Busch, 1998). The "atypical" antidepressants bupropion (Ascher et al., 1995) and amineptine (Garattini, 1997) are relatively weak antagonists of the DA transporter, and this action is considered to be central to their action as antidepressants. Remarkably, the high potency of sertraline as a DA transporter antagonist has been largely overlooked. Thus agents that enhance DA transmission, atypical antidepressants, and stimulants can elevate mood in depressed and euthymic individuals. Moreover, nomifensine, a clinically effective antidepressant which acts by blocking DA reuptake, was removed from the market because of an unacceptably high rate of hemolytic anemia in patients receiving the drug. This suggests that enhanced DA neurotransmission might be associated with antidepressant action.

Although not as much attention has been paid to DA neural circuits as to serotonin and norepinephrine systems in the pathogenesis of depression, there is some evidence that DA systems are altered in depression. Some reduced activity of certain DA circuits may take place in major depression, though it is not clear whether this is the cause or effect of this mood state. Disorders associated with decreased DA neurotransmission, such as Parkinson's disease, are often associated with profound alterations of mood, alterations that are often, but not always, corrected by restoring DA levels.

### Neuropeptides

Many different peptide neurotransmitters have been scrutinized in major depression. In particular, those peptides that regulate the hypothalamic-pituitary-adrenal (HPA) axis and the hypothalamic-pituitary-thyroid (HPT) axis have been hypothesized to be candidates for a role in the pathophysiology of mood disorders (Plotsky, Owens, &

Nemeroff, 1995). The changes in neuroendocrine function that have been repeatedly documented in major depression have led several different research groups to propose that the peptide neurotransmitter systems that regulate the endocrine axes are pathologically involved in depression and may even represent the fundamental, causative defect. Corticotropin-releasing factor (CRF), which regulates the HPA axis; somatostatin, which regulates the secretion of GH from somatotrophs; and thyrotropin-releasing hormone (TRH), which regulates the HPT axis, have all been intensively studied in major depression and other mood disorders.

## Corticotropin-Releasing Factor

CRF is the major physiological secretogogue that controls the release of adrenocorticotropic hormone (ACTH) from the corticotrophs in the anterior pituitary and is also a neurotransmitter in extrahypothalamic brain regions. There is considerable evidence that the extrahypothalamic CRF system orchestrates stress responses, coordinating endocrine, autonomic, immune, and behavioral responses. In this capacity, and as the principal regulator of ACTH secretion, hyperactivity of the CRF system has been hypothesized to be central to the pathophysiology of depression (Arborelius, Owens, Plotsky, & Nemeroff, 1999; Nemeroff, 1996). Hypercortisolinemia, DST nonsuppression, and other indices of pituitary-adrenal axis activity suggest dysregulation of the CRF system in major depression.

The CSF concentration of CRF in untreated depressed patients is increased compared with healthy controls (Nemeroff et al., 1984). Different, independent research groups have replicated this observation. Intracisternally collected CSF concentrations of CRF are elevated in suicide victims, who presumably were suffering from depression (Arato, Banki, Bissette, & Nemeroff, 1989). Higher concentrations of plasma CRF have been reported in depressed patients compared with controls (Catalan, Gallart, Castellanos, & Galard, 1998). In this sample, a relationship appeared to exist between severity of depression and plasma CRF concentration, with the more severely depressed participants exhibiting the highest CRF concentrations. The increased CRF levels in major depression appear to be due to increased production and release, because there is increased expression of the mRNA that encodes CRF in the hypothalamus of depressed suicide victims (Plotsky et al., 1995; Raadsheer et al., 1995).

The CSF concentration of CRF has also been shown to be elevated in patients with anorexia nervosa (Kaye et al., 1987). In these patients, CRF levels normalize with restoration of normal weight. The relationship, if any, between the regulation of CRF expression in depression and anorexia nervosa remains obscure. Two studies have reported elevated CSF CRF concentrations in PTSD patients (Baker et al., 1999; Bremner, Licinio, et al., 1997). The increased

CSF CRF level appears to be relatively specific for depression, PTSD, and anorexia nervosa; it has not been observed in patients with schizophrenia, neurological disorders, or dementia, nor in those with mania, panic, or other psychiatric disorders, except in those who also suffer from comorbid depression.

The CSF CRF concentration in depression appears to be a state-dependent measure because the levels normalize after treatment with ECT, fluoxetine, and other antidepressants (DeBellis, Gold, Geracioti, Listwak, & Kling, 1993; Nemeroff, Bissette, Akil, & Fink, 1991). In a cohort of elderly depressives treated with amitriptyline, CSF CRF concentrations decreased in those patients who responded to treatment (Heuser et al., 1998). A control cohort also treated with amitriptyline showed a nonsignificant decrease in CSF CRF concentrations. This finding suggests a general down regulation of CRF neuronal activity in response to antidepressant treatment. Curiously, the depressives in this particular cohort did not differ from controls in baseline CSF CRF concentrations. Normalization of CSF CRF may be predictive of long-term remission, whereas failure to normalize may predict early relapse (Banki, Karmacsi, Bissette, & Nemeroff, 1992).

In two studies, we observed decreased $B_{max}$ values for CRF receptors in the frontal cortex of depressed suicide victims (Nemeroff, Owens, Bissette, Andorn, & Stanley, 1988). Another report shows no difference in CRF receptor $B_{max}$ values in depression (Hucks, Lowther, Crompton, Katona, & Horton, 1997). In this study of suicide victims with "firm" antemortem diagnoses of depression, there were no differences in CRF receptor density, nor did exposure to antidepressants or method of suicide correlate with CRF receptor $B_{max}$.

One interpretation of the finding of decreased CRF receptor $B_{max}$ is down regulation of CRF receptors in response to the chronic hypersecretion of CRF in depression. Concordant with this are results of the CRF stimulation test, in which secretion of ACTH is measured in response to a standard intravenous dose of CRF. Depressed participants show blunting of the ACTH response to intravenously administered CRF compared with controls (Holsboer, Gerken, Stalla, & Muller, 1987; Young et al., 1990). As in the case of CSF CRF concentrations, the ACTH response to CRF challenge in depressed patients has been reported to normalize with treatment and syndrome resolution (Amsterdam et al., 1988).

There may be a correlation between the blunted ACTH response to CRF challenge and DST nonsuppression (Krishnan et al., 1993). Both of these measures normalize with treatment and syndrome resolution. There may be a subtype of major depression in which the patients experience the mood and cognitive symptoms of depression with hypercortisolinemia, DST nonsuppression, blunted ACTH response to CRF challenge, adrenal gland hypertrophy, and increased CSF concentrations of CRF. All of the peripheral manifestations of HPA dysregulation in these patients could be accounted for by hyperactivity of the CNS CRF neurons. What remains obscure is whether the CRF system is subject to a higher level of regulation that is also altered in depression, by 5-HT or NE systems, for example, or whether the dysfunction of the CRF system is the primary pathophysiological alteration in major depression.

### Somatostatin and the Growth Hormone Axis

Somatostatin is a tetradecapeptide that inhibits the secretion of growth hormone from the anterior pituitary. This peptide has also been referred to as growth-hormone-release-inhibiting hormone or somatotropin-release-inhibiting factor, or SRIF. As was the case for CRF, somatostatin has been clearly demonstrated to be a neurotransmitter, with a heterogeneous distribution outside of the hypothalamus. At least four different somatostatin receptor types have been cloned, with overlapping affinities and effector couplings. Somatostatin has been shown to affect sleep, ingestive behaviors, activity state, memory and cognition, and nociception. Growth hormone secretion is blunted in major depression in the clonidine, sumatriptan, and apomorphine challenge assays. These are probes of the NE, 5-HT, and DA systems, respectively, which suggests possible dysfunction of the somatostatin-growth hormone axis in major depression, revealed by each of these neuroendocrine challenge assays. The GH response to GHRF is blunted in depressed patients in most but not all studies.

The CSF concentration of somatostatin is decreased in major depression, an observation reported by numerous independent research groups (Bissette et al., 1986; Gerner & Yamada, 1982; Rubinow, 1986; Rubinow, Gold, & Post, 1983). CSF somatostatin has been reported to be decreased in unipolar depression and in bipolar disorder during the depressed phase of the illness. There are conflicting reports as to whether CSF somatostatin concentrations are correlated with the severity of depressive symptoms (Agren & Lundqvist, 1984). As was the case for CRF, CSF somatostatin levels appear to be a state marker of depression because they normalize with successful treatment and symptom resolution. This effect has been observed in patients with both unipolar and bipolar depression. CSF somatostatin concentrations are not altered in schizophrenia, anorexia nervosa, euthymic bipolars, or remitted depressives. Remarkably, CSF somatostatin levels have been reported to be increased in patients with OCD (Altemus et al., 1993). The relationship, if any, between somatostatin neuronal dysfunction in depression and OCD remains obscure.

The finding of decreased CSF somatostatin concentrations is not specific to major depression. The same finding has been reported in a number of neurological diseases without prominent comorbid psychiatric symptoms. Thus decreased CSF somatostatin levels have been reported in dementing diseases, including Alzheimer's disease, Parkinson's disease, and multiple sclerosis. In contrast, increased levels of CSF somatostatin have been reported in traumatic or inflammatory neurological processes, including compression injuries, meningitis, and encephalopathies. Although decreased CSF somatostatin concentration represents a state-dependent marker of depression, it appears to be relatively nonspecific, as it occurs in a number of unrelated, nonpsychiatric conditions. Whether the decreased somatostatin levels play a role in the pathophysiology of depression or are an epiphenomenon of the generalized HPA dysfunction that occurs in depression remains to be determined.

### Hypothalamic-Pituitary-Thyroid Axis

The manifestations of hypothyroidism can appear indistinguishable from those of major depression. The symptoms of both conditions include depressed mood, impaired cognition, and multiple neurovegetative symptoms. For this reason, the hypothalamic-pituitary-thyroid (HPT) axis has been studied exhaustively in major depression. Approximately 20% to 30% of patients with major depression have discernible HPT dysfunction. Secretion of thyroid-stimulating hormone (TSH) from the anterior pituitary gland is primarily regulated by thyrotropin-releasing hormone (TRH), a tripeptide, that is released into the hypothalamic-hypophyseal-portal system from hypothalamic neurons that terminate in the median eminence. TSH induces the secretion of l-triiodothyroxine ($T_3$) and thyroxin ($T_4$) from the thyroid gland.

Like other peptide neurotransmitters, the CSF concentration of TRH has been measured in patients with major depression. In two studies, the concentration of TRH was reported to be increased in depressives compared with neurological and nondepressed controls (Banki, Bissette, Arato, & Nemeroff, 1988; Kirkegaard, Faber, Hummer, & Rogowski, 1979). A negative study has also appeared (Roy, Wolkowitz, Bissette, & Nemeroff, 1994). The CSF concentration of TRH has been reported to be unaltered in Alzheimer's disease, anxiety disorders, and alcoholism. Therefore, the increased TRH level observed in the depressed patients may be specific to depression, but, given the relatively small sample size of these two studies, larger replications are warranted.

The CSF concentration of transthyretin has been reported to be decreased in major depression (Sullivan et al., 1999). Transthyretin transports and distributes thyroid hormones in the CNS. Decreased availability of this molecule in the CNS could result in a hypometabolic state in the neurons of affected individuals. This finding could account for observations of "normal" concentrations of thyroid hormones in depression, as well as for the utility of thyroid hormone augmentation in antidepressant nonresponders. Decreased transthyretin would functionally result in hypothyroidism within the CNS.

The TRH stimulation test is generally considered to be one of the most sensitive measures of HPT axis function. In this test, plasma TSH concentrations are measured at baseline and serially after a challenge dose of TRH. This test has been administered to a large number of depressed and control participants in many independent studies (Kastin, Ehrensing, Schlach, & Anderson, 1972; Prange, Lara, Wilson, Alltop, & Breese, 1972). Across all of these studies, 25%–30% of the depressed patients exhibit a blunted TSH response to TRH challenge. This is apparently not due to primary hypothyroidism, because these depressed patients were euthyroid at the time of assessment. In one study, participants were specifically identified as being depressed but having "high-normal" baseline circulating TSH levels (Kraus et al., 1997). In this particular cohort of depressives, 38% demonstrated exaggerated TSH secretion in response to TRH challenge. The magnitude of the TSH response was not related to the baseline TSH value. The authors of this study suggest that there may be a subset of depressives who are in fact hypothyroid, which is only revealed by the TRH challenge assay. A possible explanation is the presence of "asymptomatic" autoimmune thyroiditis in these depressed patients (Haggerty et al., 1990). In a related study, 26% of depressed patients were reported to have abnormal concentration of circulating thyroid hormones ($T_3$ and/or $T_4$) that normalized with treatment and syndrome resolution (Shelton, Winn, Ekhatore, & Loosen, 1993).

One possible explanation for the blunted TSH response to TRH challenge is down regulation of TRH receptors in the pituitary in response to the increased levels of TRH secreted into the hypophyseal-portal circulation. Unfortunately, there have been no studies reported that measured CSF TRH and performed TRH challenge tests in the same depressive participants, though this has been reported in alcoholism (Adinoff, Nemeroff, Bissette, Martin, & Linnoila, 1991). The significance of alteration of the HPT axis in the pathogenesis of depression remains to be completely elucidated. Certainly one could postulate a subtype of depression (or hypothyroidism) in which there was disruption of the HPT axis that could be revealed only by the TRH challenge test. Whether this represents a distinct disease entity has not been determined, nor is it clear that the patients with depression and altered TRH challenge respond preferentially to any particular treatment regimen. Potentially relevant to these findings are the studies that have demonstrated the efficacy of $T_3$ both in accelerating antidepressant response and in converting antidepressant partial responders into full responders (Aronson, Offman, Joffe, & Naylor, 1996).

One intriguing observation that suggests a role for HPT system dysfunction in major depression comes from the

antidepressant actions of TRH. In two small studies, reported by the same research group, TRH appeared to have antidepressant actions in patients with treatment refractory depression (Callahan et al., 1997; Marangell et al., 1997). In one report, two patients responded to intravenous and intrathecal administration of TRH, though tolerance developed to the intravenous route (Callahan et al., 1997). In a second study, eight patients with treatment refractory depression were treated with intrathecal TRH in a double-blind trial (Marangell et al., 1997). Five of the eight participants had a 50% or greater reduction in HDRS, but the responses were transient. These results are clearly preliminary, but they further support a role for HPT system dysfunction in major depression and may point the way to a novel treatment strategy.

## Summary

Despite 40 years of concerted research, the primary etiopathology of major depression has not been identified. Although many alterations in different neurotransmitter systems have been documented, no one system or one alteration has clearly emerged as the fundamental pathology in major depression. Reconciling the discrepancy between the relatively homogeneous clinical manifestations of depression with the disparate neurochemical manifestations of depression is one of the great challenges that face psychiatric researchers in the future.

The brain is obviously the most complex of all organs, and its structure and function is considerably more complex than current models can explain. Many different neurotransmitter systems interact with and regulate each other at many different levels of the neuraxis. There is clearly a great deal of redundancy and functional reserve within the CNS, such that pathological changes that result in depression would be quickly and diffusely compensated for by other neurochemical systems. Another expectation would be that gross changes in neuronal function would not occur in depression, as these types of changes would result in clear neurological deficits. Thus it is not surprising that the primary defect has not been identified in depression. A disease such as major depression that manifests symptoms in many different neurobehavioral domains—including mood and emotion, cognition, perception, autonomic function, homeostatic function, and stress responsiveness—would be expected to cause disruption of the neurochemical systems that regulate these diverse processes.

There are alterations in many different neurotransmitter systems in depression, principally in those that utilize NE, 5-HT, and DA. There are alterations of the NE system in patients suffering from depression and from mania. Three main neurohormonal axes, namely the HPA, hypothalamic-pituitary-growth hormone, and the HPT are altered in depression. The neuropeptide secretagogue/neurotransmitter systems that regulate these axes are disrupted in depression. Many of the changes in the different systems observed in depression appear to be state markers because they tend to normalize with successful treatment and syndrome resolution.

Many avenues exist for future research into the pathophysiology of major depression. With the emergence of functional neuroimaging modalities, the opportunity to study patients across the course of their illness is now available. The development of well-characterized and consistently acquired banks of postmortem tissues will further allow the study of the changes that major depression causes in the CNS. The other major intellectual resource that will illuminate the search for the etiopathology of depression is the rapidly evolving human genome initiative. As knowledge of the molecular genetics of the nervous system advances and new technologies, such as high density microarray systems, become available, new insights into the function and dysfunction of the brain will further our knowledge of the pathophysiology of major depression.

Steven J. Garlow is supported by National Institute of Health Grant Nos. K23 RR15531 and RO1 MH60745 and by a Young Investigator Award from the National Alliance for Research on Schizophrenia and Depression. Charles B. Nemeroff is supported by National Institute of Health Grant Nos. MH-42088, MH-39415, and MH-58922 and is the recipient of an Established Investigator Award from the National Alliance for Research on Schizophrenia and Depression.

## REFERENCES

Adinoff, B., Nemeroff, C. B., Bissette, G., Martin, P. R., & Linnoila, M. (1991). Inverse relationship between CSF TRH concentrations and the TSH response to TRH in abstinent alcohol-dependent patients. *American Journal of Psychiatry, 148*(11), 1586–1588.

Agren, H., & Lundqvist, G. (1984). Low levels of somatostatin in human CSF mark depressive episodes. *Psychoneuroendocrinology, 9*, 233–248.

Allard, P., & Norlen, M. (1997). Unchanged density of caudate nucleus dopamine uptake sites in depressed suicide victims. *Journal of Neural Transmission, 104*(11–12), 1353–1360.

Altemus, M., Pigott, T., L'Heureux, F., Davis, C. L., Rubinow, D. R., Murphy, D. L., & Gold, P. W. (1993). CSF somatostatin in obsessive-compulsive disorder. *American Journal of Psychiatry, 150*(3), 460–464.

American Psychiatric Association (1994). *Diagnostic and statistical manual of mental disorders* (4th ed.). Washington, DC: Author.

Amsterdam, J. D., Maislin, G., Skolnick, B., Berwish, N., & Winokur, A. (1989). Multiple hormone responses to clonidine administration in depressed patients and healthy volunteers. *Biological Psychiatry, 26*(3), 265–278.

Amsterdam, J. D., Maislin, G., Winokur, A., Berwish, N., Kling, M., & Gold, P. (1988). The oCRH test before and after clinical recovery from depression. *Journal of Affective Disorders, 14*, 213–222.

Ansseau, M., von Frenckell, R., Cerfontaine, J. L., Papart, P., Franck, G., Timsit-Berthier, M., Geenen, V., & Legros, J. J. (1987). Neuroendocrine evaluation of catecholamine neurotransmission in mania. *Psychiatry Research, 22*(3), 193–206.

Arango, V., Ernsberger, P., Marzuk, P., Chen, J., Tirney, H., Stanley, M., Reis, D., & Mann, J. (1990). Autoradiographic demonstration of increased serotonin 5-HT2 and ß-adrenergic receptor binding sites in the brains of suicide victims. *Archives of General Psychiatry, 47*, 1038–1047.

Arango, V., Underwood, M. D., & Mann, J. J. (1996). Fewer pigmented locus coeruleus neurons in suicide victims: Preliminary results. *Biological Psychiatry, 39*(2), 112–120.

Arato, M., Banki, C. M., Bissette, G., & Nemeroff, C. B. (1989). Elevated CSF CRF in suicide victims. *Biological Psychiatry, 25*, 355–359.

Arborelius, L., Owens, M. J., Plotsky, P. M., & Nemeroff, C. B. (1999). The role of corticotropin-releasing factor in depression and anxiety disorders. *Journal of Endocrinology, 160*(1), 1–12.

Aronson, R., Offman, H. J., Joffe, R. T., & Naylor, C. D. (1996). Triiodothyronine augmentation in the treatment of refractory depression: A meta-analysis. *Archives of General Psychiatry, 53*(9), 842–848.

Arora, R., & Meltzer, H. (1989a). Increased serotonin2 (5-HT2) receptor binding as measured by 3H-lysergic diethylamide (3H-LSD) in the blood platelets of depressed patients. *Life Sciences, 44*, 725–734.

Arora, R. C., & Meltzer, H. Y. (1989b). Serotonergic measures in the brains of suicide victims: 5-HT2 binding sites in the frontal cortex of suicide victims and control subjects. *American Journal of Psychiatry, 146*(6), 730–736.

Arora, R. C., & Meltzer, H. Y. (1993). Serotonin2 receptor binding in blood platelets of schizophrenic patients. *Psychiatric Research, 47*, 111–119.

Asberg, M., Traskman, L., & Thoren, P. (1976). 5-HIAA in the cerebrospinal fluid: A biochemical suicide predictor? *Archives of General Psychiatry, 33*, 1193–1197.

Ascher, J. A., Cole, J. O., Colin, J. N., Feighner, J. P., Ferris, R. M., Fibiger, H. C., Golden, R. N., Martin, P., Potter, W. Z., Richelson, E., & Sulser, F. (1995). Bupropion: A review of its mechanism of antidepressant activity. *Journal of Clinical Psychiatry, 56*, 395–401.

Attar-Levy, D., Martinot, J. L., Blin, J., Dao-Castellana, M. H., Crouzel, C., Mazoyer, B., Poirier, M. F., Bourdel, M. C., Aymard, N., Syrota, A., & Feline, A. (1999). The cortical serotonin2 receptors studied with positron-emission tomography and [18F]-setoperone during depressive illness and antidepressant treatment with clomipramine. *Biological Psychiatry, 45*(2), 180–186.

Baker, D. G., West, S. A., Nicholson, W. E., Ekhator, N. N., Kasckow, J. W., Hill, K. K., Bruce, A. B., Orth, D. N., & Geracioti, T. D. (1999). Serial CSF corticotropin-releasing hormone levels and adrenocortical activity in combat veterans with posttraumatic stress disorder. *American Journal of Psychiatry, 156*(4), 585–588.

Bakish, D., Cavazzoni, P., Chudzik, J., Ravindran, A., & Hrdina, P. D. (1997). Effects of selective serotonin reuptake inhibitors on platelet serotonin parameters in major depressive disorders. *Biological Psychiatry, 41*(2), 184–190.

Banki, C. M., Bissette, G., Arato, M., & Nemeroff, C. B. (1988). Elevation of immunoreactive CSF TRH in depressed patients. *American Journal of Psychiatry, 145*, 1526–1531.

Banki, C. M., Karmacsi, L., Bissette, G., & Nemeroff, C. B. (1992). CSF corticotropin-releasing hormone and somatostatin in major depression: Response to antidepressant treatment and relapse. *European Neuropsychopharmacology, 2*, 107–113.

Benkelfat, C., Ellenbogen, M. A., Dean, P., Palmour, R. M., & Young, S. N. (1994). Mood-lowering effect of tryptophan depletion: Enhanced susceptibility in young men at genetic risk for major affective disorders. *Archives of General Psychiatry, 51*(9), 687–697.

Berman, R. M., Narasimhan, M., Miller, H. L., Anand, A., Cappiello, A., Oren, D. A., Heninger, G. R., & Charney, D. S. (1999). Transient depressive relapse induced by catecholamine depletion: Potential phenotypic vulnerability marker? *Archives of General Psychiatry, 56*(5), 395–403.

Biegon, A., Essar, N., Israeli, M., Elizur, A., Bruch, S., & Bar-Nathan, A. (1990). Serotonin 5-HT2 receptor binding on blood platelets as a state dependent marker in major affective disorder. *Psychopharmacology, 102*, 73–75.

Biegon, A., Grinspoon, A., Blumenfeld, B., Bleich, A., Apter, A., & Mester, R. (1990). Increased serotonin 5-HT2 receptor binding on blood platelets of suicidal men. *Psychopharmacology, 100*, 165–167.

Biegon, A., Weizman, A., Karp, L., Ram, A., Tiano, S., & Wolff, M. (1987). Serotonin 5-HT2 receptor binding on blood platelets: A peripheral marker for depression? *Life Sciences, 41*, 2485–2492.

Bissette, G., Widerlov, E., Walleus, H., Karlsson, I., Eklund, K., Forsman, A., & Nemeroff, C. B. (1986). Alterations in cerebrospinal fluid somatostatin-like immunoreactivity in neuropsychiatric disorders. *Archives of General Psychiatry, 43*(12), 1148–1151.

Biver, F., Wikler, D., Lotstra, F., Damhaut, P., Goldman, S., & Mendlewicz, J. (1997). Serotonin 5-HT2 receptor imaging in major depression: Focal changes in orbito-insular cortex. *British Journal of Psychiatry, 171*, 444–448.

Bowden, C., Cheetham, S. C., Lowther, S., Katona, C. L., Crompton, M. R., & Horton, R. W. (1997). Dopamine uptake sites, labelled with [3H]GBR12935, in brain samples from depressed suicides and controls. *European Neuropsychopharmacology, 7*(4), 247–252.

Bremner, J. D., Innis, R. B., Salomon, R. M., Staib, L. H., Ng, C. K., Miller, H. L., Bronen, R. A., Krystal, J. H., Duncan, J., Rich, D., Price, L. H., Malison, R., Dey, H., Soufer, R., & Charney, D. S. (1997). Positron emission tomography measurement of cerebral metabolic correlates of tryptophan depletion-induced depressive relapse. *Archives of General Psychiatry, 54*(4), 364–374.

Bremner, J. D., Licinio, J., Darnell, A., Krystal, J. H., Owens, M. J., Southwick, S. M., Nemeroff, C. B., & Charney, D. S. (1997). Elevated CSF corticotropin-releasing factor concentrations in posttraumatic stress disorder. *American Journal of Psychiatry, 154*(5), 624–629.

Briley, M., Langer, S., Raisman, R., Sechter, D., & Zarifian, E. (1980a). High-affinity binding of [3H]-imipramine to human platelets: Differences between untreated depressed patients and healthy volunteers. *Proceedings of the British Pharmacological Society,* 152P–153P.

Briley, M. S., Langer, S. Z., Raisman, R., Sechter, D., & Zarifian, E. (1980b). Tritated imipramine binding sites are decreased in platelets of untreated depressed patients. *Science, 209*, 303–305.

Brogden, R. N., Heel, R. C., Speight, T. M., & Avery, G. S. (1981). Trazodone: A review of its pharmacological properties and therapeutic use in depression and anxiety. *Drugs, 21*(6), 401–429.

Brown, R. G., & Gershon, S. (1993). Dopamine and depression. *Journal of Neural Transmission, 91*, 75–109.

Brown, W. A., Johnston, R., & Mayfield, D. (1979). The 24-hour dexamethasone suppression test in a clinical setting: Relationship to diagnosis, symptoms, and response to treatment. *American Journal of Psychiatry, 136*(4B), 543–547.

Bryant, S. G., & Ereshefsky, L. (1982). Antidepressant profile of trazodone. *Clinical Pharmacology, 1*(5), 406–417.

Bunney, W. E., & Davis, M. (1965). Norepinephrine in depressive reactions. *Archives of General Psychiatry, 13*, 137–152.

Callahan, A. M., Frye, M. A., Marangell, L. B., George, M. S., Ketter, T. A., L'Herrou, T.,& Post, R. M. (1997). Comparative antidepressant effects of intravenous and intrathecal thyrotropin-releasing hormone: Confounding effects of tolerance and implications for therapeutics. *Biological Psychiatry, 41*(3), 264–272.

Cappiello, A., Malison, R. T., McDougle, C. J., Vegso, S. J., Charney, D. S., Heninger, G. R., & Price, L. H. (1996). Seasonal variation in neuroendocrine and mood response to iv L-tryptophan in depressed patients and healthy subjects. *Neuropsychpharmacology, 15*(5), 475–483.

Carpenter, L. L., Anderson, G. M., Pelton, G. H., Gudin, J. A., Kirwin, P. D., Price, L. H., Henninger, G. R., & McDougle, C. J. (1998). Tryptophan depletion during continuous CSF sampling in healthy human subjects. *Neuropsychopharmacology, 19*(1), 26–35.

Carroll, B. J. (1982). Use of the dexamethasone test in depression. *Journal of Clinical Psychiatry, 43*, 44–50.

Carroll, B. J., & Davies, B. (1970). Clinical association of 11-hydroxy-corticosteroid suppression and nonsuppression in severe depressive illness. *British Medical Journal, 3*, 285–287.

Cassidy, F., Murry, E., & Carrol, B. J. (1998). Tryptophan depletion in recently manic patients treated with lithium. *Biological Psychiatry, 43*(3), 230–232.

Cassidy, F., Murry, E., Weiner, R. D., & Carroll, B. J. (1997). Lack of relapse with tryptophan depletion following successful treatment with ECT. *American Journal of Psychiatry, 154*(8), 1151–1152.

Catalan, R., Gallart, J. M., Castellanos, J. M., & Galard, R. (1998). Plasma corticotropin-releasing factor in depressive disorders. *Biological Psychiatry, 44*(1), 15–20.

Cheetham, S., Crompton, M., Katona, C., & Horton, R. (1988). Brain5-HT2 receptor binding sites in depressed suicide victims. *Brain Research, 443*, 272–280.

Cheetham, S. C., Crompton, M. R., Katona, C. L. E., & Horton, R. W. (1990). Brain 5-HT1 binding sites in depressed suicides. *Psychopharmacology, 102*, 544–548.

Cleare, A. J., Murray, R. M., Sherwood, R. A., & O'Keane, V. (1998). Abnormal 5-HT1D receptor function in major depression: A neuropharmacological challenge study using sumatriptan. *Psychological Medicine, 28*(2), 295–300.

Cowen, P., Charig, E., Frasier, S., & Elliot, J. (1987). Platelet 5-HT receptor binding during depressive illness and tricyclic antidepressant treatment. *Journal of Affective Disorders, 13*, 45–50.

Crow, T., Cross, A., Cooper, S., Deakin, J., Terrier, I., Johnson, J., Joseph, M., Owen, F., Poulter, M., Lofthouse, R., Corsellis, J., Chambers, D., Blessed, G., Perry, E., Perry, R., & Tomlinson, B. (1984). Neurotransmitter receptors and monoamine metabolites in the brains of patients with Alzheimer-type dementia and depression, and suicides. *Neuropharm., 23*(12B), 1561–1569.

Da Prada, M., Cesura, A. M., Launay, J. M., & Richards, J. G. (1988). Platelets as model for neurones. *Experentia, 44*, 115–126.

DeBellis, M. D., Gold, P. W., Geracioti, T. D., Listwak, S., & Kling, M. A. (1993). Fluoxetine significantly reduces CSF CRH and AVP concentrations in patients with major depression. *American Journal of Psychiatry, 150*, 656–657.

Delgado, P. L., Charney, D. S., Price, L. H., Landis, H., & Henninger, G. R. (1990). Neuroendocrine and behavioral effects of dietary tryptophan restriction in healthy subjects. *Life Sciences, 45*, 2323–2332.

Delgado, P. L., Miller, H. L., Salomon, R. M., Licinio, J., Krystal, J. H., Moreno, F. A., Heninger, G. R., & Charney, D. S. (1999). Tryptophan-depletion challenge in depressed patients treated with desipramine or fluoxetine: Implications for the role of serotonin in the mechanism of antidepressant action. *Biological Psychiatry, 46*(2), 212–220.

Delgado, P. L., Price, L. H., Miller, H. L., Salomon, R. M., Aghajanian, G. K., Heninger, G. R., & Charney, D. S. (1994). Serotonin and the neurobiology of depression: Effects of tryptophan depletion in drug-free depressed patients. *Archives of General Psychiatry, 51*(11), 865–874.

De Paermentier, F., Cheetham, S. C., Crompton, M. R., Katona, C. L., & Horton, R. W. (1990). Brain beta-adrenoceptor binding sites in antidepressant-free depressed suicide victims. *Brain Research, 525*(1), 71–77.

De Paermentier, F., Cheetham, S. C., Crompton, M. R., Katona, C. L., & Horton, R. W. (1991). Brain beta-adrenoceptor binding sites in depressed suicide victims: Effects of antidepressant treatment. *Psychopharmacology, 105*(2), 283–288.

De Paermentier, F., Lowther, S., Crompton, M. R., Katona, C. L., & Horton, R. W. (1997). Beta-adrenoceptors in human pineal glands are unaltered in depressed suicides. *Journal of Psychopharmocology, 11*(4), 295–299.

De Paermentier, F., Mauger, J. M., Lowther, S., Crompton, M. R., Katona, C. L., & Horton, R. W. (1997). Brain alpha-adrenoceptors in depressed suicides. *Brain Research, 757*(1), 60–68.

Devanand, D. P., Bowers, M. B., Hoffman, F. J., & Nelson, J. C. (1985). Elevated plasma homovanillic acid in depressed females with melancholia and psychosis. *Psychiatry Research, 15*(1), 1–4.

D'haenen, H. A., & Bossuyt, A. (1994). Dopamine D2 receptors in depression measured with single photon emission computed tomography. *Biological Psychiatry, 35*(2), 128–132.

Ellenbogen, M. A., Young, S. N., Dean, P., Palmour, R. M., & Benkelfat, C. (1996). Mood response to acute tryptophan depletion in healthy volunteers: Sex differences and temporal stability. *Neuropsychopharmacology, 15*(5), 465–474.

Ellis, P. M., & Salmond, C. (1994). Is platelet imipramine binding reduced in depression? A meta-analysis. *Biological Psychiatry, 36*, 292–299.

Extein, I., Tallman, J., Smith, C. C., & Goodwin, F. K. (1979). Changes in lymphocyte beta-adrenergic receptors in depression and mania. *Psychiatry Research, 1*(2), 191–197.

Fawcett, J., & Busch, K. A. (1998). Stimulants in psychiatry. In A. F. Schatzberg & C. B. Nemeroff (Eds.), *Textbook of psychopharmacology*, 2nd ed. (pp. 503–522). Washington, DC: American Psychiatric Press.

Flory, J. D., Mann, J. J., Manuck, S. B., & Muldoon, M. F. (1998). Recovery from major depression is not associated with normalization of serotonergic function. *Biological Psychiatry, 43*(5), 320–326.

Garattini, S. (1997). Pharmacology of amineptine, an antidepressant agent acting on the dopaminergic system: A review. *International Clinical Psychopharmacology, 12*(Suppl. 3), S15–19.

Garcia-Sevilla, J. A., Padro, D., Giralt, M. T., Guimon, J., & Areso, P. (1990). Alpha 2-adrenoceptor-mediated inhibition of platelet adenylate cyclase and induction of aggregation in major depression: Effect of long-term cyclic antidepressant drug treatment. *Archives of General Psychiatry, 47*(2), 125–132.

Garcia-Sevilla, J. A., Udina, C., Fuster, M. J., Alvarez, E., & Casas, M. (1987). Enhanced binding of [3H]-adrenaline to platelets of depressed patients with melancholia: Effect of long-term clomipramine treatment. *Acta Psychiat Scand, 75*(2), 150–157.

Gerner, R. H., & Yamada, T. (1982). Altered neuropeptide concentrations in cerebrospinal fluid of psychiatric patients. *Brain Research, 238*, 298–302.

Gibbons, R. D., & Davis, J. M. (1986). Consistent evidence for a biological subtype of depression characterized by low CSF monoamine levels. *Acta Psychiatr Scand, 74*, 8–12.

Gjerris, A., Werdelin, L., Rafaelson, O. J., Alling, C., & Christensen, N. J. (1987). CSF dopamine increased in depression: CSF dopamine, noradrenaline and their metabolites in depressed patients and controls. *Journal of Affective Disorders, 13*(3), 279–286.

Glennon, R. A., & Dukat, M. (1995). Serotonin receptor subtypes. In F. E. Bloom & D. J. Kupfer (Eds.), *Psychopharmacology: The fourth generation of progress* (pp. 415–429). New York: Raven Press.

Glowinski, J., & Axelrod, J. (1966). Effects of drugs on the disposition of H-3-norepinephrine in the rat brain. *Pharmacological Reviews, 18*(1), 775–785.

Glowinski, J., Axelrod, J., Kopin, I., & Wurtman, R. (1964). Physiological disposition of ³H-norepinephrine in the developing rat. *J. Pharmacol. Exp. Therap., 146*, 48–53.

Glowinski, J., & Iverson, L. L. (1966). Regional studies of catecholamines in the rat brain. *Journal of Neurochemistry, 13*, 665–669.

Glowinski, J., Snyder, S., & Axelrod, J. (1966). Subcellular localization of H3-norepinephrine in the rat brain and the effect of drugs. *J Pharmacol Exp Ther, 152*(2), 282–292.

Gross-Isseroff, R., Israeli, M., & Biegon, A. (1989). Autoradiographic analysis of tritiated imipramine binding in the human brain post-mortem: Effects of suicide. *Archives of General Psychiatry, 46*, 237–241.

Guze, B. H., & Barrio, J. C. (1991). The etiology of depression in Parkinson's disease patients. *Psychosomatics, 32*, 390–394.

Haggerty, J. J., Evans, D. L., Golden, R. N., Pedersen, C. A.,

Simon, J. S., & Nemeroff, C. B. (1990). The presence of antithyroid antibodies in patients with affective and nonaffective psychiatric disorders. *Biological Psychiatry, 27*(1), 51–60.

Halaris, A. (1978). 3-methoxy-4-hydroxyphenyl-glycol in manic psychosis. *American Journal of Psychiatry, 135,* 493–494.

Halaris, A., & Piletz, J. (1990). Platelet adrenoreceptor binding as a marker in neuropsychiatric disorders. *Abstracts 17th Collegium Internationale Neuro-Psychopharmacologicum Congress, 28.*

Healy, D., Carney, P. A., O'Halloran, A., & Leonard, B. E. (1985). Peripheral adrenoceptors and serotonin receptors in depression: Changes associated with response to treatment with trazodone or amitriptyline. *Journal of Affective Disorders, 9*(3), 285–296.

Heils, A., Teufel, A., Petri, S., Stober, G., Riederer, P., Bengel, D., & Lesch, K. P. (1996). Allelic variation of human serotonin transporter gene expression. *Journal of Neurochemistry, 66,* 2621–2624.

Heninger, G. R., Delgado, P. L., & Charney, D. S. (1996). The revised monoamine theory of depression: A modulatory role for monoamines, based on new findings from monoamine depletion experiments in humans. *Pharmacopsychiatry, 29*(1), 2–11.

Heninger, G. R., Delgado, P. L., Charney, D. S., Price, L. H., & Aghajanian, G. K. (1992). Tryptophan-deficient diet and amino acid drink deplete plasma tryptophan and induce a relapse of depression in susceptible patients. *J Chem Neuroanatomy, 5,* 347–348.

Heuser, I., Bissette, G., Dettling, M., Schweiger, U., Gotthardt, U., Schmider, J., Lammers, C. H., Nemeroff, C. B., & Holsboer, F. (1998). Cerebrospinal fluid concentrations of corticotropin-releasing hormone, vassopressin, and somatostatin in depressed patients and healthy controls: Response to amitriptyline treatment. *Depression and Anxiety, 8*(2), 71–79.

Holsboer, F., Gerken, A., Stalla, G. K., & Muller, O. A. (1987). Blunted aldosterone and ACTH release after human corticotropin-releasing factor administration in depressed patients. *American Journal of Psychiatry, 144,* 229–231.

Hrdina, P. D., Bakish, M. D., Chudzik, J., Ravindran, A., & Lapierre, Y. D. (1995). Serotonergic markers in platelets of patients with major depression: Upregulation of 5-HT$_2$ receptors. *J. Psychiatr. Neurosci., 20*(1), 11–19.

Hrdina, P., Demeter, E., Vu, T., Sotonyi, P., & Palkovits, M. (1993). 5-HT uptake sites and 5-HT$_2$ receptors in brains of antidepressant-free suicide victims/depressives: Increase in 5-HT$_2$ sites in cortex and amygdala. *Brain Research, 614,* 37–44.

Hucks, D., Lowther, S., Crompton, M. R., Katona, C. L., & Horton, R. W. (1997). Corticotropin-releasing factor binding sites in cortex of depressed suicides. *Psychopharmacology, 134*(2) 174–178.

Jacobs, D., & Silverstone, T. (1988). Dextroamphetamine arousal in human subjects as a model for mania. *Psychological Medicine, 16,* 323–329.

Kastin, A. J., Ehrensing, R. H., Schlach, D. S., & Anderson, M. S. (1972). Improvement in mental depression with decreased thyrotropin response after administration of thyrotropin-releasing hormone. *Lancet, 2*(780), 740–742.

Kaye, W. H., Gwirtsman, H. E., George, D. T., Ebert, M. H., Jimerson, D. C., Tomai, T. P., Chrousos, G. P., & Gold, P. W. (1987). Elevated cerebrospinal fluid levels of im-munoreactive corticotropin-releasing hormone in anorexia nervosa: Relation to state of nutrition, adrenal function, and intensity of depression. *J Clin Endocrinol Metab, 64*(2), 203–208.

Kirkegaard, C., Faber, J., Hummer, L., & Rogowski, P. (1979). Increased levels of TRH in cerebrospinal fluid from patients with endogenous depression. *Psychoneuroendocrinology, 4,* 227–235.

Klimek, V., Stockmeier, C., Overholser, J., Meltzer, H. Y., Kalka, S., Dilley, G., & Ordway, G. A. (1997). Reduced levels of norepinephrine transporters in the locus coeruleus in major depression. *Journal of Neurosciences, 17*(21), 8451–8458.

Kraus, R. P., Phoenix, E., Edmonds, M. W., Nicholson, I. R., Chandarana, P. C., & Tokmakejian, S. (1997). Exaggerated TSH responses to TRH in depressed patients with "normal" baseline. *Journal of Clinical Psychiatry, 58*(6), 266–270.

Krishnan, K. R. R., Rayasam, K., Reed, D., Smith, M., Chappell, P., Saunders, W., Ritchie, J., Carroll, B., & Nemeroff, C. B. (1993). The corticotropin releasing factor stimulation test in patients with major depression: Relationship to dexamethasone suppression test results. *Depression, 1,* 133–136.

Lam, R. W., Zis, A. P., Grewal, A., Delgado, P. L., Charney, D. S., & Krystal, J. H. (1996). Effects of rapid tryptophan depletion in patients with seasonal affective disorder in remission after light therapy. *Archives of General Psychiatry, 53*(1), 41–44.

Lawrence, K. M., DePaermentier, F., Cheetham, S. C., Crompton, M. R., Katona, C. L. E., & Horton, R. W. (1990). Brain 5-HT uptake sites, labelled with [3H]paroxetine, in antidepressant-free depressed suicides. *Brain Research, 526,* 17–22.

Leake, A., Fairbairn, A. F., McKeith, I. G., & Ferrier, I. N. (1991). Studies on the serotonin uptake binding site in major depressive disorder and control post-mortem brain: Neurochemical and clinical correlates. *Psychiatric Research, 39,* 155–165.

Lesch, K. P., Bengel, D., Heils, A., Sabol, S. Z., Greenberg, B. D., Petri, S., Benjamin, J., Muller, C. R., Hamer, D. H., & Murphy, D. L. (1996). Association of anxiety-related traits with a polymorphism in the serotonin transporter gene regulatory region. *Science, 274,* 1257–1231.

Lesch, K. P., Wolozin, B. L., Murphy, D. L., & Riederer, P. (1993). Primary structure of the human platelet serotonin uptake site: Identity with the brain serotonin transporter. *Journal of Neurochemistry, 60,* 2319–2322.

Leyton, M., Young, S. N., & Benkelfat, C. (1997).Relapse of depression after rapid depletion of tryptophan. *Lancet, 349,* 1840–1841.

Leyton, M., Young, S. N., Blier, P., Ellenbogen, M. A., Palmour, R. M., Ghadirian, A. M., & Benkelfat, C. (1997). The effect of tryptophan depletion on mood in medication-free, former patients with major affective disorder. *Neuropsychopharmacology, 16*(4), 294–297.

Little, K. Y. (1988). Amphetamine, but not methylphenidate, predicts antidepressant response. *Journal of Clinical Psychopharmacology, 8,* 177–183.

Little, K. Y., McLauglin, D. P., Ranc, J., Gilmore, J., Lopez, J. F., Watson, S. J., Carroll, F. I., & Butts, J. D. (1997). Serotonin transporter binding sites and mRNA levels in depressed persons committing suicide. *Biological Psychiatry, 41*(12), 1156–1164.

Lowther, S., De Paermentier, F., Cheetham, S. C., Crompton, M. R., Katona, C. L., & Horton, R. W. (1997). 5-HT1A receptor binding sites in post-mortem brain samples from depressed suicides and controls. *Journal of Affective Disorders, 42*(2–3),199–207.

Lowther, S., De Paermentier, F., Crompton, M., Katona, C., & Horton, R. (1994). Brain 5-HT2 receptors in suicide victims: Violence of death, depression and effects of antidepressant treatment. *Brain Research, 642,* 281–289.

Maas, J. W., Fawcett, J. A., & Dekirmenjian, H. (1972). Catecholamine metabolism, depressive illness and drug response. *Archives of General Psychiatry, 26,* 252–262.

Maes, M., De Ruyter, M., & Suy, E. (1987). The renal excretion of xanthurenic acid following L-tryptophan loading in depressed patients. *Human Psychopharmacology, 2,* 231–235.

Maes, M., Jacobs, M.-P., Suy, E., Minner, B., Leclercq, C., Christiaens, F., & Raus, J. (1990). Suppressant effects of dexamethasone on the availability of plasma L-tryptophan and tyrosine in healthy controls and depressed patients. *Acta Psychiatr Scand, 81,* 19–23.

Maes, M., & Meltzer, H. Y. (1995). The serotonin hypothesis of major depression. In F. E. Bloom & D. J. Kupfer (Eds.), *Psychopharmacology: The fourth generation of progress* (pp. 933–944). New York: Raven Press.

Maes, M., Van Gastel, A., Delmeire, L., & Meltzer, H. Y. (1999). Decreased platelet alpha-2 adrenoceptor density in major depression: Effects of tricyclic antidepressants and fluoxetine. *Biological Psychiatry, 45*(3), 278–284.

Maj, M., Ariano, M. G., Arena, F., & Kemali, D. (1984). Plasma cortisol, catecholamine and cyclic AMP levels, response to dexamethasone suppression test and platelet MAO activity in manic-depressive patients: A longitudinal study. *Neuropsychobiology, 11*(3), 168–173.

Malison, R. T., Price, L. H., Berman, R., van Dyck, C. H., Pelton, G. H., Carpenter, L., Sanacora, G., Owens, M. J., Nemeroff, C. B., Rajeevan, N., Baldwin, R. M., Seibyl, J. P., Innis, R. B., & Charney, D. S. (1998). Reduced brain serotonin transporter availability in major depression as measured by [123I]-2-beta-carbomethoxy-3 beta-(4-iodophenyl)tropane and single photon emission computed tomography. *Biological Psychiatry, 44*(11), 1090–1098.

Malone, K. M., Thase, M. E., Mieczkowski, T., Myers, J. E., Stull, S. D., Cooper, T. B., & Mann, J. J. (1993). Fenfluramine challenge test as predictor of outcome in major depression. *Psychopharmacology Bulletin, 29*(2), 155–161.

Mann, J., McBride, P., Brown, R., Linnoila, M., Leon, A., DeMeo, M., Mieczkowski, T., Myers, J., & Stanley, M. (1992). Relationship between central and peripheral serotonin indexes in depressed and suicidal psychiatric inpatients. *Archives of General Psychiatry, 49,* 442–446.

Mann, J., Stanley, M., McBride, A., & McEwen, B. (1986). Increased serotonin2 and ß-adrenergic receptor binding in the frontal cortices of suicide victims. *Archives of General Psychiatry, 43,* 954–959.

Mann, J. J., Malone, K. M., Diehl, D. J., Perel, J., Cooper, T. B., & Mintun, M. A. (1996). Demonstration in vivo of reduced serotonin responsivity in the brain of untreated depressed patients. *American Journal of Psychiatry, 153*(2), 174–182.

Marangell, L. B., George, M. S., Callahan, A. M., Ketter, T. A., Pazzaglia, P. J., L'Herrou, T. A., Leverich, G. S., & Post, R. M. (1997). Effects of intrathecal thyrotropin-releasing hormone (protirelin) in refractory depressed patients. *Archives of General Psychiatry, 54*(3), 214–222.

Massou, J. M., Trichard, C., Attar-Levy, D., Feline, A., Corruble, E., Beaufils, B., & Martinot, J. L. (1997). Frontal 5-HT2A receptors studied in depressive patients during chronic treatment by selective serotonin reuptake inhibitors. *Psychopharmacology, 133*(1), 99–101.

Matsubara, S., Arora, R. C., & Meltzer, H. Y. (1991). Serotonergic measures in suicide brain: 5-HT1A binding sites in frontal cortex of suicide victims. *J Neural Transm, 85,* 181–194.

McBride, P., Brown, R., DeMeo, M., Keilp, J., Mieczkowski, T., & Mann, J. (1994). The relationship of platelet 5-HT2 receptor indices to major depressive disorder, personality traits, and suicidal behavior. *Biological Psychiatry, 35,* 295–308.

McKeith, I., Marshall, E., Ferrier, I., Armstrong, M., Kennedy, W., Perry, R., Perry, E., & Eccleston, D. (1987). 5-HT receptor binding in post-mortem brain from patients with affective disorder. *Journal of Affective Disorders, 13,* 67–74.

Meana, J. J., Barturen, F., & Garcia-Sevilla, J. A. (1992). Alpha 2-adrenoceptors in the brain of suicide victims: Increased receptor density associated with major depression. *Biological Psychiatry, 31*(5), 471–490.

Meltzer, H. Y., & Lowy, M. T. (1987). The serotonin hypothesis of depression In H. Y. Meltzer (Ed.), *Psychopharmacology: The third generation of progress* (pp. 513–526). New York: Raven Press.

Meyer, J. H., Kapur, S., Houle, S., DaSilva, J., Owczarek, B., Brown, G. M., Wilson, A. A., & Kennedy, S. H. (1999). Prefrontal cortex 5-HT2 receptors in depression: An [18F]setoperone PET imaging study. *American Journal of Psychiatry, 156*(7), 1029–1034.

Miller, H. L., Delgado, P. L., Salomon, R. M., Berman, R., Krystal, J. H., Heninger, G. R., & Charney, D. S. (1996). Clinical and biochemical effects of catecholamine depletion on antidepressant-induced remission of depression. *Archives of General Psychiatry, 53*(2), 117–128.

Miller, H. L., Delgado, P. L., Salomon, R. M., Heninger, G. R., & Charney, D. S. (1996). Effects of alpha-methyl-paratyrosine (AMPT) in drug-free depressed patients. *Neuropsychopharmacology, 14*(3), 151–157.

Mitchell, P., & Smythe, G. (1990). Hormonal responses to fenfluramine in depressed and control subjects. *Journal of Affective Disorders, 19*(1), 43–51.

Mitchell, P. B., Bearn, J. A., Corn, T. H., & Checkley, S. A. (1988). Growth hormone response to clonidine after recovery in patients with endogenous depression. *British Journal of Psychiatry, 152,* 34–38.

Moore, P., Gillin, C., Bhatti, T., DeModena, A., Seifritz, E., Clark, C., Stahl, S., Rapaport, M., & Kelsoe, J. (1998). Rapid tryptophan depletion, sleep electroencephalogram, and mood in men with remitted depression on serotonin reuptake inhibitors. *Archives of General Psychiatry, 55*(6), 534–539.

Murphy, D. L. (1972). l-DOPA, behavioral activation and psychopathology. *Res Publ Ass Res Nerv Ment Dis, 50,* 430–437.

Murray, J. B. (1996). Depression in Parkinson's disease. *Journal of Psychology, 130*(6), 659–667.

Nemeroff, C. B. (1996). The corticotropin-releasing factor (CRF) hypothesis of depression: New findings and new directions. *Mol Psychiatry, 1*(4), 336–342.

Nemeroff, C. B., Bissette, G., Akil, H., & Fink, M. (1991).

Neuropeptide concentrations in cerebrospinal fluid of depressed patients treated with electroconvulsive therapy: Corticotropin-releasing factor, B-endorphin and somatostatin. *British Journal of Psychiatry, 158*, 59–63.

Nemeroff, C. B., Knight, D. L., Franks, J., Craighead, W. E., & Krishnan, K. R. (1994). Further studies on platelet serotonin transporter binding in depression. *American Journal of Psychiatry, 151*(11), 1623–1625.

Nemeroff, C. B., Knight, D. L., Krishnan, R. R., Slotkin, T. A., Bissette, G., Melville, M. L., & Blazer, D. G. (1988). Marked reduction in the number of platelet-tritiated imipramine binding sites in geriatric depression. *Archives of General Psychiatry, 45*(10), 919–923.

Nemeroff, C. B., Owens, M. J., Bissette, G., Andorn, A. C., & Stanley, M. (1988). Reduced corticotropin releasing factor binding sites in the frontal cortex of suicide victims. *Archives of General Psychiatry, 45*(6), 577–579.

Nemeroff, C. B., Widerlov, E., Bissette, G., Walleus, H., Karlsson, I., Eklund, K., Kilts, C. D., Loosen, P. T., & Vale, W. (1984). *Science, 226*(4680), 1342–1344.

O'Keane, V., & Dinan, T. G. (1991). Prolactin and cortisol responses to d-fenfluramine in major depression: Evidence of diminished responsivity of central serotonergic function. *American Journal of Psychiatry, 148*(8), 1009–1015.

Ordway, G. A. (1997). Pathophysiology of the locus coeruleus in suicide. *Annals of the New York Academy of Sciences, 836*, 233–252.

Owen, F., Chambers, D., Cooper, S., Crow, T., Johnson, J., Lofthouse, R., & Poulter, M. (1986). Serotonergic mechanisms in brains of suicide victims. *Brain Research, 362*, 185–188.

Pandey, G. N., Pandey, S. C., Dwivedi, Y., Sharma, R. P., Janicak, P. G., & Davis, J. M. (1995). Platelet serotonin-2A receptors: A potential biological marker for suicidal behavior. *American Journal of Psychiatry, 152*(6), 850–855.

Pandey, G. N., Pandey, S. C., Janicak, P. G., Marks, R. C., & Davis, J. M. (1990). Platelet serotonin-2 receptor binding sites in depression and suicide. *Biological Psychiatry, 28*, 215–222.

Perry, E. K., Marshall, E. F., Blesseo, G., Tomlinson, B. E., & Perry, R. H. (1983). Decreased imipramine binding in the brains of patients with depressive illness. *British Journal of Psychiatry, 142*, 188–192.

Pichot, W., Ansseau, M., Gonzalez Moreno, A., Hansenne, M., & von Frenckell, R. (1992). Dopaminergic function in panic disorder: Comparison with major and minor depression. *Biological Psychiatry, 32*(11), 1004–1011.

Pichot, W., Hansenne, M., Gonzalez Moreno, A., & Ansseau, M. (1995). Growth hormone response to apomorphine in panic disorder: Comparison to major depression and normal controls. *European Arch Psych Clin Neuroscience, 245*(6), 306–308.

Plotsky, P. M., Owens, M. J., & Nemeroff, C. B. (1995). Neuropeptide alterations in mood disorders. In F. E. Bloom & D. J. Kupfer (Eds.), *Psychopharmacology: The fourth generation of progress* (pp. 971–981). New York: Raven Press.

Potter, W. Z., Karoum, F., & Linnoila, M. (1984). Common mechanisms of action of biochemically "specific" antidepressants. *Prog Neuropsychopharmacol Biol Psychiatry, 8*, 153–161.

Prange, A. (1964). The pharmacology and biochemistry of depression. *Diseases of the Central Nervous System, 25*, 217–221.

Prange, A. J., Lara, P. P., Wilson, I. C., Alltop, L. B., & Breese, G. R. (1972). Effects of thyrotropin-releasing hormone in depression. *Lancet, 2*(785), 999–1002.

Price, L. H., Charney, D. S., Delgado, P. L., & Heninger, G. R. (1991). Serotonin function and depression: Neuroendocrine and mood responses to intravenous L-tryptophan in depressed patients and healthy comparison subjects. *American Journal of Psychiatry, 148*(11), 1518–1525.

Raadsheer, F. C., van Heerikhuize, J. J., Lucassen, P. J., Hoogendijk, W. J., Tilders, F. J., & Swaab, D. F. (1995). Corticotropin-releasing hormone mRNA levels in paraventricular nucleus of patients with Alzheimer's disease and depression. *American Journal of Psychiatry, 152*(9), 1372–1379.

Reddy, P. L., Khanna, S., Subash, M. N., Channabasavanna, M. N., & Sridhara Rama Rao, B. S. (1992). CSF amine metabolites in depression. *Biological Psychiatry, 31*, 112–118.

Rothschild, A. J., Langlais, P. J., Schatzberg, A. F., Walsh, F. X., Cole, J. O., & Bird, E. D. (1984). Dexamethasone increases plasma free dopamine in man. *J Psychiatr Res, 18*(3), 217–223.

Roy, A., DeJong, J., & Linnoila, M. (1989). Cerebrospinal fluid monoamine metabolites and suicidal behavior in depressed patients: A 5-year follow-up study. *Archives of General Psychiatry, 46*(7), 609–612.

Roy, A., Karoum, F., & Pollack, S. (1992). Marked reduction in indexes of dopamine transmission among patients with depression who attempted suicide. *Archives of General Psychiatry, 49*, 447–450.

Roy, A., Pickar, D., Douillet, P., Karoum, F., & Linnoila, M. (1986). Urinary monoamines and monoamine metabolites in subtypes of unipolar depressive disorder and normal controls. *Psych Medicine, 16*(3), 541–546.

Roy, A., Pickar, D., Linnoila, M., Doran, A. R., Ninan, P., & Paul, S. M. (1985). Cerebrospinal fluid monoamine and monoamine metabolite concentration in melancholia. *Psychiatric Research, 15*, 281–290.

Roy, A., Wolkowitz, O. M., Bissette, G., & Nemeroff, C. B. (1994). Differences in CSF concentrations of thyrotropin-releasing hormone in depressed patients and normal subjects: Negative findings. *American Journal of Psychiatry, 151*(4), 600–602.

Rubinow, D. R. (1986). Cerebrospinal fluid somatostatin and psychiatric illness. *Biological Psychiatry, 21*, 341–365.

Rubinow, D. R., Gold, P. W., & Post, R. M. (1983). CSF somatostatin in affective illness. *Archives of General Psychiatry, 40*, 409–412.

Salomon, R. M., Miller, H. L., Krystal, J. H., Heninger, G. R., & Charney, D. S. (1997). Lack of behavioral effects of monoamine depletion in healthy subjects. *Biological Psychiatry, 41*(1), 58–64.

Saxena, P. R. (1995). Serotonin receptors: Subtypes, functional responses, and therapeutic relevance. *Pharmacology and Therapeutics, 66*, 339–368.

Schatzberg, A. F., Orsulak, P. J., Rosenbaum, A. H., Maruta, T., Kruger, E. R., Cole, J. O., & Schildkraut, J. J. (1982). Toward a biochemical classification of depressive disorders: V. Heterogeneity of unipolar depressions. *American Journal of Psychiatry, 139*(4), 471–475.

Schatzberg, A. F., Rothschild, A. J., Langlais, P. J., Bird, E. D., & Cole, J. O. (1985). A corticosteroid/dopamine hypothesis for psychotic depression and related states. *Journal of Psychiatric Research, 19*(1), 57–64.

Schatzberg, A. F., Samson, J. A., Bloomingdale, K. L., Orsulak, P. J., Gerson, B., Kizuka, P. P., Cole, J. O., & Schildkraut, J. J. (1989). Toward a biochemical classification of depressive disorders: X. Urinary catecholamines, their metabolites, and D-type scores in subgroups of depressive disorders. *Archives of General Psychiatry, 46*(3), 260–268.

Schatzberg, A. F., & Schildkraut, J. J. (1995). Recent studies on norepinephrine systems in mood disorders. In F. E. Bloom & D. J. Kupfer (Eds.), *Psychopharmacology: The fourth generation of progress* (pp. 911–920). New York: Raven Press.

Schildkraut, J. J. (1965). The catecholamine hypothesis of affective disorders: A review of supporting evidence. *American Journal of Psychiatry, 122*, 509–522.

Schildkraut, J. J. (1973). Norepinephrine metabolites as biochemical criteria for classifying depressive disorders and predicting response to treatment: Preliminary findings. *American Journal of Psychiatry, 130*, 695–699.

Schildkraut, J. J., Orsulak, P. J., Schatzberg, A. F., Gudeman, J. E., Cole, J. O., Rohde, W. A., & LaBrie, R. A. (1978). Toward a biochemical classification of depressive disorders: I. Differences in urinary excretion of MHPG and other catecholamine metabolites in clinically defined subtypes of depression. *Archives of General Psychiatry, 35*(12), 1427–1433.

Shah, P. J., Ogilvie, A. D., Goodwin, G. M., & Ebmeier, K. P. (1997). Clinical and psychometric correlates of dopamine D2 binding in depression. *Psychological Medicine, 27*(6), 1247–1256.

Shapira, B., Cohen, J., Newman, M. E., & Lerer, B. (1993). Prolactin response to fenfluramine and placebo challenge following maintenance pharmacotherapy withdrawal in remitted depressed patients. *Biological Psychiatry, 33*(7), 531–535.

Sheline, Y., Bargett, M., Jackson, J., Newcomer, J., & Csernansky, J. (1995). Platelet serotonin markers and depressive symptomatology. *Biological Psychiatry, 37*, 442–447.

Shelton, R. C., Winn, S., Ekhatore, N., & Loosen, P. T. (1993). The effects of antidepressants on the thyroid axis in depression. *Biological Psychiatry, 33*, 120–126.

Siever, L. J., Murphy, D. L., Slater, S., de la Vega, E., & Lipper, S. (1984). Plasma prolactin changes following fenfluramine in depressed patients compared to controls: An evaluation of central serotonergic responsivity in depression. *Life Sciences, 34*(11), 1029–1039.

Siever, L. J., Trestmen, R. L., Coccaro, E., Bernstein, D., Gabriel, S. M., Owen, K., Moran, M., Lawrence, T., Rosenthal, J., & Horvath, T. B. (1992). The growth hormone response to clonidine in acute and remitted depressed male patients. *Neuropsychopharmacology, 6*(3), 165–177.

Siever, L. J., Uhde, T. W., Jimerson, D. C., Lake, C. R., Silberman, E. R., Post, R. M., & Murphy, D. L. (1984). Differential inhibitory noradrenergic responses to clonidine in 25 depressed patients and 25 normal control subjects. *American Journal of Psychiatry, 141*(6), 733–741.

Siever, L. J., Uhde, T. W., Silberman, E. K., Jimerson, D. C., Aloi, J. A., Post, R. M., & Murphy, D. L. (1982). Growth hormone response to clonidine as a probe of noradrenergic receptor responsiveness in affective disorder patients and controls. *Psychiatry Research, 7*(2), 139–144.

Silvestrini, B. (1986). Trazodone and the mental pain hypothesis of depression. *Neuropsychobiology, 15*(Suppl. 1), 2–9.

Smith, K. A., Fairburn, C. G., & Cowen, P. J. (1997). Relapse of depression after rapid depletion of tryptophan. *Lancet, 349*, 915–919.

Stahl, S. (1977). The human platelet. *Archives of General Psychiatry, 34*, 509–516.

Stanley, M., & Mann, J. J. (1983). Increased serotonin-2 binding sites in frontal cortex of suicide victims. *Lancet, 1*, 214–216.

Sullivan, G. M., Hatterer, J. A., Herbert, J., Chen, X., Roose, S. P., Attia, E., Mann, J. J., Marangell, L. B., Goetz, R. R., & Gorman, J. M. (1999). Low levels of transthyretin in CSF of depressed patients. *American Journal of Psychiatry, 156*(5), 710–715.

Swann, A. C., Koslow, S. H., Katz, M. M., Maas, J. W., Javaid, J., Secunda, S. K., & Robins, E. (1987). Lithium carbonate treatment of mania. *Archives of General Psychiatry, 44*(4), 345–354.

Thakore, J. H., O'Keane, V., & Dinan, T. G. (1996). D-fenfluramine-induced prolactin responses in mania: Evidence for serotonergic subsensitivity. *American Journal of Psychiatry, 153*(11), 1460–1463.

Traskman, L., Asberg, M., Bertilsson, L., & Sjostrand, L. (1981). Monoamine metabolites in CSF and suicidal behavior. *Archives of General Psychiatry, 38*(6), 631–636.

Van Praag, H. M. (1982). Depression, suicide, and the metabolites of serotonin in the brain. *J Affect Disord, 4*, 21–29.

Van Praag, H. M., Korf, J., Lakke, J., & Schut, T. (1975). Dopamine metabolism in depression, psychoses, and Parkinson's disease: The problem of specificity of biological variables in behavior disorders. *Psychol Med, 5*, 138–146.

Virkkunen, M., Eggert, M., Rawlings, R., & Linnoila, M. (1996). A prospective follow-up study of violent offenders and fire setters. *Archives of General Psychiatry, 53*, 523–529.

Virkkunen, M., Goldman, D., Nielsen, D. A., & Linnoila, M. (1995). Low brain serotonin turnover rate (low CSF 5-HIAA) and impulsive violence. *Journal of Psychiatry and Neuroscience, 20*, 271–275.

Virkkunen, M., Rawlings, R., Tokola, R., Poland, R. E., Guidotti, A., Nemeroff, C., Bissette, G., Kalogeras, K., Karonen, S. L., & Linnoila, M. (1994). CSF biochemistries, glucose metabolism, and diurnal activity rhythms in alcoholic, violent offenders, fire setters, and healthy volunteers. *Archives of General Psychiatry, 51*, 20–27.

Willner, P. (1983). Dopamine and depression: A review of recent evidence. *Brain Res Rev, 6*, 211–246.

Wilner, P. (1995). Dopaminergic mechanisms in depression and mania. In F. E. Bloom & D. J. Kupfer (Eds.), *Psychopharmacology: The fourth generation of progress* (pp. 921–931). New York: Raven Press.

Wirz-Justice, A. (1988). Platelet research in psychiatry. *Experientia, 44*, 145–152.

Wolfe, N., Katz, D. I., Albert, M. L., Almozlino, A., Durso, R., Smith, M. C., & Volicer, L. (1990). Neuropsychological profile linked to low dopamine: In Alzheimer's disease, major depression, and Parkinson's disease. *J Neurol Neurosurg Psychiatry, 53*(10), 915–917.

Yatham, L. N., Liddle, P. F., Dennie, J., Shiah, I., Adam, M., Lane, C. J., Lam, R. W., & Ruth, T. J. (1999). Decrease in brain serotonin 2 receptor binding in patients with major depression following desipramine treatment. *Archives of General Psychiatry, 56*, 705–711.

Yatham, L. N., Zis, A. P., Lam, R. W., Tam, E., & Shiah, I. S. (1997). *Sumatriptan-induced growth hormone release in patients with major depression, mania, and normal controls. Neuropsychopharmacology, 17*(4), 258–263.

Young, S. N., Smith, S. E., Pihl, R., & Ervin, F. R. (1985). Tryptophan depletion causes a rapid lowering of mood in normal males. *Psychopharmacology, 87*, 173–177.

Young, E. A., Watson, S. A., Kotun, J., Haskett, R. J., Grunhaus, L., Murphy-Weinberg, V., Vale, W., Rivier, J., & Akil, H. (1990). Beta-lipotropin-beta-endorphin response to low-dose ovine corticotropin releasing factor in endogenous depression. *Archives of General Psychiatry, 47*(5), 449–457.

# X

## Emotion and Health

# 55

## INTRODUCTION: EMOTION AND HEALTH

John T. Cacioppo

The proposition that emotion is a consequence of ill health is uncontroversial. A voluminous literature confirms that one of the best predictors of overall happiness in adults of all ages is health and physical fitness (Myers, 1992). This body of research further shows that emotions are especially stirred by ill health, chronic pain, fatigue, or threat of death. The underlying mechanisms for the effect of ill health on emotion are less straightforward and more fascinating than the effect itself, however. Maier and Watkins (1998), for instance, review evidence that an infection triggers a centrally orchestrated sickness response, which is mediated by vagal afferents and includes behavioral (e.g., lethargy), autonomic (e.g., fever), and neuroendocrine (e.g., cytokine) components. One's energy and affect are down when one becomes ill in part because one's cytokines (e.g., interleukin-1) are up.

The mechanisms by which cytokines affect the brain and emotion are also becoming clearer. Cytokines signal through the vagus nerve; they trigger small signal molecules that then diffuse into brain tissue, and cytokines themselves cross the blood-brain barrier. Once in the brain cytokines influence various neurotransmitters that impact moods and emotion, such as serotonin, dopamine, and norepinephrine (e.g., Dantzer, Bluthe, Laye, Bret-Dibat, Parnet, & Kelley, 1998; Weiss, Sundar, Becker, & Cierpial, 1989; cf. Sternberg, 2000).

The ill health of an individual with whom one is connected can also affect one's own emotions, which calls forth an entirely different class of mechanisms ranging from cognitive appraisals of the demands of caring for the individual to sympathic and empathic responses to emotional contagion (Hatfield, Cacioppo, & Rapson, 1994). Additional details about the various mechanisms by which emotion is a consequence of health can be expected in the coming decades. What they all have in common thus far is the notion that the emotions that result from health or ill health foster adaptive actions, self-regulation, and social coordination.

### Emotions as Determinants of Health

The proposition that emotion can influence health or disease has been more controversial in recent history. Socrates (496–399 B.C.) and Hippocrates (466–375 B.C.), however, regarded emotion as a determinant of health and disease. In the 3rd century B.C., the Greek physician Erasistratos diagnosed a young man's debilitating attacks as caused by an emotional affliction—lovesickness (Mesulam & Perry, 1972)—and to this day, across the doorway of the building housing one of the first pharmacies in Switzerland, is an inscription that proclaims cures for all but lovesickness. In contrast, for most of the 20th century, "medical" maladies of the ilk suffered by Erasistratos's patient have been viewed as falling in the realm of mental (see Part 9 this volume) rather than physical health, a view fostered ironically by Sigmund Freud's seminal work on the role of "psychic determinism" in somatic conversion hysteria.

Bodily symptoms thought to be caused by mental or

emotional disturbances came to be labeled as psychosomatic disorders (Alexander, 1950), to distinguish them from disorders that were more amenable to the extant medical knowledge and technology. Included in psychosomatic disorders was an assortment of disorders that shared the absence of a coherent biological etiology (e.g., essential hypertension, gastric and duodenal ulcers, migraine headaches; eating disorders, asthma, arthritis).

"Stress" seemed to have something to do with these disorders, but the concept of stress itself was vaguely (or circularly) defined. Operationalizations and measures across studies, especially across animal and human studies, were regularly so different (e.g., restraint, hypoglycemic, orthostatic, mathematic stressors) that results were difficult to compare or reconcile (Lovallo, 1997). Stressors were not always negative since positive as well as negative events were considered stressors in studies focused on predicting ill health (Holmes & Rahe, 1967). Further complicating matters, the measurements of stress within a given study were often so weakly correlated that they provided poor convergent validity for the construct of stress (e.g., Lacey, 1959). In short, neither emotion nor health was a simple, unitary concept, and the search for a singular universal mechanism relating emotion to health was doomed to failure.

## The Changing Landscape of Health and Disease

The beginning of the 20th century was a period when antibiotics were nonexistent, public health was underdeveloped, and germ-based diseases were among the major causes of adult morbidity and mortality. Only 4% of the U.S. population lived to be over 65 years of age, compared to over 17% today. Medical scientists at the turn of the 20th century focused on the major health problems of the day about which they could do something, with a remarkable record of success. By the end of the 20th century, public health improvements, widespread vaccinations, and advances in medical and pharmacological treatments had greatly diminished the ravages of infectious diseases. The fastest growing segment of the population is now older adults, with the number of persons under the age 65 in the United States tripling during the 20th century while the number of persons 65 and over increasing by a factor of 11 (U.S. Department of Health and Human Services, 1990).

While threats from infectious diseases demand continued vigilance (Garrett, 2000) and research and advances in molecular biology provide powerful new weapons with which to combat the devastation of genetic diseases (Kandel & Squire, 2000), entry into the 21st century has brought into prominence a new and looming set of health problems. The leading causes of death in industrialized nations are heart disease, cancer, cerebrovascular disease, accidents, chronic lung disease, pneumonia and influenza, diabetes, suicide, HIV infection, and chronic liver disease/cirrhosis (e.g., Blumenthal, Matthews, & Weiss, 1994). Chronic diseases are now the most frequent sources of complaints and the largest causes of morbidity and mortality in older adults. According to estimates by Luskin and Newell (1997), by the early 1990s individuals 65 and older accounted for 36% of all hospital stays and 48% of total days of doctor care in the United States. These percentages and the absolute costs are expected to increase as the elderly increase in numbers and in percent of the total population. Neither the paradigm of germ-based diseases nor the paradigm of simple genetic defects provides the best platform from which to attack chronic disorders with complex social, psychological, environmental, and behavioral determinants.

## The Emergence of a New Paradigm

The dramatic theoretical and methodological developments in the affective sciences enjoyed over the last two decades coincided propitiously with the increasingly apparent need for a better paradigm for health and disease in the 21st century. This convergence was not announced by a single individual or event but rather was realized independently by researchers worldwide from multiple disciplines. The cumulative growth and potential synergisms are astounding. Figure 55.1 depicts the number of published articles uncovered by Medline searches on the terms "emotion" and "health" of the National Library of Medicine database from 1966 to 2000. As can be seen, the increase in scientific interest in emotion and health coincides nicely with the changing landscape of health problems. From this work, a paradigm shift can be identified in which environmental stimuli and events affect health not by a direct effect on the body (e.g., germ theory) but through their effects on affect (e.g., "stress") and behavior.

Within this new paradigm, one of the most powerful

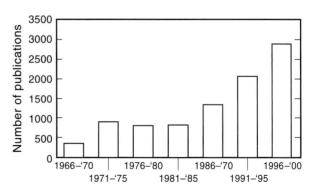

Figure 55.1 Number of publications per 5-year period from 1966 to 2000 on the topic of "emotion and health."

conceptual ideas to emerge is that the physiological systems activated by quotidian events can not only protect and restore but also damage the body. Claude Bernard (1878/1974) observed that the extracellular fluid constitutes the immediate environment—the internalized sea—for plants and animals. He noted the relative constancy of this internal milieu and regarded this constancy, and the physiological mechanisms that served to maintain it, as providing protection against the powerful entropic forces that threaten to disrupt the biological order essential for life. Without mechanisms to stabilize the cellular environment, organisms to survive would be confined to a limited ecological niche. In Claude Bernard's (1878/1974) terms, therefore, the existence of these mechanisms permitted warm-blooded creatures to live a free and independent existence.

Extending this perspective, Walter Cannon (1939) equated adaptive reactions with homeostatic processes that maintained the constancy of the fluid matrix (cf. Berntson & Cacioppo, 2000). Cannon argued that the variations from basal physiological levels ("set points") do not reach the dangerous extremes that impair the functions of the cells or threaten the existence of the organism because adaptive reactions are automatically triggered to return the affected physiological system to a basal state. In the past couple decades, the mechanisms by which such adaptive reactions are achieved have been elaborated (e.g., Berntson, Cacioppo, & Quigley, 1991), and the concept of homeostasis has been extended to the notion of allostasis—the ability to achieve stability in the internal milieu through change (McEwen & Stellar, 1993; Sterling & Eyer, 1988).

Cannon focused primarily on the physiological basis of homeostasis, but he also studied the influence of emotional disturbances on various physiological processes. This latter work focused on what he termed the emergency reaction. In Cannon's formulation, autonomic and neuroendocrine activation associated with emotional disturbances serve to mobilize metabolic resources to support the requirements of fight or flight, thereby promoting the protection and survival of the organism.

Many of the powerful elicitors of emotion in contemporary society—personal affronts, traffic congestion, pressing deadlines, computer viruses, perceived injustices—do not require or even allow behavioral fight or flight, and the reactions in response to these events can substantially exceed metabolic requirements. Thus, a design for the brain and stress physiology that worked well in human evolution in terms of maintaining a constant internal milieu may have maladaptive aspects that have become discernible as civilized societies developed and life expectancy increased well beyond the reproductive years (Lithgow & Kirkwood, 1996). Hans Selye's (1956) pullulating work on the general adaptation syndrome provided early support for the notion that physiological activation in response to stressors is beneficial up to a point but excessive or prolonged activation may indeed have hidden costs.

Selye studied physical stressors in animals, but subsequent work underscored the importance of idiosyncratic construals (i.e., cognitive appraisals) of an event for the feelings, autonomic adjustments, and behavioral responses to the event (e.g., Lazarus & Folkman, 1984; Mason, 1975; cf. Scherer, Schorr, & Johnstone, 2001) as well as the temporal dynamics of the elicited emotions (Davidson, 1998). Acute (e.g., major life events) and chronic (e.g., daily threats and challenges) psychological stressors can have short-term protective and long-term detrimental consequences. The latter costs have been termed allostatic load, which represents an overarching mechanism by which emotions may influence health. Berntson and colleagues (in chapter 58) review the neurobehavioral processes underlying the idiosyncratic construal of acute and chronic events, and McEwen and Seeman (in chapter 59) review evidence of the value of the concepts of allostasis and allostatic load in research on emotions and health.

Ceteris paribus, negative emotions have a larger impact on the brain (Ito, Larsen, Smith, & Cacioppo, 1998), the viscera (Cannon, 1939; cf. Cacioppo, Berntson, Larsen, Poehlmann, & Ito, 2000), and social cognition and behavior (Cacioppo, Gardner, & Bernston 1997; Skowronski & Carlston, 1989; Taylor, 1991). With positive and negative emotions and their underlying substrates conceptualized as falling at the opposite ends of a single bipolar evaluative mechanism, focusing on the relatively potent and disruptive negative emotional processes to the exclusion of positive emotional processes made some sense. It followed from the putative reciprocity of positive and negative hedonic processes that reducing negative feelings was equivalent to increasing positive feelings, that what was learned from the study of negative emotional processes transferred directly and completely to positive emotional processes (but see Cacioppo, Gardner, & Berntson, 1999).

Understandably, given this historical context, the vast majority of research on health and emotion has studied the impact of negative emotional experiences on disease processes, with such studies outnumbering those studying positive, health-promoting factors 11 to 1 (Mayne, 1999). A long-standing area of interest has focused on the impact of psychological stress on cardiovascular activity (e.g., Tomaka, Blascovich, Kibler, & Ernst, 1997), neuroendocrine response (e.g., Cacioppo et al., 1995), and immune function (Glaser & Kiecolt-Glaser, 1994) as well as on mental (Folkman, Lazarus, Gruen, & DeLongis, 1986) and physical health (Cohen, Tyrrell, & Smith, 1991). A second major area of research has focused on the effects on physical health of negative emotions such as depression, anxiety, loneliness, hostility, and anger, as well as on emotional personality traits (e.g., neuroticism; e.g., Friedman &

Booth-Kewley, 1987; Miller, Smith, Turner, Guijarro, & Hallet, 1996). These areas of study have been productive in identifying negative emotional factors that act as health risk factors, and for developing models explicating how such factors may contribute to disease outcomes.

This research has tended to focus on the impact of negative emotional experiences (e.g., "stress") on disease processes. Accordingly, one view to emerge from this work is that negative emotions are something to be avoided or, when aroused, to be diminished rather than to be made a kernel for brown study. It is not that negative emotions were thought to have no value in everyday life; it is that human fight or flight responses evolved in such a different ecological niche that the daily events in contemporary society were triggering maladaptive negative affective (stress) reactions. Indeed, many of the contemporary health problems have affective bases ranging from anxiety, anger, and depression to unrealistic or drug-induced feelings of euphoria and invulnerability.

The early stages of emotional processing involve attentional deployment, cognitive appraisals, and reappraisals (Gross & Levenson, 1997). As an emotion unfolds, action tendencies emerge along with supportive peripheral physiological adjustments. At this point, emotional regulation becomes response focused, largely through the suppression of the expression of the response tendencies that have been activated. Gross and colleagues have shown that suppressing one's natural expressions of an emotion results in more autonomic activation than either changing the meaning of the emotionally evocative event or simply expressing one's disgust naturally. Because suppressing one's emotional expression requires self-monitoring and self-adjustments, it also requires cognitive resources that could otherwise be allocated to other tasks such as solving the immediate problem or encoding associated events for future reference. Geise-Davis and Spiegel (in chapter 56) review evidence that the expression of emotions, even negative emotions, is also healthier than the denial or suppression of emotional expression.

In addition, emotions can foster health and well-being. Emotions are not disembodied abstractions without purpose or import, but rather they motivate and guide attention, thought, and action. What is it about the circumstances in which emotions enhance rather than diminish health? Factors such as self-esteem, self-efficacy, and resilience predict positive mental and physical health (O'Leary, 1990, 1992), dispositional optimism speeds recovery from breast cancer and heart surgery (Scheier et al., 1989), social support and hardiness facilitate well-being even in times of stress (Cohen & Wills, 1985; Wiebe & Williams, 1992), and greater social integration predicts longer mortality (House, Landis, & Umberson, 1988). Ryff and Singer (in chapter 57) note that emotions that foster health contribute to life meaning and purpose, quality social relationships, self-esteem, or mastery. They build on

this observation to examine the various roles in which emotion can promote health and well-being.

The past two decades have seen a dramatic rise in research on emotion and health. Investigations have moved from a paradigm in which environmental stimuli and events have a direct damaging effect on the body (e.g., germ theory) to one in which stimuli and events act on physical health through effects on emotion and behavior. Understanding the ways in which emotion influences health requires an integrative multilevel approach. Interest in integrative systems analyses fell out of vogue in the latter half of the 20th century, however, because it sits at the other end of the scientific spectrum from reductionistic molecular biology. The confluence of a changing landscape of health problems worldwide and the emergence of powerful multidisciplinary studies of emotion and health portend a return to integrative analyses spanning the cellular to the cultural levels of organization (Anderson, 1998; Cacioppo & Berntson, 1992). In this sense, the chapters in this part of the *Handbook* represent the wave of the future.

## REFERENCES

Alexander, F. (1950). *Psychosomatic medicine, its principles and applications.* New York: Norton.

Anderson, N. B. (1998). Levels of analysis in health science: A framework for integrating sociobehavioral and biomedical research. *Annals of the New York Academy of Sciences, 840,* 563–576.

Bernard, C. (1878/1974). *Lecons sur les phenomenes de la vie communes aux animaux et aux vegetaux.* Paris: B. Bailliere et Fils [Lectures on the phenomena of life common to animals and plants] (Translated by H. E. Hoff, R. Guillemin, & L. Guillemin). Springfield, IL: Thomas.

Berntson, G. G., & Cacioppo, J. T. (2000). From homeostasis to allodynamic regulation. In J. T. Cacioppo, L. G. Tassinary, & G. G. Berntson (Eds.), *Handbook of psychophysiology* (2nd ed., pp. 459–481). New York: Cambridge University Press.

Berntson, G. G., Cacioppo, J. T., & Quigley, K. S. (1991). Autonomic determinism: The modes of autonomic control, the doctrine of autonomic space, and the laws of autonomic constraint. *Psychological Review, 98,* 459–487.

Blumenthal, S., Matthews, K. A., & Weiss, S. (1994). *New research frontiers in behavioral medicine: Proceedings of the national conference.* Washington, DC: NIH Publications.

Cacioppo, J. T., & Berntson, G. G. (1992). Social psychological contributions to the decade of the brain: The doctrine of multilevel analysis. *American Psychologist, 47,* 1019–1028.

Cacioppo, J. T., Berntson, G. G., Larsen, J. T., Poehlmann, K. M., & Ito, T. A. (2000). The psychophysiology of emotion. In R. Lewis & J. M. Haviland-Jones (Eds.), *The handbook of emotion* (2nd ed., pp. 173–191). New York: Guilford Press.

Cacioppo, J. T., Gardner, W. L., & Berntson, G. G. (1997): Beyond bipolar conceptualizations and measures: The case of attitudes and evaluative space. *Personality and Social Psychology Review, 1,* 3–25.

Cacioppo, J. T., Gardner, W. L., & Berntson, G. G. (1999). The affect system has parallel and integrative processing components: Form follows function. *Journal of Personality and Social Psychology, 76,* 839–855.

Cacioppo, J. T., Malarkey, W. B., Kiecolt-Glaser, J. K., Uchino, B. N., Sgoutas-Emch, S. A., Sheridan, J. F., Berntson, G. G., & Glaser, R. (1995). Heterogeneity in neuroendocrine and immune responses to brief psychological stressors as a function of autonomic cardiac activation. *Psychosomatic Medicine, 57,* 154–164.

Cannon, W. B. (1939). *The wisdom of the body* (2nd ed.). London: Kegan Paul, Trench, Trubner & Co.

Cohen, S., & Wills, T. A. (1985). Stress, social support, and the buffering hypothesis. *Psychological Bulletin, 98,* 310–357.

Cohen, S., Tyrrell, D. A., & Smith, A. P. (1991). Psychological stress and susceptibility to the common cold. *New England Journal of Medicine, 325,* 606–612.

Dantzer, R., Bluthe, R., Laye, S., Bret-Dibat, J., Parnet, P., & Kelley, K. W. (1998). Cytokines and sickness behavior. *Annals of the New York Academy of Sciences, 840,* 586–590.

Davidson, R. J. (1998). Affective style and affective disorders: Perspectives from affective neuroscience. *Cognition and Emotion, 12,* 307–330.

Folkman, S., Lazarus, R. S., Gruen, R. J., & DeLongis, A. (1986). Appraisal, coping, health status, and psychological symptoms. *Journal of Personality and Social Psychology, 50,* 571–579.

Friedman, H. S., & Booth-Kewley, S. (1987). Personality, Type A behavior, and coronary heart disease: The role of emotional expression. *Journal of Personality and Social Psychology, 53,* 783–792.

Garrett, L. (2000). *Betrayal of trust: The collapse of global public health.* New York: Hyperion.

Glaser, R., & Kiecolt-Glaser, J. K. (1994). *Handbook of human stress and immunity.* San Diego: Academic Press.

Glaser, R., Pearl, D. K., Kiecolt-Glaser, J. K., & Malarkey, W. B. (1994). Plasma cortisol levels and reactivation of latent Epstein-Barr virus in response to examination stress. *Psychoneuroendocrinology, 19,* 765–772.

Gross, J. J., & Levenson, R. W. (1997). Hiding feelings: The acute effects of inhibiting negative and positive emotions. *Journal of Abnormal Psychology, 106,* 95–103.

Hatfield, E., Cacioppo, J. T., & Rapson, R. L. (1994). *Emotional contagion.* New York: Cambridge University Press.

Holmes, T. H., & Rahe, R. H. (1967). The social readjustment rating scale. *Journal of Psychosomatic Research, 11,* 213–218.

House, J. S., Landis, K. R., & Umberson, D. (1988). Social relationships and health. *Science, 241,* 540–545.

Ito, T. A., Larsen, J. T., Smith, N. K., & Cacioppo, J. T. (1998). Negative information weighs more heavily on the brain: The negativity bias in evaluative categorizations. *Journal of Personality and Social Psychology, 75,* 887–900.

Kandel, E. R., & Squire, L. R. (2000). Breaking down scientific barriers to the study of brain and mind. *Science, 290,* 1113–1120.

Kiecolt-Glaser, J. K., Page, G. G., Marucha, P. T., MacCallum, R. C., & Glaser, R. (1998). Psychological influences on surgical recovery. *American Psychologist, 53,* 1209–1218.

Lacey, J. I. (1959). Psychophysiological approaches to the evaluation of psychotherapeutic process and outcome. In E. A. Rubinstein & M. B. Parloff (Eds.), *Research in psychotherapy* (pp. 160–208). Washington, DC: American Psychological Association.

Lazarus, R. S., & Folkman, S. (1984). *Stress, appraisal, and coping.* New York: Springer.

Lithgow, G. J., & Kirkwood, T. B. L. (1996). Mechanisms and evolution of aging. *Science, 273,* 80–81.

Lovallo, W. R. (1997). *Stress and health.* Thousand Oaks, CA: Sage Publications.

Luskin, F., & Newell, K. (1997). Mind-body approaches to successful aging. In A. Watkins (Ed.), *Mind-body medicine: A clinician's guide to psychoneuroimmunology* (pp. 251–268). New York: Churchill Livingstone.

Maier, S. F., & Watkins, L. R. (1998). Cytokines for psychologists: Implications of bidirectional immune-to-brain communication for understanding behavior, mood, and cognition. *Psychological Review, 105,* 83–107.

Maslow, A. (1955). Deficiency motivation and growth motivation. In M. R. Jones (Ed.), *Nebraska symposium on motivation* (pp. 1–30). Lincoln: University of Nebraska Press.

Mason, J. W. (1975). An historical view of the stress field. Part II. *Journal of Human Stress, 1,* 22–35.

Mayne, T. J. (1999). Negative affect and health: The importance of being earnest. *Cognition and Emotion, 13,* 601–635.

McEwen, B. S., & Stellar, E. (1993). Stress and the individual: Mechanisms leading to disease. *Archives of Internal Medicine, 153,* 2093–2101.

Mesulam, M. M., & Perry, J. (1972). The diagnosis of love-sickness: Experimental psychophysiology without the polygraph. *Psychophysiology, 9,* 546–551.

Miller, T. Q., Smith, T. W., Turner, C. W., Guijarro, M. L., & Hallet, A. J. (1996). Meta-analytic review of research on hostility and physical health. *Psychological Bulletin, 119,* 322–348.

Myers, D. G. (1992). *The pursuit of happiness: Who is happy—and why?* New York: Aquarian Press.

O'Leary, A. (1990). Stress, emotion, and human immune function. *Psychological Bulletin, 108,* 363–382.

O'Leary, A. (1992). Self-efficacy and health: Behavioral and stress-physiological mediation. *Cognitive Therapy & Research, 16,* 229–245.

Scheier, M. F., Matthews, K. A., Owens, J. F., Magovern, G. J., Sr., Lefebvre, R. C., Abbott, R. A., & Carver, C. S. (1989). Dispositional optimism and recovery from coronary artery bypass surgery: The beneficial effects on physical and psychological well-being. *Journal of Personality and Social Psychology, 57,* 1024–1040.

Scherer, K., Schorr, A., & Johnstone, T. (Eds.). (2001). *Appraisal processes in emotion.* New York: Oxford University Press.

Selye, H. (1956). *The stress of life.* New York: McGraw-Hill.

Skowronski, J. J., & Carlson, D. E. (1989). Negativity and extremity biases in impression formation: A review of explanations. *Psychological Bulletin, 105,* 131–142.

Sterling, P., & Eyer, J. (1988). Allostasis: A new paradigm to explain arousal pathology. In S. Fisher & J. Reason (Eds.), *Handbook of life stress, cognition and health* (pp. 629–649). New York: Wiley.

Sternberg, E. (2000). *The balance within.* New York: Freeman.

Taylor, S. E. (1991). Asymmetrical effects of positive and negative events: The mobilization-minimization hypothesis. *Psychological Bulletin, 110,* 67–85.

Tomaka, J., Blascovich, J., Kibler, J., & Ernst, J. M. (1997). Cognitive and physiological antecedents of threat and challenge appraisal. *Journal of Personality and Social Psychology, 73,* 63–72.

U.S. Department of Health and Human Services. (1990). *Healthy people 2000: National health promotion and disease prevention objectives* (DHHS Publication No. (PHS) 91-50212.) Washington, DC: U.S. Government Printing Office.

Weiss, J., Sundar, S., Becker, K., & Cierpial, M. (1989). Behavioral and neural influences on cellular immune responses: Effects of stress and interleukin-1. *Journal of Clinical Psychiatry, 50,* 43–55.

Wiebe, D. J., & Williams, P. G. (1992). Hardiness and health: A social psychophysiological perspective on stress and adaptation. *Journal of Social and Clinical Psychology, 11,* 238–262.

# 56

## EMOTIONAL EXPRESSION AND CANCER PROGRESSION

Janine Giese-Davis and David Spiegel

Interest in the relationship between emotion and cancer began as far back as Galen's observation that cancer patients seemed melancholy, a term used for someone who was both depressed and emotionally reserved and nonassertive. More recently, there has been a literature suggesting that cancer patients or those likely to develop cancer are emotionally suppressive, especially of negative emotions such as anger. They have been characterized as the converse of "type A" personalities—hostile and impatient—who are at risk for heart disease. Cancer patients have been labeled as "type C"—unassuming and nonassertive, prone to suppress awareness and expression of their own feelings in the service of making others feel better (Temoshok, 1987), or human shock absorbers. This picture has been further complicated by a popular literature recommending a kind of emotional straitjacket for cancer patients, maintaining a "positive attitude." The implication is that giving in to fear, anger, or sadness constitutes yielding to the illness, and might actually promote progression of the disease in the body, a distortion of the Cartesian dictum *Cogito ergo sum* (I think therefore I am) to *Senti ergo sum* (I feel sick—distressed—therefore I am sick).

These popular misconceptions highlight the importance of solid empirical information about the relationship between emotion and cancer, and the delivery of clear messages to the lay public about these findings. Patients are actually struggling to suppress natural reactions to their illness or are avoiding discussion of these emotions with loved ones and physicians, out of fear that they may worsen their condition. Cancer necessarily evokes strong emotions in relation to existential issues, body damage, treatment side effects, loss of abilities, pain, fatigue, and a host of other problems. Research linking coping with these emotions and survival is easily misconstrued in ways that further burden patients.

In the current review, we will present a perspective on the associations between emotional state/emotional expression and its relationship to cancer incidence, progression, and survival. This review is not meant to be comprehensive, but is intended to highlight consistent themes, point out statistical and methodological shortcomings, and provide suggestions for future research in this area. Though our initial intention was to review only the cancer progression associations, many of the relevant epidemiological and prospective studies examine hypotheses that involve cancer incidence or onset, as well as progression or mortality, so we present both. Our conclusion is that the most consistent findings from converging sources highlight the importance of two constructs—depression and repression. Research largely supports the associations between (1) depression and/or closely related constructs of helplessness and hopelessness and faster progression of cancer or shorter survival, and (2) repression and cancer incidence or onset.

## Flexibility of Affect Regulation

Though not all studies agree, inflexible affect regulation skill may be the most parsimonious construct linking the results of many studies that have examined affect management and survival time with cancer. We assume that the ability to resolve depression demonstrates a flexible affect regulation system and coping skills. Likewise repressive-defensiveness is a rigid style that does not enable the working through of intense and changeable emotions. Our review of studies provides the following model:

1. Depression at diagnosis is normal and a denial of depression at this time (repression) is a risk factor associated with shorter survival.
2. The ability to change, to move from a genuine distress at diagnosis to lower distress over time, is a protective factor associated with longer survival. We hypothesize that lowering distress is not at all the same as repressing the affect or pretending to be happy. Instead, it is a genuine ability to experience the emotion but move beyond it.
3. However, staying depressed or in a helpless/hopeless and passive state is likely to be dangerous and associated with shorter survival. Chronic depression of this sort may reflect and also affect physiology, potentially weakening defenses against cancer progression.
4. Chronic affect suppression is likely to be a risk factor either mediating chronic depression or directly predicting shorter survival.
5. Self-efficacy with emotion may be a teachable skill allowing greater affect regulation flexibility. Greater self-efficacy with one's emotion regulation system may affect physiology directly and lengthen survival.

## Methodological Issues

### General Issues

Four principal weaknesses in the cancer survival literature have contributed to the conflicting conclusions in past reviews of studies measuring the associations between psychosocial variables and cancer incidence, progression, and survival (Fox, 1978, 1983; Gross, 1989; Holland, 1989; McKenna, Zevon, Corn, & Rounds, 1999; Mulder, van der Pompe, Spiegel, & Antoni, 1992; Spiegel & Kato, 1996):

1. Each study uses differing measurement scales, populations, control variables, and statistical methods, often not carefully assessing the multicollinearity of measured constructs.

2. Not only are measures inconsistent and often not replicated in these studies, but the same measurement tool is often called contradictory things in differing studies. For instance, depression as measured by the Minnesota Multiphasic Personality Inventory (MMPI) will be called depression in some studies, but in others called emotional expression because the participant was able to self-report a distressed emotional state. In addition, little attention has been given to clarifying how many separable dimensions these many measures reflect. For instance, it is unclear from this literature whether repression and suppression are overlapping constructs and likewise depression and helplessness/hopelessness.

3. Too much weight is given to one-time assessments rather than making use of multiple measures over time. If multiple evaluations were used, it would be possible to test whether the individual is able to change over time on these psychological dimensions (e.g., whether the measure reflects a state) or whether the response reflects a chronic style or trait. It is unfortunately the case in this literature that studies that measure psychosocial variables at multiple time points generally make no use of these additional data points or do so in a way that reduces statistical power so that finding associations would be quite difficult. Because of this limitation, there is not a single study that tests a process that reflects flexibility in coping response. We are advocating the use of the baseline (intercept) and rate of change over several measurements (slope) of a psychosocial variable. Though these measurements are often correlated they are not multicollinear (for example, correlations of slope and intercept of psychosocial variables in our randomized trial of metatastatic breast cancer patients were within a range of $r = .48\ -.51$). Calculating slopes in this way reduces error variance, minimizes the effect of missing data (Gibbons, Hedeker, Waternaux, Kraemer, & Greenhouse, 1993), and allows the investigator to predict survival from the intercept as well as the overall rate of change in the dimension. The intercept is also a preferable proxy for baseline assessment as it reduces the error variance inherent in a one-time assessment. We also advocate that this slope be calculated from multiple points prior to the targeted prediction period (as in assessing three time points prior to the "baseline") so that rather than being coincident in time, the slope precedes the predicted survival period.

4. There are wide discrepancies between results from studies relying solely on the self-report of participants compared to those assessing behavior (such

as those conducting clinical interviews with ratings, using the rated impressions of hospital staff, and collecting behavioral measures of compliance). This distinction is especially important when attempting to assess hypotheses regarding emotional expression or repression. For instance, repressors are persons who are hypothesized to be self-deceived (Weinberger, 1990) and, by definition, will report only positive things about themselves, will never rate a depression or anxiety scale high (Weinberger, Schwartz, & Davidson, 1979), and will have poor memory for emotional events in their past (Davis & Schwartz, 1987; Davis, 1990). Clearly, their self-reports will tend to skew the data from paper-and-pencil instruments or make interpretation confusing. However, because repressors are not particularly skillful at fooling others (Weinberger, 1990), behavioral measures are often more successful at achieving significant associations in prognostic studies (Temoshok et al., 1985).

## Separability of Constructs

In the history of research testing associations among emotional expression constructs and cancer incidence and progression, three main aspects of emotion have accounted for significance: (1) depression and helplessness/hopelessness; (2) fighting spirit; and (3) a category loosely combining repression, suppression, denial, restraint or conformity, and expression of emotion (Greer, 1985; Gross, 1989; McKenna et al., 1999; Temoshok & Fox, 1984; Watson, Haviland, Greer, Davidson, & Bliss, 1999). Though these may be potentially separable constructs, they also have undeniable linkages in most models of coping with a stressful life experience. For instance, just after a diagnosis of cancer, a normal grieving or period of depression might be expected (Dean & Surtees, 1989). However, if one's affect regulation style is to repress, deny, or ignore this dysphoria so that its existence is outside awareness, one may not report any feelings of depression. Without an acknowledgment or expression of this negative affect, anxiety may build to the point of outbursts of emotionality (Greer & Morris, 1975). Previously repressed affect may be more disruptive both because it seems alien and unbidden, separated from its initiating context, and because such a person is less likely to elicit social support. Additionally, if a person's style is to chronically suppress expression of these negative feelings with others around, the depression may be more intense (Classen, Koopman, Angell, & Spiegel, 1996; Giese-Davis, Hermanson, Koopman, Weibel, & Spiegel, 2000), or may linger longer than for those who have more balanced and expressive affect regulation styles.

In prior studies, it was difficult to construct a causal model to test because these interactions are possible and

most authors do not make use of longitudinal psychosocial data to establish a course of adaptation. A number of reviews have concluded that little can be made of the results because there are many inconsistencies in studies linking psychosocial variables with incidence, progression, and survival, (Holland, 1989; Petticrew, Fraser, & Regan, 1999). Temoshok (1987) and others (Greer & Watson, 1985) have proposed that confusion in the survival results may be secondary to measuring these constructs at differing points along the coping trajectory. There is little research that actually tests change over time in any of these variables, so it is difficult to disconfirm this interpretation. Likewise, there is also little evidence to support this claim.

### Separability of Depression From Helplessness/Hopelessness

Within the cancer literature, a distinction has existed between measured depression and coping involving a helpless/hopeless attitude, despite significant correlations between these scales demonstrated by the authors of the coping scale (Watson et al., 1991). Theoretically, a helpless/hopeless stance has always been part and parcel of the definition of depression (DSM-IV; American Psychiatric Association, 1994), with some self-report scales leaning more toward a balance of somatic and psychological symptoms, others leaning one way or the other. In studies where survival or cancer incidence results for depression parallel those for helplessness/hopelessness, one could make the case that the two constructs simply measure the same symptoms. In the cases in which the results do not, either there is a subtle distinction—such as between a behaviorally rated helpless/hopeless attitude and self-reported depression—or the psychometric properties of the measures may simply limit the ability to find significant differences.

Correlations and a factor analysis within our own current data among metastatic breast cancer patients enrolled in a randomized group psychotherapy trial ($N = 125$) using four scales that repeatedly appear in this cancer survival literature—(1) Profile of Mood States Total Mood Disturbance (POMS TMD); McNair, Lorr, & Drappelman, 1992, 1971); (2) Center for Epidemiology Studies—Depression (CES-D); Comstock & Helsing, 1976; Radloff, 1977); (3) Mental Adjustment to Cancer (MAC) Helpless/ Hopeless; and (4) MAC Fighting Spirit (Watson et al., 1988)—indicate that these variables are highly interrelated. Zero-order correlations show that CES-D and TMD correlate $r = .80$, and MAC Helpless/Hopeless and MAC Fighting Spirit $r = -.62$. Relationships between the MAC scales and the depressive symptom measures are also significantly related (each $p < .01$) but have a lower proportion of shared variance: CES-D with Helpless/Hopeless $r = .48$, with Fighting Spirit $r = -.35$, TMD with

Helpless/Hopeless $r = .37$, with Fighting Spirit $r = -.34$. A principal components analysis with oblique rotation using these four variables, however, found only one component with each of these loading above .70 (or $-.70$ for Fighting Spirit). Thus, while conceptually distinct, the scales appeared to be measuring overlapping constructs of distress, with about 50% shared variance. This is only one analysis based on 125 metastatic breast cancer patients. It does nevertheless illustrate the necessity for clarity with regard to these constructs when predicting survival, and caution when interpreting results for depressive symptoms, helpless/hopeless, and fighting spirit within the same data set without the presentation of a correlation matrix.

As a final note on the doubtfulness of the separability of depression from helpless/hoplessness, the researchers who initiated the measurement constructs of fighting spirit and helpless/hopeless coping (Greer, 1985, 1991; Greer, Morris, Pettingale, & Haybittle, 1990; Watson et al., 1988; Watson et al., 1994) have recently published the results of a large prospective trial utilizing both depression and their coping measures (MAC). Results indicate that their coping results (helplessness/hopelessness predicting lower 5-year event-free survival) are paralleled by depression results (Hospital Anxiety and Depression: HADS; Zigmond & Snaith, 1983), but that fighting spirit was unrelated to subsequent survival (Watson et al., 1999).

### Separability of Repression, Suppression and Related Constructs

Confusion about emotion inhibition concepts has always existed. For example, in his earliest writings, Freud interchanged the terms suppression and repression (in Erdelyi, 1990). Anna Freud (1966) and others later articulated the distinctions between conscious and unconscious processing that we have come to use as working definitions of the two terms. Suppression is a defense mechanism in which the person intentionally avoids thinking about disturbing problems, desires, feelings, or experiences; and repression is a defense mechanism in which the person is unable to remember or be cognitively aware of disturbing wishes, feelings, thoughts, or experiences (APA, 1994, pp. 756–757). Some have hypothesized that conscious suppression precedes automatic repression, as in recent research on trauma survivors suggesting that thought suppression of the traumatic event eventually becomes repression of trauma-related information (Koutstaal & Schacter, 1997). However, empirical evidence demonstrating this relationship is scarce. In lieu of such evidence, a number of empirical studies confuse the concepts and terms. This confusion is sometimes semantic, as when a researcher measures an intentional avoidance strategy for affect expression (suppression) but discusses results using the term repression (Fox, Harper, Hyner, & Lyle, 1994; Kune, Kune, Watson, & Bahnson, 1991; Petrie, Booth, & Davison, 1995).

However, some have argued that these distinctions are simply semantic (Erdelyi, 1990) and not likely to be predictive.

In a recent analysis addressing this separability issue, we demonstrated that, within a sample of 125 metastatic breast cancer patients, scales thought to measure distress, suppression, repression, and restraint were separable in a factor analysis and a multitrait, multi-occasion matrix (Giese-Davis & Spiegel, 2001). Our conclusion was that, at least in this sample, measures of distress, suppression, repression, and restraint could be used simultaneously as independent variables predicting survival without problems of multicollinearity.

## Outline of Our Review of Cancer Literature

In this review we focus on two areas: (1) findings relevant to *depression*; and (2) findings relevant to *repression*. Within each of these areas, we review studies predicting (1) *onset or incidence of cancer*, (2) *recurrence of cancer*, and (3) *mortality*. We then discuss whether intervening with education or psychotherapy affects survival, and possible mechanisms that may be responsible for the associations between psychological state and cancer progression.

### Types of Studies

The literature contains four types of studies that test associations between psychosocial variables and cancer incidence and progression: (1) long-term epidemiological studies in which psychosocial measures were obtained once and used to predict cancer incidence and mortality 5 to 30 years later; (2) studies assessing subjects just prior to a diagnostic evaluation and then comparing those whose diagnosis was malignant with the nonmalignant groups on psychosocial measures; (3) studies that compare subjects just after a diagnosis of cancer with other noncancer illness control groups; and (4) studies assessing psychosocial variables just following diagnosis of primary or metastatic cancer and predicting recurrence or survival from that baseline measurement.

#### Incidence or Onset

Establishing psychosocial links with cancer incidence or onset is theoretically tenuous unless large cohorts are followed prospectively. Even in such cases, psychosocial measurement issues may threaten the validity of the findings. For instance, most of these studies measure a psychosocial construct once and use it to predict cancer onset many years later. Trusting the validity of these associations would make sense only if that one-time measurement was a proxy for a chronic response style; however, in most studies there are no data that establish such chronicity (Penninx et al., 1998). In addition, researchers have sought to establish psychosocial links with cancer onset by assessing subjects at the time of biopsy and predicting subsequent diagnosis. These studies are potentially contaminated by the inability to control for subjects' differential internal expectation of a malignant diagnosis. Some subjects may already be in a reactive mode when answering questions prior to biopsy. In addition, subjects in the nonmalignant groups may be at risk for malignancies at later dates. A number of studies comparing cancer patients' emotional style just after diagnosis with other illness groups have found emotional expression differences purported to predispose cancer patients to the development of cancer. A methodological flaw has been pointed out dramatically by a study demonstrating a shift toward a repressive coping style following the diagnosis of breast cancer (Kreitler, Chaitchik, & Kreitler, 1993). This leaves open the possibility that what is being measured is merely a response to diagnosis or to the fear of diagnosis rather than a predisposing factor.

### Progression to Recurrence and Survival

Associating psychosocial variables at diagnosis with later cancer recurrence or survival has fewer methodological drawbacks. However, these associations are tested inconsistently in the articles available. Results are clearest in articles utilizing survival analysis techniques such as Kaplan-Meier (Kaplan & Meier, 1985) or Cox regression and life-table (Cox, 1972). However, a number of studies have significantly reduced their power to find results by dichotomizing their sample into groups of short and long survivors at arbitrary time points and conducting $t$-tests. Additionally, rather than conduct survival analyses strictly within the cohort studied, many of these studies utilize nationally published norms for particular cancers and sociodemographic groups to assess whether longer than usual survival has taken place. Lastly, we reiterate that only four studies make any use of longitudinal psychosocial data to predict incidence or survival (despite having collected it), and there is no case in which a slope of change over time has been utilized.

## Depression and Helplessness/Hopelessness

### Predicting Cancer Incidence: Depression Linked with Greater Incidence or Onset

There are at least 30 studies reported in the literature in which depression has been tested as a predictor of cancer incidence or onset, or in which comparisons between cancer and noncancer patients in levels of prediagnosis depression were assessed (see reviews by Cwikel, Behar, & Zabora, 1997; Hilakivi-Clarke, Rowland, Clarke, & Lipp-

man, 1993; McKenna et al., 1999). In at least six of these studies, higher depression level is significantly associated with increased incidence (three studies are reviewed). There are at least 14 studies in which depression was not significantly associated with incidence (5 of which are reviewed). Our choice of articles to review is based on our goal of highlighting specific theoretical or methodological issues and on a selection bias toward the greater validity of epidemiological studies to illustrate cancer incidence predictions.

In a prospective epidemiological study used to predict both cancer incidence and cancer mortality, Shekelle, (Shekelle et al., 1981) and later Persky (Persky, Kempthorne-Rawson, & Shekelle, 1987) reported on data collected in the Western Electric Study. In this study, 2,020 randomly selected middle-aged men employed by Western Electric Company in 1957–58 were assessed at baseline with medical and family history, a complete physical examination, chest X-ray, various laboratory measurements, physical activity, diet, and personality. Personality was assessed using the MMPI and Catell's 16 Personality Factor Questionnaire. With 17 years of follow-up, Shekelle showed that men who were depressed at baseline on the MMPI had a twofold increase in the odds of death from cancer compared with those who were not depressed. Persky extended these findings by utilizing 3 additional years of follow-up (20 years). She replicated the relationship between baseline depression and cancer mortality found in the Shekelle study using the depression score, but she also established a significant relationship between baseline depression and cancer incidence.

Although mean MMPI depression scores were only marginally significant in predicting cancer incidence, when she modified the depression measure to reflect a "High-D" profile, it did significantly predict incidence. This modification is important conceptually because it selected men for whom depression was greater than the other standardized MMPI scores on the nine clinical scales, and came closer to replicating a pattern of "High-D" scores tested by Blumberg (Blumberg, West, & Ellis, 1954). In this way, a primarily depressive symptom picture was being tested rather than depression secondary to other psychopathology. These results remained significant after controlling for age, family history of cancer, cigarette smoking, alcohol, occupational status, Body Mass Index, and serum cholesterol. Depression at baseline was more strongly related to cancer incidence and mortality within the first 10 to 14 years, than the final 6 to 10 of the 20-year span. This "High-D" profile was also associated with deaths owing to causes other than cancer. However, Fox (1989) has argued that the relationship between depression and later cancer in the original Shekelle study was actually due to a small cluster of cases involving workers employed in a confined space with exposure to polychlorinated biphenols, which are potent carcinogens. Thus he proposes that the work environment may have triggered both depression and later cancers.

Persky also tested the relationship between the MMPI Repression scale and additional personality factors from the 16PF, though found no significant personality associations. Critics have found her use of the Welsh repression scale (Watson, Plemel, Vassar, Manifold, & Kucala, 1987) and her control for defensiveness while testing these relationships a difficulty in interpreting these findings (Kune et al., 1991).

In a well-designed prospective study of 4,825 male and female subjects aged 71 and older from East Boston, Iowa, and New Haven, Connecticut, Penninx and colleagues (Penninx et al., 1998) assessed subjects at interviews in 1982, 1985, and 1988. Results of the interviews in 1988 were used as baseline measures of depression predicting cancer incidence 10 years later. The beauty of this study is that they did not assume that depression measured at one time point in 1988 would predict cancer incidence (and in fact, it did not). Instead, they used the two prior assessments to establish chronicity of depression. Only subjects who met a criterion of above a 20 on the CES-D at each of the three time points were deemed chronically depressed. In their sample, 146 people met this criterion. These people were significantly more likely to develop cancer than nonchronically depressed people. Importantly, they point out that in a number of prior studies depression and smoking were confounded. In their study they were able to separate smoking and chronic depression. In fact, the risk for developing cancer was higher for the nonsmokers than for the smokers. They comment that a single measure of depression is "not particularly stable and is more likely to misclassify persons as being depressed as a result of temporary stressful life circumstances or health problems present at that moment" (p. 1891). They document this inference with their result that only 25% of the 575 persons depressed at baseline were also depressed 3 and 6 years before their baseline. It is also likely that the physiological effects of depression (and other stressors) are cumulative (McEwen, 1998), so the stronger association of cancer incidence with chronic rather than acute depression may relate to severity as well as possible misclassification.

Lastly, in a pre-biopsy prospective study, Antoni and Goodkin (1989) investigated coping style and its association with diagnosis of cervical dysplasia. They studied 75 women from outpatient gynecology clinics and inpatient hospital wards who came to these facilities for workup for an abnormal pap smear including biopsy. After examination but before results were given to these women, they were interviewed and they filled out the Millon Behavioral Health Inventory (MBHI). It was their intention to replicate and extend their previous study (Goodkin, Antoni, & Blaney, 1986), predicting that personalities characterized by high levels of pessimism, hopelessness, social alienation, and somatic anxiety would be associated with diagnostic severity.

The cancer group had a significantly higher percentage of passive/helpless approaches to coping. In addition, MBHI scales of premorbid pessimism, future despair, somatic anxiety, and life-threat reactivity were all significantly higher in the cancer group. Because all of these scales were highly correlated (similar to our observation of coping and depression scales in our own study), authors combined these scores into a summative index. This index distinguished the cancer group from each other diagnostic group (benign, mild dysplasia, moderate dysplasia, severe dysplasia) except the severe dysplasia group (closest to a cancer diagnosis). Using this summative index, they show a remarkably linear relationship between this passive/distressed stance and their diagnostic categorization.

In addition, cancer patients were significantly higher on "respectful" style that emerged as the strongest predictor in a stepwise multiple regression analysis with all other variables. In summary, the greater the reported helpless distress the more likely the diagnosis was cancer. In addition, the more respectful or "conforming and cooperative, yet also likely to deny symptoms, repress emotions, and procrastinate on health matters" (p. 334), the more likely to have been diagnosed with cancer.

These articles illustrate several of our main theoretical/methodological points: (1) establishing chronicity of a psychological variable may change and clarify results as in the Persky and Penninix studies (Penninx et al., 1998; Persky et al., 1987), and (2) separating the construct of helplessness/hoplessness from depression may be unlikely to improve predictions and in fact combinations of such scales may improve predictions as in the Antoni and Goodkin study (Antoni & Goodkin, 1989).

### Predicting Cancer Incidence: Nonsignificant Findings

Although a thorough read of the literature confirms that the greater number of studies fail to find associations between depression and cancer incidence, we provide several criticisms utilizing the following examples. In the first two demonstrations authors utilized a one-time measurement of depression and failed to find an association with cancer incidence. Additionally, studies that attempted to link hospital admission for diagnosable depressive disorder failed to find associations with later cancer incidence. This effect may have been due to a combination of small sample size and short prediction period. And lastly, a meta-analysis using studies that compared breast cancer patients to controls failed to find a significant effect size. This analysis was for breast cancer alone and did not utilize large-scale epidemiological data.

Similar to our present argument, Zonderman et al. (Zonderman, Costa, & McCrae, 1989) also asserted that an assumption must be made that depression at baseline is predictive of depressive outlook, or a chronic coping style in order for an association with cancer incidence to be meaningful. They argued that depression measures may be "providing a relatively stable measure of depressive symptoms" and that if chronic depression is related to cancer, these scales should be predictive (Zonderman et al., 1989, pp. 1192–1193). In their epidemiological prospective study of the relationship between depression and cancer incidence and mortality they claim high test-retest reliability: a follow-up interview 10 years later confirmed that 83% of their subjects received the same CES-D classification, a finding at great variance with those of others (Dean & Surtees, 1989; Penninx et al., 1998).

In their study, however, they used a single (rather than an over-time) measurement of depression and found no significant associations between depression and cancer incidence or mortality as measured by either the CES-D or a few items from a General Well-Being Questionnaire (Dupuy, 1977). Their study differed from Shekelle's and Persky's in studying men and women ages 25–75, rather than just middle-aged men. Their sample was a nationally representative random sample, rather than a random sample from the same employer in the same geographic region. Because these studies used differing measures of depression it is difficult to compare them; however, Zonderman's sample size was sufficiently large ($N = 6913$) that it would appear adequately powered to detect differences that were quite small. Neither of these studies made use of a study design that measured change in depression status over time; therefore, we have no sense for the affect regulation or coping skills that might have intervened between a depressive symptom picture at baseline and the development of cancer.

Kaplan and Reynolds, in two prospective epidemiological analyses, tested the associations between depression (Kaplan & Reynolds, 1988) and social isolation (Reynolds & Kaplan, 1990) and cancer incidence and mortality. This study was based on the Alameda County study in which 6,928 adults were tested in the depression model and 6,848 in the social isolation model. Depression was tested using a measure created by Roberts (for example, Roberts, 1981). This scale is not a standard measure of depression, though it correlates with the Beck Depression Inventory. To be considered depressed, a person had to have a symptom score at least one standard deviation above the mean. Again, a one-time measurement was used. The incidence and mortality of cancer for this sample was compared with that for all of Alameda County and no differences were found. However, in their subsequent analysis, women who felt socially isolated were at greater risk for cancer incidence and mortality. This was especially true for women with hormone-sensitive tumors.

No associations were found in several of the prospective studies testing the association between admission to a psychiatric unit with an affective disorder and later cancer incidence. Evans et al. (Evans, Baldwin, & Gath, 1974) attempted to replicate a significant finding of higher cancer deaths in a psychiatric affective disorders population (Kerr, Schapira, & Roth, 1969). Both studies took place in the United Kingdom. Though they used similar methods, and utilized a sample of 823 patients, the 1 man and 3 women who subsequently died of cancer following their depressive episode did not exceed expected numbers in the local population. Criticism of this study includes the use of only a 4-year prospective window from the time of hospitalization, a very short time in which to develop and die from cancer. Classifications of affective disorders and quality of the hospitals from which the records were taken differed substantially. In a second study in Finland, Niemi and Jääskeläinen (1978), 191 patients, including 48 patients with bipolar and 143 unipolar diagnoses, were followed prospectively for an average of 10 years. No significant differences were found between observed and expected cancer incidence except for male unipolar depressives. In this group 7 as opposed to the expected 4.9 patients developed cancer.

McKenna et al. (1999) published a meta-analysis of studies measuring the associations between psychosocial factors and the development of breast cancer. This analysis included studies in which breast cancer patients were compared either pre- or post-biopsy to either a benign breast disease or a healthy control group. It did not include any of the epidemiological studies we have reviewed above. They concluded that for the 22 depression/anxiety studies included in the analysis, the mean effect size did not reach significance.

In summary, few studies find significant associations between depression and cancer incidence. However, this sampling of nonsignificant studies illustrates methodological shortcomings, making it difficult to trust that conclusion. In addition, because the association between depression and cancer incidence has often been tested without regard to coping strategy, an unclear picture may have developed.

## Predicting Cancer Incidence: Depression with Emotional Expression Linked with Lower Incidence

In our final review in this cancer incidence section, we include the possibility that higher levels of depression when accompanied by greater emotional expression and communication with supportive others may predict lower incidence. We include this study to illustrate that assessing levels of depression without the additional assessment of coping or emotion-regulation style may also mask or attenuate associations.

In another prospective cohort, 972 physicians were followed over a 30-year period (Shaffer, Graves, Swank, &

Pearson, 1987). All subjects were given a series of psychological tests and questionnaires when beginning medical school at Johns Hopkins University. An unusual clustering (hierarchical analysis) of these personality variables was used to produce five profiles. These profiles were then used to predict cancer incidence. A grouping comprised of those with both depressive symptoms and a greater use of emotional expression of anger had by far the least incidence of cancer (less than 1% of 151 subjects over 30 years). They called this group "acting out/emotional" and it combined higher parental control, depression, anxiety, and acting out. Subjects with the highest incidence of cancer were described as the "loner cluster." They were poor at forming interpersonal relationships and were considerably below the mean on good maternal relationships, average intensity of positive interaction potential, and intellectual interests. These "loners" were 16 times more likely to have developed cancer. None of these analyses controlled for demographic or medical variables. Because depression was not tested separately, it is impossible to sort out its relationship with cancer incidence in this sample. It appears as if it would be negatively associated with cancer incidence, however, since the acknowledgment of depression and anxiety at baseline were associated with less cancer 30 years later. Though the analyses are not traditional and the profiles unusual, this finding points to a distinction the other prospective studies have not anticipated. It is likely to be a far different experience physiologically and psychologically to become depressed but to have an expressive or angry coping style as in this clustering. To become depressed and retreat may lead to more dire consequences.

In summary, researchers have not found a convincingly strong association between depression and cancer incidence; however, the methodological issues we have highlighted also indicate that future research must more carefully address chronicity of depression, separability of similar constructs, and the addition of coping variables within prospective models before conclusions can be drawn.

### Predicting Cancer Recurrence and Survival: Depression Associated with Shorter Time to Recurrence, Greater Level of Recurrence, or Shorter Survival

We turn now to the prediction that higher levels of depression will be associated with greater cancer recurrence and shorter survival. Of at least 24 published studies, 15 find a significant association between higher depression and shorter time to recurrence or shorter survival. We review seven of these in this section and reviewed two of these (Persky et al., 1987; Shekelle et al., 1981) in preceding sections. Again, we also provide an example of one study in which higher depression with an emotionally ex-

pressive coping style predicted longer rather than shorter survival. At least eight studies find no significant associations, and we have reviewed two of these. Again our selection of studies to review will point out theoretical/methodological issues that future research could address.

First, in a small-scale prospective study, Levy and colleagues (Levy, Herberman, Lippman, D'Angelo, & Lee, 1991) assessed 90 women with early-stage breast cancer at baseline (5–7 days following surgery) and at 3 and 15 months postsurgery. They were then followed for a minimum of 5 (maximum 8) years. The role of social support, total mood disturbance (POMS TMD), and NK cell activity, along with standard prognostic variables such as age, number of positive nodes, tumor size, and estrogen receptor activity, were tested in path analysis models predicting both time to and presence of recurrence by the last follow-up. Although the strongest predictor of the presence of recurrence was low NK cell activity at the 15-month follow-up, time to recurrence was best predicted by a path from TMD at baseline, to TMD at 15 months. TMD was also negatively associated with NK cell activity at 15 months. Social support did not enter their model in either case. Levy's model shows the importance of chronicity of depression in predicting time to recurrence. When she utilized a model that integrated two measurements of depression, it predicted time to recurrence more potently than a physiological marker.

Second, in a prospective study of 69 female early breast cancer patients, Greer and colleagues (Greer, Morris, & Pettingale, 1979; Pettingale, Morris, Greer, & Haybittle, 1985), assessed patients through interview about their initial reactions to discovering the breast lump, characteristic response to stressful events, ability to express anger and other feelings, occurrence of depression, and loss of a significant person during the 5 years prior to the appearance of the breast lump. Data were obtained prior to surgery and at a follow-up examination 3 months postsurgery. Independent ratings of the follow-up interviews by two observers placed these women into four mutually exclusive categories: denial, fighting spirit, stoic acceptance, and helplessness/hopelessness. These assessments were associated with 5- (Greer et al., 1979), 10- (Pettingale et al., 1985), and 15-year (Greer et al., 1990) cancer progression and survival.

These four groups of women were distinguished by their coping: the deniers ($N = 10$) showed no distress and minimized discussion and acknowledgment of the seriousness of the diagnosis; women with fighting spirit ($N = 10$) maintained highly optimistic attitudes, actively sought information, and were also not distressed; women with stoic acceptance ($N = 32$) acknowledged the diagnosis but carried on with their lives and had overcome initial distress through their stoic attitude; and helpless/hopeless women ($N = 5$) were engulfed by knowledge of the diagnosis, felt as if they were dying, were preoccupied with cancer and death, were devoid of hope, and in obvious distress.

Five-year outcome was unrelated to many previously hypothesized constructs including depression as measured by the Hamilton Rating Scale, ability to express anger and other feelings, depressive illness during previous 5 years, extroversion and neuroticism, hostility scores, and delay in seeking treatment. However, favorable outcomes were more frequent at 5, 10, and 15 years in patients who were rated either in the denial or fighting-spirit categories, whereas unfavorable outcome was more common in stoic acceptance or helpless/hopeless categories (similar to endogenous depression). Very few subjects were categorized as helpless/hopeless in this study and many subjects categorized as stoic. Chi square analyses rather than survival analysis was used in the 5-year study; however, the 10- and 15-year studies utilized survival analysis and came to the same conclusions. Since no correlations between patient coping style and physiological markers were offered, it is not possible to sort out the alternate hypothesis that women were hopeless due to a poor prognosis. Though all subjects had the same TNM (a system of staging the tumor) ratings, little can be said about the realistic expectations of each woman given her particular tumor. No information on number of positive lymph nodes or disease-free interval, that have been shown to be powerful prognostic indicators, is reported.

Additionally, there are no correlations reported between the Hamilton Depression ratings, emotional expression, and these four general categories. Lastly, though psychological assessments were made longitudinally, there was no effort to use these measurements to establish chronicity or to show that change over time occurred. However, in a previous article describing change over time (possibly in this same cohort; Morris, Greer, & White, 1977), they indicated that denial and fighting spirit became less common by 2 years, whereas stoic acceptance was even more common at 2 years and was more stable over time. Patients in other categories of response tended to change category (p. 2385). This leaves open another interpretation to their findings. It is possible that those people in the denial and fighting-spirit categories are inherently more flexible in their coping style, utilizing a variety of affect regulation skills in a time-appropriate way. Others in the study may be more chronically set in rigid, unproductive, and unskilled affect-regulation patterns, such as chronic passive helplessness. A commonality between the women rated as fighting spirit and denial is that they reported no distress by 3-month follow-up. A commonality in their description of stoic acceptance and helpless/hopeless is a lasting acknowledgment of distress.

DiClemente and Temoshok (1985) successfully replicated Greer et al. (1979) by finding that in 117 patients with malignant melanoma, coping coded from an interview shortly after diagnosis predicted unfavorable outcome. Stoicism among women and helplessness/hopelessness among men predicted clinical status. However, Dean and Surtees attempted replication of their work (1989) and concluded that the interview ratings were insufficiently clear, and the ratings have since been revised into a self-report scale (Watson et al., 1988).

In this prospective replication study, Dean and Surtees (1989) found that higher levels of depression at diagnosis, but lower reported depression 3 months later predicted longer life in 125 primary breast cancer patients. All women had mastectomies and were interviewed prior to the operation. These women were interviewed and diagnosed using Spitzer's RDC criteria for major and minor depressive disorder, generalized anxiety, and phobic disorders. They were also asked about their marital and social relationships and coping styles. These assessments were repeated 3 months later. Six to 8 years after mastectomy, 37 women had recurrences and 22 had died. Using survival analyses, controlling for medical and prognostic variables, relationships between the psychosocial and demographic variables and (1) first recurrence of the disease and (2) deaths from breast cancer were examined.

These women were *less likely to have had a recurrence* if preoperatively they had been diagnosed as an RDC case—in other words, they met criteria for a psychological diagnosis, or they were rated as either helpless/hopeless or stoic, or they were unemployed. However, denial at the 3-month assessment also predicted a better chance to remain recurrence-free. *Survival was more likely* if women had been an RDC case preoperatively and were of higher social class. General Health Questionnaire distress at 3-month assessment was predictive of shorter survival. This is one of the only studies assessing a change over time and its association with survival. It found that distress indicated by RDC, GHQ, and coping styles preoperatively were associated with better outcomes; however, distress as indicated by GHQ and coping style 3 months postoperatively was associated with worse outcomes.

It may be that becoming depressed shortly after diagnosis is a normal, necessary, and healthy experience of grieving and adjustment; however, if the depression lingers it may indicate that there are not adequate coping mechanisms for its resolution. This latter more chronic depression could have more toxic endocrine and immune consequences than an acute episode. This study (Dean & Surtees, 1989) demonstrated that associations between depression and survival were not stable over time. They also observed that they could not differentiate survival results for categories of helplessness/hopelessness, stoic acceptance, and fighting spirit. This result mirrors our own correlations at baseline between measures of depression and MAC categories of helpless/hopeless and fighting spirit, showing a large degree of overlap with measures of depressive symptoms.

As mentioned earlier, a recent replication and larger-sample extension of their previous findings (Greer et al., 1979), Watson et al. (1999) assessed 578 women with early-stage breast cancer 4 to 12 weeks postdiagnosis and 1 year later. These psychosocial measures were then associated with time to recurrence and survival at 5 years. Helplessness/hopelessness was significantly associated with shorter event-free survival, though only marginally related to overall survival. High depression (HADS) was significantly associated with overall survival and became stronger when adjusted for prognostic factors. However, depression was not associated with event-free survival. Though not exact, these results indicate that their extended results are highly similar for both helplessness/hopelessness and depression, and they do not attempt to distinguish them.

In a study measuring symptom distress, psychosocial variables and lung cancer survival, Kukull et al. (Kukull, McCorkle, & Driever, 1986) assessed 53 patients with inoperable lung cancer with interviews and self-report measures 1 and 2 months following diagnosis. Survival was measured 4 years later, at which time 45 had died of lung cancer. The strongest predictor of shortened survival was the symptom distress score. This score measured a combination of physical symptoms (e.g., presence of nausea) and distress reactions to symptoms (e.g., level of concentration, appetite, insomnia). Those in the high-distress category lived an average of 13 months less than those in the low-distress group. They interpreted their finding as evidence that a depressive response to coping with diagnosis and treatment was a risk factor for early death.

In summary, a number of studies show strong associations between greater depression and faster cancer progression or shorter survival that appear, on balance, much stronger than associations between depression and cancer incidence. The studies reviewed in this section have utilized either clinical ratings or self-report of depressive symptoms. Few studies have utilized a diagnostic interview to establish an actual diagnosis, though several studies (which follow) have prospectively studied patients hospitalized for affective disorder.

Two studies utilizing patients hospitalized for affective disorder found that 4 years later these patients experienced a higher mortality from cancer than national norms would predict, though these are small numbers accrued in a short time span. Kerr et al. (1969) followed 135 patients diagnosed with affective disorders in the United Kingdom and found that 5 men compared with the expected .73 died from cancer. Mean survival time was 2.5 years beyond hospitalization. None of these patients had a history of chronic depression.

Whitlock and Siskind (1979) selected all patients over age 40 who had been admitted to a Brisbane, Australia, psychiatric unit for an affective disorder during a 1-year period. This affective disorder diagnosis could not be secondary to another condition. Four years later researchers attempted to contact these people or their relatives to discover possible deaths and their reasons. Deaths were checked against hospital and postmortem records. It was found that male depressed patients died of cancer ($N = 5$) more frequently than would be expected in the normal population. Females could not be adequately assessed as only one had died of cancer during the follow-up period. They comment that all patients who died had shown good response to antidepressant treatment.

Importantly, they speculate on the associations between depression and cancer, and we will close this section of depression review with their cautions: (1) depression may be the first sign of a small cerebral metastasis that has not yet caused any physical symptoms; (2) depression might be a nonmetastatic symptom of a hidden cancer; (3) neoplasms can cause endocrine disturbances that can cause biochemical changes similar to affective illness; (4) breast cancer can cause hypercalcaemia suggesting hyperparathyroidism; (5) parathyroid tumors are associated with depression; (6) pancreatic cancer can produce Cushinglike syndromes in which depression is a feature; (7) the effect of a developing cancer on general physical and psychological health may include depression; (8) depression compromises the individual's immunocompetence; (9) genetic research may ultimately find a common source for both cancer and depression. As future research progresses, it will be important to consider such etiology of depressive symptoms in cancer patients. Though studies have established relatively strong indications that depression and survival are related, the measured depression may reflect a physiological change secondary to disease status. It will be important to find ways to rule out this alternative hypothesis, and to assess whether changing depression status through psychosocial intervention affects survival.

### Predicting Cancer Survival: Nonsignificant Findings

Again, we present an example to illustrate methodological shortcomings in a study that failed to find associations between depression and cancer survival. Cassileth and colleagues (Cassileth, Lusk, Miller, Brown, & Miller, 1985), in a widely cited study, found no associations between a measure of hopelessness (and a number of other variables) and survival in a sample of 204 advanced cancers, and time to recurrence in a sample of 155 people with melanoma or stage 2 breast cancer. Cassileth chose psychosocial variables based on general population studies rather than prior cancer studies. The only variables tested that had been predictive of cancer survival in previous research were hopelessness and patient perception of amount of adjustment to the disease. Analyses conducted additionally dichotomized and combined variables in equations in such a way that multicollinearity is likely and power would be significantly reduced to find associations. This study was followed by a reanalysis in 1988 (Cassileth, Walsh, & Lusk, 1988) giving the subjects a few more years of follow-up and using better statistical controls and techniques. In this analysis, they found that those who indicated that more adjustment was required to cope with their illness (or possibly were not repressed) and those in the midrange of the hopelessness scale lived longer. It is interesting to note that those in the midrange of depression or hopelessness would likely be neither depressed nor repressive. Repressors would score in the lowest quartile, indicating that they are not distressed at all, while depressed would score on the high end. Not many studies have tested such a curvilinear relationship.

### Predicting Cancer Survival: Depression with Emotional Expression Linked with Longer Survival

Lastly, we again include an example in which higher depression but with an expressive coping style was associated with positive outcomes. Derogatis and colleagues (Derogatis, Abeloff, & Melisaratos, 1979) assessed 35 women with metastatic breast cancer at the second visit to the outpatient department following diagnosis of metastasis. The women participated in a 40-minute structured interview about their psychosocial adjustment and attitudes and expectancies toward the disease and treatment. In addition, they completed self-report inventories on adjustment (SCL-90) and mood (Affect Balance Scale). The interviewer completed several global ratings of her assessment of the patient's functioning, knowledge, and attitudes toward cancer. The treating oncologist also completed the same global ratings. They used these psychosocial variables to predict survival time of less or more than one year from baseline psychological evaluation. The women who had higher psychological distress at baseline survived longer. They reported higher levels of anxiety, hostility, and psychoticism and general symptom total on the SCL-90. Long-term survivors were significantly higher on all four negative affect dimensions on the Affect Balance Scale: depression, guilt, hostility, anxiety, and total score. The short-term survivors had higher scores on three of four positive mood states: joy, contentment, and affection. Oncologists' and interviewers' global ratings also mirrored these results, indicating long-term survivors had a "poorer" attitude toward their illness and their physicians, and were "more unpleasant and uncooperative," suggesting a greater ability to express anger. Though these psychosocial results were significant, no medical factors differentiated between the short- and long-term survivors in this study. Authors commented that the short-term survivors had a particular lack of hostile symptoms and generally higher levels of positive mood states but lower lev-

els of vigor. They conclude that the long-term survivors were distressed, expressed this distress, were more capable of externalizing their negative feelings, and did not suffer any self-image loss as a result of communicating in this manner. Short-term survivors were "distinctly less able to communicate dysphoric feelings—particularly those of anger and hostility" (p. 1507). These results are similar to Dean and Surtees (1989) in finding that baseline distress was associated with longer survival; however, it is not possible to ascertain whether this high level of anger and distress remained over the course of the survival period.

In summary, though there are some inconsistencies in study results, our conclusion is that a continuing state of depression once a person is diagnosed with cancer is a risk factor for shorter survival. Future research could profitably test whether the longer survival is associated with the ability to experience time-limited and event-appropriate depression upon diagnosis, but resolve that depression over the course of time. Future research could also profitably test whether depression mediated by higher emotional expression or greater emotion regulation skill is associated with longer rather than shorter survival.

## Repressive-Defensiveness

Clinical observation and empirical research have linked the incidence and progression of cancer with greater repression or suppression of affect (anger in particular; Bacon, Renneker, & Cutler, 1952; Bahnson, 1981; Blumberg et al., 1954; Fox et al., 1994; Greer & Morris, 1975; Greer & Watson, 1985; Gross, 1989; Jensen, 1987; Kneier & Temoshok, 1984), compliance (Goldstein & Antoni, 1989; Trunnell, 1952), unassertiveness (Kune et al., 1991), hopelessness (Bahnson, 1980; Schmale & Iker, 1966), denial (Bahnson & Bahnson, 1969; Derogatis et al., 1979; Schonfield, 1975), distress (Gendron, 1701; Greene & Swisher, 1969; Guy, 1759; LeShan, 1966; Paget, 1870; Parker, 1865; Schmale & Iker, 1966; Varsamis, Zuckhowski, & Maini, 1972), and recent life stresses or losses (Evans, 1926; Guy, 1759).

Until recently a valid and reliable repression scale did not exist (Weinberger et al., 1979), though clinicians have long observed and attempted to classify certain consistencies in behavior (Blumberg et al., 1954; Hagnell, 1966; Kissen & Eysenck, 1962; Kneier & Temoshok, 1984; Rogentine et al., 1979). These researchers' models lack clarity distinguishing between repression and suppression of affect, traits of overresponsibility, consideration of and conformity with others, and melancholy or distress (Fox et al., 1994), though there are consistent threads or constellations of symptoms in numerous studies. Replication of these findings has been limited both by the validity of measurement strategies and this lack of model clarity.

Several methodological issues are worth discussing before reviewing this literature.

## Self-Report Versus Behavior

Much of the research successfully documenting emotional expression/suppression and incidence or progression of cancer was based on interviewing patients and subsequently categorizing them into personality or coping styles that were assumed to stay constant over time (Abse et al., 1974; Derogatis et al., 1979; DiClemente & Temoshok, 1985; Greer, 1985; Greer & Morris, 1975; Greer et al., 1979; Grossarth-Maticek, Bastiaans, & Kanaziv, 1985; Hagnell, 1966; Morris, Greer, Pettingale, & Watson, 1981; Temoshok, 1985; Temoshok et al., 1985; Weisman & Worden, 1976). Additionally, studies in which the researcher has made a profile judgement based on a self-report scale have also been fairly successful at linking emotion-related variables and cancer incidence or progression (Blumberg et al., 1954; Graves, Phil, Mead, & Pearson, 1986; Persky et al., 1987; Thomas, Duszanski, & Shaffer, 1979). Studies using one-time self-report scales have often failed to find associations (Buddeberg et al., 1991; Cassileth et al., 1985; Zonderman et al., 1989).

Some of the studies reviewed below have tested connections with cancer progression using repression self-report scales and others test a clinical description encompassing many of the characteristics of the classic repressor. We take the time to discuss definitions of repression because it is often confused conceptually with a simple suppression of the expression of negative affect. Psychological and physiological distinctions between nonrepressors and repressors are more profound than this often inconsistently observed or reported trait. Because far more studies have found significant links between classic repression and cancer progression, we discuss its measurement first. We follow it with a discussion of emotional suppression.

Repression is an inherently difficult construct to measure since it theoretically derives from "unconscious processes" that make the individual unaware of, and therefore unable to self-report about, the connections between his or her affect and cognitions, disturbing wishes, and experiences (Weinberger & Davidson, 1994). It involves expelling disturbing wishes, thoughts, or experiences from conscious awareness through this lack of connection between the affect, which may remain apparent to others, and the person's own integration of that affect into a self-concept. As Weinberger (1990, p. 341) states, "repressive individuals are hypothesized to be persons who often believe that they are not upset despite objective evidence to the contrary." Measurement of this construct evolved from an earlier repression-sensitization scale (Byrne, 1961), which had methodological drawbacks. It correlated highly with trait anxiety and did not exclude people who were genuinely low in anxiety from the repression category. Weinberger et al. (1979) argued for the use of two scales to accomplish this goal of separating truly low anxious subjects from repressors—high scores on the Marlowe-Crowne (Crowne & Marlowe, 1960) to establish defensiveness, and low scores on the Taylor Manifest Anxiety Scale (Taylor, 1953) to establish low anxiety. And more recently, Weinberger (Weinberger Adjustment Inventory, Weinberger, 1990; Weinberger & Schwartz, 1990) created a scale measuring distress, repressive-defensiveness, and restraint. This scale circumvented difficulties in categorizing repressors who Weinberger hypothesized were not simply people who reported low distress and high need for social approval (Crowne & Marlowe, 1964) but were also high on defensiveness and restraint (Weinberger, 1990; Weinberger et al., 1979). Included in the restraint composite of the WAI are subscales measuring impulse control, suppression of aggression, consideration of others, and responsibility. Included in the repressive defensiveness composite are subscales measuring repressive defensiveness and denial of distress.

A wealth of empirical studies has established that "repressors" differ from the normal population in predictable ways, all involving this disconnection between their affective experiences and cognitive or ideational integration of those experiences into their self-concept. They have been found to have poor memories for negative emotional experiences (Crowne & Marlowe, 1964; Davis, 1990; Valliant, 1990), to rigidly self-report low distress (Kahn & Schill, 1971; Watson & Clark, 1984) regardless of direct physiological feedback to the contrary, to rigidly self-report even higher self-esteem in the face of negative feedback (Schneider & Turkat, 1975) or stressful tasks (Kiecolt-Glaser & Greenberg, 1983; Weinberger et al., 1979) than under resting or calm conditions, to avoid in an effortful way any disconfirming evidence that their self-concept is not accurate (Altrocchi, Parsons, & Dickoff, 1960; Weinberger et al., 1979), to define themselves as people who do not become upset (Weinberger et al., 1979), to have difficulty in consistently and accurately self-monitoring their behavior (Kiecolt-Glaser & Murray, 1980), to be primarily self-deceptive rather than other-deceptive (Crowne & Marlowe, 1964; Milham & Kellogg, 1980), to be more gullible (Crowne & Marlowe, 1964), less empathic (Weinberger, 1990), and to be particularly unresponsive to psychotherapy not only by dropping out early (Crowne & Marlowe, 1964) but also by failing to believe that there is any reason for them to change (Kiecolt-Glaser & Murray, 1980).

It is clear that the style of measurement used is crucial in studies testing the hypothesis that repression is linked to cancer progression. Psychometrically weak and unreliable scales (Watson et al., 1987), those not controlling for anxiety (Byrne, 1961), and those which would require a person to self-report accurately about this trait are very unlikely to accurately test this hypothesis. Repressive-defensiveness as measured by the Weinberger (Weinberger, 1990) or the combination of the Marlowe-Crowne and the Taylor Manifest Anxiety scales (Weinberger et al., 1979) is likely to have the greatest psychometric validity and reliability (Turvey & Salovey, 1993–94) in tests of this hypothesis.

In lieu of these scales, the construct can be identified clinically through a constellation of indicators including (1) poor memory for emotional events (making self-report about stressful life events invalid for these people); (2) unwillingness to self-report distress or anxiety (making depression scales invalid or findings reversed as in super-low distress predicting faster progression), though behaviorally they may appear distressed to the casual observer (making interviews potentially more valid assessments of actual distress); (3) unwillingness to indicate the need for change or adjustment, or help coping with their difficulties; (4) increased physiological stress though a calm exterior; (5) a higher likelihood that they will assert that "they have never in their lives been angry" or other extreme statements regarding negative emotion; (6) a higher probability that they actually do not express much negative emotion; (7) excessive altruism, though little genuine empathy; and (8) the ability to self-report in an unrealistically positive manner on lie scales that are similar conceptually to the Marlowe-Crowne social desirability scale (making lie scales for standardized measures perhaps more sensitive measures of true repression than some "repression scales").

## Repression

### Predicting Cancer Incidence: High Repression (Super-Low Depression), Linked with Greater Incidence

Of at least 19 published studies testing associations between repression and cancer incidence or onset, we have reviewed five, with significant results. Of the pool of studies, there are a number that seem to measure emotional suppression rather than repression. We review four of these studies, with significant or equivocal results. In addition, there are a number of postdiagnosis studies comparing cancer patients with either a benign disease, alternate disease, or healthy control group on levels of repression and suppression. We review three of these. The choice of the studies to review was based on the goal of illustrating the range of measurement strategies and consistent themes in clinical descriptions that seem to emphasize repression as the important underlying construct. At least 10 studies test associations between repression

and recurrence and survival. We have reviewed three finding significant results and one finding null results in this section. Several were reviewed in the depression section previously.

In a prospective study, Dattore and colleagues (Dattore, Shantz, & Coyne, 1980) matched 200 male cancer (75) and noncancer (125) veterans. MMPI records had been obtained a mean of 55.6 months prior to analysis for incidence of cancer for the cancer sample and 35.9 months prior to inclusion for the noncancer sample from male domiciliary residents at the Leavenworth, Kansas, VA Hospital through routine testing not associated with health risk for cancer. These profiles were collected from a sample of 3,000 records and carefully matched. Cancer groups consisted of men with lung, prostate, and multiple carcinomas. The noncancer group was composed of individuals with benign neoplasms, essential hypertension, gastrointestinal ulcers, schizophrenia, and no diagnosis. A total of 25 records in each of these subgroups were obtained. All subjects had no significant medical or psychiatric diagnosis when testing was administered.

MMPI scales included the 3 validity scales (L, F, and K), and 10 clinical scales (Hypochondriasis, Depression, Hysteria, Psychopathic Deviance, Masculinity-Femininity, Paranoia, Psychasthenia, Schizophrenia, Hypomania, and Social Introversion), and 4 additional scales (Byrne's Repression-Sensitization (Byrne, 1961), Barron's Ego-Strength (Barron, 1953), William's Caudality, and Little & Fisher's Denial of Hysteria scales. Age was found to be significantly different between the cancer and noncancer groups, and was subsequently controlled in the analyses. An analysis was performed using baseline MMPI scores to test differences between men who developed cancer and those who did not. A stepwise discriminant function analysis revealed a significant discrimination between the groups using seven variables: paranoia, masculinity-femininity, denial of hysteria, repression-sensitization, caudality, depression, and hysteria.

Using the size of discriminant function coefficients, they concluded that the most important predictors were Repression-Sensitization, Depression, and Denial of Hysteria. However, less rather than greater depression was associated with cancer. In their discussion, they note that the Repression-Sensitization scale contains most of the items from the Depression scale, yet it was also selected as a predictor. They conclude that "since depression represents such a threatening emotion to the cancer patient, one would expect to see relatively little acknowledgment of depression by subjects" (Dattore, Shantz, & Coyne, 1980, p. 392). These results support the hypothesis that repression is linked with cancer incidence, both because the single largest predictor was the repression scale and because, secondarily, the finding that those lower on depression (which is how the repressors would score) were also at risk; however, multicollinearity between their measure of depression and repression could have compromised the equation.

J. Hahn and colleagues (Hahn & Petitti, 1988) studied 8,932 women who were enrolled through Kaiser Permanente in a study for other purposes in 1977 and followed for 10 years. They completed an MMPI. Cox regresssion utilizing MMPI depression, repression/sensitization, and lie-scale scores were used to predict breast cancer incidence. Though their study found no significant associations between depression and repression/sensitization and later breast cancer incidence, they did find a significant association between an elevated lie scale and later incidence. Such lie scales may adequately assess repression (Watson et al., 1987), but they dismiss this finding in their conclusions. This study utilized a prospective design but a short time frame for an epidemiological sample. Cancer incidence is rare enough that a long-term follow-up will be necessary to evaluate these results.

In a study of 56 women just prior to breast biopsy, Wirsching and colleagues (Wirsching, Stierlin, Hoffman, Weber, & Wirsching, 1982) conducted structured interviews and rated the audiotapes for each woman on dimensions thought to be typical of women with cancer: (1) being inaccessible or overwhelmed, (2) emotional suppression with sudden outbursts, (3) rationalization, (4) little or no anxiety before the operation, (5) demonstrations of optimism, (6) super-autonomous self-sufficiency, (7) altruistic behavior, and (8) harmonization and avoidance of conflicts.

Raters correctly identified which women would be diagnosed versus not diagnosed with breast cancer at a rate that was significant (83–94% of cancer diagnoses and 71–68% noncancer). Interviewer reactions included a sense that it was more difficult to establish contact with the cancer patients. Their interpersonal and emotion regulation responses were at either end of the continuum, either aloof, self-sufficient, distant, or "overwhelming." In either case, these women refused to acknowledge their feelings during the conversation. Many of them displayed a "heroic" attitude that was never found in the control subjects, and many consistently disavowed their own interests in the service of others. They were found to be excessively altruistic. The authors consider these heroic and excessively altruistic behaviors to be "reaction formations to massive underlying anxiety, despair, and helplessness (reflecting a complete reversal of affects)" (Wirsching et al., 1982, p. 9).

These results are compromised by the fact that 17% of the cancer patients and 34% of those with benign nodes knew their diagnosis at the time of the interview and that the comparison groups were confounded by age, the cancer patients being on average 10 years older. No corrections were made for these two confounds. However, the descriptions of the cancer patients reflect characteristics found consistently in research on repressors (Crowne & Marlowe, 1964; Weinberger, 1990).

Kissen and colleagues (Kissen, Brown, & Kissen, 1969; Kissen & Eysenck, 1962) found that lung cancer patients had significantly lower scores on neuroticism on the Maudsley Personality Inventory (Eysenck, 1959). They concluded that this demonstrated a lower outlet for emotionality among cancer patients. Additionally in 489 patients, 221 with lung cancer and 268 controls, the neuroticism scores were again significantly lower using the newer Eysenck Personality Inventory. This also held true when they controlled for social desirability. They also gave 120 lung cancer patients and 167 controls an Awareness of Autonomic Activity (AAA) scale and found that cancer patients were less aware than controls. They conclude that they may have low arousal and low emotional lability, and that a psychological mechanism similar to repression could be operating.

In a recent meta-analysis (described earlier), McKenna and colleagues (1999) compared effect sizes across studies comparing either pre- or post-biopsy breast cancer patients to either a benign breast disease or a healthy control group. Their categories included anxiety/depression, childhood environment, conflict-avoidant style, denial/repression coping, expression of anger, extroversion, separation/loss, and stressful life events. They concluded that for the 15 repression studies included in the analysis, repression was the single most significant predictor of cancer onset. They report that 218 studies would need to find null results to reduce the significance of this effect size. In addition, they found that separation/loss and stressful life events were significant predictors of cancer onset. In their analysis of repression, they combined studies assessing repression—for instance, (Hahn & Petitti, 1988)—and those assessing a deliberate suppression of affect—for instance (Morris et al., 1981). Since distinctions between these constructs have not been clarified, it is difficult to assess the wisdom of their decision to collapse the categories. We review below the studies assessing suppression and cancer onset.

In the studies above, a greater number of patients with a repressive style were diagnosed with cancer across differing measurement strategies. McKenna et al.'s (1999) finding that repression was the best predictor in a meta-analysis is a strong indication that this construct may predict risk for the development of cancer; however, it as well the Wirshing (1982) and Kissen (1962) studies can be challenged because measurements were made proximal to the time of diagnosis and repression may increase at this time (Kreitler et al., 1993).

## Emotional Suppression

We review four studies assessing suppression prior to biopsy for cancer. In three of the studies, deliberate suppression was related to later diagnosis with breast cancer, but in the last study results are less clear due to the use of a nonstandardized questionnaire and inconclusive findings.

Greer and colleagues conducted a series of studies investigating emotional control in women with breast cancer (Greer & Morris, 1975). In their initial pre-biopsy study, they interviewed a consecutive series of 160 women presenting for breast biopsy, and wives' self-descriptions were verified by husbands or close relatives. The women also filled out self-report questionnaires including the Hamilton Rating Scale, Eysenck Personality Inventory, Caine and Foulds Hostility and Direction of Hostility, and an intelligence test. The 69 patients with breast cancer differed from the 91 with benign disease in their expression of emotions, particularly anger. Cancer patients were more likely to report extreme suppression ("had never or not more than twice during their adult lives openly shown anger and nearly always concealed other feelings") or extreme expression (history of frequent temper outbursts and never or very rarely concealed other feelings), and less likely to be rated as "apparently normal" (emotional release falling between the extremes). However, the same percentage of cancer and benign patients (35 and 36%) suffered from depressive illness for which they had sought treatment, and they did not differ on Hamilton Depression, Intelligence, Hostility, Extroversion, Neuroticism, Lie Scale, and Marital Relations. Their coded ratings of anger were correlated with Acting Out Hostility and with EPQ Extroversion. When they controlled for age, their results were substantially the same, though reduced in magnitude due to the smaller sample.

They replicated this study (Morris et al., 1981) in a new sample of 50 subjects interviewed pre-biopsy. Interviews focused on the frequency with which patients expressed affection, unhappiness as evidenced by crying, or anger manifested by loss of control. They also completed the EPQ and Spielberger State-Trait Anxiety questionnaires. Analysis was by coded transcription of the taped interview. Cancer patients were rated significantly lower on anger expression than the benign disease group. This result seemed to be strongest in the younger age group. Again there were no significant differences on EPQ L, E, or P scales, or on State Anxiety; however, cancer patients were significantly lower in Neuroticism and Trait Anxiety. In addition, those women reporting the least anger in their interview were also the same women with high Lie-Scale scores.

These results can be interpreted in three ways: (1) that the abnormally low expression of anger measured is really akin to a suppression of emotion because the women were reporting on instances of anger expression and in some cases acknowledging the emotion; (2) that the women who reported extreme emotional control ("does not admit to feeling anger ever since age 21" and "admits feeling anger, but no loss of control in anger ever since age 21") are likely to be repressors rather than suppressors due to the extreme nature of the claim which is similar to items on repression scales; or (3) that their results do not indicate evidence for suppression or repression, but rather indicate a poor affect regulation system in which women have few skills for successful release and resolution of intense emotion at both ends of the continuum. These studies culminated in the development of an "emotional control" questionnaire (Watson & Greer, 1983), the Courtauld Emotional Control Scale (CECS).

These two pre-biopsy studies were replicated by Fox (Fox et al., 1994) using the questionnaire rather than the interview. Fox asked women to fill out questionnaires pre-mammography in a large sample from a regional center. Some 826 women completed the packet that included the CECS, UCLA Loneliness Scale, Social Readjustment Rating Scale, and Dyadic Adjustment. After controlling for demographic and medical variables, they found that the newly diagnosed breast cancer group was significantly higher in emotional control on the CECS and significantly more lonely than the other groups ($N = 266$ normal breast tissue, 488 fibrocystic, 20 new breast cancer, 52 previous breast cancer). Unlike the previous study, no clinical ratings indicated the affect regulation styles of these women; however, the self-report scale measured a deliberate suppression of negative affect.

In a study plagued by equivocal results, Scherg and colleagues (Scherg, Cramer, & Blohmke, 1981) asked 200 women to fill out a questionnaire prior to examination at a gynecology clinic. They then compared 100 women with a subsequent diagnosis of breast cancer and 100 matched controls presenting at the same clinic but without a subsequent diagnosis of cancer. Only one significant finding relates to this review: in younger women (less than 50), the cancer patients were significantly more likely to suppress anger than the controls. This did not hold true for the older cohort. It is likely that their questionnaire lacked appropriate psychometric properties that compromised their ability to trust their findings.

Though each of these studies set out to study deliberate suppression, it also remains unclear in some results whether the construct of repression or suppression is accounting for the findings. The development of the CECS as a standardized questionnaire has been an important step in separating the two constructs; however, the initial interview studies upon which its development was based gave behavioral descriptions of women more likely to develop cancer that resonate more soundly with descriptions of repressors. Future research will be necessary before clarity is achieved.

## Predicting Cancer Correlates: Repression and Suppression in Cancer Patients Postdiagnosis and Matched Controls

Owing to long-standing hypotheses relating affect inhibition with cancer, a number of postdiagnosis studies have been conducted comparing cancer patients to either healthy, other-illness, or benign disease control groups. We review three of these.

In a follow-up study to validate their CECS questionnaire (Watson, Pettingale, & Greer, 1984), breast cancer patients were compared with other women attending a breast screening clinic. They filled out the CECS, Spielberger State-Trait Personality Inventory, and the Marlowe-Crowne Social Desirability Scale. Women watched three videotapes: (1) emotional upheaval of parents and children separated by the courts; (2) industrial accidents; and (3) a neutral tape. They filled out mood ratings during the viewing. Tapes were rated for global expressiveness and frequency of change in facial expressions. Breast cancer patients had significantly higher scores on the Marlowe-Crowne and Anger Control on the CECs, and lower scores on STPI Curiosity. Cancer patients were significantly less expressive during the two stress tapes. There were no differences between groups on ratings of frequency of expressions. Though they were less expressive during the stress tapes, the breast cancer patients were significantly higher on anxiety following the industrial accident tape, though they were significantly more likely than controls to hide their feelings during this tape viewing. They were more likely to hide their feelings the more involved they were in the viewing—an association not found in the control group. Skin conductance and heart rate measures collected during this trial were not different between the two groups; however, breast cancer patients' scores on the Marlowe-Crowne were significantly associated with their increased skin conductance fluctuations during the stress tapes (Watson et al., 1984).

In their conclusions they comment on affect regulation in the breast cancer patients: "Despite this tendency toward emotional control, some evidence suggests that breast cancer patients may be more emotionally labile. When we compared the anxiety and disturbance reported by patients and controls, we found that the patients' feelings were more generalized and had increased during both stress tapes, whereas the control group reported these negative feelings during only one of the stress tapes. Thus we concluded that the breast cancer group seemed more inclined toward emotional lability while presenting a controlled outer face" (Watson, Pettingale, & Greer, 1984, p. 28). Their interpretation supports our hypothesis that differences may be attributable to lower affect regulation ability.

Goldstein and Antoni (1989) compared three groups of women in a cross-sectional study just following diagnosis: (1) nonmetastatic, (2) metastatic breast cancer patients, and (3) women seen at a culposcopy clinic for follow-up of a suspicious Pap smear who were found to have benign or mild dysplasia. These women completed the Millon Behavioral Health Inventory. Goldstein and Antoni divided

the MBHI into the subscales they believed represented "repressive coping": the Introversive, Cooperative, and Respectful scales. They predicted that the cancer patients would score higher on these scales whereas the noncancer patients would score higher on the more expressive scales referred to as "sensitized coping": Inhibited, Forceful, and Sensitive. Taking the highest points on two scales and dividing into the just-described "repressors" or "sensitizers," that cancer patients were significantly more often categorized as repressors. Each repressive subscale also showed a similar significant difference when controlled for age (age correlated strongly with each of these scales and the cancer groups were significantly older than the the noncancer group). Likewise the sensitizer scales "inhibited" and "sensitive" were significantly higher for the noncancer controls. Additionally, women with cancer scored significantly lower on premorbid pessimism and future despair scales than the control group, which was interpreted as a greater denial of the impact of their cancer diagnoses. The nonmetastatic women were particularly low on these two scales.

Goldstein and Antoni (1989) concluded, like others using the more conventional repression scales such as the Weinberger, or the M-C and MAS, that higher repressive coping was highly correlated with lower distress on these scales. In fact, nonmetastatic cancer patients reported less distress than the controls. They interpreted their findings as supporting the hypothesis that cancer patients evidence more repressive coping. Each of their three repression scales has in common a passive coping response that they describe as "a tendency to engage in denial, act compliant with authority figures, keep their feelings under tight control . . . and hide their true feelings from conscious awareness" (p. 255). They also describe those scoring high on the "Respectful" scale as desiring social approval and to be viewed by others as responsible, conforming, and serious-minded, but harboring hostility or resentment at feeling compelled to conform and meet the requirements of others. They did find that metastatic patients were more likely to express distress than nonmetastatic patients. In this study, though they measure a number of constructs requiring a deliberate act of affect inhibition, the groupings appear to resonate more closely with traditional repression than merely suppression.

Lastly, in a large case-control study of colorectal cancer in Australia, Kune and colleagues (1991) compared 637 cases of colorectal cancer to 714 matched controls on a set of unvalidated questions that closely approximate suppression or denial of anger, conformity, and unhappiness in childhood and adult life. This was a cross-sectional study in which they predicted presence versus absence of cancer. Although they attempted to rule out the possibility that knowledge of a diagnosis of cancer contributed to their findings, their study design did not allow them to appropriately assess that question. When they combined their items into a single scale, they found significant differences between the cases and controls in the predicted directions (cancer patients with more suppression). This finding was especially true for the anger-suppression questions in both males and females. Females did report denial or suppression of anger at higher rates than males across both cases and controls. Postdiagnosis studies are remarkably consistent in finding greater suppression of affect in cancer patients. However, it is again unclear whether suppression of affect is a response shift in reaction to diagnosis (Kreitler et al., 1993; Schwartz & Geyer, 1984), or whether the intensity of affect to contain is simply greater in cancer patients who know their diagnosis.

## Predicting Cancer Progression and Survival: High Repression, Faster Progression, and Shorter Survival

We review three studies investigating repression and cancer progression, two of which find a significant association. Despite the overwhelming evidence of association with cancer incidence, repression has not been linked conclusively with cancer progression. Fewer studies of cancer progression have included this construct; however, thorough research by Temoshok (Kneier & Temoshok, 1984; Temoshok, 1985) failed to find such an association. Future research using clearly defined methods will be necessary to understand this discrepancy.

A study using the suggested Marlowe Crowne and the Taylor Manifest Anxiety Scale to categorize repressors found significant associations between women whose breast cancer had recurred and those whose had not, and between all breast cancer patients and healthy controls (Jensen, 1987). Jensen selected three groups of women: (1) those treated for breast cancer with mastectomy, radiation, and chemotherapy who had recurred or metastasized; (2) women receiving the same diagnosis and treatment but were in remission, and (3) a healthy control group seen at a clinic for minor surgery. A psychological test battery was administered, but not at the time of diagnosis. Repression was a significant predictor of time to recurrence (1,204 days for repressors and 1,755 days for nonrepressors). It also predicted the clinical staging at follow-up over and above the clinical staging at the time of this initial questionnaire assessment. He used a composite staging variable that assessed progression toward death.

Repression was the strongest predictor of progression along with a variable he created for "positive constructive daydreaming," which was a risk factor as well. He had some interesting ideas concerning the use of "positive constructive daydreaming" by repressors, as opposed to nonrepressive people. He theorized that the same behavior serves different purposes: it helps to facilitate a rigid per-

sonality style and is a risk factor for repressors, but facilitates temporary coping relief and is a protective factor in nonrepressors. He also observed that lower (rather than higher) hopelessness in repressors was associated with faster progression—in fact, it was somewhat more associated than the higher hopelessness in the nonrepressors.

This means that previous studies that did not control for repression would be likely to find odd or inconsistent results. We can, in fact, look to the literature for examples of just such confusion—for instance, Cassileth et al., (1988) found that a mid-range hopelessness value was associated with longer survival. Her results actually mirror the Jensen (1987) results and both support a conclusion of the important review by James Gross (1989): that both an overcontrol and an undercontrol of emotion are problematic, whereas the midrange may represent appropriate and flexible emotion regulation.

Ratcliffe, Dawson, and Walker (1995) recruited 63 patients with Hodgkin's disease or non-Hodgkin's lymphoma into a randomized trial of relaxation training to alleviate chemotherapy side effects. They were assessed using the Hospital Anxiety and Depression Scale (HADS) and the Eysenck Personality Inventory within 48 hours of diagnosis and were followed for 5 years. At 5 years, 27 of 63 patients had died. Thirty-one (49%) of the cancer patients scored above the cut-off of 4 for L-score, and the mean L-score of 4.68 is significantly higher than the mean L-score of 2.26 found in Eysenck's norm group ($N = 651$). L-scores and age were significantly positively related, though depression and anxiety were not associated with L-scores. In this study using univariate predictors and log-rank tests, L-scores, age, stage, performance status, and depression were all related to survival. L-scores were still significantly related to survival after controlling for age. Multivariate stepwise procedures identified three significant variables: L-score, Depression, and stage of disease at diagnosis. The best two-variable model was found to be L-score and HADS Depression. A patient obtaining an L-score of 9 was 16 times more likely to die within 5 years than a patient scoring 1, and a patient scoring in the abnormal range on depression was 11 times more likely to die.

In a series of studies with malignant melanoma patients, Temoshok found differences supporting her hypothesized "Type C" cancer personality. In an innovative study, she and her colleagues (Kneier & Temoshok, 1984) defined repression as a high discrepancy between a physiological response (skin conductance) and a self-report of distress. This measure is consistent with noncancer research findings regarding repressors (Weinberger et al., 1979). Although this measure did not correlate with the Marlowe-Crowne (a standard measure of repressive-defensiveness at the time), it did correlate with three other repression measures and did differentiate cancer patients from cardiac patients. She also found melanoma tumor thickness to be lower in subjects rated by an interviewer as more able to differentiate affective expression, elaborate on bodily sensations of sadness, articulate their sadness and anger, and minimize the seriousness of their disease.

Though she found these associations, she did not find a significant relationship with Byrne's Repression-Sensitization Scale. As in other research studies, when a repression scale has been used without the corresponding correction for anxiety (Weinberger et al., 1979), it is difficult to interpret a null result. Although repressors do score high on such scales, the corresponding highly distressed and highly defensive subjects score high as well.

In a later study, she found that a prognostically hopeful tumor-specific host response factor (desmoplasia) for melanoma was associated with greater depression (POMS), anxiety (MAS), social desirability (Marlowe-Crowne), and patient understanding of treatment; whereas, mitotic rate (a negative prognostic factor) was positively associated with 6 of 8 interview-rated variables measuring restrained expression of emotion (Temoshok, 1985). Despite this prior research finding that greater emotional expression of distress was related to better prognostic variables, when she compared 16 matched subjects (those who had died or had severe disease progression with those who had not), it was higher POMS Depression, Anger, Tension, Confusion, Taylor MAS, and the MMPI Distress scales that negatively predicted progression. It appears to be the case in this series of studies, as well as in others, that although repression is more often associated with cancer patients in pre- and postdiagnosis studies, and is often related to negative prognostic variables, it is less often significantly associated with survival in longitudinal studies.

In this section, the Jensen (1987) study using the clearest measurement strategies for repression found a significant association with cancer progression. Our conclusions are that a great deal more research will have to be done before a convincing association between repression and cancer survival will be demonstrated.

## Summary of Review of Depression and Repression Studies

We have highlighted throughout this review the methodological drawbacks to many of the studies we have cited. Our survey indicates that a predominance of studies find that repression is associated with cancer onset and differences between cancer patients and controls and that fewer studies find that repression is a risk factor for cancer progression or survival. We also find that, though few studies find that depression is predictive of cancer incidence or onset, a predominance of studies find that it is predictive of cancer survival. It is the case that a number of studies

find inconsistent or counterintuitive results. We see these inconsistencies as inherent when there is no clear theoretical framework informing this work. Measuring repression is difficult and this category will always include those subjects who score super-low on depression scales. In some ways the two constructs are at either end of a continuum. Midway between these poles may lie those subjects who have flexible efficacious emotion-regulation skill—subjects who may have the ability to shift in and out of affective states—but few studies test such a curvilinear model and virtually no studies test change over time.

For both constructs, the validity of the findings is threatened by both methodological and theoretical issues. We do not currently know whether the repression differences found at cancer onset are simply cancer patients' response to diagnosis as was found by Kreitler (Kreitler et al., 1993). Additionally, we do not know whether the association between depression and cancer survival is genuinely a psychosocial state preceding a physiological one, or whether disease progression directly causes physiological symptoms that are reported as depression (Whitlock & Siskund, 1979). Future research is necessary that will carefully address psychometric issues, insert appropriate controls, and use sophisticated theoretical frameworks to create appropriate designs before these highly suggestive results gain validity.

## Effects of Interventions That Encourage Emotional Expression or Communication with Family or Peers

Researchers providing emotionally supportive interventions for isolated individuals under stress have improved health outcomes for those individuals (Fawzy et al., 1993; Fawzy, Kemeny, et al., 1990; Raphael, 1977; Richardson, Shelton, Krailo, & Levine, 1990; Rodin, 1980, 1986; Spiegel, Bloom, Kraemer, & Gottheil, 1989; Turner, 1981). Emotional support has been shown to be an important factor in mediating individuals' ability to cope with stress. For example, Rodin (1980, 1986) observed decreases in urinary-free cortisol levels in geriatric patients exposed to education in stress management. Moreover, she found that subjects who received this experimental coping intervention were not only rated as happier and more sociable but also had longer survival times than groups that were not treated. In a sample of 48 cancer patients who participated in individual psychotherapy for 10 weeks, Forester et al. (Forester, Kornfeld, & Fleiss, 1985) found that both mood disturbance and physical symptoms of anorexia, fatigue, and nausea and vomiting were significantly improved compared to those of a matched control group. And in a sample of malignant melanoma patients participating in short-term group therapy, Fawzy et al. (1993) found that reductions in distress and increases in active coping were significantly associated with survival.

Prior work in our laboratory (Spiegel et al., 1989) has shown that participation in supportive-expressive group therapy for metastatic cancer patients prolongs survival time twofold from the point of randomization. Fifty women with metastatic breast cancer randomly assigned to a year of weekly support groups with training in self-hypnosis for pain control survived an average of 18 months longer than 36 control patients who had been randomly assigned to routine care. This difference is clinically as well as statistically significant. Further analyses suggested that these findings of associations between the intervention and increased survival occurred independent of differences between groups in subsequent medical treatment or health behaviors (Kogon, Biswas, Pearl, Carlson, & Spiegel, 1997).

Many of the psychotherapies that have shown promise in improving emotional adjustment and influencing survival time involve encouraging open expression of emotion and assertiveness in assuming control over the course of treatment, life decisions, and relationships (Fawzy, 1991; Spiegel et al., 1989; Spiegel, Bloom, & Yalom, 1981; Spiegel & Yalom, 1978). Supportive-expressive group therapy for metastatic breast cancer patients has been shown to result in better mood, fewer maladaptive coping responses, fewer phobic symptoms (Spiegel et al., 1981), reduced pain (Spiegel & Bloom, 1983), and a decrease in trauma symptoms (Classen et al., 2001).

One mechanism by which our group intervention may have these positive effects is through the direct facilitation of expression of negative affect, particularly fears of death and suffering, anger, regret, and sadness. Rather than attempting to eliminate negative affect through cognitive restructuring, this style of therapy teaches emotion-regulation skills and allows group members to have experiences of genuine emotional support during moments of intense negative affect. As skills in understanding and tolerating these intense emotions develop, this therapy may also reduce the need for defensive or repressive responding. In addition to the therapists' facilitation, the group members model emotional expression and encourage each other to express their deepest negative (and positive) feelings.

In order to navigate the aversive emotional arousal and these existential issues without debilitating dysfunction, patients must marshal their inner resources to balance the hope of life with the fear of death (Classen et al., 1998; Gotay, 1984; Mages & Mendelsohn, 1979; Spiegel, 1995; Tross, Hirsch, Rabkin, Berry, & Hololand, 1987; Yalom, 1980; Yalom & Greaves, 1977). Many support groups focus on coping successfully with natural levels of negative affect; however, supportive-expressive therapy's goals for

this expression are more direct (Classen et al., 1993; Spiegel & Spira, 1991). Processing and recovering from intense emotions is necessary for those facing a life-threatening illness so that they will be able to participate actively in the treatment process (Ferrero, Barreto, & Toledo, 1994; Watson et al., 1991), persevere in obtaining the best medical treatment, and maintain important relationships that provide support. It may be particularly important to maintaining those relationships that patients are able to communicate their emotional distress (Giese-Davis et al., 2000; Pennebaker, 1995). In addition, emotional expression combined with active coping may be associated with lowering depression (Classen et al., 1996). Such active coping may involve a patient's ability to acknowledge the reality of the threat by tolerating and expressing the sadness, anger, and anxiety it provokes while retaining a sense of self-efficacy about the management of this affect, which allows positive action to go forward (Classen et al. 1996, 1998; Jensen, 1987). These tasks draw upon cognitive strategies for coping and facility with emotion regulation. One particularly informative study conducted among HIV-infected patients utilized a randomized design to compare supportive-expressive group therapy with a cognitive-behavioral approach (Kelly et al., 1993). They found improvement with both, but an advantage for the supportive-expressive approach was a reduction of the distress about existential issues.

Studies are currently under way at Stanford and in Toronto by Goodwin and colleagues (Goodwin et al., 1996; Leszcz & Goodwin, 1998) to replicate these findings with metastatic breast cancer patients, and to investigate mediating variables in the relationship between psychotherapy and survival. Some studies show no effect of psychosocial treatment on medical outcome. The apparent beneficial effect of psychosocial support on survival time of 34 breast cancer patients in another study (Morgenstern, Gellert, Walter, Ostfeld, & Siegel, 1984) disappeared when time from cancer diagnosis to program entry was controlled. This lack of difference has recently been confirmed in a long-term follow-up of the same sample (Gellert, Maxwell, & Siegel, 1993). Three other randomized trials also found no survival benefit to psychotherapy for cancer patients. Linn, Linn, and Harris (1982) offered individual psychotherapy to a group of patients with a variety of cancers, including those of lung and pancreas, in a randomized protocol. There was no difference in survival time. It may be that since virtually all of the patients died during the follow-up year, their disease was too advanced to be significantly influenced by psychotherapeutic support. Similarly, Ilnyckyj, Farber, Cheang, and Weinerman (1994) found no survival advantage for breast cancer patients randomly assigned to one of several group psychotherapies, some peer led. Neither was there any demonstrable psychological benefit. In two of the studies demonstrating a survival impact, depression or mood disturbance was reduced significantly in the treatment condition. Thus, the relative inefficacy of the intervention may account for the lack of medical effect in those studies with null findings.

This may also have been the case in a recent study by Cunningham and colleagues (1998; Edmonds, Lockwood, & Cunningham, 1999), who provided both an unstructured long-term intervention (35 weeks), described as based on the supportive-expressive group therapy model, but combined it with a 20-week cognitive-behavioral course with homework assignments and a 2-day coping skills training course. In addition, control participants were provided with the course material from the cognitive-behavioral course along with two audiotapes for home study. This difference in therapy style, along with the relatively small sample size ($N = 66$), would have limited power to detect a difference in both psychological and medical outcome. Indeed, they found no overall improvement in mood or quality of life as a result of this hybrid treatment and no difference in survival time, although those patients from either treatment or control groups who attended community support groups did live significantly longer.

However, in addition to our own work (Spiegel et al., 1989), two other randomized trials have demonstrated a psychosocial effect on survival time among cancer patients. Richardson et al. (1990) utilized a 4-cell design among patients with lymphomas and leukemias. Patients were assigned either to a routine care condition or to one of three educational and home-visiting supportive interventions. The control group had significantly shorter survival time than patients allocated to the intervention. There were also differences in patients' adherence to medical treatment as measured by allopurinol intake. The survival differences held even when differences in medication adherence were controlled. The authors suggested that the psychosocial support may mediate this finding.

Fawzy and colleagues published psychosocial, immunological, recurrence, and survival results of a randomized trial involving 80 patients with malignant melanoma. Half were assigned to routine care and the other half to a structured series of 12 support groups. These weekly meetings were designed to help patients better cope with the illness and its effects on their families. In the first reports (Fawzy, Cousins, et al., 1990), they found significant reductions in mood disturbance on the POMS and the use of more active coping strategies in the intervention sample. In a companion report (Fawzy, Kemeny, et al., 1990), they observed significant differences in immune function at 3-month follow-up but not earlier. They found a predicted increase in natural killer cytotoxicity and an increase in LEU56 cells in the intervention sample. A 6-year follow-up (Fawzy et al., 1993) demonstrated a significantly lower rate of mortality among intervention patients (3 of 34 vs. 10 of 34), consistent with the findings among breast cancer patients in our laboratory.

## Possible Physiological Mechanisms Linking Emotional Distress and Expression to Disease Progression

A certain amount of the variance in cancer outcome (rate of disease progression, site of metastasis, and survival time) must be accounted for by host resistance factors, which may include immune response, angiogenesis, and endocrine activity. Other possibilities range from body maintenance activities such as diet, sleep, and exercise to interaction with physicians (Spiegel & Kato, 1996). We know, for example, that breast cancer is a hormone-sensitive tumor, hence the effectiveness of weak estrogen agonists that block estrogen receptors such as tamoxifen in improving survival and reducing the incidence of new primary cancers in women with breast cancer. Thus, the hormonal environment is a critical host-resistance factor in breast cancer progression. Indeed, we found in an analysis of survival data from our original randomized trial of the effects of supportive-expressive group therapy (Spiegel et al., 1989) that women who had been adrenalectomized had significantly shorter survival time (Kogon et al., 1997). Thus, those on artificial schedules of replacement corticosteroids had poorer outcome, suggesting that dysregulation of the HPA might mediate disease progression.

## Stress Response

The rationale for a focus on stress and endocrine function begins at least as far back as Riley's classic experiments in rats (Riley, 1975, 1981), which showed that crowded living conditions accelerated the rate of tumor growth and mortality. In a recent authoritative review of the human stress literature, McEwen (1998) documents the adverse health effects of cumulative stressors and the body's failure to adapt its stress response system to them. Allostatic load has been defined as the price that the body has to pay for maintaining allostasis, or stability, through physiologic change. Recently, it has been suggested that increased allostatic load, which may occur through cumulative buildup of stress over a life span, may significantly hinder the functioning of different physiologic systems (McEwen, 1998; Seeman, Singer, Rowe, Horowitz, & McEwen, 1997). Cancer itself constitutes a series of stressors: the threat to life and health, the disruption of social activities, the rigors and side effects of treatment. A given individual's psychological and physiological response pattern to stress in general is likely to be exacerbated by the diagnosis and treatment of cancer, thereby intensifying mind-body connections mediated by the stress response system. Furthermore, the impact of the stressor is likely to be determined in part by the individual's pattern of response to it. Emotional suppression or repression may make it difficult for people to acknowledge and respond to stressors, making their delayed or indirect emotional responses more problematic and less informative, an additional stress rather than a guide to action.

Indeed, prior research has found higher levels of stress physiology associated with repression. Although people categorized as repressors say that they are not distressed, they have been found to have higher mean cortisol (Brown et al., 1996), diminished immune function (Jamner, Schwartz, & Leigh, 1988; Levy, Herberman, Maluish, Schlien, & Lippman, 1985; Shea, Burton, & Girgis, 1993), and stressed autonomic functioning (Watson et al., 1984; Weinberger et al., 1979). Additionally, research with active deliberate suppression of emotion has shown increased autonomic arousal (Gross & Levenson, 1993, 1997).

Although many steps are missing in the logical process linking repression with physiology associated with shorter cancer survival, it is clear that to repress or suppress emotion may burden one's physiological system unnecessarily. Likewise, depression has been associated with higher cortisol and diminished immune function, although not consistently in all studies (Stein, Miller, & Trestman, 1991). Research does show that each of these potentially chronic states could place people at some physiological risk.

While acute activation of the hypothalamic-pituitary-adrenal axis (HPA) is an adaptive and necessary response to stress, repeated "hits" to this system over time can result in a poorly functioning HPA (McEwen, 1998). In response to cumulative stress brought on either by repeated severe life events or a chronic coping style that heightens rather than reduces physiological stress, the system's signal to noise ratio can be degraded, so that it is partially "on" all the time, leading to adverse physiological consequences, including abnormalities of glucose metabolism (Sapolsky & Donnelly, 1985), hippocampal damage (Sapolsky, Krey, & McEwen, 1985), accumulation of abdominal fat (Epel, McEwen, Seeman, Matthews, & Ickovics, 1999; Jayo & Shively, 1993), and depression (Plotsky, Owens, & Nemeroff, 1998; Posener, Schildkraut, Samson, & Schatzberg, 1996). Different but related abnormalities of HPA function, including glucocorticoid receptor hypersensitivity, have also been found to be associated with posttraumatic stress disorder (Yehuda et al., 1993; Yehuda, Teicher, Trestman, Levengood, & Siever, 1996). Thus, adverse events, ranging from traumatic stressors to cumulative minor ones, are associated with HPA dysregulation.

Persistently elevated or relatively invariant levels of cortisol may, in turn, stimulate tumor proliferation (Sapolsky & Donnelly, 1985). Possible mechanisms include differential gluconeogenesis. That is, normal and tumor cells respond differently to glucocorticoid signals to secrete glucose into the blood, selectively depriving normal cells of metabolic resources. Other possible effects include activation of hormone receptors in tumors and immunosuppression (Ben-Eliyahu, Yirmiya, Liebeskind, Taylor, & Gale, 1991; Sapolsky & Donnelly, 1985; Spiegel, 1996; Spiegel, 1999). Indeed, glucocorticoids are potently immunosuppressive, so the effects of acute and chronic stress and resulting hypercortisolemia may include functional immunosuppression as well, as has been shown extensively in animals (Padgett, Loria, & Sheridan, 1997; Sheridan, Dobbs, Brown, & Zwilling, 1994; Sheridan et al., 1998; Sternberg, Chrousos, Wilder, & Gold, 1992). There is a growing body of evidence of stress-induced immunosuppression in humans as well (Glaser, Kiecolt-Glaser, Malarkey, & Sheridan, 1998; Kiecolt-Glaser, Glaser, Cacioppo, & Malarkey, 1998). This in turn could influence the rate of cancer progression (Andersen et al., 1998; Baltrusch, Stangel, & Titze, 1991; Head, Elliott, & McCoy, 1993; Levy et al., 1985).

High levels of stress hormones such as cortisol may be associated with worse disease prognosis, since breast cancers are often hormone sensitive (Sephton, Sapolsky, Kraemer, & Spiegel, 2000). In a study of patients who had operations for breast and stomach carcinoma, the failure of morning cortisol levels to decrease within two weeks after admission was associated with shorter survival times (Audier, 1988). For example, direct evidence for effects of the HPA axis in the development of breast cancer comes from a study in which high serum levels of DHEA, a correlate of HPA axis activity, predicted the subsequent development of breast cancer 9 years later in normal postmenopausal women who had donated blood for a serum bank (Gordon, Bush, Helzlsouer, Miller, & Comstock, 1990). Thus, correlational evidence suggests that physiological stress responses associated with poor adjustment to cancer may, indeed, speed disease progression (Chrousos & Gold, 1992; McEwen, 1993; Nemeroff et al., 1984).

Many of these hormones are immunosuppressive when elevated. Acute medical illness is associated with increased secretion of ACTH (Drucker & McLaughlin, 1986) and cortisol (Parker, Levin, & Lifrak, 1985), and surgical stress is associated with lower dehydroepiandrosterone (DHEA)/cortisol ratios (i.e., a combination of relatively low DHEA and relatively high cortisol; Ozasa, Kita, Inoue, & Mori, 1990) and higher prolactin levels (Barni et al., 1987). In spousal bereavement, cortisol levels are elevated, while NK cytotoxicity is decreased (Irwin, Daniels, Risch, Bloom, & Weiner, 1988). Furthermore, there is no reason disease-related stresses, which include social isolation, death anxiety, pain, and sleep disturbance, should not affect immune function at the clinically observable level—for example, defenses against the progression of viral infection. Yet little is known about the effects of these mechanisms on clinical infection. Recently, Cohen, Tyrrell, and Smith (1991) showed that vulnerability to systemic infection by rhinovirus is significantly mediated by stress. This model might apply as well to vulnerability to cancer progression, to the extent that immune function modulates it (Spiegel, 1999). Levine, Coe, and Wiener (1989) have shown in squirrel monkeys that social support buffers the endocrine response to stress (a shock paired with a light flash). The elevation in plasma cortisol seen when the animal is stressed alone is reduced by 50% when the animal has one "friend" with him, and there is no elevation in cortisol at all in response to the same stressor when the animal has five "friends" present. Thus, a change in the social environment profoundly alters the physiological consequences of a stressor. This would plausibly apply to humans coping with stressors as well. Suppression or repression of distress may increase social isolation rather than mobilize needed social support. The interrelationships among social and psychophysiological stress-response factors is an important mediating system that bears examination in future research on cancer progression.

### Psychoneuroimmune Mechanisms

The burgeoning field of psychoneuroimmunology has provided increasing evidence of CNS-immune interactions that could also affect the course of cancer progression. It is clear that the CNS influences the immune system—for example, via circulating catecholamines and heavy autonomic innervation of the spleen (Felten, Felton, Carlson, Olschowka, & Livnat, 1985). Likewise, the immune system influences the brain via the release of pro-inflammatory cytokines. The HPA can influence immune function, since corticosteroids are potently immunosuppressive (Sheridan et al., 1998; Sternberg et al., 1992), so the mechanisms described above can influence immune function.

Natural killer (NK) cells have been implicated as having a role in cancer progression (Andersen, Kiecolt-Glaser, & Glaser, 1994; Bovbjerg, 1989; Herberman, 1991). NK cells are known to kill tumor cells of many different types when tested either in vitro or in animal studies (Herberman, 1985). NK cells are similar to lymphokine-activated killer (LAK) cells in having antitumor activity without recognition of tumor-specific antigens (Rosenberg & Lotze, 1986). The clinical salience of these findings is illustrated by the associations among breast cancer progression, axillary lymph node and estrogen receptor status, and sustained psychosocial stress and decreased natural killer cell activity (Levy, Herberman, Lippman, & d'Angelo, 1987; Levy, Fernstrom, et al., 1991; Levy, Herberman, Lee, et al., 1990; Levy et al., 1985; Levy, Herberman, Whiteside, 1990). In addition, Levy found that high-quality emotional support from a spouse or intimate other, perceived social support from one's physician, and actively seeking social support were related to higher NK activity.

In a randomized trial of the effect of group psychotherapy on patients with malignant melanoma, Fawzy, Kemeny, and colleagues (1990) found that participation in the group was associated with significantly higher alpha-interferon induced NKCA at 6-month follow-up. Analysis of outcome 6 years later (Fawzy et al., 1993) indicated that baseline NKCA levels significantly predicted relapse, and that psychotherapeutically treated patients had lower rates of recurrence and mortality. It is thus plausible that the kind of social support that results from and also encourages emotional expression could be linked to better NK function and possibly to slower cancer progression.

### Social Support as a Means of Emotional Expression and a Buffer of Stress

The social environment can have a buffering effect on stress and the physiological responses to it, potentially by allowing for disclosure and the expression and integration of emotion (Greenberg, Wortman, & Stone, 1996; Pennebaker, 1995; Pennebaker, Kiecolt-Glaser, & Glaser, 1988). Being socially "imbedded" is associated with less autonomic arousal than social isolation (Cacioppo, 1994). Indeed, social connection has profound consequences for health. Being well integrated socially reduces all-cause age-adjusted mortality twofold, about as much as having low serum cholesterol levels or being a nonsmoker (House, Landis, & Umberson, 1988). Furthermore, the nature of one's position in the social hierarchy has health consequences, including having relatively higher status within the same social class (Marmot et al., 1998). Also, people are statistically more likely to die after rather than before their birthdays and important holidays (Phillips, Ruth, & Wagner, 1993), which are usually important times for social bonding and companionship.

Thus, the presence of adverse emotional events such as traumatic stressors seems to have negative potential health consequences, while good social relations seem to be associated with positive health outcomes. One component of the effective interventions may be dealing directly with emotional distress associated with fears regarding disease progression (Spiegel, 1993), consistent with the development of "fighting spirit" (Greer, 1991). There is evidence that resilience to stress, including disease-related distress, is associated with emotional style (Davidson & Sutton, 1995). Indeed, finding meaning in the midst of experiencing a distressing situation has been linked with a positive psychological state (Folkman, 1997). Our clinical experience indicates that better adaptation does not involve being persistently upbeat or rigidly maintaining a positive attitude, but rather dealing directly with negative affect as well. Positive and negative emotions are not merely opposite sides of one dimension (Lane et al., 1997). Rather, suppression of negative emotion tends to reduce experience of all emotion, positive and negative. This is consistent with the evidence reviewed above that breast cancer patients who express more "negative" emotion, including anger and uncooperativeness, live longer (Derogatis et al., 1979).

## Conclusions

There is considerable evidence that suppression or repression of uncomfortable emotion is associated with higher risk of developing cancer and having it progress, while persistent depression is also predictive of poorer outcomes. That there is evidence for both of these connections with emotional state is interesting, especially since they may at first appear to be inconsistent. Yet there is evidence that those who suppress emotion are actually more anxious and depressed (Classen et al., 1996). Such a coping style may add to the transformation of an acute, reactive, and appropriate emotional response to a stressful situation into a chronic, maladaptive response that contributes to the nonspecific anxiety and negative self-evaluation typical of depression.

Effective psychotherapy for cancer patients typically targets this response style, encouraging emotional expression in the context of strong social support, directed toward developing greater self-efficacy with emotion-regulation skills and more active coping strategies. Existentially oriented psychotherapy seeks to help patients confront their most feared emotional reactions to awareness of their mortality by invoking the emotion and then to teach one how to think and express while experiencing emotion. Cognitive-behavioral therapy teaches control over the mistaken thoughts that lead to excessive distress, with the goal of not experiencing the distress. This is a rational playing down of the emotion. Perhaps both approaches lead to a lowering of depression, but through different pathways. Research conclusions from this rather large literature make it plausible that changes in a patient's emotional expression and regulation could affect cancer progression. Some of the literature would seem to confirm this perspective, while other studies would not.

Emotional distress goes with the territory of cancer. Yet many cancer patients report that they learn to experience more intense joy and life satisfaction after their diagnosis than they had ever had before: "My life has never been the same since I got cancer," said one woman with metastatic breast cancer, "but in many ways it is better." Coping effectively with stress, anger, fear, and sadness may liberate pleasure as well as pain, while suppressing emotional response to these negative emotions may constrain all emotion. The literature reviewed above indicates that there is at least some connection between mental and physical state among cancer patients, and that overt expression of emotion is helpful rather than hurtful. This does not in any way mean that people give themselves cancer or are responsible for its progression. Rather, it suggests that one's emotional response to a biological disorder provides an opportunity for maximizing one's chances. This research should be a source of hope and an opportunity for control, rather than a cause for blame, which increases feelings of helplessness. We advocate an interpretation in which flexible emotion regulation skill appears protective. Future research and intervention trials will assess whether this skill is responsive to change. We believe that emotion-regulation skill can be taught and that emotional change may be one important therapeutic mechanism in cancer interventions. We cannot help our feelings, but there is growing evidence that expression of our feelings may help us.

## NOTE

This review was made possible by NIMH Grant MN47226 with additional funding from NCI, The MacArthur Foundation, and California Breast Cancer Research Program Grant #1FB-0383 and 4BB-2901. We appreciate the help of Jessica Kathleen Quinn Donaghy and Melinda Manley, and the intellectual contributions of Helena C. Kraemer, biostatistician, Sandra Sephton, Ph.D., psychoneuroimmunologist on our metastatic breast cancer study, and the MacArthur Foundation Mind/Body Network to this work.

## REFERENCES

Abse, D. W., Wilkins, M. M., van de Castle, R. L., Buxton, W. D., Demars, J. P., Brown, R. S., & Kirschner, L. G. (1974). Personality and behavioral characteristics of lung cancer patients. *Journal of Psychosomatic Research, 18*, 101–113.

Altrocchi, J., Parsons, O. A., & Dickoff, H. (1960). Changes in self-ideal discrepancy in repressors and sensitizers. *Journal of Social Psychology, 61*, 67–72.

American Psychiatric Association. *Diagnostic and statistical manual of mental disorders* (4th ed.). (DSM IV). (1994). Washington, DC: Author.

Andersen, B. L., Farrar, W. B., Golden-Kreutz, D., Kutz, L. A., Courtney, M. E., & Glaser, R. (1998). Stress and immune responses after surgical treatment for regional breast cancer. *Journal of the National Cancer Institute, 90*(1), 30–36.

Andersen, B. L., Kiecolt-Glaser, J. K., & Glaser, R. (1994). A biobehavioral model of cancer stress and disease course. *American Psychologist, 49*(5), 389–404.

Antoni, M. H., & Goodkin, K. (1989). Host moderator variables in the promotion of cervical neoplasia-II. Dimensions of life stress. *Journal of Psychosomatic Research, 33*(4), 457–467.

Audier, A. G. (1988). Determination of a constitutional neuroendocrine factor probably influencing tumor development in man: Prophylactic and therapeutic aspects. *Cancer Detection and Prevention, 11*, 203–208.

Bacon, C. L., Renneker, R., & Cutler, M. (1952). A psychosomatic survey of cancer of the breast. *Psychosomatic Medicine, 14*, 453–460.

Bahnson, C. B. (1980). Stress and cancer: The state of the art part 1. *Psychosomatics, 21*(12), 975–981.

Bahnson, C. B. (1981). Stress and cancer: The state of the art, Part 2. *Psychosomatics, 22*(3), 207–220.

Bahnson, M. B., & Bahnson, C. B. (1969). Ego defenses in cancer patients. *Annals of the New York Academy of Sciences, 164*(2), 546–559.

Baltrusch, H. J., Stangel, W., & Titze, I. (1991). Stress, cancer and immunity. New developments in biopsychosocial and psychoneuroimmunologic research. *Acta Neurologia, 13*(4), 315–327.

Barni, S., Lissoni, P., Paolorossi, F., Crispino, S., Rovelli, F., Ferri, L., Sormani, A., D'Alonso, U., Bugatti, A., Nociti, V., & et al. (1987). Effects of radical mastectomy on prolactin blood levels in patients with breast cancer. *European Journal of Cancer and Clinical Oncology, 23*(8), 1141–1145.

Barron, F. (1953). An Ego-Strength Scale which predicts response to psychotherapy. *Journal of Consulting Psychology, 17*, 327–333.

Ben-Eliyahu, S., Yirmiya, R., Liebeskind, J. C., Taylor, A. N., & Gale, R. P. (1991). Stress increases metastatic spread of a mammary tumor in rats: evidence for mediation by the immune system. *Brain Behavior and Immunity, 5*(2), 193–205.

Blumberg, E., West, P., & Ellis, F. (1954). A possible relationship between psychological factors and human cancer. *Psychosomatic Medicine, 16*, 277–286.

Bovbjerg, D. (1989). Psychoneuroimmunology and cancer. In J. C. Holland & J. H. Rowland (Eds.), *Handbook of psychooncology: Psychological care of the patient with cancer* (pp. 727–754). New York: Oxford University Press.

Brown, L., Tomarken, A., Orth, D., Loosen, P., Kalin, N., & Davidson, R. (1996). Individual differences in repressive-defensiveness predict basal salivary cortisol levels. *Journal of Personality and Social Psychology, 70*(2), 362–371.

Buddeberg, C., Wolf, C., Sieber, M., Riehl-Emde, A., Bergant, A., Steiner, R., Landolt-Ritter, C., & Richter, D. (1991). Coping strategies and course of disease of breast cancer patients. Results of a 3-year longitudinal study. *Psychotherapy and Psychosomatics, 55*(2–4), 151–157.

Byrne, D. (1961). The repression-sensitization scale: Rationale, reliability, and validity. *Journal of Personality, 29*, 334–349.

Cacioppo, J. T. (1994). Social neuroscience: autonomic, neuroendocrine, and immune responses to stress. *Psychophysiology, 31*(2), 113–128.

Cassileth, B. R., Lusk, E. J., Miller, D. S., Brown, L. L., & Miller, C. (1985). Psychosocial correlates of survival in advanced malignant disease? *New England Journal of Medicine, 312*(24), 1551–1555.

Cassileth, B., Walsh, W., & Lusk, E. (1988). Psychosocial correlates of cancer survival: A subsequent report 3 to 8 years after cancer diagnosis. *Journal of Clinical Oncology, 6*(11), 1753–1759.

Chrousos, G. P., & Gold, P. W. (1992). The concepts of stress and stress system disorders. Overview of physical and behavioral homeostasis [published erratum appears in *JAMA* 1992 Jul 8;268(2):200]. *Journal of the American Medical Association, 267*(9), 1244–1252.

Classen, C. Butler, L. D., Koopman, C., Miller, E., Dimiceli, S., Giese-Davis, J., Carlson, R., Kraemer, H. C., & Spiegel, D. (2001). Supportive-expressive group therapy and distress in patients with metastatic breast cancer: A randomized clinical intervention trial. *General Archives of Psychiatry, 58*, 494–501.

Classen, C., Diamond, S., Soleman, A., Fobair, P., Spira, J., & Spiegel, D. (1993). *Brief supportive-expressive group therapy for women with primary breast cancer: A treatment manual.* Stanford, CA: Stanford University School of Medicine.

Classen, C., Giese-Davis, J., Angell, K., Michel, B., Brennan-O'Neill, E., Morrow, G., & Spiegel, D. (1998). *The delicate balance of coping with primary breast cancer: Expressing emotion while maintaining a fighting spirit.* Manuscript submitted for publication.

Classen, C., Koopman, C., Angell, K., & Spiegel, D. (1996). Coping styles associated with psychological adjustment to advanced breast cancer. *Health Psychology, 15*(6), 434–437.

Cohen, S., Tyrrell, D. A., & Smith, A. P. (1991). Psychological stress and susceptibility to the common cold. *New England Journal of Medicine, 325*, 606–612.

Comstock, G. W., & Helsing, K. J. (1976). Symptoms of depressive symptoms in patients and community populations. *Psychological Medicine, 6*, 551.

Cox, D. R. (1972). Regression models and life tables. *Journal of the Royal Statistical Society, Series B, 34*, 187–220.

Crowne, D. P., & Marlowe, D. A. (1960). A new scale of social desirability independent of psychopathology. *Journal of Consulting Psychology, 24*, 349–354.

Crowne, D. P., & Marlowe, D. (1964). *The approval motive: Studies in evaluative dependence.* New York: Wiley.

Cunningham, A. J., Edmonds, C. V. I., Jenkins, G. P., Pollack, H., Lockwood, G. A., & Warr, D. (1998). A randomized controlled trial of the effects of group psychological therapy on survival in women with metastatic breast cancer. *Psycho-Oncology, 7*, 508–517.

Cwikel, J. G., Behar, L. C., & Zabora, J. R. (1997). Psychosocial factors that affect the survival of adult cancer patients: a review of research. *Journal of Psychosocial Oncology, 15*(3/4), 1–34.

Dattore, P. J., Shantz, R. C., & Coyne, L. (1980). Premorbid personality differentiation of cancer and noncancer groups: a test of the hypothesis of cancer proneness. *Journal of Consulting and Clinical Psychology, 43*, 388–394.

Davidson, R. J., & Sutton, S. K. (1995). Affective neuroscience: the emergence of a discipline. *Current Opinion in Neurobiology, 5*(2), 217–224.

Davis, P. J., & Schwartz, E. G. (1987). Repression and the inaccessibility of affective memories. *Journal of Personality and Social Psychology, 52*(1), 155–162.

Davis, P. J. (1990). Repression and the inaccessibility of emotional memories. In J. L. Singer (Ed.), *Repression and dissociation: Implications for personality theory, psychopathology, and health* (pp. 387–403). Chicago: University of Chicago Press.

Dean, C., & Surtees, P. G. (1989). Do psychological factors predict survival in breast cancer? *Journal of Psychosomatic Research, 33*(5), 561–569.

Derogatis, L. R., Abeloff, M. D., & Melisaratos, N. (1979). Psychological coping mechanisms and survival time in metastatic breast cancer. *Journal of the American Medical Association, 242*(14), 1504–1508.

DiClemente, R. J., & Temoshok, L. (1985). Psychological adjustment to having cutaneous malignant melanoma as a predictor of follow-up clinical status. *Psychosomatic Medicine, 47*(1), 81.

Dollard, J., & Miller, N. E. (1950). *Personality and psychotherapy: An analysis in terms of learning, thinking, and culture.* New York: McGraw-Hill.

Drucker, D., & McLaughlin, J. (1986). Adrenocortical dysfunction in acute medical illness. *Critical Care Medicine, 14*(9), 789–791.

Dupuy, H. J. (1977). A concurrent validational study of the NCHS General Well-Being Schedule. *Vital and Health Statistics* (Vol. 2). Washington, DC: U.S. Dept. of Health, Education, and Welfare.

Edmonds, C. V. I., Lockwood, G. A., & Cunningham, A. J. (1999). Psychological response to long term group therapy: A randomized trial with metastatic breast cancer patients. *Psycho-Oncology, 8,* 74–91.

Epel, E. B., McEwen, B. S., Seeman, T., Matthews, K., & Ickovics, J. (1999). Psychological stress and lack of cortisol habituation among women with abdominal fat distribution. *Psychosomatic Medicine, 61,* 107.

Erdelyi, M. H. (1990). Repression, reconstruction, and defense: History and integration of the psychoanalytic and experimental frameworks. In J. L. Singer (Ed.), *Repression and dissociation: Implications for personality theory, psychopathology, and health* (pp. 1–32). Chicago: University of Chicago Press.

Evans, E. (1926). *A psychological study of cancer.* New York: Dodd, Mead and Co.

Evans, N., Baldwin, J., & Gath, D. (1974). The incidence of cancer among patients with affective disorders. *British Journal of Psychiatry, 124,* 518–525.

Eysenck, H. J. (1959, May). The differentiation between normal and various neurotic groups on the Maudsley Personality Inventory. *British Journal of Psychology, 1959,* 176–177.

Fawzy, F. (1991, October). *Effects of group support on malignant melanoma patients.* Paper presented at the Memorial Sloan-Kettering Conference on Psychosocial Oncology, New York.

Fawzy, F. I., Cousins, N., Fawzy, N. W., Kemeny, M. E., Elashoff, R., & Morton, D. (1990). A structured psychiatric intervention for cancer patients. I. Changes over time in methods of coping and affective disturbance. *Archives of General Psychiatry, 47,* 720–725.

Fawzy, F. I., Fawzy, N. W., Hyun, C. S., Elashoff, R., Guthrie, D., Fahey, J. L., & Morton, D. L. (1993). Malignant melanoma. Effects of an early structured psychiatric intervention, coping, and affective state on recurrence and survival 6 years later. *Archives of General Psychiatry, 50,* 681–689.

Fawzy, F. I., Kemeny, M. E., Fawzy, N. W., Elashoff, R., Morton, D., Cousins, N., & Fahey, J. L. (1990). A structured psychiatric intervention for cancer patients. II. Changes over time in immunological measures. *Archives of General Psychiatry, 47,* 729–735.

Felten, D. L., Felton, S. Y., Carlson, S. L., Olschowka, J. A., & Livnat, S. (1985). Noradrenergic and peptidergic innervation of lymphoid tissue. *Journal of Immunology, 135,* 775s–765s.

Ferrero, J., Barreto, M., & Toledo, M. (1994). Mental adjustment to cancer and quality of life in breast cancer patients: An exploratory study. *Psycho-Oncology, 3,* 223–232.

Folkman, S. (1997). Positive psychological states and coping with severe stress. *Social Science Medicine, 45*(8), 1207–1221.

Forester, B., Kornfeld, D. S., & Fleiss, J. L. (1985). Psychotherapy during radiotherapy: Effects on emotional and physical distress. *American Journal of Psychiatry, 142,* 22–27.

Fox, B. H. (1978). Premorbid psychological factors as related to cancer incidence. *Journal of Behavioral Medicine, 1,* 45–133.

Fox, B. H. (1983). Current theory of psychogenic effects on cancer incidence and prognosis. *Journal of Psychosocial Oncology, 1,* 17–31.

Fox, B. H. (1989). Depressive symptoms and risk of cancer [editorial]. *Journal of the American Medical Association, 262*(9), 1231.

Fox, C. M., Harper, P., Hyner, G. C., & Lyle, R. M. (1994). Loneliness, emotional repression, marital quality, and major life events in women who develop breast cancer. *Journal of Community Health, 19,* 467–482.

Freud, A. (1966). *The ego and the mechanisms of defense.* New York: International Universities Press.

Gellert, G. A., Maxwell, R. M., & Siegel, B. S. (1993). Survival of breast cancer patients receiving adjunctive psychosocial support therapy: A 10-year follow-up study. *Journal of Clinical Oncology, 11,* 66–69.

Gendron, D. (1701). *Enquiries into the nature, knowledge and cure of cancer.* London: J. Taylor.

Gibbons, R. D., Hedeker, D., Waternaux, C., Kraemer, H. C., & Greenhouse, J. B. (1993). Some conceptual and statistical issues in the analysis of longitudinal psychiatric data. *Archives of General Psychiatry, 50,* 730–750.

Giese-Davis, J., Hermanson, K., Koopman, C., Weibel, D., & Spiegel, D. (2000). Quality of couples' relationship and adjustment to metastatic breast cancer. *Journal of Family Psychology, 14,* 251–266.

Giese-Davis, J., & Spiegel, D. (2001). Suppression, repressive-defensiveness, restraint, and distress in metastatic breast cancer: Separable or inseparable constructs? *Journal of Personality, 69,* 417–449.

Glaser, R., Kiecolt-Glaser, J. K., Malarkey, W. B., & Sheridan, J. F. (1998). The influence of psychological stress on the immune response to vaccines. *Annals of the New York Academy of Science, 840,* 649–655.

Goldstein, D., & Antoni, M. (1989). The distribution of repressive copying styles among non-metastatic and metastatic breast cancer patients as compared to non-cancer patients. *Psychology and Health, 3,* 245–258.

Goodkin, K., Antoni, M. H., & Blaney, P. H. (1986). Stress and hopelessness in the promotion of cervical intraepithelial neoplasia to invasive squamous cell carcinoma of the cervix [published erratum appears in J Psychosom Res 1987;31(5):659]. *Journal of Psychosomatic Research, 30*(1), 67–76.

Goodwin, P. J., Leszcz, M., Koopmana, J., Arnold, A., Doll, R., Chochinov, H., Nsvarro, M., Butler, K., & Pritchard, K. I. (1996). Randomized trial of group psychosocial support in metastatic breast cancer; the BEST (Breast-Expressive Supportive Therapy) study. *Cancer Treatment, 22*(Suppl. A), 91–96.

Gordon, G. B., Bush, T. L., Helzlsouer, K. J., Miller, S. R., & Comstock, G. W. (1990). Relationship of serum levels of dehydroepiandrosterone and dehydroepiandrosteron sulfate to the risk of developing postmenopausal breast cancer. *Cancer Research, 50,* 3859–3862.

Gotay, C. C. (1984). The experience of cancer during early and advanced stages: The views of patients and their mates. *Social Science and Medicine, 18,* 605–613.

Graves, P. L., Phil, M., Mead, L. A., & Pearson, T. A. (1986). The Rorschach interaction scale as a potential predictor of cancer. *Psychosomatic Medicine, 48,* 549–563.

Greenberg, M. A., Wortman, C. B., & Stone, A. A. (1996). Emotional expression and physical health: revising traumatic memories or fostering self-regulation? *Journal of Personality and Social Psychology, 71*, 588–602.

Greene, W. A., & Swisher, S. N. (1969). Psychological and somatic variables associated with the development and course of monozygotic twins discordant for leukemia. *Annals of the New York Academy of Sciences, 164*, 394–408.

Greer, S. (1985). Mental attitudes to cancer: An additional prognostic factor. *Lancet, I,* 750.

Greer, S. (1991). Psychological response to cancer and survival. *Psychological Medicine, 21*, 43–49.

Greer, S., & Morris, T. (1975). Psychological attributes of women who develop breast cancer: a controlled study. *Journal of Psychosomatic Research, 19*, 147–153.

Greer, S., Morris, T., & Pettingale, K. W. (1979). Psychological response to breast cancer: Effect on outcome. *Lancet, 2*(8146), 785–787.

Greer, S., Morris, T., Pettingale, K. W., & Haybittle, J. L. (1990). Psychological response to breast cancer and 15-year outcome. *Lancet, 335*(8680), 49–50.

Greer, S., & Watson, M. (1985). Towards a psychobiological model of cancer: Psychological considerations. *Social Science Medicine, 20*, 773–777.

Gross, J. (1989). Emotional expression in cancer onset and progression. *Social Science Medicine, 28*, 1239–1248.

Gross, J. J., & Levenson, R. W. (1993). Emotional suppression: Physiology, self-report, and expressive behavior. *Journal of Personality and Social Psychology, 64*, 970–986.

Gross, J. J., & Levenson, R. W. (1997). Hiding feelings: The acute effects of inhibiting negative and positive emotion. *Journal of Abnormal Psychology, 106*, 95–103.

Grossarth-Maticek, R., Bastiaans, J., & Kanaziv, D. T. (1985). Psychosocial factors as strong predictors of mortality from cancer, ischaemic heart disease and stroke: The Yugoslav prospective study. *Journal of Psychosomatic Research, 29*, 167–176.

Guy, R. (1759). *An essay on schirrhous tumours and cancer.* London: W. Owen.

Hagnell, D. (1966). The premorbid personality of persons who developed cancer in a total population investigated in 1947 and 1957. *Annals of the New York Academy of Sciences, 125*, 846–855.

Hahn, R. C., & Petitti, D. B. (1988). Minnesota Multiphasic Personality Inventory-rated depression and the incidence of breast cancer. *Cancer, 61*, 845–848.

Head, J. F., Elliott, R. L., & McCoy, J. L. (1993). Evaluation of lymphocyte immunity in breast cancer patients. *Breast Cancer Research and Treatment, 26*, 77–88.

Herberman, R. (1985). Natural killer cells: Characteristics and possible role in resistance against tumor growth. In A. E. Reif & M. S. Mitchell (Eds.), *Immunity to cancer* (pp. 217–229). San Diego: Academic Press.

Herberman, R. (1991). Principles of tumor immunology. In A. I. Holleb, D. J. Fink, & F. P. Murphy (Eds.), *Textbook of clinical oncology* (pp. 69–79). Atlanta, GA: American Cancer Society.

Hilakivi-Clarke, L., Rowland, J., Clarke, R., & Lippman, M. E. (1993). Psychosocial factors in the development and progression of breast cancer. *Breast Cancer Research and Treatment, 29*, 141–160.

Holland, J. C. (1989). Behavioral and psychosocial risk factors in cancer: Human studies. In J. C. Holland & J. H. Rowland (Eds.), *Handbook of psychooncology: Psycho-logical care of the patient with cancer* (pp. 705–726). New York: Oxford University Press.

House, J. S., Landis, K. R., & Umberson, D. (1988). Social relationships and health. *Science, 241*(4865), 540–545.

Ilnyckyj, A., Farber, J., Cheang, M., & Weinerman, B. (1994). A randomized controlled trial of psychotherapeutic intervention in cancer patients. *Annals of the Royal College of Physicians and Surgeons of Canada, 27*, 93–96.

Irwin, M., Daniels, M., Risch, S. C., Bloom, E., & Weiner, H. (1988). Plasma cortisol and natural killer cell activity during bereavement. *Biological Psychiatry, 24*, 173–178.

Jamner, L. D., Schwartz, G. E., & Leigh, H. (1988). Repressive coping predicts monocyte, eosinophile, and serum glucose levels: Support for the opioid-peptide hypothesis. *Psychosomatic Medicine, 55*, 567–577.

Jayo, J. M., & Shively, C. (1993). Effects of exercise and stress on body fat distribution in male cynomolgus monkeys. *International Journal of Obesity and Related Metabolic Disorders, 17*, 597–604.

Jensen, M. R. (1987). Psychobiological factors predicting the course of breast cancer. *Journal of Personality, 55*, 317–342.

Kahn, M., & Schill, T. (1971). Anxiety report in defensive and nondefensive repressors. *Journal of Consulting and Clinical Psychology, 36*, 300.

Kaplan, E. L., & Meier. (1958). Non-parametric estimates from incomplete observations. *Journal of the American Statistical Association, 5*, 457–481.

Kaplan, G. A., & Reynolds, P. (1988). Depression and cancer mortality and morbidity: Prospective evidence from the Alameda County study. *Journal of Behavioral Medicine, 11*, 1–13.

Kelly, J. A., Murphy, D. A., Bahr, G. R., Kalichman, S. C., Morgan, M. G., Stevenson, L. Y., Koob, J. J., Brasfield, T. L., & Bernstein, B. M. (1993). Outcome of cognitive-behavioral and support group brief therapies for depressed, HIV-infected persons. *American Journal of Psychiatry, 150*, (1679–1686.

Kerr, T. A., Schapira, K., & Roth, M. (1969). The relationship between premature death and affective disorder. *British Journal of Psychiatry, 115*, 1277–1282.

Kiecolt-Glaser, J. K., Glaser, R., Cacioppo, J. T., & Malarkey, W. B. (1998). Marital stress: immunologic, neuroendocrine, and autonomic correlates. *Annals of the New York Academy of Science, 840*, 656–663.

Kiecolt-Glaser, J. K., & Greenberg, B. (1983). On the use of physiological measures in assertion research. *Journal of Behavioral Assessment, 5*, 97–109.

Kiecolt-Glaser, J. K., & Murray, J. A. (1980). Social desirability bias in self-monitoring data. *Journal of Behavioral Assessment, 2*, 239–247.

Kissen, D. M., Brown, R. I. F., & Kissen, M. A. (1969). A further report on the personality and psychological factors in lung cancer. *Annals of the New York Academy of Sciences, 164*, 535–545.

Kissen, D. M., & Eysenck, H. J. (1962). Personality in male lung patients. *Journal of Psychosomatic Research, 6*, 123–127.

Kneier, A. W., & Temoshok, L. (1984). Repressive coping reactions in patients with malignant melanoma as compared to cardiovascular disease patients. *Journal of Psychosomatic Research, 28*, 145–155.

Kogon, M. M., Biswas, A., Pearl, D., Carlson, R. W., & Spiegel, D. (1997). Effects of medical and psychotherapeutic treatment on the survival of women with metastatic breast carcinoma. *Cancer, 80*, 225–230.

Koutstaal, W., & Schacter, D. (1997). Intentional forgetting and voluntary thought suppression: Two potential methods for coping with childhood trauma. In L. Dickstein, R. M., & J. Oldham (Eds.), *Review of psychiatry* (Vol. 16, pp. II-79–II-121). Washington, DC: American Psychiatric Press.

Kreitler, S., Chaitchik, S., & Kreitler, H. (1993). Repressiveness: Cause or result of cancer? *Psychological Oncology, 2*, 43–54.

Kukull, W. A., McCorkle, R., & Driever, M. (1986). Symptom distress, psychosocial variables, and survival from lung cancer. *Journal of Psychosocial Oncology, 4*, 91–104.

Kune, G. A., Kune, S., Watson, L. F., & Bahnson, C. B. (1991). Personality as a risk factor in large bowel cancer: Data from the Melbourne Colorectal Cancer Study. *Psychological Medicine, 21*, 29–41.

Lane, R. D., Reiman, E. M., Bradley, M. M., Lang, P. J., Ahern, G. L., Davidson, R. J., & Schwartz, G. E. (1997). Neuroanatomical correlates of pleasant and unpleasant emotion. *Neuropsychologia, 35*, 1437–1444.

LeShan, L. L. (1966). An emotional life-history pattern associated with newoplastic disease. *Annals of the New York Academy of Sciences, 125*, 780–793.

Leszcz, M., & Goodwin, P. J. (1998). The rationale and foundations of group psychotherapy for women with metastatic breast cancer. *International Journal of Group Psychotherapy, 48*(2), 245–273.

Levine, S., Coe, C., & Wiener, S. G. (1989). Psychoneuroendocrinology of stress: A psychobiological perspective. In F. R. Brush & S. Levine (Eds.), *Psychoendocrinology* (pp. 341–377). New York: Academic Press.

Levy, S. M., Fernstrom, J., Herberman, R. B., Whiteside, T., Lee, J., Ward, M., & Massoudi, M. (1991). Persistently low natural killer cell activity and circulating levels of plasma beta endorphin: Risk factors for infectious disease. *Life Sciences, 48*(2), 107–116.

Levy, S. M., Herberman, R. B., Lee, J., Whiteside, T., Kirkwood, J., & McFeeley, S. (1990). Estrogen receptor concentration and social factors as predictors of natural killer cell activity in early-stage breast cancer patients. Confirmation of a model. *Natural Immunity and Cell Growth Regulation, 9*, 313–324.

Levy, S. M., Herberman, R., Lippman, M., & d'Angelo, T. (1987). Correlation of stress factors with sustained depression of natural killer cell activity and predicted prognosis in patients with breast cancer. *Journal of Clinical Oncology, 5*, 348–353.

Levy, S. M., Herberman, R. B., Lippman, M., & D'Angelo, T., & Lee, J. (1991). Immunological and psychosocial predictors of disease recurrence in patients with early-stage breast cancer. *Behavioral Medicine, 17*, 67–75.

Levy, S. M., Herberman, R. B., Maluish, A. M., Schlien, B., & Lippman, M. (1985). Prognostic risk assessment in primary breast cancer by behavioral and immunological parameters. *Health Psychology, 4*, 99–113.

Levy, S. M., Herberman, R. B., Whiteside, T., Sanzo, K., Lee, J., & Kirkwood, J. (1990). Perceived social support and tumor estrogen/progesterone receptor status as predictors of natural killer cell activity in breast cancer patients. *Psychosomatic Medicine 52*, 73–85.

Linn, M. W., Linn, B. S., & Harris, R. (1982). Effects of counseling for late stage cancer. *Cancer, 49*, 1048–1055.

Mages, N. L., & Mendelsohn, G. A. (1979). *Effects of cancer on patients' lives: A personological approach.* San Francisco, CA: Jossey-Bass.

Marmot, M. G., Fuhrer, R., Ettner, S. L., Marks, N. F., Bumpass, L. L., & Ryff, C. D. (1998). Contribution of psychosocial factors to socioeconomic differences in health. *Milbank Quarterly, 76*, 403–448.

McEwen, B. S. (1993). Stress and the individual: Mechanisms leading to disease. *Archives of Internal Medicine, 153*, 2093–2101.

McEwen, B. S. (1998). Protective and Damaging Effects of Stress Mediators. *New England Journal of Medicine, 338*, 171–179.

McKenna, M. C., Zevon, M. A., Corn, B., & Rounds, J. (1999). Psychosocial factors and the development of breast cancer: A meta-analysis. *Health Psychology, 18*, 520–531.

McNair, D. M., Lorr, M., & Drappelman, L. (1971). *POMS manual.* San Diego: San Diego Education and Industrial Testing Services.

McNair, D. M., Lorr, M., & Drappelman, L. (1992). *Edits manual for the profile of mood states*: Educational and Industrial Testing Service.

Milham, J., & Kellogg, R. W. (1980). Need for social approval: Impression management or self-deception? *Journal of Research in Personality, 14*, 445–457.

Morgenstern, H., Gellert, G. A., Walter, S. D., Ostfeld, A. M., & Siegel, B. S. (1984). The impact of a psychosocial support program on survival with breast cancer: the importance of selection bias in program evaluation. *Journal of Chronic Disease, 37*, 273–282.

Morris, T., Greer, H. S., & White, P. (1977). Psychological and social adjustment to mastectomy: A two-year follow-up study. *Cancer, 40*, 2381–2387.

Morris, T., Greer, S., Pettingale, K. W., & Watson, M. (1981). Patterns of expression of anger and their psychological correlates in women with breast cancer. *Journal of Psychosomatic Research, 25*, 111–117.

Mulder, C., van der Pompe, G., Spiegel, D., & Antoni, M. (1992). Do psychosocial factors influence the course of breast cancer? A review of recent literature methodological problems and future directions. *Psychooncology, 1*, 155–167.

Nemeroff, C. B., Widerlov, E., Bissette, G., Walleus, H., Karlsson, I., Eklund, K., Kilts, C. D., Loosen, P. T., & Vale, W. (1984). Elevated concentrations of CSF corticotropin-releasing factor-like immunoreactivity in depressed patients. *Science, 226*(4680), 1342–1344.

Niemi, T., & Jaaskelainen, J. (1978). Cancer morbidity in depressive persons. *Journal of Psychosomatic Research, 22*, 117–120.

Ozasa, H., Kita, M., Inoue, T., & Mori, T. (1990). Plasma dehydroepiandrosterone-to-cortisol ratios as an indicator of stress in gynecologic patients. *Gynecological Oncology, 37*, 178–182.

Padgett, D. A., Loria, R. M., & Sheridan, J. F. (1997). Endocrine regulation of the immune response to influenza virus infection with a metabolite of DHEA-androstenediol. *Journal of Neuroimmunology, 78*, 203–211.

Paget, J. (1870). *Surgical pathology* (2nd ed.). London: Longmans Green.

Parker, L. N., Levin, E. R., & Lifrak, E. T. (1985). Evidence for adrenocortical adaptation to severe illness. *Journal of Clinical Endocrinology and Metabolism, 60*, 947–1952.

Parker, W. (1865). *Cancer: A study of 397 cases of cancer of the female breast*. New York: G. P. Putnam.

Pennebaker, J. W. (Ed.) (1995). *Emotion, disclosure, and health*. Washington, DC: American Psychological Association.

Pennebaker, J. W., Kiecolt-Glaser, J. K., & Glaser, R. (1988). Disclosure of traumas and immune function: Health implications for psychotherapy. *Journal of Consulting and Clinical Psychology, 56*, 239–245.

Penninx, B. W. J. H., Guralnik, M. P., Pahor, M., Ferrucci, L., Cerhan, J. R., Wallace, R. B., & Havlik, R. J. (1998). Chronically depressed mood and cancer risk in older persons. *Journal of the National Cancer Institute, 90*, 1888–1893.

Persky, V. W., Kempthorne-Rawson, J., & Shekelle, R. B. (1987). Personality and risk of cancer: 20-year follow-up of the Western Electric Study. *Psychosomatic Medicine, 49*, 435–449.

Petrie, K. J., Booth, R. J., & Davison, K. P. (1995). Repression, disclosure, and immune function: Recent findings and methodological issues. In J. W. Pennebaker (Ed.), *Emotion, disclosure, and health* (pp. 223–237). Washington, DC: American Psychological Association.

Petticrew, M., Fraser, J., & Regan, M. F. (1999). Adverse life-events and risk of breast cancer: A meta-analysis. *British Journal of Health Psychology, 4*, 1–17.

Pettingale, K. W., Morris, T., Greer, S., & Haybittle, J. L. (1985). Mental attitudes to cancer: an additional prognostic factor. *Lancet, 8431*(1), 750.

Phillips, D. P., Ruth, T.E., & Wagner, L. M. (1993). Psychology and survival [see comments]. *Lancet, 342*(8880), 1142–1145.

Plotsky, P. M., Owens, M. J., & Nemeroff, C. B. (1998). Psychoneuroendocrinology of depression. Hypothalamic-pituitary-adrenal axis. *Psychiatric Clinics of North America, 21*, 293–307.

Posener, J. A., Schildkraut, J. J., Samson, J. A., & Schatzberg, A. F. (1996). Diurnal variation of plasma cortisol and homovanillic acid in healthy subjects. *Psychoneuroendocrinology, 21*, 33–38.

Radloff, L. S. (1977). The CES-D Scale: A self-report depression scale for research in the general population. *Applied Psychological Measurement, 1*, 385–401.

Raphael, B. (1977). Preventive intervention with the recently bereaved. *Archives of General Psychiatry, 34*, 1450–1454.

Ratcliffe, M. A., Dawson, A. A., & Walker, L. G. (1995). Eysenck Personality Inventory L-scores in patients with Hodgkin's disease and non-Hodgkin's lymphoma. *Psycho-Oncology, 4*, 39–45.

Reynolds, P., & Kaplan, G. A. (1990). Social connections and risk for cancer: Prospective evidence from the Alameda County Study. *Behavioral Medicine, 16*, 101–110.

Richardson, J. L., Shelton, D. R., Krailo, M., & Levine, A. M. (1990). The effect of compliance with treatment on survival among patients with hematologic malignancies. *Journal of Clinical Oncology, 8*, 356–364.

Riley, V. (1975). Mouse mammary tumors: Alteration of incidence as apparent function of stress. *Science, 189*(4201), 465–467.

Riley, V. (1981). Psychoneuroendocrine influences on immunocompetence and neoplasia. *Science, 212*(4499), 1100–1109.

Roberts, R. E. (1981). Prevalence of depressive symptoms among Mexican Americans. *Journal of Nervous Mental Disorder, 169*, 213–219.

Rodin, J. (1980). *Managing the stress of aging: The role of control and coping*. New York: Plenum.

Rodin, J. (1986). *Health, control and aging*. Hillsdale, NJ: Erlbaum.

Rogentine, S. N., Van Kammen, D. P., Fox, B. H., Docherty, J. P., Rosenblatt, J. E., Boyd, S. C., & Bunney, W. E. (1979). Psychological factors in the prognosis of malignant melanoma: A prospective study. *Psychosomatic Medicine, 41*, 647–655.

Rosenberg, S. A., & Lotze, M. T. (1986). Cancer immunotherapy using interleukin-2 and interleukin-2-activated lymphocytes. *Annual Review of Immunology, 4*, 681–709.

Sapolsky, R. M., & Donnelly, T. M. (1985). Vulnerability to stress-induced tumor growth increases with age in rats: role of glucocorticoids. *Endocrinology, 117*, 662–666.

Sapolsky, R., Krey, L., & McEwen, B. S. (1985). Prolonged glucocorticoid exposure reduces hippocampal neuron number: implication for aging. *Journal of Neuroscience, 5*, 1222–1227.

Scherg, H., Cramer, I., & Blohmke, M. (1981). Psychosocial factors and breast cancer: A critical evaluation of established hypotheses. *Cancer Detection and Prevention, 4*, 165–171.

Schmale, A., & Iker, H. (1966). The psychological setting of uterine cervical cancer. *Annals of the New York Academy of Sciences, 125*, 807–813.

Schneider, D. J., & Turkat, D. (1975). Self-presentation following success or failure: Defensive self-esteem models. *Journal of Personality, 43*, 127–135.

Schonfield, J. (1975). Psychological and life-experience differences between Israeli women with benign and cancerous breast lesions. *Journal of Psychosomatic Research, 19*, 229–234.

Schwartz, R., & Geyer, S. (1984). Social and psychological differences between cancer and noncancer patients: Cause or consequence of the disease? *Psychotherapy and Psychosomatics, 41*, 195–199.

Seeman, T., Singer, B. H., Rowe, J. W., Horowitz, R. I., & McEwen, B. S. (1997). Price of adaptation—allostatic load and its health consequences. MacArthur studies of successful aging. *Archives of Internal Medicine, 157*, 2259–2268.

Shaffer, J. W., Graves, P. L., Swank, R. T., & Pearson, T. A. (1987). Clustering of personality traits in youth and the subsequent development of cancer among physicians. *Journal of Behavioral Medicine, 10*, 441–447.

Shea, J. D., Burton, R., & Girgis, A. (1993). Negative affect, absorption, and immunity. *Physiological Behavior, 53*, 449–457.

Shekelle, R. B., Raynor, W., Jr., Ostfeld, A. M., Garron, D. C., Bieliauskas, L. A., Liu, S. C., Maliza, C., & Paul, O. (1981). Psychological depression and 17-year risk of death from cancer. *Psychosomatic Medicine, 43*, 117–25.

Sheridan, J. F., Dobbs, C., Brown, D., & Zwilling, B. (1994). Psychoneuroimmunology: Stress effects on pathogenesis and immunity during infection. *Clinical Microbiology Review, 7*, 200–212.

Sheridan, J. F., Dobbs, C., Jung, J., Chu, K., Konstantinos, A., Padgett, D., & Glaser, R. D. (1998). Stress-induced neuroendocrine modulation of viral pathogenesis and immunity. *Annals of the New York Academy of Sciences, 840*, 803–808.

Spiegel, D. (1993). Psychosocial intervention in cancer.

*Journal of the National Cancer Institute, 85*(5), 1198–1205.

Spiegel, D. (1995). Essentials of psychotherapeutic intervention for cancer patients. *Support Care Cancer, 3*, 252–256.

Spiegel, D. (1996). Psychological distress and disease course for women with breast cancer: one answer, many questions [editorial; comment]. *Journal of the National Cancer Institute, 88*, 629–631.

Spiegel, D. (1999). Healing words: Emotional expression and disease outcome. *Journal of the American Medical Association, 281*, 1328–1329.

Spiegel, D., & Bloom, J. R. (1983). Group therapy and hypnosis reduce metastatic breast carcinoma pain. *Psychosomatic Medicine, 45*, 333–339.

Spiegel, D., Bloom, J. R., Kraemer, H. C., & Gottheil, E. (1989). Effect of psychosocial treatment on survival of patients with metastatic breast cancer. *Lancet, 2*(8668), 888–891.

Spiegel, D., Bloom, J. R., & Yalom, I. (1981). Group support for patients with metastatic cancer. A randomized outcome study. *Archives of General Psychiatry, 38*, 527–533.

Spiegel, D., & Kato, P. (1996). Psychosocial influences on cancer incidence and progression. *Harvard Review of Psychiatry, 4*, 10–26.

Spiegel, D., & Spira, J. (1991). *Supportive/expressive group therapy: A treatment manual of psychosocial intervention for women with recurrent breast cancer.* Unpublished manuscript, Stanford University School of Medicine.

Spiegel, D., & Yalom, I. (1978). A support group for dying patients. *International Journal of Group Psychotherapy, 28*, 233–245.

Stein, M., Miller, A. H., & Trestman, R. L. (1991). Depression, the immune system, and health and illness. Findings in search of meaning. *Archives of General Psychiatry, 48*, 171–177.

Sternberg, E. M., Chrousos, G. P., Wilder, R. L., & Gold, P. W. (1992). The stress response and the regulation of inflammatory disease. *Annals of Internal Medicine, 117*, 854–866.

Taylor, J. A. (1953). A personality scale of manifest anxiety. *Journal of Abnormal and Social Psychology, 48*, 285–290.

Temoshok, L. (1985). Biopsychosocial studies on cutaneous malignant melanoma: psychosocial factors associated with prognostic indicators, progression, psychophysiology and tumor-host response. *Social Science Medicine, 20*, 833–840.

Temoshok, L. (1987). Personality, coping style, emotion and cancer: towards an integrative model. *Cancer Survival, 6*, 545–567.

Temoshok, L., & Fox, B. H. (1984). Coping styles and other psychosocial factors related to medical status and to prognosis in patients with cutaneous malignant melanoma. In B. H. Fox & B. H. Newberry (Eds.), *Impact of psychoendocrine systems in cancer and immunity* (pp. 258–287). New York: Hogrefe, C. J.

Temoshok, L., Heller, B. W., Sagebiel, R. W., Blois, M. S., Sweet, D. M., DiClemente, R. J., & Gold, M. L. (1985). The relationship of psychosocial factors to prognostic indicators in cutaneous malignant melanoma. *Journal of Psychosomatic Research, 29*, 139–153.

Thomas, C. B., Duszanski, K. R., & Shaffer, J. W. (1979). Family attitudes reported in youth as potential predictors of cancer. *Psychosomatic Medicine, 41*, 287–301.

Tross, S., Hirsch, D., Rabkin, J., Berry, C., & Holland, J. (1987). *Determinants of current psychiatric disorders in AIDS spectrum patients.* Paper presented at the Third International Conference on AIDS, Washington, DC.

Trunnell, J. B. (1952). *Second report on institutional research grants of the American Cancer Society.* New York: American Cancer Society.

Turner, R. J. (1981). Social support as a contingency to psychological well-being. *Journal of Health and Social Behavior, 22*, 357–367.

Turvey, C., & Salovey, P. (1993–94). Measures of repression: converging on the same construct? *Imagination, Cognition, and Personality, 13*(4), 279–289.

Valliant, G. E. (Ed.). (1990). *Repression in college men followed for half a century.* Chicago: University of Chicago Press.

Varsamis, J., Zuckhowski, T., & Maini, K. K. (1972). Survival rates of death in geriatric psychiatric patients: A six-year follow-up. *Canadian Psychiatric Association Journal, 7*, 17–22.

Watson, C. G., Plemel, D., Vassar, P., Manifold, V., & Kucala, T. (1987). The comparative validities of six MMPI repression scales. *Journal of Clinical Psychology, 43*, 472–477.

Watson, D., & Clark, L. A. (1984). Negative affectivity: The disposition to experience aversive emotional states. *Psychological Bulletin, 96*, 465–490.

Watson, M., & Greer, S. (1983). Development of a questionnaire measure of emotional control. *Journal of Psychosomatic Research, 27*, 299–305.

Watson, M., Greer, S., Rowden, L., Gorman, C., Robertson, B., Bliss, J. M., & Tunmore, R. (1991). Relationships between emotional control, adjustment to cancer and depression and anxiety in breast cancer patients. *Psychological Medicine, 21*, 51–57.

Watson, M., Greer, S., Young, J., Inayat, Q., Burgess, C., & Robertson, B. (1988). Development of a questionnaire measure of adjustment to cancer: the MAC scale. *Psychological Medicine, 18*, 203–209.

Watson, M., Haviland, J. S., Greer, S., Davidson, J., & Bliss, J. M. (1999). Influence of psychological response on survival in breast cancer: A population-based cohort study. *Lancet, 354*, 1331–1336.

Watson, M., Law, M., dos Santos, M., Greer, S., Baruch, J., & Bliss, J. (1994). The Mini-MAC: Further development of the Mental Adjustment to Cancer Scale. *Journal of Psychosocial Oncology, 12*, 33–46.

Watson, M., Pettingale, K. W., & Greer, S. (1984). Emotional control and autonomic arousal in breast cancer patients. *Journal of Psychosomatic Research, 28*, 467–474.

Weinberger, D. A. (1990). The construct validity of the repressive coping style. In J. L. Singer (Ed.), *Repression and dissociation: Implications for personality theory, psychopathology, and health* (pp. 337–386). Chicago: University of Chicago Press.

Weinberger, D. A., & Davidson, M. N. (1994). Styles of inhibiting emotional expression: Distinguishing repressive coping from impression management. *Journal of Personality, 62*, 587–612.

Weinberger, D. A., & Schwartz, G. E. (1990). Distress and restraint as superordinate dimensions of self-reported adjustment: A typological perspective. *Journal of Personality, 58*, 381–417.

Weinberger, D. A., Schwartz, G. E., & Davidson, R. J. (1979). Low-anxious, high anxious, and repressive coping styles: Psychometric patterns and behavioral and physiological responses to stress. *Journal of Abnormal Psychology, 88*, 369–380.

Weisman, A. D., & Worden, J. W. (1976). The existential plight in cancer: significance of the first 100 days. *International Journal of Psychiatry in Medicine, 7*(1), 1–15.

Whitlock, F., & Siskund, M. (1979). Depression and cancer: A followup study. *Psychological Medicine, 9*, 747–752.

Wirsching, M., Stierlin, H., Hoffman, F., Weber, G., & Wirsching, B. (1982). Psychological identification of breast cancer patients before biopsy. *Journal of Psychosomatic Research, 26*, 1–10.

Yalom, I. D. (1980). *Existential psychotherapy.* New York: Basic Books.

Yalom, I. D., & Greaves, C. (1977). Group therapy with the terminally ill. *American Journal of Psychiatry, 134*, 396–400.

Yehuda, R., Southwick, S. M., Krystal, J. H., Bremner, D., Charney, D. S., & Mason, J. W. (1993). Enhanced suppression of cortisol following dexamethasone administration in posttraumatic stress disorder. *American Journal of Psychiatry, 150*, 83–86.

Yehuda, R., Teicher, M. H., Trestman, R. L., Levengood, R. A., & Siever, L. J. (1996). Cortisol regulation in posttraumatic stress disorder and major depression: A chronobiological analysis. *Biological Psychiatry, 40*, 79–88.

Zigmond, A. S., & Snaith, R. P. (1983). The hospital anxiety and depression scale. *Acta Psychiatrica Scandinavica, 67*, 361–370.

Zonderman, A. B., Costa, P., Jr., & McCrae, R. R. (1989). Depression as a risk for cancer morbidity and mortality in a nationally representative sample. *Journal of the American Medical Association, 262*, 1191–1195.

# THE ROLE OF EMOTION ON PATHWAYS TO POSITIVE HEALTH

Carol D. Ryff and Burton H. Singer

Many of the core questions in affective science (e.g., Are there basic emotions? What are the antecedents and functions of emotion? How do individuals differ in emotional reactivity?) have developed without explicit connection to the realm of human health. Alternatively, when emotion has entered the health realm (e.g., Does anger increase cardiovascular risk? Is optimism protective?), it has frequently been with little connection to mainstream research in affective science. This separation is not a state of affairs to lament, but rather represents opportunities for the future in which the fields of emotion and health can enrich and extend each other.

Our objective in this chapter is to bring the nexus between these realms into focus via discussion of five guiding premises for relating emotion to health. These serve as conceptual guideposts for examining past, current, and future empirical studies, and do so with an emphasis on testable hypotheses. The five premises are: (1) emotions consequential for health are about something; (2) health requires a focus on co-occurring discrete emotions; (3) health is biopsychosocial in nature and necessitates integration of phenomenology and neurophysiology; (4) cumulative, chronic emotions are consequential for health; and (5) emotion can be protective and promote positive health. Each premise is illustrated via separate substantive studies, although a unifying theme across them is the need for integrative endeavors that put together psychosocial experience, underlying biological mechanisms, and health outcomes.

A second generic observation setting the stage for what follows is the relative paucity of knowledge about positive emotion-health linkages. Our goal is to bring greater attention to salubrious connections between affective experience and health, mental and physical. An emphasis on positive health, we note, does not translate simplistically to a focus on exclusively positive affective experience. As we will argue, one of the intriguing challenges of future work is to unearth basic processes whereby negative emotions, ubiquitous in human experience, can be transformed into benign, or even beneficial, influences on health. Finally, while we seek to underscore the positive health theme, much in our chapter deals with the role of emotion in illness as that is where most prior work has been conducted.

## Premise I. Emotions Consequential for Health Are *About Something*

In building connections between affective experience and health, we propose that it is particularly valuable to anchor emotion in the life contexts in which they occur. This is a call for greater emphasis on what gives rise to emotion. Ekman's (1992) description of basic emotions emphasized that they "evolved for their adaptive value in dealing with fundamental life-tasks" (p. 171). He drew on numerous works of others to summarize the universal predicaments (achievements, losses, frustrations), the common adaptational tasks (facing danger, progressing toward a goal), the recurrent situations (fighting, falling in love, escaping predators, confronting sexual infidelity) that catalyze emotion. Simply put, emotions are designed to deal with "inter-organismic encounters" (p. 171)—they are fundamentally *about something*.

To those outside the field of affective science, calling for attention to what emotions are about may seem gratuitous—indeed, an obvious point. However, extant work in the affective field reveals that it is the exception, not the rule, to focus on the fundamental life-tasks described above. In examining the origins and functions of positive and negative affect, Carver and Scheier (1990) make the point that how good and bad feelings arise is a pervasively neglected question: "Indeed, it is remarkable how rarely anyone ever asks where affect comes from" (p. 22), and go on to note that many formulations discuss only what happens once affect is already present. Likewise, the literature addressing the basic structure of emotion and affect (Green, Salovey, & Truax, 1999; Russell & Barrett, 1999; Watson, Wiese, Vaidya, & Tellegen, 1999; Yik, Russell, & Barrett, 1999) is primarily about momentary, free-floating assessments of reported feelings. At the level of neural substrates the focus is also "more on the architecture and operating characteristics of the affect system than on the antecedent condition for arousing positive or negative affect" (Cacioppo, Gardner, & Berntson, 1999, p. 849).

Drawing on these distinctions, Russell and Barrett (1999) distinguish between *core affect* as the most elementary consciously accessible affective feelings (and their neurophysiological counterparts) that "need not be directed at anything" (p. 806), and *prototypical emotion episodes*, which are feelings concerned with a specific object—"one is afraid *of*, is angry *with*, is in love *with*, or has pity *for* something" (p. 806). Most parsing of affective space has been about the former, not the latter (see later discussion of discrete versus dimensional models in Premise II). Moreover, when feelings about something have been considered, the focus is typically on "temporary events and slices of time" (p. 805). They note that love and hate, prototypical exemplars of emotion, as in lifelong love of an offspring, are not part of their purview.

Why do we advocate for greater focus on the fundamental life tasks that give rise to emotion in building bridges to health? A first reason is that emotional reactions to core life challenges are, we propose, powerful elicitors of affect—both phenomenologically and physiologically. It is grinding feelings of defeat or exhilarating triumph in pursuing sought-after goals, along with the comforting security or tormenting despair in primary social relationships, that leave a great imprint on psyche and soma. Further, given our advanced cognitive capacities, these poignant, sometimes elevating, sometimes debasing human feelings may well be reactivated simply by thinking about them. Elie Wiesel (1999) wrote about being haunted

over the course of his life by his inability to come to the assistance of his father as he called for help in the concentration camp. He was, in fact, unable to speak at the Nobel Peace Prize ceremony in his honor in 1986 because of the following recollection.

> I see myself once again with my father on the last day of his life, the last night. I was near him as he agonized, but not at the hour of his death. I speak of it in "Night." He called me. My father called me, gently, weakly. I heard him moaning. I heard him calling. His cries tore me apart; they tear me apart still. In spite of the danger I should have gone to him, run to him. I should have said to him: "I'm here Father. Your son will never leave you." I should have told him something, anything. But we were forbidden to speak. I would have been beaten, beaten to death. I would have been killed. I was afraid then. I am afraid now. (pp. 270–271)

Early on in the affective field, Darwin asked whether we can feel anger, fear, sadness, and enjoyment when we are alone (1872/1998). For the human species, the answer seems a resounding yes; we suggest that this capacity is consequential for health.

A further reason for focusing on what emotions are about intersects with studies of life stressors that have been previously linked to intervening neuroendocrine, cardiovascular, and immunological mechanisms implicated in health outcomes (McEwen & Schmeck, 1994; Sapolsky, 1992; Weiner, 1992). That is, notable benefits regarding the explication of mechanisms follow from focusing on the fundamental life-tasks that give rise to emotion. This interface between the psychobiology of life stress and the emergent field of affective science represents another promising nexus for cross-fertilization and interdisciplinary inquiry. Emotion, it can be argued, has been insufficiently elaborated in the stress literature. Concomitantly, anchoring the study of affect in fundamental life-tasks provides connection to neurophysiological mechanisms implicated in stress.

Yet another reason for emphasizing what emotions are about pertains to the challenge of discerning whether particular emotional responses are adaptive, maladaptive, healthy, unhealthy, warranted, or unwarranted. Davidson, Jackson, and Kalin (2000) argue that to answer these questions, it is critical to know the context in which the affect is experienced—that is, what the feelings are about. They further suggest that "context-inappropriate responding," a hypothesized product of hippocampal dysfunction, is a hallmark of certain forms of psychopathology.

To illustrate the consequential nature (for health) of feelings *about something*, we offer two examples below. The first pertains to emotions about significant others, and the second involves emotions about racism. We select these examples because they bring into high relief the extent to which health questions may lead to distinct ways of organizing affective experience from currently available models. For example, most key social emotions (e.g., love, hate, affection, attachment, jealousy, envy) are notably absent in formulations of core affect (Russell & Barrett, 1999; Watson, Wiese, Vaidya, & Tellegen, 1999; Yik et al., 1999). Similarly, the experience of racism may not be fruitfully captured by two-dimensional models of valence (positive, negative) and activation (low, high). This is not a criticism of such models, as they were not designed with health questions in mind, but rather an observation that pushing forward agendas on emotions and health may require novel conceptualizations of the affective realm. A further reason for selecting these two illustrations is that both have been previously linked to health outcomes.

## Emotions About Significant Others

By significant others, we refer to those individuals (children, parents, spouses, co-workers, friends) deemed central players in one's life. Affective experience surrounding interaction with such individuals constitutes a primary category of the inter-organismic encounters described by Ekman. Moreover, a large and growing literature has documented links between the social relational realm and morbidity and mortality (Berkman & Breslow, 1983; House, Landis, & Umberson, 1988; Ryff & Singer, 2000; Seeman, 1996; Seeman, Berkman, Blazer & Rowe, 1994; Uchino, Cacioppo, & Kiecolt-Glaser, 1996). A review of eight major epidemiological studies (Berkman, 1995) indicated that, in each case, mortality was significantly lower among persons who were more socially integrated.

This research has frequently emphasized structural features of social relationships, such as the size and proximity of one's social network (e.g., whether one is married or living alone, whether one has a close confidant; number of close friends or relatives and frequency of contact with them). Notably less concern has been given to the emotional texture and depth of such social relations, although limited questions about emotional support are sometimes included (e.g., Berkman, Leo-Summers, & Horwitz, 1992; Glass & Maddox, 1992). The nature of the emotions that actually constitute such emotional support is rarely elaborated.

There are nonetheless separate literatures dealing with intimacy, attachment, marital interaction, and parent-child relations, wherein the emotional texture of key social relationships is extensively probed (e.g., Berscheid & Reis, 1998; Carstensen, Gottman, & Levenson, 1995; Carstensen, Graff, Levenson, & Gottman, 1996; Cassidy & Shaver, 1999; Fitness, 1996; Fitness & Fletcher, 1993; Hazan & Shaver, 1994; Reis & Patrick, 1996; Ryff, Singer, Wing, & Love, 2001). These agendas are, however, rarely connected to studies of health (Ryff & Singer, 2000).

Still other literatures map the biological processes associated with social interactions, be they affiliative experiences, social isolation, or social conflict (e.g., Carter, 1998; Coe, 1993; Cohen & Herbert, 1996; Kiecolt-Glaser et al., 1997; Knox & Uvnäs-Moberg, 1998: Panksepp, 1998b; Seeman & McEwen, 1996; Uchino et al., 1996; Uvnäs-Moberg, 1998). This is where biological sequelae at multiple physiological levels (cardiovascular, neuroendocrine, immunological) are examined.

Illustrating what emotion is about *and* its links to physiology is the growing literature on marital conflict. Kiecolt-Glaser et al. (1997) have shown that among adults in long-term marriages, 30 minutes of conflict discussion was associated with changes in cortisol, adrenocorticotropic hormone (ACTH), and norepinephrine in women, but not men. Both husbands and wives showed poorer immunological response during conflict. Among newlyweds, Kiecolt-Glaser et al. (1996) also found higher cortisol and epinephrine levels among wives, but only those whose husbands had high probabilities of withdrawal response in their negative communication. More frequent positive behaviors were also associated with lower epinephrine and higher prolactin levels among wives, but not husbands. Other studies have linked marital conflict with high blood pressure (Ewart, Taylor, Kraemer, & Agras, 1991), pituitary and adrenal hormones (Malarkey, Kiecolt-Glaser, Pearl, & Glaser, 1994), and physiological arousal (Levenson, Carstensen, & Gottman (1994).

Taylor, Repetti, and Seeman (1997) have also explored the nature of "unhealthy environments" at the family level and how they get under the skin. Their review points to three characteristics of the social environments that undermine the health of children and adolescents: a social climate that is conflictual and angry, or even violent and abusive; parent-child relationships that are unresponsive and lacking in cohesiveness, warmth, and emotional support; and a parenting style that is either overly controlling and dominating, or uninvolved with little imposition of rules and structure. Such characteristics were linked to depression and maladaptive ways of coping in children as well as health-threatening behaviors in adolescents.

Emotion is a critical ingredient in putting together the pieces of social experience and biology. That is, the affective experiences in proximal and primary social relationships—that is, feelings of love, nurturance, intimacy, affection, and attachment in the positive scenario, or experiences of anger, bitterness, resentment, humiliation, and withdrawal in the negative case—are likely central activators of physiological mechanisms that subsequently feed into health outcomes. This is not to overlook the important behavioral routes through which social support impacts health, such as how significant others promote and encourage positive health practices (Berkman, 1995; Spiegel & Kimerling, 2001; Taylor et al., 1997). Rather, it is a call to sharpen and heighten the emphasis on the emotional features of key social interactions and their attendant neurophysiological underpinnings.

## Emotions of Oppression: The Affective Experience of Racism

A second illustration draws on broader social structural influences on affective experience, a realm largely missing in current studies of emotion. Here we consider the emotions associated with being a member of a group that is socially denigrated and denied fair opportunities in life. These are the feelings tied to the experience of racism. An emergent literature is exploring the stress associated with racism and its biopsychosocial sequelae (Clark, Anderson, Clark, & Williams, 1999). African Americans are disproportionately exposed to environmental stimuli that are sources of stress (chronic and acute), and they have a higher prevalence of hypertension and all-cause mortality than do Caucasians of comparable levels of education (Pappas, Queen, Hadden, & Fisher, 1993). While such differences may reflect an unequal distribution of wealth, they are also likely linked to differential exposure to stressors like racism and unfair treatment (Krieger, 1990; Williams, Yu, Jackson, & Anderson, 1997). Perceived racial discrimination, we note, has also been investigated with other ethnic minority groups, such as Southeast Asian refugees (Noh, Beiser, Kaspar, Hou, & Rummens, 1999).

Numerous responses may follow the perception that one has been subjected to racism, such as anger, anxiety, frustration, fear, helplessness-hopelessness, paranoia, and resentment. The ways in which African Americans cope with anger—the affective state most commonly reported to follow perceptions of racism—have been related to cardiovascular reactivity and resting blood pressure (Armstead, Lawler, Gorden, Cross, & Gibbons, 1989; Johnson & Browman, 1987). Investigating the efficacy of general coping strategies as moderators of perceived racism, Armstead et al. (1989) found that as outward expression of anger increased, blood pressure levels decreased after viewing racist video scenes, Other responses to racism include suppression of anger and use of alcohol or other substances to blunt angry feelings (Armstead et al., 1989). Chronic feelings of helplessness or hopelessness may evoke depression and other feelings of frustration, resentment, and distrust, themselves leading to maladaptive health behaviors (overeating, passivity, avoidance).

Recent work by McNeilly et al. (1996) outlines a broad range of emotional and coping responses to racism and methods for measuring them. One hypothesis is that over time, chronic perceptions of racism coupled with more passive coping may lead to frequent increases in and prolonged activation of sympathetic functioning, resulting in higher resting systolic blood pressure levels. Krieger (1990) found that African-American women (more than 45 years old) who responded to unfair treatment (racism and gender discrimination) with passive coping responses (e.g., keeping quiet and accepting treatment) were 4.4 times more likely to have self-reported hypertension than African-American women whose coping techniques were more active. The links between the emotional reactions to racism, coping styles, and subsequent health sequelae in the immune system and stress-induced neuroendocrine responses (see Clark et al., 1999) constitute important directions for future inquiry.

Our objective in including racism as an illustration of the importance of assessing what emotions are *about* underscores the need to anchor affective experience in the challenges, sometimes chronic, of individual lives. We posit that these are what elicit powerful, and frequently recurrent, human emotions. It is the purported intensity and persistence (both subject to empirical scrutiny) that makes these affective experiences relevant starting points for building bridges to health outcomes via diverse neurophysiological mechanisms.

Although our emphasis has been on emotions about racism, we note that such inquiry has broader relevance. Gallo and Matthews (1999), for example, have proposed that negative emotions (specifically, depression, hopelessness, anxiety, hostile attitudes, and affect) may mediate the association between socioeconomic status and health. Thus, it is not ethnic/racial status, but rather social inequalities, even among minority groups, that are consequential for health. Carroll et al. (1997) also emphasize the links between socioeconomic status, hostility, and blood pressure reactions to mental stress.

Finally, underscoring the high prevalence of perceived discrimination in the general U.S. population and its strong associations with mental health, Kessler, Mickelson, and Williams (1999) argue that perceived discrimination needs to be taken much more seriously in future studies of stress and mental health. The perception that one has been discriminated against is, we submit, an experience prompting significant, perhaps powerful, emotional response.

## Premise II. Health Requires a Focus on *Co-Occurrence* of Discrete Emotions

### Dimensional and Categorical Models of Emotion

Those who study affect give considerable attention to structural questions, such as whether positive and negative affect are best construed as independent or bipolar dimensions (e.g., Diener, Smith, & Fujita, 1995; Russell & Barrett, 1999; Watson et al., 1999; Yik et al., 1999), and the extent to which measurement error obscures understanding of these questions (Green, Goldman, & Salovey, 1993; Green et al., 1999). Comparison of multiple models (e.g., Barrett & Russell, 1998; Larsen & Diener, 1992; Watson & Tellegen, 1985; Thayer, 1989) reveals a convergent emphasis on two dimensions of valence (positive and negative) and two dimensions of activation (high and low), with differing positions as to where to place the axes in this dimensional space (Russell & Barrett, 1999).

Juxtaposed with such dimensional models are models of discrete or basic emotions, which focus on distinguishable (by their facial signals, temporal profiles, presence in other primates) features of anger, fear, sadness, enjoyment, disgust, surprise, and possibly contempt, shame, guilt, embarrassment, and awe. The question thus arises as to whether those who study links between emotion and health are best served by dimensional or discrete models. Watson and Pennebaker (1989) advocated a dimensional model, arguing that a substantial body of data show positive correlations between measures of negative affect and reports of somatic symptoms, with the further suggestion that this correlation is independent of various components (anxiety, depression, anger) constituting the affective pole. Leventhal and Patrick-Miller (1993) challenged this position, arguing that it is essential to disaggregate the negative affect pole. Differential models do a better job of accounting for changes in symptomatology over time (e.g., depression shows a positive association with increases in symptoms, but anxiety does not).

Additionally, Leventhal and Patrick-Miller (1993) pointed out that differential negative affects are necessary to understand the mediation of stress-disease relationships. Although measured in different ways, hostility is implicated in the long-term development of atherosclerosis leading to coronary occlusions and increased probability of acute coronary events during environmental crises (see Matthews, 1988; Smith, 1992). Depression, however, is not predictive of coronary disease (Matthews, 1988), although depression, hopelessness-helplessness, repressive coping style, and deficient social support have been associated with cancer outcomes, such as cancer diagnosis, patient prognosis at time of diagnosis, rate of cancer recurrence, years survived, and patient mortality (Contrada, Leventhal, & O'Leary, 1990). Drawing on animal models, Leventhal and Patrick-Miller (1993) offer possible formulations of physiological mechanisms: Helpless animals show depletion of brain norepinephrine and activation of the hypothalamic-pituitary-adrenal axis, resulting in release of corticosteroids in the bloodstream, with the latter linked to increased growth of implanted tumors, decreased T-lymphocyte proliferation, and decreased natural killer (NK) cell activity.

As these summaries indicate, legitimate arguments can be made for bringing both dimensional and discrete models of emotion to the study of health. To some extent, however, the dichotomy itself is problematic. That is, dimensional approaches cover wide territory, but for health purposes, they reduce affective experience to overly generic components (e.g., feeling good or bad, feeling

aroused or unaroused) that may be of limited value for probing differentiated responses to fundamental life-tasks. Alternatively, discrete models offer greater focus on differentiated emotional states, but lack scope regarding a larger panoply of responses that may ensue from engagement in life challenges. Thus, what may be critical for health outcomes is a third alternative—namely, the *co-occurrence of discrete emotions*. Further, recalling our prior emphasis on what gives rise to emotion in the course of living, we suggest that few significant experiences prompt only single emotions or can be adequately captured by only two dimensions (valence and activation).

Racism, for example, likely prompts a constellation of affective experiences that include diverse emotions—anger, fear, resentment, perhaps along with sadness and hopelessness (see prior discussion of Clark et al., 1999). Alienation, a likely component of discrimination, itself involves multiple feelings, including the sense of powerlessness, social isolation, normlessness, and lack of meaning (Seeman, 1959, 1975). Moreover, different individuals likely have different combinations of these negative responses, and these variations can be empirically exploited by assessing co-occurring discrete emotions.

Similarly, emotions about significant others (spouse, children, parents), when they are positive, may involve love, affection, pride, intimacy, security. Fredrickson (1998) argues that love involves a fusion of many positive emotions, the combination of which broadens the scope of thought and action as well as builds personal, social, and physical resources. Alternatively, negative family dynamics may involve combinations of hostility, bitterness, and anger, or despair, detachment, and loneliness, with differing configurations having different physiological sequelae. Miller, Dopp, Myers, et al. (1999), in studying marital conflict, found that displays of anger in husbands high in cynical hostility were associated with greater elevations in systolic and diastolic blood pressure, cortisol, and increases in natural killer cell numbers and cytotoxicity, whereas for men low in cynical hostility, anger was associated with smaller increases in heart rate and natural killer cell cytotoxicity. None of women's affect scores were related to cardiovascular, neuroendocrine, or immunologic outcomes, leading the authors to suggest that other emotions (e.g., sadness) may be more relevant for wives' physiological responses. Finally, the affective experience of illness (e.g., cancer, heart disease) may also involve blends of discrete emotions (fear, anger, sadness combined with heightened levels of intimacy and connection—see Spiegel & Kimerling, 2001).

Thus, a key reason for attending to co-occurring affective responses to life challenges is that they provide more accurate rendering of the subjective experiences—the emotional phenomenology—prompted by fundamental life-tasks. A second reason relates to mapping the neurophysiological mechanisms on the route to health and the argument that more differentiated assessment of subjective experience will provide greater precision in understanding individual differences in the neural substrates and downstream endocrinological and immunological sequelae of emotion. (See Premise III on the phenomenology and physiology of emotion for further elaboration of this point).

### What of Emotional Dispositions and Affective Style?

Our advocacy for the study of co-occurring discrete emotions, anchored in fundamental life tasks, may seem at odds with the emerging evidence of the links between personality traits and affect, such as neuroticism and negative affect, or extraversion and positive affect (Emmons & Diener, 1985; Watson & Clark, 1992), or dispositional optimism (Scheier & Carver, 1992), characterizations of affective style (Davidson, 1998). Collectively, these formulations emphasize the stable, recurrent ways in which individuals experience affect and respond to stimuli from the environment. From this perspective, a focus on co-occurring discrete emotions may seem empirically unwieldy and even unnecessary. Knowledge of an individual's characteristic way of reacting to life challenges may be all that is required, thereby obviating the need for more tedious assessment of diverse, person-specific combinations of affective response to life tasks.

To this issue we bring insight from another realm regarding the question of whether personality is stable or changing (Block, 1982). Drawing on years of longitudinal data, Block empirically documented that some individuals are stable in their personality profiles over time and others are not. Given established connections between personality and affect, it is likely that in the affective realm, some individuals will similarly show stable, dispositional affective profiles, while others will reveal more affective variability, depending on the life challenges confronted. Mapping detailed emotional responses to different tasks will thus be fundamental to distinguish between the two.

Parenthetically, this observation raises the question as to whether prior claims that emotional responses are dispositional and traitlike have been premature. Why might this be the case? At the level of self-report, studies of affect variability (Watson & Walker, 1996) and related arguments for the traitlike nature of intra-individual variability in affect (Eid & Diener, 1999) may overstate the case for stability by virtue of the free-floating assessments of affect. That is, respondents are not asked to report their subjective feelings *about anything*, but rather to indicate how often they felt particular emotions at particular temporal intervals. For some, this may be a particularly difficult task, given that on a specific day, or at a specific moment, one might have a host of different feelings depending on whether they were about the current situation at work, recent family dynamics, new developments in the stock market, or the weather. Similarly, laboratory studies of affective style may inflate profiles of dispositional differences as a function of the standardized nature of the stimuli employed. Such standardization is, of course, necessary to draw meaningful conclusions across respondents, but it may at the same time mask the variability evident in emotional reactivity to challenges of daily life.

From the health vantage point, stable, traitlike affective dispositions are nonetheless likely to be of consequence in the recurrence, or chronicity, of emotional experience and its neurophysiological substrates. The above observations do not dispute this point; rather, they underscore the need to attend to what emotions are about in the interest of better discerning those who are, and are not, stable in their affective responses.

## Premise III. Health Is Biopsychosocial in Nature and Requires Integration of Phenomenology *and* Neurophysiology

From multiple vantage points comes the argument that human health is fundamentally a matter of interacting biological and psychosocial processes. In the field of psychosomatic medicine, Engel's (1977) biopsychosocial model of illness emphasized interacting systems at cellular, tissue, organismic, interpersonal, and environmental levels. Similarly, Liposki (1986; see also Fava, 1999a) defined the scope of psychosomatic medicine as a scientific discipline concerned with the study of the relationships of biological, psychological, and social determinants of health and disease. Fava and Sonino's (2000) history of the psychosomatic field clarifies its dramatic growth in recent decades, now spanning numerous realms at the interface of behavioral science, basic biology, and clinical medicine. They underscore the leitmotif of this work—namely, that the mind and body are two inseparably linked aspects of health that, although distinguished for methodological and communicative purposes, require integrated points of observation.

Within clinical medicine, Engel (1998) also understood, with remarkable depth and eloquence, that the physician, as scientist, must operate concurrently in two modes, one observational, the other relational. The observational mode is where data are collected in the classical empirical-analytic approach with its emphasis on careful measurement and accurate description. The relational mode, however, requires attending to the human realm, in which language, symbols, thoughts, and feelings are the means by which private experience is organized and communicated. "It is through dialogue that the physician learns the nature and history of the patient's experiences and clarifies on the one hand what they mean for the patient, and on the other, what they might mean in terms of other systems in the natural hierarchy, be they biochemical and physiological, or psychological and social" (p. 8). Engel's wisdom was in understanding that the two modes constitute, not separate alternatives, but a single, integrated means for data disclosure, clarification, and interpretation.

Among those studying health from more mechanistic, biological corners there is also recognition that phenomenology and physiology must ultimately be linked. Walter Cannon (1942), using observations from other cultures and centuries, clarified that the experience of fear can, in itself, induce death. Selye (1956) emphasized environmental stressors that produce a disease-producing adaptational syndrome, with subsequent researchers elaborating wide variability in the extent to which environmental changes are appraised as threatening or stressful (Folkman et al., 1986; Pearlin, Lieberman, Menaghan, & Mullan, 1981; Thoits, 1995). Recently, the concept of allostatic load (McEwen, 1998; McEwen & Stellar, 1993; McEwen & Seeman, 1999) has been described as the price paid by the body for chronic overactivity or underactivity of multiple physiological systems (autonomic, HPA axis, cardiovascular, metabolic, and immune). Central to the formulation of allostatic load is the *interpretation of and reaction to* life challenge as benign or threatening. That is, while primary emphasis is given to the interacting physiological systems that constitute the response to challenge, the process begins with the perception of the challenge—a pivotal juncture that determines, depending on the construal, whether physiological systems will be activated.

In the field of affective science, Davidson (1998) also draws attention to "one of the most striking features of human emotion" (p. 307), which is the variability across individuals in the quality and intensity of dispositional mood and emotional reactions to *similar* incentives and challenges. He then elaborates features of "affective style" to organize these individual differences. Parameters of affective chronometry include: threshold for reactivity, peak amplitude of response, rise time to peak, and recovery time. These neural substrates are core components of emotion regulation and are consequential for understanding what underlies, at the level of brain function, psychopathology. Activation of these responses begins with subjective experience—sometimes conscious, other times not, sometimes expressed in words, other times in behavior (e.g., the face) and physiology (e.g., heart rate). Probing the phenomenology of how individuals experience their life challenges is thus essential to understand what sets this chronometry in motion.

Parenthetically, it is useful to recall that the emotion field has not always been receptive to the phenomenological realm as a fundamental part of its purview. Ekman (1992) acknowledged that "the subjective experience of emotion, how each emotion feels, is for some at the centre of what an emotion is" (p. 175), but he nonetheless excluded subjective experience from the core characteristics that distinguish basic emotions on the grounds that "too little is known about how subjectivity maps on to other aspects of an emotional experience" (p. 175). This line of reasoning and related criticisms, or dismissal, or self-reported emotion, are problematic for the study of human health, which requires attending simultaneously to phenomenology *and* neurophysiology. Accordingly, we examine below the issues revolving around self-reported emotion, underscoring its essential role in the process linking the psychosocial realm to health. In addition, we call for explicit examination of points of convergence and discrepancy between the felt experience of emotion and underlying neurophysiological substrates. The fit, or lack thereof, between these two constitutes a critical nexus for understanding individual differences in how emotion influences health. Further, the juxtaposition of the phenomenology and neurophysiology offers important opportunities to understand how one side might afford protective features to offset the vulnerabilities of the other.

## The Perils of Self-Reported Affect

Despite the fact that much of the work on the structure of the affective domain has been conducted with self-report measures (Watson et al., 1999; Yik et al., 1999), recurrent criticisms plague these data. The call to "move beyond self-report data in exploring the structure of affect" (Diener, 1999, p. 804) reflects concerns with self-report biases, motivational influences, and the fact that language does not always capture affective experience (Cacioppo et al., 1999; Green et al., 1999). Thus, individuals are viewed as unreliable reporters of their own affect because they engage in distortion (conscious or unconscious), sometimes responding carelessly or randomly, or even not actually knowing (or remembering) how they feel, or felt.

Those who study emotion via language only further complicate matters. English emotion words have been described as falling into 25 categories of synonyms (Shaver, Schwartz, Kirson, & O'Connor, 1987). This taxonomy has been used to probe emotion nomenclature universals in major geographical and linguistic groupings (Hupka, Lenton, & Hutchison, 1999). Four basic linguistic emotion categories were identified—the first pertaining to categories of anger and guilt (which exist in all languages); the second to categories of adoration, alarm, amusement, and depression (which also exist in all languages); the third to categories of alienation, arousal, and agony; and the fourth to the category eagerness. Many of these linguistic basics (e.g., guilt, adoration, alienation, agony) are, we note, missing in current self-report instruments of affect.

In addition to the linguistic parsing of affective space, individual differences in language use, referred to as linguistic styles, have also been put forth as an independent and meaningful way to study personality (Pennebaker & King, 1999).

That is, people verbally express themselves in stable and unique ways. This observation raises the further wrinkle that structured, self-report inventories of affect may not include the terms spontaneously selected by individuals to describe their feelings, thus forcing ratings on a host of terms that may exist outside an individual's linguistic style. Even if individuals choose similar terms to describe their feelings as those on self-report instruments, there is the additional quandary of not knowing whether particular words *mean* the same thing to different individuals.

Given these difficulties, it is not surprising that attempts to build knowledge of emotion on a foundation of words (the affective tower of Babel?) are greeted with suspicion. Some argue for alternative approaches to the assessment of subjective states, such as measures of "objective happiness" (Kahneman, 1999, 2000), which seek to minimize the biases of self-report. Using the example of "How happy was Helen in March?" Kahneman argues that Helen's retrospective judgment is a "fallible estimate of her objective well-being" (1999, p. 4), which is contrasted with objective happiness defined as the cumulative record of "instant utility" (i.e., being pleased or distressed at a particular moment) over the relevant period of time.

This bottom-up construction of happiness requires that momentary experiences be characterized on a good/bad dimension. Kahneman further suggests that a promising approach to the measurement of this dimension may reside in neuropsychology and the psychophysiology of affect:

> It is conceivable, if not likely, that a composite physiological measurement of the good/bad response could eventually be constructed, and that this measurement would be quite highly correlated with subjective experience of pleasure and distress. Continuous records of affective state could possibly be derived from non-invasive measures of localized brain activity eventually leading to accurate assessments of well-being over time. The movement from science fiction to practical application is likely to be rapid in this domain. (1999, p. 10)

Regarding the fallibility of Helen's retrospective account of her happiness in March, we note that the prior field of subjective well-being has rarely, if ever, been interested in recalled accounts of particular prior moments or periods (see Diener, 1984; Diener, Suh, Lucas, & Smith, 1999; Veroff, Douvan, & Kulka, 1981). The self-report questions that constitute this realm pertain to how individuals feel *now*, or how they feel *generally*. The former cannot suffer from retrospective bias because they are not retrospective. Global or general assessments are also not retrospective, although some individuals may draw on past feelings to make such judgments, or others may be influenced by current mood states (Schwarz & Clore,

1983). Moreover, when asked, retrospective questions have typically been comparative (e.g., how would you rate your happiness/life satisfaction now compared to five years ago?).

For present purposes, the central question is the extent to which such data (whether based on current, global, or retrospective reports) are plagued by distortion. Remarkably little research has actually documented the scope of this problem. Note that studies showing the variability of well-being depending on external factors, such as whether it is a rainy or sunny day, or whether the individual is in a pleasant or unpleasant room (Schwarz & Strack, 1999), are not in themselves evidence for the fallibility of self-reported subjective states, but rather may be testimony to finely tuned human capacities for discerning subjective states. Nonetheless, some have advocated for the use of informant reports or aggregated daily emotion reports (Diener, Smith, & Fujita, 1995) to address potential bias, while others have focused on behavioral assessments (e.g., facial expressions of emotion). Kahneman, as noted above, calls for measures based in neurophysiology. There are difficulties, however, with each alternative. Regarding the use of informants, the major challenge is deciding what to do when there are discrepancies, which frequently occurs, between the targeted respondent and his or her informant. Who to believe in such cases—whose report is to be taken as *true*? Observational tools are extremely valuable, but some emotional experiences (e.g., love, despair, alienation) may not have clear facial or behavioral displays. Moreover, many core life challenges involve co-occurring emotions. Other biologically based measures suffer from the same conundrum as informant reports—namely, what to do when the measures inside the skin, or brain, do not square with self-reported states? What, in such contexts, constitutes the *true* measure of the affective state—what people say they feel, or what the EEG readings show?

We raise these diverse questions to underscore the point that there is no single, final arbiter of affective experience. Human emotion is both internal and external, phenomenological and physiological—both are ultimately required to capture the phenomena. Moreover, the two are jointly needed to clarify the significance of the other. Whatever their failings, self-report measures have been, and will continue to be, *essential* to validate newly emergent assessments of affect on the biological side. Kahneman, in fact, noted that for the brain-based measures of momentary affect to work they would need to be highly correlated with subjective reports. Less hypothetically, Davidson and colleagues (Davidson, 1998; Sutton & Davidson, 1997; Tomarken, Davidson, Wheeler, & Doss, 1992) have dramatically advanced the interpretive significance of asymmetric prefrontal activation by showing that left-frontally activated people report more positive and less negative affect than their right-frontally activated counterparts, and similarly that those with greater left-sided prefrontal activation report more behavioral activation (relative to behavioral inhibition) compared to those exhibiting more right-sided prefrontal activation. Measures of prefrontal asymmetry also predict reactivity to elicitors of emotion—those with more left-sided prefrontal activation at baseline report more positive affect to positive film clips, while those with more right-sided activation reported more negative affect to the negative film clips (Wheeler, Davidson, & Tomarken, 1993).

Thus, across these studies, it is the *correspondence* between the reported states (via self-report instruments) and the electrical signals in the brain that are key to advancing understanding of the neural substrates of affective vulnerability or affective strengths. In fact, it is not possible to make sense of the affective system at the biological level *without* showing meaningful connections at the level of subjectively experienced and reported emotion. The conundrum is that the two levels rarely perfectly match. Thus, it is the *discrepancies* between the self-reported states and the biological indicators that are cause for concern. It is to these that we now turn.

### Probing the Discrepancies Between Self-Reported Affect and Biology

When phenomenological and neurophysiological data do not line up, what does it mean? We suggest that it is useful to make distinctions between discrepancies that are the result of measurement problems, on either, or both sides, and discrepancies that are meaningful and substantive. Larsen and Fredrickson (1999) provide a comprehensive overview of the reliability and validity of numerous techniques (self-report, observer ratings, facial measures, autonomic measures, brain-based measures, vocal measures). These issues are consequential; Green, Goldman, and Salovey (1993) showed that claims that positive and negative affect are independent were obscured by measurement error that, once taken into account, revealed a bipolar structure. We concur with Larsen and Fredrickson that the emotion field is advanced by increased emphasis on simultaneous use of multiple measures. As noted above, much of the validation of assessments in one realm (self-report, behavioral, autonomic, brain-based) requires showing convergence with the others.

Nonetheless, there are instances in which the self-report data do not square with the neurophysiological measures, and the discrepancy is meaningful. In fact, we submit that the degree of "fit" between these two levels may be a useful dimension of individual differences in affective experience. For example, one instance of poor correspondence pertains to the situation in which the individual, via self-report, puts forth a strongly positive evaluation, but clinical judgments suggest otherwise. Shedler, Mayman, and Manis (1993) refer to this as the "illusion of mental health." They argue that the defensive denial of distress is, however,

physiologically costly, and further show that those with illusory mental health have greater coronary reactivity to laboratory tasks than those with genuine mental health. The point we draw attention to is that the biological (heart rate) measures are essential to distinguish between the two types of self-reported mental health. That is, distortion of true subjective states becomes evident via the nexus with physiology. Similarly, Weinberger, Schwartz, and Davidson (1979) probed the phenomenon of repression (experiencing little anxiety on a conscious level but adopting a highly defensive approach to life) by juxtaposing self-reported levels of anxiety and social desirability with physiological measures of arousal.

Alternatively, it is useful to consider the possible juxtaposition of those who have biological (perhaps genetic) predispositions to show greater right-sided prefrontal activation (Davidson, 1998) in response to environmental stimuli, but who have psychosocial strengths and generally positive phenomenology. A useful question in this instance is whether these compensating influences on the psychosocial side afford protective benefits offsetting otherwise adverse downstream consequences (endocrinological, immunological). To push forward scientific agendas that follow from the convergence or divergence of phenomenology and neurophysiology, we present the cross-classification summarized in Figure 57.1. This two-by-two scheme illustrates various mind/body types for which useful predictions regarding health outcomes can be made. The rows of the table make a distinction between those showing generally positive versus negative profiles at the phenomenological (self-report) level; the columns pertain to distinctions between positive versus negative profiles at the neurophysiological level. We consider cerebral activation asymmetry from the work of Davidson, with its distinctions between greater left (+) versus right (−) activation (Davidson, 1998; Sutton & Davidson, 1997) as an example of brain-based assessment, while distinctions between low (+) versus high (−) levels of allostatic load (McEwen & Stellar, 1993; Seeman, Singer, Rowe, Horwitz, & McEwen, 1997) serve as instances of downstream physiological processes.

The convergent cells, positive and negative fit, correspond to those whose phenomenology and physiology match at equivalently valenced levels. These constitute the most straightforward cases from which to make predictions about health, with the positive subjective states, greater left-sided activation, and low allostatic load constituting a mind/body integration, described as positive fit, which predicts positive health outcomes (resistance to disease, delayed onset of disease, quicker recovery from acute health challenges). Alternatively, negative fit refers to those with the configuration of negative phenomenology, greater right-sided activation, and high allostatic load, which is predictive of poor health (vulnerability to mental and physical pathology).

**Neurophysiology***

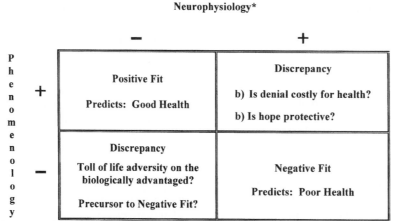

*\*At the level of brain-based assessment, "+" refers to greater left-sided prefrontal activation and "–" to greater right-sided activation. At the level of downstream physiology, "+" refers to low allostatic load and "–" refers to high allostatic load.*

Figure 57.1 Mind/body typology neurophysiology. At the level of brain-based assessment, + refers to greater left-sided prefrontal activation and − refers to greater right-sided activation. At the level of downstream physiology, + refers to low allostatic load and − refers to high allostatic load.

The off-diagonal, discrepant cells are also informative for making health predictions. Among those reporting positive subjective states, but showing negative neurophysiology, there are potentially two important types. The first corresponds to individuals engaged (consciously or unconsciously) in defensive denial and distortion (Shedler, Mayman, & Manis, 1993; Weinberger, 1990), and the second to those with dispositional optimism (Scheier & Carver, 1992; Taylor, Kemeny, Reed, Bower, & Gruenewald, 2000). Both have adverse biological profiles, but with possibly distinctive long-term health sequelae. That is, defensive denial may be physiologically costly and thus ultimately predict physical health problems, whereas positive phenomenology of the hope variety may be a protective factor. Taylor et al. (2000) document that HIV patients with greater hope show slower disease progression and delayed mortality. In both instances, what needs to be elaborated are the mechanisms whereby denial or suppression of distress can contribute to disease progression or help provide protection against it.

Alternatively, there can be discrepant types wherein individuals report negative emotions and low well-being, but their biological measures appear generally positive (i.e., left-sided prefrontal activation, low allostatic load). These may be individuals who are biologically hardy or genetically advantaged, but who, because of profiles of cumulative life adversity, have come to have negative psychological outlooks. Those who are biologically advantaged, but phenomenologically disadvantaged, would be expected to have more positive health profiles over the long term than individuals having negative profiles on both. However, given the likely plasticity of the neurophysiology (Davidson et al., 2000), what may be the relevant prediction for this cell is that it is a *precursor* to negative fit. That is, the central question is whether persistent negative phenomenology can ultimately shift neuophysiology in comparably negative directions.

Are these types believable? Indeed, they are. In the Wisconsin Longitudinal Study where we have obtained data on asymmetry, allostatic load, and reported well-being on a biological subsample, we have identified individuals who reside in each of these cells. Figure 57.2 summarizes the frequencies for those who are in the top, middle, and bottom quartiles of purpose in life (one dimension of self-reported well-being), and are also classified as having greater left-, or right-sided prefrontal activation. Figure 57.3, in turn, summarizes the frequencies of those having high or low levels of allostatic load, along with high, medium, or low levels of life purpose. Thus,

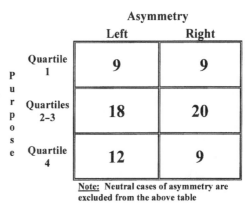

*Note: Neutral cases of asymmetry are excluded from the above table*

Figure 57.2 Cerebral activation asymmetry and purpose in life (frequencies). *Note*: Neutral cases of asymmetry are excluded from this figure.

**Allostatic Load**

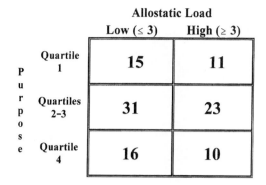

Figure 57.3 Allostatic load and purpose in life (frequencies).

the convergent types are evident, but discrepancies are also part of the empirical reality. Longitudinally, our objective is to track the health predictions following from the preceding typology. The work underscores the importance of constructing life pathways that simultaneously monitor what is occurring phenomenologically and neurophysiologically, as the different combinations may provide routes to understanding variation in health trajectories through time.

## Premise IV. Cumulative, Chronic Emotions Are Consequential for Health

To date, much of the field of affective science has focused on momentary, short-term emotions. Ekman (1992), in fact, defined basic emotions in part by their temporal profiles—namely, that they have quick onset and brief duration. He argued that it is adaptive for the organism to be able to mobilize quickly and for such mobilization to not last very long. "If one emotion-arousing event typically produced a set of response changes which endure for hours regardless of what was occurring in the external world, emotion would be less responsive than I think they are to rapidly changing circumstances" (p. 185). Ekman further distinguished emotions from moods, which last for hours or days, noting that moods are "highly saturated with one or another emotion—irritability with anger, dysphoria with sadness, apprehensiveness with fear, euphoria with a type of enjoyment" (p. 186). States that endure for weeks or months were not moods, however, but more properly identified as affective disorders (Ekman, 1994). Significantly, enduring positive feelings (e.g., love) were omitted from this classification scheme.

The persistent emphasis on emotion as brief experience is illustrated by Russell and Barrett's (1999) formulation of prototypical emotional episodes, which are "limited to temporary events and slices in time. We omit temperament, attitudes, sentiments, emotional dispositions of any kind, prolonged mood states, psychiatric symptoms, simple evaluative responses, perception of emotion in others,

perception of emotion-eliciting qualities of events, and even emotional episodes that are not prototypical" (p. 805). Despite this pervasive and long-standing emphasis on emotions of brief duration, we suggest that the linkage to health *requires* a shift to a different time scale. That is, what is consequential for health are those features of affective experience of long duration: *prolonged mood states and emotional dispositions, and more important, chronic, recurrent emotions and their cumulation over time.* Why does a focus on health call for this temporal shift? Primarily, it is because the neurophysiological mechanisms that are the nexus between the emotional experience and health outcomes will be chronically, or repeatedly, activated. It is this physiological wear and tear that is hypothesized to be costly for the organism. To illustrate these ideas, we summarize an emerging program of research on the topic of allostatic load and its connection to emotion via assessment of cumulative relationship profiles.

Allostatic load is derived from the concept of allostasis, which captures at the biological level the capacity of the organism to adapt to oncoming challenges and thereby prevent the unfolding of pathophysiological processes (Sterling & Eyer, 1988). Emphasis is on the dynamism of internal physiology and the fact that healthy functioning requires ongoing adjustments and adaptations to the internal physiological milieu. Through allostasis, the autonomic nervous system, the hypothalamic-pituitary-adrenal (HPA) axis, the cardiovascular, and metabolic systems protect the body by responding to internal and external stress. The long-term price of overactivity or underactivity of these systems is referred to as allostatic load (McEwen & Stellar, 1993), representing the cumulative wear and tear from chronic stress. Allostatic load has been operationalized with multiple indicators from the above systems, including blood pressure, waist-hip ratio, total and HDL cholesterol, glycosylated hemoglobin, cortisol, epinephrine, norepinephrine, and DHEA-S (Seeman, Singer, Rowe, Horwitz, & McEwen, 1997).

Allostatic load has been shown in longitudinal research to predict incident cardiovascular disease and later life decline in physical functioning and memory loss (Seeman et al., 1997). Recent findings over a 7.5-year period further show that high allostatic load was predictive of subsequent mortality (Seeman, McEwen, Rowe, & Singer, 2001). Such findings document the linkage from this multiple-system construct to morbidity and mortality. The question on the other side of the equation is, What *contributes to, or protects one from,* high allostatic load? We hypothesized that social relational experiences—in particular the emotional features of key significant relationships (i.e., parents, spouse)—*and* their cumulation over time would contribute to differences in allostatic load; with those on more negative relationship pathways more likely to have high load than those on more positive relationship pathways. This formulation illustrates the need to focus on emotions that are about something as well as the importance of tracking recurrent, cumulative profiles of emotion.

These questions were examined in the context of a longitudinal study of midlife adults (Ryff, Singer, Wing, & Love, 2001). For a biological subsample of members of the Wisconsin Longitudinal Study on whom measures of allostatic load were obtained, we created relationship pathways based on self-reported assessments of quality of relationships with mother and father (in childhood) and with spouse in adulthood. The Parental Bonding Scale (Parker, Tupling, & Brown, 1979) probes multiple aspects of caring and warmth in the mother/child and father/child bond (e.g., "S/he was affectionate to me. S/he spoke to me with a warm and friendly voice. S/he seemed emotionally cold to me. S/he frequently smiled at me. S/he made me feel I wasn't wanted."). For adult spousal relationships, four different aspects of intimacy were assessed with the Personal Assessment of Intimacy Relationships (PAIR, Schaefer & Olson, 1981). The emotional and sexual subscales included the most intimate forms of connection between spouses, while the intellectual and recreational subscales emphasized mutually enjoyed experiences, companionship, and the scope of shared communication.

We defined the individual to be on a negative relationship pathway if she or he had large negative evaluations of both mother and father in childhood and/or had largely negative evaluations of emotional/sexual and intellectual/recreational ties to spouse. The majority of those who experienced negative childhood ties (both men and women) also reported negative spousal ties. We defined an individual to be on a positive pathway if she or he rated at least one parent as caring and reported at least one combined category of intimacy (emotional/sexual; intellectual/recreational) with spouse.

Using a sample of 101 midlife adults (46 women, 55 men), we found that, indeed, those on the negative relationship pathway were significantly more likely to have high allostatic load than those on the positive relationship pathway (see Figure 57.4). The effects were stronger for men than women, but nonetheless supported the guiding hypothesis in both cases. In a subsequent analysis (Singer & Ryff, 1999), the potentially protective features of persistently good social relationships vis-à-vis life adversity was examined. The targeted life challenge was economic disadvantage. Drawing on the growing interest in the health consequences of socioeconomic inequalities (see Adler et al., 1994), we hypothesized that persistent economic disadvantage would increase the likelihood of high allostatic load, thereby illuminating possible mechanisms in the SES-health link.

Again, with the WLS biological subsample, diverse economic pathways were constructed depending on whether respondents were above or below the median on household

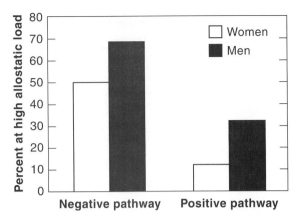

Figure 57.4 Social relationship pathways and allostatic load.

income in childhood and/or adulthood. Those with persistently low economic profiles had greater likelihood of high allostatic load compared to those with persistently high economic profiles, although the differences were not statistically significant. When cumulative relationship profiles were combined with economic data, clear patterns emerged. Specifically, those with economic disadvantage in childhood *and* on the negative relationship pathway were significantly more likely to have high allostatic load than those with economic advantage in childhood *and* on the positive relationship pathway. Illustrating the protective role of good social relationships, we also found that those with economic disadvantage in childhood *but* persistently positive social relationships were also significantly less likely to have high allostatic load than those with similar economic beginnings but negative relational experiences. These findings underscore the possible socioemotional routes through which health resilience vis-à-vis life challenge is achieved.

The above findings represent but one attempt to link cumulative emotional experience to a composite of physiological mechanisms implicated in later life morbidity and mortality. They also illustrate the use of more person-centered analytic methods (Singer, Ryff, Carr, & Magee, 1998), which may be critical in establishing biopsychosocial models of health. Typological, person-centered analyses are, we note, of growing interest in the behavioral sciences (Bergman, 1998; Magnusson, 1998; Robins, John, & Caspi, 1998). There are, in addition, numerous important avenues for extending these preliminary results. At the level of the emotional experience, there is need for improved measures that probe the relevant depths of significant social ties. We drew on the lives of famous couples (i.e., Leo and Sonya Tolstoy, Elizabeth Barrett Browning and Robert Browning, Freida Kahlo and Diego Rivera) to illustrate the texture and detail required to capture the lived experience of emotion (both positive and negative) with significant others (see Ryff, Singer, Wing, & Love, 2001).

At the level of intervening biological mechanisms, we also underscored the need to examine brain oxytocin, opioids, and prolactin systems as key participants in experiences of social solidarity, warmth, and nurturance. Oxytocin, in particular, has been shown to increase in response to the onset of pair-bonding in adults, maternal attachment, infant attachment, maternal responsivity, positive social behaviors or contact, onset of sexual behavior, and exploration or approach to novelty (Carter, 1998; Panksepp, 1998a; Uvnäs-Moberg, 1998). As an underscore to the theme of cumulative effects, social bonds lead to repeated exposures to positive social stimuli and, thereby, to repeated release of oxytocin (Uvnäs-Moberg, 1998). In humans, such positive experiences can be stored in memories, which in themselves may reactivate physiological processes. Pertinent to health outcomes, evidence from animal models further suggests that chronic oxytocin release is capable of producing long-term reductions in blood pressure and heart rate (Petersson, Alster, Lundeberg, & Uvnäs-Moberg, 1996). Such findings point to a host of new research directions at the human level.

Finally, while our focus on the health significance of cumulative emotional experience has been elaborated with a focus on social ties, we emphasize the need to extend this formulation to a wider realm. Chronic emotional experience in the workplace, where most hours of the day are spent, constitutes one important domain. Occupational stress has, of course, been linked to physical and mental health (Jackson & Warr, 1984; Link, Lennon, & Dohrenwend, 1993; Lundberg, 1999; Karasek, Baker, Marxer, Ahlbom, & Theorell, 1981), but the emotional features of work life (e.g., feeling harassed, demeaned, or chronically criticized on the job; feeling energized and engaged by work demands; worrying about hazardous work conditions) are not well understood. Our prior emphasis on emotions associated with racism and discrimination are another direction for probing prominent and likely persistent feelings of daily life that may be consequential for health.

## Premise V. Emotion Can Be Protective and Promote Positive Health

Extensive prior emphasis has been given to the links between emotion and illness (see Leventhal & Patrick-Miller, 1993). The topic of how anger, anxiety, dysphoric affect and depression, and hopelessness-helplessness contribute to dysfunction of various biological systems and, thereby, to disease has constituted a large segment of the science to date. Moreover, the pathways through which affective disturbances influence physical disorders have been increasingly specified (Cohen & Rodriguez, 1995). These pathways include biological, behavioral, cognitive, and social processes. An important message in current

work is the likely bidirectionality between affective responses and illness behavior or disease.

Emphasis on the adverse consequences of negative emotion neglects the potentially consequential influences of emotion on positive health promotion (Ryff & Singer, 1998a, 1998b, 2000, 2001). Salubrious psychosocial factors, such as having good-quality relations with others or a sense of engagement and purpose in one's life, may be central contributors to the "physiological substrates of flourishing" that, in turn, help maintain the optimal human functioning of the organism. New interest surrounds questions of what it means to thrive (Ickovics & Park, 1998) and what the possible benefits are of positive emotions (Fredrickson, 1998). Our final premise thus is that emotion can, in fact, be protective and promote positive health.

We divide this section into three parts. The first examines extant research on recovery and resilience, probing the extent to which emotion (phenomenologically and neurophysiologically) may be a part of the story. The second addresses positive health promotion and the extent to which emotional experience can be protective, aiding in the prevention or delay of mental and physical health problems. The third section considers the "intermingling" of positive and negative emotion in understanding optimal mental and physical health. The argument is that good health does not ensue from simplistic models wherein positive emotions are maximized and negative emotions minimized. Rather, optimal functioning requires refined formulations of how the two work beneficially together.

### The Role of Emotion in Recovery and Resilience

Mounting evidence points to the importance of *optimism* and *hope* in the face of health challenge. Positive expectations have been shown to predict better health after heart transplantation (Leedham, Meyerowitz, Muirhead, & Frist, 1995), and optimists show more rapid recovery from coronary bypass surgery and have less severe anginal pain than pessimists (Fitzgerald, Tenn, Affleck, & Pransky, 1993). In the HIV model, optimism predicts disease course and mortality. HIV men who were asymptomatic and did not have negative expectations showed less likelihood of symptom development in the follow-up period (Reed, Kemeny, Taylor, & Visscher, 1999). Importantly, HIV men with unrealistically optimistic beliefs about their own survival actually lived longer (Reed, Kemeny, Taylor, Wang, & Visscher, 1994). Moreover, those who were able to find meaning in their loss of a close partner maintained CD4 T help cells over the follow-up period and were less likely to die (Bower, Kemeny, Taylor, & Fahey, 1998). Thus, optimism, hope, and meaning emerge as resources that may preserve not only mental but also physical health (Scheier & Carver, 1992; Taylor, Kemeny, Reed, Bower, & Gruenewald, 2000).

What is the link between optimism and the affective realm? Dispositional optimists (who expect positive outcomes) show less mood disturbance in response to various stressors, including adaptation to college (Aspinwall & Taylor, 1992; Scheier & Carver, 1992), breast cancer biopsy (Stanton & Snider, 1993), and breast cancer surgery (Carver, Pozo, Harris et al., 1993). Exploring the relationship between optimism and immune parameters, Segerstrom, Taylor, Kemeny, and Fahey (1998) found that in a sample of law students in their first semester of study, mood (measured with the Profile of Mood States, POMS; McNair, Lorr, & Droppleman, 1971) partially accounted for the relationship between optimism and helper T cells. Avoidant coping also partially accounted for the relationship between optimism and mood. This line of reasoning thus views optimism as a largely cognitive phenomenon, which is linked to affect via mood assessments. Alternatively, a hopeful life outlook might be viewed as affective experience in its own right—this observation draws on the recognition that positive emotions may have their own defining features and time course (Fredrikson, 1998).

Other factors contributing to differential survival profiles pertain to *social and emotional support*. Group psychotherapy programs, which promote support and emotional expression among women with breast cancer, show multiple effects: reductions in anxiety and depression as well as increased survival time and lower rates of recurrence (Spiegel, 1998; Spiegel & Kimerling, 2001). Survival after myocardial infarction has also been significantly associated with emotional support, after controlling for severity of disease, comorbidity, and functional status (Berkman, Leo-Summers, & Horwitz, 1992). The role of emotional factors in survival processes has also been shown with regard to negative factors, such as anger in the context of coronary heart disease (Kawachi, Sparrow, Spiro, Vokonas, & Weiss, 1996), or depression among post-myocardial infarction patients (Frasure-Smith, Lesperance, & Talajic, 1993).

Regarding major depression, Fava and colleagues (Fava, 1999b; Fava, Rafanelli, Grandi, Conti, & Belluardo, 1998) have shown the power of positive factors in promoting recovery. During the residual phase of treatment, when major debilitating symptoms have subsided but well-being is not fully regained, the risk for relapse is especially high. It is during this period that Fava implements "well-being therapy" designed to increase awareness of and participation in positive aspects of daily life. Fava uses the multidimensional model of psychological well-being developed by Ryff (1989, 1995) as a framework for increasing the focus on positive experience. Those participating in such treatment showed dramatically higher remission profiles over a two-year period compared to those receiving standard clinical treatment. This work underscores the need to promote positive psychological, social, and emotional experience as a key route to sustained recovery from depression.

With regard to resilience, studies of children growing up under adverse conditions (e.g., parental psychopathology, parental alcoholism, extreme poverty) have shown that many evidence healthy development and avoid the disorders of their parents (Garmezy, 1991; Glanz & Johnson, 1999; Rutter, 1990; Werner, 1995). Numerous protective factors have been suggested to explain such resilience (e.g., having bonds with at least one nurturing and supportive parent, receiving external support in the community, having an affectionate and outgoing temperament). Emotion thus pervades the formulation of why some children are resilient in the face of difficult life circumstances.

Our studies have approached resilience from a life history perspective. At the biographical level, we have summarized Mark Mathabane's account of surviving the horrors of poverty and apartheid in South Africa (see Singer & Ryff, 1997), which speaks eloquently to the sustaining power of a committed and tenacious mother and a nurturing grandmother who saved him from a violent street life that destined him for early drug and alcohol use, sexual abuse, and high risk of mortality. In the context of longitudinal survey research, we have studied women who experienced depression at some point in their lives, but regained high well-being in their early fifties (Singer et al. 1998). The characterizations of adversity and advantage in these women's lives underscores the prominence of emotional factors, with regard to both persistent life challenges (i.e., growing up with an alcoholic parent, losing a parent to death in early life) and compensating life strengths (e.g., having close ties with a spouse in adulthood, purposeful engagement as exemplified by upward mobility in the workplace).

In later life, we have studied women who have maintained or regained positive levels of physical and mental health following a major life transition (community relocation); Ryff, Singer, Love, & Essex, 1998). Numerous protective factors constitute such resilience, including social structural influences (e.g., level of education; Ryff, Magee, Kling, & Wing, 1999) and diverse psychosocial influences (e.g., social comparison processes, coping processes, changing self-definitions, emotional adaptation; Kling, Ryff, & Essex, 1997; Kling, Seltzer, & Ryff, 1997; Smider, Essex, & Ryff, 1997). More differentiated assessment of the discrete emotions that constitute reactions to the challenges of aging are important future directions.

Across the above examples, investigations are needed to establish the neurobiological mechanisms through which health protection occurs. As noted earlier, we have probed the benefits of nurturing emotionally rewarding social relationships vis-à-vis economic adversity to reduce the likelihood of having high allostatic load, a known risk factor for subsequent morbidity and mortality. While adverse outcomes, particularly under conditions of high risk, have been avoided, what is unknown is whether such avoidance represents a reversal of neurophysiological systems, or compensatory responses, or both. In animal models, those reared in emotionally impoverished environments have been shown to react to stress more radically throughout their lives than those reared in enriched environments (Caldji et al., 1998). However, these effects have been shown to be *reversible*—those exposed to inadequate nurturing in early life can, if subsequently reared by a high licking and grooming foster mother, show normal functioning and healthy adult lives. What these models offer is critically needed understanding of *how* such behavioral interventions regulate the development of neural systems.

## Emotion in Health Promotion and Prevention

With regard to positive health promotion, we reiterate the importance of optimism and hope as well as social and emotional support. Optimists and minimally anxious adults have been shown to have lower ambulatory blood pressure and more positive moods than pessimistic and anxious adults (Räikkönen, Matthews, Flory, Owens, & Gump, 1999). Individuals growing up with feelings of warmth and closeness with parents had, 35 years later, decreased incidence of diagnosed diseases in midlife (coronary artery disease, hypertension, duodenal ulcers, alcoholism (Russek & Schwartz, 1997). Earlier we summarized epidemiological studies that have mapped contributions of the social ties and integration to host resistance, reduced morbidity, and delayed mortality (Berkman, 1995; Cassel, 1976; Cohen, Doyle, Skoner, Rabin, & Gwaltney, 1997; House et al., 1988).

Elsewhere we have juxtaposed the extensive literatures on the health benefits of good social supports with the extensive literatures on attachment, close and personal relationships, and marital quality (Ryff & Singer, 2000, 2001). What is notable is the missing interchange between these realms. Those in the social support arena have been explicitly concerned with health outcomes and, as such, have contributed advances regarding social influences on morbidity and mortality. Extant assessments of social relationships, however, have not probed the depths of relational flourishing, particularly emotional features—what it means to have loving, intimate, fulfilling, and enjoyable ties to others (Ryff & Singer, 2000). Alternatively, social relationship researchers who probe early and later life attachments and close personal relationships, including marital and family ties, elaborate some features of deep, meaningful, loving human connection, but these agendas are rarely connected to health.

Moreover, when social relationship researchers have probed the health significance of key social ties, inquiries have been heavily weighted on the side of relational conflict and dysfunction as risk factors for behavioral, mental, and physical health problems. In the prior section on what emotions are about (see Premise I), we reviewed findings that are mapping the physiological sequelae of marital conflict, a richly expanding area of inquiry. The counterpart agenda (i.e., mapping the physiological substrates of relational flourishing) has received dramatically less attention. The emotional upside of significant social ties and how they impact health is thus a major priority for future inquiry.

It is animal models, particularly studies of positive affiliation (Carter, 1998; Panksepp, 1998a) that may lead the way with regard to the neurobiology of relational flourishing. Animal attachment can be operationalized as selective socioemotional bonds, and thus facilitate observation and experimentation connecting these bonds to physiological substrates. A review of caregiver-infant and adult-heterosexual pair bonds revealed recurrent associations between activity in the HPA axis and expression of social behaviors. Central neuropeptides, especially oxytocin and vasopressin, are implicated in social bonding and social interaction. Uvnäs-Moberg (1997, 1998; Petersson et al., 1996) suggests that oxytocin may mediate the benefits of positive social interaction on health. Oxytocin levels are raised by somatosensory stimulation (e.g., breast-feeding, suckling) as well as touch and warm temperatures. In both male and female rats, oxytocin exerts potent antistress effects, such as decreases in blood pressure, heart rate, and cortisol levels, with effects lasting from one to several weeks. Viewed over the long term, and underscoring our theme of cumulation, social bonds lead to repeated exposure to positive social stimuli and, thereby, repeated release of oxytocin. And, as we noted earlier, such positive experiences in humans may be stored in memories, which in themselves may reactivate these physiological processes.

Further innovative avenues for linking positive experience, particularly of the relational variety, to health pertain to interest in nerve growth factors (Panksepp, 1998b) and the anabolic growth-promoting hormones that embody thriving (Epel, McEwen, & Ickovics, 1998) and help maintain or repair the body. At the behavioral level, there is also much room for expanding the positive focus. Laughter and humor—significant social and emotional experiences—may have important health-promoting substrates, as Norman Cousins (1979/1995) advocated some time ago. We would also underscore the need for expanded emphasis on what Solomon (1993) referred to as the "passions"—those central, defining goals and pursuits of our lives. "Our passions are not the animal intrusions and physiologically based disruptions that they have always been thought to be" (p. xiv). Rather, our passions are the very sources of our interests, meaning, and purposes—

"they are the high court of consciousness to which all else, even reason, must pay tribute" (p. xvii). Advances in affective neuroscience, especially interest in "approach-related affect" (Davidson et al., 1990), add further importance to bringing human passions, purposes, and pursuits into the phenomenology and neurophysiology of positive human health. These constitute an especially promising, and possibly health-promoting, realm of what emotions are about (see Premise I).

## Salutogenesis and the Intermingling of Positive and Negative Emotion

At first glance, it appears that optimal health, the process of which Antonovsky (1987) referred to as salutogenesis, would be nurtured by an abundance of positive emotional experiences and a dearth of negative. Numerous lines of inquiry challenge the simplistic notion that positive emotions heal and negative emotions are pathogenic (Dafter, 1996). We briefly highlight multiple realms of study that focused instead on how positive and negative emotions work fruitfully together.

Gottman (2001) argues that negative emotions are a fundamental part of "healthy" social relationships. He distinguishes between "emotion-coaching" versus "emotion-dismissing" parents, which characterizes the emotional styles they bring to the task of rearing children (Gottman, Katz, & Hooven, 1996). A major difference between the two parenting types is their distinctive modes of responding to children's negative emotions, such as anger, sadness, or fear. Emotion-coaching parents help children understand and label their own negative affect, which contributes, in Gottman's view, to the child's developing sense of control and optimism, and more generally, to effective emotion regulation. Emotion-dismissing parents, in contrast, equate such emotions with selfishness, loss of control, passivity, cowardice, and failure. From the health angle, Gottman suggests that children with emotion-coaching parents have higher vagal tone that conveys greater capacity for self-calming after emotional upset. Such children were reported to have fewer infectious illnesses compared to children with emotion-dismissing parents. Thus, the emotion-coaching parent sees negative affect as sometimes legitimate and even valuable, because it provides an opportunity for intimacy and/or teaching, which in turn can strengthen the bond between parent and child.

Further emphasis on the interface of positive and negative emotion comes from studies of naturally occurring, day-to-day social interactions within frameworks of attachment and intimacy (Berscheid & Reis, 1998; Reis & Patrick, 1996; Sheldon, Ryan, & Reis, 1996). The guiding assumption is that emotional well-being follows from the nourishment one obtains from daily social contact with others. Reis (2001) argues that intimacy interactions are

those in which self-disclosure occurs *and* there is a partner responsiveness to such disclosure. This can be, and frequently is, in the context of difficult, negative, painful topics, including relational conflict. While conflict may be affectively unpleasant, Reis underscores that it does not necessarily undermine satisfaction of relatedness needs. It is *meaningful*, not uniformly positive, social ties that promote emotional well-being. These are nurtured by how individuals cope constructively with negative emotion and relationship conflict. Indeed, as Gottman emphasized above, difficult or conflictual interactions may, paradoxically, be instrumental in generating enhanced closeness. Reis's work is valuable for illuminating, at the microanalytic level, the nature of social interactions that accomplish these ends.

Another example pertains to group psychotherapy with cancer patients (Spiegel, 1998). These interventions promote social support and emotional expression. Patients are encouraged to access, express, and work through their emotional reactions to the stresses of cancer. Suppression of emotion reduces intimacy in families and social networks, limiting opportunities for direct expression of affection and concern (Spiegel & Kimerling, 2001). Importantly, emotional expression decreases psychiatric and physical symptoms, reduces medical visits, and is linked with enhanced immune response and decreased viral replication. Much of this expression is about negative or traumatic events, and the prospect of dying. It is the intermingling of tears and laughter in dealing with trauma of the disease, in families that have adopted an atmosphere of open and shared problem solving, that helps reduce anxiety and depression, and thereby possibly influencing behavioral and biological pathways of survival.

Fredrickson (1998) also emphasizes how positive emotions may undo the aftereffects of negative emotions. That is, positive emotions are efficient antidotes that may restore autonomic quiescence following negative emotional arousal. Eliciting positive emotions by films or marked smiles, Fredrickson and Levenson (1998) show that positive emotions speed recovery from the cardiovascular aftereffects of fear, anxiety, and sadness. Further, Folkman (1997) underscores the importance of positive meanings and emotion in coping with severe stress (e.g., caregiving, bereavement). Coping theory, she underscores, has been overly focused management of distress and thus overlooked the consequential roles of positive psychological states in dealing with life challenges. Finally, an extensive literature is emerging on possible health benefits of emotional disclosure—that is, expressing (typically via writing) feelings about past traumatic experiences (Cameron & Nicholls, 1998; Kelley, Leisen, & Lumley, 1997; Pennebaker & Beall, 1986; Pennebaker, 1995).

Taken as a whole, the above findings converge on the important message that negative emotion is not singularly bad for health, but rather it is *how* negative emotion is expressed and responded to that arbitrates its deleterious or beneficial effects. Positive emotion is deeply entangled in such processes, both as an antidote to negative feelings and as a consequence of working through (frequently with significant others) difficult emotions. Thus, it is the nature of how positive and negative emotion are entwined that is critical for future health research.

## Conclusion

How emotion makes its way to health outcomes is, we believe, well conceptualized via the metaphor of a *pathway*. The reason is that numerous kinds of information must be put together to understand how human feelings come to be consequential for mental and physical illness, or well-being. We have emphasized that a critical ingredient of what goes on this pathway is what emotions are about—that is, the fundamental life challenges that give rise to affective experience. With regard to the feelings themselves, we call for greater emphasis on co-occurring discrete emotions as a route to sharpening understanding of what life tasks prompt within us. Capturing the emotional experience itself is, we argue, unavoidably about the need to blend phenomenology and neurophysiology. Although emotion has largely been construed as a short-term phenomenon, we proposed that building linkages to health requires focus on recurring, cumulative emotional experience. Finally, because far more is known about how emotion undermines health and well-being, we advocate for a counterpoint agenda that clarifies the protective and health-promoting features of salubrious affective experience.

## REFERENCES

Adler, N. E., Boyce, T., Chesney, M. A., Cohen, S., Folkman, S., Kahn, R. L., & Syme, S. L. (1994). Socioeconomic status and health: The challenge of the gradient. *American Psychologist, 49*, 15–24.

Antonovsky, A. (1987). *Unraveling the mysteries of health: How people manage stress and stay well.* San Francisco, CA: Jossey-Bass Publishers.

Armstead, C. A., Lawler, K. A., Gorden, G., Cross, J., & Gibbons, J. (1989). Relationship of racial stressors to blood pressure responses and anger expression in Black college students. *Health Psychology, 8*, 541–556.

Aspinwall, L. G., & Taylor, S. E. (1992). Individual differences, coping, and psychological adjustment: A longitudinal study of college adjustment and performance. *Journal of Personality and Social Psychology, 63*, 989–1003.

Barrett, L. F., & Russell, J. A. (1998). Independence and bipolarity in the structure of affect. *Journal of Personality and Social Psychology, 74*, 967–984.

Bergman, L. R. (1998). A pattern-oriented approach to studying individual development. In R. B. Cairns, L. R. Bergman, & J. Kagan (Eds.), *Methods and models for*

*studying the individual* (pp. 83–122). London: Sage Publications.

Berkman, L. F. (1995). The role of social relations in health promotion. *Psychosomatic Medicine, 57*, 245–254.

Berkman, L. F., & Breslow, L. (1983). *Health and ways of living.* New York: Oxford University.

Berkman, L. F., Leo-Summers, L., & Horwitz, R. I. (1992). Emotional support and survival after myocardial infarction. *Annals of Internal Medicine, 117*, 1003–1009.

Berscheid, E., & Reis, H. T. (1998). Attraction and close relationships. In D. T. Gilbert, S. T. Fiske, & Gl Lindzey (Eds.), *Handbook of social psychology* (Vol. 2, 4th ed., pp. 193–281). Boston, MA: McGraw-Hill.

Block, J. (1982). Some enduring and consequential structures of personality. In A. I. Rabin, J. Aronoff, A. M. Barclay, & R. A. Zucker (Eds.), *Further explorations in personality* (pp. 27–43). New York: Wiley.

Bower, J. E., Kemeny, M. E., Taylor, S. E., & Fahey, J. L. (1998). Cognitive processing, discovery of meaning, CD4 decline, and AIDS-related mortality among bereaved HIV seropositive men. *Journal of Consulting and Clinical Psychology, 66*, 979–986.

Cacioppo, J. T., Gardner, W. L., Berntson, G. G. (1999). The affect system has parallel and integrative processing components: Form follows function. *Journal of Personality and Social Psychology, 76*, 839–855.

Caldji, C., Tannenbaum, B., Sharma, S., Francis, D., Plotsky, P., & Meaney, M. (1998). Maternal care during infancy regulates the development of neural systems mediating the expression of fearfulness in the rat. *Proceedings of the National Academy of Sciences, 95*, 5335–5340.

Cameron, L. D. & Nicholls, G. (1998). Expression of stressful experiences through writing: Effects of a self-regulation manipulation for pessimists and optimists. *Health Psychology, 17*, 84–92.

Cannon, W. (1942). Voodoo death. *American Anthropologist, 44*, 169–181.

Carroll, D., Smith, G. D., Sheffield, D., Shipley, M. J., & Marmot, M. G. (1997). The relationship between socioeconomic status, hostility, and blood pressure reactions to mental stress in men: Data from the Whitehall II Study. *Health Psychology, 16*, 131–136.

Carstensen, L. L., Gottman, J. M., & Levenson, R. W. (1995). Emotional behavior in long-term marriage. *Psychology and Aging, 10*, 140–149.

Carstensen, L. L., Graff, J., Levenson, R. W., & Gottman, J. M. (1996). Affect in intimate relationships: The developmental course of marriage. In C. Magai & S. H. McFadden (Eds.), *Handbook of emotion, adult development, and aging* (pp. 227–247). San Diego, CA: Academic Press.

Carter, C. S. (1998). Neuroendocrine perspectives on social attachment and love. *Psychoneuroendocrinology, 23*, 779–818.

Carver, C. S., & Scheier, M. F. (1990). Origins and functions of positive and negative affect: A control-process view. *Psychological Review, 97*, 19–35.

Carver, C. S., Pozo, C., Harris, S. D., Noriega, V., Scheier, M. F., Robinson, D. S., Ketcham, A. S., Moffat, F. L., Jr., & Clark, K. C. (1993). How coping mediates the effect of optimism on distress: A study of women with early stage breast cancer. *Journal of Personality and Social Psychology, 65*, 375–390.

Cassel, J. (1976). The contribution of the social environment to host resistance. *American Journal of Epidemiology, 104,* 107–123.

Cassidy, J., & Shaver, P. R. (1999). *Handbook of attachment: Theory, research, and clinical applications.* New York: Guilford.

Clark, R., Anderson, N. B., Clark, V. R., Williams, D. R. (1999). Racism as a stressor for African Americans. *American Psychologist, 54,* 805–816.

Coe, C. L. (1993). Psychosocial factors and immunity in nonhuman primates: A review. *Psychosomatic Medicine, 55,* 298–308.

Coe, C. L., & Lubach, G. R. (2001). Social context and other psychological influences on the development of immunity. In C. D. Ryff & B. Singer (Eds.), *Emotion, social relationships, and health* (pp. 243–261). New York: Oxford University Press.

Cohen, S., Doyle, W. J., Skoner, D. P., Rabin, B. S., & Gwaltney, J. M. Jr. (1997). Social ties and susceptibility to the common cold. *Journal of the American Medical Association, 227,* 1940–1944.

Cohen, S., & Herbert, T. B. (1996). Health psychology: Psychological factors and physical disease from the perspective of human psychoneuroimmunology. *Annual Review of Psychology, 47,* 113–142.

Cohen, S., & Rodriguez, M. S. (1995). Pathways linking affective disturbances and physical disorders. *Health Psychology, 14,* 374–380.

Contrada, R. J., Leventhal, H., & O'Leary, A. (1990). Personality and health. In L. A. Pervin (Ed.), *Handbook of personality: Theory and research* (pp. 638–669). New York: Guilford Press.

Cousins, N. (1979/1995). *Anatomy of an illness as perceived by the patient: Reflections on healing and regeneration.* New York: W. W. Norton.

Dafter, R. E. (1996). Why "negative" emotions can sometimes be positive: The spectrum model of emotions and their role in mind-body healing. *Advances: The Journal of Mind-Body Health, 12,* 6–51.

Darwin, C. (1998). *The expression of the emotions in man and animals.* New York: Oxford University Press. (Original published in 1872)

Davidson, R. J. (1998). Affective style and affective disorders: Perspectives from affective neuroscience. *Cognition and Emotion, 12,* 307–330.

Davidson, R. J., Ekman, P., Saron, C. D., Senulis, J., & Friesen, W. (1990). Approach-withdrawal and cerebral asymmetry: Emotional expression and brain physiology. *Journal of Personality and Social Psychology, 58,* 330–341.

Davidson, R. J., Jackson, D. C., & Kalin, N. H. (2000). Emotion, plasticity, context, and regulation. *Psychological Bulletin, Special Millennium Issue, 126,* 891–909.

Diener, E. (1984). Subjective well-being. *Psychological Bulletin, 95,* 542–575.

Diener, E. (1999). Introduction to the special section on the structure of emotion. *Journal of Personality and Social Psychology, 76,* 803–804.

Diener, E., Sandvik, E., Pavot, W., & Gallaher, D. (1991). Response artifacts in the measurement of subjective well-being. *Social Indicators Research, 20,* 355–381.

Diener, E., Smith, H., & Fujita, F. (1995). The personality structure of affect. *Journal of Personality and Social Psychology, 69,* 130–141.

Diener, E., Suh, E. M., Lucas, R. E., & Smith, H. L. (1999). Subjective well-being: Three decades of progress. *Psychological Bulletin, 125,* 276–302.

Eid, M., & Diener, E. (1999). Intraindividual variability in affect: Reliability, validity, and personality correlates. *Journal of Personality and Social Psychology, 76,* 662–676.

Ekman, P. (1992). An argument for basic emotions. *Cognition and Emotion, 6,* 169–200.

Ekman, P. (1994). Moods, emotions, and traits. In P. Ekman & R. J. Davidson (Eds.), *The nature of emotion: Fundamental questions* (pp. 56–59). New York: Oxford University Press.

Emmons, R. A., & Diener, E. (1985). Personality correlates of subjective well-being. *Personality and Social Psychology Bulletin, 11,* 89–97.

Engel, G. L. (1997). The need for a new medical model: A challenge for biomedicine. *Science, 196,* 129–136

Engel, G. L. (1998). Introduction: How much longer must medicine's science be bound by a seventeenth century world view? In G. A. Fava & H. Freyberger (Eds.), *Handbook of psychosomatic medicine* (pp. 1–21). Madison, CT: International Universities Press.

Epel, E. S., McEwen, B. S., & Ickovics, J. R. (1998). Embodying psychological thriving: Physical thriving in response to stress. *Journal of Social Issues, 54,* 301–322.

Ewart, C. K., Taylor, C. B., Kraemer, H. C., & Agras, W. S. (1991). High blood pressure and marital discord: Not being nasty matters more than being nice. *Health Psychology, 10,* 155–163.

Fava, G. A. (1999a). Lipowski's legacy: The psychosomatic spirit. *Psychotherapy Psychosomatics, 68,* 1–2.

Fava, G. A. (1999b). Well-being therapy: Conceptual and technical issues. *Psychotherapy and Psychosomatics, 68,* 171–179.

Fava, G. A., Rafanelli, C., Grandi, S., Conti, S., & Belluardo, P. (1998). Prevention of recurrent depression with cognitive behavioral therapy. *Archives of General Psychiatry, 55,* 816–821.

Fava, G. A., & Sonino, N. (2000). Psychosomatic medicine: Emerging trends and perspectives. *Psychotherapy Psychosomatics, 69.*

Fitness, J. (1996). Emotion knowledge structures in close relationships. In G. J. O. Fletcher (Eds.), *Knowledge structures in close relationships: A social psychological approach* (pp. 195–217). Hillsdale, NJ: Erlbaum.

Fitness, J., & Fletcher, G. J. O. (1993). Love, hate, anger, and jealousy in close relationships: A prototype and cognitive appraisal analysis. *Journal of Personality and Social Psychology, 65,* 942–958.

Fitzgerald, T. E., Tenn, H., Affleck, G., & Pransky, G. S. (1993). The relative importance of dispositional optimism and control appraisals in quality of life after coronary artery bypass surgery. *Journal of Behavioral Medicine, 16,* 25–43.

Folkman, S. (1997). Positive psychological states and coping with severe stress. *Social Science and Medicine, 45,* 1207–1221.

Folkman, S., Lazarus, R. S., Dunkel-Schetter, C., DeLongis, A., & Gruen, R. J. (1986). The dynamics of a stressful encounter: Cognitive appraisal, coping, and encounter outcomes. *Journal of Personality and Social Psychology, 50,* 922–1003.

Frasure-Smith, N., Lesperance, M. D., & Talajic, M. (1993). Depression following myocardial infarction: Impact on 6-month survival. *Journal of the American Medical Association, 270,* 1819–1825.

Fredrickson, B. L. (1998). What good are positive emotions? *Review of General Psychology, 2,* 300–319.

Fredrickson, B. L., Levenson, R. W. (1998). Positive emotions speed recovery from the cardiovascular sequelae of negative emotions. *Cognition and Emotion, 12,* 191–220.

Gallo, L. C. & Matthews K. A. (1999). Do negative emotions mediate the association between socioeconomic status and health? *Annals of the New York Academy of Sciences, 896,* 226–245.

Garmezy, N. (1991). Resiliency and vulnerability of adverse developmental outcomes associated with poverty. *Behavioral Scientist, 34,* 416–430.

Glanz, M. D., & Johnson, J. L. (1999). *Resilience and development: Positive life adaptations.* New York: Plenum.

Glass, T. A., & Maddox, G. L. (1992). The quality and quantity of social support: Stroke recovery as psychosocial transition. *Social Science and Medicine, 34,* 1249–1261.

Gottman, J. M. (2001). Meta-emotion, children's emotional intelligence, and buffering children from marital conflict. In C. D. Ryff & B. Singer (Eds.), *Emotion, social relationships, and health* (pp. 23–40). New York: Oxford University Press.

Gottman, J. M., Katz, L.F., & Hooven, C. (1996). Parental meta-emotion philosophy and the emotional life of families: Theoretical models and preliminary data. *Journal of Family Psychology, 10,* 243–268.

Green, D. P., Goldman, S. L., & Salovey, P. (1993). Measurement error masks bipolarity in affect ratings. *Journal of Personality and Social Psychology, 64,* 1029–1041.

Green, D. P., Salovey, P., Truax, K. M. (1999). Static, dynamic, and causative bipolarity of affect. *Journal of Personality and Social Psychology, 76,* 856–867.

Hazan, C., & Shaver, P. R. (1994). Attachment as an organization framework for research on close relationships. *Psychological Inquiry, 5,* 1–22.

House, J. S., Landis, K. R., & Umberson, D. (1988). Social relationships and health. *Science, 241,* 540–545.

Hupka, R. B., Lenton, A. P., & Hutchison, K. A. (1999). Universal development of emotion categories in natural language. *Journal of Personality and Social Psychology, 77,* 247–278.

Ickovics, J. R., & Park, C. L. (1998). Paradigm shift: Why a focus on health is important. *Journal of Social Issues, 54,* 237–244.

Jackson, P. R., & Warr, P. B. (1984). Unemployment and psychological ill-health: The moderating role of duration and age. *Psychological Medicine, 14,* 605–614.

Johnson, E. H., & Browman, C. L. (1987). The relationship of anger expression to health problems among Black Americans in a national survey. *Journal of Behavioral Medicine, 10,* 103–116.

Kahneman, D. (1999). Objective happiness. In D. Kahneman, E. Diener, & N. Schwarz (Eds.). *Well-being: The foundations of hedonic psychology* (pp 3–25). New York: Russell Sage Foundation.

Kahneman, D. (2000). Experienced utility and objective happiness: A moment-based approach. In D. Kahneman & A. Tversky (Eds.). *Choices, values & frames* (pp. 673–692). New York: Cambridge University Press and the Russell Sage Foundation.

Karasek, R., Baker, R., Marxer, F., Ahlbom, A., & Theorell, T. (1981). Job latitude, job demands and cardiovascular disease: A prospective study of Swedish men. *American Journal of Public Health, 71,* 694–705.

Kawachi, I., Sparrow, D., Spiro, A., Vokonas, P., & Weiss, S. T. (1996). A prospective study of anger and coronary heart disease: The Normative Aging Study. *Circulation, 94,* 2090–2095.

Kelley, J. E., Leisen, J. C. C., & Lumley, M. A. (1997). Health effects of emotional disclosure in rheumatoid arthritis patients. *Health Psychology, 16,* 331–340.

Kessler, R. C., Mickelson, K. D., Williams, D. R. (1999). The prevalence, distribution, and mental health correlates of perceived discrimination in the United States. *Journal of Health and Social Behavior, 40,* 208–230.

Kiecolt-Glaser, J. K., Glaser, R., Cacioppo, J. T., MacCallum, R. C., Snydersmith, M., Cheongtag, K., & Malarkey, W. B. (1997). Marital conflict in older adults: Endocrinological and immunological correlates. *Psychosomatic Medicine, 59,* 339–349.

Kiecolt-Glaser, J. K., Newton, T., Cacioppo, J. T., MacCallum, R. C., Glaser, R., & Malarkey, W. B. (1996). Marital conflict and endocrine function: Are men really more physiociallly affected than women? *Journal of Consulting and Clinical Psychology, 64,* 324–332.

Kling, K. C., Ryff, C. D., & Essex, M. J. (1997). Adaptive changes in the self-concept during a life transition. *Personality and Social Psychology Bulletin, 23,* 989–998.

Kling, K. C., Seltzer, M. M., & Ryff, C. D. (1997). Distinctive late life challenges: Implications for coping and well-being. *Psychology and Aging, 12,* 288–295.

Knox, S. S., & Uvnäs-Moberg, K. (1998). Social isolation and cardiovascular disease: An atherosclerotic pathway? *Psychoneuroendocrinology, 23,* 877–890.

Krieger, N. (1990). Racial and gender discrimination: Risk factors for high blood pressure? *Social Science Medicine, 12,* 1273–1281.

Larsen, R. J., & Diener, E. (1992). Promises and problems with the circumplex model of emotion. In M. S. Clark (Ed.), *Review of personality and social psychology: Emotion* (Vol. 13, pp. 25–59). Newbury Park, CA: Sage.

Larsen, R. J., & Fredrickson, B. L. (1999). Measurement issues in emotion research. In D. Kahneman, E. Diener, & N. Schwarz (Eds.). *Well-being: The foundations of hedonic psychology* (pp. 40–60). New York: Russell Sage Foundation.

Leedham, B., Meyerowitz, B. E., Muirhead, J., & Frist, M. H. (1995). Positive expectations predict health after heart transplantation. *Health Psychology, 14,* 74–79.

Levenson, R. W., Carstensen, L. L., & Gottman, J. M. (1994). The influence of age and gender on affect, physiology, and their interrelations: A study of long-term marriage. *Journal of Personality and Social Psychology, 67,* 56–68.

Leventhal, H., Patrick-Miller, L. (1993). Emotion and illness: The mind is in the body. In M. Lewis, J. M. Haviland (Eds.). *Handbook of emotions* (pp. 365–379). New York: The Guilford Press.

Link, B. G., Lennon, M. C., & Dohrenwend, B. P. (1993). Socioeconomic status and depression: The role of occupations involving direction, control, and planning. *American Journal of Sociology, 98,* 1351–1387.

Lipowski, Z. J. (1986). Psychosomatic medicine: Past and present. *Canadian Journal of Psychiatry, 31,* 2–21.

Lundberg, U. L. F. (1999). Stress responses in low-status jobs and their relationship to health risks: Musculoskeletal disorders. *Annals of the New York Academy of Sciences, 896,* 162–172.

Magnusson, D. (1998). The logic and implications of a person-oriented approach. In R. B. Cairns, L. R. Bergman, & J. Kagan (Eds.), *Methods and models for studying the individual* (pp. 33–64). London: Sage Publications.

Malarkey, W., Kiecolt-Glaser, J. K., Pearl, D. & Glaser, R. (1994). Hostile behavior during marital conflict alters pituitary and adrenal hormones. *Psychosomatic Medicine, 56,* 41–51.

Matthews, K. A. (1988). Coronary heart disease and type A behavior: Update on an alternative to the Booth Kewley and Friedman quantitative review. *Psychological Bulletin, 104,* 373–380.

McEwen, B. S. (1998). Protective and damaging effects of stress mediators. *New England Journal of Medicine, 338,* 171–179.

McEwen, B. S., & Schmeck, H. (1994). *The hostage brain.* New York: Rockefeller University Press.

McEwen, B. S. & Seeman, T. (1999). Protective and damaging effects of mediators of stress: Elaborating and testing the concepts of allostasis and allostatic load. *Annals of the New York Academy of Sciences, 896,* 30–47.

McEwen, B. S., & Stellar, E. (1993). Stress and the individual: Mechanisms leading to disease. *Archives of Internal Medicine, 153,* 2093–2101.

McKenna, M. C., Zevon, M. A., Corn, B., & Rounds, J. (1999). Psychosocial factors and the development of breast cancer: A meta-analysis. *Health Psychology, 18,* 520–531.

McNair, D. M., Lorr, M., & Droppleman, L. F. (1971). *Profile of mood states.* San Diego: Educational and Industrial Testing Service.

McNeilly, M. D., Anderson, N. B., Armstead, C. A., Clark, R., Corbett, M. O., Robinson, E. L., Pieper, C. F., & Lipisto, M. (1996). The perceived racism scale: A multidimensional assessment of the perception of White racism among African Americans. *Racism and Health, Ethnicity, and Disease, 6,* 154–166.

Miller, G. E., Dopp, J. M., Myers, H. F., Stevens, S. Y., & Fahey, J. L. (1999). Psychosocial predictors of natural killer cell mobilization during marital conflict. *Health Psychology, 18,* 262–271.

Noh, S., Beiser, M., Kaspar, V., Hou, F., Rummens, J. (1999). Perceived racial discrimination, depression, and coping: A study of Southeast Asian refugees in Canada. *Journal of Health and Social Behavior, 40,* 193–207.

Panksepp, J. (1998a). *Affective neuroscience: The foundations of human and animal emotions.* New York: Oxford University Press.

Panksepp, J. (1998b). The quest for long-term health and happiness: To play or not to play, that is the question. *Psychological Inquiry, 9,* 56–65.

Pappas G., Queen, S., Hadden, W., & Fisher, G. (1993). The increasing disparity and mortality between socioeconomic groups in the United States, 1960 and 1986. *New England Journal of Medicine, 329,* 103–109.

Parker, G., Tupling, H., & Brown, L. B. (1979). A parental bonding instrument. *British Journal of Medical Psychology, 52,* 1–10.

Pearlin, L. I., Lieberman, M. A., Menaghan, E. G., & Mullan, J. T. (1981). The stress process. *Journal of Health and Social Behavior, 22,* 337–356.

Pennebaker, J. W. (Ed.). (1995). *Emotion, disclosure, and health.* Washington, DC: American Psychological Association.

Pennebaker, J. W., & Beall, S. K. (1986). Confronting a traumatic event: Toward an understanding of inhibition and disease. *Journal of Abnormal Psychology, 95,* 274–281.

Pennebaker, J. W., & King, L. A. (1999). Linguistic styles: Language use as an individual difference. *Journal of Personality and Social Psychology, 77,* 1296–1312.

Petersson, M., Alster, P., Lundeberg, T., & Uvnäs-Moberg, K. (1996). Oxytocin causes long-term decrease of blood pressure in female and male rats. *Physiology and Behavior, 60,* 1311–1315.

Räikkönen, K., Matthews, K. A., Flory, J. D., Owens, J. F., & Gump, B. B. (1999). Effects of optimism, pessimism, and trait anxiety on ambulatory blood pressure and mood during everyday life. *Journal of Personality and Social Psychology, 76,* 104–113.

Reed, G. M., Kemeny, M. E., Taylor, S. E., & Visscher, B. R. (1999). Negative HIV-specific expectancies and AIDS-related bereavement as predictors of symptom onset in asymptomatic HIV-positive gay men. *Health Psychology, 18,* 354–363.

Reed, G. M., Kemeny, M. E., Taylor, S. E., Wang, H.-Y. J., & Visscher, B. R. (1994). "Realistic acceptance" as a predictor of decreased survival time in gay men with AIDS. *Health Psychology, 13,* 299–307.

Reis, H. T. (2001). Relationship experiences and emotional well-being. In C. D. Ryff & B. Singer (Eds.), *Emotion, social relationships, and health* (pp. 57–86). New York: Oxford University Press.

Reis, H. T., & Patrick, B. C. (1996). Attachment and intimacy: Component processes. In E. T. Higgins and A. Kruglanski (Eds.), *Social psychology: Handbook of basic principles* (pp. 367–389). Chichester, England: Wiley.

Robins, R. W., John, O. P., & Caspi, A. (1998). The typological approach to studying personality. In R. B. Cairns, L. R. Bergman, & J. Kagan (Eds.), *Methods and models for studying the individual* (pp. 135–160). London: Sage Publications.

Russek, L. G., & Schwartz, G. E. (1997). Feelings of parental caring predict health status in midlife: A 35-year follow-up of the Harvard Mastery of Stress Study. *Journal of Behavioral Medicine, 20,* 1–13.

Russell, J. A., & Barrett, L. (1999). Core affect, prototypical emotional episodes, and other things called emotion: Dissecting the elephant. *Journal of Personality and Social Psychology, 76,* 805–819.

Rutter, M. (1990). Psychosocial resilience and protective mechanisms. In J. Rolf, A. S. Masten, D. Cicchetti, K. H. Neuchterlein, & S. Weintraub (Eds.), *Risk and protective factors in the development of psychopathology* (pp. 181–214). New York: Cambridge University Press.

Ryff, C. D. (1989). Happiness is everything, or is it? Explorations on the meaning of psychological well-being. *Journal of Personality and Social Psychology, 57,* 1069–1081.

Ryff, C. D. (1995). Psychological well-being in adult life. *Current Directions in Psychological Science, 4,* 99–104.

Ryff, C. D., & Keyes, C.L.M. (1995). The structure of psychological well-being revisited. *Journal of Personality and Social Psychology, 69,* 719–727.

Ryff, C. D., Magee, W. J., Kling, K. C., & Wing, E. H. (1999). Forging macro-micro linkages in the study of psychological well-being. In C. D. Ryff & V. W. Marshall (Eds.), *The self and society in aging processes* (pp. 247–278). New York: Springer

Ryff, C. D., & Singer, B. (2000). Interpersonal flourishing:

A positive health agenda for the new millennium. *Personality and Social Psychology Review, 4*, 30–44.

Ryff, C. D., & Singer, B. (2001). Integrating emotion into the study of social relationships and health. In C. D. Ryff & B. Singer (Eds.), *Emotion, social relationships, and health* (pp. 3–22). New York: Oxford University Press.

Ryff, C. D., & Singer, B. (1998a). The contours of positive human health. *Psychological Inquiry, 9*, 1–28.

Ryff, C. D., & Singer, B. (1998b). Human health: New directions for the next millennium. *Psychological Inquiry, 9*, 69–85.

Ryff, C. D., Singer, B., Love, G. D., & Essex, M. J. (1998). Resilience in adulthood and later life: Defining features and dynamic processes. In J.Lomranz (Ed.), *Handbook of Aging and Mental Health: An Integrative Approach* (pp. 69–96). New York: Plenum.

Ryff, C. D., Singer, B., Wing, E. H., & Love, G. D. (2001). Elective affinities and uninvited agonies: Mapping emotion with significant others onto health. In C. D. Ryff & B. Singer (Eds.), *Emotion, social relationships, and health* (pp. 133–175). New York: Oxford University Press.

Sapolsky, R. M. (1992). *Stress, the aging brain, and the mechanisms of neuron death.* Cambridge, MA: MIT Press.

Schaefer, M. T., & Olson, D. (1981). Assessing intimacy: The PAIR Inventory. *Journal of Marriage and Family Therapy, 7*, 47–60.

Scheier, M. F., & Carver, C. S. (1992). Effects of optimism on psychological and physical well-being: Theoretical overview and empirical update. *Cognitive Therapy and Research, 16*, 201–228.

Schwarz, N., & Clore, G. L. (1983). Mood, misattribution, and judgments of judgments of well-being: Informative and directive functions of affect stress. *Journal of Personality and Social Psychology, 45*, 513–523.

Schwarz, N., & Strack, F. (1999). Reports of subjective well-being: Judgmental processes and their methodological implications. In D. Kahneman, E. Diener, & N Schwarz (Eds.), *Well-being: The foundations of hedonic psychology* (pp. 40–60). New York: Russell Sage Foundation.

Seeman, M. (1959). On the meaning of alienation. *American Sociological Review, 24*, 783–791.

Seeman, M. (1975). Alienation studies. *Annual Review of Sociology, 1*, 91–123.

Seeman, T. B., Singer, C., Wilkinson, & McEwen, B. (1999). *Exploring a new concept of cumulative biological risk—allostatic load and its health consequences: MacArthur studies of successful aging.* Unpublished manuscript.

Seeman, T. E. (1996). Social ties and health: The benefits of social integration. *Annals of Epidemiology, 6*, 442–451.

Seeman, T. E., Berkman, L. F., Blazer, D., & Rowe, J. (1994). Social ties and support and neuroendocrine function: The MacArthur studies of successful aging. *Annals of Behavioral Medicine, 16*, 95–106.

Seeman, T. E., & McEwen, B. S. (1996). Impact of social environment characteristics on neuroendocrine regulation. *Psychosomatic Medicine, 58*, 459–471.

Seeman, T. E., McEwen, B. S., Rowe, J. W., & Singer, B. H. (2001). Allostatic load as a marker of cumulative biological risk. *Proceedings of the National Academy of Sciences, 98*, 4770–4775.

Seeman, T. E., Singer, B., Rowe, J. W., Horwitz, R., &

McEwen, B. S. (1997). The price of adaptation: Allostatic load and its health consequences, MacArthur studies of successful aging. *Archives of Internal Medicine, 157*, 2259–2268.

Segerstrom, S. C., Taylor, S. E., Kemeny, M. E., & Fahey, J. L. (1998). Optimism is associated with mood, coping, and immune change in response to stress. *Journal of Personality and Social Psychology 74*, 1646–1655.

Selye, H. (1956). *The stress of life.* New York: McGraw-Hill.

Shaver, P., Schwartz, J., Kirson, D., & O'Connor, C. (1987). Emotion knowledge: Further exploration of a prototype approach. *Journal of Personality and Social Psychology, 52*, 1061–1086.

Shedler, J., Mayman, M., & Manis, M. (1993). The illusion of mental health. *American Psychologist, 48*, 1117–1131.

Sheldon, K. M., Ryan, R., & Reis, H. T. (1996). What makes for a good day? Competence and autonomy in the day and in the person. *Personality and Social Psychology Bulletin, 22*, 1270–1279.

Singer, B., & Ryff, C. D. (1997). Racial and ethnic inequalities in health: Environmental, psychosocial, and physiological pathways. In B. Devlin, S. E. Feinberg, D. Resnick, & K. Roeder (Eds.), *Intelligence, genes, and success: Scientists' response to the Bell Curve* (pp. 89–122). New York: Springer-Verlag Publications.

Singer, B., & Ryff, C. D. (1999). Hierarchies of life histories and health risk. *Annals of the New York Academy of Sciences, 896*, 96–115.

Singer, B., Ryff, C. D., Carr, D., & Magee, W. J. (1998). Life histories and mental health: A person-centered strategy. In A. Raftery (Ed.), *Sociological Methodology, 1998* (pp. 1–51). Washington, D.C.: American Sociological Association.

Singer, B., Ryff, C. D., Davidson, R. J., Muller, D., Love, G. D., & Seeman, T. E. (2000). *Pathways to positive health: Connecting psychosocial factors with cerebral activation asymmetry and allostatic load.* Unpublished manuscript.

Smider, N. A., Essex, M. J., & Ryff, C. D. (1996). Adaptation to community relocation: The interactive influence of psychological resources and contextual factors. *Psychology and Aging, 11*, 362–371.

Smith, T. W. (1992). Hostility and health: Current status of a psychosomatic hypothesis. *Health Psychology, 11*, 139–150.

Solomon, R. C. (1993). *The passions: Emotions and the meaning of life.* Indianapolis: Hackett Publishing.

Spiegel, D. (1998). Effects of psychosocial treatment in prolonging cancer survival may be mediated by neuroimmune pathways. *Annals of the New York Academy of Sciences, 840*, 674–683.

Spiegel, D., & Kimerling, R. (2001). Group psychotherapy for women with breast cancer: Relationships among social support, emotional expression, and survival. In C. D. Ryff & B. Singer (Eds.), *Emotion, social relationships, and health* (pp. 97–123). New York: Oxford University Press.

Stanton, A. L., & Snider, P. R. (1993). Coping with a breast cancer diagnosis: A prospective study. *Health Psychology, 12*, 16–23.

Sterling, P. & Eyer, J. (1988). Allostasis: A new paradigm to explain arousal pathology. In J. Fisher & J. Reason (Eds.), *Handbook of life stress, cognition, and health* (pp. 629–649). New York: Wiley.

Sutton, S. K., & Davidson, R. J. (1997). Prefrontal brain asymmetry: A biological substrate of the behavioral approach and inhibition systems. *Psychological Science, 8*, 204–210.

Taylor, S. E., Kemeny, M. E., Reed, G. M., Bower, J. E., & Gruenewald, T. L. (2000) Psychological resources, positive illusions, and health. *American Psychologist, 55*, 99–109.

Taylor, S. E., Repetti, R. L., & Seeman, T. (1997). Health psychology: What is an unhealthy environment and how does it get under the skin? *Annual Review of Psychology, 48*, 411–47.

Thayer, R. E. (1989). *The biopsychology of mood and activation.* New York: Oxford University Press.

Thoits, P. A. (1995). Stress, coping, and social support processes: Where are we? What next? *Journal of Health and Social Behavior, Extra Issue,* 53–79.

Tomarken, A. J., Davidson, R. J., Wheeler, R. E., & Doss, R. C. (1992). Individual differences in anterior brain asymmetry and fundamental dimensions of emotion. *Journal of Personality and Social Psychology, 62*, 676–687.

Uchino, B. N., Cacioppo, J. T., & Kiecolt-Glaser, J. K. (1996). The relationship between social support and physiological processes: A review with emphasis on underlying mechanisms and implications for health. *Psychological Bulletin, 119*, 488–531.

Uvnäs-Moberg, K. (1997). Physiological and endocrine effects of social contact. *Annals of the New York Academy of Science, 807*, 146–163.

Uvnäs-Moberg, K. (1998). Oxytocin may mediate the benefits of positive social interaction and emotions. *Psychoneuroendocrinology, 23*, 819–835.

Veroff, J., Douvan, E., & Kulka, R. A. (1981). *The inner American: A self-portrait from 1957 to 1976.* New York: Basic Books.

Watson, D., & Clark, L. A. (1992). On traits and temperament: General and specific factors of emotional experience and their relation to the five-factor model. *Journal of Personality, 60*, 441–476.

Watson, D., & Walker, L. M. (1996). The long-term stability and predictive validity of trait measures of affect. *Journal of Personality and Social Psychology, 70*, 567–577.

Watson, D., & Pennebaker, J. W. (1989). Health complaints, stress, and distress: Exploring the central role of negative affectivity. *Psychological Review, 96*, 234–254.

Watson, D., & Tellegen, A. (1985). Toward a consensual structure of mood. *Psychological Bulletin, 98*, 219–235.

Watson, D., Wiese, D., Vaidya, J., & Tellegen, A. (1999). The two general activation systems of affect: Structural findings, evolutionary considerations, and psychobiological evidence. *Journal of Personality and Social Psychology, 76*, 830–838.

Weinberger, D. A. (1990). The construct validity of the repressive coping style. In J. L. Singer (Ed.), Repression and dissociation: Implications for personality theory, psychopathology, and health (pp. 337–385). Chicago: University of Chicago Press.

Weinberger, D. A., Schwartz, G. E., & Davidson, R. J. (1979). Low-anxious, high-anxious, and repressive coping styles: Psychometric patterns and behavioral and physiological responses to stress. *Journal of Abnormal Psychology, 88*, 369–380.

Weiner, H. (1992). *Perturbing the organism: The biology of stressful experience.* Chicago: University of Chicago Press.

Werner, E. (1995). Resilience in development. *Current Directions in Psychological Science, 4*, 81–85.

Wheeler, R. E., Davison, R. J., & Tomarken, A. J. (1993) Frontal brain asymmetry and emotional reactivity: A biological substrate of affect style. *Psychophysiology, 30*, 82–89.

Wiesel, E. (1999). *And the sea is never full.* New York: Knopf.

Williams, D. R., Yu, Y., Jackson, J., & Anderson, N. (1997). Racial differences in physical and mental health: Socioeconomic status, stress, and discrimination. *Journal of Health Psychology, 2*, 335–351.

Yik, M.S.M. & Russell, J. A., Feldman Barrett, L (1999). Structure of self-reported current affect: Integration and beyond. *Journal of Personality and Social Psychology 77*, 600–619.

# 58

## BOTTOM-UP: IMPLICATIONS FOR NEUROBEHAVIORAL MODELS OF ANXIETY AND AUTONOMIC REGULATION

Gary G. Berntson, John T. Cacioppo, and Martin Sarter

The cerebral cortex is a crucial neural substrate for higher level behavioral and cognitive processes. Given the prevailing recognition of the hierarchical structure of central neural organization, it is tempting to consider lower levels of the neuraxis as fundamentally subservient to higher level influences. This view is not baseless, but it is incomplete. Recent developments in behavioral neuroscience reveal that lower neural levels can powerfully prime, bias, or otherwise regulate processing by higher neural structures. Moreover, it is increasingly recognized that central and peripheral processes constitute reciprocally linked dimensions of neurobehavioral function. Although reciprocal interactions among levels of neural organization have been recognized historically, contemporary research has now begun to clarify and solidify this concept, and embody this pattern of interaction in documented neurobehavioral systems.

This chapter considers the reciprocal "top-down" and "bottom-up" interactions within neurobehavioral systems, as revealed by current research on anxiety and autonomic control. These data mandate a broader perspective on psychological states such as anxiety and on associated psychophysiological relations. They further suggest that a traditional approach to defining invariant behavioral-autonomic relations may not be particularly fruitful in the ultimate understanding of psychophysiological relationships. Current research increasingly focuses on the multiple interacting levels of processing within neurobehavioral systems, and the complex behavioral and autonomic manifestations of these levels of organization. Although disciplinary perspectives may distinguish between the domains of behavioral, autonomic, and neuroendocrine function, nature does not respect these artificial distinctions. Therefore, contemporary research might more fruitfully focus on specifying the components and operating characteristics of neurobehavioral systems, integrating data on the multiple levels of processing within these systems and elucidating the interactions among levels of organization.

Although we use a specific line of research for illustrative purposes, the present chapter is not primarily about anxiety or psychophysiology, but about a fundamental principle of neurobehavioral organization: the powerful ascending controls of cognitive/behavioral processing that arise from *bottom-up*, including peripheral, influences. These influences have fundamental implications for neurobehavioral models of affect and autonomic control, and their relations to health.

## Some Perspectives on Central Neural Organization

### Heterarchical Organization

A basic hierarchical structure to the functional organization of the nervous system was recognized by early researchers such as John Hughlings Jackson (1884) and Sir Charles Sherrington (1906). The hierarchical model has been widely applied in classical analyses of sensory processing (Hubel & Weisel, 1979), motor control (Bard, 1975), and neurobehavioral organization (Berntson & Micco, 1976); and continues as an important organizing concept in contemporary studies of sensorimotor and neurobehavioral processes (Berntson, Boysen, & Cacioppo, 1993; Loeb, Brown, & Cheng, 1999; Scannell, Burns, Hilgetag, O'Neil, & Young, 1999). Although there appears to be a fundamental hierarchical dimension to central neural organization, this model is not complete.

Both neuroanatomical and functional data reveal that central processing systems do not adhere to a strict hierarchical pattern of organization. Rather than operating through intermediate levels, in a hierarchical fashion, many higher brain systems project directly to lower levels, and vice versa, effectively bypassing intermediate levels of organization. This is apparent in motor systems, for example, where cortical motor neurons have been shown to project not only to brainstem somatomotor reflex circuits but also directly onto spinal motor neurons (Edgley, Eyre, Lemon, & Miller., 1997; Porter, 1987). Similarly, forebrain areas implicated in affective and behavioral processes can modulate autonomic outflow by direct monosynaptic projections to autonomic source nuclei, in addition to more conventional hierarchical influences on reflex circuits of hypothalamic and brainstem origin (see Berntson, Sarter, & Cacioppo, 1998). Further, central networks are replete with lateral interactions within organizational levels, and with parallel processing routes between levels. This more complex pattern of interaction among levels has been termed a *heterarchical* organization (Berntson et al., 1993; Cohen, 1992).

### Multiple Levels of Processing

One implication of this heterarchical structure is the existence of multiple interacting levels of organization at which stimuli can be processed and responses generated. Neurobehavioral mechanisms are not localized to a single neuraxial level, but are represented at diverse levels of the nervous system. At progressively higher levels of organization, there is a general expansion in the range and relational complexity of contextual controls and in the breadth and flexibility of discriminative and adaptive responses (Berntson et al., 1993). Adaptive flexibility has

costs, however, given the finite information-processing capacity of neural networks. Greater flexibility implies a less rigid relationship between inputs and outputs, a greater range of information that must be processed, and a wider diversity of behavioral and autonomic reactions that can be generated—all of which may tax processing capacities. Consequently, the evolutionary layering of higher processing levels onto lower substrates has considerable advantage, in that lower and more efficient processing levels continue to be utilized and may be sufficient in some circumstances.

Primitive protective responses to aversive stimuli are organized at the level of the spinal cord, as is apparent in flexor (pain) withdrawal reflexes and sympathetic responses to noxious stimuli, even after spinal transections (Berntson et al., 1993; Levin, Martin, & Natelson, 1980). These primitive protective reactions are expanded and embellished at higher levels of the neuraxis. This is documented by the wider range of behavioral and autonomic responses to sensory stimuli, including escape and aggressive reactions, that can be mediated at the level of the brain stem in decerebrate organisms (see Berntson et al., 1993). Higher neural structures, such as the amygdala, appear to be important in acquired fear responses. Stimulation of the amygdala can induce fearlike behaviors and autonomic reactions (Davis, 1992), and lesions or functional inactivation of this structure can block the acquisition and expression of conditioned autonomic and behavioral responses to a fear stimulus (Davis, 1992; LeDoux, 1995; Muller, Corodimas, Fridel, & LeDoux, 1997). A direct pathway from the thalamic auditory relay nucleus to the lateral nucleus of the amygdala appears to be sufficient for the development of a simple conditioned fear response to an auditory stimulus, in the absence of higher cortical processing of the stimulus (LeDoux, 1995). Moreover, descending projections from the amygdala to lower level behavioral, autonomic, and neuroendocrine systems appear capable of an integrated response to a simple fear stimulus.

Cortical mechanisms, however, appear to be particularly important for the processing of more complex stimuli and for contextual fear conditioning (LeDoux, 1995; Phillips & LeDoux, 1992). In fact, cortical/cognitive processing mechanisms are capable of a *top-down* activation of lower mechanisms involved in fear and anxiety, even in the absence of a relevant environmental fear stimulus. Mental imagery of aversive or anxiogenic contexts is associated with cortical activation, especially in limbic, paralimbic, and associated cortical areas as evidenced by PET studies (Kosslyn et al., 1996; Rauch et al., 1995, 1996; Rauch, Savage, Alpert, Fischman, & Jenike, 1997; Shin et al., 1999). Such imagery can evoke autonomic responses characteristic of anxiety (Witvliet & Vrana, 1995), potentiate startle responses in a fashion similar to a conditioned fear CS (Vrana, 1995), and trigger anxiety symptoms in patients with phobias or posttraumatic stress disorder (McNeil, Urana, Melamed, Cuthbert, & Lang, 1993; Rauch et al., 1995, 1996).

These findings document multiple levels at which anxiogenic stimuli may be processed. The existence of multiple processing substrates introduces considerable complexity for conceptual models of autonomic function in anxiety states, as the relative contributions of these substrates may vary depending on the stimulus context and associative processes. Conditioned fear stimuli have been shown to increase activity in both the amygdala and the cortex, as revealed by PET and fMRI studies (Hugdahl et al., 1995; LeBar, Gatenby, Gore, LeDoux, & Phelps, 1998; Morris, Ohman, & Dolan, 1999). When visually masked, fear stimuli continue to trigger autonomic reactivity in humans, despite the fact that the stimuli are no longer consciously seen or recognized (Ohman, 1996). The autonomic responses clearly indicate that the masked stimuli continue to be processed, but at a level that is not accessible to verbal report. Visual masking appears to diminish cortical/cognitive processing of the stimulus, and thus fosters a lower level of processing. In this regard, a recent fMRI study revealed that masked fear stimuli, relative to nonmasked stimuli, preferentially enhance activity in thalamic-amygdala circuits and decrease amygdala-cortical activity (Morris et al., 1999). These findings are consistent with the view that processing of fear- and anxiety-related stimuli and associations can occur at multiple interrelated levels of the neuraxis.

### Bottom-Up Influences

Higher level neural systems are often considered to be executive *top-down* regulators of lower output mechanisms. Consistent with this view, higher level systems are not mere passive recipients of sensory signals from lower levels, but via descending influences can fundamentally shape and regulate the ascending information that is relayed from lower level sensory systems (e.g., Palmeri, Bellomo, Giuffrida, & Sapienza, 1999).

Conversely, lower levels in neural heterarchies do not merely transmit preprocessed sensory information, but may also strongly bias higher level cognitive, attentional, and affective processes in a *bottom-up* fashion (Berntson et al., 1998; Ohman, 1996). Since William James's suggestion that strong emotions represent the perceptual consequences of visceral afferent feedback, there has been a continuing history of research and theory on the role of visceral afference in affective reactions (for review, see Cacioppo, Berntson, & Klein, 1992). Although it now appears that visceral feedback does not constitute the sole basis for emotional reactions, visceral afference may play an important role in the priming of central systems underlying affective response (Cacioppo et al., 1992). Recent research

offers considerable support to the view that visceral afferent input can exert important modulatory influence over rostral neural systems.

Stimulation of the vagus nerve has been shown to enhance memory in both animal and human subjects (Clark et al., 1998, 1999). Moreover, this effect persists even after inactivation of vagal afferent axons, indicating that it is vagal afferent activity that underlies these memory effects (Clark et al., 1998). In addition, systemic administration of epinephrine or substance P has been shown to potentiate "emotional" memories in rats—effects that are blocked by vagotomy or inactivation of the major visceral receiving area in the nucleus tractus solitarius (Nogueir, Tomaz, & Williams, 1994; Williams & McGaugh, 1993). These findings suggest an important modulatory effect of visceral afferent information on higher cognitive and affective processes. Additional findings suggest that visceral afference may bias, more generally, the cognitive/attentional processing of fear- and anxiety-related stimuli, as well as the associative/memorial systems that contribute to affective response (Berntson et al., 1998).

The significance of this perspective is that it focuses on important biological influences on psychological processes that arise not from the inherent organizational features of higher level cognitive substrates but on the functional biases on these higher level processing substrates that arise from lower level influences. There is now an emerging recognition of a symmetry in the reciprocal interplay among levels of organization, entailing both direct and indirect mutual interactions (top-down and bottom-up) that impact both biological and psychological processes.

## Anxiety and Autonomic Control

Anxiogenic or fear-eliciting contexts are often associated with robust autonomic responses, and the *DSM-IV* recognizes abnormal visceral reactivity as a common feature of anxiety disorders (APA, 1994). The empirical research on the specific autonomic correlates of anxiety has yielded mixed results, however, and the behavioral significance of the autonomic correlates of fear and anxiety remain uncertain (Berntson et al., 1998; Cacioppo et al., 1992). These are important issues, as anxiety disorders represent a clear risk factor for cardiovascular disease and sudden cardiac death (Hayward, 1995; Kawachi et al., 1994; Kubzansky, Kawachi, Weiss, & Sparrow, 1998), and because they bear on the fundamental nature of anxiety and the underlying neural mechanisms that link behavioral processes and autonomic function.

The autonomic nervous system is often considered to be a homeostatic regulatory system, and brain stem autonomic reflexes serve important functions in the maintenance of internal states. Limbic and forebrain areas implicated in behavioral processes, however, project directly to the nucleus tractus solitarius and other brain stem autonomic substrates, as well as monosynaptically onto autonomic source nuclei, and can powerfully modulate autonomic outflow in a heterarchical fashion. Psychological stressors, even as mild as mental arithmetic, can lead to an inhibition and/or a shift in set point of homeostatic reflexes, such as the baroreceptor-heart rate reflex (see Berntson & Cacioppo, 2000). Moreover, in contrast to the reciprocal control of the autonomic branches typical of brain stem reflexes, descending systems can yield more complex patterns of regulation, including independent activation or coactivation of the sympathetic and parasympathetic divisions (Berntson & Cacioppo, 2000).

Heart rate acceleration to standard psychological stressors, for example, has been reported to predict immune reactions to stress (Manuck, Cohen, Rabin, & Muldoon, 1991), although the amount of variance accounted for may be modest. But an increase in heart rate in behavioral contexts can arise from sympathetic activation, parasympathetic withdrawal, reciprocal sympathetic activation together with parasympathetic withdrawal, or even sympathetically dominant coactivation of both autonomic branches. These varied patterns may be related to distinct psychological states, and may have differential implications for immune function.

Whereas lower levels of neural organization are generally characterized by relatively fixed response patterns, higher levels foster a broader and more flexible range of responses. Thus, orthostatic reflexes manifest in a relatively rigid reciprocal pattern of autonomic control with little variation among subjects (Berntson et al., 1994; Cacioppo et al., 1994); whereas psychological stressors yield a more variable pattern of response, characterized by notable, but stable, individual differences (Berntson et al., 1994; see also Malarkey, Lipkus, & Cacioppo, 1995). This is important because it is the sympathetic component of heart rate reactivity, rather than heart rate reactivity per se, that is most predictive of immune responses (Cacioppo, 1994). This feature of psychophysiological relations would not have been apparent without the inclusion of higher level analyses.

The complex modulatory influences from rostral neural systems on basic brain stem autonomic substrates, which include *feed-forward* control, have necessitated expansion of the simple negative-feedback homeostatic model of autonomic regulation (Berntson & Cacioppo, 2000; Schulkin, McEwen, & Gold, 1994). The complexities of higher level influences on autonomic control may underlie apparent inconsistencies in the literature on anxiety and autonomic function. Behavioral manifestations vary widely among subcategories of anxiety disorders, and even between subjects within a given category (see Berntson et al., 1998). Consequently, it may be unrealistic to expect a simple iso-

morphism between behavioral and autonomic functions, or a universal pattern of altered autonomic control in anxiety states.

Rather than reflecting rigid stimulus-response relationships, autonomic responses to fear- or anxiety-relevant stimuli may reflect the actions of multiple processing levels, and the variety of cognitive processes and functional reaction associated with these states (Berntson et al., 1998). A meaningful understanding of the relationships between cognitive processes, anxiety, and autonomic function will depend on a greater appreciation of the role of rostral neurobehavioral systems.

Of equal importance in understanding the links between anxiety and autonomic control will be a further elucidation of the functional consequences of autonomic states, not just for visceral end organs but also for the *bottom-up* impact of these states on higher neural processes. We will return to this issue below.

## The Basal Forebrain Cholinergic System and Anxiety

The basal forebrain cholinergic system projects widely to telencephalic structures and constitutes the primary source of cholinergic innervation of the cerebral cortex. Acetylcholine has been shown to enhance the signal-to-noise ratio of the responses of cortical neurons to sensory input (Metherate & Weinberger, 1990), and more generally to enhance cortical processing of sensory and associational stimuli (Everitt & Robbins, 1997; Sarter & Bruno, 1997). The degeneration of the basal forebrain cholinergic system in Alzheimer's disease likely underlies in part the broad cognitive deficits and dementia associated with this disorder (Sarter & Bruno, 1999). We have proposed that the basal forebrain cholinergic system also plays an important mediating role in the cognitive contributions to anxiety and its autonomic manifestations, via an enhanced attentional processing of fear- and anxiety-associated stimuli and associations (Berntson et al., 1998). We will further consider this model and its implications after a brief overview of the empirical support for this view.

### Anxiety and Benzodiazepine Receptor Ligands

Benzodiazepine receptor (BZR) agonists, such as chlordiazepoxide (Librium), interact with a specific binding domain on the GABA$_A$ receptor complex, and potentiate the inhibitory actions of GABA. BZR agonists have sedative, anticonvulsant, and anticonflict effects, and are generally considered to be prototypic anxiolytic agents (Shepard, 1986). In contrast, BZR inverse agonists act via allosteric inhibition of GABA-binding, and generally exert actions opposite those of BZR agonists, including proconvulsive, proconflict, and anxiogenic effects. An intriguing subclass of these compounds is the BZR *partial* inverse agonists, which display a differential potency for the multiple actions of full inverse agonists. An example is the β-carboline FG 7142, which has potent proconflict and anxiogenic effects but minimal convulsive actions when compared to full inverse agonists (Thiebot, Soubrie, & Sanger, 1988).

In human subjects, FG 7142 (FG) has been reported to induce a variety of autonomic reactions and self-reports of severe anxiety, which were interpreted to reflect the "anxiogenic" effects of the drug (Dorow, Horowski, Paschelke, Amin, & Braestrup, 1983). Although this was an open, uncontrolled study, anxiogenic effects of FG have been repeatedly demonstrated in more controlled animal research (see Berntson et al., 1998; Thiebot et al., 1988). Moreover, consistent with the putative anxiogenic actions of FG, exposure to novel contexts has been reported to increase the selection of the FG-lever in drug discrimination experiments (Leidenheimer & Schechter, 1988), and antipanic drugs have been reported to block the anxiogenic effects of FG (Pellow & File, 1987). Thus, the available data support the view that FG is a potent anxiogenic agent, and that this drug model of anxiety may generalize to natural mechanisms of anxiety.

In accord with this view, we have found that FG increases operant suppression in a conditioned suppression paradigm (Stowell, Berntson, & Sarter, 1999), and significantly potentiates the cardioacceleratory "defensive-like" response to a moderately intense, nonsignal auditory stimulus (Berntson et al., 1998; Quigley, Sarter, Hart, & Berntson, 1994). The latter is similar to the response enhancement observed in aversive contexts, or with an increase in stimulus intensity, both of which promote a shift from orienting-like to defensive-like responses (Berntson, Boysen, & Cacioppo, 1992; Hart, Sarter, & Berntson, 1998). These findings are consistent with the enhanced cardiovascular reactivity after FG, as reported for humans (Dorow et al., 1983) and monkeys (Ninan, et al., 1982).

## Cortical Cholinergic Basis of BZR Actions

Considerable data now indicate that the anxiogenic and anxiolytic actions of BZR ligands, as reflected in both somatic and autonomic reactions, are mediated in part by the basal forebrain cholinergic system, via a GABAergic link on cholinergic neurons (for review see Sarter & Bruno, 1994). Using in vivo microdialysis, for example, we have demonstrated that cortical acetylcholine (ACh) release is subject to bidirectional modulation by BZR agonists and inverse agonists (Moore, Sarter, & Bruno, 1995; Moore, Stuckman, Sarter, & Bruno, 1995). BZR agonists block activated cortical ACh release, whereas inverse agonists enhance release, with FG being particularly potent (Moore et al., 1995). Moreover, the effects of systemically

administered BZR-ligands on ACh release can be mimicked by infusions of low doses of these compounds directly into the basal forebrain (Moore et al., 1995). Similarly, the effects of systemic administration of BZR ligands on cognitive functions, which appear to depend on forebrain ACh, can be duplicated by direct infusions into the basal forebrain (Holley, Turchi, Apple, & Sarter, 1995). These and other findings indicate that forebrain ACh is controlled in part by GABAergic mechanisms, and available data point to the basal forebrain GABAergic system as a major anatomical substrate of this interaction.

A similar pattern has emerged for the anxiety-modulating effects of BZR ligands, which also appear to depend on the basal forebrain cholinergic system. First, the potentiating effects of FG on the cardiac defensive response can be mimicked by intracerebroventricular infusions of a cholinergic agonist (carbachol), and blocked by infusions of a cholinergic antagonist (atropine), or by selective immunotoxic lesions (192 IgG saporin) of basal forebrain cholinergic neurons (Berntson, Hart, Ruland, & Sarter, 1996). Similarly, these lesions also attenuate the suppressive effects of aversive stimuli on operant performance, and block the modulating effects of BZR agonists and partial inverse agonists on operant suppression and cardiac reactivity in a conditioned suppression paradigm (Stowell et al., 1999).

These results suggest an important role of the basal forebrain cholinergic system in anxiety and the anxiety-modulating effects of BZR ligands. Although BZR agonists can also yield antianxiety effects when infused directly into the amygdala (Menard & Treit, 1999), systemically administered BZR agonists continue to exert anxiolytic effects even after lesions of the amygdala (File, Gonzalez, & Gallant, 1998). Moreover, though basal forebrain cholinergic neurons project to the amygdala as well as the cortex, additional findings indicate that it is the cortical projection, specifically to the medial prefrontal cortex (mPFC), that is the most relevant for the anxiogenic actions of FG.

First, cholinergic-specific lesions of the basal forebrain (by 192-IgG saporin) that effectively block FG-induced potentiation of the cardioacceleratory response largely spare the cholinergic projections to the amygdala (Heckers et al., 1994). Additionally, stressors are known to increase ACh release in the mPFC (Mark, Rada, & Shors, 1996). Moreover, local infusions of a cholinergic agonist into the mPFC, but not the amygdala, mimicked the effects of FG administration; and local infusions of a cholinergic antagonist into the mPFC, but not the amygdala, blocked the actions of FG (Hart, Sarter, & Berntson, 1999). Finally, local immunotoxic lesions of the cholinergic inputs to the mPFC were also found to block the effects of FG on the cardiovascular defensive response (Hart et al., 1999). These findings strongly suggest that the anxiogenic actions of FG are dependent in part on basal forebrain cholinergic projections to the mPFC, a cortical area that has been consistently implicated in anxiety and autonomic control (e.g., Barbas, 1995; Frysztak & Neafsey, 1994; Jinks & McGregor, 1997; Neafsey, 1990).

## A Neurobiological Model

As discussed above, BZR agonists and inverse agonists bidirectionally modulate the somatic and autonomic manifestations of anxiety in both humans and animals, and the neural systems underlying these effects are beginning to be elucidated. Despite these advances, and the widespread clinical application of BZR agonists in anxiety disorders, the specific behavioral and cognitive mechanisms mediating these actions remain unsettled. Here we outline a neurobiological framework that offers an organizing perspective on this complex issue (see Berntson et al., 1998).

### Cortical/Cognitive Contributions to Anxiety

Cognitive factors in anxiety disorders are widely recognized. Cognitive theories of anxiety emphasize the importance of attentional abnormalities as major contributors to the development and persistence of anxiety disorders (Beck & Clark, 1997; Eysenck, 1991; Ohman, 1996). Anxious subjects are described as more likely to attend to threat-related stimuli and to have more narrowly focused attention (Eysenck, 1991). This may arise from a *bottom-up* priming of attention toward threat-related stimuli by early stimulus processing stages (Beck & Clark, 1997; Ohman, 1996), or by a *top-down* bias on perceptual or cognitive processes (Schmidt, Lerew, & Trakowski, 1997). Because BZR agonists reduce activity in the basal forebrain cortical cholinergic system, they would be expected to attenuate cognitive/attentional processing. According to this view, antianxiety drugs may produce therapeutic effects largely via their attention-reducing properties (Curran, 1991). In Gray's neuropsychological model, for example, anxiety is considered a manifestation of a *behavioral inhibition system* that normally responds to signals of punishment, nonreward, and novelty by inhibiting ongoing behavior and by increasing arousal and attention to anxiety-related stimuli (see Gray & McNaughton, 1996). Antianxiety drugs, such as BZR agonists, are seen as antagonizing this behavioral inhibition system. Conversely, the anxiogenic effects of FG 7142 and other BZR inverse or partial inverse agonists may augment the actions of this system and lead to hyperarousal and hyperattentional processing of fear and anxiety-associated stimuli.

In this regard, the basal forebrain cortical cholinergic system has been hypothesized to play an important role in the priming of cognitive/attentional processing of threat-related stimuli and associations, and may be a major substrate for the actions of anxiogenic and anxiolytic agents (Berntson et al., 1998). This system may play a par-

ticularly salient role in those anxiety-related contexts that most heavily depend on cortical processing substrates.

## The Basal Forebrain Cortical Cholinergic System Modulates Selective Aspects of Anxiety

The basal forebrain cortical cholinergic system does not appear to impact uniformly on fear and anxiety, but rather may be more specific in its actions. This may relate to distinctions in the levels of processing. Simple aversive conditioning can be mediated at the level of the amygdala, and does not require extensive cortical processing (LeDoux, 1995). Consequently, the basal forebrain cortical cholinergic system may have minimal impact on such conditioning. This has been confirmed, as lesions of the basal forebrain do not block simple conditioned somatic or cardiovascular responses, although they do slow acquisition at a point when attentional demands would be expected to be maximal (Buchanan, Beylotte, & Powell, 1997; Ginn & Powell, 1992). Moreover, by a basal forebrain cortical cholinergic pathway, FG 7142 potentiates the cardiac defensive response to a moderately intense acoustic stimulus, a stimulus context that would likely entail evaluative cortical processing (for review see Berntson et al., 1998). In contrast, FG does not enhance somatic or cardiac startle responses to an acoustic stimulus, as the basic startle circuit is organized at the level of the brain stem (Davis, Gendelman, Tischler, & Gendelman, 1982). Nor does it enhance fear-potentiated startle to a simple aversive-conditioned stimulus (Hart et al., 1998), which can be mediated by a direct thalamic-amygdala pathway (Campeau & Davis, 1995).

Additional findings further support the selective role of the basal forebrain cholinergic system in anxiety-related processing that depends on cortical/cognitive mechanisms. Although simple conditioned fear responses can be mediated by the amygdala, contextual conditioning is more dependent on cortical processes (Phillips & LeDoux, 1992). Consistent with this distinction, BZR agonists and partial inverse agonists have greater bidirectional modulatory effects on the cardioacceleratory defensive response in contextually conditioned, compared to explicitly conditioned, animals (Berntson, Hart, & Sarter, 1997; see also Hart et al., 1998). Similarly, BZR ligands were found to have greater bidirectional modulatory effects on operant suppression to a contextually conditioned aversive stimulus, compared to an explicitly conditioned stimulus (Stowell et al., 1999).

These findings are consistent with multiple levels of processing of fear-and anxiety-related stimuli, and support the view that the basal forebrain cholinergic system plays a particularly important role in those aspects of anxiety that arise from cortical processing. As such, the basal forebrain corticopetal cholinergic system may represent an important neural substrate linking cognitive and attentional factors with subcortical mechanisms that have been implicated in fear and anxiety.

### Top-Down Influences

Figure 58.1 depicts the cerebral cortex, the amygdala, and selected descending routes by which these structures may contribute to the expression of anxiety and its autonomic features. The descending branch of the present neurobiological model conceptualizes subcortical structures previously implicated in anxiety and autonomic control, such as the amygdala, hypothalamus, and midbrain central gray, as essential elements of a descending multilevel heterarchical system (see Berntson et al., 1998). Figure 58.1 is intended to be illustrative rather than exhaustive, however, and for simplicity only the amygdala is depicted. Traditional neuropsychological models have often focused on the amygdala and its descending connections, and have rarely attempted to integrate the role of cognitive processes in neuropsychological theories of anxiety. More recent models, however, are increasingly recognizing the role of higher level influences in anxiety (see LeDoux, 1995; Gray & McNaughton, 1996; McNaughton, 1997). The inclusion of the cerebral cortical component in figure 58.1 recognizes the potentially powerful contributions of cognitive/attentional factors to anxiety and autonomic control.

The cortex and the amygdala have ample routes, through this descending heterarchical system, whereby these structures can modulate autonomic functions. As illustrated in Figure 58.1, however, both the amygdala and the medial prefrontal cortex also issue more direct projections to brain stem autonomic mechanisms, such as the nucleus of the tractus solitarius and the nucleus paragigantocellularis (see below), as well as to lower autonomic source nuclei (for review, see Berntson et al., 1998). Although the precise contributions of direct and indirect projections to the autonomic manifestations remain to be clarified, the direct projections in Figure 58.1 represent a sufficient set of pathways by which telencephalic structures can regulate autonomic states.

The present model incorporates long-standing hypotheses about the role of the amygdala in the emotional coloring of sensory stimuli in general and in the acquisition and expression of anxiety. A central feature of the present model is that major cortical inputs to the amygdala can supply the sensory stimuli and associations that may then gain emotional significance via processing within amygdalo-telencephalic circuits (Berntson et al., 1998). Importantly, the efficiency and extent of processing of such stimuli and associations by these circuits would be expected to depend on cortical acetylcholine (Berntson et al., 1998; Sarter & Bruno, 1997). Thereby, basal forebrain cortical cholinergic activity could modulate the descend-

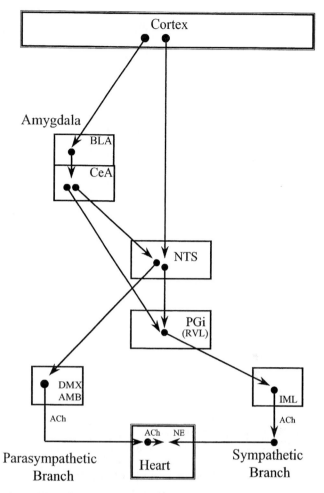

Figure 58.1 Descending arm of a neurobehavioral model by which cortical/cognitive processes may contribute to the development and expression of anxiety and its autonomic features. The model is not intended to be anatomically complete, but to illustrate concepts and hypotheses derived in part from experimental evidence (see Berntson et al., 1998). *Abbreviations:* ACh, acetylcholine; AMB, nucleus ambiguus; BLA, basolateral amygdala; CeA, central nucleus of the amygdala; DMX, dorsal motor nucleus of the vagus; IML, sympathetic preganglionic neurons of the intermediolateral cell column; NE, norepinephrine; NTS, nucleus tractus solitarius; PGi, nucleus paragigantocellularis; RVL, rostral ventrolateral medullary "pressor" area. From Berntson et al. (1998), with permission of Elsevier Science.

ing circuit (Figure 58.1) implicated in the acquisition and expression of fear and anxiety.

### Bottom-Up Influences

Figure 58.2 illustrates the ascending components of the present model, through which lower levels of the heterarchical system can influence higher level processes. Cholinergic neurons in the basal forebrain receive several af-

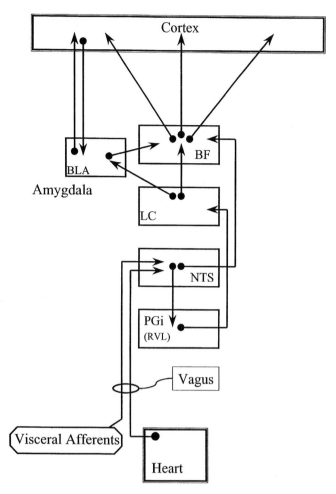

Figure 58.2 Ascending arm of a neurobehavioral model by which cortical/cognitive processes may contribute to the development and expression of anxiety and its autonomic features. Ascending pathways illustrate the potential routes by which sympathetic activity and visceral afference may modulate rostral systems. *Abbreviations:* BF, basal forebrain cortical cholinergic system; BLA, basolateral amygdala; LC, locus coeruleus; NTS, nucleus tractus solitarius; PGi, nucleus paragigantocellularis; RVL, rostral ventrolateral medullary "pressor" area. From Berntson et al. (1998), with permission of Elsevier Science.

ferent projections that modulate the activity of the cortical cholinergic projection. Excitatory noradrenergic projections to basal forebrain cholinergic neurons, as well as to the cortex directly, arise from the locus coeruleus, a structure that has been consistently implicated in emotional and behavioral activation (Aston-Jones et al., 1996; Berntson et al., 1998). The regulation of cortical acetylcholine by basal forebrain noradrenergic afferents represents an important route by which ascending noradrenergic projections could mediate potential feedback effects of cardiovascular reactivity in the modulation of cortical processing of anxiogenic stimuli.

Activity of locus coeruleus neurons is greatly enhanced by the presentation of stress-, fear-, and anxiety-inducing stimuli, leading to the hypothesis that ascending noradrenergic projections may be an important mediator of emotional activation (Aston-Jones et al., 1996), possibly in interaction with effects of corticotropin releasing hormone (Curtis, Pavcovich, Grigoriadis, & Valentino, 1995). Rewarding stimuli also increase activity of the locus coeruleus, however, suggesting that emotional valence is not encoded in locus coeruleus activation, per se (Aston-Jones et al., 1996; Berntson et al., 1998). Rather, locus coeruleus activity may represent a state-setting mechanism that enhances the processing of stimulus contexts and associative networks by more rostral structures. According to the present model, the basal forebrain cholinergic system represents a major mediator of this enhanced cortical processing, whereas the amygdala may represent an important switch for determination of the valence of the affective response.

The ability of emotional stimuli to activate the noradrenergic ascending system appears to be a direct function of the state of the sympathetic branch of the autonomic nervous system (Aston-Jones et al., 1996; Berntson et al., 1998). A major afferent to the locus coeruleus originates from the nucleus paragigantocellularis (PGi) in the medulla (Aston-Jones et al., 1991). The PGi is partially coextensive with the rostral ventrolateral medullary pressor area, a region that directly innervates sympathetic motor neurons and receives input from a variety of sources including the nucleus tractus solitarius (the primary receiving site for peripheral visceral afferents). Collectively, these considerations suggest that PGi projections to the locus coeruleus transmit information reflecting autonomic activity and visceral afference (see Aston-Jones et al., 1991, 1996; Berntson et al., 1998). Because PGi neurons activate both the locus coeruleus and the sympathetic motor neurons, they may modulate both the autonomic and cognitive aspects of emotional activation. Additionally, the medial prefrontal cortex exerts a potent excitatory influence on the locus coeruleus (Jodo, Chiang, & Aston-Jones, 1998), which could provide for *top-down* activation of this system.

## Integration of Top-Down and Bottom-Up Influences

Although ascending and descending limbs of the proposed model are separated for conceptual and descriptive clarity, the functional significance of this model lies in the interactions between the ascending and descending branches of the heterarchical system underlying fear and anxiety. A question arises as to the causal sequence of events in emotional activation. Clearly, ascending modulation of cognitive processing by autonomic states requires an initiation of those states (generally via descending projections). The present model considers reciprocal amygdalo-cortical connections as essential in mediating the classification and processing of fear- and anxiety-associated stimuli, which therefore represent an integral element of both the ascending (anxiety modulating) and the descending (anxiety expressing) components of the model. In addition, neuronal circuits that include the connections between the amygdala and the bed nucleus of the stria terminalis with the hippocampus have been speculated to mediate the evaluation of anxiety contexts and the cognitive biases that characterize pathological states of anxiety (Davis & Shi, 1999; LeDoux, 1995). Thus several limbic circuits, which are organized in parallel with the ascending network illustrated in Figure 58.2, may be essential for the cognitive processing of anxiety-associated stimuli and associations. The present model hypothesizes that the ascending recruitment of these limbic circuits, via noradrenergic-cholinergic activation, serves to prime rostral substrates for processing of the cognitive aspects fear and anxiety.

The proposed neurobiological model also provides for a cognitively driven *top-down* activation of the descending arm of the system. The importance of this possibility is that such a *top-down* activation could trigger a feedback cascade associated with the ascending component of the model. Such a reciprocal cascade may underlie the persistence and apparent irrationality of much anxiety-related ideation in anxiety disorders.

## Overview and Implications for Health

The present model offers a more comprehensive perspective on the neuropsychology of fear and anxiety by emphasizing the multiple levels of function within neurobehavioral substrates, the role of cognitive and attentional processes, and the potential impact of bottom-up influences in these states. A neurobiological model of anxiety that excludes cognitive contributions is incomplete, as a primary feature of clinical anxiety disorders is disordered cognition. The model proposes a neural system, the basal forebrain cortical cholinergic system, that may underlie the links between cognitive processes, anxiety, and autonomic function. The broader significance of the model lies not in a particular set of structures or pathways, however, but in the recognition of the existence of multiple ascending routes by which autonomic states and lower neural levels can modulate the highest level cognitive processes.

Ascending information concerning autonomic states may bias cognitive processes by its perceptual consequences (see Cacioppo et al., 1992; Schmidt et al., 1997), but the ascending pathways of Figure 58.2 also suggest more pervasive and subtle influences on higher processing levels. In quadriplegia, the spinal sympathetic outflow is disconnected from higher centers, and ascending spinal visceral afferents are transected. Despite having sustained

more severe injuries and disabilities than paraplegics, however, quadriplegics are less likely to display posttraumatic stress disorder (Radnitz et al., 1998). Although this cannot be attributable necessarily to the reduction in visceral afference, it does highlight the need for further research on the role of ascending systems in anxiety.

Although the present chapter focuses on anxiety and autonomic control, the model has far broader implications. As a substrate for the acquisition of fear and emotional memories, the amygdala likely plays an important role in a variety of psychopathological states (LeDoux & Muller, 1997). Moreover, the broad role of the basal forebrain cholinergic system in cognition has implicated this substrate in cognitive disorders ranging from schizophrenia to dementia of the Alzheimer's type (Sarter, 1994; Sarter, Bruno, & Turchi, 1999). Although these conditions may represent extremes of disordered function in the basal forebrain cholinergic system, the centrality of this system in cognitive and attentional processing suggests a much wider involvement in psychopathological states, autonomic and neuroendocrine regulation, and health.

## NOTE

Preparation of this chapter was supported in part by a grant from the National Heart, Lung and Blood Institute (HL 54428), and by a grant from the MacArthur Foundation.

## REFERENCES

American Psychiatric Association. (1994). *Diagnostic and statistical manual of mental disorders* (4th ed). Washington, DC: Author.

Aston-Jones, G., Rajkowski, J., Kubiak, P., Valentino, R. J., & Shipley, M. T. (1996). Role of the locus coeruleus in emotional activation. *Progress in Brain Research, 107,* 379–402.

Aston-Jones, G., Shipley, M. T., Chouvet, G., Ennis, M., van Bockstaele, E., Pieribone, V., Shiekhattar, R., Akaoka, H., Drolet, G., Astier, B., Charlety, P., Valentino, R. J., & Williams, J. T. (1991). Afferent regulation of locus coeruleus neurons: Anatomy, physiology, and pharmacology. *Progress in Brain Research*, 88, 47–75.

Barbas, H. (1995). Anatomic basis of cognitive-emotional interactions in the primate prefrontal cortex. *Neuroscience and Biobehavioral Reviews, 19*, 499–510.

Bard, P. (1975). Postural coordination and locomotion and their central control. In V. B. Mountcastle (Ed.), *Medical physiology*. St. Louis: C. V. Mosby.

Beck, A. T., & Clark, D. A. (1997). An information processing model of anxiety: Automatic and strategic processes. *Behaviour Research and Therapy, 33*, 49–58.

Berntson, G. G., Boysen, S. T., & Cacioppo, J. T. (1992). Cardiac orienting and defensive reactions: Potential origins in autonomic space. In B. A. Campbell, H. Hayne, & R. Richardson (Eds.), *Attention and information processing in infants and adults: Perspectives from human and animal research* (pp. 163–200). New York: Erlbaum.

Berntson, G. G., Boysen, S. T., & Cacioppo, J. T. (1993). Neurobehavioral organization and the cardinal principle of evaluative bivalence. *Annals of the New York Academy of Sciences, 702,* 75–102.

Berntson, G. G., & Cacioppo, J. T. (2000). From homeostasis to allodynamic regulation. In J. T. Cacioppo, L. G. Tassinary, & G. G. Berntson (Eds.), *Handbook of psychophysiology* (pp. 459–481). Cambridge, England: Cambridge University Press.

Berntson, G. G., Cacioppo, J. T., Binkley, P. F., Uchino, B. N., Quigley, K. S., & Fieldstone, A. (1994). Autonomic cardiac control: III. Psychological stress and cardiac response in autonomic space as revealed by pharmacological blockades. *Psychophysiology, 31,* 599–608.

Berntson, G. G., Hart, S., Ruland, S., & Sarter, M. (1996). A central cholinergic link in the cardiovascular effects of the benzodiazepine receptor partial inverse agonist FG 7142. *Behavioural Brain Research, 74,* 91–103.

Berntson, G. G., Hart, S., & Sarter, M. (1997). The cardiovascular startle response: Anxiety and the benzodiazepine receptor complex. *Psychophysiology, 34,* 348–357.

Berntson, G. G., & Micco, D. J. (1976). Organization of brainstem behavioral systems. *Brain Research Bulletin, 1,* 471–483.

Berntson, G. G., Sarter, M., & Cacioppo, J. T. (1998). Anxiety and cardiovascular reactivity: The basal forebrain cholinergic link. *Behavioral Brain Research, 94,* 225–248.

Buchanan, S. L., Beylotte, F. M., & Powell, D. A. (1997). Lesions of the thalamic reticular nucleus or the basal forebrain impair Pavlovian eyeblink conditioning and attenuate learning-related multiple-unit activity in the mediodorsal nucleus of the thalamus. *Psychobiology, 25,* 48–58.

Cacioppo, J. T. (1994). Social neuroscience: Autonomic, neuroendocrine, and immune responses to stress. *Psychophysiology, 31,* 113–128.

Cacioppo, J. T., Berntson, G. G., Binkley, P. F., Quigley, K. S., Uchino, B. N., & Fieldstone, A. (1994). Autonomic cardiac control. II. Basal response, noninvasive indices, and autonomic space as revealed by autonomic blockades. *Psychophysiology, 31,* 586–598.

Cacioppo, J. T., Berntson, G. G., & Klein, D. J. (1992). What is an emotion? The role of somatovisceral afference, with special emphasis on somatovisceral "illusions." *Review of Personality and Social Psychology, 14,* 63–98.

Campeau, S., & Davis, M. (1995). Involvement of subcortical and cortical afferents to the lateral nucleus of the amygdala in fear conditioning measured with fear-potentiated startle in rats trained concurrently with auditory and visual conditioned stimuli. *Journal of Neuroscience, 15,* 2312–2327.

Clark, K. B., Smith, D. C., Hassert, D. L., Browning, R. A., Naritoku, D. K., & Jensen, R. A. (1998). Posttraining electrical stimulation of vagal afferents with concomitant vagal efferent inactivation enhances memory storage processes in the rat. *Neurobiology of Learning and Memory, 70,* 364–373.

Clark, K. B., Naritoku, D. K., Smith, D. C., Browning, R. A., & Jensen, R. A. (1999). Enhanced recognition memory following vagus nerve stimulation in human subjects. *Nature Neuroscience, 1,* 94–98.

Cohen, A. H. (1992). The role of heterarchical control in the evolution of central pattern generators. *Brain Behavior and Evolution, 40,* 112–124.

Curran, V. H. (1991). Benzodiazepines, memory and mood: a review. *Psychopharmacology, 105,* 1–8.

Curtis, A. L., Pavcovich, L. A., Grigoriadis, D. E., & Valentino, R. J. (1995). Previous stress alters corticotropin-releasing factor neurotransmission in the locus coeruleus. *Neuroscience, 65,* 541–550.

Davis, M. (1992). The role of amygdala in fear and anxiety. *Annual Review of Neuroscience, 15,* 353–375.

Davis, M., Gendelman, D. S., Tischler, M. D., & Gendelman, P. M. (1982). A primary acoustic startle circuit: Lesion and stimulation studies. *Journal of Neuroscience, 2,* 791–805.

Davis, M., & Shi, C. (1999). The extended amygdala: are the central nucleus of the amygdala and the bed nucleus of the stria terminalis differentially involved in fear versus anxiety? *Annals of the New York Academy of Sciences, 877,* 281–291.

Dorow, R., Horowski, R., Paschelke, G., Amin, M., & Braestrup, C. (1983). Severe anxiety induced by FG 7142, a β-carboline ligand for benzodiazepine receptors. *Lancet, 8,* 98–99.

Edgley, S. A., Eyre, J. A., Lemon, R. N., & Miller, S. (1997). Comparison of activation of corticospinal neurons and spinal motor neurons by magnetic and electrical transcranial stimulation in the lumbosacral cord of the anaesthetized monkey. *Brain, 120,* 839–853.

Everitt, B. J., & Robbins, T. W. (1997). Central cholinergic systems and cognition. *Annual Review of Psychology, 48,* 649–684.

Eysenck, M. W. (1991). Cognitive factors in clinical anxiety: potential relevance to therapy. In M. Briley & S. E. File (Eds.), *New concepts in anxiety* (pp. 418–433). Boca Raton, FL: CRC Press.

File, S. E., Gonzalez, L. E., & Gallant, R. (1998). Role of the basolateral nucleus of the amygdala in the formation of a phobia. *Neuropsychopharmacology, 19,* 397–405.

Frysztak, R. J., & Neafsey, R. J. (1994). The effect of medial frontal cortex lesions on cardiovascular conditioned emotional responses in the rat. *Brain Research, 643,* 181–193.

Ginn, S. R., & Powell, D. A. (1992). Nucleus basalis lesions attenuate acquisition, but not retention, of Pavlovian heart rate conditioning and have no effect on eyeblink conditioning. *Experimental Brain Research, 89,* 501–510.

Gray, J. A., & McNaughton, N. (1996). The neuropsychology of anxiety: Reprise. *Nebraska Symposium on Motivation, 43,* 61–134.

Hart, S., Sarter, M., & Berntson, G. G. (1998). Cardiovascular and somatic startle and defense: Concordant and discordant actions of benzodiazepine receptor agonists and inverse agonists. *Behavioural Brain Research, 90,* 175–186.

Hart, S., Sarter, M., & Berntson, G. G. (1999). Cholinergic inputs to the medial prefrontal cortex mediate potentiation of the cardiovascular defensive response by the anxiogenic benzodiazepine receptor partial inverse agonist FG 7142. *Neuroscience, 94,* 1029–1038.

Hayward, C. (1995). Psychiatric illness and cardiovascular disease risk. *Epidemiology Review, 17,* 129–138

Heckers, S., Ohtake, T., Wiley, R. G., Lappi, D. A., Geula, C., & Mesulam, M. M. (1994). Complete and selective cholinergic denervation of rat neocortex and hippocampus but not amygdala by an immunotoxin against the p75 NGF receptor. *Journal of Neuroscience, 14,* 1271–1289.

Holley, L. A., Turchi, J., Apple, C., & Sarter, M. (1995).

Dissociation between the attentional effects of infusions of a benzodiazepine receptor agonist and an inverse agonist into the basal forebrain. *Psychopharmacology, 120*, 99–108.

Hubel, D. H., & Wiesel, T. N. (1979). Brain mechanisms of vision. *Scientific American, 241*, 150–162.

Hugdahl, K., Berardi, A., Thompson, W. L., Kosslyn, S. M., Macy, R., Baker, D. P., Alpert, N. M., & LeDoux, J. E. (1995). Brain mechanisms in human classical conditioning: A PET blood flow study. *Neuroreport, 6*, 1723–1728.

Jackson, J. H. (1884). Evolution and dissolution of the nervous system (Croonian Lectures). In J. Taylor (Ed.), *Selected writings of John Hughlings Jackson.* New York: Basic Books.

Jinks, A. L., & McGregor, I. S. (1997). Modulation of anxiety-related behaviours following lesions of the prelimbic or infralimbic cortex in the rat. *Brain Research, 772*, 181–190.

Jodo, E., Chiang, C., & Aston-Jones, G. (1998). Potent excitatory influence of prefrontal cortex activity on noradrenergic locus coeruleus neurons. *Neuroscience, 83*, 63–79.

Kawachi, I., Colditz, G. A., Ascherio, A., Rimm, E. B., Giovannucci, E., Stampfer, M. J., & Willett, W. C. (1994). Prospective study of phobic anxiety and risk of coronary heart disease in men. *Circulation, 89*, 1992–1997.

Kosslyn, S. M., Shin, L. M., Thompson, W. L., McNally, R. J., Rauch, S. L., Pitman, R. K., & Albert, N. M. (1996). Neural effects of visualizing and perceiving aversive stimuli: A PET investigation. *Neuroreport, 7*, 1569–1576.

Kubzansky, L. D., Kawachi, I., Weiss, S. T., & Sparrow, D. (1998). Anxiety and coronary heart disease: A synthesis of epidemiological, psychological, and experimental evidence. *Annals of Behavioral Medicine, 20*, 47–58.

LeBar, K. S., Gatenby, J. C., Gore, J. C., LeDoux, J. E., & Phelps, E. A. (1998). Human amygdala activation during conditioned fear acquisition and extinction: A mixed trial fMRI study. *Neuron, 20*, 937–945.

LeDoux, J. E. (1995). Emotion: Clues from the brain. *Annual Review of Psychology, 46*, 209–235.

LeDoux, J. E., & Muller, J. (1997). Emotional memory and psychopathology. *Philosophical Transactions of the Royal Society of London, B, Biological Sciience, 352*, 1719–1726.

Leidenheimer, N. J., & Schechter, M. D. (1988). Discriminative stimulus control by the anxiogenic β-carboline FG 7142: Generalization to a physiological stressor. *Pharmacology, Biochemistry, and Behavior, 30*, 351–355.

Levin, B. E., Martin, B. F., & Natelson, B. H. (1980). Basal sympatho-adrenal function in quadriplegic man. *Journal of the Autonomic Nervous System, 2*, 327–326.

Loeb, G. E., Brown, I. E., & Cheng, E. J. (1999). A hierarchical foundation for models of sensorimotor control. *Experimental Brain Research, 126*, 1–18.

Malarkey, W. B., Lipkus, I. M., & Cacioppo, J. T. (1995). The dissociation of catecholamine and hypothalamic-pituitary-adrenal responses to daily stressors using dexamethasone. *Journal of Clinical Endocrinology and Metabolism, 80*, 2458–2463.

Manuck, S. B., Cohen, S., Rabin, B. S., & Muldoon, M. F. (1991). Individual differences in cellular immune responses to stress. *Psychological Science, 2*, 111–115.

Mark, G. P., Rada, P. V., Shors, T. J. (1996). Inescapable stress enhances extracellular acetylcholine in the rat hippocampus and prefrontal cortex but not the nucleus accumbens or amygdala. *Neuroscience, 74*, 767–774.

Menard, J., & Treit, D. (1999). Effects of centrally administered anxiolytic compounds in animal models of anxiety. *Neuroscience and Biobehavioral Reviews, 23*, 591–613.

McNaughton, N. (1997). Cognitive dysfunction resulting from hippocampal hyperactivity—A possible cause of anxiety disorder? *Pharmacology Biochemistry and Behavior, 56*, 603–611.

McNeil, D. W., Vrana, S. R., Melamed, B. G., Cuthbert, B. N., & Lang, P. J. (1993). Emotional imagery in simple and social phobia: Fear versus anxiety. *Journal of Abnormal Psychology, 102*, 212–225.

Metherate, R., & Weinberger, N. M. (1990). Cholinergic modulation of responses to single tones produces tone-specific receptive field alterations in cat auditory cortex. *Synapse, 6*, 133–145.

Moore, H., Sarter, M., & Bruno, J. P. (1995). Bidirectional modulation of cortical acetylcholine efflux by infusion of benzodiazepine receptor ligands into the basal forebrain. *Neuroscience Letters, 189*, 31–34.

Moore, H., Stuckman, S., Sarter, M., & Bruno, J. P. (1995). Stimulation of cortical acetylcholine efflux by FG 7142 measured with repeated microdialysis sampling. *Synapse, 21*, 324–331.

Morris, J. S., Ohman, A., & Dolan, R. J. (1999). A subcortical pathway to the right amygdala mediating "unseen" fear. *Proceedings of the National Academy of Sciences, 96*, 1680–1685.

Muller, J., Corodimas, K. P., Fridel, Z., & LeDoux, J. E. (1997). Functional inactivation of the lateral and basal nuclei of the amygdala by muscimol infusion prevents fear conditioning to an explicit conditioned stimulus and to contextual stimuli. *Behavioral Neuroscience, 111*, 638–691.

Neafsey, E. J. (1990). Prefrontal cortical control of the autonomic nervous system: Anatomical and physiological observations. *Progress in Brain Research, 85*, 147–166.

Ninan, P. T., Insel, T. M., Cohen, R. M., Cook, J. M., Skolnick, P., & Saul, S. M. (1982). Benzodiazepine receptor-mediated experimental "anxiety" in primates. *Science, 218*, 1332–1334.

Nogueira, P. J., Tomaz, C., & Williams, C. L. (1994) Contribution of the vagus nerve in mediating the memory-facilitating effects of substance P. *Behavioral Brain Research, 62*, 165–169.

Ohman, A. (1996). Preferential preattentive processing of threat in anxiety: Preparedness and attentional biases. In R. M. Rapee (Ed.), *Current controversies in the anxiety disorders* (pp. 253–290). New York: Guilford Press.

Palmeri, A., Bellomo, M., Giuffrida, R., & Sapienza, S. (1999). Motor cortex modulation of exteroceptive information at bulbar and thalamic lemniscal relays in the cat. *Neuroscience, 88*, 135–150.

Pellow, S., & File, S. E. (1987). Can anti-panic drugs antagonize anxiety produced in the rat by drugs acting at the GABA-benzodiazepine receptor complex? *Neuropsychobiology, 17*, 60–65.

Phillips, R. G., & LeDoux, J. E. (1992). Differential contribution of amygdala and hippocampus to cued and contextual fear conditioning. *Behavioral Neuroscience, 106*, 274–285.

Porter, R. (1987). Functional studies of motor cortex. *Ciba Foundation Symposium, 132*, 83–97.

Quigley, K. S., Sarter, M., Hart, S. L., & Berntson, G. G. (1994). Cardiovascular effects of the benzodiazepine receptor partial inverse agonist FG 7142 in rats. *Behavioural Brain Research, 62*, 11–20.

Radnitz, C. L., Hsu, L., Tirch, D. D., Willard, J., Walczak, S., Festra, J., Perez-Strumolo, L., Broderick, C. P., Binks, M., Schlein, I., Bockian, N., Green, L., & Cytryn, A. (1998). A comparison of posttraumatic stress disorder in veterans with and without spinal cord injury. *Journal of Abnormal Psychology, 107*, 676–680.

Rauch, S. L., Savage, C. R., Alpert, N. M., Fischman, A. J., & Jenike, M. A. (1997). The functional neuroanatomy of anxiety: A study of three disorders using positron emission tomography and symptom provocation. *Biological Psychiatry, 42*, 446–452.

Rauch, S. L., Savage, C. R., Alpert, N. M., Miguel, E. C., Baer, L., Breiter, H. C., Fischman, A. J., Manzo, P. A., Moretti, C., & Jenike, M. A. (1995). A positron emission tomographic study of simple phobic symptom provocation. *Archives of General Psychiatry, 52*, 20–28.

Rauch, S. L., van der Kolk, B. A., Fisler, R. E., Alpert, N. M., Orr, S. P., Savage, C. R., Fischman, A. J., Jenike, M. A., & Pitman, R. K. (1996). A symptom provocation study of posttraumatic stress disorder using positron emission tomography and script-driven imagery. *Archives of General Psychiatry, 53*, 380–387.

Sarter, M. (1994). Neuronal mechanisms of the attentional dysfunctions in senile dementia and schizophrenia: Two sides of the same coin? *Psychopharmacology, 114*, 534–550.

Sarter, M., Bruno, J. P. (1994). Cognitive functions of cortical ACh [acetylcholine]: Lessons from studies on the trans-synaptic modulation of activated efflux. *Trends in Neuroscience, 17*, 217–221.

Sarter, M., & Bruno, J. P. (1997). Cognitive functions of cortical acetylcholine: Toward a unifying hypothesis. *Brain Research Reviews, 23*, 28–46.

Sarter, M., & Bruno, J. P. (1999). Abnormal regulation of corticopetal cholinergic neurons and impaired information processing in neuropsychiatric disorders. *Trends in Neurosciences, 22*, 67–74.

Sarter, M., Bruno, J. P., & Turchi, J. (1999). Basal forebrain afferent projections modulating cortical acetylcholine, attention, and implications for neuropsychiatric disorders. *Annals of the New York Academy of Sciences, 877*, 368–382.

Scannell, J. W., Burns, G. A., Hilgetag, C. C., O; Neil, M. A., & Young, M. P. (1999). The connectional organization of the cortico-thalamic system of the cat. *Cerebral Cortex, 9*, 277–299.

Schmidt, N. B., Lerew, D. R., & Trakowski, J. H. (1997). Body vigilance in panic disorder evaluation attention to bodily disturbances. *Journal of Consulting and Clinical Psychology, 65*, 214–220.

Schulkin, J., McEwen, B. S., & Gold, P. W. (1994). Allostasis, amygdala, and anticipatory angst. *Neuroscience and Biobehavioral Reviews, 18*, 385–396.

Shepard, R. A. (1986). Neurotransmitters, anxiety and benzodiazepines: A behavioral review. *Neuroscience and Biobehavioral Reviews, 10*, 449–461.

Sherrington, C. S. (1906). *The integrative action of the nervous system.* New Haven: Yale University Press.

Shin, L. M., McNally, R. J., Kosslyn, S. M., Thompson, W. L., Rauch, S. L., Alpert, N. M., Metzger, L. J., Lasko, N. B., Orr, S. P., & Pitman, R. K. (1999). Regional cerebral blood flow during script-driven imagery in childhood sexual abuse-related PTSD: A PET investigation. *American Journal of Psychiatry, 156*, 575–584.

Stowell, J. R., Berntson, G. G., & Sarter, M. (1999). *Attenuation of the bidirectional effects of chlordiazepoxide and FG 7142 on conditioned response suppression and associated cardiovascular reactivity by loss of cortical cholinergic inputs.* Manuscript submitted for publication.

Thiebot, M. H., Soubrie, P., & Sanger, D. (1988). Anxiogenic properties of beta-CCE and FG 7142: A review of promises and pitfalls. *Psychopharmacology, 94*, 452–463.

Williams, C. L., & McGaugh, J. L. (1993). Reversible lesions of the nucleus of the solitary tract attenuate the memory-modulating effects of posttraining epinephrine. *Behavioral Neuroscience, 107*, 955–962.

Witvliet, C. V., & Vrana, S. R. (1995). Psychophysiological responses as indices of affective dimensions. *Psychophysiology, 32*, 436–443.

Vrana, S. R. (1995). Emotional modulation of skin conductance and eyeblink responses to startle probe. *Psychophysiology, 32*, 351–357.

# 59

# STRESS AND AFFECT: APPLICABILITY OF THE CONCEPTS OF ALLOSTASIS AND ALLOSTATIC LOAD

Bruce S. McEwen and Teresa Seeman

Affective and anxiety disorders are estimated to account for half of the more than $74 billion cost burden of diagnosable mental disorders in the United States (Rupp, Gause, & Regier, 1998). Stressful life experiences play a significant role in mental disorders, not only as a causal or precipitating factor but also as an outcome of disordered thought and disrupted interpersonal relationships that lead to further stress on the individual and additional exacerbation of symptoms (e.g., see Kessler, 1997). Because of this and other connections between life experiences and health, medical science has been struggling for decades to understand the relationship between stress and disease.

Stress may be defined as a threat, real or implied, to the psychological or physiological integrity of an individual. Yet the widespread use of the term *stress* in popular culture makes this word an imprecise and ambiguous means of describing how the body copes with psychosocial, environmental, and physical challenges. For example, the subjective experience of stress does not always predict the elevation of the physiological "stress mediators," particularly cortisol and catecholamines (Kirschbaum, Kudielka, Gaab, Schommer, Hellhammer, 1999), and this leads into another aspect of the problem—namely, the tendency to dichotomize and separate "mind" from "body."

Indeed, we do need multiple levels of explanation and must often separately measure psychological and biological processes. Yet an integrated view of psychobiology

maintains that there is no such thing as a purely psychological process and that the activity and structural and chemical plasticity of nerve cells underlies all forms of experience, thought, and action (Cacioppo et al., 2000). Moreover, these two levels of analysis feed into each other and interact in a reciprocal fashion—that is, behavior and experience regulate biological processes and the biological state of the brain determines behavior and reactions to situations. Furthermore, there are three principal ways that these interactions can affect health. The first is through overt acts, like aggression, substance abuse, risky behavior, eating the wrong things, drinking, exercising or not exercising, and so on. The second is via the neural regulation of autonomic and endocrine function that leads to a long-term cost to the body (defined below as "allostatic load"). The third involves the interactions between the first two—for example, how eating a rich diet, or not exercising, or being sleep deprived increases the metabolic allostatic load and enhances insulin resistance and the processes that lead to abdominal obesity and cardiovascular disease. Thus, with the exception of behaviors that directly damage the body, the physiological mediators such as cortisol and catecholamines, but also including many other hormones and neurochemicals, provide the final common path connecting experience with both adaptation and pathophysiology. The regulation of these chemical mediators is complex and involves not only what is referred to as stress but also other aspects of brain function such as the diurnal clock residing in the hypothalamus that is synchronized by the daily rhythm of light and dark and results in the daily cycle of activity and sleep.

Thus, the basal secretion of the stress mediators also varies according to a diurnal rhythm that is coordinated by the light-dark cycle and sleep-waking patterns. Perturbations in this pattern are also linked to pathophysiological outcomes. Therefore, the challenge for investigators is to separate aspects of temporal patterning and intensity that discriminate between the protective and damaging actions of the stress mediators whether they change in their diurnal pattern or as a result of clearly defined environmental challenges—that is, "stressors" in the classical sense.

Finally, there is the important issue of the adaptive role of the stress mediators versus their participation in pathophysiology. Since the description by Hans Selye of the "general adaptation syndrome" in response to stressors (Selye, 1936), there has been an inherent paradox—namely, that the systems that react to stress—the autonomic nervous system and the adrenocortical system—are important protectors of the body in the short run, but cause damage and accelerate disease when they are active over long periods of time. What has been lacking is a comprehensive model that links these seemingly contradictory effects and provides at the same time insights into how individuals differ in their vulnerability to develop diseases.

This chapter describes such a model (McEwen, 1998; McEwen & Stellar, 1993) and discusses its applicability to affective disorders, in which altered states of brain chemistry and function make the afflicted individual more susceptible to the physiological impact of life events and, in turn, more vulnerable to the impact of the stress hormones themselves. The impact of allostatic load on the brain is discussed, followed by a discussion of the role of genetics, early life events, and the physical and social environment throughout life on the risk for a variety of diseases. The gradients of health seen across the range of income and education, known as socioeconomic status or SES, provides a natural laboratory in which to see how these factors interact to affect human health and risk for disease.

## Protective and Damaging Effects of Stress Mediators

### Secretion of the Physiological Mediators of Stress

The mediators associated with the stress response, principally the catecholamines and the glucocorticoids, are secreted according to a diurnal pattern coordinated with the cycle of waking and sleeping activity and also in response to environmental challenges that are physiological stres-

sors. In the short run, the function of these hormonal mediators is to promote adaptation and enhance survival of the individual. Yet, over longer time intervals, these same mediators contribute to pathophysiological processees. These two concepts are captured by the terms allostasis, referring to the process of adaptation, and allostatic load, pertaining to the cost to the body of being forced to adapt repeatedly to challenges.

### Allostasis and Allostatic Load

Allostasis, meaning literally "maintaining stability (or homeostasis) through change," was introduced (Sterling & Eyer, 1988) to describe how the cardiovascular system adjusts to resting and active states of the body. This notion can be applied to other physiological mediators, such as the secretion of cortisol as well as catecholamines (McEwen & Stellar, 1993). The term allostatic load refers to the wear and tear that the body experiences due to repeated cycles of allostasis, as well as the inefficient turning on or shutting off of these responses (McEwen, 1998; McEwen & Stellar, 1993). As an illustration of allostatic load, the persistent activation of blood pressure in dominant male cynomologus monkeys vying for position in an unstable dominance hierarchy accelerates atherosclerotic plaque formation (Manuck, Kaplan, Adams, & Clarkson, 1995). The mechanism for these effects involve blood pressure surges, along with elevated catecholamines, that accompany the social confrontations. Together, the blood pressure and catecholamine elevations accelerate atherosclerosis, as shown by the fact that the acceleration of atherosclerosis in dominant monkeys was prevented by beta adrenergic blocking drugs (Manuck, Kaplan, Muldoon, Adams, & Clarkson, 1991).

The concepts of allostasis and allostatic load envision a cascade of cause and effect that begins with primary stress mediators, such as catecholamines and cortisol, and leading to primary effects and then to secondary and tertiary outcomes, as will be described below. As summarized in Figure 59.1, the brain is the integrative center for coordinating the behavioral and neuroendocrine responses (hormonal, autonomic) to challenges, some of which qualify as "stressful" but others of which are related to the diurnal rhythm and its ability to coordinate waking and sleeping functions with the environment. In addition, there are also other aspects of lifestyle such as diet and exercise that contribute to allostatic load.

Figure 59.1 also notes that there are considerable individual differences in coping with challenges, based upon interacting genetic, developmental, and experiential factors. There is a cascading effect of genetic predisposition and early developmental events, such as abuse and neglect or other forms of early life stress, to predispose the organism to overreact physiologically and behaviorally to events throughout life. By the same token, a supportive

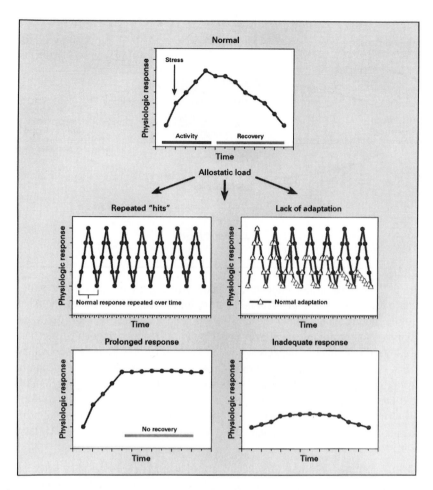

Figure 59.1 The stress response and development of allostatic load. Perception of stress is influenced by one's experiences, genetics, and behavior. When the brain perceives an experience as stressful, physiologic and behavioral responses are initiated leading to allostasis and adaptation. Over time, allostatic load can accumulate, and the overexposure to neural, endocrine, and immune stress mediators can have adverse effects on various organ systems, leading to disease. From McEwen (1998) by permission, copyright © 1998, Massachusetts Medical Society.

early life environment has the opposite effect and results in a less reactive physiological and behavioral profile.

Inherent within the neuroendocrine and behavioral responses to challenge is the capacity to adapt (allostasis); and, indeed, the neuroendocrine responses are set up to be protective in the short run. For the neuroendocrine system, turning on and turning off responses efficiently is vital (see Figure 59.2). However, inefficiency in allostasis leads to cumulative negative effects over long time intervals, as will be described below. Thus allostasis can exact a price (allostatic load) that is related to how inefficient the response is or how many challenges an individual experiences (i.e., many stressful events).

Allostatic load is more than "chronic stress" and encompasses many aspects of an individual's life that affect the regulation and level of the mediators of allostasis. Among the many factors that contribute to allostatic load

are genes and early development, as well as learned behaviors reflecting life style choices of diet, exercise, smoking, and alcohol comsumption. All of these factors influence the reactivity of the systems that produce the physiological stress mediators. Thus, allostatic load reflects, in part, genetically—and/or developmentally-programmed—inefficiency in handling the normal challenges of daily life related to the sleep-wake cycle and other daily experiences, as well as the adverse physiological consequences of a fat-rich diet, drinking, or smoking.

## Allostasis and Allostatic Load in Relation to Behavioral Processes

Behavioral responses to challenge also lead to protective and damaging effects and produce a form of allostatic load. An individual's behavior can increase or decrease

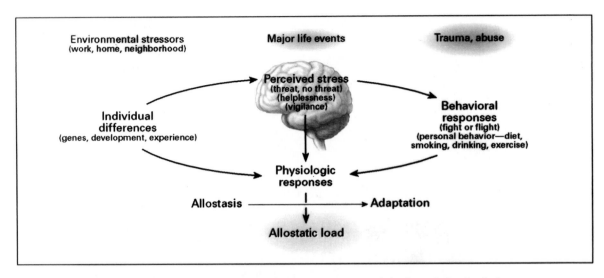

Figure 59.2 Allostasis in the autonomic nervous system and the hypothalamic-pituitary-adrenal axis. Allostatic systems respond to stress (*upper panel*) by initiating the adaptive response, sustaining it until the stress ceases, and then shutting it off (recovery). Allostatic responses are initiated (*lower panel*) by an increase in circulating catecholamines from the autonomic nervous system and glucocorticoids from the adrenal cortex. This sets into motion adaptive processes that alter the structure and function of a variety of cells and tissues. These processes are initiated via intracellular receptors for steroid hormones, plasma membrane receptors, and second messenger systems for catecholamines. Cross-talk between catecholamines and glucocorticoid receptor signaling systems can occur. From McEwen (1998) by permission, copyright © 1998, Massachusetts Medical Society.

further risk for harm or disease—for example, antisocial responses such as hostility and aggression versus cooperation and conciliation; risk-taking behaviors such as smoking, drinking, and physical risk taking versus self-protection; poor diet and health practices versus good diet and exercise. Insofar as the behavioral response, such as smoking or alcohol consumption, may have at least perceived adaptive effects in the short run but damaging effects in the long run, the linkage of allostasis and allostatic load is applicable to behavioral responses as well as to physiological responses to challenge.

However, there is another important role of behavior in relation to allostatic load—namely, that behavior and cognition play an important role in determining what is stressful, and individuals differ in at least three principal ways in how they respond to potentially stressful situations (see Figure 59.2). The first is interpretation of an event: If a situation is viewed as threatening, then the brain may initiate behaviors that avoid the threat or, alternatively, it may produce behaviors that can increase danger. The brain also regulates the hormonal physiological responses that, as discussed above, protect in the short run, but when overactive over months or years, are able to cause wear and tear on the body. On the other hand, perceiving an event as nonthreatening keeps physiological responses minimized and may have very little cost, unless the event actually turns out to be dangerous. Perceiving a

situation as threatening, particularly when it is not, can lead to high levels of stress mediators and behaviors that can lead to a high cost. In two examples cited above, those individuals who failed to habituate their cortisol response in a public-speaking challenge lacked in self-confidence and felt continually threatened (Kirschbaum et al., 1995); they reacted and produced cortisol longer than was necessary for optimal adaptation. Individual differences in cardiovascular activity are also likely to reflect the perception of danger or apparent threat in a situation (Matthews, Owens, Allen, & Stoney, 1992) as well as genetic factors such as a parental history of hypertension (Gerin & Pickering, 1995).

Another relevant aspect of individual differences concerns the condition of the body itself. People who are in good physical condition can handle strenuous exercise far better physiologically than those not in shape. Thus, personal behaviors involving regular exercise are very important for long-term health. Besides the well-known effects upon heart rate and blood pressure, exercise can have a rapid effect to increase muscle glucose utilization (Perseghin et al., 1996) and counteract the progression in a sedentary lifestyle toward insulin resistance. Moreover, metabolic imbalances that lead to obesity and diabetes can increase the vulnerability of an individual to stress, and these may have a genetic component (Brindley & Rolland, 1989). For Type I diabetes, as an example, life stressors increase the incidence and severity of the disease in children (Hagglof, Bloom, Dahlquist, Lonnberg, & Sahlin, 1991) and the BB rat model of Type I diabetes responds to stress by increasing the number of individuals that become diabetic (Lehman, Rodin, McEwen, & Brinton, 1991). There are also connections between stress and Type II diabetes, in that repeated psychosocial stress increases fat deposition in experimental animals (Jayo, Shively, Kaplan, & Manuck, 1993), and data for humans indicates that stressful life events promote abdominal obesity (Bjorntorp, 1990) and accelerate the course of the cardiovascular and other pathophysiological consequences (Cox & Gonder-Frederick, 1991; Surwit, Ross, & Feinglos, 1991).

A further role of behavior in allostatic load can be seen in the fact that certain personal behaviors, such as choice of diet, smoking, alcohol intake, and exercise, are likely to be altered in response to stressors because they are important for some individuals in coping with stress. And it is well known that such behaviors influence health outcomes over long periods of time, contributing to the physiological allostatic load.

In other words, the brain not only controls the interpretation of events as threatening or nonthreatening but also determines the behaviors and habits that can make life more or less dangerous to the individual in both the short run and increase allostatic load over a lifetime.

## Examples of Allostatic Load

Although allostasis and allostatic load are general concepts to be applied across physiological and behavioral responses, they require in each case an understanding of underlying mechanisms in each system of the body. This understanding begins with the mediators that produce organ- and tissue-specific effects by acting via receptors that are common throughout the body (see Figure 59.2). The primary mediators of allostasis (for further definitions of terms, see below) include adrenal steroids and catecholamines, but also other hormones like DHEA, prolactin, growth hormones, and the cytokines related to the immune system, as well as local tissue mediators like the excitatory amino acids. In Figure 59.2, the actions of two mediators, the glucocorticoids and the catecholamines, are shown, acting via receptors that trigger changes throughout the target cell in processes, including both rapid effects and changes in gene expression that have long-lasting consequences for cell function. Thus, whenever a hormone is secreted, there are to be considered both the short-term and long-term consequences of hormone action on cell function. For each system of the body, there are both short-term adaptive actions (allostasis) that are protective and long-term effects that can be damaging (allostatic load), and some examples are summarized in Table 59.1.

## Categories of Allostatic Load

There are four subtypes of allostatic load that result in overexposure of the body to the stress mediators, as summarized in Figure 59.3. The first type is simply too much "stress" in the form of repeated, novel events that cause repeated elevations of stress mediators over long periods of time. For example, the amount and frequency of economic hardship predicts decline of physical and mental functioning as well as increased mortality (Lynch, Kaplan, & Shema, 1997). Yet not all types of allostatic load deal with chronic stress. A second type of allostatic load depicted in Figure 59.3 involves a failure to habituate or adapt to the same stressor. This leads to the overexposure to stress mediators because of the failure of the body to dampen or eliminate the hormonal stress response to a repeated event. An example of this is the finding that repeated public-speaking challenges, in which most individuals habituated their cortisol response, led a significant minority of individuals to fail to habituate and continue to show cortisol response (Kirschbaum et al., 1995).

A third and related type of allostatic load, also depicted in Figure 59.3, involves either the failure to shut off the hormonal stress response or the failure to display the normal trough of the diurnal cortisol pattern. One example of this is blood pressure elevations in work-related stress that turn off slowly in some individuals with a family history of hypertension (Gerin & Pickering, 1995). Another example, involving the perturbation of the normal diurnal rhythm, is that sleep deprivation lasting 6 days decreases glucose tolerance and thyrotropin levels, raises evening cortisol concentrations, and elevates sympathetic nervous system activity (Van Cauter, Polonsky, & Scheen, 1997; Spiegel, Leproult, & Van Cauter, 1999). This is particularly significant because cortisol elevations in the evening result in more pronounced hyperglycemia than similar cortisol elevations in the morning (Plat et al., 1999). Moreover, depressive illness, which leads in many cases to chronically elevated cortisol, particularly in the evening, is associated with a loss of bone mineral mass (Michelson, et al., 1996).

The fourth type of allostatic load depicted in Figure 59.3 involves an inadequate hormonal stress response, which allows other systems, such as the inflammatory cytokines, to become overactive. The Lewis rat is an example of an animal strain in which increased susceptibility to inflammatory and autoimmune disturbances is related to inadequate levels of cortisol (Sternberg, 1997; Sternberg, Hill, & Chrousos, 1996).

## Measurement of Allostatic Load

Allostatic load can be measured, but thus far the measurements have been based upon parameters that, on the one hand, are generalized mediators of allostasis and, on

Table 59.1. Examples of Allostatic Load in Four Body Systems

---

*Cardiovascular system*

| | |
|---|---|
| Allostasis | Role of catecholamines in promoting adaptation by adjusting heart rate and blood pressure to sleeping, waking, physical exertion (Sterling & Eyer, 1988). |
| Allostatic load | Repeated surges of blood pressure in the face of job stress or the failure to shut off blood pressure surges efficiently accelerates atherosclerosis and synergizes with metabolic hormones to produce Type II diabetes (see McEwen, 1998). |

*Metabolism*

| | |
|---|---|
| Allostasis | Adrenal steroids increase food intake and facilitate the replenishment of energy reserves. |
| Allostatic load | Repeated HPA activity in stress or elevated evening cortisol leads to insulin resistance, accelerating progression toward Type II diabetes, including abdominal obesity, atherosclerosis, and hypertension (Bjorntorp, 1990; Bjorntorp, 1990; Brindley & Rolland, 1989). |

*Brain*

| | |
|---|---|
| Allostasis | Adrenal steroids and catecholamines promote retention of memories of emotionally charged events, both positive and negative. |
| Allostatic load | Overactivity of the HPA axis together with overactivity of the excitatory amino acid neurotransmitters promotes cognitive dysfunction by a variety of mechanisms that involve reduced neuronal excitability, neuronal atrophy, and, in extreme cases, death of brain cells, particularly in the hippocampus (McEwen, 1997; McEwen, 1999). |

*Immune system*

| | |
|---|---|
| Allostasis | Adrenal steroids together with catecholamines promote "trafficking," or movement, of immune cells to organs and tissues where they are needed to fight an infection or other challenge, and they also modulate the expression of the hormones of the immune systems, the cytokines and chemokines (McEwen et al., 1997). |
| Allostatic load | Chronic overactivity of these same mediators produces immunosuppressive effects when these mediators are secreted chronically or not shut off properly (McEwen et al., 1997). Yet, some optimal levels of these mediators are required to maintain a functional balance within the competing forces of the immune system, and the absence of sufficient levels of glucocorticoids and catecholamines allows other immune mediators to overreact and increases the risk of autoimmune and inflammatory disorders (Sternberg, 1997). Therefore, an inadequate response of the HPA axis and autonomic nervous system is another type of allostatic load, in which the disregulation of other mediators, normally contained by cortisol and catecholamines, is a primary factor in a disorder. |

---

the other hand, are predisease markers related to cardiovascular disease. These parameters were collected as part of the MacArthur Successful Aging Study and consisted of information on levels of physiologic activity across a range of important regulatory systems, including the hypothalamic-pituitary-adrenal and sympathetic nervous systems, as well as the cardiovascular system and metabolic processes (Seeman, Singer, Rowe, Horwitz, & McEwen, 1997). These measures of allostatic load, summarized in Table 59.2, represent single measures of activity levels, or measures reflecting cumulative change, rather than assessments of the dynamics of these systems in response to challenge.

The initial measure of allostatic load was created by summing across indices of subjects' status with respect to these 10 components of allostatic load. For each of the 10 indicators, subjects were classified into quartiles based on the distribution of scores (see Seeman et al., 1997). Allostatic load was measured by summing the number of parameters for which the subject fell into the "highest" risk quartile (i.e., top quartile for all parameters except HDL cholesterol and DHEA-S for which membership in the lowest quartile corresponds to highest risk).

Several alternative criteria for calculating allostatic load were also examined. One such alternative using a stricter criterion was based on a sum of the number of parameters for which the subject fell into the top (or bottom) 10% of the distribution (i.e., the group at highest "risk"). Another measure of allostatic load was based on averaging z-scores for each of the parameters. In each case, analyses yielded essentially the same results as the measure based on the quartile criteria, though the latter showed the strongest effects (Seeman et al., 1997).

These results suggest that the disease risks associated with allostatic load derive from being relatively higher on various measures of physiologic regulation rather than only at the most extreme levels. This is exactly what the concept of allostatic load would predict (McEwen, 1998; McEwen & Stellar, 1993). At the same time, simply averaging levels of activity across systems may tend to obscure the impact of elevations in a subset of systems that contribute to higher allostatic load. Thus, an algorithm for allostatic load was selected that avoids the problem of averaging, using instead a count of the number of parameters for which subjects exhibited relatively elevated levels. The 10 components were equally weighted since, based on factor analysis, indicators from physiologic systems defined different factors, and the component loadings on the rel-

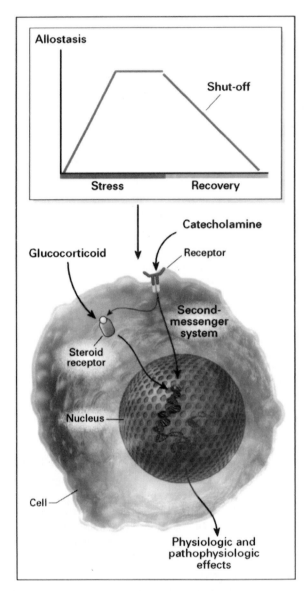

Figure 59.3 Four types of allostatic load. The top panel illustrates the normal allostatic response, in which a response is initiated by a stressor, sustained for an appropriate interval, and then turned off. The remaining panels illustrate four conditions that lead to allostatic load: (1) Repeated "hits" from multiple novel stressors; (2) Lack of adaptation; (3) Prolonged response due to delayed shut down; and (4) Inadequate response that leads to compensatory hyperactivity of other mediators: e.g., inadequate secretion of glucocorticoid, resulting in increased levels of cytokines that are normally counter-regulated by glucocorticoids. Figure drawn by Dr. Firdaus Dhabhar, Rockefeller University. From McEwen (1998) by permission, copyright © 1998, Massachusetts Medical Society.

Table 59.2 Summary of Allostatic Load Markers Used in the Initial Validation Study

**Secondary Outcome Measures***

Systolic and diastolic blood pressure, indices of cardiovascular activity.

Waist-hip ratio, an index of more chronic levels of metabolism and adipose tissue deposition, thought to be influenced by increased glucocorticoid activity.

Serum HDL and total cholesterol, related to the development of atherosclerosis—increased risks being seen with higher levels in the case of total cholesterol and lower levels in the case of HDL.

Blood plasma levels of glycosylated hemoglobin, an integrated measure of glucose metabolism over several days' time.

**Primary Mediators***

Serum dihydroepiandrosterone sulfate (DHEA-S), a functional HPA axis antagonist.

Overnight urinary cortisol excretion, an integrated measure of 12-hr HPA axis activity.

Overnight urinary norepinephrine and epinephrine excretion levels, integrated indices of 12-hour SNS activity.

*See text and Tables 59.3 and 59.4 for definition and more discussion. For details, see Seeman et al., 1997.

evant factors were virtually the same. This measure of allostatic load was then examined for its ability to predict health outcomes over a 2.5-year follow-up. Higher baseline allostatic load scores were found to predict significantly increased risks for incident cardiovascular disease as well as increased risks for decline in physical and cognitive functioning and for mortality (Seeman et al., 1997).

### Further Refinement of Allostatic Load

One of the problems with the original conceptualization of allostatic load and its measurement is that the components were not organized and categorized with regard to what each measure represents in the cascade of events that lead from allostasis to allostatic load. Nor was there any suggested organization in choosing those original measures that would facilitate systematically relating measures to specific disease outcomes or systematically adding new measures. Allostasis and allostatic load are concepts that are mechanistically based and only as good as the information about mechanisms that lead to disease. Tables 59.3 and 59.4 present a new way of classifying the measures that provides a handle for relating what is measured to a pathophysiological process and allow for the incorporation of new measures as more is known about underlying mechanisms leading to disease (McEwen & Seeman, 1999). This new formulation is based upon the notion of *primary mediators* leading to *primary effects* and then to *secondary outcomes*, which lead, finally, to *tertiary outcomes* that represent actual diseases. In the original allostatic load measures, the bottom group listed

Table 59.3.  Organization of Measures of Allostatic Load: Primary Mediators and Effects

---

***Primary mediators***—*chemical messengers that are released as part of allostasis*

As listed in table 59.2, there are presently four such mediators (cortisol, noradrenalin, epinephrine, DHEA). Primary mediators have very widespread influences throughout the body and are very useful, when measured correctly, in predicting a variety of secondary and tertiary outcomes. *Cortisol* is a glucocorticoid with wide-ranging effects throughout the body. Glucocorticoid receptors are present in virtually every tissue and organ in the body and mediate effects ranging from induction of liver enzymes involved in energy metabolism to regulating trafficking of immune cells and cytokine production to facilitating formation of fear-related memories (McEwen et al., 1993; Quirarte et al., 1997). *DHEA* is a functional antagonist of cortisol (May et al., 1990; Wright et al., 1992) which may also have effects via other signaling pathways (Araneo & Daynes, 1995); generally, low DHEA is considered deleterious, as is chronically high cortisol (Morales et al., 1994). NOTE: the acute effects of stress mediators are generally adaptive (allostasis) and it is the chronic elevation or disregulation of these mediators over long times that causes problems—ie., allostatic load.

*Catecholamines* (adrenalin, noradrenalin) are released by the adrenal medulla and sympathetic nervous system, respectively, and they produce widespread effects throughout the body, ranging from vasoconstriction and acceleration of heart rate to trafficking of immune cells to targets, as well as enhancement of fear-related memory formation (Cahill et al., 1994). Adrenergic receptors are widespread throughout the body, in blood vessels and target organs such as the liver, pancreas, as well as the brain which is not accessible to circulating catecholamines. However, catecholamines signal the brain through the sensory vagus and the nucleus of the solitary tract, as in learned fear (Cahill et al., 1994).

***Primary effects***—*cellular events, like enzymes, receptors, ion channels, or structural proteins induced genomically or phosphorylated via second messenger systems, that are regulated as part of allostasis by the primary mediators*

Primary effects are not measured as part of allostatic load assessments. Yet it may be desirable to study primary effects as the basis for the secondary and tertiary outcomes. Glucocorticoids regulate gene expression via several pathways, involving interactions with DNA via the glucocorticoid response elements (GRE's) and also via protein-protein interactions with other transcriptional regulators (Miner et al., 1991). As noted above, DHEA antagonizes glucocorticoid actions in a number of systems. Catecholamines act via alpha and beta adrenergic receptors, and beta receptors stimulate the formation of the intracellular second messenger, cyclic AMP, which, in turn, regulates intracellular events via phosphorylation, including transcription regulators via the CREB family of proteins.

In some cases, the glucocorticoid and cAMP pathways converge at the level of gene expression (e.g., see Yamada et al., 1999). Therefore it is not surprising that secondary outcomes are the result of more than one primary mediator. Primary effects are organ and tissue specific in many cases. Hence, at this level and even more for the secondary and tertiary outcomes we must become more organ and disease specific!

---

in Table 59.2 are primary mediators and the top group represent secondary outcomes. In a recent series of analyses of the MacArthur study data, the four primary mediators predicted both mortality over four years just as powerfully as the six secondary outcomes (Seeman et al., 2001).

Because the secondary outcomes are the reflection of the integrated actions of primary mediators and primary effects, these are the most useful indicators of progression toward disease. The secondary outcomes are also more organ and disease specific than the primary effects. Thus, these secondary outcomes need to be extended in at least two directions. In the first place, there is need for more specific outcomes related to the damage pathway in cardiovascular disease and risk for MI (e.g., nitric oxide, fibrinogen). Fibrinogen has already been used as an allostatic load measure in relation to job stress and socioeconomic status (Markowe et al., 1985). Another secondary outcome measure that may be useful is heart rate variability, which has been associated with the risk for cardiovascular disease and depressive illness (Krittayaphong et al., 1997).

In the second place, the identification of secondary outcomes needs to include other systems such as the brain and the immune system. For the immune system, integrated measures of the immune response such as delayed type hypersensitivity (Dhabhar & McEwen, 1999; Dhabhar & McEwen, 1996) and immunization challenge (Kiecolt-Glaser et al., 1996) should reveal the impact of allostatic load on cellular and humoral immune function and help distinguish between the immunoenhancing effects of acute stress and immunosuppressive effects of chronic stress. Moreover, assessment of the frequency and severity of the common cold (Cohen et al., 1997; Cohen, Tyrrell, & Smith, 1991) is another indirect way of assessing immune function, and this might be considered a marker of secondary outcomes related to immune function. What is needed is more information about the specific primary immune mediators that are involved in the initial phases of innate immunity (e.g., the acute phase response; the activity of NK cells) and which, if any, of these mediators or components can be measured systemically as an assessment of immune system-specific allostatic load.

For the brain, assessments of declarative and spatial memory have been employed to see individual differences in brain aging, having been shown to be related to atrophy of the hippocampus and progressive elevation of cortisol (Lupien et al., 1998). What is needed, however, is more information regarding pathways of disease—for example, secondary outcomes that are associated with the progression of psychiatric illnesses such as depression and schizophrenia. One example, to be discussed at the end of

Table 59.4.  Organization of Measures of Allostatic Load: Secondary and Tertiary Outcomes.

*Secondary outcomes—integrated processes that reflect the cumulative outcome of the primary effects in a tissue/organ specific manner in response to the primary mediators, often reflecting the actions of more than one primary mediator, including the ones described above as well as others not yet measured.*

As noted in table 59.2, allostatic load measures to date include the following secondary outcomes, which are all related to abnormal metabolism and risk for cardiovascular disease: WHR, blood pressure, glycosylated hemoglobin, cholesterol/HDL ratio, HDL cholesterol. WHR and glycosylated hemoglobin both reflect the effects of sustained elevations in glucose and the insulin resistance that develops as a result of elevated cortisol and elevated sympathetic nervous system activity. Blood pressure elevation is part of the pathophysiological pathway of the metabolic syndrome, but is also a more primary indication of the allostatic load that can lead to accelerated atherosclerosis as well as insulin resistance. Cholesterol and HDL cholesterol are measures of metabolic imbalance in relation to obesity and atherosclerosis and also reflect the operation of the same primary mediators as well as other metabolic hormones.

*Teritary outcomes—these are the actual diseases or disorders which are the result of the allostatic load that is predicted from the extreme values of the secondary outcomes and of the primary mediators.*

Thus far, allostatic load measures have focused on cardiovascular disease, decreased physical capacity and severe cognitive decline as outcomes in the successful aging studies (Seeman et al., 1997; Seeman et al., 1997), but some redefinition of outcomes is needed. That is, a stricter criterion based upon the new definitions of primary, secondary and tertiary outcomes would assign cognitive decline as a secondary outcome, although Alzheimer's disease or vascular dementia would be a tertiary outcome when there is clearly a serious and permanent disease. By the same token, cancer would be a tertiary outcome, whereas the common cold would be a secondary outcome and an indirect measure, in part, of immune system efficacy, as discussed in the text.

the next section, is atrophy of brain structures such as the hippocampus, amygdala, and prefrontal cortex in recurrent depressive illness. Since the brain is both a key controller of behavioral and physiological allostasis and a target of allostatic load, we return now to a consideration of the impact of allostatic load on the brain.

## Allostasis and Allostatic Load in the Brain

The brain is the key to allostasis and allostatic load because of its role as central controller of the autonomic nervous system and neuroendocrine system. Besides its role as a controller of stress mediators, the brain is also a target of those same mediators. In particular, glucocorticoid and catecholamine feedback are involved in regulating two key adaptive aspects of the stress response. The first is the containment of neurochemical responses to challenge, related to the CRF, noradrenergic, and serotonergic systems; the second is promoting adaptive responses such as the formation of memories for situations with a strong emotional content. Within the framework of adaptation, the overactivity or imbalances among these systems can be seen as leading to allostatic load. Yet even as allostatic load develops, there appear to be protective mechanisms that prevent irreversible damage by slowing down or counterregulating potentially damaging processes. The metaphor is that the force of the wind on a tree causes the bows to bend but not to break.

### Containment of Neurochemical Responses

Glucocorticoid secretion is one of the most frequent responses to stressful events. Adrenal steroid secretion as a

result of stress has multiple actions on the brain and body that have been characterized as "containing" or "counter-regulating" other responses to stress and trauma such as inflammations, fever, edema, and immune responses (Munck, Guyre, & Holbrook, 1984). "Containment" implies that glucocorticoids prevent responses from being excessive. In the brain, glucocorticoids contain the synthesis of CRF and vasopressin, two neuropeptide releasing hormones for ACTH; in doing this they prevent hypothalamic CRF from becoming hyperactive; the CRF system has anxiogenic, arousing, immunosuppressive, and anorexigenic effects (Gold, Licinio, Wong & Chrousos, 1995; Webster, Elenkov, & Chrousos, 1997; Heinrichs, Menzaghi, Pich, Haruger, & Koob, 1993). Other examples of containment will be discussed below in conjunction with the noradrenergic and serotonergic systems.

### Stress and Noradrenalin

Stressors of many kinds activate the release and turnover of noradrenalin, along with the release of catecholamines from the autonomic nervous system. Uncontrollable stressors tend to have more prolonged effects on noradrenalin turnover (Tsuda & Tanaka, 1985; Goodman, Losito, Corigan, Charry, Bailey, & Weiss, 1981). One of the consequences of repeated stress is the induction of tyrosine hydroxylase (TH), rate-limiting enzyme for noradrenalin and epinephrine formation, in both the locus coeruleus and the adrenal medulla (see Nisenbaum, Zigmond, Sued, & Abercrombie, 1991). Stress-induced activation of catecholamine biosynthesis also increases the catalytic efficiency of TH and leads to increased catecholamine formation (see Nisenbaum et al., 1991). Thus, in the face of increased TH amount and activity, there is a need for various forms of containment. Glucocorticoids play this role in several ways, reducing cAMP formation in cerebral cortex in response to NA (see McEwen et al., 1992, for summary), and decreasing catecholamine biosynthesis and release (Pacak et al., 1992; Pacak et al., 1993).

In view of the importance of noradrenalin in promoting excitability and disinhibition of hippocampal neurons (Doze, Cohen, & Madison, 1991; Dunwiddie, Taylor, Heginbotham, & Proctor, 1992), it is interesting that, after repeated stress, noradrenergic terminals in the hippocampus retain the potential to release larger amounts of NA in response to a novel stressor (Nisenbaum et al., 1991). Yet they are contained to a large extent by presynaptic alpha adrenergic mechanisms (Nisenbaum & Abercrombie, 1993) that may also be aided by circulating glucocorticoids (Pacak et al., 1992; Pacak et al., 1993). A similar situation exists with respect to ACTH and glucocorticoid secretion in response to novel stressors in animals that have been repeatedly stressed, as will be discussed below.

### Stress and Serotonin

Stressors also activate serotonin turnover and thus activate a system that has both anxiogenic and anxiolytic pathways within the forebrain (Deakin & Graeff, 1991; Graeff, 1993). Serotonin has a powerful role in the learning and retention of fear (Archer, 1982). A primary distinction in the qualitative nature of serotonin actions is between the dorsal raphe and median raphe nuclei: dorsal raphe innervation of amygdala and hippocampus is believed to have anxiogenic effects, very likely via 5-HT2 receptors; whereas median raphe innervation of the hippocampus reaches 5-HT1A receptors, stimulation of which facilitates the disconnection of previously learned associations with aversive events, or suppresses formation of new associations, thus providing a resilience to aversive events (Deakin & Graeff, 1991; Graeff, 1993).

Glucocorticoids play a complex role in regulating the 5-HT system. Circulating glucocorticoids acutely facilitate 5-HT turnover provoked by a wide variety of stressors (Azmitia & McEwen, 1974; Neckers & Sze, 1975; Singh, Corley, Phan, & Boadle-Biber, 1990), and repeated ACTH or glucocorticoid treatment, or chronic stress, increase 5-HT2 receptors in cerebral cortex (Kuroda, Mikuni, Ogawa, & Takahashi, 1992; Kuroda, Mikuni, Nomura, & Takahashi, 1993; McKittrick, Blanchard, Blanchard, McEwen, & Sakai, 1995) while reducing 5-HT1A receptors in hippocampus (Chalmers, Kwak, Mansour, Akil, & Watson, 1993; McKittrick et al., 1995; Mendelson & McEwen 1991, 1992). Thus, while glucocorticoids acutely facilitate the activity of the whole 5-HT system during stress, glucocorticoids chronically tip the balance in favor of 5-HT2-mediated actions of 5-HT, at least in cerebral cortex, and suppress 5-HT1A-mediated responses in hippocampus.

These changes have implications for the pathophysiology of depression (Deakin & Graeff, 1991; Graeff, 1993). Moreover, the inadequate operation of the serotonergic system has been linked to pathophysiology of anger and hostility, and suicide and myocardial infarcts are among the consequences of the hypoactivity of reduced serotonergic activity (Williams & Chesney 1993; Williams & Williams, 1993). There is also a reported link between low fat and cholesterol and violent death, and there are indications that reduced serotonergic function may be involved (Muldoon, Kaplan, Manuck, & Mann, 1992; Muldoon, Manuck, & Matthews, 1990).

### Containment of HPA Axis

A key to successful adaptation as opposed to maladaptive effects of stress is the self-containment of the hypothalamo-pituitary-adrenal (HPA) axis—that is, the ability of the HPA axis to shut itself down as well as to contain other neurochemical responses to stress such as CRF and noradrenalin release (see above). The paraventricular nuclei, which produce the CRF and vasopressin that stimulate ACTH release, are innervated by catecholaminergic and serotonergic inputs. Catecholaminergic input acts via alpha adrenergic receptors to facilitate HPA activity and via beta adrenergic receptors to inhibit it (Al-Damluji & White, 1992; Saphier 1992). In contrast, serotonergic input to PVN via 5-HT1A receptors is reported to inhibit HPA activity (Welch, Farrar, Dunn, & Saphier, 1993).

In response to repeated stressors, HPA activity tends to habituate if the stressor is the same, but tends to become hypersensitive to novel stressors (Akana et al., 1992; McEwen et al., 1992). Partial inhibition of glucocorticoid secretion in response to stress unmasks a strong facilitation, indicating that containment by glucocorticoids plays an important role (Akana et al., 1992). As noted, glucocorticoids contain the release of catecholamines by stress in the PVN (Pacak et al., 1993). Moreover, the role of glucocorticoids in enhancing 5-HT release in stress (see above) may play a role in maintaining inhibition via 5-HT1A receptors (Welch et al., 1993). It thus appears likely that the relative strengths of catecholaminergic and serotonergic input as a result of the same or different stressors may determine whether or not the HPA axis will habituate or be enhanced by repeated application of the same stressor. Moreover, the relative densities of the various adrenergic and serotonergic receptor types will play an important role in the net HPA response—that is, to what degree it remains contained. Finally, the efficacy of glucocorticoid feedback on the containment mechanisms will be an important factor in the containment response. In this connection, it is interesting that depressed patients show a larger elevation of ACTH in response to Ru486 compared to control subjects (Krishnan et al., 1992). Ru486 is an antagonist of the Type II adrenal steroid receptors, and its effect in depressed subjects indicates that there is an increased drive to release ACTH that is held partially in check by glucocorticoid feedback acting via Type II receptors (Krishnan et al., 1992).

### Role of Catecholamines and Glucocorticoids in Fear-Related Memories

Besides containment of responses, glucocorticoids and catecholamines also work together in the formation of memories of events associated with strong emotions, and this constitutes one form of allostasis—that is, adaptation in the form of learning. These so-called flashbulb memories, including both fear and also positive emotions, involve the amygdala (Le Doux, 1996). The pathway for encoding these memories involves the interaction between neurotransmitters in the amygdala and the hippocampus, facilitated by circulating stress hormones of the adrenal cortex and adrenal medulla. Indeed, encoding of these memories is strengthened by glucocorticoids acting in the amygdala and hippocampus, among other brain regions, and epinephrine acting in the sensory vagus outside of the blood-brain barrier, with information transmitted into the brain via the nucleus of the solitary tract (Cahill, Prins, Weber, & McGaugh, 1994; McGaugh, Cahill, & Roozendaal, 1996; deQuervain, Roozendaal, & McGaugh, 1998; Roozendaal, Portillo-Marquez, & McGaugh, 1996).

The formation of such memories is an adaptive process by allowing the individual to store information pertaining to important negative and positive events. Nevertheless, excessive activity of this system is not beneficial, and the role of glucocorticoids and catecholamines in the activity of the amygdala is relevant to posttraumatic stress disorder and also to symptoms of depression, in which an overactive amygdala appears to be involved (Cahill & McGaugh 1998; Drevets et al., 1997; Drevets et al., 1992; Sheline, Gado & Price, 1998). Allostatic load in the brain has implications not only for neurochemistry but also for brain structure and function, and in each case chemical imbalances lead to behavioral and structural changes that may be long lasting, but not necessarily irreversible.

### The Brain as a Target of Allostatic Load

#### Chemical Imbalances

Mental disorders such as depression are related to chemical imbalances in the central nervous system that alter interpretations of stimuli and influence behavioral responses to potentially stressful situations. These chemical imbalances constitute a form of allostatic load (Schulkin, McEwen, & Gold, 1994). There are multiple neurotrans-

mitters that may be subject to such imbalances, but two of them, serotonin and corticotrophin releasing factor (CRF), are particularly relevant for discussions of anxiety and depression, which are manifestations of allostatic load in the brain. Low brain serotonin is linked to impulsive aggression, suicide, and alcohol and substance abuse (Brown, Ebert, & Goyer, 1982; Higley et al., 1996; Mann, 1998; Williams, 1994). In addition, testosterone increases aggression and may be reciprocally linked to serotonin—that is, testosterone is involved in reducing the actions of serotonin, while serotonin inhibits testosterone-facilitated behaviors (Higley et al., 1996). In support of this notion, the serotonin behavioral syndrome (a stereotyped set of postural and motor responses elicited by tryptophan administered in the presence of pargylline) in rats is higher in females than in males and is increased in males by castration and suppressed by dihydrotestosterone administration, suggesting an effect mediated by androgen receptors (Fischette, Biegon, & McEwen, 1984).

At the same time, social ordering in animals changes brain chemistry, as seen in dominance hierarchies among laboratory animals. For example, the CRF gene is expressed in elevated amounts in both dominant and subordinate rats after chronic psychosocial stress in the amygdala (Albeck et al., 1997), a brain area associated with fear-related memory (LeDoux, 1996). Yet hypothalamic CRF expression, which controls the pituitary production of ACTH, is deficient in subordinate rats that are most severely affected by the psychosocial stress experience, as indicated by their having extremely low levels of testosterone (Albeck et al., 1997; Blanchard, Sakai, McEwen, Weiss, & Blanchard, 1993). This reduced hypothalamic CRF is linked to a failure to show a hormonal stress response in this subgroup of subordinate rats (Albeck et al., 1997). On the other hand, the increase in amygdala CRF mRNA levels is important in light of the finding that amygdala CRF is known to be involved in stress-induced anxiety behaviors (Swiergiel, Takahashi, & Kalin, 1993; Wiersma, Baauw, Bohus, & Koolhass, 1995). Moreover, amygdala CRF targets the locus coeruleus (Van Bockstaele, Colago, & Valentino, 1998). Blockade of the CRF system by alpha helical CRF infused into the locus coeruleus was found to prevent effects of intermittent stress to induce tyrosine hydroxylase (Melia & Duman, 1991).

The amygdala and extended amygdala provide one source of extra-hypothalamic CRF, which is known to be elevated in primates that are anxious as a result of deprivation of maternal care (Coplan, et al., 1996) and in individuals with posttraumatic stress disorder, PTSD (Bremner et al., 1997). In contrast to the hypothalamic CRF system, which is suppressed by glucocorticoids, stress and glucocorticoids enhance expression of the amygdala and extended amygdala CRF system (for review, see Schulkin, Gold, & McEwen, 1998).

## Structural Plasticity

At the same time as the brain encodes information and controls the behavioral responses, it is also changed structurally and chemically by those experiences (Greenough & Bailey, 1988; Guzowski & McGaugh, 1997; Martin & Kandel, 1996). While short-term response of the brain to novel and potentially threatening situations may be adaptive and result in new learning and acquired behavioral strategies for coping, as may be the case for certain types of fear-related memories, repeated stress can cause cognitive impairment via at least four different mechanisms (McEwen, 1997; 1999). The first is the compromising of neuronal excitability, which is a relatively rapid and reversible process (Joels & Vreugdenhil, 1998; Pavlides, Kimura, Magarinos, & McEwen, 1995). The second is by causing atrophy of nerve cells in the Ammon's horn region of the hippocampus by a process that is again reversible, although over days or weeks rather than hours (Magarinos, Verdugo Garcia, & McEwen 1997; McEwen, 1999). A third process involves the inhibition of neurogenesis in the dentate gyrus region of the hippocampus (Gould, Tanapat, McEwen, Flugge, & Fuchs, 1998). Fourth, prolonged and extreme psychosocial stress can lead, over months and years, to permanent loss of nerve cells in hippocampus (Uno, Ross, Else, Suleman, & Sapolsky, 1989). Each of these processes may be occurring somewhat independently of each other and contribute in various degrees to different pathophysiological situations involving traumatic stress, depression, or aging.

The hippocampus is important in declarative, spatial, and contextual memory and plays a role in processing of the contextual associations of strong emotions (Eichenbaum, 1997; Gray, 1982a; Kim & Fanselow, 1992; Phillips & LeDoux, 1992; Pugh, Tremblay, Fleshner, & Rudy, 1997). Atrophy of the human hippocampus is reported in some individual animals (Meaney, Aitken, Berkel, Bhatnager, & Sapolsky, 1998) and humans (Lupien et al., 1994; Lupien et al., 1998) as they age and is accompanied by cognitive impairment. Hippocampal atrophy and cognitive impairment is also reported in Cushing's syndrome, posttraumatic stress disorder, and recurrent major depression (for reviews, see McEwen, 1997; Sapolsky, 1996). Hippocampal atrophy in recurrent depressive illness is a progressively developing feature of the disorder, increasing with days of depression rather than age of the patient (Sheline, Sanghaui, Mintun, & Gado, 1999; Sheline, Wang, Gado, Csernansky, & Vannier, 1996), and this indicates that atrophy of the hippocampus may be an example of allostatic load that points to a progressive degeneration of cognitive function.

The hippocampus is likely not to be the only brain area affected in this way, since atrophy of the amygdala and prefrontal cortex have also been reported in depressive illness (Sheline et al., 1998; Sheline et al., 1999). Reversi-

bility and/or preventability of such atrophy is a major topic for future research, as is the implication of such treatment for cognitive function and the symptoms of depressive illness. It is conceivable, for example, that treatments that improve the affective components of depression may not arrest the progressive atrophy of brain structures that lead to cognitive impairment.

## What Are the Factors That Regulate Allostatic Load?

Having considered how the brain participates in allostasis and is itself a target of allostatic load, we now turn to the factors that contribute to individual differences in susceptibility. These include genetic constitution, early life events, and the experiences throughout life that collectively determine how the brain processes events in daily life and reacts to them. In particular, from the standpoint of epidemiology, the social and physical environment has a pervasive influence that can be seen in gradients of health across the range of income and education, referred to as socioeconomic status or SES.

### Genetic Risk Factors

Genetic factors play a major role in the risk for stress-related disorders and allostatic load, and this is particularly true for psychiatric disorders, which are also inextricably linked to an individual's experiences and behavior. Genes exist in allelic variants, some of which confer risk for certain types of diseases. For example, the concordances among identical twins for a number of psychiatric disorders is on the order of 40–60%, less than 100% but higher than that for nonidentical twins and much higher than between unrelated individuals (Plomin, 1990; Plomin, Owen, McGuffin, 1994). Yet many diseases, including psychiatric disorders, are suspected to reflect defects, or allelic variants, in more than one gene, and this increases the complexity of the analysis of such disorders (see Vogel & Motulsky, 1986). The complexity is compounded by considerations of the lifelong behavioral factors that play a role in the etiology of disorders such as depression (see Kendler, 1998; Kendler & Karkowski-Shuman, 1997).

### Early Life Experiences

Besides the genetic predisposition, the susceptibility of an individual to allostatic load also reflects developmental influences. Indeed, early life experiences play a powerful role in determining allostatic load over a lifetime in experimental animals, and these animals provide an attractive model for understanding some environmental and developmental influences upon individual differences in human stress reactivity. Neonatal "handling" of newborn rats produces animals that have lower HPA reactivity and slower rates of brain aging, measured in terms of loss of cognitive function, whereas prenatal or postnatal stress is suspected of causing increased HPA reactivity over a lifetime and leading to increased rates of brain aging (see Dellu, Mayo, Vallec, LeMoal, & Simon, 1994; Liu et al., 1997; Meaney et al., 1988). A likely mechanism for the effects of "handling" is the maternal licking and grooming behavior toward the pup, which is enhanced by the brief separation of pup from mother; pups from mothers showing higher amounts of licking and grooming show lower levels of stress hormone reactivity as adults (Liu et al., 1997). More prolonged maternal separation (180 ft) fails to have this effect and, in fact, shows signs of producing the opposite effect, namely, to increase stress hormone production later in life (Plotsky & Meaney, 1993).

There are individual differences in human brain aging related to elevated cortisol levels (see Lupien et al., 1994; Lupien et al., 1998; Seeman et al., 1997), although their connection to early life events is unknown. Yet there are beginning to be indications in studies on human development for long-term influences of events early in life on the activity of systems producing hormonal stress mediators. Although the evidence is not extensive, the initial reports encourage further investigation. For example, phenomena such as low birthweight and various types of early life trauma may influence stress hormone responsiveness over a lifetime. Evidence that extremely low birthweight, which may be caused, at least in part, by stress to the mother, is a risk factor for Type II diabetes as one indication of a lifelong influence of early life events (see Barker, 1997; Wadhwa, 1998; Wadhwa, Sandman, Porto, Dunkel, Schetter, & Garite, 1993).

Moreover, experiences in childhood have other deleterious consequences—for example, a recent report indicates that a history of sexual and physical abuse in childhood is a risk factor not only for posttraumatic stress disorder but also for hippocampal atrophy and cognitive impairment in adulthood (Bremner et al., 1997). A very recent study on adolescents with a history of childhood physical and sexual abuse has revealed a pattern of elevated urinary secretion of catecholamines in those with PTSD compared to two control groups—nontraumatized children with overanxious disorder and healthy controls; in addition, urinary free cortisol was higher in PTSD children than in healthy controls (DeBellis et al., 1999). These results point to an increased activity, or allostatic load within the stress hormone axis. A related study on maltreated children with PTSD showed smaller intracranial and cerebral volumes compared to matched controls; there was no indication of smaller hippocampal volumes in these subjects, in contrast to the adult PTSD subjects with a history of childhood abuse, described above (DeBellis et

al., 1999). These findings are consistent with a previous, qualitative study that reported electrophysiological abnormalities from EEG records in children with a history of psychological, physical, and sexual abuse (Ito et al., 1993).

There are also indications that abuse and neglect in childhood are risk factors for increased mortality and morbidity from a variety of disorders during adult life, including depression, suicide, substance abuse, cardiovascular disease, and extreme obesity (Felitti et al., 1998). In other words, the reported effects of trauma and other childhood adversities are very broad and do not appear specific for any one type of psychiatric or other disorder (Kessler et al., 1997); and the breadth and strength of the effects of such trauma is reminiscent of the broad systemic effects of alterations of the responsiveness of physiological mediators that is embodied in the concept of allostatic load (McEwen, 1998) and consistent with the elevation of stress hormone activity noted above in the abused children.

Neglect and trauma in childhood presents symptoms that are associated in other animal and human studies showing low serotonin and risk for hostility, aggression, substance abuse, and suicide. Studies in infrahuman primates have shown that early maternal deprivation reduces brain serotonin levels and increases alcohol preference and aggressive behavior and decreases affiliative behaviors, thus increasing the risk for elevated allostatic load (Higley, Hasert, Suomi, & Linnoila, 1991; for discussion see Higley et al., 1993).

## Socioeconomic Status and Health

The brain processes experiences in daily life on the basis of its predispositions that have been set by genetic factors, early developmental events, and experiences throughout life. One way of seeing the collective impact of these factors is to look at populations that differ according to income and education, which is collectively referred to as socioeconomic status or SES. This is because there is growing evidence for gradients of mortality and morbidity across the full range of SES that cannot be explained simply by access to health care or individual factors such as amount of smoking (Adler, Boyce, Chesney, Folkman, & Syme, 1993; Adler et al., 1994). The gradients of health across the range of socioeconomic status relate to a complex array of risk factors that are differentially distributed in human society and that have a cumulative impact on behavioral and physiological allostatic load; cardiovascular disease is among the most prominent disorders showing an SES gradient. Certainly, among the underlying causal factors for the SES gradient are economic hardship and early childhood experiences. For example, a study of elderly people who had a lifetime of sustained economic hardship pointed to a more rapid decline of physical and mental functioning (Lynch, Kaplan, & Shema, 1997). Moreover, as noted, individuals with a history of childhood abuse suffer greater mortality and morbidity from a range of diseases (Felitti et al., 1998).

Undoubtedly the best example of SES influences upon health is the Whitehall studies of the British Civil Service, in which stepwise gradients of mortality and morbidity were found across all six grades of the British Civil Service in spite of the fact that all of the studied individuals had jobs and access to health care (Marmot et al., 1991). There are many factors that undoubtedly contribute to these gradients, including factors in the living and working environment. Not surprisingly, cardiovascular disease is a frequent outcome of these gradients and the psychosocial and environmental factors that are responsible for the allostatic load.

Based upon the discussion of depression and cardiovascular disease, one must also consider depression as a major factor in the allostatic load that results in hypertension, abdominal obesity, and atherosclerosis. Hypertension was a sensitive index of job stress, particularly in factory workers, and in other workers with repetitive jobs and time pressures (Melin, Lundberg, Soderlund, & Granquist, 1997), and in workers whose jobs were unstable due to departmental privatization (Marmot, personal communication). "Vital exhaustion" is another work-related behavioral state, reflecting lack of perceived control and a sense of helplessness, that correlates strongly with increased risk for cardiovascular disease (Everson et al., 1997; Keltikangas-Jarvinen, Raikkonen, Hautanen, & Adlercreutz, 1996; Kop, Hamulyak, Perrot, & Appels, 1998; Lynch et al., 1997; Raikkonen, Hautanen, & Keltikangas-Jarvinen, 1996). Among indices of allostatic load, plasma fibrinogen, which also predicts increased risk of death from CHD, is elevated in men in lower British Civil Service grades (Markowe et al., 1985). Helplessness and lack of control may be factors that help to explain the gradients of health in the Whitehall studies.

Another stress-linked parameter of allostatic load that varies across SES is abdominal obesity, measured as increased waist/hip ratio (WHR). Abdominal obesity is linked to Type II diabetes and cardiovascular disease (Brindley & Rolland, 1989) and can be enhanced by psychosocial stress (Manuck, Kaplan, Muldoon, Adams, & Clarkson, 1991). WHR is increased at the lower end of the SES gradient in Swedish males (Larsson et al., 1989), and WHR also increases with decreasing civil service grade in the Whitehall studies (Brunner et al., 1997). Immune system function is also a likely target of psychosocial stress, increasing vulnerability to infections such as the common cold (Cohen, Doyle, Skoner, Rabin, & Gwaltney, 1997; Cohen et al., 1991).

With regard to psychiatric disorders, there is some evidence that low SES is associated with mental distress and depression, as well as other disorders such as schizophrenia and substance abuse (Brown & Adler, 1998). However, there are questions of causality—that is, does SES cause the disorder or does the disorder lead to low SES? In the case of schizophrenia, personality disorders, substance abuse, and severe cognitive impairment, it is very likely that the conditions themselves lead to a lower SES position (Brown & Adler, 1998; Dohrenwend et al., 1992). On the other hand, a low SES position, reflecting poor resources, living environment, and an unsatisfying job are likely to be a cause of depression and anxiety (Brown & Adler, 1998; Dohrenwend et al., 1992).

However, considerations of allostatic load and social organization go beyond the confines of organized, stable social structures. In less stable societies, conflict and social instability have been found to accelerate pathophysiological processes and increase morbidity and mortality. For example, cardiovascular disease is a major contributor to the almost 40% increase in the death rate among Russian males in the social collapse following the fall of communism; and in these studies, cardiovascular disease is a prominent cause of death, along with alcoholism, suicide, and homicide (Bobak & Marmot, 1996; Notzon et al., 1998). In addition, self-reported health was related inversely to material deprivation and positively related to education level and perceived control (Bobak, Pikhart, Hertzman, Rose, & Marmot, 1998). As noted above, blood pressure surges and sustained blood pressure elevations that are likely to occur in unstable and stressful social environments are linked to accelerated atherosclerosis, as well as increased risk for myocardial infarction (Manuck et al., 1995; Muller & Tofler, 1990).

## Conclusions

The model of allostasis and allostatic load has directed our attention to the delicate balance between the adaptive and damaging effects of stress mediators, not only in the body as a whole but specifically in the brain, where they play an important role in affective state and in the psychopathology associated with affective disturbances such as excessive anxiety, depression, and posttraumatic stress disorder. We focus on the brain because it is the interpreter of experiences and the controller of behavior as well as the neuroendocrine and autonomic output of hormonal and neural stress mediators. As noted in the introduction, it is those mediators, along with specific behavioral responses, that interact to promote successful adaptation to sustain health or enhance allostatic load and the progression toward disease.

In discussing allostatic load in the brain we have emphasized new information on the hippocampal region. This is because an increased understanding of the cellular and molecular basis of hormonally and environmentally regulated structural remodeling of the hippocampus provides a new window into processes that are undoubtedly involved in the etiology and treatment of major psychiatric illnesses, as well as providing yet another link between organic brain dysfunction and behavior. We have seen that not all of these changes are irreversible and that there is considerable latitude for treatment that may either reverse or prevent structural changes and functional impairment.

In the case of the hippocampus, there are three major contributions to brain function made by this structure: first, the well-known role in declarative, spatial, and contextual memory; second, the role of the hippocampus in shutting off the HPA response to stress and in maintaining the normal diurnal rhythm (Herman & Cullinan 1997; Jacobson & Sapolsky, 1991); third, the role of the hippocampus in the processing of emotional information (Gray, 1982). Impairment of each of these functions can be seen in psychiatric illnesses such as depression, schizophrenia, and posttraumatic stress disorder, in which hippocampal atrophy is also reported. It should also be emphasized that the hippocampus may be only the tip of the iceberg and that other brain regions, including amygdala and prefrontal cortex, may be subject to some degree of structural plasticity.

We have also seen that genetic factors and early developmental events play an important role in determining how the brain processes information. In general, and especially in the case of the hippocampus, our knowledge of genetic factors is very poor. In part, this is because our knowledge of genetics is limited in relation to its role in brain structure and function, except for certain major neurological mutations. In part, it is also because genetic factors in major psychiatric illnesses such as depression are complex, involving more than one genetic determinant and a host of causal factors (Kendler, 1998). For early developmental events, there is some information regarding the influences of early experience on the hippocampus and its influence upon the stress hormone axis, in which prenatal stress, including lack of adequate maternal care, can increase reactivity of the stress hormone axis throughout adult life. Besides increasing the rate of certain aspects of the aging process, these early life events increase the predisposition to substance abuse. More extreme forms of maternal deprivation in primate models result in antisocial behaviors, including increased hostility and depression as well as increased propensity for substance abuse. It is tempting to relate these findings in rodent and primate models of early life experience to the consequences of neglect and abuse in children, where there is now increasing evidence for specific behavioral outcomes such as hostility, social isolation, and depression that are similar to those in the primate models as well as broader health outcomes related to a cumulative allostatic load such as extreme obesity and cardiovascular disease.

Finally, there is the impact of the physical and social environment on human health that is seen in the gradients of health across SES. Cardiovascular and other diseases, as well as the distribution of some of the measures of allostatic load, follow a gradient across the full range of socioeconomic status (SES) and are associated with a stepwise gradient of morbidity and mortality across the full range of SES. On the other hand, depression is more prevalent at the lower end of the SES ladder. One possible contributing factor may be childhood abuse and neglect, which are suspected to be more prevalent in individuals at the lower end of the SES ladder. Yet new data indicate that the specific consequences of childhood neglect and abuse include both specific and more general consequences for health, and these more general consequences overlap with those related to the full gradient of health across SES. Clearly, the SES gradient of health is complex and made up of many of the factors that have been discussed in this article that influence how the brain processes experiences and controls both the affective state and overt behavior as well as the neuroendocrine and autonomic responses that contribute to allostatic load.

## NOTE

The concepts of allostasis and allostatic load have grown out of interactions within networks of the MacArthur Foundation Health Programs headed by Robert Rose, beginning with the Health and Behavior Network (Judith Rodin, Chair), the Successful Aging Network (Jack Rowe, Chair) and the Mind Body Network (Robert Rose, Chair). The authors are especially indebted to their colleagues within the Socioeconomic Status and Health Research Network (Nancy Adler, Chair). We also wish to acknowledge important contributions of a number of colleagues, especially Burton Singer (Office of Population Studies, Princeton). Research support for other aspects of this article in the authors laboratories has come from NIMH Grant MH41256 to BMc and grant support from the Health Foundation (New York) and Servier (France).

## REFERENCES

Adler, N. E., Boyce, T., Chesney, M. A., Cohen, S., Folkman, S., Kahn, R. L., & Syme, L. S. (1994). Socioeconomic status and health: The challenge of the gradient. *American Psychologist, 49,* 15–24.

Adler, N., Boyce, W. T., Chesney, M., Folkman, S., & Syme, L. (1993). Socioeconomic inequalities in health: No easy solution. *Journal of the American Medical Association, 269,* 3140–3145.

Akana, S. F., Dallman, M. F., Bradbury, M. J., Scribner, K. A., Strack, A. M., & Walker, C-D (1992). Feedback and facilitation in the adrenocortical system: Unmasking facilitation by partial inhibition of the glucocorticoid response to prior stress. *Endocrinology, 131,* 57–68.

Al-Dumluji, S., & White, A. (1992). Central noradrenergic lesion impairs the adrenocorticotrophin response to release of endogenous catecholamines. *Journal of Neuroendocrinology, 4,* 318–323.

Albeck, D. S., McKittrick, C. R., Blanchard, D. C., Blanchard, R. J., Nikulina, J., McEwen, B. S., & Sakai, R. R. (1997). Chronic social stress alters levels of corticotropin-releasing factor and arginine vasopressin mRNA in rat brain. *Journal of Neuroscience, 17*, 4895–4903.

Araneo, B., & Daynes, R. (1995). Dehydroepiandrosterone functions as more than an antiglucocorticoid in preserving immunocompetence after thermal injury. *Endocrinology, 136*, 393–401.

Archer, T. (1982). Serotonin and fear retention in the rat. *Journal Comp. Physiol. Psychol, 96*, 491–516.

Azmitia, E., & McEwen, B. S. (1974). Adrenocortical influence on rat brain tryptophan hydroxylase activity. *Brain Research, 78*, 291–302.

Barker, D. J. P. (1997). The fetal origins of coronary heart disease. *Acta Paediatr Suppl, 422*, 78–82.

Bjorntorp, P. (1990). Editorial: "Portal" adipose tissue as a generator of risk factors for cardiovascular disease and diabetes. *Atherosclerosis, 10*, 493–496.

Blanchard, D. C., Sakai, R. R., McEwen, B. S., Weiss, S. M., & Blanchard, R. J. (1993). Subordination stress: Behavioral, brain and neuroendocrine correlates. *Behavior and Brain Research, 58*, 113–121.

Bobak, M., & Marmot, M. (1996). East-west mortality divide and its potential explanations: Proposed research agenda. *British Medical Journal, 312*, 421–425.

Bobak, M., Pikhart, H., Hertzman, C., Rose, R., & Marmot, M. (1998). Socioeconomic factors, perceived control and self-reported health in Russia. A cross-sectional survey. *Social Science Medicine, 47*, 269–279.

Bremner, J. D., Licinio, J., Darnell, A., Krystal, J. H., Owens, M. J., Southwick, S. M., Nemeroff, C. B., & Charney, D. S. (1997). Elevated CSF corticotropin-releasing factor concentrations in posttraumatic stress disorder. *American Journal of Psychiatry, 154*, 624–629.

Bremner, J. D., Randall, P., Vermetten, E., Staib, L., Bronen, R. A., Mazure, C., Capelli, S., McCarthy, G., Innis, R. B., & Charney, D. S. (1997). Magnetic resonance imaging-based measurement of hippocampal volume in posttraumatic stress disorder related to childhood physical and sexual abuse—a preliminary report. *Biological Psychiatry, 41*, 23–32.

Brindley, D., & Rolland, Y. (1989). Possible connections between stress, diabetes, obesity, hypertension and altered lipoprotein metabolism that may result in atherosclerosis. *Clinical Science, 77*, 453–461.

Brown, G. L., Ebert, M. H., & Goyer, D. C. (1982). Aggression, suicide and serotonin: relationships to CSF amine metabolites. *American Journal of Psychiatry, 139*, 741–746.

Brown, H. D., & Adler, N. E. (1998). Socioeconomic status. In H. S. Friedman (Ed.), *Encyclopedia of mental health* (pp. 555–561). San Diego: Academic Press.

Brunner, E. J., Marmot, M., Nanchahal, K., Shipley, M. J., Stansfeld, S. A., Juneja, M., & Alberti, K. G. M. M. (1997). Social inequality in coronary risk: Central obesity and the metabolic syndrome. Evidence from the Whitehall II study. *Diabetologia, 40*, 1341–1349.

Cacioppo, J. T., Ernst, J. M., Burleson, M. H., McClintock, M. K., Malarkey, W. B., Hawkley, L. C., Kawalewski, R. B., Paulsen, A., Hobson, J. A., Hugdahl, K., Spiegel, D., & Berntson, G. G. (2000). Lonely traits and concomitant physiological processes: The MacArthur social neuroscience studies. *International Journal of Psychophysiology, 35*, 143–154.

Cahill, L., & McGaugh, J. L. (1998). Mechanisms of emotional arousal and lasting declarative memory. *TINS, 21*, 294–299.

Cahill, L., Prins, B., Weber, M., & McGaugh, J. L. (1994). Beta-adrenergic activation and memory for emotional events. *Nature, 371*, 702–704.

Chalmers, D. T., Kwak, S. P., Mansour, A., Akil, H., & Watson, S. J. (1993). Corticosteroids regulate brain hippocampal 5-HT receptor mRNA expression. *Journal of Neuroscience, 13*, 914–923.

Cohen, S., Doyle, W. J., Skoner, D. P., Rabin, B. S., & Gwaltney, J. M., Jr. (1997). Social ties and susceptibility to the common cold. *Journal of the American Medical Association, 277*, 1940–1944.

Cohen, S., Line, S., Manuck, S. B., Rabin, B. S., Heise, E. R., & Kaplan, J. R. (1997). Chronic social stress, social status, and susceptibility to upper respiratory infections in nonhuman primates. *Psychosomatic Medicine, 59*, 213–221.

Cohen, S., Tyrrell, D. A. J., & Smith, A. P. (1991). Psychological stress and susceptibility to the common cold. *New England Journal of Medicine, 325*, 606–612.

Coplan, J. D., Andrews, M. W., Rosenblum, L. A., Owens, M. J., Friedman, S., Gorman, J. M., & Nemeroff, C. B. (1996). Persistent elevations of cerebrospinal fluid concentrations of corticotropin-releasing factor in adult nonhuman primates exposed to early-life stressors: Implications for the pathophysiology of mood and anxiety disorders. *Proceedings of the National Academy of Science USA, 93*, 1619–l623.

Cox, D. J., & Gonder-Frederick, L. A. (1991). The role of stress in diabetes mellitus. In P. M. McCabe, N. Schneiderman, T. M. Field, & J. S. Skyler (Eds.), *Stress, coping, and disease* (pp. 118–134). Hillsdale, NJ: Erlbaum.

Deakin, W., & Graeff, F. (1991). 5-HT and mechanisms of defense. *Journal of Psychopharmacology, 5*, 305–315.

DeBellis, M. D., Baum, A. S, Birmaher, B., Keshavan, M. D., Eccard, C. H., Boring, A. M., Jenkins, F. J., & Ryan, N. D. (1999). Developmental traumatology Part I: Biological stress systems. *Biological Psychiatry, 45*, 1259–1270.

DeBellis, M. D., Keshavan, M. S., Clark, D. B., Casey, B. J., Giedd, J. N., Boring, A. M., Frustaci, K., & Ryan, N. D. (1999). Developmental traumatology Part II: Brain development. *Biological Psychiatry, 45*, 1271–1284.

Dellu, F., Mayo, W., Vallee, M., LeMoal, M., & Simon, H. (1994). Reactivity to novelty during youth as a predictive factor of cognitive impairment in the elderly: A longitudinal study in rats. *Brain Research, 653*, 51–56.

deQuervain, D. J. F., Roozendaal, B., & McGaugh, J. L. (1998). Stress and glucocorticoids impair retrieval of long-term spatial memory. *Nature, 394*, 787–790.

Dhabhar, F. S., & McEwen, B. S. (1996). Moderate stress enhances, and chronic stress suppresses, cell-mediated immunity in vivo. Abstracts, *Soc. Neurosci., 22*, #536.3-p. 1350.

Dhabhar, F., & McEwen, B. (1999). Enhancing versus suppressive effects of stress hormones on skin immune function. *Proceedings of the National Academy of Science USA, 96*, 1059–1064.

Dohrenwend, B. P., Levav, I., Shrout, P. E., Schwartz, S., Naveh, G., Link, B. G., Skodol, A. E., & Stueve, A. (1992). Socioeconomic status and psychiatric disorders: The causation-selection issue. *Science, 255,* 946–952.

Doze, V. A., Cohen, G., & Madison, D. (1991). Synaptic localization of adrenergic disinhibition in the rat hippocampus. *Neuron, 6,* 889–900.

Drevets, W. C., Price, J. L., Simpson, J. R. Jr., Todd, R. D., Reich, T., Vannier, M., & Raichle, M. E. (1997). Subgenual prefrontal cortex abnormalities in mood disorders. *Nature, 386,* 824–827.

Drevets, W. C., Videen, T. O., Price, J. L., Preskorn, S. H., Carmichael, S. T., & Raichle, M. E. (1992). A functional anatomical study of unipolar depression. *Journal of Neuroscience, 12,* 3628–3641.

Dunwiddie, T., Taylor, M., Heginbotham, L., & Proctor, W. (1992). Long-term increases in excitability in the CA1 region of rat hippocampus induced by beta-adrenergic stimulation: Possible mediation by cAMP. *Journal of Neuroscience,* 506–517.

Eichenbaum, H. (1997). How does the brain organize memories? *Science, 277,* 330–332.

Everson, S. A., Lynch, J. W., Chesney, M. A., Kaplan, G. A., Goldberg, D. E., Shade, S. B., Cohen, R. D., Salonen, R., & Salonen, J. T. (1997). Interaction of workplace demands and cardiovascular reactivity in progression of carotid atherosclerosis: Population based study. *British Medical Journal, 314,* 553–558.

Felitti, V. J., Anda, R. F., Nordenberg, D., Williamson, D. F., Spitz, A. M., Edwards, V., Koss, M. P., & Marks, J. S. (1998). Relationship of childhood abuse and household dysfunction to many of the leading causes of death in adults. The adverse childhood experiences (ACE) study. *Am.J.Prev.Med, 14,* 245–258.

Fischette, C., Biegon, A., & McEwen, B. S. (1984). Sex steroid modulation of the serotonin behavior syndrome. *Life Sciences, 35,* 1197–1206.

Gerin, W., & Pickering, T. G. (1995). Association between delayed recovery of blood pressure after acute mental stress and parental history of hypertension. *Journal of Hypertension, 13,* 603–610.

Gold, P. W., Licinio, J., Wong, M. L., & Chrousos, G. P. (1995). Corticotropin releasing hormone in the pathophysiology of melancholic and atypical depression and in the mechanism of action of antidepressant drugs. *Annals of the New York Academy of Sciences, 771,* 716–729.

Gould, E., Tanapat, P., McEwen, B. S., Flugge, G., & Fuchs, E. (1998). Proliferation of granule cell precursors in the dentate gyrus of adult monkeys is diminished by stress. *Proceedings of the National Academy of Sciences USA, 95,* 3168–3171.

Graeff, F. (1993). Role of 5-HT in defensive behavior and anxiety. *Rev. Neurosci, 4,* 181–211.

Gray, J. (1982). Precis of the neuropsychology of anxiety: an enquiry into the functions of the septo-hippocampal system. *Behavioral Brain Science, 5,* 469–534.

Greenough, W. T., & Bailey, C. H. (1988). The anatomy of a memory: Convergence of results across a diversity of tests. *TINS, 11,* 142–147.

Guzowski, J. F., & McGaugh, J. L. (1997). Antisense oligodeoxynucleotide-mediated disruption of hippocampal cAMP response element binding protein levels impairs consolidation of memory for water maze training. *Proceedings of the National Academy of Sciences USA, 94,* 2693–2698.

Hagglof, B., Bloom, L., Dahlquist, G., Lonnberg, G., & Sahlin, B. (1991). The Swedish childhood diabetes study:

Indications of severe psychological stress as a risk factor for Type I (insulin-dependent) diabetes mellitus in childhood. *Diabetologia, 34,* 579–583.

Heinrichs, S. C., Menzaghi, F., Pich, E. M., Hauger, R. L., & Koob, G. F. (1993). Corticotropin-releasing factor in the paraventricular nucleus modulates feeding induced by neuropeptide Y. *Brain Research, 611,* 18–24.

Herman, J. P., & Cullinan, W. E. (1997). Neurocircuitry of stress: Central control of the hypothalamo-pituitary-adrenocortical axis. *Trends in Neuroscience, 20,* 78–84.

Higley, J. D., Hasert, M. F., Suomi, S. J., & Linnoila, M. (1991). Nonhuman primate model of alcohol abuse: Effects of early experience, personality, and stress on alcohol consumption. *Proceedings of the National Academy of Science USA, 88,* 7261–7265.

Higley, J. D., Mehlman, P. T., Higley, S. B., Fernald, B., Vickers, J., Lindell, S. G., Taub, D. M., Suomi, S. J., Linnoila, M. (1996). Excessive mortality in young free-ranging male nonhuman primates with low cerebrospinal fluid 5-hydroxyindoleacetic acid concentrations. *Archives of General Psychiatry, 53,* 537–543.

Higley, J. D., Mehlman, P. T., Poland, R. E., Taub, D. M., Vickers, J., Suomi, S. J., & Linnoila, M. (1996). CSF testosterone and 5-HIAA correlate with different types of aggressive behaviors. *Biological Psychiatry, 40,* 1067–1082.

Higley, J. D., Thompson, W. W., Champoux, M., Goldman, D., Hasert, M. F., Kraemer, G. W., Scanlan, J. M., Suomi, S. J., & Linnoila, M. (1993). Paternal and maternal genetic and environmental contributions to cerebrospinal fluid monoamine metabolites in Rhesus monkeys (Macaca mulatta). *Archives of General Psychiatry, 50,* 615–623.

Ito, Y., Teicher, M. H., Glod, C. A., Harper, D., Magnus, E., & Gelbard, H.A. (1993). Increased prevalence of electrophysiological abnormalities in children with psychological, physical, and sexual abuse. *Journal of Neuropsychiatry, 5,* 401–408.

Jacobson, L., & Sapolsky, R. (1991). The role of the hippocampus in feedback regulation of the hypothalamic-pituitary-adrenocortical axis. *Endocrine Reviews, 12,* 118–134.

Jayo, J. M., Shively, C. A., Kaplan, J. R., & Manuck, S. B., (1993). Effects of exercise and stress on body fat distribution in male cynomolgus monkeys. *International Journal of Obesity, 17,* 597–604.

Joels, M., & Vreugdenhil E. (1998). Corticosteroids in the brain. *Molecular Neurobiology, 17,* 87–198.

Keltikangas-Jarvinen, L., Raikkonen, K., Hautanen, A. & Adlercreutz, H. (1996). Vital exhaustion, anger expression, and pituitary and adrenocortical hormones: Implications for the insulin resistance syndrome. *Arteriosclerosis, Thrombosis, and Vascular Biology, 16,* 275–280.

Kendler, K. S. (1998). Major depression and the environment: A psychiatric genetic perspective. *Pharmacopsychiatry, 31,* 5–9.

Kendler, K. S., & Karkowski-Shuman, L., (1997). Stressful life events and genetic liability to major depression: Genetic control of exposure to the environment? *Psychological Medicine, 27,* 539–547.

Kessler, R. C. (1997). The effects of stressful life events on depression. *Annual Review of Physiology, 48,* 191–214.

Kessler, R. C., Davis, C. G., & Kendler, K. S. (1997). Childhood adversity and adult psychiatric disorder in the US

National Comorbidity Survey. *Psychological Medicine,* *27*, 1101–1119.

Kiecolt-Glaser, J. K., Glaser, R., Gravenstein, S., Malarkey, W. B., & Sheridan, J. (1996). Chronic stress alters the immune response to influenza virus vaccine in older adults. *Proceedings of the National Academy of Science USA, 93*, 3043–3047.

Kim, J. J., & Fanselow, M. S., (1992). Modality-specific retrograde amnesia of fear. *Science, 256*, 675–677.

Kirschbaum, C., Kudielka, B. M., Gaab, J., Schommer, N. C., & Hellhammer, D. H. (1999). Impact of gender, menstrual cycle phase and oral contraceptive use on the activity of the hypothalamo-pituitary-adrenal axis. *Psychosomatic Medicine, 61*, 154–162.

Kirschbaum, C., Prussner, J. C., Stone, A. A., Federenko, I., Gaab, J., Lintz, D., Schommer, N., & Hellhammer, D. H. (1995). Persistent high cortisol responses to repeated psychological stress in a subpopulation of healthy men. *Psychosomatic Medicine, 57*, 468–474.

Kop, W. J., Hamulyak, K., Pernot, C., & Appels, A. (1998). Relationship of blood coagulation and fibrinolysis to vital exhaustation. *Psychosomatic Medicine, 60*, 352–358.

Krishnan, K. R. R., Reed, B., Wilson, W. H., Saunders, W. B., Ritchie, J. C., Nemeroff, C. B., & Carroll, B. J. (1992). RU486 in depression. *Progess in Neuro-Psychopharmacology and Biological Psychiatry, 16*, 913–920.

Krittayaphong, R., Cascio, W. E., Light, K. C., Sheffield, D., Golden., R. N., Finkel, J. B., Glekas, G. Koch, G. G., & Sheps, D. S., (1997). Heart rate variability in patients with coronary artery disease: Differences in patients with higher and lower depression scores. *Psychological Medicine, 59*, 231–235.

Kuroda, Y., Mikuni, M., Nomura, N., & Takahashi, K. (1993). Differential effect of subchronic dexamethasone treatment on serotonin-2 and beta-adrenergic receptors in the rat cerebral cortex and hippocampus. *Neuroscience Letters, 155*, 195–198.

Kuroda, Y., Mikuni, M., Ogawa, T., & Takahashi, K. (1992). Effect of ACTH, adrenalectomy and the combination treatment on the density of 5-HT$_2$ receptor binding sites in neocortex of rat forebrain and 5-HT$_2$ receptor-mediated wet-dog shake behaviors. *Psychopharmacology, 108*, 27–32.

Larsson, B., Seidell, J., Svardsudd, K., Welin, L., Tibblin, G., Wilhelmesen, L., & Bjorntorp, P. (1989). Obesity, adipose tissue distribution and health in men: The study of men born in 1913. *Appetite, 13*, 37–44.

LeDoux, J. E. (1996). *The emotional brain.* New York: Simon & Schuster.

Lehman, C., Rodin, J., McEwen, B. S., & Brinton, R. (1991) Impact of environmental stress on the expression of insulin-dependent diabetes mellitus. *Behav. Neurosci, 105*, 241–245.

Liu, D., Diorio, J., Tannenbaum, B., Caldji, C., Francis, D., Freedman, A., Sharma, S., Pearson, D., Plotsky, P. M., & Meaney, M. J. (1997). Maternal care, hippocampal glucocorticoid receptors, and hypothalamic-pituitary-adrenal responses to stress. *Science, 277*, 1659–1662.

Lupien, S. J., DeLeon, M. J., De Santi, S., Convit, A., Tarshish, C., Nair, N. P. V., Thakur, M., McEwen, B. S., Hauger, R. L., & Meaney, M. J. (1998). Cortisol levels during human aging predict hippocampal atrophy and memory deficits. *Nature Neuroscience, 1*, 69–73.

Lupien, S., Lecours, A. R., Lussier, I., Schwartz, G., Nair, N. P. V., & Meaney, M. J. (1994). Basal cortisol levels and cognitive deficits in human aging. *Journal of Neuroscience, 14*, 2893–2903.

Lynch, J. W., Kaplan, G. A., & Shema, S. J. (1997). Cumulative impact of sustained economic hardship on physical, cognitive, psychological, and social functioning. *New England Journal of Medicine, 337*, 1889–1895.

Lynch, J., Krause, N., Kaplan, G. A., Tuomilehto, J., & Salonen, J. T. (1997). Workplace conditions, socioeconomic status, and the risk of mortality and acute myocardial infarction: The kuopio ischemic heart disease risk factor study. *American Journal of Public Health, 87*, 617–622.

Magarinos, A. M., Verdugo Garcia, J. M., & McEwen, B. S. (1997). Chronic restraint stress alters synaptic terminal structure in hippocampus. *Proceedings of the National Academy of Sciences—USA, 94*, 14002–14008.

Mann, J. J. (1998). The neurobiology of suicide. *Nature Medicine, 4*, 25–30.

Manuck, S. B., Kaplan, J. R., Adams, M. R., & Clarkson, T. B. (1995). Studies of psychosocial influences on coronary artery atherosclerosis in cynomolgus monkeys. *Health Psychology, 7*, 113–124.

Manuck, S. B., Kaplan, J. R., Muldoon, M. F., Adams, M. R., & Clarkson, T. B. (1991). The behavioral exacerbation of atherosclerosis and its inhibition by propranolol. In P. M. McCabe, N. Schneiderman, T. M. Field, & J. S. Skyler (Eds.), *Stress, coping and disease* (pp. 51–72). Hove and London: Erlbaum.

Markowe, H. L. J., Marmot, M. G., Shipley, M. J., Bulpitt, C. J., Meade, T. W., Stirling, Y., Vickers, M. V., & Semmence, A. (1985). Fibrinogen: A possible link between social class and coronary heart disease. *British Medical Journal, 291*, 1312–1314.

Marmot, M. G., Davey Smith, G., Stanfeld, S., Patel, C., North, F., Head, J., White, I., Brunner, E., & Feeney, A. (1991). Health inequalities among British civil servants: The Whitehall II study. *Lancet, 337*, 1387–1393.

Martin, K. C., & Kandel, E. R. (1996). Cell adhesion molecules, CREB, and the formation of new synaptic connections. *Neuron, 17*, 567–570.

Matthews, K. A., Owens, J. F., Allen, M. k. T., & Stoney, C. M. (1992). Do cardiovascular responses to laboratory stress relate to ambulatory blood pressure levels: Yes, in some of the people, some of the time. *Psychosomatic Medicine, 54*, 686–697.

May, M., Holmes, E., Rogers, W., & Poth, M. (1990). Protection from glucocorticoid induced thymic involution by dehydroepiandrosterone. *Life Sciences, 46*, 1627–1631.

McEwen, B. S. (1997). Possible mechanisms for atrophy of the human hippocampus. *Molecular Psychiatry, 2*, 255–262.

McEwen, B. S. (1998). Protective and damaging effects of stress mediators. *New England Journal of Medicine, 338*, 171–179.

McEwen, B. S. (1999). Stress and hippocampal plasticity. *Annual Review of Neuroscience, 22*, 105–122.

McEwen, B. S., Angulo, J., Cameron, H., Chao, H., Daniels, D., Gannon, M., Gould, E., Mendelson, S., Sakai, R., Spencer, R., & Woolley, C. (1992). Paradoxical effects of adrenal steroids on the brain: Protection versus degeneration. *Biological Psychiatry, 31*, 177–179.

McEwen, B. S., Biron, C. A., Brunson, K. W., Bulloch, K., Chambers, W. H., Dhabhar, F. S., Goldfarb, R. H., Kitson, R. P., Miller, A. H., Spencer, R. L., & Weiss, J. M.

(1997). Neural-endocrine-immune interactions: The role of adrenocorticoids as modulators of immune function in health and disease. *Brain Research Reviews, 23,* 79–133.

McEwen, B. S., Sakai, R. R., & Spencer, R. L. (1993). Adrenal steroid effects on the brain: Versatile hormones with good and bad effects. In J. Schulkin (Ed.), *Hormonally induced changes in mind and brain* (pp. 157–189). San Diego: Academic Press.

McEwen, B. S., & Seeman, T. (1999). Protective and damaging effects of mediators of stress: Elaborating and testing the concepts of allostasis and allostatic load. *Annals of the New York Academy of Sciences.*

McEwen, B. S., & Stellar, E. (1993). Stress and the individual: Mechanisms leading to disease. *Archives of Internal Medicine, 153,* 2093–2101.

McGaugh, J. L., Cahill, L., & Roozendaal, B. (1996). Involvement of the amygdala in memory storage: Interaction with other brain systems. *Proceedings of the National Academy of Science USA, 93,* 13508–13514.

McKittrick, C. R., Blanchard, D. C., Blanchard, R. J., McEwen, B. S., & Sakai, R. R. (1995). Serotonin receptor binding in a colony model of chronic social stress. *Biological Psychiatry, 37,* 383–393.

Meaney, M., Aitken, D., Berkel, H., Bhatnager, S., & Sapolsky, R. (1988). Effect of neonatal handling of age-related impairments associated with the hippocampus. *Science, 239,* 766–768.

Melia, K. R., &., Duman, R. S. (1991). Involvement of corticotropin-releasing factor in chronic stress regulation of the brain noradrenergic system. *Proceedings of the National Academy of Science USA, 88,* 8382–8386.

Melin, B., Lundberg, U., Soderlund, J., & Granqvist, M. (1999). Psychological and physiological stress reactions of male and female assembly workers: A comparison between two different forms of work organization. *Journal of Organizational Behavior, 20,* 47–61.

Mendelson, S., & McEwen, B. S. (1991). Autoradiographic analyses of the effects of restraint-induced stress on 5-HTIA, 5-HTIC and 5-HT2 receptors in the dorsal hippocampus of male and female rats. *Neuroendocrinology, 54,* 454–461.

Mendelson, S., &., McEwen, B. S. (1992). Autoradiographic analyses of the effects of adrenalectomy and corticosterone on 5-HT1A and 5-HT1B receptors in the dorsal hippocampus and cortex of the rat. *Neuroendocrinology, 55,* 444–450.

Michelson, D., Stratakis, C., Hill, L., Reynolds, J., Galliven, E., Chrousos, G., & Gold, P. (1996). Bone mineral density in women with depression. *New England Journal of Medicine, 335,* 1176–1181.

Miner, J. N., Diamond, M. I., &., Yamamoto, K. R. (1991). Joints in the regulatory lattice: Composite regulation by steroid receptor-AP1 complexes. *Cell Growth and Differentiation, 2,* 525–530.

Morales, A. J., Nolan, J. J., Nelson, J. C., & Yen, S. S. C. (1994). Effects of replacement dose of dehydroepiandrosterone in men and women of advancing age. *Journal of Clinical Endocrinology and Metabolism, 78,* 1360–1367.

Muldoon, M., Kaplan, J., Manuck, S., &., Mann, J. (1992). Effects of a low-fat diet on brain serotonergic responsivity in cynomolgus monkey. *Biological Psychiatry, 31,* 739–742.

Muldoon, M. F., Manuck, S. B., & Matthews, K. A. (1990). Lowering cholesterol concentrations and mortality: A quantitative review of primary prevention trials. *British Medical Journal, 301,* 309–314.

Muller, J. E., & Tofler, G. H. (1990). A symposium: Triggering and circadian variation of onset of acute cardiovascular disease. *American Journal of Cardiology, 66,* 1–70.

Munck, A., Guyre, P. M., & Holbrook, N. (1984). Physiological functions of glucocorticoids in stress and their relation to pharmacological actions. *Endocrine Reviews, 5,* 25–44.

Neckers, L., & Sze, P. (1975). Regulation of 5-hydroxytryptamine metabolism in mouse brain by adrenal glucocorticoids. *Brain Research, 93,* 123–132.

Nisenbaum, L., &., Abercrombie, E. (1993). Presynaptic alterations associated with enhancement of evoked release and synthesis of norepinephrine in hippocampus of chronically cold-stressed rats. *Brain Research, 608,* 280–287.

Nisenbaum, L., Zigmond, M., Sved, A., & Abercrombie, E. (1991). Prior exposure to chronic stress results in enhanced synthesis and release of hippocampal norephinephrine in response to a novel stressor. *Journal of Neuroscience, 11,* 1478–1484.

Notzon, F. C., Komarov, Y. M., Ermakov, S. P., Sempos, C. T., Marks, J. S., & Sempos, E. V. (1998). Causes of declining life expectancy in Russia. *Journal of the American Medical Association, 279,* 793–800.

Pacak, K., Armando, I., Komoly, S., Fukuhara, K., Weise, V., Holmes, C., Kopin, I., & Goldstein, D. (1992). Hypercortisolemia inhibits yohimbine-induced release of norepinephrine in the posterolateral hypothalamus of conscious rats. *Endocrinology,* 1369–1376.

Pacak, K., Kvetnansky, R., Palkovits, M., Fukuhara, K., Yadid, G., Kopin, I. J., & Goldstein, D. S. (1993). Adrenalectomy augments in vivo release of norepinephrine in the paraventricular nucleus during immobilization stress. *Endocrinology, 133,* 1404–1410.

Pavlides, C., Kimura, A., Magarinos, A. M., & McEwen, B. S. (1995). Hippocampal homosynaptic long-term depression/depotentiation induced by adrenal steroids. *Neuroscience, 68,* 379–385.

Perseghin, G., Price, T. B., Petersen, K. F., Roden, M., Cline, G. W., Gerow, K., Rothman, D. L., & Shulman, G. I. (1996). Increased glucose transport-phosphorylation and muscle glycogen synthesis after exercise training in insulin-resistant subjects. *New England Journal of Medicine, 335,* 1357–1362.

Phillips, R. G., & LeDoux, J. E. (1992). Differential contribution of amygdala and hippocampus to cued and contextual fear conditioning. *Behav. Neurosci, 106,* 274–285.

Plat, L., Leproult, R., L-Hermite-Baleriaux, M., Fery, F., Mockel, J., Polonsky, K. S., & Van Cauter, E. (1999). Metabolic effects of short-term elevations of plasma cortisol are more pronounced in the evening than in the morning. *Journal of Clinical Endocrinology and Metabolism, 84.*

Plomin, R. (1990). The role of inheritance in behavior. *Science, 48,* 183–188.

Plomin, R., Owen, M. J., & McGuffin, P. (1994). The genetic basis of complex human behaviors. *Science, 264,* 1733–1739.

Plotsky, P. M., & Meaney, M. J. (1993). Early, postnatal experience alters hypothalamic corticotropin-releasing factor (CRF) mRNA, median eminence CRF content and stress-induced release in adult rats. *Mol. Brain Res, 18*, 195–200.

Pugh, C. R., Tremblay, D., Fleshner, M., & Rudy, J. W. (1997). A selective role for corticosterone in contextual-fear conditioning. *Behav. Neurosci, 111*, 503–511.

Quirarte, G. L., Roozendaal, B., & McGaugh, J. L. (1997). Glucocorticoid enhancement of memory storage involves noradrenergic activation in the basolateral amygdala. *Proceedings of the National Academy of Sciences USA, 94*, 14048–14053.

Raikkonen, K., Hautanen, A., & Keltikangas-Jarvinen, L. (1996). Feelings of exhaustion, emotional distress, and pituitary and adrenocortical hormones in borderline hypertension. *Journal of Hypertension, 14*, 713–718.

Roozendaal, B., Portillo-Marquez, G., & McGaugh, J. L. (1996). Basolateral amygdala lesions block glucocorticoid-induced modulation of memory for spatial learning. *Behav. Neurosci, 110*, 1074–1083.

Rupp, A., Gause, E. M., Regier, D. A. (1998). Research policy implications of cost-of-illness studies for mental disorders. *British Journal of Psychiatry, 173*, 19–25.

Saphier, D. (1992). Adrenoceptor regulation of paraventricular nucleus neuronal activity as related to hypothalamo-pituitary adrenocortical responses. In R. Kvetnansky, R. McCarty, & J. Axelrod, (Eds.), *Stress: Neuroendocrine and molecular approaches* (pp. 481–488). New York: Gordon and Breach.

Sapolsky, R. M. (1996). Why stress is bad for your brain. *Science, 273*, 749–750.

Schulkin, J., Gold, P. W., McEwen, B. S. (1998). Induction of corticotropin-releasing hormone gene expression by glucocorticoids: Implication for understanding the states of fear and anxiety and allostatic load. *Psychoneuroendocrinology, 23*, 219–243.

Schulkin, J., McEwen, B. S., Gold, P. W. (1994). Allostasis, amygdala, and anticipatory angst. *Neurosci. Biobehav. Rev, 18*, 385–396.

Seeman, T. E., McEwen, B. S., Singer, B. H., Albert, M. S., & Rowe, J. W. (1997). Increase in urinary cortisol excretion and memory declines: MacArthur studies of successful aging. *Journal of Clinical Endocrinology and Metabolism, 82*, 2458–2465.

Seeman, T. E., Singer B. H., Rowe, J. W., Horwitz, R. I., & McEwen, B. S. (1997). Price of adaptation—allostatic load and its health consequences: MacArthur studies of successful aging. *Archives of Internal Medicine, 157*, 2259–2268.

Seeman, T. E., McEwen, B. S., Rowe, J. W., & Singer, B. H. (2001). Allostatic load as a marker of cumulative biological risk: MacArthur studies of successful aging. *Proceedings of the National Academy of Sciences USA, 98*, 4770–4775.

Selye, H. (1936). A syndrome produced by diverse nocuous agents. *Nature, 138*, 32.

Sheline, Y. I., Gado, M. H., Price, J. L. (1998). Amygdala core nuclei volumes are decreased in recurrent major depression. *NeuroReport, 9*, 2023–2028.

Sheline, Y. I., Sanghavi, M., Mintun, M. A., & Gado, M. H. (1999). Depression duration but not age predicts hippocampal volume loss in medically healthy women with recurrent major depression. *Journal of Neuroscience, 19*, 5034–5043.

Sheline, Y. I., Wang, P. W., Gado, M. H., Csernansky, J. C., & Vannier, M. W. (1996). Hippocampal atrophy in re-

current major depression. *Proceedings of the National Academy of Sciences USA, 93*, 3908–3913.

Singh, V., Corley, K., Phan, T-H, & Boadle-Biber, M. (1990). Increases in the activity of tryptophan hydroxylase from rat cortex and midbrain in response to acute or repeated sound stress are blocked by adrenalectomy and restored by dexamethasone treatment. *Brain Research, 516*, 66–76.

Spiegel, K., Leproult, R., & Van Cauter, E. (1999). Impact of sleep debt on metabolic and endocrine function. *Lancet 354*, 1435–1439.

Sterling, P., & Eyer, J. (1988). Allostasis: A new paradigm to explain arousal pathology. In S. Fisher & J. Reason (Eds.). *Handbook of life stress, cognition and health*, (pp. 629–649). New York: Wiley.

Sternberg, E. M. (1997). Neural-immune interactions in health and disease. *Journal of Clinical Investigation, 100*, 2641–2647.

Sternberg, E. M., Hill, J. M., & Chrousos, G. P. (1996). Inflammatory mediator-induced hypothalamic-pituitary-adrenal axis activation is defective in streptococcal cell wall arthritis susceptible Lewis rats. *Proceedings of the National Academy of Sciences USA, 86*, 2374–2378.

Surwit, R. S., Ross, S. L., & Feinglos, M. N. (1991). Stress, behavior and glucose control in diabetes mellitus. In P. M. McCabe, N. Schneiderman, T. M. Field, & J. S. Skyler (Eds.), *Stress, coping and disease* (pp. 97–117). Hillsdale, NJ: Erlbaum.

Swiergiel, A. H., Takahashi, L. K., Kalin, N. H. (1993). Attention of stress-induced behavior by antagonism of corticotropin-releasing factor receptors in the central amygdala in the rat. *Brain Research, 623*, 229–234.

Tsuda, A., & Tanaka, M. (1985). Differential changes in noradrenaline turnover in specific regions of rat brain produced by controllable and uncontrollable shocks. *Behav. Neurosci, 99*, 802–817.

Uno, H., Ross, T., Else, J., Suleman, M., & Sapolsky R. (1989). Hippocampal damage associated with prolonged and fatal stress in primates. *Journal of Neuroscience, 9*, 1705–1711.

Van Bockstaele, E. J., Colago, E. E. O., & Valentino, R. J. (1998). Amygdaloid corticotropin-releasing factor targets locus coeruleus dendrites: Substrate for the coordination of emotional and cognitive limbs of the stress response. *Journal of Neuroendocrinology, 10*, 743–757.

Van Cauter, E., Polonsky, K. S., & Scheen, A. J. (1997). Roles of circadian rhythmicity and sleep in human glucose regulation. *Endocr. Rev, 18*, 716–738.

Vogel, F., & Motulsky, A. G. (1986). *Human genetics.* Berlin and Heidelberg: Springer-Verlag.

Wadhwa, P. D. (1998). Prenatal stress and life-span development. In H. S. Friedman (Ed.), *Encylopedia of mental health* (pp. 265–280). San Diego: Academic Press.

Wadhwa, P. D., Sandman, C. A., Porto, M., Dunkel-Schetter, C., & Garite, T. J. (1993). The association between prenatal stress and infant birth weight and gestational age at birth: A prospective investigation. *Am. J. Ob. Gyn, 169*, 858–865.

Webster, E. L., Elenkov, I. J., & Chrousos, G. P. (1997). The role of corticotropin-releasing hormone in neuroendocrine-immune interactions. *Molecular Psychiatry, 2*, 368–372.

Weiss, J., Goodman, P., Losito, B., Corigan, S., Charry, J., & Bailey W. (1981). Behavioral depression produced by an uncontrollable stressor: Relationship to norepinephrine, dopamine and serotonin levels in various regions of rat brain. *Brain Res. Rev, 3,* 167–205.

Welch, J. E., Farrar, G. E., Dunn, A. J., & Saphier, D. (1993). Central 5-HT receptors inhibit adrenocortical secretion. *Neuroendo, 57,* 272–281.

Wiersma, A., Baauw, A. D., Bohus, B., & Koolhaas, J. M. (1995). Behavioural activation produced by CRH but not a-helical CRH (CRH-receptor antagonist) when microinfused into the central nucleus of the amygdala under stress-free conditions. *Psychoneuroendocrinology, 20,* 423–432.

Williams, R. B. (1994). Neurobiology, cellular and molecular biology, and psychosomatic medicine. *Psychosomatic Medicine, 56,* 308–315.

Williams, R. B., & Chesney, M. A. (1993). Psychosocial factors and prognosis in established coronary artery disease. The need for research on interventions. *Journal of the American Medical Association, 270,* 1860–1861.

Williams, R. B., & Williams, V. P. (1993). *Anger kills: Seventeen strategies for controlling the hostility that can harm your health.* New York: Harper Perennial.

Wright, B. E., Porter, J. R., Browne, E., & Svec, F. (1992). Antiglucocorticoid action of dehydroepiandrosterone in young obese Zucker rats. *International Journal of Obesity, 16,* 579–593.

Yamada, K., Duong, D. T., Scott, D. K., Wang, J.-C., & Granner, D. K. (1999). CCAAT/Enhancer-binding protein is an accessory factor for the glucocorticoid response from the cAMP response element in the rat phosphoenolpyruvate carboxykinase gene promoter. *Journal of Biological Chemistry, 274,* 5880–5887.

# INDEX

## A

Abele, A., 601
Abend, T. A., 759
Abrams, M. H., 497
Abramson, L. Y., 992
absolute music, 505
absolutists, musical, 505
abstractions, dynamic skill theory, 388, 393, 394, 400
abstract thinking, 774, 775, 777
abuse
  of children, 813, 967, 1129–30, 1131
  memories of, 643, 645
  posttraumatic stress syndrome and, 967, 1129
  sexual, 643, 967, 968, 1129
  substance. *See* substance abuse
ACad. *See* ventral affective division
ACcd. *See* dorsal cognitive division
accent intonation models, 448
accessibility, emotional response, 873
accomplishment, 389–94, 402
acetylcholine, 142, 143, 153, 162–64, 1108, 1109, 1111–12
achievement
  American view of, 384, 386–87, 393
  attribution emotion theory and, 580
  behavioral inhibition system and, 683
  pride in, 862–63
Ackerman, P., 830
Ackermann, H., 450
Ackermann, R., 993
acoustic analyses, 446
acoustic cues, 442, 445–46, 451
acoustic parameters, 433–43, 446–51

acoustic-phonetic parameters, 437, 438*t*, 451
acoustic startle response, 199, 207n.2, 323, 1110
acquired sociopathy, 83
ACTH. *See* adrenocorticotropic hormone
action
  in dynamic component systems, 376–78, 380–81, 401
  emotion and, 296
action potentials, 160, 161, 162
action readiness, 816, 871, 872, 876–79, 883
action tendencies, 1050
  anger and, 856–57
  in appraisal theory, 573, 575, 582, 586, 628
  awe, elevation, and, 863, 864
  compassion and, 862
  contempt and, 858
  decision making and, 566, 628, 633
  disgust and, 857–58
  emotions and, 257, 378–80, 572
  facial expression and, 416
  gratitude and, 863
  guilt and, 861
  prosocial, 854, 858, 862, 864
  shame, embarrassment, and, 860
  vocal expression and, 435, 446
activation
  automatic, 690–91, 692, 694
  in dimensional emotion theories, 574, 1085, 1087
  direct, 690, 694
  emotional influences on, 679, 685, 687
  individual differences in, 699, 701, 705, 729

of mental representations, 989–90
  of responses, 872
  spreading, 687, 690, 691, 694, 994
  tonic, 692
activation dimension, 189
activation outcomes, 872
active coping, 259, 1071, 1072
activity
  genetic factors in, 727
  as temperament type, 327
Adachi, M., 527
*adagio* (music tempo), 504
Adams, R. D., 987
adaptation
  allostasis, 1118, 1119, 1121, 1125, 1130
  attitudes and, 596–97
  as decision-making consideration, 625–26, 635
  as emotion goal, 748
  evolutionary and cultural perspectives on, 840, 842
  health issues and, 1047, 1048, 1050
  personality development and, 727
adaptive rationality, 892–96
adaptive value
  aesthetic emotions, 848
  affect, 840, 842–44, 849
  basic emotions, 1083–84, 1093
addiction, 588, 634, 846. *See also* substance abuse
addictive drugs, 28, 30, 33, 34, 579, 634
Adelson, E., 524
adenylate cyclase, 98, 1023, 1025, 1029
adjective checklist methodology, 678
adjective circles, 517, 519*f*, 528
Adler, A., 774
admiration, 325, 569, 864

adolescents
    antisocial behavior and, 804
    antisocial personality disorder and, 309
    behavioral inhibition and, 330–31
    guilt feelings and, 792, 793
    health issues and, 1085
    humor and, 340
    social honor development by, 394, 400
Adolphs, R., 31, 66–87, 474
adoption studies, 15, 301, 304, 305, 307, 728
adrenal cortex, 93, 151, 1127
adrenalectomy, 98, 1072
adrenal gland hypertrophy, 1033
adrenaline. See epinephrine
adrenal medulla, 93, 94, 140, 151, 152, 174–75, 1125, 1127
adrenal steroids, 1121, 1125, 1127
adrenergic system, memory and, 105–7
adrenoceptors, 153, 162, 163, 164, 173
adrenocortical system, 1118
adrenocorticotropic hormone, 13, 1033–34, 1073, 1085, 1125–27
adults
    antisocial personality disorder and, 309
    Chinese shame/guilt and, 400–401
    emotional development of, 297, 733–34
    guilt and, 750, 793
    linguistic and emotional expression and, 536, 537–43, 548, 552, 553
    personality issues, 297, 679, 727–29, 731–39
    prosocial behavior studies of, 790, 791, 793–98
    temperament types, 327
    See also older adults
advertising, 484, 529, 750, 755
aesthetic affect, 847–48
aesthetic emotions, 569, 577–78, 580, 848
aesthetic pleasures, 841, 845
aesthetics, 488–90, 529, 569, 685
aesthetic values, 635
affect, 565–67
    adaptive value of, 840, 842–44, 848, 849
    aggression, antisocial behavior, and, 750, 804–19
    as attitude and judgment influence, 566, 596–613, 752–66
    cancer patients and regulation of, 1054, 1055, 1059, 1060, 1067, 1068
    core, 1084, 1085
    decision making and, 566, 619–36
    definition of, 323–25, 805, 840–42
    evolutionary and cultural perspectives on, 839–49
    incidental, 619, 629
    intensity of, 566–67, 603, 609
    lack of, 118
    musical expression of, 504
    negative-positive dimension of, 844–45

on-line, remembered, and anticipated types of, 841–42, 843, 846
    personality and, 678, 1088
    physiological and pharmacological induction of, 930, 939–52, 965
    prosocial behavior and, 297, 749, 750, 787–98
    temporal domains of, 930–31, 933, 954
    See also emotion; negative affect; positive affect
affect-as-information model, 600–601, 612, 627, 628, 636–37n.8, 760–61, 765–66, 767
Affect Balance Scale, 1063
affect bursts, 449, 568
affect-free decision making, 566
Affect Grid, 81
affect infusion, 599–600, 603–5, 608, 610–13, 668
    attitude change and, 759, 764–65
affect infusion model, 566, 611–13, 636–37nn.3, 8, 668, 691
    attitudes and, 764–65, 766
affection, 482, 1087
affectional emotional systems, 683
affective disorders, 9, 843, 1093
    therapeutic treatments, 901–3, 908, 925
    tripartite model of, 992
    See also emotional disorders; psychopathology; specific disorders
affective forecasting, 621, 625–26
affective imagery, 630, 631, 632
affective maps, 691
affective neuroscience, 3–7, 671
    depression neuroimaging, 4, 117–25
    emotional learning circuits, 4, 52–62
    emotion and emotion regulation, 8–19
    emotion and memory, 4, 93–109
    human vs. animal emotional brain, 4, 25–43
    lesion study contributions to, 4, 66–87
    memory and, 4, 93–109
affective priming, 566, 599–602, 604–5, 608, 610–12, 636–37n.8, 668
affective space, semantic, 678, 1089
affective startle modulation, 203–5, 207, 917–19
affective states, 11, 731–32
affective style, 4, 5, 8, 9, 17, 729, 1089
    anterior cingulate cortex and, 12
    context's role in, 298
    frontal brain asymmetry and, 701, 932
    health and, 1088
    prefrontal cortex and, 10
affective tags, 606
affect lexicon, 568
affect maintenance-affect repair hypothesis, 602
affect programs, 506
affect space. See emotional space

affect subdivision, 11, 12, 18
affect systems, 377–80, 401, 402
afferent signals, brain and, 135
affettuoso (musical direction), 504
AFFEX, 350
affiliation, 1010–19
    animal expression of, 464, 469, 472, 473, 475
    animal models of, 902, 1010–12, 1097
    autism and, 902, 1010, 1017–18
    neural system considerations, 1012–14
Africa, 538, 874, 875
African-Americans, 811, 812, 820nn.14, 16, 1086
agape love, 864–65
age. See adolescents; adults; children; infants; older adults; toddlers
age, 14, 16, 136, 583, 954
agency
    as appraisal dimension, 573–75, 580, 585, 587, 588, 874–75
    cultural differences in, 846, 874–75, 876
    personality development and, 726, 728, 739
aggression, 804, 1127, 1129
    animal expression of, 458, 460, 461, 464, 465, 466, 472, 806–7, 1012, 1014
    antisocial behavior and, 750, 804–19
    appraisal theory view of, 580–81
    cultural considerations, 879
    defensive, 683, 684, 685
    displaced, 805, 811, 815, 820n.9
    effortful control and, 693
    emotional attractiveness and, 489
    environmental instigators of, 806–10
    frustration-aggression hypothesis, 606, 811–13
    goal obstruction and, 683, 811–13
    hostile vs. instrumental, 805
    hypothalamus's role in, 34
    inhibition of, 817–19
    male guarding behavior and, 1012, 1015–16
    negative affect and, 813–19, 1019
    septal rage, 35–36
    See also violence
aging, 297, 1096, 1128, 1131
agitation, 779, 995, 1031
Agnew, R., 812
agnosia, 900, 931
agoraphobia, 627, 686, 899, 970, 988
agreeableness, 683, 731, 732, 738, 739
agriculture, 775–76
Ahadi, S. A., 730
Ahern, G. L., 947
Ainsworth, M., 730
air, 325
air pollution, 810
Aitken, P. G., 473
Akerlof, George, 895

Alameda County study, 1059
alarm calls, 459–62, 466, 474
alarm odors, 472, 475
Alberts, J. R., 457, 458
alcohol (liquor), 226, 950–51, 1086, 1119–21
    abuse of, 728–29, 1127
alcoholics, 924, 1034, 1035
    attentional issues of, 287–89
    deficient response modulation and, 905
    emotion induction study findings, 951
    maladaptive self-awareness attenuation by, 782
Aldwin, C. M., 737
Alessandri, S., 393
Alexander, F., 212, 216
Alexander, G. E., 931
alienation, 1087
*allegro* (music tempo), 504
alleles, 302, 310, 311–12, 1128
allele-sharing analysis methods, 311
alliesthesia, 34, 842
allopurinol, 1072
allostasis, 5, 1049, 1072, 1093, 1117–31
allostatic load, 1049, 1072, 1089, 1091–94, 1096, 1117–31
Alloy, L. B., 992, 998
Allport, D. A., 663
Allport, Floyd, 415
Allport, G. W., 677
Alpert, N. M., 969
alpha-methyl-para-tyrosine, 1025
alpha power, frontal area, 320, 323
*Also Sprach Zarathustra* (Strauss), 516
altanserin, 1030
Altenmüller, E., 450
altruism, 787, 788, 862
    adaptive rationality and, 893–94
    cancer patients and, 1066
    reciprocal, 854, 855, 863
Alveario, M. C., 473
Alzheimer's disease, 108, 1031, 1034, 1108, 1113
*amae* (Japanese emotion), 847
ambiguity, 714, 717–19, 891–92, 896, 988, 1001n.5
ambiguous emotions, 579
ambivalent emotions, 337
American Academy of Pediatrics, 348
American Psychiatric Association, 909
American Revolution, 481, 811
American Sign Language, 297, 536–42, 544–51
amineptine, 1032
amino acids, 1024, 1026, 1121
amitriptyline, 1033
Ammon's horn, 1128
amnesia, 97, 198, 647–48, 665, 983
    amygdala damage and, 107
    fear conditioning and, 59, 61, 654

*amoroso* (musical direction), 504
AMPA receptors, 57
amphetamine, 33, 34, 37, 103, 105, 1032
amphibians, 258, 1011
amplitude, 463, 520, 538
    as acoustic measurement, 434, 437, 440, 442
AMPT. *See* alpha-methyl-para-tyrosine
Amsterdam, J. B., 666
amusement, 412, 417, 420, 424, 425
    art vs., 485
    as basic emotion, 862
    expression of, 706
amygdala, 10*f*, 28, 118, 194, 729
    alliesthesia and, 34
    allostatic load and, 1125
    anterior cingulate cortex and, 11, 12
    anxiety and, 31, 38, 76, 972, 1109–13, 1127
    automatic emotion processing role of, 648, 649
    aversive learning and, 99, 100, 1110
    basal nuclei, 900
    basolateral complex, 97–105, 109, 900
    corticomedial, 900
    damage to, 31–32, 59, 73–82, 107–8, 931
    depression and, 15–16, 18, 900, 1127, 1128
    as emotional physiological state trigger, 87
    emotion evaluation study findings, 934–39
    emotion induction study findings, 939–49, 951, 952
    emotion processing role of, 933, 934, 938, 943, 964
    emotion regulation role of, 4, 9, 15–18, 25, 27, 31–32, 39, 41, 42, 265
    epilepsy and, 16, 41
    facial expression and, 31, 76, 78–80, 82, 423, 474, 900, 931, 934–37, 938, 939
    fear role of. *See under* fear
    fight-or-flight response and, 327
    hemisphere specialization and, 38
    lesions to. *See under* lesions/lesion studies
    mediobasal nuclei, 900
    memory and, 4, 13, 16, 75–78, 93–105, 107–9, 648, 649, 651, 654, 933, 1127
    neuroimaging of, 31, 76, 108–9, 648, 651, 934, 936, 940, 952–54
    panic disorder and, 970, 971, 972
    perception role of, 933
    phobias and, 969, 972
    posttraumatic stress disorder and, 76, 966–67, 968, 972, 1127
    psychopathology and, 900, 901, 1113
    reactivity of children and, 328, 329
    reminiscence effect and, 651

startle reflex and, 199–200, 201, 206, 329, 1110
    visceral afferent neurons and, 144
    vocal expression and, 31, 449
    *See also* extended amygdala; lateral amygdala
analgesia systems, 36
analogical representations, 669
analogue-I, 774–77, 779, 783
analysis of covariance, 242–44
analysis of variance, 243–44, 322
ancestors, African cultures, 874
ancient Greece. *See* Greece, ancient
ancient Rome. *See* Rome, ancient
ANCOVA. *See* analysis of covariance
Andersen, S. M., 996
Anderson, C. A., 807, 808, 809–10, 813–14, 815, 816, 817, 819–20nn.4, 6, 7, 10, 11, 15, 18
Anderson, K. B., 807, 808, 820n.10
Anderson, Marian, 393
Andersson, J. L., 971
Andreason, P. J., 952
Andrew, R. J., 464
androgen, 1014, 1127
anesthesia, pain and, 30
Angelman syndrome, 310
anger, 5, 412, 589n.5, 748, 840, 849
    aggression and, 812, 813, 818–19, 820n.18
    animal expression of, 458, 460
    anterior cingulate cortex and, 119
    appraisal theory view of, 574, 575, 576, 580, 581, 585, 688
    as attitude and judgment influence, 607
    as attitude change factor, 759
    as basic emotion, 68, 176, 333, 669, 1087
    blame and, 816, 818
    cancer patients and, 1053, 1063, 1067, 1069, 1071, 1075
    children's control of, 337
    cognitive-neoassociationistic aggression model, 815, 816
    cultural perspectives on, 875, 879, 882, 883, 885, 886
    developmental perspective, 364, 365*t*, 732
    emotional reactivity and, 683, 684
    emotional response research findings, 192
    emotion-specific goal attainment and, 628
    environmental causes of, 807, 809, 810
    experience of, 378, 379*t*
    expression of in interpersonal relationships, 829, 832
    facial expression and, 417, 419, 420, 423, 424, 425, 463–64

anger (*continued*)
    frustration-aggression thesis view of, 812, 813
    genetic and environmental factors in, 306
    incidental emotions' impact on, 632
    induction research issues and, 229–33, 236, 248–50
    infants' expression of, 334, 353, 357, 364, 365*t*, 421, 543, 780, 812
    as information-processing factor, 630
    journal articles published on, 852, 853*t*
    metaphors for, 215
    moral emotion issues of, 854, 855, 856–57, 858–59, 866
    music and perception of, 515, 520, 526
    neural substrates of, 936–37
    personality and, 733
    physical health and, 1049, 1050, 1087, 1096
    preparedness theory testing and, 267–68
    as prosocial behavior influence, 797–98
    as racism response, 1086, 1087
    self-attention impact on, 782
    self-generation of, 776
    serotonin and, 327, 1126
    in sibling interactions, 341
    sign language expression of, 539
    toddlers' expression of, 333, 335, 364
    universalist view of, 216
    vocal expression of, 438, 439*t*, 440, 443, 444, 446, 448
anger disorders, 819
anger to frustration, 325
anger to personal attack, 325
angular gyrus, 941
anhedonia, 33
anima, 329
animals, 3, 637n.12, 839, 1049
    affiliation models, 902, 1010–12, 1097
    aggression and, 458, 460, 461, 464, 465, 466, 472, 806–7, 1012, 1014
    amygdala lesion studies, 74–75
    anticipatory affect and, 631–32
    appeasement displays, 859
    appraisal issues, 583
    approach-withdrawal processes, 577
    behavioral genetic studies of, 312–15
    behavior-genetic research paradigm, 301
    cardiovascular responses to threat by, 188
    communication conceptual and organizing principles and, 460–63
    communication developmental processes and, 474–75
    distress expression by, 458, 469, 470, 1011
    emotional brain of, 4, 25–43
    emotional experience of, 774–77, 848, 1010

emotional learning circuits of, 4, 52–62
emotion programs and, 849
expression of emotion by, 187, 411–14, 457–76
    facial expression and, 457, 458, 459*f*, 463–65, 474, 583
    fear expression by, 458–60, 464, 465, 466, 472, 474, 475, 774
    food aversion learning, 843
    human expression similarities, 415, 425
    human intruder paradigm, 14
    human phobias toward, 259–60
    implicit knowledge of, 843
    jealous responses by, 776–77
    lack of self-reflection in, 774, 775, 776, 779, 781
    limbic system dysfunction and, 904
    mastery motivation/emotion systems, 848
    memory and, 644, 645, 651, 775
    mirror neurons, 72
    negativity bias in, 844
    parent-child relationships, 458, 469, 470–71, 473, 474, 1011
    pleasure and pain and, 842
    reciprocal altruism and, 855
    resilience studies and, 1097
    self-awareness and, 774, 780
    sensitivity to suffering by, 861–62
    septal rage and, 35–36
    stress and, 1074
    vocal expression and, 412, 449, 457–63, 465–76, 507, 583
*Anna Karenina* (Tolstoy), 486
annoyance, 815
anorexia nervosa, 1033, 1034
ANOVA. *See* analysis of variance
antelope, 472
anterior attentional system, 693, 694
anterior cingulate cortex, 117, 122
    animal vocalizations and, 473
    arousal and, 30
    controlled emotion processing and, 648–649
    depression and, 12, 17–18, 118, 121–25, 1030
    emotion and emotion regulation by, 4, 9–12, 16, 17, 27, 30
    emotion evaluation study findings, 936–39
    emotion induction study findings, 941–49
    emotion processing role of, 933, 934, 936
    facial expression and, 119, 934, 936–39
    mood and, 120, 953
    neuroimaging of, 119, 121, 934–38, 953, 954
    obsessive-compulsive disorder and, 12, 965, 966

panic disorder and, 971
    posttraumatic stress syndrome and, 12, 967, 968
    vocal expression and, 449
anterior hypothalamus, 471
anterior insula, 11, 423, 936, 941, 947
anterior paralimbic structures, 964, 968, 969, 972
    neural substrates of affect and, 930, 932, 933, 935*t*, 938, 939, 945, 951–53
anterior prefrontal cortex, 968
anterior temporal cortex, 967, 968, 971
anterior temporal lobe, 69, 71, 947
anterior temporal poles, 971
anterior temporopolar cortex, 969
anterolateral orbitofrontal cortex, 938
anthropology, 748
antiandrogens, 464
antianxiety drugs, 312, 1110
antibodies, 187
anticipated affect, 842, 843, 846
anticipation, 9, 17, 775–76, 777
anticipatory anxiety, 630, 683, 775–76
    hippocampus and, 13
    negative affect and, 988
    panic disorder and, 971
anticipatory influences, decision-making, 566, 620, 621, 630–32, 633
anticonvulsants, 201
antidepressants, 124, 226, 312, 902, 950, 964
    depression neurobiology and, 1021–28, 1030–33, 1035
    *See also specific drugs*
antidiuretic hormone. *See* vasopressin
antisocial behavior, 30, 344, 750, 804–19
antisocial personality disorder, 309, 315, 909
antithesis principle, 458, 475
Antoni, M. H., 1058, 1068
Antonis, B., 663
Antonovsky, A., 1098
anxiety, 75, 121–22, 298, 324, 933
    activation-elaboration model, 990
    as affective reaction, 598
    aggression and, 818
    amygdala and, 31, 38, 76, 972, 1109–13, 1127
    animal behavioral genetics studies and, 313–14
    animal expression of, 464
    anterior cingulate cortex and, 119
    anticipatory, 13, 630, 683, 775–76, 971, 988
    associative network theory and, 668
    attachment theory and, 489, 997
    attention and, 693–94, 978–82, 989, 990
    as attitude and judgment influence, 606, 607, 608
    avoidance goals and, 995

belief disconfirmation and, 609
cancer patients and, 1064, 1066, 1070, 1071, 1075, 1098
cingulate cortex and, 30
cognitive processing biases, 977–81, 985–90
content-specificity effect and, 992
coping processes, 714–16
emotional reactivity and, 683, 684, 686, 690, 692–94
evolutionary perspectives on, 685–86, 775–76, 977, 990, 992, 1001
fear conditioning models and, 61, 1106–7
fear of, 714
frontal brain asymmetry and, 701
genetic and environmental factors in, 306
hot/cold empathy gaps and, 629
incidental situational affect and, 632–33
judgmental/interpretive biases and, 988–89
memory biases and, 982–83, 985–88, 990
molecular genetics findings on, 311–12
mood and, 899
neurobehavioral models of, 1105–13
panic disorder and, 970
personal distress and, 788
pessimism and, 737
physical health and, 1049, 1050, 1097
preattentive bias for threat and, 264
reactivity of children and, 328, 329, 330
selective information processing and, 663–64
self-generation of, 775–76
separation-related, 683
simultaneous information processing and, 666
social, 260, 329, 688, 689, 780, 781, 970
social relationships and, 344, 606
temperamental vulnerability to, 320
threat appraisal, 264, 689, 963–64, 1110
trait-related. *See* trait anxiety
vocal expression of, 440, 443, 446
anxiety disorders, 4, 207, 899, 900
amygdala and, 16, 31
anterior cingulate cortex and, 12
attentional biases and, 977–81
cognitive interference and, 277, 979, 980, 982
cognitive processing and, 565, 666, 1110
emotional reactivity and, 683
emotion induction study findings on, 951
fear response and, 963–64, 1107
impaired recall and, 650
judgmental/interpretive biases and, 988–89

memory biases and, 982–83, 985–88
neurobehavioral systems and, 1113
neuroimaging and neurobiology of, 963–73, 1034
psychodynamic view of, 1021
social cognitive biases and, 990–1000
stress and, 1117
therapeutic treatments of, 902
threat and, 264, 689, 963–64, 979–81, 985–90
*See also* generalized anxiety disorder; phobias
Anxiety Sensitivity Index, 686
anxiety to threat, 325
anxiolytic medications, 964. *See also specific types*
aortic glomeruli, 148
apathy, 29
apes, 470, 472
AP5, 102
aphasia, 198
apology, 861
apomorphine, 1032, 1034
a posteriori research participant selection, 238–39, 240f, 246
appealingness, 687
appeasement, 849, 859
Appenzeller, O., 137
appetite, depression and, 118
appetitive motivational system, 188–89, 651
emotional priming and, 198, 206
emotional systems and, 682–84, 687, 691
startle response and, 201
appetitive motives, 579
Appleton, J., 489, 493, 495
appraisal
of accomplishments, 393, 394
action tendencies and, 573, 575, 582, 586, 628
aesthetics and, 488–89
of affect intensity and duration, 567
attachment as factor in, 730
automatic and controlled emotion processing and, 648–49, 710, 9057
of challenge, 238
children's use of, 583, 732–33
Chinese shame/guilt and, 400, 401
cognition and, 377, 567–68, 572–89, 977, 1047, 1049, 1050
component dimensions, 573, 574, 576–82, 587
conceptual emotion influences and, 687–90
culture and, 577, 579, 583–85, 588, 845, 846, 848, 849, 860, 872, 874–76, 879–80
direct sensory responses vs., 841
in dynamic component systems, 376–81, 401, 402

emotional memory and, 644
emotional role of, 296, 564–65, 572–89, 684, 709–10, 747–48
of emotional scenarios, 86–87
emotion-antecedent, 687, 690
emotion information processing and, 669, 670, 906, 1050
emotion tasks and, 132
facial expression issues, 416–19
individual differences in, 699, 700, 709–10, 719
mood and, 575, 749
negative affect-produced aggression and, 814–16, 818–19
primary and secondary, 573, 578, 580, 585, 687–90, 693–94, 709, 814
processing levels, 576, 577, 578, 583, 589
process operation, 574–76
psychopaths and, 914
reflected, 780–81
of self-attributions, 780
stimulus evaluation check model, 709–10
sympathy emotions and, 498
theoretical emotion prediction and, 582–83
theories of, 564, 572–73, 573–74
theory criticisms and issues, 585–89
of threat, 238, 269, 572, 580, 689, 1089
unconscious, 564, 568, 574, 710
universality of, 871
vocal expression and, 435–36, 441, 442, 446, 448, 449
appraisal tendencies, 628, 632, 633
appraised inputs, affect and, 841
approach, 840, 1098
appetitive motivational system and, 189
in appraisal process, 577, 579
in behavioral approach system, 327
deficient response modulation and, 905
emotion tasks and, 132
frontal brain asymmetry and, 701, 932
personality development issues and, 730
prefrontal cortex role of, 9, 17, 729
psychological disorders and, 738
temperament emotional systems and, 682–83
approach-avoidance conflict, 285–89, 716, 994–95
approach-withdrawal framework, 577, 738, 840
apraxia, emotional, 900
a priori research participant selection, 238
arbitrariness, language, 536
architecture, 411, 481–84, 495–97, 569
psychological perspectives, 487, 489, 490
Arcus, Doreen, 327

Aristotle, 411, 483, 490, 493, 497, 504, 563, 572, 596, 628, 748, 752, 756, 783, 852, 856
Armstead, C. A., 1086
Arnett, P. A., 915
Arnheim, R., 485, 487–88, 491
Arnold, Magda B., 488, 564, 572–73, 578, 709
arousal, emotional, 5, 30, 35, 187, 189, 377–78
    aggression and, 814, 817–18
    amygdala and, 74, 79, 81–82, 105–9, 964
    anticipation as factor in, 630
    attention and, 711
    coping and, 714–16
    defense responses and, 287
    dysregulatory psychopathology and, 921–26
    emotional reactivity individual differences and, 681, 682, 684–86, 691–92, 694, 1089
    emotional response research findings, 190–92, 194, 197, 198, 205, 648
    emotion regulation and, 360, 364, 793–96, 798
    empathy and, 793
    experiment design considerations, 242
    individual differences in, 706, 707
    in infants, 356, 360, 364
    interpersonal relationships and, 826, 827, 833
    magic and, 484
    memory and, 93, 105–9, 644–45, 651
    music and, 503, 514, 515, 520
    nonspecific, 905, 923, 924, 926n.2
    personality development issues and, 730, 733–34
    preattentive emotion activation and, 263
    prosody and, 538
    response modulation issues and, 905, 909, 921–23, 926n.4
    social behavior and, 749
    sympathy and, 793–94
    temperament and, 698
    vocal expression and, 433–35, 438–41, 446, 448
    See also sexual arousal
arousal-motivated behavior, 715
art. See narrative arts; visual arts
art criticism, 483, 493
arterial baroreceptor reflexes, 166–67, 168f, 173
arterial blood sampling, 934
arteriovenous anastomoses, 329
articulation, 538
    in music, 520, 524, 526
    speech production and, 434, 437, 440, 442, 443

articulatory loop, information processing paradigm, 663
articulographs, 437
arts, emotion and the, 411–13, 481–99, 569, 577–78. See also literature; music
ascending reticulocortical activating system, 933
Asendorpf, J. B., 706
Ash, R. L., 514
Ashbrook, T. W., 602
Asmus, E. P., 515
Asperger's syndrome, 366
Aspinwall, L. G., 604
aspiration level, 623
asset integration, 622–23
assimilation effect. See mood-congruence effect
associationism, 564, 566, 598–99, 600
association studies, 310–12, 313
associative memory, 650, 651, 654
associative network theory, 759, 982, 989
    dysregulatory psychopathology and, 923–25
    emotion information processing and, 599, 667–68, 671, 711, 905–6, 908, 925–26
    psychopathy perspectives, 913–14, 916, 917, 920, 925
associative representations, 670
assortative mating, 303
asthenic temperament, 326
Astrachan, D. I., 199
atenolol, 97, 99, 103
atherosclerosis, 1087, 1118, 1130
athletic temperament, 326
ATP, 162
atropine, 105, 1109
attachment, 343, 353, 360, 1095, 1097, 1098
    adults and, 679
    affiliation and, 1010–12, 1097
    anxiety-based theory of, 489, 997
    cognitive interpersonal dynamics and, 997
    compassion and, 862
    cultural perspectives on, 730, 886
    emotional attractiveness and, 489
    guilt and, 861
    parent-child relationships and, 340–42, 489, 729, 736, 886, 1010, 1011
    personality development and, 297, 304, 730, 736
    selective, 729, 1011, 1017
attachment disorganization, 312
attachment styles, 730, 997
attention, 256
    aggression and influences on, 817–18
    amygdala and, 75
    anterior cingulate cortex and, 10–11, 12
    anxiety disorders and, 1110

in appraisal process, 574, 576–77, 586, 588, 689–90
cognition and, 276–77, 565, 666, 977–82
in coping, 714–15
divided, 649
dysregulatory psychopathology and, 921–26
emotional memory and, 565, 644, 645
emotional reactivity individual differences and, 681, 682, 684, 687, 689–94
emotion processing and, 906–7, 1050
emotion regulation and, 649–50
fear-relevant stimuli and, 260
infants and, 354, 364
information processing paradigm, 661, 681
mood and, 711, 818
other-related, 997
preattentive emotion activation, 262–65
priming of, 662–63, 1110
psychopathy issues, 910–11, 914, 916–19
P3 wave modulation and, 205
refocusing of, 132
response modulation issues, 905, 907–8, 916–17, 919, 921–26
selective. See selective attention
selective information processing and, 664
self-focused, 994, 995–96, 1001
threat imminence and, 259, 269, 286, 649
attentional bias, 277, 977
    anxiety and depression and, 977–82, 989, 990
    for threat, 264, 668, 692–94
attentional control, 693–94
attentional processing, 679
attentional style, 703
attention deficit hyperactivity disorder, 304, 312, 315, 905, 951
attention deployment, 710
attention-orienting task. See cue-target paradigm
attention/rejection concept, 714
attitude-cognitive consistency, 754, 767n.2
attitudes, 750, 752–67
    affect infusion model, 566, 611–13, 759, 764–65, 766
    affect's impact on, 566, 596–613, 752–55
    bases of, 753–56, 757, 766, 767nn.1, 2
    behavior link, 610–11, 752–55
    changes in, 756–61, 766
    cognitive basis of, 752, 753–55
    contemporary cognitive theories, 599–602
    correction of, 761–63, 764, 765, 766

emotional factors in, 752–67
empirical study findings, 602–9
expectancy-value theories of, 757, 760
persistence and resistance of, 755–56, 766
research history overview, 597–99
structure of, 752–56, 767n.1
theory overviews, 599–602, 763–66
tripartite theory of, 752–53
attractiveness, emotional, 488–89
attributional style, 688, 737, 997–99, 1001
attribution theory of emotion, 227, 580, 797–98, 816
audience, arts and, 483, 484, 498
auditory cortex, 53–55, 57–59, 102, 474, 1106
auditory hallucinations, 900
auditory signaling, 462–63
auditory stimulation, 13, 68, 70–71, 937
auditory thalamus, 53, 58, 1106
Augustine, Saint, 504
Austen, Jane, 491, 497
autism, 306, 311, 423, 899, 903
affiliation and, 902, 1010, 1017–18
autobiographical memory, 679, 735, 983–87
automatic activation, 690–91, 692, 694
automatic emotion processing, 648, 649, 651, 654, 669, 670, 685
appraisal and, 710
response modulation and, 905–7, 908, 909
automatic information processing, 565, 665, 666, 667
automatic negative thoughts, 689
Automatic Thoughts Questionnaire, 991
autonomic balance, 699
autonomic brainstem motor nuclei, 11
autonomic ganglia, 154, 155, 160–64. See also specific types
Autonomic Lability Score, 246–47
autonomic nervous system, 118, 133–34, 1033
affect systems and, 377–78
allostatic load and, 1093
anterior cingulate cortex and, 11, 119
anxiety neurobehavioral models, 1105–13
appraisal and, 378, 584, 586, 684
arousal of and interpersonal relationships, 826
body protection and, 170–77, 222n.2
brain's coordination of, 135–77
central nervous system and, 4, 136, 137, 143, 144, 154, 164, 169–70, 458, 1074, 1106–7
Darwin's direct action principle and, 458
definition of, 137–38
emergency reaction and, 1049

emotion motivational organization and, 187–207, 228–29
emotion self-perception and, 567
emotion suppression's impact on, 1050
evolutionary perspectives on, 213, 256–71
expression and experience of emotion and, 73, 175–77
facial expression and, 417, 423–24
functional anatomy of, 137–43
function theories, 149–54
individual differences in, 134, 699, 702–3
peripheral pathway functional organization, 154–64, 173–74
prefrontal cortex damage and, 29
spinal and supraspinal pathway control, 164–70
stress and, 1073, 1118, 1125
visceral afferent neurons, 143–49, 155–56, 165, 166, 1107, 1112
vocal expression and, 434
See also subjective-autonomic response dissociation
autonomic psychophysiology, 131–34, 377–78
amygdala and, 82
autonomic response automaticity, 256–71
autonomic specificity, 132–33, 212–22
brain's coordinating role of, 135–77
emotion functions and tasks, 131–33
emotion motivational organization, 187–207, 228–29
emotion regulation and, 6
evolutionary perspectives on, 256–71
future research considerations, 133–34
methodological considerations, 216–20, 225–50
new concepts in, 133
selective attention modulation, 276–90
autonomic specificity, 132–33, 212–22
autonomy
as depression risk factor, 992
emotion regulation issues and, 363
ethics of, 858, 875, 876
toddlers and, 357
well-being and, 734
Averill, J. R., 485, 487, 489
aversion, 577, 685
aversive complex stimuli, 13
aversive emotion-related information, 699
aversive learning, 99, 100, 104, 105, 1110
aversive motivational system, 188–89, 190
aversive motives, 579
aversive stimuli, 74, 714–16, 806–10
avoidance, 133, 840
anxiety disorders and, 963, 970, 990, 995
in appraisal process, 577, 579

attentional disengagement and, 282, 285–87, 288f, 289
attentional style and, 703
behavioral inhibition and, 327, 994–95
cognitive. See cognitive avoidance
cultural models of, 878–79, 883–84
of danger, 327, 775
emotional, 581
emotional reactivity and, 683, 684, 693
emotion tasks and, 132
evolutionary issues in, 257
individual differences in, 706–7
inhibitory learning and, 99–104
pain recall and, 653
personality development issues and, 730
shame and, 792
avoidance of harm, 489
avoidant coping, 679, 712, 714–19, 1096
awareness, altered states of, 654
Awareness of Autonomic Activity scale, 1066
awe, 848, 862–64, 1087
Awlad 'Ali Bedouins, 872, 883, 884
Ax, A. F., 212, 213, 218, 220
Aylward, E. H., 965

**B**

babbling, 461, 475, 544
animal-human parallels, 470, 471–72, 476
babies. See infants; toddlers
baboons, 470
baby schema, 489
Bach, Carl Philipp Emanuel, 504
"back channel" facial expressions, 540
backward masking, 263–64, 265
Baddeley, A., 663
Bain, Alexander, 326
Baker, Simon C., 120, 948
Baker-Shenk, C., 546
Balaban, M. T., 203
balance, as cultural goal, 882
Baldwin, D., 335
Baldwin, M. W., 997
Balinese, 878, 879, 883, 884
Bamberg, M., 548, 549
Bandler, R., 172
Bandura, Albert, 581, 730, 739, 999, 1000
Bannister, R., 137
Banse, R., 440, 441, 443, 444, 445, 446
Barbaranelli, C., 999
Barchas, J. D., 469
Bard, Philip, 151, 900
bared-teeth display, 464
Bargh, J. A., 996
Barlow, D. H., 631, 686, 779, 999
Barnard, P. J., 576

Barnes, C. D., 137
Baron, J., 665
Baron, R. A., 633, 806, 807, 809, 819n.7
Barrett, K., 295
Barrett, L., 1084, 1093
Barrett, L. F., 829
Barriga, A. Q., 819n.1
Barron, F., 1065
Bartha, R., 966
Barthes, R., 484
Bartlett, F. C., 485, 489
Barton, A., 524
Bartsch, K., 336, 339, 343
basal forebrain, 73, 75, 85, 102, 109
    cholinergic system and, 1108–13
    emotion evaluation studies and, 937,
        938–39
    emotion induction study findings, 947
    neuroimaging studies of, 953
basal ganglia, 73, 85
    automatic emotion processing role of,
        648
    behavioral approach system and, 327
    damage to, 31, 648
    depression and, 932
    emotion induction study findings, 945,
        947
    facial expression and, 423
    language role of, 542
    memory and, 75, 648, 651, 654
    mood disorders and, 932
basal nuclei (amygdala), 900
basal physiological states, 1049
bases of attitudes, 753–56, 757, 766,
    767nn.1, 2
basic emotions, 68, 175–77, 261, 539, 573,
    1093
    affect programs and, 506
    appraisal patterns and, 709, 710
    autonomic specificity issues and, 215
    in categorical emotion theories, 574
    cultural issues and, 68, 847, 848
    facial expression and, 415–16, 435
    health-related issues and, 1083–84,
        1087
    induction nonselectivity and, 228
    infants and, 333
    lexical emotion encoding of, 541
    moral emotion issues and, 855, 862–63
    musical expression of, 526–29
    in Oatley and Johnson-Laird's emotion
        theory, 669
    research variables and, 235
    vocal expression and, 435, 441, 448,
        507
    See also specific emotions
basolateral amygdala complex, 97–105,
    109, 900
basolateral nuclei, 56
Batel, G., 515

Bateson, Gregory, 747
Batra, R., 755
Batson, C. D., 788, 830
Bauers, K. A., 469
Bauhaus, 484
Baumeister, R. F., 712, 782, 831, 844, 856,
    861
Baumgarten-Tramer, F., 863
Bayart, F. E. S., 469
Bayley, Nancy, 304, 349
Baylis, J. R., 471, 474
Bayon, C., 737
Beauregard, Mario, 120, 938, 947
beauty
    art and, 486, 489, 494
    awe of, 863
    moral, 864
    perception of, 569
Beauvois, M.-F., 664
Bechara, Antoine, 29, 84, 118, 634
Beck, A. T., 689, 982, 989, 990–91, 992,
    997, 1000
Beck Anxiety Inventory, 982
Beck Depression Inventory, 982, 1059
Becker muscular dystrophy, 308
bed nucleus, stria terminalis, 901, 1113
Beer, Jennifer, 412, 415–27
bees, 457
Beethoven, Ludwig van, 505
behavior
    affect's impact on, 596, 843
    allostasis, allostatic load, and, 1119–21,
        1127, 1130
    amygdala role in, 74
    antisocial, 30, 344, 750, 804–19
    approach-avoidance effects on, 327, 994–
        95
    attitude and, 752, 753, 754–55
    consummatory, 755
    convention-violating, 819n.2, 860
    cultural perspectives on, 878–80
    defensive. See defense reaction; defense
        systems; defense response
    delinquent, 811, 812, 813, 819n.1
    emotional expressivity and, 705–6
    emotion as organizer of, 677
    emotion regulation issues and, 362–63,
        649–50
    emotion tasks and, 132
    genetic factors in, 727–29
    goal-directed, 727, 905, 912, 919–20,
        925, 994–95
    implicit aspects of, 5
    infant predispositions, 362, 729, 789
    instrumental, 755
    intentional, 334, 354, 425, 875
    prosocial. See prosocial behavior
    selective attention modulation and, 276–
        90
    self-destructive, 635

self-referential, 774
    sexual. See sexual behavior
    social. See social behavior
    socially inappropriate, 648, 818
    territorial, 462, 472, 473, 1014
    ventromedial frontal lobe damage and,
        83
Behavioral Activation Scale, 701
behavioral activation system, 682, 685,
    687, 688
behavioral approach system, 327, 738
behavioral decision theory, 619
behavioral genetics, 301–10, 312–15, 355,
    727–29
behavioral inhibition, 133, 298, 354, 356
    avoidance goals and, 327, 994–95
    genetic factors in, 305–6, 328
    prefrontal cortex and, 9, 17, 354
    temperament and, 296, 305–6, 320–31,
        728, 729, 933
Behavioral Inhibition Scale, 701
behavioral inhibition system, 327, 683–85,
    687, 688, 1110
behavioral self-blame, 780
behavior-genetic research paradigm, 300–
    301, 307
behaviorism, 597, 598, 774, 839. See also
    classical conditioning; conditioning;
    fear conditioning
belief disconfirmation, 609
beliefs, 726, 753, 892
Belknap, J. K., 313
Bell, P. A., 807, 809, 819n.4
Bench, C. J., 121
beneceptive valenced systems, 841
Benestad, F., 530n.1
benevolence, 384–86
Benkelfat, C., 971
Bentham, Jeremy, 840, 892
benzodiazepine receptor agonists, 1108–
    10
benzodiazepines, 36, 39, 97, 226, 950,
    951, 964
benzodiazepine system, 971, 972, 1017
bereavement, 707, 848
Berkowitz, Leonard, 226, 599, 601, 750,
    762, 804–19
Berlin, B., 541
Berlin, Isaiah, 483–84
Berlioz, Hector, 505
Berlyne, D. E., 488, 489, 577, 685, 687
Berman, R., 549
Bernard, Claude, 149, 1049
Berntson, Gary G., 189, 260, 378, 465,
    1049, 1105–13
Berridge, Kent C., 4, 25–43, 588, 840
Berry, M., 630
Berscheid, E., 825–26, 827, 828, 832, 833
betrayal, 857
bias, in memory recall, 652, 653

bias signals, 9, 17
Biber, D., 541
bicuculline, 96
Biek, M., 755
bilateral temporal lobe resection, 931
bile (humor), 325, 326, 933
binge eating, 782
biological approaches, to individual
    differences, 699–702, 719
Biondi, F., 970
biopsychosocial illness model, 1088, 1094
bipolar disorder, 14, 16, 899, 900
    genetic factors, 315
    incidence of, 903
    neurobiological aspects, 1024, 1027,
        1028, 1034
Birbaumer, N., 205, 969
Birch, K., 830
birds, 459, 461, 462, 465–66, 471, 472,
    474
    affiliative behavior, 1011
    schematic patterns and, 489
Birdwhistell, R. L., 419
Birnbaum, D., 611
birth. See parturition
Bisaga, A., 970
biting behavior, 435
bitter (taste), 577
black bile (humor), 325, 326, 933
bladder, need to empty, 841
bladder ganglia, 162
Blair, R. J. R., 914, 915
Blake, William, 493
blame, 709, 780, 816, 818
Blanchard, D. C., 683
Blanchard, R. J., 683
Blascovich, J., 238
Blau, J. R., 812
Blau, P. M., 812
blending emotions, 529
Bless, H., 602, 629, 760, 765, 766
Blessing, W. W., 137
blindness, 902
blink reflex, 323–24. See also startle reflex
Block, J., 993, 1088
Block, R., 806
Blood, Anne, 938
blood
    as bodily humor, 325, 326, 932–33
    depression studies, 1023, 1025–30
blood-brain barrier, 1026, 1027, 1047,
    1127
blood feuds, 856
blood-oxygenation-level-dependent signal
    changes, 964
Blount, B. G., 469
Bluck, S., 735
Blumberg, E., 1057
Blumberg, M. S., 457, 458
blushing, 424, 425

Boden, J. M., 712
Bodenhausen, G. V., 606, 629, 630, 636n.4
bodily responses, emotion and, 187
body posture
    animal emotional expression and, 458
    communicative function of, 747
    emotion induction and, 226
    emotion-typical action tendencies and,
        380
    infant responsiveness to, 335
    signed languages and, 537, 542, 551
    universality in emotion expression of,
        871
body type, temperament and, 326
Bolero (Ravel), 515
Boles, T. L., 624
Bolles, R. C., 259
Bolte, M. C., 1000
Bonanno, G. A., 707
Bond, R. N., 445
bonding. See attachment; pair bonding
bonobos, 862
Bonte, F. J., 970
Book of Rites (Chinese text), 385
border collies, 471
borderline personality disorder, 14, 899
boredom, 438–40, 446
Borgida, E., 754
Borod, J. C., 542, 543
Bosse, R., 737
Botticelli, Sandro, 493–94
bottom-up information processing, 666–
    67, 681
    neurobehavioral systems and, 1105,
        1107, 1108, 1110–13
Bouchard, B., 520
Bower, G. H., 198, 599, 667–68, 679, 690,
    711, 982, 989
Bowlby, J., 489, 730
Boyd, J. H., 903
Boysen, S. T., 260, 465
Bradley, B. P., 264, 986, 1001nn.2, 4
Bradley, M. M., 189, 192, 194, 200, 203,
    205, 259, 645, 914, 915, 918
bradycardia, fear-related, 258–59
bradykinin, 174
Brahmins, 847
brain, 132, 134, 377, 678, 844
    aging of, 1129
    allostasis and allostatic load, 1124–28,
        1130–31
    autonomic nervous system
        coordination, 135–77
    behavioral inhibition and, 329, 356
    callosal white matter, 68
    circuitry of emotion, 9–18
    emotional reactivity individual
        differences and, 679, 684
    encephalization of, 41–42, 43, 849
    facial expressions and, 417, 422–23, 543

frontal asymmetry, 700–701, 719, 932,
    1090–92
hemisphere specialization, 31, 37–38,
    450, 729
infant functioning and, 354, 355–56,
    366
left hemisphere, 68, 71, 73, 422–23, 449–
    50, 542, 729, 941
memory storage and retrieval, 565, 646–
    49, 651, 654–55
modular organization of, 664
psychopathology and, 899–902
repeated transcranial magnetic
    stimulation and, 901
right hemisphere, 67–73, 87, 417, 422,
    449–50, 542–43, 647, 703, 729, 931,
    941
specificity research and, 222
spoken language role of, 542–43
synaptic cleft, 1022
in temperament concept history, 326,
    327
traumatic injury to, 932
tumors of, 932
vocal expression and, 449–50
See also affective neuroscience;
    cognition; neuroimaging; specific
    components
brain, emotional
    human vs. animal, 4, 25–43
    limbic system as, 27
brain atlas analysis, 934, 936–41, 943,
    945, 947, 948, 952, 954
brain damage studies, 26, 41, 66–87
brain imaging. See neuroimaging
brain manipulation techniques, 26–27
brain stem, 25, 36–37, 39, 42, 85, 118,
    1106
    acoustic startle response and, 199, 329
    anxiety disorders and, 972
    autonomic nervous system and, 140,
        149, 150t, 154, 155, 163, 164, 166–70,
        174–75, 1107–8, 1111
    depression and, 1029
    emotional systems and, 682, 685, 933
    emotion induction study findings on,
        945, 947
    neural substrates of affect and, 930–31,
        933
    panic disorder and, 970, 972
    reactivity of children and, 328
    temperament neuroimaging research
        and, 954
    visceral afferent neurons and, 143, 144,
        146
    vocal expression and, 449
brain stimulation, 572, 588
Brandt, C. A., 971
Braque, Georges, 484
Bratslavsky, E., 844

Braudel, F., 496
Braungart, J. M., 305
Brazelton, T. Berry, 350
breast cancer. *See* cancer
Breckler, S. J., 755
Breimer, N., 716
Breiter, Hans, 934, 936, 952
Bremner, J. D., 967, 968
Bremner, J. G., 362–64
Breton, G., 970
Brewin, C. R., 984
Bridges, Katherine, 349
Briggs, J. L., 568, 883
Brissette, Ian, 750, 824–33
British Civil Service, 1130
Brittlebank, A. D., 984
Broadbent, D. E., 565, 661
broadcast transmission, spoken language, 537
Broca, Paul, 27, 931
Broca's area, 68, 449, 900, 954
    panic disorder and, 971
    posttraumatic stress syndrome and, 967, 968
Brodmann's area 9, 10, 117, 940
Brody, A. L., 965–66
"Brokeback Mountain" (Proulx), 498, 499
Bromberger, J. T., 737
Brooks, D. J., 954
Brooks-Gunn, J., 353
Brothers, L., 474
Brown, Capability, 489
Brown, G. P., 993
Brown, J. D., 603
Brown, J. R., 338, 339
Brown, J. S., 199
Brown, R., 514, 529
Brown, S., 931
Brown, T. A., 686
brown adipose tissue, 458
brows, facial expression and, 417, 540, 543
Brügner, G., 702
Bruner, J. S., 416, 497
Brunswik, E., 507
Brunswikian lens model, 433, 434*f*, 442, 443, 446, 451
    musical performance and, 507–8, 527
Bryant, J., 553, 711
Bucan, M., 313
Buchsbaum, M. S., 124
Buck, R., 705
Buckley, T., 830
Bucy, P. C., 32, 75, 931
Buddhism, 846
Bugental, D. E., 553
Bühler, K., 446
Bühler, Millicent, 349

Bunge, S. A., 649
Buonocore, Michael, 937
bupropion, 1032
Burgess, S. L., 713
*burlesco* (musical direction), 504
Burn, D. J., 954
Burns, L. R., 716
Burns, T., 649
Burr, Aaron, 402
Bushnell, M. C., 119
business. *See* workplace
Buss, A. H., 327
Butler, G., 988, 996
Byrne, A., 986, 988
Byrne, D., 598, 600, 604, 714, 806, 1065, 1070

## C

Cabanac, Michel, 34, 842
Cacioppo, John T., 189, 190, 195, 378, 487, 1047–50, 1105–13
CAD-triad hypothesis, 858
caffeine, 950
Cahill, Larry, 4, 93–109, 952, 953
Caine and Foulds Hostility and Direction of Hostility, 1067
calcarine, 948
California, 367n.1
California mouse, 473
California Psychological Inventory, 732
Calkins, S. D., 320
callosal white matter, 68
Cameron, James, 498
Cameron, P., 733
Campbell, I. G., 514
Campos, J. J., 295, 321, 353, 354, 367n.6, 543, 677
Camras, L. A., 418
Canada, 886
cancer, 1048, 1050, 1053–75, 1087, 1098
Canli, Turhan, 108, 940
Cannon, Walter Bradford, 3, 133, 138, 149–52, 153, 174, 175–76, 177, 212, 566, 702, 900, 931, 1049, 1089
CA1 hippocampus subfield, 900
capacity, as cognitive resource, 662–64, 667, 671
capital punishment, 817
Caplan, N., 811, 820n.14
Caprara, G. V., 999
*capriccioso* (musical direction), 504
Capurso, A., 508
carbachol, 1109
carbon dioxide, 970, 972
carbon-11-labeled flumazenil, 971
cardiac-somatic coupling hypothesis, 258, 259
cardiomotor neurons, 166–70

cardiovascular system, 1118
    allostatic load and, 1093, 1123, 1124
    anger arousal and, 236
    anxiety disorder impact on, 1107
    autonomic nervous system and, 166–71, 257, 258, 417, 424
    behavioral inhibitions and, 328
    circadian rhythm and, 702
    defense vs. orienting responses, 287–88
    diseases of, 132, 150, 306, 311, 1048, 1123, 1124, 1129–31
    emotional response research findings on, 188, 193
    emotion suppression impact on, 216, 881
    evolutionary development of, 258
    fear's impact on, 188, 258–59, 267
    interoceptive information and, 686
    research variables, 236–38
    startle reflex and, 200, 323
    stress's impact on, 1049, 1084, 1126
card-playing tasks, 911–12
caregivers
    children's communication with, 332, 334–35, 358
    emotion coregulation and, 395
    emotion regulation inputs by, 363–66
    gene-environment correlations and, 307
    ideal/ought self development role of, 688
    ill health and, 1047
    infants and, 296, 304, 312, 332, 333, 347–50, 355–58, 363–66, 472
    personality development role of, 730–31
    *See also* parent-child relationship
Carlo, G., 795
Carlsmith, J. M., 819n.7
Carlson, M., 797
Carolina wrens, 461
carotid glomeruli, 148
Carr, W. J., 472
Carroll, D., 1086
Carstensen, L. L., 297, 679, 726–39
Carver, C. S., 287, 711, 779, 782, 1084
"Cask of Amontillado, The" (Poe), 490
Caspi, A., 366, 728
Cassatt, Mary, 494
Cassiday, K. L., 979
Cassileth, B. R., 738, 1062, 1069
caste system, 857, 880
Castle Goring (England), 482, 490
Castro, N. A., 475
catastrophizing, 689
catecholamines, 152, 238, 258, 1074, 1117
    allostasis, allostatic load, and, 1118, 1121, 1125–27, 1129
    depression and, 1021–22, 1024–25
    memory and, 105–6
    *See also specific types*
categorical information processing, 629
categorical judgments, 416, 422

categorical model of emotion, 233, 235, 574, 1086–88
catharsis, 504
Catholic Church, 504
cats, 458, 469, 471, 1010
Caudality Scale, 1065
caudal pontine reticular nucleus, 199, 329
caudal raphe nuclei, 165
caudal ventrolateral medulla, 167
caudate, 945, 948
  phobias and, 969
caudate, left, 938, 940, 942, 943, 954
caudate nucleus, 103, 104t, 118, 965, 966
caudate-putamen, 936, 937
causal locus, self-attributions and, 780
causal studies, of emotion, 39, 42
causation, as appraisal dimension, 580
cave paintings, 493
Cebul, M. S., 473
cellular environment, health and, 1049
cellular studies, animal affiliative behavior, 1016–17, 1019
Center for Epidemiology Studies-Depression, 1055, 1058, 1059
central gray matter, 56, 153, 327, 328, 1111
central nervous system, 5, 327, 378
  affect systems and, 377
  appraisal process role of, 572, 575, 584
  autonomic nervous system and, 4, 136, 137, 143, 144, 154, 164, 169–70, 458, 1074
  Darwin's direct action principle and, 458
  depression and, 1022–36, 1127
  emotion, memory, and, 4, 93–109
  emotional development and, 296
  emotional specificity research on, 222
  emotion expression and, 411, 747
  emotion perception and, 413
  facial expression and, 417, 422–23
  immune system and, 1074
  information processing and, 635
  organization of, 1106–7
  personality processes and, 678
central self-judgments, 603, 604
centroids, 248–49
cerebellar vermis, 938, 947
cerebellum
  animal vocalizations and, 473
  emotion induction study findings on, 940, 941, 945, 947, 948, 951
  panic disorder and, 971
  psychopathology issues, 901
  temperament neuroimaging research, 954
cerebral blood flow
  anxiety disorders and, 972
  neural substrates of affect and, 933–34, 937, 938, 940, 941, 943, 945–52, 954

panic disorder and, 970–71
phobias and, 969
posttraumatic stress syndrome and, 967–68
cerebral cortex, 572, 1105–8, 1111, 1126
cerebral glucose metabolism, 933, 950–53
cerebral palsy, 902
cerebrospinal fluid, 1014, 1017, 1022, 1027–28, 1030, 1032–34
cerebrum, 969
certainty
  as appraisal dimension, 573, 574, 575, 579, 687, 689
  decision making and, 629–30, 631
certainty of punishment, as crime deterrent, 817
Cervone, D., 603
Cesaro, P., 118
cetaceans, 41
c-Fos expression, 27, 28, 31, 103
Chaiken, S., 755
Chaiyasit, W., 322
challenge appraisals, 238
Challenging Situation Task, 880
change
  appraisal of, 687
  in attitude, 756–61
  as developmental science concern, 298–99
  remembered affect and, 842
  stability of, 708
characterological self-blame, 780
Charles, S. T., 726–39
Chauvet, France, 493
Cheang, M., 1071
cheerfulness, 306, 880
chemical signaling, 462–63, 472–73, 475, 476
Chen, R., 387
Cheney, D. L., 474, 475
Cheng, M.-F., 471
Cherny, S. S., 309
Chesney, G. L., 205
Chess, Stella, 321, 322, 326–27, 727
Chevalier-Skolnikoff, S., 463
Chhetri-Brahmins, 880–81, 882, 883
ch'i (Chinese concept), 326
"chickening out" phenomenon, 631
child abuse, 813, 967, 1129–30, 1131
children
  appraisal processes of, 583, 732–33
  autobiographical memories of, 735
  behavioral inhibition in, 305–6, 327–30, 354, 356, 729
  conduct disorder and, 309, 315
  deaf, 297
  depression in, 315
  depression transmission to, 738
  "difficult" vs. "easy," 327
  dispositional emotionality and, 795–96

economic status of, 1094, 1129–30
emotional development and, 332–44
emotional understanding development and, 732–33
empathy and, 336, 364, 788–91
filial piety and, 385, 386, 388, 400, 402
gene-environment correlation and, 307
guilt and, 750, 792–93
health issues and, 1085
high- vs. low-reactive, 320–21, 328–30
intentional behavior by, 334, 354, 425
language and emotion and, 297
language development and, 332, 336, 338, 354, 536, 543–53
moral development and, 852, 865
music perception and, 515, 524–25, 527, 529
parental emotional style and, 1098
parental relationship with. See parent-child relationship
personality development and, 297, 304, 727–31, 735
prosocial behavior development of, 297, 353, 358, 363, 545, 780, 787–98, 861
in psychodynamic theory, 1021
resilience of, 1096
self-report research and, 306, 315
self's development and, 332, 338, 353, 356, 357, 363–64, 777
shame and, 792–93
sign language acquisition by, 536, 543, 544–47, 549–51
social relationships and, 296, 332–44, 347, 353, 354, 355, 357, 360–61
temperament of, 296, 315, 320–23, 326–27, 347–48, 350, 353, 736
See also adolescents; infants; toddlers
Children's Behavior Questionnaire, 303, 304
child study centers, 349
chimpanzees, 463–64, 465, 470, 773, 774, 862
China, 326
  language and, 448–49, 538
  pride, shame, and guilt development in, 297, 375–403
chirp vocalizations, 475
chlordiazepoxide, 1108
chlorpromazine, 1021
choleric temperament, 326, 698, 933
Chomsky, N., 543
Chovil, N., 540, 550
Christal, R. E., 677
Christianity, music's role in, 504
Christianson, S.-A., 105, 649
Chrysoloras, Manuel, 483
Chua, P. M., 119
Chugani, H. T., 355
Church, M. A., 995
Cialdini, R. B., 797

Cicchetti, Dante, 360

cigarette smoke, 810. *See also* smoking

cinema. *See* films

cingulate cortex, 27, 37, 39, 42, 649, 729
  auditory emotion evaluation studies of, 938
  depression and, 121
  emotion-induction study findings on, 951
  facial expression and, 30–31, 423
  hemisphere specialization theories and, 38
  reactivity of children and, 328
  temperament neuroimaging research on, 954
  *See also* anterior cingulate cortex

cingulate gyrus, 901

Cioffi, D., 703

circadian rhythm, 701–2, 1117–18, 1119, 1121, 1131

citalopram, 1022

city planning, 496

civilization disorders, 169

c-jun expression, 27

Clark, D. A., 689, 992

Clark, D. M., 984

Clark, F., 915

Clark, L. A., 677, 705, 992

Clark, Margaret S., 750, 824–33

classical conditioning, 53f, 280, 686, 842
  attitude change and, 759, 764
  emotion elicitation and, 564, 775
  fear and, 13, 32, 52, 256, 265, 564
  *See also* fear conditioning

claustrum, 971

Cleckley, Hervey, 909

clenbuterol, 95, 97, 98

climate, as aggression instigator, 807–10, 819–20nn.4, 7, 8

clinical depression. *See* depression

clinical group differences, 298

clinical medicine, 1088–89

clinical problems. *See* emotional disorders

clinical psychology, 451

clomipramine, 965, 1030

clonidine, 96, 1022, 1026, 1034

Cloninger, C. Robert, 327, 737, 933, 953, 954

Clore, G. L., 598, 600, 601, 604, 608, 628, 632, 760, 761, 765–66

closeness, in interpersonal relationships, 824–33

cluster analysis, 442, 515, 528

Clynes, M., 506, 508, 524

cocaine, 28, 30, 33–35, 952

cochlear root neurons, 199

Cochran, S., 810, 816

coding system, facial expression as, 350, 366, 416, 417, 424

Coe, C. L., 469, 995, 1074

Cofer, L. F., 702

cognition, 565–66
  affect's decision-making role in, 619–36
  affect's impact on attitudes and judgments in, 596–613
  affect state's impact on, 379
  aggression role of, 814–16, 817, 819
  animal communication and, 459, 475
  anxiety disorders and, 277, 565, 666, 979, 980, 982, 1110
  appraisal processes and, 377, 572–89, 977, 1047, 1049, 1050
  attention and, 276–77, 565, 977–82
  attitude and, 752, 753–57, 761
  cholinergic modulation of, 75
  differential emotions theory and, 733
  emotional development and, 295, 296, 332, 338–39, 343, 545, 792
  emotional disorders and, 564–65, 976–1001
  emotional influences on, 690–94
  emotional reactivity individual differences in, 679, 681, 682, 684–85, 687–94
  emotion and, 5, 39, 41–43, 215, 222n.3, 563–69, 976–77, 989
  emotion induction via, 226–27
  emotion information processing and, 565, 661–71, 906, 1050
  emotion regulation and, 361
  as empathy component, 787
  fear module activation and, 256, 269–70, 271
  "frozen" structures, 568–69
  goal-directed, 994–95
  information processing paradigm in, 662–64, 668–69, 671
  lesion study concerns and, 66–67
  mood and, 566, 977
  morality and, 852, 865
  need for, 766
  perception and, 565, 566–67
  Plato's concept of, 563
  psychopathology issues and, 899, 900, 901, 908, 913, 977
  recursive processes in, 567–68
  selfhood and, 356, 792774
  sympathy and, 788
  violence role of, 806
  *See also* emotional cognition; social cognition

cognitive activation studies, 122–24, 965, 966, 968

cognitive-affective personality system, 699, 708–9

cognitive-appraisal theories of emotion, 622, 977

cognitive avoidance, 282, 285–89, 703, 706–7, 714–19

cognitive behavior therapy, 901, 966, 977, 1071, 1072, 1075

cognitive capacity, 613

cognitive change, emotion regulation and, 710

cognitive coping, 713

cognitive dissonance, 609, 761, 778

cognitive incongruity, 714

cognitive interference, 277, 285, 287, 289
  anxiety disorders and depression and, 979, 980, 982

cognitive interrupts, emotions as, 635

cognitive lateralization hypothesis, 37

cognitive-learning model of psychotherapy, 1000

cognitive loop hypothesis, 711–12

cognitive-motivational-relational theory, 367n.6

cognitive-neoassociationistic aggression model, 814–16, 817, 819

cognitive neuropsychology, 664

cognitive neuroscience, 8, 662
  emotional memory and, 643–55

*Cognitive Neurosciences, The* (Gazzaniga), 565

cognitive-perceptual model of somatic interpretation, 703

cognitive psychology, 589, 774
  information processing paradigm and, 661–62, 666, 671

*Cognitive Psychology* (Neisser), 661

cognitive reframing, 736

cognitive responses, 767n.3

cognitive subdivision, 11–12

cognitive theory of depression, 990–91, 992

cognitive therapy, 662, 902

cognitive tuning, 602, 760–61

Cohen, D., 807

Cohen, D. J., 818

Cohen, J. D., 9, 11

Cohen, R. A., 118

Cohen, S., 1074

Cohn, E. G., 808–9, 819–20n.8

cold anger, 440, 444

"cold" cognition, 565

Cole, P. M., 880

Coleman, Alice, 496, 497

Coleridge, Samuel Taylor, 482, 483, 491, 499

Colishaw, G., 470

collative properties, 488, 685

collectivism, 402, 880

Collingwood, R. G., 484–85, 490

Collins, P. F., 683

colon, need to empty, 841

color naming interference task. *See* Stroop paradigm

Columbine High School shootings (1999), 812

coma, 41
commissural pathway (hippocampus), 900
commitment problems, 893–96
communal relationships, 750, 825, 827–33, 861, 862
communal strength of relationships, 825, 827–29
communication
  affective influences on, 610
  affect's adaptive value and, 843
  animals and, 457–76
  art as, 481, 490
  autism and, 902, 1017
  between children and caregivers, 332, 334–35, 358, 364, 472
  cultural models and, 879
  Darwin's direct action principle and, 358
  depression therapeutic treatments and, 901
  about emotion, 336, 338, 339, 341, 342
  emotion as, 297, 332–33, 747, 828, 831, 832
  of emotions, 187, 214, 507, 705
  essentic forms and, 506
  facial expression as, 418, 425, 537, 539–41, 543, 550–51
  infant gestural, 354
  language acquisition and, 535–36, 543–47
  linguistic, 535–53
  musical performance as, 507–8, 525–27
  nonlinguistic, 536, 538–43, 552, 553
  nonverbal. See nonverbal communication
  paralinguistic, 536, 539, 548, 549–50, 553
  persuasive, 755–60, 766, 767n.3
  See also language; signed language; speech
communicative pressure, 339
community, ethics of, 858, 875
comorbid disorders, 684, 688, 1033
  cognitive processing biases and, 982, 985, 987, 998–99
compassion, 830, 831, 845
  as moral emotion, 855, 858, 862, 866
compatibility with standards, 573, 574, 581, 709
competence assessment, decision making and, 566
competition monitoring hypothesis, 11–12
competitive arousal, 30, 35
complex cognitive processing, 566
complex inheritance, 310–12
complexity, appraisal stimuli, 577
compliance, 355, 1063
componential theory
  emotion cultural models, 872–81, 887
  facial expression, 415, 416, 417

component process theory, appraisal and, 582, 709
components system approach. See dynamic component systems approach
compression injuries, 1034
computed axial tomography, 964
computer graphics systems, experimental methods using, 476
conation, 563, 597. See also behavior
conceptual influences, emotion and, 679, 681–82, 684, 686–90, 694
conceptual processing level, appraisal and, 576, 577, 583, 589, 689
concern, 787, 788
concern relevance, in appraisal theory, 574, 578, 687
concerns
  appraisal processes and, 377, 380
  third-party, 856, 858–59
concrete operations, domain-bound, 849
conditional (conditioned) stimuli
  behavioral inhibition system and, 327
  emotional cuing and, 280–82, 284, 285, 286
  fear conditioning and, 52–59, 100, 265–66, 267–69, 644
  feedback during conditioning and, 270, 271
  human startle response studies, 200–201
conditioning, 564
  amygdala damage and, 32
  attitudes, judgments, and, 598–99, 600, 606, 608
  emotional cuing and, 278–85, 289
  emotion biphasic organization and, 189
  shock expectancy, 270–71
  See also classical conditioning; fear conditioning
conduct disorder, 309, 315, 344, 683
confession, 861
Confessions (Augustine), 504
Confessions (Rousseau), 482
confidence, 598
configuration principle, emotion coding in speech and, 447
conflict
  children and, 337, 341, 342, 343, 347, 354, 364
  emotional, 579
  marital, 1085, 1087, 1097
  psychodynamic, 1021
  relational, 1098
conflicting emotions, 529
conflict management, by parents, 736
conflict monitoring, 11–12, 17–18
conformity, cancer patients and, 1055
confrontational defense, 171
Confucianism, 384–88, 393, 402

confusion patterns, vocal expression research, 444–45, 446
connectionist systems, 661, 690, 759
conscience, 693, 731, 792
conscientiousness, 731, 732, 738, 739
conscious memory, 647
consciousness
  affect's adaptive value and, 843
  of appraisal process, 574, 586
  attention and, 692
  development of, 848
  emotion and, 271
conscious processes, 377, 773–75
consequences, decision making and, 566, 620–26, 628, 630, 631, 633–36
consequentialist decision theories, 622–26
consonance, in music, 520, 524
Constable, John, 493
constructed anxiety, 324
constructive memory framework, 646–48
constructive processing, 599–600, 604, 605, 611, 612
constructivist theory, facial expression and, 420–21
consumer psychology, 750
consummatory behavior, 755
contact hypothesis, out-group members and, 606
contact senses, 841
contagion
  emotional, 487, 1047
  psychology of, 845
containment, neurochemical, 1125–27
contamination, negative vs. positive, 864
contempt, 412, 420, 424, 581, 1087
  cultural considerations, 845, 848, 875
  moral emotions and, 855, 856, 858–59, 860, 866, 875
content, social cognition and, 991–93, 996
content analysis, 492
contentment, 862
content-specificity effect, 992
context
  affective experience role of, 679, 1084
  affective style and, 298
  as autonomic psychophysiology, 133–34
  of cultural models, 873, 879, 880, 881, 883, 884–87
  in dynamic component systems, 376
  in dynamic skill theory, 389
  efficacy beliefs and, 999
  as emotional response factor, 189
  emotion expression and, 413
  emotion induction research and, 228, 233, 234f, 241, 242
  emotion regulation and, 364, 366
  as experiment design factor, 241, 242
  psychopathology role of, 901, 920–21, 923, 1084
  in relationships, 824–25, 833

context (*continued*)
  response modulation and, 905, 907, 908, 913, 919, 923–24
  stimulus evaluation check model, 906, 920
  *See also* social context
context conditioning, 1110
  amygdala and, 100–102
  hippocampus's role in, 13, 18, 55, 56, 59, 61
context-inappropriate emotional responding, 13–14, 15, 18, 1084
context-regulation of affect, 13, 15
contexts of practice, 338
continuity, as developmental science concern, 298–99
continuous recording response methodology, 516–17, 518f, 529
Continuous Response Digital Interface, 516
Contrada, R. J., 707
contrapuntal music, 505
control
  anticipatory emotions and, 631, 632
  appraisal theory view of, 574, 576, 580–81, 582, 689, 691, 874–75
  attention and, 693
  children's sense of, 337, 354, 355f, 356, 360, 1098
  Chinese view of, 386
  cultural perspectives on, 846, 874–75, 877–78, 879, 883
  as health factor, 738, 1130
  illusions of, 993
  incidental emotions and, 632, 633
  as memory recall issue, 653
  other-related attention and, 997
  perceived, 999, 1000
  personality development and, 730
  positional vs. personal, 883
  predictive, 781–82
  primary vs. secondary, 877–78
  self-efficacy and, 999–1000
  stimulus evaluation check model, 906, 920
controllability
  future-related cognition and, 999–1000
  as self-attribution aspect, 780
controlled emotion processing, 648–49, 654, 905–9, 921, 923, 924
controlled information processing, 565, 664, 665, 667, 668
controls (experiment design), 241
control theory, 380, 805
convention-violating behavior, 819n.2, 860
convergent validity, 242
cooing
  by birds, 471
  by infants, 333, 334
  by macaques, 468–69, 470, 474

Cook, E. W., III, 203
Cook, M., 465, 988
Cooke, Deryck, 503, 505–6, 508, 523–24
Cooper, J., 761
cooperation, adaptive rationality and, 893–95
cooperativeness, 737
COPE (assessment tool), 714
coping, 132
  active, 259, 1071, 1072
  anterior cingulate cortex and, 119
  as appraisal dimension, 573, 580–81, 584, 688–90
  avoidant, 679, 712, 714–19, 1096
  by cancer patients, 1053–63, 1068, 1071, 1072, 1074, 1075, 1087
  by children, 1085
  cognitive, 713
  defense behaviors and, 258–59
  definitions and conceptions of, 713–14
  dysregulatory psychopathology and, 924–25
  emotional development and, 295, 296
  emotion-focused, 707, 713
  emotion induction research issues and, 227–28
  emotion regulation vs., 713
  as health factor, 727
  individual differences in, 679, 681, 687, 688–90, 693–94, 698–719
  by infants, 350
  passive, 258, 1086
  periaqueductal gray and, 172
  personality issues in, 736–37
  positive emotion role of, 1098
  problem-focused, 713
  with racism, 1086
  repressive, 652–53, 707, 715–18, 1068, 1087
  self-efficacy theory and, 999, 1000
  social support and, 902
  stress and, 713–15, 1098, 1121
  uncertainty-motivated, 713, 715
  vocal expression and, 435
coping modes, 714–19
coping potential, 581, 709
Coplan, R. J., 320
copulation, 1012
copulation calls, 460, 461, 470
Corbusier, Le, Charles-Edward, 484, 495–96
core affect, 1084, 1085
core consciousness, 271
core emotional expressivity, 706
core relational themes, 628, 709, 748
Corley, R., 305, 309
cornered rat phenomenon, 809
coronary artery disease, 306, 311, 417, 1087
coronary heart disease, 132, 1096, 1130

corporal punishment, 386
correlation coefficients, 322
correlation studies, 39, 42
correspondence analysis, 515, 528
corrugator muscle, 192, 193, 265, 435, 582, 587
cortex, 25, 1107
  appraisal process and, 576, 586, 589
  arousal and, 692
  emotional systems and, 682, 685
  emotion motivational organization and, 187–207
  maternally derived genes and, 310
  neural substrates of affect and, 930–31, 933, 943, 951, 953–54
  *See also specific structures*
corticomedial amygdala, 900
corticosteroids, 1072, 1074, 1087
corticosterone, 93, 151, 1011
cortico-striato-thalamic circuits, 964, 965, 966, 972
corticotropin-releasing factor, 902, 1033–34, 1125, 1126, 1127
corticotropin-releasing hormone, 16, 313, 1112
cortisol, 314, 469, 995, 1085, 1087, 1097, 1118
  hippocampus and, 14, 15, 18, 1124
  stress and, 1070, 1073, 1074, 1117, 1120, 1121
  temperament differences and, 729
Cosmides, L., 976
Costa, P. T., 731–32, 733
Costa Rica, 880
cotton-top tamarins, 464, 466–70, 472, 473, 475
counterfactual emotions, 623–24, 626
count-up to shock/noise procedure, 916
Courtauld Emotional Control Scale, 1067, 1068
courtship, animal, 464, 470
Cousins, Norman, 1097
covariation, judgments of, 988–89
covariation accuracy, 702, 703
covariation principle, 447
Covert, M. V., 779
covert-overt continuum, 804, 819n.1
Cox regression analysis, 1057, 1066
Coyle, K., 986
Coyne, J. C., 992
craft, art vs., 484, 485, 490, 492
Craig, A. D., 119
Crane-Ross, D., 819n.2
cranial autonomic outflow, 137
craniosacral system. *See* parasympathetic nervous system
"crankcase-oil problem," 891, 896
*Cratylus* (Plato), 535
craving, 840
Crawley, J. N., 301

creative expression. *See* arts, emotion and the
credit, secondary appraisal and, 709
CRH. *See* corticotropin-releasing hormone
crime, architecture and, 496–97
criminal behavior
  causes of, 805–6, 810–13, 819–20nn.4–8
  psychopathy and, 920
  psychosurgery for, 30
  punishment of, 817
criminal justice system, 817
crises, psychosocial, 736
Crites, S. L., Jr., 754
criticism
  art, 483, 493
  literary, 488, 497
  perception of, 997
crocodiles, 258
cross-fostering studies, 474
Crowder, R. G., 523
cruelty, 857
crying
  animal-human parallels, 470, 476
  cultural perspectives on, 886
  by infants, 333, 334, 349, 354, 544, 552, 730, 748, 789, 828
CSF. *See* cerebrospinal fluid
Csikszentmihalyi, M., 485, 492
Cubells, J. F., 312
cubism, 484
cues
  aggression and, 817–18
  attitudes, judgments, and, 600, 608, 759, 764
  of autonomic activity, 702–3
  memory retrieval and, 651–52
  music performance and, 507–8, 526–27
  response modulation and, 905, 907–8, 909, 912–17, 919, 921–25
  social, 564
  vocal expression and, 433, 442, 445–46, 451
cue-target paradigm, 277–78, 285
cuing, emotional, 278–85, 289, 909
  dysregulatory psychopathology and, 921–25
  psychopaths and, 913–17, 919, 925
"cultural big bang," 773
cultural psychology, 846
cultural relativism, 416
culture
  affect and, 839–41, 845–49
  affect lexicon and, 568
  appraisal and, 577, 579, 583–85, 588, 845, 846, 848, 849, 860, 872, 874–76, 879–80
  attachment patterns and, 730, 886
  autonomic specificity and, 215–16
  basic emotions and, 68, 847, 848
  development of human, 773

disgust and, 857
emotional development and, 296–97, 357
emotional practice and, 871–87
emotion expression and, 411–13, 552, 678, 729, 846, 878–81
emotion families and, 381–83
emotion perception/attribution and, 538
empathy-related responding and, 791–92
as facial expression influence, 539
facial expression universality and, 216, 416, 419–20, 422
facial expression variation and, 420–22
morality and moral emotions and, 386–88, 840, 843, 848, 855–57, 859, 860, 865, 866n.3, 875
musical expression and, 507, 525, 527, 529
personality development and, 730–31
pride, shame, and guilt perspectives and, 297, 375–76, 379t, 381–403
sign language acquisition and, 536
social relationships and, 296, 339, 340, 344
temperament and, 322, 729
vocal expression and, 445, 538
cultures of honor, 807–8, 819nn.5–6, 846–47, 872, 884
culture-specific interpersonal cycles, 886
Cummings, J., 450
cuneus, 945, 948
Cunningham, A. J., 1072
Cupchik, G., 489, 494–95
curiosity, 488, 489, 629
Cushing's disease, 15, 1128
Cuthbert, B. N., 194, 203, 205, 259, 285, 914, 918
cytokines, 173, 1047, 1074, 1121

### D

da Fonseca, N., 118
Dager, S. R., 971
Dalgleish, Tim, 565, 661–71, 986
Daly, K., 806
Damasio, Antonio R., 3, 4, 5, 27, 29, 30, 37, 66–87, 118, 120, 134, 270, 271, 347, 474, 584, 634, 635, 691, 947
Damasio, H., 66–87, 118, 474
Damhuis, I., 792–93
d-amphetamine, 1032
Damrad-Frye, R., 549
dance, 488, 516
danger, 327, 714, 775, 843, 992
Darby, D. G., 68
Darwin, Charles, 131, 151, 176, 233, 257, 333, 349, 411, 414, 415, 419, 435, 446, 457, 458, 463, 475, 481, 485, 486, 492,

535, 609, 636n.2, 747, 775, 839, 847, 854, 857, 871, 892, 931, 1084
date rape, 920
Dattore, P. J., 1065
David, Jacques, 493
Davidson, J. R., 969
Davidson, Richard J., 3–7, 8–19, 31, 37, 38, 296, 320, 329, 354, 356, 677–79, 683, 701, 706, 729, 844, 1084, 1089, 1091
Davies, J. C., 811
Davis, M., 13, 199, 207n.2
Dawson, A. A., 1069
Dawson, G., 354, 355, 356
Deaf community, 297, 503, 537, 539, 543–51
Dean, C., 1061, 1063
Dearing, M. F., 189
Deater-Deckard, K., 306, 308
death, 845, 1047, 1126
  from cancer, 1057–58, 1059, 1062, 1072, 1087
  mortality and, 738–39, 1048, 1050, 1085, 1086, 1093, 1097, 1129–31
  *See also* homicide; suicide
*Death and Life of Great American Cities, The* (Jacobs), 496–97
death penalty, 817
deautomization, of maladaptive behavior, 908, 909, 925
*décalage*, 849
deceit, 843, 849
Deci, E. L., 994
decision making, 117, 563
  affect's role in, 5, 9, 566, 619–36, 843
  emotion benefits and pitfalls in, 633–36
  emotion processing and, 905
  expected emotions and, 566, 620–26, 628, 630, 632, 633–36
  immediate emotions and, 566, 620–21, 625, 626–36
  lesion impact on, 5, 9, 84, 118, 648
  somatic marker hypothesis, 270, 271, 634, 635, 691
  ventromedial frontal lobe and, 83, 84
Declaration of Independence (1776), 481
declarative knowledge, 990, 991, 994, 1000
decoding in vocal expression, 433, 443–46, 450, 451, 538
  musical performance and, 507, 526–27
DeCristofaro, M. T., 970
deductive analysis, 708
deductive reasoning, 84–85
"deep" cognitive processing. *See* complex cognitive processing
defeat reaction, 169, 170
defection, adaptive rationality and, 893–96

defense reaction, 133, 152, 167, 169, 170, 1109
  active and passive responses, 258–59
  aversive motivational system and, 189
  cardiovascular responses, 188, 258–59
  emotional priming and, 198, 206
  evolutionary perspective on, 257–61
  from pain and stress, 171–72
  startle reflex as, 189, 198–205, 206, 259
  threat imminence and, 259, 260f
defense response, 287–89
defense systems, emotional reactivity and, 683, 685, 687, 691
defensive aggression, 683, 684, 685
defensiveness, 1054, 1058, 1063–65, 1092
defensive pessimism, 782
defensive processing, 757
DeFries, J. C., 305, 306, 309
Degas, Edgar, 494
Degos, J. D., 118
degree of relationship interdependence, 825–27, 833
dejection-related emotions, 779, 995
Delacroix, Eugène, 493
de la Torre, S., 462
delay, as decision-making consideration, 566, 619, 622, 624–26
delayed-return environments, 776
deliberation, 633, 635
delinquent behavior, 811, 812, 813, 819n.1
delusional depressives, 1031
dementia, 423, 1033, 1034, 1108, 1113
dendrites, 28, 900
denial, 1091, 1092
  in cancer patients, 1055, 1060, 1061, 1063, 1068–69
Denial of Hysteria Scale, 1065
dense sensor arrays, 195–97
Dent, J., 984
dentate gyrus, 13, 103–4, 1128
dependency, 683, 992
depression, 5, 298, 325, 719, 899
  activation-elaboration model, 990
  activation mechanisms and, 690
  affect-guided anticipation abnormalities and, 9
  allostatic load and, 1127–30
  amygdala and, 15–16, 18, 900, 1127, 1128
  anterior cingulate cortex and, 12, 17–18, 118, 121–25, 1030
  appraisal malfunctioning and, 584
  associative network theory and, 668
  attachment theory and, 997
  attentional biases and, 977, 981–82, 990
  avoidance goals and, 995
  bipolar. See bipolar disorder
  cancer patients and, 1053–63, 1065–66, 1069–72, 1075, 1087, 1098

characterological self-blame and, 780
childhood abuse and, 1129
cingulate cortex and, 30
cognitive interference and, 277
cognitive processing biases and, 977–90
cognitive theory of, 990–91, 992
content-specificity effect and, 992
emotional priming and, 198
emotional reactivity and, 683, 684
emotion expression and, 413
emotion induction study findings on, 947–48, 949
emotion regulation and, 712
evolutionary perspectives on, 977, 990, 992, 1001
facial expression and, 427, 900
frontal brain asymmetry and, 701
genetic factors in, 308, 315, 1029, 1131
hippocampus and, 14, 15, 18, 19, 1128, 1131
hopelessness theory of, 997–99
incidence of, 903
as information-processing factor, 601, 990
judgmental/interpretive biases and, 984, 988–89, 993
maternal transmission of, 738
medial prefrontal cortex and, 4, 117–25
memory biases and, 982–85, 989, 990
mood and, 899, 900, 953, 992
neuroimaging of, 4, 117–25, 1023–25, 1027–32, 1036
pathogenesis theories of, 1021–22
pessimism and, 688, 737, 998
physical health and, 1049, 1050, 1096
predispositions for, 737
prefrontal cortex and, 9–10
pre-goal attainment positive affect and, 6
racism and, 1086
self-schemas and, 650, 652
self view and, 900
serotonin and, 327, 1022, 1023, 1026–31, 1126, 1127
social cognitive biases and, 990–1000
stress and, 1022, 1025, 1033, 1073
stroke linked with, 932
surgical treatments for, 121
therapeutic treatments for, 901, 1021, 1027, 1030–31
vocal expression and, 451
depressive disorders
  allostatic load and, 1124, 1125
  emotion induction study findings on, 943
  mood neuroimaging studies on, 952–53
  neurobiology of, 1021–36
  positive affect loss and, 1010
  See also specific disorders
depressive realism, 124, 993

depressive schemas, 991–92
deprivation, emotional, 902
Depue, R. A., 683
Deputte, B. L., 464
De Raedt, Rudt, 948
de Rivera, J., 380
Derogatis, L. R., 1063
Derousne, J., 664
Derry, P. A., 991–92, 1000
Derryberry, Douglas, 678–79, 681–94
DeRubeis, R. J., 993
Dery, R., 970
Desai, J. R., 194
Descartes, René, 563–64, 572, 596
descriptive perspective, individual differences in, 698–708, 719
deservedness, 581
desipramine, 1025, 1030
desirability, 620, 622, 635, 687, 707
desire, 588, 683
DeSteno, D. A., 604, 763
details, memory of, 644, 650
Deutsch, J. A., 691
development, emotional. See emotional development
developmental behavioral genetics, 309
developmental disorders. See specific disorders
developmental influences, allostatic load and, 1128–29, 1131
developmental instability, 310
developmental science, 297–98
development/mastery goals, 994
Devine, J. A., 812
Devine, P. G., 756
Devous, M. D., 970
de Waal, Frans B. M., 465, 1010
dexamethasone, 98, 104, 1022
dextroamphetamine, 951, 952
Dhammapada (Buddhist text), 846
DHEA, 1073, 1121
diabetes, 1018, 1048, 1120–21, 1129, 1130
Diagnostic and Statistical Manual of Mental Disorders, 1023, 1107
dialects, animal language, 475
Diamond, A., 354, 356
diazepam, 38
Dick, D. M., 728–29
Dickens, Charles, 486
Dickinson, A., 189
DiClemente, R. J., 1061
diencephalon, 152–53
Diener, E., 733
diet, 1118–21
different-experiences hypothesis, 984
differential conditioning tasks, 266–67
Differential Emotions Scale, 235, 705
differential emotions theory, 402, 733
"differential sensitivity" hypothesis, 603
differentiation, cognitive, 993

difficult child, the, 327
diffusion tensor imaging, 6, 17
digestive system, 686
Dighton, K., 986
digital photography, 457
digital speech analysis, 446
dignity, 884
dihydrotestosterone, 1127
DiLalla, L. F., 305
Dill, J. C., 813
Dimberg, U., 259, 264–65, 266, 267, 425
dimensional models of emotion, 216, 233,
    235, 568, 698, 933, 1085
    appraisal theories vs., 574
    emotional reactivity individual
        differences and, 682
    facial expression and, 416, 422–25,
        539
    health issues and, 1086–88
    musical expression and, 515–17, 528
    vocal expression and, 434–35, 441
Dinnerstein, D., 494
direct access processing, 612, 613, 764,
    765
direct action of excited nervous system
    principle, 458
direct activation, 690, 694
directed facial action, 218–20, 226, 424
direct sensory affect, 841, 845–46
disabilities, children with, 344
disappointment, 440, 623, 624
disclosure
    emotional, 750, 1098
    of self, 336, 341
discomfort, 598, 788
discounted utility model, 624–25
discrete emotions, 216, 222, 297, 353,
    411, 539, 541
    development of, 732
    facial expression and, 415, 416, 417,
        422–25
    health and, 1083, 1086–88, 1096, 1099
    shame and embarrassment as, 859
    vocal expression and, 435, 436, 440,
        441, 442, 446, 448
discriminant analysis, 248, 249, 440, 446
discriminant validity, 242
discrimination studies, 443
discursive symbolism, 506
disease
    allostatic load and, 1123–24, 1128–31
    emotion's role in, 1047–48, 1050, 1087
    infectious, 136, 1048
    stress linked with, 1117, 1118
    susceptibility to, 611, 738
    See also health, physical; illness;
        specific diseases
disease studies, 423
disengagement, attentional, 277, 278, 282,
    285–87, 289, 693–94

disgrace, 383
disgust, 5, 257, 353, 412, 686
    animal expression of, 464
    appraisal patterns for, 585
    in associative network theory, 667
    as basic emotion, 68, 176, 333, 669,
        1087
    cardiovascular responses to, 188, 417
    emotional response research findings
        on, 192
    expression of in interpersonal
        relationships, 829
    facial expression and, 417, 420, 423,
        424, 444, 857, 936
    infants and, 780
    journal articles published on, 852, 853t
    moral emotions and, 855, 856, 857–59,
        860, 865, 866, 875
    neural substrates of, 936–37
    personality and, 733
    preadaptation and, 849
    social, 857, 864
    universalist view of, 216
    vocal expression of, 443, 444, 937
dishonor, 400–401
disinhibition, 648, 905
disinterested elicitors, moral emotions,
    853–54, 864
dislikes, 847
displaced aggression, 805, 811, 815,
    820n.9
displacement
    intergroup attitudes and, 606
    as language feature, 536
display rules, 419, 421, 436, 539, 552
    cultural perspectives on, 880
    shyness issues and, 729
displays, emotion expression and, 413–
    14
disposition, emotional
    affective experience and, 737
    affect's adaptive value and, 843
    coping processes and, 679, 714, 715
    health and, 1088, 1092
    individual differences and, 708–9, 1089
    information processing paradigm, 663
    prosocial behavior and, 750, 787, 791–
        96
dispositional affect, 632, 701
dissonance
    cognitive, 609, 761, 778
    in music, 13, 520, 524
dissonance reduction, 892
distaste, 843, 857
distortion
    animal vocal communication and, 462
    self-reports and, 1092
distractability, genetic factors in, 727
distraction, self-awareness and, 782
distractive coping, 690

distress
    animals' expression of, 458, 469, 470,
        1011
    cancer patients and, 1054, 1056, 1060–
        63, 1065, 1068, 1070–72, 1074, 1075
    children's control of, 337
    children's empathetic concern for, 336,
        364, 788–91, 792
    cingulate cortex's role in, 30
    as communication of needs, 828
    denial of, 1091
    facial expression and, 424, 425, 791
    individual differences and, 707
    infants' expression of, 333, 334, 353,
        470, 544, 828, 862
    personal, 750, 788, 790, 791, 793–96
    prosocial behavior and, 750, 788, 790,
        791, 793–96
    from relationship breakup, 827
    social, 395
distress at another's distress, 862
distress-panic system, 683
distrust, 1086
Dittus, W. P. J., 469
diurnal cycle. See circadian rhythm
divided attention, 649
diving response, 169–70, 188, 258
divinity, ethics of, 858, 875
DLPFC, 11–12
DNA, 310, 1016, 1017
Doctrine of the Affections (musical
    theory), 504, 508
dogs, 458, 471
Dolan, Raymond J., 4, 5, 109, 117–25, 269
dolce (musical direction), 504
Dolgin, K., 524
Dollard, J., 811
domestic violence, 805, 806, 808, 810
dominance
    in genetics, 302
    social, 748
    violations of, 623
dominance hierarchies, 260, 464, 859,
    1118, 1127
Donald, M., 487
Donchin, E., 205
Donnerstein, E., 810
Doob, L., 811
DOPAC (metabolite), 1031
dopamine, 35, 42, 105, 125, 933, 1047
    animal behavioral genetics studies of,
        315
    arousal systems and, 692
    automatic emotion processing and, 648
    behavioral approach system and, 327
    depressive disorders and, 1024, 1031–
        32, 1034, 1035
    emotion induction and, 226, 952
    molecular genetics studies of, 312
    nucleus accumbens and, 32–34

dopamine (*continued*)
  phobias and, 969
    prefrontal cortex and, 28, 38
    reward and, 32–34, 38, 625, 933
    stimulant drugs and, 686
dopamine-β-hydroxylase, 136, 1024
dopamine hydroxylase, 327
Dopp, J. M., 1087
Doraiswamy, P. M., 969
Dorian mode, music and, 504
dorsal anterior cingulate, 938
dorsal cognitive division, anterior
    cingulate, 933, 934, 936, 938, 941, 942,
    945, 947, 948
dorsal striatum, 75
dorsolateral frontal cortices, 83
dorsolateral prefrontal circuit, 931
dorsolateral prefrontal cortex, 10*f*, 118,
    120, 354, 356
    depressive disorders and, 1027
    emotion induction study findings on,
      947, 948
    facial expression neuroimaging, 936
    lesions to, 932
dorsomedial prefrontal cortex, 104
Doss, R. C., 701
dot-probe task. *See* visual dot-probe
    methodology
Dougherty, D. D., 119
Dove, T., 465
doves, 471
Dovidio, J. F., 607
Downey, J. E., 508
Down syndrome, 366
Drabble, M., 482
drama, 483, 497, 498
dreaming, 76
Dreman, D., 630
Drevets, W. C., 16, 121
drive summation, 926n.3
drugs, 153, 297
    addictive, 28, 30, 33, 34, 579, 634
    affect induction, 588, 930, 939, 950–52,
      965
    animal affiliative behavior studies, 1014–
      16
    antisocial behavior and, 804
    emotions produced by, 572, 588
    maladaptive self-awareness attenuation
      and, 782
    memory issues and, 94–98, 101–7
    nucleus accumbens and, 33, 34
    pedunculopontine nucleus and, 37
    pharmacological emotion/mood
      induction studies, 950–52
    psychoactive, 226
    psychotherapeutic, 1021
    public health issues and, 1048
    stimulants, 686, 951–52
    *See also specific drugs and drug types*

DSP4, 95
DST nonsuppression, 1033
Duchenne muscular dystrophy, 308
Duchenne smiles, 381, 417, 418, 421, 422
ducks, 774
dueling, 402
dullness, music and perception of, 515,
    520
Dumais, S. T., 906
Duncan, B. D., 830
Duncan, E., 486
Duncan, Isadora, 493
Duncan, Todd, 393
Duncker, K., 841
Dunn, J., 296, 332–44
duration
    acoustic, 437, 443
    affect intensity and, 567
Durner, M., 306
D'Urso, V., 515
duty focus, memory retrieval and, 652
Dweck, C. S., 994
Dyadic Adjustment scale, 1067
Dykman, R. A., 992
dynamic component systems approach,
    emotional development and, 296–97,
    376–83, 401–3
dynamics, in music, 504
dynamic skill theory, 376, 388–89, 393,
    394
dynamic systems theory, 362
Dysfunctional Attitudes Scale, 991
dyslexia, phonological, 664
dysphoria, 426, 899, 943
    cognitive biases and, 981, 983, 985,
      993, 996, 997
dysregulatory psychopathology, 921–26
dysthymia, 899

E

eagerness, 683
Eagly, A. H., 754
earth, 325, 326
Eastman, K. L., 322
easy child, the, 327
eating disorders, 782, 1033, 1034
Ebert, D., 966
eccrine sweat glands, 280
Eckhardt, C. I., 818
ecological motivation models, 894
ecological properties, 685
economic issues
    allostatic load, 1094, 1096
    criminal behavior, 811–12, 820nn.14–16
    health, 1086, 1118, 1129–31
*Economist* (magazine), 819n.3
ECT. *See* electroconvulsive therapy
ectomorphs, 326

Edwards, J. A., 996
Edwards, K., 652, 816
EEGs. *See* electroencephalographs
effacement, 375, 394, 395, 400, 402
efferent signals, brain and, 135
efficacy expectation, 581
effortful control, 304, 693–94
egalitarian societies, 858, 859, 883
ego, 326, 777, 778, 865, 931
egocentric empathy, 788–89
ego-ideal, 710
ego involvement, primary appraisal and,
    709
egoistic motivation, 793
Ego-Strength Scale, 1065
ego-threatening frustration, 811, 812
Eich, Eric, 599, 652
8-bromo-cAMP, 98
[18]FDG PET. *See* fluorine-18 deoxyglucose
    PET
Eindhoven, J. E., 492
*Einfühlung. See* empathy
Eisenberg, Nancy, 297, 750, 787–98
Ekman, Paul, 176–77, 215, 219, 226, 235,
    296, 367n.5, 411–14, 415–27, 435, 444,
    449, 458, 486, 539, 540, 543, 574, 705,
    747, 846, 848, 855, 858, 862, 1083–84,
    1085, 1089, 1093
elaboration, 989–90
elaboration likelihood model, 758–61, 763–
    65, 766
elation, 380, 439*t*, 440, 443, 444, 684
    as counterfactual emotion, 623
    phasic arousal and, 692
elderly people. *See* older adults
electrical stimulation
    animal studies utilizing, 26, 34–37, 152–
      53, 473
    emotion induction via, 226, 588
    reward and, 33
electroacupuncture, 901
electroconvulsive therapy, 901, 1027,
    1033
electrodermal response system, 191, 197–
    98, 201, 914–17. *See also* skin
conductance response
electroencephalographs, 26, 325, 329,
    1129
    emotion verification and, 219
    of frontal lobe asymmetry, 320, 354,
      356, 377, 701
    of infant emotional expression, 354
    of vocal expression, 450
electromyography, 264–65, 416, 418, 582
electron microscope techniques, 356
elephants, 462
elevation, emotional, 848–49, 855, 863–
    64, 866
Elfman, L., 704

elicitation of emotion. *See* induction/
  elicitation of emotion
elicitors, of moral emotions, 866n.1
  anger as, 856
  compassion as, 862
  contempt as, 858
  disgust as, 857
  disinterested, 853–54, 864
  elevation as, 864
  gratitude as, 863
  guilt as, 861
  shame and disgust as, 860
Elie, R., 970
Eliot, George, 486, 497, 499
Eliot, T. S., 485, 488, 498
Ellgring, H., 451
Elliot, A. J., 995
Elliott, Rebecca, 4, 5, 117–25
Ellis, A. W., 664
Ellis, H. C., 601, 602
Ellsworth, Phoebe C., 564, 572–89, 669,
  816
Elmehed, K., 265
Elowson, A. M., 469–70
Elster, J., 588
embarrassment, 412, 1087
  in Chinese culture, 375, 383
  cultural perspectives on, 848, 849, 860,
    872
  development of, 338, 780, 781
  facial expression and, 417, 419, 420,
    421, 424, 425
  hot/cold empathy gaps and, 629
  moral emotions and, 855, 859–61, 865,
    866
  as praise response, 375
  reflected appraisal of, 781
  toddlers and, 335, 336, 353
Embree, M., 810, 816
Emde, Robert, 306, 350, 352, 902
emergency reaction, 1049
EMG. *See* electromyography
Emmons, R. A., 995
Emmorey, K., 554n.2
emotion
  adaptive nature of, 572, 574, 579, 609,
    636n.2, 682, 684, 1083–84, 1093
  aesthetic, 569, 577–78, 580, 848
  agitation-related, 779, 995
  ambiguous, 579
  anterior cingulate cortex and, 10–11
  antithesis principle of, 458, 475
  appraisal processes of. *See* appraisal
  approach-related, 9
  attribution theory of, 227, 580
  automatic vs. controlled processing of,
    648–49, 651, 654, 710, 905–9, 921,
    923, 924
  autonomic response automaticity of,
    256–71

autonomic specificity of, 132–33, 212–
  22
autonomic systems and, 175–77
basic. *See* basic emotions
as behavior organizer, 677
biphasic organization of, 188–89
brain circuitry of, 9–18, 27–38, 684
brain stem sites and, 37
brain structure mediation of, 40
categorical model of, 233, 235, 574,
  1086–88
children's understanding of, 337–44,
  347
cognition and, 5, 39, 41–43, 215,
  222n.3, 563–69, 976–77, 989
cognitive-appraisal theories of, 622
as cognitive interrupt, 635
as communication, 297, 332–33, 747,
  828, 831, 832
conceptual influences on, 679, 681–82,
  684, 686–90, 694
constructive systems for, 648–49
counterfactual, 623–24, 626
cultural prevalence of, 881–82
culture's impact on, 846–49
culture-specific, 847, 876
decision making and, 5, 9, 619–36
definition of, 323–25, 536, 841
dejection-related, 779, 995
dimensional models. *See* dimensional
  models of emotion
discrete. *See* discrete emotions
disorders of. *See* emotional disorders
elicitation of. *See* induction/elicitation
  of emotion
evolutionary perspectives on, 256–71,
  333, 358, 839
expected, 566, 620–26, 628, 630, 632,
  633–36
facial feedback hypothesis of, 487
fiction and generation of, 497–98
focality of, 881, 883–84
folk language of, 296
functionalist view of, 353, 354, 402, 609
functions and tasks of, 131–33, 213
health and, 3, 5, 727, 1047–50, 1083–99
hemisphere specialization of, 31, 37–38,
  729
hypercognized vs. hypocognized, 884
immediate, 566, 620–21, 625, 626–33
individual differences in, 134
induction of. *See* induction/elicitation
  of emotion
induction studies of, 939–52
infant responsiveness to, 334–35
information processing approaches to,
  565, 661–71
interdependent vs. independent, 886
interpersonal coregulation of, 381, 395,
  402

interpersonal functions of, 637n.13
interpersonal relationships and, 750,
  824–33
James-Lange theory of, 29, 149–50, 175–
  76, 188, 330
language and, 297, 347, 358, 535–53
learned, 589
learning theories of, 564
memory and, 4, 93–109, 132, 563–65,
  643–55
misunderstood, 411, 412
mixed, 337, 342, 579
modal, 589n.1
modulation of, 848
moral, 792–93, 798, 843, 845, 847, 848,
  852–66, 875, 891–96
motivational organization of, 187–207,
  228–29, 257, 367n.6
multilevel theories of, 669–71
neural substrates of, 931–32, 1084,
  1088, 1091
neuroimaging studies of, 933–52
opioid receptors and, 37
opponent process theory of, 588
orientation, attention, and, 256, 261–62,
  269, 276–87, 289
perceptual influences on, 679, 681–82,
  684–86, 687, 689, 690, 694
personality development and, 297, 726–
  39
Plato's concept of, 563
polyvagal theory of, 449
preattentive activation mechanisms for,
  262–65
prefrontal cortex damage and, 29–30
as prosocial behavior factor, 750, 787–
  98
prospective, 579
prototypical elicitors of, 418
psychopathology and, 5, 899–903
recursive processes of, 567–68
regulation of. *See* emotion regulation
right brain hemisphere and, 67–73
in romantic hypothesis of art, 490–93
romanticism's view of, 481–88
Schachter-Singer theory of, 564
selective attention modulation of, 276–
  90
self and, 773–83
self-evaluative, 386–401
self-generated, 775–77
self-organization of, 378, 381–83, 401,
  402
self-reflexive, 581
social, 296, 333, 335, 354, 356, 357, 358
as social process, 747–49
somatic marker hypothesis of, 29–30,
  83, 134, 270–71, 634, 635, 691
study methodological considerations,
  216–20, 225–50

emotion (*continued*)
 as superordinate program, 976
 temporal domains of, 930–31, 933, 954
 thalamic theory of, 151
 unconscious, 586
 universalist view of, 215–16, 871
 vicarious, 580
 visceral afferent neurons and, 149
 withdrawal-related, 9
 *See also* affect; *specific emotions*
emotion, experience of
 age-related findings on, 733, 737
 animals and, 774–77, 848, 1010
 in appraisal theory, 573, 574, 585
 autonomic nervous system and, 73, 175–
  77
 cultural perspectives on, 871–73, 875,
  881
 in dynamic component systems, 377,
  378, 402–3, 403n.1
 emotional development and, 295, 347,
  733–34
 emotion processing's effect on, 906
 facial expression and, 416–17, 418
 health issues and, 1089, 1094–95, 1099
 in interpersonal relationships, 825, 826–
  27, 828, 830–33
 limbic system role of, 939
 personality development and, 726, 727,
  732, 733, 737
 self's role in, 774, 775–76, 779–83
emotion, expression of, 411–14, 1098
 appraisal issues and, 583
 autonomic nervous system and, 73, 175–
  77
 autonomic specificity and, 214
 in cancer patients, 1053–75
 in communal relationships, 750
 cultural perspectives on, 411–13, 552,
  678, 729, 846, 878–81, 886
 Darwin's theories of, 457–59, 747, 931
 display rules of, 419, 421, 436, 539,
  552, 729
 displays and, 413–14
 emotional development and, 295, 296,
  347
 evolutionary perspectives on, 411, 747,
  931
 facial expressions as. *See* facial
  expression
 genetic factors in, 304
 implicit aspects of, 5
 individual differences in, 413, 698–99,
  705–6
 by infants, 333, 334, 347, 350, 353, 356
 in interpersonal relationships, 414, 824–
  25, 828–33
 language acquisition and, 297, 535–36,
  543–47

language and, 411, 535–53
music and, 411, 503–29
nonhuman animals and, 187, 457–76
in parent-child relationships, 341, 350
perception of, 412–13, 422–23, 442–43,
 445, 451, 476, 536
personality development and, 726, 729
signaling and, 446, 452
theoretical developments in, 413–14
universality of, 216, 415, 416, 419–22,
 445, 539, 540, 871
in visual and narrative arts, 411, 481–
 99
vocal expression of. *See* vocal
 expression
emotional behavior, 563
emotional cognition, 39, 40, 42
emotional conflict, 579
emotional contagion, 487, 1047
Emotional Counting Stroop, 938
emotional development, 3, 4, 295–99, 679
 appraisal processes and, 583, 732–33
 behavioral inhibition and temperament
  and, 296, 298, 305–6, 320–31, 354,
  729
 dynamic component systems approach
  and, 296–97, 376–83, 401–3
 in early childhood, 332–44
 emotional systems and, 684
 emotion regulation and, 296, 337, 344,
  347, 349, 354, 355, 357–66
 facial expression charting of, 427
 frontal brain asymmetry and, 701
 genetics of, 296, 300–316
 in infancy, 296, 298, 303–5, 332–35,
  347–66
 key research findings on, 357–58
 life-span perspective on, 297, 732–35
 organizational perspective on, 352–53,
  360
 of pride, shame, guilt, 297, 375–403,
  792–93
 prosocial behavior and, 750, 780, 788–
  89, 792, 861
 reactivity individual differences and,
  694
 research challenges, 297–99, 366
 research history overview, 348–57
 social relationship issues and, 332–44,
  347, 353, 354, 355, 357, 360–61
 socioemotional selectivity theory on,
  679, 734
emotional disorders, 7, 931
 affective neuroscience perspectives on,
  4, 8–19
 appraisal malfunctioning and, 584
 cognitive biases in, 976–1001
 comorbid, 684, 688, 982, 985, 987, 998–
  99

depression neuroimaging and, 4, 117–
 25
emotional reactivity and, 682, 683–84
emotion expression and, 413, 426–27
information processing and, 565, 662–
 64, 666, 667, 669–71
intentional or directed forgetting and,
 650
stress and, 1117
therapeutic treatments for, 901–3, 908,
 925
*See also* psychopathology; *specific
 disorders*
emotional expressivity. *See* emotion,
 expression of
emotional intelligence, 712
*Emotional Intelligence: Why It Can Matter
 More Than IQ* (Goleman), 633
emotionality
 appraisal theory of, 575
 attentional biases and, 979–80
 behaviorist research on, 597
 effortful control and, 693
 genetic factors in, 727
 as mental health factor, 737
 prosocial behavior and, 787, 793–96,
  798
 as temperament type, 327
emotional learning, 201
 amygdala and, 32, 74, 901
 by humans and animals, 4, 52–62
 implicit aspects of, 5
 neuroscientific perspectives on, 4, 52–
  62
 norepinephrine and, 16
emotional memories, 498, 1107
emotional perseveration, 59
emotional practice, 872–80
 cultural differences in, 874–81
 cultural models of, 871–73
 patterning differences in, 881–87
emotional preoccupation, 488
emotional priming model, 198–205
emotional responses
 as animal study focus, 39–40, 42
 individual differences in, 679, 698–719,
  1089
 personality and, 678, 1088
 psychopathology issues and, 901, 904–
  26
 reactivity individual differences and,
  681, 682, 684, 689, 691, 1089
emotional space, 216, 233, 235
emotional states
 activation mechanisms and, 690
 appraisal theory view of, 575, 709–12
 arousal and, 692
 assessment of, 705
 behavioral disposition bias and, 380

children's development and, 296, 347, 357, 366, 545
in dynamic component systems, 376–78, 401, 403n.1
empathy for, 750
information processing and, 663, 760–61
information processing paradigm and, 663
ritualization and, 457, 461–62
emotional stimuli
   appraisal processes and, 564
   attention orienting and, 278, 286–87
   fear module and, 270
   memory and, 565
   orienting responses to, 262, 276, 789, 905, 907
   skin conductance responses to, 264
emotional style, 881, 1074
emotional syndrome anatomy, 379t, 402
emotional systems, 353, 648, 976–77
   reactivity individual differences, 681–94
emotion-antecedent appraisals, 687, 690
emotion coping, 132
emotion-emotion activation principle, 226, 228
emotion evaluation studies, 934–39
emotion families
   in categorical emotion theories, 574
   moral emotions and, 855
   self-organization of, 381–83
   vocal expression and, 440, 444
emotion-focused coping, 707, 713
emotion-focused coping potential, 581
emotion goals, 131–33
emotion induction studies, 939–50
emotion-in-relationships model, 826–27
emotion-like phenomena, 588
emotion metaphors, 568
emotion phenotypes, 300–301, 306–8, 310, 312, 315
emotion potentials, 872
emotion processing
   adaptive, 904, 907, 909
   amygdala and, 933, 934, 938, 943, 964
   anterior paralimbic structure and, 933, 935t
   automatic, 648, 649, 651, 654, 669, 670, 685, 710, 905–7, 908, 909
   controlled, 648–49, 654, 905–9, 921, 923, 924
   health issues and, 1050
   lateralization and, 73
   response modulation and, 904–26
   short-circuiting of, 907, 909, 919, 921, 923, 926n.4
emotion programs, 846, 848, 849
emotion regulation, 4, 6, 8–19, 298

adults and, 679, 733–34, 795–96
amygdala and, 4, 9, 15–18, 25, 27, 31–32, 39, 41, 42
attention and, 649–50, 710–11
cancer patients and, 1054, 1063, 1066, 1069–71, 1075
children and, 296, 337, 344, 347, 349, 354, 355, 357–66, 730, 731, 795, 1098
coping processes and, 736
coping vs., 713
culture's impact on, 846, 872, 879–81, 882–83, 887
definitions of, 359–60, 710
developmental model of, 362–66
genetic contribution to, 304, 727
goals and, 713
health issues and, 1050
individual differences in, 712, 1089
information processing paradigm and, 671
intrinsic influences on, 360, 361t
lateral prefrontal cortex and, 649
mechanisms and processes of, 710–12
personality development and, 726, 727, 730, 731
personality issues and, 678, 736
prefrontal cortex damage and, 30
prosocial behavior and, 297, 363, 787–98, 793–96, 798
psychopathology and, 899
purpose of, 360–62
push and pull effects in, 567
self-perception and, 566
self's role in, 781–83
emotion signals, 668–69
emotion strategies, 131–32
emotion suppression, 132, 598
   cancer patients and, 1053–56, 1063–64, 1066–70, 1073, 1075
   cardiovascular system effects of, 216, 881
   decision-making issues and, 627, 636
   health issues and, 1050, 1092, 1098
   memory and, 649–50, 881
   mood and, 664
   as research concern, 221–222
   sympathetic nervous system arousal and, 627
emotion tactics, 131, 132
emotion tasks, 131–34
emotion-typical action tendencies, 378, 380
emotion words, 678, 883, 1089
emotion work, 879–80
emotivism, 865
empathetic concern, 296, 336
empathy, 325, 353, 545, 780
   affectional emotional systems and, 683
   as communication of caring, 828

definition of, 787–88
egocentric, 788–89
gene-environment interaction in, 308
genetic factors in, 306, 340, 794
global, 788, 789
guilt and, 792, 793
health issues and, 1047
interpersonal relationships and, 828–31, 833
journal articles published on, 852, 853t
Lipps's theory of, 487
as moral emotion, 862
personality development and, 730
prosocial behavior and, 297, 750, 787–96, 797, 798
Empfindungsästhetik (musical theory), 504
encephalitis, 75
encephalization, brain, 41–42, 43, 849
encephalopathies, 1034
encoding, emotion's role in, 565
   memory and, 644–55, 718, 719, 985, 986, 990, 1101n.3
encoding, in vocal expression, 433–42, 451, 538, 843
   empirical research on, 436–42
   lexical, 541–42
   musical performance and, 507, 526, 527
   theoretical models of, 434–36
endocrine systems, 87, 135–36, 187, 684, 686, 1033, 1074
   individual emotional differences and, 1088
endomorphs, 326
endophenotypes, 301, 306–7, 312–13, 315
endorphins, 327
energetic arousal, 686, 692
energetic components, 187
energy
   as appraisal influence, 691
   arousal states, 686, 692
   as coping factor, 689
   investment of, 707
   as temperament factor, 326
energy distribution, acoustic, 437, 440, 441, 450
engagement, attentional, 277, 285
Engberg-Pedersen, E., 554n.2
Engel, G. L., 1088–89
England, 807, 1130
English (American) language, 297, 448–49, 548, 550
engrams, 901
enjoyment, 1087
ensemble strategy, in infant development, 354
enteric nervous system, 136–38, 140, 143, 146, 149, 161–62
entertainment, art and, 484, 485, 490

enthusiasm, 683
entorhinal cortex, 104, 118, 948
envelope, music and, 520
environment, 826
    aesthetic preferences and, 488–89
    as affective state influence, 598–99
    as aggression cause, 806–10
    allostatic load and, 1128–31
    animal communication constraints and,
        461–63
    antisocial behavior instigators from, 806–
        10
    appraisal process and, 572–76, 748
    as decision making factor, 623
    disease linkage with, 1118
    as emotionality factor, 794
    facial expression and, 417, 425
    Freudian view of, 326
    genetics and, 301–9, 315
    as health factor, 1048–49, 1050
    immediate- vs. delayed-return from, 776
    as incidental affect factor, 633
    mood as informational cue and, 760,
        765
    nature-nuture debate and, 298, 541
    personality development and, 726–31,
        739
    as personality disorder factor, 309
    psychopathology issues and, 904, 908,
        920, 925
    sleep-wake patterns and, 702
    sound transmission factors and, 442
    well-being from mastery of, 734
envy, 325, 748, 780
Epictetus, 783
Epicurus, 596
epilepsy, 75, 306, 311
    mood disorders and, 932
    startle response research, 201
    temporal lobe and, 16, 41
epinephrine (adrenaline), 140, 151, 152,
        843, 1024, 1085, 1125
    memory and, 93–97, 105–7, 1107, 1127
EPI-Q (assessment tool), 737
episodic memory, 647, 650, 651, 654
epistasis, 302
Eppinger, H., 699
Epple, G., 473
equanimity, 879
equipotentiality premise, 266
equity, appraisal and, 581
Erasistratos, 1047
Erber, R., 664
ergotropic reaction, 153, 236
Erikson, E., 735–36
error detection and correction, 649, 693
error variance. See within-group
    variability
Escalona, Sibylle, 350, 367n.4
escape, 132–33, 188, 258

aggression issues and, 809
distress at another's distress and, 862
emotional reactivity and, 683, 685
evolutionary perspective on, 257
shame and, 72
espressivo (musical direction), 504
essentic forms, emotion communication
    and, 506
Esses, V. M., 607
Estes, D., 339, 343
Esteves, F., 260, 261, 267, 268, 270
esthetics. See aesthetic entries
estrogen, 1012, 1014, 1072
ethanol, 950–51
ethical issues, emotion induction research
    and, 227
ethics of autonomy, 858, 875, 876
ethics of community, 858, 875
ethics of divinity, 858, 875
ethnic cleansing, 856
ethos, 881
euphoria, 28–30, 118, 1050
euthymia, 902, 1034
evaluation
    in appraisal, 564, 567–68, 572–73, 576–
        82
    emotion elicitation and, 563–64
    language acquisition and, 297, 541, 547–
        51
evaluative responses, 755, 756–57, 759–
    60, 767n.3
Evans, A., 119
Evans, N., 1059
evening-type (E-type) individuals, 702
event coding, 866n.1
event-related potentials, 324
    affective picture processing findings on,
        194–97
    emotional cuing and, 278–80, 282, 283f,
        286
    facial expression findings on, 423
    P3 wave and startle response, 205, 206f
Everitt, B. J., 32
evolutionary perspectives, 256–71, 357,
    839–49
    affect and information processing, 602
    anxiety, 685–86, 775–76, 977, 990, 992,
        1001
    appraisal processes, 583
    attachment, 1010–11
    autonomic nervous system, 213, 256–71
    basic emotions, 176, 177
    brain encephalization, 41–42, 43
    brain stem functions, 37
    decision-making issues, 631–32, 635,
        637n.12
    depression, 977, 990, 992, 1001
    discrete emotions theory, 353, 422
    emotional systems, 684, 976
    emotion effects, 256–57, 333, 609

emotion expression, 411, 747, 931
emotion perception, 572
emotion regulation, 358
facial expression, 416, 418, 426
fear, 256, 257, 265–71, 631–32, 637n.12,
    685, 977
gratitude, 863
health and physiology, 1049
morality and moral emotions, 840, 843,
    848, 855
motivation, 892, 893–94, 895
music performance as communication,
    507
orienting responses, 256, 259, 261–62,
    264–66, 269
preattentive emotion activation, 262–65
priming, 188, 206
vocal expression, 444, 449
exaptation, affect and, 849
excitability, 328, 329, 1128
excitation, 327
excitatory connections, 690
excitement
    as basic emotion, 862
    music and perception of, 515, 520
executive neurons, 167, 169f
executive systems, 684, 689
exercise, 1118–21
expansive behavior, 878
expectancy, 709, 710, 999
expectancy effect, 228
expectancy system, 263
expectancy-value theories of attitudes,
    757, 760
expectation
    appraisal of, 687
    frustration-aggression hypothesis view,
        811–12
    of imminent reward, 625
    outcome vs. efficacy, 581
    predictive control and, 781
expectations, acquired, 726
expected emotions, 566, 620–26, 628, 630,
    632–36
expected utility model, 620, 622–25, 630,
    895
experience
    emotional. See emotion, experience of
    openness to, 731, 732, 737
experienced affect. See on-line affect
experience sampling methodology, 678,
    679, 733, 734, 750
explanatory style. See attributional style
explanatory style training, 1000
explicative perspective, individual
    differences, 698–99, 708–19
explicit knowledge, 362–64, 365t
explicit memory, 198, 647, 648
    cognitive processing biases and, 983,
        985, 987, 989–90

explicit recall, 198, 985
exploitation, 856
exploration, 489–90
expressed sequence arrays, 311
expression in vocalization. *See* encoding
expressionism, 486
expression marks, musical, 504
*Expression of Emotion in Man and Animals, The* (Darwin), 176, 411, 415, 457, 481, 486, 839
expressive confidence, 706
expressive displays, 187, 257, 421, 426
expressivity, emotional. *See* emotion, expression of
extended amygdala, 35, 1127
extended consciousness, 271
externalizers, 705
external self representations, 688
exteroceptive information, perceptual inputs and, 681, 685–86
extinction, 118
    of conditioned fear, 56, 59, 61, 102
extrastriate visual cortex, 647
extraversion, 322, 426, 698, 704, 719, 933
    circadian rhythm and, 702
    emotional reactivity and, 683, 685, 689, 692, 693
    emotion regulation and, 712
    as mental health factor, 737
    personality and, 729, 731, 732, 737
    positive affect link with, 731
    response modulation and emotion processing, 921, 923
    temperament neuroimaging findings on, 953–54
extrinsic goals, 994
eyebrows, facial expression and, 540
eye gaze, signed languages and, 537, 542, 551
Eysenck, Hans J., 683, 685, 698, 922–23, 933, 953, 954
Eysenck, M. W., 664, 717, 980, 986, 988
Eysenck Personality Inventory, 1066, 1067, 1069
Eysenck Personality Questionnaire, 921
Eyssell, K. M., 829

**F**

Fabes, R. A., 789, 791, 793, 794, 795
Fabrigar, Leandre R., 750, 752–67
face
    in Chinese culture, 383, 385, 400
    embarrassment and, 860
Facial Action Coding System, 546, 705
facial expression, 5, 17, 187, 411, 412, 415–27, 444
    as accurate emotional indicator, 416–19, 526

amygdala and, 31, 76, 78–80, 82, 423, 474, 900, 931, 934–37, 938, 939
animals and, 457, 458, 459f, 463–65, 474, 583
anterior cingulate cortex and, 119, 934, 936–39
antithesis principle and, 458, 475
appraisal effects on, 582, 586, 587
art vs., 486, 491
cingulate cortex and, 30–31, 423
coding systems for, 350, 366, 416, 417, 424
communicative function of, 747
componential theories of, 415, 416, 417
cultural variations in, 420–22
depression and recognition deficits of, 900
directed facial action task, 218–19, 220f, 226
in discrete and dimensional emotion models, 415, 416, 417, 422–25
of disgust, 417, 420, 423, 424, 444, 857
in dominance contests, 260–61
emotional response research findings on, 191–92, 198
emotion and, 5, 415–27
emotion duration and, 219–20
emotion evaluation studies of, 934–37
emotion individual differences and, 705
emotion induction and, 226
emotion-typical action tendencies and, 378, 380
hardwired preferences for, 577
hemisphere specialization and, 38
individual differences in, 426–27
infants and, 333, 350, 358, 366, 539, 543
language and, 297, 535, 537, 539–53
lesion studies of, 68–72, 76, 78–79, 80f
of pain, 417, 841
perception of, 412, 413, 422
preparedness theory testing and, 267–68
research history overview, 415–16
signed languages and, 50–51, 537, 540–47
social context factors in, 418, 420–22, 425–27, 539
social interaction and, 381
universality of, 216, 415, 416, 419–20, 422, 539, 543, 871
in visual art, 486
vocal expression and, 440, 442
*See also* smiling
facial feedback hypothesis of emotions, 487
facial muscle responses, 192–94, 264–65
factor analysis, 442, 515, 528, 678, 754
Fagen, J. W., 361
Fahey, J. L., 1096
Fahrenberg, J., 700, 702

failure
    abnormal response to, 123
    children's emotions and, 356, 792
    cognitions of and depression, 992, 997
    pessimistic attributional style and, 688
    self-attributions of, 780
Fairbrother, N., 995
fairness, 875–76
Falconer, D. S., 304
Falconer equation, 304
false memories, 644
false modesty, 387
false suffocation alarm, 970
familiarity, appraisal and, 576, 687, 710
family, 1085, 1087, 1097
    affectional emotional systems and, 683
    in Chinese culture, 385, 386, 387, 394, 400, 402
    filial piety and, 385, 386, 388, 400, 402
    interpersonal relationships with, 827–28, 829, 831–33
    social relationships in early childhood and, 332–40
    *See also* parent-child relationships; siblings
family studies, 301, 315
Fanselow, M. S., 259
Faravelli, C., 970
Farber, I. E., 199
Farber, J., 1071
Farnsworth, P. R., 517
Farrar, M. J., 445
Farrington, D. P., 804
Farver, J., 789
fat, abdominal, 1073
fate, 874
fatigue, 325, 1047
Faull, F., 469
Fava, G. A., 1088, 1096
fawning, 857
Fawzy, F. I., 1071, 1072, 1074
fear, 5, 75, 323, 354, 412, 589n.5, 849, 1010, 1019, 1089
    active and passive defenses for, 258–59
    amygdala's role in, 4, 31, 32, 53–62, 74–77, 79, 82, 99–101, 201, 265, 269, 270, 377, 654, 729, 937, 938, 939, 964, 1106–7, 1113
    animal behavioral genetics studies of, 314
    animal expression of, 458–60, 464, 465, 466, 472, 474, 475, 774
    anxiety disorders and, 963–64, 972
    appraisal theory view of, 574, 575, 585, 633
    as basic emotion, 68, 176, 333, 669, 1087
    cancer patients and, 1053, 1071, 1074
    cardiovascular responses to, 188, 258–59, 267

fear (*continued*)
  cognitive-neoassociationistic aggression model, 815, 816
  cognitive processing biases and, 977, 986–87, 988–89
  as communication of needs, 828
  cultural perspectives on, 878
  emotional development issues and, 298
  emotional reactivity and, 683, 684, 686, 687
  emotional response research findings on, 192, 648
  evolutionary perspectives on, 256, 257, 265–71, 631–32, 637n.12, 685, 977
  expression of in interpersonal relationships, 828
  facial expression of, 417, 420, 423, 424, 425, 464, 931
  fight-or-flight response and, 133, 258
  Freudian view of, 326
  glucocorticoid levels and, 327
  hemisphere specialization theories of, 37–38
  human innate preparation for, 774–75
  induction research issues, 227, 229–31, 232*f*, 248–50
  infants and, 328, 330, 348, 350, 353, 354, 356, 357, 543, 780
  lesion studies of, 69, 79
  metaphors for, 215
  moral emotion issues and, 853, 864
  music and perception of, 515
  neural substrates of, 936–37
  of pain, 653
  personality and, 733
  preattentive activation mechanisms and, 262–65
  predatory defense system and, 259–60
  psychopath deficit of, 910, 914–19
  reactivity of children and, 328, 330
  as risk-perception factor, 632, 634
  selective attention and, 285, 287, 289
  self-imagining of, 775
  skin conductance response link with, 917
  social, 859
  social submissiveness system and, 260–61
  SPAARS emotion model and, 670–71
  startle reflex and, 203, 204*f*, 206–7, 259, 1106–7, 1110
  suppression of, 598
  universalist view of, 216
  vocal expressions of, 13, 438, 439*t*, 440, 443, 444
  *See also* phobias
fear appeals, 756–58, 766, 767nn.4, 5
fear-arousing messages, 608
fear conditioning, 4, 564, 1106–7

amygdala and, 4, 31, 32, 53–62, 74, 75–76, 77*f*, 99–101, 201, 269, 1107
  cellular and molecular mechanisms, 57–59
  circuitry in humans, 59–61
  concept basics, 52–53
  contextual control of, 55, 56–57, 61
  emotional learning and, 4, 52–62
  evolutionary perspectives on, 256, 265–70, 631–32, 637n.12
  hippocampus's role in, 13, 56, 59, 61, 62
  in infants, 349
  lesion studies of, 75–76, 77*f*, 654
  memory and, 644, 645, 654
  neural pathways and, 53–56
  phobias and, 61, 968
  psychopathology and, 61–62, 914–15, 916
  startle reflex and, 199–201
feared self, 779
fearfulness, genetic factors in, 727
fear module, 256, 269–70, 271
fear of anxiety, 714
fear of danger, 714
fear of fear, 686
fear of the unfamiliar, 325
Federoff, J. P., 68
feedback
  in cognition and emotion recursive processes, 567–68
  during conditioning, 270–71
  depressed patients and, 123
  in dynamic component systems, 378, 380
  in emotion theory, 175–76, 270, 330, 487
  facial expressions as, 540
  positive affect as mediator in, 604
  response modulation and, 905
  self-image issues and, 778
feed-forward control, 1108
*Feeling and Form* (Langer), 506
feeling qualia, 871
feelings
  antisocial behavior and, 805–6
  as attitude and behavior influence, 596
  children's talk about, 336, 338, 339, 341, 342
  definition of, 805
  emotions and, 187, 206, 257, 566, 572
  music and, 505, 506
feelings-as-information theory. *See* affect-as-information model
feeling states, 324, 353, 644, 714
Fein, D., 1017
Feldstein, S., 445
females
  animal affiliative behavior, 1011–17
  animal copulation calls, 470

animal reproductive behavior, 471, 473, 1011
animal scent-marking behavior, 472
cultural segregation of, 872, 884
depression and, 14, 451
emotional expressivity and, 705, 706
emotion regulation and, 366
expressive behavior and, 421, 427
interoception and, 703
menstruation, 472, 476
parturition, 1012, 1014
symptom reporting differences, 704
veiling of, 884
*See also* maternal behavior; sex differences
fenfluramine, 1022, 1028
fentanyl, 30, 33
Ferguson, T. J., 792–93
Fernald, A., 335, 470
Fernandez, E., 807
Fesbach, N., 789
Feshbach, S., 598, 604, 806
Fessler, D. T., 849, 859
Festinger, L., 609, 761
FG 7142, 1109, 1110
fibrinogen, 1124, 1130
Ficino, Marsilio, 493–94
fiction. *See* literature
Fiedler, K., 599–600, 602
Field, N., 287
fighting spirit, cancer patients and, 1055–56, 1060, 1061, 1074
fight-or-flight response, 133, 152, 256, 258, 750, 809, 814–15, 817, 967, 972
  amygdala and, 964
  appraisal and, 580, 581
  emotional reactivity and, 683, 685, 691
  health issues and, 150, 1049
  temperament type and, 327
  threat imminence and, 259, 260*f*, 267, 580
filial piety, 385, 386, 388, 400, 402
films, 497, 498
  as attitude research subject, 600
  emotion induction via, 227, 701
  empathy-inducing, 790–91, 794
  musical accompaniment to, 503
  musical expression in, 529
  psychological perspectives on, 486, 487, 488
  *See also* picture-viewing paradigm
final autonomic pathway, 155–56, 160–63
final pitch movements, 447
Finegan, E., 541
Fink, G. R., 119
Finkenauer, C., 844
fire, 325, 326
Fischer, H., 120, 967, 971
Fischer, Kurt W., 296, 297, 375–403

fish, 472, 1011
Fiske, S. T., 606
Fitness, J., 825, 829
Fitzsimmons, J. R., 194
5-hydroxyindole acetic acid (5-HIAA), 1026, 1027–28
5-hydroxytryptamine (5-HT), 1022, 1023, 1025, 1027–35, 1126
Five Factor model of personality, 677, 683, 731, 732, 734–35, 736
Fivush, R., 735
flashbulb memories, 644, 645, 1127
Flaubert, Gustave, 497
flexible correction model, 609, 762–64, 765
flight-fight system. *See* fight-or-flight response
flight response, 133, 188
   as defense behavior, 171
flow masks, 437
fluid matrix, 149
flumazenil, 97, 951, 971
fluorine-18 deoxyglucose PET, 964
   neural substrates of affect, 933, 947, 952, 953, 954
   obsessive-compulsive disorder, 965
   panic disorder, 970, 971
fluoxetine, 966, 1022, 1025, 1033
flutamide, 464
fluvoxamine, 1022
Flykt, A., 260, 261, 270
Flynn, R. A., 666
fMRI. *See* functional magnetic resonance imaging
focality
   appraisal of, 578, 579, 687
   of emotions, 881, 883–84
focusing, in memory retrieval, 646
Foerster, F., 246, 247, 699–700, 702
Fogarty, S. J., 663, 668
Fogel, A., 381
folk language, of emotion, 296
Folkman, S., 708, 1098
folk songs, 525
Fontaine, R., 970
Fontaine, S., 970
food
   animal vocalizations and, 460, 461, 469–70, 475
   brain stem sites and, 36–37, 39
   diet and, 1118–21
   disgust concerning, 849, 857
   eating disorders and, 782, 1033, 1034
   emergence of agriculture and, 775–76
   hunger and, 34, 170, 629, 841
   hypothalamus and response to, 34
   motivational systems and, 842
   orbitofrontal cortex and, 28
   preferences for, 577
   ventral pallidum and, 35

food aversion learning, 842–43
foraging, 489
Fore, 420
forebrain, 1025, 1106
   autonomic nervous system and, 149, 154, 166, 167, 169, 171–72, 175, 1108–13
   basal. *See* basal forebrain
Forester, B., 1070
Forgas, Joseph P., 566, 596–613, 629, 636–37nn.3, 8, 668, 691, 759, 764
forgetting, 650
forgiveness, 425, 792
formal operations, domain-free, 849
*forte* (music direction), 504
forward genetics, 313
Fowles, D. C., 917
Fox, B. H., 1057
Fox, C. M., 1067
Fox, N. A., 320, 329, 354, 356
Fragile X disorder, 309
fragmentation, 993
frames (concept), 666
France, 481, 493, 807
Frank, Robert H., 843, 848, 849, 865, 891–96
Frederick, S., 626
Fredrickson, B. L., 221, 862, 864, 1087, 1091, 1098
Fredrickson, W. E., 516
Fredrikson, M., 120, 266, 700, 967, 971
Freeman, B. J., 902
free-rider hypothesis, 895–96
freeze behavior, 104, 685, 691, 840
   fear and, 99–100, 102, 258–59
   threat imminence and, 259, 260*f*
Frege, G., 322
French, C. C., 666
French, J. A., 472
French Revolution, 481, 811
frequency, of animal vocal signaling, 462, 463
Freud, Anna, 1056
Freud, Sigmund, 257, 326, 358, 488, 596, 598, 710, 716, 865, 931, 1021, 1047, 1056
Frey, J., 810
Fridlund, A. J., 418, 446
Friedman, H. S., 738
Friend, M., 445, 553
friends, 341–43, 828–29, 831–33
fright, fight, and flight response, 152
Frijda, N. H., 487, 578, 582, 586, 709, 816, 863, 866n.1, 876
Friston, K., 109
Frith, C. D., 120
*Frog, Where Are You?* (Mayer), 548, 549
frontal brain asymmetry, 700–701, 719, 932, 1090–92

frontal cortex, 934, 936–37, 947, 949
   depression and, 1029, 1030, 1033
   medial, 964
   panic disorder and, 970, 971
frontal gyrus, 936, 937, 938–39, 941–43, 945, 947, 949, 953
frontal lobes, 82–83
   alpha power, 320, 323
   EEG asymmetry findings on, 320, 354, 356, 377
   emotion induction study findings on, 951
   facial expression and, 423
   in infant brain functioning, 354, 355, 356
   language production and, 542
   psychopathology and, 901
   reactivity of children and, 329
   temperament neuroimaging research on, 954
   *See also specific areas*
frontal pole, 938, 943
frontotemporal dementia, 423
"frozen" cognitive structures, 568–69
frustration
   anger and, 856
   as antisocial behavior cause, 806, 810–13
   children's control of, 337, 354
   as decision-making issue, 630
   emotional reactivity and, 684, 687, 691
   of goals/needs, 579
   racism and, 1086
frustration-aggression hypothesis, 606, 811–13
Fulker, D. W., 305, 309
functional brain imaging. *See* neuroimaging
functional encephalization, 41–42, 43
functionalist theories of emotions, 353, 354, 402, 609
   musical performance and, 507, 526–27
functional magnetic resonance imaging, 26, 964, 973
   of affective picture processing, 194
   of amygdala, 31, 59, 60*f*, 108–9, 265, 936, 940, 1107
   animal emotional expression studies and, 476
   of anterior cingulate cortex, 119
   in attention-emotion research, 289–90
   auditory evaluation studies of, 937
   of cingulate cortex, 30–31
   depression neuroimaging and, 117
   emotion induction studies and, 940–43, 945, 947, 951
   emotion neuroimaging and, 933, 934, 936–38
   facial expression research and, 423, 936, 937
   of frontal brain asymmetry, 701

functional magnetic resonance imaging
   (*continued*)
   lexical emotion evaluation studies and,
      938
   of medial orbitofrontal cortex, 119
   musical expression research and, 529
   obsessive-compulsive disorder and, 966
   olfactory emotion evaluation studies
      and, 938
   phobias and, 969
   research concerns, 222
   resting state studies and, 121
   technique biases, 40–41
   unconscious cognitive processes
      findings on, 1021
   vocal expression study and, 450
fundamental frequency, 538, 544
   as acoustic measurement, 434, 437, 438,
      440–43, 446–51
Funkenstein, D. H., 218, 220
*fureai* (Japanese emotion), 876
Furmark, T., 971
furrowed brows, facial expression and,
   417, 540, 543
fusiform, 936, 937, 948
fusiform gyrus, 968
Futterweit, L. R., 361
future, worry about, 775–76
future expectations, secondary appraisal
   and, 709
future-related cognition, 977, 988, 991,
   997–1001

# G

GABA. *See* gamma-amino-butyric acid
GABAergic neurons, 964, 971
Gabriel, C., 523
Gabrielsson, Alf, 411, 412, 413, 503–29
Gaelick, L., 908
Gaensbauer, T. J., 350
Gaertner, S. L., 607
Gage, Phineas, 82
Gagnon, L., 520
Galen, 325–26, 331, 933, 1053
Gall, Franz, 326
Gallagher, M., 95, 97
Gallo, L. C., 1086
gambling task studies, 911
game theory, 854, 895
gamma-amino-butyric acid, 36, 167, 1108,
   1109
   agonists and antagonists, 96, 97
Gangestad, S. W., 310
ganglion cells, 139. *See also specific types*
Gans, C., 188
Gara, M. A., 996
Garcia-Coll, Cynthia, 327

gardens, landscape, 489, 496
Gardiner, J. M., 654
Gardner, H., 491
Garlow, Steven J., 902, 1021–36
Gasper, K., 628, 632
Gasson, J. A., 488
gastric ulcers, 38
gastrointestinal tract, 137–38, 140, 143,
   146, 149, 153
   defense behavior and, 171
   hypothalamic hunger center and, 170
   reflex pathways, 166, 167, 169*f*
Gaunt, A. S., 188
Gautama Buddha, 783
Gauthier, David, 895
gaze, signed languages and, 537, 542, 551
Geen, R. G., 812
Geertz, H., 879
Gelernter, J., 312
Gellhorn, E., 236
Gemar, Michael, 945, 946
gender. *See* females; males; sex
   differences
Gendolla, G. H. E., 749
gene chips, 6, 311
gene-environment covariance, 307–8
gene-environment interaction, 307, 308
gene expression, 6, 1121
gene mapping, 313, 315
general adaptation syndrome, 1049, 1089,
   1118
general affective aggression model, 813–
   14, 816, 817, 820nn.11, 18
general arousal model, 692
general expressivity, 706
General Health Questionnaire, 1061
generalizability, as research concern, 221,
   242
generalized anxiety disorder, 277, 650,
   663, 683, 686
   attentional biases and, 978, 979, 980
   evolutionary perspectives on, 992
   memory biases and, 985, 986
   other-related cognition and, 996
General Well-Being Questionnaire, 1059
genes
   aesthetic preference bias and, 488–89
   allostatic load and, 1119, 1121, 1128,
      1131
   animal affiliation studies, 1017, 1019
   behavioral inhibition issues and, 305–6,
      328
   depression and, 1029, 1131
   evolution and, 256–57
   homozygosity, 309, 310
   imprinting of, 309, 310
   nonpolymorphic, 309
   progressive amplification, 309–10
   *See also* genetics

gene therapy, 1018
genetic diseases, 1048
genetic epidemiology, 301
genetic heterogeneity, 308–9, 311
genetic probes, 311
genetics
   aggression responses and, 809, 814,
      817
   animal behavioral, 312–15
   autism and, 1017, 1018
   behavior-genetic research paradigm, 300–
      301, 307
   depression and, 308, 315, 1029, 1131
   as disease factor, 1118, 1128
   emotional development and, 296, 300–
      316, 355
   health and mortality and, 739
   human behavioral, 302–10, 727–29
   maternal behavior and, 298, 340
   molecular, 6, 7, 296, 297, 300, 310–12,
      315, 1036
   nature-nuture debate and, 298, 541
   perceptual processing issues and, 686
   as personality factor, 726–29, 739
   sleep-wake patterns and, 702
   temperament and, 296, 300, 302–10,
      315, 340, 726–28
genital sensations, 846
genome scans, 306, 311
genome screens, 300–301, 313
genre fiction, 490
George IV, king of England, 483
George, Mark S., 120, 450, 934, 936, 945,
   946, 948, 954
Gerard, R. W., 94–95
Germany, 445, 791, 886
Gershon, E. S., 903
Gervai, J., 312
Gestalt theory, 487–88, 881
gestures
   animal communication and, 463
   as communication, 354
   signed languages and, 536, 537, 539
   in visual art, 486
   vocal expression and, 442
GH. *See* growth hormone
Ghent, P. R., 492
Gholamain, M., 498
Gibbard, Allan, 865
Gibbs, J. C., 819n.1
Gibson, J. J., 485
Giese-Davis, Janine, 1050, 1053–75
*Gift of Fear, The: Survival Signals That
   Protect Us From Violence* (DeBecker),
   633
Gilbert, D. T., 626
Gilbert, P., 683
Gilboa, E., 992
Gilman, B. I., 508, 528

Gilovich, T., 623, 779, 893, 895, 896
girn vocalizations, 469, 470
gladness, 380
Glass, D., 810
glial cells, 121
glissando threshold, 442–43
global empathy, 788, 789
Globisch, J., 285
globus pallidus, 35, 943
glucocorticoids, 15, 16, 18, 327
    allostasis, allostatic load, and, 1118,
        1121, 1125–27
    depression and, 1023, 1032, 1073
    memory and, 94, 97, 98, 103
glucose, 97, 355–56, 1028, 1073, 1120,
    1121
glutamate, 57, 966
goal blockage, anger and, 856
goal congruence, 709
goal-directed behavior, 727, 905, 912, 919–
    20, 925, 994–95
goal-directed cognition, 994–95
goal/need conduciveness, 574, 578–80,
    584, 588, 687, 689, 691
goal obstructiveness, 435, 579, 683, 811–
    13
goal relevance, 709, 879–80, 906, 920
goals, 748
    action readiness and, 876, 877
    adaptive rationality and, 892, 893, 894,
        896
    of aggression, 805
    appraisal processes and, 377, 380, 573–
        75, 577–80, 687–88, 689, 709, 710,
        732
    automatic activation issues and, 691
    cultural perspectives on, 876–79, 881,
        882, 887
    decision-making and, 628
    emotional memory and, 646, 652–53,
        655
    emotion information processing and,
        668–69, 670, 671
    emotion regulation and, 712–13
    extrinsic vs. intrinsic, 994
    frustration-aggression hypothesis view
        of, 811–13
    in hunter-gatherer societies, 776
    individual differences in, 699, 700, 719
    infants and, 353, 354, 360, 362, 363
    instrumental behavior and, 755
    interpersonal relationships and, 824,
        825
    judgment/performance vs. development/
        mastery, 994
    mastery pleasures and, 841
    mood disorders and, 994–95
    pre- and post-goal attainment positive
        affect, 6, 17

prefrontal cortex and, 9–10, 17, 18
response modulation issues, 905
self-discrepancy theory, 994–95
self-relevant, 778–79
goal significance, 709
Goddard, G. V., 94
Goethe, Johann von, 482
Goffman, E., 490, 498
Gold, P. E., 94, 97
Goldbeck, T., 443
Goldman, S. L., 1091
Goldsmith, H. Hill, 295–99, 300–316, 321,
    677–79
Goldstein, D., 1068
Gombrich, Ernst, 485, 493
gonadal mosaicism, 309
Gonder-Frederick, L., 704
Gonzaga, Gian C., 412, 415–27
Gonzalez, C., 815
Goodenough, Florence L., 335, 349
good forms (Gestalt concept), 487
Goodkin, K., 1058
Goodman, S. H., 738
Goodwin, P. J., 1071
Gorenstein, E. E., 904–5
gorillas, 470
Gotlib, I. H., 738, 981, 992
Gottesman, I. I., 301, 304, 309, 310
Gottman, J. M., 486, 1098
Goya, Francisco, 486
Graf, P., 989, 990
Graham, D. T., 216
Graham, Martha, 492
grammar, 412, 447
    language acquisition and, 544
    signed languages and, 537–38, 540–41,
        544–47
Grant, H., 994
Grant, J. D., 305
gratitude, 855, 863, 864, 866
Gray, F., 118
Gray, Jeffrey A., 327, 377, 679, 683, 684,
    685, 687, 688, 921, 922, 926n.2, 933,
    976, 1110
gray rami, 139, 140
great apes, 470
Great Depression, 812, 820n.16
great limbic lode, 931, 932f
Greece, ancient, 325, 504, 508, 535, 636,
    932–33
Green, D. P., 819–20nn.3, 16, 1091
Green, J., 759
Green, S., 468–69
Greenberg, B., 707
Greenberg, D. A., 306
Greenberg, J., 711, 712, 995
Greenwald, M. K., 200, 645
Greer, S., 1060, 1061, 1067
Greger, R., 137

Gregory, A. H., 525
grief, 192
Griffit, W., 604, 806
Groans of Pain theory, 459
Grodd, W., 943
Gross, James, 1069
Gross, J. J., 705–6, 710, 734, 881, 1050
group membership, 1010
group therapy, 1071–72, 1074, 1096, 1098
growth hormone, 1022, 1026, 1028, 1032–
    36, 1097, 1121
Gruber, H., 492
guarding behavior, 1012, 1014–16
Gudjonsson, G. H., 707
Guernica (painting), 491
guided imagery mood induction, 603
guilt, 325, 330, 1087
    appraisal theory view of, 580, 581, 585,
        690, 861
    attributional style for, 688
    as communication of caring, 828
    cultural views of, 846, 848
    development of, 297, 338, 356, 375–76,
        375–403, 383–403, 780, 792–93
    interpersonal relationships and, 828,
        829, 831, 833
    journal articles published on, 852, 853t
    moral emotion issues and, 855, 859,
        860–61, 862, 865, 866
    prosocial behavior and, 750, 792–93,
        798, 861
    reflected or self-appraisal of, 781
    as stereotype correction influence, 607
    toddlers and, 335, 336, 353, 356, 792
    as warning, 778
Gulley, B. L., 728
gun control, 805–6
Gundlach, R. H., 508, 525
Gunnar, M. R., 354, 355
Gunnar-von Gnechten, M. R., 353
Gur, R. C., 943
Gur, R. E., 943
Guroff, J. J., 903
Gurvits, T. V., 967
gustatory stimuli, 937, 938
"gut" feelings, 566, 621, 636

## H

habit memory, 901
habitual actions, 774
habituation, 287, 1121, 1126
habituation effect, 941, 942, 953
Hagan, R., 979
Hahn, R. C., 1066
Haidt, Jonathan, 843, 845, 848–49, 852–66
haji (Japanese concept), 884
Halberstadt, J., 598

Hall, Stanley, 856

hallucinations, 900, 952

Hama, H., 524

Hamann, S. B., 651

Hamilton, Alexander, 402

Hamilton Depression Rating Scale, 900, 1025, 1061, 1067

Hamm, Alfons O., 187–207, 285

Hamovit, J. H., 903

Hampson, P., 523

Hampton, P. J., 508

hands, signed languages and, 536, 537, 539

Hanslick, Eduard, 505, 506

*hao-xue-xin* (Chinese concept), 400

happiness, 5, 412
  in American cultural model, 871, 880, 884, 885
  as attitude and judgment influence, 602–5, 608, 609, 611, 761, 765
  as basic emotion, 68, 176, 333, 669
  as communication of caring, 828
  cultural perspectives on, 871, 878, 879, 880, 884, 885
  expression of in interpersonal relationships, 828, 830, 831
  facial expression of, 420, 423, 424
  health as factor in, 1047
  induction studies of, 939, 943–50
  as information-processing factor, 601, 629, 761, 765
  memory's impact on, 653
  moral emotion issues and, 853
  music and perception of, 515, 520, 523, 524–25, 527, 529
  objective, 1090
  self-generation of, 776
  suppressed expression of, 847
  vocal expression of, 438, 439*t*, 440, 444, 448
  *See also* joy

hardiness, 1050

Harding, D. W., 491

*Hard Times* (Dickens), 486

Hare, R. D., 913, 914, 926n.5

harm, 861, 992

harm avoidance, 322, 933, 954

Harmon, R. J., 350

harmonics, 434, 442, 443, 544

Harmon-Jones, E., 609

harmony
  Confucian view of, 385, 386, 387
  cultural models of, 877–80, 883
  in music, 519, 520, 527
  relational, 877, 878, 879
  social, 843

Harpur, T. J., 913

Harris, L. M., 987

Harris, R., 1071

*hasham* (Bedouin concept), 859, 883, 884

Hasselmo, M. E., 474

hate, 1010, 1084

hate crimes, 812, 820n.16

Hatfield, E., 487

Hatoh, T., 516

Hauser, M. D., 470, 474

Haviland, J. M., 334, 492

Hawk, L. W., 203

Hayashi, K. T., 469

Haydn, Franz Joseph, 516

Hayes, B. K., 987

Haynes, K. N., 780

Head, Henry, 909

head-hunting, 879

healing songs, 525

health, physical
  anxiety neurobehavioral models, 1105–13
  attitudes and judgments about, 611
  autonomic specificity issues and, 216
  cancer patients' emotional expression and, 1053–75
  disease susceptibility and, 611, 738
  emotion and, 3, 5, 727, 1047–50, 1083–99
  emotion processing and, 679
  fear appeals and, 757
  hot/cold empathy gap and, 634–35
  memory's impact on, 653
  music's therapeutic effects on, 504
  personality, emotion, and, 738–39, 1057, 1058, 1060
  stress and, 5, 1049–50, 1074, 1084, 1087, 1117–31
  *See also* illness; mental health; well-being

hearing (sense), 13, 31. *See also* Deaf community

heart, 258. *See also* cardiovascular system

heart rate response, 191, 192, 323, 1108
  prosocial behavior studies, 791, 793, 794

heat. *See* temperature (environmental)

Heath, R. G., 36

Heatherton, T. F., 831, 861

Hebb, Donald O., 583, 900

Hecht, M. A., 421

Heckhausen, H., 393

Heckhausen, J., 393

hedonia, dopamine and, 33

hedonic contingency model, 760–61, 766

hedonic experiences, 843, 844

hedonic tone, 577

hedonic valence, 805

Heerwagen, J. H., 488–89

Heffner, H. E., 474

Heffner, R. S., 474

Heimberg, R. G., 688, 689

Heinlein, C. P., 523

helping behavior, 793

facial expression and, 425, 790

moral emotions and, 855, 861

motivation for, 750, 787, 796–97

*See also* prosocial behavior

helplessness, 780, 1086, 1130
  animals and, 1010
  appraisal malfunctioning and, 584
  cancer patients and, 1053–58, 1060–62, 1075, 1087
  cognitive theories of psychopathology and, 997–99
  learned, 123, 124, 901, 997, 999

hemispheric lateralization. *See* lateralization

Henderson, C., 524

Henriques, J. B., 701

Herbener, E. S., 728

heredity. *See* genes; genetics; nature-nurture debate

heritability, 302. *See also* genes; genetics

heroin, 28, 33, 34

Herrnstein, R. J., 805

Hess, L., 699

Hess, Walter Rudolf, 133, 138, 152–53, 226

heterarchical organization, central nervous system, 1106, 1108, 1111, 1112

heterozygosity, genetic, 310

Heuer, F., 645

heuristic processing, 612, 613, 764–65

heuristic-systematic model, 758

Hevner, K., 517, 519–20, 528

Hewitt, J. K., 306

hierarchically organized intonation models, 448

hierarchical societies, 858, 859–60, 883

hierarchy of needs/goals, 578, 579

Higgins, E. T., 652, 688, 689, 994, 995, 996, 1000

high-anxious copers, 716, 718

high density microarray systems, 1036

higher-level thought, 661, 990–1001

high-reactive children, 320–21, 328–30

Hilgard, E. R., 597

Hilton, S. M., 238

Hinde, R. A., 339, 340, 468, 469

Hinduism, 844, 846, 847, 865

hippocampus, 10*f*, 27, 73, 964, 1073
  allostatic load and, 1124–26, 1128, 1130–31
  amygdala and, 964, 966, 970, 972
  anxiety and, 972, 1113
  behavioral inhibition system and, 327
  conditioning role, 13, 55, 56, 59, 61, 62
  depression and, 14, 15, 18, 19, 1128, 1131
  emotion and emotion regulation, 4, 6, 9, 13–15, 17, 18, 19
  emotion induction study findings on, 940, 948

facial expression neuroimaging, 936
gene expression and, 313
gustatory emotion evaluation studies and, 938
maternally derived genes and, 310
memory and. *See under* memory
panic disorder and, 970, 971, 972
phobias and, 969
posttraumatic stress disorder and, 14, 966–67, 968, 972, 1128, 1131
psychopathology and, 900, 901, 1084
hippocampus subiculum, 104
Hippocrates, 698, 1047
Hirsch, S. M., 259
Hirschsprung's disease, 136
Hirshleifer, Jack, 895
Hitler, Adolf, 483, 857
HIV virus, 1095
Ho, A. P., 16
Ho, K., 624
Hobbes, Thomas, 572
Hochschild, A. R., 880
Hock, M., 713, 716, 717
Hodapp, V., 703
Hoffman, M. L., 787, 788, 789, 792, 793
Hoffmann, H., 649
Holen, A., 707
Hollan, D., 879
Holst, E. von, 153
homeostasis, 149, 151, 154, 155, 164, 166–70, 172
    as experiment design factor, 241
    health issues and, 1049
    survival concerns and, 257
Homer, Winslow, 494
homicide, 805–8, 812, 813, 817, 819n.4
*Homo economicus*, 854–56, 864, 866, 866n.2, 894
homosexuality, 858
homovanillic acid, 1031–32
homozygosity, genetic, 309, 310
Hong Kong, 388
honor
    anger and, 856
    Chinese view of, 387, 389–94, 400–401
    cultural perspectives on, 871, 872, 883, 884
    cultures of, 807–8, 819nn.5–6, 846–47, 872, 884
Hook-Costigan, M. A., 38
Hooley, J. M., 997
hope, 611, 683, 687, 811
    health and, 1092, 1095, 1097
Hope, D. A., 980
hopelessness
    cancer patients and, 1053–58, 1060–63, 1069, 1087
    racism and, 1086, 1087
hopelessness cognitions, 998
hopelessness theory of depression, 997–99

Hopkins, W. D., 465
hormones, 135, 167, 169, 1073
    allostasis, allostatic load, and, 1121
    corticotropin-releasing, 16, 313, 1112
    emotion expression and, 187, 572
    stress, 4, 38, 61, 93, 94, 95, 109, 1118, 1127, 1129, 1131
    thyroid, 1034–35
    *See also other specific hormones and hormone types*
Horne, J. A., 702
Horney, K., 774
Horowitz, M., 287
Horowitz, M. J., 707
horses, 471
Hoshino, E., 525
Hosoi, H., 450
Hospital Anxiety and Depression Scale, 1056, 1062, 1069
hostile affect, 820n.18
hostile aggression, 805, 806
hostility, 1126, 1131
    cancer patients and, 1063, 1068
    environmental causes of, 807, 809, 810, 820n.13
    as health factor, 739, 1049, 1087
    negative affect and, 815–16, 820n.18
hot anger, 440, 444, 446
"hot" cognition, 565
hot/cold empathy gap, 629, 634
hot emotions, 879
Houston, D. M., 999
Hovland, C. I., 812, 820n.16
"How do I feel about it?" heuristic, 600, 608, 612, 627
    attitude change and, 759, 764
Howland, E. W., 912
HPA axis. *See* hypothalamic-pituitary-adrenal axis
HPT axis. *See* hypothalamic-pituitary-thyroid axis
Hsieh, J. C., 119
Hsu, L. M., 246
H$_2$O$^{15}$O PET. *See* oxygen-15 water positron emission tomography
Hu, H. C., 385
Hubel, D. H., 902
Huber, K., 506, 508
huddling behavior, 1010
Hudson, R., 530n.1
Hugdahl, Kenneth, 266, 276–90
Hughlings Jackson, John, 42, 449, 900, 931, 1106
Human Genome Project, 301, 310, 315
human intruder paradigm, 13–14
humanism, 484, 774
humans
    animal emotion expression compared with, 463–64, 465, 470–72, 474, 476, 583

animal phobias of, 259–60, 969
behavioral genetics and, 302–10
emotional brain of, 4, 25–43
emotional learning circuits of, 4, 52–62
fear conditioning circuitry of, 59–61
fear-potentiated startle reflex of, 200–201, 202f, 203
preparedness theory and, 266–68
self-reflection and, 773–83
speech and, 433–52
Hume, David, 563–64, 572, 748, 861, 865
humor, 685, 711, 1097
    brain's processing of, 68
    facial expression and, 417
    genetic factors in, 340
    shared, 336, 337, 341
    *See also* laughter
humors (bodily), 325–26, 535, 698, 932–33
hunger, 34, 170, 629, 841
hunter-gatherer societies, 775–76
Huntington's disease, 85, 310, 423, 648, 932
Hunziker, J., 736
Hupka, R. M., 541
hurt, 781, 805, 816
Hutchinson, K. A., 541
Huttenlocher, P. R., 356
hyperalgesia, 174–75
hyperbolic time discounting, 625
hypercognized emotions, 884
hypercortisolemia, 14, 15, 1073
hypercortisolinemia, 1022, 1033
hyperglycemia, 1121
hypermetabolism, 125
hypermutability, 1017
hypertension, 169, 170, 1085–87, 1121, 1130
hyperventilation, 61
hypervigilance, 18
hypnosis, 30, 227, 667
hypocognized emotions, 884
hypocrisy, 857
hypomania (bipolar II), 899, 1024
hypometabolism, 124, 125
hypothalamic-pituitary-adrenal axis, 15, 171, 174, 175, 1072, 1087
    allostatic load and, 1093, 1126–27, 1129, 1131
    depression and, 1022, 1032–36
    immune system and, 1074
    pair bonding and, 1097
    stress and, 1073
hypothalamic-pituitary-thyroid axis, 1032–36
hypothalamus, 27, 28, 42, 73, 85, 118, 1106, 1111, 1117–18
    anterior cingulate cortex and, 11
    autonomic nervous system and, 149, 150t, 152–53, 154, 155, 163–67, 169–70, 172, 174, 175

hypothalamus (*continued*)
  bird cooing and, 471
  depression and, 1032–36
  emotion induction study findings on, 940, 947, 949
  fight-or-flight response and, 327
  functional impairment of, 136
  hunger role of, 34, 170
  immune system and, 173
  lateral, 34–35, 36, 37
  medial tumors, 41
  oxytocin and vasopressin production, 1012
  panic disorder and, 971
  paternally derived genes and, 310
  reactivity of children and, 328
  ventromedial, 34, 41
  visceral afferent neurons and, 144
  vocal expression and, 449
hypothesis generation, 649
hypothyroidism, 1034, 1035

**I**

Iacono, W. G., 683
id, 326, 865, 931
ideal focus, memory retrieval and, 652
ideal self, 688, 689, 779, 995, 996
identification, as literary experience, 488, 497, 498
identity
  autobiographical memory's role in, 735
  fragmentation and, 993
  politics of, 483–84
  sense of, 776–78
  social, 581
ideoaffective organizations, 736
idiopathic generalized epilepsies, 306, 311
idiosyncratic construals, 1049, 1089
Ifaluk, 880
Ikegaya, Y., 103
illness
  biopsychosocial model of, 1088, 1094
  emotion and, 1047, 1083, 1087, 1095
  hot/cold empathy gap and, 634–35
  *See also* disease; *specific conditions*
illusion of mental health, 1091
illusions of control, 993
Ilnyckyj, A., 1071
Ilongot, 879
imagery
  decision-making and, 630, 631, 632
  emotion induction via, 227, 228, 233
  experiment design and, 241
  *See also* mental images
imagination
  human capacity for, 775–77, 779, 780, 781, 783
  mental schemas and, 485

Imaizumi, S., 450
imipramine, 971, 1022, 1023–24, 1028–29
imitation, 354, 487, 504, 505
IML, 167
immediate emotions, 566, 620–21, 625, 626–36
immediate-return environments, 776
immorality, 875–76, 892
immune system, 169, 170, 1029, 1096
  affect's influence on, 611
  allostatic load and, 1124, 1130
  emotional expression and, 187
  evolutionary issues, 257
  individual differences in emotion and, 1088
  stress and, 738, 1033, 1049, 1073–74, 1084, 1086, 1108, 1124
  sympathetic nervous system and, 172–74
imperfect signaling, 895
implicit cognitive processing, 566
implicit knowledge, 362–64, 365*t*, 647, 843
implicit memory, 198, 647–48, 983–87, 990
importance, in appraisal theory, 574, 578, 579
impression, in vocalization. *See* decoding
impression formation paradigm, 762
impressionism, 482, 490, 494
impression management, 840
imprinting, genomic, 309, 310
impulse strength, emotional expressivity and, 706
impulse to aggression, 816
impulsive disorders, 683
impulsive/expressive aggression, 806
impulsivity, 933
  antisocial behavior and, 804, 805–6, 1027–28
  deficient response modulation and, 905
  dopamine level as factor in, 327
  effortful control and, 693
  emotional reactivity and, 683, 689, 693
  genetic factors in, 727
  health and mortality and, 739
  hyperbolic time discounting and, 625
  prefrontal cortex damage and, 29
incidental affect, 619, 629
incidental influences, decision making and, 566, 619, 620–21, 628, 630, 632–33, 635
incidental recall, 1000
indebtedness, 863
indelibility, of memory, 643–44
independent emotions, 886
India
  caste system in, 857
  cultural-specific emotions in, 847

expression universality findings on, 420, 421, 422
Indians, North American, 525
indignation, 855
individual differences, 298
  in affective development, 296, 353, 355, 356, 357
  allostatic load and, 1120, 1128–30
  in appraisal, 583, 584–85
  children's social relationships and, 296, 333, 338, 339–43
  in emotion, 134, 1088
  in emotional reactions and coping, 679, 698–719
  in emotional reactivity, 678–79, 681–94, 1089
  in emotion regulation, 347, 358, 362, 364–66
  in facial expression of emotion, 426–27
  information processing emotion model and, 671
  interpersonal relationship considerations and, 832–33
  in music perception, 508, 526
  personality and, 678, 726–27, 729, 736, 737, 739
  in response modulation, 908
  in temperament, 303, 729
individualism, 384, 386–87, 402
individualist cultures, negative emotion expression in, 880
individual-specific response patterns, 699–700, 704, 719
indoleamines, 1022
Indonesia
  cultural models in, 876–77
  shame perspective in, 859
  vocal expression findings on, 445
  *See also specific peoples*
induction/elicitation of emotion, 216–18, 221, 225–33
  appraisal process and, 573, 577, 588, 589
  in attitude and judgment studies, 602, 603, 610, 611
  in autonomic specificity research, 216–20, 221
  cognitive factors in, 563–65
  context effects and, 233, 234*f*
  evaluation criteria, 227–28
  experiment design issues, 241–43
  in individual differences research, 706
  information processing theory research, 667
  interpersonal relationships and, 824, 827
  methods of, 226–27, 588
  physiological and pharmacological studies of, 588, 930, 939–52, 965
  relative nonselectivity and, 228–33

research participant selection issues and, 238–39, 240*f*

vocal expression research and, 436

inductive analysis, 708

*Infant Behavior Questionnaire,* 303

*Infant Behavior Record,* 304–5

Infant Laboratory Assessment Battery, 552

infant psychopathology, 349

infants

anger expression by, 334, 353, 357, 364, 365*t*, 421, 543, 780, 812

appraisal processes for, 583

attachment and, 312, 489, 730, 1010, 1095

babbling by, 471–72, 475, 476, 544

behavioral inhibition and, 327–29, 354, 356

cooing by, 333, 334, 469

crying by, 333, 334, 349, 354, 470, 476, 544, 552, 730, 748, 789, 828

deaf, 543

developmental continuity in, 298–99

distress expression by, 333, 334, 353, 470, 544, 828, 862

emotional development of, 296, 298, 303–5, 332–35, 347–66, 732

emotion coregulation and, 381, 395

emotion expression by, 333, 334, 347, 350, 353, 356

emotion regulation by, 347, 349, 357–66

emotion research overview, 348–57

empathy and, 788, 789

facial expressions of, 333, 350, 358, 366, 539, 543

fear and, 328, 330, 348, 350, 353, 354, 357, 543

frustration reactions by, 812

gestural communication by, 354

lack of self in, 777, 781

language acquisition in, 535, 545–47

learning and, 361–62

music perception and, 524

personality development, 727–31, 736, 739

prosody sensitivity of, 335, 447, 507, 544

reactivity of, 320–21, 328–30, 353

smiling by, 333, 334, 364, 417, 425, 543, 552

social referencing and, 335, 353, 354, 363, 425, 543, 730–31, 789

social relationships and, 332–35, 342, 347, 353, 354, 355, 357, 360–61

temperament of, 320–23, 326–27, 347–48, 350, 353, 354, 727, 729

vocal expression development in, 544, 552

*See also* toddlers

infection, 1047, 1073–74, 1130

infectious diseases, 136, 1048

inference, 563

attitudes, judgments, and, 600–601

mood and, 566

inferior colliculus, 329

inferior frontal cortex. *See* Broca's area

inferior frontal gyrus, 942, 945

inferior mesenteric ganglion, 155

inferior parietal region, panic disorder and, 970

inferior temporal cortex, 118

inferior temporal gyrus, 474

inflammation, sympatho-adrenal system and, 174–75

information processing, 565, 661–71

affect and, 597, 605, 608, 610–13

in appraisal process, 574, 576

for attitudes and judgments, 597, 599–602, 605, 607, 759–62, 764–65

aversive emotion-related, 699

deficient response modulation and, 905

emotional disorder cognitive biases and, 976–1001

emotional disorders and, 565, 662–64, 666, 667, 669–71, 976–1001

emotional reactivity individual differences and, 678–79, 681–94

emotion theories concerning, 565, 667–71

immediate emotions' impact on, 629–30, 633, 635, 636

individual differences in, 708

key paradigm concepts, 662–67

memory and, 646–51, 661

mood and, 566, 759–62, 764–66, 767n.6

psychopaths and, 913, 918–19

vocal expression and, 435

information theory, animal communication and, 460–61

infrasound, animal use of, 462

Ingram, R. E., 690, 995–96

Ingvar, M., 119

inheritance. *See* genetics

inhibited temperament, 728, 729

inhibition

of aggression, 817–19

behavioral. *See* behavioral inhibition

conceptual emotion influences and, 687

inhibitory avoidance learning, 99–104

inhibitory control, children and, 304, 354

initial value dependency, 246, 247

injuries

counteraction of, 132

hostile aggression and, 805

injustice

anger concerning, 856

in appraisal theory, 581

cultural perspectives on, 875

inositol trisphosphate system, 1023

Insel, Thomas R., 5, 297, 315, 902, 1010–19

in situ hybridization histochemistry, 1029

instability of change, 708

Institute of Child Welfare (University of California, Berkeley), 349

instrumental action, emotion-typical tendencies, 380

instrumental aggression, 805, 806

instrumental behavior, 755

instrumental music, 504–5, 588

instruments, musical, 507, 525, 526

insular cortex, 11, 104–5, 937

emotion induction study findings on, 941, 942, 943, 945, 947

facial expression and, 423, 936

mood neuroimaging findings on, 953

panic disorder and, 971, 972

posttraumatic stress syndrome and, 967

temperament neuroimaging research, 954

insulin resistance, 1117, 1120

integration

of activated concepts, 687

cognitive, 993–94

of mental representations, 989–90

intensity

acoustical. *See* amplitude

of affect, 566–67, 603, 609

in decision-making theories, 623, 624, 627–28, 630, 633, 636, 637n.9

emotionality and prosocial behavior, 794–96

genetic factors in, 727

as memory recall factor, 653–54

of stimuli in appraisal, 577

intentional behavior

children and, 334, 354, 425

fairness appraisal and, 875

intentions

affect's adaptive value and, 843

goals and, 732

interdependent emotions, 886

interdependent relationships, 750, 825–27, 832, 833

interest

as basic emotion, 862

personality and, 733

vocal expression of, 443

intergroup attitudes, 605–8

interjections, 568

intermediate-type (I-type) individuals, 702

internalizers, 705

internal tone, 324, 329–30

International Affective Picture System, 191, 192, 200, 217, 939–41

international style of architecture, 495

interneurons, 164–67

interoception, 567, 702–3

interoceptive information

as cognition influence, 691

perceptual inputs and, 681, 682, 686, 694

interpersonal disgust, 857
interpersonal engagement, 585, 876, 877, 882
interpersonal relationships, 750, 824–33, 1097
   affection and, 482
   attitudes and judgments in, 597, 605, 610–11, 613
   business and, 832
   cognitive dynamics of, 997
   communal, 750, 825, 827–33, 861, 862
   emotional expression and, 414, 824–25
   emotional issues with significant others and, 1084–86, 1087, 1093
   family and, 827–28, 829, 831–33
   friendships and, 828–29, 831–33
   individual differences in, 832–33
   interdependent, 750, 825–27, 832, 833
   romantic, 827, 831–33
   See also parent-child relationships; social behavior; social relationships
interpretive biases. See judgmental/interpretive biases
intersubjectivity, 332
intertemporal choice, decision making and, 622, 624–26
interviews
   as research method, 227, 492
   temperament measurement and, 321–22
intimacy, 598, 1087, 1094, 1098
   children's development of, 336, 337
intonation. See prosody
intrinsic goals, 994
intrinsic pleasantness, as appraisal dimension, 573, 574, 576–79, 584, 586, 588, 687, 691, 709
introversion, 698, 704, 933
   circadian rhythm and, 702
   emotional reactivity issues and, 683, 685, 692, 693
   response modulation and emotion processing and, 921
   temperament neuroimaging findings on, 954
intrusive memories, 984, 987
Inuit language, 568
invalid trials, attention tasks and, 277–78, 281–82, 284, 285, 289
inversion effect, face processing and, 465
invulnerability, feelings of, 1050
I-123-labeled-beta CIT, 969
I-123-labeled-iomazenil, 971
Iowa Child Study group, 349
iproniazid, 1023
irrationality, 892
irritability, of infants, 357
irritation, 855
   cognitive-neoassociationistic aggression model, 815
   vocal expression of, 440

Irwin, William, 939, 940
Isaacowitz, D. M., 726–39
Isbell, L., 763, 765–66
ischemia, 417
Isen, A. M., 379, 599, 601, 607, 637n.10, 711, 712
isolation, as repressive defense mechanism, 716
Israel, 813
Isreal, J. B., 205
Italian language, 541
Italy
   cultural models in, 886
   music history and, 504
   violent crime rates in, 807
Ito, T. A., 190, 195
Izard, C. E., 226, 235, 261, 350, 353, 367n.5, 416, 418, 420, 435, 449, 543, 574, 711, 727, 816

J

Jääskeläinen, J., 1059
jackknifing (algorithm), 446
Jackson, D. C., 1084
Jackson, E. W., 322
Jacobs, Jane, 496–97
Jaggi, J. L., 943
James, William, 3, 4, 93, 109, 149–50, 175, 212, 213, 225, 270, 330, 564, 566, 567, 572, 575, 702, 776, 778, 847, 931, 1107
James-Lange theory of emotion, 29, 149–50, 175–76, 188, 330, 566, 931
Jänig, Wilfrid, 133, 135–77, 222n.2
Janis, I. L., 636n.1
Jankowski, J. J., 361
Janoff-Bulman, R., 780
Janowsky, A., 315
Japan
   appraisal patterns in, 585, 874, 875, 876
   cultural models in, 874–78, 881–82, 885–86
   culture-specific emotions in, 847, 876
   emotional expression and behavior in, 878, 880
   empathy-related responding in, 791–92
   expression universality findings on, 419, 421
   focal emotion avoidance in, 884
   musical expression studies and, 525
   reported emotion frequency in, 846
Japanese macaques, 468–69, 473, 474
Javanese, 878–79, 883
Javanmard, M., 971
jealousy, 325, 748, 776–77, 778
Jefferson, Thomas, 481, 483, 496
Jenike, M. A., 965
Jenkins, J. M., 486

Jenkins, M. A., 118
Jensen, M. R., 1069, 1070
John, B., 301
John, O. P., 705–6
Johnson, Debra, 954
Johnson, E. J., 631
Johnson, Marcia K., 576, 665
Johnson, M. H., 356
Johnson, P., 471
Johnson, Philip, 496
Johnson-Laird, P. N., 487, 668–69, 670, 671, 692, 990
Johnston, R. E., 418
Johnstone, Tom, 412, 413, 433–52, 589
Jolly, J. D., 992
Jones, Harold, 349
Jones, H. E., 705
Jones, Mary Cover, 349
Jones, R. L., 915
Jordan, D., 137
Josephson, B. R., 652, 712
joy, 325, 353, 356, 589n.5, 1010, 1019
   animals and, 774
   appraisal patterns for, 585
   as commonly reported emotion, 846
   cultural development of, 389, 393, 394
   facial expression of, 444
   infants and, 780
   music and perception of, 514, 515, 520
   personality and, 733
   vocal expression of, 443, 444
Joyce, James, 484, 497
judgment, 563
   affect infusion model of, 566, 611–13, 636–37nn.3, 8, 691, 764–65
   affect's impact on, 413, 566, 596–613
   attitudes and, 753
   behavior linked with, 610–11
   cognitive processing biases and, 977
   contemporary cognitive theories and, 599–602
   empirical study findings on, 602–9
   health-related, 611
   immediate emotions' impact on, 627, 628, 632, 633
   information processing paradigm and, 661
   mood's effect on, 628, 749
   moral, 865–66, 866n.4
   research history overview, 597–99
   selective information processing and, 664
judgmental/interpretive biases, 977, 984, 988–89, 993
judgment/performance goals, 994
judgment studies, of expression, 412, 420, 424–25
Julius Caesar (Shakespeare), 775
Jung, Carl, 329
Jürgens, U., 449, 466, 470, 473

Juslin, Patrik N., 411, 412, 413, 441, 503–29
justice, appraisal and, 581
juvenile myoclonic epilepsy, 306, 311

# K

Kaada, B. R., 103
Kafka, Franz, 497
Kagan, Jerome, 31, 296, 305, 306, 320–31, 355, 393, 678, 710, 728, 729, 865
Kahneman, Daniel, 566, 622, 626, 842, 988, 1090
Kaiser, H. A., 995
Kaler, S. R., 902
Kalin, Ned H., 8–19, 469, 940, 1084
Kalish, H. I., 199
Kalnok, M., 733
Kames, L., 472
Kaminska, Z., 523
Kanazawa, S., 465
Kanfer, F. H., 908
Kanfer, R., 999
Kant, Immanuel, 596
Kaplan, G. A., 1059
Kaplan, R. F., 118
Kaplan, S., 490
Kaplan-Meier analysis technique, 1057
Kappas, A., 587
Käppler, C., 702
Kaprio, J., 728–29
Karasawa, M., 875, 882
Karoly, P., 709
Kasser, T., 994
Katkin, E. S., 270, 271
Kato, M., 516
Katz, A. N., 981
Kavanagh, D. J., 999
Kawasaki, H., 10
Kay, P., 541
Keats, John, 484, 491, 499
Keenan, K., 366
Kelley, H. H., 825
Kelly, G. A., 993
Keltner, Dacher, 411–14, 415–27, 632, 636n.5, 707, 816, 849, 859
Kemeny, M. E., 1074, 1096
Kendall, M. G., 247
Kendler, K. S., 308
Kennedy, Q., 726–39
Kentish, J., 1001n.2
Kerr, T. A., 1062
Kessler, R. C., 1086
Ketter, Terence A., 900, 930–54
Kety, S., 93
Kidd, J. R., 312
Kidd, K. K., 312
kidneys, 170, 173, 1012
Kiecolt-Glaser, J. K., 706, 1085

King, D. W. M., 194
King, L. A., 995
Kinney, L., 701
Kipsigis, 886
Kiritani, S., 450
Kirson, D., 541, 856
Kissen, D. M., 1066
Kitayama, S., 387, 582, 585, 847, 876, 881, 882, 885
Klaaren, K. J., 776
Klasmeyer, Gudrun, 412, 413, 433–52
Klein, D. J., 608
Klein, M., 863
Kleinen, G., 525, 528
Klineberg, O., 419
Kling, A., 474
Klos, K. L., 306
Klose, U., 943
Klug, F., 979, 980
Kluver, H., 32, 75, 931
KN-62, 103
Kneier, A. W., 707
knockout genetics, 313–14
Knoll, J. F., 703
Knoll, N., 716
knowledge
    declarative vs. procedural, 990, 991, 994, 1000
    explicit, 362–64, 365t
    implicit, 362–64, 365t, 647, 843
    of self, 604, 652, 991, 993
Koch, M., 199
Kochanska, G., 350, 731, 792
Kohlberg, L., 852, 865
Kohlmann, C.-W., 703, 704, 707
Konorski, J., 189, 198
Kopp, Claire B., 296, 297, 347–66
Kopp, D. A., 603
Kosslyn, Stephen M., 666, 941
Kosson, D. S., 910, 911, 912
Kotlyar, G. M., 525
Koutstaal, W., 646
Kovecses, Z., 215
Kraepelin, Emil, 1021
Kramer, G., 630
Kratus, J., 524
Kraut, R. E., 418
Kreiman, J., 450
Kreitler, H., 487, 488
Kreitler, S., 487, 488, 1070
Kretschmer, Ernst, 326
Krieger, N., 1086
Krishnan, K. R., 969
Kroenke, K., 704
Krohne, Heinz Walter, 679, 698–719
Krumhansl, C. L., 516
Kubey, R., 485
"Kubla Kahn" (Coleridge), 482, 491
Kubzansky, L., 587
Kudoh, T., 874, 875

Kuiken, D., 488, 499
Kuikka, J. T., 971
Kuiper, N. A., 991–92, 1000
Kukull, W. A., 1062
Kune, G. A., 1068–69
Kurokawa, M., 876
Kuwano, S., 516

# L

LaBar, Kevin S., 4, 52–62, 201, 651, 939–40
La Barre, W., 419
Laberg, J. C., 288
lability, emotional. See neuroticism
labor (birth process). See parturition
Labouvie-Vief, Gisela, 733
Labov, W., 541, 548
Lacey, J. I., 246, 288, 289, 698, 699
lactation, 950, 970–72, 1012, 1014
Ladd, D. R., 445, 447
La France, M., 421
lajya (Hindu emotion), 847, 859
Lakatos, K., 312
Lakoff, G., 215
Lamb, M. E., 295
landscape gardening, 489, 496
landscape painting, 493
Lane, A. J., 970
Lane, Richard D., 11, 119, 940, 947
Lang, James, 900
Lang, Peter, 19, 189, 190, 194, 198, 200, 201, 203, 205, 259, 940
Lang, P. J., 645, 914, 915, 917, 918
Lange, Carl G., 149, 150, 330, 567, 931
Langer, Susanne K., 503, 506, 508
Langley, J. N., 137–38, 152, 153
language, 411, 412, 1089
    affective aspects of, 568
    animal dialects and, 475
    animal-human parallels, 470–71
    appraisal theory and, 588
    autism and, 902
    communication channel integration and, 551–53
    definition of, 536
    developmental processes, 332, 336, 338, 354, 543–45, 548–53
    as discursive symbolism, 506
    disgust-related, 857
    emotional, 215
    emotion and, 297, 347, 358, 535–53
    emotion encoding, 541–42
    emotion words and, 678, 883, 1089
    as "frozen" cognitive structure, 568
    grammatical facial expression and, 415, 537–38, 540–41, 544–47, 551
    information processing paradigm, 661
    linguistic systems, 537–38

language (*continued*)
　literary, 499
　moral emotion issues and, 855
　motherese, 470–71, 538
　mouth's role in, 849
　music vs., 503
　narratives' evaluative function and, 297, 541, 547–51
　neurological foundations for, 542–43
　nonlinguistic emotional expression and, 538–43, 552, 553
　pathological disorders of, 900
　perceptual representation system and, 647
　positive biases in, 845
　problems with, 344
　self-report methodology issues and, 1089–90
　signed, 297, 536–51
　spoken. *See* speech
　temperament measurement issues and, 321–22
　tone-oriented, 446, 448–49, 538
　*See also specific languages*
language acquisition, 297, 535–36, 543–47
*Language of Music, The* (Cooke), 505–6
Larrick, R. P., 624
Larsen, J. T., 195
Larsen, R. J., 733, 1091
Larsen, S. F., 499
Larson, C. R., 473
laryngographs, 437
larynx, 437, 440, 442, 449, 473, 544
Lascaux (France) cave paintings, 493
Lashley, Karl, 900
latent avoidance contingencies, 910–11
latent class analysis, 323
late positive potentials, 194–95
lateral amygdala, 53–55, 57–59, 61, 101, 102
lateral hypothalamus, 34–35, 36, 37, 56
lateralization, 37–38, 73, 450, 703, 932
lateral orbitofrontal circuits, 931
lateral prefrontal cortex, 649. *See also* dorsolateral prefrontal cortex
lateral temporal lobe, 901
laughter, 381, 1097
　facial expression and, 417, 419, 423–26, 464, 476
Laukka, P., 441
Lavine, H., 754
Law of Initial Value, 246, 247
Lawson, C., 988
Lawton, M. P., 733
Lazarus, Richard S., 367n.6, 564, 573, 578, 580, 581, 628, 679, 687, 706, 708, 709, 710, 713, 736, 747–48, 780, 857, 862, 863, 977
L-dopa, 1024, 1031–32
learned emotions, 589

learned helplessness, 123, 124, 901, 997, 999
learning, 564, 901
　aggression responses and, 809, 814, 817
　amygdala damage impact on, 32, 95
　as associative network factor, 906
　cross-species, 474
　emotional. *See* emotional learning
　emotion regulation's importance and, 361
　facial expression's role in, 425–26
　fear-related, 4, 31, 32
　food aversion, 842–43
　hippocampus's role in, 13, 55, 56, 901
　instrumental, 842
　observational, 686
　passive avoidance, 910–13, 923, 926n.5
　pattern-association, 27
　social, 507
Leary, Mark R., 749–50, 773–83
LeDoux, Joseph E., 3, 4, 52–62, 101, 201, 262, 263, 269, 377, 564, 587
Leech, G. N., 387
Leeper, R. W., 677
left anterior orbitofrontal cortex, 938
left caudate, 938, 940, 942, 943, 954
left fusiform, 948
left hemisphere, 68, 71, 73, 422–23, 449–50, 542, 729, 941
left medial temporal gyrus, 936
left orbitofrontal cortex, 938
left posterior cingulate, 938
left pulvinar, 936
legitimacy, 581
*lek* (Balinese concept), 884
Lelwica, M., 334
Lembke, Anna, 930–54
Lemery, K. S., 306, 309
Lemieux, A. M., 995
lemurs, 470, 474
lens model. *See* Brunswikian lens model
Lenton, A. P., 541
Lerner, Jennifer S., 566, 619–36, 843
Lesch, K-P., 312
Leschinger, A., 123
lesions/lesion studies, 3, 4, 66–87, 297
　amygdala, 31–32, 55f, 56, 59, 67, 73–82, 85, 95, 99–100, 102, 104, 199, 423, 648, 651, 654, 934, 1106, 1109
　animal brain-manipulation, 26
　animal vocalization, 473, 474
　anterior cingulate, 118
　basal forebrain, 1109
　basal ganglia, 932
　basolateral amygdala complex, 97–100, 103, 104
　caudate nucleus, 103
　cortical study biases, 41
　dorsolateral prefrontal, 932

　facial expression findings from, 423
　hemisphere specialization, 38
　hippocampus, 55f, 59, 61
　hypothalamus, 34, 35
　logic of, 66–67
　medial prefrontal cortex, 117, 118–19, 654
　mood disorder findings from, 932
　nucleus accumbens, 104
　orbitofrontal cortex, 118, 119, 931
　pedunculopontine nucleus, 37
　perirhinal cortex, 55
　prefrontal cortex, 29, 104
　right hemisphere, 67–73
　septum, 35
　single structure/region, 67
　spinal cord, 136
　stria terminalis, 103, 104
　subcortical, 41
　temporal pole, 931
　ventral pallidum, 35
　ventromedial frontal cortex, 82–85, 86f
　vocal expression findings from, 449–50, 450
　Wernicke's area, 449
letter-number discrimination tasks, 921–22
leukocytes, 1025
level accuracy, 702, 703
Levenson, R. L., 906, 907, 909
Levenson, Robert W., 212–22, 226, 486, 737, 878, 1098
Levenston, G. K., 915, 918, 919
Leventhal, H., 576, 671, 703, 1087
Levine, L. J., 652, 713, 735
Levine, S., 469, 1074
Levy, R. I., 568, 884
Levy, S. M., 1060, 1074
Lewin, Kurt, 350
Lewis, K. R., 301
Lewis, Marc, 335, 353, 355, 356, 393, 812
lexical decision tasks, 913–14, 917
lexical emotion evaluation studies, 938–39
Leyhausen, P., 451
*li* (ritual propriety), 384
Li, Jin, 296, 375–403
*lian*, 385, 394, 400
Liang, K. C., 97–98
Liau, A. K., 819n.1
Liberman, N., 631
Liberzon, I., 968
libido, 326
Librium, 1108
lidocaine, 96, 97, 101, 102, 103
life expectancy, 1048, 1049
Life Orientation Test, 737
ligands, 1030–32
　benzodiazepine receptor, 1108–10
　radiolabeled high affinity, 965
　SERT-specific, 1028

*liget* (Ilongot concept), 879, 884
light therapy, 1027
likelihood, appraisal of, 687
liking, 840, 842, 846, 847
Lillehei, R. A., 469
limbic system, 5, 117, 118, 120, 931, 932*f*, 1106
 animal vocalizations and, 473
 autonomic nervous system and, 154, 155, 167, 169–70, 1108, 1113
 basic emotions and, 176
 dysfunction of and psychopathology, 904–5
 as emotional brain, 27
 emotional systems and, 682, 685, 933, 964
 emotion induction study findings on, 939, 940, 947
 memory role of, 94
 temperament neuroimaging study findings on, 953–54
 vocal expression and, 449
 *See also specific components*
Lindeman, R. C., 473
Lindström, E., 520, 523
linguistic anthropology, 568
linguistic systems, 537–538. *See also* language
lingular gyrus, 941
linkage analysis, genetics, 310–11, 313
Linn, B. S., 1071
Linn, M. W., 1071
Linton, S., 629, 636n.5
Linville, P. W., 993, 994
lipoid proteinosis. *See* Urbach-Wiethe disease
Lipowski, Z. J., 1088
Lippman, E. A., 530n.1
Lipps, T., 487
lip smacking, by animals, 464
listening
 emotion evaluation studies, 937
 emotion inference and, 442, 443–46
 to music, 503, 504, 507–29
 spoken language and, 537, 538, 540
 vocal expression perception from, 442–43, 451
literary criticism, 488, 497
Literary Reading Questionnaire, 488
literature, 411, 413, 481–84, 497–99
 identification by reader and, 488, 497, 498
 modernism and, 484
 psychological perspectives in, 486, 487, 489–93
 romanticism and, 482, 483, 497, 499
 *Sturm und Drang* movement and, 504
lithium, 1024
"Little Albert" studies, 349, 598, 775
liver, 326, 1048

*Lives of the Artists, The* (Vasari), 493
Livingston, R. B., 93
Liwag, M., 732–33
loathing, 855
Locke, J. L., 471, 472
locomotor development, infants and, 353, 354, 362
locus coeruleus, 96, 98, 464, 1025, 1026, 1112, 1125, 1127
Loeber, R., 804
Loewenstein, George, 566, 619–36, 842, 843
Loewy, A. D., 137
Loftus, D. A., 651
Loftus, E. F., 649
Loftus, G. R., 649
Logan, G. D., 576, 670
*London Symphony* (Haydn), 516
loneliness, health and, 1049, 1087
longitudinal studies
 depression, 451
 emotional development, 348, 366
 emotion understanding individual differences, 342
 genetics-related, 301, 304–5, 315
 interpersonal relationships, 826–27
 social understanding development, 339
 unipolar depression risk, 998
long-term memory, 107–9
long-term potentiation, 55, 58–59, 62, 103–5
Lopes, L. L., 623
Lorenz, Amanda R., 899–900, 904–26
losing of face, 383, 400
Losoya, Sandra, 297, 750, 787–98
loss, social, 1011
loss aversion, 844
loss cognitions, depression and, 992, 997
loudness, 442, 443
 in music, 520, 524, 526, 527
Louisville Twin Study, 304, 305
love, 325, 412, 424, 1010, 1084, 1087
 appraisal theory and, 588
 cultural views of, 382
 literary portrayals of, 498–99
 moral emotion and, 864–865
lovesickness, 1047
love songs, 525
Low, P., 137
low-level thinking, 703
Lowrance, R., 607
low-reactive children, 320–21, 328–29
l-tryptophan, 1026–27
Lundholm, H., 492
Lundqvist, D., 261
Luskin, F., 1048
luteinizing hormone, 471
Lutkenhaus, P., 393
Lutz, C., 880
Lykken, D. T., 910, 926n.4

lymph, 326
lymphocytes, 173, 1023, 1029, 1087
lymphoid tissues, 173–74
lymphokine-activated killer cells, 1074
lynchings, 812, 820n.16
Lynn Schenk, D., 516
Lyons, M. J., 309
*Lyrical Ballads* (Wordsworth), 483

# M

Macaluso, C., 515
macaques, 458, 459*f*, 463–65, 468–70, 473, 474
MacArthur Longitudinal Twin Study, 304–6, 309
MacArthur Successful Aging Study, 1122, 1124
MacDonald, K., 683
MacFarlane, Jean, 349
MacGregor, D. G., 630
Macintosh, Charles Rennie, 495
Mackie, D. M., 601, 602
MacLean, Paul, 1019
MacLean, P. D., 27, 931
MacLeod, A., 988
MacLeod, C., 277, 666, 978, 979, 981, 988, 1001n.4
macrophages, 173
Maddock, Richard, 937
Madey, S. E., 779
Madison, G., 527
Madley, S. F., 623
Madsen, C. K., 516, 517
Magai, C., 297, 367n.2, 736
magic, art vs., 484–85, 490
magnetic resonance spectroscopy, 965, 966, 968, 971–72
magnetoencephalography, 450
Mahapatra, M., 875
Maier, S. F., 631, 1047
Mainz Coping Inventory, 716, 717
major affective disorder, 731–32
major depressive disorder, 16
Malatesta, C. Z., 733
males
 animal affiliative behavior, 1011–17
 animal copulation calls, 470
 animal sexual behavior, 473, 1011
 bird song and, 466
 emotional expressivity and, 705, 706
 guarding behavior, 1012, 1014–16
 interoception and, 703
 symptom reporting differences, 704
Malizia, A. L., 971
Malmo, R. B., 699
*malu* (Indonesian term), 859
mammals, 258, 259, 1012
management/assessment theory, 461, 476

Mandarin Chinese language, 448–49, 538
Mandler, G., 212, 826, 989, 990
mangabeys, 462
mania (bipolar I), 899, 1024
manic disorders, 35, 683, 900, 932
    neurobiology of, 1024, 1028, 1031–33, 1035
    *See also* bipolar disorder
manipulation theory, 461
Manis, M., 1091
Manke, B., 305
Mankowski, T. A., 603
Mann, L., 636n.1
Mannle, S., 339
MANOVA. *See* multivariate analysis of variance
MAOIs. *See* monoamine oxidase inhibitors
mapping, gene, 313, 315
marijuana, 28, 30, 951
Mark, M. H., 954
Mark, M. M., 608
Markam, S., 876
marketing, emotion-based, 750
Markow, T. A., 310
Markowitz, H., 622
Marks, I. M., 685
Markus, H. R., 387, 582, 585, 847, 876, 885
Marlowe-Crowne scale, 1064, 1065
Marlowe-Crowne Social Desirability Scale, 1068, 1069
marmosets, 461, 462, 464, 470, 472, 473, 475, 476
Marquardt, T. P., 553
marriage, 735, 1085, 1087, 1094, 1097
Martin, L., 601, 612, 775, 776
Martin, L. L., 487, 759, 763, 765
Martin, M., 978
Martorano, R. D., 472
Martz, G.-E., 989
Marwitz, M., 700
Masataka, N., 474
Mascolo, Michael F., 296, 375–403
masked stimuli, 263–65, 267–71, 1107
masking, 445, 706, 791, 880–81, 882
*Mask of Sanity, The* (Cleckley), 909
Maslow, A., 774
masochism, 782
mastery, 847–48, 1050
mastery pleasures, 841
maternal behavior, 350, 1131
    of animals, 458, 473, 474, 1129
    attachment, 342, 489, 886, 1095
    cultural perspectives on, 886
    depression transmission, 738
    genetic link with, 298, 340
    infants' responsiveness to, 334–35, 544, 789
    motherese, 470–71, 507, 538

oxytocin and, 1012, 1014
    parent-child relationship and, 340, 342, 350, 352, 473
    personality development and, 731
    scent of mother preference, 473
    talk about feelings, 338, 341, 342
    as temperament influence, 304, 306, 356
Mathabane, Mark, 1096
Matheny, A. P., 305
Mathew, Roy, 954
Mathews, A., 277, 285, 664, 666, 692, 717, 979, 980, 981, 985, 986, 988, 990, 996, 1001n.2
Mathias, C. J., 137
mating behavior
    emotional attractiveness and, 489
    pair bonding and, 297, 315, 1010–15, 1017, 1019, 1095
    partner preference and, 1012–16
    social organization and, 1011
Matsumoto, D., 421, 874, 875, 885
Matt, G., 985
Mattheson, Johann, 504
Matthews, G., 689, 690, 692, 694
Matthews, K. A., 287, 737, 1086
Maudsley Personality Inventory, 1066
Mauro, R., 585, 874, 875
Mauss, M., 884–85
Mawson, A. R., 820n.17
Maximally Discriminative Facial Movement, 350
May, J., 717
Mayberg, Helen S., 12, 120, 124, 947, 953
Mayer, J. D., 712
Mayer, Mercer, 548
Mayman, M., 1091
Mayr, E., 259
mazindol, 1025
McCabe, A., 548
McCann, C. D., 981
McCartney, K., 307
McCauley, C. R., 857
McClintic, S., 393
McConnell, P. B., 471
McCrae, R. R., 731–32, 733
McCullough, M. E., 863
McDermott, K., 985, 987
McEwen, Bruce S., 1049, 1072, 1117–31
McFadden, S. H., 297, 367n.2
McGaugh, James L., 4, 93–109
McGuire, W. J., 756
McIntosh, D. N., 213
McKenna, M. C., 1059, 1066
McLachlan, A. L., 981
McLaughlin, L., 1001n.4
McLean, J., 645
McManis, Mark, 327
McNally, R. J., 686
McNaughton, N., 683

McNeilly, M. D., 1086
meadow voles, 1017
measurement issues
    allostatic load, 1121–25
    attitude research, 754
    infant emotions, 366
    self-report methodology, 1091–93
    temperament, 321–22
medial amygdala, 474
medial frontal cortex, 964
medial frontal gyrus, 936–39, 941–43, 945, 947, 949
medial geniculate body, 53
medial geniculate nucleus, 101
medial hypothalamic tumors, 41
medial orbitofrontal cortex, 56, 117–20, 125
medial prefrontal cortex, 28, 62, 104
    anxiety and, 1109, 1111, 1112
    cognitive activation studies of, 122–24
    definition of, 117–18
    depression neuroimaging and, 4, 117–25
    depression treatment and, 124, 125
    emotion induction study findings on, 940, 945, 947, 949
    lesions to, 117, 118–19, 654
    mood induction and, 120, 953
    posttraumatic stress syndrome and, 966–67, 968, 972
    resting state studies and, 120
    temperament neuroimaging research and, 954
medial temporal gyrus, 936
medial temporal lobe, 198, 647–48, 901, 969–70, 972
medial thalamus, 938
mediators of personality, 708–9
Medici, Lorenzo di Pierfrancesco de,' 493, 494
Medici family, 493
medieval art, 483, 494
mediobasal nuclei (amygdala), 900
meditation, 782, 865
Mediterranean cultures, 871, 872
medulla oblongata, 165, 171, 1112
Medvec, V. H., 623, 779
Meehl, P. E., 322
MEG. *See* magnetoencephalography
megakaryocytes, 1023
Mehrabian, A., 190
Meins, E., 342
melancholic temperament, 326, 698, 737, 933
Mellers, B. A., 624
melody, music and, 520, 524–25
Melville, Herman, 497
Melzoff, A. N., 487
memory, 1095, 1097
    allostatic load and, 1093

amygdala and, 4, 13, 16, 75–78, 93–105, 107–9, 648, 649, 651, 654, 933, 1127
animals and, 775
appraisal theory and, 564, 586, 587
associative, 650, 651, 654
attitudes, judgments, and, 599–600, 604–5, 612, 755
autobiographical, 679, 735, 983–87
cognitive processing biases and, 977
coping issues and, 717–19
emotional, 498
emotional arousal and, 93, 105–7, 644–45
emotional learning and, 52, 58, 61, 74
emotional priming and, 198
emotion and, 4, 93–109, 132, 563–65, 643–55
emotion processing and, 906
emotion regulation and, 711, 712
episodic, 647, 650, 651, 654
expectancy system and, 263
explicit, 198, 647, 648, 983, 985, 987, 989–90
fear-related, 1127, 1128
flashbulb, 644, 645, 1127
habit and, 901
hippocampal role in, 13, 75–77, 85, 103, 104, 109, 198, 651, 1127, 1128, 1131
implicit, 198, 647–48, 983–87, 990
infants and, 334, 354
information processing paradigm and, 646–51, 661, 663
intrusive, 984, 987
mood and, 566, 599–600, 652–53, 667–68, 735, 953, 983
mood-congruent vs. mood-dependent, 983
on-line affect, anticipated affect, and, 841–42, 843
orienting responses and, 261, 262
recall, 600, 610, 645, 650, 651–54, 735
recognition, 600, 645, 651, 654
representational, 901
repressed, 643–44
retrieval of, 565, 644, 646–48, 651–55, 712, 716
selective information processing and, 664
semantic, 647, 651
short-term, 663, 693
single step direct-access retrieval of past solutions from, 670
social, 297, 1014
social cognitive neuroscience approach to, 646–51
in SPAARS emotion model, 669
stress hormones and, 4, 93, 94, 95, 109
traumatic, 643–44, 645, 653
vagus nerve and, 107, 1107
working, 6, 83, 649, 663, 683, 702

memory biases, emotional disorders and, 977, 982–90
memory theory, historical overview of, 643–45
men. See males; sex differences
menarche, age at, 727–28
meningitis, 1034
Menninger Foundation, 350
menstruation, 472, 476, 728–29
Mental Adjustment to Cancer Fighting Spirit, 1055–56, 1061
Mental Adjustment to Cancer Helpless/ Hopeless, 1055–56, 1061
mental health, 1047
    emotional processing and, 679
    illusion of, 1091
    personality, emotion, and, 727, 736–38
    stress's impact on, 1049–50, 1086
    See also emotional disorders; psychological disorders; psychopathology
mental illness. See psychopathology
mental images, 630, 631, 632, 649, 1106
mental models (concept), 666
mental retardation, 309
mental schemas, 485–86, 489–90, 492, 498
Menza, M. A., 954
Menzies, R. G., 987
Merton, R. K., 811, 812
Mervaala, E., 16
mesencephalon, 171–72
mesomorphs, 326
Mesquita, Batja, 845, 846–47, 848, 866n.1, 871–87
metabolic syndrome, 169, 170
metabolism, allostatic load and, 1093
metal, 326
metaphors, emotion, 568
methodology, research, 216–20, 225–50
    appraisal and, 583, 586–88
    for cancer survival studies, 1054–56
    for emotion elicitation/induction, 216–18, 221, 225–33, 241–43, 436, 588
    for emotion timing, 219–20, 228
    for emotion verification, 218–19
    experiment designs and, 239–44
    for musical expression studies, 527–28
    for research participant selection, 238–39, 240f, 246
    sampling variables and, 233, 235–38, 239, 240f, 247–48
    for self-reports, 218, 219, 220f, 228–35, 1088, 1089–93
    statistical analysis and, 244–50
    for vocal expression studies, 436
methylphenidate, 1032
metoprolol, 107
Mexican cultural models, 877, 878
Meyer, L. B., 505, 568, 848

MHPG. See 3-methoxy-4-hydroxyphenylglycol
Miall, D. S., 488, 499
mianzi, 385, 394, 401
mice, 472–75, 1011, 1014, 1017
Michael, R. P., 808
Mickelson, K. D., 1086
microadrenomectomy, 15
microdialysis, 27
microelectrode implantation, 27
microtine rodents. See montane voles; prairie voles
midbrain, 940, 947, 949
Middle Ages, 483, 494, 504
Middlemarch (Eliot), 486
middle prefrontal gyrus, 968
midline thalamus, 449
Mikula, G., 581
Milberg, S., 830
Millar, M. G., 755
Miller, E. K., 9
Miller, G. E., 1087
Miller, N., 797, 811, 815
Miller, N. E., 207n.3, 261, 811, 820n.9
Miller, R. E., 465, 474
Miller, S. M., 714
Miller, W. I., 857, 858
Millon Behavioral Health Inventory, 1058, 1068
Mills, J., 825, 827, 828
Milner, P., 34, 36
mimesis, 483, 497, 504, 487
mimicry, 895
Minangkabau, 420, 883
mind-body connection, 1088, 1091
mind-mindedness, 342
mind-reading abilities, 340, 342, 343
Mineka, Susan, 269, 465, 678, 686, 901, 976–1001
Minnesota Multiphasic Personality Inventory, 1054, 1057, 1058, 1065, 1066, 1070
Miranda, J., 991, 992
mirror neurons, 72
misattribution, 600
Mischel, W., 679, 699, 708–9, 719
Mistlin, A. J., 474
Mithen, S., 773
mitochondrial inheritance, 309
mixed emotions, 337, 342, 579
MMPI. See Minnesota Multiphasic Personality Inventory
mMRI. See morphometric magnetic resonance imaging
mobbing calls, birds and, 466
Modahl, C., 1017
modal emotions, 589n.1
mode, in music, 517, 520, 523–25
model of coping modes, 714–19
modernism, 484

modesty, 387, 394, 859, 863
modularity, information processing and, 663, 664–65, 667, 668, 669, 671
Mogg, K., 264, 277, 717, 980, 986, 1001n.2
molecular genetics, 6, 7, 297, 300, 1036
  human emotion-related behavior and, 296, 310–12, 315
molecular studies, of animal affiliative behavior, 1017, 1019
monetary penalties, 13
monetary rewards, 28
monitoring/blunting concept, 714
monkeys, 931, 1011, 1074, 1118
  fear communication, 465, 474, 774
  maternal scent and, 473
  reproductive behavior, 461, 472
  scent-marking behavior, 472–73
  visual signaling and, 464–65
  vocalizations, 459, 461, 462, 466–70, 473, 474
  yawning by, 464
  See also specific species
monoamine oxidase inhibitors, 964, 1021, 1022, 1023
monoaminergic transmitters, 970, 972, 1025
monody, Italian, 504
monogamy, 1011, 1017
  copulation calls and, 470
Monroe, Marilyn, 489
montane voles, 1011–13, 1015–16, 1018
Monticello, Va., 483
Montoya, P., 989
mood, 4, 5, 637n.11
  ancient Chinese view of, 326
  appraisal and, 575, 749
  approach-related, 9
  associative network theory view of, 667–68, 711
  attention and, 711, 818, 977
  as attitude formation and change factor, 750, 759–66, 767nn.6,7
  attitudes, judgments, and, 597, 599–608, 610–13
  behavioral disposition bias and, 380
  cognition and, 566, 977
  dimensional emotion model and, 424
  direct activation and, 690
  dopamine and, 1031
  duration of, 219
  emotion regulation and, 711–12
  emotion vs., 325, 1093
  genetic factors in, 727
  as information-processing factor, 566, 601–2, 759–62, 764–66
  as judgment factor, 628, 749
  medial prefrontal cortex and, 117, 119, 124
  memory and, 599–600, 652–53, 667–68, 735, 953, 983

motivational consequences of, 602, 749
negative affect and, 8, 198
neural substrates of, 931–32
neuroimaging of, 120, 952–53
as nonsensory affect, 841–42
optimism and, 1096
personality research issues and, 678
pharmacological induction studies of, 950–52
prosocial behavior and, 750, 787, 796–98, 830–31
psychodynamic view of, 1021
psychopathology and, 899, 900
as self-concept factor, 602–3
septum and, 36
serotonin levels and, 327
social behavior and, 749
social-cognitive biases and, 977
as social comparison factor, 779
suppression of, 664
temperament as predictor of, 728
temporal domains of, 930–31, 954
transcranial magnetic stimulation research and, 6
Velten method and, 120, 227, 228
ventral pallidum and, 35
vocal expression as indicator of, 451
withdrawal-related, 9
mood-as-a-resource hypothesis, 604
mood-behavior model, 749
mood-congruence effect, 761–62, 764, 767n.7, 818, 983
mood disorders, 6, 8, 899, 932, 1032–33
  anterior cingulate cortex and, 12, 17–18
  attentional biases and, 977–82
  cognitive biases and, 976–1001
  negative affect and, 8–9, 994–95
  neuroimaging studies of, 952–53, 954
  predispositions for, 737
  serotonin and, 1028
  therapeutic treatments for, 902
  See also specific disorders
mood induction, 120, 603, 900
"mood management" hypothesis, 604, 761, 766, 797
mood regulation, 8
mood repair, 712, 713, 716
Moore, M. K., 487
Mor, N., 996
Moradi, A. R., 663
moral concern, 846
moral development, 297, 342, 343
moral-emotional correction, 865
moral emotions, 843, 845, 847, 848, 852–66
  adaptive rationality and, 892–96
  cultural models and, 875
  definition of, 853
  emotion families and, 855–64
  other-condemning, 848, 855–59

other-praising, 848, 855, 862–64
other-suffering, 848, 855, 861–62
prosocial behavior and, 792–93, 798, 861, 864
prototypical features of, 853–54
reason and, 852, 865–66, 866n.4
self and, 853–55, 859–61, 863
self-conscious, 848, 855, 859–61, 866n.3
morality, 852, 853, 855
  adaptive rationality and, 894, 895–96
  ambiguity and, 891, 892, 896
  animals and, 848
  in appraisal theory, 581, 584, 875–76
  cultural views of, 386–88, 875–76
  evolutionary and cultural perspectives on, 840, 843, 848, 855
moral philosophy, 852
moral psychology, 852
Morals by Agreement (Gauthier), 895
moral values, 635, 787
More, T., 485
Moretti, M., 995
Morey, R., 525
Morgan, M. A., 101
Morgenstern, O., 622
Mori, K., 450
"morning after" syndrome, 629
morning-type individuals, 702
Morozov, V. P., 525
morphine, 34, 37, 97
morphology, American Sign Language, 537, 539, 542, 545–46
morphometric magnetic resonance imaging, 964–70
Morris, J., 109, 269
Morris, J. S., 474, 936
mortality. See death
Morton, E. S., 458
Moser, D. J., 118
Moses, L. J., 335
motherese, 470–71, 507, 538
mothers. See maternal behavior; parent-child relationship
motility-regulating neurons, 156, 165
motion, musical perception of, 505, 506
motivated processing, 612, 613, 764
motivation, 545
  affect as factor in, 602, 603–4, 609
  affective working memory and, 6
  appraisal processes and, 377, 380, 577, 578–80, 584, 589n.5, 709
  for attitude change, 763, 764
  brain structures involved in, 27, 34, 35, 36
  cognition and, 565
  decision making and, 566, 635, 637n.11
  dopamine's role in, 34
  ecological stimulus properties and, 685
  emotion induction via, 226
  emotion regulation and, 711–12, 713

emotions' adaptive nature and, 572, 579, 682
emotion tasks and, 132
evolutionary perspectives on, 892, 893–94, 895
for helping behavior, 750, 787, 796–97
hypothalamus's role in, 34, 35
mood and, 602, 749, 763
moral emotion action tendencies and, 856–63
opioid receptors and, 37
personality development and, 726, 733
Plato's concept of, 563
as processing style factor, 613
for prosocial behavior, 787–88, 790–93
motivational organization of emotions, 187–207, 257, 367n.6, 748
emotional priming model, 198–205
emotional systems and, 682, 690
emotion induction research issues, 228–29
picture-viewing paradigm, 189–98
motive consistency, 578
motives, appetitive vs. aversive, 579
motor activity, emotional expressivity and, 705
motor cortex, 118, 648, 684, 968, 1106
motor-dominance, 38
motor function, 458, 843
motor mimicry, facial expression and, 540
motor programs, 221, 487
motor systems, 1106
Motte-Haber, H. de la, 520, 530n.1
Moulder, B., 194
Mountz, J. M., 969
mouth, 841, 849, 857
movement, sign language role of, 539, 542
movies. See films
Mowrer, O., 811
Mozart, Wolfgang Amadeus, 516, 841, 848, 849
MRI. See functional magnetic resonance imaging
mRNA, 154, 311, 1016, 1017, 1029, 1032, 1127
MRS. See magnetic resonance spectroscopy
Mrs. Dalloway (Woolf), 486
Much, N. C., 875
Mueller-Preuss, P., 473
Mulhern, R. K., Jr., 813
Mullen, B., 714
Muller, S., 985
Müller, W., 700
Multhaup, K. S., 576, 665
multidimensional scaling, 515, 528, 678
Multiple Affect Adjective Check List, 705
multiple entry modular memory system, 665, 671
multiple regression analysis, 520

multiple sclerosis, 932, 1034
multistage discriminant analysis, 248
multivariate analysis, 303, 309, 515, 517, 528
multivariate analysis of variance, 248
Mumme, D. L., 335
Munch, Edvard, 486
mu opiate receptors, 1017
murder. See homicide
Murphy, B., 793, 794, 795
muscarinic receptors, 153, 163, 164
muscimol, 96
muscles
facial, 192–94, 264–65, 415, 417, 419, 440, 444, 486, 543, 582, 585–86, 587
voice-related, 437, 440, 442, 449
See also specific muscles
muscular dystrophy, 308
music, 28, 411, 412, 503–29
aesthetic affect and, 847, 848
emotion induction via, 227, 588, 564
as "frozen" symbol system, 568–69
perception of, 413, 503, 508–28
music dissonance, 13, 520, 524
music psychology, 569
music therapy, 504, 529
Mussorgsky, Modest, 516–17
mutations, 310, 1017, 1018, 1131
mutuality, parent-child, 307–8
mutual regulation, 376, 378–81, 401, 402
Myers, H. F., 1087
Myrtek, M., 700
m. zygomaticus. See zygomatic muscle

# N

N-acetyl-aspartate, 965, 966, 968
nadolol, 106–7
Nägele, T., 943
Nairn, Ian, 482
naloxone, 95–96, 98, 950
Namba, S., 516
Nangia, V., 194
Napoleon, 483
Narayan, M., 968
Narmour, E., 848
narrative arts. See arts, emotion and the; literature
narratives, 297, 339, 541, 547–51
Nasby, W., 602
Nash, John, 483
National Academy of Sciences, 817
National Institute of Mental Health, 934
National Library of Medicine, 1048
Native Americans, 525
natural killer cells, 995, 1060, 1072–74, 1087
natural selection, 849, 854, 892
natural sounds, musical imitation of, 505

natural vocal expression, 436
nature-nurture debate, 298, 541
Nature of the Child, The (Kagan), 865
nature phobias, 259
Natyasastra (Hindu text), 844, 847, 865
Nebel, L. E., 702
need for cognition, 766
needs, 578–80, 827–31, 833
Neese, R. M., 685
negative affect, 379, 1019, 1084
aggression and, 813–19
amygdala and, 15, 17, 18, 79, 81–82
animal signaling of, 476
animal vocalizations and, 470
anticipatory anxiety and, 988
as antisocial aggression cause, 750, 805–7, 809
arousal level and, 685
attitudes, judgments, and, 598, 599, 601–10, 628, 691, 755
avoidance goals and, 994–95
cancer patients and, 1055, 1067, 1071
as decision-making factor, 629, 630, 637n.11
emotional priming and, 198
emotion regulation issues and, 361
genetic factors in, 303–4
health-related issues and, 611, 1087
hemisphere specialization theories on, 37–38, 729, 932, 941
induction studies of, 939–43
as information-processing factor, 601–2, 608–9, 613, 629, 760–61, 765–66
intergroup attitudes and, 606–7
memories and, 644–45
mood and, 8, 198
mood disorders and, 8–9, 994–95
motivational consequences of, 602, 603–4
neuroticism and, 731
older adults and, 733
personality issues and, 729, 731–32
pessimism and, 737
as self-concept factor, 602, 604
self-focused attention and, 996
semantic affective space and, 678
social comparisons and, 779
startle reflex and, 323–24
negative affectivity, 704–5, 712, 719
negative cognitive triad, 990–91, 997, 1000
negative differentiation, 844, 845
negative dominance, 844, 845
negative emotions, 221, 235t, 1010
affect and, 844–45, 847
agency attribution and, 580
appraisal and, 377, 577, 580, 874
arousal recognition and, 79, 81–82, 645
attention and, 711
cancer patients and, 1053, 1074–75

negative emotions (*continued*)
coping and, 713
cultural perspectives on, 880, 881–82
decision making and, 620, 621
dispositional emotionality and, 794–96
distraction from, 664
ego-threatening events and, 777, 778
emotion families and, 381–83
emotion regulation and, 711–12, 794
empathy and, 793
facial expression and, 422, 423, 424
frontal brain asymmetry and, 701, 1090–91
goals and, 778–79
health and, 1049–50, 1074–75, 1083, 1086, 1092, 1095, 1098–99
incidental situational affect and, 632–33
infants and, 334, 395, 552
interpersonal relationships and, 826, 828, 830, 833
music and perception of, 508, 514, 515, 524–25
prosocial behavior and, 794–96, 798
reactivity and, 683
reflected appraisals and, 781
sign language expression of, 539
strain theory view of, 812
toddlers and, 337
withdrawal behavior and, 738
See also specific emotions
negative expressivity, 706
negative gradient dominance, 844
negatively toned affect, aggression and, 806
negative-positive dimension, in affect, 844–45
negative potency, 844
negative self-talk, 782
negative surprise, 714
negativity bias, 844–45, 847
negotiation, 610–11, 613
Neisser, U., 661
Nemeroff, Charles B., 902, 1021–36
Nemoda, Z., 312
neoassociationism, 564, 599
neocortex, 154, 171
basic emotions and, 176
behavioral approach system and, 327, 933
emotion and, 25, 26f, 27, 542
emotion induction study findings on, 947
encephalization of, 41–42, 43
evolutionary development and, 258
hemisphere specialization theories and, 38
re-representation in, 42, 43
study biases toward, 40–43
See also specific components

neo-Pavlovianism, 678
Nepal, 880–81, 882, 883
nerve growth, 1097
nervousness, 704
Neshat-Doost, H. T., 663
Neter, E., 604
Netherlands, 876–77
Nettelbeck, T., 524
Nettheim, N., 524
Neufeld, Susan J., 296, 297, 347–66
neurasthenia, 326
neuroanatomy, 4, 27, 66–87, 596, 930–33.
See also brain; specific brain structures
neurobiology, 583, 899
of affiliation, 1010–19
of anxiety disorders, 963–73
of depressive disorders, 1021–36
neurochemical coding, 142–43
neurochemical systems
allostasis, allostatic load, and, 1125–27
autism and, 902, 1017–18
neuroimaging of, 902, 965
obsessive-compulsive disorder and, 966
panic disorder and, 971–72
phobias and, 969–70
positive affect and, 1010
posttraumatic stress syndrome and, 968
psychopathology and, 901, 902
neuroeffector junctions, autonomic, 162–64
neuroendocrine system, 135, 149, 153, 154, 170, 172, 174
depression and, 1022, 1028–29, 1032–34
emergency reaction and, 1049
stress's impact on, 1049, 1084, 1086, 1119, 1131
neurofibromatosis, 308
neuroimaging, 3, 4, 6, 7, 298, 902
affective picture processing and, 194–98
amygdala, 31, 76, 108–9, 648, 651, 934, 936, 940, 1107
anterior cingulate cortex, 119, 121, 934, 936
anxiety disorder findings from, 963–73
cingulate cortex, 30–31
depression findings from, 4, 117–25, 1023–25, 1027–32, 1036
facial expression studies, 423, 934–37
frontal brain asymmetry, 701
human affective neuroscience and, 26, 39, 40–41
lesion method vs. brain imaging, 66
memory research and, 647, 649
methods used, 964–65
musical expression research and, 529
neural substrates of affect and, 930, 931, 933–48, 951–54

orbitofrontal cortex, 119–20, 936
vocal expression findings from, 450
See also specific types
neuroimmune dysfunction, 1029
neuromodulators, 964
neuromotor programs, 435, 440, 574
neuronal model theory of orienting response, 261, 262
neurons
animal studies of, 26–27, 28, 34, 473–74, 476
autonomic, 136, 139, 154–67, 171, 173–76
brain imaging of, 40–41
cardiomotor, 166–70
cochlear root, 199
executive, 167, 169f
lateral hypothalamus, 34
mirror, 72
motility-regulating, 156, 165
neurochemical coding of, 142–43
orbitofrontal, 28, 34
peripheral autonomic, 136, 139
pilomotor, 173
presynaptic, 1022, 1028, 1032
sudomotor, 156, 157, 158f, 161f, 162, 173
vasoconstrictor, 156, 157–58, 161f, 165–70, 173
vasodilator, 157, 162, 173
ventral pallidum, 35
visceral afferent, 143–49, 155–56, 165, 166, 1107, 1112
See also specific neurons
neuropeptides, 142–43, 146, 153–54, 162, 163
affiliative behavior role of, 1012–19, 1097
depressive disorders and, 1032–36
emotion induction utilizing, 226
See also specific neuropeptides
neuropeptide Y, 142, 143
neurophysiological social psychology, 589
neuropsychology, 449–50, 648
neuroticism, 426, 698, 704, 719, 933
avoidance goals and, 995
cancer patients and, 1066
emotional reactivity and, 683, 690, 691, 693, 923–24, 926
emotion regulation and, 712
negative affect linked with, 731
personality and, 731, 732, 737
response modulation and emotion processing and, 921, 923–24, 926
as social comparison factor, 779
temperament neuroimaging findings on, 953–54
neurotransmitter receptors, 26
neurotransmitters, 142, 1047

depressive disorders and, 1022–36, 1127

emotion induction and, 226, 236–38

opioid, 32–34

*See also specific neurotransmitters*

neutral state paradigms, functional imaging, 964

neutroceptive valenced systems, 841

New Age music, 525

Newell, K., 1048

"new look in perception" approach, 565

Newman, J. D., 470, 473–74

Newman, Joseph P., 678, 899–900, 904–26

Newman, Oscar, 496, 497

Newton, T. L., 707

New World monkeys, 472

Ney, K., 312

niceness, 855, 858

Nichols, S. L., 912

nicotine, 951

Niedenthal, P. M., 598, 779

Nielsen, F. V., 516

Niemi, T., 1059

Nietzsche, F., 499

nigrostriatal system, 41

⁹⁹ᵐTc-HMPAO SPECT. *See* technetium-99m hexamethyl-propylene-amine-oxime SPECT

Nisbett, R. E., 587, 807, 865

nitric oxide, 162

nitrous oxide anesthesia, 30

Nitschke, Jack B., 8–19

Nix, G., 711

NK cells. *See* natural killer cells

NMDA receptors, 56, 57, 58

N-methyl-D-aspartate, 103

nociceptive valenced systems, 841

nociceptor sensitization, 174–75

nodose ganglion, 144

noise

as aggression instigator, 810

animal signaling and, 462

Nolen-Hoeksema, S., 996

nomifensine, 1032

nonapeptides, 1012. *See also specific types*

nonconscious memory, 647

nonconscious processes, appraisal and, 377, 378

nondefensives, 716, 718

non-Duchenne smiles, 417, 418, 421

nonhuman animals. *See* animals

nonlinear probability weighting, 624, 630–31

nonlinguistic communication, 536, 538–43, 552, 553

non-Mendelizing genetic influences, 309–10

nonpolymorphic genes, 309

nonshared environmental variance, 302–3, 306

nonspecific arousal, 905, 923, 924, 926n.2

nonthreat appraisals, 717

nonverbal communication, 132, 705

appraisal research, 583, 586–87

*See also* body posture; facial expression; gestures

noradrenalin. *See* norepinephrine

Norasakkunkit, V., 885

Nordahl, T. E., 970, 971

Nordby, H., 278

norepinephrine (noradrenaline), 16, 94, 95–97, 100, 102, 105, 843, 1047, 1087

anxiety physiology and, 964

arousal systems and, 692

autonomic nervous system and, 136, 140, 142, 151–53, 162–64, 1112, 1113, 1125

depression and, 1022, 1023

depressive disorders and, 1021–26, 1031–33, 1035

emotional information encoding and, 651

emotion induction and, 226

marital conflict and, 1085

panic disorder and, 970

stress and, 1125–26

in temperament theory, 327, 933

Norman, D. A., 665, 668

Norman, K. A., 646

norms, 859–60, 906, 920

social, 567, 581, 584, 587

nostrils, 841

novelty, 683, 1095, 1121, 1126

as appraisal dimension, 573–77, 584, 586, 588, 687, 709–10

orienting response to, 259, 261, 262, 269, 905

stimulus evaluation check model, 906, 919

novelty-seeking, 312, 327, 933, 954

Novocain (procaine), 13, 952

nucleus accumbens, 36, 104

anterior cingulate cortex and, 11

emotion induction study findings on, 941, 951

emotions and, 32–34, 42

oxytocin and, 1016

posttraumatic stress syndrome and, 968

ventromedial prefrontal cortex and, 29

nucleus ambiguus, 145

nucleus basalis, 75

nucleus paragigantaocellularis, 96, 1111, 1112

nucleus tractus solitarius, 96–99, 1107, 1127

autonomic nervous system and, 143, 144, 148, 154, 167, 1108, 1111, 1112

Nugent, K., 986

Nunley, E. P., 487

Nurnberger, J. I., 903

# O

Oatley, Keith, 411, 412, 413, 481–99, 668–69, 670, 671, 692, 990

Oba, R., 474

obesity, 1117, 1120, 1121, 1129–31

objective correlatives, 488, 489, 498

objective happiness, 1090

Obrist, P. A., 258, 259

obsessive-compulsive disorder, 963, 1034

anterior cingulate cortex and, 12, 965, 966

attentional biases and, 978, 980

cingulate cortex and, 30

cognitive-behavioral therapies for, 901

cognitive interference and, 277

cognitive processing biases and, 978, 980, 987

emotional reactivity and, 683

memory biases and, 987

neurobiology and neuroimaging of, 965–66, 972, 973

oxytocin levels and, 1017

personal responsibility issues, 992–93

simultaneous information processing and, 666

occipital cortex, 938, 941, 948, 952, 970

occipital-parietal activation, 940

occipital-parietal-temporal activation, 947

occipital-temporal activation, 940, 943

occipito-cerebellar activation, 940

occupational stress, 1095, 1121, 1124, 1130

OCD. *See* obsessive-compulsive disorder

Ochsner, Kevin N., 565, 643–55

O'Connell, S. M., 470

O'Connor, T. G., 308

O'Connor, C., 541, 856

odors

as affect and decision-making influence, 633

as aggression instigator, 810, 820n.12

animal communication and, 462–63, 472–73, 475

animal reproductive behavior and, 414, 472, 473

direct sensory affect and, 846

emotion expression and, 412

hardwired preferences for, 577

human reactions to, 476

limbic system and, 931

olfactory emotion evaluation studies and, 937, 938

sense of smell and, 28, 29, 31

Öhman, Arne, 256–71, 425, 564, 576, 686
older adults, 1129
    coping processes and, 736, 737
    life expectancy and, 1048
    personality issues and, 728, 732, 733–34
Olds, J., 34, 36
Old World monkeys, 472
olfactory communication. *See* odors
olfactory stimuli, 937, 938
O'Malley, A., 524
one-shot prisoner's dilemma, 893–96
[133]Xe SPECT. *See* xenon-133 gas single photon emission computed tomography
"On First Looking into Chapman's Homer" (Keats), 491
on-line (experienced) affect, 841–42, 846
on-line experience sampling, 678, 679
*On the Study of Character* (Bain), 326
open-closed, as appraisal dimension, 687
open-ended thinking, 668
openness to experience, 731, 732, 737
opera, 504
opiates, 28, 30, 95–96, 97
opioid neurotransmitters, 32–34, 37, 39, 42, 327, 1095
opponent process theory of emotion, 588
oppression, 856
optimism, 719, 993, 1098
    dispositional, 737, 1092, 1096
    as health factor, 611, 1050, 1092, 1095–97
    as judgment factor, 628, 632, 633
    as social comparison factor, 779
orangutans, 773, 774, 1010
*orbicularis oris* (muscle), 440
orbital prefrontal cortex, 10, 654
orbitofrontal cortex, 10
    alliesthesia and, 34
    anterior cingulate cortex and, 11
    auditory emotion evaluation studies and, 938
    basic emotions and, 176
    conditioned fear extinction and, 56, 59
    controlled emotion processing and, 648
    depressive disorders and, 1027, 1030
    emotional learning and, 74
    emotion development role of, 356
    emotion induction study findings on, 947, 948
    emotions and, 27–30, 42
    facial expression and, 423, 936, 937
    lesions to, 118, 119, 931
    mood and, 120, 953
    neuroimaging of, 119–20, 936–38
    obsessive-compulsive disorder and, 965–66, 972
    olfactory emotion evaluation studies of, 938

panic disorder and, 971
posttraumatic stress syndrome and, 967, 968
reinforcement and, 120, 123–24
Orians, G. H., 488–89, 496
Oribe, E., 137
oribi, 472
orienting, 276–87, 289
orienting response, 256, 259, 261–62, 264–66, 269, 789
    in appraisal process, 574, 576, 586
    automatic emotion processing and, 648
    defense response vs., 287–89
    to novel stimuli, 259, 261, 262, 269, 905
    response modulation and, 907
Ortony, A., 215, 582
Osborne, J. W., 515
Osgood, C. E., 321, 568
O'Shaughnessy, M., 645
Oshinsky, J. S., 520
Öst, L.-G., 259
Östberg, O., 702
ostracism, 855, 858, 860
other-condemning moral emotions, 848, 855–59
other-orientation, 791, 793
other-praising moral emotions, 848, 855, 862–64
other-related cognition, 977, 991, 996–97, 1000
other-suffering moral emotions, 848, 855, 861–62
Ott, J., 311
Ouellette, R., 830
ought-focus, in memory retrieval, 652
ought self, 688, 689, 779, 995, 996
outcome expectancies, 999, 581
outcome probability, 687, 688
ovulation, 471, 473
Owings, D. H., 458
oxotremorine, 101, 103
oxygen, lack of, 841
oxygen-15-labeled carbon dioxide, 964
oxygen-15 water positron emission tomography, 933, 934, 936–38, 940, 941, 943, 945–48, 952, 954
oxytocin, 297, 1012–19, 1095, 1097
ozone level, 810

# P

pain
    affect evolutionary and cultural perspectives on, 840–42, 845–46, 849
    as aggression instigator, 806–7, 820n.11
    anterior cingulate cortex and, 119
    brain stem sites and, 36, 37, 39

cingulate cortex and, 30, 649
defense behavior and, 171–72
emotion and, 1047
emotion induction via, 226
facial expression of, 417, 841
hot/cold empathy gaps and, 629
memories of, 652, 653
perceptual emotion influences and, 685, 686
prevention focus and, 994
visceral afferent neurons and, 144, 146, 148
painting, 484–87, 490–91, 493–95, 569
pair bonding, 297, 315, 1010–15, 1017, 1019, 1095
paired-associate paradigm, 651
Pakstis, A. J., 312
palatographs, 437
Palladio, Andrea, 482
panic, 133, 259, 439t, 440
panic attacks, 683, 686, 963, 970, 971
panic disorders, 686, 899, 963
    amygdala and, 76
    attentional biases and, 978, 980
    cognitive-behavioral therapies for, 901
    cognitive interference and, 277
    cognitive processing biases and, 978, 980, 987–88
    fear conditioning models and, 61
    incidence of, 903
    judgmental/interpretive biases and, 988
    memory biases and, 987–88
    neurobiology and neuroimaging of, 970–72, 973, 1032, 1033
    perceived control research findings on, 999
    SPAARS emotion model and, 670–71
Panksepp, J., 3, 37, 176, 377, 679, 683, 684
Papez, J. W., 27, 931
parabrachial nucleus (pons), 36–37
Paradiso, Sergio, 120, 941, 948
parahippocampal cortex, 109, 938, 940, 970
paralimbic cortex, 947, 966, 1106
    anterior, 930, 932, 933, 935t, 938, 939, 945, 951, 952, 964
    *See also specific structures*
paralinguistic communication, 536, 539, 548, 549–50, 553
paralinguistic cues, 476, 553
parallel enrichment procedure, 526
paralysis, 902
paranoia, 692
parasubiculum, 104
parasympathetic ganglia, 161–62
parasympathetic nervous system, 137–42, 151, 153, 155, 158–72, 176, 257, 1108
    emotion identification with, 235
    evolutionary perspectives on, 258

individual-specific response patterns and, 699
paraventricular hypothalamic nuclei, 165, 1126
paravertebral ganglia, 139, 155, 160
parcel-item scales, 235
Pardo, José, 943, 945, 946
Parental Bonding Scale, 1094
parent-child mutuality, 307–8
parent-child relationships
    affectional emotional systems and, 683
    allostatic load and, 1094
    animals and, 297, 315, 458, 469, 470–71, 473, 474, 1011
    attachment and, 340–42, 489, 729, 736, 886, 1010, 1011
    child's arousal control and, 361
    child's empathetic concerns and, 336
    child's health and, 1085
    as communal relationships, 827–28, 829
    cross-fostering animal studies, 474
    in early childhood, 340–42, 343, 350, 356, 357, 361
    emotional expressiveness and responsiveness in, 332, 334–35, 337, 343, 358
    emotion-coaching vs. emotion-dismissing in, 1098
    emotion coregulation and, 381, 361
    facial expression and, 425
    family studies and, 301
    filial piety and, 385, 386, 388, 400, 402
    gene-environment covariance and, 307
    genetic imprinting and, 309, 310
    health issues and, 1085
    mothers and. See maternal behavior
    personality development through, 730–31, 735
    prairie vole behavior and, 297, 315, 1011
    temperament and, 296, 303, 304, 306, 315, 321–22
parenting education programs, 348, 367n.1
parietal cortex, 11, 947, 948
parietal lobe, posterior, 289
parieto-occipital activation, 940
Park, L., 875
Parkinson, B., 820n.19
Parkinson's disease, 35, 41, 85, 932, 1031–32, 1034
paroxetine, 124, 966, 1022, 1028, 1029
Parr, L. A., 465
Parra, C., 270
Parrott, W. G., 713
Partiot, Arnaud, 948
partner preference, 1012–16
parturition, 1012, 1014

Pascal, Blaise, 596
passion, 563, 572, 619, 852, 865, 1097–98
    crimes of, 805
Passions Within Reason (Frank), 895
passive avoidance learning, 910–13, 923, 926n.5
passive coping, 258, 1086
Passman, R. H., 813
Pastoral Symphony (Beethoven), 505
Pastorelli, C., 999
Patrick, Catherine, 492
Patrick, C. J., 914, 915, 917–18
Patrick-Miller, L., 1087
pattern-association learning, 27
pattern completion, memory retrieval and, 646–47
patterning, emotional, 873, 881–87
patterns, collative properties of, 488
pattern separation, memory and, 646, 647
Patterson, C. J., 905, 907
Patterson, C. M., 911, 912
Pauli, P. P., 989
Pavelchak, M. A., 606
Pavlov, I. P., 52, 265, 266
Pavlovian conditioning. See classical conditioning; fear conditioning
PCP, 34
peace, 847
peacefulness, 515, 520
peak experiences, 567
Peciña, Susana, 34
Pedersen, Cort, 1012
Pedersen, W. C., 815
pedigree analysis, 311
pedunculopontine nucleus (pons), 37
peer relations, children and, 342–43
Peeters, G., 844
pelvic organs, 144, 153, 162, 165
Peng, J. P., 471
Pennebaker, J. W., 703–4, 995, 1087
Pennebaker Inventory of Limbic Languidness, 704
Penninx, B. W. J. H., 1058
people concerns, 589n.5
perceived control, 999, 1000
perceived obstacles, 578
perception
    affective influences on, 596
    appraisal processes and, 572, 576, 687–88, 709
    emotional influences on, 690–94
    in Gestalt theory, 487–88
    selective information processing and, 664
    of self, 566–68, 778, 783
    of threat, 685, 1120
    visceral. See interoception
    visual, 666
    vocal, 468–69, 473–74, 538

Perception and Communication (Broadbent), 661
perception of emotion, 412–13, 476, 536
    cognition and, 565, 566–67
    facial expression and, 412, 413, 422–23, 526
    influences on, 679, 681–82, 684–87, 689, 690, 694
    linguistic, 542
    music and, 413, 503, 508–28
    vocal expression and, 413, 442–43, 445, 451, 526
perceptual memory modules, 665
perceptual priming, 198
perceptual representation system, 647
Peretz, I., 520
perfection, awe of, 863
perforant pathway (hippocampus), 900
performance
    musical expression and, 506–7, 525–27
    social anxiety concerns, 688
periaqueductal gray
    anterior cingulate cortex and, 11
    defensive behavior and, 171–72, 222n.2
    opioid neurotransmitter receptors, 37, 39
    pain and, 36
    startle reflex and, 199
    vocal expression and, 449
peripheral afferent neurons, 146, 155–56
peripheral nervous system, 5
    appraisal process role of, 572, 575, 684
    autonomic nervous system and, 136, 154–66, 686
    behavioral inhibition and, 329
    emotion, memory, and, 4, 93–109
    gross anatomy of, 138–40
    vocal expression and, 435
peripheral orientation, 277
peripheral psychophysiology, 700
peripheral self-judgments, 603, 604
perirhinal cortex, 55
permissive hypothesis of depression, 1022
Perot, Ross, 652, 735
Perrett, D. I., 474
Perrier, I. N., 984
Persky, V. W., 1057, 1058, 1059
persona, 329
Personal Assessment of Intimacy Relationships, 1094
personal distress, 750, 788, 790, 791, 793–96
personal growth, well-being and, 734
personality, 5, 298, 677–79, 933, 1130
    antisocial behaviors and, 804
    as appraisal factor, 584, 709
    childhood and development of, 297, 304, 727–31, 735
    cognitive-affective system of, 699

personality (*continued*)
emotional expression and, 413
empathy and, 794
facial expression of emotion and, 426–27
Five Factor model of, 677, 683, 731, 732, 734–735, 736
health issues and, 1049–50, 1057, 1058, 1060, 1088
as individual differences in emotional reactivity and coping factor, 678–79, 681–94, 698–719
life-span development of, 297, 679, 726–39
linguistic style and, 1089–90
neural substrates and, 3
as processing style factor, 613
social cognitive theory of, 728
theoretical development models of, 735–36
*See also* temperament
personal responsibility, 992–93
Persons, J. B., 991, 992
persuasion, 608–9, 752–67
Pervin, L. A., 598
pessimism
defensive, 782
depression and, 688, 737, 998, 999
dispositional, 737
as health factor, 738, 1097
as judgment factor, 628, 632
PET. *See* positron emission tomography
Petersen, M., 473
Peterson, C., 548
Peterson, J., 490
PET-FDG. *See* fluorine-18 deoxyglucose PET
petrosal ganglion, 144
Petruzzi, D. C., 1000
Petry, M. C., 645
Petty, Richard E., 603, 608, 609, 750, 752–67
Petzold, P., 601
Pham, M. T., 632–33
pharmacological stimulation, animal studies of, 26
pharmacotherapy, 931, 991. *See also* drugs; *specific drugs and drug types*
pharynx, 849
phasic arousal, 692
Phelps, E. A., 201, 651
phenocopies, 310
phenotypes, emotion, 300–301, 306–8, 310, 312, 315
phentolamine, 97
phenylephrine, 97
phenylketonuria, 366
pheromones, 476
Philippines, 879
Phillips, M. L., 936, 937

*Philosophy in a New Key* (Langer), 506
Phinney, J., 789
phlegm (humor), 325, 326, 932–33
phlegmatic temperament, 326, 698, 933
phobias, 285, 963
agoraphobia, 627, 686, 899, 970, 988
animal-related, 259–60, 969
anterior cingulate cortex and, 12
attentional biases and, 978
cognitive interference and, 277, 285
cognitive processing biases and, 977, 978, 986–89
emotional reactivity and, 683
evolutionary perspectives on, 977
fear conditioning models and, 61, 968, 1107
Freudian view of, 326
judgmental/interpretive biases and, 988–89
memory biases and, 986–87
neurobiology and neuroimaging of, 968–70, 972
psychophysiological response to, 264–65
self-efficacy beliefs and, 1000
simultaneous information processing and, 666
snake, 969, 980–81, 988–89, 1001n.2
social. *See* social phobias
SPAARS emotion model and, 670
spider, 906, 969, 977, 980, 986–87
phonation, 435, 437, 440
phonemes, 437, 443, 447
phonological dyslexia, 664
phonological information processing, 665
phonology, American Sign Language, 537, 539
photography, 457
physical abuse, 643
physical fitness, 1047
physical health. *See* health, physical
physiognomy, 426, 486
physiological anxiety, 324
physiology, 748
affect induction and, 930, 939–50
animal emotion expression and, 458
animal reproductive, 473
behavioral inhibition and, 329, 729
cancer survival and, 1054, 1070, 1072–73
as emotional expression factor, 457
emotion expression and, 457, 747
of emotion processing, 905–6, 1050
emotion self-perception and, 567
emotion universality and, 871
facial expression and, 416
health issues and, 739, 1049, 1085, 1087–97
individual differences in, 679, 681, 685, 698, 699–700, 702–7

prosocial behavior responses and, 791, 793, 794
stress and, 1117–18, 1120
temperament and, 323–25, 729
*See also* autonomic psychophysiology; psychophysiology
Piaget, Jean, 354, 389, 492, 849, 852, 861
*piano* (music direction), 504
Piano Sonata K. 282 (Mozart), 516
Picasso, Pablo, 484, 491
picrotoxin, 102
pictorial arts. *See* arts, emotion and the; visual arts
*Pictures at an Exhibition* (Mussorgsky), 516–17
Pictures of Facial Affect, 934, 936, 937
picture-viewing paradigm, 189–98, 201, 203–5, 207n.3, 226–28
Pieper, M., 716
Pietromonaco, P. R., 829
Pihan, H., 450
*Pilgrimage to San Isodore* (painting), 486
pilomotor neurons, 173
pineal glands, 1026
pine voles, 1017
piriform cortex, 938
pitch variation
in motherese, 470–71
in music, 519, 520, 523, 525
tone languages and, 448–49
pituitary-adrenocortical regulation system, 238
pituitary gland, 471, 1012, 1026, 1032–35
pity, 688
Pizzagalli, Diego, 8–19
plant genetics, 311
plasma, 1026–27
platelets, 1023, 1025–26, 1028–30
Plato, 504, 535, 563, 596, 852, 865
play, 342, 354, 464
playing dead. *See* tonic immobility
plays
musical accompaniment to, 503
*See also* drama
play smiles, 381
pleasantness, 881–82, 906, 919–20
as appraisal dimension, 573, 574, 576–79, 584, 586, 588
pleasure, 354, 357
affect evolutionary and cultural perspectives on, 840–46, 848, 849
as affective reaction, 598
brain stem sites and, 36, 37
Duchenne smiles and, 418, 421
in emotional response research, 189, 190–92, 194–97
lateral hypothalamus and, 35
as learning factor, 361–62

nucleus accumbens and, 32–34
promotion focus and, 994
septum and, 36
Plomin, R., 305, 306, 308, 309, 327
Ploog, D., 466
Plutchik, R., 235, 416, 976
Poe, Edgar Allan, 490
*Poetics* (Aristotle), 483
poetry, 483, 484, 491, 499
poignancy, 734
point of view, in narratives, 550
poison-avoidance systems, 257
Polak, P. R., 902
politeness, 387, 445
polite smiles, 418, 421
political science, 819n.3
politics, art and, 481–82, 483
pollution, 810
polygamy/polygyny, 470, 1011
polymerase chain reaction, 1029
polyvagal theory of emotion, 449
Pomerantz, E. M., 604
pons, 36–37, 947
pontine A5 area, 165
Pope, L. K., 780
Porges, S. W., 449
portrayal paradigm, 443, 444
positive affect, 379, 1019, 1084
    approach goals and, 994
    arousal level and, 685
    attitudes, judgments, and, 598, 599, 601–
        11, 628
    as decision-making factor, 629, 630,
        633, 637nn.10, 11
    emotional priming and, 198
    emotion regulation and, 361
    extraversion and, 731
    genetic factors in, 303–4
    health-related outcomes and, 611
    hemisphere specialization theories of,
        37–38, 729, 932, 940
    hippocampal activation and, 13
    induction studies of, 939–43
    as information-processing factor, 601–2,
        604, 608–9, 613, 629, 760–61, 765–
        66
    intergroup attitudes and, 606–7
    memories and, 644–45
    mood and, 198
    motivational consequences of, 602
    nucleus accumbens and, 32, 33
    older adults and, 733
    persuasion and induction of, 608
    post-goal attainment, 6
    pre-goal attainment, 6, 17, 683
    primate vocalizations and, 470
    psychological disorders and loss of,
        1010
    as self-concept factor, 602, 604
    semantic affective space and, 678

septum and, 36
social comparisons and, 779
ventral pallidum and, 35
positive affectivity, 705, 712
Positive and Negative Affect Scale, 678,
    701, 704, 705, 844, 953
positive constructive daydreaming, 1069
positive emotions, 235t, 412
    affect and, 844, 847
    appraisal and, 377, 577, 874
    approach behavior and, 738
    attention and, 711
    autonomic specificity research on, 220–
        21
    cultural perspectives on, 381–82, 387,
        874, 881–82
    as decision-making outcome, 620, 621,
        626
    ego affirmation and, 777
    emotion families and, 381–82
    emotion regulation and, 711–12
    facial expressions and, 417, 425, 427,
        444
    frontal brain asymmetry and, 701, 1090–
        91
    goals and, 778–79
    health and, 1049, 1074–75, 1083, 1095–
        99
    infant expression of, 552
    interpersonal relationships and, 828,
        833
    moral emotion and, 862–64
    music and perception of, 508, 515, 524–
        25
    reflected appraisals and, 781
    sibling interactions and, 341
    *See also specific emotions*
positive expressivity, 706
positive psychology, 862, 863
positive relations, 734
positive self-talk, 782
positive time discounting, 625
positron emission tomography, 26, 964,
    965, 973, 1106
    affective picture processing and, 194
    amygdala, 31, 59, 108, 109, 269, 1107
    anterior cingulate cortex, 119, 121
    cingulate cortex, 30
    for depression studies, 117, 121–23,
        1023, 1027–30
    emotion neuroimaging with, 933, 943
    for facial expression research, 423
    frontal brain asymmetry, 701
    of infant brain functioning, 355
    mood neuroimaging with, 120, 953
    for musical expression research, 529
    for obsessive-compulsive disorder, 965,
        966
    for panic disorder, 970–71
    for phobias, 969

for posttraumatic stress disorder, 967–
    68
technique biases, 40–41
of vocal expression, 450
Posner, M. I., 276, 277, 280, 285, 289,
    679, 693
Post, Robert M., 899–903
postdecisional dissonance, 609
posterior attentional system, 693
posterior cingulate
    anterior cingulate cortex and, 11, 12
    auditory emotion evaluation studies
        and, 938
    emotion induction study findings on,
        941–43, 945, 947–49
    facial expression neuroimaging and,
        936
    phobias and, 969
    posttraumatic stress syndrome and, 968
posterior frontal lobe, 542
posterior inferior frontal cortex, 971
posterior intralaminar nucleus, 53
posterior parietal lobe, 289
posterior subcallosal gyrus, 953
posteromedial orbitofrontal cortex, 938
postganglionic neurons, 139–40, 142, 143,
    151, 152, 154–64, 173
post-goal attainment positive affect, 6
postmodernism, 484
postmortem studies, of depression, 1022,
    1025, 1026, 1029–33, 1036
posttraumatic stress disorder, 899, 901,
    963, 1113, 1129
    amygdala and, 76, 966–67, 968, 972,
        1127
    anterior cingulate cortex and, 12, 967,
        968
    attentional biases and, 978, 979, 980
    cognitive interference and, 277, 979
    cognitive processing biases and, 978,
        979, 980, 984, 987
    fear conditioning models and, 61, 1107
    future research considerations, 973
    hippocampus and, 14, 966–67, 968,
        972, 1128, 1131
    incidence of, 903
    memory biases and, 984, 987
    memory retrieval and, 655
    neurobiology and neuroimaging of, 966–
        68, 972, 973, 1033, 1073
    prefrontal cortex changes and, 28
posture. *See* body posture
Potts, N. L., 969
poverty, 811, 813, 820n.15
Powell, M., 830
power, 574, 576, 580–81, 691
Prader-Willi syndrome, 310
prairie voles, 297, 315, 1011–17
praise, 375, 387, 393–94, 400, 402
Prange, A., 1022

Pratt, C., 506
Pratt, R., 473
prazosin, 97, 98
preadaptation, 849, 857
preappraisals, 575
preattentive emotion activation, 262–65
precentral gyrus, 942, 945
precuneus, 938, 941, 942, 948
predators, 459–62, 466, 474, 685, 689, 748
predatory defense system, 259–60, 267, 268
predatory imminence, 259
predictability, 573, 574, 576, 687, 710
prediction, in decision making, 566, 620, 621, 625–26, 629, 634–36
predictive control, 781–82
predispositions
    behavioral, 362, 729, 789, 893, 895
    emotional, 727, 739
    neurobiological, 901
    for psychological disorders, 737–38
prefrontal asymmetry, 701, 1090–91
prefrontal cortex, 27–30, 37, 39, 42, 354, 729
    affective working memory and, 6
    allostatic load and, 1125
    amygdala and, 18
    anterior cingulate cortex and, 12, 18
    atrophy of, 1128
    damage to, 28–30, 932
    emotion and emotion regulation and, 4, 9–10, 16, 17, 542
    emotion induction study findings on, 940, 941, 946–49, 951
    fear conditioning and, 56, 59, 60f, 62
    hemisphere specialization theories and, 38, 720
    hippocampus and, 18
    infant brain functioning and, 355, 356
    medial. See medial prefrontal cortex
    memory and, 647
    mirror neurons, 77
    mood disorders and, 952
    neural substrates of affect and, 932, 933, 934, 952, 954
    panic disorder and, 971, 972
    phobias and, 969
    posttraumatic stress syndrome and, 968
    pre-goal attainment positive affect and, 6, 17
    psychopathology and, 900
    ventromedial, 5, 9, 10, 27, 29, 56, 59, 118, 329, 947
    See also orbitofrontal cortex
prefrontal gyrus, middle, 968
prefrontal neocortex, 930
preganglionic neurons, 139, 140, 142–43, 145, 146, 151, 152, 154–67, 174, 175
pregenual cingulate, 938
pre-goal attainment positive affect, 6, 17, 683

prejudice, 597, 605–8
prelimbic region, 971, 1016
premotor cortex, 118, 947, 948, 949
preparedness, evolutionary, 266–68, 631–32, 637n.12, 686
prepotent responses, 921, 924
presence, appraisal of, 687
present-aim standard, 891, 892, 894, 896
presentational symbolism, 506
presympathetic neurons, 165, 167, 171
pretend play, 342
Preuschoft, S., 464
prevention focus, pain and, 994
prevertebral ganglia, 139, 140, 143, 146, 155
    sympathetic, 160–61, 164
Preyer, Wilhelm, 349
Pribram, Karl, 900
Price, T. R., 68
pride, 325, 335, 849, 1087
    appraisal theory view of, 582, 585
    cultural perspectives on, 845, 848, 859
    development of, 297, 356, 375–76, 375–403, 379t, 383–403, 780
    as self-conscious emotion, 859, 860
Pride and Prejudice (Austen), 491
pride in achievement, 862–63
Priester, J. R., 378
primary acoustic startle pathway, 199
primary affective disorders, 899, 900, 902
primary appraisals, 573, 578, 580
    aggression and, 814
    attention and, 693–94
    perceptual input assessment and, 687–88, 709
primary control, 877–78
primary overstimulation, 714
primary psychopathy, 683
primates
    chemical signaling and, 472–73
    sensitivity to suffering, 861–62
    visual signaling, 463–65
    vocalizations, 47, 466–70, 473–75
    See also specific species
Primavera, The (painting), 493–94
priming, 329
    affective, 566, 599–602, 604–5, 608, 610–12, 636–37n.8, 668
    of attention, 662–63, 1110
    automatic activation and, 691
    emotional states and, 816
    emotion model, 198–205
    emotion regulation and, 361
    during evolution, 188, 206
    perceptual representation system and, 647
    response modulation and, 907
Principles of Art (Collingwood), 484
printing, invention of, 481, 497
private self-focus, 996

privations, aggression and, 813
probability
    appraisal and, 576, 579, 687, 688
    as decision-making consideration, 620, 622, 624, 630–31, 632, 636
    in future-event judgments, 988
problem-focused coping, 713
problem solving, 563, 668, 735
procaine, 13, 952
procedural knowledge, 990, 991, 1000
procedural memory, 647–48
process
    individual differences and, 699, 708
    self-related cognition and, 994–96, 1000
    social cognition and, 991
procreation, evolution and, 256, 257
productivity, as language feature, 536
Profile of Mood States, 705, 1070, 1072, 1096
Profile of Mood States Total Mood Disturbance, 1055–56, 1060
profiles
    appraisal, 575, 582–83, 586, 589n.1
    statistical analysis and, 247–50
program music, 505, 515
progressive amplification, 309–10
projection, intergroup attitudes and, 606
prolactin, 1022, 1028, 1073, 1085, 1095, 1121
promiscuity, 1011
promotion focus, pleasure and, 994
propositional representations, 669–71
propranolol, 94, 95, 96, 97, 106–7
prosocial action tendencies, 854, 858, 861, 864
prosocial behavior, 749, 750, 1095
    communal interpersonal relationships and, 830–31
    definitions of, 787–88
    development of, 297, 353, 358, 363, 545, 787–98, 861
    emotion regulation and, 297, 363, 793–96, 798
    empathy's role in, 297, 750, 787–96, 798
    mood's relationship to, 750, 787, 796–98, 830–31
    moral emotions and, 792–93, 798, 861, 864
    self-awareness and, 780
prosody, 412
    auditory emotion evaluation studies, 937
    emotion recognition and, 68, 69, 70–72
    infants' sensitivity to, 335, 447, 507, 544
    in motherese, 470, 507, 538
    in signed language, 538–39, 549–50
    in spoken language, 538, 543, 548–49, 552–53
    vocal expression role of, 446–48, 450

prospective emotions, 579
prospect realization appraisal, 687
protection motivation theory, 758
protective behavior, 189
proteins, genes and, 310, 311, 312
protoemotions, 575
protoshame, 849, 859–60
prototypical emotion episodes, 1084, 1093
Proulx, Annie, 498
Proust, Marcel, 484
Provine, R. R., 464
proxemics, 549
proximity, appraisal of, 687
Psammetichus, king of Egypt, 535
pseudo-psychopathy, 83
psychiatric disorders. *See* affective
    disorders; emotional disorders;
    psychopathology; *specific disorders*
psychiatric genetics, 301
psychiatry, vocal expression applications
    to, 451
psychic determinism, 1047
psychoacoustic parameters, 437, 438*t*
psychoactive drugs, 226. *See also specific
    types*
psychoanalytic theory, 326, 931
psycho-biography method, 490–91
psychodynamic theory, 566, 596, 598,
    606, 1021
psycholinguistics, 665
psychological disorders
    facial expression and, 426
    predispositions for, 737–38
    *See also* emotional disorders;
        psychopathology
psychology
    art theories and, 486–93, 483
    attitude and judgment research, 597
    crime causation theories and, 805, 810–
        11
    emotion perception/attribution factors,
        538
    individual difference perspectives, 698,
        699, 700, 706
    mental schemas theory, 485–86, 489–90,
        492, 498
    of music, 529
    self construct, 773–74
psychonalysis, 484, 488
psychoneuroimmunology, 1074
psychopathology, 298, 391
    anterior cingulate cortex and, 11
    anxiety disorder neuroimaging and
        neurobiology, 963–73
    autism and, 306, 311, 423, 899, 902,
        903, 1010, 1017–18
    cognition and emotional disorders, 564–
        65, 976–1001
    depressive disorder neurobiology, 1021–
        36

dysregulatory, 921–26
emotion and, 5, 899–903
facial expression charting of, 427
fear conditioning models and, 61–62
genetics and, 300, 301, 310, 315, 316
hippocampus and, 13
homozygosity degree and, 310
in infants, 349
negative emotions and, 1010
neural substrate link with, 3, 5
personality's role in, 678, 731–32, 737–
    38
physiological and pharmacological
    affect induction and, 930–54
response modulation and, 904–26
self-focused attention and, 996
self-regulation's role in, 899–900, 904,
    908–9, 911–12, 919–25, 994–95
temperament and, 321
therapeutic treatments, 901–3, 908, 925,
    1000, 1021, 1027, 1030–31
triplet repeat mutation implications for,
    310
*See also specific disorders*
psychopathy, 683, 738, 861
    emotion processing deficiency and, 904,
        909–21, 923, 925
    pseudo, 83
Psychopathy Checklist, 926n.5
Psychopathy Checklist-Revised, 918
psychopharmacology, 931
psychophysical stimulus properties, 685
psychophysiology, 596
    individual-specific response patterns,
        700
    infant emotions, 353, 356
*Psychophysiology* (journal), 233
psychophysiology
    neurobehavioral models and, 1105,
        1108
    psychopath emotion processing and,
        914–17
    *See also* autonomic psychophysiology
psychosexual development, 358
psychosis, 1021, 1032
psychosocial crises, 736
psychosomatic disorders, 212, 216, 700,
    718, 1047–48
psychosomatic medicine, 1088
psychosurgery, 30
psychotherapy, 920, 1000, 1064, 1096
    cancer patients and, 1056, 1070–72,
        1074, 1075, 1098
psychoticism, 683, 954
P3 wave, 205, 206*f*, 278, 324
PTSD. *See* posttraumatic stress disorder
puberty, 473
public health issues, 1048
public housing, 496–97
public self-focus, 996

pull effects
    in emotion regulation, 567
    vocal expression and, 433–34, 447, 448,
        451
pulvinar, 13, 269, 289, 936, 937
punishment
    in African cultural models, 874
    aversive environment as factor in, 810,
        820n.10
    emotional reactivity and, 683, 685
    emotion tasks and, 132
    frustration-aggression hypothesis view
        of, 811
    guilt and, 861
    neurotic introverts and, 921, 922*f*
    ought self and, 688
    prefrontal cortex and, 10
    psychopathy issues in, 910–12, 915–
        16
    threat of and aggression inhibition, 817
Pupi, A., 970
pure music. *See* absolute music
Puritanism, 402
purposefulness, 356
purpose in life, 734, 1092, 1095
purring, 469
Pury, C., 989
push effects
    in emotion regulation, 567
    vocal expression and, 433–34, 436, 447,
        448, 451
putamen, 936, 937, 969, 971
pygmy marmosets, 461, 462, 472, 473,
    475, 476
pyknic temperament, 326
Pyszczynski, T., 711, 712, 995

## Q

quadriplegia, 1113
*qualia,* 574, 588, 843, 872
quantitative trait loci, 308, 311, 313–15
Quantz, Johann Joachim, 504
Quay, H. C., 819n.1
quiescence, 171, 172*f*
Quigley, B. M., 816
Quinn, M. J., 914
Quirk, G. J., 102

## R

racial segregation, 857
racism, 856, 1084–86, 1087
Radiant City (architectural concept), 495–
    97
radiolabeled high affinity ligands, 965
radioligand autoradiography, 1029
radio plays, 227

Radke-Yarrow, Marian, 336, 337, 350, 789
Rafaeli, Eshkol, 976–1001
rage, 439t, 440, 443, 855
　animals and, 774, 1010
　emotional reactivity and, 683, 684
　homicide and, 805–6, 817
　shame as factor in, 750, 792
Raghunathan, R., 604, 632–33
Ragozzino, M. E., 97
Raichle, M. E., 289
Ramey, C. T., 389
Randall, W. C., 137
Rapee, R. M., 631, 688, 689, 999
raphe nuclei, 165, 964, 1026, 1029, 1126
rapid fading, spoken language, 537
rapid relevance detection, 578, 907
Rapson, R. L., 487
Ratcliffe, M. A., 1069
rational choice theory, 566, 633, 805, 819n.3, 892, 894
rationality, moral emotions and, 843, 891–96
rational thought, 563, 596, 843
rats, 458, 843, 1011, 1012, 1014, 1097, 1107, 1127, 1129
rattlesnakes, 457–58, 461
Rauch, Scott L., 5, 900, 963–73
Rauschecker, J. P., 474
Ravel, Maurice, 515
Ray, M. L., 755
Razran, G. H. S., 598
reaction stereotyping, 700
reaction time, in attention tasks, 277, 278, 280f, 282, 284–89
reactivity
　individual differences in, 678–79, 681–94
　of infants, 320–21, 328–30, 353
　psychopathology and, 901
Reader, The (Schlink), 498, 499
readers' perspective, 483–84, 487–90, 498, 499
reading, 664, 665
real-life emotion inductions, 218, 227, 228, 233, 238–39
reappraisal, 567, 573, 574, 576, 588, 735, 1050
reason, 572, 633, 852, 865–66
reasoning, 84–86, 661, 664
　moral, 852, 853, 865–66, 866n.4
　rational thought, 563, 596, 843
reautomization, of maladaptive behavior, 908, 925
Rebecca, Biagio, 482
recall memory, 564, 600, 610, 645, 650–54, 735, 767n.7, 1000
Recchia, S., 393
receptor characterization studies, 965

reciprocal altruism, 854, 855, 863
reciprocity, animal communication and, 460–61
recognition memory, 600, 645, 651, 654
recognition studies, 443, 444, 446
reconstructed memories, 643–44
reconstructive thinking, 599–600, 612
recovered memories, 643–44
recovery, emotion's role in, 1095–96
recrimination, 623–24
recursive processes, cognition-emotion interaction, 567–68
Reed, Marjorie A., 678–79, 681–94
referential communication, 459–60, 473, 475
referential function, of narratives, 547, 548
referentialists, musical, 505
reflected appraisals, 780–81
reflective memory modules, 665
reflexes, 388, 389, 1106
　autonomic nervous system and, 154, 156–58, 159t, 161, 162t, 163–67, 173–75
　emotion motivational organization and, 187–207
Regan, D., 893, 895, 896
regional cerebral metabolic rates for glucose, 965–66, 970, 971
regression analysis, 242–43, 322, 517
regression toward the mean, 244, 246
regret
　cancer patients and, 1071
　as counterfactual emotion, 623–24, 636n.6
　cultural views of, 846
　guilt and, 792–93
　postdecisional dissonance and, 609
regulatory foci, 994–95, 1000
regulatory responses, 873
rehearsal
　cognitive, 565
　of emotional events, 650–51
Reilly, Judy, 297, 412, 535–53
Reiman, E. M., 119, 942, 947, 970
reinforcement, 120, 123
reinstatement, 56, 61
reintegration, shaming and, 388, 395, 400, 401
Reis, H. T., 1098
Reisberg, D., 645
rejection, depression and, 992
relational harmony, 877, 878, 879
relational intent, 876, 877
relational themes, 573, 578–79, 628, 709, 748
relationship closeness, 825, 826
Relationship Closeness Inventory, 827
relationship concerns, 589n.5

relationships. See interpersonal relationships; parent-child relationships; social relationships
relaxation, anger reduction, 819
relevance detection, 578, 907
relief, 683, 684, 687, 689, 862
religion
　agape love and, 864–65
　awe and, 863
　elevation and, 864
　morality and, 852, 856
　music's role in, 504
remembered affect, 841–42, 843, 846
remember/know method, 645, 654
reminiscence effect, 651, 735
remitted depressives, 1034
remorse, 920
REM sleep, 76
ren (benevolence), 384–86
Renaissance, 481, 483–84, 489, 493, 494
reorganization, behavioral, 362
reparations, 356, 792, 792–93, 860
repeated transcranial magnetic stimulation, 901
Repetti, R. L., 1085
representational memory, 901
representations, dynamic skill theory and, 388, 393, 394, 395, 400
repressed memory, 643–44
repression, 1091
　cancer patients and, 1053–57, 1063–70, 1073, 1075
repression-sensitization dimension, 714
Repression-Sensitization Scale, 1064, 1065, 1070
repressive coping, 652–53, 707, 715–18, 1068, 1087
repressive discontinuity hypothesis, 718
repressive emotional discreteness, 716–17
reproductive behavior, 414, 460, 461, 470, 472, 473, 1011
reptiles, 258, 259, 1011. See also snakes
reputation, 843, 849, 855–56
re-representation, 42, 43
resentment, 811, 1068, 1086, 1087
reserpine, 1023, 1025
resignation (emotion), 846
resilience, 1050, 1074, 1094, 1096–97
respect, 864
respiration, 437, 449, 473
respiratory system, 686
response activation, 872–74
response modulation, 710, 904–26
response styles theory, 996
responsibility
　as appraisal dimension, 580, 874–75
　personal, 992–93
　social, 797
responsiveness, to emotions, 334–37, 358

resting state studies, 121, 122
restraint, cancer patients and, 1055, 1070
restriction of range principle, 238
reticular activation system, 685
reticulo-septal-hippocampal-orbitofrontal cortical network, 933
Revelle, W., 651, 692
revelry, 569
revenge, 856
reverberation, 462
reversal learning, 59, 118
reverse genetics, 313
revolutions, Davies's theory of, 811
reward
    consummatory behavior and, 755
    as decision-making consideration, 625
    dopamine and, 32–34, 38, 625
    emotional systems and, 683
    emotion tasks and, 132
    facial expression and, 425–26
    hemisphere specialization theories and, 38
    ideal self and, 688
    instrumental learning and, 842
    lateral hypothalamus and, 34–35, 36, 37
    neurotic extraverts and, 921, 922f, 923
    nucleus accumbens and, 32–33, 1016
    orbitofrontal cortex and, 28, 118
    oxytocin and, 1016
    pedunculopontine nucleus and, 37
    perceptual emotion influences and, 685
    prefrontal cortex and, 10, 39
    prosocial behavior and, 787, 797
    psychopathy issues and, 910–12, 916, 923, 970
    temperament type issues and, 327
    ventral pallidum and, 35
    ventromedial frontal cortex and, 82
reward dependence, 933
reward learning, 32, 118
Reynolds, P., 663, 1059
Reznick, J. S., 305
Reznick, Steven, 327
rhesus macaques, 464, 465, 469, 473, 474
rhesus monkeys, 461, 465, 1011
Rhetoric (Aristotle), 752, 756
rhetorical figures, in music, 504, 506
rhinal cortex, 74, 75
rhythm
    music and, 519, 520, 524
    speech and, 443
Ribot, T. A., 492
Richards, A., 664, 666, 717
Richards, J. M., 881
Richardson, J. L., 1072
Richman, S. A., 608
Rigg, M. G., 508, 514, 520
right caudate, 945, 948
righteousness, 384

righteous rejection, 581
right fornix, 948
right fusiform, 936, 948
right gyrus rectus, 940
right hemisphere, 67–73, 87, 417, 422, 449–50, 542–43, 647, 703, 729, 931, 941
right parahippocampal gyrus, 938
right posterior cingulate, 936
right pulvinar, 269
right putamen, 936
right temporal lobe, 423, 970
Riley, V., 1072
"Rime of the Ancient Mariner, The" (Coleridge), 491, 499
Rimmö, P. A., 266
Ring, B., 474
ring doves, 471
Riordan, C., 820n.13
riots, 811, 819n.7, 820n.14
Risberg, J., 954
risk, 622–24, 630, 632, 634, 683
risk-taking, 1120
Ritov, I., 624
Ritter, R. C., 137
Ritter, S., 137
ritual, 879, 884–85, 886
ritualization, 457, 461–62
ritual propriety, 384
Robazza, C., 515
robbery, 806
Robbins, T. W., 32
Roberts, R. E., 1059
Roberts, R. J., 218
Roberts, T.-A., 703
Robin, L., 829
Robinson, D., 965
Robinson, J. L., 305
Robinson, R. G., 68
Robinson, T. E., 588
Robinson-Whelen, S., 737
Robitaille, B., 515, 520
Rocking of the Cradle and the Ruling of the World, The (Dinnerstein), 494
rococo art, 483
rodents, 458
Rodin, J., 1070
Roediger, H. L., 985, 987
Rogers, R. W., 758, 774
ROI analysis, 936, 937, 943, 945, 948, 952, 953
role shift, in narratives, 550–51, 554n.2
role stability, 993
Rolls, E. T., 3, 27–28, 29, 34, 118, 119, 323, 474, 628
Roman Catholic Church, 504
romance novels, 490
romantic hypothesis, art and, 490–93
romanticism
    in music, 505

in visual and narrative arts, 481–88, 493, 495, 497, 499
romantic relationships, 827, 831–33
Rome, ancient, 325
Rose, R. J., 728–29
Rose, S. A., 361
Roselli, F., 756
Roseman, I. J., 578, 579, 582, 816
Rosén, I., 954
Rosenberg, D. R., 965
Rosenberg, E. L., 420, 486
Rosenthal, R., 445
Ross, E. D., 68, 448, 449
Rossi, P. H., 806
rostral ventrolateral medulla, 165, 167, 1112
rostral ventromedial medulla, 165
Rothbart, M. K., 350, 353, 355, 356, 361, 693, 727, 730
Rottman, S. J., 472, 474
Rotton, J., 808–9, 810, 819–20nn.4, 6, 8
Rousseau, Jean-Jacques, 481, 482, 483, 495
routine-activity theory, 808, 819–20n.8
Rowe, D., 728
Rowell, L. B., 137
Rowell, T. E., 468, 469
Royal Pavilion (England), 483
Royzman, E., 844
Rozin, Paul, 577–78, 839–49, 857, 858
Ru486, 1126–27
RU 28362, 98–99
Rubin, K. H., 320
Ruckmick, C. A., 844
rukun (Javanese concept), 878
ruminative coping, 690
ruminative self-focus, 996
Rush, M. D., Sr., 970
Ruskin, John, 490–91
Russell, J. A., 190, 216, 529, 1084, 1093
Russian language, 541
Russian Revolution, 811
Rusted, J. L., 986
Rusting, C. L., 712
Ryan, R. M., 994
Ryff, Carol D., 297, 734, 1050, 1083–99

## S

Sabatinelli, D., 194
Sabini, J., 856
Sachs, Nadia, 930–54
sacral spinal cord, 143, 145, 146, 165
SAD. See seasonal affective disorder
saddleback tamarins, 473
Sadie, S., 530n.2
sadness, 5, 18, 325, 412, 589n.5, 692, 1010, 1087
    animals and, 774

sadness (*continued*)
  appraisal patterns for, 585, 633, 732
  as attitude and judgment influence, 602–5, 607–9, 611
  as attitude change factor, 759, 761
  as basic emotion, 68, 176, 333, 669, 1087
  cancer patients and, 1071
  cingulate cortex and, 30
  as communication of caring, 828
  dispositional emotionality and, 795
  as emotion family, 381
  expression of, 706, 828, 830
  facial expression of, 417, 420, 423, 424
  incidental situational affect and, 632–33
  induction studies of, 939, 943–50
  infants and, 780
  as information-processing factor, 629, 630
  medial prefrontal cortex and, 120
  musical expression of, 514
  music and perception of, 515, 520, 523–27, 529
  personality and, 733
  self-generation of, 776
  sign language expression of, 539
  universalist view of, 216
  vocal expression of, 438, 439*t*, 440, 443, 444, 446
safety, 689, 691, 693–94
St. Paul, U., 153
Salk, L., 349
Salkovskis, P. M., 992
Salovey, Peter, 604, 611, 652, 711, 712, 747–50, 819n.3, 1091
salutogenesis, 1098–99
*sama* (Hindu emotion), 865
Sanchez, H., 650
Sanderson, W. C., 631, 999
Sandvik, E., 733
sanguine temperament, 326, 698, 933
Sarge, A., 525
Sarter, Martin, 1105–13
Sasvari-Szekely, M., 312
Sato, K., 874, 876
*satru* (Javanese concept), 878–79
*Saturn* (painting), 486
Saudino, K. J., 305, 736–37
Savage, C. R., 969
Savitsky, K., 623
Saxena, S., 966
Scarone, S., 965
Scarr, S., 307
scent glands, animal, 472–73
scent marking, 472–73
Schachter, S., 212, 215, 222n.3, 702, 711, 779
Schachter-Singer theory of emotion, 564
Schacter, Daniel L., 565, 566, 643–55
*schadenfreude*, 864

Schäfer, E. A., 931
Schaffer, H. R., 350
Schagat, K. D., 818
Schaumann, L., 603
scheduling, automatic information processing and, 668
Scheff, T. J., 498
Scheier, M. F., 711, 782, 1084
Schelling, Thomas, 892–93, 895
schemas, 666, 982, 989
  depressive, 991–92
  memory and, 650, 651, 652–54
  mental, 485–86, 489–90, 492, 498
  self, 650, 652, 1001
schematic model level, 669–70
schematic patterns, emotional attractiveness and, 489
schematic processing, 576, 577, 578, 583, 726
schemes, affectively charged, 565
Scherer, Klaus R., 86, 412, 413, 433–52, 520, 553, 563–69, 572–89, 669, 671, 679, 706, 709, 710, 713, 856, 874–75, 876, 906, 907, 919–20, 923
Scherg, H., 1067
Schieffelin, E. L., 881
Schildkraut, J. J., 1022, 1024
schizophrenia, 123, 301, 306, 309, 315, 899, 1033, 1034, 1113
  cognitive-behavioral therapies, 901
  dopamine and, 1031, 1032
  emotional processing impairment and, 738, 945
  emotion induction study findings on, 945, 951
  facial expression and, 426
  hippocampus and, 1131
  incidence of, 903
  positive affect loss and, 1010
  socioeconomic status and, 1130
Schkade, D. A., 626
Schlink, Bernard, 498
Schlosberg, H., 416
Schmaling, K. B., 804
Schmid, A., 199
Schmidt, L. A., 320
Schmitt, W. A., 915
Schmitz, S., 306
Schmukle, S. C., 716
Schmutte, P. S., 734
Schneider, F., 943, 945, 946, 969
Schneider, H. J., 699–700
Schneider, W., 906
Schneirla, T. C., 577
Schnitzler, H.-U., 199
school, peer relations in, 342, 343
Schore, A. N., 349, 355, 356
Schorr, A., 573, 589
Schubert, E., 517
Schuff, N., 968

Schulkin, J., 31
Schumann, D. W., 608
Schupp, Harald T., 187–207
Schwann cells, 162
Schwartz, A., 624
Schwartz, G. E., 218, 220, 706, 1091
Schwartz, J., 541, 856
Schwartz, J. C., 381
Schwarz, N., 600, 601, 602, 608, 760, 761, 765
science, beginnings of, 481. *See also specific fields*
SCL-90 (scale), 1063
scopolamine, 102
Scott, J., 984
Scott, J. D., 194
Scott, W. D., 603
*Scream* (painting), 486
scripts (concept), 666
sculpture, 486, 487, 503, 569
search behavior, 683
Sears, R. R., 811, 812, 820n.16
Seashore Measures of Musical Talents, 515, 519
seasonal affective disorder, 124, 1027
Sebastian, S., 285, 980, 1001n.2
secondary appraisals, 573, 580, 585
  aggression and, 814
  attention and, 693–94
  coping and, 687, 688–90, 709
secondary control, 877–78
security/contentment, 846, 1087
security/potential, decision making and, 623
Sedikides, C., 603, 759
Seeman, Teresa, 1049, 1085, 1117–31
Segal, Z. V., 982
Segerstrom, S. C., 1096
segregation
  racial, 857
  sex-based, 872, 884
Seibert, Laura, 297, 412, 535–53
Seilman, U., 499
selective abstraction, 689
selective attachments, 729, 1011, 1017
selective attention
  anterior cingulate cortex and, 11
  approach-avoidance conflict, 285–87, 288*f*, 289
  cue conditioning, 278, 280–85, 289
  cue-target paradigm, 277–78, 285
  disengagement and, 277, 278, 282, 285–87, 289, 693–94
  emotional cuing with words, 278, 279*f*, 280*f*, 285–87, 289
  emotional modulation of, 276–90
  future research considerations, 289–90
  information processing paradigm and, 662–64
  orienting vs. defense responses, 287–89

priming and, 662–63
response automization and, 285
startle reflex and, 205, 207
Stroop paradigm, 276–77, 278, 285, 286, 288, 289
to threat, 269, 277
*See also* attentional bias
selective engagement, 277
selective information processing, 629, 633, 662–64, 666, 668, 669, 671
selective serotonin reuptake inhibitors, 1022, 1025, 1027, 1030, 1032
self, 482, 495
    appraisal theory view of, 581–82, 688, 689–90, 874
    attention and, 711
    attitudes and judgments about, 597, 602–4, 612
    attributions of, 600, 779–80
    in cultural models, 874, 879, 881, 885
    development of, 332, 338, 353, 356, 357, 363–64, 777, 792
    emotion and, 749–50, 773–83
    empathic overarousal and, 793
    guilt and, 792
    ideal vs. ought, 688, 689, 779, 995, 996
    imagining of oneself, 775–76, 779
    imagining of significant others, 776–77
    interdependent vs. dependent, 846
    memory retrieval and, 652
    moral emotions and, 853–55, 859–61, 863
    nature of, 773–74
    personality and, 726–27, 730, 734–35, 774
    reflected appraisals and, 780–81
    shame and, 792
    in SPAARS emotion model, 670
    symbolic threats to, 777–79
self-absorption, 996
self-acceptance, 734
Self-Assessment Manikin, 190, 191
self-attribution, 600, 779–80
self-awareness, 356, 358, 362, 363–64, 773–83
    animals and, 774, 780
    attenuation of, 782
    brain stem systems and, 37
    children's development of, 777, 780, 788, 789, 792
    emotion reorganization role of, 347
self-blame, 780
self-competence, 750
self-concept, 906, 920
self-confidence, 340
self-conscious emotions. *See* social emotions
self-conscious moral emotions, 848, 855, 859–61, 866n.3
self-consciousness, 781

self-consistency, 778
self-control, 633, 635, 636, 818, 880–81, 886
self-criticism, 885–86, 992, 997
self-cultivation, 384–86, 401
self-destructive behavior, 635
self-directedness, 737
self-disclosure, 336, 341
self-discrepancy theory, 609, 734, 779, 994–95, 996
self-distress, 788, 790
self-effacement, 375, 376, 385–87, 394, 400
self-efficacy, 581, 689, 783
    appraisal and, 709, 710
    cancer patients and, 1054, 1071, 1075
    expectancies, 999
    future-related cognition and, 999–1000
    health issues, 611, 1050
self-enhancement, 777–78, 885–86
self-esteem, 340, 384, 386, 401, 585
    in American cultural model, 871, 872, 885–86
    appraisal issues, 710
    as cognitive dissonance mediator, 609
    cultural perspectives on, 871, 872, 883
    as decision-making consideration, 624
    emotion regulation and, 712
    health issues and, 1050
    memory retrieval and, 652–53
    as motivation factor, 604
    as processing style factor, 613
    self-image and, 778
    self-judgments and, 603, 993
    as social comparison factor, 779
self-evaluation, 356, 774, 777, 779
self-evaluative emotions, 386–401
self-focused attention, 994, 995–96, 1001
self-harmonization, 386, 387–88, 389–94, 402
selfhood. *See* self
self-image, 567, 652, 777–79
self-interest, 633, 636, 787, 891–96
selfishness, 804, 893–94
self-knowledge, 604, 652, 991, 993
self-organization, 378, 381–83, 401, 402
self-perception, 566–68, 778, 783
self-perfection, 384–85
self-recognition, 774, 789
self-referent executive function, 689, 690
self-referential behavior, 774
self-reflexive emotions, 581
self-reflexive thinking, 773–83
self-regulation
    children and, 357
    emotional experience modification and, 781–83
    as emotion goal, 748
    health issues and, 1047

individual differences and, 699, 707, 708, 711, 719
    personality development and, 730, 731, 739
    psychopathology and response modulation and, 899–900, 904, 905, 908–9, 911–12, 919–25
    self-related cognition and, 994–95
self-related cognition, 977, 991–96, 1000
self-relevant thought, 775–77
self-report methodology, 5, 9, 19
    ambiguity interpretation studies and, 988, 1001n.5
    in appraisal research, 586–87
    cancer patient studies and, 1054–55, 1064–65
    children and, 306, 315
    facial expression research and, 416, 417, 419, 426
    prosocial behavior studies and, 790
    research concerns, 218, 219, 220f, 228–35, 1088, 1089–93
    self-related cognition research and, 991–92, 995, 1000
    subjective experience and, 566–67
    temperament measurement and, 321–22
self-rewards, 787
self-schemas, 650, 652, 1001
self-system therapy program, 1000
self-talk, 782, 783
self-transcendence, 737
Seligman, M. E. P., 266, 268, 631, 1000
Selves questionnaire, 922
Selye, Hans, 1049, 1089, 1118
semantic affective space, 678
semantic associative network theory, 982, 989
semantic differential, 190, 515, 844
semantic displays, facial expression and, 540
semanticity, as language feature, 536
semantic memory, 647, 651
semantic priming, 198
semantic processing, 909, 913–14
semi-ipsatization, of data matrices, 248, 249
semiotics, musical, 529
Semon, R., 651
Semple, S., 470
Semple, W. E., 967
Sen, Amartya, 895
sensations, 574
senses, 28, 633, 841. *See also specific senses*
sensitization, 565
sensitizers, 707, 715, 718–19, 1068
sensorimotor processes, 226, 1106
    appraisals and, 576, 577, 583, 589
    in dynamic skill theory, 388, 389, 393, 394, 395

sensory cortex, 969, 972
sensory inputs, 841, 842, 845–46, 849
sensory pleasure, 862
sentimental art and literature, 489, 490
sentograph, 506, 524, 528
separate appraisals, 586
separation anxiety, 683
septal nuclei, 729
septal rage, 35–36
septohippocampal circuits, 327
septum, 35–36, 449
serotonin, 16, 125, 311–13, 1047, 1129
    anxiety physiology and, 964
    depressive disorders and, 327, 1022,
        1023, 1026–31, 1126, 1127
    emotion induction and, 226
    panic disorder and, 970
    stress and, 1126
    as temperament factor, 327, 933
    violence and levels of, 327, 1027–28
serotonin reuptake inhibitors, 953, 964,
    966
    selective, 1022, 1025, 1027, 1030, 1032
serotonin-selective compounds, 902
serotonin transporter, 1028–29
sertraline, 124, 1022, 1025, 1032
serviceable associated habits principle,
    457
serviceable habits, 747
Sessarego, A., 970
setoperone, 1030
set points, 1049, 1108
sex differences
    animal copulation calls, 470
    behavioral inhibition, 328
    bird song, 466
    emotional expressivity, 705, 706
    emotional prevalence, 882
    emotion induction study findings and,
        943, 945, 950
    as emotion regulation factor, 366, 796
    interoception, 703
    music perception, 529
    symptom reporting, 704
    temperament neuroimaging research,
        954
    vocal expression variation, 451
    See also females; males
sex offenders, 30
sex segregation, 872, 884
sexual abuse, 643, 967, 968, 1129
sexual arousal, 30, 35, 470, 472, 629
sexual behavior, 34, 36, 1011, 1095
sexual desire, 325
sexual reproduction. See procreation;
    reproductive behavior
Seyfarth, R. M., 474, 475
Shagass, C., 699
Shahn, Ben, 485
Shakespeare, William, 483, 775

Shallice, T., 665, 668, 689
shame, 297, 325, 1087
    antisocial behavior and, 750
    appraisal theory view of, 581, 585, 690,
        860
    attributional style for, 688
    cultural perspectives on, 845, 846–47,
        848, 860, 883, 884
    in cultures of honor, 846–47, 872, 884
    development of, 297, 338, 356, 375–76,
        375–403, 379t, 381–403, 780, 792
    facial expression of, 420, 424, 425
    journal articles published on, 852, 853t
    moral emotion and, 849, 855, 859–61,
        862, 865, 866
    prosocial behavior and, 792–93
    reflected or self-appraisal of, 781
    toddlers and, 335, 336, 353, 356
    vocal expression of, 443
shamelessness, 383
shaming, 386, 388, 394–95, 400–402, 855
sham rage behavior, 151
Shapiro, D., 910, 913
Shapiro, I., 819n.3
shared environmental variance, 302–4,
    306
shared meaning, 332
Sharrock, R., 986
Shaver, P. R., 381, 382, 541, 856
Shaw, D., 366
Shedler, J., 1091
sheep, 1014
Shekelle, R. B., 1057, 1059
Sheldon, K. M., 994, 995
Sheldon, W. H., 326
Sheley, J. F., 812
Sheline, Y. I., 14
Shelley, Percy Bysshe, 485
Shelton, S. E., 469
Shepherd, J. Z., 137
Sheppard, L., 630
Shereck, L., 495
Sherman, M. and I. C., 349
Sherrington, Charles, 841, 1106
Shields, J., 301, 309
Shiffrin, R. M., 906
shifting emotions, 529
Shin, L. M., 654–55, 968
Shin, M., 863
shing (Surinamese concept), 883
Shinn, Millicent, 349
Shizgal, P., 33
Shnek, Z. M., 999
Shoda, Y., 699, 708–9, 719
short-term memory, 663, 693
Shweder, R. A., 847, 858, 875
shyness, 306, 309, 320, 327
    cultural perspectives on, 884
    life-span development and, 728, 729,
        730

reactivity of children and, 328, 330
    as self-conscious emotion, 859
    See also behavioral inhibition; social
        phobia
siblings
    child's empathetic concern for, 336
    cooperative play among, 342
    emotional communication among, 332,
        334, 341
    environmental variance and, 302–3,
        306
    gene-environment covariance and, 307
    parental interactions, 337
    substance abuse among, 728
    See also twin studies
sickness response, 1047
side-by-side behavior, 1010
Sidtis, J. J., 450
Siegel, R. A., 911
Siegle, G. J., 690
Siegler, R. S., 364, 366
signal-detection methodologies, 702, 703
signaling
    animals and, 412, 449, 457–76
    imperfect, 895
    systems, 747
signed languages, 297, 536–51
significant others, emotions about, 1084–
    86, 1087, 1093
significant stimuli, 259, 261–62
Sikora, S., 499
Silverman, K. E. A., 445
Simon, H. A., 635
Simpson, J., 826–27
simulated vocal expressions, 436
simulation, fiction as, 497–98, 499
simultaneous information processing, 665–
    66, 667, 668, 669
Sinclair, R. C., 608
Singer, Burton H., 297, 1050, 1083–99
Singer, J., 810
Singer, J. A., 652, 711, 712
Singer, J. E., 212, 215, 222n.3, 702, 779
Singer, R. D., 598, 604
singing, 504, 507–8, 525–27
single photon emission tomography, 964,
    965, 973
    for depression, 1029, 1032
    for obsessive-compulsive disorder, 965
    for panic disorder, 970, 971
    for phobias, 969
    for posttraumatic stress disorder, 968
single step direct-access retrieval of past
    solutions from memory, 670
Siskind, M., 1062
situational affect, 632–33
situational change, 566
situational factors
    in aggression responses, 809, 814, 817–
        18

in appraisal, 709
individual differences and, 700, 706
situation modification, 710
situation selection, 710
16 Personality Factor Questionnaire, 1057, 1058
skeletal structure, facial, 328
Skelton, J. A., 704
skin
  fibroblasts, 1023, 1029
  immune system and, 173
  temperature of, 328–29
skin conductance response, 29, 76, 83, 117–18
  cue conditioning and, 280–81, 282, 284f, 285
  differential conditioning tasks and, 266–67
  emotional response research findings on, 191, 192, 194
  orienting responses and, 264, 265
  prosocial behavior studies of, 791, 793, 794
  psychopath emotion processing and, 914–17
  startle reflex and, 201
  threat imminence and, 259
Skyrms, Brian, 895
sleep, 76
sleep deprivation, 124, 1121
sleep-wake cycle, 701–2, 1117–18, 1119, 1121, 1131
Slovic, P., 630
slow-to-warm-up child, the, 327
smell (sense), 28, 29, 31. See also odors
Smiley, P., 545
smiling, 381, 393
  facial expression and, 417, 418, 424, 425, 476
  by infants, 333, 334, 364, 417, 425, 543, 552
Smith, Adam, 861
Smith, A. P., 1074
Smith, C. A., 417, 435, 578, 582, 587, 780
Smith, G. S., 124
Smith, L. B., 362
Smith, M., 915
Smith, M. D., 812
Smith, N. K., 195
Smith, S. M., 603, 761
Smith, S. S., 915
Smith, W. J., 463
smoking, 810, 1119–21
  nicotine and, 951
snakes
  animal fear of, 465
  phobias to, 969, 980–81, 988–89, 1001n.2
  rattlers, 457–58, 461
Snidman, Nancy, 327

Snowdon, Charles T., 412, 413–14, 457–76
Soares, J. J. F., 263, 264, 267, 268, 270, 271
sociability, 327, 727
social affiliation. See affiliation
social anxiety, 260, 329, 688, 689, 780
  reflected appraisal of, 781
  social phobics and, 970
social behavior, 297, 747–50, 1049
  animal affiliation and, 315, 1010–17
  attitude and persuasion emotional factors in, 752–67
  attitudes, judgments, and, 596–98, 604–5, 610–11, 613
  cognition and emotion interactions in, 563
  depression's impact on, 118
  emotion as process of, 747–49
  emotion's interpersonal functions in, 637n.13
  inappropriate, 648, 818
  intergroup attitudes and, 605–8
  interpersonal. See interpersonal relationships
  mood and, 749
  self and emotion and, 773–83
  ventromedial frontal lobe damage and, 83
  See also antisocial behavior; prosocial behavior
social class. See socioeconomic status
social cognition, 565–66, 596, 599, 613, 1049
  attitude formation and change and, 750, 752–66
  emotional disorder cognitive biases and, 976–77, 990–1001
  information processing paradigm and, 671
  memory and, 565, 643, 646–51, 654
  moral emotions and, 855, 858
  self and emotion and, 749–50, 773–83
social cognitive theory of personality, 728
social comparisons, 779, 782
social constructionist theory, 402
social context, 402
  animal development processes and, 475
  appraisal and, 581–82, 584
  behavioral inhibition system operation and, 683
  communication channel bias and, 553
  cultural perspectives on, 883
  in dynamic skill theory, 389
  emotion expression and, 413, 748
  facial expression and, 418, 420–22, 425–27, 539
  macaque cooing and, 468–69
social coordination, 748, 1047
social cues, 564

social desirability, 707
social development, 750
social disgust, 857, 864
social distress, 395
social emotions, 296, 335, 354, 356–58
  core affect and, 1085
  development of, 780
  prosocial behavior and, 750, 787, 792–93
  self-evaluative, 386–401
  See also specific emotions
social harmony, 385, 386, 387, 843, 877–80, 883
social hierarchy, 846
social honor, 389–94, 400–401
social identity, 581, 860
social impairment, autism and, 1017
social integration, 1050, 1074, 1085, 1097
social intentions, 418, 425
social intuitionist model of moral judgment, 865–66, 866n.4
social irresponsibility, 118
social isolation, 474, 475, 1059, 1060, 1131
sociality, affiliation and, 1010
socialization, 849
  appraisal theory and, 581
  cultural differences in, 375, 386, 394–95, 402, 883
  of desirable behavior, 750
  emotional development and, 296, 356, 357
  hedonic reversal of negative responses and, 846
  helping behavior and, 797
  as personality factor, 730–31, 739
socialized delinquent behavior, 819n.1
social judgment, 413
social learning, 507
social memory, 297, 1014
social norms, 567, 581, 584, 587
social-order concerns, 589n.5
social organization, 1011, 1017
social phobias, 259, 260, 686, 963
  attentional biases and, 978, 980, 981
  cognitive interference and, 277
  memory biases and, 987
  neurobiology and neuroimaging of, 968–70, 972
social process theory, 402
social psychology, 749, 840
  appraisal theory and, 589
  attitude concept, 596
  emotion-memory link studies, 655
  environmental factors in aggression, 806
  moral emotion and, 865
  "new look in perception" approach, 565
Social Readjustment Rating scale, 1067

social referencing
    emotion regulation and, 567
    infants and, 335, 353, 354, 363, 425,
      543, 730–31, 789
social regulation, 881, 886–87
social relationships
    allostatic load and, 1093–94, 1096
    animals and, 848
    arousal control importance, 360–61
    autism and, 1017
    Confucian view of, 385
    early childhood emotional development
      and, 332–44, 347, 353, 354, 355, 357,
      360–61
    emotions about significant others, 1084–
      86, 1087, 1093
    future research considerations, 343–44
    health and, 1050, 1093–94, 1096, 1097
    individual differences in, 296, 333, 338,
      339–43
    in individualist cultures, 384
    normative developmental processes,
      333–39
    *See also* interpersonal relationships
social responsibility, 797
social signals, 446
social status, 421
social strains, criminal behavior and, 806,
    810–13
social submissiveness system, 260–61,
    267–68
social support, 902, 1050, 1085, 1096,
    1097
    cancer patients and, 1055, 1070–72,
      1074–75, 1087, 1098
social understanding, 339, 343, 344
Society for Psychiatric Genetics, 312
socioeconomic status, 322, 344
    allostatic load and, 1094, 1096, 1124,
      1128–30
    health issues and, 1086, 1118, 1129–31
socioemotional selectivity theory, 679,
    734
sociology, 748, 805, 810
sociometer theory, 778
sociotropy, depression risk, 992
Socrates, 1047
Sokolov, E. N., 261–62
solitary tract, nucleus of. *See* nucleus
    tractus solitarius
Solomon, R. C., 347, 748, 1097–98
Solomon, R. L., 588
somatic activity, cultural differences in,
    878
somatic conversion hysteria, 1047
somatic marker hypothesis, 29–30, 83,
    134, 270–71
    decision making and, 270, 271, 634,
      635, 691
somatic nervous system, 567

somatic processes, 900
somatic representation, 71–73
somatization disorder, 905
somatomotor system, 135–36, 154, 155,
    165, 167, 170, 171
    emotion expression and, 175, 177
somatosensory cortex, 969
somatostatin, 902, 1033, 1034
somatovisceral emotion responses, 134,
    378, 931
    emotion induction research and, 233–
      38, 241
    experiment design issues, 241, 242
    statistical analysis of, 247–50
somatovisceral emotion specificity, 132
songbirds, 462, 465–66, 472, 474
Sonino, N., 1088
soothability, infant, 349, 354
Sopchak, A. L., 508
sophisticated processing, 366
sorrow, 515, 580
*Sorrows of the Young Werther, The*
    (Goethe), 482
soul, 563
sound, 462, 505, 633, 665
    vocal expression and, 433, 442–43
    *See also* music
sound synthesis, 529
SPAARS model of emotion and emotional
    disorder, 669–71
spatial contexts, 55, 56, 61
spatiotemporal patterns, 506, 524
specialization, spoken language and, 537
species constant learning theory, 415
SPECT. *See* single photon emission
    tomography
spectators' perspective, 483–84, 487, 489–
    90
speech, 536–38, 540
    babbling, 470, 471–72, 476, 544
    developmental processes, 544–45, 548–
      49, 552–53
    emotion encoding, 541
    facial expression and, 540
    future research considerations, 476
    information processing paradigm, 661
    linguistic systems, 537
    prosody. *See* prosody
    vocal expression and, 433–52
speech rate. *See* articulation
speech recognition technology, 457
speech synthesis/resynthesis, 445, 447,
    538
Speer, A. L., 795
Spence, E. L., 203
Spencer, D. D., 201
spider phobia, 906, 969, 977, 980, 986–
    87
Spiegel, David, 1050, 1053–75
Spielberger, C. D., 716, 816

Spielberger State-Trait Anxiety
    Questionnaire, 1067
Spielberger State-Trait Personality
    Inventory, 1068
Spielman, L. A., 996
spinal autonomic motor programs, 166
spinal autonomic outflow, 137
spinal cord, 11, 136, 1106
    autonomic nervous system and, 139,
      140, 149, 150*t*, 154, 155, 163, 164–66,
      174–75
    sacral, 143, 145, 146, 165
spinal tendinous reflex, 205
spinal visceral afferent neurons, 143–46,
    148, 155–56, 165, 166, 1113
Spinoza, Baruch, 563–64, 572
Spinrad, Tracy, 297, 750, 787–98
Spiro, A., 737
Spitz, R. A., 902
Spitz, Rene, 349
Spitzer, R. L., 704, 1061
splanchnic ganglia, 139
spleen, 173, 1074
split-brain patient studies, 37
spoken language. *See* speech
spreading activation, 687, 690, 691, 694,
    994
Sprengelmeyer, R., 936, 937
Spurzheim, J. G., 326
Spyer, K. M., 137
squirrel monkeys, 466, 470, 473, 474,
    1074
squirrels, 457–61
Sroufe, L. Alan, 350, 352, 355, 360
Srull, T. K., 599
SSRIs. *See* selective serotonin reuptake
    inhibitors
stability
    in attachment styles, 730
    of attitudes, 755, 766
    emotional, 698, 933
    of interpersonal relationships, 827
    of personality, 732, 1088
    role-related, 993
    as self-attribution aspect, 780
    of temperament, 727–28, 731
    *See also* allostasis
stability of change, 708
stage model of development, 735–36
Staib, L. H., 968
Stanat, P., 485
stance, in communication, 541, 547
standards
    as appraisal concern, 688, 689
    compatibility with, 573, 574, 581, 709
    internalization of, 792
    living up to, 797
    self-relevant, 778–79
Stanislaski technique, 440
Starkstein, S. E., 68

Starling, E. H., 149
starlings, 474
startle reflex, 133, 189, 323–24
    amygdala and, 199–200, 201, 206, 329
    emotional priming and, 198–205
    fear-potentiated, 100, 199–204, 206–7,
        259, 1106–7, 1110
    psychopaths and, 738, 917–19
state, personality and, 677–78
state affect. *See* situational affect
State-Trait Anxiety Inventory, 980
statistical analysis, 244–50, 322
Statistical IVD, 246, 247
Steer, R. A., 992
Stegge, H., 792–93
Stein, M. B., 967
Stein, N., 338
Stein, N. L., 732–33
stellate ganglion, 139, 140
Stemmler, Gerhard, 131–34, 220, 221, 225–
    50, 700
Stenberg, C., 295, 543
Stenberg, G., 954
Stephan, C. W., 880
Stephan, G. S., 880
Stephan, W. G., 880
Stepper, S., 487
stereotyping, 597, 605–8, 629
Stern, Daniel, 332, 350, 360
Stern, D. N., 529
Sternbach, R. A., 218
Stevenson, Robert Louis, 497
Stewart, H., 704
Stewart, R. S., 970
Stillwell, A. M., 831, 856, 861
stimulant drugs, 686, 951–52
stimuli processing
    amygdala's role in, 15, 18
    in appraisal, 577, 586
    emotional memory and, 644, 645, 649,
        651
stimulus evaluation check model, 709–10,
    906, 919–20, 923
stimulus-onset asynchrony, 263
Stipek, D. J., 393
stoic acceptance, cancer patients and,
    1060, 1061
Stone-Elander, S., 119
"storage bin" model, 599
Stormark, Kjell Morten, 276–90
Strack, F., 487, 653
strain theories of crime, 806, 810–13
Strange Situation, 340
*Strategy of Conflict, The* (Schelling), 895
Strathman, A. J., 608, 754
Stratton, George, 93
Strauman, T. J., 995, 1000
Straus, M. A., 813
Strauss, Richard, 516
Stravinsky, Igor, 505

Strelau, J., 678
stress
    allostasis and allostatic load and, 1072,
        1093, 1117–31
    amygdala and, 74
    as antisocial behavior cause, 806, 810–
        13
    attentional biases and, 980–81
    cancer patients and, 1063, 1070–75
    as commonly reported emotion, 846
    coping and, 713–15, 1098, 1121
    defense behavior and, 171–72
    depression and, 1022, 1025, 1033
    health and, 5, 1049–50, 1074, 1084,
        1087, 1089, 1117–31
    hippocampus and, 15, 18
    in hopelessness depression theory, 998
    immune system and, 738, 1033, 1049,
        1073–74, 1084, 1108
    individual-specific responses to, 699–
        700, 706, 708
    infants and, 354
    language breakdown and, 552
    mediators of, 1117–21, 1125, 1129, 1130
    occupational, 1095, 1121, 1124, 1130
    orbitofrontal cortex and, 120
    pessimism and, 737
    posttraumatic stress syndrome and, 967
    psychosomatic disorders and, 1048
    racism and, 1086
    spreaded activation of affect and, 994
    uncontrollable, 999
    vocal expression and, 439*t*, 440
stress hormones, 38, 61, 1118, 1129, 1131
    memory and, 4, 93–95, 109, 1127
stress reduction, 902
stria terminalis, 74, 75, 103, 104
    bed nucleus, 901, 1113
striatum, 103
    anxiety disorders and, 972
    depression and, 1032
    dorsal, 75
    maternally derived genes and, 310
    obsessive-compulsive disorder and, 965,
        966, 972
    phobias and, 969
    psychopathology issues, 901
    ventral, 33, 74, 328, 947
stroke, 932
Stroop, J. R., 276
Stroop paradigm, 119, 276–78, 285, 286,
    288, 289, 649
    cognitive bias research, 978–82
    psychopathy studies, 913, 917
structure
    individual differences and, 708
    self-related cognition and, 993–94,
        1000
    social cognition and, 991
Stuart, A., 247

stumptail macaques, 458, 459*f*, 463–64,
    469
*Sturm und Drang* movement, 504
subcallosal gyrus, 953, 968
subcaudate tractotomy, 121
subcortical brain structures
    appraisal process and, 576, 586
    emotion and, 25, 26*f*, 39
    in hierarchical system, 42, 43
    neural substrates of affect and, 930–31,
        933, 943, 946, 948, 951, 953–54
    *See also specific structures*
subgenual cingulate, 120, 125
subgenual prefrontal cortex, 121
subjective-autonomic response
    dissociation, 699, 705, 706–8, 719
subjective experience, 566–67, 574, 575,
    586, 1087–92
subjective judgment, 324
subjective re-experiencing of events, 654
subjective self-awareness, 774
sublenticular substantia innominata
    activation, 937
submission
    animal expression of, 458, 460, 461,
        464, 472
    social, 748
substance abuse, 1086, 1127, 1130, 1131
    antisocial behavior and, 804
    childhood abuse and, 1129
    environmental facilitation of, 739
    maladaptive self-awareness attenuation
        and, 782
    mood and, 899
    among siblings, 728–29
    *See also* addictive drugs; alcoholics
substance P, 902, 1107
substantia innominata. *See* ventral
    pallidum
substantia nigra, 75
substantive processing, 612–13, 764–65,
    767n.7
success
    American cultural model of, 871, 885
    children's emotions and, 356
    self-image issues of, 777–78
Suci, G. J., 321
suddenness, appraisal of, 687, 710
sudomotor neurons, 156, 157, 158*f*, 161*f*,
    162, 173
suffering, 861–62
Sugden, R., 623–24
suicide, 737, 782, 860, 1048, 1126, 1127
    attempt factors, 1028, 1030, 1031
    childhood abuse and, 1129
    postmortem studies, 1022, 1025, 1026,
        1029–33
Sullivan, M. W., 393
Suls, J., 714
sumatriptan, 1028, 1034

sums of squares, 243
superego, 326, 840, 931
superior cervical ganglion, 139–40
superior colliculus, 269, 289, 937
superior frontal gyrus, 945
superior temporal cortex, 473–74, 970
superior temporal gyrus, 936, 937, 948
superior temporal lobe, 542
superior temporal sulcus, 474
supernatural forces, cultural views of,
    874, 875, 879–80
superordinate programs, emotions as, 976
supervisory attentional system, 689
supplementary motor area, 11
support groups, 1071–72
suppression of mood. *See* emotion
    suppression
supramarginal gyrus, 968
supraorbital frontal cortex, 970, 971
surprise, 412
    as basic emotion, 68, 176, 261, 1087
    as counterfactual emotion, 624
    facial expression of, 418, 420, 424, 543
    infants and, 780
    negative, 714
    orienting and, 261
    personality and, 733
    to the unexpected, 325
    universalist view of, 216
    vocal expression of, 443
Surtees, P. G., 1061, 1063
survival, 748, 1095–97
    cancer patients and, 1053–57, 1060–63,
        1069–72, 1087
    as evolutionary goal, 256, 257, 265
sustained-sadness technique, 953
Sutton, D., 473
Sutton, S. K., 701, 918
Svrakic, D. M., 737
Swann, W. B., Jr., 778
Swartz, T. S., 816
sweat glands, 472
Swedo, S. E., 965
sweet (taste), 35, 36, 577
Switzer, G., 795
symbolic self-awareness, 774
symbolic thinking, 774, 775
symbolism, 506
symbol processing systems, 661
symbol systems, 568–69
Symmes, D., 474
sympathetic-adrenomedullary regulation
    system, 238
sympathetic emotions, 497, 498
sympathetic nervous system, 95, 137–42,
    151–53, 155–60, 163–77, 257, 1108,
    1111, 1121
    behavioral inhibition and, 328–29, 729
    emotional suppression's effect on, 627
    emotion identification with, 235

evolutionary perspectives on, 258, 259
immune system and, 172–74
individual-specific response patterns,
    699
racism's impact on, 1086
skin conductance response and, 280
startle reflex and, 323
temperament and, 323, 327, 729
vocal expression and, 434, 435–36, 439–
    40, 538
sympathetic tone, 152, 167
sympathetic trunks, 139
sympatho-adrenal system, 149–53, 174–
    75
sympathy, 412, 417, 424, 425, 748
    definition of, 788
    health issues and, 1047
    moral emotion and, 854, 861, 862
    prosocial behavior and, 750, 790, 791,
        793–96, 798
*Symphonie Fantastique* (Berlioz), 505
symptom provocation paradigms, 964–65
symptom reporting, 703–4
symptom specificity, 699
synapses, 356, 1022
syntax, 468, 537
systematic desensitization, 819
systematic information processing, 629

**T**

Tafrate, R. C., 819
Taghavi, R., 663, 666, 668
Tagiuri, R., 416
Tahitians, 883
Taiwanese language, 448–49
Talairach, J., 934
Tamang (Nepali cultural group), 882, 883,
    886
Tamang, B. L., 880
tamarins, 464, 466–70, 472, 473, 475
tamoxifen, 1072
Tan, E. S., 486
Tangney, J. P., 688, 779
Tanksley, S. D., 311
Tannenbaum, P. H., 321
tape-recording equipment, 457
Taraban, C. B., 828, 829
Tarantino, L. M., 313
targeting, amygdala damage and, 32
target tissue, 154, 155, 156
taste (sense)
    amygdala and, 31, 32
    aversive, 13
    brain stem sites and, 36–37, 39
    cingulate cortex and, 30
    emotion evaluation studies of, 937, 938
    hardwired preferences for, 577
    hedonic impact and, 33, 36

lateral hypothalamus and, 34
nucleus accumbens and, 34
orbitofrontal cortex and, 28, 29, 119
ventral pallidum and, 35
tastes, changes in, 625
Taylor, John, 484
Taylor, S. E., 844, 1085, 1092, 1096
Taylor, Stephan F., 941
Taylor Manifest Anxiety Scale, 1064,
    1065, 1068, 1069, 1070
TcHMPAO. *See* technetium-99-labeled
    hexamethyl propylene amine oxime
Teasdale, John D., 576, 663, 668, 671, 941–
    42, 984, 997
technetium-99-labeled hexamethyl
    propylene amine oxime, 964
technetium-99m hexamethyl-propylene-
    amine-oxime SPECT, 933, 934, 948
Tedeschi, J. T., 816, 820n.13
teeth chattering, animal, 464
Telch, M. J., 1000
television, 485, 497, 503
Temoshok, L., 707, 1055, 1061, 1069–70
temperament, 4, 347–48, 350, 353, 726–
    31, 739
    adults and, 327, 679, 727–29
    affect definition and, 323–25
    behavioral inhibition and, 296, 305–6,
        320–31, 354, 729, 933
    of children, 296, 315, 320–23, 326–27,
        347–48, 350, 353, 736
    constraining aspects of, 330
    continua or category distinction, 322–23
    definition of, 320–21, 677
    emotional reactivity individual
        differences and, 681–83, 684, 688,
        689
    emotion expression and, 413
    emotion regulation and, 360
    genetic factors in, 296, 300, 302–10,
        315, 340, 726–29
    as health factor, 738–39
    history of concept of, 325–27, 535
    humors concept and, 325–26, 535, 698,
        932–33
    of infants, 320–23, 326–27, 347–48, 350,
        353–55, 727, 729
    inhibition concept and, 327–29
    internal tone and, 324, 329–30
    measurement of, 321–22
    as mood state predictor, 728
    nature-nurture debate and, 298
    neural substrates of, 932–33
    neuroimaging studies of, 953–54
    parental reports of, 296, 303, 304, 306,
        315, 321–22
    as parent-child relationship factor, 340
    as personality's emotional aspect, 677
    prosocial behavior and, 297, 794
    as sibling relationship factor, 341

temporal domains of, 930–31, 954
Wundt's dimensional view of, 698
temperature (emotional)
    in metaphorical emotional language, 215
    motivational systems and, 842
    as sympathetic activity indicator, 328–29
temperature (environmental), 807–10, 819–20nn.4, 7, 8, 10
temper tantrums, 728
tempo, music, 504, 517, 520, 524–27
temporal basal polar lesions, 932
temporal contexts, fear conditioning and, 56, 59, 61
temporal cortex, 967, 968, 971
temporal gyrus, 474, 936, 937, 941, 948
temporal lobe
    bilateral resection of, 931
    emotion induction study findings on, 946–49
    emotion recognition and, 69, 71
    facial expression and, 423, 934
    language comprehension and, 542
    memory and, 198, 647–48
    panic disorder and, 970, 972
    phobias and, 969–70
    psychopathology and, 901
    temperament neuroimaging research, 954
temporal lobe epilepsy, 16, 41
temporal polar cortex, 74, 75, 969, 971
temporal pole, 931, 936, 938, 943, 971
temporal visual cortex, 474
tense arousal, 686
tenseness, 464
tensions, 704
tension states, larynx and, 437
Teresa, Mother, 892
"terrible twos" (toddlers), 333, 335, 364
territorial behavior, animal, 462, 472, 473, 1014
Tesser, A., 755
Test-Operate-Test-Exit cycle, 994
testosterone, 464, 1014, 1127
tetrodotoxin, 104
text, music in support of, 504
Thai language, 448–49
thalamic theory of emotions, 151
thalamus, 17, 27, 101, 118, 194, 269, 931
    amygdala and, 964, 1106, 1110
    automatic emotion processing and, 648
    depressive disorders and, 1027
    emotional systems and, 685
    emotion induction study findings on, 940, 942, 943, 945, 947–49
    gustatory emotion evaluation studies of, 938
    language and, 542
    mood neuroimaging findings on, 953

obsessive-compulsive disorder and, 965, 966
phobias and, 969
temperament neuroimaging research, 954
vocal expression and, 449
Thayer, J. F., 11
Thayer, R. E., 686
THC (delta 9-tetrahydrocannabinol), 28, 30, 951
theater, 497, 498
Thelen, E., 362
thematic abstraction units (concept), 666
theory of mind, 338, 339
thermal grille illusion, 119
thinking
    abstract, 774, 775, 777
    low-level, 703
    open-ended, 668
    selective information processing and, 664
    self-reflexive, 773–83
    symbolic, 774, 775
thinking aloud research method, 492
third-party concerns, moral emotions and, 856, 858–59
thirst, 30, 31, 841
Thoits, P. A., 826
Thomas, Alexander, 321, 322, 326–27, 727
Thomas, W. I., 596–97
Thompson, Ross A., 355, 356, 360, 364, 710, 793
Thompson, W. F., 515, 520
Thomsen, C. J., 754
thoraco-lumbar spinal visceral afferent neurons, 144–45, 146, 148
thoracolumbar system. See sympathetic nervous system
thought, higher-level, 661, 990–1001
thought patterns, 417, 485
threat, 133
    animal expression of, 458, 459f, 460f, 463, 465, 466, 472, 475, 774
    anticipation's role in, 775
    anxiety and, 264, 689, 963–64, 979–81, 985–90, 1001n.1, 1110
    appraisal of, 238, 269, 572, 580, 689, 717, 1089
    attentional bias for, 264, 668, 692–94
    attention to, 269, 277, 649
    automatic activation and, 691, 694
    automatic emotion processing and, 648
    coping with, 715–19
    evolutionary perspectives on, 257, 259–61, 265–66
    fear appeals and, 757–58
    fear conditioning to, 56, 62
    panic disorder and, 970, 972
    perceptual processing of, 685, 1120
    phobias and, 969, 970, 972

psychopath response to, 914–16, 919, 925
psychophysiological responses to, 259, 260f, 914–16
startle reflex and, 206–7
unconscious cognitive processing of, 565
weapon focus and, 649
threat imminence, 259, 260f, 265–67, 269, 286, 649
threat words, 13, 663–64, 666, 978–81, 986
3-methoxy-4-hydroxyphenylglycol, 1024–25, 1031
thrillers (novels), 490
Thunberg, M., 265
thwarted expectations. See frustration-aggression hypothesis
thyroid gland, 1032–35
thyroid-stimulating hormone, 1034, 1035
thyrotropin-releasing hormone, 902, 1033, 1034, 1035, 1121
Tian, B., 474
Tiedemann, Dietrich, 349
Tiedens, L. Z., 629, 636n.5
Tiihonen, J., 969
timbre, music, 520, 524, 526, 527
time, 133, 219–21, 734, 1093
    decision-making considerations, 566, 619, 622, 624–26, 631, 632
    diurnal clock. See circadian rhythm
time series analysis, 517
Tinbergen, N., 489
Tisak, J., 819n.2
Tisak, M. S., 819n.2
Titanic (film), 498, 499
T lymphocytes, 173, 1087
Toddler Behavior Assessment Questionnaire, 303, 304
toddlers, 296, 298, 353, 354
    autonomy seeking by, 357
    behavioral inhibition in, 305–6, 729, 730
    emotional expression by, 333, 335–37, 356, 364
    emotion regulation by, 354, 357, 358, 361, 363–66
    empathy and, 788–89
    guilt and, 792
    language development in, 544–45, 553
    learning and, 361–62
    moral emotions and, 792
    personality development in, 728
    prosocial behavior development in, 297, 353, 358, 363, 545, 788–90
    talk about feelings of, 336, 342
    temperament development in, 304, 305, 729
    "terrible twos," 333, 335, 364
Tolstoy, Leo, 491, 497

Tomaka, J., 238

Tomalin, C., 491

Tomarken, A. J., 701, 988

Tomasello, M., 339

Tomkins, S. S., 367n.5, 416, 435, 506, 574, 577, 711, 736

tone languages, 446, 448–49, 538

tones (musical), 503, 526

tongue, 544
    bite expression, 421
    flicking of, 464
    protrusion expression, 425, 464, 476

tonic activation, 692

tonic immobility, 169, 188, 685, 691

Tonoike, M., 450

Tooby, J., 976

top-down information processing, 666–69, 671, 681, 682, 964
    neurobehavioral systems and, 1105, 1107, 1110–13

Torajan, 879–80, 883, 886

Toth, I., 312

Totterdell, P., 820n.19

touch (sense), 28, 119

Tourette's syndrome, 315

Tower of London task, 122, 123

town planning, 496

Trabasso, T., 732–33

trace conditioning, 13, 109

traditional transmission, language, 536

tragic drama, 483

trait anxiety, 690, 692, 700, 704–5, 707, 719
    attentional biases and, 978, 980, 982, 1001nn.1, 2
    memory biases and, 985–86
    psychopaths and, 915–16
    repression and, 1064

traits, emotional
    adaptive value of, 840
    individual differences in, 699, 701, 708, 714
    information processing paradigm and, 663
    as mental health factor, 737
    personality and, 677–78, 679, 727, 731–33, 737, 738, 1088

Tranel, D., 118, 474

transcranial magnetic stimulation, 6

transitional objects, 354

transitivity, in decision making, 622, 623

transmission
    as language feature, 536, 537
    in vocalization, 433, 442–43, 451

transthyretin, 1034–35

trauma, 1056, 1098, 1129. See also posttraumatic stress disorder

traumatic brain injury, 932

traumatic memory, 643–44, 645, 653

trazodone, 1022

Trehub, S. E., 527

Trezise, L., 986

TRH. See thyrotropin-releasing hormone

tricyclic antidepressants, 1021, 1022, 1023–24, 1030

trigeminal cranial nerve, 37

trill vocalizations, 475

tripartite model of affective disorders, 992

tripartite theory of attitudes, 752–53

triplet repeat mutations, 310

Trivers, R. L., 854

Troccoli, B. T., 762, 818

Troland, L. T., 841

Tronick, E. Z., 350, 352

Trope, Y., 604, 631

trophotropic reaction, 153, 236

Trower, P., 683

Troyer, D., 795

True IVD, 246, 247

Trussoni, S. J., 524

tryptophan, 953, 1026–27, 1028

Tsai, J. L., 878

TSH. See thyroid-stimulating hormone

Tsuda, K., 524

t-tests, 322, 1057

Tu, W. M., 385

Tucker, D. M., 692

Tucker, J., 874

Tulving, E., 646, 647, 651–52, 654

tumors, 932, 1059, 1061, 1072–74, 1087

Tupes, E. C., 677

Turk, D. C., 807

Turkheimer, E., 729

Turner, J. M. W., 493

Turner, T., 582

Turner, T. J., 215

Tversky, A., 566, 622, 631, 988

twin studies
    attachment, 340
    disease, 1128
    genetics-related, 300–308, 315, 727, 728–29, 737
    temperament heritability, 727, 728
    temperament measurement, 321

twitters, animals and, 470

two-component models of intonation, 448

Type C cancer personality, 069, 10531

tyrosine hydroxylase, 1024, 1025, 1125–26, 1127

Tyrrell, D. A., 1074


# U

UCLA Loneliness Scale, 1067

ultrasonic vocalizations, 458

uncertainty
    coping and, 714–16
    decision making and, 566, 619, 622–25, 629–30

uncertainty-motivated coping, 713, 715

unconditional (unconditioned) stimuli, 842
    emotional cuing and, 278, 280, 282, 285
    emotion biphasic organization and, 189
    fear conditioning and, 52–56, 59, 100, 265–66, 268, 269
    feedback during conditioning and, 270
    human startle response studies, 201, 202f

unconscious appraisal, 564, 568, 574, 710

unconscious cognitive processes, 565, 1021

unconscious emotions, 586

undersocialized delinquent behavior, 819n.1

unemployment, 812

unexpectedness, 687, 906

unfamiliarity, 328, 333–34, 350

uninhibited temperament, 728, 729

uninhibition, 327–28, 329, 330

unipolar disorder, 899, 900, 903, 998
    neurobiological issues, 1024, 1028, 1034

United States
    American Revolution, 481, 811
    appraisal patterns in, 584–85
    criminal violence in, 807–8, 811–12, 819–20nn.5–8, 14, 15, 20
    cultural models, 871, 874, 875, 878, 880–82, 884–86
    emotional disorder incidence, 903
    expression universality findings on, 419–22
    Great Depression, 812, 820n.16
    1960s riots, 811, 819n.7, 820n.14
    pride, shame, and guilt views in, 297, 375–76, 379t, 381–403, 584–85
    racial segregation, 857
    reported emotion frequency, 846
    Southern culture of honor, 807–8, 819nn.5–6
    "walk to Emmaus" retreat, 885

universal contingencies hypothesis, 584–85

universality of emotions, 419–22, 445, 871
    facial expression, 216, 415, 416, 419–20, 422, 539, 543, 871
    linguistic expression, 539, 540, 1089

University of California, Berkeley, 349

University of Pennsylvania, 934, 943

unpleasantness, 761, 782, 813, 881–82
    as affective aggression cause, 750, 805, 806–10, 814, 816, 817–18
    intrinsic, 574, 577
    stimulus evaluation check model, 906, 919–20

unsuccessful copers. See high-anxious copers

upward contempt, 858

Urbach-Wiethe disease, 75, 78

urgency, appraisal of, 579, 687, 688
urine, chemical signaling, 472, 473
utility, decision making and, 620, 622–26, 630
Utku Inuits, 420–21, 883
Uvnäs-Moberg, K., 1097

## V

Vache, K., 985
Vagg, J., 388
vagina, 841
vagus nerve, 167, 169*f*, 257, 258, 1047
   afferent neurons and, 144, 145, 148–49, 174–75
   memory and, 107, 1107, 1127
vagus nerve stimulators, 901
Vaillant, George, 735
Vaitl, D., 201, 285
valence, 5, 882, 1085, 1087
   affect and, 840, 841, 932
   in appraisal process. *See* intrinsic pleasantness
   emotional memories and, 644–45, 651
   *See also* negative emotions; positive emotions
Valenstein, E. S., 34
Valentiner, D. P., 1000
validity, in research experiments, 239, 241–42
valid trials, 277–78, 281–82, 284, 285
value relevance, 581
values
   aesthetic, 635
   appraisal and, 581, 709
   evolutionary and cultural perspectives on, 840, 847, 849
   as helping behavior motivation, 787
   moral, 635, 787
van Bezooijen, R., 443
VanBoven, L., 631
van Buskirk, R., 94
Van Hooff, J. A. R. A. M., 464
Van Lancker, D., 450
van Reekum, C. M., 435, 441, 584
variables
   sampling, 233, 235–40, 247–48
   temperament analysis issues, 322–23
Varney, N., 525
Vasari, G., 493
Vasile, R. G., 124
vasoactive intestinal peptide, 142, 143
vasoconstrictor neurons, 156–58, 161*f*, 165–70, 173
vasodilator neurons, 157, 162, 173
vasopressin, 297, 1012–19, 1097, 1125, 1126
Vatner, S. F., 137
vegetarianism, 857

vegetative nervous system, 137
veiling of women, 884
Velten, E., 602, 603
Velten method, 120, 227, 228, 601, 602, 948
vengeance, 855, 856
venlafaxine, 940
ventral affective division, anterior cingulate, 933, 938, 941, 945, 947, 948, 953, 954
ventral amygdalofugal pathway, 329
ventral anterior cingulate, 120, 124
ventral medial frontal cortex. *See* ventromedial frontal cortex
ventral pallidum, 35, 36, 42, 75, 109, 1016
ventral prefrontal cortex, 968
ventral striatum, 33, 74, 328, 947
ventral tegmental area, 118
ventral vagal complex, 449
ventromedial frontal cortex, 73, 82–86, 87, 648, 649, 947
ventromedial hypothalamus, 34, 41
ventromedial prefrontal cortex, 5, 9, 10, 27
   conditioned fear extinction and, 56, 59
   damage to, 29, 118
   emotion induction study findings on, 947
   internal tone and, 329
   memory retrieval and, 654
verbal behavior, 705
verbs, American Sign Language, 537
Verney, S. P., 985
vervet monkeys, 459, 470, 473, 474
vestibular system, 686
vicarious emotions, 580
videos, 503
vigilance, 169, 679, 714–19
vigilants, 703, 707
Viken, R. J., 728–29
Vinacke, W. E., 492
Vincenzo Galilei, 504
violence
   antisocial behavior and, 804–19
   climate/weather as factor in, 807–10, 819–20nn.4, 7, 8
   culture of honor and, 807–8, 819nn.5, 6
   serotonin levels and, 327, 1027–28
viral vector technology, 1018
virtual persona, music as, 514
visceral afferent neurons, 143–49, 155–56, 165, 166, 1107, 1112
vision (sense), 661, 666, 902
*vis nervosa*, 326
visual arts, 411, 413, 503, 569
   emotion communication in, 481, 483–87, 489–97
   *See also* architecture; painting; sculpture

visual association cortex, 968
visual communication, signed language and, 536, 537, 543, 545–47
visual cortex, 194
   emotion induction study findings on, 940, 941
   facial expression role of, 474
   in Gestalt theory, 487
   memory retrieval and, 655
   panic disorder and, 971
   phobias and, 969
   posttraumatic stress syndrome and, 967, 968
   priming and, 647
   synaptogenesis, 356
visual dot-probe methodology, 264, 977–82
visual hallucinations, 900, 952
visual object perception, 666
visual search tasks, 260, 261
visual signaling, animal, 458, 459*f*, 462–65, 475–76
visual thinking, 485
visuo-spatial scratch pad, 663
Vitale, J. E., 918
vitality affects, 529
vocal-acoustic-auditory channel, 433
vocal expression, 68, 187, 411, 412, 433–52
   amygdala and, 31, 449
   by animals, 412, 449, 457–63, 465–76, 507, 583
   appraisal effects on, 582, 587
   art vs., 491
   clinical applications of, 450–51
   decoding of, 433, 443–46, 450, 451, 507, 526–27, 538
   developmental issues in, 544–45, 548–49, 552–53
   of disgust, 443, 444, 937
   in dominance contests, 261
   emotion, language, and, 297, 535
   emotion evaluation studies and, 937–38
   emotion-typical action tendencies and, 378, 380
   encoding of, 433–42, 451, 507, 526, 527, 538, 541–42, 843
   fear conditioning and, 53–55
   infant responsiveness to, 335, 447
   by infants, 333, 334, 544, 552
   lesion studies of, 68, 69, 70–72
   music performance and, 504, 507–8, 525–27
   neuropsychological study of, 449–50
   perception of, 413, 442–43, 445, 526, 538
   prosody's role, 446–48, 450, 538, 543, 548–49, 552–53
   reproductive behavior and, 414
   tone languages, 446, 448–49, 538
   universality of, 871

vocal parameters. *See* acoustic parameters
Vohs, K., 844
voice, vocal expression and, 433–46
voles, 297, 315, 1010–18
*Vollkommene Capellmeister, Der*
     (Mattheson), 504
voltammetry, 27
vomeronasal organ, 472
*Vom musikalisch Schönen* (Hanslick),
     505
von Frisch, K., 472
von Neumann, J., 622
"voodoo causation," 895
Vrana, S. R., 203
Vries, B. de, 524

# W

Wagner, Richard, 503
Waletzky, J., 541, 548
Walker, L. G., 1069
"walk to Emmaus" retreat, 885
Wallace, George, 819n.5
Wallace, J. F., 915, 921
Wallbott, H. G., 443, 445, 874, 875
Walschburger, P., 699–700
Wang, G., 666
Wang, L., 382
Wang, Po W., 930–54
wanting, 34, 35, 840
*War and Peace* (Tolstoy), 491
wariness, 729
Warkentin, S., 954
Warren, S. L., 306
war songs, 525
Wason selection task, 84–85
*Waste Land, The* (Eliot), 485, 491
water, 325, 326
Watkins, L. R., 1047
Watkins, P. C., 985
Watson, C., 711
Watson, D., 677–78, 704, 705, 992, 1087
Watson, John B., 349, 598, 775
Watson, J. S., 389
Watson, K. B., 515
Watson, M., 1062
Watt, R. J., 514
Watts, F., 986
Wave 5, 329
Way, the (Confucian concept), 384, 385
Ways of Coping Checklist, 714
weapon focus, 649
Weary, G., 996, 997
weather, 807–10, 819nn.4, 7
Wedin, L., 520, 528
Weerts, T. C., 218
Wegener, Duane T., 608, 609, 750, 752–
     67

Wegner, D. M., 664
weight
     effects of depression on, 118
     obesity, 1117, 1120, 1121, 1129–31
Weike, Almut I., 187–207
Weinberger, D. A., 706, 1064, 1091
Weinberger, N. M., 102
Weinberger Adjustment Inventory, 1064,
     1065, 1068
Weiner, B., 580, 688, 780
Weiner, S. G., 469
Weinerman, B., 1071
Weinman, J., 277
Weinstein, J., 706
Weiskrantz, L., 32
Weiss, B., 322
Weissman, M. M., 903
Weisz, J. R., 322
welfare, 750, 825, 827–28, 830–31, 853
well-being, 1098
     affective forecasting of, 626, 636n.7
     communal relationship role, 750
     emotion's role in, 1050
     integration as marker of, 993
     life-span perspective, 734–35, 736
     subjective, 1090, 1092
well-being therapy, 1096
Wellman, H. M., 336
Welsh anxiety scale, 918
Welsh repression scale, 1058
Wenger, M. A., 235, 699
Werner, H., 354
Wernicke's aphasia, 198
Wernicke's area, 449, 900
Western Electric Company, 1057
Western Electric Study, 1057
Whalen, Paul J., 13, 119, 265, 937, 938
Wheeler, R. E., 701
Whiffen, V. E., 992
Whistler, James McNeill, 485, 490–91,
     494
whistles, animal control via, 471
White, G. M., 748
Whitehall studies, British Civil Service,
     1130
white rami, 139
Whitlock, F., 1062
Wickens, C. P., 205
Wiener, S. G., 1074
Wiens, Stefan, 256–71
Wiers, R., 876
Wiesel, Elie, 1084
Wiesel, T. N., 902
Wiest, C., 816
wife battering. *See* domestic violence
Wiggins, E. C., 755
Wik, G., 120, 967, 969
Wilde, Oscar, 485
Wilder, J., 246

Wilkinson, H., 118
Williams, D. R., 1086
Williams, J. M. G., 668, 981, 984, 985,
     986, 989, 990, 1001n.4
Williams, R., 986
Williams, R. H., 244
Williamson, G. M., 830
Williamson, S., 913, 914
Williams syndrome, 321
Willson, R., 524
Wilmers, F., 700
Wilson, D. W., 810
Wilson, James Q., 805, 865
Wilson, P. H., 999
Wilson, R. S., 305
Wilson, T. D., 587, 634, 776, 865
Windhorst, U., 137
Winquist, J. R., 996
Winston, A. S., 489, 494–95
Winton, W. M., 216
Wirsching, M., 1066
Wisconsin Longitudinal Study, 1092,
     1094
*Wisdom of the Body, The* (Cannon), 149,
     151
withdrawal, 840
     in appraisal process, 577
     emotional reactivity and, 683
     frontal brain asymmetry and, 701, 932
     glucocorticoid levels and, 327
     prefrontal cortex and, 9, 729
     psychological disorders and, 738
     shame and, 860
within-group variability, 242–44
Wolff, P. H., 333
Wolff, W., 426
Wolfgang, M. E., 806
women. *See* females; sex differences
wonder, 863
wood, 326
Wood, J. V., 711
Wood, W., 755
Woods, S. W., 970
Woodward, Sue, 327
Woodworth, R. S., 415–16
Woolf, J., 523
Woolf, Virginia, 484, 492, 497
words
     emotional cuing and, 278, 279*f*, 280*f*,
          285–87, 289
     emotion-related, 678, 883, 1089
     threat-related, 13, 663–64, 666, 978–81,
          986
Wordsworth, William, 483, 485
working memory
     affective, 6
     cingulate cortex and, 649
     circadian rhythm and, 702
     dorsolateral frontal cortices and, 83

information processing paradigm and, 663

pre-goal attainment of positive affect and, 683

workplace
health issues and, 1095, 1121, 1130
interpersonal relationships in, 832

Worrall, L., 525

worry, 704, 775–76

Worth, L. T., 601, 602

Wotman, S. R., 856

Woulbroun, J. E., 728

Wrangham, R. W., 470

Wright, Frank Lloyd, 495

Wright, J. D., 806

Wright, John, 495

Wu, J., 124

Wu, S., 381

Wundt, Wilhelm, 233, 567, 568, 577, 698

Wyer, R. S., 599, 763, 765–66

## X

xenon-133 gas single photon emission computed tomography, 933–34, 943, 954

## Y

Yang, J., 732

yawning, 464, 476

yellow bile (humor), 325, 933

Yeo, R. A., 310

*yi* (righteousness), 384

yin-yang, 326

yoga, 782

yohimbine, 96, 97, 107, 226, 970

Young, A. W., 664

Young, P. T., 839

Yovel, Iftah, 976–1001

Yule, W., 663

Yurgelun-Todd, D. A., 16

## Z

Zahn-Waxler, C., 336, 337, 789, 790, 791

Zajonc, R. B., 39, 213, 575, 577, 586, 597, 598, 993

Zanakos, S., 664

Zanna, M. P., 607, 754, 761

zazen, 782

Zeiss, A. M., 999

Ziegler, T. E., 473

Zillmann, D., 711, 810

Zimmerman, D. W., 244

Zinbarg, R. E., 686

Znaniecki, F., 596–97

zona incerta, 165

Zonderman, A. B., 1058–59

Zumpe, D., 808

Zuwerink, J. R., 756

zygomatic muscle, 192, 194, 265, 440, 444